# Basic Standard Deduction Amounts

| Filing Status | 2009 Deduction | 2010 Deduction |
|---|---|---|
| Single | $ 5,700 | $ 5,700 |
| Surviving spouse | $11,400 | $11,400 |
| Married filing jointly | $11,400 | $11,400 |
| Married filing separately | $ 5,700 | $ 5,700 |
| Head of household | $ 8,350 | $ 8,400 |

# Amount of Each Additional Standard Deduction

| | 2009 Deduction | 2010 Deduction |
|---|---|---|
| Married taxpayers 65 or over or blind | $1,100 | $1,100 |
| Single taxpayer or head of household who is 65 or over or blind | $1,400 | $1,400 |

# Personal and Dependency Exemption

| 2009 Exemption | 2010 Exemption |
|---|---|
| $3,650 | $3,650 |

# Corporate Income Tax Rates

| Taxable Income | Tax |
|---|---|
| < $50,000 | 15% of the taxable income |
| $50,000–$75,000 | $7,500 + 25% of taxable income over $50,000 |
| $75,000–$100,000 | $13,750 + 34% of taxable income over $75,000 |
| $100,000–$335,000 | $22,250 + 39% of taxable income over $100,000 |
| $335,000–$10,000,000 | $113,900 + 34% of taxable income over $335,000 |
| $10,000,000–$15,000,000 | $3,400,000 + 35% of taxable income over $10,000,000 |
| $15,000,000–$18,333,333 | $5,150,000 + 38% of taxable income over $15,000,000 |
| Over $18,333,333 | 35% of the taxable income |

# McGraw-Hill's
# TAXATION *of* INDIVIDUALS AND BUSINESS ENTITIES

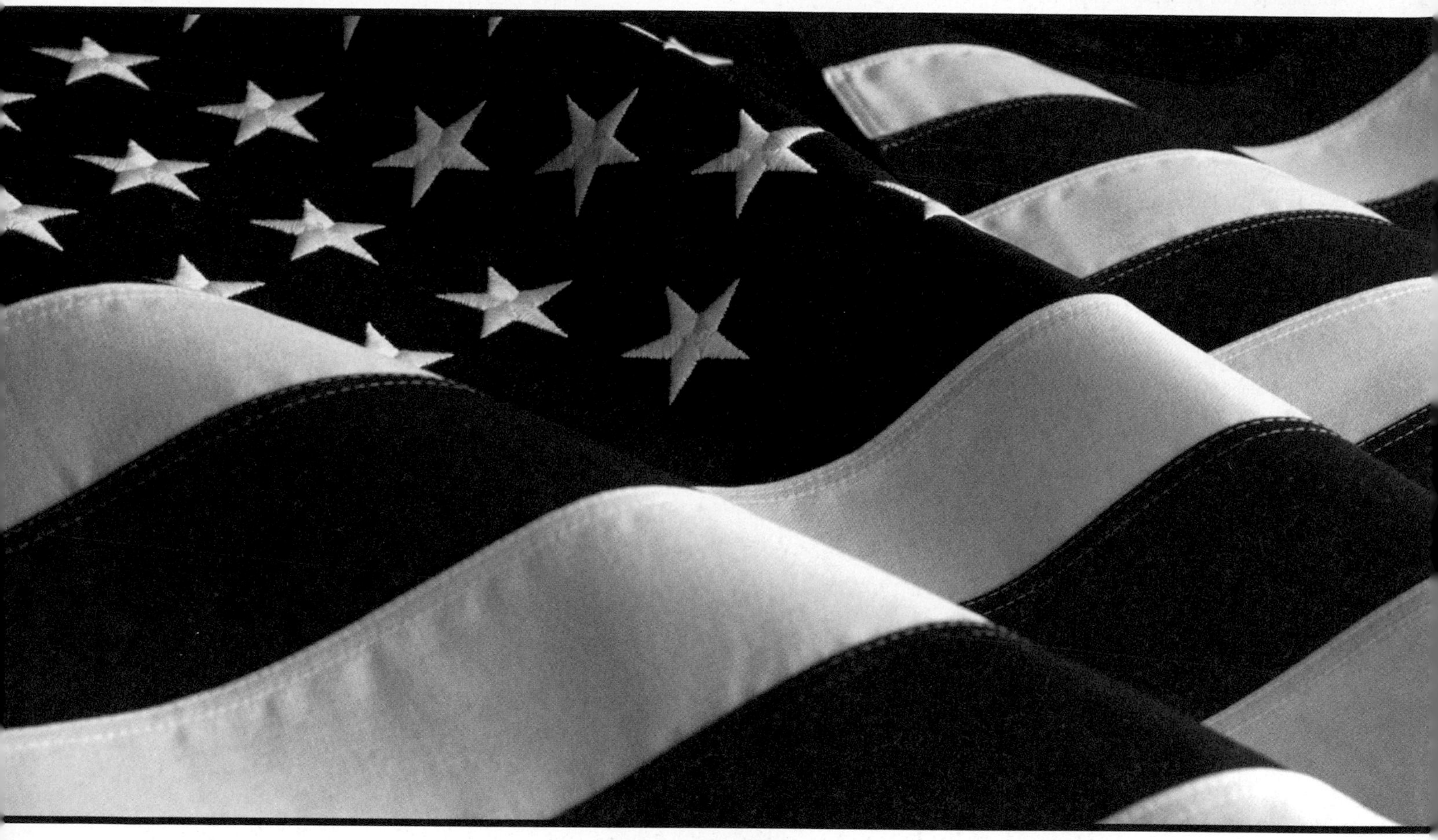

**Brian C. Spilker**
*Brigham Young University*
**Editor**

**Benjamin C. Ayers**
*The University of Georgia*

**John R. Robinson**
*The University of Texas – Austin*

**Edmund Outslay**
*Michigan State University*

**Ron G. Worsham**
*Brigham Young University*

**John A. Barrick**
*Brigham Young University*

**Connie D. Weaver**
*Texas A&M University*

The McGraw-Hill Companies

TAXATION OF INDIVIDUALS AND BUSINESS ENTITIES, 2011 EDITION

Published by McGraw-Hill/Irwin, a business unit of The McGraw-Hill Companies, Inc., 1221 Avenue of the Americas, New York, NY, 10020. Copyright © 2011, 2010 by The McGraw-Hill Companies, Inc. All rights reserved. No part of this publication may be reproduced or distributed in any form or by any means, or stored in a database or retrieval system, without the prior written consent of The McGraw-Hill Companies, Inc., including, but not limited to, in any network or other electronic storage or transmission, or broadcast for distance learning.

Some ancillaries, including electronic and print components, may not be available to customers outside the United States.

This book is printed on acid-free paper.

1 2 3 4 5 6 7 8 9 0 DOW/DOW 1 0 9 8 7 6 5 4 3 2 1 0

ISBN 978-0-07-813670-2
MHID 0-07-813670-9
ISSN 1946-7745

Vice president and editor-in-chief: *Brent Gordon*
Editorial director: *Stewart Mattson*
Publisher: *Tim Vertovec*
Director of development: *Ann Torbert*
Senior development editor: *Daryl Horrocks*
Vice president and director of marketing: *Robin J. Zwettler*
Marketing director: *Sankha Basu*
Associate marketing manager: *Dean Karampelas*
Vice president of editing, design, and production: *Sesha Bolisetty*

Lead project manager: *Pat Frederickson*
Lead production supervisor: *Michael R. McCormick*
Lead designer: *Matthew Baldwin*
Senior photo research coordinator: *Jeremy Cheshareck*
Senior media project manager: *Susan Lombardi*
Senior media project manager: *Allison Souter*
Interior designer: *Laurie Entringer*
Cover image: ©*Getty Images*
Typeface: *10.5/12 Times New Roman*
Compositor: *Aptara®, Inc.*
Printer: *R. R. Donnelley*

www.mhhe.com

# Dedications

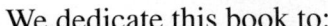

We dedicate this book to:

My children Braxton, Cameron, Ethan, and Lauren and to my parents Ray and Janet. Last but not least, to my wife Kim for allowing me to take up valuable kitchen space while I was working on the project. I love you all.

*Brian Spilker*

Wife Marilyn, daughters Margaret Lindley and Georgia, son Benjamin, and parents Bill and Linda.

*Ben Ayers*

JES, Tommy, Michelle, and Laura.

*John Robinson*

Family Jane, Mark, Sarah, and Jeff and to Professor James E. Wheeler, my mentor and friend.

*Ed Outslay*

Wife Anne, sons Matthew and Daniel, and daughters Whitney and Hayley.

*Ron Worsham*

Daughters Annika, Corinne, and Lina.

*John Barrick*

Husband Dan, son Travis, daughter Alix, and parents Charles and Helen.

*Connie Weaver*

# ABOUT THE AUTHORS

**Brian Spilker** (Ph.D., University of Texas at Austin, 1993) is the tax group coordinator and the Georgia White Professor in the School of Accountancy at Brigham Young University. He teaches taxation in the graduate and undergraduate programs at Brigham Young University. He received both B.S. and M.Acc. (tax emphasis) degrees from Brigham Young University before working as a tax consultant for Arthur Young & Co. (now Ernst & Young). After his professional work experience, Brian earned his Ph.D. at the University of Texas at Austin. In 1996, he was selected as one of two nationwide recipients of the Price Waterhouse Fellowship in Tax award. In 1998, he was a winner of the American Taxation Association and Arthur Andersen Teaching Innovation award for his work in the classroom; he has also been honored for his use of technology in the classroom at Brigham Young University. Brian researches issues relating to tax information search and professional tax judgment. His research has been published in such journals as *The Accounting Review, Organizational Behavior and Human Decision Processes, Journal of the American Taxation Association, Behavioral Research in Accounting, Journal of Accounting Education, Journal of Corporate Taxation,* and *Journal of Accountancy.*

**Ben Ayers** (Ph.D., University of Texas at Austin, 1996) holds the Earl Davis Chair in Taxation and is the Director of the J.M. Tull School of Accounting at the University of Georgia. He received a Ph.D. from the University of Texas at Austin and an M.T.A and B.S. from the University of Alabama. Prior to entering the Ph.D. program at the University of Texas, Professor Ayers was a tax manager at KPMG in Tampa, Florida, and a contract manager with Complete Health, Inc. in Birmingham, Alabama.

Professor Ayers teaches tax planning and research courses in the undergraduate and graduate programs at the University of Georgia. He is the recipient of 11 teaching awards at the school, college, and university levels, including the Richard B. Russell Undergraduate Teaching Award, the highest teaching honor for University of Georgia junior faculty members. Professor Ayers's current research interests include the effects of taxation on firm structure, mergers and acquisitions, and capital markets and the effects of accounting information on security returns. He has published articles in journals such as the *Accounting Review, Journal of Finance, Journal of Accounting and Economics, Contemporary Accounting Research, Review of Accounting Studies, Journal of Law and Economics, Journal of the American Taxation Association,* and *National Tax Journal.* Professor Ayers was the 1997 recipient of the American Accounting Association's Competitive Manuscript Award and the 2003 and 2008 recipient of the American Taxation Association's Outstanding Manuscript Award.

**John Robinson** (Ph.D., University of Michigan, 1981) is the C. Aubrey Smith Professor of Accounting in the McCombs School of Business at the University of Texas at Austin and is currently serving as an Academic Accounting fellow at the Securities and Exchange Commission's Division of Corporation Finance. Professor Robinson received his J.D. (*Cum Laude*) from the University of Michigan in 1979, and he was awarded his Ph.D. in accounting from the University of Michigan in 1981. Prior to joining the faculty at Texas in 1985, he taught at the University of Kansas where he was the Arthur Young Faculty Scholar from 1982–1984. John teaches introductory taxation, corporate tax, taxation of partnerships, and tax planning. He is the recipient of the Henry A. Bubb Award for Outstanding Teaching, the Texas Blazer's Faculty Excellence Award and the MPA Council Outstanding Professor Award. John conducts research in a broad variety of topics involving financial accounting, mergers and acquisitions, and the influence of taxes on financial structures and performance. His scholarly articles have appeared in *Accounting Review, Journal of Finance, National Tax Journal, Journal of Law and Economics, Journal of the American Taxation Association, The Journal of the American Bar Association,* and *The Journal of Taxation.* In addition, John was the editor of *The Journal of the American Taxation Association,* from 2002 through 2005, and he was a co-author of the articles honored with the 2003 and 2008 ATA Outstanding Manuscript Awards.

**Ed Outslay** (Ph.D., University of Michigan, 1981) is a professor of accounting and the Deloitte/ Michael Licata Endowed Professor of Taxation in the Department of Accounting and Information Systems at Michigan State University, where he has taught since 1981. He received a B.A. from Furman University in 1974 and an MBA and Ph.D. from the University of Michigan in 1977 and 1981. Ed currently teaches graduate classes in corporate taxation, multiunit enterprises, accounting for income taxes, and international taxation. In February 2003, Ed testified before the Senate Finance Committee on the Joint Committee on Taxation's Report on Enron Corporation. MSU has honored Ed with the Presidential Award for Outstanding Community Service, Distinguished Faculty Award, John D. Withrow Teacher-Scholar Award, Roland H. Salmonson Outstanding Teaching Award, Senior Class Council Distinguished Faculty Award, MSU Teacher-Scholar Award, and MSU's 1st Annual Curricular Service-Learning and Civic Engagement Award in 2008. Ed received the Ray M. Sommerfeld Outstanding Tax Educator Award in 2004 from the American Taxation Association. He has also received the ATA Outstanding Manuscript Award twice, the ATA/Deloitte Teaching Innovations Award, and the 2004 Distinguished Achievement in Accounting Education Award from the Michigan Association of CPAs. Ed has been recognized for his community service by the Greater Lansing Chapter of the Association of Government Accountants, the City of East Lansing (Crystal Award), and the East Lansing Education Foundation. He received a National Assistant Coach of the Year Award in 2003 from AFLAC and was named an Assistant High School Baseball Coach of the Year in 2002 by the Michigan High School Baseball Coaches Association.

## ABOUT THE AUTHORS

**Ron Worsham** (Ph.D., University of Florida, 1994) is an associate professor in the School of Accountancy at Brigham Young University. He teaches taxation in the graduate, undergraduate, MBA, and Executive MBA programs at Brigham Young University. He has also taught as a visiting professor at the University of Chicago. He received both B.S. and M.Acc. (tax emphasis) degrees from Brigham Young University before working as a tax consultant for Arthur Young & Co. (now Ernst & Young) in Dallas, Texas. While in Texas, he became licensed to practice as a CPA. After his professional work experience, Ron earned his Ph.D. at the University of Florida. He has been honored for outstanding innovation in the classroom at Brigham Young University. Ron has published academic research in the areas of taxpayer compliance and professional tax judgment. He has also published legal research in a variety of areas. His work has been published in such journals as *The Journal of the American Taxation Association, The Journal of International Taxation, The Tax Executive, The Journal of Accountancy,* and *Practical Tax Strategies.*

**John Barrick** (Ph.D., University of Nebraska at Lincoln, 1998) is currently an associate professor in the Marriott School at Brigham Young University. He served as an accountant at the United States Congress Joint Committee on Taxation for the 110th and 111th Congresses. He teaches taxation in the graduate and undergraduate programs at Brigham Young University. He received both B.S. and M.Acc. (tax emphasis) degrees from Brigham Young University before working as a tax consultant for Price Waterhouse (now PricewaterhouseCoopers). After his professional work experience, John earned his Ph.D. at the University of Nebraska at Lincoln. Professor Barrick was the 1998 recipient of the American Accounting Association, Accounting, Behavior, and Organization Section's Outstanding Dissertation Award. John researches issues relating to professional tax judgment and tax information search. His research has been published in such journals as *Organizational Behavior and Human Decision Processes, Contemporary Accounting Research,* and the *Journal of the American Taxation Association.*

**Connie Weaver** (Ph.D., Arizona State University, 1996) is an associate professor in the Mays Business School at Texas A&M University and a certified public accountant. She holds a Ph.D. from Arizona State University, a Masters of Professional Accounting from the University of Texas at Arlington, and a Bachelors of Science in Chemical Engineering from the University of Texas at Austin. Prior to obtaining her Ph.D., Professor Weaver was a tax manager at Ernst & Young in Dallas, TX.

Professor Weaver teaches introductory taxation in the undergraduate program at Texas A&M University. She has also taught undergraduates and graduate students at the University of Texas at Austin and the University of Wisconsin–Madison. She is the recipient of several teaching awards, including the 2006 American Taxation Association/Deloitte Teaching Innovations Award. Connie's current research interests include the effects of tax and financial incentives on corporate decisions and reporting. She has published articles in journals such as the *Accounting Review, Contemporary Accounting Research, Journal of the American Taxation Association,* and *Tax Notes.* She serves on the editorial board of *The Journal of the American Taxation Association* and was the 1997 recipient of the American Taxation Association/Price Waterhouse Outstanding Dissertation Award.

# TEACHING THE CODE IN CONTEXT

*The basic approach to teaching taxation hasn't changed in decades.* **Today's student deserves a new approach.** McGraw-Hill's Taxation of Individuals and Business Entities *is a bold and innovative new textbook that has already been adopted by over 100 schools across the country.*

*McGraw-Hill's Taxation* is designed to provide a unique, innovative, and engaging learning experience for students studying taxation. The breadth of the topical coverage, **the storyline approach to presenting the material,** the emphasis on the tax and nontax consequences of multiple parties involved in transactions, and the integration of financial and tax accounting topics make this book ideal for the modern tax curriculum.

> Students have a better understanding of the material when they get to class. This results in a more animated classroom experience and affords time to discuss the exceptions to the general rules.
>
> – Lynn C. Jones, University of North Florida

> A lot of thought and planning went into the structure and content of the text, and a great product was achieved. One of the most unique and helpful features is the common storyline throughout each chapter.
>
> – Raymond J. Shaffer, Youngstown State University

Since the first manuscript was written in 2005, 214 professors have contributed 190 book reviews, in addition to 13 focus groups and symposia. Throughout this preface, their comments on the book's organization, pedagogy, and unique features are a testament to the **grassroots nature of *Taxation*'s development.**

> This is a **very thorough tax textbook** covering many details about corporate tax. The authors include real life examples and several stories that make the **materials more understandable and "accessible" to students.**
>
> – Sonja Pippin, University of Nevada – Reno

# A MODERN APPROACH FOR TODAY'S STUDENT

> **This text is one of the best written textbooks I have ever read.** It covers the material using real world examples. It is easy to understand but provides the student with everything they need for the course. This textbook would make teaching the class easy.
>
> — Hughlene Burton, University of North Carolina – Charlotte

Key to this new tax series' remarkably positive reception are the five core precepts around which the text is built:

**1** **Storyline Approach:** Each chapter begins with a storyline that introduces a set of characters or a business entity facing specific tax-related situations. Each chapter's examples are related to the storyline, giving students the opportunities to **learn the code in context.**

**2** **Conversational Writing Style:** The authors took special care to write a textbook that fosters a friendly dialogue between the text and each individual student. The tone of the presentation is intentionally conversational—creating the impression of *speaking with* **the student,** as opposed to *teaching to* the student.

**3** **Superior Organization of Related Topics:** *McGraw-Hill's Taxation* takes a fresh approach to taxation by grouping related topics together in **theme chapters,** including separate chapters on home ownership, compensation, investments, and retirement savings & deferred compensation.

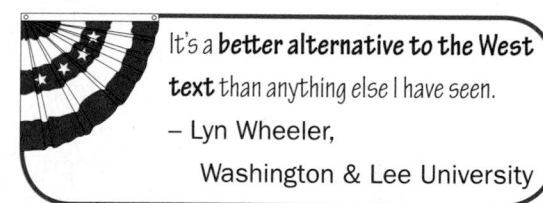

> It's a **better alternative to the West text** than anything else I have seen.
>
> — Lyn Wheeler,
> Washington & Lee University

**4** **Real World Focus:** Students learn best when they see how concepts are applied in the real world. For that reason, real-world examples and articles are included in **"Taxes in the Real World"** boxes throughout the book. These vignettes demonstrate current issues in taxation and show the relevance of tax issues in all areas of business.

**5** **Integrated Examples:** The examples used throughout the chapter relate directly to the storyline presented at the beginning of each chapter, so students become familiar with one set of facts and learn how to apply those facts to different scenarios. In addition to providing in-context examples, we provide **"What if"** scenarios within many examples to **illustrate how variations in the facts might or might not change the answers.**

> This is the most concise yet most comprehensive tax textbook I have ever seen. The text covers all pertinent information without going too deep into unimportant issues. Most importantly, it does so in a way that is **easily digestible for the reader and doesn't cause discouragement.**
>
> — Michaele Morrow,
> Northeastern University

# A STORYLINE APPROACH THAT WILL RESONATE WITH STUDENTS

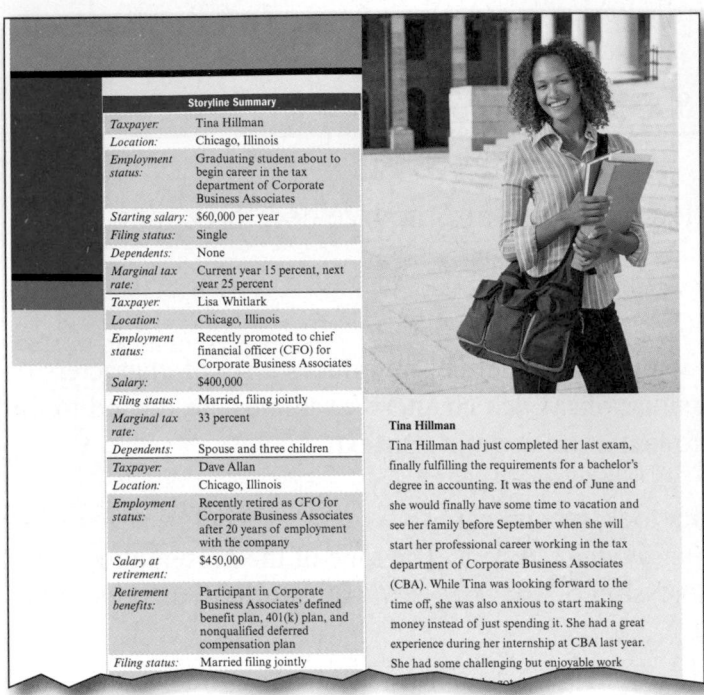

| Storyline Summary | |
|---|---|
| *Taxpayer:* | Tina Hillman |
| *Location:* | Chicago, Illinois |
| *Employment status:* | Graduating student about to begin career in the tax department of Corporate Business Associates |
| *Starting salary:* | $60,000 per year |
| *Filing status:* | Single |
| *Dependents:* | None |
| *Marginal tax rate:* | Current year 15 percent, next year 25 percent |
| *Taxpayer:* | Lisa Whitlark |
| *Location:* | Chicago, Illinois |
| *Employment status:* | Recently promoted to chief financial officer (CFO) for Corporate Business Associates |
| *Salary:* | $400,000 |
| *Filing status:* | Married, filing jointly |
| *Marginal tax rate:* | 33 percent |
| *Dependents:* | Spouse and three children |
| *Taxpayer:* | Dave Allan |
| *Location:* | Chicago, Illinois |
| *Employment status:* | Recently retired as CFO for Corporate Business Associates after 20 years of employment with the company |
| *Salary at retirement:* | $450,000 |
| *Retirement benefits:* | Participant in Corporate Business Associates' defined benefit plan, 401(k) plan, and nonqualified deferred compensation plan |
| *Filing status:* | Married filing jointly |

**Tina Hillman**

Tina Hillman had just completed her last exam, finally fulfilling the requirements for a bachelor's degree in accounting. It was the end of June and she would finally have some time to vacation and see her family before September when she will start her professional career working in the tax department of Corporate Business Associates (CBA). While Tina was looking forward to the time off, she was also anxious to start making money instead of just spending it. She had a great experience during her internship at CBA last year. She had some challenging but enjoyable work

Each chapter begins with a storyline that introduces a set of characters facing specific tax-related situations. This revolutionary approach to teaching tax emphasizes real people facing real tax dilemmas. Students learn to apply practical tax information to specific business and personal situations.

> **I really like the use of the chapter storylines** that tie together the different examples and exhibits. It definitely accomplishes the goal of providing a big picture background and allowing tax rules to be applied in real world settings.
>
> – Scott White,
> Lindenwood University

## Examples

Examples are the cornerstone of any textbook covering taxation. For this reason, *McGraw-Hill's Taxation* took special care to create clear and helpful examples that relate to the storyline of the chapter. Students learn to refer to the facts presented in the storyline and apply them to other scenarios—in this way, they build a greater base of knowledge through application. Many examples also include "What if?" scenarios that add more complexity to the example or explore related tax concepts.

**Example 8-13**

Rick is a calendar-year taxpayer. What tax year should Rick use to report income from his business Green Acres?

**Answer:** Calendar year. This is true even though Rick began his business in May of this year. He will calculate income and expense for his landscaping business over the calendar year and include the net business income from May through December of this year on Schedule C of his individual tax return.

**What If:** Suppose that Rick incorporated Green Acres at the time he began his business. What tax year could Green Acres adopt?

**Answer:** If Green Acres was operated as a C corporation, it could elect a calendar year-end, a fiscal year-end, or a 52/53 week year-end. If it were an S corporation, it likely would have a calendar year-end.

> The **case study approach is excellent** as you follow the taxpayers through the chapters.
>
> – Irwin Uhr,
> Hunter College

# THE PEDAGOGY YOUR STUDENTS NEED TO PUT THE CODE IN CONTEXT

## Taxes in the Real World

Taxes in the Real World are short boxes used throughout the book to demonstrate the real-world use of tax concepts. Current articles on tax issues, real-world application of chapter-specific tax rules, and short vignettes on popular news in tax are some of the issues covered in Taxes in the Real World boxes.

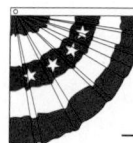

**Best I've seen in giving real world explanations** and examples that apply the complex IRS rules.

— James E. Racic, Lakeland Community College

plans, defined contribution plans shift the funding responsibility and investment risk from the employer to the employee.

| Taxes in the Real World | Retirement Benefits |

**Pension Losses Could Whack 2009 Corporate Profits**
*Time in partnership with CNN*
**By Steven Gray**

In 2008, the Standard & Poor's index declined 37 percent. Because employers with defined benefit plans (pension plans) tend to invest heavily in equities, the decline in the stock market took its toll on funds employers who have invested to fund the pension plans. In fact, the pension plans of the country's largest 1,500 companies lost more than $400 billion in 2008. Further, due to decreasing returns on Treasury bonds, the pension funding requirements (and financial accounting pension expense) for many companies is dramatically increasing. In 2008, in the aggregate, companies were required to contribute approximately $10 billion to their defined benefit plans. Estimates for 2009 suggest that these companies will be required to contribute approximately $70 billion to fund their pension plans.

Nevertheless, employees with defined benefit plans are not subject to the same level of investment risk as employees invested primarily in defined contribution plans such as 401(k) plans. The reason? When the market tanks, employees invested in 401(k)s bear the entire loss. However, employers are still required to pay employees retirement benefits even when the balance in employer pension funds drop. Further, even when an economic downturn causes an employer to become bankrupt, the retirement benefits of participants in defined benefit plans are still somewhat protected by the federal government's Pension Benefits Guaranty Corporation.

Employers may provide different types of defined contribution plans such as 401(k) (used by for-profit companies), 403(b) plans (used by nonprofit organizations,

## Key Facts

The Key Facts provide quick synopses of the critical pieces of information presented throughout each chapter.

### Roth 401(k) Plans

Employers that provide **traditional 401(k)** plans to employees may also provide **Roth 401(k)** plans. As we discuss below, employee tax consequences for Roth 401(k) plans differ from tax consequences of other traditional defined contribution plans.

When employers provide a Roth 401(k) plan, *employees* may elect to contribute to the Roth 401(k) *instead of or in addition to* contributing to a traditional 401(k) plan. However, *employer* contributions to an employee's 401(k) account must go to the employee's *traditional* 401(k) account rather than the employee's Roth 401(k) account. Consequently, the balance in an employee's Roth 401(k) account must consist of only the employee's contributions and the earnings on those contributions. Because employers providing Roth 401(k) plans to employees are not allowed to contribute to the Roth plans, these employers are required to maintain traditional 401(k) accounts for each employee participating in the Roth 401(k) plan.

**THE KEY FACTS**

**Roth 401(k) Defined Contribution Plans**

- **Employees but not employers may contribute.**
  · Employers contribute to traditional 401(k).
- **Contributions are not deductible.**
  · Employees contribute after-tax dollars.
  · Same contribution limits as traditional 401(k) plans.

## Exhibits

Today's students are visual learners, and *McGraw-Hill's Taxation* delivers with a textbook that makes appropriate use of charts, diagrams, and tabular demonstrations of key material.

taxes are levied on individuals (maximum rate of 35 percent), corporations (maximum rate of 39 percent), estates (maximum rate of 35 percent), and trusts (maximum rate of 35 percent). As Exhibit 1-4 illustrates, the individual income tax represents the largest source of federal tax revenues followed by employment taxes and the corporate income tax. We discuss each of these taxes in greater detail later in the text.

**EXHIBIT 1-4    U.S. Federal Tax Revenues**

- Excise taxes 2.1%
- Estate & gift taxes 1.2%
- Corporate income tax 13.0%
- Individual income tax 45.8%
- Employment taxes 37.9%

Source: Internal Revenue Service

U.S. government.
· Employment taxes consist of the Old Age, Survivors, and Disability Insurance (OASDI) tax, commonly called the Social Security tax, and the Medical Health Insurance (MHI) tax known as the Medicare tax.
· Unemployment taxes fund temporary unemployment benefits for individuals terminated from their jobs without cause.
- Excise taxes
  · Third largest group of taxes imposed by the U.S. government.
  · Levied on the quantity of products sold.
- Estate and gift taxes
  · Levied on the fair market values of wealth transfers upon death or by gift.

Spilker's text adds **examples that flow through the chapter** with "Key Facts" boxes.

— Debra Oden,
Missouri State University

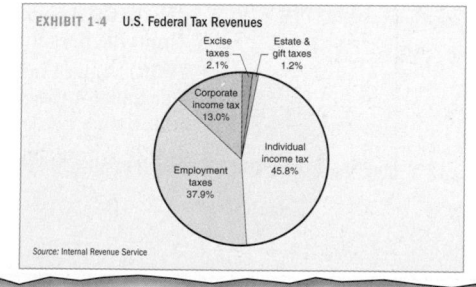

Spilker's use of examples immediately following the concept is a **great way to reinforce the concepts.**

— Karen Wisniewski, County College of Morris

# PRACTICE MAKES PERFECT WITH A...

## Summary

**SUMMARY**

**LO1** Describe the tax and nontax aspects of employer-provided defined benefit plans from both the employer's and employee's perspective.

- Benefits are determined based on years of service and salary. The maximum annual benefit is capped and adjusted upward annually for inflation.
- Benefits vest over time using either a five-year cliff or seven-year graded vesting schedule.
- Employers deduct cash contributions to fund the plan and employees treat cash distributions as ordinary income in the year received.
- Employers bear market risk with defined benefit plans.
- Premature distribution and minimum distribution penalties don't typically apply to defined benefit distributions.
- Because of the high cost of funding and maintaining defined benefit plans, they are waning in popularity.

**LO2** Explain and determine the tax consequences associated with employer-provided defined contribution plans, including traditional 401(k) and Roth 401(k) plans.

**Summary**

A unique feature of *McGraw-Hill's Taxation* is the end of chapter summary organized around learning objectives. Each objective has a brief, bullet-point summary that covers the major topics and concepts for that chapter, including references to critical exhibits and examples.

All end of chapter material is tied to learning objectives:

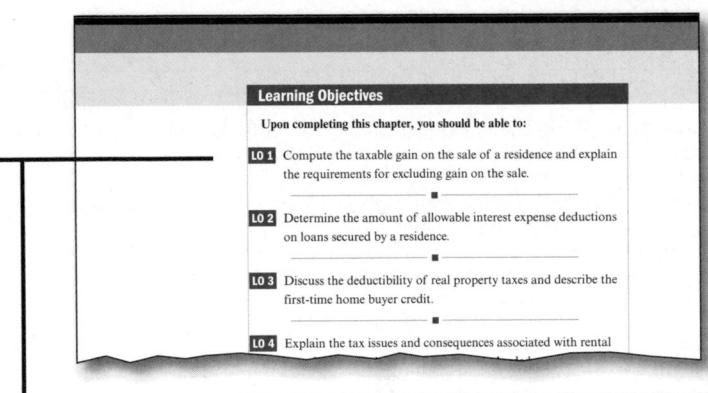

**Learning Objectives**

Upon completing this chapter, you should be able to:

**LO 1** Compute the taxable gain on the sale of a residence and explain the requirements for excluding gain on the sale.

**LO 2** Determine the amount of allowable interest expense deductions on loans secured by a residence.

**LO 3** Discuss the deductibility of real property taxes and describe the first-time home buyer credit.

**LO 4** Explain the tax issues and consequences associated with rental

> The readability is excellent and all of the students really like the continued story pattern for examples throughout each chapter and the text. **The students like it much more than the [previous] text used.**
> – Chuck Pier, Angelo State University

## DISCUSSION QUESTIONS

1. **(LO1)** Name three factors that determine w a tax return.
2. **(LO1)** Benita is concerned that she will not by April 15. Can she request an extension to she do so? Assuming she requests an extens could file her return this year without penal
3. **(LO1)** Agua Linda, Inc., is a calendar-year due date for the corporate tax return? What falls on a Saturday?
4. **(LO2)** Approximately what percentage of t

**Questions** are provided for each of the major concepts in each chapter, providing students with an opportunity to review key parts of the chapter and answer evocative questions about what they have learned. Each question is linked to a learning objective.

> [The] end of chapter material relates to the text of each chapter; the chapter coverage emphasizes only the most important concepts for each topic. **Chapter summary eliminates need for study guide.**
> – David B. Bojarsky, California State University, Long Beach

# ...WIDE VARIETY OF ASSIGNMENT MATERIAL

**Problems** are designed to test the comprehension of more complex topics. Each problem at the end of the chapter is tied to one of that chapter's learning objectives, with multiple problems for critical topics.

> **PROBLEMS**
>
> 54. **(LO1)** Whitney received $75,000 of taxable income in 2009. All of the income was salary from her employer. What is her income tax liability in each of the following alternative situations?
>    a. She files under the single filing status.
>    b. She files a joint tax return with her spouse. Together their taxable income is $75,000.

> It is a great book that will help students develop the tax foundation they need. Several of my **students last year commented that the storyline, writing style, and examples made tax concepts much easier to understand** than other tax textbooks they had used.
> — Anne Christensen, Montana State University

**Research Problems** are special problems throughout the end of the chapter's assignment material. These require students to do both basic and

> research
>
> 47. **(LO2)** Jennifer has been living in her current principal residence for three years. Six months ago Jennifer decided that she would like to purchase a second home near a beach so she can vacation there for part of the year. Despite her best efforts, Jennifer has been unable to find what she is looking for. Consequently, Jennifer recently decided to change plans. She purchased a parcel of land for $200,000 with the intention of building her second home on the property. To acquire the land, she borrowed $200,000 secured by the land. Jennifer would

more complex research on topics outside of the scope of the book. Each Research Problem includes an icon to differentiate it from regular problems.

> The questions and problems associated with the text are good and of varying levels. There are also **more questions and problems to choose from.**
> — Laurie Hagberg, Trident Technical College

**Planning Problems** are another unique set of problems, also located at the end of the chapter's assignment material. These require students to test their tax planning skills after

> home but doesn't plan to live in the home for 37 months?
>
> planning
>
> 48. **(LO2)** Rajiv and Laurie Amin are recent college graduates looking to purchase a new home. They are purchasing a $200,000 home by paying $20,000 down and borrowing the other $180,000 with a 30-year loan secured by the home. The Amins have the option of (1) paying no discount points on the loan and paying interest at 8 percent or (2) paying one discount point on the loan and paying interest of 7.5 percent. Both loans require the Amins to make interest-only payments for the first five years. Unless otherwise stated, the

covering the chapter's topics. Each Planning Problem includes an icon to differentiate it from regular problems.

**Comprehensive and Tax Return Problems** address multiple concepts in a single problem. Comprehensive problems are ideal for cumulative topics; for this reason, they are located at the end of all chapters. In the end of book Appendix C, we include Tax Return Problems that cover multiple chapters.

> **COMPREHENSIVE PROBLEMS**
>
> 40. Marc and Michelle are married and earned salaries this year (2009) of $64,000 and $12,000, respectively. In addition to their salaries, they received interest of $350 from municipal bonds and $500 from corporate bonds. Marc and Michelle also paid $2,500 of qualifying moving expenses, and Marc paid alimony to a prior spouse in the amount of $1,500. Marc and Michelle have a 10-year-old son, Matthew, who lived with them throughout the entire year. Thus, Marc and Michelle are allowed to claim a $1,000 child tax credit for Matthew. Marc and Michelle paid $6,000 of expenditures that qualify as itemized deductions and they had a total of $5,500 in federal income taxes withheld from their paychecks during the course of the year.
>    a. What is Marc and Michelle's gross income?
>    b. What is Marc and Michelle's adjusted gross income?
>    c. What is the total amount of Marc and Michelle's deductions *from* AGI?

# A Logical Organization

McGraw-Hill's *Taxation of Individuals* is organized to maximize topical efficiency and to emphasize topics that are most important to undergraduates taking their first tax course. The first three chapters provide an introduction to taxation and then carefully guide students through tax research and tax planning. Part II discusses the fundamental elements of individual income tax, starting with the tax formula in Chapter 4 and then proceeding to more depth on individual topics in Chapters 5–7. Part III then discusses tax issues associated with business and investment activities. On the business side, it addresses business income and deductions, accounting methods, and tax consequences associated with purchasing assets, property dispositions (sales, trades, or other dispositions). For investments it covers portfolio-type investments such as stocks and bonds and business investments including loss limitations associated with these investments. Part IV is unique among tax textbooks; this section combines related tax issues for compensation, retirement savings, and home ownership. The storylines in all of these chapters show how realistic individuals and business owners benefit from a clear understanding of the tax code.

Part I:  Introduction to Taxation
1. An Introduction to Tax
2. Tax Compliance, the IRS, and Tax Authorities
3. Tax Planning Strategies and Related Limitations

Part II: Basic Individual Taxation
4. Individual Income Tax Overview
5. Gross Income and Exclusions
6. Individual Deductions
7. Individual Income Tax Computation and Tax Credits

Part III: Business and Investment–Related Transactions
8. Business Income, Deductions, and Accounting Methods
9. Property Acquisition and Cost Recovery
10. Property Dispositions
11. Investments

Part IV: Specialized Topics
12. Compensation
13. Retirement Savings and Deferred Compensation
14. Tax Consequences of Home Ownership

# Makes Learning Efficient

*McGraw-Hill's Taxation of Business Entities* begins with the process for determining gross income and deductions for businesses, and the tax consequences associated with purchasing assets, property dispositions (sales, trades, or other dispositions). Part II provides a comprehensive overview of entities, and the formation, reorganization and liquidation of corporations. Unique to this series is a complete chapter on accounting for income taxes, which provides a primer on the basics of calculating the income tax provision. Included in the narrative is a discussion of temporary and permanent differences and their impact on a company's book "effective tax rate." Part III provides a detailed discussion of partnerships and S corporations. The last part of the book covers state and local taxation, multinational taxation and transfer taxes and wealth planning.

Part I: Business and Investment–Related Transactions
1. Business Income, Deductions, and Accounting Methods
2. Property Acquisition and Cost Recovery
3. Property Dispositions

Part II: Entity Overview and Taxation of C Corporations
4. Entities Overview
5. Corporate Operations
6. Accounting for Income Taxes
7. Corporate Taxation: Nonliquidating Distributions
8. Corporate Taxation: Formation, Reorganization, and Liquidation

Part III: Taxation of Flow-Through Entities
9. Forming and Operating Partnerships
10. Dispositions of Partnership Interests and Partnership Distributions
11. S Corporations

Part IV: Multijurisdictional Taxation and Transfer Taxes
12. State and Local Taxes
13. The U.S. Taxation of Multinational Transactions
14. Transfer Taxes and Wealth Planning

*McGraw-Hill's Taxation of Individuals and Business Entities* covers all chapters included in the two split volumes in one convenient volume.

# AUTHOR-WRITTEN SUPPLEMENTS ENSURE QUALITY AND CONSISTENCY

The authors write all of the supplements for *McGraw-Hill's Taxation,* including the Testbank, Solutions Manual, PowerPoints® and Instructor's Manual. Each supplement has been reviewed by the author team to ensure consistency with the text material and accuracy. With the author's personal involvement in each supplement, you can be assured that *McGraw-Hill's Taxation's* supplements are the same high quality as the book.

## Instructor's Resource Manual

This manual provides for each chapter: (a) a chapter overview; (b) a comprehensive lecture outline; (c) a variety of suggested class activities (real-world, ethics, professional development activities including research, analysis, communication and judgment, and others); and (d) an assignment chart indicating topic, learning objective, and difficulty for every question and problem.

## Solutions Manual

The Solutions Manual includes detailed solutions for every question, problem, and comprehensive problem in the text.

## Testbank

Written by the authors, this comprehensive Testbank contains over 2,500 true/false questions, multiple-choice questions, and problems.

## PowerPoints®

The PowerPoint® slides are available on the Online Learning Center (OLC). Separate sets of PowerPoints® are available for instructors and students.

## TaxACT®

*McGraw-Hill's Taxation* can be packaged with tax software from TaxACT, one of the leading preparation software companies in the market today. New to the 2011 edition is the availability of both Individuals and Business Entities software, including the 1040 forms and TaxACT Preparer's Business 3-Pack (with forms 1065, 1120, and 1120S).

TaxACT.

# ONLINE LEARNING OPPORTUNITIES THAT ACCOMMODATE A VARIETY OF LEARNING STYLES
## www.mhhe.com/spilker2011

Today's students are every bit as comfortable using a Web browser as they are reading a printed book. That's why we offer an Online Learning Center (OLC) that follows *McGraw-Hill's Taxation* chapter-by-chapter. It requires no building or maintenance on your part and is ready to go the moment you and your students type in the URL. You and your students can access the OLC Web site for such benefits as:

- Self-grading quizzes
- Kaplan CPA Simulations
- Tax forms
- Student PowerPoint® Presentations
- Text updates

- Instructor's Resource Manual
- Solutions Manual
- Instructor PowerPoint® Presentations
- EZ Test
- Sample syllabi

## ASSURANCE OF LEARNING READY

Many educational institutions today are focused on the notion of *assurance of learning,* an important element of some accreditation standards. *McGraw-Hill's Taxation* is designed specifically to support your assurance of learning initiatives with a simple, yet powerful solution.

Each test bank question for *McGraw-Hill's Taxation* maps to a specific chapter learning objective listed in the text. You can use our test bank software, EZ Test and EZ Test Online, or *Connect Accounting* to easily query for learning objectives that directly relate to the learning objectives for your course. You can then use the reporting features of EZ Test to aggregate student results in similar fashion, making the collection and presentation of assurance of learning data simple and easy.

## AACSB STATEMENT

The McGraw-Hill Companies is a proud corporate member of AACSB International. Understanding the importance and value of AACSB accreditation, *McGraw-Hill's Taxation* recognizes the curricula guidelines detailed in the AACSB standards for business accreditation by connecting selected questions in the text and the test bank to the six general knowledge and skill guidelines in the AACSB standards.

The statements contained in *McGraw-Hill's Taxation* are provided only as a guide for the users of this textbook. The AACSB leaves content coverage and assessment within the purview of individual schools, the mission of the school, and the faculty. While *McGraw-Hill's Taxation* and the teaching package make no claim of any specific AACSB qualification or evaluation, we have within *McGraw-Hill's Taxation* labeled selected questions according to the six general knowledge and skills areas.

## McGRAW-HILL CUSTOMER CARE CONTACT INFORMATION

At McGraw-Hill, we understand that getting the most from new technology can be challenging. That's why our services don't stop after you purchase our products. You can e-mail our Product Specialists 24 hours a day to get product-training online. Or you can search our knowledge bank of Frequently Asked Questions on our support Web site. For Customer Support, call **800-331-5094**, e-mail **hmsupport@mcgraw-hill.com,** or visit **www.mhhe.com/support.** One of our Technical Support Analysts will be able to assist you in a timely fashion.

## KAPLAN SIMULATIONS

Apply the knowledge you've gained through *McGraw-Hill's Taxation* with CPA Review simulations from Kaplan and McGraw-Hill Higher Education! Each CPA simulation demonstrates taxation concepts in a Web-based interface, identical to that used in the actual CPA exam. CPA simulations are found in the homework material after the very last case in selected chapters in your book.

# McGRAW-HILL *CONNECT ACCOUNTING*

## Less Managing. More Teaching. Greater Learning.

McGraw-Hill *Connect Accounting* is an online assignment and assessment solution that connects students with the tools and resources they'll need to achieve success.

McGraw-Hill *Connect Accounting* helps prepare students for their future by enabling faster learning, more efficient studying, and higher retention of knowledge.

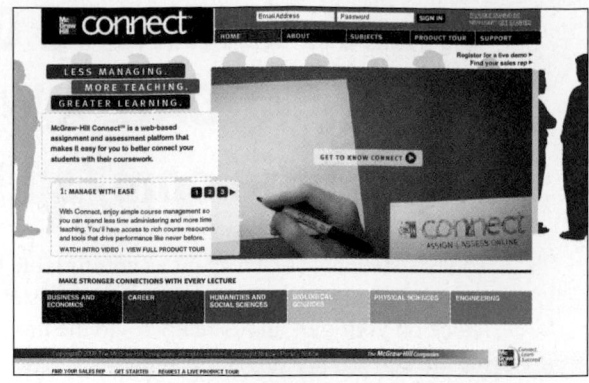

**McGraw-Hill *Connect Accounting* features**  *Connect Accounting* offers a number of powerful tools and features to make managing assignments easier, so faculty can spend more time teaching. With *Connect Accounting,* students can engage with their coursework anytime and anywhere, making the learning process more accessible and efficient. *Connect Accounting* offers you the features described below.

**Simple assignment management**  With *Connect Accounting,* creating assignments is easier than ever, so you can spend more time teaching and less time managing. The assignment management function enables you to:

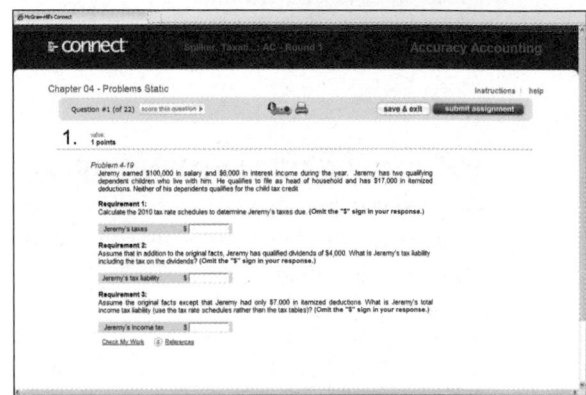

- Create and deliver assignments easily with selectable end-of-chapter questions and test bank items.
- Streamline lesson planning, student progress reporting, and assignment grading to make classroom management more efficient than ever.
- Go paperless with the eBook and online submission and grading of student assignments.

**Smart grading**  When it comes to studying, time is precious. *Connect Accounting* helps students learn more efficiently by providing feedback and practice material when they need it, where they need it. When it comes to teaching, your time also is precious. The grading function enables you to:

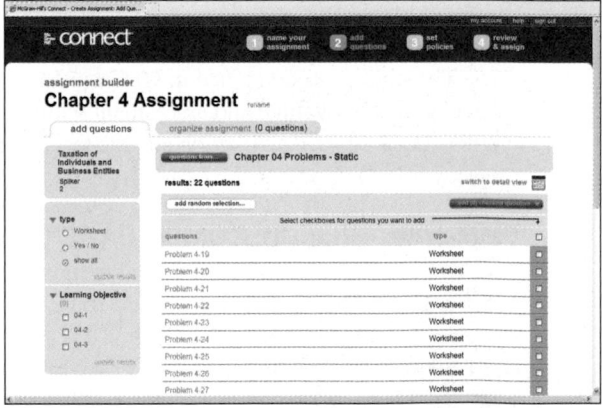

- Have assignments scored automatically, giving students immediate feedback on their work and side-by-side comparisons with correct answers.
- Access and review each response; manually change grades or leave comments for students to review.
- Reinforce classroom concepts with practice tests and instant quizzes.

**Instructor library**  The *Connect Accounting* Instructor Library is your repository for additional resources to improve student engagement in and out of class. You can select and use any asset that enhances your lecture. The *Connect Accounting* Instructor Library includes:

- *eBook*
- *PowerPoints*
- *Online quizzes*

**Student study center**   The *Connect Accounting* Student Study Center is the place for students to access additional resources. The Student Study Center:

- Offers students quick access to lectures, practice materials, eBooks, and more.
- Provides instant practice material and study questions, easily accessible on the go.

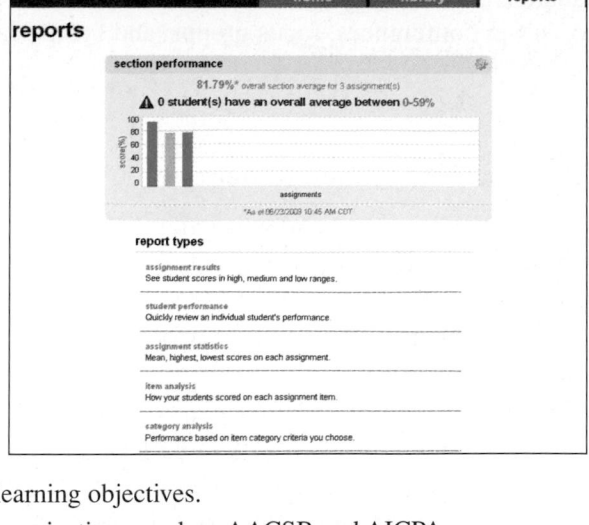

**Student progress tracking**   *Connect Accounting* keeps instructors informed about how each student, section, and class is performing, allowing for more productive use of lecture and office hours. The progress-tracking function enables you to:

- View scored work immediately and track individual or group performance with assignment and grade reports.
- Access an instant view of student or class performance relative to learning objectives.
- Collect data and generate reports required by many accreditation organizations, such as AACSB and AICPA.

**McGraw-Hill *Connect Plus Taxation***   McGraw-Hill reinvents the textbook learning experience for the modern student with *Connect Plus Taxation*. A seamless integration of an eBook and *Connect Accounting*, *Connect Plus Taxation* provides all of the *Connect Accounting* features plus the following:

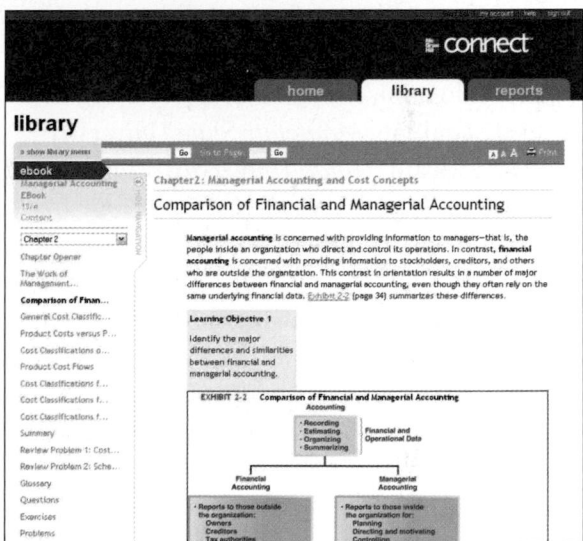

- An integrated eBook, allowing for anytime, anywhere access to the textbook.
- Dynamic links between the problems or questions you assign to your students and the location in the eBook where that problem or question is covered.
- A powerful search function to pinpoint and connect key concepts in a snap.

In short, *Connect Accounting* offers you and your students powerful tools and features that optimize your time and energies, enabling you to focus on course content, teaching, and student learning. *Connect Accounting* also offers a wealth of content resources for both instructors and students. This state-of-the-art, thoroughly tested system supports you in preparing students for the world that awaits.

For more information about Connect, go to **www.mcgrawhillconnect.com,** or contact your local McGraw-Hill sales representative.

## TEGRITY CAMPUS: LECTURES 24/7

Tegrity Campus is a service that makes class time available 24/7 by automatically capturing every lecture in a searchable format for students to review when they study and complete assignments. With a simple one-click start-and-stop process, you capture all computer screens and corresponding audio. Students can replay any part of any class with easy-to-use browser-based viewing on a PC or Mac.

Educators know that the more students can see, hear, and experience class resources, the better they learn. In fact, studies prove it. With Tegrity Campus, students quickly recall key moments by using Tegrity Campus's unique search feature. This search helps students efficiently find what they need, when they need it, across an entire semester of class recordings. Help turn all your students' study time into learning moments immediately supported by your lecture.

To learn more about Tegrity watch a 2-minute Flash demo at **http://tegritycampus.mhhe.com.**

## A HEARTFELT THANKS TO THE MANY VOICES WHO SHAPED THIS BOOK

The version of the book you are reading would not be the same book without the valuable suggestions, keen insights, and constructive criticisms of the list of reviewers below. Each professor listed here contributed in substantive ways to the organization of chapters, coverage of topics, and the use of pedagogy. We are grateful to them for taking the time to read chapters or attend reviewer conferences, focus groups, and symposia in support of the development for the book:

### 2010 and 2011 Edition Reviewers

Robert Adkins, *Clark State Community College*

Arthur Agulnek, *University of Texas at Dallas*

Robert Ahonen, *University of Akron*

Akinloye Akindayomi, *University of Massachusetts – Dartmouth*

Glenn Alan, *University of Arizona*

Susan Albring, *University of South Florida*

Raquel Alexander, *University of Kansas*

David L. Allen, *Harding University*

Amy An, *University of Iowa – Iowa City*

Mary Anderson, *University of Southern Mississippi*

Susan Anderson, *Appalachian State University*

Walter Antognini, *Pace University*

Frank J. Aquilino, *Montclair State University*

A. David Austill, *Union University – Jackson*

Jeff Austin, *Southern Methodist University*

Timothy Baker, *California State University – Fresno*

Anthony Basile, *Hofstra University*

Terry W. Bechtel, *Northwestern State University*

Kathy Black, *Utah Valley State College*

Robert Blatz, *University of Michigan – Dearborn*

Leon Blazey, *Case Western Reserve University*

Israel Blumenfrucht, *Queens College*

David Bojarsky, *California State University*

Patrick Borja, *Citrus College*

Jesse Boyles, *University of Florida – Gainesville*

Darryl Brown, *Illinois State University*

Michael Brown, *University of Missouri*

Ronald Bruce, *Gwynedd-Mercy College*

Hughlene Burton, *University of North Carolina – Charlotte*

Sandra Callaghan, *Texas Christian University*

Julia M. Camp, *University of Massachusetts – Boston*

Alan Campbell, *Troy University*

Lloyd Carroll, *Borough of Manhattan Community College*

A. J. Castillo, *West Chester University of Pennsylvania*

Valrie Chambers, *Texas A&M University – Corpus Christi*

Anne Christensen, *Montana State University*

Cathy Claiborne, *University of Colorado – Colorado Springs*

Roy Clemons, *Florida Atlantic University – Boca Raton*

Robert Clovey, *York College*

Robert Cockrum, *University of South Florida – Sarasota*

Ann Burstein Cohen, *University at Buffalo (SUNY)*

Lisa Cole, *Johnson County Community College*

Caroline K. Craig, *Illinois State University*

Terry L. Crain, *University of Oklahoma*

Stephen Crow, *California State University – Sacramento*

Anthony Curatola, *Drexel University*

Charles D'Alessandro, *Dowling College*

John Darcy, *University of Texas Pan American*

Alan Davis, *Truman State University*

James DeSimpelare, *University of Michigan – Ann Arbor*

John Dexter, *Northwood University*

Vicky Dominguez, *College of Southern Nevada – North Las Vegas*

Melanie James Earles, *Tennessee Tech University*

Rafi Efrat, *California State University – Northridge*

Elizabeth Ekmekjian, *William Paterson University*

Charles Enis, *Penn State University – University Park*

Allison L. Evans, *Wake Forest University*

Michael Fagan, *Raritan Valley Community College*

Ramon Fernandez, *University of Saint Thomas*

Philip R. Fink, *University of Toledo*

Gary Fleischman, *University of Wyoming – Laramie*

Ira Kaye Frashier, *Eastern New Mexico University*

Peter Frischmann, *Idaho State University*

Stephen Gara, *Drake University*

Greg Geisler, *University of Missouri*

Mesfin Genanaw, *Houston Community College – Central College*

Steve Gill, *San Diego State University*

Ruth Goran, *Northeastern Illinois University*

Diane Green, *Sam Houston State University*

Sanjay Gupta, *Arizona State University*

Roger W. Guyette, *University of West Florida*

Laurie Hagberg, *Trident Technical College*

Ronald W. Halsac, *Community College Allegheny County*

Marcye Hampton, *University of Central Florida*

Jerry W. Hanwell, *Robert Morris University*

Phil Harper, *Middle Tennessee State University*

Dave Harris, *Syracuse University*

Charles Hartman, *Cedarville University*

John W. Hatcher, *Purdue University*

Keith Hendrick, *DeKalb Technical College*

Cherie Hennig, *University of North Carolina – Wilmington*

Daniel Holder, *University of Illinois – Champaign*

William C. Hood, *Central Michigan University*

Bambi A. Hora, *University of Central Oklahoma*

Jana Hosmer, *Blue Ridge Community College*

Kim Hurt, *Central Community College – Grand Island*

Patrice Johnson, *University of Georgia*

Anne Jones, *University of Massachusetts*

Lynn C. Jones, *University of North Florida*

Jessica Jourdan, *Georgia Southwestern State University*

Susan Jurney, *University of Alabama – Tuscaloosa*

Elliot Kamlet, *Binghamton University*

John E. Karayan, *California Polytechnic State University*

Jocelyn Kauffunger, *University of Pittsburgh – Pittsburgh*

Carl Keller, *Indiana University/Purdue University – Ft. Wayne*

Connie Kertz, *Emory University*

Kim Key, *Auburn University – Auburn*

Dieter Kiefer, *American River College*

Charles Konkol, *University of Wisconsin – Milwaukee*

Paul Krazeise, *Bellarmine University*

Bud Lacy, *Oklahoma State University*

Teresa Lang, *Columbus State University*

David Lanning, *Tompkins Cortland Community College*

Ernest R. Larkins, *Georgia State University*

Melissa P. Larson, *Brigham Young University*

Sharon Lassar, *Florida Atlantic University*

William Lathen, *Boise State University*

Leonard Lauricella, *Montclair State University*

Rick Leaman, *University of Denver*

Christy Lefevers-Land, *Catawba Valley Community College*

Alvin Lieberman, *University of Akron*

Teresa Lightner, *University of North Texas*

Bruce Lindsey, *Genesee Community College*

Avi Liveson, *Hunter College*

Mariah Lynch, *University of South Carolina*

Richard Malamud, *California State University – Dominguez Hills*

Linda Mallory, *Central Virginia Community College*

Kate Mantzke, *Northern Illinois University*

Bobbie Martindale, *Dallas Baptist University*

Kathleen Masterson, *Flagler College*

Bruce W. McClain, *Cleveland State University*

Debra McGilsky, *Central Michigan University*

Janet Meade, *University of Houston*

Gerard Mellnick, *Schoolcraft College*

Don Mercier, *Regis University*

Melicent Middlebrook, *Trident Technical College*

Valerie C. Milliron, *California State University – Chico*

Lillian F. Mills, *University of Arizona*

Alfonsina Minchella, *Roxbury Community College*

Marc Mittleman, *William Paterson University*

Walter Montgomery, *Alabama State University*

Tom Moore, *Georgia College & State University*

Michaele Morrow, *Northeastern University*

Bill Moser, *University of Missouri*

Patricia Mounce, *University of Central Arkansas*

Brigitte W. Muehlmann, *Suffolk University*

Cathryn Nash, *DeKalb Technical College*

Adolph Neidermeyer, *West Virginia University – Morgantown*

Richard Newmark, *University of Northern Colorado*

Anthony Newton, *Highline Community College*

Quoc Nguyen, *Raritan Valley Community College*
Nancy Nichols, *James Madison University*
Mark Nixon, *Bentley University*
Patricia Nodoushani, *University of Hartford*
Tracy Noga, *Bentley College*
Priscilla O'Clock, *Xavier University*
Debra Oden, *Missouri State University*
Thomas C. Omer, *Texas A&M University*
Simon R. Pearlman, *California State University – Long Beach*
Dennis Pelzek, *Waukesha County Technical*
Deb Petrizzo, *Franklin University*
Chuck Pier, *Texas State University*
Sonja Pippin, *University of Nevada – Reno*
J. Kent Poff, *North Georgia College*
Thomas Purcell, *Creighton University*
James E. Racic, *Lakeland Community College*
David W. Randolph, *University of Dayton*
Tommy Raulston, *Midwestern State University*
Ian J. Redpath, *Canisius College*
Ramon P. Rodriguez Jr., *Southern Illinois University – Carbondale*
Patrick Rogan, *Cosumnes River College*
Tim Rupert, *Northeastern University*
R. Wayne R. Saubert, *Radford University*
Michael Schadewald, *University of Wisconsin – Milwaukee*
Paul Schloemer, *Ashland University*
Ananth Seetharaman, *Saint Louis University*
Mark Sellner, *University of Minnesota – Minneapolis*
Ray Shaffer, *Youngstown State University*
J. Riley Shaw, *University of Mississippi*
James Shimko, *Sinclair Community College*
Paul Shoemaker, *University of Nebraska – Lincoln*
Harold Silverman, *Bridgewater State College*
Georgi Smatrakalev, *Florida Atlantic University – Ft. Lauderdale*
Lucia Smeals, *Georgia State University*
Gene Smith, *Eastern New Mexico University*

Jim Smith, *University of San Diego*
Keith E. Smith, *George Washington University*
Pamela Smith, *University of Texas – San Antonio*
Will Snyder, *San Diego State University – San Diego*
Andrew Somers, *University of California – San Diego*
Susan Sorensen, *University of Houston – Clear Lake*
Pamela A. Spikes, *University of Central Arkansas*
Roxanne Spindle, *Virginia Commonwealth University*
Joe Standridge, *Sonoma State University*
Douglas Stives, *Monmouth University*
W. Joey Styron, *Augusta State University*
Judyth Swingen, *University of Arkansas – Little Rock*
Ulysses Taylor, *Fayetteville State University*
William D. Terando, *Iowa State University*
D. James Tiburzi, *University of Missouri*
James Trebby, *Marquette University*
Karen Trott, *University of North Carolina – Chapel Hill*
Ski VanderLaan, *Delta College*
Anupama Varadharajan, *University of Illinois – Champaign*
George R. Violette, *University of Southern Maine*
Sharon Walters, *Morehead State University*
Mark Washburn, *University of Texas – Tyler*
Richard Weber, *Michigan State University – East Lansing*
Len Weld, *Valdosta State University*
Delores Wellman, *Saint Ambrose University*
Wayne Wells, *St. Cloud State University*
Lyn F. Wheeler, *Washington & Lee University*
Scott White, *Lindenwood University*
Marvin Williams, *University of Houston – Downtown*
Karen Wisniewski, *Thomas Edison State College*
Jennifer Wright, *Drexel University*
Timothy Yoder, *Mississippi State University*
Marilyn Young, *Belmont University*
Charlie Yuan, *California State University – East Bay*
Michael Zaidel, *Fairleigh Dickinson University*
Charles C. Zalonka, *Oklahoma State University*

# Acknowledgments

We would like to thank the many talented people who made valuable contributions to the creation of this second edition. Patrice Johnson of the University of Georgia, Cherie Hennig of the University of North Carolina – Wilmington, and Teressa Farough checked the page proof, Testbank, and Solutions Manual for accuracy; we greatly appreciate the hours they spent checking tax forms and double-checking our calculations throughout the book. Many thanks also to Jim Young for providing the tax numbers for 2010 well before the IRS made them available. William A. Padley of Madison Area Technical College, Teresa Lang of Columbus State University, and Douglas P. Stives of Monmouth University greatly contributed to the accuracy of *McGraw-Hill's Connect Accounting* for the 2011 edition.

We also appreciate the expert attention given to this project by the staff at McGraw-Hill/Irwin, especially Stewart Mattson, Editorial Director; Tim Vertovec, Publisher; Daryl Horrocks, Senior Developmental Editor; Pat Frederickson, Lead Project Manager; Dean Karampelas, Marketing Manager; Susan Lombardi, Media Product Manager; Allison Souter, Senior Media Project Manager; Matthew Baldwin, Lead Designer; and Michael McCormick, Lead Production Supervisor.

# Changes in *Taxation of Individuals and Business Entities,* 2011 Edition

For the 2011 edition of *Taxation of Individuals and Business Entities,* the Spilker author team has spent considerable time making careful revisions to the textbook and its supplements. These specific enhancements have been made in the 2011 edition:

- All chapters and tax forms have been updated for new tax law, making them current through January of 2010. Other updates beyond January can be found on the book's Online Learning Center, www.mhhe.com/spilker2011.

- An independent accuracy checker read every page of page proof and solutions manual to ensure that there were no errors. Each tax return problem, exhibit, and example was carefully checked to make sure that the calculations and form references were accurate.

- In addition, in the Testbank, every multiple choice question, true/false question, and problem was checked for accuracy by an independent reviewer.

- Several new problems were added to Chapters 4, 6, 7, 13, 16, and 17.

- A new sample client letter has been added to Chapter 2. This chapter now includes an explanation of the components of a client letter, and guidance for what types of supporting evidence to include. Also, select problems now require students to draft client letters.

- The summary of the AICPA statement on standards for tax services (Exhibit 2-11) has been revised to correspond with recent changes from the AICPA.

- A new Key Facts box has been added to Chapter 4 explaining *for* and *from* AGI deductions.

- More detail has been added to the Support Test section of the Qualifying Relative part of Chapter 4 (LO2).

- A new "What If?" has been added to Example 4-9; the What If covers multiple support agreements.

- A new Taxes in the Real World box has been added to Chapter 4, explaining unique circumstances for the filing status of same-sex married couples.

- Several "What If?" examples were added to Example 6-33 (for standard deductions).

- Example 7-6 and two Taxes in the Real World boxes (for AMT and late payment penalties) from the 2010 edition have been deleted. A new Taxes in the Real World box for FedEx employees has been added in its place.

- New coverage of the recurring item exception, and a corresponding "What If?" example has been added to Chapter 8.

- A new Taxes in the Real World box has been added to Chapter 11, discussing mutual fund after-tax return reports to the SEC.

- A new section has been added to Chapter 11 for Passive Activity Income and Loss; this new section appears just below learning objective 5.

- A new Taxes in the Real World box discussing the employee 401(k) match at Starbucks has been added to Chapter 13.

- In Chapter 14, more detail has been added to the section on mortgage points, and the sections discussing a residence with significant rental use and deductible home business expenses have both been replaced.

- A new appendix B has been added to Chapter 14 that details the tax rules relating to a home used for rental purposes.
- In Chapter 15, a new Key Facts box has been added for the legal classification and nontax characteristics of entities.
- In Chapter 16, toward the end of learning objective 2, the Net Operating Loss section has been replaced with new Examples 8, 9 and 10. Also, the coverage of ACE Adjustments has been replaced in learning objective 4.
- As a result of the recent FASB codification changes, Chapter 17 is now entitled "Accounting for Income Taxes."
- A new exhibit has been added to Chapter 17 demonstrating the UTP disclosure from the Microsoft Corporation for 2008 and 2009.

- A new Taxes in the Real World box has been added to Chapter 18, discussing a recent quarterly cash dividend increase for McDonald's.
- In Chapter 19, some additional explanation has been added for Section 1244 stock when it is issued by a corporation in exchange for property that has an adjusted basis.
- In Chapter 19, a new Taxes in the Real World box has been added to discuss Disney's acquisition of Marvel Entertainment in August 2009.
- In Chapter 24, a new Taxes in the Real World box has been added to discuss a growing trend of companies moving their headquarters to Switzerland to avoid high corporate taxes.
- Upcoming potential changes in the taxing of multinational corporations are discussed in a new paragraph before the Conclusion of Chapter 24.

 **AS WE GO TO PRESS**

This book is current through March 8, 2010. You can go to our Web site (www.mhhe.com/spilker2011) for updates that occur after this date.

# Table of Contents

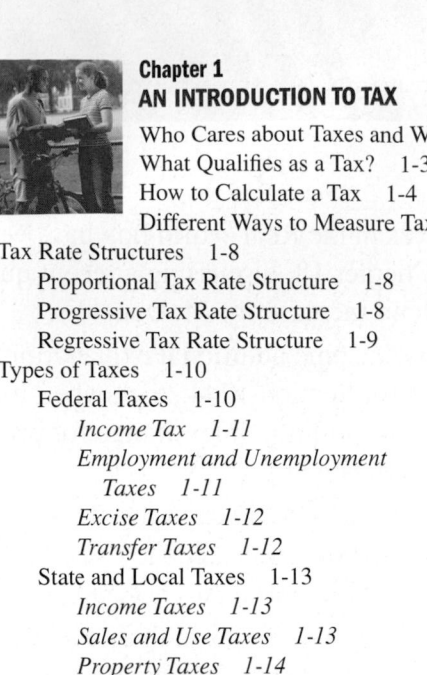

**Chapter 1**
**AN INTRODUCTION TO TAX**

Who Cares about Taxes and Why?   1-2
What Qualifies as a Tax?   1-3
How to Calculate a Tax   1-4
Different Ways to Measure Tax Rates   1-4
Tax Rate Structures   1-8
Proportional Tax Rate Structure   1-8
Progressive Tax Rate Structure   1-8
Regressive Tax Rate Structure   1-9
Types of Taxes   1-10
Federal Taxes   1-10
*Income Tax   1-11*
*Employment and Unemployment*
*Taxes   1-11*
*Excise Taxes   1-12*
*Transfer Taxes   1-12*
State and Local Taxes   1-13
*Income Taxes   1-13*
*Sales and Use Taxes   1-13*
*Property Taxes   1-14*
*Excise Taxes   1-14*
Implicit Taxes   1-14
Evaluating Alternative Tax Systems   1-16
Sufficiency   1-16
*Static vs. Dynamic Forecasting   1-17*
*Income vs. Substitution Effects   1-17*
Equity   1-19
*Horizontal vs. Vertical Equity   1-19*
Certainty   1-20
Convenience   1-20
Economy   1-21
Evaluating Tax Systems—The Trade-off   1-21
Conclusion   1-21

**Chapter 2**
**TAX COMPLIANCE, THE IRS, AND**
**TAX AUTHORITIES**

Taxpayer Filing Requirements   2-2
Tax Return Due Date and Extensions   2-2
Statute of Limitations   2-3
IRS Audit Selection   2-4
Types of Audits   2-5
*After the Audit   2-6*
Tax Law Sources   2-9
Legislative Sources: Congress and the Constitution   2-11
*Internal Revenue Code   2-11*
*The Legislative Process for Tax Laws   2-11*
*Basic Organization of the Code   2-13*
*Tax Treaties   2-13*
Judicial Sources: The Courts   2-14
Administrative Sources: The U.S. Treasury   2-15
*Regulations, Revenue Rulings, and Revenue*
*Procedures   2-15*
*Letter Rulings   2-16*

Tax Research   2-17
Step 1: Understand Facts   2-17
Step 2: Identify Issues   2-17
Step 3: Locate Relevant Authorities   2-18
Step 4: Analyze Tax Authorities   2-19
Step 5: Communicate the Results   2-20
*Facts   2-20*
*Issues   2-20*
*Authorities   2-22*
*Conclusion   2-22*
*Analysis   2-22*
*Client Letters   2-22*
*Research Question and Limitations   2-22*
*Facts   2-22*
*Analysis   2-22*
*Closing   2-22*
Tax Professional Responsibilities   2-23
Taxpayer and Tax Practitioner Penalties   2-26
Conclusion   2-27

**Chapter 3**
**TAX PLANNING STRATEGIES AND RELATED**
**LIMITATIONS**

Basic Tax Planning Overview   3-2
Timing Strategies   3-2
Present Value of Money   3-3
The Timing Strategy When Tax Rates Are Constant   3-4
The Timing Strategy When Tax Rates Change   3-8
*Limitations to Timing Strategies   3-10*
Income-Shifting Strategies   3-11
Transactions between Family Members and Limitations   3-12
Transactions between Owners and Their Businesses
and Limitations   3-13
Income Shifting across Jurisdictions and Limitations   3-15
Conversion Strategies   3-16
Limitations of Conversion Strategies   3-17
Additional Limitations to Tax Planning Strategies: Judicial
Doctrines   3-18
Tax Avoidance Versus Tax Evasion   3-18
Conclusion   3-19

**Chapter 4**
**INDIVIDUAL INCOME TAX OVERVIEW**

The Individual Income Tax Formula   4-2
Realized Income, Exclusions,
Deferrals, and Gross Income   4-2
Deductions   4-6
*Deductions for AGI   4-6*
*Deductions from AGI   4-7*
Income Tax Calculation   4-8
Other Taxes   4-9
Tax Credits   4-9
Tax Prepayments   4-10
Personal and Dependency Exemptions   4-10
Dependency Requirements   4-11
*Qualifying Child   4-11*
*Qualifying Relative   4-13*

Filing Status  4-16
    Married Filing Jointly and Married Filing Separately  4-16
    Qualifying Widow or Widower  4-17
    Head of Household  4-18
    Single  4-20
Summary of Income Tax Formula  4-20
Conclusion  4-20

### Chapter 5
### GROSS INCOME AND EXCLUSIONS

Realization and Recognition of Income  5-2
    What Is Included in Gross Income?  5-3
        *Economic Benefit  5-3*
        *Realization Principle  5-3*
    *Recognition  5-4*
Other Income Concepts  5-4
    *Form of Receipt  5-4*
    *Return of Capital Principle  5-4*
    *Recovery of Amounts Previously Deducted  5-5*
When Do Taxpayers Recognize Income?  5-6
    *Accounting Methods  5-6*
    *Constructive Receipt  5-7*
Who Recognizes the Income?  5-7
    *Assignment of Income  5-8*
    *Community Property Systems  5-8*
Types of Income  5-9
Income from Services  5-9
Income from Property  5-10
    *Annuities  5-11*
    *Property Dispositions  5-13*
Other Sources of Gross Income  5-14
    *Income from Flow-through Entities  5-14*
    *Alimony  5-14*
    *Prizes, Awards, and Gambling Winnings  5-16*
    *Social Security Benefits  5-17*
    *Imputed Income  5-18*
    *Discharge of Indebtedness  5-19*
Exclusion Provisions  5-20
Common Exclusions  5-20
    *Municipal Interest  5-20*
    *Fringe Benefits  5-21*
Education-Related Exclusions  5-22
    *Scholarships  5-22*
    *Other Educational Subsidies  5-22*
Exclusions to Mitigate Double Taxation  5-23
    *Gifts and Inheritances  5-23*
    *Life Insurance Proceeds  5-23*
    *Foreign-Earned Income  5-24*
Sickness and Injury-Related Exclusions  5-24
    *Workers' Compensation  5-24*
    *Payments Associated with Personal Injury  5-25*
    *Health Care Reimbursement  5-25*
    *Disability Insurance  5-25*
Deferral Provisions  5-26
Gross Income Summary  5-26
Conclusion  5-28

### Chapter 6
### INDIVIDUAL DEDUCTIONS

Deductions for AGI  6-2
    Deductions Directly Related to Business
        Activities  6-3
        *Trade or Business Expenses  6-4*
        *Rental and Royalty Expenses  6-5*
        *Losses  6-6*
        *Flow-Through Entities  6-6*
    Deductions Indirectly Related to Business Activities  6-6
        *Moving Expenses  6-6*
        *Health Insurance Deduction by Self-Employed*
            *Taxpayers  6-8*
        *Self-Employment Tax Deduction  6-8*
        *Penalty for Early Withdrawal of Savings  6-9*
    Deductions Subsidizing Specific Activities  6-9
        *Deduction for Interest on Qualified Education*
            *Loans  6-10*
        *Deduction for Qualified Education Expenses  6-11*
    Summary: Deductions for AGI  6-12
Deductions from AGI: Itemized Deductions  6-13
    Medical Expenses  6-13
        *Transportation and Travel for Medical Purposes  6-14*
        *Hospitals and Long-Term Care Facilities  6-15*
        *Medical Expense Deduction Limitation  6-15*
    Taxes  6-16
    Interest  6-17
    Charitable Contributions  6-18
        *Contributions of Money  6-18*
        *Contributions of Property Other Than Money  6-19*
        *Charitable Contribution Deduction Limitations  6-21*
    Casualty and Theft Losses on Personal-Use Assets  6-23
        *Tax Loss from Casualties  6-23*
        *Casualty Loss Deduction Floor Limitations  6-23*
    Miscellaneous Itemized Deductions Subject to AGI
        Floor  6-25
        *Employee Business Expenses  6-25*
        *Investment Expenses  6-27*
        *Tax Preparation Fees  6-27*
        *Hobby Losses  6-27*
        *Limitation on Miscellaneous Itemized Deductions*
            *(2 percent of AGI Floor)  6-29*
    Miscellaneous Itemized Deductions Not Subject to AGI
        Floor  6-30
    Phase-out of Itemized Deductions  6-30
    Summary of Itemized Deductions  6-30
The Standard Deduction and Exemptions  6-32
    Standard Deduction  6-32
        *Bunching Itemized Deductions  6-33*
    Deduction for Personal and Dependency Exemptions  6-34
    Taxable Income Summary  6-35
Conclusion  6-36
Appendix A: Calculation of Itemized Deduction Phase-out  6-36
Appendix B: Personal Exemption Phase-out  6-37

### Chapter 7
### INDIVIDUAL INCOME TAX COMPUTATION AND TAX CREDITS

Regular Federal Income Tax Computation  7-2
    Tax Rate Schedules  7-2
        Marriage Penalty or Benefit  7-3
Exceptions to the Basic Tax Computation  7-4
    *Preferential Tax Rates for Capital Gains and*
        *Dividends  7-4*
    *Kiddie Tax  7-6*
Alternative Minimum Tax  7-8
    Alternative Minimum Tax Formula  7-9
        *Alternative Minimum Taxable Income (AMTI)  7-9*
        *AMT Exemption  7-12*
        *Tentative Minimum Tax and AMT Computation  7-12*

Other AMT Considerations 7-13
  General AMT Planning Strategies 7-14
Employment and Self-Employment Taxes 7-14
  Employee FICA Taxes Payable 7-14
  Self-Employment Taxes 7-16
  Employee vs. Self-Employed (Independent Contractor) 7-19
    Employee vs. Independent Contractor Comparison 7-20
Tax Credits 7-22
  Nonrefundable Personal Credits 7-22
    Child Tax Credit 7-22
    Child and Dependent Care Credit 7-24
    Education Credits 7-25
  Refundable Personal Credits 7-28
    Making Work Pay Credit 7-28
    Earned Income Credit 7-29
    Other Refundable Personal Credits 7-30
  Business Tax Credits 7-30
    Foreign Tax Credit 7-31
  Tax Credit Summary 7-31
  Credit Application Sequence 7-31
Taxpayer Prepayments and Filing Requirements 7-33
  Prepayments 7-33
    Underpayment Penalties 7-34
  Filing Requirements 7-36
    Late Filing Penalty 7-36
    Late Payment Penalty 7-36
Tax Summary 7-37
Conclusion 7-37
Appendix: Excerpt from Single Tax Table 7-39

## Chapter 8
## BUSINESS INCOME, DEDUCTIONS, AND ACCOUNTING METHODS

Business Gross Income 8-2
Business Deductions 8-2
  Ordinary and Necessary 8-3
  Reasonable in Amount 8-3
Limitations on Business Deductions 8-4
  Expenditures against Public Policy 8-4
  Political Contributions and Lobbying Costs 8-5
  Capital Expenditures 8-5
  Expenses Associated with the Production of Tax-Exempt Income 8-5
  Personal Expenditures 8-6
  Mixed-Motive Expenditures 8-7
    Meals and Entertainment 8-7
    Travel and Transportation 8-8
    Property Use 8-10
    Record Keeping and Other Requirements 8-11
Specific Business Deductions 8-11
  Start-Up Costs and Organizational Expenditures 8-11
  Bad Debt Expense 8-11
  Domestic Production Activities Deduction 8-11
  Losses on Dispositions of Business Property 8-13
  Business Casualty Losses 8-14
Accounting Periods 8-15
Accounting Methods 8-16
  Financial and Tax Accounting Methods 8-17
  Overall Accounting Method 8-17
    Cash Method 8-17
    Accrual Method 8-18
  Accrual Income 8-19
    All-Events Test for Income 8-19

  Taxation of Advance Payments of Income
    (Prepaid Income) 8-19
    Advance Payment for Services 8-20
    Advance Payment for Goods 8-20
  Inventories 8-21
    Uniform Capitalization 8-21
    Inventory Cost-Flow Methods 8-22
  Accrual Deductions 8-24
    All-Events Test for Deductions 8-24
    Economic Performance 8-24
    Bad Debt Expense 8-27
    Limitations on Accruals to Related Parties 8-28
  Comparison of Accrual and Cash Methods 8-29
  Adopting an Accounting Method 8-30
  Changing Accounting Methods 8-33
    Tax Consequences of Changing Accounting Method 8-33
Conclusion 8-34

## Chapter 9
## PROPERTY ACQUISITION AND COST RECOVERY

Cost Recovery 9-2
  Basis for Cost Recovery 9-3
Depreciation 9-5
  Personal Property Depreciation 9-5
  Depreciation Method 9-5
  Depreciation Recovery Period 9-6
  Depreciation Conventions 9-8
  Calculating Depreciation for Personal Property 9-10
  Applying the Half-Year Convention 9-11
  Applying the Mid-Quarter Convention 9-13
  Immediate Expensing 9-15
  Listed Property 9-20
  Luxury Automobiles 9-23
  Real Property 9-25
    Applicable Method 9-26
    Applicable Convention 9-26
    Depreciation Tables 9-26
  Depreciation for the Alternative Minimum Tax 9-28
  Depreciation Summary 9-28
Amortization 9-30
  Section 197 Intangibles 9-30
  Organizational Expenditures and Start-Up Costs 9-32
  Research and Experimentation Expenditures 9-34
  Patents and Copyrights 9-35
  Amortizable Intangible Asset Summary 9-36
Depletion 9-37
Conclusion 9-39

## Chapter 10
## PROPERTY DISPOSITIONS

Dispositions 10-2
  Amount Realized 10-2
  Adjusted Basis 10-3
  Realized Gain or Loss on Disposition 10-3
  Recognized Gain or Loss on Disposition 10-4
Character of Gain or Loss 10-4
  Ordinary Assets 10-5
  Capital Assets 10-5
  §1231 Assets 10-6
Depreciation Recapture 10-7
  §1245 Property 10-8
    Scenario 1: Gain Created Solely through Cost Recovery
      Deductions 10-9

*Scenario 2: Gain Due to Both Cost Recovery Deductions and Asset Appreciation* 10-9
    *Scenario 3: Asset Sold at a Loss* 10-10
  §1250 Depreciation Recapture for Real Property 10-11
Other Provisions Affecting the Rate at Which Gains Are Taxed 10-12
  Unrecaptured §1250 Gain for Individuals 10-12
  Characterizing Gains on the Sale of Depreciable Property to Related Parties 10-13
Calculating Net §1231 Gains or Losses 10-14
  §1231 Look-Back Rule 10-15
Gain or Loss Summary 10-16
Nonrecognition Transactions 10-17
  Like-Kind Exchanges 10-17
  Definition of Like-Kind Property 10-21
    *Real Property* 10-21
    *Personal Property* 10-21
    *Property Ineligible for Like-Kind Treatment* 10-21
  Property Use 10-22
  Timing Requirements for A Like-Kind Exchange 10-22
  Tax Consequences When Like-Kind Property Is Exchanged Solely for Like-Kind Property 10-24
  Tax Consequences of Transfers Involving Like-Kind and Non-Like-Kind Property (Boot) 10-24
  Reporting Like-Kind Exchanges 10-26
  Involuntary Conversions 10-26
  Installment Sales 10-29
  Gains Ineligible for Installment Reporting 10-30
  Other Nonrecognition Provisions 10-31
  Related-Party Loss Disallowance Rules 10-32
Conclusion 10-33

### Chapter 11
### INVESTMENTS

Investments Overview 11-2
Portfolio Income: Interest and Dividends 11-2
    Interest 11-3
      *Corporate and U.S. Treasury Bonds* 11-4
  *U.S. Savings Bonds* 11-5
  Dividends 11-7
Portfolio Income: Capital Gains and Losses 11-8
  Types of Capital Gains and Losses 11-11
    *Unrecaptured §1250 Gain* 11-11
    *Collectibles and §1202 Gain* 11-11
    *Netting Process for Gains and Losses* 11-13
  Limitations on Capital Losses 11-18
    *Losses on the Sale of Personal-Use Assets* 11-19
    *Capital Losses on Sales to Related Parties* 11-19
    *Wash Sales* 11-19
  Balancing Tax Planning Strategies for Capital Assets with Other Goals 11-20
Portfolio Income: Tax Exempt 11-22
  Municipal Bonds 11-22
  Life Insurance 11-23
  Educational Savings Plans 11-25
Portfolio Income Summary 11-26
Portfolio Investment Expenses 11-28
  Investment Expenses 11-28
  Investment Interest Expense 11-30
    *Net Investment Income* 11-30
    *Election to Include Long-Term Capital Gains and Qualified Dividends in Investment Income* 11-31

Passive Activity Income and Losses 11-32
  Passive Activity Definition 11-36
  Income And Loss Categories 11-36
  Rental Real Estate Exception to the Passive Activity Loss Rules 11-38
Conclusion 11-39

### Chapter 12
### COMPENSATION

Salary and Wages 12-2
    Employee Considerations for Salary and Wages 12-2
      *Withholding Taxes* 12-2
  *FICA (Payroll Taxes)* 12-5
  Employer Considerations for Salary and Wages 12-6
    *Deductibility of Salary Payments* 12-6
Equity-Based Compensation 12-10
  Stock Options 12-11
    *Employee Considerations for Stock Options* 12-13
    *Employer Considerations for Stock Options* 12-15
  Restricted Stock 12-17
    *Employee Considerations for Restricted Stock* 12-18
    *Employer Considerations for Restricted Stock* 12-20
  Equity-Based Compensation Summary 12-21
Fringe Benefits 12-22
  Taxable Fringe Benefits 12-22
    *Employee Considerations for Taxable Fringe Benefits* 12-22
    *Employer Considerations for Taxable Fringe Benefits* 12-25
  Nontaxable Fringe Benefits 12-26
    *Group-Term Life Insurances* 12-27
    *Health and Accident Insurance and Benefits* 12-27
    *Meals and Lodging for the Convenience of the Employer* 12-27
    *Employee Educational Assistance* 12-28
    *Dependent Care Benefits* 12-28
    *No-Additional-Cost Services* 12-28
    *Qualified Employee Discounts* 12-29
    *Working Condition Fringe Benefit* 12-29
    De Minimis *Fringe Benefits* 12-30
    *Qualified Transportation Fringe* 12-30
    *Qualified Moving Expense Reimbursement* 12-30
    *Cafeteria Plans and Flexible Spending Accounts (FSAs)* 12-31
    *Employee and Employer Considerations for Nontaxable Fringe Benefits* 12-31
  Tax Planning with Fringe Benefits 12-32
  Fringe Benefits Summary 12-33
Conclusion 12-35

### Chapter 13
### RETIREMENT SAVINGS AND DEFERRED COMPENSATION

Employer-Provided Qualified Plans 13-3
  Defined Benefit Plans 13-3
    Vesting 13-4
  Funding, Accounting, and Plan Maintenance 13-5
  Distributions 13-5
Defined Contribution Plans 13-5
  Employer Matching 13-6
  Contribution Limits 13-7

Vesting   13-8
After-Tax Cost of Contributions   13-9
Distributions   13-9
After-Tax Rates of Return   13-11
Roth 401(k) Plans   13-13
Comparing Traditional Defined Contribution Plans and
    Roth 401(k) Plans   13-15
Nonqualified Deferred Compensation   13-15
    Nonqualified Plans vs. Qualified Defined Contribution
        Plans   13-15
    Employee Considerations   13-16
    Employer Considerations   13-18
Individually Managed Qualified Retirement Plans   13-19
Individual Retirement Accounts   13-19
    Traditional IRAs   13-20
        *Distributions   13-22*
    Roth IRAs   13-22
        *Distributions   13-22*
    Rollover from Traditional to Roth IRA   13-23
    Comparing Traditional and Roth IRAs   13-24
Self-Employed Retirement Accounts   13-24
    Simplified Employee Pension (SEP) IRA   13-26
        *Nontax Considerations   13-26*
    Individual 401(k)s   13-26
        *Nontax Considerations   13-28*
Saver's Credit   13-28
Conclusion   13-29

### Chapter 14
### TAX CONSEQUENCES OF HOME OWNERSHIP

Personal Use of the Home   14-2
    Exclusion of Gain on Sale of Personal
        Residence   14-2
            *Requirements   14-3*
    *Amount of Limitations on Exclusion   14-5*
    *Exclusion of Gain from Debt Forgiveness on Foreclosure
        of Home Mortgage   14-7*
    Interest Expense on Home-Related Debt   14-7
        *Limitations on Home-Related Debt   14-9*
        *Mortgage Insurance   14-12*
        *Points   14-12*
    Real Property Taxes   14-15
    First-Time Home Buyer Tax Credit   14-16
Rental Use of the Home   14-18
    Residence with Minimal Rental Use   14-18
    Residence with Significant Rental Use (Vacation
        Home)   14-19
    Nonresidence (Rental Property)   14-24
        *Losses on Rental Property   14-24*
Business Use of the Home   14-26
    Direct vs. Indirect Expenses   14-27
    Limitations on Deductibility of Expenses   14-28
Conclusion   14-29
Appendix A: Settlement Statement   14-30
Appendix B: Flowchart of Tax Rules Relating to Home
    Used for Rental Purposes   14-32

### Chapter 15
### ENTITIES OVERVIEW

Entity Legal Classification and Nontax
    Characteristics   15-2
    Legal Classification   15-2
    Nontax Characteristics   15-3
        *Responsibility for Liabilities   15-3*

        *Rights, Responsibilities, and Legal Arrangement
            among Owners   15-3*
Entity Tax Classification   15-5
Entity Tax Characteristics   15-6
    Double Taxation   15-7
        *After-Tax Earnings Distributed   15-7*
        *Some or All After-Tax Earnings Retained   15-11*
        *Mitigating the Double Tax   15-11*
    Limitations on Number and Type of Owners   15-13
    Contributions of Property and Services   15-13
    Accounting Periods   15-15
    Accounting Methods   15-15
    Special Allocations   15-16
    FICA and Self-Employment Tax   15-16
    Basis Computation   15-19
    Distributions   15-20
    Deductibility of Entity Losses   15-21
    Selling Ownership Interests   15-22
    Liquidating Entities   15-23
    Converting to Other Entity Types   15-24
Entity Choice Summary   15-26
Conclusion   15-27

### Chapter 16
### CORPORATE OPERATIONS

Corporate Taxable Income Formula   16-2
    Accounting Periods and  Methods   16-3
    Computing Corporate Regular Taxable
        Income   16-3
Book-Tax Differences   16-4
    *Common Permanent Book-Tax Differences   16-4*
    *Common Temporary Book-Tax Differences   16-6*
Corporate-Specific Deductions and Associated Book-Tax
    Differences   16-9
    *Stock Options   16-9*
    *Net Capital Losses   16-11*
    *Net Operating Losses   16-13*
    *Charitable Contributions   16-15*
    *Dividends Received Deduction   16-18*
Taxable Income Summary   16-22
Regular Tax Liability   16-22
    *Controlled Groups   16-24*
Compliance   16-25
    *Consolidated Tax Returns   16-28*
Corporate Tax Return Due Dates and Estimated
    Taxes   16-28
Corporate Alternative Minimum Tax   16-33
    Preference Items   16-33
    Adjustments   16-34
        *Depreciation Adjustment   16-34*
        *Gain or Loss on Disposition of Depreciable Assets   16-35*
        *ACE Adjustment   16-35*
        *Alternative Minimum Taxable Income (AMTI)   16-37*
        *AMT Exemption   16-37*
        *Alternative Minimum Tax   16-38*
    AMT Tax Planning   16-39
Conclusion   16-39

### Chapter 17
### ACCOUNTING FOR INCOME TAXES

Objectives of Accounting for Income Taxes and
    the Income Tax Provision Process   17-2
Why Is Accounting for Income Taxes So
    Complex?   17-3

Objectives of ASC 740   17-3
The Income Tax Provision Process   17-6
Calculating the Current and Deferred Income Tax Expense or
  Benefit Components of a Company's Income Tax Provision   17-6
  Step 1: Adjust Pretax Net Income for All Permanent
    Differences   17-6
  Step 2: Identify All Temporary Differences and Tax
    Carryforward Amounts   17-8
    *Revenues or Gains that Are Taxable after They Are*
      *Recognized in Financial Income*   17-8
    *Expenses or Losses that Are Deductible after They Are*
      *Recognized in Financial Income*   17-8
    *Revenues or Gains that Are Taxable before They Are*
      *Recognized in Financial Income*   17-9
    *Expenses or Losses that Are Deductible before They Are*
      *Recognized in Financial Income*   17-9
  Identifying Taxable and Deductible Temporary
    Differences   17-10
    *Taxable Temporary Difference*   17-10
    *Deductible Temporary Difference*   17-10
  Step 3: Compute the Current Income Tax Expense or
    Benefit   17-11
  Step 4: Determine the Ending Balances in the Balance
    Sheet Deferred Tax Asset and Liability Accounts   17-12
Determining Whether a Valuation Allowance Is Needed   17-18
  Step 5: Evaluate the Need for a Valuation Allowance for
    Gross Deferred Tax Assets   17-18
  Determining the Need for a Valuation Allowance   17-18
    *Future Reversals of Existing Taxable Temporary*
      *Differences*   17-18
    *Taxable Income in Prior Carryback Year(s)*   17-19
    *Expected Future Taxable Income Exclusive of Reversing*
      *Temporary Differences and Carryforwards*   17-19
    *Tax Planning Strategies*   17-19
    *Negative Evidence that a Valuation Allowance Is*
      *Needed*   17-19
  Step 6: Calculate the Deferred Income Tax Expense or
    Benefit   17-22
Accounting for Uncertainty in Income Tax Positions   17-23
  Application of ASC 740 to Uncertain Tax Positions   17-24
    *Step 1: Recognition*   17-24
    *Step 2: Measurement*   17-24
  Subsequent Events   17-26
  Interest and Penalties   17-26
  Disclosures of Uncertain Tax Positions   17-26
Financial Statement Disclosure and the Computation of a
  Corporation's Effective Tax Rate   17-27
  Balance Sheet Classification   17-27
  Income Tax Footnote Disclosure   17-28
    *Computation and Reconciliation of the Income Tax Provision*
      *with a Company's* Hypothetical *Tax Provision*   17-30
    *Importance of a Company's Effective Tax Rate*   17-31
  Interim Period Effective Tax Rates   17-32
Convergence of ASC 740 with International Financial Reporting
  Standards   17-32
Conclusion   17-32

## Chapter 18
## CORPORATE TAXATION: NONLIQUIDATING DISTRIBUTIONS

The Basic Tax Law Framework that Applies to
  Property Distributions   18-3
Computing Earnings and Profits and Determining the
  Dividend Amount Received by a Shareholder   18-3

Overview of the Shareholder Taxation of Corporate Dividends   18-3
The Tax Law Definition of a Dividend   18-4
Computing Earnings and Profits   18-4
  *Inclusion of Income that Is Excluded from Taxable*
    *Income*   18-5
  *Disallowance of Certain Expenses that Are Deducted in*
    *Computing Taxable Income but Do Not Require an*
    *Economic Outflow*   18-5
  *Deduction of Certain Expenses that Are Excluded from the*
    *Computation of Taxable Income but Do Require an*
    *Economic Outflow*   18-6
  *Deferral of Deductions or Acceleration of Income Due to*
    *Separate Accounting Methods Required for E&P*
    *Purposes*   18-6
Ordering of E&P Distributions   18-7
  *Positive Current E&P and Positive Accumulated E&P*   18-7
  *Positive Current E&P and Negative Accumulated E&P*   18-9
  *Negative Current E&P and Positive Accumulated E&P*   18-9
  *Negative Current E&P and Negative Accumulated E&P*   18-10
Distributions of Noncash Property to Shareholders   18-11
  *The Tax Consequences to a Corporation Paying Noncash*
    *Property as a Dividend*   18-12
  *Liabilities*   18-12
  *Effect of Noncash Property Distributions on E&P*   18-13
Constructive Dividends   18-14
The Motivation to Pay Dividends   18-17
Stock Dividends   18-18
  Tax Consequences to Shareholders Receiving a Stock
    Dividend   18-18
    *Nontaxable Stock Dividends*   18-18
    *Taxable Stock Dividends*   18-19
Stock Redemptions   18-20
  The Form of a Stock Redemption   18-21
  Redemptions that Contract the Shareholder's Stock
    Ownership Interest   18-22
    *Redemptions that Are Substantially Disproportionate with*
      *Respect to the Shareholder*   18-22
    *Redemptions in Complete Redemption of all of the Stock of*
      *the Corporation Owned by the Shareholder*   18-25
    *Redemptions that Are Not Essentially Equivalent to a*
      *Dividend*   18-26
  Tax Consequences to the Distributing Corporation   18-28
  Trends in Stock Redemptions by Publicly Traded
    Corporations   18-28
Partial Liquidations   18-29
Conclusion   18-30

## Chapter 19
## CORPORATE FORMATION, REORGANIZATION, AND LIQUIDATION

The General Tax Rules that Apply to Property
  Transactions   19-3
Tax-Deferred Transfers of Property to a Corporation   19-4
Transactions Subject to Tax Deferral   19-5
Meeting the Section 351 Tax Deferral Requirements   19-6
  *Section 351 Applies Only to the Transfer of Property to*
    *the Corporation*   19-6
  *The Property Transferred to the Corporation Must Be*
    *Exchanged Solely for Stock of the Corporation*   19-6
  *The Transferor(s) of Property to the Corporation Must*
    *Be in Control, in the Aggregate, of the Corporation*
    *Immediately after the Transfer*   19-7
Tax Consequences to Shareholders in a Section 351
  Transaction   19-9

Tax Consequences When a Shareholder Receives Boot   19-10
Assumption of Shareholder Liabilities by the Corporation   19-12
  *Tax-Avoidance Transactions   19-12*
  *Liabilities in Excess of Basis   19-13*
Tax Consequences to the Transferee Corporation in a
  Section 351 Transaction   19-14
Other Issues Related to Incorporating an Ongoing
  Business   19-17
  *Depreciable Assets Transferred to a Corporation   19-17*
Contributions to Capital   19-18
Section 1244 Stock   19-18
Taxable and Tax-Deferred Corporate Acquisitions   19-20
Motivation for Business Acquisitions   19-21
The Acquisition Tax Model   19-21
Computing the Tax Consequences to the Parties to a Corporate
  Acquisition   19-23
Taxable Acquisitions   19-23
Tax-Deferred Acquisitions   19-26
Judicial Principles that Underlie All Tax-Deferred
  Reorganizations   19-26
  *Continuity of Interest (COI)   19-26*
  *Continuity of Business Enterprise (COBE)   19-27*
  *Business Purpose Test   19-27*
Type A Asset Acquisitions   19-27
  *Forward Triangular Type A Merger   19-29*
  *Reverse Triangular Type A Merger   19-30*
Type B Stock-for-Stock Reorganizations   19-31
Complete Liquidation of a Corporation   19-34
Tax Consequences to the Shareholders in a Complete
  Liquidation   19-35
Tax Consequences to the Liquidating Corporation in a
  Complete Liquidation   19-36
  *Taxable Liquidating Distributions   19-36*
  *Nontaxable Liquidating Distributions   19-39*
Conclusion   19-40

**Chapter 20**
**FORMING AND OPERATING PARTNERSHIPS**
Flow-through Entities Overview   20-2
  Aggregate and Entity Concepts   20-2
Partnership Formations and Acquisitions of Partnership
  Interests   20-3
Acquiring Partnership Interests When Partnerships Are
  Formed   20-3
  *Contributions of Property   20-3*
  *Contribution of Services   20-9*
  *Organization, Start-up, and Syndication
    Costs   20-12*
Acquisitions of Partnership Interests   20-12
Partnership Accounting Periods, Methods, and Tax Elections   20-13
Tax Elections   20-13
Accounting Periods   20-14
  *Required Year-Ends   20-14*
Accounting Methods   20-16
Reporting the Results of Partnership Operations   20-17
Ordinary Business Income (Loss) and Separately Stated
  Items   20-17
  *Guaranteed Payments   20-19*
  *Self-Employment Tax   20-20*
Allocating Partners' Shares of Income and Loss   20-22
Partnership Compliance Issues   20-23
Partner's Adjusted Tax Basis in Partnership Interest   20-26
Cash Distributions in Operating Partnerships   20-28

Loss Limitations   20-29
Tax Basis Limitation   20-29
At-Risk Limitation   20-30
Passive Activity Loss Limitation   20-31
  *Passive Activity Defined   20-32*
  *Income and Loss Baskets   20-32*
Conclusion   20-34

**Chapter 21**
**DISPOSITIONS OF PARTNERSHIP INTERESTS AND
PARTNERSHIP DISTRIBUTIONS**
Basics of Sales of Partnership Interests   21-2
  Seller Issues   21-3
    *Hot Assets   21-4*
  Buyer and Partnership Issues   21-7
    *Varying Interest Rule   21-8*
  Basics of Partnership Distributions   21-9
Operating Distributions   21-9
  *Operating Distributions of Money Only   21-9*
  *Operating Distributions that Include Property Other Than
    Money   21-10*
Liquidating Distributions   21-12
  *Gain or Loss Recognition in Liquidating Distributions   21-13*
  *Basis in Distributed Property   21-13*
  *Partner's Outside Basis Is Greater Than Inside Basis of
    Distributed Assets   21-14*
  *Partner's Outside Basis Is Less Than Inside Basis of
    Distributed Assets   21-17*
  *Character and Holding Period of Distributed Assets   21-21*
Disproportionate Distributions   21-24
Special Basis Adjustments   21-26
Special Basis Adjustments for Dispositions   21-27
Special Basis Adjustments for Distributions   21-28
Conclusion   21-29

**Chapter 22**
**S CORPORATIONS**
S Corporation Elections   22-2
  Formations   22-2
S Corporation Qualification Requirements   22-2
S Corporation Election   22-3
S Corporation Terminations   22-5
Voluntary Terminations   22-5
Involuntary Terminations   22-5
  *Failure to Meet Requirements   22-5*
  *Excess of Passive Investment Income   22-6*
Short Tax Years   22-6
S Corporation Reelections   22-7
Operating Issues   22-8
Accounting Methods and Periods   22-8
Income and Loss Allocations   22-8
Separately Stated Items   22-9
Shareholder's Basis   22-11
  *Initial Basis   22-11*
  *Annual Basis Adjustments   22-12*
Loss Limitations   22-13
  *Tax Basis Limitation   22-13*
  *At-Risk Limitation   22-14*
  *Post-Termination Transition Period Loss Limitation   22-14*
  *Passive Activity Loss Limitation   22-15*
Self-Employment Income   22-15
Fringe Benefits   22-16
Distributions   22-17

Operating Distributions   22-17
    *S Corporation with No C Corporation Accumulated*
      *Earnings and Profits   22-17*
    *S Corporations with C Corporation Accumulated*
      *Earnings and Profits   22-18*
    *Property Distributions   22-20*
    *Post-Termination Transition Period Distributions   22-20*
Liquidating Distributions   22-21
S Corporation Taxes, Accounting Periods and Methods,
  and Filing Requirements   22-21
  Built-in Gains Tax   22-21
  Excess Net Passive Income Tax   22-23
  LIFO Recapture Tax   22-25
  Estimated Taxes   22-26
  Filing Requirements   22-28
Comparing C and S Corporations and Partnerships   22-30
Conclusion   22-31

### Chapter 23
### STATE AND LOCAL TAXES

State and Local Taxes   23-2
Sales and Use Taxes   23-5
    Nexus   23-5
    Sales and Use Tax Liability   23-7
    Income Taxes   23-8
Nexus   23-9
  *Public Law 86-272   23-9*
  *Income Tax Nexus for Other Business Types or*
    *Nonincome-Based Taxes   23-11*
  *Economic Nexus   23-12*
Entities Included on Income Tax Return   23-13
  *Separate Tax Returns   23-13*
  *Unitary Tax Returns   23-14*
State Taxable Income   23-15
Dividing State Tax Base among States   23-16
  *Business Income   23-17*
  *Nonbusiness Income   23-21*
State Income Tax Liability   23-22
Non (Net) Income-Based Taxes   23-22
Conclusion   23-23

### Chapter 24
### THE U.S. TAXATION OF MULTINATIONAL
### TRANSACTIONS

The U.S. Framework for Taxing Multinational
    Transactions   24-2
U.S. Taxation of a Nonresident   24-3
Definition of a Resident for U.S. Tax Purposes   24-4
Overview of the U.S. Foreign Tax Credit System   24-5
U.S. Source Rules for Gross Income and Deductions   24-6
Source of Income Rules   24-7
  *Interest   24-7*
  *Dividends   24-8*
  *Compensation for Services   24-8*
  *Rents and Royalties   24-9*
  *Gain or Loss from Sale of Real Property   24-10*
  *Gain or Loss from Sale of Purchased Personal*
    *Property   24-10*
  *Inventory Manufactured within the United States and Sold*
    *Outside the United States (§863 Sales)   24-10*
Source of Deduction Rules   24-11
  *General Principles of Allocation and Apportionment   24-11*
  *Special Apportionment Rules   24-12*
Treaties   24-14

Foreign Tax Credits   24-19
  FTC Limitation Categories of Taxable Income   24-19
    *Passive Category Income   24-19*
    *General Category Income   24-19*
  Creditable Foreign Taxes   24-20
    *Direct Taxes   24-21*
    *In Lieu of Taxes   24-21*
    *Indirect (Deemed Paid) Taxes   24-21*
Planning for International Operations   24-24
  Check-the-Box Hybrid Entities   24-25
U.S. Anti-Deferral Rules   24-26
  Definition of a Controlled Foreign Corporation   24-27
  Definition of Subpart F Income   24-28
  Planning to Avoid Subpart F Income   24-30
Proposals for Change   24-31
Conclusion   24-32

### Chapter 25
### TRANSFER TAXES AND WEALTH PLANNING

Introduction to Federal Transfer Taxes   25-2
    Beginnings   25-2
    Common Features of Integrated Transfer
      Taxes   25-2
    The Federal Estate Tax   25-3
The Gross Estate   25-3
  *Specific Inclusions   25-4*
  *Valuation   25-7*
  *Gross Estate Summary   25-10*
The Taxable Estate   25-11
  *Administrative Expenses, Debts, Losses, and State*
    *Death Taxes   25-11*
  *Marital and Charitable Deductions   25-12*
Computation of the Estate Tax   25-13
  *Adjusted Taxable Gifts   25-13*
  *Unified Credit   25-14*
The Federal Gift Tax   25-17
  Transfers Subject to Gift Tax   25-18
  *Valuation   25-19*
  *The Annual Exclusion   25-19*
  Taxable Gifts   25-20
  *Gift-Splitting Election   25-21*
  *Marital Deduction   25-22*
  *Charitable Deduction   25-23*
  Computation of the Gift Tax   25-23
  *Prior Taxable Gifts   25-24*
  *Unified Credit   25-24*
Wealth Planning Concepts   25-27
  The Generation-Skipping Tax   25-27
  Income Tax Considerations   25-27
  Transfer Tax Planning Techniques   25-27
  *Serial Gifts   25-28*
  *Bypass Provisions   25-28*
  *The Step-Up in Tax Basis   25-29*
  Integrated Wealth Plans   25-31
Conclusion   25-32

**APPENDIX A**   **Tax Forms   A-1**
**APPENDIX B**   **Tax Terms Glossary   B-0**
**APPENDIX C**   **Comprehensive Tax Return Problems   C-0**
**APPENDIX D**   **Code Index   D-0**

**PHOTO CREDITS   P-1**
**SUBJECT INDEX   I-0**

# An Introduction to Tax

## Learning Objectives

**Upon completing this chapter, you should be able to:**

**LO 1** Demonstrate how taxes influence basic business, investment, personal, and political decisions.

———————————————— ■ ————————————————

**LO 2** Discuss what constitutes a tax and the general objectives of taxes.

———————————————— ■ ————————————————

**LO 3** Describe the different tax rate structures and calculate a tax.

———————————————— ■ ————————————————

**LO 4** Identify the various federal, state, and local taxes.

———————————————— ■ ————————————————

**LO 5** Apply appropriate criteria to evaluate alternate tax systems.

**M**argaret is a junior beginning her first tax course. She is excited about her career prospects as an accounting major but hasn't had much exposure to taxes. On her way to campus she runs into an old friend, Eddy, who is going to Washington, D.C., to protest recent proposed changes to the U.S. tax system. Eddy is convinced the IRS is evil and that the current tax system is blatantly unfair and corrupt. He advocates a simpler, fairer way of taxation. Margaret is intrigued by Eddy's passion but questions whether he has a complete understanding of the U.S. tax system. She decides to withhold all judgments about it (or about pursuing a career in taxation) until the end of her tax course. ■

| Storyline Summary | |
|---|---|
| *Taxpayer:* | Margaret |
| *Employment status:* | Margaret is a full-time student at the University of Georgia. |
| *Current situation:* | She is beginning her first tax class. |

## LO1 WHO CARES ABOUT TAXES AND WHY?

A clear understanding of the role of taxes in everyday decisions will help you make an informed decision about the value of studying taxation or pursuing a career in taxation. One view of taxation is that it represents an inconvenience every April 15th (the annual due date for filing federal individual tax returns without extensions). However, the role of taxation is much more pervasive than this view suggests. Your study of this subject will provide you a unique opportunity to develop an informed opinion about taxation. As a business student, you can overcome the mystery that pervades popular impressions of the tax system and perhaps, one day, share your expertise with friends or clients.

What are some common decisions you face that taxes may influence? In this course, we alert you to situations in which you can increase your return on investments by up to one third! Even the best lessons in finance courses can't approach the increase in risk-adjusted return that smart tax planning provides. Would you like to own your home someday? Tax deductions for home mortgage interest and real estate taxes can reduce the after-tax costs of owning a home relative to renting. Thus, when you face the decision to buy or rent, you can make an informed choice if you understand the relative tax advantages of home ownership. Would you like to retire someday? Understanding the tax-advantaged methods of saving for retirement can increase the after-tax value of your retirement nest egg—and thus increase the likelihood that you can afford to retire, and do so in style. Other common personal financial decisions that taxes influence include: choosing investments, evaluating alternative job offers, saving for education expenses, and doing gift or estate planning. Indeed, taxes are a part of everyday life and have a significant effect on many of the personal financial decisions all of us face.

The role of taxes is not limited to personal finance. Taxes play an equally important role in fundamental business decisions such as the following:

- What organizational form should a business use?
- Where should the business locate?
- How should business acquisitions be structured?
- How should the business compensate employees?
- What is the appropriate mix of debt and equity for the business?
- Should the business rent or own its equipment and property?
- How should the business distribute profits to its owners?

Savvy business decisions require owners and managers to consider all costs and benefits in order to evaluate the merits of a transaction. Although taxes don't necessarily dominate these decisions, they do represent large transaction costs that businesses should factor into the financial decision-making process.

Taxes also play a major part in the political process. U.S. presidential candidates often distinguish themselves from their opponents based upon their tax rhetoric. Indeed, the major political parties generally have very diverse views of the appropriate way to tax the public.[1] Determining who is taxed, what is taxed, and how much is taxed are tough questions with nontrivial answers. Voters must have a basic understanding of taxes to evaluate the merits of alternative tax proposals. Later in this chapter, we'll introduce criteria you can use to evaluate alternative tax proposals.

---

[1]The U.S. Department of the Treasury provides a "history of taxation" on its Web site (www.treas.gov/education/fact-sheets/taxes/ustax.shtml). You may find it interesting to read this history in light of the various political parties in office at the time.

---

**Taxes in the Real World**  *No New Taxes*

George H. W. Bush famously stated in his 1988 presidential election campaign, "Read my lips, no new taxes." In 1990, he signed legislation increasing individual income tax rates. Political observers cite this as one reason he lost the 1992 presidential election to Bill Clinton.

---

In summary, taxes affect many aspects of personal, business, and political decisions. Developing a solid understanding of taxation should allow you to make informed decisions in these areas. Thus, Margaret can take comfort that her semester will likely prove useful to her personally. Who knows? Depending on her interest in business, investment, retirement planning, and the like, she may ultimately decide to pursue a career in taxation.

# WHAT QUALIFIES AS A TAX?

**LO2**

Taxes have been described in many terms, some positive, some negative, some printable, some not. Let's go directly to a formal definition of a tax, which should prove useful in identifying alternative taxes and discussing alternative tax systems.

*A **tax** is a payment required by a government that is unrelated to any specific benefit or service received from the government.* The general purpose of a tax is to fund the operations of the government (to raise revenue). Taxes differ from fines and penalties in that taxes are not intended to punish or prevent illegal behavior. Nonetheless, by allowing deductions from income, our federal tax system does encourage certain behaviors like charitable contributions, retirement savings, and research and development, and we can view it as discouraging other legal behavior. For example, "**sin taxes**" impose relatively high surcharges on alcohol and tobacco products.[2]

Key components of the definition of a tax are that

- the payment is required (it is not voluntary),
- the payment is imposed by a government agency (federal, state, or local), and
- the payment is not tied directly to the benefit received by the taxpayer.

This last point is not to say that taxpayers receive no benefits from the taxes they pay. They benefit from national defense, a judicial system, law enforcement, government-sponsored social programs, an interstate highway system, public schools, and many other government-provided programs and services. The distinction is that taxes paid are not *directly* related to any specific benefit received by the taxpayer.

Can taxes be assessed for special purposes, such as a 1 percent sales tax for education? Yes. Why is an **earmarked tax,** a tax that *is* assessed for a specific purpose, still considered a tax? Because the payment made by the taxpayer does not directly relate to the specific benefit *received by the taxpayer.*

> **THE KEY FACTS**
>
> **What Qualifies as a Tax?**
>
> ■ The general purpose of taxes is to fund government agencies.
>
> ■ Unlike fines or penalties, taxes are not meant to punish or prevent illegal behavior; but *"sin taxes"* are meant to discourage some behaviors.
>
> ■ The three criteria necessary to be a tax are that the payment is
> · required
> · imposed by a government
> · and not tied directly to the benefit received by the taxpayer.

---

**Example 1-1**

Margaret travels to Birmingham, Alabama, where she rents a hotel room and dines at several restaurants. The price she pays for her hotel room and meals includes an additional 2 percent city surcharge to fund roadway construction in Birmingham. Is this a tax?

**Answer:** Yes. The payment is required by a local government and does not directly relate to a specific benefit that Margaret receives.

---

[2]Sin taxes represent an interesting confluence of incentives. On the one hand, demand for such products as alcohol, tobacco, and gambling is often relatively inelastic because of their addictive quality. Thus, taxing such a product can raise substantial revenues. On the other hand, one of the arguments for sin taxes is frequently the social goal of *reducing* demand for such products.

**Example 1-2**

Margaret's parents, Bill and Mercedes, recently built a house and were assessed $1,000 by their county government to connect to the county sewer system. Is this a tax?

**Answer:** No. The assessment was mandatory and it was paid to a local government. However, the third criterion was not met since the payment directly relates to a specific benefit (sewer service) received by the payees. For the same reason, tolls, parking meter fees, and annual licensing fees are also not considered taxes.

**L03**

## HOW TO CALCULATE A TAX

In its simplest form, the amount of tax equals the tax base multiplied by the tax rate:

$$\text{Tax} = \text{Tax Base} \times \text{Tax Rate} \qquad \textbf{Eq. 1-1}$$

> ### THE KEY FACTS
> **How to Calculate a Tax**
> - Tax = Tax Base × Tax Rate
> - The tax base defines what is actually taxed and is usually expressed in monetary terms.
> - The tax rate determines the level of taxes imposed on the tax base and is usually expressed as a percentage.
> - Different portions of a tax base may be taxed at different rates.

The **tax base** defines what is actually taxed and is usually expressed in monetary terms, whereas the **tax rate** determines the level of taxes imposed on the tax base and is usually expressed as a percentage. For example, a sales tax rate of 6 percent on a purchase of $30 yields a tax of $1.80 ($1.80 = $30 × .06).

Federal, state, and local jurisdictions use a large variety of tax bases to collect tax. Some common tax bases (and related taxes) include taxable income (federal and state income taxes), purchases (sales tax), real estate values (real estate tax), and personal property values (personal property tax).

Different portions of a tax base may be taxed at different rates. A single tax applied to an entire base constitutes a **flat tax.** In the case of **graduated taxes,** the base is divided into a series of monetary amounts, or **brackets,** and each successive bracket is taxed at a different (gradually higher or gradually lower) percentage rate.

Calculating some taxes—income taxes for individuals or corporations, for example—can be quite complex. Advocates of flat taxes argue that the process should be simpler. But as we'll see throughout the text, most of the difficulty in calculating a tax rests in determining the tax *base,* not the tax rate. Indeed, there are only three basic tax rate structures (proportional, progressive, and regressive), and each can be mastered without much difficulty.

## DIFFERENT WAYS TO MEASURE TAX RATES

Before we discuss the alternative tax rate structures, let's first define three different tax rates that will be useful in contrasting the different tax rate structures: the marginal, average, and effective tax rates.

The **marginal tax rate** is the tax rate that applies to the *next additional increment* of a taxpayer's taxable income (or deductions). Specifically,

$$\text{Marginal Tax Rate} = \frac{\Delta\text{Tax}^*}{\Delta\text{Taxable Income}} = \frac{(\text{New Total Tax} - \text{Old Total Tax})}{(\text{New Taxable Income} - \text{Old Taxable Income})} \qquad \textbf{Eq. 1-2}$$

*$\Delta$ means *change in*.

where "old" refers to the current tax and "new" refers to the revised tax after incorporating the additional income (or deductions) in question. In graduated income tax systems, additional income (deductions) can push a taxpayer into a higher (lower) tax bracket, thus changing the marginal tax rate.

### Example 1-3

Margaret's parents, Bill and Mercedes, file a joint tax return. They have $140,000 of taxable income this year (after all tax deductions). Assuming the following federal tax rate schedule applies, how much federal income tax will they owe this year?[3]

**2010 Federal Married Filing Jointly Tax Rate Schedule**

| If taxable income is over- | But not over | The tax is: |
|---|---|---|
| $ 0 | 16,750 | 10% of the amount over $0 |
| 16,750 | 68,000 | 1,675 plus 15% of the amount over 16,750 |
| 68,000 | 137,300 | 9,362.50 plus 25% of the amount over 68,000 |
| 137,300 | 209,250 | 26,687.50 plus 28% of the amount over 137,300 |
| 209,250 | 373,650 | 46,833.50 plus 33% of the amount over 209,250 |
| 373,650 | no limit | 101,085.50 plus 35% of the amount over 373,650 |

**Answer:** Bill and Mercedes will owe $27,443.50 computed as follows:

$$\$27,443.50 = \$26,687.50 + 28\% \, (\$140,000 - \$137,300).$$

Note that in this graduated tax rate structure, the first $16,750 of taxable income is taxed at 10 percent, the next $51,250 of taxable income (between $16,750 and $68,000) is taxed at 15 percent, the next $69,300 of taxable income (between $68,000 and $137,300) is taxed at 25 percent. Bill and Mercedes' last $2,700 of taxable income (between $137,300 and $140,000) is taxed at 28 percent.

Many taxpayers incorrectly believe that all their income is taxed at their marginal rate. This mistake leads people to say, "I don't want to earn any additional money because it will put me in a higher tax bracket." Bill and Mercedes are currently in the 28 percent marginal tax rate bracket, but notice that *not* all their income is taxed at this rate. Their *marginal* tax rate is 28 percent. This means that small increases in income will be taxed at 28 percent, and small increases in tax deductions will generate tax *savings* of 28 percent. If Bill and Mercedes receive a large increase in income (or in deductions) such that they would change tax rate brackets, we cannot identify their marginal tax rate by simply identifying their current tax bracket.

### Example 1-4

Bill, a well-known economics professor, signs a publishing contract with an $80,000 royalty advance. Using the rate schedule from Example 1-3, what would Bill and Mercedes' marginal tax rate be on this additional $80,000 of taxable income?

*(continued on page 1-6...)*

---

[3]The tax rate schedules for single, married filing jointly, married filing separately, and head of household are included inside the front cover of the text.

**Answer:** 28.67 percent, computed as follows:

| Description | Amount | Explanation |
|---|---|---|
| (1) Taxable income with additional $80,000 of taxable income | $ 220,000 | $80,000 plus $140,000 taxable income stated in Example 1-3. |
| (2) Tax on $220,000 taxable income | $ 50,381 | Using the rate schedule in Example 1-3. $50,381 = $46,833.50 + 33% (10,750). |
| (3) Taxable income before additional $80,000 of taxable income | $ 140,000 | Example 1-3. |
| (4) Tax on $140,000 taxable income | $27,443.50 | Example 1-3. |
| Marginal tax rate on additional $80,000 of taxable income | 28.67% | $\frac{\Delta \text{Tax}}{\Delta \text{Taxable Income}} = [(2) - (4)]/[(1) - (3)]$ |

Note that Bill and Mercedes' marginal tax rate on the $80,000 increase in taxable income rests *between* the 28 percent and 33 percent bracket rates because a portion of the additional income ($209,250 − $140,000 = $69,250) is taxed at 28 percent with the remaining income ($220,000 − $209,250 = 10,750) taxed at 33 percent.

### Example 1-5

Assume now that, instead of receiving a book advance, Bill and Mercedes start a new business that *loses* $80,000 this year (it results in $80,000 of additional tax deductions). What would be their marginal tax rate for these deductions?

**Answer:** 24.10 percent, computed as follows:

| Description | Amount | Explanation |
|---|---|---|
| (1) Taxable income with additional $80,000 of tax deductions | $ 60,000 | $140,000 taxable income stated in Example 1-3 less $80,000. |
| (2) Tax on $60,000 taxable income | $ 8,162.50 | Using the rate schedule in Example 1-3. $8,162.50 = $1,675 + 15% ($60,000 − $16,750). |
| (3) Taxable income before additional $80,000 of tax deductions | $ 140,000 | Example 1-3. |
| (4) Tax on $140,000 taxable income | $27,443.50 | Example 1-3. |
| Marginal tax rate on additional $80,000 of tax deductions | 24.10% | $\frac{\Delta \text{Tax}}{\Delta \text{Taxable Income}} = [(2) - (4)]/[(1) - (3)]$ |

Bill and Mercedes' marginal tax rate on $80,000 of additional deductions (24.10 percent) differs from their marginal tax rate on $80,000 of additional taxable income (28.67 percent) in these scenarios because of the relatively large increase in income and deductions. Taxpayers often will face the same marginal tax rates for small changes in income and deductions.

**THE KEY FACTS**

**Different Ways to Measure Tax Rates**

■ **Marginal tax rate**
· The tax that applies to next increment of income or deduction.
· $= \dfrac{\Delta \text{Tax}}{\Delta \text{Taxable Income}}$
· Useful in tax planning.

■ **Average tax rate**
· A taxpayer's average level of taxation on each dollar of *taxable* income.
· $= \dfrac{\text{Total Tax}}{\text{Taxable Income}}$
· Useful in budgeting tax expense.

*(continued)*

The marginal tax rate is particularly useful in tax planning because it represents the rate of taxation or savings that would apply to additional taxable income (or tax deductions). In Chapter 3, we discuss basic tax planning strategies that use the marginal tax rate.

The **average tax rate** represents a taxpayer's average level of taxation on each dollar of taxable income. Specifically,

$$\text{Average Tax Rate} = \frac{\text{Total Tax}}{\text{Taxable Income}}$$   **Eq. 1-3**

The average tax rate is often used in budgeting tax expense as a portion of income (what percent of taxable income earned is paid in tax).

The **effective tax rate** represents the taxpayer's average rate of taxation on each dollar of total income, including taxable *and* nontaxable income. Specifically,

$$\text{Effective Tax Rate} = \frac{\text{Total Tax}}{\text{Total Income}}$$   **Eq. 1-4**

Relative to the average tax rate, the effective tax rate provides a better depiction of a taxpayer's tax burden because it depicts the taxpayer's total tax paid as a ratio of the sum of both taxable and nontaxable income earned.

(*concluded*)

▮ **Effective tax rate**
- A taxpayer's average rate of taxation on each dollar of *total* income (taxable *and* nontaxable income).
- $= \dfrac{\text{Total Tax}}{\text{Total Income}}$
- Useful in comparing the relative tax burdens of taxpayers.

---

**Example 1-6**

Assuming Bill and Mercedes have $140,000 of taxable income and $10,000 of nontaxable income, what is their average tax rate?

**Answer:** 19.60 percent, computed as follows:

| Description | Amount | Explanation |
|---|---|---|
| (1) Taxable income | $ 140,000 | |
| (2) Tax on $140,000 taxable income | $27,443.50 | Example 1-3. |
| Average tax rate | 19.60% | $\dfrac{\text{Total Tax}}{\text{Taxable Income}} = (2)/(1)$ |

We should not be surprised that Bill and Mercedes' average tax rate is *lower* than their marginal tax rate because although they are currently in the 28 percent tax rate bracket, not all of their taxable income is subject to tax at 28 percent. The first $16,750 of their taxable income is taxed at 10 percent, their next $51,250 is taxed at 15 percent, their next $69,300 is taxed at 25 percent, and only their last $2,700 of taxable income is taxed at 28 percent. Thus, their average tax rate is considerably lower than their marginal tax rate.

---

**Example 1-7**

Again, given the same income figures as in Example 1-6 ($140,000 of taxable income and $10,000 of nontaxable income), what is Bill and Mercedes' effective tax rate?

**Answer:** 18.30 percent, computed as follows:

| Description | Amount | Explanation |
|---|---|---|
| (1) Total income | $ 150,000 | $140,000 taxable income plus $10,000 in nontaxable income (Example 1-6). |
| (2) Tax on $140,000 taxable income | $27,443.50 | Example 1-3. |
| Effective tax rate | 18.30% | $\dfrac{\text{Total Tax}}{\text{Total Income}} = (2)/(1)$ |

Should we be surprised that the effective tax rate is lower than the *average* tax rate? No, because except when the taxpayer has more nondeductible expenses (such as fines or penalties) than nontaxable income (such as tax-exempt interest), the effective tax rate will be equal to or less than the average tax rate.

## TAX RATE STRUCTURES

There are three basic tax rate structures used to determine a tax: proportional, progressive, and regressive.

### Proportional Tax Rate Structure

A **proportional tax rate structure,** also known as a flat tax, imposes a constant tax rate throughout the tax base. As the tax base increases, the taxes paid increase proportionally. Because this rate stays the same throughout all levels of the tax base, the marginal tax rate remains constant and, in fact, equals the average tax rate (see Exhibit 1-1). The most common example of a proportional tax is a sales tax.

To calculate the tax owed for a proportional tax, simply use Equation 1-1 to multiply the tax base by the tax rate.

$$\text{Tax} = \text{Tax Base} \times \text{Tax Rate}$$

**Example 1-8**

Knowing her dad is a serious Bulldog fan, Margaret buys a $100 sweatshirt in downtown Athens. The city of Athens imposes a sales tax rate of 7 percent. How much tax does Margaret pay on the purchase?

**Answer:** $100 purchase (tax base) × 7% (tax rate) = $7

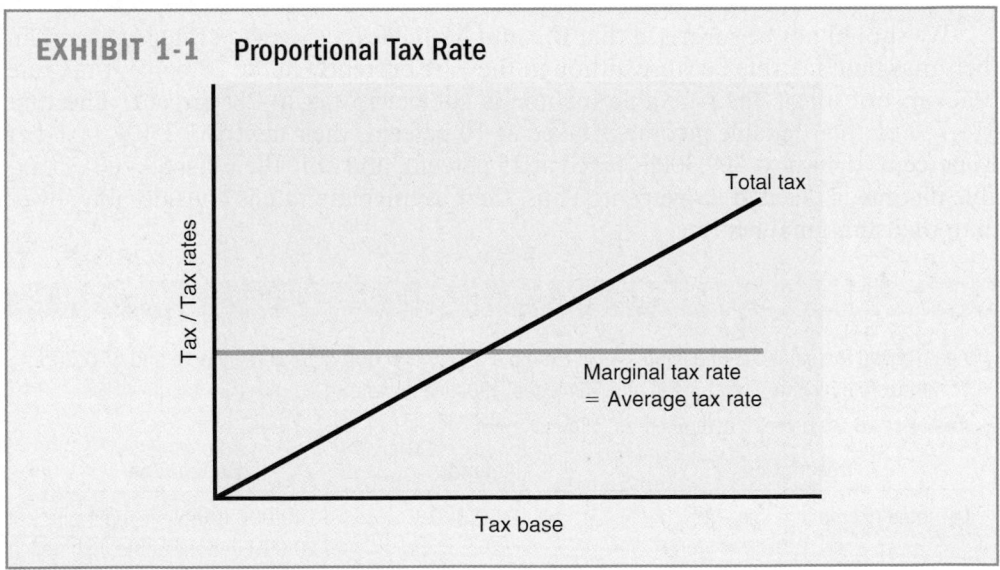

EXHIBIT 1-1    Proportional Tax Rate

### Progressive Tax Rate Structure

A **progressive tax rate structure** imposes an increasing marginal tax rate as the tax base increases. Thus as the tax base increases, both the marginal tax rate and the taxes paid increase. Common examples of progressive tax rate structures include

federal and state income taxes. The tax rate schedule in Example 1-3 is a progressive tax rate structure. As illustrated in Exhibit 1-2, the average tax rate in a progressive tax rate structure will always be less than or equal to the marginal tax rate.

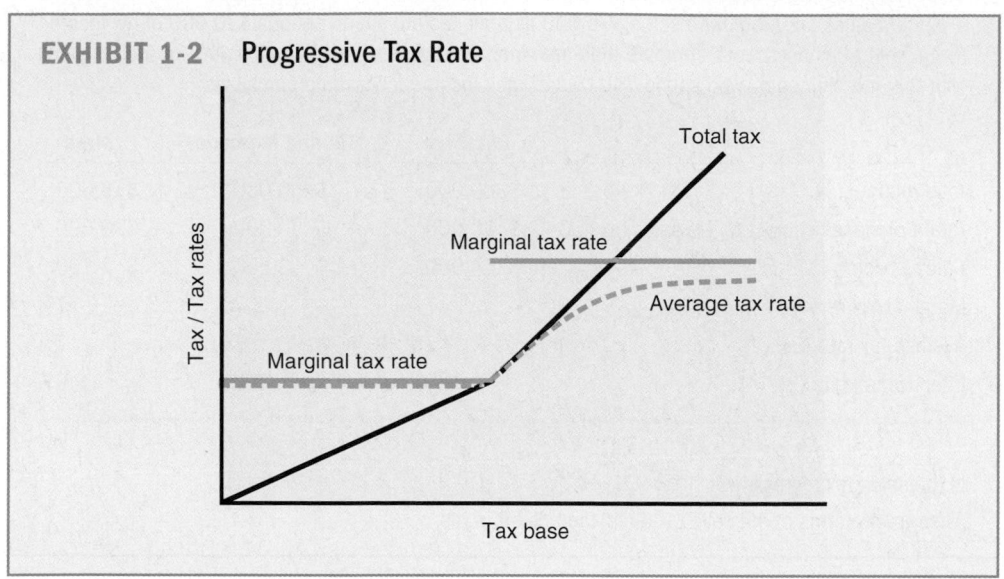

**EXHIBIT 1-2   Progressive Tax Rate**

### Regressive Tax Rate Structure

A **regressive tax rate structure** imposes a decreasing marginal tax rate as the tax base increases (see Exhibit 1-3). As the tax base increases, the taxes paid increases, but the marginal tax rate decreases. Regressive tax rate structures are not common. In the United States, the Social Security tax and federal and state unemployment taxes employ a regressive tax rate structure.[4]

However, some taxes are regressive when viewed in terms of effective tax rates. For example, a sales tax is a proportional tax by definition, because as taxable purchases increase, the sales tax rate remains constant. Nonetheless, when you consider that the proportion of your total income spent on taxable purchases likely decreases as your total income increases, you can see the sales tax as a regressive tax.

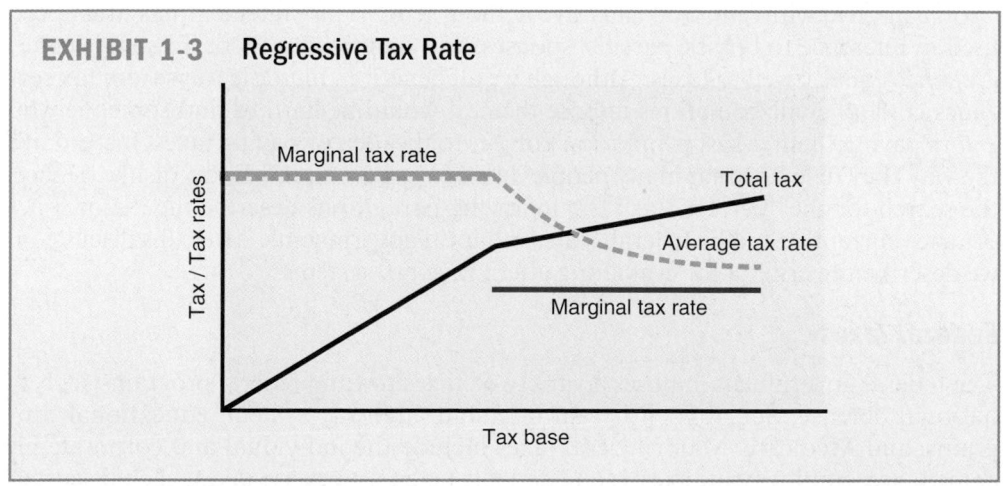

**EXHIBIT 1-3   Regressive Tax Rate**

[4]Wages subject to the Social Security tax (6.2 percent tax rate) are capped each year ($106,800 in 2010). Wages in excess of the cap are not subject to the tax. As might be expected, the maximum Social Security retirement benefit is capped as a function of the maximum wage base. Likewise, the federal and state unemployment tax bases and related unemployment benefits are capped.

## Example 1-9

Bill and Mercedes have two single friends, Elizabeth and Marc, over for dinner. Elizabeth earns $300,000 as CFO of a company and spends $70,000 for purchases subject to the 7 percent sales tax. Marc, who earns $75,000 as a real estate agent, spends $30,000 of his income for taxable purchases. Let's compare their marginal, average, and effective tax rates for the sales tax with Bill and Mercedes, who spend $50,000 of their income for taxable purchases:

|  | **Elizabeth** | **Bill and Mercedes** | **Marc** |
|---|---|---|---|
| Total income (1) | $300,000 | $150,000 | $75,000 |
| Total purchases subject to 7% sales tax (2) | $ 70,000 | $ 50,000 | $30,000 |
| Sales tax paid (3) | $ 4,900 | $ 3,500 | $ 2,100 |
| Marginal tax rate | 7% | 7% | 7% |
| Average tax rate (3)/(2) | 7% | 7% | 7% |
| Effective tax rate (3)/(1) | 1.6% | 2.3% | 2.8% |

Is the sales tax regressive?

**Answer:** In terms of *effective* tax rates, the answer is yes.

When we consider the marginal and average tax rates in Example 1-9, the sales tax has a proportional tax rate structure. But when we look at the *effective* tax rates, the sales tax is a regressive tax. Indeed, Marc, who has the smallest total income, bears the highest effective tax rate, despite all three taxpayers being subject to the same marginal and average tax rates. Why do we see such a different picture when considering the effective tax rate? Because unlike the marginal and average tax rates, the effective tax rate captures the *incidence* of taxation, which relates to the ultimate economic burden of a tax. Thus, a comparison of effective tax rates is more informative about taxpayers' relative tax burdens.

# TYPES OF TAXES

"You can't live with 'em. You can't live without 'em." This statement has often been used in reference to bosses, parents, spouses, and significant others. To some degree, it applies equally well to taxes. Although we all benefit in multiple ways from tax revenues, and all civilized nations impose them, it would be hard to find someone who *enjoys* paying them. Most people don't object to the idea of paying taxes. Instead, it's the way they're levied that many people, like Margaret's friend Eddy, dislike. Hence, the search for the "perfect" tax. The following paragraphs describe the major types of taxes currently used by federal, state, and local governments. After this discussion, we describe the criteria for evaluating alternative tax systems.

## Federal Taxes

The federal government imposes a variety of taxes to fund federal programs such as national defense, Social Security, an interstate highway system, educational programs, and Medicare. Major federal taxes include the individual and corporate income taxes, employment taxes, estate and gift taxes, and excise taxes (each discussed in detail in the following paragraphs). Noticeably absent from this list are a sales tax (a common tax for most state and local governments) and a **value-added tax** (a type of sales tax). Value-added taxes are imposed on the producers of goods and services based on the value added to the goods and services at each stage of production. They are quite common in Europe.

**Income Tax**   The most significant tax assessed by the U.S. government is the **income tax,** representing approximately 59 percent of all tax revenues collected in the United States in 2008. Despite the magnitude and importance of the federal income tax, its history is relatively short. Congress enacted the first U.S. personal income tax in 1861 to help fund the Civil War. This relatively minor tax (maximum tax rate of 5 percent) was allowed to expire in 1872. In 1892, Congress resurrected the income tax, but not without dissension among the states. In 1895, the income tax was challenged in *Pollock v. Farmers' Loan and Trust Company,* 157 U.S. 429 (1895). The U.S. Supreme Court ruled that the income tax was unconstitutional because direct taxes were prohibited by the Constitution unless the taxes were apportioned across states based upon their populations. This ruling, however, did not deter Congress. In July 1909, Congress sent a proposed constitutional amendment to the states to remove any doubt as to whether income taxes were allowed by the Constitution—and in February 1913, the 16th amendment was ratified.

Congress then enacted the Revenue Act of 1913, which included a graduated income tax structure with a maximum rate of 7 percent. The income tax has been an important source of tax revenues for the U.S. government ever since. Today, income taxes are levied on individuals (maximum rate of 35 percent), corporations (maximum rate of 39 percent), estates (maximum rate of 35 percent), and trusts (maximum rate of 35 percent). As Exhibit 1-4 illustrates, the individual income tax represents the largest source of federal tax revenues followed by employment taxes and the corporate income tax. We discuss each of these taxes in greater detail later in the text.

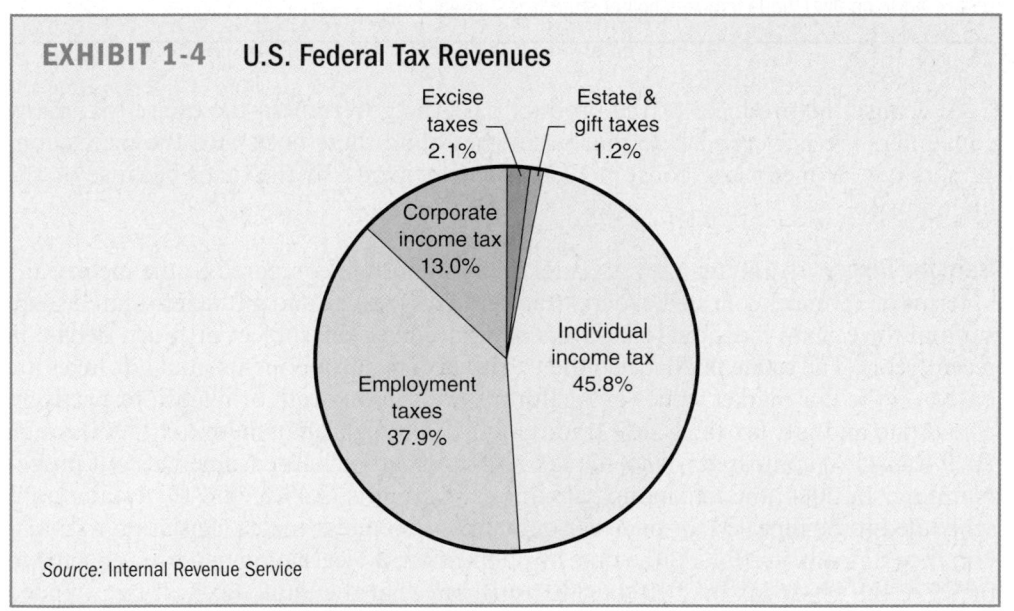

**EXHIBIT 1-4**   **U.S. Federal Tax Revenues**

- Excise taxes 2.1%
- Estate & gift taxes 1.2%
- Corporate income tax 13.0%
- Individual income tax 45.8%
- Employment taxes 37.9%

*Source:* Internal Revenue Service

**Employment and Unemployment Taxes**   Employment and unemployment taxes are the second largest group of taxes imposed by the U.S. government. **Employment taxes** consist of the Old Age, Survivors, and Disability Insurance (OASDI) tax, commonly called the Social Security tax, and the Medical Health Insurance (MHI) tax known as the Medicare tax. The **Social Security tax** pays the monthly retirement, survivor, and disability benefits for qualifying individuals, whereas the **Medicare tax** pays for medical insurance for individuals who are elderly or disabled. The tax base for the Social Security and Medicare taxes is wages or salary, and the rates are 12.4 percent and 2.9 percent, respectively. In 2010, the tax base for the Social Security tax is capped at $106,800. The tax base for the Medicare tax is not capped. Employers *and* employees split these taxes equally. Self-employed individuals, however, must pay these taxes in their entirety. In this case, the tax is often referred to as the **self-employment tax.** We discuss these taxes in more depth later in the text.

In addition to the Social Security and Medicare taxes, employers are also required to pay federal and state **unemployment taxes,** which fund temporary unemployment benefits for individuals terminated from their jobs without cause. As you might expect, the tax base for the unemployment taxes is also wages or salary. Currently, the Federal Unemployment Tax rate is 6.2 percent on the first $7,000 of wages. The U.S. government allows a credit for state unemployment taxes paid up to 5.4 percent. Thus, the Federal Unemployment Tax rate may be as low as 0.8 percent (6.2% − 5.4% = 0.8%).[5]

**Excise Taxes**   **Excise taxes** are taxes levied on the retail sale of particular products. They differ from other taxes in that the tax base for an excise tax typically depends on the *quantity* purchased, rather than a monetary amount. The federal government imposes a number of excise taxes on goods such as alcohol, diesel fuel, gasoline, and tobacco products and on services such as telephone use and air transportation. In addition, states often impose excise taxes on these same items.

---

**Example 1-10**

On the drive home from Athens, Georgia, Margaret stops at Gasup-n-Go. On each gallon of gasoline she buys, Margaret pays 18.4 cents of federal excise tax and 7.5 cents of state excise tax (plus 4 percent sales tax). Could Margaret have avoided paying excise tax had she stopped in Florida instead?

**Answer:**  No. Had she stopped in Florida instead, Margaret would have paid the same federal excise tax. Additionally, Florida imposes higher state taxes on gas.

---

Because the producer of the product pays the government the excise tax, many consumers are not even aware that businesses build these taxes into the prices consumers pay. Nonetheless, consumers bear the incidence of the taxes because of the higher price.

**Transfer Taxes**   Although they are a relatively minor tax compared to the income tax in terms of revenues collected, federal **transfer taxes**—estate and gift taxes—can be substantial for certain individual taxpayers and have been the subject of much debate in recent years. The **estate tax** (labeled the "death tax" by its opponents) and **gift taxes** are based on the fair market values of wealth transfers upon death or by gift, respectively. The estate and gift tax rates have traditionally been high (maximum tax rate through 2009 was 45%) compared to income tax rates and can be burdensome without proper planning. In 2010, the maximum rate imposed on gifts is 45%, and the estate tax is scheduled to be repealed for one year only unless Congress enacts legislation to maintain the estate tax in 2010. At the time of publication, no legislation had been enacted to preserve the estate tax in 2010, but we anticipate that the estate tax will be extended through 2010. Most taxpayers, however, are not subject to estate and gift taxation because of the annual gift exclusion and gift and estate unified tax credits. The annual gift exclusion allows a taxpayer to transfer $13,000 of gifts per donee (gift recipient) each year without gift taxation. The unified tax credit exempts from taxation up to $1,000,000 in lifetime gifts and in 2009, up to $3,500,000 in bequests (transfers upon death) and gifts.[6] Thus, only large transfers are subject to the gift and estate taxes.

---

[5]Although employers pay both federal and state unemployment taxes, all unemployment benefits actually are administered and paid by state governments.

[6]In 2010, the gift tax credit is $330,800 which exempts $1,000,000 of lifetime gifts from taxation. In 2009, the estate tax credit was $1,455,800, which exempted $3,500,000 of bequests and gifts from taxation. At the time of publication, the estate tax was scheduled for repeal in 2010 for one year. We anticipate that Congress will enact legislation to preserve the estate tax in 2010 and the credit that exempts $3,500,000 of bequests and gifts from taxation.

## State and Local Taxes

Like the federal government, state and local governments (such as counties, cities, and school districts) use a variety of taxes to generate revenues for their programs (such as education, highways, and police and fire departments). Some of the more common **state and local taxes** include income taxes, sales and use taxes, excise taxes, and property taxes. Typically, as shown in Exhibit 1-5, the largest state and local revenues are generated by state sales taxes and local property taxes.

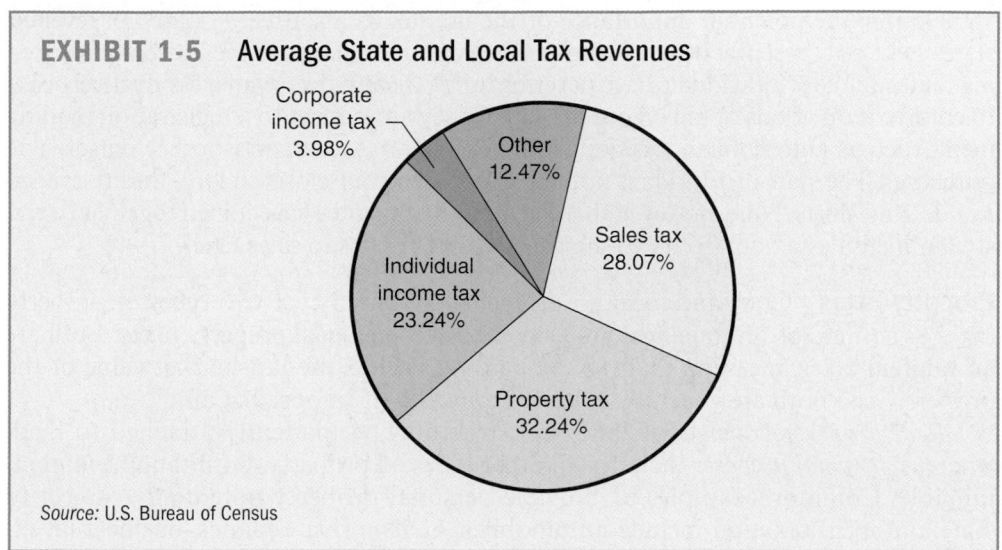

**EXHIBIT 1-5    Average State and Local Tax Revenues**

Corporate income tax 3.98%
Other 12.47%
Sales tax 28.07%
Individual income tax 23.24%
Property tax 32.24%

*Source:* U.S. Bureau of Census

**Income Taxes**   Currently, most states and the District of Columbia impose income taxes on individuals and corporations who either reside in or earn income within the state.[7] Calculations of individual and corporate taxable income vary with state law. Nonetheless, most state taxable income calculations largely conform to the federal taxable income calculations, with a limited number of modifications. The state of California is a notable exception. Certain local governments such as New York City also impose an income tax, and again, these generally follow the respective state taxable income calculation.

**Sales and Use Taxes**   Most states, the District of Columbia, and local governments impose sales and use taxes. The tax base for a **sales tax** is the retail sales of goods and some services, and retailers are responsible for collecting and remitting the tax; typically, sales tax is collected at the point of sale. The tax base for the **use tax** is the retail price of goods owned, possessed, or consumed within a state that were *not* purchased within the state. The purpose of a use tax is to discourage taxpayers from buying goods out of state in order to avoid or minimize the sales tax in their home state. At the same time, by eliminating the incentive to purchase goods out of state, a use tax removes any competitive disadvantage a retailer may incur from operating in a state with a high sales tax. States with a sales tax allow taxpayers to take a use tax credit on goods purchased out of state to mitigate the potential for double taxation on goods subject to sales tax in another state.

[7]Currently, Alaska, Florida, Nevada, South Dakota, Texas, Washington, and Wyoming have no personal income tax, and New Hampshire and Tennessee only tax individual dividend and interest income. Nevada and Wyoming do not impose taxes on corporate income, and South Dakota only taxes banks. Washington imposes a gross receipts tax instead of a corporate income tax. Texas and Ohio have an activity based tax that is based on net income or gross receipts.

---

**THE KEY FACTS**

**State and Local Taxes**

▪ **Sales and use taxes**
· The tax base for a sales tax is the retail sales of goods and some services.
· The tax base for the use tax is the retail price of goods owned, possessed, or consumed within a state that were *not* purchased within the state.

▪ **Property taxes**
· Property taxes are ad valorem taxes, meaning that the tax base for each is the fair market value of the property.
· Real property taxes consist of taxes on land and structures permanently attached to land.
· Personal property taxes include taxes on all other types of property, both tangible and intangible.

▪ **Income taxes**
· Most state taxable income calculations largely conform to the federal taxable income calculations, with a limited number of modifications.

▪ **Excise taxes**
· States typically impose excise taxes on items subject to federal excise tax.

**Example 1-11**

Margaret buys three new Lands' End shirts for her dad for $100. Because Lands' End does not have a business presence in Florida, it does not collect Florida sales tax on the $100 purchase. Does Margaret's purchase escape Florida taxation?

**Answer:** No. Because Florida has a 6 percent use tax, Margaret is liable for $6 in use tax on the purchase ($6 = $100 × .06).

Despite the potential importance of the use tax as a source of state tax revenue, states have only recently begun to enforce it. Poor compliance is therefore not surprising; indeed, many individuals have never heard of the use tax. While it is relatively easy to enforce it on goods obtained out of state if they are subject to a registration requirement, such as automobiles, it is quite difficult for states to tax most other out-of-state purchases. The state of Florida is not likely to search your closet to look for tax-evaded Lands' End shirts. Note, however, that the majority of states have joined together (www.streamlinedsalestax.org) to try to subject all Internet sales to sales taxes.

**Property Taxes**    State and local governments commonly use two types of property taxes as sources of revenue: **real property taxes** and **personal property taxes.** Both are **ad valorem** taxes, meaning that the tax base for each is the fair market value of the property, and both are generally collected annually (if imposed at all).

*Real property* consists of land and structures permanently attached to land, whereas *personal property* includes all other types of property, both tangible and intangible. Common examples of tangible personal property potentially subject to state and local taxation include automobiles, boats, private planes, business inventory, equipment, and furniture. Intangible personal property potentially subject to state and local taxation includes stocks, bonds, and intellectual property. Relative to personal property tax, real property taxes are easier to administer because real property is not moveable and purchases often have to be registered with the state, thereby making it easy to identify the tax base and taxpayer. Furthermore, the taxing body can estimate market values for real property without much difficulty. In contrast, personal property is generally mobile (easier to hide) and may be more difficult to value, which make personal property taxes difficult to enforce. Accordingly, whereas all states and the District of Columbia provide for a real property tax, only a majority of states currently impose personal property taxes, most of which are assessed at the time of licensing or registration.

**Excise Taxes**    We've said that the tax base for excise taxes is typically based on the quantity of an item or service purchased. States typically impose excise taxes on items subject to federal excise tax. Transactions subject to state excise tax often include the sale of alcohol, diesel fuel, gasoline, tobacco products, and telephone services.

### Implicit Taxes

All the taxes discussed above are **explicit taxes;** that is, they are taxes directly imposed by a government and are easily quantified. **Implicit taxes,** on the other hand, are indirect taxes—not paid directly to the government—that result from a tax advantage the government grants to certain transactions to satisfy social, economic, or other objectives. Implicit taxes are defined as the reduced before-tax return that a tax-favored asset produces because of its tax-advantaged status. Let's examine this concept more closely.

First of all, what does it mean to be *tax-favored?* An asset is said to be tax-favored when the income the asset produces is either excluded from the tax base or subject to a lower (preferential) tax rate, or if the asset generates some other tax benefit such as large tax deductions. These tax benefits, *all other things equal,* result in higher after-tax profits (or lower after-tax costs) from investing in the tax-advantaged assets.

Why do tax-advantaged assets bear an implicit tax, or a reduced before-tax return as a result of the tax advantage? The answer is simple economics. The tax benefits associated with the tax-favored asset increase the demand for the asset. Increased demand drives up the price of the asset, which in turn, reduces its before-tax return, which is an implicit tax by definition. Consider Example 1-12.

Example 1-12

Consider two bonds, one issued by the Coca-Cola Co. and the other issued by the state of Georgia. Both bonds have similar nontax characteristics (risk, for example), the same face value of $10,000, and the same market interest rate of 10 percent. The only difference between the two bonds is that the interest income from the Coca-Cola Co. bond is subject to a 20 percent income tax rate, whereas the interest income from the State of Georgia bond is tax-exempt with a 0 percent tax rate. Which of the two bonds is a better investment and should therefore have a higher demand?

| | Price | Before-Tax* Return | Interest Income | Income[†] Tax | After-Tax Income | After-Tax[†] Return |
|---|---|---|---|---|---|---|
| Coca-Cola Bond | $10,000 | 10% | $1,000 | $200 | $  800 | 8% |
| State of GA Bond | $10,000 | 10% | $1,000 | 0 | $1,000 | 10% |

*Before-tax return is calculated as the before-tax income divided by the price of the bond. Likewise, after-tax return is calculated as the after-tax income divided by the price of the bond.
[†]Income tax equals the taxable interest income ($1,000) multiplied by the assumed income marginal tax rate (20 percent).

**Answer:** Compare the after-tax returns of the bonds. Given the difference between the return after taxes (10 percent vs. 8 percent), the better investment—again, all other investment features being equal—is the State of Georgia bond because it provides a higher *after*-tax return. Because all investors in this example should prefer to buy the State of Georgia bond, the demand for the bond will be high, and its price should increase. This increase in price leads to a lower before-tax return due to the bond's tax-favored status (this is an implicit tax).

Example 1-12 is a basic illustration of the need to consider the role of taxes in investment decisions. Without understanding the relative tax effects associated with each bond, we cannot correctly compare their after-tax returns.

At what point in Example 1-12 would you be indifferent between investing in the Coca-Cola Co. bond and the State of Georgia bond? Assuming each bond has the same nontax characteristics, you would be indifferent between them when they both provide the same after-tax rate of return. This could occur if the state of Georgia raised the price of its bond from $10,000 to $12,500 ($1,000 interest/$12,500 price = 8% return). Or the state of Georgia could lower its bond interest payment from $1,000 to $800 ($800 interest/$10,000 price = 8% return). Either way, the state of Georgia benefits from selling the tax-exempt bonds—either at a higher price or at a lower interest rate relative to other bonds. Let's look more closely at this latter option, because it is, in fact, what many tax-exempt bond issuers choose to do.

| | Price | Before-Tax Return | Interest Income | Income Tax | After-Tax Income | After-Tax Return |
|---|---|---|---|---|---|---|
| Coca-Cola Bond | $10,000 | 10% | $1,000 | $200 | $800 | 8% |
| State of GA Bond | $10,000 | 8% | $  800 | 0 | $800 | 8% |

At this point, assuming each bond has the same nontax characteristics, an investor should be indifferent between the Coca-Cola Co. bond and the State of Georgia bond. What is the tax burden on investors choosing the Coca-Cola Co. bond? Coca-Cola Co. bond investors are paying $200 of income taxes (explicit taxes). What is the tax burden on investors choosing the State of Georgia bond? While it is true they are subject to zero income taxes (explicit taxes), they are subject to implicit taxes in the form of the $200 less in interest income they accept. This $200 reduced interest income (2 percent reduced before-tax rate of return) is an implicit tax. Although the investors in the State of Georgia bond are not paying this tax directly, they are paying it indirectly.

Does this happen in real life? Yes. Municipal bond interest income (interest income paid on bonds issued by state and local governments) generally is not subject to federal income taxation. Because of their tax-advantaged status, municipalities are able to pay a lower interest rate on their bond issuances and investors are willing to accept the lower rate. This type of indirect federal subsidy allows municipalities to raise money at a reduced cost without the need of direct federal subsidy or approval.

Although we were able to quantify the implicit taxes paid in the above example, in reality it is very difficult to estimate the amount of implicit taxes paid. For example, the federal government subsidizes housing by allowing taxpayers to deduct mortgage interest on their principal residence. Does this subsidy result in an implicit tax in the form of higher housing prices? Probably. Nonetheless, it would be difficult to quantify this implicit tax.

Despite the difficulty in quantifying implicit taxes, you should understand the concept of implicit taxes so you can make informed judgments about the attractiveness of alternative investments, and about the relative total tax burdens of tax-advantaged investments (considering both explicit and implicit taxes).

## L05 EVALUATING ALTERNATIVE TAX SYSTEMS

Although it may appear that tax systems are designed without much forethought, in truth lawmakers engage in continuous debate over the basic questions of whom to tax, what to tax, and how much to tax. Margaret's friend Eddy is obviously upset with what he views as an unfair tax system. But fairness, as we will discuss shortly, is often like beauty—it is in the eye of the beholder. What is fair to one may seem blatantly unfair to others. In the following paragraphs, we offer various criteria (sufficiency, equity, certainty, convenience, and economy) you can use to evaluate alternative tax systems.[8] Satisfying everyone at the same time is difficult. Hence, the spirited debate on tax reform.

### Sufficiency

Judging the **sufficiency** of a tax system means assessing the size of the tax revenues it must generate and ensuring that it provides them. For a tax system to be successful, it must provide sufficient revenues to pay for governmental expenditures for a defense system, social services, and so on. This sounds easy enough: Estimate the amount of government expenditures that will be required, and then design the system to generate enough revenues to pay for these expenses. In reality, however, accurately estimating governmental expenditures and revenues is a rather daunting and imprecise process. Estimating governmental expenditures is difficult because it is impossible to predict the unknown. For example, in recent years governmental expenditures have increased due to the terrorist attacks of September 11, 2001, the Iraq

---

[8]Adam Smith identified and described the latter four criteria in *The Wealth of Nations*.

War, and natural disasters such as the hurricanes in the Gulf Coast area. Likewise, estimating governmental revenues is difficult because tax revenues are the result of transactions influenced by these same national events, the economy, and other factors. Thus, precisely estimating and matching governmental expenditures with tax revenues is nearly impossible.

The task of estimating tax revenues becomes even more daunting when the government attempts to make significant changes to the existing tax system or design a new one. Whenever Congress proposes changing who is taxed, what is taxed, or how much is taxed, its members must consider the taxpayer response to the change. That affects the amount of tax collected, and how forecasters predict what taxpayers will do affects how much revenue they estimate.

**Static vs. Dynamic Forecasting**   One option in forecasting revenue is to ignore how taxpayers may alter their activities in response to a tax law change and to base projected tax revenues on the existing state of transactions, a process referred to as **static forecasting.** However, this type of forecasting may result in a large discrepancy in projected versus actual tax revenues if taxpayers do change their behavior. The other choice is to attempt to account for possible taxpayer responses to the tax law change, a process referred to as **dynamic forecasting.** Dynamic forecasting is ultimately only as good as the assumptions underlying the forecasts and does not guarantee accurate results. Nonetheless, considering how taxpayers may alter their activities in response to a tax law change is a useful exercise to identify the potential ramifications of the change, even if the revenue projections ultimately miss the mark.

---

### Example 1-13

The city of Heflin would like to increase tax revenues by $2,000,000 to pay for needed roadwork. A concerned taxpayer recently proposed increasing the cigarette excise tax from $1.00 per pack of cigarettes to $6.00 per pack to raise the additional needed revenue. Last year, 400,000 packs of cigarettes were sold in the city. Will the tax be successful in raising the $2,000,000 revenue?

**Answer:** Not likely. The proposed tax increase of $5, and the assumption that 400,000 packs will still be sold, is an example of static forecasting: it ignores that many taxpayers may respond to the tax change by quitting, cutting down, or buying cheaper cigarettes in the next town.

---

In some cases, static forecasting can lead to a tax consequence opposite the desired outcome. In Example 1-13, we might estimate that given Heflin's close proximity to other cities with a $1.00 cigarette tax, the number of packs of cigarettes sold within the city would drop significantly to, say, 50,000. In this case, the tax increase would actually *decrease* tax revenues by $100,000 ($400,000 existing tax − $300,000 new tax), not a good outcome if the goal was to increase tax revenues.

**Income vs. Substitution Effects**   The example above described proposed changes in an excise tax, which is a proportional tax. In terms of a progressive tax such as an *income* tax, a tax rate increase or an expansion of the tax base can result in one of two taxpayer responses, both of which are important for dynamic forecasting. The **income effect** predicts that when taxpayers are taxed more (when, say, a tax rate increases from 25 to 28 percent), they will work harder to generate the same after-tax dollars. The **substitution effect** predicts that when taxpayers are taxed more, rather than work more, they will substitute nontaxable activities like leisure pursuits for taxable ones because the marginal value of taxable activities has decreased. Which view is accurate? The answer depends on the taxpayer. Consider the following examples.

**Example 1-14**

Margaret's friend George, who earns $40,000 taxable income as a mechanic, is taxed at an average rate of 10 percent ($4,000 of tax). If Congress increases the income tax rate such that George's average tax rate increases from 10 percent to 25 percent, how much more income tax will he pay?

**Answer:** It depends on whether the income effect or the substitution effect is operating. Assuming George is single and cannot afford a net decrease in his after-tax income, he will likely work more (the income effect rules). Prior to the tax rate increase, George had $36,000 of after-tax income ($40,000 taxable income less $4,000 tax). With the increased tax rate, George will have to earn $48,000 of taxable income to keep $36,000 after taxes [$48,000 − ($48,000 × .25) = $36,000]. Thus, if the income effect rules, the government will collect $12,000 of federal income tax from George, or $8,000 more than under the previous lower tax rate. In this scenario, the tax change increases government revenues because of the increased tax rate *and* the increased tax base.

Whether the substitution effect or the income effect will describe any individual taxpayer's reaction to a tax increase is something we can only guess. But some factors—such as having higher disposable income—are likely to correlate with the substitution effect.

**Example 1-15**

***What if:*** Now let's assume that George is married and has two young children, both he and his wife work, and they file a tax return jointly with a 10 percent average tax rate. Either of their incomes is sufficient to meet necessities, even after the tax rate increase. But fixed child care costs make the marginal wage rate (the after-tax hourly wage less hourly child care cost) more sensitive to tax rate increases. In this case, the lower-earning spouse may choose to work less. Suppose George quits his full-time job and takes a part-time position that pays $20,000 to spend more time with his kids and to pursue his passion, reading sports novels. What are the taxes on George's income?

**Answer:** In this case, George will owe $5,000 tax ($20,000 × .25 = $5,000). Here, the substitution effect operates, and the government collects much less than it would have if George had maintained his full-time position, because the tax rate increase had a negative effect on the tax base.

As the previous examples illustrate, the response to a tax law change can vary by taxpayer and can greatly affect the magnitude of tax revenues generated by the change. Herein lies one of the challenges in significantly changing an existing tax system or designing a new one. If a tax system fails to generate sufficient revenues, the government must seek other sources to pay for governmental expenditures. The most common source of these additional funds for the federal government is the issuance of debt instruments such as Treasury bonds. This, however, is only a short-term solution to a budget deficit. Debt issuances require both interest and principal payments, which require the federal government to identify even more sources of revenue to service the debt issued, or to cut governmental spending (both of which may be unpopular choices with voters). A third option is for the government to default on its debt obligations. However, the costs of this option are potentially devastating. If the historical examples of Mexico, Brazil, and Argentina are any guide, a U.S. government default on its debt obligations would likely devalue the U.S. dollar severely and have extreme negative consequences for the U.S. capital markets.

The best option is for the government to match its revenues with its expenses—that is, not to spend more than it collects. State governments seem to be more

successful in this endeavor than the U.S. federal government. Indeed, all states except Vermont require a balanced budget each year, whereas the federal government has had deficit spending for most of the last 40 years.

## Equity

We've looked at the challenges of designing a tax system that provides sufficient revenues to pay for governmental expenditures. An equally challenging issue is how the tax burden should be distributed across taxpayers. At the heart of this issue is the concept of **equity** or fairness. Fairness is inherently subject to personal interpretation, and informed minds often disagree about what is fair. There is no "one-size-fits-all" definition of equity or fairness. Nonetheless, it is informative to consider in broad terms what makes a fair or equitable tax system.

In general terms, a tax system is considered fair or equitable if the tax is based on the taxpayer's ability to pay. Taxpayers with a greater ability to pay tax, pay more tax. In broad terms, each of the federal, state, and local taxes we've discussed satisfies this criterion. For example, those individuals with greater taxable income, purchases, property, and estates (upon death) generally pay higher dollar amounts in federal income tax, sales tax, property tax, and estate tax. If this is the case, why is there so much debate over the fairness of the U.S. income tax system? The answer is that equity is more complex than our first definition suggests. Let's take a closer look.

**Horizontal vs. Vertical Equity**    Two basic types of equity are relevant to tax systems. **Horizontal equity** means that two taxpayers in similar situations pay the same tax. In broad terms, each of the federal, state, and local taxes discussed satisfy this definition. Two individual taxpayers with the same taxable income, same purchases, same value of property, and same estate value pay the same federal income tax, sales tax, property tax, and estate tax. However, on closer inspection we might argue that each of these tax systems is *not* horizontally equitable. Here are some examples:

- Two individual taxpayers with the same income will not pay the same federal income tax if one individual's income was earned as salary and the other individual's income was tax-exempt municipal bond interest income, dividend income, or capital gain income, which can be subject to a lower tax rate.
- Two individuals with the same dollar amount of purchases will not pay the same sales tax if one buys a higher proportion of goods that are subject to a lower sales tax rate, such as groceries.
- Two individuals with real estate of the same value will not pay the same property tax if one individual owns farmland, which is generally subject to a lower property tax rate.
- Finally, two individuals with estates of the same value will not pay the same estate tax if one individual bequeaths more of her property to charity or a spouse, because these transfers are not subject to estate tax.

These failures of horizontal equity are due to what we call *tax preferences*. Governments provide tax preferences for a variety of reasons, such as to encourage investment or further social objectives. Whether we view these tax preferences as appropriate greatly influences whether we consider a tax system to be fair in general and horizontally equitable in particular.

The second type of equity to consider in evaluating a tax system is **vertical equity.** Vertical equity is achieved when taxpayers with greater ability to pay tax, pay more tax than taxpayers with less ability to pay. We can think of vertical equity in terms of tax dollars paid or in terms of tax rates. Proponents of a flat income tax or of a sales

---

**THE KEY FACTS**

**Evaluating Alternative Taxes—Equity**

▪ Equity considers how the tax burden should be distributed across taxpayers.

▪ Horizontal equity means that two taxpayers in similar situations pay the same tax.

▪ Vertical equity is achieved when taxpayers with greater ability to pay tax, pay more tax relative to taxpayers with a lesser ability to pay tax.

tax—both of which are proportional tax rate structures—are more likely to argue that vertical equity is achieved when taxpayers with a greater ability to pay tax, simply pay more in tax *dollars*. Proponents of a progressive tax system are more likely to argue that taxpayers with a greater ability to pay should be subject to a higher tax *rate*. This view is based upon the argument that the *relative* burden of a flat tax rate decreases as a taxpayer's income increases. Which is the correct answer? There is no correct answer. Nonetheless, many feel very strongly regarding one view or the other.

Our discussion has focused on how we can view alternative tax rate structures in terms of vertical equity, ignoring the role that the tax base plays in determining vertical equity. Indeed, focusing on the tax rate structure in evaluating a tax system is appropriate only if the tax base chosen—whether it's taxable income, purchases, property owned, or something else—accurately portrays a taxpayer's ability to pay. This can be a rather strong assumption. Consider the sales tax in Example 1-9. Although taxable purchases in this example increase as the taxpayers' total incomes increase, total incomes increase at a much faster rate than taxable purchases. Thus, the gap between taxable purchases and total income widens as total income increases. The end result is that the effective tax rates for those with a greater ability to pay are *lower* than for those taxpayers with a lesser ability to pay, making this tax regressive. Regressive tax rate structures are generally considered not to satisfy vertical equity, unless you strongly believe that those with a greater ability to pay do so simply by paying more tax dollars, albeit at a lower tax rate. In sum, evaluating vertical equity in terms of effective tax rates may be much more informative than simply evaluating tax rate structures.

### Certainty

**Certainty** means that taxpayers should be able to determine when to pay the tax, where to pay the tax, and how to determine the tax. Determining when and where to pay each of the taxes previously discussed is relatively easy. For example, individual federal income tax returns and the remaining balance of taxes owed must be filed with the Internal Revenue Service each year on or before April 15th. Likewise, sales taxes, property taxes, and excise taxes are each determined with relative ease: Sales taxes are based on the value of taxable purchases, property taxes are generally based on assessed property values, and excise taxes are based on the number of taxable units purchased. Indeed, these taxes are calculated for the taxpayer and often charged at regular intervals or at the point of purchase; they do not require a tax return.

In contrast, income taxes are often criticized as too complex. What are taxable vs. nontaxable forms of income? What are deductible/nondeductible expenses? When should income or expenses be reported? For wage earners with few investments, the answers to these questions are straightforward. For business owners and individuals with a lot of investments, the answers are nontrivial. Yearly tax law changes enacted by Congress can make it more difficult to determine a taxpayer's current tax liability, much less plan for the future.

### Convenience

**Convenience** suggests that a tax system should be designed to facilitate the collection of tax revenues without undue hardship on the taxpayer or the government. Various tax systems meet this criterion by tying the collection of the tax as closely as possible to the transaction that generates it. For example, retailers collect sales taxes when buyers purchase goods. Thus, it is difficult for the buyer to avoid paying sales tax, assuming she is transacting with an ethical retailer. Likewise, employers withhold federal income and Social Security taxes directly from wage earners' paychecks, which

speeds the government's collection of the taxes and makes it difficult for the taxpayer to evade the taxes. If tax withholdings are not sufficient relative to the taxpayer's anticipated income tax liability, the taxpayer is required to make quarterly estimated tax installments. Individual quarterly estimated payments are due on April 15, June 15, September 15, and January 15, whereas corporate estimated tax payments are due on the 15th day of the third, sixth, ninth, and twelfth months of the corporation's fiscal year.

### Economy

**Economy** requires that a good tax system should minimize the compliance and administration costs associated with the tax system. We can view economy from both the taxpayers' and the government's perspectives. Believe it or not, most tax systems fare well in terms of economy, at least from the government's perspective. For example, the current IRS budget represents approximately 1/2 of a percent of every tax dollar collected. Compared to the typical costs of a collection agency, this is quite low.

How about from the taxpayer's perspective? Here the picture is a bit different. The sales tax imposes no administrative burden on the taxpayer and only small administrative costs on the local retailer. However, out-of-state sellers argue that collecting and remitting use taxes for thousands of state and city jurisdictions would be a substantial burden. Other taxes such as excise taxes and property taxes also impose minimal administrative costs on the taxpayer. In contrast, as we've seen, the income tax is often criticized for the compliance costs imposed on the taxpayer. Indeed, for certain taxpayers, record-keeping costs, accountant fees, attorney fees, and so on can be substantial. Advocates of alternative tax systems often challenge the income tax on this criterion.

### Evaluating Tax Systems—The Trade-off

At the heart of any debate on tax reform are fundamental decisions and concessions based on the five criteria we've just discussed. Interestingly enough, much of the debate regarding alternative tax systems reduces to a choice between simplicity and fairness. Those taxes that generally are simpler and easier to administer, such as the sales tax, are typically viewed as less fair. Those taxes that may be viewed as more fair, such as the federal income tax, often are more complex to administer. Thus, Margaret's friend Eddy faces a difficult choice about which type of tax system to advocate, as do all taxpayers. An understanding of the evaluative criteria should be helpful to anyone trying to reconcile the trade-offs among alternative tax proposals.

## CONCLUSION

In almost any society taxes are a part of life. They influence decisions about personal finance, investment, business, and politics. In this chapter, we introduced the basic concepts of why one should study tax, what is a tax, and how to calculate a tax. We also discussed various tax rates, tax rate structures, and different types of taxes imposed by federal, state, and local governments. Finally, we discussed the criteria that one might use to evaluate alternative tax rate systems. To make informed personal finance, investment, business, and political decisions, one must have a basic understanding of these items. In the following chapters we expand the discussion of how taxes influence these decisions while providing a basic understanding of our federal income tax system. Read on and learn more!

## SUMMARY

**LO1**  Demonstrate how taxes influence basic business, investment, personal, and political decisions.

- Taxes are significant costs that influence many basic business, investment, and personal decisions.
  - *Business decisions:* what organization form to take; where to locate; how to compensate employees; appropriate debt mix; owning vs. renting equipment; how to distribute profits, and so forth.
  - *Investment decisions:* alternative methods for saving for education or retirement, and so forth.
  - *Personal finance decisions:* evaluating job offers; gift or estate planning; owning vs. renting home, and so forth.
- Taxes also play a major part in the political process. Major parties typically have very diverse views on whom, what, and how much to tax.

**LO2**  Discuss what constitutes a tax and the general objectives of taxes.

- The general purpose of taxes is to fund the government. Unlike fines or penalties, taxes are not meant to punish or prevent illegal behavior; but "*sin taxes*" (on alcohol, tobacco, etc.) are meant to discourage some behaviors.
- The three criteria necessary to be a tax are that the payment is (1) required (it is not voluntary), (2) imposed by a government (federal, state, or local), and (3) not tied directly to the benefit received by the taxpayer.

**LO3**  Describe the different tax rate structures and calculate a tax.

- Tax = tax rate $\times$ tax base, where the tax base is what is taxed and the tax rate is the level of taxes imposed on the base. Different portions of a tax base may be taxed at different rates.
- There are three different tax rates that are useful in contrasting the different tax rate structures, tax planning, and/or assessing the tax burden of a taxpayer: the marginal, average, and effective tax rates.
- The marginal tax rate is the tax that applies to the next increment of income or deduction. The average tax rate represents a taxpayer's average level of taxation on each dollar of taxable income. The effective tax rate represents the taxpayer's average rate of taxation on each dollar of total income (taxable *and* nontaxable income).
- The three basic tax rate structures are proportional, progressive, and regressive.
  - A *proportional tax rate* structure imposes a constant tax rate throughout the tax base. As a taxpayer's tax base increases, the taxpayer's taxes increase proportionally. The marginal tax rate remains constant and always equals the average tax rate. A common example is a sales tax.
  - A *progressive tax rate* imposes an increasing marginal tax rate as the tax base increases. As a taxpayer's tax base increases, both the marginal tax rate and the taxes paid increase. A common example is the U.S. federal income tax.
  - A *regressive tax rate* imposes a decreasing marginal tax rate as the tax base increases. As a taxpayer's tax base increases, the marginal tax rate decreases while the total taxes paid increases.

**LO4**  Identify the various federal, state, and local taxes.

- Federal taxes include the income tax, employment taxes (Social Security and Medicare taxes), unemployment taxes, excise taxes (levied on quantity purchased), and transfer taxes (estate and gift taxes).
- State and local taxes include the income tax (levied by most states), sales tax (levied on retail sales of goods and some services), use tax (levied on the retail price of goods owned or consumed within a state that were purchased out of state), property taxes (levied on fair market value of real and personal property), and excise taxes.

- Implicit taxes are indirect taxes that result from a tax advantage the government grants to certain transactions to satisfy social, economic, or other objectives. They are defined as the reduced before-tax return that a tax-favored asset produces because of its tax-advantaged status.

Apply appropriate criteria to evaluate alternate tax systems.                    **LO5**

- Sufficiency involves assessing the aggregate size of the tax revenues that must be generated and ensuring that the tax system provides these revenues. Static forecasting ignores how taxpayers may alter their activities in response to a proposed tax law change and bases projected tax revenues on the existing state of transactions. Dynamic forecasting attempts to account for possible taxpayer responses to a proposed tax law change.
- Equity considers how the tax burden should be distributed across taxpayers. Generally, a tax system is considered fair or equitable if the tax is based on the taxpayer's ability to pay—that is, taxpayers with a greater ability to pay tax, pay more tax. Horizontal equity means that two taxpayers in similar situations pay the same tax. Vertical equity is achieved when taxpayers with greater ability to pay tax, pay more tax relative to taxpayers with a lesser ability to pay tax.
- Certainty means taxpayers should be able to determine when, where, and how much tax to pay.
- Convenience means a tax system should be designed to facilitate the collection of tax revenues without undue hardship on the taxpayer or the government.
- Economy means a tax system should minimize its compliance and administration costs.

## KEY TERMS

| | | |
|---|---|---|
| ad valorem (1-14) | graduated taxes (1-4) | self-employment tax (1-11) |
| average tax rate (1-7) | horizontal equity (1-19) | sin taxes (1-3) |
| bracket (1-4) | implicit tax (1-14) | Social Security tax (1-11) |
| certainty (1-20) | income effect (1-17) | state tax (1-13) |
| convenience (1-20) | income tax (1-11) | static forecasting (1-17) |
| dynamic forecasting (1-17) | local tax (1-13) | substitution effect (1-17) |
| earmarked tax (1-3) | marginal tax rate (1-4) | sufficiency (1-16) |
| economy (1-20) | Medicare tax (1-11) | tax (1-3) |
| effective tax rate (1-7) | personal property tax (1-14) | tax base (1-4) |
| employment taxes (1-11) | progressive tax rate structure (1-8) | tax rate (1-4) |
| equity (1-19) | proportional tax rate structure (1-8) | transfer taxes (1-12) |
| estate tax (1-12) | | unemployment tax (1-12) |
| excise taxes (1-12) | real property tax (1-14) | use tax (1-13) |
| explicit tax (1-14) | regressive tax rate structure (1-8) | value-added tax (1-10) |
| flat tax (1-4) | sales tax (1-13) | vertical equity (1-19) |
| gift tax (1-12) | | |

## DISCUSSION QUESTIONS

1. **(LO1)** Jessica's friend Zachary once stated that he couldn't understand why someone would take a tax course. Why is this a rather naïve view?

2. **(LO1)** What are some aspects of business that require knowledge of taxation? What are some aspects of personal finance that require knowledge of taxation?

3. **(LO1)** Describe some ways in which taxes affect the political process in the United States.

4. **(LO2)** Courtney recently received a speeding ticket on her way to the university. Her fine was $200. Is this considered a tax? Why or why not?

5. **(LO2)** Marlon and Latoya recently started building a house. They had to pay $300 to the county government for a building permit. Is the $300 payment a tax? Why or why not?

6. **(LO2)** The city of Birmingham recently enacted a 1 percent surcharge on hotel rooms that will help pay for the city's new stadium. Is this a tax? Why or why not?

7. **(LO2)** As noted in Example 1-2, tolls, parking meter fees, and annual licensing fees are not considered taxes. Can you identify other fees that are similar?

8. **(LO2)** If the general objective of our tax system is to raise revenue, why does the income tax allow deductions for charitable contributions and retirement plan contributions?

9. **(LO2)** One common argument for imposing so-called sin taxes is the social goal of *reducing* demand for such products. Using cigarettes as an example, is there a segment of the population that might be sensitive to price and for whom high taxes might discourage purchases?

10. **(LO3)** Dontae stated that he didn't want to earn any more money because it would "put him in a higher tax bracket." What is wrong with Dontae's reasoning?

11. **(LO3)** Describe the three different tax rates discussed in the chapter and how taxpayers might use them.

12. **(LO3)** Which is a more appropriate tax rate to use to compare taxpayers' tax burdens—the average or the effective tax rate? Why?

13. **(LO3)** Describe the differences between a proportional, progressive, and regressive tax rate structure.

14. **(LO3)** Arnold and Lilly have recently had a heated discussion about whether a sales tax is a proportional tax or a regressive tax. Arnold argues that a sales tax is regressive. Lilly counters that the sales tax is a flat tax. Who is correct?

15. **(LO4)** Which is the largest tax collected by the U.S. government? What types of taxpayers are subject to this tax?

16. **(LO4)** What is the tax base for the Social Security and Medicare taxes for an employee or employer? What is the tax base for Social Security and Medicare taxes for a self-employed individual? Is the self-employment tax in addition to or in lieu of federal income tax?

17. **(LO4)** What are unemployment taxes?

18. **(LO4)** What is the distinguishing feature of an excise tax?

19. **(LO4)** What are some of the taxes that currently are unique to state and local governments? What are some of the taxes that the federal, state, and local governments each utilize?

20. **(LO4)** The state of Georgia recently increased its tax on a pack of cigarettes by $2.00. What type of tax is this? Why might Georgia choose this type of tax?

21. **(LO4)** What is the difference between a sales tax and a use tax?

22. **(LO4)** What is an ad valorem tax? Name an example of this type of tax.

23. **(LO4)** What are the differences between an explicit and an implicit tax?

24. **(LO4)** When we calculate average and effective tax rates, do we consider implicit taxes? What effect does this have on taxpayers' perception of equity?

25. **(LO4)** Benjamin recently bought a truck in Alabama for his business in Georgia. What different types of federal and state taxes may affect this transaction?

26. **(LO5)** Kobe strongly dislikes SUVs and is appalled that so many are on the road. He proposes to eliminate the federal income tax and replace it with a $50,000 annual tax per SUV. Based on the number of SUVs currently owned in the United States, he estimates the tax will generate exactly the amount of tax revenue currently collected from the income tax. What is wrong with Kobe's proposal? What type of forecasting is Kobe likely using?

27. **(LO5)** What is the difference between the income and substitution effects? For which types of taxpayers is the income effect more likely descriptive? For which types of taxpayers is the substitution effect more likely descriptive?

28. **(LO5)** What is the difference between horizontal and vertical equity? How do tax preferences affect people's view of horizontal equity?

29. **(LO3, LO5)** Montel argues that a flat income tax rate system is vertically equitable. Oprah argues that a progressive tax rate structure is vertically equitable. How do their arguments differ? Who is correct?

30. **(LO3, LO5)** Discuss why evaluating vertical equity simply based on tax rate structure may be less than optimal.

31. **(LO4, LO5)** Compare the federal income tax to sales taxes using the "certainty" criterion.

32. **(LO5)** Many years ago a famous member of Congress proposed eliminating federal income tax withholding. What criterion for evaluating tax systems did this proposal violate? What would likely have been the result of eliminating withholding?

33. **(LO5)** "The federal income tax scores very high on the economy criterion because the current IRS budget is relatively low compared to the costs of a typical collection agency." Explain why this statement may be considered wrong.

## PROBLEMS

34. **(LO3)** Chuck, a single taxpayer, earns $75,000 in taxable income and $10,000 in interest from an investment in City of Heflin bonds. Using the U.S. tax rate schedule, how much federal tax will he owe? What is his average tax rate? What is his effective tax rate? What is his current marginal tax rate?

35. **(LO3)** Using the facts in the previous problem, if Chuck earns an additional $40,000 of taxable income, what is his marginal tax rate on this income? What is his marginal rate if, instead, he had $40,000 of additional deductions?

36. **(LO3)** In reviewing the tax rate schedule for a single taxpayer, Chuck notes that the tax on $75,000 is $4,681.25 plus 25 percent of the taxable income over $34,000. What does the $4,681.25 represent?

37. **(LO3)** Campbell, a single taxpayer, earns $400,000 in taxable income and $2,000 in interest from an investment in State of New York bonds. Using the U.S. tax rate schedule, how much federal tax will she owe? What is her average tax rate? What is her effective tax rate? What is her current marginal tax rate?

38. **(LO3)** Using the facts in the previous problem, if Campbell earns an additional $15,000 of taxable income, what is her marginal tax rate on this income? What is her marginal rate if, instead, she had $15,000 of additional deductions?

39. **(LO3)** Jorge and Anita, married taxpayers, earn $150,000 in taxable income and $40,000 in interest from an investment in City of Heflin bonds. Using the U.S. tax rate schedule for married filing jointly, how much federal tax will they owe? What is their average tax rate? What is their effective tax rate? What is their current marginal tax rate?

40. **(LO3)** Using the facts in the previous problem, if Jorge and Anita earn an additional $100,000 of taxable income, what is their marginal tax rate on this income? What is their marginal rate if, instead, they reported an additional $100,000 in deductions?

41. **(LO3)** In reviewing the tax rate schedule for married filing jointly, Jorge and Anita note that the tax on $150,000 is $26,687.50 plus 28 percent of the taxable income over $137,300. What does the $26,687.50 represent?

42. **(LO3)** Scot and Vidia, married taxpayers, earn $240,000 in taxable income and $5,000 in interest from an investment in City of Tampa bonds. Using the U.S. tax rate schedule for married filing jointly, how much federal tax will they owe? What is their average tax rate? What is their effective tax rate? What is their current marginal tax rate?

43. **(LO3)** Using the facts in the previous problem, if Scot and Vidia earn an additional $70,000 of taxable income, what is their marginal tax rate on this income? How would your answer differ if they, instead, had $70,000 of additional deductions?

44. **(LO4)** Melinda invests $200,000 in a City of Heflin bond that pays 6 percent interest. Alternatively, Melinda could have invested the $200,000 in a bond recently issued by Surething, Inc., that pays 8 percent interest with similar risk and other nontax characteristics to the City of Heflin bond. Assume Melinda's marginal tax rate is 25 percent.

    a. What is her after-tax rate of return for the City of Heflin bond?
    b. How much explicit tax does Melinda pay on the City of Heflin bond?
    c. How much implicit tax does she pay on the City of Heflin bond?
    d. How much explicit tax would she have paid on the Surething, Inc., bond?
    e. What is her after-tax rate of return on the Surething, Inc. bond?

■ planning    45. **(LO4)** Hugh has the choice between investing in a City of Heflin bond at 6 percent or a Surething bond at 9 percent. Assuming that both bonds have the same nontax characteristics and that Hugh has a 40 percent marginal tax rate, in which bond should he invest?

■ planning    46. **(LO4)** Using the facts in the previous problem, what interest rate does Surething, Inc., need to offer to make Hugh indifferent between investing in the two bonds?

■ planning    47. **(LO3, LO4)** Fergie has the choice between investing in a State of New York bond at 5 percent and a Surething bond at 8 percent. Assuming that both bonds have the same nontax characteristics and that Fergie has a 30 percent marginal tax rate, in which bond should she invest?

■ planning    48. **(LO4)** Using the facts in the previous problem, what interest rate does the state of New York need to offer to make Fergie indifferent between investing in the two bonds?

49. **(LO3)** Given the following tax structure, what minimum tax would need to be assessed on Shameika to make the tax progressive with respect to average tax rates?

| Taxpayer | Salary | Muni-Bond Interest | Total Tax |
|----------|--------|--------------------|-----------|
| Mihwah   | $10,000 | $10,000 | $600 |
| Shameika | $50,000 | $30,000 | ??? |

50. **(LO3)** Using the facts in the previous problem, what minimum tax would need to be assessed on Shameika to make the tax progressive with respect to effective tax rates?

51. **(LO5)** Song earns $100,000 taxable income as an interior designer and is taxed at an average rate of 20 percent (i.e., $20,000 of tax). If Congress increases the income tax rate such that Song's average tax rate increases from 20 percent to 25 percent, how much more income tax will she pay assuming that the income effect is descriptive? What effect will this tax rate change have on the tax base and tax collected?

52. **(LO5)** Using the facts from the previous problem, what will happen to the government's tax revenues if Song chooses to spend more time pursuing her other passions besides work in response to the tax rate change and earns only $75,000 in taxable income? What is the term that describes this type of reaction to a tax rate increase? What types of taxpayers are likely to respond in this manner?

53. **(LO5)** Given the following tax structure, what tax would need to be assessed on Venita to make the tax horizontally equitable?

| Taxpayer | Salary | Total Tax |
|---|---|---|
| Mae | $10,000 | $ 600 |
| Pedro | $20,000 | $1,500 |
| Venita | $10,000 | ??? |

54. **(LO5)** Using the facts in the previous problem, what is the minimum tax that Pedro should pay to make the tax structure vertically equitable based on the tax rate paid? This would result in what type of tax rate structure?

55. **(LO5)** Using the facts in the previous problem, what is the minimum tax that Pedro should pay to make the tax structure vertically equitable with respect to the amount of tax paid? This would result in what type of tax rate structure?

56. **(LO5)** Consider the following tax rate structure. Is it horizontally equitable? Why or why not? Is it vertically equitable? Why or why not?

| Taxpayer | Salary | Total Tax |
|---|---|---|
| Rajiv | $10,000 | $600 |
| LaMarcus | $20,000 | $600 |
| Dory | $10,000 | $600 |

57. **(LO5)** Consider the following tax rate structure. Is it horizontally equitable? Why or why not? Is it vertically equitable? Why or why not?

| Taxpayer | Salary | Total Tax |
|---|---|---|
| Marilyn | $10,000 | $ 600 |
| Kobe | $20,000 | $3,000 |
| Alfonso | $30,000 | $6,000 |

58. **(LO5)** Consider the following tax rate structure. Is it horizontally equitable? Why or why not? Is it vertically equitable? Why or why not?

| Taxpayer | Salary | Total Tax |
|---|---|---|
| Rodney | $10,000 | $600 |
| Keisha | $10,000 | $600 |

59. **(LO1, LO4)** Lorenzo is considering starting a trucking company either in Texas or Oklahoma. He will relocate his family, which includes his wife, children, and parents, to reside in the same state as his business. What types of taxes may influence his decision of where to locate his business?

■ planning

■ planning    60. **(LO5)** Congress would like to increase tax revenues by 10 percent. Assume that the average taxpayer in the United States earns $65,000 and pays an average tax rate of 15 percent. If the income effect is in effect for all taxpayers, what average tax rate will result in a 10 percent increase in tax revenues? This is an example of what type of forecasting?

■ research    61. **(LO5)** Locate the IRS Web site at www.irs.gov/index.html. For every $100 the IRS collected, how much was spent on the IRS collection efforts? What tax system criterion does this information help you to evaluate with respect to the current U.S. tax system?

■ research    62. **(LO4)** Using the Internet, find a comparison of income tax rates across states. What state currently has the highest income tax rate? In considering individual tax burdens across states, what other taxes should you consider?

# Tax Compliance, the IRS, and Tax Authorities

## Learning Objectives

**Upon completing this chapter, you should be able to:**

**LO 1** Identify the filing requirements for income tax returns and the statute of limitations for assessment.

■

**LO 2** Outline the IRS audit process, how returns are selected, the different types of audits, and what happens after the audit.

■

**LO 3** Evaluate the relative weights of the various tax law sources.

■

**LO 4** Describe the legislative process as it pertains to taxation.

■

**LO 5** Perform the basic steps in tax research and evaluate various tax law sources when faced with ambiguous statutes.

■

**LO 6** Describe tax professional responsibilities in providing tax advice.

■

**LO 7** Identify taxpayer and tax professional penalties.

B ill and Mercedes received a notice from the Internal Revenue Service (IRS) that their return is under audit for certain interest deductions. As you might expect, they are quite concerned, especially because it has been several years since they claimed the deductions and they worry that all their supporting documentation may not be in place. Several questions run through their minds. How could the IRS audit a return that was filed so long ago? Why was their tax return selected, and what should they expect during the audit? The interest deductions they reported were based on advice from their CPA. What would cause the IRS and a CPA to interpret the law differently? What is their financial exposure if the deductions are ultimately disallowed?

Will they have to pay interest and penalties in addition to the tax they might owe? ∎

| Storyline Summary | |
| --- | --- |
| *Taxpayers:* | Bill and Mercedes |
| *Family description:* | Bill and Mercedes are married with one daughter, Margaret. |
| *Employment status:* | Bill is an economics professor; Mercedes is a small business owner. |
| *Filing status:* | Married, filing jointly |
| *Current situation:* | Bill and Mercedes face an IRS audit involving a previous year's interest deductions. |

Even the most conservative taxpayer is likely to feel anxiety after receiving an IRS notice. This chapter will help answer Bill and Mercedes' questions and provide an overview of the audit process and tax research. While all taxpayers should understand these basics of our tax system, aspiring accountants should be especially familiar with them.

## LO1  TAXPAYER FILING REQUIREMENTS

To file or not to file? Unlike Hamlet's "to be or not to be," this question has a pretty straightforward answer. Filing requirements are specified by law for each type of taxpayer. All corporations must file a tax return annually regardless of their taxable income. Estates and trusts are required to file annual income tax returns if their gross income exceeds $600.[1]

The filing requirements for individual taxpayers are a little more complex. Specifically, they depend on the taxpayer's filing status (single, married filing jointly, and so on, discussed in more detail in Chapter 4), age, and gross income (income before deductions). Exhibit 2-1 lists the 2010 gross income thresholds for taxpayers based on their filing status, gross income, and age.[2] These amounts are indexed for inflation and thus change each year. For certain taxpayers such as the self-employed and those claimed as dependents by another taxpayer, lower gross income thresholds apply.

### EXHIBIT 2-1   2010 Gross Income Thresholds by Filing Status

| Filing Status and Age (in 2010) | 2010 Gross Income |
|---|---|
| Single | $ 9,350 |
| Single, 65 or older | $10,750 |
| Married, filing a joint return | $18,700 |
| Married, filing a joint return, one spouse 65 or older | $19,800 |
| Married, filing a joint return, both spouses 65 or older | $20,900 |
| Married, filing a separate return | $ 3,650 |
| Head of household | $12,050 |
| Head of household, 65 or older | $13,450 |
| Surviving spouse with a dependent child | $15,050 |
| Surviving spouse, 65 or older, with a dependent child | $16,150 |

Whether a taxpayer is due a refund (which occurs when taxes paid exceed tax liability) does *not* determine whether a taxpayer must file a tax return. Gross income determines whether a tax return is required. Further, note that a taxpayer whose gross income falls below the respective threshold is not precluded from filing a tax return. Indeed, taxpayers due a refund *should* file a tax return to receive the refund (or claim a refundable tax credit), even if they are not required to file a tax return.

### Tax Return Due Date and Extensions

Like the filing requirements, due dates for tax returns vary based on the type of taxpayer. Individual tax returns are due on the fifteenth day of the fourth month following year-end—that is, April 15 for calendar year individuals. (Due dates that fall on

---

[1]Estates file income tax returns during the administration period (i.e., before all of the estate assets are distributed).

[2]The gross income thresholds are calculated as the sum of the standard deduction and personal exemption(s) that apply to each respective filing status. We describe the standard deduction and personal exemptions in detail later in the text. IRC §6012.

a Saturday, Sunday, or holidays are automatically extended to the next day that is not a Saturday, Sunday, or holiday.) Similarly, partnership returns are also due on the fifteenth day of the fourth month following the partnership's year-end. For corporations, tax returns must be filed by the fifteenth day of the third month following the corporation's year-end (March 15 for calendar-year corporations). Any individual or corporation unable to file a tax return by the original due date can, by that same deadline, request a six-month extension to file, which is granted automatically by the IRS. Similarly, partnerships may request an automatic five-month extension to file.

An extension allows the taxpayer to delay filing a tax return but does *not* extend the due date for tax payments. Thus, when a taxpayer files an extension, she must estimate how much tax will be owed. If a taxpayer fails to pay the entire balance of tax owed by the original due date of the tax return, the IRS charges the taxpayer interest on the underpayment from the due date of the return until the taxpayer pays the tax.[3] The interest rate charged depends on taxpayer type (individual or corporation) and varies quarterly with the federal short-term interest rate.[4] For example, the interest rate for tax underpayments for individuals equals the federal short-term rate plus three percentage points.[5]

What happens if the taxpayer does not file a tax return by the time required, whether April 15 or an extended deadline? As you might guess, the IRS imposes penalties on taxpayers failing to comply with the tax law. In many cases, the penalties can be quite substantial (see later discussion in this chapter). In the case of failure to file a tax return, the penalty equals 5 percent of the tax due for each month (or partial month) that the return is late. However, the maximum penalty is generally 25 percent of the tax owed, and the failure to file penalty does not apply if the taxpayer owes no tax.

## Statute of Limitations

Despite the diligent efforts of taxpayers and tax professionals, it is quite common for tax returns to contain mistakes. Some may be to the taxpayer's advantage and others may be to the government's advantage. Regardless of the nature of the mistake, the taxpayer is obligated to file an amended return to correct the error (and request a refund or pay a deficiency) if the statute of limitations has not expired for the tax return. Likewise, the IRS can propose adjustments to the taxpayer's return if the statute of limitations for the return has not expired.

By law, the **statute of limitations** defines the period in which the taxpayer can file an amended tax return or the IRS can assess a tax deficiency for a specific tax year. For both amended tax returns filed by a taxpayer and proposed tax assessments by the IRS, the statute of limitations generally ends three years from the *later* of (1) the date the tax return was actually filed or (2) the tax return's original due date.

The statute of limitations for IRS assessment can be extended in certain circumstances. For example, a six-year statute of limitations applies to IRS assessments if the taxpayer omits items of gross income that exceed 25 percent of the gross income reported on the tax return. For fraudulent returns, or if the taxpayer fails to file a tax return, the news is understandably worse. The statute of limitations remains open indefinitely in these cases.

---

[3]The tax law also imposes a penalty for late payment in addition to the interest charged on the underpayment. We briefly discuss this penalty later in the chapter and in Chapter 7.

[4]The federal short-term rate is determined from a one-month average of the market yields from marketable obligations of the United States with maturities of three years or less.

[5]This same interest rate applies to individuals who overpay their taxes (i.e., receive a tax refund and interest payment as a result of an IRS audit or from filing an amended tax return).

---

> Bill and Mercedes file their 2006 federal tax return on September 6, 2007, after receiving an automatic extension to file their return by October 15, 2007. In 2010, the IRS selects their 2006 tax return for audit. When does the statute of limitations end for Bill and Mercedes' 2006 tax return?
>
> **Answer:** Assuming the six-year and "unlimited" statute of limitation rules do not apply, the statute of limitations ends on September 6, 2010 (three years after the later of the actual filing date and the *original* due date).
>
> **What if:** When would the statute of limitations end for Bill and Mercedes for their 2006 tax return if the couple filed the return on March 22, 2007 (before the original due date of April 15, 2007)?
>
> **Answer:** In this scenario the statute of limitations would end on April 15, 2010, because the later of the actual filing date and the original due date is April 15, 2007.

Taxpayers should prepare for the possibility of an audit by retaining all supporting documents (receipts, cancelled checks, etc.) for a tax return until the statute of limitations expires. After the statute of limitations expires, taxpayers can discard much but should still keep a copy of the tax return itself, as well as any documents that may have on-going significance, such as those establishing the taxpayer's *basis* or original investment in existing assets like personal residences and long-term investments.

## IRS AUDIT SELECTION

**L02**

Why me? This is a recurring question in life and definitely a common taxpayer question after receiving an IRS audit notice. The answer, in general, is that a taxpayer's return is selected for audit because the IRS has data suggesting the taxpayer's tax return has a high probability of a significant understated tax liability. Budget constraints limit the IRS's ability to audit a majority or even a large minority of tax returns. Currently, fewer than 2 percent of all tax returns are audited. Thus, the IRS must be strategic in selecting returns for audit in an effort to promote the highest level of voluntary taxpayer compliance and increase tax revenues.

Specifically, how does the IRS select tax returns for audit? The IRS uses a number of computer programs and outside data sources (newspapers, financial statement disclosures, informants, and other public and private sources) to identify tax returns that may have an understated tax liability. Common computer initiatives include the **DIF (Discriminant Function) system, document perfection program,** and **information matching program.** The most important of these initiatives is the DIF system. The DIF system assigns a score to each tax return that represents the probability the tax liability on the return has been underreported (a higher score = a higher likelihood of underreporting). The IRS derives the weights assigned to specific tax return attributes from historical IRS audit adjustment data from the National Research Program.[6] The DIF system then uses these (undisclosed) weights to score each tax return based on the tax return's characteristics. Returns with higher DIF scores are then reviewed to determine whether an audit is the best course of action.

---

[6]Similar to its predecessor, the Taxpayer Compliance Measurement Program, the National Research Program (NRP) analyzes a large sample of tax returns that are randomly selected for audit. From these randomly selected returns, the IRS identifies tax return characteristics (e.g., deductions for a home office, unusually high tax deductions relative to a taxpayer's income) associated with underreported liabilities, weights these characteristics, and then incorporates them into the DIF system. The NRP analyzes randomly selected returns to ensure that the DIF scorings are representative of the population of tax returns.

All returns are checked for mathematical and tax calculation errors, a process referred to as the document perfection program. Individual returns are also subject to the information matching program. This program compares the taxpayer's tax return to information submitted to the IRS from other taxpayers like banks, employers, mutual funds, brokerage companies, and mortgage companies. Information matched includes items such as wages (Form W-2 submitted by employers), interest income (Form 1099-INT submitted by banks), and dividend income (Form 1099-DIV submitted by brokerage companies). For tax returns identified as incorrect via the document perfection and information matching programs, the IRS recalculates the taxpayer's tax liability and sends a notice explaining the adjustment. If the taxpayer owes tax, the IRS will request payment of the tax due. If the taxpayer overpaid tax, the IRS will send the taxpayer a refund of the overpayment.

In addition to computer-based methods for identifying tax returns for audit, the IRS may use a number of other audit initiatives that target taxpayers in certain industries, engaged in certain transactions like the acquisition of other companies, or having specific attributes like home office deductions. Taxpayers of a given size and complexity, such as large publicly traded companies, may be audited every year.

---

**THE KEY FACTS**

**IRS Audit Selection**

■ The IRS uses a number of computer programs and outside data sources to identify tax returns that may have an understated tax liability.

■ Common computer initiatives include the DIF (Discriminant Function) system, document perfection program, and information matching program.

■ The DIF system assigns a score to each tax return that represents the probability the tax liability on the return has been underreported.

■ The document perfection program checks all returns for mathematical and tax calculation errors.

■ The information matching program compares the taxpayer's tax return to information submitted to the IRS from other taxpayers.

---

### Taxes in the Real World — *Survivor Winner Can't Outwit and Outsmart the IRS*

The IRS appears to have stepped up its use of television as an audit source in recent years. In 2006, the original winner of the CBS reality show *Survivor*, Richard Hatch, was convicted of tax evasion for failing to report his $1,000,000 prize. Also in 2006, the IRS targeted the much-publicized Academy Awards gift baskets (aka Oscar Swag). Prior to the 2006 Academy Awards, IRS Commissioner Mark Everson issued a press release stating, "there's no special red-carpet tax loophole for the stars. The gift basket industry has exploded, and it's important that the groups running these events keep in mind the tax consequences." Although termed "gift baskets," the famous Oscar baskets do not meet the definition of nontaxable gifts for federal tax purposes (a transfer made solely out of detached and disinterested generosity, out of affection, respect, admiration, charity or like impulses). Later in 2006, the IRS and Academy settled the tax obligations for gift baskets awarded through 2005 and agreed that 2006 recipients of the gift baskets (estimated to be worth more than $100,000) would be fully responsible for taxes on the gift baskets. The Academy also decided to discontinue the practice of awarding gift baskets.

---

How was Bill and Mercedes' tax return selected for audit? Given the audit focus on certain deductions, the IRS likely selected their return for audit because the amount or type of the deductions resulted in a high DIF score. IRS personnel then determined that the deductions warranted further review and, thus, selected the tax return for audit.

### Types of Audits

The three types of IRS audits are correspondence, office, and field examinations. **Correspondence examinations** are the most common. These audits, as the name suggests, are conducted by mail and generally are limited to one or two items on the taxpayer's return. Of the three types of audits, correspondence audits are generally the narrowest in scope and the least complex. The IRS typically requests supporting documentation for one or more items on the taxpayer's return, like charitable contributions deducted, for example. When appropriate documentation is promptly

supplied, these audits typically can be concluded relatively quickly. Of course, they can also be expanded to address other issues that arise as a result of the IRS's inspection of taxpayer documents.

**Office examinations** are the second most common audit. As the name suggests, the IRS conducts them at its local office. These audits are typically broader in scope and more complex than correspondence examinations. Small businesses, taxpayers operating sole proprietorships, and middle- to high-income individual taxpayers are more likely, if audited, to have office examinations. In these examinations, the taxpayer receives a notice that identifies the items subject to audit; requests substantiation for these items as necessary; and notifies the taxpayer of the date, time, and location of the exam. Taxpayers may attend the examination alone or with representation, such as their tax adviser or attorney.

**Field examinations** are the least common audit. The IRS conducts these at the taxpayer's place of business or the location where the taxpayer's books, records, and source documents are maintained. Field examinations are generally the broadest in scope and the most complex of the three audit types. They can last months to years and generally are limited to business returns and the most complex individual returns.

What type of exam do you think Bill and Mercedes will have? Because their return is an individual tax return and the audit is restricted to a relatively narrow set of deductions, their return will likely be subject to a correspondence audit. If the audit were broader in scope, an office examination would be more likely.

<table>
<tr><td>
**THE KEY FACTS**

**IRS Audits**

▪ The three types of IRS audits are correspondence, office, and field examinations.

▪ After the audit, the IRS will send the taxpayer a 30-day letter, which provides the taxpayer the opportunity to pay the proposed assessment or request an appeals conference.

▪ If an agreement is not reached at appeals or the taxpayer does not pay the proposed assessment, the IRS will send the taxpayer a 90-day letter.

▪ After receiving the 90-day letter, the taxpayer may pay the tax or petition the U.S. Tax Court to hear the case.

▪ If the taxpayer chooses to pay the tax, the taxpayer may then request a refund of the tax and eventually sue the IRS for refund in the U.S. District Court or the U.S. Court of Federal Claims.
</td></tr>
</table>

**After the Audit**    After the examination, the IRS agent provides a list of proposed adjustments (if any) to the taxpayer for review. If he or she agrees to the proposed changes, the taxpayer signs an agreement form (Form 870) and pays the additional tax owed or receives the proposed refund. If the taxpayer disputes the proposed changes, the taxpayer will receive a **30-day letter** giving him or her 30 days to either (1) request a conference with an appeals officer, who is independent and resides in a separate IRS division from the examining agent, or (2) agree to the proposed adjustment. An appeals officer would consider the merits of the unresolved issues as well as the "hazards of litigation"—that is, the probability that the IRS will lose if the case is brought to court and the resulting costs of a taxpayer-favorable ruling. If the taxpayer chooses the appeals conference and reaches an agreement with the IRS there, the taxpayer can then sign the Form 870. If the taxpayer and IRS still do not agree on the proposed adjustment at the appeals conference, or the taxpayer chooses not to request an appeals conference, the IRS will send the taxpayer a 90-day letter. See Exhibit 2-2.

The **90-day letter** (also known as a *statutory notice of deficiency*) explains that the taxpayer has 90 days to either (1) pay the proposed deficiency or (2) file a petition in the U.S. Tax Court to hear the case. The **U.S. Tax Court** is a national court whose judges are tax experts and who hear only tax cases. If the taxpayer would like to litigate the case but prefers it to be heard in the local **U.S. District Court** or the **U.S. Court of Federal Claims,** the taxpayer must pay the tax deficiency first and then sue the IRS for refund in the court.

Why would a taxpayer prefer one trial court over others? To understand this, we must appreciate the basic distinguishing factors of each. First and foremost, it is relatively common for the U.S. Tax Court, local U.S. District Court, or the U.S. Court of Federal Claims to interpret and rule differently on the same basic tax issue. Given a choice of courts, the taxpayer should prefer the court most likely to rule favorably on his or her particular issues. The courts also differ in other ways. For example, the U.S. District Court is the only court that provides for a jury trial; the U.S. Tax Court is the only court that allows tax cases to be heard *before* the taxpayer pays the disputed liability and the only court with a small claims division

**EXHIBIT 2-2    IRS Appeals/Litigation Process**

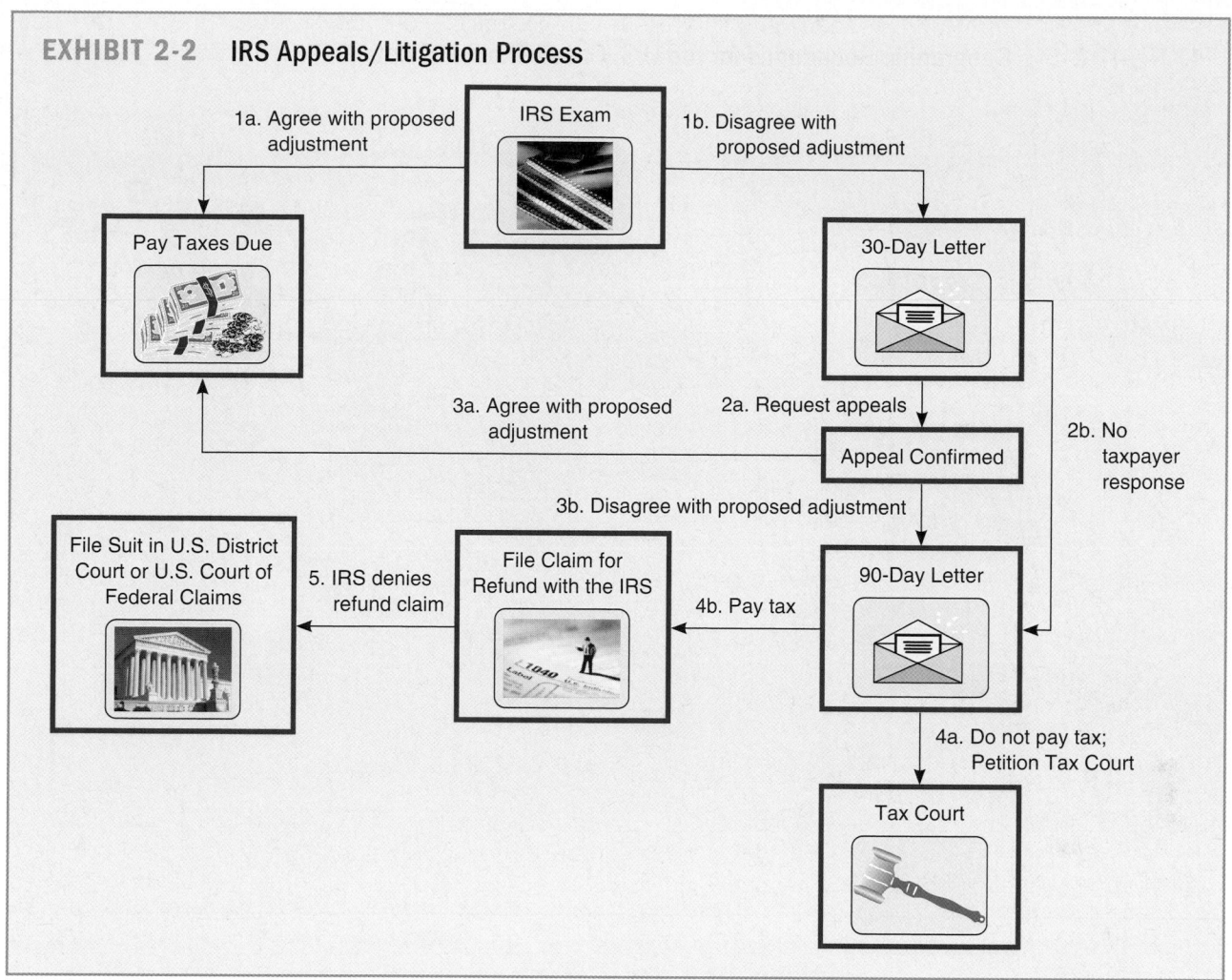

(hearing claims involving disputed liabilities of $50,000 or less); the U.S. Tax Court judges are tax experts, whereas the U.S. District Court and U.S. Court of Federal Claims judges are generalists. The taxpayer should consider each of these factors in choosing a trial court. For example, if the taxpayer feels very confident in her tax return position but does not have sufficient funds to pay the disputed liability, she will prefer the U.S. Tax Court. If, instead, the taxpayer is litigating a tax return position that is low on technical merit but high on emotional appeal, a jury trial in the local U.S. District Court may be the best option.

What happens after the taxpayer's case is decided in a trial court? The process may not be quite finished. After the trial court's verdict, the losing party has the right to request one of the 13 **U.S. Circuit Courts of Appeal** to hear the case. Both the U.S. Tax Court and local U.S. District Court cases are appealed to the specific U.S. Circuit Court of Appeals based on the taxpayer's residence. Cases litigated in Alabama, Florida, and Georgia, for example, appeal to the U.S. Circuit Court of Appeals for the 11th Circuit; whereas those tried in Louisiana, Mississippi, and Texas appeal to the 5th Circuit. In contrast, all U.S. Court of Federal Claims cases appeal to the U.S. Circuit Court of Appeals for the Federal Circuit (located in Washington, D.C.). Exhibit 2-3 depicts the geographic regions for each of the 11 U.S. Circuit Courts of Appeal defined by numerical region. Not depicted are the U.S. Circuit Court of Appeals for the District of Columbia and the U.S. Circuit Court of Appeals for the Federal Circuit.

**EXHIBIT 2-3    Geographic Boundaries for the U.S. Circuit Courts of Appeal**

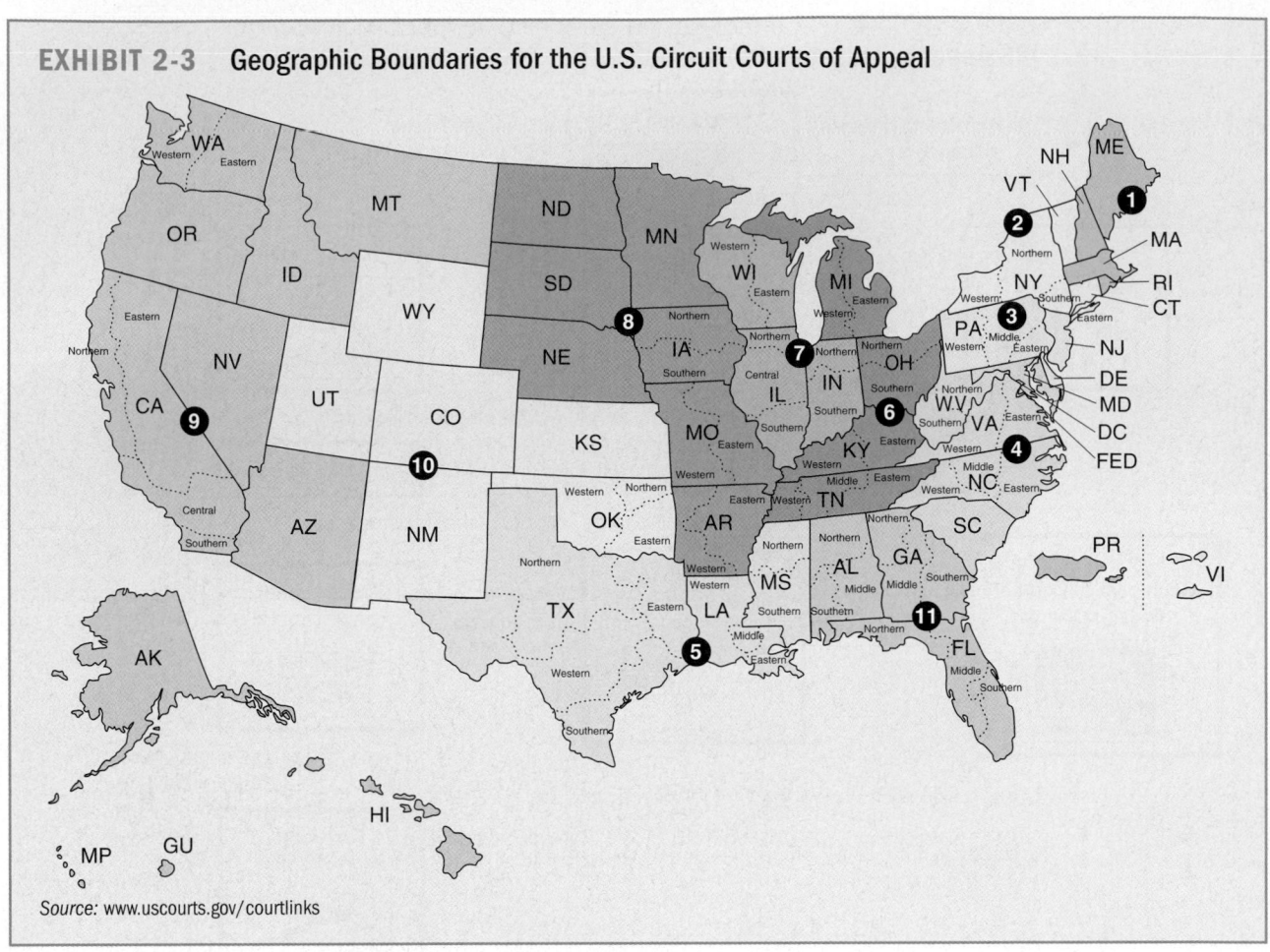

*Source:* www.uscourts.gov/courtlinks

Through the initial selection of a trial court—U.S. District Court, U.S. Tax Court, or U.S. Court of Federal Claims—the taxpayer has the ability to determine which circuit court would hear an appeal of the case (the U.S Circuit Court of Appeals based on residence or the U.S. Circuit Court of Appeals for the Federal Circuit). Because alternative circuit courts may interpret the law differently, the taxpayer should consider in choosing a trial-level court the relevant circuit courts' judicial histories to determine which circuit court (and thus, which trial court) would be more likely to rule in his or her favor.

After an appeals court hears a case, the losing party has one last option to receive a favorable ruling: a petition to the **U.S. Supreme Court** to hear the case. However, given the quantity of other cases appealed to the U.S. Supreme Court that are of national importance, the Supreme Court agrees to hear only a few tax cases a year with great significance to a broad cross-section of taxpayers, or cases litigating issues in which there has been disagreement among the circuit courts. For most tax cases, the Supreme Court refuses to hear the case (denies the ***writ of certiorari***) and litigation ends with the circuit court decision.

Although litigation of tax disputes is quite common, taxpayers should carefully consider the pros and cons. Litigation can be very costly financially and emotionally, and thus it is more appropriately used as an option of last resort, after all other appeal efforts have been exhausted.

What is the likely course of action for Bill and Mercedes' audit? It is too soon to tell. Before you can assess the likely outcome of their audit, you need a better

understanding of both the audit issue and the relevant tax laws that apply to the issue. The next section explains alternative tax law sources. After we discuss the various sources of our tax laws, we'll describe how Bill and Mercedes (or their CPA) can research the sources to identify the best possible course of action.[7]

# TAX LAW SOURCES

**L03**  **L04**

There are two broad categories of tax authorities: primary authorities and secondary authorities. **Primary authorities** are official sources of the tax law generated by the legislative branch (statutory authority issued by Congress), judicial branch (rulings by the U.S. District Court, U.S. Tax Court, U.S. Court of Federal Claims, U.S. Circuit Court of Appeals, or U.S. Supreme Court), and executive/administrative branch (Treasury and IRS pronouncements). Exhibit 2-4 displays the most common primary sources, and their relative authoritative weight (precedential

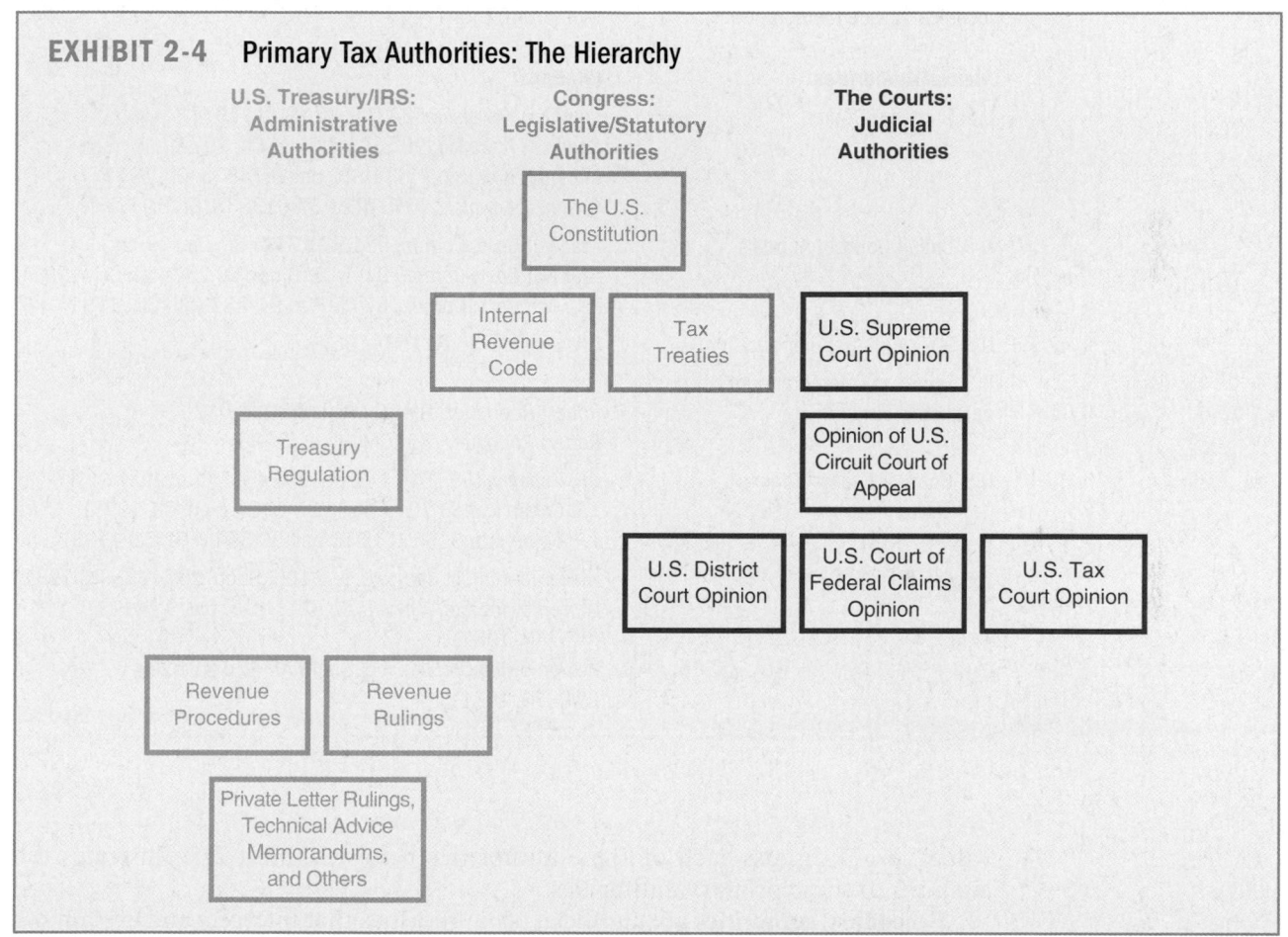

**EXHIBIT 2-4    Primary Tax Authorities: The Hierarchy**

U.S. Treasury/IRS:
Administrative
Authorities

Congress:
Legislative/Statutory
Authorities

The Courts:
Judicial
Authorities

The U.S.
Constitution

Internal
Revenue
Code

Tax
Treaties

U.S. Supreme
Court Opinion

Treasury
Regulation

Opinion of U.S.
Circuit Court of
Appeal

U.S. District
Court Opinion

U.S. Court of
Federal Claims
Opinion

U.S. Tax
Court Opinion

Revenue
Procedures

Revenue
Rulings

Private Letter Rulings,
Technical Advice
Memorandums,
and Others

---

[7]Accountants should be mindful to not engage in the unauthorized practice of law. In years past, several court cases have addressed this issue without providing a clear understanding between practicing tax accounting and the unauthorized practice of law. At present, tax accountants are not likely to overstep their responsibilities if they limit their advice to tax issues and leave the general legal advice and drafting of legal documents to attorneys.

**EXHIBIT 2-5** Citations to Common Primary Authorities

| *Statutory Authorities:* | *Citation:* |
|---|---|
| Internal Revenue Code | IRC Sec. 162(e)(1)(A) |
| Committee Reports: | |
| Senate Finance Committee Report | S. Rep. No. 353, 82d Cong., 1st Sess. 14 (1951). |
| House Ways and Means Committee Report | H. Rep. No. 242, 82d Cong., 1st Sess. 40 (1951). |
| | |
| *Administrative Authorities:* | *Citation:* |
| Final Regulation | Reg. Sec. 1.217-2(c)(1) |
| Temporary Regulation | Temp. Reg. Sec. 1.217-2(c)(1) |
| Proposed Regulation | Prop. Reg. Sec. 1.217-2(c)(1) |
| Revenue Ruling | Rev. Rul. 77-262, 1977-2 C.B. 42 |
| Revenue Procedure | Rev. Proc. 99-10, 1999-1 C.B. 272 |
| Private Letter Ruling | PLR 200601001 |
| Technical Advice Memorandum | TAM 200402004 |
| | |
| *Judicial Authorities:* | *Citation:* |
| U.S. Supreme Court | *Comm. v. Kowalski*, 434 U.S. 77 (S. Ct., 1977) |
| | *Comm. v. Kowalski*, 98 S. Ct. 315 (S. Ct., 1977) |
| | *Comm. v. Kowalski*, 77-2 USTC par. 9,748 (S. Ct., 1977) |
| | *Comm. v. Kowalski*, 40 AFTR2d 77-6128 (S. Ct., 1977) |
| U.S. Circuit Court of Appeals | *Azar Nut Co. v. Comm.*, 931 F.2d 314 (5th Cir., 1991) |
| | *Azar Nut Co. v. Comm.*, 91-1 USTC par. 50,257 (5th Cir., 1991) |
| | *Azar Nut Co. v. Comm.*, 67 AFTR2d 91-987 (5th Cir., 1991) |
| U.S. Tax Court—Regular decision | *L.A. Beeghly*, 36 TC 154 (1962) |
| U.S. Tax Court—Memorandum decision | *Robert Rodriguez*, RIA TC Memo ¶2005-012 |
| | *Robert Rodriguez*, 85 TCM 1162 (2005) |
| U.S. Court of Federal Claims | *J.R. Cohen v. U.S.*, 510 F. Supp. 297 (Fed. Cl., 1993) |
| | *J.R. Cohen v. U.S.*, 72 AFTR 2d 93-5124 (Fed. Cl., 1993) |
| | *J.R. Cohen v. U.S.*, 93-1 USTC par. 50,354 (Fed. Cl., 1993) |
| U.S. District Court | *Waxler Towing Co., Inc. v. U.S.*, 510 F. Supp. 297 (W.D, TN, 1981) |
| | *Waxler Towing Co., Inc. v. U.S.*, 81-2 USTC par. 9,541 (W.D., TN, 1981) |
| | *Waxler Towing Co., Inc. v. U.S.*, 48 AFTR2d 81-5274 (W.D., TN, 1981) |

value). We'll discuss each of these authorities below. Exhibit 2-5 illustrates the citations to these primary authorities.

**Secondary authorities** are unofficial tax authorities that interpret and explain the primary authorities, such as tax research services (discussed below), tax articles from professional journals and law reviews, and newsletters. For quick questions, practitioners often use the *CCH Master Tax Guide* or *RIA Federal Tax Handbook*. Secondary authorities may be very helpful in understanding a tax issue, but they hold little weight in a tax dispute (hence their "unofficial" status). Thus, tax advisers should always be careful to verify their understanding of tax law by examining primary authorities directly. Exhibit 2-6 lists some of the common sources of secondary authority.

**EXHIBIT 2-6**   Common Secondary Tax Authorities

**Tax Research Services:**

BNA Tax Management Portfolios

CCH Standard Federal Tax Reporter

CCH Tax Research Consultant

RIA Federal Tax Coordinator

RIA United States Tax Reporter

**Newsletters:**

Daily Tax Report

Federal Tax Weekly Alert

Tax Notes

**Law Reviews:**

Tax Law Review (New York University
School of Law)

Virginia Tax Review (University of
Virginia School of Law)

**Professional Journals:**

Journal of Accountancy

Journal of Taxation

Practical Tax Strategies

Taxes

Tax Adviser

**Quick Reference Sources:**

IRS Publications

CCH Master Tax Guide

RIA Federal Tax Handbook

## Legislative Sources: Congress and the Constitution

The three legislative or statutory tax authorities are the U.S. Constitution, the Internal Revenue Code, and tax treaties. The **U.S. Constitution** is the highest authority in the United States, but it provides very little in the way of tax law since it contains no discussion of tax rates, taxable income, or other details. Instead, the 16th Amendment provides Congress the ability to tax income directly, from whatever source derived, without apportionment across the states.

Various attempts to amend the U.S. Constitution with regard to taxation—for example, one effort to repeal the 16th amendment entirely and one to require a two-thirds majority in both houses to raise taxes—have so far met with failure.

**Internal Revenue Code**   The second (and main) statutory authority is the **Internal Revenue Code of 1986,** as amended, known as the Code. As indicated in Exhibit 2-4, the Internal Revenue Code has the same authoritative weight as tax treaties and Supreme Court rulings. Thus, a taxpayer should feel very confident in a tax return position, such as taking a deduction that is specifically allowed by the Code. The Internal Revenue Code is unique in that every other authority—all administrative and judicial authorities except tax treaties and the Constitution—can be seen as an interpretation of it. Hence, understanding the relevant code section(s) is critical to being an efficient and effective tax professional.

Congress enacts tax legislation virtually every year that changes the Code; 1986 was simply the last major overhaul. Prior to 1986, tax law changes were incorporated into the Internal Revenue Code of 1954, the year a new numbering system and other significant changes were introduced. Before that, tax law changes were incorporated into the Internal Revenue Code of 1939, which was the year of the first Code.

**The Legislative Process for Tax Laws**   Exhibit 2-7 illustrates the legislative process for enacting tax laws. As required by the U.S. Constitution (Article 1, Section 7), "All bills for raising revenue shall originate in the House of Representatives." The Senate may propose tax legislation, but the first to formally consider a bill will be the House, typically within its Ways and Means Committee. After the committee debates

**EXHIBIT 2-7** **Tax Legislation Process**

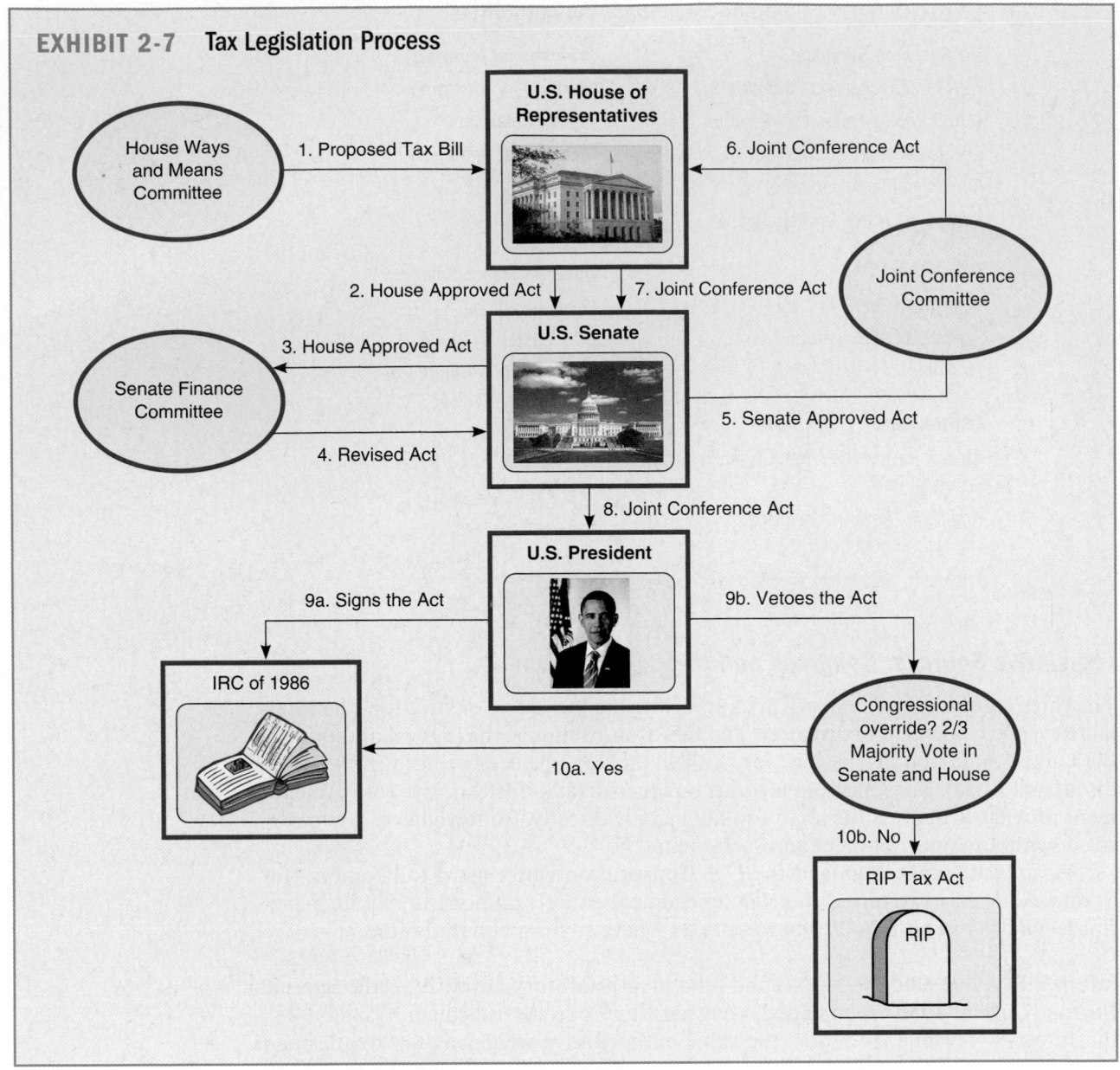

the proposed legislation and drafts a bill, the bill goes to the House of Representatives floor for debate and ultimately a vote (either yea or nay without modification). If the bill is approved, it becomes an *act* and is sent to the Senate, which typically refers the act to the Senate Finance Committee. Not to be outdone by the House, the Senate Finance Committee usually amends the act during its deliberations. After the revised act passes the Senate Finance Committee, it goes to the Senate for debate and vote. Unlike representatives, senators may modify the proposed legislation during their debate.

If the Senate passes the act, both the House and Senate versions of the legislation are sent to the Joint Conference Committee, which consists of members of the House Ways and Means Committee and the Senate Finance Committee. During the Joint Conference Committee deliberations, committee members debate the two versions of the proposed legislation. Possible outcomes for any specific provision in the proposed legislation include adoption of the Senate version, the House version, or some compromise version of the two acts. Likewise, the Joint

Conference Committee may simply choose to eliminate specific provisions from the proposed legislation or fail to reach a compromise, thereby terminating the legislation.

After the Joint Conference Committee approves the act, the revised legislation is sent to the House and Senate for vote. If both the House and Senate approve it, the act is sent to the president for his or her signature. If the president signs the act, it becomes law and is incorporated into the Internal Revenue Code of 1986 (Title 26 of the U.S. Code, which contains *all* codified laws of the United States). If the president vetoes the legislation, Congress may override the veto with a two-thirds positive vote in both the House and the Senate.

The House Ways and Means Committee, Senate Finance Committee, and Joint Conference Committee each produce a committee report that explains the current tax law, proposed change in the law, and reasons for the change. These committee reports are considered statutory sources of the tax law and may be very useful in interpreting tax law changes and understanding Congressional intent. This is especially important after new legislation has been enacted because, with the exception of the Code, there will be very little authority interpreting the new law (that is, no judicial or administrative authorities because of the time it takes for the new law to be litigated or for the IRS to issue interpretative guidance).

**Basic Organization of the Code**   The Internal Revenue Code is segregated into subtitles, chapters, subchapters, parts, subparts, and sections. All existing and any new tax laws are placed in the Code within a specific subtitle, chapter, subchapter, part, subpart, and section of the Code. When referencing a tax law, the researcher generally refers to the law simply by its code section. Code sections are numbered from 1 to 9833, with gaps in the section numbers to allow new code sections to be added to the appropriate parts of the Code as needed. Each code section is further segregated into subsections, paragraphs, subparagraphs, and clauses to allow more specific reference or citation.

Memorizing the various subtitles and chapters of the Code has limited value (except to impress your friends at cocktail parties). However, understanding the *organization* of the Code is important, especially for the aspiring tax accountant. First, you must understand the organization of a code section, its subsections, paragraphs, subparagraphs, and clauses to be able to cite the respective law correctly as, for example, IRC Sec. 162(b)(2). Second, note that many provisions in the Code apply only to specific parts of the Code. For example, it is quite common for a code section to include the phrase "for purposes of this chapter, . . . ." If you do not understand what laws are encompassed in the chapter, it would be very difficult for you to interpret the code section and determine its applicability to a research question.

Finally, remember that code sections addressing similar transactions, such as deductions, or topics, such as taxable corporations, are grouped together. Consider a researcher faced with the question of whether an item of income is taxable. If the researcher understands the organization of the Code, she can quickly focus her research on code sections 61–140, which provide a broad definition of gross income, list items specifically included in gross income, and identify items specifically excluded from gross income.

**Tax Treaties**   **Tax treaties** are negotiated agreements between countries that describe the tax treatment of entities subject to tax in both countries, such as U.S. citizens earning investment income in Spain. The U.S. president has the authority to enter into a tax treaty with another country after receiving the Senate's advice. If you are a U.S. citizen earning income abroad or an accountant with international clients, you

**EXHIBIT 2-8    Example of Code Organization**

**Subtitle A—Income Taxes**

Chapter 1—Income Taxes

**Subchapter A—Determination of Tax Liability**

Part I—Definition of Gross Income, Adjusted Gross Income, Taxable Income, etc. (Sec. 61-68)

**Sec. 61—Gross Income Defined**

**Sec. 62—Adjusted Gross Income Defined**

**Sec. 63—Taxable Income Defined**

Subsection 63(c)—Standard Deduction

**Paragraph 63(c)(2)—Basic Standard Deduction**

Subparagraph 63(c)(2)(A) . . .

**Clause 63(c)(2)(A)(i) . . .**

Part II—Items Specifically Included in Gross Income (Sec. 71-90)

**Sec. 71—Alimony**

**Sec. 72—Annuities**

**Sec. 73—Services of Child**

**Sec. 74—Prizes & Awards - . . .**

Part III—Items Specifically Excluded from Gross Income (Sec. 101-140)

**Sec. 101—Certain Death Benefits**

**Sec. 102—Gifts and Inheritances**

**Sec. 103—Interest on State & Local Bonds**

---

need knowledge of U.S. tax laws, the foreign country's tax laws, and the respective tax treaty between the U.S. and the foreign country for efficient tax planning. Because the focus in this text is on U.S. tax laws, we only briefly mention the importance of tax treaties as a statutory authority.

**Example 2-2**

Bill recently spent a summer in Milan, Italy, teaching a graduate level economics course. While in Italy he earned a $20,000 stipend from Bocconi University and some interest in a temporary banking account that he established for the trip. What tax laws must Bill consider to determine the taxation of his $20,000 stipend?

**Answer:** U.S. tax laws, Italian tax laws, and the U.S.-Italy tax treaty will determine the tax consequences of the amounts Bill earned in Italy.

**THE KEY FACTS**

**Judicial Authorities**

■ Our judicial system is tasked with the ultimate authority to interpret the Internal Revenue Code and settle disputes between taxpayers and the IRS.

■ The Supreme Court is the highest judicial authority.

■ Beneath the Supreme Court, the decisions of the 13 Circuit Courts of Appeal represent the next highest judicial authority.

*(continued)*

## Judicial Sources: The Courts

Our judicial system has the ultimate authority to interpret the Internal Revenue Code and settle disputes between the IRS and taxpayers. As Exhibit 2-4 illustrates, there are five basic sources of judicial authority (three trial-level courts, 13 U.S. Circuit Courts of Appeal, and the Supreme Court). We've noted that the Supreme Court, along with the Code, represents the highest tax-specific authority. An important distinction between the two, however, is that the Supreme Court does not establish law, but instead simply interprets and applies the Code (along with other authorities). Thus, the Code and the Supreme Court should never be in conflict.[8]

[8]The Supreme Court does have the authority to declare a Code provision unconstitutional.

Below the Supreme Court, the decisions of the 13 U.S. Circuit Courts of Appeal represent the next highest judicial authority. The lowest level of judicial authority consists of three different types of trial-level courts (U.S. District Courts, U.S. Court of Federal Claims, and the U.S. Tax Court). Given that the U.S. Tax Court hears only tax cases and that its judges are "tax experts," its decisions typically have more weight than those rendered by a district court or the U.S. Court of Federal Claims.[9] Likewise, because the U.S. Court of Federal Claims hears a much narrower set of issues than U.S. District Courts (only monetary claims against the U.S. government), its decisions have more weight than district court decisions.

In rendering court decisions, all courts apply the judicial doctrine of ***stare decisis.*** This doctrine means that a court will rule consistently with (a) its previous rulings (unless, due to evolving interpretations of the tax law over time, the court decides to overturn an earlier decision) and (b) the rulings of higher courts with appellate jurisdiction (the courts its cases are appealed to). The implication of *stare decisis* is that a circuit court will abide by Supreme Court rulings and its own rulings, whereas a trial-level court will abide by Supreme Court rulings, its respective circuit court's rulings, and its own rulings. For example, a district court in California would follow U.S. 9th Circuit and Supreme Court rulings as well as the court's own rulings.

The doctrine of *stare decisis* presents a special problem for the U.S. Tax Court because it appeals to different circuit courts based on the taxpayer's residence. To implement the doctrine of *stare decisis,* the tax court applies the **Golsen rule.** The Golsen rule simply states that the tax court will abide by rulings of the circuit court that has appellate jurisdiction for a case.

---

*(concluded)*

■ The lowest level of judicial authority consists of three different types of trial-level courts (U.S. District Courts, U.S. Court of Federal Claims, and the U.S. Tax Court).

■ U.S. Tax Court decisions typically are considered to have more authoritative weight than decisions rendered by a district court or the U.S. Court of Federal Claims.

■ All courts apply the judicial doctrine of *stare decisis*, which means that a court will rule consistently with its previous rulings and the rulings of higher courts with appellate jurisdiction.

---

**Example 2-3**

***What if:*** If Bill and Mercedes opt to litigate their case in tax court, by which circuit court's rulings will the tax court abide?

**Answer:** Because Bill and Mercedes live in Florida, the U.S. Tax Court will abide the circuit court with appellate jurisdiction in Florida, which happens to be U.S. 11th Circuit Court.

---

### Administrative Sources: The U.S. Treasury

**Regulations, Revenue Rulings, and Revenue Procedures** The Treasury Department, of which the IRS is a bureau, is charged with administering and interpreting the tax laws of the United States, among other duties such as printing money and advising the president on economic issues. **Regulations** are the Treasury Department's official interpretation of the Internal Revenue Code, have the highest authoritative weight, and often contain examples of the application of the Code that may be particularly helpful to the tax researcher. Regulations are issued in three different forms: final, temporary, and proposed. The names are very descriptive. **Final regulations** are regulations that have been issued in final form, and thus, unless or until revoked, they represent the Treasury's interpretation of the Code. **Temporary regulations** have a limited life (three years for regulations issued after November 20, 1988). Nonetheless, during their life, they carry the same authoritative weight as final regulations.

---

**THE KEY FACTS**

**Administrative Authorities**

■ The Treasury Department is charged with administering and interpreting the tax laws.

■ Regulations
· Regulations are the Treasury Department's official interpretation of the Internal Revenue Code and have the highest authoritative weight.
· Regulations are issued in three different forms (proposed, temporary, and final) and serve three basic purposes (interpretative, procedural, and legislative).

*(continued)*

---

[9]The Tax Court renders both "regular" and "memorandum" decisions. Regular decisions involve new or unusual points of law, whereas memorandum decisions involve questions of fact or the application of existing law. Both decisions have similar authoritative weight. Decisions issued by the Tax Court's Small Claims division may not be cited as precedent.

*(concluded)*

■ **Revenue rulings and revenue procedures**

· Revenue rulings and revenue procedures are second in administrative authoritative weight after regulations.

· Revenue rulings address the application of the Code and regulations to a specific factual situation.

· Revenue procedures explain in greater detail IRS practice and procedures in administering the tax law.

■ **Letter rulings**

· Letter rulings are less authoritative but more specific than revenue rulings and regulations.

· Private letter rulings represent the IRS' application of the Code and other tax authorities to a specific transaction and taxpayer.

Finally, all regulations are issued in the form of **proposed regulations** first, to allow public comment on them. Proposed regulations do not carry the same authoritative weight as temporary or final regulations.

In addition to being issued in three different forms, regulations also serve three basic purposes: interpretative, procedural, and legislative. Most regulations are issued as interpretative or procedural regulations. As the names suggest, **interpretative regulations** represent the Treasury's interpretation of the Code. In Bill and Mercedes' case, these might be the regulations issued under IRC Sec. 163, which discuss interest deductions. **Procedural regulations** explain Treasury Department procedures as they relate to administering the Code. Again, for Bill and Mercedes' case, these might be the regulations issued under IRC Sec. 6501 regarding the statute of limitations for IRS assessment and collection. **Legislative regulations,** the rarest type, are issued when Congress specifically directs the Treasury Department to create regulations to address an issue in an area of law. In these instances, the Treasury is actually writing the law instead of interpreting the Code. Because legislative regulations represent tax law instead of interpretation of tax law, legislative regulations have more authoritative weight than interpretative and procedural regulations. Nonetheless, it is a very difficult process to challenge any regulation and thus, taxpayers are cautioned not to take tax return positions inconsistent with regulations.

As illustrated in Exhibit 2-4, revenue rulings and revenue procedures are second in administrative authoritative weight after regulations. But unlike regulations, revenue rulings address the application of the Code and regulations to a specific factual situation. Thus, while **revenue rulings** have less authoritative weight, they provide a much more detailed interpretation of the Code as it applies to a specific transaction and fact pattern. For example, Rev. Rul. 87-22 discusses the deductions of prepaid interest (points) a taxpayer may claim when refinancing the mortgage for a principal residence, whereas the Code and regulations do not specifically address this issue. **Revenue procedures** are also much more detailed than regulations. They explain in greater detail IRS practice and procedures in administering the tax law. For example, Rev. Proc. 87-56 provides the specific depreciation lives for depreciable assets (discussed in Chapter 9).

**Letter Rulings**   Below revenue rulings and revenue procedures in authoritative weight rest letter rulings. As you might guess, letter rulings are less authoritative but more specific than revenue rulings and regulations. Indeed, **private letter rulings** represent the IRS's application of the Code and other tax authorities to a specific transaction and taxpayer. Private letter rulings are issued in response to a taxpayer request and are common for proposed transactions with potentially large tax implications. For example, companies commonly request a private letter ruling to ensure that a proposed corporate acquisition meets the definition of a tax-free exchange. However, the IRS also maintains a list of certain issues on which it refuses to rule, such as the tax consequences of proposed federal tax legislation. Each year, the IRS publishes an updated list of these transactions in a revenue procedure.

Other types of letter rulings include determination letters and technical advice memorandums. **Determination letters,** issued by local IRS directors, are generally not controversial. An example of a determination letter is the request by an employer for the IRS to rule that the taxpayer's retirement plan is a "qualified plan." **Technical advice memorandums** differ from private letter rulings in that they are generated for completed transactions and usually are requested by an IRS agent during an IRS audit.

Is this a comprehensive list of IRS pronouncements? No. In addition to the pronouncements listed above, the IRS issues several less common types, which are beyond the scope of this text. A couple of other pronouncements, however, warrant some discussion. As we mentioned above, the IRS and taxpayers litigate tax cases in

a number of courts and jurisdictions. Obviously, the IRS wins some and loses some of these cases. Except for Supreme Court cases, whenever the IRS loses, it may issue an **acquiescence** or **nonacquiescence** as guidance for how the IRS intends to respond to the loss. Although an acquiescence indicates that the IRS has decided to *follow* the court's adverse ruling in the future, it does not mean that the IRS *agrees* with it. Instead, it simply means that the IRS will no longer litigate this issue. A nonacquiescence has the exact opposite implications and alerts taxpayers that the IRS does plan to continue to litigate this issue. Finally, the IRS also issues **actions on decisions,** which explain the background reasoning behind an IRS acquiescence or nonacquiescence.

# TAX RESEARCH

L05

Now that you have a basic understanding of the different types of tax authority, why do you think that the IRS and taxpayers disagree with respect to the tax treatment of a transaction? In other words, why would the IRS and Bill and Mercedes' CPA reach different conclusions regarding the deductibility of certain expenses? The answer is that, because the Code does not specifically address the tax consequences of each transaction type or every possible variation of a particular transaction, the application of the tax law is subject to debate and differing interpretations by the IRS, courts, tax professionals, taxpayers, and so on. Tax research, therefore, plays a vital role in allowing us to identify and understand the varying authorities that provide guidance on an issue, to assess the relative weights of differing authorities, to understand the risks associated with different tax return positions, and ultimately to draw an appropriate conclusion regarding the application of the tax law to the issue. The following paragraphs describe the basic process of tax research that tax professionals use to identify and analyze tax authorities to answer tax questions. We will then revisit Bill and Mercedes' issue and view the research memo prepared by their CPA.

## Step 1: Understand Facts

To answer a tax question, you must understand the question. To understand the question, you must know the facts. There are two basic types of facts: open facts and closed facts. Open facts have not yet occurred, such as the facts associated with a proposed transaction. Closed facts have already occurred. The distinction between open and closed facts is important because unlike closed facts, open facts can be altered, and different facts may result in very different tax consequences. Open facts allow the taxpayer to arrange a transaction to achieve the most advantageous outcome. Thus, they are especially important in tax planning.

How do you determine the facts for a research question? Interview clients, speak with third parties such as attorneys and brokers, and review client documents such as contracts, prior tax returns, wills, trust documents, deeds, and corporate minutes. When interviewing clients, remember that not many are tax experts. Thus, it is up to the tax professional to ask the correct initial and follow-up questions to obtain all the relevant facts. Also consider nontax factors, such as a client's personal values or objectives, as these often put constraints on tax planning strategies.

## Step 2: Identify Issues

A tax professional's ability to identify issues is largely a function of his or her type of tax expertise. A tax expert in a particular area will typically be able to identify quickly the specific tax issues that relate to transactions in that area. For example, an expert in corporate acquisitions would quickly identify the tax consequences and specific issues of alternative acquisition types. A novice, on the other hand, would likely

---

**THE KEY FACTS**

**Tax Research**

■ The five steps in tax research are (1) understand the facts, (2) identify issues, (3) locate relevant authorities, (4) analyze the tax authorities, and (5) communicate research results.

■ The two types of tax services that tax professionals use in tax research are annotated tax services, arranged by code section, and topical services, arranged by topic.

■ Research questions often consist of questions of fact or questions of law.
· The answer to a question of fact hinges upon the facts and circumstances of the taxpayer's transaction.
· The answer to a question of law hinges upon the interpretation of the law, such as interpreting a particular phrase in a code section.

■ When the researcher identifies that different authorities have conflicting views, she should evaluate the "hierarchy," jurisdiction, and age of the authorities.

*(continued)*

identify broader issues first and then more specific issues as he or she researched the relevant tax law.

What's the best method to identify tax issues? First of all, get a good understanding of the client's facts. Then, combine your understanding of the facts with your knowledge of the tax law. Let's consider the example of Bill and Mercedes' interest deduction. For an expert in this particular area, the issues will be immediately evident. For a novice, the initial response may take the form of a series of general questions: (1) Is this item of expense deductible? (2) Is that item of income taxable? (3) In what year should the expense be deducted? (4) In what year should the item of income be taxed? After you identify these types of general issues, your research will enable you to identify the more specific issues that ultimately determine the tax ramifications of the transaction.

---

### Example 2-4

*(concluded)*

■ Once the tax researcher has identified relevant authorities, she must make sure that the authorities are still valid and up to date

■ The most common end product of a research question is a research memo, which has five basic parts: (1) facts, (2) issues, (3) authority list, (4) conclusion, and (5) analysis.

Elizabeth, Bill and Mercedes' friend who is a shareholder and the CFO of a company, loaned money to her company to help prevent the company from declaring bankruptcy. Despite Elizabeth's loan, the company did file bankruptcy, and Elizabeth was not repaid the loan. What issues would a researcher consider?

**Answer:** The first questions to ask are whether Elizabeth can deduct the bad debt expense and if so, as what type of deduction? As the researcher delves more into the general issue, he would identify that the type of deduction depends on whether Elizabeth's debt is considered a business or nonbusiness bad debt. This more specific issue depends on whether Elizabeth loaned the money to the company to protect her job (business bad debt) or to protect her stock investment in the company (nonbusiness bad debt). Bad debt expenses incurred for nonbusiness debts (investment-related debts) are deducted as capital losses and thus subject to limitations (discussed in Chapter 11), whereas bad debt expenses for business debts (business-related debts) are ordinary deductions and not limited.

Why might this case be a good one to litigate in U.S. District Court?

**Answer:** Because a jury might be more likely to be convinced to assess Elizabeth's motives favorably.

---

### Step 3: Locate Relevant Authorities

Step three in the research process is to locate the relevant authorities (code sections, regulations, court cases, revenue rulings) that address the tax issue. Luckily, tax services can aid the researcher in identifying relevant authorities. Most, if not all, of these services are available on the Internet (with a subscription), and thus offer the flexibility to conduct research almost anywhere.[10]

There are two basic types of tax services: annotated and topical. **Annotated tax services** are arranged by Internal Revenue Code Section. That is, for each code section, an annotated service includes the code section; a listing of the code section history; copies of congressional committee reports that explain changes to the code section; a copy of all the regulations issued for the specific code section; the service's unofficial explanation of the code section; and brief summaries (called annotations) of relevant court cases, revenue rulings, revenue procedures, and letter rulings that address issues specific to the code section. Two examples of annotated tax services are Commerce Clearing House's (CCH) Standard Federal Tax Reporter and Research Institute of America's (RIA) United States Tax Reporter.

---

[10]www.IRS.gov contains a lot of information (tax forms, IRS publications, etc.) that may be especially useful for answering basic tax questions. In addition, tax publishers, such as CCH and RIA, produce quick reference tax guides (e.g., the *CCH Master Tax Guide* or the *RIA Tax Handbook*) that may be used to answer basic tax questions.

**Topical tax services** are arranged by topic, such as taxable forms of income, tax-exempt income, and trade or business expenses. For each topic, the services identify tax issues that relate to each topic, and then explain and cite authorities relevant to the issue (code sections, regulations, court cases, revenue rulings, etc.). Beginning tax researchers often prefer topical services, because they generally are easier to read. Some examples of topical federal tax services include BNA's Tax Management Portfolios, CCH's Tax Research Consultant, and RIA's Federal Tax Coordinator.

How does a researcher use these services? An expert would probably go directly to the relevant portions of an annotated or topical service. A novice may conduct a keyword search in the service, use the tax service's topical index, or "browse" the tax service to identify the relevant portions. Some suggestions for identifying keywords: Try to describe the transaction in three to five words. An ideal keyword search typically includes (1) the relevant area of law and (2) a fact or two that describes the transaction. Try to avoid keywords that are too broad (income, deduction, taxable) or that may be too narrow.

---

**Example 2-5**

Bill and Mercedes refinanced the mortgage on their principal residence a couple of years ago when their original mortgage's four-year balloon payment came due. Their mortgage institution charged Bill and Mercedes $3,000 of points (prepaid interest) upon the refinancing in order to give them a reduced interest rate. On their CPA's advice, Bill and Mercedes deducted the $3,000 in the year they paid it, but upon audit, the IRS disallowed the deduction. What is the research issue?

**Answer:** The issue is, should Bill and Mercedes have deducted the $3,000 of points in the year they paid it?

What are some keywords that could identify relevant tax authority?

**Answer:** Points (area of law), interest (area of law), refinancing (fact that describes the transaction).

---

Keyword searching is more an art than an exact science. As you gain a better understanding of different areas of the tax law, you'll become much more efficient at using keywords. If keyword searching is not proving beneficial, check your spelling, make sure you're searching within the correct database, rethink your keywords, use another research method, use another tax service, or as a last resort, take a break.

While utilizing keyword searches or other research methods to identify potentially relevant areas of law and tax authorities, constantly ask yourself whether you are indeed in the correct area of law. Once the answer to this question is an authoritative yes, you can delve deeper into the area of law and related authorities to answer the question.

### Step 4: Analyze Tax Authorities

Once a researcher identifies relevant authorities, she must read carefully to ensure she fully understands them, as well as their application to the research problem. Two basic types of issues researchers will encounter are questions of fact and questions of law.

The answer to a **question of fact** hinges upon the facts and circumstances of the taxpayer's transaction. For example, whether a trade or business expense is "ordinary," "necessary," "reasonable," and thus deductible, is a question of fact. If you're researching a question of fact, understand *which* facts determine the answer—in this case, which facts make an expense "ordinary," "necessary," and "reasonable" and which do not. In this type of question, the researcher will focus on understanding how various facts affect the research answer and identifying authorities with fact patterns similar to her client's.

The answer to a **question of law** hinges upon the interpretation of the law, such as interpreting a particular phrase in a code section. If a researcher is faced with this

type of question, she will spend much of her time researching the various interpretations of the code section and take note of which authorities interpret the code differently and why.

For many tax questions, the answer is clear with no opposing interpretations or contrary authorities. For other questions, the researcher may identify that different authorities have conflicting views. In this situation, the tax researcher should evaluate the hierarchical level, jurisdiction, and age of the authorities, placing more weight on higher and newer authorities that have jurisdiction over the taxpayer. A tax researcher will become more adept at this process as she gains experience.

Once the tax researcher has identified relevant authorities, she must make sure the authorities are still valid and up to date. For court cases, a **citator,** which is a research tool that allows you to check the status of several types of tax authorities, will review the history of the case to find out, for example, whether it was subsequently appealed and overturned, and to identify subsequent cases that cite the case. Favorable citations strengthen a case, while unfavorable ones weaken it. Citators can also check the status of revenue rulings, revenue procedures, and other IRS pronouncements. Checking the status of the Code is fairly simple: just locate the current version. Checking the status of regulations is a little more complicated. Most tax services alert researchers if a regulation has not been updated for certain changes in the Code. If this is the case, the researcher should evaluate whether the changes in the Code make the regulation obsolete.

As you will see in the analysis section of the sample research memo drafted by Bill and Mercedes' CPA (see Exhibit 2-9, below), the question whether they should amortize or currently deduct the points paid to refinance the mortgage on their principal residence ultimately depends upon the interpretation of a particular phrase: "in connection with the purchase or improvement of" found in IRC Sec. 461(g)(2). Is there a correct answer to this question? No. There is no clear-cut answer. Rather, this is a situation where the tax professional must use professional judgment. Because there is substantial authority supporting the current deduction of the points (discussed in detail in the sample memo), Bill and Mercedes should be able to deduct the points currently without risk of penalty. However, Bill and Mercedes should be aware that the IRS has clearly stated in an action on decision that it will fight this issue outside the 8th Circuit—for example, in the 11th Circuit, where Bill and Mercedes live.

## Step 5: Communicate the Results

After a researcher finishes her research, the final step of the process is to communicate the results. The most common end product of a research question is the internal research memo the researcher drafts for her supervisor's attention. The memo has five basic parts: (1) facts, (2) issues, (3) authority list, (4) conclusion, and (5) analysis. The purpose of the memo is to inform the reader of the answer to a research question, and thus, it should be written in an objective manner by discussing all relevant authorities to the research question, including those authorities that support, as well as those that conflict with, the answer. Below are some suggestions for each part of the memo. Compare these to the execution within the sample internal research memo presented in Exhibit 2-9.

**Facts**    Discuss facts relevant to the question presented—that is, facts that provide necessary background of the transaction and those facts that may influence the research answer. Keeping the fact discussion relatively brief will focus the reader's attention on the relevant characteristics of the transaction.

**Issues**    State the specific issues that the memo addresses. This section confirms that you understand the research question, reminds the reader of the question being analyzed, and allows future researchers to determine whether the analysis in the memo

**EXHIBIT 2-9   Sample Research Memo**

Below is the memo that Bill and Mercedes' CPA drafted after researching their issue.

| | |
|---|---|
| **Facts:** | Four years ago Bill and Mercedes' credit union provided them a $250,000 mortgage loan for their new home. The mortgage loan was a four-year interest-only note with a balloon payment at the end of four years. Bill and Mercedes (Floridians residing in the 11th Circuit) chose this type of loan to allow them to minimize their mortgage payment until their previous house was sold. After 18 months, Bill and Mercedes sold their previous house and refinanced their original short-term loan with a 15-year conventional mortgage. The credit union charged Bill and Mercedes $3,000 in points (prepaid interest) upon the refinancing. |
| **Issue:** | Can Bill and Mercedes deduct the points in the year they paid them? |
| **Authorities:** | IRC Sec. 461(g) |
| | Rev. Rul. 87-22, 1987-1 CB 146. |
| | *J.R. Huntsman v. Comm.* (8 Cir., 1990), 90-2 USTC par. 50,340, rev'g 91 TC 917 (1988). |
| | AOD 1991-002. |
| | *P.G. Cao v. Comm.* (9 Cir., 1996), 96-1 USTC par. 50,167, aff'g 67 TCM 2171 (1994) |
| **Conclusion:** | Because Bill and Mercedes' refinancing represents an integrated step in securing permanent financing for their home, substantial authority supports their deduction of the $3,000 points this year. |
| **Analysis:** | IRC Sec. 461(g)(1) provides that cash-method taxpayers (Bill and Mercedes) must amortize prepaid interest (points) over the life of the loan instead of receiving a current deduction. IRC Sec. 461(g)(2) provides an exception to the general rule of Sec. 461(g)(1). Specifically, IRC Sec. 461(g)(2) allows cash-method taxpayers to deduct points in the year paid if the related debt was incurred "in connection with the purchase or improvement of," and secured by, the taxpayer's principal residence. The question whether Bill and Mercedes should amortize or currently deduct the points paid to refinance the mortgage on the their principal residence depends upon the interpretation of "in connection with the purchase or improvement of" found in IRC Sec. 461(g)(2). |
| | There are two basic interpretations of "in connection with the purchase or improvement of." In Revenue Ruling 87-22, the IRS rules that points incurred in refinancing a mortgage on a taxpayer's residence are deductible in the year paid to the extent that the taxpayer uses the loan proceeds to improve the taxpayer's residence. Thus, points paid to simply refinance an existing mortgage without improving the residence must be amortized over the life of the loan. In contrast, in *J.R. Huntsman v. Comm.*, the 8th Circuit Court interpreted the phrase "in connection with the purchase or improvement of" much more broadly and held that points incurred to refinance a mortgage on the taxpayer's principal residence are currently deductible if the refinancing represents an *integrated step to secure permanent financing* for the taxpayer's residence. The facts in *J.R. Huntsman v. Comm.* are very similar to Bill and Mercedes' facts. Like Bill and Mercedes, the taxpayers in *J.R. Huntsman v. Comm.* also purchased their principal residence using a short-term loan with a "balloon" payment. When the balloon payment came due, the taxpayers obtained a permanent mortgage on their home (a 30-year conventional mortgage). The 8th Circuit Court held that in this case the permanent mortgage was acquired to extinguish the short-term financing and finalize the purchase of the home. "Thus, where taxpayers purchase a principal residence with a short-term three-year loan secured by a mortgage on the residence, and replace the loan with permanent financing . . . , the permanent mortgage obtained is sufficiently in connection with the purchase of the home to fall within the exception provided for by section 461(g)(2)." In Action on Decision 1991-002, the IRS has indicated that it will not follow the *J.R. Huntsman v. Comm.* decision outside the 8th Circuit (in the 11th Circuit where Bill and Mercedes live). Nonetheless, other courts (the 9th Circuit in *P.G. Cao v. Comm.*) have indicated a willingness to apply the 8th Circuit's interpretation of IRC Sec. 461(g)(2). That is, they have allowed deductibility of points incurred in refinancing if the refinancing occurred to secure permanent financing, instead of for some other reason such as to secure a lower interest rate. |
| | Given the similarity in facts between Bill and Mercedes' refinancing and those in *J.R. Huntsman v. Comm.* (refinancing of a short-term note to secure permanent financing), substantial authority supports a current deduction of the points paid. |

is relevant. Issues should be written as specifically as possible and be limited to one or two sentences per issue.

**Authorities** In this section, the researcher cites the relevant tax authorities that apply to the issue, such as the IRC, court cases, and revenue rulings. How many authorities should you cite? Enough to provide a clear understanding of the issue and interpretation of the law. Remember, in order to reach an accurate assessment of the strength of your conclusion, you should consider authorities that may support your desired conclusion, as well as those that may go against it.

**Conclusion** There should be one conclusion per issue. Each conclusion should answer the question as briefly as possible, and preferably indicate why the answer is what it is.

**Analysis** The goal of the analysis is for the researcher to provide the reader a clear understanding of the area of law and specific authorities that apply. Typically, an analysis will be organized to discuss the general area(s) of law first (the code section) and then the specific authorities (court cases, revenue rulings) that apply to the research question. How many authorities should you discuss? As many as necessary to provide the reader an understanding of the issue and relevant authorities. After you discuss the relevant authorities, apply the authorities to your client's transaction and explain how the authorities result in your conclusion.

**Client Letters** In addition to internal research memos, tax professionals often send their clients letters that summarize their research and recommendations. Basic components of the client letter include: (1) research question and limitations, (2) facts, (3) analysis, and (4) closing. Below are some suggestions for each part of the client letter. Compare these to the execution within the sample client letter presented in Exhibit 2-10.

**Research Question and Limitations** After the salutation (Dear Bill and Mercedes) and social graces (I enjoyed seeing you last week at the Tampa Bay Boys and Girls Clubs charity auction. What a great event for such a worthy cause!), clearly state the research question addressed and any disclaimers related to the work performed. This portion of the letter ensures that the tax professional and client have a mutual understanding of the question researched and any limitations on the research performed. As with a memo, issues should be written as specifically as possible and be limited to one or two sentences. Most accounting firms have standard boilerplate language regarding the limitations on work performed that is included in every client letter.

**Facts** Briefly summarize the facts relevant to the question presented—that is, facts that provide necessary background of the transaction and those facts that may influence the research answer. Keeping the fact discussion relatively brief will focus the client's attention on the relevant characteristics of the transaction.

**Analysis** Summarize the relevant authorities (including citations in most situations) and their implications for the client's research question using precise language appropriate for the client's level of tax expertise. The length of this portion of the letter will vary with the complexity of the research question and client's interest in understanding the specific research details.

**Closing** In this section, summarize the key outcome(s) of the research conducted and any recommended client action, thank the client for requesting your service, and remind the client to contact you with additional questions or for further assistance.

In the case of Bill and Mercedes' interest deduction, their CPA recommended a tax return position that the IRS disallowed upon audit. Did their CPA violate her professional responsibilities by recommending a position the IRS disallowed? Good question. Let's take a look at the rules governing tax professional responsibilities.

**EXHIBIT 2-10    Sample Client Letter**

Below is the client letter that Bill and Mercedes' CPA sent to them.

Dear Bill and Mercedes,

I enjoyed seeing you last week at the Tampa Bay Boys and Girls Clubs charity auction. What a great event for such a worthy cause! Thank you for requesting my advice concerning the tax treatment of the points paid when refinancing your mortgage.

My research is based upon the federal income tax laws that apply as of the date of this letter and the facts that you have provided as follows. Four years ago your credit union provided you a $250,000 interest-only note on your home that required a balloon payment at the end of four years. You chose this type of loan to minimize your mortgage payment until your previous house sold. After 18 months, you sold your previous house and refinanced the original short-term loan with a 15-year conventional mortgage. The credit union charged you $3,000 in points upon the refinancing.

After a thorough review of the applicable tax authority, there is substantial authority that supports a current deduction of the $3,000 points paid. IRC Sec. 461(g)(2) allows cash-method taxpayers to deduct points in the year paid if the related debt was incurred "in connection with the purchase or improvement of," and secured by, the taxpayer's principal residence. There are two basic interpretations of "in connection with the purchase or improvement of." The IRS has ruled (Revenue Ruling 87-22) that points paid to simply refinance an existing mortgage without improving the residence must be amortized over the life of the loan. In contrast, in *J.R. Huntsman v. Comm.*, the 8th Circuit Court held that points incurred to refinance a mortgage on the taxpayer's principal residence are currently deductible if the refinancing represents an *integrated step to secure permanent financing* for the taxpayer's residence.

The facts in *J.R. Huntsman v. Comm.* are very similar to your facts. Like you, the taxpayers in *J.R. Huntsman v. Comm.* purchased their principal residence using a short-term loan with a "balloon" payment. When the balloon payment came due, the taxpayers obtained a permanent mortgage on their home. The 8th Circuit Court held that in this case the permanent mortgage was acquired to finalize the purchase of the home and allowed the current deduction of the points.

*J.R. Huntsman v. Comm.* provides substantial authority to support a current deduction of the $3,000 points paid to refinance your initial short-term mortgage. In addition, other courts have applied the 8th Circuit's interpretation of IRC Sec. 461(g)(2), which adds "strength" to the 8th Circuit decision. However, the IRS has indicated that it will not follow the *J.R. Huntsman v. Comm.* decision outside the 8th Circuit (in the 11th Circuit where you live). Accordingly, the IRS would likely disallow the $3,000 deduction upon audit, and thus, while you have substantial authority to deduct the points currently, there is risk in doing so.

I would be happy to discuss this issue with you in more depth as these types of issues are always difficult. Likewise, if you have any other questions or issues with which I may assist you, please do not hesitate to contact me. Thank you again for requesting my advice.

Sincerely,


Sandra Miller, CPA

# TAX PROFESSIONAL RESPONSIBILITIES

**LO6**

Tax practitioners are subject to a variety of statutes, rules, and codes of professional conduct. Some examples include the American Institute of CPAs (AICPA) Code of Professional Conduct, the AICPA Statements on Standards for Tax Services (SSTS), the IRS's Circular 230, and statutes enacted by a CPA's specific state board of accountancy. Tax practitioners should absolutely have a working knowledge of these statutes, rules, and guidelines because (1) they establish the professional standards for the practitioner and (2) failure to comply with the standards

could result in adverse consequences for the tax professional, such as being admonished, suspended, or barred from practicing before the IRS; being admonished, suspended, or expelled from the AICPA; or suffering suspension or revocation of the CPA license. Given the voluminous nature of applicable statutes, rules, and codes, we will simply provide a brief overview of the major common sources of tax professional standards.

CPAs who are members of the AICPA are bound by the AICPA Code of Professional Conduct and Statements on Standards for Tax Services. Other tax professionals use these provisions as guidance of professional standards. The AICPA Code of Professional Conduct is not specific to tax practice and provides broader professional standards that are especially relevant for auditors—that is, for those independent CPAs charged with examining an entity's financial statements. Provisions included in the Code of Professional Conduct address the importance of a CPA maintaining independence from the client and using due professional care in carrying out responsibilities. Additional provisions limit the acceptance of contingent fees, preclude discreditable acts such as signing a false return, and prohibit false advertising and charging commissions. Most of these provisions rightly fall under the heading of common sense. Nonetheless, a regular review should prove useful to the practicing CPA.

The AICPA's Statements on Standards for Tax Services (**SSTS**) recommend appropriate standards of practice for tax professionals. One objective of these standards is to encourage increased understanding by the Treasury, IRS, and the public of a CPA's professional standards. Many state boards of accountancy have adopted similar standards, thus making the SSTS especially important. Currently, seven SSTS describe the tax professional standards when recommending a tax return position, answering questions on a tax return, preparing a tax return using data supplied by a client, using estimates on a tax return, taking a tax return position inconsistent with a previous year's tax return, discovering a tax return error, and giving tax advice to taxpayers. Exhibit 2-11 provides a brief summary of each SSTS.[11] Most important from a research perspective, SSTS No. 1 provides that a tax professional must comply with the standards imposed by the applicable tax authority when recommending a tax return position or preparing or signing a tax return. IRC Sec. 6694 provides these standards for federal tax purposes.

IRC Sec. 6694 imposes a penalty on a *tax practitioner* for any position that is not supported by **substantial authority**.[12] A good tax professional evaluates whether supporting authority is substantial based upon the supporting and opposing authorities' weight and relevance. Substantial authority suggests the probability that the taxpayer's position is sustained upon audit or litigation is in the 40 plus percent range or above. The tax practitioner can also avoid penalty under IRC Sec. 6694 if the tax return position has at least a reasonable basis (i.e., supported by one or more tax authorities) and the position is disclosed on the taxpayer's return.

---

**Example 2-6**

Did Bill and Mercedes' CPA meet her professional standards as provided by SSTS No. 1?

**Answer:** Yes. Based on *J.R. Huntsman v. Comm.*, it is safe to conclude that there is a 40+ percent or greater probability that the current points deduction will be sustained upon judicial review. Specifically, Bill and Mercedes' facts are very similar to those in *J.R. Huntsman v. Comm.*, and subsequent courts have interpreted the phrase "in connection with" consistently with *J.R. Huntsman v. Comm.*

---

[11]At publication time, the AICPA had proposed revising the SSTS to reflect the seven standards described in Exhibit 2-11.

[12]The "more likely than not" standard, defined as a greater than 50 percent chance of a position being sustained on its merits, applies to tax shelters and other reportable transactions specified by the IRS.

**EXHIBIT 2-11    Summary of the AICPA Statements on Standards for Tax Services**

### SSTS No 1: Tax Return Positions

A tax professional should comply with the standards, if any, imposed by the applicable tax authority for recommending a tax return position, or preparing or signing a tax return. If the tax authority has no written standards (or if they are lower than the following standard), the tax professional may recommend a tax return position or prepare or sign a return when she has a good-faith belief that the position has a realistic possibility of being sustained if challenged, or if there is a reasonable basis for the position and it is *adequately disclosed* on the tax return.

### SSTS No. 2: Answers to Questions on Returns

A tax professional should make a reasonable effort to obtain from the taxpayer the information necessary to answer all questions on a tax return.

### SSTS No. 3: Certain Procedural Aspects of Preparing Returns

In preparing or signing a tax return, a tax professional may rely without verification on information that a taxpayer or a third party has provided, unless the information appears to be incorrect, incomplete, or inconsistent.

### SSTS No. 4: Use of Estimates

Unless prohibited by statute or rule, a tax professional may use taxpayer estimates in preparing a tax return if it is impractical to obtain exact data and if the estimated amounts appear reasonable based on the facts and circumstances known by the professional.

### SSTS No. 5: Departure from a Position Previously Concluded in an Administrative Proceeding or Court Decision

A tax professional may sign a tax return that contains a departure from a position previously concluded in an administrative or court proceeding if the tax professional adheres to the standards of SSTS No. 1. This rule does not apply if the taxpayer is bound to a specific tax treatment in the later year, such as by a formal closing agreement with the IRS.

### SSTS No. 6: Knowledge of Error: Return Preparation and Administrative Proceedings

A tax professional must advise the taxpayer promptly of an error and its potential consequences when she learns of an error in a previously filed tax return, an administrative hearing (such as an audit), or the taxpayer's failure to file a required return. The tax professional should include a recommendation for appropriate measures the taxpayer should take. The professional is not obligated to inform the IRS of the error, nor may she do so without the taxpayer's permission, except when required by law. However, in an administrative proceeding only, the tax professional should request the taxpayer's agreement to disclose the error to the IRS. If the taxpayer refuses to disclose the error to the IRS, the professional may consider terminating the professional relationship with the taxpayer.

### SSTS No. 7: Form and Content of Advice to Taxpayers

In providing advice to taxpayers, tax professionals must use judgment that reflects professional competence and serves the taxpayer's needs. The professional should ensure that the standards under SSTS No. 1 are satisfied for all advice rendered. The professional is not obligated to communicate with a taxpayer when subsequent events affect advice previously provided except when implementing plans associated with the advice provided or when the professional is obligated to do so by specific agreement.

---

> **THE KEY FACTS**
>
> **Tax Professional Responsibilities**
>
> ■ Tax practitioners are subject to a variety of statutes, rules, and codes of professional conduct.
>
> ■ The AICPA's seven Statements on Standards for Tax Services (SSTS) recommend appropriate standards of practice for tax professionals.
> · Many state boards of accountancy have adopted similar standards to the SSTS standards.
>
> ■ Circular 230 provides regulations governing tax practice and applies to all persons practicing before the IRS.
> · There is a good bit of overlap between Circular 230 and the AICPA SSTS.

**Circular 230,** issued by the IRS, provides regulations governing tax practice and applies to all persons practicing before the IRS. There are three parts of Circular 230: Subpart A describes who may practice before the IRS (CPAs, attorneys, enrolled agents) and what practicing before the IRS means (tax return preparation, representing clients before the IRS, and so on).[13] Subpart B describes the duties and restrictions that apply to individuals governed by Circular 230. Included in Subpart B are provisions discussing the submission of records to the IRS, guidelines when a

---

[13]Similar to attorneys and CPAs, enrolled agents can represent taxpayers before the IRS. To become an enrolled agent, you must have either worked for the IRS for five years or pass a comprehensive examination.

practitioner discovers a tax return error, restrictions on charging contingency fees, prohibition of sharing employment with someone suspended from practicing before the IRS, stringent rules relating to providing advice for tax shelters, and standards for when a practitioner can recommend a tax return position.[14] Subpart C explains disciplinary proceedings for practitioners violating the Circular 230 provisions. There is a good bit of overlap between Circular 230 and the AICPA SSTS.

## TAXPAYER AND TAX PRACTITIONER PENALTIES

In addition to motivating good behavior via tax professional standards, the IRS can impose both criminal and civil penalties to encourage tax compliance by both tax professionals and taxpayers. **Civil penalties** are much more common, generally come in the form of monetary penalties, and may be imposed when tax practitioners or taxpayers violate tax statutes without reasonable cause—say, as the result of negligence, intentional disregard of pertinent rules, willful disobedience, or outright fraud. Some common examples of civil penalties are listed in Exhibit 2-12.

**Criminal penalties** are much less common than civil penalties, although they have been used to incarcerate some of the most notorious criminals. (Notorious mobster Al Capone was convicted and put in prison for tax evasion.) They are commonly charged in tax evasion cases, which include willful intent to defraud the government, but are imposed only after normal due process, including a trial. Compared to civil cases, the standard of conviction is higher in a criminal trial; guilt must be proven beyond a reasonable doubt (versus a "clear and convincing evidence" standard for civil tax fraud). However, the penalties are also much higher, such as fines up to $100,000 for individuals plus a prison sentence.

Assuming the IRS assesses additional tax upon audit, will the taxpayer always be subject to penalty? No. While the taxpayer will have to pay interest on the underpayment, he or she will *not* be subject to an underpayment penalty *if there is* substantial authority *that supports the tax return position*.[15] As previously discussed, substantial authority suggests the probability that the taxpayer's position is sustained upon audit or litigation is in the 40 plus percent range or above.

### Example 2-7

What is Bill and Mercedes' exposure to penalties in their IRS audit?

**Answer:** None. Why? Because "substantial tax authority" supports their tax return position and the disputed tax liability is relatively small (the tax savings on a $3,000 tax deduction), Bill and Mercedes have no penalty exposure. Nonetheless, Bill and Mercedes will owe interest on the disputed tax liability unless the IRS recants its position in the audit or appeals process (or if the case is litigated and Bill and Mercedes win).

As we explained in Example 2-6, Bill and Mercedes' CPA met her professional standards (as defined currently in SSTS No. 1) by recommending a tax return position that meets the "Substantial Authority" standard. Likewise, because substantial tax authority supports the tax return position, Bill and Mercedes' CPA should also not have penalty exposure under IRC Sec. 6694.

[14]Circular 230 has not yet been revised to reflect the new tax practitioner standards in IRC Sec. 6694 for when a tax practitioner generally may recommend a tax return position (substantial authority and no disclosure of reasonable basis with disclosure). We expect that Circular 230 will be revised eventually to reflect these new standards.

[15]The taxpayer can also avoid penalty if the tax return position has at least a reasonable basis (i.e., supported by one or more tax authorities) and the position is disclosed on the taxpayer's return.

**EXHIBIT 2-12**    Civil Penalties Imposed for Tax Violations

| Taxpayers | | Tax Practitioners | |
|---|---|---|---|
| Failure to file a tax return. | 5% of tax due per month. | Failure to provide a copy of the tax return to a taxpayer. | $50 per violation. |
| Failure to pay tax owed. | .5% of tax due per month. Reduces the failure to file a tax return penalty, if applicable. Maximum failure to file and failure to pay tax penalty is 5% of tax due per month. | Failure to sign a tax return. | $50 per violation. |
| Failure to make estimated payments. | Penalty varies with federal short-term interest rate and underpayment. | Failure to include the tax practitioner's ID number on the tax return. | $50 per violation. |
| Substantial understatement of tax. | 20% of understatement. | Failure to keep a listing of taxpayers or tax returns. | $50 per violation. |
| Providing false withholding information. | $500. | Failure to keep a listing of employees. | $50 per violation. |
| Fraud. | 75% of liability attributable to fraud. | Understatement due to unreasonable position. | Greater of $1,000 or 50% of income derived from preparing the taxpayer's tax return. |
| | | Willful understatement of tax. | Greater of $5,000 or 50% of income derived from preparing the taxpayer's tax return. |
| | | Organizing, promoting, etc. an abusive tax shelter. | Lesser of $1,000 or 100% of gross income derived from tax shelter. If activity is based on fraudulent statements, the penalty equals 50% of gross income derived from tax shelter. |
| | | Aiding and abetting the understatement of a tax liability. | $1,000. |

---

**Taxes in the Real World**    *Even the Largest Tax Return Preparers Can't Escape Scrutiny*

In spring of 2007, the federal government investigated Jackson Hewitt, the nation's second largest tax return preparer, on charges that certain franchisees helped their customers file fraudulent tax returns to get bigger refunds. The government alleges a wide range of fraudulent actions, such as filing returns claiming re- funds based on phony wage forms and using fabri- cated businesses and business expenses on returns to claim bogus deductions. The IRS estimates that the fraud resulted in more than $70 million in combined losses to the Treasury. Upon news of the charges, Jackson Hewitt's stock price fell 18 percent.

# CONCLUSION

Now that we have a full understanding of the issue under audit for Bill and Mercedes, what is their likely outcome? Another good question. The IRS has stated that it will continue to disallow a current deduction for points incurred for refinanced mortgages.

Nonetheless, the courts appear to follow *J.R. Huntsman v. Comm.,* and therefore, the IRS stands a strong possibility of losing this case if litigated. In an IRS appeals conference, the appeals officer may consider the hazards of litigation. Accordingly, Bill and Mercedes have a good likelihood of a favorable resolution at the appeals conference.

In this chapter we discussed several of the fundamentals of tax practice and procedure: taxpayer filing requirements, the statute of limitations, the IRS audit process, the primary tax authorities, tax research, tax professional standards, and taxpayer and tax practitioner penalties. For the tax accountant, these fundamentals form the basis for much of her work. Likewise, tax research forms the basis of much of a tax professional's compliance and planning services. Even for the accountant who doesn't specialize in tax accounting, gaining a basic understanding of tax practice and procedure is important, as assisting clients with the IRS audit process is a valued service that accountants provide, and clients expect all accountants to understand basic tax procedure issues and how to research basic tax issues.

## SUMMARY

**LO1**   Identify the filing requirements for income tax returns and the statute of limitations for assessment.

- All corporations must file a tax return annually regardless of their taxable income. Estates and trusts are required to file annual income tax returns if their gross income exceeds $600. The filing requirements for individual taxpayers depend on the taxpayer's filing status, age, and gross income.

- Individual and partnership tax returns are due on the fifteenth day of the fourth month following year-end. For corporations, tax returns must be filed by the fifteenth day of the third month following the corporation's fiscal year end. Any taxpayer unable to file a tax return by the original due date can request an extension to file.

- For both amended tax returns filed by a taxpayer and proposed tax assessments by the IRS, the statute of limitations generally ends three years from the *later* of (1) the date the tax return was actually filed or (2) the tax return's original due date.

**LO2**   Outline the IRS audit process, how returns are selected, the different types of audits, and what happens after the audit.

- The IRS uses a number of computer programs and outside data sources to identify tax returns that may have an understated tax liability. Common computer initiatives include the DIF (Discriminant Function) system, document perfection program, and information matching program.

- The three types of IRS audits consist of correspondence, office, and field examinations.

- After the audit, the IRS will send the taxpayer a 30-day letter, which provides the taxpayer the opportunity to pay the proposed assessment or request an appeals conference. If an agreement is not reached at appeals or the taxpayer does not pay the proposed assessment, the IRS will send the taxpayer a 90-day letter. At this time, the taxpayer may pay the tax or petition the U.S. Tax Court to hear the case. If the taxpayer chooses to pay the tax, the taxpayer may then request a refund of the tax and eventually sue the IRS for a refund in the U.S. District Court or the U.S. Court of Federal Claims.

**LO3**   Evaluate the relative weights of the various tax law sources.

- Primary authorities are official sources of the tax law generated by the legislative branch (statutory authority issued by Congress), judicial branch (rulings by the U.S. District Court, U.S. Tax Court, U.S. Court of Federal Claims, U.S. Circuit Court of Appeals, or U.S. Supreme Court), or executive/administrative branch (Treasury and IRS pronouncements).

Exhibit 2-4 in the chapter displays the most common primary sources and their relative authoritative weight. Secondary authorities are unofficial tax authorities that interpret and explain the primary authorities.

Describe the legislative process as it pertains to taxation.    **LO4**

- Exhibit 2-7 illustrates the legislative process for enacting tax law changes. Bills proceed from the House Ways and Means Committee to the House of Representatives. If approved, the act is sent to the Senate Finance Committee with a revised version then sent to the U.S. Senate. If approved, the Joint Conference Committee considers the acts passed by the House of Representative and Senate. If a compromise is reached, the revised act is sent to the House of Representatives, if approved then to the Senate, and if approved then to the president. If signed by the president, the act is incorporated into the IRC of 1986. If the president vetoes the legislation, Congress may override the veto with a two-thirds positive vote in both the House of Representatives and Senate.

Perform the basic steps in tax research and evaluate various tax law sources when faced with ambiguous statutes.    **LO5**

- The five basic steps in tax research are (1) understand the facts, (2) identify issues, (3) locate relevant authorities, (4) analyze the tax authorities, and (5) communicate research results.

- When the researcher identifies that different authorities have conflicting views, she should evaluate the "hierarchy," jurisdiction, and age of the authorities, placing more weight on higher and newer authorities that have jurisdiction over the taxpayer.

Describe tax professional responsibilities in providing tax advice.    **LO6**

- Tax practitioners are subject to a variety of statutes, rules, and codes of professional conduct. Some examples include the American Institute of CPAs (AICPA) Code of Professional Conduct, the AICPA Statements on Standards for Tax Services (SSTS), the IRS's Circular 230, and statutes enacted by a CPA's specific state board of accountancy.

- The AICPA's Statements on Standards for Tax Services (SSTS) recommend appropriate standards of practice for tax professionals. Many state boards of accountancy have adopted similar standards, thus making the SSTS especially important. Currently, there are seven SSTS summarized in Exhibit 2-11 that describe the tax professional standards.

- Circular 230 provides regulations governing tax practice and applies to all persons practicing before the IRS. There is a good bit of overlap between Circular 230 and the AICPA SSTS.

Identify taxpayer and tax professional penalties.    **LO7**

- The IRS can impose both criminal and civil penalties to encourage tax compliance by both tax professionals and taxpayers. Civil penalties are much more common, generally come in the form of monetary penalties, and may be imposed when tax practitioners or taxpayers violate tax statutes without reasonable cause. Some common examples of civil penalties are listed in Exhibit 2-12.

- Criminal penalties are much less common than civil penalties and are commonly charged in tax evasion cases. Compared to civil cases, the standard of conviction is higher in a criminal trial, but the penalties are also much higher.

- A taxpayer will not be subject to an underpayment penalty if there is substantial authority that supports the tax return position.

- A tax practitioner will also not be subject to penalty for recommending a tax return position if there is substantial authority that supports the position.

## KEY TERMS

30-day letter (2-6)
90-day letter (2-6)
acquiescence (2-17)
action on decision (2-17)
annotated tax service (2-18)
Circular 230 (2-25)
citator (2-20)
civil penalties (2-26)
correspondence examination (2-5)
criminal penalties (2-26)
determination letters (2-16)
DIF (Discriminant Function)
system (2-4)
document perfection program (2-4)
field examination (2-6)
final regulations (2-15)
Golsen rule (2-15)

information matching program (2-4)
Internal Revenue Code of 1986 (2-11)
interpretative regulations (2-16)
legislative regulations (2-16)
nonacquiescence (2-17)
office examination (2-6)
primary authority (2-9)
private letter rulings (2-16)
procedural regulations (2-16)
proposed regulations (2-16)
question of fact (2-19)
question of law (2-19)
regulations (2-15)
revenue procedures (2-16)
revenue rulings (2-16)
secondary authority (2-10)
*stare decisis* (2-15)

Statements on Standards for Tax
Services (SSTS) (2-15)
statute of limitations (2-3)
substantial authority (2-24)
tax treaties (2-13)
technical advice memorandum (2-16)
temporary regulations (2-15)
topical tax service (2-19)
U.S. Circuit Courts of Appeal (2-7)
U.S. Constitution (2-11)
U.S. Court of Federal Claims (2-6)
U.S. District Court (2-6)
U.S. Supreme Court (2-8)
U.S. Tax Court (2-6)
*writ of certiorari* (2-8)

## DISCUSSION QUESTIONS

1. **(LO1)** Name three factors that determine whether a taxpayer is required to file a tax return.

2. **(LO1)** Benita is concerned that she will not be able to complete her tax return by April 15. Can she request an extension to file her return? By what date must she do so? Assuming she requests an extension, what is the latest date that she could file her return this year without penalty?

3. **(LO1)** Agua Linda, Inc., is a calendar-year corporation. What is the original due date for the corporate tax return? What happens if the original due date falls on a Saturday?

4. **(LO2)** Approximately what percentage of tax returns does the IRS audit? What are the implications of this number for the IRS's strategy in selecting returns for audit?

5. **(LO2)** Explain the difference between the DIF system and the National Research Program? How do they relate to each other?

6. **(LO2)** Describe the differences between the three types of audits in terms of their scope and taxpayer type.

7. **(LO2)** Simon just received a 30-day letter from the IRS indicating a proposed assessment. Does he have to pay the additional tax? What are his options?

8. **(LO2)** Compare and contrast the three trial-level courts.

9. **(LO3)** Compare and contrast the three types of tax law sources and give examples of each.

10. **(LO3)** The U.S. Constitution is the highest tax authority but provides very little in the way of tax laws. What are the next highest tax authorities beneath the U.S. Constitution?

11. **(LO3)** Jackie has just opened her copy of the Code for the first time. She looks at the table of contents and wonders why it is organized the way it is. She

questions whether it makes sense to try and understand the Code's organization. What are some reasons why understanding the organization of the Internal Revenue Code may prove useful?

12. **(LO3)** Laura Li, a U.S. resident, works for three months this summer in Hong Kong. What type of tax authority may be especially useful in determining the tax consequences of her foreign income?

13. **(LO3)** What are the basic differences between regulations, revenue rulings, and private letter rulings?

14. **(LO3)** Under what circumstance would the IRS issue an acquiescence? a non-acquiescence? An action on decision?

15. **(LO3)** Carlos has located a regulation that appears to answer his tax research question. He is concerned because the regulation is a temporary regulation. Evaluate the authoritative weight of this type of regulation. Should he feel more or less confident in his answer if the regulation was a proposed regulation?

16. **(LO3)** Tyrone recently read a regulation that Congress specifically requested the IRS to issue. What type of regulation is this? How does this regulation's authoritative weight compare to other regulations?

17. **(LO3)** In researching a tax question, you find only one authority (a trial-level court opinion) that is directly on point. Which court would you least prefer to have heard this case and why?

18. **(LO3)** What is *stare decisis* and how does it relate to the Golsen rule?

19. **(LO3)** Mason was shocked to learn that the current Code is the Internal Revenue Code of 1986. He thought that U.S. tax laws change more frequently. What is wrong with Mason's perception?

20. **(LO4)** Describe in general the process by which new tax legislation is enacted.

21. **(LO4)** What are the three committees that debate proposed tax legislation? What documents do these committees generate, and how might they be used?

22. **(LO4)** The president recently vetoed a tax act passed by the House and Senate. Is the tax act dead? If not, what will it take for the act to be passed?

23. **(LO5)** What are the five basic parts of an internal research memo?

24. **(LO5)** What is the difference between primary and secondary authorities? Explain the role of each authority type in conducting tax research.

25. **(LO5)** Jorge is puzzled that the IRS and his CPA could legitimately reach different conclusions on a tax issue. Why does this happen?

26. **(LO5)** What is the difference between open and closed facts? How is this distinction important in conducting tax research?

27. **(LO5)** In writing a research memo, what types of facts should be included in the memo?

28. **(LO5)** Amber is a tax expert, whereas Rob is a tax novice. Explain how their process in identifying tax issues may differ.

29. **(LO5)** Discuss the basic differences between annotated and topical tax services. How are these services used in tax research?

30. **(LO5)** In constructing a keyword search, what should the keyword search include?

31. **(LO5)** Lindley has become very frustrated in researching a tax issue using keyword searches. What suggestions can you give her?

32. **(LO5)** Nola, a tax novice, has a fairly simple tax question. Besides tax services, what are some sources that she can use to answer her question?

33. **(LO5)** Armando identifies a tax research question as being a question of fact. What types of authorities should he attempt to locate in his research?

34. **(LO5)** How are citators used in tax research?

35. **(LO5)** What is the general rule for how many authorities a research memo should discuss?
36. **(LO6)** Identify some of the sources for tax professional standards. What are the potential ramifications of failing to comply with these standards?
37. **(LO6)** Levi is recommending a tax return position to his client. What standard must he meet to satisfy his professional standards? What is the source of this professional standard?
38. **(LO6)** What is Circular 230?
39. **(LO7)** What are the basic differences between civil and criminal tax penalties?
40. **(LO7)** What are some of the most common civil penalties imposed on taxpayers?
41. **(LO7)** What are the taxpayer's standards to avoid the substantial understatement of tax penalty?
42. **(LO7)** What are the tax practitioner's standards to avoid a penalty for recommending a tax return position?

# PROBLEMS

43. **(LO1)** Ahmed does not have enough cash on hand to pay his taxes. He was excited to hear that he can request an extension to file his tax return. Does this solve his problem? What are the ramifications if he doesn't pay his tax liability by April 15?
44. **(LO1)** Molto Stancha Corporation had zero earnings this fiscal year; in fact, they lost money. Must they file a tax return?
45. **(LO1)** The estate of Monique Chablis earned $450 of income this year. Is the estate required to file an income tax return?
46. **(LO1)** Jamarcus, a full-time student, earned $2,500 this year from a summer job. He had no other income this year and will have zero federal income tax liability this year. His employer withheld $300 of federal income tax from his summer pay. Is Jamarcus required to file a tax return? Should Jamarcus file a tax return?
47. **(LO1)** Shane has never filed a tax return despite earning excessive sums of money as a gambler. When does the statute of limitations expire for the years in which Shane has not filed a tax return?
48. **(LO1)** Latoya filed her tax return on February 10 this year. When will the statute of limitations expire for this tax return?
49. **(LO1)** Using the facts from the previous problem, how would your answer change if Latoya understated her income by 40 percent? How would your answer change if Latoya intentionally failed to report as taxable income any cash payments she received from her clients?
50. **(LO2)** Paula could not reach an agreement with the IRS at her appeals conference and has just received a 90-day letter. If she wants to litigate the issue but does not have sufficient cash to pay the proposed deficiency, what is her best court choice?
51. **(LO2)** In choosing a trial-level court, how should a court's previous rulings influence the choice? How should circuit court rulings influence the taxpayer's choice of a trial-level court?
52. **(LO2)** Sophia recently won a tax case litigated in the 7th Circuit. She recently heard that the Supreme Court denied the *writ of certiorari*. Should she be happy or not, and why?

53. **(LO2)** Campbell's tax return was audited because she failed to report interest she earned on her tax return. What IRS audit selection method identified her tax return?

54. **(LO2)** Yong's tax return was audited because he calculated his tax liability incorrectly. What IRS audit procedure identified his tax return for audit?

55. **(LO2)** Randy deducted a high level of itemized deductions two years ago relative to his income level. He recently received an IRS notice requesting documentation for his itemized deductions. What audit procedure likely identified his tax return for audit?

56. **(LO2)** Jackie has a corporate client that has recently received a 30 day notice from the IRS with a $100,000 tax assessment. Her client is considering requesting an appeals conference to contest the assessment. What factors should Jackie advise her client to consider before requesting an appeals conference?

■ planning

57. **(LO2)** The IRS recently completed an audit of Shea's tax return and assessed $15,000 additional tax. Shea requested an appeals conference but was unable to settle the case at the conference. She is contemplating which trial court to choose to hear her case. Provide her a recommendation based on the following alternative facts:

■ planning

   a. Shea resides in the 2nd Circuit, and the 2nd Circuit has recently ruled against the position Shea is litigating.

   b. The Federal Circuit Court of Appeals has recently ruled in favor of Shea's position.

   c. The issue being litigated involves a question of fact. Shea has a very appealing story to tell but little favorable case law to support her position.

   d. The issue being litigated is highly technical, and Shea believes strongly in her interpretation of the law.

   e. Shea is a local elected official and would prefer to minimize any local publicity regarding the case.

58. **(LO3)** Juanita, a Texas resident (5th Circuit), is researching a tax question and finds a 5th Circuit case ruling that is favorable and a 9th Circuit case that is unfavorable. Which circuit case has more "authoritative weight" and why? How would your answer change if Juanita were a Kentucky resident (6th Circuit)?

59. **(LO3)** Faith, a resident of Florida (11th Circuit) recently found a circuit court case that is favorable to her research question. Which two circuits would she prefer to have issued the opinion?

60. **(LO3)** Robert has found a "favorable" authority directly on point for his tax question. If the authority is a court case, which court would he prefer to have issued the opinion? Which court would he least prefer to have issued the opinion?

61. **(LO3)** Jamareo has found a "favorable" authority directly on point for his tax question. If the authority is an administrative authority, which specific type of authority would he prefer to answer his question? Which administrative authority would he least prefer to answer his question?

62. **(LO4)** Justine would like to clarify her understanding of a code section recently enacted by Congress. What tax law sources are available to assist Justine?

63. **(LO5)** Aldina has identified conflicting authorities that address her research question. How should she evaluate these authorities to make a conclusion?

64. **(LO5)** Georgette has identified a 1983 court case that appears to answer her research question. What must she do to determine if the case still represents "current" law?

65. **(LO5)** Sandy has determined that her research question depends upon the interpretation of the phrase "not compensated by insurance." What type of research question is this?

66. **(LO5)** J. C. has been a professional gambler for many years. He loves this line of work and believes the income is tax-free.

    a. Use an available tax research service to determine whether J. C.'s thinking is correct. Is the answer to this question found in the Internal Revenue Code? If not, what type of authority answers this question?

    b. Write a memo communicating the results of your research.

67. **(LO5)** Katie recently won a ceramic dalmatian valued at $800 on a television game show. She questions whether this prize is taxable since it was a "gift" she won on the show.

    a. Use an available tax research service to answer Katie's question.

    b. Write a letter to Katie communicating the results of your research.

68. **(LO5)** Pierre recently received a tax penalty for failing to file a tax return. He was upset to receive the penalty, but he was comforted by the thought that he will get a tax deduction for paying the penalty.

    a. Use an available tax research service to determine if Pierre is correct.

    b. Write a memo communicating the results of your research.

69. **(LO5)** Paris was happy to provide a contribution to her friend Nicole's campaign for mayor, especially after she learned that charitable contributions are tax deductible.

    a. Use an available tax service to determine whether Paris can deduct this contribution.

    b. Write a memo communicating the results of your research.

70. **(LO5)** Matt and Lori recently were divorced. Although grief stricken, Matt was at least partially comforted by his monthly receipt of $10,000 alimony. He was particularly excited to learn from his friend, Denzel, that the alimony was not taxable. Use an available tax service to determine if Denzel is correct. Would your answer change if Matt and Lori continued to live together?

71. **(LO5)** Shaun is a huge college football fan. In the past, he has always bought football tickets on the street from ticket scalpers. This year, he decided to join the university's ticket program, which requires a $2,000 contribution to the university for the "right" to purchase tickets. Shaun will then pay $400 per season ticket. Shaun understands that the price paid for the season tickets is not tax deductible as a charitable contribution. However, contributions to a university are typically tax deductible.

    a. Use an available tax service to determine how much, if any, of Shaun's $2,000 contribution for the right to purchase tickets is tax deductible.

    b. Write a letter to Shaun communicating the results of your research.

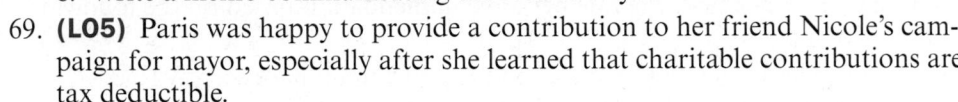

72. **(LO5)** Latrell recently used his Delta Skymiles to purchase a free roundtrip ticket to Milan, Italy (value $1,200). The frequent flyer miles used to purchase the ticket were generated from Latrell's business travel as a CPA. Latrell's employer paid for his business trips, and he was not taxed on the travel reimbursement.

    a. Use an available tax research service to determine how much income, if any, does Latrell have to recognize as a result of purchasing an airline ticket with Skymiles earned from business travel.

    b. Write a memo communicating the results of your research.

73. **(LO6)** Randy has found conflicting authorities that address a research question for one of his clients. The majority of the authorities provide an unfavorable answer for his client. Randy estimates that if the client takes the more favorable position on its tax return that there is approximately a 48 percent chance that the position will be sustained upon audit or judicial proceeding. If the client takes this position on its tax return, will Randy be subject to penalty? Will the client potentially be subject to penalty?

74. **(LO6)** Using the same facts from the previous problem, how would your answer change if Randy estimates that there is only a 20 percent chance that the position will be sustained upon audit or judicial proceeding?

75. **(LO7)** Sasha owes additional tax imposed in a recent audit. In addition to the tax, will she be assessed other amounts? If so, how will these amounts be determined?

76. **(LO7)** Maurice has a client that recently asked him about the odds of the IRS detecting cash transactions not reported on a tax return. What are some of the issues that Maurice should discuss with his client?

# Tax Planning Strategies and Related Limitations

## Learning Objectives

**Upon completing this chapter, you should be able to:**

**LO 1** Identify the objectives of basic tax planning strategies.

———————————— ■ ————————————

**LO 2** Apply the timing strategy and describe its applications and limitations.

———————————— ■ ————————————

**LO 3** Apply the concept of present value to tax planning.

———————————— ■ ————————————

**LO 4** Apply the strategy of income shifting, provide examples, and describe its limitations.

———————————— ■ ————————————

**LO 5** Apply the conversion strategy, provide examples, and describe its limitations.

———————————— ■ ————————————

**LO 6** Describe basic judicial doctrines that limit tax planning strategies.

———————————— ■ ————————————

**LO 7** Contrast tax avoidance and tax evasion.

**W**hile working with their CPA during their audit, Bill and Mercedes decide to inquire about less risky tax planning opportunities. Specifically, they would like to gain a better understanding of how to maximize their after-tax returns without increasing their potential for another audit. (Although it was fun and educational, one audit is enough!) Mercedes is convinced that, as a small-business owner (Lavish Interior Designs, Inc.), she feels she pays more than her fair share of taxes. Likewise, Bill, an avid investor, wonders whether he is missing the mark by not considering taxes in his investment decisions. ■

| Storyline Summary | |
| --- | --- |
| *Taxpayers:* | Bill and Mercedes |
| *Family description:* | Bill and Mercedes are married with one daughter, Margaret. |
| *Employment status:* | Bill is an economics professor; Mercedes is a small-business owner. |
| *Filing status:* | Married, filing jointly |
| *Current situation:* | Bill and Mercedes want to engage in less risky tax planning strategies. |

Bill and Mercedes have come to the right place. This chapter describes the basic tax planning concepts that form the basis of the simplest to most complex tax planning transactions. In the process we also discuss the judicial doctrines that serve as basic limits on tax planning.

## LO1 BASIC TAX PLANNING OVERVIEW

Effective tax planning requires a basic understanding of the roles that taxes and nontax factors play in structuring business, investment, and personal decisions. Although taxes may not be the sole or even the primary determinant of a transaction or its structure, taxes can significantly affect the costs or benefits associated with business, investment, and personal transactions. Thus, the tax implications of competing transactions warrant careful consideration. Likewise, nontax factors, such as the taxpayer's financial goals or legal constraints, are an integral part of every transaction.

In general terms, effective tax planning maximizes the taxpayer's after-tax wealth while achieving the taxpayer's nontax goals. Maximizing after-tax wealth is not necessarily the same as minimizing taxes. Specifically, maximizing after-tax wealth requires us to consider both the tax and nontax costs and benefits of alternative transactions, whereas tax minimization focuses solely on a single cost—taxes. Indeed, if the goal of tax planning were simply to minimize taxes, the simplest way to achieve it would be to earn no income at all. Obviously, this strategy has potential limitations—most notably, the unattractive nontax consequence of poverty. Thus, it is necessary to consider the nontax ramifications of any planning strategy.

Virtually every transaction includes three parties: the taxpayer, the other transacting party, and the uninvited silent party that specifies the tax consequences of the transaction—the government. Astute tax planning requires an understanding of the tax and nontax costs from the taxpayer's *and* the other party's perspective. For example, as discussed in Chapter 12, it would be impossible for an employer to develop an effective compensation plan without considering the tax and nontax costs associated with different compensation arrangements from both the employer's and the employees' perspectives. With sound tax planning, the employer can design a compensation package that generates value for employees while reducing costs for the employer. (One way to achieve this goal is through the use of nontaxable fringe benefits, such as health insurance, which are deductible by the employer but not taxable income to employees.) Throughout the text, we highlight situations where this multilateral approach to tax planning is especially important.

In this chapter we discuss three basic tax planning strategies that represent the building blocks of tax planning:

1. *Timing* (deferring or accelerating taxable income and tax deductions**)**.
2. *Income shifting* (shifting income from high to low tax rate taxpayers).
3. *Conversion* (converting income from high to low tax rate activities).

## LO2 LO3 LO6 TIMING STRATEGIES

One of the cornerstones of basic tax planning is the idea of *timing*. *When* income is taxed or an expense is deducted affects the associated "real" tax costs or savings. This is true for two reasons. First, the timing of when income is taxed or an expense is deducted affects the *present value* of the taxes paid on income or the tax savings on deductions. Second, the tax costs of income and tax savings of deductions vary as *tax rates* change. The tax costs on income are higher when tax rates are higher and

lower when tax rates are lower. Likewise, the tax savings on deductions are higher when tax rates are higher and lower when tax rates are lower. Let's look at the effects of present value and tax rates on the timing strategy.

### Present Value of Money

The concept of **present value**—also known as the time value of money—basically states that $1 today is worth *more* than $1 in the future. Is this true or is this some type of new math?

It's true. Assuming an investor can earn a positive after-tax rate of return such as 5 percent, $1 invested today should be worth $1.05 in one year.[1] Specifically

$$\text{Future Value} = \text{Present Value} \times (1 + r)^n$$
$$= \$1 \times (1 + .05)^1 = \$1.05$$

**Eq. 3-1**

where $1 is the present value, $r$ is the after-tax rate of return (5 percent), and $n$ is the investment period (1 year). Hence, $1 today is equivalent to $1.05 in one year. The implication of the time value of money for tax planning is that the timing of a cash inflow or a cash outflow affects the present value of the income or expense.

---

**Example 3-1**

Bill is given the choice of receiving a $1,000 nontaxable gift today or a $1,000 nontaxable gift in one year. Which would Bill prefer? Assume Bill could invest $1,000 today and earn an 8 percent return after taxes in one year. If he receives the gift today, how much would the $1,000 be worth in one year?

**Answer:** The $1,000 gift today would be worth $1,080 in one year and thus, Bill should prefer to receive the gift today. Specifically,

$$\text{Future Value} = \text{Present Value} \times (1 + r)^n$$
$$= \$1,000 \times (1 + .08)^1 = \$1,080$$

---

In terms of *future value,* the choice in the above example of receiving either $1,000 today or $1,000 in one year simplifies to a choice of $1,080 or $1,000. For even the least materialistic individual, choosing $1,080—that is, $1,000 *today*—should be straightforward.

Often tax planners find it useful to consider sums not in terms of future value, but rather in terms of present value. How would we restate the choice in Example 3-1 in terms of present value? Obviously, the present value of receiving $1,000 today is $1,000, but what is the *present value* of $1,000 received in one year? The answer depends on the **discount factor,** which we derive from the taxpayer's expected after-tax rate of return. The discount factor is very useful for calculating the present value of future inflows or outflows of cash. We can derive the discount factor for a given rate of return simply by rearranging the future value equation (Eq. 3-1) from above:

$$\text{Present Value} = \text{Future Value}/(1 + r)^n$$
$$= \$1/(1 + .08)^1 = \$0.926$$

**Eq. 3-2**

Therefore, the discount factor = 0.926

---

**THE KEY FACTS**

**Present Value of Money**

- The concept of present value—also known as the time value of money—states that $1 today is worth *more* than $1 in the future.

- The implication of the time value of money for tax planning is that the timing of a cash inflow or a cash outflow affects the present value of the income or expense.

- When considering cash inflows, higher present values are preferred; when considering cash outflows, lower present values are preferred.

- Present Value = Future Value/$(1 + r)^n$.

---

[1]Assuming a constant marginal tax rate (*tr*), after-tax rate of return (*r*) may be calculated as follows. $r = R \times (1 - tr)$, where R is the taxpayer's before-tax rate of return.

**EXHIBIT 3-1** **Present Value of a Single Payment at Various Annual Rates of Return**

| Year | 4% | 5% | 6% | 7% | 8% | 9% | 10% | 11% | 12% |
|------|------|------|------|------|------|------|------|------|------|
| 1 | .962 | .952 | .943 | .935 | .926 | .917 | .909 | .901 | .893 |
| 2 | .925 | .907 | .890 | .873 | .857 | .842 | .826 | .812 | .797 |
| 3 | .889 | .864 | .840 | .816 | .794 | .772 | .751 | .731 | .712 |
| 4 | .855 | .823 | .792 | .763 | .735 | .708 | .683 | .659 | .636 |
| 5 | .822 | .784 | .747 | .713 | .681 | .650 | .621 | .593 | .567 |
| 6 | .790 | .746 | .705 | .666 | .630 | .596 | .564 | .535 | .507 |
| 7 | .760 | .711 | .665 | .623 | .583 | .547 | .513 | .482 | .452 |
| 8 | .731 | .677 | .627 | .582 | .540 | .502 | .467 | .434 | .404 |
| 9 | .703 | .645 | .592 | .544 | .500 | .460 | .424 | .391 | .361 |
| 10 | .676 | .614 | .558 | .508 | .463 | .422 | .386 | .352 | .322 |
| 11 | .650 | .585 | .527 | .475 | .429 | .388 | .350 | .317 | .287 |
| 12 | .625 | .557 | .497 | .444 | .397 | .356 | .319 | .286 | .257 |
| 13 | .601 | .530 | .469 | .415 | .368 | .326 | .290 | .258 | .229 |
| 14 | .577 | .505 | .442 | .388 | .340 | .299 | .263 | .232 | .205 |
| 15 | .555 | .481 | .417 | .362 | .315 | .275 | .239 | .209 | .183 |

Applying the discount factor, we can see that $1,000 received in one year is worth $926 in today's dollars. Thus, in terms of present value, Bill's choice in Example 3-1 simplifies to a choice between a cash inflow of $1,000 today and a cash inflow worth $926 today. Again, choosing $1,000 today is pretty straight-forward.

Exhibit 3-1 provides the discount factors for a lump sum (single payment) received in *n* periods using various rates of return. Tax planners frequently utilize such tables for quick reference in calculating present value for sums under consideration.

**Example 3-2**

At a recent holiday sale, Bill and Mercedes purchased $1,000 worth of furniture with "no money down and no payments for one year!" How much money is this deal really worth? (Assume their after-tax rate of return on investments is 10 percent.)

**Answer:** The discount factor of .909 (Exhibit 3-1, 10% Rate of Return column, Year 1 row) means the present value of $1,000 is $909 ($1,000 × .909 = $909)—so Bill and Mercedes save $91 ($1,000 − $909 = $91).

While Example 3-1 considers a $1,000 cash inflow, Example 3-2 addresses a $1,000 cash *outflow*. In terms of present value, a choice between $1,000 paid today and $1,000 paid in a year simplifies to incurring a cash outflow of either $1,000 (by paying today) or $909 (by paying in one year). Most people would prefer to pay $909. Indeed, financial planners always keep the following general rule of thumb in mind: When considering *cash inflows, prefer higher present values;* when considering *cash outflows, prefer lower present values.*

### The Timing Strategy When Tax Rates Are Constant

In terms of tax planning, remember that *taxes paid* represent cash *outflows,* while *tax savings* generated from tax deductions are cash *inflows.* This perspective leads us to two basic tax-related timing strategies when tax rates are constant (not changing):

1. Accelerate tax deductions (deduct in an earlier period).
2. Defer recognizing taxable income (recognize in a later period).

Accelerating tax deductions to an earlier period increases the present value of the tax savings from the deduction. That is, tax savings received now have a higher present value than the same amount received a year from now.

Deferring income to a later period decreases the present value of the tax cost of the income. That is, taxes paid a year from now have a lower present value than taxes paid today. These two strategies are summarized in Exhibit 3-2.

**EXHIBIT 3-2    The Timing Tax Strategy When Tax Rates Are Constant**

| Item | Recommendation | Why? |
|---|---|---|
| Tax deductions | Accelerate tax deductions into earlier years. | Maximizes the present value of tax savings from deductions. |
| Taxable income | Defer taxable income into later tax years. | Minimizes the present value of taxes paid. |

**Example 3-3**

Mercedes, a calendar-year taxpayer, uses the cash method of accounting for her small business.[2] On December 28, she receives a $10,000 bill from her accountant for consulting services related to her small business. She can avoid late payment charges by paying the $10,000 bill before January 10 of next year. Let's assume that Mercedes' marginal tax rate is 30 percent *this year and next* and that she can earn an after-tax rate of return of 10 percent on her investments. When should she pay the $10,000 bill—this year or next?

**Answer:** If Mercedes pays the bill this year, she will receive a tax deduction on this year's tax return.[3] If she pays the bill in January, she will receive a tax deduction on next year's tax return (one year later). She needs to compare the after-tax cost of the accounting service using the present value of the tax savings for each scenario:

| | Present Value Comparison | |
|---|---|---|
| **Description** | **Option 1: Pay $10,000 bill *this year*** | **Option 2: Pay $10,000 bill *next year*** |
| Tax deduction | $10,000 | $10,000 |
| Marginal tax rate | × 30% | × 30% |
| Tax savings | $ 3,000 | $ 3,000 |
| Discount factor | × 1 | × .909 |
| Present value tax savings | $ 3,000 | $ 2,727 |
| *After-tax cost of accounting services:* | | |
| Before-tax cost | $10,000 | $10,000 |
| Less: Present value tax savings | −$ 3,000 | −$ 2,727 |
| After-tax cost of accounting services | $ 7,000 | $ 7,273 |

Since Mercedes would surely rather spend $7,000 than $7,273 for accounting services, paying the bill in December is the clear winner.

---

[2]In Chapter 8, we discuss the basic accounting methods (e.g., cash vs. the accrual method), which influence the timing of when income and deductions are recognized for tax purposes.

[3]Accelerating her payment from January 10 to December 31 will increase the present value of the $10,000 cash outflow by 10 days. Thus, there is a minor present value cost associated with accelerating her payment.

In terms of accelerating deductions, the intent of the timing strategy is to accelerate the tax deduction significantly *without* accelerating the actual cash outflow that generates the expense. Indeed, if we assume a marginal rate of 30 percent and an after-tax return of 8 percent, accelerating a $1,000 cash outflow by one year to realize $300 in tax savings actually *increases* the after-tax *cost* of the expense from $648.20 to $700.

| | **Present Value Comparison** | |
|---|---|---|
| **Description** | **Present value of net cash outflow *today*** | **Present value of net cash outflow in *one year*** |
| Cash outflow | $1,000 | $ 1,000 |
| Less: Tax savings (outflow × 30% tax rate) | – $ 300 | – $ 300 |
| Net cash outflow | $ 700 | $ 700 |
| Present value factor | × 1 | × .926 |
| Present value of net cash outflow today | $ 700 | $648.20 |

Generally speaking, whenever a taxpayer can accelerate a deduction without also accelerating the cash outflow, the timing strategy will be more beneficial.

Is the accelerating deductions strategy utilized in the real world? Yes. While the strategy is particularly effective for cash-method taxpayers who can often control the year in which they pay their expenses, all taxpayers have *some* latitude in timing deductions. Common examples of the timing strategy include accelerating depreciation deductions for depreciable assets, using LIFO instead of FIFO for inventory, and accelerating the deduction of certain prepaid expenses.[4] For large corporations, the benefits associated with this timing strategy can be quite substantial. Thus, tax planners spend considerable time evaluating the proper period in which to recognize expenses and identifying opportunities to accelerate deductions.

Are there certain taxpayer or transaction attributes that enhance the advantages of accelerating deductions? Absolutely. Higher tax rates, higher rates of return, larger transaction amounts, and the ability to accelerate deductions by two or more years all increase the benefits of accelerating deductions. To demonstrate this for yourself, simply rework Example 3-3 and substitute any of the following: 50 percent tax rate, 12 percent after-tax rate of return, $100,000 expense, or a five-year period difference in the timing of the expense deduction. The benefits of accelerating deductions become much more prominent with these changes.

Deferring income recognition is an equally beneficial timing strategy, especially when the taxpayer can defer the recognition of income significantly without deferring the actual receipt of income very much. Consider the following example.

## Example 3-4

In early December, Bill decides he would like to sell $100,000 of his Dell Inc. stock, which cost $20,000 10 years ago. Assume Bill's tax rate on the $80,000 gain will be 15 percent and his typical after-tax rate of return on investments is 7 percent. What effect would deferring the sale to January have on Bill's after-tax income on the sale?

[4]See the discussion of accounting methods in Chapter 8.

**Answer:**

| | Present Value Comparison | |
| --- | --- | --- |
| **Description** | **Option 1: Sell the $100,000 stock in December[5]** | **Option 2: Sell the $100,000 stock in January[6]** |
| Sales price | $100,000 | $100,000 |
| Less: Cost of stock | − $ 20,000 | − $ 20,000 |
| Gain on sale | $ 80,000 | $ 80,000 |
| Marginal tax rate | × 15% | × 15% |
| Tax on gain | $ 12,000 | $ 12,000 |
| Discount factor | × 1 | × .935 |
| Present value tax cost | $ 12,000 | $ 11,220 |
| *After-tax income from sale:* | | |
| Before-tax income | $100,000 | $100,000 |
| Less: Present value tax cost | − $ 12,000 | − $ 11,220 |
| After-tax income from sale | $ 88,000 | $ 88,780 |

Bill would doubtlessly prefer to earn $88,780 to $88,000, so from a tax perspective, selling the Dell Inc. stock in January is preferable.

Income deferral represents an important aspect of investment planning (Chapter 11), retirement planning (Chapter 13), and certain property transactions (Chapter 10). Income-related timing considerations also affect tax planning for everyday business operations, such as determining the appropriate period in which to recognize sales income (upon product shipment, on delivery, or on customer acceptance).

**Taxes in the Real World**   *The Timing Strategy and the Daimler-Chrysler Merger*

Although the two firms have since broken apart again, the 1998 Daimler–Chrysler merger provides a good example of the importance of the timing strategy for major business transactions. By structuring the acquisition as a stock-for-stock tax-free exchange, Chrysler allowed investors to defer paying tax on their gains from the acquisition, thereby reducing the present value of the tax to them. To ensure the acquisition qualified as a tax-free exchange, Chrysler requested a private letter ruling from the IRS regarding the tax ramifications of the proposed acquisition. The following excerpts from the Daimler–Chrysler Merger Prospectus (Form F-4, filed August 6, 1998, pages 47–48) describe the role of taxes in the merger discussions.

> During the course of these discussions and thereafter [referring to discussions between Daimler and Chrysler representatives the week of February 17, 1998, and thereafter], representatives of Chrysler stated that it was important to Chrysler that any potential transaction maximize value for its shareholders, that it be tax-free to Chrysler's U.S. stockholders and tax efficient for DaimlerChrysler AG, . . .

*(continued on page 3-8...)*

[5]This will require Bill to pay the tax on the gain no later than April 15 of the following year (i.e., three months after the sale). If Bill and Mercedes' current-year withholding and estimated payments do not equal or exceed 110 percent of their previous year's tax liability, they will have to make an estimated payment by January 15 to avoid the failure to make estimated tax payment penalty discussed later in Chapter 7. This example assumes that Bill and Mercedes can avoid the underpayment of estimated tax penalty discussed in Chapter 7 by paying 110 percent of their previous year's tax liability in both options 1 and 2. Thus, they can defer paying the tax on the gain until April 15 of the year following the sale.

[6]This will require Bill to pay the tax on the gain no later than April 15 of the following year (i.e., 15 months after the sale).

> Representatives of Daimler-Benz indicated that it was important to Daimler-Benz that any potential transaction maximize value for its stockholders, that it be tax-free to Daimler-Benz' German stockholders and tax efficient for DaimlerChrysler AG and . . .
>
> The prospectus later describes discussions on April 7 and 9 and states: "Major points of discussion during that period and thereafter involved: . . . (c) finding a structure that would (i) result in a tax-free transaction in the United States and Germany for both companies' stockholders and result in ongoing tax efficiency . . ."

Do certain taxpayer or transaction attributes enhance the advantages of deferring income? Yes. The list is very similar to that for accelerating deductions: Higher tax rates, higher rates of return, larger transaction amounts, and the ability to defer revenue recognition for longer periods of time increase the benefits of deferral. To demonstrate this for yourself, simply rework Example 3-4 using any of the following: 50 percent tax rate, 12 percent after-tax rate of return on investments, or $200,000 gain.[7]

### The Timing Strategy When Tax Rates Change

**THE KEY FACTS**

**The Timing Strategy**

- The timing of when income is taxed or an expense is deducted affects the *present value* of the taxes paid on income or tax savings on deductions.

- The tax costs of income and tax savings of deductions vary as *tax rates* change.

- When tax rates are constant, tax planners prefer to defer income and accelerate deductions.

- When tax rates are increasing, the taxpayer must calculate the optimal tax strategies for deductions and income.

- When tax rates are decreasing, taxpayers should accelerate tax deductions into earlier years and defer taxable income to later years.

When tax rates change, the timing strategy requires a little more consideration because the tax costs of income and the tax savings from deductions will now vary. The higher the tax rate, the higher the tax savings for a tax deduction. The lower the tax rate, the lower the tax costs for taxable income. *All other things being equal, taxpayers should prefer to recognize deductions during high-tax-rate years and income during low-tax-rate years.* The implication is that before a taxpayer implements the timing strategies suggested above (accelerate deductions, defer income), she should consider whether her tax rates are likely to change. In fact, as we discuss below, increasing tax rates may even suggest the taxpayer should *accelerate* income and *defer* deductions.

What would cause a taxpayer's marginal tax rate to change? The taxpayer's taxable income can change, perhaps due to changing jobs, retiring, or starting a new business. Indeed, in Chapter 1, we demonstrated how a taxpayer's marginal tax rate changes as income or deductions change. Marginal tax rates can also change because of tax legislation. We discussed the tax legislative process in Chapter 2 and noted that Congress frequently enacts tax legislation, because lawmakers use taxes to raise revenue, stimulate the economy, and so on. In the last 25 years, Congress has changed the maximum statutory tax rates that apply to ordinary income, such as wages and business income, or capital gains, such as gains from the sale of stock, for individual taxpayers no fewer than nine times (see Exhibit 3-3).

Let's take a look at how changing tax rates affect the timing strategy recommendations. Exhibit 3-4 presents recommendations when tax rates are increasing. The taxpayer must actually calculate the optimal tax strategies for deductions and income when tax rates are increasing. Specifically, because accelerating deductions causes them to be recognized in a *lower*-tax-rate year, the taxpayer must calculate whether the benefit of accelerating the deduction outweighs the disadvantage. Likewise, because deferring income causes income to be recognized in a *higher*-tax-rate year, the taxpayer must calculate whether the benefit of deferring it outweighs the disadvantage.

---

[7]In Example 3-4, increasing the deferral period (e.g., from one to five years) also increases the benefits of tax deferral but requires additional assumptions regarding the expected five-year return of the Dell Inc. stock (assuming he does not sell the stock for five years) and his new investment (assuming he sells the Dell Inc. stock and immediately reinvests the after-tax proceeds).

**EXHIBIT 3-3**   Historical Maximum Ordinary and Capital Gains Tax Rates for Individuals Since 1982

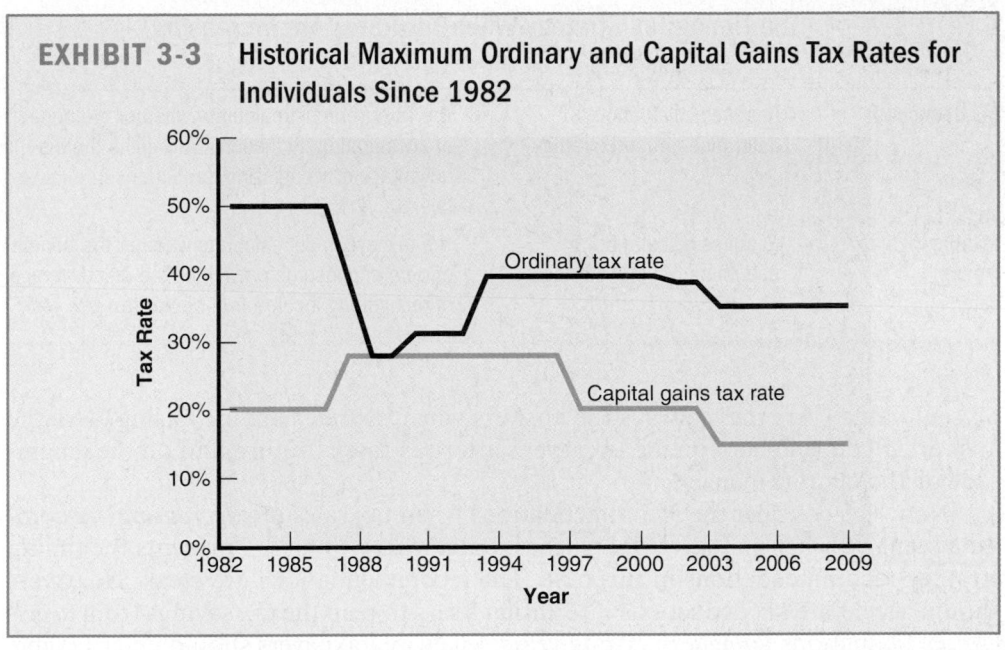

Example 3-5

Having decided she needs new equipment for her business, Mercedes is now considering whether to make the purchase and claim a corresponding $10,000 deduction at year-end or next year. Mercedes anticipates that, with the new machinery, her business income will rise such that her marginal rate will increase from 20 percent this year to 28 percent next year. Assuming her after-tax rate of return is 8 percent, what should Mercedes do?

**Answer:**  Given rising tax rates, Mercedes must calculate the after-tax cost of the equipment for *both* options and compare present values.

**Present Value Comparison**

| Description | Option 1: Pay $10,000 bill *this year* | Option 2: Pay $10,000 bill *next year* |
|---|---|---|
| Tax deduction | $10,000 | $10,000 |
| Marginal tax rate | × 20% | × 28% |
| Tax savings | $ 2,000 | $ 2,800 |
| Discount factor | × 1 | × .926 |
| Present value tax savings | $ 2,000 | $ 2,593 |
| *After-tax cost of equipment:* | | |
| Before-tax cost | $10,000 | $10,000 |
| Less: Present value tax savings | –$ 2,000 | –$ 2,593 |
| After-tax cost of equipment | $ 8,000 | $ 7,407 |

Paying the $10,000 in January is the clear winner.

In the above example, if the choice were either to recognize $10,000 of *income* this year or next, the *amounts* would be exactly the same but the conclusion would be different, and Mercedes would prefer to receive $8,000 of after-tax income this year instead of $7,407. (Remember, when considering cash *inflows,* we prefer the *higher*

**EXHIBIT 3-4** **The Timing Tax Strategy When Tax Rates Are *Increasing***

| Item | Recommendation | Why? |
| --- | --- | --- |
| Tax deductions | Requires calculation to determine optimal strategy. | The taxpayer must calculate whether the benefit of accelerating deductions outweighs the disadvantage of recognizing deductions in a *lower*-tax-rate year. |
| Taxable income | Requires calculation to determine optimal strategy. | The taxpayer must calculate whether the benefit of deferring income outweighs the disadvantage of recognizing income in a *higher*-tax-rate year. |

present value.) Are these always the answers when tax rates are increasing? No, the answer will depend both on the taxpayer's after-tax rate of return and on the magnitude of the tax rate increase.

Now let's consider the recommendations when tax rates are *decreasing*—a common scenario when an individual reaches retirement. Exhibit 3-5 presents the timing strategy recommendations in this case. The recommendations are clear. Taxpayers should accelerate tax deductions into earlier years to reap the tax savings from *accelerating* deductions to *higher*-tax-rate years. Likewise, taxpayers should defer taxable income to later years to enjoy the tax benefits of *deferring* taxable income to *lower*-tax-rate years.

**EXHIBIT 3-5** **The Timing Tax Strategy When Tax Rates Are *Decreasing***

| Item | Recommendation | Why? |
| --- | --- | --- |
| Tax deductions | Accelerate tax deductions into earlier years. | Maximizes the present value of tax savings from deductions due to the acceleration of the deductions into *earlier* years with a *higher*-tax-rate year. |
| Taxable income | Defer taxable income into later tax years. | Minimizes the present value of taxes paid due to the deferral of the income to later years with a *lower* tax rate. |

**Limitations to Timing Strategies** Timing strategies contain certain inherent limitations. First, tax laws generally require taxpayers to continue their investment in an asset in order to defer income recognition for tax purposes. In other words, deferral is generally not an option if a taxpayer has "cashed out" of an investment.[8] For example, Bill could not sell his Dell stock in December and then choose not to recognize the income until January. A deferral strategy may not be optimal (1) if the taxpayer has severe cash flow needs, (2) if continuing the investment would generate a low rate of return compared to other investments, or (3) if the current investment would subject the taxpayer to unnecessary risk. For example, the risk that the value of Bill's investment in Dell Inc. will decline from December to January in Example 3-4 may lead Bill to forgo deferring his stock sale until January. Again, the astute taxpayer considers both the tax *and* nontax ramifications of deferring income.

A second limitation results from the **constructive receipt doctrine,** which also restricts income deferral for cash-method taxpayers.[9] Unlike accrual-method taxpayers,

---

[8]See the discussions of like-kind exchanges in Chapter 10, investment planning in Chapter 11, and retirement planning in Chapter 13.

[9]Later in this chapter we discuss other judicial doctrines that apply to all planning strategies.

cash-method taxpayers report income for tax purposes when the income is *received,* whether it is in the form of cash, property, or services.[10] The cash method affords taxpayers some leeway in determining when to recognize income because such taxpayers can control when they bill their clients. However, the constructive receipt doctrine provides that a taxpayer must recognize income when it is actually *or* constructively received. Constructive receipt is deemed to have occurred if the income has been credited to the taxpayer's account or if the income is unconditionally available to the taxpayer, the taxpayer is aware of the income's availability, and there are no restrictions on the taxpayer's control over the income.

---

**Example 3-6**

Mercedes' brother-in-law, Carlos, works for King Acura, which recently instituted a bonus plan that pays year-end bonuses each December to employees rated above average for their customer service. Carlos is expecting a $10,000 bonus this year that will be paid on December 31. Thinking he'd prefer to defer this income until next year, Carlos plans to take a vacation on December 30 so that he will not receive his bonus check until January. Will Carlos's strategy work?

**Answer:** No, the constructive receipt doctrine applies here. Because Carlos's check was unconditionally available to him on December 31, he was aware of its availability, and there were no restrictions on his control over the income on that date, Carlos must report the income in the current year.

---

What could taxpayers do to avoid Carlos's problem in the future? They could request that their employer institute a company policy of paying bonuses on January 1, which would allow all employees to report the bonus income in that year. However, if the employer is a cash-method taxpayer, this creates a potential conflict with its employees.[11] Such an employer would most likely prefer to deduct the bonus in the current year, which requires the bonuses to be paid in December. This conflict would not exist if the employer were an accrual-method taxpayer, because paying the bonuses in January would not affect its ability to deduct the bonuses in the previous year.[12]

## INCOME-SHIFTING STRATEGIES

LO4 LO6

We've seen that the value of a tax deduction, or the tax cost of income, varies with the marginal tax rate. We've also seen that tax rates can vary across time, which leads to basic tax planning strategies regarding when to recognize deductions and income. Tax rates can also vary across *taxpayers* or *jurisdictions* (states, countries), which leads to still other tax planning strategies—for example, shifting income from high-tax-rate taxpayers to low-tax-rate taxpayers or shifting deductions from low-tax-rate taxpayers to high-tax-rate taxpayers.

---

[10]As we discuss in depth in Chapter 8, accrual-basis taxpayers report income when it is earned. In general, income is deemed earned when all events have occurred that fix the taxpayer's right to the income and the income can be estimated with reasonable accuracy. Thus, income recognition for accrual-basis taxpayers generally is not tied to payment. Receipt of prepaid income by accrual-basis taxpayers may trigger income recognition in certain circumstances. The constructive receipt doctrine may apply in these situations.

[11]Because King Acura carries inventory, the cash method is not allowed for transactions related to its inventory (e.g., cost of goods sold, sales, etc.). However, King Acura is permitted to use the cash method for other transactions. This mixed method is referred to the "hybrid" method of accounting.

[12]When an employee/shareholder and an employer/corporation are related (i.e., the employee/shareholder owns more than 50 percent of the value of the employer corporation), the corporation is not allowed to deduct the compensation expense until the employee/shareholder includes the payment in income. §267(a)(2).

The type of taxpayers who benefit most from this strategy are (1) related parties, such as family members or businesses and their owners, who have varying marginal tax rates and are willing to shift income for the benefit of the group; and (2) taxpayers operating in multiple jurisdictions with different marginal tax rates. In any case, tax planners should seek only legitimate methods of shifting income that will withstand IRS scrutiny. In the following section we discuss transactions between family members, followed by a discussion of transactions between owners and their businesses, and finally a discussion of income shifting across jurisdictions.

### Transactions between Family Members and Limitations

One of the most common examples of income shifting is high-tax-rate parents shifting income to low-tax-rate children. For example, Bill and Mercedes have a 30 percent marginal tax rate, whereas their daughter, Margaret, has a 10 percent marginal tax rate. Assuming their marginal tax rates remain constant with relatively modest changes in income, every $1 of income that Bill and Mercedes shift to Margaret reduces the family's tax liability by 20 cents [$1 × (30% − 10%)]. Thus, if Bill and Mercedes shift $10,000 of taxable income to Margaret, the family's after-tax income will increase by $2,000. Can taxpayers legally do this? Yes and no. As you might expect, there are limitations on this type of income shifting.

The **assignment of income doctrine** requires income to be taxed to the taxpayer who actually earns it.[13] Merely attributing your paycheck or dividend to another taxpayer does not transfer the tax liability associated with the income. The assignment of income doctrine implies that, in order to shift income to a taxpayer, that taxpayer must actually earn the income. For example, if Mercedes would like to shift some of her business income to Margaret, Margaret must actually earn it. One way to accomplish this would be for Mercedes to employ Margaret in her business and pay her a $10,000 salary. The effects of this transaction are to decrease Mercedes' taxable income by $10,000 because of tax-deductible salary expense, and increase Margaret's income by the $10,000 taxable salary. What if Margaret is paid $10,000 to answer Mercedes' business phone one Saturday afternoon every month? Does this seem reasonable? Not likely. The IRS frowns upon this type of aggressive strategy.

Indeed, the IRS closely scrutinizes such **related-party transactions**—that is, financial activities among family members (also among owners and their businesses, or among businesses owned by the same owners). Unlike **arm's-length transactions,** where each transacting party negotiates for his or her own benefit, related-party transactions involve taxpayers who are much more willing to negotiate for their own common good to the detriment of the IRS. For example, would Mercedes pay an unrelated party $10,000 to answer the phone once a month? Doubtful.[14]

Are there other ways to shift income to children? For example, could Bill shift some of his investment income to Margaret? Yes, but there's a catch. The assignment of income applies what is referred to as the "fruit and the tree" analogy (*Lucas v. Earl* (S. Ct., 1930), 8 AFTR 10287). For the owner to avoid being taxed on the fruit from the tree (the income), the owner must transfer the tree. Thus, to shift investment income, Bill would also have to transfer ownership in the underlying investment assets to Margaret.[15] Is there a problem with this requirement? Not for Margaret. However, Bill would likely prefer to maintain his wealth. The nontax disadvantages

---

[13]Later in this chapter we discuss other judicial doctrines that apply to all planning strategies.

[14]The Internal Revenue Code also contains specific provisions to curtail benefits from related-party transactions. For example, as we discuss in Chapter 10, §267 disallows a tax deduction for losses on sales to related parties (even if the sale was consummated at the asset's fair market value).

[15]Further, as we discuss in Chapter 7, the "kiddie tax" may apply when parents shift too much investment income to children. The kiddie tax restricts the amount of a child's investment income that can be taxed at the child's (lower) tax rate instead of the parents' (higher) tax rate.

of transferring wealth to implement the income-shifting strategy often outweigh the tax benefits of the transfer. For example, most parents either could not afford to or would have serious reservations about transferring significant wealth to their children—a prime example of how nontax costs may override tax considerations.

### Transactions between Owners and Their Businesses and Limitations

Income shifting is not limited to transactions within a family unit. One of the most common examples occurs between owners and their businesses. Let's consider Mercedes' interior design business. Currently, Mercedes operates her business as a sole proprietorship. A sole proprietorship (unlike a taxable corporation) is not a separate reporting entity, and thus, Mercedes reports her business income and deductions on her individual tax return. Shifting income to or from her sole proprietorship offers little benefit, because all of her sole proprietorship income is reported on her tax return regardless of whether it is attributed to her personally or to her business. On the other hand, if Mercedes operated her interior design business as a taxable corporation, shifting income to or from the taxable corporation may make good financial sense because the corporation would be a separate entity with tax rates distinct from Mercedes' individual tax rate. Shifting income to herself may allow Mercedes to decrease the tax on her business profits, thereby increasing her after-tax income. Example 3-7 illustrates the savings obtainable from this strategy.

In order to shift income from the corporation to the owner, the corporation must create a tax deduction for itself in the process. Compensation paid to employee–owners is the most common method of shifting income from corporations to their owners. Compensation expense is deductible by the corporation and is generally taxable to the employee. (See Chapter 12 for a broader discussion of nontaxable compensation benefits.) Having the business owner rent property to the corporation or loan money to the corporation are also effective income-shifting methods, because both transactions generate tax deductions for the corporation and income for the shareholder. Because corporations don't get a tax deduction for dividends paid, paying dividends is *not* an effective way to shift income. Having a business pay dividends actually results in "double taxation"—the profits generating the dividends are taxed first at the corporate level, and then at the shareholder level. Recommending this tax planning strategy may not be a good way to keep your job as a tax consultant.

---

**Example 3-7**

Mercedes is considering incorporating her interior design business. She projects $200,000 of business profit next year. Excluding this profit, Bill and Mercedes expect $140,000 of taxable income next year. If Mercedes would like to minimize her current-year tax liability, should she incorporate her business? [Use the married filing jointly and corporate tax rates inside the front cover of the book to answer this question.]

**Answer:** If Mercedes does not incorporate her business, the first $69,250 of her business profits will be taxed at 28 percent (from $140,000 to $209,250 of taxable income, the marginal tax rate is 28 percent). The remaining $130,750 (from $209,250 to $340,000 of taxable income) would be taxed at 33 percent. Upon reviewing the above corporate tax rate schedule, you should note that the first two corporate tax rates (15 percent and 25 percent) are lower than Bill and Mercedes' current marginal tax rate of 33 percent. Thus, there appears to be some opportunity for Mercedes to reduce her current year tax exposure by incorporating her business.[16]

---

[16]Note that this is a simplified discussion of one of many tax issues associated with incorporating a business.

After a taxpayer identifies the opportunity and appropriate method to shift income (compensation paid to a related party), he or she can easily determine the optimal amount to shift depending on the taxpayers' marginal tax rates.

### Example 3-8

Assuming Mercedes' goal is to minimize her current year federal income tax liability, how much of the $200,000 business income should her corporation report?

**Answer:** It should report $75,000. Comparing the two tax rate schedules reveals how to calculate this number.

**Step 1:** Would Mercedes rather have income taxed at 15 percent (the corporation's marginal tax rate from zero to $50,000 taxable income) or 28 percent (Bill and Mercedes' marginal tax rate before recognizing any profit from Mercedes' business)? 15 percent is the obvious answer. To take advantage of the 15 percent corporate tax bracket, Mercedes should retain $50,000 of the expected $200,000 in profits in the corporation, because $50,000 is the width of the 15 percent corporate tax bracket.

**Step 2:** Assuming the corporation reports $50,000 of income, its marginal tax rate will now be 25 percent, and thus Mercedes' choice is to have income taxed at 25 percent (the corporation's marginal tax rate) or at 28 percent (Bill and Mercedes' marginal tax rate before recognizing any profit from Mercedes' business). Twenty-five percent is the clear answer. To take advantage of the 25 percent corporate tax bracket, the corporation should retain another $25,000 of the expected $200,000 in profits. ($25,000 is the width of the 25 percent corporate tax bracket.) The corporation's marginal tax rate will now be 34 percent.

**Step 3:** Continuing this same decision process, Mercedes should shift the remaining $125,000 of profits ($69,250 taxed at 28 percent and $55,750 taxed at 33 percent) to herself and Bill—via a salary paid to Mercedes—because their marginal tax rates (28 percent and 33 percent) will be lower than the corporation's marginal tax rate (34 percent).

How much current federal income tax does this strategy save Bill and Mercedes? The corporation's and Bill and Mercedes' combined federal income tax liability will be $78,981 ($13,750 for the corporation plus $65,231 for Bill and Mercedes) compared to $89,981 for Bill and Mercedes if the business is operated as a sole proprietorship. Thus, they will save $11,000.[17]

Are there nontax disadvantages of the income-shifting-via-incorporating strategy? Yes. For example, one nontax disadvantage for Mercedes is that her new corporation now has $61,250 of her after-tax profits ($75,000 profits less $13,750 of corporate tax). If Mercedes has personal cash flow needs that require use of the $61,250, this is not a viable strategy. Indeed, it's advantageous only if the business owner intends to reinvest the business profits into the business. Furthermore, any subsequent transactions between Mercedes and the corporation would clearly be related-party transactions. Thus, Mercedes should be prepared for IRS scrutiny.[18] If the salary, rent, and other costs are deemed to be unreasonable, the IRS may reclassify any excess payments above the value of services and property provided as nondeductible corporate dividends. In this scenario, the corporation and Mercedes would both pay income tax on each dollar of deemed dividend payment. This is not a good outcome for Mercedes or any business owner.

---

[17]This strategy will result in the eventual double taxation of the income retained in Mercedes' corporation. Specifically, Mercedes will eventually have to pay tax on the income retained by the corporation, either in the form of taxable dividends from the corporation or a taxable gain when she sells or liquidates the corporation. The present value of this additional layer of tax reduces the tax savings from this strategy. The longer that the second layer of tax is deferred, the more advantageous this strategy will be. This calculation is beyond the scope of this chapter.

[18]The taxpayer should maintain documentation for related-party transactions (e.g., notes for related-party loans and contemporaneous documentation of reasonable compensation paid to related parties).

**Example 3-9**

Upon reviewing Bill and Mercedes' tax return, the IRS reclassifies $65,000 of Mercedes's $125,000 salary in Example 3-8 as a dividend. What are the tax consequences of this reclassification?

**Answer:** (1) The corporation's taxable income will increase from $75,000 to $140,000 because dividends are not deductible, thereby increasing the corporation's tax liability from $13,750 to $37,850; and (2) Bill and Mercedes' taxable income will remain the same, except $65,000 of their $265,000 of taxable income will be dividends taxed at a preferential 15 percent tax rate. Thus, Bill and Mercedes will have $200,000 of taxable income taxed at their ordinary tax rates ($44,243.50 of tax) and $65,000 of dividend income taxed at 15 percent ($9,750 of tax), resulting in a tax liability of $53,993.50.

Under this scenario, the combined tax liabilities of the corporation and Bill and Mercedes will be $91,843.50, which is $1,862.50 *higher* than Bill and Mercedes' $89,981 tax liability had they not incorporated Mercedes' business.[19]

As the above examples illustrate, tax-avoiding strategies can be quite beneficial, but they also entail some financial risks if the structure fails to pass muster with the IRS.

## Income Shifting across Jurisdictions and Limitations

Taxpayers that operate in multiple jurisdictions (states, countries) also apply the income-shifting strategy. Specifically, income earned in different jurisdictions—whether in the United States or abroad, and for state income tax purposes, income earned in different states—is often taxed very differently. With a proper understanding of the differences in tax laws across jurisdictions, taxpayers can use these differences to maximize their after-tax wealth.

**Example 3-10**

Carlos's employer, King Acura, has two locations. Its main location is in South Dakota (a state with no corporate tax), with a secondary location in North Dakota (maximum corporate state tax rate of 6.5 percent). What tax planning strategy may save money for King Acura?

**Answer:** The most obvious strategy is to shift income from the North Dakota location to the South Dakota location, thereby reducing King Acura's state income tax liability by seven cents for every dollar of income shifted.[20]

A number of possibilities exist to execute a strategy such as King Acura's in Example 3-10. Assuming that the North Dakota and South Dakota locations exchange cars, the firm could shift income via *transfer pricing* (using the price the South Dakota location charges the North Dakota location for cars transferred to North Dakota). Likewise, if the South Dakota location (the corporate headquarters) provides a legitimate support function for the North Dakota location, the firm should allocate a portion of the overhead and administrative expenses from the South Dakota location to the North Dakota location.

---

[19]Chapter 12 discusses the consequences of unreasonable compensation to employee–owners.

[20]Because state taxes are deductible for federal tax purposes, every dollar of state taxes reduced with this strategy will increase King Acura's federal income tax liability by its federal marginal tax rate (e.g., 35 percent). Thus, the net tax savings for every dollar of income shifted from North Dakota to South Dakota will be 4.23 percent, which equals the state tax savings (6.5 percent) less the federal tax increase resulting from the lost state tax deduction (6.5 percent × 35 percent).

What are some of the limitations of income shifting across jurisdictions? First, taxing authorities are fully aware of the tax benefits of strategically structuring transactions across tax borders (across countries or states). Thus, the IRS closely examines transfer pricing on international transactions. Similarly, state tax authorities scrutinize interstate transactions between related taxpayers. Second, when taxpayers locate in low-tax-rate jurisdictions to, in effect, shift income to a tax-advantaged jurisdiction, they may bear *implicit* taxes (that is, additional costs attributable to the jurisdiction's tax advantage). For example, the demand for workers, services, or property in low-tax-rate jurisdictions, whether a foreign country or a low-tax state, may increase the nontax costs associated with operating a business there enough to offset the tax advantages. Finally, negative publicity from moving operations (and jobs) from the United States to a lower-tax jurisdiction may more than offset any tax benefits associated with these strategies.

---

**Taxes in the Real World**    *Corporate Inversions and Income Shifting*

In the ultimate income-shifting strategy, several high-profile U.S. companies—including Cooper Industries, Fruit of the Loom, Helen of Troy, and Ingersoll-Rand—executed corporate "inversions" in the 1990s and early 2000s to escape U.S. taxation of foreign income. In a corporate inversion, a U.S. company becomes a subsidiary of a foreign company organized in a tax haven (a low-tax jurisdiction). The end result is that the former U.S. company avoids U.S. taxation on its foreign income.

Cooper Industries estimated that its corporate inversion saved the company (and cost the U.S. government) approximately $55 million in U.S. taxes per year. Not surprisingly, corporate inversions were not well received by Congress and the IRS. Congress acted swiftly to eliminate the tax benefits of these transactions.

The public also reacted very negatively to corporate inversions, which may have deterred other companies from utilizing this strategy. Indeed, Stanley Works abandoned its planned corporate inversion (expected to generate annual tax savings of $30 million) after heavy public and political pressure.

---

## CONVERSION STRATEGIES

We've now seen how tax rates can vary across time and taxpayers. They can also vary across different *activities*. For example, ordinary income such as salary, interest income, and business income received by individual taxpayers is taxed at their ordinary marginal tax rates, whereas long-term capital gains, which are gains from the sale of investment assets held longer than one year, and dividends are taxed at lower tax rates (currently a maximum of 15 percent), and still other forms of income like nontaxable compensation benefits and municipal bond interest are tax-exempt. Expenses from different types of activities may also be treated very differently for tax purposes. Business expenses are generally fully tax deductible, whereas tax deductions for investment expenses may be limited, and tax deductions for personal expenses may be completely disallowed. In sum, the tax law does not treat all types of income or deductions the same. This understanding forms the basis for the conversion strategy— recasting income and expenses to receive the most favorable tax treatment.

To implement the conversion strategy, the taxpayer must be aware of the underlying differences in tax treatment across various types of income, expenses, and activities and have some ability to alter the nature of the income or expense to receive the more advantageous tax treatment. What are some common examples of the conversion strategy? In Chapter 11, we consider investment planning and the advantages of investing in assets that generate preferentially taxed income. In Chapter 8, we explain the basic differences between business and investment activities and what characteristics result in the more favorable "business" designation for expense deductions.

In Chapters 12 and 13, we discuss compensation planning and the benefits of restructuring employee compensation from currently taxable compensation to nontaxable or tax-deferred forms of compensation, such as employer-provided health insurance and retirement contributions.

To analyze the benefits of the conversion strategy, you often compare the after-tax returns of alternative investments. Given a stationary marginal tax rate, you can calculate an investment's after-tax rate of return as follows:

$$\text{After-Tax Return} = \text{Before-Tax Return} - (\text{Before-Tax Return} \times \text{Marginal Tax Rate})$$

**Eq. 3-3**

which simplifies to:

$$\text{After-Tax Return} = \text{Before-Tax Return} \times (1 - \text{Marginal Tax Rate})$$

**Eq. 3-4**

*(concluded)*

■ The Internal Revenue Code contains specific provisions that prevent the taxpayer from changing the nature of expenses, income, or activities to a more tax-advantaged status.

■ Implicit taxes may also reduce or eliminate the advantages of conversion strategies.

---

## Example 3-11

Bill is contemplating three different investments, each with the same amount of risk:

1. A high-dividend stock that pays 8 percent dividends annually but has no appreciation potential.

2. Taxable corporate bonds that pay 9 percent interest annually.

3. Tax-exempt municipal bonds that pay 6 percent interest annually.

Assuming that dividends are taxed at 15 percent and that Bill's marginal tax rate on ordinary income is 30 percent, which investment should Bill choose?

**Answer:** To answer this question, we must compute Bill's after-tax rate of return for each investment. The after-tax returns for the 3 investments are:

| Investment Choice | Computation | After-Tax Return |
|---|---|---|
| High-dividend stock | 8% × (1 – 15%) = | 6.8% |
| Corporate bond | 9% × (1 – 30%) = | 6.3% |
| Municipal bond | 6% × (1 – 0%) = | 6.0% |

Accordingly, Bill should choose the dividend-yielding stock.

What marginal tax rate on ordinary income would make Bill indifferent between the dividend-yielding stock and the corporate bond?

**Answer:** The dividend-yielding stock has an after-tax rate return of 6.8 percent. For Bill to be indifferent between this stock and the corporate bond, the corporate bond would need a 6.8 percent after-tax rate of return. We can use Eq. 3-4 above to solve for the marginal tax rate.

$$\text{After-Tax Return} = \text{Before-Tax Return} \times (1 - \text{Marginal Tax Rate})$$
$$6.8\% = 9\% \times (1 - \text{Marginal Tax Rate})$$
$$\text{Marginal Tax Rate} = 24.44\%$$

Let's check this answer: After-Tax Return = 9% × (1 – 24.44%) = 6.8%

---

## Limitations of Conversion Strategies

Like other tax planning strategies, conversion strategies face potential limitations. The Code itself also contains several specific provisions that prevent the taxpayer from changing the nature of expenses, income, or activities to a more

**LO6**

tax-advantaged status, including (among many others) the depreciation recapture rules discussed in Chapter 10 and the luxury auto depreciation rules discussed in Chapter 9. In addition, as discussed in Chapter 1, implicit taxes may reduce or eliminate the advantages of tax-preferred investments (such as municipal bonds or any investment taxed at preferential tax rates) by decreasing their before-tax rate of returns. Thus, implicit taxes may reduce the advantages of the conversion strategy.

## ADDITIONAL LIMITATIONS TO TAX PLANNING STRATEGIES: JUDICIAL DOCTRINES

The IRS also has several other doctrines at its disposal for situations where it expects taxpayer abuse. These doctrines apply across a wide variety of transactions and planning strategies (timing, income shifting, and conversion). The **business purpose doctrine,** for instance, allows the IRS to challenge and disallow business expenses for transactions with no underlying business motivation, such as the travel cost of a spouse accompanying a taxpayer on a business trip. The **step-transaction doctrine** allows the IRS to collapse a series of related transactions into one transaction to determine the tax consequences of the transaction. Finally, the **substance-over-form doctrine** allows the IRS to consider the transaction's substance regardless of its form, and where appropriate, to reclassify the transaction according to its substance. In Chapter 2, we noted that the Internal Revenue Code is the ultimate tax authority. The business purpose, step-transaction, and substance-over-form doctrines allow the IRS to determine the tax consequences of transactions that follow only the form of the Internal Revenue Code and not the spirit.

You can often assess whether the business purpose, step-transaction, or substance-over-form doctrines apply by using the "smell test": If the transaction "smells bad," one of these doctrines likely applies. (Transactions usually smell bad when the primary purpose is to avoid taxes and not to accomplish an independent business objective.) For example, using the substance-over-form doctrine, the IRS would likely reclassify most of the $10,000 paid to Margaret for answering the phone one Saturday afternoon a month as a gift from Mercedes to Margaret (see the earlier discussion of income shifting and transactions between family members), even though the transaction was structured as compensation and Margaret did do some work for her mother. This recharacterization would unwind the income-shifting benefits for the amount considered to be a gift, as gifts to family members are not tax deductible. In sum, the *substance* of the transaction must be justifiable, not just the form.

**LO7**

## TAX AVOIDANCE VERSUS TAX EVASION

Each of the tax planning strategies discussed in this book falls within the confines of legal **tax avoidance.** Tax avoidance has long been endorsed by the courts and even Congress. For example, remember that Congress specifically encouraged tax avoidance by excluding municipal bond income from taxation, preferentially taxing dividend and capital gain income, and other strategies. Likewise, the courts have often made it quite clear that taxpayers are under no moral obligation to pay more taxes than required by law. As an example, in *Commissioner v. Newman,* 159 F.2d 848 (2 Cir., 1947), which considered a taxpayer's ability to shift income to his

children using trusts, Judge Learned Hand included the following statement in his dissenting opinion:

> Over and over again courts have said that there is nothing sinister in so arranging one's affairs as to keep taxes as low as possible. Everybody does so, rich or poor; and all do right, for nobody owes any public duty to pay more than the law demands: taxes are enforced exactions, not voluntary contributions. To demand more in the name of morals is mere cant.

In contrast to tax avoidance, **tax evasion**—that is, the willful attempt to defraud the government—falls outside the confines of legal tax avoidance and thus may land the perpetrator within the confines of a federal prison. (Recall from Chapter 2 that the rewards of tax evasion include stiff monetary penalties and imprisonment.) When does tax avoidance become tax evasion? Very good question. In many cases a clear distinction exists between avoidance (such as not paying tax on municipal bond interest) and evasion (not paying tax on a $1,000,000 game show prize). In other cases, the line is less clear. In these situations, professional judgment, the use of a smell test, and consideration of the business purpose, step-transaction, and substance-over-form doctrines may prove useful.

As you might expect, tax evasion is a major area of concern and focus for the IRS. While the IRS vigorously prosecutes suspected tax evaders, its actions alone have not been able to solve this problem. Is tax evasion a victimless crime? No. Because the federal government must replace lost tax revenues by imposing higher taxes on others, honest taxpayers are the true victims of tax evasion. Currently, the federal government estimates that tax evasion costs the federal government annually more than $200 billion in lost tax revenues. As citizens and residents of the United States, each of us must recognize our obligation to support our country. As future accountants and business professionals, we also must recognize the inherent value of high ethical standards, which call for us to do the right thing in *all* situations. As business professionals have learned over and over, the costs of doing otherwise far exceed any short-term gains.

> **THE KEY FACTS**
>
> **Tax Evasion versus Tax Avoidance**
>
> - Tax avoidance is the legal act of arranging one's transactions to minimize taxes paid.
> - Tax evasion is the willful attempt to defraud the government by not paying taxes legally owed.
> - Tax evasion falls outside the confines of legal tax avoidance.

## CONCLUSION

In this chapter we discussed three basic tax planning strategies—timing, income shifting, and conversion—and their related limitations. Each of these strategies exploits the variation in taxation across different dimensions. The timing strategy exploits the variation in taxation across time: The "real" tax costs of income decrease as taxation is deferred; the "real" tax savings associated with tax deductions increase as tax deductions are accelerated. However, because tax rates may change over time and the tax costs of income and tax savings of deductions vary with tax rates, tax planning should consider the effects of such changes on the timing strategy. The income-shifting strategy exploits the variation in taxation across taxpayers or jurisdictions. The assignment of income doctrine limits aggressive attempts to shift income across taxpayers. In addition, related-party transactions receive close IRS attention given the increased likelihood of taxpayer abuses in these transactions. Finally, the conversion strategy exploits the variation in taxation rates across activities although implicit taxes may reduce the advantages of this strategy. In addition to limitations specific to each planning strategy, the judicial doctrines of business purpose, step-transaction, and substance-over-form broadly apply to a wide range of transactions and planning strategies.

The timing, income-shifting, and conversion strategies represent the building blocks for the more sophisticated tax strategies that tax professionals employ on a daily basis. Combining an understanding of these basic tax planning strategies with knowledge of our tax law will provide you with the tools necessary to identify, evaluate, and implement tax planning strategies. Throughout the remainder of the text, we will discuss how these strategies can be applied to different transactions.

## SUMMARY

**LO1** Identify the objectives of basic tax planning strategies.

- Effective tax planning maximizes the taxpayer's after-tax wealth while achieving the taxpayer's nontax goals. Maximizing after-tax wealth is not necessarily the same as tax minimization. Maximizing after-tax wealth requires one to consider both the tax and nontax costs and benefits of alternative transactions, whereas tax minimization focuses solely on a single cost (i.e., taxes).

- Virtually every transaction involves three parties: the taxpayer, the other transacting party, and the uninvited silent party that specifies the tax consequences of the transaction (i.e., the government). Astute tax planning requires an understanding of the tax and nontax costs from the taxpayer's *and* the other party's perspectives.

**LO2** Apply the timing strategy and describe its applications and limitations.

- One of the cornerstones of basic tax planning involves the idea of *timing*—that is, *when* income is taxed or an expense is deducted affects the associated "real" tax costs or savings. This is true for two reasons. First, the timing of when income is taxed or an expense is deducted affects the *present value* of the taxes paid on income or tax savings on deductions. Second, the tax costs of income and tax savings income vary as *tax rates* change.

- When tax rates are constant, tax planners prefer to defer income (i.e., to reduce the present value of taxes paid) and accelerate deductions (i.e., to increase the present value of tax savings). Higher tax rates, higher rates of return, larger transaction amounts, and the ability to accelerate deductions or defer income by two or more years increase the benefits of the timing strategy.

- When tax rates change, the timing strategy requires a little more consideration because the tax costs of income and the tax savings from deductions vary as *tax rates* change. When tax rates are increasing, the taxpayer must calculate the optimal tax strategies for deductions and income. When tax rates are decreasing, the recommendations are clear. Taxpayers should accelerate tax deductions into earlier years and defer taxable income to later years.

- Timing strategies contain several inherent limitations. Generally speaking, whenever a taxpayer must accelerate a cash outflow to accelerate a deduction, the timing strategy will be less beneficial. Tax law generally requires taxpayers to continue their investment in an asset in order to defer income recognition for tax purposes. A deferral strategy may not be optimal if the taxpayer has severe cash flow needs, if continuing the investment would generate a low rate of return compared to other investments, if the current investment would subject the taxpayer to unnecessary risk, and so on. The constructive receipt doctrine, which provides that a taxpayer must recognize income when it is actually or constructively received, also restricts income deferral for cash-method taxpayers.

**LO3** Apply the concept of present value to tax planning.

- The concept of present value—also known as the time value of money—basically states that $1 today is worth *more* than $1 in the future. For example, assuming an investor can earn a positive return (e.g., 5 percent after taxes), $1 invested today should be worth $1.05 in one year. Hence, $1 today is equivalent to $1.05 in one year.

- The implication of the time value of money for tax planning is that the timing of a cash inflow or a cash outflow affects the present value of the income or expense.

**LO4** Apply the strategy of income shifting, provide examples, and describe its limitations.

- The income-shifting strategy exploits the differences in tax rates across taxpayers or jurisdictions. Three of the most common examples of income shifting are high-tax-rate parents shifting income to low-tax-rate children, businesses shifting income to their owners, and taxpayers shifting income from high-tax jurisdictions to low-tax jurisdictions.

- The assignment of income doctrine requires income to be taxed to the taxpayer who actually earns the income. In addition, the IRS closely monitors such related-party transactions—that is, financial activities among family members, among owners and their businesses, or among businesses owned by the same owners. Implicit taxes may also limit the benefits of income shifting via locating in tax-advantaged jurisdictions.

Apply the conversion strategy, provide examples, and describe its limitations.
**LO5**

- Tax law does not treat all types of income or deductions the same. This understanding forms the basis for the conversion strategy—recasting income and expenses to receive the most favorable tax treatment. To implement the conversion strategy, one must be aware of the underlying differences in tax treatment across various types of income, expenses, and activities, and have some ability to alter the nature of the income or expense to receive the more advantageous tax treatment.

- Common examples of the conversion strategy include investment planning to invest in assets that generate preferentially taxed income, compensation planning to restructure employee compensation from currently taxable compensation to nontaxable or tax-deferred forms of compensation, and corporate distribution planning to structure corporate distributions to receive the most advantageous tax treatment.

- The Internal Revenue Code contains specific provisions that prevent the taxpayer from changing the nature of expenses, income, or activities to a more tax-advantaged status. Implicit taxes may also reduce or eliminate the advantages of conversion strategies.

Describe basic judicial doctrines that limit tax planning strategies.
**LO6**

- The constructive receipt doctrine, which may limit the timing strategy, provides that a taxpayer must recognize income when it is actually *or* constructively received. Constructive receipt is deemed to have occurred if the income has been credited to the taxpayer's account or if the income is unconditionally available to the taxpayer, the taxpayer is aware of the income's availability, and there are no restrictions on the taxpayer's control over the income.

- The assignment of income doctrine requires income to be taxed to the taxpayer who actually earns the income. The assignment of income doctrine implies that, in order to shift income to a taxpayer, that taxpayer must actually earn the income.

- The business purpose, step-transaction, and substance-over-form doctrines apply across a wide variety of transactions and planning strategies (timing, income shifting, and conversion).

- The business purpose doctrine allows the IRS to challenge and disallow business expenses for transactions with no underlying business motivation, such as a travel cost of a spouse accompanying a taxpayer on a business trip.

- The step-transaction doctrine allows the IRS to collapse a series of related transactions into one transaction to determine the tax consequences of the transaction.

- The substance-over-form doctrine allows the IRS to consider the transaction's substance regardless of its form, and where appropriate, reclassify the transaction according to its substance.

Contrast tax avoidance and tax evasion.
**LO7**

- Tax avoidance is the legal act of arranging one's transactions, and so on, to minimize taxes paid. Tax evasion is the willful attempt to defraud the government (i.e., by not paying taxes legally owed). Tax evasion falls outside the confines of legal tax avoidance.

- In many cases a clear distinction exists between avoidance (e.g., not paying tax on municipal bond interest) and evasion (e.g., not paying tax on a $1,000,000 game show prize). In other cases, the line between tax avoidance and evasion is less clear. In these situations, professional judgment, the use of a "smell test," and consideration of the business purpose, step-transaction, and substance-over-form doctrines may prove useful.

# KEY TERMS

arm's-length transaction (3-12)

assignment of income doctrine (3-12)

business purpose doctrine (3-18)

constructive receipt doctrine (3-10)

discount factor (3-3)

present value (3-3)

related-party transaction (3-12)

step-transaction doctrine (3-18)

substance-over-form doctrine (3-18)

tax avoidance (3-18)

tax evasion (3-19)

# DISCUSSION QUESTIONS

1. **(LO1)** "The goal of tax planning is to minimize taxes." Explain why this statement is not true.

2. **(LO1)** Describe the three parties engaged in every business transaction and how understanding taxes may aid in structuring transactions.

3. **(LO1)** In this chapter we discuss three basic tax-planning strategies. What different features of taxation does each of these strategies exploit?

4. **(LO2)** What are the two basic timing strategies? What is the intent of each?

5. **(LO2)** Why is the timing strategy particularly effective for cash-method taxpayers?

6. **(LO2)** What are some common examples of the timing strategy?

7. **(LO2)** What factors increase the benefits of accelerating deductions or deferring income?

8. **(LO2, LO3)** How do changing tax rates affect the timing strategy? What information do you need to determine the appropriate timing strategy when tax rates change?

9. **(LO2, LO6)** Describe the ways in which the timing strategy has limitations.

10. **(LO3)** The concept of the time value of money suggests that $1 today is not equal to $1 in the future. Explain why this is true.

11. **(LO3)** Why is understanding the time value of money important for tax planning?

12. **(LO3)** What two factors increase the difference between present and future values?

13. **(LO4)** What factors have to be present for income shifting to be a viable strategy?

14. **(LO4)** Name three common types of income shifting.

15. **(LO4)** What are some ways that a parent could effectively shift income to a child? What are some of the disadvantages of these methods?

16. **(LO4)** What is the key factor in shifting income from a business to its owners? What are some methods of shifting income in this context?

17. **(LO4)** Explain why paying dividends is not an effective way to shift income from a corporation to its owners.

18. **(LO5)** What are some of the common examples of the conversion strategy?

19. **(LO5)** What is needed to implement the conversion strategy?

20. **(LO5)** Explain how implicit taxes may limit the benefits of the conversion strategy.

21. **(LO6)** Several judicial doctrines limit basic tax planning strategies. What are they? Which planning strategies do they limit?

22. **(LO6)** What is the constructive receipt doctrine? What types of taxpayers does this doctrine generally affect? For what tax planning strategy is the constructive receipt doctrine a potential limitation?

23. **(LO6)** Explain the assignment of income doctrine. In what situations would this doctrine potentially apply?

24. **(LO6)** Relative to arm's-length transactions, why do related-party transactions receive more IRS scrutiny?

25. **(LO6)** Describe the business purpose, step-transaction, and substance-over-form doctrines. What types of tax planning strategies may these doctrines inhibit?

26. **(LO7)** What is the difference between tax avoidance and tax evasion?

27. **(LO7)** What are the rewards of tax avoidance? What are the rewards of tax evasion?

28. **(LO7)** "Tax avoidance is discouraged by the courts and Congress." Is this statement true or false? Please explain.

## PROBLEMS

29. **(LO2)** Yong recently paid his accountant $10,000 for elaborate tax planning strategies that exploit the timing strategy. Assuming this is an election year and there could be a power shift in the White House and Congress, what is a potential risk associated with Yong's strategies?    ■ planning

30. **(LO2, LO3)** Billups, a physician and cash-method taxpayer, is new to the concept of tax planning and recently learned of the timing strategy. To implement the timing strategy, Billups plans to establish a new policy that allows all his clients to wait two years to pay their co-pays. Assume that Billups does not expect his marginal tax rates to change. What is wrong with his strategy?    ■ planning

31. **(LO2, LO3)** Tesha works for a company that pays a year-end bonus in January of each year (instead of December of the preceding year) to allow employees to defer the bonus income. Assume Congress recently passed tax legislation that decreases individual tax rates as of next year. Does this increase or decrease the benefits of the bonus deferral this year? What if Congress passed legislation that increased tax rates next year? Should Tesha ask the company to change its policy this year? What additional information do you need to answer this question?    ■ planning

32. **(LO2, LO3)** Isabel, a calendar-year taxpayer, uses the cash method of accounting for her sole proprietorship. In late December she received a $20,000 bill from her accountant for consulting services related to her small business. Isabel can pay the $20,000 bill anytime before January 30 of next year without penalty. Assume her marginal tax rate is 40 percent this year and next year, and that she can earn an after-tax rate of return of 12 percent on her investments. When should she pay the $20,000 bill—this year or next?    ■ planning

33. **(LO2, LO3)** Using the facts from the previous problem, how would your answer change if Isabel's after-tax rate of return were 8 percent?    ■ planning

34. **(LO2, LO3)** Manny, a calendar-year taxpayer, uses the cash method of accounting for his sole proprietorship. In late December he performed $20,000 of legal services for a client. Manny typically requires his clients to pay his bills immediately upon receipt. Assume Manny's marginal tax rate is 40 percent this year and next year, and that he can earn an after-tax rate of return of 12 percent on his investments. Should Manny send his client the bill in December or January?    ■ planning

35. **(LO2, LO3)** Using the facts from the previous problem, how would your answer change if Manny's after-tax rate of return were 8 percent?    ■ planning

36. **(LO2, LO3)** Reese, a calendar-year taxpayer, uses the cash method of accounting for her sole proprietorship. In late December, she received a $20,000    ■ planning

bill from her accountant for consulting services related to her small business. Reese can pay the $20,000 bill anytime before January 30 of next year without penalty. Assume Reese's marginal tax rate is 30 percent this year and will be 40 percent next year, and that she can earn an after-tax rate of return of 12 percent on her investments. When should she pay the $20,000 bill—this year or next?

■ **planning**   37. **(LO2, LO3)**  Using the facts from the previous problem, when should Reese pay the bill if she expects her marginal tax rate to be 33 percent next year? 25 percent next year?

■ **planning**   38. **(LO2, LO3)**  Hank, a calendar-year taxpayer, uses the cash method of accounting for his sole proprietorship. In late December, he performed $20,000 of legal services for a client. Hank typically requires his clients to pay his bills immediately upon receipt. Assume his marginal tax rate is 30 percent this year and will be 40 percent next year, and that he can earn an after-tax rate of return of 12 percent on his investments. Should Hank send his client the bill in December or January?

■ **planning**   39. **(LO2, LO3)**  Using the facts from the previous problem, when should Hank send the bill if he expects his marginal tax rate to be 33 percent next year? 25 percent next year?

40. **(LO3)**  Geraldo recently won a lottery and chose to receive $100,000 today instead of an equivalent amount in 10 years, computed using an 8 percent rate of return. Today, he learned that interest rates are expected to increase in the future. Is this good news for Geraldo given his decision?

■ **planning**   41. **(LO3)**  Assume Rafael can earn an 8 percent after-tax rate of return. Would he prefer $1,000 today or $1,500 in five years?

■ **planning**   42. **(LO3)**  Assume Ellina earns a 10 percent after-tax rate of return, and that she owes a friend $1,200. Would she prefer to pay the friend $1,200 today or $1,750 in four years?

■ **planning**   43. **(LO3)**  Jonah has the choice of paying Rita $10,000 today or $40,000 in 10 years. Assume Jonah can earn a 12 percent after-tax rate of return. Which should he choose?

■ **planning**   44. **(LO3)**  Bob's Lottery, Inc., has decided to offer winners a choice of $100,000 in 10 years or some amount currently. Assume that Bob's Lottery, Inc., earns a 10 percent after-tax rate of return. What amount should Bob offer lottery winners currently, in order for him to be indifferent between the two choices?

■ **planning**   45. **(LO4)**  Tawana owns and operates a sole proprietorship and has a 40 percent marginal tax rate. She provides her son, Jonathon, $8,000 a year for college expenses. Jonathon works as a pizza delivery person every fall, and has a marginal tax rate of 15 percent. What could Tawana do to reduce her family tax burden? How much pretax income does it currently take Tawana to generate the $8,000 after taxes given to Jonathon? If Jonathon worked for his mother's sole proprietorship, what salary would she have to pay him to generate $8,000 after taxes (ignoring any Social Security, Medicare, or self-employment tax issues)? How much money would this strategy save?

■ **planning**   46. **(LO4)**  Moana is a single taxpayer who operates a sole proprietorship. She expects her taxable income next year to be $250,000, of which $200,000 is attributed to her sole proprietorship. Moana is contemplating incorporating her sole proprietorship. Using the single individual tax brackets and the corporate tax brackets inside the book's front cover, find out how much current tax this strategy could save Moana (ignore any Social Security, Medicare, or self-employment tax issues). How much income should be left in the corporation?

■ **planning**   47. **(LO4)**  Orie and Jane, husband and wife, operate a sole proprietorship. They expect their taxable income next year to be $275,000, of which $125,000 is

attributed to the sole proprietorship. Orie and Jane are contemplating incorporating their sole proprietorship. Using the married-joint tax brackets and the corporate tax brackets inside the book's front cover, find out how much current tax this strategy could save Orie and Jane. How much income should be left in the corporation?

48. **(LO4)** Hyundai is considering opening a plant in two neighboring states. One state has a corporate tax rate of 10 percent. If operated in this state, the plant is expected to generate $1,000,000 pretax profit. The other state has a corporate tax rate of 2 percent. If operated in this state, the plant is expected to generate $930,000 of pretax profit. Which state should Hyundai choose? Why do you think the plant in the state with a lower tax rate would produce a lower before-tax income? ■ **planning**

49. **(LO4, LO6)** Bendetta, a high-tax-rate taxpayer, owns several rental properties and would like to shift some income to her daughter, Jenine. Bendetta instructs her tenants to send their rent checks to Jenine so Jenine can report the rental income. Will this shift the income from Bendetta to Jenine? Why, or why not? ■ **planning**

50. **(LO4, LO6)** Using the facts in the previous problem, what are some ways that Bendetta could shift some of the rental income to Jenine? What are the disadvantages associated with these income-shifting strategies? ■ **planning**

51. **(LO5)** Dennis is currently considering investing in municipal bonds that earn 6 percent interest, or in taxable bonds issued by the Coca-Cola Company that pay 8 percent. If Dennis's tax rate is 20 percent, which bond should he choose? Which bond should he choose if his tax rate is 30 percent? At what tax rate would he be indifferent between the bonds? What strategy is this decision based upon? ■ **planning**

52. **(LO7)** Duff is really interested in decreasing his tax liability, and by his very nature he is somewhat aggressive. A friend of a friend told him that cash transactions are more difficult for the IRS to identify and, thus, tax. Duff is contemplating using this "strategy" of not reporting cash collected in his business to minimize his tax liability. Is this tax planning? What are the risks with this strategy?

53. **(LO7)** Using the facts from the previous problem, how would your answer change if instead, Duff adopted the cash method of accounting to allow him to better control the timing of his cash receipts and disbursements?

54. **(LO2, LO4, LO5)** Using an available tax service or the Internet, identify three basic tax planning ideas or tax tips suggested for year-end tax planning. Which basic tax strategy from this chapter does each planning idea employ? ■ **planning**
■ **research** ■■

55. **(LO7)** Jayanna, an advertising consultant, is contemplating instructing some of her clients to pay her in cash so that she does not have to report the income on her tax return. Use an available tax service to identify the three basic elements of tax evasion and penalties associated with tax evasion. Write a memo to Jayanna explaining tax evasion and the risks associated with her actions. ■ **research** ■■

56. **(LO7)** Using the IRS Web site (www.irs.gov/index.html), how large is the current estimated "tax gap" (i.e., the amount of tax underpaid by taxpayers annually)? What group of taxpayers represents the largest "contributors" to the tax gap? ■ **research** ■■

# Individual Income Tax Overview

## Learning Objectives

**Upon completing this chapter, you should be able to:**

**LO 1** Describe the formula for calculating an individual taxpayer's taxes payable or refund and generally explain each formula component.

■

**LO 2** Explain the requirements for determining a taxpayer's personal and dependency exemptions.

■

**LO 3** Determine a taxpayer's filing status.

| Storyline Summary | |
| --- | --- |
| *Taxpayer:* | Rodney and Anita Hall |
| *Other household members:* | Tara, their 21-year-old daughter, and Braxton, their 12-year-old son. Shawn, Rodney's brother, also lives with the Halls. |
| *Location:* | Brookings, South Dakota |
| *Employment status:* | Rodney is a manager for a regional grocery chain. His salary is $64,000. Anita works part-time as a purchasing-card auditor at South Dakota State University. Her salary is $46,000. |
| *Current situation:* | Determining their tax liability |

T ara Hall just completed a unit on individual taxation in her undergraduate tax class at South Dakota State University. She was excited to share her knowledge with her parents, Rodney and Anita Hall, as they prepared their tax return. Rodney and Anita have been married for over 25 years, and they have filed a joint tax return each year. The Halls' 12-year-old son Braxton lives at home but Tara, who is 21, lives nearby in the university dorms. Further, in January of this year, Rodney's younger brother Shawn moved in with the Halls. They expect Shawn to live with them for at least one year and maybe two. Every year Rodney and Anita use tax-preparation software to complete their tax return, but they are not always sure they understand the final result. This year, with Tara's help, they hope that will change. ∎

This chapter and the next three discuss the fundamental elements of the individual income tax formula. This is the overview chapter; the other chapters provide more depth on individual income tax topics. Here we introduce the individual income tax formula, summarize its components, describe requirements for dependency exemptions, and explain how to determine a taxpayer's filing status. Chapter 5 explains gross income, and Chapter 6 describes deductible expenses to determine adjusted gross income and taxable income. Finally, Chapter 7 addresses issues associated with calculating a taxpayer's tax liability and discusses tax return filing concerns.

## LO1 THE INDIVIDUAL INCOME TAX FORMULA

Each year, individuals file tax returns to report their **taxable income,** the tax base for the individual income tax, to the Internal Revenue Service. Exhibit 4-1 presents a simplified formula for calculating taxable income.

**EXHIBIT 4-1** Individual Tax Formula

|  | Realized income from whatever source derived |
|---|---|
| Minus: | Excluded or deferred income |
| Equals: | Gross income |
| Minus: | *For* AGI deductions |
| Equals: | Adjusted gross income (AGI) |
| Minus: | *From* AGI deductions: |
|  | (1) *Greater* of |
|  |     (a) Standard deduction or |
|  |     (b) Itemized deductions and |
|  | (2) Personal and dependency exemptions |
| Equals: | Taxable income |
| Times: | Tax rates |
| Equals: | Income tax liability |
| Plus: | Other taxes |
| Equals: | Total tax |
| Minus: | Credits |
| Minus: | Prepayments |
| Equals: | Taxes due or (refund) |

Beginning with gross income, this formula is imbedded in the first two pages of the individual income tax Form 1040, the form individuals generally use to report their taxable income. Exhibit 4-2 presents the first two pages from the form. Note that income excluded from taxation is usually not reported on the tax return (though line 8b asks for tax-exempt interest). However, deferred income is generally reported on the tax return, but it is usually provided on supporting schedules rather than on the first two pages of the tax return. Also, note that the last line on page 1 of Form 1040 is adjusted gross income (AGI), an important reference point in the income tax formula.

Let's look at the components of the individual tax formula and provide a brief description of each of the key elements.

### Realized Income, Exclusions, Deferrals, and Gross Income

The U.S. tax laws are based on the **all-inclusive income concept.** Under this concept, taxpayers generally must include in taxable income *all* **realized income** *from whatever source derived.*[1] Realized income is income generated in a transaction with a second party in which there is a measurable change in property rights between parties.

[1]§61(a).

**EXHIBIT 4-2**    Form 1040, pages 1 and 2

Form **1040**   Department of the Treasury—Internal Revenue Service
**U.S. Individual Income Tax Return**   20**09**   (99)   IRS Use Only—Do not write or staple in this space.

For the year Jan. 1–Dec. 31, 2009, or other tax year beginning _____ , 2009, ending _____ , 20 ___    OMB No. 1545-0074

**Label** (See instructions on page 14.) **Use the IRS label.** Otherwise, please print or type.

L A B E L   H E R E

- Your first name and initial | Last name | Your social security number
- If a joint return, spouse's first name and initial | Last name | Spouse's social security number
- Home address (number and street). If you have a P.O. box, see page 14. | Apt. no.
- City, town or post office, state, and ZIP code. If you have a foreign address, see page 14.

▲ You **must** enter your SSN(s) above. ▲

Checking a box below will not change your tax or refund.

**Presidential Election Campaign** ► Check here if you, or your spouse if filing jointly, want $3 to go to this fund (see page 14) ► ☐ You ☐ Spouse

**Filing Status** — Check only one box.
1 ☐ Single
2 ☐ Married filing jointly (even if only one had income)
3 ☐ Married filing separately. Enter spouse's SSN above and full name here. ►
4 ☐ Head of household (with qualifying person). (See page 15.) If the qualifying person is a child but not your dependent, enter this child's name here. ►
5 ☐ Qualifying widow(er) with dependent child (see page 16)

**Exemptions**
6a ☐ **Yourself.** If someone can claim you as a dependent, **do not** check box 6a
b ☐ **Spouse**
c **Dependents:**

| (1) First name   Last name | (2) Dependent's social security number | (3) Dependent's relationship to you | (4) ✓ if qualifying child for child tax credit (see page 17) |
|---|---|---|---|
| | | | ☐ |
| | | | ☐ |
| | | | ☐ |
| | | | ☐ |

Boxes checked on 6a and 6b ___
No. of children on 6c who:
● lived with you ___
● did not live with you due to divorce or separation (see page 18) ___
Dependents on 6c not entered above ___

If more than four dependents, see page 17 and check here ► ☐

d Total number of exemptions claimed ...........   Add numbers on lines above ► ___

**Income**

Attach Form(s) W-2 here. Also attach Forms W-2G and 1099-R if tax was withheld.

If you did not get a W-2, see page 22.

Enclose, but do not attach, any payment. Also, please use Form 1040-V.

| | | |
|---|---|---|
| 7 | Wages, salaries, tips, etc. Attach Form(s) W-2 | 7 |
| 8a | **Taxable** interest. Attach Schedule B if required | 8a |
| b | **Tax-exempt** interest. **Do not** include on line 8a | 8b |
| 9a | Ordinary dividends. Attach Schedule B if required | 9a |
| b | Qualified dividends (see page 22) | 9b |
| 10 | Taxable refunds, credits, or offsets of state and local income taxes (see page 23) | 10 |
| 11 | Alimony received | 11 |
| 12 | Business income or (loss). Attach Schedule C or C-EZ | 12 |
| 13 | Capital gain or (loss). Attach Schedule D if required. If not required, check here ► ☐ | 13 |
| 14 | Other gains or (losses). Attach Form 4797 | 14 |
| 15a | IRA distributions   15a   b Taxable amount (see page 24) | 15b |
| 16a | Pensions and annuities   16a   b Taxable amount (see page 25) | 16b |
| 17 | Rental real estate, royalties, partnerships, S corporations, trusts, etc. Attach Schedule E | 17 |
| 18 | Farm income or (loss). Attach Schedule F | 18 |
| 19 | Unemployment compensation in excess of $2,400 per recipient (see page 27) | 19 |
| 20a | Social security benefits   20a   b Taxable amount (see page 27) | 20b |
| 21 | Other income. List type and amount (see page 29) | 21 |
| 22 | Add the amounts in the far right column for lines 7 through 21. This is your **total income** ► | 22 |

**Adjusted Gross Income**

| | | |
|---|---|---|
| 23 | Educator expenses (see page 29) | 23 |
| 24 | Certain business expenses of reservists, performing artists, and fee-basis government officials. Attach Form 2106 or 2106-EZ | 24 |
| 25 | Health savings account deduction. Attach Form 8889 | 25 |
| 26 | Moving expenses. Attach Form 3903 | 26 |
| 27 | One-half of self-employment tax. Attach Schedule SE | 27 |
| 28 | Self-employed SEP, SIMPLE, and qualified plans | 28 |
| 29 | Self-employed health insurance deduction (see page 30) | 29 |
| 30 | Penalty on early withdrawal of savings | 30 |
| 31a | Alimony paid   b Recipient's SSN ► | 31a |
| 32 | IRA deduction (see page 31) | 32 |
| 33 | Student loan interest deduction (see page 34) | 33 |
| 34 | Tuition and fees deduction. Attach Form 8917 | 34 |
| 35 | Domestic production activities deduction. Attach Form 8903 | 35 |
| 36 | Add lines 23 through 31a and 32 through 35 | 36 |
| 37 | Subtract line 36 from line 22. This is your **adjusted gross income** ► | 37 |

**For Disclosure, Privacy Act, and Paperwork Reduction Act Notice, see page 97.**    Cat. No. 11320B    Form **1040** (2009)

*(continued)*

**EXHIBIT 4-2    Form 1040, pages 1 and 2 (*continued*)**

Form 1040 (2009)                                                                                                          Page **2**

| | | | | |
|---|---|---|---|---|
| **Tax and Credits** | 38 | Amount from line 37 (adjusted gross income) . . . . . . . . . | 38 | |
| | 39a | Check if: { **You** were born before January 2, 1945, ☐ Blind. **Spouse** was born before January 2, 1945, ☐ Blind. } Total boxes checked ▶ 39a | | |

**Standard Deduction for—**
- People who check any box on line 39a, 39b, or 40b **or** who can be claimed as a dependent, see page 35.
- All others:

Single or Married filing separately, $5,700

Married filing jointly or Qualifying widow(er), $11,400

Head of household, $8,350

| | | | | |
|---|---|---|---|---|
| | b | If your spouse itemizes on a separate return or you were a dual-status alien, see page 35 and check here ▶ 39b ☐ | | |
| | 40a | **Itemized deductions** (from Schedule A) **or** your **standard deduction** (see left margin) . . | 40a | |
| | b | If you are increasing your standard deduction by certain real estate taxes, new motor vehicle taxes, or a net disaster loss, attach Schedule L and check here (see page 35) . ▶ 40b ☐ | | |
| | 41 | Subtract line 40a from line 38 . . . . . . . . . . . . . . | 41 | |
| | 42 | **Exemptions.** If line 38 is $125,100 or less and you did not provide housing to a Midwestern displaced individual, multiply $3,650 by the number on line 6d. Otherwise, see page 37 . . | 42 | |
| | 43 | **Taxable income.** Subtract line 42 from line 41. If line 42 is more than line 41, enter -0- | 43 | |
| | 44 | **Tax** (see page 37). Check if any tax is from:  **a** ☐ Form(s) 8814  **b** ☐ Form 4972 . | 44 | |
| | 45 | **Alternative minimum tax** (see page 40). Attach Form 6251 . . . . . . . | 45 | |
| | 46 | Add lines 44 and 45 . . . . . . . . . . . . . . . . ▶ | 46 | |
| | 47 | Foreign tax credit. Attach Form 1116 if required . . . [47] | | |
| | 48 | Credit for child and dependent care expenses. Attach Form 2441 [48] | | |
| | 49 | Education credits from Form 8863, line 29 . . . . [49] | | |
| | 50 | Retirement savings contributions credit. Attach Form 8880 [50] | | |
| | 51 | Child tax credit (see page 42) . . . . . . . . [51] | | |
| | 52 | Credits from Form: **a** ☐ 8396  **b** ☐ 8839  **c** ☐ 5695 [52] | | |
| | 53 | Other credits from Form: **a** ☐ 3800 **b** ☐ 8801 **c** ☐ [53] | | |
| | 54 | Add lines 47 through 53. These are your **total credits** . . . . . . . | 54 | |
| | 55 | Subtract line 54 from line 46. If line 54 is more than line 46, enter -0- . . . . . ▶ | 55 | |
| **Other Taxes** | 56 | Self-employment tax. Attach Schedule SE . . . . . . . . . . | 56 | |
| | 57 | Unreported social security and Medicare tax from Form: **a** ☐ 4137 **b** ☐ 8919 . . | 57 | |
| | 58 | Additional tax on IRAs, other qualified retirement plans, etc. Attach Form 5329 if required . . | 58 | |
| | 59 | Additional taxes: **a** ☐ AEIC payments  **b** ☐ Household employment taxes. Attach Schedule H | 59 | |
| | 60 | Add lines 55 through 59. This is your **total tax** . . . . . . . . . ▶ | 60 | |
| **Payments** | 61 | Federal income tax withheld from Forms W-2 and 1099 [61] | | |
| | 62 | 2009 estimated tax payments and amount applied from 2008 return [62] | | |
| | 63 | Making work pay and government retiree credits. Attach Schedule M [63] | | |

If you have a qualifying child, attach Schedule EIC.

| | | | | |
|---|---|---|---|---|
| | 64a | **Earned income credit (EIC)** . . . . . . [64a] | | |
| | b | Nontaxable combat pay election [64b] | | |
| | 65 | Additional child tax credit. Attach Form 8812 . . . [65] | | |
| | 66 | Refundable education credit from Form 8863, line 16 . . . [66] | | |
| | 67 | First-time homebuyer credit. Attach Form 5405 . . . [67] | | |
| | 68 | Amount paid with request for extension to file (see page 72) . [68] | | |
| | 69 | Excess social security and tier 1 RRTA tax withheld (see page 72) [69] | | |
| | 70 | Credits from Form: **a** ☐ 2439 **b** ☐ 4136 **c** ☐ 8801 **d** ☐ 8885 [70] | | |
| | 71 | Add lines 61, 62, 63, 64a, and 65 through 70. These are your **total payments** . . . . ▶ | 71 | |
| **Refund** | 72 | If line 71 is more than line 60, subtract line 60 from line 71. This is the amount you **overpaid** | 72 | |
| Direct deposit? See page 73 and fill in 73b, 73c, and 73d, or Form 8888. | 73a | Amount of line 72 you want **refunded to you.** If Form 8888 is attached, check here . ▶ ☐ | 73a | |
| | ▶ b | Routing number _____  ▶ c Type: ☐ Checking  ☐ Savings | | |
| | ▶ d | Account number _____ | | |
| | 74 | Amount of line 72 you want **applied to your 2010 estimated tax** ▶ [74] | | |
| **Amount You Owe** | 75 | **Amount you owe.** Subtract line 71 from line 60. For details on how to pay, see page 74 . ▶ | 75 | |
| | 76 | Estimated tax penalty (see page 74) . . . . . . . . [76] | | |

**Third Party Designee**

Do you want to allow another person to discuss this return with the IRS (see page 75)? ☐ **Yes.** Complete the following. ☐ **No**

Designee's name ▶ _____  Phone no. ▶ _____  Personal identification number (PIN) ▶ ☐☐☐☐☐

**Sign Here**

Joint return? See page 15. Keep a copy for your records.

Under penalties of perjury, I declare that I have examined this return and accompanying schedules and statements, and to the best of my knowledge and belief, they are true, correct, and complete. Declaration of preparer (other than taxpayer) is based on all information of which preparer has any knowledge.

| Your signature | Date | Your occupation | Daytime phone number |
|---|---|---|---|
| Spouse's signature. If a joint return, **both** must sign. | Date | Spouse's occupation | |

**Paid Preparer's Use Only**

| Preparer's signature ▶ | Date | Check if self-employed ☐ | Preparer's SSN or PTIN |
|---|---|---|---|
| Firm's name (or yours if self-employed), address, and ZIP code ▶ | | EIN | |
| | | Phone no. | |

Form **1040** (2009)

Exhibit 4-3 provides a listing of common income items that meet the realization threshold and indicates where in the text we provide more detail on each income item.

**EXHIBIT 4-3   Common Income Items**

| Income Item | Discussed in More Detail in |
|---|---|
| Compensation for services including fringe benefits | Chapter 12 |
| Business income | Chapter 8 |
| Gains from selling property | Chapters 10 and 11 |
| Interest and dividends | Chapters 5 and 11 |
| Rents and royalties | Chapters 5, 11, and 14 |
| Alimony received and annuities | Chapter 5 |
| Retirement income | Chapter 13 |
| Income from the discharge of indebtedness | Chapter 5 |

Taxpayers are allowed to permanently exclude certain types of realized income from taxation or defer paying taxes to a later year on certain types of realized income if, and only if, *a specific tax provision allows them to do so.* Income items that taxpayers permanently exclude from taxation are referred to as **excluded income** or **exclusions.** Income items that taxpayers realize in one year, but are allowed to defer paying taxes on until a later year, are called **deferral items, deferred income,** or simply **deferrals.** Exhibit 4-4 provides a listing of common exclusions and deferrals and indicates where in the text we discuss each in more detail. **Gross income** is realized income minus exclusions and deferrals. That is, gross income is the income that taxpayers actually report on their tax returns.

**EXHIBIT 4-4   Common Exclusions and Deferrals**

| Exclusion or Deferral Item | Exclusion or Deferral | Discussed in |
|---|---|---|
| Interest income from municipal bonds | Exclusion | Chapters 5 and 11 |
| Gifts and inheritances | Exclusion | Chapter 5 |
| Gain on sale of personal residence | Exclusion | Chapter 14 |
| Life insurance proceeds | Exclusion | Chapters 5 and 11 |
| Installment sale | Deferral | Chapter 10 |
| Like-kind exchange | Deferral | Chapter 10 |

**Example 4-1**

In 2010, Rodney earned a salary of $64,000, and Anita earned a salary of $46,000 working part-time. The Halls also received $600 of interest income from investments in corporate bonds and $300 of interest income from investments in municipal bonds. This was their only income during the year. What is the Halls' 2010 gross income?

**Answer:** $110,600, computed as follows:

| Description | Amount | Explanation |
|---|---|---|
| (1) Rodney's salary | $ 64,000 | |
| (2) Anita's salary | 46,000 | |
| (3) Interest from corporate bonds | 600 | |
| (4) Interest from municipal bonds | 300 | |
| (5) Realized income | $110,900 | (1) + (2) + (3) + (4). |
| (6) Exclusions and deferrals | (300) | (4) Exclusion for municipal bond interest. |
| **Gross income** | **$110,600** | (5) + (6). |

## Deductions

Taxpayers subtract their **deductions** from gross income to determine their taxable income. In stark contrast to the all-inclusive treatment of income, taxpayers are *not allowed to deduct anything unless a specific tax provision allows them to do so.* Thus, deductions are a matter of **legislative grace.** The tax laws provide for two distinct types of deductions in the individual tax formula: **deductions *for* AGI** and **deductions *from* AGI.** Deductions *for* AGI are also referred to as **deductions above the line,** while deductions *from* AGI are referred to as **deductions below the line.** In both cases, the "line" is **adjusted gross income (AGI).** AGI is the last line on the front page of the individual tax return Form 1040 (see Exhibit 4-2) and is defined as gross income minus *for* AGI deductions. When it enacts new legislation that grants deductions, Congress typically identifies whether the deductions are for or from AGI. In general, deductions *for* AGI tend to be related to business activities and certain investing activities, whereas deductions *from* AGI tend to be more personal in nature.

**Deductions for AGI**   Taxpayers first reduce their gross income by deductions *for* AGI, so we discuss these first. They are called *for* AGI deductions because they are used *for* calculating AGI, or come *before* AGI in the tax formula. In contrast to *from* AGI deductions, which may be limited or may generate no tax benefit, *for* AGI deductions *always* reduce gross income and therefore reduce taxable income dollar for dollar. For these reasons, deductions *for* AGI are typically considered more valuable than deductions *from* AGI. Exhibit 4-5 provides a listing of common for AGI deductions and indicates where in the text we discuss them.

---

**THE KEY FACTS**

*For* and *From* AGI Deductions

■ *For* AGI deductions
· Deduct in determining AGI.
· "Above the line" deduction.
· Generally more valuable than *from* AGI deductions.
■ *From* AGI deductions
· Deducted *from* AGI to determine taxable income.
· "Below the line" deduction.
· Generally less valuable than *for* AGI deductions.

---

**EXHIBIT 4-5   Common *for* AGI Deductions**

| *For* AGI Deduction | Discussed in |
|---|---|
| Alimony paid | Chapter 6 |
| Health insurance deduction for self-employed taxpayers | Chapter 6 |
| Moving expenses | Chapter 6 |
| Rental and royalty expenses | Chapter 6 |
| One-half of self-employment taxes paid | Chapter 7 |
| Business expenses | Chapter 8 |
| Losses on dispositions of assets used in a trade or business | Chapter 10 |
| Losses from flow-through entities | Chapter 11 |
| Losses on dispositions of investment assets (*net* losses limited to $3,000 for the year). | Chapter 11 |
| Contributions to qualified retirement accounts | Chapter 13 |

---

**Example 4-2**

In 2010, the Halls paid $5,000 of deductible moving expenses when the family relocated due to an employment transfer for Rodney. What is the Halls' 2010 adjusted gross income?

**Answer:** $105,600, computed as follows:

| Description | Amount | Explanation |
|---|---|---|
| (1) Gross income | $110,600 | Example 4-1. |
| (2) Moving expenses | (5,000) | *For* AGI deduction (see Exhibit 4-5). |
| **Adjusted gross income** | **$105,600** | (1) + (2). |

AGI is an important reference point in the tax formula because it is often used in other tax-related calculations. Specifically, limits on certain *from* AGI expenses depend on AGI (certain from AGI deductions are reduced for taxpayers with high AGI). Because *for* AGI deductions decrease AGI, they *increase* the deductibility of the *from* AGI deductions subject to AGI limitations.

**Deductions from AGI**   Taxpayers reduce their AGI by deductions *from* AGI to determine their taxable income. Deductions from AGI include **itemized deductions,** the **standard deduction,** and **exemptions.** Individuals have the choice of deducting their itemized deductions *or* deducting a fixed amount called the standard deduction amount. They generally deduct the higher of the two. Exhibit 4-6 identifies the primary categories of itemized deductions.

### EXHIBIT 4-6   Primary Categories of Itemized Deductions

- *Medical and dental expenses:* Deductible to the extent these expenses exceed 7.5 percent of AGI.
- *Taxes:* State and local income taxes, real estate taxes, personal property taxes, and other taxes.
- *Interest expense:* Mortgage, home equity, and investment interest expense.
- *Gifts to charity (charitable contributions).*
- *Casualty and theft losses:* Deductible to the extent they exceed 10 percent of AGI.
- *Job expenses and certain miscellaneous deductions:* Deductible to the extent the sum of these expenses exceeds 2 percent of AGI.
- *Other miscellaneous deductions:* Gambling losses (to the extent of gambling winnings) and certain other deductions not subject to AGI limitation.

*Note:* Itemized deductions are discussed in more detail in Chapter 6.

The amount of the standard deduction varies by taxpayer filing status (we discuss filing status in more detail later in the chapter); the government indexes this deduction for inflation. Exhibit 4-7 presents the standard deduction amounts by filing status for 2009 and 2010. In addition to the amounts presented in Exhibit 4-7, taxpayers 65 years of age and/or blind taxpayers are entitled to additional standard deduction amounts. The additional standard deduction for age and for blindness is $1,100 for married taxpayers and qualifying widows and widowers and $1,400 for other taxpayers. A blind taxpayer who is 65 years old or older is entitled to two additional standard deduction amounts.[2] Finally, the standard deduction for individuals who are claimed as a dependent on another tax return is limited to the greater of (1) $950 or (2) $300 plus the dependent's earned income.[3]

### EXHIBIT 4-7   Standard Deduction Amounts by Filing Status

|  | 2009 | 2010 |
|---|---|---|
| Married filing jointly | $11,400 | $11,400 |
| Qualifying widow or widower | $11,400 | $11,400 |
| Married filing separately | $ 5,700 | $ 5,700 |
| Head of household | $ 8,350 | $ 8,400 |
| Single | $ 5,700 | $ 5,700 |

Exemptions are the final amount taxpayers deduct *from* AGI in determining their taxable income. An exemption is a flat deduction allowed for the taxpayer, the

---

[2]We discuss additional standard deductions in more detail in Chapter 6.

[3]The standard deduction cannot exceed the basic standard deduction amount. We discuss the standard deduction for taxpayers claimed as a dependent on another return in more detail in Chapter 6.

taxpayer's spouse, and each person who qualifies as a dependent of the taxpayer. The exemptions for the taxpayer(s) filing the tax return are called **personal exemptions,** while the others are referred to as **dependency exemptions.** In 2010 the amount of the exemption deduction is $3,650 for both exemption types. We discuss the dependency qualification requirements later in this chapter.

| Example 4-3 | |
|---|---|

Tara's parents, Rodney and Anita, annually file a joint tax return. Tara determined that during 2010 her parents paid a total of $14,000 for expenditures that qualify as itemized deductions. Assuming Tara and her younger brother Braxton qualify as Rodney and Anita's dependents, what is the total amount of *from* AGI deductions Rodney and Anita are allowed to deduct on their 2010 tax return?

**Answer:** $28,600, computed as follows:

| Description | Amount | Explanation |
|---|---|---|
| (1) Standard deduction | $11,400 | Married filing joint filing status (see Exhibit 4-7). |
| (2) Itemized deductions | 14,000 | |
| (3) Greater of (1) or (2) | 14,000 | Itemized deductions exceed the standard deduction. |
| (4) Personal and dependency exemptions | 14,600 | ($3,650 × 4) One exemption each for Rodney, Anita, Tara, and Braxton. |
| **Total deductions from AGI** | **$28,600** | (3) + (4). (Also referred to as deductions "below the line.") |

**What if:** What would be the amount of the Halls' from AGI deductions for 2010 if, instead of the original facts, Rodney and Anita had paid a total of $8,000 in expenditures that qualified as itemized deductions, such as interest expense and gifts to charity?

**Answer:** $26,000, computed as follows:

| Description | Amount | Explanation |
|---|---|---|
| (1) Standard deduction | $11,400 | Married filing joint filing status (see Exhibit 4-7). |
| (2) Itemized deductions | 8,000 | |
| (3) Greater of (1) or (2) | 11,400 | The standard deduction exceeds itemized deductions. |
| (4) Personal and dependency exemptions | 14,600 | ($3,650 × 4) One personal exemption each for Rodney, Anita, Tara, and Braxton. |
| **Total deductions from AGI** | **$26,000** | (3) + (4). |

### Income Tax Calculation

After determining taxable income, taxpayers can generally calculate their regular income tax liability using either a **tax table** or a **tax rate schedule,** depending on their filing status and income level (see inside front cover for the regular tax rate schedule and see Appendix A to this chapter for an excerpt from a tax table). Taxpayers with taxable income under $100,000 generally must use the tax tables.[4] However, as we discuss in other chapters, certain types of income that are included in taxable income are taxed at rates different from the rates embedded in the tables or published in the tax rate schedules. Exhibit 4-8 identifies these income items and indicates where in the text we discuss the income items in more detail.

---

[4]For administrative convenience and to prevent low- and middle-income taxpayers from making mathematical errors using a rate schedule, the IRS provides tax tables that present the gross tax for various amounts of taxable income. For simplicity, we use the tax rate schedule to determine tax liabilities in the examples presented in this text.

**EXHIBIT 4-8**   Income Taxed at Rate Other Than Rate from Tax Rate Schedule for That Taxpayer

| Income Item | Applicable Tax Rate | Discussed in |
|---|---|---|
| Unearned income of dependent child | Portion may be taxed at parents' marginal tax rate | Chapter 7 |
| Long-term capital gains* | Generally 15%. Can be as low as 0% and as high as 28%.[5] | Chapters 10 and 11 |
| Qualified dividends | Generally 15%. Can be as low as 0%. | Chapter 11 |

*Generally, these are gains on assets held for investments for more than one year before selling.

---

**Example 4-4**

With Tara's help, the Halls determined their 2010 taxable income to be $77,000 as follows:

| Description | Amount | Explanation |
|---|---|---|
| (1) Adjusted gross income | $105,600 | Example 4-2. |
| (2) From AGI deductions | (28,600) | Example 4-3. |
| Taxable income | $ 77,000 | (1) + (2). |

They have also determined that all of their income is taxed at the rates provided in the tax rate schedule. What is their tax liability for 2010 (use the tax rate schedule rather than the tax tables to answer the question)?

**Answer:** $11,612.50. See the married filing jointly tax rate schedule inside the front cover. [$9,362.50 + $2,250 {25% × (77,000 − 68,000)}].

**What if:** Suppose the Halls reported $77,000 of taxable income in 2009; what would be their 2009 tax liability using the tax tables (see Appendix A at the end of this chapter. Note there we use a 2009 tax table because the 2010 tax table was unavailable at press time).

**Answer:** $11,619.

**What if:** What would the Halls' tax liability be if their 2010 taxable income was $12,000 (all taxed at the ordinary rates in the tax rate schedule)?

**Answer:** $1,200 ($12,000 × 10%).

**What if:** Assume that in addition to the $77,000 of income taxed at the normal rates described in the original facts, the Halls also reported $5,000 of qualified dividends subject to a 15 percent tax rate. How much tax would they pay on the additional $5,000 dividend?

**Answer:** $750 ($5,000 × 15%). Qualifying dividends are generally taxed at a 15 percent rate. Note that the Halls' taxable income is $82,000. $77,000 of the income is taxed at the normal rates and $5,000 is taxed at the preferential 15 percent rate.

## Other Taxes

In addition to the individual income tax, individuals may also be required to pay other taxes such as the **alternative minimum tax (AMT)** or **self-employment taxes.** These taxes are imposed on tax bases other than the individual's regular taxable income. We discuss both taxes in more detail in Chapter 7.

## Tax Credits

Individual taxpayers may reduce their tax liabilities by **tax credits** to determine their total taxes payable. Like deductions, tax credits are specifically granted by Congress

[5]§1(h).

and are narrowly defined. Unlike deductions, which reduce *taxable income,* tax credits *directly reduce taxes payable.* Thus, a $1 deduction reduces taxes payable by $1 times the marginal tax rate while a $1 credit reduces taxes payable by $1. Common credits include the child tax credit ($1,000 per child that qualifies for the credit), the child and dependent care credit, the earned income credit, American opportunity credit, and the lifetime learning credit. We discuss credits in more detail in Chapter 7.

### Tax Prepayments

After calculating the total tax and subtracting their available credits, taxpayers determine their taxes due (or tax refund) by subtracting tax prepayments from the total tax remaining after credits. Tax prepayments include (1) **withholdings,** or income taxes withheld from the taxpayer's salary or wages by her employer; (2) **estimated tax payments** the taxpayer makes for the year; and (3) taxes the taxpayer overpaid in the previous year that the taxpayer elects to apply as an estimated payment for the current year.

If tax prepayments exceed the total tax after subtracting credits, the taxpayer receives a tax refund for the difference. If tax prepayments are less than the total tax after credits, the taxpayer owes additional tax and potentially a penalty for the underpayment.

---

**Example 4-5**

Based on their calculation in Example 4-4, Rodney and Anita Hall's tax liability for 2010 is $11,612.50. The Halls had $10,552 of federal income taxes withheld by their employers from their 2010 paychecks and are able to claim a $1,000 child tax credit for their 12-year-old son Braxton (Tara is too old to qualify). What is the Halls' tax due or tax refund for 2010?

**Answer:** $60.50 taxes due, computed as follows:

| Description | Amount | Explanation |
|---|---|---|
| (1) Tax liability | $ 11,612.50 | Example 4-4. |
| (2) Tax credits | (1,000) | $1,000 child tax credit for 12-year old son Braxton. |
| (3) Tax prepayments | (10,552) | |
| **Tax due** | $ 60.50 | (1) + (2) + (3). |

---

Although not explicitly stated in the individual tax formula, a taxpayer's filing status affects many parts of the tax formula, including the standard deduction amount and the applicable income tax rate schedule among others. Below, we describe the rules for determining a taxpayer's filing status. However, because a taxpayer's filing status may depend on whether the taxpayer has dependents for tax purposes, we discuss how to determine who qualifies as a taxpayer's dependent before we address filing status.

**L02**

## PERSONAL AND DEPENDENCY EXEMPTIONS

In 2010, taxpayers are allowed to deduct $3,650 for each personal and dependency exemption they are entitled to claim.[6] Individual taxpayers generally may deduct a personal exemption for themselves. Married couples filing jointly may claim two personal exemptions (one for each spouse).[7] Further, to provide some tax relief for taxpayers supporting others, individuals may claim additional exemptions for each person who qualifies as the taxpayer's dependent.[8] Individuals who qualify as a

---

[6]The amount of the exemption is indexed for inflation.

[7]§151(b).

[8]§151(c).

dependent of another taxpayer may *not* claim a personal exemption for themselves on their own individual tax returns.[9]

Example 4-6

Assume that Tara (the Halls' 21-year-old daughter who is a full-time college student) qualifies as Rodney and Anita's dependent. Tara earned $9,000 at a summer job this year, and she files her own tax return. Is Tara allowed to claim a personal exemption for herself on her own tax return?

**Answer:** No. Because Tara qualifies as the Halls' dependent, the Halls may deduct a dependency exemption for Tara, but Tara may *not* deduct a personal exemption for herself.

## Dependency Requirements

Taxpayers may claim exemptions only for persons qualifying as their **dependents.** To qualify as a dependent of another, an individual

1.  Must be a resident of the United States, Canada, or Mexico.
2.  Must *not* file a joint return with the individual's spouse unless there is no tax liability on the couple's joint return and there would not have been any tax liability on either spouse's tax return if they had filed separately.[10]
3.  Must be considered either a **qualifying child** of the taxpayer *or* a **qualifying relative** of the taxpayer.[11]

While the requirements for determining a qualifying child and a qualifying relative have some similarities, the qualifying relative requirements are broader in scope than the qualifying child requirements.

**Qualifying Child**    To be considered a qualifying child of a taxpayer, an individual must satisfy the following four tests: (1) relationship, (2) age, (3) residence, and (4) support.[12]

*Relationship test.*    A qualifying child must be a relative of the taxpayer. Eligible relatives include the taxpayer's son, daughter, stepchild, an eligible foster child, brother, sister, half-brother, half-sister, stepbrother, stepsister, or a descendant of any of these relatives. This definition does not include cousins.

*Age test.*    A qualifying child must be younger than the taxpayer claiming such individual as a qualifying child and *either* (1) under age 19 at the end of the year or (2) under age 24 at the end of the year *and* a full-time student.[13] A person is a full-time student if she was in school full-time during any part of each of five calendar months during the calendar year.[14] An individual who is permanently and totally disabled is deemed to have met the age test.[15]

*Residence test.*    A qualifying child must have the same principal residence as the taxpayer for *more* than half the year. Time that a child (or the taxpayer) is temporarily away from the taxpayer's home because the child (or taxpayer) is ill, is pursuing an education, or has other special circumstances is counted as though the child (or taxpayer) were living in the taxpayer's home.[16]

[9]See Publication 17, "Your Federal Income Tax," for information relating to personal and dependency exemptions.
[10]Rev. Rul. 54-567, 1954-2 C.B. 108.
[11]§152.
[12]Technically, an individual is not eligible to be a qualifying child of another if she filed a joint return with her spouse (other than to claim a refund) [see §151(c)(2)(e)]. However, because this is also a requirement to be claimed as a dependent, we do not discuss the requirement separately here.
[13]§152(c)(3)(A).
[14]§152(f)(2).
[15]§151(c)(3)(B).
[16]Reg. §1.152-1(b).

***Support test.*** A qualifying child must *not* have provided more than half his or her *own* support (living expenses) for the year. When determining who provided the support for a *child* of the taxpayer who is a full-time student, scholarships are excluded from the computation.[17] Otherwise, support generally includes:

- Food, school lunches, toilet articles, and haircuts.
- Clothing.
- Recreation—including toys, summer camp, horseback riding, entertainment, and vacation expenses.
- Medical and dental care.
- Child care expenses.
- Allowances and gifts.
- Wedding costs.
- Lodging.
- Education—including board, uniforms at military schools, and tuition.

---

**Example 4-7**

Rodney and Anita have two children: Braxton, age 12, who lives at home and Tara, age 21, who is a full-time student and does not live at home. While Tara earned $9,000 in a summer job (see previous example), she did *not* provide more than half of her own support during the year. Are Braxton and Tara qualifying children to Rodney and Anita?

**Answer:** Yes, see analysis of factors below:

| Test | Braxton | Tara |
|---|---|---|
| Relationship | Yes, son. | Yes, daughter. |
| Age | Yes, under age 19 at end of year (and younger than his parents). | Yes, under age 24 at year-end *and* full-time student (and younger than her parents). |
| Residence | Yes, lived at home entire year. | Yes, time away at college is considered as time at home. |
| Support | Yes, does not provide more than half of own support. | Yes, does not provide more than half of own support. |

Because they both meet all the requirements, Braxton and Tara are qualifying children to the Halls. So, the Halls may claim one dependency exemption for Braxton and one for Tara.

---

***Tiebreaking rules.*** The requirements for determining who is a qualifying child leave open the possibility that one person could be a qualifying child to more than one taxpayer. In these circumstances, the taxpayer who has priority for claiming the dependency exemption is based on the following tiebreaking rules:

1. If the person is a qualifying child of a parent, the parent is entitled to the dependency exemption for the child. This situation could arise, for example, when a child lives with her mother *and* her grandparents. In this case, the mother has priority for claiming the dependency exemption over the grandparents.

2. If the individual is a qualifying child to both parents, the parent with whom the child has resided for the longest period of time during the year has priority for claiming the dependency exemption. This situation may arise in a year when the child lives with both parents for more than half of the year, but the parents

---

[17]§152(f)(5) and §152(f)(1). This provision requires that the student be a son, daughter, stepson, stepdaughter, or an eligible foster child of the taxpayer.

divorce in the latter part of the year. Note, however, that the dependency exemption for a child of divorced parents can be specifically allocated in the divorce decree or separation agreement to the noncustodial parent.[18]

3.  Finally, if the child resides with both parents for the same amount of time or the qualifying child resides with taxpayers who are not the parents, the taxpayer with the *highest AGI* has priority for claiming the dependency exemption for the child.[19]

### Example 4-8

In the previous example, we determined that Braxton (Rodney and Anita's son) is Rodney and Anita's qualifying child. Braxton's Uncle Shawn (Rodney's brother) lived in the Halls' home (the same home Braxton lived in) for more than 11 months during 2010. Does Braxton meet the requirements to be considered Shawn's qualifying child?

**Answer:** Yes, see analysis of factors below.

| Test | Braxton |
| --- | --- |
| Relationship | Yes, son of Shawn's brother. |
| Age | Yes, under age 19 at end of year (and younger than Shawn). |
| Residence | Yes, lived in same residence as Shawn for more than half the year. |
| Support | Yes, does not provide more than half of own support. |

Thus, Braxton is considered to be Rodney and Anita's qualifying child *and* he is considered to be Shawn's qualifying child. Under the tiebreaker rules, who is allowed to claim Braxton as a dependent for the year?

**Answer:** Rodney and Anita. Under the first tiebreaking rule, Rodney and Anita are allowed to claim the dependency exemption for Braxton because they are Braxton's parents.

**Qualifying Relative**   A qualifying relative is a person who is *not* a qualifying child *and* satisfies (1) a relationship test, (2) a support test, and (3) a gross income test.

*Relationship test.*   As you might expect, the relationship test for a qualifying relative is more inclusive than the relationship test for a qualifying child. In fact, it even includes people who are *unrelated* to the taxpayer if the unrelated person lived as a member of the taxpayer's household for the *entire* year.[20] A person is "related" to the taxpayer if the person is a descendant or ancestor of the taxpayer (child, grandchild, parent, or grandparent), a sibling of the taxpayer, or a stepmother, stepfather, stepbrother, stepsister, nephew, niece, aunt, uncle, or in-law (mother-in law, father-in-law, sister-in-law, brother-in-law, son-in-law, and daughter-in-law) of the taxpayer.[21] Cousins are *not* considered related to the taxpayer for purposes of this test.

*Support test.*   The support test generally requires that the taxpayer pay more than half the qualifying relative's living expenses. As we discussed above, living expenses include rent, food, medicine, and clothes, among other things. Just as with the qualifying child support test, scholarships of children of a taxpayer who are full-time students

---

[18]See §152(e). The custodial parent releases the exemption to the noncustodial parent with a signature on Form 8332.

[19]However, if the parents may claim the child as a qualifying child but no parent does so, another taxpayer may claim the individual as a qualifying child but only if the other individual's AGI is higher than the AGI of any parent of the child [§152(c)(4)(C)].

[20]A person is considered to live with the taxpayer for the entire year if he or she was either born during the year or died during the year and resided with the taxpayer for the remaining part of the year. For example, a person who dies in March is deemed to live with the taxpayer for the entire year if the person resided with the taxpayer from the beginning of the year.

[21]Persons who are adopted qualify as if they are blood relatives.

are excluded from the support test.[22] Under a multiple support agreement, taxpayers who don't pay over half of an individual's support may still be allowed to claim him or her as a dependent under the qualifying relative rules if the following apply.[23]

1. No one taxpayer paid over one-half of the individual's support.
2. The taxpayer and at least one other person provided more than half the support of the individual, and the taxpayer and the other person(s) would have been allowed to claim the individual as a dependent except for the fact that they did not provide over half of the support of the individual.
3. The taxpayer contributed *over* 10 percent of the individual's support for the year.
4. Each other person who provided *over* 10 percent of the individual's support (see requirement (2) above) provides a signed statement to the taxpayer agreeing not to claim the individual as a dependent. The taxpayer includes the names, addresses, and Social Security numbers of each other person on a Form 2120, which the taxpayer attaches to her Form 1040.

***Gross income test.***   The gross income test requires that a qualifying relative's gross income for the year be *less* than the personal exemption amount. As we noted above, the personal exemption amount for 2010 is $3,650.

**Example 4-9**

In determining their dependency exemptions for the year, Rodney and Anita evaluated whether Shawn is their *qualifying relative*. Assuming Shawn's gross income for the year is $42,000, the Halls provided food and lodging for Shawn valued at $8,000, and Shawn paid for his other living expenses valued at $14,000, is Shawn a qualifying relative of the Halls?

**Answer:** No, as analyzed below.

| Test | Explanation |
|---|---|
| Relationship | Yes, Rodney's brother. |
| Support | No, the Halls provided $8,000 of support to Shawn, but Shawn provided $14,000 of his own support. Because the Halls provided less than half of Shawn's support, Shawn does not pass the support test. |
| Gross income | No, Shawn's gross income for the year is $42,000, which exceeds the exemption amount, so Shawn fails the gross income test. |

Because Shawn fails the support test and the gross income test, he is not a qualifying relative of the Halls. Consequently, they cannot claim a dependency exemption for him. Thus, Shawn can claim a personal exemption for himself on his own tax return.

***What if:***  Assume that Shawn received $5,000 of tax-exempt interest during the year and that this is his only source of income. Does he fail the gross income test?

**Answer:** No. Because tax-exempt interest is excluded from gross income Shawn's gross income is $0, so he passes the gross income test.

***What if:***  Assume the original facts in the example except that Shawn paid for his $14,000 of living expenses with interest he had received from tax-exempt bonds. Would Shawn pass the support test?

**Answer:** No. The Halls would not have provided more than half of Shawn's support. The fact that Shawn received the money he spent on his support from tax-exempt income does not matter. All that matters is that he provided more than half of his own support with his own funds.

---

[22]§152(f)(5) and §152(f)(1). Just as with a qualifying child, this provision requires that the student be a son, daughter, stepson, stepdaughter, or an eligible foster child of the taxpayer.
[23]§152(d)(3).

**What if:** Assume that in 2010 Anita's 92-year-old grandfather Juan lives in an apartment by himself near the Halls' residence. His gross income for the year is $3,000. Assuming the Halls provide more than half of Juan's living expenses for the year, would Juan be a qualifying relative of the Halls?

**Answer:** Yes, as analyzed below.

| Test | Explanation |
|---|---|
| Relationship | Yes, Anita's father. |
| Support | Yes, as assumed in the facts, the Halls provide more than half of Juan's support. |
| Gross income | Yes, Juan's gross income for the year is $3,000, which is below the $3,650 exemption amount, so Juan passes the gross income test. |

**What if:** Assume that in 2010 Anita's 92-year-old grandfather Juan lives in an apartment by himself and reports gross income for the year of $3,000. Anita provided 40 percent of Juan's support, Juan provided 25 percent of his own support, Anita's brother Carlos provides 30 percent of the support, and Anita's sister Kamella provided 5 percent of Juan's support. Who is eligible to claim Juan as a dependent under a multiple support agreement?

**Answer:** Anita and Carlos. Anita and Carlos are eligible because (1) no one taxpayer provided more than half of Juan's support, (2) Anita and Carlos together provided more than half of Juan's support and Juan would have been both Anita's and Carlos's qualifying relative except for the fact that neither provided over half of Juan's support, and (3) Anita and Carlos each provided over 10 percent of Juan's support (Kamella provided only 5 percent of Juan's support so she is not eligible). Anita and Carlos would need to agree on who would claim the dependency exemption for Juan. Assuming they agree that Anita would claim the exemption, she would need to receive a signed statement from Carlos agreeing not to claim the exemption and she would need to attach a Form 2120 to her (and Rodney's) tax return providing Carlos's name, address, and Social Security number.

**What if:** Assume Juan was a friend of the family but was not related to either Rodney or Anita, that his gross income is $3,000, and that the Halls provided over half of his support. Is Juan a qualifying relative of the Halls?

**Answer:** No, as analyzed below.

| Test | Explanation |
|---|---|
| Relationship | No, not related to Halls and did not live as a member of the Halls' household for the *entire* year. If he had lived with the Halls, he would have met the relationship test even though he's not actually related to anyone in the Hall family. |
| Support | Yes, as assumed in the facts, the Halls provide more than half of Juan's support. |
| Gross income | Yes, Juan's gross income for the year is $3,000, which is below the $3,650 exemption amount, so Juan passes the gross income test. |

The Halls would not be able to claim an exemption for Juan as a qualifying relative because he fails the relationship test under this set of facts.

The rules for determining who qualifies as a dependent as a qualifying child and who qualifies as a dependent as a qualifying relative overlap to some extent. The primary differences between the two are (1) the relationship requirement is more broadly defined for qualifying relatives than qualifying children, (2) qualifying children are subject to age restrictions while qualifying relatives are not, (3) qualifying relatives are subject to a

gross income restriction while qualifying children are not, and (4) taxpayers need not provide more than half a qualifying child's support (though the child cannot provide more than half of her own support), but they must provide more than half the support of a qualifying relative. Exhibit 4-9 summarizes the dependency requirements.

**EXHIBIT 4-9    Summary of Dependency Requirements**

| Test | Qualifying Child | Qualifying Relative |
|---|---|---|
| Relationship | Taxpayer's child, stepchild, foster child, sibling, half-brother or sister, stepbrother or sister, or a descendant of any of these relatives. | Taxpayer's descendant or ancestor, sibling, stepmother, stepfather, stepbrother or sister, nephews, nieces, aunts, uncles, in-laws, and anyone else who lives with the taxpayer for the entire year. |
| Age | Younger than the taxpayer claiming the individual as a qualifying child and under age 19 or a full-time student under age 24. Also anyone totally and permanently disabled. | Not applicable. |
| Residence | Lives with taxpayer for more than half of the year (includes temporary absences for things such as illness and education). | Not applicable. |
| Support | The qualifying child must not provide more than half of his or her own support. | Taxpayer must have provided more than half of the support for the qualifying relative. |
| Gross income | Not applicable. | Gross income less than exemption amount ($3,650 in 2010). |
| Other | Not applicable. | Not a qualifying child. |

## FILING STATUS

Each year taxpayers determine their **filing status** according to their marital status at year-end and whether they have any dependents. A taxpayer's filing status is important because, as we discussed above, it determines:

1. The applicable tax rate schedule for determining the taxpayer's tax liability.
2. The taxpayer's standard deduction amount.
3. The AGI threshold for reductions in certain tax benefits such as certain itemized deductions and certain tax credits, among others.

Each year, all taxpayers filing tax returns file under one of the following five filing statuses:

- Married filing jointly
- Married filing separately
- Qualifying widow or widower (surviving spouse)
- Head of household
- Single

### Married Filing Jointly and Married Filing Separately

Married couples may file tax returns jointly **(married filing jointly)** or separately **(married filing separately).** To be married for filing status purposes, taxpayers must be married on the last day of the year. When one spouse dies during the year, the surviving spouse is

considered to be *married* to the decedent spouse at the end of the year unless the surviving spouse remarries during the year. Married couples filing joint returns combine their income and deductions and agree to share joint and several liability for the resulting tax. That is, they are both ultimately responsible to see that the tax is paid.

When married couples file separately, each spouse reports the income he or she received during the year and the deductions he or she paid on a tax return separate from that of the other spouse.[24] So that married taxpayers can't file separately to gain more combined tax benefits than they are entitled to if they filed jointly, tax-related items for married filing separate (MFS) taxpayers—such as tax rate schedules and standard deduction amounts, among others—are generally *one-half* what they are for married filing joint (MFJ) taxpayers. Also, if one spouse deducts itemized deductions, the other spouse is required to deduct itemized deductions even if his or her itemized deductions are less than the standard deduction. Thus, only in unusual circumstances does it make sense for *tax* purposes for married couples to file separately.

However, it may be wise for married couples to file separately for *nontax* reasons. For example, a spouse who does not want to be liable for the other spouse's income tax liability, or a spouse who is not in contact with the other spouse, may want to file separately (see abandoned spouse discussion below).

*(concluded)*

· Each spouse is ultimately responsible for paying own tax.
· Couples may choose to file separately (generally for nontax reasons).

■ **Qualifying widow or widower**
· When a taxpayer's spouse dies, the surviving spouse can file as qualifying widow or widower for two years after the year of the spouse's death if the surviving spouse remains unmarried and maintains a household for a dependent child.

**Example 4-10**

Rodney and Anita Hall are married at the end of the year. What is their filing status?

**Answer:** Married filing jointly, unless they choose to file separately.

**What if:** Assume that in 2010 the Halls file a joint return. In 2011, Rodney and Anita divorce and the IRS audits their 2010 tax return and determines that due to overstating their deductions, the Halls underpaid their taxes by $2,000. Who must pay the tax?

**Answer:** Both Rodney and Anita are responsible for paying. If the IRS can't locate Rodney, it can require Anita to pay the full $2,000 even though Anita earned $40,000 and Rodney earned $59,000.

**What if:** Assume that in 2010 the Halls file separate tax returns. In 2011, Rodney and Anita divorce and the IRS audits the Halls' separate tax returns. It determines that by overstating deductions, Rodney understated his tax liability by $1,500 and Anita understated her tax liability by $500. Further, the IRS cannot locate Rodney. What is the maximum amount of taxes Anita is liable for?

**Answer:** $500. Because she filed a separate return, she is responsible for the tax liability associated with her separate tax return and she is not responsible for the taxes associated with Rodney's tax return.

**Taxes in the Real World** · *Filing Status for Same-Sex Married Couples*

Some states recognize same-sex marriages. These states allow same-sex married couples to file as married filing jointly on their state income tax returns. However, for federal income tax purposes the federal "Defense of Marriage Act" does not allow any federal agency, including the IRS, to recognize same-sex marriages. The end result? A same-sex married couple may file as married filing jointly for state income tax purposes but be required to file as single or head of household taxpayers for federal income tax purposes.

*Source:* "Defense of Marriage Act." United States Government Printing Office. 1996-09-21.

## Qualifying Widow or Widower

When a taxpayer's spouse dies during the year, the taxpayer is no longer legally married. However, to provide tax relief for widows and widowers *with dependents,* taxpayers who qualify for the **qualifying widow or widower** filing status may file as though

---

[24]As we discuss in the next chapter, under community property laws of certain states, one spouse may be treated as receiving income earned by the other spouse.

they are married filing jointly for up to two years *after* the end of the year in which the other spouse died (recall that for tax purposes, they are still considered to be married for the year of the spouse's death).[25] Taxpayers qualify for this exception as long as they (1) remain unmarried and (2) paid over half the cost of maintaining a household where a dependent child lived for the entire year (except for temporary absences). The dependent child must be a child or stepchild (including an adopted child) for whom the taxpayer may claim an exemption (not a foster child).

---

**Example 4-11**

**What if:** Assume that last year Rodney passed away, and during the current year Anita did not remarry but maintained a household for Braxton and Tara, her dependent children. Under these circumstances, what would Anita's filing status be?

**Answer:** Qualifying widow. Last year, the year of Rodney's death, Anita qualified to file a joint return with Rodney. This year, Anita qualifies as a qualifying widow (also referred to as a surviving spouse) because she has not remarried and she maintains a household for the entire year for her dependent children. She will qualify as a surviving spouse next year (two years after Rodney's death) if she does not remarry and she continues to maintain a household for Braxton and/or Tara for the entire year.

---

### THE KEY FACTS

**Filing Status for Unmarried Taxpayers**

▪ **Head of household**
  · Unmarried taxpayers or abandoned spouses.
  · Must pay more than half of the costs of maintaining a household in which a qualifying dependent lives for more than half of the tax year or must pay more than half of the costs for maintaining a separate household for a parent who qualifies as taxpayer's dependent.

▪ **Single**
  · Unmarried taxpayers at year-end who do not qualify for head of household.

## Head of Household

A taxpayer who is unmarried at the end of the year and who is not a qualifying widow or widower may be able to file as a **head of household.** To qualify for head of household filing status, the taxpayer must pay more than half the costs of maintaining a household, and a "qualifying person" must live with the taxpayer in that household for *more* than half the taxable year.[26] If, however, the qualifying person is the taxpayer's parent, the parent does not need to live with the taxpayer. A qualifying person includes (the person need meet only one of the following tests):

1. A qualifying child who qualifies as the taxpayer's dependent.
2. An individual whom the taxpayer would be able to claim as a *dependent* qualifying child except that the taxpayer released the exemption to the noncustodial parent.
3. A mother or father who qualifies as the taxpayer's dependent.
4. An individual who is not required to live with the taxpayer in order to meet the qualifying relative test (the individual is actually related to the taxpayer). However, this does not include individuals who qualify as the taxpayer's dependent under a multiple support agreement. Note also that these individuals may qualify as the taxpayer's dependent as a qualifying relative even if they do not live with the taxpayer during more than half the year. Even though the individual qualifies as the taxpayer's dependent, unless she lives with the taxpayer for more than half the year, she is not a qualifying person for purposes of the head of household test.

---

**Example 4-12**

**What if:** Assume Rodney and Anita divorced last year. During the current year, Braxton lives with Anita and Anita pays all the costs of maintaining the household for herself and Braxton. Under these circumstances, what is Anita's filing status for the current year?

**Answer:** Head of household. Anita is unmarried at the end of the year, and she provides more than half the costs of maintaining her household and Braxton, who is her qualifying child, lives with her for more than half the year.

---

[25]The qualifying widow or widower is not allowed to claim a dependency exemption for the deceased spouse for the two years after the spouse's death.
[26]§2(b).

---

***What if:*** Assume Shawn (Rodney's brother) lived with the Halls, but Shawn paid more than half the costs of maintaining a separate apartment that is the principal residence of his mother, Sharon, whose gross income is $1,500. Because Shawn provided more than half of Sharon's support during the year, and because Sharon's gross income was only $1,500, she qualifies as Shawn's dependent (as a qualifying relative). In these circumstances, what is Shawn's filing status?

**Answer:** Head of household. Shawn paid more than half the costs of maintaining a separate household where his mother resides, and his mother qualifies as his dependent.

If Sharon's gross income exceeded $3,650 she would fail the dependency gross income test and would not qualify as Shawn's dependent. If she did not qualify as his dependent she would not be a qualifying person and Shawn would not qualify for the head of household filing status. Also, if Sharon were Shawn's grandmother rather than his mother, she would not be a qualifying person and Shawn would not qualify for head of household status—Sharon must be Shawn's parent for him to qualify as a head of household.

---

In certain situations a couple may be legally married at the end of the year, but living apart. Although the couple could technically file a joint tax return, this is often not desirable from a nontax perspective, because each spouse would be assuming responsibility for paying tax on income earned by either spouse whether it was reported or not. However, because both spouses are married at the end of the year, their only other option is to file under the tax unfavorable status of married filing separately.

To provide tax relief in these situations, the tax laws treat married taxpayers who qualify as **abandoned spouses** *as though they were unmarried* at the end of the year. This allows them to qualify for the more favorable head of household filing status. An abandoned spouse is a taxpayer who meets all of the following requirements:

1. Is married at the end of the year (or is not *legally* separated from the other spouse).
2. Files a tax return for the year separate from the other spouse's.
3. Pays *more than half* the costs of maintaining his or her home for the entire year, and this home is the principal residence for a child (who qualifies as the taxpayer's dependent[27]) for *more than* half the year (the child must be a child (including adopted child), stepchild, or eligible foster child[28]).
4. Whose spouse does not live in the taxpayer's home for the last six months of the year.

---

**Example 4-13**

***What if:*** Assume that last year, Rodney and Anita informally separated (they did not legally separate). Rodney moved out of the home and into his own apartment. Anita stayed in the Halls' home with Braxton. During the current year, Anita paid more than half the cost of maintaining the home for herself and Braxton. Even though Rodney and Anita were legally married at the end of the year, they filed separate tax returns. Under these circumstances, what is Anita's filing status for the current year?

**Answer:** Head of household, determined as follows (see numbered requirements above):

1. Anita is married to Rodney at the end of the year.
2. Anita filed a tax return separate from Rodney's.
3. Anita paid more than half the costs of maintaining her home, and her home was the principal residence for Braxton who is her dependent child.

*(continued on page 4-20 ...)*

---

[27]Taxpayer meets this test if the taxpayer (custodial parent) cannot claim an exemption for the child only because he or she released the exemption to the noncustodial parent under a divorce agreement.
[28]§152(f).

4. Rodney did not live in Anita's home for the last six months of the year (in fact, he didn't live there at any time during the entire year).

Without the abandoned spouse rule, Anita would have been required to file as married filing separately. Rodney's filing status, however, is married filing separately.

### Single

Unmarried taxpayers who do not qualify for head of household status file as **single** taxpayers.

**Example 4-14**

Shawn Hall, Rodney's brother, was divorced in January and is unmarried at the end of the year. What is his filing status?

**Answer:** Single. Because Shawn is unmarried at the end of the year, and he did not maintain a household for any other person, his filing status is single.

## SUMMARY OF INCOME TAX FORMULA

Tara crunched some numbers and put together a summary of her parents' taxable income calculation. She determined that her parents will be required to pay $60.50 of tax when they file their 2010 tax return. Tara's summary is provided in Exhibit 4-10.

**EXHIBIT 4-10** 2010 Taxable Income and Tax Calculation Summary for Rodney and Anita Hall

| Description | Amount | Explanation |
|---|---|---|
| (1) Realized income from all sources | $ 110,900 | Example 4-1, line (5). |
| (2) Excluded or deferred income | (300) | Example 4-1, line (6). |
| (3) Gross income | 110,600 | (1) + (2). |
| (4) For AGI deductions | (5,000) | Example 4-2, line (2). |
| (5) Adjusted gross income | $ 105,600 | (3) + (4). |
| (6) Itemized deductions | (14,000) | Example 4-3, line (2). |
| (7) Personal and dependency exemptions | (14,600) | Example 4-3, line (4). |
| (8) Taxable income | $ 77,000 | (5) + (6) + (7). |
| (9) Income tax liability | $ 11,612.50 | Example 4-4. |
| (10) Other taxes | 0 | |
| (11) Total tax | $ 11,612.50 | (9) + (10). |
| (12) Credits | (1,000) | Example 4-5, line (2). |
| (13) Prepayments | (10,552) | Example 4-5, line (3). |
| Tax due with return | $ 60.50 | (11) + (12) + (13). |

Exhibit 4-11 presents pages 1 and 2 of the Halls' Form 1040.

## CONCLUSION

This chapter presents an overview of the individual income tax formula and provides rules for determining a taxpayer's filing status and who qualifies as a taxpayer's dependents. In Chapter 5, we turn our attention to determining gross income. In Chapter 6, we describe deductions available to taxpayers when computing their taxable income. In Chapter 7, we conclude our review of the individual income tax formula by determining how to compute a taxpayer's tax liability and her taxes due or tax refund.

**EXHIBIT 4-11**

Form **1040**  Department of the Treasury—Internal Revenue Service
**U.S. Individual Income Tax Return**  20**09**  (99)  IRS Use Only—Do not write or staple in this space.

OMB No. 1545-0074

For the year Jan. 1–Dec. 31, 2009, or other tax year beginning _____ , 2009, ending _____ , 20 ____

**Label** (See instructions on page 14.) Use the IRS label. Otherwise, please print or type.

| | |
|---|---|
| Your first name and initial: **Rodney** | Last name: **Hall** |
| If a joint return, spouse's first name and initial: **Anita** | Last name: **Hall** |

Home address (number and street). If you have a P.O. box, see page 14.  **655 Henry Avenue**  Apt. no.

City, town or post office, state, and ZIP code. If you have a foreign address, see page 14.  **Brookings, SD 57007**

Your social security number: 2 2 4 5 6 1 2 4 5
Spouse's social security number: 3 2 4 4 3 3 4 7 8

▲ You **must** enter your SSN(s) above. ▲

Checking a box below will not change your tax or refund.

**Presidential Election Campaign** ► Check here if you, or your spouse if filing jointly, want $3 to go to this fund (see page 14) ► ☐ You ☐ Spouse

**Filing Status**
Check only one box.

1 ☐ Single
2 ☑ Married filing jointly (even if only one had income)
3 ☐ Married filing separately. Enter spouse's SSN above and full name here. ►
4 ☐ Head of household (with qualifying person). (See page 15.) If the qualifying person is a child but not your dependent, enter this child's name here. ►
5 ☐ Qualifying widow(er) with dependent child (see page 16)

**Exemptions**

6a ☑ **Yourself.** If someone can claim you as a dependent, **do not** check box 6a . . . . .
b ☑ **Spouse**
c Dependents:

| (1) First name   Last name | (2) Dependent's social security number | (3) Dependent's relationship to you | (4) ✓ if qualifying child for child tax credit (see page 17) |
|---|---|---|---|
| Tara Hall | 2 4 2 6 8 9 9 4 5 | Daughter | ☐ |
| Braxton Hall | 2 4 2 2 3 7 8 4 5 | Son | ☑ |
| | | | ☐ |
| | | | ☐ |

If more than four dependents, see page 17 and check here ► ☐

d Total number of exemptions claimed . . . . . . . . . .

Boxes checked on 6a and 6b: **2**
No. of children on 6c who:
• lived with you: **1**
• did not live with you due to divorce or separation (see page 18):
Dependents on 6c not entered above: **1**
Add numbers on lines above ►: **4**

**Income**

Attach Form(s) W-2 here. Also attach Forms W-2G and 1099-R if tax was withheld.

If you did not get a W-2, see page 22.

Enclose, but do not attach, any payment. Also, please use Form 1040-V.

| | | | |
|---|---|---|---|
| 7 | Wages, salaries, tips, etc. Attach Form(s) W-2 . . . . . . . . | 7 | 110,000 |
| 8a | **Taxable** interest. Attach Schedule B if required . . . . . . | 8a | 600 |
| b | Tax-exempt interest. **Do not** include on line 8a . . . 8b | 300 | |
| 9a | Ordinary dividends. Attach Schedule B if required . . . . . | 9a | |
| b | Qualified dividends (see page 22) . . . . . . . 9b | | |
| 10 | Taxable refunds, credits, or offsets of state and local income taxes (see page 23) . . | 10 | |
| 11 | Alimony received . . . . . . . . . . . . . . . | 11 | |
| 12 | Business income or (loss). Attach Schedule C or C-EZ . . . . . . | 12 | |
| 13 | Capital gain or (loss). Attach Schedule D if required. If not required, check here ► ☐ | 13 | |
| 14 | Other gains or (losses). Attach Form 4797 . . . . . . . . | 14 | |
| 15a | IRA distributions . 15a | b Taxable amount (see page 24) | 15b |
| 16a | Pensions and annuities 16a | b Taxable amount (see page 25) | 16b |
| 17 | Rental real estate, royalties, partnerships, S corporations, trusts, etc. Attach Schedule E | 17 | |
| 18 | Farm income or (loss). Attach Schedule F . . . . . . . . | 18 | |
| 19 | Unemployment compensation in excess of $2,400 per recipient (see page 27) . . . | 19 | |
| 20a | Social security benefits 20a | b Taxable amount (see page 27) | 20b |
| 21 | Other income. List type and amount (see page 29) _____ | 21 | |
| 22 | Add the amounts in the far right column for lines 7 through 21. This is your **total income** ► | 22 | 110,600 |

**Adjusted Gross Income**

| | | | |
|---|---|---|---|
| 23 | Educator expenses (see page 29) . . . . . . . | 23 | |
| 24 | Certain business expenses of reservists, performing artists, and fee-basis government officials. Attach Form 2106 or 2106-EZ | 24 | |
| 25 | Health savings account deduction. Attach Form 8889 . | 25 | |
| 26 | Moving expenses. Attach Form 3903 . . . . | 26 | 5,000 |
| 27 | One-half of self-employment tax. Attach Schedule SE . | 27 | |
| 28 | Self-employed SEP, SIMPLE, and qualified plans . | 28 | |
| 29 | Self-employed health insurance deduction (see page 30) | 29 | |
| 30 | Penalty on early withdrawal of savings . . . . . | 30 | |
| 31a | Alimony paid  b Recipient's SSN ► ___ | 31a | |
| 32 | IRA deduction (see page 31) . . . . . . | 32 | |
| 33 | Student loan interest deduction (see page 34) . . | 33 | |
| 34 | Tuition and fees deduction. Attach Form 8917 . . | 34 | |
| 35 | Domestic production activities deduction. Attach Form 8903 | 35 | |
| 36 | Add lines 23 through 31a and 32 through 35 . . . . . . . | 36 | 5,000 |
| 37 | Subtract line 36 from line 22. This is your **adjusted gross income** . . . . . ► | 37 | 105,600 |

**For Disclosure, Privacy Act, and Paperwork Reduction Act Notice, see page 97.**  Cat. No. 11320B  Form **1040** (2009)

*(continued)*

## EXHIBIT 4-11   *(continued)*

Form 1040 (2009)                                                                                                    Page **2**

| | | | | |
|---|---|---|---|---|
| **Tax and Credits** | 38 | Amount from line 37 (adjusted gross income) . . . . . . . . . . | 38 | 105,600 |
| | 39a | Check if: ☐ **You** were born before January 2, 1945, ☐ Blind. ☐ **Spouse** was born before January 2, 1945, ☐ Blind. } Total boxes checked ▶ 39a | | |

**Standard Deduction for—**
- People who check any box on line 39a, 39b, or 40b **or** who can be claimed as a dependent, see page 35.
- All others:

Single or Married filing separately, $5,700

Married filing jointly or Qualifying widow(er), $11,400

Head of household, $8,350

| | | | |
|---|---|---|---|
| b | If your spouse itemizes on a separate return or you were a dual-status alien, see page 35 and check here ▶ 39b☐ | | |
| 40a | Itemized deductions (from Schedule A) **or** your **standard deduction** (see left margin) . . | 40a | 14,000 |
| b | If you are increasing your standard deduction by certain real estate taxes, new motor vehicle taxes, or a net disaster loss, attach Schedule L and check here (see page 35) . ▶ 40b☐ | | |
| 41 | Subtract line 40a from line 38 . . . . . . . . . . . . . . | 41 | 91,600 |
| 42 | **Exemptions.** If line 38 is $125,100 or less and you did not provide housing to a Midwestern displaced individual, multiply $3,650 by the number on line 6d. Otherwise, see page 37 . . | 42 | 14,600 |
| 43 | **Taxable income.** Subtract line 42 from line 41. If line 42 is more than line 41, enter -0- . . | 43 | 77,000 |
| 44 | **Tax** (see page 37). Check if any tax is from: **a** ☐ Form(s) 8814  **b** ☐ Form 4972 . | 44 | 11,612 50 |
| 45 | **Alternative minimum tax** (see page 40). Attach Form 6251 . . . . . . | 45 | |
| 46 | Add lines 44 and 45 . . . . . . . . . . . . . . . . ▶ | 46 | 11,612 50 |

| | | | | |
|---|---|---|---|---|
| 47 | Foreign tax credit. Attach Form 1116 if required . . . | 47 | | |
| 48 | Credit for child and dependent care expenses. Attach Form 2441 | 48 | | |
| 49 | Education credits from Form 8863, line 29 . . . . . | 49 | | |
| 50 | Retirement savings contributions credit. Attach Form 8880 | 50 | | |
| 51 | Child tax credit (see page 42) . . . . . | 51 | 1,000 | |
| 52 | Credits from Form: **a** ☐ 8396 **b** ☐ 8839 **c** ☐ 5695 | 52 | | |
| 53 | Other credits from Form: **a** ☐ 3800 **b** ☐ 8801 **c** ☐ | 53 | | |
| 54 | Add lines 47 through 53. These are your **total credits** . . . . . . . | 54 | 1,000 | |
| 55 | Subtract line 54 from line 46. If line 54 is more than line 46, enter -0- . . . . ▶ | 55 | 10,612 | 50 |

| | | | |
|---|---|---|---|
| **Other Taxes** | 56 | Self-employment tax. Attach Schedule SE . . . . . . . . . . | 56 |
| | 57 | Unreported social security and Medicare tax from Form: **a** ☐ 4137 **b** ☐ 8919 | 57 |
| | 58 | Additional tax on IRAs, other qualified retirement plans, etc. Attach Form 5329 if required . . | 58 |
| | 59 | Additional taxes: **a** ☐ AEIC payments **b** ☐ Household employment taxes. Attach Schedule H | 59 |
| | 60 | Add lines 55 through 59. This is your **total tax** . . . . . . . . ▶ | 60 | 10,612 50 |

| | | | | |
|---|---|---|---|---|
| **Payments** | 61 | Federal income tax withheld from Forms W-2 and 1099 . . . | 61 | 10,552 |
| | 62 | 2009 estimated tax payments and amount applied from 2008 return | 62 | |
| | 63 | Making work pay and government retiree credits. Attach Schedule M | 63 | |
| If you have a qualifying child, attach Schedule EIC. | 64a | **Earned income credit (EIC)** . . . . . . . | 64a | |
| | b | Nontaxable combat pay election  64b | | |
| | 65 | Additional child tax credit. Attach Form 8812 . . . . | 65 | |
| | 66 | Refundable education credit from Form 8863, line 16 . . . | 66 | |
| | 67 | First-time homebuyer credit. Attach Form 5405 . . . . | 67 | |
| | 68 | Amount paid with request for extension to file (see page 72) . | 68 | |
| | 69 | Excess social security and tier 1 RRTA tax withheld (see page 72) | 69 | |
| | 70 | Credits from Form: **a** ☐ 2439 **b** ☐ 4136 **c** ☐ 8801 **d** ☐ 8885 | 70 | |
| | 71 | Add lines 61, 62, 63, 64a, and 65 through 70. These are your **total payments** . . . . ▶ | 71 | 10,552 |

| | | | |
|---|---|---|---|
| **Refund** | 72 | If line 71 is more than line 60, subtract line 60 from line 71. This is the amount you **overpaid** | 72 |
| Direct deposit? See page 73 and fill in 73b, 73c, and 73d, or Form 8888. | 73a | Amount of line 72 you want **refunded to you.** If Form 8888 is attached, check here . ▶ ☐ | 73a |
| | ▶ b | Routing number ☐☐☐☐☐☐☐☐☐  ▶ c Type: ☐ Checking ☐ Savings | |
| | ▶ d | Account number ☐☐☐☐☐☐☐☐☐☐☐☐☐ | |
| | 74 | Amount of line 72 you want **applied to your 2010 estimated tax** ▶ 74 | |
| **Amount You Owe** | 75 | **Amount you owe.** Subtract line 71 from line 60. For details on how to pay, see page 74 . ▶ | 75 | 60 50 |
| | 76 | Estimated tax penalty (see page 74) . . . . . . . 76 | |

| | |
|---|---|
| **Third Party Designee** | Do you want to allow another person to discuss this return with the IRS (see page 75)? ☐ **Yes.** Complete the following.   ☐ **No** |
| | Designee's name ▶ | Phone no. ▶ | Personal identification number (PIN) ▶ ☐☐☐☐☐ |

**Sign Here**
Joint return? See page 15.
Keep a copy for your records.

Under penalties of perjury, I declare that I have examined this return and accompanying schedules and statements, and to the best of my knowledge and belief, they are true, correct, and complete. Declaration of preparer (other than taxpayer) is based on all information of which preparer has any knowledge.

| Your signature | Date | Your occupation | Daytime phone number |
|---|---|---|---|
| Spouse's signature. If a joint return, **both** must sign. | Date | Spouse's occupation | |

**Paid Preparer's Use Only**

| Preparer's signature ▶ | Date | Check if self-employed ☐ | Preparer's SSN or PTIN |
|---|---|---|---|
| Firm's name (or yours if self-employed), address, and ZIP code ▶ | | EIN | |
| | | Phone no. | |

Form **1040** (2009)

# APPENDIX A EXCERPT FROM 2009 TAX TABLE

**2009 Tax Table–*Continued***

| If line 43 (taxable income) is— | | And you are— | | | |
|---|---|---|---|---|---|
| At least | But less than | Single | Married filing jointly * | Married filing separately | Head of a household |
| | | Your tax is— | | | |
| **68,000** | | | | | |
| **68,000** | **68,050** | 13,194 | 9,381 | 13,194 | 11,859 |
| **68,050** | **68,100** | 13,206 | 9,394 | 13,206 | 11,871 |
| **68,100** | **68,150** | 13,219 | 9,406 | 13,219 | 11,884 |
| **68,150** | **68,200** | 13,231 | 9,419 | 13,231 | 11,896 |
| **68,200** | **68,250** | 13,244 | 9,431 | 13,244 | 11,909 |
| **68,250** | **68,300** | 13,256 | 9,444 | 13,256 | 11,921 |
| **68,300** | **68,350** | 13,269 | 9,456 | 13,269 | 11,934 |
| **68,350** | **68,400** | 13,281 | 9,469 | 13,281 | 11,946 |
| **68,400** | **68,450** | 13,294 | 9,481 | 13,294 | 11,959 |
| **68,450** | **68,500** | 13,306 | 9,494 | 13,306 | 11,971 |
| **68,500** | **68,550** | 13,319 | 9,506 | 13,319 | 11,984 |
| **68,550** | **68,600** | 13,331 | 9,519 | 13,333 | 11,996 |
| **68,600** | **68,650** | 13,344 | 9,531 | 13,347 | 12,009 |
| **68,650** | **68,700** | 13,356 | 9,544 | 13,361 | 12,021 |
| **68,700** | **68,750** | 13,369 | 9,556 | 13,375 | 12,034 |
| **68,750** | **68,800** | 13,381 | 9,569 | 13,389 | 12,046 |
| **68,800** | **68,850** | 13,394 | 9,581 | 13,403 | 12,059 |
| **68,850** | **68,900** | 13,406 | 9,594 | 13,417 | 12,071 |
| **68,900** | **68,950** | 13,419 | 9,606 | 13,431 | 12,084 |
| **68,950** | **69,000** | 13,431 | 9,619 | 13,445 | 12,096 |
| **69,000** | | | | | |
| **69,000** | **69,050** | 13,444 | 9,631 | 13,459 | 12,109 |
| **69,050** | **69,100** | 13,456 | 9,644 | 13,473 | 12,121 |
| **69,100** | **69,150** | 13,469 | 9,656 | 13,487 | 12,134 |
| **69,150** | **69,200** | 13,481 | 9,669 | 13,501 | 12,146 |
| **69,200** | **69,250** | 13,494 | 9,681 | 13,515 | 12,159 |
| **69,250** | **69,300** | 13,506 | 9,694 | 13,529 | 12,171 |
| **69,300** | **69,350** | 13,519 | 9,706 | 13,543 | 12,184 |
| **69,350** | **69,400** | 13,531 | 9,719 | 13,557 | 12,196 |
| **69,400** | **69,450** | 13,544 | 9,731 | 13,571 | 12,209 |
| **69,450** | **69,500** | 13,556 | 9,744 | 13,585 | 12,221 |
| **69,500** | **69,550** | 13,569 | 9,756 | 13,599 | 12,234 |
| **69,550** | **69,600** | 13,581 | 9,769 | 13,613 | 12,246 |
| **69,600** | **69,650** | 13,594 | 9,781 | 13,627 | 12,259 |
| **69,650** | **69,700** | 13,606 | 9,794 | 13,641 | 12,271 |
| **69,700** | **69,750** | 13,619 | 9,806 | 13,655 | 12,284 |
| **69,750** | **69,800** | 13,631 | 9,819 | 13,669 | 12,296 |
| **69,800** | **69,850** | 13,644 | 9,831 | 13,683 | 12,309 |
| **69,850** | **69,900** | 13,656 | 9,844 | 13,697 | 12,321 |
| **69,900** | **69,950** | 13,669 | 9,856 | 13,711 | 12,334 |
| **69,950** | **70,000** | 13,681 | 9,869 | 13,725 | 12,346 |
| **70,000** | | | | | |
| **70,000** | **70,050** | 13,694 | 9,881 | 13,739 | 12,359 |
| **70,050** | **70,100** | 13,706 | 9,894 | 13,753 | 12,371 |
| **70,100** | **70,150** | 13,719 | 9,906 | 13,767 | 12,384 |
| **70,150** | **70,200** | 13,731 | 9,919 | 13,781 | 12,396 |
| **70,200** | **70,250** | 13,744 | 9,931 | 13,795 | 12,409 |
| **70,250** | **70,300** | 13,756 | 9,944 | 13,809 | 12,421 |
| **70,300** | **70,350** | 13,769 | 9,956 | 13,823 | 12,434 |
| **70,350** | **70,400** | 13,781 | 9,969 | 13,837 | 12,446 |
| **70,400** | **70,450** | 13,794 | 9,981 | 13,851 | 12,459 |
| **70,450** | **70,500** | 13,806 | 9,994 | 13,865 | 12,471 |
| **70,500** | **70,550** | 13,819 | 10,006 | 13,879 | 12,484 |
| **70,550** | **70,600** | 13,831 | 10,019 | 13,893 | 12,496 |
| **70,600** | **70,650** | 13,844 | 10,031 | 13,907 | 12,509 |
| **70,650** | **70,700** | 13,856 | 10,044 | 13,921 | 12,521 |
| **70,700** | **70,750** | 13,869 | 10,056 | 13,935 | 12,534 |
| **70,750** | **70,800** | 13,881 | 10,069 | 13,949 | 12,546 |
| **70,800** | **70,850** | 13,894 | 10,081 | 13,963 | 12,559 |
| **70,850** | **70,900** | 13,906 | 10,094 | 13,977 | 12,571 |
| **70,900** | **70,950** | 13,919 | 10,106 | 13,991 | 12,584 |
| **70,950** | **71,000** | 13,931 | 10,119 | 14,005 | 12,596 |

| If line 43 (taxable income) is— | | And you are— | | | |
|---|---|---|---|---|---|
| At least | But less than | Single | Married filing jointly * | Married filing separately | Head of a household |
| | | Your tax is— | | | |
| **71,000** | | | | | |
| **71,000** | **71,050** | 13,944 | 10,131 | 14,019 | 12,609 |
| **71,050** | **71,100** | 13,956 | 10,144 | 14,033 | 12,621 |
| **71,100** | **71,150** | 13,969 | 10,156 | 14,047 | 12,634 |
| **71,150** | **71,200** | 13,981 | 10,169 | 14,061 | 12,646 |
| **71,200** | **71,250** | 13,994 | 10,181 | 14,075 | 12,659 |
| **71,250** | **71,300** | 14,006 | 10,194 | 14,089 | 12,671 |
| **71,300** | **71,350** | 14,019 | 10,206 | 14,103 | 12,684 |
| **71,350** | **71,400** | 14,031 | 10,219 | 14,117 | 12,696 |
| **71,400** | **71,450** | 14,044 | 10,231 | 14,131 | 12,709 |
| **71,450** | **71,500** | 14,056 | 10,244 | 14,145 | 12,721 |
| **71,500** | **71,550** | 14,069 | 10,256 | 14,159 | 12,734 |
| **71,550** | **71,600** | 14,081 | 10,269 | 14,173 | 12,746 |
| **71,600** | **71,650** | 14,094 | 10,281 | 14,187 | 12,759 |
| **71,650** | **71,700** | 14,106 | 10,294 | 14,201 | 12,771 |
| **71,700** | **71,750** | 14,119 | 10,306 | 14,215 | 12,784 |
| **71,750** | **71,800** | 14,131 | 10,319 | 14,229 | 12,796 |
| **71,800** | **71,850** | 14,144 | 10,331 | 14,243 | 12,809 |
| **71,850** | **71,900** | 14,156 | 10,344 | 14,257 | 12,821 |
| **71,900** | **71,950** | 14,169 | 10,356 | 14,271 | 12,834 |
| **71,950** | **72,000** | 14,181 | 10,369 | 14,285 | 12,846 |
| **72,000** | | | | | |
| **72,000** | **72,050** | 14,194 | 10,381 | 14,299 | 12,859 |
| **72,050** | **72,100** | 14,206 | 10,394 | 14,313 | 12,871 |
| **72,100** | **72,150** | 14,219 | 10,406 | 14,327 | 12,884 |
| **72,150** | **72,200** | 14,231 | 10,419 | 14,341 | 12,896 |
| **72,200** | **72,250** | 14,244 | 10,431 | 14,355 | 12,909 |
| **72,250** | **72,300** | 14,256 | 10,444 | 14,369 | 12,921 |
| **72,300** | **72,350** | 14,269 | 10,456 | 14,383 | 12,934 |
| **72,350** | **72,400** | 14,281 | 10,469 | 14,397 | 12,946 |
| **72,400** | **72,450** | 14,294 | 10,481 | 14,411 | 12,959 |
| **72,450** | **72,500** | 14,306 | 10,494 | 14,425 | 12,971 |
| **72,500** | **72,550** | 14,319 | 10,506 | 14,439 | 12,984 |
| **72,550** | **72,600** | 14,331 | 10,519 | 14,453 | 12,996 |
| **72,600** | **72,650** | 14,344 | 10,531 | 14,467 | 13,009 |
| **72,650** | **72,700** | 14,356 | 10,544 | 14,481 | 13,021 |
| **72,700** | **72,750** | 14,369 | 10,556 | 14,495 | 13,034 |
| **72,750** | **72,800** | 14,381 | 10,569 | 14,509 | 13,046 |
| **72,800** | **72,850** | 14,394 | 10,581 | 14,523 | 13,059 |
| **72,850** | **72,900** | 14,406 | 10,594 | 14,537 | 13,071 |
| **72,900** | **72,950** | 14,419 | 10,606 | 14,551 | 13,084 |
| **72,950** | **73,000** | 14,431 | 10,619 | 14,565 | 13,096 |
| **73,000** | | | | | |
| **73,000** | **73,050** | 14,444 | 10,631 | 14,579 | 13,109 |
| **73,050** | **73,100** | 14,456 | 10,644 | 14,593 | 13,121 |
| **73,100** | **73,150** | 14,469 | 10,656 | 14,607 | 13,134 |
| **73,150** | **73,200** | 14,481 | 10,669 | 14,621 | 13,146 |
| **73,200** | **73,250** | 14,494 | 10,681 | 14,635 | 13,159 |
| **73,250** | **73,300** | 14,506 | 10,694 | 14,649 | 13,171 |
| **73,300** | **73,350** | 14,519 | 10,706 | 14,663 | 13,184 |
| **73,350** | **73,400** | 14,531 | 10,719 | 14,677 | 13,196 |
| **73,400** | **73,450** | 14,544 | 10,731 | 14,691 | 13,209 |
| **73,450** | **73,500** | 14,556 | 10,744 | 14,705 | 13,221 |
| **73,500** | **73,550** | 14,569 | 10,756 | 14,719 | 13,234 |
| **73,550** | **73,600** | 14,581 | 10,769 | 14,733 | 13,246 |
| **73,600** | **73,650** | 14,594 | 10,781 | 14,747 | 13,259 |
| **73,650** | **73,700** | 14,606 | 10,794 | 14,761 | 13,271 |
| **73,700** | **73,750** | 14,619 | 10,806 | 14,775 | 13,284 |
| **73,750** | **73,800** | 14,631 | 10,819 | 14,789 | 13,296 |
| **73,800** | **73,850** | 14,644 | 10,831 | 14,803 | 13,309 |
| **73,850** | **73,900** | 14,656 | 10,844 | 14,817 | 13,321 |
| **73,900** | **73,950** | 14,669 | 10,856 | 14,831 | 13,334 |
| **73,950** | **74,000** | 14,681 | 10,869 | 14,845 | 13,346 |

| If line 43 (taxable income) is— | | And you are— | | | |
|---|---|---|---|---|---|
| At least | But less than | Single | Married filing jointly * | Married filing separately | Head of a household |
| | | Your tax is— | | | |
| **74,000** | | | | | |
| **74,000** | **74,050** | 14,694 | 10,881 | 14,859 | 13,359 |
| **74,050** | **74,100** | 14,706 | 10,894 | 14,873 | 13,371 |
| **74,100** | **74,150** | 14,719 | 10,906 | 14,887 | 13,384 |
| **74,150** | **74,200** | 14,731 | 10,919 | 14,901 | 13,396 |
| **74,200** | **74,250** | 14,744 | 10,931 | 14,915 | 13,409 |
| **74,250** | **74,300** | 14,756 | 10,944 | 14,929 | 13,421 |
| **74,300** | **74,350** | 14,769 | 10,956 | 14,943 | 13,434 |
| **74,350** | **74,400** | 14,781 | 10,969 | 14,957 | 13,446 |
| **74,400** | **74,450** | 14,794 | 10,981 | 14,971 | 13,459 |
| **74,450** | **74,500** | 14,806 | 10,994 | 14,985 | 13,471 |
| **74,500** | **74,550** | 14,819 | 11,006 | 14,999 | 13,484 |
| **74,550** | **74,600** | 14,831 | 11,019 | 15,013 | 13,496 |
| **74,600** | **74,650** | 14,844 | 11,031 | 15,027 | 13,509 |
| **74,650** | **74,700** | 14,856 | 11,044 | 15,041 | 13,521 |
| **74,700** | **74,750** | 14,869 | 11,056 | 15,055 | 13,534 |
| **74,750** | **74,800** | 14,881 | 11,069 | 15,069 | 13,546 |
| **74,800** | **74,850** | 14,894 | 11,081 | 15,083 | 13,559 |
| **74,850** | **74,900** | 14,906 | 11,094 | 15,097 | 13,571 |
| **74,900** | **74,950** | 14,919 | 11,106 | 15,111 | 13,584 |
| **74,950** | **75,000** | 14,931 | 11,119 | 15,125 | 13,596 |
| **75,000** | | | | | |
| **75,000** | **75,050** | 14,944 | 11,131 | 15,139 | 13,609 |
| **75,050** | **75,100** | 14,956 | 11,144 | 15,153 | 13,621 |
| **75,100** | **75,150** | 14,969 | 11,156 | 15,167 | 13,634 |
| **75,150** | **75,200** | 14,981 | 11,169 | 15,181 | 13,646 |
| **75,200** | **75,250** | 14,994 | 11,181 | 15,195 | 13,659 |
| **75,250** | **75,300** | 15,006 | 11,194 | 15,209 | 13,671 |
| **75,300** | **75,350** | 15,019 | 11,206 | 15,223 | 13,684 |
| **75,350** | **75,400** | 15,031 | 11,219 | 15,237 | 13,696 |
| **75,400** | **75,450** | 15,044 | 11,231 | 15,251 | 13,709 |
| **75,450** | **75,500** | 15,056 | 11,244 | 15,265 | 13,721 |
| **75,500** | **75,550** | 15,069 | 11,256 | 15,279 | 13,734 |
| **75,550** | **75,600** | 15,081 | 11,269 | 15,293 | 13,746 |
| **75,600** | **75,650** | 15,094 | 11,281 | 15,307 | 13,759 |
| **75,650** | **75,700** | 15,106 | 11,294 | 15,321 | 13,771 |
| **75,700** | **75,750** | 15,119 | 11,306 | 15,335 | 13,784 |
| **75,750** | **75,800** | 15,131 | 11,319 | 15,349 | 13,796 |
| **75,800** | **75,850** | 15,144 | 11,331 | 15,363 | 13,809 |
| **75,850** | **75,900** | 15,156 | 11,344 | 15,377 | 13,821 |
| **75,900** | **75,950** | 15,169 | 11,356 | 15,391 | 13,834 |
| **75,950** | **76,000** | 15,181 | 11,369 | 15,405 | 13,846 |
| **76,000** | | | | | |
| **76,000** | **76,050** | 15,194 | 11,381 | 15,419 | 13,859 |
| **76,050** | **76,100** | 15,206 | 11,394 | 15,433 | 13,871 |
| **76,100** | **76,150** | 15,219 | 11,406 | 15,447 | 13,884 |
| **76,150** | **76,200** | 15,231 | 11,419 | 15,461 | 13,896 |
| **76,200** | **76,250** | 15,244 | 11,431 | 15,475 | 13,909 |
| **76,250** | **76,300** | 15,256 | 11,444 | 15,489 | 13,921 |
| **76,300** | **76,350** | 15,269 | 11,456 | 15,503 | 13,934 |
| **76,350** | **76,400** | 15,281 | 11,469 | 15,517 | 13,946 |
| **76,400** | **76,450** | 15,294 | 11,481 | 15,531 | 13,959 |
| **76,450** | **76,500** | 15,306 | 11,494 | 15,545 | 13,971 |
| **76,500** | **76,550** | 15,319 | 11,506 | 15,559 | 13,984 |
| **76,550** | **76,600** | 15,331 | 11,519 | 15,573 | 13,996 |
| **76,600** | **76,650** | 15,344 | 11,531 | 15,587 | 14,009 |
| **76,650** | **76,700** | 15,356 | 11,544 | 15,601 | 14,021 |
| **76,700** | **76,750** | 15,369 | 11,556 | 15,615 | 14,034 |
| **76,750** | **76,800** | 15,381 | 11,569 | 15,629 | 14,046 |
| **76,800** | **76,850** | 15,394 | 11,581 | 15,643 | 14,059 |
| **76,850** | **76,900** | 15,406 | 11,594 | 15,657 | 14,071 |
| **76,900** | **76,950** | 15,419 | 11,606 | 15,671 | 14,084 |
| **76,950** | **77,000** | 15,431 | 11,619 | 15,685 | 14,096 |

* This column must also be used by a qualifying widow(er).

## SUMMARY

**L01**    Describe the formula for calculating an individual taxpayer's taxes payable or refund and generally explain each formula component.

- Generally, taxpayers are taxed on all income they realize during the year, no matter the source. However, the tax laws allow taxpayers to permanently exclude or defer to a later year certain types of income they realize during the year.

- Income items that taxpayers are allowed to permanently exclude from income are called exclusions. Realized income items that taxpayers are not taxed on until a future period are called deferrals.

- Taxpayers include gross income on their tax returns. Gross income is realized income minus exclusions and deferrals.

- Taxpayers subtract deductions from their gross income to determine their taxable income. Taxpayers are not allowed to reduce income for any deductions unless a specific provision in the tax laws provides for the deduction.

- *For* AGI deductions tend to relate to business activities and certain investment activities. These deductions always reduce taxable income, dollar for dollar. *For* AGI deductions are deductions "above the line," the line being the last line on the front page of the individual tax Form 1040.

- Gross income minus *for* AGI deductions equals adjusted gross income (AGI).

- AGI is an important reference point in the individual tax formula because it is often used in other tax-related calculations, including determining limitations on from AGI deductions.

- *From* AGI deductions are subtracted from AGI to determine taxable income. *From* AGI deductions include itemized deductions, the standard deduction, and exemptions. *From* AGI deductions are referred to as "deductions below the line."

- Taxpayers generally deduct itemized deductions when the amount of the itemized deductions exceeds the standard deduction. The standard deduction varies by filing status and is indexed for inflation. Taxpayers receive additional standard deduction amounts for blindness and old age.

- The standard deduction for taxpayers claimed as a dependent on another's tax return is the greater of (1) $950 or (2) $300 plus the dependent's earned income, not to exceed the normal standard deduction amount.

- Taxpayers are allowed to deduct personal exemptions for themselves and their spouses (if any) and dependency exemptions for those who qualify as their dependents.

- Taxpayers generally calculate the tax on their taxable income by referring to tax tables or tax rate schedules. However, certain types of income such as long-term capital gains and qualifying dividends may be taxed at rates lower than the rates provided in the tax rate schedule.

- Taxpayers may be required to pay the alternative minimum tax (AMT) or self-employment tax in addition to their regular income tax.

- Tax credits reduce taxpayers' tax liability dollar for dollar, while deduction decrease taxable income dollar for dollar.

- Taxpayers prepay taxes during the year through withholdings by employers, estimated tax payments, or a prior year overpayment applied toward the current year tax liability.

- If tax prepayments exceed the taxpayer's total tax after credits, the taxpayer receives a refund. If tax prepayments are less than the total tax after credits, the taxpayer owes additional tax with his or her tax return.

**L02**    Explain the requirements for determining a taxpayer's personal and dependency exemptions.

- In 2010, taxpayers are allowed to deduct $3,650 for each personal and dependency exemption they are entitled to claim.

- Individuals may claim an exemption for themselves and their spouses if they are married and file jointly. They may also claim dependency exemptions for each person who qualifies as their dependent.

- If an individual qualifies as a dependent of another taxpayer, the dependent may not deduct a personal exemption for him- or herself on his or her individual return.
- Taxpayers may claim dependency exemptions for those qualifying as their qualifying child or qualifying relative.
- A child must meet a relationship test, an age test, a residence test, and a support test to qualify as a qualifying child.
- A person may be considered a qualifying relative by meeting a relationship test, a support test, and a gross income test.

Determine a taxpayer's filing status  **LO3**

- Taxpayers may file their tax returns as married filing jointly, married filing separately, qualifying widow or widower (or surviving spouse), head of household, or single.
- Married taxpayers may file a joint return or they may choose to file separately. It is generally more advantageous for tax purposes to file jointly if married. However, for nontax reasons, it may be advantageous to file separately.
- Each spouse is ultimately responsible for paying the tax on a joint return.
- For two years after the year in which one spouse dies, qualifying widows or widowers may file as if they were married filing jointly as long as they (1) remain unmarried and (2) maintain a household for a dependent child (child, stepchild, or adopted child). However, they are not allowed to claim a dependency exemption for the deceased spouse beyond the year of the spouse's death.
- An unmarried taxpayer who is not a qualifying widow or widower may file as head of household if the person either (1) pays more than half the costs of maintaining a household that is, for *more* than half the taxable year, the principal place of abode for a qualifying person (if the qualifying person is a parent, the parent need not reside with the taxpayer). A qualifying person must be a relative of the taxpayer.
- Unmarried taxpayers who do not qualify for head of household status file as single taxpayers.

## KEY TERMS

abandoned spouse (4-19)

adjusted gross income (AGI) (4-6)

all-inclusive income concept (4-2)

alternative minimum tax (AMT) (4-9)

deductions (4-6)

deductions above the line (4-6)

deductions below the line (4-6)

deductions *for* AGI (4-6)

deductions *from* AGI (4-6)

deferral items, deferred income, or deferrals (4-5)

dependency exemptions (4-8)

dependent (4-11)

estimated tax payments (4-10)

excluded income or exclusions (4-5)

exemptions (4-7)

filing status (4-16)

gross income (4-5)

head of household (4-18)

itemized deductions (4-7)

legislative grace (4-6)

married filing jointly (4-16)

married filing separately (4-16)

personal exemptions (4-8)

qualifying child (4-11)

qualifying relative (4-11)

qualifying widow or widower (4-17)

realized income (4-2)

single (4-20)

self-employment taxes (4-9)

standard deduction (4-7)

taxable income (4-2)

tax credits (4-9)

tax rate schedule (4-8)

tax tables (4-8)

withholdings (4-10)

## DISCUSSION QUESTIONS

1. **(LO1)** How are realized income, gross income, and taxable income similar, and how are they different?
2. **(LO1)** Are taxpayers required to include all realized income in gross income? Explain.

3. **(LO1)** All else equal, should taxpayers prefer to exclude income or to defer it? Why?

4. **(LO1)** Compare and contrast *for* and *from* AGI deductions. Why are *for* AGI deductions likely more valuable to taxpayers than *from* AGI deductions?

5. **(LO1)** What is the difference between gross income and adjusted gross income, and what is the difference between adjusted gross income and taxable income?

6. **(LO1)** How do taxpayers determine whether they should deduct their itemized deductions or utilize the standard deduction?

7. **(LO1)** Why are some deductions called "above the line" deductions and others are called "below the line" deductions? What is the "line"?

8. **(LO1)** What is the difference between a tax deduction and a tax credit? Is one more beneficial than the other? Explain.

9. **(LO1)** What types of income are taxed at rates different than the rates provided in tax rate schedules and tax tables?

10. **(LO1)** What types of federal income-based taxes, other than the regular income tax, might taxpayers be required to pay? In general terms, what is the tax base for each of these other taxes on income?

11. **(LO1)** Identify three ways taxpayers can pay their income taxes to the government.

12. **(LO2)** Emily and Tony are recently married college students. Can Emily qualify as her parents' dependent? Explain.

13. **(LO2)** In general terms, what are the differences in the rules for determining who is a qualifying child and who qualifies as a dependent as a qualifying relative? Is it possible for someone to be a qualifying child and a qualifying relative of the same taxpayer? Why or why not?

14. **(LO2)** How do two taxpayers determine who has priority to claim the dependency exemption for a qualifying child of both taxpayers when neither taxpayer is a parent of the child (assume the child does not qualify as a qualifying child of either parent)? How do parents determine who gets to deduct the dependency exemption for a qualifying child of both parents when the parents are divorced or file separate returns?

15. **(LO2)** Isabella provides 30 percent of the support for her father Hastings who lives in an apartment by himself and has no gross income. Is it possible for Isabella to claim a dependency exemption for her father? Explain.

16. **(LO3)** What requirements do the abandoned spouse and qualifying widow or widower have in common?

17. **(LO3)** For tax purposes, why is the married filing jointly tax status generally preferable to the married filing separately filing status? Why might a married taxpayer prefer *not* to file a joint return with the taxpayer's spouse?

18. **(LO3)** What does it mean to say that a married couple filing a joint tax return has joint and several liability for the taxes associated with the return?

## PROBLEMS

19. **(LO1)** Jeremy earned $100,000 in salary and $6,000 in interest income during the year. Jeremy has two qualifying dependent children who live with him. He qualifies to file as head of household and has $17,000 in itemized deductions. Neither of his dependents qualifies for the child tax credit.

   a. Use the 2010 tax rate schedules to determine Jeremy's taxes due.

   b. Assume that in addition to the original facts, Jeremy has qualified dividends of $4,000. What is Jeremy's tax liability including the tax on the dividends (use the tax rate schedules rather than the tax tables)?

c. Assume the original facts except that Jeremy had only $7,000 in itemized deductions. What is Jeremy's total income tax liability (use the tax rate schedules rather than the tax tables)?

20. **(LO1)** David and Lilly Fernandez have determined their tax liability on their joint tax return to be $1,700. They have made prepayments of $1,500 and also have a child tax credit of $1,000. What is the amount of their tax refund or taxes due?

21. **(LO1)** In 2010, Rick, who is single, has been offered a position as a city land-scape consultant. The position pays $125,000 in cash wages. Assume Rick files single and is entitled to one personal exemption. Rick deducts the standard deduction instead of itemized deductions.

    ■ **planning**

a. What is the amount of Rick's after-tax compensation (ignore payroll taxes)?

b. Suppose Rick receives a competing job offer of $120,000 in cash compensation and nontaxable (excluded) benefits worth $4,000. What is the amount of Rick's after-tax compensation for the competing offer? Which job should he take if taxes were the only concern?

22. **(LO1)** Through November 2010, Tex has received gross income of $120,000. For December, Tex is considering whether to accept one more work engagement for the year. Engagement 1 will generate $7,000 of revenue at a cost of $4,000 which is deductible for AGI. In contrast, engagement 2 will generate $7,000 of revenue at a cost of $3,000, which is deductible as an itemized deduction. Tex files a single tax return.

a. Calculate Tex's taxable income assuming he chooses engagement 1 and assuming he chooses engagement 2. Assume he has no itemized deductions other than those generated by engagement 2.

b. Calculate Tex's taxable income assuming he chooses engagement 1 and assuming he chooses engagement 2. Assume he has $4,500 of itemized deductions other than those generated by engagement 2.

c. Calculate Tex's taxable income assuming he chooses engagement 1 and assuming he chooses engagement 2. Assume he has $7,000 of itemized deductions other than those generated by engagement 2.

23. **(LO1)** Matteo, who is single and has no dependents, was planning on spend-ing the weekend repairing his car. On Friday, Matteo's employer called and offered him $500 in overtime pay if he would agree to work over the weekend. Matteo could get his car repaired over the weekend at Autofix for $400. If Matteo works over the weekend, he will have to pay the $400 to have his car repaired but he will earn $500. Assume Matteo pays a tax at a flat rate of 15 percent rate.

    ■ **planning**

a. Strictly considering tax factors, should Matteo work or repair his car if the $400 he must pay to have his car fixed is not deductible?

b. Strictly considering tax factors, should Matteo work or repair his car if the $400 he must pay to have his car fixed is deductible for AGI?

24. **(LO1, LO2)** Rank the following three single taxpayers in order of the magnitude of taxable income for 2010 (from lowest to highest) and explain your results.

| | Ahmed | Baker | Chin |
|---|---|---|---|
| Gross income | $80,000 | $80,000 | $80,000 |
| Deductions *for* AGI | 8,000 | 4,000 | 0 |
| Itemized deductions | 0 | 4,000 | 8,000 |

25. **(LO2)** The Samsons are trying to determine whether they can claim their 22-year-old adopted son, Jason, as a dependent. Jason is currently a full-time student at an out-of-state university. Jason lived in his parents' home for three months of

the year and he was away at school for the rest of the year. He received $9,500 in scholarships this year for his outstanding academic performance and earned $3,900 of income working a part-time job during the year. The Samsons paid a total of $4,000 to support Jason while he was away at college. Jason used the scholarship, the earnings from the part-time job, and the money from the Samsons as his only sources of support.

a. Can the Samsons claim Jason as their dependent?

b. Assume the original facts except that Jason's grandparents, not the Samsons, provided him with the $4,000 worth of support. Can the Samsons (Jason's parents) claim Jason as their dependent? Why or why not?

c. Assume the original facts except substitute Jason's grandparents for his parents. Determine whether Jason's grandparents can claim Jason as a dependent.

d. Assume the original facts except that Jason earned $4,500 while working part-time and used this amount for his support. Can the Samsons claim Jason as their dependent? Why or why not?

26. **(LO2)** John and Tara Smith are married and have lived in the same home for over 20 years. John's uncle Tim, who is 64 years old, has lived with the Smiths since March of this year. Tim is searching for employment but has been unable to find any—his gross income for the year is $2,000. Tim used all $2,000 toward his own support. The Smiths provided the rest of Tim's support by providing him with lodging valued at $5,000 and food valued at $2,200.

a. Are the Smiths able to claim a dependency exemption for Tim?

b. Assume the original facts except that Tim earned $10,000 and used all the funds for his own support. Are the Smiths able to claim Tim as a dependent?

c. Assume the original facts except that Tim is a friend of the family and not John's uncle.

d. Assume the original facts except that Tim is a friend of the family and not John's uncle and Tim lived with the Smiths for the entire year.

27. **(LO2)** Francine's mother Donna and her father Darren separated and divorced in September of this year. Francine lived with both parents until the separation. Francine does *not* provide more than half of her own support. Francine is 15 years old at the end of the year.

a. Is Francine a qualifying child to Donna?

b. Is Francine a qualifying child to Darren?

c. Assume Francine spends more time living with Darren than Donna after the separation. Who may claim Francine as a dependency exemption for tax purposes?

d. Assume Francine spends an equal number of days with her mother and her father and that Donna has AGI of $52,000 and Darren has AGI of $50,000. Who may claim a dependency exemption for Francine?

28. **(LO2)** By the end of 2010, Jamel and Jennifer have been married 30 years and have filed a joint return every year of their marriage. Their three daughters, Jade, Lindsay, and Abbi, are ages 12, 17, and 22 respectively and all live at home. None of the daughters provides more than half of her own support. Abbi is a full-time student at a local university and does not have any gross income.

a. How many personal and dependency exemptions are Jamel and Jennifer allowed to claim?

b. Assume the original facts except that Abbi is married. She and her husband live with Jamel and Jennifer while attending school and they file a joint return. Abbi and her husband reported a $1,000 tax liability on their 2010

tax return. If all parties are willing, can Jamel and Jennifer claim Abbi as a dependent on their 2010 tax return? Why or why not?

c. Assume the same facts as part b., except that Abbi and her husband report a $0 tax liability on their 2010 joint tax return. Also, if the couple had filed separately, Abbi would have not had a tax liability on her return but her husband would owe $250 of tax on his separate return. Can Jamel and Jennifer claim Abbi as a dependent on their 2010 tax return? Why or why not?

d. Assume the original facts except that Abbi is married. Abbi files a separate tax return for 2010. Abbi's husband files a separate tax return and owes $250 in taxes. Can Jamel and Jennifer claim Abbi as a dependent in 2010?

29. **(LO2)** Dean Kastner is 78 years old and lives by himself in an apartment in Chicago. Dean's gross income for the year is $2,500. Dean's support is provided as follows: Himself (5 percent), his daughters Camille (25 percent) and Rachel (30 percent), his son Zander (5 percent), his friend Frankie (15 percent), and his niece Sharon (20 percent).

a. Absent a multiple support agreement, of the parties mentioned in the problem, who may claim a dependency exemption for Dean as a qualifying relative?

b. Under a multiple support agreement, who is eligible to claim a dependency exemption for Dean as a qualifying relative? Explain.

30. **(LO2)** Mel and Cindy Gibson's 12-year-old daughter Rachel was abducted on her way home from school on March 15, 2010. Police reports indicated that a stranger had physically dragged Rachel into a waiting car and sped away. Everyone hoped that the kidnapper and Rachel would be located quickly. However, as of the end of the year, Rachel was still missing. The police were still pursuing several promising leads and had every reason to believe that Rachel was still alive. In 2011, Rachel was returned safely to her parents.

■ research

a. Are the Gibsons allowed to claim an exemption deduction for Rachel in 2010 even though she only lived in the Gibson's home for two-and-one-half months? Explain and cite your authority.

b. Assume the original facts except that Rachel is unrelated to the Gibsons but she has been living with them since January 2005. The Gibsons have claimed a dependency exemption for Rachel for the years 2005 through 2009. Are the Gibsons allowed to claim a dependency exemption for Rachel in 2010? Explain and cite your authority.

31. **(LO2)** Bob Ryan filed his 2010 tax return and claimed a dependency exemption for his 16-year-old son Dylan. Both Bob and Dylan are citizens and residents of the United States. Dylan meets all the necessary requirements to be considered a qualifying child; however, when Bob filed the tax return he didn't know Dylan's Social Security number and, therefore, didn't include an identifying number for his son on the tax return. Instead, Bob submitted an affidavit with his tax return stating he had requested Dylan's Social Security number from Dylan's birth state. Is Bob allowed to claim a dependency exemption for Dylan without including Dylan's identifying number on the return?

■ research

32. **(LO2, LO3)** Kimberly is divorced and the custodial parent of 5-year-old twins, Bailey and Cameron. All three live with Kimberly's parents, who pay all the costs of maintaining the household (such as mortgage, property taxes, and food). Kimberly pays for and the children's clothing, entertainment, and health insurance costs. These costs comprised only a small part of the total costs of maintaining the household.

a. Determine the appropriate filing status for Kimberly.

b. What if Kimberly lived in her own home and provided all the costs of maintaining the household?

33. **(LO3)** Juan and Bonita are married and have two dependent children living at home. This year, Juan is killed in an avalanche while skiing.

    a. What is Bonita's filing status this year?

    b. Assuming Bonita doesn't remarry and still has two dependent children living at home, what will her filing status be next year?

    c. Assuming Bonita doesn't remarry and doesn't have any dependents next year, what will her filing status be next year?

34. **(LO3)** Gary and Lakesha were married on December 31 last year. They are now preparing their taxes for the April 15 deadline and are unsure of their filing status.

    a. What filing status options do Gary and Lakesha have for last year?

    b. Assume instead that Gary and Lakesha were married on January 1 of this year. What is their filing status for last year (neither has been married before and neither had any dependents last year)?

35. **(LO3)** Elroy, who is single, has taken over the care of his mother Irene in her old age. Elroy pays the bills relating to Irene's home. He also buys all her groceries and provides the rest of her support. Irene has no gross income.

    a. What is Elroy's filing status?

    b. Assume the original facts except that Elroy has taken over the care of his grandmother, Renae, instead of his mother. What is Elroy's filing status?

    c. Assume the original facts except that Elroy's mother, Irene, lives with him and that she receives an annual $4,000 taxable distribution from her retirement account. Elroy still pays all the costs to maintain the household. What is his filing status?

36. **(LO3)** Kano and his wife, Hoshi, have been married for 10 years and have two children under the age of 12. The couple has been living apart for the last two years and both children live with Kano. Kano has provided all the means necessary to support himself and his children. Kano and Hoshi do not file a joint return.

    a. What is Kano's filing status?

    b. Assume the original facts except that Kano and Hoshi separated in May of the current year. What is Kano's filing status?

    c. Assume the original facts except that Kano and Hoshi separated in November of this year. What is Kano's filing status?

    d. Assume the original facts except that Kano's parents, not Kano, paid more than half of the cost of maintaining the home in which Kano and his children live. What is Kano's filing status?

37. **(LO3)** Horatio and Kelly were divorced at the end of 2009. Neither Horatio nor Kelly remarried during 2010 and Horatio moved out of state. Determine the filing status of Horatio and Kelly for 2010 in the following independent situations:

    a. Horatio and Kelly did not have any children and neither reported any dependents in 2010.

    b. Horatio and Kelly had one child, Amy, who turned 10 years of age in 2010. Amy lived with Kelly for all of 2010 and kelly provided all of her support.

    c. Assume the same facts as in b. But the divorce decree allocated the exemption for Amy to Horatio even though Amy did not reside with him at all during 2010.

    d. Assume the original facts except that during 2010 Madison, a 17-year-old friend of the family, lived with (for the entire year) and was fully supported by Kelly.

    e. Assume the original facts except that during 2010 Kelly's mother, Janet, lived with Kelly. For 2010, Kelly was able to claim a dependency exemption for her mother under a multiple support agreement.

38. **(LO2, LO3)** In each of the following *independent* situations, determine the tax-payer's filing status and the number of personal and dependency exemptions the taxpayer is allowed to claim.

    a. Frank is single and supports his 17-year-old brother, Bill. Bill earned $3,000 and did not live with Frank.

    b. Geneva and her spouse reside with their son, Steve, who is a 20-year-old undergraduate student at State University. Steve earned $13,100 at a part-time summer job, but he deposited this money in a savings account for graduate school. Geneva paid all of the $12,000 cost of supporting Steve.

    c. Hamish's spouse died last year and Hamish has not remarried. Hamish supports his father, Reggie, age 78, who lives in a nursing home and had interest income this year of $2,500.

    d. Irene is married but has not seen her spouse since February. She supports her spouse's 18-year-old child, Dolores, who lives with Irene. Dolores earned $4,500 this year.

39. **(LO2, LO3)** In each of the following *independent* cases, determine the taxpayer's filing status and the number of personal and dependency exemptions the taxpayer is allowed to claim.

    a. Alexandra is a blind widow who provides a home for her 18-year-old nephew, Newt. Newt's parents are dead and so Newt supports himself. Newt's gross income is $5,000.

    b. Bharati supports and maintains a home for her daughter, Daru, and son-in-law, Sam. Sam earned $15,000 and filed a joint return with Daru, who had no income.

    c. Charlie intended to file a joint return with his spouse, Sally. However, Sally died in December. Charlie has not remarried.

    d. Deshi cannot convince his spouse to consent to signing a joint return. The couple has not separated.

    e. Edith and her spouse support their 35-year-old son, Slim. Slim is a full-time college student who earned $5,500 over the summer in part-time work.

40. **(LO3)** Jasper and Crewella Dahvill were married in year 0. They filed joint tax returns in years 1 and 2. In year 3, their relationship was strained and Jasper insisted on filing a separate tax return. In year 4, the couple divorced. Both Jasper and Crewella filed single tax returns in year 4. In year 5, the IRS audited the couple's joint year 2 tax return and each spouse's separate year 3 tax returns. The IRS determined that the year 2 joint return and Crewella's separate year 3 tax return understated Crewella's self-employment income causing the joint return year 2 tax liability to be understated by $4,000 and Crewella's year 3 separate return tax liability to be understated by $6,000. The IRS also assessed penalties and interest on both of these tax returns. Try as it might, the IRS has not been able to locate Crewella, but they have been able to find Jasper.

    a. What amount of tax can the IRS require Jasper to pay for the Dahvill's year 2 joint return? Explain.

    b. What amount of tax can the IRS require Jasper to pay for Crewella's year 3 separate tax return? Explain.

41. **(LO3)** Janice Traylor is single. She has an 18-year-old son named Marty. Marty is Janice's only child. Marty has lived with Janice his entire life. However, Marty recently joined the Marines and was sent on a special assignment to Australia. During 2010, Marty spent nine months in Australia. Marty was extremely homesick while in Australia, since he had never lived away from home. However, Marty knew this assignment was only temporary, and he couldn't wait to

come home and find his room just the way he left it. Janice has always filed as head of household, and Marty has always been considered a qualifying child (and he continues to meet all the tests with the possible exception of the residence test due to his stay in Australia). However, this year Janice is unsure whether she qualifies as head of household due to Marty's nine-month absence during the year. Janice has come to you for advice on whether she qualifies for head of household filing status in 2010. What do you tell her?

42. **(LO3)** Doug Jones timely submitted his 2010 tax return and elected married filing jointly status with his wife, Darlene. Doug and Darlene did not request an extension for their 2010 tax return. Doug and Darlene owed and paid the IRS $124,000 for their 2010 tax year. Two years later, Doug amended his return and claimed married filing separate status. By changing his filing status, Doug sought a refund for an overpayment for the tax year 2010 (he paid more tax in the original joint return than he owed on a separate return). Is Doug allowed to change his filing status for the 2010 tax year and receive a tax refund with his amended return?

## COMPREHENSIVE PROBLEMS

43. Marc and Michelle are married and earned salaries this year (2010) of $64,000 and $12,000, respectively. In addition to their salaries, they received interest of $350 from municipal bonds and $500 from corporate bonds. Marc and Michelle also paid $2,500 of qualifying moving expenses, and Marc paid alimony to a prior spouse in the amount of $1,500. Marc and Michelle have a 10-year-old son, Matthew, who lived with them throughout the entire year. Thus, Marc and Michelle are allowed to claim a $1,000 child tax credit for Matthew. Marc and Michelle paid $6,000 of expenditures that qualify as itemized deductions and they had a total of $5,500 in federal income taxes withheld from their paychecks during the course of the year.

   a. What is Marc and Michelle's gross income?

   b. What is Marc and Michelle's adjusted gross income?

   c. What is the total amount of Marc and Michelle's deductions *from* AGI?

   d. What is Marc and Michelle's taxable income?

   e. What is Marc and Michelle's taxes payable or refund due for the year? (Use the tax rate schedules.)

44. Demarco and Janine Jackson have been married for 20 years and have four children who qualify as their dependents. Their income from all sources this year (2010) totaled $200,000 and included a gain from the sale of their home, which they purchased a few years ago for $200,000 and sold this year for $250,000. The gain on the sale qualified for the exclusion from the sale of a principal residence. The Jacksons incurred $16,500 of itemized deductions.

   a. What is the Jackson's taxable income?

   b. What would their taxable income be if their itemized deductions totaled $6,000 instead of $16,500?

   c. What would their taxable income be if they had $0 itemized deductions and $6,000 of for AGI deductions?

   d. Assume the original facts except that they also incurred a loss of $5,000 on the sale of some of their investment assets. What effect does the $5,000 loss have on their *taxable income?*

e. Assume the original facts except that the Jacksons owned investments that appreciated by $10,000 during the year. The Jacksons believe the investments will continue to appreciate, so they did not sell the investments during this year. What is the Jackson's taxable income?

45. Camille Sikorski was divorced last year. She currently owns and provides a home for her 15-year-old daughter, Kaly, and 18-year-old son, Parker. Both children lived in Camille's home for the entire year, and Camille paid for all the costs of maintaining the home. She received a salary of $105,000 and contributed $6,000 of it to a qualified retirement account. She also received $10,000 of alimony from her former husband. Finally, Camille paid $5,000 of expenditures that qualified as itemized deductions. (The current year is 2010.)

a. What is Camille's taxable income?

b. What would Camille's taxable income be if she incurred $14,000 of itemized deductions instead of $5,000?

c. Assume the original facts except that Camille's daughter, Kaly, is 25 years old and a full-time student. Kaly's gross income for the year was $5,000. Kaly provided $3,000 of her own support, and Camille provided $5,000 of support. What is Camille's taxable income?

46. In 2010, Tiffany is unmarried and has a 15-year-old qualifying child. Tiffany has determined her tax liability to be $3,525, and her employer has withheld $1,500 of federal taxes from her paycheck. Tiffany is allowed to claim a $1,000 child credit for her qualifying child. What amount of taxes will Tiffany owe (or what amount will she receive as a refund) when she files her tax return?

# Gross Income and Exclusions

**Upon completing this chapter, you should be able to:**

**LO 1** Apply the concept of realization and explain when taxpayers recognize gross income.

■

**LO 2** Understand the distinctions between the various sources of income, including income from services and property.

■

**LO 3** Apply basic income exclusion provisions to compute gross income.

T he past year was a year of change for Courtney Wilson. After her divorce from Al Wilson, Courtney assumed sole custody of their 10-year-old son, Deron, and their 20-year-old daughter, Ellen. Looking for a fresh start in January, Courtney quit her job as an architect in Cincinnati, Ohio, and moved to Kansas City, Missouri. Courtney wanted to pursue several promising job opportunities in Kansas City and be close to Ellen while she attends the University of Missouri-Kansas City. Courtney's 70-year-old mother "Gram" also lives in Kansas City and is in relatively good health. However, Courtney's father, "Gramps," passed away last December from cancer. At Courtney's insistence, Gram moved in with Courtney and Deron in April.

In late April, Courtney broke her wrist in a mountain biking accident and was unable to work for two weeks. Thankfully, Courtney's disability insurance paid her for lost wages during her time away from work.

While her personal life has been in disarray, Courtney's financial prospects have been improving. Shortly after arriving in Kansas City, Courtney was fortunate to land a job as an architect with Earth Wise Design (EWD). EWD provided Courtney the following compensation and benefits this year:

- Salary $98,000.
- Medical and life insurance premiums.
- Contribution of 10 percent of her base salary to her qualified retirement account.
- No-interest loan with a promise to forgive the loan principal over time if she continues her employment with EWD.
- Performance bonus for her first year on the job.

| Storyline Summary | |
|---|---|
| *Taxpayers:* | Courtney Wilson, age 40 Courtney's mother, Dorothy "Gram" Weiss, age 70 |
| *Family description:* | Courtney is divorced with a son, Deron, age 10, and a daughter, Ellen, age 20. Gram is currently residing with Courtney. |
| *Location:* | Kansas City, Missouri |
| *Employment status:* | Courtney works as an architect for EWD. Her salary is $98,000. Gram is unemployed. |
| *Current situation:* | Determining what income is taxable |

Courtney also received other payments unrelated to her employment with EWD as follows:

- Alimony from her ex-husband Al.
- Child support from her ex-husband Al.
- Consulting income.
- Dividend, interest, and rental income.
- Refund of state taxes she paid last year.

Before Gram moved in with Courtney, she lived alone in an apartment in Kansas City. After Gramps died, Gram was dependent on her Social Security benefits. In March, Gram's landlord agreed to allow Gram to babysit his infant son in lieu of paying rent. In early April, Gram received the proceeds from Gramp's life insurance policy. She invested part of the proceeds in an annuity contract that will pay Gram a fixed amount per year. Gram also invested some of the proceeds in the stock of a local corporation. She used the rest of the life insurance proceeds to purchase a certificate of deposit and start a savings account. Gram also spent some of her spare time completing sweepstakes entries. Her hard work paid off when she won a WaveRunner in a sweepstakes contest.

Until their divorce, Courtney's husband always prepared their income tax return. Since EWD hired her, Courtney has become anxious about her income tax and whether her withholding will be sufficient to cover her tax bill. Courtney is also worried about Gram's tax situation, because Gram did not make any tax payments this year. ■

In the previous chapter, we presented an overview of individual taxation. In this chapter, we begin to dig deeper into the tax formula to determine a taxpayer's gross income. We focus on whether income is included or excluded from a taxpayer's gross income rather than the rate at which the income is taxed. In the next two chapters, we continue to work through the individual tax formula to determine the tax liabilities for Courtney and Gram. Chapter 6 describes deductible expenses to determine adjusted gross income and taxable income, and Chapter 7 addresses issues associated with calculating the tax liability, tax credits, and tax return filing concerns.

## LO1 REALIZATION AND RECOGNITION OF INCOME

As we learned in the previous chapter, **gross income** is income that taxpayers realize and recognize and report on their tax returns for the year. In the individual tax formula, gross income is computed as income *realized* during the year, minus realized income that is either **excluded** from taxation or **deferred** until a subsequent year. In the previous chapter, we discussed gross income in general terms. In this chapter we

explain the requirements for taxpayers to recognize gross income, and we discuss the most common sources of gross income.

## What Is Included in Gross Income?

The definition of gross income for tax purposes is provided in §61(a) as follows:

> GENERAL DEFINITION.—Except as otherwise provided in this subtitle, gross income means all income *from whatever source derived* (emphasis added).

In addition to providing this **all-inclusive definition of income,** §61 includes a list of examples of gross income such as compensation for services, business income, rents, royalties, interest, and dividends. However, it is clear that unless a tax provision says otherwise, gross income includes *all* income. Thus, gross income is *broadly* defined. Reg. §1.61-(a) provides further insight into the definition of gross income as follows:

> Gross income means all income from whatever source derived, unless excluded by law. Gross income includes income realized in any form, whether in money, property, or services.

Based on §61(a), Reg. §1.61-(a), and various judicial rulings, taxpayers *recognize* gross income when (1) they receive an economic benefit, (2) they realize the income, *and* (3) no tax provision allows them to exclude or defer the income from gross income for that year.[1] Let's address each of these three requirements for recognizing gross income.

**Economic Benefit**   Taxpayers must receive an economic benefit to have gross income. Thus, when a taxpayer borrows money, the borrowed funds do *not* represent gross income because the increase in the taxpayer's assets from receiving the borrowed funds is completely offset by the liability the taxpayer is required to pay from borrowing the funds.

**Realization Principle**   As indicated in Reg. §1.61-(a), the tax definition of income adopts the **realization principle.** Under this principle, income is realized when (1) a taxpayer engages in a transaction with another party, and (2) the transaction results in a measurable change in property rights. In other words, assets or services are exchanged for cash, claims to cash, or other assets with determinable value.

The concept of realization for tax purposes closely parallels the concept of realization for financial accounting purposes. A transaction has the benefit of reducing the uncertainty associated with determining the *amount* of income because a change in rights can typically be traced to a specific moment in time and is generally accompanied by legal documentation.

---

**Example 5-1**

In April, Gram used part of the life insurance proceeds she received from Gramps's death to purchase 50 shares in Acme Corporation for $30 per share. From April to the end of December, the value of the shares fluctuated between $40 and $25, but on December 31, the shares were worth $35. If Gram does *not* sell the shares, how much income from her stockholdings in Acme Corporation does she *realize for* the year?

**Answer:** $0. Unless Gram sells the stock, she does not enter into a transaction resulting in a measurable change of property rights with a second party. Thus, she does not realize income even though she experienced an economic benefit from the appreciation of the stock from $30 per share to $35 per share.

---

[1]For tax purposes it matters not whether income is obtained through legal or illegal activities.

Adopting the realization principle for defining gross income provides two major advantages. First, because parties to the transaction must agree to the value of the exchanged property rights, the transaction allows the income to be measured objectively. Second, the transaction generally provides the taxpayer with the **wherewithal to pay** taxes. That is, the transaction itself provides the taxpayer with the funds to pay taxes on income generated by the transaction. Thus, it reduces the possibility that the taxpayer will be required to sell other assets to pay the taxes on the income from the transaction.

**Recognition**  Taxpayers who realize an economic benefit must include the benefit in gross income unless a specific provision of the tax code says otherwise. That is, taxpayers are generally required to *recognize* all realized income by reporting it as gross income on their tax returns. However, as we describe later in this chapter, through exclusions Congress allows taxpayers to permanently exclude certain types of income from gross income and through deferrals they allow taxpayers to defer certain types of income from gross income until a subsequent year. Thus, it is important to distinguish between realized and recognized income.

### Other Income Concepts

The tax laws, administrative authority, and judicial rulings have established several other concepts important for determining an individual's gross income.

**Form of Receipt**  A common misperception is that taxpayers must receive cash to realize and recognize gross income. However, Reg. §1.61-(a) indicates that taxpayers realize income whether they receive money, property, *or* services in a transaction. For example, **barter clubs** facilitate the exchange of rights to goods and services between members, many of whom have the mistaken belief that they need not recognize income on the exchanges. However, when members exchange property, they realize and recognize income at the market price, the amount that outsiders are willing to pay for the goods or services. Also, other taxpayers who exchange or trade goods or services with each other must recognize the value of the goods or services as income, even when they do not receive any cash. Indeed, taxpayers have the legal and ethical responsibility to report realized income no matter the form of its receipt or whether the IRS knows the taxpayer received the income.

---

**Example 5-2**

During March, Gram paid no rent to her neighbor (also her landlord). Although the neighbor typically charges $350 per month for rent, he allowed Gram to live rent free in exchange for babysitting his infant son. What income must Gram and Gram's neighbor realize and recognize on this exchange?

**Answer:** $350. Gram and the neighbor each must recognize $350 of income for March. The neighbor recognizes $350 of rental receipts because this is the value of the babysitting services the neighbor received in lieu of a cash payment for rent from Gram (an economic benefit the neighbor realized through the exchange). Gram recognizes $350 of babysitting income, because this is the value of the services provided to her neighbor (an economic benefit was realized because Gram was not required to pay rent).

---

**Return of Capital Principle**  When taxpayers sell assets, they must determine the extent to which they include the sale proceeds in gross income. Initially, the IRS was convinced that Congress's all-inclusive definition of income required taxpayers to include *all* sale proceeds in gross income. Taxpayers, on the other hand, argued that a portion of proceeds from a sale represented a return of the cost or capital investment in the underlying property (called **tax basis**). The courts determined that when receiving

a payment for property, taxpayers are allowed to recover the cost of the property tax free. Consequently, when taxpayers sell property, they are allowed to reduce the sale proceeds by their unrecovered investment in the property to determine the realized gain from the sale.[2] When the tax basis exceeds the sale proceeds, the **return of capital** principle generally applies to the extent of the sale proceeds. The excess of basis over sale proceeds is generally not considered to be a return of capital, but rather a loss that is deductible only if specifically authorized by a specific provision of the tax code. Below, we revisit the return of capital principle when we discuss asset dispositions.

The return of capital principle gets complicated when taxpayers sell assets and collect the sale proceeds over several periods. In these cases, the principle is usually modified by law to provide that the return of capital occurs evenly (pro rata) over the collection period. We discuss this issue in more detail later in this chapter when we discuss the taxation of annuities.

**Recovery of Amounts Previously Deducted**   A refund is not typically included in gross income because it usually represents a return of capital. For example, a refund of $1,000 on an auto purchased for $12,000 simply reduces the net cost of the vehicle to $11,000. Likewise, a $200 refund of a $700 business expense is not included in gross income but instead reduces the net expense to $500. However, if the refund is made for an expenditure deducted in a *previous* year, then under the **tax benefit rule** the refund is included in gross income to the extent that the prior deduction produced a tax benefit.[3] For example, suppose an individual paid a $1,000 expense claimed as an itemized deduction in 2010, but $250 of the expense was subsequently reimbursed in 2011. The $250 would *not* be included in income in 2011 *unless* the individual itemized deductions in 2010. Without electing to itemize deductions, the expense could not produce any tax benefit.

The application of the tax benefit rule is more complex for individuals who itemize deductions. An itemized deduction only produces a tax benefit to the extent that total itemized deductions exceed the standard deduction. For example, suppose that an individual's total itemized deductions exceeded the standard deduction by $100. A refund of $150 of itemized deductions would cause the individual's itemized deductions to fall $50 beneath the standard deduction. If the refund occurred in the same year as the expense, the individual would have elected the standard deduction, and the refund would have only caused taxable income to decline by $100 (the difference between claiming the standard deduction and the total itemized deductions that would have been claimed in the absence of any refund). If the refund occurs the year after the deduction is claimed, then only $100 of the $150 refund would be included in gross income under the tax benefit rule. The $100 is added to taxable income in the year of the refund because this is the increment in taxable income that would have resulted if the refund was issued in the year the itemized deduction was claimed.

---

**Example 5-3**

In 2009 Courtney paid $3,500 in Ohio state income taxes, and she included this payment with her other itemized deductions when she filed her federal income tax return in March of 2010. Courtney filed her 2009 federal return as a head of household and claimed $15,500 of itemized deductions. She also filed an Ohio state income tax return in March of 2010 and discovered she only owed $3,080 in Ohio income tax for 2009. Hence, Courtney received a $420 refund of her Ohio income tax in June of 2010. How much of the $420 refund, if any, is Courtney required to include in her gross income in 2010? The answer depends upon the standard deduction for 2009. Help Courtney apply the tax benefit rule (the standard deduction for head of household filling status in 2009 was $8,350).

*(continued on page 5-6...)*

---

[2]§1001(a).
[3]§111.

**Answer:** All $420. Courtney is required to include the entire refund in her 2010 gross income because her itemized deduction for the $420 of state income taxes that she overpaid last year reduced her taxable income by $420. Accordingly, because she received a tax benefit (deduction) for the entire $420 overpayment, she must include it all in gross income in 2010. See the following for the calculation of the amount of tax benefit Courtney received from the $420 overpayment of taxes in 2009.

| Deduction | Amount | Explanation |
|---|---|---|
| (1) Itemized deduction | $15,500 | |
| (2) Standard deduction | 8,350 | Head of household filing status. |
| (3) Reduction in taxable income | 15,500 | Greater of (1) and (2). |
| (4) Itemized deductions adjusted for the $420 refund | 15,080 | (1) − $420. |
| (5) Reduction in taxable income after adjustment for the $420 refund | 15,080 | Greater of (2) and (4). |
| Tax benefit due to prior deduction or $420 refund | $  420 | (3) − (5). |

**What if:** Let's consider *alternative* fact patterns provided in Scenarios A and B to further illustrate the application of the tax benefit rule.

**Scenario A:** In 2009 Courtney's itemized deductions, including $3,500 in state taxes, were $5,500.

**Scenario B:** In 2009 Courtney's itemized deductions, including $3,500 in state taxes, were $8,600.

How much of the $420 refund would Courtney include in her 2010 gross income in Scenarios A and B?

**Answer Scenario A:** $0. As computed below, Courtney received $0 tax benefit from the $420 tax overpayment in 2009, so she need not include any of the refund in her gross income.

**Answer Scenario B:** $250. As computed below, Courtney received a $250 tax benefit (reduction in taxable income) from the $420 state tax overpayment in 2009, so she must include $250 of the refund in her 2010 gross income.

| Deduction | Scenario A Amount | Scenario B Amount | Explanation |
|---|---|---|---|
| (1) Itemized deductions | $5,500 | $8,600 | |
| (2) 2009 standard deduction | 8,350 | 8,350 | Head of household filing status. |
| (3) Reduction in taxable income | 8,350 | 8,600 | Greater of (1) and (2). |
| (4) Itemized deductions adjusted for the $420 refund | 5,080 | 8,180 | (1) − $420. |
| (5) Reduction in taxable income adjusted for the $420 refund | 8,350 | 8,350 | Greater of (2) and (4). |
| Tax benefit due to prior deduction of $420 refund | $  0 | $  250 | (3) − (5). |

## When Do Taxpayers Recognize Income?

Individual taxpayers generally file tax returns reporting their taxable income for a calendar-year period, whereas corporations often use a fiscal year-end. In either case, the taxpayer's method of accounting generally determines the year in which realized income is recognized and included in gross income.

**Accounting Methods**   Most large corporations use the accrual method of accounting. Under the **accrual method,** income is generally recognized when earned,

and expenses are generally deducted in the period when liabilities are incurred. In contrast, most individuals use the **cash method** as their overall method of accounting.[4] Under the cash method, taxpayers recognize income in the period they receive it (in the form of cash, property, or services), rather than when they actually earn it. Likewise, cash-method taxpayers claim deductions when they make expenditures, rather than when they incur liabilities. The cash method greatly simplifies the computation of income for the overwhelming majority of individuals, many of whom have neither the time nor the training to apply the accrual method. Another advantage of the cash method is that taxpayers may have some control over when income is received and expenses are paid. Because of this control, taxpayers can more easily use the timing tax planning strategy (described in Chapter 3) to lower the present value of their tax bill.

**Constructive Receipt**   Taxpayers using the cash method of accounting may try to shift income from the current year to the next year when they receive payments near year-end. For instance, taxpayers may merely delay cashing a check or avoid picking up a compensation payment until after year-end. The courts responded to this ploy by devising the **constructive receipt doctrine.**[5] The constructive receipt doctrine states that a taxpayer must realize and recognize income when it is actually or *constructively* received. Constructive receipt is deemed to occur when the income has been credited to the taxpayer's account or when the income is unconditionally available to the taxpayer, the taxpayer is aware of the income's availability, and there are no restrictions on the taxpayer's control over the income.

> ### THE KEY FACTS
> **Income Recognition**
>
> ■ Cash-method taxpayers recognize income when it is received.
>
> ■ Income is realized regardless of whether payments are received in money, property, *or* services.
>
> ■ Income is taxed in the period in which a cash-method taxpayer has a right to receive payment without substantial restrictions.

### Example 5-4

Courtney is a cash-method taxpayer. Based on her outstanding performance, Courtney earned a $4,800 year-end bonus. On December 28, Courtney's supervisor told her that her bonus was issued as a separate check and that Courtney could pick up the check in the accounting office anytime. Courtney did not pick up the check until January 2 of next year, and she did not cash it until late January. When does Courtney realize and recognize the $4,800 income?

**Answer:** On December 28 of the current year. Courtney *constructively* received the check this year because it was unconditionally available to her on December 28, she was aware of the check's availability, and there were no restrictions on her control over the check. Courtney must include the $4,800 bonus in gross income this year, even though she did not actually receive the funds until late January of next year.[6]

## Who Recognizes the Income?

In addition to determining when taxpayers realize and recognize income, it is important to consider *who* (which taxpayer) recognizes the income. This question often arises when taxpayers attempt to shift income to other related taxpayers through the income-shifting strategy. For example, a father (with a high marginal income tax rate) might wish to assign his paycheck to his baby daughter (with a low marginal income tax rate) to minimize their collective tax burden.

---

[4]Taxpayers involved in a business may use the accrual or hybrid overall method of accounting. We discuss these methods in Chapter 8.

[5]Justice Holmes summarized this doctrine as follows: "The income that is subject to a man's unfettered command and that he is free to enjoy at his own option may be taxed to him as his income, whether he sees fit to enjoy it or not." *Corliss v. Bowers,* 281 US 378 (1930).

[6]Note also that Courtney's employer would include her bonus on Courtney's W-2 for the year in which it issued the check.

**Assignment of Income**    The courts developed the **assignment of income doctrine** to prevent taxpayers from arbitrarily transferring the taxation on their income to others. In essence, the assignment of income doctrine holds that the taxpayer who earns income from services must recognize the income. Likewise, income from property, such as dividends and interest, is taxable to the person who actually owns the income-producing property.[7] For example, interest income from a bond is taxable to the person who owns the bond during the time the interest income accrues. Thus, to shift income from property to another person, a taxpayer must also transfer the *ownership* in the property to the other person.

## Example 5-5

*What if:* Courtney would like to begin saving for Deron's college tuition. If Courtney were to direct EWD to deposit part of her salary in Deron's bank account, who would pay tax on the salary income?

**Answer:** Courtney would be taxed on her entire salary as income because she earned the income.[8] The payment to Deron would be treated as a gift and would not be taxable to him (gifts are excluded from the recipient's income as discussed later in the chapter).

*What if:* Suppose that Courtney wanted to shift her rental income to Deron. What would Courtney need to do to ensure that her rental income is taxed to Deron?

**Answer:** Courtney would have to transfer her ownership in the rental property to Deron in order for Deron to be taxed on the rental income.[9]

**Community Property Systems**    The state laws of nine states (Arizona, California, Idaho, Louisiana, Nevada, New Mexico, Texas, Washington, and Wisconsin) implement **community property systems.** Under community property systems, the income earned from services by one spouse is treated as though it was earned equally by both spouses. Also, property acquired by either spouse during the marriage is usually community property and is treated as though it is owned equally by each spouse. Property that a spouse brings into a marriage is treated as that spouse's separate property. For federal income tax purposes, the community property system has the following consequences:

- Half of the income earned from the services of one spouse is included in the gross income of the other spouse. In contrast, in common law states, all of the income earned by one spouse is included in the gross income of the spouse who earned it.
- Half of the income from property held as community property by the married couple is included in the gross income of each spouse.
- In all common law states and in five community property states (Arizona, California, Nevada, New Mexico, and Washington), all of the income from property owned separately by one spouse is included in that spouse's gross income.
- In Texas, Louisiana, Wisconsin, and Idaho, half of the income from property owned separately by one spouse is included in the gross income of each spouse.

---

[7]This rule of thumb is also referred to as the "fruit and the tree" doctrine because of the analogy to fruit belonging the tree upon which it was grown. See *Lucas v. Earl* (1930) 281 US 111 and *Helvering v. Horst* (1940) 311 US 112.

[8]Note also, that EWD has the responsibility of issuing a W-2 to the taxpayer who provided the services—Courtney in this case.

[9]As explained in Chapter 7, the tax savings from such a transfer would be mitigated in the calculation of Deron's tax by the so-called "kiddie" tax.

**Example 5-6**

In the year of their divorce, Courtney and Al Wilson lived in Ohio, a common law state. The divorce was finalized on October 1 of that year, and up to that date Al had earned $90,000 of annual salary and Courtney had earned $60,000. How much of the income earned by Al and by Courtney in the year of the divorce did Al report on his individual tax return? How much income did Courtney report on her individual tax return?

**Answer:** Because they resided in a common law state, Al reports the $90,000 that he earned through September (and all the income he earned through the end of the year) on his own return, and Courtney reports the entire $60,000 she earned through September (and all the income she earned through the rest of the year) on her own tax return.

**What if:** How much of this income would Al have been required to include on his individual tax return and how much of this income would Courtney have been required to report on her individual tax return if they lived in California, a community property state?

**Answer:** If they resided in a community property state, both Al and Courtney would have included $75,000 of the $150,000 the couple had jointly earned through September [(Al's $90,000 + Courtney's $60,000)/2] on their respective individual tax returns. Whether they resided in a community property state or not, Al and Courtney also would have included on their respective individual tax returns the income they individually earned and received from October through December.

If a couple files a joint tax return, the community property rules do not affect the aggregate taxes payable by the couple, because the income of both spouses is aggregated on the return. However, when couples file separate tax returns, their combined tax liability may depend on whether they live in a common law state, a community property state that shares income from separate property equally between spouses, or a community property state that does not split income from separate property between spouses.[10]

The treatment of income from property is relatively simple when the property is jointly owned in a common law state. In this instance, each co-owner is taxed on the income attributable to his share of the property. For example, suppose that a parcel of property is jointly owned by three individuals in equal shares. One-third of the income from this property will be included in the gross income of each co-owner.

## TYPES OF INCOME

**L02**

Now that we have a basic understanding of the general definition of gross income and related concepts, let's turn our attention to specific *types* of income subject to taxation. Our discussion is organized around income from services, income from property, and other sources of income.

### Income from Services

Income from labor is one of the most common sources of gross income, and it is rarely exempt from taxation. Payments for services including salary, wages, and fees that a taxpayer earns through services in a nonemployee capacity are all considered

---

[10]§66 provides rules that allow spouses living apart in community property states to be taxed on his or her own income from services if (1) the taxpayers live apart for the entire year, (2) they do not file a joint tax return with each other, and (3) they do not transfer any of the income from services between each other.

income from services.[11] Income from services is also referred to as **earned income** because it is generated by the efforts of the taxpayer (this also includes business income earned by a taxpayer even if the taxpayer's business is selling inventory).

## Example 5-7

EWD pays Courtney a salary of $98,000. In addition, Courtney earned and received $19,500 of fees from consulting work she did on weekends independent of her employment with EWD. She incurred $1,500 of miscellaneous expenses for supplies and transportation while doing the consulting work. What is Courtney's *gross income* from services (earned income) from her employment and her self-employment activities?

**Answer:** $117,500, consisting of her $98,000 of salary and $19,500 of her business income from her consulting activities. Note that Courtney's $1,500 of expenses will be used to calculate her net income from the business but not her gross income from the business (these expenses are deductions *for* AGI and are not a reduction in Courtney's gross income).

### Income from Property

Income from property, often referred to as **unearned income,** may take different forms, such as gain or losses from the sale of property, dividends, interest, rents, royalties, and annuities.[12] The tax treatment of unearned income depends upon the type of income and, in some circumstances, the type of the transaction generating the income. For example, while gains or losses are typically recognized in the current period, certain types of gains and losses are postponed indefinitely. We discuss annuity income and property dispositions briefly in the following paragraphs. We discuss income from property in more detail in subsequent chapters.

## Example 5-8

**Dividends:** Courtney owns 1,000 shares of GE stock that she registered in a dividend reinvestment plan. Under this plan, all dividends are automatically used to purchase more shares of the stock. This year, GE declared and paid $700 in dividends on Courtney's stock. Must Courtney include the dividend in her gross income for the year?

**Answer:** Yes. Courtney includes the $700 of dividends (unearned income) in her gross income.

## Example 5-9

**Interest income:** Gram purchased a $100,000, three-year certificate of deposit (CD) with a portion of the life insurance proceeds she received on Gramps's death. At year-end, her CD account is credited with $4,100 of interest, and her savings account is credited with $300 of interest. Courtney had a total of $550 of interest credited to her savings account and $50 credited to her checking account during the year. How much interest must Gram and Courtney include in their gross income for the year?

**Answer:** Gram must include the $4,100 of interest credited to her CD account and the $300 of interest credited to her savings account this year regardless of whether she withdraws the interest or not. Courtney must include the $600 of interest credited to her savings account ($550) and her checking account ($50) regardless of whether she withdraws it or not.

---

[11]This includes unemployment compensation. Up to $2,400 of unemployment compensation was excluded from the recipient's gross income in 2009. As of press time, this exclusion does not apply to unemployment compensation received in 2010.

[12]The tax definition of unearned income is different from the financial accounting definition. Unearned income for financial accounting purposes is a liability that represents advance payments for goods or services.

**Example 5-10**

*Rental income:* Courtney owns a condo in town that she rents to tenants. This year, the condo generated $14,000 of rental revenue. Courtney incurred $4,000 in real estate taxes, $2,500 in utility expenses, $500 in advertising expenses, and $2,000 of depreciation and other expenses associated with the rental. What effect does the rental have on Courtney's *gross income*? What effect does the rental have on Courtney's *taxable income*?

**Answer:** The rent increases Courtney's *gross income* by $14,000. However, after considering her allowable deductions for the rental, Courtney will only report $5,000 of *taxable income* from rental activities computed as follows:

| Description | Amount | |
|---|---|---|
| Rental revenue | | $14,000 |
| Less allowable deductions: | | |
|     Real estate taxes | (4,000) | |
|     Utilities | (2,500) | |
|     Advertising | (500) | |
|     Depreciation and other expenses | (2,000) | |
| Total rental expenses | | (9,000) |
| Net rental income | | $ 5,000 |

**Annuities**  An **annuity** is an investment that pays a stream of equal payments over time. Individuals often purchase annuities as a means of generating a fixed income stream during retirement. There are two basic types of annuities: (1) annuities paid over a fixed period and (2) annuities paid over a person's life (for as long as the person lives). The challenge from a tax perspective is to determine how much of each annuity payment represents gross income (income taxed at ordinary tax rates) and how much represents a nontaxable *return of capital* (return of the original investment). For both types of annuities, the tax law deems a *portion* of each annuity payment as a nontaxable return of capital and the remainder as gross income. Taxpayers use the annuity *exclusion* ratio to determine the portion of each payment that is a nontaxable return of capital.

$$\text{Annuity exclusion ratio} = \frac{Original\ investment}{Expected\ value\ of\ annuity} = \text{Return of capital } percentage$$

For fixed annuities, the expected value is the number of payments times the amount of the payment. In other words, for an annuity payable over a fixed term the return of capital is simply the original investment divided by the number of payments. The number of payments, however, is uncertain for annuities paid over a person's life. For these annuities, taxpayers must use IRS tables to determine the expected value based upon the taxpayer's life expectancy at the start of the annuity.[13] To calculate the expected value of the annuity, the number of annual payments from the table (referred to as the expected return multiple) is multiplied by the annual payment amount. Taxpayers with an annuity paid over the life of one person (a single-life annuity) use the expected return multiple from the table, a portion of which is presented in Exhibit 5-1.

---

[13]See Reg. §1.72-9. Special rules under §72(d) apply to annuities from qualified retirement plans.

**EXHIBIT 5-1**     Table for Expected Return Multiple for Ordinary Single-Life Annuity

| Age at Annuity Starting Date | Expected Return Multiple |
|---|---|
| 68 | 17.6 |
| 69 | 16.8 |
| 70 | 16.0 |
| 71 | 15.3 |
| 72 | 14.6 |

Some annuities provide payments over the lives of two people. For example, a taxpayer may purchase an annuity that provides an annual payment each year until both the taxpayer *and* the taxpayer's spouse pass away. This type of annuity is called a joint-life annuity. The IRS provides a separate table for determining the expected number of payments from joint-life annuities.

A taxpayer who lives longer than his or her estimated life expectancy will ultimately receive more than the expected number of payments. The entire amount of these "extra" payments is included in the taxpayer's gross income because the taxpayer has completely recovered her investment in the annuity by the time she receives them. If the taxpayer dies *before* receiving the expected number of payments, the amount of the unrecovered investment (the initial investment less the amounts received that is treated as a nontaxable return of capital) is deducted on the taxpayer's final income tax return.[14]

**Example 5-11**

In January of this year, Gram purchased an annuity from UBET Insurance Co. that will pay her $10,000 per year for the next 15 years. Gram received the first $10,000 payment in December. Gram paid $99,000 for the annuity and will receive $150,000 over the life of the annuity (15 years × $10,000 per year). How much of the $10,000 payment Gram receives in December should she include in her gross income?

**Answer:** $3,400. Because Gram purchased a fixed-payment annuity, the portion of the annuity payment included in gross income is calculated as follows:

| Description | Amount | Explanation |
|---|---|---|
| (1) Investment in annuity contract | $99,000 | |
| (2) Number of payments | 15 | |
| (3) Return of capital per payment | $ 6,600 | (1)/(2). |
| (4) Amount of each payment: | $10,000 | |
| **Gross income per payment** | **$ 3,400** | (4) − (3). |

**What if:** Assume the annuity Gram purchased pays her $1,000 per month over the remainder of her life. Gram (70 years old) paid $99,000 for the annuity, and she received her first $1,000 payment in December of this year. How much income would she recognize on the $1,000 payment?

(continued on page 5-13...)

[14]The unrecovered cost of the annuity is deducted as a miscellaneous itemized deduction not subject to the 2 percent of AGI floor. See §72(a)(3) and §67(b)(10).

**Answer:** $484.40, computed as follows:

| Description | Amount | Explanation |
|---|---|---|
| (1) Investment in annuity contract | $ 99,000 | |
| (2) Expected return multiple | 16 | Exhibit 5-1, 70 years old. |
| (3) Amount of each payment | $1,000 | |
| (4) Expected return | $192,000 | (2) × (3) × 12 months. |
| (5) Return of capital percentage | 51.56% | (1)/(4). |
| (6) Return of capital per payment | $ 515.60 | (3) × (5). |
| (7) Taxable income per payment | $ 484.40 | (3) − (6). |

After Gram receives her entire $99,000 as a return of capital, each subsequent $1,000 annuity payment would be fully taxable.

**Property Dispositions**   Taxpayers can realize a gain or loss when disposing of an asset. Consistent with the return of capital principle we discussed above, taxpayers are allowed to recover their investment in property (tax basis) before they realize any gain. A loss is realized when the proceeds are less than the tax basis in the property. Because the return of capital principle generally applies only to the extent of the sale proceeds, a loss does not necessarily reduce the taxpayer's taxable income. A loss will only reduce the taxpayer's taxable income if the loss is deductible. Exhibit 5-2 presents a general formula for computing the gain or loss from a sale of an asset.

**THE KEY FACTS**

*Return of Capital*

- Taxpayers are allowed to recover the capital invested in property tax free.

- Payments from purchased annuities are part income and part return of capital.

- When property is sold or disposed, the realized gain or loss equals the sale proceeds reduced by the tax basis of the property.

**EXHIBIT 5-2**   **Formula for Calculating Gain (Loss) from Sale of an Asset**

Sales proceeds
Less: Selling expenses
= Amount realized
Less: Basis (investment) in property sold
= Gain (Loss) on sale

The rate at which taxpayers are taxed on *gains* from property dispositions and the extent to which they can deduct *losses* from property dispositions depends on whether the taxpayer used the asset for business purposes, investment purposes, or personal purposes. We discuss specific rules associated with property dispositions in Chapters 10 and 11.

**Example 5-12**

On December 31, Gram sold her 50 shares of Acme Corporation stock for $40 per share. Gram also paid $150 of broker's commissions on the sale. Gram originally purchased the shares in April of this year for $30 per share. How much gross income does Gram recognize from the stock sale?

**Answer:** Gram recognizes $350 gross income on the sale, computed as follows:

| | |
|---|---|
| Sales proceeds ($40 × 50 shares) | $2,000 |
| Less: Selling expenses | −150 |
| = Amount realized | $1,850 |
| Less: Tax basis (investment) in property sold ($30 × 50 shares) | −1,500 |
| Gain (Loss) on sale | $   350 |

### Other Sources of Gross Income

Taxpayers may receive income from sources other than their efforts (earned income from wages or business) and their property (unearned income such as dividends and interest). In this section we briefly summarize other common types of gross income. If by chance you encounter other types of income that are not specifically discussed here, remember that the tax law is based upon the all-inclusive income concept. That is, unless a specific provision grants exclusion or deferral, economic benefits that are realized generate gross income. This basic understanding of the structure of our tax law (and research skills to investigate the taxability of specific income types) will serve you well as you evaluate whether realized income should be included in gross income.

**Income from Flow-through Entities** Individuals may invest in various business entities. The legal form of the business affects how the income generated by the business is taxed. If the entity is a **flow-through entity** such as a partnership or S corporation, the income and deductions of the entity "flow through" to the owners of the entity (partners or shareholders). That is, the owners report income as though they operated a portion of the business personally. Specifically, each partner or S corporation shareholder reports his or her share of the entity's income and deductions, generally in proportion to his or her ownership percentage, on his or her individual tax return.[15]

Because different types of income and deductions may be treated differently for tax purposes (for example, dividends may be eligible for a special low tax rate), each item the partners or shareholders report on their tax returns retains its underlying tax characteristics. That is, the partners are treated as if they personally received their share of each item of the flow-through entity's income. For example, corporate dividend income paid to a partnership is reported and taxed as dividend income on the partners' individual tax returns.[16] Also, it is important to note that owners of flow-through entities are taxed on their share of the entity's income whether or not cash is distributed to them. When owners receive cash distributions from the entity, the distributions are generally treated as a return of capital and, therefore, not included in the owner's gross income.

| Example 5-13 | |
|---|---|

**What if:** Suppose that Courtney is a 40 percent partner in KJZ partnership. KJZ reported $20,000 of business income and $3,000 of interest income for the year. KJZ also distributed $1,000 of cash to Courtney. What amount of gross income from her ownership in KJZ partnership would Courtney report for the current year?

**Answer:** $9,200, consisting of $8,000 of business income ($20,000 × 40%) and $1,200 of interest income ($3,000 × 40%). Courtney would not include the $1,000 distribution in her gross income because it was a return of her investment.

**Alimony** When couples legally separate or divorce, one spouse may be required to provide financial support to the other in the form of **alimony.** The tax law defines

---

[15]The deduction of losses from partnerships and S corporations are subject to several limitations that we discuss in Chapter 11.

[16]Partnerships and S corporations report to each partner or shareholder, that partner's or shareholder's share of partnership and S corporation income (or loss) on Schedule K-1 filed with the partnership and S corporation's annual information returns (Form 1065 and 1120S, respectively). See the Forms 1065 and 1120S on the IRS Web site, www.IRS.gov.

alimony as (1) a transfer of *cash* made under a written separation agreement or divorce decree, (2) the separation or divorce decree does not designate the payment as something other than alimony, and (3) the payments cannot continue after the death of the recipient.[17]

For tax purposes, a transfer between former spouses represents alimony only if it meets this definition. If the payment is alimony, then the amount of the payment is included in the gross income of the person receiving it and is deductible *for* AGI by the person paying it. Thus, alimony shifts income from one spouse to the other.

**Example 5-14**

In addition to paying child support, under the divorce decree Al is required to pay Courtney $20,000 cash each year until she dies. The decree does not designate the payment as a payment for something other than alimony. Does this payment qualify as alimony?

**Answer:** Yes. These payments qualify as alimony for tax purposes because they are (1) cash payments made under a divorce decree, (2) the payments are not designated as something other than alimony, and (3) the payments cease on Courtney's death. In the current year, Al made a $20,000 alimony payment to Courtney. Courtney includes all $20,000 in her gross income. To ensure that the income is taxed only once, Al is allowed to deduct the entire payment as a deduction *for* AGI.

There may be other types of payments that *do not qualify as alimony*. These include (1) property divisions (for example, who gets the car, house, or china?) and (2) child support payments fixed by the divorce or separation agreement.[18] In any event, if a transfer of property between spouses does *not* meet the definition of alimony, the *recipient* of the transfer *excludes* the value of the transfer from income, and the person transferring the property is not allowed to deduct the value of the property transferred.

**Example 5-15**

As required by the divorce decree, Al made $10,000 in child support payments during the year to Courtney to help her support Deron. Al is required to make child support payments until Deron is 18 years old. Is the current-year payment considered alimony?

**Answer:** No. The $10,000 of child support payments are not income to Courtney. The payments are not alimony because the divorce decree specifies that the payments are for child support. Consequently, Courtney does not include these payments in gross income, and Al does not deduct them.

The objective definition of alimony eliminates uncertainty regarding which transfers are treated as alimony. However, it creates a second problem. Since the purpose of the transfer is irrelevant to the tax consequences, it is possible to use alimony transfers to assign income from the (higher tax rate) payer of the alimony to the (lower tax rate) recipient. For example, instead of transferring ownership of an asset to the recipient as a nondeductible/nontaxable property settlement, the payer could claim an alimony

[17]§71(b). Another requirement for alimony is that spouses who are legally separated (but not divorced) may not live in the same household. In addition, certain payments to third parties on behalf of the spouse, such as mortgage payments, can also qualify as payments in cash.

[18]§71(c). A payment that is not specifically designated as child support may nonetheless be treated as child support if the payment is reduced on the happening of a specific contingency related to the child. For example, a payment that ceases once a child reaches the age of 18 would be treated as child support.

deduction by making a transfer that meets the alimony requirements. The spouses can share the tax savings from this transaction if they can agree on structuring the payments to qualify as alimony (although cooperations may be a little difficult for a couple going through a divorce). To address this tax-avoidance opportunity, Congress enacted a complex set of restrictions called *front loading* that make it difficult for taxpayers to disguise property payments as alimony payments. In general terms, when taxpayers attempt to disguise property payments as alimony payments (large alimony payments shortly after the divorce, followed by smaller alimony payments in subsequent years), the tax laws may require the taxpayers to recharacterize (or "recapture") part of the alimony payments as nondeductible property transfers.[19]

### Example 5-16

As part of the divorce agreement, Al transferred his interest in their joint residence to Courtney. The couple did not have any outstanding debt on the home. At the time of the divorce, the home was valued at $500,000 and Al's share was valued at $250,000. What are the tax consequences of the home ownership transfer to Courtney?

**Answer:** Because the transfer is not a cash transfer, it does not qualify as alimony. Consequently, Courtney does not recognize the $250,000 as income, and Al is not allowed to deduct the $250,000 transfer.

***What if:*** Assume that Al's marginal tax rate is 35 percent and Courtney's marginal tax rate is 15 percent. To generate tax savings, in lieu of transferring his share of the ownership in the home, Al and Courtney agreed that Al would make a $250,000 cash transfer to Courtney. The divorce agreement stipulated that this payment was alimony. What are Al and Courtney trying to accomplish under this arrangement? Will they be successful?

**Answer:** They are trying to convert a property payment into alimony that is deductible by Al (at a high tax rate) and includible in Courtney's income (at a lower tax rate). As we discussed above, under a complex set of alimony recapture rules, it is likely that a portion of this payment will be treated as a nonalimony property settlement.

**Prizes, Awards, and Gambling Winnings**  Prizes, awards, and gambling winnings, such as raffle or sweepstake prizes or lottery winnings, are included in gross income.

### Example 5-17

After devoting much of her free time during the year to filling out sweepstakes entries, Gram hit the jackpot. She won a WaveRunner worth $7,500 in a sweepstakes sponsored by *Reader's Digest*. How much of the prize, if any, must Gram include in her gross income?

**Answer:** Gram must include the full $7,500 value of the WaveRunner in her gross income. Note that because she must pay taxes on the winnings, she's not really getting the WaveRunner for "free."

There are two specific, narrowly defined exceptions to this rule. First, awards for scientific, literary, or charitable achievement such as the Nobel prize are excluded from gross income, *but only if* the taxpayer *immediately* transfers the award to a federal, state, or local governmental unit or qualified charity such as a church, school, or charitable organization.[20] The obvious downside of this exception is that the award recipient does not actually get to keep the award. However, for tax purposes it is more

[19]See §71(f) for details. The specifics of these provisions are beyond the scope of this text.
[20]§74(b).

beneficial for the recipient to exclude the award from income entirely by immediately transferring it to a charitable organization than it is to receive the award, recognize the income, and then contribute funds to a charity for a charitable deduction. Transferring the award has the same effect as claiming the transfer as a deduction *for* AGI. However, by receiving the award, recognizing the income, and then contributing funds to a charity, the taxpayer is deducting the donation as a deduction *from* AGI. As we discussed in Chapter 4, deductions *for* AGI are likely more advantageous than deductions *from* AGI.

The second exception is for employee *awards for length of service or safety achievement.*[21] These nontaxable awards are limited to $400 of tangible property *other than cash* per employee per year.[22] The award is not excluded from the employee's income if circumstances suggest it is disguised compensation.[23]

---

**Taxes in the Real World**   *Oprah Car Winners Hit with Hefty Tax*

Like any prize, the value is counted as income; winners must pay up to $7,000 or forfeit the car.

**September 22, 2004: 7:05 PM EDT**
**NEW YORK (CNN/Money)—Leave it to Uncle Sam to spoil the party.**
When Oprah Winfrey gave away 276 cars last week to the audience of her show, images of people laughing, jumping, crying—some hysterically—filled the airwaves and the give-away became stuff of legend. Late night talk show hosts and newspaper columnists are still talking about it. But now some of those eager prize-winners have a choice: Fork over $7,000 or give up the car.

According to a spokeswoman for Harpo Productions Inc., Oprah's company, the recipients must pay a tax on the winnings, just like any prize. For a brand new Pontiac G-Six, the model given away on the show, the sticker price is $28,500. The $28,500 would need to be claimed as income so, depending on the individual's tax bracket, the tax could be as high as $7,000. And that was after Pontiac agreed to pay most of the local charges, including state sales tax and licensing fees. The Harpo Spokeswomen said winners had three choices. They could keep the car and pay the tax, sell the car and pay the tax with the profits, or forfeit the car.

*Source: http://money.cnn.com/2004/09/ 22/news/ newsmakers/oprah_car_tax/*

---

Taxpayers must include the *gross* amount of their gambling winnings for the year in gross income. Taxpayers are allowed to deduct their gambling losses to the extent of their gambling winnings, but the losses are usually deductible as miscellaneous itemized deductions.[24] For professional gamblers, however, the losses are deductible (to the extent of gambling winnings) *for* AGI.

**Social Security Benefits**   Over the last 30 years, the taxation of Social Security benefits has changed considerably. Thirty years ago, Social Security benefits were completely excluded from income. Today, taxpayers may be required to include *up to* 85 percent of the benefits in gross income *depending* on the amount of the taxpayer's Social Security benefits and the taxpayer's *modified* AGI.[25] Modified AGI is regular

---

[21]Prizes or awards from an employer-sponsored contest are fully taxable.

[22]§74(c).

[23]The $400 limit is increased to $1,600 for qualified award plans (written plans that do not discriminate in favor of highly compensated employees). However, the *average* cost of all qualified plan awards from an employer is limited to $400.

[24]See Rev. Rul. 83-130, 1983-2 CB 148.

[25]§86(d) applies to monthly benefits under title II of the Social Security Act and tier 1 railroad retirement benefits.

AGI (without including Social Security benefits) plus tax-exempt interest income and certain other deductions *for* AGI.[26] The calculation of the amount of Social Security benefits to be included in income is depicted on the IRS worksheet in Appendix A at the end of this chapter.[27] The calculation is complex, to say the least. However, the taxability of Social Security benefits can be summarized as follows:

1.  Low income individuals exclude all Social Security benefits from gross income. Low income is defined to include single taxpayers whose modified AGI plus one-half of their Social Security benefits are $25,000 or less and married taxpayers whose modified AGI plus one-half of their Social Security benefits is $32,000 or less.

2.  High-income individuals include a portion of their benefits up to a maximum of 85 percent of the total Social Security benefits. High income is defined to include single taxpayers whose modified AGI plus one-half of their Social Security benefits is above $34,000 and married taxpayers whose modified AGI plus one-half of their Social Security benefits is above $44,000.

3.  Taxpayers not in groups (1) and (2) above include a portion of their benefits up to 50 percent of the total Social Security benefits.

## Example 5-18

Gram received $7,200 of Social Security benefits this year. Suppose that Gram's modified AGI is $16,000. What amount of the Social Security benefits must Gram include in her gross income?

**Answer:** $0. Gram's modified AGI plus one-half of her Social Security benefits is $19,600, which is below $25,000. Hence, Gram may *exclude* the entire $7,200 of Social Security income from gross income.

**What if:** Assume that Gram received $7,200 of Social Security benefits this year and that her modified AGI is $50,000. What amount of benefits must Gram include in her gross income?

**Answer:** $6,120 ($7,200 × 85%).

**Imputed Income**    Besides realizing *direct* economic benefits like wages and interest, taxpayers sometimes realize *indirect* economic benefits that they must include in gross income. For example, taxpayers realize an economic benefit when (1) they are allowed to purchase products or services from an employer at less than the market price or (2) they are allowed to borrow money at less than the market rate of interest. Even though these types of transactions provide an indirect economic benefit, taxpayers receiving such benefits may be required to include a certain amount of **imputed income** from these transactions in their gross income. For example, employees must recognize income to the extent they receive a greater than 20 percent discount from their employer for the employer's services or purchase goods from their employer at a price below the employer's cost.

## Example 5-19

As part of her compensation package, EWD agreed to provide Courtney with EWD architectural design services (to create more space for Gram) at a substantial discount. EWD provided Courtney with

*(continued on page 5-19...)*

[26]See §86(b)(2)(A).

[27]Because the 2010 worksheet was not available at the time the book went to press, we include the 2009 worksheet in Appendix A. The 2009 worksheet can be used to determine the taxable portion of Social Security benefits received in 2010.

services valued at $35,000 but charged her only $22,000 for the services. How much of the discount must Courtney include in gross income?

**Answer:** $6,000, computed as follows:

| Description | Amount | Explanation |
|---|---|---|
| (1) Value of services EWD provided to Courtney | $35,000 | |
| (2) Courtney's cost of the services | 22,000 | |
| (3) Discount on services | $13,000 | (1) − (2). |
| (4) Excludable discount | 7,000 | (1) × 20%. |
| **Discount in excess of 20% is included in gross income** | **$ 6,000** | (3) − (4). |

Employees may also recognize imputed income when they borrow money from an employer at a below-market interest rate. The amount of imputed income is the difference between the amount of the loan multiplied by an applicable federal interest rate (compounded semiannually) and the amount of interest the taxpayer actually pays. The imputed interest rules do not apply to loans of $10,000 or less [§7872(c)(2)].

### Example 5-20

At the beginning of January, EWD provides Courtney with a $100,000 zero-interest loan. Assume that the applicable federal interest rate (compounded semiannually) is 4 percent. Courtney used the loan proceeds to acquire several personal-use assets (an automobile and other items). What amount is Courtney required to include in gross income in the current year?

**Answer:** $4,000, computed as follows:

| Description | Amount | Explanation |
|---|---|---|
| (1) Loan principal | $100,000 | |
| (2) Applicable federal interest rate compounded semiannually | 4% | |
| (3) Interest on loan principal at federal rate | $ 4,000 | (1) × (2). |
| (4) Interest paid by Courtney | 0 | |
| (5) Imputed interest included in Courtney's gross income[28] | $ 4,000 | (3) − (4). |

**What if:** Assume the same facts except that EWD had loaned Courtney $10,000 at a zero-interest rate, how much imputed interest income would Courtney be required to include in her gross income for the year?

**Answer:** $0. The imputed interest rules don't apply because the loan did not exceed $10,000.

**THE KEY FACTS**

**Other Sources of Income**

- Alimony is taxed to recipient when paid in cash, pursuant to written agreement or decree and contingent on life of the recipient.
- Awards are included in gross income unless made for scientific, literary, or charitable achievement and transferred to a qualified charity.
- A maximum of 85% of Social Security benefits are included in gross income depending on level of AGI.
- Discharge of debt is included in gross income unless taxpayer is insolvent before and after forgiveness.

**Discharge of Indebtedness**   In general, when a taxpayer's debt is forgiven by a lender (the debt is discharged), the taxpayer must include the amount of debt relief in gross income.[29]

---

[28]Courtney will also incur an imputed interest expense of $4,000 for the year and EWD will also deduct $4,000 of compensation expense. As we learn in the next chapter, business interest expense is a deduction *for* AGI, investment interest expense is an itemized deduction subject to limitations, and personal interest is generally not deductible. In this example, we assume Courtney used the proceeds for personal purposes so she is not allowed to deduct the interest expense.

[29]§61(a)(12). Income from discharge of indebtedness is also realized when debt is forgiven by lenders other than employers such as banks and credit card companies.

**Example 5-21**

> In the previous example, Courtney borrowed $100,000 from EWD. Because EWD wants to keep Courtney as an employee, it agreed to forgive $10,000 of loan principal at the end of each year that Courtney stays on board. On December 31 of this year, EWD formally cancels $10,000 of Courtney's indebtedness. How much of this debt relief is Courtney required to include in gross income?
>
> **Answer:** All $10,000 is included in Courtney's gross income.

To provide tax relief for insolvent taxpayers—taxpayers with liabilities, including tax liabilities, exceeding their assets—a **discharge of indebtedness** is *not* taxable if the taxpayer is insolvent before *and* after the debt forgiveness.[30] If the discharge of indebtedness makes the taxpayer solvent, the taxpayer recognizes gross income to the extent of his solvency.[31] For example if a taxpayer is discharged of $30,000 of debt and this causes him to be solvent by $10,000 (after the debt relief, the taxpayer's assets exceed his liabilities by $10,000), the taxpayer must include $10,000 in gross income.[32]

## L03  EXCLUSION PROVISIONS

So far in this chapter, we've discussed various types of income taxpayers must realize and recognize by reporting it on their tax returns in the current year. However, there are specific types of income that taxpayers realize but are allowed to permanently *exclude* from gross income or temporarily defer from gross income until a subsequent period. As we discussed in the previous chapter, *exclusions* and *deferrals* are the result of *specific Congressional action* and are *narrowly defined*. Because taxpayers are not required to recognize income that is excluded or deferred, we refer to tax laws allowing exclusions or deferrals as **nonrecognition provisions.** Nonrecognition provisions result from various policy objectives. In very general terms, Congress allows most exclusions and deferrals for two primary reasons: (1) to subsidize or encourage particular activities or (2) to be fair to taxpayers (such as mitigating the inequity of double taxation). Our discussion in this chapter focuses on exclusions.

### Common Exclusions

Because exclusion provisions allow taxpayers to permanently remove certain income items from their tax base, they are particularly taxpayer friendly. We begin by introducing two common exclusion provisions, the exclusion of municipal interest and fringe benefits. We continue with a survey of other exclusion provisions based on their underlying purpose: education, double taxation, and sickness and injury.[33]

**Municipal Interest**  The most common example of an exclusion provision is the exclusion of interest on **municipal bonds.** Municipal bonds include bonds issued by state and local governments located in the United States, and this exclusion is generally recognized as a subsidy to state and local governments.

---

[30]§108(a)(1)(B).

[31]§108(a)(3).

[32]Other circumstances in which taxpayers may exclude a discharge of indebtedness are beyond the scope of this chapter.

[33]Two other common exclusions we discuss in detail in subsequent chapters include the exclusion of gain on the sale of a personal residence (Chapter 14) and the exclusion of earnings on "Roth" retirement savings accounts (Chapter 13).

**Example 5-22**

Courtney holds a $10,000 City of Cincinnati municipal bond. The bond pays 5 percent interest annually. Courtney acquired the bond a few years ago. The city used the proceeds from the bond issuance to help pay for renovations on a major league baseball stadium. In late December, Courtney received $500 of interest income from the bond for the year. How much of the $500 interest from the municipal bond may Courtney *exclude* from her gross income?

**Answer:** All $500 because the interest is from a municipal bond.

**Fringe Benefits** In addition to paying salary and wages, many employers provide employees with **fringe benefits.** For example, an employer may provide an employee with an automobile to use for personal purposes, pay for an employee to join a health club, or pay for an employee's home security. In general, the value of these benefits is *included* in the employee's gross income as compensation for services. However, certain fringe benefits, called "qualifying" fringe benefits, are excluded from gross income.[34] Exhibit 5-3 lists some of the most common fringe benefits that are excluded from an employee's gross income. We discuss fringe benefits in more depth in Chapter 12.

**EXHIBIT 5-3    Common Qualifying Fringe Benefits**
(excluded from employee's gross income)

| Item | Description |
|------|-------------|
| Medical and dental health insurance coverage | An employee may exclude from income the cost of medical and dental health insurance premiums the employer pays on an employee's behalf. |
| Life insurance coverage | Employees may exclude from income the value of life insurance premiums the employer pays on an employee's behalf for up to $50,000 of group-term life insurance. |
| De minimis (small) benefits | As a matter of administrative convenience, Congress allows employees to exclude from income relatively small and infrequent benefits employees receive at work (such as limited use of a business copy machine). |

**Example 5-23**

EWD paid $6,000 this year for Courtney's health insurance premiums and $150 in premiums for her $40,000 group-term life insurance policy. How much of the $6,150 in benefits can Courtney exclude from her gross income?

**Answer:** Courtney can exclude all $6,150 in benefits from her gross income. All health insurance premiums paid by an employer on an employee's behalf are excluded from the employee's income. In addition, premiums employers pay on an employee's behalf for group-term life insurance (up to $50,000 of coverage) are also excluded from the employee's gross income.

[34]Most nontaxable fringe benefits are listed with "items specifically excluded from gross income" in §§101-140 of the Internal Revenue Code. Employers are generally prohibited from discriminating among employees with respect to nontaxable fringe benefits (that is, they cannot offer them only to executives).

## Example 5-24

In December, Courtney mailed a newsletter to several dozen friends and relatives with a recent picture of her son, daughter, and grandmother. Courtney printed both the newsletter and the photos on printers at work (with permission of EWD). Courtney would have paid $55 for the duplicate newsletters and photos at a nearby copy center. How much of this $55 benefit that Courtney received from EWD may Courtney *exclude* from her gross income?

**Answer:**  All $55 is excluded. The $55 benefit is considered a nontaxable de minimis fringe benefit because it is small in amount and infrequent.

### Education-Related Exclusions

As an incentive for taxpayers to participate in higher education (education beyond high school), Congress excludes certain types of income if the funds are used for higher education. In the following paragraphs, we discuss exclusions for scholarships and exclusions for certain types of investment plans used to save for college.[35]

**Scholarships**    College students seeking a degree can exclude from gross income scholarships that pay for tuition, fees, books, supplies, and other equipment *required* for the student's courses.[36] Any excess scholarship amounts (such as for room or meals) are fully taxable. The scholarship exclusion applies only if the recipient is *not* required to perform services in exchange for receiving the scholarship. "Scholarships" that represent compensation for past, current, or future services are fully taxable. Consequently, students working at school for compensation must include these payments in gross income.

## Example 5-25

Ellen, Courtney's daughter, received a $700 scholarship from the University of Missouri–Kansas City that pays $400 of her tuition and provides $300 cash for books. Ellen spent $350 on books. How much of the scholarship may she exclude from gross income?

**Answer:**  All $700 is excluded. Ellen may exclude all of the scholarship for tuition and she may exclude the $300 cash she received for books because she spent all $300 purchasing her books for school.

*What if:*  How much is Ellen allowed to exclude if she spent only $250 on books?

**Answer:**  $650 is excluded. Ellen excludes all of the scholarship for her tuition and $250 of the $300 in cash payments because she spent $250 on books. She must include the excess cash payment of $50 ($300 − $250) in her gross income.

---

**Other Educational Subsidies**    Taxpayers are allowed to exclude from gross income earnings on investments in qualified education plans such as 529 plans and Coverdell education savings accounts as long as they use the earnings to pay for qualifying educational expenditures. We discuss these plans in more detail in Chapter 11.

The federal government issues bonds that allow taxpayers to acquire the bonds at a discount and redeem the bonds for a fixed amount over stated time intervals. These bonds don't generate any cash in the form of interest until the taxpayer redeems the bond. At redemption, the amount of the redemption price in excess of the acquisition price is interest included in gross income.[37] U.S. Series EE bonds fall into this category.

---

**THE KEY FACTS**

**Education Exclusions**

■ Students seeking a college degree can exclude scholarships that pay for required tuition, fees, books, and supplies.

■ Taxpayers can elect to exclude interest earned on Series EE savings bonds when the redemption proceeds are used to pay qualified higher education expenses.

■ The exclusion of interest on Series EE savings bonds is restricted to taxpayers with modified AGI below specific limits.

---

[35]A detailed explanation is available in IRS Publication 970 *Tax Benefits for Education* available on the Web at www.IRS.gov.

[36]§177(b)(2).

[37]Alternatively, taxpayers can elect to include the annual increase in the redemption value in gross income rather than waiting to recognize all the income on redemption. See §454(a).

However, an exclusion is available for interest from Series EE bonds. This exclusion requires that the redemption proceeds be used to pay for higher education expenses of the taxpayer, the taxpayer's spouse, or a dependent of the taxpayer. Qualified higher education expenses include the tuition and fees required for enrollment or attendance at an eligible educational institution. Taxpayers may also exclude the interest income if they contribute the proceeds to a qualified tuition program.

The exclusion is partially reduced or eliminated for taxpayers exceeding a fixed level of modified adjusted gross income (adjusted gross income before the educational savings bond exclusion, the foreign earned income exclusion, and certain other deductions).[38] If the taxpayer's modified AGI exceeds the thresholds in the redemption year, the exclusion is phased out (gradually reduced) until all of the interest from the bonds is taxed.[39]

### Exclusions to Mitigate Double Taxation

Congress provides certain exclusions to eliminate the potential double tax that may arise for gifts, inheritances, and life insurance proceeds.

**Gifts and Inheritances**    Individuals may transfer property to other taxpayers without receiving or expecting to receive value in return. If the *transferor* is alive at the time of the transfer, the property transfer is called a **gift.** If the property is transferred from the decedent's estate (*transferor* is deceased), it is called an **inheritance.** These transfers are generally subject to a federal transfer tax, *not* the income tax. Gifts are typically subject to the federal gift tax and inheritances are typically subject to a federal estate tax.[40] Thus, gift and estate taxes are imposed on *transfer* of the property and not included in income by the recipient. Congress excludes property transferred as gifts and inheritances from income taxation to avoid the potential double taxation (transfer and income taxation) on these transfers.

**Example 5-26**

Ellen graduated from high school last year. As a graduation present, Gram purchased a $1,500 travel package for Ellen, so that Ellen could go on a Caribbean cruise. Last year, Ellen also received an inheritance of $2,000 from Gramps's estate. How much gross income does Ellen recognize on the $1,500 gift she received from Gram and the $2,000 inheritance she received from Gramps's estate?

**Answer:** $0. Ellen is allowed to exclude the entire gift and the entire amount of the inheritance from her gross income. Consequently, she does not recognize any gross income from these transactions.

**Life Insurance Proceeds**    In some ways, life insurance proceeds are similar to inheritances. When the owner of the life insurance policy dies, the beneficiary receives the death benefit proceeds. The decedent (or the decedent's estate) is generally subject to estate taxation on the amount of the insurance proceeds. In order to avoid potential double taxation on the life insurance proceeds, the tax laws allow taxpayers receiving life insurance proceeds to exclude the proceeds from taxable income.[41] However, when the insurance proceeds are paid over a period of time rather than in a lump sum, a portion of the payments represents interest and must be included in gross income.

[38]§135(c)(4).

[39]In 2010, the phase-out range begins at $105,100 of modified adjusted gross income for married taxpayers filing joint returns. For all other taxpayers, the phase-out range begins at $70,100.

[40]As a general rule, the federal gift tax does not apply to relatively small gifts ($13,000 or less), and the federal estate tax does not apply to transfers from relatively small estates (under $3.5 million).

[41]§101. The exclusion does not apply if the insurance policy is sold by the owner.

**Foreign-Earned Income**    U.S. citizens are subject to tax on all income whether it is generated in the United States or in foreign countries. Because most foreign countries also impose tax on income earned within their borders, U.S. citizens could be subject to both U.S. and foreign taxation on income earned abroad. To provide relief from this potential double taxation, Congress allows taxpayers to exclude foreign earned income up to an annual maximum amount. The maximum exclusion is indexed for inflation, and in 2010 the maximum is $91,500. Rather than claim this exclusion, taxpayers may deduct foreign taxes paid as itemized deductions or they may claim the foreign tax credit for foreign taxes paid on their foreign earned income.[42] Thus, each year taxpayers must choose to (1) exclude the income from U.S. taxation, (2) deduct the taxes, *or* (3) claim the foreign tax credit to offset their U.S. income tax liability. To determine whether claiming the annual exclusion, the deduction, or the foreign tax credit is most advantageous, taxpayers should compare the tax effects of each option on an annual basis.

As you might expect, individuals must meet certain requirements to qualify for the foreign earned income exclusion. To be eligible for the annual exclusion, a taxpayer must (1) be considered a resident of the foreign country or (2) live in the foreign country for 330 days in a consecutive 12-month period. However, because the exclusion is computed on a *daily* basis, the *maximum* exclusion is reduced pro rata for each day during the calendar year the taxpayer is not considered to be a resident of the foreign country or does not actually live in the foreign country.

**Example 5-27**

**What if:** Assume that Courtney is considering a one-year rotation in one of EWD's overseas offices. If Courtney agrees to do the rotation, she anticipates she will earn approximately $120,000 in salary. How much of her expected $120,000 salary will Courtney be allowed to exclude from her gross income assuming she meets the residency requirements?

**Answer:** She is eligible to exclude $91,500 of her $120,000 of compensation from U.S. taxation in 2010. However, her entire $120,000 salary may be subject to the foreign country's income tax.

**What if:** Assume that Courtney agrees to the rotation but she expects to live in the foreign country for only 340 days. How much of her expected $120,000 salary will she be allowed to exclude from gross income?

**Answer:** $85,233 [$91,500 full exclusion × 340/365 (days in foreign country/days in year)].

**What if:** Assume that Courtney expects to live in the foreign country for 340 days and that she expects her salary to be $60,000. How much of her expected $60,000 salary will she be allowed to exclude from gross income?

**Answer:** All $60,000. She can exclude up to $85,233 of salary from income (see above computation).

### Sickness and Injury-Related Exclusions

The tax laws provide several exclusion provisions for taxpayers who are sick or injured. One explanation for these exclusions is that payments for sickness or injury.

**Workers' Compensation**    The provision for workers' compensation is relatively straightforward. Taxpayers receive workers' compensation benefits when they are unable to work because of a work-related injury. Any payments a taxpayer receives from a state-sponsored workers' compensation plan are excluded from the taxpayer's

[42]See §911(b)(2) and Chapters 6 and 7.

income.[43] Note that this treatment is *opposite* that of *unemployment* compensation, which is fully taxable.

**Payments Associated with Personal Injury**   Historically, the question of which payments associated with a personal injury were excludible was controversial. In 1996 Congress settled the matter by deciding that all payments associated with compensating a taxpayer for a *physical* injury are excluded from gross income. That is, the tax laws specify that any payments on account of a *physical injury* or *physical sickness* are nontaxable. Thus, damages taxpayers receive for emotional distress associated with a physical injury are excluded. In contrast, punitive damages are *fully taxable,* because they are intended to punish the harm-doer rather than to compensate the taxpayer for injuries. Likewise, taxpayers receiving damages for emotional distress that are not associated with a physical injury must include those payments in income. In general, all other awards (those that do not relate to physical injury or sickness or are payments for the medical costs of treating emotional distress) are included in gross income.

---

### Example 5-28

In February, Courtney's cousin, Kelsey, was struck and injured by a bus while walking in a crosswalk. Because the bus driver was negligent, the bus company settled Kelsey's claim by paying her $1,500 for medical expenses and $500 for emotional distress associated with the accident. How much of the $2,000 Kelsey received from the bus company may she *exclude* from her gross income?

**Answer:** All $2,000. Kelsey may exclude the $1,500 she received for medical expenses and the $500 payment she received for emotional distress because these damages were associated with Kelsey's physical injury.

***What if:*** Assume Kelsey sued the bus company and was awarded $5,000 in punitive damages. How much of the $5,000 would Kelsey be able to exclude from her gross income?

**Answer:** $0. Payments for punitive damages are not excludable. Kelsey would be required to include the entire $5,000 in her gross income.

---

**Health Care Reimbursement**   Any reimbursement a taxpayer receives from a health and accident insurance policy for medical expenses paid by the taxpayer during the current year is excluded from gross income. Of course, the tax benefit rule may require inclusion of reimbursements of medical expenses deducted in a prior year.

**Disability Insurance**   The exclusion provisions for **disability insurance** are more restrictive than those for workers' compensation payments or reimbursements from a health and accident insurance plan. Disability insurance, sometimes called wage replacement insurance, pays the insured individual for wages lost when the individual misses work due to injury or disability. If an individual purchases disability insurance directly, the cost of the policy is not deductible, but any disability benefits are excluded from gross income.

Disability insurance may also be purchased on an individual's behalf by an employer. When an employer pays disability insurance premiums, the employer may allow employees to choose whether the payments on their behalf are to be considered taxable compensation or a nontaxable fringe benefit. If the premiums paid on the employee's behalf are taxable compensation to the employee, the policy is considered to have been purchased by the employee. If the premium paid for by the employer is a nontaxable fringe benefit to the employee, the policy is considered to have been purchased by the employer. This distinction is important because only payments taxpayers

---

**THE KEY FACTS**

**Exclusions Related to Sickness and Injury**

- Payments from workers' compensation plans are excluded from gross income.

- Payments received as compensation for a *physical* injury are excluded from gross income, but punitive damages are included in gross income.

- Reimbursements by health and accident insurance policies for medical expenses paid by the taxpayer are excluded from gross income.

- Disability payments received from an *employee-purchased* policy are excluded from gross income.

---

[43]§104.

receive from an *employee-purchased* policy are excluded from an employee's gross income. If the employer pays the premiums for an employee as a nontaxable fringe benefit, the employee must include all disability benefits in gross income.

**Example 5-29**

Courtney purchased disability insurance last year. In late April of this year, she broke her wrist in a mountain biking accident and could not work for two weeks. Courtney's doctor bills totaled $2,000, of which $1,600 were reimbursed by her health insurance purchased by EWD. How much of the $1,600 health insurance reimbursement for medical expenses is Courtney allowed to *exclude* from her gross income?

**Answer:** All $1,600 is excluded. All medical expense reimbursements from health insurance are excluded from a taxpayer's gross income.

Courtney also received $600 for lost wages due to the accident from her disability insurance policy. How much of the $600 is Courtney allowed to exclude from her gross income?

**Answer:** All $600 is excluded. Courtney can exclude the entire amount because she paid the premiums on the policy.

*What if:* How much of the $600 payment for lost wages from the disability insurance policy would Courtney exclude if EWD paid the disability insurance premium on her behalf as a nontaxable fringe benefit?

**Answer:** $0 is excluded. In this circumstance the policy would be considered to be purchased by the employer, so Courtney would not be allowed to exclude any of the payment from gross income. She would include the payment in gross income and be taxed on the entire $600.

*What if:* How much of the $600 payment for lost wages from the disability insurance policy would Courtney be allowed to exclude if she paid half the cost of the policy with after-tax dollars and EWD paid the other half as a nontaxable fringe benefit?

**Answer:** $300 is excluded. Because Courtney paid for half the cost of the policy with after-tax dollars, she is allowed to exclude half of the disability insurance benefit.

### Deferral Provisions

We've described exclusion provisions that allow taxpayers to permanently eliminate certain types of income from their tax base. Other code sections, called *deferral provisions,* allow taxpayers to defer (but not permanently exclude) the recognition of certain types of realized income. Transactions generating deferred income include **installment sales,** like-kind exchanges, involuntary conversions, and contributions to non-Roth **qualified retirement accounts.** We "defer" our detailed discussion of these transactions to subsequent chapters.

## GROSS INCOME SUMMARY

At the end of the year, Courtney calculated her gross income and Gram's gross income. Exhibit 5-4 presents Courtney's gross income calculation and Exhibit 5-5 displays how this income would be reported on the front page of Courtney's tax return. Note that line 22 of the first page of the Form 1040 sums to "total income" not gross income. The difference between these two numbers is that "total income" is gross income minus certain deductions *for* AGI such as business expenses and deductible capital losses. Exhibit 5-4 reconciles from Courtney's gross income to her total income as displayed on her tax return.

Exhibit 5-6 presents Gram's gross income calculation. Because Gram doesn't have any business, rental, or royalty deductions, her gross income is equal to her total income on line 22 of page 1 of her tax return.

**EXHIBIT 5-4    Courtney's Gross Income**

| Description | Amount | Reference |
|---|---|---|
| (1) Salary (line 7, 1040 page 1) | $ 98,000 | Example 5-7. |
| (2) Employment bonus award (line 7, 1040 page 1) | 4,800 | Example 5-4. |
| (3) Discount architectural design services (line 7, 1040 page 1) | 6,000 | Example 5-19. |
| (4) Compensation on below market loan from EWD (line 7, 1040 page 1) | 4,000 | Example 5-20. |
| (5) Discharge of indebtedness (line 7, 1040 page 1) | 10,000 | Example 5-21. |
| (6) Interest income (line 8a, 1040 page 1) | 600 | Example 5-9. |
| (7) Dividends (lines 9a and 9b, 1040, page 1) | 700 | Example 5-8. |
| (8) State tax refund (line 10, 1040 page 1) | 420 | Example 5-3. |
| (9) Alimony (line 11, 1040 page 1) | 20,000 | Example 5-14. |
| (10) Gross business income (line 12, 1040 page 1) | 19,500 | Example 5-7. |
| (11) Gross rental income (line 17, 1040 page 1) | 14,000 | Example 5-10. |
| (12) Gross income for current year | **$178,020** | Sum of (1) through (11). |
| (13) Business expenses associated with consulting activities (line 12, 1040 page 1) | (1,500) | Example 5-7. |
| (14) Rental expenses (line 17, 1040 page 1) | (9,000) | Example 5-10. |
| Total income as presented on line 22 of front page of 1040 (see Exhibit 5-5) | **$167,520** | (12) + (13) + (14). |

**EXHIBIT 5-5    Courtney's Tax Return**

**(total income as reported on 1040 page 1, lines 7–22)**

| | | | | |
|---|---|---|---|---|
| **Income** | **7** | Wages, salaries, tips, etc. Attach Form(s) W-2 . . . . . . . . . . . . . | **7** | 122,800 |
| | **8a** | **Taxable** interest. Attach Schedule B if required . . . . . . . . . . | **8a** | 600 |
| **Attach Form(s) W-2 here. Also attach Forms W-2G and 1099-R if tax was withheld.** | **b** | **Tax-exempt** interest. **Do not** include on line 8a . . . **8b** 500 | | |
| | **9a** | Ordinary dividends. Attach Schedule B if required . . . . . . . . . | **9a** | 700 |
| | **b** | Qualified dividends (see page 22) . . . . . . . . **9b** 700 | | |
| | **10** | Taxable refunds, credits, or offsets of state and local income taxes (see page 23) . . | **10** | 420 |
| | **11** | Alimony received . . . . . . . . . . . . . . . . . . . | **11** | 20,000 |
| **If you did not get a W-2, see page 22.** | **12** | Business income or (loss). Attach Schedule C or C-EZ . . . . . . . . . | **12** | 18,000 |
| | **13** | Capital gain or (loss). Attach Schedule D if required. If not required, check here ▶ ☐ | **13** | |
| | **14** | Other gains or (losses). Attach Form 4797 . . . . . . . . . . . . | **14** | |
| | **15a** | IRA distributions . **15a** | **b** Taxable amount (see page 24) | **15b** | |
| | **16a** | Pensions and annuities **16a** | **b** Taxable amount (see page 25) | **16b** | |
| **Enclose, but do not attach, any payment. Also, please use Form 1040-V.** | **17** | Rental real estate, royalties, partnerships, S corporations, trusts, etc. Attach Schedule E | **17** | 5,000 |
| | **18** | Farm income or (loss). Attach Schedule F . . . . . . . . . . . . | **18** | |
| | **19** | Unemployment compensation in excess of $2,400 per recipient (see page 27) . . . | **19** | |
| | **20a** | Social security benefits **20a** | **b** Taxable amount (see page 27) | **20b** | |
| | **21** | Other income. List type and amount (see page 29) _____ | **21** | |
| | **22** | Add the amounts in the far right column for lines 7 through 21. This is your **total income** ▶ | **22** | 167,520 |

**EXHIBIT 5-6    Gram's Gross Income and Total Income**

| Description | Amount | Reference |
|---|---|---|
| Babysitting services | $ 350 | Example 5-2. |
| Interest income | 4,400 | Example 5-9. |
| Annuity income | 3,400 | Example 5-11. |
| Gain on stock sale | 350 | Example 5-12. |
| Sweepstakes winnings (WaveRunner) | 7,500 | Example 5-17. |
| **Gross (and total) income for current year** | $16,000 | |

## CONCLUSION

In this chapter we explained the basic concepts of income realization and recognition, identified and discussed the major types of income, and described the most common income exclusions. We discovered that many exclusions are related to specific Congressional objectives, but that absent an specific exclusion, realized income should be included in gross income. In the next two chapters, we turn our attention to the deductions available to taxpayers when computing their taxable income, and we conclude our review of the individual income tax formula by determining how to compute taxpayers' tax liability and their taxes due or tax refund. We will continue to follow Courtney and Gram in their quest to determine their taxable income and corresponding tax liability.

# 2009 SOCIAL SECURITY WORKSHEET FROM IRS PUBLICATION 915

**APPENDIX A**

---

Worksheet 1.    **Figuring Your Taxable Benefits**

---

**Before you begin:**

- If you are married filing separately and you lived apart from your spouse for all of 2009, enter "D" to the right of the word "benefits" on Form 1040, line 20a, or Form 1040A, line 14a.
- Do not use this worksheet if you repaid benefits in 2009 and your total repayments (box 4 of Forms SSA-1099 and RRB-1099) were more than your gross benefits for 2009 (box 3 of Forms SSA-1099 and RRB-1099). None of your benefits are taxable for 2009. For more information, see *Repayments More Than Gross Benefits.*

---

1. Enter the total amount from box 5 of ALL your Forms SSA-1099 and RRB-1099. Also
   enter this amount on Form 1040, line 20a, or Form 1040A, line 14a . . . . . . . . . . . . . .    **1.** _____

2. Enter one-half of line 1 . . . . . . . . . . . . . . . . . . . . . . . . . . . . . . . . . . . . . . . . . . . . .    **2.** _____

3. Enter the total of the amounts from:
   **Form 1040:** Lines 7, 8a, 9a, 10 through 14, 15b, 16b, 17 through 19, and 21
   **Form 1040A:** Lines 7, 8a, 9a, 10, 11b, 12b, and 13 . . . . . . . . . . . . . . . . . . . . .    **3.** _____

4. Enter the amount, if any, from Form 1040 or 1040A, line 8b . . . . . . . . . . . . . . . . . . . . . . . . . . . .    **4.** _____

5. **Form 1040 filers:** Enter the total of any exclusions/adjustments for:
   - Qualified U.S. savings bond interest (Form 8815, line 14)
   - Adoption benefits (Form 8839, line 30)
   - Foreign earned income or housing (Form 2555, lines 45 and 50, or Form 2555-EZ, line 18), and
   - Certain income of bona fide residents of American Samoa (Form 4563, line 15) or Puerto Rico
     **Form 1040A filers:** Enter the total of any exclusions for:
   - Qualified U.S. savings bond interest (Form 8815, line 14)
   - Adoption benefits (Form 8839, line 30) . . . . . . . . . . . . . . . . . . . . . . . . . . . . . .    **5.** _____

6. Add lines 2, 3, 4, and 5 . . . . . . . . . . . . . . . . . . . . . . . . . . . . . . . . . . . . . . . . . . . . . . . . . . . .    **6.** _____

7. **Form 1040 filers:** Enter the amounts from Form 1040, lines 23 through 32, and any write-in adjustments you entered on the dotted line next to line 36. **Form 1040A filers:** Enter the amounts from Form 1040A, lines 16 and 17 . . . . . . . . . . . . . . . . . . . . . . . . . . . . . . . . . . . . . . . . . . . . . . . . . . . . . . . .    **7.** _____

8. Is the amount on line 7 less than the amount on line 6?

   **No.** (STOP)    None of your social security benefits are taxable. Enter -0- on Form 1040, line 20b, or
   Form 1040A, line 14b.

   **Yes.**    Subtract line 7 from line 6 . . . . . . . . . . . . . . . . . . . . . . . . . . . . . . . .    **8.** _____

9. If you are:
   - Married filing jointly, enter $32,000
   - Single, head of household, qualifying widow(er), or married filing separately and you **lived apart** from your spouse for all of 2009, enter $25,000 . . . . . . . . . . . . . . . . . . . . . . . . . . . . . .    **9.** _____

   **Note.** If you are married filing separately and you lived with your spouse at any time in 2009, skip lines 9 through 16; multiply line 8 by 85% (.85) and enter the result on line 17. Then go to line 18.

10. Is the amount on line 9 less than the amount on line 8?

    **No.** (STOP)    None of your benefits are taxable. Enter -0- on Form 1040, line 20b, or on Form 1040A,
    line 14b. If you are married filing separately and you **lived apart** from your spouse for all
    of 2009, be sure you entered "D" to the right of the word "benefits" on Form 1040, line
    20a, or on Form 1040A, line 14a.

    **Yes.**    Subtract line 9 from line 8 . . . . . . . . . . . . . . . . . . . . . . . . . . . . . . . . . . . .    **10.** _____

11. Enter $12,000 if married filing jointly; $9,000 if single, head of household, qualifying widow(er), or married
    filing separately and you **lived apart** from your spouse for all of 2009 . . . . . . . . . . . . . . . . . . . . . . .    **11.** _____

12. Subtract line 11 from line 10. If zero or less, enter -0- . . . . . . . . . . . . . . . . . . . . . . . . . . . . . . . .    **12.** _____

13. Enter the **smaller** of line 10 or line 11 . . . . . . . . . . . . . . . . . . . . . . . . . . . . . . . . . . . . . . . . . .    **13.** _____

14. Enter one-half of line 13 . . . . . . . . . . . . . . . . . . . . . . . . . . . . . . . . . . . . . . . . . . . . . . . . . . . .    **14.** _____

15. Enter the **smaller** of line 2 or line 14 . . . . . . . . . . . . . . . . . . . . . . . . . . . . . . . . . . . . . . . . . . .    **15.** _____

16. Multiply line 12 by 85% (.85). If line 12 is zero, enter -0- . . . . . . . . . . . . . . . . . . . . . . . . . . . . . . .    **16.** _____

17. Add lines 15 and 16 . . . . . . . . . . . . . . . . . . . . . . . . . . . . . . . . . . . . . . . . . . . . . . . . . . . . . . .    **17.** _____

18. Multiply line 1 by 85% (.85) . . . . . . . . . . . . . . . . . . . . . . . . . . . . . . . . . . . . . . . . . . . . . . . . . .    **18.** _____

19. **Taxable benefits.** Enter the **smaller** of line 17 or line 18. Also enter this amount on Form 1040, line 20b, or
    Form 1040A, line 14b . . . . . . . . . . . . . . . . . . . . . . . . . . . . . . . . . . . . . . . . . . . . . . . . . . . . .    **19.** _____

---

**TIP**    *If you received a lump-sum payment in 2009 that was for an earlier year, also complete Worksheet 2 or 3 and Worksheet 4 to see if you can report a lower taxable benefit.*

## SUMMARY

**L01**   Apply the concept of realization and explain when taxpayers recognize gross income.

- Income is typically realized with a transaction that allows economic benefit to be identified and measured.
- Unless realized income is deferred or excluded, it is included in gross income in the period dictated by the taxpayer's accounting method.
- The accrual method of accounting recognizes income in the period it is earned, and this method is typically used by large corporations.
- The cash method of accounting recognizes income in the period received, and this method offers a simple and flexible method of accounting typically used by individuals.
- The return of capital principle, constructive receipt doctrine, and assignment of income doctrine affect how much income is recognized, when income is recognized, and who recognizes income, respectively.

**L02**   Understand the distinctions between the various sources of income, including income from services and property.

- Income from services is called earned income, whereas income from property is called unearned income.
- A portion of annuity payments and proceeds from sales of property is a nontaxable return of capital.
- Earned and unearned income generated by flow-through business entities is reported by partners and Subchapter S shareholders.
- Other sources of income include alimony payments, unemployment compensation, Social Security benefits, prizes and awards, bargain purchases, imputed interest on below-market loans, and discharge of indebtedness.

**L03**   Apply basic income exclusion provisions to compute gross income.

- Interest received from holding state and local indebtedness (municipal interest) is excluded from gross income.
- Employment-related nonrecognition provisions include a variety of excludable fringe benefits.
- Gifts, inheritances, life insurance proceeds, and foreign earned income are excluded from gross income in order to mitigate the effects of double taxation.
- Common injury-related nonrecognition provisions include the exclusions for worker's compensation, personal injury payments and reimbursements from health insurance policies, and certain payments from disability policies.

# KEY TERMS

accrual method (5-6)

alimony (5-14)

all-inclusive definition of income (5-3)

annuity (5-11)

assignment of income doctrine (5-8)

barter clubs (5-4)

cash method (5-7)

community property systems (5-8)

constructive receipt doctrine (5-7)

deferred income (5-2)

disability insurance (5-25)

discharge of indebtedness (5-20)

earned income (5-10)

excluded income (5-2)

flow-through entity (5-14)

fringe benefits (5-21)

gift (5-23)

gross income (5-2)

imputed income (5-18)

inheritance (5-23)

installment sale (5-26)

municipal bond (5-20)

nonrecognition provisions (5-20)

qualified retirement accounts (5-26)

realization principle (5-3)

return of capital (5-5)

tax basis (5-4)

tax benefit rule (5-5)

unearned income (5-10)

wherewithal to pay (5-4)

# DISCUSSION QUESTIONS

1. **(LO1)** Explain how the definition of gross income in §61 might influence whether a specific cash flow is included in gross income.

2. **(LO1)** Discuss why it might be difficult to determine taxable income using an economist's definition of income.

3. **(LO1)** Describe the concept of realization for tax purposes.

4. **(LO1)** Explain why the definition of gross income for tax purposes might vary from the definition of income for financial accounting income.

5. **(LO1)** Compare and contrast realization of income with recognition of income.

6. **(LO1)** Tim is a plumber who joined a barter club. This year Tim exchanges plumbing services for a new roof. The roof is properly valued at $2,500, but Tim would have only billed $2,200 for the plumbing services. What amount of income should Tim recognize on the exchange of his services for a roof? Would your answer change if Tim would have normally billed $3,000 for his services?

7. **(LO1)** Andre constructs and installs cabinets in homes. Blair sells and installs carpet in apartments. Andre and Blair worked out an arrangement whereby Andre installed cabinets in Blair's home and Blair installed carpet in Andre's home. Neither Andre nor Blair believes they are required to recognize any gross income on this exchange because neither received cash. Do you agree with them? Explain.

8. **(LO1)** What issue precipitated the return of capital principle? Explain.

9. **(LO1)** Compare how the return of capital principle applies when (1) a taxpayer sells an asset and collects the sale proceeds immediately and (2) a taxpayer sells an asset and collects the sale proceeds over several periods (an installment sale). If Congress wanted to maximize revenue from installment sales, how would they have applied the return of capital principle for installment sales?

10. **(LO1)** This year Jorge received a refund of property taxes that he deducted on his tax return last year. Jorge is not sure whether he should include the refund in his gross income. What would you tell him?

11. **(LO1)** Describe in general how the cash method of accounting differs from the accrual method of accounting.

12. **(LO1)** Janet is a cash-method calendar-year taxpayer. She received a check for services provided in the mail during the last week of December. However, rather than cash the check, Janet decided to wait until the following January because she believes that her delay will cause the income to be realized and recognized next year. What would you tell her? Would it matter if she didn't open the envelope? Would it matter if she refused to check her mail during the last week of December? Explain.

13. **(LO1)** The cash method of accounting means that taxpayers don't recognize income unless they receive cash or cash equivalents. True or false? Explain.

14. **(LO1)** Dewey is a lawyer who uses the cash method of accounting. Last year Dewey provided a client with legal services worth $55,000, but the client could not pay the fee. This year Dewey requested that in lieu of paying Dewey $55,000 for the services, the client could make a $45,000 gift to Dewey's daughter. Dewey's daughter received the check for $45,000 and deposited it in her bank account. How much of this income is taxed, if any, to Dewey? Explain.

15. **(LO1)** Clyde and Bonnie were married this year. Clyde has a steady job that will pay him about $37,000, while Bonnie does odd jobs that will produce about $28,000 of income. They also have a joint savings account that will pay about $400 of interest. If Clyde and Bonnie reside in a community property state and

file married-separate tax returns, how much gross income will Clyde and Bonnie each report? Any difference if they reside in a common law state? Explain.

16. **(LO2)** Distinguish earned income from unearned income, and provide an example of each.

17. **(LO2)** Jim purchased 100 shares of stock this year and elected to participate in a dividend reinvestment program. This program automatically uses dividends to purchase additional shares of stock. This year Jim's shares paid $350 of dividends and he used these funds to purchase additional shares of stock. These additional shares are worth $375 at year-end. What amount of dividends, if any, should Jim declare as income this year? Explain.

18. **(LO2)** Jerry has a certificate of deposit at the local bank. The interest on this certificate was credited to his account on December 31 of last year, but he didn't withdraw the interest until January of this year. Explain to Jerry when the interest income is taxed to him.

19. **(LO2)** Conceptually, when taxpayers receive annuity payments, how do they determine the amount of the payment they must include in gross income?

20. **(LO2)** George purchased a life annuity to provide him monthly payments for as long as he lives. Based on IRS tables, George's life expectancy is 100 months. Is George able to recover his cost of the annuity if he dies before he receives 100 monthly payments? Explain. What happens for tax purposes if George receives more than 100 payments?

21. **(LO2)** Brad purchased land for $45,000 this year. At year-end Brad sold the land for $51,700 and paid a sales commission of $450. What effect does this transaction have on Brad's gross income? Explain.

22. **(LO2)** Tomiko is a 50 percent owner (partner) in the Tanaka partnership. During the year, the partnership reported $1,000 of interest income and $2,000 of dividends. How much of this income must Tomiko include in her gross income?

23. **(LO2)** Clem and Ida have been married for several years, but this year they decided to get divorced. In the divorce decree, Clem agreed to deed his car to Ida and pay Ida $10,000 per year for four years. Will either of these transfers qualify as alimony for tax purposes? Explain.

24. **(LO2)** Otto and Fiona are negotiating the terms of their divorce. Otto has agreed to transfer property to Fiona over the next two years, but he has reserved the right to make cash payments in lieu of property transfers. Will tax considerations play a role in Otto's decision to transfer property or pay cash? How will Otto's choice affect the combined gross income and income taxes paid by Otto and Fiona? Explain.

25. **(LO2)** Larry Bounds has won the gold bat award for hitting the longest home run in major league baseball this year. The bat is worth almost $35,000. Under what conditions can Larry exclude the award from his gross income? Explain.

26. **(LO2)** Both Rory and Nicholi each annually receive Social Security benefits of $15,000. Rory's taxable income from sources other than Social Security exceeds $200,000. In contrast, the Social Security benefits are Nicholi's only source of income. What percentage of the Social Security benefits must Rory include in his gross income? What percentage of Social Security benefits is Nicholi required to include in his gross income?

27. **(LO2)** Explain why taxpayers are required to include indirect benefits, such as imputed interest, in gross income. Provide an example of how imputed interest can increase a taxpayer's gross income.

28. **(LO2)** Explain why an insolvent taxpayer is allowed to exclude income from the discharge of indebtedness if the taxpayer remains insolvent after receiving the debt relief.

29. **(LO3)** Cassie works in an office and has access to several professional color printers. Her employer allows Cassie and her fellow employees to use the printers to print color postcards for the holidays. This year Cassie printed out two dozen postcards worth almost $76. Must Cassie include this amount in her gross income this year? Explain your answer.

30. **(LO3)** Describe a policy reason for allowing taxpayers to exclude certain fringe benefits from gross income?

31. **(LO3)** Explain how state and local governments benefit from the provisions that allow taxpayers to exclude interest on state and local bonds from their gross income.

32. **(LO3)** Explain why taxpayers are allowed to exclude gifts and inheritances from gross income even though these payments are realized and clearly provide taxpayers with wherewithal to pay.

33. **(LO3)** Describe the kinds of insurance premiums an employer can pay on behalf of an employee without triggering includible compensation to the employee.

34. **(LO3)** Jim was injured in an accident and his surgeon botched the medical procedure. Jim recovered $5,000 from the doctors for pain and suffering and $2,000 for emotional distress. Determine the taxability of these payments and briefly explain to Jim the apparent rationale for including or excluding these payments from gross income.

35. **(LO3)** Tom was just hired by Acme Corporation and has decided to purchase disability insurance. This insurance promises to pay him weekly benefits to replace his salary should he be unable to work because of disability. Disability insurance is also available through Acme as part of its compensation plan. Acme pays these premiums as a nontaxable fringe benefit, but the plan promises to pay about 10 percent less in benefits. If Tom elects to have Acme pay the premiums, then his compensation will be reduced by an equivalent amount. Should tax considerations play a role in Tom's choice to buy disability insurance through Acme or on his own? Explain.

36. **(LO3)** Describe a rationale for allowing taxpayers to defer recognizing certain types of realized income?

## PROBLEMS

37. **(LO1)** For the following independent cases, determine whether economic income is present and, if so, whether it must be included in gross income (that is, is it realized and recognized for tax purposes?).

   a. Asia owns stock that is listed on the New York Stock Exchange, and this year the stock increased in value by $20,000.

   b. Ben sold stock for $10,000 and paid a sales commission of $250. Ben purchased the stock several years ago for $4,000.

   c. Devon owns 1,000 shares of stock worth $10,000. This year he received 200 additional shares of this stock from a stock dividend. His 1,200 shares are now worth $12,500.

   d. Bessie is a partner in SULU Enterprises LLC. This year SULU reported that Bessie's share of rental income was $2,700 and her share of municipal interest was $750.

38. **(LO1)** XYZ declared a $1 per share dividend on August 15. The date of record for the dividend was September 1 (the stock began selling *ex-dividend* on September 2). The dividend was paid on September 10. Ellis is a cash-method

**research**

taxpayer. Determine if he must include the dividends in gross income under the following independent circumstances.

a. Ellis bought 100 shares of XYZ stock on August 1 for $21 per share. Ellis received $100 on September 10. Ellis still owns the shares at year-end.

b. Ellis bought 100 shares of XYZ stock on August 1 for $21 per share. Ellis sold his XYZ shares on September 5 for $23 per share. Ellis received the $100 dividend on September 10 (note that even though Ellis didn't own the stock on September 10, he still received the dividend because he was the shareholder on the record date).

c. Ellis bought 100 shares of XYZ stock for $22 per share on August 20. Ellis received the $100 dividend on September 10. Ellis still owns the shares at year-end.

■ research ■■    39. **(LO1)** For the following independent cases, determine whether economic income is present and, if so, whether it must be included in gross income. Identify a tax authority that supports your analysis.

a. Hermione discovered a gold nugget (valued at $10,000) on her land.

b. Jay embezzled $20,000 from his employer and has not yet been apprehended.

c. Keisha found $1,000 inside an old dresser. She purchased the dresser at a discount furniture store at the end of last year and found the money after the beginning of the new year. No one has claimed the money.

40. **(LO1)** Although Hank is retired, he is an excellent handyman and often works part-time on small projects for neighbors and friends. Last week his neighbor, Mike, offered to pay Hank $500 for minor repairs to his house. Hank completed the repairs in December of this year. Hank uses the cash method of accounting and is a calendar-year taxpayer. Compute Hank's gross income for this year from each of the following alternative transactions:

a. Mike paid Hank $200 in cash in December of this year and promised to pay the remaining $300 with interest in three months.

b. Mike paid Hank $100 in cash in December of this year and gave him a negotiable promissory note for $400 due in three months with interest. Hank sold the note in January for $350.

c. Mike gave Hank tickets to the big game in January. The tickets have a face value of $50 but Hank could sell them for $400. Hank went to the game with his son.

d. Mike bought Hank a new set of snow tires. The tires typically sell for $500, but Mike bought them on sale for $450.

41. **(LO1)** Jim recently joined the Austin Barter Club, an organization that facilitates the exchange of services between its members. This year Jim provided lawn-mowing services to other club members. Jim received the following from the barter club. Determine the amount, if any, Jim should include in his gross income in each of the following situations:

a. Jim received $275 of car repair services from another member of the club.

b. Jim received a $150 credit that gave him the option of receiving a season pass at a local ski resort from another member of the club. However, he forgot to request the pass by the end of the ski season and his credit expired.

c. Jim received a $450 credit that can only be applied for goods or services from club members next year.

■ research ■■    42. **(LO1)** Last year Acme paid Ralph $15,000 to install a new air-conditioning unit at its headquarters building. The air conditioner did not function properly, and this year Acme requested that Ralph return the payment. Because Ralph could

not repair one critical part in the unit, he refunded the cost of the repair, $5,000, to Acme.

   a. Is Ralph required to include the $15,000 payment he received last year in his gross income from last year?

   b. What are the tax implications of the repayment if Ralph was in the 35 percent tax bracket when he received the $15,000 payment from Acme, but was in the 28 percent tax bracket when he refunded $5,000 to Acme?

   c. How would you answer the question in part (b) if Ralph refunded $2,500 to Acme and not $5,000?

43. **(LO1)** Louis files as a single taxpayer. In April of this year he received a $900 refund of state income taxes that he paid last year. How much of the refund, if any, must Louis include in gross income under the following independent scenarios? Assume the standard deduction last year was $5,700.

   a. Last year Louis claimed itemized deductions of $6,050. Louis's itemized deductions included state income taxes paid of $1,750.

   b. Last year Louis had itemized deductions of $4,800 and he chose to claim the standard deduction. Louis's itemized deductions included state income taxes paid of $1,750.

   c. Last year Louis claimed itemized deductions of $7,540. Louis's itemized deductions included state income taxes paid of $2,750.

44. **(LO1)** Clyde is a cash-method taxpayer who reports on a calendar-year basis. This year Paylate Corporation has decided to pay Clyde a year-end bonus of $1,000. Determine the amount Clyde should include in his gross income this year under the following circumstances:

   a. Paylate Corporation wrote the check and put it in his office mail slot on December 30 of this year, but Clyde did not bother to stop by the office to pick it up until after year-end.

   b. Paylate Corporation mistakenly wrote the check for $100. Clyde received the remaining $900 after year-end.

   c. Paylate Corporation mailed the check to Clyde before the end of the year, but although he expected the bonus payment, he decided not to collect his mail until after year-end.

   d. Clyde picked up the check in December, but the check could not be cashed immediately because it was postdated January 10.

45. **(LO1)** Identify the amount, if any, that these individuals must include in gross income in the following independent cases. Assume that the individuals are on the cash method of accounting and report income on a calendar-year basis.

   a. Elmer was an extremely diligent employee this year and his employer gave him three additional days off with pay (Elmer's gross pay for the three days totaled $1,200, but his net pay was only $948).

   b. Amax purchased new office furniture and allowed each employee to take home $250 of old office furniture.

46. **(LO2)** Ralph owns a building that he is trying to lease. Ralph is a calendar-year, cash-method taxpayer and is trying to evaluate the tax consequences of three different lease arrangements. Under lease 1 the building rents for $500 per month, payable on the first of the next month, and the tenant must make a $500 security deposit that is refunded at the end of the lease. Under lease 2 the building rents for $5,500 per year, payable at the time the lease is signed, but no security deposit is required. Under lease 3 the building rents for $500 per month, payable at the beginning of each month, and the tenant must pay a security deposit of $1,000 that is to be applied toward the rent for the last two months of the lease.

**research**

   a. What amounts are included in Ralph's gross income this year if a tenant signs lease 1 on December 1 and makes timely payments under that lease?

   b. What amounts are included in Ralph's gross income this year if the tenant signs lease 2 on December 31 and makes timely payments under that lease?

   c. What amounts are included in Ralph's gross income this year if the tenant signs lease 3 on November 30 and makes timely payments under that lease?

47. **(LO2)** Anne purchased an annuity from an insurance company that promised to pay her $20,000 per year for the next ten years. Anne paid $145,000 for the annuity, and in exchange she will receive $200,000 over term of the annuity.

   a. How much of the first $20,000 payment should Anne include in gross income?

   b. How much income will Anne recognize over the term of the annuity?

48. **(LO2)** Larry purchased an annuity from an insurance company that promises to pay him $1,000 per month for the rest of his life. Larry paid $170,820 for the annuity. Larry is in good health and he is 72 years old. Larry received the first annuity payment of $1,500 this month. Use the expected number of payments in Exhibit 5-1 for this problem.

   a. How much of the first payment should Larry include in gross income?

   b. If Larry lives 16 years, how much of each payment should he include in gross income?

   c. What are the tax consequences if Larry dies just after he receives the 100th payment?

**research**

49. **(LO2)** Gramps purchased a joint survivor annuity that pays $500 monthly over his remaining life and that of his wife, Gram. Gramps is 70 years old and Gram is 65 years old. Gramps paid $97,020 for the contract. How much income will Gramps recognize on the first payment?

50. **(LO2)** Lanny and Shirley are recently divorced. Shirley has custody of their child, Art, and Lanny pays Shirley $22,000 per year. All property was divided equally.

   a. How much should Shirley include in income if Lanny's payments are made in cash but will cease if Shirley dies or remarries?

   b. How much should Shirley include in income if only $12,000 of Lanny's payments is designated as "nonalimony" in the divorce decree?

   c. How much should Shirley include in income if Lanny's payments drop to $15,000 once Art reaches the age of 18?

**planning**

51. **(LO2)** Todd and Margo are seeking a divorce. Margo has offered to pay Todd $42,000 per year for five years if Margo receives sole title to the art collection. This collection cost them $100,000, but is now worth $360,000. All other property is to be divided equally.

   a. If Margo's payments cease in the event of Todd's death, how are the payments treated for tax purposes?

   b. How much of the gain would be taxed to Todd if Margo sells the art at the end of five years?

   c. Compute the tax cost (benefit) to Todd (Margo) if the payments qualify as alimony. Assume that Todd (Margo) has a marginal tax rate of 15 percent (35 percent), and ignore the time value of money.

   d. How much more should Todd demand in order to agree to allow the payments to cease in the event of his death?

52. **(LO2)** For each of the following independent situations, indicate the amount the taxpayer must include in gross income and explain your answer:

   a. Phil won $500 in the scratch-off state lottery. There is no state income tax.

   b. Ted won a compact car worth $17,000 in a TV game show. Ted plans to sell the car next year.

   c. Al Bore won the Nobel Peace Prize of $500,000 this year. Rather than take the prize, Al designated that the entire award should go to Weatherhead Charity, a tax-exempt organization.

   d. Jerry was awarded $2,500 from his employer, Acme Toons, when he was selected most handsome employee for Valentine's Day this year.

   e. Ellen won a $1,000 cash prize in a school essay contest. The school is a tax-exempt entity, and Ellen plans to use the funds to pay her college education.

   f. Gene won $400 in the office March Madness pool. He paid $40 to join the pool.

53. **(LO2)** Grady received $8,205 of Social Security benefits this year. Grady also reported salary and interest income this year. What amount of the benefits must Grady include in his gross income under the following two independent situations?

   a. Grady files single and reports salary of $12,100 and interest income of $245.

   b. Grady files married joint and reports salary of $75,000 and interest income of $500.

54. **(LO2)** Wally is employed as an executive with Pay More Incorporated. To entice Wally to work for Pay More, the corporation loaned him $20,000 at the beginning of the year at a simple interest rate of 1 percent. Wally would have paid interest of $2,400 this year if the interest rate on the loan had been set at the prevailing federal interest rate.

   a. Wally used the funds as a down payment on a vacation home and repaid the $20,000 loan (including $200 of interest) at year-end. Does this loan result in any income to either party, and if so, how much?

   b. Assume that in addition to the facts described in part (a), Pay More forgave the loan and interest on December 31. What amount of gross income does Wally recognize this year? Explain.

55. **(LO3)** Jimmy has fallen on hard times recently. Last year he borrowed $250,000 and added an additional $50,000 of his own funds to purchase $300,000 of undeveloped real estate. This year the value of the real estate dropped dramatically, and Jimmy's lender agreed to reduce the loan amount to $230,000. For each of the following independent situations, indicate the amount Jimmy must include in gross income and explain your answer:

   a. The real estate is worth $175,000 and Jimmy has no other assets or liabilities.

   b. The real estate is worth $235,000 and Jimmy has no other assets or liabilities.

   c. The real estate is worth $200,000 and Jimmy has $45,000 in other assets but no other liabilities.

56. **(LO3)** Grady is a 45-year-old employee with AMUCK Garbage Corporation. AMUCK pays group-term life insurance premiums for employees, and Grady chose the maximum face amount of $120,000. What amount, if any, of the premium AMUCK paid on his behalf, must Grady include in his gross income for the year? Provide a tax authority to support your answer.

   **research**

57. **(LO3)** Fred currently earns $9,000 per month. Fred has been offered the chance to work overseas on a temporary assignment next year. His employer is willing to pay Fred $10,000 per month if he accepts the assignment. Assume that the maximum foreign earned income exclusion for next year is $91,500.

   a. How much U.S. gross income will Fred report if he accepts the assignment abroad on January 1 of next year and works overseas for the entire year?

b. Suppose that Fred's employer has offered Fred only a six-month overseas assignment beginning on January 1 of next year. How much U.S. gross income will Fred report next year if he accepts the six-month assignment abroad and returns home on July 1 of next year?

c. Suppose that Fred's employer offers Fred a permanent overseas assignment beginning on March 1 of next year. How much U.S. gross income will Fred report next year if he accepts the permanent assignment abroad? Assume that Fred will be abroad for 305 days next year.

58. **(LO3)** For each of the following situations, indicate how much the taxpayer is required to include in gross income and explain your answer:

a. Steve was awarded a $5,000 scholarship to attend State Law School. The scholarship pays Steve's tuition and fees.

b. Hal was awarded a $15,000 scholarship to attend State Hotel School. All scholarship students must work 20 hours per week at the school residency during the term.

c. Bill was the recipient of an athletic scholarship that pays his $12,000 tuition to State University and provides him with a $500 per month stipend to pay for food and housing. The scholarship requires Bill to participate in athletic competition each term.

59. **(LO3)** Cecil cashed in a Series EE savings bond with a redemption value of $14,000 and an original cost of $9,800. For each of the following independent scenarios, calculate the amount of interest Cecil will include in his gross income assuming he files as a single taxpayer:

a. Cecil plans to spend all of the proceeds to pay his tuition at State University and estimates his modified adjusted gross income at $63,100.

b. Cecil plans to spend $4,200 of the proceeds to pay his tuition at State University and estimates his modified adjusted gross income at $60,600.

60. **(LO3)** Grady is a member of a large family and received the following payments this year. For each payment, determine whether the payment constitutes realized income and determine the amount of each payment Grady must include in his gross income.

a. A gift of $20,000 from Grady's grandfather.

b. 1,000 shares of GM stock worth $120 per share inherited from Grady's uncle. The uncle purchased the shares for $25 each, and the shares are worth $125 at year-end.

c. A gift of $50,000 of Ford Motor Bonds. Grady received the bonds on October 31, and he received $1,500 of semiannual interest from the bonds on December 31.

d. A loan of $5,000 for school expenses from Grady's aunt.

61. **(LO3)** Bart is the favorite nephew of his aunt Thelma. Thelma transferred several items of value to Bart. For each of the following transactions, determine the effect on Bart's gross income.

a. Thelma gave Bart an auto worth $22,000. Thelma purchased the auto three years ago for $17,000.

b. Bart eventually sold the automobile he received in part (a) for $15,000 (assume his basis in the auto was $17,000).

c. Thelma elects to cancel her life insurance policy, and she gives the cash surrender value of $15,000 to Bart.

d. Bart is the beneficiary of a $100,000 whole life insurance policy on the life of Thelma. Thelma died this year, and Bart received $100,000 in cash.

e. Bart inherited 500 shares of stock from Thelma's estate. Thelma purchased the shares many years ago for $1,200, and the shares are worth $45,000 at her death.

62. **(LO3)** Terry was ill for three months and missed work during this period. During his illness, Terry received $4,500 in sick pay from a disability insurance policy. What amounts are included in Terry's gross income under the following independent circumstances?

    a. Terry has disability insurance provided by his employer as a nontaxable fringe benefit. Terry's employer paid $2,800 in disability premiums for Terry this year.

    b. Terry paid $2,800 in premiums for his disability insurance this year.

    c. Terry's employer paid the $2,800 in premiums for Terry, but Terry elected to have his employer include the $2,800 as compensation on Terry's W-2.

    d. Terry has disability insurance whose cost is shared with his employer. Terry's employer paid $1,800 in disability premiums for Terry this year as a nontaxable fringe benefit, and Terry paid the remaining $1,000 of premiums from his after-tax salary.

63. **(LO3)** Tim's parents plan to provide him with $50,000 to support him while he establishes a new landscaping business. In exchange for the support, Tim will maintain the landscape at his father's business. Under what conditions will the transfer of $50,000 be included in Tim's gross income? Explain. Do you have a recommendation for Tim and his parents?

■ **planning**

64. **(LO3)** What amounts are included in gross income for the following taxpayers? Explain your answers.

    a. Janus sued Tiny Toys for personal injuries from swallowing a toy. Janus was paid $30,000 for medical costs and $250,000 for punitive damages.

    b. Carl was injured in a car accident. Carl's insurance paid him $500 to reimburse his medical expenses and an additional $250 for the emotional distress Carl suffered as a result of the accident.

    c. Ajax published a story about Pete and as a result Pete sued Ajax for damage to his reputation. Ajax lost in court and paid Pete an award of $20,000.

    d. Bevis was laid off from his job last month. This month he drew $800 in unemployment benefits.

## COMPREHENSIVE PROBLEMS

65. Charlie was hired by Ajax this year as a corporate executive and a member of the board of directors. During the current year, Charlie received the following payments or benefits paid on his behalf.

| | |
|---|---:|
| Salary payments | $92,000 |
| Contributions to qualified pension plan | 10,200 |
| Qualified health insurance premiums | 8,400 |
| Year-end bonus | 15,000 |
| Annual director's fee | 10,000 |
| Group-term life insurance premiums (face = $40,000) | 750 |
| Whole life insurance premiums (face = $100,000) | 1,420 |
| Disability insurance premiums (no special elections) | 4,350 |

    a. Charlie uses the cash method and calendar year for tax purposes. Calculate Charlie's gross income for the current year.

b. Suppose that Ajax agrees to pay Charlie an additional $100,000 once Charlie completes five years of employment. Will this agreement alter Charlie's gross income this year relative to your part (a) answer? Explain.

c. Suppose that in exchange for his promise to remain with the firm for the next four years, Ajax paid Charlie four years of director's fees in advance. Will this arrangement alter Charlie's gross income this year relative to your part (a) answer? Explain.

d. Assume that in lieu of a year-end bonus Ajax transferred 500 shares of Bell stock to Charlie as compensation. Further assume that the stock was listed at $35 per share and Charlie would sell the shares by year-end, at which time he expected the price to be $37 per share. Will this arrangement alter Charlie's gross income this year relative to your part (a) answer? Explain.

e. Suppose that in lieu of a year-end bonus Ajax made Charlie's house payments (a total of $23,000). Will this arrangement alter Charlie's gross income this year relative to your part (a) answer? Explain.

66. Irene is disabled and receives payments from a number of sources. The interest payments are from bonds that Irene purchased over past years and a disability insurance policy that Irene purchased herself. Calculate Irene's gross income.

| | |
|---|---|
| Interest, bonds issued by City of Austin, Texas | $2,000 |
| Social Security benefits | 8,200 |
| Interest, U.S. Treasury bills | 1,300 |
| Interest, bonds issued by Ford Motor Company | 1,500 |
| Interest, bonds issued by City of Quebec, Canada | 750 |
| Disability insurance benefits | 19,500 |
| Distributions from qualified pension plan | 5,400 |

67. Ken is 63 years old and unmarried. He retired at age 55 when he sold his business, Understock.com. Though Ken is retired, he is still very active. Ken reported the following financial information this year. *Assume* Ken's modified adjusted gross income for purposes of the bond interest exclusion and for determining the taxability of his Social Security benefits is $70,000 and that Ken files as a single taxpayer. Determine Ken's gross income.

a. Ken won $1,200 in an illegal game of poker (the game was played in Utah, where gambling is illegal).

b. Ken sold 1,000 shares of stock for $32 a share. He inherited the stock two years ago. His tax basis (or investment) in the stock was $31 per share.

c. Ken received $25,000 from an annuity he purchased eight years ago. He purchased the annuity, to be paid annually for 20 years, for $210,000.

d. Ken received $13,000 in disability benefits for the year. He purchased the disability insurance policy last year.

e. Ken resided in Ireland from July 1, 2009, through June 30, 2010, visiting relatives. While he was there he earned $35,000 working in his cousin's pub. He was paid $17,000 for his services in 2009 and $18,000 for his services in 2010. Assume Ken elects to use the foreign-earned income exclusion to the extent he is eligible.

f. Ken decided to go back to school to learn about European history. He received a $500 cash scholarship to attend. He used $300 to pay for his books and he applied the rest toward his new car payment.

g. Ken's son, Mike, instructed his employer to make half of his final paycheck of the year payable to Ken. Ken received the check on December 30 in the amount of $1,100.

h. Ken received a $610 refund of the $3,600 in state income taxes his employer withheld from his pay last year. Ken claimed $5,750 in itemized deductions last year (the standard deduction for a single filer was $5,700).

i. Ken received $30,000 of interest from corporate bonds and money market accounts.

68. Consider the following letter and answer Shady's question.

**To my friendly student tax preparer:**

Hello, my name is Shady Slim. I understand you are going to help me figure out my gross income for the year . . . whatever that means. It's been a busy year and I'm a busy man, so let me give you the lowdown on my life and you can do your thing.

I was unemployed at the beginning of the year and got $2,000 in unemployment compensation. I later got a job as a manager for Roca Cola. I earned $55,000 in base salary this year. My boss gave me a $5,000 Christmas bonus check on December 22. I decided to hold on to that check and not cash it until next year, so I won't have to pay taxes on it this year. Pretty smart, huh? My job's pretty cool. I get a lot of fringe benefits like a membership to the gym that costs $400 a year and all the Roca Cola I can drink, although I can't really drink a whole lot. I also got an award for having the department with the least number of accidents. My boss gave me a gold watch worth $300!

As part of my manager duties, I get to decide on certain things like contracts for the company. My good buddy, Eddie, runs a bottling company. I made sure that he won the bottling contract for Roca Cola for this year (even though his contract wasn't quite the best). Eddie bought me a Corvette this year for being such a good friend. The Corvette cost $50,000 and he bought it for me out of the goodness of his own heart. What a great guy!

Here's a bit of good luck for the year. Upon leaving my office one day, I found $10,000 lying in the street! Well, one person's bad luck is my good luck, right?

I like to gamble a lot. I won a $22,000 poker tournament in Las Vegas this year. I also won about $5,000 over the year playing the guys at our Friday night poker game. Can you believe that I didn't lose anything this year?

Speaking of the guys, one of them hit me with his car as we were leaving the game one night. He must have been pretty ticked that he lost! I broke my right leg and my left arm. I sued the guy and got $11,000 for my medical expenses, $3,000 to pay my psychotherapist for the emotional problems I had relating to the injuries (I got really depressed!), and I won $10,000 in punitive damages. That'll teach him that he's not so tough without his car!

Another bit of bad luck. My uncle Monty died this year. I really liked the guy, but the $200,000 inheritance I received from him made me feel a little better about the loss. I did the smart thing with the money and invested it in stocks and bonds and socked a little into my savings account. As a result, I received $600 in dividends from the stock, $400 in interest from the municipal bonds, and $300 in interest from my savings account.

My ex-wife, Alice, is still paying me alimony. She's a lawyer who divorced me a few years ago because I was "unethical" or something like that. Since she was making so much money and I was unemployed at the time, the judge ruled that she had to pay ME alimony. Isn't that something? She sent me $3,000 in alimony payments this year. She still kind of likes me, though. She sent me a check for $500 as a Christmas gift this year. I didn't get her anything, though.

So there you go. That's this year in a nutshell. Can you figure out my gross income for me? And since you're a student, this is free, right? Thanks, I owe you one! Let me know if I can get you a six-pack of Roca Cola or something.

69. Diana and Ryan Workman were married on January 1 of last year. Diana has an eight-year-old son, Jorge, from her previous marriage. Ryan works as a computer programmer at Datafile Inc. (DI) earning a salary of $96,000. Diana is self-employed and runs a day care center. The Workmans reported the following financial information pertaining to their activities during the current year.

a. Ryan earned a $96,000 salary for the year.

b. Ryan borrowed $12,000 from DI to purchase a car. DI charged him 2 percent interest on the loan, which Ryan paid on December 31. DT would have charged Ryan $720 if interest had been calculated at the applicable federal interest rate.

c. Diana received $2,000 in alimony and $4,500 in child support payments from her former husband.

d. Diana won a $900 cash prize at her church-sponsored Bingo game.

e. The Workmans received $500 of interest from corporate bonds and $250 of interest from a municipal bond. Diana owned these bonds before she married Ryan.

f. The couple bought 50 shares of ABC Inc. stock for $40 per share on July 2. The stock was worth $47 a share on December 31. The stock paid a dividend of $1.00 per share on December 1.

g. Diana's father passed away on April 14. She inherited cash of $50,000 and his baseball card collection, valued at $2,000. As the beneficiary of her father's life insurance policy, Diana also received $150,000.

h. The couple spent a weekend in Atlantic City in November and came home with gambling winnings of $1,200.

i. Ryan received $400 cash for reaching 10 years of continuous service at DI.

j. Ryan was hit and injured by a drunk driver while crossing a street at a crosswalk. He was unable to work for a month. He received $6,000 from his disability insurance. DI paid the premiums for Ryan, but they reported the amount of the premiums as compensation to Ryan on his year-end W-2.

k. The drunk driver who hit Ryan in part (j) was required to pay his $2,000 medical costs, $1,500 for the emotional trauma he suffered from the accident, and $5,000 for punitive damages.

l. For meeting his performance goals this year, Ryan was informed on December 27 that he would receive a $5,000 year-end bonus. DI mailed the check to Ryan on December 30 but Ryan didn't receive the check at his home until January 2.

m. Diana is a 10 percent owner of MNO Inc., a Subchapter S corporation. The company reported ordinary business income for the year of $92,000. Diana acquired the MNO stock last year.

n. Diana's day care business received $35,000 in revenues. In addition, customers owed her $3,000 at year-end. During the year, Diana spent $5,500 for supplies, $1,500 for utilities, $15,000 for rent, and $500 for miscellaneous expenses. One customer gave her free advertising (worth $2,500) on a local radio station he owned in exchange for Diana allowing his child to attend the day care center free of charge. Diana accounts for her business activities using the cash method of accounting.

o. Ryan's employer pays the couple's annual health insurance premiums of $5,500.

**Required:**

A. Assuming the Workmans file a joint tax return, determine their gross income.

B. Assuming the Workmans live in California, a community property state, and that Diana and Ryan file separately, what is Ryan's gross income?

chapter

# 6

# Individual Deductions

## Learning Objectives

**Upon completing this chapter, you should be able to:**

**LO 1** Identify the common deductions necessary for calculating adjusted gross income (AGI).

---- ■ ----

**LO 2** Describe the different types of itemized deductions available to individuals and compute itemized deductions.

---- ■ ----

**LO 3** Explain the operation of the standard deduction, determine the deduction for personal and dependency exemptions, and compute taxable income.

ow that Courtney has determined her gross income, she still must determine her deductions to compute taxable income. Fortunately, Courtney keeps detailed records of all the expenditures she believes to be deductible. Besides expenses associated with her weekend consulting work and rental property, Courtney incurred some significant costs moving from Cincinnati to Kansas City. She also paid self-employment taxes on her consulting income and paid tuition for Ellen to attend summer school. Courtney is confident most of these items are deductible, but she isn't quite sure about the tuition.

Based on her review of prior-year tax returns, Courtney has a pretty good handle on her itemized deductions. She incurred some extra medical expenses to treat a broken wrist from a mountain biking accident and had additional state income taxes withheld from her paycheck. Courtney paid real estate taxes for her personal residence and investment property and interest expense on loans secured by her new home. She also donated (cash and property) to her favorite charities. Courtney experienced losses when her purse was stolen and when she damaged her car in an accident. She isn't sure if these losses are deductible.

In a push to improve her job performance, Courtney incurred costs to attend motivational seminars and travel to

| Storyline Summary | |
|---|---|
| *Taxpayers:* | Courtney Wilson, age 40 Courtney's mother Dorothy "Gram" Weiss, age 70 |
| *Family description:* | Courtney is divorced with a son, Deron, age 10, and a daughter, Ellen, age 20. Gram is currently residing with Courtney. Ellen is currently a full-time student. |
| *Location:* | Kansas City, Missouri |
| *Employment status:* | Courtney works as an architect for EWD. Gram is retired. |
| *Filing status:* | Courtney files as head-of-household. Gram files as a single taxpayer. |
| *Current situation:* | Determining allowable deductions and computing taxable income |

other parts of the country to study different architectural designs. Despite the fact that she was trying to improve her job performance, EWD did not reimburse her for these costs.

Gram wasn't as busy as Courtney this year. Gram paid a penalty for cashing in her certificate of deposit early. She also paid some medical expenses and donated money to her local church. Gram is a little frustrated because she doesn't incur enough itemized deductions to exceed the standard deduction amount. Gram recently heard that she might be able to save taxes by "bunching" her itemized deductions into one year. She's hoping to learn a little bit more about this technique. In any event, Gram didn't pay any taxes during the year and she wants to learn how much she's going to owe. ∎

In the previous chapter, we determined *gross income* for both Courtney and Gram. To compute their taxable income, however, we need to identify their deductions. As emphasized previously, taxpayers are not allowed to deduct expenditures unless there is a specific tax law authorizing the deductions. And as we learn in this chapter, Congress grants many deductions for taxpayers for a variety of reasons.

As we discussed in Chapter 4, deductions appear in one of two places in the individual income tax formula. Deductions "for AGI" (also called deductions "above the line") are subtracted directly from gross income.[1] Next, deductions "from AGI" (also called deductions "below the line" or "itemized" deductions) are subtracted directly from AGI, resulting in taxable income. Deductions for AGI are generally preferred over deductions from AGI because deductions above the line reduce taxable income dollar for dollar. In contrast, deductions from AGI sometimes have no effect on taxable income. Further, because many of the limitations on tax benefits for higher income taxpayers are based upon AGI, deductions for AGI often reduce these limitations thereby increasing potential tax benefits. Thus, it's important to determine both the amount of the deduction and whether it's a deduction *for* AGI or *from* AGI. We begin our discussion of deductions by describing deductions for AGI, and we conclude by tackling itemized deductions, the standard deduction, and exemptions.

## L01 DEDUCTIONS FOR AGI

Congress allows taxpayers to claim a variety of deductions for AGI.[2] To provide an overview, we select a cross section of deductions for AGI and classify them into three categories:

1. Deductions *directly* related to **business activities.**
2. Deductions *indirectly* related to business activities.
3. Deductions subsidizing specific activities.

[1]Most, but not all, deductions for AGI appear on lines 23 through 35 on page 1 of Form 1040. The term "above the line" refers to the placement of deductions for AGI before the last line of the first page of Form 1040. This last line is the taxpayer's AGI.

[2]§63(d) identifies deductions for AGI.

We've organized our discussion around these categories to illustrate the variety of deductions for AGI and explain why Congress provides preferential treatment for certain deductions.

## Deductions Directly Related to Business Activities

As a matter of equity, Congress allows taxpayers involved in business activities to deduct expenses incurred to generate business income. That is, because taxpayers include the revenue they receive from doing business in gross income, they should be allowed to deduct against gross income the expenses they incur to generate those revenues.

To begin, we must define "business activities" and, for reasons we discuss below, we must distinguish business activities from **investment activities.** In general, for tax purposes activities are either *profit-motivated* or motivated by personal objectives. Profit-motivated activities are, in turn, classified as either (1) business activities or (2) investment activities. Business activities are sometimes referred to as a **trade or business,** and these activities require a relatively high level of involvement or effort from the taxpayer. For example, if an individual is a full-time employee, the individual is in the business of being an employee. Self-employed individuals are also engaged in business activities. Unlike business activities, investment activities are profit-motivated activities that *don't* require a high degree of taxpayer involvement or effort.[3] Instead, investment activities involve investing in property for appreciation or for income payments. An individual who occasionally buys land or stock in anticipation of appreciation or dividend payments would be engaged in an investment activity.

---

**Example 6-1**

Suppose that Courtney purchased a parcel of land for its appreciation potential. Would her ownership in the land be considered a business or investment activity?

**Answer:** Courtney's activity would most likely be considered an investment activity, because she acquired the land for its appreciation potential and she does not plan to exercise any special effort to develop the property or to become actively involved in other real estate speculation.

*What if:* Suppose that Courtney frequently buys and sells land or develops land to sell in small parcels to those wanting to build homes. Would Courtney's activity be considered a business or investment activity?

**Answer:** Courtney's activity would most likely be considered a business activity because she is actively involved in generating profits from the land by developing it rather than simply holding the land for appreciation.

---

The distinction between business and investment activities is critical for determining whether a deduction associated with the activity is above the line or below. With one exception, business expenses are deducted for AGI. The lone exception is unreimbursed employee business expenses, which are deductible as itemized (from AGI) deductions.[4] In contrast, investment expenses are deductible as itemized deductions, with one exception. Expenses associated with rental and royalty activities are deductible for AGI regardless of whether the activity qualifies as an investment or a business. Exhibit 6-1 summarizes the rules for classifying business and investment expenses as for and from AGI deductions.

---

[3]§162 authorizes trade or business expense deductions, while §212 authorizes deductions for investment activities. The distinction between these activities is discussed in Chapter 8.

[4]For example, an employee may use her own automobile to make a business delivery for her employer. The expenses she incurs to make the delivery (cost of operating the automobile and parking) are business expenses that are deducted from AGI as miscellaneous itemized deductions.

**EXHIBIT 6-1** Individual Business and Investment Expense Deductions for AGI and from AGI

| | Deduction Type | |
|---|---|---|
| **Activity Type** | **Deduction for AGI** | **Deduction from AGI** (itemized deduction) |
| Business activities | Self-employed business expenses | Employee business expenses |
| Investment activities | Rental and royalty expenses | Other investment expenses |

**Trade or Business Expenses** Congress limits business deductions to expenses directly related to the business activity and those that are **ordinary and necessary** for the activity.[5] This means that deductible expenses must be appropriate and helpful for generating a profit. Although business deductions are one of the most common deductions for AGI, they are not readily visible on the front page of Form 1040. Instead, these deductions are reported with business revenues on Schedule C of Form 1040. Schedule C, presented in Exhibit 6-2, is essentially an income statement for the business that identifies typical ordinary and necessary business expenses.

**EXHIBIT 6-2** Parts I and II from Schedule C Profit or Loss from Business

**Part I  Income**

1 Gross receipts or sales. **Caution.** See page C-4 and check the box if:
   • This income was reported to you on Form W-2 and the "Statutory employee" box on that form was checked, or
   • You are a member of a qualified joint venture reporting only rental real estate income not subject to self-employment tax. Also see page C-3 for limit on losses. ▸ ☐  1
2 Returns and allowances . . . . . . . . . . . . . . . . . . . . . . .  2
3 Subtract line 2 from line 1 . . . . . . . . . . . . . . . . . . . . .  3
4 Cost of goods sold (from line 42 on page 2) . . . . . . . . . . . . . .  4
5 **Gross profit.** Subtract line 4 from line 3 . . . . . . . . . . . . . .  5
6 Other income, including federal and state gasoline or fuel tax credit or refund (see page C-4) . . .  6
7 **Gross income.** Add lines 5 and 6 . . . . . . . . . . . . . . . . . ▸  7

**Part II  Expenses.** Enter expenses for business use of your home **only** on line 30.

| 8 | Advertising . . . . . . | 8 | | 18 | Office expense . . . . . | 18 | |
|---|---|---|---|---|---|---|---|
| 9 | Car and truck expenses (see page C-4) . . . . . | 9 | | 19 | Pension and profit-sharing plans . | 19 | |
| 10 | Commissions and fees . | 10 | | 20 | Rent or lease (see page C-6): | | |
| 11 | Contract labor (see page C-4) | 11 | | a | Vehicles, machinery, and equipment | 20a | |
| 12 | Depletion . . . . . | 12 | | b | Other business property . . . . | 20b | |
| 13 | Depreciation and section 179 expense deduction (not included in Part III) (see page C-5) . . . . . | 13 | | 21 | Repairs and maintenance . . . | 21 | |
| | | | | 22 | Supplies (not included in Part III) . | 22 | |
| | | | | 23 | Taxes and licenses . . . . . | 23 | |
| | | | | 24 | Travel, meals, and entertainment: | | |
| 14 | Employee benefit programs (other than on line 19) . . | 14 | | a | Travel . . . . . . . . . | 24a | |
| 15 | Insurance (other than health) | 15 | | b | Deductible meals and entertainment (see page C-6) . | 24b | |
| 16 | Interest: | | | 25 | Utilities . . . . . . . . | 25 | |
| a | Mortgage (paid to banks, etc.) | 16a | | 26 | Wages (less employment credits) . | 26 | |
| b | Other . . . . . . | 16b | | 27 | Other expenses (from line 48 on page 2) . . . . . . . | 27 | |
| 17 | Legal and professional services . . . . . . | 17 | | | | | |

28 **Total expenses** before expenses for business use of home. Add lines 8 through 27 . . . . . . ▸  28
29 Tentative profit or (loss). Subtract line 28 from line 7 . . . . . . . . . . . . . . . .  29
30 Expenses for business use of your home. Attach **Form 8829** . . . . . . . . . . . . . .  30
31 **Net profit or (loss).** Subtract line 30 from line 29.
   • If a profit, enter on both **Form 1040, line 12,** and **Schedule SE, line 2,** or on **Form 1040NR, line 13** (if you checked the box on line 1, see page C-7). Estates and trusts, enter on **Form 1041, line 3.**  31
   • If a loss, you **must** go to line 32.
32 If you have a loss, check the box that describes your investment in this activity (see page C-7).
   • If you checked 32a, enter the loss on both **Form 1040, line 12,** and **Schedule SE, line 2,** or on **Form 1040NR, line 13** (if you checked the box on line 1, see the line 31 instructions on page C-7). Estates and trusts, enter on **Form 1041, line 3.**   32a ☐ All investment is at risk.
   • If you checked 32b, you **must** attach **Form 6198.** Your loss may be limited.   32b ☐ Some investment is not at risk.

For Paperwork Reduction Act Notice, see page C-9 of the instructions.   Cat. No. 11334P   Schedule C (Form 1040) 2009

Taxpayers transfer the *net* income or loss from Schedule C to Form 1040 (page 1), line 12. Business deductions are not listed on the front of Form 1040, because these expenses reduce the net income on Schedule C that is reported on page 1 of Form 1040.

[5]§162. In Chapter 8, we address the requirements for deductible business expenses in detail.

**Example 6-2**

Besides being employed by EWD, Courtney is also a self-employed consultant (a business activity). This year her consulting activity generated $19,500 of revenue and incurred $1,500 in expenses (primarily travel and transportation expenses). How does she report the revenue and deductions from the activity?

**Answer:** Courtney reports the $19,500 of revenue and deducts the $1,500 of business expenses for AGI on her Schedule C. Her net income of $18,000 from her consulting activities is included on the front page (line 12) of her individual tax return.

**Rental and Royalty Expenses**    Taxpayers are allowed to deduct their expenses associated with generating rental or royalty income for AGI.[6] Similar to business expenses, rental and royalty expenses do not appear directly on the front page of Form 1040. Instead, rental and royalty deductions are reported with rental and royalty revenues on Schedule E of Form 1040. Schedule E, presented in Exhibit 6-3, is

**EXHIBIT 6-3    Page 1 of Schedule E Rental or Royalty Income**

| Income: | | | Properties A | B | C |
|---|---|---|---|---|---|
| 3 | Rents received | 3 | | | |
| 4 | Royalties received | 4 | | | |
| **Expenses:** | | | | | |
| 5 | Advertising | 5 | | | |
| 6 | Auto and travel (see page E-4) | 6 | | | |
| 7 | Cleaning and maintenance | 7 | | | |
| 8 | Commissions | 8 | | | |
| 9 | Insurance | 9 | | | |
| 10 | Legal and other professional fees | 10 | | | |
| 11 | Management fees | 11 | | | |
| 12 | Mortgage interest paid to banks, etc. (see page E-5) | 12 | | | |
| 13 | Other interest | 13 | | | |
| 14 | Repairs | 14 | | | |
| 15 | Supplies | 15 | | | |
| 16 | Taxes | 16 | | | |
| 17 | Utilities | 17 | | | |
| 18 | Other (list) ▶ _____ | 18 | | | |
| 19 | Add lines 5 through 18 | 19 | | | |
| 20 | Depreciation expense or depletion (see page E-5) | 20 | | | |
| 21 | Total expenses. Add lines 19 and 20 | 21 | | | |
| 22 | Income or (loss) from rental real estate or royalty properties. Subtract line 21 from line 3 (rents) or line 4 (royalties). If the result is a (loss), see page E-5 to find out if you must file **Form 6198** | 22 | | | |
| 23 | Deductible rental real estate loss. **Caution.** Your rental real estate loss on line 22 may be limited. See page E-5 to find out if you must file **Form 8582.** Real estate professionals **must** complete line 43 on page 2 | 23 ( | )( | )( | ) |
| 24 | **Income.** Add positive amounts shown on line 22. **Do not** include any losses | | | | |
| 25 | **Losses.** Add royalty losses from line 22 and rental real estate losses from line 23. Enter total losses here. | | | | |
| 26 | **Total rental real estate and royalty income or (loss).** Combine lines 24 and 25. Enter the result here. If Parts II, III, IV, and line 40 on page 2 do not apply to you, also enter this amount on Form 1040, line 17, or Form 1040NR, line 18. Otherwise, include this amount in the total on line 41 on page 2. | | | | |

**For Paperwork Reduction Act Notice, see page E-8 of the instructions.**    Cat. No. 11344L

[6] §212(a)(4).

essentially an income statement for the taxpayer's rental or royalty activities. Taxpayers transfer the *net* income or loss from Schedule E to Form 1040 (page 1), line 17.

Rental and royalty endeavors are most commonly considered to be investment activities, but like trade or business expenses, rental and royalty deductions are claimed above the line.[7] Perhaps rental and royalty expenses are deductible for AGI because Congress believed that these activities usually require more taxpayer involvement than other types of investment activities.

---

**Example 6-3**

Courtney owns a condominium that she rents to tenants. This year she received $14,000 in rental revenue and incurred $9,000 of expenses associated with the rental, including management fees, maintenance, and depreciation. How does she report the revenue and expenses for tax purposes?

**Answer:** Courtney reports the $14,000 of rental receipts and deducts the $9,000 of rental expenses for AGI on Schedule E. The net rental income of $5,000 is reported on the front page (line 17) of her individual tax return.

---

**Losses**    As we discuss in more detail in Chapter 10, taxpayers disposing of business assets at a loss are allowed to deduct the losses for AGI. Also, individual taxpayers selling investment (capital) assets at a loss are allowed to deduct the "capital" losses against other capital gains. If the capital losses exceed the capital gains, they can deduct up to $3,000 as a net capital loss in a particular year. Losses in excess of the $3,000 limit are carried forward indefinitely to subsequent years when they are deductible subject to the same limitations.

**Flow-through Entities**    Income from flow-through entities such as partnerships, LLCs, and S corporations passes through to the owners of those entities and is reported on Schedule E of the tax returns of the owners. Similarly, any expenses and losses incurred by the entity pass through to the entity owners, who typically treat them as deductions for AGI, subject to certain restrictions that we discuss in Chapter 11.

### Deductions Indirectly Related to Business Activities

Taxpayers can incur expenses in activities that are not directly related to making money but that they would not have incurred if they were not involved in a business activity. Taxpayers are allowed to deduct several of these expenses that are indirectly related to business activities as deductions for AGI. We describe several of these deductions below.

**Moving Expenses**    The cost of moving personal possessions is not a direct cost of doing business or being employed. Nonetheless, individuals qualify for a moving expense deduction if they move *and* change their principal place of work. Specifically, individuals can deduct moving expenses as deductions for AGI if they meet two tests: (1) a distance test and (2) a business test associated with the move.[8]

---

[7]Royalties are received for allowing others to use property or rights to property. For example, royalties are paid for allowing others to use or sell copyrighted material such as books or plays, or extract natural resources from property. The amount of the royalty is often a percentage of total revenues derived from the property or rights to property.

[8]§217. Moving expenses are deducted on Form 3903.

To satisfy the distance test, the distance from the taxpayer's old residence to the new place of work must be at least 50 miles more than the distance from the old residence to the old place of work. In other words, if the taxpayer were staying in her old home, the new place of work must increase her commute by at least 50 miles, thereby justifying a move to a new residence. To satisfy the business test, the taxpayer must either be employed full-time for 39 of the first 52 weeks after the move or be self-employed for 78 of the first 104 weeks after the move.

Individuals need not change employers if they meet both tests. Indeed, taxpayers can qualify for a moving expense deduction by beginning their first job, by beginning a job after a prolonged absence from the workforce, or by changing locations with the same employer. In addition, a taxpayer's reasons for moving may be entirely personal, such as wanting to move to a milder climate; business-related, such as wanting to change jobs or start a new business; or some of both.

---

**Example 6-4**

Before moving to Kansas City, Courtney lived in Cincinnati, Ohio, where she commuted 10 miles to her place of work. The distance from Courtney's home in Cincinnati to EWD in Kansas City, her new place of work, is 580 miles. Can Courtney deduct the expenses of moving her residence to Kansas City?

**Answer:** Yes. Courtney meets both the distance and the business tests because 580 miles is more than 60 miles (her original 10-mile commute from her former residence to her former place of work, plus 50 miles), and because she worked for EWD for the requisite 39 weeks during her first 52 weeks after her move (she worked from mid-January through December 31).

**What if:** Suppose that Courtney started a new job at an office just outside of Cincinnati and she moved into a new residence. The distance from Courtney's former residence to her former place of work was 12 miles. The distance from Courtney's former residence to her new place of work is 55 miles. Does Courtney meet the distance test for moving expenses?

**Answer:** No, because if she had stayed in her former residence her commute would have increased by only 43 miles. To qualify, the commute from her former residence to her new work must be at least 50 miles longer than her commute from her former residence to her former place of work. Note that the location of her new residence is irrelevant to the distance test.

**What if:** Suppose that Courtney started a new job at an office just outside of Cincinnati and she moved into a new residence. If the distance from Courtney's former residence to her former place of work was 12 miles, and the distance from her former residence to her new work place was 80 miles, would Courtney meet the distance test for moving expenses?

**Answer:** Yes, the commute from her former residence to her new job is 68 miles longer than the commute from her former residence to her old job.

---

Deductible moving expenses are limited to reasonable expenses associated with moving personal possessions and traveling to the new residence, including transportation and lodging. Taxpayers are allowed to deduct a mileage rate in lieu of the actual costs of driving their personal automobiles during the move. In 2010, taxpayers are allowed to deduct 16.5 cents a mile for driving their personal automobiles during a move. Taxpayers may also deduct the cost of moving their personal belongings and the belongings of members of their households. Taxpayers are *not* allowed to deduct costs such as meals during the move or costs associated with house-hunting trips. Taxpayers who are reimbursed by their employers for actual moving expenses exclude the reimbursement from income but do not deduct the reimbursed expenses. However, taxpayers who receive a flat amount as a moving allowance from their employers are required to include the allowance in gross income, and can deduct their actual moving expenses for AGI.

---

**THE KEY FACTS**

**Moving Expenses**

- Deductible for AGI for individuals who pass a mileage test and a business test.

- Mileage test: New job site must extend existing commute by at least 50 miles.

- Business test: Taxpayer must be employed at least 39 of 52 weeks or be self-employed for 78 of the 104 weeks following the move.

**Example 6-5**

Courtney drove 691 miles in her move from Cincinnati to Kansas City and incurred the following expenses related to the move:

| Description | Amount |
|---|---|
| Moving company (personal belongings) | $5,000 |
| Lodging (one night en route) | 165 |
| Meals en route | 75 |
| House-hunting trip | 520 |

What amount can Courtney deduct as moving expenses?

**Answer:** Courtney can deduct $5,279 computed as follows:

| Description | Deduction |
|---|---|
| Transportation (16.5¢ per mile times 691 miles) | $ 114 |
| Moving company (personal belongings) | 5,000 |
| Lodging (one night en route) | 165 |
| **Total deduction** | **$5,279** |

The meals and house-hunting are not deductible.

**What if:** Suppose that EWD agreed to reimburse Courtney for a maximum of $2,000 of actual moving expenses. What amount would Courtney deduct for moving expenses?

**Answer:** $3,279. Courtney would deduct $3,279 in moving expenses ($5,279 minus $2,000 reimbursement). She would not include the reimbursement in income and she would not deduct the $2,000 of expenses for which she was reimbursed.

**Health Insurance Deduction by Self-Employed Taxpayers**   The cost of health insurance is essentially a personal expense. However, *employers* often pay a portion of health insurance premiums for employees as a qualified fringe benefit. Employers are allowed to deduct health insurance premiums as compensation expense while employees are allowed to *exclude* these premiums from gross income. In contrast to employees, the health insurance fringe benefit does not apply to self-employed taxpayers because they are not "employees." To provide equitable treatment, Congress allows self-employed taxpayers to claim personal health insurance premiums as deductions for AGI.[9]

This deduction is intended to help self-employed taxpayers who must pay their own insurance premiums. Consequently, self-employed taxpayers are *not* allowed to deduct health care insurance premiums if the taxpayer is *eligible* to participate in an employer-provided health plan. This restriction applies regardless of whether the health plan is sponsored by either an employer of the taxpayer or an employer of the taxpayer's spouse, and it is irrelevant whether the taxpayer actually participates in the plan.[10]

**Self-Employment Tax Deduction**   Employees and employers each pay one-half of employees' Social Security tax liability. Employers deduct the Social Security taxes on the half they pay for employees. In contrast, because self-employed individuals do not have an employer, these individuals are required to pay self-employment

[9]§162(l). As we'll explain shortly, health insurance premiums also qualify as itemized deductions as medical expenses, but itemizing these deductions may not produce any tax benefits.
[10]§162(l)(2)(B).

tax. This tax is double that paid by employees because it represents both the employee's *and* the employer's share of the Social Security tax. Unfortunately for the self-employed, the self-employment tax is *not* considered a business expense. To put self-employed individuals on somewhat equal footing with other employers who are allowed to deduct the *employer's* share of the Social Security tax, self-employed taxpayers are allowed to deduct one-half of the self-employment tax they pay.

<br>

**Example 6-6**

As we indicated in Example 6-2, Courtney reported $18,000 of net income from her self-employed consulting activities. She paid $482 in self-employment taxes on this income.[11] What amount of self-employment tax can she deduct this year?

**Answer:** $241. ($482 × 50% = $241).

<br>

**Penalty for Early Withdrawal of Savings**    This provision allows a deduction for AGI for any interest income an individual forfeits to a bank as a penalty for prematurely withdrawing a certificate of deposit or similar deposit. This deduction reduces the taxpayer's net interest income to the amount she actually received. Otherwise, taxpayers would be required to report the full amount of interest income as taxable income and could deduct only the forfeited interest as an investment-expense itemized deduction. As we discuss below, investment expenses deducted as itemized deductions are subject to limitations that substantially reduce their tax benefits.

<br>

**Example 6-7**

Gram invested $100,000 in a three-year certificate of deposit (CD). On December 31, she decided to cash out the certificate of deposit after holding it for less than a year. She receives the $4,100 of interest income the CD had generated up to the withdrawal date, less a $410 early withdrawal penalty. How will Gram report the interest and early withdrawal for tax purposes?

**Answer:** Gram reports $4,100 as interest income this year and deducts the $410 early withdrawal penalty as a deduction for AGI.

<br>

### Deductions Subsidizing Specific Activities

To address specific policy objectives, Congress provides that certain expenditures are deductible for AGI. For example, alimony payments are deductible for AGI to maintain equity and contributions to retirement savings are deductible for AGI to encourage savings.[12] Further, Congress created two important deductions for AGI to encourage and subsidize higher education. Taxpayers are allowed to deduct for AGI, subject to certain limitations, (1) interest expense on **qualified educational loans** and (2) **qualified educational expenses**.[13] As we discuss throughout the text, Congress has also created a number of related provisions, including education tax credits, to encourage and subsidize higher education.

---

[11]In this case, Courtney uses the following equation to determine her self-employment tax $18,000 × .9235 × .029 (Courtney's business income is subject to the Medicare tax but not the Social Security tax due to the level of her salary). We discuss how to compute the self-employment tax in detail in Chapter 7.

[12]See Chapter 5 for detailed discussion of alimony and Chapter 13 for detailed discussion of the tax consequences of retirement savings.

[13]See §221 and §222. At press time, the deduction for qualified education expenses is scheduled to expire at the end of 2009. However, we discuss it here because it may be extended to 2010.

**Deduction for Interest on Qualified Education Loans**   Qualified education loans are loans whose proceeds are used to pay qualified education expenses.[14] Qualified education expenses encompass expenses paid for the education of the taxpayer, the taxpayer's spouse, or a taxpayer's dependent to attend a postsecondary institution of higher education.[15] These expenses include tuition and fees, books and expenses required for enrollment, room and board, and other necessary supplies and expenses including travel.

The maximum deduction for interest expense on qualified education loans is $2,500. However, the maximum deduction is reduced (phased-out) for taxpayers depending on the taxpayer's filing status and **modified AGI.** Modified AGI for this purpose is AGI *before* deducting interest expense on the qualified education loans and *before* deducting qualified education expenses (discussed below). Married individuals who file separately are not allowed to deduct this expense under any circumstance. The deduction limitations for other taxpayers are summarized in Exhibit 6-4 as follows:

**EXHIBIT 6-4**   Summary of Limitations on Deduction of Interest on Education Loans

| Panel A: AGI limitations | |
| --- | --- |
| **Modified AGI Level** | **Maximum Deduction** |
| Not over $60,000 ($120,000 for married filing jointly) | Amount paid up to $2,500 |
| Above $60,000 ($120,000 for married filing jointly) but below $75,000 ($150,000 for married filing jointly) | Lesser of (1) amount paid or (2) $2,500 minus the phase-out amount. The phase-out amount is $2,500 times the phase-out percentage (see Panel B for the phase-out percentage computation). |
| Equal to or above $75,000 ($150,000 for married filing jointly) | Zero |

| Panel B: Phase-out Percentage* | |
| --- | --- |
| **Filing Status** | **Phase-out Percentage** |
| Single or head of household | (Modified AGI − $60,000)/$15,000 |
| Married filing jointly | (Modified AGI − $120,000)/$30,000 |

*Married taxpayers filing separately are ineligible for the deduction.

**Example 6-8**

*What if:* Assume that Courtney's brother Jason paid interest on a qualified education loan that he used to pay the tuition and fees for his three daughters to attend State University. In 2010, Jason was married and filed a joint return, paid $3,000 of interest expense on the loan, and reported modified AGI of $132,000. What amount of interest expense on the education loan is Jason allowed to deduct as a for AGI deduction?

(continued on page 6-11...)

[14]Home equity loans cannot qualify as education loans regardless of how the loan proceeds are spent.

[15]Postsecondary education includes courses at a university, college, or vocational school including internship programs leading to a degree or certificate. Qualifying costs claimed as deductions for AGI cannot be reimbursed by scholarships or Coverdell education savings accounts and are also ineligible for American opportunity and lifetime learning credit purposes.

**Answer:** $1,500, computed as follows:

| Description | Amount | Explanation |
|---|---|---|
| (1) Modified AGI | $132,000 | AGI before higher education deductions. |
| (2) Actual interest expense on loan | 3,000 | Amount paid. |
| (3) Maximum interest expense deduction before phase-out | 2,500 | |
| (4) Phase-out (reduction) percentage | 40% | [(1) − 120,000]/30,000. |
| (5) Phase-out amount (reduction in maximum) | 1,000 | (3) × (4). |
| (6) Maximum deduction after phase-out | 1,500 | (3) − (5). |
| (7) Deductible interest expense | $   1,500 | Lesser of (2) and (6). |

**Deduction for Qualified Education Expenses**   This deduction subsidizes tuition payments for higher education. For purposes of this deduction, qualified education expenses are limited to the tuition and fees required for enrollment at a postsecondary institution of higher education. Thus, the definition of qualifying expenses is more restrictive for the qualified education expense deduction than it is for the education loan interest expense deduction. However, similar to the education interest expense deduction, the amount of the maximum education expense deduction depends on filing status and level of modified AGI. For purposes of the qualified education expense deduction, modified AGI is AGI *after* deducting the education loan interest expense but *before* deducting qualified education expenses. Just as with the qualified education loan interest deduction, married individuals filing separately are ineligible for the qualified education expense deduction. The rules for determining the allowable education expense deduction for taxpayers who qualify for the deduction in 2009 are summarized in Exhibit 6-5. (At press time, this deduction had not been extended to 2010.)

**EXHIBIT 6-5**   **Summary of Limitations on Qualified Education Expenses**

| Modified AGI Level | Deduction |
|---|---|
| Not over $65,000 ($130,000 for married filing jointly) | Amount paid up to $4,000 |
| Above $65,000 ($130,000 for married filing jointly) but below $80,000 ($160,000) | Lesser of amount paid or $2,000 |
| Equal to or above 80,000 ($160,000 for married filing jointly) | Zero |

There are two important differences between the AGI limits on the interest on education loans deduction (summarized in Exhibit 6-4) and the AGI limits on the educational expense deduction (summarized in Exhibit 6-5). First, the definition of modified AGI for qualified education expenses in Exhibit 6-5 includes the deduction for interest on education loans. Second, the interest expense on education loans is phased out gradually over a range of AGI but the deduction for qualified education expenses is phased out in specific AGI increments (the phase-out applies in steps).

**Example 6-9**

Courtney paid $2,100 of tuition for Ellen to attend the University of Missouri–Kansas City during the summer. How much of this payment can Courtney deduct as a qualifying education expense?

**Answer:** None. The cost of the tuition is a qualified education expense but Courtney's modified AGI exceeds $80,000 (Courtney files as a head of household). Hence, Courtney is not allowed to deduct any of the cost of the tuition she paid for Ellen.

(*continued on page 6-12...*)

**THE KEY FACTS**

**Education Expenses**

▮ Up to $4,000 of qualified education expenses can be deducted for AGI.

▮ Qualified education expenses include tuition and related costs for postsecondary or higher education.

▮ The deduction is reduced for taxpayers with modified AGI over $65,000 ($130,000 married filing jointly) and eliminated for taxpayers with modified AGI of $80,000 ($160,000 married filing jointly) or more.

*What if:* Assume the same facts except that Courtney is married filing jointly and her modified AGI is $57,000. What amount can Courtney deduct as a qualifying education expense in this situation?

**Answer:** $2,100. She can deduct the full amount of the expenditure (limited to $4,000) because she is married filing jointly and her modified AGI is less than $65,000.

*What if:* Assume the original facts except that Courtney's modified AGI is $77,000. How much of the $2,100 tuition for Ellen would Courtney be allowed to deduct as a for AGI qualified education expense?

**Answer:** $2,000. Because Courtney's AGI is greater than $65,000 but not greater than $80,000 (she files as head of household) her deduction is the lesser of (1) her actual qualified education expenditures and (2) $2,000. Since Courtney's actual education expenditures were $2,100, her deduction is $2,000.

Because there are several education-related tax incentives, individuals can sometimes select among different tax benefits. For example, certain education expenses that qualify as deductions for AGI may also qualify for an education tax credit. Typically, a single expenditure *cannot* generate multiple tax benefits. Consequently, individuals should select the tax provision to apply to the expenses that generates the most benefit.

### Summary: Deductions for AGI

Business expenses and rental and royalty expenses are two of the most important deductions for AGI. There are a variety of other important deductions for AGI that are indirectly related to business or provided to subsidize certain activities. After we have determined the deductions for AGI, we can compute AGI. Exhibits 6-6 and 6-7 summarize the computation of AGI for Courtney and for Gram, respectively. Exhibit 6-8 shows Courtney's AGI calculation as presented on the front page of her Form 1040.

**EXHIBIT 6-6    Courtney's Adjusted Gross Income**

| Description | Amount | Reference |
|---|---|---|
| Gross income for current year | $178,020 | Exhibit 5-4 |
| Deductions for AGI: | | |
|     Business expenses | (1,500) | Example 6-2 |
|     Rental expenses | (9,000) | Example 6-3 |
|     Moving expenses | (5,279) | Example 6-5 |
|     One-half of self-employment taxes | (241) | Example 6-6 |
| Adjusted gross income | $162,000 | |

**EXHIBIT 6-7    Gram's Adjusted Gross Income**

| Description | Amount | Reference |
|---|---|---|
| Gross income for current year | $16,000 | Exhibit 5-6 |
| Deduction for AGI: | | |
|     Penalty for early withdrawal of savings | (410) | Example 6-7 |
| Adjusted gross income | $15,590 | |

**EXHIBIT 6-8    Courtney's AGI Computation on Form 1040, Page 1**

| | |  | |  |
|---|---|---|---|---|
| **Income** | 7 | Wages, salaries, tips, etc. Attach Form(s) W-2 | 7 | 122,800 |
| | 8a | Taxable interest. Attach Schedule B if required | 8a | 600 |
| Attach Form(s) W-2 here. Also attach Forms W-2G and 1099-R if tax was withheld. | b | Tax-exempt interest. **Do not** include on line 8a   `8b` 500 | | |
| | 9a | Ordinary dividends. Attach Schedule B if required | 9a | 700 |
| | b | Qualified dividends (see page 21)   `9b` 700 | | |
| | 10 | Taxable refunds, credits, or offsets of state and local income taxes (see page 22) | 10 | 420 |
| | 11 | Alimony received | 11 | 20,000 |
| | 12 | Business income or (loss). Attach Schedule C or C-EZ | 12 | 18,000 |
| | 13 | Capital gain or (loss). Attach Schedule D if required. If not required, check here ▶ ☐ | 13 | |
| If you did not get a W-2, see page 21. | 14 | Other gains or (losses). Attach Form 4797 | 14 | |
| | 15a | IRA distributions `15a`   b Taxable amount (see page 23) | 15b | |
| | 16a | Pensions and annuities `16a`   b Taxable amount (see page 24) | 16b | |
| Enclose, but do not attach, any payment. Also, please use Form 1040-V. | 17 | Rental real estate, royalties, partnerships, S corporations, trusts, etc. Attach Schedule E | 17 | 5,000 |
| | 18 | Farm income or (loss). Attach Schedule F | 18 | |
| | 19 | Unemployment compensation | 19 | |
| | 20a | Social security benefits `20a`   b Taxable amount (see page 26) | 20b | |
| | 21 | Other income. List type and amount (see page 28) | 21 | |
| | 22 | Add the amounts in the far right column for lines 7 through 21. This is your **total income** ▶ | 22 | 167,520 |
| **Adjusted Gross Income** | 23 | Educator expenses (see page 28) `23` | | |
| | 24 | Certain business expenses of reservists, performing artists, and fee-basis government officials. Attach Form 2106 or 2106-EZ `24` | | |
| | 25 | Health savings account deduction. Attach Form 8889 `25` | | |
| | 26 | Moving expenses. Attach Form 3903 `26` 5,279 | | |
| | 27 | One-half of self-employment tax. Attach Schedule SE `27` 241 | | |
| | 28 | Self-employed SEP, SIMPLE, and qualified plans `28` | | |
| | 29 | Self-employed health insurance deduction (see page 29) `29` | | |
| | 30 | Penalty on early withdrawal of savings `30` | | |
| | 31a | Alimony paid   b Recipient's SSN ▶ `31a` | | |
| | 32 | IRA deduction (see page 30) `32` | | |
| | 33 | Student loan interest deduction (see page 33) `33` | | |
| | 34 | Tuition and fees deduction. Attach Form 8917 `34` | | |
| | 35 | Domestic production activities deduction. Attach Form 8903 `35` | | |
| | 36 | Add lines 23 through 31a and 32 through 35 | 36 | 5,520 |
| | 37 | Subtract line 36 from line 22. This is your **adjusted gross income** ▶ | 37 | 162,000 |

Once we have determined AGI, we calculate taxable income by identifying deductions *from* AGI. These deductions consist of (1) the greater of itemized deductions or the standard deduction and (2) personal and dependency exemption deductions. We address itemized deductions next.

# DEDUCTIONS FROM AGI: ITEMIZED DEDUCTIONS                                         LO2

There is a variety of itemized deductions, a few of which relate to profit-motivated activities (employee business expenses and investment expenses that are unrelated to rental or royalty activities). Many itemized deductions are personal in nature but are allowed to subsidize desirable activities such as home ownership and charitable giving. Other itemized deductions, such as medical expenses and casualty losses, provide relief for taxpayers whose ability to pay taxes has been involuntarily reduced. We discuss itemized deductions in the order they appear on the individual tax return, Form 1040, Schedule A.

## Medical Expenses

The medical expense deduction is designed to provide relief for taxpayers whose ability to pay taxes is seriously hindered by health-related circumstances. Qualifying medical expenses include any payments for the care, prevention, diagnosis, or cure of injury, disease, or bodily function that are not reimbursed by health insurance or are not paid for through a "flexible spending account."[16] Taxpayers may also deduct

[16]Taxpayers participating in flexible spending accounts are allowed to direct that a fixed amount of their salary be placed in an account to pay for medical expenses. The salary paid into these accounts is excluded from gross income and used to pay for medical expenses. See Chapter 12.

medical expenses incurred to treat their spouses and their dependents.[17] Common medical expenses include:

- Prescription medication and medical aids such as eyeglasses, contact lenses, and wheel chairs.
- Payments to medical care *providers* such as doctors, dentists, and nurses and medical care *facilities* such as hospitals.
- Transportation for medical purposes.
- Long-term care facilities.
- Health insurance premiums (if not deducted for AGI by self-employed taxpayers) and insurance for long-term care services.[18]

---

**Example 6-10**

In April, Courtney broke her wrist in a mountain biking accident. She paid $2,000 for a visit to the hospital emergency room and follow-up visits with her doctor. While she recuperated, Courtney paid $300 for prescription medicine and $700 to a therapist for rehabilitation. Courtney's insurance reimbursed her $1,840 for these expenses. What is the amount of Courtney's qualifying medical expenses?

**Answer:** $1,160, computed as follows:

| Description | Deduction |
|---|---|
| Emergency room and doctor visits | $2,000 |
| Prescription medication | 300 |
| Physical therapy | 700 |
| Total qualifying medical expenses | $3,000 |
| Less insurance reimbursement | −1,840 |
| Qualifying medical expenses from the accident | $1,160 |

---

Medical expenses for cosmetic surgery or other similar procedures are not deductible unless the surgery or procedure is necessary to ameliorate a deformity arising from, or directly related to, a congenital abnormality, a personal injury resulting from an accident or trauma, or disfiguring disease.[19]

**Transportation and Travel for Medical Purposes**   Taxpayers traveling for the primary purpose of receiving essential and deductible medical care may deduct the cost of lodging while away from home overnight (with certain restrictions) and transportation.[20] Taxpayers using personal automobiles for medical transportation purposes may deduct a standard mileage allowance in lieu of actual costs. For 2010, the mileage rate is 16.5 cents a mile.

---

[17]For the purpose of deducting medical expenses, a dependent need not meet the gross income test (§213(a)) and a child of divorced parents is considered a dependent of both parents [§213(d)(5)]. We discuss the general requirements for dependency in Chapter 4.

[18]This includes the annual cost of Medicare and prescription insurance withheld from Social Security recipient's benefits checks.

[19]§213(d)(9)(A).

[20]The cost of travel for and essential to medical care, including lodging (with certain limitations) is also deductible if the expense is not extravagant and the travel has no significant element of personal pleasure. However, under §213(d)(2) the deduction for the cost of lodging is limited to $50 per night per individual.

**Example 6-11**

Gram drove Courtney, *in Courtney's car,* 110 miles back and forth from the doctor's office and the physical therapist's facility during the period Courtney was being treated for her broken wrist. What is the amount of Courtney's qualifying medical expense for her trips to the doctor's office?

**Answer:** $18 (110 miles × $0.165 rounded)

**Hospitals and Long-Term Care Facilities**   Taxpayers may deduct the cost of meals and lodging at hospitals. However, the costs of meals and lodging at other types of facilities such as nursing homes are deductible only when the principal purpose for the stay is medical care rather than convenience. Of course, taxpayers may deduct the costs of actual medical care whether the care is provided at hospitals or other long-term care facilities.

**Example 6-12**

Gram considered moving into a long-term care facility before she decided she would move in with Courtney. The facility was not primarily for medical care and would have cost Gram $36,000 a year. During discussions with facility administrators, Gram learned that typically 20 percent of the total cost for the facility is allocable to medical care. If Gram were to stay in the facility for an entire year, what amount of the long-term care costs would qualify as a medical expense for Gram?

**Answer:** $7,200 ($36,000 × 20% allocable to medical care)

**Medical Expense Deduction Limitation**   The deduction for medical expenses is limited to the amount of unreimbursed qualifying medical expenses paid during the year (no matter when the services were provided) *reduced* by 7.5 percent of the taxpayer's AGI. This restriction is called a **floor limitation** because it eliminates any deduction for amounts below the floor. The purpose of a floor limitation is to restrict a deduction to taxpayers with substantial qualifying expenses. Because this floor limitation is set at a high percentage of AGI, unreimbursed medical expenses rarely produce tax benefits, especially for high income taxpayers.

**Example 6-13**

This year Courtney incurred $2,400 in unreimbursed qualifying medical expenses (including the $1,160 of qualifying medical expenses associated with the accident and the $18 transportation deduction for mileage). Given that Courtney's AGI is $162,000, what is the amount of Courtney's itemized medical expense deduction?

**Answer:** $0 computed as follows:

| Description | Expense |
|---|---|
| Total unreimbursed qualifying medical expenses | $ 2,400 |
| Minus: 7.5% of AGI ($162,000 × 7.5%) | (12,150) |
| Medical expense itemized deduction | $     0 |

*What if:* What amount of medical expenses would Courtney be allowed to deduct if her AGI was $30,000?

*(continued on page 6-16...)*

**Answer:** $150, computed as follows:

| Description | Expense |
| --- | --- |
| Total unreimbursed qualifying medical expenses | $ 2,400 |
| Minus: 7.5% of AGI ($30,000 × 7.5%) | (2,250) |
| Medical expense itemized deduction | $ 150 |

## Taxes

Individuals may deduct as itemized deductions payments made during the year for the following taxes:

- State, local, and foreign *income* taxes, including state and local taxes paid during the year through employer withholding, estimated tax payments, and overpayments on the prior year return that the taxpayer applies to the current year (the taxpayer asks the state to keep the overpayment rather than refund it).
- Real estate taxes on property held for personal or investment purposes.
- Personal property taxes that are assessed on the *value* of the specific property.[21]

In 2009, taxpayers who did not itemize deductions were allowed to increase their standard deduction amount for (1) real property taxes they paid during the year and (2) sales taxes they paid during the year on purchases of qualified motor vehicles (passenger cars, light trucks, motorcycles, and new motor homes).[22]

For real property taxes, the additional standard deduction amount is limited to the lesser of:

1. The amount of real property taxes paid during the year.
2. $500 ($1,000 for a married couple filing jointly).[23]

For sales taxes, the additional standard deduction amount is limited to the tax on up to $49,500 of the purchase price of qualified motor vehicles ($24,750 if married filing separately).[24] In addition, the additional standard deduction for sales taxes was phased out ratably for taxpayers with modified AGI between $125,000 and $135,000 ($250,000 and $260,000 on a joint return). Finally, the itemized deduction for qualified motor vehicle taxes was not available to a taxpayer who elected to deduct state and local sales taxes in lieu of state income taxes.

---

[21]§164.

[22]At press time, the option to deduct state and local sales tax in lieu of state and local income tax had not been extended to 2010. The deduction was based upon either the amount paid or the amount published in the IRS tables (IRS Publication 600) based upon the state of residence, income, and number of exemptions. The states with no income tax are Alaska, Florida, Nevada, South Dakota, Texas, Washington, and Wyoming. Tennessee and New Hampshire have no state income tax on wages, but do impose a tax on unearned income.

[23]§63(c)(1)(C). At press time, this deduction had not been extended to 2010.

[24]§63(c)(1)(E). At press time, the increase in the standard deduction for sales taxes on qualified motor vehicle purchases had not been extended to 2010.

**Example 6-14**

During the year, Courtney paid $6,700 of state income taxes through withholding from her paycheck. She also paid $2,700 of real estate taxes on her personal residence and $850 of real estate taxes on an investment property she owns in Oklahoma. Finally, Courtney paid $180 as a registration fee for her automobile (the fee is based on the year the automobile was manufactured, not its value). What amount of these payments can Courtney deduct as itemized deductions?

**Answer:** $10,250 ($6,700 state taxes + $2,700 real estate taxes on residence + $850 real estate taxes on investment property). Courtney is not allowed to deduct the registration fee for her car because the fee is not based on the value of the automobile.

*What if:* Suppose that on April 15, 2010, Courtney filed her 2009 state tax return and was due a refund from the state in the amount of $420. However, Courtney elected to have the state keep the overpayment and apply it to her 2010 tax payments. What amount of state income taxes is Courtney allowed to deduct as an itemized deduction in 2010?

**Answer:** $7,120 ($6,700 withholding + $420 overpayment applied to 2010). The treatment of the overpayment is the same as if Courtney had received the refund in 2010 and then remitted it to the state as payment of 2010 taxes. Because she paid the tax in 2010, she is allowed to deduct the tax in 2010. Recall that under the tax benefit rule (see Chapter 5), Courtney was required to include the $420 in her 2010 gross income.

## Interest

There are two itemized deductions for interest expense.[25] Subject to limitations discussed in Chapter 14, individuals can deduct interest paid on loans secured by a personal residence. As we discuss in more detail in Chapter 11, individuals can also deduct interest paid on loans used to purchase investment assets such as stocks, bonds, or land (investment interest expense). The deduction of investment interest is limited to a taxpayer's net investment income (investment income minus investment expenses). Any investment interest in excess of the net investment income limitation carries forward to the subsequent year. Taxpayers are not allowed to deduct interest on personal credit card debt or on loans to acquire (and secured by) personal-use automobiles.

**Example 6-15**

Courtney acquired her home in Kansas City in January of this year for $300,000 (also its value throughout the year). She purchased it by paying $40,000 as a down payment and borrowing $260,000 from a credit union. Her home is the collateral for the loan. During the year, Courtney paid $15,800 in interest on the loan. How much of this interest may Courtney deduct?

**Answer:** $15,800. Because Courtney's home mortgage is secured by her home, she is allowed to deduct the interest expense on the home as an itemized deduction.

*What if:* Suppose that Courtney borrowed $26,000 to purchase a new car (the loan was secured by the car). Would she be allowed to deduct the interest on the loan?

**Answer:** No, the loan was not used to purchase a personal residence or investment assets.

---

[25]Interest paid on loans where the proceeds are used in a trade or business is fully deductible as a business expense deduction for AGI.

**Example 6-16**

In March, Courtney borrowed $2,000 from her bank to purchase stock in Delta, Inc. During the year, she paid $130 of interest expense on the loan and realized $600 of investment income. What amount of the $130 in interest expense can Courtney deduct as an itemized deduction this year?

**Answer:** $130. Courtney can deduct investment interest expense as an itemized deduction to the extent of her net investment income. Courtney recognized $600 of investment income, but she had no deductible investment expenses (investment interest expense is not an investment expense). Hence, Courtney's net investment income is $600. Because net investment income exceeds the amount of Courtney's investment interest expense, she can deduct the entire $130 of investment interest expense on her return.[26]

**What if:** Suppose that Courtney received net investment income of only $100 this year. How much of the $130 investment interest expense would she be allowed to deduct?

**Answer:** $100. Her deduction is limited to the net investment income of $100. Courtney would be allowed to carry over the $30 of interest expense that was not deductible to deduct in a future year when she has net investment income.

## Charitable Contributions

Congress encourages donations to charities by allowing taxpayers to deduct contributions of money and other property to *qualified* charitable organizations. Qualifying charitable organizations include organizations that engage in educational, religious, scientific, governmental, and other public activities.[27]

**Example 6-17**

This year Courtney donated $1,700 to the Red Cross. She also gave $200 in cash to various homeless people she met on the streets during the year. What amount of these donations is Courtney allowed to deduct as a charitable contribution?

**Answer:** $1,700. Because the Red Cross is a public charity recognized by the IRS, Courtney may deduct her $1,700 charitable contribution to it as an itemized deduction. However, despite Courtney's charitable intent, her donations to the homeless are not deductible as charitable contributions because individuals do not qualify as charitable organizations.

**What if:** Suppose that instead of transferring cash to homeless people on the streets, Courtney donated $200 cash to a local food bank that is listed in IRS Publication 78 as a qualified charity. The food bank provides meals to those in need. Would Courtney be allowed to deduct this contribution?

**Answer:** Yes, because the food bank is a qualified charity.

The *amount* of the charitable contribution deduction depends on whether the taxpayer contributes money or other property to the charity. Note that in virtually all circumstances, donations are only deductible if the contribution is substantiated by written records.[28]

**Contributions of Money** Cash contributions are deductible in the year paid, including donations of cash or by check, electronic funds transfers, credit card charges, and payroll deductions.[29] Taxpayers are also considered as making monetary contributions

---

[26] Recall from Chapter 5 that Courtney also had $700 of investment income in the form of dividends on her 1,000 shares of GE stock. However, this income is subject to a preferential tax rate, and absent a special election, it would not qualify as net investment income. We describe this election in Chapter 11.

[27] §170(c). IRS Publication 78 lists the organizations that the IRS has determined to be qualified charities.

[28] For example, to deduct monetary donations, taxpayers must keep a bank record or a written communication from the charity showing the name of the charity and the date and amount of the contribution. See Publication 526 for more information.

[29] When individual taxpayers mail a contribution, they are allowed to deduct the contribution when they place the payment in the mail. When they pay via credit card, they are allowed to deduct the contribution on the day of the charge. Rev. Rul. 78-38, 1978-1 CB 67.

for the cost of transportation and travel for charitable purposes if there is no significant element of pleasure or entertainment in the travel. When taxpayers use their personal vehicles for charitable transportation purposes, they may deduct, as a cash contribution, a standard mileage allowance for each mile driven (14 cents a mile in 2010). While taxpayers are allowed to deduct their transportation costs and other out-of-pocket costs of providing services for charities, they are not allowed to deduct the value of the services they provide for charities.

**Example 6-18**

Once a month, Courtney does volunteer work at a Goodwill Industries outlet about 20 miles from her home. Altogether, Courtney traveled 500 miles during the year driving to and from the Goodwill outlet. Courtney has determined that the services she provided during the year are reasonably valued at $1,500. What amount is Courtney allowed to deduct for her volunteer work with Goodwill Industries?

**Answer:** $70. Courtney is *not* allowed to deduct the value of the services she provides to Goodwill. However, she is allowed to deduct the $70 cost of her transportation to and from the Goodwill outlet (500 miles × 14 cents per mile).

Taxpayers receiving goods or services from a charity in exchange for a contribution may only deduct the amount of the contribution *in excess of the fair market value of the goods or services they receive* in exchange for their contribution.[30]

**Contributions of Property Other Than Money**   When a taxpayer donates *property* to charity, the *amount* the taxpayer is allowed to deduct depends on whether the property is **capital gain property** or **ordinary income property.**

*Capital gain property.*   In general, taxpayers are allowed to deduct the *fair market value* of capital gain property on the date of the donation. Capital gain property is any appreciated asset that would have generated a *long-term* capital gain if the taxpayer had sold the property for its fair market value instead of contributing the asset to charity. To qualify as long-term, the taxpayer must have held the asset for more than a year. Capital assets include the following assets:

- Investment assets (stocks, bonds, land held for investment, paintings, etc.).
- Business assets (to the extent that gain on the sale of the business asset would *not* have been considered ordinary income).[31]
- Personal-use assets.

Contributing capital gain property is a particularly tax efficient way to make charitable contributions, because taxpayers are allowed to deduct the fair market value of the property, and they are *not* required to include the appreciation on the asset in gross income.

**Example 6-19**

In December of the current year, Courtney donated 100 shares of stock in JBD Corp. to her church, a qualified charity. Courtney purchased the stock several years ago for $2,600, but the shares were worth $10,600 at the time of the donation. What is the amount of Courtney's charitable deduction for donating the stock?

*(continued on page 6-20…)*

[30]Reg. §1.170A-1(h). To help with this determination, a charity that provides goods or services in return for a contribution of more than $75 must provide contributors with a written statement estimating the value of goods and services that the charity has provided to the donor.

[31]These assets are considered to be §1231(b) assets. We discuss the tax treatment of dispositions of business assets in Chapter 10.

> **Answer:** $10,600. Because the stock is an appreciated investment asset held for more than a year, it qualifies as capital gain property. Hence, Courtney is allowed to deduct the $10,600 fair market value of the stock, and she is *not* required to recognize any of the $8,000 realized gain ($10,600 − $2,600).

Certain contributions of capital gain property do not qualify for a fair market value deduction. The deduction for capital gain property that is *tangible personal property* is limited to the *adjusted basis* of the property if the charity uses the property for a purpose that is *unrelated* to its charitable purpose.[32] That is, this restriction applies to capital gains property that is (1) tangible, (2) personal property (not realty), and (3) unrelated to the charity's operations. The third requirement does not apply if, at the time of the donation, the taxpayer reasonably anticipates that the charity will put the property to a related use.

### Example 6-20

> **What if:** Suppose that Courtney donated a religious-themed painting to her church. Courtney purchased the painting several years ago for $2,600, but the painting was worth $10,600 at the time of the donation. When Courtney contributed the painting, she reasonably expected the church to hang the painting in the church chapel. What would be the amount of Courtney's charitable contribution deduction?
>
> **Answer:** $10,600. Because Courtney reasonably expected the church to use the painting in a manner related to its tax-exempt purpose, Courtney is allowed to deduct the full fair market value of the painting without recognizing the $8,000 realized gain.
>
> **What if:** Suppose that Courtney was told at the time she donated the painting that the church intended to sell it and use the cash to help fund expansion of the church building. What would be Courtney's charitable contribution deduction?
>
> **Answer:** $2,600, the adjusted basis of the property. Because the church expects to sell it, the painting is being used for a purpose unrelated to the charitable purpose of the church. Thus, Courtney may deduct only the tax basis of the painting.
>
> **What if:** Suppose that Courtney donated stock to her church and the church informed her that it intended to immediately sell the stock. What would be the amount of Courtney's charitable contribution deduction?
>
> **Answer:** $10,600. Stock is intangible property, not tangible personal property. Hence, Courtney would deduct the fair market value of the stock.

***Ordinary income property.*** Taxpayers contributing ordinary income property can only deduct the *lesser* of (1) the property's fair market value or (2) the property's adjusted basis. Ordinary income property consists of all assets other than capital gain property. That is, ordinary income property is property that if sold would generate income taxed at ordinary rates. This includes the following types of assets:

- Assets the taxpayer has held for a year or less.
- Inventory the taxpayer sells in a trade or business.
- Business assets held for more than a year to the extent the taxpayer would recognize ordinary income under the depreciation recapture rules if the taxpayer had sold the property.[33]
- Assets, including investment assets and personal-use assets, with a value *less than* the taxpayer's basis in the assets (assets that have declined in value).

---

[32]Reg. §1.170A-4(b)(2). The taxpayer's deduction for donating capital gain property is also limited to basis if the taxpayer contributes capital gain property other than publicly-traded stock to a private nonoperating foundation. There are also other exceptions in which capital gain property might not otherwise qualify for deduction at value such as the subsequent sales of donated property by the charity. These exceptions are beyond the scope of this text.

[33]We discuss depreciation recapture in Chapter 9.

**Example 6-21**

Before her move from Cincinnati, Courtney decided to donate her excess possessions to Goodwill Industries. Courtney estimated that she paid over $900 for these items, including clothing, a table, and a couch. However, although the items were in excellent condition, they were worth only $160. What amount can Courtney deduct for her donation of these items?

**Answer:** $160. Because Courtney's possessions have declined in value, they are considered to be ordinary income property. Consequently, Courtney may deduct the lesser of (1) the fair market value of $160 or (2) her tax basis in the property of $900.

**Charitable Contribution Deduction Limitations**   The amount of a taxpayer's charitable contribution deduction for the year is limited to a **ceiling** or maximum deduction. The ceiling depends upon the type of property the taxpayer donates and the nature of the charity receiving the donation; donations to public charities (charities that are publicly supported such as churches and schools) and **private operating foundations** (privately sponsored foundations that actually fund and conduct charitable activities) are subject to less stringent restrictions than other charities. In general, cash and property donations to public charities and private operating foundations are limited to 50 percent of the taxpayer's AGI. Deductions for contributions of capital gain property to public charities and private operating foundations are generally limited to 30 percent of the taxpayer's AGI. Deductions for cash and property contributions to **private nonoperating foundations** (privately sponsored foundations that disburse funds to other charities) are limited to 30 percent of the taxpayer's AGI. Finally, deductions for contributions of capital gain property to private nonoperating foundations are limited to 20 percent of the taxpayer's AGI. Exhibit 6-9 summarizes the charitable contribution limitations for individual taxpayers.

**EXHIBIT 6-9**   Summary of Charitable Contribution Limitation Rules

| Contribution Type | Public Charity and Private Operating Foundation | Private Nonoperating Foundation |
|---|---|---|
| Cash: | | |
| Amount | Cash amount | Cash amount |
| AGI limit | 50% | 30% |
| Capital gain property: | | |
| Amount | FMV | Basis* |
| AGI limit | 30% | 20% |
| Ordinary income property: | | |
| Amount | Lesser of Basis or FMV | Lesser of Basis or FMV |
| AGI limit | 50% | 30% |

*FMV if the stock is publicly traded [§170(e)(5)].

When taxpayers make contributions that are subject to different percentage limitations, they apply the AGI limitations in the following sequence:

**Step 1:** Determine the limitation for the 50 percent contributions.

**Step 2:** Apply the limitations to the 30 percent contributions. The 30 percent contribution limit is the *lesser* of (a) AGI × 30% or (b) AGI × 50% minus the amount of contributions deducted in Step 1.

**Step 3:** Apply the limitations to the 20 percent contributions. The 20 percent contribution limit is the *lesser* of (a) AGI × 20% or (b) AGI × 30% minus the amount of contributions from Step 2.

When a taxpayer's contributions exceed the AGI ceiling limitation for the year, the excess contribution is treated as though it were made in the subsequent tax year

and is subject to the same AGI limitations in the next year. The excess contribution can be carried forward for five years before it expires. However, because the ceiling limitations are fairly generous, taxpayers exceed the ceiling limitations only in unusual circumstances.

---

**Example 6-22**

This year Courtney made the following contributions to qualified charities:

| Organization | Amount | Type | AGI Limitation | Reference |
|---|---|---|---|---|
| Red Cross | $ 1,700 | Cash | 50% | Example 6-17. |
| Goodwill Industries | 70 | Cash-mileage | 50% | Example 6-18. |
| Goodwill | 160 | Ordinary income property | 50% | Example 6-21. |
| Church | 10,600 | Capital gain property | 30% | Example 6-19. |
| Total contributions | $12,530 | | | |

After applying the AGI limitations, how much of the $12,530 in contributions is Courtney allowed to deduct?

**Answer:** $12,530, computed as follows:

| Description | Amount | Explanation |
|---|---|---|
| (1) AGI | $162,000 | Exhibit 6-6. |
| (2) 50% contributions | 1,930 | ($1,700 + 70 + 160). |
| (3) 50% AGI contribution limit | 81,000 | (1) × 50%. |
| **(4) Allowable 50% deductions** | **1,930** | Lesser of (2) or (3). |
| (5) 30% contributions | 10,600 | |
| (6) 30% AGI contribution limit | 48,600 | (1) × 30%. |
| (7) Remaining 50% AGI limitation | 79,070 | (3) − (4). |
| **(8) Allowable 30% deductions** | **10,600** | Least of (5), (6), or (7). |
| Deductible charitable contributions | $ 12,530 | (4) + (8). |

*What if:* Suppose that Courtney's AGI was $30,000. After applying the AGI limitations, how much of the $12,530 in contributions would Courtney be allowed to deduct?

**Answer:** $10,930, computed as follows:

| Description | Amount | Explanation |
|---|---|---|
| (1) AGI | $30,000 | |
| (2) 50% contributions | 1,930 | |
| (3) 50% AGI contribution limit | 15,000 | (1) × 50%. |
| **(4) Allowable 50% deductions** | **1,930** | Lesser of (2) and (3). |
| (5) 30% contributions | 10,600 | |
| (6) 30% AGI contribution limit | 9,000 | (1) × 30%. |
| (7) Remaining 50% AGI limitation | 13,070 | (3) − (4). |
| **(8) Allowable 30% deductions** | **9,000** | Least of (5), (6), or (7). |
| Deductible charitable contributions | $10,930 | (4) + (8). |

Courtney would not be allowed to deduct this year $1,600 of her $10,600 capital gain property contribution to her church. However, she will carry forward the $1,600 to next year (and upto four years after that, if necessary) and treat it as though she made a $1,600 contribution next year subject to the 30 percent of AGI limitation.

## Casualty and Theft Losses on Personal-Use Assets

Individuals cannot deduct losses they realize when they sell or dispose of assets used for personal purposes (personal-use assets as opposed to business or investment assets). However, individuals *are* allowed to deduct casualty and theft losses realized on personal-use assets.[34] A **casualty loss** is defined as a loss arising from a *sudden, unexpected,* or *unusual* event such as a "fire, storm, or shipwreck" or loss from theft.[35]

**Tax Loss from Casualties**    Congress allows deductions for unreimbursed casualty and theft losses because these losses may substantially reduce a taxpayer's ability to pay taxes. However, limitations on the deduction generally ensure that taxpayers receive a tax benefit from such losses only when the losses are relatively large. The *amount* of the tax loss from any *specific casualty event* (including theft) is the *lesser* of (1) the decline in value of the property caused by the casualty or (2) the taxpayer's tax basis in the damaged or stolen asset. The loss is reduced by any reimbursements the individual is eligible to receive, such as insurance reimbursements.

### Example 6-23

In June, Courtney had a bad day at a nearby lake. Her purse containing $200 in cash was stolen, and she wrecked her car on the way home. Courtney purchased her purse for $150 and it was worth $125 at the time of the theft ($325 in total value was stolen). Courtney purchased her car earlier in the year for $22,000 and had to pay $2,000 to have it repaired. Courtney's insurance company reimbursed her $1,400 for the repairs. What is the amount of Courtney's casualty tax loss before considering deductibility limitations?

**Answer:** $925 ($325 theft + $600 accident). The theft and the automobile accident are considered to be two separate casualty events generating two different casualty losses. The amount of each casualty loss, before considering deductibility limitations, is computed as follows:

|  | Theft | Accident |
|---|---|---|
| Fair market value (FMV) before casualty | $325 | |
| FMV after the casualty | −0 | |
| (1) Decline in FMV (cost to repair) | 325 | $ 2,000 |
| (2) Tax basis in property before casualty | 350 | 22,000 |
| Loss before reimbursement [lesser of (1) or (2)] | 325 | 2,000 |
| Insurance reimbursement | −0 | −1,400 |
| Unreimbursed casualty losses | $325 | $  600 |

**Casualty Loss Deduction Floor Limitations**    Casualty losses must exceed two separate floor limitations to qualify as itemized deductions. The first floor is $100 for *each* casualty event during the year.[36] This floor eliminates deductions for small losses. The second floor limitation is 10 percent of AGI and it applies to the sum of all casualty losses for the year (after applying the $100 floor). In other words, the itemized deduction is the aggregate amount of casualty losses that exceeds 10 percent of AGI.

### Example 6-24

Courtney's total casualty loss before applying the deduction limitations is $925. What amount of the $925 loss is Courtney allowed to deduct after applying the two floor limitations?

*(continued on page 6-24...)*

---

[34]§165. As we discuss in more detail in Chapter 8, businesses may deduct casualty and theft losses of business property as a deduction for AGI. Further, casualty or theft losses on investment assets are deductible as a miscellaneous itemized deduction not subject to the 2 percent of AGI floor.

[35]§165(c)(3). See also IRS Publication No. 547 (Casualties, Disasters, and Thefts), 2006, p. 2.

[36] In 2009 the first casualty loss floor was $500 per casualty. At press time, the $500 limit is scheduled to drop to $100 after 2009.

**Answer:** $0 Computed as follows:

|  | Theft | Accident | Total |
|---|---|---|---|
| Losses before limitations | $325 | $600 | |
| Less $100 per casualty floor | −100 | −100 | |
| Casualty loss before AGI limit | $225 | $500 | $    725 |
| Less 10% of $162,000 | | | −16,200 |
| Casualty loss deduction after AGI limit | | | $       0 |

***What if:*** Suppose that Courtney's automobile was worth $20,000, and that it was completely destroyed in the accident. What would be Courtney's casualty loss deduction if she received only $3,100 of insurance reimbursement for her loss?

**Answer:** $825, computed as follows:

|  | Theft | Accident | Total |
|---|---|---|---|
| Fair market value (FMV) before casualty | $325 | $20,000 | |
| FMV after the casualty | 0 | 0 | |
| (1) Decline in FMV (cost to repair) | $325 | $20,000 | |
| (2) Tax basis in property before casualty | $350 | $22,000 | |
| Loss before reimbursement [lesser of (1) or (2)] | $325 | $20,000 | |
| Less Insurance reimbursement | −0 | −3,100 | |
| Less $100 per casualty floor | −100 | −100 | |
| Unreimbursed casualty losses | $225 | $16,800 | $17,025 |
| Less 10% of $162,000 | | | −16,200 |
| Casualty loss deduction after AGI limit | | | $    825 |

## Taxes in the Real World

In order to qualify for a casualty loss deduction, a taxpayer's personal loss must be sudden or unexpected. Taxpayers and the IRS sometimes disagree about what is a casualty. Consider the following three case summaries (sometimes called the "trilogy of the rings") and, for each case, see whether you can determine whether the taxpayer or the IRS was victorious.

### Case 1

Nancy Carpenter cleaned her wedding ring by placing it in some ammonia near the kitchen sink. Nancy's husband, William, later emptied the ammonia into the drain along with the ring while doing the dishes. He then turned on the garbage disposal, destroying the ring [*William H. Carpenter*, decided by the Tax Court in 1966, 25 TCM 1186].

### Case 2

John lovingly helped his wife Agnes from the car and started to shut the door. Agnes, upon realizing she had left something on the seat, reached her hand back toward the car only to have the door shut directly on her engagement ring. The setting of the ring broke on impact and the diamond was flung into the leaf-covered driveway as she retracted her hand. Despite all their efforts, John and Agnes never found the stone [*John P. White,* decided by the Tax Court in 1967, 48 TC 430].

### Case 3

Mr. and Mrs. Keenan spent the night at a hotel. Mr. Keenan, who was suffering from a stuffy nose, used tissues he had placed near his bed throughout the night. During the night Mrs. Keenan removed her rings and placed them within a tissue at the bedside. Mr. Keenan awoke before his wife the following morning, and he gathered the tissues, including the ring, and flushed them down the toilet [*Keenan v. Bowers*, decided in 1950 by the South Carolina District Court, 50-2 USTC ¶9444].

So, what do you think?

The taxpayers won Case 1 and Case 2 because the losses were deemed to be "sudden and unexpected" in nature. However, the taxpayer lost Case 3 because the loss was due to a "chain of events on the parts of Mrs. Keenan and Mr. Keenan." Thus, the loss was not considered to be sudden in nature.

### *Miscellaneous Itemized Deductions Subject to AGI Floor*

There are a variety of deductions that address specific objectives but do not fit easily into any category. Congress called these deductions **miscellaneous itemized deductions** and subjected most of these deductions to an AGI floor (only amounts over the floor are deductible). Miscellaneous itemized deductions subject to the floor limitation include employee business expenses, investment expenses, and certain other expenses. These miscellaneous deductions are summed together and are deductible only to the extent that their sum *exceeds* 2 percent of the taxpayer's AGI.

**Employee Business Expenses**   While most business expenses are typically deductible as deductions for AGI, employee business expenses are deductible as miscellaneous itemized deductions. Expenses that qualify include those that are appropriate and helpful for the employee's work such as the cost of professional dues, uniforms (unless suitable as normal attire), and subscriptions to publications related to employment.

---

**Example 6-25**

Courtney subscribes to several architectural publications at an annual cost of $410. She finds these publications helpful, and it is certainly appropriate that an architect read current publications to keep up with new trends. Her employer does not reimburse Courtney for the cost of the subscriptions. What amount, if any, qualifies as a deductible employee business expense?

**Answer:** All $410 qualifies as a deductible employee business expense because the expense is appropriate and helpful to Courtney's employment.

---

Several types of employee expenses are restricted. For example, the costs of job hunting qualify if the job is in the employee's current trade or business, but not for the individual's first job. In addition, the cost of education qualifies if it serves to maintain or improve the employee's skill in the business, but not if the education is *required* to qualify for a new business or profession. Thus, a high school teacher would not be able to deduct the cost of attending law school because a law degree would qualify him for a different profession.

---

**Example 6-26**

During the year, Courtney paid $1,550 to attend motivational seminars sponsored by a continuing education provider. Courtney has found these seminars helpful, and her employer has encouraged Courtney to attend. How much of the cost of the seminars qualifies as a deductible employee business expense?

**Answer:** All $1,550. The cost qualifies as an employee business expense because the courses are appropriate and helpful and do not qualify Courtney for a new business.

---

*Travel and transportation.*   The cost of travel and transportation associated with the employee's work responsibilities may also qualify as miscellaneous itemized deductions. The cost of travel is deductible if the primary purpose of the trip is business. However, the cost of **commuting**—traveling from a residence to the place of business—is personal and never deductible.[37] When employees drive their personal

---

[37]Costs of commuting to and from a temporary place of work are deductible and costs of commuting from a first job to a second job are deductible. Employees may take *temporary* business trips that last for months. For these trips, the costs of the travel, including meals and lodging, are deductible for the duration of the trip. However, because trips in excess of one year are deemed to be *permanent,* the cost of travel on indefinite trips is *not* deductible.

automobiles for business purposes, they may deduct a standard mileage rate in lieu of deducting actual costs. In 2010, the standard business mileage rate is 50 cents per mile. When employees travel on business trips long enough to be away from home overnight, meals and lodging also qualify as employee business expenses. Although meals and lodging are deductible employee business expenses, employees are allowed to deduct only half the cost of the meals.

---

**Example 6-27**

Because Courtney is extremely motivated to reach her potential as an architect (the seminars are doing wonders), she spent a week in September, at her own expense, driving her personal car to several large cities to study different architectural designs. During the trip, she drove a total of 2,134 miles, spent $796 on lodging, and paid $500 for meals. What amount can Courtney deduct as unreimbursed employee business expenses before considering the 2 percent of AGI floor?

**Answer:** $2,113, computed as follows:

| Description | Expense | Calculation |
|---|---|---|
| Transportation | $1,067 | 2,134 miles × 50 cents |
| Lodging | 796 | |
| Meals | 250 | $500 × 50% |
| Total employee business expense from trip | $2,113 | |

---

***Employee expense reimbursements.***    Many employees are reimbursed for their business expenses by their employers. As a general rule, employees *include* reimbursements in gross income and deduct employee business expenses as miscellaneous itemized deductions. However, if an employee is required to submit documentation supporting expenses to receive reimbursement and the employer reimburses only legitimate business expenses, then the employer's reimbursement plan qualifies as an **accountable plan.** Under an accountable plan employees *exclude* expense reimbursements from gross income and do *not* deduct the reimbursed expenses. If the expenses exceed the reimbursements, the excess (unreimbursed) portion is deductible as an employee business expense. Thus, miscellaneous itemized deductions for employee business expenses are commonly referred to as deductions for *unreimbursed* employee business expenses.

---

**Example 6-28**

In November, Courtney went on a business trip to Los Angeles to meet with a prospective client and spent $1,700 on business travel including meals and lodging. EWD reimbursed Courtney for the entire $1,700 cost of the trip under an accountable plan. What amount can Courtney deduct?

**Answer:** $0. Because EWD's reimbursement is made under an accountable plan, Courtney ignores the reimbursement and the expenses for tax purposes; the reimbursement and expenses completely offset each other.

*What if:* Suppose that EWD provided Courtney with a flat amount of $2,000 to cover her expenses for the trip and did not require her to account for expenditures. How would Courtney treat the reimbursement and the expenses for tax purposes?

**Answer:** Courtney would include the $2,000 in gross income and claim the $1,700 from the trip from AGI as an employee business expense, miscellaneous itemized deduction subject to the 2 percent of AGI floor (and 50 percent meals limitation). The reimbursement was not made under an accountable plan because Courtney was not required to substantiate her expenses.

**Investment Expenses**    As previously explained, investment expenses are itemized deductions. These expenses are classified as miscellaneous itemized deductions and include expenditures necessary for the production or collection of income, or for the management, conservation, or maintenance of property held for the production of income.[38] Common investment expenses include:

- Expenses associated with investment income or property.
- Investment advisory fees.
- Safe-deposit box fees.
- Subscriptions to investment-related publications.

**Tax Preparation Fees**    Ordinary and necessary expenses incurred in connection with determining tax obligations imposed by federal, state, municipal, or foreign authorities are also deductible as miscellaneous itemized deductions subject to the 2 percent of AGI floor.[39] While the most common tax preparation fees are the costs of preparing taxpayers' tax returns, taxpayers may also deduct other related expenses such as the cost of property appraisals for tax purposes and the costs of contesting tax liabilities.

**Example 6-29**

In 2010, Courtney paid Quick Taxes, Inc., $250 to prepare her 2009 income tax return. What amount of this expenditure can Courtney deduct before considering the 2 percent of AGI floor?

**Answer:** $250. The entire amount qualifies as a miscellaneous itemized deduction for 2010.

**Hobby Losses**    As stated previously, individuals engaged in *business* activities are allowed to deduct their business expenses as deductions for AGI. However, taxpayers may engage in certain activities for primarily personal enjoyment but these activities may also generate revenue. For tax purposes, this type of activity is considered a **hobby** rather than a business. Hobby expenses are deductible only to the extent of the revenue generated by the hobby. Sometimes referred to as the *hobby loss limitation,* this limit is less taxpayer-friendly for a hobby than the limits on business expenses. Thus, it's important to determine whether an activity should be considered a business or a hobby for tax purposes. This determination hinges upon whether the taxpayer is engaged in the activity *primarily* to make a profit or *primarily* for personal enjoyment.

To help make this subjective determination, the regulations provide a list of following factors to consider.[40]

- The manner in which the taxpayer carries on the activity.
- The expertise of the taxpayer or his advisors.
- The time and effort expended by the taxpayer in carrying on the activity.
- The expectation that assets used in the activity may appreciate in value.
- The success of the taxpayer in carrying on other, similar activities.
- The taxpayer's history of income or losses with respect to the activity.
- The amount of occasional profits, if any.
- The financial status of the taxpayer.
- The elements of personal pleasure or recreation.

---

[38]§212. As we discussed earlier in the chapter, rental and royalty expenses are the only investment expenses that qualify as a deduction for AGI.

[39]§212.

[40]See Reg. §1.183-2.

One of the most important factors is the taxpayer's history of income or loss in the activity. In fact, the tax law explicitly presumes that an activity is a business if it generates a profit in three of five consecutive years.[41] This presumption is difficult for the IRS to overcome in disputes with taxpayers.

If an activity is determined to be a hobby, the taxpayer must *include* the revenue from the activity in gross income and may deduct the expenses, to the extent of the gross income from the activity, *as miscellaneous itemized deductions* (see discussion below).[42] Thus, the revenue from the activity increases the taxpayer's AGI (and taxable income) dollar for dollar. However, the deductions may or may not decrease taxable income depending on whether and the extent to which they exceed the 2 percent of AGI floor.

### Example 6-30

Courtney's cousin, Phil T. Thrill, played golf at Arizona State University. He turned pro and tried to qualify for the PGA tour when he graduated from college. Unfortunately, he couldn't support his family playing golf and is currently employed as a high school physical education instructor. Every summer, Phil plays in several local and a few regional professional golf tournaments. His only source of revenue from golf is the prize money he wins in these tournaments. Phil has managed to earn prize money in excess of his expenses in only one of the previous five years. This year Phil received golf revenues of $3,200 and incurred golf-related expenses of $8,800 consisting of tournament entry fees, equipment, food, transportation, clothing, and lodging. For tax purposes, are Phil's golf activities considered to be a business or a hobby? If Phil's golfing activities are determined to be a *hobby,* how does Phil account for his revenues and expenses for tax purposes?

**Answer:** Most likely a hobby. Because Phil has only generated golf revenue in excess of expenses in one of the past five years, the activity is not presumed to be a business activity. To qualify as a business, Phil would have to convince the IRS that he is primarily engaging in golf activities to make a profit rather than for personal enjoyment. If the activity is determined to be a hobby, Phil includes the $3,200 of revenue in gross income as miscellaneous income. He is allowed to deduct $3,200 of his expenses as miscellaneous itemized deductions subject to the 2 percent floor (the deduction is limited to gross income from the activity).

**What if:** Suppose that Phil's golfing activities are determined to be a hobby and (1) his AGI is $70,000 before considering the effects of his golfing activity and (2) he has no miscellaneous itemized deductions other than his golfing expenses. What is the effect of his golfing activities on his AGI and taxable income this year?

**Answer:** The golfing activities will increase Phil's AGI by $3,200 and his taxable income by $1,464 because the full amount of the revenue is included in gross income but his expense deductions are limited. Phil's AGI and taxable income are computed as follows:

| Description | Amount | Explanation |
|---|---|---|
| (1) AGI before activity | $70,000 | |
| (2) Golf revenue (increase in AGI) | 3,200 | |
| (3) AGI after activity | 73,200 | (1) + (2). |
| (4) Golf expenses | 8,800 | |
| (5) Golf expenses after revenue limit | 3,200 | Lesser of (2) or (4). |
| (6) 2% of AGI floor | 1,464 | (3) × 2%. |
| (7) Deductible golf expenses (as itemized deduction) | 1,736 | (5) − (6). |
| Increase in taxable income | $ 1,464 | (2) − (7). |

[41]For activities involving breeding, training, or racing horses, the taxpayer need show a profit in only two of seven years for the activity to be presumed to be a business.

[42]When expenses of a hobby exceed revenue, the expenses must be deducted in a particular sequence. Taxpayers first deduct expenses that are deductible anyway, such as mortgage interest or property taxes. Second, taxpayers deduct all other expenses except depreciation expense. Finally, they deduct depreciation expense. A similar sequence is applied to deductions associated with offices in the home and rental homes.

**Limitation on Miscellaneous Itemized Deductions (2 percent of AGI Floor)**   To apply the 2 percent floor limit and determine the miscellaneous itemized deduction, the sum of all deductions subject to the 2 percent floor limitation is reduced by 2 percent of AGI. If the 2 percent floor equals or exceeds the sum of miscellaneous itemized deductions, the deductions do not increase the taxpayer's itemized deductions (they don't provide any tax benefit). The 2 percent floor limitation makes it likely that most taxpayers will receive limited, if any, tax benefit from the deductions subject to the floor.

---

**Example 6-31**

What amount is Courtney's deduction for miscellaneous itemized deductions that are subject to the 2 percent floor?

**Answer:** $1,083, computed as follows:

| Description | Amount | Reference |
|---|---|---|
| Subscriptions to publications | $   410 | Example 6-25. |
| Educational costs | 1,550 | Example 6-26. |
| Business trip to observe architecture | 2,113 | Example 6-27. |
| Tax preparation fees | 250 | Example 6-29. |
| Total deductions subject to 2% floor | $4,323 | |
| 2% of AGI floor (162,000 × 2%) | −3,240 | |
| Total miscellaneous itemized deductions | $1,083 | |

Courtney incurred a total of $4,323 of miscellaneous itemized deductions, but she can deduct only $1,083 of them due to the 2 percent of AGI restriction.

**THE KEY FACTS**

Miscellaneous Itemized Deductions

■ Employee business expenses not reimbursed by an accountable plan.

■ Investment expenses if not in a rental or royalty activity.

■ Tax preparation fees and allowable hobby expenses.

■ Total miscellaneous itemized deductions are subject to a 2 percent of AGI floor limit.

---

**Taxes in the Real World**

Mrs. Tschetschot was a database project engineer residing in Cedar Rapids, Iowa, but she was also a professional tournament poker player. In 2000, Mrs. Tschetschot participated in nine poker tournament series, winning in excess of $11,000. In contrast, Mr. Tschetschot occasionally played slot machines and blackjack while accompanying his wife on her poker tournament trips. In 2000, Mr. and Mrs. Tschetschot claimed a net loss of $29,933 on Schedule C from "professional" (business) gambling activities. The IRS assessed a deficiency of $10,071 based on the view that the deductions were not appropriately Schedule C deductions, but rather should be claimed as miscellaneous itemized deductions on Schedule A and limited to the extent of gambling winnings.

Mr. and Mrs. Tschetschot petitioned the Tax Court, and at trial the IRS conceded Mrs. Tschetschot's status as a professional and allowed her deductions. The IRS, however, disputed Mr. Tschetschot's deductions.

In deciding the case, the Tax Court noted that "a player's tournament success depends on a combination of both luck and skill. A player might have a decent hand, but as Kenny Rogers tells us in 'The Gambler,' he or she would still have to 'know when to hold 'em, know when to fold 'em, know when to walk away and know when to run' to actually be a success." Despite that, the Tax Court decided that Congress made a policy decision to treat businesses based on wagering activities differently than other businesses, and that the court was not free to rewrite the Internal Revenue Code. Accordingly, the court held that tournament poker is a "wagering" activity and that deductions are limited by gambling winnings. Given this decision, do you think the IRS regrets conceding Mrs. Tschetschot's deductions?

*Source: George E. Tschetschot, TC Memo 2007-38*

### Miscellaneous Itemized Deductions Not Subject to AGI Floor

Several deductions are considered to be miscellaneous itemized deductions but are not subject to the 2 percent of AGI floor. Perhaps because gambling includes a significant element of personal enjoyment (losers may think otherwise), individuals include all gambling winnings for the year in gross income but may also deduct gambling losses *to the extent of gambling winnings* for the year. The deductible gambling losses are miscellaneous itemized deductions; therefore, *losses don't directly offset winnings.* However, unlike other miscellaneous itemized deductions, gambling losses are *not* subject to the 2 percent of AGI floor. Casualty and theft losses on property held for investment and the unrecovered cost of a life annuity (the taxpayer died before recovering the full cost of the annuity) also qualify as miscellaneous itemized deductions not subject to the AGI floor.

### Phase-out of Itemized Deductions

In addition to limits on specific deductions, the amount of a taxpayer's *total* itemized deductions *other than* medical expenses, casualty losses, investment *interest* expense, and gambling losses is subject to phase-out.[43] That is, when AGI exceeds a certain threshold, itemized deductions are reduced. At press time, the phase-out of certain itemized deductions was scheduled to expire at the end of 2009 and re-emerge in 2011 [§68(g) added by P.L. 107-16 (2001) §103(a)]. The computational details of the phase-out are provided in Appendix A to this chapter.

### Summary of Itemized Deductions

This part of the chapter examined the various itemized deductions (deductions from AGI). We found that both medical expense and casualty loss deductions are designed to reduce the tax burden on individuals whose ability to pay has been involuntarily impaired, but because of large floor limitations these itemized deductions are unlikely to produce tax benefits. Most miscellaneous itemized deductions, including unreimbursed employee business expense and investment expenses (excluding rental and royalty expenses), are likewise hampered by a relatively large floor limitation.

---

**Example 6-32**

Given Courtney's current year AGI of $162,000, what is the amount of her total itemized deductions she may claim on her tax return after computing the itemized deduction phase-out?

**Answer:** Courtney's itemized deductions for the year are $39,793 calculated as follows:

| Description | Amount | Reference |
|---|---|---|
| Taxes | $10,250 | Example 6-14. |
| Interest on loans secured by residence | 15,800 | Example 6-15. |
| Charitable contributions | 12,530 | Example 6-22. |
| Miscellaneous itemized deductions | +1,083 | Example 6-31. |
| Total itemized deductions subject to phase-out | $39,663 | |
| Less phase-out of itemized deductions* | −0 | |
| Plus investment interest expense | +130 | Example 6-16. |
| Total itemized deductions | $39,793 | |

*Because Courtney's AGI of $162,000 is below the beginning of the phase-out threshold for taxpayers filing as a head of household, none of her itemized deductions is phased out.

---

[43]§68. Certain charitable contributions made for hurricane relief are also exempt from the phase-out.

Exhibit 6-10 presents Courtney's itemized deductions on Form 1040, Schedule A.

**EXHIBIT 6-10**    Courtney's Form 1040, Schedule A

| SCHEDULE A (Form 1040) | **Itemized Deductions** | OMB No. 1545-0074 |
|---|---|---|

Department of the Treasury
Internal Revenue Service (99)

▶ Attach to Form 1040.    ▶ See Instructions for Schedule A (Form 1040).

20**09**

Attachment Sequence No. **07**

Name(s) shown on Form 1040 — COURTNEY WILSON    Your social security number

| | | | | | |
|---|---|---|---|---|---|
| **Medical and Dental Expenses** | | **Caution.** Do not include expenses reimbursed or paid by others. | | | |
| | 1 | Medical and dental expenses (see page A-1) | 1 | 2,400 | |
| | 2 | Enter amount from Form 1040, line 38 **2** | | | |
| | 3 | Multiply line 2 by 7.5% (.075) | 3 | 12,150 | |
| | 4 | Subtract line 3 from line 1. If line 3 is more than line 1, enter -0- | 4 | | 0 |
| **Taxes You Paid** (See page A-2.) | 5 | State and local (check only one box): a ☑ Income taxes, or  b ☐ General sales taxes | 5 | 6,700 | |
| | 6 | Real estate taxes (see page A-5) | 6 | 3,550 | |
| | 7 | New motor vehicle taxes from line 11 of the worksheet on back. Skip this line if you checked box 5b | 7 | | |
| | 8 | Other taxes. List type and amount ▶ _____ | 8 | | |
| | 9 | Add lines 5 through 8 | 9 | | 10,250 |
| **Interest You Paid** (See page A-6.) | 10 | Home mortgage interest and points reported to you on Form 1098 | 10 | 15,800 | |
| | 11 | Home mortgage interest not reported to you on Form 1098. If paid to the person from whom you bought the home, see page A-7 and show that person's name, identifying no., and address ▶ _____ | 11 | | |
| **Note.** Personal interest is not deductible. | 12 | Points not reported to you on Form 1098. See page A-7 for special rules | 12 | | |
| | 13 | Qualified mortgage insurance premiums (see page A-7) | 13 | | |
| | 14 | Investment interest. Attach Form 4952 if required. (See page A-8.) | 14 | 130 | |
| | 15 | Add lines 10 through 14 | 15 | | 15,930 |
| **Gifts to Charity** If you made a gift and got a benefit for it, see page A-8. | 16 | Gifts by cash or check. If you made any gift of $250 or more, see page A-8 | 16 | 1,770 | |
| | 17 | Other than by cash or check. If any gift of $250 or more, see page A-8. You **must** attach Form 8283 if over $500 | 17 | 10,760 | |
| | 18 | Carryover from prior year | 18 | | |
| | 19 | Add lines 16 through 18 | 19 | | 12,530 |
| **Casualty and Theft Losses** | 20 | Casualty or theft loss(es). Attach Form 4684. (See page A-10.) | 20 | | |
| **Job Expenses and Certain Miscellaneous Deductions** (See page A-10.) | 21 | Unreimbursed employee expenses—job travel, union dues, job education, etc. Attach Form 2106 or 2106-EZ if required. (See page A-10.) ▶ _____ | 21 | 3,663 | |
| | 22 | Tax preparation fees | 22 | 250 | |
| | 23 | Other expenses—investment, safe deposit box, etc. List type and amount ▶ _____ | 23 | 410 | |
| | 24 | Add lines 21 through 23 | 24 | 4,323 | |
| | 25 | Enter amount from Form 1040, line 38 **25** | | | |
| | 26 | Multiply line 25 by 2% (.02) | 26 | 3,240 | |
| | 27 | Subtract line 26 from line 24. If line 26 is more than line 24, enter -0- | 27 | | 1,083 |
| **Other Miscellaneous Deductions** | 28 | Other—from list on page A-11. List type and amount ▶ _____ | 28 | | |
| **Total Itemized Deductions** | 29 | Is Form 1040, line 38, over $166,800 (over $83,400 if married filing separately)? ☐ **No.** Your deduction is not limited. Add the amounts in the far right column for lines 4 through 28. Also, enter this amount on Form 1040, line 40a. ☐ **Yes.** Your deduction may be limited. See page A-11 for the amount to enter. | 29 | | 39,793 |
| | 30 | If you elect to itemize deductions even though they are less than your standard deduction, check here ▶ ☐ | | | |

For Paperwork Reduction Act Notice, see Form 1040 instructions.    Cat. No. 17145C    Schedule A (Form 1040) 2009

**L03**

# THE STANDARD DEDUCTION AND EXEMPTIONS

## Standard Deduction

The **standard deduction** is a flat amount that most individuals can elect to deduct *instead* of deducting their itemized deductions (if any). That is, taxpayers generally *deduct the greater of their standard deduction or their itemized deductions.*

The amount of the standard deduction varies according to the taxpayer's filing status, age, and eyesight. The basic standard deduction is greater for married taxpayers filing jointly and those supporting a family (head of household) than it is for married taxpayers filing separately and unmarried taxpayers not supporting a family. Taxpayers who are at least 65 years of age on the last day of the year or blind are entitled to additional standard deduction amounts above and beyond their basic standard deduction.[44] Exhibit 6-11 summarizes the standard deduction amounts.[45]

### EXHIBIT 6-11    Standard Deduction Amounts*

| 2009 Amounts | | |
| --- | --- | --- |
| **Filing Status** | **Basic Standard Deduction** | **Additional Standard Deduction for Age and/or Blindness at End of Year** |
| Married filing jointly | $11,400 | $1,100 |
| Head of household | 8,350 | 1,400 |
| Single | 5,700 | 1,400 |
| Married filing separately | 5,700 | 1,100 |

| 2010 Amounts | | |
| --- | --- | --- |
| **Filing Status** | **Basic Standard Deduction** | **Additional Standard Deduction for Age and/or Blindness at End of Year** |
| Married filing jointly | $11,400 | $1,100 |
| Head of household | 8,400 | 1,400 |
| Single | 5,700 | 1,400 |
| Married filing separately | 5,700 | 1,100 |

*For individuals claimed as a dependent on another return, the 2010 standard deduction is the greater of (1) $950 or (2) $300 plus earned income not to exceed the standard deduction amount of those who are not dependents.

For 2010, the additional standard deduction for either age and/or blindness is $1,100 for married taxpayers and $1,400 for taxpayers who are not married. Thus, a blind individual who is 65 years old and single is entitled to a standard deduction of $8,500 (5,700 + 1,400 + 1,400). A married couple filing a joint return with one spouse over age 65 and one spouse considered legally blind is entitled to a standard deduction of $13,600 (11,400 + 1,100 + 1,100). Finally, for an individual who is claimed as a dependent on another's return, the standard deduction is the greater of (1) $950 or (2) $300 plus the individual's earned income limited to the regular standard deduction (including the additional standard deduction amounts, if any).

---

[44]Taxpayers are considered to be blind if they have a certified statement from their eye doctor or registered optometrist that their corrected vision of their better eye is no better than 20/200 or their field of vision is 20 degrees or less.

[45]The standard deduction amount is indexed for inflation.

**Example 6-33**

What is Courtney's standard deduction for the year?

**Answer:** $8,400. Because Courtney is unmarried at the end of the year and she maintains a household for more than six months for Deron and Ellen who both qualify as her dependents (as qualifying children), Courtney's filing status is head of household, which allows her to claim a standard deduction of $8,400.

Given that Courtney's itemized deductions are $39,793, will Courtney deduct her itemized deductions or her standard deduction?

**Answer:** She will deduct her itemized deductions because they exceed her standard deduction.

*What if:* Suppose that Courtney's 10-year-old son, Deron, earned $600 this summer by mowing lawns for neighbors. If Courtney claims a dependency exemption for Deron, what amount of standard deduction can Deron claim on his individual return?

**Answer:** Deron claims a minimum standard deduction of $950 because he is claimed as a dependent on Courtney's return. Hence, Deron would not pay any income tax because his taxable income is reduced to zero by the standard deduction.[46]

*What if:* Any difference in amount of the standard deduction if Deron earned $2,100?

**Answer:** Because the amount of his earnings, Deron claims a standard deduction in the amount of his earned income plus $300. Hence, Deron claims a standard deduction of $2,400 and he would not pay any income tax.

*What if:* Suppose that Deron earned $8,500?

**Answer:** Again, Deron claims a standard deduction in the amount of his earned income plus $300. However, Deron's standard deduction is limited to $5,700, the maximum allowable standard deduction for a taxpayer filing single and claimed as a dependent on another return. Hence, Deron would report taxable income of $2,800.

From the government's standpoint, the standard deduction serves two purposes. First, to help taxpayers with lower income, it automatically provides a minimum amount of income that is not subject to taxation. Second, it eliminates the need for the IRS to verify and audit itemized deductions for those taxpayers who chose to deduct the standard deduction. From the taxpayers' perspective, the standard deduction allows them to avoid taxation on a portion of their income, and for those not planning to itemize deductions, it eliminates the need to substantiate and collect information about them. The standard deduction, however, is a double-edged sword. While it reduces taxes by offsetting income with an automatic deduction, it eliminates the tax benefits of itemized deductions up to the amount of the standard deduction. This is a very important point to consider when evaluating the tax benefits of itemized deductions.

**Example 6-34**

In Example 6-32, we determined that Courtney is entitled to deduct $39,793 of itemized deductions this year. How much do Courtney's itemized deductions reduce her taxable income relative to a situation in which she had $0 itemized deductions?

**Answer:** $31,393. Because Courtney files as a head of household, she would have been able to deduct $8,400 as a standard deduction even if she had not incurred *any* itemized deductions. Consequently, her itemized deductions reduce her taxable income by only $31,393 ($39,793 − $8,400) beyond what her taxable income would have been if she did not itemize deductions.

[46]Deron will need to file a tax return because his self-employment income exceeds $400 and, as explained in Chapter 7, he will likely owe self-employment tax.

**Bunching Itemized Deductions** Some taxpayers may deduct the standard deduction every year because their itemized deductions always fall just short of the standard deduction amount and thus never produce any tax benefit. They may gain some tax benefit from their itemized deductions by implementing a simple timing tax planning strategy called **bunching itemized deductions.** The basic strategy consists of shifting itemized deductions into one year such that the amount of itemized deductions exceeds the standard deduction for the year, and then deducting the standard deduction in the next year (or vice versa).

Because individuals are cash-method taxpayers, they may shift certain itemized deductions by accelerating payment into the current year. For example, a taxpayer could make charitable contributions at the end of December rather than at the beginning of January in the following year. Taxpayers' ability to shift itemized deductions is limited because the timing of these payments is not completely discretionary. For example, real estate taxes have due dates, state taxes are generally paid throughout the year via withholding, and employees may incur and be required to pay business expenses throughout the year. However, taxpayers who annually make a certain amount of charitable contributions, for example, may consider lumping contributions for two years into one year and not contributing in the next year.[47]

---

## Example 6-35

**What if:** Gram is 70 years old and files as a single taxpayer. Last year Gram paid deductible medical expenses (after the 7.5 percent AGI floor) of $4,000. She also contributed $2,000 to her local church. Last year her total itemized deductions were $6,000 ($4,000 medical + 2,000 charitable). Assuming Gram has similar expenditures this year, what amount of additional deductions would Gram have been able to deduct last year if she had bunched her deductions by making her 2009 and 2010 charitable contributions in 2010?

**Answer:** $900, computed as follows:

| | No Bunching | | Bunching | |
| --- | --- | --- | --- | --- |
| | **2009** | **2010** | **2009** | **2010** |
| (1) Standard deduction* | $7,100 | $7,100 | $7,100 | $7,100 |
| (2) Itemized deductions | 6,000 | 6,000 | 4,000 | 8,000 |
| Greater of (1) and (2) | $7,100 | $7,100 | $7,100 | $8,000 |
| Total deductions (combined years) | $14,200 ($7,100 + 7,100) | | $15,100 ($7,100 + 8,000) | |
| Deductions gained through bunching | $900 ($15,100 bunching deductions − $14,200 nonbunching deductions) | | | |

*For both 2009 and 2010, her standard deduction is the $5,700 standard deduction for single taxpayers plus an additional $1,400 standard deduction amount for age.

---

## Deduction for Personal and Dependency Exemptions

As we learned in Chapter 4, taxpayers are generally allowed to deduct $3,650 in 2010 for each **personal** and **dependency exemption.** In general, then, a taxpayer's

---

[47]Of course, as we discussed in Chapter 3, taxpayers adopting this strategy must also consider the time value of money for the contributions amounts they pay in advance to determine whether a tax planning strategy designed to save taxes makes economic sense.

from AGI deduction for personal and dependency exemptions is $3,650 multiplied by the number of the taxpayer's **exemptions.** In 2009, a taxpayer's total exemption deduction was phased out based on AGI for relatively high income taxpayers. At press time, the phase-out of personal exemptions was scheduled to expire at the end of 2009 and re-emerge in 2011 (§151(d)(3)(F) added by P.L. 107-16 (2001) §102(a)). We discuss the computational details of the phase-out in Appendix B to this chapter.

---

**Example 6-36**

This year, Courtney is allowed to claim a personal exemption for herself and dependency exemptions for her daughter Ellen and her son Deron. Courtney's filing status is head of household. What amount is Courtney allowed to deduct for her personal and dependency exemptions?

**Answer:** $10,950 ($3,650 × 3).

---

## Taxable Income Summary

We now have enough information to calculate Courtney's and Gram's taxable income. Exhibit 6-12 shows Courtney's taxable income calculation and Exhibit 6-13 illustrates how this information would be displayed on page 2 of Courtney's Form 1040.

Exhibit 6-14 provides Gram's taxable income calculation.

**EXHIBIT 6-12    Courtney's Taxable Income**

| Description | Amount | Reference |
|---|---|---|
| AGI | $162,000 | Exhibit 6-6. |
| Less: Greater of (1) itemized deductions ($39,793) or (2) standard deduction ($8,400) | (39,793) | Example 6-32. |
| Less: Personal and dependency exemptions | (10,950) | Example 6-36. |
| Taxable income | $111,257 | |

**EXHIBIT 6-13    Courtney's Taxable Income Computation as Presented on Form 1040, Page 2**

| | | | | |
|---|---|---|---|---|
| Form 1040 (2009) | | | | Page **2** |
| **Tax and Credits** | **38** | Amount from line 37 (adjusted gross income) . . . . . . . . . . . . | **38** | 162,000 |
| | **39a** | Check { ☐ **You** were born before January 2, 1945, ☐ Blind. } Total boxes if: { ☐ **Spouse** was born before January 2, 1945, ☐ Blind. } checked ▶ **39a** | | |
| **Standard Deduction for—** | **b** | If your spouse itemizes on a separate return or you were a dual-status alien, see page 35 and check here ▶ **39b**☐ | | |
| ● People who check any box on line 39a, 39b, or 40b **or** who can be claimed as a dependent, see page 35 | **40a** | **Itemized deductions** (from Schedule A) **or** your **standard deduction** (see left margin) . . | **40a** | 39,793 |
| | **b** | If you are increasing your standard deduction by certain real estate taxes, new motor vehicle taxes, or a net disaster loss, attach Schedule L and check here (see page 35) . ▶ **40b**☐ | | |
| | **41** | Subtract line 40a from line 38 . . . . . . . . . . . . . . . | **41** | 122,207 |
| | **42** | **Exemptions.** If line 38 is $125,100 or less and you did not provide housing to a Midwestern displaced individual, multiply $3,650 by the number on line 6d. Otherwise, see page 37 . . | **42** | 10,950 |
| | **43** | **Taxable income.** Subtract line 42 from line 41. If line 42 is more than line 41, enter -0- . . | **43** | 111,257 |

**EXHIBIT 6-14**    Gram's Taxable Income

| Description | Amount | Explanation |
|---|---|---|
| (1) AGI | $15,590 | Exhibit 6-7. |
| (2) Greater of (a) itemized deductions ($6,000) or (b) standard deduction ($7,100) | (7,100) | Example 6-35. |
| (3) Personal and dependency exemptions | (3,650) | One exemption. |
| Taxable income | $ 4,840 | (1) + (2) + (3). |

Note that because Gram's gross income of $16,150 (Exhibit 5-6) is more than the sum of her basic standard deduction amount plus her personal and dependency exemption ($10,750), therefore, she is required to file a tax return.

## CONCLUSION

We started this chapter with Courtney's and Gram's gross incomes. In this chapter, we first identified the duo's separate *deductions for AGI* and we computed their AGI. We then determined their *from* AGI deductions. Courtney deducted her itemized deductions because they exceeded her standard deduction. Gram, on the other hand, deducted her standard deduction. Finally, Courtney deducted three exemptions: a personal exemption for herself and dependency exemptions for each of her two children, Deron and Ellen. Gram deducted one personal exemption for herself. By subtracting their *from* AGI deductions from their AGI, we determined taxable income for both Courtney and Gram. With this knowledge, we proceed to the next chapter and address issues relating to determining the amount of tax Courtney and Gram are required to pay on their taxable income. As we'll discover, it's not always as simple as applying taxable income to a tax rate schedule to determine the tax liability.

## APPENDIX A    CALCULATION OF ITEMIZED DEDUCTION PHASE-OUT

Taxpayers with AGI in excess of the threshold amount determine the phase-out by comparing the lesser of the following two numbers:[48]

> 3 percent × (AGI in excess of the threshold amount)
> 80 percent of the those itemized deductions subject to phase-out.

Because itemized deductions can be reduced but not completely eliminated, the phase-out provision is sometimes referred to as a **cutback** or **haircut.**

**Example 6-1A**

*What if:* Suppose that the phase-out of excess itemized deductions was applicable this year and that Courtney's AGI was $100,000 over the threshold amount. All else equal, what would be the amount of her total itemized deductions she may claim on her tax return after computing the itemized deduction phase-out?

(continued on page 6-37...)

[48]For years ending after 2005 and before 2010, §68(f) limited the actual phase-out to a fraction of the total amount subject to phase-out.

**Answer:** Courtney would be able to claim itemized deductions for the year of $36,793, calculated as follows:

| Description | Amount | Reference |
|---|---:|---|
| Taxes | $10,250 | Example 6-14. |
| Interest on loans secured by residence | 15,800 | Example 6-15. |
| Charitable contributions | 12,530 | Example 6-22. |
| Miscellaneous itemized deduction | + 1,083 | Example 6-31. |
| Total itemized deductions subject to phase-out | $39,663 | |
| Less phase-out of itemized deductions | − 3,000 | See calculation below. |
| Plus investment interest expense (not subject to phase-out) | + 130 | Example 6-16. |
| Total itemized deductions | $36,793 | |

The phase-out is the lesser of (1) 3 percent × (AGI minus threshold amount) or (2) 80 percent of the deductions subject to the phase-out ($39,663) as follows:

> Step 1: Phase-out amount is $3,000. This is the lesser of:
>
> | | |
> |---|---|
> | 3% × ($100,000) | $3,000 |
> | 80% × 39,663 | $31,730 |

# PERSONAL EXEMPTION PHASE-OUT COMPUTATION

**APPENDIX B**

The process of determining the amount of the phase-out involves several steps. First, in general terms, the phase-out requires the taxpayer to reduce her *total* amount of personal and dependency deductions by a percentage that depends on the extent to which the taxpayer's AGI exceeds the threshold. Specifically, the process to determine the taxpayer's allowable personal and dependency exemptions after the phase-out involves the following five steps.

**Step 1:** Subtract the taxpayer's AGI from the AGI threshold based on the taxpayer's filing status. If the threshold equals or exceeds the taxpayer's AGI, the taxpayer deducts her full personal and dependency exemptions.

**Step 2:** Divide the excess AGI (the amount from Step 1) by 2,500. If the result is not a whole number (i.e., the excess AGI is not evenly divisible by 2,500), round *up* to the next whole number.[49]

**Step 3:** Multiply the outcome of Step 3 by 2 percent, but limit the product to 100 percent. This is the *full* phase-out percentage.

**Step 4:** Multiply the percentage determined in Step 3 by the taxpayer's total personal and dependency exemptions (number of personal and dependent exemptions times the exemption amount for that year). The product is the amount of personal and dependency exemption deductions that is phased-out (the taxpayer is *not* allowed to deduct this amount).

**Step 5:** Subtract the Step 4 result from the taxpayer's total personal and dependency exemptions that would be deductible without any phase-out (i.e., number of personal and dependent exemptions times the exemption amount for that year).

[49]For married filing separate taxpayers, replace the $2,500 amount with $1,250.

## Example 6-1B

*What if:* Assume Courtney files as a head of household with three personal and dependency exemptions in a year that the phase-out of personal exemptions is applicable. Assume further that Courtney's AGI is $51,500 over the threshold amount for this phase-out and that the exemption amount for the year is $3,650. What is Courtney's *from* AGI deduction for personal and dependency exemptions?

**Answer:** $6,351, computed as follows:

|         | Amount   | Explanation |
|---------|----------|-------------|
| Step 1: | $51,500  | Excess AGI over applicable threshold amount. |
| Step 2: | 21       | Divide $51,500 by 2,500 and round up to nearest whole number $51,500/2,500 = 20.6 → 21. |
| Step 3: | 42%      | Multiply the amount in Step 2 by 2% (21 × 2%). This is the full phase-out percentage. |
| Step 4: | $ 4,599  | Multiply the Step 4 result by total exemption amount ($10,950 × 42%). This is the amount of the phase-out. |
| Step 5: | $ 6,351  | Subtract the Step 4 result from total exemption amounts ($10,950 − $4,599). This is the deductible exemption amount. |

## SUMMARY

**LO1**   Identify the common deductions necessary for calculating adjusted gross income (AGI).

- Deductions for AGI may be categorized into those that are directly or indirectly business-related and those that address specific policy issues.
- The business-related deductions for AGI include business expenses, rent and royalty expenses, self-employment taxes, moving expenses, medical and health insurance by self-employed taxpayers, and forfeited interest.
- Other common deductions for AGI include the deductions for alimony, interest on student loans, for qualified education expenses and early withdrawal penalties.

**LO2**   Describe the different types of itemized deductions available to individuals and compute itemized deductions.

- The medical expense and casualty loss deductions are designed to provide tax benefits to needy individuals but both are subject to significant floor limitations.
- The itemized deduction for interest is limited to interest related to a personal residence and investment interest, and the latter is limited by net investment income.
- The deduction for charitable contributions extends to contributions of money and property to qualifying charities. The charitable deduction is subject to ceiling limitations, which are more restrictive for donations of property.
- The deduction for taxes includes state income and property taxes. Sales taxes can be deducted in lieu of deducting state and local income taxes.
- Employee business expenses and investment expenses (except rental and royalty expenses) are miscellaneous itemized deductions subject to a 2 percent of AGI floor limitation.

**LO3**   Explain the operation of the standard deduction, determine the deduction for personal and dependency exemptions, and compute taxable income.

- Itemized deductions do not produce any tax benefit unless the total itemized deductions exceed the standard deduction.
- Personal exemptions are allowed for the taxpayer and spouse (if married filing jointly).

# KEY TERMS

accountable plan (6-26)
bunching itemized deductions (6-34)
business activities (6-2)
capital gain property (6-20)
casualty loss (6-23)
ceiling (6-21)
commuting (6-25)
cutback (6-36)
dependency exemption (6-34)

exemption (6-34)
floor limitation (6-15)
haircut (6-36)
hobby (6-27)
investment activities (6-3)
miscellaneous itemized
deductions (6-25)
modified AGI (6-10)
ordinary and necessary (6-4)

ordinary income property (6-20)
personal exemption (6-34)
private nonoperating foundations (6-21)
private operating foundations (6-21)
qualified educational expenses (6-9)
qualified educational loans (6-9)
standard deduction (6-32)
trade or business (6-3)

# DISCUSSION QUESTIONS

1. **(LO1)** It has been suggested that tax policy favors deductions for AGI compared to itemized deductions. Describe two ways in which deductions for AGI are treated more favorably than itemized deductions.

2. **(LO1)** How is a business activity distinguished from an investment activity? Why is this distinction important for the purpose of calculating federal income taxes?

3. **(LO1)** Describe how a business element is reflected in the requirements to deduct moving expenses and how Congress limited this deduction to substantial moves.

4. **(LO1)** Explain why Congress allows self-employed taxpayers to deduct the cost of health insurance above the line (for AGI) when employees can only itemize this cost as a medical expense. Would a self-employed taxpayer ever prefer to claim health insurance premiums as an itemized deductions rather than a deduction for AGI? Explain.

5. **(LO1)** Explain why Congress allows self-employed taxpayers to deduct half of their self-employment tax.

6. **(LO1)** Using the Internal Revenue Code, describe two deductions for AGI that are not discussed in this chapter.

7. **(LO1)** Explain why Congress allows taxpayers to deduct interest forfeited as a penalty on the premature withdrawal from a certificate of deposit.

8. **(LO1)** Describe the mechanical limitation on the deduction for interest on qualified educational loans.

9. **(LO1)** Congress has tried to subsidize certain expenditures through the federal income tax system. Compare and contrast the operation of the deduction interest on qualified educational loans with the deduction for medical expenses.

10. **(LO2)** Explain why the medical expense and casualty loss provisions are sometimes referred to as "wherewithal" deductions and how this rationale is reflected in the limits on these deductions.

11. **(LO2)** Describe the type of medical expenditures that qualify for the medical expense deduction. Will the cost of meals consumed while hospitalized qualify for the deduction? Will over-the-counter drugs and medicines qualify for the deduction? Why or why not?

12. **(LO2)** Under what circumstances can a taxpayer deduct medical expenses paid for a member of his family? Does it matter if the family member reports significant amounts of gross income and cannot be claimed as a dependent?

13. **(LO2)** What types of taxes qualify to be deducted as itemized deductions? What sort of taxes don't qualify for the deduction? Would a vehicle registration fee qualify as a deductible tax? Why or why not?

*research*

14. **(LO2)** Compare and contrast the limits on the deduction of interest on home acquisition indebtedness versus home equity loans. Are these limits consistent with horizontal equity? Explain.

15. **(LO2)** Explain the argument that the deductions for charitable contributions, home mortgage interest, and state and local taxes all represent indirect subsidies for these activities.

*research*

16. **(LO2)** Cash donations to charity are subject to a number of very specific substantiation requirements. Describe these requirements and how charitable gifts can be substantiated. Describe the substantiation requirements for property donations.

17. **(LO2)** Describe the conditions in which a donation of property to a charity will result in a charitable contribution deduction of fair market value and when it will result in a deduction of the tax basis of the property.

18. **(LO2)** Describe the type of event that qualifies as a casualty for tax purposes.

19. **(LO2)** A casualty loss from the complete destruction of a personal asset is limited to the lesser of fair market value or the property's adjusted basis. Explain the rationale for this rule as opposed to just allowing a deduction for the basis of the asset.

*research*

20. **(LO2)** This week Jim's residence was heavily damaged by a storm system that spread destruction throughout the region. While Jim's property insurance covers some of the damage, there is a significant amount of uninsured loss. The governor of Jim's state has requested that the president declare the region a federal disaster area and provide federal disaster assistance. Explain to Jim the income tax implications of such a declaration and any associated tax planning possibilities.

21. **(LO2)** Describe the types of expenses that constitute miscellaneous itemized deductions and explain why these expenses rarely produce any tax benefits.

22. **(LO2)** Explain why the cost of commuting from home to work is not deductible as a business expense.

23. **(LO2)** When is the cost of education deductible as an employee business expense?

24. **(LO2)** How might the reimbursement of a portion of an employee expense influence the deductibility of the expense for the employee?

25. **(LO2)** Explain why an employee should be concerned about whether his employer reimburses business expenses using an "accountable" plan?

26. **(LO2)** Jake is a retired jockey who takes monthly trips to Las Vegas to gamble on horse races. Jake also trains race horses part time at his Louisville ranch. So far this year, Jake has won almost $47,500 during his trips to Las Vegas while spending $27,250 on travel expenses and incurring $62,400 of gambling losses. Jake also received $60,000 in revenue from his training activities and he incurred $72,000 of associated costs. Explain how Jake's gambling winnings and related costs will be treated for tax purposes. Describe the factors that will influence how Jake's ranch expenses are treated for tax purposes.

*research*

27. **(LO2)** Frank paid $3,700 in fees for an accountant to tabulate business information (Frank operates as a self-employed contractor and files a Schedule C). The accountant also spent time tabulating Frank's income from his investments and determining Frank's personal itemized deductions. Explain to Frank whether or not he can deduct the $3,700 as a business expense or as an itemized deduction, and provide a citation to an authority that supports your conclusion.

28. **(LO2)** Contrast ceiling and floor limitations, and give an example of each.

29. **(LO2)** Identify which itemized deductions are subject to floor limitations, ceiling limitations, phase-out limitations (for years after 2010), or some combination of these limits.

30. **(LO3)** Describe the tax benefits from "bunching" itemized deductions in one year. Describe the characteristics of the taxpayers who are most likely to benefit from using bunching and explain why this is so.

31. **(LO3)** Explain how the standard deduction is rationalized and why the standard deduction might be viewed as a floor limit on itemized deductions.

32. **(LO3)** Explain how the calculation of the standard deduction limits the ability to shift income to a dependent.

33. **(LO3)** Explain why the overall phase-out of itemized deductions has been described as both a "stealth" tax and a "haircut" of itemized deductions. Explain whether it is possible for a taxpayer to lose all itemized deductions under the phase-out rules scheduled to apply after 2010.

34. **(LO3)** Describe the mechanism for phasing out exemptions for years after 2010. Can a taxpayer lose the benefit of all of her personal and dependency exemptions?

35. **(LO3)** Determine if a taxpayer can change his election to itemize deductions once a return is filed. (*Hint:* Read about itemization under Reg. §1.63-1.)

36. **(LO3)** Determine whether a taxpayer who is claimed as a dependent on another return is entitled to an addition to the standard deduction for age or blindness. (*Hint:* Read the calculation of the standard deduction under IRC §63.)

## PROBLEMS

37. **(LO1)** Clem is married and is a skilled carpenter. Clem's wife, Wanda, works part-time as a substitute grade school teacher. Determine the amount of Clem's expenses that are deductible *for AGI* this year (if any) under the following circumstances:

    a. Clem is self-employed and this year he incurred $525 for tools and supplies related to his job. Since neither were covered by a qualified health plan, Wanda paid health insurance premiums of $3,600 to provide coverage for herself and Clem.

    b. Clem and Wanda own a garage downtown that they rent to a local business for storage. This year they incurred $1,250 in utilities and depreciation of $780.

    c. Clem paid self-employment tax of $14,200 and Wanda had $3,000 of Social Security taxes withheld from her pay.

    d. Clem paid $45 to rent a safe deposit box to store his coin collection. Clem has collected coins intermittently since he was a boy, and he expects to sell his collection when he retires.

38. **(LO1)** Clyde currently commutes 55 miles to work in the city. He is considering a new assignment in the suburbs on the other side of the city that would increase his commute considerably. He would like to accept the assignment, but he thinks it might require that he move to the other side of the city. Determine if Clyde's move qualifies for a moving expense deduction and calculate the amount (if any) under the following circumstances:

    a. Clyde estimates that unless he moves across town, his new commute would be almost 70 miles. He also estimates the costs of a move as follows:

| | |
|---|---:|
| Lodging while searching for an apartment | $  125 |
| Transportation—auto | 75 |
| Mover's fee (furniture and possessions) | 1,500 |
| Lodging while en route | 210 |
| Meals while en route | 35 |

b. Same as (a) above, except Clyde estimates that unless he moves across town, his new commute would be almost 115 miles.

c. Same as (a) above, except Clyde's new commute would be almost 150 miles and the movers intend to impose a $450 surcharge on the moving fee for the additional distance.

39. **(LO1)** Smithers is a self-employed individual who earns $30,000 per year in self-employment income. Smithers pays $2,200 in annual health insurance premiums for his own medical care. In each of the following situations, determine the amount of the deductible health insurance premium for Smithers.

a. Smithers is single and the self-employment income is his only source of income.

b. Smithers is single, but besides being self-employed, Smithers is also employed part-time by SF Power Corporation. This year Smithers elected not to participate in SF's health plan.

c. Smithers is self-employed and he is also married. Smithers's spouse, Samantha, is employed full-time by SF Power Corporation and is covered by SF's health plan. Smithers is not eligible to participate in SF's health plan.

d. Smithers is self-employed and he is also married. Smithers' spouse, Samantha, is employed full-time by SF Power Corporation and is covered by SF's health plan. Smithers elected not to participate in SF's health plan.

40. **(LO1)** Hardaway earned $100,000 of compensation this year. He also paid (or had paid for him) $3,000 of health insurance. What is Hardaway's AGI in each of the following situations (ignore the effects of Social Security and self-employment taxes)?

a. Hardaway is an employee and his employer paid Hardaway's $3,000 of health insurance for him as a nontaxable fringe benefit. Consequently, Hardaway received $97,000 of taxable compensation and $3,000 of nontaxable compensation.

b. Hardaway is a self-employed taxpayer, and he paid $3,000 of health insurance himself. He is not eligible to participate in an employer-sponsored plan.

41. **(LO1)** Betty operates a beauty salon as a sole proprietorship. Betty also owns other property including a half interest in a partnership that operates a delivery service, a half interest in a partnership that operates a movie theatre, and an apartment building. This year Betty paid or reported the following expenses related to her salon and her share of other businesses. Determine Betty's AGI.

| | |
|---|---|
| Interest income | $11,255 |
| Salon sales and revenue | 86,360 |
| Salaries paid to beauticians | 45,250 |
| Beauty salon supplies | 23,400 |
| Revenues from delivery service partnership | 18,200 |
| Expenses from delivery service partnership | 5,200 |
| Operating income for theatre partnership | 17,250 |
| Rental revenue from apartment building | 31,220 |
| Depreciation on apartment building | 12,900 |
| Real estate taxes paid on apartment building | 11,100 |
| Real estate taxes paid on personal residence | 6,241 |
| Contributions to charity | 4,237 |

42. **(LO1)** Lionel is an unmarried law student at State University Law School, a qualified educational institution. This year Lionel borrowed $24,000 from Counti Bank and paid interest of $1,440. Lionel used the loan proceeds to pay

his law school tuition. Calculate the amounts Lionel can deduct for higher education expenses and interest on higher education loans under the following circumstances (assume the 2009 rules apply for purposes of the qualified education expense deduction):

a. Lionel's AGI before deducting interest on higher education loans is $50,000.
b. Lionel's AGI before deducting interest on higher education loans is $69,000.
c. Lionel's AGI before deducting interest on higher education loans is $90,000.
d. Lionel's AGI is $50,000 before deducting interest on higher education loans. Lionel used $16,000 of the loan to pay law school tuition and $8,000 of the loan to purchase a car.

43. **(LO1)** This year Jack intends to file a married-joint return with two dependents. Jack received $157,500 of salary and paid $5,000 of interest on loans used to pay qualified tuition costs for his dependent daughter, Deb. This year Jack has also paid qualified moving expenses of $4,300 and $24,000 of alimony.

■ planning

a. What is Jack's adjusted gross income? Assume that Jack will opt to treat tax items in a manner to minimize his AGI.
b. Suppose that Jack also reported income of $8,800 from a half share of profits from a partnership. What AGI would Jack report under these circumstances? Again, assume that Jack will opt to treat tax items in a manner to minimize his AGI.

44. **(LO1, LO2)** In each of the following independent cases, indicate the amount (1) deductible *for* AGI, (2) deductible *from* AGI, or (3) not deductible at all.

a. Ted paid $8 rent on a safety deposit box at the bank. In this box he kept the few shares of stock that he owned.
b. Tyler paid $85 for minor repairs to the fence at a rental house he owned.
c. Timmy paid $545 for health insurance premiums this year. Timmy is employed full-time and his employer paid the remaining premiums as a qualified fringe benefit.
d. Tess paid $850 for self-employment taxes and $1,150 of state income taxes on her consulting income.

45. **(LO1, LO2)** In each of the following independent cases, indicate the amount (1) deductible *for* AGI, (2) deductible *from* AGI, or (3) not deductible at all.

a. Fran spent $90 for uniforms for use on her job. Her employer reimbursed her for $75 of this amount under an accountable plan.
b. Timothy, a plumber employed by ACE Plumbing, spent $65 for small tools to be used on his job, but he was not reimbursed by ACE.
c. Jake is a perfume salesperson. Because of his high pay, he receives no allowance or reimbursement from his employer for advertising expenses even though his position requires him to advertise frequently. During the year, he spent $2,200 on legitimate business advertisements.
d. Trey is a self-employed special-duty nurse. He spent $120 for uniforms.
e. Mary, a professor at a community college, spent $340 for magazine subscriptions. The magazines were helpful for her research activities, but she was not reimbursed for the expenditures.
f. Wayne lost $325 on the bets he made at the race track, but he won $57 playing online poker.

46. **(LO2)** Ted is a successful attorney, but when he turned 50 years old he decided to retire from his law practice and become a professional golfer. Ted has been a very successful amateur golfer, so beginning this year Ted began competing

in professional golf tournaments. At year-end, Ted reported the following expenses associated with competing in 15 professional events:

| | |
|---|---:|
| Transportation from his home to various tournaments | $25,000 |
| Lodging for the 15 weeks on the road | 18,200 |
| Meals while traveling and during golf tournaments | 5,200 |
| Entry fees | 7,500 |
| Lessons from various golf teachers | 12,500 |
| Golf supplies (balls, tees, etc.) | 783 |
| Total expenses | $69,183 |

a. Suppose that Ted reports $275,000 in gross income from his pension and various investments. Describe the various considerations that will dictate the extent to which Ted can deduct the expenses associated with professional golf.

b. Calculate the maximum amount of his golf expenses that Ted could deduct if the IRS and the courts are convinced that Ted engages in competitive golf primarily for enjoyment rather than the expectation of making a profit. Assume Ted's AGI is $275,000.

47. **(LO2)**  Simpson is a single individual who is employed full-time by Duff Corporation. This year Simpson reports AGI of $50,000 and has incurred the following medical expenses:

| | |
|---|---:|
| Dentist charges | $ 900 |
| Physician's charges | 1,800 |
| Optical charges | 500 |
| Cost of eyeglasses | 300 |
| Hospital charges | 2,100 |
| Prescription drugs | 250 |
| Over-the-counter drugs | 450 |
| Medical insurance premiums | 775 |

a. Calculate the amount of medical expenses that will be included with Simpson's itemized deductions.

b. Suppose that Simpson was reimbursed for $650 of the physician's charges and $1,200 for the hospital costs. Calculate the amount of medical expenses that will be included with Simpson's itemized deductions.

**research**

48. **(LO2)**  This year Tim is age 45 and is considering enrolling in an insurance program that provides for long-term care insurance. He is curious about whether the insurance premiums are deductible as a medical expense and, if so, what is the maximum amount that can be deducted in any year.

**research**

49. **(LO2)**  Doctor Bones prescribed physical therapy in a pool to treat Jack's broken back. In response to this advice (and for no other reason), Jack built a swimming pool in his backyard and strictly limited use of the pool to physical therapy. Jack paid $25,000 to build the pool, but he wondered if this amount could be deducted as a medical expenses? Determine if a capital expenditure such as the cost of a swimming pool qualifies for the medical expense deduction.

50. **(LO1, LO2)**  Charles has AGI of $50,000 and has made the following payments related to (1) land he inherited from his deceased aunt and (2) a personal vacation taken last year. Calculate the amount of taxes Charles may include in his itemized deductions for the year under the following circumstances:

| | |
|---|---|
| State inheritance tax on the land | $1,200 |
| County real estate tax on the land | 1,500 |
| School district tax on the land | 690 |
| City special assessment on the land (replacing curbs and gutters) | 700 |
| State tax on airline tickets (paid on vacation) | 125 |
| Local hotel tax (paid during vacation) | 195 |

a. Suppose that Charles holds the land for appreciation.

b. Suppose that Charles holds the land for rent.

c. Suppose that the vacation was actually a business trip for his employes.

51. **(LO2)** Dan has AGI of $50,000 and paid the following taxes during this tax year. Calculate the amount of taxes Dan may include in his itemized deductions for the year.

| | |
|---|---|
| State income tax withholding | $1,400 |
| State income tax estimated payments | 750 |
| Federal income tax withholding | 3,000 |
| Social Security tax withheld from wages | 2,100 |
| State excise tax on liquor | 400 |
| Automobile license (based on the car's weight) | 300 |
| State sales tax paid | 475 |

52. **(LO1, LO2)** Tim is a single, cash method taxpayer with one personal exemption. In April of this year Tim paid $1,020 with his state income tax return for the previous year. During the year, Tim had $5,400 of state income tax and $18,250 of federal income tax withheld from his salary. In addition, Tim made estimated payments of $1,360 and $1,900 of state and federal income taxes, respectively. Finally, Tim expects to receive a refund of $500 for state income taxes when he files his state tax return for this year in April next year. What is the amount of taxes that Tim can deduct as an itemized deduction?

53. **(LO2)** This year Randy paid $28,000 of interest (Randy borrowed $450,000 to buy his residence and it is currently worth $500,000). Randy also paid $2,500 of interest on his car loan and $4,200 of margin interest to his stockbroker (investment interest expense). How much of this interest can Randy deduct as an itemized deduction under the following circumstances?

a. Randy received $2,200 of interest this year and no other investment income or expenses.

b. Randy had no investment income this year.

54. **(LO2)** Calvin reviewed his cancelled checks and receipts this year for charitable contributions. Calculate Calvin's charitable contribution deduction and carryover (if any) under the following circumstances:

| Donee | Item | Cost | FMV |
|---|---|---|---|
| Hobbs Medical Center | IBM stock | $5,000 | $22,000 |
| State Museum | painting | 5,000 | 3,000 |
| A needy family | food and clothes | 400 | 250 |
| United Way | cash | 8,000 | 8,000 |

a. Calvin's AGI is $100,000.

b. Calvin's AGI is $100,000 but the State Museum told Calvin that it plans to sell the painting.

c. Calvin's AGI is $50,000.

d. Calvin's AGI is $100,000 and Hobbs is a nonoperating private foundation.

e. Calvin's AGI is $100,000 but the painting is worth $10,000.

55. **(LO2)** In addition to cash contributions to charity, Dean decided to donate shares of stock and a portrait painted during the earlier part of the last century. Dean purchased the stock and portrait many years ago as investments. Dean reported the following recipients:

| Charity | Property | Cost | FMV |
|---|---|---|---|
| State University | cash | $15,000 | $15,000 |
| Red Cross | cash | 14,500 | 14,500 |
| State History Museum | painting | 5,000 | $82,000 |
| City Medical Center | Dell stock | 28,000 | 17,000 |

    a. Determine the maximum amount of charitable deduction for each of these contributions *ignoring* the AGI ceiling on charitable contributions.

    b. Assume that Dean's AGI this year is $150,000. Determine Dean's itemized deduction for his charitable contributions this year and any carryover.

    c. Assume that Dean's AGI this year is $240,000. Determine Dean's itemized deduction for his charitable contributions this year and any carryover.

    d. Suppose Dean is a dealer in antique paintings and he held the paintings for sale before the contribution. Determine Dean's itemized deduction for his charitable contributions this year and any carryover.

    e. Suppose that Dean's objective with the donation to the museum was to finance expansion of the historical collection. Hence, Dean was not surprised when the museum announced the sale of the portrait because of its limited historical value. What is Dean's charitable contribution for the paintings in this situation (ignoring AGI limitations)?

56. **(LO2)** Tim suffered greatly this year. In January a freak storm damaged his sailboat and in July Tim's motorcycle was stolen from his vacation home. Tim originally paid $27,000 for the boat, but he was able to repair the damage for $6,200. Tim paid $15,500 for the motorcycle, but it was worth $17,000 before it was stolen. Insurance reimbursed $1,000 for the boat repairs and the cycle was uninsured.

    a. Calculate Tim's deductible casualty loss if his AGI is $50,000.

    b. Calculate Tim's deductible casualty loss if his AGI is $150,000.

    c. How would you answer (a) if Tim received an additional $65,000 in interest from municipal bonds this year?

57. **(LO2)** Trevor is a single individual who is a cash-method calendar-year taxpayer. For each of the next two years (year 1 and year 2), Trevor expects to report AGI of $80,000, contribute $3,000 to charity, and pay $2,200 in state income taxes.

    a. Estimate Trevor's taxable income for year 1 and year 2 using the current amounts for the standard deduction and personal exemption for both years.

    b. Now assume that Trevor combines his anticipated charitable contributions for the next two years and makes the combined contribution in December of year 1. Estimate Trevor's taxable income for each of the next two years using the current amounts for the standard deduction and personal exemption. Reconcile the total taxable income to your solution to (a) above.

    c. Trevor plans to purchase a residence next year, and he estimates that additional property taxes and residential interest will each cost $4,000 annually ($8,000 in total). Estimate Trevor's taxable income for each of the next two years (year 1 and year 2) using the current amounts for the standard deduction and personal exemption.

    d. Assume that Trevor makes the charitable contribution for year 2 and pays the real estate taxes for year 2 in December of year 1. Estimate Trevor's taxable income for year 1 and year 2 using the current amounts for the standard

deduction and personal exemption. Reconcile the total taxable income to your solution to (c) above.

e. Explain the conditions in which the bunching strategy in part (d) will generate tax savings for Trevor.

58. **(LO2)** Baker paid $775 for the preparation of his tax return and incurred $375 of employee business expenses, of which $60 was reimbursed by his employer through an accountable plan. Baker also paid a $100 fee for investment advice. Calculate the amount of these expenses that Baker is able to deduct assuming he itemizes his deductions in each of the following situations:

a. Baker's AGI is $50,000.

b. Baker's AGI is $100,000.

59. **(LO2)** Zack is employed as a full-time airport security guard. This year Zack's employer transferred him from Dallas to Houston. At year-end, Zack discovered a number of unreimbursed expenses related to his employment in Dallas prior to his move to Houston. Identify which expenses are deductible and whether the deductions are *for* or *from* AGI.

| | |
|---|---:|
| Cost of bus transportation from his home to the airport | $ 150 |
| Subscription to *Journal of Security Guards* | 52 |
| Lunch with colleagues | 195 |
| Cost of self-defense course at local college | 500 |
| Lunch with supervisor during evaluations | 383 |
| Total | $1,280 |

60. **(LO3)** This year Jeff, who is single, is entitled to the following deductions before phase-outs:

| | |
|---|---:|
| State income taxes | $7,850 |
| Real estate taxes | 1,900 |
| Home mortgage interest | 8,200 |
| Charitable contributions | 1,700 |

a. Assume that the phase-out of itemized deductions applies to Jeff and that his AGI is $30,000 over the threshold amount. Calculate Jeff's itemized deductions after considering the overall phase-out of itemized deductions.

b. Suppose that in a. above, Jeff's AGI increases by $1 million. Calculate Jeff's itemized deductions after considering the overall phase-out of itemized deductions.

61. **(LO3)** Jim who is single is considering expending $30,000 that will be deductible. He is eligible to claim the standard deduction and one personal exemption. Assuming the year is 2009, Jim has no other deductions, and his taxable income is subject to a tax rate of 25 percent, calculate the amount of tax savings Jim will gain from the deduction under the following independent conditions:

research

a. Jim has AGI of $150,000 (without the deduction) and the deduction is *for AGI*.

b. Jim has AGI of $150,000 and the deduction is *from AGI*. Assume that the deduction is a charitable contribution and Jim has no other itemized deductions.

c. Jim has AGI of $250,000 (without the deduction) and the deduction is *for AGI*.

62. **(LO3)** Stephanie is a twelve-year-old who often assists neighbors on weekends by babysitting their children. Calculate the standard deduction Stephanie will claim under the following independent circumstances (assume that Stephanie's parents will claim her as a dependent).

a. Stephanie reported $850 of earnings from her babysitting.

b. Stephanie reported $1,500 of earnings from her babysitting.

c. Stephanie reported $6,200 of earnings from her babysitting.

**research**

63. **(LO1, LO2, LO3)** Tammy teaches elementary school history for the Metro School District. This year she has incurred the following expenses associated with her job:

| | |
|---|---:|
| Noncredit correspondence course on history | $ 900 |
| Teaching publications | 1,800 |
| Tuition for university graduate course in physics | 1,200 |
| Transportation between school and home | 750 |
| Photocopying class materials | 100 |
| Transportation from school to extracurricular activities | 110 |
| Cost of lunches eaten during study halls | 540 |

Tammy's base salary is $45,000 and she receives a $200 salary supplement to help her cover expenses associated with her school extracurricular activities.

a. Identify the amount and type (*for* AGI or *from* AGI) of deductible expenses.

b. Calculate Tammy's AGI and taxable income for 2010 assuming she files single with one personal exemption.

c. Calculate Tammy's AGI and taxable income assuming she files single with one personal exemption and the year is 2009.

## COMPREHENSIVE PROBLEMS

64. Evan graduated from college, and took a job as a deliveryman in the city. Evan was paid a salary of $63,500 and he received $700 in hourly pay for part-time work over the weekends. Evan summarized his expenses below.

| | |
|---|---:|
| Cost of moving his possessions to the city | $1,200 |
| Interest paid on accumulated student loans | 2,800 |
| Cost of purchasing a delivery uniform | 1,100 |
| Contribution to State University deliveryman program | 1,300 |

Calculate Evan's AGI and taxable income if he files single with one personal exemption.

65. Read the following letter and help Shady Slim with his tax situation. Please assume that gross income is $172,900 for purposes of this problem.

**December 31, 2010**

**To the friendly student tax preparer:**

Hi, it's Shady Slim again. I'm told that you need some more information from me in order to complete my tax return. I'm an open book! I'll tell you whatever I think you need to know.

Let me tell you a few more things about my life. As you may recall, I am divorced from my wife, Alice. I know that it's unusual, but I have custody of my son, Shady, Jr. The judge owed me a few favors and I really love the kid. He lives with me full-time and my wife gets him every other weekend. I pay the vast majority of my son's expenses. I think Alice should have to pay some child support, but she doesn't have to pay a dime. The judge didn't owe me that much, I guess.

I had to move this year after getting my job at Roca Cola. We moved on February 3 of this year, and I worked my job at Roca Cola for the rest of the year. I still live in the same state, but I moved 500 miles away from my old house. I left a little bit early to go on a house-hunting trip that cost me a total of $450. I hired a moving company to move our stuff at a cost of $2,300. Junior and I got a hotel room along the way that cost us $40 (I love Super 8!). We spent $35 on meals on the way to our new home. Oh yeah, I took Junior to a movie on the way and that cost $20.

Can you believe I'm still paying off my student loans, even after 15 years? I paid a total of $900 in interest on my old student loans this year.

Remember when I told you about that guy that hit me with his car? I had a bunch of medical expenses that were not reimbursed to me by the lawsuit or by my

insurance. I incurred a total of $20,000 in medical expenses, and I was only reimbursed for $11,000. Good thing I can write off medical expenses, right?

I contributed a lot of money to charity this year. I'm such a nice guy! I gave $1,000 in cash to the March of Dimes. I contributed some of my old furniture to the church. It was some good stuff! I contributed a red velvet couch and my old recliner. The furniture is considered vintage and is worth $5,000 today (the appraiser surprised me!), even though I only paid $1,000 for it back in the day. When I contributed the furniture, the pastor said he didn't like the fabric and was going to sell the furniture to pay for some more pews in the church. Oh well, some people just have no taste, right? Roca Cola had a charity drive for the United Way this year and I contributed $90. Turns out, I don't even miss it, because Roca Cola takes it right off my paycheck every month . . . $15 a month starting in July. My pay stub verifies that I contributed the $90 to the United Way. Oh, one other bit of charity from me this year. An old buddy of mine was down on his luck. He lost his job and his house. I gave him $500 to help him out.

I paid a lot of money in interest this year. I paid a total of $950 in personal credit card interest. I also paid $13,000 in interest on my home mortgage. I also paid $2,000 in real estate taxes for my new house.

A few other things I want to tell you about last year. Someone broke into my house and stole my kid's brand new bicycle and my set of golf clubs. The total loss from theft was $900. I paid $100 in union dues this year. I had to pay $1,000 for new suits for my job. Roca Cola requires its managers to wear suits every day on the job. I spent a total of $1,300 to pay for gas to commute to my job this year.

Oh, this is pretty cool. I've always wanted to be a firefighter. I spent $1,000 in tuition to go to the local firefighter's school. I did this because someone told me that I can deduct the tuition as an itemized deduction, so the money would be coming back to me.

That should be all the information you need right now. Please calculate my taxable income. You're still doing this for free, right?

66. Jeremy and Alyssa Johnson have been married for five years and do not have any children. Jeremy was married previously and has one child from the prior marriage. He is self-employed and operates his own computer parts store. For the first two months of the year, Alyssa worked for Staples, Inc., as an employee. In March, Alyssa accepted a new job with Super Toys, Inc. (ST), where she worked for the remainder of the year. This year, the Johnsons received $255,000 of gross income. Determine the Johnson's AGI given the following information:

a. Expenses associated with Jeremy's store include $40,000 in salary (and employment taxes) to employees, $45,000 of cost of goods sold, and $18,000 in rent and other administrative expenses.

b. As a salesperson, Alyssa incurred $2,000 in travel expenses related to her employment that were not reimbursed by her employer.

c. The Johnsons own a piece of investment real estate. They paid $500 of real property taxes on the property and they incurred $200 of expenses in travel costs to see the property and to evaluate other similar potential investment properties.

d. The Johnsons own a rental home. They incurred $8,500 of expenses associated with the property.

e. The Johnson's home was only five miles from the Staples store where Alyssa worked in January and February. The ST store was 60 miles from their home, so the Johnsons decided to move to make the commute easier for Alyssa. The Johnson's new home was only ten miles from the ST store. However, it was 50 miles from their former residence. The Johnsons paid a moving company $2,000 to move their possessions to the new location. They also drove the 50 miles to their new residence. They stopped along the way for lunch and spent $60 eating at Denny's. None of the moving expenses were reimbursed by ST.

f.   Jeremy paid $4,500 for health insurance coverage for himself. Alyssa was covered by health plans provided by her employer, but Jeremy is not eligible for the plan until next year.

g.   Jeremy paid $2,500 in self-employment taxes.

h.   Jeremy paid $5,000 in alimony and $3,000 in child support from his prior marriage.

i.   Alyssa paid $3,100 of tuition and fees to attend night classes at a local university. The Johnsons would like to deduct as much of this expenditure as possible rather than claim a credit. (Assume the 2009 qualified education expense deduction rules apply.)

j.   The Johnsons donated $2,000 to their favorite charity.

67.   Shauna Coleman is single. She works as an architectural designer for Streamline Design (SD). Shauna wanted to determine her taxable income for this year. She correctly calculated her AGI. However, she wasn't sure how to compute the rest of her taxable income. She provided the following information with hopes that you could use it to determine her taxable income.

a.   Shauna paid $2,000 for medical expenses and Blake, Shauna's boyfriend, drove Shauna (in her car) a total of 115 miles so that she could receive care for a broken ankle she sustained in a biking accident.

b.   Shauna paid a total of $3,400 in health insurance premiums during the year. SD did not reimburse any of this expense. Besides the health insurance premiums and the medical expenses for her broken ankle, Shauna had Lasik eye surgery last year and she paid $3,000 for the surgery (she received no insurance reimbursement). She also incurred $450 of other medical expenses for the year.

c.   SD withheld $1,800 of state income tax, $7,495 of Social Security tax, and $14,500 of federal income tax from Shauna's paychecks throughout the year.

d.   In 2010, Shauna was due a refund of $250 for overpaying her 2009 state taxes. On her 2009 state tax return that she filed in April 2010, she applied the overpayment toward her 2010 state tax liability. She estimated that her state tax liability for 2010 will be $2,300.

e.   Shauna paid $3,200 of property taxes on her personal residence. She also paid $500 to the developer of her subdivision, because he had to replace the sidewalk in certain areas of the subdivision.

f.   Shauna paid a $200 property tax based on the state's estimate of the value of her car.

g.   Shauna has a home mortgage loan in the amount of $220,000. The home is worth about $400,000. Shauna paid interest of $12,300 on the loan this year. She also paid $1,000 of interest on a home equity loan.

h.   Shauna made several charitable contributions throughout the year. She contributed stock in ZYX Corp. to the Red Cross. On the date of the contribution, the fair market value of the donated shares was $1,000 and her basis in the shares was $400. Shauna also contributed $300 cash to State University and religious artifacts she has held for several years to her church. The artifacts were valued at $500 and Shauna's basis in the items was $300. Shauna had every reason to believe the church would keep them on display indefinitely. Shauna also drove 200 miles doing church-related errands for her minister. Finally, Shauna contributed $1,200 of services to her church last year.

i.   Shauna's car was totaled in a wreck in January. The car was worth $14,000 and her cost basis in the car was $16,000. The car was a complete loss. Shauna received $2,000 in insurance reimbursements for the loss.

j.  Shauna paid $300 for architectural design publications, $100 for continuing education courses to keep her up to date on the latest design technology, and $200 for professional dues to maintain her status in a professional designer's organization.

k.  Shauna paid $250 in investment advisory fees and another $150 to have her tax return prepared (that is, she paid $150 in 2010 to have her 2009 tax return prepared).

l.  Shauna is involved in horse racing as a hobby. During the year, she won $2,500 in prize money and incurred $10,000 in expenses. She has never had a profitable year with her horse racing activities, so she acknowledges that this is a hobby for federal income tax purposes.

m.  Shauna sustained $2,000 in gambling losses over the year (mostly horse-racing bets) and only had $200 in winnings.

### Required

A.  Determine Shauna's taxable income assuming her AGI is $107,000.

B.  Determine Shauna's taxable income assuming her AGI is $207,000.

68.  Joe and Jessie are married and have one dependent child, Lizzie. Lizzie is currently in college at State University. Joe works as a design engineer for a manufacturing firm while Jessie runs a craft business from their home. Jessie's craft business consists of making craft items for sale at craft shows that are held periodically at various locations. Jessie spends considerable time and effort on her craft business and it has been consistently profitable over the years. Joe and Jessie own a home and pay interest on their home loan (balance of $220,000) and a personal loan to pay for Lizzie's college expenses (balance of $35,000). Neither Joe nor Jessie is blind or over age 65, and they plan to file as married-joint. Based on their estimates, determine Joe and Jessie's AGI and taxable income for the year. They have summarized the income and expenses they expect to report this year as follows:

Income:

| | |
|---|---:|
| Joe's salary | $109,100 |
| Jessie's craft sales | 18,400 |
| Interest from certificate of deposit | 1,650 |
| Interest from Treasury bond funds | 730 |
| Interest from municipal bond funds | 920 |

Expenditures:

| | |
|---|---:|
| Federal income tax withheld from Joe's wages | $13,700 |
| State income tax withheld from Joe's wages | 6,400 |
| Social Security tax withheld from Joe's wages | 7,482 |
| Real estate taxes on residence | 6,200 |
| Automobile licenses (based on weight) | 310 |
| State sales tax paid | 1,150 |
| Home mortgage interest | 14,000 |
| Interest on Masterdebt credit card | 2,300 |
| Medical expenses (unreimbursed) | 1,690 |
| Joe's employee expenses (unreimbursed) | 2,400 |
| Cost of Jessie's craft supplies | 4,260 |
| Postage for mailing crafts | 145 |
| Travel and lodging for craft shows | 2,230 |
| Meals during craft shows | 670 |
| Self-employment tax on Jessie's craft income | 1,620 |
| College tuition paid for Lizzie | 5,780 |
| Interest on loans to pay Lizzie's tuition | 3,200 |
| Lizzie's room and board at college | 12,620 |
| Cash contributions to the Red Cross | 525 |

chapter

7

# Individual Income Tax Computation and Tax Credits

## Learning Objectives

**Upon completing this chapter, you should be able to:**

**LO 1** Determine a taxpayer's regular tax liability and identify tax issues associated with the process.

**LO 2** Compute a taxpayer's alternative minimum tax liability and describe the tax characteristics of taxpayers most likely to owe the alternative minimum tax.

**LO 3** Calculate a taxpayer's employment and self-employment taxes payable and explain tax considerations relating to whether a taxpayer is considered to be an employee or a self-employed independent contractor.

**LO 4** Describe the different general types of tax credits, identify specific tax credits, and compute a taxpayer's allowable child tax credit, child and dependent care credit, American opportunity credit, lifetime learning credit, making work pay credit, and earned income credit.

**LO 5** Explain taxpayer filing and tax payment requirements and describe in general terms how to compute a taxpayer's underpayment, late filing, and late payment penalties.

C ourtney has already determined her taxable income. Now she's working on computing her tax liability. She knows she owes a significant amount of regular income tax on her employment and business activities. However, she's not sure how to compute the tax on the qualified dividends she received from General Electric. Courtney is worried that she may be subject to the alternative minimum tax this year because she's heard that an increasing number of taxpayers in her income range must pay the tax. Finally, Courtney knows she owes some self-employment taxes on her business income. Courtney would like to determine whether she is eligible to claim any tax credits such as the child tax credit for her two children and education credits because she paid for a portion of her daughter Ellen's tuition at the University of Missouri–Kansas City this year. Courtney is hoping that she has paid enough in taxes during the year to avoid underpayment penalties. She's planning on filing her tax return and paying her taxes on time.

Gram's tax situation is much more straightforward. She needs to determine the regular income tax on her taxable income. Her income is so low she knows she need not worry about the alternative minimum tax, and she believes she doesn't owe any self-employment tax. Gram didn't prepay any taxes this year, so she is concerned that she might be required to pay an underpayment penalty. She also expects to file her tax return and pay her taxes by the looming due date.

*to be continued . . .*

| Storyline Summary | |
|---|---|
| *Taxpayers:* | Courtney Wilson, age 40 Courtney's mother Dorothy "Gram" Weiss, age 70 |
| *Family description:* | Courtney is divorced with a son, Deron, age 10, and a daughter, Ellen, age 20. Gram is currently residing with Courtney. |
| *Location:* | Kansas City, Missouri |
| *Employment status:* | Courtney works as an architect for EWD. Gram is retired. |
| *Filing status:* | Courtney is head of household. Gram is single. |
| *Current situation:* | Courtney and Gram have computed their taxable income. Now they are trying to determine their tax liability, tax refund or additional taxes due, and whether they owe any payment-related penalties. |

In prior chapters we've learned how to compute taxable income for taxpayers such as Courtney and Gram. This chapter describes how to determine a taxpayer's tax liability for the year. We discover that the process is not as easy as simply applying taxable income to the applicable tax rate schedule or tax table. Taxpayers may generate taxable income that is taxed at rates not provided in the tax rate schedules or tax tables. We will learn that they may also be required to pay taxes in addition to the regular income tax. We also describe tax credits taxpayers may use to reduce their gross taxes payable. We conclude the chapter by describing taxpayer filing requirements and identifying certain penalties taxpayers may be required to pay when they underpay or are late paying their taxes. We start our coverage by explaining how to compute one's regular tax liability.

## LO1 REGULAR FEDERAL INCOME TAX COMPUTATION

When taxpayers have determined their taxable income, they are ready to compute their gross tax from a series of progressive tax rates called a **tax rate schedule.**

### Tax Rate Schedules

Congress has constructed four different tax rate schedules for individuals. The applicable tax rate schedule is determined by the taxpayer's filing status, which we discussed in depth in Chapter 4. Recall that a taxpayer's filing status is one of the following:

1. Married filing jointly.
2. Qualifying widow or widower, also referred to as surviving spouse.
3. Married filing separately.
4. Head of household.
5. Single.

As we describe in Chapter 1, a tax rate schedule is composed of several ranges of income taxed at different (increasing) rates. Each separate range of income subject to a different tax rate is referred to as a **tax bracket.** While each filing status has its own tax rate schedule (married filing jointly and qualifying widow or widower use the same rate schedule), all tax rate schedules consist of tax brackets taxed at 10 percent, 15 percent, 25 percent, 28 percent, 33 percent, and 35 percent. However, the width or range of income within each bracket varies by filing status. In general, the tax brackets are widest and higher levels of income are taxed at the lowest rates for the married filing jointly filing status, followed by the head of household filing status, single filing status, and finally, the married filing separately filing status.

The tax rate schedule for each filing status is provided inside the front cover of this book. Notice that the married filing separately schedule is the same as the married filing jointly schedule except that the taxable income levels listed in the schedule are exactly one-half the taxable income levels for married filing jointly.

### Example 7-1

As we determined in Chapter 6, Courtney files under the head of household filing status and her 2010 taxable income is $111,257 (see Exhibit 6-13).

**What if:** For now, let's *assume* that all of Courtney's income is taxed as ordinary income. That is, assume that none of her income is taxed at a preferential rate (some is, but we'll address this in a bit). What is the tax on her taxable income?

**Answer:** $22,661.75 Using the head of household tax rate schedule, her taxable income falls in the 25 percent marginal tax rate bracket, in between $45,550 and $117,650, so her tax is computed as follows:

| Description | Amount | Explanation |
|---|---|---|
| (1) Base tax | $ 6,235 | From head of household tax rate schedule for taxpayer with taxable income in 25 percent bracket. |
| (2) Income taxed at marginal tax rate | 65,707 | ($111,257 − 45,550) from head of household tax rate schedule. |
| (3) Marginal tax rate | 25% | From head of household tax rate schedule. |
| (4) Tax on income at marginal tax rate | 16,426.75 | (2) × (3). |
| **Tax on taxable income** | **$22,661.75** | (1) + (4). |

**Example 7-2**

As we determined in Chapter 6, Gram files under the single filing status. In Chapter 6 we calculated her 2010 taxable income to be $4,840 (see Exhibit 6-15). None of her income is taxed at a preferential rate. What is the tax on her taxable income using the tax rate schedules?

**Answer:** $484. ($4,840 × 10%).

For administrative convenience and to prevent low and middle income taxpayers from making mathematical errors using a tax rate schedule, the IRS provides **tax tables** that present the gross tax for various amounts of taxable income under $100,000 and filing status (it's impractical to provide a table for essentially unlimited amounts of income).

Because the tax tables generate nearly the same tax as calculated from the tax rate schedule, we use the tax rate schedules throughout this chapter.

## Marriage Penalty or Benefit

An interesting artifact of the tax rate schedules is that they can impose what some refer to as a **marriage penalty,** but they may actually produce a **marriage benefit.** A marriage penalty (benefit) occurs when, for a given level of income, a married couple has a greater (lesser) tax liability when they use the married filing jointly tax rate schedule to determine the tax on their joint income than they would have owed (in total) if each spouse would have used the single tax rate schedule to compute the tax on each spouse's individual income. Exhibit 7-1 explores the marriage penalty in a scenario in which both spouses earn income and another in which only one spouse earns income. As the exhibit illustrates, the marriage penalty applies to couples with two wage earners, but a marriage benefit applies to couples with single breadwinners.

**EXHIBIT 7-1** 2010 Marriage Penalty (Benefit) Two Income vs. Single Income Married Couple*

| Married Couple | Taxable Income | Tax if File Jointly (1) | Tax if File Single† (2) | Marriage Penalty (Benefit) (1) − (2) |
|---|---|---|---|---|
| **Scenario 1:** *Two wage-earners* | | | | |
| Wife | $100,000 | | $21,709.25 | |
| Husband | 100,000 | | 21,709.25 | |
| **Combined** | $200,000 | $44,243.50 | $43,418.50 | $825 |
| **Scenario 2:** *One wage-earner* | | | | |
| Wife | $200,000 | | $51,116.75 | |
| Husband | 0 | | 0 | |
| **Combined** | $200,000 | $44,243.50 | $51,116.75 | ($6,879) |

*This analysis assumes the taxpayers do not owe any alternative minimum tax (discussed below).
†Married couples do not actually have the option of filing as single. If they choose not to file jointly they must file as married filing separately.

## Exceptions to the Basic Tax Computation

In certain circumstances, taxpayers cannot completely determine their final tax liability from their tax rate schedule or tax table. Taxpayers must perform additional computations to determine their tax liability (1) when they recognize long-term capital gains or receive dividends that are taxed at preferential (lower) rates and/or (2) when the taxpayer is a child and the child's unearned income is taxed at her parent's **marginal tax rate.** We describe these additional computations in detail below.

**Preferential Tax Rates for Capital Gains and Dividends**    As we describe in detail in Chapter 11, certain capital gains and certain dividends are taxed at a lower or **preferential tax rate** relative to other types of income. In general, the preferential tax rate is 15 percent.[1] While we discuss this in more depth in Chapter 11, let's briefly introduce the capital gains and dividends that are taxed at preferential rates. A capital gain is the gain recognized on the disposition of a capital asset. In general terms, a capital asset is any asset *other than*

- Accounts receivable from the sale of goods or services.
- Inventory and other assets held for sale in the ordinary course of business.
- Assets used in a trade or business, including supplies.

Thus, assets held for investment, such as stocks or bonds, are capital assets. When a taxpayer sells a capital asset at a gain or loss, the gain or loss is considered to be a long-term capital gain or loss if the taxpayer owned the asset for *more than* a year before selling it. Otherwise, the capital gain or loss is considered to be a short-term capital gain or loss. Only net long-term capital gains in excess of net short-term capital losses are taxed at preferential rates.

Qualified dividends (distributions from corporations to shareholders) are also taxed at preferential tax rates. Qualified dividends generally include dividends paid by a U.S. corporation (including mutual funds)[2] on stock that the taxpayer has held for a certain amount of time.[3] In Chapter 11, we describe in more depth

---

[1]As we discover in Chapter 11, some types of income may be taxed at a preferential rate of 28 percent or 25 percent. Further, as we discuss below, income that would otherwise be taxed at the 15 percent preferential rate is taxed at 0 percent if it would have been taxed at a 15 percent or lower rate if it were ordinary income taxed at the rates in the tax rate schedule.

[2]Dividends from "qualified foreign corporations" may also qualify [see §1(h)(11)(B)].

[3]We discuss the holding period in Chapter 11. See §1(h)(11)(B)(iii).

how to determine the amount of capital gains and dividends that qualify for the preferential tax rate. Here, we focus on how to determine a taxpayer's tax liability when the taxpayer recognizes income taxed at a preferential tax rate.

The tax rate tables and tax rate schedules allow taxpayers to compute their tax on ordinary but not **preferentially taxed income.** This is true even though preferentially taxed income is included in adjusted gross income (AGI) and in taxable income. Taxpayers with income subject to the preferential rate (long-term capital gains and qualified dividends) can use the following three-step process to determine their tax liability.

**Step 1:** Split taxable income into the portion that is subject to the preferential rate and the portion taxed at the ordinary rates.

**Step 2:** Compute the tax separately on each type of income. Note that the income that is not taxed at the preferential rate is taxed at the ordinary tax rates using the tax rate schedule for the taxpayer's filing status.

**Step 3:** Add the tax on the income subject to the preferential tax rates and the tax on the income subject to the ordinary rates. This is the taxpayer's regular tax liability.

### Example 7-3

Courtney's taxable income of $111,257 includes $700 of qualified dividends from GE (Exhibit 5-4). What is her tax liability on her taxable income?

**Answer:** $22,591.75, computed at head of household rates as follows:

| Description | Amount | Explanation |
|---|---|---|
| (1) Taxable income | $111,257 | Exhibit 6-13. |
| (2) Preferentially taxed income | 700 | Exhibit 5-4. |
| (3) Income taxed at ordinary rates | 110,557 | (1) − (2). |
| (4) Tax on income taxed at ordinary rates | 22,486.75 | [$6,235 + (110,557 − 45,550) × 25%]. |
| (5) Tax on preferentially taxed income | 105 | (2) × 15% [Note that if (2) were ordinary income it would have been taxed at 25 percent]. |
| Tax on taxable income | $22,591.75 | (4) + (5). |

In this example, what is Courtney's tax savings from having the dividends taxed at the preferential rate rather than the ordinary rate?

**Answer:** $70. $700 × (25% − 15%). This is the amount of the dividend times the difference in the ordinary and preferential tax rate.

To ensure that taxpayers receive some tax benefit from preferentially taxed income, *to the extent* that this income would have been taxed at 15 percent or 10 percent if it were ordinary income, it is taxed at a 0 percent preferential rate.

### Example 7-4

**What if:** Gram's taxable income is $4,840. We computed her tax on this income in Example 7-2. Suppose that Gram's taxable income included $350 of long-term capital gains taxable at the preferential rate (the $350 capital gain she *actually* recognized was a short-term gain not subject to the preferential rate). What is Gram's tax liability under these circumstances?

*(continued on page 7-6...)*

**Answer:** $449, calculated as follows:

| Description | Amount | Explanation |
|---|---|---|
| (1) Taxable income | $4,840 | Exhibit 6-15. |
| (2) Preferentially taxed income | 350 | |
| (3) Income taxed at ordinary rates | 4,490 | (1) − (2). |
| (4) Tax on income taxed at ordinary rates | 449 | (3) × 10% (see tax rate schedule for single taxpayers). |
| (5) Tax on preferentially taxed income | 0 | (2) × 0% [Note that if (2) were ordinary income it would have been taxed at 10 percent; since this is equal to or less than 15 percent the income is taxed at 0 percent]. |
| Tax | $ 449 | (4) + (5). |

## Example 7-5

**What if:** Assume that Gram's taxable income is $35,000 including $4,000 of qualified dividends taxed at the preferential rate. What would be Gram's tax liability on her income under these circumstances?

**Answer:** $4,381.50, computed using the single tax rate schedule as follows:

| Description | Amount | Explanation |
|---|---|---|
| (1) Taxable income | $35,000 | |
| (2) Preferentially taxed income | 4,000 | |
| (3) Income taxed at ordinary rates | 31,000 | (1) − (2). |
| (4) Tax on income taxed at ordinary rates | 4,231.50 | $837.50 + [(31,000 − 8,375) × 15%] (see tax rate schedule for single taxpayers). |
| (5) Tax on preferentially taxed income | 150 | [($3,000 × 0%) + (1,000 × 15%)].* |
| Tax | $ 4,381.50 | (4) + (5). |

*Gram had $4,000 of preferentially taxed income. If this income was ordinary income, $3,000 of the income would have been taxed at 15 percent [$34,000 (end of 15 percent bracket) − $31,000 (ordinary taxable income)] and the remaining $1,000 would have been taxed at 25 percent [$35,000 (total taxable income) − $34,000 (end of 15 percent bracket)]. Consequently, $3,000 of the preferential income is taxed at 0 percent and the remaining $1,000 is taxed at 15 percent.

**Kiddie Tax** Parents can reduce their family's income tax bill by shifting income that would otherwise be taxed at their higher tax rates to their children whose income is taxed at lower rates. However, as we described in Chapter 5, under the assignment of income doctrine, taxpayers cannot simply assign or transfer income to other parties. Earned income, or income from services or labor, is taxed to the person who earns it. Thus, it's difficult for a parent to shift *earned* income to a child. However, unearned income or income from property such as dividends from stocks or interest from bonds is taxed to the *owner* of the property. Thus, a parent can shift unearned income to a child by transferring actual ownership of the income-producing property to the child. By transferring ownership, the parent runs the risk that the child will sell the asset or use it in a way unintended by the parent. However, this risk is relatively small for parents transferring property ownership to younger children.

The tax laws reduce parents' ability to shift unearned income to children through the so-called **kiddie tax.** The kiddie tax provisions apply (or potentially apply) to a

child if (1) the child is under 18 years old at year end, (2) the child is 18 at year end but her earned income does *not* exceed half of her support, or (3) the child is over age 18 but under age 24 at year end, is a full-time student during the year, and her earned income does not exceed half of her support (excluding scholarships).[4]

In general terms, if the kiddie tax applies, children must pay tax on a certain amount of their unearned income (their **net unearned income,** discussed below) at their parents' marginal tax rate rather than at their own marginal tax rate, unless the parents' marginal tax rate on the income (the preferential tax rate if the income is long-term capital gain or qualified dividends) would be lower than the child's marginal tax rate.[5] When the parents of the child are not married, this provision applies to the custodial parent.[6] That is, the kiddie tax will never allow children to pay less tax than they would have been required to pay without the kiddie tax provision.

The kiddie tax base is the child's net unearned income. Net unearned income is the *lesser* of (1) the child's gross *unearned income* minus $1,900[7] or (2) the child's taxable income (the child is not taxed on more than her taxable income).[8] Consequently, the kiddie tax does not apply unless the child has *unearned* income in *excess* of $1,900.[9] Thus the kiddie tax significantly limits, but does not eliminate, the tax benefit gained by a family unit when parents transfer income-producing assets to children.

---

### Example 7-6

**What if:** Suppose that during 2010, Deron received $1,000 in interest from the IBM bond, and he received another $2,100 in interest income from a money market account that his parents have been contributing to over the years. Is Deron potentially subject to the kiddie tax?

**Answer:** Yes, Deron is younger than 18 years old at the end of the year and his net unearned income exceeds $1,900.

What is Deron's taxable income and corresponding tax liability?

**Answer:** $2,150 taxable income and $395 tax liability, calculated as follows:

| Description | Amount | Explanation |
|---|---|---|
| (1) Gross income/AGI | $3,100 | $1,000 interest from IBM bond + $2,100 interest. All unearned income. |
| (2) Standard deduction | 950 | Minimum for taxpayer claimed as a dependent on another return (no earned income, so must use minimum. See Chapter 6). |
| (3) Personal exemption | 0 | Claimed as a dependent on Courtney's return. |
| **(4) Taxable income** | **$2,150** | (1) − (2) − (3). |
| (5) Gross unearned income minus $1,900 | 1,200 | (1) − $1,900. |
| (6) Net unearned income | $1,200 | Lesser of (4) or (5). |
| (7) Courtney's ordinary marginal rate | 25% | See Example 7-3 (use Courtney's rate because she is the custodial parent). |

(*continued on page 7-8...*)

---

[4]§1(g)(2)(A).

[5]§1(g).

[6]§1(g)(5).

[7]The $1,900 consists of $950 of the child's standard deduction (even if the child is entitled to a larger standard deduction) plus an *extra* $950. See Chapter 6 for a discussion of the standard deduction for the dependent of another taxpayer. If the child itemizes deductions, then the calculation becomes more complex and is beyond the scope of this text.

[8]§1(g)(4).

[9]Under §1(g)(7), subject to certain requirements, parents may elect to include their child's unearned income on their own tax return (on Form 8814).

| | | |
|---|---|---|
| (8) Kiddie tax | $ 300 | (6) × (7) (Deron's income taxed at Courtney's marginal rate). |
| (9) Taxable income taxed at Deron's rate | 950 | (4) − (6). |
| (10) Tax on taxable income using Deron's tax rates | $ 95 | (9) × 10% (See single filing status, $950 taxable income). |
| **Deron's total tax liability** | **$ 395** | (8) + (10). |

**What if:** Assume Deron's only source of income is qualified dividends of $2,100 (unearned income). What is his taxable income and tax liability?

**Answer:** Taxable income is $1,150; tax liability is $30, computed as follows:

| Description | Amount | Explanation |
|---|---|---|
| (1) Gross income/(AGI) | $2,100 | Qualified dividends, all unearned income |
| (2) Minimum standard deduction | 950 | Minimum for taxpayer claimed as a dependent on another return (all unearned income, so must use minimum. See Chapter 6). |
| (3) Personal exemption | 0 | Claimed as a dependent on Courtney's return. |
| **(4) Taxable income** | **$1,150** | (1) − (2) − (3). |
| (5) Gross unearned income minus $1,900 | 200 | (1) − $1,900. |
| (6) Net unearned income | $ 200 | Lesser of (4) or (5). |
| (7) Courtney's marginal tax rate on qualified dividend income | 15% | See Example 7-3 (her marginal rate on ordinary income is 25 percent, so her marginal rate on preferentially taxed income is 15 percent). |
| (8) Kiddie tax | $ 30 | (6) × (7) (Deron's income taxed at Courtney's marginal rate on the dividend income). |
| (9) Taxable income taxed at Deron's rate | 950 | (4) − (6). |
| (10) Tax on taxable income using Deron's tax rates | $ 0 | (9) × 0% (Deron's marginal rate on the dividend would be 10 percent if it were ordinary income, so he qualifies for 0 percent rate on dividend). |
| **Deron's total tax liability** | **$ 30** | (8) + (10). |

As we've just described, all individual taxpayers must pay federal income taxes on their federal taxable income. However, taxpayers may be liable for other federal taxes in addition to the regular tax liability. Many taxpayers are also required to pay the alternative minimum tax, and some working taxpayers are required to pay employment or self-employment taxes. We delve into these additional taxes below.

**LO2**

## ALTERNATIVE MINIMUM TAX

Each year, an increasing number of taxpayers are required to pay the **alternative minimum tax (AMT)** in *addition to* their *regular* tax liability. The **alternative minimum tax system** was implemented in 1986 (earlier variations date back to the late 1960s) to ensure that taxpayers generating income pay some *minimum* amount of income tax each year. The tax was originally targeted at higher-income taxpayers who were benefiting from or were perceived by the public to be benefiting from the *excessive* use (more than Congress intended) of tax preference items such as exclusions,

deferrals, and deductions to reduce or even eliminate their tax liabilities. However, for reasons we discuss below, the tax is forcing many taxpayers who don't fit this description to pay the tax. While in 2002, only about 2 million taxpayers paid AMT, estimates indicate that nearly 30 million taxpayers will pay the AMT in 2010 if Congress does not increase the current law AMT exemption amounts.[10]

In general terms, the alternative minimum tax is a tax on an *alternative* tax base meant to more closely reflect economic income than the regular income tax base. Thus the **AMT base** is more inclusive (or more broadly defined) than is the regular income tax base. To compute their AMT, taxpayers first compute their regular income tax liability. Then, they compute the AMT base and multiply the base by the applicable alternative tax rate.[11] They must pay the AMT only when the tax on the AMT base exceeds their regular tax liability.

### Alternative Minimum Tax Formula

Regular taxable income is the starting point for determining the alternative minimum tax. As the AMT formula in Exhibit 7-2 illustrates, taxpayers make several "plus" and "minus" adjustments to regular taxable income to compute alternative minimum taxable income (AMTI). They then arrive at the AMT base by subtracting an AMT exemption from AMTI. Taxpayers multiply the AMT base by the AMT rate to determine their **tentative minimum tax.** Finally, to determine their alternative minimum tax, taxpayers subtract their regular tax liability from the tentative minimum tax. The alternative minimum tax is the *excess* of the tentative minimum tax over the regular tax. If the regular tax liability equals or exceeds the tentative minimum tax, taxpayers need not pay any AMT. Individual taxpayers compute their AMT on Form 6251.

**EXHIBIT 7-2    Formula for Computing the Alternative Minimum Tax**

|  |  |
|---|---|
| | Regular Taxable Income |
| *Plus:* | Personal exemptions and standard deduction if taxpayer deducted the standard deduction in computing regular taxable income |
| *Minus:* | Phase-out of itemized deductions for regular tax purposes (if applicable) |
| *Plus or Minus:* | Other adjustments* |
| | Alternative minimum taxable income |
| *Minus:* | AMT exemption amount (if any) |
| *Equals:* | Tax base for AMT |
| *Times:* | AMT rate |
| *Equals:* | Tentative minimum tax |
| *Minus:* | Regular tax |
| *Equals:* | Alternative minimum tax |

*Technically, some of these adjustments are referred to as preference items and some are referred to as adjustments. We refer to all of these items as adjustments for simplicity's sake.

**Alternative Minimum Taxable Income (AMTI)**   In order to compute alternative minimum taxable income (AMTI), taxpayers make several **alternative minimum tax adjustments** to regular taxable income. Many of these are plus adjustments that are added to regular taxable income to reach AMTI and some are minus adjustments that are subtracted from regular taxable income to determine AMTI. Consequently, these adjustments tend to expand the regular income tax base to more closely reflect economic income.

[10]See "Aggregate AMT Projections, 2008–2019." Urbans-Brookings Tax Policy Center: March 27, 2009 (http://www.taxpolicycenter.org).

[11]The rate of the alternative minimum tax (AMT) was set below that of the income tax with the objective of avoiding the perception that the AMT was an additional assessment.

***Exemptions and standard deduction.***    Taxpayers first add back to regular taxable income the amount of personal and dependency exemptions they actually deducted, after considering phase-outs, in determining their regular taxable income. The exemption deduction is added back because it does not represent an actual economic outflow. Next, taxpayers add back the standard deduction amount, but only *if they deducted it* in determining taxable income. Again, just like exemptions, taxpayers add back the standard deduction because it is a deduction that does not reflect an actual economic outflow from the taxpayer.

---

**Example 7-7**

Courtney started the process of determining whether she owed any AMT by adjusting her regular taxable income for her exemptions. What is Courtney's AMTI before other adjustments?

**Answer:** $122,207, computed as follows:

| Description | Amount | Explanation |
| --- | --- | --- |
| (1) Taxable income | $111,257 | Exhibit 6-13. |
| (2) Exemptions | 10,950 | Exhibit 6-13. |
| AMTI before other adjustments | $122,207 | (1) + (2). |

---

***Other adjustments.***    Taxpayers are required to make several other adjustments to compute AMTI. Exhibit 7-3 describes the most common of these adjustments.

As Exhibit 7-3 indicates, several itemized deductions are not deductible for AMT purposes. The major itemized deductions that are deductible for both regular tax and AMT purposes using the *same limitations* are

- Casualty and theft losses.
- Charitable contributions.
- Home mortgage interest expenses.
- Gambling losses.

Deductions that are deductible for regular tax and AMT purposes but have *different limitations* are

- Medical expenses (10 percent of AGI floor rather than 7.5 percent of AGI).
- Home-equity interest (interest not deductible unless loan proceeds used to acquire or substantially improve the home).
- Investment interest expense (interest income that is tax exempt for regular tax purposes but included in the AMT base is included in investment income for determining the AMT investment interest expense deduction).

---

**Example 7-8**

Courtney continued to work on her AMT computation by determining the other adjustments she needs to make to determine her alternative minimum taxable income (AMTI). What is Courtney's AMTI?

**Answer:** $133,620, computed as follows:

| Description | Amount | Explanation |
| --- | --- | --- |
| (1) AMTI before other adjustments | $122,207 | Example 7-7. |
| Plus adjustments: | | |
| (2) Tax-exempt interest on Cincinnati bond used to pay for renovations to major league baseball stadium (Private activity bond: issued in 2005) | 500 | Example 5-22. |

(*continued on page 7-11...*)

*(continued from page 7-10...)*

| Description | Amount | Explanation |
|---|---|---|
| (3) Real estate property taxes | 3,550 | Example 6-14. |
| (4) State income taxes | 6,700 | Example 6-14. |
| (5) Miscellaneous itemized deductions in excess of 2 percent floor | 1,083 | Example 6-31. |
| Minus adjustments: | | |
| (6) State income tax refund | (420) | Example 5-3. |
| Alternative minimum taxable income | $133,620 | Sum of (1) through (6). |

## EXHIBIT 7-3  Common AMT Adjustments

| Adjustment | Description |
|---|---|
| **Plus adjustments:**<br>Tax-exempt interest from private activity bonds | Taxpayers must add back interest income that was excluded for regular tax purposes if the bonds were used to fund private activities (privately owned baseball stadium or private business subsidies) and not for the public good (build or repair public roads). However, taxpayers do not add back interest income from private activity bonds if the bonds were issued in either 2009 or 2010. |
| Real property and personal property taxes deducted as itemized deductions | Deductible for regular tax purposes, but not for AMT purposes. |
| State income or sales taxes | Deductible for regular tax purposes, but not for AMT purposes. |
| Home-equity interest expense | This is *not deductible* for AMT purposes if the proceeds from the loan are used for *purposes other than to acquire or substantially improve the home.* |
| Miscellaneous itemized deductions (subject to the 2 percent floor) in excess of the 2 percent floor | Deductible for regular tax purposes but not for AMT purposes. |
| **Plus or Minus adjustment:** | |
| Depreciation | Taxpayers must compute their depreciation expense for AMT purposes. For certain types of assets, the regular tax method is more accelerated than the AMT method. In any event, if the regular tax depreciation exceeds the AMT depreciation, this is a plus adjustment. If the AMT depreciation exceeds the regular tax depreciation, this is a minus adjustment. |
| **Minus adjustments:**<br>State income tax refunds included in regular taxable income | Because state income taxes paid are not deductible for AMT purposes, refunds are not taxable (they do not increase the AMT base). |
| Gain or loss on sale of depreciable assets | Due to differences in regular tax and AMT depreciation methods, taxpayers may have a different adjusted basis (cost minus accumulated depreciation) for regular tax and for AMT purposes. Thus, they may have a different gain or loss for regular tax purposes than they do for AMT purposes. If regular tax gain exceeds AMT gain, this is a minus adjustment. Because AMT accumulated depreciation will never exceed regular tax accumulated depreciation, this would never be a plus adjustment. |

**AMT Exemption**   To help ensure that low-income taxpayers aren't required to pay the alternative minimum tax, Congress allows taxpayers to deduct an **AMT exemption** amount to determine their alternative minimum tax base.[12] The amount of the exemption depends on the taxpayer's filing status. The exemption is phased-out (reduced) by 25 cents for every dollar the AMTI exceeds the threshold amount. Exhibit 7-4 identifies, by filing status, the base exemption amount, the phase-out threshold, and the range of AMTI over which the exemption is phased out for 2009.

**EXHIBIT 7-4   2009 AMT Exemptions**

| Filing Status | Exemption* | Phase-out Begins at This Level of AMTI | Phase-out Complete for This Level of AMTI |
|---|---|---|---|
| Married filing jointly | $70,950 | $150,000 | $433,800 |
| Married filing separately | 35,475 | 75,000 | 216,900 |
| Head of household and Single | 46,700 | 112,500 | 299,300 |

*At press time, for tax years beginning after 2009, the AMT exemption amounts were scheduled to return to their original levels of $45,000 for taxpayers who are married filing jointly, $33,750 for head of household and single taxpayers, and $22,500 for married taxpayers filing separate returns. However, because the original exemption amounts have been consistently modified over the years to reflect inflation, we use the 2009 exemption amounts in this chapter as an approximation of the modified 2010 exemption amounts given expected Congressional action.

**Example 7-9**

What is Courtney's AMT base?

**Answer:** $92,200 computed by subtracting her allowable exemption amount from her AMTI as follows:

| Description | Amount | Explanation |
|---|---|---|
| (1) AMTI | $133,620 | Example 7-8. |
| (2) Full AMT Exemption (head of household): | 46,700 | Exhibit 7-4. |
| (3) Exemption phase-out threshold | 112,500 | |
| (4) AMTI in excess of exemption phase-out threshold | 21,120 | (1) − (3). |
| (5) Exemption phase-out percentage | 25% | |
| (6) Exemption phase-out amount | 5,280 | (4) × (5). |
| (7) Deductible exemption amount | 41,420 | (2) − (6). |
| AMT base | $ 92,200 | (1) − (7). |

**Tentative Minimum Tax and AMT Computation**   Taxpayers compute the tentative minimum tax by multiplying the AMT base by the applicable AMT rates. The AMT rate schedule consists of just two regular brackets as follows:

- 26 percent on the first $175,000 of AMT base ($87,500 for married taxpayers filing separately).
- 28 percent on AMT base in excess of $175,000.

However, for AMT purposes long-term capital gains and dividends are taxed at the same preferential rate as they were taxed for regular tax purposes (generally 15 percent).

**Example 7-10**

Courtney's AMT base is $92,200 However, Courtney also received $700 in dividends that are included in the base but are subject to a maximum tax rate of 15 percent even under the AMT system. The remaining $91,500 ($92,200 − 700) is taxed at the normal AMT rates. What is Courtney's tentative minimum tax?

(*continued on page 7-13...*)

---

[12]Unlike exemption and standard deduction amounts, the AMT exemption is not indexed for inflation. However, Congress usually increases the exemption amount for that particular year.

**Answer:** $23,895, computed as follows:

| Description | Amount | Reference |
|---|---|---|
| (1) AMT base | $92,200 | Example 7-9. |
| (2) Dividends taxed at preferential rate | 700 | Example 7-3. |
| (3) Tax rate applicable to dividends | 15% | |
| (4) Tax on dividends | 105 | (2) × (3). |
| (5) AMT base taxed at regular AMT rates | 91,500 | (1) − (2). |
| (6) Regular AMT tax rate | 26% | For AMT base below $175,000. |
| (7) Tax on AMT base taxed at regular AMT rates | 23,790 | (5) × (6). |
| **Tentative minimum tax** | **$23,895** | (4) + (7). |

Taxpayers subtract their regular tax liability from their tentative minimum tax to determine their AMT. If the taxpayer's regular tax liability is equal to or exceeds the tentative minimum tax liability, the taxpayer does not owe any AMT.

**Example 7-11**

What is Courtney's alternative minimum tax liability?

**Answer:** $1,303.25, computed as follows:

| Description | Amount | Reference |
|---|---|---|
| (1) Tentative minimum tax | $ 23,895 | Example 7-10. |
| (2) Regular tax liability | 22,591.75 | Example 7-3. |
| **Alternative minimum tax** | $ 1,303.25 | (1) − (2). |

Courtney owes $1,303.25 of alternative minimum tax in addition to her regular tax liability.

In some situations, taxpayers who pay the AMT are entitled to a **minimum tax credit** to use when the regular tax exceeds the tentative minimum tax. They can use the credit to offset regular tax but not below the tentative minimum tax for that year.[13]

## Other AMT Considerations

Above we mentioned that the number of taxpayers subject to the AMT is increasing over time and is projected to continue to increase through 2011. Why is this happening? Contributing factors are

1. The AMT exemption amount is not indexed for inflation. Consequently, as taxpayers' incomes increase over time through inflation, the exemption amount does not. Increasing income combined with a stable exemption exposes more income to the AMT (income over exemption amount). Congress has been applying a temporary fix to this problem each year by increasing the exemption amount for that particular year. However, there are no guarantees that Congress will continue this trend.

[13]The credit only applies when the taxpayer has positive adjustments that will reverse and become negative adjustments in the future. For example, depreciation, gain or loss on asset sales, and incentive stock option bargain element adjustments (see Chapter 12) fall into this category. Due to the nature of her adjustments, Courtney does not qualify for the minimum tax credit.

**L03**

2. Individual tax rates have been decreasing while AMT rates have remained constant. For example, the top tax rate from 1993 through 2000 was 39.6 percent, in 2001 it was 39.1 percent, in 2002 it was 38.6 percent, and from 2003 to today it is 35 percent. Further, the lowest tax bracket was reduced from 15 percent to 10 percent with no corresponding reduction in the AMT rates. Because taxpayers pay the AMT only when the tax on the AMT base exceeds the regular tax liability, taxpayers may owe the AMT because their regular tax is decreasing (due to lower rates) and not necessarily because their tentative minimum tax is increasing.

Based on the nature of the adjustments we've explained, it's clear that the taxpayers who tend to get hit the hardest by AMT are taxpayers who (1) have many dependents, (2) live in a high-income-tax state (they deduct state taxes for regular tax purposes but not AMT purposes), (3) pay high real estate or other property taxes, and/or (4) have relatively high capital gains (the capital gains increase AMTI, which reduces the exemption amount and thus exposes more income to the AMT).

**General AMT Planning Strategies** In certain circumstances, taxpayers can implement tax planning strategies to mitigate the impact of the AMT. For example, consistent with the tax rate timing strategy we discussed in Chapter 3, taxpayers who pay AMT at 26 percent (or 28 percent) one year and expect to pay regular tax at 35 percent in the next year may want to consider accelerating income into the AMT year to ensure that it is taxed at a lower rate than it would be in a regular tax year. In any event, taxpayers who either pay or may pay the AMT should consider their tax situation to determine whether and how to use timing tax planning strategies to reduce their combined tax burden (regular tax and AMT) given their circumstances.

# EMPLOYMENT AND SELF-EMPLOYMENT TAXES

As we discussed in Chapter 1, employees and self-employed taxpayers must pay employment (or self-employment) taxes known as FICA taxes.[14] The FICA tax consists of a Social Security and a Medicare component that are payable by both employees and employers. The **Social Security tax** is intended to provide basic pension coverage for the retired and disabled. The **Medicare tax** helps pay medical costs for qualifying individuals. Because Social Security and Medicare taxes are paid by working taxpayers but received by retired taxpayers, Social Security and Medicare taxes represent intergenerational transfers. The Social Security tax rate is 12.4 percent on the tax base (limited to $106,800 in 2010), and the Medicare tax rate is 2.9 percent on the tax base. The party responsible for paying the tax and the tax base depends on whether the taxpayer is an employee or whether the taxpayer is self-employed.

## Employee FICA Taxes Payable

Employees must pay **FICA taxes** on their salary, wages, and other compensation provided to them by their employer. However, employers are responsible for paying one-half of employees' FICA tax liabilities. Consequently, the Social Security tax rate for employees is 6.2 percent (12.4% × 1/2) of their salary or wages and the Medicare tax rate for employees is 1.45 percent (2.9% × 1/2) of their salary or wages. Employers withhold the employees' FICA tax liabilities from the employees' paychecks.

[14]FICA stands for Federal Insurance Contributions Act.

**Example 7-12**

While she was attending school full-time, Ellen received $15,000 in wages working part-time for an off-campus employer during 2010. How much in FICA taxes should Ellen's employer have withheld from her paychecks during the year?

**Answer:** $1,148, computed as follows:

| Description | Amount | Reference |
|---|---|---|
| (1) Wages | $15,000 | |
| (2) Social Security tax rate | 6.2% | |
| (3) Social Security tax | 930 | (1) × (2). |
| (4) Medicare tax rate | 1.45% | |
| (5) Medicare tax | 218 | (1) × (4). |
| FICA taxes withheld | $ 1,148 | (3) + (5). |

The wage base on which employees pay Social Security taxes is limited to an annually determined amount, reflecting the fact that the benefits the employee may ultimately receive are also capped. The limits apply to *each* taxpayer's wages regardless of marital or tax filing status. That is, the earnings of each spouse are subject to a *separate* limit. The 2010 limit is $106,800, which is the same as the 2009 limit. There is no wage base limit for the Medicare component of the FICA tax (all wages are subject to the 1.45 percent Medicare tax).

**Example 7-13**

During 2010, Courtney received a total of $122,800 in employee compensation from EWD. Recall that the compensation consisted of $98,000 in wages, $4,800 performance bonus, $6,000 discount for architectural design services, $4,000 compensation for a below-market loan, and $10,000 forgiveness of debt (see Exhibit 5-4). What is her FICA tax liability on this income?

**Answer:** $8,403, computed as follows:

| Description | Amount | Reference |
|---|---|---|
| (1) Compensation subject to FICA tax | $122,800 | |
| (2) Social Security tax base limit for 2009 | 106,800 | |
| (3) Compensation subject to Social Security tax | 106,800 | Lesser of (1) or (2). |
| (4) Social Security tax rate | 6.2% | |
| (5) Social Security tax | 6,622 | (3) × (4). |
| (6) Medicare tax rate | 1.45% | |
| (7) Medicare tax* | 1,781 | (1) × (6). |
| FICA taxes | $ 8,403 | (5) + (7). |

*Note that Courtney's compensation subject to the Social Security tax wage base is capped at $106,800, but her Medicare tax wage base is not.

What amount of FICA taxes for the year must EWD pay on Courtney's behalf?

**Answer:** $8,403. Courtney paid one-half of her FICA tax liability and EWD is required to pay the other half. Consequently, EWD would calculate its liability exactly as Courtney calculated hers.

Employees who work for multiple employers within a calendar year may receive aggregate compensation that exceeds the Social Security wage base. Because each employer is required to withhold Social Security taxes on the employee's wages until the employee has reached the wage base limit *with that employer,* the employee may end

up paying Social Security tax in *excess* of the required maximum. In such cases, the IRS treats the excess Social Security tax paid through withholding as an additional federal income tax payment (or credit) on Page 2 of Form 1040. The government refunds the excess withholding to the employee through either lower taxes payable with the tax return or a greater tax refund.[15] Employers, on the other hand, are *not* able to recover excess Social Security taxes paid on behalf of their employees.

---

**Example 7-14**

**What if:** Suppose that Courtney worked for her former employer Landmark Architects, Inc. (LA), in Cincinnati for two weeks in January 2010 before moving to Kansas City. During those two weeks, Courtney would have earned $4,000 in salary. LA would have withheld $306 in FICA taxes from her final paycheck consisting of $248 of Social Security taxes ($4,000 × 6.2%) and $58 of Medicare taxes ($4,000 × 1.45%). How much excess Social Security tax would have been withheld from Courtney's combined salaries from LA and EWD during 2010?

**Answer:** $248 ($4,000 wages earned with LA × 6.2 percent Social Security rate). Due to the $106,800 Social Security tax wage base for the year, Courtney's Social Security tax liability is limited to $6,622 ($106,800 × 6.2%). However, through employer withholding, she would have paid a total of $6,870 in Social Security taxes, consisting of $248 withheld by LA ($4,000 × 6.2%) and $6,622 withheld by EWD ($106,800 × 6.2%). Thus, given these facts, Courtney's *excess* Social Security tax withheld was $248 ($6,870 − 6,622). Courtney would get this amount back from the government through either lower taxes payable with her tax return or a greater tax refund. Because there is no limit on Medicare taxes, Courtney's entire 2010 compensation from both employers would be subject to the 1.45 percent Medicare tax.

---

## Self-Employment Taxes

While employees equally share their FICA (Social Security and Medicare) tax burden with employers, self-employed taxpayers must pay the *entire* FICA tax burden on their self-employment earnings.[16] Just as it is with FICA taxes for employees, self-employment taxes consist of both Social Security and Medicare taxes. Because their FICA taxes are based on their self-employment earnings, FICA taxes for self-employed taxpayers are referred to as **self-employment taxes.** Just as it is with employees, the base for the Social Security component of the self-employment tax is limited to $106,800. The base for the Medicare portion of the self-employment tax is unlimited. The process for determining the taxpayer's self-employment taxes payable requires the following three steps:

**Step 1:** Compute the amount of the taxpayer's net income from self-employment activities (this is generally the taxpayer's net income from **Schedule C** of Form 1040—Schedule C reports the taxpayers self-employment-related income and expenses) that is subject to self-employment taxes.

**Step 2:** Multiply the amount from Step (1) by 92.35 percent. The product is called **net earnings from self-employment.** Because self-employed taxpayers are responsible for paying the *entire* amount of their FICA taxes, they are allowed an implicit deduction for the 7.65 percent "employer's portion" of the taxes, leaving 92.35 percent (100% − 7.65%) of the full amount subject to self-employment taxes. Note that the 7.65 percent consists of the 6.2 percent Social Security tax and 1.45 percent Medicare tax. Net earnings from self-employment is the base for the self-employment tax.

---

[15]Because employees meet their FICA tax payment obligations through withholding, no FICA taxes are due with their returns.

[16]As we discussed in Chapters 5 and 6, self-employed taxpayers report their self-employment earnings on Schedule C of Form 1040. Individuals who are partners in partnerships and who are actively involved in the partnerships' business activities may be required to pay self-employment taxes on the income they are allocated from the partnerships. They would report these earnings on Schedule E of Form 1040.

**Step 3:** The computation of the self-employment tax depends on the amount of the taxpayer's net earnings from self-employment as follows:

- If the taxpayer's net earnings from self-employment are less than $400, the taxpayer is not required to pay *any* self-employment tax. [Note that a taxpayer can have $433 of net income from self-employment before paying self-employment tax ($433 × .9235 = $400)].
- If the taxpayer's net earnings from self-employment are $106,800 or less, multiply the amount from Step (2) by 15.3 percent.
- If the taxpayer's net earnings from self-employment exceeds $106,800, multiply the amount from Step (2) by 2.9 percent and add $13,243 ($106,800 × 12.4%). This reflects the fact that the Medicare tax base is unlimited but the Social Security tax base is limited to $106,800.

Note that as we discussed in Chapter 6, taxpayers are allowed to deduct one-half of their self-employment taxes as a *for* AGI deduction.

---

### Example 7-15

**What if:** *Assume* that Courtney's only income for the year is her $18,000 in net self-employment income from her weekend consulting business. What amount of self-employment taxes would Courtney be required to pay on this income?

**Answer:** $2,543, computed as follows:

Step 1:   $18,000 of net self-employment income subject to self-employment taxes.

Step 2:   $18,000 × .9235 = $16,623. This is net earnings from self-employment.

Step 3:   $16,623 × 15.3% = $2,543. This is the Courtney's self-employment taxes payable.

Under these circumstances, Courtney would be able to deduct $1,272 as a *for* AGI deduction for one-half of the self-employment taxes she paid ($2,543 × 50%).

---

When a taxpayer receives *both* employee compensation and self-employment earnings in the same year, the taxpayer's *total earnings* subject to the Social Security tax is capped at $106,800 and the earnings subject to Medicare tax is unlimited. In these situations, the taxpayer's FICA tax liability on the employee compensation is determined as if the employee had no self-employment income. The taxpayer then computes her self-employment tax liability. This ordering is favorable for taxpayers because it allows them to use up all or a portion of the Social Security wage base limit with their employee income (taxed at 6.2 percent) before they determine the Social Security tax on their net earnings from self-employment (taxed at 12.4 percent). Consequently, if an employee's wages exceed the Social Security tax wage base limitation, she would not be required to pay any Social Security tax on her self-employment earnings. After calculating the FICA taxes on the taxpayer's employee wages, the taxpayer's self-employment taxes payable are determined as follows:

**Step 1:** Determine the limit on the Social Security portion of the self-employment tax base by subtracting the employee compensation from the Social Security wage base ($106,800 in 2010) (not below $0).

**Step 2:** Determine the net earnings from self-employment (self-employment earnings times 92.35 percent).

**Step 3:** Multiply the *lesser* of Step (1) and Step (2) by 12.4 percent. This is the amount of Social Security taxes due on the self-employment income.

**Step 4:** Multiply Step (2) by 2.9 percent. This is the amount of Medicare taxes due on the self-employment income.

**Step 5:** Add the amounts from Steps (3) and (4).

**Example 7-16**

In 2010, Courtney received $122,800 in taxable compensation from EWD (see Example 7-13) and $18,000 in self-employment income from her weekend consulting activities (see Example 6-2). What are Courtney's *self-employment taxes* payable on her $18,000 of income from self-employment?

**Answer:** $482, computed as follows:

| Description | Amount | Explanation |
|---|---|---|
| (1) Limit on Social Security wage base | $106,800 | |
| (2) Employee compensation | 122,800 | |
| (3) Limit on Social Security base for self-employment tax purposes | 0 | Step 1: (1) − (2), limited to $0. |
| (4) Self-employment income | 18,000 | |
| (5) Net earnings from self-employment percentage | 92.35% | |
| (6) Net earnings from self-employment | 16,623 | Step 2: (4) × (5). |
| (7) Social Security portion of self-employment tax | 0 | Step 3: [Lesser of (3) or (6)] × 12.4%. |
| (8) Medicare portion of self-employment tax | 482 | Step 4: (6) × 2.9%. |
| **Total self-employment taxes** | **$ 482** | Step 5: (7) + (8). |

As we reported in Chapter 6, Courtney is entitled to a $241 *for* AGI deduction for one half of her $482 self-employment taxes she incurred during the year ($482 × 50%).

**Example 7-17**

*What if:* Let's change the facts and assume that Courtney received $100,000 of taxable compensation from EWD in 2010, and she received $18,000 in self-employment income from her weekend consulting activities. What amount of self-employment taxes is Courtney required to pay on her $18,000 of business income?

**Answer:** $1,325 computed as follows:

| Description | Amount | Explanation |
|---|---|---|
| (1) Limit on Social Security wage base | $106,800 | |
| (2) Employee compensation | 100,000 | |
| (3) Limit on Social Security base for self-employment tax purposes | 6,800 | Step 1: (1) − (2). |
| (4) Self-employment income | 18,000 | |
| (5) Net earnings from self employment percentage | 92.35% | |
| (6) Net earnings from self employment | 16,623 | Step 2: (4) × (5). |
| (7) Social Security portion of self-employment tax | 843 | Step 3: [Lesser of (3) or (6)] × 12.4%. |
| (8) Medicare portion of self-employment tax | 482 | Step 4: (6) × 2.9%. |
| **Total self-employment taxes** | **$ 1,325** | Step 5: (7) + (8). |

Because the extra FICA taxes paid by the self-employed represent an incremental cost of doing business for them, as we discussed in Chapter 6, self-employed taxpayers are allowed to deduct half of the self-employment taxes they pay as a *for* AGI deduction.

Unlike employees, whose employers withhold tax throughout the year on their behalf, self-employed taxpayers must satisfy their self-employment tax obligations through periodic, usually quarterly, estimated tax payments. Taxpayers who are employed and self-employed (an employee with a business on the side, like Courtney) may have their employers withhold enough taxes to cover both their income and self-employment tax obligations.[17] Any self-employment taxes not paid through these mechanisms must be paid with the self-employed taxpayer's individual tax return.

*continued from page 7-1 . . .*

Courtney was enjoying her work with EWD but she also really liked her weekend consulting work. A couple of months ago, after Courtney had played an integral part in completing a successful project, Courtney's boss jokingly mentioned that if Courtney ever decided to leave EWD to work for herself as a full-time consultant that EWD would love to hire her back for contract work. This caused Courtney to start thinking about the possibilities of starting her own consulting business. She's always had some interest in working for herself, but she is not at a point in her life where she can take significant financial risks even if it might mean a more satisfying career. Courtney knew that before making such a move she would need to seriously consider the non-tax issues associated with self-employment and she would need to learn more about the tax consequences of working as an independent contractor. She was particularly interested in the tax consequences of working for EWD as an independent contractor (contract worker) relative to working for EWD as an employee. ■

### Employee vs. Self-Employed (Independent Contractor)

Determining whether an individual is taxed as an **employee** or as an **independent contractor** can be straightforward or quite complex, depending on the specific arrangement between the parties. In its published guidance, the IRS stipulates that an employer/employee relationship exists when the party for whom services are performed has the right to direct or control the individual performing services.[18] To assist taxpayers in deciding whether the party receiving services has the requisite amount of control over the individual providing services, the IRS has published a list of 20 factors to consider.[19] A few of the factors suggesting independent contractor rather than employee status include the contractor's ability to

1. Set her own working hours.
2. Work part-time.
3. Work for more than one firm.
4. Realize either a profit or a loss from the activities.
5. Perform work somewhere other than on an employer's premises.
6. Work without frequent oversight.

When these factors are absent, individuals are more likely to be classified as employees. Rather than simply summing the number of factors in favor of independent contractor status and those in favor of employee status, however, taxpayers and their

[17]As we describe in Chapter 12, employees can manage their employer withholdings with Form W-4.

[18]IRS Publication 1779. Independent Contractor or Employee brochure.

[19]Rev. Rul. 87-41, 1987-1 CB 296.

advisors should use the factors as guides in determining the overall substance of the contractual relationship.

Whether a taxpayer is classified as an employee or as an independent contractor (self-employed) has both tax and nontax consequences to the employer and the taxpayer. The best classification for the taxpayer is situation specific.

**Employee vs. Independent Contractor Comparison**   The two primary *tax* differences between independent contractors and employees relate to (1) the amount of their FICA taxes payable and (2) the deductibility of their business expenses.[20] However, there are several nontax factors to consider as well. In the previous section, we detailed how to determine the FICA taxes payable for employees and independent contractors (self-employed taxpayers). In terms of the deductibility of business expenses, as we discussed in Chapter 6, *employees* who incur unreimbursed business expenses relating to their employment can deduct these expenses as miscellaneous itemized deductions subject to a 2 percent of AGI floor. This floor means, in many cases, that employees receive little or no tax benefit for their employee business expenses. In contrast, as we also described in Chapter 6, self-employed independent contractors are able to deduct expenses relating to their business activities as *for* AGI deductions, which they can deduct without restriction. While these factors appear to favor independent contractor status over employee status, note that employees generally don't incur many unreimbursed expenses relating to their employment. Thus, even though independent contractors may be able to deduct more expenses than employees, they typically incur more costs in doing business.

When taxpayers are classified as independent contractors rather than employees, they are not eligible for nontaxable fringe benefits available to employees, such as health care insurance, retirement plan benefits, and other fringe benefits provided to employees. Further, independent contractors are responsible for paying their estimated tax liability throughout the year through estimated tax payments because the employer does not withhold taxes from an independent contractor's pay. However, as we mentioned above, taxpayers are allowed to deduct one-half of the self-employment taxes they pay.

---

| Taxes in the Real World | *Delivery by Employee or Independent Contractor? FedEx and IRS Disagree* |
|---|---|

While both UPS and FedEx deliver packages, these two delivery companies have different models for their workers. UPS hires employees to deliver its packages. The company provides the drivers with trucks, gas, and supplies to complete their tasks. The company also provides benefits packages to their employees. In contrast, FedEx delivery persons must pay for and maintain their own trucks, uniforms, supplies, gas, maintenance, and other costs. They receive no company benefits. In contrast to UPS, FedEx treats its contract drivers as independent contractors for tax purposes. However, in its Form 8K

it filed with the SEC on September 9, 2009, FedEx reports the following tax issue:

On September 9, 2009, the Internal Revenue Service's audit team ("Audit Team") fully informed us of the results of their employment tax audit for the 2002 calendar year regarding the classification of independent contractors at FedEx Ground Package System, Inc. ("FedEx Ground"), a wholly owned subsidiary of FedEx Corporation. The Audit Team has proposed that no assessment of federal employment tax be made with respect to FedEx Ground's independent contractors, with the exception of

(continued on page 7-21...)

---

[20]Also, independent contractors generally receive a Form 1099 from each client reporting the gross income they received from the client during the year. Employees receive Form W-2 reporting the compensation the employee received from the employer during the year.

independent contractors providing the FedEx Home Delivery service. With respect to those independent contractors, the Audit Team has notified us that they propose to assess tax and penalties of $14 million plus interest for 2002. Substantially all of the proposed assessment relates to employment and withholding taxes for the 2002 calendar year.

We intend to contest the erroneous conclusions in the audit. We expect that a final resolution may not occur for some time. We believe that we have strong defenses to the proposed assessment and will vigorously defend our position, as we continue to believe that all of FedEx Ground's independent contractors, including those providing the FedEx Home Delivery service, are independent contractors.

This disagreement highlights the subjective nature of the employee vs. independent contractor determination.

From the employer's perspective, it is generally less costly to hire an independent contractor than an employee because the employer need not provide these benefits and the employer need not withhold or pay any FICA taxes on behalf of an independent contractor. As a result, an employer may be willing to offer an apparently higher level of taxable compensation to an independent contractor than a similarly situated employee. However, after considering all relevant factors, the taxpayer may do better receiving less compensation as an employee than slightly higher compensation as an independent contractor.

**Example 7-18**

**What if:** Let's compare Courtney's compensation as an employee with EWD to her compensation if she were to work for EWD as an independent contractor. *Assume* that Courtney works an average of 40 hours per week for 50 weeks per year to earn a salary of $100,000; in addition she receives fringe benefits including a 5 percent contribution to her retirement plan, life insurance coverage, and health insurance coverage. Would Courtney be "made whole" in terms of her hourly rate if EWD agreed to pay her $55 an hour for her contract work (10 percent more than her hourly rate as an employee)?

**Answer:** Not very likely. As an independent contractor, Courtney must pay more costly self-employment taxes (at nearly twice the rate of employment taxes) under the new arrangement. In addition, she will be ineligible for the nontaxable fringe benefits (retirement plan contributions, life insurance, and health coverage) she was receiving as an employee and will not receive as a contractor.

We've described how to calculate a taxpayer's regular tax liability, alternative minimum tax liability, and self-employment tax liability. These tax liabilities sum to a taxpayer's gross tax liability. While Gram's gross tax is simply her regular income tax liability of $484 (see Example 7-2), Courtney's gross tax includes other taxes. Courtney's gross tax liability is calculated in Exhibit 7-5.

**EXHIBIT 7-5  Courtney's Gross Tax**

| Description | Amount | Explanation |
|---|---|---|
| (1) Regular federal income tax | $22,591.75 | Example 7-3. |
| (2) Alternative minimum tax | 1,303.25 | Example 7-11. |
| (3) Self-employment tax | 482 | Example 7-16. |
| Gross tax | $24,377 | (1) + (2) + (3). |

Taxpayers reduce their gross tax by tax credits and tax prepayments (withholding and estimated tax payments) for the year. As indicated in Exhibit 7-6, if the gross

**EXHIBIT 7-6  Formula for Computing Net Tax Due or Refund**

Gross tax
Minus: Tax credits
Minus: Prepayments
**Net tax due (refund)**

**THE KEY FACTS**

**Employee vs. Independent Contractor**

■ Employees
· Less control over how, when, and where to perform duties.
· Pay 6.2 percent Social Security tax subject to limit.
· Pay 1.45 percent Medicare tax.

■ Independent contractors
· More control over how, when, and where to perform duties.
· Report income and expenses on Form 1040, Schedule C.
· Pay 12.4 percent self-employment (Social Security) tax subject to limit.
· Pay 2.9 percent self-employment (Medicare tax) tax (no limit).
· Self-employment tax base is 92.35 percent of net self-employment income.
· Deduct half of self-employment taxes paid for AGI.

tax exceeds the tax credits and prepayments, the taxpayer owes additional taxes when she files her tax return. In contrast, if the prepayments exceed the gross tax after applying tax credits, the taxpayer is entitled to a tax refund. We next explore available tax credits and conclude the chapter by dealing with taxpayer prepayments.

## LO4    TAX CREDITS

Congress provides a considerable number of credits for taxpayers. **Tax credits** reduce a taxpayer's *tax liability* dollar for dollar. In contrast, deductions reduce *taxable income* dollar for dollar, but the tax savings deductions generate depend on the taxpayer's marginal tax rate. Because tax credits generate tax savings *independent of* a taxpayer's marginal tax rate, they are a popular tax policy tool for avoiding the perception that tax benefits for certain tax policies are distributed disproportionately to taxpayers with higher incomes and corresponding higher marginal tax rates. Further, tax credits are powerful tax policy tools because they directly affect taxes due. By using tax credits, policy makers can adjust the magnitude of the tax effects of tax policy without changing tax rates.

Tax credits may be either nonrefundable or refundable. A **nonrefundable credit** may reduce a taxpayer's gross tax liability to zero, but if the amount of the credit exceeds the amount of the taxpayer's gross tax liability, the credit in excess of the gross tax liability is not refunded to the taxpayer and expires without ever providing tax benefits (unless the unused credit can be carried over to a different year). Refundable credits in excess of a taxpayer's gross tax liability are refunded to the taxpayer.

Tax credits are generally classified into one of three categories: nonrefundable personal, refundable personal, or business credits, depending on the nature of the credit. The primary exception to this general rule is the foreign tax credit. The foreign tax credit is a hybrid between personal and business credits because, like nonrefundable personal credits, it reduces the taxpayer's liability before business credits but, like business credits, unused foreign tax credits can be carried over to use in other years.

### Nonrefundable Personal Credits

Congress provides many nonrefundable personal tax credits to generate tax relief for certain groups of individuals. For example, the child tax credit provides tax relief for taxpayers who provide a home for dependent children and the child and dependent care credit provides tax relief for taxpayers who incur expenses to care for their children and other dependents in order to work. The adoption expense credit helps parents pay the cost of adopting children. The American opportunity credit (partially refundable) and the lifetime learning credit help taxpayers pay for the cost of higher education. Because the child tax credit, the child and dependent care credit, and the American opportunity and lifetime learning credits are some of the most common nonrefundable personal credits, we discuss them in detail.

**Child Tax Credit**    Taxpayers may claim a $1,000 **child tax credit** for *each qualifying child* (same definition for dependency exemption purposes—see §152(c) and Chapter 4) who is under age 17 at the end of the year and who is claimed as their dependent.[21] The credit is subject to phase-out based on the taxpayer's AGI. The phase-out threshold depends on the taxpayer's filing status and is provided in Exhibit 7-7.

> **THE KEY FACTS**
>
> Child Tax Credit
>
> ▪ Taxpayers may claim a $1,000 credit for each qualifying child under age 17.
>
> ▪ Credit is phased out for taxpayers with AGI above $110,000.
> · Lose $50 for every $1,000 or portion thereof that AGI exceeds $110,000.

[21]§24(a).

**EXHIBIT 7-7    Child Tax Credit Phase-out Threshold**

| Filing Status | Phase-out Threshold |
|---|---|
| Married filing jointly | $110,000 |
| Married filing separately | 55,000 |
| Head of household and single | 75,000 |

The total amount of the credit ($1,000 × number of qualifying children) is phased-out, but not below zero, by $50 for each $1,000 *or portion thereof* by which the taxpayer's AGI exceeds the applicable threshold. Taxpayers can determine their allowable child tax credit after the phase-out by using the following four steps:

**Step 1:** Determine the excess AGI by subtracting the threshold amount (see Exhibit 7-7) from the taxpayer's AGI.

**Step 2:** Divide the excess AGI from step (1) by 1,000 and round up to the next whole number.

**Step 3:** Multiply the amount from step (2) by $50. This is the amount of the total credit that is phased-out or disallowed.

**Step 4:** Subtract the amount from step (3) from the total credit before phase-out (limited to $0) to determine the allowable child tax credit.

Because the phase-out is based upon a fixed amount ($50) rather than a percentage, the phase-out range varies according to the amount of credit claimed.[22]

**Example 7-19**

Both Ellen and Deron are Courtney's qualifying children. Courtney may claim a child tax credit for Deron but she may *not* claim a child tax credit for Ellen because Ellen is not under age 17 at the end of the year. What amount of child tax credit is Courtney allowed to claim for Deron after accounting for the credit phase-out?

**Answer:** $0. Because Courtney's AGI of $162,000 exceeds the $75,000 AGI phase-out threshold, she must determine her credit after the phase-out. Her phase-out is computed as follows:

1. $162,000 AGI (Exhibit 6-6) − $75,000 head of household threshold (Exhibit 7-7) = $87,000.
2. $87,000 excess AGI divided by 1,000 = 87 (if her AGI was $87,001, this would be 88)
3. 87 × $50 = $4,350. This is the amount of the phase-out.
4. $1,000 allowable credit minus $4,350 = $0 (limited to $0).

Courtney is *not able to claim any child tax credit* because the entire amount is phased out.

**What if:** How much child tax credit would Courtney be able to claim after the phase-out if she had claimed five qualifying children under the age of 17 as dependents?

**Answer:** $650. Her total child tax credit before phase-outs would be $5,000 ($1,000 × 5). Assuming the same AGI of $162,000, she would be required to phase-out $4,350 of the credit. Consequently, she would still be able to reduce her taxes by the $650 portion of the credit that was not phased-out ($5,000 − $4,350).

[22]The child tax credit is partially refundable. In 2010, the refundable portion of the credit is the lesser of (1) the taxpayer's earned income in excess of $3,000 times 15 percent, or (2) the amount of the unclaimed portion of the otherwise nonrefundable credit. Thus, if a taxpayer has enough tax liability to absorb the nonrefundable portion of the credit, the refundable portion is reduced to zero. The computation is modified for taxpayers with three or more qualifying children. See IRS Publication 972 for more information relating to the child tax credit.

**Child and Dependent Care Credit**   The child and dependent care credit is a tax subsidy to help taxpayers pay the cost of providing care for their dependents to allow taxpayers to work or look for work. The amount of the credit is based on the amount of the taxpayer's expenditures to provide care for one or more qualifying persons. A qualifying person includes (1) a dependent under the age of 13, and (2) a dependent or spouse who is physically or mentally incapable of caring for herself or himself and who lives in the taxpayer's home for more than half the year.

The amount of expenditures eligible for the credit is the *least* of the following three amounts:

1.   The total amount of dependent care expenditures for the year.
2.   $3,000 for one qualifying person or $6,000 for two or more qualifying persons.
3.   The taxpayer's earned income including wage, salary, or other taxable employee compensation, or net earnings from self-employment. Married taxpayers must file a joint tax return and the amount of earned income for purposes of the dependent care credit limitation is the earned income of the lesser-earning spouse.[23]

Expenditures for care qualify whether the care is provided outside or within the home. But, expenditures for care do *not* qualify if the caregiver is a dependent relative or child of the taxpayer.[24] The amount of the credit is calculated by multiplying qualifying expenditures by the appropriate credit percentage. The credit percentage is based upon the taxpayer's AGI level and begins at 35 percent for taxpayers with AGI of $15,000 or less. The minimum dependent care credit is 20 percent for taxpayers with AGI over $43,000. Exhibit 7-8 provides the dependent care credit percentage for different levels of AGI.

**EXHIBIT 7-8**   **Child and Dependent Care Credit Percentage**

| If AGI is over | but not over | then the percentage is |
|---|---|---|
| $     0 | 15,000 | 35% |
| 15,000 | 17,000 | 34% |
| 17,000 | 19,000 | 33% |
| 19,000 | 21,000 | 32% |
| 21,000 | 23,000 | 31% |
| 23,000 | 25,000 | 30% |
| 25,000 | 27,000 | 29% |
| 27,000 | 29,000 | 28% |
| 29,000 | 31,000 | 27% |
| 31,000 | 33,000 | 26% |
| 33,000 | 35,000 | 25% |
| 35,000 | 37,000 | 24% |
| 37,000 | 39,000 | 23% |
| 39,000 | 41,000 | 22% |
| 41,000 | 43,000 | 21% |
| 43,000 | No limit | 20% |

[23]If the lesser-earning spouse cannot work due to a disability or is a full-time student, the lesser-earning spouse is *deemed* to have earned $250 a month if the couple is computing the credit for one qualifying person or $500 a month if the couple is computing the credit for more than one qualifying person.

[24]§21(e)(6). Also, the regulations indicate that the costs of summer school and tutoring programs are indistinguishable from general education and, therefore, do not qualify for the credit [See Reg. §1.21-1(b)].

**Example 7-20**

**What if:** Suppose that this year, Courtney paid a neighbor $3,200 to care for her 10-year-old son, Deron, so Courtney could work. Would Courtney be allowed to claim the child and dependent care credit for the expenditures she made for Deron's care?

**Answer:** Yes. (1) Courtney paid for Deron's care to allow her to work, and (2) Deron is a qualifying person for purposes of the credit because (a) he is Courtney's dependent and (b) he is under 13 years of age at the end of the year.

What amount of child and dependent care credit, if any, would Courtney be allowed to claim for the $3,200 she spent to provide Deron's care given her AGI is $162,000?

**Answer:** $600, computed as follows:

| Description | Amount | Explanation |
|---|---|---|
| (1) Dependent care expenditures | $ 3,200 | |
| (2) Limit on qualifying expenditures for one dependent | 3,000 | |
| (3) Courtney's earned income | 140,800 | $122,800 compensation from EWD + $18,000 business income (see Example 7-16). |
| (4) Expenditures eligible for credit | 3,000 | Least of (1), (2), and (3). |
| (5) Credit percentage rate | 20% | AGI over $43,000. See Exhibit 7-8. |
| **Dependent care credit** | $ 600 | (4) × (5). |

**What if:** If Courtney's AGI (and her earned income) was only $31,500, what would be her child and dependent care credit?

**Answer:** $780, computed as follows:

| Description | Amount | Explanation |
|---|---|---|
| (1) Dependent care expenditures | $ 3,200 | |
| (2) Limit on qualifying expenditures for one dependent | 3,000 | |
| (3) Courtney's earned income | 31,500 | |
| (4) Expenditures eligible for credit | 3,000 | Least of (1), (2), and (3). |
| (5) Credit percentage rate | 26% | See table for AGI between $31,000 and $33,000. |
| **Dependent care credit** | $ 780 | (4) × (5). |

**Education Credits**    Congress provides the American opportunity credit (AOC) (formerly called the Hope scholarship credit) and the lifetime learning credit to encourage taxpayers and their dependents to obtain higher education by reducing the costs of the education. Taxpayers may claim credits for eligible expenditures made by them personally, their dependents, and third parties on behalf of the taxpayers' dependents.[25] Married taxpayers filing separate returns are not eligible for the AOC or the lifetime learning credit.

The AOC is available for students in their *first four years* of postsecondary (post high school) education. To qualify, students must be enrolled in a qualified postsecondary educational institution at least half time.[26] For 2010, the amount of the credit is 100 percent of the first $2,000 of eligible expenses paid by the taxpayer plus

[25]§25A(g)(3).

[26]§25A(b). Generally, eligible institutions are those eligible to participate in the federal student loan program [§25A(f)(2)].

25 percent of the next $2,000 of eligible expenses paid by the taxpayer. Thus, the maximum AOC for eligible expenses paid in 2010 for any one person is $2,500 [$2,000 + (25% × $2,000)].[27] To be eligible for the 2010 credit, taxpayers must pay the eligible expenses in 2010 for any academic period beginning in 2010 or in the first three months of 2011.[28] Eligible expenses for the AOC include tuition, fees, and course materials (cost of books and other materials) needed for courses of instruction at an eligible educational institution.[29] The AOC is applied on a *per student* basis. Consequently, a taxpayer with three eligible dependents can claim a maximum AOC of $2,500 for *each* dependent. The AOC is subject to phase-out based on the taxpayer's AGI. For 2010, the credit is phased out pro rata for taxpayers with AGI between $80,000 and $90,000 ($160,000 – $180,000 for married taxpayers filing jointly).[30] For 2010, 40 percent of a taxpayer's allowable AOC is refundable.[31]

## Example 7-21

### THE KEY FACTS

#### Education Credits

■ **American opportunity credit**
· Qualifying expenses include tuition for a qualifying student incurred during the first four years at a qualifying institution of higher education.
· In 2010, maximum credit of $2,500 per student calculated as percentage of maximum of $4,000 qualifying expenses.
· Subject to phase-out for taxpayers with AGI in excess of $80,000 ($160,000 MFJ).

■ **Lifetime learning credit**
· Qualifying expenses include costs at a qualifying institution associated with acquiring or improving job skills.
· Maximum credit of $2,000 per taxpayer calculated as percentage of maximum of $10,000 in annual expenses.
· Subject to phase-out for taxpayers with AGI in excess of $50,000 ($100,000 MFJ).

Courtney paid $2,000 of tuition and $300 for books for Ellen to attend the University of Missouri-Kansas City during the summer at the end of her freshman year. What is the maximum American opportunity credit (AOC) (before phase-out) Courtney may claim for these expenses?

**Answer:** $2,075. Because the cost of tuition and books is an eligible expense Courtney may claim a maximum AOC before phase-out of $2,075 [($2,000 × 100%) + ($2,300 − $2,000) × 25%].

How much AOC is Courtney allowed to claim on her 2010 tax return (how much can she claim after applying the phase-out)?

**Answer:** $0. Because Courtney's AGI exceeds the head of household limit of $90,000, she is not allowed to claim any AOC.

**What if:** How much AOC would Courtney have been allowed to claim on her 2010 tax return if she were married and filed a joint return with her husband (assuming the couple's AGI is $162,000)?

**Answer:** $1,867, computed as follows:

| Description | Amount | Explanation |
|---|---|---|
| (1) AOC before phase-out | $ 2,075 | |
| (2) AGI | 162,000 | |
| (3) Phase-out threshold | 160,000 | |
| (4) Excess AGI | 2,000 | (2) − (3). |
| (5) Phase-out range for taxpayer filing for married filing jointly | 20,000 | $180,000 − 160,000. |
| (6) Phase-out percentage | 10% | (4)/(5). |
| (7) Phase-out amount | 208 | (1) × (6). |
| AOC after phase-out | $ 1,867 | (1) − (7). |

**What if:** Suppose Courtney could claim a $1,867 AOC in 2010 (after phase-out). How much of this credit would be refundable?

**Answer:** $747 ($1,867 × 40%).

[27]The maximum American opportunity credit for eligible expenses paid in 2009 is $2,500.

[28]Reg. §1.25A-3(e).

[29]§25A(i)(3). Eligible expenses for both the AOC and the lifetime learning credit must be reduced by scholarships received to pay for these expenses or other amounts received as reimbursements for the expenses (employer-sponsored reimbursement plans, Educational IRAs, 529 plans, and the like). The cost of room and board or other personal expenses do not qualify as eligible expenses for either the AOC or the lifetime learning credit.

[30]§25A(i)(4).

[31]§25A(i)(6).

The lifetime learning credit is a nonrefundable credit that applies to the cost of tuition and fees (but generally not books) for any course of instruction to acquire or improve a taxpayer's job skills.[32] This includes the cost of professional or graduate school tuition (expenses are not limited to those incurred in the first four years of postsecondary education). The credit is equal to 20 percent of eligible expenses up to an annual maximum of $10,000 of eligible expenses (maximum of $2,000). The credit for a year is based on the amount paid during that year for an academic period beginning in that year or the first three months of the following year. In contrast to the American opportunity credit, the lifetime learning credit limit applies to the taxpayer (a married couple filing a joint return may claim only $2,000 of lifetime learning credit). Thus, a taxpayer with multiple eligible dependents can claim a maximum lifetime learning credit of only $2,000. Finally, the credit is phased out pro rata for taxpayers with AGI between $50,000 and $60,000 ($100,000 – $120,000 for married taxpayers filing jointly).[33]

---

**Example 7-22**

Courtney paid $1,550 to attend motivational seminars to help her improve her job skills. Courtney could elect to claim the lifetime learning credit for these expenses instead of deducting them as miscellaneous itemized deductions. If Courtney decided to claim a credit for these expenditures, what would be her maximum lifetime learning credit (before phase-out)?

**Answer:** $310 ($1,550 × 20%)

How much lifetime learning credit is Courtney allowed to claim on her 2010 tax return (how much can she claim after applying the phase-out)?

**Answer:** $0. Because Courtney's AGI exceeds the head of household limit of $60,000 she is not allowed to claim any lifetime learning credit.

---

For expenses that qualify for both the AOC and lifetime learning credit (tuition and fees during the first four years of postsecondary education), taxpayers may choose which credit to use, but they may not claim both credits for the same student in the same year. In addition, taxpayers may choose to *either* (1) deduct qualifying education expenses of an individual as a *for* AGI deduction if the deduction is extended to 2010 (see discussion of this *for* AGI deduction in Chapter 6) or claim an education credit for the individual's expenses. However, if a taxpayer claims *any* educational credit for an individual's educational expenditures, the taxpayer may not claim *any* for AGI deduction for that individual's qualifying expenditures (and vice versa).[34]

---

**Example 7-23**

***What if:*** Suppose Courtney paid $5,000 of tuition for Ellen to attend the University of Missouri–Kansas City during the summer at the end of her freshman year. Further assume that Courtney's AGI is $45,000, so her education credits are not subject to phase-out. Courtney would be allowed to claim the maximum AOC of $2,500 on the first $4,000 of the qualifying educational expenditures. Assuming Courtney used $4,000 of the educational expenses to claim the maximum AOC, would she be allowed to deduct (or claim the lifetime credit on) the remaining $1,000 of tuition costs ($5,000 total expenses — $4,000 maximum AOC expenses)?

(*continued on page 7-28...*)

---

[32]§25A(f)(1).
[33]§25A(d).
[34]§222(c)(2)(A).

**Answer:** No. If Courtney claims any AOC for Ellen's expenditures, she is not allowed to deduct or claim a lifetime learning credit for Ellen's expenditures (even for the expenses not used in computing the AOC).

*What if:* Assume that both Ellen and Deron were in their first year of college, and that Courtney paid tuition for both Ellen and Deron. Further, assume that Courtney's AGI is below the phase-out threshold. Is Courtney allowed to claim a AOC for Ellen's expenses and claim a *for* AGI educational expense deduction for Deron's expenses? (Assume the *for* AGI deduction is extended to 2010.)

**Answer:** Yes. Courtney may claim a AOC or a deduction for Ellen's expenses, and she may claim a AOC or a deduction for Deron's expenses.

## Example 7-24

*What if:* Assume the qualified education expense deduction is extended to 2010 and that Courtney paid $8,000 tuition for Ellen to attend graduate school at the University of Missouri–Kansas City (assume this is her fifth year at the university and that Ellen still qualifies as Courtney's dependent). Further assume that Courtney's AGI is $55,000, so her potential lifetime learning credit for Ellen would be phased-out by 50 percent (assume Courtney did not claim the credit for herself). Before phase-out, Courtney would be allowed to claim a $1,600 lifetime learning credit ($8,000 tuition × 20% credit percentage). After the phase-out, however, Courtney would be able to claim an $800 lifetime learning credit ($1,600 full credit × 50% phase-out percentage). If Courtney claims the $800 lifetime learning credit for Ellen's tuition, is she allowed to claim any for AGI deduction for Ellen's tuition since half of the lifetime learning credit is phased-out based on Courtney's AGI?

**Answer:** No. As we discussed above, if Courtney claims *any* lifetime learning credit for Ellen's expenditures, she is not allowed to deduct any *for* AGI deduction for Ellen's expenditures (even the portion of the expenses that provided no tax benefit because the credit was partially phased out).

*What if:* Assume the same facts as above and that Courtney's marginal tax rate is 15%. Would Courtney be better off claiming an $800 lifetime learning credit or a $4,000 *for* AGI qualified education expense deduction for the cost of Ellen's tuition?

**Answer:** The $800 lifetime learning credit. The credit saves Courtney $800 while the qualified education expense deduction would save her $600 ($4,000 × 15%).

### Refundable Personal Credits

Several personal credits are refundable, the most common of which are the making work pay credit, the earned income credit, and the first-time home buyer credit. We discuss the making work pay credit and earned income credit in this chapter. We discuss the first-time home buyer credit in Chapter 14.

**Making Work Pay Credit**    The making work pay credit (MWPC) is a **refundable credit** designed to mitigate the Social Security tax burden on qualifying taxpayers. The amount of the credit is the lesser of (1) 6.2 percent of the taxpayer's earned income or (2) $400 ($800 for married couples filing a joint tax return).[35]

Taxpayers must reduce the credit (but not below zero) by 2 percent of their AGI in excess of $75,000 ($150,000 for married filing jointly). Consequently, the $400 credit is phased out completely at $95,000 of AGI and the $800 credit is phased out completely at $190,000 of AGI. Taxpayers who are dependents of other taxpayers are not eligible for the credit. We learned in Chapter 5 (see Exhibit 5-6) that Gram reported $350 of earned income for providing babysitting service. Based on this earned income, she is entitled to a $22 making work pay credit ($350 × 6.2%). On the other hand, based on her ample earned income, Courtney is eligible for a

[35]§36A.

$400 making work pay credit before phase-out. However, because her AGI exceeds $95,000 she may not claim the credit.

**Earned Income Credit**   The **earned income credit** is a refundable credit that is designed to help offset the effect of employment taxes on compensation paid to low-income taxpayers and to encourage lower-income taxpayers to seek employment. Because it is refundable (if the credit exceeds the tax after considering nonrefundable credits the taxpayer receives a refund for the excess), it is sometimes referred to as a *negative income tax.* The credit is available for qualified individuals who have earned income for the year.[36] Qualified individuals generally include (1) any individual who has at least one qualifying child (same definition of qualifying child for dependent purposes—see Chapter 4) or (2) any individual who does not have a qualifying child for the taxable year, but who lives in the United States for more than half the year, is at least 25 years old but younger than 65 years old at the end of the year, and is not a dependent of another taxpayer. Earned income includes wages, salaries, tips, and other employee compensation included in gross income and net earnings from self-employment. Taxpayers with investment income such as interest, dividends, and capital gains in excess of $3,100 are ineligible for the credit.[37]

The amount of the credit depends on the taxpayer's filing status, the number of the taxpayer's qualifying children who live in the home for more than half of the year, and the amount of the taxpayer's earned income. To be eligible for the credit, married taxpayers must file a joint tax return. The credit is computed by multiplying the appropriate credit percentage times the taxpayer's earned income up to a maximum amount. The credit percentage depends upon the number of qualifying children in the home and is subject to a phase-out based upon AGI (or earned income if greater). As summarized in Exhibit 7-9, the earned income credit increases as taxpayers receive earned income up to the maximum amount of earned income eligible for the credit. However, as taxpayers earn more income, the credit begins to phase-out and is completely eliminated once taxpayers' earned income reaches established levels.

**EXHIBIT 7-9   2010 Earned Income Credit Table**

| Qualifying children | (1) Maximum earned income eligible for credit | (2) Credit % | (3) Maximum credit (1) × (2) | (4) Credit phase-out for AGI (or earned income if greater) over this amount | (5) Phase-out percentage | No credit when AGI (or earned income if greater) equals or exceeds this amount (4) + [(3)/(5)] |
|---|---|---|---|---|---|---|
| \multicolumn{7}{c}{Married taxpayers filing joint returns} |
| 0 | $ 5,980 | 7.65% | $ 457 | $ 12,490 | 7.65% | $18,470 |
| 1 | 8,970 | 34% | 3,050 | 21,460 | 15.98% | 40,545 |
| 2 | 12,590 | 40% | 5,036 | 21,460 | 21.06% | 45,372 |
| 3+ | 12,590 | 45% | 5,666 | 21,460 | 21.06% | 48,362 |
| \multicolumn{7}{c}{All taxpayers *except* married taxpayers filing joint returns} |
| 0 | $ 5,980 | 7.65% | $ 457 | $ 7,480 | 7.65% | $13,460 |
| 1 | 8,970 | 34% | 3,050 | 16,450 | 15.98% | 35,535 |
| 2 | 12,590 | 40% | 5,036 | 16,450 | 21.06% | 40,363 |
| 3+ | 12,590 | 45% | 5,666 | 16,450 | 21.06% | 43,352 |

[36] §32.
[37] §32(i).

## Example 7-25

Courtney's earned income for the year is $140,800 and her AGI is $162,000. Deron and Ellen both qualify as Courtney's qualifying children. What amount of earned income credit is Courtney entitled to claim on her 2010 tax return?

**Answer:** $0. Courtney's AGI (which is greater than her earned income) exceeds the $40,363 limit for unmarried taxpayers with two or more qualifying children. Consequently, Courtney is not allowed to claim any earned income credit.

**What if:** Assume that Courtney's only source of income for the year was $30,000 in salary. Also assume Courtney's AGI for the year was $30,000. What would be Courtney's earned income credit in these circumstances?

**Answer:** $2,182.40, computed as follows

| Description | Amount | Explanation |
|---|---|---|
| (1) AGI and earned income | $30,000 | |
| (2) Maximum earned income eligible for earned income credit for taxpayers filing as head of household with two qualifying children | 12,590 | Exhibit 7-9. |
| (3) Earned income eligible for credit | 12,590 | Lesser of (1) and (2). |
| (4) Earned income credit percentage for taxpayer with two qualifying children | 40% | |
| (5) Earned income credit before phase-out | 5,036 | (3) × (4). |
| (6) Phase-out threshold begins at this level of AGI (or earned income if greater) | 16,450 | See Exhibit 7-9 for head of household filing status and two qualifying children. |
| (7) AGI in excess of phase-out threshold | 13,550 | (1) − (6). |
| (8) Phase-out percentage | 21.06% | See Exhibit 7-9. |
| (9) Credit phase-out amount | 2,853.60 | (7) × (8). |
| **Earned income credit after phase-out** | **$ 2,182.40** | (5) − (9). |

**Other Refundable Personal Credits** Other refundable personal tax credits include a portion of the child tax credit (discussed above), excess FICA withholdings (see discussion above under FICA taxes), and taxes withheld on wages and estimated tax payments. We address withholdings and estimated taxes below when we discuss tax prepayments.

### Business Tax Credits

**Business tax credits** are designed to provide incentives for taxpayers to hire certain types of individuals or to participate in certain business activities. For example, Congress provides the employment tax credit to encourage businesses to hire certain unemployed individuals, and it provides the research and development credit to encourage businesses to expend funds to develop new technology. Business tax credits are *nonrefundable* credits. However, when business credits other than the foreign tax credit (discussed below), exceed the taxpayer's gross tax for the year, the credits are carried *back* one year and forward 20 years to use in years when the taxpayer has sufficient gross tax liability to use the credits.

Why discuss business credits in an individual tax chapter? We discuss business credits here because self-employed individuals may qualify for these credits. Also, individuals may be allocated business credits from flow-through entities (partnerships, LLCs, and S corporations). Finally, individuals working as employees overseas or receiving dividends from investments in foreign securities may qualify for the foreign tax credit.

**Foreign Tax Credit** U.S. citizens must pay U.S. tax on their worldwide income. However, when they generate some or all of their income in other countries, they generally are required to pay income taxes to the foreign country where they earned their income. Without some form of tax relief, taxpayers earning income overseas would be double-taxed on this income. When taxpayers pay income taxes to foreign countries, for U.S. tax purposes, they may treat the payment in one of three ways: (1) as we discussed in Chapter 5 when we introduced the foreign earned income exclusion, taxpayers may exclude the foreign earned income from U.S. taxation (in which case they would *not* deduct or receive a credit for any foreign taxes paid); (2) taxpayers may include the foreign income in their gross income and deduct the foreign taxes paid as itemized deductions; or (3) taxpayers may include foreign income in gross income and claim a foreign tax credit for the foreign taxes paid. Here, we discuss the foreign tax credit.

The foreign tax credit helps reduce the double tax taxpayers may pay when they pay income taxes on foreign earned income to the United States and to foreign countries. Taxpayers are allowed to claim a foreign tax credit, against their U.S. tax liability, for the income taxes they pay to foreign countries.[38] In certain situations, taxpayers may not be able to claim the full amount of foreign tax paid as a credit. This restriction may apply when the taxpayer's effective foreign tax rate is higher than the effective U.S. tax rate on the foreign earnings. Taxpayers generally benefit from claiming credits rather than deductions for foreign taxes paid because credits reduce their liabilities dollar for dollar. However, in circumstances when the foreign tax credit is restricted (see above), taxpayers may benefit by claiming deductions for the taxes paid instead of credits.

As we discussed above, the foreign tax credit may be limited in circumstances where a taxpayer's effective foreign tax rate exceeds her U.S. tax rate. Further, the foreign tax credit offsets an individual's tax liability *after* all nonrefundable credits *except* for the adoption credit and the child tax credit.[39] As a nonrefundable credit, it may only reduce the taxpayer's tax liability to zero. When the use of a foreign tax credit is limited, taxpayers may carry back their unused credits one year and carry forward the credits up to 10 years.[40]

### Tax Credit Summary

Exhibit 7-10 identifies several tax credits and for each credit identifies the credit type, notes the IRC section allowing the credit, and describes the credit.

### Credit Application Sequence

As we've discussed, credits are applied against a taxpayer's gross tax. However, we still must describe what happens when the taxpayer's allowable credits exceed the taxpayer's gross tax. To set up this discussion, it is important to understand that non-refundable personal credits and business credits may be used to reduce a taxpayer's gross tax to zero, but not below zero.[41] In contrast, by definition, a refundable credit may reduce a taxpayer's gross tax below zero. This excess refundable credit generates a tax refund for the taxpayer.

When a nonrefundable personal credit exceeds the taxpayer's gross tax, it reduces the gross tax to zero, but the excess credit (credit in excess of the taxpayer's gross tax) disappears. That is, the taxpayer may *not* carry over any excess nonrefundable personal credits to use in other years. However, when a business credit or foreign tax credit exceeds the gross tax, it reduces the taxpayer's gross tax to zero, but the excess credit may

---

[38]§904.

[39]The foreign tax credit also offsets an individual's liability after the saver's credit. We discuss the saver's credit in Chapter 13.

[40]See IRS Publication 514 "Foreign Tax Credit for Individuals" for more information about the foreign tax credit.

[41]In general, nonrefundable personal credits can offset a taxpayer's regular tax and AMT (§26) but not self-employment tax. The limitation on business credits is more complex. We limit our discussion here to basic concepts. See §38(c) for the detailed limitations.

**EXHIBIT 7-10    Summary of Selected Tax Credits**

| Credit | Type of Credit | IRC | Description |
|---|---|---|---|
| Child and dependent care credit | Nonrefundable personal | §21 | Credit for taxpayers who pay dependent care expenses due to their employment activities. |
| Credit for elderly and disabled | Nonrefundable personal | §22 | Credit for elderly low-income taxpayers who retired because of a disability. |
| Adoption expense credit | Nonrefundable personal | §23 | Credit for qualified adoption-related expenses. |
| Child tax credit | Nonrefundable and refundable personal | §24 | Credit for providing home for dependent children under the age of 17. |
| American opportunity credit | Nonrefundable and refundable personal | §25A | Credit for higher education expenses for the first four years of postsecondary education. |
| Lifetime learning credit | Nonrefundable personal | §25A | Credit for higher education expenses. |
| Saver's credit | Nonrefundable personal | §25B | Credit for contributing to qualified retirement plans. See Chapter 13 for details. |
| Residential energy efficient property credit | Nonrefundable personal | §25D | Credit for qualified expenditures for solar water heating property, fuel cell property, wind energy property, and qualified geothermal heat pump property. |
| Earned income credit | Refundable personal | §32 | Credit to encourage low-income taxpayers to work. |
| First-time home buyer credit | Refundable personal | §36 | Credit for certain principal residence purchases. |
| Making work pay credit | Refundable personal | §36A | Credit to offset some of cost of Social Security tax. |
| Credit for increasing research activities | Business | §41 | Credit to encourage research and development. |
| Employer-provided child care credit | Business | §45F | Credit for providing child care for employees. |
| Rehabilitation credit | Business | §47 | Credit for expenditures to renovate or restore older business buildings. |
| Energy credit | Business | §48 | Credit for businesses that invest in energy conservation measures. |
| Work opportunity credit | Business | §51 | Credit for hiring certain economically disadvantaged individuals. |
| Welfare to work credit | Business | §51A | Credit for hiring those on welfare. |
| Foreign tax credit | Hybrid business and personal | §904 | Credit to reduce effects of double taxation of foreign income. |

be carried forward or back to be used in other years when the taxpayer has sufficient gross tax to use the credit (subject to certain time restrictions discussed above).

Because the tax treatment of excess credits depends on the type of credit, it is important to identify the sequence in which taxpayers apply the credits when they have more than one type of credit for the year. When taxpayers have multiple credit types in the same year, they apply the credits against their gross tax in the following

order: (1) nonrefundable personal credits, (2) business credits, and (3) refundable credits. This sequence maximizes the chances that taxpayers will receive full benefit for their tax credits.

Because, as we discuss above, the foreign tax credit is a hybrid credit subject to a unique set of application rules, we exclude it from our general discussion on applying credits. Exhibit 7-11 summarizes the order in which the credits are applied against gross tax and indicates the tax treatment of any excess credits.

**EXHIBIT 7-11**  Credit Application

| Credit Type | Order Applied | Excess Credit |
|---|---|---|
| Nonrefundable personal | First | Lost |
| Business | Second | Carryback and carryover |
| Refundable personal | Last | Refunded |

**Example 7-26**

**What if:** As we describe in Example 7-2, Gram's gross tax liability is $484. For illustrative purposes, let's *assume* that Gram is entitled to an $800 nonrefundable personal tax credit, a $700 business tax credit, and a $600 refundable personal tax credit. What is the amount of Gram's refund or taxes due?

**Answer:** $600 refund. Gram would apply these credits as follows:

| Description | Amount | Treatment of excess credit |
|---|---|---|
| Gross tax liability | $ 484 | Example 7-2. |
| Nonrefundable personal credits | (484) | $316 ($800 − 484) excess credit expires unused. |
| Business credits | 0 | $700 carried back one year or forward 20 years (10 years for foreign tax credit). |
| Refundable personal credits | (600) | Generates $600 tax refund to Gram. |

# TAXPAYER PREPAYMENTS AND FILING REQUIREMENTS

**LO5**

Even after determining their tax liabilities, taxpayers must still file a tax return and pay any additional tax due or receive a refund. When taxpayers don't pay enough taxes during the year or when they are late filing their tax return or late paying their taxes due, they may be subject to certain penalties.

## Prepayments

The income tax must be paid on a *pay-as-you-go* basis. This means that the tax must be prepaid via **withholding** from salary or through periodic **estimated tax payments** during the tax year. Employees pay tax through withholding, and self-employed taxpayers generally pay taxes through estimated tax payments. Employers are required to withhold taxes from an employee's wages based upon the employee's marital status, exemptions, and estimated annual pay. Wages include both cash and noncash remuneration for services, and employers remit withholdings to the government on behalf of employees. At the end of the year employers report the amounts withheld to each employee via Form W-2. Estimated tax payments are required only if withholdings are insufficient to meet the taxpayer's tax liability. For calendar-year taxpayers, estimated tax payments are due on April 15, June 15, and September 15 of the current year and January 15 of the following year.

**Example 7-27**

Courtney's gross tax liability for the year including federal income tax, alternative minimum tax, and self-employment taxes is $24,377 (see Exhibit 7-5). However, because she had only $21,439 withheld from her paycheck by EWD, she underpaid $2,938 for the year ($24,377 – $21,439). If she had been aware that her withholding would be insufficient, she could have increased her withholding at any time during the year (even in her December paycheck) or made estimated tax payments of $735 on April 15, June 15, and September 15 of 2010 and January 15, 2011 ($2,938/4).

*What if:* If Courtney was self-employed (instead of employed by EWD) and thus had no tax withholdings by an employer, she would be *required* to pay quarterly estimated tax payments. In this scenario, she would need to pay $6,094 ($24,377/4 = $6,094) by April 15, June 15, and September 15 of 2010 and $6,094 by January 15 of 2011 to cover her gross tax liability of $24,377.

**Underpayment Penalties**    When taxpayers like Courtney fall behind on their tax prepayments, they may be subject to an **underpayment penalty.**[42] Taxpayers with unpredictable income streams may be particularly susceptible to this penalty because it is difficult for them to accurately estimate their tax liability for the year. To help taxpayers who may not be able to predict their earnings for the year and to provide some margin of error for those who can, the tax laws provide some **safe-harbor provisions.** Under these provisions taxpayers can avoid underpayment penalties if their withholdings and estimated tax payments equal or exceed one of the following two safe harbors: (1) 90 percent of their *current tax liability* or (2) 100 percent of their *previous year tax liability* (110 percent for individuals with AGI greater than $150,000).

These two safe harbors determine on a quarterly basis the minimum tax prepayments that a taxpayer must have made to avoid the underpayment penalty. The first safe harbor requires that a taxpayer must have paid at least 22.5 percent (90 percent/4 = 22.5 percent) of the *current* year liability via withholdings or estimated tax payments by April 15 to avoid the underpayment penalty for the first quarter. Similarly by June 15, September 15, and January 15, the taxpayer must have paid 45 percent (22.5 percent × 2), 67.5 percent (22.5 percent × 3), and 90 percent (22.5 percent × 4), respectively, of the current year liability via withholding or estimated tax payments to avoid the underpayment penalty in the second, third, and fourth quarters.[43] In determining taxpayers' prepayments for a quarter, tax withholdings are generally treated as though they are withheld evenly through the year. In contrast, estimated tax payments are credited to the taxpayer's account when they are remitted.

**Example 7-28**

Because all of Courtney's prepayments were made through withholding by EWD, the payments are treated as though they were made evenly throughout the year. What are Courtney's actual and required withholdings under the 90 percent safe-harbor provision throughout the year?

*(continued in on page 7-35...)*

---

[42]§6654.

[43]As an alternative method of estimating safe harbor, (1) taxpayers can compute 90 percent of the current liability using the seasonal method. This method allows the taxpayer to estimate 90 percent of their current tax liability by annualizing their taxable income earned through the month prior to the payment date (e.g., through March for April 15, May for June 15, and August for September 15). Taxpayers with uneven taxable income throughout the year with smaller taxable income earlier in the year benefit from this method.

**Answer:** See the following table:

| Dates | (1)<br>Actual Withholding | (2)<br>Required Withholding | (1) − (2)<br>Over (Under) Withheld |
|---|---|---|---|
| April 15, 2010 | $5,360<br>($21,439 × .25) | $5,485<br>($24,377 × .9 × .25) | ($125) |
| June 15, 2010 | $10,720<br>($21,439 × .50) | $10,970<br>($24,377 × .9 × .50) | (250) |
| September 15, 2010 | $16,079<br>($21,439 × .75) | $16,454<br>($24,377 × .9 × .75) | (375) |
| January 15, 2011 | $21,439 | $21,939<br>($24,377 × .9 × 1) | (500) |

It looks like Courtney is underwithheld in each quarter.

The second safe harbor requires that by April 15, June 15, September 15, and January 15, the taxpayer must have paid 25 percent, 50 percent (25 percent × 2), 75 percent (25 percent × 3), and 100 percent (25 percent × 4), respectively, of the *previous* year tax liability via withholding or estimated tax payments to avoid the underpayment penalty in the first, second, third, and fourth quarters.

If the taxpayer does not satisfy either of the safe harbor provisions, the taxpayer can compute the underpayment penalty owed using Form 2210. The underpayment penalty is determined by multiplying the **federal short-term interest rate** plus 3 percentage points by the amount of tax underpayment per quarter. For purposes of this computation, the quarterly tax underpayment is the difference between the taxpayer's quarterly withholding and estimated tax payments and the required minimum tax payment under the first or second safe harbor (whichever is less). If the taxpayer does not complete Form 2210 and remit the underpayment penalty with the taxpayer's tax return, the IRS will compute and assess the penalty for the taxpayer.

**Example 7-29**

In the previous example, we discovered that Courtney was underwithheld in each quarter based on the first (90 percent of current year) safe-harbor provision. Assuming Courtney was underwithheld by even more under the second (100 percent of prior year) safe-harbor provision, she is required to pay an underpayment penalty based on the underpayments determined using the first safe harbor. Assuming the federal short-term rate is 5 percent, what is Courtney's underpayment penalty for 2010?

**Answer:** $26, computed as follows:

| Description | First<br>Quarter | Second<br>Quarter | Third<br>Quarter | Fourth<br>Quarter |
|---|---|---|---|---|
| Underpayment | $ 125 | $250 | $375 | $ 500 |
| Times: federal rate + 3% (5% + 3%) | × 8% | × 8% | × 8% | × 8% |
| | $ 10 | $ 20 | $ 30 | $ 40 |
| Times one quarter of a year[44] | × 25% | × 25% | × 25% | × 25% |
| Underpayment penalty per quarter | $ 3 | $ 5 | $ 8 | $ 10 |

That's a lot of work to figure out a $26 penalty (3 + 5 + 8 + 10 = $26).

[44]Form 2210 actually computes the penalty per quarter based on the number of days in the quarter divided by the number of days in the year. For simplicity, we assume this ratio is 1/4 per quarter.

As a matter of administrative convenience, taxpayers who either (1) had no tax liability in the previous year or (2) whose tax payable after subtracting their withholding amounts (but not estimated payments) is less than $1,000 are not subject to underpayment penalties.

**Example 7-30**

Gram's tax liability for the year is $462 (Example 7-2 amount of $484 less $22 Making work pay credit), but she did not have any taxes withheld during the year, and she did not make any estimated tax payments. What is Gram's underpayment penalty?

**Answer:** $0. Because Gram's $462 tax payable after subtracting her withholding amounts ($462 tax — $0 withholding) is less than $1,000, she is not subject to an underpayment penalty.

---

**THE KEY FACTS**

**Taxpayer Prepayments and Underpayment Penalties**

- Taxpayers prepay their tax via withholding from salary or through periodic estimated tax payments during the tax year.
- Estimated tax payments are required only if withholdings are insufficient to meet the taxpayer's tax liability.
- For calendar-year taxpayers, estimated tax payments are due on April 15, June 15, and September 15 of the current year and January 15 of the following year.
- Taxpayers can avoid an underpayment penalty if their withholdings and estimated tax payments equal or exceed one of two safe harbors.
- The underpayment penalty is determined by multiplying the federal short-term interest rate plus 3 percentage points by the amount of tax underpayment per quarter.

## Filing Requirements

Individual taxpayers are required to file a tax return only if their *gross income* exceeds certain thresholds, which vary based on the taxpayer's filing status and age. However, a taxpayer may prefer to file a tax return even when she is not required to do so. For example, a taxpayer with gross income less than the threshold may want to file a tax return to receive a refund of income taxes withheld. In general, the thresholds are simply the applicable standard deduction amount for the different filing statuses plus the personal exemption amount (twice the personal exemption amount of married taxpayers filing jointly).[45]

Individual tax returns are due on April 15 for calendar-year individuals (the fifteenth day of the fourth month following year-end). If the due date falls on a Saturday, Sunday, or holiday, it is automatically extended to the next day that is not a Saturday, Sunday, or holiday. Taxpayers unable to file a tax return by the original due date can request (by that same deadline) a six-month extension to file, which is granted automatically by the IRS. The extension gives the taxpayer additional time to file the tax return, but does *not* extend the due date for paying the tax.

**Late Filing Penalty**   The tax law imposes a penalty on taxpayers that do not file a tax return by the required date (the original due date plus extension).[46] The penalty equals 5 percent of the amount of tax owed for each month (or fraction thereof) that the tax return is late, with a maximum penalty of 25 percent. For fraudulent failure to file, the penalty is 15 percent of the amount of tax owed per month with a maximum penalty of 75 percent. If the taxpayer owes no tax as of the due date of the tax return (plus extension), the tax law does not impose a **late filing penalty.**

**Late Payment Penalty**   An extension allows the taxpayer to delay filing a tax return but does *not* extend the due date for tax payments. If a taxpayer fails to pay the entire balance of tax owed by the original due date of the tax return, the tax law imposes a **late payment penalty** from the due date of the return until the taxpayer pays the tax.[47] The late payment penalty equals .5 percent of the amount of tax owed for each month (or fraction thereof) that the tax is not paid.

---

[45]§6012. Filing requirements for individuals who are dependents of other taxpayers are subject to special rules that consider the individual's unearned income, earned income, and gross income. See IRS Publication 17 "Your Federal Income Tax."

[46]§6651.

[47]§6651. As we discussed in Chapter 2, the tax law also assesses interest on any tax underpayments until the tax is paid (§6601).

The *combined* maximum penalty that may be imposed for late payment and late filing (nonfraudulent) is 5 percent per month (25 percent in total). For late payment and filing due to fraud, the combined maximum penalty for late payment and late filing is 15 percent per month (75 percent in total).

---

**Example 7-31**

Courtney filed her tax return on April 10 and included a check with the return for $2,964 made payable to the United States Treasury. The $2,964 consisted of her underpaid tax liability of $2,938 (Example 7-27) and her $26 underpayment penalty (Example 7-29).

**What if:** If Courtney had waited until May 1 to file her return and pay her taxes, what late filing and late payment penalties would she owe?

**Answer:** Her combined *late filing penalty* and *late payment penalty* would be $147 ($2,938 late payment × 5 percent × 1 month or portion thereof—the combined penalty is limited to 5 percent per month).

---

## TAX SUMMARY

Courtney's and Gram's net taxes due, including an underpayment penalty for Courtney, are provided in Exhibits 7-12 and 7-14, respectively. Exhibit 7-13 illustrates how this information would be presented on Courtney's tax return by providing Courtney's Form 1040, page 2.

### EXHIBIT 7-12    Courtney's Net Tax Payable

| Description | Amount | Reference |
|---|---|---|
| (1) Regular federal income tax | $22,591.75 | Example 7-3. |
| (2) Alternative minimum tax | 1,303.25 | Example 7-11. |
| (3) Self-employment tax | 482 | Example 7-16. |
| (4) Gross tax | $24,377 | (1) + (2) + (3). |
| (5) Tax credits | 0 | Examples 7-19, 7-23, and 7-25. |
| (6) Prepayments | (21,439) | Example 7-28. |
| (7) Underpayment penalties | 26 | Example 7-30. |
| Tax and penalties due with tax return | $ 2,964 | |

## CONCLUSION

This chapter reviewed the process for determining an individual's gross and net tax liability. We discovered that taxpayers may be required to pay regular federal income tax, alternative minimum tax, and employment-related tax. Taxpayers are able to offset their gross tax liability dollar for dollar with various types of tax credits and by the amount of tax they prepay during the year. Taxpayers must pay additional taxes with their tax return or they may receive a refund when they file their tax return depending on their gross tax liability and their available tax credits and tax prepayments. The prior three chapters have covered the basic individual tax formula. The next three chapters (8–10) address issues relevant for taxpayers involved in business activities. In Chapters 11–14, we dig a little deeper into certain individual income taxation issues.

**EXHIBIT 7-13**    Courtney's Net Tax Payable (as presented on her Form 1040, page 2)

Form 1040 (2009)    Page **2**

| | | | | |
|---|---|---|---|---|
| **Tax and Credits** | 38 | Amount from line 37 (adjusted gross income) | 38 | 162,000 |
| | 39a | Check if: ☐ You were born before January 2, 1945, ☐ Blind. ☐ Spouse was born before January 2, 1945, ☐ Blind. Total boxes checked ▶ 39a | | |
| **Standard Deduction for—** ● People who check any box on line 39a, 39b, or 40b or who can be claimed as a dependent, see page 35. ● All others: Single or Married filing separately, $5,700 Married filing jointly or Qualifying widow(er), $11,400 Head of household, $8,350 | b | If your spouse itemizes on a separate return or you were a dual-status alien, see page 35 and check here ▶ 39b ☑ | | |
| | 40a | **Itemized deductions** (from Schedule A) **or** your **standard deduction** (see left margin) | 40a | 39,793 |
| | b | If you are increasing your standard deduction by certain real estate taxes, new motor vehicle taxes, or a net disaster loss, attach Schedule L and check here (see page 35) . ▶ 40b ☐ | | |
| | 41 | Subtract line 40a from line 38 | 41 | 122,207 |
| | 42 | **Exemptions.** If line 38 is $125,100 or less and you did not provide housing to a Midwestern displaced individual, multiply $3,650 by the number on line 6d. Otherwise, see page 37 | 42 | 10,950 |
| | 43 | **Taxable income.** Subtract line 42 from line 41. If line 42 is more than line 41, enter -0- | 43 | 111,257 |
| | 44 | **Tax** (see page 37). Check if any tax is from: **a** ☐ Form(s) 8814 **b** ☐ Form 4972 | 44 | 22,592 |
| | 45 | **Alternative minimum tax** (see page 40). Attach Form 6251 | 45 | 1,303 |
| | 46 | Add lines 44 and 45 ▶ | 46 | 23,895 |
| | 47 | Foreign tax credit. Attach Form 1116 if required . . . 47 | | |
| | 48 | Credit for child and dependent care expenses. Attach Form 2441 . 48 | | |
| | 49 | Education credits from Form 8863, line 29 . . . 49 | | |
| | 50 | Retirement savings contributions credit. Attach Form 8880 50 | | |
| | 51 | Child tax credit (see page 42) . . . . . . 51 | | |
| | 52 | Credits from Form: **a** ☐ 8396 **b** ☐ 8839 **c** ☐ 5695 52 | | |
| | 53 | Other credits from Form: **a** ☐ 3800 **b** ☐ 8801 **c** ☐ 53 | | |
| | 54 | Add lines 47 through 53. These are your **total credits** | 54 | |
| | 55 | Subtract line 54 from line 46. If line 54 is more than line 46, enter -0- ▶ | 55 | 23,895 |
| **Other Taxes** | 56 | Self-employment tax. Attach Schedule SE | 56 | 482 |
| | 57 | Unreported social security and Medicare tax from Form: **a** ☐ 4137 **b** ☐ 8919 | 57 | |
| | 58 | Additional tax on IRAs, other qualified retirement plans, etc. Attach Form 5329 if required | 58 | |
| | 59 | Additional taxes: **a** ☐ AEIC payments **b** ☐ Household employment taxes. Attach Schedule H | 59 | |
| | 60 | Add lines 55 through 59. This is your **total tax** ▶ | 60 | 24,377 |
| **Payments** If you have a qualifying child, attach Schedule EIC. | 61 | Federal income tax withheld from Forms W-2 and 1099 . . 61 21,439 | | |
| | 62 | 2009 estimated tax payments and amount applied from 2008 return 62 | | |
| | 63 | Making work pay and government retiree credits. Attach Schedule M 63 | | |
| | 64a | **Earned income credit (EIC)** . . . . . 64a | | |
| | b | Nontaxable combat pay election 64b | | |
| | 65 | Additional child tax credit. Attach Form 8812 . . . 65 | | |
| | 66 | Refundable education credit from Form 8863, line 16 . . 66 | | |
| | 67 | First-time homebuyer credit. Attach Form 5405 . . . 67 | | |
| | 68 | Amount paid with request for extension to file (see page 72) . 68 | | |
| | 69 | Excess social security and tier 1 RRTA tax withheld (see page 72) 69 | | |
| | 70 | Credits from Form: **a** ☐ 2439 **b** ☐ 4136 **c** ☐ 8801 **d** ☐ 8885 70 | | |
| | 71 | Add lines 61, 62, 63, 64a, and 65 through 70. These are your **total payments** ▶ | 71 | 21,439 |
| **Refund** Direct deposit? See page 73 and fill in 73b, 73c, and 73d, or Form 8888. | 72 | If line 71 is more than line 60, subtract line 60 from line 71. This is the amount you **overpaid** | 72 | |
| | 73a | Amount of line 72 you want **refunded to you.** If Form 8888 is attached, check here ▶ ☐ | 73a | |
| | b | Routing number ▶ c Type: ☐ Checking ☐ Savings | | |
| | d | Account number | | |
| | 74 | Amount of line 72 you want **applied to your 2010 estimated tax** ▶ 74 | | |
| **Amount You Owe** | 75 | **Amount you owe.** Subtract line 71 from line 60. For details on how to pay, see page 74 ▶ | 75 | 2,938 |
| | 76 | Estimated tax penalty (see page 74) . . . . 76 26 | | |

**Third Party Designee**    Do you want to allow another person to discuss this return with the IRS (see page 75)? ☐ **Yes.** Complete the following. ☐ **No**
Designee's name ▶    Phone no. ▶    Personal identification number (PIN)

**Sign Here**    Under penalties of perjury, I declare that I have examined this return and accompanying schedules and statements, and to the best of my knowledge and belief, they are true, correct, and complete. Declaration of preparer (other than taxpayer) is based on all information of which preparer has any knowledge.
Joint return? See page 15. Keep a copy for your records.
Your signature | Date | Your occupation | Daytime phone number
Spouse's signature. If a joint return, **both** must sign. | Date | Spouse's occupation

**Paid Preparer's Use Only**
Preparer's signature ▶ | Date | Check if self-employed ☐ | Preparer's SSN or PTIN
Firm's name (or yours if self-employed), address, and ZIP code ▶ | EIN | Phone no.

Form **1040** (2009)

**EXHIBIT 7-14**    Gram's Tax Payable

| Description | Amount | Explanation |
|---|---|---|
| (1) Gross tax | $484 | Example 7-2. |
| (2) Alternative minimum tax | 0 | |
| (3) Self-employment tax | 0 | |
| (4) Gross tax | $484 | (1) + (2) + (3). |
| (5) Tax Credits | 22 | Making work pay credit ($350 × .062) |
| (6) Prepayments | 0 | |
| (7) Penalties | 0 | |
| Tax due with return | $462 | (4) − (5) − (6) − (7). |

## SUMMARY

Determine a taxpayer's regular tax liability and identify tax issues associated with the process.

**L01**

- Individual income is taxed using progressive tax rate schedules with rates ranging from 10 percent to 35 percent.
- Marginal tax rates depend on filing status and amount of taxable income.
- Progressive tax rate schedules may lead to either a marriage penalty or a marriage benefit for married taxpayers.
- Long-term capital gains and qualified dividends are taxed at either a 0 percent or 15 percent rate, depending on the amount of taxable income.
- Strategies to shift investment income from parents to children are limited by the "kiddic tax" whereby children's investment income is taxed at the parents' marginal tax rate.

Compute a taxpayer's alternative minimum tax liability and describe the tax characteristics of taxpayers most likely to owe the alternative minimum tax.

**L02**

- The AMT was designed to ensure that higher-income taxpayers pay some minimum level of income tax.
- The AMT base is broader than the regular income tax base. The AMT base is designed to more closely reflect economic income than is regular taxable income.
- The starting point for calculating AMT is regular taxable income. To compute AMTI, taxpayers add back items not deductible for AMT purposes. In some cases, taxpayers may subtract items not includible in AMTI and items deductible for AMT but not for regular tax purposes. Taxpayers then subtract the allowable AMT exemption to generate the AMT base. They then apply the AMT rates and compare the product (the tentative minimum tax) to their regular tax liability. They owe AMT if the tentative minimum tax exceeds the regular tax liability.
- The AMT exemption depends on the taxpayer's filing status and is subject to phase-out of 25 cents for each dollar of AMTI over the specific thresholds based on filing status.
- The AMT tax rates are 26 percent (up to $175,000 of AMT base) and 28 percent thereafter. However, long-term capital gains and qualified dividends are subject to the same preferential rate they are taxed at for regular tax purposes.
- The amount of the AMT is the excess of the tentative minimum tax over the taxpayer's regular tax liability.

Calculate a taxpayer's employment and self-employment taxes payable and explain tax considerations relating to whether a taxpayer is considered to be an employee or a self-employed independent contractor.

**L03**

- Employees' wages are subject to FICA tax. The Social Security component is 6.2 percent and the Medicare component is 1.45 percent. The Social Security tax applies to the first $106,800 of income in 2010. The wage base on the Medicare tax is unlimited.
- Self-employed taxpayers pay self-employment tax on their net self-employment income (92.35 percent of their net Schedule C income). They pay Social Security tax of 12.4 percent and Medicare tax of 2.9 percent on their net self-employment income. The Social Security tax applies to the first $106,800 of net Schedule C income in 2010. The base for the Medicare tax is unlimited.
- The decision of whether a worker should be treated as an independent contractor or as an employee for tax purposes is a subjective test based in large part on the extent of control the worker has over things such as the nature, timing, and location of work performed.
- Independent contractors are able to deduct ordinary and necessary business expenses as *for* AGI deductions. Employees incurring unreimbursed business expenses must

deduct the items as miscellaneous itemized deductions subject to the 2 percent of AGI floor.

- Independent contractors may deduct one-half of their self-employment taxes paid during the year. Employees may not deduct their FICA taxes.

- Independent contractors are required to pay self-employment tax, which is nearly double the amount they must pay in FICA taxes as employees. Further, independent contractors must pay estimated taxes on their income because the employer does not withhold taxes from the independent contractor's paychecks.

- Hiring independent contractors is generally less costly for employers than is hiring employees. Employers do not pay FICA taxes, withhold taxes, or provide fringe benefits for independent contractors.

**LO4** Describe the different general types of tax credits, identify specific tax credits, and compute a taxpayer's allowable child tax credit, child and dependent care credit, American opportunity credit, lifetime learning credit, making work pay credit, and earned income credit.

- Tax credits are generally classified into one of three categories, business, nonrefundable personal, or refundable personal credits.

- Nonrefundable personal tax credits provide tax relief to specified groups of individuals.

- The child tax credit is a $1,000 credit for low-income taxpayers who provide a home for dependent children under the age of 17.

- The child and dependent care credit is provided to help taxpayers pay the cost of providing care for their dependents to allow taxpayers to work or to look for work.

- The American opportunity credit provides a credit for a percentage of the costs of the first four years of a student's college education. Forty percent of the credit is refundable.

- The lifetime learning credit provides a credit for a percentage of the costs for instruction in a postsecondary degree program, or to acquire or improve a taxpayer's job skills.

- Nonrefundable credits are first used to reduce a taxpayer's gross tax but cannot reduce the gross tax below zero. Any excess credit is lost unless it is allowed to be carried to a different tax year.

- The making work pay credit is a refundable credit designed to offset a limited amount of a taxpayer's Social Security tax.

- The earned income credit is refundable but subject to a very complex calculation.

- Business credits reduce the tax after applying nonrefundable credits. Any credit in excess of the remaining tax is generally allowed to be carried over or back to be used in other years.

- Refundable credits are the last credit applied to the tax after applying nonrefundable and business credits. Any refundable credit in excess of the remaining tax is treated as an overpayment and refunded to the taxpayer.

**LO5** Explain taxpayer filing and tax payment requirements and describe in general terms how to compute a taxpayer's underpayment, late filing, and late payment penalties.

- The income tax must be prepaid via withholding from salary or through periodic estimated tax payments during the tax year. Estimated tax payments are required only if withholdings are insufficient to meet the taxpayer's tax liability. For calendar-year taxpayers, estimated tax payments are due on April 15, June 15, and September 15 of the current year and January 15 of the following year.

- Taxpayers can avoid an underpayment penalty if their withholdings and estimated tax payments equal or exceed one of two safe harbors (90 percent of current year tax, 100 percent of previous year tax, or 110% if AGI exceeds $150,000). If the taxpayer does not satisfy either of the safe-harbor provisions, the underpayment penalty is determined by multiplying the federal short-term interest rate plus 3 percentage points by the amount of tax underpayment per quarter.

- Individual taxpayers are required to file a tax return only if their *gross income* exceeds certain thresholds, which vary based on the taxpayer's filing status, age, and gross income.

- Individual tax returns are due on April 15 for calendar-year individuals. Taxpayers unable to file a tax return by the original due date can request a six-month extension to file.
- The tax law imposes penalties on taxpayers that do not file a tax return (by the original due date plus extension) or pay the tax owed (by the original due date). The failure to file penalty equals 5 percent of the amount of tax owed for each month (or fraction thereof) that the tax return is late with a maximum penalty of 25 percent. The late payment penalty equals .5 percent of the amount of tax owed for each month (or fraction thereof) that the tax is not paid. The combined maximum penalty that may be imposed for late filing and late payment is 5 percent per month (25 percent in total). The late filing and late payment penalties are higher if fraud is involved.

## KEY TERMS

alternative minimum tax (AMT) (7-8)

alternative minimum tax adjustments (7-9)

alternative minimum tax base (AMT base) (7-9)

alternative minimum tax exemption (7-11)

alternative minimum tax system (7-8)

business tax credits (7-30)

child tax credits (7-22)

earned income credit (7-29)

employee (7-19)

estimated tax payments (7-33)

federal short-term interest rate (7-35)

FICA taxes (7-14)

independent contractor (7-19)

kiddie tax (7-6)

late filing penalty (7-36)

late payment penalty (7-36)

marginal tax rate (7-4)

marriage benefit (7-3)

marriage penalty (7-3)

Medicare tax (7-14)

minimum tax credit (7-13)

net earnings from self-employment (7-16)

net unearned income (7-7)

nonrefundable credit (7-22)

preferential tax rate (7-4)

preferentially taxed income (7-5)

refundable credits (7-28)

safe-harbor provisions (7-34)

Schedule C (7-16)

self-employment taxes (7-16)

Social Security tax (7-14)

tax bracket (7-2)

tax credits (7-22)

tax rate schedule (7-2)

tax tables (7-3)

tentative minimum tax (7-9)

underpayment penalty (7-34)

withholding (7-33)

## DISCUSSION QUESTIONS

1. **(LO1)** What is a tax bracket? What is the relationship between filing status and the width of the tax brackets in the tax rate schedule?

2. **(LO1)** In 2010, for a taxpayer with $50,000 of taxable income, without doing any actual computations, which filing status do you expect to provide the lowest tax liability? Which filing status provides the highest tax liability?

3. **(LO1)** What is the tax marriage penalty and when does it apply? Under what circumstances would a couple experience a tax marriage benefit?

4. **(LO1)** Once they've computed their taxable income, how do taxpayers determine their regular tax liability? What additional steps must taxpayers take to compute their tax liability when they have preferentially taxed income?

5. **(LO1)** Are there circumstances in which preferentially taxed income (long-term capital gains and qualified dividends) is taxed at the same rate as ordinary income? Explain.

6. **(LO1)** Augustana received $10,000 of qualified dividends this year. Under what circumstances would all $10,000 be taxed at the same rate? Under

what circumstances might the entire $10,000 of income not be taxed at the same rate?

7. **(LO1)** What is the difference between earned and unearned income?

8. **(LO1)** Does the kiddie tax eliminate the tax benefits gained by a family when parents transfer income-producing assets to children? Explain.

9. **(LO1)** Does the kiddie tax apply to all children no matter their age? Explain.

10. **(LO1)** What is the kiddie tax and on whose tax return is the kiddie tax liability reported? Explain.

11. **(LO1)** Lauren is 17 years old. She reports earned income of $3,000 and unearned income of $2,000. Is it likely that she is subject to the kiddie tax? Explain.

12. **(LO2)** In very general terms, how is the alternative minimum tax system different from the regular income tax system? How is it similar?

13. **(LO2)** Describe, in general terms, why Congress implemented the AMT.

14. **(LO2)** Do taxpayers always add back the standard deduction when computing alternative minimum taxable income? Explain.

15. **(LO2)** The starting point for computing alternative minimum taxable income is regular taxable income. What are some of the plus adjustments, plus or minus adjustments, and minus adjustments to regular taxable income to compute alternative minimum taxable income?

16. **(LO2)** Describe what the AMT exemption is and who is and isn't allowed to deduct the exemption. How is it similar to the standard deduction and how is it dissimilar?

17. **(LO1, LO2)** How do the AMT tax rates compare to the regular income tax rates?

18. **(LO2)** Is it possible for a taxpayer who pays AMT to have a marginal tax rate higher than the stated AMT rate? Explain.

19. **(LO2)** What is the difference between the tentative minimum tax (TMT) and the AMT?

20. **(LO2)** Why is it that an increasing number of taxpayers are forced to pay the AMT?

■ planning     21. **(LO2)** Lee is single and he runs his own business. He uses the cash method of accounting to determine his business income. Near the end of the year, Lee performed work that he needs to bill a client for. The value of his services is $5,000. Lee figures that if he immediately takes the time to put the bill together and send it out, the client will pay him before year-end. However, if he doesn't send out the bill for one week, he won't receive the client's payment until the beginning of next year. Lee expects that he will owe AMT this year and that his AMT base will be around $200,000 before counting any of the additional business income. Further, Lee anticipates that he will not owe AMT next year. He anticipates his regular taxable income next year will be in the $200,000 range. Would you advise Lee to immediately bill his client or to wait? What factors would you consider in making your recommendation?

22. **(LO3)** Are an employee's entire wages subject to the FICA tax? Explain.

23. **(LO3)** Bobbie works as an employee for Altron Corp. for the first half of the year and for Betel Inc. for rest of the year. She is relatively well paid. What FICA tax issues is she likely to encounter? What FICA tax issues do Altron Corp. and Betel Inc. need to consider?

24. **(LO3)** Compare and contrast an employee's FICA tax payment responsibilities with those of a self-employed taxpayer.

25. **(LO3)** When a taxpayer works as an employee and as a self-employed independent contractor during the year, how does the taxpayer determine her employment and self-employment taxes payable?

26. **(LO3)** What are the primary factors to consider when deciding whether a worker should be considered an employee or a self-employed taxpayer for tax purposes?

27. **(LO3)** How do the tax consequences of being an employee differ from those of being self-employed?

28. **(LO3)** Mike wanted to work for a CPA firm but he also wanted to work on his father's farm in Montana. Because the CPA firm wanted Mike to be happy, they offered to let him work for them as an independent contractor during the fall and winter and let him return to Montana to work for his father during the spring and summer. He was very excited to hear that they were also going to give him a 5 percent higher "salary" for the six months he would be working for the firm over what he would have made over the same six-month period if he worked full-time as an employee. Should Mike be excited about his 5 percent raise? Why or why not? What counter offer could Mike reasonably suggest?    ■ **planning**

29. **(LO4)** How are tax credits and tax deductions similar? How are they dissimilar?

30. **(LO4)** What are the three types of tax credits, and explain why it is important to distinguish between the different types of tax credits.

31. **(LO4)** Explain why there is such a large number and variety of tax credits.

32. **(LO4)** What is the difference between a refundable and nonrefundable tax credit?

33. **(LO4)** Is the child tax credit a refundable or nonrefundable credit? Explain.

34. **(LO4)** Diane has a job working three-quarter time. She hired her mother to take care of her two small children so Diane could work. Do Diane's child care payments to her mother qualify for the child and dependent care credit? Explain.

35. **(LO4)** The amount of the child and dependent care credit is based on the amount of the taxpayer's expenditures to provide care for one or more qualifying persons. Who is considered to be a qualifying person for this purpose?

36. **(LO4)** Compare and contrast the lifetime learning credit with the American opportunity credit.

37. **(LO4)** Jennie's grandfather paid her tuition this fall to State University (an eligible educational institution). Jennie is claimed as a dependent by her parents, but she also files her own tax return. Can Jennie claim an education credit for the tuition paid by her grandfather? What difference would it make, if any, if Jennie did not qualify as a dependent of her parents (or anyone else)?    ■ **research**

38. **(LO4)** True or False? The making work pay credit is designed to eliminate the burden of Social Security tax on a certain amount of income. Explain.

39. **(LO4)** Why is the earned income credit referred to as a negative income tax?

40. **(LO4)** Under what circumstances can a college student qualify for the earned income credit?

41. **(LO4)** How are business credits similar to personal credits? How are they dissimilar?

42. **(LO4)** Is the foreign tax credit a personal credit or a business credit? Explain.

43. **(LO4)** When a U.S. taxpayer pays income taxes to a foreign government, what options does the taxpayer have when determining how to treat the expenditure on her U.S. individual income tax return?

44. **(LO4)** Describe the order in which different types of tax credits are applied to reduce a taxpayer's tax liability.

45. **(LO5)** Describe the two methods that taxpayers use to prepay their taxes.

46. **(LO5)** What are the consequences of a taxpayer underpaying his or her tax liability throughout the year? Explain the safe-harbor provisions that may apply in this situation.

47. **(LO5)** Describe how the underpayment penalty is calculated.

48. **(LO5)** What determines if a taxpayer is required to file a tax return? If a taxpayer is not required to file a tax return, does this mean that the taxpayer should not file a tax return?

49. **(LO5)** What is the due date for individual tax returns? What extensions are available?

50. **(LO5)** Describe the consequences for failing to file a tax return and for paying tax owed late.

## PROBLEMS

51. **(LO1)** Whitney received $75,000 of taxable income in 2010. All of the income was salary from her employer. What is her income tax liability in each of the following alternative situations?

    a. She files under the single filing status.
    b. She files a joint tax return with her spouse. Together their taxable income is $75,000.
    c. She is married but files a separate tax return. Her taxable income is $75,000.
    d. She files as a head of household.

52. **(LO1)** In 2010, Lisa and Fred, a married couple, have taxable income of $300,000. If they were to file separate tax returns, Lisa would have reported taxable income of $125,000 and Fred would have reported taxable income of $175,000. What is the couple's marriage penalty or benefit?

53. **(LO1)** In 2010, Jasmine and Thomas, a married couple, have taxable income of $150,000. If they were to file separate tax returns, Jasmine would have reported taxable income of $140,000 and Thomas would have reported taxable income of $10,000. What is the couple's marriage penalty or benefit?

54. **(LO1)** Lacy is a single taxpayer. In 2010, her taxable income is $37,000. What is her tax liability in each of the following alternative situations?

    a. All of her income is salary from her employer.
    b. Her $37,000 of taxable income includes $2,000 of qualified dividends.
    c. Her $37,000 of taxable income includes $5,000 of qualified dividends.

55. **(LO1)** Henrich is a single taxpayer. In 2010, his taxable income is $85,000. What is his tax liability in each of the following alternative scenarios?

    a. All of his income is salary from his employer.
    b. His $85,000 of taxable income includes $2,000 of long-term capital gain that is taxed at preferential rates.
    c. His $85,000 of taxable income includes $55,000 of long-term capital gain that is taxed at preferential rates.

56. **(LO1)** In 2010, Sheryl is claimed as a dependent on her parents' tax return. Her parents' ordinary income marginal tax rate is 35 percent. Sheryl did not provide more than half her own support. What is Sheryl's tax liability for the year in each of the following alternative circumstances?

   a. She received $7,000 from a part-time job. This was her only source of income. She is 16 years old at year-end.

   b. She received $7,000 of interest income from corporate bonds she received several years ago. This is her only source of income. She is 16 years old at year-end.

   c. She received $7,000 of interest income from corporate bonds she received several years ago. This is her only source of income. She is 20 years old at year-end and is a full-time student.

   d. She received $7,000 of qualified dividend income. This is her only source of income. She is 16 years old at year-end.

57. **(LO2)** Brooklyn files as a head of household for 2010 and claims a total of three personal exemptions (3 × $3,650 = $10,950). She claimed the standard deduction of $8,400 for regular tax purposes. Her regular taxable income was $80,000. What is Brooklyn's AMTI?

58. **(LO2)** Sylvester files as a single taxpayer during 2010 and claims one personal exemption. He itemizes deductions for regular tax purposes. He paid charitable contributions of $7,000, real estate taxes of $1,000, state income taxes of $4,000, and interest on a home-equity loan of $2,000. Sylvester's regular taxable income is $100,000.

   a. What is Sylvester's AMTI if he used the home-equity proceeds to purchase a car?

   b. What is Sylvester's AMTI if he used the home-equity loan proceeds to build a new garage next to his home?

59. **(LO2)** In 2010, Nadia has $100,000 of regular taxable income. She itemizes her deductions as follows: real property taxes of $1,500, state income taxes of $2,000, and mortgage interest expense of $10,000 (not a home-equity loan). In addition, she receives tax-exempt interest of $1,000 from a municipal bond (issued in 2006) that was used to fund a new business building for a (formerly) out-of-state employer. Finally, she received a state tax refund of $300 from the prior year.

   a. What is Nadia's AMTI this year if she deducted $15,000 of itemized deductions last year (she did not owe any AMT last year)?

   b. What is Nadia's AMTI this year if she deducted the standard deduction last year (she did not owe any AMT last year)?

60. **(LO2)** In 2010, Sven is single and has $120,000 of regular taxable income. He itemizes his deductions as follows: real property tax of $2,000, state income tax of $4,000, mortgage interest expense of $15,000 (not a home-equity loan). He also paid $2,000 in tax preparation fees and has a positive AMT depreciation adjustment of $500. What is Sven's alternative minimum taxable income (AMTI)?

61. **(LO2)** Olga is married and files a joint tax return with her husband. What amount of AMT exemption may she deduct under each of the following alternative circumstances? (Use 2009 exemption amounts.)

   a. Her AMTI is $90,000.

   b. Her AMTI is $180,000.

   c. Her AMTI is $450,000.

62. **(LO2)** Corbett's AMTI is $130,000. What is his AMT exemption under the following alternative circumstances? (Use 2009 exemption amounts.)

a. He is married and files a joint return.

b. He is married and files a separate return.

c. His filing status is single.

d. His filing status is head of household.

63. **(LO2)** In 2010, Juanita is married and files a joint tax return with her husband. What is her tentative minimum tax in each of the following alternative circumstances?

a. Her AMT base is $100,000, all ordinary income.

b. Her AMT base is $250,000, all ordinary income.

c. Her AMT base is $100,000, which includes $10,000 of qualified dividends.

d. Her AMT base is $250,000, which includes $10,000 of qualified dividends.

64. **(LO2)** Steve's tentative minimum tax (TMT) for 2010 is $15,000. What is his AMT if

a. His regular tax is $10,000?

b. His regular tax is $20,000?

65. **(LO2)** In 2010, Janet and Ray are married filing jointly. They have five dependent children under 18 years of age. The couple's AGI is $180,000 and their taxable income is $140,000. They itemize their deductions as follows: real property taxes of $5,000, state income taxes of $9,000, and mortgage interest expense of $15,000 (not a home-equity loan). What is Janet and Ray's AMT? (Use 2009 exemption amounts.)

66. **(LO3)** Brooke works for Company A for all of 2010, earning a salary of $50,000.

a. What is her FICA tax obligation for the year?

b. Assume Brooke works for Company A for half of 2010, earning $50,000 in salary, and she works for Company B for the second half of 2010, earning $70,000 in salary. What is Brooke's FICA tax obligation for the year?

67. **(LO3)** Rasheed works for Company A, earning $350,000 in salary during 2010. Assuming he has no other sources of income, what amount of FICA tax will Rasheed pay for the year?

68. **(LO3)** Alice is self-employed in 2010. Her net business profit on her Schedule C for the year is $140,000. What is her self-employment tax liability for 2010?

69. **(LO3)** Kyle worked as a free-lance software engineer for the first three months of 2010. During that time, he earned $44,000 of self-employment income. On April 1, 2010, Kyle took a job as a full-time software engineer with one of his former clients, Hoogle Inc. From April through the end of the year, Kyle earned $78,000 in salary. What amount of self-employment/FICA tax does Kyle owe for the year?

70. **(LO3)** Eva received $60,000 in compensation payments from JAZZ Corp. during 2010. Eva incurred $5,000 in business expenses relating to her work for JAZZ Corp. JAZZ did not reimburse Eva for any of these expenses. Eva is single and she deducts a standard deduction of $5,700 and a personal exemption of $3,650. Based on these facts answer the following questions:

a. Assume that Eva is considered to be an *employee*. What amount of FICA taxes is she required to pay for the year?

b. Assume that Eva is considered to be an *employee*. What is her regular income tax liability for the year?

c. Assume that Eva is considered to be a *self-employed contractor*. What is her self-employment tax liability for the year?

d. Assume that Eva is considered to be a *self-employed contractor*. What is her regular tax liability for the year?

71. **(LO3)** Terry Hutchison worked as a self-employed lawyer until two years ago when he retired. He used the cash method of accounting in his business for tax purposes. Five years ago, Terry represented his client ABC corporation in an antitrust lawsuit against XYZ corporation. During that year, Terry paid self-employment taxes on all of his income. ABC won the lawsuit but Terry and ABC could not agree on the amount of his earnings. Finally, this year, the issue got resolved and ABC paid Terry $90,000 for the services he provided five years ago. Terry plans to include the payment in his gross income, but because he spends most of his time playing golf and absolutely no time working on legal matters, he does not intend to pay self-employment taxes on the income. Is Terry subject to self-employment taxes on this income? ■ research

72. **(LO4)** Trey claims a dependency exemption for both of his two daughters, ages 14 and 17, at year-end. Trey files a joint return with his wife. What amount of child credit will Trey be able to claim for his daughters under each of the following alternative situations?

a. His AGI is $100,000.

b. His AGI is $120,000.

c. His AGI is $122,100, and his daughters are ages 10 and 12.

73. **(LO4)** Julie paid a day care center to watch her two-year-old son while she worked as a computer programmer for a local start-up company. What amount of child and dependent care credit can Julie claim in each of the following alternative scenarios?

a. Julie paid $2,000 to the day care center and her AGI is $50,000 (all salary).

b. Julie paid $5,000 to the day care center and her AGI is $50,000 (all salary).

c. Julie paid $4,000 to the day care center and her AGI is $25,000 (all salary).

d. Julie paid $2,000 to the day care center and her AGI is $14,000 (all salary).

e. Julie paid $4,000 to the day care center and her AGI is $14,000 ($2,000 salary and $12,000 unearned income).

74. **(LO4)** In 2010, Elaine paid $2,800 of tuition and $600 for books for her dependent son to attend State University this past fall as a freshman. Elaine files a joint return with her husband. What is the maximum American opportunity credit that Elaine can claim for the tuition payment in each of the following alternative situations?

a. Elaine's AGI is $80,000.

b. Elaine's AGI is $168,000.

c. Elaine's AGI is $184,000.

75. **(LO4)** Amy paid $3,200 of qualified tuition and related expenses for her son Bryan to attend State University as a freshman. Can Amy claim a American opportunity credit for part of the tuition costs and a lifetime learning credit for the remaining tuition costs?

76. **(LO4)** In 2010, Laureen is currently single. She paid $2,800 of qualified tuition and related expenses for each of her twin daughters Sheri and Meri to attend State University as freshmen ($2,800 each for a total of $5,600). Sheri and Meri qualify as Laureen's dependents. Laureen also paid $1,900 for her son Ryan's (also ■ planning

Laureen's dependent) tuition and related expenses to attend his junior year at State University. Finally, Laureen paid $1,200 for herself to attend seminars at a community college to help her improve her job skills. What is the maximum amount of education credits Laureen can claim for these expenditures in each of the following alternative scenarios? (Assume the for AGI deduction for qualified education expenses is extended to 2010.)

a. Laureen's AGI is $45,000. If Laureen claims education credits is she allowed to deduct as *for* AGI expenses tuition costs for her daughters that do not generate credits? Explain.

b. Laureen's AGI is $95,000. What options does Laureen have for deducting her continuing education costs to the extent the costs don't generate a credit?

c. Laureen's AGI is $45,000 and Laureen paid $12,000 (not $1,900) for Ryan to attend graduate school (his fifth year not his junior year).

77. **(LO4)** What is Karen's making work pay credit in each of the following alternative scenarios?

a. Karen is single. For the year, she received a salary of $30,000 and reported dividend income of $6,000 (AGI is $36,000).

b. Karen is single. For the year, she received a salary of $4,000 (also AGI).

c. Karen is single. For the year, she received a salary of $90,000 (also AGI).

d. Karen is single. For the year, she received a salary of $150,000 (also AGI).

e. Karen is married and files a joint return. For the year, she received a salary of $70,000 and her husband Craig received a salary of $60,000 (the couple's AGI is $130,000).

78. **(LO4)** In 2010, Amanda and Jaxon Stuart have a daughter who is one year old. The Stuarts are full-time students and they are both 23 years old. Their only sources of income are gains from stock they held for three years before selling and wages from part-time jobs. What is their earned income credit in the following alternative scenarios?

a. Their AGI is $15,000, consisting of $5,000 of capital gains and $10,000 of wages.

b. Their AGI is $15,000, consisting of $10,000 of alimony (unearned income) and $5,000 of wages.

c. Their AGI is $25,000, consisting of $20,000 of wages and $5,000 of alimony (unearned income).

d. Their AGI is $25,000, consisting of $5,000 of wages and $20,000 of alimony (unearned income).

e. Their AGI is $10,000, consisting of $10,000 of alimony (unearned income).

79. **(LO4)** In 2010, Zach is single with no dependents. He is not claimed as a dependent on another's return. All of his income is from salary and he does not have any *for* AGI deductions. What is his earned income credit in the following alternative scenarios?

a. Zach is 29 years old and his AGI is $5,000.

b. Zach is 29 years old and his AGI is $10,000.

c. Zach is 29 years old and his AGI is $19,000.

d. Zach is 24 years old and his AGI is $5,000.

80. **(LO4)** This year Luke has calculated his gross tax liability at $1,800. Luke is entitled to a $2,400 nonrefundable personal tax credit, a $1,500 business tax credit, and a $600 refundable personal tax credit. In addition, Luke has had $2,300 of income taxes withheld from his salary. What is Luke's net tax due or refund?

81. **(LO5)** This year Lloyd, a single taxpayer, estimates that his tax liability will be $10,000. Last year, his total tax liability was $15,000. He estimates that his tax withholding from his employer will be $7,800.      ■ planning

    a. Is Lloyd required to increase his withholding or make estimated tax payments this year to avoid the underpayment penalty? If so, how much?

    b. Assuming Lloyd does not make any additional payments, what is the amount of his underpayment penalty? Assume the federal short-term rate is 5 percent.

82. **(LO5)** This year, Paula and Simon (married filing jointly) estimate that their tax liability will be $200,000. Last year, their total tax liability was $170,000. They estimate that their tax withholding from their employers will be $175,000. Are Paula and Simon required to increase their withholdings or make estimated tax payments this year to avoid the underpayment penalty? If so, how much?      ■ planning

83. **(LO5)** This year, Santhosh, a single taxpayer, estimates that his tax liability will be $100,000. Last year, his total tax liability was $15,000. He estimates that his tax withholding from his employer will be $35,000. Is Santhosh required to increase his withholding or make estimated tax payments this year to avoid the underpayment penalty? If so, how much?      ■ planning

84. **(LO5)** For the following taxpayers, determine if they are required to file a tax return in 2010.

    a. Ricko, single taxpayer, with gross income of $12,000.

    b. Fantasia, head of household, with gross income of $17,500.

    c. Ken and Barbie, married taxpayers with no dependents, with gross income of $12,000.

    d. Dorothy and Rudolf, married taxpayers, both age 68, with gross income of $19,000.

    e. Janyce, single taxpayer, age 73, with gross income of $12,500.

85. **(LO5)** For the following taxpayers, determine the due date of their tax returns.

    a. Jerome, a single taxpayer, is not requesting an extension this year. Assume the due date falls on a Tuesday.

    b. Lashaunda, a single taxpayer, requests an extension this year. Assume the extended due date falls on a Wednesday.

    c. Barney and Betty, married taxpayers, do not request an extension this year. Assume the due date falls on a Sunday.

    d. Fred and Wilma, married taxpayers, request an extension this year. Assume the extended date falls on a Saturday.

86. **(LO5)** Determine the amount of the late filing and late payment penalties that apply for the following taxpayers.      ■ planning

    a. Jolene filed her tax return by its original due date but did not pay the $2,000 in taxes she owed with the return until one and a half months later.

    b. Oscar filed his tax return and paid his $3,000 tax liability seven months late.

    c. Wilfred, attempting to evade his taxes, did not file a tax return or pay his $10,000 in taxes for several years.

# COMPREHENSIVE PROBLEMS

87. In 2010, Jack and Diane Heart are married with two children, ages 10 and 12. Jack works full-time and earns an annual salary of $75,000, while Diane works as a substitute teacher and earns approximately $25,000 per year. Jack and Diane expect to file jointly and do not itemize their deductions. In the fall of

this year, Diane was offered a full-time teaching position that would pay her an additional $20,000.

a. Calculate the marginal tax rate on the additional income, *excluding employment taxes,* to help Jack and Diane evaluate the offer.

b. Calculate the marginal tax rate on the additional income, *including employment taxes,* to help Jack and Diane evaluate the offer.

c. Calculate the marginal tax rate on the additional income, *including self-employment taxes,* if Diane earned an additional $20,000 as self-employed contractor instead of as an employee.

■ planning

88. Matt and Carrie are married, have two children, and file a joint return. Their daughter Katie is 19 years old and was a full-time student at State University. During 2010, she completed her freshman year and one semester as a sophomore. Katie's expenses while she was away at school during the year were as follows:

| Tuition | $5,000 |
|---|---|
| Class fees | 300 |
| Books | 500 |
| Room and board | 4,500 |

Katie received a half-tuition scholarship that paid for $2,500 of her tuition costs. Katie's parents paid the rest of these expenses. Matt and Carrie are able to claim Carrie as a dependent on their tax return.

Matt and Carrie's 23-year-old son Todd also attended graduate school (fifth year of college) full time at a nearby college. Todd's expenses while away at school were as follows:

| Tuition | $3,000 |
|---|---|
| Class fees | 0 |
| Books | 250 |
| Room and board | 4,000 |

Todd paid for his own tuition and books, but Matt and Carrie paid for his room and board.

Since Matt and Carrie still benefit from claiming Todd as a dependent on their tax return, they decided to provide Todd with additional financial assistance by making the payments on Todd's outstanding loans. Todd used the proceeds from these loans to pay his tuition costs. Besides paying off some of the loan principal, Matt and Carrie paid a total of $900 of interest on the loan.

This year Carrie decided to take some classes at the local community college to help improve her skills as a schoolteacher. The community college is considered to be a qualifying postsecondary institution of higher education. Carrie spent a total of $1,300 on tuition for the classes, and she was not reimbursed by her employer. Matt and Carrie's AGI for 2010 before any education-related tax deductions is $112,000 and their taxable income before considering any education-related tax benefits is $80,000. Matt and Carrie incurred $2,300 of miscellaneous itemized deductions subject to the 2 percent floor not counting any education-related expenses.

**Required:**

Determine the mix of tax benefits that maximize tax savings for Matt and Carrie. Their options for credits for each student are as follows (assume the for AGI deduction for qualified education expenses is extended to 2010):

a. They may claim either a credit or a qualified education deduction for Katie's expenses.

b. They may claim either a credit or a qualified education deduction for Todd.

c. They may claim (1) a credit or (2) a qualified education deduction for Carrie. They may deduct any amount not included in (1) or (2) as a miscellaneous itemized deduction subject to the 2 percent of AGI floor.

Remember to apply any applicable limits or phase-outs in your computations. Also, be sure to include the interest deduction for qualified educational loans in your computations.

89. Reba Dixon is a fifth grade school teacher who earned a salary of $38,000 in 2010. She is 45 years old and has been divorced for four years. She received $1,200 of alimony payments each month from her former husband. Reba also rents out a small apartment building. This year Reba received $30,000 of rental payments from tenants and she incurred $19,500 of expenses associated with the rental.

Reba and her daughter Heather (20 years old at the end of the year) moved to Georgia in January of this year. Reba provides more than one half of Heather's support. They had been living in Colorado for the past 15 years, but ever since her divorce, Reba has been wanting to move back to Georgia to be closer to her family. Luckily, last December, a teaching position opened up and Reba and Heather decided to make the move. Reba paid a moving company $2,010 to move their personal belongings, and she and Heather spent two days driving the 1,395 miles to Georgia. During the trip, Reba paid $150 for lodging and $85 for meals. Reba's mother was so excited to have her daughter and granddaughter move back to Georgia that she gave Reba $3,000 to help out with the moving costs.

Reba rented a home in Georgia. Heather decided to continue living at home with her mom, but she started attending school full-time at a nearby university. She was awarded a $3,000 partial tuition scholarship this year, and Reba helped out by paying the remaining $500 tuition cost. If possible, Reba thought it would be best to claim the education credit for these expenses.

Reba wasn't sure if she would have enough items to help her benefit from itemizing on her tax return. However, she kept track of several expenses this year that she thought might qualify if she was able to itemize. Reba paid $2,400 in state income taxes and $6,500 in charitable contributions during the year. She also paid the following medical-related expenses for her and Heather:

| | |
|---|---|
| Insurance premiums | $3,200 |
| Medical care expenses | 1,100 |
| Prescription medicine | 350 |
| Nonprescription medicine | 100 |
| New contact lenses for Heather | 200 |

Shortly after the move, Reba got distracted while driving and she ran into a street sign. The accident caused $900 in damage to the car and gave her whiplash. Because the repairs were less than her insurance deductible, she paid the entire cost of the repairs. Reba wasn't able to work for two months after the accident. Fortunately, she received $2,000 from her disability insurance. Her employer, the Central Georgia School District, paid 60 percent of the premiums on the policy as a nontaxable fringe benefit and Reba paid the remaining 40 percent portion.

A few years ago, Reba acquired several investments with her portion of the divorce settlement. This year she reported the following income from her investments: $2,200 of interest income from corporate bonds and $1,500 interest

income from City of Denver municipal bonds. Overall, Reba's stock portfolio appreciated by $12,000 but she did not sell any of her stocks.

Heather reported $3,200 of interest income from corporate bonds she received as gifts from her father over the last several years. This was Heather's only source of income for the year.

Reba had $10,000 of federal income taxes withheld by her employer. Heather made $500 of estimated tax payments during the year. Reba did not make any estimated payments.

**Required:**

a. Determine Reba's federal income taxes due or taxes payable for the current year.

b. Is Reba allowed to file as a head of household or single?

c. Determine the amount of FICA taxes Reba was required to pay on her salary.

d. Determine Heather's federal income taxes due or payable.

90. John and Sandy Ferguson got married eight years ago and have a seven-year-old daughter Samantha. In 2010, John worked as a computer technician at a local university earning a salary of $52,000, and Sandy worked part-time as a receptionist for a law firm earning a salary of $29,000. John also does some Web design work on the side and reported revenues of $4,000 and associated expenses of $750. The Fergusons received $800 in qualified dividends and a $200 refund of their state income taxes. The Fergusons always itemize their deductions and their itemized deductions were well over the standard deduction amount last year.

The Fergusons reported making the following payments during the year:

- State income taxes of $4,400.
- Alimony payments to John's former wife of $10,000.
- Child support payments for John's child with his former wife of $4,100.
- $3,200 of real property taxes.
- Sandy was reimbursed $600 for employee business expenses she incurred. She was required to provide documentation for her expenses to her employer.
- In addition to the $750 of Web design expenses, John attended a conference to improve his skills associated with his Web design work. His trip was for three days and he incurred the following expenses: airfare $370, total taxi fares for trip $180, meals $80, and conference fee of $200.
- $3,600 to Kid Care day care center for Samantha's care while John and Sandy worked.
- $14,000 interest on their home mortgage.
- $3,000 interest on a home-equity loan. They used the loan to pay for family vacation and new car.
- $6,000 cash charitable contributions to qualified charities.
- Donation of used furniture to Goodwill. The furniture had a fair market value of $400 and cost $2,000.

**Required:**

What is the Fergus on's 2010 federal income taxes payable or refund, including any self-employment tax and AMT, if applicable? (Use the 2009 AMT exemption amounts.)

# KAPLAN CPA SIMULATIONS

**KAPLAN** CPA REVIEW

**Please visit the Online Learning Center**  (www.mhhe.com/spilker2011) to access the following Kaplan CPA Simulation:

The simulation for **Lisa Harrison** covers individual income tax issues, including filing status and exemptions over two years; calculation of AGI; and tax treatment of numerous items.

**Please visit the Online Learning Center**  (www.mhhe.com/spilker2011) to access the following Kaplan CPA Simulation:

The simulation for **Steve and Raelene Sutton** covers individual income tax issues, including filing status and exemptions; job expenses and other miscellaneous deductions; casualty/theft; dependents and exemptions; capital gains and losses; and earned income.

**Please visit the Online Learning Center**  (www.mhhe.com/spilker2011) to access the following Kaplan CPA Simulation:

The simulation for **Michael and Marshall Morgan** covers individual income tax issues, including itemized deductions; rental income and expenses; deductions for AGI; filing requirements; AMT; and dependents with summer job income.

Intentionally blank

Intentionally blank

# chapter 8

# Business Income, Deductions, and Accounting Methods

## Learning Objectives

**Upon completing this chapter, you should be able to:**

**LO 1** Describe the general requirements for deducting business expenses and identify common business deductions.

---■---

**LO 2** Apply the limitations on business deductions to distinguish between deductible and nondeductible business expenses.

---■---

**LO 3** Identify and explain special business deductions specifically permitted under the tax laws.

---■---

**LO 4** Explain the concept of an accounting period and describe accounting periods available to businesses.

---■---

**LO 5** Identify and describe accounting methods available to businesses and apply cash and accrual methods to determine business income and expense deductions.

| Storyline Summary | |
|---|---|
| *Taxpayer:* | Rick Grime |
| *Location:* | San Antonio, Texas |
| *Family description:* | Unmarried |
| *Employment status:* | Rick quit his landscaping job in Dallas and moved to San Antonio to start a business as a self-employed landscaper. |

R ick Grime graduated from Texas State University with a degree in agronomy, and for the past few years he has been employed by a landscape architect in Dallas. Nearly every day that Rick went to work, he shared ideas with his employer about improving the business. In April, Rick finally decided he should take his ideas and start his own landscaping business in his hometown of San Antonio, Texas. In mid-April, Rick left his job and moved his belongings to San Antonio. Once in town, Rick discovered he had to do a lot of things to start his business. First, he registered his new business name (Green Acres Landscaping) and established a bank account for the business. Next, he rented a used sport utility vehicle (SUV) and a shop for his place of business. Rick didn't know much about accounting for business activities, so he hired a CPA, Jane Bronson, to help him. Jane and Rick decided that Rick should initially operate Green Acres as a sole proprietorship, but Jane suggested that as the business grew, he might want to consider organizing it as a different type of legal entity. Operating as a corporation, for instance, would allow him to invite new investors or business partners to help fund future expansion. Rick formally started his business on May 1. He spent a lot of time attracting new customers, and he figured he would hire employees as he needed them.

*to be continued . . .*

In previous chapters, we've emphasized the process of determining gross income and deductions for *individuals*. This chapter describes the process for determining gross income and deductions for *businesses*. Keep in mind that the concepts we discuss in this chapter generally apply to all types of business entities including sole proprietorships (such as Rick's company, Green Acres), partnerships, hybrid entities (such as LLCs), S corporations, and C corporations.[1] Because Rick is a sole proprietor, our examples emphasize business income and deductions from a proprietor's perspective. Proprietors report business income and deductions on Schedule C of their individual income tax returns. Schedule C income is subject to both individual income and self-employment taxes. Entities other than sole proprietorships report income on tax forms separate from the owners' tax returns. For example, partnerships report taxable income on Form 1065, S corporations report taxable income on Form 1120S, and C corporations report taxable income on Form 1120. Of all these entity types, generally only C corporations pay taxes on their income.

## BUSINESS GROSS INCOME

In most respects, the rules for determining business gross income are the same as for determining gross income for individuals. Gross income includes "all income from whatever source derived."[2] Further, the tax laws specifically indicate that this definition includes gross income from "business." Generally speaking, income from business includes gross profit from inventory sales (sales minus cost of goods sold), income from services provided to customers, and income from renting property to customers. Just like individuals, businesses are allowed to exclude certain types of realized income from gross income, such as municipal bond interest.

**LO1**

## BUSINESS DEDUCTIONS

Because Congress intended for taxable income to reflect the *net* increase in wealth from a business, it is only fair that businesses be allowed to deduct expenses incurred to generate business income. Typically, Congress provides *specific* statutory rules authorizing deductions. However, as you can see from the following excerpt from IRC §162, the provision authorizing business deductions is relatively broad and ambiguous:

> There shall be allowed as a deduction all the ordinary and necessary expenses paid or incurred during the taxable year in carrying on any trade or business . . .

This provision authorizes taxpayers to deduct expenses for "trade or business" activities.[3] The tax code does not define the phrase "trade or business," but it's clear that the objective of business activities is to make a profit. Thus, the tax law requires that a business expense be made in the pursuit of profits rather than the pursuit of other, presumably personal, motives.

When a taxpayer's activity does not meet the "for profit" requirement, it is treated as a hobby (an activity motivated by personal objectives). A taxpayer engaged in a

---

[1] Both S corporations and C corporations are incorporated for state law purposes. However, S corporations are taxed as flow-through entities (S corporation income is taxed to its owners) while C corporations (or taxable corporations) are taxed as separate taxable entities. Hybrid entities may opt to be taxed as either flow-through entities or taxable corporations.

[2] §61(a).

[3] §212 contains a sister provision to §162 allowing deductions for ordinary and necessary expenses incurred for the production of income ("investment expenses") and for the management and maintenance of property (including expenses incurred in renting property in situations when the rental activity is not considered to be a trade or business). Recall from Chapter 6 that a business activity, sometimes referred to as a trade or business, requires a relatively high level of involvement or effort from the taxpayer. Unlike business activities, investments are profit-motivated activities that don't require a high degree of taxpayer involvement or effort.

hobby that generates revenues includes all revenues from the activity in gross income and deducts associated expenses to the extent of gross income from the activity as *miscellaneous itemized deductions* (subject to the 2 percent of AGI floor).

### Ordinary and Necessary

Business expenditures must be both **ordinary and necessary** to be deductible. An *ordinary* expense is an expense that is normal or appropriate for the business under the circumstances.[4] An expense is *not* necessarily required to be typical or repetitive in nature to be considered ordinary. For example, a business could deduct the legal fees it expends to defend itself in an antitrust suit. Although an antitrust suit would be atypical and unusual for most businesses, defending the suit would probably be deemed ordinary, because it would be expected under the circumstances. A *necessary* expense is an expense that is helpful or conducive to the business activity, but the expenditure need not be essential or indispensable. For example, a deduction for metric tools would qualify as ordinary and necessary even if there was only a small chance that a repairman might need these tools. The "ordinary and necessary" requirements are applied on a case-by-case basis, and while the deduction depends on individual circumstances, the IRS is often reluctant to second-guess business decisions. Exhibit 8-1 presents examples of expenditures that are ordinary and necessary for typical businesses.

### EXHIBIT 8-1 Examples of Typical Ordinary and Necessary Business Expenses

| | |
|---|---|
| • Advertising | • Office expenses |
| • Car and truck expenses | • Rent |
| • Depreciation | • Repairs |
| • Employee compensation and benefits | • Supplies |
| • Insurance | • Travel |
| • Interest | • Utilities |
| • Legal fees | • Wages |

### Example 8-1

Rick paid $50 to attend a two-week, nighttime meditation course ("Meditation for Dummies") to learn how to meditate. He is considering whether this expenditure qualifies as an ordinary and necessary business expense. Rick believes that meditation will improve his ability to produce innovative landscape designs and, thus, increase the demand for his business services. Further, he plans to meditate only for business purposes. Rick decides that the cost of the course is a deductible business expense, so he deducts the $50 cost as an ordinary and necessary business expense. Is he correct?

**Answer:** Under the regulations, educational expenses are deductible if they help the taxpayer maintain or improve skills in an existing trade or business. It is difficult, however, to know whether the IRS or a court would agree that meditation is ordinary and necessary. What do you think?

### Reasonable in Amount

Ordinary and necessary business expenses are deductible only *to the extent* they are also **reasonable in amount.** The courts have interpreted this requirement to mean that an expenditure is not reasonable when it is extravagant or exorbitant.[5] If the expenditure is extravagant in amount, the courts presume the excess amount was spent for personal rather than business reasons and, thus, is not deductible.

---

[4] *Welch v. Helvering* (1933), 290 US 111.

[5] §162(a) and *Comm. v. Lincoln Electric Co.* (CA-6, 1949), 176 F.2d 815.

Determining whether an expenditure is reasonable is not an exact science and, not surprisingly, taxpayers and the IRS may have different opinions. Generally, the courts and the IRS test for extravagance by comparing the amount of the expense to a market price or an **arm's length amount.** If the amount of the expense is the amount typically charged in the market by unrelated parties, the amount is considered to be reasonable. Because the underlying issue is *why* a profit-motivated taxpayer would pay an extravagant amount, reasonableness is most likely to be an issue when a payment is made to an individual related to the taxpayer, or the taxpayer enjoys some incidental benefit from the expenditure, such as entertainment value.

---

**Example 8-2**

During the busy part of the year, Rick could not keep up with all the work. Therefore, he hired four part-time employees and paid them $10 an hour to mow lawns and pull weeds for an average of 20 hours a week. When things finally slowed down in late fall, Rick released his four part-time employees. Rick paid a total of $22,000 in compensation to the four employees. He still needed some extra help now and then, so he hired his brother, Tom, on a part-time basis. Tom performed the same duties as the prior part-time employees (his quality of work was about the same). However, Rick paid Tom $25 per hour because Tom is a college student and Rick wanted to provide some additional support for Tom's education. At year-end, Tom had worked a total of 100 hours and received $2,500 from Rick. What amount can Rick deduct for the compensation he paid to his employees?

**Answer:** $23,000. Rick can deduct the $22,000 paid to part-time employees. However, he can only deduct $10 an hour for Tom's compensation because the extra $15 per hour Rick paid Tom is unreasonable in amount.[6] The remaining $15 per hour is considered a personal (nondeductible) gift from Rick to Tom. Hence, Rick can deduct a total of $23,000 for compensation expense this year [$22,000 + ($10 × 100)].

---

**L02**

## LIMITATIONS ON BUSINESS DEDUCTIONS

For a variety of reasons, Congress specifically prohibits or limits a business's ability to deduct certain expenditures that appear to otherwise meet the general business expense deductibility requirements.

### Expenditures against Public Policy

Even though they incur the expenses as part of their business activities, businesses are not allowed to deduct fines, penalties, illegal bribes, or illegal kickbacks.[7] Congress disallows these expenditures under the rationale that allowing them would subsidize illegal activities and frustrate public policy. Interestingly enough, businesses conducting illegal activities (selling stolen goods or conducting illegal gambling activities) are allowed to deduct their cost of goods sold and their ordinary and necessary business expenses in conducting the business activities (note, however, that they are not allowed to deduct fines, penalties, illegal bribes, or illegal kickbacks).[8] Of course, the IRS is probably more concerned that many illegal businesses fail to report *any* income than that illegal businesses overstate deductions.[9]

**THE KEY FACTS**

Limitations on Business Deductions

■ No business deductions are allowable for expenditures against public policy (bribes) or political contributions.

■ Expenditures that benefit a period longer than 12 months generally must be capitalized.

■ No deductions are allowable for expenditures associated with the production of tax-exempt income.

■ Personal expenditures are not deductible.

---

[6]In practice, this distinction is rarely cut and dried. Rick may be able to argue for various reasons that Tom's work is worth more than $10 an hour but perhaps not as much as $25 per hour. We use this example to illustrate the issue of reasonable expenses and not to discuss the merits of what actually is reasonable compensation to Tom.

[7]§162(c) and Reg. §1.162-21.

[8]*Comm. v. Sullivan* (1958), 356 US 27.

[9]§280E explicitly prohibits drug dealers from deducting any business expenses associated with this "business" activity. However, drug dealers are able to deduct cost of goods sold because cost of goods sold is technically a reduction in gross income and not a business expense. See Reg. §1.61-3(a).

---

**Taxes in the Real World** *Al Capone Put Away—By the IRS*

Al Capone, the notorious Chicago crime boss, wasn't put behind bars for murder, extortion, drug dealing, or even bootlegging. He went to prison because he didn't pay taxes on his illegal income. In the summer of 1929, Capone was alleged to owe more than $250,000 in taxes and over $150,000 in penalties and he was charged with 24 counts of income tax evasion and failure to file tax returns. Capone was ultimately convicted on three charges of tax evasion in 1925, 1926, and 1927 and two charges of failing

to file a tax return in 1928 and 1929. He was sentenced to 11 years in prison and assessed fines totaling $80,000. Capone was brought to justice by the work of IRS agent Frank J. Wilson, who was able to follow Capone's money trail and establish that Capone's income required him to file tax returns and pay taxes.

*Source: IN DEPTH: Crime: Al Capone.* Last Updated March 20, 2007, by Robin Rowland, CBC News, http://www.cbc.ca/news/background/crime/capone.html.

---

## Political Contributions and Lobbying Costs

Perhaps to avoid the perception that the federal government subsidizes taxpayer efforts to influence politics, the tax laws disallow deductions for political contributions and most lobbying expenses.[10]

---

**Example 8-3**

In July, the city fined Rick $200 for violating the city's watering ban when he watered a newly installed landscape. Later, Rick donated $250 to the mayor's campaign for reelection. Can Rick deduct these expenditures?

**Answer:** No. Rick cannot deduct either the fine or the political contribution as business expenses because the tax laws specifically prohibit deductions for these expenditures.

---

## Capital Expenditures

Whether a business uses the cash or the accrual method of accounting, it generally must capitalize expenditures for *tangible* assets such as buildings, machinery and equipment, furniture and fixtures, and similar property that have useful lives of more than one year (12 months).[11] For tax purposes, businesses generally recover the cost of capitalized tangible assets (other than land) through depreciation.

Businesses also generally must capitalize the cost to create or acquire *intangible* assets such as patents, goodwill, start-up costs, and organizational expenditures.[12] They recover the costs of capitalized intangible assets either through amortization (when the tax laws allow them to do so) or upon disposition of the assets.[13]

## Expenses Associated with the Production of Tax-Exempt Income

Expenses that do not help businesses generate *taxable* income are not allowed to offset taxable income. For example, this restriction disallows interest expense deductions for businesses that borrow money and invest the loan proceeds in municipal

---

[10]§162(e). Exceptions under §162(e) allow the deduction of certain *de minimis* expenditures and reasonable costs incurred in conjunction with the submission of statements to a local council with respect to proposed legislation of direct interest to the taxpayer.

[11]Reg. §1.263(a)-2(d)(4). The act of recording the asset is sometimes referred to as *capitalizing* the expenditure.

[12]Reg. §1.263(a)-4(b). The extent to which expenditures for intangible assets must be capitalized is explored in *Indopco v. Comm.* (1992), 503 US 79.

[13]See §195, §197, and §248 for provisions that allow taxpayers to amortize the cost of certain intangible assets.

(tax-exempt) bonds. It also disallows deductions for life insurance premiums businesses pay on policies that cover the lives of officers or other key employees and compensate the business for the disruption and lost income they may experience due to a key employee's death. Because the death benefit from the life insurance policy is not taxable, the business is not allowed to deduct the insurance premium expense associated with this nontaxable income.

---

**Example 8-4**

Rick employs Joan, an arborist who specializes in trimming trees and treating local tree ailments. Joan generates a great deal of revenue for Rick's business, but is in her mid-60s and suffers from diabetes. In November, Rick purchased a "key-employee" term-life insurance policy on Joan's life. The policy cost Rick $720 and will pay him a $20,000 death benefit if Joan passes away during the next 12 months. What amount of life insurance policy premium can Rick deduct?

**Answer:** $0. Rick cannot deduct the $720 premium on the life insurance policy because the life insurance proceeds from the policy are tax-exempt.

**What if:** Suppose Rick purchased the life insurance policy on Joan's life and allowed Joan to name the beneficiary. The policy cost Rick $720 and will pay the beneficiary a $20,000 death benefit if Joan passes away during the next 12 months. What amount of life insurance policy premium can Rick deduct?

**Answer:** $720. In this scenario, Rick can deduct the entire premium of $720 as a *compensation* expense because the benefit of the policy inures to Joan and not to Rick's business.

---

### Personal Expenditures

Taxpayers are not allowed to deduct **personal expenses** unless the expenses are "expressly" authorized by a provision in the law.[14] While the tax laws do not define personal expenses, they imply the scope of personal expenses by stating that "personal, living, or family expenses" are not deductible. Therefore, at a minimum, the costs of food, clothing, and shelter are assumed to be personal and nondeductible. Of course, there are the inevitable exceptions when otherwise personal items are specially adapted to business use. For example, taxpayers may deduct the cost of uniforms or special clothing they purchase for use in their business, if the clothing is not appropriate to wear as ordinary clothing outside the place of business. When the clothing is adaptable as ordinary clothing, the cost of the clothing is a nondeductible personal expenditure.[15]

---

**Example 8-5**

Rick spent $500 to purchase special coveralls that identify his landscaping service and provide a professional appearance. How much of the cost for the clothing can Rick deduct as a business expense?

**Answer:** All $500. While the cost of clothing is inherently personal, Rick can deduct the $500 cost of the coveralls because, due to the design and labeling on the coveralls, they are not suitable for ordinary use.

---

Many business owners, particularly small business owners such as sole proprietors, may be in a position to use business funds to pay for items that are entirely personal in nature. For example, a sole proprietor could use the business checking account to pay for family groceries. These expenditures, even though funded by the business, are not deductible.

---

[14]§262(a).

[15]An employee who purchases clothing for work would go through a similar analysis to determine if the cost of the clothing qualifies as an employee business expense.

## Mixed-Motive Expenditures

Business owners in general, and owners of small or closely held businesses in particular, often make expenditures that are motivated by *both* business and personal concerns. These **mixed-motive expenditures** are of particular concern to lawmakers and the IRS because of the tax incentive to disguise nondeductible personal expenses as deductible business expenses. Thus, deductions for business expenditures with potential personal motives are closely monitored and restricted. The rules for determining the amount of *deductible* mixed-motive expenditures depend on the type of the expenditure. Here we review the rules for determining the deductible portion of mixed-motive expenditures for meals and entertainment, travel and transportation, and the use of property for both business and personal purposes.

**Meals and Entertainment**   Because everyone needs to eat, even business meals contain a significant personal element. To allow for this personal element, taxpayers may only deduct 50 percent of actual business meals. In addition, to deduct any portion of the cost of a meal as a business expense, (1) the amount must be reasonable under the circumstances, (2) the taxpayer (or an employee) must be present when the meal is furnished, and (3) the meal must be directly associated with the active conduct of the taxpayer's business.

Similar to business meals, entertainment associated with business activities contains a significant element of enjoyment. Hence, only 50 percent of allowable business entertainment may be deducted as a business expense.[16] Further, entertainment deductions are allowable only if (1) "business associates" are entertained, (2) the amounts paid are reasonable in amount, and (3) the entertainment is either "directly related" or "associated with" the active conduct of business.

Business associates are individuals with whom the taxpayer reasonably expects to do business, such as customers, suppliers, employees, or advisors. Entertainment is directly related to business if there is an active discussion aimed at generating revenue or fees or the discussion occurs in a clear business setting (such as a hospitality room). The cost of entertainment that occurs in a setting with little possibility of conducting a business discussion, such as a theatre or sports venue, will only be deductible if the entertainment directly precedes or follows a substantial business discussion, thereby satisfying the "associated with" test. In addition, to deduct the cost of meals and entertainment, taxpayers generally must meet strict record-keeping requirements we discuss below.[17]

> **THE KEY FACTS**
>
> Mixed-Motive Expenditures
>
> ■ Only 50 percent of business meals and entertainment are deductible.
>
> ■ Special limits are imposed on expenditures that have both personal and business benefits.
>
> ■ Contemporaneous written records of business purpose are required.

---

**Example 8-6**

Rick went out to dinner with a prospective client to discuss Rick's ideas for landscaping the homeowner's yard. After dinner, Rick and the prospective client attended the theatre. Rick paid $190 for the meal and $350 for the tickets, amounts that were reasonable under the circumstances. What amount of these expenditures can Rick deduct as a business expense?

**Answer:** Rick can deduct $270 [($190 + $350) × 50%], representing half the cost of the meal and entertainment, as a business expense, as long as Rick can substantiate the business purpose and substantial nature of the dinner discussion.

(*continued on page 8-8...*)

---

[16]§274 also provides some exceptions to the 50 percent reduction for meals and entertainment, such as meals and entertainment provided for special events or as employee compensation. Taxpayers can also use a *per diem* rate (an automatic, flat amount per meal) in lieu of actual expenditures to determine the amount of the deduction. There are special limits placed on entertainment expenses associated with spouses.

[17]Under §274, there are special limits placed on certain entertainment expenditures, such as those related to spouses, club dues and entertainment facilities, skyboxes, and entertainment associated with corporate officers, directors, and large shareholders.

> **What if:** Suppose that Rick did not discuss business with the client either before, during, or after the meal. What amount of the expenditures can Rick deduct as a business expense?
>
> **Answer:** $0. In this scenario, Rick cannot deduct the costs of the meal or entertainment because the activity was not directly related to or associated with a substantial business discussion.

**Travel and Transportation** Under certain conditions, sole proprietors and self-employed taxpayers may deduct the cost of travel and transportation for business purposes. Transportation expenses include the direct cost of transporting the taxpayer to and from business sites. However, the cost of commuting between the taxpayer's home and regular place of business is personal and, therefore, not deductible. If the taxpayer uses a vehicle for business, the taxpayer can deduct the costs of operating the vehicle plus depreciation on the vehicle's tax basis. Alternatively, in lieu of deducting these costs, the taxpayer may simply deduct a standard amount for each business mile she drives. The standard mileage rate represents the per-mile cost of operating an automobile (including depreciation or lease payments).[18] For 2010 the standard mileage rate has been set at 50 cents per mile. Once a taxpayer uses the mileage rate to claim deductions for automobile expenses, she must continue to do so in subsequent years. To be deductible, the transportation must be for business reasons. If the transportation is primarily for personal purposes, the cost is not deductible.

---

**Example 8-7**

Rick leases an SUV to drive between his shop and various work sites. Rick carefully documents the business use of the SUV (8,100 miles in 2010) and his $5,335 of operating expenses ($3,935 for gas, oil, and repairs and $1,400 for lease payments). At no time does Rick use the SUV for personal purposes. What amount of these expenses may Rick deduct as business expenses?

**Answer:** $5,335. Since Rick uses the SUV in his business activities, he can deduct (1) the $5,335 cost of operating and leasing the SUV or (2) $4,050 for the 8,100 business miles he drove (50 cents per mile × 8,100 miles). Assuming Rick chooses to deduct operating expenses and lease payments in lieu of using the mileage rate, he can deduct $5,335. Note that if Rick chose the mileage rate this year, he would be required to continue to use the mileage rate for the SUV's business use in future years.

---

In contrast to transportation expenses, travel expenses are only deductible if the taxpayer is away from home overnight while traveling. This distinction is important because besides the cost of transportation, the deduction for **travel expenses** includes meals (50 percent), lodging, and incidental expenses. A taxpayer is considered to be away from home overnight if she has left her primary place of business on a trip of sufficient duration to require sleep or rest. When a taxpayer travels solely for business purposes, *all* of the costs of travel are deductible (but only 50 percent of meals). When the travel has both business and personal aspects, the deductibility of the transportation costs depends upon whether business is the *primary* purpose for the trip. If the primary purpose of a trip is business, the transportation costs are fully deductible, but meals (50 percent), lodging, and incidental expenditures are limited to those incurred during the business portion of the travel.[19] If the taxpayer's primary purpose for the trip is personal, the

---

[18]This mileage rate is updated periodically (sometimes two or three times within a year) to reflect changes in the cost of operating a vehicle. For example, the mileage rate was 50.5 cents per mile for the first half of 2008 and 58.5 cents per mile from July 1, 2008 until year-end. The mileage option is only available for vehicles not previously depreciated, vehicles previously depreciated on the straight-line method, or for leased vehicles where this method has been used throughout the term of the lease.

[19]Special limitations apply to a number of travel expenses that are potentially abusive, such as luxury water travel, foreign conventions, conventions on cruise ships, and travel expenses associated with taking a companion.

taxpayer may not deduct *any* transportation costs to arrive at the location but may deduct meals (50 percent), lodging, transportation, and incidental expenditures for the *business* portion of the trip.

The rule for business travel is modified somewhat if a trip abroad includes both business and personal activities. Like the rule for domestic travel, if foreign travel is primarily for personal purposes, then only those expenses directly associated with business activities are deductible. However, unlike the rule for domestic travel, when foreign travel is primarily for business purposes, a portion of the transportation costs to arrive abroad is not deductible. The nondeductible portion is typically computed based on a time ratio such as the proportion of personal days to total days (travel days count as business days).[20]

---

**Example 8-8**

Rick paid a $300 registration fee for a three-day course in landscape design. The course was held in New York (Rick paid $700 for airfare to attend) and he spent four days in New York. He spent the last day sightseeing. During the trip, Rick paid $150 a night for three nights' lodging, $50 a day for meals, and $70 a day for a rental car. What amount of these travel-related expenditures may Rick deduct as business expenses?

**Answer:** $1,435 for travel and $300 for business education. The primary purpose for the trip appears to be business because Rick spent three days on business activities versus one personal day. He can deduct travel costs, computed as follows:

**Deductible Travel Costs**

| Description | Amount | Explanation |
|---|---|---|
| Airfare to New York | $ 700 | Primary purposes is business |
| Lodging in New York | 450 | 3 business days × $150 a day |
| Meals | 75 | 3 business days × $50 a day × 50% limit |
| Rental car | 210 | 3 business days × $70 a day |
| Total business travel expenses | $1,435 | |

---

**What if:** Assume Rick stayed in New York for ten days, spending three days at the seminar and seven days sightseeing. What amount could he deduct?

**Answer:** In this scenario Rick can deduct $735 for travel and $300 for business education. Rick would not be able to deduct the $700 cost of airfare because the trip is primarily personal, as evidenced by the seven days of personal activities compared to only three days of business activities.

**Deductible Travel Costs**

| Description | Amount | Explanation |
|---|---|---|
| Airfare to New York | $ 0 | Primary purposes is personal |
| Lodging in New York | 450 | 3 business days × $150 a day |
| Meals | 75 | 3 business days × $50 a day × 50% limit |
| Rental car | 210 | 3 business days × $70 a day |
| Total business travel expenses | $735 | |

(*continued on page 8-10…*)

---

[20]Foreign transportation expense is deductible without prorating under special circumstances authorized in §274(c). For example, the cost of getting abroad is fully deductible if the travel is for one week or less or if the personal activity constitutes less than one-fourth of the travel time.

*What if:* Assume the original facts in the example except Rick traveled to London (rather than New York) for ten days spending six days at the seminar and four days sightseeing. What amount could he deduct?

**Answer:** In this scenario Rick can deduct $1,890 for travel (computed below) and $300 for business education.

| Deductible Travel Costs | | |
|---|---|---|
| **Description** | **Amount** | **Explanation** |
| Airfare to London | $ 420 | 6 business days/10 total days × $700 |
| Lodging in London | 900 | 6 business days × $150 a day |
| Meals | 150 | 6 business days × $50 a day × 50% limit |
| Rental car | 420 | 6 business days × $70 a day |
| Total business travel expenses | $1,890 | |

Rick is allowed to deduct $420 of the $700 airfare (60 percent) because he spent six of the ten days on the trip conducting business activities.

**Property Use**    Several types of property may be used for both business and personal purposes. For example, business owners often use automobiles, computers, or cell phones for both business and personal purposes.[21] However, because expenses relating to these assets are deductible only to the extent the assets are used for business purposes, taxpayers must allocate the expenses between the business and personal use portions.

### Example 8-9

Rick occasionally uses his personal auto (a BMW) to drive to interviews with prospective clients and to drive back and forth between his shop and various work sites. This year Rick carefully recorded that the BMW was driven 412 miles for business activities and 10,500 miles in total. What expenses associated with the BMW may Rick deduct?

**Answer:** $206. Based on the 2010 standard mileage rate of 50 cents per mile, Rick can deduct $206 (412 × 50 cents) for business use of his BMW. Alternatively, Rick can track the operating expenses of the BMW (including depreciation) and deduct the business portion [based upon the percentage of business miles driven to total miles driven (412 business miles/10,500 total miles)].

When taxpayers use other business assets for both business and personal purposes, the deductible business expense is determined by prorating the expenses based upon the percentage of the time the asset is used for business purposes. For example, if a full year's expense for a business asset is $1,000, but the asset is only used for business purposes 90 percent of the time, then only $900 of expense can be deducted ($1,000 × 90%). Special rules apply when the business usage for an asset drops below 50 percent. We discuss these issues in the next chapter.

---

[21]These types of assets are referred to as "listed property."

**Record Keeping and Other Requirements**    Because distinguishing business purposes from personal purposes is a difficult and subjective task, the tax laws include provisions designed to help the courts and the IRS determine the business element of mixed-motive transactions. Under these provisions, taxpayers must maintain specific, written, contemporaneous records (of time, amount, and business purpose) for mixed-motive expenses. For example, as we discussed above, the tax laws prohibit any deductions for business meals and entertainment unless substantial business discussions accompany the entertainment activity. Consequently, when taxpayers incur meals and entertainment expenses, they must document the business purpose and the extent of the discussion to deduct any of the expenditures.[22]

# SPECIFIC BUSINESS DEDUCTIONS

L03

As we discuss above, the tax code provides general guidelines for determining whether business expenditures are deductible. We learned that to be deductible, business expenditures must be ordinary, necessary, and reasonable in amount. In some cases, however, the tax laws identify *specific* items businesses are allowed to deduct. We discuss several of these deductions below.

## Start-Up Costs and Organizational Expenditures

Businesses may make expenditures to create, establish, or organize new trades or businesses. These expenditures are typically immediately expensed for financial accounting purposes. The tax rules associated with these expenditures are summarized in Exhibit 8-2. We summarize the rules in the exhibit because we discuss the tax treatment of these expenditures in depth in the next chapter.

## Bad Debt Expense

Businesses are allowed to deduct bad debt expense when a debt owed to the business becomes worthless or uncollectible.[23] While this business deduction is specifically allowed by the tax laws, it is available only to businesses using the accrual method of accounting for tax purposes. Thus, we defer a detailed discussion of bad debt expense until we discuss accrual method deductions.

## Domestic Production Activities Deduction

Businesses that manufacture goods are allowed to deduct an *artificial* business deduction for tax purposes called the U.S. **domestic production activities deduction (DPAD).** This deduction is designed to reduce the tax burden on domestic manufacturers to make investments in domestic manufacturing facilities more attractive. The DPAD provides a special tax deduction for businesses, large and small, that "manufacture, produce, grow or extract" tangible products entirely or in significant part within the United States.[24] This deduction is artificial because it does not represent an

---

[22]§274 requires substantiation of all elements of travel and entertainment including sufficient corroborating evidence. Although there are a few exceptions to this rule, approximations and estimates are generally not sufficient. Also, taxpayers must maintain records to deduct the business portion of mixed-use assets such as cars used for both business and personal purposes.

[23]§166(a). Nonbusiness bad debts are deductible as short-term capital losses in the year of complete worthlessness (no deduction for partial worthlessness).

[24]§199 also allows this deduction for qualifying taxpayers in the domestic film and sound recording industries, those engaged in a construction business in the United States, and engineering and architectural firms providing services for U.S. construction projects. Because the domestic manufacturing deduction does not represent a real expenditure, the deduction is not an expense for financial accounting purposes.

---

**THE KEY FACTS**

**Domestic Production Activities Deduction**

- A subsidy for the cost of producing goods or certain construction services within the United States.
- 9 percent of qualified production activity income.
- Limited to overall income (AGI for individuals) and 50 percent of wages associated with the production.

**EXHIBIT 8-2    Start-Up Costs and Organizational Expenditures**

| Item | Description | Discussed in |
|---|---|---|
| Start-up costs | • Costs associated with investigating and creating or acquiring a business.<br>• Normal business expenditures before business actually begins.<br>• Immediately expense up to $5,000.<br>• If start-up costs exceed $50,000, immediate expense is reduced dollar for dollar. Once start-up costs reach $55,000, no immediate expense.<br>• Amount not immediately expensed is amortized over 180 months on straight-line basis beginning in the month the business begins.<br>• Applies to any business regardless of form. | Chapter 9 |
| Organizational expenditures | • Expenditures to organize business, including: cost of organizational meetings, state fees, accounting service costs, and legal service expenditures incident to the organization.<br>• Costs of selling or marketing stock or ownership interests are not deductible.<br>• Same rules for immediate expensing and amortizing as start-up costs.<br>• Applies to corporations (§248) and to partnerships (§709). | Chapter 9 |

expenditure per se, but merely serves to reduce the income taxes the business must pay and thereby increase the after-tax profitability of domestic manufacturing.

The formula for computing the DPAD is 9 percent times the *lesser* of (1) the business's taxable income before the deduction (or modified AGI for individuals) or (2) **qualified production activities income (QPAI).**[25] Generally speaking, QPAI is the *net* income from selling or leasing property that was manufactured in the United States. Thus, to compute QPAI, businesses need to determine the amount of revenues, cost of goods sold, and expenses attributable to U.S. production activities. Obviously, the calculation of the income allocable to domestic production can be exceedingly complex, especially in the case of large multinational businesses. The final deduction cannot exceed 50 percent of the wages the business paid to employees for working in qualifying production activities during the year.[26]

---

**Example 8-10**

This fall Rick constructed a greenhouse that qualified for the domestic production activities deduction. Rick received $5,000 for the construction project from his client and allocated $4,000 in expenses to the project. These expenses included $2,000 of qualified wages. Thus, the greenhouse project generated $1,000 of qualified production activity income (QPAI) for Rick ($5,000 minus $4,000). What is Rick's domestic production activities deduction for this project?

**Answer:** $90. Assuming Rick's QPAI of $1,000 is less than his modified AGI, the DPAD is $90, calculated by multiplying 9 percent times $1,000 of QPAI. The entire computation is summarized as follows:

(continued on page 8-13...)

---

[25]See §199(d)(2). Modified AGI is AGI before the DPAD and certain other specified deductions.
[26]Taxpayers show the deduction computations on Form 8903.

**DPAD Calculation**

| Description | Amount | Explanation |
|---|---|---|
| Qualified domestic gross receipts | $5,000 | Must be a qualified activity |
| Allocable costs and expenses | −4,000 | Allocate to qualified activity |
| Qualified production activity income | $1,000 | Limited to modified AGI |
| Statutory percentage for 2010 | × 9% | |
| Domestic production activities deduction | $  90 | Limited to 50% of wages |

The 50 percent wage limitation is $1,000 (50% × $2,000 in wages Rick paid to employees working on the project). Thus, Rick is allowed to deduct the entire $90 domestic production activities deduction even though the $90 deduction doesn't represent a specific liability or payment to anyone.

**Taxes in the Real World**    *Starbucks the Manufacturer?*

When you think of Starbucks, do you think of a manufacturing company? Apparently Congress does. The tax law describing business activities that qualify for the domestic production activities deduction explicitly states that "the sale of food and beverages prepared by the taxpayer at a retail establishment" is *not* a qualifying activity. However, a footnote in the House-Senate Conference Committee report of the tax act creating the deduction explicitly indicates that *roasting* coffee beans is a qualifying activity but *brewing* coffee is not. Since the retail price of brewed coffee includes the cost of roasted beans, businesses that roast and brew coffee are able to claim a domestic production activities deduction for the profit they make from directly selling roasted beans to walk-up customers (and other retailers), and for a portion of the profit they make from selling brewed coffee to customers attributable to the value of the coffee beans. The footnote describing the proper classification of roasted coffee beans for purposes of determining the domestic production activities deduction is frequently referred to as the "Starbucks footnote" due to the influence Starbucks had in helping lawmakers see things its way.

*Sources: Janet Novack, "Business in the Beltway: Domestic Help," Forbes, May 10, 2006. www.forbes.com/taxes/ 2006/05/10/intel-aol-ge-; §199(c)(4)(B)(i).*

## Losses on Dispositions of Business Property

Besides operating expenses, businesses are generally allowed to deduct losses incurred when selling or disposing of business assets.[27] The calculation of losses from business property dispositions can be complex, but the main idea is that businesses realize and recognize a loss when the asset's tax basis exceeds the sale proceeds. We discuss the rules governing the tax treatment of gains and losses on asset disposition in more detail in Chapter 10.

**Example 8-11**

***What if:*** Assume that in late October, Rick purchased a used trailer to transport equipment to work sites. Rick bought the trailer for what he thought was a bargain price of $1,000. However, shortly after Rick acquired it, the axle snapped and was not repairable. Rick was forced to sell the trailer to a parts shop for $325. What amount can Rick deduct as a loss from the trailer sale?

(continued on page 8-14...)

---

[27]In most circumstances businesses may *not* deduct losses on assets sold to related parties.

> **Answer:** $675, because the trailer was a business asset (amount realized of $325 minus adjusted basis of $1,000). (Note, as we discuss in the next chapter, Rick is not allowed to deduct depreciation on the trailer because he disposed of it in the same year he acquired it.)

### Business Casualty Losses

Besides selling assets, businesses can incur losses when their assets are stolen, damaged, or completely destroyed by a force outside the control of the business.[28] These events are called casualty losses. Businesses may deduct casualty losses in the year the casualty occurs or in the year the theft of an asset is discovered. The amount of the loss deduction depends on whether the asset is (1) completely destroyed or stolen or (2) only partially destroyed. When its asset is *completely* destroyed or stolen, the business calculates the amount of the loss as though it sold the asset for the insurance proceeds, if any. That is, the loss is the amount of insurance proceeds minus the adjusted tax basis of the asset. If the asset is damaged but not completely destroyed, the amount of the loss is the amount of the insurance proceeds minus the *lesser* of (1) the asset's tax basis or (2) the decline in the value of the asset due to the casualty. While individuals deduct business casualty losses and casualty losses associated with rentals and royalties as deductions *for* AGI, casualty and theft losses of assets used for the production of income (investments) and personal-use assets are generally deductible as itemized deductions.[29] We summarize the casualty and theft loss rules for business, production of income, and personal-use assets in Exhibit 8-3, which appears on the following page.

---

**Example 8-12**

*What if:* Suppose Rick acquired a personal-use asset several years ago for $9,000. Suppose further that a casualty event destroyed the asset, and at that time the asset was worth $1,000 and insured for $250. What is the amount of Rick's casualty loss (before applying the per casualty floor and the AGI restriction)?

**Answer:** $750, computed as follows:

| | | |
|---|---|---|
| Insurance proceeds | | $250 |
| Minus the *lesser* of: | | |
| (1) adjusted tax basis or | $9,000 | |
| (2) value at time of casualty | $1,000 | −1,000 |
| Casualty loss deduction (before limitations) | | ($750) |

Suppose instead that Rick's asset was a business-use asset and Rick had deducted $4,000 of depreciation expense against the asset. Hence, the asset's tax basis was $5,000 ($9,000 − $4,000), what would be the amount of his business casualty loss?

**Answer:** $4,750, computed as follows:

| | |
|---|---|
| Insurance proceeds | $ 250 |
| Minus adjusted tax basis | −5,000 |
| Casualty loss deduction | ($4,750) |

---

[28]Casualties can be described as unexpected events driven by forces outside the control of the taxpayer that damage or destroy a taxpayer's property. For example, §165 lists "fire, storm, and shipwreck" as examples of casualties.

[29]For example, a taxpayer with a coin collection that is stolen or valuable antique collection that burns is potentially eligible for a casualty loss deduction on assets used for the production of income. Under §165(h)(5), personal casualty losses are allowed to offset personal casualty gains in computing AGI.

**EXHIBIT 8-3**    Comparison of Casualty and Theft Loss Rules for Property Used in Business, for Production of Income, and for Personal Purposes

|  | Property Used in Business (including losses from rental and royalty property) | Property Used for the Production of Income | Property Used for Personal Purposes |
|---|---|---|---|
| Amount of loss if property completely destroyed or stolen | Insurance proceeds minus adjusted basis | Same as business | Insurance proceeds minus lesser of (1) adjusted basis or (2) decline in asset's value due to casualty or theft |
| Amount of loss if property is not completely destroyed | Insurance proceeds minus lesser of (1) adjusted basis or (2) decline in asset's value | Same as business | Same as business |
| Loss limitation | None | None | A $100 per casualty floor limitation and 10 percent of AGI floor for total casualty losses for year |
| Type of deduction | For AGI | Miscellaneous itemized deduction (not subject to 2 percent floor) | Itemized deduction |

# ACCOUNTING PERIODS

**LO4**

So far we've discussed how to determine a business's income and how to determine its deductible business expenses. In this section, we discuss accounting periods, which affect when taxpayers determine their income and deductions. Businesses must report their income and deductions over a fixed **accounting period** or **tax year.** A full tax year consists of 12 full months. A tax year can consist of a period less than 12 months (a short tax year) in certain circumstances. For instance, a business may report income for such a short year in its first year of existence (for example, it reports income on a calendar year-end and starts business after January 1) or in its final year of existence (for example, a calendar-year business ends its business before December 31). Short tax years in a business's initial or final year are treated the same as full years. A business may also have a short year when it changes its tax year, and this can occur when the business is acquired by new owners. In these situations, special rules may apply for computing the tax liability of the business.[30]

There are three types of tax years, each with different year-ends:

- A calendar year ends on December 31.
- A **fiscal year** ends on the last day of a month other than December.
- A 52/53 week year ends on the same day of the week every year. In other words, a 52/53 week year could end on the same day of the week that is the last such day in the month or on the same day of the week nearest the end of the month. For example, a business could adopt a 52/53 week fiscal year that (1) ends on the last Saturday in July each year or (2) ends on the Saturday closest to the end of July (although this Saturday might be in August rather than July).[31]

> **THE KEY FACTS**
>
> *Accounting Periods*
>
> - Individuals and proprietorships account for income on a calendar year.
> - Corporations are allowed to choose a fiscal year.
> - Partnerships and other flow-through entities generally use a required year.

[30]§443. Discussion of tax consequences associated with these short years is beyond the scope of this text.

[31]Businesses with inventories may benefit from 52/53 year-ends to facilitate an inventory count when the store is closed (e.g., over a weekend).

Not all types of tax years are available to all types of businesses. The rules for determining the tax years available to the business depends on whether the business is a sole proprietorship, a **flow-through entity,** or a C corporation. These rules are summarized as follows:

- *Sole proprietorships:* Because individual proprietors must report their business income on their individual returns, proprietorships use a calendar year-end to report their business income.[32]
- *Flow-through entities:* Because partnerships and S corporations are flow-through entities (partners and S corporation owners report the entity's income directly on their own tax returns), these entities generally must adopt tax years consistent with the owners' tax years.[33] Because owners are allocated income from flow-through entities on the last day of the entity's taxable year, the tax laws impose the tax year consistency requirement to minimize income tax deferral opportunities for the owners.
- *C corporations:* C corporations are generally allowed to select a calendar, fiscal, or 52/53 week year-end.

A business adopts a calendar year-end or fiscal year-end by filing its initial tax return. In contrast, a business adopts a 52/53 week year-end by filing a special election with the IRS. Once a business establishes its tax year, it generally must receive permission from the IRS to change.

### Example 8-13

Rick is a calendar-year taxpayer. What tax year should Rick use to report income from his business Green Acres?

**Answer:** Calendar year. This is true even though Rick began his business in May of this year. He will calculate income and expense for his landscaping business over the calendar year and include the net business income from May through December of this year on Schedule C of his individual tax return.

*What if:* Suppose that Rick incorporated Green Acres at the time he began his business. What tax year could Green Acres adopt?

**Answer:** If Green Acres was operated as a C corporation, it could elect a calendar year-end, a fiscal year-end, or a 52/53 week year-end. If it were an S corporation, it likely would have a calendar year-end.

### LO5

## ACCOUNTING METHODS

Once a business adopts a tax year, it must determine which items of income and deduction to recognize during a *particular* year. Generally speaking, the taxpayer's **accounting methods** determine the tax year in which a business recognizes a particular item of income or deduction. Because accounting methods affect the *timing* of when a taxpayer reports income and deductions, accounting methods are very important for taxpayers using a timing tax strategy to defer income or accelerate deductions.[34]

---

[32]Virtually all individual taxpayers use a calendar year tax year.

[33]See §706 for the specific restrictions on year-ends for partnerships and §1378 for restrictions on S corporations. If they can show a business purpose (not easy to do), both partnerships and S corporations may adopt year-ends other than those used by their owners. Recall that hybrid entities have the option to be treated as either flow-through entities or taxable corporations for tax purposes.

[34]Accounting methods do not determine *whether* an item of income is taxable or an expense is deductible. Accordingly, accounting methods generally do not affect the total income or deductions recognized over the taxpayer's lifetime.

## Financial and Tax Accounting Methods

Many businesses are required to generate financial statements for nontax reasons. For example, publicly traded corporations must file financial statements with the Securities and Exchange Commission (SEC) based on generally accepted accounting principles (GAAP). Also, privately owned businesses borrowing money from banks are often required to generate financial statements under GAAP, so that the lender can evaluate the business's creditworthiness. In reporting financial statement income, businesses have incentives to select accounting methods permissible under GAAP that accelerate income and defer deductions. In contrast, for tax planning purposes, businesses have incentives to choose accounting methods that *defer income* and *accelerate deductions*. This natural tension between financial reporting incentives and tax reporting incentives may be the reason the tax laws sometimes require businesses to use the same accounting methods for tax purposes that they use for financial accounting purposes. In other words, in many circumstances, if businesses want to defer taxable income, they must also defer book income.[35]

However, sometimes the tax laws require businesses to use different, presumably more appropriate, accounting methods for tax purposes. Consequently, for policy and administrative reasons, the tax laws also identify several circumstances when businesses must use specific tax accounting methods to determine taxable income no matter what accounting method they use for financial reporting purposes. We now turn our attention to accounting methods prescribed by the tax laws. With certain restrictions, businesses are able to select their *overall* accounting methods and accounting methods for *specific* items or transactions. We cover each of these in turn.

## Overall Accounting Method

Businesses must choose an overall method of accounting to track and report their business activities for tax purposes. The overriding requirement for any tax accounting method is that the method must "clearly reflect income" and be applied consistently.[36] The two primary overall methods are the cash method and the accrual method. Businesses may also choose a hybrid method (some accounts on the cash method and others on the accrual method).

**Cash Method**   A taxpayer (or business) using the cash method of accounting recognizes revenue when property or services are actually or constructively received. This is generally true no matter when the business sells the good or performs the service that generates the revenue. Likewise, a business adopting the cash method generally recognizes deductions when the expense is paid. Thus, the timing of the liability giving rise to the expense is usually irrelevant.

Keep in mind that a cash-method business receiving payments in *noncash* form (as property or services) must recognize the noncash payments as gross income. Also, in certain circumstances, a business expending cash on ordinary and necessary business expenses may not be allowed to *currently* deduct the expense at the time of the payment. For example, cash-method taxpayers (and accrual-method taxpayers) are not allowed to deduct prepaid interest expense and cannot usually deduct prepaid expenses or payments that create a tangible or intangible asset.[37] However, the regulations provide a **12-month rule** for prepaid business expenses to simplify the process of determining whether to capitalize or immediately expense payments that create benefits for a relatively brief period of time, such as insurance, security, rent, and

---

[35]§446(a).
[36]§446(b).
[37]§461(g).

warranty service contracts. When a business prepays business expenses, it may *immediately* deduct the prepayment if (1) the contract period does not last more than a year *and* (2) the contract period does not extend beyond the end of the taxable year following the tax year in which the taxpayer makes the payment.[38] If the prepaid expense does not meet both of these criteria, the business must capitalize the prepaid amount and amortize it over the length of the contract whether the business uses the cash or accrual method of accounting.[39]

---

**Example 8-14**

On July 1, 2010, Rick paid $1,200 for a 12-month insurance policy that covers his business property from accidents and casualties from July 1, 2010, through June 30, 2011. How much of the $1,200 expenditure may Rick deduct in 2010 if he uses the cash method of accounting for his business activities?

**Answer:** $1,200. Because the insurance coverage does not exceed 12 months and does not extend beyond the end of 2011, Rick is allowed to deduct the entire premium payment under the 12-month rule.

*What if:* Suppose the insurance policy was for 12 months but the policy ran from February 1, 2011, through January 31, 2012. How much of the expenditure may Rick deduct in 2010 if he uses the cash method of accounting for his business activities?

**Answer:** $0. Even though the contract period is 12 months or less, Rick is required to capitalize the cost of the prepayment for the insurance policy because the contract period extends beyond the end of 2011.

*What if:* Suppose Rick had paid $1,200 for an *18-month* policy beginning July 1, 2010 and ending December 31, 2011. How much may he deduct in 2010 if he uses the cash method of accounting for his business activities?

**Answer:** $400. In this scenario, because the policy exceeds 12 months, Rick is allowed to deduct the portion of the premium pertaining to 2010. In 2010, he would deduct $400 (6 months/ 18 months × $1,200). He would deduct the remaining $800 in 2011.

---

**Accrual Method**   Businesses using the accrual method to determine taxable income follow rules similar to GAAP with two basic differences. First, as we discuss below, requirements for recognizing taxable income tend to be structured to recognize income earlier than the recognition rules for financial accounting. Second, requirements for accruing tax deductions tend to be structured to recognize less accrued expenses than the recognition rules for financial reporting purposes. These differences reflect the underlying objectives of financial accounting income and taxable income. The objective of financial accounting is to provide useful information to stakeholders such as creditors, prospective investors, and shareholders. Because financial accounting methods are designed to guard against businesses overstating their profitability to these users, financial accounting tends to bias *against overstating* income. In contrast, the government's main objective for writing tax laws is to collect revenues. Thus, tax accounting rules for accrual-method businesses tend to bias *against understating* income. These differences should be apparent as we describe tax accounting rules for businesses.

---

[38]This 12-month rule applies to both cash-method and accrual-method taxpayers. However, for accrual-method taxpayers to deduct prepaid expenses, they must meet both the 12-month rule requirements and the economic performance requirements that we discuss in the next section.

[39]Reg. §1.263(a)-4(f).

*continued from page 8-1...*

Rick's CPA, Jane, informed him that he needs to select an overall method of accounting for Green Acres to compute its taxable income. Jane advised Rick to use the cash method. However, Rick wanted to prepare GAAP financial statements and use the accrual method of accounting. He decided that if Green Acres was going to become a big business, it needed to act like a big business. Finally, after much discussion, Rick and Jane reached a compromise. For the first year, they would track Green Acres' business activities using both the cash *and* the accrual methods. In addition, they would also keep GAAP-based books for financial purposes. When filing time comes, Rick would decide which method to use in reporting taxable income. Jane told Rick that he could wait until he filed his tax return to select the accounting method for tax purposes. ∎

### Accrual Income

Businesses using the accrual method of accounting generally recognize income when they meet the "all-events test."

**All-Events Test for Income**   The all-events test requires that businesses recognize income when (1) all events have occurred that determine or fix their right to receive the income and (2) the amount of the income can be determined with reasonable accuracy.[40] Assuming the amount of income can be determined with reasonable accuracy, businesses meet the all-events requirement on the *earliest* of the following three dates:

1. When they complete the task required to earn the income. Businesses earn income for services as they provide the services, and they generally earn income from selling property when the title of the property passes to the buyer.
2. When the payment for the task is due from the customer.
3. When the business receives payment for the task.

**Example 8-15**

In early fall, Rick contracted with a dozen homeowners to landscape their yards. Rick agreed to do the work for an aggregate of $11,000. Rick and his crew started in the fall and completed the jobs in December 2010. However, he didn't mail the bills until after the holidays and didn't receive any payments until January 2011. When must Rick recognize the income from this work?

**Answer:** Under the accrual method, Rick must recognize the entire $11,000 as income in 2010 because his right to the income is fixed when Rick and his crew had completed the work by year-end. Under the cash method, however, Rick would not recognize the $11,000 as income until 2011 when he received it.

### Taxation of Advance Payments of Income (Prepaid Income)

In some cases, businesses receive income payments *before* they actually earn the income (they receive a prepayment). *When* the business must recognize a prepayment as income depends on the type of income. The rule for interest and rental income is

[40]Reg. §1.451-1(a).

relatively strict. Businesses must recognize prepaid rental and prepaid interest income *immediately* upon receipt (the income is recognized before it is earned). However, businesses are not required to recognize security deposits received from rental customers because they incur a liability to return security deposits when they receive the payments.[41] The income recognition rules are less strict when businesses receive advance payments for services or goods.

**Advance Payment for Services** For financial reporting purposes, a business does not immediately recognize income on advance payments it receives for services to be provided in the future. For financial reporting purposes, an advance payment for services is recorded as a debit for cash received and a credit to a liability account (unearned financial accounting income). The business then recognizes the *financial* income from the services as it performs the services. In contrast, for tax purposes, the all-events test generally requires businesses receiving *advance* payments for services to recognize the income when they receive the payment, rather than when they perform the services.

The IRS provides an exception to this immediate recognition general rule. Specifically, businesses receiving advance payments for services may *defer* recognizing the *prepayment* as income until the tax year *following* the year they receive the payment.[42] This one-year deferral does *not* apply (1) if (or the extent to which) the income is actually earned by the end of the year of receipt, (2) if the prepayment was included in financial reporting income, or (3) if the prepayment was for interest or rent (taxpayers must recognize prepaid interest and rental income on receipt).

**Advance Payment for Goods** When an accrual-method business receives an advance payment for *goods* it will provide to customers in the future, the business may account for the prepayment for tax purposes under the **full-inclusion method** or the **deferral method**.[43] Businesses electing the full-inclusion method *immediately* recognize the advance payment as income. Businesses using the deferral method recognize advance payments for goods by the earlier of (1) when the business would recognize the income for tax purposes if it had not received the *advance* payment or (2) when it recognizes the income for financial reporting purposes. Thus, the deferral method is comparable to the deferral allowed for advance payments received for future services. However, unlike the treatment of advance payments for services, advance payments for goods could be deferred for more than a year, if the business defers the income for financial reporting purposes for more than a year.

**Example 8-16**

In late November 2010, Rick received a $7,200 payment from a client for monthly landscaping services from December 1, 2010, through November 30, 2012 ($300 a month for 24 months). When must Rick recognize the income from the advance payment for services?

**Answer:** Under the accrual method, Rick would initially recognize the $300 income he earned in December 2010. In 2011, he would recognize the remaining $6,900 (rather than only the $3,600

(*continued on page 8-21...*)

---

[41]*Comm. v. Indianapolis Power & Light Co.* (1990), 493 US 203.
[42]Rev Proc. 2004-34, 2004-1 CB 991.
[43]Reg. §1.141-5

related to 2011) because he is not allowed to defer the prepayments for services for more than a year. Under the cash method, Rick must recognize the entire prepayment, $7,200, as income upon receipt in 2010.

*What if:* Suppose the $7,200 prepayment was for the delivery of 15 pallets of sod at a cost to Rick of $1,800. Suppose further that five pallets were to be delivered in 2011 and the remainder was to be delivered in 2012. When would Rick recognize the income from the advance payment of goods under the accrual method?

**Answer:** If Rick elected the full-inclusion method, then he would recognize the entire prepayment of $7,200 as income (minus his cost of goods sold of $1,800) in 2010. However, if Rick elected the deferral method, then he would recognize the income as the sod is delivered, $2,400 in 2011 (minus $600 cost of goods sold) and $4,800 in 2012 (minus $1,200 cost of goods sold).

## Inventories

Many businesses generate income by selling products they acquire for resale or products they manufacture. Businesses for which selling inventory is a material income-producing factor generally must account for gross profit (sales minus cost of goods sold) using the accrual method, even when they are otherwise cash-method taxpayers.

An exception to this general rule is that a cash-method business is allowed to use the cash method to account for gross profit if the average annual gross receipts for the three-year period prior to the current year do not exceed $10 million. In addition, the primary business activity must be to provide services to customers and the sales of products is a secondary or small part of its services.[44] However, the business is not allowed to deduct the cost of the inventory to the extent it has the product at the end of the year. How does this exception benefit a cash-method business if the business is not allowed to fully deduct the cost of inventory until it sells the inventory? It may benefit the business because it allows it to use the cash method to account for sales revenue. Without the exception, cash-method service businesses would be required to account for sales revenue from inventory sales on the accrual method, which means they may be required to recognize revenue before they actually receive it. With the exception, they are allowed to defer the revenue recognition until they receive the payments from customers.

Businesses selling inventory must determine their inventory costs to accurately compute taxable income. This requires businesses to maintain records of balances for finished goods inventory and, if applicable, for partially finished goods and raw materials. Inventory costs include the purchase price of raw materials (minus any discounts), shipping costs, and any indirect costs it allocates to the inventory under the **uniform cost capitalization rules (UNICAP rules).**[45]

**Uniform Capitalization**   The tax laws require businesses to capitalize in the cost of inventory certain direct and indirect costs associated with inventories.[46] Congress enacted these rules primarily for two reasons. First, the rules accelerate tax revenues for the government by deferring deductions for the capitalized costs until the business sells the associated inventory. Thus, there is generally a one-year lag between when businesses initially capitalize the costs and when they deduct them. Second, Congress designed the "uniform" rules to reduce variation in the costs businesses

> **THE KEY FACTS**
>
> **Inventories**
>
> ■ Businesses must use the accrual method to account for substantial inventories.
>
> ■ The UNICAP rules require capitalization of most indirect costs of production.
>
> ■ The LIFO method is allowed if also used for financial reporting purposes.

---

[44]Rev. Proc. 2002-28, 2002-1 CB 815. There are other exceptions to this general rule. For example, certain cash-method taxpayers (average annual receipts of $1 million or less) can qualify to account for merchandise for sale as materials and supplies under Rev. Proc. 2001-10, 2001-1 CB 272.

[45]Inventory valuation allowances are generally not allowed, but taxpayers can adopt the lower of cost or market method of inventory valuation. In addition, specific goods not salable at normal prices can be valued at bona fide selling prices less direct cost of disposition.

[46]§263A(a).

include in inventory. Congress intended the UNICAP provisions to apply to large businesses. Consequently, businesses with average annual gross receipts of $10 million or less over the three-year period ending with the taxable year prior to the current year are not *required* to use the UNICAP rules.

Under these uniform cost capitalization rules, large businesses are generally required to capitalize more costs to inventory for tax purposes than they capitalize under financial accounting rules. Under GAAP, businesses generally include in inventory only those costs incurred within their production facility. In contrast, the UNICAP rules require businesses to allocate to inventory the costs they incur inside the production facility and the costs they incur outside the facility to support production (or inventory acquisition) activities. For example, under the UNICAP provisions, a business must capitalize at least a portion of the compensation paid to employees in its purchasing department, general and administrative department, and even its information technology department, to the extent these groups provide support for the production process. In contrast, businesses immediately expense these costs as period costs for financial accounting purposes. The regulations provide guidance on the costs that must be allocated to inventory. Selling, advertising, and research costs are specifically identified as costs that do not have to be allocated to inventory under the UNICAP provisions.[47]

---

**Example 8-17**

**What if:** Green Acres sells trees but Rick anticipates selling flowers, shrubs, and other plants in future years. Ken is Rick's employee in charge of purchasing inventory. Ken's compensation this year is $30,000, and Rick estimates that Ken spends about 5 percent of his time acquiring inventory and the remaining time working on landscaping projects. How would Rick allocate Ken's compensation under the UNICAP rules?

**Answer:** If the UNICAP rules applied to Green Acres, Rick would allocate $1,500 ($30,000 × 5%) of Ken's compensation to the cost of the inventory Green Acres acquired this year. (Note, however, because Green Acres' gross receipts for the year are under $10,000,000, it is not *required* to apply the UNICAP rules.) In contrast, Ken's entire salary would be expensed as a period cost for financial accounting purposes.

---

**Inventory Cost-Flow Methods** Once a business determines the cost of its inventory, it must use an inventory cost-flow method to determine its cost of goods sold. Three primary cost-flow methods are (1) first-in, first-out (**FIFO**), (2) last-in, first-out (**LIFO**), and (3) **specific identification.** Businesses might be inclined to use FIFO or LIFO methods when they sell similar, relatively low-cost, high-volume products such as cans of soup or barrels of oil. These methods simplify inventory accounting because the business need not track the individual cost of each item it sells. In contrast, businesses that sell distinct, relatively high-cost, low-volume products might be more likely to adopt the specific identification method. For example, jewelry and used-car businesses would likely use the specific identification method to account for their cost of sales. In general terms, when costs are increasing, a business using the FIFO method will report a higher gross margin than if it used the LIFO method. The opposite is true if costs are decreasing.

---

[47]Reg. §1.263A–1(e)(3)(iii).

**Example 8-18**

In late August, Rick purchased 10 oak saplings (immature trees) for a total purchase price of $3,000. In September, he purchased 12 more for a total price of $3,900, and in late October, he purchased 15 more for $5,000. The total cost of each lot of trees was determined as follows:

| Purchase Date | Trees | Direct Cost | Other Costs | Total Cost |
|---|---|---|---|---|
| August 20 | 10 | $ 3,000 | $200 | $ 3,200 |
| September 15 | 12 | 3,900 | 300 | 4,200 |
| October 22 | 15 | 5,000 | 400 | 5,400 |
| Totals | 37 | $11,900 | $900 | $12,800 |

Before the end of the year, Green Acres sold 20 of the oak saplings (5 from the August lot, 5 from the September lot, and 10 from the October lot) for cash. What is Green Acres' gross profit from sales of oak saplings if the sales revenue totaled $14,000 (all collected by year-end), and what is its ending oak sapling inventory under the accrual and the cash method of accounting?

**Answer:** Under the accrual method, Green Acres' gross profit from sapling sales and its ending inventory balance for the remaining oak saplings under the FIFO, LIFO, and specific identification cost-flow methods is as follows:

| | FIFO | LIFO | Specific ID |
|---|---|---|---|
| Sales | $14,000 | $14,000 | $14,000 |
| Cost of goods sold | −6,700 | −7,150 | −6,950 |
| Gross profit | $ 7,300 | $ 6,850 | $ 7,050 |
| Ending inventory: | | | |
| August 20 trees | $ 0 | $ 3,200 | $ 1,600 |
| September 15 trees | 700 | 2,450 | 2,450 |
| October 22 trees | 5,400 | 0 | 1,800 |
| Total ending inventory | $ 6,100 | $ 5,650 | $ 5,850 |

Using the cash method, the answer is the same as it is under the accrual method. Green Acres is not allowed to deduct the cost of its ending inventory even if it qualifies to use the cash method to account for gross profit under the small business ($10M) exception.

**What if:** Assume the same original facts except that Green Acres received $10,000 sales revenue from customers this year and the remaining $4,000 early next year. Assuming Green Acres qualifies to use the cash method to account for gross profit under the small business ($10M) exception, what is the amount of Green Acres' gross profit this year if it uses the specific identification method of accounting for its ending inventory?

**Answer:** $3,050 ($10,000 revenue minus $6,950 cost of goods sold). In this situation Green Acres would be allowed to defer $4,000 of the sales revenue until it collected it next year.

When costs are subject to inflation over time, a business would get the best of both worlds if it adopted the FIFO method for financial reporting purposes and the LIFO method for tax purposes. Not surprisingly, the tax laws require that a business can use LIFO for tax purposes only if it also uses LIFO for financial reporting purposes.[48] While this "consistency" requirement may not matter to entities not required to generate financial reports, it can be very restrictive to publicly traded corporations.

[48]§472(c).

### Accrual Deductions

Generally, when accrual-method businesses incur a liability relating to a business expense, they account for it by crediting a liability account (or cash if they pay the liability at the time they incur it) and debiting an expense account. However, to record an expense and the corresponding deduction for tax purposes, the business must meet (1) an all-events test for the liability *and* (2) an **economic performance test** with respect to the liability.[49] While the all-events test for recognizing deductions is similar to the all-events test for recognizing income, the additional economic performance requirement makes the deduction recognition rules more stringent than the income recognition rules. The deduction rules generally preclude businesses from deducting estimated expenses or reserves.

**All-Events Test for Deductions**   For a business to recognize a deduction, all events that establish its liability giving rise to the deduction must have occurred, and it must be able to determine the amount of the liability with reasonable accuracy.[50]

| **Example 8-19** | |
|---|---|

On November of this year, Rick agreed to a one-year $6,000 contract with Ace Advertising to produce a radio ad campaign. Ace agreed that Rick would owe nothing under the contract unless his sales increase a minimum of 25 percent over the next six months. What amount, if any, may Rick deduct this year for this contract under the accrual and cash methods?

**Answer:** Under the accrual method, Green Acres is not allowed to recognize *any* deduction this year for the liability. Even though Ace will have completed two months of advertising for Green Acres by the end of the year, its guarantee means that Rick's liability is not fixed until and unless his sales increase by 25 percent.

Under the cash method, Rick would not deduct any of the cost of the campaign this year because he has not paid anything to Ace.

**Economic Performance**   Even when businesses meet the all-events test, they still must clear the economic performance hurdle to recognize the tax deduction. This requirement specifies that businesses may not recognize a deduction for an expense until the underlying activity generating the associated liability (called *economic performance*) has occurred. Thus, an accrual-method business would not be allowed to deduct a prepaid business expense even if it qualified to do so under the 12-month rule (discussed above) unless it also met the economic performance test with respect to the liability associated with the expense.

The specific requirements for the economic performance test differ based on whether the liability arose from:

- Receiving goods or services *from* another party.
- Renting or leasing property *from* another party.
- Providing goods or services *to* another party.
- Certain activities creating **payment liabilities.**

*Receiving goods and (or) services from another party.*   When a business agrees to pay another party for goods or services the other party will provide, the business deducts the expense associated with the liability as the other party provides the goods or

[49]§461(h).
[50]§461.

services (assuming the all-events test is met for the liability). As an exception to this general rule, when a business hires another party to provide goods or services, and in this situation the business actually *pays* the liability before the other party provides the goods or services, the business may treat the *actual payment as economic performance* as long as it *reasonably expects* the other party to provide the goods or all of the services within three and one-half months after it makes the payment.[51]

**Example 8-20**

On December 15, 2010, Rick hires Your New Fence, LLC (YNF), to install a concrete wall for one of his clients by paying $1,000 of the cost as a down payment and agreeing to pay the remaining $7,000 when YNF finishes the wall. YNF was not going to start building the wall until early 2011, so as of the end of the year Rick has not billed his client for the wall. Rick expects YNF to finish the wall by the end of April. What amount associated with his liability to YNF is Rick allowed to deduct in 2010 and 2011?

**Answer:** Rick is not entitled to a deduction in 2010. Under the accrual method, Rick will deduct his full $8,000 cost of the wall in 2011 when YNF builds the wall, because economic performance occurs as YNF provides the services, even though Rick paid for part of the goods and services in 2010. Under the cash method, Rick would deduct $1,000 (his down payment) in 2010 and the remainder in 2011 when he pays the remainder on the contract.

**What if:** Assume that Rick expected YNF to finish building the wall by the end of January 2011. What amount associated with this liability to YNF is Rick allowed to deduct in 2010 and 2011?

**Answer:** Under the accrual method, Rick is allowed to deduct $1,000 in 2010 because Rick actually paid this amount in 2010 and he reasonably expected YNF to finish its work on the wall within 3½ months after he made the payment to YNF on December 15. Rick would deduct the remaining $7,000 cost of the wall in 2011 when YNF builds the wall.

Under the cash method, Rick deducts the $1,000 down payment in 2010 and the remaining $7,000 when he makes the payment in 2011.

***Renting or leasing property from another party.*** When a business enters into an agreement to rent or lease property from another party, economic performance occurs over the rental period. Thus, the business is allowed to deduct the rental expense over the rental period.

**Example 8-21**

On May 1, 2010, Rick paid $7,200 in advance to rent his shop for 12 months ($600 per month). What amount may Rick deduct for rent in 2010 if he accounts for his business activities using the accrual method?

**Answer:** $4,800 ($600 × 8 months use in 2010). Even though the rent is a prepaid business expense under the 12-month rule (the contract period is for 12 months and the contract period does not extend beyond 2011), he must deduct the rent expense over the term of the lease because that is when economic performance occurs.

**What if:** Assuming the original facts, what amount of the $7,200 rental payment may Rick deduct in 2010 if he is using the cash method of accounting for his business?

**Answer:** $7,200. In this case, Rick may deduct the expense under the 12-month rule. He does not have to meet the economic performance requirement to deduct the expense because the economic performance requirements apply to accrual—not cash-method taxpayers.

[51]Reg. §1.461-4(d)(6).

| Example 8-22 | |
|---|---|

On November 1, 2010, Rick paid $2,400 to rent a trailer for 24 months. What amount of this payment may Rick deduct and when may he deduct it?

**Answer:** Under the accrual method, even though Rick paid the entire rental fee in advance, economic performance occurs over the 24-month rental period. Thus, Green Acres deducts $200 for the trailer rental in 2010, $1,200 in 2011, and $1,000 in 2012. Because the rental period exceeds 12 months, the amount and timing of the deductions are the same under the cash method.

***Providing goods and services to another party.*** Businesses liable for providing goods and services to other parties meet the economic performance test for these liabilities as they incur costs in satisfying the liabilities.

| Example 8-23 | |
|---|---|

In the summer, Rick landscaped a city park. As part of this service, Rick agreed to remove a fountain from the park at the option of the city parks committee. In December 2010, the committee decided to have Rick remove the fountain. Rick began the removal in December and completed the removal in the spring of 2011. Rick paid a part-time employee $850 for the removal work in December and an additional $685 to complete the removal the following spring. What is the amount and timing of Rick's deductions for the removal project?

**Answer:** Under the accrual method, Rick is allowed to deduct his payments for services to others as he incurs costs to satisfy his liability for removing the fountain. Consequently, Rick can deduct the $850 payment to meet this obligation in 2010 and the remaining $685 in 2011. Under the cash method, the amount and timing of his deductions would be the same as it is under the accrual method.

***What if:*** Suppose that in December 2010, Rick paid $1,000 to a subcontractor to remove the fountain and the subcontractor removed the fountain in 2011. What is the amount and timing of Rick's deductions for the removal project in this situation?

**Answer:** Under the accrual method, because Rick is hiring another person to provide the service that he is liable to perform, economic performance occurs once the service is provided (rather than as costs are incurred). Hence, Rick can only deduct the $1,000 payment once the fountain has been removed in 2011.[52] Under the cash method, however, Rick can deduct $1,000 in 2010 when he makes the payment to the subcontractor.

***Payment liabilities.*** Economic performance occurs for certain liabilities only when the business actually *pays* the liability. Thus, accrual-method businesses incurring payment liabilities are essentially on the *cash method* for deducting the associated expenses. Exhibit 8-4 describes different categories of these payment liabilities.

### EXHIBIT 8-4    Categories of Payment Liabilities

Economic performance occurs when taxpayer pays liability associated with:

- Worker's compensation, tort, breach of contract, or violation of law.
- Rebates and refunds.
- Awards, prizes, and jackpots.
- Insurance, warranties, and service contracts provided *to* the business. (Note: This is insurance, warranties, and product service contracts that cover the taxpayer and *not* a warranty like the one in Example 8-24 that the taxpayer provides to others.)
- Taxes.[53]
- Other liabilities not provided for elsewhere.

---

[52]Reg. §1.461-4(d)(4) and Reg. §1.461-4(d)(7), Example 1. Under Reg. §1.461-d(6), Rick could deduct the $1,000 in 2010 if he reasonably expected the subcontractor to complete the removal of the fountain within 3½ months of year-end.

[53]While taxes are generally not deducted until they are paid, §461(c) allows businesses to elect to accrue the deduction for real property taxes as time passes instead of deducting them when they actually pay them.

***Recurring item exception.***   One of the most common exceptions to economic performance is the recurring item exception. Under §461(h)(3), accrual method taxpayers can deduct certain accrued expenses even if economic performance has not occurred by year-end. A recurring item is a liability that is expected to persist in future years, and is either not material in amount or deducting the expense currently matches with revenue. In addition, the all-events test must be satisfied at year-end and actual economic performance must occur within a reasonable time or 8½ months of year-end. As a final note, the recurring item exception does not apply to worker's compensation or tort liabilities.

---

**Example 8-24**

If clients are not completely satisfied with Green Acres' landscaping work, Rick offers a $200 refund with no questions asked. Near the end of the year, Rick had four clients request refunds. Rick incurred the liability for the refunds this year. However, Rick was busy during the holiday season, so he didn't pay the refunds until January 2011. When should Rick deduct the customer refunds?

**Answer:** Because refunds are payment liabilities, economic performance does not occur until Rick actually pays the refunds. Consequently, Rick deducts the $800 of refunds in 2011 even though the liability for the refunds met the all-events test in 2010. Under the cash method, Rick would not deduct the refunds until he paid them in 2011.

***What if:*** Suppose that Rick expected that $800 of refunds would typically be accrued at year-end. Under what conditions could Rick deduct the refunds in 2010 if he elects to use accrual accounting?

**Answer:** If the accrued refunds are not material in amount and Rick expects actual economic performance within a reasonable time after year-end (but not longer than 8½ months), then Rick can elect to deduct the refunds in 2010 using the recurring item exception.

---

Accrual-method taxpayers that prepay business expenses for *payment liabilities* (insurance contracts, warranties, and product service contracts provided to the taxpayer) are allowed to immediately deduct the prepayments subject to the 12-month rule for prepaid expenses. Thus, the deductible amounts for Rick's prepaid insurance contracts in Example 8-14 are the same for both the cash method and accrual method of accounting. Exhibit 8-5 describes the requirements for economic performance for the different types of liabilities.

## EXHIBIT 8-5   Economic Performance

| Taxpayer incurs liability from | Economic performance occurs |
|---|---|
| Receiving goods and services *from* another party | When the goods or services are provided to the taxpayer or with payment if the taxpayer reasonably expects actual performance within 3½ months. |
| Renting or leasing property *from* another party | Ratably over the time period during which the taxpayer is entitled to use the property or money. |
| Providing goods and services *to* another party | When the taxpayer incurs costs to satisfy the liability or provide the goods and services. |
| Activities creating "payment" liabilities | When the business actually makes payment. |
| Interest expense | As accrued. This technically does not fall within the economic performance rules but it is a similar concept. |

**Bad Debt Expense**   When accrual method businesses sell a product or a service on credit, they debit accounts receivable and credit sales revenue for both financial and tax purposes. However, because businesses usually are unable to collect the full amount of their accounts receivable, they incur bad debt expense (a customer owes them a debt that the customer will not pay). For financial reporting purposes, the business estimates the amount of the bad debt, debits bad debt expense, and credits

an allowance for doubtful accounts. However, for tax purposes, businesses are allowed to deduct bad debt expense only when the debt actually becomes worthless within the taxable year.[54] Consequently, for tax purposes, businesses determine which debts are uncollectible and write them off by debiting bad debt expense and *directly* crediting the actual account receivable account that is uncollectible. This required method of determining bad debt expense for tax purposes is called the **direct write-off method.** In contrast, the method used for financial reporting purposes is called the **allowance method.** Businesses reporting taxable income on the cash method of accounting are *not* allowed to deduct bad debt expenses, because they do not include receivables in taxable income (they do not credit revenue until they actually receive payment).

---

**Example 8-25**

At year-end, Rick estimates that about $900 of the receivables from his landscaping services will be uncollectible, but he has identified only one client, Jared, who will definitely not pay his bill. Jared, who has skipped town, owes Rick $280 for landscaping this fall. What amount of bad debt expense may Rick deduct for the year?

**Answer:** For financial reporting purposes, Rick recognizes a $900 bad debt expense. However, for tax purposes, under the accrual method, Rick can only deduct $280—the amount associated with specifically writing off Jared's receivable. Under the cash method, Rick would not be able to claim any deduction, because he did not receive a payment from Jared and thus did not recognize income on the amount Jared owed him.

---

**Limitations on Accruals to Related Parties**    To prevent businesses and related parties from working together to defer taxes, the tax laws prevent an accrual-method business from accruing (and deducting) an expense for a liability owed to a related party using the cash method until the related party recognizes the income associated with the payment.[55] For this purpose, related parties include:

- Family members including parents, siblings, and spouses.
- Shareholders and C corporations when the shareholder owns more than 50 percent of the corporation's stock.[56]
- Owners of partnerships and S corporations no matter the ownership percentage.[57]

This issue frequently arises in situations in which a business employs the owner or a relative of an owner. The business is not allowed to deduct compensation expense owed to the related party until the year in which the related party includes the compensation in income. However, this related-party limit extends beyond compensation to *any* accrued expense the business owes to a related cash-method taxpayer.

---

**Example 8-26**

In December, Rick asked his retired father, Henry, to help him finish a landscaping job. By the end of the year, Rick owed Henry $2,000 of (reasonable) compensation for his efforts, which he paid in January 2011. What amount of this compensation may Rick deduct and when may he deduct it?

**Answer:** If Rick uses the accrual method and Henry the cash method, Rick will not be able to deduct the $2,000 compensation expense until 2011. Rick is Henry's son, so Rick and Henry are "related" parties for tax purposes. Consequently, Rick can deduct the compensation only when Henry includes the payment in his taxable income in 2011. If Rick uses the cash method, he will deduct the expense when he pays it in January 2011.

---

[54]§166(a).

[55]§267(a).

[56]Certain constructive ownership rules apply in determining ownership percentages for this purpose. See §267(c).

[57]See §267(b) for related-party definitions.

## Comparison of Accrual and Cash Methods

From a business perspective, the two primary advantages of adopting the cash method over the accrual method are that (1) the cash method provides the business with more flexibility to time income and deductions by accelerating or deferring payments (timing tax planning strategy) and (2) bookkeeping for the cash method is easier. For example, a cash-method taxpayer could defer revenue by waiting to bill clients for goods or services until after year-end, thereby increasing the likelihood that customers would send payment after year-end. There are some concerns with this tax strategy. For example, delaying the bills might increase the likelihood that the customers will not pay their bills at all.

The primary advantage of the accrual method over the cash method is that it better matches revenues and expenses. For that reason, external financial statement users who want to evaluate a business's financial performance prefer the accrual method. Consistent with this idea, the cash method is not allowed for financial reporting under GAAP.

Although the cash method is by far the predominate accounting method among sole proprietors, it is less common in other types of businesses. In fact, tax laws generally prohibit C corporations and partnerships with corporate partners from using the cash method of accounting.[58] Exhibit 8-6 details the basic differences in accounting for income and deductions under the accrual and the cash method of accounting.

### EXHIBIT 8-6   Comparison of Cash and Accrual Methods

| Income or Expense Item | Cash Method | Accrual Method |
|---|---|---|
| Income recognition | Actually or constructively received. | Earned under the all-events test. |
| Prepaid rental and interest income | Taxable on receipt. | Taxable on receipt. |
| Prepaid income for services | Taxable on receipt. | Taxed when earned or in the following year of receipt if not earned by end of year of receipt. |
| Prepaid income for goods | Taxable on receipt. | Full-inclusion is taxed on receipt but deferral election allows taxation when earned. |
| Deduction recognition | Deduct when paid; economic performance does not apply. | Deduct under all-events test and economic performance test. |
| Expenditures for tangible assets with a useful life more than one year | Capitalize and apply cost recovery. | Same as cash method. |
| Expenditures for intangible assets other than prepaid business expenses | Capitalize and amortize if provision in code allows it. | Same as the cash method. |
| Prepaid business expenses | Immediately deductible unless contract period exceeds 12 months or extends beyond the end of the next taxable year. | Same as cash method if payment liability, otherwise, capitalize and apply economic performance rules to determine timing of deduction. |
| Prepaid interest expense | Not deductible until interest accrues. | Same as the cash method. |
| Bad debt expense | Not deductible because sales on account not included in income. | Deduct under direct write-off method. |

---

[58]These entities are able to adopt the cash method if their average annual gross receipts for the three tax years ending with the prior tax year do not exceed $5 million (see §448).

**Example 8-27**

At year-end, Rick determined that Green Acres had collected a total of $71,000 of service revenue (not described elsewhere in examples). Rick is debating whether to adopt the cash or accrual method. To help him resolve his dilemma, Jane includes these revenues in a calculation of Green Acres' taxable income under the cash and accrual methods (Exhibit 8-7). What are the differences between the two calculations?

**Answer:** Jane provided the following summary of the differences between taxable income under the cash method and taxable income under the accrual method:

| Description | (1)<br>Cash | (2)<br>Accrual | (1) - (2)<br>Difference | Example |
|---|---|---|---|---|
| Revenue: | | | | |
|    Credit sales | 0 | 11,000 | −11,000 | 8-15 |
|    Prepaid revenue | 7,200 | 300 | +6,900 | 8-16 |
| Expenses: | | | | |
|    Prepaid services | −1,000 | 0 | −1,000 | 8-20 |
|    Prepaid rent expense | −7,200 | −4,800 | −2,400 | 8-21 |
|    Bad debts | 0 | −280 | +280 | 8-25 |
| Total difference (accrual income > cash income) | | | −7,220 | |

Jane explains that by comparing the revenue and expenses recognized under the two accounting methods, the selection of the accrual method for Green Acres means that Rick will be taxed on an additional $7,220 of income this year than if Green Acres adopts the cash method.

The business income for Green Acres under the accrual and cash methods is summarized in Exhibit 8-7. After reflecting on these numbers and realizing that he would recognize $7,220 more taxable income (and self-employment income subject to self-employment tax) this year under the accrual method than under the cash method, Rick decided it made sense to adopt the cash method of accounting for Green Acres' first tax return. He figured Green Acres could always act like a big business next year. Meanwhile, he knew he had to include Green Acres' business income on Schedule C of his individual tax return. Exhibit 8-8 presents Rick's Schedule C for Green Acres using the cash method of accounting.

## Adopting an Accounting Method

We've seen that businesses use overall accounting methods (cash, accrual, or hybrid) and many specific accounting methods (inventory cost-flow assumption, methods of accounting for prepaid income for goods, and methods for accounting for prepaid expenses, among other methods) to account for their business activities. For tax purposes, it's important to understand how and when a business technically *adopts* an accounting method because once it does so, it must get the IRS's permission to change the method.

Businesses generally elect their accounting methods by using the methods on their tax returns. However, *when* the business technically adopts a method depends on whether the method it uses on its tax return is a **permissible accounting method** or an **impermissible accounting method.** So far, our discussion has emphasized accounting methods permissible under the tax laws. However, businesses may unwittingly (or

**EXHIBIT 8-7    Green Acres' Net Business Income**

| Description | Cash | Accrual | Example |
|---|---|---|---|
| **Income** | | | |
| Service revenue: | | | |
| Greenhouse construction | $ 5,000 | $ 5,000 | 8-10 |
| December landscape service | 0 | 11,000 | 8-15 |
| Prepaid landscape services | 7,200 | 300 | 8-16 |
| Landscaping revenue | 71,000 | 71,000 | 8-27 |
| Sales of inventory: | | | |
| Trees sales | 14,000 | 14,000 | 8-18 |
| Cost of goods sold (LIFO method) | −7,150 | −7,150 | 8-18 |
| **Gross Profit** | **$90,050** | **$94,150** | |
| Car and truck expense: | | | |
| SUV operating expense | 5,335 | 5,335 | 8-7 |
| BMW operating expense | 206 | 206 | 8-9 |
| Insurance | 1,200 | 1,200 | 8-14 |
| Rent | | | |
| Shop | 7,200 | 4,800 | 8-21 |
| Trailer | 200 | 200 | 8-22 |
| Travel, meals, and entertainment: | | | |
| Travel to NY seminar | 1,435 | 1,435 | 8-8 |
| Dinner and Theatre with client | 270 | 270 | 8-6 |
| Wages and subcontractor fees: | | | |
| Part-time employees | 23,000 | 23,000 | 8-2 |
| Full time employee (Ken) | 30,000 | 30,000 | 8-17 |
| Fountain removal | 850 | 850 | 8-23 |
| Fence installation (prepaid subcontractor) | 1,000 | 0 | 8-20 |
| Other expenses: | | | |
| Education—meditation class | 50 | 50 | 8-1 |
| Education—seminar | 300 | 300 | 8-8 |
| Domestic manufacturing deduction | 90 | 90 | 8-10 |
| Uniforms | 500 | 500 | 8-5 |
| Bad debts | 0 | 280 | 8-25 |
| Other expenses not in examples: | | | |
| Advertising | 1,200 | 1,200 | |
| Depreciation | 4,000 | 4,000 | |
| Interest | 300 | 300 | |
| Legal and professional services | 1,100 | 1,100 | |
| Office expense | 1,500 | 1,500 | |
| Repairs and maintenance | 1,975 | 1,975 | |
| Taxes and licenses | 400 | 400 | |
| Utilities | 2,200 | 2,200 | |
| **Total deductions** | **$84,311** | **$81,191** | |
| **Net Business Income** | **$ 5,739** | **$12,959** | |

intentionally) use impermissible accounting methods. For example, a business using the allowance method for determining bad debt expense for tax purposes is using an impermissible accounting method because the tax laws prescribe the use of the direct write-off method for determining bad debt expense. A business *adopts* a *permissible* accounting method by using and reporting the tax results of the method for at least *one year*. A business *adopts* an *impermissible* method by using and reporting the results of the method for *two consecutive years*.

**EXHIBIT 8-8    Green Acres Schedule C**

| SCHEDULE C (Form 1040) | **Profit or Loss From Business** (Sole Proprietorship) | OMB No. 1545-0074 |
| --- | --- | --- |
| Department of the Treasury Internal Revenue Service (99) | ▶ Partnerships, joint ventures, etc., generally must file Form 1065 or 1065-B. ▶ Attach to Form 1040, 1040NR, or 1041.    ▶ See Instructions for Schedule C (Form 1040). | **20 09** Attachment Sequence No. **09** |

Name of proprietor | Social security number (SSN)

**RICK GRIME** ⊞

| A | Principal business or profession, including product or service (see page C-2 of the instructions) | | B Enter code from pages C-9, 10, & 11 |
| --- | --- | --- | --- |

**LANDSCAPER** ⊞    ▶ 5 7 1 6 3 0

| C | Business name. If no separate business name, leave blank. | D Employer ID number (EIN), if any |
| --- | --- | --- |

**GREEN ACRES LANDSCAPING** ⊞

| E | Business address (including suite or room no.) ▶ SAN ANTONIO, TEXAS |
| --- | --- |
| | City, town or post office, state, and ZIP code |

| F | Accounting method:    (1) ☑ Cash    (2) ☐ Accrual    (3) ☐ Other (specify) ▶ _____ |
| --- | --- |
| G | Did you "materially participate" in the operation of this business during 2009? If "No," see page C-3 for limit on losses    ☑ Yes    ☐ No |
| H | If you started or acquired this business during 2009, check here . . . . . . . . . . . . . . . . ▶ ☑ |

**Part I    Income**

| 1 | Gross receipts or sales. **Caution.** See page C-4 and check the box if: | | |
| --- | --- | --- | --- |
| | ● This income was reported to you on Form W-2 and the "Statutory employee" box on that form was checked, or | ▶ ☐ | |
| | ● You are a member of a qualified joint venture reporting only rental real estate income not subject to self-employment tax. Also see page C-3 for limit on losses. | 1 | 97,200 |
| 2 | Returns and allowances . . . . . . | 2 | |
| 3 | Subtract line 2 from line 1 . . . . . . | 3 | 97,200 |
| 4 | Cost of goods sold (from line 42 on page 2) . . . . . | 4 | 7,150 |
| 5 | **Gross profit.** Subtract line 4 from line 3 . . . . . . | 5 | 90,050 |
| 6 | Other income, including federal and state gasoline or fuel tax credit or refund (see page C-4) . . . . | 6 | |
| 7 | **Gross income.** Add lines 5 and 6 . . . . . . . . . . . . . . . . . . . ▶ | 7 | 90,050 |

**Part II    Expenses.** Enter expenses for business use of your home **only** on line 30.

| 8 | Advertising . . . . . | 8 | 1,200 | 18 | Office expense . . . . . . | 18 | 1,500 |
| --- | --- | --- | --- | --- | --- | --- | --- |
| 9 | Car and truck expenses (see page C-4) . . . . . | 9 | 5,541 | 19 | Pension and profit-sharing plans . | 19 | |
| 10 | Commissions and fees . | 10 | | 20 | Rent or lease (see page C-6): | | |
| 11 | Contract labor (see page C-4) | 11 | 1,000 | a | Vehicles, machinery, and equipment | 20a | 7,400 |
| 12 | Depletion . . . . | 12 | | b | Other business property . . . | 20b | |
| 13 | Depreciation and section 179 expense deduction (not included in Part III) (see page C-5) . . . . . | 13 | 4,000 | 21 | Repairs and maintenance . . . | 21 | 1,975 |
| | | | | 22 | Supplies (not included in Part III) . | 22 | |
| | | | | 23 | Taxes and licenses . . . . | 23 | 400 |
| | | | | 24 | Travel, meals, and entertainment: | | |
| | | | | a | Travel . . . . . . . . . | 24a | 1,435 |
| 14 | Employee benefit programs (other than on line 19) . . | 14 | | b | Deductible meals and entertainment (see page C-6) . . | 24b | 270 |
| 15 | Insurance (other than health) | 15 | 1,200 | 25 | Utilities . . . . . . | 25 | 2,200 |
| 16 | Interest: | | | 26 | Wages (less employment credits) . | 26 | 53,850 |
| a | Mortgage (paid to banks, etc.) | 16a | | 27 | Other expenses (from line 48 on page 2) . . . . . . . | 27 | 940 |
| b | Other . . . . . . | 16b | 300 | | | | |
| 17 | Legal and professional services . . . . . . | 17 | 1,100 | | | | |

| 28 | **Total expenses** before expenses for business use of home. Add lines 8 through 27 . . . . ▶ | 28 | 84,311 |
| --- | --- | --- | --- |
| 29 | Tentative profit or (loss). Subtract line 28 from line 7 . . . . . . . . . . | 29 | 5,739 |
| 30 | Expenses for business use of your home. Attach **Form 8829** . . . . . . . . | 30 | |
| 31 | **Net profit or (loss).** Subtract line 30 from line 29. | | |
| | ● If a profit, enter on both **Form 1040, line 12,** and **Schedule SE, line 2,** or on **Form 1040NR, line 13** (if you checked the box on line 1, see page C-7). Estates and trusts, enter on **Form 1041, line 3.** ● If a loss, you **must** go to line 32. | 31 | 5,739 |
| 32 | If you have a loss, check the box that describes your investment in this activity (see page C-7). | | |
| | ● If you checked 32a, enter the loss on both **Form 1040, line 12,** and **Schedule SE, line 2,** or on **Form 1040NR, line 13** (if you checked the box on line 1, see the line 31 instructions on page C-7). Estates and trusts, enter on **Form 1041, line 3.** ● If you checked 32b, you **must** attach **Form 6198.** Your loss may be limited. | 32a ☑ All investment is at risk. 32b ☐ Some investment is not at risk. | |

For Paperwork Reduction Act Notice, see page C-9 of the instructions.    Cat. No. 11334P    Schedule C (Form 1040) 2009

## Changing Accounting Methods

Once a business has adopted an accounting method, it must receive permission to change the method, regardless of whether the existing method is a permissible method or an impermissible method. A taxpayer requests permission to change accounting methods by filing Form 3115 with the IRS. The IRS automatically approves certain types of accounting method changes, but for others the business must provide a good business purpose for the change and pay a fee. The IRS also requires permission when a business must change from using an impermissible method; this requirement helps the IRS to certify that the business properly makes the transition to a permissible method. In essence, the IRS requires the business to report its own noncompliance. Why would a business do so? Besides complying with the tax laws, a business might report its own noncompliance to receive leniency from the IRS. Without getting into the details, the IRS is likely to assess fewer penalties and less interest expense for noncompliance when the business reports the noncompliance before the IRS discovers it on its own.

**Tax Consequences of Changing Accounting Method**  When a business changes from one accounting method to another, the business determines its taxable income for the year of change using the new method. Further, the business must make an adjustment to taxable income that effectively represents the *cumulative difference,* as of the beginning of the tax year, between the amount of income (or deductions) recognized under the old accounting method and the amount that would have been recognized for all prior years if the new method had been applied. This adjustment is called a **Section 481 adjustment.** The §481 adjustment prevents the duplication or omission of items of income or deduction due to a change in accounting method. If the §481 adjustment *increases* taxable income, the taxpayer recognizes it over *four years* beginning with the year of the change (25 percent of the full adjustment each year). If the adjustment *decreases* taxable income, the taxpayer recognizes it *entirely in the year of change.*

---

**Example 8-28**

***What if:*** Suppose that at the end of 2010, Green Acres has $24,000 of accounts receivable. Assuming Green Acres uses the cash method of accounting in 2010, it would not include the $24,000 of receivables in income in determining its 2010 taxable income. Suppose further that Rick decides to switch Green Acres to the accrual method of accounting in 2011 by filing a Form 3115 and receiving permission from the IRS. What is Rick's §481 adjustment for his change in accounting method from the cash to the accrual method?

**Answer:** $24,000 increase to income ($6,000 in 2011 and each of the subsequent three years). Since Rick would use the accrual method in 2011, he would *not* include payments he receives for the $24,000 receivables as income because he earned this income in 2010 (not 2011). Instead, Rick would be required to make a §481 adjustment to ensure that he does not *omit* these items from taxable income. His total §481 adjustment is to increase net income by $24,000. Because this is an income-increasing adjustment, Rick includes $6,000 of the adjustment (25 percent) in Green Acres' taxable income in 2011. He would likewise include a $6,000 §481 adjustment in each of the subsequent three years.

***What if:*** Suppose that at the end of 2010, Green Acres has $4,000 of accounts payable instead of $24,000 of accounts receivable. What is Rick's §481 adjustment for his change in accounting method from the cash to the accrual method?

**Answer:** In this instance Green Acres would have a negative (income-decreasing) §481 adjustment of $4,000 because the $4,000 of expenses would have accrued in 2010 but would not have been deducted. Hence, Green Acres would be entitled to deduct the full $4,000 as a negative §481 adjustment amount in 2011.

# CONCLUSION

This chapter discussed issues relating to business income and deductions. We learned that the income rules for businesses are very similar to those for individuals, and that businesses may deduct only ordinary and necessary business expenses and other business expenses specifically authorized by law. We also described several business expense limitations. Finally, we discussed the accounting periods and methods businesses may use in reporting taxable income to the IRS. The issues described in this chapter are widely applicable to all types of business entities including sole proprietorships, partnerships, S corporations, and C corporations. In the next chapter, we determine how businesses recover the costs of assets they use in their business activities.

## SUMMARY

**LO1**   Describe the general requirements for deducting business expenses and identify common business deductions.

- Ordinary and necessary business expenses are allowed as deductions to calculate net income from activities entered into with a profit motive.
- Only reasonable amounts are allowed as business expense deductions. Extravagant or excessive amounts are likely to be characterized by personal motives and are disallowed.

**LO2**   Apply the limitations on business deductions to distinguish between deductible and nondeductible business expenses.

- The law specifically prohibits deducting expenses against public policy (such as fines or bribes) and expenses that produce tax-exempt income.
- Expenses benefiting multiple periods must be capitalized and special limits and record-keeping requirements are applied to business expenses that may have personal benefits, such as entertainment and meals.

**LO3**   Identify and explain special business deductions specifically permitted under the tax laws.

- Special calculations are necessary for deductions such as bad debt expenses, the domestic production activities deduction, and casualty losses.

**LO4**   Explain the concept of an accounting period and describe accounting periods available to businesses.

- Accounting periods and methods are chosen at the time of filing the first tax return.
- There are three types of tax years, calendar year, fiscal year, and 52/53 week year, and each tax year is distinguished by year-end.

**LO5**   Identify and describe accounting methods available to businesses and apply cash and accrual methods to determine business income and expense deductions.

- Under the cash method, taxpayers recognize revenue when they actually or constructively receive property or services and recognize deductions when they actually pay the expense.
- Under the accrual method, the all-events test requires that income be recognized when all the events have occurred that are necessary to fix the right to receive payments and the amount of the payments can be determined with reasonable accuracy.
- The accrual method must be used to account for sales and purchases for businesses where inventories are an income-producing factor.
- Under the accrual method, accrued expenses can only be deducted once both the all-events test and the economic performance tests are met. The application of the economic performance test depends, in part, on the type of business expense.
- Changes in accounting method or accounting period typically require the consent of the IRS and a §481 adjustment to taxable income.

## KEY TERMS

12-month rule (8-17)
accounting method (8-16)
accounting period (8-15)
allowance method (8-28)
arm's length amount (8-4)
deferral method (8-20)
direct write-off method (8-28)
domestic production activities deduction (DPAD) (8-11)
economic performance test (8-24)
FIFO (8-22)

fiscal year (8-15)
flow-through entities (8-16)
full-inclusion method (8-20)
impermissible accounting method (8-30)
LIFO (8-22)
mixed-motive expenditures (8-7)
ordinary and necessary (8-3)
payment liability (8-24)
permissible accounting method (8-30)
personal expenses (8-6)

qualified production activities income (QPAI) (8-12)
reasonable in amount (8-3)
Section 481 adjustment (8-33)
specific identification (8-22)
tax year (8-15)
travel expenses (8-8)
uniform cost capitalization rules (UNICAP rules) (8-21)

## DISCUSSION QUESTIONS

1. **(LO1)** What is an "ordinary and necessary" business expenditure?
2. **(LO1)** Is cost of goods sold deductible as a business expense for a business selling inventory? Explain.
3. **(LO1)** Tom is an attorney who often represents individuals injured while working (worker liability claims). This year Tom spent $50 on a book entitled *Plumbing for Dummies* and paid $500 to take a course on plumbing residences and rental housing. Can you imagine circumstances in which these expenditures would be deductible as "ordinary and necessary" for an attorney. Explain.
4. **(LO1)** Jake is a professional dog trainer who purchases and trains dogs for use by law enforcement agencies. Last year Jake purchased 500 bags of dog food from a large pet food company at an average cost of $30 per bag. This year, however, Jake purchased 500 bags of dog food from a local pet food company at an average cost of $45 per bag. Under what circumstances would the IRS likely challenge the cost of Jake's dog food as unreasonable?
5. **(LO2)** What kinds of deductions are prohibited as a matter of public policy? Why might Congress deem it important to disallow deductions for expenditures against public policy?
6. **(LO2)** Provide an example of an expense associated with the production of tax-exempt income, and explain what might happen if Congress repealed the prohibition against deducting expenses incurred to produce tax-exempt income.
7. **(LO2)** Jerry is a self-employed rock star and this year he expended $1,000 on special "flashy" clothes and outfits. Jerry would like to deduct the cost of these clothes as work-related because the clothes are not acceptable to Jerry's sense of fashion. Under what circumstances can Jerry deduct the cost of these work clothes?
8. **(LO2)** Jimmy is a sole proprietor of a small dry cleaning business. This month Jimmy paid for his groceries by writing checks from the checking account dedicated to the dry cleaning business. Why do you suppose Jimmy is using his business checking account rather than his personal checking account to pay for personal expenditures?
9. **(LO2)** Tim employs three sales representatives who often take clients to dinner and provide entertainment in order to increase sales. This year Tim reimbursed the representatives $2,500 for the cost of meals and $8,250 for the cost of

**research**

entertaining clients. Describe the conditions under which Tim can claim deductions for meals and entertainment.

10. **(LO2)** Jenny uses her car for both business and personal purposes. She purchased the auto this year and drove 11,000 miles on business trips and 9,000 miles for personal transportation. Describe how Jenny will determine the amount of deductible expenses associated with the auto.

11. **(LO1, LO2)** What expenses are deductible when a taxpayer combines both business and personal activities on a trip? How do the rules for international travel differ from the rules for domestic travel?

12. **(LO2)** Clyde lives and operates a sole proprietorship in Dallas, Texas. This year Clyde found it necessary to travel to Fort Worth (about 25 miles away) for legitimate business reasons. Is Clyde's trip likely to qualify as "away from home," and why would this designation matter?

13. **(LO2)** Describe the record-keeping requirements for business deductions expenses including mixed-motive expenditures.

14. **(LO3)** Explain why the domestic production activities deduction is sometimes described as an "artificial" expense and the apparent rationale for this deduction. How might a business begin to determine the domestic portion of revenues and expenses for products that are assembled in the United States from parts made overseas?

15. **(LO3)** Describe the two limitations placed on the calculation of the domestic production activities deduction and explain the apparent reason for each limitation.

16. **(LO3)** Compare and contrast start-up costs and organizational expenditures. Describe how the tax treatment of these expenditures differs from the treatment for financial accounting purposes.

17. **(LO3)** Explain the difference between calculating a loss deduction for a business asset that was partially damaged in an accident and a loss deduction for a business asset that was stolen or completely destroyed in an accident.

18. **(LO3)** How do casualty loss deductions differ when a business asset is completely destroyed as opposed to the destruction of a personal-use asset?

19. **(LO4)** What is the difference between a full tax year and a short tax year? Describe circumstances in which a business may have a short tax year.

20. **(LO4)** Explain why a taxpayer might choose one tax year over another if given a choice.

21. **(LO4)** Compare and contrast the different year-ends available to sole proprietorships, flow-through entities, and C corporations.

22. **(LO4)** Why does the law generally require partnerships to adopt a tax year consistent with the year used by the partners?

23. **(LO4)** How does an entity choose its tax year? Is it the same process no matter the type of tax year-end the taxpayer adopts?

24. **(LO5)** Explain when an expenditure should be "capitalized" rather than expensed based upon accounting principles. From time to time, it is suggested that all business expenditures should be expensed for tax purposes. Do you agree with this proposition, and if so, why?

25. **(LO5)** Describe the 12-month rule for determining whether and to what extent businesses should capitalize or immediately deduct prepaid expenses such as insurance or security contracts. Explain the apparent rationale for this rule.

26. **(LO5)** Explain why Congress sometimes mandates that businesses use particular accounting methods while other times Congress is content to require businesses to use the same accounting methods for tax purposes that they use for financial accounting purposes.

27. **(LO5)** Why is it not surprising that specific rules differ between tax accounting and financial accounting?

28. **(LO5)** Fred is considering using the accrual method for his next business venture. Explain to Fred the conditions for recognizing income for tax purposes under the accrual method.

29. **(LO5)** Describe the all-events test for determining income and describe how to determine the date on which the all-events test has been met.

30. **(LO5)** Compare and contrast the tax treatment for rental income received in advance and advance payments for services.

31. **(LO5)** Compare and contrast the rules for determining the tax treatment of advance payments for services versus advance payments for goods.

32. **(LO5)** Jack operates a plumbing business as a sole proprietorship on the cash method. Besides providing plumbing services, Jack also sells plumbing supplies to homeowners and other plumbers. The sales of plumbing supplies constitute less than $20,000 per year, and this is such a small portion of Jack's income that he does not keep physical inventories for the supplies. Describe the conditions in which Jack must account for sales and purchases of plumbing supplies on the accrual method.

33. **(LO5)** Explain why Congress enacted the UNICAP rules and describe the burdens these rules place on taxpayers.

34. **(LO5)** Compare and contrast financial accounting rules with the tax rules under UNICAP (§263A). Explain whether the UNICAP rules tend to accelerate or defer income relative to the financial accounting rules.

35. **(LO5)** Compare and contrast the tests for accruing income and those for accruing deductions for tax purposes.

36. **(LO5)** Compare and contrast when taxpayers are allowed to deduct amounts for warranties provided by others to the taxpayer and when taxpayers are allowed to deduct expenses associated with warranties they provide to others.

37. **(LO5)** Describe when economic performance occurs for the following expenses:
    Worker's compensation
    Rebates and refunds
    Insurance, warranties, and service contracts provided *to* the business
    Taxes

38. **(LO5)** On December 31 of the current year, a taxpayer prepays an advertising company to provide advertising services for the next 10 months. Using the 12-month rule and the economic performance rules, contrast when the taxpayer would be able to deduct the expenditure if the taxpayer uses the cash method of accounting versus if the taxpayer uses the accrual method of accounting.

39. **(LO5)** Compare and contrast how bad debt expense is determined for financial accounting purposes and how the deduction for bad debts is determined for accrual-method taxpayers. How do cash-method taxpayers determine their bad debt expense for accounts receivable?

40. **(LO5)** Describe the related-party limitation on accrued deductions. What tax savings strategy is this limitation designed to thwart?

41. **(LO5)** What are the relative advantages of the cash and accrual methods of accounting?

42. **(LO5)** Describe how a business adopts a permissible accounting method. Explain whether a taxpayer can adopt an impermissible accounting method.

43. **(LO5)** Describe why the IRS might be skeptical of permitting requests for changes in accounting method without a good business purpose?

44. **(LO5)** What is a §481 adjustment and what is its purpose?

## PROBLEMS

45. **(LO1)** Manny hired his brother's firm to provide accounting services to his business. During the current year, Manny paid his brother's firm $82,000 for services even though other firms were willing to provide the same services for $40,000. How much of this expenditure, if any, is deductible as an ordinary and necessary business expenditure?

46. **(LO1, LO2)** Indicate the amount (if any) that Michael can deduct as ordinary and necessary business deductions in each of the following situations and explain your solution.

    a. From time to time, Michael rents a dump truck for his business. While hauling gravel to a job site, Michael was stopped for speeding. He paid a fine of $125 for speeding and a fine of $80 for carrying an overweight load.

    b. Michael paid a part-time employee $750 to drive his rented dump truck. Michael reimbursed the employee $35 for gasoline for the truck.

    c. Michael gave a member of the city council a new watch, which cost $200. He hopes that the city councilman will "throw" some contracts to his business.

47. **(LO1, LO2)** Indicate the amount (if any) that Josh can deduct as ordinary and necessary business deductions in each of the following situations and explain your solution.

    a. Josh borrowed $50,000 from the First State Bank using his business assets as collateral. He used the money to buy City of Blanksville bonds. Over the course of a year, Josh paid interest of $4,200 on the borrowed funds, but he received $3,500 of interest on the bonds.

    b. Josh purchased a piece of land for $45,000 in order to get a location to expand his business. He also paid $3,200 to construct a new driveway for access to the property.

    c. This year Josh paid $15,000 to employ the mayor's son in the business. Josh would typically pay an employee with these responsibilities about $10,000 but the mayor assured Josh that after his son was hired, some city business would be coming his way.

    d. Josh paid his brother, a mechanic, $3,000 to install a robotic machine for Josh's business. The amount he paid to his brother is comparable to what he would have paid to an unrelated party to do the same work. Once the installation was completed by his brother, Josh began calibrating the machine for operation. However, by the end of the year, he had not started using the machine in his business.

48. **(LO2)** Ralph invited a potential client to dinner and the theatre. Ralph paid $250 for the dinner and $220 for the theatre tickets in advance. They first went to dinner and then they went to the theatre.

    a. What amount can Ralph deduct if, prior to the dinner, he met with the potential client to discuss future business prospects?

    b. What amount can Ralph deduct if he and the client only discussed business during the course of the dinner?

    c. What amount can Ralph deduct if he and the potential client tried to discuss business during the course of the theatre performance but did not discuss business at any other time?

    d. What amount can Ralph deduct if the potential client declined Ralph's invitation, so Ralph took his accountant to dinner and the theatre to reward his accountant for a hard day at work? At dinner, they discussed the accountant's workload and upcoming assignments.

49. **(LO2)** Melissa recently paid $400 for round-trip airfare to San Francisco to attend a business conference for three days. Melissa also paid the following expenses: $250 fee to register for the conference, $300 per night for three night's lodging, $200 for meals, and $150 for cab fare.

    a. What amount of the travel costs can Melissa deduct as business expenses?

    b. Suppose that while Melissa was on the coast, she also spent two days sightseeing the national parks in the area. To do the sightseeing, she paid $1,000 for transportation, $800 for lodging, and $450 for meals during this part of her trip, which she considers personal in nature. What amount of the travel costs can Melissa deduct as business expenses?

    c. Suppose that Melissa made the trip to San Francisco primarily to visit the national parks and only attended the business conference as an incidental benefit of being present on the coast at that time. What amount of the travel costs (airfare) can Melissa deduct as business expenses?

    d. Suppose that Melissa's permanent residence and business was located in San Francisco. She attended the conference in San Francisco and paid $250 for the registration fee. She drove 100 miles over the course of three days and paid $90 for parking at the conference hotel. In addition, she spent $150 for breakfast and dinner over the three days of the conference. She bought breakfast on the way to the conference hotel and she bought dinner on her way home each night from the conference. What amount of the travel costs can Melissa deduct as business expenses?

50. **(LO2)** Kimberly is a self-employed taxpayer. She recently spent $1,000 for airfare to travel to Italy. What amount of the airfare is she allowed to deduct in each of the following alternative scenarios?

    a. Her trip was entirely for personal purposes.

    b. On the trip, she spent eight days on personal activities and two days on business activities.

    c. On the trip, she spent eight days on business activities and two days on personal activities.

    d. Her trip was entirely for business purposes.

51. **(LO2)** Ryan is self-employed. This year Ryan used his personal auto for several long business trips. Ryan paid $1,500 for gasoline on these trips. His depreciation on the car if he was using it fully for business purposes would be $3,000. During the year, he drove his car a total of 12,000 miles (a combination of business and personal travel).

    a. Ryan can provide written documentation of the business purpose for trips totaling 3,000 miles. What business expense amount can Ryan deduct (if any) for these trips?

    b. Ryan estimates that he drove approximately 1,300 miles on business trips, but he can only provide written documentation of the business purpose for trips totaling 820 miles. What business expense amount can Ryan deduct (if any) for these trips?

52. **(LO1, LO2)** Christopher is a cash-method, calendar-year taxpayer, and he made the following cash payments related to his business this year. Calculate the after-tax cost of each payment assuming he has a 30 percent marginal tax rate.

    a. $500 fine for speeding while traveling to a client meeting.

    b. $240 of interest on a short-term loan incurred in September and repaid in November. Half of the loan proceeds were used immediately to pay salaries and the other half was invested in municipal bonds until November.

c. $600 for office supplies in May of this year. He used half of the supplies this year and he will use the remaining half by February of next year.

d. $450 for several pair of work boots. Christopher expects to use the boots about 80 percent of the time in his business and the remainder of the time for hiking. Consider the boots to be a form of clothing.

■
**research**
■■

53. **(LO2)**  Heather paid $15,000 to join a country club in order to meet potential clients. This year she paid $4,300 in greens fees when golfing with clients. Under what circumstances, if any, can Heather deduct the $15,000 cost of country club dues and the costs of the golf played with clients?

54. **(LO1, LO2)**  Assume Sarah is a cash-method, calendar-year taxpayer, and she is considering making the following cash payments related to her business. Calculate the after-tax cost of each payment assuming she has a 25 percent marginal tax rate.

a. $2,000 payment for next year's property taxes on her place of business.

b. $800 to reimburse the cost of meals incurred by employees while traveling for the business.

c. $1,200 for football tickets to entertain out-of-town clients during contract negotiations.

d. $500 contribution to the mayor's re-election campaign.

55. **(LO3)**  Renee manufactured and sold a "gadget," a specialized asset used by auto manufacturers that qualifies for the domestic production activities deduction. Renee incurred $15,000 in direct expenses in the project, which includes $2,000 of wages Renee paid to employees in the manufacturing of the gadget. What is Renee's domestic production activities deduction for the gadget in each of the following alternative scenarios?

a. Renee sold the gadget for $25,000 and she reported AGI of $75,000 before considering the manufacturing deduction.

b. Renee sold the gadget for $25,000 and she reported AGI of $5,000 before considering the manufacturing deduction.

c. Renee sold the gadget for $40,000 and she reported AGI of $50,000 before considering the manufacturing deduction.

■ **planning**

56. **(LO3)**  Andrew is considering starting a business of constructing and selling prefabricated greenhouses. There are three very different methods to constructing these greenhouses, and each method results in different revenue and cost projections. Below, Andrew has projected the qualifying revenue and costs for each method. The selling price includes qualifying receipts. The allocable expenses include wages and allocable expenses are included in total costs.

| Method | Selling Price | Qualifying Receipts | Total Cost | Allocable Expenses | Allocable Wages |
|--------|--------------|--------------------|-----------|-------------------|-----------------|
| #1 | $13,000 | $ 9,000 | $6,500 | $2,500 | $2,000 |
| #2 | 14,000 | 9,000 | 7,400 | 5,500 | 1,500 |
| #3 | 15,000 | 14,000 | 8,600 | 2,000 | 1,000 |

a. Estimate the tax benefit from the domestic production activities deduction for each construction technique. You may assume that Andrew has sufficient AGI to utilize the deduction.

b. Which construction technique should Andrew use if his marginal tax rate is 30 percent?

57. **(LO3)** This year Amy purchased $2,000 of equipment for use in her business. However, the machine was damaged in a traffic accident while Amy was transporting the equipment to her business. Note that because Amy did not place the equipment into service during the year, she does not claim any depreciation expense for the equipment.

   a. After the accident, Amy had the choice of repairing the equipment for $1,800 or selling the equipment to a junk shop for $300. Amy sold the equipment. What amount can Amy deduct for the loss of the equipment?

   b. After the accident, Amy repaired the equipment for $800. What amount can Amy deduct for the loss of the equipment?

   c. After the accident, Amy could not replace the equipment so she had the equipment repaired for $2,300. What amount can Amy deduct for the loss of the equipment?

58. **(LO3)** Stephen operates a small hardware store on the cash method. On July 1 of this year, Stephen purchased a "key-employee" term-life policy that insures the life of his best store clerk. The policy cost Stephen $1,220 and will pay him a $40,000 death benefit if his clerk passes away any time during the next 12 months.

   a. What amount of the $1,220 life insurance policy premium can Stephen deduct this year?

   b. Suppose that Stephen purchased the life insurance policy on the clerk's life but allowed the clerk to name the clerk's wife as the beneficiary. What amount of the life insurance policy can Stephen deduct this year?

59. **(LO5)** Nicole is a calendar-year taxpayer who accounts for her business using the cash method. On average, Nicole sends out bills for about $12,000 of her services at the first of each month. The bills are due by the end of the month, and typically 70 percent of the bills are paid on time and 98 percent are paid within 60 days.

■ **planning**

   a. Suppose that Nicole is expecting a 2 percent reduction in her marginal tax rate next year. Ignoring the time value of money, estimate the tax savings for Nicole if she postpones mailing of bills for December until January 1 of next year.

   b. Describe how the time value of money affects your calculations.

   c. Would this tax savings strategy create any additional business risks? Explain.

60. **(LO5)** Jeremy is a calendar-year taxpayer who sometimes leases his business equipment to local organizations. He recorded the following receipts this year. Indicate the extent to which these payments are taxable income to Jeremy this year if Jeremy is (1) a cash-method taxpayer and (2) he is an accrual-method taxpayer.

   a. $1,000 deposit from the Ladies' Club, which wants to lease a trailer. The club will receive the entire deposit back when the trailer is returned undamaged.

   b. $800 from the Ladies' Club for leasing the trailer from December of this year through March of next year ($200 per month).

   c. $300 lease payment received from the Men's Club this year for renting Jeremy's trailer last year. Jeremy billed the club last year but by year-end of last year he determined that the Men's Club would never pay him, so he was surprised when he received the check.

61. **(LO5)** Brown Thumb Landscaping is a calendar-year, accrual-method taxpayer. In September, Brown Thumb negotiated a $14,000 contract for services it would provide to the city in November of the current year. The contract specifies that Brown Thumb will receive $4,000 in October as a down payment

for these services and it will receive the remaining $10,000 in January of next year when the city budget is reviewed.

a. How much income from this $14,000 contract will Brown Thumb recognize in the current year? Explain.

b. How much income from this $14,000 contract will Brown Thumb recognize in the current year if it uses the cash method of accounting?

c. Suppose that the total amount to be paid under the contract with the city is estimated at $14,000 but may be adjusted to $12,000 next year during the review of the city budget. What amount from the contract, if any, should Brown Thumb recognize as income this year? Explain.

d. Suppose that in addition to the basic contract, Brown Thumb will be paid an additional $3,000 if its city landscape design wins the annual design competition next year. Should Brown Thumb accrue a $3,000 revenue this year? Why or why not?

62. **(LO5)** In January of year 0, Justin paid $4,800 for an insurance policy that covers his business property for accidents and casualties. Justin is a calendar-year taxpayer who uses the cash method of accounting. What amount of the insurance premium may Justin deduct in year 0 in each of the following alternative scenarios?

a. The policy covers the business property from April 1 of year 0 through March 31 of year 1.

b. The policy begins on February 1 of year 1 and extends through January 31 of year 2.

c. Assume Justin paid $6,000 for a 24-month policy that covers from April 1, year 0 through March 31, year 2.

d. Assume that instead of paying an insurance premium, Justin paid $4,800 to rent his business property from April 1 of year 0 through March 31 of year 1.

research

63. **(LO5)** Tiffany decided to promise her full-time employees a two-week paid vacation. When, if ever, may Tiffany deduct the expense for the vacation pay? {*Hint: See Reg. §1.404b.-1T, Q&A-2(b)(1).*}

a. Assume Tiffany's business uses the cash method of accounting.

b. Assume Tiffany's business uses the accrual method of accounting.

64. **(LO5)** On April 1 of year 0 Stephanie received a $9,000 payment for full payment on a three-year service contract (under the contract Stephanie is obligated to provide advisory services for the next three years).

a. What amount of income should Stephanie recognize in year 0 if she uses the accrual method of accounting (she recognized $2,250 for financial accounting purposes)?

b. What amount of income will Stephanie recognize in year 1 if she uses the accrual method of accounting?

c. What amount of income will Stephanie recognize in year 2 if she uses the accrual method of accounting?

d. What amount of income will Stephanie recognize in year 0 if she recognizes $5,000 of income from the contract for financial statement purposes?

65. **(LO5)** In October of year 0, Janine received a $6,000 payment from a client for 25 months of security services she will provide starting on November 1 of year 0. This amounts to $240 per month.

a. When must Janine recognize the income from the $6,000 advance payment for services if she uses the cash method of accounting?

b. When must Janine recognize the income from the $6,000 advance payment for services if she uses the accrual method of accounting?

c. Suppose that instead of services, Janine received the payment for a security system (inventory) that she will deliver and install in year 2. When would Janine recognize the income from the advance payment for inventory sale if she uses the accrual method of accounting and she uses the deferral method for reporting income from advance payments? For financial accounting purposes, she reports the income when the inventory is delivered.

d. Suppose that instead of services, Janine received the payment for the delivery of inventory to be delivered next year. When would Janine recognize the income from the advance payment for sale of goods if she uses the accrual method of accounting and she uses the full-inclusion method for advance payments?

66. **(LO5)** Nicole's business uses the accrual method of accounting and accounts for inventory with specific identification. In year 0, Nicole received a $4,500 payment with an order for inventory to be delivered to the client early next year. Nicole has the inventory ready for delivery at the end of year 0 (she purchased the inventory in year 0 for $2,300).

a. When does Nicole recognize the $2,200 of gross profit ($4,500 revenue minus $2,300 cost of the inventory) if she uses the full-inclusion method?

b. When does Nicole recognize the $2,200 of gross profit from the inventory sale if she if she uses the deferral method?

c. How would Nicole account for the inventory-related transactions if she uses the cash method of accounting and her annual sales are usually less than $100,000?

d. How would Nicole account for the inventory-related transactions if she uses the cash method of accounting and her annual sales are usually over $2,000,000 per year?

67. **(LO5)** This year Amber opened a factory to process and package landscape mulch. At the end of the year, Amber's accountant prepared the following schedule for allocating manufacturing costs to the mulch inventory, but her accountant is unsure of what costs need to be allocated to the inventory under UNICAP. Approximately 20 percent of management time, space, and expenses are spent on this manufacturing process.

| | | Costs | Tax Inventory |
|---|---|---|---|
| Material: | Mulch and packaging | $ 5,000 | ? |
| | Administrative supplies | 250 | ? |
| Salaries: | Factory labor | 12,000 | ? |
| | Sales & advertising | 3,500 | ? |
| | Administration | 5,200 | ? |
| Property taxes: | Factory | 4,600 | ? |
| | Offices | 2,700 | ? |
| Depreciation: | Factory | 8,000 | ? |
| | Offices | 1,500 | ? |

a. At the end of the year, Amber's accountant indicated that the business had processed 10,000 bags of mulch but only 1,000 bags remained in the ending inventory. What is Amber's tax basis in her ending inventory after applying the UNICAP rules to allocate indirect costs to inventory? (Assume direct costs are allocated to inventory according to the level of ending inventory. In contrast, indirect costs are first allocated by time spent and then according to level of ending inventory.)

b. Under what conditions could Amber's business avoid having to apply UNICAP to allocate indirect costs to inventory for tax purposes?

68. **(LO5)** Suppose that David adopted the last-in, first-out (LIFO) inventory-flow method for his business inventory of widgets (purchase prices below).

| Widget | Purchase Date | Direct Cost | Other Costs | Total Cost |
|--------|---------------|-------------|-------------|------------|
| #1 | August 15 | $2,100 | $100 | $2,200 |
| #2 | October 30 | $2,200 | $150 | $2,350 |
| #3 | November 10 | $2,300 | $100 | $2,400 |

In late December, David sold widget #2 and next year David expects to purchase three more widgets at the following estimated prices:

| Widget | Purchase Date | Estimated Cost |
|--------|---------------|----------------|
| #4 | Early spring | $2,600 |
| #5 | Summer | $2,260 |
| #6 | Fall | $2,400 |

a. What cost of goods sold and ending inventory would David record if he elects to use the LIFO method this year?

b. If David sells two widgets next year, what will be his cost of goods sold and ending inventory next year under the LIFO method?

c. How would you answer (a) and (b) if David had initially selected the first-in, first-out (FIFO) method instead of LIFO?

d. Suppose that David initially adopted the LIFO method, but wants to apply for a change to FIFO next year. What would be his §481 adjustment for this change, and in what year(s) would he make the adjustment?

69. **(LO5)** On November 1 of year 0, Jaxon borrowed $50,000 from Bucksnort Savings and Loan for use in his business. In December, Jaxon paid interest of $4,500 relating to the 12-month period from November of year 0 through October of year 1.

a. How much interest, if any, can Jaxon deduct in year 0 if his business uses the cash method of accounting for tax purposes?

b. How much interest, if any, can Jaxon deduct in year 0 if his business uses the accrual method of accounting for tax purposes?

70. **(LO5)** Matt has contracted with Apex Services to provide routine repair and maintenance services for several pieces of his business equipment. On November 1 of year 0, Matt paid $2,000 for the repairs that he expects will begin in early March of year 1.

a. What amount of the cost of the repairs can Matt deduct in year 0 if he uses the cash method of accounting for his business?

b. What amount of the cost of the repairs can Matt deduct in year 0 if he uses the accrual method of accounting for his business?

c. What amount of the cost of the repairs can Matt deduct in year 0 if he uses the accrual method and he expects the repairs to be done by early February?

d. What amount of the cost of the repairs can Matt deduct in year 0 if he uses the cash method of accounting and he expects the repairs to be done by early February?

71. **(LO5)** Circuit Corporation (CC) is a calendar-year, accrual-method taxpayer. CC manufactures and sells electronic circuitry. On November 15, year 0, CC enters into a contract with Equip Corp (EC) that provides CC with exclusive use of EC's specialized manufacturing equipment for the five-year period beginning on January 1 of year 1. Pursuant to the contract, CC pays EC

$1,000,000 on December 30, year 0. How much of this $1,000,000 expenditure is CC allowed to deduct in year 0 and in year 1?

72. **(LO5)** This year (year 0) Elizabeth agreed to a three-year service contract with an engineering consulting firm to improve efficiency in her factory. The contract pays the consulting firm $1,500 for each instance that Elizabeth requests their assistance. The contract also provides that Elizabeth only pays the consultants if its advice increases efficiency as measured 12 months from the date of service. This year Elizabeth requested advice on three occasions and she has not yet made any payments to the consultants.

   a. How much should Elizabeth deduct in year 0 under this service contract if she uses the accrual method of accounting?

   b. How much should Elizabeth deduct in year 0 under this service contract if she uses the cash method of accounting?

73. **(LO5)** Travis is a professional landscaper. He provides his clients with a one-year (12-month) warranty for retaining walls he installs. In June of year 1, Travis installed a wall for an important client, Sheila. In early November, Sheila informed Travis that the retaining wall had failed. To repair the wall, Travis paid $700 cash for additional stone that he delivered to Sheila's location. Travis also offered to pay a mason $800 to repair the wall. Due to some bad weather and the mason's work backlog, the mason agreed to finish the work by the end of January of year 2. Even though Travis expected the mason to finish the project as agreed (end of January), Travis informed the mason that he would pay the mason the $800 when he completed the job.

   a. Assuming Travis is an accrual-method taxpayer, how much can he deduct in year 1 from these activities?

   b. Assuming Travis is a cash-method taxpayer, how much can he deduct in year 1 from these activities?

74. **(LO5)** Adam elects the accrual method of accounting for his business. What amount of deductions does Adam recognize in year 0 for the following transactions?

   a. Adam guarantees that he will refund the cost of any goods sold to a client if the goods fail within a year of delivery. In December of year 0, Adam agreed to refund $2,400 to clients, and he expects to make payment in January of year 1.

   b. On December 1 of year 0, Adam paid $480 for a one-year contract with CleanUP Services to clean his store. The agreement calls for services to be provided on a weekly basis.

   c. Adam was billed $240 for annual personal property taxes on his delivery van. Because this was the first time Adam was billed for these taxes, he did not make payment until January. However, he considers the amounts immaterial.

75. **(LO5)** Rebecca is a calendar-year taxpayer who operates a business. She made the following business-related expenditures in December of year 0. Indicate the amount of these payments that she may deduct in year 0 under both the cash method of accounting and the accrual method of accounting.

   a. $2,000 for an accountant to evaluate the accounting system of Rebecca's business. The accountant spent three weeks in January of year 1 working on the evaluation.

   b. $2,500 for new office furniture. The furniture was delivered on January 15.

   c. $3,000 for property taxes payable on her factory.

   d. $1,500 for interest on a short-term bank loan relating to the period from November 1 through March 31.

76. **(LO5)** BCS Corporation is a calendar-year, accrual-method taxpayer. BCS was formed and started its business activities on January 1, year 0. It reported the following information for year 0. Indicate BCS's deductible amount for year 0 in each of the following alternative scenarios.

    a. BCS provides two-year warranties on products it sells to customers. For its year 0 sales, BCS estimated and accrued $200,000 in warranty expense for financial accounting purposes. During year 0, BCS actually spent $30,000 repairing its product under the warranty.

    b. BCS accrued an expense for $50,000 for amounts it anticipated it would be required to pay *under* the worker compensation act. During year 0, BCS actually paid $10,000 for workers' compensation–related liabilities.

    c. In June of year 0, a display of BCS's product located in its showroom fell on and injured a customer. The customer sued BCS for $500,000. The case is scheduled to go to trial next year. BCS anticipates that it will lose the case and accrued a $500,000 expense on its financial statements.

    d. Assume the same facts as in (c) except that BCS was required to pay $500,000 to a court-appointed escrow fund in year 0. If BCS loses the case in year 1, the money from the escrow fund will be transferred to the customer suing BCS.

    e. On December 1 of year 0, BCS acquired equipment from Equip Company. As part of the purchase, BCS signed a warranty agreement with Equip so that Equip would warranty the equipment for two years (from December 1 of year 0 through November 30 of year 2). The cost of the warranty was $12,000. BCS paid Equip for the warranty in January of year 1.

77. **(LO5)** This year William provided $4,200 of services to a large client on credit. Unfortunately, this client has recently encountered financial difficulties and has been unable to pay William for the services. Moreover, William does not expect to collect for his services for at least a year. William has "written off" the account and would like to claim a deduction for tax purposes.

    a. What amount of deduction for bad debt expense can William claim this year if he uses the accrual method?

    b. What amount of deduction for bad debt expense can William claim this year if he uses the cash method?

78. **(LO5)** Dustin has a contract to provide services to Dado Enterprises. In November of year 0, Dustin billed Dado $10,000 for the services he rendered during the year. Dado is an accrual-method proprietorship that is owned and operated by Dustin's father.

    a. What amount of revenue must Dustin recognize in year 0 if Dustin uses the cash method and Dado remits payment for the services in December of year 0? What amount can Dado deduct in year 0?

    b. What amount of revenue must Dustin recognize in year 0 if Dustin uses the accrual method and Dado remits payment for the services in December of year 0? What amount can Dado deduct in year 0?

    c. What amount of revenue must Dustin recognize in year 0 if Dustin uses the cash method and Dado remits payment for the services in January of year 1? What amount can Dado deduct in year 0?

    d. What amount of revenue must Dustin recognize in year 0 if Dustin uses the accrual method and Dado remits payment for the services in January of year 1? What amount can Dado deduct in year 0?

79. **(LO5)** Nancy operates a business that uses the accrual method of accounting. In December, Nancy asked her brother, Hank, to provide her business with consulting advice. Hank billed Nancy for $5,000 of consulting services in year 0

(a reasonable amount), but Nancy was only able to pay $3,000 of the bill by the end of year 0. However, Nancy paid the remainder of the bill in year 1.

   a. How much of the $5,000 consulting services will Hank include in his income in year 0 if he uses the cash method of accounting? What amount can Nancy deduct in year 0 for the consulting services?

   b. How much of the $5,000 consulting services will Hank include in his income in year 0 if he uses the accrual method of accounting? What amount can Nancy deduct in year 0 for the consulting services?

80. **(LO5)** Erin is considering switching her business from the cash method to the accrual method at the beginning of next year (year 1). Determine the amount and timing of her §481 adjustment assuming the IRS grants Erin's request in the following alternative scenarios.

   a. At the end of year 0/beginning of year 1, Erin's business has $15,000 of accounts receivables and $18,000 of accounts payables that have not been recorded for tax purposes.

   b. At the end of year 0/beginning of year 1, Erin's business reports $25,000 of accounts receivables and $9,000 of accounts payables that have not been recorded for tax purposes.

## COMPREHENSIVE PROBLEMS

81. Joe operates a business that locates and purchases specialized assets for clients, among other activities. Joe uses the accrual method of accounting but he doesn't keep any significant inventories of the specialized assets that he sells. Joe reported the following financial information for his business activities during year 0. Determine the effect of each of the following transactions on the taxable business income.

   a. Joe has signed a contract to sell gadgets to the city. The contract provides that sales of gadgets are dependent upon a test sample of gadgets operating successfully. In December, Joe delivers $12,000 worth of gadgets to the city that will be tested in March. Joe purchased the gadgets especially for this contract and paid $8,500.

   b. Joe paid $180 for entertaining a visiting out-of-town client. The client didn't discuss business with Joe during this visit, but Joe wants to maintain good relations to encourage additional business next year.

   c. On November 1, Joe paid $600 for premiums providing for $40,000 of "key man" insurance on the life of Joe's accountant over the next 12 months.

   d. At the end of the year (year 0), Joe's business reports $9,000 of accounts receivable. Based upon past experience, Joe believes that at least $2,000 of his new receivables will be uncollectible.

   e. In December of year 0, Joe rented equipment to complete a large job. Joe paid $3,000 in December because the rental agency required a minimum rental of three months ($1,000 per month). Joe completed the job before year-end and returned the equipment to the rental agency.

   f. Joe hired a new sales representative as an employee and sent her to Dallas for a week to contact prospective out-of-state clients. Joe ended up reimbursing his employee $300 for airfare, $350 for lodging, $250 for meals, and $150 for entertainment (Joe provided adequate documentation to substantiate the business purpose for the meals and entertainment). Joe requires the employee to account for all expenditures in order to be reimbursed.

   g. Joe uses his BMW (a personal auto) to travel to and from his residence to his factory. However, he switches to a business vehicle if he needs to travel

after he reaches the factory. Last month, the business vehicle broke down and he was forced to use the BMW both to travel to and from the factory and to visit work sites. He drove 120 miles visiting work sites and 46 miles driving to and from the factory from his home. Joe uses the standard mileage rate to determine his auto-related business expenses.

h. Joe paid a visit to his parents in Dallas over the Christmas holidays. While he was in the city, Joe spent $50 to attend a half-day business symposium. Joe paid $200 for airfare, $50 for meals during the symposium, and $20 on cab fare to the symposium.

82. Jack, a geologist, had been debating for years whether or not to venture out on his own and operate his own business. He had developed a lot of solid relationships with clients and he believed that many of them would follow him if he were to leave his current employer. As part of a New Year's resolution, Jack decided he would finally do it. In January, Jack put his business plan together and in February opened his doors for business as a C corporation called Geo-Jack (GJ). Jack is the sole shareholder. Jack reported the following financial information for the year (assume GJ reports on a calendar year and uses the accrual method of accounting).

a. GJ incurred $3,000 of organizational expenditures in January.

b. GJ earned and collected $290,000 performing geological-related services and selling its specialized digging tool [see part (i)].

c. GJ received $50 interest from municipal bonds and $2,100 interest from other investments.

d. GJ purchased some new equipment in February for $42,500. It claimed depreciation on these assets during the year in the amount of $6,540.

e. GJ paid $7,000 to buy luxury season tickets for Jack's parents for State U football games.

f. GJ paid Jack's father $10,000 for services that would have cost no more than $6,000 if Jack had hired any other local business to perform the services. While Jack's dad was competent, he does not command such a premium from his other clients.

g. In an attempt to get his name and new business recognized, GJ paid $7,000 for a one-page ad in the *Geologic Survey*. It also paid $15,000 in radio ads to be run through the end of December.

h. GJ leased office space in a building downtown. GJ paid rent of $27,000 for the year.

i. In August, GJ began manufacturing a special geological digging tool that it sells to wholesalers. GJ's QPAI from the activity for the year is $100,000 [included in revenues reported in part (b)]. GJ paid $10,000 of wages to the employees working on the project during the year and its cost of goods sold on the sales is $15,000. (Assume that taxable income does not limit the amount of the DPAD, and that no wages should be included in cost of goods sold.) Remember that cost of goods sold and wages reduce taxable income.

j. In November, Jack's office was broken into and equipment valued at $5,000 was stolen. The tax basis of the equipment was $5,500. Jack received $2,000 of insurance proceeds from the theft.

k. GJ incurred a $4,000 fine from the state government for digging in an unauthorized digging zone.

l. GJ contributed $3,000 to lobbyists for their help in persuading the state government to authorize certain unauthorized digging zones.

m. On July 1, GJ paid $1,800 for an 18-month insurance policy for its business equipment. The policy covers the period July 1 of this year through December 31 of next year.

n. GJ borrowed $20,000 to help with the company's initial funding needs. GJ used $2,000 of funds to invest in municipal bonds. At the end of the year, GJ paid the $1,200 of interest expense that accrued on the loan during the year.

o. Jack lives 12 miles from the office. He carefully tracked his mileage and drove his truck 6,280 miles between the office and his home. He also drove an additional 7,200 miles between the office and traveling to client sites. Jack did not use the truck for any other purposes. He did not keep track of the specific expenses associated with the truck. However, while traveling to a client site, Jack received a $150 speeding ticket. GJ reimbursed Jack for business mileage and for the speeding ticket.

p. GJ purchased two season tickets (20 games) to attend State U baseball games for a total of $1,100. Jack took existing and prospective clients to the games to maintain contact and find further work. This was very successful for Jack as GJ gained many new projects through substantial discussions with the clients following the games.

q. GJ reimbursed employee-salespersons $3,500 for meals involving substantial business discussion.

r. GJ had a client who needed Jack to perform work in Florida. Because Jack had never been to Florida before, he booked an extra day and night for sight-seeing. Jack spent $400 for airfare and booked a hotel for 3 nights ($120/ night). (Jack stayed two days for business purposes and one day for personal purposes.) He also rented a car for $45 per day. The client arranged for Jack's meals while Jack was doing business. GJ reimbursed Jack for all expenses.

**Required:**

A. What is GJ's net business income for tax purposes for the year?

B. As a C corporation, does GJ have a required tax year? If so, what would it be?

C. If GJ were a sole proprietorship, would it have a required tax year-end? If so, what would it be?

D. If GJ were an S corporation, would it have a required tax year-end? If so, what would it be?

83. Rex loves to work with his hands and is very good at making small figurines. In 2005, Rex opened Bronze Age Miniatures (BAM) for business as a sole proprietor-ship. BAM produces miniature characters ranging from sci-fi characters (his favorite) to historical characters like George Washington (the most popular). Business has been going very well for him, and he has provided the following information relating to his business. Calculate the business taxable income for BAM.

a. Rex received approval from the IRS to switch from the cash method of accounting to the accrual method of accounting effective January 1 of this year. At year-end of last year, BAM reported accounts receivable that had not been included in income under the accrual method of $14,000 and accounts payable that had not been deducted under the accrual method of $5,000.

b. In March, BAM sold 5,000 miniature historical figures to History R Us, Inc. (HRU), a retailer of historical artifacts and figurines, for $75,000.

c. HRU was so impressed with the figurines that it purchased in March that it wanted to contract with BAM to continue to produce the figurines for them for the next three years. HRU paid BAM $216,000 ($12 per figurine) on October 30 of this year, to produce 500 figurines per month for 36 months beginning on November 1 of this year. BAM delivered 500 figurines on November 30 and again on December 30. Rex elects to use the deferral method to account for the transaction.

d. Though the sci-fi figurines were not quite as popular, BAM sold 400 figurines at a sci-fi convention in April. Rex accepted cash only and received $11,000 for these sales.

e.  In January, BAM determined that it would not be able to collect on $2,000 of its beginning-of-the-year receivables, so it wrote off $2,000 of specific receivables. BAM sold 100,000 other figurines on credit for $120,000. BAM estimates that it will be unable to collect 5 percent of the sales revenue from these sales but it has not been able to specifically identify any accounts to write off.

f.  Assume that BAM correctly determined that its cost of goods sold this year is $54,000.

g.  The sci-fi convention in April was held in Chicago, Illinois. Rex attended the convention because he felt it was a good opportunity to gain new customers and to get new ideas for figurines. He paid $350 round-trip airfare, $100 for entrance to the convention, $210 for lodging, $65 for cab fare, and $110 for meals during the trip. He was busy with business activities the entire trip.

h.  On August 1, BAM purchased a 12-month insurance policy that covers its business property for accidents and casualties through July 31 of next year. The policy cost BAM $3,600.

i.  BAM reported depreciation expense of $8,200 for this year.

j.  Rex had previously operated his business out of his garage, but in January he decided to rent a larger space. He entered into a lease agreement on February 1 and paid $14,400 ($1,200 per month) to possess the space for the next 12 months (February of this year through January of next year).

k.  Before he opened his doors for business in 2005, Rex spent $30,000 investigating and otherwise getting ready to do business. He expensed $5,000 immediately and is amortizing the remainder using the straight-line method over 180 months.

l.  In December, BAM agreed to a 12-month $8,000 contract with Advertise-With-Us (AWU) to produce a radio ad campaign. BAM paid $3,000 up front (in December of this year) and AWU agreed that BAM would owe the remaining $5,000 only if BAM's sales increased by 15 percent over the nine-month period after the contract was signed.

m.  In November of this year, BAM paid $2,500 in business property taxes (based on asset values) covering the period December 1 of this year through November 30 of next year. In November of last year, BAM paid $1,500 for business property taxes (based on asset values) covering the period December 1 of last year through November 30 of this year.

84.  Bryan followed in his father's footsteps and entered into the carpet business. He owns and operates I Do Carpet (IDC). Bryan prefers to install carpet only, but in order to earn additional revenue, he also cleans carpets and sells carpet cleaning supplies. Compute his taxable income considering the following items:

a.  IDC contracted with a homebuilder in December of last year to install carpet in 10 new homes being built. The contract price of $80,000 includes $50,000 for materials (carpet). The remaining $30,000 is for IDC's service of installing the carpet. The contract also stated that all money was to be paid upfront. The homebuilder paid IDC in full on December 28 of last year. The contract required IDC to complete the work by January 31 of this year. Bryan purchased the necessary carpet on January 2 and began working on the first home January 4. He completed the last home on January 27 of this year.

b.  IDC entered into several other contracts this year and completed the work before year-end. The work cost $130,000 in materials. Bryan billed out

$240,000 but only collected $220,000 by year-end. Of the $20,000 still owed to him, Bryan wrote off $3,000 he didn't expect to collect as a bad debt from a customer experiencing extreme financial difficulties.

c. IDC entered into a three-year contract to clean the carpets of an office building. The contract specified that IDC would clean the carpets monthly from July 1 of this year through June 30 three years hence. IDC received payment in full of $8,640 ($240 a month for 36 months) on June 30 of this year.

d. IDC sold 100 bottles of carpet stain remover this year for $5 per bottle (it collected $500). Rex sold 40 bottles on June 1 and 60 bottles on November 2. IDC had the following carpet cleaning supplies on hand for this year and it uses the LIFO method of accounting for inventory:

| Purchase Date | Bottles | Total Cost |
|---|---|---|
| November last year | 40 | $120 |
| February this year | 35 | $112 |
| July this year | 25 | $ 85 |
| August this year | 40 | $140 |
| Totals | 140 | $457 |

e. On August 1 of this year, IDC needed more room for storage and paid $900 to rent a garage for 12 months.

f. On November 30 of this year, Bryan decided it was time to get his logo on the sides of his work van. IDC hired We Paint Anything, Inc. (WPA), to do the job. It paid $500 down and agreed to pay the remaining $1,500 upon completion of the job. WPA indicated it wouldn't be able to begin the job until January 15 of next year, but the job would only take one week to complete. Due to circumstances beyond its control, WPA wasn't able to complete the job until April 1 of next year, at which time IDC paid the remaining $1,500.

g. In December, Bryan's son, Aiden, helped him finish some carpeting jobs. IDC owed Aiden $600 (reasonable) compensation for his work. However, Aiden did not receive the payment until January of next year.

h. IDC also paid $1,000 for interest on a short-term bank loan relating to the period from November 1 of this year through March 31 of next year.

85. Hank started a new business in June of last year, Hank's Donut World (HW for short). He has requested your advice on the following specific tax matters associated with HW's first year of operations. Hank has estimated HW's income for the first year as follows:

| | | |
|---|---|---|
| Revenue: | | |
| Donut sales | $252,000 | |
| Catering revenues | 71,550 | $323,550 |
| Expenditures: | | |
| Donut supplies | $124,240 | |
| Catering expense | 27,910 | |
| Salaries to shop employees | 52,500 | |
| Rent expense | 40,050 | |
| Accident insurance premiums | 8,400 | |
| Other business expenditures | 6,850 | −259,950 |
| Net Income | | $ 63,600 |

HW operates as a sole proprietorship and Hank reports on a calendar-year. Hank uses the cash method of accounting and plans to do the same with HW (HW has no inventory of donuts because unsold donuts are not salable). HW does not purchase donut supplies on credit nor does it generally make sales on credit. Hank has provided the following details for specific first-year transactions.

- A small minority of HW clients complained about the catering service. To mitigate these complaints, Hank's policy is to refund dissatisfied clients 50 percent of the catering fee. By the end of the first year, only two HW clients had complained but had not yet been paid refunds. The expected refunds amount to $1,700, and Hank reduced the reported catering fees for the first year to reflect the expected refund.

- In the first year, HW received a $6,750 payment from a client for catering a monthly breakfast for 30 consecutive months beginning in December. Because the payment didn't relate to last year, Hank excluded the entire amount when he calculated catering revenues.

- In July, HW paid $1,500 to ADMAN Co. for an advertising campaign to distribute fliers advertising HW's catering service. Unfortunately, this campaign violated a city code restricting advertising by fliers, and the city fined HW $250 for the violation. HW paid the fine, and Hank included the fine and the cost of the campaign in "other business" expenditures.

- In July, HW also paid $8,400 for a 24-month insurance policy that covers HW for accidents and casualties beginning on August 1 of the first year. Hank deducted the entire $8,400 as accident insurance premiums. In his estimate, Hank deducted these amounts ($40,050 in total) as rent expense.

- On May of the first year, Hank signed a contract to lease the HW donut shop for 10 months. In conjunction with the contract, Hank paid $2,000 as a damage deposit and $8,050 for rent ($805 per month). Hank explained that the damage deposit was refundable at the end of the lease. At this time, Hank also paid $30,000 to lease kitchen equipment for 24 months ($1,250 per month). Both leases began on June 1 of the first year.

- Hank signed a contract hiring WEGO Catering to help cater breakfasts. At year-end, WEGO asked Hank to hold the last catering payment for the year, $9,250, until after January 1 (apparently because WEGO didn't want to report the income on its tax return). The last check was delivered to WEGO in January after the end of the first year. However, because the payment related to the first year of operations, Hank included the $9,250 in last year's catering expense.

- Hank believes that the key to the success of HW has been hiring Jimbo Jones to supervise the donut production and manage the shop. Because Jimbo is such an important employee, HW purchased a "key-employee" term-life insurance policy on his life. HW paid a $5,100 premium for this policy and it will pay HW a $40,000 death benefit if Jimbo passes away any time during the next 12 months. The term of the policy began on September 1 of last year and this payment was included in "other business" expenditures.

- In the first year, HW catered a large breakfast event to celebrate the city's anniversary. The city agreed to pay $7,100 for the event, but Hank forgot to notify the city of the outstanding bill until January of this year. When he mailed the bill in January, Hank decided to discount the charge to $5,500. On the bill, Hank thanked the mayor and the city council for their patronage and asked them to "send a little more business our way." This bill is not reflected in Hank's estimate of HW's income for the first year of operations.

**Required:**

A. Hank files his personal tax return on a calendar year, but he has not yet filed last year's personal tax return nor has he filed a tax return reporting HW's results for the first year of operations. Explain when Hank should file the tax return for HW and calculate the amount of taxable income generated by HW last year.

B. Determine the taxable income that HW will generate if Hank chooses to account for the business under the accrual method.

C. Describe how your solution might change if Hank incorporated HW before he commenced business last year.

86. R.E.M., a calendar-year corporation and Athens, Georgia, band, recently sold tickets ($20,000,000) for concerts scheduled in the United States for next year and the following year. For financial statement purposes, R.E.M. will recognize the income from the ticket sales when it perform the concerts. For tax purposes, it uses the accrual method and would prefer to defer the income from the ticket sales until it performs the concerts. This is the first time that it has sold tickets one or two years in advance. Michael Stipe has asked your advice. Write a memo to Michael explaining your findings.

research

# KAPLAN CPA SIMULATIONS

KAPLAN CPA REVIEW

**Please visit the Online Learning Center**   (www.mhhe.com/spilker2011) to access the following Kaplan CPA Simulation:

The simulation for **Colt and Cara West** covers individual income tax issues, including business income/expense; home office deduction; NOL; charitable donations; and capital expenditures.

# chapter

# 9

# Property Acquisition and Cost Recovery

## Learning Objectives

**Upon completing this chapter, you should be able to:**

**LO 1** Explain the concept of basis and adjusted basis and describe the cost recovery methods used under the tax law to recover the cost of personal property, real property, intangible assets, and natural resources.

■

**LO 2** Determine the applicable cost recovery (depreciation) life, method, and convention for tangible personal and real property and calculate the deduction allowable under MACRS.

■

**LO 3** Explain the rationale behind amortization, describe the four categories of amortizable intangible assets, and calculate amortization expense.

■

**LO 4** Explain cost recovery of natural resources and the allowable depletion methods.

| Storyline Summary | |
|---|---|
| *Taxpayer:* | Teton Mountaineering Technology, LLC (Teton)—a calendar-year single-member LLC (treated as a sole proprietorship for tax purposes) |
| *Location:* | Cody, Wyoming |
| *President/ Founder:* | Steve Dallimore |
| *Current situation:* | Teton must acquire property to start manufacturing operations and wants to understand the tax consequences of property acquisitions. |

T wo years ago while climbing the Black Ice Couloir (pronounced "cool-wahr") in Grand Teton National Park, Steve Dallimore and his buddy got into a desperate situation. The climbers planned to move fast and light and to be home before an approaching storm reached the Teton. But just shy of the summit, climbing conditions forced them to turn back. Huddled in a wet sleeping bag in a dark snow cave waiting for the tempest to pass, Steve had an epiphany—a design for a better ice-climbing tool. Since that moment, Steve has been quietly consumed with making his dream— designing and selling his own line of climbing equipment—a reality. Although his current sales career is challenging and financially rewarding, Steve has too often found himself watching the clock and dreaming of a more fulfilling and adventurous career based upon his early training as a mechanical engineer. Steve decided to exercise his stock options, leave his current position, and start Teton. The only problem is that Steve has no employees, no business location, and no manufacturing equipment.

*to be continued . . .*

Steve obviously has many issues to resolve and decisions to make. In this chapter, we focus on issues dealing with the assets Steve will acquire for use in his new business. In particular, we explain how Teton will determine its cost recovery (depreciation, amortization, and depletion) deductions for the assets in the year the business begins and in subsequent years. These deductions can generate significant tax savings for companies in capital-intensive industries.

This chapter explores the tax consequences of acquiring new or used property, depreciation methods businesses may use to recover the cost of their assets, and special cost recovery incentives for small businesses such as Teton. Along the way, we compare and contrast the process of computing depreciation for tax purposes and for financial accounting purposes. We also address the tax consequences of using intangible assets and natural resources in business activities.

**L01**

# COST RECOVERY

Most businesses make a significant investment in property, plant, and equipment that is expected to provide benefits over a number of years. For both financial accounting and tax accounting purposes, businesses must capitalize the cost of assets with a useful life of more than one year (on the balance sheet) rather than expense the cost immediately. Businesses are allowed to use various methods to recover the cost of these assets over time because the assets are subject to wear, tear, and obsolescence.

The method of **cost recovery** is referred to as **depreciation, amortization,** or **depletion**—depending on the nature of the underlying asset. Depreciation is the method of deducting the cost of *tangible* personal and real property (other than land) over a specific time period. Amortization is the method of deducting the cost of **intangible assets** over a specific time period. Finally, depletion is the method of deducting the cost of natural resources over time. Exhibit 9-1 summarizes these concepts.

Generally, a significant portion of a firm's assets is comprised of property, plant, equipment, intangibles, or even natural resources. In most cases, this holds true for small businesses like Teton and also for large publicly traded companies. For example, Exhibit 9-2 describes the assets held by Weyerhaeuser, a publicly traded timber company. As indicated in Exhibit 9-2, Weyerhaeuser has almost $3.8 billion in property and equipment (net of depreciation), $4.2 billion in timber (net of depletion), and $4 billion in goodwill.

Businesses must choose accounting methods for the assets acquired during the year from among the allowable cost recovery alternatives we describe in this chapter.

**EXHIBIT 9-1** Assets and Cost Recovery

| Asset Type | Cost Recovery Method |
|---|---|
| *Personal property* is comprised of tangible assets such as automobiles, equipment, and machinery. | Depreciation |
| *Real property* is comprised of buildings and land (although land is nondepreciable). | Depreciation |
| *Intangible assets* are nonphysical assets such as goodwill and patents. | Amortization |
| *Natural resources* are commodities that are considered valuable in their natural form such as oil, coal, timber, and gold. | Depletion |

**EXHIBIT 9-2   Weyerhaeuser Assets**

| Assets (in millions) per 10-K Statement | 2008 | 2007 |
|---|---|---|
| Total current assets | $ 4,133 | $ 3,014 |
| Property and equipment, net (Note 6) | 3,858 | 4,112 |
| Construction in progress | 104 | 289 |
| Timber and timberlands at cost, less depletion charged to disposals | 4,205 | 3,769 |
| Investments in and advances to equity affiliates (Note 7) | 202 | 285 |
| Goodwill (Note 8) | 43 | 941 |
| Deferred pension and other assets (Note 9) | 608 | 2,445 |
| Restricted assets held by special purpose entities (Note 10) | 916 | 916 |
| Noncurrent assets of discontinued operations (Note 3) | 11 | 4,255 |
| | $14,080 | $20,026 |

Attention to detail is important because the basis of an asset must be reduced by the cost recovery deductions allowed or *allowable*.[1]

## Basis for Cost Recovery

Businesses may begin recouping the cost of purchased business assets (cost basis) once they begin using the asset in their business (they place it in service).[2] Once the business establishes its cost basis in an asset, the basis is reduced as the business recovers the cost of the asset through cost recovery deductions such as depreciation, amortization, or depletion. The amount of an asset's cost that has yet to be recovered through cost recovery deductions is called the asset's **adjusted basis** or **tax basis.** An asset's adjusted basis can be computed by subtracting the accumulated depreciation (or amortization or depletion) from the asset's initial cost or historical basis.[3]

An asset's *cost basis* includes all of the expenses to purchase, prepare it for use, and begin using the asset. These costs may include sales tax, shipping, and installation. The financial accounting and tax rules for computing an asset's basis are very similar. Thus, a purchased asset's initial basis for both tax and book purposes is generally the same.[4]

When a business incurs additional costs associated with an asset after the asset has been placed in service, how are the additional costs treated for tax purposes? The answer depends on whether the expense constitutes routine maintenance on the asset or whether it significantly extends the useful life of the asset. Routine maintenance costs are immediately deductible as ordinary business expenses. For example, if Teton spent $35 to have a delivery truck's oil changed, it would immediately deduct the cost as routine maintenance. Alternatively, if an additional cost significantly extends an

> **THE KEY FACTS**
>
> **Cost Basis**
>
> ■ An asset's cost basis includes all expenses needed to purchase the asset, prepare it for use, and begin using it.
>
> ■ Cost basis is usually the same for book and tax purposes.
>
> ■ Special basis rules apply when personal use assets are converted to business use and when assets are acquired through nontaxable transactions, gifts, or inheritances.

---

[1]This means that if a business fails to deduct (by mistake or error) the allowable amount of depreciation expense for the year, the business must still reduce the asset's basis by the depreciation expense the taxpayer could have deducted under the method the business is using to depreciate the asset (this reduces the future depreciation deductions for the asset). If a business discovers that it failed to claim allowable depreciation in a previous year, it cannot currently deduct the depreciation attributable to prior years. Rather, the business must file amended returns—assuming the statute of limitations is still open—to claim the depreciation expense. Additionally, Reg. §1.446-1 indicates other situations that will result in an accounting method change.

[2]Cost basis is defined under §1012. The mere purchase of an asset does not trigger cost recovery deductions. A business must begin using the asset for business purposes (place it in service) in order to depreciate the asset. However, because businesses generally acquire and place assets in service at the same time, we refer to these terms interchangeably throughout the chapter.

[3]§1011.

[4]However, special basis rules apply when an asset is acquired through a nontaxable transaction. See discussion below.

asset's useful life, the expenditure generates a new asset (for cost recovery purposes) separate from the original asset.[5] For example, if Teton spends $3,000 on a rebuilt engine for a delivery truck in an attempt to add 50,000 miles to the truck's useful life, the cost of the engine would be accounted for as a separate, new asset.

When a business acquires multiple assets for one purchase price, the tax laws require the business to determine a cost basis for each separate asset. For example, if Teton were to acquire land and a building on the land, Teton must treat the building and land as separate assets. In these types of acquisitions, businesses determine the cost basis of each asset by allocating a portion of the purchase price to each asset based on that asset's value relative to the total value of all the assets the business acquired in the same purchase. The asset values are generally determined by an appraisal.[6]

## Example 9-1

Steve determined that he needed machinery and office furniture for a manufacturing facility and a design studio (located in Cody, Wyoming). During the year, Steve purchased the following assets and incurred the following costs to prepare the assets for business use. His cost basis in each asset is determined as follows:

| Asset | Date Acquired | (1) Purchase Price | (2) Business Preparation Costs | (1) + (2) Cost Basis |
|---|---|---|---|---|
| Office furniture | 2/3/10 | $ 10,000 | | $ 10,000 |
| Warehouse | 5/1/10 | $270,000* | $5,000 (minor modifications) | $275,000 |
| Land (10 acres) | 5/1/10 | $ 75,000* | | $ 75,000 |
| Machinery | 7/22/10 | $250,000 | $10,000 (delivery and setup) | $260,000 |
| Delivery truck (used) | 8/17/10 | $ 15,000 | | $ 15,000 |

*Note that the warehouse and the land were purchased together for $345,000. Steve and the seller determined that the value (and cost) of the warehouse was $270,000 and the value (and cost) of the land was $75,000.

Special rules apply when determining the tax basis of assets converted from personal to business use or assets acquired through a nontaxable exchange, gift, or inheritance. If an asset is used for personal purposes and is later converted to business (or rental) use, the basis is the *lesser* of (1) the cost basis of the asset or (2) the fair market value of the asset on the date of conversion to business use.[7] This rule prevents taxpayers from converting a nondeductible personal loss into a deductible business loss. For example, if Steve had purchased a truck for $20,000 several years ago and decided to use it as a delivery truck when its value had declined to $15,000, his cost basis (or tax basis) in the truck for tax purposes would be $15,000. The $5,000 decline in the truck's value from $20,000 to $15,000 would be a nondeductible personal loss to Steve, and the reduction in basis ensures that he will not ever be allowed to deduct the loss. Assets acquired through a nontaxable exchange such as a like-kind exchange take the same basis the taxpayer had in the property the taxpayer transferred in the transaction. Assets acquired by gift have a carryover basis. This means that the taxpayer's basis in property received through a gift is generally the same basis the transferor had in the property.[8] For example, if Steve's parents gave him stock worth $45,000 to help him start his business and his parents had purchased the stock 10 years earlier for $25,000, Steve's basis in the stock would be $25,000 (the same basis his parents had in the stock). Assets acquired through

[5]§168(i)(6).
[6]Reg. §1.167(a)-5.
[7]Reg. §§1.168-2(j)(6) and 1.168(i)-4(b).
[8]§1015. The basis may be increased if the transferor is required to pay gift tax on the transfer [see §1015(d)].

inheritance generally receive a basis equal to the fair market value on the transferor's date of death.[9] For example, if Steve inherited a 1957 Porsche Speedster worth $90,000 from his grandfather who originally paid $3,500 for it, Steve's basis would be $90,000 (its fair market value at date of death) because Steve acquired it through an inheritance.

# DEPRECIATION

**L02**

Before 1981, tax depreciation methods closely resembled financial accounting methods. For both financial accounting and tax purposes, businesses were allowed to choose from among a wide range of depreciation methods and **recovery periods.** Computing both tax and financial accounting depreciation required businesses to determine the assets' useful lives and "salvage values." In 1981, tax and financial accounting depreciation methods parted ways when Congress introduced the **Accelerated Cost Recovery System (ACRS)** for computing depreciation expense. Under ACRS, businesses used accelerated depreciation methods to depreciate assets over predetermined, fixed recovery periods.

> **THE KEY FACTS**
>
> **Tax Depreciation**
>
> ▮ To depreciate an asset, a business must determine:
> · Original basis
> · Depreciation method
> · Recovery period
> · Depreciation convention

Today, businesses calculate their tax depreciation using the **Modified Accelerated Cost Recovery System (MACRS)**—which is pronounced "makers" by tax accountants.[10] Compared to financial (book) depreciation, MACRS tax depreciation is quite simple. To compute MACRS depreciation for an asset, the business need only know the asset's *original cost,* the applicable *depreciation method,* the asset's *recovery period* (or depreciable "life"), and the applicable depreciation *convention* (the amount of depreciation deductible in the year of acquisition and the year of disposition). The method, recovery, period, and convention vary based on whether the asset is **personal property** or **real property.** We first turn our attention to determining depreciation expense for personal property.

## Personal Property Depreciation

Personal property includes all tangible property, such as computers, automobiles, furniture, machinery, and equipment, other than real property. Note that personal property and *personal-use* property are *not* the same thing. Personal property denotes any property that is not real property (e.g., building and land) while personal-use property is any property used for personal purposes (for example, a personal residence is personal-use property even though it is real property). Personal property is relatively short-lived and subject to obsolescence as compared to real property.

**Depreciation Method**   MACRS provides three acceptable methods for depreciating personal property: 200 percent (double) declining balance, 150 percent declining balance, and straight-line.[11] The 200 percent declining balance method is the default method. This method takes twice the straight-line amount of depreciation in the first year and continues to take twice the straight-line percentage on the asset's declining basis until switching to the straight-line method in the year that the straight-line method over the remaining life provides a greater depreciation expense. Fortunately, as we describe below, the IRS provides depreciation tables to simplify the calculations.

Profitable businesses with relatively high marginal tax rates generally choose to use the 200 percent declining balance method because it generates the largest depreciation expense in the early years of the assets' lives and, thus, the highest current

---

[9]§1014. The date for determining the fair market value is later if the alternate valuation date is elected by the estate. Based on the tax law at the time we went to press, in certain circumstances, the the basis of property acquired through inheritance could take a basis equal to the lesser of fair market value at date of death or the decedent's basis in the property immediately before death.

[10]IRS Publication 946 provides a useful summary of MACRS depreciation.

[11]For personal property, the 200 percent DB is often referred to as the General Depreciation System (GDS) while the 150 percent DB or straight-line methods are referred to as the Alternative Depreciation System (ADS).

year after-tax cash flows. For tax planning purposes, companies that currently have lower marginal tax rates but expect their marginal tax rates to increase in the near future may elect the straight-line method because that method generates less depreciation expense in the early years of the asset's life, relatively, and more depreciation expense in the later years when their marginal tax rates may increase.

**Example 9-2**

> If Teton wants to accelerate its current depreciation deductions to the extent possible, what method should it use to depreciate its office furniture, machinery, and delivery truck?
>
> **Answer:** The 200 percent declining balance method (switching to straight-line). Teton could have elected to use either the 150 percent declining balance or the straight-line method, if it wanted a less accelerated method for determining its depreciation deductions.

Each year, businesses elect the depreciation method for the assets placed in service during *that year*. Specifically, businesses elect one depreciation method for all similar assets they acquired that year.[12] Thus, if a business acquires several different machines during the year, it must use the same method to depreciate all of the machines.

**Depreciation Recovery Period**    For financial accounting purposes, an asset's recovery period (depreciable life) is based on its taxpayer-determined estimated useful life. In contrast, for tax purposes an asset's recovery period is predetermined by the IRS in Rev. Proc. 87-56. This revenue procedure helps taxpayers categorize each of their assets based upon the property's description. Once the business has determined the appropriate categories for its assets, it can use the Revenue Procedure to identify the recovery period for all assets in a particular category. For example, Teton placed office furniture in service during the year. By examining the excerpt from Rev. Proc. 87-56 provided in Exhibit 9-3, you can see that Category or Asset Class 00.11 includes office furniture and that assets in this category, including Teton's office furniture, have a recovery period of seven years (emphasis in excerpt added through bold text).[13]

**EXHIBIT 9-3    Excerpt from Revenue Procedure 87-56**

| Description of Assets Included | | Years | |
| --- | --- | --- | --- |
| Specific depreciable assets used in all business activities, except as noted: | Class Life | General Recovery Period | Alternative Recovery Period |
| 00.11 **Office Furniture**, Fixtures, and Equipment: Includes furniture and fixtures that are not a structural component of a building. Includes such assets as desks, files, safes, and communications equipment. Does not include communications equipment that is included in other classes. | 10 | 7 | 10 |
| 00.241 Light General Purpose Trucks: Includes trucks for use over the road (actual unloaded weight less than 13,000 pounds) . . . | 4 | 5 | 5 |
| 34.0 Manufacture of Fabricated Metal Products Special Tools: Includes assets used in the production of metal cans, tinware . . . | 12 | 7 | 12 |

[12]Technically, similar assets are assets in the same asset class. We discuss asset classes below.

[13]The "alternative" recovery period in Rev. Proc. 87-56 refers to an asset's life under the alternative depreciation system (which was discussed earlier under depreciation methods). The Class Life referred to in Rev. Proc. 87-56 refers to the midpoint of asset depreciation range (ADR) applicable under pre-ACRS and has little or no meaning under MACRS.

While even this excerpt from Rev. Proc. 87-56 may seem a bit intimidating, you can classify the vast majority of business assets acquired by knowing a few common recovery periods. You should know the recovery period for the commonly purchased assets described in Exhibit 9-4.

**EXHIBIT 9-4**   Recovery Period for Most Common Business Assets

| Asset Description (summary of Rev. Proc. 87-57) | Recovery Period* |
|---|---|
| Cars, light general-purpose trucks, and computers and peripheral equipment. | 5-year |
| Office furniture, fixtures, machinery, and equipment. | 7-year |

*Using 200 percent declining balance, switching to straight-line.

To this point, our discussion has emphasized computing depreciation for new assets. Does the process change when businesses acquire used assets? No, it is exactly the same. For example, Teton purchased a *used* delivery truck. The fact that the truck is used does not change its MACRS recovery period. No matter how long the previous owner used the truck, Teton will restart the five-year recovery period for light general purpose trucks (see Exhibit 9-4).

Compare this to the process of determining the life of each *individual* asset as required by financial accounting rules. Exhibit 9-5 provides an excerpt from

**EXHIBIT 9-5**   Weyerhaeuser Asset Depreciable Lives for Financial Accounting Purposes

| Weyerhaeuser NOTE 6: PROPERTY AND EQUIPMENT | | | |
|---|---|---|---|
| *(Dollar amounts in millions)* | **Range of Lives** | **December 31, 2008** | **December 30, 2007** |
| Property and equipment, at cost: | | | |
| Land | N/A | $    177 | $    282 |
| Buildings and improvements | 10–40 | 1,643 | 2,449 |
| Machinery and equipment | 2–25 | 7,358 | 12,640 |
| Rail and truck roads | 10–20 | 562 | 585 |
| Other | 3–10 | 381 | 391 |
| Total cost | | 10,121 | 16,347 |
| Less discontinued operations | | (72) | (5,914) |
| | | 10,049 | 10,433 |
| Allowance for depreciation and amortization | | (6,252) | (9,529) |
| Less discontinued operations | | 61 | 3,208 |
| | | (6,191) | (6,321) |
| Property and equipment, net | | $ 3,858 | $ 4,112 |

**Weyerhaeuser, a portion of**
**NOTE 1. SUMMARY OF SIGNIFICANT ACCOUNTING POLICIES**

**Property and Equipment**
We maintain property accounts on an individual asset basis.
Here's how we handle major items:

- Improvements to and replacements of major units of property are capitalized.
- Maintenance, repairs and minor replacements are expensed.
- Depreciation is calculated using a straight-line method at rates based on estimated service lives.
- Logging railroads and truck roads are generally amortized—as timber is harvested—at rates based on the volume of timber estimated to be removed.
- Cost and accumulated depreciation of property sold or retired are removed from the accounts and the gain or loss is included in earnings.

Weyerhaeuser's financial statements illustrating the complexities of financial accounting depreciation.

Notice that, for financial statement purposes, Weyerhaeuser has determined that the life of its machinery and equipment ranges from 2 to 25 years. Determining the tax recovery periods for these assets is very simple. Under MACRS, the tax recovery period for machinery and equipment is seven years. Using Rev. Proc. 87-56, Teton has determined the cost recovery periods for the personal property it purchased and placed in service during the year. Exhibit 9-6 summarizes this information.

**EXHIBIT 9-6**  Teton Personal Property Summary (Base Scenario)

| Asset | Date Acquired | Quarter Acquired | Cost Basis | Recovery Period | Reference |
|---|---|---|---|---|---|
| Machinery | 7/22/10 | 3rd | $260,000 | 7 | Example 9-1; Exhibit 9-3. |
| Office furniture | 2/3/10 | 1st | 10,000 | 7 | Example-9-1; Exhibit 9-3. |
| Delivery truck | 8/17/10 | 3rd | 15,000 | 5 | Example 9-1; Exhibit 9-3. |
| Total personal property | | | $285,000 | | |

**Depreciation Conventions**  Once a business has determined the depreciation methods and recovery periods for the assets it placed in service during the year, it must also determine the applicable depreciation conventions. The depreciation convention specifies the portion of a full year's depreciation the business can deduct for an asset in the year the asset is first placed in service *and* in the year the asset is sold. For *personal property,* taxpayers must use either the **half-year convention** or the **mid-quarter convention.** But, as we discuss below, taxpayers are *not* free to choose the convention that applies.

*Half-year convention.*  The half-year convention allows one-half of a full year's depreciation in the year the asset is placed in service, regardless of when it was actually placed in service. For example, when the half-year convention applies to a calendar-year business, an asset placed in service on either February 3 or August 17 is treated as though it was placed in service on July 1, which is the middle of the calendar year. Thus, under this convention, Teton would deduct one-half of a year's worth of depreciation for the machinery, office furniture, and delivery truck even though it acquired the machinery, delivery truck, and office furniture at various times during the year (see Exhibit 9-6). The half-year convention is built into the depreciation tables provided by the IRS, which simplifies the depreciation calculation for the year the asset is placed into service.

The original ACRS system required the use of the half-year convention for all personal property placed in service during the year. However, Congress believed that many businesses took unfair advantage of the half-year convention by purposely acquiring assets at the end of the year that they otherwise would have acquired at the beginning of the next taxable year. Thus, businesses received one-half of a year's worth of depreciation for assets that they only used for a small portion of the year. Even though the half-year convention is the default convention, policy makers introduced the *mid-quarter convention* under MACRS to limit or prevent this type of opportunistic behavior.

*Mid-quarter convention.*  Under the mid-quarter convention, businesses treat assets *as though* they were placed in service during the middle of the *quarter* in which the business actually placed the assets into service. For example, when the

mid-quarter convention applies, if a business places an asset in service on December 1 (in the fourth quarter) it must treat the asset as though it was placed in service on November 15, which is the middle of the fourth quarter. Consequently, the business would only be able to deduct one-half of a quarter's worth of depreciation in the year the asset was placed in service (depreciation for the second half of November and the entire month of December).

Businesses must use the mid-quarter convention when *more* than 40 percent of their total *tangible personal property* that they place in service during the year is placed in service during the *fourth* quarter. Thus, the steps to determine whether the mid-quarter convention applies are the following:

**Step 1:** Sum the total basis of the tangible personal property that was placed in service during the year.

**Step 2:** Sum the total basis of the tangible personal property that was place in service in the fourth quarter.

**Step 3:** Divide the outcome of Step 2 by the outcome of Step 1. If the quotient is greater than 40 percent, the business must use the mid-quarter convention to determine the depreciation for all tangible personal property the business places in service during the year. Otherwise, the business uses the half-year convention for depreciating this property.

In accordance with Reg. §1.168(d)-1(b)(4), property expensed under §179 (discussed later in the chapter) is not included in the numerator or denominator of the mid-quarter test. The mid-quarter test is applied after the §179 expense but before bonus depreciation.

---

## Example 9-3

The following excerpt from the base scenario in Exhibit 9-6 provides the information we need to determine if Teton must use the mid-quarter convention to compute depreciation:

| Asset | Date Acquired | Quarter Acquired | Cost Basis |
|---|---|---|---|
| Office furniture | 2/3/10 | First | $ 10,000 |
| Machinery | 7/22/10 | Third | 260,000 |
| Delivery truck | 8/17/10 | Third | 15,000 |
| **Total personal property** | | | $285,000 |

Is Teton required to use the mid-quarter convention to depreciate its personal property?

**Answer:** No. See computation below.

| Description | Amount | Explanation |
|---|---|---|
| (1) Total basis of tangible personal property placed in service during year | $285,000 | |
| (2) Total basis of tangible personal property placed in service in fourth quarter | $ 0 | |
| (3) Percentage of basis of total tangible personal property placed in service during fourth quarter | 0% | (2)/(1). |

Teton is not required to use the mid-quarter convention because it did not place more than 40 percent of its assets in service during the fourth quarter. (In fact, Teton did not place any assets in service in the fourth quarter.) Consequently, Teton will use the half-year convention to calculate its depreciation expense.

---

**THE KEY FACTS**

**Mid-Quarter Convention**

▪ The mid-quarter convention is required when more than 40 percent of a taxpayer's personal property placed in service during the year was placed during the fourth quarter.

▪ Each quarter has its own depreciation table. Once you begin using a table, you must use the table over the asset's whole life.

▪ If an asset is disposed of before it is fully depreciated, use the formula given to determine the allowable depreciation in the year of disposition.

| Example 9-4 |
|---|

**What if:** Let's replace the facts from the base scenario presented in Exhibit 9-6 with the following alternative scenario 1 facts. In this alternative set of facts, we assume the machinery was acquired during the fourth quarter on October 25 as follows:

| Asset | Date Acquired | Quarter Acquired | Cost Basis |
|---|---|---|---|
| Office furniture | 2/3/10 | First | $ 10,000 |
| Delivery truck | 8/17/10 | Third | 15,000 |
| Machinery | 10/25/10 | Fourth | 260,000 |
| **Total personal property** | | | **$285,000** |

Under alternative scenario 1, is Teton required to use the mid-quarter convention?

**Answer:** Yes. Of the personal property it placed in service during the year, it placed 91.2 percent in service in the last quarter (this is greater than 40 percent). See the calculations below:

| Description | Amount | Explanation |
|---|---|---|
| (1) Cost of all personal property placed in service during current year. | $285,000 | |
| (2) Cost of personal property placed in service in the fourth quarter during current year. | $260,000 | |
| (3) Percentage of all personal property placed in service during current year that was placed in service in the fourth quarter. | 91.2% | (2)/(1). |

**What if:** Assume that Teton also placed in service on July 1 a building costing $500,000. Is Teton subject to the mid-quarter convention?

**Answer:** Yes. Because the building is real property (not personal property), it is not included in the mid-quarter calculation. The calculation is exactly the same as the calculation in alternative scenario 1 above.

**Calculating Depreciation for Personal Property** Once a business has identified the applicable method, recovery period, and convention for personal property, tax depreciation is relatively easy to calculate because the Internal Revenue Service provides depreciation percentage tables in Rev. Proc. 87-57. The percentages in the depreciation tables for tangible personal property incorporate the method and convention [accordingly there are separate tables for each combination of depreciation method (200 percent declining balance, 150 percent declining balance, and straight-line) and convention (half-year and mid-quarter; each quarter has its own table)]. To determine the depreciation for an asset for the year, use the following three steps:

**Step 1:** Locate the applicable table provided in Rev. Proc. 87-57.

**Step 2:** Select the column that corresponds with the asset's recovery period.

**Step 3:** Find the row identifying the year of the asset's recovery period.

The tables are constructed so that the intersection of the row and column provides the percentage of the asset's *original basis* that is deductible as depreciation expense for the particular year. Thus, depreciation expense for a particular asset is the product of the percentage from the table and the asset's *original basis*.

**Applying the Half-Year Convention**   Consider the excerpt from Rev. Proc. 87-57 provided in Exhibit 9-7 that shows the depreciation percentages for MACRS 200 percent declining balance using the half-year convention.[14] If a seven-year asset is placed into service during the current year, the depreciation percentage is 14.29 percent (the intersection of row 1 (year 1) and the seven-year property column).

**EXHIBIT 9-7    MACRS 200 Percent Declining Balance Using the Half-Year Convention**

| Year | Depreciation Rate for Recovery Period | |
| | 5-Year Property | 7-Year Property |
| --- | --- | --- |
| 1 | 20.00% | 14.29% |
| 2 | 32.00 | 24.49 |
| 3 | 19.20 | 17.49 |
| 4 | 11.52 | 12.49 |
| 5 | 11.52 | 8.93 |
| 6 | 5.76 | 8.92 |
| 7 | N/A | 8.93 |
| 8 | N/A | 4.46 |

Notice that the depreciation percentages for five-year property extend for six years and the percentages for seven-year property extend for eight years. Why does it take six years to fully depreciate an asset with a five-year recovery period and eight years for a seven-year asset? Because the business does not deduct a full year's depreciation in the first year (businesses must use either the half-year or mid-quarter convention), an entire year of depreciation is effectively split between the first and last year. For example, when the half-year convention applies to a five-year asset, the taxpayer deducts one-half of a year's depreciation in year 1 and one-half of a year's depreciation in year 6.

**Example 9-5**

Teton is using the 200 percent declining balance method and half-year convention to compute depreciation expense on its current year personal property additions. What is Teton's depreciation expense for these assets?

**Answer:** $41,583, computed as follows:

| Asset | Date Placed in Service | (1) Original Basis | (2) Rate | (1) × (2) Depreciation |
| --- | --- | --- | --- | --- |
| Office furniture | February 3 | $ 10,000 | 14.29% | $ 1,429 |
| Machinery | July 22 | $260,000 | 14.29% | $37,154 |
| Used delivery truck | August 17 | $ 15,000 | 20.00% | $ 3,000 |
| Total | | | | $41,583 |

Because the office furniture and machinery have a seven-year recovery period and it is the first year for depreciation, the depreciation rate is 14.29 percent (see Exhibit 9-7). The depreciation rate for the used delivery truck (five-year property) is determined in a similar manner.

[14]MACRS tables for the half-year and mid-quarter convention are also provided in Appendix A at the end of this chapter.

Calculating depreciation for assets in years after the year of acquisition is also relatively simple. Again, using the MACRS Half-Year Convention Table (see Exhibit 9-7) to compute depreciation for the second year, the taxpayer would multiply the asset's original basis times the rate factor in the *year 2* row and the *year 3* row in the following year and so on.

## Example 9-6

**What if:** Assume that Teton holds the tangible personal property it acquired and placed in service this year until the assets are fully depreciated. Using the IRS provided tables (see Exhibit 9-7) how would Teton determine its depreciation expense for years 1 through 8?

**Answer:** See the following table:

**Depreciation Over Asset Recovery Period**

| Year | 7-Year Machinery | 7-Year Office Furniture | 5-Year Delivery Truck | Yearly Total |
|---|---|---|---|---|
| 1 | $ 37,154 | $ 1,429 | $ 3,000 | $ 41,583 |
| 2 | $ 63,674 | $ 2,449 | $ 4,800 | $ 70,923 |
| 3 | $ 45,474 | $ 1,749 | $ 2,880 | $ 50,103 |
| 4 | $ 32,474 | $ 1,249 | $ 1,728 | $ 35,451 |
| 5 | $ 23,218 | $ 893 | $ 1,728 | $ 25,839 |
| 6 | $ 23,192 | $ 892 | $ 864 | $ 24,948 |
| 7 | $ 23,218 | $ 893 | N/A | $ 24,111 |
| 8 | $ 11,596 | $ 446 | N/A | $ 12,042 |
| Accumulated Depreciation | $260,000 | $10,000 | $15,000 | $285,000 |

***Half-year convention for year of disposition.*** Businesses often sell or dispose of assets before they fully depreciate them. Recall that the half-year convention applies in both the year of acquisition and the year of disposition. Note, however, that the tables can't anticipate when a business may dispose of an asset. Accordingly, the tables only provide depreciation percentages for assets assuming the asset won't be disposed of before it is fully depreciated. That is, for each year in the asset's recovery period, the tables provide a percentage for an entire year's worth of depreciation. So, to calculate the depreciation for the year of disposition, the business first calculates depreciation for the *entire year* as if the property had not been disposed of. Then the business applies the half-year convention by multiplying the full year's depreciation by 50 percent (one-half of a year's depreciation). Note, however, that if a business acquires and disposes of an asset in the same year, it is not allowed to claim any depreciation on the asset.[15]

## Example 9-7

**What if:** Assume that Teton sells all of its office furniture in year 2 (the year after it buys it). What is Teton's depreciation for the office furniture in the year of disposition (year 2)?

*(continued on page 9-13...)*

---

[15]Reg. §1.168(d)-1(b)(3).

**Answer:** $1,225, calculated using the MACRS Half-Year Convention Table as follows:

| Asset | Amount | Explanation |
|---|---|---|
| (1) Office furniture | $10,000 | Original basis. |
| (2) Depreciation percentage | 24.49% | Seven-year property, year 2. |
| (3) Full year of depreciation | $ 2,449 | (1) × (2). |
| (4) Half-year convention percentage | 50% | Depreciation limit in year of disposal. |
| Depreciation in year of disposal | $ 1,225 | (3) × (4). |

**What if:** Assume that Teton sold all of its office furniture in year 1 (the year it bought it and placed it in service). How much deprecation expense can Teton deduct for the office furniture in year 1?

**Answer:** $0. A business is not allowed to claim any depreciation expense for assets it acquires and disposes of in the same year.

**Applying the Mid-Quarter Convention**   When the mid-quarter convention applies, the process for computing depreciation is the same as it is when the half-year convention applies, except that businesses use a different set of depreciation tables (a separate table for each quarter). After categorizing the assets by recovery period and grouping them into quarters, businesses consult the Mid-Quarter Convention Tables (which have been consolidated into Exhibit 9-8) to determine the depreciation rate for each asset group.

**EXHIBIT 9-8**   Mid-Quarter Depreciation Table for Personal Property by Quarter Placed in Service and Recovery Period (Excerpts from Rev. Proc. 87-57)

| Year | First Quarter 5-year | First Quarter 7-year | Second Quarter 5-year | Second Quarter 7-year | Third Quarter 5-year | Third Quarter 7-year | Fourth Quarter 5-year | Fourth Quarter 7-year |
|---|---|---|---|---|---|---|---|---|
| 1 | 35.00% | 25.00% | 25.00% | 17.85% | 15.00% | 10.71% | 5.00% | 3.57% |
| 2 | 26.00 | 21.43 | 30.00 | 23.47 | 34.00 | 25.51 | 38.00 | 27.55 |
| 3 | 15.60 | 15.31 | 18.00 | 16.76 | 20.40 | 18.22 | 22.80 | 19.68 |
| 4 | 11.01 | 10.93 | 11.37 | 11.97 | 12.24 | 13.02 | 13.68 | 14.06 |
| 5 | 11.01 | 8.75 | 11.37 | 8.87 | 11.30 | 9.30 | 10.94 | 10.04 |
| 6 | 1.38 | 8.74 | 4.26 | 8.87 | 7.06 | 8.85 | 9.58 | 8.73 |
| 7 | | 8.75 | | 8.87 | | 8.86 | | 8.73 |
| 8 | | 1.09 | | 3.33 | | 5.53 | | 7.64 |

The depreciation expense for an asset is the product of the asset's original basis and the percentage from the table.

**Example 9-8**

**What if:** For this example, we assume the facts from alternative scenario 1 presented in Example 9-4 (see table below). What is Teton's year 1 depreciation expense for its personal property additions under the alternative scenario 1 presented in Example 9-4?

(continued on page 9-14...)

**Answer:** $14,032, computed as follows:

| Asset | Purchase Date | Quarter | Original Basis | Rate | Depreciation |
|---|---|---|---|---|---|
| Office furniture (7-year) | February 3 | First | $ 10,000 | 25.00% | $ 2,500 |
| Delivery truck (5-year) | August 17 | Third | $ 15,000 | 15.00% | $ 2,250 |
| Machinery (7-year) | October 25 | Fourth | $260,000 | 3.57% | $ 9,282 |
| | | | | | $14,032 |

The office furniture factor of 25.00 percent is located in Exhibit 9-8. See the columns for property placed into service during the first quarter (first two columns), select the 7-year recovery period column (last column), and the year 1 row. The process for determining the rate factor for the delivery truck and machinery follows the same methodology using the third and fourth quarter columns, respectively.

Teton's $41,583 depreciation expense under the half-year convention (see Example 9-5) is significantly higher than its $14,032 depreciation expense under the mid-quarter convention (see Example 9-8). Why the big disparity? Because the (high cost) machinery was placed into service during the fourth quarter and thus generated significantly less current depreciation expense (one-half of one quarter's depreciation) than it would have under the half-year convention. It is important to note, however, that when using the mid-quarter convention, assets placed in service in the first or second quarter will generate more depreciation than they would have under the half-year convention (10.5/12ths and 7.5/12ths of a full year, respectively). However, because the mid-quarter convention only applies when a large percentage of the cost of the assets was placed in service in the fourth quarter, the mid-quarter convention tends to generate less overall depreciation expense for new additions than the half-year convention.

The process for calculating depreciation for assets in years after the year of acquisition under the mid-quarter convention is nearly identical to the process we described for making this computation under the half-year convention. The only difference is that the business looks to the MACRS Mid-Quarter Convention Table (Exhibit 9-8) for the appropriate quarter rather than the MACRS Half-Year Convention Table (Exhibit 9-7).

## Example 9-9

**What if:** Assume that Teton held and fully depreciated the tangible personal property it placed in service this year under the mid-quarter convention (alternative scenario 1). What would be Teton's depreciation expense for its personal property additions for years 1 through 8 using the mid-quarter tables provided in Exhibit 9-8?

**Answer:** See table below*:

| Year | 7-year Machinery 4th Quarter | 7-year Office Furniture 1st Quarter | 5-year Delivery Truck 3rd Quarter | Yearly Total |
|---|---|---|---|---|
| 1 | $ 9,282 | $ 2,500 | $ 2,250 | $ 14,032 |
| 2 | $ 71,630 | $ 2,143 | $ 5,100 | $ 78,873 |
| 3 | $ 51,168 | $ 1,531 | $ 3,060 | $ 55,759 |
| 4 | $ 36,556 | $ 1,093 | $ 1,836 | $ 39,485 |
| 5 | $ 26,104 | $ 875 | $ 1,695 | $ 28,674 |
| 6 | $ 22,698 | $ 874 | $ 1,059 | $ 24,631 |
| 7 | $ 22,698 | $ 875 | N/A | $ 23,573 |
| 8 | $ 19,864 | $ 109 | N/A | $ 19,973 |
| | $260,000 | $10,000 | $15,000 | $285,000 |

*See Exhibit 9-8; the depreciation is calculated by multiplying the applicable rate by the cost basis.

***Mid-quarter convention for year of disposition.*** Calculating depreciation expense in the year of sale or disposition is a bit more involved when the mid-quarter convention applies than when it does not. When the mid-quarter convention applies, the asset is treated as though it is sold in the middle of the quarter of which it was actually sold. The process for calculating mid-quarter convention depreciation for the year of sale is exactly the same as the process for using the half-year convention, except that *instead of* multiplying the full year's depreciation by 50 percent, the business multiplies the amount of depreciation it would have been able to claim on the asset if it had not sold the asset (a full year's depreciation) by the applicable percentage in Exhibit 9-9 below.

**EXHIBIT 9-9** Mid-Quarter Convention Percentage of Full Year's Depreciation in Year of Disposition

| Quarter of Disposition | Percentage | Calculation* |
|---|---|---|
| First | 12.5% | 1.5/12 |
| Second | 37.5% | 4.5/12 |
| Third | 62.5% | 7.5/12 |
| Fourth | 87.5% | 10.5/12 |

*The calculation is the number of months the taxpayer held or is deemed to have held the asset in the year of disposition divided by 12 months in the year.

**Example 9-10**

***What if:*** Assume that Teton depreciates its personal property under the mid-quarter convention (alternative scenario 1, see Example 9-4) and that it sells its office furniture in the third quarter of year 2. The office furniture ($10,000 original basis) was placed into service during the first quarter of year 1 and has a seven-year recovery period. What depreciation expense can Teton deduct for the office furniture in year 2, the year of sale?

**Answer:** $1,339. Computed as follows:

| Description | Amount | Explanation |
|---|---|---|
| (1) Original basis | $10,000 | Example 9-4. |
| (2) Year 2 depreciation percentage | 21.43% | Exhibit 9-8; Mid-quarter, first quarter table, 7-year property, year 2. |
| (3) Full year 2 depreciation | 2,143 | (1) × (2). |
| (4) Percentage of full year's depreciation in year of disposition if mid-quarter convention applies | 62.5% | From Exhibit 9-9; asset disposed of in third quarter. |
| Depreciation in year of disposition | $ 1,339 | (3) × (4). |

***What if:*** Assume Teton disposed of the office furniture on January 2 of year 2. How much depreciation expense would it be able to claim on the furniture in year 2?

**Answer:** $268 ($2,143 full year's depreciation × 12.5% from Exhibit 9-9).

**Immediate Expensing** Policy makers created an important tax incentive designed to help small businesses purchasing new or used tangible personal property. This incentive is commonly referred to as the **§179 expense** or *immediate expensing* election.[16]

---

[16]Real property, intangibles, and tangible personal property that are used less than 50 percent for business are not eligible for immediate expensing.

As discussed earlier in the chapter, businesses must generally depreciate assets over the assets' recovery periods. However, under §179, businesses may elect to immediately expense up to $250,000 of tangible personal property placed in service during 2010 (also $250,000 in 2009).[17] They may also elect to deduct less than the maximum. When businesses elect to deduct a certain amount of §179 expense, they immediately expense all or a portion of an asset's basis or several assets' bases. To reflect this immediate depreciation expense, they must reduce the basis of the asset or assets (to which they applied the expense) *before* they compute the MACRS depreciation expense.

## Example 9-11

***What if:*** Assume Teton is eligible for and elects to immediately deduct $80,000 of §179 expense against the basis of the machinery. (Note that Teton could have elected to deduct up to $250,000.) What is the amount of Teton's current year depreciation expense, including regular MACRS depreciation and the §179 expense on its machinery (assuming half-year convention applies)?

**Answer:** $105,722, computed as follows:

| Description | Amount | Explanation |
|---|---|---|
| (1) Machinery | $260,000 | Example 9-1. |
| (2) §179 expense | $ 80,000 | |
| (3) Remaining basis in machinery | $180,000 | (1) − (2). |
| (4) MACRS depreciation rate for 7-year machinery | 14.29% | Rate from Exhibit 9-7. |
| (5) MACRS deprecation expense on machinery | $ 25,722 | (3) × (4). |
| Total depreciation on machinery | $105,722 | (2) + (5). |

***What if:*** Assume that Teton was eligible for and elected to claim the maximum amount of §179 expense. What would be its total current-year depreciation expense, including MACRS depreciation and §179 expense (assuming half-year convention applies)?

**Answer:** $251,429, computed as follows:

| Description | Amount | Explanation |
|---|---|---|
| (1) Machinery | $260,000 | Example 9-1. |
| (2) §179 expense | $250,000 | Maximum expense in 2009. |
| (3) Remaining basis in machinery | $ 10,000 | (1) − (2). |
| (4) MACRS depreciation rate for 7-year machinery | 14.29% | Rate from Exhibit 9-7. |
| (5) MACRS deprecation expense on machinery | $ 1,429 | (3) × (4). |
| Total depreciation on machinery | $251,429 | (2) + (5). |

***Limits on immediate expensing.*** The maximum amount of §179 expense a business may elect to claim for the year is subject to a phase-out limitation. Under the phase-out limitation, businesses must reduce the $250,000 maximum available expense

[17]The maximum allowable expense under §179 is indexed for inflation and changes annually. Generally, the annual amount is released in a Revenue Procedure at the beginning of the taxable year. The 2010 amount assumes extension of the American Reinvestment and Recovery Act of 2009; absent this proposed legislation, the 2010 amount would be $133,000. At press time, the Senate had approved the extension of the 2009 amount but the bill was waiting for approval from the House.

dollar for dollar for the amount of *tangible personal property* purchased and placed in service during 2010 *over* an $800,000 threshold (also $800,000 in 2009).[18] Thus if a business places more than $1,050,000 ($800,000 threshold plus $250,000) expense of tangible personal property into service during 2010, its maximum available §179 expense for the year is $0. The phased-out portion of the maximum expense disappears and does *not* carry over to another year.

**Example 9-12**

**What if:** Let's assume that during 2010, Teton placed into service $900,000 of machinery (up from the base scenario amount of $260,000), $10,000 of office furniture, and a $10,000 truck for a total of $920,000 of tangible *personal* property placed in service for the year. What is Teton's maximum §179 expense after applying the phase-out limitation?

**Answer:** $130,000 computed as follows:

| Description | Amount | Explanation |
|---|---|---|
| (1) Property placed in service in 2010 | $920,000 | |
| (2) Threshold for §179 phase-out | (800,000) | 2010 amount [§179(b)(1)]. |
| (3) Phase-out of maximum §179 expense | $120,000 | (1) − (2) (permanently disallowed). |
| (4) Maximum §179 expense before phase-out | $250,000 | §179(b)(2). |
| (5) Phase-out of maximum §179 expense | 120,000 | From (3). |
| Maximum §179 expense after phase-out* | $130,000 | (4) − (5). |

*Note that this is the maximum expense after phase-out but *before* the taxable income limitation we discuss next.

**What if:** Assume further that Teton acquired and placed in service a warehouse costing $275,000. Taking the warehouse into account, what is Teton's maximum §179 expense after the phase-out?

**Answer:** $130,000. The same answer as above. The phase-out is based on the amount of tangible personal property placed in service during the year. Because the warehouse is *real property*, its acquisition has no effect on Teton's maximum §179 expense.

Businesses may elect to claim the §179 expense for the year up to the maximum amount available (after computing the phase-out—see the previous example). When a business elects to claim a certain amount of §179 expense, it must reduce the basis of the asset(s) to which the expense is applied. It then computes regular depreciation on the remaining basis after reducing the basis of the asset(s) for the §179 expense.

The business's *deductible* §179 expense is limited to the business's net income after deducting all expenses (including regular depreciation expense) except the §179 expense. Consequently, the §179 expense cannot create or extend a business's net operating loss. If a business claims more §179 expense than it is allowed to deduct due to the taxable income limitation, it carries the excess forward and deducts it in a subsequent year, subject to the taxable income limitation (but not the phase-out limitation) in the subsequent year.[19]

---

[18]The threshold under §179 is indexed for inflation and changes annually. Generally, the annual amount is released in a Revenue Procedure at the beginning of the taxable year. The 2010 amount assumes extension of the American Reinvestment and Recovery Act of 2009; absent this proposed legislation, the 2010 amount would be $530,000. At press time, the Senate had approved the extension of the 2009 amount but the bill was waiting for approval from the House.

[19]Businesses typically elect only to expense the currently deductible amount since the taxable income limitation may also limit their §179 expense in future years just as it does for the current year.

## Example 9-13

**What if:** Let's assume the facts of the previous example, where Teton's maximum §179 expense after applying the phase-out limitation is $130,000. Also assume that Teton elects to claim the entire $130,000 expense and it chooses to apply it against the machinery. Further assume that Teton reports $50,000 of taxable income before deducting any §179 expense [note that this is after deducting all regular (non-§179) depreciation (including the amount on line (5) in the table below]. What amount of total depreciation (including §179 expense) is Teton able to deduct on the machinery for the year?

**Answer:** $160,033 computed as follows:

| Description | Amount | Explanation |
|---|---|---|
| (1) Machinery | $900,000 | Example 9-12. |
| (2) Elected §179 expense | 130,000 | |
| (3) Remaining basis | 770,000 | (1) − (2). |
| (4) MACRS depreciation rate for 7-year machinery, year 1 | 14.29% | See Exhibit 9-7. |
| (5) MACRS deprecation expense on machinery | $110,033 | (3) × (4). |
| (6) Deductible §179 expense | $ 50,000 | Taxable income limitation. |
| (7) Total depreciation expense on machinery for the year | $160,033 | (5) + (6). |
| (8) Excess §179 expense | $ 80,000 | (2) − (6). |

What is the amount of Teton's excess §179 expense (elected expense in excess of the deductible amount due to the taxable income limitation), and what does it do with it for tax purposes?

**Answer:** $80,000. See the above table for the computation (line 8). Teton carries this $80,000 excess §179 expense forward to future years and may deduct it subject to the taxable income limitation.

---

### THE KEY FACTS

**§179 Expenses**

▪ $250,000 of tangible personal property can be immediately expensed in 2010 (assuming the 2009 amounts are extended to 2010).

▪ Businesses are eligible for the full amount of this expense when tangible personal property placed in service is less than $800,000 (assuming the 2009 amount is extended to 2010). Beginning at $800,000, the §179 expense is phased out, dollar-for-dollar. When assets placed in service exceed $1,050,000, no §179 expense can be taken.

▪ §179 expenses are also limited to a business's taxable income before the §179 expense. §179 expenses cannot create losses.

---

***Choosing the assets to immediately expense.***   Businesses qualifying for immediate expensing are allowed to choose the asset or assets (from tangible personal property placed in service during the year) they immediately expense under §179. If a business's objective is to maximize its current depreciation expense and the half-year convention applies, it should immediately expense the property with the *longest recovery period.* For example, it should immediately expense a seven-year asset before a five-year asset. However, if the mid-quarter convention applies, the business should apply the §179 expense on the asset or assets with the *lowest first year depreciation percentage,* which might mean applying it against the shorter-lived asset if it was placed in service in a later quarter than the longer-lived asset. For example, looking at Exhibit 9-8, if a business had to choose between immediately expensing seven-year property placed in service in the first quarter or five-year property placed in service in the third quarter, which asset should it elect to expense under §179 if it wanted to maximize its current year depreciation expense? The five-year asset because its first year depreciation percentage is 15 percent, while the seven-year asset's first year depreciation percentage is 25 percent. Finally, it is important to note that businesses reduce the basis of the assets for the §179 expense before computing whether the mid-quarter convention applies.[20]

[20]§168(d)(3)(B)(ii).

**Example 9-14**

***What if:*** Let's assume that Teton placed into service on June 1, five-year property costing $350,000 and seven-year property costing $350,000. Further assume that Teton is not subject to the taxable income limitation for the §179 expense. What is Teton's depreciation expense (including §179 expense) if it elects to apply the full §179 expense against the five-year property (Scenario A)? What is its depreciation expense if it applies it against its seven-year property (Scenario B)?

**Answer:** $320,015 if it applies the §179 to the five-year property (Scenario A) and $334,290 it applies it to the seven-year property (Scenario B). See the computations below:

| Description | (Scenario A) §179 Expense on 5-year Property | (Scenario B) §179 Expense on 7-year Property | Explanation |
|---|---|---|---|
| (1) Original basis | $350,000 | $350,000 | |
| (2) Elected §179 expense | 250,000 | 250,000 | Maximum expense. |
| (3) Remaining basis | 100,000 | 100,000 | (1) − (2). |
| (4) MACRS depreciation rate | 20% | 14.29% | See Exhibit 9-7. |
| (5) MACRS deprecation expense | $ 20,000 | $ 14,290 | (3) × (4). |
| (6) Deductible §179 expense | $250,000 | $250,000 | Example 9-12. |
| (7) MACRS depreciation on other property | $ 50,015 | $ 70,000 | This is the depreciation on the $350,000 seven-year property in the five-year column and on the $350,000 five-year property in the seven-year column. |
| Total depreciation expense | $320,015 | $334,290 | (5) + (6) + (7). |

Note that Teton deducts $14,275 more in depreciation expense if it applies the §179 expense to the seven-year property.

***What if:*** Assume the same facts, except that Teton placed the five-year property in service on December 1. Absent any §179 expense, Teton would be subject to the mid-quarter convention because 50 percent of its tangible personal property was placed in service in the fourth quarter. Assuming Teton wanted to avoid the mid-quarter convention, how should it apply its §179 expense?

**Answer:** It should apply the §179 expense against the five-year property. By doing so, the basis of the assets placed in service in the fourth quarter is $100,000 ($350,000 minus $250,000 §179 expense) and the basis of the assets placed in service in total is $450,000 ($350,000 7-year property + $100,000 5-year property). Thus, the percentage of tangible personal property placed in service in the fourth quarter is 22.22 percent ($100,000/$450,000), and the mid-quarter convention does not apply. If, however, it applies the §179 expense against the seven-year property, the mid-quarter convention would apply because the percentage of tangible personal property placed in service in the fourth quarter increases to 77.78 percent ($350,000/$450,000). Because this exceeds 40 percent, the mid-quarter convention applies. Teton could also expense just enough 5-year property to avoid the mid-quarter convention and elect the rest of the §179 expense against the seven-year property to maximize its total depreciation.

***Bonus Depreciation.***   To stimulate the economy, policy makers occasionally implement **bonus depreciation.**[21] In 2008 and 2009, taxpayers could elect to immediately expense 50 percent of qualified property. Qualified property must have a recovery period of 20 years or less (no real property), the original use of the property must

---

[21]§168(k)(2)(6). Bonus depreciation, if applicable, is also allowable for purposes of the AMT.

commence with the taxpayer (the property must be new rather than used), and the property must be placed in service during 2008 through 2009.[22] The bonus depreciation is calculated after the §179 expense but before MACRS depreciation.[23]

---

## Example 9-15

**What if:** Assume that the bonus depreciation provisions apply to 2010 and that Teton elected bonus depreciation for the tangible personal property acquired in Exhibit 9-6.

| Asset | Date Acquired | Quarter Acquired | Cost Basis | Recovery Period |
|---|---|---|---|---|
| Office furniture | 2/3/10 | 1st | $ 10,000 | 7 |
| Machinery | 7/22/10 | 3rd | 260,000 | 7 |
| Delivery truck | 8/17/10 | 3rd | 15,000 | 5 |
| Total | | | $285,000 | |

Assuming Teton elects no §179 expensing, what is Teton's bonus depreciation?

**Answer:** $142,500 computed as follows:

| Description | Amount | Explanation |
|---|---|---|
| (1) Qualified property | $285,000 | |
| (2) Bonus depreciation rate | 50% | §168(k)(1)(A). |
| Bonus depreciation | $142,500 | (1) × (2). |

**What if:** Assuming Teton elects §179 expensing, what is Teton's bonus depreciation?

**Answer:** $17,500 computed as follows:

| Description | Amount | Explanation |
|---|---|---|
| (1) Qualified property | $285,000 | |
| (2) §179 expense | $250,000 | Maximum expense. |
| (3) Remaining amount eligible for bonus depreciation | $ 35,000 | (1) − (2). |
| (4) Bonus depreciation rate | 50% | §168(k)(1)(A). |
| Bonus depreciation | $ 17,500 | (3) × (4). |

---

**THE KEY FACTS**

**Listed Property**

∎ When an asset is used for both personal and business use, calculate what percentage was used for business purposes.

∎ If the business-use percentage is above 50 percent, the allowable depreciation is limited to the business-use percentage.

*(continued)*

**Listed Property**    Most business-owned assets are used for business rather than personal purposes. For example, Weyerhaeuser employees probably have little or no personal interest in using Weyerhaeuser's timber-harvesting equipment during their free time. In contrast, business owners and employees may find some business assets, such as company automobiles or laptop computers, conducive for personal use.

Business assets that tend to be used for both business and personal purposes are referred to as **listed property.** For example, automobiles, other means of transportation (planes, boats, and recreation vehicles), computer equipment, and even cell phones are considered to be listed property. The tax law limits the allowable depreciation on listed property to the portion of the asset used for business purposes.

[22]§168(k)(2)(A)(iv). At press time the bonus depreciation provisions had not been extended to 2010. We discuss them here in case they are eventually extended to include 2010.

[23]Reg. §1.168(k)-1(a)(2)(iii) and Reg. §1.168(k)-1(d)(3) Example (2).

How do taxpayers compute depreciation for listed property? First, they must determine the percentage of business vs. personal use of the asset for the year. If the business-use percentage for the year *exceeds* 50 percent, the deductible depreciation is limited to the full annual depreciation multiplied by the *business-use* percentage for the year. Listed property used in trade or business more than 50% is eligible for the §179 expensing election and bonus depreciation (if bonus depreciation is applicable for year asset was placed into service).

> (*concluded*)
> ■ If a listed property's business-use percentage ever falls below 50 percent, depreciation for all previous years is retroactively restated using MACRS straight-line method.

### Example 9-16

**What if:** Assume that, in addition to the assets Teton purchased in the base scenario presented in Exhibit 9-6, it also purchased a new computer projector for $2,000 that its employees use for business presentations on weekdays. On weekends, Steve uses the projector as an integral part of his high-definition home theater system. Since the computer projector is listed property, Teton must assess the business-use percentage to properly calculate its deductible depreciation for the projector. Assuming that Teton determines the business-use percentage to be 75 percent, what is Teton's depreciation deduction on the projector for the year?

**Answer:** $300, computed as follows:

| Description | Amount | Explanation |
|---|---|---|
| (1) Original basis of projector | $2,000 | |
| (2) MACRS depreciation rate | 20% | 5-year property, year 1, half-year convention. |
| (3) Full MACRS depreciation expense | 400 | (1) × (2). |
| (4) Business-use percentage | 75% | |
| Depreciation deduction for year | $  300 | (3) × (4). |

When the business-use percentage of an asset is 50 percent or less, the business must compute depreciation for the asset using the MACRS *straight-line* method over the MACRS ADS (alternative depreciation system) recovery period.[24] For five-year assets such as automobiles and computers, the assets on which the personal use limitation is most common, the MACRS ADS recovery period is also five years. However, for seven-year assets, the ADS recovery period is generally 10 years.[25]

If a business initially uses an asset more than 50 percent of the time for business (and appropriately adopts the 200 percent declining balance method) but subsequently its business use drops to 50 percent or below, the *depreciation expense for all prior years must be recomputed* as if it had been using the straight-line depreciation over the ADS recovery period the entire time. It must then make up for any excess of accelerated depreciation it did deduct over the straight-line depreciation it should have deducted by adjusting the current year depreciation. In practical terms, the business can use the following five steps to determine its current depreciation expense for the asset:

**Step 1:** Compute depreciation for the year it drops to 50 percent or below using the straight-line method (this method also applies to all subsequent years).

**Step 2:** Compute the amount of depreciation the taxpayer would have deducted if the taxpayer had used the straight-line method over the ADS recovery period for all prior years (recall that depreciation is limited to the business-use percentage in those years).

[24]This is the alternative recovery period listed in Rev. Proc. 87-56. See §168(g)(3)(C) and Reg. §1.280F-3T(d)(1).

[25]However, there are exceptions to this general rule. For example, the ADS recovery period for certain machinery for food and beverages is 12 years and the ADS recovery period for machinery for tobacco products is 15 years. Thus, it is important to check Rev. Proc. 87-56 to verify the ADS recovery period in these situations.

**Step 3:** Compute the amount of depreciation the taxpayer had actually deducted on the asset for all prior years.

**Step 4:** Subtract the amount from Step 2 from the amount in Step 3. The difference is the prior year accelerated depreciation in excess of straight-line depreciation.

**Step 5:** Subtract the excess accelerated depreciation from Step 4 from the current year straight-line depreciation in Step 1. This is the business's allowable depreciation expense on the asset for the year. If the prior year excess depreciation from Step 4 exceeds the current year straight-line depreciation in Step 1, the business is not allowed to deduct any depreciation on the asset for the year and must actually recognize additional ordinary income for the amount of the excess.

This five-step process is designed to place the business in the same position it would have been in if it had used straight-line depreciation during all years of the asset's life.

## Example 9-17

*What if:* Assume that, consistent with the previous example, in year 1 Teton used the projector 75 percent of the time for business purposes and deducted $300 depreciation expense on the projector. However, in year 2, Teton's business-use percentage falls to 40 percent. What is Teton's depreciation deduction for the projector in year 2?

*Answer:* $10, computed using the five-step process described above as follows:

| Description | Amount | Explanation* |
|---|---|---|
| (1) Straight-line depreciation in current year | $160 | $2,000/5 years × 40 percent business use percentage (Step 1). |
| (2) Prior year straight-line depreciation | 150 | $2,000/5 × 50 percent (half-year convention) × 75 percent business-use percentage (Step 2). |
| (3) Prior year accelerated depreciation | 300 | Example 9-16 (prior example) (Step 3). |
| (4) Excess accelerated depreciation | 150 | (3) − (2) (Step 4). |
| **Allowable current year depreciation** | **$ 10** | (1) − (4) (Step 5). |

*Note that the MACRS ADS recovery period (five years) for computers and peripherals (qualified technological equipment) is the same as the standard MACRS recovery period (five years).

*What if:* Now assume that, in year 1 Teton used the projector 85 percent of the time for business purposes and deducted $340 depreciation expense on the projector. However, in year 2, Teton's business-use percentage falls to 40 percent. What is Teton's depreciation deduction for the projector in year 2?

*Answer:* $0 depreciation deduction and $10 of ordinary income because excess accelerated depreciative exceeds current year straight-line depreciation, computed as follows:

| Description | Amount | Explanation |
|---|---|---|
| (1) Straight-line depreciation in current year | $160 | $2,000/5 years × 40 percent business use. |
| (2) Prior year straight-line depreciation | 170 | $2,000/5 × 50 percent (half-year convention) × 85 percent business-use percentage. |
| (3) Prior year accelerated depreciation | 340 | Example 9-16 (prior example, if 85%). |
| (4) Excess accelerated depreciation | 170 | (3) − (2). |
| **Allowable current year depreciation (income)** | **($10)** | (1) − (4). |

**Luxury Automobiles**   For good reason, policy makers believe that an element of personal pleasure or benefit is derived from passenger automobiles.[26] As we discussed in Chapter 8, §162 limits business deductions to those considered to be "ordinary, necessary, and reasonable" to prevent subsidizing (giving a tax deduction for) unwarranted business expenses. Although these terms are subject to interpretation, most taxpayers probably agree that for purposes of simply transporting passengers for business-related purposes, the cost of acquiring and using a Ford Focus is more likely to be ordinary, necessary, and reasonable than the cost of acquiring and using a Ferrari California—although not as exhilarating. Since either vehicle should be able to transport an employee or business owner from the office to a business meeting, the Ford Focus should be just as effective at accomplishing the business purpose as the Ferrari. If this is true, why should the government help taxpayers pay for expensive cars with tax savings from large depreciation deductions associated with automobiles? Congress decided it shouldn't. Therefore, with certain exceptions we discuss below, the tax laws generally limit the annual depreciation expense for automobiles.[27] Each year, the IRS provides a maximum depreciation schedule for automobiles placed in service during that particular year.[28] For 2008 and 2009, taxpayers were allowed to expense $8,000 of bonus depreciation above the otherwise allowable maximum depreciation.[29] Exhibit 9-10 summarizes these schedules for automobiles placed in service for each year from 2010 back to 2007.

> **THE KEY FACTS**
>
> **Luxury Vehicles**
>
> ■ Depreciation on automobiles weighing less than 6,000 lbs. is subject to luxury auto provisions.
>
> ■ Luxury automobiles have a maximum depreciation limit for each year.
>
> ■ Listed property rules are also applicable to luxury automobiles.

**EXHIBIT 9-10   Automobile Depreciation Limits**

| Recovery Year | Year Placed in Service | | | |
|---|---|---|---|---|
| | 2010 | 2009 | 2008 | 2007 |
| 1 | $3,060 | $2,960* | $2,960* | $3,060 |
| 2 | 4,900 | 4,800 | 4,800 | 4,900 |
| 3 | 2,950 | 2,850 | 2,850 | 2,850 |
| 4 and after | 1,775 | 1,775 | 1,775 | 1,775 |

*$10,960 for automobiles for which the 50 percent bonus depreciation is elected.

Businesses placing automobiles into service during the year determine depreciation expense for the automobiles by first computing the regular MACRS depreciation expense (using the appropriate convention). They then compare it to the maximum depreciation amount for the first year of the recovery period based on the IRS-provided tables. Businesses are allowed to deduct the lesser of the two. If the automobile depreciation limits apply in the first year, the taxpayer must use the IRS maximum automobile depreciation table to compute depreciation for the asset(s) in all subsequent years. In 2010, if the half-year convention applies, the table limits the depreciation on automobiles placed in service during the year costing more than $15,300.[30] Automobiles to which the depreciation limits apply are commonly referred

---

[26]The passenger automobile definition excludes vehicles that charge for transportation such as taxi cabs, limousines, and hearses. It also excludes delivery trucks and vans.

[27]The tax law also limits the deduction for leased autos, which closed the leasing loophole that circumvented the luxury auto depreciation rules.

[28]The luxury automobile limitations are indexed for inflation and change annually. Generally, the annual amount is released in a Revenue Procedure at the beginning of the taxable year. The annual Rev. Proc. also provides slightly higher limits for hybrids, trucks, and SUVs.

[29]§168(k)(2)(F)(i).

[30]In 2010, the full first-year depreciation on an automobile costing $15,300 is $3,060 ($15,300 × 20%). This is the amount of the first year limit for automobiles placed in service in 2010.

to as **luxury automobiles.**[31] For any two such luxury cars—say, a 2011 Honda Civic and a 2011 Porsche 911—the annual depreciation limit is the same, regardless of the cost of the vehicles. The only difference is the length of time it will take to fully depreciate the vehicle.

**Example 9-18**

What is the maximum annual depreciation expense available for 2010 (year 1) on a 2011 Honda Civic costing $15,860 and a 2011 Porsche 911 costing $97,400?

**Answer:** $2,960 for both. See the following depreciation schedules for each automobile.

### Luxury Auto Depreciation

| Year/Make | 2011 Honda Civic | 2011 Porsche 911 |
|---|---|---|
| Model | DX 2dr Coupe | Carrera 4S |
| Price | $15,460 | $97,100 |
| **Depreciation** | | |
| Year 1 | $ 3,060 | $ 3,060 |
| Year 2 | $ 4,900 | $ 4,900 |
| Year 3 | $ 2,950 | $ 2,950 |
| Year 4 | $ 1,775 | $ 1,775 |
| Year 5 | $ 1,775 | $ 1,775 |
| Year 6 | $ 1,400 | $ 1,775 |
| Years 7–51 | | $ 1,775 |
| Year 52 | | $ 1,290 |

Given the maximum deduction limitations, the depreciation of the Honda and Porsche are identical in years 1–5. However, beginning in year 6 the Porsche is depreciated at a maximum of $1,775 per year until fully depreciated in year 52—however, it is unlikely the business will actually hold the Porsche through year 52.

The luxury automobile limitations don't apply to vehicles weighing more than 6,000 pounds. Thus, businesses owning these vehicles are allowed to compute regular MACRS depreciation expense for these vehicles.[32]

Just like businesses using other types of listed property, businesses using luxury automobiles for business and personal purposes may only deduct depreciation on the asset to the extent of business use. Business use is determined by miles driven for business purposes relative to total miles driven for the year.[33] Consequently, if a business places a luxury automobile into service in 2010 and uses the automobile 90 percent of the time for business purposes during the year (9,000 miles for business and 1,000 miles of personal use), the owner's depreciation (ignoring bonus depreciation) on the auto for the year is limited to $2,754 (year 1 full depreciation of $3,060 × 90 percent

---

[31]Correspondingly, the depreciation limits on automobiles are commonly referred to as the *luxury auto depreciation limits.*

[32]§280F(d)(5)(A). Congress regularly considers closing this loophole; however, it has not followed through (most recently it was considered as part of the 2007 Energy Bill).

[33]As an alternative to deducting depreciation expense and other costs of operating an automobile, taxpayers using automobiles for both personal and business purposes may deduct a standard mileage rate for each mile of business use. In 2010, the business mileage rate is 50 cents per mile. In 2009, the business mileage rate was 55 cents per mile.

business use—see Exhibit 9-10).[34] Further, if the business use falls below 50 percent in any subsequent year, just as with other listed property, the taxpayer must use the straight-line method of depreciation and reduce depreciation expense by the amount of excess accelerated depreciation (see Example 9-16). However, because straight-line depreciation is also limited by the luxury auto depreciation limits, it may turn out that the business doesn't have any excess accelerated depreciation.

Are businesses allowed to deduct §179 expensing on luxury automobiles? Yes, but the maximum depreciation *including* §179 expense is subject to the luxury auto limits ($3,960 for 2010). Thus, using the §179 expense on a luxury auto is unlikely to provide any tax benefit beyond the regular depreciation for most automobiles. However, businesses may deduct $25,000 of §179 expense for trucks and SUVs weighing over 6,000 pounds.[35] This $25,000 is part of the overall $250,000 maximum amount in 2010 (assuming 2009 amount is extended to 2010). Some companies use the §179 benefits to sell customers on purchasing automobiles that qualify for these tax benefits.

---

**Taxes in the Real World**   *Marketing Tax Advantages*

**Small-Business Tax Advantage**

Using your Range Rover for business purposes can provide significant tax advantages. Consult your tax advisor to learn more about the financial benefits and calculate your potential savings.

Source: http://www.landroverusa.com/us/en/Vehicles/new-range-rover/a-resource-for-owners.htm?page=3

---

## Real Property

For depreciation purposes, real property is classified as land, *residential rental* property, or *nonresidential property*. Land is nondepreciable. Residential rental property consists of dwelling units such as houses, condominiums, and apartment complexes. Residential property has a 27.5-year recovery period. Nonresidential property consists of all other buildings (office buildings, manufacturing facilities, shopping malls, and the like). Nonresidential property placed in service on or after May 13, 1993, has a 39-year recovery period and nonresidential property placed in service after December 31, 1986, and before May 13, 1993, has a 31.5-year recovery period. Exhibit 9-11 summarizes the recovery periods for real property.

**THE KEY FACTS**

**Real Property Depreciation**

- Real property is depreciated using the straight-line method.
- Real property uses the mid-month convention.
- Residential property has a recovery period of 27.5 years.
- Nonresidential property placed in service after 1993 has a life of 39 years.

**EXHIBIT 9-11**   **Recovery Period for Real Property**

| Asset Description (summary from Rev. Proc. 87-57) | Recovery Period |
| --- | --- |
| Residential | 27.5 years |
| Nonresidential property placed in service on or after May 13, 1993 | 39 years |
| Nonresidential property placed in service before May 13, 1993 | 31.5 years |

If a building is substantially improved (not a minor repair) at some point after the initial purchase, the building addition is treated as a new asset with the same recovery period of the original building. For example, if Teton expanded its warehouse 10 years after the building was placed in service, the expansion or building addition would be depreciated over 39 years because it is nonresidential property.

---

[34]Even if the business-use percentage multiplied by the MACRS depreciation is greater than the $3,060 maximum, the depreciation amount is limited to the maximum depreciation amount times the business-use percentage.

[35]§179(b)(6).

An important area of tax practice related to real property is cost segregation. This practice attempts to partition or divide the costs of a building into two or more categories. The first category is the building itself, which has a recovery period as noted in Exhibit 9-11. The second category is building components (tangible personal property associated with the building such as electrical and plumbing fixtures that have a shorter recovery period and accelerated depreciation method). Cost segregation utilizes engineers and construction experts who divide the costs between real and tangible personal property. This can generate significant tax savings due to the difference in the present value of the tax savings from the accelerated depreciation deductions associated with personal property relative to real property.

**Applicable Method** All depreciable real property is depreciated for tax purposes using the straight-line method. This is generally consistent with depreciation methods used for financial accounting purposes.

**Applicable Convention** All real property is depreciated using the mid-month convention. The **mid-month convention** allows the owner of real property to expense one-half of a month's depreciation for the month in which the property was placed in service (and in the month of the year it is sold as well). This is true regardless of whether the asset was placed in service at the beginning or at the end of the month. For example, if Teton placed its warehouse into service on May 1 (or on *any* other day in May), it would deduct *one-half* a month's depreciation for May and then full depreciation for the months June through December.

**Depreciation Tables** Just as it does for personal property, the IRS provides depreciation tables for real property. The depreciation tables for 27.5 year, 31.5 year, and 39 year real property are reproduced in this chapter's Appendix A. The percentage of the asset's original basis that is depreciated in a particular year is located at the intersection of the month the asset was placed in service (column) and the year of depreciation (row—first, second, etc.).

---

**Example 9-19**

As indicated in Example 9-1, Teton's basis in the warehouse it purchased on May 1 of year 1 is $275,000. What is Teton's year 1 depreciation on its warehouse?

**Answer:** $4,414, computed as follows:

| Asset | Method | Recovery Period | Date Placed in Service | (1) Basis | (2) Rate* | (1) × (2) Depreciation |
|-------|--------|-----------------|------------------------|-----------|-----------|------------------------|
| Warehouse | SL | 39 | May 1 | $275,000 | 1.605% | $4,414 |

**What if:** What would be Teton's year 1 depreciation expense if the building was not a warehouse but was an apartment building that it rented to Teton's employees?

**Answer:** $6,251, computed as follows:

| Asset | Method | Recovery Period | Date Placed in Service | (1) Basis | (2) Rate† | (1) × (2) Depreciation |
|-------|--------|-----------------|------------------------|-----------|-----------|------------------------|
| Apt. Bldg. | SL | 27.5 | May 1 | $275,000 | 2.273% | $6,251 |

\* The 1.605 percent tax rate factor for the year is found in the 39-year table (see Appendix A to this chapter) in the fifth column (fifth month) and first row (first year).
† The 2.273 percent tax rate factor for the year is found in the 27.5-year table (see Appendix A to this chapter) in the fifth column (fifth month) and first row (first year).

When using depreciation tables for real property it is important to stay in the month column corresponding with the month the property was originally placed in service.[36] Thus, to calculate depreciation for a piece of real property placed in service in May (the fifth month), businesses will *always* (for each year of depreciation) find the current year rate factor in the fifth column for that asset. This is true even if the asset is sold in a subsequent year in July (it's easy to make the mistake of using the seventh column to calculate the depreciation for the year of disposition in this situation).

***Mid-month convention for year of disposition.***   Businesses deduct one-half of a month's depreciation in the month they sell or otherwise dispose of real property. For example, if Teton sold its warehouse on March 5 of year 2, it would deduct two and one-half months of depreciation in that year for the warehouse (depreciation for January, February, and one-half of March). Calculating depreciation expense in the year of sale or disposition for mid-month convention assets is similar to the calculation under the mid-quarter convention. When the mid-month convention applies, the asset is treated as though it is sold in the *middle of the month* of which it was actually sold. The simplest process for calculating mid-month convention depreciation for the year of sale consists of the following four steps:

**Step 1:** Determine the amount of depreciation expense for the asset as if the asset was held for the entire year,

**Step 2:** Subtract one-half of a month from the month in which the asset was sold (if sold in third month, subtract .5 from 3 to get 2.5). (Subtract half of a month because the business is treated as though the asset was disposed of in the middle of the third month—not the end),

**Step 3:** Divide the amount determined in Step 2 by 12 months (2.5/12). This is the fraction of the full year's depreciation the business is eligible to deduct.

**Step 4:** Multiply the Step 3 outcome by the full depreciation determined in Step 1.

These steps are summarized in the following formula:

Mid-month depreciation for year of disposition

$$= \text{Full year's depreciation} \times \frac{(\text{Month in which asset was disposed of} - .5)}{12}$$

**Example 9-20**

**What if:**   Assume that Teton sells its warehouse on March 5 in year 2 (the year after Teton buys it). What is Teton's depreciation for the warehouse in the year of disposition (year 2)?

**Answer:**   $1,469, computed using the four-step procedure outlined above as follows.

**Step 1:** Determine full year's depreciation: $275,000 × 2.564%* = $7,051

**Step 2:** 3 (month sold) − .5 = 2.5

**Step 3:** 2.5/12

**Step 4:** $7,051 × 2.5/12 = $1,469 (see formula above).

*The 2.564 percent rate factor (full year percentage) in Step 1 is obtained from the MACRS Mid-Month Table for 39-year property placed in service during the fifth month (year 2 row).

---

[36]Failure to do so will result in the wrong depreciation expense and is technically a change in accounting method (which requires filing of a Form 3115 with the IRS).

### *Depreciation for the Alternative Minimum Tax*

Both individuals and corporations are subject to tax under the Alternative Minimum Tax (AMT) system. In determining their alternative minimum taxable income, individuals and corporations may be required to recalculate their depreciation expense. For AMT purposes, the allowable recovery period and conventions are the same for all depreciable assets as they are for regular tax purposes.[37] However, for AMT purposes, businesses are not allowed to use the 200 percent declining balance method to depreciate tangible personal property. Rather, they must choose from the 150 percent declining balance method or the straight-line method to depreciate the property for AMT purposes. The difference between regular tax depreciation and AMT depreciation is an adjustment that is either added to or subtracted from regular taxable income in computing the alternative minimum tax base.[38] In contrast, the §179 expense is equally deductible for both regular tax and AMT purposes. Depreciation of real property is the same for both regular tax and AMT purposes. Exhibit 9-12 summarizes the recovery periods for assets for regular tax purposes and AMT purposes.

**EXHIBIT 9-12**    **MACRS Recovery Periods for Regular Tax and AMT Purposes**

|  | Regular Tax | AMT |
|---|---|---|
| Software | 3-Year | 3-Year |
| Cars, light general purpose trucks, and computers and peripheral equipment | 5-Year | 5-Year |
| Office furniture, fixtures, machinery, and equipment | 7-Year | 7-Year |
| Residential real property | 27.5-Year | 27.5-Year |
| Nonresidential real property | 39-Year | 39-Year |

### *Depreciation Summary*

Teton's depreciation for the year is summarized in Exhibit 9-13 and Exhibit 9-14 presents Teton's depreciation expense as it would be reported on its tax return on Form 4562.

**EXHIBIT 9-13**    **Tax Depreciation Expense Summary**

| Asset | Original Basis | §179 Expense | Remaining Basis* | Depreciation Expense | Reference |
|---|---|---|---|---|---|
| Machinery | $260,000 | $80,000 | $180,000 | $ 25,722 | Example 9-11 (What-if scenario). |
| Office furniture | $ 10,000 | | $ 10,000 | $ 1,429 | Example 9-5. |
| Delivery truck | $ 15,000 | $ 0 | $ 15,000 | $ 3,000 | Example 9-5. |
| Warehouse | $275,000 | N/A | $275,000 | $ 4,414 | Example 9-19. |
| Land | $ 75,000 | N/A | $ 75,000 | $ 0 | N/A. |
| §179 Expense | | | | $ 80,000 | Example 9-11. |
| Total Depreciation Expense | | | | $114,565 | |

*Note that Teton's remaining basis is the original cost less the §179 expense.

---

[37]This is true for assets placed in service after 1998.

[38]If the taxpayer elected either the 150 percent declining balance or the straight-line method for regular tax depreciation of tangible personal property, then there is no AMT adjustment with respect to that property.

**EXHIBIT 9-14**   Teton's Form 4562 Parts I – IV for Depreciation
(Assumes $100,000 of taxable income before the §179 expense)

| Form **4562** | **Depreciation and Amortization** | OMB No. 1545-0172 |
|---|---|---|
| | (Including Information on Listed Property) | **2009** |
| Department of the Treasury Internal Revenue Service (99) | ▶ See separate instructions.   ▶ Attach to your tax return. | Attachment Sequence No. **67** |

| Name(s) shown on return | Business or activity to which this form relates | Identifying number |
|---|---|---|
| | | |

**Part I**   Election To Expense Certain Property Under Section 179
**Note:** *If you have any listed property, complete Part V before you complete Part I.*

| | | | |
|---|---|---|---|
| 1 | Maximum amount. See the instructions for a higher limit for certain businesses . . . . . . . . . . | **1** | $250,000 |
| 2 | Total cost of section 179 property placed in service (see instructions) . . . . . . . . . . | **2** | 285,000 |
| 3 | Threshold cost of section 179 property before reduction in limitation (see instructions) . . . . . . | **3** | $800,000 |
| 4 | Reduction in limitation. Subtract line 3 from line 2. If zero or less, enter -0- . . . . . . . . . | **4** | |
| 5 | Dollar limitation for tax year. Subtract line 4 from line 1. If zero or less, enter -0-. If married filing separately, see instructions . . . . . . . . . . . . . . . . . . . . . . | **5** | 250,000 |

| **6** | **(a)** Description of property | **(b)** Cost (business use only) | **(c)** Elected cost | | |
|---|---|---|---|---|---|
| Machinery | | 260,000 | 80,000 | | |
| | | | | | |

| | | | |
|---|---|---|---|
| 7 | Listed property. Enter the amount from line 29 . . . . . . . . **7** | | |
| 8 | Total elected cost of section 179 property. Add amounts in column (c), lines 6 and 7 . . . . . . | **8** | 80,000 |
| 9 | Tentative deduction. Enter the **smaller** of line 5 or line 8 . . . . . . . . . . | **9** | 80,000 |
| 10 | Carryover of disallowed deduction from line 13 of your 2008 Form 4562 . . . . . . . | **10** | |
| 11 | Business income limitation. Enter the smaller of business income (not less than zero) or line 5 (see instructions) . . . | **11** | 100,000 |
| 12 | Section 179 expense deduction. Add lines 9 and 10, but do not enter more than line 11 . . . . . | **12** | 80,000 |
| 13 | Carryover of disallowed deduction to 2010. Add lines 9 and 10, less line 12 ▶ **13** | | |

**Note:** *Do not use Part II or Part III below for listed property. Instead, use Part V.*

**Part II**   Special Depreciation Allowance and Other Depreciation (Do not include listed property.) (See instructions.)

| | | | |
|---|---|---|---|
| 14 | Special depreciation allowance for qualified property (other than listed property) placed in service during the tax year (see instructions) . . . . . . . . . . . . . . . . . | **14** | |
| 15 | Property subject to section 168(f)(1) election . . . . . . . . . . . . . | **15** | |
| 16 | Other depreciation (including ACRS) . . . . . . . . . . . . . . . | **16** | |

**Part III**   MACRS Depreciation (Do not include listed property.) (See instructions.)

**Section A**

| | | | |
|---|---|---|---|
| 17 | MACRS deductions for assets placed in service in tax years beginning before 2009 . . . . . . . | **17** | |
| 18 | If you are electing to group any assets placed in service during the tax year into one or more general asset accounts, check here . . . . . . . . . . . . . . . . . . . . ▶ ☐ | | |

**Section B—Assets Placed in Service During 2009 Tax Year Using the General Depreciation System**

| (a) Classification of property | (b) Month and year placed in service | (c) Basis for depreciation (business/investment use only—see instructions) | (d) Recovery period | (e) Convention | (f) Method | (g) Depreciation deduction |
|---|---|---|---|---|---|---|
| **19a** 3-year property | | | | | | |
| **b** 5-year property | | 15,000 | 5 year | HY | DDB | 3,000 |
| **c** 7-year property | | 190,000 | 7 year | HY | DDB | 27,151 |
| **d** 10-year property | | | | | | |
| **e** 15-year property | | | | | | |
| **f** 20-year property | | | | | | |
| **g** 25-year property | | | 25 yrs. | | S/L | |
| **h** Residential rental property | | | 27.5 yrs. | MM | S/L | |
| | | | 27.5 yrs. | MM | S/L | |
| **i** Nonresidential real property | May 2009 | 275,000 | 39 yrs. | MM | S/L | 4,414 |
| | | | | MM | S/L | |

**Section C—Assets Placed in Service During 2009 Tax Year Using the Alternative Depreciation System**

| | | | | | | |
|---|---|---|---|---|---|---|
| **20a** Class life | | | | | S/L | |
| **b** 12-year | | | 12 yrs. | | S/L | |
| **c** 40-year | | | 40 yrs. | MM | S/L | |

**Part IV**   Summary (See instructions.)

| | | | |
|---|---|---|---|
| 21 | Listed property. Enter amount from line 28 . . . . . . . . . . . . . . . . | **21** | |
| 22 | **Total.** Add amounts from line 12, lines 14 through 17, lines 19 and 20 in column (g), and line 21. Enter here and on the appropriate lines of your return. Partnerships and S corporations—see instructions . . . . . | **22** | 114,565 |
| 23 | For assets shown above and placed in service during the current year, enter the portion of the basis attributable to section 263A costs . . . . . . . . **23** | | |

**For Paperwork Reduction Act Notice, see separate instructions.**       Cat. No. 12906N       Form **4562** (2009)

# AMORTIZATION

Businesses recover the cost of intangible assets through amortization rather than depreciation expense. Intangible assets in the form of capitalized expenditures, such as capitalized **research and experimentation (R&E) costs** or **covenants not to compete,** do not have physical characteristics. Nonetheless, they may have determinable lives. While research and experimentation costs may have an indeterminate life, a covenant not to compete, for example, would have a life equal to the stated term of the contractual agreement. When the life of intangible assets cannot be determined, taxpayers recover the cost of the assets when they dispose of them—unless they are assigned a specific tax recovery period.

For tax purposes, an intangible asset can be placed into one of the following four general categories:

1. §197 purchased intangibles.
2. Start-up expenditures and organizational costs.
3. Research and experimentation costs.
4. Patents and copyrights.

Businesses amortize all intangible assets in these categories using the straight-line method for both book and tax purposes.

---

**THE KEY FACTS**

**§197 Intangible Assets**

- Purchased intangibles are amortized over a period of 180 months, regardless of their explicitly stated lifetimes.

- The full-month convention applies to amortizable assets.

---

## Section 197 Intangibles

When a business purchases the *assets* of another business for a single purchase price, the business must determine the basis of each of the assets it acquired in the transaction. To determine basis, the business must allocate a portion of the purchase price to each of the individual assets acquired in the transaction. Generally, under this approach, each asset acquired in the purchase (cash, machinery, and real property, for example) takes a basis equal to its fair market value. However, some of the assets acquired in the transaction may not appear on the seller's balance sheet. In fact, a substantial portion of a business's value may exist in the form of intangible assets such as customer lists, patents, trademarks, trade names, goodwill, going-concern value, covenants not to compete, and so forth. Nearly all of these assets are amortized according to §197 of the Internal Revenue Code—hence, they are often referred to as **§197 purchased intangibles.** According to §197, these assets have a recovery period of 180 months (15 years), *regardless of their actual life*.[39] For example, when a business buys an existing business, the owner selling the business often signs a covenant not to compete for a specified period such as five years.[40] Even though a five-year covenant not to compete clearly has a fixed and determinable life, it must be amortized over 180 months (15 years). The **full-month convention** applies to the amortization of purchased intangibles. This convention allows taxpayers to deduct an entire month's worth of amortization for the month of purchase and all subsequent months in the year. The full-month convention also applies in the month of sale or disposition.

Special rules apply when a taxpayer sells a §197 intangible or the intangible becomes worthless and the taxpayer's basis in the asset exceeds the sale proceeds (if any). A business may recognize a loss on the sale or disposition only when the business does not hold any other §197 assets that the business acquired in the *same initial transaction.* Otherwise, the taxpayer may not deduct the loss on the sale or disposition until the business sells or disposes of *all* of the other §197 intangibles that

---

[39]§197 was Congress's response to taxpayers manipulating the valuation and recovery periods assigned to these purchased intangibles.

[40]A covenant not to compete is a contract between the seller of a business and its buyer that the seller will not operate a similar business that would compete with the previous business for a specified period of time.

it purchased in the same initial transaction.[41] The same loss disallowance rule applies if a §197 intangible expires before it is fully amortized. For example, a business would not be allowed to deduct a loss on a five-year covenant not to compete when it expires even though the covenant is worthless and still would have two-thirds of its original cost remaining (10 years left to amortize over a 15-year recovery period). In either case, the remaining basis (basis in excess of sale proceeds or basis in excess of worthless intangible asset) is allocated to the remaining §197 intangibles that were initially acquired in the same transaction (this allocation is on a pro rata basis), based on the relative adjusted bases of the remaining §197 intangibles. The new basis allocated to each remaining §197 intangible is amortized over the remaining years of the initial 15-year recovery period.

**Example 9-21**

***What if:*** Assume that at the beginning of year 1, Teton acquires a competitor's assets for $350,000.[42] Of the $350,000 purchase price, $125,000 is allocated to tangible assets and $225,000 is allocated to §197 intangible assets (patent, goodwill, and a customer list with a three-year life).[43] For each of the first three years, Teton would deduct one-fifteenth of the basis of each asset as amortization expense. What is Teton's accumulated amortization and remaining basis in each of these §197 intangibles after three years?

**Answer:** See the table below:

| Description | Patent | Goodwill | Customer List |
|---|---|---|---|
| Basis | $25,000 | $150,000 | $50,000 |
| Accumulated amortization (3/15ths of original basis) | ($5,000) | ($30,000) | ($10,000) |
| Remaining basis | $20,000 | $120,000 | $40,000 |

At the end of year 3, Teton's customer list is worthless (it has expired), but it still has a remaining basis of $40,000. Rather than deducting the $40,000 loss on the customer list, Teton must allocate it to the other §197 intangible assets that were initially purchased in the same transaction. After this allocation what is Teton's new basis in the patent and the goodwill?[44]

**Answer:** Teton's new basis in the patent is $25,716 and its new basis in the goodwill is $154,284, computed as follows:

| Description | (A) Remaining basis | (B) Percentage of remaining basis | (C) Allocated portion of remaining basis in customer list [(B) × $40,000] | (A) + (C) New basis |
|---|---|---|---|---|
| (1) Patent | $ 20,000 | 14.29% [(1)/(3)] | $ 5,716 | $ 25,716 |
| (2) Goodwill | 120,000 | 85.71% [(2)/(3)] | 34,284 | 154,284 |
| (3) Total basis | $140,000 | 100% | $40,000 | $180,000 |

The new basis of the patent and goodwill are amortized over the remaining 12-year (144-month) recovery period.

[41]Reg. §1.197-2(g)(1)(i).

[42]If a business acquires another business's stock (rather than assets) there is no goodwill assigned for tax purposes, and the purchase price simply becomes the basis of the stock purchased.

[43]A customer base is the value assigned to current customers (i.e., the lists that will allow the new owner to capture future benefits from the current customers).

[44]Reg. §1.197-2(g)(1)(i).

When a taxpayer sells a §197 intangible for more than its basis, the taxpayer recognizes gain. We describe how to characterize this type of gain in the next chapter.

## Organizational Expenditures and Start-Up Costs

**Organizational expenditures** include expenditures to form and organize a business in the form of a corporation or a partnership.[45] Organizational expenditures typically include costs of organizational meetings, state fees, accounting service costs incident to organization, and legal service expenditures such as document drafting, taking minutes of organizational meetings, and creating terms of the original stock certificates. These costs are generally incurred prior to the starting of business (or shortly thereafter) but relate to creating the business entity. The costs of selling or marketing stock do *not* qualify as organizational expenditures and cannot be amortized.[46]

---

**Example 9-22**

**What if:** Suppose Teton was organized as a corporation rather than a sole proprietorship (recall that sole proprietorships cannot expense organizational expenditures). Steve paid $35,000 of legal costs to Scott, Tang, and Malan to draft the corporate charter and articles of incorporation; $10,000 to Harvey and Stratford for accounting fees related to the organization; and $7,000 for organizational meetings, $5,000 for stock issuance costs, and $1,000 for state fees related to the incorporation. What amounts of these expenditures qualify as organizational costs?

**Answer:** $53,000 computed as follows (with the exception of the stock issuance costs, each of Teton's expenses qualify as amortizable organizational expenditures):

| Description | Qualifying Organizational Expenditures |
|---|---|
| Legal drafting of corporate charter and articles of incorporation | $35,000 |
| Accounting fees related to organization | 10,000 |
| Organizational meetings | 7,000 |
| Stock issuance costs | 0 |
| State incorporation fees | 1,000 |
| Totals | $53,000 |

---

**THE KEY FACTS**

*Organizational Expenditures and Start-up Costs*

■ Taxpayers may immediately expense up to $5,000 of organizational expenditures and $5,000 of start-up costs.

■ The $5,000 immediate expense rule has a dollar-for-dollar phase-out that begins at $50,000, so that when expenses exceed $55,000, there is no immediate expensing.

---

Businesses may *immediately expense* up to $5,000 of organizational expenditures.[47] However, businesses incurring more than $50,000 in organizational expenditures must phase-out (reduce) the $5,000 immediate expense amount dollar for dollar for expenditures exceeding $50,000. Thus, businesses incurring at least $55,000 of organizational expenditures are not allowed to immediately expense any of the expenditures.

---

**Example 9-23**

**What if:** Suppose Teton is a corporation and it wants to maximize its current year organizational expenditure deduction. As described in Example 9-22, Teton incurred $53,000 of organizational expenditures in year 1. How much of the organizational expenditures can Teton immediately expense in year 1?

(*continued on page 9-33...*)

---

[45]§248 for corporations and §709 for partnerships. Sole proprietorships cannot deduct organizational expenditures.

[46]These costs are capitalized and deducted on the final tax return a business files.

[47]§248(a)(1) for corporations or §709 for partnerships.

**Answer:** $2,000, computed as follows:

| Description | Amount | Explanation |
|---|---|---|
| (1) Maximum immediate expense | $ 5,000 | §248(a)(1). |
| (2) Total organizational expenditures | 53,000 | Example 9-22. |
| (3) Phase-out threshold | 50,000 | §248(a)(1)(B). |
| (4) Immediate expense phase-out | 3,000 | (2) − (3). |
| **(5) Allowable immediate expense** | **2,000** | (1) − (4). |
| Remaining organizational expenditures | $51,000* | (2) − (5). |

**What if:** Assuming that Teton is a corporation and that it incurred $41,000 of organizational expenditures in year 1. How much of the organizational expenditures could Teton immediately expense in year 1?

**Answer:** $5,000, computed as follows:

| Description | Amount | Explanation |
|---|---|---|
| (1) Maximum immediate expense | $ 5,000 | §248(a)(1). |
| (2) Total organizational expenditures | 41,000 | |
| (3) Phase-out threshold | 50,000 | §248(a)(1)(B). |
| (4) Immediate expense phase-out | 0 | Limit to zero. |
| **(5) Allowable immediate expense** | **5,000** | (1) − (4). |
| Remaining organizational expenditures | $36,000* | (2) − (5). |

**What if:** Assuming that Teton is a corporation and it incurred $60,000 of organizational expenditures in year 1, how much of the organizational expenditures could Teton immediately expense in year 1?

**Answer:** $0, computed as follows:

| Description | Amount | Explanation |
|---|---|---|
| (1) Maximum immediate expense | $ 5,000 | §248(a)(1). |
| (2) Total organizational expenditures | 60,000 | |
| (3) Phase-out threshold | 50,000 | §248(a)(1)(B). |
| (4) Immediate expense phase-out | 10,000 | (2) − (3). |
| **(5) Allowable immediate expense** | **0** | (1) − (4). |
| Remaining organizational expenditures | $60,000* | (2) − (5). |

*As we discuss below, Teton amortizes the remaining organizational costs.

Businesses amortize organizational expenditures that they do not immediately expense using the straight-line method over a recovery period of 15 years (180 months).[48]

**Example 9-24**

**What if:** Assume Teton is a corporation and it amortizes the $51,000 of organizational expenditures remaining after it immediately expenses $2,000 of the costs (see Example 9-23). If Teton began business on February 1 of year 1, how much total cost recovery expense for the organizational expenditures is Teton able to deduct in year 1?

(continued on page 9-34...)

[48]§248(a)(2) prior to amendment by the American Jobs Creation Act of 2004. Businesses incurring organizational expenditures on or before October 22, 2004, are allowed to amortize the expenditures on a straight-line basis over five years (60 months).

**Answer:** $5,117, computed as follows:

| Description | Amount | Explanation |
|---|---|---|
| (1) Total organizational expenditures | $53,000 | Example 9-21. |
| (2) Amount immediately expensed | 2,000 | Example 9-22. |
| (3) Expenditures subject to straight-line amortization | $51,000 | (1) − (2). |
| (4) Recovery period in months | 180 | 15 years §248(a)(2). |
| (5) Monthly straight-line amortization | 283.33 | (3)/(4). |
| (6) Teton business months during year 1 | × 11 | February through December. |
| (7) Year 1 straight-line amortization | 3,117 | (5) × (6). |
| **Total year 1 cost recovery expense for organizational expenditures.** | **$ 5,117** | (2) + (7). |

**Start-up costs** are costs businesses incur to, not surprisingly, start up a business.[49] Start-up costs apply to all types of business forms.[50] These costs include costs associated with investigating the possibilities of and actually creating or acquiring a trade or business. For example, costs Teton incurs in deciding whether to locate the business in Cody, Wyoming, or Bozeman, Montana, are start-up costs. Start-up costs also include costs that would normally be deductible as ordinary business expenses except that they don't qualify as business expenses because they are incurred before the trade or business activity actually begins. For example, costs Teton incurs to train its employees before the business begins are start-up costs. The rules for immediately expensing and amortizing start-up costs are identical to those for immediately expensing and amortizing organizational expenditures (see discussion above). While the rules are the same, the limitations are computed separately for organizational expenditures and for start-up costs. Consequently, a business could immediately expense $5,000 of organizational expenditures and $5,000 of start-up costs in its first year of business.

---

**Example 9-25**

*What if:* Assume that in January of year 1 (before it began business on February 1) Teton spent $4,500 investigating the climbing hardware market, creating company logos, and determining the locations for both the office and manufacturing facility. The $4,500 of expenditures qualifies as start-up costs. How much of the $4,500 of start-up costs is Teton allowed to immediately expense?

**Answer:** All $4,500. Teton is allowed to immediately expense the entire $4,500 because its total start-up costs do not exceed $50,000. Teton could have immediately expensed up to $5,000 of start-up costs as long as its total start-up costs did not exceed $50,000.

---

Exhibit 9-15 illustrates the timing of organizational expenditures, start-up costs, and normal trade or business expenses.

### Research and Experimentation Expenditures

To stay competitive, businesses often invest in activities they believe will generate innovative products or significantly improve their current products or processes. These research and experimentation costs include expenditures for research laboratories including salaries, materials, and other related expenses. Businesses may immediately expense these costs or they may *elect* to capitalize these costs and amortize them

---

[49]§195.

[50]Recall that rules for amortizing organizational expenditures apply only to corporations and partnerships.

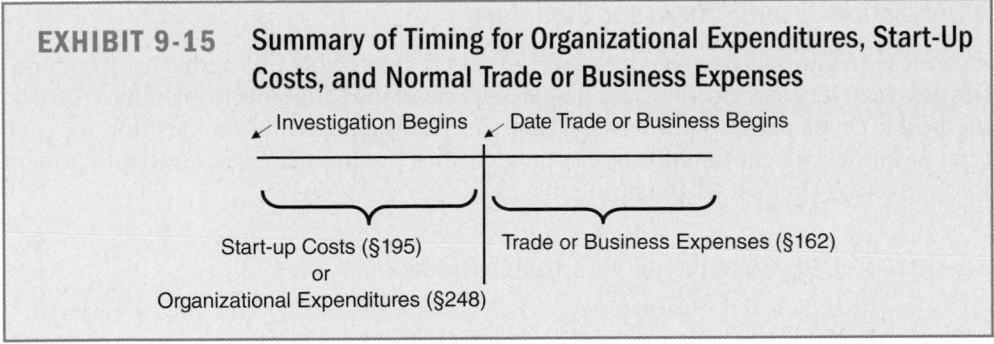

**EXHIBIT 9-15**   Summary of Timing for Organizational Expenditures, Start-Up Costs, and Normal Trade or Business Expenses

using the straight-line method over the determinable useful life or, if there is no determinable useful life, over a period of not less than 60 months, beginning in the month benefits are first derived from the research.[51] However, if a business elects to capitalize and amortize the costs, it must stop amortizing the costs if and when the business receives a patent relating to the expenditures. When the business obtains a patent, it adds any remaining basis in the costs to the basis of the patent and it amortizes the basis of the patent over the patent's life (see discussion below).

### Patents and Copyrights

The manner in which a business amortizes a patent or copyright depends on whether the business directly purchases the patent or copyright or whether it self-creates the intangibles. Businesses directly purchasing patents or copyrights (not in an asset acquisition to which §197 applies) amortize the cost over the remaining life of the patents or copyrights.[52] Businesses receiving "self-created" patents or copyrights amortize the cost or basis of the self-created intangible assets over their legal lives—up to a maximum of 17 years for patents and 28 years for copyrights. The costs included in the basis of a self-created patent or copyright include legal costs, fees, and, as we discussed above, unamortized research and experimentation expenditures associated with the creation of the patent or copyright. However, because the patent approval process is slow, the unamortized research and experimentation costs included in the patent's basis are likely to be relatively small because, with a five-year recovery period, the research and experimentation costs would likely be mostly or even fully amortized by the time the patent is approved.

**Example 9-26**

In September of year 1, Teton purchased a patent with a remaining life of 10 years from Chouinard Equipment for $60,000. What amount of amortization expense is Teton allowed to deduct for the patent in year 1?

**Answer:**  $2,000, computed as follows:

| Description | Amount | Explanation |
|---|---|---|
| (1) Cost of patent | $60,000 | |
| (2) Remaining life of patent in months | 120 | 10 years. |
| (3) Monthly amortization | $    500 | (1)/(2). |
| (4) Months in year 1 Teton held patent | × 4 | September through December. |
| **(5) Monthly straight-line amortization** | **$ 2,000** | (3) × (4). |
| Unamortized cost of patent at end of year 1 | $58,000 | (1) − (5). |

[51]See §174. High tax rate taxpayers may choose to deduct these costs while low tax rate taxpayers may prefer to capitalize and amortize them so that they will have more future deductions when they are hopefully generating more income. There is also the research and experimentation credit which is available to some businesses.

[52]§167(f).

### Amortizable Intangible Asset Summary

Exhibit 9-16 summarizes the different types of amortizable intangible assets, identifies the recovery period of these assets, and describes the applicable amortization method for each asset. Exhibit 9-16 also identifies the applicable convention for each type of amortizable intangible asset and identifies the financial accounting treatment for recovering the cost of the intangible assets under GAAP.

**EXHIBIT 9-16   Summary of Amortizable Assets**

| Asset Description | Recovery Period (months) | Applicable Method | Applicable Convention | Financial Accounting Treatment |
|---|---|---|---|---|
| §197 purchased intangibles including goodwill, trademarks, patents, and covenants not to compete.[53] | 180 | Straight-line | Full-month beginning with month of purchase. | ISC 350 tests for annual impairment. |
| Organizational expenditures and start-up costs are required to be capitalized. | 180 | Straight-line | Full-month in month business begins. | AICPA SOP 98-5. |
| Research and experimentation costs that are capitalized. | Determinable useful life, or 60 (not less than); ceases when patent is issued. | Straight-line | Full-month in first month that benefits from research are obtained. | Expensed. |
| Self-created patents (17 years maximum) and copyrights (28 years maximum). | Actual life. | Straight-line | Full-month month intangible is obtained. | Expensed. |
| Purchased patents and copyrights | Remaining life | Straight-line | Full-month in month intangible is obtained. | Expensed |

Exhibit 9-17 presents Teton's amortization expense as it would be reported on its tax return on Form 4562.

**EXHIBIT 9-17   Teton Form 4562, Part VI Amortization of Organizational Expenditures and Patent**

**Part VI   Amortization**

| (a) Description of costs | (b) Date amortization begins | (c) Amortizable amount | (d) Code section | (e) Amortization period or percentage | (f) Amortization for this year |
|---|---|---|---|---|---|
| **42** Amortization of costs that begins during your 2009 tax year (see instructions): | | | | | |
| Organizational Expenditures | 2/1/2009 | 53,000 | 248 | 15 yrs | 5,117 |
| Patent | 9/1/2009 | 60,000 | 167 | 10 yrs | 2,000 |
| **43** Amortization of costs that began before your 2009 tax year . . . . . . . . . . . . . | | | | **43** | |
| **44 Total.** Add amounts in column (f). See the instructions for where to report . . . . . . . . . | | | | **44** | 7,117 |

Form **4562** (2009)

[53]A patent or copyright that is part of a basket purchase (several assets together) is treated as a §197 intangible. A patent or copyright that is purchased separately is simply amortized over its remaining life (§167(f)).

*continued from page 9-1...*
Teton was developing some additional employee parking on a lot adjacent to the warehouse when the excavation crew discovered a small gold deposit. Steve called his friend Ken, who had some experience in mining precious metals, to see what Ken thought of the find. Ken was impressed and offered Steve $150,000 for the rights to the gold. Steve accepted the offer on Teton's behalf. ∎

# DEPLETION

LO4

*Depletion* is the method taxpayers use to recover their capital investment in natural resources. Depletion is a particularly significant deduction for businesses in the mining, oil and gas, and forestry industries. These businesses generally incur depletion expense as they use the natural resource. Specifically, businesses compute annual depletion expense under both the cost and percentage depletion methods and they deduct the larger of the two.[54]

Under **cost depletion,** taxpayers must estimate or determine the number of units or reserves (tons of coal, barrels of oil, board feet of timber, for example) that remain at the beginning of the year and allocate a pro rata share of that basis to each unit that is extracted during the year.[55]

### Example 9-27

Ken's cost basis in the gold is the $150,000 he paid for it. Based on a mining engineer's estimate that the gold deposit probably holds 1,000 ounces of gold, Ken can determine his cost depletion. What is Ken's cost depletion for year 1 and year 2, assuming he extracts 300 and 700 ounces of gold in year 1 and year 2, respectively?

**Answer:** $45,000 in year 1 and $105,000 in year 2, computed as follows:

| Description | Amount | Explanation |
|---|---|---|
| (1) Cost basis in gold | $150,000 | |
| (2) Estimated ounces of gold | 1,000 | |
| (3) Per ounce cost depletion rate | 150 | (1)/(2). |
| (4) Year 1 ounces extracted | 300 | |
| **(5) Year 1 cost depletion** | **$ 45,000** | (3) × (4). |
| (6) Basis remaining after year 1 depletion | 105,000 | (1) − (5). |
| (7) Year 2 ounces extracted | 700 | |
| **(8) Year 2 cost depletion** | **$105,000** | (7) × (3). |
| Basis remaining after year 2 depletion | $    0 | (6) − (8). |

Ken is not eligible for cost depletion after year 2 because as of the end of year 2, his cost basis has been reduced to $0.

Because the cost depletion method of depletion requires businesses to estimate the number of units of the resource they will actually extract, it is possible that their estimate will prove to be inaccurate. If they underestimate the number of units, they will fully deplete the cost basis of the resource before they have fully extracted the resource. Once they have recovered the entire cost basis of the resource, businesses are not allowed to use cost depletion to determine depletion expense. Businesses,

---

[54]Depletion of timber and major integrated oil companies must be calculated using only the cost depletion method (no percentage depletion is available).
[55]§612.

> **THE KEY FACTS**
>
> **Depletion**
>
> ■ Cost depletion involves estimating resource reserves and allocating a pro-rata share of basis based on the number of units extracted.
>
> ■ Percentage depletion is determined by a statutory percentage of gross income that is permitted to be expensed each year. Different resources have different statutory percentages (i.e., gold, tin, coal).
>
> ■ Taxpayers may expense the larger of cost or percentage depletion.

however, may continue to use percentage depletion (see discussion below). If a business overestimates the number of units to be extracted, it will still have basis remaining after the resource has been fully extracted. In these situations, the business would deduct the unrecovered basis once it had sold all the remaining units.

The amount of **percentage depletion** for a natural resource business activity is determined by multiplying the *gross income* from the resource extraction activity by a fixed percentage based on the type of natural resource as indicated in Exhibit 9-18.[56]

**EXHIBIT 9-18** Applicable Percentage Depletion Rates

| Statutory Percentage | Natural Resources (Partial list) |
|---|---|
| 5 percent [§613(b)(6)] | Gravel, pumice, and stone. |
| 14 percent [§613(b)(3)] | Asphalt rock, clay, and other metals. |
| 15 percent [§613(b)(2)] | Gold, copper, oil shale, and silver. |
| 22 percent [§613(b)(1)] | Platinum, sulfur, uranium, and titanium. |

In many cases, percentage depletion may generate *larger* depletion deductions than does cost depletion. Recall that taxpayers are allowed to deduct the greater of cost and percentage depletion. Businesses reduce their cost basis in the resource when they deduct percentage depletion. However, once the cost basis is exhausted, they are allowed to continue to deduct percentage (but not cost) depletion. This provides a potentially significant governmental subsidy to extraction businesses that have completely recovered their costs in a natural resource.[57]

It is important to note that businesses deduct percentage depletion when they *sell* the natural resource and they deduct cost depletion in the year they *produce* or extract the natural resource. Also, percentage depletion cannot exceed 50 percent of the *net income* from the natural resource business activity before considering the depletion expense, while cost depletion has no such limitation.

**Example 9-28**

In Example 9-27, Ken determined his cost depletion expense for the gold. However, because he is allowed to deduct the greater of cost or percentage depletion each year, he set out to determine his percentage depletion for year 2. Assuming that Ken has gross (net) income from the gold mining activity before depletion expense of $200,000 ($50,000), $600,000 ($450,000), and $600,000 ($500,000) in year 1, year 2, and year 3, respectively, what is his percentage depletion expense for each of these three years?

**Answer:** $25,000, $90,000, and $90,000 for years 1, 2, and 3, respectively, computed as follows:

| | Year 1 | Year 2 | Year 3 | Explanation |
|---|---|---|---|---|
| (1) Net income from activity (before depletion expense) | $ 50,000 | $450,000 | $500,000 | |
| (2) Gross income | $200,000 | $600,000 | $600,000 | |
| (3) Percentage | × 15% | × 15% | × 15% | Exhibit 9-18. |
| (4) Percentage depletion expense before limit | $ 30,000 | $ 90,000 | $ 90,000 | (2) × (3). |
| (5) 50 percent of net income limitation | $ 25,000 | $225,000 | $250,000 | (1) × 50%. |
| **Allowable percentage depletion** | **$ 25,000** | **$ 90,000** | **$ 90,000** | Lesser of (4) or (5). |

Finally, as we discussed above, a business's depletion expense deduction is the greater of either the annual cost or percentage depletion.

---

[56]§613.

[57]Percentage depletion in excess of basis is an AMT preference item.

**Example 9-29**

Based on his computations of cost depletion and percentage depletion, Ken was able to determine his deductible depletion expense. Using the cost and percentage depletion computations from Examples 9-27 and 9-28, what is Ken's deductible depletion expense for years 1, 2, and 3?

**Answer:** $45,000 for year 1, $105,000 for year 2, and $90,000 for year 3, computed as follows:

| Tax Depletion Expense | Year 1 | Year 2 | Year 3 | Explanation |
|---|---|---|---|---|
| (1) Cost depletion | $45,000 | $105,000 | $   0 | Example 9-27. |
| (2) Percentage depletion | $30,000 | $ 90,000 | $90,000 | Example 9-28. |
| Allowable expense | $45,000 | $105,000 | $90,000 | Greater of (1) or (2). |

# CONCLUSION

This chapter describes and discusses how businesses recover the costs of their tangible and intangible assets. Cost recovery expenses are important because they represent a significant tax deduction for many businesses. Businesses must routinely make choices that affect the amount and timing of these deductions. Further understanding cost recovery basics helps businesses determine how to compute and characterize gain and loss they recognize when they sell or otherwise dispose of business assets. We address the interaction between cost recovery expenses and gain and loss on property dispositions in the next chapter.

# MACRS TABLES

**APPENDIX A**

## MACRS Half-Year Convention

| | Depreciation Rate for Recovery Period | |
|---|---|---|
| Year | 5-year | 7-year |
| 1 | 20.00% | 14.29% |
| 2 | 32.00 | 24.49 |
| 3 | 19.20 | 17.49 |
| 4 | 11.52 | 12.49 |
| 5 | 11.52 | 8.93 |
| 6 | 5.76 | 8.92 |
| 7 | | 8.93 |
| 8 | | 4.46 |

## MACRS Mid-Quarter Convention: *For property placed in service during the first quarter*

| | Depreciation Rate for Recovery Period | |
|---|---|---|
| Year | 5-year | 7-year |
| 1 | 35.00% | 25.00% |
| 2 | 26.00 | 21.43 |
| 3 | 15.60 | 15.31 |
| 4 | 11.01 | 10.93 |
| 5 | 11.01 | 8.75 |
| 6 | 1.38 | 8.74 |
| 7 | | 8.75 |
| 8 | | 1.09 |

## MACRS Mid-Quarter Convention: *For property placed in service during the second quarter*

| Year | Depreciation Rate for Recovery Period | |
|------|-------------|--------|
|      | 5-year | 7-year |
| 1 | 25.00% | 17.85% |
| 2 | 30.00 | 23.47 |
| 3 | 18.00 | 16.76 |
| 4 | 11.37 | 11.97 |
| 5 | 11.37 | 8.87 |
| 6 | 4.26 | 8.87 |
| 7 |  | 8.87 |
| 8 |  | 3.33 |

## MACRS Mid-Quarter Convention: *For property placed in service during the third quarter*

| Year | Depreciation Rate for Recovery Period | |
|------|-------------|--------|
|      | 5-year | 7-year |
| 1 | 15.00% | 10.71% |
| 2 | 34.00 | 25.51 |
| 3 | 20.40 | 18.22 |
| 4 | 12.24 | 13.02 |
| 5 | 11.30 | 9.30 |
| 6 | 7.06 | 8.85 |
| 7 |  | 8.86 |
| 8 |  | 5.53 |

## MACRS-Mid Quarter Convention: *For property placed in service during the fourth quarter*

| Year | Depreciation Rate for Recovery Period | |
|------|-------------|--------|
|      | 5-year | 7-year |
| 1 | 5.00% | 3.57% |
| 2 | 38.00 | 27.55 |
| 3 | 22.80 | 19.68 |
| 4 | 13.68 | 14.06 |
| 5 | 10.94 | 10.04 |
| 6 | 9.58 | 8.73 |
| 7 |  | 8.73 |
| 8 |  | 7.64 |

Residential Rental Property Mid-Month Convention Straight Line—27.5 Years

| Year | 1 | 2 | 3 | 4 | 5 | 6 | 7 | 8 | 9 | 10 | 11 | 12 |
|------|------|------|------|------|------|------|------|------|------|------|------|------|
| | | | | | | Month Property Placed in Service | | | | | | |
| 1 | 3.485% | 3.182% | 2.879% | 2.576% | 2.273% | 1.970% | 1.667% | 1.364% | 1.061% | 0.758% | 0.455% | 0.152% |
| 2-9 | 3.636 | 3.636 | 3.636 | 3.636 | 3.636 | 3.636 | 3.636 | 3.636 | 3.636 | 3.636 | 3.636 | 3.636 |
| 10 | 3.637 | 3.637 | 3.637 | 3.637 | 3.637 | 3.637 | 3.636 | 3.636 | 3.636 | 3.636 | 3.636 | 3.636 |
| 11 | 3.636 | 3.636 | 3.636 | 3.636 | 3.636 | 3.636 | 3.637 | 3.637 | 3.636 | 3.637 | 3.637 | 3.637 |
| 12 | 3.637 | 3.637 | 3.637 | 3.637 | 3.637 | 3.637 | 3.636 | 3.636 | 3.637 | 3.636 | 3.636 | 3.636 |
| 13 | 3.636 | 3.636 | 3.636 | 3.636 | 3.636 | 3.636 | 3.637 | 3.637 | 3.636 | 3.637 | 3.637 | 3.637 |
| 14 | 3.637 | 3.637 | 3.637 | 3.637 | 3.637 | 3.637 | 3.636 | 3.636 | 3.637 | 3.636 | 3.636 | 3.636 |
| 15 | 3.636 | 3.636 | 3.636 | 3.636 | 3.636 | 3.636 | 3.637 | 3.637 | 3.636 | 3.637 | 3.637 | 3.637 |
| 16 | 3.637 | 3.637 | 3.637 | 3.637 | 3.637 | 3.637 | 3.636 | 3.636 | 3.637 | 3.636 | 3.636 | 3.636 |
| 17 | 3.636 | 3.636 | 3.636 | 3.636 | 3.636 | 3.636 | 3.637 | 3.637 | 3.636 | 3.637 | 3.637 | 3.637 |
| 18 | 3.637 | 3.637 | 3.637 | 3.637 | 3.637 | 3.637 | 3.636 | 3.636 | 3.637 | 3.636 | 3.636 | 3.636 |
| 19 | 3.636 | 3.636 | 3.636 | 3.636 | 3.636 | 3.636 | 3.637 | 3.637 | 3.636 | 3.637 | 3.637 | 3.637 |
| 20 | 3.637 | 3.637 | 3.637 | 3.637 | 3.637 | 3.637 | 3.636 | 3.636 | 3.637 | 3.636 | 3.636 | 3.636 |
| 21 | 3.636 | 3.636 | 3.636 | 3.636 | 3.636 | 3.636 | 3.637 | 3.637 | 3.636 | 3.637 | 3.637 | 3.637 |
| 22 | 3.637 | 3.637 | 3.637 | 3.637 | 3.637 | 3.637 | 3.636 | 3.636 | 3.637 | 3.636 | 3.636 | 3.636 |
| 23 | 3.636 | 3.636 | 3.636 | 3.636 | 3.636 | 3.636 | 3.637 | 3.637 | 3.636 | 3.637 | 3.637 | 3.637 |
| 24 | 3.637 | 3.637 | 3.637 | 3.637 | 3.637 | 3.637 | 3.636 | 3.636 | 3.637 | 3.636 | 3.636 | 3.636 |
| 25 | 3.636 | 3.636 | 3.636 | 3.636 | 3.636 | 3.636 | 3.637 | 3.637 | 3.636 | 3.637 | 3.637 | 3.637 |
| 26 | 3.637 | 3.637 | 3.637 | 3.637 | 3.637 | 3.637 | 3.636 | 3.636 | 3.637 | 3.636 | 3.636 | 3.636 |
| 27 | 3.636 | 3.636 | 3.636 | 3.636 | 3.636 | 3.636 | 3.637 | 3.637 | 3.636 | 3.637 | 3.637 | 3.637 |
| 28 | 1.97 | 2.273 | 2.576 | 2.879 | 3.182 | 3.485 | 3.636 | 3.636 | 3.636 | 3.636 | 3.636 | 3.636 |
| 29 | | | | | | | 0.152 | 0.455 | 0.758 | 1.061 | 1.364 | 1.667 |

## Nonresidential Real Property Mid-Month Convention Straight Line—31.5 Years

| Year | Month Property Placed in Service | | | | | | | | | | | |
|------|-------|-------|-------|-------|-------|-------|-------|-------|-------|-------|-------|-------|
|      | 1 | 2 | 3 | 4 | 5 | 6 | 7 | 8 | 9 | 10 | 11 | 12 |
| 1 | 3.042% | 2.778% | 2.513% | 2.249% | 1.984% | 1.720% | 1.455% | 1.190% | 0.926% | 0.661% | 0.397% | 0.132% |
| 2-7 | 3.175 | 3.175 | 3.175 | 3.175 | 3.175 | 3.175 | 3.175 | 3.175 | 3.175 | 3.175 | 3.175 | 3.175 |
| 8 | 3.175 | 3.174 | 3.175 | 3.174 | 3.175 | 3.174 | 3.175 | 3.175 | 3.175 | 3.175 | 3.175 | 3.175 |
| 9 | 3.174 | 3.175 | 3.174 | 3.175 | 3.174 | 3.175 | 3.174 | 3.175 | 3.174 | 3.175 | 3.174 | 3.175 |
| 10 | 3.175 | 3.174 | 3.175 | 3.174 | 3.175 | 3.174 | 3.175 | 3.174 | 3.175 | 3.174 | 3.175 | 3.174 |
| 11 | 3.174 | 3.175 | 3.174 | 3.175 | 3.174 | 3.174 | 3.175 | 3.175 | 3.175 | 3.175 | 3.174 | 3.175 |
| 12 | 3.175 | 3.174 | 3.175 | 3.174 | 3.175 | 3.175 | 3.174 | 3.174 | 3.175 | 3.174 | 3.175 | 3.174 |
| 13 | 3.174 | 3.175 | 3.174 | 3.175 | 3.174 | 3.175 | 3.175 | 3.175 | 3.174 | 3.175 | 3.174 | 3.175 |
| 14 | 3.175 | 3.174 | 3.175 | 3.174 | 3.175 | 3.175 | 3.174 | 3.174 | 3.175 | 3.174 | 3.175 | 3.174 |
| 15 | 3.174 | 3.175 | 3.174 | 3.175 | 3.174 | 3.175 | 3.174 | 3.175 | 3.174 | 3.175 | 3.174 | 3.175 |
| 16 | 3.175 | 3.175 | 3.175 | 3.174 | 3.175 | 3.175 | 3.175 | 3.174 | 3.175 | 3.175 | 3.174 | 3.174 |
| 17 | 3.174 | 3.175 | 3.174 | 3.175 | 3.174 | 3.175 | 3.174 | 3.175 | 3.175 | 3.175 | 3.174 | 3.175 |
| 18 | 3.175 | 3.175 | 3.175 | 3.174 | 3.175 | 3.175 | 3.175 | 3.174 | 3.175 | 3.175 | 3.174 | 3.174 |
| 19 | 3.174 | 3.175 | 3.174 | 3.175 | 3.174 | 3.175 | 3.174 | 3.175 | 3.175 | 3.175 | 3.174 | 3.174 |
| 20 | 3.175 | 3.174 | 3.175 | 3.174 | 3.175 | 3.174 | 3.175 | 3.174 | 3.174 | 3.174 | 3.174 | 3.174 |
| 21 | 3.175 | 3.175 | 3.174 | 3.175 | 3.174 | 3.174 | 3.175 | 3.175 | 3.175 | 3.175 | 3.174 | 3.175 |
| 22 | 3.175 | 3.175 | 3.175 | 3.174 | 3.175 | 3.175 | 3.175 | 3.175 | 3.175 | 3.174 | 3.175 | 3.175 |
| 23 | 3.174 | 3.175 | 3.174 | 3.175 | 3.174 | 3.175 | 3.174 | 3.115 | 3.175 | 3.175 | 3.174 | 3.175 |
| 24 | 3.175 | 3.174 | 3.175 | 3.174 | 3.175 | 3.175 | 3.175 | 3.174 | 3.175 | 3.174 | 3.175 | 3.175 |
| 25 | 3.174 | 3.175 | 3.174 | 3.175 | 3.174 | 3.175 | 3.174 | 3.175 | 3.174 | 3.175 | 3.174 | 3.175 |
| 26 | 3.175 | 3.174 | 3.175 | 3.174 | 3.175 | 3.174 | 3.175 | 3.175 | 3.174 | 3.175 | 3.175 | 3.175 |
| 27 | 3.174 | 3.175 | 3.174 | 3.175 | 3.174 | 3.175 | 3.174 | 3.175 | 3.175 | 3.174 | 3.174 | 3.175 |
| 28 | 3.175 | 3.174 | 3.175 | 3.174 | 3.175 | 3.175 | 3.175 | 3.174 | 3.175 | 3.175 | 3.175 | 3.174 |
| 29 | 3.174 | 3.175 | 3.174 | 3.175 | 3.174 | 3.175 | 3.174 | 3.175 | 3.175 | 3.175 | 3.175 | 3.175 |
| 30 | 3.175 | 3.174 | 3.175 | 3.174 | 3.175 | 3.174 | 3.175 | 3.174 | 3.174 | 3.174 | 3.175 | 3.174 |
| 31 | 3.174 | 3.175 | 3.174 | 3.175 | 3.174 | 3.175 | 3.174 | 3.175 | 3.175 | 3.174 | 3.174 | 3.175 |
| 32 | 1.720 | 1.984 | 2.249 | 2.513 | 2.778 | 3.042 | 3.175 | 3.174 | 3.175 | 3.174 | 3.175 | 3.174 |
| 33 | | | | | | | 0.132 | 0.397 | 0.661 | 0.926 | 1.190 | 1.455 |

## Nonresidential Real Property Mid-Month Convention Straight Line—39 Years

| Year | Month property placed in service | | | | | | | | | | | |
|------|-------|-------|-------|-------|-------|-------|-------|-------|-------|-------|-------|-------|
|      | 1 | 2 | 3 | 4 | 5 | 6 | 7 | 8 | 9 | 10 | 11 | 12 |
| 1 | 2.461% | 2.247% | 2.033% | 1.819% | 1.605% | 1.391% | 1.177% | 0.963% | 0.749% | 0.535% | 0.321% | 0.107% |
| 2-39 | 2.564 | 2.564 | 2.564 | 2.564 | 2.564 | 2.564 | 2.564 | 2.564 | 2.564 | 2.564 | 2.564 | 2.564 |
| 40 | 0.107 | 0.321 | 0.535 | 0.749 | 0.963 | 1.177 | 1.391 | 1.605 | 1.819 | 2.033 | 2.247 | 2.461 |

## SUMMARY

**LO1** Explain the concept of basis and adjusted basis and describe the cost recovery methods used under the tax law to recover the cost of personal property, real property, intangible assets, and natural resources.

- Tangible personal and real property (depreciation), intangibles (amortization), and natural resources (depletion) are all subject to cost recovery.
- An asset's basis is the amount that is subject to cost recovery. Generally, an asset's initial basis is its purchase price, plus the cost of any other expenses incurred to get the asset in working condition.
- The taxpayer's basis of assets acquired in a nontaxable exchange is the same basis the taxpayer transferred to acquire the property received.
- Expenditures on an asset are either expensed currently or capitalized as a new asset. Expenditures for routine or general maintenance of the asset are expensed currently. Expenditures that extend the useful life of the asset are capitalized.
- When acquiring a business and purchasing a bundle of property, the basis of each asset is determined as the fair market value of the asset.

**LO2** Determine the applicable cost recovery (depreciation) life, method, and convention for tangible personal and real property and calculate the deduction allowable under MACRS.

- Tax depreciation is currently calculated under the Modified Accelerated Cost Recovery System (MACRS).
- MACRS for tangible personal property is based upon recovery period (Rev. Proc. 87-56), method (200 percent declining balance, 150 percent declining balance, and straight-line), and convention (half-year or mid-quarter).
- §179 allows taxpayers to expense tangible personal property. The expense is limited by the amount of property placed in service and taxable income.
- Listed property includes automobiles, other means of transportation, computer equipment, and cell phones. Depreciation is limited to the expense multiplied by business-use percentage. Special rules apply if business use is less than 50 percent.
- Additional limitations apply to luxury automobiles.
- Real property is divided into two groups for tax purposes: residential rental and nonresidential. The recovery period is 27.5 years for residential property and 31.5 years or 39 years for nonresidential property, depending on when the property was placed in service. The depreciation method is straight-line and the convention is mid-month.

**LO3** Explain the rationale behind amortization, describe the four categories of amortizable intangible assets, and calculate amortization expense.

- Intangible assets (such as patents, goodwill, and trademarks) have their costs recovered through amortization.
- Intangible assets are amortized (straight-line method) using the full-month convention.
- Intangibles are divided into four types (§197 purchased intangibles, start-up costs and organizational expenditures, research and experimentation, and self-created intangibles).

**LO4** Explain cost recovery of natural resources and the allowable depletion methods.

- Depletion allows a taxpayer to recover his or her capital investment in natural resources.
- Two methods of depletion are available, and the taxpayer must calculate both and take the one that results in the larger depletion deduction each year.
- Cost depletion allows taxpayers to estimate number of units and then allocate a pro rata share of the basis to each unit extracted during the year.
- Percentage depletion allows the taxpayer to take a statutory determined percentage of gross income as an expense. Deductions are not limited to basis.

# KEY TERMS

Accelerated Cost Recovery System (ACRS) (9-5)
adjusted basis (9-3)
amortization (9-2)
bonus depreciation (9-19)
cost depletion (9-37)
cost recovery (9-2)
covenant not to compete (9-30)
depletion (9-2)
depreciation (9-2)

full-month convention (9-30)
half-year convention (9-8)
intangible assets (9-2)
listed property (9-20)
luxury automobile (9-24)
mid-month convention (9-26)
mid-quarter convention (9-8)
Modified Cost Recovery System (MACRS) (9-5)
organizational expenditures (9-32)

percentage depletion (9-38)
personal property (9-5)
real property (9-5)
recovery period (9-5)
research and experimentation (R&E) costs (9-30)
§179 expense (9-15)
§197 purchased intangibles (9-30)
start-up costs (9-34)
tax basis (9-3)

# DISCUSSION QUESTIONS

1. **(LO1)** Explain the reasoning why the tax laws require the cost of certain assets to be capitalized and recovered over time rather than immediately expensed.

2. **(LO1)** Explain the differences and similarities between personal property, real property, intangible property, and natural resources. Also, provide an example of each type of asset.

3. **(LO1)** Explain the similarities and dissimilarities between depreciation, amortization, and depletion. Describe the cost recovery method used for each of the four asset types (personal property, real property, intangible property, and natural resources).

4. **(LO1)** Is an asset's initial or cost basis simply its purchase price? Explain.

5. **(LO1)** Compare and contrast the basis of property acquired via purchase, conversion from personal use to business or rental use, a nontaxable exchange, gift, and inheritance.

6. **(LO1)** Explain why the expenses incurred to get an asset in place and operable should be included in the asset's basis.

7. **(LO1)** Graber Corporation runs a long-haul trucking business. Graber incurs the following expenses: replacement tires, oil changes, and a transmission overhaul. Which of these expenditures may be deducted currently and which must be capitalized? Explain.

8. **(LO2)** MACRS depreciation requires the use of a recovery period, method, and convention to depreciate tangible personal property assets. Briefly explain why each is important to the calculation.

9. **(LO2)** Can a taxpayer with very little current year income choose to not claim any depreciation expense for the current year and thus save depreciation deductions for the future when the taxpayer expects to be more profitable?

 planning

10. **(LO2)** What depreciation methods are available for tangible personal property? Explain the characteristics of a business likely to adopt each method.

11. **(LO2)** If a business places several different assets in service during the year, must it use the same depreciation method for all assets? If not, what restrictions apply to the business's choices of depreciation methods?

12. **(LO2)** Describe how you would determine the MACRS recovery period for an asset if you did not already know it.

research 13. **(LO2)** Compare and contrast the recovery periods used by MACRS and those used under generally accepted accounting principles (GAAP).

14. **(LO2)** Fast and Furious Corporation (F&F) decided that it should cash in on the current popularity of stock car racing. F&F designed and built a track and related facilities including grandstands, garages, concession stands, landscaping, and a hotel on the property. ■research

    a. What does Rev. Proc. 87-56 list for the recovery period of the land improvements such as landscaping?

    b. Now, conduct research (*hint:* use a tax service and the term "motorsports entertainment complex") to determine the recovery period for the various assets if the entire project was completed in July 2007 and the first race was held on October 10, 2007.

    c. Would your answers change if there were a one-year delay in construction? If so, how would it change and why?

15. **(LO2)** What are the two depreciation conventions that apply to tangible personal property under MACRS? Explain why Congress provides two methods.

16. **(LO2)** A business buys two identical tangible personal property assets for the same identical price. It buys one at the beginning of the year and one at the end of year. Under what conditions would the taxpayer's depreciation on each asset be exactly the same? Under what conditions would it be different?

17. **(LO2)** AAA, Inc., acquired a machine in year 1. In May of year 3, it sold the asset. Can AAA find its year 3 depreciation percentage for the machine on the MACRS table? If not, what adjustment must AAA make to its full year depreciation percentage to determine its year 3 depreciation?

18. **(LO2)** Discuss why a small business might be able to deduct a greater percentage of the assets it places in service during the year than a larger business.

19. **(LO2)** Explain the two limitations placed on the §179 expense deduction. How are they similar? How are they different?

20. **(LO2)** Compare and contrast the types of businesses that would benefit from and those that would not benefit from the §179 expense.

21. **(LO2)** What strategies will help a business maximize its current depreciation deductions (including §179)? Why might a taxpayer choose not to maximize its current depreciation deductions?

22. **(LO2)** Why might a business elect only the §179 expense it can deduct in the current year rather than claiming the full amount available?

23. **(LO2)** Describe assets that are considered to be listed property. Why do you think Congress requires them to be "listed"?

24. **(LO2)** Are taxpayers allowed to claim deprecation expense on assets they use for both business and personal purposes? What are the tax consequences if the business use drops from above 50 percent in one year to below 50 percent in the next?

25. **(LO2)** Discuss why Congress limits the amount of depreciation expense businesses may claim on certain automobiles.

26. **(LO2)** Compare and contrast how a Land Rover SUV and a Mercedes Benz sedan are treated under the luxury auto rules. Also include a discussion of the similarities and differences in available §179 expense.

27. **(LO2)** There are two recovery period classifications for real property. What reasons might Congress have to allow residential real estate a shorter recovery period than nonresidential real property?

28. **(LO2)** Discuss why Congress has instructed taxpayers that real property be depreciated using the mid-month convention as opposed to the half-year or mid-quarter conventions used for tangible personal property.

29. **(LO2)** If a taxpayer has owned a building for 10 years and decides that it should make significant improvements to the building, what is the recovery period for the improvements?

30. **(LO2)** Compare and contrast the differences between computing depreciation expense for tangible personal property and depreciation expense for real property under both the regular tax and alternative tax systems.

31. **(LO3)** What is a §197 intangible? How do taxpayers recover the costs of these intangibles? How do taxpayers recover the cost of a §197 intangible that expires (such as a covenant not to compete)?

32. **(LO3)** Compare and contrast the tax and financial accounting treatment of goodwill. Are taxpayers allowed to deduct amounts associated with self-created goodwill?

33. **(LO3)** Compare and contrast the similarities and differences between organizational expenditures and start-up costs for tax purposes.

34. **(LO3)** Discuss the methodology used to determine the amount of organizational expenditures or start-up costs that may be immediately expensed in the year a taxpayer begins business.

35. **(LO3)** Explain the amortization convention applicable to intangible assets.

36. **(LO3)** Compare and contrast the recovery periods of §197 intangibles, organizational expenditures, start-up costs, and research and experimentation expenses.

37. **(LO4)** Compare and contrast the cost and percentage depletion methods for recovering the costs of natural resources. What are the similarities and differences between the two methods?

38. **(LO4)** Explain why percentage depletion has been referred to as a government subsidy.

## PROBLEMS

39. **(LO1)** Jose purchased a delivery van for his business through an online auction. His winning bid for the van was $24,500. In addition, Jose incurred the following expenses before using the van: shipping costs of $650; paint to match the other fleet vehicles at a cost of $1,000; registration costs of $3,200 which included $3,000 of sales tax and a registration fee of $200; wash and detailing for $50; and an engine tune-up for $250. What is Jose's cost basis for the delivery van?

40. **(LO1)** Emily purchased a building to store inventory for her business. The purchase price was $760,000. Beyond this, Emily incurred the following necessary expenses to get the building ready for use: $10,000 to repair the roof, $5,000 to make the interior suitable for her finished goods, and $300 in legal fees. What is Emily's cost basis in the new building?

41. **(LO1)** Dennis contributed business assets to a new business in exchange for stock in the company. The exchange did not qualify as a nontaxable exchange. The fair market value of these assets was $287,000 on the contribution date. Dennis's original basis in the assets he contributed was $143,000, and the accumulated depreciation on the assets was $78,000.

    a. What is the business's basis in the assets it received from Dennis?

    b. What would be the business's basis if the transaction qualified as a nontaxable exchange?

42. **(LO1)** Brittany started a law practice as a sole proprietor. She owned a computer, printer, desk, and file cabinet she purchased during law school (several years ago)

that she is planning to use in her business. What is the depreciable basis that Brittany should use in her business for each asset, given the following information?

| Asset | Purchase Price | FMV at Time Converted to Business Use |
|---|---|---|
| Computer | $2,500 | $ 800 |
| Printer | $ 300 | $ 150 |
| Desk | $1,200 | $1,000 |
| File cabinet | $ 200 | $ 225 |

43. **(LO1)** Meg O'Brien received a gift of some small-scale jewelry manufacturing equipment that her father had used for personal purposes for many years. Her father originally purchased the equipment for $1,500. Because the equipment is out of production and no longer available, the property is currently worth $4,000. Meg has decided to begin a new jewelry manufacturing trade or business. What is her depreciable basis for depreciating the equipment?

44. **(LO1)** Gary inherited a Maine summer cabin on 10 acres from his grandmother. His grandparents originally purchased the property for $500 in 1950 and built the cabin at a cost of $10,000 in 1965. His grandfather died in 1980 and when his grandmother recently passed away, the property was appraised at $500,000 for the land and $700,000 for the cabin. Since Gary doesn't currently live in New England, he decided that it would be best to put the property to use as a rental. What is Gary's basis in the land and in the cabin?

45. **(LO1)** Wanting to finalize a sale before year-end, on December 29, WR Outfitters discounted and sold to Bob a warehouse and the land it was built on for $125,000. The appraised fair market value of the warehouse was $75,000, and the appraised value of the land was $100,000.

   a. What is Bob's basis in the warehouse and in the land?

   b. What would be Bob's basis in the warehouse and in the land if the appraised value of the warehouse is $50,000, and the appraised value of the land is $125,000?

   c. Which appraisal would Bob likely prefer?

46. **(LO2)** At the beginning of the year, Poplock began a calendar-year dog boarding business called Griff's Palace. Poplock bought and placed in service the following assets during the year:

| Asset | Placed in Service Date | Cost Basis |
|---|---|---|
| Computer equipment | 3/23 | $ 5,000 |
| Dog grooming furniture | 5/12 | $ 7,000 |
| Pickup truck | 9/17 | $ 10,000 |
| Commercial building | 10/11 | $270,000 |
| Land (one acre) | 10/11 | $ 80,000 |

Assuming Poplock does not elect §179 expensing or bonus depreciation, answer the following questions:

   a. What is Poplock's year 1 depreciation expense for each asset?

   b. What is Poplock's year 2 depreciation expense for each asset?

   c. What is Poplock's year 1 depreciation expense for each asset if the pickup truck was purchased and placed in service on 11/15 instead of 9/17?

   d. Assuming the pickup truck was purchased and placed in service on 11/15, what is Poplock's year 2 depreciation expense for each asset?

47. **(LO2)** Evergreen Corporation acquired the following assets during the current year (ignore §179 expense and bonus depreciation for this problem):

| Asset | Placed in Service Date | Original Basis |
|---|---|---|
| Machinery | October 25 | $ 70,000 |
| Computer equipment | February 3 | $ 10,000 |
| Used delivery truck* | August 17 | $ 23,000 |
| Furniture | April 22 | $150,000 |

*The delivery truck is not a luxury automobile.

a. What is the allowable MACRS depreciation on Evergreen's property in the current year?

b. What is the allowable MACRS depreciation on Evergreen's property in the current year if bonus depreciation is taken? (Assume 2009 rules apply to 2010.)

c. What is the allowable MACRS depreciation on Evergreen's property in the current year if the machinery had a basis of $170,000 rather than $70,000?

d. What is the allowable MACRS depreciation on Evergreen's property in the current year if the machinery had a basis of $270,000 rather than $170,000?

■ **planning**
48. **(LO2)** Parley needs a new truck to help him expand Parley's Plumbing Palace. Business has been booming and Parley would like to accelerate his tax deductions as much as possible (ignore §179 expense and bonus depreciation for this problem). On April 1, Parley purchased a new delivery van for $25,000. It is now September 26 and Parley, already in need of another vehicle, has found a deal on buying a truck for $22,000 (all fees included). The dealer tells him if he doesn't buy the truck (Option 1), it will be gone tomorrow. There is an auction (Option 2) scheduled for October 5 where Parley believes he can get a similar truck for $21,500, but there is also a $500 auction fee.

a. Which option allows Parley to generate more depreciation expense deductions this year (the vehicles are not considered to be luxury autos)?

b. Assume the original facts, except that the delivery van was placed in service one day earlier on March 31 rather than April 1. Which option generates more depreciation expense?

49. **(LO2)** Way Corporation disposed of the following tangible personal property assets in the current year. Assume that the delivery truck is not a luxury auto. Calculate Way Corporation's 2010 depreciation expense (assuming it elected no §179 expense or bonus depreciation in the prior or current year).

| Asset | Date Acquired | Date Sold | Convention | Original Basis |
|---|---|---|---|---|
| Furniture (7-year) | 5/12/06 | 7/15/10 | HY | $ 55,000 |
| Machinery (7-year) | 3/23/07 | 3/15/10 | MQ | $ 72,000 |
| Delivery truck* (5-year) | 9/17/08 | 3/13/10 | HY | $ 20,000 |
| Machinery (7-year) | 10/11/09 | 8/11/10 | MQ | $270,000 |
| Computer (5-year) | 10/11/10 | 12/15/10 | HY | $ 80,000 |

*Used 100 percent for business.

■ **planning**
50. **(LO2)** Assume that Green Corporation has 2010 taxable income of $350,000 before the §179 expense (assume no bonus depreciation) and acquired the following assets during 2010:

| Asset | Placed in Service | Basis |
|---|---|---|
| Machinery | October 12 | $ 470,000 |
| Computer equipment | February 10 | $ 70,000 |
| Delivery truck | August 21 | $ 93,000 |
| Furniture | April 2 | $ 380,000 |
| Total | | $1,013,000 |

a. What is the maximum amount of §179 expense Green may deduct for 2010?

b. What is the maximum total depreciation expense, including §179 expense, that Green may deduct in 2010 on the assets it placed in service in 2010?

c. What is the maximum total depreciation expense, including §179 expense, that Green may deduct in 2010 on the assets it placed in service in 2010 if it does use bonus depreciation? (Assume the 2009 rules apply to 2010.)

d. What is the maximum total depreciation expense, including §179 expense, Green may deduct in 2010 on the assets it placed in service in 2010 if the delivery truck was purchased and placed in service on October 21 instead of August 21?

51. **(LO2)** Assume that Timberline Corporation has 2010 taxable income of $25,000 before the §179 expense (assume no bonus depreciation).

| Asset | Purchase Date | Basis |
|---|---|---|
| Furniture (7-year) | December 1 | $150,000 |
| Computer equipment (5-year) | February 28 | $ 90,000 |
| Copier (5-year) | July 15 | $ 30,000 |
| Machinery (7-year) | May 22 | $280,000 |
| Total | | $550,000 |

a. What is the maximum amount of §179 expense Timberline may deduct for 2010?

b. What would Timberline's maximum depreciation expense be for 2010?

c. What would Timberline's maximum depreciation expense be for 2010 if the furniture cost $750,000 instead of $150,000?

52. **(LO2)** Dain's Diamond Bit Drilling purchased the following assets during 2010. Assume its taxable income for the year was $53,000 before deducting any §179 expense (assume no bonus depreciation).

■ planning

| Asset | Purchase Date | Original Basis |
|---|---|---|
| Drill bits (5-year) | January 25 | $ 90,000 |
| Drill bits (5-year) | July 25 | $ 95,000 |
| Commercial building | April 22 | $220,000 |

a. What is Dain's maximum §179 expense for the year 2010?

b. What is Dain's maximum depreciation expense for the year 2010 (including §179 expense)?

c. If the January drill bits' original basis was $925,000, what is Dain's maximum §179 expense for the year 2010?

d. If the January drill bits' basis was $1,000,000, what is Dain's maximum §179 expense for the year 2010?

53. **(LO2)** Phil owns a ranch business and uses four-wheelers to do much of his work. Occasionally, though, he and his boys will go for a ride together as a family activity. During year 1, Phil put 765 miles on the four-wheeler that he bought on January 15 for $6,500. Of the miles driven, only 175 miles were for personal use. Assume four-wheelers qualify to be depreciated according to the five-year MACRS schedule and the four-wheeler was the only asset Phil purchased this year.

a. Calculate the allowable depreciation for year 1 (ignore the §179 expense and bonus depreciation).

b. Calculate the allowable depreciation for year 2 if total miles were 930 and personal-use miles were 400 (ignore the §179 expense and bonus depreciation).

54. **(LO2)** Assume that Ernesto purchased a laptop computer on July 10 of year 1 for $3,000. In year 1, 80 percent of his computer usage was for his business and 20 percent was for computer gaming with his friends. This was the only asset he placed in service during year 1. Ignoring any potential §179 expense and bonus depreciation, answer the questions for each of the following alternative scenarios:

    a. What is Ernesto's depreciation deduction for the computer in year 1?

    b. What would be Ernesto's depreciation deduction for the computer in year 2 if his year 2 usage was 75 percent business and 25 percent for computer gaming?

    c. What would be Ernesto's depreciation deduction for the computer in year 2 if his year 2 usage was 45 percent business and 55 percent for computer gaming?

    d. What would be Ernesto's depreciation deduction for the computer in year 2 if his year 2 usage was 30 percent business and 70 percent for computer gaming?

55. **(LO2)** Lina purchased a new car for use in her business during 2009. The auto was the only business asset she purchased during the year and her business was extremely profitable. Calculate her maximum depreciation deductions (including §179 expense unless stated otherwise) for the automobile in 2009 (Lina didn't elect bonus depreciation for 2009) and 2010 in the following alternative scenarios (assuming half-year convention for all):

    a. The vehicle cost $15,000 and business use is 100 percent (ignore §179 expense).

    b. The vehicle cost $40,000, and business use is 100 percent.

    c. The vehicle cost $40,000, and she used it 80 percent for business.

    d. The vehicle cost $40,000, and she used it 80 percent for business. She sold it on March 1 of year 2.

    e. The vehicle cost $40,000, and she used it 20 percent for business.

    f. The vehicle cost $40,000, and is an SUV that weighed 6,500 pounds. Business use was 100 percent.

56. **(LO2)** On November 10 of year 1 Javier purchased a building, including the land it was on, to assemble his new equipment. The total cost of the purchase was $1,200,000; $300,000 was allocated to the basis of the land and the remaining $900,000 was allocated to the basis of the building.

    a. Using MACRS, what is Javier's depreciation expense on the building for years 1 through 3?

    b. What would be the year 3 depreciation expense if the building was sold on August 1 of year 3?

    c. Answer the question in part (a), except assume the building was purchased and placed in service on March 3 instead of November 10.

    d. Answer the question in part (a), except assume that the building is residential property.

    e. What would be the depreciation for 2009, 2010, and 2011 if the property were nonresidential property purchased and placed in service November 10, 1992 (assume the same original basis)?

57. **(LO2)** Carl purchased an apartment complex for $1.1 million on March 17 of year 1. $300,000 of the purchase price was attributable to the land the complex sits on. He also installed new furniture into half of the units at a cost of $60,000.

    a. What is Carl's allowable depreciation expense for his real property for years 1 and 2?

    b. What is Carl's allowable depreciation expense for year 3 if the property is sold on January 2 of year 3?

58. **(LO2)** Paul Vote purchased the following business assets this year (ignore §179 expensing and bonus depreciation when answering the questions below):

| Asset | Purchase Date | Basis |
|---|---|---|
| Machinery | May 12 | $ 23,500 |
| Computers | August 13 | $ 20,000 |
| Warehouse | December 13 | $180,000 |

a. What is Paul's allowable MACRS depreciation expense for the property?

b. What is Paul's allowable alternative minimum tax (AMT) depreciation expense for the property? You will need to find the AMT depreciation tables to compute the depreciation.

59. **(LO3)** After several profitable years running her business, Ingrid decided to acquire a small competing business. On May 1 of year 1, Ingrid acquired the competing business for $300,000. Ingrid allocated $50,000 of the purchase price to goodwill. Ingrid's business reports its taxable income on a calendar-year basis.

a. How much amortization expense on the goodwill can Ingrid deduct in year 1, year 2, and year 3?

b. In lieu of the original facts, assume that $40,000 of the purchase price was allocated to goodwill and $10,000 of the purchase price was allocated to a customer phone list that has an expected life of two years. How much amortization expense on the goodwill and the phone list can Ingrid deduct in year 1, year 2, and year 3?

c. Assume that the only intangible asset Ingrid acquired was the customer phone list with a useful life of two years and that $10,000 of the purchase price was allocated to the customer list. How much amortization expense for the customer phone list can Ingrid deduct in year 1, year 2, and year 3, and how will she account for the fact that the phone list is no longer useful after April of year 3?

60. **(LO3)** Juliette formed a new business to sell sporting goods this year. The business opened its doors to customers on June 1. Determine the amount of start-up costs Juliette can immediately expense (not including amortization) this year in the following alternative scenarios.

a. She incurred start-up costs of $2,000.

b. She incurred start-up costs of $45,000.

c. She incurred start-up costs of $53,500.

d. She incurred start-up costs of $60,000.

e. How would you answer parts (a–d) if she formed a partnership or a corporation and she incurred the same amount of organizational expenditures rather than start-up costs (how much of the organizational expenditures would be immediately deductible)?

61. **(LO3)** Nicole organized a new corporation. The corporation began business on April 1 of year 1. She made the following expenditures associated with getting the corporation started:

| Expense | Date | Amount |
|---|---|---|
| Attorney fees for articles of incorporation | February 10 | $32,000 |
| March 1–March 30 wages | March 30 | $ 4,500 |
| March 1–March 30 rent | March 30 | $ 2,000 |
| Stock issuance costs | April 1 | $20,000 |
| April 1–May 30 wages | May 30 | $12,000 |

a. What is the total amount of the start-up costs and organizational expenditures for Nicole's corporation?

b. What amount of the start-up costs and organizational expenditures may the corporation immediately expense in year 1?

c. What amount can the corporation deduct as amortization expense for the organizational expenditures and for the start-up costs for year 1 (not including the amount it immediately expensed)?

d. What would be the allowable organizational expenditures, including immediate expensing and amortization, if Ingrid started a sole proprietorship instead?

62. **(LO3)** Bethany incurred $20,000 in research and experimental costs for developing a specialized product during July of year 1. Bethany went through a lot of trouble and spent $10,000 in legal fees to receive a patent for the product in August of year 3.

a. What amount of research and experimental expenses for year 1, year 2, and year 3 may Bethany deduct if she elects to amortize the expenses over 60 months?

b. How much *patent* amortization expense would Bethany deduct in year 3 assuming she elected to amortize the research and experimental costs over 60 months?

c. If Bethany chose to capitalize but *not* amortize the research and experimental expenses she incurred in year 1, how much patent amortization expense would Bethany deduct in year 3?

63. **(LO4)** Last Chance Mine (LC) purchased a coal deposit for $750,000. It estimated it would extract 12,000 tons of coal from the deposit. LC mined the coal and sold it, reporting gross receipts of $1 million, $3 million, and $2 million for years 1 through 3, respectively. During years 1–3, LC reported net income (loss) from the coal deposit activity in the amount of ($20,000), $500,000, and $450,000, respectively. In years 1–3, LC actually extracted 13,000 tons of coal as follows:

| (1)<br>Tons of Coal | (2)<br>Basis | Depletion (2)/(1)<br>Rate | Tons Extracted per Year | | |
| --- | --- | --- | --- | --- | --- |
| | | | Year 1 | Year 2 | Year 3 |
| 12,000 | $750,000 | $62.50 | 2,000 | 7,200 | 3,800 |

a. What is Last Chance's cost depletion for years 1, 2, and 3?

b. What is Last Chance's percentage depletion for each year (the applicable percentage for coal is 10 percent)?

c. Using the cost and percentage depletion computations from the previous parts, what is Last Chance's actual depletion expense for each year?

## COMPREHENSIVE PROBLEMS

64. Back in Boston, Steve has been busy creating and managing his new company, Teton Mountaineering (TM), which is based out of a small town in Wyoming. In the process of doing so, TM has acquired various types of assets. Below is a list of assets acquired during 2009:

| Asset | Cost | Date Place in Service |
| --- | --- | --- |
| Office equipment | $ 10,000 | 02/03/2009 |
| Machinery | $260,000 | 07/22/2009 |
| Used delivery truck* | $ 15,000 | 08/17/2009 |

*Not considered a luxury automobile, thus not subject to the luxury automobile limitations

During 2009, TM had huge success (and no §179 limitations) and Steve acquired more assets the next year to increase its production capacity. These are the assets that were acquired during 2010:

| Asset | Cost | Date Place in Service |
|---|---|---|
| Computers & info. system | $ 40,000 | 03/31/2010 |
| Luxury auto† | $ 80,000 | 05/26/2010 |
| Assembly equipment | $175,000 | 08/15/2010 |
| Storage building | $400,000 | 11/13/2010 |

†Used 100 percent for business purposes.

TM did extremely well during 2010 by generating a taxable income before any §179 expense of $432,500.

**Required**

a. Compute 2009 depreciation deductions including §179 expense (ignoring bonus depreciation).

b. Compute 2010 depreciation deductions including §179 expense (ignoring bonus depreciation).

c. Compute 2010 depreciation deductions including §179 expense (ignoring bonus depreciation), but now assume that Steve acquired a new machine on October 2nd for $300,000 plus $20,000 for delivery and setup costs.

d. Ignoring part c, now assume that during 2010, Steve decides to buy a competitor's assets for a purchase price of $350,000. Steve purchased the following assets for the lump-sum purchase price.

| Asset | Cost | Date Placed in Service |
|---|---|---|
| Inventory | $ 20,000 | 09/15/2010 |
| Office furniture | $ 30,000 | 09/15/2010 |
| Machinery | $ 50,000 | 09/15/2010 |
| Patent | $ 98,000 | 09/15/2010 |
| Goodwill | $  2,000 | 09/15/2010 |
| Building | $130,000 | 09/15/2010 |
| Land | $ 20,000 | 09/15/2010 |

e. Complete Part I of Form 4562 for part b (Use 2009 form if 2010 form is unavailable.)

65. While completing undergraduate work in information systems, Dallin Bourne and Michael Banks decided to start a business called ISys Answers, which was a technology support company. During 2009, they bought the following assets and incurred the following fees at start up:

| 2009 Assets | Purchase Date | Basis |
|---|---|---|
| Computers (5-year) | October 30, 2009 | $15,000 |
| Office equipment (7-year) | October 30, 2009 | $10,000 |
| Furniture (7-year) | October 30, 2009 | $ 3,000 |
| Start-up costs | October 30, 2009 | $ 7,000 |

In April of 2010, they decided to purchase a customer list from a company started by fellow information systems students preparing to graduate that provided virtually the same services. The customer list cost $10,000, and the sale was completed on April 30. During their summer break, Dallin and Michael passed on internship opportunities in an attempt to really grow their business

into something they could do full-time after graduation. In the summer, they purchased a small van (for transportation, not considered a luxury auto) and a pinball machine (to help attract new employees). They bought the van on June 15 of 2010 for $15,000, and spent $3,000 getting it ready to put into service. The pinball machine cost $4,000, and was placed in service on July 1 of 2010.

| 2010 Assets | Purchase Date | Basis |
| --- | --- | --- |
| Van | June 15, 2010 | $18,000 |
| Pinball machine (7-year) | July 1, 2010 | $ 4,000 |
| Customer list | April 30, 2010 | $10,000 |

Assume that ISys Answers does not elect any §179 expense or bonus depreciation.

a. What are the maximum cost recovery deductions for ISys Answers (excluding §179 expensing) for 2009 and 2010?

b. What is ISys Answers' basis in each of its assets at the end of 2009 and 2010?

66. Diamond Mountain was originally thought to be one of the few places in North America to contain diamonds, so Diamond Mountain Inc. (DM) purchased the land for $1,000,000. Later, DM discovered that the only diamonds on the mountain had been planted there and the land was worthless for mining. DM engineers discovered a new survey technology and discovered a silver deposit estimated at 5,000 pounds on Diamond Mountain. DM bought new drilling equipment and immediately began mining the silver.

In years 1–3 following the opening of the mine, DM had net (gross) income of $200,000 ($700,000), $400,000 ($1,100,000), and $600,000 ($1,450,000), respectively. Mining amounts for each year were as follows: 750 pounds (year 1), 1,450 pounds (year 2), and 1,800 pounds (year 3). At the end of year 2, engineers used the new technology (which had been improving over time) and estimated there was still an estimated 6,000 pounds of silver deposits.

DM also began a research and experimentation project with the hopes of gaining a patent for its new survey technology. Diamond Mountain Inc. chooses to capitalize research and experimentation expenditures and amortize the costs over 60 months or until it obtains a patent on its technology. In March of year 1, DM spent $95,000 on research and experimentation. DM spent another $75,000 in February of year 2 for research and experimentation. In September of year 2, DM paid $20,000 of legal fees and was granted the patent in October of year 2 (the entire process of obtaining a patent was unusually fast).

Answer the following questions regarding DM's activities (assume that DM tries to maximize its deductions if given a choice).

a. What is DM's depletion expense for years 1–3?

b. What is DM's research and experimentation amortization for years 1 and 2?

c. What is DM's basis in its patent and what is its amortization for the patent in year 2?

# Property Dispositions

## Learning Objectives

**Upon completing this chapter, you should be able to:**

**LO 1** Calculate the amount of gain or loss recognized on the disposition of assets used in a trade or business.

■

**LO 2** Describe the general character types of gain or loss recognized on property dispositions.

■

**LO 3** Explain the rationale for and calculate depreciation recapture.

■

**LO 4** Describe the tax treatment of unrecaptured §1250 gains and determine the character of gains on property sold to related parties.

■

**LO 5** Describe the tax treatment of §1231 gains or losses, including the §1231 netting process.

■

**LO 6** Explain common exceptions to the general rule that realized gains and losses are recognized currently.

| Storyline Summary | |
| --- | --- |
| *Taxpayer:* | Teton Mountaineering Technologies, LLC (Teton)—a calendar-year, single-member LLC (treated as a sole proprietorship for tax purposes) |
| *President:* | Steve Dallimore |
| *Location:* | Cody, Wyoming |

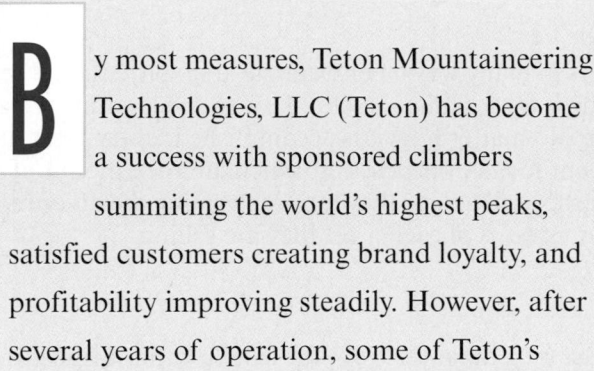

**B**y most measures, Teton Mountaineering Technologies, LLC (Teton) has become a success with sponsored climbers summiting the world's highest peaks, satisfied customers creating brand loyalty, and profitability improving steadily. However, after several years of operation, some of Teton's machinery is wearing out and must be replaced. Further, because Teton has outgrown its manufacturing capacity, Steve is considering whether to expand the company's current facility or sell it and build a new one in a different location. Steve would like to know how any asset dispositions will affect Teton's tax bill.

Steve has found a willing buyer for Teton's machinery, and he has options for trading the equipment. For tax purposes, does it matter whether he sells or trades the equipment? Steve also has questions about how to best manage Teton's acquisitions and dispositions of real property. It all seems a bit overwhelming. . . . He picks up the phone and dials his tax accountant's number. ∎

You can imagine why Steve might be eager to reach his accountant. Tax accounting widely impacts business decisions: What are the tax consequences of selling, trading, or even abandoning business assets? Are the tax consequences the same whether taxpayers sell machinery, inventory, or investment assets? Does it matter for tax purposes whether Teton is structured as a sole proprietorship or a corporation when its sells its warehouse? If Steve sells his personal sailboat, car, or furniture, what are the tax consequences?

In the previous chapter we explained the tax consequences associated with purchasing assets and recovering the cost of the assets through depreciation, amortization, or depletion. This chapter explores fundamental tax issues associated with property dispositions (sales, trades, or other dispositions). We focus on the disposition of depreciable assets, but the same principles apply to the sale of intangible assets and natural resources.

**LO1**

# DISPOSITIONS

Taxpayers can dispose of assets in many ways. For example, a taxpayer could sell an asset, donate it to charity, trade it for a similar asset, take it to the landfill, or have it destroyed in a natural disaster. No matter how it is accomplished, every asset disposition triggers a realization event for tax purposes. To calculate the amount of gain or loss taxpayers realize when they sell assets, they must determine the amount realized on the sale and their *adjusted basis* in each asset they are selling.

## Amount Realized

Simply put, the **amount realized** by a taxpayer from the sale or other disposition of an asset is everything of *value* received from the buyer *less* any selling costs.[1] While taxpayers typically receive cash when they sell property, they may also accept marketable securities, notes receivable, similar assets, or any combination of these items as payment. Additionally, taxpayers selling assets such as real property subject to loans or mortgages must increase their amount realized by the amount of debt relief (the buyer's assumption of the seller's liability increases the seller's amount realized). The amount realized computation is captured in the following formula:

$$\text{Amount realized} = \text{Cash received} + \text{Fair market value of other property} \\ + \text{Buyer's assumption of liabilities} - \text{Seller's expenses}$$

---

**Example 10-1**

Teton wants to upgrade its old manufacturing machinery that is wearing out. On November 1 of the current year, Teton sells the old machinery for $30,000 cash and marketable securities valued at $70,500. Teton paid a broker $500 to find a buyer. What is Teton's amount realized on the sale of the machinery?

**Answer:** $100,000, computed as follows:

| Description | Amount | Explanation |
|---|---|---|
| (1) Cash received | $ 30,000 | |
| (2) Marketable securities received | 70,500 | |
| (3) Broker commission paid | (500) | |
| Amount realized | $100,000 | (1) + (2) + (3). |

---

[1] *S. C. Chapin,* CA-8, 50-1 USTC ¶9171.

## Adjusted Basis

Recall from the previous chapter that an asset's *cost basis* is the amount *subject to* cost recovery. The **adjusted basis** however, is the original basis reduced by depreciation or other types of cost recovery deductions taken against the property. The adjusted basis of an asset can be determined using the following formula:

$$\text{Adjusted basis} = \text{Cost basis} - \text{Cost recovery deductions}$$

**Example 10-2**

To determine its realized gain or loss on the sale, Teton must calculate the adjusted basis of the machinery it sold in Example 10-1 for $100,000. Teton originally purchased the machinery for $260,000 three years ago. For tax purposes, Teton depreciated the machinery using MACRS (seven-year recovery period, 200 percent declining balance method, and half-year convention). The machinery's adjusted basis at the time of the sale is $97,461, computed as follows:

| Description | Tax | Explanation |
|---|---|---|
| (1) Original basis | $260,000 | Example 9-1. |
| (2) Year 1 | (37,154) | Example 9-6. |
| (3) Year 2 | (63,674) | Example 9-6. |
| (4) Year 3 | (45,474) | Example 9-6. |
| (5) Year 4 | (16,237) | $32,474 (Example 9-6) × 50% (half-year convention). |
| (6) Accumulated depreciation | ($162,539) | (2) + (3) + (4) + (5). |
| Adjusted basis | $ 97,461 | (1) + (6). |

Because businesses generally use more highly accelerated depreciation methods for tax purposes than they do for book purposes, the tax-adjusted basis of a particular asset is likely to be lower than the book-adjusted basis.

## Realized Gain or Loss on Disposition

The amount of gain or loss taxpayers realize on a sale or other disposition of assets is simply the amount they realize minus their adjusted basis in the disposed assets.[2] The formula for computing **realized gain or loss** is as follows:

$$\text{Gain or (loss) realized} = \text{Amount realized} - \text{Adjusted basis}$$

**Example 10-3**

In Example 10-1, we learned that Teton sold machinery for a total amount realized of $100,000, and in Example 10-2 we learned that its basis in the machinery was $97,461. What is Teton's realized gain or loss on the sale of the machinery?

**Answer:** $2,539, computed as follows:

| Description | Amount | Explanation |
|---|---|---|
| (1) Amount realized | $100,000 | Example 10-1. |
| (2) Adjusted basis | (97,461) | Example 10-2. |
| Gain realized | $ 2,539 | (1) + (2). |

[2]§1001(a).

Exhibit 10-1 details the important formulas necessary to determine realized tax gains and losses.

### EXHIBIT 10-1   Summary of Formulas for Computing Gain or Loss Realized on an Asset Disposition

- Gain (loss) realized = Amount realized − Adjusted basis
- Amount realized = Cash received + Fair market value of other property + Buyer's assumption of seller's liabilities − Seller's expenses
- Adjusted basis = Cost basis − Cost recovery deductions

So far, our examples have used one of Teton's asset sales to demonstrate how to compute gain or loss realized when property is sold. However, as we describe in Exhibit 10-2, Teton disposed of several assets during the year. We refer to this exhibit throughout the chapter as a reference point for discussing the tax issues associated with property dispositions.

### EXHIBIT 10-2   Teton's Asset Dispositions* Realized Gain (Loss) for Tax Purposes

| Asset | (1) Amount Realized | (2) Cost | (3) Accumulated Depreciation | (4) [(2) − (3)] Adjusted Basis | (5) [(1) − (4)] Gain (Loss) Realized |
|---|---|---|---|---|---|
| Machinery | $100,000 | $260,000 | $162,539 | $ 97,461 | $  2,539 |
| Office furniture | 12,000 | 10,000 | 7,000 | 3,000 | 9,000 |
| Delivery truck | 2,000 | 15,000 | 10,500 | 4,500 | (2,500) |
| Warehouse | 350,000 | 275,000 | 15,000 | 260,000 | 90,000 |
| Land | 175,000 | 75,000 | 0 | 75,000 | 100,000 |
| Total gain realized | | | | | $199,039 |

*These are the assets initially purchased by Teton in Example 9-1. Chapter 10 generally assumes that Teton has been in business for four years. For simplicity, this chapter assumes Teton did not previously elect any §179 immediate expensing or bonus depreciation.

### Recognized Gain or Loss on Disposition

As a general rule, taxpayers realizing gains and losses during a year must recognize the gains or losses. **Recognized gains or losses** are gains (losses) that increase (decrease) taxpayers' gross income.[3] Thus, taxpayers must report recognized gains and losses on their tax returns. Although taxpayers must immediately recognize the vast majority of realized gains and losses, in certain circumstances they may be allowed to defer recognizing gains to subsequent periods, or they may be allowed to permanently exclude the gains from taxable income. However, taxpayers may also be required to defer losses to later periods and, in more extreme cases, they may have their realized losses permanently disallowed. We address certain nonrecognition provisions later in the chapter.

### L02   CHARACTER OF GAIN OR LOSS

In order to determine how a recognized gain or loss affects a taxpayer's income tax liability, the taxpayer must determine the *character* or type of gain or loss recognized. Ultimately, every gain or loss is characterized as either ordinary or capital

---

[3]Recall under the return of capital principle we discussed in Chapter 5, when a taxpayer sells an asset, the taxpayer's adjusted basis is a return of capital and not a deductible expense.

(long-term or short-term). As described below, businesses may recognize §1231 gains or losses on property dispositions but even the §1231 gains or losses are eventually characterized as ordinary or capital (long-term). The character of a gain or loss is important because gains and losses of different characters are treated differently for tax purposes. For example, ordinary income (loss) is generally taxed at ordinary rates (fully deductible against ordinary income). However, capital gains may be taxed at preferential (lower) rates while deductions for capital losses are subject to certain restrictions. The character of the gains or losses taxpayers recognize when they sell assets depends on the character of the assets they are selling. The character of an asset depends on how the taxpayer used the asset and how long the taxpayer owned the asset (the holding period) before selling it.

In general terms, property may be used in a trade or business, treated as inventory or accounts receivable of a business, held for investment, or used for personal purposes. The holding period may be short-term (one year or less) or long-term (more than a year). Exhibit 10-3 provides a matrix of the character of assets (ordinary, capital, or §1231) depending on how taxpayers used the assets and the length of time they held the property before selling it.

> **THE KEY FACTS**
>
> Character of Assets
>
> ■ Ordinary assets
> · Assets created or used in a taxpayer's trade or business.
> · Business assets held for less than a year.
>
> ■ Capital assets
> · Assets held for investment purposes.
> · Assets held for personal-use purposes.
>
> ■ §1231 assets
> · Depreciable assets and land used in a trade or business held for *more* than one year.

**EXHIBIT 10-3**   Character of Assets Depending on Property Use and Holding Period

| | Property Use | | |
| --- | --- | --- | --- |
| **Holding Period** | **Trade or Business** | **Investment or Personal-Use Assets** | **Inventory and Accounts Receivable** |
| Short-term (One year or less) | Ordinary | Short-term Capital | Ordinary |
| Long-term (More than one year) | §1231† | Long-term Capital | Ordinary |

*Gains on the sale of personal-use assets are taxable capital gains but losses on the sale of personal-use assets are not deductible.

†As we describe later in the chapter, gain or loss is eventually characterized as ordinary or capital (long-term).

## Ordinary Assets

Ordinary assets are generally assets created or used in a taxpayer's trade or business. For example, inventory is an **ordinary asset** because it is held for sale to customers in the ordinary course of business. Accounts receivable are ordinary assets because receivables are generated from the sale of inventory or business services. Other assets used in a trade or business such as machinery and equipment are also considered to be ordinary assets if they have been used in a business for *one year or less*. For example, if Teton purchased a forklift for the warehouse but sold it six months later, the gain or loss would be ordinary. When taxpayers sell ordinary assets at a gain, they recognize an ordinary gain that is taxed at ordinary rates. When taxpayers sell ordinary assets at a loss, they deduct the loss against other ordinary income.

## Capital Assets

A **capital asset** is generally something held for investment (stocks and bonds), for the **production of income** (a for-profit activity that doesn't rise to the level of a trade or business), or for personal use (your car, house, or personal computer).[4] Whether an asset qualifies as a capital asset depends on the purpose for which the taxpayer uses the asset. Thus, the same asset may be considered a capital asset to one taxpayer and

---

[4]§1221 defines what is not a capital asset. Broadly speaking, a *capital asset* is any property *other than* property used in a trade or business (e.g., inventory, manufacturing equipment) or accounts (or notes) receivable acquired in a business from the sale of services or property.

an ordinary asset to another taxpayer. For example, a piece of land held as an investment because it is expected to appreciate in value over time is a capital asset to that taxpayer. However, the same piece of land held as inventory by a real estate developer would be an ordinary asset. Finally, the same piece of land would be a §1231 asset if the taxpayer held it for more than one year and used it in a trade or business (e.g., as a parking lot).

Individual taxpayers generally prefer capital gains to ordinary income because certain capital gains are taxed at lower rates and capital gains may offset capital losses that cannot be deducted against ordinary income. Individuals also prefer ordinary losses to capital losses because ordinary losses are deductible without limit while individuals may deduct only $3,000 of net capital losses against ordinary income each year. Corporate taxpayers may prefer capital gains to ordinary income because capital gains may offset capital losses that they would not be allowed to offset otherwise. Corporations are not allowed to offset any net capital losses, but they are allowed to carry capital losses back three years and forward five years. Exhibit 10-4 reviews the treatment of capital gains and losses for individuals and corporations.

**EXHIBIT 10-4** **Review of Capital Gains and Losses**

| Taxpayer Type | Preferential Rates | Loss Limitations |
|---|---|---|
| Individuals | • Most capital gains taxed at 15 percent (0 percent to the extent the gain would have been taxed at a 15 percent or lower rate if it were ordinary income).<br>• Unrecaptured §1250 gains taxed at a maximum rate of 25 percent.<br>• Gains on collectibles held for more than a year taxed at a maximum rate of 28 percent. | • Individuals may annually deduct up to $3,000 of net capital losses against ordinary income.<br>• Losses carried forward indefinitely but not carried back. |
| Corporations | • No preferential rates, taxed at ordinary rates. | • No offset against ordinary income.<br>• Net capital losses can generally be carried back three years and forward five years to offset gains in those years. |

## §1231 Assets

**Section 1231 assets** are depreciable assets and land used in a trade or business (including rental property) held by taxpayers for *more* than one year.[5] At a general level, when a taxpayer sells a §1231 asset, the taxpayer recognizes a §1231 gain or loss. As discussed above, however, ultimately §1231 gains or losses are characterized as ordinary or capital on a taxpayer's return. When taxpayers sell multiple §1231 assets during the year, they combine or "net" their §1231 gains and §1231 losses together. If the taxpayer recognizes a net §1231 gain, the net gain is treated as a long-term capital gain. If the taxpayer recognizes a net §1231 loss, the net loss is treated as an ordinary loss. Because net §1231 gains are treated as capital gains and §1231 losses are treated as ordinary losses, §1231 assets are tax favored relative to other types of assets.

As we discuss below, §1231 gains on individual depreciable assets may be recharacterized as ordinary income under the depreciation recapture rules. However,

---

[5]As noted above, property used in a trade or business and held for *one year or less* is ordinary income property.

because land is not depreciable, when taxpayers sell or otherwise dispose of land that qualifies as §1231 property, the gain or loss from the sale is always characterized as §1231 gain or loss. Thus, we refer to land as a pure §1231 asset.

---

**Example 10-4**

So that it can acquire another parcel of land to expand its manufacturing capabilities, Teton sold five acres of land that it has been using in its trade or business for $175,000. Teton purchased the land several years ago for $75,000. What is the amount and character of Teton's gain recognized on the land?

**Answer:** $100,000 §1231 gain, calculated as follows:

| Description | Amount | Explanation |
|---|---|---|
| (1) Amount realized | $175,000 | Exhibit 10-2. |
| (2) Original basis and current adjusted basis | 75,000 | Example 9-1. |
| Gain (Loss) realized and recognized | $100,000 | (1) − (2) §1231 gain. |

**What if:** Assume that Teton sold the land for $50,000. What would be the character of the ($25,000) loss it would recognize?

**Answer:** §1231 loss.

**What if:** Assume that the land was the only asset Teton sold during the year. How would the §1231 gain or §1231 loss on the sale ultimately be characterized on its tax return?

**Answer:** If Teton recognized a §1231 gain on the sale, it would be characterized as a long-term capital gain on its return. If Teton recognized a §1231 loss on the sale, it would be characterized as an ordinary loss.

---

## DEPRECIATION RECAPTURE

**L03**

Because all §1231 assets except land are subject to cost recovery, it is possible that a §1231 asset other than land could be sold at a gain in situations when the asset has not appreciated in value and even in situations when the asset has *declined* in value since it was placed in service. How does this happen? It happens because depreciation deductions relating to the asset could reduce the adjusted basis of the asset by more than the actual economic decline in the asset's value. In this situation, absent tax rules to the contrary, taxpayers selling these assets would recognize §1231 gains (likely treated as long-term capital gains) even though the gain was created by depreciation deductions (against ordinary income) that reduced the basis of the asset being sold.

While Congress intended for businesses to receive favorable treatment on economic gains from the *appreciation* of §1231 assets, it did not intend for this favorable treatment to apply to gains that were created artificially through depreciation deductions that offset ordinary income.[6] In response to this concern, Congress introduced the concept of **depreciation recapture.** Depreciation recapture potentially applies to gains (but not losses) on the sale of depreciable or amortizable business property. When depreciation recapture applies, it recharacterizes the gain on the sale of a §1231 asset (all or a portion of the gain) from §1231 gain into ordinary income. Note, however, that depreciation recapture does not affect §1231 losses.

The method for computing the amount of depreciation recapture depends on the type of §1231 asset the taxpayer is selling (personal property or real property). As

---

[6]Due to accelerated methods for determining depreciation expense, many assets are depreciated faster for tax purposes than their true economic decline in value.

presented in Exhibit 10-5, §1231 assets can be categorized as pure §1231 assets (land), §1245 assets (personal property), or §1250 assets (real property). Whether personal or real property is sold, it is important to understand that depreciation recapture changes only the *character* but not the *amount* of gain.

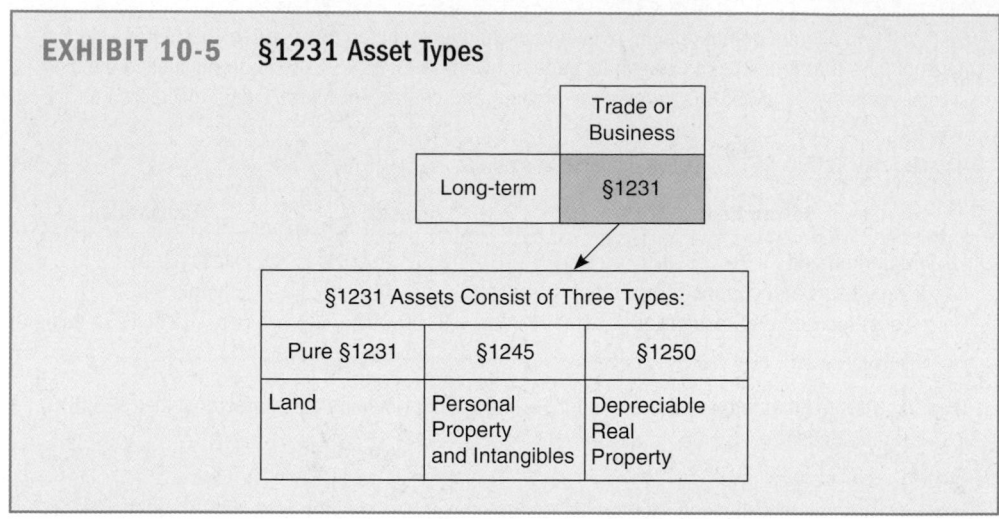

**EXHIBIT 10-5   §1231 Asset Types**

| Trade or Business | |
|---|---|
| Long-term | §1231 |

| §1231 Assets Consist of Three Types: | | |
|---|---|---|
| Pure §1231 | §1245 | §1250 |
| Land | Personal Property and Intangibles | Depreciable Real Property |

**THE KEY FACTS**

**§1245 Assets**

- Personal property and amortizable intangible assets are §1245 assets.
- The lesser of (1) gain recognized or (2) accumulated depreciation is recaptured (characterized) as ordinary income under §1245.
- Any remaining gain is §1231 gain.
- There is no depreciation recapture on assets sold at a loss.

## §1245 Property

Tangible personal property (machinery, equipment, and automobiles) and amortizable intangible property (patents, copyrights, and purchased goodwill) are a subset of §1231 property known as **§1245 property.**[7] The gain from the sale of §1245 property is characterized as ordinary income to the extent the gain was created by depreciation or amortization deductions. The amount of *ordinary income* (§1245 depreciation recapture) taxpayers recognize when they sell §1245 property is the lesser of (1) recognized gain on the sale *or* (2) total accumulated depreciation (or amortization) on the asset.[8] The remainder of any recognized gain is characterized as §1231 gain.[9] The sum of the ordinary income (due to depreciation recapture) and the §1231 gain on the sale equals the *total* gain recognized because depreciation recapture changes only the character of the gain, not the amount.

When taxpayers sell or dispose of §1245 property, they encounter one of the following three scenarios involving gain or loss:

*Scenario 1:* They recognize a gain created solely through depreciation deductions.

*Scenario 2:* They recognize a gain created through both depreciation deductions and actual asset appreciation.

*Scenario 3:* They recognize a loss.

---

[7]An exception in the law is that §1245 property also includes nonresidential real property placed in service between 1981 and 1986 (ACRS) for which the taxpayer elected accelerated depreciation.

[8]§1245 recapture is commonly referred to as "full" depreciation recapture because it may cause a taxpayer to recapture the entire accumulated depreciation amount as ordinary income. §1245 recapture applies notwithstanding any other provision of the IRS Code (depreciation recapture trumps all other tax rules).

[9]As a practical matter, taxpayers are unlikely to recognize any §1231 gain on the disposition of personal property because the real economic value of most tangible personal property does not increase over time as the property is used.

The following discussion considers each of these scenarios.

### Scenario 1: Gain Created Solely through Cost Recovery Deductions

Most §1231 assets that experience wear and tear or obsolescence generally do not appreciate in value. Thus, when a taxpayer sells these types of assets at a gain, the gain is usually created because the taxpayer's depreciation deductions associated with the asset reduced the asset's adjusted basis faster than the real decline in the asset's economic value. In other words, the entire gain is artificially generated through depreciation the taxpayer claims before disposing of the asset. That is, absent depreciation deductions, the taxpayer would recognize a loss on the sale of the asset. Therefore, the entire gain on the disposition is recaptured (or characterized) as ordinary income under §1245 (recall that without depreciation recapture the gain would be §1231 gain, which can generate long-term capital gain and could create a double benefit for the taxpayer: ordinary depreciation deductions and capital gain upon disposition).

---

**Example 10-5**

As indicated in Exhibit 10-2, Teton sold machinery for $100,000. What is the amount and character of the gain Teton recognizes on the sale?

**Answer:** $2,539 of ordinary income under the §1245 depreciation recapture rules and $0 of §1231 gain, computed as follows:

**Machinery Sale: Scenario 1**
**(Original scenario sales price = $100,000)**

| Description | Amount | Explanation |
|---|---|---|
| (1) Amount realized | $100,000 | Exhibit 10-2. |
| (2) Original basis | 260,000 | Exhibit 10-2. |
| (3) Accumulated depreciation | 162,539 | Exhibit 10-2. |
| (4) Adjusted basis | 97,461 | (2) − (3). |
| (5) Gain (loss) recognized | 2,539 | (1) − (4). |
| (6) Ordinary income (§1245 depreciation recapture) | $  2,539 | Lesser of (3) or (5). |
| §1231 gain | $     0 | (5) − (6). |

Note that in this situation, because Teton's entire gain is created through depreciation deductions, the entire gain is treated as ordinary income under §1245.

**What if:** What would be the amount and character of Teton's gain without the depreciation recapture rules?

**Answer:** $2,539 of §1231 gain. Note that the recapture rules change the character of the gain but not the amount of the gain.

---

### Scenario 2: Gain Due to Both Cost Recovery Deductions and Asset Appreciation

Assets subject to cost recovery deductions may actually *appreciate* in value over time. When these assets are sold, the recognized gain must be divided into ordinary gain from depreciation recapture and §1231 gain. The portion of the gain created through cost recovery deductions is **recaptured** as ordinary income. The remaining gain (the gain due to economic appreciation) is §1231 gain.

**Example 10-6**

**What if:** Let's assume the same facts as in the previous example and in Exhibit 10-2, except that Teton sells the machinery for $270,000. What is the amount and character of the gain Teton would recognize on this sale?

**Answer:** $162,539 of ordinary income under the §1245 depreciation recapture rules and $10,000 of §1231 gain due to the asset's economic appreciation, computed as follows:

**Machinery Sale: Scenario 2**
**(Assumed sales price = $270,000)**

| Description | Amount | Explanation |
|---|---|---|
| (1) Amount realized | $270,000 | |
| (2) Original basis | 260,000 | Exhibit 10-2. |
| (3) Accumulated depreciation | 162,539 | Exhibit 10-2. |
| (4) Adjusted basis | 97,461 | (2) − (3). |
| (5) Gain (loss) recognized | 172,539 | (1) − (4). |
| (6) Ordinary income (§1245 depreciation recapture) | $162,539 | Lesser of (3) or (5). |
| §1231 gain | $ 10,000 | (5) − (6). |

Note that taxpayers can quickly determine their §1231 gain (if any) when they sell §1245 property by subtracting the asset's *original* basis from the amount realized. In Scenario 2, presented above (Example 10-6), the §1231 gain is $10,000 ($270,000 amount realized less the $260,000 original basis).

**Scenario 3: Asset Sold at a Loss**    Many §1231 assets, such as computer equipment or automobiles, tend to decline in value faster than the corresponding depreciation deductions reduce the asset's adjusted basis. When taxpayers sell or dispose of these assets before the assets are fully depreciated, they recognize a loss on the disposition. Because the depreciation recapture rules don't apply to losses, taxpayers selling §1245 property at a loss recognize §1231 loss.

**Example 10-7**

**What if:** Let's assume the same facts as in Example 10-5 and in Exhibit 10-2, except that Teton sells the machinery for $90,000. What is the amount and character of the gain or loss Teton would recognize on this sale?

**Answer:** A $7,461 §1231 loss, computed as follows:

**Machinery Sale: Scenario 3**
**(Assumed sales price = $90,000)**

| Description | Amount | Explanation |
|---|---|---|
| (1) Amount realized | $ 90,000 | |
| (2) Original basis | 260,000 | Exhibit 10-2. |
| (3) Accumulated depreciation | 162,539 | Exhibit 10-2. |
| (4) Adjusted basis | 97,461 | (2) − (3). |
| (5) Gain (loss) recognized | (7,461) | (1) − (4). |
| (6) Ordinary income (§1245 depreciation recapture) | $ 0 | Lesser of (3) or (5) (limited to $0). |
| §1231 (loss) | ($7,461) | (5) − (6). |

Exhibit 10-6 graphically illustrates the §1245 depreciation recapture computations for the machinery sold in Scenarios 1, 2, and 3, presented in Examples 10-5, 10-6, and 10-7, respectively.[10]

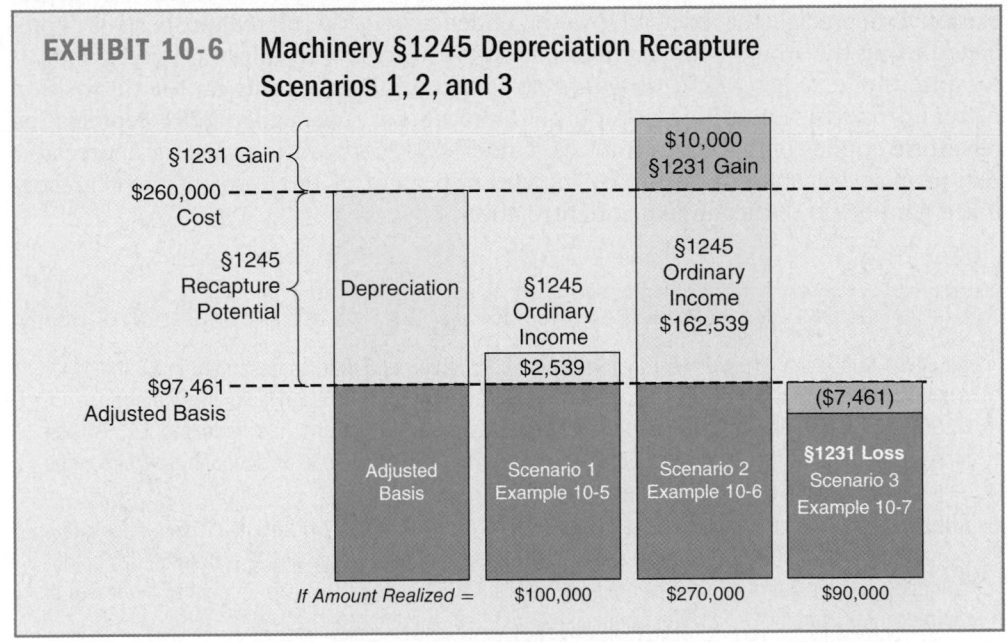

**EXHIBIT 10-6    Machinery §1245 Depreciation Recapture Scenarios 1, 2, and 3**

---

**Example 10-8**

In Example 10-5 (Scenario 1), we characterized the gain Teton recognized when it sold its machinery. For completeness, let's characterize the gain or loss Teton recognized on the other two §1245 assets it sold during the year (see Exhibit 10-2). Teton sold its office furniture for $12,000 and its delivery truck for $2,000. What is the amount and character of gain or loss Teton recognizes on the sales of the office furniture and delivery truck?

**Answer:** Office furniture: $7,000 ordinary income and $2,000 §1231 gain. Delivery truck: $2,500 §1231 loss.

The computations supporting the answers are as follows:

| Description | Office Furniture | Delivery Truck | Explanation |
|---|---|---|---|
| (1) Amount realized | $12,000 | $ 2,000 | Exhibit 10-2. |
| (2) Original basis | 10,000 | 15,000 | Exhibit 10-2. |
| (3) Accumulated depreciation | 7,000 | 10,500 | Exhibit 10-2. |
| (4) Adjusted basis | 3,000 | 4,500 | (2) − (3). |
| (5) Gain (loss) recognized | 9,000 | (2,500) | (1) − (4). |
| (6) Ordinary income (§1245 depreciation recapture) | $ 7,000 | $ 0 | Lesser of (3) or (5), limited to $0. |
| §1231 gain (loss) | $ 2,000 | ($2,500) | (5) − (6). |

## §1250 Depreciation Recapture for Real Property

Depreciable real property, such as an office building or a warehouse, sold at a gain is *not* subject to §1245 depreciation recapture. Rather, it is subject to a different type of recapture called §1250 depreciation recapture. Thus, depreciable real property is

[10]The authors thank PricewaterhouseCoopers for allowing us to use these figures.

frequently referred to as **§1250 property.** Under §1250, when depreciable real property is sold at a gain, the amount of gain recaptured as ordinary income is limited to the excess of *accelerated* depreciation deductions on the property over the amount that would have been deducted if the taxpayer had used the straight-line method of depreciation to depreciate the asset.[11] However, under current law, all real property is depreciated using the straight-line method so the §1250 recapture rules no longer apply.[12] Despite the fact that *§1250 recapture* no longer applies to gains on the disposition of real property, a modified version of the recapture rules called **§291 depreciation recapture** applies only to corporations. Under §291, corporations selling depreciable real property recapture as ordinary income 20 percent of the lesser of the (1) recognized gain or (2) the accumulated depreciation.

| Example 10-9 | |
|---|---|

**What if:**  Suppose that Teton was organized as a corporation and that, as described in Exhibit 10-2, it sold its existing warehouse. Let's assume the same facts: that Teton sold the warehouse for $350,000, that it initially purchased the warehouse for $275,000, and has deducted $15,000 of straight-line depreciation deductions as of the date of the sale. What is Teton's recognized gain on the sale and what is the character of its gain on the sale?

**Answer:**  $90,000 gain recognized; $3,000 ordinary income and $87,000 §1231 gain. Teton's recognized gain is $90,000 ($350,000 − $260,000 adjusted basis). Under §291, if Teton is a corporation, it must recapture $3,000 as ordinary income (20% × $15,000) [20 percent of the lesser of (1) recognized gain of $90,000 or (2) accumulated depreciation of $15,000].

**LO4**

## OTHER PROVISIONS AFFECTING THE RATE AT WHICH GAINS ARE TAXED

Other provisions, other than depreciation recapture, may affect the rate at which taxpayer gains are taxed. The first potentially applies when individuals sell §1250 property at a gain and the second potentially applies when taxpayers sell property to related parties at a gain.

### Unrecaptured §1250 Gain for Individuals

When individual taxpayers sell §1250 property at a gain, they are not required to recapture any of the gain as ordinary income under the depreciation recapture rules. Consequently, a gain resulting from the disposition of §1250 property is a §1231 gain and is netted with other §1231 gains and losses to determine whether the taxpayer has a net §1231 gain for the year or a net §1231 loss for the year.

If, after the §1231 netting process (described below), the gain on the sale of the §1250 property is ultimately determined to be a long-term capital gain, the taxpayer must determine the rate at which the gain will be taxed. Tax policy makers determined that the portion of the gain caused by depreciation deductions reducing the basis (called **unrecaptured §1250 gain**) should be taxed at a maximum rate of 25 percent (taxed at the ordinary rate if the ordinary rate is lower than 25 percent) and not the 15 percent rate generally applicable to other types of long-term capital gains.

> **THE KEY FACTS**
>
> Unrecaptured §1250 Gains
>
> ■ Depreciable real property sold at a gain is §1250 property, but is no longer subject to §1250 recapture.
>
> ■ The gain that would be §1245 recapture if the asset were §1245 property is called *unrecaptured §1250 gain.*
>
> ■ Unrecaptured §1250 gain is §1231 gain that, if ultimately characterized as a long-term capital gain, is taxed at a maximum rate of 25 percent.

[11]§1250 recapture is commonly referred to as *partial depreciation recapture.*

[12]Accelerated depreciation was allowed for real property placed in service before 1987. Such property had a maximum recovery period of 19 years, which means that as of 2005 all of this property is now fully depreciated under both the accelerated and straight-line depreciation methods—so §1250 recapture does not apply.

Consequently, when an individual sells §1250 property at a gain, the amount of the gain taxed at a maximum rate of 25 percent is the *lesser* of the (1) recognized gain or (2) the accumulated depreciation on the asset.[13] The remainder of the gain is taxed at a maximum rate of 15 percent.

Teton bought its warehouse for $275,000, depreciated it $15,000, and sold it for $350,000. What is the amount and character of the gain Teton (and thus Steve) reports on the sale (recall that income of sole proprietorships is taxed directly to the owner of the business)?

**Answer:** $90,000 of §1231 gain, which includes $15,000 of unrecaptured §1250 gain, computed as follows:

| Description | Amount | Explanation |
|---|---|---|
| (1) Amount realized | $350,000 | |
| (2) Original basis | 275,000 | |
| (3) Accumulated depreciation | 15,000 | |
| (4) Adjusted basis | 260,000 | (2) − (3). |
| (5) Gain (Loss) recognized | 90,000 | (1) − (4). |
| (6) Unrecaptured §1250 gain | 15,000 | Lesser of (3) or (5). |
| (7) Remaining §1231 gain | 75,000 | (5) − (6). |
| Total §1231 gain | $ 90,000 | (6) + (7). |

**What if:** Suppose Steve's marginal ordinary tax rate is 35 percent. What amount of tax will he pay on the gain (assuming no other asset dispositions)?

**Answer:** $15,000, computed as follows:

| Description | (1) Gain | (2) Rate | (1) × (2) Tax | Explanation |
|---|---|---|---|---|
| Long-term capital gain (unrecaptured §1250 gain portion) | $15,000 | 25% | $ 3,750 | This is the gain due to depreciation deductions. |
| Long-term capital gain (15 percent portion) | 75,000 | 15% | 11,250 | |
| Totals | $90,000 | | $15,000 | |

Because Steve did not sell any other §1231 assets during the year, the entire §1231 gain is treated as a long-term capital gain that is split into a portion taxed at 25 percent and a portion taxed at 15 percent.

## Characterizing Gains on the Sale of Depreciable Property to Related Parties

Under §1239, when a taxpayer sells property to a *related party* and the property is depreciable property to the *buyer,* the entire gain on the sale is characterized as ordinary income to the *seller*.[14] In these situations, the tax laws essentially treat the related parties (the buyer and the seller) as the same person. Because the buyer will be offsetting ordinary income with future depreciation deductions associated with the property, the tax laws require the seller to currently recognize ordinary income.

[13]The amount taxed at a maximum rate of 25 percent cannot exceed the amount of the taxpayer's net §1231 gain.

[14]§707(b)(2) contains a similar provision for partnerships.

**THE KEY FACTS**

Related-Party Transactions

■ All gain recognized from selling property that is a depreciable asset to a related-party buyer is ordinary income (regardless of the character of the asset to the seller).

■ Related parties include an individual and
· Siblings, spouses, ancestors, lineal descendants, and
· Corporations in which the individual owns more than 50 percent of the stock.
· See §267(b) for others.

Without this provision, related parties could create tax savings by currently generating capital or §1231 gains through selling appreciated assets to related parties and receiving future ordinary deductions through depreciation expense on the basis of the property (stepped up to fair market value through the sale) acquired in the transaction.

The §1239 recapture provision is different from depreciation recapture in the sense that the seller is required to recognize ordinary income *for depreciation deductions the buyer will receive in the future,* while depreciation recapture requires taxpayers to recognize ordinary income *for depreciation deductions they have received in the past.* In both cases, however, the tax laws are designed to provide symmetry between the character of deductions an asset generates and the character of income the asset generates when it is sold. When depreciation recapture and the §1239 recapture provision apply to the same gain, the depreciation recapture rule applies first.

For purposes of §1239, §267 provides the definition of related parties. The definition includes family relationships including siblings, spouses, ancestors, and lineal descendants. It also includes an individual and a corporation if the individual owns more than 50 percent of the stock of the corporation, a partnership and any of its partners, and an S corporation and any of its shareholders.[15]

---

**Example 10-11**

**What if:** Suppose that Teton is organized as a corporation and Steve is the sole shareholder. Steve sells equipment that he was using for personal purposes to Teton for $90,000 (he originally purchased the equipment for $80,000). The equipment was a capital asset to Steve because he had been using it for personal purposes (he did not depreciate it). What is the amount and character of the gain Steve would recognize on the sale?

**Answer:** $10,000 of ordinary income (amount realized $90,000 − $80,000 adjusted basis). Even though Steve is selling what is a capital asset to him, because it is a depreciable asset to Teton and because Steve and Teton are considered to be related parties, Steve is required to characterize the entire amount of gain as ordinary under §1239. Without the §1239 provision, Steve would have recognized a capital gain.

---

**L05**

## CALCULATING NET §1231 GAINS OR LOSSES

Once taxpayers determine the amount and character of gain or loss they recognize on *each* §1231 asset they sell during the year, they still have work to do to determine whether the gains or losses will be treated as ordinary or capital. After recharacterizing §1231 gain as ordinary income under the §1245 and §291 (if applicable) depreciation recapture rules and the §1239 related-party rules, the remaining §1231 gains and losses are netted together. If the gains exceed the losses, the net gain becomes a long-term capital gain (a portion of which may be taxed at maximum rate of 25 percent). If the losses exceed the gains, the net loss is treated as an ordinary loss.

A taxpayer could gain significant tax benefits by discovering a way to have all §1231 gains treated as long-term capital gains and all §1231 losses treated as ordinary losses. The *annual* netting process makes this task impossible for a *particular* year. However, a taxpayer who owns multiple §1231 assets could sell the §1231 loss assets at the end of year 1 and the §1231 gain assets at the beginning of year 2. The taxpayer could benefit from this strategy in three ways: (1) accelerating losses into

---

[15]See §267(b) for more related-party relationships. This section also details the constructive ownership rules where the taxpayer is deemed to own what another related taxpayer owns (for example a married taxpayer is considered to own what her spouse owns).

year 1, (2) deferring gains until year 2, and (3) characterizing the gains and losses due to the §1231 netting process. The **§1231 look-back rule** prevents this strategy.

### §1231 Look-Back Rule

The §1231 look-back rule is a *nondepreciation* recapture rule that applies in situations like the one we just described to turn what would otherwise be §1231 gain into ordinary income. That is, the rule affects the character but not the amount of gains on which a taxpayer is taxed. In general terms, the §1231 look-back rule is designed to require taxpayers who recognize net §1231 gains in the current year to recapture (recharacterize) those gains as ordinary gains to the extent they recognized §1231 losses that were treated as ordinary losses in prior years. Without the look-back rule, taxpayers could carefully time the year in which the §1231 assets are sold to maximize the tax benefits.

In specific terms, the §1231 look-back rule indicates that anytime a taxpayer recognizes a net §1231 gain for a year, the taxpayer must "look-back" to the *five-year* period preceding the current tax year to determine if, during that period, the taxpayer recognized any **unrecaptured §1231 losses** (losses that were deducted as ordinary losses that have not caused subsequent §1231 gains to be recharacterized as ordinary income). The taxpayer starts the process by looking back to the year five years prior to the beginning of the current year. If the taxpayer recognized a net §1231 loss in that period, and had not previously recaptured the loss (by causing a subsequent §1231 gain to be recharacterized as ordinary) in a subsequent year (but prior to the current year), the taxpayer must recharacterize the *current year* net §1231 gain as ordinary income to the extent of that prior year unrecaptured §1231 loss. The prior year loss is then "recaptured," to the extent it caused the current year gain to be treated as ordinary income. If the current year net §1231 gain exceeds the unrecaptured §1231 loss from the year five-years prior, the taxpayer repeats the process for the year four-years prior, and then three-years prior, and so on. It is important to note that a prior year's unrecaptured losses are not netted against the current year's gains (they don't offset the current year gains); rather, they cause the taxpayer to recharacterize a net §1231 gain or a portion of that gain (that would otherwise be characterized as a long-term capital gain) as ordinary income.[16]

> **THE KEY FACTS**
>
> Netting and
> Look-Back Rule
>
> ▌ §1231 gains and losses from individual asset dispositions are annually netted together.
>
> ▌ Net §1231 gains may be recharacterized as ordinary income under the §1231 look-back rule.

---

## Example 10-12

**What if:** Suppose that Teton began business in year 1 and that it recognized a $7,000 net §1231 loss in year 1. Assume that the current year is year 6 and that Teton reports a *net* §1231 gain of $25,000 for the year. Teton did not recognize any §1231 gains or losses in years 2–5. For year 6, what would be the ultimate character of the $25,000 net §1231 gain?

**Answer:** $7,000 ordinary income and $18,000 long-term capital gain. Because it recognized a net §1231 loss in year 1, it must recharacterize $7,000 of its net §1231 gain in year 6 as ordinary income. The remaining $18,000 §1231 gain is taxed as long-term capital gain.

**What if:** Assume the same facts as above, except that Teton also recognized a $2,000 net §1231 loss in year 5. For year 6, what would be the ultimate character of the $25,000 net §1231 gain?

**Answer:** $9,000 ordinary income and $16,000 long-term capital gain. Note that the overall gain is still $25,000, but to the extent of the $7,000 loss in year 1 and the $2,000 loss in year 5, the §1231 gain is recharacterized as ordinary income under the §1231 look-back rule.

---

[16]If the taxpayer's net §1231 gains include unrecaptured §1250 gains and other 15 percent long-term capital gains, the unrecaptured §1231 losses first recharacterize the unrecaptured §1250 gains as ordinary income.

As we've mentioned several times, ultimately, all of a taxpayer's §1231 gains and losses must be characterized as ordinary or capital for purposes of determining a taxpayer's tax liability. Exhibit 10-7 summarizes the process of characterizing §1231 gains and losses as ordinary or capital.

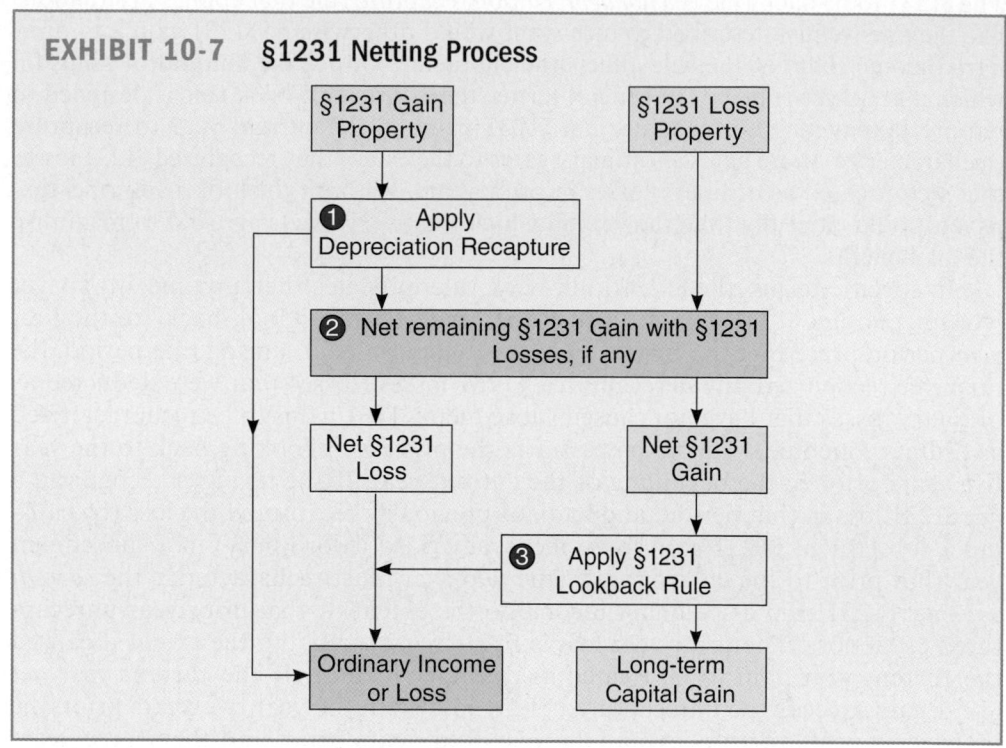

**EXHIBIT 10-7** **§1231 Netting Process**

The following provides details on Steps 1–3 from Exhibit 10-7:

**Step 1:** Apply the *depreciation* recapture rules (and the §1239 recapture rules) to §1231 assets sold at a gain (any recaptured amounts become ordinary).

**Step 2:** Net the remaining §1231 gains with the §1231 losses. If the netting process yields a §1231 loss, the net §1231 loss becomes an ordinary loss.

**Step 3:** If the netting process produces a net §1231 gain, the taxpayer applies the §1231 look-back rule to determine if any of the remaining §1231 gain should be recharacterized as ordinary gain. Any gain remaining after applying the look-back rule is treated as long-term capital gain (including unrecaptured §1250 gain). This gain is included in the capital gains netting process, which is discussed in Chapter 11.

## GAIN OR LOSS SUMMARY

As indicated in Exhibit 10-2, Teton sold several assets during the year. Exhibit 10-8 summarizes the character of the gain or loss Teton (and thus Steve) recognized on each asset sale.

So, how would this information be reported on Steve's tax return? Exhibit 10-9 (see page 10-18) provides Steve's Form 4797, which summarizes Teton's property transactions and divides the gain and losses between the ordinary gain of $19,539 and the §1231 gain of $179,500. Because the net §1231 gain is treated as a long-term capital gain, it flows to Steve's Schedule D (the form for reporting capital gains and losses). Steve's Schedule D is presented in Exhibit 10-10 (see page 10-20).

**EXHIBIT 10-8    Summary of Teton Gains and Losses on Property Dispositions**

| Asset | (1) §1245 Ordinary Gain | (2) Total Ordinary Gain | (3) §1231 Gain (Loss) | (2) + (3) Total Gain |
|---|---|---|---|---|
| Machinery | $2,539 | $ 2,539 | $    0 | $  2,539 |
| Office furniture | 7,000 | 7,000 | 2,000 | 9,000 |
| Delivery truck | 0 | 0 | (2,500) | (2,500) |
| Warehouse | 0 | 0 | 90,000* | 90,000 |
| Land | 0 | 0 | 100,000 | 100,000 |
| §1231 look-back | | 10,000 | (10,000)† | 0 |
| Totals | $9,539 | $19,539 | $179,500* | $199,039 |

*Because the warehouse is §1231 property, the $90,000 gain is included in the §1231 gain (loss) column. Further, $15,000 of the $90,000 gain is considered unrecaptured §1250 gain (see Example 10-10).
†This exhibit assumes that Teton had $10,000 of net §1231 losses in the prior five years.

# NONRECOGNITION TRANSACTIONS

LO6

Taxpayers realizing gains and losses when they sell or exchange property must immediately recognize the gain for tax purposes unless a specific provision in the tax code says otherwise. Under certain tax provisions, taxpayers defer or delay recognizing a gain or loss until a subsequent period. We first explore tax provisions that allow taxpayers to defer recognizing realized gains. Congress allows taxpayers to defer recognizing gains in certain types of exchanges because the exchange itself does not provide the taxpayers with the wherewithal (cash) to pay taxes on the realized gain if the taxpayers were required to immediately recognize the gain. In particular, we discuss common **nonrecognition transactions** such as like-kind exchanges, involuntary conversions, installment sales, and other business-related transactions such as business formations and reorganizations.

## Like-Kind Exchanges

Taxpayers involved in a business may have valid reasons to trade business assets to others for similar business assets. For example, to increase productivity a taxpayer may want to trade machinery used in the business for the latest model. As we discussed earlier in this chapter, taxpayers exchanging property *realize* gains (or losses) on exchanges just as taxpayers do by selling property for cash. However, taxpayers exchanging property for property are in a different situation than taxpayers selling the same property for cash. Taxpayers exchanging one piece of business property for another haven't changed their relative economic position in the sense that both before and after the exchange they hold an asset for use in their business. Further, exchanges of property do not generate the wherewithal (cash) for the taxpayers to pay taxes on the gain they realize on the exchanges. While taxpayers selling property for cash must immediately recognize gain on the sale, taxpayers exchanging property for assets other than cash must defer recognizing gain (or loss) realized on the exchange if they meet certain requirements. This type of deferred gain (or loss) transaction is commonly referred to as a **like-kind exchange** or §1031 exchange.[17]

---

[17]Like-kind exchanges are defined in §1031 of the Internal Revenue Code.

**EXHIBIT 10-9** Teton's (On Steve's return) Form 4797

| | | |
|---|---|---|
| Form **4797** | **Sales of Business Property** | OMB No. 1545-0184 |

Form **4797**

Department of the Treasury
Internal Revenue Service (99)

**Sales of Business Property**
**(Also Involuntary Conversions and Recapture Amounts**
**Under Sections 179 and 280F(b)(2))**
► Attach to your tax return. ► See separate instructions.

20**09**
Attachment
Sequence No. **27**

Name(s) shown on return

**Steve Dallimore (Teton Mountaineering Technologies, LLC)**

Identifying number

**1** Enter the gross proceeds from sales or exchanges reported to you for 2009 on Form(s) 1099-B or 1099-S (or substitute statement) that you are including on line 2, 10, or 20 (see instructions) . . . . . . . . . . | **1** |

**Part I** **Sales or Exchanges of Property Used in a Trade or Business and Involuntary Conversions From Other Than Casualty or Theft—Most Property Held More Than 1 Year** (see instructions)

| 2 | **(a)** Description of property | **(b)** Date acquired (mo., day, yr.) | **(c)** Date sold (mo., day, yr.) | **(d)** Gross sales price | **(e)** Depreciation allowed or allowable since acquisition | **(f)** Cost or other basis, plus improvements and expense of sale | **(g)** Gain or (loss) Subtract (f) from the sum of (d) and (e) |
|---|---|---|---|---|---|---|---|
| | Delivery Truck | Yr 0 | Yr 4 | 2,000 | 10,500 | 15,000 | (2,500) |
| | Land | Yr 0 | Yr 4 | 175,000 | 0 | 75,000 | 100,000 |
| | | | | | | | |
| | | | | | | | |

| | | | |
|---|---|---|---|
| **3** | Gain, if any, from Form 4684, line 43 . . . . . . . . . . . . . . . . . . . . . . | **3** | |
| **4** | Section 1231 gain from installment sales from Form 6252, line 26 or 37 . . . . . . . . . . . | **4** | |
| **5** | Section 1231 gain or (loss) from like-kind exchanges from Form 8824 . . . . . . . . . . . | **5** | |
| **6** | Gain, if any, from line 32, from other than casualty or theft. . . . . . . . . . . . . . | **6** | 92,000 |
| **7** | Combine lines 2 through 6. Enter the gain or (loss) here and on the appropriate line as follows: . . . . | **7** | 189,500 |

**Partnerships (except electing large partnerships) and S corporations.** Report the gain or (loss) following the instructions for Form 1065, Schedule K, line 10, or Form 1120S, Schedule K, line 9. Skip lines 8, 9, 11, and 12 below.

**Individuals, partners, S corporation shareholders, and all others.** If line 7 is zero or a loss, enter the amount from line 7 on line 11 below and skip lines 8 and 9. If line 7 is a gain and you did not have any prior year section 1231 losses, or they were recaptured in an earlier year, enter the gain from line 7 as a long-term capital gain on the Schedule D filed with your return and skip lines 8, 9, 11, and 12 below.

| | | | |
|---|---|---|---|
| **8** | Nonrecaptured net section 1231 losses from prior years (see instructions) . . . . . . . . . . | **8** | 10,000 |
| **9** | Subtract line 8 from line 7. If zero or less, enter -0-. If line 9 is zero, enter the gain from line 7 on line 12 below. If line 9 is more than zero, enter the amount from line 8 on line 12 below and enter the gain from line 9 as a long-term capital gain on the Schedule D filed with your return (see instructions) . . . . . . . . . . . . | **9** | 179,500 |

**Part II** **Ordinary Gains and Losses** (see instructions)

| | | | |
|---|---|---|---|
| **10** | Ordinary gains and losses not included on lines 11 through 16 (include property held 1 year or less): | | |
| | | | |
| | | | |
| | | | |
| | | | |

| | | | |
|---|---|---|---|
| **11** | Loss, if any, from line 7 . . . . . . . . . . . . . . . . . . . . . . . . . | **11** | ( ) |
| **12** | Gain, if any, from line 7 or amount from line 8, if applicable . . . . . . . . . . . . . | **12** | 10,000 |
| **13** | Gain, if any, from line 31 . . . . . . . . . . . . . . . . . . . . . . . . . | **13** | 9,539 |
| **14** | Net gain or (loss) from Form 4684, lines 35 and 42a . . . . . . . . . . . . . . . . | **14** | |
| **15** | Ordinary gain from installment sales from Form 6252, line 25 or 36 . . . . . . . . . . . | **15** | |
| **16** | Ordinary gain or (loss) from like-kind exchanges from Form 8824. . . . . . . . . . . . | **16** | |
| **17** | Combine lines 10 through 16 . . . . . . . . . . . . . . . . . . . . . . . . | **17** | 19,539 |
| **18** | For all except individual returns, enter the amount from line 17 on the appropriate line of your return and skip lines a and b below. For individual returns, complete lines a and b below: | | |
| **a** | If the loss on line 11 includes a loss from Form 4684, line 39, column (b)(ii), enter that part of the loss here. Enter the part of the loss from income-producing property on Schedule A (Form 1040), line 28, and the part of the loss from property used as an employee on Schedule A (Form 1040), line 23. Identify as from "Form 4797, line 18a." See instructions . . | **18a** | |
| **b** | Redetermine the gain or (loss) on line 17 excluding the loss, if any, on line 18a. Enter here and on Form 1040, line 14 | **18b** | 19,539 |

**For Paperwork Reduction Act Notice, see separate instructions.**        Cat. No. 13086I        Form **4797** (2009)

**EXHIBIT 10-9    Teton's (On Steve's return) Form 4797 (*continued*)**

Form 4797 (2009)                                                                                                            Page **2**

| Part III | Gain From Disposition of Property Under Sections 1245, 1250, 1252, 1254, and 1255 (see instructions) |
|---|---|

| 19 | (a) Description of section 1245, 1250, 1252, 1254, or 1255 property: | (b) Date acquired (mo., day, yr.) | (c) Date sold (mo., day, yr.) |
|---|---|---|---|
| A | Machinery | Yr 0 | 11/1/Yr 4 |
| B | Office Furniture | Yr 0 | Yr 4 |
| C | Warehouse | Yr 0 | Yr 4 |
| D | | | |

| These columns relate to the properties on lines 19A through 19D. ► | | Property A | Property B | Property C | Property D |
|---|---|---|---|---|---|
| 20 | Gross sales price (**Note:** *See line 1 before completing.*) . | **20** | 100,000 | 12,000 | 350,000 | |
| 21 | Cost or other basis plus expense of sale . . . . . | **21** | 260,000 | 10,000 | 275,000 | |
| 22 | Depreciation (or depletion) allowed or allowable. . . | **22** | 162,539 | 7,000 | 15,000 | |
| 23 | Adjusted basis. Subtract line 22 from line 21. . . . | **23** | 97,461 | 3,000 | 260,000 | |
| 24 | Total gain. Subtract line 23 from line 20 . . . . . | **24** | 2,539 | 9,000 | 90,000 | |
| 25 | **If section 1245 property:** | | | | | |
| a | Depreciation allowed or allowable from line 22 . . . | **25a** | 162,539 | 7,000 | | |
| b | Enter the **smaller** of line 24 or 25a . . . . . . | **25b** | 2,539 | 7,000 | | |
| 26 | **If section 1250 property:** If straight line depreciation was used, enter -0- on line 26g, except for a corporation subject to section 291. | | | | | |
| a | Additional depreciation after 1975 (see instructions) . | **26a** | | | | |
| b | Applicable percentage multiplied by the **smaller** of line 24 or line 26a (see instructions) . . . . . . | **26b** | | | | |
| c | Subtract line 26a from line 24. If residential rental property **or** line 24 is not more than line 26a, skip lines 26d and 26e | **26c** | | | | |
| d | Additional depreciation after 1969 and before 1976. . | **26d** | | | | |
| e | Enter the **smaller** of line 26c or 26d . . . . . . | **26e** | | | | |
| f | Section 291 amount (corporations only) . . . . . | **26f** | | | | |
| g | Add lines 26b, 26e, and 26f. . . . . . . . . . | **26g** | | | | |
| 27 | **If section 1252 property:** Skip this section if you did not dispose of farmland or if this form is being completed for a partnership (other than an electing large partnership). | | | | | |
| a | Soil, water, and land clearing expenses . . . . . | **27a** | | | | |
| b | Line 27a multiplied by applicable percentage (see instructions) | **27b** | | | | |
| c | Enter the **smaller** of line 24 or 27b . . . . . . | **27c** | | | | |
| 28 | **If section 1254 property:** | | | | | |
| a | Intangible drilling and development costs, expenditures for development of mines and other natural deposits, mining exploration costs, and depletion (see instructions) . . . . . . . . . . . . . . | **28a** | | | | |
| b | Enter the **smaller** of line 24 or 28a . . . . . . | **28b** | | | | |
| 29 | **If section 1255 property:** | | | | | |
| a | Applicable percentage of payments excluded from income under section 126 (see instructions) . . . . | **29a** | | | | |
| b | Enter the **smaller** of line 24 or 29a (see instructions) . | **29b** | | | | |

**Summary of Part III Gains.** Complete property columns A through D through line 29b before going to line 30.

| 30 | Total gains for all properties. Add property columns A through D, line 24 . . . . . . . . . . . . . | **30** | 101,539 |
|---|---|---|---|
| 31 | Add property columns A through D, lines 25b, 26g, 27c, 28b, and 29b. Enter here and on line 13 . . . . . . . | **31** | 9,539 |
| 32 | Subtract line 31 from line 30. Enter the portion from casualty or theft on Form 4684, line 37. Enter the portion from other than casualty or theft on Form 4797, line 6 . . . . . . . . . . . . . . . . . . . . . . | **32** | 92,000 |

| Part IV | Recapture Amounts Under Sections 179 and 280F(b)(2) When Business Use Drops to 50% or Less (see instructions) |
|---|---|

| | | | (a) Section 179 | (b) Section 280F(b)(2) |
|---|---|---|---|---|
| 33 | Section 179 expense deduction or depreciation allowable in prior years. . . . . . . . . | **33** | | |
| 34 | Recomputed depreciation (see instructions) . . . . . . . . . . . . . . . . . | **34** | | |
| 35 | Recapture amount. Subtract line 34 from line 33. See the instructions for where to report . . | **35** | | |

Form **4797** (2009)

**EXHIBIT 10-10    Steve's Schedule D (Assumes Steve had no other capital gains and losses other than those incurred by Teton)**

| SCHEDULE D (Form 1040) | Capital Gains and Losses | OMB No. 1545-0074 |
|---|---|---|
| Department of the Treasury Internal Revenue Service (99) | ► Attach to Form 1040 or Form 1040NR.  ► See Instructions for Schedule D (Form 1040).  ► Use Schedule D-1 to list additional transactions for lines 1 and 8. | 2009  Attachment Sequence No. 12 |

Name(s) shown on return: **Steve Dallimore**

Your social security number

### Part I    Short-Term Capital Gains and Losses—Assets Held One Year or Less

| (a) Description of property (Example: 100 sh. XYZ Co.) | (b) Date acquired (Mo., day, yr.) | (c) Date sold (Mo., day, yr.) | (d) Sales price (see page D-7 of the instructions) | (e) Cost or other basis (see page D-7 of the instructions) | (f) Gain or (loss) Subtract (e) from (d) |
|---|---|---|---|---|---|
| 1 | | | | | |
| | | | | | |
| | | | | | |
| | | | | | |
| | | | | | |

2  Enter your short-term totals, if any, from Schedule D-1, line 2 . . . . . . . . . . . . . . . . .   **2**

3  **Total short-term sales price amounts.** Add lines 1 and 2 in column (d) . . . . . . . . . . . . .   **3**

4  Short-term gain from Form 6252 and short-term gain or (loss) from Forms 4684, 6781, and 8824   **4**

5  Net short-term gain or (loss) from partnerships, S corporations, estates, and trusts from Schedule(s) K-1 . . . . . . . . . . . . . . . . . . . . . .   **5**

6  Short-term capital loss carryover. Enter the amount, if any, from line 10 of your **Capital Loss Carryover Worksheet** on page D-7 of the instructions . . . . . . . . . . . . . .   **6** (                    )

7  **Net short-term capital gain or (loss).** Combine lines 1 through 6 in column (f) . . . . . .   **7**

### Part II    Long-Term Capital Gains and Losses—Assets Held More Than One Year

| (a) Description of property (Example: 100 sh. XYZ Co.) | (b) Date acquired (Mo., day, yr.) | (c) Date sold (Mo., day, yr.) | (d) Sales price (see page D-7 of the instructions) | (e) Cost or other basis (see page D-7 of the instructions) | (f) Gain or (loss) Subtract (e) from (d) |
|---|---|---|---|---|---|
| 8 | | | | | |
| | | | | | |
| | | | | | |
| | | | | | |
| | | | | | |

9  Enter your long-term totals, if any, from Schedule D-1, line 9 . . . . . . . . . . . . . . . . .   **9**

10  **Total long-term sales price amounts.** Add lines 8 and 9 in column (d) . . . . . . . . . . . . .   **10**

11  Gain from Form 4797, Part I; long-term gain from Forms 2439 and 6252; and long-term gain or (loss) from Forms 4684, 6781, and 8824 . . . . . . . .   **11**    179,500

12  Net long-term gain or (loss) from partnerships, S corporations, estates, and trusts from Schedule(s) K-1 . . . . . . . . . . . . . . . . . . . . . .   **12**

13  Capital gain distributions. See page D-2 of the instructions . . . . . . . . . . . .   **13**

14  Long-term capital loss carryover. Enter the amount, if any, from line 15 of your **Capital Loss Carryover Worksheet** on page D-7 of the instructions . . . . . . . . . . . .   **14** (                    )

15  **Net long-term capital gain or (loss).** Combine lines 8 through 14 in column (f). Then go to Part III on the back . . . . . . . . . . . . . . . . . .   **15**    179,500

For Paperwork Reduction Act Notice, see Form 1040 or Form 1040NR instructions.     Cat. No. 11338H     Schedule D (Form 1040) 2009

Like-kind exchange treatment can provide taxpayers with significant tax advantages by allowing them to defer gain (and current taxes payable) that would otherwise be recognized immediately.[18] For an exchange to qualify as a like-kind exchange for tax purposes, the transaction must meet the following three criteria:

1. The property is exchanged "solely for like-kind" property.
2. Both the property given up and the property received in the exchange by the taxpayer are either "used in a trade or business" or are "held for investment," by the taxpayer.
3. The "exchange" must meet certain time restrictions.

Below, we discuss each of these requirements in detail.

### Definition of Like-Kind Property

The definition of like-kind property depends on whether the property exchanged is real property or tangible personal property. Generally, the definition of like-kind *real* property is much less restrictive than it is for like-kind *personal* property.

**Real Property**   All real property is considered to be "like-kind" with any other type of real property as long as the real property is used in a trade or business or held for investment. For example, from Teton's perspective, its warehouse on 10 acres would be considered to be like-kind with a nearby condominium complex, a 20-acre parcel of raw land for sale across town, or even a Manhattan skyscraper.

**Personal Property**   Determining what qualifies as like-kind property for tangible personal property is a little more involved. The Treasury regulations explain that tangible personal property qualifies as "like-kind" if the property transferred and the property received in the exchange is in the same general asset class in Rev. Proc. 87-56 (this is the concept we use in the previous chapter to determine the recovery period for MACRS depreciation).[19] In simpler terms, for personal property to qualify as like-kind property the property given in the exchange and the property received in the exchange must have the same general use to the taxpayer. For example, if Teton were to trade some machinery used in its manufacturing operations for some new machinery to be used in its manufacturing process, the transaction would qualify as a like-kind exchange. However, if Teton were to trade some machinery used in its manufacturing operations for a new delivery truck, the exchange would not qualify as a like-kind exchange.

**Property Ineligible for Like-Kind Treatment**   Certain types of property are, by definition, excluded from the definition of like-kind property and thus, are not eligible for like-kind treatment.[20] This property includes inventory held for resale (including land held by a developer), most financial instruments (such as stocks, bonds, or notes), domestic property exchanged for foreign property, and partnership interests.[21]

---

[18]In contrast, financial accounting rules require businesses to recognize (for financial accounting purposes) any gain they realize in a like-kind exchange transaction.

[19]Like-kind is defined in Reg. §1.1031(a)-2(b).

[20]§1031(a)(2).

[21]Property used more than 50 percent of the time in a foreign country is not like-kind with domestic or with other foreign property.

---

**THE KEY FACTS**

**Like-Kind Property**

▌**Real property**
· All real property used in a trade or business or held for investment is considered "like-kind" with other real property used in a trade or business or held for investment.

▌**Personal property**
· Personal property is considered "like-kind" if it has the same general use and is used in a business or held for investment.

▌**Ineligible property**
· Inventory.
· Most financial instruments.
· Partnerships interests.
· Domestic property exchanged for property used in a foreign country and all property used in a foreign country.

---

**Taxes in the Real World**    *A Super Like-Kind Exchange*

Long before the Indianapolis Colts won the 2007 NFL Super Bowl, they were called the Baltimore Colts. Back in 1972, Carrol Rosenbloom, the owner of the Baltimore Colts, wanted to move the Colts franchise to another city. When the NFL blocked the move, Mr. Rosenbloom wanted to sell the Colts franchise and buy another NFL franchise in a different city. However, if he sold the Colts, he would be required to pay a significant amount of tax on the capital gain he would recognize on the sale because the value of the franchise had appreciated significantly from the time he initially acquired the Colts. So, with the help of attorney Hugh Culverhouse, Mr. Rosenbloom engaged in an unprecedented NFL franchise swap. Mr. Culverhouse found Bob Irsay who was willing to buy and then trade the Los Angeles Rams to Mr. Rosenbloom for the Baltimore Colts in a qualifying like-kind exchange. When the dust had settled, Mr. Rosenbloom had acquired a different NFL franchise without having to currently pay tax on the exchange. How's that for a super tax planning strategy?

---

## Property Use

Even when property meets the definition of like-kind property, taxpayers can only exchange the property in a qualifying like-kind exchange if the taxpayer used the transferred property in a trade or business or for investment *and* the taxpayer will use the property received in the exchange in a trade or business or for investment. For example, Teton could exchange its warehouse on 10 acres for a 200-acre parcel of land it intends to hold as an investment in a qualifying like-kind exchange because Teton was using the warehouse in its business and it would hold the land as an investment. However, if Steve exchanged his personal-use cabin in Maine for a personal residence in Wyoming, the exchange would not qualify because Steve used the residence for personal purposes, and he would be using the Wyoming property for personal rather than business or investment purposes. In fact, even if Steve was renting his Maine cabin (it qualifies as investment property) when he exchanged it for his principal residence in Wyoming, the exchange would not qualify for like-kind exchange treatment because *both* properties (the property the taxpayer is giving up and the property the taxpayer is receiving in the exchange) must meet the use test (the personal residence does not qualify as business or investment property). Likewise, if Teton exchanged a business computer for Steve's personal computer, which he uses for playing Halo and Warcraft with his friends, Teton would qualify for like-kind exchange treatment because Teton was using its computer equipment in its business and it will use Steve's computer in its business. However, the exchange would not qualify as a like-kind exchange for Steve because Steve used the computer for personal (not business or investment) purposes. A key takeaway here is that due to the use and other requirements, one party to an exchange may qualify for like-kind treatment and the other party may not. Each party to the exchange must individually determine whether or not the exchange qualifies as a like-kind exchange to her.

## Timing Requirements for a Like-Kind Exchange

Many like-kind exchanges involve a simultaneous exchange of like-kind assets. For example, Teton could take its used machinery to a dealer and pick up its new machinery at the same time. However, a simultaneous exchange may not be practical or possible. For example, taxpayers may not always be able to immediately (or even eventually) find another party who is willing to exchange properties with the taxpayer. In these situations taxpayers often use **third-party intermediaries** to facilitate like-kind exchanges. When a third party is involved, the taxpayer transfers the like-kind property to the intermediary and the intermediary sells the property and uses the

---

**THE KEY FACTS**

**Timing Requirements**

- Like-kind property exchanges may involve intermediaries.

- Taxpayers must identify replacement like-kind property within 45 days of giving up their property.

- Like-kind property must be received within 180 days of when the taxpayer transfers property in a like-kind exchange.

proceeds to acquire the new property for the taxpayer.[22] Because the third party must sell the taxpayer's old property and locate and purchase suitable replacement property, this process is subject to delay. In these types of situations, does a delay in the completion of the exchange disqualify an otherwise allowable like-kind exchange? Not necessarily. The tax laws do not require a simultaneous exchange of assets, but they do impose some timing requirements to ensure that a transaction is completed within a reasonable time in order to qualify as a **deferred** (not simultaneous) **like-kind exchange**—often referred to as a *Starker exchange*.[23]

The two timing rules applicable to like-kind exchanges are (1) the taxpayer must *identify* the like-kind replacement property within 45 days after transferring the property given up in the exchange, and (2) the taxpayer must receive the replacement like-kind property within 180 days (or the due date of the tax return including extensions) after the taxpayer initially transfers property in the exchange.[24] The time limits force the taxpayer to close the transaction within a specified time period, so that the taxpayers can report the tax consequences of the transaction. Exhibit 10-11 provides a diagram of a like-kind exchange involving a third-party intermediary.

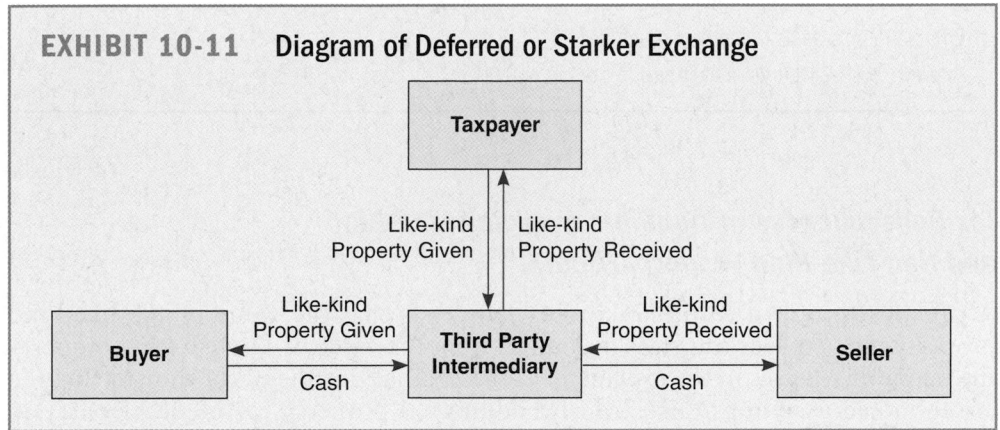

**EXHIBIT 10-11**   Diagram of Deferred or Starker Exchange

When a taxpayer fails to meet the timing requirements, the exchange fails to qualify for like-kind treatment and it thus fully taxable.

**Example 10-13**

**What if:** Suppose that on July 1 of year 1 Steve transferred a parcel of real property that he was holding as an investment to a third-party intermediary with the intention of exchanging the property for another suitable investment property. By what date does Steve need to identify the replacement property?

**Answer:** August 16 of year 1, which is 45 days after Steve transferred the property to the intermediary.

Assuming Steve identifies the replacement property within the 45-day time period, by what date does he need to receive the replacement property in order to qualify for like-kind exchange treatment?

**Answer:** December 21 of year 1, which is 180 days from July 1, the date he transferred the property to the intermediary.

[22]Exchanges involving third-party intermediaries are very common with real estate exchanges. For real estate, taxpayers must use a "qualified exchange intermediary," such as a title company, and cannot use a personal attorney (because attorneys are considered to be the taxpayer's agent).

[23]The term *Starker exchange* refers to a landmark court case that first allowed deferred exchanges (*T.J. Starker, Appellant v. United States of America,* 79-2 USTC ¶9541). The rules for deferred exchanges are found in §1031(a)(3). The tax laws also allow for reverse like-kind exchanges where replacement property is acquired before the taxpayer transfers the like-kind property.

[24]The taxpayer must identify at least one like-kind asset; however, since failure to obtain the asset disqualifies the transaction from having deferred like-kind exchange status, the taxpayer may identify up to three alternatives to hedge against the inability to obtain the first identified asset. Generally, a taxpayer must obtain only one to facilitate the exchange [see Reg. §1.1031(k)-1(c)(4)].

### Tax Consequences When Like-Kind Property Is Exchanged Solely for Like-Kind Property

As we've discussed, when taxpayers exchanging property meet the like-kind exchange requirements, they do not recognize gain or loss on the exchange. They also establish or receive an **exchanged basis** in the like-kind property they receive. That is, they exchange the basis they had in the property given up and transfer it to the basis of the property received.[25]

---

**Example 10-14**

Teton would like to trade machinery worth $29,500 (adjusted basis of $18,742), for new machinery worth $29,500. How much gain does Teton recognize on this exchange?

**Answer:** $0. Teton's exchange qualifies as a like-kind exchange and the $10,758 realized gain ($29,500 amount realized minus $18,742 adjusted basis) is deferred.

What is Teton's basis in the new machinery?

**Answer:** $18,742, the basis it had in the old machinery it traded in.

---

**THE KEY FACTS**

**Like-Kind Exchanges Involving Boot**

■ Non-like-kind property is known as boot.

■ When boot is given as part of a like-kind transaction:
· The asset received is recorded in two parts: property received in exchange for like-kind property and property received in a sale (bought by the boot).

■ When boot is received:
· Boot received usually creates recognized gain.
· Gain recognized is lesser of gain realized or boot received.

### Tax Consequences of Transfers Involving Like-Kind and Non-Like-Kind Property (Boot)

A practical problem with like-kind exchanges is that the value of the like-kind property the taxpayer transfers may differ from the value of the like-kind property the taxpayer receives in the exchange. In these situations the party transferring the lesser-valued asset must also transfer additional property to the other party to equate the values. When this additional property or **"boot"** (non-like-kind property) is transferred, the party receiving it apparently fails the first like-kind exchange requirement that like-kind property be exchanged solely for like-kind property. Nevertheless, if a taxpayer receives boot in addition to like-kind property, the transaction can still qualify for like-kind exchange treatment, but the taxpayer is required to recognize realized gain *to the extent of the boot received*.[26] As a practical matter, this means the taxpayer's recognized gain is the *lesser of* (1) gain realized or (2) boot received.

The reason a taxpayer must recognize gain is that the taxpayer is essentially selling a portion of the like-kind property for the boot in a taxable exchange. The receipt of boot triggers taxable gain (but not a taxable loss) in an otherwise qualifying like-kind exchange. If the taxpayer transfers loss property (adjusted basis is greater than fair market value) in a qualifying like-kind exchange, the taxpayer defers recognition of the loss until the taxpayer sells or disposes of the loss property in a taxable transaction—so it may be important for tax planning purposes to avoid the like-kind exchange rules if the taxpayer wishes to currently recognize the loss.[27] When a taxpayer recognizes gain in a like-kind exchange, the character of the gain depends on the character of the asset transferred by the taxpayer (the depreciation recapture rules apply when characterizing gains).

---

[25]If the asset is a depreciable asset, the taxpayer continues to depreciate the new asset as if it were the old asset.

[26]§1031(b).

[27]§1031(a) states that no gain or loss is recognized in a qualifying like-kind exchange.

**Example 10-15**

**What if:** Suppose that Teton trades its used machinery with a value of $29,500 and an adjusted basis of $18,742 ($30,615 historical cost less $11,873 of accumulated depreciation) to the dealer for new machinery valued at $27,500. To equate the value of the property exchanged, the dealer also pays Teton $2,000. What gain or loss does Teton realize on the exchange and what gain or loss does Teton recognize on the exchange?

**Answer:** $10,758 realized gain and $2,000 recognized gain, calculated as follows:

| Description | Amount | Explanation |
|---|---|---|
| (1) Amount realized from machine | $27,500 | |
| (2) Amount realized from boot (cash) | 2,000 | |
| (3) Total amount realized | $29,500 | (1) + (2). |
| (4) Adjusted basis | 18,742 | |
| (5) Gain realized | $10,758 | (3) − (4). |
| Gain recognized | $ 2,000 | Lesser of (2) or (5). |

What is the character of Teton's $2,000 gain?

**Answer:** Ordinary income. Because Teton's accumulated depreciation on the asset exceeds its $2,000 gain, Teton must treat the gain as ordinary gain under the §1245 depreciation recapture rules discussed earlier.

**What if:** Suppose the same facts as above, except that Teton's adjusted basis in the machinery was $29,000. What amount of gain would Teton recognize on the exchange?

**Answer:** $500. Teton recognizes the lesser of (1) $500 gain realized ($29,500 minus $29,000) or (2) $2,000 boot received.

When taxpayers receive like-kind property and boot in a like-kind exchange, their basis in the like-kind property is computed using the following formula:

$$\text{Basis in like-kind property} = \text{Fair market value of like-kind property received} - \text{Deferred gain} + \text{Deferred loss}$$

The basis of boot received in the exchange is always the boot's fair market value. This formula for computing basis ensures that the taxpayer's deferred gain or loss on the exchange (the gain or loss realized that is not recognized) is captured in the difference between the value and the basis of the new property received. Consequently, taxpayers defer realized gain or loss on qualifying like-kind exchanges; they do not exclude them. Taxpayers will ultimately recognize the gain or loss when they dispose of the new asset in a taxable transaction.[28]

**Example 10-16**

**What if:** Assume the facts in the previous example where Teton traded its used machinery with a value of $29,500 and an adjusted basis of $18,742 to the dealer for new machinery valued at $27,500 and $2,000 cash. Teton recognized $2,000 on the exchange. What is Teton's basis in the new machinery it received from the dealer?

(continued on page 10-26)

---

[28]Additionally, the deferred gain is subject to depreciation recapture when the asset is eventually disposed of in a taxable disposition.

**Answer:** $18,742, computed as follows:

| Description | Amount | Explanation |
|---|---|---|
| (1) Amount realized from machine | $27,500 | Fair market value of new machine. |
| (2) Amount realized from boot (cash) | 2,000 | |
| (3) Total amount realized | $29,500 | (1) + (2). |
| (4) Adjusted basis of used machinery | 18,742 | |
| (5) Gain realized | $10,758 | (3) − (4). |
| (6) Gain recognized | $ 2,000 | Lesser of (2) or (5). |
| (7) Deferred gain | $ 8,758 | (5) − (6). |
| Adjusted basis in new property | $18,742 | (1) − (7). |

It is important to note that anything a taxpayer receives in an exchange other than like-kind property is considered boot. This includes cash, other property, or even the amount of a taxpayer's liability transferred to (assumed by) the other party in the exchange. For example, let's return to the previous example. If instead of paying Teton $2,000 of cash, the dealer assumed Teton's $2,000 liability secured by Teton's old machinery, the tax consequences would have been identical. The dealer relieved Teton of $2,000 of debt and the debt relief is treated the same as if the dealer had paid Teton cash and Teton had paid off its $2,000 liability. Generally, when a taxpayer both transfers and receives boot in an otherwise qualifying like-kind exchange, the taxpayer must recognize any realized gain to the extent of the boot received. That is, the taxpayer is not allowed to offset boot received with boot paid.[29] However, when the taxpayer gives and receives boot in the form of liabilities, the taxpayer is allowed to net the boot received and the boot paid.[30]

### Reporting Like-Kind Exchanges

Like-kind exchange transactions are reported on Form 8824. Exhibit 10-12 presents the computations from Form 8824 reflecting the like-kind exchange of the machinery in Example 10-14.

### Involuntary Conversions

Usually, when taxpayers sell, exchange, or abandon property they intend to do so. However, in certain situations taxpayers may involuntarily dispose of property due to circumstances beyond their control. Thus, the tax law refers to these types of property dispositions as **involuntary conversions.**[31] Involuntary conversions occur when property is partially or wholly destroyed by a natural disaster or accident, stolen, condemned, or seized via eminent domain by a governmental agency. Tragic examples of this include the results of the September 11, 2001, terrorist attacks and the Hurricane Katrina-related events in 2005. Even in situations when taxpayers

[29]However, Reg. §1.1031(j)-1 provides an exception where multiple like-kind exchanges are made in a single exchange.

[30]Further details of this important exception are beyond the scope of our discussion. See the examples provided in Reg. §1.1031(d)-2 for further guidance.

[31]§1033.

**EXHIBIT 10-12** Form 8824, Part III (From machine exchange in Example 10-14)

Form 8824 (2009)                                                                                          Page **2**

| Name(s) shown on tax return. Do not enter name and social security number if shown on other side. | Your social security number |
|---|---|
| Steve Dallimore (Teton Mountaineering Technologies, LLC) | |

**Part III**     Realized Gain or (Loss), Recognized Gain, and Basis of Like-Kind Property Received

**Caution:** *If you transferred **and** received **(a)** more than one group of like-kind properties or **(b)** cash or other (not like-kind) property,* see **Reporting of multi-asset exchanges** *in the instructions.*

**Note:** *Complete lines 12 through 14 **only** if you gave up property that was not like-kind. Otherwise, go to line 15.*

| | | | |
|---|---|---|---|
| 12 | Fair market value (FMV) of other property given up | 12 | 0 |
| 13 | Adjusted basis of other property given up | 13 | 0 |
| 14 | Gain or (loss) recognized on other property given up. Subtract line 13 from line 12. Report the gain or (loss) in the same manner as if the exchange had been a sale | 14 | 0 |
| | **Caution:** *If the property given up was used previously or partly as a home, see* **Property used as home** *in the instructions.* | | |
| 15 | Cash received, FMV of other property received, plus net liabilities assumed by other party, reduced (but not below zero) by any exchange expenses you incurred (see instructions) | 15 | 0 |
| 16 | FMV of like-kind property you received | 16 | 29,500 |
| 17 | Add lines 15 and 16 | 17 | 29,500 |
| 18 | Adjusted basis of like-kind property you gave up, net amounts paid to other party, plus any exchange expenses **not** used on line 15 (see instructions) | 18 | 18,742 |
| 19 | **Realized gain or (loss).** Subtract line 18 from line 17 | 19 | 10,758 |
| 20 | Enter the smaller of line 15 or line 19, but not less than zero | 20 | |
| 21 | Ordinary income under recapture rules. Enter here and on Form 4797, line 16 (see instructions) | 21 | |
| 22 | Subtract line 21 from line 20. If zero or less, enter -0-. If more than zero, enter here and on Schedule D or Form 4797, unless the installment method applies (see instructions) | 22 | |
| 23 | **Recognized gain.** Add lines 21 and 22 | 23 | |
| 24 | Deferred gain or (loss). Subtract line 23 from line 19. If a related party exchange, see instructions | 24 | 10,758 |
| 25 | **Basis of like-kind property received.** Subtract line 15 from the sum of lines 18 and 23 | 25 | 18,742 |

experience a loss of property due to theft, disaster, or other circumstances, they might realize a gain for tax purposes if they receive replacement property or insurance proceeds in excess of their basis in the property that was stolen or destroyed.

Taxpayers may experience a tremendous financial hardship if they were required to recognize the realized gain in these circumstances. For example, let's consider a business that acquired a building for $100,000. The building appreciates in value and when the building is worth $150,000 it is destroyed by fire. The building is fully insured at its replacement cost, so the business receives a check from the insurance company for $150,000. The problem for the business is that it realizes a $50,000 gain on this involuntary conversion ($150,000 insurance proceeds minus $100,000 basis in property without considering depreciation). Assuming the business's income is taxed at a 30 percent marginal rate, it must pay $15,000 of tax on the insurance money it receives. This leaves the business with only $135,000 to replace property worth $150,000. This hardly seems equitable. Congress provides special tax laws to allow taxpayers to defer the gains on such *involuntary* conversions.

Taxpayers may defer realized gains on both direct and indirect involuntary conversions. **Direct conversions** involve taxpayers receiving a direct property replacement for the involuntarily converted property. For example, a municipality that is widening its streets may seize land from a taxpayer through its eminent domain and compensate the taxpayer with another parcel of similar value. In this case, the taxpayer would not recognize gain on the exchange of property and would take an adjusted basis in the new parcel of land equal to the taxpayer's basis in the land that was claimed by the municipality. Just as with like-kind exchanges, an exchanged basis

(basis of old property exchanged for basis of new property) ensures that the gain built into the new property (fair market value minus adjusted basis) includes the same gain that was built into the old property.

**Indirect conversions** involve taxpayers receiving money for the involuntarily converted property through insurance reimbursement or some other type of settlement. Taxpayers meeting the involuntary conversion requirements may *elect* to either recognize or defer realized gain on the conversions. Indirect conversions are more common than direct conversions. Taxpayers can defer realized gains on indirect conversions *if* they acquire **qualified replacement property** within a prescribed time limit, which is generally two years (three years in case of condemnation) after the close of the tax year in which they receive the proceeds.[32]

For both personal and real property, qualified replacement property for an involuntary conversion is defined more narrowly than is like-kind property in a like-kind exchange. The property must be similar *and* related in service or use to qualify.[33] For example, a bowling alley is not qualified replacement property for a pool hall, even though both are real properties used for entertainment purposes. This is stricter than the like-kind exchange rules that would allow the bowling alley to be exchanged for any other real property including a pool hall. Taxpayers recognize realized gain to the extent that they do not reinvest the reimbursement proceeds in qualified property. However, just like in like-kind exchanges, taxpayers do not recognize more gain than they realize on involuntary conversions. That is, a taxpayer's recognized gain on an involuntary conversion can be determined by the following formula: Recognized gain on involuntary conversion = the *lesser of* (1) the gain realized on the conversion or (2) the amount of reimbursement the taxpayer does *not reinvest* in qualified property.

The character of any gain recognized in an involuntary conversion depends on the nature of the asset that was converted—including depreciation recapture if applicable. The basis of the replacement property in an involuntary conversion is calculated in the same way it is for like-kind exchange property. That is, the basis of the replacement property is the fair market value of the new property minus the deferred gain on the conversion.

---

**Example 10-17**

**What if:** *Assume* that one of Teton's employees was involved in a traffic accident while driving a delivery van. The employee escaped without serious injury but the van was totally destroyed. Before the accident, Teton's delivery van had a fair market value of $15,000 and an adjusted basis of $11,000 (the cost basis was $15,000 and accumulated depreciation on the van was $4,000). Teton received $15,000 of insurance proceeds to cover the loss. Teton was considering two alternatives for replacing the van: Alternative 1 was to purchase a new delivery van for $20,000 and Alternative 2 was to purchase a used delivery van for $14,000. What gain or loss does Teton recognize under Alternative 1 and Alternative 2?

**Answer:** $0 gain recognized under Alternative 1 and $1,000 gain recognized under Alternative 2 (see computations below). Teton qualifies for a deferral because the new property (delivery van) has a similar and related use to the old property (delivery van). But it must recognize gain under Alternative 2 because it did not reinvest all of the insurance proceeds in a replacement van.

(continued on page 10-29...)

---

[32]§1033(a)(2)(B). The time period varies depending on the type of property converted. Additionally, the IRS may consent to an extension of the time period for replacement.

[33]The similar and related-use test has been developed through a variety of administrative pronouncements and judicial law.

What is Teton's basis in the replacement property it acquired under Alternative 1 and Alternative 2?

**Answer:** $16,000 in Alternative 1 and $11,000 in Alternative 2, computed as follows:

| Description | Alternative 1 Amount | Alternative 2 Amount | Explanation |
|---|---|---|---|
| (1) Amount realized | $15,000 | $15,000 | |
| (2) Adjusted basis | 11,000 | 11,000 | |
| (3) Gain realized | 4,000 | 4,000 | (1) − (2). |
| (4) Insurance proceeds | 15,000 | 15,000 | |
| (5) Proceeds reinvested | 15,000 | 14,000 | |
| (6) Amount not reinvested | 0 | 1,000 | (4) − (5). |
| (7) **Gain recognized** | 0 | 1,000 | Lesser of (3) or (6).* |
| (8) Deferred gain | 4,000 | 3,000 | (3) − (7). |
| (9) Value of replacement property | 20,000 | 14,000 | |
| **Basis of replacement property** | **$16,000** | **$11,000** | (9) − (8). |

*The character of the $1,000 recognized gain is ordinary income under §1245 (lesser of gain recognized or accumulated depreciation).

Involuntary conversions share several similar concepts with like-kind exchanges such as the concept of qualified property, time period restrictions, the method of computing gain recognized (lesser of realized gain or cash received in addition to qualifying property), and basis calculation (gain or loss from old property remains built into new property). However, one important difference between the two is that taxpayers experiencing a loss from involuntary conversion may immediately deduct the loss as a casualty loss (either personal or business depending on the nature of the loss).

## Installment Sales

In general, when taxpayers sell property for cash and collect the entire sale proceeds in one lump-sum payment, they immediately recognize gain or loss for tax purposes. However, taxpayers selling property don't always collect the sale proceeds in one lump sum from the buyer. For example, the buyer may make a down payment in the year of sale and then agree to pay the remainder of the sale proceeds over a period of time. This type of arrangement is termed an **installment sale.** Technically, an installment sale is any sale of property where the seller receives at least one payment in a taxable year subsequent to the year of disposition of the property.[34] Taxpayers selling property via an installment sale realize gains to the extent the selling price (the amount realized) exceeds their adjusted basis in the property sold. The installment sale rules stay true to the wherewithal-to-pay concept and allow taxpayers selling property in this manner to use the installment method of recognizing *gain* on the sale over time.[35] The installment method does not apply to property sold at a loss. Under the installment method taxpayers determine the amount of realized gain on the transaction, and they recognize the gain pro rata as they receive the installment payments. So, by the time they have received all of the installment payments, they will have recognized all of the initial realized gain.[36] For financial accounting purposes,

> **THE KEY FACTS**
>
> **Installment Sales**
>
> ■ Sale of property where the seller receives at least one payment in a taxable year subsequent to the year of disposition of the property.
>
> ■ Must recognize a portion of gain on each installment payment received.
>
> ■ Gains from installments sales are calculated as follows:
>   · Gross profit percentage = Gain realized/Amount realized.
>
> ■ Inventory, marketable securities, and depreciation recapture cannot be accounted for under installment sale rules.
>
> ■ Does not apply to losses.

[34]§453(b)(1).

[35]Technically, a taxpayer selling property on an installment basis at a gain is required to use the installment method of reporting the recognized gain from the transaction. However, taxpayers are allowed to *elect* out of using the installment method §453(d).

[36]Because the seller in an installment sale is essentially lending money to the buyer, the buyer makes the required installment payments to the seller and the buyer pays interest to the seller for the money the buyer is borrowing. Any interest income received by the seller is immediately taxable as ordinary income. Special rules apply regarding interest for installment sales of more than $150,000 (see §453A).

businesses selling property on an installment basis generally immediately recognize the realized gain on their financial statements.[37]

To determine the amount of gain the taxpayer (seller) must recognize on each installment payment received, the seller must compute the gross profit percentage on the transaction. The gross profit percentage is calculated as follows:

$$\text{Gross profit percentage} = \frac{\text{Gain realized}}{\text{Amount realized}}$$

The gross profit percentage indicates the percentage of the total sales proceeds (or amount realized) that will ultimately be recognized as gain. To determine the portion of a particular payment that is currently recognized as gain, the seller multiplies the amount of the payments received during the year (including the year of sale) by the gross profit percentage (note that once established, the gross profit percentage does not change). Similar to fully taxable transactions, the character of gain taxpayers recognize using the installment method is determined by the character of the asset they sell.

| Example 10-18 | |
|---|---|

**What if:** Suppose Teton decides to sell 5 acres of land adjacent to the warehouse for $100,000. The cost basis for the land is $37,500. Teton agrees to sell the property for four equal payments of $25,000—one now (in year 1) and the other three on January 1 of the next three years—plus interest. What amount of gain does Teton realize on the sale and what amount of gain does it recognize in year 1?

**Answer:** The realized gain on the transaction is $62,500 ($100,000 amount realized less $37,500 adjusted basis), and the year 1 recognized gain is $15,625, computed as follows:

| Description | Amount | Explanation |
|---|---|---|
| (1) Amount realized | $100,000 | |
| (2) Adjusted basis | 37,500 | |
| (3) Gain realized | 62,500 | (1) − (2). |
| (4) Gross profit percentage | 62.5% | (3)/(1). |
| (5) Payment received in year 1 | 25,000 | |
| Gain recognized in year 1 | $ 15,625 | (5) × (4). |

Because Teton used the land in its trade or business and it held the land for more than a year, the character of the gain is §1231 gain.

The formula for determining the basis of an installment note receivable is (1 − gross profit percentage) × remaining payments on note. Because the gross profit percentage reflects the percentage of the installment payments that will be recognized as gain, (1 − gross profit percentage) is the percentage that is not recognized as gain because it reflects a return of capital (basis).

### Gains Ineligible for Installment Reporting

Not all gains are eligible for installment sale reporting. Taxpayers selling marketable securities or inventory on an installment basis may not use the installment method to report gain on the sales. Similarly, any §1245 depreciation recapture is

[37]One exception is that the installment sale method similar to the tax installment method is used for financial accounting purposes when there is doubt that the business will collect the receivable.

not eligible for installment reporting and must be recognized in the year of sale.[38] However, the §1231 gain remaining after the §1245 depreciation recapture can be recognized using the installment method. To ensure that any §1245 depreciation recapture is not taxed twice (once immediately and then a second time as payments are received), immediately taxable recapture-related gains are *added to* the adjusted basis of the property sold to determine the gross profit percentage. The increase in basis reduces the gain realized, which also reduces the gross profit percentage and the amount of future gain that will ultimately be recognized as the taxpayer receives the installment payments.

**Example 10-19**

**What if:** Assume that Teton agrees to sell some of its machinery for $90,000 for two equal payments of $45,000 plus interest. Teton's original basis was $80,000 and accumulated depreciation on the machinery was $30,000. Teton will receive one payment in year 1 (the current year) and the other payment in year 2. What is the amount and character of the gain Teton recognizes on the sale in year 1?

**Answer:** $30,000 ordinary income and $5,000 of §1231 gain, computed as follows:

| Description | Amount | Explanation |
|---|---|---|
| (1) Amount realized | $90,000 | |
| (2) Original basis | 80,000 | |
| (3) Accumulated depreciation | (30,000) | |
| (4) Adjusted basis | 50,000 | (2) + (3). |
| (5) Realized gain (loss) | 40,000 | (1) − (4). |
| (6) Ordinary income from depreciation recapture (not eligible for installment reporting) | **30,000** | Ordinary income. Lesser of (3) or (5). |
| (7) Gain eligible for installment reporting | 10,000 | (5) − (6). |
| (8) Gross profit percentage | 11.11% | (7)/(1). |
| (9) Payment received in year 1 | 45,000 | |
| Installment gain recognized in year 1 | $ 5,000 | (9) × (8) §1231 gain. |

What is the amount and character of the gain Teton recognized upon receipt of the payment in year 2?

**Answer:** $5,000 of §1231 gain ($45,000 payment received times the gross profit percentage of 11.11 percent).

## Other Nonrecognition Provisions

There are several tax law provisions that allow businesses to change the form or organization of their business while deferring the realized gains for tax purposes. For example, a sole proprietor can form his business as a corporation or contribute assets to an existing corporation and defer the gain realized on the exchange of assets for an ownership interest in the business entity.[39] Without the nonrecognition provision, the tax cost of forming a corporation may be large enough to deter taxpayers from doing so. Nonrecognition rules also apply to taxpayers forming partnerships or contributing assets to partnerships.[40] In still other corporate transactions, such as mergers, divisions (spin-offs or split-ups), or reorganizations,

[38]§453(i).
[39]§351.
[40]§721.

corporations can often do so in tax deferred transactions.[41] While these transactions generally result in deferred gain or loss for the involved parties, the specific details of these topics can easily fill chapters worth of material, and are not considered further in this chapter.

### Related-Party Loss Disallowance Rules

For equity reasons, the tax laws limit or disallow deductions for losses taxpayers realize when they sell property to related parties. Taxpayers selling business or investment property at a loss to unrelated parties are generally able to deduct the loss.[42] This makes sense in most situations because taxpayers are selling the property for less than their remaining investment (adjusted basis) in the property and after the sale, the taxpayer's investment in the property is completely terminated. In contrast, when a taxpayer sells property at a loss to a related party, she effectively retains some element of control over the property through the related party. Consistent with this idea, the tax laws essentially treat related parties as though they are the same taxpayer and, accordingly, disallow recognition of losses on sales to related parties. Related taxpayers include individuals with family relationships including siblings, spouses, ancestors, and lineal descendants. Related parties also include an individual and a corporation if the individual owns more than 50 percent of the stock of the corporation and a partner and the partnership no matter the partner's ownership percentage.[43]

---

**Example 10-20**

***What if:*** Suppose Teton is formed as a corporation and Steve is its sole shareholder. Teton is looking to make some long-term investments to fund its anticipated purchase of a new manufacturing facility. Steve currently owns 1,000 shares of stock in his previous company Northeastern Corp., which he intends to sell in the near future. Steve initially paid $40 a share for the stock but the stock is currently valued at $30 a share. While Steve believes the stock has good long-term potential, he needs cash now to purchase a personal residence in Cody, Wyoming. Steve believes selling the shares to Teton makes good sense because he can deduct the loss and save taxes now and Teton can benefit from the expected long-term appreciation of the stock. If Steve sells 1,000 shares of Northeastern Corp. stock to Teton for $30 per share, what amount of loss will he realize and what amount of loss will he recognize for tax purposes?

**Answer:** $10,000 loss realized and $0 loss recognized, determined as follows:

| Description | Amount | Explanation |
|---|---|---|
| (1) Amount realized on sale | $30,000 | (1,000 × $30). |
| (2) Adjusted basis in stock | 40,000 | (1,000 × $40). |
| (3) **Loss realized on sale** | ($10,000) | (1) − (2). |
| **Loss recognized on sale** | $ 0 | Losses on sales to related parties are disallowed. |

Because Steve owns more than 50 percent of Teton (he owns 100 percent), Steve and Teton are considered to be related parties. Consequently, Steve is not allowed to recognize any loss on the sale.

---

[41]§368 contains the numerous variations and requirements of these tax-deferred reorganizations.

[42]Capital losses are subject to certain limitations for individuals and corporate taxpayers (§1211).

[43]§267(a). The related-party rules include both direct ownership as well as indirect ownership (ownership attributed to the taxpayer from related parties). See §267(c) for a description of the indirect ownership rules.

As we discussed above, the tax laws essentially treat related sellers and buyers as a single entity. Thus, while taxpayers are not allowed to immediately deduct losses when they sell property to the related party, the related-party buyer may be able to subsequently deduct the disallowed loss by selling the property to an *unrelated* third party at a gain. The rules follow:

- If the related buyer sells the property at a gain (the related-party buyer sells it for more than she purchased it for) greater than the disallowed loss, the entire loss that was disallowed for the related-party seller is deductible by the buyer.
- If the related-party buyer subsequently sells the property and the related-party seller's disallowed loss exceeds the related party's gain on the subsequent sale, the related-party buyer may only deduct or offset the previously disallowed loss *to the extent of the gain* on the sale to the unrelated third party—the remaining disallowed loss expires unused.
- If the related-party buyer sells the property for less than her purchase price from the related seller, the disallowed loss expires unused.

---

**Example 10-21**

**What if:** Let's return to the previous example where Steve sold 1,000 shares of Northeastern Corp. stock to Teton (a corporation) for $30,000. As we discovered in that example, Steve realized a $10,000 loss on the sale, but he was not allowed to deduct it because Steve and Teton are related parties. Let's assume that a few years after Teton purchased the stock from Steve, Teton sells the Northeastern Corp. stock to an unrelated third party. What gain or loss does *Teton* recognize when it sells the stock in each of three scenarios, assuming it sells the stock for $37,000 in Scenario 1, $55,000 in Scenario 2, and $25,000 in Scenario 3?

**Answer:** $0 gain or loss in Scenario 1, $15,000 gain in Scenario 2, and $5,000 loss in Scenario 3, computed as follows:

| Description | Scenario 1 | Scenario 2 | Scenario 3 | Explanation |
|---|---|---|---|---|
| (1) Amount realized | $37,000 | $55,000 | $25,000 | |
| (2) Adjusted basis | $30,000 | $30,000 | $30,000 | Example 10-20 (Teton's purchase price). |
| (3) Realized gain (loss) | $ 7,000 | $25,000 | ($5,000) | (1) − (2). |
| (4) Benefit of Steve's ($10,000) disallowed loss | ($7,000) | ($10,000) | $    0 | Loss benefit limited to realized gain. |
| Recognized gain (loss) | $    0 | $15,000 | ($5,000) | (3) + (4). |

In Scenario 1 $3,000 of Steve's $10,000 remaining disallowed loss expires unused. In Scenario 3, Steve's entire $10,000 disallowed loss expires unused.

---

## CONCLUSION

This chapter describes and discusses the tax consequences associated with sales and other types of property dispositions. We've learned how to determine the amount of gain or loss taxpayers recognize when they sell or otherwise dispose of property, and we've learned how to determine the character of these gains and losses. Tax accountants who understand the rules and concepts of property dispositions are able to comply with the tax law and advise clients of potential tax-planning opportunities and avoid pitfalls associated with various nonrecognition provisions.

## SUMMARY

**LO1**  Calculate the amount of gain or loss recognized on the disposition of assets used in a trade or business.

- Dispositions occur in the form of sales, trades, or other realization events.
- Gain realized is the amount realized less the adjusted basis of an asset.
- Amount realized is everything of value received in the transaction less any selling costs.
- Adjusted basis is the historical cost or basis of an asset less any cost recovery deductions applied against the asset.
- Gain realized on asset dispositions is not always recognized.

**LO2**  Describe the general character types of gain or loss recognized on property dispositions.

- Recognized gains must be characterized as ordinary, capital, or §1231. An asset's character is a function of the asset's use and holding period.
- Ordinary assets are derived from normal transactions of the business (revenues and accounts receivable), sale of short-term trade or business assets, and depreciation recapture.
- Capital assets are assets that are held either for investment or for personal use (a taxpayer's principal residence).
- §1231 assets consist of property used in a taxpayer's trade or business that has been held for more than one year.
- Net §1231 assets receive the best of both worlds—net §1231 gains become capital and net §1231 losses become ordinary.

**LO3**  Explain the rationale for and calculate depreciation recapture.

- §1231 assets, other than land, are subject to cost recovery deductions (depreciation), which generate ordinary deductions.
- Gains that are created through depreciation deductions are subject to depreciation recapture. Any remaining gain is §1231 gain.
- Depreciation recapture does not change the amount of the gain but simply converts or recharacterizes the gain from §1231 to ordinary.
- Different recapture rules apply to tangible personal property (§1245) and real property (§291 corporations only).

**LO4**  Describe the tax treatment of unrecaptured §1250 gains and determine the character of gains on property sold to related parties.

- When individuals sell §1250 property at a gain, the portion of the gain generated by depreciation deductions is called unrecaptured §1250 gain.
- This gain is a §1231 gain that, if treated as a capital gain after the netting process, is taxed at a maximum rate of 25 percent.
- If a taxpayer sells an asset at a gain to a related party and the asset is a depreciable asset to the related party, the seller must characterize the entire gain as ordinary income.

**LO5**  Describe the tax treatment of §1231 gains or losses, including the §1231 netting process.

- After applying the depreciation recapture rules, taxpayers calculate the net §1231 gain or loss.
- If a net §1231 loss results, the loss will become ordinary and offset ordinary income.
- If a net §1231 gain results, the §1231 look-back rule must be applied.
- After applying the look-back rule, any remaining net §1231 gain is a long-term capital gain.

**LO6**  Explain common exceptions to the general rule that realized gains and losses are recognized currently.

- Like-kind exchanges involve trading or exchanging business assets for similar business assets. The gain is deferred unless boot or non-like-kind property is received.

- Involuntary conversions are the losses on property through circumstances beyond taxpayers' control. Reasons include natural disasters, accidents, theft, or condemnation.
- Installment sales occur when any portion of the amount realized is received in a year subsequent to the disposition.
- §267 related-party losses are disallowed but the related-party buyer may be able to deduct the disallowed loss if she subsequently sells the property at a gain.

## KEY TERMS

| | | |
|---|---|---|
| adjusted basis (10-3) | installment sale (10-29) | recognized gain or loss (10-4) |
| amount realized (10-2) | involuntary conversion (10-26) | §291 depreciation recapture (10-12) |
| boot (10-24) | like-kind exchange (10-17) | §1231 assets (10-6) |
| capital asset (10-5) | nonrecognition transaction (10-17) | §1231 look-back rule (10-15) |
| deferred like-kind exchange (10-23) | ordinary asset (10-5) | §1245 property (10-8) |
| depreciation recapture (10-7) | production of income (10-5) | §1250 property (10-12) |
| direct conversion (10-27) | qualified replacement property (10-28) | third-party intermediaries (10-22) |
| exchanged basis (10-24) | realized gain or loss (10-3) | unrecaptured §1231 losses (10-15) |
| indirect conversion (10-28) | recapture (10-9) | unrecaptured §1250 gain (10-12) |

## DISCUSSION QUESTIONS

1. **(LO1)** Compare and contrast different ways in which a taxpayer triggers a realization event by disposing of an asset.

2. **(LO1)** Potomac Corporation wants to sell a warehouse that it has used in its business for 10 years. Potomac is asking $450,000 for the property. The warehouse is subject to a mortgage of $125,000. If Potomac accepts Wyden Inc.'s offer to give Potomac $325,000 in cash and assume full responsibility for the mortgage on the property, what amount does Potomac realize on the sale?

3. **(LO1)** Montana Max sells a 2,500-acre ranch for $1,000,000 in cash, a note receivable of $1,000,000, and debt relief of $2,400,000. He also pays selling commissions of $60,000. In addition, Max agrees to build a new barn on the property (cost $250,000) and spend $100,000 upgrading the fence on the property before the sale. What is Max's amount realized on the sale?

4. **(LO1)** Hawkeye sold farming equipment for $55,000. It bought the equipment four years ago for $75,000, and it has since claimed a total of $42,000 in depreciation deductions against the asset. Explain how to calculate Hawkeye's adjusted basis in the farming equipment.

5. **(LO1)** When a taxpayer sells an asset, what is the difference between realized and recognized gain or loss on the sale?

6. **(LO2)** What does it mean to characterize a gain or loss? Why is characterizing a gain or loss important?

7. **(LO2)** Explain the difference between ordinary, capital, and §1231 assets.

8. **(LO2)** Discuss the reasons why individuals generally prefer capital gains over ordinary gains. Explain why corporate taxpayers might prefer capital gains over ordinary gains.

9. **(LO2)** Dakota Conrad owns a parcel of land he would like to sell. Describe the circumstances in which the sale of the land would generate §1231 gain or loss, ordinary gain or loss, or capital gain or loss. Also, describe the circumstances where Dakota would not be allowed to deduct a loss on the sale.

10. **(LO2)** Lincoln has used a piece of land in her business for the past five years. The land qualifies as §1231 property. It is unclear whether Lincoln will have to recognize a gain or loss when she eventually sells the asset. She asks her accountant how the gain or loss would be characterized if she decides to sell. Her accountant said that selling §1231 assets gives sellers "the best of both worlds." Explain what her accountant means by "the best of both worlds."

11. **(LO3)** Explain Congress's rationale for depreciation recapture.

12. **(LO3)** Compare and contrast §1245 recapture and §1250 recapture.

13. **(LO3)** Why is depreciation recapture not required when assets are sold at a loss?

14. **(LO3)** What are the similarities and differences between the tax benefit rule and depreciation recapture?

15. **(LO3, LO4)** Are both corporations and individuals subject to depreciation recapture when they sell depreciable real property at a gain? Explain.

16. **(LO4)** How is unrecaptured §1250 gain for individuals similar to depreciation recapture? How is it different?

17. **(LO4)** Explain why gains from depreciable property sold to a related taxpayer are treated as ordinary income under §1239.

18. **(LO5)** Bingaman Resources sold two depreciable §1231 assets during the year. One asset resulted in a large gain (the asset was sold for more than it was purchased for) and the other resulted in a small loss. Describe the §1231 netting process for Bingaman.

19. **(LO5)** Jeraldine believes that when the §1231 look-back rule applies, the taxpayer deducts a §1231 loss in a previous year against §1231 gains in the current year. Explain whether Jeraldine's description is correct.

20. **(LO5)** Explain the purpose behind the §1231 look-back rule.

21. **(LO5)** Does a taxpayer apply the §1231 look-back rule in a year when the taxpayer recognizes a net §1231 loss? Explain.

22. **(LO5)** How would you describe the application of the §1231 look-back rule to a friend who knows little about taxation?

23. **(LO4, LO5)** Describe the circumstances in which an individual taxpayer with a net §1231 gain will have different portions of the gain taxed at different rates.

24. **(LO6)** Rocky and Bullwinkle Partnership sold a parcel of land during the current year and realized a gain of $250,000. Rocky and Bullwinkle did not recognize gain related to the sale of the land on its tax return. Is this possible? Explain how a taxpayer could realize a gain but not recognize it.

25. **(LO6)** Why does Congress allow taxpayers to defer gains on like-kind exchanges? How do the tax laws ensure that the gains (or losses) are deferred and not permanently excluded from a taxpayer's income?

26. **(LO6)** Compare and contrast the like-kind property requirements for real property and for personal property for purposes of qualifying for a like-kind exchange. Explain whether a car held by a corporation for delivering documents will qualify as like-kind property with a car held by an individual for personal use.

27. **(LO6)** Salazar Inc., a Colorado company, is relocating to a nearby town. It would like to trade its real property for some real property in the new location. While Salazar has found several prospective buyers for its real property and has also located several properties that are acceptable in the new location, it cannot find anyone that is willing to trade Salazar Inc. for its property in a like-kind exchange. Explain how a third-party intermediary could facilitate Salazar's like-kind exchange.

28. **(LO6)** Minuteman wants to enter into a like-kind exchange by exchanging its old New England manufacturing facility for a ranch in Wyoming. Minuteman is using a third-party intermediary to facilitate the exchange. The purchaser of

the manufacturing facility wants to complete the transaction immediately but, for various reasons, the ranch transaction will not be completed for three to four months. Will this delay cause a problem for Minuteman's desire to accomplish this through a like-kind exchange? Explain.

29. **(LO6)** Olympia Corporation, of Kittery, Maine, wants to exchange its manufacturing machinery for Bangor Company's machinery. Both parties agree that Olympia's machinery is worth $100,000 and that Bangor's machinery is worth $95,000. Olympia would like the transaction to qualify as a like-kind exchange. What could the parties do to equalize the value exchanged but still allow the exchange to qualify as a like-kind exchange? How would the necessary change affect the tax consequences of the transaction?

30. **(LO6)** Compare and contrast the similarities and differences between like-kind exchanges and involuntary conversions for tax purposes?

31. **(LO6)** What is an installment sale? How do the tax laws ensure that taxpayers recognize all the gain they realize on an installment sale? How is depreciation recapture treated in an installment sale? Explain the gross profit ratio and how it relates to gains recognized under installment method sales.

32. **(LO6)** Mr. Kyle owns stock in a local publicly traded company. Although the stock price has declined since he purchased it two years ago, he likes the long-term prospects for the company. If Kyle sells the stock to his sister because he needs some cash for a down payment on a new home, is the loss deductible? If Kyle is right and the stock price increases in the future, how is his sister's gain computed if she sells the stock?

## PROBLEMS

33. **(LO1)** Rafael sold an asset to Jamal. What is Rafael's amount realized on the sale in each of the following alternative scenarios?

   a. Rafael received $80,000 of cash and a vehicle worth $10,000. Rafael also pays $5,000 in selling expenses.

   b. Rafael received $80,000 of cash and was relieved of a $30,000 mortgage on the asset he sold to Jamal. Rafael also paid a commission of $5,000 on the transaction.

   c. Rafael received $20,000 of cash, a parcel of land worth $50,000, and marketable securities of $10,000. Rafael also paid a commission of $8,000 on the transaction.

34. **(LO1)** Shasta Corporation sold a piece of land to Bill for $45,000. Shasta bought the land two years ago for $30,600. What gain or loss does Shasta realize on the transaction?

35. **(LO1)** Lassen Corporation sold a machine to a machine dealer for $25,000. Lassen bought the machine for $55,000 and has claimed $15,000 of depreciation expense on the machine. What gain or loss does Lassen realize on the transaction?

36. **(LO2)** Identify each of White Corporation's following assets as an ordinary, capital, or §1231 asset.

   a. Two years ago, White used its excess cash to purchase a piece of land as an investment.

   b. Two years ago, White purchased land and a warehouse. It uses these assets in its business.

   c. Manufacturing machinery White purchased earlier this year.

   d. Inventory White purchased 13 months ago, but is ready to be shipped to a customer.

    e. Office equipment White has used in its business for the past three years.

    f. 1,000 shares of stock in Black corporation that White purchased two years ago because it was a good investment.

    g. Account receivable from a customer with terms 2/10 net 30.

    h. Machinery White held for three years and then sold at a loss of $10,000.

37. **(LO3, LO4)** In year 0, Canon purchased a machine to use in its business for $56,000. In year 3, Canon sold the machine for $42,000. Between the date of the purchase and the date of the sale, Canon depreciated the machine by $32,000.

    a. What is the amount and character of the gain Canon will recognize on the sale, assuming that it is a partnership?

    b. What is the amount and character of the gain Canon will recognize on the sale, assuming that it is a corporation?

    c. What is the amount and character of the gain Canon will recognize on the sale, assuming that it is a corporation and the sale proceeds were increased to $60,000?

    d. What is the amount and character of the gain Canon will recognize on the sale, assuming that it is a corporation and the sale proceeds were decreased to $20,000?

38. **(LO3, LO4)** In year 0, Longworth Partnership purchased a machine for $40,000 to use in its business. In year 3, Longworth sold the machine for $35,000. Between the date of the purchase and the date of the sale, Longworth depreciated the machine by $22,000.

    a. What is the amount and character of the gain Longworth will recognize on the sale?

    b. What is the amount and character of the gain Longworth will recognize on the sale if the sale proceeds were increased to $45,000?

    c. What is the amount and character of the gain Longworth will recognize on the sale if the sale proceeds were decreased to $15,000?

39. **(LO3, LO4)** On August 1 of year 0, Dirksen purchased a machine for $20,000 to use in its business. On December 4 of year 0, Dirksen sold the machine for $18,000.

    a. What is the amount and character of the gain Dirksen will recognize on the sale?

    b. What is the amount and character of the gain Dirksen will recognize on the sale if the machine was sold on January 15 of year 1 instead?

40. **(LO3, LO4)** Rayburn Corporation has a building that it bought during year 0 for $850,000. It sold the building in year 5. During the time it held the building Rayburn depreciated it by $100,000. What is the amount and character of the gain or loss Rayburn will recognize on the sale in each of the following alternative situations?

    a. Rayburn receives $840,000.

    b. Rayburn receives $900,000.

    c. Rayburn receives $700,000.

41. **(LO3, LO4)** Moran owns a building he bought during year 0 for $150,000. He sold the building in year 6. During the time he held the building he depreciated it by $32,000. What is the amount and character of the gain or loss Moran will recognize on the sale in each of the following alternative situations?

    a. Moran received $145,000.

    b. Moran received $170,000.

    c. Moran received $110,000.

 **planning**

42. **(LO3, LO4, LO5)** Hart, an individual, bought an asset for $500,000 and has claimed $100,000 of depreciation deductions against the asset. Hart has a marginal tax rate of 30 percent. Answer the questions presented in the following alternative scenarios (assume Hart had no property transactions other than those described in the problem):

  a. What is the amount and character of Hart's recognized gain if the asset is tangible personal property sold for $450,000? What effect does the sale have on Hart's tax liability for the year?

  b. What is the amount and character of Hart's recognized gain if the asset is tangible personal property sold for $550,000? What effect does the sale have on Hart's tax liability for the year?

  c. What is the amount and character of Hart's recognized gain if the asset is tangible personal property sold for $350,000? What effect does the sale have on Hart's tax liability for the year?

  d. What is the amount and character of Hart's recognized gain if the asset is a nonresidential building sold for $450,000? What effect does the sale have on Hart's tax liability for the year?

  e. Now assume that Hart is a corporation. What is the amount and character of its recognized gain if the asset is a nonresidential building sold for $450,000? What effect does the sale have on Hart's tax liability for the year (assume the same 30 percent marginal tax rate)?

  f. Now assuming that the asset is real property, which entity type should be used to minimize the taxes paid on real estate gains?

43. **(LO4)** Luke sold a building and the parcel of land the building is built on to his brother at fair market value. The fair market value of the building was determined to be $325,000; Luke built the building several years ago at a cost of $200,000. Luke had claimed $45,000 of depreciation expense on the building. The fair market value of the land was determined to be $210,000; Luke purchased the land many years ago for $130,000. Luke's brother will use the building in his business.

  a. What is the amount and character of Luke's recognized gain or loss on the building?

  b. What is the amount and character of Luke's recognized gain or loss on the land?

44. **(LO5)** Buckley, an individual, began business two years ago and has never sold a §1231 asset. Buckley owned each of the assets for several years. In the current year, Buckley sold the following business assets:

| Asset | Original Cost | Accumulated Depreciation | §1231 Gain/Loss |
|---|---|---|---|
| Computers | $  6,000 | $  2,000 | ($3,000) |
| Machinery | $ 10,000 | $  4,000 | ($2,000) |
| Furniture | $ 20,000 | $12,000 | $7,000 |
| Building | $100,000 | $10,000 | ($1,000) |

Assuming Buckley's marginal ordinary income tax rate is 35 percent, answer the questions for the following alternative scenarios:

  a. What are Buckley's gains or losses for the current year? What effect do the gains and losses have on Buckley's tax liability?

  b. Assume that the amount realized increased so that the building was sold at a $6,000 gain instead. What are Buckley's gains or losses for the current year? What effect do the gains and losses have on Buckley's tax liability?

c. Assume that the amount realized increased so that the building was sold at a $15,000 gain instead. What are Buckley's gains or losses for the current year? What effect do the gains and losses have on Buckley's tax liability?

**■ planning**   45. **(LO5)** Aruna, a sole proprietor, wants to sell two assets that she no longer needs for her business. Both assets qualify as §1231 assets. The first is machinery and will generate a $10,000 §1231 loss on the sale. The second is land that will generate a $7,000 §1231 gain on the sale. Aruna's ordinary marginal tax rate is 30 percent.

a. Assuming she sells both assets in December of year 1 (the current year), what effect will the sales have on Aruna's tax liability?

b. Assuming that Aruna sells the land in December of year 1 and the machinery in January of year 2, what effect will the sales have on Aruna's tax liability for each year?

c. Explain why selling the assets in separate years will result in tax savings for Aruna.

46. **(LO5)** Bourne Guitars, a corporation, reported a $157,000 net §1231 gain for year 6.

a. Assuming Bourne reported $50,000 of unrecaptured §1231 losses during years 1–5, what amount of Bourne's net §1231 gain for year 6, if any, is treated as ordinary income?

b. Assuming Bourne's unrecaptured §1231 losses from years 1–5 were $200,000, what amount of Bourne's net §1231 gain for year 6, if any, is treated as ordinary income?

**■ planning**   47. **(LO5)** Tonya Jefferson, a sole proprietor, runs a successful lobbying business in Washington, DC. She doesn't sell many business assets, but she is planning on retiring and selling her historic townhouse, which she runs her business from, in order to buy a place somewhere sunny and warm. Tonya's townhouse is worth $1,000,000 and the land is worth another $1,000,000. The original basis in the townhouse was $600,000, and she has claimed $250,000 of depreciation deductions against the asset over the years. The original basis in the land was $500,000. Tonya has located a buyer that would like to finalize the transaction in December of the current year. Tonya's marginal ordinary income tax rate is 35 percent.

a. What amount of gain or loss does Tonya recognize on the sale? What is the character of the gain or loss? What effect does the gain and loss have on her tax liability?

b. In additional to the original facts, assume that Tonya reports the following unrecaptured 1231 loss:

| Year | Net §1231 Gains/(Losses) |
| --- | --- |
| Year 1 | ($200,000) |
| Year 2 | $0 |
| Year 3 | $0 |
| Year 4 | $0 |
| Year 5 | $0 |
| Year 6 (current year) | ? |

What amount of gain or loss does Tonya recognize on the sale? What is the character of the gain or loss? What effect does the gain or loss have on her year 6 (the current year) tax liability?

c. Assuming the unrecaptured 1231 loss in part (b), as Tonya's tax advisor could you make a suggestion as to when Tonya should sell the townhouse in order to reduce her taxes? What would Tonya's tax liability be if she adopts your recommendation?

48. **(LO5)** Morgan's Water World (MWW), an LLC, opened several years ago and reports the following net §1231 gains and losses since it began business.

| Year | Net §1231 Gains/(Losses) |
|---|---|
| Year 1 | ($11,000) |
| Year 2 | $ 5,000 |
| Year 3 | ($21,000) |
| Year 4 | ($4,000) |
| Year 5 | $ 17,000 |
| Year 6 | ($43,000) |
| Year 7 (current year) | $113,000 |

What amount, if any, of the year 7 $113,000 net §1231 gain is treated as ordinary income?

49. **(LO5)** Hans runs a sole proprietorship. Hans reported the following net §1231 gains and losses since he began business:

| Year | Net §1231 Gains/(Losses) |
|---|---|
| Year 1 | ($110,000) |
| Year 2 | $15,000 |
| Year 3 | $ 0 |
| Year 4 | $ 0 |
| Year 5 | $10,000 |
| Year 6 | $ 0 |
| Year 7 (current year) | $50,000 |

a. What amount, if any, of the year 7 (current year) $50,000 net §1231 gain is treated as ordinary income?

b. Assume that the $50,000 net §1231 gain occurs in year 6 instead of year 7. What amount of the gain would be treated as ordinary income in year 6?

50. **(LO6)** Independence Corporation needs to replace some of the assets used in its trade or business and is contemplating the following exchanges:

| Exchange | Asset Given Up by Independence | Asset Received by Independence |
|---|---|---|
| a | Band saw | Band saw |
| b | Machinery used in textiles | Machinery used for wood working |
| c | Passenger automobile used for deliveries | Heavy duty van that seats two and has a large cargo box |
| d | Large warehouse on two acres | Small warehouse on twenty-two acres |
| e | Office building in Green Bay, WI, used in the business | Apartment complex in Newport Beach, CA, that will be held as an investment |

Determine whether each exchange qualifies as a like-kind exchange. Also, explain the rationale for why each qualifies or does not qualify as a like-kind exchange.

51. **(LO6)** Kase, an individual, purchased some property in Potomac, Maryland, for $150,000 approximately 10 years ago. Kase is approached by a real estate agent representing a client who would like to exchange a parcel of

land in North Carolina for Kase's Maryland property. Kase agrees to the exchange. What is Kase's realized gain or loss, recognized gain or loss, and basis in the North Carolina property in each of the following alternative scenarios?

a. The transaction qualifies as a like-kind exchange and the fair market value of each property is $675,000.

b. The transaction qualifies as a like-kind exchange and the fair market value of each property is $100,000.

**research**

52. **(LO6)** Longhaul Trucking traded two smaller trucks (each had a 10,000-pound gross weight) for one larger truck (18,000-pound gross weight). Do the trucks qualify as like-kind property (*Hint:* because the trucks are tangible personal property they must be the same asset class to be like-kind assets). You should use Rev. Proc. 87-56 to determine the asset classes for the trucks.

**research**

53. **(LO6)** Twinbrook Corporation needed to upgrade to a larger manufacturing facility. Twinbrook first acquired a new manufacturing facility for $2,100,000 cash, and then transferred the facility it was using (building and land) to White Flint Corporation for $2,000,000 three months later. Does the exchange qualify for like-kind exchange treatment (*Hint:* examine Revenue Procedures 2000-37 and 2004-51)? If not, can you propose a change in the transaction that will allow it to qualify?

**research**

54. **(LO6)** Woodley Park Corporation currently owns two parcels of land (parcel 1 and parcel 2). It owns a warehouse facility on parcel 1. Woodley needs to acquire a new and larger manufacturing facility. Woodley was approached by Blazing Fast Construction (who specializes in prefabricated warehouses) about acquiring Woodley's existing warehouse on parcel 1. Woodley indicated that it prefers to exchange its existing facility for a new and larger facility in a qualifying like-kind exchange. Blazing Fast indicated that it could construct a new manufacturing facility on parcel 2 to Woodley's specification within four months. Woodley and Blazing Fast agreed to the following arrangement. First, Blazing Fast would construct the new warehouse on parcel 2 and then relinquish the property to Woodley within four months. Woodley would then transfer the warehouse facility and land parcel 1 to Blazing Fast. All of the property exchanged in the deal was identified immediately and the construction was completed within 180 days. Does the exchange of the new building for the old building and parcel 1 qualify as a like-kind exchange (see *DeCleene v. Commissioner,* 115 TC 457)?

55. **(LO6)** Metro Corp. traded machine A for machine B. Metro originally purchased machine A for $50,000 and machine A's adjusted basis was $25,000 at the time of the exchange. What is Metro's realized gain or loss, recognized gain or loss, and adjusted basis in machine B in each of the following alternative scenarios?

a. The fair market value of machine A and of machine B is $40,000 at the time of the exchange. The exchange does not qualify as a like-kind exchange.

b. The fair market value of machine A and of machine B is $40,000. The exchange qualifies as a like-kind exchange.

c. The fair market value of machine A is $35,000 and machine B is valued at $40,000. Metro exchanges machine A and $5,000 cash for machine B. Machine A and machine B are like-kind property.

d. The fair market value of machine A is $45,000 and Metro trades machine A for machine B valued at $40,000 and $5,000 cash. Machine A and machine B are like-kind property.

56. **(LO6)** Prater Inc. enters into an exchange in which it gives up its warehouse on 10 acres of land and receives a tract of land. A summary of the exchange is as follows:

| Transferred | FMV | Original Basis | Accumulated Depreciation |
|---|---|---|---|
| Warehouse | $300,000 | $225,000 | $45,000 |
| Land | $ 50,000 | $ 50,000 | |
| Mortgage on warehouse | $ 30,000 | | |
| Cash | $ 20,000 | $ 20,000 | |
| | | | |
| Assets Received | FMV | | |
| Land | $340,000 | | |

What is Prater's realized and recognized gain on the exchange and its basis in the assets it received in the exchange?

57. **(LO6)** Baker Corporation owned a building located in Kansas. Baker used the building for its business operations. Last year a tornado hit the property and completely destroyed it. This year, Baker received an insurance settlement. Baker had originally purchased the building for $350,000 and had claimed a total of $100,000 of depreciation deductions against the property. What is Baker's realized and recognized gain or (loss) on this transaction and what is its basis in the new building in the following alternative scenarios?

 a. Baker received $450,000 in insurance proceeds and spent $450,000 rebuilding the building during the current year.

 b. Baker received $450,000 in insurance proceeds and spent $500,000 rebuilding the building during the current year.

 c. Baker received $450,000 in insurance proceeds and spent $400,000 rebuilding the building during the current year.

 d. Baker received $450,000 in insurance proceeds and spent $450,000 rebuilding the building during the next three years.

58. **(LO6)** Russell Corporation sold a parcel of land valued at $400,000. Its basis in the land was $275,000. For the land, Russell received $50,000 in cash in year 0 and a note providing that Russell will receive $175,000 in year 1 and $175,000 in year 2 from the buyer.

 a. What is Russell's realized gain on the transaction?

 b. What is Russell's recognized gain in year 0, year 1, and year 2?

59. **(LO6)** In year 0, Javens Inc. sold machinery with a fair market value of $400,000 to Chris. The machinery's original basis was $317,000 and Javens's accumulated depreciation on the machinery was $50,000, so its adjusted basis to Javens was $267,000. Chris paid Javens $40,000 immediately (in year 0) and provided a note to Javens indicating that Chris would pay Javens $60,000 a year for six years beginning in year 1. What is the amount and character of the gain that Javens will recognize in year 0? What amount and character of the gain will Javens recognize in years 1 through 6?

60. **(LO6)** Ken sold a rental property for $500,000. He received $100,000 in the current year and $100,000 each year for the next four years. $400,000 of the sales price was allocated to the building and the remaining $100,000 was allocated to the land. Ken purchased the property several years ago for $300,000. When he initially purchased the property, he allocated $225,000 of the purchase

■ **research**

price to the building and $75,000 to the land. Ken has claimed $25,000 of depreciation deductions over the years against the building. If Ken had no other sales of §1231 or capital assets in the current year, determine what Ken's recognized gain or loss is, the character of Ken's gain, and calculate Ken's tax due because of the sale (assuming his marginal ordinary tax rate is 35 percent). (**Hint:** see the examples in Reg. §1.453-12.)

■ planning

61. **(LO6)** Hillary is in the leasing business and faces a marginal tax rate of 35 percent. She has leased equipment to Whitewater Corporation for several years. Hillary bought the equipment for $50,000 and claimed $20,000 of depreciation deductions against the asset. The lease term is about to expire and Whitewater would like to acquire the equipment. Hillary has been offered two options to choose from:

| Option | Details |
| --- | --- |
| Like-kind exchange | Whitewater would provide Hillary with like-kind equipment. The like-kind equipment has a fair market value of $35,000. |
| Installment sale | Whitewater would provide Hillary with two payments of $19,000. She would use the proceeds to purchase equipment that she could also lease. |

Ignoring time value of money, which option provides the greatest after-tax value for Hillary, assuming she is indifferent between the proposals based on nontax factors?

62. **(LO6)** Deirdre sold 100 shares of stock to her brother, James, for $2,400. Deirdre purchased the stock several years ago for $3,000.

   a. What gain or loss does Deirdre recognize on the sale?

   b. What amount of gain or loss does James recognize if he sells the stock for $3,200?

   c. What amount of gain or loss does James recognize if he sells the stock for $2,600?

   d. What amount of gain or loss does James recognize if he sells the stock for $2,000?

# COMPREHENSIVE PROBLEMS

63. Two years ago, Bethesda Corporation bought a delivery truck for $30,000 (not subject to the luxury auto depreciation limits). Bethesda used MACRS 200 percent declining balance and the half-year convention to recover the cost of the truck, but it did not elect §179 expensing or any eligible bonus depreciation. Answer the questions for the following alternative scenarios.

   a. Assuming Bethesda used the truck until March of year 3, what depreciation expense can it claim on the truck for years 1 through 3?

   b. Assume that Bethesda claimed $18,500 of depreciation expense on the truck before it sold it in year 3. What is the amount and character of the gain or loss if Bethesda sold the truck in year 3 for $17,000, and incurred $2,000 of selling expenses on the sale?

   c. Assume that Bethesda claimed $18,500 of depreciation expense on the truck before it sold it in year 3. What is the amount and character of the gain or loss if Bethesda sold the truck in year 3 for $35,000, and incurred $3,000 of selling expenses on the sale?

64. Hauswirth Corporation sold (or exchanged) some manufacturing equipment in year 0. Hauswirth bought the machinery several years ago for $65,000 and it has claimed $23,000 of depreciation expense against the equipment.

   a. Assuming that Hauswirth receives $50,000 in cash for the equipment, compute the amount and character of Hauswirth's recognized gain or loss on the sale.

   b. Assuming that Hauswirth receives like-kind equipment with a fair market value of $50,000 in exchange for its equipment, compute Hauswirth's gain realized, gain recognized, deferred gain, and basis in the new equipment.

   c. Assuming that Hauswirth receives $20,000 in cash in year 0 and a $50,000 note receivable that is payable in year 1, compute the amount and character of Hauswirth's gain in year 0 and in year 1.

65. Fontenot Corporation sold some machinery to its majority owner Gray (an individual who owns 60 percent of Fontenot). Fontenot purchased the machinery for $100,000 and has claimed a total of $40,000 of depreciation expense deductions against the property. Gray will provide Fontenot with $10,000 of cash today and provide a $100,000 note that will pay Fontenot $50,000 one year from now and $50,000 two years from now.

   ■ research

   a. What gain does Fontenot's realize on the sale?

   b. What is the amount and character of the gain that Fontenot must recognize in the year of sale (if any) and each of the two subsequent years? (*Hint:* use the Internal Revenue Code and start with §453; please give appropriate citations.)

66. Moab Inc. manufactures and distributes high-tech biking gadgets. It has decided to streamline some of its operations so that it will be able to be more productive and efficient. Because of this decision it has entered into several transactions during the year.

   Part (1) Determine the gain/loss realized and recognized in the current year for each of these events. Also determine whether the gain/loss recognized will be §1231, capital, or ordinary.

   a. Moab Inc. sold a machine that it used to make computerized gadgets for $27,300 cash. It originally bought the machine for $19,200 three years ago and has taken $8,000 depreciation.

   b. Moab Inc. held stock in ABC Corp., which had a value of $12,000 at the beginning of the year. That same stock had a value of $15,230 at the end of the year.

   c. Moab Inc. sold some of its inventory for $7,000 cash. This inventory had a basis of $5,000.

   d. Moab Inc. disposed of an office building with a fair market value of $75,000 for another office building with a fair market value of $55,000 and $20,000 in cash. It originally bought the office building seven years ago for $62,000 and has taken $15,000 in depreciation.

   e. Moab Inc. sold some land held for investment for $28,000. It originally bought the land for $32,000.

   f. Moab Inc. sold another machine for a note payable in four annual installments of $12,000. The first payment was received in the current year. It originally bought the machine two years ago for $32,000 and has claimed $9,000 in depreciation expense against the machine.

   g. Moab Inc. sold stock it held for eight years for $2,750. It originally purchased the stock for $2,100.

   h. Moab Inc. sold another machine for $7,300. It originally purchased this machine six months ago for $9,000 and has claimed $830 in depreciation expense against the asset.

Part (2) From the recognized gains/losses determined in part 1, determine the net §1231 gain/loss and the net ordinary gain/loss Moab will recognize on its tax return. Moab Inc. also has $2,000 of unrecaptured §1231 losses from previous years.

■
■ research
■■

67. Vertovec Inc., a large local consulting firm in Utah, hired several new consultants from out of state last year to help service their expanding list of clients. To aide in relocating the consultants, Vertovec Inc. purchased the consultants' homes in their prior location if the consultants were unable to sell their homes within 30 days of listing them for sale. Vertovec Inc. bought the homes from the consultants for 5 percent less than the list price and then continued to list the homes for sale. Each home Vertovec Inc. purchased was sold at a loss. By the end of last year, Vertovec had suffered a loss totaling $250,000 from the homes. How should Vertovec treat the loss for tax purposes? Write a memo to Vertovec Inc. explaining your findings and any planning suggestions that you may have if Vertovec Inc. continues to offer this type of relocation benefit to newly hired consultants.

# Investments

## Learning Objectives

**Upon completing this chapter, you should be able to:**

**LO 1** Explain how interest income and dividend income are taxed.

---

**LO 2** Compute the tax consequences associated with the disposition of capital assets, including the netting process for calculating gains and losses.

---

**LO 3** Describe common sources of tax-exempt investment income and explain the rationale for exempting some investments from taxation.

---

**LO 4** Calculate the deduction for portfolio investment-related expenses, including investment expenses and investment interest expense.

---

**LO 5** Understand the distinction between portfolio investments and passive investments and apply tax basis, at-risk, and passive activity loss limits to losses from passive investments.

| Storyline Summary | |
|---|---|
| *Taxpayers:* | Nick and Rachel Sutton |
| *Home:* | Scottsdale, Arizona |
| *Employment status:* | Rachel—Software developer for national software company; current salary $120,000 Nick—High school science teacher; current salary $50,000 |
| *Filing status:* | Married filing jointly |
| *Dependents:* | None currently, but they are expecting a baby girl |
| *Marginal tax rate for ordinary income:* | 30 percent |
| *Current situation:* | Nick recently received an inheritance, and the Suttons are deciding how to invest it. |

N ick and Rachel Sutton live in Scottsdale, Arizona. The couple has been married for 10 years and is expecting their first child, a girl, next month. Nick is a high school science teacher, earning an annual salary of $50,000, and Rachel is a software developer, earning an annual salary of $120,000. With their above-average family income, the Suttons invest in retirement accounts through their employers but have no other investments.

When Nick's grandmother recently passed away, he learned that she had left him an inheritance of $100,000 with the stipulation that he "invest it to financially benefit his family."

After considerable discussion, Nick and Rachel decide to invest the inheritance to help the family accomplish two financial goals. First, they want to save for their daughter's college education. They figure that if they immediately invest $50,000 of the inheritance for her college education, they should have a significant sum accumulated when Lea (yes, they've decided on the baby's name) starts college in 18 years. Second, they decided they will immediately invest the remaining $50,000 for five years and use the accumulation to make a significant down payment on a vacation home in Park City, Utah, a town they fell in love with while attending the 2002 Winter Olympics. The Suttons have a marginal income tax rate of 30 percent, and they have investment opportunities that earn an 8 percent **before-tax rate of return.**[1] Their objective is to devise an investment strategy that will maximize the **after-tax rate of return** on their investments while accomplishing their nontax objectives. ■

[1]Unless otherwise noted, all the investments discussed in the chapter are assumed to yield an 8 percent before-tax return. Although this rate may be somewhat unrealistic, this assumption is made to facilitate a comparison of investments based on their tax characteristics alone.

# INVESTMENTS OVERVIEW

Investors are attracted to certain investments according to their investment philosophy and their appetite for risk, among other things. Some prefer investments that provide a consistent income stream. Others prefer investments that have significant appreciation potential but provide no current cash flows. These investment attributes affect the before-tax returns on investments. However, taxes are levied on **investment income,** and thus, it would be unwise to make an investment without considering the tax cost. For example, it is possible that two investments with identical before-tax rates of return will generate different after-tax rates of return because the investments are taxed differently. Indeed, it is possible that an investment with a lower before-tax rate of return compared to an alternative investment will have a higher after-tax rate of return because income from the investment is taxed at a later date or taxed at a lower rate than the alternative investment.

Two key tax characteristics that affect after-tax returns from investments are (1) the timing of tax payments or tax benefits and (2) the rate at which investment income or gains are taxed or deductible expenses or losses generate tax savings. Not surprisingly, these variables are directly related to the timing and conversion tax planning strategies introduced in Chapter 3.

Income from **portfolio investments** (investments producing **dividends,** interest, royalties, annuities, or capital gains) may be taxed at ordinary rates, preferential rates, or may be exempt from taxation. Further, depending on the type of investment, tax on income from a portfolio investment may be imposed annually or may be deferred until the taxpayer sells the investment. Losses from portfolio investments are deferred until the investment is sold and are typically subject to limitations.

In contrast to portfolio investments, **passive investments** generate **operating income** and **operating losses.** Operating income is always taxed annually at ordinary rates while operating losses are either deducted annually at ordinary rates or deferred and deducted later at ordinary rates depending on the investor's circumstances. Losses from passive investments are also subject to limitations.

This chapter explores several common portfolio and passive investments, discusses important tax and nontax considerations relevant for those investments, and compares investment returns on an after-tax basis.

| Taxes in the Real World   *Helping Investors Make Better Decisions* |
| --- |

Since 2002, the Securities and Exchange Commission has required mutual funds—large, professionally managed investment funds—to disclose after-tax returns in addition to pretax returns in their prospectuses. The disclosure requirements were changed in 2002 to provide mutual fund investors with a better understanding of the impact of taxes on their investment returns.

**LO1**

# PORTFOLIO INCOME: INTEREST AND DIVIDENDS

Taxpayers who desire current cash flows from their investments may choose investments that generate interest or regular dividends. Investments generating interest income include **certificates of deposit** (CDs), savings accounts, corporate **bonds,** and governmental bonds. Investments generating dividend income include direct equity investments in corporate stocks or investments in **mutual funds** that invest in corporate stock.[2] Although all of these investments generate current cash flows, they differ significantly in terms of their economic and tax consequences.

---

[2]Mutual funds are portfolios of investment assets managed by professional money managers. Generally, the income earned by mutual funds flows through to the owners of mutual fund shares who pay the resulting taxes due. The nature of the assets held by the mutual fund determines the character of the income.

By lending money to banks, governmental entities, or corporations, investors essentially become debt holders. As such, they are legally entitled to receive periodic interest payments *and* to recover the amount of principal loaned (in the case of bonds, principal is the **maturity value** or **face value** of the bonds). Interest payments and the time and manner of repayment of the loan principal are defined either contractually for CDs and savings accounts or by bond covenants for loans made either to governments or corporations. In contrast, investors who purchase stocks become shareholders (also called equity holders) of a corporation. As shareholders, they are entitled to receive dividends if the company declares dividends and to *indirectly* share in either the future appreciation or depreciation in the value of a corporation through stock ownership. Unlike debt holders, shareholders are not legally entitled to receive dividend payments or to recover their initial investment. Thus, from an investor's perspective, debt tends to be less risky than equity.

For tax purposes, individual investors typically are taxed on both interest and dividend income when they receive it. However, interest income is taxed at ordinary rates while dividend income is generally taxed at lower capital gains rates.

## Interest

In general, taxpayers recognize interest income from investments when they receive the interest payments.[3] Taxpayers investing in savings accounts, money market accounts, CDs, and most bonds receive interest payments based on a stated annual rate of return at yearly or more frequent intervals. When interest is paid annually at a stated rate of return, it is relatively straightforward to modify the rate of return and time value of money formulas you have seen in finance-type courses to account for taxes on interest income. Indeed, assuming constant tax rates, the after-tax rate of return and the future value of an investment *paying* interest *annually* at a *constant before-tax rate of return* can be determined after any number of years using the formulas provided in Exhibit 11-1. For bonds, the formulas assume the bonds are purchased at face value.

**EXHIBIT 11-1**   **Formulas for the After-Tax Rate of Return and the After-Tax Future Value of Investment with *Constant Rate of Return***

Annual after-tax rate of return = before-tax rate of return × (1 − marginal tax rate)

After-tax future value = $I \times (1 + r)^n$ where

$I$ = the amount of the original investment,
$r$ = the annual *after-tax rate* of return, and
$n$ = the number of years the investment is maintained.

> **THE KEY FACTS**
>
> Interest and Dividend Income
>
> ∎ **Interest**
> · Interest is taxed at ordinary rates.
> · Cash interest payments are taxed annually.
> · Accrued market discount is taxed at sale or maturity.
> · Savings bonds are taxed at sale or maturity.
> · Original issue discount is taxed annually.
>
> ∎ **Dividends**
> · Dividends are taxed annually.
> · Qualified dividends are taxed at preferential rates.
>
> ∎ **Interest vs. dividends**
> · Time horizon does not affect after-tax rate of return on investments taxed annually.
> · The dividend tax rate is lower than the ordinary tax rate on interest; all else equal, dividends generate higher after-tax rates of return than interest.

**Example 11-1**

Assume on January 1 of year 1 the Suttons invest the $50,000 earmarked for the Park City vacation home in General Electric (GE) bonds that mature in exactly five years and the $50,000 designated for Lea's education in GE bonds that mature in exactly 18 years. They will purchase both bonds at face value, and both bonds will pay 8 percent interest annually. How much interest income will Nick and Rachel report from this investment at the end of the first year?

**Answer:** $8,000. $4,000 of interest income ($50,000 × .08) from each bond in the first year of the investment.

Assuming they reinvest their annual after-tax interest payments in the GE bonds, what annual after-tax rate of return will they earn on the bonds over the 5- and 18-year investment periods, and what (continued on page 11-4...)

[3]Interest income is reported on Part I of Schedule B filed with taxpayers' Form 1040.

amount will the Suttons receive 5 and 18 years from now when the bonds mature? (Remember from the opening story-line, the Sutton's marginal tax rate is 30%.)

**Answer:** See (1) and (2) in the table below.

| Time to Maturity | 5 Years | 18 Years |
|---|---|---|
| (1) Annual after-tax rates of return = 8% × (1 − .3) | 5.6% | 5.6% |
| (2) Nick and Rachel will receive after-tax: $50,000 (1 + .056)$^n$, where n is 5 and 18 years, respectively. | $65,658 | $133,328 |

Why are the after-tax returns the same for both bonds? Because the investments are taxed annually, the investment horizon does not affect after-tax rates of return.

Special rules apply for determining the timing and amount of interest from bonds when there is a **bond discount** (bonds are issued at an amount below the maturity value) or a **bond premium** (bonds are issued at an amount above the maturity value). Below we discuss these rules as they apply to corporate, U.S. Treasury bonds, and **U.S. savings bonds.**

**Corporate and U.S. Treasury Bonds**    Both corporations and the U.S. Treasury raise money from debt markets by issuing bonds.[4] Corporate bonds, **Treasury bonds,** and **Treasury notes** are issued at maturity value, at a discount, or at a premium, depending on prevailing interest rates.[5] Treasury bonds and Treasury notes pay a stated rate of interest semiannually.[6] However, corporate bonds may pay interest at a stated "coupon" rate or they may not provide any periodic interest payments. Corporate bonds that do not pay periodic interest are called **zero-coupon bonds.** Overall, the consequences of holding corporate or Treasury bonds are very similar. The two primary differences are that (1) interest from Treasury bonds is exempt from *state* taxation while interest from corporate bonds is not and (2) Treasury bonds always pay interest periodically while corporate bonds may or may not. The tax rules for determining the timing and amount of interest income from corporate and U.S. Treasury bonds are as follows:

- Taxpayers include the actual interest payments they receive in gross income.
- If the bond was issued at a discount, special **original issue discount** (OID) rules apply. Taxpayers are required to amortize the discount and include the amount of the current year **amortization** in gross income in addition to any interest payments the taxpayer actually receives.[7] In the case of corporate zero-coupon bonds, this means taxpayers must report and pay taxes on income related to the bonds even though they did not receive *any* payments from the bonds. Bond issuers or brokers are responsible for calculating the yearly amortization of original issue discount and providing this information to investors using Form 1099-OID.

---

[4]Investors in corporate bonds assume more risk than investors in Treasury securities because they are relying on the creditworthiness of the corporation issuing the bonds. To compensate bondholders for this additional risk, corporate bonds usually yield higher before-tax rates of return than Treasury securities.

[5]The bonds are issued at a discount (premium) if the market interest rate is higher (lower) than the stated rate on the bonds.

[6]Treasury notes and bonds differ in terms of their maturities. Treasury notes are issued with two, five, and ten year maturities. In contrast, Treasury bonds are issued with maturities greater than ten years. From this point forward, we use the term Treasury bonds to refer to both Treasury notes and Treasury bonds.

[7]§1272. Original issue discount is amortized semiannually under the constant yield method, which is consistent with the approach used to amortize bond discount under GAAP.

- If the bond was issued at a premium, taxpayers may *elect* to amortize the premium.[8] Taxpayers or their advisors are responsible for determining the yearly amortization of bond premium if the election to amortize the premium has been made. The amount of the current year amortization offsets a portion of the actual interest payments that taxpayers must include in gross income. The original tax basis of the bond includes the premium and is reduced by any amortization of bond premium over the life of the bond.

- If the bond is purchased in the secondary bond market at a discount, the taxpayer treats some of or all of the **market discount** as interest income *when she sells the bond or the bond matures.*[9] If the bond is sold prior to **maturity,** a ratable amount of the market discount (based on the number of days the bond is held over the number of days until maturity when the bond is purchased), called the **accrued market discount,** is treated as interest income on the date of sale.[10] If the bond is held to maturity, the entire bond discount is treated as interest income at maturity.

- If the bond is purchased in the secondary bond market at a premium, the premium is treated exactly like original issue bond premiums. As a result, the taxpayer may elect to amortize the **market premium** to reduce the annual interest income received from the bond. Otherwise, the premium remains as part of the tax basis of the bond and affects the capital gain or loss the taxpayer recognizes when the taxpayer sells or redeems the bond.

**U.S. Savings Bonds**   U.S. savings bonds such as Series EE or Series I bonds are issued at either face value or at a discount. These bonds do not pay periodic interest; rather, interest accumulates over the term of the bonds and is paid when investors redeem them at maturity or earlier.[11] That is, the amount of interest income taxpayers recognize *when they redeem* the bonds is the excess of the bond proceeds over the taxpayer's **basis** (purchase price) in the bonds. Taxpayers may elect to include the increase in the bond redemption value in income each year, but this is generally not advisable because it accelerates the income from the bond without providing any cash to pay the taxes.[12] Finally, interest from Series EE and Series I bonds may be excluded from gross income to the extent the bond proceeds are used to pay qualifying educational expenses. However, this exclusion benefit is subject to phase-out based on the taxpayer's AGI.

---

**Example 11-2**

*What if:* Assume that instead of buying GE bonds, Nick and Rachel were deciding whether to invest the $50,000 earmarked for the Park City vacation home in (1) Series EE savings bonds that mature in exactly five years, (2) original issue AMD Corporation *zero-coupon* bonds that mature in exactly five years, or (3) U.S. Treasury bonds that pay $46,250 at maturity in five years trading in the secondary bond market with a stated annual interest rate of 10 percent. Further, assume that all bonds yield 8 (*continued on page 11-6...*)

---

[8]§171. Like an original issue discount, a bond premium is amortized semiannually under the constant yield method—the same method used to amortize bond premiums under GAAP. Unlike premiums on taxable bonds, premiums on tax-exempt bonds must always be amortized.

[9]§1276(a). Under §1278(b)(1), taxpayers may elect to include the amortization of market discount in their income annually. However, this election accelerates the recognition of income from the market discount and is therefore usually not advisable.

[10]§1276(b).

[11]Series EE savings bonds are issued at a discount and Series I savings bonds are issued at maturity value. EE bonds provide a constant rate of return while Series I bonds provides a return that is indexed for inflation and thus increases over time.

[12]§454(a). Investors that make this election report the annual increase in the redemption value of their savings bonds using savings bond redemption tables published by the Treasury Department.

percent annual before-tax returns compounded semiannually. At the end of the first year, the redemption value of the EE savings bond would be $54,080, or the Suttons would receive a Form 1099-OID from AMD reporting $4,080 of OID amortization for the year, or they would receive two semiannual interest payments of $2,312.50 from the Treasury bonds. Under the general rules, how much interest income from each bond would Nick and Rachel report at the end of the first year?

**Answer:** $0 from the Series EE savings bonds, $4,080 from the AMD bonds, and $4,625 (two semi-annual payments of $2,312.50) from the Treasury bonds. Note, however, that the Suttons could *elect* to include the $4,080 increase in redemption value of the Series EE bond in interest income even though they did not receive any interest payments on the bond (probably not optimal). They also could *elect* to amortize $637.50 of the $3,750 premium ($50,000 purchase price less the $46,250 maturity value) on the Treasury bond to offset the $4,625 in actual interest payments they received on the bond (probably a good idea). The calculations required to amortize the premium on the Treasury bond for the first year are reflected in the following table:

| Semiannual Period | (A)<br>Adjusted Basis of Bond at Beginning of Semiannual Period | (B)<br>Interest Received and Reported<br>($46,250 × 10% × .5) | (C)<br>Interest Earned<br>(A) × 8% × .5 | Premium Amortization<br>(B) − (C) |
|---|---|---|---|---|
| 1 | $50,000.00 | $2,312.50 | $2,000.00 | $312.50 |
| 2 | $49,687.50 | $2,312.50 | $1,987.50 | $325.00 |
| Yearly Total | | $4,625.00 | $3,987.50 | $637.50 |

Intuitively, would the Suttons be better or worse off purchasing the Series EE savings bonds rather than the GE bonds (see Example 11-1) to save for the Park City home?

**Answer:** They would better off in two respects. First, they wouldn't have to pay state income taxes on the interest earned from the savings bonds. Second, they would be able to defer paying taxes on the accumulated interest from the savings bonds until the savings bonds are cashed in at maturity. This will increase the after-tax returns from the savings bonds relative to the GE bonds.

Intuitively, would the Suttons be better or worse off purchasing the AMD zero-coupon bonds rather than the GE bonds (see Example 11-1) to save for the Park City home?

**Answer:** They will be worse off because they will have to pay taxes currently from the OID amortization on the AMD bonds without receiving any cash flow from the bonds to pay the taxes due. This will reduce the after-tax returns from the AMD bonds relative to the GE bonds.

## Example 11-3

*What if:* Assume that on January 1, Nick and Rachel use the $50,000 earmarked for the Park City vacation home to purchase AMD zero-coupon bonds in the *secondary bond market* almost immediately after they were originally issued. If the bonds mature in exactly five years and have a maturity value of $74,000, how much interest income will Nick and Rachel report at the end of the first year and in the year the bonds mature?

**Answer:** $0 in the first year and $24,000 in the year the bonds mature. Because the AMD zero-coupon bonds were not purchased at original issue, the entire $24,000 market discount on the bonds will be reported as interest income when the bonds mature. Thus, the Suttons will not report any income related to the AMD bonds until the year the bonds mature.

*What if:* Assume the same facts as above, except the Suttons purchased a U.S. Series EE bond instead of an AMD zero-coupon bond to fund the Park City vacation home in five years. How much interest income will the Suttons report at the end of the first year and in the year the bonds mature?

**Answer:** $0 in the first year and $24,000 in the year the EE savings bonds mature; exactly the same outcome as the investment in the AMD zero-coupon bonds.

As our discussion suggests, for certain types of investments such as savings accounts, money market accounts, and CDs, computing the annual taxable interest income is relatively straightforward. However, for investments in bonds, the process is much more involved. Exhibit 11-2 summarizes the general rule and exceptions for the timing of interest payments and related tax payments.

**EXHIBIT 11-2    Timing of Interest Payments and Taxes**

| General Rule | Exception | Exception |
|---|---|---|
| **Interest Received Annually and Taxed Annually** | **Interest Received at Sale or Maturity and Taxed at Sale or Maturity** | **Interest Received at Sale or Maturity but Taxed Annually** |
| • Savings accounts.<br>• CDs.<br>• Money market accounts.<br>• Bond interest payments actually received in the year. | • Accrued market discount on bonds.<br>• Interest earned on U.S. savings bonds. | • Original issue discount (OID) on corporate and Treasury bonds. |

## Dividends

Historically, dividends received by investors have been taxed at the same rate as interest income. However, in 2003, Congress changed the law for dividends to mitigate the so-called "double tax" on dividend income.[13] Consistent with the general rule for taxing interest income, dividend payments (including reinvested dividends) are taxed annually.[14] However, **qualified dividends** generally are taxed at a 15 percent preferential rate (in some circumstances, qualified dividends may be taxed at rate as low as 0 percent depending on the taxpayer's ordinary income tax rate).[15] Qualified dividends are those paid by domestic or certain qualified foreign corporations provided investors hold the dividend-paying stock for *more than* 60 days during the 121-day period that begins 60 days before the **ex-dividend date** (the first day on which the purchaser of the stock would not be entitled to receive a declared dividend on the stock).[16] Nonqualified dividends are not eligible for the reduced rate and are therefore, taxed at ordinary rates. Corporations normally indicate whether their dividends are potentially eligible for the preferential rate when they send Form 1099-DIV to shareholders after year-end. However, shareholders ultimately must determine if they qualify for the preferential rate by confirming they held the stock for the required number of days around the ex-dividend date.

**Example 11-4**

*What if:* Assume that Nick and Rachel decide to purchase dividend-paying stocks to achieve their short- and long-term financial objectives. They invest $50,000 in Xerox stock, intend to hold the stock for five years, and then sell it to fund the Park City home down payment. They invest another $50,000

(*continued on page 11-8...*)

---

[13]Because corporations pay income taxes, dividends are taxed once at the corporate level when the income used to pay dividends is earned by the corporation, and a second time when dividends are received by investors.

[14]Dividends are reported on Part II of Schedule B filed with taxpayers' Form 1040.

[15]Certain dividends paid in the form of additional stock shares (stock dividends) are not taxable (see §305).

[16]Qualified foreign corporations are those incorporated in a U.S. possession (e.g., Puerto Rico, U.S. Virgin Islands), those eligible for the benefits of a comprehensive income tax treaty with the United States, or those whose shares are readily traded on an established U.S. securities market.

in Xerox stock, intend to hold it for 18 years, and then sell it to fund their daughter's education. How much dividend income will Nick and Rachel report at the end of the first year if the dividend payments provide an 8 percent return on their investments?[17]

**Answer:** Nick and Rachel will report $4,000 ($50,000 × .08) of dividend income from each block of the Xerox stock for the first year of their investment.

*What if:* Assume that Xerox dividends continue to provide an 8 percent return for 5 and 18 years, respectively, that Nick and Rachel reinvest their after-tax dividends each year, and that the share price of Xerox remains constant. Given these assumptions, what will be their after-tax rate of return over the 5- and 18-year investment periods, and what will be the value of their investment in the Xerox 5-year block and the Xerox 18-year block of stock 5 and 18 years from now?

**Answer:** See (1) and (2) in the table below.

| Time to Maturity | 5 years | 18 years |
|---|---|---|
| (1) Annual after-tax rates of return: 8% × (1 − .15)<br>Note that qualified dividends are taxed at 15% | 6.80% | 6.80% |
| (2) Nick and Rachel will receive after-tax:<br>$50,000 (1 + .068)^n$, where $n$ is 5 and<br>18 years, respectively. | $69,475 | $163,400 |

Note that the formula for determining the after-tax rate of return and the after-tax accumulation is identical to the formula used in Example 11-1 to determine the after-tax rate of return and accumulation on the bond investments. The only difference is that the dividends are taxed at a 15 percent rate, which is *half the rate* at which the interest on the bonds was taxed to the Suttons.

Because dividend income is taxed generally at lower rates than interest income, it appears that taxpayers seeking current cash flows from their investments should favor dividend-paying investments over interest-paying investments. This raises the question of why anyone would ever prefer investments paying interest over those paying dividends. Remember, though, that savvy investors also should consider non-tax factors such as before-tax rates of return, risk, and liquidity needs when choosing among alternative investments. These fundamental differences explain why investors may continue to seek out interest income in spite of the associated tax disadvantages.

## **LO2** PORTFOLIO INCOME: CAPITAL GAINS AND LOSSES

Investors who don't need annual cash flows from their investments may prefer to invest in assets with the expectation that the investments will appreciate in value over time, providing cash at some point in the future when they sell the assets. Investors also may be willing to assume greater risk in exchange for greater returns than those provided by interest or dividend-paying investments. For example, they might purchase raw land, fine art, rare coins, precious gems or metals, growth stocks (stock in corporations that reinvest their earnings to grow the company as opposed to distributing earnings to shareholders in the form of dividends), mutual fund shares, or even vintage automobiles. Purchasing any such asset is

---

[17]Annual returns from dividend-paying stocks are typically lower than the return from taxable bonds. However, it is assumed here that the returns are equal for the sake of comparability.

not without risk. Indeed, investments held solely for appreciation potential *may* actually decline in value.

When taxpayers buy and hold assets with appreciation potential, they typically are investing in **capital assets.** As we discussed in the previous chapter, capital assets are typically investment-type assets and personal-use assets.[18] Thus, artwork, corporate stock, bonds, your personal residence, and even your iPod are capital assets.

While it may be enjoyable to view collectible fine art in your home or watch a stock portfolio grow in value on quarterly brokerage statements, from a tax perspective the real advantages of investing in capital assets are (1) gains are deferred for tax purposes until the taxpayer sells or otherwise disposes of the assets[19] and (2) gains generally are taxed at preferential rates relative to ordinary income.[20] Why the favorable treatment? One reason is that taxpayers may not have the wherewithal (cash) to pay the tax on their gains until they sell the investment. Another is that the preferential tax rate provides an incentive for taxpayers to invest in assets that may stimulate the economy. Investors can capture these tax benefits when they sell capital assets at a gain. However, when they sell capital assets at a loss, their ability to deduct the loss may be limited.

When a taxpayer sells a capital asset for more than its **tax basis,** the taxpayer recognizes a capital gain; if a taxpayer sells a capital asset for less than its tax basis, the taxpayer recognizes a capital loss (to the extent the loss is deductible).[21] The amount realized or selling price of a capital asset includes the cash and fair market value of other property received, less broker's fees and other selling costs. The basis of any asset, including a capital asset, is generally the taxpayer's "cost" of acquiring the asset, including the initial purchase price and other costs incurred to purchase or improve the asset.[22] Thus, the tax basis of corporate stock purchased from a stockbroker includes the cost of the stock and any additional brokerage fees paid by the taxpayer to acquire the stock. Also, the tax basis in a personal residence includes the initial purchase price plus the cost of subsequent improvements to the home.

Because a taxpayer cannot accurately compute the gain or loss on the sale of a capital asset without knowing its basis, it is important for taxpayers to maintain accurate records to track their basis in capital assets. This process is relatively straightforward for unique assets such as a taxpayer's personal residence or individual jewels in a taxpayer's jewelry collection. However, capital assets such as shares of stock are much more homogeneous and difficult to track. For example, a taxpayer may purchase blocks of stock in a given corporation at different times over a period of several years, paying a different price per share for each block of stock acquired. When the taxpayer sells shares of this stock in subsequent years, what basis does she use to compute gain or loss? Taxpayers who haven't adequately

---

[18]§1221 defines capital assets in the negative. This code section excludes inventory, depreciable property or real property used in a trade or business, certain self-created intangibles, accounts or notes receivable, U.S. government publications, certain commodities derivative financial instruments, certain hedging transactions, and supplies from the definition of a capital asset.

[19]Similarly, interest related to market discount on bonds and the original issue discount on U.S. EE savings bonds accumulates free of tax until the bonds mature or are sold. However, ordinary rather than capital gains rates apply when the tax must finally be paid.

[20]Mutual funds that generate current income by regularly selling capital assets or by holding income-producing securities are an exception to this general rule. However, tax-efficient mutual funds that only buy and hold growth stocks are treated more like other capital assets for tax purposes (capital gains are deferred until mutual fund shares are sold).

[21]As discussed below, losses on personal assets are not deductible for tax purposes.

[22]Currently, brokers must file annual information returns reporting the proceeds their customers realize from the sale of securities. However, for stocks acquired on or after January 1, 2011 (later for other specialized securities), brokers will also be required to report the tax basis of securities their customers sell.

tracked the basis in their stock are required to use the **first-in first-out (FIFO) method** of determining the basis of the shares they sell.[23] However, if they maintain good records, they can use the **specific identification method** to determine the basis of the shares they sell. Taxpayers using the specific identification method can choose to sell their high-basis stock first, minimizing their gains or increasing their losses on stock dispositions.

**Example 11-5**

After Rachel's car broke down, Nick and Rachel decided to buy a new one. To fund the down payment, they sold 200 shares of Cisco stock at the current market price of $40 per share for a total amount realized of $8,000. The Suttons held the following blocks of Cisco stock at the time of the sale:

**Cisco Corporation Stock Ownership**

| Holding Period | (1) Cost per share | (2) Shares | (1) × (2) Basis | Basis of 200 shares sold | Explanation |
|---|---|---|---|---|---|
| 5 years | $25 | 250 | $6,250 | $5,000 | FIFO basis ($25 × 200) |
| 2 years | $32 | 250 | $8,000 | $6,400 | Specific ID basis ($32 × 200) |

How much capital gain will the Suttons recognize if they use the FIFO method of computing the basis in the Cisco shares sold?

**Answer:** $3,000. $8,000 amount realized ($40 × 200) minus $5,000 FIFO basis ($25 × 200). As indicated in the table above, under the FIFO (oldest first) method, they are treated as though they sold the stock held for five years.

**What if:** How much capital gain will the Suttons recognize if they use the specific identification method of computing the basis in the shares sold to minimize the taxable gain on the sale?

**Answer:** $1,600. $8,000 amount realized ($40 × 200) minus $6,400 ($32 × 200). To minimize their gain on the sale under the specific identification method, the Suttons would choose to sell the 200 shares with the highest basis. As indicated in the table above, the shares with the higher basis are those acquired and held two years for $32 per share.

Note in the above example that the Suttons receive $8,000 from the stock sale ($40 per share × 200 shares sold) regardless of the method they use to compute the basis of the shares they sell. The difference between the FIFO and specific identification methods lies in the amount of taxable gain on the *current* sale. Over time, as taxpayers sell all of their stock, both methods will ultimately allow taxpayers to fully recover their cost in the investments. However, applying the specific identification method will result in lower capital gains taxes currently and thereby minimize the present value of the taxes paid on stock sales.

[23]Reg. §1.1012-1(c)(1).

## Types of Capital Gains and Losses

Taxpayers selling capital assets that they hold for a year or less recognize **short-term capital gains or losses.**[24] Alternatively, taxpayers selling capital assets they hold for more than a year recognize **long-term capital gains or losses.** Short-term capital gains are taxed at ordinary rather than preferential rates. In contrast, long-term capital gains are taxed at preferential rates. However, not all long-term capital gains are created equal. Although most long-term capital gains are taxed at a maximum 15 percent rate, certain long-term capital gains are taxed at a maximum rate of 25 percent and others are taxed at a maximum 28 percent rate for tax policy reasons.

**Unrecaptured §1250 Gain**    When individuals sell depreciable real property at a gain, some or all of the gain is subject to a maximum tax rate of 25 percent. As we discussed in Chapter 10, the amount of this **unrecaptured §1250 gain** is generally the *lesser* of (1) the recognized gain or (2) the accumulated depreciation on the property. Gains from depreciable real property in excess of this unrecaptured §1250 gain amount may be treated as long-term capital gains subject to a maximum 15 percent tax rate. Thus, even though unrecaptured §1250 gains are treated as long-term capital gains, they are taxed at a rate higher than most other long-term capital gains.[25] Unrecaptured §1250 gains are taxed at higher capital gains rates because the depreciation deductions responsible for these gains previously reduced the seller's ordinary income taxable at higher ordinary rates.

---

**Example 11-6**

**What if:** Assume Jeb Landers, Rachel's father, recently sold a rental home for $160,000. He originally acquired the home many years ago for $100,000, and he has fully depreciated it for tax purposes. Assuming Jeb's marginal ordinary tax rate is 35 percent, what tax does he owe on the gain if he did not sell any other property during the year?

**Answer:** $34,000. Because Jeb's tax basis in the home is $0 (he has fully depreciated it), his gain on the sale is $160,000. As we pointed out in Chapter 10, all of the gain qualifies as §1231 gain because Jeb held the rental home for more than one year. This gain will ultimately be treated as long-term capital gain because Jeb does not have any §1231 losses during the year. The unrecaptured §1250 gain is $100,000, which is the lesser of (1) the $160,000 gain recognized on the sale or (2) the $100,000 accumulated depreciation. Thus, Jeb must pay $25,000 in tax on this portion of the gain ($100,000 × 25%). The remaining $60,000 of gain is taxed at 15 percent, so he owes $9,000 of tax on this portion ($60,000 × 15%). In total, he owes $34,000 of tax on the sale ($25,000 + $9,000).

---

**Collectibles and §1202 Gain**    Gains from two types of capital assets are taxable at a maximum 28 percent rate. The first type, **collectibles,** consists of works of art, any rug or antique, any metal or gem, any stamp or coin, any alcoholic beverage, or other similar items held for more than one year.[26] The second type is **qualified small business stock**

---

[24]Nonbusiness bad debt is treated as a short-term capital loss no matter how long the debt was outstanding before it became worthless. Whether a bad debt is considered to be a business bad debt for individuals depends on the facts and circumstances. In general, if the taxpayer experiencing the loss is in the business of loaning money, the bad debt should be considered to be business bad debt; otherwise, the bad debt will likely be considered nonbusiness bad debt.

[25]As we discussed in Chapter 10, unrecaptured §1250 gain is technically a §1231 gain.

[26]§408(m).

held for *more than five years*.[27] In general, §1202 defines qualified small business stock as stock received at *original issue* from a C corporation with a gross tax basis in its assets both before and after the issuance of no more than $50,000,000 and with at least 80 percent of the value of its assets used in the active conduct of certain qualified trades or businesses. Under this definition, many investors and employees who hold stock in closely held corporations are likely to hold qualified small business stock. When taxpayers sell qualified small business stock after holding it for more than five years, they may exclude half of the gain on the sale from regular taxable income (75 percent if the stock was acquired after February 17, 2009, and before January 1, 2011).[28] However, the capital gain not excluded from income is taxed at 28 percent. Thus, the effective maximum capital gains rate on the total gain from the sale is 14 percent (7 percent for stock acquired after February 17, 2009, and before January 1, 2011)—less than the usual long-term capital gains rate of 15 percent. The 28 percent rate imposed on qualified small business stock was motivated by a desire in Congress to recapture a portion of the benefit from the 50 percent exclusion available when such stock is sold after five years.

## Example 11-7

**What if:** Assume that Jeb sold his stock in Gangbusters, Inc., a qualified small business stock, for $200,000 after holding it for six years. His basis in the stock is $50,000. How much tax will he owe on the sale if his ordinary marginal rate is 35 percent, the stock was acquired before February 17, 2009, and he is not subject to the alternative minimum tax?

**Answer:** $21,000. Because Jeb held the qualified small business stock for more than five years, he will exclude $75,000 of the gain from income (one-half), and he will be taxed on the other $75,000 at 28 percent.

**What if:** Assume instead that Jeb sold his Gangbusters stock after holding it for only two years, how much tax will he owe on the sale?

**Answer:** $22,500. Because Jeb didn't hold the stock for more than five years, he must recognize all $150,000 of long-term capital gain. This gain is taxed at 15 percent, yielding a total tax due of $22,500.

Exhibit 11-3 presents the maximum tax rates applicable to capital gains.

**EXHIBIT 11-3** **Classification of Capital Gains by Maximum Applicable Tax Rates**

| Short-Term or Long-Term | Type | Maximum Rate |
|---|---|---|
| Short-Term | All | 35% |
| Long-Term | Collectibles | 28%* |
| Held > 5 years | Qualified Small Business Stock | 28%* |
| Long-Term | Unrecaptured §1250 Gain from Depreciable Realty | 25%* |
| Long-Term | All Remaining Capital (and §1231 Gains) Gain Not Included Elsewhere | 15%† |

*Lower rates will apply when the taxpayer's ordinary rate is less than the rates reflected in this exhibit.
†This gain is taxed at 0 percent to the extent it would have been taxed at a rate of 15 percent or less if it were ordinary income.

[27]§1(h)(7).

[28]The maximum exclusion is the lesser of $10,000,000 ($5,000,000 for married taxpayers filing separately) or 10 times the adjusted basis of the stock [see §1202(b)(1)]. The amount of gain excluded from the sale of qualified small business stock is an AMT preference item. Consequently, the gain otherwise excludable for regular tax purposes may be taxed under the AMT system.

**Netting Process for Gains and Losses** To this point, our discussion of applicable tax rates for capital gains hasn't considered situations in which taxpayers recognize both capital gains and capital losses in the same year. To determine the appropriate tax treatment for the capital gains and losses recognized during the year, the taxpayer must engage in a netting process. This netting process can be complex when taxpayers recognize capital losses and long-term capital gains subject to different maximum tax rates. We first describe the netting steps for taxpayers *who do not recognize any 25 percent or 28 percent rate long-term capital gains.*

**Step 1:** Net all short-term gains and short-term losses, including any short-term capital loss carried forward from a prior year. If the net amount is positive, it is termed a **net short-term capital gain** (NSTCG). If the net amount is negative, it is called a **net short-term capital loss** (NSTCL).

**Step 2:** Net long-term gains and losses, including any long-term capital loss carried forward from a prior year. If the net amount is positive, the amount is called a **net long-term capital gain** (NLTCG). If negative, the amount is termed a **net long-term capital loss** (NLTCL).

**Step 3:** If Step 1 and Step 2 both yield gains—*or* if they both yield losses—the netting process ends. Otherwise, net the short- and long-term outcomes against each other to yield a final net gain or net loss, which may be either classified as short-term (if the NSTCG exceeds the NLTCL or if the NSTCL exceeds the NLTCG) or long-term (if the NLTCG exceeds the NSTCL or if the NLTCL exceeds the NSTCG). When net long-term capital gains exceed net short-term capital losses, if any, the taxpayer is said to have a **net capital gain.**

---

### Example 11-8

Jeb Landers has recently retired and now wants to pursue his life-long dream of owning a sailboat. To come up with the necessary cash, he sells the following investments:

| Stock | Market Value | Basis | Capital Gain/Loss | Scenario 1 Type | Scenario 2 Type |
|-------|-------------|--------|-------------------|-----------------|-----------------|
| A | $40,000 | $ 5,000 | $35,000 | Long | Short |
| B | $20,000 | $30,000 | ($10,000) | Long | Short |
| C | $20,000 | $12,000 | $ 8,000 | Short | Long |
| D | $17,000 | $28,000 | ($11,000) | Short | Long |

What is the amount and nature of Jeb's capital gains and losses (Scenario 1)?

**Answer:** $22,000 net capital gain (treated as long-term capital gain), computed as follows:

**Step 1:** Net short-term gains and short-term losses. The $8,000 short-term gain on stock C is netted against the $11,000 short-term loss on stock D, yielding a NSTCL of $3,000.

**Step 2:** Net long-term gains and long-term losses. The $35,000 long-term gain on stock A is netted against the $10,000 long-term loss on stock B, producing a NLTCG of $25,000.

**Step 3:** Net the results of Step 1 and Step 2. The NSTCL from Step 1 is netted with the NLTCG from Step 2 yielding a $22,000 net capital gain [($3,000) + $25,000] taxable at long-term capital gains rates.

**What if:** Consider the original facts, except that Scenario 2 dictates the long- and short-term capital gains. What is the amount and character of Jeb's net gain (or loss) on the sale of the shares in this situation?

(continued on page 11-14...)

**Answer:** $22,000 net short-term capital gain computed as follows:

**Step 1:** The gain from stock A would first be netted with the loss from stock B to produce a $25,000 NSTCG [$35,000 + ($10,000)]

**Step 2:** The loss from stock D and the gain from stock C are combined to provide a $3,000 NLTCL [($11,000) + $8,000].

**Step 3:** The results from Step 1 and Step 2 are netted to reach a $22,000 net short-term capital gain [$25,000 NSTCG + ($3,000) NLTCL].

**What if:** Assume the original facts (Scenario 1), except that stocks B and C were the only investments Jeb sold during the year. Walk through the outlined steps and see if you determine that Jeb would recognize a ($2,000) net long-term capital loss.

After completing the netting process, taxpayers must calculate the tax consequences of the resulting outcomes. Net short-term capital gains are taxed as ordinary income. As we discussed and illustrated in Chapter 7, net long-term capital gains generally are taxed at 15 percent to the extent the gains would have been taxed at a rate higher if they were ordinary income, and they are taxed at 0 percent to the extent they would have been taxed at a rate of 15 percent or lower if they were ordinary income. Taxpayers can deduct up to $3,000 ($1,500 if married filing separately) of net capital losses against ordinary income. Net capital losses in excess of $3,000 ($1,500 if married filing separately) retain their short- or long-term character and are carried forward and treated as though they were incurred in the subsequent year. Short-term losses are applied first to reduce ordinary income when the taxpayer recognizes both short- and long-term net capital losses. Capital loss carryovers for individuals never expire.

***Reporting Capital Gains.*** When taxpayers sell capital assets, they report their sales on Schedule D of Form 1040 (dates of sale and purchase are additional items provided on Schedule D). After listing their sales, taxpayers then use Schedule D to apply the basic capital gains netting process. Exhibit 11-4 illustrates how Jeb would report his stock sales in Example 11-8, Scenario 1.

***Netting Gains and Losses from 15 Percent, 25 Percent, and 28 Percent Capital Assets***
When taxpayers sell long-term capital assets and recognize gains subject to the 25 percent and/or 28 percent capital gains rates, we must expand the basic netting process we've just described.[29] In these situations, apply the following steps to determine the amount of gain taxable at the different tax rates:

**Step 1:** Net all short-term gains and short-term losses, including any short-term capital loss carried forward from a prior year. If the net amount is positive, it is a net short-term capital gain. If the net amount is negative, it is a net short-term capital loss.

**Step 2:** Determine whether long-term capital losses, including any long-term capital losses carried forward from a prior year, exceed long-term capital gains. If they do, proceed to Step 3; otherwise, ignore Step 3 and proceed to Step 4.

**Step 3:** If Step 1 generated a gain, net the gain against the loss from Step 2. If the outcome is a gain, the gain is a net short-term gain and you can ignore Steps 4–9. If the outcome is a loss, it is a net long-term capital

[29]§1(h).

**EXHIBIT 11-4**  Jeb's Schedule D

| SCHEDULE D<br>(Form 1040) | **Capital Gains and Losses** | OMB No. 1545-0074 |
|---|---|---|
| Department of the Treasury<br>Internal Revenue Service (99) | ► Attach to Form 1040 or Form 1040NR.  ► See Instructions for Schedule D (Form 1040).<br>► Use Schedule D-1 to list additional transactions for lines 1 and 8. | **20**09<br>Attachment<br>Sequence No. **12** |

| Name(s) shown on return | Your social security number |
|---|---|
| Jeb Landers | 450-28-2934 |

**Part I**  Short-Term Capital Gains and Losses—Assets Held One Year or Less

| (a) Description of property<br>(Example: 100 sh. XYZ Co.) | (b) Date acquired<br>(Mo., day, yr.) | (c) Date sold<br>(Mo., day, yr.) | (d) Sales price<br>(see page D-7 of<br>the instructions) | (e) Cost or other basis<br>(see page D-7 of<br>the instructions) | (f) Gain or (loss)<br>Subtract (e) from (d) |
|---|---|---|---|---|---|
| **1** Stock C | 3/01/09 | 11/05/09 | 20,000 | 12,000 | 8,000 |
| Stock D | 2/07/09 | 6/09/09 | 17,000 | 28,000 | (11,000) |
| | | | | | |
| | | | | | |
| | | | | | |

| | | |
|---|---|---|
| **2** Enter your short-term totals, if any, from Schedule D-1, line 2 . . . . . . . . . . . . . . . . . . . | **2** | |
| **3** **Total short-term sales price amounts.** Add lines 1 and 2 in column (d) . . . . . . . . . . . . . . . . | **3** | |
| **4** Short-term gain from Form 6252 and short-term gain or (loss) from Forms 4684, 6781, and 8824 | **4** | |
| **5** Net short-term gain or (loss) from partnerships, S corporations, estates, and trusts from Schedule(s) K-1 | **5** | |
| **6** Short-term capital loss carryover. Enter the amount, if any, from line 10 of your **Capital Loss Carryover Worksheet** on page D-7 of the instructions . . . . . . . . . . . . . | **6** | (          ) |
| **7** **Net short-term capital gain or (loss).** Combine lines 1 through 6 in column (f) . . . . . | **7** | (3,000) |

**Part II**  Long-Term Capital Gains and Losses—Assets Held More Than One Year

| (a) Description of property<br>(Example: 100 sh. XYZ Co.) | (b) Date acquired<br>(Mo., day, yr.) | (c) Date sold<br>(Mo., day, yr.) | (d) Sales price<br>(see page D-7 of<br>the instructions) | (e) Cost or other basis<br>(see page D-7 of<br>the instructions) | (f) Gain or (loss)<br>Subtract (e) from (d) |
|---|---|---|---|---|---|
| **8** Stock A | 11/07/07 | 3/06/09 | 40,000 | 5,000 | 35,000 |
| Stock B | 7/09/06 | 9/01/09 | 20,000 | 30,000 | (10,000) |
| | | | | | |
| | | | | | |
| | | | | | |

| | | |
|---|---|---|
| **9** Enter your long-term totals, if any, from Schedule D-1, line 9 . . . . . . . . . . . . . . . . . . . | **9** | |
| **10** **Total long-term sales price amounts.** Add lines 8 and 9 in column (d) . . . . . . . . . . . . . . | **10** | 60,000 |
| **11** Gain from Form 4797, Part I; long-term gain from Forms 2439 and 6252; and long-term gain or (loss) from Forms 4684, 6781, and 8824 . . . . . . . . . . . . | **11** | |
| **12** Net long-term gain or (loss) from partnerships, S corporations, estates, and trusts from Schedule(s) K-1 . . . . . . . . . . . . | **12** | |
| **13** Capital gain distributions. See page D-2 of the instructions . . . . . . . . . . . . | **13** | |
| **14** Long-term capital loss carryover. Enter the amount, if any, from line 15 of your **Capital Loss Carryover Worksheet** on page D-7 of the instructions . . . . . . . . . | **14** | (          ) |
| **15** **Net long-term capital gain or (loss).** Combine lines 8 through 14 in column (f). Then go to Part III on the back . . . . . . . . . . . . . . . . . . . | **15** | 25,000 |

For Paperwork Reduction Act Notice, see Form 1040 or Form 1040NR instructions.  Cat. No. 11338H  Schedule D (Form 1040) 2009

loss and you can ignore steps 4-9. If Step 1 generated a loss, you have both a net short-term and net long-term capital loss; apply the capital loss deduction limitations we described previously, and ignore Steps 4–9.

**Step 4:** Separate all long-term capital gains and losses into the three separate rate groups. Any long-term capital loss carried forward from the previous year is placed in the 28 percent group. Also, note that by definition the 25 percent group includes only gains.

**Step 5:** Net the gains and losses in the 15 percent group. If the result is a net loss, move the net loss into the 28 percent group. If the result is a net gain, leave the net gain in the 15 percent group and proceed to Step 9.

**Step 6:** *If the Step 1 result is a short-term capital loss,* move the loss into the 28 percent rate group. Otherwise, ignore this step.

**Step 7:** Net the gains and losses in the 28 percent rate group to determine if there is a net gain or loss in this group. Net gains in this group are taxed at a maximum rate of 28 percent. Net losses move to the 25 percent group.

**Step 8:** Net the 25 percent gains with the net loss determined in Step 7. Net gains are taxed at a maximum rate of 25 percent. Net losses move to the 15 percent rate group.

**Step 9:** Net the 15 percent net gain from Step 5 with the net loss from Step 8. This gain is taxed at a maximum 15 percent rate.

Steps 4 through 9 are designed to maximize the tax benefits of net short-term capital losses, long-term capital loss carryovers, and current year net losses in the 15 percent and 28 percent rate groups.

---

### Example 11-9

*What if:* Assume that in addition to selling stocks, Jeb sold gold coins and a rental home (with $50,000 of accumulated depreciation) as follows:

| Capital Asset | Market Value | Tax Basis | Capital Gain/Loss | Scenario 1 Type |
|---|---|---|---|---|
| A stock | $ 40,000 | $ 5,000 | $ 35,000 | Long 15% |
| B stock | 20,000 | 30,000 | (10,000) | Long 15% |
| C stock | 20,000 | 12,000 | 8,000 | Short |
| D stock | 17,000 | 28,000 | (11,000) | Short |
| Gold coins | 4,000 | 3,000 | 1,000 | Long 28% |
| Rental home | 200,000 | 80,000 | 120,000 | Long 25% and 15%* |
| Overall gain | | | $143,000 | |

*$50,000 of the gain is 25 percent gain (from accumulated depreciation on the property) and the remaining $70,000 is 15 percent gain.

Assuming Jeb did not sell any other capital assets during the year, he recognizes an overall capital gain of $143,000. What is (are) the maximum tax rate(s) applicable to this gain?

**Answer:** $95,000 of gain subject to a 15 percent maximum rate and $48,000 of gain is subject to a 25 percent rate, computed as follows:

**Step 1:** $3,000 net short-term capital loss [$8,000 + ($11,000)].

**Step 2:** $146,000 overall net long-term capital gain, so ignore Step 3 and proceed to Step 4.

**Step 4:** The $35,000 gain on the A stock, the $10,000 loss on the B stock, and $70,000 ($120,000 − $50,000) of gain from the rental home are placed in the 15 percent group. $50,000 of the gain from the rental property is placed in the 25 percent group, and $1,000 gain on the gold coins is placed in the 28 percent group.

**Step 5:** *$95,000 net gain in the 15 percent group* [$35,000 A stock + (10,000) B stock + $70,000 rental property].

**Step 6:** Move the $3,000 loss from Step 1 into the 28 percent group.

**Step 7:** *$2,000 net loss in 28 percent group* [$1,000 gain on gold + ($3,000) short term loss from Step 1]. Move the $2,000 net loss to the 25 percent group.

**Step 8:** *$48,000 net gain in the 25 percent group* [$50,000 25 percent gain on rental + ($2,000) loss from Step 7].

**Step 9:** Not required.

Jeb's netting process is reflected in the following table:

| Description | Short-Term | Long-Term Overall | Long-Term 28% | Long-Term 25% | Long-Term 15% |
|---|---|---|---|---|---|
| Stock C | $8,000 | | | | |
| Stock D | (11,000) | | | | |
| Step 1: | (3,000) | | | | |
| Coins | | $ 1,000 | 1,000 | | |
| Unrecaptured §1250 Gain | | 50,000 | | 50,000 | |
| Remaining Gain from Rental Property | | 70,000 | | | 70,000 |
| Stock A | | 35,000 | | | 35,000 |
| Stock B | | (10,000) | | | (10,000) |
| Step 2: | | $146,000 | | | |
| Steps 4 and 5: | | | $1,000 | $50,000 | $95,000 |
| Step 6: | (3,000) | | (3,000) | | |
| Step 7 | | | (2,000) | (2,000) | |
| Step 8 | | | | 48,000 | |
| Summary | | | | $48,000 | $95,000 |
| Applicable Rate | | | | 25% | 15% |

So, we've learned how to determine the *maximum* tax rates applicable to different types of capital gains. How do we go about actually calculating the effect these gains have on the taxpayer's tax liability? Follow these basic guidelines:

- If the long-term capital gains would have been taxed at a rate of 28 percent or higher if they were ordinary income, the gain is taxed at the maximum rate for their group (15 percent, 25 percent, or 28 percent).
- If the long-term capital gains would have been taxed at a rate of 15 percent or lower if they were ordinary income, the 15 percent gains are taxed at 0 percent, and the 25 percent and 28 percent gains are taxed at the taxpayer's ordinary rate.
- For other situations, use the following steps to determine the tax on the gains:[30]

  **Step 1:** Fill up the 10 percent and 15 percent tax rate brackets with taxable income, exclusive of long-term capital gains subject to preferential rates.

  **Step 2:** Next, add any 25 percent rate capital gains to either the 10 percent or 15 percent brackets to the extent room remains in either of these brackets after Step 1. Twenty-five percent rate capital gains included in these brackets are taxed at the ordinary rates applicable to these brackets.

[30]§1(h).

---

**THE KEY FACTS**

**28 Percent and 25 Percent Rate Capital Gains**

- Certain capital gains are taxable at maximum rates of 25 percent or 28 percent.
  · Unrecaptured §1250 gains are taxed at a maximum rate of 25 percent.
  · Gains from collectibles and from qualified small business stock (after the 50 percent exclusion) held for longer than five years are taxed at a maximum rate of 28 percent.

- When taxpayers have 25 percent or 28 percent rate capital gains, an expanded netting process applies.
  · The expanded netting process generally requires that losses be applied to higher rate groups before lower rate groups.

- When taxable income without long-term capital gains would be taxed in the 28 percent or higher ordinary income rate bracket, the capital gains in each rate group are simply taxed according to the capital gains rate applicable to each group. Otherwise applicable capital gains rates must be adjusted to reflect their inclusion in lower ordinary income rate brackets.

**Step 3:** Next, add any 28 percent rate capital gains to either the 10 percent or 15 percent brackets to the extent room remains in either of these brackets after Step 2. Twenty-eight percent rate capital gains included in these brackets are taxed at the ordinary rates applicable to these brackets.

**Step 4:** Next, add any 15 percent rate capital gains to either the 10 percent or 15 percent brackets to the extent room remains in either of these brackets after Step 3. Fifteen percent rate capital gains included in these brackets are taxed at 0 percent.

**Step 5:** Any capital gains remaining after Steps 1 through 4 are taxed at the lesser of the applicable ordinary rate or maximum rate applicable to the gains (15 percent, 25 percent, or 28 percent).

---

### Example 11-10

***What if:*** Let's return to the facts of the previous example where Jeb recognized a $48,000 25 percent net capital gain and a $95,000 15 percent net capital gain. Also, assume that Jeb's taxable income for 2010 before considering the net capital gains is $10,000. Jeb's filing status is single. What is Jeb's gross tax liability for the year?

**Answer:** $24,931.25, computed as follows:

| Amount and Type of Income | Applicable Rate | Tax | Explanation |
|---|---|---|---|
| $8,375; ordinary | 10% | $ 837.50 | $8,375 × 10%<br>The first $8,375 of Jeb's $10,000 of ordinary income is taxed at 10 percent (see single tax rate schedule for this and other computations). |
| $1,625; ordinary | 15% | 243.75 | $1,625 × 15%.<br>Jeb's remaining $1,625 of ordinary income ($10,000 − $8,375) is taxed at 15 percent. |
| $24,000;<br>25 percent rate capital gains | 15% | 3,600 | 23,950 × 15%<br>The end of the 15 percent bracket is $34,000 minus $10,000 ($8,375 + $1,625) already taxed. |
| $24,000;<br>25 percent rate capital gains | 25% | 6,000 | $24,000 × 25%<br>$48,000 total 25 percent gain minus $24,000 25 percent gain already taxed at 15 percent. |
| $95,000; 15 percent rate capital gains | 15% | 14,250 | $95,000 × 15%<br>All of the 15 percent gain would have been taxed at a rate higher than 15 percent, so it is all taxed at 15 percent. |
| Gross tax liability | | $24,931.25 | |

---

## Limitations on Capital Losses

We've previously discussed the general rule that taxpayers may deduct capital losses against capital gains in the netting process and that individual taxpayers may deduct up to $3,000 ($1,500 if married filing separately) of net capital losses against ordinary income in a given year. This general rule, however, is subject to certain exceptions as described below.

**Losses on the Sale of Personal-Use Assets**    As previously described, personal-use assets fall within the category of capital assets. When taxpayers sell personal-use assets, what are the tax consequences? Consider an engaged taxpayer who calls off the wedding plans. After getting the ring back from his former fiancée, the taxpayer sells the engagement ring for more than its purchase price. Does he recognize a taxable gain? Absolutely—the gain from the sale of a personal-use asset is taxable even though it was not purchased for its appreciation potential. The tax rate on the gain depends on the amount of time between the date the taxpayer purchased the ring and the date he sold it and on the netting process involving the seller's other capital gains and losses during the year. What if a taxpayer sold her car for less than she paid for it? Does she get to deduct the capital loss? Unfortunately, no—losses on the sale of personal-use assets are *not* deductible, and therefore never become part of the netting process.

**Capital Losses on Sales to Related Parties**    When taxpayers sell capital assets at a loss to related parties, they are not able to deduct the loss.[31] As we described in detail in Chapter 10, the related party acquiring the asset may eventually be allowed to deduct all, a portion, or none of the disallowed loss on a subsequent sale.

**Wash Sales**    Consider the case of a taxpayer attempting to do some tax planning near the end of the year: She has invested in the stock of several corporations; some of these investments have appreciated while others have declined in value. The taxpayer wants to capture the tax benefit of the stock losses in the current year to offset ordinary income (up to $3,000) or to offset other capital gains she has already recognized during the year. However, she can't deduct the losses until she sells the stock. Why might this be a problem? If the taxpayer believes that the stocks with unrealized losses are likely to appreciate in the near future, she may prefer *not* to sell those stocks but rather to keep them in her investment portfolio. What might this taxpayer do to deduct the losses while continuing to hold the investment in the stocks? For one, she might be tempted to sell the stocks and then immediately buy them back. Or, she might buy more of the same stock and then sell the stock she originally held to recognize the losses. With this strategy, she hopes to realize (and then recognize or deduct) the losses and, at the end of the day, still hold the stocks in her investment portfolio.

Although this might sound like a great plan, certain **wash sale** tax rules prevent this strategy from accomplishing the taxpayer's objective. A wash sale occurs when an investor sells or trades stock or securities at a loss *and* within 30 days *either before or after* the day of sale buys substantially identical stocks or securities.[32] Because the day of sale is included, the 30 days before and after period creates a 61-day window during which the wash sale provisions may apply.[33] When the wash sale provisions apply to a sale of stock, realized losses are not recognized; instead, the amount of *the unrecognized loss is added to the basis of the newly acquired stock.* Congress created this rule to prevent taxpayers from accelerating losses on securities that have declined in value without actually altering their investment in the securities. The 61-day period ensures that taxpayers cannot deduct losses from stock sales without exposing themselves to the risk that the stock they sold will subsequently increase in value.

---

[31]§267(a). §267(b) defines related parties and limits related-party losses. Because we described this concept in detail in Chapter 10, we merely raise the issue here.

[32]Substantially identical stocks or securities include contracts or options to buy substantially identical securities. However, corporate bonds and preferred stock are not generally considered substantially identical to common stock of the same corporation.

[33]§1091.

## Example 11-11

Nick and Rachel Sutton own 100 shares of Cisco stock that they purchased in June 2009 for $50 a share. On December 21, 2010, Nick and Rachel sell the shares for $40 a share to generate cash for the holidays. This sale generates a capital loss of $1,000 [$4,000 sale proceeds (100 × $40) − $5,000 tax basis ($50 × 100)]. Later, however, Nick and Rachel decide that Cisco might be a good long-term investment. On January 3, 2011 (13 days later), the Suttons purchase 100 shares of Cisco stock for $41 a share ($4,100). Do the Suttons *realize* a short- or long-term capital loss on the December 21 sale?

**Answer:** Long-term capital loss. They held the stock for more than one year (June 2009 to December 2010) before selling.

How much of the realized $1,000 long-term capital loss can the Suttons recognize or deduct on their 2010 tax return?

**Answer:** Zero. Because the Suttons sold the stock at a loss and purchased the same stock within the 61-day period centered on the date of sale (30 days before December 21, and 30 days after December 21), the wash sale rules disallow the loss in 2010. Had the Suttons waited just another 18 days to repurchase the Cisco shares, they could have avoided the wash sale rules. In that case, under the general rules for capital loss deductibility, the Suttons *would* be able to deduct the $1,000 capital loss from the sale against their ordinary income on their 2010 income tax return.

What tax basis will the Suttons have in the Cisco stock they purchased (or repurchased) on January 3, 2011?

**Answer:** $5,100. Under the wash sale rules, the Suttons add the $1,000 disallowed loss to the basis of the stock they purchased on January 3. Thus, they now own 100 shares of Cisco stock with a $5,100 basis in the shares, which is $1,000 more than they paid for it.

*What if:* How much of the $1,000 realized loss would the Suttons have recognized if they had only purchased 40 shares of Cisco stock instead of 100 shares on January 3, 2011?

**Answer:** $600. The wash sale rules disallow the loss to the extent taxpayers acquire other shares in the 61-day window. In this situation, the Suttons only acquired 40 percent (40 of 100) of the shares they sold at a loss within the window. Consequently, they must disallow 40 percent, or $400, of the loss, and they are allowed to deduct the remaining $600 loss.

## Balancing Tax Planning Strategies for Capital Assets with Other Goals

When taxpayers invest in capital assets and hold the assets for more than a year, they receive at least two benefits. First, they are able to defer recognizing gains on the assets until they sell them—the longer the deferral period, the lower the present value of the capital gains tax when taxpayers ultimately sell the assets. Second, they pay taxes on the gains at preferential rates. These tax advantages provide taxpayers with a greater after-tax rate of return on these investments than they would obtain from less tax-favored assets that earn equivalent before-tax rates of return. Investors who quickly sell investments pay taxes on gains at higher, ordinary rates and incur significantly greater transaction costs. Nevertheless, taxpayers should balance the tax benefits available for holding assets with the risk that the asset values will have declined by the time they want to sell the assets.

## Example 11-12

*What if:* Assume the Suttons decide to purchase Intel stock for $100,000 and hold half of the shares for 5 years to purchase the Park City home and the other half for 18 years to pay for Lea's education. If the Intel stock grows at a constant 8 percent before-tax rate and does not pay any dividends, how much cash will the Suttons accumulate after taxes for the Park City home?

**Answer:** $69,946, computed as follows:

| Description | Amount | Explanation |
|---|---|---|
| (1) Proceeds from sale | $73,466 | [$50,000 × $(1 + .08)^5$]. |
| (2) Basis in fund shares | 50,000 | This is the nondeductible investment in the shares. |
| (3) Gain realized on sale | $23,466 | (1) − (2). |
| (4) Tax rate on gain | × 15% | Low rate for long-term capital gain.* |
| (5) Tax on gain | $ 3,520 | (3) × (4). |
| **After-tax cash for Park City home** | **$69,946** | (1) − (5). |

*Assumes the Suttons don't have any capital losses.

What annual after-tax rate of return will the Suttons earn on the money invested for the Park City home?
**Answer:**[34] 6.94 percent [($69,946/$50,000)$^{1/5}$ − 1].

How much cash will the Suttons accumulate after taxes for Lea's education?
**Answer:** $177,331, computed as follows:

| Description | Amount | Explanation |
|---|---|---|
| (1) Proceeds from sale | $199,801 | [$50,000 × $(1 + .08)^{18}$]. |
| (2) Basis in fund shares | 50,000 | This is the nondeductible investment in the shares. |
| (3) Gain realized on sale | $149,801 | (1) − (2). |
| (4) Tax rate on gain | × 15% | Low rate for long-term capital gain.* |
| (5) Tax on gain | $ 22,470 | (3) × (4). |
| **After-tax cash for education goal** | **$177,331** | (1) − (5). |

*Assumes the Suttons don't have capital losses.

What annual after-tax rate of return will the Suttons earn on the money invested for Lea's education?
**Answer:** 7.29 percent. [($177,331/$50,000)$^{1/18}$ − 1].

Intuitively, why is the annual after-tax rate of return greater for the 18-year investment than for the 5-year investment?
**Answer:** Although both the 5-year and the 18-year investments are taxed at preferential capital gains rates, taxes are deferred a longer period of time for the 18-year investment and, as a result, are less on a present value basis.

---

**Taxes in the Real World**    *Seeking Long-Term Capital Gains and Diversification*

Investors seeking long-term capital gains and diversification of their investments frequently invest in so-called tax efficient mutual funds. Like other mutual funds, tax efficient mutual funds invest in a portfolio of stock and other securities; but, unlike other mutual funds, they actively employ tax planning strategies to reduce current distributions and to increase the likelihood that recognized investment gains will be taxed at favorable long-term capital gains rates. One basic tax planning strategy they employ is a simple buy and hold strategy rather than frequently trading securities the way other mutual funds do. Exchange traded funds, or ETFs, are also popular among traditional investors in tax efficient mutual

(continued on page 11-22...)

---

[34]In general, the formula for computing the after-tax rate of return on any investment is $(FV/I)^{1/n} - 1$ where $FV$ is the future value after taxes, $I$ is the investment, and $n$ is the number of investment periods. Financial calculators designate this calculation as the IRR or internal rate of return.

funds. ETFs are securities that typically derive their value from an investment index such as the S&P 500. Thus, like tax efficient mutual funds, they provide a measure of investment diversification. However, unlike tax efficient mutual funds whose actions determine when and how investment returns are taxed, investors in ETFs have greater control over the timing and character of investment returns from ETFs because they are treated like individual stocks for tax purposes.

*Source:* Katy Marquardt, "Building a Better Mousetrap: Exchange Traded Funds are Low Cost, Tax Efficient, and Highly Versatile," U.S. News & World Report, December 15, 2008.

When investing in capital assets, taxpayers run the risk that some of their investments may decline in value. Thus, a productive strategy for managing investments in capital assets is to sell investments with built-in losses. This strategy is commonly referred to as "loss harvesting." By selectively selling loss assets, taxpayers can reduce their taxes by deducting up to $3,000 against their ordinary income and by reducing the amount of capital gains that would otherwise be subject to tax during the year. This is particularly beneficial for taxpayers who have short-term capital gains that will be taxed at higher ordinary rates absent offsetting capital losses. Note, however, that taxpayers should not sell investments to gain tax benefits if they believe that the potential economic benefit of holding the investment outweighs the tax benefits of selling the stock. Also, keep in mind that capital losses on stock sales may not be deductible due to the wash sale rules discussed above.

## PORTFOLIO INCOME: TAX-EXEMPT

So far in this chapter, we have discussed investments that are taxed at different rates and at different times depending on the nature of the investment. Some other investments are, for policy reasons, never explicitly taxed. Among these tax-favored investments are municipal bonds, life insurance, and educational savings plans. Other tax-exempt vehicles meant to stimulate retirement savings are discussed in Chapter 13.

### Municipal Bonds

Municipal bonds are debt instruments issued by state and local governments to build roads, schools, and for other governmental needs.[35] Similar to U.S. Treasury securities, municipal bonds are generally considered to be less risky than corporate bonds. In most cases, municipal bond interest is not subject to federal income tax.[36] However, it may be subject to state income taxes if the bondholder holds municipal bonds from a state that is not the state of his primary residence.[37] For example, a taxpayer residing in Arizona would not pay Arizona state income tax on the interest from municipal bonds issued by the state of Arizona, but she would for municipal bonds issued by Utah.

Why does the federal government grant municipal bonds tax-favored status? The answer is, to subsidize the expenditures of state and local governments. Investors are attracted to municipal bonds because they are tax favored relative to similar

[35]The District of Columbia as well as U.S. possessions such as Puerto Rico may also issue tax-exempt municipal bonds.

[36]Interest from certain municipal bonds issued before 2009 or after 2010 to fund activities of a more private nature, such as redevelopment and stadium construction, is included as a preference item in the alternative minimum tax calculation. These bonds are referred to as *private activity bonds*.

[37]States determine residency status by such factors as voter registration, property ownership, and amount of time spent in the state.

taxable bonds. Increased demand drives the price up—and conversely the yield, or interest rate, down—for municipal bonds relative to taxable bonds. The yield on municipal bonds represents the rate that a state, in effect, pays to borrow money. In essence, the federal government is willing to forgo tax revenues so that state and local governments may borrow from bond investors at a lower rate.

Viewed from an investor's perspective, the subsidy state and local governments receive when issuing municipal bonds is reflected as lower rates of return relative to alternative rates of return available on taxable bonds. These lower rates of return are economically similar to other taxes on investment income because they subsidize municipal governments while leaving investors in municipal bonds with lower investment returns than they would have received otherwise. As we described in Chapter 1, differences in rates of return on municipal bonds relative to taxable bonds are sometimes referred to as **implicit taxes** as opposed to **explicit taxes,** which are actually levied by and paid to governmental entities. To make correct investment choices, investors must consider implicit taxes when comparing investment alternatives.

---

### Example 11-13

In addition to their other investment options, Nick and Rachel are considering investing in Arizona municipal bonds paying interest of 5 percent annually because they heard they are "tax free." They decide to compare the General Electric corporate bonds with the Arizona municipal bonds. Assume the Arizona bonds are similar to the GE bonds in all respects except for how they are taxed and the rate of return on the Arizona bonds. Recall that when Nick and Rachel previously considered purchasing the taxable GE bonds, they learned that the bonds paid interest annually at a before-tax rate of 8 percent. Given this information, should Nick and Rachel invest in Arizona municipal bonds?

**Answer:** No. With a 30 percent marginal tax rate, they would earn a 5.6 percent annual after-tax rate of return on the GE bonds (see Example 11-1), but only a 5 percent after-tax return on the Arizona bonds.

Would their decision change if they expected their marginal tax rate to increase to 40 percent?

**Answer:** Yes. With a 40 percent marginal tax rate, their annual after-tax rate of return on the GE bonds decreases to 4.8 percent [8% × (1 − 40%)]. If they expected their rate to increase to 40 percent, the Arizona bonds would be the superior investment!

---

This example illustrates an important truism: taxpayers with high marginal tax rates prefer tax-favored investments like municipal bonds. Why? Because the explicit tax that taxpayers with high marginal tax rates avoid is greater than the implicit tax they incur when purchasing municipal bonds. The converse also is true—taxpayers with low marginal tax rates prefer explicitly taxed investments like corporate bonds because the explicit taxes they actually pay are less than the implicit taxes they avoid on tax-favored assets like municipal bonds.

### Life Insurance

Many people think of life insurance solely as a product designed to financially protect a family in the event of an untimely death of another family member. In addition to insuring one's own life or the life of a family member, however, it is possible to purchase an insurance policy on the life of a nonfamily member such as a business partner. Moreover, companies frequently insure the lives of their key executives and name themselves as beneficiaries.

Although you may not have previously thought of life insurance as an investment, life insurance companies also offer life insurance policies with an investment component in addition to the insurance component. This type of insurance often is referred to as **whole life insurance** whereas insurance without a savings component is

called **term insurance.** The premiums paid for whole life policies—minus various insurers' costs—are invested by the insurance company in stocks, bonds, and other securities. In the event the policy is cashed in before the death of the insured individual, the beneficiary receives the **cash surrender value** of the policy, which approximates the value of the invested premiums and the associated investment gains. In reality, the cash surrender value is somewhat less than this amount because of the administrative and other fees insurance companies charge to provide their products.

As we described in Chapter 5, taxpayers receiving life insurance proceeds on the death of the insured exclude the proceeds from gross income. To some extent, the tax-advantaged treatment of life insurance permits individuals to use life insurance policies as tax-favored vehicles to acquire investments that would be taxed if held in normal investment accounts.[38] As long as the investment gains within the life insurance policy remain untapped until the death of the insured, they are tax-exempt. However, if a policy is cashed in early for its surrender value, the proceeds are not tax-exempt. The policy owner is taxed at *ordinary rates* on the total investment *gains* from the policy—that is, the difference between the cash surrender value of the policy and the premiums paid.[39]

| Example 11-14 | |
|---|---|

Nick's father, Dale, recently purchased a whole life policy to insure his life and named Nick and Rachel as beneficiaries. The policy, at a one-time cost of $50,000, promises returns of 8 percent per year. How much will Nick and Rachel receive after-tax if Dale dies in 18 years and what would be their after-tax rate of return?

**Answer:** $199,801. [$50,000 × (1 + .08)$^{18}$]. Proceeds paid on the death of the insured are not taxable, so the life insurance policy generates an 8 percent before- and after-tax rate of return.

How much will they receive after-tax if Dale dies prematurely in five years and what would be their after-tax rate of return?[40]

**Answer:** $73,466. [$50,000 × (1 + .08)$^{5}$]. Proceeds paid on the death of the insured are not taxable, so the life insurance policy generates an 8 percent before- and after-tax rate of return.

How much will *Dale* receive after-tax if he decides to cash in the policy for a cash surrender value of $73,466 after five years while he is still living (his marginal ordinary rate is 30%) and what will be his after-tax rate of return?

**Answer:** $66,426 and 5.8 percent, computed as follows:

| Description | Amount | Explanation |
|---|---|---|
| (1) Cash surrender value received | $73,466 | [$50,000 × (1 + .08)$^{5}$]. |
| (2) Premiums paid | 50,000 | Investment in policy. |
| (3) Gain on surrender | $23,466 | (1) − (2). |
| (4) Ordinary marginal rate | × 30% | |
| (5) Taxes payable on surrender | 7,040 | (3) × (4). |
| (6) After-tax proceeds | $66,426 | (1) − (5). |
| After-tax rate of return | 5.8% | $[(66,246/50,000)^{1/5} - 1]$. |

[38]Tax rules require life insurance policies to provide minimum levels of actual life insurance to prevent life insurance from being used by investors solely as tax-exempt investment vehicles.

[39]Rev. Rul. 2009-13, 2009-21 IRB 1029.

[40]For the sake of simplicity, we assume the life insurance purchased in this example functions as a pure investment contract. That is, we assume the life insurance policy will generate a before-tax rate of return of 8 percent regardless of when Dale dies. In reality, if Dale were to die prematurely, the rate of return on the policy would likely be greater than 8 percent because life insurance contracts typically specify a fixed payout regardless of when the insured dies.

Although life insurance, with its tax-favored status, might appear to be an ideal investment, various aspects of life insurance limit its desirability as an investment vehicle. Life insurance products tend to be weighed down with high commissions and fees that reduce before-tax returns relative to other investment alternatives. Moreover, investors who purchase life insurance are constrained because they must wait until the insured individual dies to minimize the tax burden on their investment.

## Educational Savings Plans

To encourage families to save for their children's college education, Congress has created tax-favored educational savings accounts that shield investment returns from income taxes.[41] When donors contribute to these plans, they designate how their contributions will be invested within the plans. The investment returns then accumulate tax-free. When distributions are made from these plans, earnings are distributed tax-free provided they are used for qualified education costs. One well-known tax-advantaged account is the Coverdell Educational Savings Account. With a Coverdell account, yearly contributions to the account are limited to $2,000 for each beneficiary, and distributions may be used to pay for qualified educational costs of kindergarten through 12th grade and qualified higher education expenses such as tuition, books, fees, supplies, and reasonable room and board.[42] The $2,000 contribution limit for Coverdell accounts phases out as AGI (modified to include certain types of excluded foreign income) increases from $190,000 to $220,000 for married filing jointly taxpayers, and from $95,000 to $110,000 for all other taxpayers.

Another tax-advantaged educational savings vehicle gaining in popularity is the **qualified tuition program** or **529 plan.** 529 plans allow parents, grandparents, and other individuals to contribute up to the maximum allowed by state-sponsored 529 plans to fund the qualified educational costs of future *college* students.[43] Earnings in 529 plans are distributed tax-free provided they are used for qualified *higher* education expenses. If, on the other hand, distributions are made to the beneficiary for other purposes, investment returns are taxed to the beneficiary at the beneficiary's tax rate and are subject to an additional 10 percent penalty while distributions to the beneficiary in excess of investment returns are treated as gifts.[44] Distributions to contributors (e.g., parents, grandparents) in excess of their contributions are included in contributors' gross income and also subject to the 10 percent penalty.

---

**Example 11-15**

Assume Nick and Rachel decide to invest $50,000 in the state of Arizona 529 plan to fund Lea's college education. Assuming an 8 percent annual return, how much money, after-taxes, would this investment produce for Lea's college education in 18 years, and what after-tax rate of return would the investment earn?

*(continued on page 11-26...)*

---

[41] Taxpayers may also use U.S. savings bonds as a tax efficient means of saving for higher education. Interest from U.S. savings bonds (series EE and I) is excluded from taxable income to the extent it is used to pay for certain higher education costs.

[42] §530(b). This definition of qualified higher education expenses is consistent with the definition used in §221(d)(2) to determine if interest paid on education-related loans is deductible (see Chapter 6).

[43] Contribution limits vary according to the state administering the 529 plan. The median contribution limit is approximately $235,000. In addition, more than half the states offer a state tax deduction or credit to residents contributing to the 529 plan sponsored by the state in which the contributors reside.

[44] Under §529(c)(3), multiple distributions received under these circumstances are treated as annuities. As a result, a portion of each distribution would be treated as a gift with the remainder treated as income.

**THE KEY FACTS**

Tax-Exempt
Investment Income

■ Before-tax rate of
return = After-tax rate
of return.

■ Municipal bonds gener-
ate tax-exempt income.
· Investors generally earn
a lower rate of return
(implicit tax) than on
comparable corporate
bonds.

■ Life insurance.
· Proceeds received at
death of insured are
tax-exempt.
· If cashed out before
insured's death, excess
of cash surrender value
over premiums paid is
taxed as ordinary income.

■ Educational savings
plans generate tax-
exempt income if the
proceeds are used to
pay for certain educa-
tion costs.
· Qualified tuition pro-
grams (529 plans) for
higher education.
· 529 plan distributions
that are not used for
education are taxed at
the beneficiary's ordi-
nary income rates and
are subject to a 10 per-
cent penalty.
· Coverdell accounts are
for K–12 and higher edu-
cation costs. Maximum
$2,000 contribution
phases out for high AGI
between $190,000 and
$220,000 for married
filing jointly taxpayers
and $95,000 and
$110,000 for other
taxpayers.

**Answer:** $199,801. [$50,000 × (1 + .08)$^{18}$]. Because the income is tax exempt, the before- and after-tax rate of return is 8 percent. This calculation is exactly the same as the calculation we used to determine what the value of the life insurance policy on Dale's life would be if he dies in 18 years. If used to cover Lea's qualified higher educational expenses, none of the $149,801 in earnings on the $50,000 investment would ever be taxed![45]

What amount would the Suttons have after taxes if they withdrew the balance of their 529 account after five years to use the money to help fund the Park City home and what after-tax (and penalty) rate of return would they earn?

**Answer:** $64,079 proceeds after-tax and penalty and 5.1 percent after-tax and penalty rate of return.

| Description | Amount | Explanation |
|---|---|---|
| (1) Total proceeds before taxes and penalties | $73,466 | $50,000 × (1 + .08)$^5$. |
| (2) Total investment in plan | 50,000 | Amount initially invested in plan. |
| (3) Gain on distribution | $23,466 | (1) − (2). |
| (4) The Suttons' marginal ordinary tax rate | × 30% | |
| (5) Taxes payable on distribution of proceeds | ($7,040) | (3) × (4) taxed because proceeds not used for education. |
| (6) After-tax proceeds | $66,426 | (1) + (5). |
| (7) Penalty rate for noneducational use | 10% | |
| (8) Penalty for noneducational use of proceeds | (2,347) | (3) × (7). |
| (9) Proceeds after taxes and penalties | $64,079 | (1) + (5) + (8). |
| After-tax and penalty rate of return | 5.1% | [($64,079/50,000)$^{1/5}$ − 1]. |

529 plans and other tax-advantaged educational savings vehicles compare favorably with other investment alternatives when it comes to saving for educational costs. While Coverdell plans allow investors some latitude in deciding how to invest contributed funds, the states and organizations that administer 529 plans provide limited investment options. Families looking for greater flexibility when investing for higher education may be willing to trade the tax advantages of these vehicles for the possibility of greater investment returns elsewhere. Investors should consider these plans within the context of their overall investment philosophy.

529 plans and Coverdell savings accounts also offer significant nontax advantages relative to some alternative education savings strategies. In calculating eligibility for financial aid, colleges and universities weight assets held by students more heavily than those held by parents. Because 529 and Coverdell accounts are generally considered parental assets, they are less likely to affect the amount of financial aid a student receives compared to investments held in the student's name.

## PORTFOLIO INCOME SUMMARY

As we've discussed the tax consequences of various investments up to this point in the chapter, we have proceeded from the least tax-advantaged (taxed annually at ordinary rates) to the most tax-advantaged (tax-exempt). By moving along this

[45]This analysis reflects the federal income tax impications of investing in a 529 plan. State income taxes as well as state and federal gift taxes may also be an important consideration.

continuum from investments taxed annually at ordinary rates (corporate bonds[46]) to investments taxed annually at capital gains rates (dividend-paying stock), investors are in essence employing the conversion planning strategy referred to repeatedly throughout this text. As taxpayers move from dividend-paying stock to growth stock, which provides tax deferral in addition to preferential tax rates, taxpayers combine the conversion strategy with the basic strategy of shifting income from one time period to another. Finally, taxpayers also rely on conversion when they choose to purchase either tax-exempt municipal bonds or when they invest in tax-exempt vehicles like insurance and educational savings plans.

Exhibit 11-5 reviews and ranks investments from best to worst based solely on their tax characteristics. With the exception of the municipal bond investment, the differences in after-tax returns are driven solely by the tax treatment of each investment.

**EXHIBIT 11-5    Portfolio Income Summary**

| Rank | Income Type | Timing of Taxation | Tax Rate | Example of Investment |
|------|-------------|--------------------|----------|-----------------------|
| 1 | Tax-exempt income | Never | Zero | Municipal bonds |
| 2 | Appreciation in capital assets | Deferred | Capital gains | Growth stock |
| 3 | Dividends | Current | Capital gains | Stock in electric utility company |
| 4 | Taxable interest | Current | Ordinary | Certificate of deposit |

In this chapter and elsewhere in this text, we emphasize that tax planning must not be done in a vacuum without considering all relevant parties and taxpayers' economic and personal objectives. Because investments typically are not designed to accommodate the specific needs of each individual investor, considering the other party in the deal is not as relevant when investing as it is in other transactions. However, it is vital that investors carefully balance the tax characteristics of their investment options with the other attributes of their investment options such as risk and liquidity. Similarly, investors must be sure to consider implicit taxes when purchasing tax-favored assets like municipal bonds.

**Example 11-16**

After doing some basic research on investments that might be suitable savings vehicles for the Park City vacation home and Lea's Ivy League education, Nick and Rachel must now decide how to invest $50,000 for 5 years and another $50,000 for 18 years. Given the following summary information from prior examples, how should Nick and Rachel invest their money if they were to base their decision on the tax characteristics of these investments alone?

| Investment | 5 Years After-Tax Rate of Return | 18 Years After-Tax Rate of Return | Reference |
|------------|----------------------------------|-----------------------------------|-----------|
| Corporate bonds (GE) | 5.6% | 5.6% | Example 11-1. |
| Dividend-paying stocks (Xerox) | 6.80% | 6.80% | Example 11-4. |
| Growth stock (Intel) | 6.94% | 7.29% | Example 11-12. |
| Municipal bonds (Arizona 5% yield) | 5% | 5% | Example 11-13. |
| 529 college savings plan (Arizona) | N/A | 8% | Example 11-15. |

Note: Except for the Arizona municipal bonds, all other investments are assumed to yield 8 percent before tax. Because of implicit taxes, the Arizona bond only yields 5 percent.

(continued on page 11-28...)

[46]We refer here to corporate bonds issued or acquired at face value.

**Answer:** To save for the Park City home, the best alternative would be an investment in the Intel stock. This option is superior to the other remaining alternatives from a tax perspective because it combines the power of tax deferral with the conversion of ordinary income into capital gains. Note, however, that the tax deferral benefit in this instance is limited given the short deferral period.

To save for Lea's education, the Suttons would do best to use the Arizona 529 plan because it generates the greatest after-tax rate of return among the alternatives. Purchasing the Intel stock would be the next best alternative for the Suttons because the power of conversion and deferral over an 18-year time horizon generates after-tax returns that are close to being tax-exempt. Recall that 529 plans limit the range of investments savers may select relative to a privately managed investment account. If the Suttons feel this is a significant constraint, they may decide to invest in growth stocks and either forgo or limit their contributions to the 529 plan.

**L04**

# PORTFOLIO INVESTMENT EXPENSES

Now that we've discussed how *income* from various forms of investments is taxed and how tax rules affect after-tax returns, let's explore the deductibility of expenses taxpayers incur to acquire or maintain their investments. We first discuss tax consequences associated with **investment expenses,** and we conclude by discussing the deductibility of **investment interest expense.** Even though the names of these two deductions sound very similar, investment expenses and investment interest expense are two *different* deductions with different deductibility limitations. So, when you are reading about an investment-related expense, pay careful attention to whether the expense is an *investment expense* or *investment interest expense.* Exhibit 11-6 provides a description of these expenses and the limitations on the deductibility of the expenses.

**EXHIBIT 11-6**    Summary of Investment-Related Expenses

| Item | Investment Expense | Investment *Interest* Expense |
|---|---|---|
| Description | Expenses (other than interest) incurred to generate investment income. | Interest expense on loans used to acquire investments. |
| Deduction type | Miscellaneous itemized deduction (subject to 2 percent of AGI floor). | Interest expense itemized deduction. |
| Deduction limitations | Deductible only when investment expenses and other miscellaneous itemized deductions exceed 2 percent of AGI floor. | Deduction limited to taxpayer's net investment income for the year. Net investment income is gross investment income reduced by *deductible investment expenses.* |
| Nondeductible amounts due to limitations | Deduct it in the year incurred or lose it. | Carryover indefinitely. |

### Investment Expenses

Just as taxpayers can deduct ordinary and necessary business expenditures when conducting business activities, individual taxpayers are allowed to deduct ordinary and necessary expenses they incur in investment activities to produce or collect income and for expenses they pay or incur to manage property held for producing

income—such as safe deposit box rental fees, attorney and accounting fees that are necessary to produce investment income, and expenses for investment advice, among other things.[47]

The arrangement makes sense if you think about it: The government taxes investment income, so it is willing to allow taxpayers to deduct expenses they incur to generate investment income. Conversely, to the extent taxpayers incur expenses to produce tax-exempt income, such as municipal bond interest, they are not allowed to deduct the related expenses.[48] For example, a taxpayer who keeps a fully taxable corporate bond in a safe deposit box would be allowed an investment expense deduction for the cost of renting the box, but one who keeps a tax-exempt municipal bond in a safe deposit box would not.

The bad news here for taxpayers is that investment expenses are treated as miscellaneous itemized deductions subject to the 2 percent of AGI floor.[49] Thus, taxpayers with investment expenses will only realize tax benefits from these expenses if they itemize deductions *and* their total miscellaneous itemized deductions (fees for investment advice, tax return preparation fees, an employee's job-related magazine subscriptions, and other unreimbursed employee business expenses—see Chapter 6)—including investment expenses—exceed 2 percent of their AGI. Consequently, it is likely that taxpayers with taxable investments and investment expenses will receive little tax benefit, if any, from the expenses.

> **THE KEY FACTS**
>
> Investment-Related Expenses
>
> ■ Investment expenses deducted as miscellaneous itemized deductions are subject to the 2 percent of AGI floor.
> · Expenses other than interest incurred to generate investment income.
> · No carryover of amounts not currently deductible.

---

**Example 11-17**

Nick and Rachel Sutton met several times with a financial planner who advised them regarding some difficult investment decisions. Nick and Rachel paid the advisor $500 for her services. Also, during the year Nick and Rachel paid a CPA $300 to prepare their tax return. The Suttons had no other miscellaneous itemized deductions for the year. Do the Suttons gain any tax benefit from the $500 they paid to the financial planner (their AGI is $170,000)?

**Answer:** No. The $500 payment is a deductible investment expense for Nick and Rachel. However, to receive any tax benefit from the payment, their total miscellaneous itemized deductions must exceed 2 percent of their AGI. The computation for their deductible investment expense is as follows:

| Description | Amount |
|---|---|
| Investment expenses | $  500 |
| Tax return preparation fees | 300 |
| Total miscellaneous itemized deductions | $  800 |
| Less: 2 percent of AGI ($170,000 × 2%) | 3,400 |
| Miscellaneous itemized deductions over 2 percent of AGI floor. | $      0 |

Because their miscellaneous itemized deductions are less than 2 percent of their AGI, the Suttons do not gain any tax benefit from the $500 investment expense (it does not offset taxable income).

In fact, the Suttons could have paid another $2,600 of investment expenses before they would have exceeded the 2 percent of AGI threshold and received *any* tax benefit from the payment ($3,400 − $800).

---

[47]IRC §212. Rental expenses are also deductible under §212 as we discuss in Chapter 6.

[48]§265.

[49]See Chapter 6 for a discussion of the tax treatment of miscellaneous itemized deductions. Also note that as we discussed in Chapter 6, investment expenses from rental and royalty-related activities are deductible as *for* AGI and not as itemized deductions.

## Investment Interest Expense

When taxpayers borrow money to acquire investments, the interest expense they pay on the loan is investment interest expense. For example, if you borrow funds to buy stock, any interest you pay on the loan would be considered investment interest expense. Investment interest expense may be deductible as an itemized deduction.[50] Unlike investment expenses, the investment interest expense deduction is *not* a miscellaneous itemized deduction subject to the 2 percent of AGI floor. It is, however, subject to a different limitation. A taxpayer's investment interest expense deduction for the year is limited to the taxpayer's **net investment income** for the year.[51]

**Net Investment Income**    Net investment income is gross investment income reduced by *deductible* investment expenses. Deductible investment expenses are investment expenses that actually reduce taxable income *after* applying the 2 percent of AGI floor.[52] Gross investment income includes interest, annuity, and royalty income not derived in the ordinary course of a trade or business. It also includes net *short*-term capital gains, net capital losses (short- and long-term), and nonqualified dividends. However, investment income generally does not include net long-term capital gains and qualified dividends because this income is taxed at a preferential rate.

---

**Example 11-18**

During the year, Nick and Rachel recognized the following income from investments: $3,000 of qualified dividends and $500 of taxable interest. What is the Suttons' gross investment income?

**Answer:**  $500. The taxable interest is included, and the qualified dividends are excluded because they are taxed at a preferential rate.

What is the Suttons' *net* investment income?

**Answer:**  $500. Recall that net investment income is gross investment income minus deductible (taxable income reducing) investment expenses. We learned in Example 11-17 that the Suttons' deductible investment expenses are $0. Thus, their net investment income is $500 ($500 − $0).

---

Taxpayers may deduct their investment interest expense up to the amount of their net investment income. Any investment interest expense in excess of net investment income is carried over and treated as though it was incurred in the next year when it is subject to the same limitations.[53] The carryover amount never expires. That is, taxpayers can carry over the excess investment interest expense until they generate sufficient net investment income to deduct it.

---

[50]§163.

[51]The investment interest expense limitation is calculated on Form 4952. Note that taxpayers can avoid the limitations on investment interest expense by acquiring the investment assets with funds from a qualified home equity loan. As we discuss in Chapter 14, interest on home equity loans is generally fully deductible.

[52]When taxpayers have both investment expenses and other miscellaneous itemized deductions subject to the 2 percent of AGI floor, deductible amounts in excess of the 2 percent of AGI floor are considered to first come from investment expenses up to the total amount of investment expenses and then from other miscellaneous itemized deductions.

[53]In lieu of deducting investment interest expense, taxpayers may elect to capitalize it to the basis of the investment property purchased with the loan generating the investment interest expense. See Reg. §1.266-1(c)(1).

**Example 11-19**

In July of this year, the Suttons purchased a parcel of undeveloped land as an investment for $120,000. They made a $20,000 down payment and financed the remaining $100,000 with a loan from their local credit union. The interest rate on the loan was 9 percent, payable annually. During the year, the Suttons paid $4,500 in interest expense on the loan. Because the loan was used to purchase an investment, the interest expense is investment interest expense. What amount of this investment interest expense are the Suttons allowed to deduct this year?

**Answer:** $500. Although they incurred $4,500 of investment interest expense, their deduction for the current year is limited to their $500 net investment income (see Example 11-18). The $4,000 of investment interest expense that is not deductible this year is carried forward until the Suttons generate enough net investment income to deduct it.

### Election to Include Long-Term Capital Gains and Qualified Dividends in Investment Income

When we described the types of income included in investment income, we mentioned that net long-term capital gains and qualified dividends generally are excluded from investment income because these types of income are taxed at a preferential rate that is lower than the ordinary income tax rate. Congress decided that it wasn't right to allow income that is taxed at a preferential rate to increase the amount of deductions that offset income taxed at an ordinary rate. However, Congress allows taxpayers to *elect to include* preferentially taxed income in investment income if they are willing to subject this income to tax at the ordinary (not preferential) tax rates.

Taxpayers who make this election benefit from increasing their net investment income and thus increasing their current year investment interest expense deduction. But, this additional deduction comes at a price because they must subject their net long-term capital gains and qualified dividends included in investment income to ordinary tax rates. Note that the election is not an all-or-nothing proposition. Taxpayers can elect to include all or only a portion of their net long-term capital gains and qualified dividends in investment income. However, whatever they include in investment income, they must subject to tax at the ordinary tax rates.

**Example 11-20**

In Examples 11-18 and 11-19, we discovered that the Suttons paid $4,500 of investment interest expense during the year but were only able to deduct $500 of the interest expense because their net investment income was only $500. However, as indicated in Example 11-18, the Suttons also received $3,000 of qualified dividends that were *excluded* from the net investment income computation. The Suttons may elect to increase their investment income by the amount of the qualified dividends (and increase their investment interest expense deduction), but by doing so, they must subject the qualified dividends to their ordinary tax rate (30 percent) instead of the preferential rate (15 percent). Thus, the Suttons are faced with a choice of whether to include the $3,000 dividend in investment income and tax it at ordinary rates (alternative 1) or to exclude it from investment income and tax it at preferential rates (alternative 2).[54] How much more investment interest expense are they allowed to deduct under alternative 1 than alternative 2?

*(continued on page 11-32...)*

**THE KEY FACTS**

Investment-Related Expenses

■ Investment *interest* expense.

· Itemized deduction not subject to the 2 percent of AGI floor.

· Interest expense on loans used to purchase taxable investments.

· Deductible to the extent of net investment income.

*(continued)*

[54]While this example presents only two options, the Suttons may elect to include any amount of the dividends in investment income.

(concluded)
· Net investment income is gross investment income minus deductible investment expenses.
· Investment income includes interest, annuity, and other investment-type income not taxed at the preferential rate (long-term capital gains and qualified dividends).
· Taxpayers can elect to include long-term capital gains and dividends in investment income but must tax them at the ordinary not the preferential rate.
· Investment interest expense not deducted carries forward indefinitely.

**Answer:** $3,000 more under alternative 1, computed as follows:

**Alternative 1:** *Include the $3,000 dividends in investment income.*

| Description | Amount | Explanation |
|---|---|---|
| (1) Increase in net investment income | $3,000 | Elect to include dividends in net investment income. |
| (2) Increase in investment interest expense deduction | $3,000 | Investment interest expense deduction increased from $500 to $3,500. |
| (3) Tax benefit from additional deduction | $ 900 | (2) × 30%. |
| (4) Tax cost of taxing dividends at ordinary rate | $ 450 | (1) × (30% − 15%). |
| (5) Current savings from election to include dividends in net investment income | $ 450 | (3) − (4). |
| Investment interest expense carryforward | $1,000 | $4,500 total − $3,500 deducted. |

**Alternative 2:** *Exclude the $3,000 dividends from investment income.*

| Description | Amount | Explanation |
|---|---|---|
| Forgone tax benefit available *this year* under alternative 1 | $ 450 | Under alternative 2, the Suttons don't receive the tax savings available under alternative 1. |
| (1) Increase in investment interest expense carryforward | $3,000 | Investment interest expense not deducted under alternative 2. |
| Total investment interest expense carryforward | $4,000 | (1) + $1,000 investment interest expense carryforward under alternative 1. |

Whether or not it makes sense to elect to include net long-term capital gains and qualified dividends in investment income depends on the taxpayers' circumstances and their personal preferences. As we see in Example 11-20, the Suttons could save $450 this year by electing to include this income in investment income. However, by doing so, they are forgoing $3,000 of investment interest expense carryforward ($4,000 − $1,000) that would be available to offset ordinary income in future years.

## L05    PASSIVE ACTIVITY INCOME AND LOSSES

Thus far we have discussed how taxpayers may invest in business- and income-producing activities and earn various forms of income that are taxed as *portfolio income*. For example, taxpayers acquiring stock in a **taxable corporation** that files tax returns and pays taxes or purchasing bonds issued by a taxable corporation are taxed on the portfolio income these investments generate in the form of dividends and interest. On the other hand, a taxpayer may invest directly in an income-producing enterprise by purchasing rental property or by forming a business as a sole proprietor. Similarly, a taxpayer could invest in a partial interest in a trade or business or rental activity by acquiring an ownership interest in a **flow-through entity** that doesn't pay taxes such as a partnership, limited liability company (taxed as a partnership), or an S corporation (taxed similar to a partnership by shareholders' election). No matter whether an investor makes a direct investment in rental property or in a sole proprietorship or makes an indirect investment in a business or rental activity through a partnership, limited liability company, or S corporation, the *actual operating income or loss* from these investments flows through

to the taxpayer as it is earned and is treated as ordinary income or ordinary loss. If trade or business or rental activities (held either directly or indirectly through flow-through entities) generate ordinary operating income, taxpayers report it on their tax returns and it is taxed at ordinary rates. However, if these activities generate operating losses, the operating losses must clear three hurdles to be deductible currently. The three loss limits are the tax basis, at-risk, and the passive loss limits.

The tax basis hurdle limits a taxpayer's deductible operating losses to the taxpayer's tax basis in the business or rental activity. This limitation is very similar to loss limitations that apply when a taxpayer sells an investment asset such as corporate stock or other similar capital asset. Recall that the formula for determining gain or loss on an exchange is the amount realized less the taxpayer's adjusted basis in the property. If a taxpayer were to sell an asset for nothing, the loss would be the amount of her tax basis in the property, but no more.

Obviously, in order to apply the tax basis loss limitation, we must first compute the taxpayer's tax basis in the business or rental activity. Assuming a taxpayer invests only cash in a business activity, the taxpayer's initial basis in the activity is the amount of cash the taxpayer invests (including borrowed funds) and possibly a share of the activity's debt.[55] In general, a taxpayer's share of the activity's debt is included in her tax basis when it is *deemed for tax purposes* to be similar to debt the taxpayer may have incurred outside of the activity to obtain cash to invest in the activity. In addition, a taxpayer's share of the undistributed income from the activity increases the taxpayer's basis because it is treated as an additional investment of cash in the activity. In a similar vein, distributions of cash and losses reduce tax basis; but if the taxpayer's losses from an activity exceed her tax basis in the activity, the losses are suspended until the taxpayer generates enough tax basis in the future to absorb the suspended losses.

---

### Example 11-21

***What if:*** Assume that instead of investing solely in assets that generate portfolio income, Nick and Rachel used $10,000 of the inheritance from Nick's grandmother to acquire a 5 percent interest in a limited partnership (a flow-through entity) called Color Comfort Sheets (CCS). CCS uses unique fabric blends to manufacture extremely comfortable bed sheets. As 5 percent owners, 5 percent of the actual income and loss of the business flows through to Nick and Rachel each year and is treated as though they received the income directly. However, as limited partners, Nick and Rachel are not involved in managing CCS's business activities and they are not personally liable for CCS's debts. Assuming CCS has no debt, what is Nick and Rachel's tax basis in their CCS limited partnership interest?

**Answer:** $10,000, the amount of cash they invested in the business.

***What if:*** Assuming CCS had total debt of $100,000 and Nick and Rachel's share of this debt was deemed to be $5,000, what would be the Suttons' tax basis in their CCS limited partnership interest?

**Answer:** $15,000, the amount of cash they invested directly plus their share of CCS's debt.

***What if:*** Assuming CCS did not have any debt and generated $300,000 of ordinary income in the first year after the Suttons invested, how much of this income would the Suttons recognize on their joint return?

**Answer:** $15,000. Because CCS is a flow-through entity, the Suttons' share of the business income ($300,000 × 5%) would be taxed to them as if they had received the income directly. Note that this income allocation would increase their tax basis in CCS by $15,000 up to $25,000 if their share of the income is not distributed to them.

(continued on page 11-34...)

---

[55]Special rules may apply when a taxpayer invests or contributes other types of property to the activity. In addition, debt from an activity is allocated to investors in varying degrees depending on the type of entity (e.g., S corporation, partnership, sole proprietorship), within which the activity is housed. These rules are beyond the scope of this discussion.

> **What if:** Assuming CCS did not have any debt and generated a $300,000 ordinary loss in the first year after the Suttons invested, how much of this loss would the Suttons be allowed to deduct based solely on the tax basis limitation?
>
> **Answer:** $10,000, because their 5 percent share of the loss, or $15,000, is limited to their tax basis in their CCS interest. This loss allocation would reduce their tax basis in CCS to $0 and they would have a suspended $5,000 loss. They must gain additional basis in the future in order to deduct this suspended loss.

When a loss from a business or business-related activity clears the tax basis hurdle, it next must clear the **at-risk** hurdle on its journey toward deductibility.[56] The at-risk rules are meant to limit the ability of investors to deduct "artificial" ordinary losses produced with certain types of debt. These rules limit ordinary losses to a taxpayer's amount at risk in an activity. Generally, a taxpayer is considered to be at risk in an activity to the extent of any cash personally contributed to the activity.[57] Additionally, a taxpayer's amount at risk also includes her share, if any, of amounts borrowed for use in the activity *if she is personally liable for repayment.* As with the tax basis calculation, a taxpayer's share of income increases the taxpayer's amount at risk in the activity and cash distributions reduce the amount at risk. Because the computation of tax basis and at-risk amount are so similar, a taxpayer's tax basis and her at-risk amount in the activity are frequently the same so that when she clears the tax basis hurdle for deducting a loss, she also clears the at-risk hurdle. However, the tax basis may exceed the at-risk amount when the taxpayer's share of the business activity's liabilities included in her tax basis includes liabilities that the taxpayer is not personally liable to repay. For example, taxpayers with limited partnership interests in a partnership are usually not at risk for their share of partnership debt because they are usually not economically at risk or responsible for paying the debts of the limited partnership.[58] Taxpayers, including limited partners, are, however, allowed to include their share of debt for "qualified nonrecourse financing" in their at-risk amount even though they are not personally liable to repay the debt.[59] Qualified nonrecourse financing is debt from the activity that (1) represents a legitimate loan and was borrowed to fund real estate used in the activity and (2) was borrowed from a person or entity actively and regularly engaged in the business of lending money. Losses that do not clear the at-risk hurdle are suspended until the taxpayer generates more at-risk amounts to absorb the loss or until the activity is sold, when they may offset the seller's gain from the disposition of the activity. Exhibit 11-7 summarizes the items included in calculating a taxpayer's tax basis and at-risk amount.

## Example 11-22

> **What if:** Assume the same facts as in the previous example. The Suttons acquired a limited partnership interest in Color Comfort Sheets (CCS) limited partnership for $10,000. What is their at-risk amount in CCS?
>
> **Answer:** $10,000, the cash they invested in the CCS limited partnership interest.
>
> (continued on page 11-35...)

[56]§465.

[57]The amount at risk also includes the tax basis of other property a taxpayer contributes to the activity.

[58]Limited partners are usually only allocated a share of the partnership's "nonrecourse" debt. Because nonrecourse debt is debt for which no partner has economic risk of loss, partners are generally not "at risk" with respect to this type of debt.

[59]§465(b)(6).

**EXHIBIT 11-7   Items Affecting Tax Basis and At-Risk Amount**

| Item | Effect on Tax Basis | Effect on At-Risk Amount |
|---|:---:|:---:|
| Cash invested | + | + |
| Share of debt responsible to repay | + | + |
| Share of debt not responsible to repay:<br>Qualified nonrecourse financing | + | + |
| Share of debt not responsible to repay: Other | + | No effect |
| Share of income | + | + |
| Cash distributions | − | − |
| Share of loss | − | − |

*(continued from previous page...)*

Assuming that CCS incurred $100,000 of debt (other than qualified nonrecourse financing) and that the Suttons' share of the debt is $5,000, what is the Suttons' at-risk amount in CCS?

**Answer:** $10,000. Even though the Suttons are allowed to include their $5,000 share of CCS's debt in their tax basis for CCS, they are not allowed to include the debt in their at-risk amount because, as limited partners, they are not personally liable for this debt, so they are not economically at risk with respect to this amount.

***What if:*** Assuming the Suttons' share of CCS's debt is $5,000 and that CCS generated a $300,000 ordinary loss in the first year after the Suttons invested, how much of the Suttons' $15,000 share of this loss would they be allowed to deduct after applying the tax basis and at-risk limitations?

**Answer:** $10,000. The Suttons' tax basis is $15,000, but their at-risk amount is only $10,000; consequently, their entire $15,000 share of loss clears the tax basis hurdle, but only $10,000 of the loss clears the at-risk hurdle. Thus, the Suttons may deduct $10,000 of the loss reducing their amount at risk to zero, but they must wait until they generate amounts at risk in order to deduct the $5,000 loss that is suspended by the at-risk limit or until they sell their limited partnership interest.

***What if:*** Assume that the Suttons' share of CCS's debt is $5,000 but that CCS is involved in rental real estate activities and that its debt is considered to be qualified nonrecourse financing. Further assume that the Suttons' share of CCS's loss for the year is $15,000. What amount of this loss are the Suttons allowed to deduct after applying the tax basis and at-risk limitations?

**Answer:** $15,000. The Suttons' tax basis in their CCS interest is $15,000, and their at-risk amount is also $15,000. Because qualified nonrecourse financing is included in their amount at risk, the Suttons may deduct the entire $15,000 loss (subject to the passive activity loss limits discussed below).

Even when a taxpayer has sufficient tax basis and sufficient amounts at risk to absorb a loss from a business-related activity, the loss may still be limited by the passive activity loss rules. Prior to 1986, investors were able to use ordinary losses from certain passive activities to offset portfolio income (interest, dividends, and capital gains), salary income, and self-employment income, including income from other trades or businesses they were actively involved in managing. During this time, a **tax shelter** industry thrived by marketing investments to wealthy investors designed primarily to generate ordinary losses that could be used to shield other income from tax. To combat this practice, Congress introduced the passive activity loss rules.[60] Specifically, these rules limit the ability of investors in certain passive activities involving interests in trade or businesses and in rental property, including real estate,

[60]§469.

to use their ordinary losses from these activities currently to reduce taxable income from other sources.[61] The passive activity loss rules are applied to any losses remaining *after* applying the tax basis and at-risk loss limits described above.

### Passive Activity Definition

The **passive activity loss rules** define a passive activity as "any activity which involves the conduct of a trade or business, and in which the taxpayer does not materially participate." According to the tax code, participants in rental activities, including rental real estate, and limited partners in partnerships are generally deemed to be passive participants, and participants in all other trade or business activities are passive unless their involvement in an activity is "regular, continuous, and substantial." Clearly, these terms are quite subjective and difficult to apply. Fortunately, regulations provide more certainty in this area by listing seven separate tests for material participation.[62] An individual, other than a limited partner, can be classified as a material participant in an activity by meeting any one of the seven tests in Exhibit 11-8. Therefore, investors who purchase rental property or an interest in a trade or business without intending to be involved in the management of the trade or business are classified as passive participants, and these activities are classified as passive activities with respect to them.

### EXHIBIT 11-8   Tests for Material Participation

**Individuals are generally considered material participants for the activity if they meet any *one* of these tests:**

1. The individual participates in the activity more than 500 hours during the year.
2. The individual's activity constitutes substantially all of the participation in such activity by all individuals including nonowners.
3. The individual participates more than 100 hours during the year, and the individual's participation is not less than any other individual's participation in the activity.
4. The activity qualifies as a "significant participation activity" (more than 100 hours spent during the year) and the aggregate of all "significant participation activities" is greater than 500 hours for the year.
5. The individual materially participated in the activity for any five of the preceding 10 taxable years.
6. The individual materially participated for any three preceding years in any personal service activity (personal services in health, law, accounting, architecture, etc.)
7. Taking into account all the facts and circumstances, the individual participates on a regular, continuous, and substantial basis during the year.

### Income and Loss Categories

Under the passive activity loss rules, each item of a taxpayer's income or loss for the year is placed in one of three categories. Losses from *the passive category* cannot offset income from other categories. The three different categories are as follows (see Exhibit 11-9):

1. *Passive activity income or loss*—income or loss from an activity in which the taxpayer is not a material participant.[63]

---

[61]Before passage of the passive activity loss rules, the "at-risk rules" in §465 were adopted in an attempt to limit the ability of investors to deduct "artificial" ordinary losses. Given the similarity of the at risk and tax basis computations, especially for real estate investments, the at-risk rules were not entirely successful at accomplishing this objective. The passive activity loss rules were adopted as a backstop to the at-risk rules and both sets of rules may potentially apply to a given activity.

[62]§1.469-5T.

[63]According to §1.163-8T, interest from debt used to purchase a passive activity is allocated to that activity and either reduces passive income or increases passive loss from the activity.

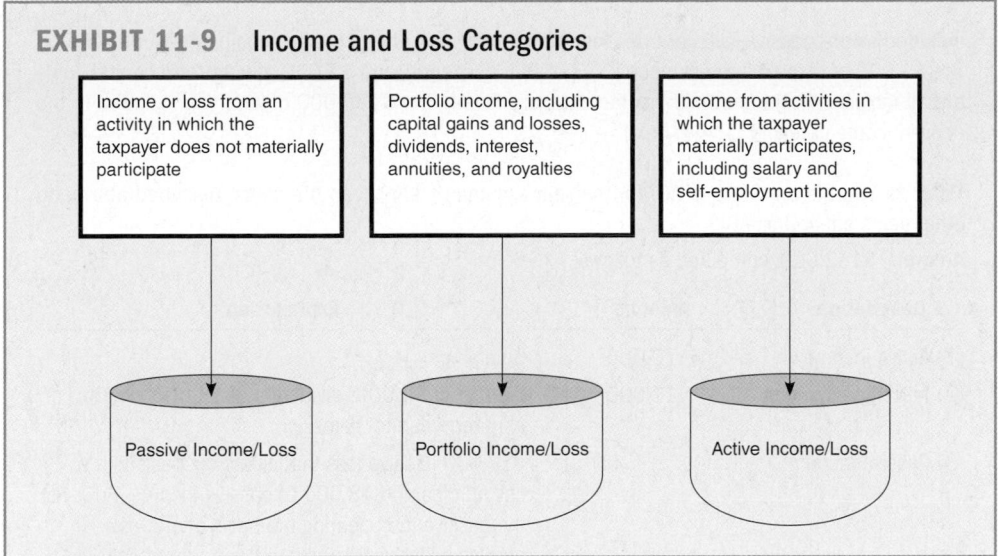

EXHIBIT 11-9     Income and Loss Categories

| Income or loss from an activity in which the taxpayer does not materially participate | Portfolio income, including capital gains and losses, dividends, interest, annuities, and royalties | Income from activities in which the taxpayer materially participates, including salary and self-employment income |
|---|---|---|

Passive Income/Loss     Portfolio Income/Loss     Active Income/Loss

2. *Portfolio income*—income from investments including capital gains and losses, dividends, interest, annuities, and royalties.

3. *Active business income*—income from sources in which the taxpayer is a material participant. For individuals, this includes salary and self-employment income. Thus, an individual with income in this category is no longer an investor with respect to this source of income given that we define investors in this chapter as individuals with portfolio and/or passive income and losses.

The impact of segregating taxpayers' income in these categories is to limit their ability to apply passive activity losses against income in the other two categories. In effect, passive activity losses are suspended and remain in the passive income or loss category until the taxpayer generates passive income, either from the passive activity producing the loss or from some other passive activity, or until the taxpayer sells the entire activity that generated the passive loss.[64] On the sale, current and suspended passive losses from the activity are first applied to reduce gain from the sale of the activity, then to reduce net passive income from other passive activities, and then to reduce nonpassive income.[65]

### Example 11-23

**What if:** Let's return to the facts in the previous example where the Suttons' share of CCS loss was $15,000, their tax basis in their CCS interest is $15,000, and their at-risk amount in the activity is $10,000. Further assume that the Suttons received $170,000 in combined salary, $4,000 of taxable interest income from corporate bonds, $3,000 of dividends, and $5,000 of long-term capital gains. Finally, assume that the Suttons also owned a rental condominium that generated $8,000 of net income. How would each of these income or loss items be allocated among the passive, portfolio, and active income and loss categories?

**Answer:** The Suttons' $10,000 loss from CCS remaining after applying the tax basis and at risk loss limits is placed in the passive category because, as limited partners, the Suttons did not materially participate in the activity. Further, their $8,000 of net income from their rental property is

(*continued on page 11-38...*)

---

[64]To utilize suspended passive losses on the disposition of a passive activity, the disposition must be a fully taxable transaction.

[65]§469(g).

included in the passive category because rental activities are generally considered to be passive. The $4,000 of taxable interest income, $3,000 of dividends, and $5,000 of long-term capital gains are all included in the portfolio income category. Finally, the $170,000 of salary is included in the active income category.

**What if:** What is the Suttons' AGI for the year assuming, other than the items described above, no other items affect their AGI?

**Answer:** $182,000, computed as follows:

| Description | Amount | Explanation |
|---|---|---|
| (1) Active income | $170,000 | Salary. |
| (2) Portfolio income | 12,000 | Interest of $4,000; dividends of $3,000; $5,000 of long-term capital gains. |
| (3) Passive income | 0 | $10,000 passive loss that clears tax basis and at-risk hurdles and $8,000 of passive income. However, the passive loss clearing the basis and at-risk hurdles is deductible only to the extent of passive income. The suspended passive loss is ($2,000). |
| AGI | $182,000 | (1) + (2) + (3). |

**What if:** Assume the facts above and that at the beginning of next year the Suttons sell their limited partnership interest for $12,000 ($7,000 in cash and $5,000 debt relief from the purchaser assuming their share of partnership debt). Given that their tax basis on the date of sale is $0, what effect does the sale have on their AGI?

**Answer:** $5,000 increase in AGI, computed as follows:

| Description | Amount | Explanation |
|---|---|---|
| (1) Capital gain | $12,000 | Gain recognized = $12,000 − $0 tax basis. |
| (2) Ordinary loss | ($5,000) | The loss that was previously suspended at the at-risk level becomes an at-risk amount on the sale (it is no longer suspended). The loss is fully deductible because the loss leaves the passive category and enters the active category on the sale of the interest in the activity. |
| (3) Ordinary loss | ($2,000) | This is the loss that was suspended at the passive loss level last year. |
| Increase in AGI | $ 5,000 | (1) + (2) + (3). |

## Rental Real Estate Exception to the Passive Activity Loss Rules

Tax laws are renowned for exceptions to rules and, not surprisingly, the general rule that passive activity losses cannot be used to offset nonpassive types of income is subject to a few important exceptions. The one we choose to discuss here applies to lower-to-middle income individuals with rental real estate.[66] A taxpayer

---

[66]§469(b)(7) provides another important exception to the general rule that all real estate activities are passive. To overcome this presumption, taxpayers must spend more than half their time working in real estate trades or businesses and for more than 750 hours during the year. This exception benefits individuals that spend a substantial amount of time in activities like real estate development and construction.

who is an **active participant in a rental activity** may be allowed to deduct up to $25,000 of the rental loss against other types of income. To be considered an active participant, the taxpayer must (1) own at least 10 percent of the rental property, and (2) participate in the process of making management decisions such as approving new tenants, deciding on rental terms, and approving repairs and capital expenditures.

Consistent with a number of tax benefits, the exception amount for active owners is phased out as adjusted gross income increases: The $25,000 maximum exception amount is phased out by 50 cents for every dollar the taxpayer's adjusted gross income (before considering the rental loss) exceeds $100,000. Consequently, the entire $25,000 deduction is phased-out when the taxpayer's adjusted gross income reaches $150,000.

## Example 11-24

**What if:** Assume that Jeb Landers, Rachel's father, owns and rents a condominium. Jeb is involved in approving new tenants for the rental home and in managing its maintenance. During the year, he reported a net loss of $5,000 from the rental activity, and he had sufficient tax basis and at-risk amounts to absorb the loss. Further, his only sources of income during the year were $126,000 of salary and $22,000 of long-term capital gains. Given Jeb's $5,000 loss from his rental home, how much of the loss could he deduct currently?

**Answer:** $1,000. Because Jeb meets the definition of an "active participant" and has adjusted gross income of less than $150,000, before considering his rental loss, he may deduct a portion of the loss against his other income. His $1,000 deduction is computed as follows:

| Description | Amount | Explanation |
|---|---|---|
| (1) Maximum deduction available before phase-out | $25,000 | |
| (2) Phase-out of maximum deduction | $24,000 | [($148,000 − 100,000) × .5]. |
| (3) Maximum deduction in current year | $ 1,000 | (1) − (2). |
| (4) Rental loss in current year | $ 5,000 | |
| (5) Rental loss deductible in current year | $ 1,000 | Lesser of (3) or (4). |
| Passive loss carryforward | $ 4,000 | (4) − (3). |

**What if:** Assume that Jeb's salary for the year had been $50,000 and he reported $22,000 from the sale of his stock, how much of his rental loss could he deduct currently?

**Answer:** Because Jeb's adjusted gross income would only be $72,000 under this scenario, he could deduct his entire $5,000 rental loss during the year.

---

**THE KEY FACTS**

**Rental Real Estate Losses**

■ Rental real estate exception to passive loss rules.
· Applies to active participants in rental property.
· Deduct up to $25,000 of rental real estate loss against ordinary income.
· $25,000 maximum deduction phased out by 50 cents for every dollar of AGI over $100,000 (excluding the rental loss deduction).
· Fully phased out at $150,000 of AGI.

---

## CONCLUSION

Investors and their advisors face numerous tax rules that apply to investment income and expenses. Understanding these rules is important, not only to comply with the tax law, but also to make wise investment choices. Investments differ in terms of their potential for implementing the conversion and shifting tax planning strategies. Failing to consider these strategies when investing will lead to less than optimal results. By carefully weighing nontax investment objectives along with the tax characteristics of different investment options, informed investors will be better equipped to select investments appropriate for them.

# SUMMARY

**LO1**    Explain how interest income and dividend income are taxed.

- Investors seeking current income invest in interest-bearing securities or dividend-paying stocks.
- Interest income received from certificates of deposit, U.S. Treasury securities, corporate bonds, and other similar investments is typically taxed annually at ordinary rates.
- Accrued market discount on bonds and interest earned on U.S. savings bonds is taxed at sale or maturity, while original issue discount on bonds is taxed annually.
- Bond premiums increase the tax basis of bonds and affect the amount of capital gains or losses investors report.
- Taxpayers may elect to amortize bond premiums to reduce the amount of annual interest reported on bonds purchased at a premium.
- Dividend income, like interest income, is taxed annually when it is received. However, most dividend income currently is taxed at preferential capital gains rates.
- Explicit tax rates favor dividend income over interest income.
- After-tax returns from interest and dividend-paying investments are not affected by an investor's investment horizon because the income they generate is taxed annually.

**LO2**    Compute the tax consequences associated with the disposition of capital assets, including the netting process for calculating gains and losses.

- When taxpayers sell stock, they may determine the basis of the stock using the specific identification method or the FIFO method.
- Capital assets held for more than one year generate long-term capital gains or losses on sale or disposition. Other capital assets generate short-term capital gains or losses on sale or disposition.
- Generally, net long-term capital gains in excess of net short-term losses are taxed at a maximum 15 percent tax rate.
- Unrecaptured §1250 gain is taxed at a maximum 25 percent rate, and gains from collectibles and §1202 stock are taxed at a maximum 28 percent rate.
- Up to $3,000 of net capital losses are deductible against ordinary income for the year.
- A taxpayer's capital gains and losses for the year are reported on Schedule D of Form 1040.
- Wash sale provisions prevent taxpayers from selling stock at a loss, deducting the loss, and replacing the stock sold with the same stock or substantially identical securities within 30 days either before or after the day of sale.
- Losses on the disposition of property held for personal use are not deductible.
- Because of the deferral of the capital gains tax, after-tax returns from capital assets will increase as an investor's investment horizon increases.

**LO3**    Describe common sources of tax-exempt investment income and explain the rationale for exempting some investments from taxation.

- To promote certain social goals, the income from some investments and investment vehicles is exempt from federal income taxes.
- Interest from municipal bonds issued by state and local governments is exempt from federal income tax. However, states tax municipal bond interest their residents receive from other states.
- Because of their tax-exempt status, municipal bonds yield lower pretax rates of return relative to similar taxable bonds. This lower relative rate of return is referred to as an *implicit tax*.
- Proceeds from life insurance policies are tax-exempt unless the policy has been cashed in early for its cash surrender value. In that case, the recipient is taxed on the difference between the amount invested in the policy and the premiums paid.
- Investment income earned within a 529 or other education savings plan is tax-exempt provided it is used to pay for certain qualified educational expenses.

Calculate the deduction for portfolio investment-related expenses, including investment expenses and investment interest expense.

**L04**

- Investment expenses are miscellaneous itemized deductions subject to the 2 percent of AGI floor.
- Investment interest expense is deductible to the extent of net investment income.
- Net investment income is investment income minus deductible investment expenses.
- Net long-term capital gains and qualified dividends are not included in investment income unless the taxpayer elects to tax them as ordinary income.

Understand the distinction between portfolio investments and passive investments and apply tax basis, at-risk, and passive activity loss limits to losses from passive investments.

**L05**

- A taxpayer's share of operating losses from flow-through entities and other trade or business activities are deductible to the extent they clear the tax basis, at-risk, and passive activity loss hurdles.
- A taxpayer's ordinary losses from flow-through entities and other trade or business activities may be classified as passive if the taxpayer's involvement is not regular, continuous, and substantial.
- A taxpayer's operating losses from rental activities are, with limited exceptions, deemed to be passive regardless of taxpayer's activity level.
- A taxpayer's passive losses from an activity are limited to passive income from all other sources until disposition of the activity. On disposition, current and prior passive losses from an activity can be used without limitation.
- A rental real estate exception allows taxpayers to deduct up to $25,000 of operating losses from rental real estate annually provided they are actively involved in managing the rental real estate and have adjusted gross income of less than $150,000.

# KEY TERMS

accrued market discount (11-5)

active participant in a rental activity (11-39)

after-tax rate of return (11-1)

amortization (11-4)

at risk (11-34)

basis (11-5)

before-tax rate of return (11-1)

bond (11-2)

bond discount (11-4)

bond premium (11-4)

capital asset (11-9)

cash surrender value (11-24)

certificate of deposit (11-2)

collectibles (11-11)

dividend (11-2)

ex-dividend date (11-7)

explicit tax (11-23)

face value (11-3)

first-in first-out (FIFO) method (11-10)

flow-through entity (11-32)

implicit tax (11-23)

investment expenses (11-28)

investment income (11-2)

investment interest expense (11-28)

long-term capital gains or losses (11-11)

market discount (11-5)

market premium (11-5)

maturity (11-5)

maturity value (11-3)

mutual fund (11-2)

net capital gain (11-13)

net investment income (11-30)

net long-term capital gain (11-13)

net long-term capital loss (11-13)

net short-term capital gain (11-13)

net short-term capital loss (11-13)

operating income (11-2)

operating loss (11-2)

original issue discount (11-4)

passive activity loss rules (11-36)

passive investments (11-2)

portfolio investments (11-2)

qualified dividends (11-7)

qualified small business stock (11-11)

qualified tuition plans (529 plans) (11-25)

short-term capital gains or losses (11-11)

specific identification method (11-10)

tax basis (11-9)

tax shelter (11-35)

taxable corporations (11-32)

term insurance (11-24)

Treasury bond (11-4)

Treasury note (11-4)

unrecaptured §1250 gain (11-11)

U.S. savings bonds (11-4)

wash sale (11-19)

whole life insurance (11-23)

zero-coupon bonds (11-4)

# DISCUSSION QUESTIONS

1. **(LO1)** Describe how interest income and dividend income are taxed. What are the similarities and differences in their tax treatment?

2. **(LO1)** What is the underlying policy rationale for the current tax rules applicable to interest income and dividend income?

3. **(LO1)** Compare and contrast the tax treatment of interest from a Treasury bond and qualified dividends from corporate stock.

4. **(LO1)** How are Treasury notes and Treasury bonds treated for federal and state income tax purposes?

5. **(LO1)** Why would taxpayers generally prefer the tax treatment of market discount to the treatment of original issue discount on corporate bonds?

6. **(LO1)** In what ways are U.S. savings bonds treated more favorably for tax purposes than corporate bonds?

7. **(LO1)** When should investors consider making an election to amortize market discount on a bond into income annually? [*Hint:* see §1278(b).]

8. **(LO1)** Why might investors purchase interest-paying securities rather than dividend-paying stocks?

9. **(LO1)** Compare and contrast the tax treatment of dividend-paying stocks and growth stocks.

10. **(LO1)** Do after-tax rates of return for investments in either interest- or dividend-paying securities increase with the length of the investment? Why or why not?

11. **(LO2)** What is the definition of a capital asset? Give three examples of capital assets.

12. **(LO2)** Why does the tax law allow a taxpayer to defer gains accrued on a capital asset until the taxpayer actually sells the asset?

13. **(LO2)** Why does the tax law provide preferential rates on certain capital gains?

14. **(LO2)** Cameron purchases stock in Corporation X and in Corporation Y. Neither corporation pays dividends. The stocks both earn an identical before-tax rate of return. Cameron sells stock in Corporation X after three years and he sells the stock in Corporation Y after five years. Which investment likely earned a greater after-tax return? Why?

15. **(LO2)** What is the deciding factor in determining whether a capital gain is a short-term or long-term capital gain?

16. **(LO2)** What methods may taxpayers use to determine the adjusted basis of stock they have sold?

17. **(LO2)** What tax rate applies to net short-term capital gains?

18. **(LO2)** What limitations are placed on the deductibility of capital losses for individual taxpayers?

19. **(LO2)** What happens to capital losses that are not deductible in the current year?

20. **(LO2)** Are all long-term capital gains taxable at the same maximum rate? If not, what rates may apply to long-term capital gains?

21. **(LO2)** David, a taxpayer currently in the highest tax rate bracket, has the option to purchase either stock in a Fortune 500 company or qualified small business stock in his friend's corporation. All else equal, which of the two will he prefer from a tax perspective if he intends to hold the stock for six years? Which would he prefer if he only plans to hold the stock for two years?

22. **(LO2)** What is a "wash sale"? What is the purpose of the wash sale tax rules?

23. **(LO2)** Nick does not use his car for business purposes. If he sells his car for less than he paid for it, does he get to deduct the loss for tax purposes? Why or why not?

24. **(LO2)** Describe three basic tax planning strategies available to taxpayers investing in capital assets.

25. **(LO2)** Clark owns stock in BCS Corporation that he purchased in January of the current year. The stock has appreciated significantly during the year. It is now December of the current year, and Clark is deciding whether or not he should sell the stock. What tax and nontax factors should Clark consider before making the decision on whether to sell the stock now?    ■ planning

26. **(LO2)** Under what circumstances would you expect the after-tax return from an investment in a capital asset to approach that of tax-exempt assets assuming equal before-tax rates of return?

27. **(LO3)** Why does the federal government exempt municipal bond interest from federal income tax?

28. **(LO3)** Why do taxpayers have an incentive to purchase municipal bonds from within their own states?

29. **(LO3)** What is an "implicit tax" and how does it affect a taxpayer's decision to purchase municipal bonds?

30. **(LO3)** How do taxpayers' explicit marginal tax rates affect their decision to purchase municipal bonds?

31. **(LO3)** Is there a natural clientele for municipal bonds? Why or why not?

32. **(LO3)** In what sense can life insurance be viewed as an investment?

33. **(LO3)** How are life insurance proceeds taxed when paid after the insured individual's death?

34. **(LO3)** How are life insurance proceeds taxed if a policy is cashed out early?

35. **(LO3)** List the important nontax issues to consider when purchasing life insurance as an investment.

36. **(LO3)** How are state-sponsored 529 educational savings plans taxed if investment returns are used for educational purposes? Are the returns taxed differently if they are not ultimately used to pay for education costs?

37. **(LO3)** Why would someone saving for college consider investing in something other than a 529 plan?    ■ planning

38. **(LO4)** Are dividends and capital gains considered to be investment income for purposes of determining the amount of a taxpayer's deductible investment interest expense for the year?

39. **(LO4)** How is the amount of net investment income determined for a taxpayer with investment expenses and other noninvestment miscellaneous itemized deductions?

40. **(LO4)** What limitations are placed on the deductibility of investment interest expense? What happens to investment interest expense that is not deductible because of the limitations?

41. **(LO4)** When taxpayers borrow money to buy municipal bonds, are they allowed to deduct interest expense on the loan? Why or why not?

42. **(LO5)** What types of losses may potentially be characterized as passive losses?

43. **(LO5)** What are the implications of treating losses as passive?

44. **(LO5)** What tests are applied to determine if losses should be characterized as passive?

45. **(LO5)** All else being equal, would a taxpayer with passive losses rather have wage income or passive income?    ■ planning

■ planning

46. **(LO1, LO2, LO3)** Laurie is thinking about investing in one or several of the following investment options:

Corporate bonds
529 plan
Dividend-paying stock
Life insurance
Savings account
Treasury bonds
Growth stock

a. Assuming all seven options earn similar returns before taxes, rank Laurie's investment options from highest to lowest according to their after-tax returns.

b. Which of the investments employ the deferral and/or conversion tax planning strategies?

c. How does the time period of the investment affect the returns from these alternatives?

d. How do these alternative investments differ in terms of their nontax characteristics?

## PROBLEMS

47. **(LO1)** Anne's marginal income tax rate is 30 percent. She purchases a corporate bond for $10,000 and the maturity, or face value, of the bond is $10,000. If the bond pays 5 percent per year before taxes, what is Anne's annual after-tax rate of return from the bond if the bond matures in one year? What is her annual after-tax rate of return if the bond matures in 10 years?

48. **(LO1)** Matt recently deposited $20,000 in a savings account paying a guaranteed interest rate of 4 percent for the next 10 years. If Matt expects his marginal tax rate to be 20 percent for the next 10 years, how much interest will he earn after-tax for the first year of his investment? How much interest will he earn after-tax for the second year of his investment if he withdraws enough cash every year to pay the tax on the interest he earns? How much will he have in the account after four years? How much will he have in the account after seven years?

49. **(LO1)** Dana intends to invest $30,000 in either a Treasury bond or a corporate bond. The Treasury bond yields 5 percent before tax and the corporate bond yields 6 percent before tax. Assuming Dana's federal marginal rate is 25 percent and her marginal state rate is 5 percent, which of the two options should she choose? If she were to move to another state where her marginal state rate would be 10 percent, would her choice be any different? Assume that Dana itemizes deductions.

50. **(LO1)** At the beginning of his current tax year David invests $12,000 in original issue U.S. Treasury bonds with a $10,000 face value that mature in exactly 10 years. David receives $700 in interest ($350 every six months) from the Treasury bonds during the current year, and the yield to maturity on the bonds is 5 percent.

a. How much interest income will he report this year if he elects to amortize the bond premium?

b. How much interest will he report this year if he does not elect to amortize the bond premium?

51. **(LO1)** Seth invested $20,000 in Series EE savings bonds on April 1. By December 31, the published redemption value of the bonds had increased to $20,700. How much interest income will Seth report from the savings bonds in the current year absent any special election?

52. **(LO1)** At the beginning of her current tax year, Angela purchased a zero-coupon corporate bond at original issue for $30,000 with a yield to maturity of 6 percent. Given that she will not actually receive any interest payments until the bond matures in 10 years, how much interest income will she report this year assuming semiannual compounding of interest?

53. **(LO1)** At the beginning of his current tax year, Eric bought a corporate bond with a maturity value of $50,000 from the secondary market for $45,000. The bond has a stated annual interest rate of 5 percent payable on June 30 and December 31, and it matures in five years on December 31. Absent any special tax elections, how much interest income will Eric report from the bond this year and in the year the bond matures?

54. **(LO1)** Hayley recently invested $50,000 in a public utility stock paying a 3 percent annual dividend. If Hayley reinvests the annual dividend she receives net of any taxes owed on the dividend, how much will her investment be worth in four years if the dividends paid are qualified dividends? (Hayley's marginal income tax rate is 28 percent.) What will her investment be worth in four years if the dividends are nonqualified?

55. **(LO1)** Five years ago, Kate purchased a dividend-paying stock for $10,000. For all five years, the stock paid an annual dividend of 4 percent before tax and Kate's marginal tax rate was 25 percent. Every year Kate reinvested her after-tax dividends in the same stock. For the first two years of her investment, the dividends qualified for the 15 percent capital gains rate; however, for the last three years the 15 percent dividend rate was repealed and dividends were taxed at ordinary rates.

    a. What is the current value (at the beginning of year 6) of Kate's investment assuming the stock has not appreciated in value?

    b. What will Kate's investment be worth three years from now (at the beginning of year 9) assuming her marginal tax rate increases to 35 percent for the next three years?

■ **planning**

56. **(LO2)** John bought 1,000 shares of Intel stock on October 18, 2007, for $30 per share plus a $750 commission he paid to his broker. On December 12, 2010, he sells the shares for $42.50 per share. He also incurs a $1,000 fee for this transaction.

    a. What is John's adjusted basis in the 1,000 shares of Intel stock?

    b. What amount does John realize when he sells the 1,000 shares?

    c. What is the gain/loss for John on the sale of his Intel stock? What is the character of the gain/loss?

57. **(LO2)** Dahlia is in the 28 percent tax rate bracket and has purchased the following shares of Microsoft common stock over the years:

| Date Purchased | Shares | Basis |
|---|---|---|
| 7/10/2002 | 400 | $12,000 |
| 4/20/2003 | 300 | $10,750 |
| 1/29/2004 | 500 | $12,230 |
| 11/02/2006 | 250 | $ 7,300 |

If Dahlia sells 800 shares of Microsoft for $40,000 on December 20, 2010, what is her capital gain or loss in each of the following assumptions?

a. She uses the FIFO method.

b. She uses the specific identification method and she wants to minimize her current year capital gain.

**research**

58. **(LO2)** Karyn loaned $20,000 to her co-worker to begin a new business several years ago. If her co-worker declares bankruptcy on June 22nd of the current year, is Karyn allowed to deduct the bad debt loss this year? If she can deduct the loss, what is the character of the loss?

59. **(LO2)** Sue has 5,000 shares of Sony stock that has an adjusted basis of $27,500. She sold the 5,000 shares of stock for cash of $10,000, and she also received a piece of land as part of the proceeds. The land was valued at $20,000 and had an adjusted basis to the buyer of $12,000. What is Sue's gain or loss on the sale of 5,000 shares of Sony stock?

60. **(LO2)** Matt and Meg Comer are married. They do not have any children. Matt works as a history professor at a local university and earns a salary of $52,000. Meg works part-time at the same university. She earns $21,000 a year. The couple does not itemize deductions. Other than salary, the Comers's only other source of income is from the disposition of various capital assets (mostly stocks).

    a. What is the Comers' tax liability for 2010 if they report the following capital gains and losses for the year?

| | |
|---|---|
| Short-term capital gains | $ 7,000 |
| Short-term capital losses | ($2,000) |
| Long-term capital gains | $15,000 |
| Long-term capital losses | ($6,000) |

    b. What is the Comers' tax liability for 2010 if they report the following capital gains and losses for the year?

| | |
|---|---|
| Short-term capital gains | $ 1,500 |
| Short-term capital losses | $    0 |
| Long-term capital gains | $15,000 |
| Long-term capital losses | ($10,000) |

61. **(LO2)** Grayson is in the 25 percent tax rate bracket and has the sold the following stocks in 2010:

| | Date Purchased | Basis | Date Sold | Amount Realized |
|---|---|---|---|---|
| Stock A | 1/23/1986 | $ 7,250 | 7/22/2010 | $ 4,500 |
| Stock B | 4/10/2010 | $14,000 | 9/13/2010 | $17,500 |
| Stock C | 8/23/2008 | $10,750 | 10/12/2010 | $15,300 |
| Stock D | 5/19/2000 | $ 5,230 | 10/12/2010 | $12,400 |
| Stock E | 8/20/2010 | $ 7,300 | 11/14/2010 | $ 3,500 |

    a. What is Grayson's net short-term capital gain or loss from these transactions?

    b. What is Grayson's net long-term gain or loss from these transactions?

    c. What is Grayson's overall net gain or loss from these transactions?

    d. What amount of the gain, if any, is subject to the preferential rate for certain capital gains?

62. **(LO2)** George bought the following amounts of Stock A over the years:

| | Date Purchased | Number of Shares | Adjusted Basis |
|---|---|---|---|
| Stock A | 11/21/1986 | 1,000 | $24,000 |
| Stock A | 3/18/1992 | 500 | $ 9,000 |
| Stock A | 5/22/2001 | 750 | $27,000 |

On October 12, 2010, he sold 1,200 of his shares of Stock A for $38 per share.

a. How much gain/loss will George have to recognize if he uses the FIFO method of accounting for the shares sold?

b. How much gain/loss will George have to recognize if he specifically identifies the shares to be sold by telling his broker to sell all 750 shares from the 5/22/2001 purchase and 450 shares from the 11/21/1986 purchase?

63. **(LO2)** During the current year, Ron and Anne sold the following assets:

| Capital Asset | Market Value | Tax Basis | Holding Period |
|---|---|---|---|
| L stock | $ 50,000 | $41,000 | > 1 year |
| M stock | 28,000 | 39,000 | > 1 year |
| N stock | 30,000 | 22,000 | < 1 year |
| O stock | 26,000 | 33,000 | < 1 year |
| Antiques | 7,000 | 4,000 | > 1 year |
| Rental home | 300,000* | 90,000 | > 1 year |

*$30,000 of the gain is 25 percent gain (from accumulated depreciation on the property).

a. Given that Ron and Anne have taxable income of only $20,000 (all ordinary) before considering the tax effect of their asset sales, what is their gross tax liability for 2010 assuming they file a joint return?

b. Given that Ron and Anne have taxable income of $150,000 (all ordinary) before considering the tax effect of their asset sales, what is their gross tax liability for 2010 assuming they file a joint return?

64. **(LO2)** During the current year, Ken and Marie sold the following assets:

| Capital Asset | Market Value | Tax Basis | Holding Period |
|---|---|---|---|
| R stock | $ 34,000 | $48,000 | > 1 year |
| S stock | 18,000 | 27,000 | > 1 year |
| T stock | 33,000 | 31,000 | < 1 year |
| U stock | 17,000 | 18,000 | < 1 year |
| Stamp collection | 8,000 | 11,000 | > 1 year |
| Rental home | 350,000* | 90,000 | > 1 year |

*$70,000 of the gain is 25 percent gain (from accumulated depreciation on the property).

a. Given that Ken and Marie have taxable income of only $30,000 (all ordinary) before considering the tax effect of their asset sales, what is their gross tax liability for 2010 assuming they file a joint return?

b. Given that Ken and Marie have taxable income of $120,000 (all ordinary) before considering the tax effect of their asset sales, what is their gross tax liability for 2010 assuming they file a joint return?

65. **(LO2)** In 2010, Tom and Amanda Jackson (married filing jointly) have $200,000 of taxable income before considering the following events:

- On May 12, 2010, they sold a painting (art) for $110,000 that was inherited from Grandma on July 23, 2008. The fair market value on the date of Grandma's death was $90,000 and Grandma's adjusted basis of the painting was $25,000.
- Applied a long-term capital loss carryover from 2009 of $10,000.
- Recognized a $12,000 loss on 11/1/10 sale of bonds (acquired on 5/12/01).
- Recognized a $4,000 gain on 12/12/10 sale of IBM stock (acquired on 2/5/10).
- Recognized a $17,000 gain on the 10/17/10 sale of rental property (the only §1231 transaction) of which $8,000 is reportable as gain subject to the 25 percent maximum rate and the remaining $9,000 is subject to the 15 percent maximum rate (the property was acquired on 8/2/04).

- Recognized a $12,000 loss on 12/20/10 sale of bonds (acquired on 1/18/10).
- Recognized a $7,000 gain on 6/27/10 sale of BH stock (acquired on 7/30/02).
- Recognized an $11,000 loss on 6/13/10 sale of QuikCo stock (acquired on 3/20/03).
- Received $500 of qualified dividends on 7/15/10.

Complete the required capital gains netting procedures and calculate the Jacksons' 2010 tax liability.

66. **(LO2)** For 2010, Sherri has a short-term loss of $2,500 and a long-term loss of $4,750.

    a. How much loss can Sherri deduct in 2010?

    b. How much loss will Sherri carryover to 2011, and what is the character of the loss carryover?

67. **(LO2)** Jermaine has the following losses during the current year:

| Loss | Amount |
| --- | --- |
| Short-term capital loss | ($10,000) |
| Long-term capital loss | ($25,000) |

How much capital loss can Jermaine deduct this year against his ordinary income?

68. **(LO2)** Three years ago, Adrian purchased 100 shares of stock in X Corp. for $10,000. On December 30 of year 4, Adrian sells the 100 shares for $6,000.

    a. Assuming Adrian has no other capital gains or losses, how much of the loss is Adrian able to deduct on her year 4 tax return?

    b. Assume the same facts as in part (a), except that on January 20 of year 5, Adrian purchases 100 shares of X Corp. stock for $6,000. How much loss from the sale on December 30 of year 4 is deductible on Adrian's year 4 tax return? What basis does Adrian take in the stock purchased on January 20 of year 5?

69. **(LO2)** Christopher sold 100 shares of Cisco stock for $5,500 in the current year. He purchased the shares several years ago for $2,200. Assuming his marginal ordinary income tax rate is 28 percent, and he has no other capital gains or losses, how much tax will he pay on this gain?

70. **(LO2)** Christina, who is single, purchased 100 shares of Apple Inc. stock several years ago for $3,500. During her year-end tax planning, she decided to sell 50 shares of Apple for $1,500 on December 30. However, two weeks later, Apple introduced the iPhone, and she decided that she should buy the 50 shares (cost of $1,600) of Apple back before prices skyrocket.

    a. What is Christina's deductible loss on the sale of 50 shares? What is her basis in the 50 new shares?

    b. Assume the same facts, except that Christina repurchased only 25 shares for $800. What is Christina's deductible loss on the sale of 50 shares? What is her basis in the 25 new shares?

**research**

71. **(LO2)** Arden purchased 300 shares of AMC common stock several years ago for $1,500. On April 30, Arden sold the shares of AMC common for $500 and then purchased 250 shares of AMC preferred stock two days later for $700. The AMC preferred stock is not convertible into AMC common stock. What is Arden's deductible loss from the sale of the 300 shares of AMC common stock?

72. **(LO2)** Shaun bought 300 shares of Dental Equipment, Inc., several years ago for $10,000. Currently the stock is worth $8,000. Shaun's marginal tax rate this year is 25 percent, and he has no other capital gains or losses. Shaun expects to have a marginal rate of 30 percent next year, but also expects to have a long-term capital gain of $10,000. To minimize taxes, should Shaun sell the stock on December 31 of this year or January 1 of next year (ignore the time value of money)?

■ planning

73. **(LO2)** Irene is saving for a new car she hopes to purchase either four or six years from now. Irene invests $10,000 in a growth stock that does not pay dividends and expects a 6 percent annual before-tax return (the investment is tax deferred). When she cashes in the investment after either four or six years, she expects the applicable marginal tax rate on long-term capital gains to be 25 percent.

■ planning

   a. What will be the value of this investment four and six years from now?

   b. When Irene sells the investment, how much cash will she have after taxes to purchase the new car (four and six years from now)?

74. **(LO2)** Komiko Tanaka invests $12,000 in LymaBean, Inc. LymaBean does not pay any dividends. Komiko projects that her investment will generate a 10 percent before-tax rate of return. She plans to invest for the long term.

■ planning

   a. How much cash will Komiko retain, after taxes, if she holds the investment for 5 years and then she sells it when the long-term capital gains rate is 15 percent?

   b. What is Komiko's after-tax rate of return on her investment in part (a)?

   c. How much cash will Komiko retain, after taxes, if she holds the investment for 5 years and then sells when the long-term capital gains rate is 25 percent?

   d. What is Komiko's after-tax rate of return on her investment in part (c)?

   e. How much cash will Komiko retain, after taxes, if she holds the investment for 15 years and then she sells when the long-term capital gains rate is 15 percent?

   f. What is Komiko's after-tax rate of return on her investment in part (e)?

75. **(LO2)** Becky recently discovered some high-tech cooking technology that has advantages over microwave and traditional ovens. She received a patent on the technology that gives her exclusive rights to the technology for 20 years. Becky would prefer to retain the patent, but she doesn't want to deal with the manufacturing and marketing of the technology. She was able to reach a compromise. A little over a year after she secured the patent, Becky signed a contract with DEF Company giving DEF control to manufacture and market the technology. In exchange, Becky is to receive a royalty based on the sales of the technology. For tax purposes, Becky is not sure how to treat her arrangement with DEF. If the exchange with DEF is treated as a sale, she will recognize long-term capital gain because the patent is a capital asset held for more than a year. If the exchange is not treated as a sale, Becky will recognize ordinary income as she receives the royalties. (*Hint:* IRC §1235 and www.aicpa.org/pubs/taxadv/online/aug2000/clinic5a.htm)

■ research

   a. Is it possible for Becky to treat the exchange with DEF as a sale even though she never relinquishes actual title of the patent? If so, what requirements must she meet to treat the contract as a sale for tax purposes?

   b. Does your answer to the question above change if Becky's contract with DEF gave DEF Company control over the income from the patent for the next 10 years of the patent's remaining 19-year life?

76. **(LO3)** The Johnsons recently decided to invest in municipal bonds because their marginal tax rate is 40 percent. The return on municipal bonds is currently

■ planning

3.5 percent and the return on similar taxable bonds is 5 percent. Compare the after-tax returns of the municipal and taxable bonds.

a. Which type of bond should the Johnsons select?

b. What type of bond should the Johnsons select if their marginal tax rate was 20 percent?

c. At what marginal tax rate would the Johnsons be indifferent between investing in either taxable or municipal bonds?

77. **(LO3)** Lynette VanWagoner purchased a life insurance policy to insure her mother Idon. Idon is currently 64. Insurance companies predict that women in her condition will live, on average, to be 81 years old. Lynette makes a one-time payment of $100,000 to purchase a life insurance policy on Idon's life. The policy provides for a $1,000,000 death benefit and a cash surrender value equal to the original $100,000 premium plus a 7 percent annual rate of return on the premium.

a. How much will Lynette receive after taxes if Idon dies in 14 years?

b. How much will Lynette receive after taxes if Idon dies in seven years?

c. How much will Lynette receive after taxes if Lynette decides to cash in the policy after four years when Idon is still living and Lynette's marginal tax rate is 28 percent?

78. **(LO3)** Ben recently made a one-time investment of $20,000 in the Florida 529 educational savings plan for his three-year-old son, Mitch. Assume the plan yields a constant 6 percent return for the next 15 years.

a. How much money will be available for Mitch after taxes when he begins college at age 18?

b. Assume, instead, that when Mitch turns 18, he decides to forgo college and spend his time as a traveling artist. If Mitch's parents give him the amount in the 529 plan to pursue his dreams, how much will he keep after taxes if his marginal tax rate is 10 percent?

79. **(LO4)** Rich and Shauna Nielson file a joint tax return, and they itemize deductions. Assume their marginal tax rate on ordinary income is 25 percent. The Nielsons incur $2,000 in miscellaneous itemized deductions, excluding investment expenses. They also incur $1,000 in noninterest investment expenses during the year. What tax savings do they receive from the investment expenses under the following assumptions:

a. Their AGI is $90,000.

b. Their AGI is $130,000.

80. **(LO4)** Mickey and Jenny Porter file a joint tax return, and they itemize deductions. The Porters incur $2,000 in employment-related miscellaneous itemized deductions. They also incur $3,000 of investment interest expense during the year. The Porters' income for the year consists of $150,000 in salary, and $2,500 of interest income.

a. What is the amount of the Porters' investment interest expense deduction for the year?

b. What would their investment interest expense deduction be if they also had a ($2,000) long-term capital loss?

**■ planning**    81. **(LO4)** On January 1 of year 1, Nick and Rachel Sutton purchased a parcel of undeveloped land as an investment. The purchase price of the land was $150,000. They paid for the property by making a down payment of $50,000

and borrowing $100,000 from the bank at an interest rate of 6 percent per year. At the end of the first year, the Suttons paid $6,000 of interest to the bank. During year 1, the Suttons only source of income was salary. On December 31 of year 2, the Suttons paid $6,000 of interest to the bank and sold the land for $210,000. They used $100,000 of the sale proceeds to pay off the $100,000 loan. The Suttons itemize deductions and are subject to a marginal ordinary income tax rate of 35 percent.

a. Should the Suttons treat the capital gain from the land sale as investment income in year 2 in order to minimize their year 2 tax bill?

b. How much does this cost or save them in year 2?

82. **(LO4)** George recently received a great stock tip from his friend, Mason. George didn't have any cash on hand to invest, so he decided to take out a $20,000 loan to facilitate the stock acquisition. The loan terms are 8 percent interest with interest-only payments due each year for five years. At the end of the five-year period the entire loan principal is due. When George closed on the loan on April 1, 2010, he decided to invest $16,000 in stock and to use the remaining $4,000 to purchase a four-wheel recreation vehicle. Mason is unsure how he will treat the interest paid on the $20,000 loan. In 2010, Mason paid $1,200 interest expense on the loan. For tax purposes, how should he treat the 2010 interest expense? (*Hint:* visit www.irs.gov and consider IRS Publication 550.)

83. **(LO5)** Larry recently invested $9,000 in purchasing a limited partnership interest. His share of the debt in the partnership is $11,000, but he is not personally responsible for paying the debt in the event the partnership cannot pay it. In addition, Larry's share of the limited partnership loss for the year is $2,000, his share of income from a different limited partnership was $1,000, and he had $3,000 of dividend income from the stock he owns.

a. What is Larry's tax basis in the limited partnership after considering his $2,000 loss for the year?

b. What is Larry's at-risk amount in the limited partnership after considering the $2,000 loss for the year?

c. How much of Larry's $2,000 loss from the limited partnership can he deduct in the current year?

84. **(LO5)** Joe recently invested $11,000 in purchasing a limited partnership interest. His share of the debt in the partnership is $3,000, but he is not personally responsible for paying the debt in the event the partnership cannot pay it. In addition, Joe's share of the limited partnership loss for the year is $12,000, his share of income from a different limited partnership was $3,000, and he had $7,000 of dividend income from the stock he owns.

a. What is Joe's tax basis in the limited partnership after considering his $12,000 loss for the year?

b. What is Joe's at-risk amount in the limited partnership after considering the $12,000 loss for the year?

c. How much of Joe's $12,000 loss from the limited partnership can he deduct in the current year?

85. **(LO5)** Rubio recently invested $15,000 in purchasing a limited partnership interest. His share of the debt in the partnership is $5,000, but he is not personally responsible for paying the debt in the event the partnership cannot pay it. In addition, Rubio's share of the limited partnership loss for the year is $22,000, his share of income from a different limited partnership was

$5,000, and he had $40,000 in wage income and $10,000 in long-term capital gains.

a. What is Rubio's tax basis in the limited partnership after considering his $22,000 loss for the year?

b. What is Rubio's at-risk amount in the limited partnership after considering the $22,000 loss for the year?

c. How much of Rubio's $22,000 loss from the limited partnership can he deduct in the current year?

86. **(LO5)** Anwar owns a rental home and is involved in maintaining it and approving renters. During the year he has a net loss of $8,000 from renting the home. His other sources of income during the year were a salary of $111,000 and $34,000 of long-term capital gains. How much of Anwar's $8,000 rental loss can he deduct currently if he has no sources of passive income?

## COMPREHENSIVE PROBLEMS

■ planning

87. As noted in the chapter, Nick inherited $100,000 with the stipulation that he "invest it to financially benefit his family." Nick and Rachel decided they would invest the inheritance to help them accomplish two financial goals: purchasing a Park City vacation home and saving for Lea's education.

|  | Vacation Home | Lea's Education |
|---|---|---|
| Initial investment | $50,000 | $50,000 |
| Investment horizon | 5 years | 18 years |

The Suttons have a marginal income tax rate of 30 percent (capital gains rate of 15 percent), and have decided to investigate the following investment opportunities.

|  | 5 Years | Annual After-Tax Rate of Return | 18 Years | Annual After-Tax Rate of Return |
|---|---|---|---|---|
| Corporate bonds | 5.75% |  | 4.75% |  |
| Dividend-paying stock (no appreciation) | 3.50% |  | 3.50% |  |
| Growth stock | Future value is $65,000 |  | Future value is $140,000 |  |
| Municipal bonds | 3.20% |  | 3.10% |  |
| Qualified tuition program | 5.75% |  | 5.50% |  |

Complete the two annual after-tax rates of return columns for each investment, and provide investment recommendations for the Suttons.

88. During 2010, your clients, Mr. and Mrs. Howell, owned the following investment assets:

| Investment Assets | Date Acquired | Purchase Price | Broker's Commission Paid at Time of Purchase |
|---|---|---|---|
| 300 shares of IBM common | 11/22/07 | $ 10,350 | $ 100 |
| 200 shares of IBM common | 4/3/08 | $ 43,250 | $ 300 |
| 3,000 shares of Apple preferred | 12/12/08 | $147,000 | $1,300 |
| 2,100 shares of Cisco common | 8/14/09 | $ 52,500 | $ 550 |
| 420 shares of Vanguard mutual fund | 3/2/10 | $ 14,700 | No load fund* |

*No commissions are charged when no load mutual funds are bought and sold.

Because of the downturn in the stock market, Mr. and Mrs. Howell decided to sell most of their stocks and mutual fund in 2010 and to reinvest in municipal bonds. The following investment assets were sold in 2010:

| Investment Assets | Date Sold | Sale Price | Broker's Commission Paid at Time of Sale |
| --- | --- | --- | --- |
| 300 shares of IBM common | 5/6/10 | $ 13,700 | $ 100 |
| 3,000 shares of Apple preferred | 10/5/10 | $221,400 | $2,000 |
| 2,100 shares of Cisco common | 8/15/10 | $ 63,250 | $ 650 |
| 451 Shares of Vanguard mutual fund | 12/21/10 | $ 15,700 | No load fund* |

*No commissions are charged when no load mutual funds are bought and sold.

The Howells' broker issued them a Form 1099 showing the sales proceeds net of the commissions paid. For example, the IBM sales proceeds were reported as $13,600 on the Form 1099 they received.

In addition to the sales reflected in the table above, the Howells provided you with the following additional information concerning 2010:

- The Howells received a Form 1099 from the Vanguard mutual fund reporting a $900 long-term capital gain distribution. This distribution was reinvested in 31 additional Vanguard mutual fund shares on 6/30/10.
- In 2005, Mrs. Howell loaned $6,000 to a friend who was starting a new multilevel marketing company called LD3. The friend declared bankruptcy in 2010, and Mrs. Howell has been notified she will not be receiving any repayment of the loan.
- The Howells have a $2,300 short-term capital loss carryover and a $4,800 long-term capital loss carryover from prior years.
- The Howells did not instruct their broker to sell any particular lot of IBM stock.
- The Howells earned $3,000 in municipal bond interest, $3,000 in interest from corporate bonds, and $4,000 in qualified dividends.
- The Howells paid $5,000 in investment interest expense during the year ($1,000 is attributable to their municipal bond investments).
- The Howells paid $2,000 for investment advice during the year but did not have any additional miscellaneous itemized deductions.
- Assume the Howells have $130,000 of wage income during the year.

a. Go to the IRS Web site (www.IRS.gov) and download the most current version of Schedule D. Use page 1 of Schedule D to compute net long-term and short-term capital gains. Then, compute the Howells' tax liability for the year (ignoring the alternative minimum tax and any phase-out provisions) assuming they file a joint return, they have no dependents, they don't make any special tax elections, and their itemized deductions total $25,000.

b. Are there any tax planning recommendations related to the stock sales that you should have shared with the Howells before their decision to sell?

c. Assume the Howells' short-term capital loss carryover from prior years is $82,300 rather than $2,300 as indicated above. If this is the case, how much short-term and long-term capital loss carryover remains to be carried beyond 2010 to future tax years?

89. WAR (We Are Rich) has been in business since 1980. WAR is an accrual method sole proprietorship that deals in the manufacturing and wholesaling of various

types of golf equipment. Hack & Hack CPAs have filed accurate tax returns for WAR's owner since WAR opened its doors. The managing partner of Hack & Hack (Jack) has gotten along very well with the owner of WAR—Mr. Someday Woods. However, in early 2010, Jack Hack and Someday Woods played a round of golf and Jack, for the first time ever, actually beat Mr. Woods. Mr. Woods was so upset that he fired Hack & Hack and has hired you to compute his 2010 tax liability. Mr. Woods was able to provide you with the following information from prior tax returns. The taxable income numbers reflect the results from all of Mr. Woods's activities *except for the items separately stated*. You will need to consider how to handle the separately stated items for tax purposes. Also, note that the 2005–2009 numbers do not reflect capital loss carryovers.

|  | 2005 | 2006 | 2007 | 2008 | 2009 |
|---|---|---|---|---|---|
| Ordinary taxable income | $ 4,000 | $ 2,000 | $94,000 | $170,000 | $250,000 |
| Other items not included in ordinary taxable income: | | | | | |
| Net gain (loss) on disposition of §1231 assets | $ 3,000 | $10,000 | | ($6,000) | |
| Net long-term capital gain (loss) on disposition of capital assets | ($15,000) | $ 1,000 | ($7,000) | | ($5,000) |

In 2010, Mr. Woods had taxable income in the amount of $460,000 *before* considering the following events and transactions that transpired in 2010:

a. On January 1, 2010, WAR purchased a plot of land for $100,000 with the intention of creating a driving range where patrons could test their new golf equipment. WAR never got around to building the driving range; instead, WAR sold the land on October 1, 2010, for $40,000.

b. On August 17, 2010, WAR sold its golf testing machine, "Iron Byron" and replaced it with a new machine "Iron Tiger." "Iron Byron" was purchased and installed for a total cost of $22,000 on February 5, 2006. At the time of sale, "Iron Byron" had an adjusted tax basis of $4,000. WAR sold "Iron Byron" for $25,000.

c. In the months October through December 2010, WAR sold various assets to come up with the funds necessary to invest in WAR's latest and greatest invention—the three-dimple golf ball. Data on these assets are provided below:

| Asset | Placed in Service (or purchased) | Sold | Initial Basis | Accumulated Depreciation | Selling Price |
|---|---|---|---|---|---|
| Someday's black leather sofa (used in office) | 4/4/09 | 10/16/10 | $ 3,000 | $ 540 | $ 2,900 |
| Someday's office chair | 3/1/08 | 11/8/10 | $ 8,000 | $3,000 | $ 4,000 |
| Marketable securities | 2/1/07 | 12/1/10 | $12,000 | $ 0 | $20,000 |
| Land held for investment | 7/1/09 | 11/29/10 | $45,000 | $ 0 | $48,000 |
| Other investment property | 11/30/08 | 10/15/10 | $10,000 | $ 0 | $ 8,000 |

d. Finally, on May 7, 2010, WAR sold the building where they tested their plutonium shaft, lignite head drivers. WAR purchased the building on January 5, 1998, for $190,000 ($170,000 for the building, $20,000 for the land). At the time of the sale, the accumulated depreciation on the building was $50,000. WAR sold the building (with the land) for $300,000. The fair market value of the land at the time of sale was $45,000.

Compute Mr. Woods's taxable income *after* taking into account the transactions described above. In addition, record the effects of the transactions above in Mr. Woods's Schedule D and Schedule 4797 (use the most current version of these schedules) to be attached to his Form 1040.

## KAPLAN CPA SIMULATIONS

KAPLAN CPA REVIEW

**Please visit the Online Learning Center**    (www.mhhe.com/spilker2011) to access the following Kaplan CPA Simulation:

The simulation for **Pria Patel** covers capital gains and losses; home office expenses; business income and expense; NOL; charitable contributions; and capital expenditures.

# chapter
# 12 Compensation

## Learning Objectives

**Upon completing this chapter, you should be able to:**

**LO 1** Discuss and explain the tax implications of compensation in the form of salary and wages from the employee's and employer's perspectives.

■

**LO 2** Describe and distinguish the tax implications of various forms of equity-based compensation from the employer's and employee's perspectives.

■

**LO 3** Compare and contrast taxable and nontaxable fringe benefits and explain the employee and employer tax consequences associated with fringe benefits.

J ulie and Ethan Clark and their two children have been settled into their life in San Diego, California, for some time. Julie has decided her career is at a crossroads. On the one hand, her employment as a mid-level executive for Premier Computer Corporation (PCC) is going well, but the work is not as challenging as it used to be. She suspects that, given her skills and abilities, she could put her career on the fast track with the right opportunity, engaging in more fulfilling work and gaining a significant increase in compensation.

Julie was sitting at her desk contemplating her career when she received yet another call from a corporate headhunter. While she usually quickly dismisses such calls, this time she gave her full attention. He asked if she had any interest in a vice president of marketing position with a publicly traded company located nearby. After the headhunter answered a few of her questions, Julie gave him the go-ahead to set up an interview.

A couple of weeks later, Julie had been through two rounds of interviews for the marketing VP position when she received a call informing her that she was the one Technology Products Inc. (TPI), wanted for the job and that an offer letter with the details was on its way. The letter indicated TPI was offering a $280,000 salary (a nice increase from her current salary). TPI was also offering her a choice of certain types of equity-based compensation and some nice fringe benefits. While excited by the letter, Julie knew she needed to learn more about

| Storyline Summary | |
|---|---|
| *Taxpayers:* | Julie and Ethan Clark |
| *Location:* | San Diego, California |
| *Employment status:* | Julie—mid-level executive for Premier Computer Corporation (PCC); current salary $240,000 Ethan—mechanical engineer; current salary $70,000 |
| *Filing status:* | Married filing jointly |
| *Dependents:* | Two children |
| *Marginal ordinary tax rate:* | 40 percent |
| *Current situation:* | Julie is considering an offer for the vice president of marketing position with Technology Products Inc. |

the equity-based compensation alternatives and the other forms of compensation TPI was offering before she could adequately evaluate the offer and reach her decision.

*to be continued . . .*

As TPI's letter to Julie illustrates, employers are able to offer many different forms of compensation to employees. They can also pay some compensation currently and defer some to the future. Each type of compensation has unique tax and nontax consequences.

This chapter addresses the tax and nontax consequences of current compensation from both the employee's and the employer's perspective. The next chapter addresses future compensation.

**LO1**

# SALARY AND WAGES

Current compensation paid to **employees** in the form of **salary** and **wages,** usually paid in cash, has tax consequences to both employees and employers. Below, we address the tax (and nontax) considerations of salary and wages from the employee's perspective followed by the employer's perspective.

## Employee Considerations for Salary and Wages

Employees receiving salary generally earn a fixed amount of compensation for the year no matter how many hours they work. In addition, salaried employees may be eligible for bonuses based on satisfying certain criteria. In contrast, employees receiving wages generally get paid by the hour. Salary, bonus, and wages are taxed to employees as ordinary income. Employees generally report income from salary and wages as they receive it.[1]

At the end of each year, employees receive a **Form W-2** (see Exhibit 12-1) from their employers summarizing their salary or wage compensation and the various withholding amounts during the year.[2] Employees simply report their wages on page 1, line 7 of the 1040 federal tax return and report their income taxes withheld on line 61 of page 2.

**Withholding Taxes**  When they begin employment with a firm, employees complete a **Form W-4** to supply the information the firm needs to withhold the correct amount of tax from each paycheck. Specifically, employees use Form W-4 to indicate (1) whether to withhold at the single rate or at the lower married rate, (2) the number of withholding allowances the employee chooses to claim (the more withholding allowances claimed, the less the withholding amount), and (3) whether the employee wants an additional amount of tax withheld each period above the amount based on the number of allowances claimed.

[1]Reg. §1.451-1(a).

[2]Compensation received by taxpayers who are self-employed is not considered to be salary and wages.

**EXHIBIT 12-1   2009 Form W-2**

| 22222 | a Employee's social security number | | |
|---|---|---|---|
| | OMB No. 1545-0008 | | |

| b Employer identification number (EIN) | | 1 Wages, tips, other compensation | 2 Federal income tax withheld |
|---|---|---|---|
| c Employer's name, address, and ZIP code | | 3 Social security wages | 4 Social security tax withheld |
| | | 5 Medicare wages and tips | 6 Medicare tax withheld |
| | | 7 Social security tips | 8 Allocated tips |
| d Control number | | 9 Advance EIC payment | 10 Dependent care benefits |
| e Employee's first name and initial    Last name    Suff. | | 11 Nonqualified plans | 12a |
| | 13 Statutory employee   Retirement plan   Third-party sick pay | | 12b |
| | 14 Other | | 12c |
| | | | 12d |
| f Employee's address and ZIP code | | | |

| 15 State   Employer's state ID number | 16 State wages, tips, etc. | 17 State income tax | 18 Local wages, tips, etc. | 19 Local income tax | 20 Locality name |
|---|---|---|---|---|---|
| | | | | | |

Form **W-2** Wage and Tax Statement          2009          Department of the Treasury—Internal Revenue Service

Copy 1—For State, City, or Local Tax Department

In general, the withholding tables are designed so that employers will withhold taxes fairly close to the amount of the taxpayer's actual tax liability—if the employee claims the same number of withholding allowances on her W-4 as the number of personal and dependency exemptions she claims on her tax return. However, there are special circumstances in which this general rule does not hold. Taxpayers who itemize deductions, have deductible losses, file jointly with an employed spouse, or have other special tax circumstances may need to adjust the number of withholding allowances claimed to have the desired amount of taxes withheld.[3] Thus, a married taxpayer with three dependent children would generally elect to have taxes withheld based on the married withholding table and report five withholding allowances on the W-4 (one for herself, her spouse, and each dependent). In this situation, assuming none of the special circumstances described above, the taxpayer's withholding would be very close to her actual tax liability when she files her tax return for the year. However, because the tables assume taxpayers *don't* itemize deductions, they may require employers to withhold more taxes than are necessary from taxpayers who report a significant amount of itemized deductions. Taxpayers in this situation can claim additional withholding allowances on Form W-4 above and beyond the number of their exemptions. Each extra withholding allowance claimed by taxpayers reduces the amount of income taxes their employers will withhold. Taxpayers should claim enough extra allowances to ensure that the desired amount of tax is withheld from their paychecks.[4]

Through the W-4, taxpayers can manage the withholding on their salary or wages—whether it is to *decrease* withholding through increasing the number of withholding allowances, or to *increase* withholding by either reducing withholding

---

> **THE KEY FACTS**
>
> **Employment-Related Forms**
>
> ▌**Form W-2**
> · Summarizes an employee's taxable salary and wages.
> · Provides annual federal and state withholding information.
> · Generated by employer on an annual basis.
>
> ▌**Form W-4**
> · Supplies an employee's withholding information to employer.
> · Generated by employee.
> · Numbers reported on form remain constant unless employee makes changes.

---

[3]See IRS publication 505 "Tax Withholding and Estimated Tax" for other circumstances.

[4]The taxpayer could use actual IRS withholding tables to compute the number of withholding allowances required to have the desired amount of taxes withheld, or the taxpayer could solicit help from his payroll department in determining the right number of allowances.

allowances or by specifying an additional amount to be withheld. Further, employees can revise the information on the W-4 throughout the year.[5] Taxpayers who, given their income, have underwithheld at any point during the year can increase their withholdings to catch up before the end of the year. For example, a taxpayer who has underwithheld taxes through September can increase her withholdings for October, November, and December to catch up. Because the IRS generally assumes that withholdings are made evenly throughout the year, taxpayers are treated as though most of the withholding increase was made earlier in the year, and the late withholding will likely not cause them to suffer tax underpayment penalties (see Chapter 7).[6]

Taxpayers in any of the special circumstances outlined above should complete their W-4s with care to ensure proper withholding.[7] Julie and Ethan, from our opening storyline, will together earn $310,000 of salary with their current employers. Because they itemize deductions and make deductible contributions to employer-provided retirement accounts, they project their taxable income at $280,000 for the year. Based on this projection, the Clarks will incur a $70,181 tax liability for the year. After consulting with their respective payroll departments, Julie and Ethan learn that if each files a Form W-4 with four personal allowances and has tax withheld at the married rate, Julie will have $49,604 withheld and Ethan will have $5,710 withheld. In total, they will have $55,314 withheld, leaving a withholding shortfall of $14,867. To equalize their withholding and their anticipated liability, the Clarks can reduce the number of withholding allowances they're claiming, have taxes withheld at the higher single rate, and/or have an additional amount withheld from each paycheck.[8] They decide to have an extra $1,239 withheld from Julie's monthly paycheck ($14,868 for the year) to cover their withholding. Julie's completed Form W-4 without her signature is presented in Exhibit 12-2.

**EXHIBIT 12-2    Form W-4**

| Form **W-4** | **Employee's Withholding Allowance Certificate** | OMB No. 1545-0074 |
|---|---|---|
| Department of the Treasury Internal Revenue Service | ► **Whether you are entitled to claim a certain number of allowances or exemption from withholding is subject to review by the IRS. Your employer may be required to send a copy of this form to the IRS.** | 20**10** |

| **1** Type or print your first name and middle initial. Julie | Last name Clark | **2** Your social security number 123 : 45 : 6789 |
|---|---|---|

Home address (number and street or rural route)
**1250 Beach Street**

**3** ☐ Single ☑ Married ☐ Married, but withhold at higher Single rate.
**Note.** If married, but legally separated, or spouse is a nonresident alien, check the "Single" box.

City or town, state, and ZIP code
**San Diego, CA 92101**

**4** If your last name differs from that shown on your social security card, check here. You must call 1-800-772-1213 for a replacement card. ► ☐

| **5** | Total number of allowances you are claiming (from line **H** above **or** from the applicable worksheet on page 2) | **5** | 4 |
|---|---|---|---|
| **6** | Additional amount, if any, you want withheld from each paycheck . . . . . . . . . . | **6** $ | 1,239 |

**7** I claim exemption from withholding for 2010, and I certify that I meet **both** of the following conditions for exemption.
- Last year I had a right to a refund of **all** federal income tax withheld because I had **no** tax liability **and**
- This year I expect a refund of **all** federal income tax withheld because I expect to have **no** tax liability.

If you meet both conditions, write "Exempt" here . . . . . . . . . . . ► | **7** |

Under penalties of perjury, I declare that I have examined this certificate and to the best of my knowledge and belief, it is true, correct, and complete.

**Employee's signature**
(Form is not valid unless you sign it.) ►                                           Date ►

| **8** Employer's name and address (Employer: Complete lines 8 and 10 only if sending to the IRS.) | **9** Office code (optional) | **10** Employer identification number (EIN) |
|---|---|---|

For Privacy Act and Paperwork Reduction Act Notice, see page 2.          Cat. No. 10220Q          Form **W-4** (2010)

[5]Most employers require an employee to submit a revised Form W-4 at least two weeks before the end of the pay period for which the new withholding amount is to take effect.

[6]See instructions for Form 2210: Underpayment of Estimated Tax by Individuals, Estates, and Trusts.

[7]Note the bottom of Form W-4 indicates that it is signed under penalties of perjury.

[8]While Julie and Ethan are only required to pay 90 percent of their current tax liability to avoid penalty, they prefer to not have a large liability at the end of the year—even if it is suboptimal from a time value of money perspective.

**FICA (Payroll Taxes)**  As we discuss in detail in Chapter 7, employees must pay **FICA taxes** on their wages.[9] FICA tax consists of both a Social Security and a Medicare component. Employees pay **Social Security tax** at a rate of 6.2 percent on their wage base, and **Medicare tax** at a rate of 1.45 percent on their wages.[10] As we describe in Chapter 7, the wage base on which employees pay Social Security taxes is limited to an annually determined amount, which is indexed for inflation. The wage base limitation reflects the fact that the benefits an employee may ultimately receive are also capped. The limits apply to each taxpayer's wages regardless of marital or tax filing status. The 2010 limit is $106,800, which is the same as the 2009 limit. There is no wage base for the Medicare component of the FICA tax. In other words, employees' first $106,800 of wages are subject to the Social Security tax and employees' entire wages are subject to the Medicare tax. We defer to Chapter 7 for a more detailed discussion on *employee*-related FICA tax considerations.

**Example 12-1**

In 2010, Ethan and Julie have salaries of $70,000 and $240,000, respectively. What are Ethan's and Julie's FICA taxes for the current year?

**Answer:** Ethan's FICA tax is $5,355, computed as follows:

| Description | Amount | Reference |
|---|---|---|
| (1) Compensation subject to FICA tax | $ 70,000 | |
| (2) Social Security tax base limit for 2010 | $106,800 | |
| (3) Compensation subject to Social Security tax | $ 70,000 | Lesser of (1) and (2). |
| (4) Social Security tax rate | 6.2% | |
| (5) Social Security tax | $ 4,340 | (3) × (4). |
| (6) Medicare tax rate | 1.45% | |
| (7) Medicare tax | $ 1,015 | (1) × (6). |
| FICA taxes | $ 5,355 | (5) + (7). |

**Answer:** Julie's FICA tax is $10,102, computed as follows:

| Description | Amount | Reference |
|---|---|---|
| (1) Compensation subject to FICA tax | $240,000 | |
| (2) Social Security tax base limit for 2010 | $106,800 | |
| (3) Compensation subject to Social Security tax | $106,800 | Lesser of (1) and (2). |
| (4) Social Security tax rate | 6.2% | |
| (5) Social Security tax | $ 6,622 | (3) × (4). |
| (6) Medicare tax rate | 1.45% | |
| (7) Medicare tax | $ 3,480 | (1) × (6). |
| FICA taxes | $ 10,102 | (5) + (7). |

[9]FICA stands for Federal Insurance Contributions Act.

[10]As discussed in the "employer" section, employers must also pay FICA taxes on behalf of the employee.

## Employer Considerations for Salary and Wages

| Storyline Summary | |
|---|---|
| *Taxpayer:* | TPI Corporation |
| *Location:* | San Diego, California |
| *Ownership:* | Publicly traded corporation |
| *Industry:* | Manufacturing high-technology products |
| *CEO:* | Daniel Hewitt |
| *Marginal tax rate:* | 35 percent |
| *Current Situation:* | Recruiting Julie Clark for marketing VP position |

**THE KEY FACTS**

**Compensation Deductibility for Accrual-Basis Taxpayers**

■ Compensation expense accrued at end of year is deductible in year accrued if
· Paid to an *unrelated* party within 2½ months of year-end.

■ Compensation expense accrued at end of year is *deductible when paid* if
· Paid to *related* party.
· Related party if employee owns > 50 percent of corporate employer.

**Deductibility of Salary Payments**   Employers computing taxable income under the cash method of accounting generally deduct salary and wages when they pay the employee.[11] Employers computing taxable income under the accrual method generally deduct wages payable to employees as the employees earn the wages.[12] This general rule holds even in situations when the employer accrues compensation expense in one year but actually pays the employee in the subsequent year, as long as the company makes the payment within 2½ months after the employer's year-end. If the employer pays the employee more than 2½ months after the employer's year-end, the wages are considered deferred compensation and are not deductible by the employer until the employee recognizes the salary as income (receives payment).[13] Because most employers pay regular salary and wages to employees each month (or more frequently), the 2½ month rule is likely to be more of an issue for accrued compensation, such as one-time year-end bonuses, than it is for normal wages.

In situations when the employer and employee are "related" parties, special rules apply. In this context, the definition of related parties includes an employee/shareholder who owns more than 50 percent of the value of the employer corporation.[14] When the corporation and employee/shareholder are related parties, a corporation is not allowed to deduct the compensation expense until the employee/shareholder (related party) includes the payment in income.[15] Therefore, for an accrual-method company paying compensation, such as wages or a bonus, to a related employee, the 2½ month rule does not apply. Because related parties are theoretically considered to be the same taxpayer to some extent, the tax laws limit their ability to accelerate deductions and enjoy the immediate tax benefits while at the same time deferring income and delaying the payment of taxes.

Because employers are required to match FICA taxes paid by employees (they must pay as much FICA tax on an employee's behalf as the employee is required to pay for herself), their before-tax cost of providing salary (the cost *before* subtracting the tax benefit of the deduction) is greater than the salary itself.[16]

[11]Reg. §1.461-1(a)(1).

[12]Reg. §1.461-1(a)(2). See Chapter 8 for a detailed discussion of the cash and accrual accounting methods.

[13]Reg. §1.404(b)-1T(A-2). We discuss tax issues and consequences relating to deferred compensation in Chapter 13.

[14]See §267(b) for the complete definition of "related" parties.

[15]§267(a)(2).

[16]Employers may be required to pay other expenses based on the employee wages such as workers' compensation insurance. While these other expenses are not addressed in this discussion, the concepts are the same as for the FICA taxes.

However, the after-tax cost of providing this salary is generally much less than the before-tax cost, because the employer deducts the salary and associated FICA taxes paid. The formula for computing the after-tax cost of the salary (the cost after subtracting the tax savings from the deduction), or any deductible expense, for that matter, is as follows:

$$\text{Deductible expenditure} \times (1 - \text{Marginal tax rate})$$

**Example 12-2**

What is PCC's before-tax and after-tax costs of paying Julie a $240,000 salary? (Note PCC's marginal tax rate is 35 percent.)

**Answer:** $250,102 before taxes and $162,566 after taxes, computed as follows:

| Description | Amount | Explanation |
|---|---|---|
| Before tax cost of salary: | | |
| (1) Compensation subject to FICA tax | $240,000 | |
| (2) Social Security tax base limit for 2010 | $106,800 | |
| (3) Compensation subject to Social Security tax | $106,800 | Lesser of (1) and (2). |
| (4) Social Security tax rate | 6.2% | |
| (5) Social Security tax | $ 6,622 | (3) × (4). |
| (6) Medicare tax rate | 1.45% | |
| (7) Medicare tax | $ 3,480 | (1) × (6). |
| (8) FICA taxes | $ 10,102 | (5) + (7). |
| **(9) Total before-tax cost** | $250,102 | (1) + (8). |
| (10) (1 − marginal tax rate) | × 65% | (1 − 35%). |
| **After-tax cost of salary** | **$162,566** | (9) × (10). |

*Limits on salary deductibility.* Employers are generally allowed to deduct reasonable compensation paid to employees.[17] Determining whether compensation is reasonable in amount is a **facts and circumstances test** that involves considering the duties of the employee, the complexities of the business, and the amount of salary compared with the income of the business among other things. The amount of salary in excess of the amount considered reasonable is not deductible. The reasonable compensation limit typically applies to closely held businesses where the employee is also an owner of the company or the employee is a relative of the business owner. For publicly traded corporations, another limitation applies that is generally more restrictive than the reasonableness limitation.

Responding to a growing public perception that executives of publicly traded corporations were being overpaid at the expense of shareholders and that the government was subsidizing (paying a part of) the excess by allowing corporations to deduct the high salaries, in 1993 Congress enacted §162(m) of the Internal Revenue Code.[18] This provision limits the deduction for compensation paid by publicly traded corporations to the CEO and the four other most highly compensated officers to $1,000,000 each, per year.[19] However, certain exceptions allow companies to pay and

> **THE KEY FACTS**
>
> **Limits on Salary Deductibility Publicly Traded Corporations**
>
> ■ **$1,000,000 maximum annual compensation deduction per person.**
> · Limit applies to CEO and four other highest compensated officers.
> · Does not apply to performance-based compensation.

[17]As we discussed in Chapter 8, all business expenses (not just compensation) must be reasonable in amount to be fully deductible.

[18]Nelson, Daniel, "Section 162(m) Revisited," *Tax Notes Today,* January 10, 2005, pp. 8–22.

[19]To be deductible, compensation (just like all deductible business expenses) must be "reasonable" irrespective of the $1 million deduction limitation. See Chapter 8 for a discussion of the reasonableness limitation on business expenses. Additionally, the American Recovery and Reinvestment Act of 2009 expanded executive compensation restrictions on the next 20 highly paid executives of companies receiving Troubled Asset Relief Program (TARP) assistance under the Emergency Economic Stabilization Act of 2008.

deduct compensation in excess of the $1 million limit. For example, the limit does not apply to compensation based on (1) performance (this is the most significant of the exceptions in terms of dollars and frequency of application), (2) commissions, (3) contributions to qualified retirement plans, or (4) other tax-free benefits.

While most publicly traded corporations are aware of and are sensitive to the limitation, they may take different approaches in dealing with it. For example, as described in the following excerpt from its proxy statement (see Exhibit 12-3 below), Callaway Golf attempts to maximize its compensation deduction, yet it acknowledges that there are situations when, in order to achieve its nontax goals, it may provide compensation to executives that is not deductible.

---

**EXHIBIT 12-3    Excerpt from Callaway Golf's 2009 Proxy Statement**

The tax deductibility of compensation should be maximized where appropriate. To the extent consistent with the Company's compensation strategy, the Company seeks to maximize the deductibility for tax purposes of all elements of compensation. In designing and approving the Company's executive compensation plans, the Compensation Committee considers the effect of all applicable tax regulations, including Section 162(m) of the Internal Revenue Code which generally disallows a tax deduction to public corporations for nonqualifying compensation in excess of $1.0 million paid to the chief executive officer or certain of the Company's other executive officers. Although maximizing the tax deductibility of compensation is an important consideration, the Compensation Committee may from time to time approve compensation that does not qualify for deductibility where it is appropriate to do so in light of other competing interests or objectives.

---

In contrast, State Street Corporation takes a slightly different approach. As indicated in the following excerpt from its proxy statement (see Exhibit 12-4), State Street caps its salaries at $1 million. Apparently, the firm wants to make sure salaries paid to executives are fully deductible.

---

**EXHIBIT 12-4    Excerpt from State Street Bank's 2009 Proxy Statement**

Each of our named executive officers received a base salary in 2008, which was paid periodically in cash during the year. The Committee has adopted a policy for reviewing executive base salary levels every two years. For all named executive officers, base salary historically has been a relatively small portion of total compensation, allowing us to vary annual total compensation to reflect performance and other factors deemed relevant at the time. The base salary for each named executive officer was established in February 2008, with reference to the median base salary paid to comparable executives in the peer group and mindful of the then applicable maximum level of the non-performance-based compensation deduction limitation under Section 162(m) of the Internal Revenue Code. This threshold has subsequently been reduced from $1 million to $500,000, and the exclusion for performance-based compensation has been removed, for compensation for services performed during a taxable year in which State Street participates in Treasury's TARP capital purchase program; however, the Committee did not believe it appropriate to reduce salaries to fall within this new limitation. This is consistent with our general belief that the availability of a tax deduction for compensation is a secondary consideration to the goal of providing compensation at an appropriate level based upon corporate and individual performance and other market considerations. The next review of base salary levels is scheduled to be undertaken in February 2010; however, base salary may be reconsidered prior to then as part of the Committee's 2009 review of State Street's compensation programs. Because, in particular, none of our named executive officers received any incentive compensation grants for 2008, management believes that the effect of the non-deductibility of compensation for 2008 in excess of $500,000 per named executive officer will have a relatively limited tax effect on State Street.

The difference in philosophy between Callaway and State Street may be driven by nontax considerations. To be deductible, compensation to executives in excess of $1 million generally must be performance-based. This means that the executives bear the risk that they won't receive the additional compensation if certain performance benchmarks like stock-price targets aren't met. Some companies may decide they don't want their executives to shoulder this risk, so they pay them salaries in excess of the deductible amount to guarantee a certain level of compensation. Companies may also decide to cap executive salaries at $1 million just to avoid the public perception that they are being fiscally irresponsible by paying more than the deductibility limits.

## Example 12-3

Several years ago, TPI was actively searching for a new CEO. The board of directors eventually chose Daniel Hewitt. During negotiations, Daniel indicated he wanted a $2 million salary (Option 1) in addition to the equity-based compensation the board was offering. While this level of salary could be considered reasonable, the board of directors was concerned about the $1 million limitation on deductible salary, so the board offered an alternative proposal. Under this proposal, TPI would pay Daniel a $1 million salary and offer him an additional $1.2 million of bonus, contingent on achieving realistic financial performance goals for TPI (Option 2). Confident he could meet the financial goals, Daniel accepted the offer. Assuming the performance goals are met, what is TPI's after-tax cost of providing the current year compensation under Option 1 and Option 2?

**Answer:** $1,673,154 under Option 1 and $1,455,039 under Option 2, computed as follows:

| | Option 1<br>($2,000,000 salary<br>$0 bonus) | Option 2<br>($1,000,000 salary<br>$1,200,000 bonus) | Explanation |
|---|---|---|---|
| Before-tax cost: | | | |
| (1) Total compensation | $2,000,000 | $2,200,000 | Salary + bonus. |
| (2) Social Security taxes for employee | $ 6,622 | $ 6,622 | ($106,800 × 6.2%). |
| (3) Medicare taxes for employee | $ 29,000 | $ 31,900 | (1) × 1.45%. |
| **(4) Total before-tax cost** | $2,035,622 | $2,238,522 | (1) + (2) + (3). |
| (5) Deductible amount | $1,035,622 | $2,238,522 | Option 1: $1M salary not deductible. |
| (6) Marginal tax rate | × 35% | × 35% | |
| (7) Tax savings from compensation deduction | 362,468 | 783,483 | (5) × (6). |
| **After-tax cost** | $1,673,154 | $1,455,039 | (4) − (7). |

Assuming the performance goals are met, both parties benefit from the arrangement. Daniel prefers Option 2 because it provides him with $200,000 more of before-tax compensation ($2.2M − $2M). TPI also prefers Option 2 because it costs $218,115 less after taxes than Option 1 ($1,673,154 − $1,455,039). Of course, Daniel is the one who must bear the risk of the contingent compensation in Option 2, so he must consider this risk before accepting the offer.

As this example illustrates, the $1 million deduction limitation can have a considerable impact on the after-tax cost of providing compensation to corporate executives. However, employers frequently utilize the options described above to craft offers that meet the needs of both parties.

## L02    EQUITY-BASED COMPENSATION

*continued from page 12-2...*

As she read TPI's offer letter more carefully, Julie discovered that on the first day of January following her acceptance of the offer, she would be granted 10,000 shares of restricted stock, 50 incentive stock options (ISOs), and 200 nonqualified options (NQOs). Each of the incentive and nonqualified options gives her the right to purchase 100 shares of stock at a fixed price equal to the market value of TPI stock on the date of grant. As she read on, Julie noticed that she would not be able to exercise either type of stock option (that is, purchase TPI stock for the exercise price stated in the options) until the options vested (the options become hers when they vest), which will be two years from the grant date. Further, Julie understood that, after the restricted stock vests (one year from the grant date on January 1), she would be free to do what she wanted with it. The last detail Julie noticed when reading this part of the offer letter was that both types of options will expire 10 years from the grant date. She understood this to mean that if she did not exercise her options sometime before their expiration date, she would lose them.

Although it was obvious to Julie that the value of the options and restricted stock would increase as the share price of TPI increased from the current share price of $5 per share, she remained unsure about the terminology used in this section of the letter, and she realized she needed to know more about the economic and tax implications of stock options and restricted stock before making her decision.

*to be continued...*

---

### THE KEY FACTS

**Equity-Based Compensation**

■ Stock Options
  · Allow employees to purchase stock at a discount.

■ Restricted Stock
  · Form of compensation that provides actual stock ownership to employee after restrictions lapse.

---

Equity-based compensation such as stock options and restricted stock provides risks and potential rewards not available with other forms of compensation. If the employer's stock price increases after it grants options and restricted stock, employees can be rewarded handsomely. On the other hand, if employer stock prices don't increase, the value of restricted stock will be limited and stock options will expire worthless.

Employers use equity-based compensation, in part, to motivate their employees to take ownership in their companies. When employees hold employer options and stock, their compensation is more directly tied to the fortunes of their employer and its shareholders—employees' compensation increases in tandem with their employer's stock price. This philosophy is reflected in an excerpt from Adobe's proxy statement presented in Exhibit 12-5.

In addition to its motivational effects, equity-based compensation has traditionally brought employers cash flow benefits as well. How? Unless employers purchase their own stock in a market transaction to satisfy option exercises and stock grants,

---

### THE KEY FACTS

**Stock Option Terminology**

■ *Incentive stock* options satisfy certain tax code requirements to provide favorable tax treatment to employees.

*(continued)*

---

**EXHIBIT 12-5    Excerpt from Adobe's 2009 Proxy Statement**

The equity incentive component of our executive compensation program consists of grants of annual stock options, restricted stock units and performance shares. We use equity compensation to motivate and reward strong performance and retain valued executives, as equity compensation typically vests over a period of four years after the date of grant. New-hire equity grants also act as a means to attract qualified candidates. Adobe strongly believes that equity awards serve to align the interests of its executives with those of its stockholders. By having a significant majority of the Named Executive Officer's target compensation payable as equity compensation and, thus, subject to risk of loss, our executives are motivated to align themselves with our stockholders when taking actions that will benefit us in the long-term.

there are no cash outflows associated with this form of compensation. In fact, employers actually *receive* cash from their employees in the amount of the exercise price on the options exercised. There are a couple of downsides to this benefit, however. First, employers experience the opportunity cost of selling shares at a discounted price to employees rather than selling the shares at fair market value on the open market. Second, because employers must issue new shares to satisfy option exercises and stock grants, the total number of shares outstanding increases, and, therefore, earnings per share are diluted, which is a detriment to existing shareholders. The only way for employers to mitigate this problem without increasing earnings is to use their cash reserves to acquire their own shares to satisfy the options exercise.[20] However, from a cash-flow perspective, this is no different from paying cash compensation.

## Stock Options

As a form of equity-based compensation, stock options have two important characteristics: (1) employees must use cash to purchase the employer stock once they are allowed to exercise the options and (2) employees often never exercise options when share prices are depressed. When stock options **vest,** employees are legally entitled to buy or exercise employer stock at a stipulated price, referred to as the **exercise price** or **strike price.** Options may be exercised anytime between the vesting date and the expiration date of the options.[21] If the share price does not go above the exercise price at some point during this interval, employees will not exercise their options and the options will expire without providing them any benefit.

As suggested in Exhibit 12-6, the future value of stock option awards will depend on the exercise price, the company's future share price, the exercise date of the options, and the timing for selling the shares received from the **option exercise.**

*(concluded)*

■ *Nonqualified stock options* are any options that don't meet the requirements for being classified as incentive stock options.

■ The *grant date* is the date employees are initially allocated stock options.

■ The *exercise date* is the date that employees purchase stock using their options.

■ The *exercise price* is the amount paid to acquire shares with stock options.

■ The *bargain element* is the difference between the fair market value of stock and the exercise price on the exercise date.

■ The *vesting date* is the time when stock options granted can be exercised.

---

**Example 12-4**

Given the assumptions in the stock option time line shown in Exhibit 12-6, on the next page how much will it cost Julie to exercise her options at the end of year 3 (before taxes), and how much will she have if she immediately sells the acquired shares (before taxes)?[22]

**Answer:** $125,000 cost to exercise; $375,000 remaining after sale before taxes, calculated as follows:

| Description | Amount | Explanation |
|---|---|---|
| (1) Shares acquired | 25,000 | (20,000 NQOs and 5,000 ISOs). |
| (2) Exercise price | $    5 | Exhibit 12-6. |
| (3) Cash needed to exercise | $125,000 | (1) × (2). |
| (4) Market price | $    20 | Exhibit 12-6. |
| (5) Market value of shares | $500,000 | (1) × (4). |
| Net proceeds upon sale | $375,000 | (5) − (3). |

---

[20]Because earnings per share is calculated by dividing earnings by the number of shares of stock outstanding, for a given level of earnings, earnings per share could even increase when new shares are issued to satisfy option exercises if earnings increase by an amount that more than offsets the effect of issuing new shares into the market.

[21]Vesting dates are frequently specified as future calendar dates or they may be triggered when certain events occur (i.e., predefined performance objectives are met, or the company has been sold).

[22]According to the facts presented in Exhibit 12-6, Julie could have exercised her options as early as the vesting date for her options at the end of year 2. We assume she waits one year to exercise her options to better illustrate the implications of deferring the option exercise beyond the vesting date. In reality, it is quite common for employees to exercise their stock options on the vesting date.

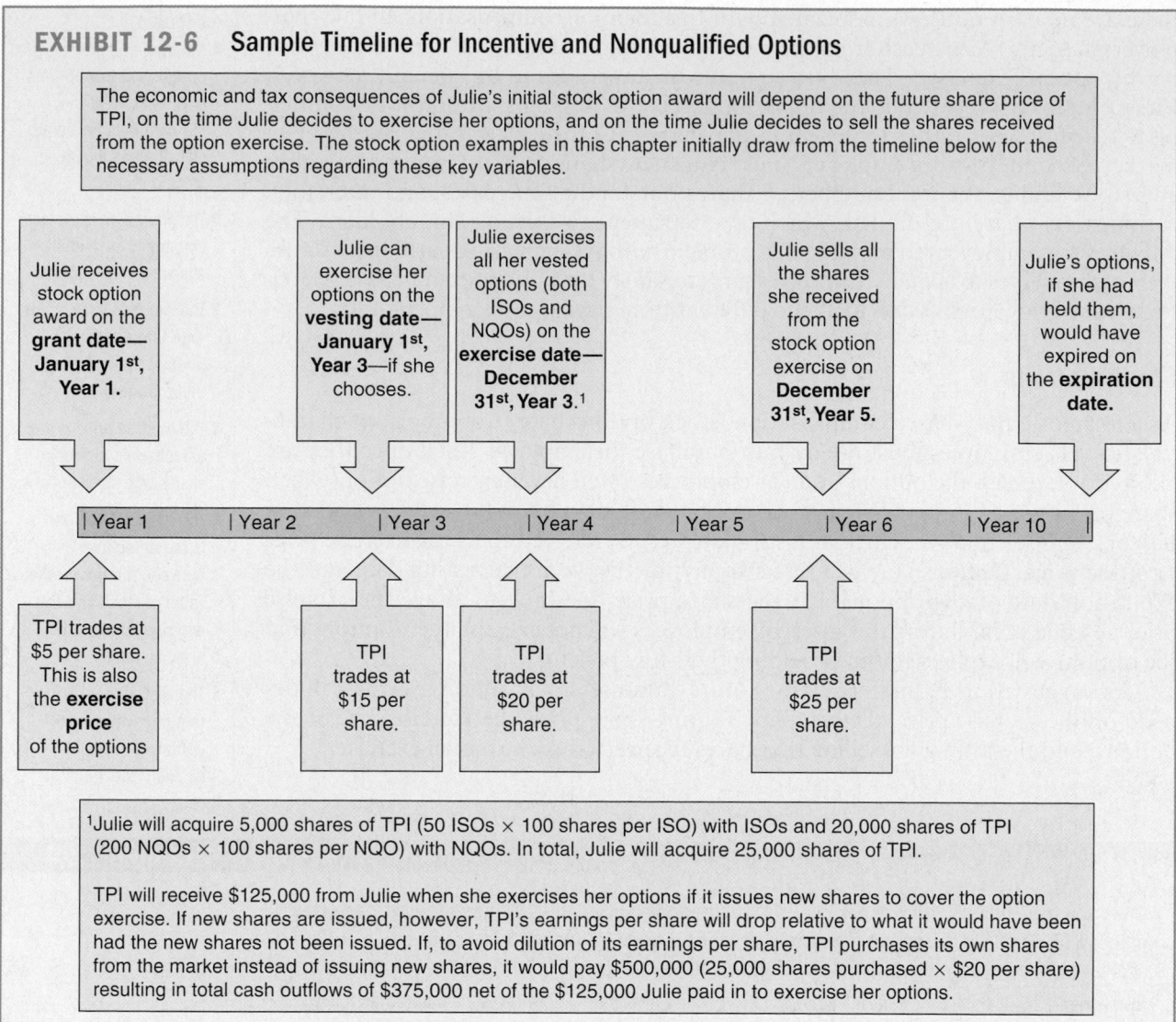

**EXHIBIT 12-6** Sample Timeline for Incentive and Nonqualified Options

The economic and tax consequences of Julie's initial stock option award will depend on the future share price of TPI, on the time Julie decides to exercise her options, and on the time Julie decides to sell the shares received from the option exercise. The stock option examples in this chapter initially draw from the timeline below for the necessary assumptions regarding these key variables.

Julie receives stock option award on the **grant date—January 1st, Year 1.**

Julie can exercise her options on the **vesting date—January 1st, Year 3**—if she chooses.

Julie exercises all her vested options (both ISOs and NQOs) on the **exercise date—December 31st, Year 3.**[1]

Julie sells all the shares she received from the stock option exercise on **December 31st, Year 5.**

Julie's options, if she had held them, would have expired on the **expiration date.**

| Year 1 | Year 2 | Year 3 | Year 4 | Year 5 | Year 6 | Year 10 |

TPI trades at $5 per share. This is also the **exercise price** of the options

TPI trades at $15 per share.

TPI trades at $20 per share.

TPI trades at $25 per share.

[1]Julie will acquire 5,000 shares of TPI (50 ISOs × 100 shares per ISO) with ISOs and 20,000 shares of TPI (200 NQOs × 100 shares per NQO) with NQOs. In total, Julie will acquire 25,000 shares of TPI.

TPI will receive $125,000 from Julie when she exercises her options if it issues new shares to cover the option exercise. If new shares are issued, however, TPI's earnings per share will drop relative to what it would have been had the new shares not been issued. If, to avoid dilution of its earnings per share, TPI purchases its own shares from the market instead of issuing new shares, it would pay $500,000 (25,000 shares purchased × $20 per share) resulting in total cash outflows of $375,000 net of the $125,000 Julie paid in to exercise her options.

If, in the prior example, Julie didn't have enough cash on hand to cover the $125,000 cost of exercising the options, she could simultaneously exercise the options and sell the stock, using $125,000 of the proceeds from the stock sale to pay for exercising the options. This so-called cashless exercise is typically facilitated using the services of an employer-provided stockbroker.

An employee who uses options to purchase shares experiences an increase in net worth equal to the difference between the exercise price and the market value of the acquired shares on the date of exercise. This difference is called the **bargain element.** In Example 12-4, the bargain element is $15 per share and the total bargain element is $375,000 (25,000 shares × $15 per share).

**Example 12-5**

***What if:*** What is Julie's economic loss from her stock options if the TPI shares fall to $3 per share and remain there after the options are granted?

**Answer:** Zero. If TPI's stock price never increases above the $5 per share exercise price before the expiration date of the options, Julie would never exercise her options to purchase TPI shares, and those options would expire worthless.

**Employee Considerations for Stock Options**    Stock options are classified for tax purposes as either **nonqualified stock options** (NQOs) or **incentive stock options** (ISOs). They differ in terms of when and how the bargain element is taxed. To appreciate these differences, it's important to understand what happens on the **grant date,** the vesting date, the **exercise date,** and the date the shares are ultimately sold.

For either type of option, employees experience no tax consequences on the grant date or vesting date. However, when they exercise *nonqualified* stock options, employees report ordinary income equal to the total bargain element on the shares of stock acquired—whether they hold the shares or sell them immediately.[23] A taxpayer's basis in nonqualified stock options acquired is the fair market value on the date of exercise. Thus the basis includes the exercise price plus the ordinary income the taxpayer recognizes on the exercise (the bargain element). In contrast, when they exercise *incentive* stock options, employees don't report any income for regular tax purposes (as long as they don't immediately sell their shares). Their basis in shares acquired with ISOs is the exercise price. The holding period for stock acquired with NQOs and ISOs begins on the exercise date.

When taxpayers exercise incentive stock options, the bargain element is added to their alternative minimum taxable income. This increases the likelihood that taxpayers exercising incentive stock options will be required to pay the alternative minimum tax—this is almost always true if the bargain element is large. We discuss the alternative minimum tax in Chapter 7.

| | **Example 12-6** |

On the date Julie exercises her options (Example 12-4), she acquires 20,000 shares of TPI with NQOs (200 NQOs × 100 shares per NQO) and 5,000 shares with ISOs (50 ISOs × 100 shares per ISO). Given that the bargain element for each share she purchased is $15, how much income will Julie report on the day she exercises the options?

**Answer:** $300,000 ordinary income from the NQOs, calculated below, and $0 for the ISOs (she must include the bargain element of $75,000 on the 5,000 ISOs in her AMT calculation).

| Description | Amount | Explanation |
|---|---|---|
| (1) Shares acquired with NQOs | 20,000 | |
| (2) Market price per share | $     20 | Exhibit 12-6. |
| (3) Exercise price | $      5 | Exhibit 12-6. |
| (4) Bargain element per share | $     15 | (2) − (3). |
| Bargain element (ordinary income) | $300,000 | (1) × (4). |

What is Julie's basis in the 20,000 shares she acquired with NQOs?

**Answer:** $400,000. [$100,000 (20,000 shares × $5 per share exercise price) + $300,000 (bargain element taxed as ordinary income).]

What is Julie's basis in the 5,000 shares she acquired through ISOs?

**Answer:** $25,000. (5,000 shares acquired × $5 per share exercise price.)

Once they've exercised their stock options, employees face different choices depending on the type of option. Employees who purchase stock with NQOs and retain the stock are in the same position for tax purposes as any other investor: their basis in the stock is the fair market value on the date they exercised the options

[23]The bargain element income is reflected on employees' Form W-2 and the applicable income and payroll taxes are withheld.

(this is the exercise price of the stock plus the bargain element), and any *future* appreciation or depreciation of the stock will be treated for tax purposes as either short-term or long-term capital gain or loss depending on the holding period, which begins on the date of exercise. Moreover, employees using nonqualified options to purchase employer stock are also in the same economic position as any other investor in that the value of the stock is subject to investment risk (the risk that the value of the stock will go down). To avoid overweighting their investment portfolios with a single stock, employees exercising nonqualified options often immediately sell all or a significant portion of the shares acquired on the exercise date, a practice referred to as a **same-day sale**.[24]

---

**Example 12-7**

*What if:* Suppose that five years after Julie exercised her NQOs and acquired 20,000 TPI shares with a basis of $20 per share, she sold all of the shares for $25 per share. What is the amount and character of the gain she will recognize on the sale?

**Answer:** $100,000 long-term capital gain, calculated as follows:

| Description | Amount | Explanation |
|---|---|---|
| (1) Amount realized (sale proceeds) | $500,000 | (20,000 × $25). |
| (2) Tax basis | 400,000 | Example 12-6. |
| Long-term capital gain recognized | $100,000 | (1) − (2). |

*What if:* If Julie sold the shares for $25 per share six months after she exercised them, what is the character of the $100,000 gain she recognizes on the sale?

**Answer:** Short-term capital gain because she held the shares for one year or less before selling.

---

> **THE KEY FACTS**
>
> **Nonqualified Stock Options (NQOs)**
>
> ▪ No tax consequences on grant date.
>
> ▪ On exercise date, bargain element is treated as ordinary (compensation) income to employee.
> · Employee holds stock with holding period beginning on date of exercise.
>
> ▪ Employers deduct bargain element as compensation expense on exercise date.

Employees who acquire shares through the exercise of ISOs also have an additional tax benefit: if they hold such shares *for at least two years after the grant date and one year after the exercise date,* they will not be taxed until they sell the stock.[25] When they sell, employees will treat the difference between the sale proceeds and the tax basis (the exercise price) as a long-term capital gain in the year of disposition. Thus, employees prefer ISOs to NQOs.

---

**Example 12-8**

*What if:* Suppose that five years after Julie exercised her ISOs and acquired 5,000 TPI shares with a basis of $5 per share, she sold all of the shares for $25 per share. What is the amount and character of the gain she will recognize on the sale?

**Answer:** Julie will recognize a $100,000 long-term capital gain, calculated as follows:

| Description | Amount | Explanation |
|---|---|---|
| (1) Amount realized | $125,000 | (5,000 × $25). |
| (2) Tax basis | 25,000 | Example 12-6. |
| Long-term capital gain recognized | $100,000 | (1) − (2). |

---

[24]In addition to limiting investment risk, employees also engage in same-day sales to cover all or a portion of the exercise price associated with the options exercised, to pay the taxes triggered when nonqualified options are exercised, and to fund planned purchases.

[25]§422(a)(1).

If the two-year and one-year requirements are not met, the premature sale of stock is classified as a **disqualifying disposition,** and the bargain element is taxed at the time of sale *as if* the option had been a nonqualified option. Thus, when holders of ISOs execute same-day sales, they forgo the benefit of taxing the bargain element at lower capital gains rates—but they do so in order to eliminate the investment risk they would otherwise have to bear if they attempted to satisfy the two-year and one-year holding period requirements.

---

### Example 12-9

**What if:** Assume that Julie exercised her ISOs and executed a same-day sale of the 5,000 shares on the vesting date (January 1, year 3) when the share price was $15, what is the amount and character of income she will recognize on these transactions?

**Answer:** $50,000 ordinary income. Because Julie's sale is a disqualifying disposition, the transactions are recast as though she exercised nonqualified options. See computations below.

| Description | Amount | Explanation |
|---|---|---|
| (1) Shares acquired with ISOs that were disqualified (became NQOs) | 5,000 | |
| (2) Market price per share | $  15 | |
| (3) Exercise price | $  5 | Exhibit 12-6. |
| (4) Bargain element per share | $  10 | (2) − (3). |
| Bargain element (ordinary income) | $50,000 | (1) × (4). |

---

#### THE KEY FACTS

**Incentive Stock Options (ISOs)**

■ No tax consequences on grant date.

■ No tax consequences on exercise date if employee holds for two years after grant date and one year after exercise date.
· If holding requirements are not met (if there is a disqualifying disposition), option becomes an NQO.

■ When employee sells stock, employee recognizes long-term capital gain on difference between selling price and exercise price.

■ No deduction for employers unless employee doesn't meet holding requirements.

---

**Employer Considerations for Stock Options**   As is true for employees, an employer's tax treatment of stock options depends on whether the options are nonqualified options (NQOs) or incentive stock options (ISOs).

*Nonqualified options.*   With nonqualified options, employers deduct the bargain element that employees recognize as income when the employees exercise the nonqualified options. From the employer's perspective, no other date is relevant for tax purposes.

---

### Example 12-10

**What if:** Suppose that in year 3, Julie exercises NQOs to acquire 20,000 shares of TPI, and she reports $300,000 of ordinary income for the bargain element of the exercise (see Example 12-6). How much compensation expense for Julie's stock option exercise can TPI deduct in year 3?

**Answer:** $300,000. TPI can deduct the bargain element of Julie's exercise.

---

Note that this tax deduction is not tied to a cash payment. Thus, unless employers purchase their own shares to satisfy their employees' stock option exercises, they'll be entitled to a tax deduction without incurring any cash outflow.

Another important tax benefit associated with nonqualified options derives from the fact that income from NQOs is usually viewed as performance-based compensation. As a result, employers frequently use these options to circumvent the $1,000,000

deduction limitation imposed by §162(m). In fact, the stock option income of key executives at publicly traded companies usually dwarfs their cash salaries.[26]

***Incentive stock options.***    Employers typically don't view incentive stock options as favorably as nonqualified options, because (1) ISOs don't provide them with the same tax benefits (no tax deduction) and (2) the IRS regulatory requirements for ISOs can be cumbersome. No matter what the circumstances, employers never receive any tax deductions related to ISOs. For this reason, firms with high marginal tax rates may lose significant tax benefits by issuing ISOs rather than NQOs. On the other hand, start-up companies or firms with net operating losses may actually benefit by issuing ISOs instead of NQOs. Due to their low or nonexistent marginal tax rates, companies in this position may not lose tax benefits by granting ISOs; however, because of the potential tax benefits ISOs provide to their employees relative to NQOs, they may be able to persuade their employees to accept relatively fewer ISOs.

***Accounting issues.***    Historically, a major reason that companies used stock options to compensate their employees was the favorable accounting treatment stock options were afforded. Before 2006, companies were not required to reflect stock options as an expense in their financial statements. Thus, before 2006, companies that used stock options in lieu of cash salary typically reported higher earnings than equally situated firms that were not heavy users of stock options. To increase the comparability of financial statements as well as to ensure that the true cost of stock options would be reflected in the financial statements, the FASB mandated the expensing of stock options for financial accounting purposes for years beginning on or after January 1, 2006.[27] Under the new rules, firms must measure the economic value of options on the grant date and then amortize this cost on a straight-line basis over the vesting period of the options.[28]

---

### Example 12-11

***What if:*** Assume that an accounting employee benefits specialist calculated the economic value of Julie's stock option grant (NQOs and ISOs) to be $32,000. Also assume that Julie's options vest 50 percent in year 1 (the year of the grant) and 50 percent in year 2. What compensation expense for book purposes would TPI report for Julie's stock options in year 1 and year 2?

**Answer:** $16,000 ($32,000 × 50%) in year 1 and $16,000 in year 2.

---

### THE KEY FACTS

**Stock Option Expense: GAAP vs. Tax**

▪ For tax purposes, employer deducts bargain element of nonqualified stock option on exercise date but receives no tax deduction for incentive stock options unless they become disqualified.

▪ For GAAP purposes, employer expenses the estimated value of the option pro rata over the vesting period.

As you probably realize by now, the tax rules governing the treatment of stock options differ markedly from generally accepted accounting principles in terms of both the amount and the timing of the stock option expense. To compare the tax and book treatment, we present TPI's book expense and tax deduction resulting from its stock option grant to Julie (given prior assumptions) in Exhibit 12-7.

The tremendous difference between the book and tax numbers presented in Exhibit 12-7 is driven by the increase in TPI's share price, from $5 on the date of grant to $20 on the date of exercise. The economic valuation of the stock options used to determine the book expense did not anticipate the extent of the stock appreciation before exercise.

[26]An extreme example of this is Barry Diller, CEO and chairman of the board at InterActiveCorp, who received $726,000 in salary and options valued at approximately $294 million in 2005.

[27]Accounting Standards Codification (ASC) 718, Stock Compensation.

[28]Although the exercise price of compensatory stock options typically equals the stock price on the date of grant, compensatory options are, nevertheless, economically valuable on the grant date. They have economic value because the stock price may eventually exceed the exercise price before the options expire. To determine economic value, firms typically use either the Black-Scholes option pricing model or the binomial option pricing model.

**EXHIBIT 12-7**    TPI's Tax Deductions and Book Expense from Stock Option
Grant to Julie

|  | Tax Deduction if Stock Price Increases | Tax Deduction if Stock Price Decreases | Book Expense |
|---|---|---|---|
| Year 1 | $ 0 | $0 | $16,000 |
| Year 2 | $ 0 | $0 | $16,000 |
| Year 3 | $300,000 | $0* | $ 0 |

*There would be no exercise because the exercise price exceeds the stock price.

## Restricted Stock

Like stock options described above, **restricted stock** can't be sold or otherwise treated
as owned by employees until they legally have the right to sell the shares on the vesting date. However, unlike the stock acquired through options exercises, employees
receive restricted stock on the vesting date *without having to pay for it,* after which
they can either sell it immediately or retain it.

As indicated in the timeline in Exhibit 12-8, the initial value of an employee's
restricted stock award depends on the share price of the stock on the vesting date.

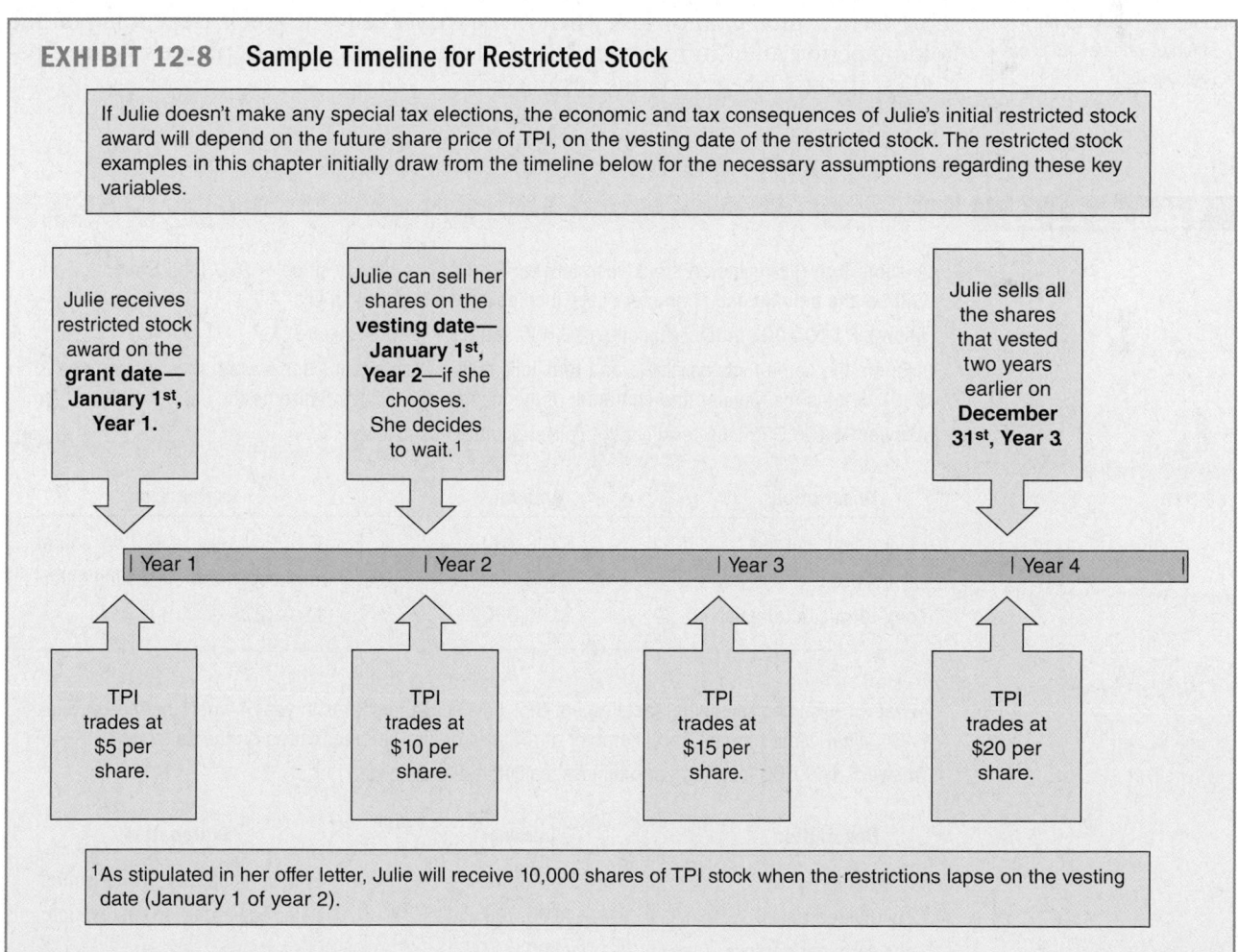

**EXHIBIT 12-8    Sample Timeline for Restricted Stock**

If Julie doesn't make any special tax elections, the economic and tax consequences of Julie's initial restricted stock award will depend on the future share price of TPI, on the vesting date of the restricted stock. The restricted stock examples in this chapter initially draw from the timeline below for the necessary assumptions regarding these key variables.

Julie receives restricted stock award on the **grant date— January 1st, Year 1.**

Julie can sell her shares on the **vesting date— January 1st, Year 2**—if she chooses. She decides to wait.[1]

Julie sells all the shares that vested two years earlier on **December 31st, Year 3**

| Year 1 | Year 2 | Year 3 | Year 4 |

TPI trades at $5 per share.

TPI trades at $10 per share.

TPI trades at $15 per share.

TPI trades at $20 per share.

[1] As stipulated in her offer letter, Julie will receive 10,000 shares of TPI stock when the restrictions lapse on the vesting date (January 1 of year 2).

**Example 12-12**

Given the assumptions regarding the restricted stock in Exhibit 12-8, by how much would Julie's wealth increase on the vesting date?

**Answer:** Julie's wealth would increase by $100,000 (10,000 shares × $10 per share).

**What if:** Assume that the stock decreased to $3 per share on the vesting date, by how much would Julie's wealth increase or decrease on the vesting date?

**Answer:** $30,000 increase ($3 × 10,000). Until the vesting date, Julie was not entitled to any economic benefit from the restricted stock. On the vesting date, however, she is entitled to stock valued at $30,000. Thus, the vesting of Julie's restricted stock increases her wealth even if the stock price decreases between the grant date and vesting date (unlike options that would be worthless).

---

**THE KEY FACTS**

**Restricted Stock *without* §83(b) Election**

- No tax consequences on grant date.
- Employee recognizes ordinary income on fair market value of stock on vesting date.
- Holding period for stock begins on vesting date.
- Employer deducts fair market value of stock on vesting date.

---

**Employee Considerations for Restricted Stock**   Restricted stock is taxed like nonqualified options with two important distinctions: while employees receiving NQOs are taxed at ordinary rates on the bargain element of the shares when they exercise their options, employees receiving restricted stock are taxed on the *full fair market value* of the shares *on the date the restricted stock vests.* They are taxed on the fair market value of the stock because they are entitled to receive the stock without any payment requirements (contrast this with the exercise price paid for stock options). Any subsequent appreciation in the value of the stock is taxed as either long-term or short-term capital gain or loss when the taxpayer sells the stock, depending on the holding period and future movement of the stock price. The employee's holding period for the stock begins on the vesting date.

---

**Example 12-13**

Assume that the restricted stock vests in year 2 when the market price is $10 (see Exhibit 12-8). What is the amount and character of the income Julie recognizes in year 2?

**Answer:** $100,000 ordinary income (10,000 shares × $10 per share).

Assume the same facts as above and that Julie sells the shares in year 4 when the market price is $20? What is the amount and character of the income she will recognize on the sale?

**Answer:** $100,000 long-term capital gain, calculated as follows:

| Description | Amount | Explanation |
|---|---|---|
| (1) Amount realized | $200,000 | 10,000 shares × $20 per share. |
| (2) Tax basis | 100,000 | Gain recognized on vesting date. |
| Long-term capital gain | $100,000 | (1) − (2). |

**What if:** Assume the original facts except that Julie sells the shares in year 4 when the market price is $4. What is the amount and character of the gain or loss she recognizes on the sale?

**Answer:** $60,000 long-term capital loss, calculated as follows:

| Description | Amount | Explanation |
|---|---|---|
| (1) Amount realized | $ 40,000 | 10,000 shares × $4 per share. |
| (2) Adjusted basis | 100,000 | Gain recognized on vesting date. |
| Long-term capital loss | ($60,000) | (1) − (2). |

*§83(b) election.*    The tax laws allow employees who receive restricted stock to make a tax election that can significantly change the tax consequences by treating the stock nearly the same as vested stock. Up until 30 days after the grant date, employees can make what is known as a **§83(b) election;** once made, however, this election is irrevocable. If the employee makes the §83(b) election, the value of the restricted stock is taxed on the grant date rather than the date on which the stock vests. The effect of the election is to accelerate the tax on the market value of the restricted shares—which, you'll recall from Chapter 3, is usually not desirable from a tax planning perspective. However, if the employee expects the share price to increase after the grant date, making the election converts ordinary income to long-term capital gain (which, assuming the shares are held for more than one year after the grant date, results in a preferential tax rate when the taxpayer sells the shares). Without the §83(b) election, the employee reports no income when the shares are granted, but is taxed on their fair market value at ordinary rates when the stock vests. With the §83(b) election, the employee simply pays tax at ordinary rates on the market value of the shares at the grant date.

## Example 12-14

*What if:* How much tax on the restricted stock would Julie pay in year 1 if she does not make a §83(b) election?

**Answer:** $0. The stock has not vested yet so she has no income.

*What if:* How much tax on the restricted stock would Julie pay in year 1 if she makes a §83(b) election?

**Answer:** $20,000 [$50,000 ordinary income (10,000 shares × $5 per share) × 40 percent marginal ordinary tax rate].

*What if:* How much tax would Julie pay in year 2 on the restricted stock (the year the restricted stock vests) if she did *not* make a §83(b) election in year 1 (the stock is trading at $10 a share on the vesting date)?

**Answer:** $40,000 [$100,000 ordinary income (10,000 shares × $10 per share) × 40 percent marginal ordinary tax rate].

*What if:* How much tax would Julie pay in year 2 on the restricted stock if she made the §83(b) election in year 1?

**Answer:** $0. With the §83(b) election, Julie treated the stock as though it vested in year 1, not year 2, so she does not have a taxable event in year 2 when the stock actually vests.

*What if:* How much tax would Julie pay in year 4 on the restricted stock when she sells the stock for $20 a share (on December 31) if she did *not* make the §83(b) election in year 1?

**Answer:** $15,000 [$200,000 (10,000 × $20) − $100,000 tax basis (fair market value on vesting date in year 2) = $100,000. $100,000 × 15 percent long-term capital gains rate = $15,000].

*What if:* How much tax would Julie pay in year 4 on the restricted stock when she sells the stock for $20 a share (on December 31) if she made the §83(b) election in year 1?

**Answer:** $22,500 [$200,000 (10,000 × $20) − $50,000 tax basis (fair market value in year 1 when made §83(b) election) = $150,000. $150,000 × 15 percent long-term capital gains rate = $22,500].

Given the analyses above what amount of taxes would Julie save by making the §83(b) election (ignore time value of money)?

**Answer:** $12,500 ($42,500 with election; $55,000 without), computed as follows:

| Taxes Payable | | |
| --- | --- | --- |
| **Description** | **With Election** | **Without Election** |
| Year 1 taxes on ordinary income | $20,000 | $    0 |
| Year 2 taxes on ordinary income | 0 | 40,000 |
| Year 4 taxes on long-term capital gains | 22,500 | 15,000 |
| **Total taxes** | $42,500 | $55,000 |

*(continued on page 12-20...)*

> Note that Julie saves taxes because the election allowed her to convert $50,000 in income from ordinary income taxed at 40 percent into long-term capital gain taxed at 15 percent.
>
> Also note that this computation overstates to some degree the benefits of making the §83(b) election because it ignores the time value of money. In order to have a greater portion of her gains taxed at capital gains rates, Julie gave up some tax deferral when she accelerated $50,000 of income from year 4 into year 1.

Employees making the §83(b) election essentially trade off some additional current tax now in order to convert ordinary income into long-term capital gains later. Accordingly, the §83(b) election is advisable when the potential for growth in the stock value is high and the amount of additional current tax is manageable. If an employee makes a §83(b) election and then forfeits the stock for any reason, the employee cannot deduct the loss on the forfeiture.[29] Thus, the risk of making the election is that if the employee forfeits the stock he would have paid taxes on value that he never receives.

**Employer Considerations for Restricted Stock**   Like the tax treatment of non-qualified options, the employer's deduction for restricted stock equals the amount of ordinary income reported by its employees. The timing of the deduction is determined by the employee's decision regarding the §83(b) election. If the employee makes a §83(b) election, the employer claims the deduction in the year the restricted stock is granted. Otherwise, the employer claims a deduction when the restrictions lapse. Some employers believe that restricted stock is a superior form of compensation to stock options. See Apple Inc.'s 2009 proxy statement in Exhibit 12-9.

### EXHIBIT 12-9   Excerpt from Apple Inc.'s 2009 Proxy Statement

Since fiscal 2004, all of the Company's equity awards to its named executive officers have been RSUs rather than stock options. A grant of RSUs gives an officer the right to receive a specified number of shares of the Company's common stock, at no cost to the officer, if the officer remains employed at the Company until the RSUs vest. Although its value may increase or decrease with changes in the stock price during the period between granting and vesting, an RSU will have value in the long term. By contrast, the entire compensation value of a stock option depends on future stock price appreciation. Accordingly, RSUs can deliver significantly greater share-for-share compensation value at grant than stock options, and the Company can offer comparable grant date compensation value with fewer shares and less dilution for its shareholders.

The accounting treatment for restricted stock is similar to the accounting treatment for stock options.[30] If restricted stock grants vest over time, the value of restricted stock on the *date of grant* is expensed pro rata over the vesting period.

---

**Example 12-15**

***What if:*** Given the assumptions in Exhibit 12-8, what amount can TPI deduct for tax purposes in year 1 and in year 2 assuming Julie does *not* make a §83(b)?

**Answer:** $0 in year 1 and $100,000 in year 2 (10,000 shares of restricted stock vested × $10 per share market price at vesting date).

[29]Reg. §1.83-2(a).
[30]ASC 718.

> **What if:** What amount can TPI deduct in year 1 and in year 2 if Julie *does* make a §83(b) election?
>
> **Answer:** $50,000 in year 1 (10,000 shares of restricted stock awarded × $5 per share market price on the grant date) and $0 in year 2.
>
> What amount is TPI's compensation expense for financial accounting purposes for Julie's restricted stock in year 1 and in year 2?
>
> **Answer:** $50,000 book expense in year 1. Because the value of Julie's restricted stock award on the date of grant is $50,000, TPI expenses the award on its books over the vesting period, which in this case is just one year (it has a one year vesting period).

*Other nontax issues.*    Since it became clear that accounting rules were changing in 2006 to require employers to record a book expense for stock option grants, as had historically been the case for restricted stock, the popularity of restricted stock has increased relative to stock options. Other factors besides the accounting rule change also help to explain this trend. For example, companies with stagnant or declining stock prices realized that stock options granted when their stock prices were higher, so-called underwater options, were no longer motivating their employees. To address this problem, they replaced some or all of their stock options with restricted stock that, unlike stock options, retains some value even when a company's stock price is falling.[31]

### Equity-Based Compensation Summary

To summarize our discussion of the tax treatment of equity-based compensation, Exhibit 12-10 highlights the general tax treatment of nonqualified options, incentive stock options, and restricted stock on a per share basis from both employee and employer perspectives given an arbitrary time series of share prices. In addition to future share prices, the exhibit assumes options are exercisable for the share price on the grant date.

> **THE KEY FACTS**
>
> **Restricted Stock Expense: GAAP vs. Tax**
>
> ■ For tax purposes, employers deduct the market value of stock when the employee recognizes income. For GAAP purposes, employers deduct the grant date value over the vesting period.

**EXHIBIT 12-10**    Reportable Income and Deductions from Equity Based Compensation (for given time frame and stock prices)

| | Party Affected | NQOs | ISOs | Restricted Stock |
|---|---|---|---|---|
| Grant Date-Year 1 Stock (exercise) Price = $1/share | Employee | No Effect | No Effect | No Effect |
| | Employer | No Effect | No Effect | No Effect |
| Vesting Date-Year 4 Stock Price = $6/share | Employee | No Effect | No Effect | $6/share Ordinary Income |
| | Employer | No Effect | No Effect | $6/share Ordinary Deduction |
| Exercise Date for Options-Year 6 Stock Price = $11/share | Employee | $10/share Ordinary Income | No Effect* | N/A |
| | Employer | $10/share Ordinary Deduction | No Effect | N/A |
| Sale Date-Year 8 Stock Price = $16/share | Employee | $5/share LT Capital Gain | $15/share LT Capital Gain | $10/share Capital Gain |
| | Employer | No Effect | No Effect | No Effect |

*$10 per share is included in alternative minimum taxable income.

[31]Microsoft is an extreme example of this trend. In July 2003, it announced it was replacing all of its employee's stock options with restricted stock.

**L03**    # FRINGE BENEFITS

*continued from page 12-10...*
The final section of TPI's offer letter indicated Julie would receive fringe benefits in the form of health and dental insurance (value of $18,000), $750,000 of group-term life insurance, a biennial $30,000 automobile allowance, monthly parking, and a flexible spending account for medical expenses. ∎

Employees generally receive most of their compensation in the form of cash salary or wages. However, employers often provide noncash benefits to employees in addition to their cash compensation. These **fringe benefits** range from the common (health insurance) to the exotic (use of a corporate aircraft). As a general rule, because fringe benefits are employee compensation, they are taxable to the employee on receipt. In fact, fringe benefits are specifically mentioned in the definition of gross income. As we indicated in Chapter 5, IRC §61(a) indicates that, "gross income means all income from whatever source derived, including . . . (1) Compensation for services, including fees, commissions, *fringe benefits,* and similar items (emphasis added)." This definition of income notwithstanding, the tax laws specifically *exclude* certain fringe benefits from an employee's gross income. Thus, some fringe benefits are taxable and others are not.

---

> ### THE KEY FACTS
>
> **Taxable Fringe Benefits**
>
> ▪ Employees recognize compensation income on all benefits received unless specifically excluded by tax laws.
>
> ▪ Employees treat benefits received like taxable cash compensation.
>
> ▪ Employer deducts cost and pays employer's share of FICA taxes on benefit.

## Taxable Fringe Benefits

**Taxable fringe benefits** are fringe benefits not specifically excluded from gross income. Congress views many of the taxable fringe benefits as luxuries and chooses not to subsidize them. Taxable fringe benefits include such things as below-market interest rate loans (see discussion in Chapter 5), gym memberships, season tickets to the local NBA team, an automobile allowance for a personal automobile, or anything else not specifically excluded by the tax laws. Employers generally provide taxable fringe benefits to executives and higher salaried employees rather than to the rank and file employees.

**Employee Considerations for Taxable Fringe Benefits**    From an employee's perspective, taxable fringe benefits are treated just like cash. Employees recognize ordinary compensation income when they receive taxable benefits and, just as they do with salary, pay FICA taxes on the value of the benefit. As a result, taxable fringe benefits cost employees the amount of tax they must pay on the benefits.

---

**Example 12-16**

Julie's offer includes a biennial auto allowance of up to $30,000. That is, every other year, TPI will reimburse Julie for an automobile purchase up to $30,000. TPI provides this benefit to executives that interact with the public on a regular basis. Julie purchases a Toyota 4Runner with a retail price of $35,000. What tax is Julie required to pay if she uses the allowance to apply toward the purchase? What is Julie's after-tax cost of the automobile if her marginal tax rate is 40 percent?

**Answer:** $12,435 in total taxes and $17,435 after-tax cost, computed as follows:

| Description | Amount | Explanation |
|---|---|---|
| (1) Fair market value of Toyota | $35,000 | |
| (2) Automobile allowance | 30,000 | Taxable fringe benefit. |
| (3) Julie's additional cost | 5,000 | (1) − (2). |
| (4) Income tax on allowance | 12,000 | (2) × 40%. |
| (5) FICA taxes on automobile allowance (Medicare) | 435 | (2) × 1.45% (Julie is over the Social Security wage base). |
| (6) Total taxes paid | 12,435 | (4) + (5). |
| **Total after-tax cost** | $17,435 | (3) + (6). |

From Julie's perspective, this is a pretty good deal—particularly if she was willing to pay the market price for the car.

Employees may prefer a taxable benefit to an equivalent amount of cash when they benefit from employer-provided quantity or group discounts associated with the benefit. For example, many companies provide (pay premiums for) **group-term life insurance** as a fringe benefit, in part, because they can purchase the insurance at a lower rate than employees can purchase it individually. However, employees must recognize a certain amount of gross income when employers pay life insurance premiums for the employee for policies with a death benefit in excess of $50,000.[32] Consequently, a portion of the group-term life insurance benefit is taxable and a portion is nontaxable. In these circumstances, the employer determines the employee's taxable amount using a table provided in the Treasury Regulations. An excerpt of this table is provided in Exhibit 12-11.[33] To compute the annual taxable benefit, taxpayers use the following steps:

*Step 1:* Subtract $50,000 from the death benefit of their employer-provided group-term life insurance policy.

*Step 2:* Divide the Step 1 result by $1,000.

**EXHIBIT 12-11    Uniform Premiums for $1,000 of Group-Term Life Insurance Protection**

| 5-year Age Bracket | Cost per $1,000 of Protection for One Month |
|---|---|
| Under 25 | $0.05 |
| 25 to 29 | .06 |
| 30 to 34 | .08 |
| 35 to 39 | .09 |
| 40 to 44 | .10 |
| 45 to 49 | .15 |
| 50 to 54 | .23 |
| 55 to 59 | .43 |
| 60 to 64 | .66 |
| 65 to 69 | 1.27 |
| 70 and above | 2.06 |

[32]§79.

[33]Reg. §1.79-3(d)(2) provides an age-based table and instructions to calculate the employee's includable amount.

*Step 3:* Multiply the result from Step 2 by the cost per $1,000 of protection for one month from the table (Exhibit 12-11) based on the taxpayer's age.

*Step 4:* Multiply the outcome of Step 3 by 12 (months).

### Example 12-17

Julie's offer from TPI includes $750,000 of group-term life insurance. TPI's cost to provide Julie the insurance is $500 per year. If Julie were to purchase the insurance herself she would pay $2,000 per year. Assume that Julie is 37 years old. Based on the Treasury's table (see Exhibit 12-11), the monthly premium per $1,000 of insurance is $.09 cents. What is Julie's taxable compensation from receiving the group-term life benefit? What does this benefit cost Julie?

**Answer:** $756 of taxable compensation and $313 cost (all taxes). Julie's cost is the income and Medicare taxes she must pay on the compensation, calculated as follows:

| Group-Term Life Insurance Description | Amount | Explanation |
|---|---|---|
| (1) Insurance coverage | $750,000 | Provided by employer. |
| (2) Excluded coverage | ($50,000) | Nontaxable portion. |
| (3) Taxable benefit | $700,000 | (1) + (2) (Step 1). |
| (4) Divide by 1,000 | 1,000 | Divide by 1,000 (Step 2) |
| (5) Result of Step 2 | 700 | (3)/(4) |
| (6) Monthly cost per $1,000 | 0.09 | Taxable portion per $1,000 from Exhibit 12-11. |
| (7) Monthly benefit | $    63 | (5) × (6) |
| (8) Months | × 12 | Annualize monthly taxable amount. |
| **(9) Annual taxable benefit** | $    756 | (7) × (8). |
| (10) Income taxes | $    302 | (9) × 40%. |
| (11) FICA taxes | $    11 | (9) × 1.45% (Julie is over Social Security wage base limit so she pays only Medicare portion of FICA taxes). |
| Tax cost of benefit | $    313 | (10) + (11). |

Note that Julie's income is not based on TPI's actual cost ($500) of providing the policy.

Taxpayers receiving taxable fringe benefits may experience some financial strain because they must pay the tax on the benefits. Frequently, when corporations provide taxable fringe benefits to senior executives, they also provide the executives enough cash to cover the taxes so the benefit costs the executive nothing.[34] This is commonly referred to as a *gross-up.* For example, GE's 2009 proxy statement reveals that it made payments of $14,403 to Keith S. Sherin, its CFO, and indicates that the additional cash is "for the payment of taxes with respect to financial counseling, tax preparation services and personal use of NBCU car service."[35] Employees can choose to forgo a benefit if they prefer not to pay taxes on it.

---

[34]Companies generally choose a formula to determine how much cash (gross up) they need to pay the employee in addition to the taxable benefit to ensure the benefit costs the employee nothing.

[35]While, based on its formula, GE reimbursed Mr. Sherin for $14,403 of taxes on taxable benefits of $61,849 (23.3 percent), this is less than some plans that provide such "gross ups" of over 60 percent in an attempt to eliminate the tax on the taxable gross up.

**Employer Considerations for Taxable Fringe Benefits**    Like employees, employers treat taxable fringe benefits just like cash compensation. That is, the employer has an outlay for the cost of the benefit and must pay the employer's share of FICA taxes on the taxable portion of benefits it provides to employees. The employer deducts its *cost* of the benefit (plus FICA taxes), *not the value* of the benefit to the employee. As we mention above, employers are often able to purchase fringe benefits at a lower cost than can individual employees. For example, employers may receive a group discount for purchasing life insurance, automobiles, financial or tax planning services, or accident insurance.

---

**Example 12-18**

In Example 12-17, TPI provided Julie with $750,000 of group-term life insurance. Its cost of providing the entire $750,000 of coverage is $500 per year. If Julie were to purchase the policy herself, it would cost her $2,000 per year. Assuming TPI's marginal tax rate is 35 percent, what is TPI's after-tax cost of the partially taxable group-term life insurance benefit it provided to Julie?

**Answer:** TPI's after-tax cost of the benefit provided is $332, calculated as follows:

| Description | Amount | Explanation |
|---|---|---|
| (1) Cost of policy | $500 | |
| (2) Income tax benefit | (175) | (1) × 35%. |
| (3) FICA taxes paid | 11 | See Julie's FICA tax in line (9) of Example 12-17. |
| (4) FICA tax benefit | (4) | (3) × 35%. |
| Total after-tax cost | $332 | Sum of (1) through (4). |

---

Finally, employers may discriminate between employees when providing taxable benefits. That is, they can select which employees receive the taxable benefits and which do not. Not surprisingly, the more highly compensated employees tend to receive these benefits. For example, as described in an excerpt from Walmart's proxy statement in Exhibit 12-12, Walmart's perquisite and supplemental benefits provides certain officers with use of the company aircraft and home security systems. Walmart is unlikely to offer these same benefits to its hourly store clerks.

---

**Taxes in the Real World**    *Fringe Benefits*

**A Perk Takes Off**

*The Wall Street Journal*
*By Christina Cheddar Berk*
*April 11, 2005*

"When Charles K. Gifford stepped down as chairman of Bank of America Corp. in January, he could look forward to a comfortable retirement. Mr. Gifford will receive an annual pension of $3.1 million for life. As the former chief executive of Fleet Financial Group, he also took home $16.4 million stemming from the 1999 merger with BankBoston that formed FleetBoston Financial Corp., which Bank of America bought last year.

And the 62-year-old former executive will receive perks, potentially for life, including choice tickets for as many as 15 Boston Red Sox baseball games a year. If Mr. Gifford isn't in Boston on game day, he needn't worry. He can summon a private jet, provided by Bank of America, to fly him and a handful of friends there in time for the first pitch. Mr. Gifford has access to as many as 120 hours of flight time a year. He doesn't even need to be on board—he can dispatch a plane to ferry his guests.

Bank of America said in filings with the Securities and Exchange Commission that this perk is in part compensation to Mr. Gifford for his continued availability to provide the Charlotte, N.C., company with services including advice and consulting. That's a common justification, along with security concerns, for giving retired executives use of corporate jets."

**EXHIBIT 12-12** **Excerpt from Walmart's 2009 Proxy Statement**

*Perquisites and supplemental benefits:* . . . Executive Officers are entitled to a limited number of perquisites and supplemental benefits. For certain Executive Officers, these include:
- Personal use of Company aircraft,
- An annual senior executive physical, and
- Equipment, maintenance, and monitoring of security systems in their homes.

## Nontaxable Fringe Benefits

For policy reasons, Congress specifically excludes certain fringe benefits, such as health insurance, from employees' gross income to encourage employers to provide the benefits.[36] We refer to excluded benefits as **nontaxable fringe benefits.** Other nontaxable fringe benefits enable taxpayers to become or stay employed, including meals or lodging for the convenience of the employer, educational assistance, dependent-care benefits, moving expense benefits, and transportation-related benefits. Finally, some benefits are excluded for simplicity's sake, such as no-additional-cost services, qualified employee discounts, and *de minimis* (small) fringe benefits. Exhibit 12-13 provides a partial list of nontaxable fringe benefits. Below, we discuss these benefits in more detail.

**EXHIBIT 12-13** **Common Forms of Nontaxable Fringe Benefits**

| Benefit | Description |
|---|---|
| Group-term life insurance (§79) | Employer-paid premiums on up to $50,000 group-term life insurance policy are excluded from employees' income. |
| Health benefits (§§ 105–106) | Employer-paid premiums covering health, medical, and dental insurance and the benefits provided through the insurance. |
| Meals or lodging for the convenience of the employer (§119)* | Meals provided on employer's premises and lodging provided by the employer as a condition of employment. |
| Employee educational assistance (§127) | Up to $5,250 exclusion for tuition, books, and fees. See IRS Publication 970, *Tax Benefits for Education.* |
| Dependent care benefits (§129) | Up to $5,000 exclusion for cost of providing care for a dependent under 13 years old or disabled. |
| No-additional-cost services [§132(a)(1)] | Benefits that don't cost the employer a material amount. |
| Qualified employee discounts [§132(a)(2)] | Reduced prices on employer's product within certain limits. |
| Working condition fringe [§132(a)(3)]* | A benefit provided by an employer that would be deductible as an ordinary and necessary business expense by the employee if the employee rather than the employer paid the expense. |
| *De minimis* fringe [§132(a)(4)]* | Relatively small and infrequently provided benefits. |
| Qualified transportation fringe benefits [§132(a)(5)]* | Mass transit passes, qualified parking, or use of company owned car pool vehicles (vans). |
| Qualified moving expense reimbursement [§132(a)(6)]* | Reimbursement for allowable moving expenses such as moving household goods and travel. |
| Cafeteria plans (§125) | A plan where employees can choose from among various nontaxable fringe benefits or cash. Taxable to the extent employees receive cash. |

*Employer may discriminate in providing this benefit.

[36]The nontaxable fringe benefits are listed with "items specifically excluded from gross income" in §§101-140 of the Internal Revenue Code. Employers are generally prohibited from discriminating among employees with respect to nontaxable fringe benefits (they cannot offer them only to executives). This chapter indicates whether or not discrimination for a particular benefit is allowed. However, the discrimination rules are complex and vary from benefit to benefit in ways too numerous to explain in detail in this text.

**Group-Term Life Insurance**    As we mentioned in the taxable benefits section, employees may exclude from income the employer-provided benefit for the first $50,000 of group-term life insurance.[37] Any remaining group-term life insurance benefit is taxable (see Example 12-17). An employer may not discriminate between employees in providing nontaxable group-term life insurance benefits.

**Health and Accident Insurance and Benefits**    When employers pay for **health and accident insurance** for an employee and the employee's spouse and dependents, the employee excludes the benefit from her gross income.[38] For example, if TPI pays health premiums of $18,000 for Julie and her family, Julie is not required to include this $18,000 fringe benefit in her gross income.[39] Further, when employees receive cash reimbursements for medical care, they can exclude the reimbursement from gross income.[40] For example, if TPI reimburses Julie for $450 of medical co-payments she makes during the year, Julie excludes the $450 from her gross income. Generally, employers may not discriminate between employees when providing health and accident insurance benefits.[41]

**Meals and Lodging for the Convenience of the Employer**    The value of certain meals and lodging the employer provides to an employee may be excluded from an employee's gross income if the benefit meets two criteria: (1) the meals and lodging are provided on the employer's business premises to the employee (and the employee's spouse and dependents, if any) and (2) the meals and lodging are provided for the convenience of the employer.[42] For example, employers may provide meals at their place of business so employees can continue working efficiently without taking time off to go out to eat. Accounting firms frequently provide meals to tax professionals working late during tax season. Employers are allowed to deduct the full cost of meals provided to employees for the convenience of the employer. That is, the cost is not subject to the 50 percent deductibility limitation on meals we discussed in Chapter 8.[43] Employers may generally discriminate between employees **for the convenience of the employer benefits.**

---

| **Example 12-19** |
| --- |

***What if:*** Assume that last year Julie purchased 25 meals, at a cost of $500, on evenings when she worked late. Julie turned in expense reports and receipts for the meals totaling $500, which PCC reimbursed. What is the amount Julie must include in income?

**Answer:** Julie will not include the value of any of the overtime meals into income because they were provided for PCC's convenience.

---

In some situations, employers may provide lodging for employees and require employees to live on the business premises as a condition of their employment. In these cases, employees may exclude the value of the lodging from gross income.[44] For

---

[37]§79.

[38]§106.

[39]If Julie were to purchase the health insurance with after-tax dollars the equivalent would be $30,743 [$18,000 / (1 − .4 marginal tax rate − .0145 Medicare portion of FICA tax)].

[40]§105(b). Although, reimbursement in excess of costs is included in income.

[41]However, employers may exclude part-time employees from participation.

[42]§119(a)(1).

[43]§274(n).

[44]§119(a)(2).

example, an employer may require an apartment complex manager to live in an apartment in the complex (free of charge) so the employee can respond to tenant needs, provide security, and handle emergencies. The apartment manager can exclude the value of the lodging from gross income.

**Employee Educational Assistance**   Employees can exclude from income up to $5,250 of employee **educational assistance benefits** covering tuition, books, and fees.[45] Amounts received in excess of this limit are taxed as compensation to the employee. (See IRS Publication 970 for details related to education benefits.) This includes amounts employers provide for employee undergraduate or graduate level courses or for courses that lead to a professional degree. Amounts excluded from income cannot qualify for educational deductions or credits (such as the American opportunity and lifetime learning credits).

**Dependent Care Benefits**   Employees can exclude up to $5,000 for benefits paid or reimbursed by employers for caring for children under age 13 or dependents or spouses who are physically or mentally unable to care for themselves.[46] Excluded amounts do not qualify for the child and dependent care credit (see Chapter 7).

**No-Additional-Cost Services**   Employees can exclude the value of **no-additional-cost services.** These are any services employers provide to employees in the ordinary course of business that generate no substantial costs to the employer (including opportunity costs).[47] For example, airline companies can provide employees with free flight benefits on a space-available basis, hoteliers can allow employees to use vacant hotel rooms, and telephone companies can provide free basic phone service to their employees—all without the employees recognizing gross income. Exhibit 12-14 (above) provides an excerpt from the JetBlue Airways Web site that describes no-cost benefits it provides to its employees.[48]

---

**EXHIBIT 12-14**   **Excerpt from JetBlue Airways' Web Site**

Flight Benefits

- Free and reduced rate standby travel on JetBlue flights.
- Discounted standby travel on other flights.

---

| Example 12-20 | |
|---|---|

**What if:** Assume that Julie's current employer, PCC, has a division that provides wireless Internet service and virus protection software. Because PCC has such a large contract with a national provider, its contract has sufficient bandwidth to allow employees to use the service without incurring additional cost. The market value of the services is $1,080 per year. What amount of this benefit must Julie include in her gross income?

**Answer:** $0. Julie may exclude the value of the wireless Internet from her income because it qualifies as a no-additional-cost service under §132.

---

[45]§127(a)(2). The discrimination and eligibility rules are provided in §127(b)(2).
[46]§129.
[47]§132(a)(1).
[48]From JetBlue Web site: www.jetblue.com/about/work/benefits.html.

**Qualified Employee Discounts**    Employers frequently allow employees to purchase their goods and services at a discount. Employees may exclude **qualified employee discounts** from income as long as they don't acquire *goods* at a price below the employer's cost or *services* at more than a 20 percent discount of the price of the services to customers.[49] This can be a fairly significant nontaxable benefit to employees, particularly for higher priced products. For example, Ford Motor Company could allow employees a substantial discount on its Ford, Land Rover, Jaguar, or Volvo brand cars. Also, Exhibit 12-15 presents an excerpt from the General Electric Web site describing the GE employee product purchase plan that allows employees to acquire home appliances at a significant discount.[50]

**EXHIBIT 12-15    Excerpt from General Electric's Web Site**

GE Employee Product Purchase Plan

An employee can receive substantial discounts on a variety of GE products. Discounts vary by product and model and apply to items such as refrigerators, clothes washers and dryers, ranges, ovens and dishwashers.

From a nontax perspective, employers can use this qualified fringe benefit to entice and retain employees who would otherwise purchase the employer's brand or product.

---

**Example 12-21**

*What if:*  Assume that Julie's current employer, PCC, allows all employees to purchase computers (both laptops and desktops) from its retail stores at a discount. Julie purchased two computers during the current year: a laptop for $1,600 (retails for $2,100, with a cost to PCC of $1,500) and a desktop for $1,300 (retails for $1,800, with a cost of $1,250). Julie saved $500 ($2,100 − $1,600) on the laptop and $500 ($1,800 − $1,300) on the desktop. What amount of the savings must Julie include in her gross income?

**Answer:**  Julie can exclude the entire savings from her income because the savings are a qualified employee discount under §132.

*What if:*  Suppose that the laptop Julie purchased for $1,600 has a cost of $1,700 (instead of $1,500 as stated above). What amount of the tax savings on the laptop must Julie include in her gross income?

**Answer:**  $100. Because Julie's cost of the computer is $100 less than PCC's cost, Julie must include $100 in her gross income.

*What if:*  Assume that Julie's current employer, PCC, allows all employees to receive one free computer each year. Julie selected the laptop (retails for $2,100, with a cost to PCC of $1,500) as her free computer. What amount must PCC include in Julie's gross income?

**Answer:**  $1,500. Julie's cost of the computer ($0) is $1,500 less than PCC's cost. Therefore, she must include $1,500 in income. Employee discounts only qualify as a qualified employee discount under §132 to the extent they don't exceed the employer's cost.

---

**Working Condition Fringe Benefits**    Employees may exclude from income any benefit or reimbursement of a benefit provided by an employer that would be deductible as an ordinary and necessary expense by the employee if the employee rather than

---

[49]§132(a)(2).

[50]General Electric's Web site: www.ge.com/research/grc_6_2_2.html

the employer paid the expense (or the employer did not reimburse the employee). For example, if a company or firm reimburses its employees for professional licensing costs or dues (CPA or bar fees or AICPA dues), the reimbursement may be excluded from an employee's income.[51] Additionally, telephones or computers provided to employees for business use may be excluded. Employers may discriminate between employees with respect to **working condition fringe benefits.**

---

**Example 12-22**

*What if:* Assume that Julie's employer reimburses executives for business-related continuing education courses as well as travel related to such education. Julie attended a certificate (nondegree program) course at the University of Chicago this year. Her costs were as follows: $2,500 for the course, $600 for airfare, $800 for hotels, and $200 for books and course materials. PCC reimbursed Julie for the entire $4,100 ($2,500 + $600 + $800 + $200). What amount of the reimbursement must Julie include in her gross income?

**Answer:** $0. The reimbursement qualifies as a working condition fringe benefit under §132.

*What if:* Assume that Ethan's employer allows all its engineers to take home products for consumer testing and evaluation. For example, Ethan is currently designing a new disc brake system for mountain bikes. So Ethan is allowed to check out up to three mountain bikes at a time to see how various different brake systems work. The annual rental value of products Ethan uses is $2,500. What amount of the annual rental value must Ethan include in his gross income?

**Answer:** $0. The value of the consumer testing products is an excludible working condition fringe benefit under §132.

---

*De Minimis* **Fringe Benefits**   Employees can also exclude from income occasional or incidental *de minimis* **fringe benefits** (very small).[52] These typically include occasional personal use of a copy machine, company-sponsored picnics, noncash traditional holiday gifts (Thanksgiving turkey or Christmas ham), and occasional tickets to sporting or theatrical events. Employers are allowed to discriminate between employees when providing *de minimis* fringe benefits. Who do you think gets to use a company's NBA tickets—the new employee or the boss?

**Qualified Transportation Fringe**   Employees may exclude from income the value of certain transportation benefits they receive from employers, whether employers pay for these benefits directly or reimburse employees for the transportation costs.[53] These **qualified transportation fringe benefits** eligible for exclusion include the value of company-owned car pool vehicles for commuting to and from work, the cost of mass transit passes, and the cost of qualified parking near the work place. In 2010, the maximum exclusion for the car pool vehicle and mass transit pass is $230 per month and the maximum exclusion for the qualified parking benefit is $230 per month.[54]

**Qualified Moving Expense Reimbursement**   Employees receiving payments (or reimbursements) from employers for **qualified moving expense reimbursements** may exclude the payments from gross income to the extent that they do not deduct the

---

[51]Employees can exclude reimbursements from their income if they properly document their expenses through expense reports, mileage logs, and receipts.

[52]§132(a)(4).

[53]§132(f)(1).

[54]Starting in March 2009, the amount was $230 per month for both qualified parking and mass transit passes.

moving expenses.[55] As we discussed in Chapter 6, qualified moving expenses include the cost of moving household items and travel, including lodging, for the employee and dependents as long as the employee's move meets certain distance and length of employment tests. Employees are, however, taxed on payments they receive from employers for house-hunting trips, temporary housing allowances, and reimbursements for expenses related to the sale of their prior residence.

### Cafeteria Plans and Flexible Spending Accounts (FSAs)

Employers choose the benefits they make available to employees. Some employers offer a standard package of benefits that employees can either take or leave. Standard benefits typically include health and dental insurance for the employee and her family, dependent care benefits, and group-term life insurance for the employee. However, a standard benefit plan is not optimal for all employees because each employee has his or her own needs. So how can employers tailor their benefits to the needs of employees? The answer is cafeteria plans and flexible spending accounts.

Under a **cafeteria plan,** employers determine the total cost of benefits they are willing to provide for each employee. Each employee then either chooses (or buys) benefits up to the determined amount from a menu of nontaxable fringe benefits or may receive a cash equivalent in lieu of forgone benefits.[56] However, cash received from a cafeteria plan is taxable compensation to employees. Cafeteria plans are popular because each employee may desire different types of nontaxable fringe benefits. For example, if an employer provides $3,000 of dependent care benefits to every employee, the benefits would be worthless to employees without dependents. Through a cafeteria plan, employees can select the benefits best suited to their needs. For example, instead of selecting dependent care benefits, an employee with no dependents could choose any combination of nontaxable benefits such as dental insurance, educational benefits, or cash if none of the benefits is desirable.

Employers can also offer **flexible spending accounts (FSAs),** which allow employees to set aside a portion of their before-tax salary for payment of either health and/or dependent-care benefits. These plans allow employees to set aside either employee contributions (on a before-tax basis) or employer contributions (a leftover cafeteria plan amount) to pay for medical-related expenses (such as co-payments and prescriptions) or dependent care. Generally, taxpayers must use amounts placed in flexible spending accounts to pay for qualified benefits they expend funds on during the FSA plan year (which is often the calendar year), or they forfeit the remaining balance of the account. However, employers may allow employees to use the remaining balance from one year within the first two and a half months of the next FSA plan year.[57]

### Employee and Employer Considerations for Nontaxable Fringe Benefits

Nontaxable fringe benefits are very attractive to employees because their after-tax cost of these benefits is zero.[58] They do not pay for the benefits and they are not taxed on the value of the benefits they receive. In contrast to taxable fringe benefits, nontaxable fringe benefits cannot, with a few exceptions noted above, be provided on a discriminatory basis (may not be provided to some employees and not others). Employers deduct the cost of providing the benefits, which (thanks to group or

> **THE KEY FACTS**
>
> **Nontaxable Fringe Benefits**
> - Specifically identified in the Code.
> - Employee excludes benefit from taxable income.
> - Employer deducts cost when benefit is paid.

---

[55]§132(a)(6).

[56]§125.

[57]Employers can elect to allow employees to use funds set aside for one year until March 15 of the following year under Notice 2005-42. If employers don't make the election, employees must use their account balance by December 31 of the current year or they lose it after year-end.

[58]Furthermore, there are nontax reasons for employees to value nontaxable benefits, such as the fact that many employer-provided group health insurance plans allow for preexisting health conditions that employees cannot obtain on their own.

quantity discounts) can be considerably lower than the cost to the employee of purchasing the benefit separately. IRS publication 15-B "Employer's Tax Guide to Fringe Benefits" (available at www.IRS.gov) provides tax guidance for employers providing fringe benefits.

### Tax Planning with Fringe Benefits

The fact that employees can exclude nontaxable fringe benefits from gross income, while employers can deduct the cost of providing them, (just as they deduct the cost of taxable fringe benefits) gives rise to compensation-related tax-planning opportunities that may benefit both employee and employer.

---

**Example 12-23**

TPI proposed to reimburse Julie $200 a month for her parking costs. What amount of this reimbursement would be a nontaxable qualified transportation fringe to Julie?

**Answer:** All $2,400. Julie can exclude up to $230 per month ($2,760 per year) as a qualified transportation fringe.

**What if:** Assume that TPI would not reimburse Julie's parking costs unless Julie is willing to accept a reduction in salary. Assuming Julie is subject to a 40 percent marginal tax rate, how much salary should Julie be willing to forgo to receive the $2,400 of nontaxable parking benefits?

**Answer:** $4,099, computed as follows:

| Description | Amount | Explanation |
|---|---|---|
| (1) Annual fringe benefit | $2,400 | |
| (2) Marginal ordinary tax rate | 40% | |
| (3) Medicare tax rate on salary | 1.45% | Julie is over Social Security tax wage base limit. |
| (4) Total marginal tax rate on income | 41.45% | (2) + (3). |
| Before-tax compensation required to pay for annual fringe benefit | $4,099 | (1)/[1 − (4)]. |

---

**Example 12-24**

**What if:** Assume that instead of a parking benefit, TPI would pay Julie $4,099 of salary that she would use to pay for her parking and FICA taxes. What would be TPI's after-tax cost of paying $4,099 of salary to Julie assuming its marginal tax rate is 35 percent?

**Answer:** $2,702, calculated as follows:

| Description | Amount | Explanation |
|---|---|---|
| (1) Taxable salary paid | $4,099 | |
| (2) Income tax benefit | (1,435) | (1) × 35%. |
| (3) FICA taxes paid | 59 | (1) × 1.45% (over the SS cap). |
| (4) FICA tax benefit | (21) | (3) × 35%. |
| Total after-tax cost of salary | $2,702 | Sum (1) through (4). |

**What if:** Assume that TPI were to provide Julie $2,400 of qualified transportation fringe benefits in the form of parking. What would be its after-tax cost of paying the $2,400 nontaxable fringe benefit to Julie assuming its marginal tax rate is 35 percent?

**Answer:** $1,560, calculated as follows:

| Description | Amount | Explanation |
|---|---|---|
| (1) Nontaxable fringe benefit paid | $2,400 | |
| (2) Income tax benefit | (840) | (1) × 35% |
| Total after-tax cost of nontaxable benefit | $1,560 | (1) + (2). |

Can an employer and an employee work together to implement the conversion tax planning strategy to make both the employee and employer better off by substituting desired nontaxable fringe benefits for taxable salary in the compensation package? The answer is yes!

Example 12-25

**What if:** As shown in Example 12-23, Julie is indifferent between receiving (1) $4,099 in salary ($2,400 after-taxes) or (2) $2,400 in nontaxable parking benefits. Consequently, if TPI paid Julie $2,400 in nontaxable benefits and any amount of additional salary she would be better off than she would be by receiving no parking and $4,099 in salary. As shown in Example 12-24, TPI would be better off after taxes by providing Julie with (1) $2,400 in nontaxable benefits (cost of $1,560) rather than (2) salary of $4,099 (after-tax cost of $2,702). What amount of salary could TPI provide in addition to the $2,400 of nontaxable benefits to make it indifferent between providing the parking and the additional salary or providing salary of $4,099?

**Answer:** $1,732 additional salary for indifference, calculated as follows:

| Description | Amount | Explanation |
|---|---|---|
| (1) After-tax cost of salary | $2,702 | Example 12-24. |
| (2) After-tax cost of fringe benefit | $1,560 | Example 12-24. |
| (3) After-tax cost of additional salary | $1,142 | (1) − (2). |
| (4) After-tax cost percentage | 65.94% | (1 + .0145) × (1 − .35).* |
| Additional before-tax salary | $1,732 | (3)/(4). |

*Where (1 + .0145) is the before-tax salary plus FICA tax and (1 − .35) is the after-tax conversion factor.

To summarize, if TPI pays Julie's parking costs and provides her with additional salary of any amount below $1,732, it will be better off than it would be by not providing the parking and paying her $4,099 in salary. Julie is better off if TPI pays her parking and gives her any additional salary than she is if it doesn't pay her parking but pays her $4,099 of salary.

## Fringe Benefits Summary

Fringe benefits, both taxable and nontaxable, can make up a significant portion of an employee's compensation. Fringe benefits are taxable unless the tax laws specifically exclude them from gross income. Taxable fringe benefits usually represent a luxury perk, while nontaxable fringe benefits are generally excluded for public policy

reasons. At this point, you should be able to distinguish between taxable and nontaxable fringe benefits. Exhibit 12-16 presents an excerpt from Disney Company's proxy statement. Read through the excerpt and see if you can determine which of the benefits Mr. Iger received are taxable and which are nontaxable.

**EXHIBIT 12-16**    **Excerpt from Disney Company's 2009 Proxy Statement Dealing with Fringe Benefits**

**The Walt Disney Company Notice of Annual Meeting and Proxy Statement**
*Benefits and perquisites*

The following table identifies the incremental cost of each perquisite or personal benefit that exceeded the greater of $25,000 or 10% of the total amount of perquisites and personal benefits for a named executive officer in fiscal 2008.

| COMPONENTS OF OTHER ANNUAL COMPENSATION | | | | |
|---|---|---|---|---|
| **Executive** | **Year** | **Personal Air Travel** | **Security** | **Other** | **Total** |
| Robert A. Iger | 2008 | $107,897 | $645,368 | 14,400 | $767,755 |

The incremental cost of the items specified above was determined as follows:

• Personal air travel: the actual catering costs, landing and ramp fees, fuel costs and costs incurred by flight crew plus a per hour charge based on the average hourly maintenance costs for the aircraft during the year for flights that were purely personal in nature, and a pro rata portion of catering costs where personal guests accompanied executives on flights that were business in nature.
• Security: actual costs incurred by the Company for providing security equipment and services.

The column labeled "Other" in the table above includes the incremental cost to the Company of the vehicle benefit and, for those named executive officers who elected to receive it, reimbursement of up to $450 for health club membership or exercise equipment, reimbursement of up to $1,500 for an annual physical exam and reimbursement of expenses for financial consulting.

Executives also are entitled to the other benefits described in the *Compensation Discussion and Analysis* under *"Benefits and Perquisites,"* which either involved no incremental cost to the Company or are offered through programs that are available to substantially all of the Company's salaried employees.

Mr. Iger's taxable benefits include the personal air travel, security, health club membership, annual physical exam, reimbursement for financial consulting, and perhaps part of the group-term life insurance. Mr. Iger's nontaxable benefits include theme park access (a no-additional-cost service), merchandise discounts (qualified employee discount), occasional sporting events (*de minimis* fringe benefit), educational expense reimbursements, health insurance, and group-term life insurance (some of this coverage may be taxable).

Recall the fringe benefits included in Julie's offer letter: health insurance (valued at $18,000), $750,000 of group-term life insurance, and a flexible spending account (no amounts given; assume she elects $1,500). She also received an annual parking benefit of $2,400. Which benefits are taxable and which are nontaxable? Exhibit 12-17 summarizes how each of these benefits is classified for tax purposes, Julie's after-tax benefit, and TPI's after-tax cost.

**EXHIBIT 12-17**   Summary of Julie's Nonsalary Benefits from TPI

| Benefit | Nontaxable Fringe | Taxable Fringe | Employee After-Tax Benefit | Employer After-Tax Cost |
|---|---|---|---|---|
| Auto allowance | | X | $17,565<br>($30,000 − 12,435) | $19,783<br>[($30,000 + 435) ×<br>(1 − .35)] |
| Health and dental insurance | X | | $18,000<br>[$18,000 × (1 − .0)] | $11,700<br>[$18,000 × (1 − .35)] |
| Flexible spending account | X | | $1,500<br>[$1,500 × (1 − .0)] | $975<br>[$1,500 × (1 − .35)] |
| Parking reimbursement | X | | $2,400<br>[$2,400 × (1 − .0)]<br>(Example 12-23) | $1,560<br>($2,400 − $840)<br>(Example 12-24) |
| Group-term life insurance | X | X | $1,687<br>($2,000 − $313)*<br>(Examples 12-17, 18) | $332<br>(Example 12-18) |
| Total | | | $41,152 | $34,348 |

*This is the fair market value of the benefit less the actual taxes payable by Julie.

# CONCLUSION

Individuals and employers routinely make choices involving compensation issues. As they do so, they must understand how alternative forms of compensation are taxed. In this chapter, we have discussed the tax compliance and planning implications associated with common types of payment including salary and wages, equity-based compensation (such as stock options and restricted stock), and taxable and nontaxable fringe benefits from both employee and employer perspectives. Throughout, we have emphasized that both tax and nontax issues must be considered in the broader context of compensation planning. Armed with the information provided in this chapter, future employees and employers can approach the compensation decisions they will undoubtedly face with more confidence and insight.

## SUMMARY

Discuss and explain the tax implications of compensation in the form of salary and wages from the employee's and employer's perspectives.   **L01**

- Employees are taxed on salary at ordinary income rates.
- Employees use Form W-4 to supply their employer with withholding information. Employees can use the W-4 to manage withholding throughout the year because withholding is treated as though it is withheld evenly throughout the year for estimated tax purposes.
- Employees' wages are subject to FICA tax. The Social Security component is 6.2 percent and the Medicare component is 1.45 percent. The Social Security tax applies to the first $106,800 of income in 2010. The wage base on the Medicare tax is unlimited.
- Cash-method employers deduct wages when paid. Accrual-method employers deduct wages when accrued as long as the wages are paid within 2.5 months of year-end. If paid after 2.5 months of year-end, wages are deductible when the employee recognizes the income (when paid). When an employer accrues wages to a related-party employee (more than 50 percent ownership), the wages are not deductible until the employee recognizes the income (when paid).

- Employers are responsible for matching employees' FICA taxes.

- Employers' after-tax cost of wages is the cost of the wages including FICA taxes minus the tax benefit of the deduction for the wages and the FICA taxes.

- For publicly traded corporations, the tax deduction for nonperformance-based compensation paid to the CEO and four other most highly compensated officers is limited to $1,000,000 per year per individual.

**LO2** Describe and distinguish the tax implications of various forms of equity-based compensation from the employee's and employer's perspectives.

- Stock options and restricted stock are common forms of equity-based compensation. Although both reward employees for increases in the stock price of their employers, there are fundamental economic differences between them.

- Stock options are treated as either nonqualified or incentive stock options for tax purposes.

- Employees recognize ordinary income equal to the bargain element on nonqualified options when they are exercised. Employers are able to deduct the bargain element when nonqualified options are exercised. Any appreciation in the value of shares subsequent to the exercise of nonqualified options is treated as capital gain by employees when the shares are sold.

- If certain holding period requirements are met, employees exercising incentive stock options don't recognize any income until the shares received from the exercised options are sold. When the shares are sold, the difference between the exercise price and the share price is long-term capital gain (assuming appreciation). Employers are not permitted a deduction for incentive stock options.

- Generally, employees prefer incentive stock options and employers prefer nonqualified options because of differences in the way the two types of options are taxed.

- Employers treat stock options differently for book and tax purposes.

- Employees recognize ordinary income from restricted stock equal to the fair market value of the stock on the vesting date. Employers receive a corresponding tax deduction.

- Employees may elect to recognize taxable income from restricted stock on the date it is received rather than on the vesting date if they make an §83(b) election. Although this election accelerates the recognition of income, it gives the employee the ability to convert ordinary income from further appreciation into capital gain.

**LO3** Compare and contrast taxable and nontaxable fringe benefits and explain the employee and employer tax consequences associated with fringe benefits.

- Fringe benefits are taxable to the employee unless the Code specifically excludes the benefit from gross income. Taxable fringe benefits are generally luxury perks, such as corporate air travel and security.

- Nontaxable fringe benefits include up to $50,000 of group-term life insurance, health benefits, meals and lodging for the convenience of the employer, educational assistance, dependent care benefits, qualified employee discounts, and qualified transportation benefits (among others).

# KEY TERMS

bargain element (12-12)
cafeteria plan (12-30)
*de minimis* fringe benefit (12-30)
disqualifying disposition (12-15)
educational assistance benefit (12-28)
employee (12-2)
exercise date (12-13)
exercise price (12-11)
facts and circumstances test (12-7)

FICA taxes (12-6)
flexible spending account (FSA) (12-30)
for the convenience of the employer benefits (12-27)
Form W-2 (12-2)
Form W-4 (12-2)
fringe benefits (12-22)
grant date (12-13)

group-term life insurance (12-23)
health and accident insurance (12-27)
incentive stock option (12-13)
Medicare tax (12-5)
no-additional-cost services (12-28)
nonqualified stock option (12-13)
nontaxable fringe benefit (12-26)
option exercise (12-11)
qualified employee discount (12-29)

qualified moving expense
reimbursement (12-30)

qualified transportation fringe
benefit (12-30)

restricted stock (12-17)

salary (12-2)

same-day sale (12-14)

§83(b) election (12-19)

Social Security tax (12-5)

strike price (12-11)

taxable fringe benefit (12-22)

vest (12-11)

wages (12-2)

working condition fringe
benefit (12-30)

## DISCUSSION QUESTIONS

1. **(LO1)** Shane is an employee who has had a relatively consistent income over the years. His withholding is pretty much right on target with his actual tax liability, so he rarely has much of a tax refund or tax due with his tax return. At the beginning of this year, Shane sold some property at a large gain. What issues relating to withholding should Shane consider? What would you advise him to do?

   ■ **planning**

2. **(LO1)** Juanita recently started employment for Maple Corporation. For tax purposes, Juanita files as a head-of-household with three dependents. Juanita needs to determine the number of "withholding exemptions" to claim on her W-4 form. Should she claim four withholding exemptions or should she claim more? What factors should she consider in making this determination?

   ■ **planning**

3. **(LO1)** Are taxpayers' entire wages subject to the FICA tax? Explain.

4. **(LO1)** Nicole and Braxton are each 50 percent shareholders of NB Corporation. Nicole is also an employee of the corporation. NB is a calendar-year taxpayer and uses the accrual method of accounting. The corporation pays its employees monthly on the first day of the month after the salary is earned by the employees. What issues must NB consider with respect to the deductibility of the wages it pays to Nicole if Nicole is Braxton's sister? What issues arise if Nicole and Braxton are unrelated?

5. **(LO1)** Holding all else equal, does an employer with a higher marginal tax rate or lower marginal tax rate have a lower after-tax cost of paying a particular employee's salary? Explain.

6. **(LO1)** What are nontax reasons for why a corporation may choose to cap its executives' salaries at $1 million?

7. **(LO1)** What are tax reasons why a corporation may choose to cap its executives' salaries at $1 million?

8. **(LO1)** Lea is a highly paid executive with MCC, Inc., a publicly traded corporation. What are the circumstances under which MCC will be able to deduct more than $1 million of compensation paid to Lea during the year?

9. **(LO2)** From an *employee* perspective, how are incentive stock options treated differently than nonqualified stock options for tax purposes? In general, for a given number of options, which type of stock option should employees prefer?

10. **(LO2)** From an *employer* perspective, how are incentive stock options treated differently than nonqualified stock options for tax purposes? In general, for a given number of options, which type of stock option should employers prefer?

11. **(LO2)** Why do employers use stock options in addition to salary to compensate their employees? For employers, are stock options treated more favorably than salary for tax purposes? Explain.

12. **(LO2)** What is a "disqualifying disposition" of incentive stock options, and how does it affect employees who have exercised incentive stock options?

13. **(LO2)** Compare and contrast how employers record book and tax expense for stock options.

14. **(LO2)** How is the tax treatment of restricted stock different from that of nonqualified options? How is it similar?

15. **(LO2)** Matt just started work with Boom Zoom, Inc., a manufacturer of credit card size devices for storing and playing back music. Due to the popularity of its devices, analysts expect Boom Zoom's stock price to increase dramatically. In addition to his salary, Matt received Boom Zoom restricted stock. How will Matt's restricted stock be treated for tax purposes? Should Matt consider making the §83(b) election? What are the factors he should consider in making this decision? From a tax perspective, would this election help or hurt Boom Zoom?

16. **(LO2)** What risks do employees making a §83(b) election on a restricted stock grant assume?

17. **(LO3)** Explain the differences and similarities between fringe benefits and salary as forms of compensation.

18. **(LO3)** When an employer provides group-term life insurance for an employee, what are the tax consequences to the employee? What are the tax consequences for the employer?

19. **(LO3)** Compare and contrast the employer's tax consequences of providing taxable versus nontaxable fringe benefits.

20. **(LO3)** Mike is working his way through college and trying to make ends meet. Tara, a friend, is graduating soon and tells Mike about a really great job opportunity. She is the onsite manager for an apartment complex catering to students. The job entails working in the office for about 10 hours a week, collecting rent each month, and answering after-hours emergency calls. The pay is $10 per hour, plus a rent-free apartment (worth about $500 per month). Tara then tells him the best part: the rent-free apartment is tax-free. Knowing that you are a tax student, Mike asks you if the rent-free apartment is really tax-free or if Tara is mistaken. Explain to Mike whether the compensation for the apartment is really a nontaxable fringe benefit.

21. **(LO3)** Assume that your friend has accepted a position working as an accountant for a large automaker. As a signing bonus, the employer provides the traditional cash incentive but also provides the employee with a vehicle not to exceed a retail price of $25,000. Explain to your friend whether the value of the vehicle is included, excluded, or partially included in the employee's gross income.

22. **(LO3)** Explain why an employee might accept a lower salary to receive a nontaxable fringe benefit. Why might an employee not accept a lower salary to receive a nontaxable fringe benefit?

23. **(LO3)** Describe a cafeteria plan and discuss why an employer would provide a cafeteria plan for its employees.

24. **(LO3)** Explain why Congress allows employees to receive certain fringe benefits tax-free but others are taxable?

25. **(LO3)** Explain the policy reason for including the value of country club memberships provided to an executive as a taxable fringe benefit.

26. **(LO3)** Describe the circumstances in which an employee may not value a nontaxable fringe benefit.

## PROBLEMS

research

27. **(LO1)** Anna is single with one four-year-old child. She earns a monthly salary in 2010 of $5,000. Her filing status is head of household.

   a. If she claims two withholding allowances, how much will her employer withhold from her monthly paycheck? (*Hint:* Go to www.irs.gov and search for withholding tables.)

   b. If she claims four withholding allowances, how much will her employer withhold from her monthly paycheck?

c. Assuming that she has no other income, claims the standard deduction, and claims one personal and one dependency deduction, what is Anna's tax liability for the year? How many withholding allowances should she claim to equalize (approximately) her withholding and her tax liability?

28. **(LO1)** Baker works for Company ATT for all of 2010. What is his FICA obligation under the following circumstances:

a. Baker is single and earns a salary of $50,000.

b. Baker is single and earns a salary of $110,000.

c. Baker is married and earns a salary of $50,000. His spouse earns $25,000 per year.

d. Baker is married and earns a salary of $50,000. His spouse earns $65,000 per year.

29. **(LO1)** Rasheed works for AD Company and earns $350,000 in salary during 2010. Assuming he has no other sources of income, what amount of Social Security taxes and what amount of Medicare taxes will Rasheed pay for the year?

30. **(LO1)** North Inc. is a calendar-year, accrual-basis taxpayer. At the end of year 1, North accrued and deducted the following bonuses for certain employees for financial accounting purposes.

- $7,500 for Lisa Tanaka, a 30 percent shareholder.
- $10,000 for Jared Zabaski, a 35 percent shareholder.
- $12,500 for Helen Talanian, a 20 percent shareholder.
- $5,000 for Steve Nielson, a 0 percent shareholder.

Unless stated otherwise, assume these shareholders are unrelated.

How much of the accrued bonuses can North Inc. deduct in year 1 under the following alternative scenarios?

a. North paid the bonuses to the employees on March 1 of year 2.

b. North paid the bonuses to the employees on April 1 of year 2.

c. North paid the bonuses to employees on March 1 of year 2 and Lisa and Jared are related to each other, so they are treated as owning each other's stock in North.

d. North paid the bonuses to employees on March 1 of year 2 and Lisa and Helen are related to each other, so they are treated as owning each other's stock in North.

31. **(LO1)** Lynette is the CEO of publicly traded TTT Corporation and earns a salary of $200,000 in 2010. Assume TTT has a 35 percent marginal tax rate.

a. What is TTT Corporation's after-tax cost of paying Lynette's salary excluding FICA taxes?

b. What is TTT Corporation's after-tax cost of paying Lynette's salary including FICA taxes?

32. **(LO1)** Marcus is the CEO of publicly traded ABC Corporation and earns a salary of $1,500,000. Assume ABC has a 35 percent marginal tax rate.

a. What is ABC's after-tax cost of paying Marcus's salary (excluding FICA taxes)?

b. Now assume that Marcus, in addition to the $1.5 million salary, earns a performance-based bonus of $500,000. What is ABC's after-tax cost of paying Marcus's salary (excluding FICA taxes)?

33. **(LO1)** Ramon has finally arrived. He has interviewed for the CEO position with MMM Corporation. They have presented him with two alternative compensation offers. Alternative 1 is for a straight salary of $2,500,000. Option 2 is

■ **planning**

for a salary of $1,000,000 and performance-based compensation of up to $2,000,000. Assume that Ramon has a marginal tax rate of 40 percent, MMM has a marginal tax rate of 35 percent, and ignore FICA taxes for this problem. Answer the questions under each of the following alternative scenarios.

a. If Ramon is 100 percent certain he can meet the qualifications for the full performance-based compensation, which offer should he choose?

b. If Ramon believes there is only a 20 percent chance that he can meet the performance-based requirements, which offer should he choose (assume he is risk neutral)?

c. What is MMM's after-tax cost of providing Ramon with Option 1?

d. What is MMM's expected after-tax cost of providing Ramon with Option 2 if it believes there is a 40 percent chance Ramon will qualify for the performance-based compensation?

34. **(LO2)** Cammie received 100 NQOs (each option provides a right to purchase 10 shares of MNL stock for $10 per share) at the time she started working for MNL Corporation four years ago when MNL's stock price was $8 per share. Now that MNL's stock price is $40 per share, she intends to exercise all of her options. After acquiring the 1,000 MNL shares with her options, she held the shares for over one year and sold them at $60 per share.

a. What are Cammie's tax consequences on the grant date, the exercise date, and the date she sold the shares, assuming her ordinary marginal rate is 30 percent and her long-term capital gains rate is 15 percent?

b. What are MNL Corporation's tax consequences on grant date, exercise date, and date of sale assuming its marginal tax rate is 35 percent?

■ planning

35. **(LO2)** Yost received 300 NQOs (each option gives Yost the right to purchase 10 shares of Cutter Corporation stock for $15 per share) at the time he started working for Cutter Corporation three years ago. Cutter's stock price was $15 per share. Yost exercises all of his options when the share price is $26 per share. Two years after acquiring the shares, he sold them at $47 per share.

a. What are Yost's tax consequences (amount of income/gain recognized and amount of taxes payable) on the grant date, the exercise date, and the date he sells the shares, assuming his ordinary marginal rate is 35 percent and his long-term capital gains rate is 15 percent?

b. What are Cutter Corporation's tax consequences (amount of deduction and tax savings from deduction) on the grant date, the exercise date, and the date Yost sells the shares assuming its marginal tax rate is 25 percent?

c. Assume that Yost is cash poor and needs to perform a same-day sale in order to buy his shares. Due to his belief that the stock price is going to increase significantly, he wants to maintain as many shares as possible. How many shares must he sell in order to cover his purchase price and taxes payable on the exercise?

d. Assume that Yost's options were exercisable at $20 and expired after five years. If the stock only reached $18 dollars during its high point during the five-year period, what are Yost's tax consequences on the grant date, the exercise date, and the date the shares are sold, assuming his ordinary marginal rate is 35 percent and his long-term capital gains rate is 15 percent?

36. **(LO2)** Haven received 200 NQOs (each option gives him the right to purchase 20 shares of Barlow Corporation stock for $7 per share) at the time he started working for Barlow Corporation three years ago when its stock price was $7 per share. Now that Barlow's share price is $50 per share, he intends to exercise all of his options. After acquiring the 4,000 Barlow shares with his options, he

intends to hold the shares for more than one year and then sell the shares when the price reaches $75 per share.

   a. What are the cash flow effects of these transactions to Haven assuming his ordinary marginal rate is 30 percent and his long-term capital gains rate is 15 percent?

   b. What are the cash flow effects for Barlow Corporation resulting from Haven's option exercise if Barlow's marginal tax rate is 35 percent?

37. **(LO2)** Mark received 10 ISOs (each option gives him the right to purchase 10 shares of Hendricks Corporation stock for $5 per share) at the time he started working for Hendricks Corporation five years ago when Hendricks's stock price was $5 per share. Now that Hendricks's share price is $35 per share, he intends to exercise all options and hold all of his shares for more than year. Assume that more than a year after exercise, Mark sells the stock for $35 a share.

   a. What are Mark's tax consequences on the grant date, the exercise date, and the date he sells the shares, assuming his ordinary marginal rate is 30 percent and his long-term capital gains rate is 15 percent?

   b. What are Hendricks's tax consequences on the grant date, the exercise date, and the date Mark sells the shares assuming its marginal tax rate is 25 percent?

38. **(LO2)** Antonio received 40 ISOs (each option gives him the right to purchase 20 shares of Zorro stock for $3 per share) at the time he started working for Zorro Corporation six years ago. Zorro's stock price was $3 per share at the time. Now that Zorro's stock price is $50 per share, he intends to exercise all of his options and immediately sell all the shares he receives from the options exercise.

   a. What are Antonio's tax consequences on the grant date, the exercise date, and the date the shares are sold, assuming his ordinary marginal rate is 30 percent and his long-term capital gains rate is 15 percent?

   b. What are Zorro's tax consequences on the grant date, the exercise date, and the date Antonio sells the shares assuming its marginal tax rate is 25 percent?

   c. What are the cash flow effects of these transactions to Antonio, assuming his ordinary marginal rate is 25 percent and his long-term capital gains rate is 15 percent?

   d. What are the cash flow effects to Zorro Corporation resulting from Antonio's option exercise if Zorro's marginal tax rate is 35 percent?

39. **(LO2)** Harmer Inc. is now a successful company. In the early days (before it became profitable), it issued incentive stock options (ISOs) to its employees. Now Harmer is trying to decide whether to issue nonqualified options (NQOs) or ISOs to its employees. Initially, Harmer would like to give each employee 20 options (each option allows the employee to acquire one share of Harmer stock). For purposes of this problem, assume that the options are exercised in three years (*three years from now*) and that the underlying stock is sold in five years (*five years from now*). Also assume the following facts:

**planning**

   • The after-tax discount rate for both Harmer Inc. and its employees is 10 percent.
   • Corporate tax rate is 35 percent.
   • Personal (employee) ordinary income rate is 40 percent.
   • Personal (employee) long-term capital gains rate is 15 percent.
   • Exercise price of the options is $7.
   • Market price of Harmer at date of grant is $5.
   • Market price of Harmer at date of exercise is $25.
   • Market price of Harmer at date of sale is $35.

Answer the following questions (disregard FICA taxes in your analysis):

a. Considering these facts, which type of option plan, nonqualified (NQO) or incentive (ISO), should Harmer Inc. prefer? Explain.

b. Assuming Harmer issues NQOs, what is Harmer's tax benefit from the options for each employee in the year each employee exercises the NQOs?

c. Assuming Harmer issues ISOs, what is the tax benefit to Harmer in the year the ISOs are exercised?

d. Which type of option plan should Harmer's employees prefer?

e. What is the present value of each employee's after-tax cash flows from year 1 through year 5 if the employees receive ISOs?

f. What is the present value of each employee's after-tax cash flows from year 1 through year 5 if the employees receive NQOs?

g. How many NQOs would Harmer have to grant to keep its employees indifferent between NQOs and 20 ISOs?

40. **(LO2)** On January 1, year 1, Dave received 1,000 shares of restricted stock from his employer, RRK Corporation. On that date, the stock price was $7 per share. Dave's restricted shares will vest at the end of year 2. He intends to hold the shares until the end of year 4 when he intends to sell them to help fund the purchase of a new home. Dave predicts the share price of RRK will be $30 per share when his shares vest and will be $40 per share when he sells them.

a. If Dave's stock price predictions are correct, what are the tax consequences of these transactions to Dave if his ordinary marginal rate is 30 percent and his long-term capital gains rate is 15 percent?

b. If Dave's stock price predictions are correct, what are the tax consequences of these transactions to RRK if its marginal rate is 35 percent?

41. **(LO2)** On January 1, year 1, Dave received 1,000 shares of restricted stock from his employer, RRK Corporation. On that date, the stock price was $7 per share. On receiving the restricted stock, Dave made the §83(b) election. Dave's restricted shares will vest at the end of year 2. He intends to hold the shares until the end of year 4 when he intends to sell them to help fund the purchase of a new home. Dave predicts the share price of RRK will be $30 per share when his shares vest and will be $40 per share when he sells them. Assume that Dave's price predictions are correct and answer the following questions:

a. What are the tax consequences of these transactions to Dave if his ordinary marginal rate is 30 percent and his long-term capital gains rate is 15 percent?

b. What are the tax consequences of these transactions to RRK if its marginal rate is 35 percent?

42. **(LO2)** On January 1, year 1, Jessica received 10,000 shares of restricted stock from her employer, Rocket Corporation. On that date, the stock price was $10 per share. On receiving the restricted stock, Jessica made the §83(b) election. Jessica's restricted shares will all vest at the end of year 4. After the shares vest, she intends to sell them immediately to fund an around-the-world cruise. Unfortunately, Jessica decided that she couldn't wait four years and she quit her job to start her cruise on January 1, year 3.

a. What are the year 1 tax consequences of these transactions to Jessica, assuming her marginal tax rate is 33 percent and her long-term capital gains rate is 15 percent?

b. What are the year 3 tax consequences of these transactions to Jessica, assuming her marginal tax rate is 33 percent and her long-term capital gains rate is 15 percent?

43. **(LO2)** On May 1, year 1, Anna received 5,000 shares of restricted stock from her employer, Jarbal Corporation. On that date, the stock price was $5 per share. On receiving the restricted stock, Anna made the §83(b) election. Anna's restricted shares will all vest on May 1, year 3. After the shares vest, she intends to sell them immediately to purchase a condo. True to her plan, Anna sold the shares immediately after they were vested.

   a. What are the tax consequences of these transactions to Anna in year 1?
   b. What are the tax consequences of these transactions to Anna in year 3 if the stock is valued at $1 per share on the day the shares vest?
   c. What are the tax consequences of these transactions to Anna in year 3 if the stock is valued at $9 per share on the day the shares vest?
   d. What are the tax consequences of these transactions to Anna in year 3 if the stock is valued at $5 per share on the day the shares vest?

44. **(LO2)** On January 1, year 1, Tyra started working for Hatch Corporation. New employees must choose immediately between receiving seven NQOs (each NQO provides the right to purchase for $5 per share 10 shares of Hatch stock) or 50 restricted shares. Hatch's stock price is $5 on Tyra's start date. Either form of equity-based compensation will vest in two years. Tyra believes that the stock will be worth $15 per share in two years and $25 in four years when she will sell the stock. Tyra's marginal tax rate is 30 percent and her long-term capital gains rate is 15 percent. Assume that Tyra's price predictions are correct, answer the following questions (ignore present value, use nominal dollars):

   ■ **planning**

   a. What are the cash-flow effects to Tyra in the year she receives the options, the year the options vest and she exercises the options, and in the year she sells the stock if she chooses the NQOs?
   b. What are the cash-flow effects to Tyra in the year she receives the restricted stock, in the year the stock vests, and in the year she sells the stock if Tyra chooses the restricted stock?
   c. What are the cash-flow effects to Tyra in the year she receives the restricted stock, the year the stock vests, and the year she sells the stock if she makes a §83(b) election?
   d. What recommendation would you give Tyra? Explain.

45. **(LO3)** Nicole's employer, Poe Corporation, provides her with an automobile allowance of $20,000 every other year. Her marginal tax rate is 30 percent. Poe Corporation has a marginal tax rate of 35 percent. Answer the following questions relating to this fringe benefit.

   a. What is Nicole's after-tax benefit if she receives the allowance this year (ignore FICA taxes)?
   b. What is Poe's after-tax cost of providing the auto allowance (ignore FICA taxes)?
   c. What is Nicole's after-tax benefit if she receives the allowance this year, and her salary is below the Social Security wage base limit (include FICA taxes in your analysis)?
   d. What is Poe's after-tax cost of providing the auto allowance, and Nicole's salary is under the Social Security wage base limit (include FICA taxes in your analysis)?
   e. What is Nicole's after-tax benefit if she receives the allowance this year, and her salary is over the Social Security wage base (include FICA taxes in your analysis)?
   f. What is Poe's after-tax cost of providing the auto allowance if Nicole's salary is over the Social Security wage base (include FICA taxes in your analysis)?

**research**

46. **(LO3)** Bills Corporation runs a defense contracting business that requires security clearance. To prevent unauthorized access to its materials, Bills requires its security personnel to be on duty except for a 15-minute break every two hours. Since the nearest restaurants are a 25-minute round trip, Bills provides free lunches to its security personnel. Bills has never included the value of these meals in its employees' compensation. Bills is currently under audit, and the IRS agent wants to deny Bills a deduction for past meals. The agent also wants Bills to begin including the value of the meals in employee compensation starting with the current year. As Bills' tax advisor, give it a recommendation on whether to appeal the agent's decision (*Hint:* see *Boyd Gaming Corp.,* CA-9, 99-1 USTC ¶50,530 (Acq.), 177 F3d 1096).

**planning**

47. **(LO3)** Lars Osberg, a single taxpayer with a 35 percent marginal tax rate, desires health insurance. The health insurance would cost Lars $8,500 to purchase if he pays for it himself (Lars's AGI is too high to receive any tax deduction for the insurance as a medical expense). Volvo, Lars's employer, has a 40 percent marginal tax rate. Answer the following questions about this benefit (ignore FICA taxes in your analysis).

    a. What is the maximum amount of before-tax salary Lars would give up to receive health insurance from Volvo?

    b. What would be the after-tax cost to Volvo to provide Lars with health insurance if it could purchase the insurance through its group plan for $5,000?

    c. Assume that Volvo could purchase the insurance for $5,000. Lars is interested in getting health insurance and he is willing to receive a lower salary in exchange for the health insurance. What is the least amount by which Volvo would be willing to reduce Lars's salary while agreeing to pay his health insurance?

    d. Will Volvo and Lars be able to reach an agreement by which Volvo will provide Lars with health insurance?

**planning**

48. **(LO3)** Seiko's current salary is $85,000. Her marginal tax rate is 30 percent and she fancies European sports cars. She purchases a new auto each year. Seiko is currently a manager for an office equipment company. Her friend, knowing of her interest in sports cars, tells her about a manager position at the local BMW and Porsche dealer. The new position pays only $75,000 per year, but it allows employees to purchase one new car per year at a discount of $15,000. This discount qualifies as a nontaxable fringe benefit. In an effort to keep Seiko as an employee, her current employer offers her a $10,000 raise. Answer the following questions about this analysis (ignore FICA taxes in your analyses).

    a. What is the annual after-tax cost to her current employer (office equipment company that has a 35 percent marginal tax rate) to provide Seiko with the $10,000 increase in salary?

    b. Financially, which offer is better for Seiko on an after-tax basis and by how much? (Assume that Seiko is going to purchase the new car whether she switches jobs or not.)

    c. What salary would Seiko need to receive from her current employer to make her financially indifferent (after taxes) between receiving additional salary from her current employer and accepting a position at the auto dealership?

49. **(LO1, LO3)** JDD Corporation provides the following benefits to its employee, Ahmed (age 47):

| | |
|---|---|
| Salary | $300,000 |
| Health insurance | $ 10,000 |
| Dental insurance | $ 2,000 |
| Life insurance | $ 3,000 |
| Dependent care | $ 5,000 |
| Professional dues | $ 500 |
| Personal use of company jet | $200,000 |

Assume the life insurance is a group-term life insurance policy that provides $200,000 of coverage for Ahmed.

a. Assuming Ahmed is subject to a marginal tax rate of 30 percent, what is his after-tax benefit of receiving each of these benefits (ignoring FICA taxes)?

b. Assuming Ahmed is subject to a marginal tax rate of 30 percent, what is his after-tax benefit of receiving each of these benefits (including FICA taxes)?

c. Assuming JDD Corp.'s marginal tax rate is 35 percent, what is its after-tax cost of providing these benefits to Ahmed ignoring FICA taxes (assume the before-tax cost of each benefit is equal to the values stated in the problem)?

d. Assuming JDD Corp.'s marginal tax rate is 35 percent, what is its after-tax cost of providing these benefits to Ahmed including FICA taxes (assume the before-tax cost of each benefit is equal to the values stated in the problem)?

50. **(LO3)** Gray's employer is now offering group-term life insurance. The company will provide each employee with $100,000 of group-term life insurance. It costs Gray's employer $300 to provide this amount of insurance to Gray each year. Assuming that Gray is 52 years old, determine the monthly premium that Gray must include in gross income as a result of receiving the group-term life benefit?

51. **(LO3)** Brady graduated from SUNY New Paltz with his bachelor's degree recently. He works for Makarov & Company CPAs. The firm pays his tuition ($10,000 per year) for him so that he can receive his Master of Science in Taxation, which will qualify him to sit for the CPA exam. How much of the $10,000 tuition benefit does Brady need to include in gross income?

52. **(LO3)** Meg works for Freedom Airlines in the accounts payable department. Meg and all other employees receive free flight benefits (for the employee, family, and 10 free buddy passes for friends per year) as part of its employee benefits package. If Meg uses 30 flights with a value of $12,350 this year, how much must she include in her compensation this year?

53. **(LO3)** Sharmilla works for Shasta Lumber, a local lumber supplier. The company annually provides each employee with a Shasta Lumber shirt so that employees look branded and advertise for the business while wearing the shirts. Are Shasta's employees required to include the value of the shirts in income?

54. **(LO3)** LaMont works for a company in downtown Chicago. The firm encourages employees to use public transportation (to save the environment) by providing them with transit passes at a cost of $250 per month.

a. If LaMont receives one pass (worth $250) each month, how much of this benefit must he include in his gross income each year?

b. If the company provides each employee with $250 per month in parking benefits, how much of the parking benefit must LaMont include in his gross income each year?

55. **(LO3)** Jasmine works in Washington, D.C. She accepts a new position with her current firm in Los Angeles. Her employer provides the following moving benefits:

- Temporary housing for one month—$3,000.
- Transportation for her household goods—$4,500.
- Flight and hotel for a house-hunting trip—$1,750.
- Flights to Los Angeles for her and her family—$2,000.

What amount of these benefits must Jasmine include in her gross income?

56. **(LO3)** Jarvie loves to bike. In fact, he has always turned down better paying jobs to work in bicycle shops where he gets an employee discount. At Jarvie's current shop, Bad Dog Cycles, each employee is allowed to purchase four bicycles a year at a discount. Because road bikes have higher profit margins, employees receive a

30 percent discount. Employees also normally receive a 20 percent discount on mountain bikes. During the current year, Jarvie bought the following bikes:

| Description | Retail Price | Cost | Employee Price |
| --- | --- | --- | --- |
| Specialized road bike | $3,200 | $2,000 | $2,240 |
| Rocky Mountain mountain bike | $3,800 | $3,200 | $3,040 |
| Trek road bike | $2,700 | $2,000 | $1,890 |
| Yeti mountain bike | $3,500 | $2,500 | $2,800 |

a. What amount is Jarvie required to include in taxable income from these purchases?

b. What amount of deductions is Bad Dog allowed to claim from these transactions?

57. **(LO1, LO3)** Matt works for Fresh Corporation. Fresh offers a cafeteria plan that allows each employee to receive $15,000 worth of benefits each year. The menu of benefits is as follows:

| Benefit | Cost |
| --- | --- |
| Health insurance–single | $ 5,000 |
| Health insurance–with spouse | $ 8,000 |
| Health insurance–with spouse and dependents | $11,000 |
| Dental and vision | $ 1,500 |
| Dependent care–any specified amount up to $5,000 | Variable |
| Adoption benefits–any specified amount up to $5,000 | Variable |
| Educational benefits–any specified amount (no limit) | Variable |
| Cash–any specified amount up to $15,000 plan benefit | Variable |
| 401(k)–any specified amount up to $10,000 | Variable |

For each of the following independent circumstances, determine the amount of income Matt must recognize and the amount of deduction Fresh may claim (ignore FICA taxes):

a. Matt selects the single health insurance and places $10,000 in his 401(k).

b. Matt selects the single health insurance, is reimbursed $5,000 for MBA tuition, and takes the remainder in cash.

c. Matt selects the single health insurance and is reimbursed for MBA tuition of $10,000.

d. Matt gets married and selects the health insurance with his spouse and takes the rest in cash to help pay for the wedding.

e. Matt elects to take all cash.

## COMPREHENSIVE PROBLEMS

■ planning

58. Pratt is ready to graduate and leave College Park. His future employer (Ferndale Corp.) offers the following four compensation packages from which Pratt may choose. Pratt will start working for Ferndale on January 1, year 1.

| Benefit Description | Option 1 | Option 2 | Option 3 | Option 4 |
| --- | --- | --- | --- | --- |
| Salary | $60,000 | $50,000 | $45,000 | $45,000 |
| Health insurance | $ 0 | $ 5,000 | $ 5,000 | $ 5,000 |
| Restricted stock | $ 0 | $ 0 | $ 5,000 | $ 0 |
| NQOs | $ 0 | $ 0 | $ 0 | $ 5,000 |

Assume that the restricted stock is 1,000 shares that trade at $5 per share on the grant date (January 1, year 1) and are expected to be worth $10 per share on the vesting date at the end of year 1. Assume that the NQOs (100 options that each allow the employee to purchase 20 shares at $5 strike price). The stock trades at $5 per share on the grant date (January 1, year 1) and is expected to be worth $10 per share on the vesting date at the end of year 1. Also assume that Pratt spends on average $3,000 on health-related costs that would be covered by insurance if he has coverage. Assume that Pratt's marginal tax rate is 35 percent.

a. What is the after-tax value of each compensation package?

b. If Pratt's sole consideration is maximizing after-tax compensation, which scheme should he select?

59. Santini's new contract for 2010 indicates the following compensation and benefits:

| Benefit Description | Amount |
|---|---|
| Salary | $130,000 |
| Health insurance | $ 9,000 |
| Restricted stock grant | $ 2,500 |
| Bonus | $ 5,000 |
| Hawaii trip | $ 4,000 |
| Group-term life insurance | $ 1,600 |
| Parking ($265 per month) | $ 3,180 |

Santini is 54 years old at the end of 2010. He is single and has no dependents. Assume that the employer matches $1 for $1 for the first $6,000 that the employee contributes to his 401(k) during the year. The 100 ISOs each allow the purchase of 10 shares of stock at a strike price of $5 (also the market price on the date of grant). The ISOs vest in two years when the stock price is expected to be $15 and Santini expects to sell the shares in three years when the market price is $20. The restricted stock grant is 500 shares granted when the market price was $5 per share. Assume that the stock vests on December 31, 2010, and that the market price on that date is $7.50 per share. Also assume that Santini is willing to make any elections to reduce equity-based compensation taxes. The Hawaii trip was given to him as the outstanding sales person for 2009. The group-term life policy gives him $150,000 of coverage. Assume that Santini does not itemize deductions for the year. Determine Santini's taxable income, income tax liability, and FICA tax liability for 2010.

60. Sylvana is given a job offer with two alternative compensation packages to choose from. The first package offers her $250,000 annual salary with no qualified fringe benefits. The second package offers $235,000 annual salary plus health and life insurance benefits. If Sylvana were required to purchase the health and life insurance benefits herself, she would need to pay $10,000 annually after taxes. Assume her marginal tax rate is 33 percent (Ignore FICA taxes in your analysis.)

■ planning

a. Which compensation package should she choose and by how much would she benefit in after-tax dollars by choosing this package?

b. Assume the second package offers $240,000 plus the benefits instead of $235,000 plus benefits. Which compensation package should she choose and by how much would she benefit in after-tax dollars by choosing this package?

## chapter

# 13

# Retirement Savings and Deferred Compensation

## Learning Objectives

**Upon completing this chapter, you should be able to:**

**LO 1** Describe the tax and nontax aspects of employer-provided defined benefit plans from both the employer's and employee's perspective.

---

**LO 2** Explain and determine the tax consequences associated with employer-provided defined contribution plans, including traditional 401(k) and Roth 401(k) plans.

---

**LO 3** Describe the tax implications of deferred compensation from both the employer's and employee's perspective.

---

**LO 4** Determine the tax consequences of traditional and Roth Individual Retirement Accounts and explain the differences between them.

---

**LO 5** Describe retirement savings options available to self-employed taxpayers and compute the limitations for deductible contributions to retirement accounts for self-employed taxpayers.

---

**LO 6** Compute the saver's credit.

| Storyline Summary | |
|---|---|
| *Taxpayer:* | Tina Hillman |
| *Location:* | Chicago, Illinois |
| *Employment status:* | Graduating student about to begin career in the tax department of Corporate Business Associates |
| *Starting salary:* | $60,000 per year |
| *Filing status:* | Single |
| *Dependents:* | None |
| *Marginal tax rate:* | Current year 15 percent, next year 25 percent |
| *Taxpayer:* | Lisa Whitlark |
| *Location:* | Chicago, Illinois |
| *Employment status:* | Recently promoted to chief financial officer (CFO) for Corporate Business Associates |
| *Salary:* | $400,000 |
| *Filing status:* | Married, filing jointly |
| *Marginal tax rate:* | 33 percent |
| *Dependents:* | Spouse and three children |
| *Taxpayer:* | Dave Allan |
| *Location:* | Chicago, Illinois |
| *Employment status:* | Recently retired as CFO for Corporate Business Associates after 20 years of employment with the company |
| *Salary at retirement:* | $450,000 |
| *Retirement benefits:* | Participant in Corporate Business Associates' defined benefit plan, 401(k) plan, and nonqualified deferred compensation plan |
| *Filing status:* | Married filing jointly |
| *Dependents:* | Spouse |
| *Marginal tax rate:* | 35 percent for current year |
| *Taxpayer:* | Corporate Business Associates (CBA) |
| *Location:* | Chicago, Illinois |
| *Marginal tax rate:* | 35 percent |
| *Status:* | Publicly traded corporation |

## Tina Hillman

Tina Hillman had just completed her last exam, finally fulfilling the requirements for a bachelor's degree in accounting. It was the end of June and she would finally have some time to vacation and see her family before September when she will start her professional career working in the tax department of Corporate Business Associates (CBA). While Tina was looking forward to the time off, she was also anxious to start making money instead of just spending it. She had a great experience during her internship at CBA last year. She had some challenging but enjoyable work assignments and she got along very well with the staff. Overall, she was excited about the work opportunities she would get at CBA.

Tina recently received an information packet on the benefits available to her as a CBA employee. The information indicated that Tina would be

eligible to participate in CBA's 401(k) plan on January 1 of next year. Tina plans on contributing to the plan as soon as she is eligible because CBA matches employee contributions to the plan such that for every dollar contributed by the employee (up to 4 percent of the employee's salary) CBA contributes two dollars. In the meantime, Tina wonders if she has any retirement savings options during the current year while waiting to participate in CBA's plan.

**Lisa Whitlark**

Lisa Whitlark was finally getting used to her new responsibilities. She was recently promoted to the position of chief financial officer (CFO) for CBA. Lisa threw her name into the ring a few months ago when CBA announced that Dave Allan, the former CFO, would be retiring. Lisa had been working as CBA's tax director for the last 10 years. As a top executive of the company, Lisa was now eligible to participate in CBA's nonqualified deferred compensation program. She didn't have this option as a tax director. Lisa knew she should consider both tax and nontax factors when deciding whether and to what extent she will participate in the plan.

**Dave Allan**

Dave Allan couldn't believe that he was actually retiring at the end of this year. Looking back, his successful career had passed so quickly. At age 72, he was now ready to move on and spend time seeing the world with his wife. Dave's retirement plans were going to be quite expensive. Fortunately, he had accumulated substantial retirement benefits during his CBA career. Dave would be receiving retirement benefits from CBA's defined benefit plan, 401(k) plan, and nonqualified deferred compensation plan. He knew he had some choices about the timing and amounts of his distributions from these plans. Dave wanted to be sure to evaluate both the tax and nontax considerations before making these decisions. ■

At different stages in their careers, taxpayers are likely to face issues similar to those confronting Tina, Lisa, and Dave. Saving for retirement is not always easy to do because it requires forgoing cash now in order to receive benefits at some point in the future. However, not saving for retirement can be a costly mistake because it's not likely that government-promised Social Security benefits alone will satisfy most taxpayers' retirement needs.[1] Many employers help employees save for retirement by sponsoring retirement plans on behalf of their employees. These plans may be "qualified" retirement plans or "nonqualified" deferred compensation plans. Qualified plans are subject to certain restrictions not applicable to nonqualified plans. Both qualified and nonqualified plans are useful tools through which employers can achieve various compensation-related goals. In this chapter, we discuss the tax and

[1]In its 2009 annual report, the Board of Trustees for the Social Security Trust Fund reported that under our current system, costs will begin to exceed tax income in 2016 and the fund will be exhausted and unable to pay promised benefits beginning in 2037. See www.ssa.gov/OACT/TR/2009/II_project.html#105057.

nontax consequences of qualified retirement plans and nonqualified plans to both employers and to employees, including issues relating to contributions to and distributions from these plans. We also discuss individually managed retirement savings plans available to certain individual taxpayers and qualified retirement plans available to self-employed taxpayers.

## EMPLOYER-PROVIDED QUALIFIED PLANS

Traditional **qualified retirement plans** grew from a Congressional concern that, if unregulated, employers might not adequately fund and protect employee pension benefits and that they might be tempted to provide lavish retirement plans to highly compensated employees such as executives and business owners to the detriment of rank-and-file employees. To address these concerns, Congress mandated that employer-provided plans only receive tax-favored qualified plan status if they meet certain requirements ensuring the plan does not discriminate against rank-and-file employees and if promised benefits are secure. Over the years, the rules addressing these issues have evolved, but the concept of a qualified plan eligible for favorable tax treatment remains the same.

Employer-provided qualified plans can be generally classified as **defined benefit plans** or **defined contribution plans.** As the name suggests, defined benefit plans spell out the specific benefit the employee will receive on retirement. In contrast, defined contribution plans specify the maximum annual contributions that employers and employees may contribute to the plan. While we explore both basic plan types below, we emphasize defined contribution plans because they are much more common than defined benefit plans.

## DEFINED BENEFIT PLANS

**LO1**

Defined benefit plans are traditional pension plans used by many older and more established companies and tax-exempt organizations. These plans provide standard retirement benefits to employees based on a fixed formula. The formula to determine the standard retirement benefit is usually a function of years of service and employees' compensation levels as they near retirement. For employees who retire in 2010, the maximum annual benefit an employee can receive is the *lesser* of (1) 100 percent of the average of the employee's three highest years of compensation or (2) $195,000.[2]

> **THE KEY FACTS**
>
> **Defined Benefit Plans**
> ∎ Employer specifies benefit employee receives on retirement based on years of service and salary.
> *(continued)*

**Example 13-1**

CBA provides a defined benefit plan for its employees. The plan uses a fixed formula to determine employee benefits. The formula specifies a benefit of 2 percent for each year of service, up to a maximum of 50 percent (25 years of service), of the average of the employee's three highest years of salary. In 2010, Dave retires from CBA. On the date of retirement, Dave had been a CBA employee for 20 years plus a couple of months. The average of his three highest years of salary was $420,000. What is Dave's annual benefit from the defined benefit plan?

**Answer:** $168,000 a year. The benefit is calculated by multiplying 40 percent (2 percent for each of his 20 years of service) by $420,000 (the average of his highest three years of salary).

**What if:** Assume the same facts except that the average of Dave's three highest years of salary was $600,000. What is the annual benefit he will receive from the plan?

**Answer:** $195,000. The lesser of (1) $240,000 ($600,000 × 40%) or (2) $195,000.

---

[2]§415(b)(1). The maximum benefit is adjusted annually for inflation.

*(concluded)*

■ Maximum annual benefit for employees who retire in 2010 is the lesser of (1) 100% of the average of the employee's three highest years of compensation or (2) $195,000.

■ Employee must vest to receive benefits using
· 5-year cliff vesting schedule
· 7-year graded vesting schedule

## Vesting

We've discussed the idea that an employee's benefit is based on the number of years she works for an employer. When an employee works for an employer for only a short time before leaving, her benefit depends on her salary, the number of full years she worked for the employer, and the employer's vesting schedule. **Vesting** is the process of becoming legally entitled to a certain right or property. Thus, a taxpayer vests in retirement benefits (becomes legally entitled to retirement benefits) as she meets certain requirements set forth by the employer. The most restrictive vesting requirements an employer can impose on a qualified defined benefit plan is either a five-year "cliff" or seven-year graded vesting schedule.[3] Under the **cliff vesting** option, after a certain period of time, benefits vest all at once. With a **graded vesting** schedule, the employee's vested benefit increases each full year she works for the employer. Exhibit 13-1 features the five-year cliff and seven-year graded vesting schedules for defined benefit plans.

### EXHIBIT 13-1    Defined Benefit Plans Minimum Vesting Schedules*

| Full Years of Service | 5-year Cliff | 7-year Graded |
|---|---|---|
| 1 | 0% | 0% |
| 2 | 0% | 0% |
| 3 | 0% | 20% |
| 4 | 0% | 40% |
| 5 | 100% | 60% |
| 6 | N/A | 80% |
| 7 | N/A | 100% |

*Percent of employee benefit no longer subject to forfeiture.

---

**Example 13-2**

*What if:* As we described in Example 13-1, CBA provides a defined benefit plan to its employees. Under the plan, employees earn a benefit equal to 2 percent for every year of service of their average salary for their three highest years of compensation. CBA implements a seven-year graded vesting schedule as part of the plan. If Tina works for CBA for four years, earning annual salaries of $60,000, $65,000, $70,000, and $75,000, and then leaves to work for another employer, what benefit would she be entitled to receive (her vested benefit)?

**Answer:** $2,240, computed as follows:

| Description | Amount | Explanation |
|---|---|---|
| (1) Average of three highest years of salary | $70,000 | ($65,000 + 70,000 + 75,000)/3. |
| (2) Benefit percentage | × 8% | Four years of service × 2 percent per year. |
| (3) Full annual benefit | $ 5,600 | (1) × (2). |
| (4) Vesting percentage | × 40% | Four years of service on 7-year graded vesting schedule (See Exhibit 13-1). |
| Vested benefit | $ 2,240 | (3) × (4) Amount that she is allowed to keep. |

Tina would forfeit her unvested benefit of $3,360 ($5,600 − $2,240 vested benefit).

*What if:* Assume the same facts except that CBA uses a five-year cliff schedule. What would be Tina's vested benefit?

**Answer:** $0. She did not work for CBA for five years so she would not vest in her benefits in CBA's defined benefit plan.

---

[3] §411(a) specifies maximum vesting periods for employer contributions to qualified plans. Employers are allowed to adopt more generous vesting requirements such as immediate vesting if they choose.

## Funding, Accounting, and Plan Maintenance

To ensure that employers are able to meet their defined benefit plan obligations, employers are required to contribute enough to the plan to fund their expected future liabilities under the plan. The amount of the required contribution for a year is based on certain assumptions about the number of participants in the plan, the life expectancies and expected retirement age of those covered under the plan, and the anticipated tax-exempt rate of return earned by contributions to the plan. The required contribution is determined on an aggregate basis rather than on an employee-by-employee basis.

To account for defined benefit plans in their *financial statements,* employers compare anticipated returns from pension assets with expected pension costs, given the attributes of plan participants, to determine the amount of pension expense (if expected costs exceed anticipated returns) or pension income (if anticipated returns exceed expected costs) to record each year. Under this approach, the measurement of anticipated returns and future pension costs is dependent on actuarial and management estimates. In contrast, for tax purposes, employers deduct *actual contributions* to the plan for a given year as long as they make the contributions by the extended tax return due date for that year.[4] Because the process for determining annual required contributions differs markedly from the method used to determine pension expense on the books, tax expense may be greater than or less than book expense from year to year, depending on the circumstances of the particular employer.

From a nontax perspective, a defined benefit plan imposes administrative burdens and risks on the employer sponsoring the plan. A significant amount of work is required to track employee benefits and to compute required contributions to the plan. Because defined benefit plans require employers to provide particular benefits to employees on retirement, the employer bears the investment risk associated with investments within the plan. Beyond the additional administrative costs and risk, defined benefit plans impose significant funding costs on employers relative to alternative retirement plans. Consequently, in recent years, many employers have begun replacing defined benefit plans with defined contribution plans.

### Distributions

When their benefits have vested, employees are entitled to receive future distributions according to the provisions of the plan—these distributions are taxable as ordinary income in the year received.[5] Distributions from defined benefit plans (and defined contribution plans) are subject to early distribution requirements and to minimum distribution requirements. Distributions violating these requirements are penalized. However, because defined benefit plans typically don't permit payout arrangements that would trigger the early distribution or minimum distribution penalties, these penalties are of greater concern to participants in defined contribution plans. Consequently, we address these penalties in more detail when we discuss distributions from defined contribution plans.

## DEFINED CONTRIBUTION PLANS

**L02**

Defined contribution plans provide an alternative approach for employers to help employees save for retirement. While defined contribution plans and defined benefit plans have similar overall objectives, they are different in important ways. First, employers maintain separate accounts for *each* employee participating in a defined contribution plan. Second, defined contribution plans specify the up-front contributions the employer will make to the employee's separate account rather than specifying the ultimate benefit the employee will receive from the plan. Third, employees are

**THE KEY FACTS**

**Defined Benefit Plans**

- Employer must fund expected future liability under plan.
  · Employer, not employee, bears investment risk of plan.
- Early and minimum distribution rules apply, but usually not restrictive.

---

[4]§404(a)(6).

[5]Distributions of both defined benefit plans and defined contribution plans are reported to taxpayers on Form 1099R.

frequently allowed to contribute to their own defined contribution plans, and in many instances they contribute more than their employers. Finally, employees are generally free to choose how amounts in their retirement accounts are invested. If investments in the plan perform well, employees benefit; if the investments perform poorly, employees suffer the financial consequences. Thus, relative to defined benefit plans, defined contribution plans shift the funding responsibility and investment risk from the employer to the employee.

---

**Taxes in the Real World**    *Retirement Benefits*

**Pension Losses Could Whack 2009 Corporate Profits**
*Time in partnership with CNN*
**By Steven Gray**
In 2008, the Standard & Poor's index declined 37 percent. Because employers with defined benefit plans (pension plans) tend to invest heavily in equities, the decline in the stock market took its toll on funds employers who have invested to fund the pension plans. In fact, the pension plans of the country's largest 1,500 companies lost more than $400 billion in 2008. Further, due to decreasing returns on Treasury bonds, the pension funding requirements (and financial accounting pension expense) for many companies is dramatically increasing. In 2008, in the aggregate, companies were required to contribute approximately $10 billion to their defined benefit plans. Estimates for 2009 suggest that these companies will be required to contribute approximately $70 billion to fund their pension plans.

Nevertheless, employees with defined benefit plans are not subject to the same level of investment risk as employees invested primarily in defined contribution plans such as 401(k) plans. The reason? When the market tanks, employees invested in 401(k)s bear the entire loss. However, employers are still required to pay employees retirement benefits even when the balance in employer pension funds drop. Further, even when an economic downturn causes an employer to become bankrupt, the retirement benefits of participants in defined benefit plans are still somewhat protected by the federal government's Pension Benefits Guaranty Corporation.

---

Employers may provide different types of defined contribution plans such as 401(k) (used by for-profit companies), 403(b) plans (used by nonprofit organizations, including educational institutions), and 457 plans (used by government agencies), profit sharing plans, and money purchase pension plans.[6] Employers may even offer multiple defined contribution plans. Because of their popularity, we use 401(k) plans here to represent the general category of defined contribution plans. However, no matter what defined contribution plan(s) employers provide, employers must ensure that they meet certain requirements relating to annual contribution limits and vesting requirements. Also, to a greater extent than with defined benefit plans, *participants* in defined contribution plans must be careful to avoid the penalties associated with either early distributions or insufficient **minimum distributions** from these plans. Although minimum distribution requirements were suspended for distributions pertaining to 2009 under legislation passed in 2008,[7] under current law the minimum distribution requirement applies to distributions pertaining to 2010 and beyond.

### Employer Matching

Employers, but not employees, typically contribute to certain defined contribution plan types such as profit sharing (contributions may be made based on a fixed formula based on profits or may be at the employer's discretion) and money purchase plans (contributions are a fixed percentage of the employee's compensation). In contrast, employees contribute to 401(k) type plans. Many employers also "match" employee

---

[6]401(k), 403(b), and 457 plans reflect the Code sections describing the plans.
[7]See The Worker, Retiree, and Employer Recovery Act of 2008.

contributions to these plans. When deciding whether to contribute to a 401(k) plan, employees should take into account their employer's matching policy. For companies matching employee contributions, the match can range from a small percentage (25 cents on the dollar) to a multiple of the employee's contribution.[8] A dollar-for-dollar match gives employees a 100 percent immediate return on their contributions. Therefore, whenever possible, employees should contribute enough to receive the full match from the employer because, subject to the employer's vesting requirements, the match represents an immediate, no-risk return on the amount contributed.

---

**Example 13-3**

Tina's offer from CBA includes participation in its 401(k) plan effective the beginning of next year. The plan's formula provides that CBA will match employee contributions on a two-for-one basis up to employee contributions of 4 percent of the employee's annual salary. Next year when she's eligible, Tina will contribute 4 percent of her salary to the plan. Assuming a $60,000 salary for next year, how much will Tina contribute and how much will CBA contribute to Tina's 401(k) account?

**Answer:** Tina will contribute $2,400 ($60,000 × 4%) to her 401(k) account and CBA will contribute $4,800 ($2,400 × 2).

---

**Taxes in the Real World**   *When Is a Match Not a Match?*

NEW YORK—Coffee shop chain Starbucks (SBUX) has informed employees it won't guarantee matching contributions to their 401(k) retirement plans next year. In a memo sent to workers last week, Starbucks said it will switch to a "fully discretionary match" program from a fixed employer match as of Jan. 1. "This means that at the end of calendar year 2009 and future years, Starbucks will make a decision whether or not to make matching contributions to plan participants," said the memo, which was emailed to Reuters.

"If a matching contribution is made, Starbucks may do so using a rate that is different than the tenure-based fixed rate currently in place for the 2008 plan year," the letter added. Starbucks spokeswoman Deb Trevino told Reuters that future company contributions would be discretionary, based on company performance. She confirmed that the letter had been sent to employees.

A growing list of U.S. companies have announced plans to suspend or cut 401(k) benefits to save costs in a recession, including FedEx and Eastman Kodak. Earlier this month, Starbucks said it does not expect to meet Wall Street estimates for its first quarter that began in late September and pledged to ramp up its cost cuts.

*Copyright 2008 Reuters Limited.*

*Source:* www.reuters.com/article/managementIssues/idUSN2354295920081223

*Note:* In 2009, Starbucks chose to make (voluntary) matching contributions to employees' 401(k) accounts (see www.reuters.com/article/companyNews/idUSN2753532620090727)

## Contribution Limits

For 2010, the sum of employer *and* employee contributions to an employee's defined contribution account(s) is limited to the *lesser* of (1) $49,000 ($54,500 for employees who are at least 50 years of age by the end of the year) or (2) 100 percent of the employee's compensation for the year.[9] *Employee* contributions to an employee's 401(k) account are limited to $16,500 (or $22,000 for employees that reach age 50 by the end of the year).[10] While this limit applies only to employee contributions, the $49,000 (or $54,500) limit still applies to the sum of employer and employee contributions.

[8]For example, Chevron contributes $4 to its 401(k) plan for every $1 contributed by its employees.
[9]§415(c)(1). The amount is indexed for inflation under §415(d)(1)(C).
[10]§402(g)(1). The amount is indexed for inflation under §402(g)(4).

For example, if an employee under age 50 contributes the maximum $16,500 to her employer-sponsored 401(k) plan in 2010, the employer's contribution would be limited to $32,500 ($49,000 − $16,500).[11] Because of this limit on employer contributions, highly compensated employees may not be able to receive the full employer match available to other employees.

**Example 13-4**

Before Dave retires at the end of 2010 he continues to contribute to his CBA-sponsored 401(k) account. CBA matches employee contributions on a two-for-one basis up to 4 percent of the employee's salary. Dave is 72 years old at the end of the year and he earned a salary of $450,000 during the year. Dave contributed $22,000 to his 401(k) account. How much would CBA contribute to Dave's 401(k) account?

**Answer:** $32,500 [$54,500 (Dave is 50+ years old) minus $22,000 (Dave's contribution)]. Without the limitation, CBA would have contributed $36,000 ($450,000 × 4% × 2) to Dave's account.

**What if:** Assume Dave contributed $20,000 to his 401(k) account. How much would CBA contribute to his account?

**Answer:** $34,500. Note that this is a better deal for Dave because $54,500 ends up in his account either way, but he only funded $20,000 of the contribution instead of $22,000.

## Vesting

When employees contribute to defined contribution plans, they are fully vested in the accrued benefit from the contributions (employee contributions plus earnings on the contributions). However, employees vest in the accrued benefit from employer contributions (employer contributions plus earnings on the contributions) based on the employer's vesting schedule. When separate employee accounts are not maintained, the accrued benefit from employee contributions is determined by multiplying the total accrued benefit in the account by the ratio of employee contributions to total contributions (employee plus employer) to the account.[12] The accrued benefit from employer contributions is the difference between the total accrued benefit and the accrued benefit from employee contributions. The minimum vesting requirements for defined contribution plans are a bit more accelerated than the five-year cliff and seven-year graded vesting schedules applicable to defined benefit plans. For defined contribution plans, employers have the option of providing three-year cliff or six-year graded vesting. These vesting schedules are presented in Exhibit 13-2.

**EXHIBIT 13-2    Defined Contribution Plans Minimum Vesting Schedules***

| Full Years of Service with Employer | 3-year Cliff | 6-year Graded |
|---|---|---|
| 1 | 0% | 0% |
| 2 | 0% | 20% |
| 3 | 100% | 40% |
| 4 | N/A | 60% |
| 5 | N/A | 80% |
| 6 | N/A | 100% |

*Percent of employer contributions no longer subject to forfeiture.

[11] If an employee participates in more than one defined contribution plan, these limits apply to the total employee and employer contributions to all defined contribution plans. Thus, in a situation where the employee participates in more than one defined contribution plan, the contribution limits for any one defined contribution plan may be less than the overall contribution limits described here.

[12] §411(c).

**Example 13-5**

***What if:*** Suppose that in three and one-half years the balance in Tina's 401(k) account is $33,000. In total, Tina had contributed $9,000 to the account and CBA had contributed $18,000. Also assume that Tina was 40 percent vested in her accrued benefit from CBA contributions. What is Tina's vested benefit?

**Answer:** $19,800 [$11,000 accrued benefit from her contributions + $8,800 ($22,000 × 40%), which is 40 percent of the $22,000 accrued benefit from CBA contributions]. Tina is fully vested in the $11,000 accrued benefit from her contributions ($33,000 total accrued benefit in account × 9,000 employee contributions/27,000 total contributions to her account) and 40 percent vested in the $22,000 accrued benefit from CBA contributions ($33,000 total accrued benefit in account minus $11,000 accrued benefit from her contributions).

## After-Tax Cost of Contributions

Employees effectively deduct their contributions to defined contribution plans, except for Roth 401(k) plans (discussed below), because contributions are removed from their taxable salary (they are, however, still subject to FICA taxes).[13] When employees contribute to traditional defined contribution plan accounts, they are contributing "before-tax" dollars because the contribution represents the cost of the contribution before considering the tax savings generated by the contribution. The employee's after-tax contribution (or after-tax cost of making the contribution) is the before-tax contribution minus the tax savings generated by the contribution.

**Example 13-6**

In Example 13-3, Tina contributed $2,400 to her CBA-sponsored traditional 401(k) account in her first full calendar year with CBA. Given Tina's marginal tax rate of 25 percent, what is the after-tax cost of her $2,400 contribution?

**Answer:** $1,800 computed as follows:

| Description | Amount | Explanation |
|---|---|---|
| (1) Before-tax contribution | $2,400 | Cost of contribution before tax savings. |
| (2) Tax savings from contribution | (600) | $2,400 deduction × 25 percent marginal tax rate. |
| After-tax cost of contribution | $1,800 | (1) + (2). |

## Distributions

When employees receive distributions from defined contribution plans (other than Roth 401(k) plans), the distributions are taxed as ordinary income. However, when employees receive distributions (or take withdrawals) from defined contribution plans either too early or too late, they must pay a penalty in addition to the ordinary income taxes they owe on the distributions. Generally, employees who receive distributions before they reach (1) 59½ years of age or (2) 55 years of age *and* have separated from service (retired or let go) are subject to a 10 percent nondeductible penalty on the amount of the early distributions.

---

[13]Employees pay the same FICA taxes no matter how much they contribute to defined contribution plans.

| **Example 13-7** |
|---|

**What if:** Assume that when she reaches 60 years of age, Lisa Whitlark retires from CBA and receives a $60,000 distribution from her 401(k) account in the year she retires. Assuming her marginal ordinary tax rate is 33 percent, what amount of tax will Lisa pay on the distribution?

**Answer:** $19,800 ($60,000 × 33%).

**What if:** Assume that when Lisa is 57 years of age and still employed by CBA, she requests and receives a $60,000 distribution from her 401(k) account. What amount of tax and penalty is Lisa required to pay on the distribution?

**Answer:** $19,800 taxes ($60,000 × 33%) + $6,000 penalty ($60,000 × 10%).

**What if:** Assume that Lisa is let go from CBA when she is 57 years old. In that same year, she requests and receives a $60,000 distribution from her 401(k) account. What amount of tax and penalty is Lisa required to pay on the distribution?

**Answer:** $19,800 taxes ($60,000 × 33%) + $0 penalty (she is over 55 years of age and has separated from service with CBA).

---

| **THE KEY FACTS** |
|---|

**Traditional Defined Contribution Plans: Distributions**

■ Taxed at ordinary rates.

■ 10 percent penalty on early distributions.
· Before 59½ years of age if not retired or
· Before 55 years of age if retired.

■ Minimum distributions requirements:
· Must receive by April 1 of the later of (1) the year after the year in which taxpayer reaches 70½ years of age or (2) the year after the year in which the employee retires.
· If retired employee waits until year after 70½ to begin receiving distributions, must receive two distributions in year of first distribution.
· 50 percent penalty on excess of required minimum distribution amounts and amount actually distributed.

Taxpayers who fail to receive minimum distributions for (pertaining to) years *other than 2009* are also penalized. (Recall that minimum distributions for 2009 are not required.) Taxpayers must receive their *first* minimum distribution from the account *for* the year in which the employee reaches 70½ years of age or the year in which the employee retires, if later (2009 excluded). Taxpayers must receive this distribution no later than April 1 of the year after the year to which the distribution pertains.[14] Taxpayers generally must receive minimum distributions for subsequent years by the end of the years to which they pertain.

The amount of the minimum required distribution for a particular year is the taxpayer's account balance at the end of the year *prior to* the year to which the distribution pertains multiplied by a percentage from an IRS Uniform Lifetime Table. The percentage is based on the taxpayer's age at the end of the year to which the distribution pertains. An abbreviated version of the table is presented in Exhibit 13-3.[15]

**EXHIBIT 13-3    Abbreviated Uniform Lifetime Table**

| Age of Participant | Distribution Period | Applicable Percentage* |
|---|---|---|
| 70 | 27.4 | 3.65% |
| 71 | 26.5 | 3.77% |
| 72 | 25.6 | 3.91% |
| 73 | 24.7 | 4.05% |
| 74 | 23.8 | 4.20% |
| 75 | 22.9 | 4.37% |
| 76 | 22.0 | 4.54% |
| 77 | 21.2 | 4.72% |

*The applicable percentage is calculated by dividing one by the relevant distribution period.

---

| **Example 13-8** |
|---|

**What if:** Suppose that Dave retires from CBA in 2009 at age 72 (also 72 at year-end). When must he receive his minimum distribution for 2009 from his 401(k) account?

**Answer:** Dave is not required to receive a minimum distribution for 2009 because the minimum distribution requirements were suspended for distributions pertaining to 2009.

(continued on page 13-11...)

---

[14]The amount of the required minimum distribution *for the year* in which a retired employee turns 70½ is the same whether the employee receives the distribution in the year she turns 70½ or whether she defers receiving the distribution until the next year (no later than April 1).

[15]See Reg. §1.401(a)(9)-9 Q&A 2 to reference the full version of the table. This table applies in most circumstances.

*What if:* Suppose that Dave retires from CBA in 2010 at age 72 (also 72 at year-end). When must he receive his minimum distribution for 2010 from his 401(k) account?

**Answer:** By April 1, 2011.

*What if:* Assuming Dave retires in 2010 and that his 401(k) account balance on December 31, 2009, was $3,500,000, what is the amount of the minimum distribution Dave must receive by April 1, 2011?

**Answer:** $136,850 ($3,500,000 × 3.91%). The percentage from the IRS table for determining this minimum distribution is based on Dave's age at the end of 2010, which is 72 years old.

*What if:* Assuming Dave's 401(k) account balance on December 31, 2010, is $3,700,000, what is the minimum distribution for 2011 Dave must receive sometime during 2011 (in addition to the $136,850 distribution by April 1)?

**Answer:** $149,850 for 2011 ($3,700,000 × 4.05%) in 2011.

The consequences for failing to receive timely minimum distributions from defined contribution plans are even more severe than receiving distributions too early. Taxpayers incur a 50 percent nondeductible penalty on the amount of a minimum distribution the employee should have received but did not. For this reason, it is vital that payouts from defined contribution plans be monitored to avoid not only the 10 percent premature distribution penalty, but also the 50 percent penalty for late withdrawals.

**Example 13-9**

*What if:* In the previous example, we determined that Dave must receive a minimum distribution of $136,850 from his 401(k) account by April 1, 2011. If Dave does not receive any distribution before April 1, 2011, what penalty will he be required to pay?

**Answer:** $68,425 ($136,850 × 50%). This nondeductible penalty is a strong incentive to take the required minimum distributions or at least to take the penalty into consideration when developing a distribution plan.

*What if:* Assume that Dave received his first distribution from his 401(k) account on March 1, 2011, in the amount of $100,000. But, he did not receive any other distributions before April 1, 2011. What penalty is Dave required to pay?

**Answer:** $18,425 [($136,850 − $100,000) × 50%]

In contrast to defined benefit plans, defined contribution plans often provide distribution options that could trigger the penalty for premature distributions for the uninformed or unwary. For example, an employee who retires (or is fired) and takes a lump-sum distribution from her defined contribution account in a year before the year in which she turns 55 will be subject to a 10 percent early distribution penalty on the entire amount of the distribution. Employees who receive such lump-sum distributions may avoid the 10 percent penalty by electing to "roll over" (deposit) the distributions into one of the individually managed retirement plans we discuss later in this chapter.

### After-Tax Rates of Return

For a given before-tax rate of return, the longer the taxpayer defers distributions from a qualified retirement account, the greater the taxpayer's after-tax rate of return on the account, because deferring the distribution reduces the present value of the taxes paid on the distribution. A taxpayer's after-tax rate of return is also sensitive to the taxpayer's marginal tax rate at the time she contributes to the plan and at the time she receives distributions from the plan. All else equal, the higher her marginal tax rate at the time she contributes to the plan, the higher the after-tax rate of return (the higher tax rate makes the deduction more valuable), and the lower her marginal tax rate at the time she receives distributions from the plan the higher the after-tax rate of return (the lower rate reduces the taxes on the income).

Of course, any employer contributions to an employee's account, such as CBA's two-for-one matching contributions to Tina's account, significantly increases the after-tax rate of return (and after-tax accumulation) because the contributions increase the employee's after-tax proceeds, but the employee's cost of these contributions is zero.

Exhibit 13-4 summarizes the tax aspects of defined benefit and defined contribution plans.

**EXHIBIT 13-4**  Defined Benefit Plan vs. Defined Contribution Plan Summary

| | Defined Benefit Plan | Defined Contribution Plan |
|---|---|---|
| Benefits | • Specifies benefit employee receives on retirement.<br>• Maximum benefit in 2010 lesser of (1) 100 percent of average of highest three years compensation or (2) $195,000. | • Specifies the amounts employer and employee contribute to the account.<br>• Ultimate benefit depends on earnings on contributions. |
| Payout type | • Life annuity.<br>• Lump sum distribution of the present value of standard benefit. | • Life annuity.<br>• Lump sum.<br>• Fixed number of years. |
| Funding requirements | • Employers fund increase in expected future liability each year. | • No funding requirement other than to make required contributions to employee accounts. |
| Employer's contributions tax deductible? | • Yes. | • Yes, but limited to 25 percent of aggregate employee annual compensation. |
| Employee's contributions tax deductible? | • No employee contributions. | • Yes, subject to limitations on the amount that can be contributed [$16,500 ($22,000 if 50 or older) maximum contribution to 401(k) plan in 2010]. |
| Contribution limits | • Not applicable. | • In 2010, lesser of (1) $49,000 ($54,500 for taxpayers at least 50 years of age at end of year) and (2) 100 percent of the employee's compensation for year. |
| Other factors | • All employees paid from same account.<br>• Heavy administrative burden.<br>• Employer assumes investment risk. | • Separate accounts for each employee.<br>• Employees make investment choices.<br>• Employees assume investment risk. |
| Vesting requirements | • 5-year cliff or<br>• 7-year graded | • 3-year cliff or<br>• 6-year graded<br>• Employee contributions vest immediately. |
| Distributions | • Taxed as ordinary income.<br>• No 10 percent penalty if 55 years of age and retired.<br>• Minimum distributions for years other than 2009 required by April 1 of year after the later of (1) year employee reaches 70½ or (2) year employee retires. | • Taxed as ordinary income (except Roth type accounts).<br>• No 10 percent penalty if 55 years of age and retired.<br>• Minimum distributions requirements same as for defined benefit plan. |

## Roth 401(k) Plans

Employers that provide **traditional 401(k)** plans to employees may also provide **Roth 401(k)** plans. As we discuss below, employee tax consequences for Roth 401(k) plans differ from tax consequences of other traditional defined contribution plans.

When employers provide a Roth 401(k) plan, *employees* may elect to contribute to the Roth 401(k) *instead of or in addition to* contributing to a traditional 401(k) plan. However, *employer* contributions to an employee's 401(k) account must go to the employee's *traditional* 401(k) account rather than the employee's Roth 401(k) account. Consequently, the balance in an employee's Roth 401(k) account must consist of only the employee's contributions and the earnings on those contributions. Because employers providing Roth 401(k) plans to employees are not allowed to contribute to the Roth plans, these employers are required to maintain traditional 401(k) accounts for each employee participating in the Roth 401(k) plan.

In contrast to contributions to traditional 401(k) plans, employee contributions to Roth 401(k) accounts are *not* deductible and, therefore, do not produce any immediate tax savings for employees. Consequently, employees contributing to Roth 401(k) plans are contributing after-tax dollars. That is, employees wanting to contribute a certain amount to a Roth 401(k) plan must earn more than that specified amount in order to have the desired contribution amount remaining *after* paying taxes on the amount they earn. For example, assume an employee in a 20 percent marginal tax bracket wants to contribute $2,000 to a Roth 401(k) plan. To earn the funds to make this contribution, the employee must earn $2,500 before taxes. The tax on the $2,500 of income is $500 ($2,500 × 20%). This leaves the taxpayer with $2,000 after taxes ($2,500 before taxes minus $500 in taxes) to contribute to the Roth 401(k) plan.

> **THE KEY FACTS**
>
> **Roth 401(k) Defined Contribution Plans**
>
> ∎ **Employees but not employers may contribute.**
> · Employers contribute to traditional 401(k).
>
> ∎ **Contributions are not deductible.**
> · Employees contribute after-tax dollars.
> · Same contribution limits as traditional 401(k) plans.

---

**Example 13-10**

*What if:* Let's assume that CBA offers a Roth 401(k) plan in addition to its traditional 401(k) plan. In her first full calendar year of employment with CBA, Tina elects to contribute 4 percent of her $60,000 salary to CBA's Roth 401(k) plan instead of CBA's traditional 401(k) plan. What is Tina's after-tax cost of this $2,400 contribution?

**Answer:** $2,400. Her after-tax cost is her $2,400 contribution because the contribution does not generate any tax savings.

What is Tina's before-tax cost of the contribution? That is, how much did Tina need to earn before taxes to fund the $2,400 after-tax contribution?

**Answer:** $3,200. Because her marginal tax rate is 25 percent, she needs to earn $3,200 before taxes [$2,400/(1 − .25)] to have $2,400 to contribute to the Roth 401(k) after taxes [$3,200 × (1 − .25)] When she contributes $2,400 *after taxes* to the Roth 401(k), she is contributing $3,200 *before taxes*.

---

While contributions to Roth 401(k) accounts are not deductible and, as a result, do not generate any current tax savings, *qualified* distributions from a Roth 401(k) account are excluded from gross income. Note, however, that Roth 401(k) accounts are subject to the same minimum distribution requirements as traditional 401(k) accounts. Because contributions to Roth 401(k) accounts are not deductible and distributions from Roth 401(k) accounts are not taxable, the after-tax rate of return on a Roth 401(k) does not depend on marginal tax rates. The after-tax rate of return on a Roth 401(k) account is the same as the before-tax rate of return.

## Example 13-11

***What if:*** In the previous example, Tina contributed $2,400 after taxes to her Roth 401(k) account in her first calendar year on the job with CBA. Let's assume that Tina leaves this contribution in the account until she retires in 40 years at the age of 63, that her contribution earns an annual 8 percent before-tax rate of return, and that her marginal tax rate will be 30 percent when she receives the distribution. How much will Tina have accumulated after taxes if she withdraws the initial contribution and all the earnings on the contribution when she retires?

**Answer:** $52,139 ($2,400 × $1.08^{40}$).

Tina's after-tax rate of return on her $2,400 after-tax contribution is exactly 8 percent, the same as the before-tax rate of return. With a Roth 401(k) the after-tax rate of return should always equal the before-tax rate return because the after-tax cost of the contribution and the after-tax accumulation on distribution are not affected by the taxpayer's marginal tax rate at the time of contribution or at the time of distribution.

Qualified distributions from Roth 401(k) accounts are those made after the employee's account has been open for five taxable years *and* the employee is at least 59½ years of age. All other distributions are nonqualified distributions. When a taxpayer receives a *non*qualified distribution from a Roth 401(k) account, the tax consequences of the distribution depends on the extent to which the distribution is from the account earnings and the extent to which it is from the employee's contributions to the account. Nonqualified distributions of the account *earnings* are fully taxable and are subject to the 10 percent early distribution penalty. Nonqualified distributions of the taxpayer's account *contributions* are not subject to tax because the taxpayer did not deduct these amounts. If less than the entire balance in the plan is distributed, the nontaxable portion of the distribution is determined by multiplying the amount of the distribution by the ratio of account contributions to the total account balance.

## Example 13-12

***What if:*** In the previous example, Tina contributed $2,400 to CBA's Roth 401(k) plan, her account generated an 8 percent before-tax return, and she withdrew the entire balance 40 years after the contribution. Let's assume that at the end of year 6, Tina needs cash, so she withdraws $1,000 from the account when her marginal tax rate is 28 percent. How much tax and penalty, if any, is Tina required to pay on this nonqualified distribution?

**Answer:** $104 tax and $37 penalty, computed as follows:

| Description | Amount | Explanation |
|---|---|---|
| (1) Nondeductible contribution to Roth 401(k) | $2,400 | Beginning of year 1. |
| (2) Account balance end of year 6 | 3,808 | $2,400 × $1.08^{6}$. |
| (3) Nonqualified distribution end of year 6 | 1,000 | |
| (4) Percentage of distribution that is not taxable | 63.03% | (1)/(2). |
| (5) Nontaxable portion of distribution | 630 | (3) × (4). |
| (6) Taxable portion of distribution | 370 | (3) − (5). |
| (7) Marginal tax rate in year 6 | 28% | |
| **(8) Regular income tax on distribution** | 104 | (6) × (7). |
| (9) Penalty tax percentage for early distributions | 10% | |
| **(10) Penalty tax on early distribution** | 37 | (6) × (9). |
| **Total tax and penalty on early distribution** | $  141 | (8) + (10). |

Finally, it is important to note that the minimum distribution requirements applicable to traditional 401(k) accounts also apply to Roth 401(k) accounts.

### Comparing Traditional Defined Contribution Plans and Roth 401(k) Plans

We've described and discussed the tax consequences associated with participating in traditional and Roth 401(k) plans. So which is better for employees? If given a choice, which type of 401(k) plan should you contribute to? As we've discussed, current and future marginal tax rates are an important factor to consider. In general terms, the traditional 401(k) plans will generate higher (lower) after-tax rates of return than Roth 401(k) plans when taxpayers' marginal tax rates *decrease* (*increase*) from the time of contribution to the time of distribution. If marginal tax rates remain the same, 401(k) plans and Roth 401(k) plans will generate the same after-tax rate of return. Exhibit 13-5 summarizes and compares traditional 401(k) plans and Roth 401(k) plans.

**EXHIBIT 13-5**   Traditional 401(k) Plan vs. Roth 401(k) Plan Summary

| | Traditional 401(k) Plans | Roth 401(k) Plans |
|---|---|---|
| Employer contributions allowed | • Yes. | • No. |
| Tax consequences to employer | • Contributions deductible when paid. | • Not applicable. |
| Tax consequences to employee | • Contributions are deductible. | • Contributions are not deductible. |
| Distributions | • Taxed as ordinary income.<br>• No 10 percent penalty if 55 years of age and retired.<br>• If life annuity or joint and survivor annuity no penalty even if not 55 years of age.<br>• Minimum distributions for years other than 2009 required by April 1 of the later of (1) the year after the year in which the employee reaches 70½ or (2) the year after the year in which the employee retires.<br>• Failure to meet minimum distribution timing and amount requirements triggers 50 percent penalty.<br>• Nonqualified distributions (early distributions) trigger ordinary tax and penalty tax on earnings. | • Qualified distributions not taxed.<br>• Qualified distributions when funds in account for 5 years and employee has reached the age of 59½.<br>• No 10 percent penalty if 55 years of age and retired.<br>• If life annuity or joint and survivor annuity, no penalty even if not 55 years of age.<br>• Minimum distribution requirements and penalties are the same as for traditional 401(k) plans.<br>• If nonqualified distribution, nontaxable percentage of distribution is the ratio of contributions to total account value. |

## NONQUALIFIED DEFERRED COMPENSATION                                  L03

So far, our discussion has emphasized the tax and nontax aspects of employer-provided *qualified* defined benefit and defined contribution plans. In addition to or perhaps in lieu of these types of qualified plans, employers may offer **nonqualified deferred compensation** plans to certain employees.

### Nonqualified Plans vs. Qualified Defined Contribution Plans

Deferred compensation plans permit employees to defer (or contribute) current salary in exchange for a future payment from the employer. From an employee's perspective, the tax consequences of contributions to and distributions from nonqualified plans receive tax treatment similar to qualified defined contribution plans. For example, just as with defined contribution plans, employee contributions

to nonqualified deferred compensation plans (NQDC) reduce an employee's taxable income in the year of contribution.[16] Also, just as with qualified plans, employees are not taxed on the balance in their accounts until they receive distributions. Finally, like distributions from qualified plans, distributions from nonqualified deferred compensation plans are taxed as ordinary income.

---

**Example 13-13**

CBA provides a nonqualified deferred compensation plan under which executives may elect to defer up to 10 percent of their salary. Dave Allan has been participating in the plan by deferring a portion of his salary each year for the last 15 years. The balance in his deferred compensation account is currently $2,000,000. In keeping with the fixed payment schedule Dave elected under the plan, he receives a $50,000 distribution. What amount of tax must Dave pay on the distribution (recall that his marginal tax rate is 35 percent)?

**Answer:** $17,500 ($50,000 × .35).

---

**THE KEY FACTS**

**Nonqualified Deferred Compensation Plans**

■ Employees defer current income in exchange for future payment.
· Employee taxed when payment received.
· Employee generally selects deemed investment choices up front to determine return on deferral.
· Just like traditional deferred compensation plans, after-tax rate of return depends on before-tax rate of return, marginal tax rate at time of deferral, and marginal tax rate at time of distribution.
· Payment not guaranteed. If employer doesn't pay, employee becomes unsecured creditor.

For employers, NQDC plans are treated differently than qualified plans. For example, because nonqualified plans are not subject to the same restrictive requirements pertaining to qualified plans, employers may discriminate in terms of whom they allow to participate in the plan. In fact, employers generally restrict participation in nonqualified plans to more highly compensated employees. Also, employers are not required to "fund" nonqualified plans. That is, employers are not required to formally set aside and accumulate funds specifically to pay the deferred compensation obligation when it comes due. Rather, employers typically retain funds deferred by employees under the plan, use the funds for business operations, and pay the deferred compensation out of their general funds when it becomes payable. Because employers retain, control, and generate income on funds deferred by employees under nonqualified plans, employers are allowed to *deduct only actual payments* of deferred compensation to employees. That is, employers cannot deduct the amount of deferred compensation they accrue each year. Thus, for tax purposes, an employer may not deduct the deferred compensation when an employee initially earns the compensation even though the employer becomes liable for the deferred compensation payment. In contrast, for financial accounting purposes, companies generally expense deferred compensation in the year employees earn it and record a corresponding deferred compensation liability.[17]

### Employee Considerations

Should employees participate in nonqualified plans when given the chance? The decision obviously involves several considerations. First, employees must decide if the benefits they expect to receive from qualified retirement plans (or other sources) will be adequate to provide for their expected costs during retirement. Next, employees should consider whether they can afford to defer current salary. This may not be a significant concern for most eligible participants, however, because nonqualified plans are generally available only to highly compensated employees who likely may not have the liquidity concerns that lower-compensated employees may face. Also, employees should consider the expected rate of return on the deferred salary relative to what they could earn on the salary by receiving it currently and personally investing it.

Generally, larger employers allow employees participating in nonqualified plans to choose how their deferred compensation will be invested from among alternative

---

[16]Technically, employees participating in NQDC plans defer the receipt of current salary and employers credit the employee's account for the amount of the deferral. This has the same effect as if the employee had actually made a deductible contribution to her account as an employee participating in a defined contribution plan would do.

[17]Employers record additional expense and liability as earnings on the deferred compensation accumulate.

investments provided under the plan (money market, various bond funds, and stock funds among others). However, because employers *do not actually invest* compensation deferred under the plan on the employee's behalf, the employer credits the employee's account "as if" the employee's contributions had been invested in the employee's *deemed* investment choices. The description of Coca-Cola Company's nonqualified retirement plan, presented in Exhibit 13-6, illustrates this concept:

## EXHIBIT 13-6    Description of Nonqualified Retirement Plan

*Excerpt from Coca-Cola Company's proxy statement*

The Deferred Compensation Plan is a non-qualified and unfunded deferred compensation program offered to approximately 600 U.S. based employees who are not International Service Associates. Eligible participants may defer up to 80% of base salary and, for 2008, up to 100% of their incentive. Gains and losses are credited based on the participant's election of a variety of deemed investment choices. The Company *does not* match any employee deferral or guarantee a return. In fact, due to the downturn in world markets, the weighted average return of the various deemed investment choices under the plan as of December 31, 2008 was negative 25%. Participants' accounts may or may not appreciate and may depreciate depending on the performance of their deemed investment choices. None of the deemed investment choices provide interest at above-market rates. All deferrals are paid out in cash upon distribution. Participants may schedule a distribution during employment, or may opt to receive their balance after separation from service.

Just as with qualified defined contribution plans, other than Roth 401(k) plans, an employee's after-tax rate of return on deferred compensation depends on the employee's investment choices *and* on the employee's marginal tax rates at the time of the contribution and at the time of the distribution.[18]

**Example 13-14**

As a new executive with CBA, Lisa Whitlark is eligible to participate in its nonqualified deferred compensation plan. Recall that CBA provides a nonqualified deferred compensation plan under which executives may elect to defer up to 10 percent of their salary. In her first year with CBA, Lisa elects to defer $40,000 of salary ($400,000 × 10%) under the plan. Because her current marginal income tax rate is 33 percent, she saves $13,200 in taxes by deferring the salary ($40,000 × 33%). Consequently, her after-tax cost of deferring the compensation is $26,800 ($40,000 − $13,200). She plans to receive a distribution from the nonqualified plan in 20 years when she expects her marginal tax rate to be 28 percent. Lisa selects a stock index fund as her "deemed" investment choice. She expects the fund to provide an 8 percent before-tax rate of return on her $40,000 deferral. What will Lisa receive after-taxes from her $40,000 deferral?

**Answer:** $134,235 after-tax accumulation, computed as follows:

| Description | Amount | Explanation |
|---|---|---|
| Before-tax contribution | $ 40,000 | Deferral of 10 percent of her current salary. |
| Times future value factor | × $1.08^{20}$ | 8 percent annual rate of return for 20 years. |
| Future value of deferred compensation | 186,438 | Value of deferral/distribution 20 years after deferral. |
| Minus: taxes payable on distribution | (52,203) | $186,438 value of account × 28 percent marginal tax rate. |
| After-tax proceeds from distributions | **$134,235** | Value of account minus taxes payable on distribution. |

[18]As discussed previously, after-tax accumulations in Roth 401(k) accounts are not dependent on current and future marginal tax rates.

Deferring salary to a future period is potentially an effective tax planning technique, particularly when the employee anticipates her marginal tax rate to be lower in the year she will receive the deferred compensation than it is in the year she defers the salary. In fact, if employees had complete flexibility as to when they could receive distributions from deferred compensation plans, they would likely accelerate distributions from deferred compensation plans into years they knew with certainty would have relatively low marginal tax rates. This strategy is limited, however, by rules requiring employees to specify the timing of the future payments at the time they decide to participate in deferred compensation plans.[19]

Employees considering participating in nonqualified deferred compensation plans should also consider potential financial risks of doing so. Recall that employers are not required to fund nonqualified plans. So, there's always the possibility that the employer will not have the funds to pay the employee on the scheduled distribution dates (e.g., the employer becomes bankrupt). If the employer is not able to make the payments, the employee becomes an unsecured creditor of the company and may never receive the full compensation owed to her. Consequently, the employee should evaluate the financial stability of the company when deciding whether to defer compensation under the employer's plan.

## Employer Considerations

It's pretty clear that nonqualified plans can provide significant benefits to employees. How might employers benefit from providing nonqualified plans? First, employers may benefit if they are able to earn a better rate of return on the deferred compensation than the rate of return they are required to pay employees participating in the plan. In addition, employers can use nonqualified plans to achieve certain compensation objectives. For example, nonqualified plans could be a component of a compensation package a company may use to attract prospective executives. Also, because deferred compensation is not deductible until it is paid, deferred compensation plans provide a potentially effective way for employers to circumvent the $1 million salary deduction limitation for executives imposed by §162(m) (see Chapter 12 discussion of the limitation).[20] That is, an employer may pay an executive $1 million of current compensation and defer compensation over $1 million to a future period. By doing this, the employer is able to deduct the full $1 million of salary and the entire amount of the deferred compensation as long as the employee has retired at the time the employer pays the deferred compensation. This is because the $1 million deductibility limitation on compensation does not apply if the executive is no longer employed by the company when the company pays the deferred compensation. However, if the executive is still an employee when the deferred compensation is paid, it is subject to the $1 million deduction limit. Exhibit 13-7 provides an excerpt from an IBM proxy statement that mentions the effectiveness of IBM's deferred compensation plan in avoiding the **§162(m) limitation.**

### EXHIBIT 13-7    Deferred Compensation and §162(m) Limitation

*Excerpt from proxy statement for IBM*

The IBM Excess 401(k) Plus Plan (formerly the Executive Deferred Compensation Plan) permits an executive officer who is subject to section 162(m) and whose salary is above $1 million to defer payment of a sufficient amount of the salary to bring it below the section 162(m) limit.

---

[19]§409A. These rules do provide, however, that specified payments from deferred compensation plans may commence while employees are still employed.

[20]Note that the $1 million salary deduction limitation applies to executives of publicly traded corporations only.

In the same vein, deferring compensation may be an important tax planning tool for employers in situations where their current marginal tax rates are low (employers currently experiencing net operating losses) and they expect their future marginal tax rates when deferred compensation is paid to be significantly higher (employers expect to return to profitability). In effect, deferring compensation into a year with a higher marginal tax rate increases the after-tax benefit of the compensation deduction, which reduces the after-tax cost of the compensation to the employer.

Exhibit 13-8 summarizes and compares qualified retirement plans and nonqualified deferred compensation plans.

**EXHIBIT 13-8    Qualified Plan vs. Nonqualified Plan Summary**

|  | Qualified Plans | Nonqualified Plans |
|---|---|---|
| Types | • Defined benefit (Pension).<br>• Defined contribution (401k). | • Deferred compensation. |
| Requirements | • May not discriminate against "rank and file" employees of the company.<br>• Funding or contribution requirements.<br>• Vesting requirements. | • May discriminate.<br>• Generally provided to executives and highly compensated.<br>• No formal funding requirements (employee essentially unsecured creditor).<br>• No formal vesting requirements. |
| Tax consequences to employers | • Immediately deduct contributions to plan (amount funded). | • No deduction until paid to employee. |
| Tax consequences to employees | • Employee contributions deductible unless to Roth-type account.<br>• Employer contributions not immediately taxed.<br>• Earnings deferred until distributed to employee.<br>• Distributions from non-Roth plans treated as ordinary income. | • Employee contributions (or deferrals) deductible.<br>• Taxed as ordinary income when received.<br>• Earnings deferred until distributed to employee. |

# INDIVIDUALLY MANAGED QUALIFIED RETIREMENT PLANS

We've covered tax and nontax issues relating to both qualified and nonqualified employer-sponsored retirement savings plans. However, not all employers provide retirement savings plans, and when they do, some employees may not be eligible to participate, while others who are eligible may elect to not participate in these plans. The tax laws provide opportunities for these taxpayers to provide for their own retirement security through individually managed retirement plans. The **Individual Retirement Account (IRA)** is the most common of the individually managed retirement plans. Other types of individually managed plans are available to self-employed taxpayers.

# INDIVIDUAL RETIREMENT ACCOUNTS

**LO4**

Taxpayers who meet certain eligibility requirements can contribute to **traditional IRAs,** to **Roth IRAs,** or to both. Just like traditional and Roth 401(k) plans, traditional IRAs and Roth IRAs have different tax characteristics. In fact, in most respects, the tax characteristics of traditional 401(k) plans mirror those of traditional IRAs and tax characteristics of Roth 401(k) plans mirror those of Roth IRA accounts. To

**THE KEY FACTS**

*Traditional IRAs*

■ **2010 Contribution limit.**
· Lesser of $5,000 or earned income.
· Taxpayers over 50, lesser of $6,000 or earned income.

■ **If taxpayers participate in employer provided plan:**
· Deduction limit phased out for single taxpayers with AGI between $56,000 and $66,000 and for married filing jointly taxpayers with AGI between $89,000 and $109,000.
· Special rules if one spouse covered by plan and other is not.

minimize redundancy in this section, we focus on the tax characteristics that differ between employer-sponsored 401(k) plans and self-managed IRAs.

### Traditional IRAs

Because the government provides IRAs primarily to help taxpayers who are not able to participate in employer-sponsored retirement plans and to help taxpayers with relatively low levels of income to save for retirement, tax laws restrict who can make *deductible* contributions to traditional IRAs. To be able to deduct contributions to traditional IRAs, taxpayers must (1) *not* be a participant in an employer-sponsored retirement plan or (2) if they are participating in an employer-sponsored plan, they must have income below the thresholds described below.

For taxpayers who do not participate in an employer-sponsored retirement plan, the limit for deductible IRA contributions is $5,000 in 2010 or the amount of *earned* income if it is less.[21, 22] As we discussed in Chapter 5, earned income generally includes income actually earned through the taxpayer's efforts such as wages, salaries, tips, and other employee compensation plus the amount of the taxpayer's net earnings from self-employment. Alimony income is also considered as earned income for this purpose. Taxpayers who are 50 years of age or older at year-end may make an additional $1,000 contribution each year in excess of the standard contribution limit. This extra $1,000 limit is granted to allow taxpayers nearing retirement age to "catch up" on contributions they may have not made in previous years.

**Example 13-15**

In the year she graduated from college, Tina earned $25,000. She earned $5,000 in salary working part-time while she was in school and she earned $20,000 in salary working for CBA from September through December. To get an early start saving for retirement, she contributed $5,000 to a *traditional* IRA. Assuming the 2010 limitations apply, how much of this contribution may Tina deduct?

**Answer:** $5,000. Because Tina is not participating in an employer-sponsored retirement plan during the current year, Tina may deduct the full $5,000 contribution as a *for* AGI deduction, reducing her AGI from $25,000 to $20,000.

Unmarried taxpayers who participate in an employer-sponsored retirement plan can still make deductible contributions to traditional IRAs subject to certain AGI restrictions. For 2010, unmarried taxpayers with AGI of $56,000 can make fully deductible contributions to an IRA account, subject to the $5,000 overall deduction limitation (or $6,000 if age 50 or older). The $5,000 deduction limitation is phased out *proportionally* for single taxpayers with AGI between $56,000 and $66,000. Married taxpayers can make deductible contributions to separate IRAs. For married couples filing jointly, when one spouse has more earned income than the other, the deduction for contributions to the traditional IRA of the spouse with the greater amount of earned income is the same as it is for unmarried taxpayers [$5,000 (plus $1,000 if at least 50 years of age at year-end) or earned income if it is less]. However for the spouse with the lesser amount of earned income, the deduction is limited to the lesser of (1) $5,000 ($6,000 if this spouse is age 50 or older at year-end) or (2) the total earned income of both spouses reduced by deductible and nondeductible contributions to the other spouse's traditional IRA and contributions to the other spouse's Roth IRA.[23] If a spouse is an active participant in an employer's retirement plan, the

---

[21]Lump-sum distributions from qualified plans other than Roth 401(k)s received prior to retirement are frequently rolled over into traditional IRA accounts to avoid the 10 percent premature distribution penalty and current taxation. Rollover contributions are not subject to normal contribution limits for traditional IRAs.

[22]The IRA contribution limit is indexed for inflation.

[23]§219(c).

deduction for that spouse is phased out proportionally over the couple's AGI between $89,000 and $109,000. If one spouse is an active participant in an employer's retirement plan and the other is not, the deduction for the spouse who is not an active participant is phased out proportionally over the couple's AGI between $167,000 and $177,000.

Married taxpayers who file separately may also make deductible contributions to an IRA. The deduction is limited to the lesser of $5,000 ($6,000 if the taxpayer is at least 50 years old at year-end) or earned income. However, if either spouse is an active participant in an employer's retirement plan, then each spouse's deductible contribution (including a nonactive participant spouse) is phased out over the couple's AGI between $0 and $10,000. If the couple files separate tax returns and did not live with each other at any time during the year, both spouses will be treated as single taxpayers for purposes of the IRA deduction limitations.

**Example 13-16**

In her first full calendar year working for CBA, Tina earns $60,000. Because she contributes $2,400 of her salary to CBA's 401(k) plan, her AGI is $57,600 ($60,000 − $2,400). Tina also would like to make the maximum deductible contribution to her IRA. Assuming the 2010 limitations apply, how much is she allowed to deduct?

**Answer:** $4,200. The deductible amount before considering AGI limitations is $5,000. However, because Tina is a participant in CBA's retirement plan, the $5,000 deduction limit is subject to phase-out. Because Tina's AGI is 16 percent of the way through the $56,000 − $66,000 phase-out range for a single taxpayer [($57,600 − 56,000)/(66,000 − 56,000)], the $5,000 deductible contribution limit is reduced by 16 percent to $4,200 [$5,000 × (1 − .16)]. So, $4,200 is the maximum deductible contribution she can make to her traditional IRA.

**What if:** Assume that Tina is married and files a joint return with her spouse Steve. Tina participates in CBA's 401(k) plan and she receives $60,000 in salary from CBA for the year. Steve is a full-time student and is unemployed. The couple's AGI before considering IRA contributions is $60,000. What is Tina's maximum deductible IRA contribution for the year? What is Steve's maximum deductible IRA contribution for the year?

**Answer:** Tina's maximum deductible contribution for the year is $5,000. Because Tina is married, files a joint return, and reports AGI under $89,000 with her husband, her contribution is not phased out at all even though she is an active participant in CBA's retirement plan.

Steve's maximum deductible contribution for the year is also $5,000. Because Steve reports less earned income than Tina (in fact he doesn't report any earned income for the year), his deductible IRA contribution is limited to the lesser of (1) $5,000 or (2) $55,000 ($60,000 − $5,000) which is the couple's earned income minus Tina's deductible IRA contribution.

**What if:** Assume the same facts as the previous what if except that Tina and Steve file separately. What is each spouse's maximum deductible IRA contribution for the year?

**Answer:** $0 for Tina and $0 for Steve. Tina is ineligible to make a deductible IRA contribution because the couple's AGI of $60,000 exceeds the $10,000 phase-out limit and Steve may not make a deductible contribution to the IRA for two reasons: (1) his spouse participates in an employer's retirement plan and the couple's AGI exceeds the $10,000 phase-out limit and (2) he does not report any earned income.

> **THE KEY FACTS**
>
> **Traditional IRAs**
>
> ◼ **If taxpayer does not participate in employer provided plan but spouse does**
> · Deduction limit phased out for AGI between $167,000 and $177,000.
>
> ◼ **Distribution taxed as ordinary income**
> · If distribution before taxpayer is 59½, 10 percent penalty generally applies.

For all taxpayers, when the $5,000 ($6,000 for taxpayers 50 years of age at year-end) deductible limitation is phased out, taxpayers can still make *nondeductible* contributions to reach the $5,000 (or $6,000) contribution limit. While these contributions are not deductible, the earnings on the contributions grow tax-free until the taxpayer receives distributions from the IRA. On distribution, the taxpayer is taxed on the earnings generated by the nondeductible contributions but not on the actual nondeductible contributions. When taxpayers take partial distributions from an IRA to which they have made deductible and nondeductible contributions, each distribution consists of a taxable and nontaxable component. The portion of the distribution that is nontaxable is the ratio of the nondeductible contributions to the entire balance in

the account at the time of the distribution (nondeductible contributions divided by the entire balance in account). This is exactly the same procedure used in Example 13-11 to determine the nontaxable portion of nonqualified distributions from Roth 401(k) accounts. Most taxpayers exceeding the deductibility limits on traditional IRAs would likely do better by contributing to a Roth IRA, if eligible, instead of making nondeductible contributions to traditional IRAs.

Taxpayers who are eligible to contribute to an IRA may contribute to the IRA up to April 15 of the subsequent year (the unextended tax return due date). That is, as long as the taxpayer makes a contribution to the IRA by April 15 of year 2, the contribution counts as though it were made during year 1 (the prior calendar year).

**Distributions** Just as with traditional 401(k) plans, distributions from traditional IRAs are taxed as ordinary income to the taxpayer. Also, taxpayers withdrawing funds from traditional IRAs before reaching the age of 59½ are subject to a 10 percent early distribution penalty on the amount of the withdrawal. The IRA rules exempt certain distributions from the 10 percent penalty for early withdrawal. Among others, these distributions include proceeds distributed in the form of a life annuity and proceeds used for qualifying medical expenses, health insurance premiums for the owner, qualified higher education expenses, or first-time home purchases.[24] Taxpayers are also subject to the same minimum distribution requirements applicable to traditional 401(k) and other qualified retirement plans. Because the distribution rules for traditional IRAs are so similar to the rules for traditional 401(k) accounts, taxpayers with traditional IRAs face virtually the same issues as participants in traditional 401(k) plans when planning for distributions. Thus, they should be careful to avoid the 10 percent penalty while at the same time taking similar steps to maximize the tax deferral on their traditional IRA account balances.

## Roth IRAs

As an alternative to deductible IRAs, taxpayers meeting certain requirements can contribute to Roth IRAs. Contributions to Roth IRAs are *not* deductible and *qualifying* distributions from Roth IRAs are *not* taxable. Roth IRAs are subject to the same annual contribution limits as traditional IRAs ($5,000 in 2010; $6,000 if 50 years of age or older).[25]

Whether or not they participate in an employer-sponsored retirement plan, taxpayers are allowed to contribute to Roth IRAs as long as their AGI does not exceed specified thresholds. For unmarried taxpayers filing for 2010, the $5,000 Roth IRA contribution limitation (or $6,000 if age 50 and older) phases out proportionally for AGI between $105,000 and $120,000. For married taxpayers filing joint returns for 2010, the contribution limit phases out for AGI between $167,000 and $177,000. For married taxpayers filing separately, the limit on Roth IRA contributions phases out between AGI of $0 and $10,000.

**Distributions** *Qualifying* distributions from Roth IRAs are not taxable. A qualifying distribution is a distribution from funds or earnings from funds in a Roth IRA *if the distribution is at least five years after the taxpayer has opened the Roth IRA*[26] *and the distribution is* (1) made on or after the date the taxpayer reaches 59½ years of age, (2) made to a beneficiary (or to the estate of the taxpayer) on or after the death of the taxpayer, (3) attributable to the taxpayer being disabled, *or* (4) used to pay

---

THE KEY FACTS

**Roth IRAs**

- Contributions not deductible.

- Same contribution limits as traditional IRAs but
  · For 2010, contribution phases out for AGI between $105,000 and $120,000 for unmarried taxpayers and between $167,000 and $177,000 for married filing jointly taxpayers.

- Qualified distributions not taxable.
  · To qualify, account must be open for at least five years before distribution and distribution made after taxpayer reaches 59½ years of age (among others).

- Nonqualified distributions of account earnings
  · Taxed at ordinary rates and subject to 10 percent penalty.
  · Distributions first from contributions and then from account earnings.

---

[24]§72(t).

[25]Participants in Roth 401(k) accounts receiving distributions subject to the 10% premature distribution penalty and current taxation may avoid this outcome by rolling their distributions into a Roth IRA account. In this event, the normal Roth IRA contribution limit does not apply.

[26]The five-year period starts on January 1 of the year in which the contribution was made and ends on the last day of the fifth taxable year. See Reg §1.408A-6, Q&A2 and Q&A-5(b).

qualified acquisition costs for first-time homebuyers (limited to $10,000).[27] All other distributions are considered to be *nonqualified* distributions.

Nonqualified distributions are not necessarily taxable, however. Because taxpayers contributing to a Roth IRA contribute after-tax dollars (they don't deduct the contribution), they are able to withdraw the contributions tax-free at any time. However, *nonqualified* distributions of the *earnings* of a Roth IRA are taxable as ordinary income and subject to a 10 percent penalty. Nonqualified distributions are deemed to come first from the taxpayer's contributions and then from the earnings after the total contributions have been distributed (note that this is different than the equivalent rule for Roth 401(k)s). Thus, taxpayers can treat the Roth IRA as an emergency savings account to the extent of their contributions without incurring any penalties.

---

**Example 13-17**

**What if:** Assume that when Tina started working for CBA, she made a one-time contribution of $4,000 to a Roth IRA. Years later, she retired at the age of 65 when the value of her Roth account was $60,000. If Tina receives a $10,000 distribution from her Roth IRA, what amount of taxes (and penalty, if applicable) must she pay on the distribution (assume her ordinary marginal rate is 30 percent)?

**Answer:** $0 taxes and $0 penalty. Qualified Roth IRA distributions are not taxable.

**What if:** Assume the same facts as above, except that Tina received a $10,000 distribution when she was 57 years of age. What amount of taxes (and penalty, if applicable) is she required to pay on the distribution (assume a 30 percent ordinary marginal rate)?

**Answer:** $2,400 in total consisting of $1,800 in taxes ($6,000 earnings distributed × 30 percent marginal tax rate) and $600 penalty ($6,000 earnings × 10 percent penalty rate). Because Tina has not reached age 59½ at the time of the distribution, this is a nonqualified distribution. Consequently, she is taxed and penalized on the $6,000 distribution of earnings ($10,000 distribution minus $4,000 contribution).

**What if:** Assume that when Tina was 62 years old, she opened a Roth IRA, contributing $4,000. Three years later, Tina withdrew the entire account balance of $5,000. What amount of taxes (and penalty, if applicable) must Tina pay on the distribution (assume her marginal tax rate is 30 percent)?

**Answer:** $400 in total consisting of $300 taxes ($1,000 earnings × 30 percent marginal tax rate) and $100 penalty ($1,000 earnings × 10 percent penalty rate). The distribution is a nonqualified distribution because Tina did not have the Roth IRA open for five years before receiving the distribution. Consequently, she must pay taxes and penalties on the $1,000 account earnings ($5,000 − $4,000).

---

In contrast to taxpayers with traditional IRAs, taxpayers are *not ever* required to take minimum distributions from Roth IRAs. Thus, taxpayers can minimize distributions from Roth IRAs to maintain a source of tax-free income for as long as they choose.

### Rollover from Traditional to Roth IRA

Many taxpayers made contributions to traditional IRAs before Roth IRAs were available. Some taxpayers may have contributed to traditional IRAs and then later decided they should have contributed to a Roth IRA. The tax laws accommodate these taxpayers by allowing them to transfer funds from a traditional IRA (and other qualified defined contribution plans) to a Roth IRA.[28] This transfer of funds is called a **rollover.** When taxpayers do this, however, the entire amount taken out of the traditional IRA is taxed at ordinary rates but is not subject to the 10 percent penalty tax as long as the taxpayer contributes the *full amount* to a Roth IRA within 60 days of the withdrawal from the traditional IRA.[29]

---

[27]§408A(d)(2). A first-time homebuyer is someone who did not own a principal residence in the two years before acquiring the new home [see §72(t)(2)(F)].

[28]See Notice 2009-75, 2009-39 IRB.

[29]§408(d)(3).

**Example 13-18**

**THE KEY FACTS**

*Roth IRAs*

■ Rollovers from traditional IRAs to Roth IRAs.
· Amount withdrawn from traditional IRA fully taxable but not penalized.
· Must contribute full amount withdrawn to Roth IRA account within 60 days of withdrawal.
· Amounts withdrawn but not contributed subject to tax and 10 percent penalty.

**What if:** Let's assume that in the year she graduated from college and began working for CBA, Tina made a fully deductible $4,000 contribution to a *traditional* IRA. Three years later, when her marginal tax rate is 25 percent, she rolls over the entire $5,000 account balance into a Roth IRA. What amount of taxes is she required to pay on the rollover?

**Answer:** $1,250 ($5,000 × 25%). The entire $5,000 transferred from the IRA to the Roth IRA is taxed at 25 percent but is not subject to the 10 percent early withdrawal penalty. Even though Tina pays $1,250 in taxes on the transfer, she is required to contribute $5,000 to the Roth IRA within 60 days from the time she withdraws the money from the traditional IRA.

**What if:** What are the tax consequences if Tina pays the $1,250 tax bill and contributes only $3,750 to the Roth IRA account?

**Answer:** She must pay a $125 penalty. The penalty is 10 percent of the $1,250 that she withdrew from the IRA and did not contribute to the Roth IRA ($5,000 − $3,750).

Why would anyone be willing to pay taxes currently in order to avoid paying taxes later? Typically, a rollover from a traditional to a Roth IRA makes sense when taxpayers' marginal rates are currently low (when the tax costs of the rollover are low) and expected to be significantly higher in the future (when the expected benefits of the rollover are great). Before 2010, taxpayers with AGI in excess of $100,000 were not allowed to roll over traditional IRAs (and other qualified defined contribution plans) into Roth IRAs. However, beginning in 2010, there is no AGI restriction and higher-income taxpayers have the option to roll over amounts in traditional IRAs (and other qualified defined contribution plans) into Roth IRAs.[30]

### Comparing Traditional and Roth IRAs

So, which type of IRA is better for taxpayers? The tax considerations are very similar to those we already discussed when we compared traditional and Roth 401(k) plans. In general, after-tax returns from traditional IRAs will exceed those from Roth IRAs when marginal tax rates decline.[31] However, after-tax rates of return from Roth IRAs will exceed those from traditional IRAs when tax rates increase.

Unrelated to marginal tax rates, Roth IRAs have several advantages relative to traditional IRAs. Taxpayers can contribute to Roth IRAs at any age. In contrast, taxpayers are not allowed to make deductible contributions to traditional IRAs once they have reached 70½ years of age. Also, as noted earlier, the minimum distribution requirements for traditional IRAs do not apply to Roth IRAs. This provision permits owners of Roth IRAs to use their accounts to generate tax-free returns long after retirement. Exhibit 13-9 summarizes tax-related requirements for traditional and Roth IRAs.

**L05**

## SELF-EMPLOYED RETIREMENT ACCOUNTS

**THE KEY FACTS**

*Self-Employed Retirement Accounts*

■ Popular plans include SEP IRAs and individual 401(k)s.

■ Similar to (non-Roth) qualified defined contribution plans.
· Contributions deductible, distributions taxable.

We've discussed retirement savings opportunities available to employees. However, many taxpayers are self-employed small business owners who do not have access to employer-sponsored plans.[32] Moreover, individually managed retirement plans such as traditional and Roth IRAs are not particularly attractive to self-employed taxpayers due to the relatively low contribution limits on these plans. What retirement savings options, then, are available to the self-employed?

[30]§408A(c)(3).

[31]Under certain conditions, after-tax returns from Roth IRAs may exceed those from traditional IRAs even when tax rates are expected to be constant or to drop. See "Trimming Your Taxes: Why Roth 401(k)s Often Beat Conventional 401(k) Plans," *The Wall Street Journal,* September 6, 2006.

[32]Because sole proprietorships with self-employment income are very common, we assume in our examples and explanations here that any self-employment income originates from a sole proprietorship. In some cases, however, partners and LLC members may also have self-employment income from a partnership or LLC.

**EXHIBIT 13-9** Traditional IRA vs. Roth IRA Summary

| | Traditional IRA | Roth IRA |
|---|---|---|
| Contributions requirements | • Taxpayer must not be a participant in an employer-sponsored plan or, if participating in an employer-provided plan, must meet certain income thresholds. Those above the threshold will have deductible portion of contribution phased out. | • No deduction allowed for contributions. Must meet certain income requirements to be able to contribute to a Roth IRA. |
| Contributions | • Deductible unless participant in employer plan and high AGI.<br>• Nondeductible contributions allowed. | • Not deductible.<br>• May not contribute if high AGI. |
| Maximum contribution | • Lesser of $5,000 per taxpayer ($6,000 for taxpayers over 50 years old) or earned income. | • Same as traditional IRA. |
| Contribution dates | • Can contribute up to unextended tax return due date—generally April 15. | • Same as traditional IRA. |
| Distributions | • Generally taxed as ordinary income.<br>• If made before 59½, generally subject to 10 percent penalty.<br>• If nondeductible contribution made, allocate distribution between taxable and nontaxable amounts similar to annuity rules.<br>• Minimum distributions for years other than 2009 required by April 1 of the later of (1) the year after the year in which the taxpayer reaches 70½ or (2) the year after the year in which the taxpayer retires.<br>• Failure to meet minimum distribution timing and amount requirements triggers 50 percent penalty. | • Qualified distributions not taxed.<br>• Generally, distributions are qualified after account open for five years and employee has reached the age of 59½.<br>• Nonqualified distributions not taxed to extent of prior contributions.<br>• Nonqualified distributions of earnings subject to tax at ordinary rates and 10 percent penalty.<br>• No minimum distribution requirements. |

Congress created a number of retirement savings plans targeted toward self-employed taxpayers. Two of the more popular plans for the self-employed are SEP IRAs and individual (or "self-employed") 401(k) plans. These are defined contribution plans that generally work the same as employer-provided plans. That is, amounts set aside in these plans are deducted from income, earnings are free from tax until distributed, and distributions from the plans are fully taxable.[33] As we discuss below, these plans differ in terms of their annual contribution limits. They also have different nontax characteristics including their suitability for businesses with employees other than the owner and their administration costs. As you might expect, these factors come into play when self-employed small business owners choose a retirement plan.[34] We describe SEP IRAs and individual 401(k) plans below.[35]

[33]"Keogh" self-employed defined benefit plans are also an option. Generally, defined benefit plans are attractive to older, self-employed individuals with profitable businesses because they allow for greater deductible contributions. However, they are usually more costly to maintain than the defined contribution plans we mention here.

[34]Many investment firms provide comparisons to help taxpayers select self-employed retirement plans. One particularly good comparison is provided by Fidelity Investments at http://personal.fidelity.com/products/retirement/getstart/newacc/smallbizintro.shtml.cvsr?refpr=rrc50

[35]A Savings Incentive Match Plans for Employees (SIMPLE) IRA is another popular form of retirement plan for the self employed. For those earning lower amounts of self-employment income, the contribution limits for a SIMPLE IRA tend to be higher than contribution limits for SEP IRAs.

## Simplified Employee Pension (SEP) IRA

A simplified employee pension (SEP) can be administered through an individual retirement account (IRA) called a **SEP IRA**.[36] The owner of a sole proprietorship can make annual contributions directly to her SEP IRA. For 2010, the annual contribution is limited to the *lesser* of (1) $49,000 or (2) 20 percent of the sole proprietor's **net earnings from self-employment**.[37] Contributions can be made up to the extended due date of the tax return.[38]

**Example 13-19**

**THE KEY FACTS**

**Self-Employed Retirement Accounts**

■ SEP IRA 2010 contribution limit.
· Lesser of (1) $49,000 or (2) 20 percent of net earnings from self-employment (Sch. C income × 92.35%).

*What if:* Dave (age 64) receives director compensation of $30,000 during the current year and is reimbursed for all relevant expenses. Due to the specifics of the work arrangement, Dave is treated as a self-employed sole proprietor for tax purposes. If Dave sets up a SEP IRA for himself, what is the maximum contribution he may make to the plan (assuming he has no other source of employee or self-employment income)?

**Answer:** $5,541, computed as follows:

| Description | Amount | Explanation |
|---|---|---|
| (1) First limit on contribution | $49,000 | |
| (2) Net earnings from self-employment | 27,705 | $30,000 (Schedule C net income) × .9235. |
| (3) Percentage for limitation based on net earnings from self-employment | 20% | |
| (4) Second limit on contribution | 5,541 | (2) × (3). |
| Maximum contribution | $ 5,541 | Lesser of (1) or (4). |

*What if:* Assume Dave is 48 years old at the end of the year. What is his maximum deductible contribution?

**Answer:** $5,541. Dave's maximum deductible contribution for a SEP IRA does not depend on his age.

*What if:* Suppose Dave received $300,000 of self-employment income rather than $30,000. What is his maximum deductible contribution to this SEP IRA account?

**Answer:** $49,000, the lesser of (1) $49,000 or (2) $54,410 [20% × ($300,000 × .9235)].

**Nontax Considerations**   If a sole proprietor has hired employees, the sole proprietor *must* contribute to their respective SEP IRAs based on their compensation. Because owners may view this requirement as being too favorable to employees, this plan is best suited for sole proprietors who do not have employees or for situations where owners are willing to provide generous benefits to their employees. From an administrative perspective, SEP IRAs are easy to set up and have relatively low administrative costs from year to year.

## Individual 401(k)s

Individual 401(k) plans are strictly for sole proprietors (and the spouse of the sole proprietor) who do not have employees. Under this type of plan, the sole proprietor can contribute the lesser of (1) $49,000 or (2) 20 percent × net earnings from self-employment (employer's contribution) + $16,500 (employee's contribution). Further, if the sole proprietor is at least 50 years of age by the end of the tax year, she may contribute an *additional* $5,500 (called a "catch-up contribution"). However, total contributions may not exceed the taxpayer's net earnings from self-employment.

[36]§408(k).

[37]This is generally calculated by multiplying the owner's net Schedule C income by 92.35%. Chapter 7 addresses self-employment taxes in more detail. Also note that for SEP IRAs no catch-up contributions are allowed for taxpayers 50 years and older.

[38]§404(h). This is September 15 for a calendar-year taxpayer.

**Example 13-20**

*What if:* Assume the same facts as in Example 13-19, except that Dave set up an individual 401(k) account. Dave is 64 years old at the end of the year, reports $30,000 of self-employment income, and has no other sources of income. What is the maximum amount he can contribute to his individual 401(k) account?

**Answer:** $27,541, computed as follows:

| Description | Amount | Explanation |
|---|---|---|
| (1) First limit on contribution | $49,000 | |
| (2) Net earnings from self-employment | 27,705 | $30,000 (Schedule C net income) × .9235. |
| (3) Percentage for limitation based on net earnings from self-employment | 20% | |
| (4) Limit on employer's contribution | 5,541 | (2) × (3). |
| (5) Limit on employee's contribution | 16,500 | |
| (6) Second limitation | 22,041 | (4) + (5). |
| (7) Maximum contribution before catch-up contribution | 22,041 | Lesser of (1) or (6). |
| (8) Catch-up contribution | 5,500 | Dave is 64 years old at year-end. |
| **Maximum contribution** | **$27,541** | (7) + (8), not to exceed (2). |

---

**THE KEY FACTS**

Self-Employed Retirement Accounts

■ Individual 401(k) 2010 contribution limit.
· Lesser of (1) $49,000 or (2) 20 percent of net earnings from self employment plus $16,500 ($22,000 for taxpayers who are at least 50 years old at the end of the year).
· Contribution cannot exceed net earnings from self employment.

---

**Example 13-21**

*What if:* Assume Dave is 48 years old at the end of the year, reports $30,000 of self-employment income, and has no other sources of income. What is his maximum deductible contribution to his individual 401(k) account?

**Answer:** $22,041. This is the same as the amount he could contribute as a 64-year-old (see prior example), minus the $5,500 catch-up adjustment ($27,541 − $5,500).

*What if:* Assume the same facts as above except that Dave (age 64) earned $10,000 of self-employment income rather than $30,000. What is his maximum deductible contribution to his individual 401(k)?

**Answer:** $9,235, computed as follows (Dave's contribution is limited to his net earnings from self-employment):

| Description | Amount | Explanation |
|---|---|---|
| (1) First limit on contribution | $49,000 | |
| (2) Net earnings from self-employment | 9,235 | $10,000 (Schedule C net income) × .9235. |
| (3) Percentage for limitation based on net earnings from self-employment | 20% | |
| (4) Limit on employer's contribution | 1,847 | (2) × (3). |
| (5) Limit on employee's contribution | 16,500 | |
| (6) Second limitation | 18,347 | (4) + (5). |
| (7) Maximum contribution before catch-up contribution | 18,347 | Lesser of (1) or (6). |
| (8) Catch-up contribution | 5,500 | Dave is 64 years old at year-end. |
| **Maximum contribution** | **$ 9,235** | (7) + (8), not to exceed (2). |

**Example 13-22**

**What if:** Assume Dave (age 64) earned $400,000 of self-employment income. What is his maximum deductible contribution to his individual 401(k)?

**Answer:** $54,500, computed as follows:

| Description | Amount | Explanation |
|---|---|---|
| (1) First limit on contribution | $ 49,000 | |
| (2) Net earnings from self-employment | 369,400 | $400,000 (Schedule C net income) × .9235. |
| (3) Percentage for limitation based on net earnings from self-employment | 20% | |
| (4) Limit on employer's contribution | 73,880 | (2) × (3). |
| (5) Limit on employee's contribution | 16,500 | |
| (6) Second limitation | 90,380 | (4) + (5). |
| (7) Maximum contribution before catch-up contribution | 49,000 | Lesser of (1) or (6). |
| (8) Catch-up contribution | 5,500 | Dave is 64 years old at year-end. |
| **Maximum contribution** | **$ 54,500** | (7) + (8), not to exceed (2). |

**Nontax Considerations**  As we mentioned above, the individual 401(k) plan is not available for sole proprietors with employees, so providing benefits to employees under the plan is not a concern. However, the administrative burden of establishing, operating, and maintaining a 401(k) plan is potentially higher than it is for the other self-employed plans.

**LO6**

## SAVER'S CREDIT

To encourage middle- and low-income taxpayers to take advantage of the retirement savings opportunities discussed in this chapter, Congress provides an additional **saver's credit** for an individual's elective contribution of up to $2,000 to any of the qualified retirement plans discussed in this chapter including employer-sponsored qualified plans, traditional and Roth IRA plans, and self-employed qualified plans. The credit is provided *in addition to* any deduction the taxpayer is allowed for contributing to a retirement account. It is calculated by multiplying the taxpayer's contribution, up to a maximum of $2,000, by the applicable percentage depending on the taxpayer's filing status and AGI. The credit is nonrefundable.[39] Exhibit 13-10 provides the applicable percentages for 2010 according to a taxpayer's filing status and AGI.[40]

In addition to restricting the credit to taxpayers with AGI below a certain amount, the credit is also restricted to individuals who are 18 years of age or older and who are not full-time students or claimed as dependents on another taxpayer's return.[41] Although limited in scope, the saver's credit provides some tax benefits for those taxpayers who qualify.

---

**THE KEY FACTS**

**Saver's Credit**

▪ Credit for taxpayers contributing to qualified plan.

▪ Credit is based on contributions up to $2,000, taxpayer's filing status, and AGI.
· Phased out as AGI increases.
· Maximum credit is $1,000.
· Unavailable for married filing jointly taxpayers with AGI over $55,500, head of household taxpayers with AGI above $41,625, and all other taxpayers with AGI above $27,750.

---

[39]According to §25B(g), the saver's credit is applied to the taxpayer's remaining tax liability after the application of certain other tax credits including the child tax credit and the American opportunity and lifetime learning credits.

[40]For this purpose, AGI is determined without considering the foreign earned income exclusion provided for U.S. residents living abroad under §911.

[41]Generally speaking, "full-time students" are those who are classified as such by the educational organizations referred to in §152(f)(2).

**EXHIBIT 13-10**   **2010 Applicable Percentages for Saver's Credit by Filing Status and AGI**

| Applicable Percentage | Joint Filers AGI | Heads of Household AGI | All Other Filers AGI |
| --- | --- | --- | --- |
| 50% | 0 to $33,500 | 0 to $25,125 | 0 to $16,750 |
| 20% | $33,500 to $36,000 | $25,125 to $27,000 | $16,750 to $18,000 |
| 10% | $36,000 to $55,500 | $27,000 to $41,625 | $18,000 to $27,750 |
| No credit available | Above $55,500 | Above $41,625 | Above $27,750 |

**Example 13-23**

*What if:* Tina earned $24,000 during the year she began working for CBA. She earned $4,000 in salary working part-time while she was in school and $20,000 in salary working for CBA from September through December. To get an early start saving for retirement, assume she contributed $4,000 to a traditional IRA. Because Tina did not participate in an employer-sponsored retirement plan during the current year she may deduct the full $4,000 contribution as a *for* AGI deduction, reducing her AGI from $24,000 to $20,000. What amount of saver's credit, if any, is Tina allowed to claim?

**Answer:** $200 ($2,000 × 10 percent applicable credit).

*What if:* What saver's credit may Tina claim if her AGI was $15,000?

**Answer:** $1,000 ($2,000 × 50 percent applicable credit).

## CONCLUSION

The decisions that employees like Tina, Lisa, and Dave must deal with highlight the role that tax issues play in this important area. Employers, like their employees, must also pay careful attention to tax considerations when deciding on retirement savings vehicles to offer their employees. Further, as has been a recurring theme throughout this book, nontax issues play an equal, if not more important, role in the retirement savings decisions of both employees and employers.

### SUMMARY

Describe the tax and nontax aspects of employer-provided defined benefit plans from both the employer's and employee's perspective.   **LO1**

- Benefits are determined based on years of service and salary. The maximum annual benefit is capped and adjusted upward annually for inflation.
- Benefits vest over time using either a five-year cliff or seven-year graded vesting schedule.
- Employers deduct cash contributions to fund the plan and employees treat cash distributions as ordinary income in the year received.
- Employers bear investment risk with defined benefit plans.
- Premature distribution and minimum distribution penalties don't typically apply to defined benefit distributions.
- Because of the high cost of funding and maintaining defined benefit plans, they are waning in popularity.

Explain and determine the tax consequences associated with employer-provided defined contribution plans, including traditional 401(k) and Roth 401(k) plans.   **LO2**

- Employers specify the amount they will contribute to defined contribution plans instead of the annual benefit. However, employers are not permitted to contribute to Roth 401(k) plans.

- Employees may contribute to either a traditional 401(k) or Roth 401(k) account, and they determine how employer and employee contributions are invested. Employees bear investment risk with defined contribution plans.
- Annual employer and employee contributions are limited and maximum contribution amounts are adjusted annually for inflation.
- Employer contributions to traditional plans vest over time using either a three-year cliff or six-year graded vesting schedule.
- Employers deduct their contributions to traditional defined contribution plans.
- Employee contributions to traditional defined contribution plans are excluded from their taxable wages on Form W-2. Employee contributions to Roth 401(k) plans are not excluded.
- Distributions from traditional 401(k) plans are taxable at ordinary rates and qualified distributions from Roth 401(k) plans are not taxable.
- Distributions from both traditional 401(k) and Roth 401(k) plans are subject to premature and minimum distribution penalties. Minimum distributions are not required for distributions pertaining to 2009.
- After-tax returns from Roth 401(k) plans are generally superior to those from traditional 401(k) plans when marginal tax rates are increasing.

**LO3**  Describe the tax implications of deferred compensation from both the employer's and employee's perspective.

- Employees elect to defer current salary in exchange for promised future payments from the employer.
- Because the employer's promise of future payment is unsecured, employees recognize ordinary income when future payments are received. Employers wait to deduct payments until cash is actually paid.
- The after-tax returns and costs from deferred compensation arrangements to employees and employers depend on the current and future marginal tax rates of both the employee and employer. They also depend on the rate of return employers promise employees on deferred salary.
- Deferred compensation is often used to overcome deductibility constraints imposed on salary and qualified pension plans.
- Employees bear more risk with deferred compensation relative to other forms of retirement savings because employees are unsecured creditors of their employers.

**LO4**  Determine the tax consequences of traditional and Roth Individual Retirement Accounts and explain the differences between them.

- The same inflation-adjusted annual contribution limits apply to both traditional IRAs and Roth IRAs.
- The deduction for traditional IRA contributions is phased out for taxpayers covered by a retirement plan at work and with AGI above certain inflation-adjusted amounts. Special rules pertain for spouses not covered by an employer plan.
- The ability to contribute to a Roth IRA is phased out for individuals with AGI above certain inflation-adjusted amounts.
- Distributions from traditional IRAs are taxed at ordinary rates. A 10 percent premature distribution penalty generally applies to distributions from traditional IRAs received before age 59½.
- Distributions from Roth IRAs received after a Roth IRA account has been open for at least five years and after the recipient reaches age 59½ are not taxable. The earnings component of any distributions not meeting these requirements is generally taxable and subject to the 10 percent premature distribution penalty.
- Taxpayers generally prefer Roth IRAs to traditional IRAs when they expect their marginal tax rates to increase.

Describe the retirement savings options available to self-employed taxpayers and compute the limitations for deductible contributions to retirement accounts for self-employed taxpayers.

**L05**

- Self-employed individuals may set up their own qualified pension plans such as SEP IRAs and individual 401(k)s.
- Contribution limits generally parallel those for employer-sponsored plans, allowing self-employed individuals to have the same access to qualified plans that employees have.
- Self-employed individuals with employees may have to incur the cost of covering their employees when they establish a qualified retirement plan.

Compute the saver's credit.

**L06**

- Individuals may receive up to a $1,000 tax credit for contributions they make to IRAs and employer-sponsored qualified plans.
- The maximum contribution eligible for the credit is $2,000, and the amount of the credit is a function of the taxpayer's filing status and AGI.

# KEY TERMS

cliff vesting (13-4)
defined benefit plan (13-3)
defined contribution plan (13-3)
graded vesting (13-4)
Individual Retirement Account (IRA) (13-19)
minimum distributions (13-6)

net earnings from self-employment (13-26)
nonqualified deferred compensation (13-15)
qualified retirement plans (13-3)
rollover (13-23)
Roth IRA (13-19)

saver's credit (13-28)
§162(m) limitation (13-18)
SEP IRA (13-26)
traditional 401(k) (13-13)
traditional IRA (13-19)
vesting (13-4)

Roth 401(k) (13-13)

# DISCUSSION QUESTIONS

1. **(LO1, LO2)** How are defined benefit plans different from defined contribution plans? How are they similar?
2. **(LO1)** Describe how an employee's benefit under a defined benefit plan is computed.
3. **(LO1, LO2)** What does it mean to vest in a defined benefit or defined contribution plan?
4. **(LO1, LO2)** Compare and contrast the minimum vesting requirements for defined benefit plans and defined contribution plans.
5. **(LO1, LO2)** What are the nontax advantages and disadvantages of defined benefit plans relative to defined contribution plans?
6. **(LO1)** Describe the maximum annual benefit that taxpayers may receive under defined benefit plans.
7. **(LO1)** Describe the distribution or payout options available to taxpayers participating in qualified defined benefit plans. How are defined benefit plan distributions to recipients taxed?
8. **(LO1, LO2)** Describe the minimum distribution requirements for defined benefit plans. Are these requirements typically an item of concern for taxpayers?
9. **(LO1, LO2)** Compare and contrast the employer's responsibilities for providing a defined benefit plan to employees relative to providing a defined contribution plan.

10. **(LO2)** Describe how an employee's benefit under a defined contribution plan is determined.

11. **(LO2)** Is there a limit to how much an employer and/or employee may contribute to an employee's defined contribution account(s) for the year? If so, describe the limit.

12. **(LO2)** Cami (age 52 and married) was recently let go as part of her employer's reduction in force program. Cami's annual AGI was usually around $50,000. Shortly after Cami's employment was terminated, her employer distributed the balance of her employer-sponsored 401(k) account to her. What could Cami do to avoid being assessed the 10 percent early distribution penalty?

13. **(LO2)** When may employees begin to receive defined contribution plan distributions without penalty?

14. **(LO2)** Describe the circumstances under which distributions from defined contribution plans are penalized. What are the penalties?

**research**

15. **(LO2)** Brady Corporation has a profit sharing plan that allocates 10 percent of all after-tax income to employees. The profit sharing is allocated to individual employees based on relative employee compensation. The profit sharing contributions vest to employees under a six-year graded plan. If an employee terminates his or her employment before fully vesting, the plan allocates the forfeited amounts among the remaining participants according to their account balances. Is this forfeiture allocation policy discriminatory, and will it cause the plan to lose its qualified status? Use Rev. Rul. 81-10 to help formulate your answer.

16. **(LO2)** What does it mean if an employer "matches" employee contributions to 401(k) plans?

**planning**

17. **(LO2)** What nontax factor(s) should an employee consider when deciding whether and to what extent to participate in an employer's 401(k) plan?

18. **(LO2)** What are the differences between a traditional 401(k) and Roth 401(k) plan?

19. **(LO2)** Can employers match employee contributions to Roth 401(k) plans? Explain.

20. **(LO2)** Describe the annual limitation on employer and employee contributions to traditional 401(k) and Roth 401(k) plans.

21. **(LO2, LO3)** When a company is limited by the tax laws in the amount it can contribute to an employee's 401(k) plan, what will it generally do to make the employee whole? Is this likely an issue for rank-and-file employees? Why or why not?

**planning**

22. **(LO2)** From a tax perspective, how would taxpayers determine whether they should contribute to a traditional 401(k) or a Roth 401(k)?

23. **(LO2)** Could a taxpayer contributing to a traditional 401(k) plan earn an after-tax return *greater* than the before-tax return? Explain.

24. **(LO2, LO3)** Explain the *tax* similarities and differences between qualified defined contribution plans and nonqualified deferred compensation plans from an *employer's* perspective.

25. **(LO2, LO3)** Explain the *tax* similarities and differences between qualified defined contribution plans and nonqualified deferred compensation plans from an *employee's* perspective.

26. **(LO2, LO3)** Explain the *nontax* similarities and differences between qualified defined contribution plans and nonqualified deferred compensation plans from an *employer's* perspective.

27. **(LO2, LO3)** Explain the *nontax* similarities and differences between qualified defined contribution plans and nonqualified deferred compensation plans from an *employee's* perspective.

**planning**

28. **(LO3)** From a *tax* perspective, what issues does an employee need to consider in deciding whether to defer compensation under a nonqualified deferred compensation plan or to receive it immediately?

29. **(LO3)** From a *nontax* perspective, what issues does an employee need to consider in deciding whether to defer compensation under a nonqualified deferred compensation plan or to receive it immediately?    ■ **planning**

30. **(LO3)** What are reasons why companies provide nonqualified deferred compensation plans for certain employees?

31. **(LO3)** How can companies use deferred compensation to avoid the §162(m) limitation on salary deductibility?    ■ **planning**

32. **(LO3)** Are companies allowed to decide who can and who cannot participate in nonqualified deferred compensation plans? Briefly explain.

33. **(LO1, LO2, LO3)** How might the ultimate benefits to an employee who participates in a qualified retirement plan of a company differ from an employee who participates in a nonqualified deferred compensation plan of the company if the company experiences bankruptcy before the employee is scheduled to receive the benefits?

34. **(LO4)** What are the primary tax differences between traditional IRAs and Roth IRAs?

35. **(LO4)** Describe the circumstances in which it would be more favorable for a taxpayer to contribute to a traditional IRA rather than a Roth IRA and vice versa.    ■ **planning**

36. **(LO4)** What are the requirements for a taxpayer to make a deductible contribution to a traditional IRA? Why do the tax laws impose these restrictions?

37. **(LO4)** What is the limitation on a deductible IRA contribution for 2010?

38. **(LO4)** Compare the minimum distribution requirements for traditional IRAs to those of Roth IRAs.

39. **(LO4)** How are qualified distributions from Roth IRAs taxed? How are nonqualified distributions taxed?

40. **(LO4)** Explain when a taxpayer will be subject to the 10 percent penalty when receiving distributions from a Roth IRA.

41. **(LO4)** Is a taxpayer who contributed to a traditional IRA able to transfer or "roll over" the money into a Roth IRA? If yes, explain the tax consequences of the transfer.

42. **(LO4)** Assume a taxpayer makes a nondeductible contribution to a traditional IRA. How does the taxpayer determine the taxability of distributions from the IRA on reaching retirement?

43. **(LO4)** When a taxpayer takes a nonqualified distribution from a Roth IRA, is the entire amount of the distribution treated as taxable income?

44. **(LO5)** What types of retirement plans are available to self-employed taxpayers?

45. **(LO5)** Compare and contrast the annual limitations on deductible contributions for self-employed taxpayers to SEP IRAs, and individual 401(k) accounts.

46 **(LO5)** What are the nontax considerations for self-employed taxpayers deciding whether to set up a SEP IRA or an individual 401(k)?    ■ **planning**

47. **(LO6)** What is the saver's credit and who is eligible to receive it?

48. **(LO6)** What is the maximum saver's credit available to taxpayers? What taxpayer characteristics are relevant to the determination?

49. **(LO6)** How is the saver's credit computed?

## PROBLEMS

50. **(LO1)** Javier recently graduated and started his career with DNL Inc. DNL provides a defined benefit plan to all employees. According to the terms of the plan, for each full year of service working for the employer, employees receive a benefit of 1.5 percent of their average salary over their highest three years of

compensation from the company. Employees may accrue only 30 years of benefit under the plan (45 percent). Determine Javier's annual benefit on retirement, before taxes, under each of the following scenarios:

a. Javier works for DNL for three years and three months before he leaves for another job. Javier's annual salary was $55,000, $65,000, $70,000, and $72,000 for years 1, 2, 3, and 4 respectively. DNL uses a five-year cliff vesting schedule.

b. Javier works for DNL for three years and three months before he leaves for another job. Javier's annual salary was $55,000, $65,000, $70,000, and $72,000 for years 1, 2, 3, and 4 respectively. DNL uses a seven-year graded vesting schedule.

c. Javier works for DNL for six years and three months before he leaves for another job. Javier's annual salary was $75,000, $85,000, $90,000, and $95,000 for years 4, 5, 6, and 7 respectively. DNL uses a five-year cliff vesting schedule.

d. Javier works for DNL for six years and three months before he leaves for another job. Javier's annual salary was $75,000, $85,000, $90,000, and $95,000 for years 4, 5, 6, and 7 respectively. DNL uses a seven-year graded vesting schedule.

e. Javier works for DNL for 32 years and three months before retiring. Javier's annual salary was $175,000, $185,000, and $190,000 for his final three years of employment.

51. **(LO1)** Alicia has been working for JMM Corp. for 32 years. Alicia participates in JMM's defined benefit plan. Under the plan, for every year of service for JMM she is to receive 2 percent of the average salary of her three highest years of compensation from JMM. She retired on January 1, 2010. Before retirement, her annual salary was $570,000, $600,000, and $630,000 for 2007, 2008, and 2009. What is the maximum benefit Alicia can receive in 2010?

52. **(LO2)** Kim has worked for one employer her entire career. While she was working, she participated in the employer's defined contribution plan [traditional 401(k)]. At the end of 2010, Kim retires and the balance in her defined contribution plan was $2,000,000 at the end of 2009.

a. What is Kim's minimum required distribution for 2010 in 2011 if she is 68 years old at the end of 2010?

b. What is Kim's minimum required distribution for 2010 if she turns 70½ during 2010 and she has not turned 71 years old by the end of 2010? When must she receive this distribution?

c. What is Kim's minimum required distribution for 2010 in 2011 if she is 73 years old at the end of 2010?

d. Assuming that Kim is 75 years old at the end of 2010 and that her marginal tax rate in 2010 is 33 percent, what will she have remaining after taxes if she receives only a distribution of $50,000 for 2010?

53. **(LO2)** Matthew (48 at year-end) develops cutting-edge technology for SV, Inc., located in Silicon Valley. In 2010, Matthew participates in SV's money purchase pension plan (a defined contribution plan) and in his company's 401(k) plan. Under the money purchase pension plan, SV contributes 15 percent of an employee's salary to a retirement account for the employee up to the amount limited by the tax code. Because it provides the money purchase pension plan, SV does not contribute to the employee's 401(k) plan. Matthew would like to maximize his contribution to his 401(k) account after SV's contribution to the money purchase plan.

a. Assuming Matthew's annual salary is $400,000, what amount will SV contribute to Matthew's money purchase plan? What can Matthew contribute to his 401(k) account in 2010?

b. Assuming Matthew's annual salary is $240,000, what amount will SV contribute to Matthew's money purchase plan? What can Matthew contribute to his 401(k) account in 2010?

c. Assuming Matthew's annual salary is $60,000, what amount will SV contribute to Matthew's money purchase plan? What amount can Matthew contribute to his 401(k) account in 2010?

d. Assume the same facts as c. except that Matthew is 54 years old at the end of 2010. What amount can Matthew contribute to his 401(k) account in 2010?

54. **(LO2)** In 2010, Maggy (34 years old) is an employee of YBU Corp. YBU provides a 401(k) plan for all its employees. According to the terms of the plan, YBU contributes 50 cents for every dollar the employee contributes. The maximum employer contribution under the plan is 15 percent of the employee's salary (if allowed, YBU contributes until the employee has contributed 30 percent of her salary).

a. Maggy has worked for YBU corporation for 3½ years before deciding to leave. Maggy's annual salary during this time was $45,000, $52,000, $55,000, and $60,000 (she only received half of her final year's salary). Assuming Maggy contributed 8 percent of her salary (including her 2010 salary) to her 401(k) account, what is Maggy's vested account balance when she leaves YBU (exclusive of account earnings)? Assume YBU uses three-year cliff vesting.

b. Same question as a. except YBU uses six-year graded vesting.

c. Maggy wants to maximize YBU's contribution to her 401(k) account in 2010. How much should Maggy contribute to her 401(k) account assuming her annual salary is $100,000 (she works for YBU for the entire year)?   ■ **planning**

d. Same question as c., except Maggy is 55 years old rather than 34 years old at the end of the year.   ■ **planning**

55. **(LO2)** In 2010, Nina contributes 10 percent of her $100,000 annual salary to her 401(k) account. She expects to earn a 7 percent before-tax rate of return. Assuming she leaves this (and any employer contributions) in the account until she retires in 25 years, what is Nina's after-tax accumulation from her 2010 contributions to her 401(k) account?

a. Assume Nina's marginal tax rate at retirement is 30 percent.

b. Assume Nina's marginal tax at retirement is 20 percent.

c. Assume Nina's marginal tax rate at retirement is 40 percent.

56. **(LO2)** In 2010, Nitai contributes 10 percent of his $100,000 annual salary to a Roth 401(k) account sponsored by his employer, AY, Inc. AY, Inc., matches employee contributions dollar for dollar up to 10 percent of the employee's salary to the employee's traditional 401(k) account. Nitai expects to earn a 7 percent before-tax rate of return. Assuming he leaves his contributions in the Roth 401(k) and traditional 401(k) accounts until he retires in 25 years, what are Nitai's after-tax proceeds from the Roth 401(k) and traditional 401(k) accounts after he receives the distributions assuming his marginal tax rate at retirement is 30%?

57. **(LO3)** Marissa participates in her employer's nonqualified deferred compensation plan. For 2010, she is deferring 10 percent of her $320,000 annual salary. Assuming this is her only source of income and her marginal income tax rate is 30 percent, how much *tax* does Marissa save in 2010 by deferring this income?   ■ **planning**

58. **(LO3)** Paris participates in her employer's nonqualified deferred compensation plan. For 2010, she is deferring 10 percent of her $320,000 annual salary. Assuming this is her only source of income and her marginal income tax rate is 30 percent, how much does deferring Paris's income save her employer (after taxes) in 2010? Paris's employer's marginal tax rate is 35 percent.

59. **(LO3)** Leslie participates in IBO's nonqualified deferred compensation plan. For 2010, she is deferring 10 percent of her $300,000 annual salary. Based on her deemed investment choice, Leslie expects to earn a 7 percent before-tax rate of return on her deferred compensation, which she plans to receive in 10 years. Leslie's marginal tax rate in 2009 is 30 percent. IBO's marginal tax rate is 35 percent.

    a. Assuming Leslie's marginal tax rate in 10 years when she receives the distribution is 33 percent, what is Leslie's after-tax accumulation on the deferred compensation?

    b. Assuming Leslie's marginal tax rate in 10 years when she receives the distribution is 20 percent, what is Leslie's after-tax accumulation on the deferred compensation?

■ planning

    c. Assuming IBO's cost of capital is 8 percent after taxes, how much deferred compensation should IBO be willing to pay Leslie that would make it indifferent between paying 10 percent of Leslie's current salary or deferring it for 10 years?

■ planning

60. **(LO3)** XYZ Corporation has a deferred compensation plan under which it allows certain employees to defer up to 40 percent of their salary for five years.

    a. Assume XYZ has a marginal tax rate of 35 percent for the foreseeable future and earns a before-tax return of 8 percent on its assets. Joel Johnson, XYZ's VP of finance, is attempting to determine what amount of deferred compensation XYZ should be willing to pay in five years that would make XYZ indifferent between paying current salary of $10,000 and paying the deferred compensation. What amount of deferred compensation would accomplish this objective?

    b. Assume Julie, an XYZ employee, has the option of participating in XYZ's deferred compensation plan. Julie's marginal tax rate is 40 percent and she expects the rate to remain constant over the next five years. Julie is trying to decide how much deferred compensation she will need to receive from XYZ in five years to make her indifferent between receiving current salary of $10,000 and receiving the deferred compensation payment. If Julie takes the salary, she will invest it in a taxable corporate bond paying interest at 5 percent annually. What amount of deferred compensation would accomplish this objective?

61. **(LO4)** John (age 51 and single) has earned income of $3,000. He has $30,000 of unearned (capital gain) income.

    a. If he does not participate in an employer-sponsored plan, what is the maximum deductible IRA contribution John can make in 2010?

    b. If he does participate in an employer-sponsored plan, what is the maximum deductible IRA contribution John can make in 2010?

    c. If he does not participate in an employer-sponsored plan, what is the maximum deductible IRA contribution John can make in 2010 if he has earned income of $10,000?

62. **(LO4)** William is a single writer (age 35) who recently decided that he needs to save more for retirement. His 2010 AGI is $61,000 (all earned income).

    a. If he does not participate in an employer-sponsored plan, what is the maximum deductible IRA contribution William can make in 2010?

b.  If he does participate in an employer-sponsored plan, what is the maximum deductible IRA contribution William can make in 2010?

c.  Assuming the same facts as in b. except his AGI is $75,000, what is the maximum deductible IRA contribution William can make in 2010?

63. **(LO4)** In 2010, Susan (44 years old) is a highly successful architect and is covered by an employee-sponsored plan. Her husband, Dan (47 years old), however, is a Ph.D. student and is unemployed. Compute the maximum deductible IRA contribution for each spouse in the following alternative situations.

a.  Susan's salary and the couple's AGI is $180,000. The couple files a joint tax return.

b.  Susan's salary and the couple's AGI is $120,000. The couple files a joint tax return.

c.  Susan's salary and the couple's AGI is $80,000. The couple files a joint tax return.

d.  Susan's salary and her AGI is $80,000. Dan reports $5,000 of AGI (earned income). The couple files separate tax returns.

64. **(LO4)** In 2010, Rashaun (62 years old) retired and planned on immediately receiving distributions (making withdrawals) from his traditional IRA account. The current balance of his IRA account is $160,000. Over the years, Rashaun has contributed $40,000 to the IRA. Of his $40,000 contributions, $30,000 was *nondeductible* and $10,000 was *deductible*.

a.  If Rashaun currently withdraws $20,000 from the IRA, how much tax will he be required to pay on the withdrawal if his marginal tax rate is 20 percent?

b.  If Rashaun currently withdraws $70,000 from the IRA, how much tax will he be required to pay on the withdrawal if his marginal tax rate is 30 percent?

65. **(LO4)** Brooklyn has been contributing to a traditional IRA for seven years (all deductible contributions) and has a total of $30,000 in the account. In 2010, she is 39 years old and has decided that she wants to get a new car. She withdraws $20,000 from the IRA to help pay for the car. She is currently in the 25 percent marginal tax bracket. What amount of the withdrawal, after tax considerations, will Brooklyn have available to purchase the car?

66. **(LO4)** Jackson and Ashley Turner (both 45 years old) are married and want to contribute to a Roth IRA for Ashley. In 2010, their AGI is $170,000. Jackson and Ashley each earned half of the income.

a.  How much can Ashley contribute to her Roth IRA if they file a joint return?

b.  How much can Ashley contribute if she files a separate return?

67. **(LO4)** Harriet and Harry Combs (both 37 years old) are married and both want to contribute to a Roth IRA. In 2010, their AGI is $50,000. Harriet earned $46,000 and Harry earned $4,000.

a.  How much can Harriet contribute to her Roth IRA if they file a joint return?

b.  How much can Harriet contribute if she files a separate return?

c.  How much can Harry contribute to his Roth IRA if they file separately?

68. **(LO4)** George (age 42 at year-end) has been contributing to a traditional IRA for years (all deductible contributions) and his IRA is now worth $25,000. He is planning on transferring (or rolling over) the entire balance into a Roth IRA account. George's marginal tax rate is 25 percent.

a.  What are the tax consequences to George if he takes $25,000 out of the traditional IRA and puts the entire amount into a Roth IRA?

b. What are the tax consequences to George if he takes $25,000 out of the traditional IRA, pays the taxes due from the IRA distribution, and contributes the remaining distribution to the Roth IRA?

c. What are the tax consequences to George if he takes $25,000 out of the traditional IRA and keeps $10,000 to pay taxes and to make a down payment on a new car?

**■ planning** 69. **(LO4)** John is trying to decide whether to contribute to a Roth IRA or a traditional IRA. He plans on making the maximum $5,000 contribution to whichever plan he decides to fund. He currently pays tax at a 30 percent marginal income tax rate but he believes that his marginal tax rate in the future will be 28 percent. He intends to leave the money in the Roth IRA or traditional IRA accounts for 30 years and he expects to earn a 6 percent before-tax rate of return on the account.

a. How much will John accumulate after taxes if he contributes to a Roth IRA?

b. How much will John accumulate after taxes if he contributes to a traditional IRA?

c. Without doing any computations, explain whether the traditional IRA or the Roth IRA will generate a greater after-tax rate of return.

70. **(LO4)** Over the past three years, Sherry has contributed a total of $12,000 to a Roth IRA account ($4,000 a year). The current value of the Roth IRA is $16,300. In the current year, Sherry withdraws $14,000 of the account balance to purchase a car. Assuming Sherry is in a 25 percent marginal tax bracket, how much of the $14,000 withdrawal will she retain after taxes to fund her car purchase?

71. **(LO4)** Seven years ago, Halle (currently age 41) contributed $4,000 to a Roth IRA account. The current value of the Roth IRA is $9,000. In the current year Halle withdraws $8,000 of the account balance to use as a down payment on her first home. Assuming Halle is in a 25 percent marginal tax bracket, how much of the $8,000 withdrawal will she retain after taxes to fund her house down payment?

**■**
**research** 72. **(LO4)** Sarah was contemplating making a contribution to her traditional
**■■** individual retirement account for 2010. She determined that she would contribute $5,000 to her IRA and she deducted $5,000 for the contribution when she completed and filed her 2010 tax return on February 15, 2011. Two months later, on April 15, Sarah realized that she had not yet actually contributed the funds to her IRA. On April 15, she went to the post office and mailed a $5,000 check to the bank holding her IRA. The bank received the payment on April 17. In which year is Sarah's $5,000 contribution deductible?

**■ planning** 73. **(LO5)** Elvira is a self-employed taxpayer who turns 42 years old at the end of the year (2010). In 2010, her net Schedule C income was $120,000. This was her only source of income. This year, Elvira is considering setting up a retirement plan. What is the maximum amount Elvira may contribute to the self-employed plan in each of the following situations?

a. She sets up a SEP IRA.

b. She sets up an individual 401(k).

**■ planning** 74. **(LO5)** Hope is a self-employed taxpayer who turns 54 years old at the end of the year (2010). In 2010, her net Schedule C income was $120,000. This was her only source of income. This year, Hope is considering setting up a retirement plan. What is the maximum amount Hope may contribute to the self-employed plan in each of the following situations?

a. She sets up a SEP IRA.

b. She sets up an individual 401(k).

75. **(LO5)** Rita is a self-employed taxpayer who turns 39 years old at the end of the year (2010). In 2010, her net Schedule C income was $300,000. This was her only source of income. This year, Rita is considering setting up a retirement plan. What is the maximum amount Rita may contribute to the self-employed plan in each of the following situations?

   a. She sets up a SEP IRA.

   b. She sets up an individual 401(k).

76. **(LO5)** Reggie is a self-employed taxpayer who turns 59 years old at the end of the year (2010). In 2010, his net Schedule C income was $300,000. This was his only source of income. This year, Reggie is considering setting up a retirement plan. What is the maximum amount he may contribute to the self-employed plan in each of the following situations?

   a. He sets up a SEP IRA.

   b. He sets up an individual 401(k).

77. **(LO6)** Desmond is 25 years old and he participates in his employer's 401(k) plan. During the year, he contributed $3,000 to his 401(k) account. What is Desmond's 2010 saver's credit in each of the following alternative scenarios?

   a. Desmond is not married and has no dependents. His AGI after deducting his 401(k) contribution is $30,000.

   b. Desmond is not married and has no dependents. His AGI after deducting his 401(k) contribution is $17,500.

   c. Desmond files as a head of household and has AGI of $39,000.

   d. Desmond and his wife file jointly and report an AGI of $30,000 for the year.

78. **(LO6)** Penny is 57 years old and she participates in her employer's 401(k) plan. During the year, she contributed $2,000 to her 401(k) account. Penny's AGI is $26,000 after deducting her 401(k) contribution. What is Penny's 2010 saver's credit in each of the following alternative scenarios?

   a. Penny is not married and has no dependents.

   b. Penny files as a head of household and she has three dependents.

   c. Penny files as a head of household and she has one dependent.

   d. Penny is married and files a joint return with her husband. They have three dependents.

   e. Penny files a separate tax return from her husband. She claims two dependent children on her return.

## COMPREHENSIVE PROBLEMS

79. Alex is 31 years old and has lived in Los Alamos, New Mexico, for the last four years where he works at the Los Alamos National Laboratory (LANL). LANL provides employees with a 401(k) plan and for every $1 an employee contributes (up to 9 percent of the employee's salary) LANL contributes $3 (a 3 to 1 match). The plan provides a six-year graded vesting schedule. Alex is now in his fifth year working for LANL, and his current year salary is $150,000. Alex's marginal tax rate is 28 percent in 2010. Answer the following questions relating to Alex's retirement savings in 2010.

   a. Assume that over the past four years, Alex has contributed $45,000 to his 401(k) and his employer has contributed $115,000 to the plan. The plan has an account balance of $175,000. What is Alex's vested account balance in his 401(k)?

b.  Because Alex considers his employer's matching contributions "free money," he wants to maximize the amount of LANL's contributions. What is the least amount Alex can contribute and still maximize LANL's contribution?

c.  In need of cash to build a home theater, Alex withdrew $30,000 from his traditional 401(k) account. What amount of the withdrawal, after taxes and penalties, will Alex have available to complete his project?

d.  Assume that Alex contributes $10,000 to his traditional 401(k) account this year. Also assume that in 30 years, Alex retires (at age 61) and withdraws the $10,000 contribution made this year *and* all the earnings generated by the contribution. Also assume that his marginal tax rate at the time he retires is 25 percent. Ignore any prior or subsequent contributions to his plan. If Alex earns a 6 percent annual before-tax rate of return, what are his after-tax proceeds from the distribution?

e.  Assume that Alex is 74 years old at the end of the year (assume the year is not 2009), retired, and that his marginal tax rate is 25 percent. His account balance in his traditional 401(k) was $1,250,000 at the end of last year. What is the minimum distribution Alex must receive from his 401(k) account for this year (not 2009)? If Alex receives a $43,000 distribution from his 401(k) account (his only distribution during the year) what amount will he be able to keep after taxes and penalties (if any)?

f.  Assume that Alex retired in 2008 but, as of the end of 2009, he had not received any distributions from his 401(k) account. Further assume that the balance in his 401(k) account at the end of 2008 was $2,000,000. Alex turned 70 years old on February 15, 2010. Is Alex required to receive a distribution for 2009? If so, what is the amount of the required distribution and when must he receive it to avoid a penalty?

80.  Tommy (age 47) and his wife, Michelle (age 49), live in Sandusky, Ohio, where Tommy works for Callahan Auto Parts (CAP) as the vice-president of the brakes division. Tommy's 2010 salary is $360,000. CAP allows Tommy to participate in its nonqualified deferred compensation plan in which participants can defer 15 percent of their salary for five years. Tommy also participates in CAP's qualified 401(k) plan. Tommy's current marginal tax rate is 28 percent and CAP's current marginal tax rate is 34 percent.

a.  Assuming Tommy earns a 6 percent *after-tax* rate of return and he expects his marginal tax rate to be 30 percent in five years, what before-tax deferred compensation payment in five years would make him indifferent between receiving the deferred compensation payment or 15 percent of his salary now (ignore payroll taxes)?

b.  Assuming CAP has an 8 percent *after-tax* rate of return and expects its marginal tax rate to be 35 percent in five years, how much would it be willing to pay in five years to be indifferent between paying the deferred compensation or paying 15 percent of Tommy's salary now (ignore payroll taxes)?

c.  Will Tommy and CAP be able to come to an agreement on deferring Tommy's salary?

d.  Assuming that Tommy has an AGI of $93,000, that Michelle earns $10,000 working part-time but she does not participate in an employer-sponsored retirement plan, and that they file a joint return, what is the maximum deductible contribution Tommy and Michelle may make to a traditional IRA?

e.  Tommy has a balance of $55,000 in his traditional IRA. Due to some recent tax cuts, his marginal tax rate is 20 percent, so he would like to roll his traditional IRA into a Roth IRA. What are the tax consequences to Tommy if he takes $55,000 out of the IRA, pays the taxes due from the traditional IRA distribution, and contributes the remaining distribution to the Roth IRA?

81. Gerry (age 56) and Elaine (age 54) have been married for 12 years and file a joint tax return. The couple lives in an apartment in downtown Manhattan. Gerry's father, Mortey, recently retired from Del Boca Vista Corporation (DBVC) where he worked for many years. Mortey participated in DBVC's defined benefit plan. Elaine is an editor and works for Pendent Publishing earning an annual $150,000 salary in 2010. Gerry is a self-employed standup comedian, and had net business income of $46,000 in 2010. At the advice of their neighbor, Gerry and Elaine have come to you to for help in answering several retirement savings-related questions.

    a. The DBVC defined benefit plan specifies a benefit of 1.5 percent for each year of service, up to a maximum of 30 percent (20 years of service), of the average of the employee's three highest years of salary. Mortey worked for the company for 25 years and earned $75,000, $78,000, and $84,000 over his final three years of service. What is Mortey's annual benefit from DBVC's defined benefit plan?

    b. Elaine has worked at Pendent Publishing since January 1, 2005. The company offers a defined contribution plan. It matches 100 percent of employee contributions to the plan up to 6 percent of her salary. Prior to 2009, Elaine had contributed $40,000 to the plan and her employer had contributed $28,000 to the plan. In 2010, Elaine contributed $16,500 to her traditional 401(k). What is the amount of her employer's matching contribution for 2010? Assuming the company uses a six-year graded vesting schedule, what is Elaine's vested balance in the plan at the end of 2010 (for simplicity, disregard the plan's earnings)?

    c. Elaine tells you that her employer has offered her $30,000 in 10 years to defer 10 percent of her current salary (defer $15,000). Assuming that the couple's marginal tax rate is currently 30 percent, they earn an after-tax rate of return of 8 percent, and they expect their marginal tax rate to be 25 percent in 10 years, should Elaine accept her company's offer? What is the minimum amount she should be willing to accept (ignoring nontax factors and payroll taxes)?

    d. Gerry has a SEP IRA and would like to contribute as much as possible to this account. What is the maximum contribution Gerry can make to his SEP IRA in 2010?

    e. Assuming Gerry had an individual 401(k), what is the maximum amount he could contribute to the plan in 2010?

    f. Gerry also has a traditional IRA with an account balance of $42,000. He would like to convert the traditional IRA to a Roth IRA. Gerry would like to pay the least amount of tax possible in rolling the account over. How should he accomplish this and what amount of tax will he owe assuming a 30 percent marginal tax rate?

    g. Assume that Gerry rolled over his traditional IRA into a Roth IRA six years ago (rather than in 2010) and that the account now has a balance of $78,000. The couple is considering buying their first home and would like to pay as much down as possible. They have heard from their friends that they can take the funds from their Roth IRA and use it to buy their first home. Are their friends correct? What would you advise them to do?

    h. Assume that Gerry and Elaine made $20,000 of total contributions to their qualified retirement accounts in 2010. Also assume that their AGI is $38,000. What would be the amount of their saver's credit for 2010?

chapter

# 14 Tax Consequences of Home Ownership

## Learning Objectives

**Upon completing this chapter, you should be able to:**

**LO 1** Compute the taxable gain on the sale of a residence and explain the requirements for excluding gain on the sale.

———————————————■———————————————

**LO 2** Determine the amount of allowable interest expense deductions on loans secured by a residence.

———————————————■———————————————

**LO 3** Discuss the deductibility of real property taxes and describe the first-time home buyer credit.

———————————————■———————————————

**LO 4** Explain the tax issues and consequences associated with rental use of the home, including determining the deductibility of residential rental real estate losses.

———————————————■———————————————

**LO 5** Describe the requirements necessary to qualify for home office deductions and compute the deduction limitations on home office deductions.

| Storyline Summary | |
|---|---|
| *Taxpayers:* | Tyler and Jasmine Jefferson |
| *Location:* | Chicago, Illinois |
| *Employment status:* | Tyler—Newly hired V.P. of Sales for GLO Corporation earning an annual salary of $225,000 per year. Jasmine—graphic designer, earning an annual salary of $40,000 per year. |
| *Filing status:* | Married filing jointly |
| *Dependents:* | Two children |
| *Marginal tax rate:* | 33 percent |

W ith the extra income Tyler Jefferson is earning in his new V.P. of Sales position for GLO Corporation, his family now has greater financial flexibility, but with the money comes new possibilities. For one, Tyler and Jasmine Jefferson would like to sell their current home and purchase a larger one closer to Tyler's work. Fortunately, the value of their home has increased considerably since they purchased it, which should allow them to make a substantial down payment on a new home. Still, they would need to acquire financing to make the purchase. Jasmine likes the idea of buying a vacation home in Scottsdale, Arizona. Besides the great weather (she and Tyler both love golf), Scottsdale has the added benefit of being near Jasmine's family. She is trying to sell the second-home idea to Tyler by suggesting that they could rent the house when they're not there to help defray the costs. Finally, Jasmine is seriously considering a transition to self-employment as a graphic designer. She believes, with her experience and contacts, she can find enough clients to keep busy most of the time—and she very much likes the idea of setting aside a room in their primary home as her workplace. ∎

When making these decisions, the Jeffersons should consider the tax consequences of their actions. Will they be required to pay taxes on the gain from the sale of their current home? Will the interest expense on the new home be fully deductible? Should they pay points to obtain a lower interest rate on the home loan? What will be the after-tax cost of the loan payments? If they use a home-equity loan to cover personal expenses, is the interest expense deductible? If they borrow money to buy a vacation home, can they deduct interest on the loan? If they rent out the vacation home for part of the year, how do they account for the related income and expenses for tax purposes? If the rental of the second home generates losses, are these losses deductible? If Jasmine sets up a home office, will the Jeffersons be allowed any tax deductions for expenses relating to their home? This chapter answers these and other relevant questions for the Jeffersons and for others interested in the tax consequences of home ownership.

## PERSONAL USE OF THE HOME

To buy or to rent? This is a difficult question with no single answer. The decision to purchase a home is a significant one that involves both nontax and tax considerations. Primary nontax factors favoring home ownership include the appreciation potential for the home as an investment. As the value of the home increases, so does the homeowner's net worth. A home is frequently an individual's most significant investment. Therefore, home ownership also involves significant potential risk. When real estate values decline, the owner's net worth declines as well. Homeowners borrowing funds to purchase their home can potentially achieve large returns on their investment due to the power of leverage, but a home is by no means a liquid asset. Furthermore, homeowners must assume the risk associated with the possible default on the loan. If the owner does not make the mortgage payments required by the terms of the loan, the lender may repossess the home. Homeowners also are responsible for the cost or effort required to repair, maintain, and landscape the home. Finally, because building, buying, or selling a home and moving in or out of a home are expensive and time-consuming tasks, home ownership reduces one's ability to relocate to take advantage of new opportunities.

On the tax side, the government clearly smiles on home ownership given the deductions available to homeowners that are unavailable to renters. In fact, in the government's listing of projected "tax expenditures" (tax breaks provided to taxpayers) for the years 2009–2013, the deductibility of mortgage interest on owner-occupied homes is ranked number two.[1] The projections indicate that in 2009 homeowners were expected to save over $100 billion in tax payments due to the mortgage interest deduction. Besides the deduction for interest payments made on home-related loans, other tax benefits of home ownership involve excluding gain on the sale of the home, deducting real estate taxes paid on the home, and deducting expenses relating to business offices in the home. Homeowners also may gain tax benefits associated with owning and renting a vacation home. We address the tax consequences of home ownership throughout the remainder of the chapter.

### THE KEY FACTS

**Tax and Nontax Consequences of Home Ownership**

■ **Nontax Consequences**
- Large investment.
- Potential for big return (or loss) on investment with use of leverage.
- Risk of default on home loan.
- Time and costs of maintenance.
- Limited mobility.

■ **Tax Consequences**
- Interest expense deductible.
- Gain on sale excludable.
- Real property taxes on home deductible.
- Rental and business-use possibilities.

**LO1**

### *Exclusion of Gain on Sale of Personal Residence*

Because a personal residence is a capital asset, any gain or loss a taxpayer realizes by selling the residence is a capital gain or loss. When a taxpayer sells a personal residence at a loss, the loss is a nondeductible personal loss.[2] However, when a taxpayer sells a personal residence at a gain, the tax consequences are generally much more

---

[1]Number one on the list is the gross income exclusion for employer-paid medical insurance premiums and medical care. See http://www.whitehouse.gov/omb/budget/fy2009/pdf/apers/receipts.pdf (see page 298).
[2]§165(c).

favorable. In fact, taxpayers meeting certain home ownership *and* use requirements can permanently exclude up to $250,000 ($500,000 if married filing jointly) of realized gain on the sale.[3] Gain in excess of the excludable amount generally qualifies as long-term capital gain subject to tax at preferential rates. Details about the exclusion requirements are provided below.

**Requirements**    To qualify for the exclusion, the taxpayer must meet both ownership and use tests for the residence:

> *Ownership test:* The taxpayer must have owned the property for a total of two or more years during the five-year period ending on the date of the sale. The ownership test prevents a taxpayer from purchasing a home, fixing it up, and soon thereafter selling it and excluding the gain—a real estate investment practice termed **flipping.** In these circumstances, the gain is primarily due to the taxpayer's efforts in remodeling the home, not to general appreciation in the value of the property.

> *Use test:* The taxpayer must have *used* the property as her **principal residence** for a total of two or more years during the five-year period ending on the date of the sale. Congress intended for the exclusion provision to provide tax benefits to homeowners rather than investors or landlords. The use test helps ensure that taxpayers using the exclusion have realized gains from selling the home they actually live in as opposed to selling an investment or rental property. What qualifies as a principal residence? By definition, a taxpayer can have only one "principal" residence. When a taxpayer lives in more than one residence during the year, the determination of which residence is the principal residence depends on the facts and circumstances such as:

- Amount of time the taxpayer spends at each residence during the year.
- The proximity of each residence to the taxpayer's employment.
- The principal place of abode of the taxpayer's immediate family.
- The taxpayer's mailing address for bills and correspondence.

A taxpayer's principal residence *could* be a houseboat, trailer, or condominium—a residence need not be in a fixed location.

Note that the periods of ownership and use need not be continuous nor do they need to cover the same two-year period. In fact, a taxpayer could rent a home and live in it as her principal residence during 2005 and then again during 2007, purchase the home and rent to someone else during 2008 and 2009, and then sell the home at the beginning of 2010—and *still* meet the ownership and use tests!

How do the ownership and use tests apply to married couples filing joint returns? Married couples filing joint returns are eligible for the full $500,000 exclusion if *either* spouse meets the ownership test and *both* spouses meet the principal-use test.

> **THE KEY FACTS**
>
> **Exclusion of Gain on Sale of Personal Residence**
>
> ▮ Must meet ownership and use tests.
> · Must own home for at least two of five years before sale.
> · Must use home as principal residence for at least two of five years before sale.
> · For married couples to qualify for exclusion on a joint return, one spouse must meet ownership test and both spouses must meet use test.

---

**Example 14-1**

When Tyler and Jasmine were married, Jasmine moved into Tyler's home located in Denver, Colorado. Tyler had purchased the home two years before the marriage. After the marriage, the couple lived in the home together as their principal residence for three years before selling the home to move to Chicago. Tyler was the sole owner of the home for the entire five years he resided in the home. Would gain on the sale of the home qualify for the $500,000 exclusion available to married couples filing jointly even though Jasmine was never an owner of the home?

(continued on page 14-4...)

---

[3]§121(a). Also see IRS Publication 523 *"Selling Your Home."*

> **Answer:** Yes. Gain on the sale qualifies for the full $500,000 exclusion available to married couples filing jointly because Tyler met the ownership test, and both Tyler and Jasmine met the use test.
>
> **What if:** Assume that Tyler and Jasmine lived in the home together for only one year before selling it. Would the couple be allowed to exclude any gain on the sale?
>
> **Answer:** Yes, but because only Tyler meets the ownership and use tests, they would qualify for the $250,000 exclusion available to *single taxpayers* even if they file a joint return.

Another issue arises when a taxpayer moves out of a home, rents it to another to occupy for a while, and then sells it. Does the taxpayer lose the exclusion because the property is technically a rental property at the time of sale? As we mention above, the tax laws accommodate the taxpayer in this situation because the taxpayer need only use the home as a principal residence for two of the five years preceding the sale. Thus, a taxpayer can still qualify if she moves out and rents the home before selling it. Interestingly, as illustrated in Exhibit 14-1, a taxpayer could technically simultaneously own two residences meeting the ownership and use tests.

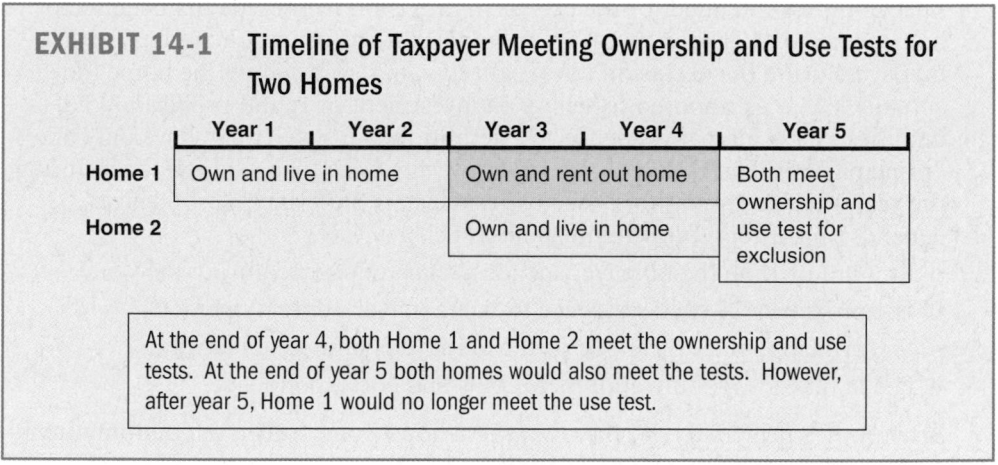

**EXHIBIT 14-1    Timeline of Taxpayer Meeting Ownership and Use Tests for Two Homes**

|  | Year 1 | Year 2 | Year 3 | Year 4 | Year 5 |
|---|---|---|---|---|---|
| **Home 1** | Own and live in home | | Own and rent out home | | Both meet ownership and use test for exclusion |
| **Home 2** | | | Own and live in home | | |

At the end of year 4, both Home 1 and Home 2 meet the ownership and use tests. At the end of year 5 both homes would also meet the tests. However, after year 5, Home 1 would no longer meet the use test.

While taxpayers may qualify for the exclusion even when they rent homes before selling them, they must consider three issues:

1.  If a taxpayer converts a home from a personal residence to a rental property, the tax basis of the home becomes the *lesser* of (a) the taxpayer's basis at the time of the conversion or (b) the fair market value of the home at the time of the conversion (any loss that accrued while the property was personal-use property disappears at the time of the conversion).[4]

2.  If a taxpayer deducts depreciation expense (and reduces the basis of the home by the amount of the depreciation expense) while renting it, either before or after using the home as a principal residence, the *gain caused by the reduction in basis from the depreciation expense* is not eligible for the exclusion.[5]

3.  If a taxpayer converts a rental home to a principal residence, the basis of the home as a principal residence is the same basis the home had as a rental at the time the rental home was converted to a principal residence. Thus, if at the time of the conversion to personal use, the value of the home is less than the basis of the home, the built-in loss will never be deductible because the rental use has ceased.[6]

---

[4]Reg. §1.167(g)-1.

[5]This gain is unrecaptured §1250 gain subject to a maximum tax rate of 25 percent. See discussion in Chapter 10 for details.

[6]To deduct the loss, the taxpayer must sell the home rather than convert it to personal use.

When taxpayers own two homes that meet the exclusion requirements and they sell both homes in the same year, can they exclude gain on both homes? Remember the old adage: If it sounds too good to be true, it probably is. Indeed, the tax law limits each taxpayer to one exclusion every two years. That is, once a taxpayer sells a residence and uses the exclusion on the sale, she will not be allowed to claim another exclusion until at least two years pass from the time of the first sale.

Finally, the exclusion of gain on a sale of a residence provides a great opportunity for contractors in the business of building homes to convert what would otherwise be ordinary income from the taxpayer's trade or business into nontaxable capital gain. Generally when a contractor builds and sells a home for a profit, the gain on the sale is taxable as ordinary business income to the contractor. However, if a contractor builds a home, lives in it for two years, and then sells the home at a profit the gain may qualify for the exclusion. One commentator has pointed out that the gain exclusion provision allows those in the business of building homes to generate the only tax-free business income under the current tax system.[7]

**Amount of Limitations on Exclusion** As we describe above, single taxpayers (or married taxpayers when only one spouse meets the requirements) may exclude up to $250,000 of gain on the sale of a principal residence. Married couples filing jointly may exclude up to $500,000 of gain.

---

**Example 14-2**

As we described in Example 14-1, the Jeffersons sold their home in Denver, Colorado, and moved to Chicago. Let's assume that Tyler initially purchased the home for $220,000 and the Jeffersons sold the home for $320,000. How much of the $100,000 gain realized on the sale ($320,000 − $220,000) are they allowed to exclude?

**Answer:** All $100,000. As we determined in Example 14-1, the Jeffersons qualified for the full exclusion available to married couples filing jointly because Tyler met the ownership test and both Tyler and Jasmine met the use test. Consequently, they are allowed to exclude the entire $100,000 of gain and could have excluded up to $500,000 of gain on the sale.

---

However, if *either* spouse is ineligible for the exclusion because he or she personally used the $250,000 exclusion on another home sale during the two years before the date of the current sale, the couple's available exclusion is reduced to $250,000. If a widow or widower sells a home that the surviving spouse owned and occupied with the other spouse, the surviving spouse is entitled to the full $500,000 exclusion provided that the surviving spouse sells the home within two years after the date of death of the spouse.

Sometimes taxpayers are unable to meet the ownership and use tests due to unusual or hardship circumstances. For example, a taxpayer may be forced to sell his home before he meets the ownership and use requirements due to a change in employment, significant health issues, or other unforeseen financial difficulties. In such cases, the *maximum* available exclusion is reduced. To qualify for the exclusion due to a change in employment, the taxpayer's new place of employment must be at least 50 miles farther from the residence that is sold than was the previous place of employment.[8] That is, the taxpayer will not qualify unless the taxpayer's commute from the old home to the new job is at least 50 miles longer than the

> **THE KEY FACTS**
>
> **Exclusion of Gain on Sale of Personal Residence**
>
> ■ **Exclusion Amount**
> · $500,000 for married couples filing joint returns.
> · $250,000 for other taxpayers.
> · Hardship provisions *maximum exclusion* = full exclusion × months of qualifying ownership and use/24 months.
> · Gain eligible for exclusion may be reduced for time home is not used as principal residence if it is being used as a principal residence at the time of the sale.

---

[7]See L. M. Stone, "Obvious Flaws Reduce Confidence in Federal Tax System," *Tax Notes,* February 23, 2004, pp. 1034–35.

[8]If there is no previous place of employment, the distance between the individual's new place of employment and the residence sold must be at least 50 miles.

taxpayer's commute from the old home to the old job.[9] The maximum exclusion available to a taxpayer selling under these circumstances is expressed in the formula presented in Exhibit 14-2.

---

**EXHIBIT 14-2** **Formula for Determining Maximum Home Sale Exclusion in Hardship Circumstances**

Maximum exclusion in hardship circumstances =
Full exclusion × Qualifying months/24 months, where

*Full exclusion* = $250,000 for single taxpayers or $500,000 for taxpayers filing a joint return.

*Qualifying months* = the number of months the taxpayer met the ownership and use requirements for the home before *selling* it.

*24 months* = the number of months taxpayer must own and use home as principal residence to qualify for the full exclusion.[10]

---

**Example 14-3**

**What if:** Let's assume that when the Jeffersons moved from Denver, they purchased a home in Chicago for $275,000 and moved into the home on July 1, 2009. In January of 2010, Tyler accepted a work opportunity with a different employer located in Miami, Florida. On February 1 of 2010, the Jeffersons sold their home for $295,000 and permanently relocated to Miami. How much of the $20,000 realized gain ($295,000 − $275,000) on their home sale can the Jeffersons *exclude* from taxable income?

**Answer:** All $20,000. The Jeffersons lived in the home for only seven months (July 1, 2009, to February 1, 2010), so they do not meet either the ownership or the use test to qualify for the full exclusion. Thus, they must compute their maximum exclusion using the formula presented in Exhibit 14-2 as follows:

$500,000 (full exclusion) × 7 (qualifying months)/24 = $145,833.

**What if:** Assume the same facts, except that the Jeffersons realized a $150,000 gain on the sale of their home. How much of the realized gain would they recognize and at what rate would this gain be taxed?

**Answer:** $150,000 gain realized minus $145,833 exclusion = $4,167 short-term capital gain (the home is a capital asset that the Jeffersons owned for one year or less).

---

Note, as the previous example illustrates, that under the so-called hardship provision, it is the *full exclusion* that is reduced, not necessarily the excludable gain. Consequently, if a taxpayer's gain on the sale of a residence is less than the maximum exclusion, the taxpayer may exclude the full amount of the gain. Finally, the rule limiting taxpayers to claiming one exclusion every two years *does not apply* to taxpayers selling under hardship circumstances.

***Limitation on exclusion for nonqualified use.*** The amount of gain eligible for exclusion may be limited for taxpayers selling homes after December 31, 2008.[11] The limitation applies if, on or after January 1, 2009, the taxpayer uses the home for something other than a principal residence for a period (termed *nonqualified use*) and then uses the home as a principal residence before selling it. The provision is designed to reduce the excludable gain for taxpayers who use the home as a vacation home or rental property for a period and then convert it to a principal residence before selling

---

[9]You may recall that this is the same test required to determine if a taxpayer qualifies for moving expenses as discussed in Chapter 6.

[10]Taxpayers may choose to use the number of days the taxpayer fully qualified for the exclusion divided by 730 days.

[11]§121(b)(4)[(5)].

in order to exclude gain (including gain accrued while it was not a principal residence) on the sale. If the limitation applies, the percentage of the gain that is not eligible for exclusion is the ratio of the amount of the nonqualified use divided by the amount of time the taxpayer owned the home (purchase date through date of sale). Note that this provision does not reduce the maximum exclusion. Rather, it reduces the amount of gain eligible for exclusion.

---

**Example 14-4**

**What if:** Suppose the Jeffersons purchased a home 1 on July 1, 2008, for $300,000. They lived in home 1 as their principal residence until July 1, 2011, when they moved to a new principal residence (home 2). They finally sold home 1 on July 1, 2013, for $400,000. What amount of the $100,000 gain on the sale of home 1 ($400,000 amount realized minus $300,000 adjusted basis) may the Jeffersons exclude from gross income?

**Answer:** All $100,000. The Jeffersons meet the ownership and use tests (they owned and used home 1 as their principal residence for at least two of the five years prior to July 1, 2013), so they qualify for a maximum exclusion of $500,000. Further, the gain eligible for the exclusion is *not* reduced because the Jeffersons stopped using home 1 as a principal residence after July 1, 2011, but they did not use it as a principal residence before they sold it.

**What if:** Assume the same facts as above, except that on July 1, 2012, the Jeffersons moved back into home 1 and used it as their principal residence until they sold it for $400,000 on July 1, 2013. What amount of the $100,000 gain on the sale of home 1 may the Jeffersons exclude from income?

**Answer:** $80,000. The Jeffersons meet the ownership and use tests for home 1 and therefore qualify for the maximum $500,000 exclusion. However, because they sold home 1 after December 31, 2008, they stopped using the home as their principal residence for a period (nonqualified use from July 1, 2011–July 1, 2012), and they again used the home as their principal residence before selling (July 1, 2012–July 1, 2013), the gain eligible for exclusion must be reduced. The percentage of the gain that is not eligible for exclusion is 20 percent, which is the amount of nonqualified use (one year; July 1, 2012–July 1, 2013) divided by the total amount of time the Jeffersons owned the home (five years; July 1, 2008–July 1, 2013). Therefore, the Jeffersons must reduce their gain eligible for exclusion by $20,000 ($100,000 gain × 20% reduction percentage), allowing them to exclude $80,000 of the $100,000 gain from gross income.

---

**Exclusion of Gain from Debt Forgiveness on Foreclosure of Home Mortgage**    Prior to 2007, if a lender foreclosed (took possession of) a taxpayer's principal residence, sold the home for less than the taxpayer's outstanding mortgage, and forgave the taxpayer of the remainder of the debt, the taxpayer was required to include the debt forgiveness in her gross income. However, from January 1, 2007, through December 31, 2012, taxpayers who realize income from this situation are allowed to exclude up to $2 million of debt forgiveness if the debt is secured by the taxpayer's principal residence (the principal residence is collateral for the loan) and the debt was incurred to acquire, construct, or substantially improve the home.[12]

### Interest Expense on Home-Related Debt

L02

A major tax benefit of owning a home is that taxpayers are generally allowed to deduct the interest they pay on their home mortgage loans as itemized (*from* AGI) deductions. Taxpayers report these itemized deductions on Schedule A of their individual tax Form 1040. For taxpayers that itemize deductions, the mortgage interest expense can generate significant tax savings and reduce the after-tax cost of mortgage payments. Often, this deduction alone exceeds the standard deduction, thus allowing taxpayers to claim other itemized deductions.

---

[12]§108(h).

**Example 14-5**

During the current year, Tyler and Jasmine own a home with an average mortgage balance of $300,000. They pay interest at 6 percent annually on the loan. The Jeffersons' marginal income tax rate is 33 percent, and before counting mortgage interest, their itemized deductions exceed the standard deduction. What is the before- and after-tax cost of their mortgage interest expense for the year?

**Answer:** $18,000 before-tax cost and $12,060 after-tax cost, computed as follows:

| Description | Amount | Explanation |
| --- | --- | --- |
| (1) Before-tax interest expense | $18,000 | $300,000 × 6%. All deductible. |
| (2) Marginal tax rate | × 33% | |
| (3) Tax savings from interest expense | 5,940 | (1) × (2). |
| After-tax cost of interest expense | $12,060 | (1) − (3). |

Note that the $5,940 tax savings generated by the mortgage interest expense deduction reduces the after-tax cost of their monthly mortgage payment by $495 ($5,940/12).

**What if:** Assume that instead of buying a home, the Jeffersons rented a home and paid $1,500 a month for rent expense. What would be the before- and after-tax cost of the $18,000 annual rental payments?

**Answer:** $18,000 before- and after-tax cost of rental payments. Because rental payments are not deductible, they do not generate any tax savings, so the before- and after-tax cost of the rental payments is the same.

Despite the apparent tax savings from buying versus renting a home, it is important to consider that nontax factors could favor renting over purchasing a home.

Taxpayers are allowed to deduct only "qualified" residence interest as an itemized deduction.[13] Qualified residence interest is interest paid on the principal amount of **acquisition indebtedness** and on the principal amount of **home-equity indebtedness.** Both types of indebtedness must be **secured** by a **qualified residence** to qualify. To understand what this means exactly, we need to define a few terms.

*Loan secured by residence:* The residence is the collateral for the loan. If the owner does not make the payments on the loan, the lender may take possession of the home to satisfy the owner's responsibility for the loan.

*Qualified residence:* The taxpayer's principal residence (as described in the previous section) *and* one other residence. For a taxpayer with *more* than two residences, which property is treated as the second qualified residence is an annual election—that is, the taxpayer can choose to deduct interest related to a particular second home one year and a different second home the next. The second residence is often a vacation home where the taxpayer resides part time. If the taxpayer rents the second residence for part of the year, the residence will qualify if the taxpayer's personal use of the home *exceeds the greater* of (1) 14 days or (2) 10 percent of the number of rental days during the year.[14] Consequently, for a second home to be considered a qualified residence, a taxpayer who rents the home for 100 days must use the home for personal purposes for at least 15 days, and a taxpayer who rents the second home for 200 days must use the home for personal purposes for at least 21 days.

---

[13]§163(h).

[14]§163(h)(4). If the taxpayer does not rent out the property, the taxpayer may choose the property as a qualified residence even if the taxpayer's personal use of the property is 14 days or less. See §163(h)(4)(A)(iii) and IRS Publication, "Home Mortgage Interest Deduction."

*Acquisition indebtedness:* Any debt secured by a qualified residence that is incurred in acquiring, constructing, or substantially improving the residence.

*Home-equity indebtedness:* Any debt, except for acquisition indebtedness, secured by the taxpayer's qualified residence to *the extent it does not exceed the fair market value of the residence minus the acquisition indebtedness.* That is, for purposes of deducting interest, total qualifying home-related debt cannot exceed the total value of the home. For example, in a rapidly appreciating real estate environment, aggressive lenders may offer "home-equity" loans that result in loan-to-value ratios up to 125 percent. To the extent that the loan exceeds the equity in the home (value minus acquisition indebtedness), the interest is not deductible.[15] The determination of the amount of home-equity debt is made at the time the loan is executed, so a subsequent decline in a home's value does not reduce the interest expense deduction.

Borrowers can use the proceeds from a home-equity loan for any purpose, as long as the loan is secured by the residence—hence, the popularity of home-equity loans to consolidate debt and lower monthly payments. However, as we note in Chapter 7, interest expense on home-equity loans not used to purchase or substantially improve the home is not deductible for AMT purposes. The use of home-equity loans to pay for non-home-related expenditures is an example of the conversion tax planning strategy described in Chapter 3.

**Limitations on Home-Related Debt** The tax laws *limit the amount of debt* on which taxpayers can deduct interest expense. Two separate considerations limit the amount of debt that generates qualifying residence (and thus deductible) interest: a limitation on the amount of acquisition indebtedness and a limitation on the amount of home-equity indebtedness.

***Limitation on amount of acquisition indebtedness.*** Interest expense of up to $1,000,000 of acquisition indebtedness is deductible as qualified residence interest. Once acquisition indebtedness is established for a qualifying residence (or for the sum of two qualifying residences), only principal payments on the loan(s) can reduce it and only additional indebtedness, secured by the residence(s) *and* incurred to substantially improve the residence(s), can increase it. (Notice the requirements to use funds to *acquire or improve the residence*, a stipulation that markedly differentiates acquisition indebtedness from home-equity indebtedness.)

When a taxpayer **refinances** a mortgage, how does the tax law treat the new loan? Assuming the taxpayer does not use the proceeds from the refinance to substantially improve her residence, the refinanced loan is treated as acquisition debt *only to the extent that the principal amount of the refinancing does not exceed the amount of the acquisition debt immediately before the refinancing.* Consequently, any amount borrowed in excess of the remaining principal on the original loan does not qualify as acquisition indebtedness. Interest on the "excess" part of this loan can only be deducted if it qualifies as home-equity indebtedness (described below).

> **THE KEY FACTS**
> Home-Related Interest Deduction
> ▪ Deduction allowed for qualified residence interest.
> · Principal residence and one other residence.
> · If rented out, personal use must exceed greater of (1) 14 days or (2) 10 percent of rental days to be qualified residence.
> · Acquisition indebtedness.
> · Home-equity indebtedness.

> **THE KEY FACTS**
> Home-Related Interest Deduction
> ▪ Acquisition Indebtedness
> · Proceeds used to acquire or substantially improve home.
> · Limited to $1,000,000.
> · Principal payments permanently reduce amount.

**Example 14-6**

*What if:* Assume that when they moved to Chicago, the Jeffersons purchased a home costing $330,000 by making a down payment of $300,000 and taking out a $30,000 loan secured by the home. During the next few years, the Jeffersons paid $10,000 of principal on the loan, thereby reducing the loan balance to $20,000. Last year, due to a decrease in interest rates and a need for cash, (continued on page 14-10...)

---

[15]This is why advertisements for these loans generally suggest borrowers consult with their tax advisors to determine the deductibility of interest on the loans.

the Jeffersons refinanced their mortgage by taking out a loan, secured by their residence, for $150,000. With the $150,000 they paid off the $20,000 balance on the original loan and used the $130,000 of extra cash for purposes unrelated to the home. After the refinance, what is the Jeffersons' acquisition indebtedness?

**Answer:** $20,000, the same amount as before the refinance. The only way to increase acquisition indebtedness is to borrow money to substantially improve the home. Thus, the Jeffersons' interest deductions on the home will be limited to the interest expense on the $20,000 acquisition indebtedness plus a limited amount of home-equity indebtedness.

**What if:** Assume the same facts as above except that the Jeffersons used $40,000 of the cash from the loan to build a new garage on their property. After the refinance, what is the Jeffersons' acquisition indebtedness?

**Answer:** $60,000 ($20,000 original loan principal + $40,000 used to substantially improve home).

---

### THE KEY FACTS

**Home-Related Interest Deduction**

▎**Home-Equity Indebtedness**
· Can use proceeds for any purpose.
· Loan must be secured by equity in home (FMV > Debt).
· $100,000 limit.

*Limitation on amount of home-equity indebtedness.* As noted earlier, interest on home-equity indebtedness is deductible as qualified residence interest. However, the amount of qualified home-equity indebtedness is limited to the *lesser* of (1) the fair market value of the qualified residence(s) in excess of the acquisition debt related to the residence(s) and (2) $100,000 ($50,000 for married filing separately). Thus, a taxpayer can deduct interest on up to $100,000 of home-related debt above and beyond acquisition debt (limited to $1,000,000) as long as the debt is secured by the equity in the home(s) no matter what the taxpayer does with the proceeds from the home-equity loan. When deciding whether to borrow money through a home-equity loan, the taxpayer must weigh the advantage of the interest deductibility against the risk of losing her home if she does not repay the loan.

### Example 14-7

**What if:** Assume that the Jeffersons' home is worth $400,000 and they have a balance of $290,000 on their original home loan. The Jeffersons are interested in purchasing a $50,000 Chevy Suburban. Wanting to finance the full purchase price, they ask you, their financial planner, whether they should borrow the money with a 6 percent automobile loan from their local credit union or use a home-equity loan at 8 percent to fund the purchase. Assuming their marginal tax rate is 33 percent, and that they itemize deductions, what is the after-tax interest rate for the automobile loan and what is the after-tax interest rate for the home-equity loan?

**Answer:** 6 percent for the automobile loan (same as the before-tax rate because the interest is not deductible) and 5.36 percent for the home equity loan [8% × (1 − 33%)]. After taxes, the home-equity loan appears to be a much better deal than the automobile loan. Before taking out the home-equity loan, however, the Jeffersons should consider the economic consequences if they are not able to repay the loan. If they don't make the payments on the automobile loan, they may lose the automobile; if they don't make the payments on the home-equity loan, they may lose their home.

**What if:** If the Jeffersons wanted to tap their home-equity loan for $110,000 so that they could buy two automobiles, would they be allowed to deduct the interest on the entire loan?

**Answer:** No. Even though the home has $110,000 of equity ($400,000 fair market value minus $290,000 acquisition indebtedness), the cap on qualifying home-equity debt is $100,000. Consequently, the Jeffersons would be able to deduct interest on only $100,000 of the $110,000 home-equity loan.

---

*Combined limitation on qualifying debt.* What is the maximum amount of debt on which a taxpayer can deduct qualified residence interest? Because the acquisition indebtedness limit of $1,000,000 and the home-equity indebtedness limit of $100,000 are two separate limits, the maximum amount of debt on which a taxpayer may

deduct qualified residence interest is $1,100,000—provided, of course, that the value of the taxpayer's qualified residence (or residences) is at least $1,100,000.

When a taxpayer's home-related debt exceeds the limitations, the amount of deductible interest can be determined in one of two ways. First, the deductible interest can be computed as the product of (1) total interest expense on debt secured by the home and (2) the ratio of **qualified debt** to total debt outstanding on the home. This average interest expense option is summarized as follows:

$$\text{Total interest expense} \times \frac{\text{Qualified debt}}{\text{Total debt}} = \text{Deductible interest}$$

The second method is based on the chronological order of when the loans were executed, rather than as a weighted average. A taxpayer can choose to deduct all interest on earlier loans up to the limit on qualifying debt. Once the limit on qualifying debt is reached, interest on debt above the limit is not deductible. Why might taxpayers opt for this ordering method? This method generates a higher deduction when the earlier loans have a higher interest rate than subsequent loans.

### Example 14-8

*What if:* Assume the Jeffersons moved to Chicago several years ago and purchased a home valued at $330,000 by paying $30,000 down and funding the remaining balance with a 30-year mortgage fixed at 6 percent. By the beginning of last year the value of their home had increased to $400,000, and the principal amount of their original loan had been paid down to $290,000. In need of extra cash for anticipated expenditures unrelated to their home, the Jeffersons borrowed $70,000 at a fixed interest rate of 7 percent with a loan secured by their home. As of the beginning of this year, the value of the Jeffersons' home had increased to $420,000. With a need for still more cash, the Jeffersons decided to take out a third loan secured by their home. The Jeffersons borrowed $50,000 on the third mortgage at an annual interest rate of 9 percent. During the year, they made interest-only payments on all three loans. The interest they paid on these loans is summarized as follows:

| Loan | Balance | Rate | Interest Paid |
|---|---|---|---|
| **Acquisition indebtedness:** | | | |
| Original home loan | $290,000 | 6% | $17,400 |
| **Home equity indebtedness:** | | | |
| Home-equity loan 1 | 70,000 | 7% | 4,900 |
| Home-equity loan 2 | 50,000 | 9% | 4,500 |
| Totals | $410,000 | | $26,800 |

How much of the $26,800 interest expense can the Jeffersons deduct this year using the average interest expense option?

**Answer:** $25,493. Plugging the numbers into the formula for this option (see above) yields the following:

$$\$26,800 \times \frac{\$390,000}{\$410,000} = \$25,493$$

Where the total interest expense is $26,800, the qualifying debt is $390,000 ($290,000 acquisition indebtedness + $100,000 limit on home-equity indebtedness), and the total debt is $410,000 ($290,000 + $70,000 + $50,000).

How much of the $26,800 interest expense can the Jeffersons deduct this year using the chronological order method of determining interest expense?

**Answer:** $25,000. The first loan is the original home loan. Because the loan is acquisition debt and is under the $1,000,000 acquisition debt limit, the entire $17,400 interest on this loan is deductible.

*(continued on page 14-12...)*

---

**THE KEY FACTS**

**Home-Related Interest Deduction**

■ If combined debt exceeds limitations
· Average method: Total interest × qualifying debt/total debt.
· Chronological method: Deduct interest on loans based on chronological order loans were executed (FIFO).

■ Acquisition debt and home-equity debt can apply to the same loan.
· Interest-deductible loan of up to $1.1M secured by the home.

> The second mortgage of $70,000 was executed next. Because this loan is a home-equity loan and is under the $100,000 home-equity limit, the entire $4,900 interest on this loan is deductible. Finally, the third mortgage of $50,000 was executed last. However, because only $30,000 of this debt is qualifying home-equity debt ($100,000 limit minus $70,000 second mortgage) only $2,700 of interest on this loan is deductible ($30,000 × 9%). Thus, under the chronological order option, the Jeffersons can deduct $25,000 of the interest expense ($17,400 + $4,900 + $2,700).
>
> Note that the $25,493 interest deduction under the first option is higher than the $25,000 interest expense under the second option because interest rate on the second home equity loan is higher than the rates on the original loan and on the first home equity loan.

Finally, even though there are separate limits on acquisition indebtedness and home-equity indebtedness, both limits can apply to the same loan.

**Example 14-9**

> Refer back to Example 14-6 where we assumed the Jeffersons refinanced their $20,000 home loan by borrowing $150,000 against their home and paying off the original $20,000 loan. Of course, the Jeffersons can deduct interest on the $20,000 acquisition debt on the loan. How much interest on the remaining $130,000 of the loan are the Jeffersons allowed to deduct?
>
> **Answer:** The Jeffersons can deduct interest on $100,000 of the remaining $130,000 loan because this is the amount that qualifies as home-equity indebtedness. Interest on the other $30,000 of loan principal is not deductible.
>
> Assuming they paid $9,000 of interest expense on these loans during the year, the Jeffersons could deduct $7,200 of the interest, computed under the average interest rate option as follows:
>
> $$\$9,000 \times \frac{\$120,000}{\$150,000} = \$7,200$$
>
> Note that because in this example the Jeffersons have only one loan (part acquisition debt and part home-equity debt, and part neither), the second (chronological order) method of deducting interest expense does not apply.

**Mortgage Insurance**    Taxpayers are allowed to deduct as qualified residence interest expense premiums paid or accrued on mortgage insurance (insurance premiums paid by the borrower to protect the lender against the borrower defaulting on the loan).[16] To qualify, the premiums for the mortgage insurance must be paid or accrued in connection with acquisition indebtedness on a qualified residence and must be paid by December 31, 2010. The deduction does not apply to mortgage insurance contracts issued before January 1, 2007. The (itemized) deduction is phased out by 10 percent for every $1,000 (or fraction thereof) that the taxpayer's AGI exceeds $100,000.

**Points**    A home buyer arranging financing for a home typically incurs several loan-related fees or expenses including charges for "points." A **point** is 1 percent of the principal amount of the loan. In general, borrowers pay points to lenders in exchange for reduced interest rates on loans. However, borrowers may also pay lenders for other purposes (for example, to compensate lenders for the service of providing the loan). In order for taxpayers to deduct points, the points must be paid for a reduced interest rate (rather than for the service of providing the loans).[17] However, to minimize possible disputes regarding the deductibility of points and as a matter of administrative

---

[16]§163(h)(3)(E). Lenders generally require borrowers to pay mortgage insurance when the loan exceeds 80% of the property's sales price. Borrowers are usually able to cancel the insurance when the loan-to-value ratio drops below 80%.

[17]§461(g)(2).

convenience, the IRS will treat points as deductible **qualified residence interest** if the following requirements are met:[18]

1.  The **settlement statement** (see Appendix A—the settlement statement details the monies paid out and received by the buyer and seller as part of the loan transaction) must clearly designate the amounts as points payable in connection with the loan, for example as "loan origination fees," "loan discount," or "discount points." (These amounts are typically provided on lines 801 and 802 of the settlement statement.)

2.  The amounts must be computed as a percentage of the stated principal amount of the loan.

3.  The amounts paid must conform to an established business general practice of charging points for loans in the area in which the residence is located, and the amount of the points paid must not exceed the amount generally charged in that area.

4.  The amounts must be paid in connection with the acquisition of the taxpayer's *principal residence* and the loan *must be secured by that residence* (the deduction for points is not available for points paid in connection with a loan for a second home).

5.  The buyer must provide enough funds in the down payment on the home to at least equal the cost of the points (the buyer is not allowed to borrow from the lender to pay the points). However, points paid by the *seller* to the lender in connection with the taxpayer's loan are treated as paid directly by the taxpayer. Consequently, such points are generally deductible by the buyer.

Note that points paid in *refinancing* a home loan are not immediately deductible by the homeowner. These points must be amortized and deducted on a straight-line basis over the life of the loan.[19]

Now that we understand how the tax laws treat points, let's consider the home buyer's decision of whether or not to pay points to obtain a lower interest rate on a home loan. From an economic standpoint, the buyer must choose between (1) paying extra money up front and having lower monthly mortgage payments or (2) paying less initially and having larger monthly payments.

When the taxpayer can afford to pay points, deciding whether or not to do so generally requires a "break-even" analysis. Essentially, the taxpayer determines how long it will take to recoup the after-tax cost of the point(s) through the after-tax interest savings on the loan. Generally speaking, the longer the taxpayer plans on staying in the home and maintaining the loan (not refinancing it), the more likely it is financially beneficial to pay points to obtain a lower interest rate. However, paying points can be costly if, after too short a time, the taxpayer sells the home or refinances the home loan. In these situations, the taxpayer may not reach the break-even point.

---

**Example 14-10**

Tyler and Jasmine are seeking financing for their new $800,000 home. They are paying $500,000 down and borrowing the remaining $300,000 to be paid back over 30 years. They have the choice of paying two discount points ($6,000) and getting a fixed interest rate of 5 percent or paying no discount points and getting a fixed interest rate of 6 percent. Assuming the points meet the immediate deductibility requirements, the Jeffersons' marginal tax rate is 33 percent, and they pay interest only for the first three years of the loan, what is the Jeffersons' break-even point for paying the points?

*(continued on page 14-14...)*

---

[18]Rev. Proc. 94-27 1994-1 C.B. 613.

[19]See Chapter 2 research memo and *J.R. Huntsman v. Comm.* (8 Cir., 1990), 90-2 USTC par. 50,340, rev'g 91 TC 917 (1988) for a limited exception to this rule.

**Answer:** Two years, calculated as follows:

**Loan summary:** $300,000; 6 percent rate with no points. 5 percent rate with two points ($6,000). Assume the Jeffersons pay interest only for the first three years.

| Description | Amounts | Calculation |
|---|---|---|
| (1) Initial cash outflow from paying points | ($6,000) | $300,000 × 2%. |
| (2) Tax benefit from deducting points | 1,980 | (1) × 33%. |
| (3) After-tax cost of points | (4,020) | (1) + (2). |
| (4) Before-tax *savings per year* from 5% vs. 6% interest rate | 3,000 | $300,000 × (6% − 5%). |
| (5) *Forgone tax benefit per year* of higher interest rate | (990) | (4) × 33%. |
| (6) After-tax savings per year of 5% vs. 6% interest rate | $2,010 | (4) + (5). |
| Break-even point in years | 2 years | (3)/(6). |

The break-even analysis in Example 14-10, while a useful exercise, oversimplifies the calculations a bit. Why? It oversimplifies because it doesn't take into account the present value of the tax savings, nor does it take into account the increasing principal that would be paid on a traditional principal-and-interest-type loan. In reality, the cost of the points is immediate while the savings comes later—so the break-even point on a present value basis is likely a little longer than two years. Also, the more principal paid on the loan, the less the amount of interest paid each month—so savings from the lower interest rate declines over time, which would also extend the break-even point.

Because points paid on a refinancing are deducted over the life of the loan, the break-even point for paying points on a refinanced mortgage is longer than the break-even point for an original mortgage of the same amount.

## Example 14-11

*What if:* Assume that due to recent interest rate declines, the Jeffersons have decided to refinance the $300,000 mortgage on their home with a new 30-year loan. The Jeffersons have the option of paying two discount points ($6,000) and obtaining a 5 percent interest rate or obtaining a 6 percent interest rate with no discount points. Assuming the Jeffersons' marginal tax rate is 33 percent and they pay interest only for the first three years of the loan, what is the Jeffersons' approximate break-even point for paying the points on the refinance?

**Answer:** 2.89 years, calculated as follows:

**Loan summary:** $300,000; 6 percent rate with no points. 30 years or 5 percent rate with two points ($6,000). Assume the Jeffersons pay interest only for the first three years.

| Description | Points | Notes |
|---|---|---|
| (1) Initial cash outflow from paying points | ($6,000) | $300,000 × 2%. |
| (2) Tax benefit from deducting points | 0 | |
| (3) After tax cost of points | (6,000) | (1) + (2). |
| (4) Before-tax savings per year from 5% vs. 6% interest rate | 3,000 | $300,000 × (6% − 5%). |
| (5) Forgone tax benefit per year of higher interest payments | (990) | (4) × 33%. |
| (6) After-tax savings per year of 5% vs. 6% interest rate | 2,010 | (4) + (5). |
| (7) Annual tax savings from amortizing points | 66 | (1)/30 years × 33%. |
| (8) Annual after-tax cash flow benefit of paying points | $2,076 | (6) + (7). |
| Break-even point in years | 2.89 years | (3)/(8). |

The reason for the longer break-even point is that the points effectively cost more because they are not immediately deductible in a refinance.

## *Real Property Taxes*

Owners of personal residences and other types of real estate such as land, rental properties, business buildings, and other types of real property are generally required to pay **real property taxes.** These taxes are assessed by local governments and are based on the fair market value of the property.[20] Real property taxes support general public welfare by providing funding for public needs such as schools and roads.

Local governments set the tax rates applied to the value of the property annually based on financial needs for the year. The applicable rates may depend on the type of real estate. For example, the tax rate for real estate used in a business may be higher than the rates for residential real property. Real property tax payments are deductible by taxpayers conducting self-employment activities against business income as *for* AGI deductions, by landlords against rental income as *for* AGI deductions, and by individuals as itemized deductions. As we discussed in Chapter 6, taxpayers who do not itemize deductions are allowed to deduct real property taxes by increasing the amount of their basic standard deduction by the lesser of (1) the amount of real property taxes paid during the year or (2) $500 ($1,000 for a married couple filing jointly).[21]

Taxpayers are not allowed to deduct fees paid for setting up water and sewer services, and assessments for local benefits such as streets and sidewalks.[22] Taxpayers generally add these expenditures to the basis of their property.

Frequently, homeowners pay their real estate taxes through an **escrow** (holding) **account** with their mortgage lender. Each monthly payment to the lender includes an amount that represents roughly one-twelfth of the anticipated real property taxes for the year. The actual tax payment (or payments if the taxes are due more than once a year) is made by the mortgage company with funds accumulated in the escrow account. When does the homeowner get to deduct the property taxes? The homeowner gets to deduct the property taxes when the actual taxes are paid to the taxing jurisdiction, not when the homeowner makes payments for taxes to the escrow account.

Because property taxes are generally payable to the government only once or twice a year, who is responsible for paying the taxes when an owner sells a personal residence or another type of real estate during the year? Is the owner at the time the taxes are due responsible for paying the full amount of the taxes? Does the person who makes the tax payment also receive the corresponding tax deduction? In most situations, the buyer and seller divide the responsibility for the tax payments based on the portion of the property tax year that each party held the property. This allocation of taxes between buyer and seller is generally spelled out on the settlement statement when the sale becomes final (see Appendix A to this chapter for a sample settlement statement for the Jeffersons). For tax purposes, it doesn't matter who actually pays the tax, although generally the current owner has the responsibility to do so. The tax deduction is based on the relative amount of time each party owned the property during the year (or period over which the property taxes are payable).[23]

> **THE KEY FACTS**
>
> **Real Estate Taxes**
>
> ▮ Applies to homes, land, business buildings, and other types of real estate.
>
> ▮ Homeowners frequently pay real property tax bill to escrow account.
>   · Deduction timing based on payment of taxes to governmental body and not escrow account.
>
> ▮ When homeowners sell home during year.
>   · Deduction is based on proportion of year taxpayer lived in home no matter who actually pays tax.

[20]Local governments tend to understate the fair market value of property when appraising it to minimize the chances that the taxpayer will contest the appraisal.

[21]§63(c)(1)(C).

[22]Reg. §1.164-4(a).

[23]The seller gets a deduction for the taxes allocable for the period of time up to and including the day *before* the date of the sale. The taxes allocable to the day of the sale through the end of the property tax year are deductible by the buyer.

| **Example 14-12** |
| --- |

On February 1, 2010, Tyler and Jasmine purchased a new home for $800,000. At the time of the purchase, it was estimated that the property tax bill on the home for the year would be $12,000 ($800,000 × 1.5%). Assuming the tax bill is paid and that the property tax bill is based on a calendar year, how much will the Jeffersons *deduct* in property taxes for 2010?

**Answer:** $11,000. Because the seller lived in the home for one-twelfth of the year (January) and the Jeffersons lived in the home for eleven-twelfths of the year (February through December), the seller will deduct $1,000 of the property taxes (one-twelfth) and the Jeffersons will deduct $11,000 (eleven-twelfths) as an itemized deduction.

**THE KEY FACTS**

**First-Time Home Buyer Credit**

■ Refundable first-time home buyer credit for first-time home buyers purchasing homes.
· If purchased home in 2008 (on or after April 9), maximum credit was $7,500 and taxpayer must pay back credit over 15 years.
· If purchased home in 2009 (through November 6), maximum credit was $8,000 and taxpayers need not pay it back.
· If purchased November 7, 2009 through April 30, 2010, maximum credit of $8,000 unless a long-time owner of principal residence then maximum credit of $6,500.

## First-Time Home Buyer Tax Credit

The first-time home buyer tax credit (FTHTC) is a refundable tax credit available to "first-time home buyers" and to certain other taxpayers purchasing homes.[24] For purposes of the credit, a first-time home buyer is a taxpayer who purchases a home but who did not own a principal residence during the three-year period immediately before the purchase. The credit was initially available to first-time home buyers purchasing a principal residence on or after April 9, 2008, through December 31, 2008. These taxpayers were allowed to claim a credit equal to the lesser of (1) 10 percent of the purchase price of a home or (2) $7,500 ($3,750 for married taxpayers filing separately). Taxpayers who claimed a credit for a 2008 home purchase are required to repay the credit over a 15-year period beginning in 2010 (with their 2010 tax return). If a taxpayer sells or ceases to use the home as her personal residence before repaying the entire credit, the balance of the credit is due in the year in which the residence is sold or is no longer used as a principal residence. The amount of the credit required to be repaid in these circumstances may not exceed the amount of gain from the sale of the residence to an unrelated person.

The tax law has been modified to allow first-time home buyers purchasing homes on or after January 1, 2009, through April 30, 2010 to claim a credit equal to (1) 10 percent of the purchase price of the home or (2) $8,000 ($4,000 for married taxpayers filing separately).[25] Taxpayers claiming the credit for purchases in 2009 or 2010 are not required to repay the credit unless they sell the home or stop using it as a principal residence within 36 months after purchasing the home. Taxpayers qualifying for the credit in 2010 may elect to report the credit on their 2009 tax returns.

| **Example 14-13** |
| --- |

**What if:** Suppose the Jeffersons purchased a home on July 1, 2008, and that they qualified for and claimed a $7,500 first-time home buyer credit. When are they required to start paying back the credit, and what is the amount of their first payback installment payment?

**Answer:** The Jeffersons are required to begin making $500 annual payments to pay back the credit when they file their 2010 tax return. They will make the $500 payments each year from 2010 through 2024.

**What if:** Assume the same facts as above and that the Jeffersons sell their home in 2011, after they had made one $500 installment payment on the credit. How much of the credit are they required to pay back when they file their 2011 tax return?

**Answer:** $7,000. They paid $500 of the $7,500 credit with their 2010 tax return and they must pay the remainder of the unpaid balance of the credit with their 2011 tax return.

(*continued on page 14-17...*)

[24]See §36.

[25]Taxpayers are also eligible for the credit if they enter into a written binding contract to purchase the home before May 1, 2010, and they close on the purchase of a principal residence before July 1, 2010 [See §36(h)].

> ***What if:*** Suppose the Jeffersons purchased a home on July 1, 2009, and they qualified for and claimed an $8,000 first-time home buyer credit. When are they required to start paying back the credit, and what is the amount of their first payback installment payment?
>
> **Answer:** The Jeffersons are not required to pay back any of the credit unless they sell the home or stop using it as their principal residence before July 1, 2012. If they do sell the home or stop using it as their principal residence before then, they will have to pay back the entire $8,000 credit with their tax return for the year in which they sold the home or stopped using it as their principal residence.

Taxpayers who purchase a home from November 7, 2009 through April 30, 2010 but are not first-time home buyers are still eligible to claim the FTHTC if they are considered to be "long-time residents of the same principal residence." To qualify as a "long-time resident," the taxpayer (and, if married, the taxpayer's spouse) must have *owned and used* the same principal residence for any 5-consecutive year period during the 8-year period ending on the date of the purchase of the principal residence that qualifies for the credit. The FTHTC available to "long-time residents" is the lesser of (1) 10% of the purchase price or (2) of $6,500 ($3,250 if married filing separately).

Whether they qualify for the credit as first-time home buyers or as long-time residents, taxpayers who purchase a home from November 7, 2009 through April 30, 2010 are ineligible for the credit if any one of the following applies:

- the taxpayer qualifies as a dependent of another in the year of the purchase
- the taxpayer is under age 18 on the date of purchase (unless the taxpayer's spouse is at least 18 year of age on the date of purchase)
- the purchase price of the home exceeds $800,000 or more[26]

The FTHTC is subject to phase-out based on modified AGI. For home purchases made in 2010, the credit the taxpayer may otherwise claim is phased out proportionally between modified AGI of $125,000 − $145,000 ($225,000 − $245,000 if married filing jointly). For this purpose, modified AGI is AGI before considering the foreign earned income exclusion and certain other exclusions.

**Example 14-14**

> ***What if:*** Suppose the Jeffersons had rented a home for the prior 4 years (they did not own a principal residence). On February 1, 2010, they purchased a home for $400,000. Their 2010 AGI is $180,000. What amount of first-time home buyer credit are they entitled to claim?
>
> **Answer:** $4,000 ($400,000 × 10%). The Jeffersons may elect to report the credit on their 2009 tax return.
>
> ***What if:*** Suppose the Jeffersons had rented a home for the prior 4 years (they did not own a principal residence). On February 1, 2010, they purchased a home for $900,000. Their 2010 AGI is $230,000. What amount of first-time home buyer credit are they entitled to claim?
>
> **Answer:** $0. Taxpayers acquiring homes for more than $800,000 after November 6, 2009 are ineligible for the credit.
>
> ***What if:*** Suppose that on March 1, 2010, the Jeffersons sold their principal residence of the last six years. They were able to exclude the entire amount of the gain on the sale from their gross income. On April 20, 2010, the Jeffersons purchased a new principal residence for $700,000. Their 2010 AGI is $210,000. What amount of first-time home buyer credit are they entitled to claim?
>
> **Answer:** $6,500. Because the Jeffersons owned a principal residence for at least 5 consecutive years in the 8-year period before their new home purchase, they are eligible for a maximum $6,500 first-time home buyer credit.

---

[26]See §36 for other eligibility limitations and exceptions to the limitations.

## LO4

# RENTAL USE OF THE HOME

A taxpayer with the financial wherewithal to do so may purchase a second home as a vacation home, a rental property, or a combination of the two. A taxpayer may own a second home outright or may share ownership with others through a time-share or fractional ownership arrangement. The nontax benefits of owning a second home include a fixed vacation destination, the ability to trade the use of the home with an owner of a home in a different destination, the opportunity for generating income through rentals, and the potential appreciation of the second home as an investment. The nontax costs of owning a second home include the initial cost of the home, the extra cost of maintaining the home, the hassle of dealing with renters or property managers, and the downside risk associated with holding the second home as an investment.

The tax consequences of owning a second home depend on the number of days the taxpayer uses the home for personal purposes and how many days the taxpayer rents the home. The personal vs. rental use can be categorized in one of three ways:

1. Residence with minimal rental use.
2. Residence with significant rental use.
3. Nonresidence.

To make these determinations, the taxpayer needs to calculate the number of days the rental property was used for personal use during the year and the number of days the property was rented out during the year. So what counts as a day of personal use and what counts as a day of rental use? Exhibit 14-3 summarizes rules for determining the days of personal use.

**EXHIBIT 14-3**   **Personal Use and Deemed Personal Use of a Home**

(1) Taxpayer stays in home.[27]
(2) Relative of an owner stays in the home, even if the relative pays full fair market value rent.
(3) A nonowner stays in the home under a vacation home exchange or swap arrangement.
(4) Taxpayer rents out the property for less than fair market value.

Rental use includes (1) days when the property is rented out at fair market value and (2) days spent repairing or maintaining the home for rental use. Days when the home is available for rent, but not actually rented out, *do not count* either as personal days or as rental days.

Just as we discussed earlier when we discussed the mortgage interest expense deduction, a home is considered to be a "residence" for tax purposes if the taxpayer uses the home for personal purposes for *more than* the greater of 14 days or 10 percent of the number of rental days during the year. For example, if a taxpayer rents her home for 200 days and uses it for personal purposes for 21 days or more, the home is considered to be a residence for tax purposes. If the same taxpayer used the home for personal purposes for 20 days, the home would not be considered to be a residence for tax purposes.

### Residence with Minimal Rental Use

The law is simple for homeowners who rent a home that qualifies as a residence for a minimal amount of time during the year. That is, they live in it for at least 15 days and they rent it for 14 or fewer days. Taxpayers are not required to include the gross receipts in rental income and are not allowed to deduct any expenses related to the rental.[28] The

[27]This includes use by a co-owner even when the co-owner pays a usage fee.
[28]§280A(g).

owner is, however, allowed to deduct qualified residence interest and real property taxes on the second home as itemized deductions.

---

**Example 14-15**

The Jeffersons purchased a vacation home in a golf community in Scottsdale, Arizona, in January of 2010. They spent 10 days vacationing in the home in early March and another 15 days vacationing in the home in mid-December. In early February, they rented the home for 14 days to a group of golfers who were in town to attend a PGA Tour golf tournament and to play golf. The Jeffersons received $6,000 in rent from the group and the Jeffersons incurred $1,000 of expenses relating to the rental home. The Jeffersons did not rent the property again for the rest of the year. How much will the $5,000 net income from the rental increase their taxable income?

**Answer:** Zero! Because the Jeffersons lived in the home for at least 15 days (25 days) and rented the home for fewer than 15 days (14 days) during 2010, they do not report the rental income to the IRS and they do not deduct expenses associated with the rental. The Jeffersons saved $1,650 in taxes by excluding the $5,000 of net rental income ($5,000 net income × 33 percent marginal tax rate). Note that the Jeffersons can also deduct the mortgage interest and real property taxes on the property for the *full year* as itemized deductions.

---

**Taxes in the Real World** *Extreme Tax Savings Strategy?*

*Newsweek* reports that *Extreme Makeover: Home Edition* signs a contract with the contestants to rent the home from the contestant for 10 days. The "makeover" or improvements of the home take the place of rental payments. Because the rental period is less than 15 days, the value of the improvements, which would otherwise be taxable income, is not reported as taxable income by the contestant.[29]

Note that this appears to be a fairly aggressive interpretation of the tax law in this situation. In fact, the IRS has suggested in a nonbinding information letter that "to the extent that the value of the improvements constitutes a prize or an award . . . it cannot also be considered rent, and therefore could not qualify for the exclusion from gross income under §280A(g) of the Code."[30]

---

A taxpayer with a strategically located second (or even first) home can take advantage of this favorable tax rule by renting the property and excluding potentially large rental payments from those in town to attend high-profile events such as certain college football games (for example, games for Notre Dame University or the University of Texas), the Olympics, the Masters golf tournament, the Super Bowl, and Mardi Gras.

## Residence with Significant Rental Use (Vacation Home)

When a home qualifies as a residence (see discussion above) and the taxpayer rents out the home for 15 days or more the rental revenue is included in gross income, expenses to obtain tenants (advertising and realtor commissions) are fully deductible as direct rental expenses, and expenses relating to the home are allocated between personal and rental use. The expenses allocated to personal use are not deductible unless they are deductible under nonrental tax provisions as itemized deductions (mortgage interest or real property taxes) or in the case of real property taxes as a limited additional standard deduction for nonitemizers.

---

**THE KEY FACTS**

**Rental Use of the Home**

■ Residence with significant rental use.
· Use home for personal purposes for greater of (1) 15 days or (2) 10 percent of rental days.
· Deduct direct rental expenses such as advertising and realtor commissions.

*(continued)*

---

[29]D. McGinn, "Television: Tax Trouble for ABC's 'Extreme' Winners?" *Newsweek,* May 17, 2004, p. 12.
[30]INFO 2006-12, release date March 31, 2006.

*(concluded)*

· Allocate home-related expenses between rental use and personal use.

· Interest and taxes allocated to personal use deducted as itemized deductions and all other expenses allocated to personal use not deductible.

· IRS method allocates interest and taxes to rental use based on rental use to total use for the year while Tax Court method allocates to rental use based on rental use to total days in entire year.

· Rental deductions other than tier-1 expenses limited to gross rental revenue. When limited deduct tier 1 (interest and taxes) first, then tier 2 (all expenses except interest, taxes, and depreciation), and then tier 3 (depreciation).

When the gross rental revenue exceeds the sum of the direct rental expenses and the expenses allocated to the rental use of the home, the taxpayer is allowed to deduct the expenses in full. However, when these expenses exceed the rental revenue, the deductibility of the expenses is limited. In these situations, taxpayers divide the rental expenses into one of three categories or "tiers." The tier 1, 2, and 3 expenses for rental property are described in Exhibit 14-4.

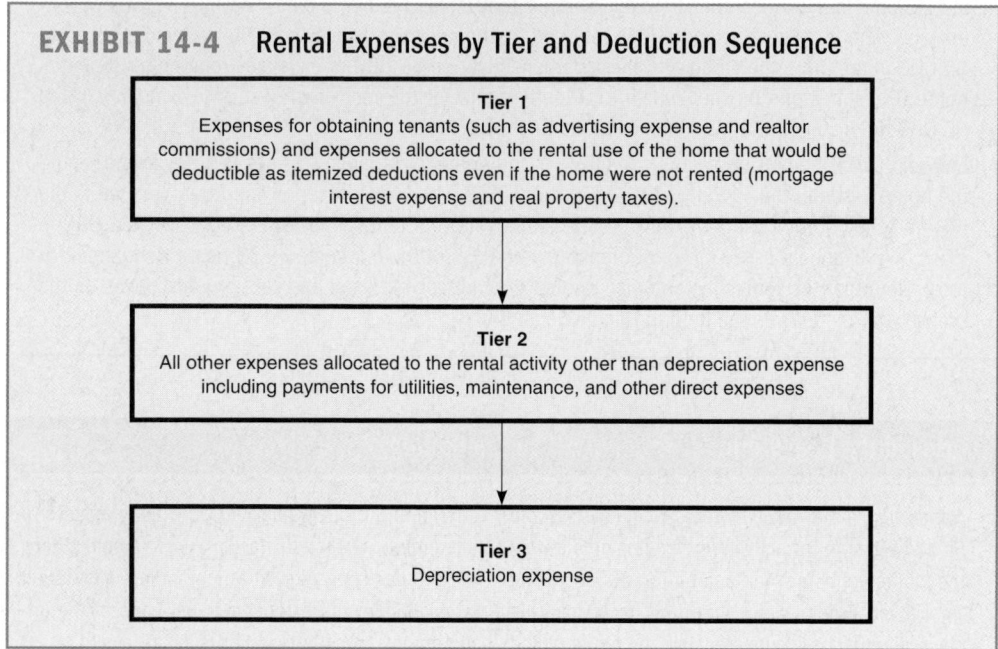

**EXHIBIT 14-4**   **Rental Expenses by Tier and Deduction Sequence**

**Tier 1**
Expenses for obtaining tenants (such as advertising expense and realtor commissions) and expenses allocated to the rental use of the home that would be deductible as itemized deductions even if the home were not rented (mortgage interest expense and real property taxes).

**Tier 2**
All other expenses allocated to the rental activity other than depreciation expense including payments for utilities, maintenance, and other direct expenses

**Tier 3**
Depreciation expense

The taxpayer first deducts tier 1 (expenses to obtain tenants and mortgage interest and real property taxes allocated to rental use[31]) expenses in full. This is true even when tier 1 expenses exceed the gross rental revenue.[32] Second, the taxpayer deducts tier 2 expenses.[33] However, the tier 2 expense deductions are limited to the gross rental revenue in excess of tier 1 expenses. Any tier 2 expenses not deducted in the current year due to the income limitation are suspended and carried forward to the next year. Finally, the taxpayer deducts tier 3 expense (depreciation). The tier 3 expense deduction is limited to the gross rental revenue in excess of tier 1 and tier 2 expenses. Any tier 3 expenses not deductible because of the income limitation are suspended and carried forward to next year. The nondeductible tier 3 expense does not reduce the basis in the home. In general terms, this deduction sequence is unfavorable for taxpayers, because it is designed to maximize taxpayer deductions for expenses that would be deductible even without any rental use of the home (mortgage interest and real property taxes) and to minimize the allowable depreciation deductions for the home.

As we mentioned above, expenses associated with the rental use of the home must be allocated between rental use and personal use of the home. These expenses

---

[31]Technically, expenses to obtain tenants (advertising and realtor commissions) are a reduction in gross rental income for tax purposes. However, we classify them as tier 1 expenses to simplify the discussion.

[32]The rental activity associated with a home falling into the residence with significant rental use category is not considered to be a passive activity, so income or loss generated from the activity is not considered to be passive income or passive loss [§469(j)]. See discussion of passive loss rules below.

[33]§280A(c)(5). Also see IRS Publication 537, "Residential Rental Property (Including Rental of Vacation Homes)."

are *generally* allocated to rental use based on the ratio of the number of days of rental use to the total number of days the property was used for rental and personal purposes (see Exhibit 14-5). All expenses not allocated to rental use are allocated to personal use.

## EXHIBIT 14-5    Tax Court vs. IRS Method of Allocating Expenses

| Rental Allocation | IRS Method | Tax Court Method |
|---|---|---|
| Mortgage interest and property taxes (tier 1 expenses) | $\text{Expense} \times \dfrac{\text{Total rental days}}{\text{Total days used}}$ | $\text{Expense} \times \dfrac{\text{Total rental days}}{365}$ |
| All other expenses | $\text{Expense} \times \dfrac{\text{Total rental days}}{\text{Total days used}}$ | $\text{Expense} \times \dfrac{\text{Total rental days}}{\text{Total days used}}$ |

The only potential exception to the general allocation rule involves the allocation of mortgage interest expense and real property taxes (both tier 1 expenses). The IRS and the Tax Court disagree on how to allocate these particular expenses. The IRS allocates these expenses the same way as all other expenses. However, the Tax Court allocates *interest* and *taxes* to rental use based on the ratio of days that the property was rented over the *number of days in the year*, rather than the number of days the property was used for any purpose during the year.[34] The IRS and Tax Court allocation methods are described in Exhibit 14-5.

The Tax Court justifies its approach by pointing out that interest expense and property taxes accrue over the entire year regardless of the level of personal or rental use. The Tax Court method generally favors the taxpayer because it tends to allocate less interest expense and real property taxes to the rental use, which reduces the tier 1 expenses and allows more tier 2 and tier 3 expenses to be deducted when the gross income limitation applies. That is, the sum of the taxpayer's deductible personal (*from* AGI) and rental expenses (*for* AGI) associated with the rental home under the Tax Court method generally will exceed the sum of personal (*from* AGI) and rental expenses (*for* AGI) associated with the home under the IRS method when the gross income limitation applies. This is because the taxpayer does not lose deductions for the extra interest and real property taxes allocated to personal use under the Tax Court method because these expenses are allowed as itemized deductions on Schedule A.

**Example 14-16**

At the beginning of 2010, the Jeffersons purchased a vacation home in Scottsdale, Arizona, for $400,000. They paid $100,000 down and financed the remaining $300,000 with a 6 percent mortgage secured by the home. During the year, the Jeffersons used the home for personal purposes for 30 days and rented the home for 200 days. Thus, the home falls in the residence with significant rental use category. They received $37,500 of rental revenue and incurred $500 of rental advertising expenses. How are their expenses allocated to the rental use under the IRS and Tax Court methods?

(continued on page 14-22...)

[34]The Tax Court method of allocating these expenses is also referred to as the Bolton method after the taxpayer in the court case in which the Tax Court approved this method of allocating deductions. While the court case initially was tried in the Tax Court, the decision in favor of the taxpayer was appealed to the Ninth Circuit Court that also ruled in favor of the taxpayer and sanctioned the use of the Tax Court or Bolton method of allocating interest expense. *Bolton v. Commissioner,* 82-2 USTC ³⁰§9699 (CA 9), Affirming Tax Court, 77 TC 104.

**Answer:** See the following summary of allocation of expenses associated with the home:

**Allocation Method to Rental Use**

| Expense | Amount | Tier | IRS Method (200/230) | Tax Court Method (200/365 Tier 1 200/230 other) |
|---|---|---|---|---|
| Advertising* | $ 500 | 1 | $ 500 | $ 500 |
| Interest | 18,000 | 1 | 15,652 | 9,863 |
| Real estate taxes | 5,000 | 1 | 4,348 | 2,740 |
| Total tier 1 expenses | $23,500 | 1 | $20,500 | $13,103 |
| Utilities | 4,500 | 2 | 3,913 | 3,913 |
| Repairs | 1,800 | 2 | 1,565 | 1,565 |
| Insurance | 3,500 | 2 | 3,043 | 3,043 |
| Maintenance | 3,200 | 2 | 2,782 | 2,782 |
| Total tier 2 expenses | $13,000 | 2 | $11,303 | $11,303 |
| Tier 3: Depreciation | 13,939 | 3 | $12,121 | $12,121 |
| Total expenses | $50,439 | | | |

*Advertising is a direct expense of the rental so it is fully deductible against rental revenue.

| Net income from rental | IRS Method | Tax Court Method |
|---|---|---|
| Rental receipts | $37,500 | $37,500 |
| Less tier 1 expenses | (20,500) | (13,103) |
| Income after tier 1 expenses | 17,000 | 24,397 |
| Less tier 2 expenses | (11,303) | (11,303) |
| Income after tier 2 expenses | 5,697 | 13,094 |
| Less: tier 3 expenses | (5,697) | (12,121) |
| Taxable rental income | $ 0 | $ 973 |
| Deductible personal expenses (interest and property taxes) | $ 3,000 | $10,397 |
| Deductible rental expenses (sum of tier 1, 2, and 3 expenses) | 37,500 | 36,527 |
| Total personal and rental expenses | $40,500 | $46,924 |

Note that under the Tax Court method, the Jeffersons are able to deduct $7,397 more in itemized deductions for interest and real property taxes than they do under the IRS method, and they deduct $973 fewer rental expenses (*for* AGI) under the Tax Court method relative to the IRS method. In total, the Jeffersons are allowed to deduct $6,424 more in total deductions under the Tax Court method than the IRS method in the current year. However, under the IRS method, the Jeffersons are allowed to carry forward to next year the $6,424 in depreciation expense that they were not allowed to deduct in the current year ($12,121– $5,697). Under the Tax Court method, they were able to deduct all of their expenses so they do not carry forward any expenses to future years.

Taxpayers would report their rental activities on Schedule E of Form 1040. The deductible tier 1, tier 2, and tier 3 expenses are *for* AGI deductions. Exhibit 14-6 displays the completed Schedule E for the Jefferson's Scottsdale vacation home using the Tax Court method.

**EXHIBIT 14-6**    Jeffersons' Schedule E for Vacation Home Rental

| SCHEDULE E | Supplemental Income and Loss | OMB No. 1545-0074 |
|---|---|---|
| (Form 1040) | (From rental real estate, royalties, partnerships, S corporations, estates, trusts, REMICs, etc.) | 20**09** |
| Department of the Treasury Internal Revenue Service (99) | ▶ **Attach to Form 1040, 1040NR, or Form 1041.**    ▶ **See Instructions for Schedule E (Form 1040).** | Attachment Sequence No. **13** |

| Name(s) shown on return | Your social security number |
|---|---|
| Tyler and Jasmine Jefferson | 321-54-9876 |

**Part I**    Income or Loss From Rental Real Estate and Royalties  **Note.** If you are in the business of renting personal property, use **Schedule C** or **C-EZ** (see page E-3). If you are an individual, report farm rental income or loss from **Form 4835** on page 2, line 40.

| | 1    List the type and address of each **rental real estate property:** | | 2  For each rental real estate property listed on line 1, did you or your family use it during the tax year for personal purposes for more than the greater of: | Yes | No |
|---|---|---|---|---|---|
| A | Residence | | | A | ✔ |
| | 3 Hole-in-One Blvd. Scottsdale, Arizona  85262 | | ● 14 days  **or** | | |
| B | | | ● 10% of the total days rented at fair rental value? | B | |
| C | | | (See page E-3) | C | |

| | Income: | | Properties | | | Totals (Add columns A, B, and C.) | |
|---|---|---|---|---|---|---|---|
| | | | A | B | C | | |
| 3 | Rents received | 3 | 37,500 | | | 3 | |
| 4 | Royalties received | 4 | | | | 4 | |
| | **Expenses:** | | | | | | |
| 5 | Advertising | 5 | 500 | | | | |
| 6 | Auto and travel (see page E-4) | 6 | | | | | |
| 7 | Cleaning and maintenance | 7 | 2,782 | | | | |
| 8 | Commissions | 8 | | | | | |
| 9 | Insurance | 9 | 3,043 | | | | |
| 10 | Legal and other professional fees | 10 | | | | | |
| 11 | Management fees | 11 | | | | | |
| 12 | Mortgage interest paid to banks, etc. (see page E-5) | 12 | 9,863 | | | 12 | |
| 13 | Other interest | 13 | | | | | |
| 14 | Repairs | 14 | 1,565 | | | | |
| 15 | Supplies | 15 | | | | | |
| 16 | Taxes | 16 | 2,740 | | | | |
| 17 | Utilities | 17 | 3,913 | | | | |
| 18 | Other (list) ▶ | 18 | | | | | |
| 19 | Add lines 5 through 18. | 19 | | | | 19 | |
| 20 | Depreciation expense or depletion (see page E-5) | 20 | 12,121 | | | 20 | |
| 21 | Total expenses. Add lines 19 and 20 | 21 | 36,527 | | | | |
| 22 | Income or (loss) from rental real estate or royalty properties. Subtract line 21 from line 3 (rents) or line 4 (royalties). If the result is a (loss), see page E-5 to find out if you must file **Form 6198**. | 22 | 973 | | | | |
| 23 | Deductible rental real estate loss. **Caution.** Your rental real estate loss on line 22 may be limited. See page E-5 to find out if you must file **Form 8582**. Real estate professionals **must** complete line 43 on page 2 | 23 | ( | )( | )( | ) | |
| 24 | **Income.** Add positive amounts shown on line 22. **Do not** include any losses | | | | | 24 | 973 |
| 25 | **Losses.** Add royalty losses from line 22 and rental real estate losses from line 23. Enter total losses here | | | | | 25 | ( ) |
| 26 | **Total rental real estate and royalty income or (loss).** Combine lines 24 and 25. Enter the result here. If Parts II, III, IV, and line 40 on page 2 do not apply to you, also enter this amount on Form 1040, line 17, or Form 1040NR, line 18. Otherwise, include this amount in the total on line 41 on page 2 | | | | | 26 | 973 |

For Paperwork Reduction Act Notice, see page E-8 of the instructions.    Cat. No. 11344L    Schedule E (Form 1040) 2009

**THE KEY FACTS**

**Rental Use of the Home**

■ **Nonresidence.**

· Personal use is no more than the *greater* of (1) 14 days or (2) 10 percent of rental days.

· Allocate expenses to rental and personal use.

· Rental deductions in excess of rental income are deductible subject to passive loss limitation rules.

· Interest expense allocated to personal use not deductible.

## Nonresidence (Rental Property)

For property in this category, the taxpayer includes the rental revenue in gross income and deducts all rental expenses *allocated to the rental use* of the property. When the property is used for even a day for personal purposes, the expenses must be allocated between the rental usage and the personal usage.[35] In this situation, however, the law does *not allow* the taxpayer to deduct mortgage interest not allocated to rental use because the taxpayer does not meet the minimum amount of personal use required for the deduction (the home is not a qualified residence—see our earlier discussion on mortgage interest expense). However, the taxpayer is still allowed to deduct real property taxes not allocated to the rental as an itemized deduction. In contrast to the residence with significant rental use category, if the rental expenses exceed the gross income from the home in this category, the deductibility of the loss is not subject to a gross income limitation but it is subject to the passive activity restrictions discussed below.[36]

**Example 14-17**

Assume the same facts we used in Example 14-16 except that the Jeffersons *did not use the home at all for personal purposes.* They received $37,500 in gross rental revenue for the year and incurred $50,439 of expenses relating to the rental property. How much can the Jeffersons deduct?

**Answer:** The good news is that the deductions are not limited to gross income from the rental so they can deduct all $50,439, generating a ($12,939) loss on the property ($37,500 − $50,439). The bad news is that, as we discuss below, the loss may not be immediately deductible due to the passive activity loss limitations.

Exhibit 14-7 summarizes the tax rules relating to a home used for rental purposes depending on the extent of rental (and personal use). Appendix B to this chapter provides a flowchart summarizing the implementation of these rules.

**Losses on Rental Property**    A rental property can be a great investment that gets the best of all worlds. It could (1) appreciate in value, (2) produce annual positive cash flow (rental receipts exceed expenses other than depreciation), and (3) generate tax losses that reduce the taxes the owner is required to pay on other sources of income. Consider the Jeffersons' second-home property, purchased for $400,000 and used primarily as a rental home (see Example 14-16), which we'll assume has appreciated to $440,000 by the end of 2010. The property has appreciated by $40,000, produced a positive cash flow of $1,000 [$37,500 rental income minus expenses other than depreciation of $36,500 ($50,439 total expenses minus depreciation expense of $13,939)], and generated a net tax loss of $12,939. This tax loss apparently saves the Jeffersons $4,270 in taxes [($12,939) × 33% marginal tax rate].

Thus, the increase in the Jeffersons' wealth from their second-home investment in 2010 appears to be $45,270 ($40,000 appreciation + $1,000 rental cash flow + $4,270 tax savings). But as noted elsewhere in this text, when a tax outcome seems too good to be true, it usually is. Read on.

***Passive activity loss rules.***    In Chapter 11, we introduced the **passive activity loss** rules that indicate taxpayers may only deduct passive losses for a year to the extent

---

[35]§280A(e).

[36]If the home rental is deemed to be a not-for-profit activity, the loss is subject to the hobby loss rules in §183.

**EXHIBIT 14-7**    Summary of Tax Rules Relating to Home Used for Rental Purposes

| | Residence with Minimal Rental Use | Residence with Significant Rental Use | Nonresidence |
|---|---|---|---|
| **Classification test** | Reside in home for at least 15 days and rent home for fewer than 15 days during the year. | Rent home for 15 days or more and use home for personal purposes for more than the greater of (1) 14 days or (2) 10 percent of the total rental days. | Rent home for at least one day, and personal use does not exceed the greater of (1) 14 days or (2) 10 percent of the rental days. |
| **Rental revenue** | Exclude from gross income. | Include in gross income. | Include in gross income. |
| **Direct rental expenses unrelated to home use** | Not deductible. | Fully deductible for AGI (loss not subject to passive activity loss rules). | Deductible for AGI but subject to passive activity loss rules. |
| **Treatment of mortgage interest and real property taxes** | Deductible as itemized deductions. | Allocate between personal-use days and rental days; interest and taxes allocated to rental days are deductible as rental expenses; interest and taxes allocated to personal-use days are deductible as itemized deductions. | Allocated between personal-use days and rental days; interest and taxes allocated to rental days are deductible as rental expenses; taxes allocated to personal-use days are deductible as itemized deductions; interest allocated to personal-use days is not deductible. |
| **Treatment of all other expenses** | Not deductible. | Allocate between personal-use days and rental days; expenses allocated to personal-use days are not deductible; expenses allocated to rental days are deductible as rental expenses to the extent of rental revenue minus sum of direct rental expenses and rental mortgage interest and real property taxes; when expenses allocated to rental days exceed the rental income. | Allocated between personal-use days and rental days; expenses allocated to personal-use days are not deductible; expenses allocated to rental days are deductible and can generate loss but loss is subject to passive activity loss rules. |
| **Excess expenses.** | Not applicable. | Rental expenses in excess of rental income minus sum of direct rental expenses and rental mortgage interest expense and real property taxes are carried forward to the next year. | Not applicable; rental expenses are deductible, even if they create a rental loss. |

**THE KEY FACTS**

**Rental Losses**

■ Losses on home rentals in nonresidence use category are passive losses.

■ Passive loss rules generally limit deductions for losses from passive activities such as rental to passive income from other sources.
  · Passive losses in excess of passive income are suspended and deductible against passive income in the future or when the taxpayer sells the passive activity generating the loss.

■ Rental real estate exception to passive loss rules
  · Applies to active participants in rental property.
  · Deduct up to $25,000 of rental real estate loss against ordinary income.
  · $25,000 maximum deduction phased out by 50 cents for every dollar of AGI over $100,000 (excluding the rental loss deduction). Fully phased out at $150,000 of AGI.

of their passive income. We also learned that, by definition, a rental activity (including a second home rental that falls in the nonresidence category) is considered to be a passive activity.[37] Because they are passive losses, losses from rental property are generally not allowed to offset other ordinary or investment type income. However, as we also discussed in Chapter 11, a taxpayer who is an **active participant in a rental activity** may be allowed to deduct up to $25,000 of the rental loss against nonpassive income.[38] Consistent with a number of tax benefits, the exception amount for active owners is phased out as income increases: the $25,000 maximum exception amount is phased out by 50 cents for every dollar the taxpayer's adjusted gross income (before considering the rental loss) exceeds $100,000. Consequently, the entire $25,000 is phased out when the taxpayer's adjusted gross income reaches $150,000.

---

**Example 14-18**

The Jeffersons incurred a $12,939 passive loss from their Scottsdale rental home, and they did not receive any passive income during the year. Assuming their current year AGI is $250,000 and that they are considered to be active participants in the rental activity, how much of the rental loss are the Jeffersons allowed to deduct this year under the rental real estate exception to the passive activity loss rules?

**Answer:** $0. Because their adjusted gross income exceeds $150,000, the $25,000 deduction exception to the passive activity loss rules is completely phased out. Consequently, the Jeffersons are not allowed to deduct any of the $12,939 rental loss from 2010.

**What if:** How much of the $12,939 loss could the Jeffersons deduct if their adjusted gross income (before considering the rental loss) was $120,000?

**Answer:** They could deduct the entire $12,939 loss. The $25,000 exception amount would be reduced by a $10,000 phase-out [50 cents × ($120,000 − $100,000)]. The maximum amount of the rental loss that can offset ordinary income would therefore be reduced from $25,000 to $15,000 ($25,000 − $10,000 phased out). However, because their loss is less than $15,000, they may deduct the entire $12,939 rental loss against their other sources of income in 2010.

---

Are passive losses from rental real estate activities that taxpayers are not allowed to deduct in the current year permanently disallowed? No, these losses are suspended until the taxpayer generates passive income or until the taxpayer sells the property that generated the passive loss. On the sale, in addition to reporting gain or loss from the sale of the property, the taxpayer will be allowed to deduct suspended passive losses against ordinary income.

## L05 BUSINESS USE OF THE HOME

Because a personal residence is a personal-use asset, utility payments and depreciation due to wear and tear are not deductible expenses. However, taxpayers who use their home—or at least part of their home—for business purposes may be able to deduct expenses associated with their home use if they meet certain stringent requirements.[39]

To qualify for **home office deductions,** a taxpayer must use her home—or part of her home—*exclusively and regularly* as either (1) the principal place of business for any of the taxpayer's trade or businesses, or (2) as a place to meet with patients, clients, or customers in the normal course of business.

---

[37] Recall that second homes falling in the significant personal and rental use category are not passive activities. See §469(j).

[38] §469(i).

[39] §280A. If taxpayers rent the home they occupy and they meet the requirements for business use of the home, they can deduct part of the rent they pay. To determine the amount of the deduction, multiply the rental payment by the percentage of the home used for business purposes.

Let's consider these requirements in turn. When a taxpayer has more than one business location, including the home, which is her principal place of business? This is a facts-and-circumstances determination based upon (a) the total time spent doing work at each location, (b) the facilities for doing work at each location, and (c) the relative amount of income derived from each location. By definition, a taxpayer's principal place of business also includes the place of business used by the taxpayer for the administrative or management activities of the taxpayer's trade or business *if there is no other fixed location of the trade or business where the taxpayer conducts substantial administrative or management activities of the trade or business.*

If a taxpayer meets with clients or patients in her home during the normal course of business, she qualifies for the home office deduction even if the home is not her principal place of business. However, the clients or patients must visit the taxpayer's home *in person*. Communication through telephone calls or other types of communication technology does not qualify.

---

### Example 14-19

Jasmine recently quit her job as an employee for an advertising firm because, with the move to the new home, the commute was too long. She has decided to go it alone as a self-employed graphic designer. She uses a large room in the basement of the Jeffersons' new home as her office. The room has been wired for all of her office needs. Does this space qualify for a home office deduction?

**Answer:** A qualified yes. While Jasmine will spend a good deal of time meeting with clients on location, she has no other fixed location for her trade or business. Consequently, as long as the office is used *exclusively* for business purposes, the Jeffersons qualify for home office deductions subject to certain limitations described below.

---

Finally, note that an *employee* (not a self-employed taxpayer) who otherwise meets these requirements qualifies for home office deductions only if the employee's use of the home is considered to be for the convenience of the employer. Generally, with such strict requirements, only self-employed taxpayers and employees such as outside salespersons or full-time telecommuters who have no office space anywhere except at home can qualify for the deductions.

### Direct vs. Indirect Expenses

When a taxpayer qualifies for home office deductions the deductions are limited to expenses that are related—either directly or indirectly—to the business. Direct expenses are expenses incurred in maintaining the room or part of the home that is set aside for business use. Direct expenses include painting or costs of other repairs to the area of the home used for business.[40] These expenses are deductible in full as home office expenses. Indirect expenses are expenses incurred in maintaining and using the home. Indirect expenses include insurance, utilities, interest, real property taxes, general repairs, and depreciation on the home as if it were used entirely for business purposes. In contrast to direct expenses, only indirect expenses *allocated* to the home office space are deductible.

How do taxpayers allocate indirect expenses to the home office space? If the rooms in the home are roughly of equal size, the taxpayer may allocate the indirect expenses to the business portion of the home based on the number of rooms. In a

---

**THE KEY FACTS**

**Home Office Deduction**

- Deductibility limits on expenses allocated to office.
  - If employee, expenses deducted as unreimbursed employee business expenses.
  - If self-employed, deducted for AGI but deductions may be subject to income limitation.
  - If deduction is limited by income limitation, apply the same tiered system as used for rental property when tier 2 and tier 3 deductions are limited to gross rental income minus tier 1 expenses.

- Depreciation expense
  - Reduces basis in home.
  - Gain on sale due to depreciation is ineligible for exclusion.
  - This gain is taxed at a maximum 25 percent rate as unrecaptured §1250 gain.

---

[40]The basic local telephone service charge, including taxes, for the first telephone line into a home is a nondeductible personal expense. However, charges for business long-distance phone calls on that line, as well as the cost of a second line into the home used exclusively for business, are deductible business expenses. However, these expenses are not deducted as home office expenses. Rather, these expenses are deducted separately on the appropriate form or schedule. Taxpayers filing Schedule C (Form 1040), would deduct these expenses as utilities.

10-room home, a taxpayer using one room for qualifying business use is allowed to deduct 10 percent of the indirect expenses. Alternatively, the taxpayer may allocate indirect expenses based on the amount of the space or square footage of the business-use room relative to the total square footage in the home. If the home is 5,000 square feet and the home office is 250 square feet, the taxpayer may deduct 5 percent of the indirect expenses. Unrelated expenses such as painting a room not used for business purposes are not deductible.

---

**Example 14-20**

The Jeffersons moved into their new $800,000, 6,000-square-foot home on February 1, 2010. Jasmine quit her job and set up a 420-square-foot home office in the basement on that same date. Through the end of the calendar year, the Jeffersons incurred several expenses relating to their home (see table below). Assuming they qualify for the home office deduction, they would sum the direct expenses and the indirect expenses allocated to the office. They would allocate the indirect expenses based on the square footage of the office compared to the rest of the home. What amount of home-related expenses would qualify as home office expenses?

**Answer:** $5,413. See allocation below. All direct expenses and 7 percent of the indirect expenses would be allocated to the home office (420 office square footage/6,000 home square footage). The Jeffersons would allocate the expenses as follows:

| Total Expense | Type | (A) Amount | (B) Office % | (A) × (B) Home Office Expense |
|---|---|---|---|---|
| Painting office | Direct | $ 200 | 100% | $ 200 |
| Real property taxes | Indirect | 11,000 | 7% | 770 |
| Home interest expense | Indirect | 27,917 | 7% | 1,954 |
| Electricity | Indirect | 2,600 | 7% | 182 |
| Gas and other utilities | Indirect | 2,500 | 7% | 175 |
| Homeowner's insurance | Indirect | 5,000 | 7% | 350 |
| Depreciation | Indirect | 25,454 | 7% | 1,782 |
| Total expenses | | $74,671 | | $5,413 |

The expenses attributable to the home office are deductible subject to the limitations discussed below.

---

## Limitations on Deductibility of Expenses

The process for determining the amount of deductible home office expenses is similar to the process used to determine the deductions for vacation homes. Gross revenue from the business is included in gross income, business expenses unrelated to the home are fully deductible (on Schedule C of Form 1040), and expenses relating to the home are allocated between business (direct and indirect expenses) and nonbusiness use of the home (see above for discussion regarding allocating expenses). The expenses allocated to nonbusiness use are not deductible unless they are deductible under nonbusiness tax provisions as itemized deductions (such as mortgage interest expense and real property taxes) or, in the case of real property taxes, as a limited additional standard deduction for nonitemizers.

When gross business revenue exceeds the sum of business expenses unrelated to the home and business expenses relating to the home, the business expenses relating to the home business are deductible in full. However, when these expenses exceed the gross business revenue, deductibility of the expenses is limited. In these situations, taxpayers divide business expenses associated with the home office into one of three categories or "tiers." Tier 1 expenses consist of mortgage interest and real property taxes allocated to the business use of the home. Tier 2 expenses consist of all other

expenses allocated to the business use of the home except for depreciation. Tier 3 expense consists of depreciation.

The taxpayer first deducts tier 1 expenses in full even when tier 1 expenses exceed gross net Schedule C income (before home office expenses).[41] Second, the taxpayer deducts tier 2 expenses. However, the amount of the deductible tier 2 expenses is limited to net Schedule C income minus tier 1 expenses. Any tier 2 expenses not deductible due to the income limitation are suspended and carried forward to the next year, subject to the same limitations. Finally, the taxpayer deducts tier 3 expense. However, the amount of the deductible tier 3 expense is limited to net Schedule C income (before home office expenses) minus tier 1 expenses minus deductible tier 2 expenses. The nondeductible portion of depreciation expense is carried forward to next year, subject to the same limitations.

It is important to note that, when a taxpayer deducts depreciation as a home office expense, the depreciation expense reduces the taxpayer's basis in the home. Consequently, when the taxpayer sells the home, the gain on the sale will be greater than it would have been had the taxpayer not deducted depreciation expense. Further, the gain on the sale of the home attributable to the depreciation deductions is *not* eligible to be excluded under the home sale exclusion provisions. Rather, this gain is treated as unrecaptured §1250 gain and is subject to a maximum 25 percent tax rate (see Chapter 10 for detailed discussion of §1250 gain).

**Example 14-21**

At the beginning of the year, the Jeffersons' basis in their home was $800,000. Jasmine's first-year home office deductions included $1,782 in depreciation expense. Let's assume that this is the only depreciation expense the Jeffersons ever deduct. What is their adjusted basis in the home?

**Answer:** The depreciation deduction reduces the basis to $798,218 ($800,000 − $1,782).

**What if:** Now, assume that after the Jeffersons meet the ownership and use tests for the home sale exclusion, they sell the home for $900,000. The Jeffersons realize a gain of $101,782 on the sale. How much of the gain are they able to exclude?

**Answer:** They can exclude $100,000 of gain. However, they are not allowed to exclude the $1,782 gain caused by the depreciation expense for the home office. The Jeffersons must pay $446 of tax on the gain ($1,782 × 25% unrecaptured §1250 gain).

Allowing taxpayers to deduct part of their home-related expenses as business expenses creates temptations for taxpayers to deduct home-related expenses that don't meet the requirements. Not surprisingly, the IRS is very concerned about taxpayers inappropriately deducting expenses relating to their home. Consequently, expenses for business use of the home are some of the most highly scrutinized deductions available to taxpayers. Self-employed taxpayers must file a separate Form 8829 "Expenses for Business Use of Your Home" when deducting home office expenses on a tax return. With the high level of scrutiny applied to home office expenses, taxpayers should be sure to have documentation available to support their deductions.

## CONCLUSION

When deciding whether to invest in a home as a primary residence, a vacation home, or even a rental home, prospective owners should consider both nontax and tax factors relating to the ownership of the property. The tax code includes several provisions favorable to homeowners. This chapter is intended to provide current and prospective homeowners with enough insight on tax and nontax consequences of home ownership to allow them to make informed investment and compliance decisions when applicable.

[41]§280A(c)(5).

# SAMPLE SETTLEMENT STATEMENT FOR THE JEFFERSONS    APPENDIX A

### A. Settlement Statement

**U.S. Department of Housing and Urban Development**

OMB Approval No. 2502-0265

### B. Type of Loan

| | | |
|---|---|---|
| 1. ☐ FHA  2. ☐ FmHA  3. ☑ Conv. Unins. | 6. File Number: **1355** | 7. Loan Number: **6788** |
| 4. ☐ VA   5. ☐ Conv. Ins. | 8. Mortgage Insurance Case Number: | |

**C. Note:** This form is furnished to give you a statement of actual settlement costs. Amounts paid to and by the settlement agent are shown. Items marked "(p.o.c.)" were paid outside the closing; they are shown here for informational purposes and are not included in the totals.

| D. Name & Address of Borrower: | E. Name & Address of Seller: | F. Name & Address of Lender: |
|---|---|---|
| Tyler Jefferson<br>Jasmine Jefferson<br>225 El Tejon Dr.<br>Chicago, IL 60612 | Ian Sabin<br>525 Roberts Ln.<br>Glencoe, IL 60022 | 125 Decatur St.<br>Chicago, IL 60612 |

| G. Property Location: | H. Settlement Agent: Beardsley Settlement Group | |
|---|---|---|
| 225 El Tejon Dr.<br>Chicago, IL 60612<br>Lot 1, Block 2, Dozier Estates<br>Cook County, Illinois | Place of Settlement:<br>425 McCray St.<br>Chicago, IL 60612 | I. Settlement Date:<br>1/31/2010 |

| J. Summary of Borrower's Transaction | | K. Summary of Seller's Transaction | |
|---|---|---|---|
| **100. Gross Amount Due From Borrower** | | **400. Gross Amount Due To Seller** | |
| 101. Contract sales price | 800,000.00 | 401. Contract sales price | 800,000.00 |
| 102. Personal property | | 402. Personal property | |
| 103. Settlement charges to borrower (line 1400) | 28,116.00 | 403. | |
| 104. | | 404. | |
| 105. | | 405. | |
| **Adjustments for items paid by seller in advance** | | **Adjustments for items paid by seller in advance** | |
| 106. City/town taxes          to | | 406. City/town taxes          to | |
| 107. County taxes          to | | 407. County taxes          to | |
| 108. Assessments          to | | 408. Assessments          to | |
| 109. | | 409. | |
| 110. | | 410. | |
| 111. | | 411. | |
| 112. | | 412. | |
| **120. Gross Amount Due From Borrower** | 828,116.00 | **420. Gross Amount Due To Seller** | 800,000.00 |
| **200. Amounts Paid By Or In Behalf Of Borrower** | | **500. Reductions In Amount Due To Seller** | |
| 201. Deposit or earnest money | 20,000.00 | 501. Excess deposit (see instructions) | |
| 202. Principal amount of new loan(s) | 300,000.00 | 502. Settlement charges to seller (line 1400) | 48,260.00 |
| 203. Existing loan(s) taken subject to | | 503. Existing loan(s) taken subject to | |
| 204. | | 504. Payoff of first mortgage loan | |
| 205. | | 505. Payoff of second mortgage loan | |
| 206. | | 506. | |
| 207. | | 507. | |
| 208. | | 508. | |
| 209. | | 509. | |
| **Adjustments for items unpaid by seller** | | **Adjustments for items unpaid by seller** | |
| 210. City/town taxes          to | | 510. City/town taxes          to | |
| 211. County taxes  1/1/2010  to  1/31/2010 | 1,000.00 | 511. County taxes  1/1/2010  to  1/31/2010 | 1,000.00 |
| 212. Assessments          to | | 512. Assessments          to | |
| 213. | | 513. | |
| 214. | | 514. | |
| 215. | | 515. | |
| 216. | | 516. | |
| 217. | | 517. | |
| 218. | | 518. | |
| 219. | | 519. | |
| **220. Total Paid By/For Borrower** | 321,000.00 | **520. Total Reduction Amount Due Seller** | 49,260.00 |
| **300. Cash At Settlement From/To Borrower** | | **600. Cash At Settlement To/From Seller** | |
| 301. Gross Amount due from borrower (line 120) | 828,116.00 | 601. Gross amount due to seller (line 420) | 800,000.00 |
| 302. Less amounts paid by/for borrower (line 220) | ( 321,000.00) | 602. Less reductions in amt. due seller (line 520) | ( 49,260.00 ) |
| **303. Cash** ☑ From  ☐ To Borrower | 507,116.00 | **603. Cash** ☑ To  ☐ From Seller | 750,740.00 |

**L.  Settlement Charges**

| 700.  Total Sales/Broker's Commission based on price $ 800,000.00 @ 6.000 % = 48,000.00 | Paid From Borrowers Funds at Settlement | Paid From Seller's Funds at Settlement |
|---|---|---|
| Division of Commission (line 700) as follows: | | |
| 701.  $ 24,000.00 to Selling Agent Co. | | |
| 702.  $ 24,000.00 to Listing Agent Co. | | |
| 703.  Commission paid at Settlement | | 48,000.00 |
| 704. | | |
| **800.  Items Payable In Connection With Loan** | | |
| 801.  Loan Origination Fee  1.000 % | 3,000.00 | |
| 802.  Loan Discount  2.000 % | 6,000.00 | |
| 803.  Appraisal Fee  to Drumgoole Apraisal Co. | 400.00 | |
| 804.  Credit Report  to O'Brien Credit Check Inc. | 40.00 | |
| 805.  Lender's Inspection Fee | | |
| 806.  Mortgage Insurance Application Fee to | | |
| 807.  Assumption Fee | | |
| 808. | | |
| 809. | | |
| 810. | | |
| 811. | | |
| **900.  Items Required By Lender To Be Paid In Advance** | | |
| 901.  Interest from 1/31/2010 to 2/10/2010 @$ 41.10 /day | 411.00 | |
| 902.  Mortgage Insurance Premium for  months to | | |
| 903.  Hazard Insurance Premium for  years to | | |
| 904.  years to | | |
| 905. | | |
| **1000.  Reserves Deposited With Lender** | | |
| 1001.  Hazard insurance  2 months @$ 100.00 per month | 200.00 | |
| 1002.  Mortgage insurance  months @$ per month | | |
| 1003.  City property taxes  months @$ per month | | |
| 1004.  County property taxes  11 months @$ 1,000.00 per month | 11,000.00 | |
| 1005.  Annual assessments  months @$ per month | | |
| 1006.  months @$ per month | | |
| 1007.  months @$ per month | | |
| 1008.  months @$ per month | | |
| **1100.  Title Charges** | | |
| 1101.  Settlement or closing fee  to Beardsley Settlement Group | 300.00 | |
| 1102.  Abstract or title search  to | | |
| 1103.  Title examination  to Title Examination Inc. | 250.00 | |
| 1104.  Title insurance binder  to | | |
| 1105.  Document preparation  to Buckles & Pitts, L.L.P | | 200.00 |
| 1106.  Notary fees  to | | |
| 1107.  Attorney's fees  to | | |
| (includes above items numbers: ) | | |
| 1108.  Title insurance  to Title Insurance Co. | 3,250.00 | |
| (includes above items numbers: ) | | |
| 1109.  Lender's coverage  $ | | |
| 1110.  Owner's coverage  $ | | |
| 1111. | | |
| 1112. | | |
| 1113. | | |
| **1200.  Government Recording and Transfer Charges** | | |
| 1201.  Recording fees:  Deed $ 40.00 ; Mortgage $ 50.00 ; Releases $ | 90.00 | |
| 1202.  City/county tax/stamps:  Deed $ 450.00 ; Mortgage $ 350.00 | 800.00 | |
| 1203.  State tax/stamps:  Deed $ 1,250.00 ; Mortgage $ 1,000.00 | 2,250.00 | |
| 1204. | | |
| 1205. | | |
| **1300.  Additional Settlement Charges** | | |
| 1301.  Survey  to Beardsley Settlement Group | 125.00 | |
| 1302.  Pest inspection to Clark's Pest Control | | 60.00 |
| 1303. | | |
| 1304. | | |
| 1305. | | |
| **1400.  Total Settlement Charges (enter on lines 103, Section J and 502, Section K)** | 28,116.00 | 48,260.00 |

# FLOWCHART OF TAX RULES RELATING TO HOME USED FOR RENTAL PURPOSES (PAGE 1)

APPENDIX B

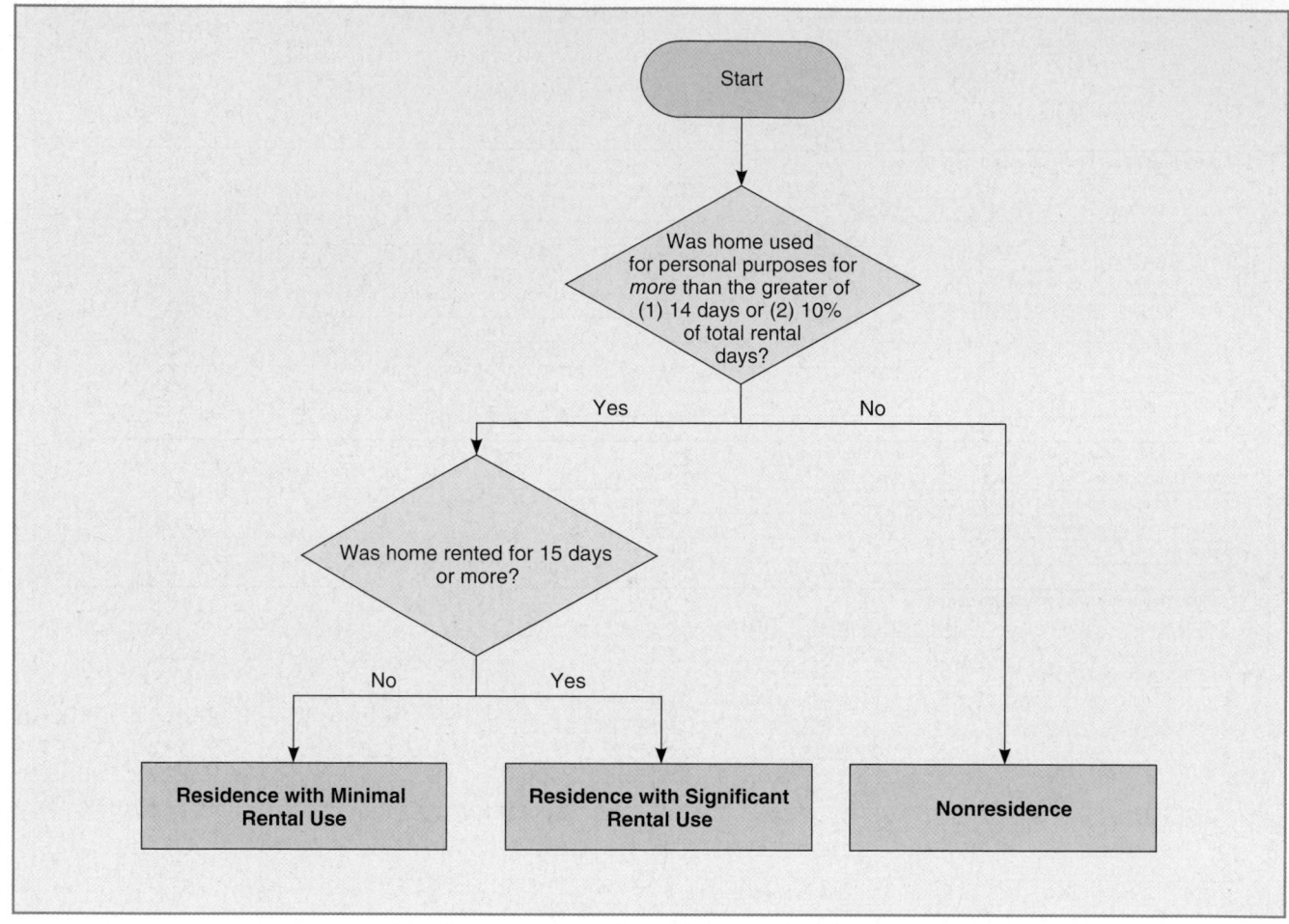

# (PAGE 2)

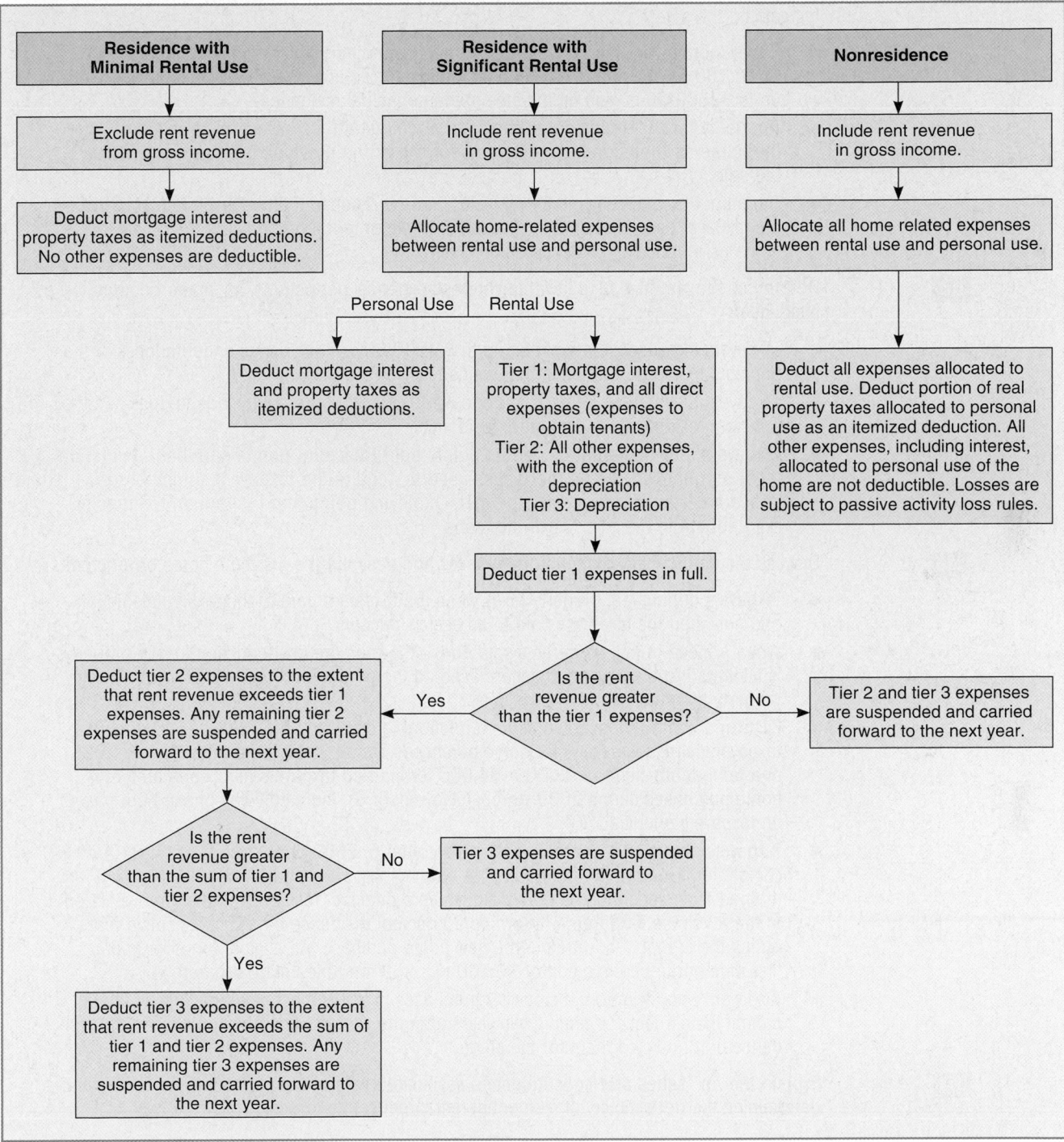

## SUMMARY

**LO1**    Compute the taxable gain on the sale of a residence and explain the requirements for excluding gain on the sale.

- If they meet ownership and use requirements, married taxpayers may exclude up to $500,000 of gain on the sale of their principal residence. Single taxpayers may exclude up to $250,000 of gain on the sale of their principal residence.

- To qualify for the exclusion on the sale of real estate, taxpayers must own and use the home as their principal residence for two of the previous five years preceding the sale.

- The amount of gain eligible for exclusion may be reduced if after December 31, 2008, the taxpayer uses the home as a vacation home or rental property and then uses the home as a principal residence before selling it.

**LO2**    Determine the amount of allowable interest expense deductions on loans secured by a residence.

- Taxpayers may deduct interest on up to $1,000,000 of acquisition indebtedness of their principal residence and one other residence.

- Taxpayers may deduct interest on up to $100,000 of home-equity indebtedness on their principal residence and one other residence.

- Taxpayers may immediately deduct points paid (discount points and loan origination fees) on qualifying home mortgages used to acquire the taxpayer's principal residence if certain requirements are met. Qualifying points paid on a loan refinancing are deductible over the life of the loan.

**LO3**    Discuss the deductibility of real property taxes and describe the first-time home buyer credit.

- Taxpayers deduct real property taxes when the taxes are paid to the taxing jurisdiction and not when the taxes are paid to an escrow account.

- When a piece of real property is sold during the year, the tax deduction for the property is allocated to the buyer and seller based on the portion of the year that each held the property no matter who pays the taxes.

- First-time home buyers could claim a refundable credit of $7,500 ($3,750 for married taxpayers filing separately) for home purchases during 2008 (on or after April 8, 2008), or a refundable credit of $8,000 ($4,000 for married taxpayers filing separately) for home purchases during 2009 (through November 6). The credit was phased-out based on taxpayers' modified AGI.

- Taxpayers acquiring a new home after November 6, 2009 but before May 1, 2010 are eligible for a maximum refundable first-time home owner credit of $8,000 ($4,000 if married filing separately) if they did not own a principal residence in the three years prior to the purchase. Taxpayers who owned a principal residence for a 5 consecutive years during the 8-year period before the new home purchase are eligible for a maximum first-time home buyers credit of $6,500 ($3,250 if married filing separately).

- Taxpayers who claimed the credit for purchases in 2008 must pay it back in 15 equal annual installments beginning two years after the year in which they purchased the residence that qualified them for the credit.

**LO4**    Explain the tax issues and consequences associated with rental use of the home, including determining the deductibility of residential rental real estate losses.

- Taxpayers who live in a home for 15 days or more and rent the home out for 14 days or less (a residence with minimal rental use) do not include gross rental receipts in taxable income and do not deduct rental expenses.

- Taxpayers who both reside in and rent out a home for a significant portion of the year (a residence with significant rental use) include rental revenue in gross income, deduct direct rental expenses not relating to the home (expenses to obtain tenants), and allocate home-related expenses between personal use and rental use of the home. They deduct

mortgage interest expense and real property taxes allocated to the rental use of the home as *for* AGI deductions and the mortgage interest expense and real property taxes allocated to the personal use of the home as itemized deductions. The remaining deductions allocated to the rental use of the home are deductible in a particular sequence and the amount of these deductions cannot exceed rental revenue in excess of direct rental expenses and rental mortgage interest and real property taxes.

- Taxpayers who rent a home with minimal or no personal use (nonresidence) include rental receipts in income and deduct all rental expenses. In this situation expenses exceeding income are subject to the passive activity loss rules.

- Taxpayers may be able to deduct up to $25,000 of passive loss on their rental home if they are active participants with respect to the property. This deduction is phased out for taxpayers with adjusted gross income between $100,000 and $150,000.

Describe the requirements necessary to qualify for home office deductions and compute the deduction limitations on home office deductions.

**LO5**

- To deduct expenses relating to a home office, the taxpayer must use the home exclusively and regularly for business purposes.

- Home-related expenses are allocated between business expenses and personal expenses based on the size of the office relative to the size of the home.

- Mortgage interest and real property taxes allocated to business use of the home are deductible in full without regard to the income of the business.

- Other expenses allocated to the business use of the home are deducted in a particular sequence. The deduction for these expenses cannot exceed the taxpayer's net Schedule C income (before home office expenses) minus the mortgage interest and real property taxes allocated to business use of the home.

## KEY TERMS

acquisition indebtedness (14-8)

active participant in a rental activity (14-26)

escrow account (14-15)

flipping (14-3)

home-equity indebtedness (14-8)

home office deductions (14-26)

passive activity income or loss (14-24)

point (14-12)

principal residence (14-3)

qualified debt (14-11)

qualified residence (14-8)

qualified residence interest (14-13)

real property taxes (14-15)

refinance (14-9)

secured loan (14-8)

settlement statement (14-13)

## DISCUSSION QUESTIONS

1. **(LO1)** A taxpayer owns a home in Salt Lake City, Utah, and a second home in St. George, Utah. The taxpayer sells the home in St. George at a gain. How does the taxpayer determine which home is her principal residence for purposes of qualifying for the exclusion of gain on the sale of a personal residence?

2. **(LO1)** What are the ownership and use requirements a taxpayer must meet to qualify for the exclusion of the gain on the sale of a residence?

3. **(LO1)** Under what circumstances, if any, can a taxpayer fail to meet the ownership and use requirements but still be able to exclude all of the gain on the sale of a principal residence?

4. **(LO1)** Under what circumstances can a taxpayer meet the ownership and use requirements for a residence but still not be allowed to exclude gain on the sale of the residence?

5. **(LO1)** A taxpayer purchases and lives in a home for a year. The home appreciates in value by $50,000. The taxpayer sells the home after her employer transfers her to an office in a nearby city. The taxpayer buys a new home. What information do you need to obtain to determine whether the taxpayer is allowed to exclude the gain on the sale of the first home?

6. **(LO2)** Juanita owns a principal residence in New Jersey, a cabin in Montana, and a houseboat in Hawaii. All of these properties have mortgages on which Juanita pays interest. What limits, if any, apply to Juanita's mortgage interest deductions? Explain whether deductible interest is deductible *for* AGI or *from* AGI.

7. **(LO2)** Barbi really wants to acquire an expensive automobile (perhaps more expensive than she can really afford). She has two options. Option 1: finance the purchase with an automobile loan from her local bank at a 7 percent interest rate, or Option 2: finance the purchase with a home-equity loan at a rate of 7 percent. Compare and contrast the tax and nontax factors Barbi should consider before deciding which loan to use to pay for the automobile. Barbi typically has more itemized deductions than the standard deduction amount.

8. **(LO2)** Lars and Leigha saved up for years before they purchased their dream home. They were considering (1) using all of their savings to make a large down payment on the home (90 percent of the value of the home) and barely scraping by without the backup savings, or (2) making a more modest down payment (50 percent of the value of the loan) and holding some of the savings in reserve as needed if funds get tight. They decided to go with the large down payment because they figured they could always refinance the home to pull some equity out of the home if things got tight. What advice would you give them about the tax consequences of their decision?

9. **(LO2)** How are acquisition indebtedness and home-equity indebtedness similar? How are they dissimilar?

10. **(LO2)** Why might it be good advice from a tax perspective to think hard before deciding to quickly pay down mortgage debt?

11. **(LO2)** Can portions of one loan secured by a residence consist of both acquisition indebtedness and home-equity indebtedness? Explain.

12. **(LO2)** When a taxpayer has multiple loans secured by her residence that in total exceed the limits for deductibility, how does the taxpayer determine the amount of the deductible interest expense?

13. **(LO2)** Compare and contrast the characteristics of a deductible point from a nondeductible point on a first home mortgage.

14. **(LO2)** Is the break-even period generally longer for points paid to reduce the interest rate on initial home loans or points paid for the same purpose on a refinance? Explain.

■ planning

15. **(LO2)** Under what circumstances is it likely economically beneficial to pay points to reduce the interest rate on a home loan?

16. **(LO2)** Harry decides to finance his new home with a 30-year fixed mortgage. Because he figures he will be in this home for a long time he decides to pay a fully deductible discount point on his mortgage to reduce the interest rate. Assuming Harry itemizes deductions and has a constant marginal tax rate over time, will the time required to recover the cost of the discount point be shorter or longer if Harry makes extra principal payments starting in the first year than it would be if he does not make any extra principal payments?

17. **(LO3)** A taxpayer sold a piece of real property in year 1. The amount of year 1 real property taxes was estimated at the closing of the sale and the amounts were allocated between the buyer and the taxpayer. At the end of year 1, the buyer receives a property tax bill that turns out to be higher than the estimate. After paying the tax bill, the buyer contacts the taxpayer at the beginning of year 2 and asks the taxpayer to pay the taxpayer's share of the shortfall. The

taxpayer sends a check to the buyer. Should the taxpayer be concerned that she won't get to deduct the extra tax payment because it was paid to the buyer and not to the taxing jurisdiction? Explain.

18. **(LO3)** Is a homeowner allowed a property tax deduction for amounts included in the monthly mortgage payment that are earmarked for property taxes? Explain.

19. **(LO3)** How is the first-time home buyer credit similar to an interest-free loan from the government? How is it different from an interest-free loan? Answer for qualifying home purchases in 2008, 2009, and 2010.

20. **(LO3)** Is it possible for a taxpayer who currently owns a principal residence to sell the residence and acquire a new principal residence with a purchase that qualifies for the first-time home buyer credit? Explain.

21. **(LO4)** For taxpayers that own second homes, how does the taxpayer distinguish a day of personal use from a day of rental use?

22. **(LO4)** Is it possible for a taxpayer to receive rental income that is not subject to taxation? Explain.

■ **planning**

23. **(LO4)** Halle just acquired a vacation home. She plans on spending several months each year vacationing in the home and on renting the property for the rest of the year. She is projecting tax losses on the rental portion of the property for the year. She is not too concerned about the losses because she is confident she will be able to use the losses to offset her income from other sources. Is her confidence misplaced? Explain.

24. **(LO4)** A taxpayer stays in a second home for the entire month of September. He would like the home to fall into the residence with significant rental use category for tax purposes. What is the maximum number of days he can rent out the home and have it qualify?

■ **planning**

25. **(LO4)** Compare and contrast the IRS method and the Tax Court method for allocating expenses between personal use and rental use for vacation homes. Include the Tax Court's justification for departing from the IRS method in your answer.

26. **(LO4)** In what circumstances is the IRS method for allocating expenses between personal use and rental use for second homes more beneficial to a taxpayer than the Tax Court method?

27. **(LO4)** Under what circumstances would a taxpayer who generates a loss from renting a home that is not a residence be able to fully deduct the loss? What potential limitations apply?

28. **(LO4)** Describe the circumstances in which a taxpayer acquires a home and rents it out and is not allowed to deduct a portion of the interest expense on the loan the taxpayer used to acquire the home.

29. **(LO4)** Is it possible for a rental property to generate a positive annual cash flow and at the same time produce a loss for tax purposes? Explain.

30. **(LO4, LO5)** How are the tax issues associated with home offices and vacation homes used as rentals similar? How are the tax issues or requirements dissimilar?

31. **(LO5)** Are employees or self-employed taxpayers more likely to qualify for the home office deduction? Explain.

32. **(LO5)** Compare and contrast the manner in which employees and employers report home office deductions on their tax returns.

33. **(LO5)** For taxpayers qualifying for home office deductions, what are considered to be indirect expenses of maintaining the home? How are these expenses allocated to personal and home office use?

34. **(LO5)** What limitations exist for self-employed taxpayers in deducting home office expenses, and how does the taxpayer determine which deductions are deductible and which are not in situations when the overall amount of the home office deduction is limited?

35. **(LO1, LO5)** A self-employed taxpayer deducts home office expenses. The tax-payer then sells the home at a $100,000 gain. Assuming the taxpayer meets the ownership and use tests, does the full gain qualify for exclusion? Explain.

## PROBLEMS

36. **(LO1)** Steve and Stephanie Pratt purchased a home in Spokane, Washington, for $400,000. They moved into the home on February 1 of year 1. They lived in the home as their primary residence until June 30 of year 5, when they sold the home for $700,000. The Pratts' marginal tax rate is 34 percent.

    a. How much in taxes will they be required to pay on the gain on the sale of the home?

    b. Assume the original facts, except that Steve and Stephanie live in the home until January 1 of year 3 when they purchased a new home and rented the original home. They finally sell the original home on June 30 of year 5 for $700,000. Ignoring any issues relating to depreciation taken on the home while it was being rented, what amount of taxes will the Pratts be required to pay on the sale of the home?

    c. Assume the same facts as in (b), except that the Pratts lived in the home until January of year 4 when they purchased a new home and rented the first home. What amount of taxes will the Pratts need to pay if they sell the first home on June 30 of year 5 for $700,000?

37. **(LO1)** Steve and Stephanie Pratt purchased a home in Spokane, Washington, for $400,000. They moved into the home on February 1 of year 1. They lived in the home as their primary residence until November 1 of year 1, when they sold the home for $500,000. The Pratts' marginal tax rate is 34 percent.

    a. Assume that the Pratts sold their home and moved because they don't like their neighbors. How much gain will the Pratts recognize on their home sale? At what rate, if any, will the gain be taxed?

    b. Assume the Pratts sell the home because Stephanie's employer transfers her to an office in Utah. How much gain will the Pratts recognize on their home sale?

    c. Assume the same facts as in (b), except that the Pratts sell their home for $700,000. How much gain will the Pratts recognize on the home sale?

    d. Assume the same facts as (b), except that on December 1 of year 0 the Pratts sold their home in Seattle and excluded the $300,000 gain from income on their year 0 tax return. How much gain will the Pratts recognize on the sale of their Spokane home?

38. **(LO1)** Steve Pratt, who is single, purchased a home in Spokane, Washington, for $400,000. He moved into the home on February 1 of year 1. He lived in the home as his primary residence until June 30 of year 5, when he sold the home for $700,000. Steve's ordinary marginal tax rate is 34 percent.

    a. What amount of gain will Steve be required to recognize on the sale of the home?

    b. Assume the original facts, except that the home is Steve's vacation home and he vacations there four months each year. Steve does not ever rent the home to others. What gain must Steve recognize on the home sale?

    c. Assume the original facts, except that Steve married Stephanie on February 1 of year 3 and the couple lived in the home until they sold it in June of year 5. Under state law, Steve owned the home by himself. How much gain must Steve and Stephanie recognize on the sale (assume they file a joint return in year 5).

d. Assume the original facts, except that Stephanie moved in with Steve on March 1 of year 3 and the couple was married on March 1 of year 4. Under state law, the couple jointly owned Steve's home beginning on the date they were married. On December 1 of year 3, Stephanie sold her home that she lived in before she moved in with Steve. She excluded the entire $50,000 gain on the sale on her individual year 3 tax return. What amount of gain must the couple recognize on the sale in June of year 5?

39. **(LO1)** Celia has been married to Daryl for 52 years. The couple has lived in their current home for the last 20 years. On October of year 0, Daryl passed away. Celia sold their home and moved into a condominium. What is the maximum exclusion Celia is entitled to if she sells the home on December 15 of year 1?

40. **(LO1)** Sarah purchased a home on January 1, 2007, for $600,000. She eventually sold the home for $800,000. What amount of the $200,000 gain on the sale may Sarah exclude from gross income in each of the following alternative situations?

   a. Sarah used the home as her principal residence until July 1, 2012. She used the home as a vacation home from July 1, 2012, until she sold it on July 1, 2014.

   b. Sarah used the property as a vacation home until July 1, 2012. She then used the home as her principal residence from July 1, 2012, until she sold it on July 1, 2014.

   c. Sarah used the home as a vacation home from January 1, 2007, until January 1, 2013. She used the home as her principal residence from January 1, 2013, until she sold it on July 1, 2014.

   d. Sarah used the home as a vacation home from January 1, 2007, until July 1, 2008. She used the home as her principal residence from July 1, 2008, until she sold it on July 1, 2011.

41. **(LO2)** Javier and Anita Sanchez purchased a home on January 1, 2010, for $500,000 by paying $200,000 down and borrowing the remaining $300,000 with a 7 percent loan secured by the home. The loan requires interest-only payments for the first five years. The Sanchezes would itemize deductions even if they did not have any deductible interest. The Sanchezes' marginal tax rate is 30 percent.

   a. What is the after-tax cost of the interest expense to the Sanchezes in 2010?

   b. Assume the original facts, except that the Sanchezes rent a home and pay $21,000 in rent during the year. What is the after-tax cost of their rental payments in 2010?

   c. Assuming the interest expense is their only itemized deduction for the year and that Javier and Anita file a joint return, have great eyesight, and are under 60 years of age, what is the after-tax cost of their 2010 interest expense?

42. **(LO2)** Javier and Anita Sanchez purchased a home on January 1 of year 1 for $500,000 by paying $50,000 down and borrowing the remaining $450,000 with a 7 percent loan secured by the home. The loan requires interest-only payments for the first five years. The Sanchezes would itemize deductions even if they did not have any deductible interest.

   a. Assume the Sanchezes also took out a second loan secured by the home for $80,000 to fund expenses unrelated to the home. The interest rate on the second loan is 8 percent. The Sanchezes make interest-only payments on the loan in year 1. What is the amount of their deductible interest expense on the second loan in year 1?

b. Assume the original facts and that the Sanchezes take out a second loan secured by the home in the amount of $50,000 to fund expenses unrelated to the home. The interest rate on the second loan is 8 percent. The Sanchezes make interest-only payments during the year. What is the amount of their deductible interest expense on the second loan in year 1?

43. **(LO2)** Javier and Anita Sanchez purchased a home on January 1 of year 1 for $500,000 by paying $200,000 down and borrowing the remaining $300,000 with a 7 percent loan secured by the home. The loan requires interest-only payments for the first five years. The Sanchezes would itemize deductions even if they did not have any deductible interest. On January 1, the Sanchezes also borrowed money on a second loan secured by the home for $75,000. The interest rate on the loan is 8 percent and the Sanchezes make interest-only payments in year 1 on the second loan.

a. Assuming the Sanchezes use the second loan to landscape the yard to their home, how much of the interest expense on the second loan are they allowed to deduct in year 1?

b. Assume the original facts and that the Sanchezes use the $75,000 loan proceeds for an extended family vacation. How much of the interest expense on the second loan are they allowed to deduct in year 1?

c. Assume the original facts, except that the Sanchezes borrow $120,000 on the second loan and they use the proceeds for an extended family vacation and other personal expenses. How much of the second loan interest expense are the Sanchezes allowed to deduct in year 1?

44. **(LO2)** On January 1 of year 1, Arthur and Aretha Franklin purchased a home for $1.5 million by paying $200,000 down and borrowing the remaining $1.3 million with a 7 percent loan secured by the home.

a. What is the amount of the interest expense the Franklins may deduct in year 1?

b. Assume that in year 2, the Franklins pay off the entire loan but at the beginning of year 3, they borrow $300,000 secured by the home at a 7 percent rate. They make interest-only payments on the loan during the year. What amount of interest expense may the Franklins deduct in year 3 on this loan? Does it matter what they do with the loan proceeds? Explain.

c. Assume the same facts as in (b), except that the Franklins borrow $80,000 secured by their home. What amount of interest expense may the Franklins deduct in year 3 on this loan? Does it matter what they do with the loan proceeds? Explain.

45. **(LO2)** In year 0, Eva took out a $50,000 home-equity loan from her local credit union. At the time she took out the loan, her home was valued $350,000. At the time of the loan, Eva's original mortgage on the home was $265,000. At the end of year 1, her original mortgage is $260,000. Unfortunately for Eva, during year 1, the value of her home dropped to $280,000. Consequently, as of the end of year 1, Eva's home secured $310,000 of home-related debt but her home is only valued at $280,000. Assuming Eva paid $15,000 of interest on the original mortgage and $3,500 of interest on the home-equity loan during the year, how much qualified residence interest can Eva deduct in year 1?

46. **(LO2)** On January 1 of year 1, Jason and Jill Marsh acquired a home for $500,000 by paying $400,000 down and borrowing $100,000 with a 7 percent loan secured by the home. On June 30 of year 1, the Marshes needed cash so they refinanced the original loan by taking out a new $250,000 7 percent loan. With the $250,000 proceeds from the new loan, the Marshes paid off the original $100,000 loan and used the remaining $150,000 to fund their son's college education.

a. What amount of interest expense on this loan may the Marshes deduct in year 1?

b. Assume the same facts as in (a), except that the Marshes use the $150,000 cash from the refinancing to add two rooms and a garage to their home. What amount of interest expense on this loan may the Marshes deduct in year 1?

47. **(LO2)** On January 1 of year 1 Brandon and Alisa Roy purchased a home for $1.5 million by paying $500,000 down and borrowing the remaining $1 million with a 7 percent loan secured by the home. On the same day, the Roys took out a second loan, secured by the home, in the amount of $300,000.

    ■ **planning**

    a. Assuming the interest rate on the second loan is 8 percent, what is the maximum amount of interest expense the Roys may deduct on these two loans in year 1?

    b. Assuming the interest rate on the second loan is 6 percent, what is the maximum amount of interest expense the Roys may deduct on these two loans in year 1?

48. **(LO2)** Jennifer has been living in her current principal residence for three years. Six months ago Jennifer decided that she would like to purchase a second home near a beach so she can vacation there for part of the year. Despite her best efforts, Jennifer has been unable to find what she is looking for. Consequently, Jennifer recently decided to change plans. She purchased a parcel of land for $200,000 with the intention of building her second home on the property. To acquire the land, she borrowed $200,000 secured by the land. Jennifer would like to know whether the interest she pays on the loan before construction on the house is completed is deductible as mortgage interest.

    ■ **research** ■■

    a. How should Jennifer treat the interest if she has begun construction on the home and plans to live in the home in 12 months?

    b. How should Jennifer treat the interest if she hasn't begun construction on the home but plans to live in the home in 15 months?

    c. How should Jennifer treat the interest if she has begun construction on the home but doesn't plan to live in the home for 37 months?

49. **(LO2)** Rajiv and Laurie Amin are recent college graduates looking to purchase a new home. They are purchasing a $200,000 home by paying $20,000 down and borrowing the other $180,000 with a 30-year loan secured by the home. The Amins have the option of (1) paying no discount points on the loan and paying interest at 8 percent or (2) paying one discount point on the loan and paying interest of 7.5 percent. Both loans require the Amins to make interest-only payments for the first five years. Unless otherwise stated, the Amins itemize deductions irrespective of the amount of interest expense. The Amins are in the 25 percent marginal ordinary income tax bracket.

    ■ **planning**

    a. Assuming the Amins *do not itemize deductions,* what is the break-even point for paying the point to get a lower interest rate?

    b. Assuming the Amins do itemize deductions, what is the break-even point for paying the point to get a lower interest rate?

    c. Assume the original facts, except that the amount of the loan is $300,000. What is the break-even point for the Amins for paying the point to get a lower interest rate?

    d. Assume the original facts, except that the $180,000 loan is a refinance instead of an original loan. What is the break-even point for paying the point to get a lower interest rate?

    e. Assume the original facts, except that the amount of the loan is $300,000 and the loan is a refinance and not an original loan. What is the break-even point for paying the point to get a lower interest rate?

50. **(LO3)** In year 1, Peter and Shaline Johnsen moved into a home in a new subdivision. Theirs was one of the first homes in the subdivision. In year 1, they paid $1,500 in property taxes to the state government, $500 to the developer of the subdivision for an assessment to pay for the sidewalks, and $900 for property taxes on land they hold as an investment. What amount of taxes are the Johnsens allowed to deduct assuming their itemized deductions exceed the standard deduction amount before considering any property tax deductions?

51. **(LO3)** Jesse Brimhall is single. In 2010, his itemized deductions were $5,000 before considering any real property taxes he paid during the year. Jesse's adjusted gross income was $70,000 (also before considering any property tax deductions). In 2010, he paid real property taxes of $3,000 on property 1 and $800 of real property taxes on property 2.

    a. If property 1 is Jesse's primary residence and property 2 is his vacation home (he does not rent it out at all), what is his taxable income after taking property taxes into account?

    b. If property 1 is Jesse's business building (he owns the property) and property 2 is his primary residence, what is his taxable income after taking property taxes into account?

    c. If property 1 is Jesse's primary residence and property 2 is a parcel of land he holds for investment, what is his taxable income after taking property taxes into account?

52. **(LO3)** Kirk and Lorna Newbold purchased a new home on August 1 of year 1 for $300,000. At the time of the purchase, it was estimated that the real property tax rate for the year would be .5 percent of the property's value. Because the taxing jurisdiction collects taxes on a July 1 year-end, it was estimated that the Newbolds would be required to pay $1,375 in property taxes for the property tax year relating to August through June of year 2 ($300,000 × .005 × 11/12). The seller would be required to pay the $125 for July of year 1. Along with their monthly payment of principal and interest, the Newbolds paid $125 to the mortgage company to cover the property taxes. The mortgage company placed the money in escrow and used the funds in the escrow account to pay the property tax bill in July of year 2. The Newbold's itemized deductions exceed the standard deduction before considering real property taxes.

    a. How much in real property taxes can the Newbolds deduct for year 1?

    b. How much in real property taxes can the Newbolds deduct for year 2?

    c. Assume the original facts, except that the Newbolds were not able to collect $125 from the seller for the property taxes for July of year 1. How much in real property taxes can the Newbolds deduct for year 1 and year 2?

    d. Assume the original facts, except that the tax bill for July 1 of year 1 through June 30 of year 2 turned out to be $1,200 instead of $1,500. How much in real property taxes can the Newbolds deduct in year 1 and year 2?

**research**

53. **(LO3)** Jenae and Terry Hutchings own a parcel of land as tenants by entirety. That is, they both own the property but when one of them dies the other becomes the sole owner of the property. For nontax reasons, Jenae and Terry decide to file separate tax returns for the current year. Jenae paid the entire $3,000 property tax bill for the land. How much of the $3,000 property tax payment is each spouse entitled to deduct in the current year?

54. **(LO3)** After renting an apartment for five years, Todd and Diane purchased a new home for $150,000 on July 1, 2008. On their 2008 joint tax return, they claimed a $7,500 first-time home buyer credit. Answer the following questions relating to the credit.

   a. Assuming they still live in the home, what amount of credit must Todd and Diane repay with their 2010 tax return?

   b. Assuming they sell the home in August 2014 for a $20,000 gain, what amount of credit must they pay back with their 2014 tax return?

   c. Assuming they sell the home in August 2014 for a $3,000 gain, what amount of credit must they pay back with their 2014 tax return?

55. **(LO3)** In 2010, Harold purchased a new condominium for $70,000 to use as his principal residence. Harold files as a single taxpayer. What is Harold's first-time home buyer credit in the following alternative situations?

   a. Harold purchased the condominium on February 1, 2010. Harold has lived in an apartment he has rented since 2002. Harold's 2010 AGI is $60,000.

   b. Harold purchased the condominium on February 1, 2010. Harold has lived in an apartment he has rented since 2002. Harold's 2010 AGI is $135,000.

   c. Harold purchased the condominium on February 1, 2010. In the six years preceding this purchase, Harold lived in another home he owned. Harold sold that other home on March 1, 2010. Harold's 2010 AGI is $60,000.

   d. Harold purchased the condominium on February 1, 2010. In the three years preceding this purchase, Harold lived in a home he owned. This was the first home Harold ever owned. Harold sold this home on March 1, 2010. Harold's 2010 AGI is $60,000.

56. **(LO3)** For her 90th birthday, Jamie (a widow) purchased a new home on September 1, 2008, and appropriately claimed a first-time home buyer credit of $7,500 on her 2008 tax return. Jamie followed the appropriate schedule for paying back the credit. However, in December 2014, Jamie passed away of old age. Is Jamie (or her estate) responsible for paying the unpaid balance of the credit? Explain.

57. **(LO4)** Several years ago, Junior acquired a home that he vacationed in part of the time and rented out part of the time. During the current year Junior:

- Personally stayed in the home for 22 days.
- Rented it to his favorite brother at a discount for 10 days.
- Rented it to his least favorite brother for eight days at the full market rate.
- Rented it to his friend at a discounted rate for four days.
- Rented the home to third parties for 58 days at the market rate.
- Did repair and maintenance work for two days.
- Marketed the property and made it available for rent for 150 days during the year.

How many days of personal use and how many days of rental use did Junior experience on the property during the year?

58. **(LO4)** Dillon rented his personal residence at Lake Tahoe for 14 days while he was vacationing in Ireland. He resided in the home for the remainder of the year. Rental income from the property was $6,500. Expenses associated with use of the home for the entire year were as follows:

| | |
|---|---|
| Real property taxes | $ 3,100 |
| Mortgage interest | 12,000 |
| Repairs | 1,500 |
| Insurance | 1,500 |
| Utilities | 3,900 |
| Depreciation | 13,000 |

   a. What effect does the rental have on Dillon's AGI?

   b. What effect does the rental have on Dillon's itemized deductions?

**Use the following facts to answer problems 59 and 60.**

Natalie owns a condominium near Cocoa Beach in Florida. This year, she incurs the following expenses in connection with her condo:

| | |
|---|---|
| Insurance | $1,000 |
| Advertising expense | 500 |
| Mortgage interest | 3,500 |
| Property taxes | 900 |
| Repairs & maintenance | 650 |
| Utilities | 950 |
| Depreciation | 8,500 |

During the year, Natalie rented out the condo for 75 days, receiving $10,000 of gross income. She personally used the condo for 35 days during her vacation.

59. **(LO4)** Assume Natalie uses the *IRS* method of allocating expenses to rental use of the property.

a. What is the total amount of *for* AGI (rental) deductions Natalie may deduct in the current year related to the condo?

b. What is the total amount of itemized deductions Natalie may deduct in the current year related to the condo?

c. If Natalie's basis in the condo at the beginning of the year was $150,000, what is her basis in the condo at the end of the year?

d. Assume that gross rental revenue was $1,000 (rather than $10,000), what amount of *for* AGI deductions may Natalie deduct in the current year related to the condo?

60. **(LO4)** Assume Natalie uses the *Tax Court* method of allocating expenses to rental use of the property.

a. What is the total amount of *for* AGI (rental) deductions Natalie may deduct in the current year related to the condo?

b. What is the total amount of itemized deductions Natalie may deduct in the current year related to the condo?

c. If Natalie's basis in the condo at the beginning of the year was $150,000, what is her basis in the condo at the end of the year?

d. Assume that gross rental revenue was $2,000 (rather than $10,000), what amount of *for* AGI deductions may Natalie deduct in the current year related to the condo?

**Use the following facts to answer problems 61–63.**

Alexa owns a condominium near Cocoa Beach in Florida. This year, she incurs the following expenses in connection with her condo:

| | |
|---|---|
| Insurance | $2,000 |
| Mortgage interest | 6,500 |
| Property taxes | 2,000 |
| Repairs & maintenance | 1,400 |
| Utilities | 2,500 |
| Depreciation | 14,500 |

During the year, Alexa rented out the condo for 100 days. She did not use the condo at all for personal purposes during the year. Alexa's AGI from all sources other than the rental property is $200,000. Unless otherwise specified, Alexa has no sources of passive income.

61. **(LO4)** Assume Alexa receives $30,000 in gross rental receipts.

    a. What effect do the expenses associated with the property have on her AGI?

    b. What effect do the expenses associated with the property have on her itemized deductions?

62. **(LO4)** Assuming Alexa receives $20,000 in gross rental receipts, answer the following questions:

    a. What effect does the rental activity have on her AGI for the year?

    b. Assuming that Alexa's AGI from other sources is $90,000, what effect does the rental activity have on Alexa's AGI? Alexa makes all decisions with respect to the property.

    c. Assuming that Alexa's AGI from other sources is $120,000, what effect does the rental activity have on Alexa's AGI? Alexa makes all decisions with respect to the property.

    d. Assume that Alexa's AGI from other sources is $200,000. This consists of $150,000 salary, $10,000 of dividends, and $25,000 of long-term capital gain, and net rental income from another rental property in the amount of $15,000. What effect does the Cocoa Beach Condo rental activity have on Alexa's AGI?

63. **(LO4)** Assume that in addition to renting the condo for 100 days, Alexa uses the condo for eight days of personal use. Also assume that Alexa receives $30,000 of gross rental receipts. Answer the following questions:

    ■ **planning**

    a. What is the total amount of *for* AGI deductions relating to the condo that Alexa may deduct in the current year? Assume she uses the IRS method of allocating expenses between rental and personal days.

    b. What is the total amount of *from* AGI deductions relating to the condo that Alexa may deduct in the current year? Assume she uses the IRS method of allocating expenses between rental and personal days.

    c. Would Alexa be better or worse off after taxes if she uses the Tax Court method of allocating expenses?

64. **(LO5)** Brooke owns a sole proprietorship in which she works as a management consultant. She maintains an office in her home where she meets with clients, prepares bills, and performs other work-related tasks. The home office is 300 square feet and the entire house is 4,500 square feet. Brooke incurred the following home-related expenses during the year.

| | |
|---|---|
| Real property taxes | $ 3,600 |
| Interest on home mortgage | 14,000 |
| Operating expenses of home | 5,000 |
| Depreciation | 12,000 |
| Repairs to home theater room | 1,000 |

What amount of each of these expenses is allocated to the home office?

**Use the following facts to answer problems 65 and 66.**

Rita owns a sole proprietorship in which she works as a management consultant. She maintains an office in her home where she meets with clients, prepares bills, and performs other work-related tasks. Her business expenses, other than home office expenses, total $5,600. The following home-related expenses have been allocated to her home office.

| | |
|---|---|
| Real property taxes | $1,600 |
| Interest on home mortgage | 5,100 |
| Operating expenses of home | 800 |
| Depreciation | 1,600 |

Also, assume that not counting the sole proprietorship, Rita's AGI is $60,000.

65. **(LO5)** Assume Rita's consulting business generated $15,000 in gross income.

    a. What is Rita's home office deduction for the current year?

    b. What would Rita's home office deduction be if her business generated $10,000 of gross income instead of $15,000?

    c. What is Rita's AGI for the year?

    d. What types and amounts of expenses will she carry over to next year?

66. **(LO5)** Assume Rita's consulting business generated $13,000 in gross income for the current year.

    a. What is Rita's home office deduction for the current year?

    b. What is Rita's AGI for the year?

    c. Assume the original facts, except that Rita is an employee and not self-employed. Consequently, she does not receive any gross income from the (sole proprietorship) business and she does not incur any business expenses unrelated to the home office. Finally, her AGI is $60,000 consisting of salary from her work as an employee. What effect do her home office expenses have on her itemized deductions?

    d. Assuming the original facts, what types and amounts of expenses will she carry over to next year?

67. **(LO1, LO5)** Alisha, who is single, owns a sole proprietorship in which she works as a management consultant. She maintains an office in her home where she meets with clients, prepares bills, and performs other work-related tasks. She purchased the home at the beginning of year 1 for $400,000. Since she purchased the home and moved into it she has been able to deduct $10,000 of depreciation expenses to offset her consulting income. At the end of year 3, Alisha sold the home for $500,000. What is the amount of taxes Alisha will be required to pay on the gain from the sale of the home? Alisha's ordinary marginal tax rate is 30 percent.

## COMPREHENSIVE PROBLEMS

■ planning

68. Derek and Meagan Jacoby recently graduated from State University and Derek accepted a job in business consulting while Meagan accepted a job in computer programming. Meagan inherited $75,000 from her grandfather who recently passed away. The couple is debating whether they should buy or rent a home. They located a rental home that meets their needs. The monthly rent is $2,250. They also found a three-bedroom home that would cost $475,000 to purchase. The Jacobys could use Meagan's inheritance for a down payment on the home. Thus, they would need to borrow $400,000 to acquire the home. They have the option of paying two discount points to receive a fixed interest rate of 4.5 percent on the loan or paying no points and receiving a fixed interest rate of 5.75 percent for a 30-year fixed loan.

    Though anything could happen, the couple expects to live in the home for no more than five years before relocating to a different region of the country. Derek and Meagan don't have any school-related debt, so they will save the $75,000 if they don't purchase a home. Also, consider the following information:

    • The couple's marginal tax rate is 25 percent.

    • Regardless of whether they buy or rent, the couple will itemize their deductions.

    • If they buy, the Jacobys would purchase and move into the home on January 1, 2010.

    • If they buy the home, the property tax year runs from July 1 through June 30. The taxes payable on the home on June 30, 2010, are $3,600. The taxes payable on the home on June 30, 2011, are $4,000.

- Disregard loan-related fees not mentioned above.
- If the couple does not buy a home, they will put their money into their savings account where they earn 5 percent annual interest.
- Assume that all unstated costs are equal between the buy and rent option.

**Required:**

Help the Jacobys with their decisions by answering the following questions:

a. If the Jacobys decide to rent the home, what is their after-tax cost of the rental for the first year?

b. What is the approximate break-even point in years (or months) for paying the points to receive a reduced interest rate (to simplify this computation, assume the Jacobys will make interest-only payments, and ignore the time value of money)?

c. What is the after-tax cost (in interest and property taxes) of living in the home for 2010? Assume that the Jacoby's interest rate is 5.75 percent, they do not pay discount points, they make interest-only payments for the first year, and the value of the home does not change during the year. Also consider the after-tax cost of the property tax (ignore the time value of money) they must pay because they lived in the home during 2010 (not necessarily payable in 2010). Finally, assume the Jacobys sell the home as described in part d.

d. Assume that on March 1, 2011, the Jacobys sold their home for $525,000, so that Derek and Meagan could accept job opportunities in a different state. The Jacobys used the sale proceeds to (1) pay off the $400,000 principal of the mortgage, (2) pay a $10,000 commission to their real estate broker, and (3) make a down payment on a new home in the different state. However, the new home cost only $300,000. What gain or loss do the Jacobys realize and recognize on the sale of their home and what amount of taxes must they pay on the gain, if any (assume they make interest only payments on the loan)?

e. Assume the same facts as in (d), except that the Jacobys sell their home for $450,000 and they pay a $7,500 commission. What effect does the sale have on their year 2 income tax liability? Recall that the Jacobys are subject to an ordinary marginal tax rate of 25 percent and assume that they do not have any other transactions involving capital assets in 2011.

69. James and Kate Sawyer were married on New Year's Eve of 2009. Before their marriage, Kate lived in New York and worked as a hair stylist for one of the city's top salons. James lives in Atlanta where he works for a public accounting firm earning an annual salary of $100,000. After their marriage, Kate left her job in New York and moved into the couple's newly purchased 3,200-square-foot home in Atlanta. Kate incurred $2,200 of qualified moving expenses. The couple purchased the home on January 3, 2010, by paying $100,000 down and obtaining a $240,000 mortgage for the remainder. The interest rate on this loan was 7 percent and the Sawyers made interest-only payments on the loan through June 30, 2010 (assume they paid exactly one-half of a year's worth of interest on this loan by June 30). On July 1, 2010, because the value of their home had increased to $400,000, the Sawyers were in need of cash, and interest rates had dropped, the Sawyers refinanced their home loan. On the refinancing, they borrowed $370,000 at 6 percent interest. They made interest-only payments on the home loan through the end of the year and they spent $20,000 of the loan proceeds improving their home (assume they paid exactly one-half of a year's worth of interest on this loan by year end).

Kate wanted to try her hand at making it on her own in business, and with James's help, she started Kate's Beauty Cuts, LLC. She set up shop in a 384-square-foot corner room of the couple's home and began to get it ready for business. The room conveniently had a door to the outside providing customers direct access to the shop. Before she opened the doors to the business, Kate paid $2,100 to have the carpet replaced with a tile floor. She also paid $1,200 to have the room painted with vibrant colors, and $650 to have the room rewired for appropriate lighting. Kate ran an ad in the local newspaper and officially opened her shop on January 24, 2010. By the end of the year, Kate's Beauty Cuts LLC generated $40,000 of *net* income before considering the home office deduction. The Sawyers incurred the following home-related expenditures during 2010:

- $4,200 of real property taxes.
- $2,000 for homeowner's insurance.
- $2,400 for electricity.
- $1,500 for gas and other utilities.

They determined depreciation expense for their entire house was $7,300.

Also, on March 2, Kate was able to finally sell her one-bedroom Manhattan condominium for $478,000. She purchased the condo, which she had lived in for six years prior to her marriage, for $205,000.

Kate owns a vacation home in Myrtle Beach, South Carolina. She purchased the home several years ago, largely as an investment opportunity. To help cover the expenses of maintaining the home, James and Kate decided to rent the home out. They rented the home for a total of 106 days at fair market value (this included eight days that they rented the home to James's brother Jack). In addition to the 106 days, Kate allowed a good friend and customer, Clair, to stay in the home for half-price for two days. James and Kate stayed in the home for six days for a romantic getaway and another three days in order to do some repair and maintenance work on the home. The rental revenues from the home in 2010 were $18,400. The Sawyers incurred the following expenses associated with the home.

- $9,100 of interest expense.
- $3,400 of real property taxes.
- $1,900 for homeowner's insurance.
- $1,200 for electricity.
- $1,600 for gas, other utilities, and landscaping.
- $5,200 for depreciation.

### Required:

Determine the Sawyer's taxable income for 2010. Disregard self-employment taxes for Kate and disregard the phase-out of itemized deductions. Assume the couple paid $4,400 in state income taxes and files a joint return. The Sawyers use the method of allocating expenses to the rental that minimizes their *overall taxable income for 2010*.

# KAPLAN CPA SIMULATIONS

**KAPLAN** CPA REVIEW

**Please visit the Online Learning Center**    (www.mhhe.com/spilker2011) to access the following Kaplan CPA simulation:

The simulation for **Michael and Marshall Morgan** covers individual income tax issues, including itemized deductions; rental income and expenses; deductions for AGI; filing requirements; AMT; and dependents with summer job income.

**Please visit the Online Learning Center**    (www.mhhe.com/spilker2011) to access the following Kaplan CPA simulation:

The simulation for **Colt and Cara West** covers individual income tax issues, including business income/expense; home office deduction; NOL; charitable donations; and capital expenditures.

# Entities Overview

## Learning Objectives

**Upon completing this chapter, you should be able to:**

**LO 1** Discuss the legal and nontax characteristics of different types of legal entities.

■

**LO 2** Describe the different types of entities for tax purposes.

■

**LO 3** Explain fundamental differences in tax characteristics across entity types.

**N**icole Johnson is currently employed by the Utah Chamber of Commerce in Salt Lake City, Utah. While she enjoys the relatively short workweeks, she eventually would like to work for herself rather than for an employer. In her current position, she deals with a lot of successful entrepreneurs who have become role models for her. Nicole has also developed an extensive list of contacts that should serve her well when she starts her own business. It has taken a while, but Nicole believes she has finally developed a viable new business idea. Her idea is to design and manufacture bed sheets that have various colored patterns and are made of unique fabric blends. The sheets look great and are extremely comfortable whether the bedroom is warm or cool. She has had several friends try out her prototype sheets and they have consistently given the sheets rave reviews. With this encouragement, Nicole started giving serious thought to making "Color Comfort Sheets" a moneymaking enterprise.

Nicole has enough business background to realize that she is embarking on a risky path, but one, she hopes, with significant potential rewards in the future. After creating some initial income projections, Nicole realized that it will take a few years for the business to become profitable. After that, she hopes the sky's the limit.

While Nicole's original plan was to start the business by herself, she is considering seeking out another equity owner for the business so that she can add financial resources and business experience to the venture. Nicole felt like she had a grasp on her business plan, but she still needed to determine how to organize the business for tax purposes. After doing some research, Nicole learned that she should consider many factors in order to determine the

| Storyline Summary | |
|---|---|
| *Taxpayer:* | Nicole Johnson |
| *Location:* | Salt Lake City, Utah |
| *Employment status:* | State government employee with entrepreneurial ambitions |
| *Filing status:* | Married |
| *Husband Tom:* | Executive with a local chemical company |
| *Dependents:* | None |
| *Marginal tax rate:* | 35 percent unless otherwise stated |

"best" entity type for her business. Each type of entity has advantages and disadvantages from both tax and nontax perspectives, and the best entity for a business depends on the goals, outlook, and strategy for that particular business and its owners. She realized she had more work to do to make an informed decision.

*. . . to be continued*

This chapter explores the various types of legal entities and then discusses entities available for tax purposes. We outline some of the pros and cons of each entity type, emphasizing both nontax and tax perspectives as we help Nicole determine how she will organize her business to best accomplish her goals. Later chapters provide additional detail concerning the tax characteristics of each entity type.

LO1

# ENTITY LEGAL CLASSIFICATION AND NONTAX CHARACTERISTICS

When forming new business ventures, entrepreneurs can choose to house their operations under one of several basic entity types. These entities differ in terms of their legal and tax considerations. In fact, as we discuss in more depth below, the legal classification of a business may be different from its tax classification. These entities differ in terms of the formalities that entrepreneurs must follow to create them, the legal rights and responsibilities conferred on the entities and their owners, and the tax rules that determine how the entities and owners will be taxed on income generated by the entities.

## Legal Classification

Generally, a business entity may be classified as a corporation, a **limited liability company** (LLC), a **general partnership** (GP), a **limited partnership** (LP), or a **sole proprietorship** under state law. State laws recognize corporations as legal entities separate from their owners (shareholders). Business owners legally form corporations by filing **articles of incorporation** with the state in which they organize the business. State laws also recognize limited liability companies (LLCs) as legal entities separate from their owners (members). Business owners create limited liability companies by filing **articles of organization** with the state in which they are organizing the businesses.

Partnerships are formed under state partnership statutes and the degree of formality required depends on the type of partnership being formed. General partnerships may be formed by written agreement among the partners, called a **partnership agreement,** or may be formed informally without a written agreement when two or more owners join together in an activity to generate profits. Although general partners are not required to file partnership agreements with the state, general partnerships are still considered to be legal entities separate from their owners under state laws. Unlike general partnerships, limited partnerships are usually organized by written agreement and must typically file a **certificate of limited partnership** to be recognized by the state.[1]

---

[1]Similar to limited partnerships, limited liability partnerships (LLPs), professional corporations (PCs), and professional limited liability companies (PLLCs) must register with the state to receive formal recognition.

Finally, for state law purposes, sole proprietorships are *not* treated as legal entities separate from their individual owners. As a result, sole proprietors are not required to formally organize their businesses with the state, and they hold title to business assets in their own names rather than in the name of their businesses.

### Nontax Characteristics

The different legal entity types may differ from or share similarities with other legal entity types with respect to certain nontax characteristics. Rather than identify and discuss all possible nontax entity characteristics, we compare and contrast several prominent characteristics across the different legal entity types.

**Responsibility for Liabilities**   Whether the entity or the owner(s) is ultimately responsible for paying the liabilities of the business depends on the type of entity. Under state law, a corporation is solely responsible for its liabilities.[2] Similarly, LLCs and not their members are responsible for the liabilities of the business.[3] For entities formed as partnerships, all general partners are ultimately responsible for the liabilities of the partnership. In contrast, limited partners are not responsible for the partnership's liabilities.[4]

Finally, if a business is conducted as a sole proprietorship, the individual owner rather than the sole proprietorship is responsible for the liabilities of the business. It is important to note, however, that individual business owners may also organize their businesses as single-member LLCs. In exchange for observing the formalities of organizing as an LLC, they receive the liability protection afforded LLC members.

**Rights, Responsibilities, and Legal Arrangement among Owners**   State corporation laws specify the rights and responsibilities of corporations and their shareholders. Consequently, shareholders have no flexibility to alter their legal treatment with respect to one another, with respect to the corporation, and with respect to outsiders. In contrast, while state laws provide *default* provisions specifying rights and responsibilities of LLCs and their members, members have the *flexibility to alter* their arrangement by spelling out the management practices of the entity and the rights and responsibilities of the members consistent with their wishes. Thus, LLCs allow more flexible business arrangements than do corporations.

Similar to LLC statutes, state partnership laws provide default provisions specifying the partners' legal rights and responsibilities for dealing with each other absent an agreement to the contrary. Because partners have the flexibility to depart from the default provisions, they frequently craft partnership agreements that are consistent with their preferences.

Although in many instances having the flexibility to customize business arrangements is desirable, sometimes inflexible governance rules mandated by state statute are needed to limit the participation of owners in management when their participation becomes impractical. For example, when businesses decide to "go public" with an **initial public offering** (IPO) on one of the public securities exchanges, they usually

---

[2]Payroll tax liabilities are an important exception to this general rule. Shareholders of closely held corporations may be held responsible for these liabilities.

[3]When closely held corporations and LLCs borrow from banks or other lenders, shareholders or members are usually asked to personally guarantee the debt. To the extent they do this, they become personally liable to repay the loan in the event the corporation or LLC is unable to repay it.

[4]Because some states don't permit professional service organizations to operate as LLCs or limited partnerships, accounting firms and other service businesses are frequently organized as limited liability partnerships (LLPs). They are very similar to LLCs or limited partnerships in that they typically insulate owners from liabilities arising from the malpractice of other partners. However, LLPs are also different because they do not provide protection against liabilities stemming from the partners' own malpractice or from the LLP's contractual liabilities.

solicit a vast pool of potential investors to become *corporate* shareholders.[5] As shareholders, state corporation laws prohibit them from directly amending corporate governance rules and from directly participating in management—they only have the right to vote for corporate directors or officers. In comparison, LLC members generally have the right to amend the LLC operating agreement, provide input, and manage LLCs. Obviously, managing a publicly traded business would be next to impossible if thousands of owners had the legal right to change operating rules and to directly participate in managing the enterprise.

Exhibit 15-1 summarizes several nontax characteristics of different types of legal entities.

### EXHIBIT 15-1    Business Types: Legal Entities and Nontax Characteristics

| Nontax Characteristics | Corporation | LLC | Partnership | Sole Proprietorship |
|---|---|---|---|---|
| Must formally organize with state | Yes | Yes | No | No |
| Responsibility for liabilities of business | Entity | Entity | General partner(s) | Owner |
| Legal arrangement among owners | Not flexible | Flexible | Flexible | Not applicable |
| Suitable for initial public offering | Yes | No | No | No |

As summarized in Exhibit 15-1, corporations and LLCs have the advantage in liability protection, LLCs and partnerships have an advantage over other entities in terms of legal flexibility, and corporations have the advantage if owners ever want to take a business public.

*continued from page 15-2 . . .*

As an initial step in the process of selecting an entity to house CCS, Nicole began to research nontax issues that might be relevant to her decision. Early on in her research she realized that the nontax benefits unique to traditional corporations were relevant primarily to large, publicly traded corporations. Although Nicole was very optimistic about CCS's prospects, she knew it would likely be a long time, if ever, before it went public. However, she remained concerned about limiting her own and other potential investors' liability in the new venture so she began to dig a little deeper. As she perused the Utah state Web site, she learned that corporations and LLCs are the only legal entities that can completely shield her and future investors from liabilities. Although Nicole doesn't anticipate any trouble from her future creditors, she decides to limit her choice of legal entity to either a corporation or LLC.

At this point in her information-gathering process, Nicole is leaning toward the LLC option because she is not sure if she wants to deal with board meetings and all the other formalities of operating a corporation; however, she decides to assemble a five-year forecast of CCS's expected operating results and to learn a little more about the way corporations and LLCs are taxed before narrowing her options any further.

*. . . to be continued*

---

[5]The vast majority of IPOs involve corporate shares; however, limited partnership interests are occasionally sold in IPOs. Like shareholders, limited partners are typically not allowed to participate in management. Limited partnerships are used for public offerings in lieu of corporations when they qualify for favorable partnership tax treatment available to some publicly traded partnerships.

# ENTITY TAX CLASSIFICATION

**LO2**

In general terms, for tax purposes business entities can be classified as either separate taxpaying entities or as **flow-through entities.** Separate taxpaying entities pay tax on their own income. In contrast, flow-through entities generally don't pay taxes because income from these entities flows through to their business owners who are responsible for paying tax on the income.

How do we determine whether a particular business entity is treated as a separate taxpaying entity or as a flow-through entity for tax purposes? According to Treasury Regulations, commonly referred to as the "check-the-box" regulations, a corporation under state law, by default, it is treated as a **taxable corporation** (also referred to as a **C corporation**).[6] Taxable corporations report their taxable income to the IRS on Form 1120. However, shareholders of *legal* corporations may qualify to make a special tax election known as an "S" election permitting the corporation to be taxed as a flow-through entity called an **S corporation.**[7] S corporations report the results of their operations to the IRS on Form 1120S.

Also under the check-the-box regulations, unincorporated entities are, by default, treated as flow-through entities.[8] However, owners of unincorporated entities can elect to have their businesses taxed as taxable corporations instead of as flow-through entities.[9] Why would this make sense? Owners may desire the legal flexibility offered by LLCs, but may prefer to treat the business as an S corporation rather than a partnership for tax purposes. To accomplish this goal, they would legally form the LLC and then elect to have it taxed as a corporation. Then, they would make a second election to treat the "corporation" as an S corporation for tax purposes. Thus, an LLC could be taxed as an S corporation if the appropriate tax elections are made. Note that these elections do not affect the legal classification of the entity.

Finally, unincorporated flow-through entities (all flow-through entities except S corporations) are *taxed* as either partnerships, sole proprietorships, or **disregarded entities** (an entity that is considered to be the same entity as the owner).[10] Unincorporated entities (including LLCs) with more than one owner are taxed as partnerships.[11] Partnerships report their operating results to the IRS on Form 1065. Unincorporated entities (including LLCs) with only one *individual* owner such as sole proprietorships and **single-member LLCs** are taxed as sole proprietorships.[12] Income from businesses taxed as sole proprietorships is reported on Schedule C of Form 1040. Similarly, unincorporated entities with only one *corporate* owner, typically a single-member LLC, are disregarded for tax purposes. Thus, income and losses from this single, corporate-member LLC is reported as if it had originated from a division of the corporation and is reported directly on the single-member corporation's return.

---

> ### THE KEY FACTS
>
> **Tax Classification of Legal Entities**
>
> ■ Corporations are taxable C corporations unless they make a valid S election.
>
> ■ Unincorporated entities are taxed as partnerships if they have more than one owner.
>
> ■ Unincorporated entities are taxed as sole proprietorships if held by an individual or as disregarded entities if held by some other entity.
>
> ■ Unincorporated entities may elect to be treated as taxable corporations.

---

[6]Reg. §301.7701-3(a). Taxable corporations are technically C corporations because these corporations and their shareholders are subject to tax provisions in Subchapter C of the Internal Revenue Code (and they are not subject to provisions in Subchapter S of the Code). Throughout the chapter we refer to C corporations as taxable corporations and we refer to corporations treated as flow-through entities for tax purposes as S corporations.

[7]§1362(a). Because §1361 limits the number and type of shareholders of corporations qualifying to make an S election, some corporations are ineligible to become S corporations.

[8]Reg. §301.7701-3(b). However, §7704 mandates that unincorporated publicly traded entities be taxed as corporations unless their income predominately consists of certain types of passive income.

[9]Reg. §301.7701-3(a).

[10]Reg. §301.7701-3(a).

[11]Reg. §301.7701-3(b)(i).

[12]Reg. §301.7701-3(b)(ii).

To summarize, although there are other types of legal entities, there are really only four categories of business entities recognized by our tax system, as follows:

- Taxable corporation (separate taxpaying entity)
- S corporation (flow-through entity)
- Partnership (flow-through entity)
- Sole proprietorship (flow-through entity)

---

**Example 15-1**

*What if:* Assume Nicole legally forms CCS as a corporation (with only common stock) by filing articles of incorporation with the state. What are Nicole's options for classifying CCS for tax purposes if she is the only shareholder of CCS?

**Answer:** Nicole may treat CCS as either a taxable corporation or as an S corporation. The default tax classification of legal corporations is as a taxable corporation for tax purposes. In addition, certain eligible corporations may elect to be treated as S corporations. Given the facts provided, CCS is eligible to make an S election.[13]

*What if:* Assume Nicole legally forms CCS as an LLC (with only one class of ownership rights) by filing articles of organization with the state. What are Nicole's options for classifying CCS for tax purposes if she is the only member of CCS?

**Answer:** Nicole may treat CCS as a taxable corporation, an S corporation, or as a sole proprietorship. CCS can be treated as a taxable corporation because unincorporated entities may elect to be taxed as corporations. Further, eligible entities taxed as corporations can elect to be treated as S corporations. Given the facts provided, CCS is eligible to make an S election after first electing to be treated as a corporation. Finally, the default tax classification of CCS is as a sole proprietorship since CCS is unincorporated with one individual member.

*What if:* Assume Nicole legally forms CCS as an LLC and allows other individuals or businesses to become members in return for contributing their cash, property, or services to CCS. What is the default tax classification of CCS under these assumptions?

**Answer:** Partnership. The default tax classification for unincorporated entities with multiple owners is a partnership.

---

It might seem at this point that owners of businesses classified as flow-through entities would be treated the same for tax purposes; however, that is only true in a general sense. We see in this and in other chapters that there are some subtle, and some not so subtle, differences in how the owners of ventures classified as S corporations, partnerships, and sole proprietorships are taxed.[14]

**L03**    # ENTITY TAX CHARACTERISTICS

In deciding among the available options for taxing business ventures, owners and their advisors must carefully consider whether tax rules that apply to a particular tax classification would be either more or less favorable than tax rules under other alternative tax classifications. The specific tax rules they must compare and contrast are

---

[13]§1361(b)

[14]Chapter 8 explains how sole proprietors are taxed, and Chapters 20 through 22 explain how partners and S corporation shareholders are taxed.

unique to their situations; however, certain key differences in the tax rules tend to be relevant in many scenarios. We now focus on these differences in terms of how the owners of entities classified as taxable corporations, S corporations, partnerships, and sole proprietorships are taxed.

## Double Taxation

Under our current system of tax rates, flow-through entities are generally considered to be superior to corporations for tax purposes because they generate income that is taxed only once while corporations produce income that is taxed twice. Flow-through entity income retains its character (ordinary, capital gain, tax exempt, etc.) and is allocated to or "flows through" to entity owners. The owners generally pay tax on their share of the income as if they had earned it themselves.

Corporations pay the first level of tax on their taxable income. The marginal rate for the first level of tax depends on where the corporation's taxable income falls in the corporate tax rate schedule (provided inside the front cover of this text). The current lowest marginal tax rate for corporations is 15 percent and the top marginal rate is 39 percent. The most profitable corporations are taxed at a flat 35 percent rate.

Shareholders are subject to **double taxation** because they pay a second level of tax. The applicable rate for the second level of tax depends on whether corporations retain their after-tax earnings and on the type of shareholder(s). We first discuss the second level of tax that shareholders pay if corporations distribute their after-tax earnings and then we discuss the second level of tax if they retain the earnings.

**After-Tax Earnings Distributed**   Assuming a corporation distributes its after-tax earnings, the second level of tax depends on whether the corporation's shareholders are individuals, other corporations, **institutional shareholders,** tax-exempt, or foreign entities.

*Individual Shareholders.*   Individual shareholders receiving distributions from corporations pay the second tax on the dividends they receive, usually at a 15 percent tax rate.[15]

---

**Example 15-2**

**What if:** Assume that Nicole did some income projections to help her in her quest to determine the taxable form of her business. She makes the following assumptions:

- CCS earns taxable income of $1,000,000.
- CCS will pay out all of its after-tax earnings annually as a dividend.
- Her ordinary marginal tax rate is 35 percent and her dividend tax rate is 15 percent.

Given these assumptions, if Nicole organizes CCS as a corporation, what would be the overall tax rate on CCS's income [(corporate-level tax + shareholder-level tax)/taxable income]?

*(continued on page 15-8...)*

---

[15]Distributions to shareholders are taxed as dividends to the extent they come from the "earnings and profits" (similar to economic income) of corporations. Section 1(h) of the Internal Revenue Code provides that qualified dividend income be taxed at a marginal rate of 15 percent for taxpayers in income tax brackets higher than 15 percent and at 0 percent otherwise. Nonqualified dividends are taxed at ordinary marginal rates.

**Answer:** 43.9 percent, computed as follows:

| Description | Amount | Explanation |
| --- | --- | --- |
| (1) Taxable income | $1,000,000 | |
| (2) Corporate tax rate | 34% | (3)/(1). |
| (3) Corporate-level tax | $ 340,000 | From tax table, inside cover. |
| (4) Income remaining after taxes and distributed as a dividend | $ 660,000 | (1) − (3). |
| (5) Dividend tax rate | 15% | |
| (6) Shareholder-level tax on dividend | $ 99,000 | (4) × (5) [second level of tax]. |
| (7) Total tax paid on corporate taxable income | $ 439,000 | (3) + (6). |
| **Overall tax rate on corporate taxable income** | **43.9%** | (7)/(1). |

Note that the overall rate is not 49 percent (34 percent corporate rate + 15 percent shareholder rate) because the amount of corporate-level tax ($340,000) is not taxed twice (not subject to the dividend tax).

**What if:** Given the same assumptions, what would be the overall tax rate on CCS's income if Nicole forms CCS as a flow-through entity?

**Answer:** 35 percent, computed as follows:

| Description | Amount | Explanation |
| --- | --- | --- |
| (1) Taxable income | $1,000,000 | |
| (2) Nicole's marginal individual tax rate | 35% | |
| (3) Owner-level tax | $ 350,000 | (1) × (2) [first and only level of tax]. |
| **Overall tax rate on CCS income** | **35%** | (3)/(1). |

Under these assumptions, CCS's income is subject to an 8.9 percent higher overall tax rate if it is organized as a corporation rather than as a flow-through entity (43.9% − 35%).

Although corporations are subject to a double tax, there may be circumstances in which the overall tax rate for corporate income is lower than the tax rate for flow-through income.

**Example 15-3**

**What if:** Assume that Nicole made the following assumptions when projecting CCS's income:

- CCS's taxable income is $50,000.
- CCS pays out all of its after-tax earnings.
- Nicole's ordinary marginal tax rate is 35 percent and her dividend tax rate is 15 percent.

Given these assumptions, if Nicole organizes CCS as a corporation, what would be the overall tax rate on CCS's income?

**Answer:** 27.75 percent, computed as follows:

| Description | Amount | Explanation |
|---|---|---|
| (1) Taxable income | $50,000 | |
| (2) Corporate tax rate | 15% | From tax table, inside cover. |
| (3) Corporate-level tax | $ 7,500 | (1) × (2) [first level of tax]. |
| (4) Income remaining after taxes and amount distributed as a dividend | $42,500 | (1) − (3). |
| (5) Dividend tax rate | 15% | |
| (6) Shareholder-level tax on dividend | $ 6,375 | (4) × (5) [second level of tax]. |
| (7) Total tax paid on corporate taxable income | $13,875 | (3) + (6). |
| Overall tax rate on corporate taxable income | 27.75% | (7)/(1). |

**What if:** Under the revised assumptions presented in this example, if Nicole forms CCS as a flow-through entity, what would be the overall tax rate on CCS's income?

**Answer:** 35 percent. CCS's income would flow through to Nicole and be taxed at her 35 percent marginal ordinary income tax rate. Under the assumptions provided in this example, CCS's income is subject to a 7.25 percent *lower* overall tax rate if it is organized as a corporation rather than as a flow-through entity (35% − 27.75%).

Examples 15-2 and 15-3 highlight the importance for business owners to accurately estimate their corporate marginal tax rate and their own individual marginal tax rates when deciding whether to have an entity taxed as a corporation or flow-through entity. These examples also suggest that individual business owners' overall tax rates will be higher with a corporation when the corporation's marginal tax rate is expected to be higher than or equal to the owners' marginal tax rates. Moreover, they suggest that overall tax rates may be lower with corporations when corporate marginal rates are substantially lower than individual shareholder marginal rates.

**Taxes in the Real World**    *U.S. Corporate Tax Rates Among the World's Highest*

The Organization for Economic Cooperation and Development (OECD) recently reported that U.S. corporate tax rates are among the world's highest, second only after Japan. Further, the report found that high U.S. corporate tax rates are a factor in limiting the economic growth of the United States. These findings have spurred business leaders and politicians from both political parties to call for a substantial reduction in corporate tax rates to make the U.S. more competitive with the rest of the world. If these appeals ultimately result in lower U.S. corporate tax rates, the current impact of the double tax will be reduced—perhaps to the point where taxable corporations can compete with flow-through entities.

*Source:* The Tax Foundation, August 5, 2009.

***Corporate Shareholders.*** Corporate shareholders receiving dividends are not entitled to the reduced dividend tax rate (15 percent) available to individual shareholders. That is, dividends are subject to the corporate shareholder's ordinary rates. Further, dividends received by a corporation are potentially subject to another (third) level of tax when the corporation receiving the dividend distributes its earnings as dividends to its shareholders. This potential for more than two levels of tax on the same before-tax

earnings prompted Congress to allow corporations to claim the **dividends received deduction** (DRD). In the next chapter, we discuss the DRD in detail but the underlying concept is that a corporation *receiving* a dividend is allowed to deduct a certain percentage of the dividend from its taxable income to offset the potential for additional layers of taxation on the dividend when the dividend-receiving corporation distributes the dividend to its shareholders. The dividends received deduction percentage is 70, 80, or 100 percent depending on the extent of the recipient corporation's ownership in the dividend-paying corporation. Thus, the DRD partially mitigates the tax burden associated with *more than two levels* of tax on corporate income.

---

### Example 15-4

**What if:** Assume that Nicole invites a corporation with a 35 percent marginal tax rate to invest in exchange for a 10 percent share in CCS. Nicole makes the following assumptions as part of her calculations:

- CCS is a taxable corporation.
- CCS earns taxable income of $1,000,000.
- CCS will pay out all of its after-tax earnings annually as a dividend.

Given these assumptions, what would be the overall tax rate on the corporate investor's share of CCS's income [(corporate-level tax + shareholder-level tax)/taxable income] given that the corporation would be eligible for a 70 percent dividends received deduction?

**Answer:** 40.9 percent, computed as follows:

| Description | Amount | Explanation |
|---|---|---|
| (1) Taxable income | $1,000,000 | |
| (2) Corporate tax rate | 34% | (3)/(1). |
| (3) Entity-level tax | $ 340,000 | From tax table, inside cover. |
| (4) After-tax income | $ 660,000 | (1) − (3). |
| (5) Corporate investor's dividend | $ 66,000 | (4) × 10%. |
| (6) Taxable dividend | $ 19,800 | (5) × (1 − 70% DRD). |
| (7) Corporate investor's share of entity-level tax | $ 34,000 | (3) × 10% investor's share. |
| (8) Corporate investor's tax on dividend | $ 6,930 | (6) × 35% assumed investor tax rate [second level of tax]. |
| (9) Total tax paid on corporate taxable income | $ 40,930 | (7) + (8). |
| Overall tax rate on corporate taxable income | 40.9% | (9)/[(1) × 10% investor's share]. |

---

***Institutional Shareholders.*** Pension and retirement funds are some of the largest institutional shareholders of corporations. However, these entities do not pay shareholder-level tax on the dividends they receive. Ultimately, retirees pay the second tax on this income when they receive retirement distributions from these funds. While retirees pay the second tax at ordinary rates, not the reduced dividend rates, they are able to defer the tax until they receive fund distributions.

***Tax-Exempt and Foreign Shareholders.*** Tax-exempt organizations such as churches and universities are exempt from tax on their investment income, including dividend income from investments in corporate stock. Similarly, foreign investors may be

eligible for reduced rates on dividend income depending on the tax treaty, if any, their country of residence has signed with the United States.

**Some or All After-Tax Earnings Retained**  We've already determined that a double tax on corporate income arises when corporations pay tax on their income, and shareholders pay a second level of tax when they receive dividends. Shareholders also pay a second level of tax when corporations *retain* their after-tax earnings. Keep in mind that shareholders should experience an increase in the value of their shares to reflect any undistributed earnings (increase in assets). Individual shareholders pay the second tax at capital gains rates (currently at a 15 percent maximum rate) on this undistributed income when they realize the appreciation in their stock (from the retained earnings) by selling their shares. Because shareholders *defer* paying this portion of the second tax until they sell their shares, taxes on capital gains must be discounted to reflect their present value.

Note, however, that other types of shareholders will face different tax consequences when they sell their shares. If a corporation with corporate shareholders retains after-tax earnings, corporate shareholders are taxed on capital gains at ordinary rates (there is no preferential tax rate on capital gains for corporations) when they eventually sell the stock. Consequently, a corporate shareholder's income from capital appreciation may be subject to *more* than two levels of taxation because income from capital appreciation doesn't qualify for the dividends received deduction. Also, institutional shareholders don't pay tax when they sell their stock and recognize capital gains. However, retirees generally pay tax on the gains at ordinary rates when they receive distributions from their retirement accounts. Finally, tax-exempt shareholders do not pay tax on capital gains from selling stock and foreign investors are generally not subject to U.S. tax on their capital gains from selling corporate stock.

**Mitigating the Double Tax**  While corporate taxable income is subject to double taxation, corporations and shareholders have options for mitigating the double tax by taking steps to reduce the corporate-level tax and/or the shareholder-level tax. These options are particularly relevant when corporations are not eligible to make an S election or when the tax and nontax costs of converting to some other legal entity are prohibitive. Let's first focus on strategies to reduce the corporate-level tax.

*Reducing the Corporate-Level Tax.*  When a corporation's marginal tax rate exceeds its *individual* shareholders' marginal tax rates the overall tax rate on corporate income will exceed the flow-through tax rate even if shareholders can defer the second tax indefinitely. In these situations, it makes sense for closely held corporations and their shareholders to consider strategies to shift income from the corporation to shareholders. These strategies are all designed to move earnings out of the corporations and to shareholders with payments that are *deductible* (dividends are not deductible payments) by the corporation and (generally) taxable to shareholders. Making tax-deductible payments to shareholders accomplishes two objectives. First, it shifts income away from (relatively) high tax rate corporations to (relatively) lower tax rate shareholders. Second, the deduction shields income from the corporate-level tax. Strategies that shift income from corporations to shareholders include:

- Paying salaries to shareholders (salaries are deductible only to the extent they are reasonable).
- Paying fringe benefits to shareholders (generally taxable to shareholders unless benefits are specifically excluded from taxation).[16]
- Leasing property from shareholders.
- Paying interest on loans from shareholders.

[16]Common fringe benefits excluded from taxation are medical insurance, group-term life insurance, dependent care assistance, tuition benefits, and so forth.

## Example 15-5

**What if:** Assume Nicole uses her own funds to purchase the equipment required to manufacture the color comfort sheets. She leases the equipment to CCS corporation for $12,000 per year, the fair rental value for the equipment. What are the tax consequences to CCS and to Nicole of this leasing arrangement?

**Answer:** CCS deducts the $12,000 paid to Nicole each year for the use of the equipment, shielding $12,000 of its earnings from the corporate-level tax. Nicole is taxed on the $12,000 lease payments at her ordinary rate. In the end, Nicole and the corporation have achieved their objective of getting earnings out of CCS and into Nicole's hands with only one level of tax on the earnings.

---

### THE KEY FACTS

**Double Taxation**

- Most profitable taxable corporations are taxed at a 35 percent rate.

- Individual taxable corporation shareholders are generally taxed at a 15 percent rate on dividends when received.

- Taxable corporation shareholders that are taxable corporations are generally eligible to receive a 70 percent or greater dividends received deduction.

- Taxable corporation shareholders who are individuals generally pay capital gains taxes when shares are sold at a gain.

- The double tax is mitigated when income is shifted from taxable corporations to shareholders and when dividends are deferred or not paid.

*Reducing the Shareholder-Level Tax.* Shareholders generally pay the second tax immediately when they receive dividends or in the future when they sell their stock and pay capital gains tax. For *individual* shareholders, the tax rate applicable to both dividend income and (long-term) capital gains is generally 15 percent under current tax laws. However, because individual shareholders defer paying the second tax on capital gains until they sell their stock, the present value of the second tax is a function of the (1) percentage of after-tax earnings the corporation retains rather than currently distributing as dividends and (2) the length of time shareholders hold the stock before selling. By retaining after-tax earnings, corporations defer the second level of tax until the shareholder sells the stock. The longer a shareholder holds stock in a corporation that retains earnings, the lower the present value of the shareholder-level tax on the corporation's earnings. Individuals who make lifetime gifts of appreciated stock to their children utilize this basic strategy. The concept is that by deferring the second level of tax until children sell the shares many years into the future, the double tax becomes very small on a present value basis.[17] Alternatively, the donor could have sold the shares, paid the resulting capital gains tax, and given the remainder to her children, but this would have immediately triggered the shareholder tax leaving her children with less after-tax wealth on a present value basis.

---

### Taxes in the Real World    *The Big Stock Giveaway*

On June 26, 2006, Warren Buffett, Berkshire Hathaway Inc. chairman, stunned the financial community when he announced that he planned to give away the bulk of his fortune, approximately $31 billion in Berkshire Hathaway stock, to the Bill and Melinda Gates Foundation. Mr. Buffett, one of the richest men in the world, built his fortune using Berkshire Hathaway as a vehicle to acquire other promising companies. Berkshire Hathaway is a textbook example of a growth stock because it has never paid its shareholders a dividend.

Did Warren Buffet ever pay the double tax on the before-tax income earned by Berkshire Hathaway Inc.? How was the size of his gift affected by his tax-planning strategy?

Because Berkshire Hathaway never paid dividends and Warren Buffett decided to give his shares away rather than sell them, he never paid the double tax on Berkshire Hathaway's corporate earnings. As a result, he was able to give more to charity than if he had sold some or all of the shares prior to his gift.

---

It is important to note that the length of time a shareholder holds stock before selling and the percentage of earnings retained are not always under the shareholder's or corporation's control. For example, a shareholder may need cash for reasons unrelated to the business and therefore may need to sell the stock before recognizing

---

[17]Shareholders who wait until death to bequeath stock along with their heirs escape the shareholder tax entirely because the tax basis of inherited shares is stepped up to fair market value on the date of death.

the deferral benefits of holding the stock. Also, certain tax laws may force corporations to distribute rather than retain earnings if the corporation does not have a business need for retaining the cash.[18]

In spite of the fact that the double tax can be reduced by careful planning at both the corporate and shareholder level, some element of the double tax will likely remain, leaving corporations disadvantaged relative to flow-through entities under our current system of individual and corporate tax rates.

### Limitations on Number and Type of Owners

Of the different types of tax entities, taxable corporations have the least restrictive ownership requirements and S corporations have the most restrictive. Taxable corporations need to have only one shareholder but they may have as many as desired. S corporations, however, may not have more than 100 unrelated shareholders nor may they have shareholders that are corporations, nonresident aliens, partnerships, or certain types of trusts.[19] Entities taxed as partnerships (limited liability companies, general partnerships, and limited partnerships) must have at least two partners. Entities taxed as partnerships have no restrictions on owner types but limited partnerships must have at least one general partner. Sole proprietorships have only one owner (an individual). In sum, limitations on the types and number of owners tend to favor taxable corporations, followed by entities taxed as partnerships, and finally S corporations.

Example 15-6

**What if:** Assume Nicole decided to seek capital for CCS from both corporate and individual investors. Which among the four available tax entities (corporation, partnership, S corporation, or sole proprietorship) can she use for CCS?

**Answer:** She could only use a corporation or an entity taxed as a partnership. She could not use a sole proprietorship because she will have more than one owner, and CCS would not be eligible to make an S election because S corporations are not allowed to have corporate shareholders.

### Contributions of Property and Services

Business owners may contribute property to a new business or to an ongoing business in exchange for ownership in the business entity. When a business owner contributes appreciated property to an entity in exchange for an ownership interest (or increased ownership interest), the business owner *realizes* a gain in the amount of the value of the ownership interest received in excess of the basis of the property transferred. Whether business owners must *recognize* this gain (or loss) depends on provisions in the tax code. Shareholders of taxable corporations and S corporations are allowed to defer this gain (or required to defer a loss) as long as the shareholders contributing *property* to the corporation "control" the corporation after the exchange (defined as 80 percent ownership).[20] In contrast, members of LLCs and partners in partnerships are allowed to defer the gain no matter their level of ownership in the business entity.[21] Thus, it is typically easier for members of LLCs and partners to defer realized gain on contributions. This is generally an advantage for entities taxed as partnerships relative to corporations.

---

[18]§531 imposes the accumulated earnings tax and §541 imposes the personal holding company tax.

[19]§1361(b). Nonresident aliens are individuals with citizenship outside the United States who don't hold a green card or who don't spend a significant amount of time in the United States. See IRS Publication 519 for additional information regarding the tax definition of nonresident aliens.

[20]§351(a).

[21]§721(a).

When an owner contributes services in exchange for ownership in a business, she will be treated differently depending on the type of ownership interest received. If the owner provides services to the business entity in exchange for an ownership interest in a taxable corporation or an S corporation, the shareholder immediately recognizes ordinary income equal to the value of the shares she receives.[22] If the owner provides services to an entity taxed as a partnership for an immediate ownership interest in the entity's *assets,* the owner is taxed on the value of the interest.[23] In contrast, if the owner provides services to an entity taxed as a partnership in exchange for an interest unique to entities taxed as partnerships, called a **profits interest,** the owner is generally not taxed immediately on the value of the profits interest but is taxed only when future profits are allocated to the owner.[24] Thus, the ability to defer recognizing income when receiving a profits interest in exchange for services is an advantage for entities taxed as partnerships relative to other entities.

## Example 15-7

**What if:** Assume that Nicole and her friend Sarah formed CCS with each taxpayer receiving a 50 percent ownership interest in the entity. For her interest valued at $50,000, Nicole contributed land valued at $50,000 with an adjusted basis of $20,000 and Sarah agreed to contribute services valued at $50,000 for her interest valued at $50,000. For each interest received, $25,000 of the value is derived from the value of the property in the entity and the remaining $25,000 reflects expectations of future profits. What amount of income do Nicole and Sarah recognize in these transactions if CCS is a corporation (taxable or S) or an LLC (an entity taxed as a partnership)?

**Answer:** If CCS is organized as a corporation, Nicole will recognize a $30,000 gain and Sarah will recognize $50,000 of ordinary income, the value of the stock she received in exchange for her services. Nicole must recognize the gain built into her land if CCS forms as a corporation because Nicole and Sarah did not meet the 80 percent control requirement. Because Sarah did not contribute property her ownership interest does not count in the 80 percent control test and Nicole's 50 percent interest does not reach the 80 percent requirement.

If CCS is organized as an LLC, Nicole will not currently recognize gain on the transfer because there is no control requirement for deferring gain on property contributed to an entity taxed as a partnership. Sarah will only recognize $25,000 attributable to the value of her indirect ownership in the entity's assets. The $25,000 value of her profits interest is not currently taxable. This is summarized below:

| Description | Corporation (Taxable or S) Gain/Income Recognized | LLC (Entity taxed as partnership) Gain/Income Recognized | Explanation |
|---|---|---|---|
| Nicole | $30,000 | $ 0 | Realized gain equals $50,000 fair market value of stock received less $20,000 basis in land. |
| Sarah | $50,000 | $25,000 | Value of interest received for services currently taxable. |

Because proprietors and their sole proprietorships are considered to be the same entity for tax purposes, proprietors do not contribute property or services to proprietorships in exchange for ownership interests. As a result, these tax provisions do not apply to sole proprietorships.

[22]§83(a).
[23]Rev. Proc. 93-27 1993-2 CB 343.
[24]Rev. Proc. 93-27 1993-2 CB 343.

## Accounting Periods

Taxable corporations may generally choose a tax year that ends on the last day of any month of the year. When determining a taxable corporation's year-end, the year-end of its owners is not relevant. This is not the case for flow-through entities. When owners of flow-through entities have different year-ends from their entities, the owners can defer reporting their income from the flow-through entity to some extent (good for the owner). Consequently, the tax laws used to determine the tax year-ends for flow-through entities generally require the flow-through entity to adopt the tax year of its owners. For example, S corporations, whose owners are typically individuals, are generally required to adopt a calendar year-end.[25] Entities taxed as partnerships are generally required to adopt year-ends consistent with the year-end of their partners.[26] Sole proprietorships adopt the same year-end as the individual proprietor. Flexibility in selecting accounting periods tends to favor taxable corporations over flow-through entities.

---

**Example 15-8**

**What if:** Assume Nicole and her friend Sarah form CCS as an LLC and each contribute property and services to CCS in exchange for their ownership interests. What tax year-end will CCS be required to use?

**Answer:** A calendar year-end. As individual taxpayers, both Nicole and Sarah have calendar year-ends. Because entities taxed as partnerships must adopt year-ends consistent with the year-end of their owners, CCS must adopt a calendar year-end.

**What if:** Assume Nicole and her friend Sarah form CCS as a corporation and do not make the S election. What tax year-end will CCS be required to use?

**Answer:** CCS does not have a required year-end. As a taxable corporation, CCS would be free to adopt any tax year-end it chooses.[27]

---

## Accounting Methods

For tax purposes, the cash method of accounting allows business entities more flexibility to defer income or to accelerate deductions. Consequently, the tax laws restrict the entities that may use the cash method. Taxable corporations are generally required to use the accrual method of accounting.[28] However, a taxable corporation may use the cash method if its annual average gross receipts do not exceed $5,000,000 for the three previous tax years. S corporations may generally choose to use the cash or the accrual method of accounting.[29] Entities taxed as partnerships (LLCs, general partnerships, and limited partnerships) generally may use the cash method of accounting unless they have a taxable corporation as a member or partner and the partnership reports annual average gross receipts in excess of $5,000,000 for the three previous tax years.[30] It should be noted, however, that entities generally eligible to use the overall cash method of accounting must nevertheless use the accrual method to account for the purchase and sale of inventory unless they meet certain procedural exceptions provided by the IRS.[31]

---

[25]§1378(b).

[26]§706(b)(1)(B).

[27]§441(e) provides that a tax year must end on the last day of the month unless taxpayers elect a 52-53 week year-end under §441(f).

[28]§448(a).

[29]§448(b)(3).

[30]§448(b)(3).

[31]Rev. Proc. 2001-10 2001-1 CB 272 and Rev. Proc. 2002-28 2002-1 CB 815 permit certain small businesses to treat inventory items as nonincidental materials and supplies.

Because flow-through entities tend to have more flexibility than taxable corporations in selecting their accounting methods, this characteristic tends to favor flow-through entities over taxable corporations in the entity selection decision.

### Special Allocations

As we've discussed, the income or loss of taxable corporations is taxed to the corporations but the income or loss of flow-through entities is taxed to the owners. The income or loss of S corporations is allocated to the shareholders based on their stock ownership percentages.[32] In contrast, the income and loss of entities taxed as partnerships is allocated to the members or partners based on the partnership agreement.[33] The agreement may specify **special allocations** that are different from the actual ownership percentages. The income from a sole proprietorship is taxed directly to the proprietor. For businesses with multiple owners choosing between flow-through entities, the ability to make special allocations of income or loss favors entities taxed as partnerships over S corporations. The ability to make special allocations is a relative strength of entities taxed as partnerships because it gives owners the freedom to be creative in terms of differentially rewarding owners based on their responsibilities, contributions, and individual needs.[34]

---

**Example 15-9**

**What if:** Assume that Nicole and her friend Sarah form and operate CCS as a flow-through entity as equal owners. In year 1, CCS opened two retail locations, one in Salt Lake City, Utah, and one in Boise, Idaho. Nicole assumed primary responsibility for the Salt Lake City store and Sarah assumed responsibility for the Boise store. In year 1, CCS reported business income of $200,000. Of the $200,000 of income, the Salt Lake City store generated $150,000 and the Boise store generated $50,000. If CCS is organized as an S corporation, how much of the $200,000 income would be allocated to Nicole and how much to Sarah?

**Answer:** Nicole and Sarah would each be allocated $100,000 of business income ($200,000 × 50 percent).

**What if:** Assume that Nicole and Sarah formed CCS as an LLC, and that Nicole and Sarah agreed that, for the year, Nicole would be allocated 75 percent of the business income from the Salt Lake City store and Sarah would be allocated 75 percent of the business income from the Boise store. They would share the rest equally. How much of CCS's business income would be allocated to Nicole and how much to Sarah under this special allocation?

**Answer:** Nicole would be allocated $137,500 [($150,000 × 75%) + ($50,000 × 50%)] and Sarah would be allocated the remaining $62,500 [($50,000 × 75%) + ($50,000 × 50%)]. Note that this arrangement gives the owners incentive to generate profits in their respective stores. Such an arrangement would not be possible for tax purposes if they had formed the entity as an S corporation.[35]

---

### FICA and Self-Employment Tax

Owners of business entities may provide services to the entities in exchange for compensation. Shareholders of C corporations and S corporations can work as employees for the corporation and receive salary in return. Employee-shareholders pay a 6.2% Social Security tax (capped at $106,800 × 6.2%, or $6,621.60 for 2010) and a 1.45% Medicare tax, and the corporation also pays an equal amount of Social Security and

---

[32]§1366(a).

[33]§704(b).

[34]Special allocations are subject to certain limitations that are beyond the scope of this chapter.

[35]Bonus arrangements among shareholders designed to accomplish the same result as special allocations would likely violate the prohibition in §1361(b) against S corporations having more than one class of stock.

Medicare taxes. Together, the Social Security and Medicare taxes paid by employees and employers are referred to as the FICA (Federal Insurance Contributions Act) tax. In addition to receiving salary from an S corporation, an employee-shareholder also receives an income allocation from the S corporation representing the shareholder's share of the S corporation business income for the year. This income allocation is *not* subject to FICA or self-employment tax.[36]

The employment tax implications are a bit different for sole proprietorships or entities taxed as partnerships. All income from sole proprietorships is subject to self-employment tax. For entities taxed as partnerships, application of the self-employment tax rules depends on whether owners are receiving compensation for services they provide or a share of the entity's operating income. Owners of entities taxed as partnerships may not work as employees, per se, for the entities. However, they may still provide services to the entities and receive compensation in return. This compensation is called a **guaranteed payment** and, like any other form of self-employment income, 92.35% of these payments are subject to self-employment taxes consisting of a 12.4% Social Security tax (capped at $106,800 × 12.4, or $13,243.20 for 2010) and a 2.9% Medicare tax.[37]

Just like S corporation shareholders, owners of entities taxed as partnerships are also allocated business income from the entity. Is this income allocation subject to self-employment tax? It depends. If the owner is a general partner, the income allocation is subject to self-employment tax and if the partner is a limited partner, the allocation is not subject to self-employment tax.[38] There are no hard-and-fast rules for determining whether income allocations to LLC members are subject to self-employment tax. If a member is treated as a limited partner, the allocation is not subject to self-employment tax. If, however, the member is not treated as a limited partner, the allocation is subject to self-employment tax. How do we determine whether a member is treated as a limited partner or not? Good question. Whether the member is treated as a limited partner depends on the amount of time the member spends working in the LLC, the member's level of authority and responsibility, and the member's amount of liability protection.

In 1997, the Treasury issued (nonbinding) proposed regulations providing bright-line tests for determining whether an LLC member should be treated as a limited partner for self-employment tax purposes but the regulations were never made final.[39] According to the proposed regulations, a member of an LLC is treated as a limited partner unless the member meets any of the following tests:

- Has personal liability for the debts of the partnership, or
- Has authority to contract on behalf of the partnership, or
- Participates in the partnership's trade or business for more than 500 hours during the year.

---

### Example 15-10

*What if:* Assume that Nicole and her friend Sarah each own 50 percent of CCS. During the year, Nicole receives $50,000 compensation for services she performs for CCS. Nicole worked about 1,000 hours and she was involved in significant management decisions of the entity. After deducting Nicole's compensation, CCS reports taxable income of $30,000. How much FICA and/or self-employment tax will be paid on Nicole's compensation and her share of the CCS income if CCS is formed as a taxable corporation, S corporation, or limited liability company?

*(continued on page 15-18...)*

---

[36]Rev. Rul. 59-221 1959-1 CB 225.

[37]Reg. §1.1402(a)-1(b). Note, that sole proprietors and partners may deduct half of their self-employment taxes as a for AGI deduction in computing their individual income tax liabilities.

[38]§1402(a).

[39]Prop. Reg. §1.1402(a)-2.

**Answer:** Taxable corporation $3,825; S corporation $3,825; and LLC $9,184, computed as follows:

| Description | Taxable Corporation | S Corporation | LLC | Explanation |
|---|---|---|---|---|
| (1) FICA | $3,825 | $3,825 | $    0 | $50,000 salary × 7.65%. |
| (2) Self-employment tax on compensation from entity | $    0 | $    0 | $7,065 | $50,000 self-employment income × 92.35% × 15.3%.* |
| (3) Self-employment tax on portion of entity business income | $    0 | $    0 | $2,119 | $30,000 × 50% × 92.35% × 15.3%.† |
| (4) Total FICA/self-employment tax paid by Nicole | $3,825 | $3,825 | $9,184 | (1) + (2) + (3). |
| (5) FICA tax paid by entity | $3,825 | $3,825 | $    0 | $50,000 salary × 7.65%. |
| Total FICA/self employment taxes | $7,650 | $7,650 | $9,184 | (4) + (5). |

* Technically, the self-employment tax is imposed on net earnings from self-employment, which is defined as 92.35 percent of self-employment income.

† This analysis assumes the rules in the proposed regulations for determining whether Nicole should be treated as a limited partner for self-employment tax purposes are followed.

According to the calculations above, how much FICA/self-employment tax must Nicole and CCS pay *combined* given that CCS is a C corporation, S corporation, or limited liability company?

**Answer:** C corporation $7,650; S corporation $7,650; LLC $9,184.

In these circumstances, the FICA/self-employment tax comparison favors the taxable and S corporation entities over the LLC because Nicole is subject to FICA/self-employment tax only on her direct compensation if CCS is organized as a corporation. However, she is subject to self-employment tax on her direct compensation *and* on her share of CCS's income if it is organized as an LLC.

*What if:* Assume that CCS is formed as an LLC and that Nicole earns $5,000 working 100 hours during the year for CCS. Further, she does not participate in management decisions and she is not personally liable for any of CCS's liabilities. CCS's taxable income for the year after deducting Nicole's compensation is $30,000, of which Nicole's share is $15,000. Is Nicole required to pay self-employment tax on her $5,000 guaranteed payment from CCS? Is she required to pay self-employment tax on her $15,000 income allocation from CCS?

**Answer:** Yes, she must pay self-employment tax on the guaranteed payment; No, she is not required to pay self-employment tax on the income allocation. Because she did not work over 500 hours for CCS during the year, she does not make management decisions, and she's not personally responsible for any liabilities of CCS, Nicole will be treated as a limited partner and is therefore not subject to self-employment tax on her income allocation.

An argument can be made that the FICA/self-employment tax characteristic favors an S corporation over an LLC. For FICA purposes, an S corporation shareholder who performs services for the business can minimize FICA taxes by paying herself a low salary that is subject to FICA and leaving a higher income allocation that is not subject to FICA. However, if the S corporation shareholder pays herself an unreasonably low salary, the IRS may enter the picture and recalculate the taxpayer's salary, thus increasing the FICA taxes payable.

## Basis Computation

The tax basis of a taxable corporation shareholder's stock is generally the purchase price minus any distributions to the shareholder in excess of the corporation's **earnings and profits** (essentially the economic earnings of the corporation).[40] The computation of an owner's tax basis for an ownership interest in a flow-through entity (S corporations and entities taxed as partnerships) is more involved.[41] An owner's tax basis in a flow-through entity interest is *increased* for contributions to the entity and income allocated from the entity to the owners. The tax basis of the interest is *decreased* by distributions to owners and for losses allocated from the entity to the owner. There is an important difference, however, in the process of computing the stock basis of an S corporation shareholder and the basis of an ownership interest in an entity taxed as a partnership. Owners of entities taxed as a partnership are allowed to increase the tax basis in their ownership interest by their share of the entity's liabilities (bank loans, accounts payable, etc.). In contrast, shareholders of S corporations are not allowed to increase the basis in their S corporation stock by liabilities of the S corporation. Because shareholders of S corporations and owners of entities taxed as partnerships receive nontaxable distributions to the extent of the basis in their ownership interests and they are not allowed to deduct losses allocated tö them in excess of their tax basis, owners of entities taxed as partnerships may, in some circumstances, enjoy an advantage over equally situated S corporation shareholders because they increase their basis by their share of the entity's debt.[42]

### Example 15-11

**What if:** Assume that Nicole invites her friend, Sarah Walker, to join her in forming CCS with each party contributing $35,000 in cash to become equal owners in all respects. CCS plans to obtain additional cash through a $100,000 small business loan from the local bank, which will be allocated equally to Nicole and Sarah. Also, assume the following about CCS's year 1 business activities:

- CCS reported a net loss of ($40,000) in year 1.
- CCS did not make any distributions during the year.

What would be Nicole's tax basis in her ownership interest if CCS was organized as a C corporation, an S corporation, or an LLC?

**Answer:** $35,000 as a C corporation, $15,000 as an S corporation, and $65,000 as an LLC, computed as follows:

| Description | C Corporation | S Corporation | LLC | Explanation |
|---|---|---|---|---|
| (1) Cash contribution | $35,000 | $35,000 | $35,000 | Cash contributions increase tax basis. |
| (2) Share of entity liabilities | 0 | 0 | 50,000 | 50% of $100,000 debt for LLC. |
| (3) Nicole's share of entity loss | 0 | (20,000) | (20,000) | Basis reduced by Nicole's share of loss for flow-through entities. |
| Basis in ownership interest at end of year 1 | $35,000 | $15,000 | $65,000 | (1) + (2) + (3). |

(continued on page 15-20...)

[40]See §1012 and §301 through §307.

[41]§705 provides the basis computation rules for partnerships and §1367 provides these rules for S corporations.

[42]As provided in §1366(b)(2), S corporation shareholders are, however, allowed to deduct losses in excess of the basis in their shares to the extent they have made shareholder loans to their S corporations.

---

*What if:* Assume the same facts as in the prior example, except for the following about CCS's year 1 business activities:

- CCS reported income of $40,000 in year 1.
- CCS distributed $10,000 to each owner during the year.

What would be Nicole's tax basis in her ownership interest if CCS was organized as a C corporation, an S corporation, or an LLC?

**Answer:** $35,000 as a C corporation, $45,000 as an S corporation, and $95,000 as an LLC, computed as follows:

| Description | C corp. | S corp. | LLC | Explanation |
|---|---|---|---|---|
| (1) Cash contribution | $35,000 | $35,000 | $35,000 | Cash contributions increase tax basis. |
| (2) Share of entity liabilities | 0 | 0 | 50,000 | 50% of $100,000 debt for LLC. |
| (3) Nicole's share of entity income | 0 | 20,000 | 20,000 | Basis increased by income from flow-through entities |
| (4) Distributions | 0 | (10,000) | (10,000) | |
| **Basis in ownership interest at end of year 1** | $35,000 | $45,000 | $95,000 | Sum of (1) through (4). |

---

## Distributions

The tax consequences of distributions from an entity to an owner depend on the type of entity. At the entity level, both taxable and S corporations recognize gain when they distribute appreciated property to shareholders.[43] However, they are not allowed to recognize loss when they distribute property with a value less than its basis (depreciated property). Entities taxed as partnerships generally do not recognize gain or loss when they distribute property (appreciated or depreciated) to owners.[44]

In terms of distributions to owners, shareholders of taxable corporations generally recognize dividend income in the amount of the fair market value of the distributions they receive. Individual shareholders generally pay tax on the dividends at 15 percent. Shareholders that are taxable corporations deduct the dividends received deduction and pay tax on the remaining dividend at ordinary rates. To the extent a C corporation distributes more than its "earnings and profits" (essentially the economic earnings of the corporation) the distribution is a nontaxable return of capital to the shareholder to the extent of the shareholder's stock basis with the remainder treated as capital gain.[45]

Distributions to S corporation shareholders and distributions to owners of entities taxed as partnerships are treated as a nontaxable return of capital, to the extent of the owner's basis in the ownership interest. Amounts in excess of basis are *generally* treated as capital gain to the owners.[46] Because property distributions don't trigger gain at the entity level for entities taxed as partnerships and because distributions are generally a nontaxable return of capital for owners of these entities, the distribution rules tend to favor entities taxed as a partnership, followed by S corporations, and then taxable corporations.

---

[43]§311(b).
[44]§731(b).
[45]§301(c).
[46]§731(a) and §1368(b).

**Example 15-12**

**What if:** Assume CCS, after operating for several years, distributes to Nicole (a 50 percent owner) land with a fair market value of $150,000. CCS purchased the land several years ago for $50,000. If Nicole's tax basis in CCS is $700,000 at the time of the distribution, and CCS has accumulated $1.2 million in earnings and profits (undistributed profits), how much gain or loss will CCS report from the distribution and how much income will Nicole report from the distribution if CCS was originally organized as a C corporation, an S corporation, or an LLC?

**Answer:** As computed in the table below, CCS reports a $100,000 gain and Nicole reports a $150,000 dividend if CCS is organized as a C corporation; CCS reports a $100,000 gain and Nicole reports a $50,000 gain if CCS is organized as an S corporation; neither CCS nor Nicole report any income or gain related to the distribution if CCS is organized as an LLC.

| Description | C Corporation | S Corporation | LLC | Explanation |
|---|---|---|---|---|
| (1) Gain recognized and taxed at entity level | $100,000 | 0 | 0 | $150,000 fair market value of land less CCS's $50,000 tax basis. Gain is taxed at entity level if CCS is a taxable corporation. |
| (2) Gain recognized at entity level but taxed at the owner level | 0 | $100,000 | 0 | $150,000 fair market value of land less CCS's $50,000 tax basis. Gain is not taxed at entity level if CCS is an S corporation. |
| (3) Nicole's 50 percent share of entity gain | 0 | 50,000 | 0 | 50% × (2). |
| (4) Other owners' share of entity gain | 0 | 50,000 | 0 | (2) − (3). |
| (5) Distribution taxed at owner level | 150,000 | 0 | 0 | Property distribution is a dividend to taxable corporation shareholders but generally not taxable to S corporation shareholders or LLC members. |
| Total amount subject to tax | $250,000 | $100,000 | 0 | For C corp. (1) + (5). For S corp. (3) + (4). |

## Deductibility of Entity Losses

When taxable corporations are reporting losses for tax purposes, double taxation (or even single taxation) is not a concern. Losses generated by taxable corporations are called **net operating losses** (NOLs). While NOLs provide no tax benefit to a corporation in the year the corporation experiences the NOL, they may only be used to reduce corporate taxes in other years. Generally, taxable corporations with a NOL for the year can carry back the loss to offset the taxable income reported in the two preceding years and carry it forward for up to 20 years.[47]

Under this approach, losses from taxable corporations are *not* available to offset their shareholders' personal income. In contrast, losses generated by flow-through entities are generally available to offset the owners' personal income, subject to certain

---

[47]Certain corporations may elect to carry back NOLs attributable to 2008, and all corporations may elect to carry back NOLs attributable to 2009 for up to five years.

restrictions. For example, the owner of a flow-through entity may only deduct losses from the entity to the extent of the owner's basis in her ownership interest in the flow-through entity.[48] The ability to deduct flow-through losses against other sources of income can be a significant issue for owners of new businesses because new businesses tend to report losses early on as the businesses get established. If owners form a new business as a taxable corporation, the corporate-level losses provide no current tax benefits to the shareholders. The fact that taxable corporation losses are trapped at the corporate level effectively imposes a higher tax cost for shareholders initially doing business as a taxable corporation relative to a flow-through entity such as an S corporation or LLC because the flow-through entity owners, subject to the limits mentioned above, can use the losses to offset other sources of income.

---

**Example 15-13**

**What if:** Assume that Nicole will organize CCS as a taxable corporation and that in spite of her best efforts as CEO of the company, CCS reports a tax loss of $50,000 in its first year of operation (year 1). Also, recall Nicole's marginal tax rate is 35 percent and assume she will have ordinary taxable income of $200,000 from other sources unrelated to CCS in year 1. How much tax will CCS pay in year 1 and how much tax will Nicole pay on her $200,000 of other taxable income if CCS is organized as a taxable corporation?

**Answer:** CCS will pay $0 in taxes because it reports a loss for tax purposes. Because Nicole may not use the CCS loss to offset her other income, she must pay $70,000 in taxes. See the computations in the table below.

How much tax will CCS pay in year 1 and how much tax will Nicole pay on her $200,000 of other income if CCS is organized as an S corporation and Nicole's basis in CCS before the year 1 loss is $100,000?

**Answer:** CCS pays $0 taxes (S corporations are not taxpaying entities) and Nicole pays $52,500 in taxes. See the computations in table below:

| Description | Taxable Corporation | S Corporation (flow-through) | Explanation |
|---|---|---|---|
| (1) Taxable income (loss) | ($50,000) | ($50,000) | |
| (2) CCS corporate-level tax | $    0 | $    0 | No taxable income. |
| (3) Nicole's other income | $200,000 | $200,000 | |
| (4) CCS loss available to offset Nicole's other income | $    0 | ($50,000) | $0 if taxable corp. (1) if flow-through entity (S corporation). |
| (5) Nicole's other income reduced by entity loss | $200,000 | $150,000 | (3) + (4). |
| (6) Nicole's marginal ordinary tax rate | 35% | 35% | |
| Nicole's tax on other income | $ 70,000 | $ 52,500 | (5) × (6). |

---

As the example above illustrates, owners' ability to immediately use start-up losses from flow-through entities to offset income from other sources further enhances the tax advantages of flow-through entities relative to corporations in many situations.

### Selling Ownership Interests

When a shareholder in either a taxable or S corporation sells stock, she generally recognizes capital gain or loss on the disposition. In certain circumstances, if a shareholder of

---

[48]In addition to this tax basis loss limitation, flow-through losses may be further limited by the "at risk" and passive activity loss limitation rules. These additional limitations on deducting losses from flow-through entities are discussed at length in Chapter 20.

a small corporation sells stock at a loss, she may be allowed to treat the loss (or at least a portion of the loss) as an ordinary loss.[49] When an owner of an entity taxed as a partnership sells an ownership interest in the entity, the tax rules characterize the gain by looking through the ownership interest to the assets of the entity.[50] Consequently, the character of the gain is based on the owner's share of ordinary income built into the entity's assets. Thus, the rules in this area tend to favor entities other than those taxed as partnerships when assets have appreciated in value.

---

**Example 15-14**

*What if:* Assume that Nicole and Sarah have owned and operated CCS for a number of years. When they formed the entity, Nicole and Sarah each contributed $50,000 to CCS. Information on CCS's assets at the end of year 4 is as follows (note: CCS does not have any liabilities):

| Assets | FMV | Adjusted Basis | Built-in Gain |
|---|---|---|---|
| Cash | $100,000 | $100,000 | $    0 |
| Inventory | 30,000 | 10,000 | 20,000 |
| Land and building | 270,000 | 130,000 | 140,000 |
| Total | $400,000 | | |

At the end of year 4, Nicole sold her 50 percent ownership interest to another investor for $200,000 when the basis in her ownership interest was $120,000. What is the amount and character of gain or loss she will recognize on the sale if CCS is organized as a taxable corporation or as an S corporation?

**Answer:** $80,000 of long-term capital gain. This is the amount realized of $200,000 minus her basis of $120,000.

What is the amount and character of gain or loss she will recognize if CCS is organized as an LLC?

**Answer:** $10,000 ordinary income and $70,000 of long-term capital gain, computed as follows:

| Description | Amount | Explanation |
|---|---|---|
| (1) Amount realized | $200,000 | |
| (2) Adjusted basis | 120,000 | |
| (3) Total gain/income on sale | 80,000 | (1) − (2). |
| (4) Ordinary income | 10,000 | One-half of ordinary income potential in inventory ($20,000 × 50%). |
| Long-term capital gain: | $  70,000 | (3) − (4). |

---

## Liquidating Entities

When a C corporation or an S corporation liquidates and distributes assets to shareholders, the corporation generally recognizes gain or loss on each of its assets as if it had sold each asset at fair market value.[51] The shareholders of the corporation also recognize gain or loss on the liquidation to the extent that the value of property they receive differs from their stock basis.[52] In the case of a taxable corporation, this generally means that the corporate gains from liquidating are subject to double taxation

---

[49]§1244. This section allows up to $100,000 of loss from the sale of "section 1244 stock" to be treated as an ordinary loss.

[50]§751(a).

[51]§336.

[52]§331.

and corporate losses from liquidating receive a double benefit. In the case of an S corporation, there is no double taxation or double benefit because the corporate-level gains or losses flow through to the owners, which increases or decreases their stock basis and reduces the gain or loss they would otherwise recognize when giving up their shares for the assets they receive in the liquidating distribution.

Liquidating an entity taxed as a partnership generally does not trigger gain or loss at the entity level or at the partner level.[53] However, in certain circumstances, a partner may recognize loss on a liquidating distribution. Because entities taxed as partnerships and the owners of those entities generally do not recognize gain on liquidating distributions while liquidating a corporation triggers two levels of tax for a C corporation and one level of tax for an S corporation, the tax rules associated with liquidations generally favor entities taxed as partnerships relative to taxable corporations and S corporations when gains from liquidating distributions are expected. However, the liquidation tax rules are a two-edged sword. When losses from liquidating distributions are expected, the tax rules in this area favor taxable corporations and S corporations because they and their shareholders are usually able to immediately deduct liquidation losses while owners of entities taxed as partnerships must generally wait to deduct liquidation losses until property received in the liquidating distribution is sold. Thus, the tax rules applicable to liquidations generally favor entities taxed as partnerships when appreciated assets are distributed and favor taxable corporations and S corporations when depreciated assets are distributed.

### Converting to Other Entity Types

As we discuss previously, taxable corporations can take steps to mitigate the double tax. For example, deductible compensation, rent, and interest payments, to the extent they are reasonable, provide a mechanism for shifting income to their shareholders. Depending on the total amount of these deductible shareholder payments relative to a corporation's income before the payments, they effectively convert or partially convert taxable corporations into flow-through entities in the sense that these payments are taxed at the owner level and not at the corporate level. If this is true, why not avoid the constraints associated with deductible shareholder payments and accomplish the same result more directly by converting an existing corporation into a flow-through entity?

Besides making deductible payments to their shareholders, existing corporations really only have two options for converting into flow-through entities. First, shareholders of taxable corporations could make an S election to treat the corporation as an S corporation (flow-through entity), if they are eligible to do so. This option is not available for many corporations due to the tax rule restrictions prohibiting certain corporations from operating as S corporations. The only other option is for the shareholders to liquidate the corporation and form the business as a partnership or LLC. This may not be a viable option, however, because the taxes imposed on liquidating corporations with appreciated assets can be very punitive. As we discuss above, liquidating corporations are taxed on the appreciation in the assets they distribute to their shareholders as part of the liquidation. Further, shareholders of liquidating corporations are also taxed on the difference between the fair market value of the assets they receive from the liquidating corporation and their tax basis in their stock. Effectively, the total double-tax cost of liquidating a corporation can swamp the expected tax savings from operating as a flow-through entity.

When feasible, S elections or corporate liquidations, like deductible payments to shareholders, are used to convert *existing* corporations into flow-through entities. Why then, didn't shareholders of *existing* corporations initially form the entities as

---

[53]§731.

flow-through entities? Perhaps, at the time of formation the corporate form was optimal from purely a tax perspective because corporate marginal tax rates were significantly lower than shareholder marginal tax rates at that time. Or, maybe, the corporations were willing to be treated as taxable corporations in order to go public but then became closely held when all their outstanding shares were purchased by a small number of shareholders.

As costly as it can be to convert corporations to flow-through entities, it is equally as easy and inexpensive to convert entities taxed as partnerships or sole proprietorships into corporations. Typically, converting entities taxed as partnerships or sole proprietorships into corporations can be accomplished tax free without any special tax elections.[54] For this reason, many businesses that plan to eventually go public will operate for a time as entities taxable as partnerships to receive the associated tax benefits and then convert to taxable corporations when they finally decide to go public.

*continued from page 15-4...*
Nicole's five-year forecast of CCS's expected operating results showed that CCS would generate losses for the first three years and then become very profitable after. With these projections in hand, Nicole then considered the basic question of whether a taxable corporation or a flow-through entity would minimize her overall tax liability. Nicole's marginal tax rate and CCS's expected marginal tax rate after three years, if it were to operate as a taxable corporation, led her to conclude that she needed to avoid the double tax by operating CCS as a flow-through entity from the start. Given her initial desire to limit her choice of legal entity to either a corporation or LLC, this left her with the option of operating CCS as either an S corporation or as an LLC taxed as a partnership.

After narrowing her choice down to either an LLC or S corporation, Nicole compared the specific tax rules applicable to LLCs and S corporations before making her final decision. As she compared them, she identified four differences that could sway her decision one way or the other. Supporting a decision to select an LLC, Nicole learned she would likely be able to deduct the projected start-up losses from CCS more quickly with an LLC compared with an S corporation because she could include a share of the LLC's debt in her tax basis. Moreover, she learned that LLC profits and losses can be specially allocated while S corporation profits and losses can only be allocated pro rata to the shareholders. Nicole was hoping to have the ability to be a little more creative with profit and loss allocations. Finally, she had hoped to possibly attract corporate investors, but discovered that S corporations are not permitted to have corporate shareholders. She did find however, that S corporations appear to have a compelling advantage over LLCs in reducing the self-employment tax of owners active in managing their businesses.

Ultimately, Nicole decided that she would be willing to incur additional payroll taxes with an LLC in exchange for the ability to deduct her losses sooner, for the flexibility she might need one day to specially allocate profits or losses, and for the freedom to solicit corporate investors. Given these considerations, she decided to organize CCS as an LLC in the state of Utah.

With this big decision out of the way, Nicole could now focus on applying for a small business loan from her local bank and on having her attorney take the necessary steps to formally organize CCS as a limited liability company. ∎

[54]§351 and Rev. Rul. 84-111 1984-2 CB 88.

# ENTITY CHOICE SUMMARY

Exhibit 15-2 identifies the tax and nontax entity characteristics we discuss in the chapter. Entities that do well on a particular characteristic relative to the others are noted to provide a high-level understanding of which characteristics tend to favor particular tax entities. It is important to note that whether a given characteristic favors a certain type of entity depends on the specific facts and circumstances of the particular situation. The exhibit presents only general rules. Further, which factors are most important to the decision also depends on the facts and circumstances of the specific situation. However, for small business owners, liability protection and double tax concerns are key drivers in their entity choice decisions.

**EXHIBIT 15-2**   Business Entities with the Most Favorable Nontax and Tax Characteristics

| | Taxable Corporations | S Corporations | Entities Taxed as Partnerships | Sole Proprietorships |
|---|---|---|---|---|
| **Nontax Characteristics:** | | | | |
| Time and cost to organize | | | X (general partnerships) | X |
| Liability protection | X | X | X (LLCs) | |
| Flexibility | | | X | N/A |
| Initial public offerings | X | | X (some limited partnerships) | N/A |
| **Tax Characteristics:** | | | | |
| Double taxation | | X | X | X |
| Limitations on number and type of owners | X | | X | |
| Contributions to entity | | | X | N/A |
| Accounting periods | X | | | |
| Accounting methods | | X | X | X |
| Special allocations | | | X | |
| FICA and self-employment taxes | | X | | |
| Entity debt in basis | | | X | N/A |
| Distributions | | | X | N/A |
| Deductibility of entity losses | | | X | X |
| Selling ownership interest at a gain | X | X | | N/A |
| Liquidating entity with gains | | | X | N/A |
| Liquidating entity with losses | X | X | | |
| Converting to other entity types | | | X | X |

Note that Exhibit 15-2 lists the nontax characteristics of business entities first to drive home the point that entity choice decisions typically are driven by nontax objectives and that taxes are typically a secondary, but important, consideration that must be in balance with these objectives.

---

**Taxes in the Real World**    *Banks and S Corporations*

A recent study by the FDIC reported that approximately 30 percent of the nation's 8,494 commercial banks and savings institutions are operating as S corporations. The remaining banks operate as taxable corporations. Why would banks choose to operate as S corporations and forgo potentially more favorable partnership tax rules available to LLCs? It turns out that state banking rules require banks to operate as legal corporations.[55] Thus, the only flow-through entity they can qualify to use is an S corporation.

*Source: FDIC Quarterly,* Volume 2, Number 2, 2008.

---

# CONCLUSION

Anytime a new business is formed and periodically thereafter as circumstances change, business owners must carefully evaluate what type of business entity will maximize the after-tax profits from their business ventures. Many of the key factors to consider in the entity selection decision-making process are outlined in this chapter. When making the entity selection decision, owners must carefully balance the tax and nontax characteristics unique to the entities available to them. This chapter explained how various legal entities are treated for tax purposes and how certain tax characteristics differ between entity types. Moreover, it also identified some of the more important nontax issues that come to bear on the choice of entity decision. With this understanding, taxpayers and their advisors will be better prepared to face this frequently encountered business decision. In Chapter 20, we return to Nicole and Color Comfort Sheets, LLC, to examine the tax rules that apply to Nicole and other members in CCS as they form the entity for tax purposes and begin business operations.

## SUMMARY

Discuss the legal and nontax characteristics of different types of legal entities.                    **LO1**

- Entities that differ in terms of their legal characteristics include corporations, limited liability companies, general partnerships, limited partnerships, and sole proprietorships.

- Corporations are formally organized by filing articles of incorporation with the state. They are legally separate entities and protect their shareholders from the liabilities of the corporation. State corporation laws dictate interactions between corporations and shareholders. As a result, shareholders have limited flexibility to customize their business arrangements with the corporation and other shareholders. State corporate governance rules do, however, facilitate initial public offerings.

- Limited liability companies are formally organized by filing articles of organization with the state. Like corporations, they are separate legal entities that shield their members from liabilities. In contrast to corporations, state LLC statutes give members a great deal of latitude in customizing their business arrangements with the LLC and other members.

- General partnerships may be organized informally without state approval, but limited partnerships must file a certificate of limited partnership with the state to organize. Although they are considered to be legally separate entities, they provide either limited or no liability protection for partners. While limited partners in limited partnerships have liability protection, general partners are fully exposed to the liabilities of the partnership. General and limited partnerships are given a great deal of latitude in customizing their partnership agreements.

---

[55]Banks also must operate as corporations to qualify for favorable bank tax accounting rules as provided in §581.

- Sole proprietorships are businesses legally indistinguishable from their sole individual owners. As such, they are very flexible but provide no liability protection. Sole proprietors can obtain liability protection by converting to a single-member LLC.

**LO2** Describe the different entities for tax purposes.

- The four categories of business entities recognized by our tax system include: taxable corporations, S corporations, partnerships, and sole proprietorships.
- Legal corporations that don't make the S election are treated as taxable corporations and therefore pay taxes. All other entities recognized for tax purposes are flow-through entities.
- Legal corporations that qualify for and make the S election are treated as S corporations.
- Unincorporated entities with more than one owner are treated as partnerships.
- Unincorporated entities with one owner are treated as sole proprietorships where the sole owner is an individual or as a disregarded entity otherwise.

**LO3** Explain fundamental differences in tax characteristics across entity types.

- Because taxable corporations and their shareholders pay taxes, taxable corporations are double taxed.
- Shareholders in taxable corporations are taxed either when they receive dividends or when they sell their shares.
- Tax planning strategies applied at the corporate level to mitigate the double taxation of taxable corporations include paying salary to shareholder-employees, paying fringe benefits to shareholder-employees, leasing property from a shareholder, and borrowing money from and paying interest to shareholders. All of these strategies provide deductions to the corporation, which reduces corporate-level taxes. Shareholders are generally taxed when they receive these payments except when they receive qualified fringe benefits. In addition, corporations also mitigate the double tax by retaining income rather than paying dividends.
- Shareholders can mitigate the double tax by increasing the time they hold shares before selling.
- Taxable corporations may have one or many shareholders. S corporations may have one shareholder and as many as 100 unrelated shareholders; but corporations, nonresident aliens, partnerships, and certain trusts may not be S corporation shareholders. Partnerships must have at least two partners but are not restricted to a maximum number of partners. Sole proprietorships may have only one owner.
- Gains and income from contributing property and services to business entities are more easily deferred with partnerships compared to taxable and S corporations.
- S corporations, partnerships, and sole proprietorships are required to use tax year-ends conforming to the tax year-ends of their owners. Taxable corporations may use any tax year-end.
- Taxable corporations must use the accrual method unless their average annual gross receipts are less than $5 million for three previous tax years. S corporations may use either the cash or accrual method of accounting. Partnerships without corporate partners may use either the cash or accrual method. If partnerships with corporate partners have average annual gross receipts greater than $5 million for three previous tax years, then they must use the accrual method.
- Income and losses may be specially allocated to partners. This gives partnerships a great deal of flexibility in determining how the risks and rewards of the enterprise are shared among partners. In contrast, income and losses must be allocated pro rata to S corporation shareholders consistent with their ownership percentages.
- Shareholder-employees of taxable corporations or S corporations pay half the FICA tax on their wages and their corporations pay the other half. Income allocated to S corporation shareholders is not subject to self-employment tax.
- Owners of entities taxed as partnerships pay self-employment taxes on guaranteed payments. General partners pay self-employment tax on their share of partnership income, but limited partners do not pay self-employment tax on their share of partnership

income. LLC members may be treated as either general partners or as limited partners for self-employment tax purposes depending on the amount of time they spend in the business, their decision-making authority, and their responsibility for the LLC's debt.

- S corporation shareholders and partners must adjust the basis of their shares or partner-ship interests periodically to reflect contributions they make, income allocated to them, distributions they receive, and losses allocated to them. Partners, but not S corporation shareholders, may add their share of partnership debt to their basis.

- Generally, distributions of appreciated property trigger gain at both the corporate and shareholder level when made to shareholders of taxable corporations, trigger gain at the corporate level when made to S corporation shareholders, and don't trigger any gain at all when made to partners.

- Losses from S corporations and partnerships are limited to the shareholder's or partner's tax basis. S corporation debt is generally not included in an S corporation shareholder's tax basis while partnership debt is included in a partner's tax basis. Thus, when compared to losses allocated to S corporation shareholders, it is less likely losses allocated to partners will be limited due to insufficient tax basis.

- When taxable or S corporation shareholders sell their shares, any gain is treated entirely as capital gain. In contrast, partners must treat a portion of any gain from selling their partnership interests as ordinary to the extent they indirectly own a share of ordinary income producing assets inside the partnership.

- On liquidation, taxable and S corporations will generally recognize gains and losses on distributed assets. In contrast, partnerships and their partners generally do not recognize gains or losses on liquidating distributions.

- Taxable corporations wanting to convert to a flow-through entity have two options. They may elect to become an S corporation if eligible, or they may liquidate the corporation and organize as a new entity. Taxes from liquidating taxable corporations are typically prohibitive when taxable corporations have appreciated assets.

# KEY TERMS

articles of incorporation (15-2)
articles of organization (15-2)
C corporation (15-5)
certificate of limited partnership (15-2)
disregarded entities (15-5)
dividends received deduction (15-10)
double taxation (15-7)

earnings and profits (15-19)
flow-through entities (15-5)
general partnership (15-2)
guaranteed payment (15-17)
initial public offering (15-3)
institutional shareholders (15-7)
limited liability company (15-2)
limited partnership (15-2)

net operating losses (15-21)
partnership agreement (15-2)
profits interest (15-14)
S corporation (15-5)
single-member LLCs (15-5)
sole proprietorship (15-2)
special allocations (15-16)
taxable corporation (15-5)

# DISCUSSION QUESTIONS

1. **(LO1)** What are the more common legal entities used for operating a business? How are these entities treated similarly and differently for state law purposes?
2. **(LO1)** How do business owners create legal entities? Is the process the same for all entities? If not, what are the differences?
3. **(LO1)** What is an operating agreement for an LLC? Are operating agreements required for limited liability companies? If not, why might it be important to have one?

4. **(LO1)** Explain how legal entities differ in terms of the liability protection they afford their owners.

5. **(LO1)** Why are taxable corporations still popular despite the double tax on their income?

6. **(LO1)** Why is it a nontax advantage for corporations to be able to trade their stock on the stock market?

7. **(LO1)** How do corporations protect shareholders from liability? If you formed a small corporation, would you be able to avoid repaying a bank loan from your community bank if the corporation went bankrupt? Explain.

8. **(LO1, LO2)** Other than corporations, are there other legal entities that offer liability protection? Are any of them taxed as flow-through entities? Explain.

9. **(LO2)** In general, how are unincorporated entities classified for tax purposes?

10. **(LO2)** Can unincorporated legal entities ever be treated as corporations for tax purposes? Can corporations ever be treated as flow-through entities for tax purposes? Explain.

11. **(LO2)** What are the differences, if any, between the legal and tax classification of business entities?

12. **(LO2)** What types of business entities does our tax system recognize?

13. **(LO3)** Who pays the first level of tax on a taxable corporation's income? What is the tax rate applicable to the first level of tax?

14. **(LO3)** Who pays the second level of tax on a taxable corporation's income? What is the tax rate applicable to the second level of tax and when is it levied?

15. **(LO3)** Is it possible for shareholders to defer or avoid the second level of tax on corporate income? Briefly explain.

16. **(LO3)** How does a corporation's decision to pay dividends affect its double-tax rate?

17. **(LO3)** Is it possible for the overall or double-tax rate on corporate income for corporations to be lower than the tax rate on flow-through entity taxable income? If so, under what conditions would you expect the overall corporate tax rate to be lower?

18. **(LO3)** Assume Congress increases individual tax rates on ordinary income while leaving all other tax rates constant. How would this change affect corporate overall or double-tax rates? How would this change affect overall tax rates for owners of flow-through entities?

19. **(LO3)** Assume Congress increases individual capital gains rates while leaving all other tax rates constant. How would this change affect the overall corporate or double-tax rate?

20. **(LO3)** Evaluate the following statements: "Dividends and long-term capital gains are generally taxed at the same rate. Therefore, the overall tax rate on corporate income is the same whether the corporation distributes its after-tax earnings as a dividend or whether it reinvests the after-tax earnings to increase the value of the corporation."

21. **(LO3)** If the reduced 15 percent dividend tax rate is repealed and increased to the ordinary rate, would the overall tax rate of corporate income tend to increase or decrease? Explain.

22. **(LO3)** If XYZ corporation is a shareholder of BCD corporation, how many levels of tax is BCD's before-tax income potentially subject to? Has Congress provided any tax relief for this result? Explain.

23. **(LO3)** How many times is income from a C corporation taxed if a retirement fund is the owner of the corporation's stock? Explain.

24. **(LO3)** List four basic tax planning strategies that corporations and shareholders can use to mitigate double taxation of a taxable corporation's taxable income.

25. **(LO3)** Explain why paying a salary to an employee-shareholder is an effective way to mitigate the double taxation of corporate income.

26. **(LO3)** What limits apply to the amount of deductible salary a corporation may pay to an employee-shareholder?

27. **(LO3)** Explain why the IRS would be concerned that a closely held taxable corporation only pay its shareholders reasonable compensation.

28. **(LO3)** When a corporation pays salary to a shareholder-employee beyond what is considered to be reasonable compensation, how is the salary in excess of what is reasonable treated for tax purposes? Is it subject to double taxation? *[Hint: See Reg. §1.162-7(b)(1).]*

29. **(LO3)** How can fringe benefits be used to mitigate the double taxation of corporate income?

30. **(LO3)** How many levels of taxation apply to corporate earnings paid out as qualified fringe benefits? Explain.

31. **(LO3)** How many levels of taxation apply to corporate earnings paid out as nonqualified fringe benefits? Explain.

32. **(LO3)** How can leasing property to a corporation be an effective method of mitigating the double tax on corporate income?

33. **(LO3)** When a corporation leases property from a shareholder and pays the shareholder at a higher than market rate, how is the excess likely to be classified by the IRS?

34. **(LO3)** How do shareholder loans to corporations mitigate the double tax of corporate income?

35. **(LO3)** Conceptually, what is the overall tax rate imposed on interest paid on loans from shareholders to corporations?

36. **(LO3)** If a corporation borrows money from a shareholder and pays the shareholder interest at a greater than market rate, how do you believe the interest in excess of the market rate will be treated by the IRS?

37. **(LO3)** Rank taxable corporations, S corporations, and LLCs in terms of their usefulness in allowing owners to defer gain or income when contributing property or services to the entity. Why is one type of entity preferred over another?

38. **(LO3)** Are taxable corporations or flow-through entities (S corporations and LLCs) more flexible in terms of selecting a tax year-end? Why are the tax rules in this area different for taxable corporations and flow-through entities?

39. **(LO3)** Rank taxable corporations, LLCs, and S corporations in terms of their flexibility to use the cash method of accounting. In general, do the tax rules in this area favor taxable corporations or flow-through entities?

40. **(LO3)** According to the tax rules, how are profits and losses allocated to LLC members? How are they allocated to S corporation shareholders? Which entity permits greater flexibility in allocating profits and losses?

41. **(LO3)** What does it mean to do a special allocation of profits and losses? Why would business owners want to be able to do a special allocation? What types of entities are allowed to specially allocate profits and losses?

42. **(LO3)** Compare and contrast the FICA tax burden of S corporation shareholder-employees and LLC members receiving guaranteed payments, assuming LLC members are treated as general partners for FICA tax purposes. How does your analysis change if LLC members are treated as limited partners for FICA tax purposes?

43. **(LO3)** A tax advisor recently recommended that her client form an LLC because distributions of appreciated property always trigger gain recognition when made from taxable corporations or S corporations, but less often when made from LLCs. Was her analysis correct? Why or why not?

44. **(LO3)** When a C corporation reports a loss for the year, can shareholders use the loss to offset their personal income? Why or why not?

45. **(LO3)** Is a current-year net operating loss of a taxable corporation available to offset income from the corporation in other years?

46. **(LO3)** A taxable corporation has a current year loss of $100,000. The corporation had paid estimated taxes for the year of $10,000 and expects to have this amount refunded when it files its tax return. Is it possible that the corporation may receive a refund larger than $10,000? If so, how is it possible? If not, why not?

47. **(LO3)** What happens to a taxable corporation's net operating loss carryforward after 20 years?

48. **(LO3)** Does a taxable corporation gain more tax benefit by using a net operating loss to offset other taxable income (1) two years after the NOL arises or (2) ten years after the loss arises? Explain.

49. **(LO3)** In its first year of existence, KES, a taxable corporation, reported a taxable loss of $10,000. Kim, KES's sole shareholder, reports $50,000 of taxable income from sources other than KES. How much of the $10,000 loss can be applied to offset her taxable income from other sources? Explain.

50. **(LO3)** Explain how liabilities of an LLC or an S corporation affect the amount of tax losses from the entity that limited liability company members and S corporation shareholders may deduct. Do the tax rules favor LLCs or S corporations?

51. **(LO3)** When shareholders of taxable corporations or S corporations sell their shares at a gain, how much of the gain is treated as capital gain and how much is treated as ordinary gain? Does this approach also apply to partners that sell their partnership interests?

52. **(LO3)** To what extent are gains and losses on distributed assets recognized when taxable corporations, S corporations, or partnerships liquidate? Do the tax rules in this area always favor certain entities over others? Why or why not?

53. **(LO3)** If limited liability companies and S corporations are both taxed as flow-through entities for tax purposes, why might an owner prefer one form over the other for tax purposes? List separately the tax factors supporting the decision to operate as either an LLC or S corporation.

54. **(LO3)** What are the tax advantages and disadvantages of converting a taxable corporation into an LLC?

## PROBLEMS

research

55. **(LO1)** Visit your state's official Web site and review the information there related to forming and operating business entities in your state. Write a short report explaining the steps for organizing a business in your state and summarizing any tax-related information you found.

56. **(LO3)** Evon would like to organize SHO as either an LLC or as a corporation generating an 11 percent annual before-tax return on a $200,000 investment. Assume individual and corporate tax rates are both 35 percent and individual capital gains and dividend tax rates are 15 percent. SHO will pay out its after-tax earnings every year to either its members or its shareholders.

   a. How much would Evon keep after taxes if SHO is organized as either an LLC or as a corporation?

   b. What are the overall tax rates if SHO is organized as either an LLC or a corporation?

57. **(LO3)** Evon would like to organize SHO as either an LLC or as a corporation generating a 9 percent annual before-tax return on a $200,000 investment.

Individual and corporate tax rates are both 30 percent and individual capital gains and dividends tax rates are 20 percent. SHO will distribute its earnings annually to either its members or shareholders.

   a. How much would Evon keep after taxes if SHO is organized as either a corporation or an LLC?

   b. What are the overall tax rates if SHO is organized as either an LLC or a corporation?

58. **(LO3)** Jack would like to organize PPS as either an LLC or as a corporation generating an 11 percent annual before-tax return on a $100,000 investment. Individual ordinary rates are 35 percent, corporate rates are 15 percent, and individual capital gains and dividends tax rates are 20 percent. PPS will distribute its earnings annually to either its members or shareholders.

   a. How much would Jack keep after taxes if PPS is organized as either a corporation or an LLC?

   b. What are the overall tax rates if PPS is organized as either an LLC or a corporation?

59. **(LO3)** Gaby would like to organize CBC as either an LLC or as a corporation generating a 7 percent annual before-tax return on a $300,000 investment. Individual and corporate tax rates are both 35 percent and individual capital gains and dividends tax rates are 10 percent. CBC will pay out its after-tax earnings every year to either its members or its shareholders. How much would Gaby keep after taxes if CBC is organized as either a corporation or an LLC?

60. **(LO3)** Gaby would like to organize CBC as either an LLC or as a corporation generating a 9 percent annual before-tax return on a $300,000 investment. Assume individual and corporate tax rates are both 35 percent and individual capital gains and dividends tax rates are 5 percent. CBC will distribute its earnings annually to either its members or shareholders.

   a. How much would Gaby keep after taxes if CBC is organized as either a corporation or an LLC?

   b. What are the overall tax rates if CBC is organized as either an LLC or a corporation?

61. **(LO3)** Anna would like to organize RLI as either an LLC or as a corporation generating a 7 percent annual before-tax return on a $250,000 investment. Assume individual ordinary rates are 30 percent, corporate rates are 15 percent, and individual capital gains and dividends tax rates are 15 percent. RLI will distribute its earnings annually to either its members or shareholders.

   a. How much would Anna keep after taxes if RLI is organized as either a corporation or an LLC?

   b. What are the overall tax rates if RLI is organized as either an LLC or a corporation?

62. **(LO3)** Using the Web as a research tool, determine which countries levy a double tax on corporate income. Based on your research, what seem to be the pros and cons of the double tax?

**research**

63. **(LO3)** LNS corporation, a taxable corporation, reports $300,000 of taxable income in the current year. Assume LNS's tax rate is 30 percent. Answer the following questions, assuming Natalie, LNS's sole shareholder, has a marginal tax rate of 35 percent on ordinary income and 15 percent on dividend income.

   a. Compute the first level of tax on LNS's taxable income for the year.

   b. Compute the second level of tax on LNS's income assuming that LNS currently distributes all of its after-tax earnings to Natalie. What is the overall corporate (double) tax rate on LNS's taxable income for the year?

■
**research**
■■

64. **(LO3)** In the current year, BCS had taxable income of $500,000 and distributed all of its after-tax earnings to Braxton, its sole shareholder. BCS's tax rate is 35 percent. Assuming Braxton's marginal tax rate on ordinary income is 35 percent and his dividend rate is 20 percent, what is the overall tax rate on BCS's $500,000 of taxable income?

65. **(LO3)** After several years of profitable operations, Javell, the sole shareholder of JBD Inc., a taxable corporation, sold 18 percent of her JBD stock to ZNO Inc., a taxable corporation in a similar industry. During the current year JBD reports $1,000,000 of after-tax income. JBD distributes all of its after-tax earnings to its two shareholders in proportion to their shareholdings. Assume ZNO's marginal tax rate is 35 percent. How much tax will ZNO pay on the dividend it receives from JBD? What is ZNO's overall tax rate on its dividend income? *[Hint: See IRC §243(a).]*

66. **(LO3)** In its first year of existence SCC corporation (a taxable corporation) reported a loss for tax purposes of $30,000. Using the corporate tax rate table, determine how much tax SCC will pay in year 2 if it reports taxable income from operations of $20,000 in year 2 before any loss carryovers.

67. **(LO3)** In its first year of existence, Willow Corp. reported a loss for tax purposes of $30,000. In year 2, it reports a $40,000 loss. For year 3, it reports taxable income from operations of $100,000 before any loss carryovers. Using the corporate tax rate table, determine how much tax Willow Corp. will pay for year 3.

68. **(LO3)** For the current year, custom Craft Services Inc. (CCS), a taxable corporation, reports taxable income of $200,000 before paying salary to Jaron the sole shareholder. Jaron's marginal tax rate on ordinary income is 35 percent and 15 percent on dividend income. Assume CCS's tax rate is 35 percent.

   a. How much total income tax will Custom Craft Services and Jaron pay on the $200,000 taxable income for the year if CCS doesn't pay any salary to Jaron and instead distributes all of its after-tax income to Jaron as a dividend?

   b. How much total income tax will Custom Craft Services and Jaron pay on the $200,000 of income if CCS pays Jaron a salary of $150,000 and distributes its remaining after-tax earnings to Jaron as a dividend?

   c. Why is the answer to part b lower than the answer to part a?

69. **(LO3)** For the current year, Maple Corporation, a taxable corporation, reports taxable income of $200,000 before paying salary to its sole shareholder, Diane. Diane's marginal tax rate on ordinary income is 35 percent and 15 percent on dividend income. If Maple pays Diane a salary of $150,000 but the IRS determines that Diane's salary in excess of $80,000 is unreasonable compensation, what is the amount of the double income tax on Maple's $200,000 presalary income? Assume Maple's tax rate is 35 percent and it distributes all after-tax earnings to Diane.

70. **(LO3)** Sandy Corp. projects that it will have taxable income of $150,000 for the year before paying any fringe benefits. Assume Karen, Sandy's sole shareholder, has a marginal tax rate of 35 percent on ordinary income and 15 percent on dividend income. Assume Sandy's tax rate is 35 percent.

   a. What is the amount of the double income tax on Sandy's $150,000 of pre-benefit income if Sandy Corp. does not pay out any fringe benefits and distributes all of its after-tax earnings to Karen?

   b. What is the amount of the double income tax on Sandy's $150,000 of pre-benefit income if Sandy Corp. pays Karen's adoption expenses of $10,000 and the payment is considered to be a nontaxable fringe benefit? Sandy Corp. distributes all of its after-tax earnings to Karen.

c.  What is the amount of the double income tax on Sandy's $150,000 of pre-benefit income if Sandy Corp. pays Karen's adoption expenses of $10,000 and the payment is considered to be a taxable fringe benefit? Sandy Corp. distributes all of its after-tax earnings to Karen.

71. **(LO3)** Jabar Corporation, a taxable corporation, projects that it will have taxable income of $300,000 before incurring any lease expenses. Jabar's tax rate is 35 percent. Abdul, Jabar's sole shareholder, has a marginal tax rate of 35 percent on ordinary income and 15 percent on dividend income. Jabar always distributes all of its after-tax earnings to Abdul.

   a.  What is the amount of the double tax on Jabar Corp.'s $300,000 prelease expense income if Jabar Corp. distributes all of its after-tax earnings to its sole shareholder, Abdul?

   b.  What is the amount of the double tax on Jabar Corp.'s $300,000 prelease expense income if Jabar leases equipment from Abdul at a cost of $30,000 for the year?

   c.  What is the amount of double tax on Jabar Corp.'s $300,000 prelease expense income if Jabar Corp. leases equipment from Abdul at a cost of $30,000 for the year but the IRS determines that the fair market value of the lease payments is $25,000?

72. **(LO3)** Nutt Corporation projects that it will have taxable income for the year of $400,000 before incurring any interest expense. Assume Nutt's tax rate is 35 percent.

   a.  What is the amount of the double tax on the $400,000 of preinterest expense earnings if Hazel, Nutt's sole shareholder, lends Nutt Corporation $30,000 at the beginning of the year, Nutt pays Hazel $8,000 of interest on the loan (interest is considered to be reasonable), and Nutt distributes all of its after-tax earnings to Hazel? Assume her ordinary marginal rate is 35 percent and dividend tax rate is 15 percent.

   b.  Assume the same facts as in part a except that the IRS determines that the fair market value of the interest should be $6,000. What is the amount of the double tax on Nutt Corporation's preinterest expense earnings?

73. **(LO3)** Ultimate Comfort Blankets, Inc., has had a great couple of years and wants to distribute its earnings while avoiding the double tax. It decides to give its sole shareholder, Laura, a salary of $1,500,000 in the current year. What factors would the courts examine to determine if Laura's salary is reasonable? *[Hint: See Elliotts, Inc. v. Commissioner, 716 F.2d 1241 (9th Cir. 1983)].*

   ■
   ■ **research**
   ■■

74. **(LO3)** Alice, the sole shareholder of QLP, decided that she would purchase a building and then lease it to QLP. She leased the building to QLP for $1,850 per month. However, the IRS determined that the fair market value of the lease payment should only be $1,600 per month. How would the lease payment be treated with respect to both Alice and QLP?

75. **(LO3)** Larry and his friend Cade formed FitQuest with each taxpayer receiving a 50 percent ownership interest in the entity. For his interest valued at $120,000, Larry contributed land valued at $120,000 with an adjusted basis of $30,000 and Cade agreed to contribute services valued at $120,000 for his interest valued at $120,000. For each interest received, $60,000 of the value is derived from the value of the property in the entity and the remaining $60,000 reflects expectations of future profits. What amount of income does Larry and Cade recognize in these transactions if CCS is a corporation (taxable or S) or is an LLC (an entity taxed as a partnership)?

76. **(LO3)** Dave and his friend Stewart each own 50 percent of KBS. During the year, Dave receives $75,000 compensation for services he performs for KBS during the

year. He worked about 1,000 hours and was involved in significant management decisions of the entity. After deducting Dave's compensation, KBS reports taxable income of $30,000. How much FICA and/or self-employment tax is Dave required to pay on his compensation and his share of the KBS income if KBS is formed as a taxable corporation, S corporation, or a limited liability company?

77. **(LO3)** Aaron and his sister Jessica each own 50 percent of PLR. During the year, Aaron receives $40,000 compensation for services he performs for PLR during the year. He worked about 100 hours, but was not involved in significant management decisions of the entity nor was he personally liable for any of PLR's debts. After deducting Aaron's compensation, PLR reports taxable income of $90,000. How much FICA and/or self-employment tax is Aaron required to pay on his compensation and his share of the PLR income if PLR is formed as a taxable corporation, S corporation, or a limited liability company?

78. **(LO3)** Daniel invites his associate, Matt, to join him in forming MDW, with each party contributing $40,000 in cash to become equal owners in all respects. MDW plans to obtain additional cash through a $200,000 small business loan from the local bank, which will be allocated equally to Daniel and Matt. For its first year of business, MDW reported a net loss of $50,000, and did not make any distributions during the year.

   a. What is Daniel's tax basis in his ownership interest at the end of MDW's first year if it was organized as a C corporation, an S corporation, or an LLC?

   b. Assuming instead that MDW reported $50,000 of profit and distributed $20,000 to each owner, what is Daniel's tax basis in his ownership interest at the end of MDW's first year if it was organized as a C corporation, an S corporation, or an LLC?

79. **(LO3)** Lazy Acres, after operating for several years, distributes to Peter (a 50 percent owner) land with a fair market value of $250,000. Lazy Acres purchased the land several years ago for $75,000. If Peter's tax basis in Lazy Acres is $600,000 at the time of the distribution, and Lazy Acres has accumulated $2.3 million in undistributed profits, how much gain or loss will Lazy Acres report from the distribution and how much income will Peter report from the distribution if Lazy Acres was originally organized as a C corporation, an S corporation, or an LLC?

80. **(LO3)** Rondo and his business associate, Larry, are considering forming a business but they are unsure about whether to form it as an S corporation or as an LLC. Each will invest $50,000 and the business will borrow $100,000. They project Rondo's share of business income and loss for the first five years of the business as follows:

| Year | Income (Loss) |
|------|---------------|
| 1 | ($25,000) |
| 2 | ($25,000) |
| 3 | ($8,000) |
| 4 | $60,000 |
| 5 | $40,000 |

If they form their new business as an LLC, they plan to allocate the debt 50 percent to each of them.

   a. What is Rondo's tax basis at the end of year 3 if he and Larry organize their business as an LLC?

   b. What is Rondo's tax basis at the end of year 3 if he and Larry organize their business as an S corporation?

   c. Will Rondo's losses be limited in year 3 if he and Larry organize their business as an S corporation? Explain.

81. **(LO3)** Tim and Manuel recently obtained a patent for a technology they invented to significantly increase the storage capacity of cell phones and other handheld electronic devices. They want to form a business to bring their idea to market but haven't decided whether to form their business as an LLC or as an S corporation. In addition to the patent, they will each contribute some cash to the new business, but most of the required funds will come from bank loans. Tim and Manuel will work full-time in the business, and they expect that the business will incur significant losses for at least three years before becoming profitable. Until then, Tim and Manuel would like to utilize their losses currently to reduce their current tax liabilities as much as possible.

    ■ planning

    ■ research

  a. Assuming that Tim and Manuel are not required to guarantee their firm's debt, will they prefer to organize as an LLC or as an S corporation?

  b. Assuming that Tim and Manuel are required to guarantee their firm's debt, will they prefer to organize as an LLC or as an S corporation? [*Hint: See Reg. §1.1367-2, Rev. Rul. 70-50, 1970-1 CB 178.*]

82. **(LO3)** Kevin and Bob have owned and operated SOA for a number of years. When they formed the entity, Kevin and Bob each contributed $100,000 to SOA. Information on SOA's assets at the end of year 5 is as follows (SOA does not have any liabilities):

    ■ planning

    ■ research

| Assets | FMV | Adjusted Basis | Built-in Gain |
|--------|-----|----------------|---------------|
| Cash | $200,000 | $200,000 | $ 0 |
| Inventory | 80,000 | 40,000 | 40,000 |
| Land and building | 360,000 | 300,000 | 60,000 |
| Total | $640,000 | | |

At the end of year 5, Kevin sold his 50 percent ownership interest to another investor for $320,000 when the basis in his ownership interest was $270,000.

  a. What is the amount and character of gain or loss Kevin will recognize on the sale if SOA is organized as a taxable corporation or as an S corporation?

  b. What is the amount and character of gain or loss Kevin will recognize on the sale if SOA is organized as an LLC?

## COMPREHENSIVE PROBLEMS

83. Dawn Taylor is currently employed by the state Chamber of Commerce. While she enjoys the relatively short workweeks, she eventually would like to work for herself rather than for an employer. In her current position, she deals with a lot of successful entrepreneurs who have become role models for her. Dawn has also developed an extensive list of contacts that should serve her well when she starts her own business.

    ■ planning

    It has taken a while but Dawn believes she has finally developed a viable new business idea. Her idea is to design and manufacture cookware that remains cool to the touch when in use. She has had several friends try out her prototype cookware and they have consistently given the cookware rave reviews. With this encouragement, Dawn started giving serious thoughts to making "Cool Touch Cookware" (CTC) a moneymaking enterprise.

    Dawn had enough business background to realize that she is embarking on a risky path, but one, she hopes, with significant potential rewards down the road. After creating some initial income projections, Dawn realized that it will take a few years for the business to become profitable. After that, she hopes the sky's the limit. She would like to grow her business and perhaps at some point "go public" or sell the business to a large retailer. This could be her ticket to the rich and famous.

Dawn, who is single, decided to quit her job with the state Chamber of Commerce so that she could focus all of her efforts on the new business. Dawn had some savings to support her for a while but she did not have any other source of income. Dawn was able to recruit Linda and Mike to join her as initial equity investors in CTC. Linda has an MBA and a law degree. She was employed as a business consultant when she decided to leave that job and work with Dawn and Mike. Linda's husband earns around $300,000 a year as an engineer (employee). Mike owns a *very* profitable used car business. Because buying and selling used cars takes all his time, he is interested in becoming only a passive investor in CTC. He wanted to get in on the ground floor because he really likes the product and believes CTC will be wildly successful. While CTC originally has three investors, Dawn and Linda have plans to grow the business and seek more owners and capital in the future.

The three owners agreed that Dawn would contribute land and cash for a 30 percent interest in CTC, Linda would contribute services (legal and business advisory) for the first two years for a 30 percent interest, and Mike would contribute cash for a 40 percent interest. The plan called for Dawn and Linda to be actively involved in managing the business while Mike would not be. The three equity owners' contributions are summarized as follows:

| Dawn Contributed | FMV | Adjusted Basis | Ownership Interest |
|---|---|---|---|
| Land (held as investment) | $120,000 | $70,000 | 30% |
| Cash | $ 30,000 | | |
| **Linda Contributed** | | | |
| Services | $150,000 | | 30% |
| **Mike Contributed** | | | |
| Cash | $200,000 | | 40% |

Working together, Dawn and Linda made the following five-year income and loss projections for CTC. They anticipate the business will be profitable and that it will continue to grow after the first five years.

| Cool Touch Cookware 5-Year Income and Loss Projections | |
|---|---|
| Year | Income (Loss) |
| 1 | ($200,000) |
| 2 | ($80,000) |
| 3 | ($20,000) |
| 4 | $60,000 |
| 5 | $180,000 |

With plans for Dawn and Linda to spend a considerable amount of their time working for and managing CTC, the owners would like to develop a compensation plan that works for all parties. Down the road, they plan to have two business locations (in different cities). Dawn would take responsibility for the activities of one location and Linda would take responsibility for the other. Finally, they would like to arrange for some performance-based financial incentives for each location.

To get the business activities started, Dawn and Linda determined CTC would need to borrow $800,000 to purchase a building to house its manufacturing facilities and its administrative offices (at least for now). Also, in need of additional cash, Dawn and Linda arranged to have CTC borrow $300,000 from a local bank and to borrow $200,000 cash from Mike. CTC would pay Mike a market rate of interest on the loan but there was no fixed date for principal repayment.

**Required:**

Identify significant tax and nontax issues or concerns that may differ across entity types and discuss how they are relevant to the choice of entity decision for CTC.

84. Cool Touch Cookware (CTC) has been in business for about 10 years now. Dawn and Linda are each 50 percent owners of the business. They initially established the business with cash contributions. CTC manufactures unique cookware that remains cool to the touch when in use. CTC has been fairly profitable over the years. Dawn and Linda have both been actively involved in managing the business. They have developed very good personal relationships with many customers (both wholesale and retail) that, Dawn and Linda believe, keep the customers coming back.

On September 30 of the current year, CTC had all of its assets appraised. Below is CTC's balance sheet, as of September 30, with the corresponding appraisals of the fair market value of all of its assets. Note that CTC has several depreciated assets. CTC uses the hybrid method of accounting. It accounts for its gross margin-related items under the accrual method and it accounts for everything else using the cash method of accounting.

| Assets | Adjusted Tax Basis | FMV |
|---|---|---|
| Cash | $150,000 | $150,000 |
| Accounts receivable | 20,000 | 15,000 |
| Inventory* | 90,000 | 300,000 |
| Equipment | 120,000 | 100,000 |
| Investment in XYZ stock | 40,000 | 120,000 |
| Land (used in the business) | 80,000 | 70,000 |
| Building | 200,000 | 180,000 |
| Total Assets | $700,000 | $935,000† |

| Liabilities | |
|---|---|
| Accounts payable | $ 40,000 |
| Bank loan | 60,000 |
| Mortgage on building | 100,000 |
| Equity | 500,000 |
| Total liabilities and equity | $700,000 |

*CTC uses the LIFO method for determining the adjusted basis of its inventory. Its basis in the inventory under the FIFO method would have been $110,000.

†In addition, Dawn and Linda had the entire business appraised at $1,135,000, which is $200,000 more than the value of the identifiable assets.

From January 1 of the current year through September 30, CTC reported the following income:

| | |
|---|---|
| Ordinary business income: | $530,000 |
| Dividends from XYZ stock: | $ 12,000 |
| Long-term capital losses: | $ 15,000 |
| Interest income: | $ 3,000 |

Dawn and Linda are considering changing the business form of CTC.

**Required:**

a. Assume CTC is organized as a C corporation. Identify significant tax and nontax issues associated with converting CTC from a C corporation to an S corporation. *[Hint: See IRC §1374 and §1363(d).]*

b. Assume CTC is organized as a C corporation. Identify significant tax and nontax issues associated with converting CTC from a C corporation to an LLC. Assume CTC coverts to an LLC by distributing its assets to its shareholders who then contribute the assets to a new LLC. [*Hint: see IRC §§331, 336, and 721(a).*]

c. Assume that CTC is a C corporation with a net operating loss carryforward as of the beginning of the year in the amount of $2,000,000. Identify significant tax and nontax issues associated with converting CTC from a C corporation to an LLC. Assume CTC coverts to an LLC by distributing its assets to its shareholders who then contribute the assets to a new LLC. [*Hint: see IRC §§172(a), 331, 336, and 721(a).*]

# chapter

# 16 Corporate Operations

## Learning Objectives

**Upon completing this chapter, you should be able to:**

**LO 1** Describe the corporate income tax formula, compare and contrast the corporate to the individual tax formula, and discuss tax considerations relating to corporations' accounting periods and accounting methods.

■

**LO 2** Identify common book-tax differences, distinguish between permanent and temporary differences, and compute a corporation's taxable income and regular tax liability.

■

**LO 3** Describe a corporation's tax return reporting and estimated tax payment obligations.

■

**LO 4** Explain how to calculate a corporation's alternative minimum tax liability.

### Storyline Summary

**Premiere Computer Corporation (PCC)**

Medium-sized publicly traded company

Manufactures and sells computer-related equipment

Calendar-year taxpayer

**Elise Brandon**

Newly hired tax consultant for large public accounting firm

Currently assigned to prepare tax return for PCC

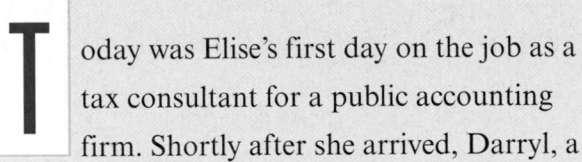

T oday was Elise's first day on the job as a tax consultant for a public accounting firm. Shortly after she arrived, Darryl, a tax manager, introduced himself and took Elise around the office to meet some of the people she would be working with. After the introductions, Darryl told Elise he would like her to work with him to prepare the tax return for Premiere Computer Corporation (PCC). He asked Elise to meet him in his office to discuss the assignment in 15 minutes.

PCC is a medium-sized publicly traded taxable corporation (C corporation) that manufactures computers and computer equipment. It has been a client of the firm for several years. Overall, PCC has been a fairly profitable company, but last year it experienced a bit of a hiccup incurring its first tax loss in many years.

Elise was excited about her opportunity, and she was confident her accounting education had adequately prepared her to successfully complete the assignment. In fact, her tax class was her favorite class. She had studied hard and learned all about computing corporate taxable income. When Elise spoke with Darryl about the assignment, he advised her to first review PCC's tax return and tax return workpapers from last year to get an idea how to prepare the return. Next, she should start with the audited numbers on the income statement and make book-to-tax adjustments for the items that are accounted for differently for book and tax purposes. Once she makes these adjustments, all she has to do is input the numbers into the firm's tax preparation software package to produce the return. Because Darryl would be reviewing the return, he told Elise to stay in close contact and let him know if she had any questions.

*to be continued . . .*

This chapter explores computing and reporting taxable income for taxable corporations (also known as *C corporations*). As we discussed in the previous chapter, taxable corporations are separate legal and taxpaying entities from their owners. Each year, corporations are required to compute their taxable income and pay tax on the income. In contrast to individuals, corporations generally compute their taxable income by starting with their book or financial accounting income and make adjustments for book-tax differences.

## LO1   CORPORATE TAXABLE INCOME FORMULA

The formula for computing corporate taxable income and individual taxable income is similar in some respects and different in others. Exhibit 16-1 presents the corporate income tax formula, and it also includes the individual tax formula for comparison purposes.

**EXHIBIT 16-1   Corporate and Individual Tax Formulas**

|  | Corporate Tax Formula | Individual Tax Formula |
|---|---|---|
|  | Realized income from whatever source derived | Realized income from whatever source derived |
| *Minus:* | Excluded or deferred income | Excluded or deferred income |
| *Equals:* | Gross income | Gross income |
| *Minus:* | Deductions | *For* AGI deductions |
| *Equals* |  | Adjusted gross income |
| *Minus:* |  | *From* AGI deductions |
|  |  | (1) *Greater* of: |
|  |  | (a) Standard deduction or |
|  |  | (b) Itemized deductions and |
|  |  | (2) Personal and dependency exemptions |
| *Equals* | Taxable income | Taxable income |
| *Times* | Tax rates | Tax rates |
| *Equals* | Regular income tax liability | Regular income tax liability |
| *Add* | Other taxes | Other taxes |
| *Equals* | Total tax | Total tax |
| *Minus* | Credits | Credits |
| *Minus* | Prepayments | Prepayments |
| *Equals* | Taxes due or (refund) | Taxes due or (refund) |

Corporations compute gross income as do other types of business entities and individual taxpayers. However, in contrast to individual taxpayers, corporations do not report adjusted gross income (AGI). Similar to other businesses, corporations are allowed to deduct ordinary and necessary business expenditures (see discussion in Chapter 8). In contrast to individual taxpayers, corporations don't itemize deductions, so they need not be concerned with standard deductions. Also, corporations don't deduct amounts for personal and dependency exemptions. In general, corporations exist to generate income through business activities. Consequently, nearly all corporate expenditures create either current tax deductions such as utilities expense or future deductions such as depreciation expense. Because corporations exist solely to do business, it is not surprising that the corporate taxable income formula is relatively straightforward.

### Accounting Periods and Methods

In Chapter 8, we discussed accounting periods and methods for all types of business entities. We learned that corporations measure their taxable income over a tax year and that their tax year must be the same as their financial accounting year. Corporations generally elect their tax year when they file their first income tax returns.

The timing of when corporations recognize income and deductions depends on their accounting methods. As we discussed in Chapter 8, accounting methods include overall methods of accounting (accrual method, cash method, or hybrid method) and accounting methods for individual items such as inventory (LIFO vs. FIFO) or depreciation (double declining balance vs. straight line). For tax purposes, corporations have some flexibility in choosing methods of accounting for individual items or transactions. However, corporations are generally required to use the accrual overall method of accounting.[1] For tax purposes, corporations with average gross receipts for the three years prior to the current tax year of $5 million or less may use the cash method of accounting.[2] Corporations that have not been in existence for at least three years may compute their average gross receipts over the prior periods they have been in existence to determine if they are allowed to use the cash method of accounting.

---

**THE KEY FACTS**

*Corporate Taxable Income Formula and Accounting Periods and Methods*

- ■ The corporate tax formula is similar to the individual tax formula, but corporations don't itemize deductions or deduct personal and dependency exemptions.

- ■ Corporations with average gross receipts of $5 million or less over the three prior tax years (or a shorter period for new corporations) may use the cash method.

---

**Taxes in the Real World**   *Choosing Tax Accounting Methods*

For certain transaction types, corporations face an interesting choice when choosing from permissible accounting methods. A corporation could choose an accounting method that tends to defer income or accelerate deductions from certain types of transactions or it could choose a method that tends to accelerate income or defer deductions. A research study by accounting professors provides evidence that when faced with this decision, publicly traded corporations tend to select income *accelerating* methods while privately held corporations tend to select income *deferring* methods.[3] Why the difference? Recall that generally speaking, the tax treatment of a transaction follows the book treatment. Publicly traded corporations are generally more concerned with increasing financial statement income in order to impress stockholders and potential investors. If corporations have to report higher levels of taxable income and pay more taxes as a result, that's OK. Privately held corporations are just the opposite. They don't need to impress the shareholders with accelerated earnings. They would rather reap the benefits of paying less current taxes even if it means reporting lower book income. This research illustrates the fact that nontax considerations may be more important than tax factors in the decision-making process. *After all, a business's objective should not be to minimize taxes but rather to maximize after-tax cash-flows.*

---

## COMPUTING CORPORATE REGULAR TAXABLE INCOME

**LO2**

To compute taxable income, corporations start with **book or financial reporting income** and then make adjustments for book-tax differences to reconcile to the tax numbers.[4] Some privately held corporations may use tax accounting rules for book purposes. These corporations need not make adjustments for book-tax differences.

---

[1]See Chapter 8 for a detailed discussion of determining the timing of taxable income and tax deductions under the accrual method.

[2]§448. Other special types of corporations such as qualified family farming corporations and qualified personal service corporations may use the cash method of accounting.

[3]See C. B. Cloyd, J. Pratt, and T. Stock, "The Use of Financial Accounting Choice to Support Aggressive Tax Positions: Public and Private Firms," *Journal of Accounting Research* 34 (Spring 1996), pp. 23–43.

[4]This chapter generally assumes that GAAP is used to determine book income numbers. In the future, many corporations will use International Financial Reporting Standards (IFRS) to determine their book income numbers.

### Book-Tax Differences

As we've been discussing in this chapter, many items of income and expense are accounted for differently for book and tax purposes. The following discussion describes several common **book-tax differences** applicable to corporations. Each book-tax difference can be considered to be "unfavorable" or "favorable" depending on its effect on taxable income relative to book income. Any book-tax difference that requires an add back to book income to compute taxable income is an **unfavorable book-tax difference** because it requires an adjustment that increases taxable income (and taxes payable) relative to book income. Any book-tax difference that requires corporations to subtract the difference from book income in computing taxable income is a **favorable book-tax difference** because it decreases taxable income (and taxes payable) relative to book income.

In addition to the favorable/unfavorable distinction, book-tax differences can also be categorized as permanent or temporary differences. **Permanent book-tax differences** arise from items that are income or deductions during the year for either book purposes or for tax purposes but not both. Permanent differences *do not reverse* over time, so over the long-run the *total* amount of income or deductions for the items are different for book and tax purposes. In contrast, **temporary book-tax differences** are those book-tax differences that reverse over time such that over the long-term, corporations recognize the same amount of income or deductions for the items on their financial statements as they recognize on their tax returns. Temporary book-tax differences arise because the income or deduction items are included in financial accounting income in one year and in taxable income in a different year. It is also important to note that temporary book-tax differences may *initially* be favorable (unfavorable) but are unfavorable (favorable) in subsequent years when they reverse.

Distinguishing between permanent and temporary book-tax differences is important for at least two reasons. First, as we discuss later in the chapter, many corporations are *required to disclose* their permanent and temporary book-tax differences on their tax returns. Second, the distinction is useful for those responsible for computing and tracking book-tax differences. For temporary book-tax differences, it is important to understand how the items were accounted for in previous years to appropriately account for current year reversals. In contrast, for permanent book-tax differences, corporations need only consider current year amounts to determine book-tax differences. While small corporations may report only a few book-tax differences, large corporations may report hundreds. Below we describe some of the most common book-tax differences.

**Common Permanent Book-Tax Differences**  As we have previously described in Chapter 8, businesses, including corporations, are allowed to exclude certain income items from gross income, and they are not allowed to deduct certain expenditures for tax purposes. Because these income items are included in book income, and the expenditures are deductible for financial reporting purposes, they generate permanent book-tax differences. Exhibit 16-2 identifies several permanent book-tax differences associated with items we discuss in Chapter 8, explains their tax treatment, and identifies whether the items create favorable or unfavorable book-tax differences.

---

**THE KEY FACTS**

**Computing Corporate Regular Taxable Income**

■ Corporations reconcile from book income to taxable income.
· Favorable (unfavorable) book-tax differences decrease (increase) book income relative to taxable income.
· Permanent book-tax differences arise in one year and never reverse.
· Temporary book-tax differences arise in one year and reverse in a subsequent year.

---

**Example 16-1**

Elise reviewed PCC's prior year tax return and its current year trial balance. She discovered that PCC earned $12,000 of interest income from City of San Diego municipal bonds (bonds issued in 2007), expensed $34,000 for premiums on key employee life insurance policies, expensed $28,000 in meals and entertainment expenses for the year, and reported a domestic production activities deduction of $465,000. What amount of permanent book-tax differences does PCC report from these transactions? Are the differences favorable or unfavorable?

**Answer:**  See Elise's summary of these items below:

| Item | Adjustment (Favorable) Unfavorable | Notes |
|---|---|---|
| Interest income from City of San Diego municipal bonds (bonds issued in 2007) | ($12,000) | Income excluded from gross income. Bond proceeds used to help fund *privately owned* baseball stadium. |
| Premiums paid for key employee life insurance policies | $34,000 | Premiums paid to insure lives of key company executives are not deductible for tax purposes. |
| Meals and entertainment | $14,000 | $28,000 expense for book purposes, but only 50 percent deductible for tax purposes. |
| Domestic production activities deduction | ($465,000) | $5,166,667 qualified production activities income (QPAI) × 9%. |

**EXHIBIT 16-2**   **Common Permanent Book-Tax Differences Associated with Items Discussed in Chapter 8**

| Description | Explanation | Difference |
|---|---|---|
| Interest income from municipal bonds | Income included in book income, excluded from taxable income | Favorable |
| Death benefit from life insurance on key employees | Income included in book income, excluded from taxable income | Favorable |
| Interest expense on loans to acquire investments generating tax-exempt income | Deductible for books, but expenses incurred to generate tax-exempt income are not deductible for tax | Unfavorable |
| Life insurance premiums for which corporation is beneficiary | Deductible for books, but expenses incurred to generate tax-exempt income (life insurance death benefit) are not deductible for tax | Unfavorable |
| Meals and entertainment expenses | Fully deductible for books, but only 50 percent deductible for tax | Unfavorable |
| Fines and penalties and political contributions | Deductible for books, but not for tax | Unfavorable |
| Domestic production activities deduction (DPAD) | Deduction for businesses involved in manufacturing activities in the U.S. equal to 9 percent of the company's qualified production activities income (QPAI) | Favorable |

*Federal income tax expense.*   Corporations deduct federal income tax expense (called a provision for income taxes) in determining their book income [determined under ASC (Accounting Standards Codification) 740 (formerly known as FAS 109)]. However, they are not allowed to deduct federal income tax expense for tax purposes.[5] Thus, the amount of federal income tax expense they deduct for book purposes is a permanent book-tax difference.

[5]§275(a)(1).

**Example 16-2**

**What if:** Assume that PCC's audited financial reporting income statement indicates that its federal income tax provision (expense) is $2,000,000.[6] What is PCC's book-tax difference for the year associated with this expense? Is the difference favorable or unfavorable? Is it permanent or temporary?

**Answer:** $2,000,000 unfavorable, permanent book-tax difference because PCC is not allowed to deduct federal income tax expense for tax purposes.

**Common Temporary Book-Tax Differences**  Corporations experience temporary book-tax differences because the accounting methods they apply to determine certain items of income and expense for financial reporting purposes differ from those they use for tax purposes. However, as we mentioned above, unlike permanent book-tax differences, over time temporary book-tax differences balance out so that corporations eventually recognize the same amount of income or deduction for the particular item. Exhibit 16-3

**EXHIBIT 16-3**  **Common Temporary Book-Tax Differences Associated with Items Discussed in Other Chapters**

| Description | Explanation | Initial Difference* |
|---|---|---|
| Depreciation expense (Chapter 9) | Difference between depreciation expense for tax purposes and depreciation expense for book purposes. | Favorable |
| Gain or loss on disposition of depreciable assets (Chapter 10) | Difference between gain or loss for tax and book purposes when corporation sells or disposes of depreciable property. Difference generally arises because depreciation expense, and thus the adjusted basis of the asset is different for tax and book purposes. This difference is essentially the reversal of the book-tax difference for the depreciation expense on the asset sold or disposed of. | Unfavorable |
| Bad debt expense (Chapter 8) | Direct write-off method for tax purposes, allowance method for book purposes. | Unfavorable |
| Unearned rent revenue (Chapter 8) | Rent revenue is taxable on receipt, but recognized when earned for book purposes. | Unfavorable |
| Deferred compensation (Chapter 8) | Deductible when accrued for book purposes, but deductible when paid for tax purposes if accrued but not paid for 2.5 months after year-end. Also, accrued compensation to shareholders owning more than 50 percent of the corporation is not deductible until paid. | Unfavorable |
| Organizational expenses and start-up costs (Chapter 9) | Immediately deducted for book purposes but capitalized and amortized for tax purposes (limited immediate expensing allowed for tax). | Unfavorable |
| Warranty expense and other estimated expenses (Chapter 8) | Estimated expenses deducted for book purposes, but actual expenses deducted for tax purposes. | Unfavorable |
| UNICAP (§263A) (Chapter 8) | Certain expenditures deducted for book purposes, but capitalized to inventory for tax purposes. Difference reverses when inventory is sold. | Unfavorable |

*Note that each of the initial book-tax differences will reverse over time [the initially favorable (unfavorable) book-tax differences will reverse to become unfavorable (favorable) book-tax differences in the future].

[6]Note that this example is presented in *what-if* form because this is not the income tax expense PCC will report in its financial statements. We compute PCC's actual income tax expense in Chapter 17.

identifies common book-tax differences associated with items we discuss in other chapters. Exhibit 16-4 summarizes PCC's temporary book-tax differences described in Exhibit 16-3.

**EXHIBIT 16-4**   PCC's Temporary Book-Tax Differences Associated with Items Discussed in Other Chapters

| Item | (1) Books (Dr) Cr | (2) Tax (Dr) Cr | (2) − (1) Difference (Favorable) Unfavorable |
|---|---|---|---|
| Depreciation expense | ($2,400,000) | ($3,100,000) | ($700,000) |
| Gain on fixed asset disposition | $54,000 | $70,000 | $ 16,000 |
| Bad debt expense | ($165,000) | ($95,000) | $ 70,000 |
| Warranty expense | ($580,000) | ($410,000) | $170,000 |
| Deferred compensation | ($300,000) | ($450,000) | ($150,000) |

***Dividends.***   Corporations receiving dividends from other corporations may account for the dividends in different ways for book and tax purposes. For tax purposes, corporations receiving dividends include the dividends in gross income.[7] For financial reporting purposes, accounting for the dividend (and investment in the corporation) depends on the level of ownership in the distributing corporation. The *general* rules for such investments are summarized as follows:

- If the receiving corporation owns less than 20 percent of the stock of the distributing corporation, the receiving corporation includes the dividend in income (same as tax; no book-tax difference).
- If the receiving corporation owns at least 20 percent but not more than 50 percent of the distributing corporation's stock, the receiving corporation includes a pro rata portion of the distributing corporation's earnings in its income and does not include the dividend in its income (temporary favorable or unfavorable book-tax difference for the difference between the pro rata share of income and the amount of the dividend).
- If the receiving corporation owns more than 50 percent of the distributing corporation's stock, the receiving corporation and the distributing corporation consolidate their financial reporting and the dividend is eliminated (book-tax difference beyond the scope of the text).[8]

---

**Example 16-3**

***What if:*** Assume that PCC owns 30 percent of the stock of BCS corporation. During 2010, BCS distributed a $40,000 dividend to PCC. BCS reported $100,000 of net income for 2010. Based on this information, what is PCC's 2010 book-tax difference relating to the dividend and its investment in BCS (ignore the dividends received deduction)? Is the difference favorable or unfavorable?

*(continued on page 16-8...)*

---

[7]As we discuss later in the chapter, corporations are entitled to deduct a certain percentage of the dividends received based on the level of the receiving corporation's ownership in the distributing corporation.

[8]Note that 80 percent ownership is required to file a consolidated tax return.

**Answer:** $10,000 unfavorable book-tax difference, computed as follows:

| Description | Amount | Explanation |
|---|---|---|
| (1) Dividend received in 2010 (included in 2010 taxable income but not in book income) | $ 40,000 | |
| (2) BCS 2010 net income | $100,000 | |
| (3) PCC's ownership in BCS stock | 30% | |
| (4) PCC's book income from BCS investment | $ 30,000 | (2) × (3). |
| Unfavorable book-tax difference associated with dividend | $ 10,000 | (1) − (4). |

*What if:* Assume the same facts as above, except that PCC owns 10 percent of BCS rather than 30 percent. What would be PCC's 2010 book-tax difference relating to the dividend and its investment in BCS (ignore the dividends received deduction)?

**Answer:** $0. PCC includes the $40,000 dividend in income for both book and tax purposes.

*Goodwill acquired in an asset acquisition.* When a corporation acquires the *assets* of another business in a taxable transaction, and it allocates part of the purchase price to goodwill (excess purchase price over the fair market value of identifiable assets acquired), the corporation is allowed to amortize this **purchased goodwill** on a straight-line basis over 15 years (180 months) for tax purposes.[9] For book purposes, corporations acquiring the assets of another business also typically allocate part of the purchase price to goodwill. Generally speaking in these asset acquisitions, the amount of goodwill corporations recognize for tax purposes is the same amount they recognize for book purposes. However, corporations amortize the goodwill over 15 years for tax purposes but recover the cost of goodwill for book purposes only when and only to the extent goodwill is impaired. Thus, to determine the *temporary* book-tax difference associated with purchased goodwill, corporations need only compare the amount of goodwill they amortize for tax purposes with the goodwill impairment expense for book purposes. If the tax amortization exceeds the book impairment expense, corporations report favorable book-tax differences. If the book impairment expense exceeds the goodwill tax amortization, corporations report unfavorable book-tax differences for goodwill.[10]

**Example 16-4**

*What if:* Suppose that on July 1, 2009, PCC acquired the assets of another business in a taxable acquisition. As part of the transaction, PCC recognized $180,000 of goodwill for both financial accounting and tax purposes. During 2009, PCC amortized $6,000 of the goodwill for tax purposes ($180,000/180 months × 6 months during year) and did not impair any of the goodwill for financial accounting purposes. What was PCC's book-tax difference associated with this goodwill in 2009? Was it a favorable or unfavorable difference? Was the difference permanent or temporary?

**Answer:** $6,000 favorable, temporary book-tax difference. The amount of capitalized goodwill is the same for book and tax purposes and PCC deducted $6,000 of the goodwill for tax purposes and none for book purposes.

(*continued on page 16-9...*)

---

[9]§197. Self-created goodwill is not amortizable for tax purposes.

[10]When corporations acquire the stock of another corporation, they may recognize book goodwill but will not recognize any tax goodwill. When this book goodwill is written off as impaired, it generates a permanent book-tax difference.

---

**What if:** Assume that at the end of 2010, PCC, with its auditors, determined that the value of the goodwill had been reduced to $150,000. That is, PCC experienced a $30,000 impairment expense to its goodwill. What is PCC's book-tax difference associated with its goodwill during 2010? Is the difference favorable or unfavorable? Is the difference permanent or temporary?

**Answer:** $18,000 unfavorable, temporary book-tax difference, computed as follows:

| Description | Amount | Explanation |
|---|---|---|
| (1) Goodwill initially recorded on 7/1/09 acquisition | $180,000 | |
| (2) Goodwill impairment recorded in 2010 | $ 30,000 | This write-down is expensed for book purposes. |
| (3) Months over which goodwill amortized for tax purposes. | 180 | 15 years × 12 months = 180 months. |
| (4) Tax goodwill amortization expense for 2010 | $ 12,000 | [(1)/(3)] × 12 months. |
| Unfavorable book-tax *temporary* difference associated with goodwill in 2010. | $ 18,000 | (2) − (4). |

---

### Corporate-Specific Deductions and Associated Book-Tax Differences

Certain deductions and corresponding limitations apply specifically to corporations. In this section, we introduce these deductions and identify book-tax differences associated with the deductions.

**Stock Options**   Corporations often compensate executives and other employees with stock options. Stock options allow recipients to acquire stock in corporations issuing the options. To acquire the stock, employees exercise the options and pay the **exercise price.** The exercise price is usually the stock price on the day the options are issued to the employee. For example, at a time when a corporation's stock is trading for $10 per share, a corporation might issue (or grant) 100 stock options to an employee that allow the employee to purchase up to 100 shares of the corporation's stock for $10 a share. Employees usually must wait a certain amount of time between when they receive the options and when they are able to exercise them (that is, they must wait until the options **vest** before they can exercise them). If employees quit working for the corporation before the options vest, they forfeit the options.

Stock options are valuable to employees when the stock price appreciates above the exercise price because, when the options vest, employees can use the options to purchase the stock at a price below the market price. Stock options are a popular form of compensation because they provide incentives for employees receiving the options to work to increase the value of the corporation and thereby benefit themselves and the stockholders.

For tax purposes, the tax treatment to the corporation (and the employee[11]) depends on whether the options are **incentive stock options** (ISOs) (less common, more administrative requirements for the corporation to qualify) or **nonqualified stock options** (NQOs) (more common, options that don't qualify as ISOs).[12] Corporations

---

[11]Employees do not recognize any income when they exercise incentive stock options. However, for nonqualified options, they recognize ordinary income for the difference between the value of the stock and the exercise price on the date of exercise. This chapter emphasizes the tax treatment of the options from the corporation's perspective.

[12]Requirements for options to qualify as incentive stock options are more restrictive than for nonqualified stock options. The formal requirements for incentive stock options are beyond the scope of this chapter.

issuing incentive stock options *never* deduct any compensation expense associated with the options for tax purposes. In contrast, for nonqualified options, corporations deduct the difference between the fair market value of the stock and the exercise price of the option (the **bargain element**) in the year in which employees exercise the stock options.

For financial accounting purposes, corporations were generally not required to expense stock options until 2006. Consequently, corporations do not report a book-tax difference for *incentive* stock options granted before 2006 and they report favorable, *permanent* book-tax differences for the bargain element of *nonqualified* stock options they granted *before* 2006 (when the options are exercised).

Under ASC 718 (formerly FAS 123R), corporations are required to recognize *book expense* for stock options they grant after 2005.[13] Corporations granting stock options *after 2005* are required to estimate the value of the options at the time they issue them. They must deduct the value of the options over the option **vesting period** as they vest. Book-tax differences for options granted after 2005 may be permanent, temporary, or both. The permanent difference is recognized in the year that post-2005 stock options are exercised. For incentive stock options, the amount of the permanent difference is the estimated value of the stock that vests during the year. The book-tax difference associated with incentive stock options is always unfavorable.

## Example 16-5

***What if:*** Assume that on January 1, 2010, PCC issued 10,000 incentive stock options (ISOs) with an estimated value of $6 per option. Each option entitles the owner to purchase one share of PCC stock for $15 a share (the per share price of PCC stock on January 1, 2010, when the options were granted). The options vest 25 percent a year for four years. What would be PCC's 2010 book-tax difference associated with the incentive stock options? Would the difference be favorable or unfavorable? Would the difference be permanent or temporary?

**Answer:** $15,000 unfavorable, permanent difference (10,000 options × 25% vesting × $6 estimated value). This is the book deduction for the ISOs. PCC does not deduct anything relating to the ISOs for tax purposes.

Nonqualified options may generate permanent and/or temporary book-tax differences. Corporations *initially* recognize *temporary* book-tax differences associated with stock options for the value of options that vest during the year but are not exercised during that year. This initial temporary difference is always *unfavorable* because the corporation deducts the value of the unexercised options that vest during the year for book purposes but not for tax purposes. This initial unfavorable temporary book-tax difference *completely reverses* when employees *actually exercise* the stock options.

The amount of the permanent difference is the difference between the estimated value of the stock options exercised (the amount associated with these stock options deducted for book purposes) minus the bargain element of the stock options exercised during the year (the amount that is deducted for tax purposes). If the estimated value of stock options exercised exceeds the bargain element of the stock options exercised, the permanent book-tax difference is unfavorable; otherwise it is favorable. The permanent book-tax difference is recognized in the year the options are exercised.

[13]ASC 718 is effective for years beginning after June 15, 2005, for large publicly traded corporations and for years beginning after December 15, 2005, for small publicly traded corporations and nonpublicly traded entities. Corporations could have elected to expense stock options for book purposes before the effective date of ASC 718.

**Example 16-6**

On January 1, 2010, PCC granted 20,000 nonqualified options with an estimated $5 value per option ($100,000 total value). Each option entitled the owner to purchase one share of PCC stock for $15 a share (the per share price of PCC stock on January 1, 2010, when the options were granted). The options vested at the end of the day on December 31, 2010 (employees could not exercise options in 2010). What is PCC's book-tax difference associated with the nonqualified options in 2010? Is the difference favorable or unfavorable? Is it permanent or temporary?

**Answer:** $100,000 unfavorable, temporary book-tax difference. PCC expensed $100,000 for book purposes and $0 for tax purposes (the options were not exercised).

*What if:* Assume the same facts as above and that on March 1, 2011, employees exercised all 20,000 options at a time when the PCC stock was trading at $20 per share. What is PCC's book-tax difference associated with the stock options in 2011? Is it a permanent difference or a temporary difference? Is it favorable or unfavorable?

**Answer:** $100,000 favorable, temporary book-tax difference in 2011. The favorable book-tax difference is a complete reversal of the unfavorable book-tax difference in 2010. The 2010 and 2011 book-tax differences completely offset each other because the estimated value of $5 per option is equal to the bargain element ($20 FMV minus $15 exercise price per share).

*What if:* Assume that on March 1, 2011, employees exercised all 20,000 options at a time when the PCC stock was trading at $24 per share. What is PCC's book-tax difference associated with the stock options in 2011? Is it a permanent difference or a temporary difference? Is it favorable or unfavorable?

**Answer:** $180,000 favorable book-tax difference in 2011. The $180,000 difference consists of a $100,000 favorable, temporary difference (the reversal of the prior year unfavorable, temporary difference) and an $80,000 permanent, favorable difference. The permanent difference is the bargain element on the 20,000 options in excess of the estimated value of the options for book purposes [($24 − $20) × 20,000 options].

Exhibit 16-5, which appears on the next page, summarizes the book and tax treatment of stock options both before and after ASC 718 became effective.

**Net Capital Losses**    For corporations, all net capital gains (long- and short-term) are taxed at ordinary income rates. Yet, corporations still generally prefer capital gains to ordinary income. Why is that? It's because corporations can only deduct capital losses *to the extent they recognize capital gains* in a particular year.[14] That is, corporations cannot deduct net capital losses. In contrast, individuals may deduct up to $3,000 of net capital losses in a year against ordinary income.[15]

When corporations recognize net capital losses for a year, they are permitted to carry the capital losses back three years (called a **capital loss carryback**) and forward five years (called a **capital loss carryover**) to offset net capital gains in the three years preceding the current tax year and then to offset net capital gains in the five years subsequent to the current tax year.[16] The capital loss carrybacks and carryovers must be applied in a particular order. If a corporation reports a net capital loss in year 4, it must first carry back the loss to year 1, then year 2, and then year 3. If the net capital loss remains after the carryback period, the corporation carries the loss forward to year 5 first, then year 6, year 7, year 8, and finally year 9. If the capital loss carryover has not been fully utilized by the end of the fifth year after it was incurred (year 9), the carryover expires unused.

[14]§1211(a).
[15]§1211(b). Individuals are also allowed to carry net capital losses forward indefinitely.
[16]§1212(a).

**EXHIBIT 16-5    Book and Tax Treatment of Stock Options Before and After ASC 718 Effective Date**

| Description | Book Deduction | Tax Deduction | Book-Tax Difference |
|---|---|---|---|
| **Pre ASC 718** | | | |
| Incentive stock option | No deduction | No deduction | None |
| Nonqualified stock option | No deduction | Bargain element* | Favorable, permanent |
| **Under ASC 718** | | | |
| Incentive stock option | Initial estimated value of stock options × percentage of options that vest during the year | No deduction | Unfavorable, permanent |
| Nonqualified stock option (in years before exercise) | Initial estimated value of stock options × percentage of options that vest during the year | No deduction until exercise | Unfavorable, temporary |
| Nonqualified stock option (in year of exercise) | Initial estimated value of stock options × percentage of options that vest during the year | Bargain element* | Favorable, temporary reversing unfavorable, temporary difference in prior years<br><br>Favorable, permanent difference if the bargain element exceeds the initial estimated value of stock options, unfavorable permanent difference otherwise |

*The bargain element is the difference between the fair market value of the stock and the exercise price on the date the employee exercises the stock options.

While corporations may carry back net capital losses, they may not *carry back* a capital loss to a year if doing so creates or increases the net operating loss of the corporation (excess of deductions over income) in the year to which it is carried back (see discussion of net operating losses in the next section).[17]

For financial reporting purposes, corporations deduct net capital losses in the year they sell the property. Thus, corporations recognizing net capital losses report unfavorable book-tax differences in the year they recognize the losses and favorable book-tax differences in the year they utilize capital loss carrybacks or carryovers.

---

**Example 16-7**

During 2010, PCC sold Intel stock at a $12,000 gain and also reported a $40,000 capital loss on the disposition of land held for investment. PCC has not recognized a net capital gain or loss since 2002. What is PCC's net capital loss for the year?

**Answer:**  $28,000 loss; [$12,000 + ($40,000)]. Because PCC had not recognized any net capital gains in 2007, 2008, or 2009 it may not carry back the loss (note that it could not carry back the loss to 2009 in any event because it recognized a net operating loss in that year as evidenced by its net operating loss carryover from 2009 (see Example 16-9).

(continued on page 16-13...)

---

[17]§1212(a)(1)(A)(ii).

What amount of book-tax difference does this loss trigger? Is the difference favorable or unfavorable? Is it temporary or permanent?

**Answer:** $28,000 unfavorable, temporary book tax difference.

**What if:** Assume that in 2010, PCC reported a net capital loss of $28,000 and that it reported a $7,000 net capital gain in 2007, no net capital gain or loss in 2008, and a $4,000 net capital gain in 2009. What is the amount of its net capital loss carryover to 2011? PCC reported a net operating loss in 2009 but did not report a net operating loss in either 2007 or 2008.

**Answer:** $21,000. PCC first carries back the $28,000 loss to 2007, offsetting the $7,000 net capital gain in that year. PCC then carries the remaining $21,000 loss [($28,000) + $7,000] back to 2009. However, because PCC reported a net operating loss in 2009, it is not allowed to offset the $4,000 net capital gain with the capital loss carryback. Consequently, the $21,000 unused capital loss carryover is carried forward to 2011.

**What if:** Suppose PCC did not recognize any net capital gains in prior years but that next year (2011) it recognizes a net capital gain of $5,000 (before considering any capital loss carryovers). What will be its book-tax difference associated with capital gains and losses next year? Is it favorable or unfavorable? Is it temporary or permanent?

**Answer:** Next year, PCC would report a $5,000 favorable, temporary book-tax difference because it would be allowed to deduct $5,000 of its $28,000 capital loss carryover for tax purposes. This is a reversal of $5,000 of the unfavorable book-tax difference from the prior year.

**Net Operating Losses**   Compare the tax burden of Corporation A and Corporation B. Corporation A reports $1,000,000 of taxable income and pays $340,000 of tax in year 1 and again in year 2 (see corporate tax rate schedule inside of front cover). In contrast, Corporation B reports $4,000,000 of taxable income in year 1 and a $2,000,000 loss in year 2. Absent any special tax provisions, Corporation B would pay $1,360,000 of tax in year 1 and no tax in year 2. Over the same two-year period both Corporation A and Corporation B reported $2,000,000 of (net) taxable income, yet Corporation B paid twice the tax Corporation A paid ($1,360,000 vs. $680,000). The problem for Corporation B is that, because it is required to report taxable income on an annual basis, it receives no tax benefit for its $2,000,000 loss (deductions in excess of gross income) in year 2. To ease the tax burden on corporations that aren't consistently profitable (for tax purposes), the tax laws allow corporations that report deductions in excess of gross income in a particular year to carry back or carry over the excess deductions to reduce taxable income and taxes payable in years when gross income exceeds deductions. This excess of deductions over gross income is referred to as a **net operating loss (NOL).** A corporation's net operating loss for the current year is the excess of its deductions over its gross income with the following adjustments:

- A corporation does not deduct a NOL generated in another year in determining its current year NOL.
- A corporation may deduct a capital loss carryover against a net capital gain arising in the current year in determining its NOL but it may not deduct a capital loss carryback against a net capital gain in determining its NOL.
- A corporation does not deduct the domestic production activities deduction in determining its NOL.

Corporations can carry current year net operating losses back **(net operating loss carrybacks)** two years and forward **(net operating loss carryovers)** 20 years to offset taxable income and reduce taxes payable (or already paid) in those

years.[18] Corporations that carry back losses to offset taxable income in prior years can file for and receive an immediate refund of taxes they paid on this income. When they carry a loss back, they must first carry it back to the year two years before the current year.

---

**Example 16-8**

**What if:** Assume that in 2010 PCC reported a $300,000 net operating loss. In addition, PCC reported the following taxable income from 2007 through 2009:

|  | 2007 | 2008 | 2009 |
|---|---|---|---|
| Taxable income | $90,000 | $45,000 | $250,000 |

If PCC carries back its NOL, what is its NOL carryover to 2011?

**Answer:** $5,000 carryover. PCC first carries the 2010 NOL back to 2008 reducing its 2008 taxable income to $0 and reducing the NOL carryback/over to $255,000 ($300,000 − $45,000). PCC receives a refund for taxes it paid in 2008. It then carries the remaining $255,000 NOL back to 2009 reducing 2009 taxable income to $0. PCC receives a refund for tax it paid in 2009. This leaves a $5,000 NOL carryover (from 2010) to 2011 ($255,000 − $250,000).

**What If:** Assume that in 2010 PCC reported $120,000 of deductions and $90,000 of gross income (including $6,000 of net capital gain). PCC also has a $15,000 NOL carryover from 2009 and an $8,000 capital loss carryover from 2009. What are PCC's net operating loss and capital loss carryovers to 2011 and when do they expire?

**Answer:** $15,000 net operating loss carryover from 2009 that expires at the end of 2029 if unused, a $36,000 net operating loss carryover from 2010 that expires at the end of 2030 if unused, and a $2,000 capital loss carryover from 2009 that expires at the end of 2014 if unused. PCC's 2009 NOL is unused in 2010 because PCC reports a NOL in 2010 and it does not deduct NOL carryovers in determining its 2010 NOL. In 2010, PCC is able to offset the $6,000 net capital gain included in gross income with $6,000 of the $8,000 capital loss carryover from 2009. This reduces PCC's gross income to $84,000 ($90,000 − $6,000) and increases its deductions in excess of gross income (its current year NOL) to $36,000 ($120,000 − $84,000). Finally, PCC's 2009 capital loss carryover is reduced by the $6,000 utilized portion to $2,000 ($8,000 minus $6,000 utilized in 2010).

---

A corporation with a current net operating loss may elect to forgo the carryback option and instead carry the net operating loss forward to future years. From a tax planning perspective, why would a corporation elect to forgo the carryback if it had taxable income in previous years? In deciding whether to forgo the carryback, corporations must evaluate the tax savings the NOL will generate if they carry the losses back and the tax savings they will generate if they carry them forward. If a carryback will offset income that was taxed at a low marginal tax rate, it may make

---

[18]For a NOL ending in 2008 (or beginning in 2008 if the corporation so elects), a corporation with average gross receipts of $15 million or less for three years prior to the year of the NOL (a "small" corporation) could elect to carry back the NOL for two, three, four, or five years. In addition, under tax legislation enacted in November 2009, other corporations (corporations that do not meet the gross receipts test or corporations that meet the gross receipts test but do not elect to carry back a 2008 NOL for more than the standard two years) may elect to carry back for up to five years NOLs incurred in 2008 or 2009 (but not for both years). If a corporation elects to carry back the NOL five years, it may offset a maximum of 50 percent of the available income from the fifth year and 100 percent of income from the remaining four carryback years. A small corporation that made the carryback election for a 2008 NOL may also elect to carry back a 2009 NOL subject to the same restrictions as the other corporations. See §172(b)(1)(H).

sense for the corporation to forgo the carryback and carry the NOL forward to offset income that would otherwise be taxed at a higher rate in upcoming years. Tax savings notwithstanding, corporations carrying back losses receive immediate cash while corporations forgoing the carryback do not.

---

**Example 16-9**

*What if:* Suppose that PCC generates a $50,000 net operating loss in the current year (year 1) and that last year (year 0) it reported taxable income of $50,000 and paid $7,500 in taxes. Next year, PCC expects to earn $335,000 of taxable income. How much more tax savings will PCC realize by electing to forgo the NOL carryback (ignore the time value of money)?

**Answer:** $12,000 [$50,000 × (39% − 15%)]. If PCC carries the loss back, it offsets $50,000 of income that was taxed at 15%. If it decides to forgo the carryback, the carryover to next year will offset $50,000 of income that would be taxed at 39%. Note, however, that PCC will immediately receive the $7,500 if it carries the loss back. It will have to wait to get its tax savings if it elects to forgo the carryback.

---

For financial reporting purposes, corporations deduct losses in the year they incur them. Consequently corporations report unfavorable temporary book-tax difference in the year they generate NOLs. However, because corporations do not deduct NOL carrybacks or NOL carryovers in determining book income they report favorable *temporary* book-tax differences in the year they deduct the NOL carrybacks or carryovers for tax purposes.

---

**Example 16-10**

*What if:* Assume that last year PCC incurred a $24,000 net operating loss. Last year's NOL becomes a NOL carryover to this year that is available to reduce its current year taxable income. What is PCC's current year book-tax difference associated with its NOL carryover? Is the difference favorable or unfavorable? Is it permanent or temporary?

**Answer:** $24,000 favorable, temporary book-tax difference. The net operating loss carryover from the prior year is deductible for tax purposes but not for book purposes.

---

**Charitable Contributions**    Similar to individuals, corporations are allowed to deduct charitable contributions to qualified charitable organizations.[19] However, the deduction and timing limitations are a little different for corporations than they are for individual taxpayers. Generally, corporations are allowed to deduct the amount of money they contribute, the fair market value of **capital gain property** they donate (property that would generate long-term capital gain if sold), and the adjusted basis of **ordinary income property** they donate (property that if sold would generate income taxed at ordinary rates). This chapter emphasizes the tax consequences of cash donations by corporations to qualified charities.[20] Generally, corporations are allowed to deduct charitable contributions at the time they make payment to charitable organizations (subject to an overall taxable income limitation we discuss below). However, corporations using the accrual method of accounting can deduct contributions in the year *before* they actually pay the contribution when (1) their board of

---

[19]In IRS Publication 78, *Cumulative List of Organizations Described in Section 170(c) of the Internal Revenue Code of 1986,* the IRS provides a list of organizations eligible to receive tax-deductible charitable contributions. The publication is searchable online at www.irs.gov/charities/article/0,,id=96136,00.html. Qualifying organizations tend to be those engaging in educational, scientific, governmental, and other public activities.

[20]For more details on the tax consequences of charitable contributions, see §170.

directors approves the payment and (2) they actually pay the contributions within two and one-half months of their tax year.[21]

---

**Example 16-11**

On December 1, 2010, the PCC board of directors approved a $110,000 cash contribution to the American Red Cross (ARC). For financial reporting purposes, PCC accrued and expensed the donation in 2010. PCC transferred the cash to the ARC on March 1, 2011. Does PCC report a book-tax difference associated with the charitable contribution (assume the taxable income limitation does not apply)?

**Answer:** No book-tax difference. For tax purposes, as an accrual-method taxpayer PCC may deduct the $110,000 contribution in 2010 because it paid the donation to the ARC within two and one-half months after year-end.

**What if:** Assume the same facts as above, except that PCC transferred the cash to the ARC on March 31, 2011. Does PCC report a book-tax difference associated with the charitable contribution (assume the taxable income limitation does not apply)?

**Answer:** Yes, it reports a $110,000 unfavorable, temporary book-tax difference in 2010. This will reverse and become a $110,000 favorable, temporary book-tax difference in 2011 when PCC deducts the contribution for tax purposes.

---

**THE KEY FACTS**

**Charitable Contributions**

■ **Charitable contribution deductions**
  · Deductible when they accrue if approved by board of directors and pay within 2.5 months of year-end.
  · Deductions limited to 10 percent of charitable contribution deduction modified taxable income.
  · Contributions in excess of 10 percent limit carried forward up to five years.

A corporation's deductible charitable contributions for the year may not exceed 10 percent of its **charitable contribution limit modified taxable income**. A corporation's charitable contribution limit modified taxable income is its taxable income *before* deducting the following:

1. *Any* charitable contributions.
2. The dividends received deduction (DRD) (discussed below).
3. NOL *carrybacks.*
4. The domestic production activities deduction (DPAD).
5. Capital loss *carrybacks.*

Note that capital loss and NOL *carryovers are deductible* in determining charitable contribution limit modified taxable income. Capital loss and NOL *carrybacks* are *not deductible* for charitable contribution limitation purposes because they are unknown when corporations must determine the limitation (they arise in a future year).

Due to the 10 percent limitation, a corporation's charitable contribution deduction for the year is the *lesser* of (1) the amount of charitable contributions to qualifying charities (including charitable contribution carryovers and carrybacks—discussed below) or (2) 10 percent of charitable contribution limit modified taxable income.

---

**Example 16-12**

**What if:** Assume that PCC's 2010 taxable income before considering the charitable contribution limitation was $100,000. The taxable income computation includes an $18,000 charitable contribution deduction, an $11,000 DRD, a $9,000 DPAD, a $24,000 NOL carryover, a $4,000 capital loss carryover (offsets $4,000 of capital gain), and $25,000 of depreciation expense. Under these circumstances, what would be PCC's 2010 deductible charitable contribution?

*(continued on page 16-17...)*

---

[21]§170(a)(2).

**Answer:** $13,800 deductible charitable contribution, computed as follows:

| Description | Amount | Explanation |
|---|---|---|
| (1) Taxable income before charitable contribution limitation | $100,000 | |
| (2) Charitable contribution deduction before limitation | $ 18,000 | Not deductible in computing limitation. |
| (3) Dividends received deduction | $ 11,000 | Not deductible in computing limitation. |
| (4) Domestic production activities deduction | $ 9,000 | Not deductible in computing limitation. |
| (5) **Charitable contribution limit modified taxable income\*** | **$138,000** | Sum of (1) through (4). |
| (6) Tax deduction limitation percentage | 10% | §170(b)(2)(A). |
| (7) Charitable contribution deduction limitation | $ 13,800 | (5) × (6). |
| (8) **Charitable contribution deduction for year** | **$ 13,800** | Lesser of (2) or (7). |
| Charitable contribution carryover | $ 4,200 | (2) − (8). |

\*Note that the NOL and capital loss carryover are not added back to compute line (5) because they are deductible in determining the charitable contribution limit modified taxable income.

Corporations making current year charitable contributions in excess of the 10 percent modified taxable limitation may carry forward the excess for up to five years after the year in which the carryover arises (FIFO order). They may deduct the carryover in future years to the extent the 10 percent limitation does not restrict deductions for charitable contributions corporations actually make in those years. Unused carryovers expire after five years.

**Example 16-13**

***What if:*** Under the assumptions provided in the previous example, we determined that PCC had a $4,200 charitable contribution carryover (it was not able to deduct $4,200 of its $18,000 contribution). Assume that in 2011, PCC contributed $10,000 to charity, and its charitable contribution limit modified taxable income was $110,000. What would be PCC's deductible charitable contribution in 2011? What would its charitable contribution carryover be at the end of 2011? When would it expire?

**Answer:** $11,000 charitable contribution deduction. This is the lesser of the charitable contribution limit of $11,000 ($110,000 × 10%) or $14,200 ($10,000 current year contribution plus $4,200 carryover from prior year). The carryover is $3,200 ($14,200 − $11,000). Because the current year contribution uses the limit first, the $3,200 carryover is from the excess contribution in 2010 and it will expire if it has not been used by the end of 2015.

Corporations report *unfavorable, temporary* book-tax differences to the extent the 10 percent modified taxable income limitation restricts the amount of their tax charitable contribution deduction. That is, they recognize unfavorable, temporary book-tax differences in the amount of the charitable contribution *carryover* they generate for the year. Conversely, corporations report *favorable, temporary* book-tax differences when they deduct charitable contribution carryovers because they deduct the carryovers for tax purposes, but not book purposes.

**Example 16-14**

In 2010, PCC donated a total of $700,000 of cash to the American Red Cross. Elise knew she still had to apply the 10 percent taxable income limitation to determine the amount PCC could deduct for tax purposes. She had determined that PCC's taxable income before the charitable contribution deduction, NOL carryover ($24,000), DRD ($21,000) (see Exhibit 16-5 below), and DPAD ($465,000) was $6,287,000. What is PCC's charitable contribution deduction for the year? What is its charitable contribution carryover to next year, if any?

**Answer:** $626,300 charitable contribution deduction and $73,700 charitable contribution carryover, computed as follows:

| Description | Amount | Explanation |
|---|---|---|
| (1) Taxable income before *any* charitable contribution, NOL carryover from previous year, DRD, and DPAD | $6,287,000 | Exhibit 16-7 |
| (2) NOL *carryover* from previous year | (24,000) | Deductible in determining taxable income limit. |
| (3) Charitable contribution limit modified taxable income | $6,263,000 | (1) + (2). |
| (4) Total charitable contributions for year | 700,000 | |
| (5) Tax deduction limitation percentage | 10% | §170(b)(2)(A) |
| (6) Charitable contribution deduction limitation | 626,300 | (3) × (5). |
| (7) **Charitable contribution deduction for year** | **$ 626,300** | Lesser of (4) or (6). |
| **Charitable contribution carryover*** | **$ 73,700** | (4) − (7). |

*As we discuss above, the carryover expires if it has not been used during the five-year period after the current year.

What is PCC's book-tax difference associated with its charitable contribution? Is the difference favorable or unfavorable? Is it permanent or temporary?

**Answer:** $73,700 unfavorable, temporary book-tax difference.

---

**Dividends Received Deduction**    When corporations receive dividends from other corporations they are taxed on the dividends at their ordinary tax rate, not the preferential 15 percent rate available to individual taxpayers. This isn't all bad news, however, because corporations are allowed to deduct a dividends received deduction (DRD) that reduces the actual tax they pay on the dividends.[22] The DRD is designed to mitigate the extent to which corporate earnings are subject to three (or perhaps even more) levels of taxation. Corporate taxable income is subject to triple taxation when a corporation pays tax on its income and then distributes its after-tax income to shareholders that are corporations. Corporate shareholders are taxed on the dividends, creating the second tax. When corporate shareholders distribute their after-tax earnings from the dividends to their shareholders the income is taxed for a third time. The dividends received deduction reduces the amount of the second-level tax and thus reduces the impact of triple taxation (or more) of earnings that corporations distribute as dividends.

Corporations generally compute their dividends received deduction by multiplying the dividend amount by 70 percent, 80 percent, or 100 percent, depending on their level of ownership in the distributing corporation's stock. Exhibit 16-6 summarizes the stock ownership thresholds and the corresponding dividends received deduction percentage.

[22]§243. Also, §246(c) describes certain dividends that are ineligible for the dividends received deduction.

**EXHIBIT 16-6    Stock Ownership and Dividends Received Deduction Percentage**

| Receiving Corporation's Stock Ownership in Distributing Corporation's Stock | Dividends Received Deduction Percentage |
|---|:---:|
| *Less than* 20 percent | 70% |
| *At least* 20 percent but less than 80 percent | 80% |
| 80 percent or more[23] | 100% |

---

**Example 16-15**

During 2010, PCC received a $30,000 dividend from IBM. PCC owns less than 1 percent of the IBM stock. What is PCC's DRD associated with the dividend?

**Answer:** $21,000 ($30,000 × 70%).

**What if:** Assume PCC's marginal tax rate on the dividend *before* considering the effect of the dividends received deduction is 34 percent. What is PCC's marginal tax rate on the IBM dividend income *after* considering the dividends received deduction?

**Answer:** 10.2 percent marginal tax rate on dividend income, computed as follows:

| Description | Amount | Explanation |
|---|---|---|
| (1) Dividend from IBM | $30,000 | |
| (2) DRD percentage | 70% | Less than 20 percent ownership in IBM. |
| **(3) Dividends received deduction** | **$21,000** | (1) × (2). |
| (4) Dividend subject to taxation after DRD | $ 9,000 | (1) − (3). |
| (5) Marginal ordinary tax rate | 34% | |
| (6) Taxes payable on dividend *after* DRD | $ 3,060 | (4) × (5). |
| **Marginal tax rate on dividend *after* DRD** | **10.20%** | (6)/(1). |

---

***Deduction limitation.***    The dividends received deduction is limited to the product of the applicable dividends received deduction percentage (see Exhibit 16-6) and **DRD modified taxable income.**[24] DRD modified taxable income is the dividend receiving corporation's taxable income *before* deducting the following:

- The DRD.
- *Any* NOL deduction (carryover or carryback).
- Capital loss *carrybacks.*
- The domestic production activities deduction (DPAD).[25]

---

**Example 16-16**

**What if:** Suppose that during 2010, PCC received a $30,000 dividend from IBM and that PCC owns less than 1 percent of the IBM stock. Further assume that PCC's taxable income before the dividends received deduction was $50,000 in Scenario A and $25,000 in Scenario B. To arrive at the taxable

(*continued on page 16-20...*)

---

[23]To qualify for the 100 percent dividends received deduction the receiving and distributing corporations must be in the same affiliated group as described in §1504. The 80 percent ownership requirement is the minimum ownership level required for inclusion in the same affiliated group.

[24]When corporations receive dividends from multiple corporations with different deduction percentages, according to §246(b)(3), the limitations first apply to the 80 percent dividends received deduction and then the 70 percent dividends received deduction.

[25]§246(b)(1).

income under both scenarios (before the DRD), PCC deducted a $2,000 NOL carryover, a $4,000 capital loss carryover, and a $1,000 DPAD. What is PCC's dividends received deduction associated with the dividend in Scenario A and in Scenario B?

**Answer:** $21,000 in Scenario A and $19,600 in Scenario B, computed as follows:

| Description | Scenario A | Scenario B | Explanation |
|---|---|---|---|
| (1) Taxable income before the dividends received deduction (includes dividend income) | $50,000 | $25,000 | |
| (2) NOL carryover | 2,000 | 2,000 | |
| (3) DMD | 1,000 | 1,000 | |
| **(4) DRD modified taxable income** | $53,000 | $28,000 | (1) + (2) + (3). |
| (5) Dividend income | 30,000 | 30,000 | |
| (6) Dividends received deduction percentage based on ownership | 70% | 70% | §243(a). |
| (7) Dividends received deduction before limitation | 21,000 | 21,000 | (5) × (6). |
| (8) Dividends received deduction limitation | 37,100 | 19,600 | (4) × (6). |
| **Deductible DRD** | **$21,000** | **$19,600** | Lesser of (7) or (8). |

Note that the capital loss carryover is deductible in determining the DRD modified taxable income so it is not added back to taxable income to arrive at DRD modified taxable income.

The modified taxable income limitation *does not apply* if after deducting the *full* dividends received deduction (dividend × DRD percentage) a corporation reports a current year net operating loss. That is, if after deducting the full dividends received deduction, the corporation has a net operating loss, the corporation is allowed to deduct the *full* dividends received deduction no matter what the modified taxable income limitation is.[26] As the following example illustrates, this rule can cause some unusual results.

---

**Example 16-17**

**What if:** Let's assume that PCC reports gross income of $80,000, *including* $30,000 of dividend income from TOU Corp. PCC owns 25 percent of TOU Corp. stock so its applicable DRD percentage is 80 percent (see Exhibit 16-6). Finally, let's consider two alternative scenarios. In Scenario A, PCC reports $56,000 of business expenses deductible in determining its DRD modified taxable income. In Scenario B, PCC reports $57,000 of business expenses deductible in determining its DRD modified taxable income. For each scenario, what is PCC's DRD modified taxable income? For each scenario, what is PCC's dividends received deduction?

(continued on page 16-21...)

---

[26]§246(b)(2).

**Scenario A Answer:** $24,000 DRD modified taxable income; $19,200 dividends received deduction (see computation below).

**Scenario B Answer:** $23,000 DRD modified taxable income; $24,000 dividends received deduction, computed as follows:

| Description | Scenario A | Scenario B | Explanation |
|---|---|---|---|
| (1) Gross income other than dividends | $50,000 | $50,000 | |
| (2) Dividend income | 30,000 | 30,000 | |
| (3) Gross income | $80,000 | $80,000 | (1) + (2). |
| (4) Business expenses deductible in determining the DRD modified taxable income | 56,000 | 57,000 | |
| (5) DRD modified taxable income (note this is taxable income before the DRD) | **$24,000** | **$23,000** | (3) − (4). |
| (6) Full dividends received deduction | $24,000 | $24,000 | (2) × 80%. |
| (7) DRD modified taxable income limitation | $19,200 | $18,400 | (5) × 80%. |
| (8) Taxable income (loss) after deducting full DRD | $     0 | ($1,000) | (5) − (6). |
| **Deductible DRD** | **$19,200** | **$24,000** | Lesser of (6) or (7) unless (8) is negative, then (6). |

Compare the results in Scenario A and Scenario B in the previous example. In Scenario B, PCC's DRD is $4,800 larger than it is in Scenario A ($24,000 − $19,200) despite the fact that the only difference in the two scenarios is that PCC reports $56,000 of business expenses in Scenario A and $57,000 of business expenses in Scenario B. Interestingly, the tax laws allow a corporation to increase its DRD by $4,800 for a $30,000 dividend simply by incurring $1,000 more in expenses (or even $1 more).

Because the dividends received deduction is strictly a tax deduction not a book deduction, *any* dividends received deduction creates a *favorable, permanent* book-tax difference.

**Example 16-18**

From her review of PCC's dividend income computations, Elise discovered that the only dividend PCC received during the year was a $30,000 dividend from IBM. Because PCC owns a very small percentage of IBM stock (less than 1 percent) Elise determined that PCC was entitled to a 70 percent dividends received deduction. What is PCC's book-tax difference associated with its dividends received deduction? Is the difference favorable or unfavorable? Is it permanent or temporary?

(continued on page 16-22...)

**Answer:** $21,000 favorable, permanent book-tax difference, computed as follows:

| Description | Amount | Explanation |
|---|---|---|
| (1) Taxable income before NOL, DRD and DMD (DRD modified taxable income) | $5,660,700 | Exhibit 16-7 ($5,636,700 + 24,000 NOL). |
| (2) Dividend income | $ 30,000 | Exhibit 16-7. |
| (3) Applicable DRD percentage | 70% | Own less that 20 percent of IBM. |
| (4) Full dividends received deduction | $ 21,000 | (2) × (3). |
| (5) Dividends received deduction taxable income limitation | $3,962,490 | (1) × (3). |
| (6) Book deductible dividends received deduction | 0 | No book DRD. |
| (7) Tax deductible dividends received deduction | $ 21,000 | Lesser of (4) or (5). |
| **(Favorable) permanent book-tax difference** | **($21,000)** | (6) − (7). |

## Taxable Income Summary

Exhibit 16-7 presents Elise's template for reconciling PCC's book and its taxable income. Note that the template does not follow the typical financial accounting format because it organizes the information to facilitate the taxable income computation. In particular, it puts the deductions in the *sequence they are deducted for tax purposes*.

## Regular Tax Liability

When corporations determine their taxable income, they can compute their tax liability from the corporate tax rate schedule. The corporate tax rate schedule is not indexed for inflation like the individual tax rate schedules are. Consequently, unlike the individual tax rate schedules, the corporate tax rate schedule does not change every year. The lowest marginal corporate tax rate bracket is 15 percent and the highest marginal tax rate bracket is 39 percent. Corporations with over $18,333,333 of taxable income pay tax at a flat 35 percent rate.

**Example 16-19**

Elise determined that PCC's taxable income is $5,150,700. What is its regular income tax liability?

**Answer:** $1,751,238, computed as follows:

| Description | Amount | Explanation |
|---|---|---|
| (1) Taxable income | $5,150,700 | Exhibit 16-7. |
| (2) Tax on first $335,000 | $ 113,900 | Corporate tax rate schedule (for taxable income between $335K and $10M). |
| (3) Taxable income above $335,000 | $4,815,700 | (1) − $335,000. |
| (4) Marginal tax rate for fifth bracket | 34% | Tax rate schedule. |
| (5) Tax on income above $335,000 | $1,637,338 | (3) × (4). |
| **Regular tax liability** | **$1,751,238** | (2) + (5). |

**EXHIBIT 16-7   PCC Book-Tax Reconciliation Template**

| Description | Book Income (Dr) Cr | Book-Tax Adjustments (Dr)† | Cr† | Taxable Income (Dr) Cr |
|---|---|---|---|---|
| Revenue from sales | $60,000,000 | | | $60,000,000 |
| Cost of goods sold | (38,000,000) | | | (38,000,000) |
| **Gross profit** | $22,000,000 | | | $22,000,000 |
| **Other income:** | | | | |
| Dividend income | 30,000 | | | 30,000 |
| Interest income | 120,000 | (12,000)ex. 1 | | 108,000 |
| Capital gains (losses) | (28,000) | | 28,000ex. 7 | 0 |
| Gain on fixed asset dispositions | 54,000 | | 16,000exh. 4 | 70,000 |
| **Gross income** | $22,176,000 | | | $22,208,000 |
| **Expenses:** | | | | |
| Compensation | (9,868,000) | | | (9,868,000) |
| Deferred compensation | (300,000) | (150,000)exh. 4 | | (450,000) |
| Stock option compensation | (100,000) | | 100,000ex. 6 | 0 |
| Bad debt expense | (165,000) | | 70,000exh. 4 | (95,000) |
| Charitable contributions | Moved below | | | |
| Depreciation | (2,400,000) | (700,000)exh. 4 | | (3,100,000) |
| Advertising | (1,920,000) | | | (1,920,000) |
| Warranty expenses | (580,000) | | 170,000exh. 4 | (410,000) |
| Meals and entertainment | (28,000) | | 14,000ex. 1 | (14,000) |
| Life insurance premiums | (34,000) | | 34,000ex. 1 | 0 |
| Other expenses | (64,000) | | | (64,000) |
| Federal income tax expense | (2,000,000)* | | 2,000,000ex. 2 | 0 |
| Total expenses *before* charitable contribution, NOL, DRD, and DPAD deduction | (17,459,000) | | | (15,921,000) |
| Income *before* charitable contribution, NOL, DRD, and DPAD | 4,717,000 | | | $6,287,000 |
| NOL carryover from prior year | | (24,000)ex. 9 | | (24,000) |
| Taxable income for charitable contribution limitation purposes | | | | 6,263,000 |
| Charitable contributions | (700,000) | | 73,700ex. 14 | (626,300) |
| Taxable income before DRD and DPAD | | | | 5,636,700 |
| Dividends received deduction (DRD) | | (21,000)ex. 18 | | (21,000) |
| Domestic production activities deduction (DPAD) | | (465,000)ex. 1 | | (465,000) |
| **Book/taxable income** | **$4,017,000** | | | **$5,150,700** |

*This number is used only for illustrative purposes. In Chapter 17, we compute the correct federal income tax expense (also referred to as the federal tax provision).

†Note that the superscript by each book-tax difference identifies the example (ex) or exhibit (exh) where the adjustment is calculated. Also note that the numbers in the debit column are favorable M adjustments while numbers in the credit column are unfavorable M adjustments.

So, why do corporate marginal tax rates increase from 15 percent to 25 percent to 34 percent to 39 percent and then drop to 34 percent and then increase again to 35 percent and then to 38 percent before settling in at 35 percent? This doesn't really look like a truly progressive tax rate schedule, does it? It turns out that the rate schedule is progressive with some modifications. When the apparent marginal rate increases to 39 percent, the marginal tax rate is really 34 percent but the tax laws impose a 5 percent add-on tax that is designed to eliminate the benefit of the rates lower than 34 percent (15 percent and 25 percent). Consequently, by the time the marginal rate from the schedule drops back down to 34 percent at $335,000 of taxable income, the entire amount of taxable income is taxed at a flat 34 percent rate. Therefore, taxable income between $335,000 and $10,000,000, is taxed at a flat 34 percent rate (verify this by referring to the previous example and dividing PCC's tax liability by its taxable income). The marginal rate then jumps to 35 percent and then to 38 percent. The 3 percent increase from 35 percent to 38 percent is also an add-on tax designed to phase-out the benefit of the 34 percent tax rate relative to the 35 percent rate. As a result, by the time taxable income hits $18,333,333, a corporation's taxable income is taxed at a flat 35 percent tax rate.

**Controlled Groups**   Corporate shareholders interested in reducing a corporation's overall tax burden may be tempted to split up an existing profitable corporation into several smaller corporations. By doing this, the group of corporations may earn the same taxable income in the aggregate but will pay less in taxes because each corporation will benefit from the low end of the corporate tax rate schedule. In the extreme, shareholders could split a corporation into enough separate corporations such that each separate corporation will report taxable income of $50,000 or lower and, consequently, pay tax on all of its income at the lowest marginal tax rate of 15 percent. Congress was concerned about this possibility and other similar abuses so they implemented special rules for **controlled groups.**

Essentially, a controlled group is a group of corporations that is controlled or owned by the same taxpayer or group of taxpayers. A controlled group could be a **parent-subsidiary controlled group,** a **brother-sister controlled group,** or a **combined controlled group.**[27] Exhibit 16-8 summarizes, in general terms, the definition of each of these controlled group types.

**EXHIBIT 16-8**   Controlled Group Definitions

| Type | Definition | Reference |
|------|-----------|-----------|
| Parent-Subsidiary | One corporation (the parent) owns at least 80 percent of the voting power or stock value of another corporation (the subsidiary) on the last day of the year. | §1563(a)(1) |
| Brother-Sister | Two or more corporations of which five or fewer persons own more than 50 percent of the voting power or stock value of each corporation on the last day of the year. | §1563(a)(2) |
| Combined | Three or more corporations, each of which is a member of either a parent-subsidiary or brother-sister controlled group and one of the corporations is the parent in the parent-subsidiary controlled group and also is in a brother-sister controlled group. | §1563(a)(3) |

The tax laws impose some complex rules for determining whether corporations meet the stock ownership requirements for controlled groups described in Exhibit 16-8.[28]

---

[27]§1563(a). The definition of a controlled group also includes certain insurance companies [§1563(a)].

[28]The ownership rules include direct and indirect (or constructive) ownership and the concept of identical ownership in each corporation in a brother-sister controlled group. The details of these rules are beyond the scope of this text. See §1563 for more detail.

No matter the type, a controlled group of corporations may use only one 15 percent tax bracket, and one 25 percent tax bracket among all the corporations in the group. That is, the controlled group is treated as one corporation for purposes of using the tax rate schedules.[29] In general, the tax provisions associated with controlled groups are designed to eliminate the benefit of splitting large corporations into smaller entities to take advantage of multiple tax benefits allowable to smaller corporations because the controlled group rules treat the entire group as though it is one entity.[30]

---

**Example 16-20**

**What if:** Assume that PCC and ACC are privately held corporations with calendar year-ends. On December 31, Jordan Michaels owns 50 percent of the stock of PCC and 50 percent of the stock of ACC. Sally Perkins owns the remaining shares of PCC and ACC. Are PCC and ACC a controlled group?

**Answer:** Yes, two persons (Jordan and Sally) own more than 50 percent of the stock of both PCC and ACC on the last day of the year (they own 100 percent of the stock of both corporations).

Assuming PCC reported $45,000 of taxable income for the year and ACC reported $40,000 of taxable income, what is the combined tax liability of PCC and ACC (given that they consist of a controlled group)?

**Answer:** $17,150 [($50,000 × 15%) + ($25,000 × 25%) + ($10,000 × 34%)].

**What if:** Assume the same taxable income for PCC and for ACC but that PCC and ACC have the same 10 owners and that each owner owns 10 percent of each corporation. What would be the combined tax liability of PCC and ACC?

**Answer:** $12,750 [PCC: $6,750 ($45,000 × 15%) + ACC: $6,000 ($40,000 × 15%)]. PCC and ACC are *not* part of a controlled group, so both corporations are allowed to take advantage of the 15 percent corporate tax bracket.

In this example, the controlled group rules would extract an additional $4,400 of tax ($17,150 − $12,750) from the entities because the rules essentially treat the two entities as one.

---

# COMPLIANCE

**L03**

Corporations report their taxable income on Form 1120.[31] Exhibit 16-9 presents the front page of PCC's current year Form 1120 through the tax liability.

Form 1120 includes a schedule for corporations to report their book-tax differences and reconcile their book and taxable income. Corporations with total assets of less than $10,000,000 report their book-tax differences on Schedule M-1. Beginning in 2005, corporations with total assets of $10,000,000 or more are required to report their book-tax differences on Schedule M-3. Because corporations report book-tax differences as adjustments to book income to compute taxable income on either Schedule M-1 or M-3, these book-to-tax adjustments are often referred to as **Schedule M adjustments, M adjustments,** and even **"Ms"** (plural version of M).

---

[29]§1561(a).

[30]The controlled group provisions require corporations in the group to share other tax benefits such as the AMT exemption discussed below. A potential benefit of having a controlled group is that if the group files a consolidated tax return, the losses of one corporation in the group can offset income from other corporations in the group.

[31]Corporations with gross receipts, total income, and total assets under $500,000 may complete Form 1120A, which is a short version of Form 1120.

**EXHIBIT 16-9    PCC Form 1120 page 1, through tax refund**

# Form 1120

Department of the Treasury
Internal Revenue Service

## U.S. Corporation Income Tax Return

For calendar year 2009 or tax year beginning _____ , 2009, ending _____ , 20 ____

▶ See separate instructions.

OMB No. 1545-0123

**2009**

**A Check if:**

1a Consolidated return (attach Form 851) ☐
b Life/nonlife consolidated return . . . ☐
2 Personal holding co. (attach Sch. PH) . ☐
3 Personal service corp. (see instructions) . ☐
4 Schedule M-3 attached ☐

Use IRS label. Otherwise, print or type.

| | |
|---|---|
| Name | **B Employer identification number** |
| **Premier Computer Corporation** | 12-3456789 |
| Number, street, and room or suite no. If a P.O. box, see instructions. | **C Date incorporated** |
| **1533 East Crown Drive** | 1/1/1994 |
| City or town, state, and ZIP code | **D Total assets (see instructions)** $ 9,500,000 |

**E Check if:** (1) ☐ Initial return (2) ☐ Final return (3) ☐ Name change (4) ☐ Address change

### Income

| | | | |
|---|---|---|---|
| 1a | Gross receipts or sales | b Less returns and allowances | c Bal ▶ |
| 1c | | | 60,000,000 |
| 2 | Cost of goods sold (Schedule A, line 8) | 2 | 38,000,000 |
| 3 | Gross profit. Subtract line 2 from line 1c | 3 | 22,000,000 |
| 4 | Dividends (Schedule C, line 19) | 4 | 30,000 |
| 5 | Interest | 5 | 108,000 |
| 6 | Gross rents | 6 | |
| 7 | Gross royalties | 7 | |
| 8 | Capital gain net income (attach Schedule D (Form 1120)) | 8 | |
| 9 | Net gain or (loss) from Form 4797, Part II, line 17 (attach Form 4797) | 9 | 70,000 |
| 10 | Other income (see instructions—attach schedule) | 10 | |
| 11 | **Total income.** Add lines 3 through 10 . . . . . ▶ | 11 | 22,208,000 |

### Deductions (See instructions for limitations on deductions.)

| | | | |
|---|---|---|---|
| 12 | Compensation of officers (Schedule E, line 4) . . . . ▶ | 12 | 1,500,000 |
| 13 | Salaries and wages (less employment credits) | 13 | 8,818,000 |
| 14 | Repairs and maintenance | 14 | |
| 15 | Bad debts | 15 | 95,000 |
| 16 | Rents | 16 | |
| 17 | Taxes and licenses | 17 | |
| 18 | Interest | 18 | |
| 19 | Charitable contributions | 19 | 626,300 |
| 20 | Depreciation from Form 4562 not claimed on Schedule A or elsewhere on return (attach Form 4562) | 20 | 3,100,000 |
| 21 | Depletion | 21 | |
| 22 | Advertising | 22 | 1,920,000 |
| 23 | Pension, profit-sharing, etc., plans | 23 | |
| 24 | Employee benefit programs | 24 | |
| 25 | Domestic production activities deduction (attach Form 8903) | 25 | 465,000 |
| 26 | Other deductions (attach schedule) | 26 | 488,000 |
| 27 | **Total deductions.** Add lines 12 through 26 . . . . . ▶ | 27 | |
| 28 | Taxable income before net operating loss deduction and special deductions. Subtract line 27 from line 11 | 28 | 17,012,300 |
| 29 | **Less: a** Net operating loss deduction (see instructions) . . . . | 29a 24,000 | |
| | **b** Special deductions (Schedule C, line 20) . . . . . | 29b 21,000 | 29c 45,000 |

### Tax, Refundable Credits, and Payments

| | | | |
|---|---|---|---|
| 30 | **Taxable income.** Subtract line 29c from line 28 (see instructions) | 30 | 5,150,700 |
| 31 | **Total tax** (Schedule J, line 10) | 31 | 1,751,238 |
| 32a | 2008 overpayment credited to 2009 . . 32a | | |
| b | 2009 estimated tax payments . . . . 32b 1,813,333 | | |
| c | 2009 refund applied for on Form 4466 . . 32c ( ) d Bal ▶ 32d | | |
| e | Tax deposited with Form 7004 . . . . . . . . . . . . 32e | | |
| f | Credits: (1) Form 2439 _____ (2) Form 4136 _____ 32f | | |
| g | Refundable credits from Form 3800, line 19c, and Form 8827, line 8c . . . 32g | 32h | 1,813,333 |
| 33 | Estimated tax penalty (see instructions). Check if Form 2220 is attached . . . ▶ ☐ | 33 | |
| 34 | **Amount owed.** If line 32h is smaller than the total of lines 31 and 33, enter amount owed | 34 | |
| 35 | **Overpayment.** If line 32h is larger than the total of lines 31 and 33, enter amount overpaid . . . . | 35 | 62,095 |
| 36 | Enter amount from line 35 you want: **Credited to 2010 estimated tax** ▶ _____ Refunded ▶ | 36 | 62,095 |

**Sign Here**

Under penalties of perjury, I declare that I have examined this return, including accompanying schedules and statements, and to the best of my knowledge and belief, it is true, correct, and complete. Declaration of preparer (other than taxpayer) is based on all information of which preparer has any knowledge.

▶ _____   ▶ _____
Signature of officer        Date        Title

May the IRS discuss this return with the preparer shown below (see instructions)? ☐ Yes ☐ No

**Paid Preparer's Use Only**

| | | | |
|---|---|---|---|
| Preparer's signature ▶ | | Date | Check if self-employed ☐ | Preparer's SSN or PTIN |
| Firm's name (or yours if self-employed), address, and ZIP code ▶ | | EIN | |
| | | Phone no. | |

**For Privacy Act and Paperwork Reduction Act Notice, see separate instructions.**    Cat. No. 11450Q    Form **1120** (2009)

Because PCC's total assets are $9,500,000 (see Exhibit 16-9, line D) it may complete a Schedule M-1 rather than a Schedule M-3. Exhibit 16-10 presents PCC's completed Schedule M-1 for 2009 based on the information provided in Exhibit 16-7. As you can see, Schedule M-1 is a relatively short schedule and it does not require corporations to provide much detail about the nature of their book-tax differences.

**EXHIBIT 16-10    Form 1120, Schedule M-1**

| **Schedule M-1** | **Reconciliation of Income (Loss) per Books With Income per Return** | | | | |
|---|---|---|---|---|---|
| | Note: Schedule M-3 required instead of Schedule M-1 if total assets are $10 million or more—see instructions | | | | |
| 1 | Net income (loss) per books . . . . . . | $4,017,000 | 7 | Income recorded on books this year not included on this return (itemize): | |
| 2 | Federal income tax per books . . . . . | 2,000,000 | | | |
| 3 | Excess of capital losses over capital gains . | 28,000 | | Tax-exempt interest   $ ____12,000____ | |
| 4 | Income subject to tax not recorded on books this year (itemize): _____ | | | _____ | 12,000 |
| | **Gain on disposition of fixed assets** | 16,000 | 8 | Deductions on this return not charged against book income this year (itemize): | |
| 5 | Expenses recorded on books this year not deducted on this return (itemize): | | a | Depreciation . . $ ___700,000___ | |
| a | Depreciation . . . . $ _____ | | b | Charitable contributions $ _____ | |
| b | Charitable contributions . $ _____73,700_____ | | | **Deferred compen. 150,000** | |
| c | Travel and entertainment . $ _____14,000_____ | | | **Dom. prod. act. ded. 465,000** | 1,315,000 |
| | **Other (see statement 1) 374,000** | 461,700 | 9 | Add lines 7 and 8 . . . . . . | 1,327,000 |
| 6 | Add lines 1 through 5 . . . . . . . | $6,522,700 | 10 | Income (page 1, line 28)—line 6 less line 9 | $5,195,700 |

**Schedule M-1**
**Statement 1**
**Other expenses recorded on books this year not deducted on this return**

| | |
|---|---|
| Compensation expense (stock options) | $100,000 |
| Bad debt expense | 70,000 |
| Warranty expense | 170,000 |
| Life insurance premiums | 34,000 |
| Total other expenses | $374,000 |

The schedule begins on line 1 with book income after taxes. The left-hand column includes all unfavorable book-tax differences (add-backs to book income to arrive at taxable income). In general, the top part of the left column is for income items and the bottom part is for expense items. The right-hand column consists of all favorable book-tax differences. The top part of the right column is for income items and the bottom part includes expense items.

Finally, it is important to note that the Schedule M-1 (and the Schedule M-3) reconcile to taxable income *before* the net operating loss deduction and the dividends received deduction.[32] Consequently, to fully reconcile book and taxable income, corporations must deduct net operating loss carryovers and dividends received deductions from line 10 on the Schedule M-1 (or the amount on line 30d on the Schedule M-3).

**Example 16-21**

In reviewing her work on PCC's tax return, Elise wanted to check to make sure that she could reconcile from the bottom line of the Schedule M-1 to PCC's taxable income. She noted that line 10 of PCC's Schedule M-1 was $5,195,700. How should Elise reconcile from this number to PCC's taxable income?

(*continued on page 16-28...*)

---

[32]Schedule M-1 (and the Schedule M-3) reconciles to line 28 on the Form 1120. Line 28 is taxable income before the net operating loss and special deductions (the dividends received deduction).

**Answer:** Start with the amount on line 10 and subtract PCC's NOL carryover and its DRD, as illustrated below:

| Description | Amount | Explanation |
|---|---|---|
| (1) Schedule M-1 taxable income reconciliation total | $5,195,700 | Form 1120, Schedule M-1, line 10. |
| (2) Net operating loss deduction | (24,000) | Exhibit 16-7. |
| (3) Dividends received deduction | (21,000) | Exhibit 16-7. |
| Taxable income | $5,150,700 | (1) + (2) + (3). |

The Schedule M-3 requires corporations to report significantly more information than the Schedule M-1 does. For example, the Schedule M-3 includes more than 60 types of book-tax differences while the Schedule M-1 includes only 10 lines. Furthermore, Schedule M-3 requires corporations to identify each book-tax difference as either temporary or permanent. The IRS created Schedule M-3 in hopes of providing a better and more efficient starting point for agents to identify and scrutinize large dollar compliance issues.

**Consolidated Tax Returns**    An **affiliated group** of corporations may elect to file a **consolidated tax return** in which the group files a tax return as if it were one entity for tax purposes. An affiliated group exists when one corporation owns at least 80 percent of (1) the total voting power and (2) the total stock value of another corporation.[33] Filing a consolidated tax return allows the losses of one group member to offset income of other members. Further, income from certain intercompany transactions is deferred until realized through a transaction outside of the affiliated group. However, losses from certain intercompany transactions are deferred until realized through a transaction outside of the affiliated group.

Affiliated groups cannot file a consolidated tax return unless they elect to do so. Because the election is binding on subsequent years, it should be made with care. Consolidated tax returns may impose additional administrative and compliance costs on the taxpayers. The consolidated tax return laws are very complex and beyond the scope of this text.[34] Further, the rules for consolidated reporting for financial statement purposes are different from the tax rules.

### Corporate Tax Return Due Dates and Estimated Taxes

The tax return due date for a taxable corporation is two and one-half months after the corporation's year-end. Thus, a calendar-year corporation's unextended tax return due date is March 15. Corporations requesting an extension can extend the due date for filing their tax returns (not for paying the taxes) for six months (September 15 for calendar-year corporations).

Corporations with a federal income tax liability of $500 or more (including the alternative minimum tax—discussed below) are required to pay their tax liability for the year in quarterly estimated installments.[35] The installments are due on the 15th day of the 4th, 6th, 9th, and 12th months of their tax year.[36] When corporations file their tax returns, they determine whether they must pay

---

[33]§1504(a).

[34]The tax rules for consolidated tax returns are provided primarily in the Regulations under §1502.

[35]§6655; §6655(e).

[36]§6655(c).

estimated tax underpayment penalties. Generally, corporations are subject to underpayment penalties if they did not pay in 25 percent, 50 percent, 75 percent, and 100 percent of their *required annual payment* with their first, second, third, and fourth installment payments, respectively.[37] The required annual payment is the *least* of:

1. 100 percent of the tax liability on the prior year's return, but only if there was a positive tax liability on the return and the prior year return covered a 12-month period (however, see discussion of "large" corporations below).
2. 100 percent of the current year tax liability (corporations usually don't rely on this method to determine the required payment because they won't know what this is until they complete their tax returns—after the estimated tax due dates).
3. 100 percent of the estimated current year tax liability using the annualized income method (discussed below).[38]

From a cash management perspective (time value of money) it generally makes sense for corporations to make the *minimum* required estimated payment installments for each quarter. Thus, as each estimated tax due date approaches, corporations will generally compute the required estimated payment under the prior year tax method (if available) and under the annualized method and pay the lesser of the two.

The **annualized income method** is perhaps the most popular method of determining estimated tax payments (particularly for corporations that can't use the prior year tax liability to determine their current year estimated tax payment obligations) because corporations can use this method as a safe harbor to avoid estimated payment penalties. Under this method, corporations determine their taxable income as of the end of each quarter and then annualize (project) the amounts to determine their estimated taxable income and tax liability for the year. The estimated annual tax liability is used at the end of each quarter to determine the minimum required estimated payment for that quarter. Corporations use the first quarter taxable income to project their annual tax liability for the *first and second quarter* estimated tax payments. They use taxable income at the end of the second quarter to determine the third quarter estimated tax payment requirement, and taxable income at the end of the third quarter to determine their fourth quarter payment requirement. Exhibit 16-11 shows the formula for computing estimated taxable income under the annualized income method.

**EXHIBIT 16-11**   **Estimated Taxable Income Computation under Annualized Income Method**

| Installment | (1) Taxable Income (first __ months of year) | (2) Annualization Factor | (1) × (2) Annual Estimated Taxable Income |
|---|---|---|---|
| First quarter | 3 | 12/3 = 4 | |
| Second quarter | 3 | 12/3 = 4 | |
| Third quarter | 6 | 12/6 = 2 | |
| Fourth quarter | 9 | 12/9 = 1.3333 | |

---

[37]§6665(d).

[38]§6655(e). Corporations may also use the adjusted seasonal income method of determining their required estimated tax payments. This method is similar in concept to the annualized method but is less common and is beyond the scope of this text.

**Example 16-22**

PCC determined its taxable income at the close of the first, second, and third quarters as follows:

| Quarter-end | Cumulative Taxable Income |
|---|---|
| First | $1,000,000 |
| Second | $3,200,000 |
| Third | $4,000,000 |

What is its annual estimated taxable income for estimated tax purposes as of the end of the first, second, third, and fourth quarters respectively?

**Answer:** $4,000,000 for the first and second quarters, $6,400,000 for the third quarter, and $5,333,333 for the fourth quarter, computed as follows:

| Installment | (1) Taxable income | (2) Annualization Factor | (1) × (2) Annual Estimated Taxable Income |
|---|---|---|---|
| First quarter | $1,000,000 | 12/3 = 4 | $4,000,000 |
| Second quarter | $1,000,000 | 12/3 = 4 | $4,000,000 |
| Third quarter | $3,200,000 | 12/6 = 2 | $6,400,000 |
| Fourth quarter | $4,000,000 | 12/9 = 1.333 | $5,333,333 |

Once corporations have determined their annual estimated taxable income for each quarter, they can use the formulas in Exhibit 16-12 to compute the required estimated tax installments for each quarter under the annualized income method.

**EXHIBIT 16-12    Estimated Taxable Income Computation under Annualized Income Method (*continued*)**

| Installment | (1) Annual Estimated Taxable Income | (2) Tax on Estimated Taxable Income | (3) Percentage of Tax Required to Be Paid | (4) (2) × (3) Required Cumulative Payment | (5) Prior Cumulative Payments | (4) − (5) Required Estimated Tax Payment |
|---|---|---|---|---|---|---|
| First quarter | | | 25% | | | |
| Second quarter | | | 50% | | | |
| Third quarter | | | 75% | | | |
| Fourth quarter | | | 100% | | | |

**Example 16-23**

Based on the estimated taxable income in the previous example, what are PCC's required estimated tax payments for the year under the annualized income method?

**Answer:** $340,000 for the first and second quarters, $952,000 for the third quarter, and $181,333 for the fourth quarter, computed as follows:

| Installment | (1) Annual Estimated Taxable Income | (2) Tax on Estimated Taxable Income (flat 34 percent) | (3) Percentage of Tax Required to Be Paid | (4) (2) × (3) Required Cumulative Payment | (5) Prior Cumulative Payments | (4) − (5) Required Estimated Tax Payment |
|---|---|---|---|---|---|---|
| First quarter | $4,000,000 | $1,360,000 | 25% | $ 340,000 | $ 0 | **$340,000** |
| Second quarter | $4,000,000 | $1,360,000 | 50% | $ 680,000 | $ 340,000 | **$340,000** |
| Third quarter | $6,400,000 | $2,176,000 | 75% | $1,632,000 | $ 680,000 | **$952,000** |
| Fourth quarter | $5,333,333 | $1,813,333 | 100% | $1,813,333 | $1,632,000 | **$181,333** |

Can PCC use its prior year tax liability to determine its current year estimated tax payments?

**Answer:** No. PCC reported a net operating loss last year and did not pay taxes so it may not use its prior year tax liability to determine its current year estimated tax payments.

Can PCC use its current year tax liability to determine its current year estimated tax payments?

**Answer:** Yes. As we determined in Example 16-19, PCC's actual tax liability for the year is $1,751,238. So, PCC could have avoided estimated tax penalties by paying in $437,810 each quarter ($1,751,238 × 25%). However, it did not know this amount when it was required to make its estimated tax payments so it would likely have used the annualized income method of determining its estimated tax payments to protect itself from penalties.

"Large" corporations, defined as corporations with over $1,000,000 of taxable income in *any* of the three years prior to the current year,[39] may use the prior year tax liability to determine their *first quarter* estimated tax payments only. If they use the prior year tax liability to determine their first quarter payment, their second quarter payment must "catch up" their estimated payments. That is, the second quarter payment must be large enough for the sum of their first and second quarter payments to equal or exceed 50 percent of their projected current year tax liability.[40]

**Example 16-24**

*What if:* Assume that last year PCC reported taxable income of $2,000,000 and a tax liability of $680,000. Further, PCC determined its required estimated tax payments under the annualized method as described in the previous example. What would be PCC's required minimum estimated tax payments for each quarter for the current year (ignore the current year tax requirement because PCC is unsure what its current year tax will be)?

(continued on page 16-32...)

[39]§6655(g)(2).
[40]§6655(d).

**Answer:** $170,000 for the first quarter, $510,000 for the second quarter, $952,000 for the third quarter, and $181,333 for the fourth quarter, computed as follows:

| Installment | (1)<br>Estimated<br>Tax Payment<br>under Prior<br>Year Tax<br>Exception | (2)<br>Estimated<br>Tax Payment<br>under<br>Annualized<br>Method | (3)<br>Required Cumulative<br>Payment for Quarter<br>×<br>[sum of the lesser of<br>(1) or (2) through<br>quarter] | (4)<br>Prior<br>Cumulative<br>Payments | (5)<br>(3) − (4)<br>Required<br>Estimated<br>Tax<br>Payment |
|---|---|---|---|---|---|
| First quarter | $170,000* | $340,000 | $  170,000 | $          0 | **$170,000** |
| Second quarter | Not applicable* | $340,000 | $  680,000 | $  170,000 | **$510,000** |
| Third quarter | Not applicable* | $952,000 | $1,632,000 | $  680,000 | **$952,000** |
| Fourth quarter | Not applicable* | $181,333 | $1,813,333 | $1,632,000 | **$181,333** |

*Because PCC is a large corporation, it may determine its first quarter estimated tax payment using its prior year liability ($680,000 × 25% = $170,000). However, it must use the annualized method to determine its second, third, and fourth quarter required payments.

With its second installment, PCC must have paid in $680,000. Because it only paid in $170,000 with the first quarter installment, it must pay $510,000 with its second quarter payment.

***What if:*** Assume the same facts as above, except that last year PCC paid $200,000 in tax and PCC is not a large corporation. What would be PCC's required minimum estimated tax payments for each quarter (ignore the current year tax requirement)?

**Answer:** $50,000 for the first quarter, $50,000 for the second quarter, $50,000 for the third quarter, and $50,000 for the fourth quarter, computed as follows:

| Installment | (1)<br>Estimated<br>Tax Payment<br>under Prior<br>Year Tax<br>Exception<br>($200,000/4) | (2)<br>Estimated Tax<br>Payment under<br>Annualized<br>Method | (3)<br>Required Cumulative<br>Payment for Quarter<br>×<br>[sum of the lesser of<br>(1) or (2) through<br>quarter ×] | (4)<br>Prior<br>Cumulative<br>Payments | (5)<br>(3) − (4)<br>Required<br>Estimated<br>Tax<br>Payment |
|---|---|---|---|---|---|
| First quarter | $50,000 | $340,000 | $  50,000 | $          0 | **$50,000** |
| Second quarter | $50,000 | $340,000 | $100,000 | $  50,000 | **$50,000** |
| Third quarter | $50,000 | $952,000 | $150,000 | $100,000 | **$50,000** |
| Fourth quarter | $50,000 | $181,333 | $200,000 | $150,000 | **$50,000** |

PCC can use the prior year tax to determine its minimum required estimated tax payments.

Corporations that have underpaid their estimated taxes for any quarter must pay an underpayment penalty determined on Form 2220. The amount of the penalty is based on the underpayment rate (or interest rate), the amount of the underpayment, and the period of the underpayment. The interest rate is generally the federal short-term interest rate plus 3 percent. The period of the underpayment is the due date for the installment through the earlier of (1) the date the payment is made or (2) the 15th day of the third month after the close of the tax year. The penalties are not deductible.[41]

[41]§6655(b)(2).

*continued from page 16-1...*

Elise figured she was done when she sat down to discuss PCC's tax return with Darryl. Darryl only had a few review comments. One of the comments sounded pretty important, though. Darryl asked Elise if PCC owed any alternative minimum tax. Elise told Darryl she would get back to him on that one. She left Darryl's office and immediately started researching the alternative minimum tax. She wasn't really sure what it was. ■

# CORPORATE ALTERNATIVE MINIMUM TAX

**L04**

Back in the early 1980s Congress was concerned that many large corporations were reporting positive financial income to shareholders, but reporting tax losses or minimal taxable income to the IRS and, as a result, not paying what the voting public perceived as their fair share of taxes. A common perception was that big businesses (and wealthy individuals) had the ability and sophistication to avoid paying taxes while middle-class taxpayers were carrying a disproportionate amount of the country's tax burden. Congress decided to do something about this perceived inequity by enacting the corporate (and individual) **alternative minimum tax** as part of the Tax Reform Act of 1986. The alternative minimum tax is a tax on a base broader than the regular tax base. The alternative minimum tax is designed to require corporations to pay some minimum level of tax even when they have low or no regular taxable income due to certain tax breaks they gain from the tax code.

Small corporations are exempt from the AMT. For this purpose, small corporations are those with average annual gross receipts *less than* $7.5 million for the three years prior to the current tax year. New corporations are automatically exempt from the AMT in their first year of existence and they are exempt from the AMT for their first three years of existence as long as their average annual gross receipts are below $5 million during the three-year period.[42] Once a corporation fails the AMT gross-receipts test, it is no longer exempt from the AMT.

Corporations compute their alternative minimum tax by multiplying their AMT base by the 20 percent AMT rate and then subtracting their regular tax liability from the product of the base and rate.[43] To determine their AMT base, corporations start with regular taxable income, add preference items, add or subtract certain adjustments, and then subtract an exemption amount. Exhibit 16-13 presents the corporate AMT formula.[44]

## *Preference Items*

When computing alternative minimum taxable income, corporations *add* preference items to taxable income. These items represent tax breaks that corporations received for regular tax purposes, but that Congress chose to eliminate for alternative minimum tax purposes. Common preference items include percentage depletion in excess

---

[42]§55(e). Note, however, that IRS Publication 542 "Corporations" and the instructions to Form 4626 indicate that (1) all corporations are exempt from the AMT in their first year of existence, (2) a corporation is exempt from the AMT in its second year of existence if the gross receipts from its first year are under $5,000,000, and (3) a corporation is exempt from the AMT if its average gross receipts for the 3-year period (or portion thereof during which the corporation was in existence) ending before its current tax year did not exceed $7,500,000. This test is more taxpayer favorable than the test specifically described in §55(e).

[43]§55(a).

[44]The formula has been simplified by leaving out an explicit adjustment for ACE, the AMT NOL deduction, and AMT foreign tax credits.

**EXHIBIT 16-13**    **Corporate AMT Formula**

Taxable income or loss before NOL deduction
Add: Preference items
Add or subtract: Adjustments
Alternative minimum taxable income (AMTI)
Subtract: Exemption
AMT base
× 20%
Tentative minimum tax
Subtract: Regular income tax
Alternative minimum tax if positive

of cost basis and tax-exempt interest income from a **private activity bond** (a municipal bond used to fund a nonpublic activity—if the bond is for a public purpose, the interest is not a preference item). Tax exempt interest on private activity bonds issued in 2009 or 2010 is not an AMT tax preference item.[45]

**Example 16-25**

Elise reviewed PCC's book-tax reconciliation provided in Exhibit 16-7 to determine if it had any preference items during the year. What preference items if any should PCC report for alternative minimum tax purposes?

**Answer:**  $12,000 tax-exempt interest income from the San Diego municipal bond issued in 2007. The bond is a private activity bond because proceeds from the bond were used to fund a privately owned and used baseball stadium.

**What if:**  Assume the San Diego municipal bond proceeds were used to construct public roads. Would the interest represent an AMT preference item?

**Answer:**  No, because the bond was not a private activity bond.

### Adjustments

Corporations may add or subtract alternative minimum tax adjustments to regular taxable income in computing alternative minimum taxable income.[46] Whether the adjustment is positive (unfavorable) or negative (favorable) for a particular item depends on the way the corporation accounts for the item for regular taxable income purposes and the way it accounts for the item for AMT purposes. In general, the most common AMT adjustments for corporations are (1) depreciation, (2) gain or loss on sale of depreciable assets, and (3) adjusted current earnings (ACE).

**Depreciation Adjustment**    Corporations with fixed assets may benefit from the highly accelerated depreciation methods allowed under the regular taxable income system. For alternative minimum tax purposes, assets aren't depreciated as quickly.[47] Consequently, in the early years of an asset's depreciable life, regular tax depreciation exceeds alternative minimum tax depreciation, and corporations must make positive adjustments to regular taxable income to compute the AMT base. However, after corporations fully depreciate assets for regular tax purposes they may

---

[45]§56(a)(5)(C)(vi).

[46]§56.

[47]Chapter 9 describes the regular tax and alternative minimum tax depreciable lives and methods.

still have basis left to depreciate for AMT purposes. In these situations, corporations make negative AMT depreciation adjustments to regular taxable income to compute the AMT base.

**Example 16-26**

Back at her desk, Elise reviewed the tax depreciation calculations. She discovered that while PCC deducted $3,100,000 of depreciation expense for regular tax purposes, it was entitled to deduct only $2,500,000 for AMT purposes. What is the amount of PCC's depreciation AMT adjustment? Is the adjustment positive or negative?

**Answer:** $600,000 positive or unfavorable adjustment, computed as follows:

| Description | Amount | Explanation |
|---|---|---|
| (1) Regular tax depreciation | $3,100,000 | Exhibit 16-7. |
| (2) AMT depreciation | 2,500,000 | |
| **Positive or unfavorable AMT adjustment** | **$ 600,000** | (1) − (2). |

**Gain or Loss on Disposition of Depreciable Assets**   Depreciation differences for regular tax and AMT purposes cause differences in the adjusted basis of the assets for regular tax purposes and AMT purposes. Consequently, when corporations sell or dispose of depreciable assets before they completely depreciate them, they will likely recognize a different gain or loss for regular tax purposes than they recognize for AMT purposes. If the regular tax gain is greater than the AMT gain, due to accelerated depreciation, corporations make negative adjustments to regular taxable income to compute the AMT base.

**Example 16-27**

Elise discovered that while PCC's regular tax gain on fixed asset dispositions for the year was $70,000, its AMT gain on fixed asset dispositions was only $55,000. What is the amount of PCC's fixed asset dispositions AMT adjustment? Is the adjustment positive or negative?

**Answer:** $15,000 negative or favorable, computed as follows:

| Description | Amount | Explanation |
|---|---|---|
| (1) AMT gain on fixed asset dispositions | $55,000 | |
| (2) Regular tax gain on fixed asset dispositions | 70,000 | Exhibit 16-7. |
| **Negative or favorable AMT adjustment** | **($15,000)** | (1) − (2). |

**THE KEY FACTS**

**Alternative Minimum Tax**

■ Corporations with average annual gross receipts less than $7.5M for three years prior to the current year are exempt from tax.
 · Corporations are exempt from tax in their first year of existence.
 · For first three years, exempt if annual average gross receipts are below $5M.
 · Once fail gross receipts test, no longer exempt.

■ Common preference items are tax-exempt interest from municipal
*(continued)*

**ACE Adjustment**   The ACE **(adjusted current earnings)** adjustment is designed to capture various sources of economic income not otherwise included in the alternative minimum tax base. Consequently, unlike other adjustments, the ACE adjustment is not tied to any one item. In order to calculate the ACE adjustment, a corporation must first compute its adjusted current earnings. Adjusted current earnings is computed by making certain modifications (designed to reflect economic income) to AMTI (discussed below). Once the corporation has computed its ACE it determines its ACE *adjustment* by subtracting AMTI (before the ACE adjustment)

*(concluded)*

bonds (unless issued in 2009 or 2010) and percentage depletion in excess of cost basis.

▪ Common adjustments are for depreciation, gain or loss on sale of depreciable assets, and adjusted current earnings.
  · ACE adjustment is sum of ACE adjustment items times 75 percent.

from ACE and multiplying the difference by 75 percent [(ACE − AMTI) × 75%].[48] Exhibit 16-14 describes several of the more common modifications to AMTI in computing ACE and indicates whether each modification is added to or subtracted from AMTI to determine ACE.

### EXHIBIT 16-14   Common Modifications to AMTI to Determine ACE

| Description | Modification to AMTI |
|---|---|
| Tax-exempt interest income from tax-exempt bond that funds a *public activity* (as opposed to private activity). If bond was issued in 2009 or 2010 it is not a modification[49] | + |
| Difference between AMT depreciation and ACE depreciation* | + or − |
| Difference between AMT and ACE gain or loss on asset disposition | + or − |
| Death benefit from life insurance contracts | + |
| 70 percent dividends received deduction (not the 80 percent or 100 percent deduction) | + |
| Organizational expenditures that were expensed during the year | + |
| Difference between gain reported under the installment method and gain otherwise reported (installment method not allowed for ACE purposes) | + or − |

*This adjustment may apply only for assets placed in service after 1989 and before 1994.

As a practical matter, the amount of the ACE adjustment can be determined by multiplying the sum of the modifications to AMTI in computing ACE by 75 percent. If the sum of the modifications is negative, the ACE adjustment may also be negative. However, negative ACE adjustments in excess of cumulative positive prior year ACE adjustments are not allowed.[50]

---

### Example 16-28

Finally, Elise focused on the ACE adjustment. She discovered that the only modification to AMTI for computing ACE was the $21,000 (70 percent) dividends received deduction. What is PCC's ACE adjustment?

**Answer:** $15,750, positive adjustment, computed as follows:

| Description | Amount | Explanation |
|---|---|---|
| (1) Dividends received deduction | $21,000 | 70 percent dividends received deduction is not deductible in determining ACE. |
| (2) ACE adjustment percentage | 75% | §56(g)(1). |
| **Positive or unfavorable ACE adjustment** | **$15,750** | (1) × (2). |

**What if:** Assume that PCC did not receive any dividends and that the San Diego bond generating $12,000 of tax-exempt interest is *not* a private activity bond. Further, assume that PCC reported $5,000 of organizational expenses this year and it reported $20,000 of gain this year from an installment sale it executed two years ago. Assuming PCC's cumulative ACE adjustment as of the beginning of the year is $100,000, what is its current year ACE adjustment under these circumstances?

*(continued on page 16-37...)*

---

[48]§56(g)(1).
[49]§56(g)(4)(B)(iv).
[50]§56(g)(2).

**Answer:** $2,250 negative ACE adjustment.

| Description | Amount | Explanation |
|---|---|---|
| (1) Tax-exempt interest | $12,000 | Public activity bond. |
| (2) Organizational expenses | $ 5,000 | Not deductible for ACE. |
| (3) Installment gain | ($20,000) | Negative modification because all gain was already included in ACE in year of sale (prior year). |
| (4) Total modification items | ($3,000) | (1) + (2) + (3). |
| (5) ACE adjustment percentage | 75% | §56(g)(1). |
| **Negative or favorable ACE adjustment** | **($2,250)** | (4) × (5). Not limited because prior year cumulated ACE adjustment is positive $100,000. |

**What if:** Assume the same facts as above except that PCC's cumulative positive ACE adjustment at the beginning of the year was $1,000 rather than $100,000. What would be PCC's ACE adjustment in these circumstances?

**Answer:** $1,000 negative ACE adjustment. PCC's current year negative ACE adjustment is limited to the cumulative positive ACE adjustment at the beginning of the year.

**Alternative Minimum Taxable Income (AMTI)**    Corporations compute their alternative minimum taxable income by adding their preference items and adding or subtracting their adjustments from regular taxable income. The alternative minimum taxable income is an important number because corporations use it to determine the amount of the AMT exemption (discussed next) they are allowed to deduct to compute their AMT base.

**Example 16-29**

After computing PCC's preference items and adjustments Elise had all the information she needed to compute PCC's AMTI. What is PCC's AMTI?

**Answer:** $5,763,450, computed as follows:

| Description | Amount | Explanation |
|---|---|---|
| (1) Regular taxable income | $5,150,700 | Exhibit 16-7. |
| (2) Preference items | 12,000 | Example 16-25. |
| (3) Depreciation adjustment | 600,000 | Example 16-26. |
| (4) Fixed asset disposition adjustment | (15,000) | Example 16-27. |
| (5) ACE adjustment | 15,750 | Example 16-28. |
| Alternative minimum taxable income (AMTI) | $5,763,450 | Sum of (1) through (5). |

**AMT Exemption**    Much like individual taxpayers are allowed to deduct standard deductions and personal exemptions in computing their taxable income, corporations are allowed to deduct a certain exemption amount in computing their alternative minimum tax base. The exemption is subject to an AMTI-based phase-out. The full exemption amount for corporations is $40,000. The exemption is phased out by 25 percent of the amount that AMTI exceeds $150,000 and is completely phased out for corporations with AMTI of at least $310,000.[51] Thus, the exemption

---

[51]§55(d)(2).

is fully phased out for only moderately profitable large corporations. However, the exemption protects many small corporations from paying the alternative minimum tax.

## Example 16-30

Because PCC's AMTI exceeds $310,000, Elise determined that PCC's deductible AMT exemption amount is $0.

*What if:* If PCC's AMTI was $200,000, what exemption amount would it deduct?

**Answer:** $27,500, computed as follows:

| Description | Amount | Explanation |
|---|---|---|
| (1) Full exemption amount | $ 40,000 | §55(d). |
| (2) Assumed AMTI | 200,000 | |
| (3) Exemption phase-out threshold | 150,000 | §55(d)(2). |
| (4) AMTI over exemption threshold. | $ 50,000 | (2) − (3). |
| (5) Phase-out percentage | 25% | §55(d)(3). |
| (6) Exemption phase-out amount | 12,500 | (4) × (5). |
| **Deductible exemption** | **$ 27,500** | (1) − (6). |

---

**THE KEY FACTS**

**Alternative Minimum Tax**

▪ AMT full exemption amount is $40,000.
· Phase-out 25 percent for each $1 of AMTI in excess of $150,000.

▪ AMT rate is 20 percent.

▪ AMT equals excess of TMT over regular tax liability.

▪ Tentative minimum tax credit reduces regular tax down to TMT in year corporation doesn't owe AMT.

---

**Alternative Minimum Tax** To determine their alternative minimum tax, corporations next compute their **tentative minimum tax** (TMT) by multiplying their AMT base (AMTI minus exemption amount) by a flat 20 percent rate. Then they compare their TMT to their regular tax liability. If a corporation's regular tax liability is greater than the TMT, it does not owe any alternative minimum tax. If its TMT is greater than its regular tax liability, it must pay its regular tax liability and the excess of the TMT over its regular tax liability. This excess is the alternative minimum tax.

## Example 16-31

Elise had enough information to compute PCC's alternative minimum tax. She knew the tax software would compute the AMT but she wanted to calculate it independent from the program to ensure the results were accurate. What is PCC's alternative minimum tax, if any?

**Answer:** $0, computed as follows:

| Description | Amount | Explanation |
|---|---|---|
| (1) AMTI | $5,763,450 | Example 16-29. |
| (2) Deductible exemption | $ 0 | Example 16-30. |
| (3) AMT base | $5,763,450 | (1) + (2). |
| (4) AMT rate | 20% | §55(b)(2). |
| (5) Tentative minimum tax | $1,152,690 | (3) × (4). |
| (6) Regular tax | $1,751,238 | Example 16-19. |
| **Alternative minimum tax** | **$ 0** | (5) − (6), but not less than $0. |

*What if:* If PCC's regular tax liability had been $1,000,000, what would be the amount of its AMT?

**Answer:** $152,690, which is the excess of the $1,152,690 TMT over the $1,000,000 regular tax liability. PCC would pay its $1,000,000 regular tax liability and $152,690 of AMT.

When corporations owe the alternative minimum tax, they generate a **minimum tax credit** that they can carry forward *indefinitely* to offset their regular tax liability down to their tentative minimum tax in years when their regular tax exceeds their tentative minimum tax. That is, they can use the tentative minimum tax credit in years when they do not owe the alternative minimum tax.

---

**Example 16-32**

*What if:* Assume that in year 1, PCC has a TMT of $1,152,690 and a regular tax liability of $1,000,000. PCC would owe $152,690 of AMT and $1,000,000 of regular tax. It would also generate a $152,690 minimum tax credit. Further, assume that in year 2 PCC reports a tentative minimum tax of $900,000 and a regular tax liability of $1,000,000. What is PCC's tax liability after applying the minimum tax credit?

**Answer:** $900,000 tax liability and $52,690 minimum tax credit carryover, computed as follows:

| Description | Amount | Explanation |
|---|---|---|
| (1) Year 1 minimum tax credit | $ 152,690 | |
| (2) Year 2 tentative minimum tax | $ 900,000 | |
| (3) Year 2 regular tax liability | $1,000,000 | |
| (4) Year 2 AMT | $ 0 | (2) − (3), but not less than $0. |
| (5) Limit on year 2 minimum tax credit | $ 100,000 | (3) − (2). |
| (6) Year 2 minimum tax credit | $ 100,000 | Lesser of (1) and (5). |
| (7) Total tax liability for year | $ 900,000 | (3) − (6). |
| Minimum credit carryover | $ 52,690 | (1) − (6). |

---

Exhibit 16-15 presents PCC's Form 4626: Alternative Minimum Tax—Corporations.

## AMT Tax Planning

So, what would you do if your corporation was paying alternative minimum tax this year but you didn't think it would be required to pay AMT next year? What is the marginal tax rate for a corporation that is required to pay AMT? Assuming the corporation's AMTI is not in the exemption phase-out range, its marginal tax rate is 20 percent. What is a corporation's marginal tax rate for regular tax purposes? This obviously depends on the level of income, but we'll assume it's 34 percent or higher. That is, we'll assume that the corporation's taxable income is at least $335,000. If your corporation has the ability to shift income or deductions between years, should it try to accelerate income or deductions into the AMT year? Recall that corporations pay less tax on income when marginal tax rates are lower and they receive more tax benefit when marginal tax rates are higher. As a result, a good general strategy is to, when possible, accelerate income into the AMT year and defer deductions into the non–AMT year. With this strategy, the corporation's accelerated income would be taxed at 20 percent instead of 34 percent and its deferred deductions would provide a benefit at 34 percent instead of 20 percent.

## CONCLUSION

A taxable or C corporation is a separate legal and taxpaying entity from its stockholders. Consequently, it must determine and report its own taxable income to the IRS. This chapter discussed and described the process of computing a corporation's taxable income and the associated tax liability for taxable corporations. We

**EXHIBIT 16-15**   **PCC's Form 4626**

| Form **4626** | | |
|---|---|---|
| Department of the Treasury Internal Revenue Service | | |

**Alternative Minimum Tax—Corporations**

▶ See separate instructions.
▶ Attach to the corporation's tax return.

OMB No. 1545-0175

20**09**

| Name | Employer identification number |
|---|---|
| Premier Computer Corporation | 123456789 |

**Part I**   **Alternative Minimum Tax Computation**

**Note:** *See the instructions to find out if the corporation is a small corporation exempt from the alternative minimum tax (AMT) under section 55(e).*

| | | | |
|---|---|---|---:|
| 1 | Taxable income or (loss) before net operating loss deduction | **1** | $5,150,700 |
| 2 | **Adjustments and preferences:** | | |
| a | Depreciation of post-1986 property | **2a** | 600,000 |
| b | Amortization of certified pollution control facilities. | **2b** | |
| c | Amortization of mining exploration and development costs | **2c** | |
| d | Amortization of circulation expenditures (personal holding companies only) | **2d** | |
| e | Adjusted gain or loss | **2e** | (15,000) |
| f | Long-term contracts | **2f** | |
| g | Merchant marine capital construction funds. | **2g** | |
| h | Section 833(b) deduction (Blue Cross, Blue Shield, and similar type organizations only) | **2h** | |
| i | Tax shelter farm activities (personal service corporations only) | **2i** | |
| j | Passive activities (closely held corporations and personal service corporations only) | **2j** | |
| k | Loss limitations | **2k** | |
| l | Depletion | **2l** | |
| m | Tax-exempt interest income from specified private activity bonds | **2m** | 12,000 |
| n | Intangible drilling costs | **2n** | |
| o | Other adjustments and preferences | **2o** | |
| 3 | Pre-adjustment alternative minimum taxable income (AMTI). Combine lines 1 through 2o. | **3** | 5,747,700 |
| 4 | **Adjusted current earnings (ACE) adjustment:** | | |

| | | | | |
|---|---|---|---:|---:|
| a | ACE from line 10 of the ACE worksheet in the instructions | **4a** | 5,768,700 | |
| b | Subtract line 3 from line 4a. If line 3 exceeds line 4a, enter the difference as a negative amount (see instructions). | **4b** | 21,000 | |
| c | Multiply line 4b by 75% (.75). Enter the result as a positive amount | **4c** | 15,750 | |
| d | Enter the excess, if any, of the corporation's total increases in AMTI from prior year ACE adjustments over its total reductions in AMTI from prior year ACE adjustments (see instructions). **Note:** *You* **must** *enter an amount on line 4d (even if line 4b is positive)* | **4d** | 0 | |

| | | | |
|---|---|---|---:|
| e | ACE adjustment. ● If line 4b is zero or more, enter the amount from line 4c ● If line 4b is less than zero, enter the **smaller** of line 4c or line 4d as a negative amount | **4e** | 15,750 |
| 5 | Combine lines 3 and 4e. If zero or less, stop here; the corporation does not owe any AMT | **5** | 5,763,450 |
| 6 | Alternative tax net operating loss deduction (see instructions). | **6** | |
| 7 | **Alternative minimum taxable income.** Subtract line 6 from line 5. If the corporation held a residual interest in a REMIC, see instructions | **7** | 5,763,450 |
| 8 | **Exemption phase-out** (if line 7 is $310,000 or more, skip lines 8a and 8b and enter -0- on line 8c): | | |
| a | Subtract $150,000 from line 7 (if completing this line for a member of a controlled group, see instructions). If zero or less, enter -0-    **8a** | | |
| b | Multiply line 8a by 25% (.25).    **8b** | | |
| c | Exemption. Subtract line 8b from $40,000 (if completing this line for a member of a controlled group, see instructions). If zero or less, enter -0- | **8c** | 0 |
| 9 | Subtract line 8c from line 7. If zero or less, enter -0- | **9** | 5,763,450 |
| 10 | If the corporation had qualified timber gain, complete Part II and enter the amount from line 24 here. Otherwise, multiply line 9 by 20% (.20) | **10** | 1,152,690 |
| 11 | Alternative minimum tax foreign tax credit (AMTFTC) (see instructions) | **11** | |
| 12 | Tentative minimum tax. Subtract line 11 from line 10. | **12** | 1,152,690 |
| 13 | Regular tax liability before applying all credits except the foreign tax credit | **13** | 1,751,238 |
| 14 | **Alternative minimum tax.** Subtract line 13 from line 12. If zero or less, enter -0-. Enter here and on Form 1120, Schedule J, line 3, or the appropriate line of the corporation's income tax return | **14** | $0 |

For Paperwork Reduction Act Notice, see the instructions.    Cat. No. 12955I    Form **4626** (2009)

learned that book income is the starting point for determining taxable income. Corporations adjust their book income for book-tax differences that arise because they account for many items of income and deduction differently for book purposes than they do for tax purposes. Some of these book-tax differences are temporary (the differences balance out over time) and some are permanent in nature (they don't balance out over the long-term). As we discover in the next chapter, the distinction between temporary and permanent book-tax differences is critical for corporations computing their income tax expense for financial accounting purposes under ASC 740 (formerly FAS 109).

## SUMMARY

Describe the corporate income tax formula, compare and contrast the corporate to the individual tax formula, and discuss tax considerations relating to corporations' accounting periods and accounting methods.    **LO1**

- A corporation's taxable income is gross income from all sources minus exclusions minus deductions.

- The corporate tax formula is similar to the individual formula except that corporations don't itemize deductions or deduct standard deductions. Corporations also don't deduct personal and dependency exemptions.

- Corporations may generally elect any tax year for reporting their taxable income, but the year must coincide with their financial accounting year.

- The timing of a corporation's income and deductions depends on the corporation's overall accounting method and its methods for specific transactions.

- Corporations are generally required to use the accrual overall method of accounting. However, smaller corporations may be allowed to use the cash method.

Identify common book-tax differences, distinguish between permanent and temporary differences, and compute a corporation's taxable income and regular tax liability.    **LO2**

- Corporations typically compute taxable income by starting with book income and adjusting for book-tax differences.

- Book-tax differences are favorable when they reduce taxable income relative to book income and unfavorable when they increase it.

- Book-tax differences are permanent when the amount of income or deduction items is different for book and tax purposes and the amount will not reverse in the future.

- Book-tax differences are temporary when the amount of income or deduction item is different for book and tax purposes in the current year but the same for book and tax purposes over the long-term. That is, temporary book-tax differences reverse over time.

- Common permanent book-tax differences include interest from municipal bonds (favorable), life insurance premiums on policies covering key employees (unfavorable), and one-half of meals and entertainment expense, among others.

- Nonqualified stock options granted before ASC 718's effective date generate favorable permanent book-tax differences when employees exercise them. The amount of the difference is the bargain element of the options that is deductible for tax but not for books.

- Common temporary book-tax differences include depreciation expense, gain or loss on sale of depreciable assets, bad-debt expense, purchased goodwill amortization, and warranty expense, among others.

- Stock options granted when ASC 718 applies can generate temporary and permanent book-tax differences.

- Corporations may not deduct net capital losses for tax purposes. However, they may carry them back three years and forward five years to offset capital gains in those other years.

- Corporations may carry net operating losses back two years and forward 20 years (in general, corporations may elect to carry back a 2008 or a 2009 NOL for two, three, four, or five years). They may elect to forgo the carryback.

- When computing their net operating losses for the year, corporations may not deduct net operating losses from other years or net capital losses from other years.

- Subject to limitation, corporations can deduct as the amount of money, the fair market value of capital gain property, and the adjusted basis of ordinary income property they donate to charity.

- The charitable contribution deduction for the year is limited to 10 percent of taxable income before deducting the charitable contribution, the dividends received deduction, NOL carrybacks, the domestic production activities deduction, and capital loss carrybacks. Amounts in excess of the limitation can be carried forward for up to five years.

- Corporations are allowed a deduction for dividends received to help mitigate potential triple taxation of the income distributed as a dividend. The amount of the deduction depends on the corporation's ownership in the distributing corporation. The deduction is 70 percent if the ownership is less than 20 percent; the deduction is 80 percent if the ownership is at least 20 percent but less than 80 percent; and finally, the deduction is 100 percent if the ownership is 80 percent or more.

- The dividends received deduction (DRD) is subject to a taxable income limitation. This limitation does not apply if the full DRD extends or creates a net operating loss for the corporation in the current year.

- A corporation's marginal tax rates range from 15 percent to 39 percent. High-income corporations are taxed at a flat 35 percent tax rate.

- Controlled groups are groups of corporations with common ownership. Special rules apply to limit the tax benefits (including lower marginal tax rates) of splitting large corporations into smaller corporations. Controlled groups can be parent-subsidiary controlled groups, brother-sister controlled groups, or combined groups.

**LO3** Describe a corporation's tax return reporting and estimated tax payment obligations.

- Corporations file their tax returns on Form 1120, which are due two and one-half months after the corporation's year-end. Corporations can apply for an extension of the due date for filing the return for six months.

- Small corporations report their book-tax differences on Schedule M-1 of Form 1120. Large corporations (assets of $10 million or more) report them on Schedule M-3. Schedule M-3 requires much more detail than Schedule M-1.

- Corporations pay income taxes through estimated tax payments. Each payment should be 25 percent of their required annual payment. The installments are due on the 15th day of the 4th, 6th, 9th, and 12th months of the corporation's taxable year.

- Corporations' required annual payment is the least of (1) 100 percent of their current year tax liability, (2) 100 percent of their prior year tax liability (but only if they had a positive tax liability in the prior year), or (3) 100 percent of the estimated current year tax liability using the annualized income method. Large corporations may rely on (2) only to compute their first quarter estimated payment requirement.

**LO4** Explain how to calculate a corporation's alternative minimum tax liability.

- The alternative minimum tax is a tax on a broader base than the regular tax. It ensures that corporations are not able to avoid taxes entirely by receiving tax-advantaged treatment for regular income tax items. The alternative minimum tax rate is a flat 20 percent for corporations.

- To compute alternative minimum taxable income, corporations start with regular taxable income and add preferences, add or subtract adjustments, and subtract an exemption amount. The AMT base is taxed at 20 percent to provide a tentative minimum tax. The AMT is the excess of the tentative minimum tax over the regular tax.

- Corporations receive a minimum tax credit in the amount of the alternative minimum tax they pay for the year. This credit can offset the corporation's regular tax liability to the extent it exceeds the tentative minimum tax in a future year.

# KEY TERMS

adjusted current
earnings (ACE) (16-35)

affiliated group (16-28)

alternative minimum tax (16-33)

annualized income method (16-29)

bargain element (16-10)

book or financial reporting
income (16-3)

book-tax differences (16-4)

brother-sister controlled group (16-24)

capital gain property (16-15)

capital loss carryback (16-11)

capital loss carryover (16-11)

charitable contribution limit modified
taxable income (16-16)

combined controlled group (16-24)

controlled groups (16-24)

consolidated tax return (16-28)

DRD modified taxable
income (16-19)

exercise price (16-9)

favorable book-tax
difference (16-4)

incentive stock options (16-9)

"Ms" (16-25)

M adjustments (16-25)

minimum tax credit (16-39)

net operating loss (NOL) (16-13)

net operating loss
carryback (16-13)

net operating loss carryover (16-13)

nonqualified stock options (16-9)

ordinary income property (16-15)

parent-subsidiary controlled
group (16-24)

permanent book-tax
differences (16-4)

private activity bond (16-34)

purchased goodwill (16-8)

Schedule M adjustments (16-25)

temporary book-tax
differences (16-4)

tentative minimum tax (16-38)

unfavorable book-tax
difference (16-4)

vest (16-9)

vesting period (16-10)

# DISCUSSION QUESTIONS

1. **(LO1)** In general terms, identify the similarities and differences between the corporate taxable income formula and the individual taxable income formula.

2. **(LO1)** Is a corporation's choice of its tax year independent from its year-end for financial accounting purposes?

3. **(LO1)** Can taxable corporations use the cash method of accounting? Explain.

4. **(LO2)** Briefly describe the process of computing a corporation's taxable income assuming the corporation must use GAAP to determine its book income. How might the process differ for corporations not required to use GAAP for book purposes?

5. **(LO2)** What role does a corporation's audited financial statements play in determining its taxable income?

6. **(LO2)** What is the difference between favorable and unfavorable book-tax differences?

7. **(LO2)** What is the difference between permanent and temporary book-tax differences?

8. **(LO2)** Why is it important to be able to determine whether a particular book-tax difference is permanent or temporary?

9. **(LO2)** Describe the relation between the book-tax differences associated with depreciation expense and with gain or loss on disposition of depreciable assets.

10. **(LO2)** When a corporation receives a dividend from another corporation, does the dividend generate a book-tax difference to the dividend-receiving corporation (ignore the dividends received deduction)? Explain.

11. **(LO2)** Describe how goodwill recognized in an asset acquisition leads to temporary book-tax differences.

12. **(LO2)** Describe the book-tax differences that arise from incentive stock options and nonqualified stock options granted before ASC 718 (formerly FAS 123R) became effective.

13. **(LO2)** Describe the book-tax differences that arise from incentive stock options granted after ASC 718 (formerly FAS 123R) became effective.

14. **(LO2)** Describe the book-tax differences that arise from nonqualified stock options granted after ASC 718 (formerly FAS 123R) became effective.

15. **(LO2)** How do corporations account for capital gains and losses for tax purposes? How is this different than the way individuals account for capital gains and losses?

16. **(LO2)** What are the common book-tax differences relating to accounting for capital gains and losses? Do these differences create favorable or unfavorable book-to-tax adjustments?

17. **(LO2)** What is the carryback and carryover period for a net operating loss? Does it depend on the size of the corporation? Explain.

18. **(LO2)** Is a corporation allowed to carry a net operating loss forward if it has income in prior years that it could offset with a carryback? Explain.

19. **(LO2)** What must a decision maker consider when deciding whether to carry back a net operating loss or to elect to forgo the carryback?

20. **(LO2)** A corporation commissioned an accounting firm to recalculate the way it accounted for leasing transactions. With the new calculations, the corporation was able to file amended tax returns for the past few years that increased the corporation's net operating loss carryover from $3,000,000 to $5,000,000. Was the corporation wise to pay the accountants for their work that led to the increase in the NOL carryover? What factors should be considered in making this determination?

21. **(LO2)** Compare and contrast the general rule for determining the amount of the charitable contribution if the corporation contributes capital gain property versus ordinary income property.

22. **(LO2)** Which limitations might restrict a corporation's deduction for a cash charitable contribution? Explain how to determine the amount of the limitation.

23. **(LO2)** For tax purposes, what happens to a corporation's charitable contributions that are not deducted in the current year because of the taxable income limitation?

24. **(LO2)** What are common book-tax differences relating to corporate charitable contributions? Are these differences favorable or unfavorable?

25. **(LO2)** Why does Congress provide the dividends received deduction for corporations receiving dividends?

26. **(LO2)** How does a corporation determine the percentage for its dividends received deduction? Explain.

27. **(LO2)** What limitations apply to the amount of the allowable dividends received deduction?

28. **(LO2)** Why do the marginal rates in the corporate tax rate schedule increase and then decrease before increasing again?

29. **(LO2)** Explain the controlled group rules in very general terms and indicate what type of behavior the rules are attempting to prevent in terms of computing a corporation's tax liability.

30. **(LO2)** Describe the three types of controlled groups.

31. **(LO3)** How is the Schedule M-1 similar to and different from a Schedule M-3? How does a corporation determine whether it must complete Schedule M-1 or Schedule M-3 when it completes its tax return?

32. **(LO3)** What is the due date for the corporation tax return Form 1120? Is it possible to extend the due date? Explain.

33. **(LO3)** How does a corporation determine the minimum amount of estimated tax payments it must make to avoid underpayment penalties? How are these rules different for large corporations than they are for other corporations?

34. **(LO3)** Describe the annualized income method for determining a corporation's required estimated tax payments. What advantages does this method have over other methods?

35. **(LO4)** Are any corporations exempt from the AMT? Briefly explain.

36. **(LO4)** Briefly describe the process of computing a corporation's AMT.

37. **(LO4)** What is the conceptual difference between adjustments and preference items for AMT purposes?

38. **(LO4)** What does the ACE adjustment attempt to capture? How does a corporation determine its ACE adjustment?

39. **(LO4)** What is the corporate AMT exemption? Is it available to all corporations? Briefly explain.

40. **(LO4)** How is it possible that a corporation's marginal AMT rate is greater than 20 percent if the stated AMT rate is 20 percent?

41. **(LO4)** Does a corporation pay the AMT in addition to or instead of the regular tax? Briefly explain.

42. **(LO4)** How does a corporation compute its minimum tax credit? How does a minimum tax credit benefit a corporation?

43. **(LO4)** What basic tax planning strategies might a corporation that is expected to owe AMT this year but not next year engage in? How would those strategies change if the corporation expected to be in AMT next year but not in the current year?                                                        ■ planning

## PROBLEMS

44. **(LO1)** LNS corporation reports book income of $2,000,000. Included in the $2,000,000 is $15,000 of tax-exempt interest income. LNS reports $1,345,000 in ordinary and necessary business expenses. What is LNS corporation's taxable income for the year?

45. **(LO1)** ATW corporation currently uses the FIFO method of accounting for its inventory for book and tax purposes. Its beginning inventory for the current year was $8,000,000. Its ending inventory for the current year was $7,000,000. If ATW had been using the LIFO method of accounting for its inventory, its beginning inventory would have been $7,000,000 and its ending inventory would have been $5,500,000. Assume ATW corporation's marginal tax rate is 34 percent.

    a. How much more in taxes did ATW corporation pay for the current year because it used the FIFO method of accounting for inventory than it would have paid if it had used the LIFO method?

    b. Why would ATW use the FIFO method of accounting if doing so causes it to pay more taxes on a present value basis? (Note that the tax laws don't allow corporations to use the LIFO method of accounting for inventory unless they also use the LIFO method of accounting for inventory for book purposes.)

46. **(LO1)** ELS corporation is about to begin its sixth year of existence. Assume that ELS reported gross receipts for each of its first five years of existence for Scenarios A, B, and C as follows:

| Year of Existence | Scenario A | Scenario B | Scenario C |
|---|---|---|---|
| 1 | $4,000,000 | $3,000,000 | $5,500,000 |
| 2 | $5,000,000 | $5,000,000 | $5,000,000 |
| 3 | $5,900,000 | $7,500,000 | $4,750,000 |
| 4 | $6,000,000 | $6,000,000 | $5,000,000 |
| 5 | $4,500,000 | $4,500,000 | $5,250,000 |

a. In what years is ELS allowed to use the cash method of accounting under Scenario A?

b. In what years is ELS allowed to use the cash method of accounting under Scenario B?

c. In what years is ELS allowed to use the cash method of accounting under Scenario C?

47. **(LO2)** On its year 1 financial statements, Seatax Corporation, an accrual-method taxpayer, reported federal income tax expense of $570,000. On its year 1 tax return, it reported a tax liability of $650,000. During year 1, Seatax made estimated tax payments of $700,000. What book-tax difference, if any, associated with its federal income tax expense should Seatax have reported when computing its year 1 taxable income? Is the difference favorable or unfavorable? Is it temporary or permanent?

48. **(LO2)** Assume Maple Corp. has just completed the third year of its existence (year 3). The table below indicates Maple's ending book inventory for each year and the additional §263A costs it was required to include in its ending inventory. Maple immediately expensed these costs for book purposes. In year 2, Maple sold all of its year 1 ending inventory, and in year 3 it sold all of its year 2 ending inventory.

|  | Year 1 | Year 2 | Year 3 |
|---|---|---|---|
| Ending book inventory | $2,400,000 | $2,700,000 | $2,040,000 |
| Additional §263A costs | 60,000 | 70,000 | 40,000 |
| Ending tax inventory | $2,460,000 | $2,770,000 | $2,080,000 |

a. What book-tax difference associated with its inventory did Maple report in year 1? Was the difference favorable or unfavorable? Was it permanent or temporary?

b. What book-tax difference associated with its inventory did Maple report in year 2? Was the difference favorable or unfavorable? Was it permanent or temporary?

c. What book-tax difference associated with its inventory did Maple report in year 3? Was the difference favorable or unfavorable? Was it permanent or temporary?

49. **(LO2)** JDog corporation owns stock in Oscar Inc. JDog received a $10,000 dividend from Oscar Inc. What temporary book-tax difference associated with the dividend will JDog report for the year in the following alternative scenarios?

a. JDog owns 5 percent of the Oscar Inc. stock. Oscar's income for the year was $500,000.

b. JDog owns 40 percent of the Oscar Inc. stock. Oscar's income for the year was $500,000.

50. **(LO2)** On July 1 of year 1, Riverside Corp. (RC), a calendar-year taxpayer, acquired the assets of another business in a taxable acquisition. When the purchase price was allocated to the assets purchased, RC determined it had purchased $1,200,000 of goodwill for both book and tax purposes. At the end of year 1, the auditors for RC determined that the goodwill had not been impaired during the year. In year 2, however, the auditors concluded that $200,000 of the goodwill had been impaired, and they required RC to write down the goodwill by $200,000 for book purposes.

a. What book-tax difference associated with its goodwill should RC report in year 1? Is it favorable or unfavorable? Is it permanent or temporary?

b. What book-tax difference associated with its goodwill should RC report in year 2? Is it favorable or unfavorable? Is it permanent or temporary?

51. **(LO2)** Assume that on January 1, year 1, ABC Inc. issued 5,000 stock options with an estimated value of $10 per option. Each option entitles the owner to purchase one share of ABC stock for $25 a share (the per share price of ABC stock on January 1, year 1, when the options were granted). The options vest 50 percent at the end of the day on December 31, year 1, and 50 percent at the end of the day on December 31, year 2. All 5,000 stock options were exercised in year 3 when the ABC stock was valued at $31 per share. Identify ABC's year 1, 2, and 3 tax deductions and book-tax differences (indicate whether permanent and/or temporary) associated with the stock options under the following alternative scenarios:

    a. The stock options are incentive stock options and ASC 718 (formerly FAS 123R) does not apply to the options.
    b. The stock options are nonqualified stock options and ASC 718 does not apply to the options.
    c. The stock options are incentive stock options and ASC 718 applies to the options.
    d. The stock options are nonqualified stock options and ASC 718 applies to the options.

52. **(LO2)** Assume that on January 1, year 1, XYZ Corp. issued 1,000 nonqualified stock options with an estimated value of $4 per option. Each option entitles the owner to purchase one share of XYZ stock for $14 a share (the per share price of XYZ stock on January 1, year 1, when the options were granted). The options vest 25 percent a year (on December 31) for four years (beginning with year 1). All 500 stock options that had vested to that point were exercised in year 3 when the XYZ stock was valued at $20 per share. No other options were exercised in year 3 or year 4. Identify XYZ's year 1, 2, 3, and 4 tax deductions and book-tax difference (identify as permanent and/or temporary) associated with the stock options under the following alternative scenarios:

    a. ASC 718 (formerly FAS 123R) does not apply to the stock options.
    b. ASC 718 applies to the stock options.

53. **(LO2)** What book-tax differences in year 1 and year 2 associated with its capital gains and losses would ABD Inc. report in the following alternative scenarios? Identify each book-tax difference as favorable or unfavorable and as permanent or temporary.

    a.

    |                | Year 1    | Year 2   |
    |----------------|-----------|----------|
    | Capital gains  | $20,000   | $5,000   |
    | Capital losses | 8,000     | 0        |

    b.

    |                | Year 1    | Year 2   |
    |----------------|-----------|----------|
    | Capital gains  | $ 8,000   | $ 5,000  |
    | Capital losses | 20,000    | 0        |

    c.

    |                | Year 1    | Year 2   |
    |----------------|-----------|----------|
    | Capital gains  | $    0    | $50,000  |
    | Capital losses | 25,000    | 30,000   |

    d.

    |                | Year 1    | Year 2   |
    |----------------|-----------|----------|
    | Capital gains  | $    0    | $40,000  |
    | Capital losses | 25,000    | 0        |

e. Answer for year 6 only.

|  | Year 1 | Years 2–5 | Year 6 |
|---|---|---|---|
| Capital gains | $    0 | $    0 | $15,000 |
| Capital losses | 10,000 | 0 | 0 |

f. Answer for year 7 only.

|  | Year 1 | Years 2–6 | Year 7 |
|---|---|---|---|
| Capital gains | $    0 | $    0 | $15,000 |
| Capital losses | 10,000 | 0 | 0 |

54. **(LO2)** What book-tax differences in year 1 and year 2 associated with its capital gains and losses would DEF Inc. report in the following alternative scenarios? Identify each book-tax difference as favorable or unfavorable and as permanent or temporary.

   a. In year 1, DEF recognized a loss of $15,000 on land that it had held for investment. In year 1, it also recognized a $30,000 gain on equipment it had purchased a few years ago. The equipment sold for $50,000 and had an adjusted basis of $20,000. DEF had deducted $40,000 of depreciation on the equipment. In year 2, DEF recognized a capital loss of $2,000.

   b. In year 1, DEF recognized a loss of $15,000 on land that it had held for investment. It also recognized a $20,000 gain on equipment it had purchased a few years ago. The equipment sold for $50,000 and had an adjusted basis of $30,000. DEF had deducted $15,000 of tax depreciation on the equipment.

55. **(LO2)** MWC Corp. is currently in the sixth year of its existence (2010). In 2005–2009, it reported the following income and (losses) (before net operating loss carryovers or carrybacks).

   > 2005: ($ 70,000)
   > 2006: ($ 30,000)
   > 2007: $ 60,000
   > 2008: $140,000
   > 2009: ($ 25,000)
   > 2010: $300,000.

   a. Assuming the original facts and that MWC elects to not carry back NOLs, what was MWC's 2008 taxable income?

   b. If MWC does not elect to forgo any NOL carrybacks, what is its 2010 taxable income after the NOL deduction?

   c. If MWC always elects to forgo NOL carrybacks, what is its 2010 taxable income after the NOL deduction? What is its 2010 book-tax difference associated with its NOL? Is it favorable or unfavorable? Is it permanent or temporary?

**■ planning**    56. **(LO2)** WCC Inc. has a current year (2010) net operating loss of $100,000. It is trying to determine whether it should carry back the loss or whether it should elect to forgo the carryback. How would you advise WCC in each of the following alternative situations (ignore the time value of money in your computations)?

a.

| | 2008 | 2009 | 2011 |
|---|---|---|---|
| Taxable income | $ 30,000 | $ 0 | $ 300,000 |

b.

| | 2008 | 2009 | 2011 |
|---|---|---|---|
| Taxable income | $900,000 | $60,000 | $ 100,000 |

c.

| | 2008 | 2009 | 2011 |
|---|---|---|---|
| Taxable income | $900,000 | $60,000 | $5,000,000 |

d.

| | 2008 | 2009 | 2011 |
|---|---|---|---|
| Taxable income | $ 50,000 | $20,000 | $2,000,000 |

57. **(LO2)** Assume that in year 1 Hill Corporation reported a net operating loss of $10,000 that it carried forward to year 2. In year 1, Hill also reported a net capital loss of $3,000 that it carried forward to year 2. In year 3, ignoring any carryovers from other years, Hill reported a loss for tax purposes of $50,000. The current year loss includes a $12,000 net capital gain. What is Hill's year 2 net operating loss?

58. **(LO2)** Golf Corp. (GC), a calendar-year accrual-method corporation, held its directors meeting on December 15 of year 1. During the meeting the board of directors authorized GC to pay a $75,000 charitable contribution to the Tiger Woods Foundation, a qualifying charity.

   a. If GC actually pays $50,000 of this contribution on January 15 of year 2 and the remaining $25,000 on March 15 of year 2, what book-tax difference will it report associated with the contribution in year 1 (assume the 10 percent limitation does not apply)? Is it favorable or unfavorable? Is it permanent or temporary?

   b. Assuming the same facts as in part a, what book-tax difference will GC report in year 2 (assuming the 10 percent limitation does not apply)? Is it favorable or unfavorable?

   c. If GC actually pays $50,000 of this contribution on January 15 of year 2 and the remaining $25,000 on April 15 of year 2, what book-tax difference will it report associated with the contribution in year 1 (assume the 10 percent limitation does not apply)? Is it favorable or unfavorable? Is it permanent or temporary?

   d. Assuming the same facts as in part c, what book-tax difference will GC report in year 2 (assuming the 10 percent limitation does not apply)? Is it favorable or unfavorable?

59. **(LO2)** In year 1 (the current year), OCC Corp. made a charitable donation of $200,000 to the Tiger Woods Foundation (a qualifying charity). For the year, OCC reported taxable income of $1,500,000 before deducting any charitable contributions, before deducting its $20,000 dividends received deduction, and before deducting its $40,000 NOL carryover from last year.

   a. What amount of the $200,000 donation is OCC allowed to deduct for tax purposes in year 1?

   b. In year 2, OCC did not make any charitable contributions. It reported taxable income of $300,000 before any charitable contribution deductions and before a $15,000 dividends received deduction. What book-tax difference associated with the charitable contributions will OCC report in year 2? Is the difference favorable or unfavorable? Is it permanent or temporary?

c. Assume the original facts and those provided in part b. In years 3, 4, and 5, OCC reported taxable losses of $50,000. Finally, in year 6 it reported $1,000,000 in taxable income before any charitable contribution deductions. It did not have any dividends received deduction. OCC did not actually make any charitable donations in year 6. What book-tax difference associated with charitable contributions will OCC report in year 6?

60. **(LO2)** In year 1 (the current year), LAA Inc. made a charitable donation of $100,000 to the American Red Cross (a qualifying charity). For the year, LAA reported taxable income of $550,000, which included a $100,000 charitable contribution deduction (before limitation), a $50,000 dividends received deduction, a $20,000 domestic production activities deduction, and a $10,000 net operating loss carryover from year 0. What is LAA Inc.'s charitable contribution deduction for year 1?

■
**research**
■■

61. **(LO2)** Coattail Corporation (CC) manufactures and sells women and children's coats. This year, CC donated 1,000 coats to a qualified public charity. The charity distributed the coats to needy women and children throughout the region. At the time of the contribution, the fair market value of each coat was $80. Determine the amount of CC's charitable contribution (the taxable income limitation does not apply) for the coats assuming the following:

a. CC's adjusted basis in each coat was $30.

b. CC's adjusted basis in each coat was $10.

■
**research**
■■

62. **(LO2)** Maple Corp. owns several pieces of highly valued paintings that are on display in the corporation's headquarters. This year, it donated one of the paintings valued at $100,000 (adjusted basis of $25,000) to a local museum for the museum to display. What is the amount of Maple Corp.'s charitable contribution deduction for the painting (assuming income limitations do not apply)? What would be Maple's deduction if the museum sold the painting one month after it received it from Maple?

63. **(LO2)** Riverbend Inc. received a $200,000 dividend from stock it held in Hobble Corporation. Riverbend's taxable income is $2,100,000 before deducting the dividends received deduction (DRD), a $40,000 NOL carryover, a $10,000 domestic production activities deduction, and a $100,000 charitable contribution.

a. What is Riverbend's deductible DRD assuming it owns 10 percent of Hobble Corporation?

b. Assuming the facts in part a, what is Riverbend's marginal tax rate on the dividend?

c. What is Riverbend's DRD assuming it owns 60 percent of Hobble Corporation?

d. Assuming the facts in part c, what is Riverbend's marginal tax rate on the dividend?

e. What is Riverbend's DRD assuming it owns 85 percent of Hobble Corporation (and is part of the same affiliated group)?

f. Assuming the facts in part e, what is Riverbend's marginal tax rate on the dividend?

64. **(LO2)** Wasatch Corp. (WC) received a $200,000 dividend from Tager Corporation (TC). WC owns 15 percent of the TC stock. Compute WC's deductible DRD in each of the following situations:

a. WC's taxable income (loss) without the dividend income or the DRD is $10,000.

b. WC's taxable income (loss) without the dividend income or the DRD is ($10,000).

   c. WC's taxable income (loss) without the dividend income or the DRD is ($59,000).

   d. WC's taxable income (loss) without the dividend income or the DRD is ($61,000).

   e. WC's taxable income (loss) without the dividend income or the DRD is ($500,000).

   f. What is WC's book-tax difference associated with its DRD in part a? Is the difference favorable or unfavorable? Is it permanent or temporary?

65. **(LO2)** Compute SWK Inc.'s tax liability for each of the following scenarios:

   a. SWK's taxable income is $60,000.

   b. SWK's taxable income is $275,000.

   c. SWK's taxable income is $15,500,000.

   d. SWK's taxable income for the year is $50,000,000.

66. **(LO2)** ABC's taxable income for the year is $200,000 and CBA's taxable income for the year is $400,000. Compute the combined tax liability of the two corporations assuming the following:

   a. Amanda, Jermaine, and O'Neil each own one-third of the stock of ABC and CBA.

   b. Amanda, Jermaine, and O'Neil each own one-third of the stock of ABC and Amanda and Dustin each own 50 percent of the stock of CBA.

   c. ABC owns 85 percent of CBA's stock on the last day of the year. ABC and CBA file separate (as opposed to consolidated) tax returns.

67. **(LO2)** ABC's taxable income for the year is $25,000 and CBA's taxable income for the year is $10,000,000. Compute the combined tax liability of the two corporations assuming the following:

   a. Amanda, Jermaine, and O'Neil each own one-third of the stock of ABC and CBA.

   b. Amanda, Jermaine, and O'Neil each own one-third of the stock of ABC and Amanda and Dustin each own 50 percent of the stock of CBA.

68. **(LO3)** Last year, TBA Corporation, a calendar-year taxpayer, reported a tax liability of $100,000. TBA confidently anticipates a current year tax liability of $240,000. What minimum estimated tax payments should TBA make for the first, second, third, and fourth quarters respectively (ignore the annualized income method) assuming the following:

   a. TBA is not considered to be a large corporation for estimated tax purposes.

   b. TBA is considered to be a large corporation for estimated tax purposes.

69. **(LO3)** Last year, BTA Corporation, a calendar-year taxpayer, reported a net operating loss of $10,000 and a $0 tax liability. BTA confidently anticipates a current year tax liability of $240,000. What minimum estimated tax payments should BTA make for the first, second, third, and fourth quarters respectively (ignore the annualized income method) assuming the following:

   a. BTA is not considered to be a large corporation for estimated tax purposes.

   b. BTA is considered to be a large corporation for estimated tax purposes.

70. **(LO3)** For the current year, LNS corporation reported the following taxable income at the end of its first, second, and third quarters. What are LNS's

minimum first, second, third, and fourth quarter estimated tax payments determined using the annualized income method?

| Quarter-end | Cumulative Taxable Income |
|---|---|
| First | $1,000,000 |
| Second | $1,600,000 |
| Third | $2,400,000 |

**■ planning**    71. **(LO3)**  Last year, JL Corporation's tax liability was $900,000. For the current year, JL Corporation reported the following taxable income at the end of its first, second, and third quarters (see table below). What are JL's minimum required first, second, third, and fourth quarter estimated tax payments (ignore the actual current year tax safe harbor)?

| Quarter-end | Cumulative Taxable Income |
|---|---|
| First | $ 500,000 |
| Second | $1,250,000 |
| Third | $2,250,000 |

72. **(LO3)**  Last year, Cougar Corp. (CC) reported a net operating loss of $25,000. In the current year, CC expected its current year tax liability to be $440,000 so it made four equal estimated tax payments of $110,000 each. Cougar closed its books at the end of each quarter. The following schedule reports CC's taxable income at the end of each quarter:

| Quarter-end | Cumulative Taxable Income |
|---|---|
| First | $ 300,000 |
| Second | $ 700,000 |
| Third | $1,000,000 |
| Fourth | $1,470,588 |

CC's current year tax liability on $1,470,588 of taxable income is $480,000. Does CC owe underpayment penalties on its estimated tax payments? If so, for which quarters does it owe the penalty?

73. **(LO2, LO4)**  For the current year, CCP Inc. received the following interest income:

- $12,000 interest from Irvine City bonds: Bonds issued in 2006 and proceeds used to fund public schools.
- $20,000 interest from Fluor Corporation bonds.
- $8,000 interest from Mission Viejo City: Bonds issued in 2008 and proceeds used to lure new business to the area.
- $6,000 interest from U.S. Treasury notes.

a.  What amount of this interest income is taxable to CCP?
b.  What amount of interest should CCP report as a preference item when calculating its alternative minimum tax liability?

74. **(LO4)**  On January 2 of year 1, XYZ Corp. acquired a piece of machinery for $50,000. The recovery period for the assets is seven years for both regular tax and AMT purposes. XYZ uses the double declining balance method to compute its tax depreciation on this asset, and it uses 150 percent declining balance to determine its depreciation for AMT purposes. The following

schedule projects the tax and AMT depreciation on the asset until it is fully depreciated:

| | Tax | | AMT | |
| --- | --- | --- | --- | --- |
| Year | Depreciation | Basis at End of Year | Depreciation | Basis at End of Year |
| 1 | $ 7,145 | $42,855 | $5,355 | $44,645 |
| 2 | $12,245 | $30,610 | $9,565 | $35,080 |
| 3 | $ 8,745 | $21,865 | $7,515 | $27,565 |
| 4 | $ 6,245 | $15,620 | $6,125 | $21,440 |
| 5 | $ 4,465 | $11,155 | $6,125 | $15,315 |
| 6 | $ 4,460 | $ 6,695 | $6,125 | $ 9,190 |
| 7 | $ 4,465 | $ 2,230 | $6,125 | $ 3,065 |
| 8 | $ 2,230 | $ 0 | $3,065 | $ 0 |

a. What AMT adjustment relating to depreciation on the equipment will XYZ make for year 1? Is the adjustment positive (unfavorable) or negative (favorable)?

b. What AMT adjustment relating to depreciation on the equipment will XYZ make for year 5? Is the adjustment positive or negative?

c. If XYZ sells the equipment for $30,000 at the beginning of year 3, what AMT adjustment will it make in year 3 to reflect the difference in the gain or loss for regular tax and for AMT purposes on the sale (assume no year 3 depreciation)? Is the adjustment positive or negative?

75. **(LO4)** During the current year, CRS Inc. reported the following tax-related information:

- $10,000 tax-exempt interest from public activity bonds issued before 2009.
- $16,000 tax-exempt interest from private activity bonds issued before 2009.
- $150,000 death benefit from life insurance policies on officers' lives.
- $6,000 70 percent dividends received deduction.
- $12,000 80 percent dividends received deduction.
- $50,000 bad debt expense.
- $20,000 tax amortization expense relating to organizational expenditures.
- $80,000 gain included in taxable income under the installment method (sale occurred in previous year).

What is CRS's current year ACE adjustment?

76. **(LO4)** During the current year, ELS Corporation reported the following tax-related information:

- $5,000 tax-exempt interest from public activity bonds issued in 2008.
- $45,000 gain included in taxable income under the installment method. The installment sale occurred two years ago.

a. What is ELS Corp.'s current year ACE adjustment assuming its cumulative ACE adjustment as of the beginning of the year is a positive $12,000?

b. What is ELS Corp.'s current year ACE adjustment assuming its cumulative ACE adjustment as of the beginning of the year is a positive $80,000?

77. **(LO4)** During the current year, FTP Corporation reported regular taxable income of $500,000. FTP used the following information in its tax-related computations:

- $12,000 interest from Irvine City bonds: Bonds issued in 2007 and proceeds used to fund public schools.

- $20,000 interest from Fluor Corporation bonds.
- $8,000 interest from Mission Viejo City bonds: Bonds issued in 2006 and proceeds used to lure new business to the area.
- $6,000 interest from U.S. Treasury notes.
- $30,000 dividends received from General Electric Corporation (FTP owns less than 1 percent of GE stock).
- $10,000 dividends received from Hobble Inc. (FTP owns 25 percent of Hobble Inc.).
- $25,000 charitable contribution to the Tiger Woods Foundation.
- $60,000 AMT depreciation (regular tax depreciation was $70,000).
- $50,000 ACE depreciation.
- $7,000 AMT gain on disposition of assets (regular tax gain on the disposition of assets was $8,000).
- $5,000 ACE gain on disposition of assets.

a. What is FTP's ACE adjustment for the current year? Is it positive or negative?

b. What is FTP's alternative minimum tax base?

c. What is FTP's alternative minimum tax liability, if any?

78. **(LO4)** What is WSS Corporation's AMT base in each of the following alternative scenarios?

a. WSS's AMTI is $50,000.

b. WSS's AMTI is $175,000.

c. WSS's AMTI is $300,000.

d. WSS's AMTI is $1,000,000.

■ **planning**    79. **(LO4)** Assume CDA corporation must pay the AMT for the current year. It is considering entering into a transaction that will generate $20,000 of income for the current year. What is CDA's after-tax benefit of receiving this income in each of the following alternative scenarios?

a. CDA's AMTI before the transaction is $50,000.

b. CDA's AMTI before the transaction is $140,000.

c. CDA's AMTI before the transaction is $200,000.

d. CDA's AMTI before the transaction is $1,000,000.

■ **planning**    80. **(LO4)** Assume JJ Inc. must pay the AMT for the current year. Near the end of the year, JJ is considering making a charitable contribution of $20,000. What is its after-tax cost of the contribution under each of the following alternative scenarios?

a. JJ's AMTI before the transaction is $50,000.

b. JJ's AMTI before the transaction is $160,000.

c. JJ's AMTI before the transaction is $200,000.

d. JJ's AMTI before the transaction is $1,000,000.

81. **(LO4)** Compute ACC Inc.'s tentative minimum tax (TMT), alternative minimum tax (AMT), and minimum tax credit (MTC) in each of the following alternative scenarios:

a. ACC's alternative minimum tax base is $500,000 and its regular tax liability is $80,000.

b. ACC's alternative minimum tax base is $300,000 and its regular tax liability is $80,000.

c. ACC's alternative minimum tax base is $1,000,000 and its regular tax liability is $250,000.

82. **(LO4)** In year 1, GSL Corp.'s alternative minimum tax base was $2,000,000 and its regular tax liability is $350,000.

   a. What is GSL's total tax liability for years 1, 2, 3, and 4 (by year) assuming the following?

      Year 2: AMT base $600,000; Regular tax liability $100,000.

      Year 3: AMT base $500,000; Regular tax liability $160,000.

      Year 4: AMT base $1,000,000; Regular tax liability $150,000.

   b. What, if any, minimum tax credit does GSL have at the end of year 4?

83. **(LO4)** In year 1, Lazy corporation reported a $500,000 net operating loss for regular tax purposes and a $450,000 net operating loss for alternative minimum tax purposes (called an *alternative tax net operating loss*). In year 2, Lazy reported $450,000 of taxable income before deducting its net operating loss carryover from year 1 (it elected to forgo the net operating loss carryback). It also reported $450,000 of alternative minimum taxable income before taking the alternative tax net operating loss carryover into account (it did not report any preference or adjustments in year 2). (Note that, subject to certain limitations, alternative tax NOLs are deducted from AMTI in the process of determining the alternative minimum tax.) What is Lazy Corporation's year 2 tax liability? Assume Lazy did not have any MTC carryover from a prior year.

## COMPREHENSIVE PROBLEMS

84. Compute MV Corp.'s 2010 taxable income given the following information relating to its year 1 activities. Also, compute MV's Schedule M-1 assuming that MV's federal income tax expense for book purposes is $100,000.

- Gross profit from inventory sales of $500,000 (no book-tax differences).
- Dividends MV received from 25 percent-owned corporation of $100,000.
- Expenses *other than* DRD, charitable contribution (CC), net operating loss (NOL), and domestic production activities deduction (DPAD) are $350,000 (no book-tax differences).
- NOL carryover from prior year of $10,000.
- Cash charitable contribution of $120,000.
- Domestic production activities deduction of $5,000 (wage limitation does not apply).

85. Compute HC Inc.'s current year taxable income given the following information relating to its 2010 activities. Also, compute HC's Schedule M-1 assuming that HC's federal income tax expense for book purposes is $30,000.

- Gross profit from inventory sales of $310,000 (no book-tax differences).
- Dividends HC received from 28 percent-owned corporation of $120,000 (this is also HC's pro rata share of corporation's earnings).
- Expenses *other than* DRD, charitable contribution (CC), net operating loss (NOL), and domestic production activities deduction (DPAD) are $300,000 (no book-tax differences).
- NOL carryover from prior year of $12,000.
- Cash charitable contribution of $50,000.
- Domestic production activities deduction of $4,000 (wage limitation does not apply).

86. Timpanogos Inc. is an accrual-method calendar-year corporation. For 2010, it reported financial statement income after taxes of $1,149,000.

Timpanogos provided the following information relating to its 2010 activities:

| | |
|---|---:|
| Life insurance proceeds as a result of CEO's death | $ 200,000 |
| Revenue from sales (for both book and tax purposes) | 2,000,000 |
| Premiums paid on the key-person life insurance policies. The policies have no cash surrender value. | 21,000 |
| Charitable contributions | 180,000 |
| Overhead costs that were expensed for book purposes but are included in ending inventory for tax purposes under §263A | 50,000 |
| Overhead costs that were expensed for book purposes in 2009 but were included in 2009 ending inventory. All 2009 ending inventory was sold in 2010. | 60,000 |
| Cost of goods sold for book purposes | 300,000 |
| Interest income on private activity tax-exempt bonds issued in 2004. | 40,000 |
| Interest paid on loan obtained to purchase tax-exempt bonds | 45,000 |
| Rental income payments received and earned in 2010 | 15,000 |
| Rental income payments received in 2009 but earned in 2010 | 10,000 |
| Rental income payments received in 2010 but not earned by year-end | 30,000 |
| MACRS depreciation | 55,000 |
| Book depreciation | 25,000 |
| Alternative minimum tax depreciation | 50,000 |
| Net capital loss | 45,000 |
| Federal income tax expense for books in 2010 | 500,000 |

Timpanogos did not qualify for the domestic production activities deduction.

**Required:**

    a. Reconcile book income to taxable income for Timpanogos Inc. Be sure to start with book income and identify all of the adjustments necessary to arrive at taxable income.

    b. Identify each book-tax difference as either permanent or temporary.

    c. Complete Schedule M-1 for Timpanogos.

    d. Compute Timpanogos Inc.'s regular tax liability for 2010.

    e. Determine Timpanogos's alternative minimum tax, if any.

87. XYZ is a calendar-year corporation that began business on January 1, 2010. For 2010, it reported the following information in its current year audited income statement. Notes with important tax information are provided below.

**Required:**

Identify the book-to-tax adjustments for XYZ.

    a. Reconcile book income to taxable income and identify each book-tax difference as temporary or permanent.

    b. Compute XYZ's regular income tax liability.

    c. Complete XYZ's Schedule M-1.

    d. Complete XYZ's Form 1120, page 1 (use 2009 form if 2010 form is unavailable). Ignore estimated tax penalties when completing this form.

    e. Compute XYZ's alternative minimum tax, if any.

f.  Complete Form 4626 for XYZ (use 2009 form if 2010 form is unavailable).

g.  Determine the quarters for which XYZ is subject to underpayment of estimated taxes penalties (see estimated tax information below).

| XYZ Corp. Income Statement for Current Year | Book Income | Book to Tax Adjustments (Dr.) | Cr. | Taxable Income |
|---|---|---|---|---|
| Revenue from sales | $40,000,000 | | | |
| Cost of goods sold | (27,000,000) | | | |
| Gross profit | $13,000,000 | | | |
| Other income: | | | | |
| Income from investment in corporate stock | 300,000[1] | | | |
| Interest income | 20,000[2] | | | |
| Capital gains (losses) | (4,000) | | | |
| Gain or loss from disposition of fixed assets | 3,000[3] | | | |
| Miscellaneous income | 50,000 | | | |
| Gross Income | $13,369,000 | | | |
| Expenses: | | | | |
| Compensation | (7,500,000)[4] | | | |
| Stock option compensation | (200,000)[5] | | | |
| Advertising | (1,350,000) | | | |
| Repairs and maintenance | (75,000) | | | |
| Rent | (22,000) | | | |
| Bad debt expense | (41,000)[6] | | | |
| Depreciation | (1,400,000)[7] | | | |
| Warranty expenses | (70,000)[8] | | | |
| Charitable donations | (500,000)[9] | | | |
| Meals and entertainment | (18,000) | | | |
| Goodwill impairment | (30,000)[10] | | | |
| Organizational expenditures | (44,000)[11] | | | |
| Other expenses | (140,000)[12] | | | |
| Total expenses | ($11,390,000) | | | |
| Income before taxes | $1,979,000 | | | |
| Provision for income taxes | (720,000)[13] | | | |
| Net Income after taxes | $1,259,000[14] | | | |

## Notes:

1.  XYZ owns 30 percent of the outstanding Hobble Corp. (HC) stock. Hobble Corp. reported $1,000,000 of income for the year. XYZ accounted for its investment in HC under the equity method and it recorded its pro rata share of HC's earnings for the year. HC also distributed a $200,000 dividend to XYZ.
2.  Of the $20,000 interest income, $5,000 was from a City of Seattle bond (issued in 2007) that was used to fund public activities, $7,000 was from a Tacoma City bond (issued in 2008) used to fund private activities, $6,000 was from a fully taxable corporate bond, and the remaining $2,000 was from a money market account.
3.  This gain is from equipment that XYZ purchased in February and sold in December (that is, it does not qualify as §1231 gain).
4.  This includes total officer compensation of $2,500,000 (no one officer received more than $1,000,000 compensation).
5.  This amount is the portion of incentive stock option compensation that vested during the year (recipients are officers).
6.  XYZ actually wrote off $27,000 of its accounts receivable as uncollectible.
7.  Regular tax depreciation was $1,900,000 and AMT (and ACE) depreciation was $1,700,000.
8.  In the current year, XYZ did not make any actual payments on warranties it provided to customers.
9.  XYZ made $500,000 of cash contributions to qualified charities during the year.
10. On July 1 of this year XYZ acquired the assets of another business. In the process it acquired $300,000 of goodwill. At the end of the year, XYZ wrote off $30,000 of the goodwill as impaired.
11. XYZ expensed all of its organizational expenditures for book purposes. It expensed the maximum amount of organizational expenditures allowed for tax purposes.
12. The other expenses do not contain any items with book-tax differences.

13. This is an estimated tax provision (federal tax expense) for the year. (In a subsequent class period, we will learn how to compute the correct tax provision.) Assume that XYZ is not subject to state income taxes.

14. XYZ calculated that its domestic production activities deduction (DPAD) is $90,000. This amount is not included on the audited income statement numbers.

### Estimated Tax Information:

XYZ made four equal estimated tax payments totaling $480,000. Assume for purposes of estimated tax liabilities, XYZ was in existence in 2009 and it reported a tax liability of $800,000. During 2010, XYZ determined its taxable income at the end of each of the four quarters as follows:

| Quarter-end | Cumulative taxable income (loss) |
|---|---|
| First | $ 350,000 |
| Second | $ 800,000 |
| Third | $1,000,000 |

Finally, assume that XYZ is not a large corporation for purposes of estimated tax calculations.

**KAPLAN** CPA REVIEW

## KAPLAN CPA SIMULATIONS

**Please visit the Online Learning Center**   (www.mhhe.com/spilker2011) to access the following Kaplan CPA Simulation:

The simulation for **Kimberly Co.** covers corporate income tax issues, including taxable and deductible amounts; reportable amounts; AMT; and dividends.

**Please visit the Online Learning Center**   (www.mhhe.com/spilker2011) to access the following Kaplan CPA Simulation:

The simulation for **Clark Co.** covers corporate tax and partnerships, including filing status; book-to-tax reconciliation; transactions with owners; and the tax impact of various partnership items.

# 17

# Accounting for Income Taxes

## Learning Objectives

**Upon completing this chapter, you should be able to:**

**LO 1** Explain the objectives behind FASB ASC Topic 740 *Income Taxes* and the income tax provision process.

■

**LO 2** Calculate the current and deferred income tax expense or benefit components of a company's income tax provision.

■

**LO 3** Recall what a valuation allowance represents and describe the process by which it is determined.

■

**LO 4** Explain how a company accounts for its uncertain income tax positions under FASB ASC Topic 740 (formerly FASB Interpretation (FIN) No. 48, *Accounting for Uncertainty in Income Taxes*).

■

**LO 5** Recognize the different components of a company's disclosure of its income tax accounts in the financial statements and footnotes and comprehend how a company computes and discloses the components of its "effective tax rate."

E lise felt a great sense of accomplishment when she completed the federal income tax return for Premiere Computer Corporation (PCC). She was glad the return was filed on time and did not need to be extended. With the tax return filed, Elise was assigned to help the PCC tax department compute the federal income tax provision for the company's soon to be published income statement and to determine the correct amounts in the company's income-tax-related balance sheet accounts. She also was given the responsibility to help prepare the income tax note to the financial statements.[1]

Elise was aware that, as a result of more stringent independence requirements imposed by the Sarbanes-Oxley Act, her colleagues in the tax department were getting a lot of new engagements to help prepare the income tax provision for nonaudit clients. In fact, her firm now considered accounting for income taxes to be a "core competency" for all tax staff. Elise even heard that individuals who understood the nuances of accounting for income taxes were being called the new "rock stars" of accounting.[2] Having recently attended firm training on accounting for income taxes, which was now required of all tax staff, Elise was eager to apply her new knowledge to an actual client situation. She knew that developing her skill set in this complex topic would make her more valuable to her firm and her clients.

*to be continued . . .*

### Storyline Summary

#### Elise Brandon

| | |
|---|---|
| *Employment status:* | Tax associate for a large public accounting firm. |

Assigned to prepare the federal income tax provision and income-tax-related balance sheet accounts and footnote disclosures for Premiere Computer Corporation, a nonaudit client.

#### Premiere Computer Corporation

Medium-sized publicly traded company.

Manufactures and sells computer-related equipment.

Calendar-year taxpayer.

| | |
|---|---|
| *Marginal tax rate:* | 34 percent, unless otherwise stated. |

[1]Publicly traded companies usually file their financial statements (Form 10-K) with the Securities and Exchange Commission well before they file their income tax returns with the Internal Revenue Service, often by as much as six months. The company must estimate its current year income tax liability when it files its financial statements and then adjust for any "provision to return" differences in the quarter (Form 10-Q) in which the tax return is filed. In today's post–Sarbanes-Oxley environment, staff from public accounting firms that are not a company's auditors often are hired to help prepare the company's income tax provision under ASC 740 because many companies do not have staff with the expertise to make this calculation.

[2]Kris Frieswick, "Too Taxing," *CFO Magazine* (November 1, 2005).

As you learned in computing PCC's taxable income in the previous chapter, many of the items of income (revenue) and deductions (expenses) that are included in a company's taxable income also are included in the company's net income before taxes. Not all of these items are included in the computations in the same accounting period, however, which creates "temporary" differences between taxable income and net income. Other items affect only one of the computations, which creates "permanent" differences between taxable income and net income. A company must take these differences into account in computing its income tax provision on the income statement and its "deferred" income taxes payable (liabilities) or refundable (assets) on the balance sheet.

FASB Accounting Standards Codification Topic 740, *Income Taxes* (hereafter, ASC 740), governs the computation and disclosure of a company's income tax provision (expense or benefit) and its expected future income tax liabilities or benefits related to "events" that have been recorded on either the financial statement or the tax return. ASC 740 codifies the "majority" of accounting and reporting guidance related to income taxes, primarily FAS 109. Accounting for income taxes related to accounting for investments under the equity method, stock compensation, business combinations, foreign currency translation, and industry subtopics such as real estate, entertainment, and oil and gas is covered within the ASC topic that deals with that issue. ASC 740 applies to interim and annual periods ending after September 15, 2009. The Emerging Issues Task Force (EITF)[3] and the Securities and Exchange Commission continue to provide guidance on issues related to accounting for income taxes. A company's failure to accurately compute the income tax provision and related balance sheet accounts can lead to the issuance of a material weakness statement by the auditor and, in some cases, a restatement of the financial statements. Not surprisingly, individuals who understand these rules are in great demand by public accounting firms and industry.

This chapter discusses the basic rules for how a company computes and discloses its current year income tax provision and its future income taxes payable or refundable using the facts related to Premiere Computer Corporation in the previous chapter. We focus on the portion of the provision that relates to federal income taxes.

## LO1 OBJECTIVES OF ACCOUNTING FOR INCOME TAXES AND THE INCOME TAX PROVISION PROCESS

In addition to filing its federal, state and local, and non-U.S. income tax returns, Premiere Computer Corporation, along with all other U.S. publicly traded corporations and many privately held corporations, must prepare financial statements in accordance with generally accepted accounting principles (GAAP) issued by the FASB. Under GAAP, a company must include as part of its income statement a "provision" for the income tax expense or benefit that is associated with the pretax net income or loss reported on the income statement. The income tax provision includes not only current year taxes payable or refundable, but also any changes to future income taxes payable or refundable that result from differences in the timing of when an item is reported on the tax return compared to the financial statement. The company records these future income taxes payable or refundable on its balance sheet as the amount the company expects to pay (**deferred tax liability**) or recover (**deferred tax asset**) in a future accounting period.

[3]The Emerging Issues Task Force is a committee of accounting practitioners who assist the FASB in providing timely guidance on emerging issues and the implementation of existing standards.

---

**Taxes in the Real World** *Why Is Accounting for Income Taxes So Important?*

Donald Nicolaisen, former Chief Accountant of the SEC, made the following remarks about the importance of the income tax accounting rules:

*Why is the accounting for income taxes so important? For most companies, income taxes typically equal 30 some percent, in some cases more, of pretax income, and significant portions of the recorded assets and liabilities are judgmental and therefore, subject to second guessing. Accurately accounting for the income tax consequences of a company's transactions is critical to the credibility of the financial statements as a whole.[4]*

---

## Why Is Accounting for Income Taxes So Complex?

ASC 740 provides the general rules that apply to the computation of a company's income tax provision. The basic principles that underlie these rules are fairly straightforward, but the application of the rules themselves can be very complex. Much of the complexity is due to the fact that the U.S. tax laws are complex and often ambiguous. In addition, companies frequently prepare their financial statements (Form 10-K) much earlier than when they file their corresponding tax returns. For example, a calendar-year corporation generally files its Form 10-K with the SEC in February or early March, but the company may not file its federal income tax return (Form 1120) with the Internal Revenue Service (IRS) until August or September.[5] As a result, a company often must exercise a high degree of judgment in estimating its income tax return positions currently and in future years when a tax return position might be challenged by the tax authorities. After the tax return is filed, it may take five years or more before the tax return is audited by the IRS and the final tax liability is determined.[6]

## Objectives of ASC 740

ASC 740 applies only to *income* taxes levied by the U.S. federal government, U.S. state and local governments, and non-U.S. ("foreign") governments. The FASB defines an *income tax* as a tax *based on income.* This definition excludes property taxes, excise taxes, sales taxes, and value-added taxes. Companies report nonincome taxes as expenses in the computation of their net income before taxes.

ASC 740 has two primary objectives. One objective is to "recognize the amount of taxes payable or refundable in the current year" (referred to as the **current tax liability or asset**).[7] A second objective is to "recognize deferred tax liabilities and assets for the future tax consequences of events that have been recognized in an entity's financial statements or tax returns."[8] Both objectives relate to reporting a company's income tax amounts on the *balance sheet,* not the *income statement.* The FASB refers

---

[4]"Expanding Disclosure Demands—Impact on Tax Accruals," Remarks of Donald Nicolaisen, Chief Accountant, SEC, February 11, 2004. Available at the SEC Web site, www.sec.gov.

[5]The due date for a federal income tax return filed by a calendar-year corporation is March 15, but corporations can request a six-month extension to September 15 by filing Form 7004 and paying any remaining tax liability.

[6]Although the statute of limitations for a filed income tax return is three years, large corporations often agree to extend the statute for a longer period of time to allow the IRS to audit the return. As a result, a corporation's tax return may not be audited for five or more years from the date it is filed.

[7]ASC 740-10-10-1(a).

[8]ASC 740-10-10-1(b).

to this method as the "asset and liability approach" to accounting for income taxes.[9] The FASB chose this approach because it felt it is most consistent with the definitions in FASB Concepts Statement No. 6, *Elements of Financial Statements,* and produces the most useful and understandable information.[10]

To compute the deferred tax liability or asset, a company must calculate the future tax effects attributable to temporary differences and **tax carryforwards.**[11] As you learned in the previous chapter, temporary differences generally can be thought of as revenue (income) or expenses (deductions) that will appear on both the income statement and the tax return but in different accounting periods. Temporary differences that are cumulatively favorable create deferred tax liabilities, while temporary differences that are cumulatively unfavorable create deferred tax assets.

---

**Example 17-1**

Before she began the income tax provision process, Elise knew she needed to get the ending balances in PCC's deferred tax accounts from the prior year. Accordingly, she retrieved PCC's prior year balance sheet (Exhibit 17-1) and the deferred tax component of the company's income tax note (Exhibit 17-2).

Looking at Exhibit 17-1, what income tax accounts appear on PCC's balance sheet from the prior year?

**Answer:** There are three deferred tax accounts on PCC's prior year balance sheet: current deferred tax assets of $271,660, noncurrent deferred tax assets of $408,000, and noncurrent deferred tax liabilities of $3,400,000.

Looking at Exhibit 17-2, is PCC in a net deferred tax asset or net deferred tax liability position at the end of the prior year (gross deferred tax assets less gross deferred tax liabilities)?

**Answer:** PCC ended the prior year with a net deferred tax liability of $2,720,340.

Since its inception, has PCC had net favorable or unfavorable temporary differences (that is, has PCC's cumulative pretax net income been greater or less than its taxable income)?

**Answer:** PCC's net deferred tax liability indicates that the company has had net cumulative favorable temporary differences, which indicates its cumulative pretax net income has exceeded its cumulative taxable income.

---

### EXHIBIT 17-1    PCC Balance Sheet at 12/31/2009

**Assets**

**Current Assets**

| | |
|---|---:|
| Cash | $10,722,380 |
| Municipal bonds | 300,000 |
| Accounts receivable | 17,250,000 |
| Less: Allowance for bad debts | (345,000) |
| Accounts receivable (net) | 16,905,000 |
| Inventory | 4,312,500 |
| Deferred tax assets | 271,660 |
| Total Current Assets | $32,511,540 |

*(continued)*

---

[9]FAS 109, ¶63. (This paragraph was not codified in ASC 740.)
[10]FAS 109, ¶63.
[11]ASC 740-10-25-2(b).

**EXHIBIT 17-1**   PCC Balance Sheet at 12/31/2009
             (*concluded*)

| Noncurrent Assets | |
|---|---:|
| Fixed assets | $60,000,000 |
| Less: Accumulated depreciation | (12,000,000) |
| Fixed assets (net) | 48,000,000 |
| Life insurance (cash surrender value) | 1,100,000 |
| Investments | 497,960 |
| Goodwill | 180,000 |
| Deferred tax assets | 408,000 |
| Total Noncurrent Assets | 50,185,960 |
| **Total Assets** | **$82,697,500** |

| Liabilities and Shareholders' Equity | |
|---|---:|
| **Current Liabilities** | |
| Accounts payable | $20,013,000 |
| Reserve for warranties | 430,000 |
| Deferred tax liabilities | — |
| Total Current Liabilities | $20,443,000 |
| **Noncurrent Liabilities** | |
| Long-term debt | $40,000,000 |
| Deferred compensation | 1,200,000 |
| Deferred tax liabilities | 3,400,000 |
| Total Noncurrent Liabilities | $44,600,000 |
| **Total Liabilities** | **$65,043,000** |
| **Shareholders' Equity** | |
| Common stock (par value = $1) | $   500,000 |
| Additional paid-in-capital | 5,000,000 |
| Retained earnings | 12,154,500 |
| Total Shareholders' Equity | $17,654,500 |
| **Total Liabilities and Shareholders' Equity** | **$82,697,500** |

**EXHIBIT 17-2**   PCC Deferred Tax Accounts at 12/31/2009

| Deferred Tax Assets | |
|---|---:|
| Allowance for bad debts | $   117,300 |
| Reserve for warranties | 146,200 |
| Net operating loss carryforward | 8,160 |
| **Current deferred tax assets** | **$   271,660** |
| Deferred compensation | 408,000 |
| Capital loss carryforward | — |
| Contribution carryforward | — |
| **Noncurrent deferred tax assets** | **$   408,000** |
| **Total deferred tax assets** | **$   679,660** |
| Valuation allowance for deferred tax assets | — |
| Deferred tax assets, net of valuation allowance | $   679,660 |
| **Deferred tax liabilities** | |
| Depreciation | (3,400,000) |
| Total deferred tax liabilities | ($3,400,000) |
| **Net deferred tax liabilities** | **($2,720,340)** |

### The Income Tax Provision Process

A company computes the two components of its income tax provision (current and deferred) separately (independently) for each category of income tax (U.S. federal, U.S. state and local, and international) and then combines the components to produce the total income tax provision. The "formula" to compute a company's total income tax provision can be summarized as:

> Total income tax provision = Current income tax expense (benefit)
> + Deferred income tax expense (benefit)

There are six steps in the computation of a company's federal income tax provision. These steps are:

1. Adjust pretax net income for all permanent differences.
2. Identify all temporary differences and tax carryforward amounts.
3. Calculate the current income tax expense or benefit (refund).
4. Determine the ending balances in the balance sheet deferred tax asset and liability accounts.
5. Evaluate the need for a valuation allowance for gross deferred tax assets.
6. Calculate the deferred income tax expense or benefit.

**L02**

## CALCULATING THE CURRENT AND DEFERRED INCOME TAX EXPENSE OR BENEFIT COMPONENTS OF A COMPANY'S INCOME TAX PROVISION

*continued from page 17-1...*
Elise gathered the financial statement and tax return data she needed to get started beginning with the workpaper template she used to compute PCC's taxable income (Exhibit 17-3 reproduces the book-tax reconciliation template before federal income taxes from Exhibit 16-7). She identified each of the book-tax adjustments as being either permanent (P) or temporary (T). She was ready to begin the process of computing PCC's federal income tax provision using the six-step process she had learned at firm training.

*to be continued...*

### Step 1: Adjust Pretax Net Income for All Permanent Differences

As you learned in the previous chapter, not all book-tax differences meet the definition of a temporary difference. Some differences will appear only on the income statement or the tax return, but not on both. Examples of the former include tax-exempt interest income and nondeductible fines. Examples of the latter include the dividends received deduction and the domestic production activities deduction. Although not defined as such in ASC 740, most accounting professionals refer to these types of book-tax differences as **permanent differences.**

A company does not take permanent differences into account in computing its deferred tax assets and liabilities (and consequently, the deferred component of its income tax provision). Permanent differences enter into the company's computation of taxable income, and thus affect the current tax expense or benefit, either increasing

## EXHIBIT 17-3 PCC Book-Tax Reconciliation Template

**Premiere Computer Corporation**

| Income Statement for Current Year | Book Income | Book-Tax Adjustments (Dr) | Book-Tax Adjustments Cr | Taxable Income |
|---|---|---|---|---|
| Revenue from sales | $ 60,000,000 | | | $60,000,000 |
| Cost of goods sold | 38,000,000 | | | 38,000,000 |
| **Gross profit** | $ 22,000,000 | | | $22,000,000 |
| **Other income:** | | | | |
| Dividend income | 30,000 | | | 30,000 |
| Interest income (P) | 120,000 | (12,000) | | 108,000 |
| Capital gains (losses) (T) | (28,000) | | 28,000 | 0 |
| Gain on fixed asset dispositions (T) | 54,000 | | 16,000 | 70,000 |
| **Gross Income** | $ 22,176,000 | | | $22,208,000 |
| **Expenses:** | | | | |
| Compensation | (9,868,000) | | | (9,868,000) |
| Deferred compensation (T) | (300,000) | (150,000) | | (450,000) |
| Stock option compensation (P) | (100,000) | | 100,000 | 0 |
| Bad debt expense (T) | (165,000) | | 70,000 | (95,000) |
| Charitable contributions (T) | (700,000) | | 73,700 | (626,300) |
| Depreciation (T) | (2,400,000) | (700,000) | | (3,100,000) |
| Advertising | (1,920,000) | | | (1,920,000) |
| Warranty expenses (T) | (580,000) | | 170,000 | (410,000) |
| Meals and entertainment (P) | (28,000) | | 14,000 | (14,000) |
| Life insurance premiums (P) | (34,000) | | 34,000 | 0 |
| Other expenses | (64,000) | | | (64,000) |
| Total expenses *before* NOL, DRD, DMD | $(16,159,000) | | | $16,547,300 |
| Income *before* NOL, DRD, DMD | $ 6,017,000 | | | $ 5,660,700 |
| NOL carryforward from prior year (T) | 0 | (24,000) | | (24,000) |
| Dividends received deduction (P) | 0 | (21,000) | | (21,000) |
| Domestic production activities deduction (P) | 0 | (465,000) | 0 | (465,000) |
| **Book/Taxable income** | $ 6,017,000 | (1,372,000) | 505,700 | $ 5,150,700 |

or decreasing it. As a result, permanent differences usually affect a company's **effective tax rate** (income tax provision/pretax net income) and appear as part of the company's reconciliation of its effective tax rate with its statutory U.S. tax rate (34 percent in PCC's case).[12] We discuss ASC 740 disclosure requirements in a subsequent section of this chapter.

Exhibit 17-4 provides a list of common permanent differences you will encounter in practice.

## EXHIBIT 17-4 Common Permanent Differences

| | |
|---|---|
| Life insurance proceeds | Disallowed meals and entertainment expenses |
| Tax-exempt interest income | Disallowed premiums on officers' life insurance |
| Nondeductible tax penalties and fines | Dividends received deduction |
| Tax credits | Domestic production activities deduction |
| Political contributions | Medicare Part D subsidies |

[12]The tax benefit from a nonqualified stock option deduction that is not treated as a temporary difference is recorded in additional paid-in capital (refer back to the previous discussion of stock option deductions in Chapter 16).

**Example 17-2**

Elise went back to the template she used to compute PCC's taxable income and identified the book-tax adjustments that were considered permanent in nature. What are PCC's permanent differences and are they favorable or unfavorable?

**Answer:** A net favorable permanent difference of $350,000, computed as follows:

| Permanent Differences | Favorable (Unfavorable) |
|---|---|
| Tax-exempt interest income | $ 12,000 |
| Stock option compensation | (100,000) |
| Meals and entertainment | (14,000) |
| Life insurance premiums | (34,000) |
| Dividends received deduction | 21,000 |
| Domestic production activities deduction | 465,000 |
| Net favorable permanent difference | $350,000 |

**Example 17-3**

Elise used the net favorable permanent difference of $350,000 to adjust PCC's pretax net income. What is PCC's pretax net income adjusted for permanent differences?

**Answer:** $5,667,000, computed as follows:

| | |
|---|---|
| PCC pretax net income | $6,017,000 |
| Net favorable permanent difference | (350,000) |
| PCC pretax net income adjusted for permanent differences | $5,667,000 |

Elise remembered that her instructor at ASC 740 training referred to this intermediate computation as a company's **book equivalent of taxable income.** That is, this amount represents the book income that will ultimately be taxable, either currently or in the future.

## Step 2: Identify All Temporary Differences and Tax Carryforward Amounts

ASC 740 formally defines a *temporary difference* as

> A difference between the tax basis of an asset or liability . . . and its reported amount in the financial statements that will result in taxable or deductible amounts in future years when the reported amount of the asset or liability is recovered or settled, respectively.[13]

As you learned in Chapter 16, temporary differences commonly arise in four instances.

**Revenues or Gains that Are Taxable after They Are Recognized in Financial Income** An example of such a "favorable" book-tax adjustment is gain from an installment sale that is recognized for financial accounting purposes in the year of sale but is recognized over the collection period for tax purposes.[14]

**Expenses or Losses that Are Deductible after They Are Recognized in Financial Income** Examples of such "unfavorable" book-tax adjustments include bad debt expenses, warranty expenses, and accrued compensation and vacation pay that are recorded using the reserve method for financial accounting purposes but can

---

[13]ASC 740-10-20 Glossary.

[14]Consistent with the terminology introduced in Chapter 16, a "favorable" book-tax adjustment is one that reduces current year taxable income compared to current year net income.

only be deducted when paid on the tax return.[15] Capitalized inventory costs under §263A also fall into this category, as do stock option compensation expenses that are recorded at the grant date for financial reporting purposes under ASC 718 [FAS 123(R)] but do not become tax deductible until the exercise date.

**Revenues or Gains that Are Taxable before They Are Recognized in Financial Income**    An example of such an "unfavorable" book-tax adjustment is a prepayment that is recognized in the year received for tax purposes but is not recognized for financial accounting purposes until the revenue is earned.

**Expenses or Losses that Are Deductible before They Are Recognized in Financial Income**    A common example of such a "favorable" book-tax adjustment is the excess of tax depreciation over financial reporting depreciation.

Temporary differences also can arise from items that cannot be associated with a particular asset or liability for financial accounting purposes but produce revenue (income) or expense (deduction) that has been recognized in the financial statement and will result in taxable or deductible amounts in future years. For example, a net operating loss carryover and a net capital loss carryover create unfavorable temporary differences without being associated with a specific asset or liability.

Exhibit 17-5 lists common temporary differences.

**EXHIBIT 17-5    Common Temporary Differences**

| | |
|---|---|
| Depreciation | Reserves for bad debts (uncollectible accounts) |
| Accrued vacation pay | Inventory costs capitalized under §263A |
| Prepayments of income | Warranty reserves |
| Installment sale income | Stock option expense under ASC 718 |
| Pension plan deductions | Accrued bonuses and other compensation |
| Accrued contingency losses | Net operating loss and net capital loss carryovers |

## Identifying Taxable and Deductible Temporary Differences

**Taxable Temporary Difference**    A temporary difference that is cumulatively *favorable* (that is, an item that has cumulatively decreased taxable income relative to book income) gives rise to what ASC 740 refers to as a **taxable temporary difference.**[16] This category of temporary difference gets its name from the fact that when the difference reverses in a future period it will *increase taxable income* relative to book income.

Taxable temporary differences generally arise when (1) revenues or gains are taxable *after* they are recognized in net income (for example, gross profit from an installment sale) and (2) expenses or losses are deductible on the tax return *before* they reduce net income (for example, excess tax depreciation over financial accounting depreciation). From a balance sheet perspective, a taxable temporary difference generally causes the financial reporting basis of an asset to exceed its corresponding tax basis or the financial reporting basis of a liability to be less than its corresponding tax basis. The future tax cost associated with a taxable temporary difference is recorded on the balance sheet as a deferred tax liability.

**Deductible Temporary Difference**    A temporary difference that is cumulatively *unfavorable* (that is, an item that has cumulatively increased taxable income relative to book income) gives rise to what ASC 740 refers to as a **deductible temporary**

---

[15]Consistent with the terminology introduced in Chapter 16, an "unfavorable" book-tax adjustment is one that increases current year taxable income compared to current year net income.
[16]ASC 740-10-25-23.

difference.[17] This category of temporary difference gets its name from the fact that when the difference reverses in a future period it will *decrease taxable income* relative to book income.

Deductible temporary differences generally arise when (1) revenues or gains are taxable *before* they are recognized in net income (for example, prepayments of subscriptions) and (2) expenses or losses are deductible on the tax return *after* they reduce net income (for example, reserves for product warranty or uncollectible accounts). From a balance sheet perspective, a deductible temporary difference generally causes the financial reporting basis of an asset to be less than its corresponding tax basis or the financial reporting basis of a liability to exceed its corresponding tax basis. The future tax benefit associated with a deductible temporary difference is recorded on the balance sheet as a deferred tax asset.

Unfavorable temporary differences that do not have balance sheet accounts, such as net operating loss carryovers, net capital loss carryovers, and charitable contribution carryovers, must be tracked to ensure that the appropriate adjustment is made to a company's deferred tax asset accounts when the carryover is used on a future tax return.

## Example 17-4

Elise decided to separate PCC's temporary differences as being cumulatively favorable or cumulatively unfavorable (see Exhibit 17-3). What are PCC's taxable (cumulatively favorable) temporary differences?

**Answer:** PCC has one taxable temporary difference that arises in the current year—the excess of tax depreciation over book depreciation in the amount of $684,000. The gain on the sale of the fixed asset appears as an unfavorable difference, but it actually represents the reversal of a previously recorded favorable difference, the excess of tax over book depreciation. This "drawdown" of a previously recorded taxable temporary difference is included with the taxable temporary differences arising in the current year. Elise summarized the taxable temporary differences as follows:

| Taxable Temporary Differences | Amount |
|---|---|
| Excess of tax over book depreciation | ($700,000) |
| Gain on fixed asset disposition | 16,000 |
| Total taxable temporary differences | ($684,000) |

What are PCC's deductible (cumulatively unfavorable) temporary differences?

**Answer:** The deduction of previously accrued deferred compensation and PCC's use of its net operating loss carryover appear as favorable temporary differences in 2010, but they are actually reversals of prior unfavorable temporary differences and are included with the deductible temporary differences. PCC has total deductible temporary differences of $167,700, computed as follows:

| Deductible Temporary Differences | Amount |
|---|---|
| Net capital loss carryforward | $ 28,000 |
| Deferred compensation | (150,000) |
| Bad debt expense | 70,000 |
| Charitable contribution carryforward | 73,700 |
| Warranty expense | 170,000 |
| NOL carryforward from prior year | (24,000) |
| Total deductible temporary differences | $167,700 |

For the year, PCC has a net taxable (favorable) temporary difference of $516,300 [($684,000) + $167,700].

---

[17]ASC 740-10-25-23.

## Step 3: Compute the Current Income Tax Expense or Benefit

In many respects, the computation of the current portion of a company's tax provision appears to be straightforward. ASC 740 defines the **current income tax expense or benefit** as

> The amount of income taxes paid or payable (or refundable) for a year as determined by applying the provisions of the enacted tax law to the taxable income or excess of deductions over revenues for that year.[18]

To be sure, the major component of a company's current income tax expense or benefit is the income tax liability or refund from its current year operations. However, there are other items that enter into the computation that do not appear on the company's income tax return (Form 1120), which adds to the complexity of the computation.

In practice, the computation of a company's current income tax expense or benefit rarely reflects the actual taxes paid on the company's current year tax returns. In particular, the current component of PCC's income tax provision also can be impacted by prior year income tax refunds from current year carrybacks of a net operating loss or net capital loss,[19] IRS audit adjustments from prior year tax returns,[20] and changes in the company's **uncertain tax positions** (a company's reserve for taxes it has not paid but expects to pay in the future for positions taken on the current and prior year income tax returns).[21]

---

### Example 17-5

Elise used her summary of permanent and temporary differences to verify her previous computation of PCC's taxable income. Does using Elise's summary of PCC's permanent and temporary differences verify her previous computation of PCC's taxable income?

**Answer:** Yes!

| | |
|---|---:|
| PCC pretax net income | $6,017,000 |
| Net favorable permanent differences (from Example 17-2) | (350,000) |
| Net favorable temporary differences (from Example 17-4) | (516,300) |
| PCC taxable income | $5,150,700 |

What is PCC's current income tax expense, assuming a tax rate of 34 percent?

**Answer:** $1,751,238, computed as follows:

| | |
|---|---:|
| PCC taxable income | $5,150,700 |
| | × 34% |
| PCC federal income tax payable | $1,751,238 |

What tax accounting journal entry does PCC make to record its current tax expense?

**Answer:**

| | | |
|---|---:|---:|
| Current income tax expense | 1,751,238 | |
| Current income taxes payable (or cash) | | 1,751,238 |

**THE KEY FACTS**

**Computing the Deferred Income Tax Expense or Benefits**

- Identify current year changes in taxable and deductible temporary differences.

- Determine ending balances in each deferred tax asset and liability balance sheet account.

- Identify carryovers (net operating loss, capital loss, charitable contributions) not on the balance sheet.

- The current year deferred income tax expense or benefit is the difference between the deferred tax asset and liability balances at the beginning of the year to the end of the year as well as changes in tax carryovers.

---

[18]ASC 740-10-20 Glossary.
[19]Requested on Form 1139 or Form 1120X.
[20]Agreed to on Form 5701.
[21]Calculated in the uncertain tax position workpapers.

### Step 4: Determine the Ending Balances in the Balance Sheet Deferred Tax Asset and Liability Accounts

*continued from page 17-6...*

Having calculated the current portion of PCC's income tax provision, Elise turned her attention to computing the deferred piece of PCC's income tax provision. She knew from training that the technically correct method to compute PCC's deferred tax provision would be to compare the financial accounting basis of each asset and liability with its corresponding tax basis. Elise had the financial accounting basis of each account from the balance sheet but, like most companies, PCC did not keep a formal **tax accounting balance sheet**.[22] She would need to use an alternative method to calculate the change in the cumulative book-tax basis differences for each account she identified as being a temporary difference.

*to be continued...*

The FASB could have decided that a company report only the "as-paid" income taxes on its income statement. Investors and policymakers might favor this approach because it would disclose the actual income taxes paid or refunded (cash outflow or inflow) in the current year. Reporting only income taxes currently payable ignores one of the basic premises underlying financial accounting, which is that the accrual method of accounting provides more relevant information to investors and creditors than the cash method of accounting.[23]

The deferred income tax expense or benefit portion of a company's income tax provision reflects the change during the year in a company's deferred tax liabilities or assets.[24] This information provides investors and other interested parties with a measure of a company's expected future income tax-related cash inflows or outflows resulting from book-tax differences that are *temporary* in nature or from tax carryovers, but its computation is more complex and time-consuming than computing the current income tax provision.

ASC 740 takes an "asset and liability" or balance sheet approach to the computation of the deferred tax expense or benefit. The computations are based on the change in the *cumulative* differences between the financial accounting basis of an asset or liability and its corresponding tax basis from the beginning of the year to the end of the year. Under GAAP, the company is presumed to recover these basis differences over time, resulting in future sacrifices of a company's resources (in the case of liabilities) or future recoveries of a company's resources (in the case of assets). These expected future recoveries of assets or future sacrifices of assets to settle liabilities give rise to future (deferred) tax payments or refunds that are recorded in the income tax provision in the year the differences arise rather than in the year in which the future taxes are paid or recovered.

The future tax cost of a taxable (cumulatively favorable) temporary difference is recorded on the balance sheet as a deferred tax liability. The company computes the deferred tax liability using the **enacted tax rate** that is expected to apply to taxable income in the period(s) in which the deferred tax liability is expected to be settled.[25]

---

[22]Schedule L to Form 1120 requests that the taxpayer report its financial statement balance sheet.

[23]ASC 230, *Statement of Cash Flows,* requires an enterprise to separately disclose income taxes paid as part of the statement itself or in a note to the financial statements (usually the income taxes note).

[24]ASC 740-10-20 Glossary.

[25]ASC 740-10-30-2. For federal income tax provision purposes, a corporation applies the regular tax rate in computing its deferred tax assets and liabilities.

**Example 17-6**

Lacking a formal tax-basis balance sheet, Elise identified the current year temporary differences and adjusted the cumulative differences at the beginning of the year to get the end of the year cumulative book-tax basis differences. She used this change in the cumulative book-tax basis difference to compute the deferred tax expense or benefit for the current year. Elise reviewed her schedules of favorable and unfavorable temporary differences (from Example 17-3). She identified one favorable temporary difference related to an asset recorded on the balance sheet—the excess of tax depreciation over book depreciation. Elise retrieved the fixed asset workpaper and recorded the changes in the financial accounting and tax accumulated depreciation balances of PCC's fixed assets from the beginning of the year to the end of the year related to current year depreciation.

| *Financial accounting change in accumulated depreciation* | |
| --- | ---: |
| Beginning of the year | $12,000,000 |
| End of the year | 14,400,000 |
| Net change | $ 2,400,000 |
| | |
| *Tax accounting change in accumulated depreciation\** | |
| Beginning of the year | $22,000,000 |
| End of the year | 25,100,000 |
| Net change | $ 3,100,000 |

*\*Not given in the original facts; assumed for purposes of this example.*

The net increase in tax accounting accumulated depreciation over the corresponding financial accounting depreciation created a current year $700,000 favorable (taxable) temporary difference (that is, the difference between the financial accounting basis of the fixed assets increased by $700,000 over their corresponding tax basis). This increase in the cumulative favorable temporary difference requires an *increase* in PCC's deferred tax liabilities.

By what amount will PCC increase its deferred tax liabilities as a result of the increase in the book over tax basis in these assets from the beginning of the year to the end of the year?

**Answer:** $238,000, computed as $700,000 × 34 percent.

What tax accounting journal entry does PCC record related to this transaction?

**Answer:**

| | | |
| --- | ---: | ---: |
| Deferred income tax expense | 238,000 | |
| Deferred income tax liability | | 238,000 |

**What if:** Assume current year book depreciation exceeded current year tax depreciation by $700,000? What adjustment to the balance sheet would PCC be required to make?

**Answer:** PCC would *decrease* its deferred tax liability on the balance sheet by $238,000.

**Example 17-7**

Elise also saw that accumulated depreciation decreased as a result of PCC's sale of a fixed asset during the year (see Exhibit 17-3). She observed from the workpapers that PCC sold the fixed asset for $100,000, its original cost (not given in the original facts, assumed for purposes of this example). The book basis of the asset was $46,000, resulting in a book gain of $54,000. The tax gain on the sale was $70,000, which corresponds to a decrease in accumulated tax depreciation of $70,000 (that is, the tax basis of the asset was $30,000). The excess of the reduction in accumulated tax

(*continued on page 17-14…*)

depreciation over accumulated book depreciation of $16,000 corresponds to the excess of the tax gain over the book gain on the sale.

| | |
|---|---|
| *Financial accounting change in accumulated depreciation on the fixed asset sold* | |
| Beginning of the year | $54,000 |
| End of the year | 0 |
| Net change | $54,000 |
| *Tax accounting change in accumulated depreciation on the fixed asset sold* | |
| Beginning of the year | $70,000 |
| End of the year | 0 |
| Net change | $70,000 |

By what amount will PCC *decrease* its deferred tax liabilities as a result of the decrease in the tax over book basis in this asset from the beginning of the year to the end of the year?

**Answer:** $5,440, computed as $16,000 × 34%

What tax accounting journal entry does PCC record *related to this transaction*?

**Answer:**

| | | |
|---|---|---|
| Deferred income tax liability | 5,440 | |
| Deferred income tax benefit | | 5,440 |

This "draw down" of the excess of tax accumulated depreciation over book accumulated depreciation requires a reduction in the previously recorded deferred tax liability that resulted from the book-tax difference created by the excess of tax depreciation over book depreciation.

By what amount will PCC increase its current income tax expense as a result of this transaction (the tax gain was $70,000)?

**Answer:** $23,800, computed as $70,000 × 34%

What tax accounting journal entry does PCC record *related to this transaction*?

**Answer:**

| | | |
|---|---|---|
| Current income tax expense | 23,800 | |
| Income taxes payable | | 23,800 |

What is the net impact of this transaction on PCC's income tax provision?

**Answer:** A net increase of $18,360, computed as:

| | |
|---|---|
| Current income tax expense | $23,800 |
| Deferred income tax benefit | (5,440) |
| Net increase in PCC's income tax provision | $18,360 |

What do these journal entries accomplish?

**Answer:** The $18,360 provision reflects the tax expense related to the book gain of $54,000, computed as follows:

| | |
|---|---|
| Book gain on sale of the fixed asset | $54,000 |
| | × 34% |
| Net increase in PCC's income tax provision | $18,360 |

The recording of a deferred tax liability for years in which tax depreciation exceeded book depreciation anticipated the difference in the book and tax gain that would result when the fixed asset eventually was recovered, either through sale or depreciation of the entire basis.

**Example 17-8**

Using her cumulative temporary differences template, Elise recorded the cumulative taxable temporary differences and the corresponding deferred tax liability at the beginning of the year (BOY) and the end of the year (EOY) to determine the change in the deferred tax liability related to accumulated depreciation.

**Premiere Computer Corporation**
**Temporary Difference Scheduling Template**

| Taxable Temporary Differences | BOY Cumulative T/D | Beginning Deferred Taxes (@ 34%) | Current Year Change | EOY Cumulative T/D | Ending Deferred Taxes (@ 34%) |
|---|---|---|---|---|---|
| *Noncurrent* Accumulated Depreciation | (10,000,000) | **(3,400,000)** | (684,000) | (10,684,000) | **(3,632,560)** |

What is the net increase in PCC's deferred tax liability related to fixed assets for 2009?

**Answer:** $232,560, the change in the cumulative deferred tax liability from the beginning of the year ($3,400,000) to the end of the year ($3,632,560).

This amount corresponds to the increase in the deferred tax liability due to the current year change in the book-tax difference related to depreciation ($700,000) less the reduction in the deferred tax liability due to the change in the book-tax difference related to accumulated depreciation written off on the sale of the fixed asset ($16,000).

What tax accounting journal entry does PCC record related to the change in total deferred tax liabilities from the beginning of the year to the end of the year?

**Answer:**

| | | |
|---|---|---|
| Deferred income tax expense | 232,560 | |
| Deferred income tax liability | | 232,560 |

Using a template that tracks the cumulative changes in the book-tax differences related to balance sheet accounts becomes especially important when a company's enacted tax rate changes. For example, if PCC's federal income tax rate increased from 34 percent to 35 percent as a result of an increase in its taxable income, and PCC expects to maintain that tax rate in future periods, the company would tax-effect its year-end cumulative book-tax difference related to fixed assets at the new tax rate, 35 percent. The increase in the deferred tax expense related to adjusting the balance sheet will reflect the current year change in the book-tax difference and also an adjustment to revalue the cumulative book-tax difference at the beginning of the year. This discussion points to the fact that the focus of ASC 740 is to have the balance sheet deferred tax accounts reflect the tax that will be due or refunded when the underlying temporary differences reverse in a future period.

**Example 17-9**

**What if:** Assume PCC's tax rate increased from 34 percent in 2009 to 35 percent in 2010. By what amount would PCC increase or decrease its balance sheet deferred tax liability related to the fixed asset account?

(*continued on page 17-16...*)

**Answer:** PCC *increases* its deferred tax liability related to fixed assets by $339,400, calculated as follows:

**Premiere Computer Corporation**
**Temporary Difference Scheduling Template**

| Taxable Temporary Differences | BOY Cumulative T/D | Beginning Deferred Taxes (@ 34%) | Current Year Change | EOY Cumulative T/D | Ending Deferred Taxes (@ 35%) |
|---|---|---|---|---|---|
| ***Noncurrent*** | | | | | |
| Accumulated depreciation | (10,000,000) | (3,400,000) | (684,000) | (10,684,000) | (3,739,400) |

PCC would use a tax rate of 35 percent to compute the ending balance in its deferred tax liability related to fixed assets. The net increase in the deferred tax liability related to accumulated depreciation is now $339,400 ($3,739,400 − $3,400,000).

What tax accounting journal entry does PCC record *related to fixed assets?*
**Answer:**

| | | |
|---|---|---|
| Deferred income tax expense | 339,400 | |
| Deferred income tax liability | | 339,400 |

This amount no longer corresponds to the increase in the deferred income tax liability due to the current year change in the book-tax difference related to depreciation ($700,000) less the reduction in the deferred income tax liability due to the change in the book-tax difference related to accumulated depreciation written off on the sale of the fixed asset ($16,000) times the new applicable tax rate of 35 percent ($684,000 × 35% = $239,400). The $100,000 difference results from increasing the beginning of the year cumulative temporary difference of $10,000,000 times the change in the tax rate of 1 percent ($10,000,000 × 1% = $100,000).

## Example 17-10

Returning to her temporary differences template, Elise recorded the deductible (cumulatively unfavorable) temporary differences and the corresponding deferred tax assets at the beginning of the year (BOY) and the end of the year (EOY) to determine the change in PCC's deferred tax assets during the current year.

**Premiere Computer Corporation**
**Temporary Difference Scheduling Template**

| Deductible Temporary Differences | BOY Cumulative T/D | Beginning Deferred Taxes (@ 34%) | Current Year Change | EOY Cumulative T/D | Ending Deferred Taxes (@ 34%) |
|---|---|---|---|---|---|
| *Current* | | | | | |
| Allowance for bad debts | $ 345,000 | $117,300 | $ 70,000 | $ 415,000 | $141,100 |
| Reserve for warranties | 430,000 | 146,200 | 170,000 | 600,000 | 204,000 |
| Net operating loss | 24,000 | 8,160 | (24,000) | 0 | 0 |
| Total current | $ 799,000 | $271,660 | $ 216,000 | $1,015,000 | $345,100 |
| *Noncurrent* | | | | | |
| Deferred compensation | $1,200,000 | $408,000 | ($150,000) | $1,050,000 | $357,000 |
| Net capital loss carryover | 0 | 0 | 28,000 | 28,000 | 9,520 |
| Contribution carryover | 0 | 0 | 73,700 | 73,700 | 25,058 |
| Total noncurrent | $1,200,000 | $408,000 | ($48,300) | $1,151,700 | $391,578 |
| Total | $1,999,000 | $679,660 | $ 167,700 | $2,166,700 | $736,678 |

What is the net increase in PCC's total deferred tax assets for 2010?

**Answer:** $57,018, the change in the cumulative deferred tax asset from the beginning of the year ($679,660) to the end of the year ($736,678).

What tax accounting journal entry does PCC record *related to deferred tax assets?*

**Answer:**

| | | |
|---|---|---|
| Deferred income tax assets | 57,018 | |
| Deferred income tax benefit | | 57,018 |

---

**Example 17-11**

*What if:* Assume PCC's tax rate increased from 34 percent in 2009 to 35 percent in 2010. By what amount would PCC increase or decrease its *total* balance sheet deferred tax assets?

**Answer:** PCC *increases* its deferred tax asset related to fixed assets by $78,685, calculated as follows:

**Premiere Computer Corporation**
**Temporary Difference Scheduling Template**

| Deductible Temporary Differences | BOY Cumulative T/D | Beginning Deferred Taxes (@ 34%) | Current Year Change | EOY Cumulative T/D | Ending Deferred Taxes (@ 35%) |
|---|---|---|---|---|---|
| *Current* | | | | | |
| Allowance for bad debts | $ 345,000 | $117,300 | $ 70,000 | $ 415,000 | $145,250 |
| Reserve for warranties | 430,000 | 146,200 | 170,000 | 600,000 | 210,000 |
| Net operating loss | 24,000 | 8,160 | (24,000) | 0 | 0 |
| Total current | $ 799,000 | $271,660 | $ 216,000 | $1,015,000 | $355,250 |
| | | | | | |
| *Noncurrent* | | | | | |
| Deferred compensation | $1,200,000 | $408,000 | ($150,000) | $1,050,000 | $367,500 |
| Net capital loss carryover | 0 | 0 | 28,000 | 28,000 | 9,800 |
| Contribution carryover | 0 | 0 | 73,700 | 73,700 | 25,795 |
| Total noncurrent | $1,200,000 | $408,000 | ($48,300) | $1,151,700 | $403,095 |
| Total | $1,999,000 | $679,660 | $ 167,700 | $2,166,700 | $758,345 |

PCC would use a tax rate of 35 percent to compute the ending balance in each of its deferred tax asset accounts. The net increase in total deferred tax assets is now $78,685 ($758,345 − $679,660).

What tax accounting journal entry does PCC record to reflect the change in its *total* deferred tax assets?

**Answer:**

| | | |
|---|---|---|
| Deferred income tax assets | 78,685 | |
| Deferred income tax benefit | | 78,685 |

This amount no longer corresponds to the increase in total deferred tax assets due to the current year change in cumulative deductible temporary differences ($167,700) times the new applicable tax rate of 35 percent ($167,700 × 35% = $58,695). The $19,990 difference results from increasing the beginning of the year cumulative temporary difference of $1,999,000 times the change in the tax rate of 1 percent ($1,999,000 × 1% = $19,990).

## LO3

# DETERMINING WHETHER A VALUATION ALLOWANCE IS NEEDED

### Step 5: Evaluate the Need for a Valuation Allowance for Gross Deferred Tax Assets

ASC 740 specifically precludes PCC or any company from discounting (recording the present value of) the deferred tax liability or asset related to a temporary difference based on when the asset is expected to be recovered or the liability settled. The FASB debated whether discounting deferred tax assets and liabilities would provide more relevant information to investors, but ultimately it decided that the complexity and cost of making the computation outweighed any benefits investors and creditors might receive from the computation.[26]

In lieu of discounting, ASC 740 requires that a company evaluate each of its gross deferred tax assets on the balance sheet and assess the likelihood the expected tax benefit will be realized in a future period. The income tax benefits reflected in the deferred tax assets can only be *realized* (converted into cash) if the company expects to have sufficient taxable income or tax liability in the future to absorb the future tax deductions or credits when they are reported on the tax return or before they expire.

### Determining the Need for a Valuation Allowance

Under ASC 740, if a company determines that it is *more likely than not* (a likelihood greater than 50 percent) that some portion or all of the deferred tax assets will not be realized in a future period, it must offset the deferred tax assets with a **valuation allowance** to reflect the amount the company does not expect to realize in the future.[27] Valuation allowances operate as *contra accounts* to the deferred tax assets on the balance sheet, much like the allowance for bad debts a company must estimate for its accounts receivable. Companies usually disclose the amount of the valuation allowance in the income tax footnote to the financial statements.

Management must assess whether it is more likely than not that a deferred tax asset will *not* be realized in the future based on all available evidence, both positive and negative. ASC 740 identifies four sources of potential future taxable income, two of which are objective and two of which are subjective (that is, determined by management judgment).[28] The objective sources include (1) future reversals of existing taxable temporary differences and (2) taxable income in prior carryback year(s). The subjective sources include (1) expected future taxable income exclusive of reversing temporary differences and carryforwards and (2) tax planning strategies.

**Future Reversals of Existing Taxable Temporary Differences** Existing taxable (cumulatively favorable) temporary differences provide taxable income when they are recovered in a future period. For example, the recovery of the excess of an asset's financial accounting basis over its tax basis, whether through sale or depreciation, will cause taxable income to be higher than net income in the periods in which the excess financial accounting basis is recovered. If the reversing taxable temporary differences provide sufficient future taxable income to absorb the reversing deductible temporary differences, the company does not record a valuation allowance against the deferred tax asset.

---

[26]FAS 109, ¶¶198–199. (These paragraphs were not codified in ASC 740.)
[27]ASC 740-10-30-5(e).
[28]ASC 740-10-30-18.

**Taxable Income in Prior Carryback Year(s)**   The company does not record a valuation allowance if the tax benefit from the realization of a deferred tax asset can be carried back to a prior year that has sufficient taxable income (or capital gain net income in the case of a net capital loss carryback) to absorb the realized tax benefit.

**Expected Future Taxable Income Exclusive of Reversing Temporary Differences and Carryforwards**   ASC 740 allows a company to consider taxable income it expects to earn in future periods in determining whether a valuation allowance is necessary. The company might support its predictions of future taxable income with evidence of existing contracts or a sales backlog that will produce enough taxable income to realize the deferred tax asset when it reverses. In addition, the company might demonstrate that it has a strong earnings history if a deferred tax asset arises from a loss that could be considered out of the ordinary and not from a continuing condition. Cyclical industries such as automobile manufacturers and airlines traditionally have cited a history of past income as evidence of expected future income.

**Tax Planning Strategies**   The most subjective source of future taxable income to support the realization of a deferred tax asset involves the company's ability and willingness to employ tax strategies in those future periods to create the taxable income needed to absorb the deferred tax asset. ASC 740 allows a company to consider actions it might take to create sufficient taxable income to absorb a deferred tax asset, provided such actions (1) are prudent and feasible; (2) are actions an enterprise might not take, but would take to prevent an operating loss or tax credit carryforward from expiring unused; and (3) would result in realization of the deferred tax assets. The company does not have to implement the strategy to avoid recording a valuation allowance, but management must be willing and able to execute the strategy if the need arises. Tax planning strategies could include (1) selling and leasing back operating assets, (2) changing inventory accounting methods (for example, from LIFO to FIFO), (3) refraining from making voluntary contributions to the company pension plan, (4) electing to capitalize certain expenditures (e.g., research and development costs) rather than deduct them currently, (5) selling noncore assets, and (6) electing the alternative depreciation system (straight line instead of declining balance).

**Negative Evidence that a Valuation Allowance Is Needed**   ASC 740 requires that a company consider *negative evidence* as well as *positive evidence* in determining whether it is more likely than not that a deferred tax asset will not be realized in the future. Negative evidence could include (1) cumulative (book) losses in recent years, (2) a history of net operating (capital) losses and credits expiring unused, (3) an expectation of losses in the near future, and (4) unsettled circumstances that, if resolved unfavorably, will result in losses from continuing operations in future years (for example, the loss of a patent on a highly profitable drug).[29] Some public accounting firms require their auditors to consult the firm's national accounting group when a company has reported a cumulative financial accounting loss (adjusted for permanent differences and nonrecurring items) over the prior 12 financial reporting quarters (that is, the company must evaluate the need for a valuation allowance every quarter).

---

[29]ASC 740-10-30-21.

**Taxes in the Real World** *A $39 Billion Headache for GM*

General Motors, the world's largest automaker, has the world's largest headache on its hands. GM announced after the bell on Tuesday that it will take a $39 billion noncash charge in the third quarter related to establishing a valuation allowance against its deferred tax assets in the United States, Canada, and Germany.

GM shares closed up 0.4 percent, or 16 cents, to $36.16, but dropped 3 percent, or $1.06, in after-hours trading after the news of the charge broke.

GM is expected to report third-quarter results on Wednesday.

The company said that in the past it had evaluated its deferred tax assets quarterly and determined that valuation allowances were not necessary in the United States, Canada, and Germany because its three-year losses were due to one-time expenses and it still expected strong earnings at GMAC Financial Services. But now the automaker said that accounting standards require it to establish a valuation allowance due to developments in the third quarter. One significant factor was the company's three-year historical cumulative loss in the United States, Canada, and Germany on an adjusted basis. Another factor was the substantial losses incurred that GMAC related to its residential capital mortgage business, of

which GM owns 49 percent. Challenges in near-term automotive market conditions in the United States and Germany also played a role.

"The establishment of a valuation allowance does not have any impact on cash, nor does such an allowance preclude us from using our loss carry forwards or other deferred tax assets in the future," said Fritz Henderson, GM's chief financial officer.

Henderson said that the establishment of a valuation allowance "does not reflect a change in the company's view of its long-term automotive financial outlook." The company still believes that its new products and the new GM-United Auto Workers agreement will improve GM's position in the United States and better position it to use tax benefits in the future, Henderson said.

But David Healy, a Burnham Securities analyst, said that the charge is an indication that GM's outlook is not as strong as it was a few months ago. "It's a deterioration in their short-term outlook," he said.

GMAC suffered a large loss in the third quarter and the provisions GM took were not sufficient, Healy said, which may mean further write-downs are expected.

*Source:* Ruthie Ackerman, Forbes.com, November 6, 2007.

**Example 17-12**

Elise created a workpaper that listed PCC's ending balances in its deferred tax assets and liabilities at December 31, 2010 (from Examples 17-8 and 17-10), as follows:

### PCC Deferred Tax Accounts at 12/31/2010

**Deferred Tax Assets**

| | |
|---|---|
| Allowance for bad debts | $ 141,100 |
| Reserve for warranties | 204,000 |
| Net operating loss carryforward | 0 |
| Deferred compensation | 357,000 |
| Capital loss carryforward | 9,520 |
| Contribution carryforward | 25,058 |
| **Total deferred tax assets** | $ 736,678 |
| **Deferred tax liabilities** | |
| Depreciation | (3,632,560) |
| Total deferred tax liabilities | $(3,632,560) |
| **Net deferred tax liabilities** | $(2,895,882) |

What *positive* evidence should Elise consider in her evaluation as to whether PCC should record a valuation allowance against some or all of the deferred tax assets?

**Answer:** PCC has an excess of deferred tax liabilities over deferred tax assets of $2,895,882. When the book-tax depreciation difference reverses in the future, this will provide PCC with enough taxable income to absorb the reversing deferred tax assets.

What *negative* evidence should Elise consider in her evaluation as to whether PCC should record a valuation allowance against some or all of the deferred tax assets?

**Answer:** The deferred tax asset related to the charitable contribution carryover has a short carryover expiration date (five years). Elise may need to schedule out when the depreciation differences will reverse to determine if the reversals alone will provide PCC with enough taxable income to absorb the contribution carryover within the next five years.

   More problematic, the net capital loss carryover has both a short carryover expiration date (five years) and requires PCC to recognize net capital gains in future periods to absorb the net capital loss. A reversal of the book-tax depreciation temporary difference will not provide PCC with net capital gain to absorb the net capital loss carryover.

What other sources of *positive* evidence should Elise consider in her evaluation as to whether PCC should record a valuation allowance against the deferred tax asset related to the net capital loss carryover?

**Answer:** Two additional sources of positive evidence are management's projections of future taxable income from sources other than reversing taxable temporary differences and future taxable income from tax planning strategies. Because PCC is in the business of manufacturing and selling computer-related equipment, any additional taxable income it generates from selling additional equipment will produce ordinary income. The company likely will have to fall back on an assertion that management has a *tax planning strategy* it would be willing to use to generate net capital gain in the future. An example of such a strategy might be management's willingness to sell a parcel of land held for investment to generate a capital gain sufficient to absorb the net capital loss.

---

**Example 17-13**

*What if:* Assume PCC has had net book losses of $5,000,000 and $2,500,000 in 2008 and 2009, respectively. How might this additional fact influence Elise's assessment about the need for a valuation allowance?

**Answer:** PCC would have a cumulative book loss of $1,483,000 over the past 12 quarters at December 31, 2010. ASC 740 states that a cumulative loss "in recent years" is considered objective negative evidence that may be hard to overcome. Elise likely would have to consult with someone in her firm's national office to consider other sources of positive evidence that will outweigh the negative evidence in this situation.

---

**Example 17-14**

*What if:* Assume PCC just lost a big account to its competitor, but the company had reported cumulative net income in the current and prior two years. How might this additional fact influence Elise's assessment about the need for a valuation allowance?

**Answer:** Expectations of future events can outweigh historic results. In this case, Elise would have to seriously consider whether a valuation allowance would be required to the extent that reversing taxable temporary differences would not absorb expected future losses.

## Step 6: Calculate the Deferred Income Tax Expense or Benefit

**Example 17-15**

After discussing with management its assessment of the company's sources of future taxable income, Elise concurred with management that the company did not need to record a valuation allowance for 2010. Elise now had the pieces to determine PCC's deferred income tax expense or benefit for 2010. What is PCC's deferred income tax provision for 2010 (use the solutions from Examples 17-8 and 17-10)?

**Answer:** $175,542 net deferred tax expense, computed as follows:

| | |
|---|---|
| Gross deferred tax expense | $232,560 |
| Gross deferred tax benefit | (57,018) |
| Net deferred tax expense | $175,542 |

What is PCC's total income tax provision for 2010?

**Answer:** $1,926,780 income tax expense, computed as follows:

| | |
|---|---|
| Current tax expense | $1,751,238 |
| Gross deferred tax expense | 232,560 |
| Gross deferred tax benefit | (57,018) |
| Income tax expense | $1,926,780 |

There is a straightforward "back-of-the-envelope" method of verifying the ASC 740 approach to calculating PCC's total tax provision. Under the assumption that all temporary differences will appear on a tax return in a current or future period, the total tax provision should reflect the tax that ultimately will be paid on pretax net income adjusted for *permanent differences*. Remember from Example 17-3 that this amount is sometimes referred to as a company's book equivalent of taxable income. The total income tax provision should equal the company's tax rate times its book equivalent of taxable income. We would emphasize that this approach to computing a company's income tax provision is not in accordance with GAAP and will not provide the correct answer when there are changes in a company's income tax rate.

**Example 17-16**

Elise retrieved her computation of PCC's book equivalent of taxable income (from Example 17-3), as follows:

| | |
|---|---|
| PCC pretax net income | $6,017,000 |
| Net favorable permanent difference | (350,000) |
| PCC book equivalent to taxable income | $5,667,000 |

What is PCC's total tax provision using book equivalent of taxable income as a base?

**Answer:** $1,926,780, computed as follows:

| | |
|---|---|
| PCC book equivalent to taxable income | $5,667,000 |
| | × 34% |
| PCC book equivalent to taxable income | $1,926,780 |

This computation confirms the computation made under ASC 740 from Example 17-15.

# ACCOUNTING FOR UNCERTAINTY IN INCOME TAX POSITIONS

**L04**

*continued from page 17-12 . . .*
Elise recalled from her calculation of PCC's taxable income that there had been some discussion about the appropriate tax treatment of certain items on the tax return. In particular, she and PCC's tax director had debated whether certain income qualified for the domestic production activities deduction. In particular, there was some uncertainty as to whether $1,000,000 of the company's QPAI would be allowed by the IRS on audit. This amount of QPAI provided the company with a domestic production activities deduction of $90,000 (9% × $1,000,000). The tax director felt "comfortable" in taking the tax return position that the income met the definition of qualified production activity income (QPAI). Elise decided she needed to know more about how to deal with accounting for this tax uncertainty. ■

As you have learned in your study of the U.S. income tax laws, the answer to every tax question is not always certain. Taxpayers and the IRS may differ in their opinions as to whether an expenditure is deductible or must be capitalized or whether income is taxable or is deferred or exempt from taxation. When irresolvable disputes arise, the taxpayer can petition the courts to resolve the tax treatment of a transaction. Taxpayers and the IRS can appeal decisions of the lower courts to the appellate courts and ultimately to the Supreme Court. Taxpayers also take tax positions that can be disputed by state and local taxing authorities and international tax authorities. For example, the taxpayer and a state (international) tax authority may differ on whether the taxpayer has earned income in that jurisdiction and should pay tax on such income. The courts may not resolve this issue for many years after the original transaction takes place. If the courts do not resolve the issue in the taxpayer's favor, the taxpayer will be subject to interest and possible penalties on the tax owed.

For financial accounting purposes, a company must determine whether it can record the current or future tax benefits from an "uncertain" tax position in its financial statement for the period in which the transaction takes place, knowing that the ultimate resolution of the tax position may not be known until some time in the future.

FAS 109 as originally written provided no specific guidance on how to deal with uncertain tax positions. As a result, companies generally applied the principles of FAS 5, *Accounting for Contingencies,* to uncertain tax positions. The FASB became concerned that companies were not applying FAS 5 uniformly, leading to diversity in practice and financial statements that were not comparable. After much debate, the FASB issued FASB Interpretation (FIN) No. 48, *Accounting for Uncertainty in Income Taxes—An Interpretation of FASB Statement No. 109,* in July 2006, effective for years beginning after December 15, 2006. FIN 48 has been codified in ASC 740. The objective of FIN 48 is to provide a uniform approach to recording and disclosing tax benefits resulting from tax positions that are considered to be uncertain.

ASC 740 (FIN 48) applies a two-step process to evaluating tax positions. ASC 740 refers to the first step as *recognition.*[30] A company must determine whether it is *more likely than not* (a greater than 50 percent probability) that a tax position will be sustained on examination by the IRS or other taxing authority, including resolution of any appeals within the court system, based on the technical merits of the position. In making this determination, the company must presume that the taxing authority (IRS) will examine the tax position with full knowledge of all relevant information.

[30]ASC 740-10-25-5 through 25-7.

---

**THE KEY FACTS**

**Accounting for Uncertain Tax Positions**

■ ASC 740 requires a two-step process in determining if a tax benefit can be recognized in the financial statements.
· A company first determines if it is more likely than not that its tax position on a particular account will be sustained on IRS examination based on its technical merits.
· A company then determines the amount it expects to be able to recognize.

■ The measurement process requires the company to make a cumulative probability assessment of all likely outcomes of the audit and litigation process.
· The company recognizes the amount that has a greater than 50 percent probability of being sustained on examination and subsequent litigation.
· The amount not recognized is recorded as a liability on the balance sheet.

In other words, the company cannot take into account the possibility that the taxing authority will not audit the uncertain tax position (play the "audit lottery").

The second step is referred to as *measurement*.[31] If the tax position meets the more-likely-than-not threshold (a subjective determination), the company must determine the amount of the benefit to record in the financial statements, or from an ASC 740 perspective, how much of its claimed tax benefit the company is not allowed to recognize. (ASC 740 refers to this unclaimed amount as "unrecognized tax benefits.") Under ASC 740, the company records the largest amount of the benefit, as calculated on a cumulative probability basis, which is more likely than not to be realized on the ultimate settlement of the tax position.

### Application of ASC 740 to Uncertain Tax Positions

ASC 740 applies to all *tax positions* dealing with income taxes. As a result, ASC 740 pertains to tax positions taken on a current or previously filed tax return or a tax position that will be taken on a future tax return that is reflected in the financial statements as a deferred tax asset or liability. ASC 740 also applies to tax positions that result in permanent differences (for example, the domestic production activities deduction and credits) and to decisions not to file a tax return in a particular jurisdiction. For example, assume a company deducts an expenditure on its current tax return, which the IRS may challenge on audit in a future period. The deduction produces a net operating loss that will be carried forward and offset against future taxable income. ASC 740 addresses whether the company can *recognize* the deferred tax asset related to the NOL carryforward on its balance sheet. Once the recognition hurdle is overcome, the company must then evaluate whether it is more likely than not that the deferred tax asset will be *realized* in the future period (that is, whether a valuation allowance should be recorded).

**Step 1: Recognition**    A company first must determine if it is more likely than not that its tax position on a particular account will be sustained on IRS examination based on its technical merits. If the company believes this threshold has been met, the company can record (recognize) the tax benefit of the tax position on its financial statements as a reduction in its current tax expense or an increase in its deferred tax benefit. The company must presume that the IRS will examine this tax position with full knowledge of all relevant information. However, in determining if the more-likely-than-not threshold has been met, the company can take into account how the tax position might be resolved if litigated. This requires the company to evaluate the sources of authority that address this issue (that is, the tax law, regulations, legislative history, IRS rulings, and court opinions).

**Step 2: Measurement**    After the company determines that the more-likely-than-not recognition threshold has been met, it must compute the amount of the tax benefit to recognize in its financial statements. ASC 740 states that the tax position is to be measured as

> the largest amount of tax benefit that is greater than 50 percent likely of being realized upon ultimate settlement with a taxing authority that has full knowledge of all relevant information.[32]

This measurement process requires the company to make a cumulative probability assessment of all likely outcomes of the audit and litigation process. The company then recognizes the amount that has a greater than 50 percent probability of being sustained on examination and subsequent litigation.

The amount of the tax benefit that is not recognized is recorded as a liability on the balance sheet (usually labeled as "Income Taxes Payable"). The corresponding

---

[31]ASC 740-10-30-7.
[32]ASC 740-10-30-7.

"debit" to record the balance sheet liability is to income tax expense (or a decrease in income tax benefit). If the company expects the uncertain tax position to be resolved in the next 12 months, the balance sheet payable is characterized as current. Otherwise, the payable is characterized as being long-term. The increase in tax expense is added to the current portion of the provision.

### Example 17-17

Elise saw in the domestic production activities deduction (DPAD) workpapers that PCC claimed $465,000 of DPAD on its tax return, computed as 9 percent times $5,166,667 of qualified production activity income (from Example 16-1). She noted that there was mention in the uncertain tax position (UTP) workpapers that there was uncertainty as to whether $1,000,000 of the $5,166,667 met the definition of qualified production activity income (QPAI). This tax position provided PCC with a current year tax benefit of $30,600 ($1,000,000 × 9% × 34%).

What threshold must be met before PCC can *recognize* any of the tax benefit from the "uncertain" portion of the DPAD on its financial statements?

**Answer:** PCC must determine that it is more likely than not that its tax position on the DPAD will be sustained by the IRS on examination based on its technical merits.

### Example 17-18

PCC determined that it was more likely than not that the tax position would be sustained on audit and litigation. The tax department calculated the probability of receiving a full or partial benefit after resolution of the issue as follows:

| Potential Estimated Tax Benefit | Individual Probability of Being Realized (%) | Cumulative Probability of Being Realized (%) |
|---|---|---|
| $30,600 | 60 | 60 |
| $22,500 | 25 | 85 |
| $18,000 | 10 | 95 |
| 0 | 5 | 100 |

Based on these probabilities, how much of the uncertain tax benefit of $30,600 can PCC recognize?

**Answer:** $30,600. PCC can recognize all $30,600 of the DPAD tax benefit because this amount is the largest amount that has a greater than 50 percent cumulative probability of being realized on the ultimate settlement of the tax position.

### Example 17-19

*What if:* Assume PCC's tax department had assessed the cumulative probabilities of sustaining the DPAD tax benefit as follows:

| Potential Estimated Tax Benefit | Individual Probability of Being Realized (%) | Cumulative Probability of Being Realized (%) |
|---|---|---|
| $30,600 | 40 | 40 |
| $22,500 | 30 | 70 |
| $18,000 | 20 | 90 |
| 0 | 10 | 100 |

(continued on page 17-26...)

Based on these probabilities, how much of the uncertain tax benefit of $30,600 can PCC recognize?

**Answer:** $22,500. PCC can recognize $22,500 of the DPAD tax benefit because this amount is the largest amount that has a greater than 50 percent cumulative probability of being realized on the ultimate settlement of the tax position.

What would be PCC's journal entry to record the portion of the tax benefit that cannot be recognized?

**Answer:** PCC would establish a liability for the $8,100 difference between the amount of the benefit received on the current year tax return ($30,600) and the amount the company ultimately expects to receive ($22,500). PCC would record the following journal entry:

| | | |
|---|---|---|
| Current income tax expense | 8,100 | |
| Income taxes payable | | 8,100 |

The income taxes payable account is characterized as long-term on the balance sheet if PCC does not expect the UTP to be resolved within the next 12 months.

## Subsequent Events

ASC 740 requires a company to monitor subsequent events (for example, the issuance of regulations, rulings, court opinions) that might change the company's assessment that a tax position will be sustained on audit and litigation. As facts and circumstances change, a company must reevaluate the tax benefit amount they expect to realize in the future. For example, the Treasury might issue a regulation or ruling that clarifies its tax position on a particular item. This regulation could change a company's assessment that its tax position meets the more-likely-than-not threshold required for recognition.

## Interest and Penalties

ASC 740 requires a company to accrue interest and any applicable penalties on liabilities it establishes for potential future tax obligations. The interest (net of the tax benefit from deducting it on a future tax return when paid) and penalties (which are not tax deductible) can be treated as part of the company's UTP-related income tax expense and income tax payable or can be recognized as interest or penalties separate from the UTP-related income tax expense. ASC 740 only requires that the company apply its election consistently from period to period. This election creates the potential for diversity in practice. For example, General Motors Corporation treats accrued interest and penalties on its uncertain tax positions as part of its selling, general, and administrative expenses, while Ford Motor Company treats accrued interest and penalties on its uncertain tax positions as part of its income tax provision.

## Disclosures of Uncertain Tax Positions

One of the most controversial aspects of ASC 740 is its expansion of the disclosure requirements related to liabilities recorded due to uncertain tax positions. ASC 740 requires the company to roll forward all unrecognized tax benefits on a worldwide aggregated basis. Specific line items must disclose (1) the gross amounts of increases and decreases in liabilities related to uncertain tax positions as a result of tax positions taken during a prior period, (2) the gross amounts of increases and decreases in liabilities related to uncertain tax positions as a result of tax positions taken during the current period, (3) the amounts of decreases in liabilities related to uncertain tax positions relating to settlements with taxing authorities, and (4) reductions in liabilities related to uncertain tax positions as a result of a lapse of the applicable statute of limitations

(the taxing authority can no longer audit the tax return on which the tax position was taken). The UTP disclosure by Microsoft Corporation is illustrated in Exhibit 17-6.

**EXHIBIT 17-6    The UTP Disclosure of Microsoft Corporation**

The aggregate changes in the balance of unrecognized tax benefits were as follows:

| | (In millions) | |
| --- | --- | --- |
| **Year Ended June 30,** | **2009** | **2008** |
| Balance, beginning of year | $3,195 | $ 7,076 |
| Decreases related to settlements | (82) | (4,787) |
| Increases for tax positions related to the current year | 2,203 | 934 |
| Increases for tax positions related to prior years | 239 | 66 |
| Decreases for tax positions related to prior years | (132) | (80) |
| Reductions due to lapsed statute of limitations | (20) | (14) |
| Balance, end of year | $5,403 | $ 3,195 |

FIN 48 became effective for years beginning after December 15, 2006. The FASB required adopters to record their initial FIN 48 cumulative effect adjustment (in the first quarter after adoption) to retained earnings or other balance sheet account rather than to the income tax provision. Subsequent adjustments must be reported as part of the income tax provision.

Opponents of FIN 48 worried that the FIN 48 disclosures would provide a "roadmap" to the IRS to a company's uncertain tax positions.[33] It remains to be seen if this fear is justified, primarily because the UTP disclosure does not identify the tax jurisdictions to which the uncertain tax positions relate.

# FINANCIAL STATEMENT DISCLOSURE AND THE COMPUTATION OF A CORPORATION'S EFFECTIVE TAX RATE

L05

## Balance Sheet Classification

ASC 740 requires publicly traded and privately held companies to disclose their deferred tax assets and liabilities on their balance sheets and classify them as either current or noncurrent.[34] A company classifies its deferred tax assets and liabilities based on the classification of the asset or liability to which the deferred tax account relates. For example, a deferred tax liability related to a long-term asset (for example, depreciation of a fixed asset) is classified as noncurrent because the related asset is classified as noncurrent on the balance sheet. Deferred tax liabilities and assets not related to a specific asset (for example, a net operating loss carryover or organizational expenditures capitalized for tax purposes) are classified based on the expected reversal date of the temporary difference.

ASC 740 requires companies to net deferred tax assets and liabilities based on their classification (current with current, noncurrent with noncurrent) and present the net amount on the balance sheet.[35] ASC 740 does not permit netting of deferred tax assets and liabilities that are attributable to different tax jurisdictions. For example, PCC cannot offset a noncurrent deferred tax asset related to a net operating loss incurred in Germany against a noncurrent deferred tax liability arising from depreciation of fixed assets within the United States. Exhibit 17-7 provides the balance sheet classification for common deferred tax assets and liabilities.

[33]Jesse Drucker, "Lifting the Veil on Tax Risk—New Accounting Rule Lays Bare A Firm's Liability if Transaction Is Later Disallowed by the IRS," *The Wall Street Journal,* May 25, 2007.
[34]ASC 740-10-45-4.
[35]ASC 740-10-45-6.

**EXHIBIT 17-7    Classification of Common Deferred Tax Assets and Liabilities**

| **Current Deferred Account** | **Related Balance Sheet Account** |
|---|---|
| Allowance for Bad Debts | Accounts Receivable |
| Reserve for Warranties | Warranty Payable (liability) |
| Inventory §263A Adjustment | Inventory |
| Revenue Recognition | Unearned Revenue (liability) |
| **Noncurrent Deferred Account** | **Related Balance Sheet Account** |
| Accumulated Depreciation | Fixed Assets |
| Amortization | Goodwill or Other Intangible |
| Deferred Compensation | Deferred Compensation (liability) |

Deferred tax assets related to net operating loss carryovers, net capital loss carryovers, and charitable contribution are classified based on when the temporary difference is expected to reverse (be deducted on a future tax return).

---

**Example 17-20**

Elise reviewed her temporary difference templates (see Examples 17-8 and 17-10). What will be the ending balance in PCC's net current deferred tax assets or liabilities at December 31, 2010?

**Answer:** $345,100 net current deferred tax assets. PCC does not have any current deferred tax liabilities to offset against its current deferred tax assets.

What will be the ending balance in PCC's net noncurrent deferred tax assets or liabilities at December 31, 2010?

**Answer:** ($3,240,982) net noncurrent deferred tax liability.

Because PCC's deferred tax accounts relate to the same tax jurisdiction (United States), PCC can net the noncurrent deferred tax liabilities of $3,632,560 with the noncurrent deferred tax assets of $391,578, resulting in a net noncurrent deferred tax liability of $3,240,982.

---

**Example 17-21**

*What if:* Assume the noncurrent deferred tax asset related to deferred compensation arose in Canada. What will be the ending balance in PCC's net noncurrent deferred tax assets or liabilities at December 31, 2010?

**Answer:** $357,000 noncurrent deferred tax asset and ($3,597,982) net noncurrent deferred tax liability.

PCC cannot net the deferred tax asset that relates to Canada with the other noncurrent deferred tax accounts that relate to the United States.

---

## Income Tax Footnote Disclosure

In addition to the above balance sheet disclosure requirements, ASC 740 mandates that a company disclose the components of the net deferred tax assets and liabilities reported on its balance sheet and the total valuation allowance recognized for deferred tax assets.[36] Most companies provide this information in a footnote to the financial statements (often referred to as the *income tax footnote*). Publicly traded companies must disclose the approximate "tax effect" of each type of temporary difference and carryforward that gives rise to a *significant* portion of the net deferred tax liabilities and deferred tax assets.[37] Privately held (nonpublic) companies only need to disclose the types of significant temporary differences without disclosing the tax effects of each

[36]ASC 740-10-50-2.
[37]ASC 740-10-50-6.

type. ASC 740 does not define the term *significant,* although the SEC requires a publicly traded company to disclose separately the components of its total deferred tax assets and liabilities that are 5 percent or more of the total balance.[38] Exhibit 17-8 provides the disclosure of PCC's deferred tax accounts in its income tax footnote.

## EXHIBIT 17-8 PCC's Income Tax Note to Its Financial Statements

**NOTE 5 INCOME TAXES**

The Company's income (loss) from continuing operations before the income tax provision by taxing jurisdiction is as follows:

|  | **2010** |
|---|---|
| United States | $6,017,000 |

The provision (benefit) for income taxes is as follows:

|  | |
|---|---|
| Current tax provision (benefit) | |
| Federal (U.S.) | $1,751,238 |
| Deferred tax expense (benefit) | |
| Federal (U.S.) | 175,542 |
| Income tax provision | $1,926,780 |

Deferred tax assets and liabilities are classified as current or noncurrent according to the classification of the related asset or liability. The significant components of the Company's deferred tax assets and liabilities as of December 31, 2010, are as follows:

|  | **2010** |
|---|---|
| Deferred tax *assets* | |
| Allowance for bad debts | $ 141,100 |
| Reserve for warranties | 204,000 |
| Deferred compensation | 357,000 |
| Capital loss carryover | 9,520 |
| Contribution carryforward | 25,058 |
| Total deferred tax assets | $ 736,678 |
| Valuation allowance | 0 |
| Net deferred tax assets | $ 736,678 |
| Deferred tax *liabilities* | |
| Depreciation | ($3,632,560) |
| Total deferred tax liabilities | ($3,632,560) |
| Net deferred tax liabilities | ($2,895,882) |

The capital loss carryforward and the contribution carryforward expire in 2013 if unused.

A reconciliation of income taxes computed by applying the statutory U.S. income tax rate to the Company's income before income taxes to the income tax provision is as follows:

|  | **2010** |
|---|---|
| Amount computed at the statutory U.S. tax rate (34 percent) | $2,045,780 |
| Tax-exempt income | (4,080) |
| Nondeductible stock option compensation | 34,000 |
| Nondeductible meals and entertainment | 4,760 |
| Nondeductible life insurance premiums | 11,560 |
| Dividends received deduction | (7,140) |
| Domestic production activities deduction | (158,100) |
| Income tax provision | $1,926,780 |

Cash amounts paid during 2010 for income taxes, net of refunds, was $1,803,938.

---

[38]ASC 740-10-50-8 and SEC Regulation S-X, §210.4-08(h).

ASC 740 also requires publicly traded companies to disclose the significant components of its income tax provision (expense or benefit) attributable to continuing operations in either the financial statements or a note thereto.[39] These components include the (1) current tax expense or benefit, (2) deferred tax expense or benefit, (3) the benefits of operating loss carryforwards, (4) adjustments of a deferred tax liability or asset for enacted changes in tax laws or rates, and (5) adjustments of the beginning-of-the-year balance of a valuation allowance because of a change in circumstances that causes a change in management's judgment about the realizability of the recognized deferred tax assets.

### Computation and Reconciliation of the Income Tax Provision with a Company's *Hypothetical* Tax Provision

ASC 740 requires a company to reconcile its (a) reported income tax provision attributable to continuing operations with (b) the amount of income tax expense that would result from applying its U.S. statutory tax rate to its pretax net income or loss from continuing operations.[40] Alternatively, a company can present the reconciliation in terms of tax rates, comparing its statutory tax rate with its effective tax rate (income tax provision/pretax income from continuing operations).

Differences between a company's income tax provision and its hypothetical tax provision can arise from several sources. Income taxes paid to a state or municipality increase a company's total income tax provision over its hypothetical income tax expense. Income taxes paid to a jurisdiction outside the United States can increase or decrease a company's total income tax provision over its hypothetical income tax expense depending on whether the jurisdiction taxes the company's income at more or less than the U.S. statutory rate. Permanent differences also affect the computation of PCC's income tax provision. Favorable permanent differences (for example, tax-exempt income) decrease the income tax provision relative to the hypothetical income tax provision. Unfavorable permanent differences (for example, nondeductible fines and penalties) increase the income tax provision relative to the hypothetical income tax provision.

ASC 740 requires a publicly traded company to disclose the estimated amount and nature of each significant reconciling item, which the SEC defines as an amount equal to or greater than 5 percent of the hypothetical provision. The SEC requires nonpublicly traded companies to disclose the nature of significant reconciling items but not the reconciling amount.

---

**Example 17-22**

Elise used her schedule of permanent differences (from Example 17-2) to reconcile PCC's income tax provision ($1,926,780, from Example 17-15) with the company's hypothetical income tax provision. The permanent differences from Example 17-2 are reproduced below:

| Permanent Differences | Favorable (Unfavorable) |
| --- | :---: |
| Tax exempt interest income | $12,000 |
| Stock option compensation | $(100,000) |
| Meals and entertainment | $(14,000) |
| Life insurance premiums | $(34,000) |
| Dividends received deduction | $21,000 |
| Domestic production activities deduction | $465,000 |

PCC's pretax net income from continuing operations in 2010 is $6,017,000.

*(continued on page 17-31...)*

---

[39] ASC 740-10-50-9.

[40] ASC 740-10-50-12. The income tax provision computed using the statutory tax rate is often referred to as the *hypothetical* income tax expense.

What is PCC's *hypothetical* income tax provision for 2010?

**Answer:** $2,045,780, computed as $6,017,000 × 34 percent.

What is PCC's *effective tax rate* for 2010?

**Answer:** 32 percent, computed as $1,926,780/$6,017,000.

Provide a reconciliation of PCC's hypothetical income tax provision with its actual income tax provision in 2010. The tax cost or benefit from each permanent difference is computed by multiplying the permanent difference (from above) times 34 percent.

**Answer:**

|  | 2010 |
|---|---|
| Amount computed at statutory U.S. tax rate (34%) | $2,045,780 |
| Tax-exempt income | (4,080) |
| Nondeductible stock compensation | 34,000 |
| Nondeductible meals and entertainment | 4,760 |
| Nondeductible life insurance premiums | 11,560 |
| Dividends received deduction | (7,140) |
| Domestic production activities deduction | (158,100) |
| Income tax provision | $1,926,780 |

The SEC requires its registrants to separately disclose only those components of their effective tax rate reconciliations that equal or exceed 5 percent of the "hypothetical" tax expense. In the above reconciliation, PCC would only be required to separately disclose the items that equal or exceed $102,289 ($2,045,780 x 5%), which, in this example, would be the domestic production activities deduction. The other items could be netted in the reconciliation.

Provide a reconciliation of PCC's statutory income tax rate (34 percent) with its actual effective tax rate (32 percent) in 2010. The percentage effect of each permanent difference is computed by dividing the tax cost or benefit from the item (from above) by PCC's pretax net income ($6,017,000).

**Answer:**

|  | 2010 |
|---|---|
| Statutory U.S. tax rate | 34.0% |
| Tax-exempt income | (0.0) |
| Nondeductible compensation | 0.6 |
| Nondeductible meals and entertainment | 0.0 |
| Nondeductible life insurance premiums | 0.2 |
| Dividends received deduction | (0.1) |
| Domestic production activities deduction | (2.6) |
| Effective tax rate | 32.0% |

Exhibit 17-8 provides the disclosure of PCC's reconciliation of its effective tax rate in its income tax footnote.

**Importance of a Company's Effective Tax Rate**    The effective tax rate often serves as a benchmark for companies in the same industry. However, nonrecurring events can sometimes have a significant impact on the effective tax rate. To mitigate the impact of such aberrational events, companies and their investors may use (at least for internal purposes) a different measure of effective tax rate that backs out one-time and nonrecurring events. This effective tax rate is referred to as the company's **structural tax rate.** The structural effective tax rate often is viewed as more representative of the

company's effective tax rate from its normal (recurring) operations. In our example, PCC does not appear to have any nonrecurring reconciling items, which would make its effective tax rate and its structural tax rate the same.

Analysts often compute a company's **cash tax rate** (cash taxes paid divided by pretax book income) in their evaluation of the company's tax status. As the name implies, the cash tax rate excludes deferred taxes. PCC's cash tax rate in 2010 is 29.1 percent ($1,751,238/$6,017,000). Companies earning income in low-tax jurisdictions outside the United States or that have significant favorable permanent differences can have a cash tax rate that is much lower than their accounting effective tax rate. For example, Amazon.com, Inc. reported an accounting effective tax rate of 27.4 percent and a cash tax rate of 5.9 percent in 2008.

### Interim Period Effective Tax Rates

In addition to annual reports (Form 10-K), PCC also must report earnings on a quarterly basis (Form 10-Q). ASC 740-270, *Interim Reporting,* governs the preparation of these quarterly statements. ASC 740-270-30-6, states that *"at the end of each interim period the entity should make its best estimate of the effective tax rate expected to be applicable for the full fiscal year"* and apply this rate to the income reported in the quarterly statement. A company must reconsider its estimate of the annual rate each quarter. When the estimate changes, the company must adjust the cumulative tax provision for the year-to-date earnings to reflect the new expected annual rate. The adjusting amount becomes the company's income tax provision for the quarter.

## CONVERGENCE OF ASC 740 WITH INTERNATIONAL FINANCIAL REPORTING STANDARDS

In 2002, the FASB and the International Accounting Standards Board (IASB) announced they would work together to develop common accounting standards for the world's capital markets. Included in this project was an effort to converge ASC 740 with its International Financial Reporting Standards (IFRS) counterpart, IAS 12, *Accounting for Income Taxes*. The convergence project currently was put on hold by the FASB after the SEC announced that it was considering allowing the adoption of all IFRS standards by U.S. companies. In March 2009, the IASB issued a proposed revision of IAS 12 that incorporates some convergence with ASC 740. IAS 12 and ASC 740 share many commonalities. The differences relate primarily to issues beyond the scope of this chapter, although there are some disclosure and measurement differences (for example, IAS 12 does not separate deferred tax accounts between current and noncurrent). It seems highly likely that the world will converge to one set of accounting standards in the next decade, in which case U.S. companies will have to comply with a modified version of IAS 12.

## CONCLUSION

In this chapter we discussed the basic rules that govern the computation of a company's U.S. income tax provision. As a result of increased SEC and PCAOB scrutiny, the need for individuals who understand these rules has increased dramatically. The FASB requires a company to take a balance sheet approach to computing its current and future (deferred) tax liabilities or benefits (assets). The income tax provision that appears on a company's income statement becomes the amount necessary to adjust the beginning balances of these accounts to their appropriate ending balances. The FASB and SEC also impose disclosure requirements for how a company reports its tax accounts in the financial statement amounts and notes to the financial statements.

## SUMMARY

Explain the objectives behind FASB ASC Topic 740, *Income Taxes,* and the income tax provision process.

- Objectives of ASC 740.
  - To recognize a current income tax liability or asset for the company's taxes payable or refundable in the current year.
  - To recognize a deferred income tax liability or asset for the income tax effects of the company's temporary differences and carryovers.
- The income tax provision process consists of six steps:
  - Adjust net income before income taxes for all permanent differences.
  - Identify all temporary differences and tax carryforward amounts.
  - Calculate the current income tax expense or benefit (refund).
  - Determine the ending balances in the balance sheet deferred tax asset and liability accounts.
  - Evaluate the need for a valuation allowance for gross deferred tax assets.
  - Calculate the deferred income tax expense or benefit.

Calculate the current and deferred income tax expense or benefit components of a company's income tax provision.

- The company first adjusts its pretax net income or loss for permanent and temporary book-tax differences to compute taxable income or loss. The company then applies the appropriate tax rate to taxable income (loss) to compute the tax return current tax expense or benefit.
- The company adjusts its tax return income tax liability or benefit for audit refunds or deficiencies from prior year tax returns, and income tax benefits from stock option exercises treated as permanent differences.
- A company computes its deferred income tax expense or benefit by applying the applicable tax rate to the change in the cumulative balance sheet temporary differences between the financial accounting basis of an asset or liability and its corresponding tax basis from the beginning of the year to the end of the year.
- The future tax benefits from deductible (cumulatively unfavorable) temporary differences are recorded as deferred tax assets.
- The future tax costs of favorable taxable (cumulatively favorable) temporary differences are recorded as deferred tax liabilities.

Recall what a valuation allowance represents and describe the process by which it is determined.

- If a company determines that it is more likely than not (a greater than 50 percent probability) that some portion or all of the deferred tax assets will not be realized in a future period, it must offset the deferred tax assets with a valuation allowance to reflect the amount the company does not expect to realize in the future.
- The determination as to whether it is more likely than not that a deferred tax asset will not be realized in the future must be based on all available evidence, both positive and negative.
- ASC 740 identifies four sources of prior and future taxable income to consider: (1) future reversals of existing taxable temporary differences, (2) taxable income in prior carryback year(s), (3) expected future taxable income exclusive of reversing temporary differences and carryforwards, and (4) expected income from tax strategies.

Explain how a company accounts for its uncertain income tax positions under ASC 740.

- A company must determine whether it can record the tax benefits from an "uncertain" tax position in its financial statement for the period in which the transaction takes place, knowing that the ultimate resolution of the tax position may not be known until some future period.

- ASC 740 applies a two-step process to evaluating uncertain tax positions:
  - Recognition: A company must determine whether it is more likely than not (a greater than 50 percent probability) that a tax position will be sustained upon examination by the IRS or other taxing authority, including resolution of any appeals within the court system, based on the technical merits of the position.
  - Measurement: If the tax position meets the more-likely-than-not threshold (a subjective determination), the company must determine the amount of the benefit to record in the financial statements.
- Under ASC 740, the amount to be recorded is the largest amount of the benefit, as calculated on a cumulative probability basis, which is more likely than not to be realized on the ultimate settlement of the tax position.

**LO5** Recognize the different components of a company's disclosure of its income tax accounts in the financial statements and footnotes and comprehend how a company computes and discloses the components of its "effective tax rate."

- ASC 740 requires a company to disclose and separate its deferred tax liabilities and assets into a current amount and a noncurrent amount on its balance sheet.
- A company also is required to present the "significant" components of the income tax provision (expense or benefit) attributable to continuing operations.
- ASC 740 requires publicly traded companies to reconcile their reported income tax expense (benefit) from continuing operations with the *hypothetical* tax expense that would have resulted from applying the domestic federal statutory rate to pretax income from continuing operations. Alternatively, the company can compute an *effective tax rate* from its continuing operations and reconcile it with the domestic federal statutory rate (34 percent or 35 percent).
- A company computes its effective tax rate by dividing its income tax provision (benefit) from continuing operations by its pretax net income from continuing operations.
- Items that cause the effective tax rate to differ from the statutory tax rate include permanent differences, audit adjustments, state and local taxes, and international taxes.

# KEY TERMS

**book equivalent of taxable income (17-8)**

**cash tax rate (17-32)**

**current income tax expense or benefit (17-11)**

**current tax liability or asset (17-3)**

**deductible temporary difference (17-10)**

**deferred tax asset (17-2)**

**deferred tax liability (17-2)**

**effective tax rate (17-7)**

**enacted tax rate (17-12)**

**permanent book-tax differences (17-6)**

**structural tax rate (17-31)**

**tax accounting balance sheet (17-12)**

**tax carryforwards (17-2)**

**taxable temporary difference (17-9)**

**uncertain tax positions (17-11)**

**valuation allowance (17-18)**

# DISCUSSION QUESTIONS

1. **(LO1)** Identify some of the reasons why accounting for income taxes is complex.
2. **(LO1)** True or False: ASC 740 applies to all taxes paid by a corporation. Explain.
3. **(LO1)** True or False: ASC 740 is the sole source for the rules that apply to accounting for income taxes. Explain.
4. **(LO1)** How does the fact that most corporations file their financial statements several months before they file their income tax returns complicate the income tax provision process?
5. **(LO1)** What distinguishes an *income tax* from other taxes?
6. **(LO1)** Briefly describe the six-step process by which a company computes its income tax provision.

7. **(LO2)** What are the two components of a company's income tax provision? What does each component represent about a company's income tax provision?

8. **(LO2)** True or False: All differences between book and taxable income, both permanent and temporary, affect a company's effective tax rate. Explain.

9. **(LO2)** When does a temporary difference resulting from an expense (deduction) create a taxable temporary difference? A deductible temporary difference?

10. **(LO2)** When does a temporary difference resulting from income create a taxable temporary difference? A deductible temporary difference?

11. **(LO2)** Briefly describe what is meant by the *asset and liability* or *balance sheet* approach taken by ASC 740 with respect to computing a corporation's deferred tax provision.

12. **(LO2)** Why are cumulatively favorable temporary differences referred to as taxable temporary differences?

13. **(LO2)** Why are cumulatively unfavorable temporary differences referred to as deductible temporary differences?

14. **(LO2)** In addition to the current year tax return taxes payable or refundable, what other transactions can affect a company's current income tax provision?

15. **(LO2,4)** What is an unrecognized tax benefit and how does it affect a company's current income tax expense?

16. **(LO2)** True or False: When Congress changes the corporate tax rates, only the current year book-tax temporary differences are measured using the new rates. Explain.

17. **(LO2)** True or False: All temporary differences have a financial accounting basis. Explain.

18. **(LO3)** What is the purpose behind a valuation allowance as it applies to deferred tax assets?

19. **(LO3)** What is the difference between *recognition* and *realization* as it applies to the recording of a deferred tax asset on a balance sheet?

20. **(LO3)** Briefly describe the four sources of taxable income a company evaluates in determining if a valuation allowance is necessary.

21. **(LO3)** Which of the four sources of taxable income are considered objective and which are considered subjective? Which of these sources generally receives the most weight in analyzing whether a valuation allowance is necessary?

22. **(LO3)** What are the elements that define a tax planning strategy as it applies to determining if a valuation allowance is necessary? Provide an example where a tax planning strategy may be necessary to avoid recording a valuation allowance.

23. **(LO3)** When does a company remove a valuation allowance from its balance sheet?

24. **(LO3)** What is a company's *book equivalent of taxable income* and how does this computation enter into the income tax provision process?

25. **(LO4)** What motivated the FASB to issue FIN 48?

26. **(LO4)** Briefly describe the two-step process a company must undertake when it evaluates whether it can record the tax benefit from an uncertain tax position under ASC 740.

27. **(LO4)** Distinguish between *recognition* and *measurement* as they relate to the computation of unrecognized tax benefits under ASC 740.

28. **(LO4)** What is a *tax position* as it relates to the application of ASC 740 to uncertain tax positions?

29. **(LO4)** True or False: A company determines its unrecognized tax benefits with respect to a transaction only at the time the transaction takes place; subsequent events are ignored. Explain.

30. **(LO4)** True or False: ASC 740 requires that a company treat potential interest and penalties related to an unrecognized tax benefit as part of its income tax provision. Explain.

31. **(LO4)** Where on the balance sheet does a company report its unrecognized tax benefits?

32. **(LO4)** Why did many companies oppose FIN 48 when it was first proposed?

33. **(LO5)** How does a company determine if a deferred tax asset or liability should be classified as current or noncurrent on its balance sheet?

34. **(LO5)** Under what conditions can a company net its current deferred tax assets with its current deferred tax liabilities on the balance sheet?

35. **(LO5)** True or False: A publicly traded company must disclose all of the components of its deferred tax assets and liabilities in a footnote to the financial statements. Explain.

36. **(LO5)** What is a company's *hypothetical* income tax provision and what is its importance in a company's disclosure of its income tax provision in the tax footnote?

37. **(LO5)** Briefly describe the difference between a company's effective tax rate, cash tax rate, and structural tax rate.

## PROBLEMS

38. **(LO1)** Which of the following taxes is *not* accounted for under ASC 740?
    a. Income taxes paid to the U.S. government.
    b. Income taxes paid to the French government.
    c. Income taxes paid to the city of Detroit.
    d. Property taxes paid to the city of Detroit.
    e. All of the above taxes are accounted for under ASC 740.

39. **(LO1)** Which of the following organizations can issue rules that govern accounting for income taxes?
    a. FASB.
    b. SEC.
    c. IRS.
    d. a and b above.
    e. All of the above organizations.

■ research ■■

40. **(LO1)** Find the paragraph(s) in ASC 740 that deal with the following items (you can access ASC 740 on the FASB Web site, www.fasb.org, and then clicking on "View the Codification"). You will need a password from your instructor.
    a. The objectives and basic principles that underlie ASC 740.
    b. Examples of book-tax differences that create temporary differences.
    c. The definition of a *tax planning strategy*.
    d. Examples of positive evidence in the valuation allowance process.
    e. Rules relating to financial statement disclosure.

41. **(LO2)** Woodward Corporation reported pretax book income of $1,000,000 in 2010. Included in the computation were favorable temporary differences of $200,000, unfavorable temporary differences of $50,000, and favorable permanent differences of $100,000. Assuming a tax rate of 34 percent, compute the company's current income tax expense or benefit for 2010.

42. **(LO2)** Cass Corporation reported pretax book income of $10,000,000 in 2010. During the current year, the reserve for bad debts increased by $100,000. In

addition, tax depreciation exceeded book depreciation by $200,000. Cass Corporation sold a fixed asset and reported book gain of $50,000 and tax gain of $75,000. Finally, the company received $250,000 of tax-exempt life insurance proceeds from the death of one of its officers. Assuming a tax rate of 34 percent, compute the company's current income tax expense or benefit for 2010.

43. **(LO2)** Grand Corporation reported pretax book income of $600,000 in 2010. Tax depreciation exceeded book depreciation by $400,000. In addition, the company received $300,000 of tax-exempt municipal bond interest. The company's prior year tax return showed taxable income of $50,000. Assuming a tax rate of 34 percent, compute the company's current income tax expense or benefit for 2010.

44. **(LO2)** Chandler Corporation reported pretax book income of $2,000,000 in 2010. Tax depreciation exceeded book depreciation by $500,000. During the year the company capitalized $250,000 into ending inventory under §263A. Capitalized inventory costs of $150,000 in beginning inventory were deducted as part of cost of goods sold on the tax return. Assuming a tax rate of 34 percent, compute the company's taxes payable or refundable for 2010.

45. **(LO2)** Davison Company determined that the book basis of its office building exceeded the tax basis by $800,000. This basis difference is properly characterized as:

   a. A permanent difference.
   b. A taxable temporary difference.
   c. A deductible temporary difference.
   d. A favorable book-tax difference.
   e. Both c and d above are correct.

46. **(LO2)** Abbot Company determined that the book basis of its allowance for bad debts is $100,000. There is no corresponding tax basis in this account. The basis difference is properly characterized as:

   a. A permanent difference.
   b. A taxable temporary difference.
   c. A deductible temporary difference.
   d. A favorable book-tax difference.
   e. Both b and d above are correct.

47. **(LO2)** Which of the following items is *not* a temporary book-tax basis difference?

   a. Warranty reserve accruals.
   b. Accelerated depreciation.
   c. Capitalized inventory costs under §263A.
   d. Nondeductible stock option compensation from exercising an ISO.
   e. All of the above are temporary differences.

48. **(LO2)** Which of the following book-tax differences does *not* create a favorable temporary book-tax basis difference?

   a. Tax depreciation for the period exceeds book depreciation.
   b. Bad debts charged off in the current period exceed the bad debts accrued in the current period.
   c. Inventory costs capitalized under §263A deducted as part of current year tax cost of goods sold are less than the inventory costs capitalized in ending inventory.
   d. Vacation pay accrued for tax purposes in a prior period is deducted in the current period.
   e. All of the above create a favorable temporary book-tax difference.

49. **(LO2)** Lodge Inc. reported pretax book income of $5,000,000 in 2010. During the year, the company increased its reserve for warranties by $200,000. The company deducted $50,000 on its 2010 tax return related to warranty payments made during the year. What is the impact on taxable income compared to pretax book income of the book-tax difference that results from these two events?

   a. Favorable (decreases taxable income).

   b. Unfavorable (increases taxable income).

   c. Neutral (no impact on taxable income).

50. **(LO2)** Which of the following book-tax basis differences results in a deductible temporary difference?

   a. Book basis of a fixed asset exceeds its tax basis.

   b. Book basis of a pension-related liability exceeds its tax basis.

   c. Prepayment of income included on the tax return but not on the income statement (the transaction is recorded as a liability on the balance sheet).

   d. All of the above result in a deductible temporary difference.

   e. Both b and c result in a deductible temporary difference.

51. **(LO2)** Shaw Corporation reported pretax book income of $1,000,000 in 2010. Included in the computation were favorable temporary differences of $200,000, unfavorable temporary differences of $50,000, and favorable permanent differences of $100,000. Assuming a tax rate of 34 percent, compute the company's deferred income tax expense or benefit for 2010.

52. **(LO2)** Shaw Inc. reported pretax book income of $10,000,000 in 2010. During the current year, the reserve for bad debts increased by $100,000. In addition, tax depreciation exceeded book depreciation by $200,000. Shaw Inc. sold a fixed asset and reported book gain of $50,000 and tax gain of $75,000. Finally, the company received $250,000 of tax-exempt life insurance proceeds from the death of one of its officers. Assuming a tax rate of 34 percent, compute the company's deferred income tax expense or benefit for 2010.

53. **(LO2)** Harrison Corporation reported pretax book income of $600,000 in 2010. Tax depreciation exceeded book depreciation by $400,000. In addition, the company received $300,000 of tax-exempt municipal bond interest. The company's prior year tax return showed taxable income of $50,000. Assuming a tax rate of 34 percent, compute the company's deferred income tax expense or benefit for 2010.

54. **(LO2)** Identify the following items as creating a temporary difference, permanent difference, or no difference.

| Item | Temporary Difference | Permanent Difference | No Difference |
|------|----------------------|----------------------|---------------|
| Reserve for warranties | | | |
| Accrued pension liability | | | |
| Goodwill not amortized for tax purposes but subject to impairment under ASC 350 | | | |
| Meal and entertainment expenses | | | |
| Life insurance proceeds | | | |
| Net capital loss carryover | | | |
| Nondeductible fines and penalties | | | |
| Accrued vacation pay liability paid within the first two and one-half months of the next tax year | | | |

55. **(LO2)** Which of the following items is *not* a permanent book-tax difference?

   a. Tax-exempt interest income.

   b. Tax-exempt insurance proceeds.

   c. Domestic production activities deduction.

   d. Nondeductible meals and entertainment expense.

   e. First-year expensing under §179.

56. **(LO2)** Ann Corporation reported pretax book income of $1,000,000 in 2010. Included in the computation were favorable temporary differences of $200,000, unfavorable temporary differences of $50,000, and favorable permanent differences of $100,000. Compute the company's book equivalent of taxable income. Use this number to compute the company's total income tax provision or benefit for 2010, assuming a tax rate of 34 percent.

57. **(LO2)** Burcham Corporation reported pretax book income of $600,000 in 2010. Tax depreciation exceeded book depreciation by $400,000. In addition, the company received $300,000 of tax-exempt municipal bond interest. The company's prior year tax return showed taxable income of $50,000. Compute the company's book equivalent of taxable income. Use this number to compute the company's total income tax provision or benefit for 2010, assuming a tax rate of 34 percent.

58. **(LO3)** Adams Corporation has total deferred tax assets of $3,000,000 at year-end. Management is assessing whether a valuation allowance must be recorded against some or all of the deferred tax assets. What level of assurance must management have, based on the weight of available evidence, that some or all of the deferred tax assets will not be realized before a valuation allowance is required?

   a. Probable.

   b. More likely than not.

   c. Realistic possibility.

   d. Reasonable.

   e. More than remote.

59. **(LO3)** Which of the following evidence would *not* be considered positive in determining whether Adams Corporation needs to record a valuation allowance for some or all of its deferred tax assets?

   a. The company forecasts future taxable income because of its backlog of orders.

   b. The company has unfavorable temporary differences that will create future taxable income when they reverse.

   c. The company has tax planning strategies that it can implement to create future taxable income.

   d. The company has cumulative net income over the current and prior two years.

   e. The company had a net operating loss carryover expire in the current year.

60. **(LO3)** As of the beginning of the year, Gratiot Company recorded a valuation allowance of $200,000 against its deferred tax assets of $1,000,000. The valuation allowance relates to a net operating loss carryover from the prior year. During the year, management concludes that the valuation allowance is no longer necessary because it forecasts sufficient taxable income to absorb the NOL carryover. What is the impact of management's reversal of the valuation allowance on the company's effective tax rate?

   a. Increases the effective tax rate

   b. Decreases the effective tax rate

   c. No impact on the effective tax rate

61. **(LO3)** Which of the following evidence would be considered negative in determining whether Gratiot Corporation needs to record a valuation allowance for some or all of its deferred tax assets?

   a. The company forecasts future taxable income because of its backlog of orders.

   b. The company has a cumulative net loss over the current and prior two years.

c. The company has unfavorable temporary differences that will create future taxable income when they reverse.

d. The company had a net operating loss carryover expire in the current year.

e. Both b and d constitute negative evidence in assessing the need for a valuation allowance.

62. **(LO3)** Saginaw Inc. completed its first year of operations with a pretax loss of $500,000. The tax return showed a net operating loss of $600,000, which the company will carry forward. The $100,000 book-tax difference results from excess tax depreciation over book depreciation. Management has determined that they should record a valuation allowance equal to the net deferred tax asset. Assuming the current tax expense is zero, prepare the journal entries to record the deferred tax provision and the valuation allowance.

research

63. **(LO3)** What reasons did General Motors management give for their establishment of a $39 billion valuation allowance in the third quarter of 2007? You can access the company's Form 10-Q for the third quarter, 2007, from the Company's Web site, www.gm.com.

64. **(LO4)** Montcalm Corporation has total deferred tax assets of $3,000,000 at year-end. Of that amount, $1,000,000 results from the current expensing of an expenditure that the IRS might assert must be capitalized on audit. Management is trying to determine if it should not recognize the deferred tax asset related to this item under ASC 740. What confidence level must management have that the item will be sustained on audit before it can recognize any portion of the deferred tax asset under ASC 740?

a. Probable.

b. More likely than not.

c. Realistic possibility.

d. Reasonable.

e. More than remote.

65. **(LO4)** Which of the following statements about uncertain tax positions (UTP) is correct?

a. UTP applies only to tax positions accounted for under ASC 740 taken on a filed tax return.

b. UTP applies to all tax positions accounted for under ASC 740, regardless of whether the item is taken on a filed tax return.

c. UTP deals with both the recognition and realization of deferred tax assets.

d. If a tax position meets the more-likely-than-not standard, the entire amount of the deferred tax asset or current tax benefit related to the tax position can be recognized under ASC 740.

e. Statements b, c, and d are correct.

66. **(LO4)** Cadillac Square Corporation determined that $1,000,000 of its domestic production activities deduction on its current year tax return was uncertain, but that it was more likely than not to be sustained on audit. Management made the following assessment of the company's potential tax benefit from the deduction and its probability of occurring.

| Potential Estimated Benefit (000s) | Individual Probability of Occurring (%) | Cumulative Probability of Occurring |
|---|---|---|
| $340,000 | 40 | 40 |
| $272,000 | 25 | 65 |
| $170,000 | 20 | 85 |
| 0 | 15 | 100 |

What amount of the tax benefit related to the uncertain tax position from the domestic production activities deduction can Cadillac Square Corporation recognize in calculating its income tax provision in the current year?

67. **(LO4)** How would your answer to Problem 67 change if management determined that there was only a 50/50 chance any portion of the $1,000,000 DPAD would be sustained on audit?

68. **(LO4)** As part of its UTP assessment, Penobscot Company records interest and penalties related to its unrecognized tax benefit of $500,000. Which of the following statements about recording this amount is most correct?

a. Penobscot must include the amount in its income tax provision.

b. Penobscot must record the amount separate from its income tax provision.

c. Penobscot can elect to allocate a portion of the amount to both its income tax provision and its general and administrative expenses provided the company discloses which option it chose.

d. Penobscot can elect to record the entire amount as part of its income tax provision or separate from its income tax provision, provided the company discloses which option it chose.

e. Statements c and d above are both correct.

69. **(LO4)** By what amount did Intel Corporation adjust its retained earnings in 2007 after adopting FIN 48? What amount of its unrecognized tax benefit did Intel reclassify as noncurrent on its balance sheet for 2007? You can access the company's 2007 Annual Report at www.intel.com.

**research**

70. **(LO5)** Beacon Corporation recorded the following deferred tax assets and liabilities:

| | |
|---|---|
| Current deferred tax assets | $ 650,000 |
| Current deferred tax liabilities | (400,000) |
| Noncurrent deferred tax assets | 1,000,000 |
| Noncurrent deferred tax liabilities | (2,500,000) |
| Net deferred tax liabilities | $(1,250,000) |

All of the deferred tax accounts relate to temporary differences that arose as a result of the company's U.S. operations. Which of the following statements describes how Beacon should disclose these accounts on its balance sheet?

a. Beacon reports a net deferred tax liability of $1,250,000 on its balance sheet.

b. Beacon nets the deferred tax assets and the deferred tax liabilities and reports a net deferred tax asset of $1,650,000 and a net deferred tax liability of $2,900,000 on its balance sheet.

c. Beacon can elect to net the current deferred tax accounts and the noncurrent tax accounts and report a net current deferred tax asset of $250,000 and a net deferred tax liability of $1,500,000 on its balance sheet.

d. Beacon is required to net the current deferred tax accounts and the noncurrent tax accounts and report a net current deferred tax asset of $250,000 and a net deferred tax liability of $1,500,000 on its balance sheet.

71. **(LO5)** ASC 740 requires a company to disclose those components of its deferred tax assets and liabilities that are considered:

a. Relevant.

b. Significant.

c. Important.

d. Major.

72. **(LO5)** Which of the following temporary differences creates a current deferred tax asset?

    a. Allowance for bad debts.
    b. Goodwill amortization.
    c. Accumulated depreciation.
    d. Inventory capitalization under §263A.
    e. Both a and d above create a current deferred tax asset.

73. **(LO5)** Which formula represents the calculation of a company's effective tax rate?

    a. Income taxes paid/Taxable income.
    b. Income taxes paid/Pretax income from continuing operations.
    c. Income tax provision/Taxable income.
    d. Income tax provision/Pretax income from continuing operations.

74. **(LO5)** Which of the following items is *not* a reconciling item in the income tax footnote?

    a. State income taxes.
    b. Foreign income taxes.
    c. Accrued pension liabilities.
    d. Dividends received deduction.
    e. Tax-exempt municipal bond interest.

75. **(LO5)** Randolph Company reported pretax net income from continuing operations of $800,000 and taxable income of $500,000. The book-tax difference of $300,000 was due to a $200,000 favorable temporary difference relating to depreciation, an unfavorable temporary difference of $80,000 due to an increase in the reserve for bad debts, and a $180,000 favorable permanent difference from the receipt of life insurance proceeds. Randolph Company's applicable tax rate is 34 percent.

    a. Compute Randolph Company's current income tax expense.
    b. Compute Randolph Company's deferred income tax expense or benefit.
    c. Compute Randolph Company's effective tax rate.
    d. Provide a reconciliation of Randolph Company's effective tax rate with its hypothetical tax rate of 34 percent.

76. **(LO5)** Which of the following pronouncements should a company consult in computing its quarterly income tax provision?

    a. ASC 740.
    b. ASC 230.
    c. ASC 718.
    d. ASC 810.
    e. SarbOX 404.

## COMPREHENSIVE PROBLEMS

77. You have been assigned to compute the income tax provision for Motown Memories Inc. (MM) as of December 31, 2010. The company's federal income tax rate is 34 percent. The company's income statement for 2010 is provided below:

|  |  |
|---|---|
| **Motown Memories Inc.** | |
| **Statement of Operations** | |
| **at December 31, 2010** | |

| | |
|---|---|
| Net sales | $50,000,000 |
| Cost of sales | 28,000,000 |
| Gross profit | $22,000,000 |
| Compensation | $ 2,000,000 |
| Selling expenses | 1,500,000 |
| Depreciation and amortization | 4,000,000 |
| Other expenses | 500,000 |
| Total operating expenses | $ 8,000,000 |
| Income from operations | $14,000,000 |
| Interest and other income | 1,000,000 |
| Income before income taxes | $15,000,000 |

You have identified the following permanent differences:

| | |
|---|---|
| Interest income from municipal bonds: | $ 50,000 |
| Nondeductible meals and entertainment expenses: | $ 20,000 |
| Domestic production activities deduction: | $250,000 |
| Nondeductible fines: | $ 5,000 |

MM prepared the following schedule of temporary differences from the beginning of the year to the end of the year:

|  |  |  |  |  |  |
|---|---|---|---|---|---|
| **Motown Memories Inc.** | | | | | |
| **Temporary Difference Scheduling Template** | | | | | |

| Taxable Temporary Differences | BOY Cumulative T/D | Beginning Deferred Taxes (@ 34%) | Current Year Change | EOY Cumulative T/D | Ending Deferred Taxes (@ 34%) |
|---|---|---|---|---|---|
| *Noncurrent* | | | | | |
| Accumulated depreciation | (8,000,000) | (2,720,000) | (1,000,000) | (9,000,000) | (3,060,000) |

| Deductible Temporary Differences | BOY Cumulative T/D | Beginning Deferred Taxes (@ 34%) | Current Year Change | EOY Cumulative T/D | Ending Deferred Taxes (@ 34%) |
|---|---|---|---|---|---|
| *Current* | | | | | |
| Allowance for bad debts | 200,000 | 68,000 | 50,000 | 250,000 | 85,000 |
| Reserve for warranties | 100,000 | 34,000 | 20,000 | 120,000 | 40,800 |
| Inventory §263A adjustment | 240,000 | 81,600 | 60,000 | 300,000 | 102,000 |
| Total current | 540,000 | 183,600 | 130,000 | 670,000 | 227,800 |
| *Noncurrent* | | | | | |
| Deferred compensation | 50,000 | 17,000 | 10,000 | 60,000 | 20,400 |
| Accrued pension liabilities | 3,000,000 | 1,020,000 | 250,000 | 3,250,000 | 1,105,000 |
| Total noncurrent | 3,050,000 | 1,037,000 | 260,000 | 3,310,000 | 1,125,400 |
| Total | 3,590,000 | 1,220,600 | 390,000 | 3,980,000 | 1,353,200 |

**Required:**

    a. Compute MM's current income tax expense or benefit for 2010.

    b. Compute MM's deferred income tax expense or benefit for 2010.

    c. Prepare a reconciliation of MM's total income tax provision with its hypothetical income tax expense in both dollars and rates.

78. You have been assigned to compute the income tax provision for Tulip City Flowers Inc. (TCF) as of December 31, 2010. The company's federal income tax rate is 34 percent. The company's income statement for 2010 is provided below:

**Tulip City Flowers Inc.**
**Statement of Operations**
**at December 31, 2010**

| | |
|---|---:|
| Net sales | $20,000,000 |
| Cost of sales | 12,000,000 |
| Gross profit | $ 8,000,000 |
| Compensation | $    500,000 |
| Selling expenses | 750,000 |
| Depreciation and amortization | 1,250,000 |
| Other expenses | 1,000,000 |
| Total operating expenses | $ 3,500,000 |
| Income from operations | $ 4,500,000 |
| Interest and other income | 25,000 |
| Income before income taxes | $ 4,525,000 |

You have identified the following permanent differences:

| | |
|---|---|
| Interest income from municipal bonds: | $10,000 |
| Nondeductible stock compensation: | $ 5,000 |
| Domestic production activities deduction: | $ 8,000 |
| Nondeductible fines: | $ 1,000 |

TCF prepared the following schedule of temporary differences from the beginning of the year to the end of the year:

**Tulip City Flowers Inc.**
**Temporary Difference Scheduling Template**

| Taxable Temporary Differences | BOY Cumulative T/D | Beginning Deferred Taxes (@ 34%) | Current Year Change | EOY Cumulative T/D | Ending Deferred Taxes (@ 34%) |
|---|---|---|---|---|---|
| *Noncurrent* | | | | | |
| Accumulated depreciation | (5,000,000) | (1,700,000) | (500,000) | (5,500,000) | (1,870,000) |

| Deductible Temporary Differences | BOY Cumulative T/D | Beginning Deferred Taxes (@ 34%) | Current Year Change | EOY Cumulative T/D | Ending Deferred Taxes (@ 34%) |
|---|---|---|---|---|---|
| *Current* | | | | | |
| Allowance for bad debts | 100,000 | 34,000 | 10,000 | 110,000 | 37,400 |
| Prepaid income | 0 | 0 | 20,000 | 20,000 | 7,000 |
| Total current | 100,000 | 34,000 | 30,000 | 130,000 | 44,400 |

(continued)

| Deductible Temporary Differences | BOY Cumulative T/D | Beginning Deferred Taxes (@ 34%) | Current Year Change | EOY Cumulative T/D | Ending Deferred Taxes (@ 34%) |
|---|---|---|---|---|---|
| *Noncurrent* | | | | | |
| Deferred compensation | 50,000 | 17,000 | 10,000 | 60,000 | 20,400 |
| Accrued pension liabilities | 500,000 | 170,000 | 100,000 | 600,000 | 204,000 |
| Total noncurrent | 550,000 | 187,000 | 110,000 | 660,000 | 224,400 |
| Total | 650,000 | 221,000 | 140,000 | 790,000 | 268,800 |

**Required:**

a. Compute TCF's current income tax expense or benefit for 2010.
b. Compute TCF's deferred income tax expense or benefit for 2010.
c. Prepare a reconciliation of TCF's total income tax provision with its hypothetical income tax expense in both dollars and rates.
d. Assume TCF's tax rate increased to 35 percent in 2010. Recompute TCF's deferred income tax expense or benefit for 2010 using the following template:

**Tulip City Flowers Inc.**
**Temporary Difference Scheduling Template**

| Taxable Temporary Differences | BOY Cumulative T/D | Beginning Deferred Taxes (@ 34%) | Current Year Change | EOY Cumulative T/D | Ending Deferred Taxes (@ 35%) |
|---|---|---|---|---|---|
| *Noncurrent* | | | | | |
| Accumulated depreciation | (5,000,000) | (1,700,000) | (500,000) | (5,500,000) | |

| Deductible Temporary Differences | BOY Cumulative T/D | Beginning Deferred Taxes (@ 34%) | Current Year Change | EOY Cumulative T/D | Ending Deferred Taxes (@ 35%) |
|---|---|---|---|---|---|
| *Current* | | | | | |
| Allowance for bad debts | 100,000 | 34,000 | 10,000 | 110,000 | |
| Prepaid income | 0 | 0 | 20,000 | 20,000 | |
| Total current | 100,000 | 34,000 | 30,000 | 130,000 | |
| *Noncurrent* | | | | | |
| Deferred compensation | 50,000 | 17,000 | 10,000 | 60,000 | |
| Accrued pension liabilities | 500,000 | 170,000 | 100,000 | 600,000 | |
| Total noncurrent | 550,000 | 187,000 | 110,000 | 660,000 | |
| Total | 650,000 | 221,000 | 140,000 | 790,000 | |

79. Access the 2008 Annual Report for Johnson & Johnson Company and answer the following questions. You can access the annual report at www.jnj.com.

**Required:**

a. Using information from the company's income statement and income taxes footnote, what was the company's effective tax rate for 2008? Show how the rate is calculated.

b. Using information from the statement of cash flows, calculate the company's cash tax rate.

c. What does the company's income taxes note tell you about where the company earns its international income? Why does earning income in these countries cause the effective tax rate to decrease?

d. What item creates the company's largest deferred tax asset? Explain why this item creates a deductible temporary difference.

e. What item creates the company's largest deferred tax liability? Explain why this item creates a taxable temporary difference.

f. How does the company classify its income taxes payable related to its unrecognized tax benefits on the balance sheet?

g. How does the company treat interest and penalties related to its unrecognized tax benefits?

80. Spartan Builders Corporation is a builder of high-end housing with locations in major metropolitan areas throughout the Midwest. At June 30, 2010, the company has deferred tax assets totaling $10 million and deferred tax liabilities of $5 million, all of which relate to U.S. temporary differences. Reversing taxable temporary differences and taxable income in the carryback period can be used to support approximately $2 million of the $10 million gross deferred tax asset. The remaining $8 million of gross deferred tax assets will have to come from future taxable income.

    The company has historically been profitable. However, significant losses were incurred in fiscal years 2008 and 2009. These two years reflect a cumulative loss of 10 million, with losses of $3 million expected in 2010. $7 million of the losses was due to a write-down of inventory. Beginning in fiscal 2011, management decided to get out of the metropolitan Chicago market, which had become oversaturated with new houses.

    Evaluate the company's need to record a valuation allowance for the $10 of gross deferred tax assets. What positive and negative evidence would you weigh?

# chapter
# 18

# Corporate Taxation: Nonliquidating Distributions

## Learning Objectives

**Upon completing this chapter, you should be able to:**

**LO 1** Explain the basic tax law framework that applies to property distributions from a corporation to a shareholder.

**LO 2** Compute a corporation's earnings and profits and calculate the dividend amount received by a shareholder.

**LO 3** Identify situations in which a corporation may be deemed to have paid a "constructive dividend" to a shareholder.

**LO 4** Comprehend the basic tax rules that apply to stock dividends.

**LO 5** Comprehend the different tax consequences that can arise from stock redemptions.

**LO 6** Contrast a partial liquidation from a stock redemption and describe the difference in tax consequences to the shareholders.

| Storyline Summary | |
| --- | --- |
| *Taxpayer:* | Jim Wheeler |
| *Location:* | East Lansing, Michigan |
| *Employment status:* | Co-owner of Spartan Cycle and Repair (75 percent) |
| *Filing status:* | Married filing jointly |
| *Dependents:* | One child |
| *Marginal tax rate:* | 40 percent |
| *Taxpayer:* | Ginny Gears |
| *Location:* | East Lansing, Michigan |
| *Employment status:* | Co-owner of Spartan Cycles and Repair (25 percent) |
| *Filing status:* | Unmarried |
| *Marginal tax rate:* | 25 percent |

J im Wheeler and Ginny Gears have been friends for many years, having met at the Mid-Michigan Cycling Club in 2000. They often talked about their shared dream of owning and operating a high-end bicycle shop in East Lansing, Michigan, on their weekly 50-mile bike trips together. Many of their friends in the club often remarked how difficult it was to get parts and have their bicycles repaired locally. Jim found himself repairing his friends' bicycles using the knowledge he gained while working at a bicycle shop in Boulder, Colorado, during his undergraduate days at the University of Colorado. Ginny had majored in marketing at Michigan State University (MSU) and was eager to put her marketing and management skills to work in her own business.

Jim and Ginny fulfilled their dream when they created Spartan Cycles and Repair (SCR) in July 2007. They began their business by leasing a vacant building on Grand River Avenue near the MSU campus. Their business had humble beginnings, as most start-up companies do. They raised the $50,000 capital they needed to purchase inventory and the necessary repair tools by borrowing from Jim's parents, Walt and Wanda. On the advice of their accountant and lawyer, Jim and Ginny organized their company as a C corporation, with Jim owning 75 percent of the corporation's stock and Ginny owning the remaining 25 percent. Jim's responsibilities include doing the bicycle repairs and deciding which bicycle brands to carry. Ginny is responsible for managing and marketing the business. Jim works approximately 20 hours per week at the store, for which he currently receives a

modest salary of $15,000 per year. Ginny works full-time at the store and currently receives a higher salary of $25,000 per year.

Since the company's inception, Jim and Ginny used most of the company's profits to pay back the loan to Jim's parents and to expand the store's inventory and marketing activities. By the end of 2010, their business had become very successful, as evidenced by the significant amount of cash ($300,000) in the company's bank accounts. Jim and Ginny made many sacrifices, both financially and socially, to make the business successful. Over a cafè latte at the local gourmet coffee shop, Jim and Ginny decided it was time to think about withdrawing some of the company's profits as a reward for their hard work. Jim admitted he had his eye on a dark green BMW 528i Sedan, which retailed for approximately $48,000, fully loaded. Ginny was a bit more restrained, hoping she could put a down payment on a condominium in the newly developed Evergreen Commons being constructed near their store. She estimated she would need approximately $16,000 for the down payment.

Jim and Ginny considered several options. One alternative was to increase their salaries or declare a year-end bonus for the amounts they desired to withdraw from the company. A second alternative was to have the company pay each of them a dividend at year-end ($48,000 to Jim and $16,000 to Ginny). A call was made to their tax accountant, Louis Tully, to ask for his evaluation of the tax consequences of each alternative.

*to be continued . . .*

As the storyline indicates, at some point during the life of a company, especially in the case of a closely held business, the owners (shareholders) likely will want to withdraw some of the company's accumulated after-tax profits. If the business is operated as a C corporation, the company can distribute its *after-tax* profits to its shareholders in the form of a **dividend, stock redemption,** or, in rare cases, a **partial liquidation.** Alternatively, if the shareholders also serve in some other capacity in the business (for example, as an employee, creditor, or lessor), the company can distribute its *before-tax* profits to these persons in the form of compensation (salary or bonus), interest, or rent.

This chapter addresses the tax consequences to the corporation and its shareholders of making nonliquidating distributions to its shareholders in these various ways. Because Jim and Ginny have chosen to operate through a C corporation, they must confront the potential double taxation of the company's earnings if distributed as a dividend. As you learned in the entities overview chapter, Jim and Ginny could have elected to operate their business through an S corporation or partnership, which would have eliminated the entity-level taxation of the company's earnings. The tax consequences of these two flow-through entity choices are discussed in more detail in subsequent chapters.

# THE BASIC TAX LAW FRAMEWORK THAT APPLIES TO PROPERTY DISTRIBUTIONS

L01

The characterization of a distribution from a corporation to a shareholder has important tax consequences to both parties to the transaction. If the tax law characterizes the distribution as a dividend, the corporation may not deduct the amount paid in computing its taxable income. In addition, the shareholder is subject to tax on the gross amount of the dividend received. The nondeductibility of the distribution by the corporation, coupled with the taxation of the distribution to the shareholder, creates *double taxation* of the corporation's income, first at the corporate level and then at the shareholder level. The double taxation of distributed corporate income is a fundamental principle of the U.S. income tax system, having been made part of the tax code in 1913. Historically, much tax planning has gone into eliminating or mitigating the second level of taxation on C corporation earnings.

Subchapter C of the Internal Revenue Code (§§301–385) provides guidelines and rules for determining the tax status of distributions from a taxable ("C") corporation to its shareholders.[1] The recipient of a dividend or payment in exchange for corporate stock (stock redemption) generally receives preferential tax treatment on the distribution, in the form of a reduced tax rate or as a tax-free return of capital or both. The reduction in the tax rate applied to dividends and capital gains received by individuals (generally 15 percent) has reduced, but not eliminated, the motivation for taxpayers to engage in creative tax strategies to avoid this second level of tax.

If the distribution can instead be characterized as salary, bonus, interest, or rent, the corporation usually can deduct the amount paid in computing its taxable income, unless the Internal Revenue Service (IRS) asserts the distribution is a **constructive dividend.** In such a case, the corporation cannot deduct the amount recharacterized as a dividend.

# COMPUTING EARNINGS AND PROFITS AND DETERMINING THE DIVIDEND AMOUNT RECEIVED BY A SHAREHOLDER

L02

### Overview of the Shareholder Taxation of Corporate Dividends

When a corporation distributes property to shareholders *in their capacity as shareholders,* the tax consequences of the distribution to the *shareholder* can be summarized as follows:

- The portion of the distribution that is a dividend is included in gross income.
- The portion of the distribution that is not a dividend reduces the shareholder's tax basis in the corporation's stock (that is, it is a nontaxable return of capital).
- The portion of the distribution that is not a dividend and is in excess of the shareholder's stock tax basis is treated as gain from sale or exchange of the stock (capital gain).[2]

Corporate distributions of "property" usually take the form of cash, but they can include debt and other tangible or intangible property. Special rules apply when a corporation distributes its own stock **(stock dividends)** to its shareholders.[3]

---

[1]Taxable corporations are referred to as *C corporations* because subchapter C describes the tax consequences of distributions between a corporation and its shareholders.

[2]§301(c).

[3]§317.

### The Tax Law Definition of a Dividend

The tax law defines a dividend as any distribution of property made by a corporation to its shareholders out of its earnings and profits (E&P) account. While earnings and profits is similar in concept to financial accounting retained earnings, its computation can be very different. Congress intended earnings and profits to be a measure of the corporation's *economic earnings* available for distribution to its shareholders.

The IRC requires a corporation to keep two separate E&P accounts: One for the current year **(current earnings and profits)** and one for undistributed earnings and profits accumulated in all prior years **(accumulated earnings and profits).** Distributions first are deemed paid out of current E&P, with any excess deemed paid from accumulated E&P. Current E&P not distributed to shareholders is added to accumulated E&P at the beginning of the next taxable year. The IRS does not require a corporation to keep contemporaneous records to track its E&P balance, provided the corporation does not pay out more than its current E&P each year. A corporation that pays a distribution in excess of its total E&P (that is, a nontaxable return of capital or capital gain) must report the distribution on Form 5452 and include a calculation of its E&P balance to support the tax treatment.

| Example 18-1 | |
|---|---|

Jim has a tax basis in his Spartan Cycles and Repair (SCR) stock of $24,000. Ginny's tax basis in her SCR stock is $10,000.

***What if:*** Assume SCR has current earnings and profits (CE&P) of $30,000 at December 31, 2010, and no accumulated earnings and profits. At year-end, SCR makes a $48,000 distribution to Jim and a $16,000 distribution to Ginny. Jim owns 75 percent of the SCR stock, while Ginny owns the remaining 25 percent.

What is the tax treatment of the distribution to Jim and Ginny?

**Answer:**

Jim treats the $48,000 distribution for tax purposes as follows:

- $22,500 is treated as a dividend (to the extent of his 75 percent share of current E&P).
- $24,000 is a nontaxable reduction in his stock tax basis (return of capital).
- $1,500 is treated as gain from the deemed sale of his stock (capital gain).

Note that a distribution cannot reduce a shareholder's stock basis below zero.

Ginny treats the $16,000 distribution for tax purposes as follows:

- $7,500 is treated as a dividend (to the extent of her 25 percent share of current E&P).
- $8,500 is a nontaxable reduction in her stock tax basis (return of capital).

What is Jim and Ginny's tax basis in their SCR stock after the distribution?

**Answer:** Jim has a remaining tax basis in his SCR stock of zero, while Ginny has a remaining tax basis of $1,500 ($10,000 − $8,500) in her SCR stock.

### Computing Earnings and Profits

The term *earnings and profits* has been part of the tax laws since 1916. Congress has never provided a precise definition of E&P, leading commentators to refer to E&P as a "concept." Since 1916, legislators have enacted "partial" adjustments that should be made to taxable income to compute E&P. Earnings and profits includes taxable and nontaxable income, reflecting the fact that Congress intended E&P to represent a corporation's economic income. As a result, shareholders may be taxed

on distributions of income not subject to tax at the corporate level, even though the shareholder would not have been taxed on such income if it were earned directly.

---

**Example 18-2**

SCR reported current earnings and profits of $100,000 related to taxable income. The company also earned $5,000 of tax-exempt interest from its investment in City of East Lansing municipal bonds. If SCR distributes all of its current year E&P to Jim and Ginny, what amount will they report as dividend income in the current year?

**Answer:** $105,000. SCR must include the $5,000 of tax-exempt interest in the computation of current E&P. The portion of the E&P that represents the tax-exempt interest will be treated as a taxable dividend even though Jim and Ginny would not have included the interest in gross income had they earned it directly.

**What if:** Assume Jim and Ginny operated SCR as an S corporation. How would that have changed your answer to the previous example?

**Answer:** Jim and Ginny would have reported their share of the tax-exempt interest on their individual tax returns as being tax-exempt and would not have been taxed on the amount.

---

To compute earnings and profits, a corporation must maintain a separate accounting system. The corporation begins its computation of current E&P with taxable income or loss. It then makes adjustments required by the Internal Revenue Code (IRC) or the accompanying regulations and IRS rulings. These adjustments fall into four broad categories:

- Inclusion of income that is excluded from taxable income.
- Disallowance of certain expenses that are deducted in computing taxable income but do not require an economic outflow.
- Deduction of certain expenses that are excluded from the computation of taxable income but do require an economic outflow.
- Deferral of deductions or acceleration of income due to separate accounting methods required for E&P purposes.[4]

**Inclusion of Income that Is Excluded from Taxable Income** The regulations state that "all income exempted by statute" must be added back to taxable income in computing current E&P. Most commentators do not interpret this phrase to mean that all statutory exclusions are included in E&P. Common examples of tax-exempt income included in E&P are tax-exempt interest and tax-exempt life insurance proceeds. Exempt income not included in E&P includes gifts and bequests and contributions to capital.

**Disallowance of Certain Expenses that Are Deducted in Computing Taxable Income But Do Not Require an Economic Outflow** Deductions that are allowed in computing taxable income but disallowed in the computation of current E&P generally are deductions that require no cash outlay by the corporation or are carryovers from a different tax year. Examples include the dividends received deduction, net capital loss carryovers from a different tax year, net operating loss carryovers from a different tax year, and charitable contribution carryovers from a prior tax year. Note, however, that the deduction allowed for employee exercises of nonqualified stock options and the domestic manufacturing deduction reduce E&P even though they do not require a cash outflow. The domestic production activities deduction is not allowed as a reduction in computing current E&P.

---

[4]§312 and the related regulations describe these adjustments.

### Deduction of Certain Expenses that Are Excluded from the Computation of Taxable Income but Do Require an Economic Outflow

A corporation reduces its current E&P for certain items that are not deductible in computing its taxable income but require a cash outflow. Examples of such expenses include:

- Federal income taxes (regular or alternative minimum tax) paid or accrued (depending on the corporation's method of accounting).
- Expenses incurred in earning tax-exempt income (such income is included in E&P).
- Current year charitable contributions in excess of 10 percent of taxable income (there is no 10 percent limitation for E&P purposes).
- Premiums on life insurance contracts in excess of the increase in the policy's cash surrender value.
- Current year net capital loss (there is no limit on capital losses).
- Meals and entertainment expenses disallowed (generally 50 percent of the total).
- Nondeductible lobbying expenses and political contributions.
- Penalties and fines.

### Deferral of Deductions or Acceleration of Income Due to Separate Accounting Methods Required for E&P Purposes

A corporation must use the same accounting method for computing E&P and taxable income unless otherwise allowed. For example, a gain or loss deferred for tax purposes under the like-kind exchange rules or the involuntary conversion rules also is deferred for E&P purposes. A corporation using the accrual method for regular income tax purposes generally must use the accrual method for E&P purposes.

Some income deferred from inclusion in the computation of current year taxable income must be included in the computation of current E&P in the year in which the transaction occurs. For example, if a corporation uses the installment sales method for tax purposes, the deferred gain from current year sales must be included in current E&P. In other cases, gain deferred from taxation is not added back in the E&P computation. Deferred gain from a like-kind exchange (§1031) and a §351 exchange (discussed in Chapter 19) fall into this category. In addition, certain expenses currently deducted in the computation of taxable income are deferred in computing E&P.[5] Organizational expenditures, which can be deducted currently or amortized for income tax purposes, must be capitalized for E&P purposes.

Depreciation must be computed using the prescribed E&P method. For property acquired after 1986, the alternative depreciation system must be used, which requires that assets be depreciated using a straight-line method over the asset's *"mid-point class life"* (40 years in the case of realty).[6] Amounts expensed under §179 (first year expensing) must be amortized over five years for E&P purposes.

---

**Example 18-3**

In 2010, SCR reported taxable income of $500,000 and paid federal income tax of $170,000. The following deductions were included in the computation of taxable income:

- $50,000 of depreciation.
- $7,000 dividends received deduction.
- $10,000 net operating loss from the prior year.

*(continued on page 18-7...)*

---

[5] §312(n). Section 312(n) was added in 1984 to "ensure that a corporation's earnings and profits more closely conform to its economic income."
[6] §168(g)(2).

Not included in the computation of taxable income were the following items:

- $5,000 of tax-exempt interest.
- $6,000 meals and entertainment expense.
- $4,000 net capital loss from the current year.

For E&P purposes, depreciation computed under the alternative depreciation method is $30,000.

What is SCR's current E&P for 2010?

**Answer:** $362,000, computed as follows:

| | |
|---|---:|
| Taxable income | $500,000 |
| **Add:** | |
| Tax-exempt interest | 5,000 |
| Dividends received deduction | 7,000 |
| NOL carryover | 10,000 |
| Excess of regular tax deprecation over E&P depreciation | 20,000 |
| **Subtract:** | |
| Federal income taxes | (170,000) |
| Nondeductible meals and entertainment | (6,000) |
| Net capital loss for the current year | (4,000) |
| **Current E&P** | **$362,000** |

**What if:** Assume SCR also reported a tax-deferred gain of $100,000 as the result of a §1031 exchange and deferred $75,000 of gain from an installment sale during the year. What is SCR's current E&P under these circumstances?

**Answer:** Current E&P would equal $437,000 ($362,000 + $75,000). Deferred gains from §1031 (like-kind) exchanges are not included in the computation of current E&P, but all gain from current year installment sales is included in current E&P. In future years, SCR would back out any deferred gain recognized in taxable income from the installment sale in its computation of current E&P.

The IRC does not impose a statute of limitations on the computation of earnings and profits. Exhibit 18-1 provides a more comprehensive summary of common adjustments made to compute current E&P.

## Ordering of E&P Distributions

As we noted above, a corporation must maintain two separate E&P accounts: current E&P and accumulated E&P. Whether a distribution is characterized as a dividend depends on whether the balances in these accounts are positive or negative. There are four possible scenarios:

1. Positive current E&P, positive accumulated E&P.
2. Positive current E&P, negative accumulated E&P.
3. Negative current E&P, positive accumulated E&P.
4. Negative current E&P, negative accumulated E&P.

**Positive Current E&P and Positive Accumulated E&P**   Corporate distributions are deemed to be paid out of current E&P first. If distributions exceed current E&P, the amount distributed out of current E&P is allocated pro rata to all of the distributions made during the year. Any distribution out of accumulated E&P is allocated to the recipients in the chronological order in which the distributions were made.[7] This

---

[7]Reg. §1.316-2(b) and Rev. Rul. 74-164, 1974-1 C.B. 74. If current E&P is negative, the corporation calculates its accumulated E&P at the date of each distribution to determine the tax status of the distribution. This situation is rare and beyond the scope of this text.

**EXHIBIT 18-1    Template for Computing Current Earnings and Profits**

**Taxable Income (Net Operating Loss)**

**Add:**    **Exclusions from Taxable Income**
- Tax-exempt bond interest.
- Life insurance proceeds.
- Federal tax refunds (if a cash-basis taxpayer).

**Add:**    **Deductions Allowed for Tax Purposes but Not for E&P**
- Dividends received deduction.
- NOL deduction carrybacks and carryforwards.
- Net capital loss carrybacks and carryforwards.
- Contribution carryforwards.
- Domestic production activities deduction.

**Add:**    **Income Deferred for Tax Purposes but Not for E&P**
- Deferred gain on installment sales.
- Deferred gain on completed contract method of accounting.
- Increase in cash surrender value of corporate-owned life insurance policies.

**Add:**    **Deductions Deferred for E&P Purposes**
- Regular tax depreciation in excess of E&P depreciation.
- Percentage depletion in excess of cost depletion.
- Capitalized construction period interest, taxes, and carrying charges.
- Amortized intangible costs of oil and gas wells over 60 months.
- Amortized mineral exploration and development costs over 120 months.
- Capitalized circulation expenditures and organizational expenditures.
- Capitalized first-year expensing and amortize over five years.
- Increases in the LIFO recapture amount (FIFO over LIFO ending inventory).

**Less:**    **Deductions Allowed for E&P Purposes but Not for Tax**
- Federal income taxes paid or accrued.
- Expenses of earning tax-exempt income.
- Current year charitable contributions in excess of the 10 percent limitation.
- Nondeductible premiums on life insurance policies.
- Current year net capital loss.
- E&P depreciation in excess of regular tax depreciation.
- Penalties and fines.
- Decreases in the LIFO recapture amount (LIFO over FIFO ending inventory).
- Disallowed entertainment expenses.
- Disallowed lobbying expenses, dues, and political contributions.

**Equals:**    **Current Earnings and Profits**

---

ordering of distributions is necessary only when distributions exceed current E&P and either the identity of the shareholders receiving the distributions changes or a shareholder's percentage ownership changes during the year.

## Example 18-4

**What if:** Assume SCR reported current E&P of $60,000 in 2010. The balance in accumulated E&P was $50,000. On December 31, 2010, SCR distributed $48,000 to Jim and $16,000 to Ginny. What amount of dividend income do Jim and Ginny report in 2010?

**Answer:** $48,000 to Jim and $16,000 to Ginny. The distribution is first deemed to be paid from current E&P ($45,000 to Jim and $15,000 to Ginny). The additional amount is deemed to be paid from accumulated E&P ($3,000 to Jim and $1,000 to Ginny). Total E&P exceeds the distribution, which makes the entire amount paid to Jim and Ginny a taxable dividend. SCR has a remaining balance in accumulated E&P of $46,000 ($50,000 − $4,000).

**What if:** Assume that SCR's current E&P is $40,000 and its accumulated E&P is $15,000. Also, assume that Jim was a 75 percent shareholder of SCR and he received a $45,000 distribution on June 1, 2010. On December 1, Ginny, a 25 percent shareholder, received a $15,000 dividend on December 31. What is the amount and the character of each distribution?

**Answer:** Jim has a $45,000 dividend. Ginny has a $10,000 dividend and a $5,000 return of capital. Of the $40,000 of current E&P, $30,000 is allocated to Jim's distribution and $10,000 is allocated to Ginny's distribution (pro rata to each distribution). However, because Jim's distribution took place before Ginny's distribution, the accumulated E&P is allocated to Jim's distribution ($15,000), leaving $0 in remaining accumulated E&P to be allocated to Ginny's distribution. Ginny is allocated only $10,000 of E&P, leaving her with an excess distribution of $5,000 ($15,000 − $10,000). This excess distribution is treated as a nontaxable reduction of her basis in the SCR stock.

**Positive Current E&P and Negative Accumulated E&P**    Distributions deemed paid out of current E&P are taxable as dividends. Distributions in excess of current E&P in this scenario would first be treated as nontaxable reductions in the shareholders' tax basis in their stock. Any excess received over their stock basis would be treated as a (capital) gain from sale of the stock.

---

**Example 18-5**

**What if:** Assume SCR reported current E&P of $60,000 in 2010. The balance in accumulated E&P at the beginning of the year was negative $20,000. On December 31, 2010, SCR distributed $48,000 to Jim and $16,000 to Ginny. Jim has a tax basis in his SCR stock of $24,000. Ginny's tax basis in her SCR stock is $10,000. What amount of dividend income do Jim and Ginny report in 2010?

**Answer:** $45,000 to Jim and $15,000 to Ginny. The distribution is first deemed to be paid from current E&P ($45,000 to Jim and $15,000 to Ginny). No additional amount is treated as a dividend because SCR has negative accumulated E&P.

What tax basis do Jim and Ginny have in their SCR stock after the distribution?

**Answer:** The amount in excess of current E&P ($3,000 to Jim, $1,000 to Ginny) would be treated as a nontaxable return of capital because Jim and Ginny have enough tax basis in their SCR stock to absorb the amount paid in excess of E&P. Jim's tax basis in his SCR stock after the distribution would be $21,000 ($24,000 − $3,000), and Ginny's tax basis in her SCR stock after the distribution would be $9,000 ($10,000 − $1,000).

What is SCR's remaining balance in accumulated E&P at the end of the year?

**Answer:** SCR has a remaining balance in accumulated E&P of negative $20,000.

**Negative Current E&P and Positive Accumulated E&P**    When current E&P is negative, the tax status of a dividend is determined by total E&P on the *date of the distribution*. This requires the corporation to prorate the negative current E&P to the distribution date and add it to accumulated E&P at the beginning of the year to determine total E&P at the distribution date. Distributions in excess of total E&P in this scenario are treated as reductions in the shareholders' tax basis in their stock. Any excess over their stock basis would be treated as a capital gain.

## Example 18-6

**What if:** Assume SCR reported current E&P of negative $20,000 in 2010. The balance in accumulated E&P at the beginning of the year was $60,000. On June 30, 2010, SCR distributed $48,000 to Jim and $16,000 to Ginny. Jim has a tax basis in his SCR stock of $24,000. Ginny's tax basis in her SCR stock is $10,000. What amount of dividend income do Jim and Ginny report in 2010?

**Answer:** $37,500 to Jim and $12,500 to Ginny. Because current E&P is negative, SCR must determine its total E&P on the distribution date. SCR prorates the full year negative current E&P to June 30 [6 months/12 months × ($20,000) = ($10,000)]. The negative current E&P of $10,000 is added to the beginning balance in accumulated E&P of $60,000 to get total E&P as of July 1 of $50,000. Because their distributions were made at the same time, Jim is allocated 75 percent of the total E&P and Ginny is allocated the remaining 25 percent.

What tax basis do Jim and Ginny have in their SCR stock after the distribution?

**Answer:** The amount in excess of total E&P ($10,500 to Jim, $3,500 to Ginny) is treated first as a nontaxable return of capital. Jim reduces the basis in his SCR stock to $13,500 ($24,000 − $10,500). Ginny reduces the basis in her SCR stock to $6,500 ($10,000 − $3,500).

What is SCR's remaining balance in accumulated E&P at the end of the year?

**Answer:** Negative $10,000, computed as follows:

| | |
|---|---:|
| Beginning balance | $60,000 |
| Prorated negative current E&P, 1/1–6/30 | (10,000) |
| Dividends | (50,000) |
| Prorated negative current E&P, 7/1–12/31 | (10,000) |
| Ending balance | ($10,000) |

**Negative Current E&P and Negative Accumulated E&P**   When current E&P and accumulated E&P are both negative, none of the distribution is treated as a dividend. Distributions in this scenario would first be treated as reductions in the shareholders' tax basis in their stock. Any excess over their stock basis would be treated as a capital gain.

## Example 18-7

**What if:** Assume SCR reported current E&P of negative $50,000 in 2010. The balance in accumulated E&P at the beginning of the year was negative $60,000. Jim has a tax basis in his SCR stock of $24,000. Ginny's tax basis in her SCR stock is $10,000. On December 31, 2010, SCR distributed $48,000 to Jim and $16,000 to Ginny. What amount of dividend income do Jim and Ginny report in 2010?

**Answer:** $0 to Jim and $0 to Ginny. Because current E&P and accumulated E&P are negative, the entire distribution would be treated as either a return of capital or capital gain.

What are Jim and Ginny's tax bases in their SCR stock after the distribution?

**Answer:** The amount in excess of total E&P ($48,000 to Jim, $16,000 to Ginny) is treated first as a nontaxable return of capital. Jim reduces the basis in his SCR stock to $0 ($24,000 − $48,000, limited to $0). Ginny reduces the basis in her SCR stock to $0 ($10,000 − $16,000, limited to $0).

What amount of capital gain do Jim and Ginny report as a result of the distribution?

**Answer:** Jim has a capital gain of $24,000, the amount by which the distribution exceeds the tax basis in his SCR stock ($48,000 − $24,000). Ginny has a capital gain of $6,000, the amount by which the distribution exceeds the tax basis in her SCR stock ($16,000 − $10,000).

What is SCR's remaining balance in accumulated E&P at the end of the year?

**Answer:** Negative $110,000, the sum of accumulated E&P of negative $60,000 plus current E&P of negative $50,000.

### Distributions of Noncash Property to Shareholders

On occasion, a shareholder will receive property other than cash in the form of a dividend. When noncash property is received, the shareholder determines the amount distributed as follows:

> Money received
> + Fair market value of other property received
> − Liabilities assumed by the shareholder on property received
> Amount distributed[8]

---

**Example 18-8**

**What if:** Assume Ginny elected to receive $15,000 in cash and a Fuji custom touring bike that had a fair market value of $1,000. SCR has current E&P of $100,000 and no accumulated E&P. What amount of dividend income will Ginny report in 2010?

**Answer:** $16,000. Ginny would include the $15,000 plus the $1,000 fair market value of the bicycle in her gross income as a dividend.

---

As a general rule, a shareholder's tax basis in noncash property received as a dividend equals the property's fair market value.[9] No downward adjustment is made for liabilities assumed by the shareholder (these are considered part of the property's cost). The shareholder determines fair market value as of the date of the distribution.

---

**Example 18-9**

What is Ginny's tax basis in the bicycle she received as a dividend in the previous example?

**Answer:** $1,000. Ginny has a tax basis in the bicycle of $1,000, the bicycle's fair market value. Ginny would pay an income tax of $150 on receipt of the bicycle (assuming the dividend qualifies for the preferential 15 percent tax rate).

---

**Example 18-10**

**What if:** Assume Jim elected to receive a parcel of land the company had previously purchased for possible expansion instead of cash. The land has a fair market value of $60,000 and a remaining mortgage of $12,000 attached to it. SCR has a tax basis in the land of $20,000. Jim will assume the mortgage on the land. SCR has current E&P of $100,000 and no accumulated E&P. How much dividend income does Jim recognize on the distribution?

**Answer:** $48,000. Jim recognizes dividend income in an amount equal to the land's fair market value ($60,000) less the mortgage he assumes on the land ($12,000).

What is Jim's tax basis in the land he receives?

**Answer:** $60,000. Jim receives a tax basis equal to the land's fair market value. The basis consists of the $48,000 taxable dividend plus the $12,000 liability Jim assumes.

---

[8]§301(b).
[9]§301(d).

### The Tax Consequences to a Corporation Paying Noncash Property as a Dividend

The IRC provides that taxable *gains (but not losses)* are recognized by a corporation on the distribution of noncash property as a dividend.[10] Specifically, to the extent the fair market value of property distributed as a dividend exceeds the corporation's tax basis in the property, the corporation recognizes a taxable gain on the distribution. This gain increases current E&P by virtue of the fact that it increases taxable income. In contrast, if the fair market value of the property distributed is less than the corporation's tax basis in the property, the corporation does not recognize a deductible loss on the distribution. E&P is subsequently reduced by the distributed property's fair market value if the property is appreciated (gain is recognized) and by the property's E&P basis if the property is depreciated (loss is not recognized). Congress made distributions of appreciated property taxable to the distributing corporation in 1986 to prevent corporations from avoiding the double taxation of corporate income by distributing appreciated property to shareholders in the form of a dividend.

---

| **Example 18-11** | |
|---|---|

**What if:** Assume SCR purchased the Fuji custom touring bike that it distributed to Ginny (see the facts in Example 18-9) from its wholesaler for $650 (that is, SCR had a tax basis in the bicycle of $650). How much gain, if any, does SCR recognize when it distributes the bicycle to Ginny as a dividend?

**Answer:** $350. SCR recognizes a taxable gain of $350 on the distribution of the bicycle to Ginny ($1,000 − $650). Because the bike is considered inventory, SCR would characterize the gain as ordinary income. Assuming a tax rate of 34 percent, SCR would pay a corporate level tax of $119 on the distribution (34% × $350). The total tax paid by SCR and Ginny would be $269 ($150 + $119). This is a high tax cost to pay to transfer the $1,000 bicycle to Ginny in the form of a dividend.

**What if:** Assume SCR purchased the Fuji custom touring bike that it distributed to Ginny for $1,200 (that is, SCR had a tax basis in the bicycle of $1,200). The bicycle's fair market value declined to $1,000 because it was an outdated model. How much loss, if any, does SCR recognize when it distributes the bicycle to Ginny as a dividend?

**Answer:** $0. SCR is not permitted to recognize a loss on the distribution of the bicycle to Ginny.

**What if:** Suppose SCR *sold* the bicycle to Ginny for $1,000. How much loss, if any, could SCR recognize if it sold the bicycle to Ginny?

**Answer:** $200. SCR is permitted to recognize a loss on the sale of the bicycle to Ginny provided it does not run afoul of the related-person loss rules found in §267 (discussed in the property dispositions chapter). To be a related person, Ginny must own *more than* 50 percent of SCR, which she does not in this scenario.

---

**Liabilities**    If the property's fair market value is less than the amount of the liability assumed, the property's fair market value is deemed to be the amount of the liability assumed by the shareholder. If the liability assumed is less than the property's fair market value, the gain recognized on the distribution is the excess of the property's fair market value over its tax basis (that is, the liability is ignored).

---

[10]§311.

**Example 18-12**

*What if:* Assume Jim received a parcel of land the company had previously purchased for possible expansion. The land has a fair market value of $60,000 and a remaining mortgage of $12,000 attached to it. SCR has a tax basis in the land of $20,000. Jim will assume the mortgage on the land. SCR has current E&P of $100,000 and no accumulated E&P. How much gain, if any, does SCR recognize when it distributes the land to Jim as a dividend?

**Answer:** $40,000 ($60,000 − $20,000). Because the mortgage assumed by Jim is less than the land's fair market value, SCR recognizes gain in an amount equal to the excess of the land's fair market value of $60,000 over its tax basis of $20,000.

*What if:* Assume the mortgage assumed by Jim was $75,000 instead of $12,000. The land has a fair market value of $60,000. SCR has a tax basis in the land of $20,000. Jim will assume the mortgage on the land. SCR has current E&P of $100,000. How much gain, if any, does SCR recognize when it distributes the land to Jim as a dividend?

**Answer:** $55,000 ($75,000 − $20,000). Because the mortgage assumed by Jim exceeds the land's fair market value, SCR treats the land's fair market value as $75,000 and recognizes gain in an amount equal to the excess of the mortgage assumed of $75,000 over its tax basis of $20,000.

**Effect of Noncash Property Distributions on E&P**   A corporation computes its current E&P without regard to any distributions made during the year. However, gain recognized by the corporation on a distribution of appreciated property (less any taxes paid) increases current E&P by virtue of the fact that such gain is included in the corporation's taxable income.

In the case of noncash property distributions, the corporation reduces current E&P by the property's E&P basis, except in the case of distributions of appreciated property.[11] When appreciated property is distributed by the corporation, the corporation recognizes gain to the extent the property's fair market value exceeds the corporation's tax basis in the property. In computing current E&P, the corporation must adjust the gain to take into account the property's E&P adjusted basis (this is likely to happen when the asset has been depreciated differently for regular tax and E&P purposes). After making the determination as to whether the distribution is a dividend, the corporation reduces E&P by the property's fair market value and adds back any mortgage or other liability assumed by the shareholders in the distribution.

Exhibit 18-2 provides a template for computing the effect of distributions on current E&P.

**EXHIBIT 18-2    Template to Compute the Effect of Distributions on E&P**

|   | Current E&P (computed before any distributions) |
|---|---|
| − | Money distributed |
| − | E&P adjusted basis of unappreciated property distributed |
| − | Fair market value of appreciated property distributed |
| + | Liabilities assumed by the shareholders |
|   | Undistributed current E&P (added to accumulated E&P from prior years) |

[11]§312.

**THE KEY FACTS**

**Adjustments to Taxable Income (Loss) to Compute Current E&P**

■ A corporation makes the following adjustments to taxable income to compute current E&P:
· Include certain income that is excluded from taxable income.
· Disallow certain expenses that are deducted in computing taxable income.
· Deduct certain expenses that are excluded from the computation of taxable income.
· Defer deductions or accelerate income due to separate accounting methods required for E&P purposes.

■ The amount distributed as a dividend equals:
· Cash received.
· Fair market value of noncash property received.
· Reduced by any liabilities assumed by the shareholder on property received.

■ E&P is reduced by distributions treated as dividends as follows:
· Cash distributed.
· E&P basis of noncash property with a fair market value less than its E&P basis.
· Fair market value of noncash appreciated property.
· Reduced by any liabilities assumed by the shareholder on property received.

In the case where a property's fair market value or E&P basis exceeds current E&P, the excess amount reduces any accumulated E&P at the beginning of the year. Note, however, that a distribution of property can only reduce E&P to the extent E&P is positive. A distribution cannot create negative E&P or increase already existing negative E&P that results from operations.

---

**Example 18-13**

***What if:*** Assume the same facts as in Example 18-12. SCR distributed land to Jim that has a fair market value of $60,000 and a remaining mortgage of $12,000 attached to it. SCR has a tax and E&P basis in the land of $20,000. Jim assumed the mortgage on the land. SCR has current E&P of $100,000, which includes the net gain of $26,400 from distribution of the land ($40,000 gain less a related tax liability of $13,600 assuming a tax rate of 34 percent), and accumulated E&P at the beginning of the year of $500,000. What is SCR's beginning balance in accumulated E&P at January 1, 2011, as a result of the distribution of the land to Jim?

**Answer:** $552,000, computed as follows:

| | |
|---|---|
| Accumulated E&P, 1/01/10 | $500,000 |
| Current E&P | 100,000 |
| Fair market value of land distributed | (60,000) |
| Liability assumed by Jim | 12,000 |
| Beginning balance, AE&P, 1/01/11 | $552,000 |

***What if:*** Assume SCR has current E&P of $40,000, which includes the net gain of $26,400 from distribution of the land ($40,000 gain less a related tax liability of $13,600 assuming a tax rate of 34 percent), and accumulated E&P of $500,000. What is SCR's beginning balance in accumulated E&P at January 1, 2011, as a result of the distribution of the land to Jim?

**Answer:** $492,000, computed as follows:

| | |
|---|---|
| Accumulated E&P, 1/01/10 | $500,000 |
| Current E&P | 40,000 |
| Fair market value of land distributed | (60,000) |
| Liability assumed by Jim | 12,000 |
| Beginning balance, AE&P, 1/01/11 | $492,000 |

***What if:*** Assume the land distributed to Jim had a tax and E&P basis to SCR of $75,000 instead of $20,000. SCR has current E&P of $100,000, which does not include the disallowed loss of $15,000 on the distribution ($60,000 fair market value less $75,000 tax basis). SCR has accumulated E&P at the beginning of the year of $500,000. What is SCR's beginning balance in accumulated E&P at January 1, 2011, as a result of the distribution of the land to Jim?

**Answer:** $537,000, computed as follows:

| | |
|---|---|
| Accumulated E&P, 1/01/10 | $500,000 |
| Current E&P | 100,000 |
| E&P basis of land distributed | (75,000) |
| Liability assumed by Jim | 12,000 |
| Beginning balance, AE&P, 1/01/11 | $537,000 |

---

**L03**

# CONSTRUCTIVE DIVIDENDS

Dividend distributions often result in double taxation to the parties to the transaction because the corporation making the distribution cannot deduct dividends paid in computing its taxable income. Corporations can avoid this second level of taxation by characterizing the distribution as being made to the shareholders in their capacity as other than a shareholder. For example, the corporation might characterize

the distribution as a payment of salary, bonus, interest, or rent to a shareholder who also is an employee, creditor, or lessor to the corporation. The corporation can deduct these types of payments, thus eliminating the double tax imposed on the distribution at the corporate level. From the recipient's perspective, the amount included in gross income no longer qualifies for preferential tax rates and would be taxed at the recipient's marginal tax rate. Payments designated to be compensation also could be subject to Social Security and Medicare payroll taxes.

The incentive for a corporation to make payments to shareholders that are deductible on the corporation's tax return arises primarily in a closely held setting, where the shareholders also interact with the corporation in other capacities, such as managers, creditors, and lessors. In this setting, the shareholders are likely to consider the combined tax to be paid by the corporation and themselves rather than just the tax they pay separate from the corporation.

The IRC and the courts provide the IRS with the ability to recharacterize the form of a transaction (the technical manner in which a transaction is conducted) between a corporation and its dual-capacity shareholders into what the IRS considers to be the transaction's substance (the manner in which a transaction is treated for tax purposes). In effect, the IRS can recharacterize what the corporation calls a deductible payment (for example, compensation) into a nondeductible "constructive" dividend distribution. Common examples of constructive dividends include:

* Excess ("unreasonable") compensation paid to shareholder/employees.
* Bargain sales of property by the corporation to shareholders.
* A bargain lease or uncompensated use of corporate property by a shareholder (for example, a company car used for personal reasons).
* An excess purchase/lease price paid to a shareholder/lessor by the corporation.
* "Loans" to a shareholder/creditor at less than market interest rates.
* Corporate payments on a shareholder's behalf (for example, legal fees paid to defend a sole shareholder of criminal charges).

The most frequent causes of disputes between corporations and the IRS over the characterization of deductible payments made to individuals who also are shareholders involve compensation and interest payments. With respect to whether compensation paid to an employee who also is a shareholder is *reasonable,* the IRS usually looks to factors that include the individual's duties and responsibilities, what individuals performing in comparable capacities at other corporations are paid, whether the corporation has a formal compensation policy, and what the individual's return on his or her investment is as a shareholder of the company.[12]

Corporate payments made on behalf of shareholders also are sources of contention between corporations and the IRS. In a recent court case, the Tax Court held that a corporation's payment of a seat license fee to purchase season tickets to Houston Texans football games, to be used exclusively by the sole shareholder, was a constructive dividend to the shareholder.[13]

> **THE KEY FACTS**
>
> **Examples of Disguised Dividends**
>
> ▪ Unreasonable compensation.
>
> ▪ Bargain sales to shareholders.
>
> ▪ Shareholder use of corporate assets without an arm's-length payment.
>
> ▪ Loans from shareholders at excessive interest rates.
>
> ▪ Corporate payments made on behalf of the shareholder.

## Example 18-14

***What if:*** Assume SCR has current E&P of $200,000. Jim and Ginny would like to withdraw $48,000 and $16,000, respectively, from the company to fulfill some personal dreams (a BMW and a condominium, respectively). If SCR pays the amounts to Jim and Ginny as dividends, it will not be able to deduct the payments in computing its taxable income. What is the total tax cost (entity and shareholder level) of distributing a dividend to Jim and Ginny?

*(continued on page 18-16...)*

---

[12]*Thomas A. Curtis, M.D., Inc.,* 67 T.C.M. 1958 (1994).

[13]*Kerns v. Comm.,* T.C. Memo 2004-63.

**Answer:** $31,360. The nondeductibility of the dividend payments will increase SCR's tax liability by $21,760 ($64,000 × 34%). Jim and Ginny will be eligible for a reduced dividend tax rate of 15 percent on the distributions, causing them to pay a shareholder-level tax of $7,200 and $2,400, respectively. The total tax cost to this strategy will be $31,360.

**What if:** Assume SCR declared a year-end bonus (additional compensation) of $48,000 and $16,000 to Jim and Ginny, respectively, to reward them for their hard work as employees. What is the total tax cost (entity and shareholder level) of paying a bonus to Jim and Ginny?

**Answer:** $23,200. By converting the dividend into compensation, SCR can deduct the $64,000 payment in computing its taxable income, saving $21,760 in taxes in the process ($64,000 × 34%). Jim and Ginny will no longer be eligible for the preferential dividend tax rate and will have to pay tax at their marginal tax rates (40 percent and 25 percent, respectively). Jim's tax cost will increase to $19,200, while Ginny's tax cost will increase to $4,000, for a combined tax cost of $23,200. This is still $8,160 less than the combined cost of the dividend strategy ($31,360).

What other tax costs will SCR and Jim and Ginny incur as a result of converting the dividend into a bonus?

**Answer:** Social Security and Medicare taxes. SCR and Jim and Ginny will have to pay Social Security and Medicare taxes on the $64,000 of compensation payments. SCR will pay a tax of 7.65 percent on the $64,000 ($4,896). In addition, Jim and Ginny will pay 7.65 percent on their compensation (collectively, $4,896). SCR will be able to deduct its share of these payroll taxes ($4,896), creating additional tax *savings* of $1,665 ($4,896 × 34%). The combined income tax and payroll tax cost of this strategy is now $31,327 ($23,200 + $9,792 − $1,665). The total tax savings from the compensation strategy is reduced to $33, which may no longer justify incurring any additional administrative costs to choose this course of action.

A summary of tax consequences of these two distribution alternatives follows:

| Description | Pay Dividend | Calculation | Pay Year-End Bonus | Calculation |
|---|---|---|---|---|
| SCR income tax cost | $21,760 | $64,000 × 34% | | |
| Shareholder-level income tax | 9,600 | 64,000 × 15% | $23,200 | 19,200 + 4,000 |
| Shareholder-level employment tax | 0 | | 4,896 | 64,000 × 7.65% |
| SCR employment tax | | | 4,896 | 64,000 × 7.65% |
| SCR deduction of employment tax | | | (1,665) | 4,896 × 34% |
| Total tax cost | $31,360 | | $31,327 | |

**What if:** If Jim and Ginny go through with the bonus compensation alternative, would the strategy be vulnerable to IRS scrutiny?

**Answer:** Possibly. The IRS could argue that the bonus is really a constructive dividend. Key facts in the determination would be Jim and Ginny's contribution to the business, the compensation paid to individuals doing similar jobs at comparable businesses, whether SCR paid any dividends, and whether SCR had a formal compensation policy for determining year-end bonuses. For example, would Jim, who works only part-time, be able to justify why his contributions as an employee are valued at four times the bonus paid to Ginny, who works full-time?

## Example 18-15

**What if:** Assume SCR sold Ginny a Fuji custom touring bike for its cost of $650. The selling price of the bicycle to customers was $1,000. What tax issues might arise in this transaction?

**Answer:** Two tax issues arise here. The transaction meets the definition of a *bargain purchase* by Ginny of the bicycle. The IRS could argue that Ginny received property worth $1,000 for $650 and

thus had a constructive dividend of $350. Because the bicycle is inventory to SCR, the sale could qualify as a nontaxable fringe benefit under the employee discount rules.[14] Assuming this "discount" is available to all SCR employees, Ginny would not have taxable income (compensation) for the bargain portion of the sale in an amount equal to SCR's gross profit percentage times the price it normally charges nonemployee customers for the bicycle. SCR's gross profit percentage is 35 percent ($350/$1,000). The maximum employee discount that would be tax-free is $350 (35% × $1,000). Ginny would not have to report any compensation in this bargain purchase under the fringe benefit rules.

**What if:** Assume SCR sold the bicycle to Ginny for $500 (that is, below cost). How might your answer change?

**Answer:** Ginny would now have taxable compensation of $150 at the very least. Depending on the circumstances, the IRS could assert that she had a constructive dividend of $500.

## The Motivation to Pay Dividends

Many publicly traded corporations regularly pay out a portion of their earnings to shareholders as a dividend. Why corporate managers would willingly pay out cash that could be reinvested in the corporation (or better yet, paid to the managers as compensation), has long intrigued corporate finance theorists. Several possible reasons have been offered to explain this "illogical" behavior (the *dividend puzzle*).

For example, "forcing" managers to pay out dividends restricts their investment activities and forces them to adopt more efficient investment policies. Some view dividends as a source of investor goodwill. Still others see dividends as a signal to the capital markets (stock market and bond market) about the health of a corporation's activities without providing explicit financial information. Many companies pride themselves on the consecutive number of quarters in which they have paid a dividend. Exhibit 18-3 reproduces McDonald's announcement of its increase in its cash dividend in 2009.

### EXHIBIT 18-3    McDonald's Raises Quarterly Cash Dividend by 10 percent

OAK BROOK, Ill., Sept. 24—McDonald's Board of Directors today declared a quarterly cash dividend of $0.55 per share of common stock payable on December 15, 2009, to shareholders of record at the close of business on December 1, 2009. This represents a 10% increase over the Company's previous quarterly dividend rate and brings the total quarterly dividend payout to about $600 million.

McDonald's Chief Executive Officer Jim Skinner said, "So far in 2009 we've returned nearly $4.0 billion to shareholders through dividends and share repurchases, bringing total cash returned since the beginning of 2007 to about $15.5 billion. With today's dividend increase, we expect to end the year near the high end of our three-year, $15 billion to $17 billion total cash return target."

Skinner continued, "This achievement reflects the success of our better, not just bigger strategy, which has helped drive sales, profits and, ultimately, cash from operations. Going forward, our philosophy on our use of capital remains unchanged. Our first priority is to reinvest to grow our business and enhance shareholder value. After these investment opportunities, we expect to return all of our free cash flow over the long term through dividends and share repurchases—while maintaining a strong financial foundation. Today's dividend increase underscores our confidence in the long-term strength of our business and ongoing commitment to returning cash to shareholders."

McDonald's has raised its dividend each and every year since paying its first dividend in 1976. The new quarterly dividend of $0.55 per share is equivalent to $2.20 per share annually—quadruple the amount paid in 2004.

---

[14]§132(c).

Closely held corporations usually are the alter egos of their shareholders. As a result, their dividend policies are much less likely to be structured. Rather, dividends may be a function of the shareholders' cash needs. The double taxation of corporate earnings plus the higher corporate tax rates provide an incentive for closely held corporations to pay out earnings in tax deductible ways, although as we saw in the case of Jim and Ginny, the additional payroll tax cost of a compensation strategy might outweigh the double tax imposed on the dividend. It makes sense to retain earnings in the corporation if the after-tax rate of return earned by the corporation exceeds the rate that could be earned by the individual shareholders. Paying dividends rather than salary can be a way to avoid Social Security taxes (in which case, the IRS may argue the dividend is really compensation). Closely held corporations also run the risk of paying a penalty tax called the *accumulated earnings tax* if they accumulate earnings in excess of $250,000 without having a documented business purpose for retaining the excess.[15]

## STOCK DIVIDENDS

**L04**

Rather than distribute cash dividends to its shareholders, a corporation may instead distribute additional shares of its own stock or rights to acquire additional shares. Publicly held corporations are likely to issue stock dividends to promote shareholder goodwill (that is, a stock dividend allows the corporation to retain cash and still provide shareholders with tangible evidence of their interest in corporate earnings) or to reduce the market price of its outstanding shares. A stock dividend increases the number of shares outstanding and thereby reduces the (value) price per share. This makes the stock more accessible to a wider range of shareholders. Most stock dividends take the form of a **stock split,** which is a 2-for-1 stock dividend. Exhibit 18-4 provides an example of the stock dividend strategy used by McDonald's Corporation to keep its stock price accessible to a diverse group of investors.

### EXHIBIT 18-4   Keeping the Stock Price Accessible to Individual Investors

Publicly traded corporations such as McDonald's Corporation often use stock splits to reduce the market price of their stock. This makes the stock accessible to a wider group of shareholders, ranging from institutional investors (pension funds) to investment clubs. A lower stock price keeps the stock widely held, which prevents a small group of investors from dominating company policy. McDonald's Corporation makes the following statement about its history of stock dividends on its Web site:

> Since going public in 1965, McDonald's has paid twelve stock splits. In fact, an investment of $2,250 in 100 shares at that time had grown to 74,360 shares worth approximately $4.6 million as of year-end market close on December 31, 2008.

### Tax Consequences to Shareholders Receiving a Stock Dividend

**Nontaxable Stock Dividends**   Stock dividends generally do not provide shareholders with any increase in value. That is, the shareholders' interest in the corporation remains unchanged except for the fact that they now own more pieces of paper (stock) than before. As a result, a stock dividend usually is not included in the shareholders' gross income.[16]

For the nontaxable general rule to apply, the stock distribution must meet two conditions: (1) it must be made with respect to the corporation's common stock, and (2) it must be pro rata with respect to all shareholders (that is, the shareholders' relative equity positions do not change as a result of the distribution).

The recipient of a nontaxable stock dividend allocates a portion of the tax basis from the stock on which the stock dividend was issued to the newly issued stock

---

[15]§§531–535.
[16]§305(a).

based on the relative fair market values (FMV) of the stock.[17] The tax basis of the newly issued stock can be determined using the following formula:

$$\text{Adjusted basis of "old stock"} \times \frac{\text{FMV of stock received}}{\text{Total FMV of all stock}} = \text{Adjusted basis of "new stock"}$$

The holding period of the new stock includes the holding period for which the shareholder held the old stock.[18]

The shareholder reduces the adjusted tax basis of the "old stock" by the tax basis allocated to the "new stock." For example, assume a shareholder owns 100 shares of McDonald's Corporation stock, for which she paid $3,000. McDonald's declares a 2-for-1 stock dividend and sends the shareholder an additional 100 shares of stock. The shareholder will now own 200 shares of stock with the same tax basis of $3,000. The basis of each share of stock decreases from its original $30 per share ($3,000/100) to $15 per share ($3,000/200).

---

**Example 18-16**

Jim has a tax basis in his SCR stock of $24,000. Ginny's tax basis in her SCR stock is $10,000. Jim owns 75 of the 100 shares of outstanding SCR stock, while Ginny owns the remaining 25 shares.

*What if:* Assume for estate and gift tax purposes, their tax accountant, Louis Tully, suggested that SCR declare a 2-for-1 stock dividend. As a result of the stock split, Jim would own 150 shares of SCR stock, and Ginny would own the remaining 50 shares. Based on a recent valuation, Jim and Ginny learned that each share of SCR was worth $5,000 prior to the stock split ($2,500 after the split). The total fair market value of Jim's SCR stock prior to and after the split is $375,000 (75 shares × $5,000). The total fair market value of Ginny's SCR stock is $125,000 (25 shares × $5,000).

Is the stock dividend taxable to Jim and Ginny?

**Answer:** No. The stock dividend to Jim and Ginny is nontaxable because it is made equally (pro rata) to the shareholders.

What is the tax basis of each share of SCR stock now held by Jim and Ginny?

**Answer:**

Jim recomputes his tax basis in the new SCR stock received as follows:

$$\frac{\$187,500 \text{ (FMV of new stock received)}}{\$375,000 \text{ (total FMV of stock)}} \times \$24,000 = \$12,000$$

His tax basis in the original shares of SCR stock is $24,000 − $12,000 = $12,000

Ginny recomputes her tax basis in the new SCR stock received as follows:

$$\frac{\$62,500 \text{ (FMV of new stock received)}}{\$125,000 \text{ (total FMV of stock)}} \times \$10,000 = \$5,000$$

Her tax basis in the original shares of SCR stock is $10,000 − $5,000 = $5,000

---

**Taxable Stock Dividends**    Non-pro rata stock dividends usually are included in the shareholder's gross income as taxable dividends to the extent of the distributing corporation's E&P.[19] This makes sense in that the recipient has now received something of value: an increase in the shareholder's claim on the corporation's income and assets. For example, a corporation may give its shareholders the choice between a cash dividend or a stock dividend. In this case, shareholders who elect the stock dividend in

**THE KEY FACTS**

Tax Consequences of Stock Dividends

▪ Pro rata distributions generally are nontaxable.

▪ Shareholders allocate basis from the "old" stock to the "new" stock based on relative fair market value.

▪ Non-pro rata stock dividends usually are taxable as dividends.

[17]§307.
[18]§1223(4).
[19]§305(b).

lieu of money will have a taxable dividend equal to the fair market value of the stock received. Because the stock dividend is taxable, the recipient will have a tax basis in the stock equal to its fair market value. A technical discussion of all of the rules that apply to determine if a stock dividend is taxable is beyond the scope of this text.

## L05   STOCK REDEMPTIONS

*continued from page 18-2 . . .*

In the original storyline, Jim and Ginny raised some of the initial capital they needed to start SCR by borrowing $50,000 from Jim's parents, Walt and Wanda. An alternative strategy would have been to issue 25 additional shares of SCR stock to Walt and Wanda in return for their $50,000. This change in facts would reduce Jim's ownership percentage in SCR to 60 percent (75 shares / 125 shares). Ginny's ownership percentage would decrease to 20 percent (25 shares / 125 shares). Walt and Wanda would own the remaining 20 percent. We will assume this change in facts to continue the storyline.

Walt and Wanda do not participate in the management of the company. In fact, Walt and Wanda were hoping to cash out of SCR when it became profitable and use the money to put a down payment on a condominium in The Villages, a retirement community near Orlando, Florida. With the SCR stock valued at $5,000 per share ($125,000 in total), Walt and Wanda saw this as an opportunity to realize their retirement dream. Jim and Ginny saw this as an opportunity to own all of the company's stock, eliminating a potential source of discord should Jim's parents disapprove of the way Jim and Ginny were managing the company.

By the end of 2011, the company had sufficient cash to buy back some or all of Walt and Wanda's shares of SCR stock. Jim and Ginny were wondering about the potential tax consequences to SCR and Walt and Wanda under various redemption plans. In particular, Jim and Ginny wanted to know if there was a tax difference in (1) buying back five of Walt and Wanda's shares in 2011 and the remaining 20 shares equally in years 2012–2015 (five shares per year), or (2) buying back all 25 shares in 2010 using an installment note that would pay them 20 percent of the purchase price in each of the next five years plus interest. Once again, they turned to their trusted tax accountant, Louis Tully, for advice. ■

Publicly held corporations buy back (redeem) their stock from existing shareholders for many and varied reasons. For example, a corporation may have excess cash and limited investment opportunities, or management may feel the stock is undervalued. Management may see a large redemption as a way to get analysts to take a closer look at their company (this action sometimes is referred to as *signaling*). Reducing the number of outstanding shares also increases earnings per share (by reducing the number of shares in the denominator of the calculation) and potentially increases the stock's market price. Stock redemptions can be used to selectively buy-out dissenting shareholders who have become disruptive to the company. Exhibit 18-5 illustrates Microsoft Corporation's use of a $40 billion stock buyback to return cash to its shareholders and signal the market that management has confidence in the company's future earnings and cash flows.

Privately held corporations engage in stock redemptions for reasons that are different from publicly traded corporations. These corporations often use stock redemptions to shift ownership control between family members (usually the older generation to the younger generation) when the acquiring family members (younger generation) do not have the liquidity (cash) to purchase shares directly from the other family members (older generation). They also use redemptions to buy out dissatisfied, disinterested, or

**EXHIBIT 18-5    Microsoft Stock Repurchase**

*Microsoft Announces Share Repurchase Program and Increases Quarterly Dividend*
*$40 billion authorized for share repurchase; Dividend increased 18 percent*

REDMOND, Wash.—September 22, 2008—Microsoft Corp. today announced that its board of directors approved a new share repurchase program authorizing up to an additional $40 billion in share repurchases with an expiration of September 30, 2013.

The board of directors also declared a quarterly dividend of $0.13 per share, reflecting a two-cent or 18 percent increase over the previous quarter's dividend. The dividend is payable December 11, 2008, to shareholders of record on November 20, 2008. The ex-dividend date will be November 18, 2008.

In addition, the company stated that it has completed its previous $40 billion stock repurchase program. Microsoft has returned over $115 billion to shareholders through a combination of share repurchases and dividends over the last five years.

"These announcements illustrate our confidence in the long-term growth of the company and our commitment to returning capital to our shareholders," said Chris Liddell, chief financial officer of Microsoft.

deceased shareholders (for example, a child who does not want to continue in the family business or a family member who has become disruptive in the management of the company). In addition, redemptions of an ex-spouse's stock can provide liquidity in a divorce agreement and eliminate the individual from management or ownership in the company. Finally, redemptions can be used to provide cash to satisfy estate taxes imposed on the estate of a deceased shareholder of the company.

Closely held corporations and their shareholders frequently have buy-sell agreements in which either the corporation or the other shareholders are obligated or given an option to purchase the shares of another shareholder when a "trigger event" occurs (usually the death or retirement of a shareholder). A buy-sell agreement in which the *corporation* is required or has the option to repurchase the shares is called a *redemption agreement*. A buy-sell agreement in which the *shareholders* are required or have the option to purchase the shares is called a *cross-purchase agreement*. Buy-sell agreements provide for the liquidation of a shareholder's stock for estate tax purposes and protection of the remaining shareholders from a sale of the stock to an undesirable shareholder.

### The Form of a Stock Redemption

The tax law defines a redemption as an acquisition by a corporation of its stock from a shareholder in exchange for property, whether or not the stock so acquired is canceled, retired, or held as treasury stock.[20] The term *property* has the same meaning as it did for dividend transactions (that is, cash and noncash property, not including the stock of the distributing corporation).

Stock redemptions take the form of an *exchange;* that is, the shareholders exchange their stock in the corporation for property, usually cash. If the *form* of the transaction is respected, shareholders compute gain or loss (usually capital) by comparing the amount realized (money and the fair market value of other property received) with their tax basis in the stock exchanged.

Form is not always respected in a redemption, however. The tax law may determine (or the IRS may argue that) the transaction is, in substance, a property distribution, the tax consequences of which should be determined under the previously discussed dividend rules.

The IRC attempts to provide both "bright line" and subjective tests to distinguish when a redemption should be treated as an exchange or a potential dividend.[21]

[20]§317(b).
[21]§302.

The result is an intricate set of rules that must be navigated carefully by the corporation and its shareholders to ensure that the shareholders receive the tax treatment they desire.[22] This is especially true in closely held, family corporations, where the majority of stock is held by people related to each other through birth or marriage.

Without any tax law restrictions, a sole shareholder of a corporation could circumvent the dividend rules by structuring distributions to have the form of an exchange (that is, a stock redemption). For example, rather than have the corporation make a $100,000 dividend distribution, the shareholder could have the corporation buy back $100,000 of stock from the shareholder. If the shareholder had a tax basis of $60,000 in the stock redeemed, the amount of income reported on the shareholder's tax return would decrease from $100,000 (dividend) to $40,000 (capital gain). Both amounts would be taxed at the same preferential tax rate (generally 15 percent), assuming the shareholder held the stock for more than a year. Similar to a dividend, however, the sole shareholder would continue to own 100 percent of the corporation before and after the stock redemption.

To frustrate this tax strategy, the tax law treats stock redemptions as exchanges only if the shareholder can show that his or her ownership interest in the corporation has been "meaningfully" reduced relative to other shareholders as a result of the redemption. A sole shareholder will never be able to satisfy this requirement.

Individuals generally are (were) motivated to seek exchange treatment in a stock redemption because of the preferential tax rates imposed on capital gains. In the 1990s, for example, dividends could be taxed as high as 39.6 percent, while capital gains were taxed at only 20 percent. This incentive diminished when Congress equalized the tax rates imposed on capital gains and dividends in 2003 (generally 15 percent). The reduction in the amount of gain recognized by the adjusted tax basis of the stock redeemed could still make a substantial difference if the stock's tax basis is high or the shareholder wants to absorb an existing capital loss with capital gains. Additionally, a shareholder with a stock tax basis greater than the amount received could potentially recognize a capital loss on the exchange compared to dividend income.[23] President Obama has proposed increasing the tax on dividends and capital gains to 20 percent.

Corporate shareholders generally have more incentive for dividend treatment. Dividends from domestic corporations are eligible for the dividends received deduction (usually 70 percent or 80 percent), whereas a capital gain is taxed at the corporation's marginal tax rate (as high as 35 percent). Again, a corporation might prefer exchange treatment if the redemption results in a loss or its stock tax basis as a percentage of the redemption price exceeds the dividends received deduction ratio.

### Redemptions that Contract the Shareholder's Stock Ownership Interest

The IRC allows a shareholder to treat a redemption as an exchange if the transaction meets one of three change-in-stock-ownership tests.[24] These stock ownership tests look at the redemption from the shareholder's perspective.

#### Redemptions that Are Substantially Disproportionate with Respect to the Shareholder
The IRC states that a redemption will be treated as an exchange if the redemption is *"substantially disproportionate with respect to the shareholder."*[25] A

---

[22]Not all taxpayers have the same tax incentives in a redemption. Corporate shareholders may desire dividend treatment to capture the dividends received deduction. Individuals, on the other hand, may desire exchange treatment to lessen the amount of gain recognized (by reducing the amount received by the basis of the stock exchanged) or to report a capital loss.

[23]This loss could be disallowed under the related-party rules discussed in Chapter 10, depending on the percentage of stock owned by the shareholder.

[24]§302(b)(1), (b)(2), and (b)(3).

[25]§302(b)(2).

shareholder meets this requirement by satisfying three mechanical *("bright line")* *stock ownership tests:*

- Immediately after the exchange, the shareholder owns less than 50 percent of the total combined voting power of all classes of stock entitled to vote.
- The shareholder's percentage ownership of voting stock after the redemption is less than 80 percent of his or her percentage ownership before the redemption.
- The shareholder's percentage ownership of the aggregate fair market value of the corporation's common stock (voting and nonvoting) after the redemption is less than 80 percent of his or her percentage ownership before the redemption.

For example, if a shareholder owns 60 percent of a corporation's stock, she must own less than 48 percent of the stock after a stock redemption to have the redemption treated as an exchange ($60\% \times 80\% = 48\%$, which is less than 50 percent). If the shareholder owns 70 percent of the stock, she must own less than 50 percent of the stock after the redemption to have the transaction treated as an exchange ($70\% \times 80\% = 56\%$, which is greater than 50 percent).

The determination as to whether a shareholder meets the 50 percent and 80 percent tests is evaluated on a shareholder-by-shareholder basis. As a result, some shareholders can satisfy the test while others do not. If a shareholder owns multiple classes (voting and nonvoting) of common stock, the less-than-80-percent of fair market value test is applied to the shareholder's aggregate ownership of the common stock rather than on a class-by-class basis.

---

**Example 18-17**

***What if:*** Assume Walt and Wanda are not related to either Jim or Ginny. In 2011, SCR redeemed five shares of their stock in exchange for $25,000. Walt and Wanda have a tax basis in the five shares of SCR stock of $10,000 ($2,000 per share). What is the tax treatment of the stock redemption to Walt and Wanda under §302(b)(2)?

**Answer:** $25,000 dividend. Prior to the redemption, Walt and Wanda owned 20 percent of SCR (25/125 shares). After the redemption, their ownership percentage in SCR drops to 16.67 percent (20/120 shares). This redemption does not satisfy the substantially disproportionate test, which would treat the redemption as an exchange. After the redemption, Walt and Wanda own less than 50 percent of SCR stock, but their ownership percentage after the redemption (16.67 percent) does not fall below 80 percent of their ownership percentage prior to the redemption ($80\% \times 20\% = 16\%$). Walt and Wanda will not be able to treat the redemption as an exchange under this change-in-ownership test. Unless they can satisfy one of the other change-in-ownership tests, Walt and Wanda will have a $25,000 dividend, assuming SCR has sufficient E&P, rather than a $15,000 capital gain ($25,000 − $10,000).

How many shares of stock would SCR have to redeem from Walt and Wanda to guarantee them exchange treatment under the substantially disproportionate test?

**Answer:** Six shares. For Walt and Wanda to meet the 80 percent test, SCR must redeem six shares of stock. The computation is made as follows:

$$\frac{25 - x}{125 - x} < 16\%, \text{ where } x \text{ is the number of shares to be redeemed}$$

Using some algebra, we can compute $x$ to be 5.95, which we must round up to six shares.[26] If SCR redeems six shares from Walt and Wanda, their ownership percentage after the redemption will be 15.97 percent (19/119 shares), which now meets the 80 percent test. The redemption of this one additional share transforms the transaction from a $30,000 dividend (6 shares × $5,000) to an $18,000 capital gain ($30,000 − $12,000).

---

[26]Multiply both sides by ($125 - x$), we get $25 - x = 20 - .16x$. Moving $x$ to the right side of the equation and the integers to the left side of the equation, we get $5 = .84x$. Solving for $x$ we get 5.95.

In determining whether Walt and Wanda meet the 50 percent and 80 percent tests, they must take into account the **constructive ownership** (stock attribution) rules found in sub-chapter C.[27] These tax law rules causes stock owned by other persons (individuals and entities) to be treated as owned by (attributed to) the shareholder for purposes of determining whether the shareholder has met the change-in-stock-ownership tests. The purpose of the attribution rules is to prevent shareholders from dispersing stock ownership to either family members who have similar economic interests or entities controlled by the shareholder to avoid having stock redemptions recharacterized as dividends.

***Family attribution.*** Individuals are treated as owning the shares of stock owned by their spouse, children, grandchildren, and parents. Stock owned constructively through the family attribution rule cannot be reattributed to another family member through the family attribution rule (this is known as *double family attribution*).

## Example 18-18

Return to the original storyline facts, where Walt and Wanda are Jim's parents. In 2011, SCR redeemed six shares of stock from them in exchange for $30,000. Walt and Wanda have a tax basis in the six shares of stock redeemed of $12,000 ($2,000 per share). What is the tax treatment of the stock redemption to Walt and Wanda under §302(b)(2)?

**Answer:** $30,000 dividend.

Prior to the redemption, Walt and Wanda owned 20 percent of SCR (25/125 shares) directly. Under the family attribution rules, they are treated as constructively owning the shares of SCR stock owned by their son Jim (75 shares). In applying the substantially disproportionate change-in-stock-ownership tests, Walt and Wanda are treated as owning 100 shares of SCR stock (25 + 75), or 80 percent of the SCR stock (100/125 shares). After the redemption, their ownership percentage in SCR drops to 79 percent (94/119 shares). This redemption does not satisfy the substantially disproportionate test because Walt and Wanda are deemed to own more than 50 percent of the SCR stock after the redemption. As a result, they will have a $30,000 dividend, assuming SCR has sufficient E&P, rather than an $18,000 capital gain ($30,000 − $12,000).

An interesting question arises as to what happens to the tax basis of stock redeemed that is not used in determining the shareholder's tax consequences. This occurs in a redemption treated as a dividend, where the tax basis of the stock redeemed is not subtracted from the amount received from the corporation. Under the current rules, the tax basis of the stock redeemed is added back to the tax basis of any shares still held by the shareholder.[28] If the shareholder no longer holds any shares, the tax basis transfers to the stock held by those persons who caused the shareholder to have dividend treatment under the attribution rules.

## Example 18-19

In the prior example, SCR redeemed six shares of stock from Walt and Wanda for $30,000, and the transaction was treated as a dividend because of the application of the family attribution rules. Walt and Wanda had a tax basis in the six shares of stock redeemed of $12,000 ($2,000 per share), but this tax basis was not used in determining their taxable income from the transaction.

What is Walt and Wanda's tax basis in their remaining 19 shares of SCR stock?

**Answer:** $50,000. Walt and Wanda add back the unused $12,000 tax basis in the six shares redeemed to the tax basis of their remaining 19 shares. Their tax basis in these remaining shares increases to $50,000, the original tax basis of their 25 shares.

[27]§318.
[28]Reg. §1.302-2.

*Attribution from entities to owners or beneficiaries.*    Owners or beneficiaries of entities can be deemed to own shares of stock owned by the entity itself. Under these rules, partners are deemed to own a pro rata share of their partnership's stock holdings (that is, a partner who has a 10 percent interest in a partnership is deemed to own 10 percent of any stock owned by the partnership). Beneficiaries are deemed to own a pro rata share of the stock owned by the trust or estate of which they are a beneficiary. Shareholders are deemed to own a pro rata share of their corporation's stock holdings, but only if they own at least 50 percent of the value of the corporation's stock. Other attribution rules, such as family attribution, apply in determining if this 50 percent test is met.

For example, assume an individual owns 100 shares of a corporation's stock directly. In addition, she is a 50 percent partner in a partnership that owns 100 shares of stock in the same corporation. Under the entity-to-owner attribution rules, the individual is deemed to own 50 percent of the partnership's 100 shares in the corporation. She is deemed to own 150 shares of stock in the corporation (100 + 50) for purposes of applying any of the change-in-stock-ownership tests in a stock redemption.

> **Example 18-20**
>
> **What if:** Assume that Walt and Wanda are not Jim's parents, and they are 50 percent partners in a partnership that owns 25 shares in SCR. The other 50 percent of the partnership is owned by their neighbors, Fred and Ethel, who are unrelated to them. How many shares of SCR are Walt and Wanda treated as constructively owning through the partnership?
>
> **Answer:** 12.5 shares. Walt and Wanda are treated as owning their pro rata share of stock owned by their partnership; in this example, 50 percent times 25 shares.

*Attribution from owners or beneficiaries to entities.*    Entities can be deemed to own all of the stock owned by their owners or beneficiaries. Under these rules, a partnership is deemed to own 100 percent of the shares owned by its partners. A trust or estate is deemed to own 100 percent of the shares owned by its beneficiaries. A corporation is deemed to own 100 percent of the shares owned by its shareholders, but only if the shareholder owns at least 50 percent of the value of the corporation's stock. Stock that is deemed owned by an entity cannot be reattributed to the other owners in the entity under the entity-to-owner rules previously discussed (this is known as *sideways attribution*).

For example, assume an individual owns 100 shares of a corporation's stock directly. In addition, she is a 50 percent partner in a partnership that owns 100 shares of stock in the same corporation. Under the owner-to-entity attribution rules, the partnership is deemed to own 100 percent of the partner's 100 shares in the corporation. The partnership is treated as owning 200 shares of stock in the corporation (100 + 100) for purposes of applying any of the change-in-stock-ownership tests in a stock redemption.

*Option attribution.*    A person having an option to purchase stock is deemed to own the stock that the option entitles the person to purchase.

### Redemptions in Complete Redemption of all of the Stock of the Corporation Owned by the Shareholder

The IRC holds that a redemption will be treated as an exchange if the redemption is in *"complete redemption of all of the stock of the corporation owned by the shareholder."*[29] This test seems redundant with the substantially disproportionate test discussed previously; after all, a complete redemption

---

[29]§302(b)(3).

automatically satisfies the 50 percent and 80 percent tests. The difference relates to the application of the stock attribution rules that apply to this form of redemption.

The stock attribution rules previously discussed also apply to a complete redemption. This presents a potential problem in family owned corporations in which the only (or majority) shareholders are parents, children, and grandchildren. Parents who have all of their stock redeemed will be treated as having received a dividend if their children or grandchildren continue to own the remaining stock in the corporation because of the operation of the family attribution rules. To provide family members with relief in these situations, the IRC allows shareholders to waive (ignore) the family attribution rules in a complete redemption of their stock.[30] As usual, there are some strings attached.

The first requirement is that the shareholder has no interest in the corporation immediately after the exchange as a *"shareholder, employee, director, officer or consultant."*[31] These relations to the corporation are referred to as **prohibited interests.** The second requirement is that the shareholder does not acquire a prohibited interest within 10 years after the redemption, unless by inheritance (this is known as the *10-year look-forward rule*). Finally, the shareholder must agree to notify the IRS district director within 30 days if he or she acquires a prohibited interest within 10 years after the redemption. These agreements are referred to as **triple i agreements.**[32] The shareholder can still be a creditor of the corporation (that is, the parents can receive a corporate note in return for their stock if the corporation does not have the cash on hand to finance the redemption).

---

**Example 18-21**

Return to the original storyline facts, where Walt and Wanda are Jim's parents. Assume SCR redeemed all of their 25 shares in 2011 for $125,000. Their tax basis in the SCR shares is $50,000 (25 × $2,000). Under the family attribution rules, Walt and Wanda would still be treated as constructively owning 75 percent of the SCR stock (Jim would own 75 of the remaining 100 shares in SCR). The $125,000 payment would be treated as a taxable dividend.

What happens to their unused $50,000 tax basis in the SCR stock redeemed?
**Answer:** Their tax basis transfers to Jim's stock, giving him a new tax basis in his SCR stock of $74,000 ($24,000 + $50,000).

How can Walt and Wanda change the tax treatment of the complete redemption?
**Answer:** Because Walt and Wanda have all of their shares redeemed, they can waive the family attribution rules provided they file a triple i agreement with the IRS and do not retain a prohibited interest in SCR (for example, as an employee or consultant). By waiving the family attribution rules, Walt and Wanda will be able to treat the redemption as an exchange and report a capital gain of $75,000 ($125,000 − $50,000).

---

**Redemptions that Are Not Essentially Equivalent to a Dividend**    The IRC provides that a redemption will be treated as an exchange if the redemption is *"not essentially equivalent to a dividend."*[33] This is a *subjective* determination that turns on the facts and circumstances of each case. To satisfy this requirement, the IRS or the court must conclude that there has been a "meaningful" reduction in the shareholder's ownership interest in the corporation as a result of the redemption. The IRS does not provide any mechanical tests to make this determination. As a result, shareholder reliance on

[30]§302(c)(2).

[31]§302(c).

[32]The agreement gets its name from the clause in which it is described [§302(c)(2)(A)(*iii*)].

[33]§302(b)(1).

this test usually is one of last resort.[34] The Supreme Court has held that the only way for a shareholder to qualify under this test is for the redemption to "result in a meaningful reduction of the shareholder's proportionate interest in the corporation."[35]

Although the courts have held that a shareholder's interest can include the right to vote and exercise control, participate in current and accumulated earnings, or share in net assets on liquidation, the IRS generally looks at the change in voting power as the key factor. The shareholder's voting power must decrease and be below 50 percent as a result of the exchange before this test can be considered.[36] As before, the stock attribution rules apply to these types of redemptions. Shareholders generally turn to this test to provide exchange treatment for redemptions when they cannot meet the "bright line" tests discussed previously.

---

**Example 18-22**

*What if:* Assume Walt and Wanda are not related to Jim or Ginny. In 2011, SCR redeemed five shares of their stock in exchange for $25,000. Walt and Wanda have a tax basis in the five shares of SCR stock of $10,000 ($2,000 per share).

What is the tax treatment of the stock redemption to Walt and Wanda under the *not essentially equivalent to a dividend* test?

**Answer:** $15,000 capital gain.

Prior to the redemption, Walt and Wanda owned 20 percent of SCR (25/125 shares). After the redemption, their ownership percentage in SCR drops to 16.67 percent (20/120 shares). This redemption does not satisfy the substantially disproportionate test, which would treat the redemption as an exchange. Walt and Wanda likely have a case that the redemption should be treated as an exchange because it was *"not essentially equal to a dividend."* After all, their ownership percentage decreased (20 percent to 16.67 percent) and is below 50 percent after the redemption. They likely have a case, although the result they seek (exchange treatment) is not guaranteed. For peace of mind, they might prefer having SCR redeem one additional share and have the certainty that the redemption will be treated as an exchange.

---

**Example 18-23**

*What if:* Assume Walt and Wanda are Jim's parents and SCR redeemed five shares of their stock in exchange for $25,000. Walt and Wanda have a tax basis in the five shares of SCR stock of $10,000 ($2,000 per share). What is the tax treatment of the stock redemption to Walt and Wanda under the *not essentially equivalent to a dividend* test?

**Answer:** $25,000 dividend.

Prior to the redemption, Walt and Wanda are treated as owning 80 percent of SCR (25 shares directly and 75 shares through Jim). After the redemption, their ownership percentage in SCR drops to 79 percent (95/120 shares). This redemption does not satisfy the *not essentially equal to a dividend* test because they are treated as owning more than 50 percent of the SCR stock.

---

[34]One set of commentators refer to this provision as the "last cloudy chance" for a taxpayer to achieve exchange treatment in a stock redemption. See Boris I. Bittker and James E. Eustice, *Federal Income Taxation of Corporations and Shareholders,* Sixth Edition (Boston, MA: Warren, Gorham & Lamont, 1998), pp. 9–31.

[35]*United States v. Davis,* 397 U.S. 301, at 313 (1970).

[36]In Rev. Rul. 76-385, 1976-2 C.B. 92, the IRS held that in the case of a "small, minority shareholder, whose relative stock interest is minimal and who exercises no control over the affairs of the corporation," any reduction in proportionate interest is "meaningful." In this ruling, the shareholder's ownership percentage decreased from .0001118% to .0001081%, which would not be considered a "meaningful" reduction by most standards. Because the reduction in stock ownership did not meet the substantially disproportionate tests of §302(b)(2), the shareholder's only hope for exchange treatment was to qualify under §302(b)(1).

### Tax Consequences to the Distributing Corporation

The corporation distributing property to shareholders in a redemption generally recognizes gain on distributions of appreciated property but is not permitted to recognize loss on distribution of property with a fair market value less than its tax basis.[37]

If the shareholder treats the redemption as a *dividend,* the corporation reduces its E&P by the cash distributed and the fair market value of other property distributed.[38] If the shareholder treats the redemption as an *exchange,* the corporation reduces E&P at the date of distribution by the percentage of stock redeemed (that is, if 50 percent of the stock is redeemed, E&P is reduced by 50 percent), not to exceed the fair market value of the property distributed.[39] The distributing corporation reduces its E&P by any dividend distributions made during the year before reducing its E&P for redemptions treated as exchanges.[40]

The distributing corporation cannot deduct expenses incurred in a stock redemption.[41] The corporation can deduct interest on debt incurred to finance a redemption, however.

| Example 18-24 | |
|---|---|

**What if:** Assume SCR redeemed all of the 25 shares owned by Walt and Wanda in exchange for $125,000. The stock redeemed represents 20 percent of the total stock outstanding. Walt and Wanda have a tax basis in their SCR shares of $50,000. Further assume that Walt and Wanda treated the redemption as an exchange because they waived the family attribution rules and filed a triple i agreement with the IRS.[42] As a result, Walt and Wanda recognized a capital gain of $75,000 ($125,000 − $50,000). The redemption took place on December 31, 2011, on which date SCR had total E&P of $500,000. SCR did not make any dividend payments during the year.

By what amount does SCR reduce its E&P as a result of this redemption?

**Answer:** $100,000. SCR reduces total E&P by the lesser of (1) $100,000 (20% × $500,000) or (2) $125,000, the amount paid to Walt and Wanda in the redemption.

**What if:** Assume total E&P was $1,000,000 at the end of 2011. By what amount does SCR reduce its E&P as a result of this redemption?

**Answer:** $125,000. SCR reduces total E&P by the lesser of (1) $200,000 (20% × $1,000,000) or (2) $125,000, the amount paid to Walt and Wanda in the redemption.

**What if:** Assume SCR paid a dividend of $100,000 to its shareholders on June 1, 2011. Total E&P was $500,000 at the end of 2011, before taking into account the dividend and redemption. By what amount does SCR reduce its E&P as a result of this redemption?

**Answer:** $80,000. SCR first reduces total E&P by the dividend paid during the year to $400,000 ($500,000 − $100,000). SCR then reduces its E&P for the redemption by the lesser of (1) $80,000 (20% × $400,000) or (2) $125,000, the amount paid to Walt and Wanda in the redemption.

---

### Trends in Stock Redemptions by Publicly Traded Corporations

Traditionally, publicly traded corporations viewed stock redemptions as a tax efficient means to return cash to their shareholders. Redemptions allow shareholders to "declare their own dividends" by voluntarily selling shares back to the corporation.

---

**THE KEY FACTS**

**Stock Redemptions Treated as Exchanges**

■ A stock redemption is treated as an exchange if it meets one of the following three tests:
· Not essentially equivalent to a dividend.
· Substantially disproportionate with respect to the shareholders.
· In complete termination of the shareholder's interest.

*(continued)*

---

[37]§311(a) and (b).
[38]§312(a).
[39]§312(n)(7).
[40]Rev. Rul. 74-338, 1974-2 C.B. 101 and Rev. Rul. 74-339, 1974-2 C.B. 103.
[41]§162(k).
[42]The requirements for filing the triple i agreement are found in Reg. §1.302-4T.

Many companies increased their dividends after Congress decreased the dividend tax rate to 15 percent or 5 percent (now 0 percent) for individuals in 2003. Anheuser-Busch Company is an example of a corporation that increased its dividend payments as a result of the reduction in the tax rate applied to dividends.

---

**Taxes in the Real World** *Changing Distribution Strategies in Light of Tax Law Changes*

**Anheuser-Busch Cos., Inc. Announces 12.8 Percent Dividend Increase and New Dividend Policy Targeting Higher Growth**

ST. LOUIS, Jul. 23, 2003 (BUSINESS WIRE)—Patrick Stokes, president and chief executive officer of Anheuser-Busch Cos., Inc., (NYSE:BUD) today announced that the Board of Directors has increased the regular quarterly dividend on the company's common stock to 22 cents, from 19½ cents per share, an increase of 12.8 percent. This marks the 27th consecutive year of Anheuser-Busch dividend increases. The new dividend rate is payable September 9, 2003, to shareholders of record on August 11, 2003.

Anheuser-Busch's average annual dividend per share increase during the past five years was 8.4 percent, which represented top quartile dividend per share growth among S&P 500 companies. The higher dividend increase in 2003 reflects a change in Anheuser-Busch's dividend policy. It is now the Board of Directors' intent to increase dividends per share in line with the company's earnings per share growth, versus a prior policy of increasing dividends per share somewhat less than the growth in earnings per share. This policy change reflects the recent reduction in the federal tax rate on corporate dividends.

---

*(concluded)*

■ **The following attribution rules are used to determine if one of the three tests is met:**
· Family attribution.
· Entity-to-owner attribution (pro rata).
· Owner-to-entity attribution (100 percent).
· Options.

■ **A corporation reduces its E&P as a result of a stock redemption as follows:**
· If the distribution is treated as an exchange, E&P is reduced by the lesser of (1) the amount distributed or (2) the percentage of stock redeemed times AE&P at the redemption date.
· If the distribution is treated as a dividend, E&P is reduced using the dividend rules.

---

Individuals have a tax incentive to participate in a redemption because gain recognized as a result of the redemption usually is capital gain (which is reduced by the basis of the stock redeemed and can absorb capital losses from other investments). Losses produced by the buyback generally can be deducted against capital gains.

## PARTIAL LIQUIDATIONS

**LO6**

Corporations can contract their operations by either distributing the stock of a subsidiary to their shareholders or by selling the business. In the case of a sale, the corporation may distribute the proceeds from the sale to its shareholders in partial liquidation of their ownership interests. The distribution may require the shareholders to tender shares of stock back to the corporation or may be pro rata to all the shareholders without an actual exchange of stock.

The tax treatment of a distribution received in a partial liquidation depends on the identity of the shareholder receiving the distribution.[43] All *noncorporate* shareholders receive exchange treatment. This entitles the individual to capital gain treatment with respect to gain or loss recognized on the actual or deemed exchange. If the shareholder is not required to tender stock to the corporation in return for the property received, the shareholder computes gain or loss recognized on the exchange by calculating the tax basis of the shares that would have been transferred to the corporation had the transaction been a stock redemption.

All *corporate* shareholders are subject to the change-in-stock-ownership rules that apply to stock redemptions. This usually results in dividend treatment because partial liquidations almost always involve pro rata distributions. Corporate shareholders generally prefer dividend treatment because of the availability of the dividends received deduction.

---

[43]§302(b)(4).

For a distribution to be in partial liquidation of the corporation, it must either be *"not essentially equivalent to a dividend"* (as determined at the corporate level) or be the result of the termination of a *"qualified trade or business."*[44] The technical requirements to meet these requirements are beyond the scope of this text.

Partial liquidations can be a tax efficient way for a corporation to satisfy both its corporate and individual shareholders. For example, in the 1990s, General Dynamics Corporation sold off several of its divisions and distributed the proceeds ($20 per share) to its shareholders in partial liquidation of the corporation. As a result, the company's largest corporate shareholder treated the distribution as a dividend and received a 70 percent dividends received deduction. The company's largest individual shareholders treated the redemption as an exchange and received preferential taxation at the capital gain tax rate. The corporation was able to distribute cash from the sale of its assets in a manner that was tax efficient to its diverse set of shareholders. Despite their beneficial tax results, partial liquidations are rare in practice.

---

### Taxes in the Real World    *Focusing on Core Competencies*

**Brown-Forman to Distribute Net Proceeds from Lenox Sale to Shareholders**

LOUISVILLE, Ky. (BUSINESS WIRE) March 22, 2007—Brown-Forman Corporation (NYSE:BFB)(NYSE:BFA) announced today that its board of directors approved a cash distribution of approximately $205 million to be distributed pro rata to the holders of its common stock. Approximately $1.66 per share will be distributed on May 10, 2007 to stockholders of record on April 5, 2007. This amount will be adjusted for the actual number of outstanding shares on April 5, 2007.

This distribution will be equal to the cash received (net of fees) for the sale of the Company's Consumer Durables segment, excluding Hartmann. Now that the Company has completed the sale of this segment, proceeds can be distributed in partial liquidation of the Company.

Brown-Forman Chief Executive Officer Paul Varga stated, "The sale of this segment reinforces our company's focus on brand-building in the thriving wine and spirits business."

The Company elected this form of distribution as a tax-efficient means of distributing cash to the Company's shareholders. Under Sections 302 (b)(4) and 302 (e)(1) of the Internal Revenue Code, each non-corporate shareholder should receive capital gains treatment as if they sold part of their stock, taking into account their tax basis in the stock. However, this statement is not intended to be, nor should it be interpreted as, tax advice by the Company. Each shareholder should consult his or her own tax advisor regarding the federal, state, local and foreign tax consequences to the shareholder of the distribution.

---

## CONCLUSION

In this chapter we learned that a corporation can distribute cash and other property to its shareholders in alternative ways. The most common forms are dividend distributions and stock buybacks (redemptions). The form chosen to make such a distribution affects the tax consequences to the recipients (shareholders) as well as the corporation itself. In some cases, the tax laws or the tax administrators can ignore the form of the transaction and assess tax based on the substance of the transaction. This is common in the case of stock redemptions that can be taxed as dividend payments or deductible payments (compensation, interest, rent) that can be treated as constructive dividends (with no deduction for the corporation). The tax rules that apply to make this distinction often are complex and must be evaluated carefully by taxpayers and their tax advisors prior to making a decision.

---

[44]§302(e).

## SUMMARY

Explain the basic tax law framework that applies to property distributions from a corporation to a shareholder.                                                                                           **L01**

- Subchapter C of the Internal Revenue Code provides guidelines and rules for determining the tax status of distributions from a taxable ("C") corporation to its shareholders.

- When a corporation distributes property to persons in their capacity as shareholders without receiving any property or services in return, the shareholder must determine if the amount received is a dividend.

- If the distribution is of property other than cash, the distributing corporation recognizes gain but not loss on the distribution.

Compute a corporation's earnings and profits and calculate the dividend amount received by a shareholder.                                                                                                 **L02**

- The IRC defines a dividend as any distribution of property made by a corporation to its shareholders out of its current or accumulated earnings and profits (E&P).

- Earnings and profits is the tax equivalent of financial accounting retained earnings, although the computations can be significantly different.

- A corporation must keep two E&P accounts: Current E&P and accumulated E&P.

- The IRC and the related regulations list four basic types of adjustments that a corporation must make to its taxable income to compute current E&P.
  - Inclusion of income that is excluded from taxable income.
  - Disallowance of certain expenses that are deducted in computing taxable income.
  - Deduction of certain expenses that are excluded from the computation of taxable income.
  - Deferral of deductions or acceleration of income due to separate accounting methods required for E&P purposes.

- The shareholder computes the dividend amount to include in gross income as the sum of cash received plus the fair market value of property received less any liabilities assumed.

- The distributing corporation recognizes gain, but not loss, on the distribution of noncash property in a dividend distribution.

- A corporation reduces its E&P by the amount of cash distributed, the E&P basis of unappreciated property distributed, and the fair market value of appreciated property distributed, net of any liability assumed by the shareholders.

Identify situations in which a corporation may be deemed to have paid a "constructive dividend" to a shareholder.                                                                                            **L03**

- A transaction between a shareholder and a corporation that does not take the form of a dividend may be treated by the IRS as a constructive dividend. Examples include:
  - Unreasonable compensation paid to shareholder/employees.
  - A bargain lease or uncompensated use of corporate property by a shareholder.
  - An excess purchase/lease price paid to a shareholder.
  - "Loans" to a shareholder who has no intent to repay the loan.
  - Corporate payments on a shareholder's behalf.
  - Unlawful diversions of corporate income to shareholders.

Comprehend the basic tax rules that apply to stock dividends.                                                                                                                                              **L04**

- The general rule is that a stock dividend is not taxable.

- The basis of the "new" stock received is computed by allocating basis from the existing stock based on relative fair market value.

- The holding period of the new stock includes the holding period of the existing stock on which the new stock was distributed.

- Non-pro rata stock dividends usually are treated as taxable dividends to the recipients.

**LO5**    Comprehend the different tax consequences that can arise from stock redemptions.

- If a redemption is treated as an exchange, the shareholder computes gain or loss by comparing the amount realized (money and property received) with the tax-adjusted basis of the stock surrendered.
  - The character of the gain or loss is capital.
  - The basis of noncash property received is its fair market value.
  - The holding period of the property received begins at the date of receipt.
- If the transaction is treated as a dividend, the shareholder has gross income in an amount equal to the cash and fair market value of other property received to the extent of the corporation's E&P.
  - The basis of the property received is its fair market value.
- The IRC treats redemptions as exchanges in transactions in which the shareholder's ownership interest in the corporation has been "meaningfully" reduced relative to other shareholders as a result of the redemption.
- There are three change-in-stock-ownership tests that entitle the shareholder to exchange treatment in a redemption.
- The IRC states that a redemption will be treated as an exchange if the redemption is "not essentially equivalent to a dividend."
  - This is a facts and circumstances determination (subjective).
  - To satisfy this requirement, the courts or IRS must conclude that there has been a "meaningful" reduction in the shareholder's ownership interest in the corporation as a result of the redemption (usually below 50 percent stock ownership).
- The IRC states that a redemption will be treated as an exchange if the redemption is "substantially disproportionate with respect to the shareholder," defined as follows:
  - Immediately after the exchange the shareholder owns less than 50 percent of the total combined voting power of all classes of stock entitled to vote.
  - The shareholder's percentage ownership of voting stock after the redemption is less than 80 percent of his or her percentage ownership before the redemption.
  - The shareholder's percentage ownership of the aggregate fair market value of the corporation's common stock (voting and nonvoting) after the redemption is less than 80 percent of his or her percentage ownership before the redemption.
- The IRC holds that a redemption will be treated as an exchange if the redemption is in "complete redemption of all of the stock of the corporation owned by the shareholder."
- In determining whether the change-in-stock-ownership tests are met, each shareholder's percentage change in ownership in the corporation before and after a redemption must take into account constructive ownership (attribution) rules.
- The attribution rules cause stock owned by other persons to be treated as owned by (attributed to) the shareholder for purposes of determining whether the shareholder has met any of the change-in-stock-ownership tests to receive exchange treatment.
  - Family attribution. Individuals are treated as owning the shares of stock owned by their spouse, children, grandchildren, and parents.
  - Attribution from entities to owners or beneficiaries.
    - Partners are deemed to own a pro rata share of their partnership's stock holdings (i.e., a partner who has a 10 percent interest in a partnership is deemed to own 10 percent of any stock owned by the partnership).
    - Shareholders are deemed to own a pro rata share of their corporation's stock holdings, but only if they own at least 50 percent of the value of the corporation's stock.
  - Attribution from owners or beneficiaries to entities.
    - Partnerships are deemed to own 100 percent of stock owned by partners (i.e., a partnership is deemed to own 100 percent of stock owned by a 10 percent partner)
    - Attribution to a corporation only applies to shareholders owning 50 percent or more of the value of the corporation's stock.

- Option attribution. A person having an option to purchase stock is deemed to own the stock that the option entitles the person to purchase.
- Shareholders can waive the family attribution rules in a complete redemption of their stock if certain conditions are met.
  - The shareholder has not retained a prohibited interest in the corporation immediately after the exchange (for example, as a shareholder, employee, director, officer, or consultant).
  - The shareholder does not acquire a prohibited interest within 10 years after the redemption, unless by inheritance (the 10-year look-forward rule).
  - The shareholder agrees to notify the IRS district director within 30 days if she acquires a prohibited interest within 10 years (sign a triple i agreement).
- If the redemption is treated as a dividend by the shareholder, the corporation generally reduces its E&P by the cash distributed and the fair market value of other property distributed.
- If the redemption is treated as an exchange by the shareholder, the corporation reduces E&P at the date of distribution by the percentage of stock redeemed (i.e., if 50 percent of the stock is redeemed, E&P is reduced by 50 percent), not to exceed the fair market value of the property distributed.

Contrast a partial liquidation from a stock redemption and describe the difference in tax consequences to the shareholders.

**LO6**

- For a distribution to be a partial liquidation, it must either be "not essentially equivalent to a dividend" (as determined at the corporate level, not the shareholder level) or is the result of the termination of a "qualified trade or business."
- The tax treatment of a distribution received in partial liquidation of a corporation depends on the identity of the shareholder receiving it.
  - All noncorporate shareholders get exchange treatment.
  - All corporate shareholders are subject to the stock redemption change in ownership rules, which usually results in dividend treatment because partial liquidations are almost always pro rata distributions.

## KEY TERMS

accumulated earnings and profits (18-4)

constructive dividend (18-3)

constructive ownership (18-24)

current earnings and profits (18-4)

dividend (18-2)

partial liquidation (18-2)

prohibited interests (18-26)

stock dividend (18-3)

stock redemption (18-2)

stock split (18-18)

triple i agreement (18-26)

## DISCUSSION QUESTIONS

1. **(LO1)** What is meant by the term *double taxation of corporate income?*
2. **(LO1)** How does the issue of double taxation arise when a corporation decides between making a distribution to a shareholder-employee as a dividend or compensation?
3. **(LO1)** Why might a shareholder who is also an employee prefer receiving a dividend instead of compensation from a corporation?
4. **(LO2)** What are the three potential tax treatments of a cash distribution to a shareholder? Are these potential tax treatments elective by the shareholder?
5. **(LO2)** In general, what is the concept of earnings and profits designed to represent?

6. **(LO2)** How does *current earnings and profits* differ from *accumulated earnings and profits?* Is there any congressional logic for keeping the two accounts separate?

7. **(LO2)** True or False: A calendar-year corporation has positive current E&P of $100 and accumulated negative E&P of $200. A cash distribution of $100 to the corporation's sole shareholder at year-end will not be treated as a dividend because total E&P is negative $100. Explain.

8. **(LO2)** True or False: A calendar-year corporation has negative current E&P of $100 and accumulated E&P of $100. A cash distribution of $100 to the corporation's sole shareholder on June 30 will not be treated as a dividend because total E&P at December 31 is $0. Explain.

9. **(LO2)** List the four basic adjustments that a corporation makes to taxable income or net loss to compute current E&P. What is the rationale for making these adjustments?

10. **(LO2)** What must a shareholder consider in computing the amount of a noncash distribution to include in her gross income?

11. **(LO2)** What income tax issues must a corporation consider before it makes a noncash distribution to a shareholder?

12. **(LO2)** Will the shareholder's tax basis in noncash property received equal the amount she includes in gross income as a dividend? Under what circumstances will the amounts be different, if any?

13. **(LO2)** A shareholder receives appreciated noncash property from his corporation and assumes a liability attached to the property. How does this assumption affect the amount of dividend he reports in gross income? From the shareholder's perspective, does it matter if the liability he assumes exceeds the property's gross fair market value?

14. **(LO2)** A shareholder receives appreciated noncash property from his corporation and assumes a liability attached to the property. How does this assumption affect the amount of gain the corporation recognizes? From the corporation's perspective, does it matter if the liability assumed by the shareholder exceeds the property's gross fair market value?

15. **(LO2)** A corporation distributes appreciated noncash property to a shareholder as a dividend. What impact does the distribution have on the corporation's earnings and profits?

16. **(LO3)** Amy is the sole shareholder of her corporation. Rather than have the corporation pay her a dividend, Amy decides to have the corporation declare a "bonus" at year-end and pay her tax-deductible compensation. What potential tax issue may arise in this situation? Which parties, Amy or the corporation or both, are affected by the classification of the payment?

17. **(LO3)** Brian is the sole shareholder of his corporation. Rather than have the corporation pay him a dividend, he had the corporation "loan" him $100,000. The loan had no required interest payments and no maturity date for repayment. What potential tax issue may arise in this situation? Which parties, Brian or the corporation or both, are affected by the classification of the payment?

18. **(LO4)** Why might a corporation issue a stock dividend to its shareholders?

19. **(LO4)** What tax issue arises when a shareholder receives a nontaxable stock dividend?

20. **(LO4)** In general, what causes a stock dividend to be taxable to the recipient?

21. **(LO5)** What are the potential tax consequences to a shareholder who participates in a stock redemption?

22. **(LO5)** What stock ownership tests must be met before a shareholder receives exchange treatment under the substantially disproportionate change-in-stock-ownership test in a stock redemption? Why is a change-in-stock-ownership test used to determine the tax status of a stock redemption?

23. **(LO5)** What are the criteria to meet the "not essentially equivalent to a dividend" change-in-stock-ownership test in a stock redemption?

24. **(LO5)** When might a shareholder have to rely on the not essentially equivalent to a dividend test in arguing that her stock redemption should be treated as an exchange for tax purposes?

25. **(LO5)** Why do you think the tax law imposes constructive stock ownership rules on stock redemptions?

26. **(LO5)** Which members of a family are included in the family attribution rules? Is there any rationale for the family members included in the test?

27. **(LO5)** Ilya and Olga are brother and sister. Ilya owns 200 shares of stock in Parker Corporation. Is Olga deemed to own Ilya's 200 shares under the family attribution rules that apply to stock redemptions?

28. **(LO5)** Maria has all of her stock in Mayan Corporation redeemed. Under what conditions will Maria treat the redemption as an exchange and recognize capital gain or loss?

29. **(LO5)** What must a shareholder do to waive the family attribution rules in a complete redemption of stock?

30. **(LO5)** How does a corporation's computation of earnings and profits differ based on the tax treatment of a stock redemption to the shareholder (that is, as either a dividend or exchange)?

31. **(LO6)** How does the tax treatment of a partial liquidation differ from a stock redemption?

32. **(LO6)** Bevo Corporation experienced a complete loss of its mill as the result of a fire. The company received $2 million from the insurance company. Rather than rebuild, Bevo decided to distribute the $2 million to its two shareholders. No stock was exchanged in return. Under what conditions will the distribution meet the requirements to be a partial liquidation and not a dividend? Why does it matter to the shareholders?

## PROBLEMS

33. **(LO1)** Gopher Corporation reported taxable income of $500,000 in 2010. Gopher paid a dividend of $100,000 to its sole shareholder, Sven Anderson. Gopher Corporation is subject to a flat-rate tax of 34 percent. The dividend meets the requirements to be a qualified dividend, and Sven is subject to a tax rate of 15 percent on the dividend. What is the total income tax imposed on the corporate income earned by Gopher and distributed to Sven as a dividend?

34. **(LO1)** Bulldog Corporation reported taxable income of $500,000 in 2010, before any deduction for any payment to its sole shareholder and employee, Georgia Brown. Bulldog chose to pay a bonus of $100,000 to Georgia at year-end. Bulldog Corporation is subject to a flat-rate tax of 34 percent. The bonus meets the requirements to be "reasonable," and is therefore deductible by Bulldog. Georgia is subject to a marginal tax rate of 35 percent on the bonus. What is the total income tax imposed on the corporate income earned by Bulldog and paid to Georgia as a bonus?

35. **(LO2)** Hawkeye Company reports current E&P of $300,000 in 2010 and accumulated E&P at the beginning of the year of $200,000. Hawkeye distributed $400,000 to its sole shareholder, Ray Kinsella, on December 31, 2010. Ray's tax basis in his Hawkeye stock is $75,000.

    a. How much of the $400,000 distribution is treated as a dividend to Ray?

    b. What is Ray's tax basis in his Hawkeye stock after the distribution?

    c. What is Hawkeye's balance in accumulated E&P as of January 1, 2011?

36. **(LO2)** Jayhawk Company reports current E&P of $300,000 and accumulated E&P of negative $200,000. Jayhawk distributed $400,000 to its sole shareholder, Christine Rock, on December 31, 2010. Christine's tax basis in her Jayhawk stock is $75,000.

    a. How much of the $400,000 distribution is treated as a dividend to Christine?

    b. What is Christine's tax basis in her Jayhawk stock after the distribution?

    c. What is Jayhawk's balance in accumulated E&P as of January 1, 2011?

37. **(LO2)** Sooner Company reports current E&P of negative $300,000 and accumulated E&P of $200,000. Sooner distributed $400,000 to its sole shareholder, Boomer Wells, on June 30, 2011. Boomer's tax basis in his Sooner stock is $75,000.

    a. How much of the $400,000 distribution is treated as a dividend to Boomer?

    b. What is Boomer's tax basis in his Sooner stock after the distribution?

    c. What is Sooner's balance in accumulated E&P as of January 1, 2011?

38. **(LO2)** Blackhawk Company reports current E&P of negative $300,000 and accumulated E&P of negative $200,000. Blackhawk distributed $400,000 to its sole shareholder, Melanie Rushmore, on June 30, 2010. Melanie's tax basis in her Blackhawk stock is $75,000.

    a. How much of the $400,000 distribution is treated as a dividend to Melanie?

    b. What is Melanie's tax basis in her Blackhawk stock after the distribution?

    c. What is Blackhawk's balance in accumulated E&P as of January 1, 2011?

39. **(LO2)** On October 3, 2006, the board of directors of Saks Inc. declared a special cash dividend of $4 per share payable on November 30, 2006, to shareholders of record as of November 15, 2006. Determine the tax status of this distribution to the shareholders using the company's Web site (www.saksincorporated.com/).

40. **(LO2)** Boilermaker Inc. reported taxable income of $500,000 in 2010 and paid federal income taxes of $170,000. Not included in the company's computation of taxable income is tax-exempt income of $20,000, disallowed meals and entertainment expenses of $30,000, and disallowed expenses related to the tax-exempt income of $1,000. Boilermaker deducted depreciation of $100,000 on its tax return. Under the alternative (E&P) depreciation method, the deduction would have been $60,000. Compute the company's current E&P for 2010.

41. **(LO2)** Gator Inc. reported taxable income of $1,000,000 in 2010 and paid federal income taxes of $340,000. Included in the company's computation of taxable income is gain from the sale of a depreciable asset of $50,000. The income tax basis of the asset was $100,000. The E&P basis of the asset using the alternative depreciation system was $175,000. Compute the company's current E&P for 2010.

42. **(LO2)** Paladin Inc. reported taxable income of $1,000,000 in 2010 and paid federal income taxes of $340,000. The company reported a capital gain from sale of investments of $150,000, which was partially offset by a $100,000 net capital loss carryover from 2009, resulting in a net capital gain of $50,000 included in taxable income. Compute the company's current E&P for 2010.

43. **(LO2)** Volunteer Corporation reported taxable income of $500,000 from operations for 2010. The company paid federal income taxes of $170,000 on this taxable income. During the year, the company made a distribution of land to its sole shareholder, Rocky Topp. The land's fair market value was $75,000 and its tax and E&P basis to Volunteer was $25,000. Rocky assumed a mortgage attached to the land of $15,000. Any gain from the distribution will be taxed at 34 percent. The company had accumulated E&P of $750,000 at the beginning of the year.

a. Compute Volunteer's total taxable income and federal income tax paid as a result of the distribution.

b. Compute Volunteer's current E&P for 2010.

c. Compute Volunteer's accumulated E&P at the beginning of 2011.

d. What amount of dividend income does Rocky report as a result of the distribution?

e. What is Rocky's income tax basis in the land received from Volunteer?

44. **(LO2)** Tiger Corporation reported taxable income of $500,000 from operations for 2010. The company paid federal income taxes of $170,000 on this taxable income. During the year, the company made a distribution of land to its sole shareholder, Mike Woods. The land's fair market value was $75,000 and its tax and E&P basis to Tiger was $125,000. Mike assumed a mortgage attached to the land of $15,000. Any gain from the distribution will be taxed at 34 percent. The company had accumulated E&P of $750,000 at the beginning of the year.

a. Compute Tiger's total taxable income and federal income tax paid as a result of the distribution.

b. Compute Tiger's current E&P for 2010.

c. Compute Tiger's accumulated E&P at the beginning of 2011.

d. What amount of dividend income does Mike report as a result of the distribution?

e. What is Mike's tax basis in the land he received from Tiger?

45. **(LO2)** Illini Corporation reported taxable income of $500,000 from operations for 2010. The company paid federal income taxes of $170,000 on this taxable income. During the year, the company made a distribution of an automobile to its sole shareholder, Carly Urbana. The auto's fair market value was $30,000 and its tax basis to Illini was $0. The auto's E&P basis was $15,000. Any gain from the distribution will be taxed at 34 percent. Illini had accumulated E&P of $1,500,000.

a. Compute Illini's total taxable income and federal income tax paid as a result of the distribution.

b. Compute Illini's current E&P for 2010.

c. Compute Illini's accumulated E&P at the beginning of 2011.

d. What amount of dividend income does Carly report as a result of the distribution?

e. What is Carly's tax basis in the auto she received from Illini?

46. **(LO3)** Beaver Corporation reported taxable income of $500,000 from operations for 2010. The company paid federal income taxes of $170,000 on this taxable income. During the year, the company made a distribution of land to its sole shareholder, Eugenia VanDam. The land's fair market value was $20,000 and its tax and E&P basis to Beaver was $50,000. Eugenia assumed a mortgage on the land of $25,000. Any gain from the distribution will be taxed at 34 percent. Beaver Corporation had accumulated E&P of $1,500,000.

a. Compute Beaver's total taxable income and federal income tax paid as a result of the distribution.

b. Compute Beaver's current E&P for 2010.

c. Compute Beaver's accumulated E&P at the beginning of 2011.

d. What amount of dividend income does Eugenia report as a result of the distribution?

e. What is Eugenia's income tax basis in the land received from Beaver?

47. **(LO3)** Nittany Company pays its sole shareholder, Joe Papa, a salary of $100,000. At the end of each year, the company pays Joe a bonus equal to the difference between the corporation's taxable income for the year (before the bonus) and $75,000. In this way, the company hopes to keep its taxable income at amounts that are taxed at either 15 percent or 25 percent. For 2010, Nittany reported prebonus taxable income of $675,000 and paid Joe a bonus of $600,000. On audit, the IRS determined that individuals working in Joe's position earned on average $300,000 per year. The company had no formal compensation policy and never paid a dividend.

    a. How much of Joe's bonus might the IRS recharacterize as a dividend?

    b. What arguments might Joe make to counter this assertion?

    c. Assuming the IRS recharacterizes $200,000 of Joe's bonus as a dividend, what additional income tax liability does Nittany Company face?

48. **(LO4)** Hoosier Corporation declared a 2-for-1 stock split to all shareholders of record on March 25, 2010. Hoosier reported current E&P of $600,000 and accumulated E&P of $3,000,000. The total fair market value of the stock distributed was $1,500,000. Barbara Bloomington owned 1,000 shares of Hoosier stock with a tax basis of $100 per share.

    a. What amount of taxable dividend income, if any, does Barbara recognize in 2010? Assume the fair market value of the stock was $150 per share on March 25, 2010.

    b. What is Barbara's income tax basis in the new and existing stock she owns in Hoosier Corporation, assuming the distribution is tax-free?

    c. How does the stock dividend affect Hoosier's accumulated E&P at the beginning of 2011?

49. **(LO4)** Badger Corporation declared a stock dividend to all shareholders of record on March 25, 2010. Shareholders will receive one share of Badger stock for each ten shares of stock they already own. Madison Cheeseman owns 1,000 shares of Badger stock with a tax basis of $100 per share. The fair market value of the Badger stock was $110 per share on March 25, 2010.

    a. What amount of taxable dividend income, if any, does Madison recognize in 2010?

    b. What is Madison's income tax basis in her new and existing stock in Badger Corporation, assuming the distribution is nontaxable?

    c. How would you answer questions a and b if Madison was offered the choice between one share of stock in Badger for each ten she owned or $100 cash for each ten shares she owned in Badger?

50. **(LO5)** Wildcat Company is owned equally by Evan Stone and his sister Sara, each of whom hold 1,000 shares in the company. Sara wants to reduce her ownership in the company, and it was decided that the company will redeem 500 of her shares for $25,000 per share on December 31, 2010. Sara's income tax basis in each share is $5,000. Wildcat has current E&P of $10,000,000 and accumulated E&P of $50,000,000.

    a. What is the amount and character (capital gain or dividend) recognized by Sara as a result of the stock redemption?

    b. What is Sara's income tax basis in the remaining 500 shares she owns in the company?

    c. Assuming the company did not make any dividend distributions during 2010, by what amount does Wildcat reduce its E&P as a result of the redemption?

51. **(LO5)** Flintstone Company is owned equally by Fred Stone and his sister Wilma, each of whom hold 1,000 shares in the company. Wilma wants to reduce her ownership in the company, and it was decided that the company will redeem 250 of her shares for $25,000 per share on December 31. Wilma's income tax basis in each share is $5,000. Flintstone has current E&P of $10,000,000 and accumulated E&P of $50,000,000.

    a. What is the amount and character (capital gain or dividend) recognized by Wilma as a result of the stock redemption, assuming only the "substantially disproportionate with respect to the shareholder" test is applied?

    b. Given your answer to question a, what is Wilma's income tax basis in the remaining 750 shares she owns in the company?

    c. Assuming the company did not make any dividend distributions during 2010, by what amount does Flintstone reduce its E&P as a result of the redemption?

    d. What other argument might Wilma make to treat the redemption as an exchange?

52. **(LO3)** Using the facts in problem 51, determine the minimum amount of stock that Flintstone must redeem from Wilma for her to treat the redemption as being "substantially disproportionate with respect to the shareholder" and receive exchange treatment.

■ **planning**

53. **(LO5)** Bedrock Inc. is owned equally by Barney Rubble and his wife Betty, each of whom hold 1,000 shares in the company. Betty wants to reduce her ownership in the company, and it was decided that the company will redeem 500 of her shares for $25,000 per share on December 31. Betty's income tax basis in each share is $5,000. Bedrock has current E&P of $10,000,000 and accumulated E&P of $50,000,000.

    a. What is the amount and character (capital gain or dividend) recognized by Betty as a result of the stock redemption, assuming only the "substantially disproportionate with respect to the shareholder" test is applied?

    b. Given your answer to question a, what is Betty's income tax basis in the remaining 500 shares she owns in the company?

    c. Assuming the company did not make any dividend distributions during 2010, by what amount does Bedrock reduce its E&P as a result of the redemption?

    d. Can Betty argue that the redemption is "not essentially equivalent to a dividend" and should be treated as an exchange?

54. **(LO5)** Assume in problem 53 that Betty and Barney are not getting along and have separated due to marital discord (although they are not legally separated). In fact, they cannot even stand to talk to each other anymore and communicate only through their accountant. Betty wants to argue that she should not be treated as owning any of Barney's stock in Bedrock because of their hostility toward each other. Can family hostility be used as an argument to void the family attribution rules? Consult Rev. Rul. 80-26, 1980-1 C.B. 66, *Robin Haft Trust v. Comm.,* 510 F.2d 43 (CA-1 1975), *Metzger Trust v. Comm.,* 693 F.2d 459 (CA-5 1982, and *Cerone v. Comm.,* 87 TC 1 (1986).

■ **research**

55. **(LO5)** Boots Inc. is owned equally by Frank Albert and his daughter Nancy, each of whom hold 1,000 shares in the company. Frank wants to retire from the company, and it was decided that the company will redeem all 1,000 of his shares for $25,000 per share on December 31, 2010. Frank's income tax basis in each share is $500. Boots Inc. has current E&P of $1,000,000 and accumulated E&P of $5,000,000.

    a. What must Frank do to ensure that the redemption will be treated as an exchange?

b. If Frank remained as the chairman of the board after the redemption, what is the amount and character (capital gain or dividend) of income that Frank will recognize in 2010?

c. If Frank treats the redemption as a dividend in 2010, what happens to his stock basis in the 1,000 shares redeemed?

**research**

56. **(LO5)** In problem 55, Nancy would like to have Frank stay on as a consultant after all of his shares are redeemed. She would pay him a modest amount of $500 per month. Nancy wants to know if there is any *de minimus* rule such that Frank would not be treated as having retained a prohibited interest in the company because he is receiving such a small amount of money. Consult *Lynch v. Comm.,* 801 F.2d 1176 (CA-9 1986), *reversing* 83 T.C. 597 (1984), *Seda,* 82 T.C. 484 (1984), and *Cerone,* 87 T.C. 1 (1986).

**planning**

57. **(LO5)** The Limited Brands recently repurchased 68,965,000 of its shares, paying $29 per share. The total number of shares outstanding before the redemption was 473,223,066. The total number of shares outstanding after the redemption was 404,258,066. Assume your client owned 20,000 shares of stock in The Limited. What is the minimum number of shares she must tender to receive exchange treatment under the "substantially disproportionate with respect to the shareholder" change-in-ownership rules?

58. **(LO5)** Cougar Company is owned equally by Cat Stevens and a partnership that is owned equally by his father and two unrelated individuals. Cat and the partnership each own 3,000 shares in the company. Cat wants to reduce his ownership in the company, and it is decided that the company will redeem 1,500 of his shares for $25,000 per share. Cat's income tax basis in each share is $5,000. What are the income tax consequences to Cat as a result of the stock redemption, assuming the company has earnings and profits of $10 million?

**planning**

59. **(LO5)** Oriole Corporation, a privately held company, has one class of voting common stock, of which 1,000 shares are issued and outstanding. The shares are owned as follows:

| | |
|---|---|
| Larry Byrd | 400 |
| Paul Byrd (Larry's son) | 200 |
| Lady Byrd (Larry's daughter) | 200 |
| Cal Rifkin (unrelated) | 200 |
| Total | 1,000 |

Larry is considering retirement and would like to have the corporation redeem all of his shares for $400,000.

a. What must Larry do or consider if he wants to guarantee that the redemption will be treated as an exchange?

b. Could Larry act as a consultant to the company and still have the redemption treated as an exchange?

**research**

60. **(LO5)** Using the facts from problem 59, Oriole Corporation proposes to pay Larry $100,000 and give him an installment note that will pay him $30,000 per year for the next 10 years plus a market rate of interest. Will this arrangement allow Larry to treat the redemption as an exchange? Consult §453(k)(2)(A).

61. **(LO5)** EG Corporation redeemed 200 shares of stock from one of its shareholders in exchange for $200,000. The redemption represented 20 percent of the corporation's outstanding stock. The redemption was treated as an exchange by the shareholder. By what amount does EG reduce its total E&P as a result of the redemption under the following E&P assumptions?

a. EG's total E&P at the time of the distribution was $2,000,000.

b. EG's total E&P at the time of the distribution was $500,000.

62. **(LO5)** Spartan Corporation redeemed 25 percent of its shares for $2,000 on July 1, 2010, in a transaction that qualified as an exchange under §302(a). Spartan's accumulated E&P on January 1, 2010, was $2,000. Its current E&P for 2010 was $12,000. During 2010, Spartan made dividend distributions of $1,000 on June 1 and $4,000 on August 31. Determine the beginning balance in Spartan's accumulated E&P at January 1, 2011. See Rev. Rul. 74-338, 1974-2 C.B. 101 and Rev. Rul. 74-339, 1974-2 C.B. 103 for help in making this calculation.

 **research**

63. **(LO6)** Spartan Corporation made a distribution of $500,000 to Rusty Cedar in partial liquidation of the company on December 31, 2010. Rusty, an individual, owns 100 percent of Spartan Corporation. The distribution was in exchange for 50 percent of Rusty's stock in the company. At the time of the distribution, the shares had a fair market value of $200 per share. Rusty's income tax basis in the shares was $50 per share. Spartan had total E&P of $8,000,000 at the time of the distribution.

    a. What is the amount and character (capital gain or dividend) of any income or gain recognized by Rusty as a result of the partial liquidation?

    b. Assuming Spartan made no other distributions to Rusty during 2010, by what amount does Spartan reduce its total E&P as a result of the partial liquidation?

64. **(LO6)** Wolverine Corporation made a distribution of $500,000 to Rich Rod Inc. in partial liquidation of the company on December 31, 2010. Rich Rod Inc. owns 100 percent of Wolverine Corporation. The distribution was in exchange for 50 percent of Rich Rod Inc.'s stock in the company. At the time of the distribution, the shares had a fair market value of $200 per share. Rich Rod Inc.'s income tax basis in the shares was $50 per share. Wolverine had total E&P of $8,000,000 at the time of the distribution.

    a. What is the amount and character (capital gain or dividend) of any income or gain recognized by Rich Rod Inc. as a result of the partial liquidation?

    b. Assuming Wolverine made no other distributions to Rich Rod Inc. during 2010, by what amount does Wolverine reduce its total E&P as a result of the partial liquidation?

## COMPREHENSIVE PROBLEMS

65. Lanco Corporation, an accrual-method corporation, reported taxable income of $1,460,000 for 2010. Included in the computation of taxable income were the following items:

    • MACRS depreciation of $200,000. Straight-line depreciation would have been $120,000.

    • A net capital loss carryover of $10,000 from 2009.

    • A net operating loss carryover of $25,000 from 2009.

    • $65,000 capital gain from the distribution of land to the company's sole shareholder (see below).

    Not included in the computation of taxable income were the following items:

    • Tax-exempt income of $5,000.

    • Life insurance proceeds of $250,000.

    • Excess current year charitable contribution of $2,500 (to be carried over to 2010).

    • Tax-deferred gain of $20,000 on a like-kind exchange.

- Federal income tax refund from 2008 of $35,000.
- Nondeductible life insurance premium of $3,500.
- Nondeductible interest expense of $1,000 on a loan used to buy tax-exempt bonds.

Lanco paid federal income taxes for 2010 of $496,400. The company's accumulated E&P at the beginning of the year was $2,400,000.

During 2010, Lanco made the following distributions to its sole shareholder, Luigi (Lug) Nutt:

- June 30, 2010: $50,000.
- September 30, 2010: Parcel of land with a fair market value of $75,000. Lanco's tax basis in the land was $10,000. Lug assumed an existing mortgage on the property of $15,000.

**Required:**

a. Compute Lanco's current E&P for 2010.

b. Compute the amount of dividend income reported by Lug Nutt in 2010 as a result of the distributions.

c. Compute Lanco's accumulated E&P at the beginning of 2011.

66. Petoskey Stone Quarry Inc. (PSQ), a calendar-year, accrual-method C corporation, provides landscaping supplies to local builders in northern Michigan. PSQ has always been a family owned business and has a single class of voting common stock outstanding. The 1,000 outstanding shares are owned as follows:

| | |
|---|---|
| Nick Adams | 150 |
| Amy Adams (Nick's wife) | 150 |
| Abigail Adams (Nick's daughter) | 50 |
| Charlie Adams (Nick's son) | 50 |
| Sandler Adams (Nick's father) | 100 |
| Total shares | 500 |

Nick Adams serves as president of PSQ, and his father Sandler serves as chairman of the board. Amy is the company's CFO, and Abigail and Charlie work as employees of the company. Sandler would like to retire and sell his shares back to the company. The fair market value of the shares is $500,000. Sandler's tax basis is $10,000.

The redemption is tentatively scheduled to take place on December 31, 2010. As of January 1, 2010, PSQ had accumulated earnings and profits of $2,500,000. The company projects current E&P for 2010 of $200,000. The company intends to pay pro rata cash dividends of $300 per share to its shareholders on December 1, 2010.

**Required:**

a. Assume the redemption takes place as planned on December 31 and no elections are made by the shareholders.

   1. What amount of dividend or capital gain will Sandler recognize as a result of the stock redemption?

   2. How, if at all, will the tax results to Sandler affect the remaining shareholders?

b. What must Sandler and the other shareholders do to change the tax results you calculated in question a?

c. Compute PSQ's accumulated earnings and profits on January 1, 2011, assuming the redemption is treated as an exchange.

67. Thriller Corporation has one class of voting common stock, of which 1,000 shares are issued and outstanding. The shares are owned as follows:

| | |
|---|---|
| Joe Jackson | 400 |
| Mike Jackson (Joe's son) | 200 |
| Jane Jackson (Joe's daughter) | 200 |
| Vinnie Price (unrelated) | 200 |
| Total | 1,000 |

Thriller Corporation has current E&P of $300,000 for 2010 and accumulated E&P at January 1, 2010, of $500,000.

During 2010, the corporation made the following distributions to its shareholders:

03/31: Paid a dividend of $10 per share to each shareholder ($10,000 in total).

06/30: Redeemed 200 shares of Joe's stock for $200,000. Joe's basis in the 200 shares redeemed was $100,000.

09/30: Redeemed 60 shares of Vinnie's stock for $60,000. His basis in the 60 shares was $36,000.

12/31: Paid a dividend of $10/share to each shareholder ($7,400 in total).

**Required:**

a. Determine the tax status of each distribution made during 2010. (*Hint:* First, consider if the redemptions are treated as dividend distributions or exchanges.)

b. Compute the corporation's accumulated E&P at January 1, 2011.

c. Joe is considering retirement and would like to have the corporation redeem all of his shares for $100,000 plus a 10-year note with a fair market value of $300,000.

1. What must Joe do or consider if he wants to ensure that the redemption will be treated as an exchange?

2. Could Joe still act as a consultant to the company?

d. Thriller Corporation must pay attorney's fees of $5,000 to facilitate the stock redemptions. Is this fee deductible?

# KAPLAN CPA SIMULATIONS

KAPLAN CPA REVIEW

**Please visit the Online Learning Center**   (www.mhhe.com/spilker2011) to access the following Kaplan CPA Simulation:

The simulation for **Clark Co.** covers corporate tax and partnerships, including filing status; book-to-tax reconciliation; transactions with owners; and the tax impact of various partnership items.

# Corporate Formation, Reorganization, and Liquidation

## Learning Objectives

**Upon completing this chapter, you should be able to:**

**LO 1** Recall the general tax rules that apply to property transactions.

**LO 2** Compute the tax consequences to the parties to a tax-deferred corporate formation.

**LO 3** Identify the different forms of taxable and tax-deferred acquisitions.

**LO 4** Compute the tax consequences to the parties to a corporate acquisition.

**LO 5** Calculate the basic tax law consequences that apply to the parties to a complete liquidation of a corporation.

## Storyline Summary

### Spartan Cycle and Repair

Privately held company located in East Lansing, Michigan

Sells and repairs high-end bicycles

### Jim Wheeler

Co-owner of Spartan Cycle and Repair (75 percent)

*Filing status:* Married filing jointly

*Dependents:* One child

*Marginal tax rate:* 40 percent

### Ginny Gears

Co-owner of Spartan Cycles and Repair (25 percent)

*Filing status:* Unmarried

*Marginal tax rate:* 25 percent

### 360 Air

Privately held company in East Lansing, Michigan

Sells snowboarding equipment

### Al Pine

Owner of 360 Air

*Filing status:* Unmarried

*Marginal tax rate:* 35 percent

J im Wheeler and Ginny Gears were excited about the growth of their business, Spartan Cycles and Repair (SCR), since its establishment in July 2006. By 2010, the business had a solid base of loyal customers and was showing a healthy profit. Jim and Ginny were ready for some new challenges. Among the opportunities they considered were expanding the bicycle business to a new geographic region or branching out into a new line of business. Given the seasonal nature of the demand for bicycle products and repair in Michigan, Jim and Ginny were searching for a complementary line of business that would provide them with a source of income during the winter months. Ginny was impressed with the growing popularity of snowboarding, especially among young people. Factors that contributed to this growth included lower equipment costs (compared to skiing), easier to master skills, a "coolness" that attracted young people, and the sport's inclusion in the Olympic games.

Jim and Ginny were aware of a small snowboarding store in East Lansing called 360 Air, which was named after a daring snowboarding maneuver. The business was owned and operated by Al Pine, a rather free-spirited individual whose enthusiasm for the sport was not matched by his business acumen.

Jim and Ginny felt that with some additional capital investment and marketing effort, they could turn Al's snowboarding business into a profitable operation. A meeting was set up with Al to discuss how they could become partners in his business enterprise.

After some negotiation, Jim, Ginny, and Al agreed to operate the snowboarding business through a C corporation. Al had been operating his business as a sole proprietorship. As part of the incorporation process, each of the three individuals would make a contribution of property or services to the corporation in return for stock. Al would contribute his existing inventory as well as the building and land on which the building was situated in return for 50 percent of the stock in 360 Air. The corporation would assume the existing mortgage on the property. Jim would contribute cash in exchange for 40 percent of the stock, and Ginny would contribute her marketing services in return for 10 percent of the stock. The business would be incorporated on July 1, 2010.

Each of the parties wanted to know the income tax implications of incorporating Al's ongoing business. In addition, Jim was wondering if the manner in which they were intending to create the corporation was tax efficient, or whether there were other issues they should consider that would lessen the tax burdens of both the corporation and its new shareholders in the future. They turned to their trusted tax accountant, Louis Tully, for his expertise.

*to be continued . . .*

When a business is created, the owners must choose the organizational form through which to operate the business. The choice of entity affects how (whether) the income or loss generated by the business is taxed at the entity level and the owner level. As the storyline indicates, at some point during the life of a business, the owners may decide to change its tax status. In the case of an ongoing business such as 360 Air, the decision to change to a corporate tax status will involve the transfer of assets and liabilities by one or more of the owners in return for stock in the corporation. These property transfers raise several tax questions, including whether the shareholders or the newly created corporation realize gain or loss on the transfer and, more importantly, whether they have to recognize that gain or loss on their tax returns. Tax basis questions also arise in the transfers; namely, what is each shareholder's tax basis in the stock received in the exchange and what tax basis does the corporation take in the assets and liabilities transferred to the corporation?

# THE GENERAL TAX RULES THAT APPLY TO PROPERTY TRANSACTIONS

**LO1**

The tax rules that apply to property transactions were discussed in detail in Chapter 10. This section provides a brief review of these tax rules as they apply to transfers of property to a corporation in the incorporation process. Before gain or loss is *recognized* (included in taxable income), it must first be *realized*. **Realization** generally occurs when a *transaction* takes place (that is, there has been an exchange of property rights between two persons).

Exhibit 19-1 provides a template for computing gain or loss realized by a party to a property transaction.

> **THE KEY FACTS**
>
> Overview of the Taxation of Property Transactions
>
> ■ Gain or loss is realized when a person engages in a transaction (an exchange of property rights with another person).
>
> ■ Gain or loss realized is computed by subtracting the transferor's tax-adjusted basis in the property exchanged from the amount realized in the exchange.
>
> ■ Gain or loss realized is recognized (included in the computation of taxable income) unless exempted or deferred by a provision of the tax laws.

**EXHIBIT 19-1**   Computing Gain or Loss Realized in a Property Transaction[1]

|   | |
|---|---|
|   | Amount realized (received) |
| − | Adjusted tax basis of the property transferred |
|   | Gain (+) or loss (−) realized |

The **amount realized** is computed using the template in Exhibit 19-2.

**EXHIBIT 19-2**   Computing the Amount Realized in a Property Transaction[2]

|   | |
|---|---|
|   | Cash received |
| + | Fair market value of other property received |
| + | Liabilities assumed by the transferee on the transferred property |
| − | Selling expenses incurred in the transaction |
| − | Liabilities assumed by the transferor on any property received in the exchange |
|   | Amount realized |

A property's **adjusted tax basis** is calculated using the template in Exhibit 19-3.

**EXHIBIT 19-3**   Computing a Property's Adjusted Tax Basis in a Property Transaction[3]

|   | |
|---|---|
|   | Acquisition basis |
| + | Capital improvements |
| − | Depreciation |
|   | Adjusted tax basis |

[1] §1001(a).
[2] §1001(b).
[3] §1011.

**Example 19-1**

As part of the incorporation of 360 Air, Al Pine will transfer inventory and a building and land to the corporation in return for 50 percent of the corporation's stock (50 shares). The property transferred to the corporation has the following fair market values and tax-adjusted bases:

|  | FMV | Tax-Adjusted Basis |
|---|---|---|
| Inventory | $ 25,000 | $ 15,000 |
| Building | 150,000 | 60,000 |
| Land | 200,000 | 100,000 |
| Total | $375,000 | $175,000 |

In addition, the corporation will assume a mortgage of $75,000 attached to the building and land. The fair market value of the 360 Air stock Al received in the exchange is $300,000. How much net gain or loss does Al *realize* in the exchange?

**Answer:** Al realizes a net gain of $200,000 on this transfer, computed as follows:

|  | | |
|---|---|---|
|  | Fair market value of 360 Air stock received | $300,000 |
| + | Mortgage assumed by 360 Air | 75,000 |
|  | Amount realized | $375,000 |
| − | Adjusted tax basis of the property transferred | 175,000 |
|  | Gain realized | $200,000 |

The tax law states that a taxpayer recognizes the entire amount of gain or loss realized unless *otherwise provided* by a different code section.[4] Gain or loss not recognized when realized falls into one of two categories: (1) the gain or loss is *excluded* from gross income (that is, the gain or loss will never be recognized) or (2) the gain or loss is *deferred* from inclusion in (or deduction from) gross income (that is, **recognition** of the gain or loss is postponed to a future period). Incorporations involving transfers of property to a corporation are transactions in which gain or loss realized may be deferred if certain tax law requirements are met.[5] A taxpayer generally recognizes gain or loss deferred in a property exchange when the property received in the exchange is later disposed of in a transaction that does not qualify for deferral (for example, Al later sells the stock in 360 Air).

**L02**

## TAX-DEFERRED TRANSFERS OF PROPERTY TO A CORPORATION

In the formation of a corporation, or in subsequent transfers of property to an existing corporation, shareholders transfer cash and noncash property to the corporation in return for stock in the corporation. The stock can be common or preferred, voting or nonvoting.[6]

Gain or loss deferred in the transfer of property to a corporation in return for stock is reflected in the shareholder's *tax basis* in the stock received in exchange for the property transferred.[7] Gain deferred *decreases* the shareholder's tax basis in the

---

[4]§1001(c).

[5]§351.

[6]A category of stock with different rights (e.g., voting rights, dividend rights, liquidation rights) is referred to as a *class* of stock.

[7]§358.

stock to an amount equal to the stock's fair market value less the gain deferred. Loss deferred *increases* the shareholder's tax basis in the stock to an amount equal to the stock's fair market value plus the loss deferred. In essence, the shareholder's tax basis in the stock received reflects the tax basis of the property transferred.

---

### Example 19-2

Assume Al meets the tax law requirements to defer recognizing the $200,000 gain realized in the property transfer to 360 Air. The fair market value of the 360 Air stock he receives in the exchange is $300,000. What is Al's tax basis in the stock received?

**Answer:** $100,000. To reflect the deferral of the gain in his tax basis in the stock, Al's tax basis must be $100,000 ($300,000 − $200,000 gain deferred). If he subsequently sells the stock for $300,000, Al will recognize the $200,000 gain deferred previously ($300,000 − $100,000).

**What if:** Assume Al realized a $100,000 loss on the exchange of his property for stock in 360 Air. What would be his tax basis in the stock received?

**Answer:** $400,000. To reflect the deferral of the loss in his tax basis in the stock, Al's tax basis must be $400,000 ($300,000 + $100,000 loss deferred). If he subsequently sells the stock for $300,000, Al will recognize the $100,000 loss deferred previously ($300,000 − $400,000).

---

**THE KEY FACTS**

**Requirements for Tax Deferral in a Corporate Formation**

- Tax deferral only applies to transfers of property to a corporation.
- The persons transferring property to a corporation must receive solely stock in the corporation in return.
- The persons transferring property to a corporation must collectively control the corporation after the transaction.
- Control is defined as ownership of 80 percent or more of the corporation's voting stock and 80 percent or more of each class of nonvoting stock.
- Stock received in exchange for services can be counted in the control test if the transferor also receives stock in exchange for property with a fair market value of 10 percent or more of the services rendered.

Congress enacted the tax laws allowing for the deferral of gain or loss on the transfer of property to a corporation in exchange for stock in the Revenue Act of 1921. The reason was to remove tax consequences as an impediment to forming a corporation and to provide taxpayers with flexibility in choosing their preferred form of doing business. In enacting this tax law, Congress considered the case of a sole proprietor similar to Al who wished to incorporate his business, either alone or with additional owners. Lawmakers felt that to impose a tax on this type of transaction would impede the creation of corporations for valid business purposes. Congress justified tax deferral because shareholders maintained an interest in the property transferred through a different form of ownership (from direct ownership to indirect ownership through stock). Taxing this type of transfer also would require a determination of each asset's fair market value, which could be difficult if the corporation was closely held.

Despite the narrow focus that led to their passage, the tax rules that Congress wrote are rather broad and protect shareholders in transactions that can stretch the "continuity of ownership interest" principle quite far. For example, a shareholder owning 1 percent of a newly formed corporation may receive the same tax deferral protection as the shareholder owning 99 percent of the corporation after the formation. One could argue that the shareholder with a 1 percent ownership interest has diversified her ownership of a portfolio of assets far more than the shareholder with a 99 percent ownership interest.

## Transactions Subject to Tax Deferral

For shareholders to receive tax deferral in a transfer of property to a corporation, either at formation or later, the transferors must meet the requirements of IRC §351. Section 351 applies to those transactions in which one or more shareholders transfer property to a corporation in return for stock, and immediately after the transfer, these same shareholders, in the aggregate, control the corporation to which they transferred the property. The deferral of gain or loss in a §351 transaction is mandatory if the requirements are met. Section 351 applies to transfers of property to both C corporations and S corporations.

Section 351 applies only to those **persons** who transfer property to the corporation in exchange for stock (that is, the shareholders). The IRC defines a person for tax purposes as including individuals, corporations, partnerships, and fiduciaries

(estates and trusts).[8] Thus, §351 allows individuals like Al to form a corporation and also allows existing corporations such as General Electric to create a subsidiary or a joint venture. The corporation receiving the property in exchange for its own stock is not subject to tax when it receives property.[9]

### Meeting the Section 351 Tax Deferral Requirements

The shareholders transferring property to a corporation must meet several requirements for the transfer to be tax deferred. Many of these requirements are not tightly defined in either the IRC or the regulations. As a result, much of what we understand about the parameters of §351 has developed over time as the IRS and the courts have attempted to discern Congressional intent with respect to the meanings of the terms and phrases used in the statute. This incremental approach to understanding the parameters within which §351 operates is very prevalent throughout all of subchapter C of the Internal Revenue Code.[10]

**Section 351 Applies Only to the Transfer of Property to the Corporation**    Most assets (tangible and intangible) meet the definition of property for purposes of §351. Property includes money, tangible assets, and intangible assets (for example, company name, patents, customer lists, trademarks, and logos). Services are excluded from the definition of property (that is, a person who receives stock in return for services generally has compensation equal to the fair market value of the stock received).[11]

---

**Example 19-3**

As part of the incorporation, Ginny received 10 percent of the stock in 360 Air valued at $60,000 in exchange for her services in setting up the corporation. Will Ginny defer recognition of the $60,000 "gain" she realizes on the transaction (assuming her services have no tax basis)?

**Answer:** No. Ginny must report compensation income of $60,000 as a result of this exchange because services are not considered property under §351.

**What if:** Suppose Ginny received 10 percent of the stock in 360 Air valued at $60,000 in exchange for artwork and a catchphrase she created to provide the company with a distinctive logo. Assume her tax basis in the artwork and the catchphrase is zero because she created them. Will Ginny defer recognition of the $60,000 gain she realizes on the transfer of the artwork and catchphrase?

**Answer:** Yes. Ginny defers recognition of the $60,000 gain realized because intangibles are considered property under §351.

---

**The Property Transferred to the Corporation Must Be Exchanged Solely for Stock of the Corporation**    To receive tax deferral on the transfer, the transferor cannot receive something other than qualifying stock from the corporation in return for the property transferred. This "something" often is referred to as **boot.** The term *boot*

---

[8]§7701(a)(1).

[9]§1032.

[10]Subchapter C encompasses IRC §§ 301–385 and provides the tax rules for the corporate transactions discussed in this chapter. Tax advisers who specialize in structuring corporate transactions often are referred to as "subchapter C experts."

[11]An individual who receives stock subject to "restrictions" (for example, she remains with the company for a certain number of years) does not report compensation income until the restrictions attached to the stock are lifted (§83) unless she elects to value the stock at the date received and report that amount as income (that is, she makes a "§83(b) election").

derives from a trading expression where a party to an exchange might throw in additional property "*to boot*" to equalize the exchange. The receipt of boot will cause the transferor to recognize gain, but not loss, realized on the exchange. We will discuss the details of this computation later in the chapter.

The type of stock a shareholder can receive in a §351 exchange is quite flexible and includes voting or nonvoting, common or preferred stock. Stock for purposes of §351 does not include stock warrants, rights, or options.[12] Property transferred in exchange for debt of the corporation is not eligible for deferral under §351.

---

**Example 19-4**

**What if:** Suppose Ginny received a five-year note (debt) in 360 Air valued at $60,000 in exchange for her artwork and catchphrase. Will Ginny defer recognition of the $60,000 gain she realizes on the transfer of the artwork and catchphrase?

**Answer:** No. Section 351 provides for deferral only when the transferor of property receives stock in return. Ginny must recognize the entire $60,000 gain.

---

### The Transferor(s) of Property to the Corporation Must Be in Control, in the Aggregate, of the Corporation Immediately after the Transfer

Control for purposes of §351 is defined as the ownership of 80 percent or more of the total combined *voting power* of all voting stock that is issued and outstanding, and 80 percent or more of the total number of shares of *each class* of nonvoting stock.[13]

Whether the control test is met is based on the collective ownership of the shareholders transferring property to the corporation immediately after the transfer. Voting power generally is defined as the ability of the shareholders to elect members of the corporation's board of directors.

---

**Example 19-5**

**What if:** Assume Ginny was hesitant to join with Jim and Al in the incorporation of 360 Air. After six months, she changed her mind and received a 10 percent interest in 360 Air stock in exchange for intangibles that qualified as property under §351. The stock was valued at $60,000, and Ginny's tax basis in the intangibles was zero. Will Ginny defer recognition of the $60,000 gain she realized on the exchange under §351?

**Answer:** No. Ginny does not control (own 80 percent or more of the stock of) 360 Air immediately after the transfer. As a result, she must recognize the $60,000 gain.

---

**Example 19-6**

**What if:** Suppose Ginny joined with Jim and Al in the incorporation of 360 Air and received 25 percent of the corporation's stock in exchange for services. The stock was valued at $150,000. Al and Jim received the remaining 75 percent of the stock in the company in exchange for appreciated property. Will Al and Jim defer recognition of gain they realize on the exchange of the appreciated property under §351?

**Answer:** No. Taking into account only the stock received in exchange for property, Al and Jim do not collectively control 360 Air immediately after the transaction. (they own 75% not 80%) Consequently, the transaction is not eligible for deferral under §351, and all gain realized is recognized.

---

[12]§351 precludes nonqualified preferred stock from qualifying as equity eligible for deferral. Nonqualified preferred stock generally has characteristics that cause it to more resemble debt than equity.
[13]§368(c).

The regulations state that if a shareholder receives stock in return for property and services in a §351 exchange, all of the stock received is included in the control test provided the fair market value of the property transferred is not of *"relatively small value in comparison to the value of the stock"* received in return for services.[14] The IRS has stated that for ruling purposes, property will not be of *"relatively small value"* if it equals at least 10 percent of the value of the services provided.[15]

---

**Example 19-7**

*What if:* Let's say Ginny joined with Jim and Al in the incorporation of 360 Air and received 25 percent of the corporation's stock in exchange for services and intangibles treated as property. The stock was valued at $150,000. The services were valued at $125,000 and the intangibles were valued at $25,000. Al and Jim received the remaining 75 percent of the stock in the company in exchange for appreciated property. Will Al and Jim defer recognition of gain they realize on the exchange of the appreciated property under §351?

**Answer:** Yes. The stock Ginny received in exchange for the intangibles exceeds 10 percent of the value of the services ($25,000/$125,000 = 20%). Ginny will treat all of the stock she received in 360 Air as having been received for property. Al, Jim, and Ginny will be treated as collectively receiving 100 percent of the 360 Air stock in exchange for property. Al and Jim will defer gain realized on their exchanges of property for stock. Ginny will recognize compensation of $125,000 on the exchange, but she will defer recognizing any gain realized on the transfer of the intangibles.

*What if:* Assume Ginny's services were valued at $140,000 and the intangibles were valued at $10,000. Will Al and Jim defer recognition of gain they realize on the exchange of the appreciated property under §351?

**Answer:** No. The fair market value of the intangibles is less than 10 percent of the fair market value of the services ($10,000/$140,000 = 7.14%). As a result, only the stock Ginny receives in exchange for the intangibles is counted in the control test ($10,000/$150,000 × 25% = 1.67%). Al, Jim, and Ginny are treated as having received collectively only 76.67 percent of 360 Air stock in exchange for property. Consequently, §351 does not apply to any of the transferors of the property to 360 Air.

---

This same 10 percent *de minimus* rule applies to subsequent transfers of property by an existing shareholder to "accommodate" a new shareholder's transfer of property to an established corporation. The regulations state that stock received for property that is of "relatively small value" in comparison to the value of the stock already owned will not be considered issued in return for property (that is, the shareholder making the contribution will not be included in the control test) if the "primary purpose" of the transfer is to qualify the exchanges of another person under §351. The IRS has stated that for ruling purposes, an existing shareholder must contribute property that has a fair market value of at least 10 percent of the value of the stock already owned to be included in the control test.[16]

---

**Example 19-8**

*What if:* Assume Jim and Ginny were 100 percent shareholders of SCR and wanted to bring Al on board as a 20 percent shareholder. Al will transfer appreciated property to SCR in return for stock in SCR valued at $100,000. Will Al defer recognizing any gain realized on the transfer under §351?

*(continued on page 19-9...)*

---

[14]Reg. §1.351-1(a)(1)(ii).
[15]Rev. Proc. 77-37, 1977-2 C.B. 568.
[16]Rev. Proc. 77-37, 1977-2 C.B. 568.

**Answer:** No. Al does not control SCR "immediately after" the exchange, taking into account only the stock he owns in SCR.

**What if:** Suppose Jim agreed to make an additional property contribution to SCR at the same time as Al's transfer. Jim's 75 percent ownership interest in SCR was valued at $300,000 at the time of Al's transfer. How much property (fair market value) must Jim contribute to SCR to have his ownership of stock in SCR counted in determining if Al qualifies for deferral under §351?

**Answer:** $30,000. For this "accommodation transfer" by Jim to be respected, he must contribute property with a fair market value of 10 percent or more of the fair market value of his existing stock in SCR (10% × $300,000).

## Tax Consequences to Shareholders in a Section 351 Transaction

The tax basis of stock received in a tax-deferred §351 exchange equals the tax basis of the property transferred.[17] Most practitioners refer to the stock as having a **substituted basis** (that is, the basis of the property transferred is substituted for the basis of the property received).[18] Exhibit 19-4 provides a template for computing the tax basis of stock received in a tax-deferred §351 transaction.

**EXHIBIT 19-4   Computing the Tax Basis of Stock Received in a Tax-Deferred Section 351 Transaction**

|   | |
|---|---|
| | Cash contributed |
| + | Tax basis of other property contributed |
| − | Liabilities assumed by the corporation on property contributed |
| | Tax basis of stock received |

**Example 19-9**

As part of the incorporation of 360 Air, Al transferred inventory and a building and land to the corporation in return for 50 percent of the corporation's stock (50 shares). The property transferred to the corporation had the following fair market values and tax-adjusted bases:

|  | FMV | Tax-Adjusted Basis |
|---|---|---|
| Inventory | $ 25,000 | $ 15,000 |
| Building | 150,000 | 60,000 |
| Land | 200,000 | 100,000 |
| Total | $375,000 | $175,000 |

In addition, the corporation assumed a mortgage of $75,000 attached to the building and land. The fair market value of the 360 Air stock Al received in the exchange was $300,000. As we computed in Example 19-1, Al realizes a gain of $200,000 on the transfer, computed as follows:

|   | | |
|---|---|---|
| | Fair market value of 360 Air stock received | $300,000 |
| + | Mortgage assumed by 360 Air | 75,000 |
| | Amount realized | $375,000 |
| − | Adjusted tax basis of the property transferred | 175,000 |
| | Gain realized | $200,000 |

(continued on page 19-10…)

[17]§358(a).
[18]§7701(a)(44) uses the term *exchanged basis property* for this type of property.

Assuming Al meets the requirements under §351 to defer recognizing the $200,000 gain realized, what is his tax basis in the 50 shares of 360 Air stock he receives in the exchange?

**Answer:** $100,000. Al's tax basis in his stock must reflect the gain he defers in the exchange. He computes his tax basis in his 360 Air stock as follows:

|   |   |   |
|---|---|---|
|   | Tax-adjusted basis of property contributed | $175,000 |
| − | Mortgage assumed by 360 Air | 75,000 |
|   | Tax basis of 360 Air stock received | $100,000 |

If Al sold his 360 Air stock for its fair market value of $300,000, he would recognize a capital gain of $200,000 ($300,000 − $100,000), an amount equal to the gain he deferred previously. In determining whether the gain is long or short term, Al includes the holding periods of capital assets and §1231 property transferred in exchange for the stock.[19]

## Example 19-10

**What if:** Assume Al did not meet the requirements under §351 and was required to recognize the $200,000 gain realized. What is his tax basis in the 50 shares of 360 Air stock he receives in the exchange?

**Answer:** $300,000. Al's tax basis in his stock equals its fair market value. If Al sold his 360 Air stock for its fair market value of $300,000, he would not recognize any further gain.

## Tax Consequences When a Shareholder Receives Boot

A shareholder who receives property other than stock (boot) in the transferee corporation recognizes gain (*but not loss*) in an amount not to exceed the *lesser of* (1) gain realized or (2) the fair market value of the boot received. The amount of gain recognized when boot is received in a §351 transaction is determined by allocating the boot received pro rata to each property using the relative fair market values of the properties.[20] The character of gain recognized (capital gain, §1231 gain, ordinary income) is determined by the type of property to which the boot is allocated.

## Example 19-11

**What if:** Suppose Al received 40 shares of 360 Air stock with a fair market value of $315,000 plus $60,000 in return for his transfer of inventory and a building and land to the corporation. The property transferred to the corporation had the following fair market values and tax-adjusted bases:

|   | FMV | Tax-Adjusted Basis | Gain Realized |
|---|---|---|---|
| Inventory | $ 25,000 | $ 15,000 | $ 10,000 |
| Building | 150,000 | 60,000 | 90,000 |
| Land | 200,000 | 100,000 | 100,000 |
| Total | $375,000 | $175,000 | $200,000 |

(*continued on page 19-11...*)

---

[19]§1223(1).

[20]Rev. Rul. 68-55, 1968-1 C.B. 140 and Rev. Rul. 85-164, 1985-2 C.B. 117.

What amount of gain does Al recognize on his receipt of the $60,000 boot and what is its character (ordinary or §1231)?

**Answer:** The $60,000 received by Al constitutes boot received and causes him to recognize some or all of the gain realized on the transfer. He apportions the $60,000 to each of the properties transferred to the corporation based on their relative fair market values. Al recognizes gain on each property transferred in an amount equal to the lesser of the gain realized or the fair market value of the boot apportioned to the property. The computation is made for each property separately as follows:

| | **Inventory** | |
|---|---|---|
| | Fair market value of 360 Air stock and cash received | $ 25,000 |
| − | Tax-adjusted basis of the inventory transferred | 15,000 |
| | (1) Gain realized | $ 10,000 |
| | (2) Boot apportioned (25/375 × $60,000) | 4,000 |
| | Gain recognized: lesser of (1) or (2) | $ 4,000 |
| | Character of gain recognized: ordinary | |

| | **Building** | |
|---|---|---|
| | Fair market value of 360 Air stock and cash received | $150,000 |
| − | Tax-adjusted basis of the building transferred | 60,000 |
| | (1) Gain realized | $ 90,000 |
| | (2) Boot apportioned (150/375 × $60,000) | 24,000 |
| | Gain recognized: lesser of (1) or (2) | $ 24,000 |
| | Character of gain recognized: §1231[21] | |

| | **Land** | |
|---|---|---|
| | Fair market value of 360 Air stock and cash received | $200,000 |
| − | Tax-adjusted basis of the building transferred | 100,000 |
| | (1) Gain realized | $100,000 |
| | (2) Boot apportioned (200/375 × $60,000) | 32,000 |
| | Gain recognized: lesser of (1) or (2) | $ 32,000 |
| | Character of gain recognized: §1231 | |

Al recognizes total gain of $60,000 on this transfer and defers recognition of $140,000 of the $200,000 gain realized ($200,000 − $60,000).

**What if:** Let's say the land had a tax-adjusted basis of $250,000. What amount of gain does Al now recognize?

**Answer:** The $60,000 received by Al still must be apportioned to the land based on its fair market value, but Al cannot recognize any of the loss realized on the exchange. Boot only causes gain realized to be recognized. The recomputation for the land is as follows:

| | **Land** | |
|---|---|---|
| | Fair market value of 360 Air stock and cash received | $200,000 |
| − | Tax-adjusted basis of the building transferred | 250,000 |
| | (1) Loss realized | $ (50,000) |
| | (2) Boot apportioned (200/375 × $60,000) | 32,000 |
| | No loss is recognized | |

Al recognizes total gain of $28,000 ($24,000 + $4,000) and defers recognition of $72,000 of gain realized ($6,000 + $66,000) and all of the $50,000 loss realized.

---

[21]If Al owned more than 50 percent of 360 Air after the transfer, the gain would be treated as ordinary income under §1239(a). §1239 converts §1231 gain to ordinary income if the transferor of the property owns more than 50 percent of the corporation and the property is depreciable in the hands of the transferee. The gain also could be unrecaptured §1250 gain subject to a maximum tax rate of 25 percent.

Boot received in a §351 transaction receives a tax basis equal to its fair market value.[22] Al must adjust the tax basis in his 360 Air stock to take into account the boot received and the gain recognized. Exhibit 19-5 provides a template for computing stock basis when boot is received in a §351 transaction.

**EXHIBIT 19-5**  **Computing the Tax Basis of Stock in a Section 351 Transaction When Boot Is Received**

|   | Cash contributed |
|---|---|
| + | Tax basis of other property contributed |
| + | Gain recognized on the transfer |
| − | Fair market value of boot received |
| − | Liabilities assumed by the corporation on property contributed |
|   | Tax basis of stock received |

**Example 19-12**

Return to the original facts in Example 19-11, in which Al received $60,000 and recognized $60,000 gain in the exchange. What is Al's tax basis in his 360 Air stock?

**Answer:** $175,000. Al computes his tax basis in the 360 Air as follows:

|   | | |
|---|---|---|
|   | Tax-adjusted basis of property contributed | $175,000 |
| + | Gain recognized on the exchange | 60,000 |
| − | Fair market value of boot (cash) received | 60,000 |
|   | Tax basis of stock received | $175,000 |

If Al sold his 360 Air stock for its current fair market value of $315,000, he would recognize a gain of $140,000 ($315,000 − $175,000), an amount equal to the gain he deferred in the exchange.

### Assumption of Shareholder Liabilities by the Corporation

When an unincorporated business (for example, Al's sole proprietorship) is incorporated or an existing corporation creates a subsidiary, the newly created corporation frequently assumes the outstanding liabilities of the business (for example, accounts payable or mortgages). An important tax issue is whether the assumption of these liabilities by the newly created corporation constitutes boot received by the shareholder transferring the liabilities to the corporation. After all, the shareholder does receive something other than stock in the transaction—that is, relief from debt.

Under the general rule, the corporation's assumption of a shareholder's liability attached to property transferred (for example, the mortgage attached to the building and land transferred by Al to 360 Air) is *not* treated as boot received by the shareholder.[23] However, as we discuss below, there is an exception to the general rule for tax avoidance transactions.

**Tax-Avoidance Transactions**   Under the exception, if *any* of the liabilities assumed by the corporation are assumed with the purpose of avoiding the federal income tax or if there is no corporate business purpose for the assumption, *all* of the liabilities assumed are treated as boot to the shareholder.[24] The "avoidance" motive may be present where shareholders leverage their appreciated assets prior to the transfer and have the corporation assume the liabilities (this could be interpreted as having the corporation pay the shareholder cash in exchange for the

[22]§358(a)(2).

[23]§357(a).

[24]§357(b).

property). The "no business purpose" motive can be present where shareholders have the corporation assume the shareholder's personal liabilities (for example, grocery bills or alimony).

**Liabilities in Excess of Basis**    Even when liabilities are not treated as boot, the taxpayer is required to recognize gain to the extent the liabilities assumed by the corporation exceed the aggregate tax basis of the properties transferred by the shareholder.[25]

---

**Example 19-13**

***What if:*** Assume Al transferred inventory and a building and land to 360 Air in return for 50 percent of the corporation's stock (50 shares) with a fair market value of $175,000 and the corporation's assumption of a mortgage of $200,000 attached to the land and building. The properties transferred have fair market values and tax bases as follows:

|  | FMV | Tax-Adjusted Basis |
|---|---|---|
| Inventory | $ 25,000 | $ 15,000 |
| Building | 150,000 | 60,000 |
| Land | 200,000 | 100,000 |
| Total | $375,000 | $175,000 |

Al realizes a gain of $200,000 on the transfer, computed as follows:

|  | | |
|---|---|---|
| | Fair market value of 360 Air stock received | $175,000 |
| + | Mortgage assumed by 360 Air | 200,000 |
| | Amount realized | $375,000 |
| − | Adjusted tax basis of the property transferred | 175,000 |
| | Gain realized | $200,000 |

What amount of gain, if any, does Al recognize on the transfer, assuming all of the other requirements of §351 are met?

**Answer:** $25,000, the excess of the mortgage assumed by 360 Air ($200,000) over the total tax-adjusted basis of the property Al transferred to the corporation ($175,000). Al defers gain of $175,000.

What is Al's tax basis in the 360 Air stock?

**Answer:** $0, computed as follows:

|  | | |
|---|---|---|
| | Tax-adjusted basis of property contributed | $175,000 |
| + | Gain recognized on the exchange | 25,000 |
| − | Mortgage assumed by 360 Air | 200,000 |
| | Tax basis of stock received | $         0 |

If Al sold his 360 Air stock for $175,000 (its current fair market value), he would recognize a gain of $175,000 ($175,000 − $0), an amount equal to the gain he deferred in the exchange.

---

The tax law provides a special exception for the assumption of liabilities, the payment of which would give rise to a deduction. The assumption of such liabilities is disregarded in determining if the liabilities assumed exceed basis.[26] Examples would be where a corporation assumes the accounts payable of a cash-method sole proprietorship or where a subsidiary assumes "payment liabilities" (for example, accrued vacation pay) of an accrual-method corporation.

---

[25]§357(c). A liability assumed by the corporation cannot reduce stock basis below zero.
[26]357(c)(3).

## Example 19-14

**What if:** Suppose Al transferred inventory and a building and land to 360 Air in return for 50 percent of the corporation's stock (50 shares) with a fair market value of $175,000 and the corporation's assumption of cash-method accounts payable of $200,000. The properties transferred have fair market values and tax bases as follows:

|  | FMV | Tax-Adjusted Basis |
|---|---|---|
| Inventory | $ 25,000 | $ 15,000 |
| Building | 150,000 | 60,000 |
| Land | 200,000 | 100,000 |
| Total | $375,000 | $175,000 |

Al realizes a gain of $200,000 on the transfer, computed as follows:

|  |  |  |
|---|---|---|
|  | Fair market value of 360 Air stock received | $175,000 |
| + | Payables assumed by 360 Air | 200,000 |
|  | Amount realized | $375,000 |
| − | Adjusted tax basis of the property transferred | 175,000 |
|  | Gain realized | $200,000 |

What amount of gain, if any, does Al recognize in the transfer, assuming all of the other requirements of §351 are met?

**Answer:** $0. Al defers recognition of the entire gain of $200,000. The assumption of the cash-method payables is disregarded in computing whether the liabilities assumed exceed the aggregate tax basis of the property transferred.

What is Al's tax basis in the 360 Air stock?

**Answer:** $0, computed as follows:

|  |  |  |
|---|---|---|
|  | Tax-adjusted basis of property contributed | $175,000 |
| + | Gain recognized on the exchange | 0 |
| − | Payables assumed by 360 Air | 0 |
|  | Tax basis of stock received | $175,000 |

If Al sold his 360 Air stock for $175,000 (its current fair market value), he would recognize a gain of $0 ($175,000 − $175,000). This result seems odd at first glance because the gain deferred previously was $200,000. However, by transferring the payables to 360 Air, Al is forgoing a $200,000 deduction that he would have received if he paid off the liabilities while operating as a sole proprietorship. This $200,000 "loss" exactly offsets the $200,000 gain he realized when 360 Air assumed the payables, resulting in a net gain of $0.

## Tax Consequences to the Transferee Corporation in a Section 351 Transaction

The corporation receiving property in exchange for its stock in a §351 transaction does not recognize (excludes) gain or loss realized on the transfer.[27] The tax basis of property received by the corporation equals the property's tax basis in the transferor's hands.[28] Most practitioners refer to the transferred property as having a **carryover basis** (that is, the corporation "carries over" the shareholder's basis in the property).[29] To the extent the shareholder's tax basis carries over to the corporation and the property

---

[27]§1032.

[28]§362(a).

[29]§7701(a)(43) refers to this type of property as *transferred basis property*.

is §1231 property or a capital asset, the shareholder's holding period also carries over (it tacks to the property).[30] This could be important in determining if subsequent gain or loss recognized on the disposition of the property qualifies as a §1231 gain or loss or a long-term capital gain or loss.

If the shareholder recognizes gain as a result of the property transfer (for example, because boot is received), the corporation increases its tax basis in the property by the gain recognized. Exhibit 19-6 provides a template for computing the tax basis of property received by the corporation in a §351 transaction.

**EXHIBIT 19-6    Computing the Tax Basis of Property Received by the Corporation in a Section 351 Transaction**

|   | Cash contributed by the shareholder |
|---|---|
| + | Tax basis of other property contributed by the shareholder |
| + | Gain recognized on the transfer by the shareholder |
|   | Tax basis of property received |

**Example 19-15**

Let's return to the facts in Example 19-11 where Al received 40 shares of 360 Air stock with a fair market value of $240,000 and $60,000 in return for his transfer of inventory and a building and land to the corporation. The $60,000 received by Al constituted boot received and caused him to recognize gain on the transfer. The $60,000 was allocated to each of the properties transferred to the corporation based on their relative fair market values. Al recognized gain on each property transferred in an amount equal to the lesser of the gain realized or the fair market value of the boot allocated to the property. Al's tax results from this transaction can be summarized as follows:

|   | Tax Basis | Gain Recognized |
|---|---|---|
| Inventory | $ 15,000 | $ 4,000 |
| Building | 60,000 | 24,000 |
| Land | 100,000 | 32,000 |
| Total | $175,000 | $60,000 |

What tax basis does 360 Air get in each of the properties it receives from Al in the exchange?

**Answer:** 360 Air will carry over Al's tax basis in the property transferred and will increase the tax basis by gain recognized by Al on the transfer. The corporation's tax basis in each of the three properties is as follows:

|   | Tax Basis | Gain Recognized | 360 Air Tax Basis |
|---|---|---|---|
| Inventory | $ 15,000 | $ 4,000 | $ 19,000 |
| Building | 60,000 | 24,000 | 84,000 |
| Land | 100,000 | 32,000 | 132,000 |
| Total | $175,000 | $60,000 | $235,000 |

360 Air also will carry over Al's holding period in the building and land transferred because they are §1231 assets.

The tax law limits the ability of a shareholder to transfer a "built-in loss" to a corporation in a §351 transaction. In particular, if the *aggregate* adjusted tax basis of property transferred to a corporation by a shareholder in a §351 transfer exceeds the aggregate fair market value of the assets, the aggregate tax basis of the assets in the hands of the

[30]§1223(1).

transferee corporation cannot exceed their aggregate fair market value.[31] The aggregate reduction in tax basis is allocated among the assets transferred in proportion to their respective built-in losses immediately before the transfer. As an alternative, the transferor and transferee can elect to have the transferor reduce her stock basis to fair market value (that is, the duplicate loss is eliminated at either the corporate or shareholder level).

## Example 19-16

**What if:** Assume Al transferred a building and land to the corporation in return for 50 percent of the corporation's stock (50 shares). The property transferred to the corporation had the following fair market values and tax-adjusted bases:

|  | FMV | Tax-Adjusted Basis |
|---|---|---|
| Building | $ 75,000 | $100,000 |
| Land | 200,000 | 100,000 |
| Total | $275,000 | $200,000 |

The fair market value of the 360 Air stock Al received in the exchange was $275,000.

Assuming Al meets the requirements under §351 to defer recognizing the $75,000 net gain realized, what is his tax basis in the 50 shares of 360 Air stock he receives in the exchange?

**Answer:** $200,000. In this case, the aggregate fair market value of the property transferred to the corporation exceeds the aggregate tax-adjusted basis of the property. As a result, Al's tax basis in the stock he receives equals the aggregate tax-adjusted bases of the property transferred.

What is the tax-adjusted basis of the building and land held by 360 Air?

**Answer:** The building has a carryover basis of $100,000, and the land has a carryover basis of $100,000. Because the aggregate fair market value of the assets transferred to the corporation exceeds the aggregate tax-adjusted basis of the property, 360 Air applies the general basis carryover rules. The building retains its built-in loss of $25,000 at the corporate level.

## Example 19-17

**What if:** Suppose Al transferred a building and land to the corporation in return for 50 percent of the corporation's stock (50 shares). The property transferred to the corporation had the following fair market values and tax-adjusted bases:

|  | FMV | Tax-Adjusted Basis |
|---|---|---|
| Building | $ 75,000 | $200,000 |
| Land | 200,000 | 100,000 |
| Total | $275,000 | $300,000 |

The fair market value of the 360 Air stock Al received in the exchange was $275,000.

Assuming Al meets the requirements under §351 to defer recognizing the $25,000 net loss realized, what is his tax basis in the 50 shares of 360 Air stock he receives in the exchange?

**Answer:** $300,000. In this case, the aggregate tax-adjusted bases of the property transferred to the corporation exceed the aggregate tax fair market value of the property. Assuming he doesn't elect to reduce his stock basis to fair market value, Al's tax basis in the stock he receives will equal the tax-adjusted basis of the assets transferred.

(*continued on page 19-17...*)

---

[31]§362(e)(2).

What is the tax-adjusted basis of the building and land held by 360 Air?

**Answer:** An aggregate tax-adjusted basis of $275,000. Because the aggregate fair market value of the property transferred to the corporation is less than the aggregate tax-adjusted bases of the property, 360 Air must reduce the aggregate tax-adjusted bases of the property to their aggregate fair market value. The allocation is made to those assets that have a built-in loss; in this example, only the building. The tax-adjusted basis of the building will be reduced to $175,000 ($200,000 − $25,000 net built-in loss). The tax-adjusted basis of the land will retain its carryover basis of $100,000. This adjustment eliminates the net $25,000 built-in loss at the corporate level.

What alternative election can Al and 360 Air make with respect to these basis reduction rules?

**Answer:** Al and the corporation can jointly elect to have Al reduce his stock basis to its fair market value of $275,000. The corporation would take a carryover basis of $200,000 in the building and a carryover basis of $100,000 in the land.

## Other Issues Related to Incorporating an Ongoing Business

**Depreciable Assets Transferred to a Corporation**    To the extent a property's tax-adjusted basis carries over from the shareholder, the corporation *steps into the shoes* of the shareholder and continues to depreciate the *carryover basis* portion of the property's tax basis using the shareholder's depreciation schedule.[32] Any additional basis (from recognition of gain due to boot received) is treated as a separate asset and is subject to a separate depreciation election (that is, this one physical asset is treated as two tax assets for depreciation purposes).

**Example 19-18**

**What if:** Assume Al received 40 shares of 360 Air stock with a fair market value of $250,000 and $50,000 in return for his transfer of a building and land to the corporation (assume for this problem that the tax basis of the assets transferred is as listed in the table below). The $50,000 received by Al constituted boot and caused him to recognize gain on the transfer. The $50,000 gain was allocated to each of the properties transferred to the corporation based on their relative fair market values, as follows:

|  | Tax Basis | Gain Recognized |
|---|---|---|
| Building | $ 89,633 | $20,000 |
| Land | 100,000 | 30,000 |
| Total | $189,633 | $50,000 |

360 Air carries over Al's tax basis in the property transferred and increases the tax basis by gain recognized by Al on the transfer. The corporation's tax basis in building and land is as follows:

|  | Tax Basis | Gain Recognized | 360 Air Tax Basis |
|---|---|---|---|
| Building | $ 89,633 | $20,000 | $119,633 |
| Land | 100,000 | 30,000 | 130,000 |
| Total | $189,633 | $50,000 | $249,633 |

The mid-month percentages for month 1, year 1, is 2.461 percent and 2.564 percent for years 2–39.

(*continued on page 19-18...*)

[32]§168(i)(7)(B)(ii).

> What is the depreciation amount that 360 Air can claim on the building in the first year?
>
> **Answer:** $2,949. 360 Air carries over Al's depreciation schedule for the building with respect to the $89,633 basis that carries over and depreciates the remaining $20,000 as a new asset. With respect to the carryover basis portion of the building, 360 Air uses Al's original $100,000 tax basis in the building to calculate the depreciation computation. For 2010, 360 Air applies the remaining depreciation rates (starting in year 5) to Al's original cost. Because Al received one-half month of depreciation in 2010, 360 Air gets 11½ months of year 5 depreciation ($100,000 × .02564 × 11.5/12 = $2,457). 360 Air treats $20,000 of the basis as a new asset and applies the month 1, year 1, depreciation rate to it ($20,000 × .02461 = $492). 360 Air has total depreciation on the building in 2010 of $2,949. This bifurcated computation often is ignored or overlooked in practice.

Practitioners often advise against transferring appreciated property (especially real estate) into a closely held corporation. By transferring the property into the corporation, the shareholder creates two assets with the same built-in gain as the original property (the stock received in the hands of the shareholder and the building owned by the corporation). The federal government can now collect taxes twice on the same gain: Once if the corporation sells the property received and a second time if the shareholder sells the stock. You will notice that Congress is not concerned by a duplication of gain result, only a duplication of loss result. By retaining the property outside the corporation, the shareholder can lease the property to the corporation, thereby reducing the corporation's taxable income through rent deductions. Note, however, that there may be valid state tax reasons to own the property inside a corporation, such as lower property taxes.

### Contributions to Capital

A **contribution to capital** is a transfer of property to a corporation by a shareholder or nonshareholder for which no stock or other property is received in return. The corporation receiving the property is not taxed on the receipt of the property.[33] If the property is contributed by a shareholder, the corporation takes a carryover tax basis in the property.[34] If the property is contributed by a nonshareholder (for example, a city contributes land to induce a corporation to locate its operations there), the corporation's tax basis in the property is zero.[35]

A capital contribution generally is not a taxable event to the shareholder because the shareholder does not receive any additional consideration in return for the transfer. A shareholder making a capital contribution gets to increase the tax basis in her existing stock in an amount equal to the tax basis of the property contributed.

### Section 1244 Stock

Stock is generally a capital asset in the hands of the shareholders, and gains or losses from sale or exchange are capital in nature. For individuals, long-term capital gains are taxed at a maximum tax rate of 15 percent. Losses can only offset capital gains plus $3,000 of ordinary income per year. Section 1244 allows a shareholder to treat a *loss* on the sale or exchange of stock that qualifies as §1244 stock as an *ordinary* loss.

Section 1244 applies only to individual shareholders who are the original recipients of the stock. The maximum amount of loss that can be treated as an ordinary

[33]§118.
[34]§362(a)(2).
[35]§362(c)(1).

loss under §1244 is $50,000 per year ($100,000 in the case of married, filing jointly shareholders). To qualify for this tax benefit, the corporation from which the stock was received must be a "small business corporation" when the stock was issued. The IRC defines a small business corporation as one in which the aggregate amount of money and other property received in return for the stock or as a contribution to capital did not exceed $1 million. In our storyline, 360 Air would qualify as a small business corporation. There is an additional requirement that for the five taxable years preceding the year in which the stock was sold, the corporation must have derived more than 50 percent of its aggregate gross receipts from an *active* trade or business. 360 Air meets this test as well. Section 1244 provides a tax benefit to entrepreneurs who create a risky start-up company that ultimately fails rather than succeeds.

---

**Example 19-19**

**What if:** Assume Al received 50 shares of 360 Air stock (50 percent of the outstanding stock) with a fair market value of $300,000 in return for his transfer of a building and land to the corporation in a transaction that qualified under §351. As a result of the transfer, Al received a tax basis in the 50 shares of $200,000 ($4,000 per share). Unfortunately for Al and his co-owners, Jim and Ginny, the snowboarding business declined due to a change in weather patterns in Michigan. As a result, Al's 50 shares were worth $50,000 ($1,000 per share) at the end of 2016. Needing some cash, Al sold all 50 of his shares to Jim for $50,000 and recognized a $150,000 loss [$50,000 − ($4,000 × 50 shares)]. 360 Air qualifies as a small business corporation under §1244. Al has no capital gains in the year of the sale. How much of the loss can Al deduct in 2016, assuming current tax rules and he is married, filing a joint tax return? What is the character of the loss (capital or ordinary)?

**Answer:** $103,000, $100,000 of which is ordinary loss and $3,000 of which is capital loss that can reduce up to $3,000 of ordinary income. The remaining $47,000 loss is carried forward as a capital loss.

What tax planning advice would you give Al to maximize the tax treatment of his loss from sale of the stock?

**Answer:** §1244 imposes an annual limit on the amount of the loss that can be treated as ordinary. To maximize the tax value of his loss, Al should sell enough shares of 360 Air stock to generate a $100,000 loss in 2010 and sell the remaining amount to generate a $50,000 loss in 2011. In that way, the entire $150,000 loss will be treated as ordinary loss.

---

A special rule applies when §1244 stock is issued by a corporation in exchange for property that, immediately before the exchange, has an adjusted basis (for determining loss) in excess of its fair market value (that is, a "built-in loss"). If §1244 stock is issued in exchange for such property and the taxpayer has elected not to reduce the stock's basis by the built-in loss, then for purposes of §1244 only, the basis of the stock is reduced by an amount equal to the built-in loss at the time of the exchange. For example, assume a taxpayer transfers property with an adjusted basis of $1,000 and a fair market value of $250 in exchange for 10 shares of §1244 stock in a §351 transaction. The total basis of the stock is $1,000, but, solely for purposes of §1244, the total basis of the stock must be reduced by $750, the excess of the adjusted basis of the property exchanged over its fair market value. The total basis of such stock for purposes of §1244 is $250. If the taxpayer sells her 10 shares for $250, she will recognize a loss of $750, all of which must be treated as a capital loss. If she sells the 10 shares for $200, then $50 of her total loss of $800 will be treated as an ordinary loss under §1244 and the remaining $750 will be a capital loss.

## **L03**   TAXABLE AND TAX-DEFERRED CORPORATE ACQUISITIONS

| Storyline Summary |
| --- |
| **Spartan Cycle and Repair** |
| Privately held company located in East Lansing, Michigan |
| Sells and repairs high-end bicycles |
| **Jim Wheeler** |
| Co-owner of Spartan Cycle and Repair (75 percent) |
| *Filing status:* Married filing jointly |
| *Dependents:* One child |
| *Marginal tax rate:* 40 percent |
| **Ginny Gears** |
| Co-owner of Spartan Cycles and Repair (25 percent) |
| *Filing status:* Unmarried |
| *Marginal tax rate:* 25 percent |
| **Wolverine Cycles and Repair** |
| Privately held company in Ann Arbor, Michigan |
| Sells and repairs high-end bicycles |
| **Pam Peloton** |
| Owner of Wolverine Cycles and Repair |
| *Filing status:* Unmarried |
| *Marginal tax rate:* 31 percent |

*continued from page 19-2 . . .*

Jim Wheeler and Ginny Gears were excited about their new business venture with Al Pine. This seemed to solve their need to find a source of revenues during the winter months, when the demand for bicycles declined significantly. With that challenge met, Jim and Ginny turned their attention to expanding their bicycle business to a new geographic region. At the recent Tour de Gaslight race sponsored by the Michigan Bicycle Racing Association, Jim struck up a conversation with Pam Peloton, owner of Wolverine Cycles and Repair (WCR) in Ann Arbor, Michigan. Pam mentioned she was planning to move to Colorado and was looking to sell her business. Jim could see lots of synergies in buying her business. He and Ginny were familiar with the biking community in Ann Arbor, and they understood the economics of operating a business in a college town. Ginny was excited about the possibility of expanding their business to Ann Arbor. Both communities had a large network of bike paths and avid biking clubs.

A meeting was set up with Pam to explore the possible acquisition of her business. Pam operated her business through a C corporation, which gave Jim and Pam the opportunity to consider buying the assets of the business directly or buying Pam's stock in the corporation. If the stock acquisition route is taken, Jim and Ginny need to consider whether they want to operate their new company as a subsidiary of Spartan Cycles and Repair or in a lateral ownership arrangement ("brother-sister" corporations). Operating WCR as a subsidiary of SCR would allow Jim and Ginny to file a consolidated tax return with SCR. Pam is concerned about the tax consequences of each of these options, as are Jim and Ginny. They know they are in over their heads, so a call was made to their tax accountant, Louis Tully, for help in sorting out their options.

*to be continued . . .*

At some point in the life of a business, the owners likely will consider expanding the scope or geographic locations of their business. Businesses can grow internally through expansion (organic growth) or externally by acquiring an existing business. This is the issue Jim and Ginny must resolve. As the storyline indicates, Jim and Ginny have the opportunity to buy Pam's existing business in a new geographic location. Because Pam operates the business through a C corporation, Jim and Ginny have several options. They can acquire the assets directly from WCR and transfer

them to a new corporation or their existing corporation, or they can acquire Pam's stock in WCR itself. These two options produce very different tax results to the buyer and the seller. In this section of the chapter, we consider the *basic* ways in which a corporation or its shareholders can acquire the stock or assets of another corporation and the tax consequences that follow the form of the acquisition. This is an extremely complicated and technical area of the tax law. A thorough discussion of all of the variations in which an acquisition can take place likely would take up most or all of a semester. As a result, our discussion is limited to basic taxable asset and stock acquisitions and tax-deferred asset (Type A) and stock (Type B) acquisitions.

## Motivation for Business Acquisitions

The decision to acquire an existing business can be motivated by many factors, including the desire to diversify, acquire a source of raw materials (vertical integration), expand into new product or geographic markets, acquire specific assets or technologies, and provide improved distribution channels. For example, Google recently acquired all of the stock of YouTube in exchange for $1.65 billion of Google stock. From Google's perspective, the acquisition would help the company expand into online video entertainment. Google, in turn, provides YouTube with its expertise in creating new models for advertising on the Internet.

---

**Taxes in the Real World**    *Google's Acquisition of YouTube*

**Google To Acquire YouTube for $1.65 Billion in Stock Combination Will Create New Opportunities for Users and Content Owners Everywhere**

MOUNTAIN VIEW, Calif., October 9, 2006—Google Inc. (NASDAQ: GOOG) announced today that it has agreed to acquire YouTube, the consumer media company for people to watch and share original videos through a Web experience, for $1.65 billion in a stock-for-stock transaction. Following the acquisition, YouTube will operate independently to preserve its successful brand and passionate community.

The acquisition combines one of the largest and fastest growing online video entertainment communities with Google's expertise in organizing information and creating new models for advertising on the

Internet. The combined companies will focus on providing a better, more comprehensive experience for users interested in uploading, watching and sharing videos, and will offer new opportunities for professional content owners to distribute their work to reach a vast new audience.

"The YouTube team has built an exciting and powerful media platform that complements Google's mission to organize the world's information and make it universally accessible and useful," said Eric Schmidt, Chief Executive Officer of Google. "Our companies share similar values; we both always put our users first and are committed to innovating to improve their experience. Together, we are natural partners to offer a compelling media entertainment service to users, content owners and advertisers."

---

> **THE KEY FACTS**
>
> **Tax Model for Corporate Acquisitions**
>
> ■ The acquiring corporation can acquire the target corporation through either a stock or asset acquisition.
>
> ■ The acquisition can be structured as either taxable or tax-deferred.
>
> ■ Taxable asset acquisitions allow the acquiring corporation to step-up the tax basis of the assets acquired to fair value.
>
> ■ In stock acquisitions and tax-deferred asset acquisitions, the tax basis of the target corporation's assets remain at their carryover basis (generally, cost less any depreciation).

## The Acquisition Tax Model

When negotiating an acquisition, management of the acquiring corporation must decide whether to acquire the target corporation's assets or stock and what consideration to use (equity, debt, and/or cash). The *form* of the transaction and the consideration used will determine the *tax status* of the transaction.[36] Nontax considerations (in particular, the effect of the acquisition on earnings per share) often dictate the

---

[36]The form of the transaction and the consideration used no longer affect the financial accounting treatment of the acquisition—ASC 805 requires that all business combinations be accounted for using the purchase method.

form of an acquisition by a publicly traded corporation. Privately held corporations are more likely to make tax considerations a priority.

The shareholders of the target company also must decide what consideration to accept in return for their stock or assets in the company. Cash provides liquidity and does not decline in value after the acquisition is announced, but it also causes the transaction to be fully or partially taxable to the seller. Receiving stock in the acquiring corporation may allow shareholders to defer paying tax on gain realized on the exchange, but the sellers now accept the risk that the acquiring corporation's stock will decline in value after the merger is announced or consummated.

Exhibit 19-7 summarizes the four basic types of transactions that can be used to effect an acquisition of another company. The *buyer* can purchase either stock or assets in a transaction that is either taxable or tax-deferred (in whole or in part) to the seller. Both sides to the transaction must decide which category they desire to be in after the transaction.

### EXHIBIT 19-7    The Acquisition Tax Model

| Taxable Asset Acquisition | Taxable Stock Acquisition |
|---|---|
| Nontaxable Asset Acquisition | Nontaxable Stock Acquisition |

Often the buyer and seller have different tax incentives (that is, they each want to be in a different "box"), which requires both sides to negotiate a compromise arrangement that satisfies both parties. For example, the buyer likely prefers to acquire the target corporation's assets in a taxable transaction. By purchasing the target corporation's assets directly, the acquiring corporation gets a "stepped-up" tax basis in the assets equal to fair market value (cost). To the extent the acquiring corporation can allocate the purchase price to depreciable or amortizable assets, this increases future depreciation or amortization deductions on the acquiring corporation's tax return. It is not uncommon in an acquisition involving publicly traded corporations for goodwill to comprise 80 percent to 90 percent of the purchase price. If the acquiring corporation can achieve a tax basis in the goodwill, the basis can be amortized over 15 years.[37] If the acquiring corporation is required to take a carryover basis in the goodwill (which occurs in a tax-deferred acquisition), the goodwill tax basis will be zero and no amortization will result.

The seller likely prefers to sell either stock (in a taxable or tax-deferred transaction) or assets in a tax-deferred transaction, either because the gain recognized is taxed at a lower capital gain tax rate (15 percent) or because the gain realized can be deferred into the future. These three options do not provide the acquiring corporation with a stepped-up tax basis in the assets acquired equal to cost (fair market value), potentially greatly reducing the tax subsidy the acquiring corporation would get from depreciating or amortizing the higher tax basis.

The technical tax (and accounting) rules that apply to mergers and acquisitions are extremely complex. Because the statutory language governing reorganizations is sparse, the IRS and courts often must decide whether the *form* of a reorganization transaction meets both the literal language of the statute and the *substance* of the judicial principles that underlie the reorganization provisions. As a result, the reorganization area is heavily laden with administrative and judicial pronouncements. Our goal is to provide you with a basic overview of the most common types of mergers and acquisitions that you will see discussed in business periodicals such as *The Wall Street Journal*.

[37]§197.

# COMPUTING THE TAX CONSEQUENCES TO THE PARTIES TO A CORPORATE ACQUISITION

**LO4**

*continued from page 19-20...*

As part of their negotiations with Pam, Jim and Ginny had their tax accountant, Louis Tully, look over WCR's **tax accounting balance sheet** along with a recent valuation of the assets' fair market values. WCR is an accrual-method taxpayer. As a result, the payables have a tax basis because the corporation deducted the expenses related to the payables when the expenses were accrued. These important facts are summarized as follows:

|  | FMV | Tax-Adjusted Basis | Appreciation |
|---|---|---|---|
| Cash | $ 10,000 | $ 10,000 | |
| Receivables | 5,000 | 5,000 | |
| Inventory | 20,000 | 10,000 | $ 10,000 |
| Building | 80,000 | 50,000 | 30,000 |
| Land | 120,000 | 60,000 | 60,000 |
| Total | $235,000 | $135,000 | $100,000 |
| | | | |
| Payables | 4,000 | 4,000 | |
| Mortgage* | 31,000 | 31,000 | |
| Total | $ 35,000 | $ 35,000 | |

*The mortgage was attached to the building and land.

Pam's tax basis in her WCR stock is $50,000 and she has held the stock for 10 years.

Jim and Ginny agreed to pay Pam $300,000 for her business, an amount that is $100,000 more than the net fair market value of the assets less the liabilities listed on the balance sheet ($235,000 − $35,000). The additional $100,000 reflects an amount to be paid for the company's customer list valued at $25,000, with the remaining $75,000 allocated to goodwill.

With the price settled, Jim, Ginny, and Pam now must agree on the form the transaction will take. Jim and Ginny asked Louis to develop some computations for each of the different ways in which the transaction could take place.

*to be continued...*

## Taxable Acquisitions

A corporation can acquire an ongoing business through the purchase of its stock or assets in return for cash, debt, or equity or a combination thereof. Cash purchases of stock are the most common form of acquisition of publicly held corporations. Using cash to acquire another company has several nontax advantages; most notably, the acquiring corporation does not "acquire" the target corporation's shareholders in the transaction and does not increase the denominator in its calculation of earnings per share. There are disadvantages to using cash, particularly if the acquiring corporation incurs additional debt to fund the purchase.

If SCR purchases the assets directly from WCR in return for cash, WCR will recognize gain or loss on the sale of each asset individually. WCR will cease to exist as a

separate corporation and will completely liquidate by transferring the net after-tax proceeds received from SCR to its shareholder, Pam. Pam recognizes gain or loss on the exchange of her WCR stock for the cash received.

---

**Example 19-20**

**What if:** Assume SCR will purchase WCR's assets for $300,000 and assume the company's liabilities of $35,000. WCR will realize $335,000 ($300,000 + $35,000), which it will allocate to each of the assets sold, as follows:

|  | **Allocation** | **Tax-Adjusted Basis** | **Gain Realized** |
|---|---|---|---|
| Cash | $ 10,000 | $ 10,000 | $      0 |
| Receivables | 5,000 | 5,000 | 0 |
| Inventory | 20,000 | 10,000 | 10,000 |
| Building | 80,000 | 50,000 | 30,000 |
| Land | 120,000 | 60,000 | 60,000 |
| Customer list | 25,000 | 0 | 25,000 |
| Goodwill | 75,000 | 0 | 75,000 |
| Total | $335,000 | $135,000 | $200,000 |

What amount of gain or loss does WCR recognize on the sale of its assets and what is the character of the gain or loss (ordinary, §1231, or capital)?

**Answer:** WCR recognizes total gain of $200,000. The character of the gain will be as follows:

|  | **Gain Recognized** | **Character** |
|---|---|---|
| Inventory | $ 10,000 | Ordinary |
| Building | 30,000 | Ordinary (§291 ) and §1231 |
| Land | 60,000 | §1231 |
| Customer list | 25,000 | §1231 |
| Goodwill | 75,000 | §1231 |
| Total | $200,000 | |

WCR pays a corporate-level tax of $68,000 (assuming a tax rate of 34 percent). WCR will go out of existence (liquidate) by exchanging the $232,000 net amount realized after taxes ($300,000 − $68,000) to Pam in return for her WCR stock.

What amount of gain or loss will Pam recognize on the exchange of her WCR stock for the after-tax proceeds from the sale ($232,000)?

**Answer:** Pam recognizes a long-term capital gain of $182,000 ($232,000 − $50,000 stock basis) and pays a shareholder-level tax of $27,300 ($182,000 × 15%). The total tax paid using this form of acquisition is $95,300. Pam is left with $204,700 after taxes ($300,000 − $68,000 − $27,300).

Although unattractive to Pam, this deal provides SCR (Jim and Ginny) with the maximum tax benefits. The building will have an increased tax basis of $30,000, which SCR can depreciate over 39 years. The customer list and goodwill will have a tax basis of $25,000 and $75,000, respectively, which SCR can amortize over 15 years on a straight-line basis.[38]

---

[38]§197.

If SCR acquires WCR through a stock acquisition for cash, WCR retains its tax and legal identity unless SCR liquidates WCR into itself or merges it into an existing subsidiary. The tax basis of WCR's assets, which will carry over, will not reflect SCR's tax basis (purchase price) in WCR's stock.

---

**Example 19-21**

*What if:* Suppose instead that SCR purchases the WCR stock from Pam for $300,000 and assumes WCR's liabilities. What amount of gain or loss does WCR recognize in this transaction?

**Answer:** WCR will not recognize gain on this form of acquisition because it has not sold any assets directly to SCR.

What amount and character of gain or loss does Pam recognize in this transaction?

**Answer:** Pam recognizes long-term capital gain of $250,000 ($300,000 − $50,000 stock basis) and pays a shareholder-level tax of $37,500 ($250,000 × 15%). Pam will be left with $262,500 after taxes ($300,000 − $37,500), which is $57,800 more than a direct asset sale ($262,500 − $204,700).

Although attractive to Pam, this deal will not be as attractive to SCR (Jim and Ginny). The building will retain its carryover tax basis of $50,000, and the customer list and goodwill will have a tax basis of zero. The customer list and goodwill have a zero tax basis to WCR because they are self-created assets. The inside tax bases of WCR's assets remain at $135,000. SCR has an outside tax basis in the WCR stock equal to the purchase price of $300,000.

---

Tax nirvana will be achieved if Pam can treat the transaction as a stock sale and pay a single level of capital gains tax on the gain recognized from the sale, while SCR can treat the transaction as an asset purchase and receive a step-up in basis of the assets to fair market value. This best of both tax worlds is available in transactions where a corporate taxpayer purchases 80 percent or more of another corporation's stock within a 12-month period. In such cases, SCR can make a **section 338 election** to treat the stock purchase as a *deemed asset purchase*.

As with most things that appear too good to be true, this election does not come without some tax costs. The actual computations involved in calculating these costs are extremely technical and beyond the scope of this text. In big-picture terms, WCR is treated as selling its assets prior to the transaction and then repurchasing them at fair market value. This deemed sale of assets causes WCR to recognize gain on assets that have appreciated in value. SCR, as the buyer, bears this tax cost because the fair market value of WCR will be reduced by the tax paid. In almost all cases, this tax cost negates the tax benefits of getting a step-up in basis in WCR's assets and is rarely ever elected. This election might be tax-efficient if WCR has net operating losses or net capital losses that can be used to offset gain from the deemed sale of its assets.

If the target corporation is a subsidiary of the seller, the acquiring corporation and seller can make a joint **section 338(h)(10) election** and have the seller report the gain from the deemed sale of the target corporation's assets on its tax return in lieu of reporting the actual gain from the sale of the target corporation stock. The technical rules that apply to §338(h)(10) elections are beyond the scope of this text. These elections, which are more common than a regular §338 election, often achieve tax savings to both parties to the transaction. For example, the Wm. Wrigley Jr. Company recently purchased Life Savers® and Altoids® from Kraft Foods. The buyer and seller made a joint §338(h)(10) election, which allowed Wrigley to record a tax basis for the intangibles and goodwill acquired in the transaction. As you can see from the announcement reproduced below, this provided Wrigley with an estimated $300 million in cash tax benefits from being able to amortize the step-up in basis.

**Taxes in the Real World** *Wrigley's "Curiously Refreshing"*
*Tax Benefits from Acquiring Altoids*

**Wrigley to Add Life Savers® and Altoids® to Its Confectionery Portfolio**

CHICAGO, Nov. 15/PRNewswire-FirstCall/—The Wm. Wrigley Jr. Company (NYSE: WWY) announced today that it has entered into an agreement to purchase certain confectionery assets of Kraft Foods for $1.48 billion. The transaction includes ownership of well-known, iconic brand franchises—such as Life Savers, Creme Savers®, and Altoids—as well as a number of high-quality local or regional brands and production facilities in the United States and Europe.

**Transaction Details**

As noted, the purchase price will be $1.48 billion, offset in part by approximately $300 million in cash

tax benefits associated with amortization of intangible assets. The net acquisition cost of $1.18 billion represents 2.4 times estimated 2004 sales. In order to complete this all-cash transaction, the Wrigley Company has received a commitment for a credit facility of $1.5 billion that, even when fully utilized, will leave the Company with a modest debt-to-market capitalization ratio. This transaction, including one-time costs, is expected to be slightly dilutive to earnings in the first full year of combined operations and accretive thereafter.

© 2008 Wm. Wrigley Jr. Company. Used with permission.

---

<table>
<tr><td>

**THE KEY FACTS**

**Forms of a Tax-Deferred Asset Acquisition**

■ **Straight Type A merger**
· Must meet state law requirements to be a merger or consolidation.
· Judicial requirements of COI, COBE, and business purpose must be met.

■ **Forward triangular Type A merger**
· Must meet requirements to be a straight Type A merger.
· The target corporation merges into an 80 percent or more owned acquisition subsidiary of the acquiring corporation.
· The acquisition subsidiary must acquire "substantially all" of the target corporation's properties in the exchange.

■ **Reverse triangular Type A merger**
· Must meet requirements to be a straight Type A merger.
· The acquisition subsidiary merges into the target corporation.
· The target corporation must hold "substantially all" of the acquisition subsidiary's properties and its own properties after the exchange.
· The acquisition subsidiary must receive in the exchange 80 percent or more of the target corporation's stock in exchange for voting stock of the acquiring corporation.

</td></tr></table>

## Tax-Deferred Acquisitions

As you learned previously in this chapter, the tax law allows taxpayers to organize a corporation in a tax-deferred manner under §351. The tax laws also allow taxpayers to *reorganize* their corporate structure in a tax-deferred manner. For tax purposes, **reorganizations** encompass acquisitions and dispositions of corporate assets (including the stock of subsidiaries) and a corporation's restructuring of its capital structure, place of incorporation, or company name. The IRC allows for tax deferral to the corporation(s) involved in the reorganization (the *parties to the reorganization*) and the shareholders provided the transaction meets one of seven statutory definitions[39] and satisfies the judicial principles that underlie the reorganization statutes. As before, tax deferral in corporate reorganizations is predicated on the seller receiving a continuing ownership interest in the assets transferred through the receipt of equity in the acquiring corporation.

The statutory language governing corporate reorganizations is rather sparse. It should not be surprising, then, that the IRS and the courts frequently must interpret how changes in the facts related to a transaction's form affect its tax status. The end result has been the development of a complex and confusing legacy of IRS rulings and court decisions that dictate how a reorganization transaction will be taxed. Corporate reorganizations are best left to the tax experts who have devoted much of their professional lives to understanding their intricacies. Our goal is to acquaint you with the basic principles that underlie all corporate reorganizations and provide you with an understanding of the most common forms of corporate acquisitions that are tax-deferred.

## Judicial Principles that Underlie All Tax-Deferred Reorganizations

**Continuity of Interest (COI)**    Tax deferral in a reorganization is based on the presumption that the shareholders of the acquired (target) corporation retain a continuing ownership (equity) interest in the target corporation's assets or historic business through ownership of stock in the acquiring corporation. The IRC does

---

[39]The "forms" of corporate reorganizations are defined in §368(a)(1).

not provide a **bright line test** for when **continuity of interest (COI)** is met, although the regulations provide an example that states that COI is satisfied when the shareholders of the target corporation, in the aggregate, receive equity equal to 40 percent or more of the total value of the consideration received.[40] The proposed acquisition of Marvel Entertainment by The Walt Disney Company involved a combination of cash and equity and was designed to be a tax-deferred reorganization. As you can see by the announcement below, the amount of cash was restricted to 60 percent of the total consideration so as to not violate the continuity of interest rules.

---

**Taxes in the Real World**   *Disney's Acquisition of Marvel Entertainment*

**Disney to Acquire Marvel Entertainment**

Burbank, CA, and New York, NY, August 31, 2009—Building on its strategy of delivering quality branded content to people around the world, The Walt Disney Company has agreed to acquire Marvel Entertainment, Inc., in a stock and cash transaction, the companies announced today.

Under the terms of the agreement and based on the closing price of Disney on August 28, 2009, Marvel shareholders would receive a total of $30 per share in cash plus approximately 0.745 Disney shares for each Marvel share they own. At closing,

the amount of cash and stock will be adjusted if necessary so that the total value of the Disney stock issued as merger consideration based on its trading value at that time is not less than 40% of the total merger consideration.

This adjustment will be made in an effort to achieve the anticipated qualification of the transaction as a "reorganization" within the meaning of Section 368(a) of the Internal Revenue Code of 1986. (From Form S-4 Registration Statement filed with the SEC.)

---

**Continuity of Business Enterprise (COBE)**   For a transaction to qualify as a tax-deferred reorganization, the acquiring corporation must continue the target corporation's historic business or continue to use a *significant* portion of the target corporation's historic business assets. Whether the historic business assets retained are "significant" is a facts and circumstances test, which adds to the administrative and judicial rulings that are part and parcel of the reorganization landscape. **Continuity of business enterprise (COBE)** does not apply to the historic business or assets of the acquiring corporation; the acquiring corporation can sell off its assets after the reorganization without violating the COBE requirement.

**Business Purpose Test**   As early as 1935, the Supreme Court stated that transactions with "no business or corporate purpose" should not receive tax deferral even if they comply with the statutory requirements.[41] To meet the business purpose test, the acquiring corporation must be able to show a significant nontax avoidance purpose for engaging in the transaction.

### Type A Asset Acquisitions

Type A reorganizations [so named because they are described in §368(a)(1)(*A*)] are statutory **mergers** or **consolidations.** In a statutory merger, SCR will acquire WCR's assets and assume its liabilities by transferring SCR stock to Pam, the shareholder of WCR, in exchange for her WCR stock. In a consolidation, SCR and WCR will transfer their assets and liabilities to a newly formed corporation in return for stock in the new corporation, after which SCR and WCR will cease to exist.

---

[40]Reg. §1.368-1T(e)(2)(v), Example 10.
[41]*Gregory v. Helvering,* 293 U.S. 465 (1935).

In a Type A reorganization, the target corporation shareholders defer recognition of gain or loss realized on the receipt of stock of the acquiring corporation. Similar to a §351 transaction, if a target corporation shareholder receives money or other property (boot) from the acquiring corporation or its acquisition subsidiary, the shareholder recognizes *gain* to the extent of the money and fair market value of other property received (not to exceed the gain realized). The shareholder's tax basis in the stock received is a *substituted basis* of the stock transferred plus any gain recognized less any money and the fair market value of other property received. The target corporation's assets remain at their carryover (historic) tax basis in a Type A merger.

Exhibit 19-8 provides an illustration of a Type A merger. The consideration that can be paid to Pam is very flexible in a Type A merger; the only limitation being that the transaction satisfy the COI requirement (that is, at least 40 percent of the consideration must be SCR stock). The stock used to satisfy the COI test can be voting or nonvoting, common or preferred.

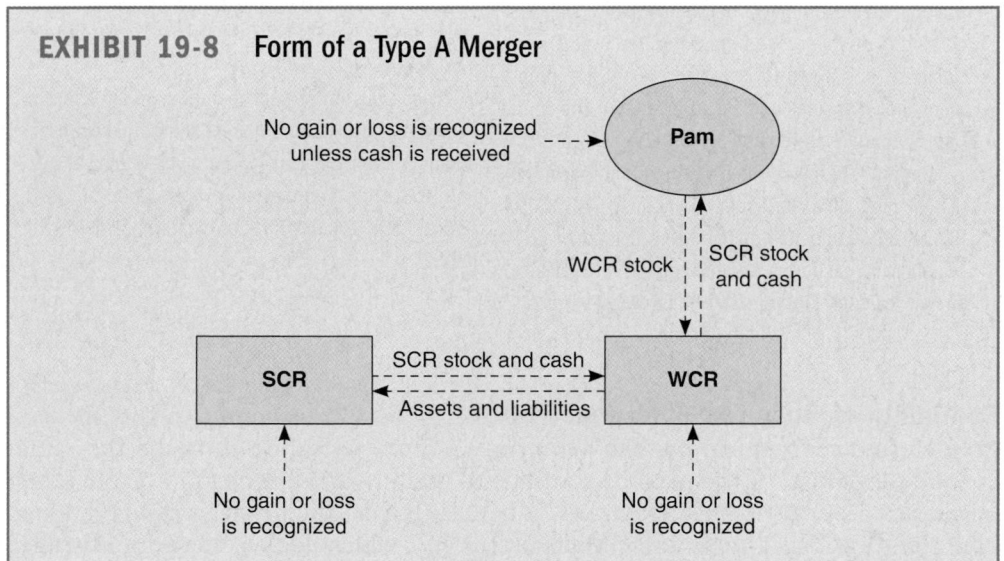

**EXHIBIT 19-8    Form of a Type A Merger**

---

**Example 19-22**

**What if:** Assume WCR will merge into SCR in a Type A reorganization. Under the terms of the deal, SCR will pay Pam $300,000 in SCR stock, after which WCR will merge into SCR. Pam's tax basis in her WCR stock is $50,000. What amount of gain will Pam realize on the exchange of her WCR stock for SCR stock?

**Answer:** $250,000 ($300,000 − $50,000)

What amount of gain will Pam recognize on the exchange of her WCR stock for SCR stock?

**Answer:** $0. Because Pam receives only SCR stock, she defers the entire $250,000 gain realized.

What is Pam's tax basis in her SCR stock?

**Answer:** $50,000. Because Pam defers the entire gain, her tax basis in the SCR stock is a substituted basis from her WCR stock. This preserves the gain deferred for future recognition if Pam sold her SCR stock in the future for its fair market value of $300,000.

What are SCR's tax bases in the assets it receives from WCR in the merger?

**Answer:** SCR receives a carryover tax basis in each of the assets received (for example, the tax basis of the goodwill and customer list will be zero).

**Example 19-23**

*What if:* Suppose instead Pam wants some cash as well as SCR stock in the transaction. What is the maximum amount of cash Pam can receive from SCR and not violate the continuity of interest rule as illustrated in the regulations?

**Answer:** $180,000 ($300,000 × 60%). Pam can receive a maximum of 60 percent of the consideration in cash and not violate the continuity of interest rule under the regulations.

*What if:* Assume Pam receives $100,000 plus $200,000 in SCR stock in exchange for all of her WCR stock in a Type A merger. What amount of gain will Pam *realize* on the exchange?

**Answer:** $250,000 ($300,000 − $50,000)

What amount of gain will Pam *recognize* on the exchange?

**Answer:** $100,000. Pam must recognize gain in an amount that is the lesser of the gain realized or the boot received. Pam defers recognizing $150,000 gain.

What is Pam's tax basis in her SCR stock?

**Answer:** $50,000, computed as follows:

|   | Tax-adjusted basis of WCR stock exchanged | $ 50,000 |
|---|---|---|
| + | Gain recognized on the exchange | 100,000 |
| − | Fair market value of boot (cash) received | 100,000 |
|   | Tax basis of stock received | $ 50,000 |

This calculation preserves the gain deferred for future recognition if Pam sold her SCR stock in the future for its fair market value of $200,000 ($200,000 − $50,000 = $150,000).

There are several potential downsides to structuring the transaction in this form. Pam will become a shareholder of SCR, which neither she nor Jim and Ginny seem to want. The historic tax basis of WCR's assets and liabilities will carry over to SCR. Going back to the original set of facts in the above example, Pam will not owe any tax on the transaction but she will not receive any cash, which she desires. Finally, WCR will cease to exist as a separate corporation. Jim and Ginny expressed a desire to operate WCR as an independent company. To accomplish this, SCR will have to transfer the WCR assets and liabilities to a newly created subsidiary under §351. SCR will incur the additional cost of retitling the assets a second time and pay any state transfer tax on the transfer of the assets.

**Forward Triangular Type A Merger**    In a forward triangular merger, WCR merges into a controlled (80 percent or more owned) subsidiary of SCR, with Pam receiving SCR stock or a combination of SCR stock and cash in exchange for her WCR stock, which will come directly from SCR or from an intermediary (bank). Exhibit 19-9 provides an illustration of the "fictional" form of a forward triangular Type A merger for determining the tax consequences to the parties to the transaction.

A forward triangular merger isolates WCR's assets and liabilities in a separate subsidiary of SCR. This type of merger is a common vehicle for effecting mergers when the parent corporation stock is publicly traded or the parent corporation is a holding company. For a forward triangular merger to be effective, the transaction must satisfy the requirements to be a straight Type A merger and one additional requirement: SCR's acquisition subsidiary must acquire "substantially all" of WCR's properties in the exchange. The IRS interprets "substantially all" to mean 90 percent of the fair market value of WCR's net properties ($300,000), and 70 percent of the fair market value of WCR's gross properties ($335,000). The technical tax rules that

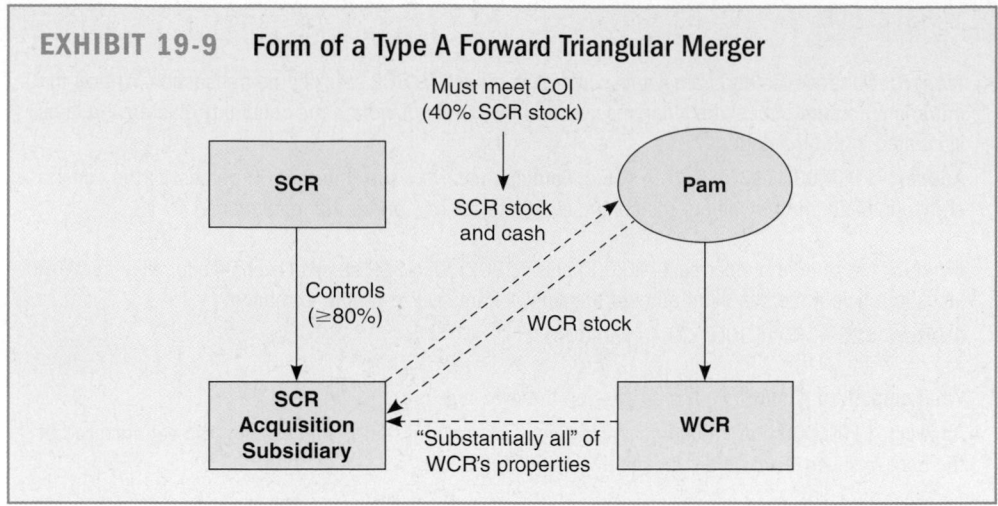

**EXHIBIT 19-9    Form of a Type A Forward Triangular Merger**

apply to determine the tax basis of WCR's assets after the merger are complex and beyond the scope of this text.

**Reverse Triangular Type A Merger**    In a reverse triangular merger, SCR's acquisition subsidiary will merge into WCR, with Pam receiving SCR stock or a combination of SCR stock and cash in exchange for her WCR stock, which will come directly from SCR or from an intermediary (bank). WCR, rather than the SCR acquisition subsidiary, survives and becomes a wholly owned subsidiary of SCR. Reverse triangular Type A mergers are desirable because the transaction preserves the target corporation's existence. Exhibit 19-10 provides an illustration of the "fictional" form of a reverse triangular Type A merger for determining the tax consequences to the parties to the transaction.

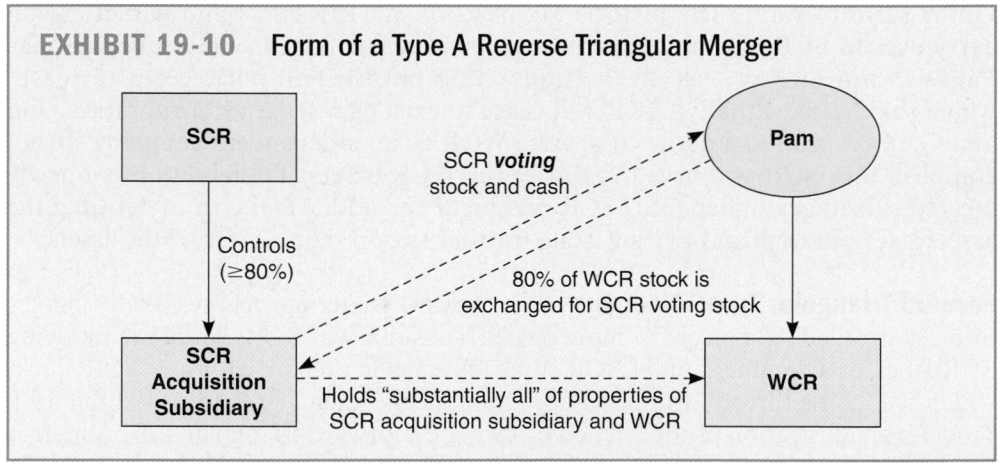

**EXHIBIT 19-10    Form of a Type A Reverse Triangular Merger**

There are three additional requirements that must be met to satisfy the requirements for tax deferral in a reverse triangular merger. First, WCR must hold "substantially all" of the properties of both WCR and the SCR Acquisition Subsidiary. Second, Pam must transfer in the exchange an amount of stock in WCR that constitutes control of WCR (80 percent or more of WCR stock). Finally, Pam must receive SCR *voting stock* in return for her WCR stock that constitutes control of WCR in the exchange. For example, if the SCR Acquisition Subsidiary acquires 100 percent of WCR's stock in the exchange, at least 80 percent of the

consideration the SCR Acquisition Subsidiary pays Pam must be in the form of SCR voting stock.

This last requirement often presents too difficult a hurdle to overcome in acquisitions in which the acquiring corporation wants to use a combination of cash and stock to acquire the target corporation. Publicly traded companies are very sensitive to the amount of stock they use in an acquisition because of the potential negative effect it can have on the company's earnings per share (that is, issuing additional stock increases the denominator in the earnings per share computation). The technical tax rules that apply to determine the tax basis of WCR's assets after the merger are complex and beyond the scope of this text.

The Walt Disney Company recently acquired Pixar in a reverse triangular merger. You can see from the excerpt below that Disney's acquisition subsidiary merged into Pixar, after which the former shareholders of Pixar received Disney stock in exchange for their Pixar stock.

---

**Taxes in the Real World**   *Disney's Acquisition of Pixar*

**Disney to Acquire Pixar** *Long-time Creative Partners Form New Worldwide Leader in Quality Family Entertainment*

Burbank, CA and Emeryville, CA (January 24, 2006)—Furthering its strategy of delivering outstanding creative content, Robert A. Iger, President and Chief Executive Officer of The Walt Disney Company (NYSE: DIS), announced today that Disney has agreed to acquire computer animation leader Pixar (NASDAQ: PIXR) in an all-stock transaction, expected to be completed by this summer. Under terms of the agreement, 2.3 Disney shares will be issued for each Pixar share. Based on Pixar's fully diluted shares outstanding, the transaction value is $7.4 billion ($6.3 billion net of Pixar's cash of just over $1 billion).

**Item 1.01. Entry into a Material Definitive Agreement.**

On January 24, 2006, The Walt Disney Company, a Delaware Corporation, ("Disney"), Lux Acquisition Corp. ("Merger Sub"), a California Corporation and a direct wholly owned subsidiary of Disney, and Pixar, a California Corporation ("Pixar"), entered into an Agreement and Plan of Merger (the "Merger Agreement"). Pursuant to the terms and subject to the conditions set forth in the Merger Agreement, Merger Sub will merge with and into Pixar (the "Merger"), with Pixar continuing as the surviving corporation after the Merger. As a result of the Merger, Pixar will become a wholly owned subsidiary of Disney. The Boards of Directors of Disney and Pixar approved the Merger and the Merger Agreement.

---

## Type B Stock-for-Stock Reorganizations

Type B reorganizations [so named because they are described in §368(a)(1)(B)] often are referred to as **stock-for-stock acquisitions.** The requirements to meet a tax-deferred Type B reorganization are very restrictive. In particular, the SCR must acquire *control* (80 percent or more ownership) of WCR using *solely* SCR *voting* stock. Additional consideration of as little as $1 can taint the transaction and cause it to be fully taxable to Pam. Not surprisingly, Type B reorganizations are rare among publicly traded companies. Exhibit 19-11 provides an illustration of the form of a Type B merger.

In a Type B reorganization, Pam will defer recognition of any gain or loss realized and take a substituted basis in the SCR stock she receives. SCR takes a *carryover basis* (from Pam) in the WCR stock received. In the case of publicly traded companies, this requires the acquiring corporation to determine the tax basis of each share of stock it receives from thousands or even millions of shareholders of the target corporation. In such cases, the IRS allows the acquiring corporation to determine its stock basis using statistical sampling.

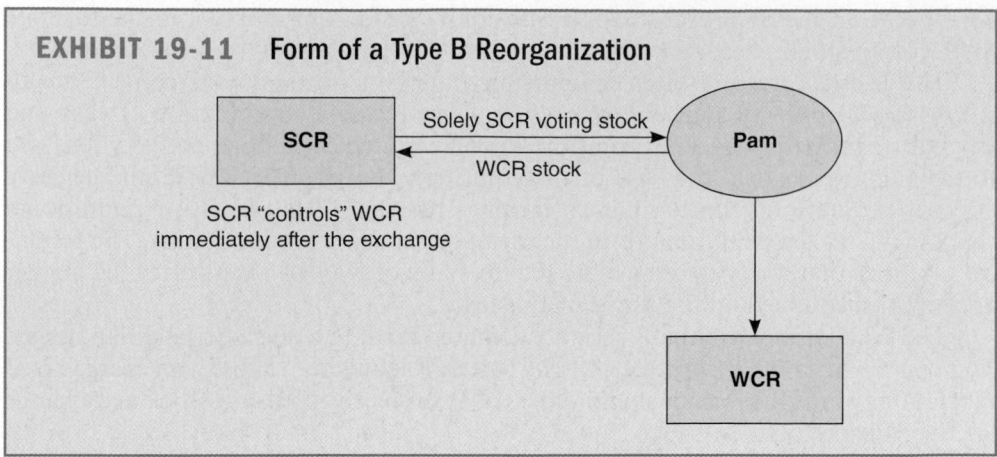

**EXHIBIT 19-11    Form of a Type B Reorganization**

---

**Example 19-24**

**What if:** Let's say SCR will exchange SCR voting stock for all of Pam's WCR stock in a Type B stock-for-stock reorganization. Pam's tax basis in her WCR stock is $50,000. The fair market value of the SCR stock is $300,000. What amount of gain will Pam *realize* on the exchange of her WCR stock for SCR stock?

**Answer:** $250,000 ($300,000 − $50,000)

What amount of gain will Pam *recognize* on the exchange of her WCR stock for SCR stock?

**Answer:** $0. Because Pam receives only SCR stock, she defers the entire $250,000 gain realized.

What is Pam's tax basis in her SCR stock?

**Answer:** $50,000. Because Pam defers the entire gain, her tax basis in the SCR stock is a substituted basis from her WCR stock. This preserves the gain deferred for future recognition if Pam sold her SCR stock in the future for its fair market value of $300,000.

What are SCR's tax bases in the WCR stock received in the exchange?

**Answer:** SCR receives a substituted tax basis equal to Pam's basis in her WCR stock.

What are WCR's tax bases in the assets after the exchange?

**Answer:** WCR retains a carryover tax basis in each of the assets (for example, the tax basis of the goodwill and customer list will be zero).

**What if:** Suppose Pam received $10,000 plus $290,000 of SCR stock in the transaction. How does this change in facts affect Pam's tax consequences?

**Answer:** The entire gain realized of $250,000 is recognized. For a Type B reorganization to be tax-deferred, Pam cannot receive any cash. Given her desire to move to Colorado, this limitation likely will be a deal breaker.

---

There are many variations of Type A and Type B acquisitions, along with other asset-type acquisitions that can be tax-deferred, that we do not discuss in this chapter because of their complexity. Suffice it to say that tax experts in mergers and acquisitions have a toolbox of ideas and alternatives that allow for a multiplicity of ways to structure a transaction and achieve tax deferral to the parties to the reorganization. For the novice entering this field of taxation, this can be both exhilarating and exasperating. Our goal in this section is to provide you with a glimpse of this intricate area of taxation. A summary of the tax-deferred reorganizations discussed above along with the other forms of tax-deferred reorganizations is provided in Exhibit 19-12.

**EXHIBIT 19-12** Summary of Tax-Deferred Corporate Reorganizations

| Form of Reorganization | Description |
|---|---|
| Type A | One corporation acquires the assets and liabilities of another corporation in return for stock or a combination of stock and cash. The acquisition is tax-deferred if the transaction satisfies the continuity of interest, continuity of business, and business purpose requirements. |
| Forward Triangular Type A | The acquiring corporation uses stock of its *parent* corporation to acquire the target corporation's stock, after which the target corporation merges into the acquiring corporation. To be tax-deferred, the transaction must meet the requirements to be a Type A merger. In addition, the acquiring corporation must use *solely* the stock of its parent corporation and acquire "substantially all" of the target corporation's property in the transaction. |
| Reverse Triangular Type A | The acquiring corporation uses stock of its parent corporation to acquire the target corporation's stock, after which the acquiring corporation merges into the target corporation (which becomes a subsidiary of the parent corporation). To be tax-deferred, the transaction must satisfy three requirements: (1) the surviving corporation must hold "substantially all" of the properties of both the surviving and the merged corporations; (2) the target shareholders must transfer in the exchange an amount of stock in the target that constitutes control of the target (80 percent or more of the target's stock); and (3) the target shareholders must receive parent corporation voting stock in return. |
| Type B | The acquiring corporation uses its voting stock (or the voting stock of its parent corporation) to acquire control (80 percent voting power and 80 percent of nonvoting stock) of the target corporation. To be tax-deferred, the target shareholders must receive *solely* voting stock of the acquiring corporation. |
| Type C | The acquiring corporation uses its voting stock (or voting stock of its parent corporation) to acquire "substantially all" of the target corporation's assets. The end result of a Type C reorganization resembles a Type A reorganization. The major difference between a Type C reorganization and a Type A reorganization is that state law governs the form of the Type A merger, while the Internal Revenue Code governs the form of the Type C reorganization. |
| Type D | A corporation transfers all or part of its assets to another corporation, and immediately after the transfer the shareholders of the transferor corporation own at least 50 percent of the voting power or value of the transferee corporation (nondivisive Type D). A corporation transfers all or part of its assets to another corporation, and immediately after the transfer the shareholders of the transferor corporation own at least 80 percent of the transferee corporation (divisive Type D). |
| Type E | Type E reorganizations are often referred to as recapitalizations. Stock in the corporation (e.g., common) is exchanged for a different class of stock (e.g., preferred) or securities (debt). Recapitalizations can range from an amendment in the corporate charter to a change in the redemption price or liquidating value of stock to an actual exchange of stock between the corporation and its shareholder(s). |
| Type F | Type F reorganizations are described as a "mere change in identity, form, or place of organization" of a single corporation. A corporation uses a Type F reorganization to change its corporate name or its state (country) of incorporation. |
| Type G | Type G reorganizations are often referred to as bankruptcy reorganizations. In a Type G reorganization, the corporation transfers all or a part of its assets to another corporation in a Title 11 case, and the stock of the corporation receiving the assets is distributed in a transaction that is tax-deferred. |

The tax law also allows corporations to divide by transferring stock of a subsidiary to shareholders in a pro rata distribution (spin-off) or a non-pro rata distribution (split-off).[42] The technical details of these transactions are beyond the scope of this text.

*continued from page 19-23 . . .*

After several years of trying to get 360 Air off the ground, it became clear to Jim, Ginny, and even Al that there was not enough demand for snowboarding products in East Lansing to make their business venture profitable. Reluctantly, the three owners decided to liquidate the corporation. Once again, they summoned their tax adviser, Louis Tully, to help them understand the tax consequences of liquidating the corporation. Louis constructed the company's tax accounting balance sheet, which is reproduced below.

|  | FMV | Tax-Adjusted Basis | Difference |
|---|---|---|---|
| Cash | $200,000 | $200,000 | |
| Receivables | 2,000 | 2,000 | |
| Inventory | 10,000 | 12,000 | $ (2,000) |
| Building | 150,000 | 48,000 | 102,000 |
| Land | 200,000 | 100,000 | 100,000 |
| Total | $562,000 | $362,000 | $200,000 |

In addition, the corporation had an outstanding mortgage of $62,000 attached to the building and land (the net fair market value of the company is $500,000). Jim wanted to acquire the building and land to use to expand SCR in East Lansing (Ginny was no longer a co-owner). The parties agreed that 360 Air would sell off the remaining inventory and collect the remaining receivables, after which the cash (net of the mortgage), building, and land would be distributed pro rata to each of the three shareholders (50 percent to Al, 40 percent to Jim, and 10 percent to Ginny). Jim would then buy Al and Ginny's interests in the building and land. The bank agreed to let Jim assume the remaining mortgage on the building. ■

As the storyline indicates, the owners of a corporation may decide at some point to discontinue the corporation's business activities. This decision may be made because the corporation is not profitable, the officers and shareholders wish to change the organizational form of the business (for example, to a flow-through entity), or the owners want to consolidate operations (for example, a subsidiary is liquidated into the parent corporation).

A complete liquidation occurs when a corporation acquires all of its stock from all of its shareholders in exchange for "all" of its net assets, after which time the corporation ceases to do business. For tax purposes, a corporation files Form 966 to inform the IRS of its intention to liquidate its tax existence. The form should be filed within 30 days after the owners (board of directors) resolve to liquidate the corporation.

---

[42]§355.

## Tax Consequences to the Shareholders in a Complete Liquidation

The tax consequences to the shareholders in a complete liquidation depend on the shareholder's (1) identity and (2) ownership percentage in the corporation. In general, all *noncorporate* shareholders receiving liquidating distributions have a fully taxable transaction.[43] The shareholders treat the property received as in "full payment in exchange for the stock" transferred. The shareholder computes capital gain or loss by subtracting the stock's tax basis from the money and fair market value of property received in return. If a shareholder assumes the corporation's liabilities on property received as a liquidating distribution, the amount realized in the computation of gain or loss is reduced by the amount of the liabilities assumed. The shareholder's tax basis in the property received equals the property's fair market value.

---

**Example 19-25**

As a result of the complete liquidation of 360 Air, Ginny received cash and an interest in the building and land valued at $50,000, representing her 10 percent ownership of the net fair market value of the company ($500,000). Her tax basis in the 360 Air stock is $60,000.

What amount of gain or loss will Ginny *realize* on the exchange of her 360 Air stock for 360 Air assets?
**Answer:** $10,000 net capital loss ($50,000 − $60,000).

What amount of loss will Ginny *recognize* on the exchange? Assume Ginny has $40,000 of long-term capital gain from the sale of investment stock during the year.
**Answer:** $10,000. The entire amount is deductible to the extent of Ginny's capital gains.

What is Ginny's tax basis in her interest in the building and land?
**Answer:** $50,000. Ginny receives a tax basis in the assets she receives equal to their fair market values.

---

**Example 19-26**

As a result of the complete liquidation of 360 Air, Al received cash and an interest in the building and land valued at $250,000, representing his 50 percent ownership of the net fair market value of the company. His tax basis in the 360 Air stock was $100,000.

What amount of gain or loss will Al *realize* on the exchange of his 360 Air stock for 360 Air assets?
**Answer:** $150,000 net capital gain ($250,000 − $100,000).

What amount of gain will Al *recognize* on the exchange?
**Answer:** $150,000. The entire amount is taxable. The $150,000 gain he recognizes is a partial restoration of the gain he deferred in the formation of 360 Air.

What is Al's tax basis in the cash and assets he receives in the liquidation?
**Answer:** $250,000. Al receives a tax basis in the assets he receives equal to their fair market values.

---

**Example 19-27**

As a result of the complete liquidation of 360 Air, Jim received cash and an interest in the building and land valued at $262,000, representing his 40 percent ownership. He also assumed the $62,000 remaining mortgage, which decreased his amount realized to $200,000. His tax basis in 360 Air is
(*continued on page 19-36...*)

---

[43]§331.

> $240,000, an amount equal to the cash he contributed when the corporation was formed. Jim has $100,000 of long-term capital gain from the sale of investments during the year.
>
> What amount of gain or loss will Jim *realize* on the exchange of his 360 Air stock for 360 Air assets?
> **Answer:** $40,000 net capital loss ($200,000 − $240,000).
>
> What amount of loss will Jim *recognize* on the exchange?
> **Answer:** $40,000.
>
> What is Jim's tax basis in the cash and assets he receives in the liquidation?
> **Answer:** $262,000. Jim receives a tax basis in the assets he receives equal to their fair market values.

*Corporate* shareholders owning 80 percent or more of the stock (voting power and value) of the liquidating corporation do not recognize gain or loss on the receipt of liquidating distributions.[44] This nonrecognition treatment is mandatory. The tax basis in the property transferred carries over to the recipient.[45] This deferral provision allows a group of corporations under common control to reorganize their organizational structure without tax consequences.

## Example 19-28

> **What if:** Suppose 360 Air was a 100 percent owned subsidiary of SCR, and SCR liquidated the company into itself. SCR has a tax basis in its 360 Air stock of $300,000. The total fair market value of 360 Air's assets is $562,000, and SCR will assume 360 Air's liabilities of $62,000. The amount realized by SCR in the liquidation is $500,000 ($562,000 − $62,000).
>
> What amount of gain or loss will SCR *realize* on the complete liquidation of 360 Air stock for 360 Air assets?
> **Answer:** $200,000 net capital gain ($500,000 − $300,000)
>
> What amount of gain will SCR *recognize* on the exchange?
> **Answer:** $0. The gain is not recognized because SCR owns 80 percent or more of 360 Air.
>
> What is SCR's tax basis in the cash and assets it receives in the liquidation?
> **Answer:** A carryover of 360 Air's tax basis in the assets and liabilities.

## Tax Consequences to the Liquidating Corporation in a Complete Liquidation

The tax consequences to the liquidating corporation depend on the tax treatment applied to the shareholder to whom the property was distributed.

**Taxable Liquidating Distributions**    The liquidating corporation recognizes all gains and certain losses on taxable distributions of property to shareholders.[46] The liquidating corporation does not recognize *loss* if the property is distributed to a *related party* and either (1) the distribution is non-pro rata, or (2) the asset distributed is *disqualified property*.[47] A *related person* generally is defined as a shareholder who

[44]§332(a).
[45]§334(b)(1).
[46]§336(a).
[47]§336(d)(1).

owns more than 50 percent of the stock of the liquidating corporation. *Disqualified property* is property acquired within five years of the date of distribution in a tax-deferred §351 transaction or as a nontaxable contribution to capital.

**Example 19-29**

360 Air made taxable liquidating distributions to Jim, Ginny, and Al during the current year. Jim owns 50 percent of the stock, Ginny owns 10 percent, and Al owns 40 percent. Assume for purposes of this example that 360 Air made a pro rata distribution of all of the assets to its three shareholders. The company's tax accounting balance sheet at the time of the distribution is reproduced below:

| | FMV | Tax-Adjusted Basis | Difference |
|---|---|---|---|
| Cash | $200,000 | $200,000 | |
| Receivables | 2,000 | 2,000 | |
| Inventory | 10,000 | 12,000 | $ (2,000) |
| Building | 150,000 | 48,000 | 102,000 |
| Land | 200,000 | 100,000 | 100,000 |
| Total | $562,000 | $362,000 | $200,000 |

What amount of gain or loss does 360 Air recognize as a result of the distribution?

**Answer:** $200,000. 360 Air recognizes all gains and losses on the distribution of its assets in the following amounts and character:

| | Gain (Loss) Recognized | Character |
|---|---|---|
| Inventory | $ (2,000) | Ordinary |
| Building | 102,000 | Ordinary (§291) and §1231 |
| Land | 100,000 | §1231 |
| Net gain | $200,000 | |

**Example 19-30**

*What if:* Assume Jim owned 60 percent of the stock, and 360 Air distributed all of the inventory to Jim in a non-pro rata distribution. The company's tax accounting balance sheet at the time of the distribution is reproduced below:

| | FMV | Tax-Adjusted Basis | Difference |
|---|---|---|---|
| Cash | $200,000 | $200,000 | |
| Receivables | 2,000 | 2,000 | |
| Inventory | 10,000 | 12,000 | $ (2,000) |
| Building | 150,000 | 48,000 | 102,000 |
| Land | 200,000 | 100,000 | 100,000 |
| Total | $562,000 | $362,000 | $200,000 |

What amount of gain or loss does 360 Air recognize as a result of the distribution?

**Answer:** $202,000 gain. 360 Air recognizes all gains but cannot recognize the inventory loss because the distribution is non-pro rata and the loss property is distributed to a related person (Jim owns more than 50 percent of the stock).

(*continued on page 19-38...*)

| | Gain (Loss) Recognized | Character |
|---|---|---|
| Inventory | $   0 | |
| Building | 102,000 | Ordinary (§291) and §1231 |
| Land | 100,000 | §1231 |
| Net gain | $202,000 | |

**What if:** Assume Jim owned 60 percent of the stock, and 360 Air distributed all of the inventory to Ginny in a non-pro rata distribution. What amount of gain or loss does 360 Air recognize as a result of the distribution?

**Answer:** $200,000. 360 Air recognizes all of the gain can now recognize the $2,000 loss on the distribution of the inventory because the property was not distributed to a related person.

A second loss disallowance rule applies to built-in loss that arises with respect to property acquired in a §351 transaction or as a contribution to capital. A loss on the complete liquidation of such property is not recognized if the property distributed was acquired in a §351 transaction or as a contribution to capital, and a *principal purpose* of the contribution was to recognize a loss by the liquidating corporation.[48] This rule prevents a built-in loss existing at the time of the distribution (basis in excess of fair market value) from being recognized by treating the basis of the property distributed as being its fair market value at the time it was contributed to the corporation. This prohibited tax avoidance purpose is presumed if the property transfer occurs within two years of the liquidation. This presumption can be overcome if the corporation can show that there was a corporate business purpose for contributing the property to the corporation. This provision is designed as an *anti-stuffing* provision to prevent shareholders from contributing property with built-in losses to a corporation shortly before a liquidation to offset gain property distributed in the liquidation. Earlier in this chapter you learned that Congress added a similar built-in loss disallowance rule that applies to §351 transfers.[49] Under this provision, if the *aggregate* adjusted tax basis of property transferred to a corporation by a shareholder in a §351 transfer exceeds the aggregate fair market value of the assets, the aggregate tax basis of the assets in the hands of the transferee corporation cannot exceed their aggregate fair market value. The loss disallowance rule that relates to liquidating distributions of built-in loss property received in a §351 transaction applies on an asset by asset basis to those assets that retained their built-in loss when contributed to the corporation.

**Example 19-31**

**What if:** Suppose Al transferred a building and land to 360 Air in return for 50 percent of the corporation's stock (50 shares) in a transaction that qualified under §351. The property transferred to the corporation had the following fair market values and tax-adjusted bases:

| | FMV | Tax-Adjusted Basis |
|---|---|---|
| Building | $  75,000 | $100,000 |
| Land | 200,000 | 100,000 |
| Total | $275,000 | $200,000 |

(*continued on page 19-39...*)

[48]§336(d)(2).
[49]§362(e)(2).

In this case, the aggregate fair market value of the property transferred to the corporation exceeds the aggregate tax-adjusted basis of the property. As a result, the building will retain its carryover basis of $100,000 and subsequent built-in loss of $25,000.

If the building and land are distributed to Al in complete liquidation of his ownership of 360 Air stock within two years of the §351 transaction, will 360 Air be able to deduct the $25,000 loss on the distribution of the building?

**Answer:** It depends. Because the liquidating distribution is made within two years of the §351 transaction, the presumption is that Al contributed the property to 360 Air for tax avoidance purposes (that is, to allow the corporation to deduct the loss). The corporation can rebut this presumption by demonstrating that the contribution of the property by Al had a corporate business purpose at the time of the §351 transaction.

**Nontaxable Liquidating Distributions**  The liquidating corporation does not recognize gain or loss on tax-free distributions of property to an 80 percent corporate shareholder.[50] If any one of the shareholders receives tax deferral in the liquidation, the liquidating corporation cannot recognize any *loss,* even on distributions to shareholders who receive taxable distributions.[51] There are exceptions to this rule that are beyond the scope of this text.

**Example 19-32**

*What if:* Assume 360 Air was a 100 percent owned subsidiary of SCR, and SCR liquidated the company into itself. SCR has a tax basis in its 360 Air stock of $300,000. The company's tax accounting balance sheet at the time of the distribution is reproduced below:

|  | FMV | Tax-Adjusted Basis | Difference |
|---|---|---|---|
| Cash | $200,000 | $200,000 |  |
| Receivables | 2,000 | 2,000 |  |
| Inventory | 10,000 | 12,000 | $ (2,000) |
| Building | 150,000 | 48,000 | 102,000 |
| Land | 200,000 | 100,000 | 100,000 |
| Total | $562,000 | $362,000 | $200,000 |

What amount of gain or loss does 360 Air *recognize* as a result of the distribution?

**Answer:** $0. 360 Air does not recognize any gain or loss on the distribution because SCR is not taxed on the liquidating distribution.

*What if:* Suppose 360 Air was 80 percent owned by SCR and 20 percent owned by Jim. 360 Air distributed the inventory plus $190,000 to Jim in complete liquidation of his stock. Can 360 Air recognize the $2,000 inventory loss?

**Answer:** No. 360 Air cannot recognize the loss even though Jim is not a related party and has a taxable distribution. When one shareholder is not taxable on a liquidating distribution (SCR), the liquidating corporation cannot recognize any losses on the distribution of property to any shareholder.

Liquidation-related expenses, including the cost of preparing and effectuating a plan of complete liquidation, are deductible by the liquidating corporation on its final Form 1120. Deferred or capitalized expenditures such as organizational expenditures also are deductible on the final tax return.

[50]§337(a).
[51]§336(d)(3).

# CONCLUSION

In this chapter we discussed some of the important tax rules that apply during the life cycle of a C corporation. As the storyline indicates, forming a corporation generally does not create any tax to any of the parties to the transaction. Gain or loss realized by the shareholders on the transfer of property to the corporation is deferred until a later date, either when the shareholder sells his ownership interest or the corporation liquidates. Subsequent acquisitions of new businesses or dispositions of existing businesses also can be achieved in a tax-deferred manner. However, failure to meet all of the requirements can convert a tax-deferred transaction into a taxable transaction. A complete liquidation of a corporation generally is a fully taxable transaction to the shareholders and the liquidating corporation, except in the case where a subsidiary is liquidated into its parent corporation.

## SUMMARY

**LO1**  Recall the general tax rules that apply to property transactions.

- A person realizes gain or loss as a result of engaging in a transaction, which is defined as an exchange of property rights with another person.
- Gain or loss realized is computed by subtracting the tax-adjusted basis of property transferred in the exchange from the amount realized in the exchange.
- The amount realized is computed as cash received plus the fair market value of other property received plus any liabilities assumed by the transferee on the property transferred, reduced by selling expenses and any liabilities assumed by the transferor on property received in the exchange.
- The general tax rule is that gain or loss realized is recognized (included in the computation of taxable income) unless a specific tax rule exempts the gain or loss from being recognized (permanently) or defers such recognition until a future date.

**LO2**  Compute the tax consequences to the parties to a tax-deferred corporate formation.

- Section 351 applies to transactions in which one or more persons transfer property to a corporation in return for stock, and immediately after the transfer, these same persons control the corporation to which they transferred the property.
- If a transaction meets these requirements, the transferors of property (shareholders) do not recognize (defer) gain or loss realized on the transfer of the property to the corporation.
  - Shareholders contributing property to a corporation in a §351 transaction compute gain or loss realized by subtracting the tax-adjusted basis of the property they contribute to the corporation from the fair market value of the consideration they receive in return (amount realized).
  - Gain, but not loss, is recognized when property other than the corporation's stock (boot) is received in the exchange.
  - Gain is recognized in an amount equal to the *lesser of* the gain realized or the fair market value of boot received.
  - The tax basis of stock received in the exchange equals the tax basis of the property transferred, less any liabilities assumed by the corporation on the property contributed (substituted basis).
  - The shareholder's stock basis is increased by any gain recognized and reduced by the fair market value of any boot received.
- The corporation receiving property for its stock in a §351 exchange does not recognize (excludes) gain or loss realized on the transfer.
  - The tax basis of the property received by the corporation equals the property's tax basis in the transferor's hands (carryover basis).
  - The asset's tax basis is increased by any gain recognized by the shareholder on the transfer of the property to the corporation.

Identify the different forms of taxable and tax-deferred acquisitions.

- Corporations can be acquired in taxable asset or stock purchases.
- Corporations can be acquired in tax-deferred asset or stock purchases.
- To be tax-deferred, an acquisition must meet certain IRC and judicial requirements to be a reorganization.
  - The judicial requirements, now summarized in the regulations, require continuity of interest, continuity of business enterprise, and business purpose.
- In a Type A tax-deferred acquisition, the target corporation's assets and liabilities are merged into the acquiring corporation (stock-for-assets exchange).
  - Type A acquisitions involving publicly traded corporations often use an acquisition subsidiary (triangular merger) to acquire the target corporation's assets and liabilities.
- In a Type B tax-deferred acquisition, the shareholders of the target corporation exchange their stock for stock of the acquiring corporation (stock-for-stock exchange).
  - Type B acquisitions prohibit the use of cash in the exchange.

Compute the tax consequences to the parties to a corporate acquisition.

- Shareholders participating in a taxable asset or stock transaction compute gain or loss realized by subtracting the tax-adjusted basis of the stock they surrender to the acquiring corporation from the fair market value of the consideration they receive in the exchange.
- Shareholders participating in a tax-deferred reorganization defer gain and loss realized in the exchange unless cash (boot) is received.
  - Shareholders receiving boot recognize gain, but not loss, in an amount equal to the lesser of the gain realized or the fair market value of the boot received.
- The corporation does not recognize gain on the distribution of its own stock in exchange for property in a reorganization.
- The stock received in return for stock in a tax-deferred reorganization has a tax basis equal to the tax basis of the stock surrendered in the exchange (substituted basis).
- The shareholder's stock basis is increased by any gain recognized and reduced by cash or other boot received.
- The assets transferred to the corporation in a tax-deferred reorganization carry over the tax basis of the shareholders contributing the property (carryover basis).

Calculate the basic tax law consequences that apply to the parties to a complete liquidation of a corporation.

- Noncorporate shareholders receiving a distribution in complete liquidation of their corporation recognize gain and (usually) loss in the exchange.
- Tax deferral is extended to corporate shareholders owning 80 percent or more of the liquidating corporation.
- The liquidating corporation recognizes gain and (usually) loss on the distribution of property to those shareholders who are taxable on the distribution.
- The liquidating corporation cannot deduct losses on property distributed in the following three situations:
  - The loss property is distributed to a related person and is non-pro rata.
  - The loss property was contributed to the corporation in a §351 transaction and the principle purpose of the contribution was tax avoidance.
  - One of the persons receiving a liquidating distribution was not taxable on the distribution (an 80 percent or more corporate shareholder).
- The liquidating corporation does not recognize gain or loss on the distribution of property to a corporate shareholder that is not taxable on the distribution.
- The tax basis of each asset received by the shareholder in a taxable complete liquidation equals the asset's fair market value on the date of the distribution.
- The tax basis of each asset received by an 80 percent or more corporate shareholder in a tax-deferred complete liquidation carries over from the liquidating corporation.

# KEY TERMS

adjusted tax basis (19-3)

amount realized (19-3)

boot (19-6)

bright line tests (19-27)

carryover basis (19-14)

consolidation (19-27)

continuity of business enterprise
(COBE) (19-27)

continuity of interest
(COI) (19-27)

contribution to capital (19-18)

merger (19-27)

person (19-5)

realization (19-3)

recognition (19-4)

reorganization (19-26)

section 338 election (19-25)

section 338(h)(10)
election (19-25)

stock-for-stock
acquisition (19-31)

substituted basis (19-9)

tax accounting balance
sheet (19-23)

# DISCUSSION QUESTIONS

1. **(LO1)** Discuss the difference between gain realization and gain recognition in a property transaction.

2. **(LO1)** What information must a taxpayer gather to determine the *amount realized* in a property transaction?

3. **(LO1)** Distinguish between exclusion and deferral as it relates to a property transaction.

4. **(LO1)** Discuss how a taxpayer's tax basis in property received in a property transaction will be affected based on whether a property transaction results in gain exclusions or gain deferral.

5. **(LO1)** What information must a taxpayer gather to determine the *tax-adjusted basis* of property exchanged in a property transaction?

6. **(LO2)** Why does Congress allow tax deferral on the formation of a corporation?

7. **(LO2)** List the key statutory requirements that must be met before a corporate formation is tax-deferred under §351.

8. **(LO2)** What is the definition of *control* for purposes of §351? Why does Congress require the shareholders to control a corporation to receive tax deferral?

9. **(LO2)** What is a *substituted basis* as it relates to stock received in exchange for property in a §351 transaction? What is the purpose of attaching a substituted basis to stock received in a §351 transaction?

10. **(LO2)** True or False. The receipt of boot by a shareholder in a §351 transaction causes the transaction to be fully taxable. Explain.

11. **(LO2)** True or False. A corporation's assumption of shareholder liabilities will always constitute boot in a §351 transaction. Explain.

12. **(LO2)** How does the tax treatment differ in cases where liabilities are assumed with a tax avoidance purpose versus where liabilities assumed exceed basis? When would this distinction cause a difference in the tax treatment of the transactions?

13. **(LO2)** What is a *carryover basis* as it relates to property received by a corporation in a §351 transaction? What is the purpose of attaching a carryover basis to property received in a §351 transaction?

14. **(LO2)** Under what circumstances does property received by a corporation in a §351 transaction not receive a carryover basis? What is the reason for this rule?

15. **(LO2)** How does a corporation depreciate an asset received in a §351 transaction in which no gain or loss is recognized by the transferor of the property?

16. **(LO2)** True or False. A shareholder receives the same tax consequences whether property is contributed to a corporation in a §351 transaction or as a capital contribution. Explain.

17. **(LO2)** Why might a corporation prefer to characterize an instrument as debt rather than equity for tax purposes? Are the holders of the instrument indifferent as to its characterization for tax purposes?

18. **(LO2)** Under what conditions is it advantageous for a shareholder to hold §1244 stock? Why did Congress bestow these tax benefits on holders of such stock?

19. **(LO3)** Why does the acquiring corporation usually prefer to buy the target corporation's assets directly in an acquisition?

20. **(LO3)** Why do the shareholders of the target corporation usually prefer to sell the stock of the target corporation to the acquiring corporation?

21. **(LO3)** What is the Congressional purpose for allowing tax deferral on transactions that meet the definition of a corporate reorganization?

22. **(LO3)** Why do publicly traded corporations use a triangular form of Type A reorganization in acquiring other corporations?

23. **(LO3)** What are the key differences in the tax law requirements that apply to forward versus reverse triangular mergers?

24. **(LO3)** What are the key differences in the tax law requirements that apply to a Type A stock-for-assets acquisition versus a Type B stock-for-stock acquisition?

25. **(LO4)** How does the form of a regular §338 election compare and contrast to a §338(h)(10) election?

26. **(LO4)** What tax benefits does the buyer hope to obtain by making a §338 or §338(h)(10) election?

27. **(LO4)** What is the difference between the *inside tax basis* and the *outside tax basis* that results from an acquisition? Why is the distinction important?

28. **(LO4)** What is the presumption behind the continuity of ownership interest (COI) requirement in a tax-deferred acquisition? How do the target shareholders determine if COI is met in a Type A reorganization?

29. **(LO4)** W Corporation will acquire all of the assets and liabilities of Z Corporation in a Type A merger, after which W Corporation will sell off all of its assets and liabilities and focus solely on Z Corporation's business. True or False: The transaction will be taxable because W Corporation fails the *continuity of business enterprise test.* Explain.

30. **(LO4)** Compare how a shareholder computes her tax basis in stock received from the acquiring corporation in a straight Type A merger versus a Type B merger.

31. **(LO5)** True or False. All shareholders receive the same tax treatment in a complete liquidation of a corporation. Explain.

32. **(LO5)** True or False. A corporation recognizes all gains and losses on liquidating distributions of property to noncorporate shareholders. Explain.

33. **(LO5)** Under what circumstances does a corporate shareholder receive tax deferral in a complete liquidation?

34. **(LO5)** Under what circumstances will a liquidating corporation be allowed to recognize loss in a non-pro rata distribution?

35. **(LO5)** Compare and contrast the built-in loss duplication rule as it relates to §351 with the built-in loss disallowance rule as it applies to a complete liquidation.

## PROBLEMS

36. **(LO2)** Ramon incorporated his sole proprietorship by transferring inventory, a building, and land to the corporation in return for 100 percent of the corporation's stock. The property transferred to the corporation had the following fair market values and tax-adjusted bases:

|  | FMV | Tax-Adjusted Basis |
|---|---|---|
| Inventory | $ 10,000 | $ 4,000 |
| Building | 50,000 | 30,000 |
| Land | 100,000 | 50,000 |
| Total | $160,000 | $84,000 |

The fair market value of the corporation's stock received in the exchange equaled the fair market value of the assets transferred to the corporation by Ramon.

a. What amount of gain or loss does Ramon *realize* on the transfer of the property to his corporation?

b. What amount of gain or loss does Ramon *recognize* on the transfer of the property to his corporation?

c. What is Ramon's basis in the stock he receives in his corporation?

37. **(LO2)** Carla incorporated her sole proprietorship by transferring inventory, a building, and land to the corporation in return for 100 percent of the corporation's stock. The property transferred to the corporation had the following fair market values and tax-adjusted bases:

|  | FMV | Tax-Adjusted Basis |
|---|---|---|
| Inventory | $ 20,000 | $ 10,000 |
| Building | 150,000 | 100,000 |
| Land | 250,000 | 300,000 |
| Total | $420,000 | $410,000 |

The corporation also assumed a mortgage of $120,000 attached to the building and land. The fair market value of the corporation's stock received in the exchange was $300,000.

a. What amount of gain or loss does Carla *realize* on the transfer of the property to her corporation?

b. What amount of gain or loss does Carla *recognize* on the transfer of the property to her corporation?

c. What is Carla's basis in the stock she receives in her corporation?

■ **planning**

d. Would you advise Carla to transfer the building and land to the corporation? What tax benefits might she and the corporation receive if she kept the building and land and leased it to the corporation?

38. **(LO2)** Ivan incorporated his sole proprietorship by transferring inventory, a building, and land to the corporation in return for 100 percent of the corporation's

stock. The property transferred to the corporation had the following fair market values and tax-adjusted bases:

| | FMV | Tax-Adjusted Basis |
|---|---|---|
| Inventory | $ 10,000 | $15,000 |
| Building | 50,000 | 40,000 |
| Land | 60,000 | 30,000 |
| Total | $120,000 | $85,000 |

The fair market value of the corporation's stock received in the exchange equaled the fair market value of the assets transferred to the corporation by Ivan. The transaction met the requirements to be tax-deferred under §351.

a. What amount of gain or loss does Ivan *realize* on the transfer of the property to his corporation?

b. What amount of gain or loss does Ivan *recognize* on the transfer of the property to his corporation?

c. What is Ivan's basis in the stock he receives in his corporation?

d. What is the corporation's tax-adjusted basis in each of the assets received in the exchange?

e. Would the stock held by Ivan qualify as §1244 stock? Why would this fact be important if he sold his stock at a loss at some future date?

39. **(LO2)** Zhang incorporated her sole proprietorship by transferring inventory, a building, and land to the corporation in return for 100 percent of the corporation's stock. The property transferred to the corporation had the following fair market values and tax-adjusted bases:

| | FMV | Tax-Adjusted Basis |
|---|---|---|
| Inventory | $ 20,000 | $ 10,000 |
| Building | 150,000 | 100,000 |
| Land | 230,000 | 300,000 |
| Total | $400,000 | $410,000 |

The corporation also assumed a mortgage of $100,000 attached to the building and land. The fair market value of the corporation's stock received in the exchange was $300,000. The transaction met the requirements to be tax-deferred under §351.

a. What amount of gain or loss does Zhang *realize* on the transfer of the property to her corporation?

b. What amount of gain or loss does Zhang *recognize* on the transfer of the property to her corporation?

c. What is Zhang's tax basis in the stock she receives in the exchange?

d. What is the corporation's tax-adjusted basis in each of the assets received in the exchange?

Assume the corporation assumed a mortgage of $500,000 attached to the building and land. Assume the fair market value of the building is now $250,000 and the fair market value of the land is $530,000. The fair market value of the stock remains $300,000.

e. How much, if any, gain or loss does Zhang recognize on the exchange assuming the revised facts?

f. What is Zhang's tax basis in the stock she receives in the exchange?

g. What is the corporation's tax-adjusted basis in each of the assets received in the exchange?

40. **(LO2)** Sam and Devon agree to go into business together selling college-licensed clothing. According to the agreement, Sam will contribute inventory valued at $100,000 in return for 80 percent of the stock in the corporation. Sam's tax basis in the inventory is $60,000. Devon will receive 20 percent of the stock in return for providing accounting services to the corporation (these qualified as organizational expenditures). The accounting services are valued at $25,000.

   a. What amount of income gain or loss does Sam *realize* on the formation of the corporation? What amount, if any, does he *recognize?*

   b. What is Sam's tax basis in the stock he receives in return for his contribution of property to the corporation?

   c. What amount of income gain or loss does Devon *realize* on the formation of the corporation? What amount, if any, does he *recognize?*

   d. What is Devon's tax basis in the stock he receives in return for his contribution of services to the corporation?

   Assume Devon received 25 percent of the stock in the corporation in return for his services.

   e. What amount of income gain or loss does Sam *recognize* on the formation of the corporation?

   f. What is Sam's tax basis in the stock he receives in return for his contribution of property to the corporation?

   g. What amount of income gain or loss does Devon *recognize* on the formation of the corporation?

   h. What is Devon's tax basis in the stock he receives in return for his contribution of services to the corporation?

■ **planning**     41. **(LO2)** What tax advice could you give Sam and Devon to change the tax consequences you identified that relate to Sam in problem 40e?

42. **(LO2)** Ron and Hermione formed Wizard Corporation on January 2. Ron contributed cash of $200,000 in return for 50 percent of the corporation's stock. Hermione contributed a building and land with the following fair market values and tax-adjusted bases in return for 50 percent of the corporation's stock:

| | FMV | Tax-Adjusted Basis |
|---|---|---|
| Building | $ 75,000 | $ 20,000 |
| Land | 175,000 | 80,000 |
| Total | $250,000 | $100,000 |

   To equalize the exchange, Wizard Corporation paid Hermione $50,000 in addition to her stock.

   a. What amount of gain or loss does Ron *realize* on the formation of the corporation? What amount, if any, does he *recognize?*

   b. What is Ron's tax basis in the stock he receives in return for his contribution of property to the corporation?

   c. What amount of gain or loss does Hermione *realize* on the formation of the corporation? What amount, if any, does she *recognize?*

   d. What is Hermione's tax basis in the stock she receives in return for her contribution of property to the corporation?

   e. What tax-adjusted basis does Wizard Corporation take in the land and building received from Hermione?

Assume Hermione's tax-adjusted basis in the land was $200,000.

f.  What amount of gain or loss does Hermione *realize* on the formation of the corporation? What amount, if any, does she *recognize?*

g.  What tax-adjusted basis does Wizard Corporation take in the land and building received from Hermione?

Assume Hermione's tax-adjusted basis in the land was $250,000.

h.  What amount of gain or loss does Hermione *realize* on the formation of the corporation? What amount, if any, does she *recognize?*

i.  What tax-adjusted basis does Wizard Corporation take in the land and building received from Hermione?

j.  What election can Hermione and Wizard Corporation make to allow Wizard Corporation to take a carryover basis in the land?

43. **(LO2)** On October 31, 2010, Jack O. Lantern incurred a $60,000 loss on the worthlessness of his stock in the Creepy Corporation (CC). The stock, which Jack purchased in 2005, met all of the §1244 stock requirements at the time of issue. In December 2010, Jack's wife Jill incurred a $75,000 loss on the sale of Eerie Corporation (EC) stock that she purchased in July 2005 and which also satisfied all of the §1244 stock requirements at the time of issue. Both corporations are operating companies.

■ **planning**

a.  How much of the losses incurred on the two stock sales can Jack and Jill deduct in 2010, assuming they do not have capital gains in the current or prior years?

b.  Assuming they did not engage in any other property transactions in 2010, how much of a net capital loss carryover to 2011 will Jack and Jill have?

c.  What would be the tax treatment for the losses if Jack and Jill reported only $60,000 of taxable income in 2010, excluding the securities transactions?

d.  What tax planning suggestions can you offer the Lanterns to increase the tax benefits of these losses?

44. **(LO2)** Breslin Inc. made a capital contribution of investment property to its 100 percent owned subsidiary, Crisler Company. The investment property had a fair market value of $3,000,000 and a tax basis to Breslin of $2,225,000.

a.  What are the tax consequences to Breslin Inc. on the contribution of the investment property to Crisler Company?

b.  What is the tax basis of the investment property to Crisler Company after the contribution to capital?

45. **(LO3)** On February 27, 2005, Federated Department Stores (Macy's) acquired The May Department Stores Company (Marshall Fields) in a tax-deferred acquisition. The Form 8-K describing the transaction was issued on February 28, 2005. You can access the Form 8-K at the company's Web site, www.federated-fds.com and accessing the company's SEC filings from its Investor Web site. Read "Item 1.01, Entry into a Material Definitive Agreement" and determine which form of merger was used to bring about the acquisition.

■ **research**

46. **(LO3)** On January 28, 2005, the Procter & Gamble Company acquired The Gillette Company in a tax-deferred acquisition. The Form 8-K describing the transaction was issued on January 28, 2005. You can access the Form 8-K at the company's Web site, www.pg.com and accessing the company's SEC filings. Read "Item 1.01, Entry into a Material Definitive Agreement" and determine which form of merger was used to effect the acquisition.

■ **research**

47. **(LO4)** Amy and Brian were investigating the acquisition of a tax accounting business, Bottom Line Inc. (BLI). As part of their discussions with the sole

shareholder of the corporation, Ernesto Young, they examined the company's tax accounting balance sheet. The relevant information is summarized as follows:

|  | FMV | Tax-Adjusted Basis | Appreciation |
|---|---|---|---|
| Cash | $ 10,000 | $ 10,000 | |
| Receivables | 15,000 | 15,000 | |
| Building | 100,000 | 50,000 | $ 50,000 |
| Land | 225,000 | 75,000 | 150,000 |
| Total | $350,000 | $150,000 | $200,000 |
| | | | |
| Payables | $ 18,000 | $ 18,000 | |
| Mortgage* | 112,000 | 112,000 | |
| Total | $130,000 | $130,000 | |

*The mortgage is attached to the building and land.

Ernesto was asking for $400,000 for the company. His tax basis in the BLI stock was $100,000. Included in the sales price was an unrecognized customer list valued at $100,000. The unallocated portion of the purchase price ($80,000) will be recorded as goodwill.

a. What amount of gain or loss does BLI recognize if the transaction is structured as a direct asset sale to Amy and Brian? What amount of corporate-level tax does BLI pay as a result of the transaction, assuming a tax rate of 34 percent?

b. What amount of gain or loss does Ernesto recognize if the transaction is structured as a direct asset sale to Amy and Brian, and BLI distributes the after-tax proceeds (computed in question a) to Ernesto in liquidation of his stock?

c. What are the tax benefits, if any, to Amy and Brian as a result of structuring the acquisition as a direct asset purchase?

48. **(LO4)** Using the same facts in problem 47, assume Ernesto agrees to sell his stock in BLI to Amy and Brian for $400,000.

a. What amount of gain or loss does BLI recognize if the transaction is structured as a stock sale to Amy and Brian? What amount of corporate-level tax does BLI pay as a result of the transaction, assuming a tax rate of 34 percent?

b. What amount of gain or loss does Ernesto recognize if the transaction is structured as a stock sale to Amy and Brian?

c. What are the tax benefits, if any, to Amy and Brian as a result of structuring the acquisition as a stock sale?

49. **(LO4)** Rather than purchase BLI directly (as in problems 47 and 48), Amy and Brian will have their corporation, Spartan Tax Services (STS), acquire the business from Ernesto in a tax-deferred Type A merger. Amy and Brian would like Ernesto to continue to run BLI, which he agreed to do if he could obtain an equity interest in STS. As part of the agreement, Amy and Brian propose to pay Ernesto $200,000 plus voting stock in STS worth $200,000. Ernesto will become a 10 percent shareholder in STS after the transaction.

a. Will the continuity of ownership interest (COI) requirements for a straight Type A merger be met? Explain.

b. What amount of gain or loss does BLI recognize if the transaction is structured as a Type A merger? What amount of corporate-level tax does BLI pay as a result of the transaction, assuming a tax rate of 34 percent?

c. What amount of gain or loss does Ernesto recognize if the transaction is structured as a Type A merger?

d. What is Ernesto's tax basis in the STS stock he receives in the exchange?

e. What are the tax bases of the BLI assets held by STS after the merger?

50. **(LO4)** Robert and Sylvia propose to have their corporation, Wolverine Universal (WU), acquire another corporation, EMU Inc., in a tax-deferred triangular Type A merger using an acquisition subsidiary of WU. The sole shareholder of EMU, Edie Eagle, will receive $225,000 plus $150,000 of WU voting stock in the transaction.

a. Can the transaction be structured as a forward triangular Type A merger? Explain why or why not.

b. Can the transaction be structured as a reverse triangular Type A merger? Explain why or why not.

51. **(LO4)** Robert and Sylvia propose to have their corporation, Wolverine Universal (WU), acquire another corporation, EMU Inc., in a stock-for-stock Type B acquisition. The sole shareholder of EMU, Edie Eagle, will receive $400,000 of WU voting stock in the transaction. Edie's tax basis in her EMU stock is $100,000.

a. What amount of gain or loss does Edie recognize if the transaction is structured as a stock-for-stock Type B acquisition?

b. What is Edie's tax basis in the WU stock she receives in the exchange?

c. What is the tax basis of the EMU stock held by WU after the exchange?

52. **(LO5)** Shauna and Danielle decided to liquidate their jointly owned corporation, Woodward Fashions Inc. (WFI). After liquidating its remaining inventory and paying off its remaining liabilities, WFI had the following tax accounting balance sheet:

|  | FMV | Tax-Adjusted Basis | Appreciation |
|---|---|---|---|
| Cash | $200,000 | $200,000 |  |
| Building | 50,000 | 10,000 | $ 40,000 |
| Land | 150,000 | 90,000 | 60,000 |
| Total | $400,000 | $300,000 | $100,000 |

Under the terms of the agreement, Shauna will receive the $200,000 cash in exchange for her 50 percent interest in WFI. Shauna's tax basis in her WFI stock is $50,000. Danielle will receive the building and land in exchange for her 50 percent interest in WFI. Danielle's tax basis in her WFI stock is $100,000.

a. What amount of gain or loss does WFI recognize in the complete liquidation?

b. What amount of gain or loss does Shauna recognize in the complete liquidation?

c. What amount of gain or loss does Danielle recognize in the complete liquidation?

d. What is Danielle's tax basis in the building and land after the complete liquidation?

53. **(LO5)** Tiffany and Carlos decided to liquidate their jointly owned corporation, Royal Oak Furniture (ROF). After liquidating its remaining inventory and paying off its remaining liabilities, ROF had the following tax accounting balance sheet:

|  | FMV | Tax-Adjusted Basis | Appreciation (Depreciation) |
|---|---|---|---|
| Cash | $200,000 | $200,000 | |
| Building | 50,000 | 10,000 | $ 40,000 |
| Land | 150,000 | 200,000 | (50,000) |
| Total | $400,000 | $410,000 | $(10,000) |

Under the terms of the agreement, Tiffany will receive the $200,000 cash in exchange for her 50 percent interest in ROF. Tiffany's tax basis in her ROF stock is $50,000. Carlos will receive the building and land in exchange for his 50 percent interest in ROF. His tax basis in the ROF stock is $100,000.

a. What amount of gain or loss does ROF recognize in the complete liquidation?

b. What amount of gain or loss does Tiffany recognize in the complete liquidation?

c. What amount of gain or loss does Carlos recognize in the complete liquidation?

d. What is Carlos's tax basis of the building and land after the complete liquidation?

Assume Tiffany owns 40 percent of the ROF stock and Carlos owns 60 percent. Tiffany will receive $160,000 in the liquidation and Carlos will receive the land and building plus $40,000.

e. What amount of gain or loss does ROF recognize in the complete liquidation?

f. What amount of gain or loss does Tiffany recognize in the complete liquidation?

g. What amount of gain or loss does Carlos recognize in the complete liquidation?

h. What is Carlos's tax basis in the building and land after the complete liquidation?

54. **(LO5)** Jefferson Millinery Inc. (JMI) decided to liquidate its wholly owned subsidiary, 8 Miles High Inc. (8MH). 8MH had the following tax accounting balance sheet:

|  | FMV | Tax-Adjusted Basis | Appreciation |
|---|---|---|---|
| Cash | $200,000 | $200,000 | |
| Building | 50,000 | 10,000 | $ 40,000 |
| Land | 150,000 | 90,000 | 60,000 |
| Total | $400,000 | $300,000 | $100,000 |

a. What amount of gain or loss does 8MH recognize in the complete liquidation?

b. What amount of gain or loss does JMI recognize in the complete liquidation?

c. What is JMI's tax basis in the building and land after the complete liquidation?

55. **(LO5)** Jefferson Millinery Inc. (JMI) decided to liquidate its wholly owned subsidiary, 8 Miles High Inc. (8MH). 8MH had the following tax accounting balance sheet:

| | FMV | Tax-Adjusted Basis | Appreciation |
|---|---|---|---|
| Cash | $200,000 | $200,000 | |
| Building | 50,000 | 10,000 | $ 40,000 |
| Land | 150,000 | 200,000 | (50,000) |
| Total | $400,000 | $410,000 | $(10,000) |

a. What amount of gain or loss does 8MH recognize in the complete liquidation?

b. What amount of gain or loss does JMI recognize in the complete liquidation?

c. What is JMI's tax basis in the building and land after the complete liquidation?

# COMPREHENSIVE PROBLEMS

56. Several years ago, your client, Brooks Robinson, started an office cleaning service. His business was very successful, owing much to his legacy as the greatest defensive third baseman in major league history and his nickname, "The Human Vacuum Cleaner." Brooks operated his business as a sole proprietorship and used the cash method of accounting. Brooks was advised by his attorney that it is too risky to operate his business as a sole proprietorship and that he should incorporate to limit his liability. Brooks has come to you for advice on the tax implications of incorporation. His balance sheet is presented below. Under the terms of the incorporation, Brooks would transfer the assets to the corporation in return for 100 percent of the company's common stock. The corporation would also assume the company's liabilities (payables and mortgage).

| Balance Sheet | | |
|---|---|---|
| | Tax Basis | FMV |
| **Assets** | | |
| Accounts receivable | $ 0 | $ 5,000 |
| Cleaning equipment (net) | 25,000 | 20,000 |
| Building | 50,000 | 75,000 |
| Land | 25,000 | 50,000 |
| Total assets | $100,000 | $150,000 |
| **Liabilities** | | |
| Accounts payable | $ 0 | $ 10,000 |
| Salaries payable | 0 | 5,000 |
| Mortgage on land and building | 35,000 | 35,000 |
| Total liabilities | $ 35,000 | $ 50,000 |

a. How much gain or loss does Brooks realize on the transfer of each asset to the corporation?

b. How much, if any, gain or loss does he recognize (on a per asset basis)?

c. How much gain or loss, if any, must the corporation recognize on the receipt of the assets of the sole proprietorship in exchange for the corporation's stock?

d. What basis does Brooks have in the corporation's stock?

e. What is the corporation's tax basis in each asset it receives from Brooks?

f. How would you answer question b if Brooks had taken back a 10-year note worth $25,000 plus stock worth $75,000 plus the liability assumption?

g. Will Brooks be able to transfer the accounts receivable to the corporation and have the corporation recognize the income when the receivable is collected?

h. Brooks was depreciating the equipment (200 percent declining balance) and building (straight-line) using MACRS when it was held inside the proprietorship. How will the corporation depreciate the equipment and building? Assume Brooks owned the equipment for four years (seven-year property) and the building for six years.

i. Will the corporation be able to deduct the liabilities when paid? Will it matter which accounting method (cash or accrual) the corporation uses?

j. Would you advise Brooks to transfer the land and building to the corporation? What other tax strategy might you suggest to Brooks with respect to the realty?

57. Your client, Midwest Products Inc. (MPI), is a closely held, calendar-year, accrual-method corporation located in Fowlerville, Michigan. MPI has two operating divisions. One division manufactures lawn and garden furniture and decorative objects (furniture division), while the other division manufactures garden tools and hardware (tool division). MPI's single class of voting common stock is owned as follows:

|  | Shares | Tax Basis | FMV |
|---|---|---|---|
| Iris Green | 300 | $2,000,000 | $3,000,000 |
| Rose Ruby | 100 | 1,200,000 | 1,000,000 |
| Lily White | 100 | 800,000 | 1,000,000 |
| Totals | 500 | $4,000,000 | $5,000,000 |

The three shareholders are unrelated.

Outdoor Living Company (OLC), a publicly held, calendar-year corporation doing business in several midwestern states, has approached MPI about acquiring its furniture division. OLC has no interest in acquiring the tool division, however. OLC's management has several strong business reasons for the acquisition, the most important of which is to expand the company's market into Michigan. Iris, Rose, and Lily are amenable to the acquisition provided it can be accomplished in a tax-deferred manner.

OLC has proposed the following transaction for acquiring MPI's furniture division. On April 30, 2009, OLC will create a 100 percent owned subsidiary, OLC Acquisition Inc (OLC-A). OLC will transfer to the subsidiary 60,000 shares of OLC voting common stock and $2,000,000. The current fair market value of the OLC voting stock is $50 per share ($3,000,000 in total). Each of the three MPI shareholders will receive a pro rata amount of OLC stock and cash.

As part of the agreement, MPI will sell the tool division before the acquisition, after which MPI will merge into OLC-A under Michigan and Ohio state laws (a forward triangular Type A merger). Pursuant to the merger agreement, OLC-A will acquire all of MPI's assets, including 100 percent of the cash received from the sale of the tool division ($2,000,000), and will assume all of MPI's liabilities. The cash from the sale of the tool division will be used to modernize and upgrade much of the furniture division's production facilities. OLC's management is convinced that the cash infusion, coupled with new management, will make MPI's furniture business profitable. OLC management has no plans to liquidate OLC-A into OLC at any time subsequent to the merger. After the merger, OLC-A will be renamed Michigan Garden Furniture Inc.

a. Determine whether the proposed transaction meets the requirements to qualify as a tax-deferred forward triangular Type A merger. Consult Rev. Rul. 88-48 and Rev. Rul. 2001-25 in thinking about the premerger sale of the tool division assets.

b. Could the proposed transaction qualify as a reverse triangular Type A merger if OLC-A merged into MPI? If not, how would the transaction have to be restructured to meet the requirements to be a reverse triangular merger?

58. Rex and Felix are the sole shareholders of the Dogs and Cats Corporation (DCC). After several years of operations, they decided to liquidate the corporation and operate the business as a partnership. Rex and Felix hired a lawyer to draw up the legal papers to dissolve the corporation, but they need some tax advice from you, their trusted accountant. They are hoping you will find a way for them to liquidate the corporation without incurring any corporate-level tax liability.

The DCC's tax accounting balance sheet at the date of liquidation is as follows:

| | Tax Basis | FMV |
|---|---|---|
| **Assets** | | |
| Cash | $ 30,000 | $ 30,000 |
| Accounts receivable | 10,000 | 10,000 |
| Inventory | 10,000 | 20,000 |
| Equipment | 30,000 | 20,000 |
| Building | 15,000 | 30,000 |
| Land | 5,000 | 40,000 |
| Total assets | $100,000 | $150,000 |
| | | |
| **Liabilities** | | |
| Accounts payable | | $ 5,000 |
| Mortgage payable–Building | | 10,000 |
| Mortgage payable–Land | | 10,000 |
| Total liabilities | | $ 25,000 |
| | | |
| **Shareholders' Equity** | | |
| Common stock–Rex (80%) | $ 60,000 | $100,000 |
| Common stock–Felix (20%) | 30,000 | 25,000 |
| Total shareholders' equity | $ 90,000 | $125,000 |

a. Compute the gain or loss recognized by Rex, Felix, and DCC on a complete liquidation of the corporation assuming each shareholder receives a pro rata distribution of the corporation's assets and assumes a pro rata amount of the liabilities.

b. Compute the gain or loss recognized by Rex, Felix, and DCC on a complete liquidation of the corporation assuming Felix receives $25,000 in cash and Rex receives the remainder of the assets and assumes all of the liabilities.

Assume Felix received the accounts receivable and equipment and assumed the accounts payable.

c. Will Felix recognize any income when he collects the accounts receivable?

d. Will Felix be able to take a deduction when he pays the accounts payable?

Assume Rex is a corporate shareholder of DCC.

e. Compute the gain or loss recognized by Rex, Felix, and DCC on a complete liquidation of the corporation assuming each shareholder receives a pro rata distribution of the corporation's assets and assumes a pro rata amount of the liabilities.

f. Compute the gain or loss recognized by Rex, Felix, and DCC on a complete liquidation of the corporation assuming Felix receives $25,000 in cash and Rex receives the remainder of the assets and assumes all of the liabilities.

Assume the equipment was contributed by Rex to DCC in a §351 transaction two months prior to the liquidation. At the time of the contribution, the property's fair market value was $25,000.

g. Would the tax result change if the property was contributed one year ago? Two years ago? Three years ago?

# Forming and Operating Partnerships

## Learning Objectives

**Upon completing this chapter, you should be able to:**

**LO 1** Determine whether a flow-through entity is taxed as a partnership or S corporation and distinguish the entity approach from the aggregate approach for taxing partnerships.

**LO 2** Resolve tax issues applicable to partnership formations and other acquisitions of partnership interests, including gain recognition to partners and tax basis for partners and partnerships.

**LO 3** Determine the appropriate accounting periods and methods for partnerships.

**LO 4** Calculate and characterize a partnership's ordinary business income or loss and its separately stated items and demonstrate how to report these items to partners.

**LO 5** Explain the importance of a partner's tax basis and the adjustments that affect it.

**LO 6** Apply the basis, at-risk, and passive activity loss limits to losses from partnerships.

### Storyline Summary

**Nicole Johnson**

| | |
|---|---|
| *Location:* | Salt Lake City, Utah |
| *Status:* | Managing member of Color Comfort Sheets, LLC |
| *Filing status:* | Married to Tom Johnson |
| *Marginal tax rate:* | 35 percent unless otherwise stated |

**Sarah Walker**

| | |
|---|---|
| *Location:* | Salt Lake City, Utah |
| *Status:* | Managing member of Color Comfort Sheets, LLC |
| *Filing status:* | Married to Blaine Walker |
| *Marginal tax rate:* | 28 percent unless otherwise stated |

**Chanzz Inc.**

| | |
|---|---|
| *Location:* | Salt Lake City, Utah |
| *Business:* | Managing sports franchises |
| *Status:* | Nonmanaging member of Color Comfort Sheets, LLC |
| *Filing status:* | C Corporation with a June 30 year-end |
| *Marginal tax rate:* | 35 percent |

In Chapter 15, we introduced you to Nicole Johnson, who decided to turn her sheet-making hobby into a full-time business called Color Comfort Sheets (CCS). Early in 2009, after deciding to organize her new enterprise as a limited liability company (LLC), she turned her attention to raising capital for the business from other investors and a bank loan. Although Nicole's limited savings would clearly not be enough to get CCS started, she was willing to contribute a parcel of land in the industrial section of town that she had inherited five years ago from her grandfather. Her friend and mentor, Sarah Walker, offered to contribute both her time and money to help CCS get off the ground.

With Sarah on board, things seemed to be coming together nicely for Nicole. However, the amount her bank was willing to loan was not enough to fully capitalize CCS, and Nicole and Sarah were unable to invest any more cash into the business to make up the shortfall. Hoping to obtain the additional funding they needed, Nicole and Sarah visited Chance Armstrong, a successful local sports-team owner who had a reputation for being willing to take a chance on new ventures. After listening to Nicole and Sarah's proposal, Chance agreed to invest the additional cash needed to fully fund CCS. Rather than use his personal funds, however, Chance planned to have his closely held corporation, Chanzz Inc., invest in CCS. Unlike Nicole and Sarah, who would take an active role in managing CCS, Chanzz Inc.—with everyone's agreement—would not play a part. By the end of March, CCS had cash, land on which to build its manufacturing facility and offices, and owners who were excited and willing to work hard to make it a successful company.

*to be continued . . .*

In this chapter, we review the options for operating a business with multiple owners as a **flow-through entity.** In addition, we explain the basic tax consequences of forming and operating business entities taxed as partnerships by examining the specific tax consequences of forming and operating Color Comfort Sheets as a limited liability company (LLC).

# FLOW-THROUGH ENTITIES OVERVIEW

**LO1**

Income earned by flow-through entities is usually not taxed at the entity level. Instead, the *owners* of flow-through entities are taxed on the share of entity-level income allocated to them. Thus, unlike income earned by **taxable corporations,** income from flow-though entities is taxed only once—when it "flows through" to owners of these entities.[1]

Owners of flow-through entities are taxed under two somewhat different sets of rules in our tax system.[2] Unincorporated business entities such as **general partnerships, limited partnerships,** and **limited liability companies (LLC)** are treated as partnerships under the rules provided in **Subchapter K** of the Internal Revenue Code.[3] In contrast, corporations whose owners elect to treat them as flow-through entities are classified as such under the rules in **Subchapter S.** These corporations are called **S corporations.**

There are many similarities and a few important differences between the tax rules for partnerships and S corporations. Our focus in this chapter and the next is on the tax rules for partnerships. Then, in Chapter 22, we turn our attention to the tax treatment of S corporations and their shareholders.

---

| **Taxes in the Real World** *Hedge Funds* | |
|---|---|
| One can scarcely read the financial press these days without encountering some reference to hedge funds. Hedge funds are private investment funds that have grown in popularity in recent years to the point where they were estimated to have $1.5 trillion in assets | under management at the beginning of 2009.[4] According to a study by the Joint Committee on Taxation, most hedge funds are organized as partnerships and their investors are taxed as limited partners.[5] |

---

## Aggregate and Entity Concepts

When Congress adopted Subchapter K in 1954, it had to decide whether to follow an **entity approach** and treat tax partnerships as entities separate from their partners, or to apply an **aggregate approach** and treat them simply as an aggregation of the partners' separate interests in the assets and liabilities of the partnership. In the end, Congress decided to apply both concepts in formulating partnership tax law. For instance, one of the most basic tenets of partnerships tax law—that partnerships don't pay taxes—reflects the aggregate approach. However, Congress also adopted other partnership tax rules that fall more squarely on the side of the entity approach. For example, the requirement that partnerships, rather than partners, make most tax elections represents the entity concept. Throughout this chapter and the following chapter, we highlight examples where one or the other basic approaches underlies a specific partnership tax rule.

[1]The "check the box" rules determine how various legal entities should be classified for tax purposes. See the discussion in Chapter 15 for a more detailed explanation of these rules.

[2]Unincorporated entities with one individual owner are taxed as *sole proprietorships.* The tax rules relevant to sole proprietorships are discussed in Chapter 8. In addition to sole proprietorships, other specialized forms of flow-through entities such as real estate investment trusts and regulated investment companies are authorized by the Code. A discussion of these entities is beyond the scope of this chapter.

[3]Publicly traded partnerships may be taxed as corporations. The tax treatment of publicly traded partnerships is more fully developed in Chapter 15.

[4]*"Hedge Funds 2009,"* International Financial Services London (www.ifsl.org.uk), July 4, 2009.

[5]*"Present Law and Analysis Relating to Tax Treatment of Partnership Carried Interests and Related Issues, Part I,"* (JCX-62-07), September 4, 2007.

# PARTNERSHIP FORMATIONS AND ACQUISITIONS OF PARTNERSHIP INTERESTS

### Acquiring Partnership Interests When Partnerships Are Formed

When a partnership is formed, and afterwards, partners may transfer cash, other tangible or intangible property, and services to it in exchange for an equity interest called a **partnership interest.** Partnership interests represent the bundle of economic rights granted to partners under the partnership agreement (or operating agreement for an LLC).[6] These rights include the right to receive a share of the partnership net assets if the partnership were to liquidate, called a **capital interest,** and the right or obligation to receive a share of *future* profits *or future* losses, called a **profits interest.**[7] It is quite common for partners contributing property to receive both capital and profits interests in exchange. Partners who contribute services instead of property frequently receive only profits interests. The distinction between capital and profits interests is important because the tax rules for partnerships are sometimes applied to them differently.

**Contributions of Property**   Partnership formations are similar to other tax-deferred transactions such as like-kind exchanges and corporate formations, because realized gains and losses from the exchange of contributed property for partnership interests are either fully or partially deferred for tax purposes depending on the specifics of the transaction. The rationale for permitting taxpayers to defer realized gains or losses on property contributed to partnerships is identical to the rationale for permitting tax deferral when corporations are formed.[8] From a practical perspective, the tax rules in this area allow entrepreneurs to organize their businesses without having to pay taxes. In addition, these rules follow the aggregate theory of partnership taxation because they recognize that partners contributing property to a partnership still own the contributed property, albeit a smaller percentage, since other partners will also indirectly own the contributed property through their partnership interests.

*Gain and loss recognition.*   As a general rule, neither partnerships nor partners recognize gain or loss when they contribute property to partnerships.[9] This applies to property contributions when a partnership is initially formed and to subsequent property contributions. In this context, the term *property* is defined broadly to include a wide variety of both tangible and intangible assets but not services. The general rule facilitates contributions of property with **built-in gains** (fair market value is greater than tax basis) but discourages contributions of property with **built-in losses** (fair market value is less than tax basis). In fact, partners holding property with built-in losses are usually better off selling the property, recognizing the related tax loss, and contributing the cash from the sale to the partnership so it can acquire property elsewhere.

**LO2**

**THE KEY FACTS**

**Property Contributions**

- Partners don't generally recognize gain or loss when they contribute property to partnerships.

- Initial tax basis for partners contributing property = basis of contributed property − debt securing contributed property + partnership debt allocated to contributing partner + gain recognized.

- Contributing partner's holding period in a partnership interest depends on the type of property contributed.

---

**Example 20-1**

*What if:* Assume Nicole contributes land to CCS with a fair market value of $120,000 and an adjusted basis of $20,000. What amount of gain or loss would she recognize on the contribution?

*Answer:* None. Under the general rule for contributions of appreciated property, Nicole will not recognize any of the $100,000 built-in gain from her land.

(continued on page 20-4...)

---

[6]The partnership books reflect partners' shares of the partnership's net assets in their individual capital accounts.

[7]An interest in the future profits or losses of a partnership is customarily referred to as a profits interest rather than a profits/loss interest.

[8]Chapter 19 discusses the tax rules related to corporate formations.

[9]§721.

> *What if:* Suppose Chanzz Inc. contributed equipment with a fair market value of $120,000 and a tax basis of $220,000 to CCS. What amount of the gain or loss would Chanzz Inc. recognize on the contribution?
>
> **Answer:** None. Chanzz Inc. would not recognize any of the $100,000 built-in loss on the equipment. However, if Chanzz Inc. sold the property to an unrelated party and contributed $120,000 in cash instead of the equipment, it could recognize the $100,000 built-in tax loss. If, for some reason, the equipment Chanzz planned to contribute was uniquely suited to CCS's operations, Chanzz could obtain the same result by selling the equipment to Sarah, who would then contribute the equipment to CCS rather than her planned $120,000 cash contribution.

*Partner's initial tax basis.* Among other things, partners need to determine the tax basis in their partnership interests to properly compute their taxable gains and losses when they sell their partnership interests. A partner's tax basis in her partnership interest is her **outside basis.** In contrast, the partnership's basis in its assets is its **inside basis.** As we progress through this and the next chapter, you'll see other important reasons for calculating a partner's outside tax basis.

Determining a partner's initial tax basis in a partnership interest acquired by contributing property and/or cash is relatively straightforward if the partnership doesn't have any debt. Partners will simply have a basis in their partnership interest equivalent to the tax basis of the property and cash they contributed.[10] This rule ensures that realized gains and losses on contributed property are merely deferred until either the contributing partner sells her partnership interest or the partnership sells the contributed property.

## Example 20-2

> *What if:* Assume that Sarah contributed $120,000 to CCS in exchange for her partnership interest and that CCS had no liabilities. What is Sarah's outside basis in her partnership interest after the contribution?
>
> **Answer:** Sarah's basis is $120,000, the amount of cash she contributed to CCS.
>
> *What if:* Assume Nicole contributed land with a fair market value of $120,000 and an adjusted basis of $20,000 and CCS had no liabilities. What is Nicole's initial tax basis in CCS?
>
> **Answer:** Nicole's basis is $20,000, the basis of the property she contributed to CCS. If Nicole immediately sold her interest in CCS for $120,000 (the value of the land she contributed), she would recognize gain of $100,000—exactly the amount she would have recognized if she had sold the land instead of contributing it to CCS.

When partnerships have debt, a few additional steps are required to determine a partner's tax basis in her partnership interest. First, each partner must include her share of the partnership's debt in calculating the tax basis in her partnership interest because partnership tax law treats each partner as borrowing her proportionate share of the partnership's debt and then contributing the borrowed cash to acquire her partnership interest.[11] You can understand the necessity for this basis increase by recalling that the basis of any purchased asset increases by the amount of any borrowed funds used to purchase it.

Partnerships may have either **recourse debt** or **nonrecourse debt** or both, and the specific approach to allocating partnership debt to individual partners differs for each. The fundamental difference between the two types of debt lies in the legal responsibility partners assume for ultimately paying the debt. Recourse debts are those for which partners have economic risk of loss—that is, they may have to

[10]§722.
[11]§752(a).

legally satisfy the debt with their own funds. For example, the unsecured debts of general partnerships, such as payables, are recourse debt because general partners are legally responsible for the debts of the partnership. Recourse debt is usually allocated to the partners who will ultimately be responsible for paying it.[12] The partners must consider their partner guarantees, other agreements, and state partnership or LLC statutes in making this determination.

Nonrecourse debts, in contrast, don't provide creditors the same level of legal recourse against partners. Nonrecourse debts such as mortgages are typically secured by real property and only give lenders the right to obtain the secured property in the event the partnership defaults on the debt. Because partners are responsible for paying nonrecourse debts only to the extent the partnership generates sufficient profits, such debts are generally allocated according to partners' profit-sharing ratios. (We discuss an exception to this general rule later in the chapter.[13]) The *basic* rules for allocating recourse and nonrecourse debt are summarized in Exhibit 20-1.

**EXHIBIT 20-1** Basic Rules for Allocating Partnership Debt to Partners

| Type of Debt | Allocation Method |
| --- | --- |
| Recourse | Allocated to partners with ultimate responsibility for paying debt |
| Nonrecourse | Allocated according to partners' profit-sharing ratios |

The legal structure of entities taxed as partnerships also influences the way partners characterize and allocate partnership debt. Recourse debts in limited partnerships are typically allocated only to general partners, because, as we discuss in Chapter 15, limited partners are legally protected from a limited partnership's recourse debt holders.[14] Limited partners, however, may be allocated recourse debt if they forgo their legal protection by guaranteeing some or all of the recourse debt. Similarly, LLC members generally treat debts as nonrecourse because of their legal protection against the LLC's creditors. However, like limited partners, LLC members may treat debt as recourse debt to the extent they contractually assume risk of loss by agreeing to be legally responsible for paying the debt.[15]

**Example 20-3**

When CCS was formed, Sarah and Chanzz Inc. initially each contributed $120,000 and CCS borrowed $60,000 from a bank. The bank required Nicole, Sarah, and Chanzz Inc. to personally guarantee the bank loan. The terms were structured so the members would each be responsible for a portion of the debt equal to the percentage of CCS losses allocated to each member (one-third each) and would have no right of reimbursement from either CCS or the other members of CCS. How much of the $60,000 bank debt was allocated to each member?

(continued on page 20-6…)

---

[12]Reg. §1.752-2. Under the regulations, partners' obligations for paying recourse debt are determined by assuming a hypothetical, worst-case scenario where partnership assets (including cash) become worthless, and the resulting losses are then allocated to partners. The partners who legally would be responsible for partnership recourse debts under this scenario must be allocated the recourse debt. A detailed description of this approach for allocating recourse debt is beyond the scope of this book.

[13]Reg. §1.752-3 provides the rules for allocating nonrecourse debt, some of which are beyond the scope of this text.

[14]Recall from Chapter 15 that, in limited partnerships, general partners' liability is unlimited whereas limited partners' liability is usually limited to the amount they have invested.

[15]It's actually quite common for banks and other lenders to require LLC members to personally guarantee loans made to LLCs.

**Answer:** Each member was allocated $20,000. The debt is treated as recourse debt because they are personally guaranteeing it. Because each guarantees one-third of the debt, the $60,000 debt is allocated equally among them.

**What if:** Assuming the $60,000 bank loan is CCS's only debt, what is Sarah's initial basis in her CCS interest after taking her share of CCS's bank debt into account?

**Answer:** Sarah's basis is $140,000 ($120,000 + $20,000) and consists of her cash contribution plus her share of CCS's $60,000 bank loan.

Another step is needed to determine a partner's outside basis when the partnership assumes *debt of the partner* secured by property the partner contributes to the partnership. Essentially, the contributing partner must treat her debt relief as a deemed cash distribution from the partnership that reduces her outside basis.[16] If the debt securing the contributed property is nonrecourse debt, the amount of the debt in excess of the basis of the contributed property is allocated solely to the contributing partner, and the remaining debt is allocated to all partners according to their profit-sharing ratios.[17]

## Example 20-4

Nicole initially contributed $10,000 of cash and land with a fair market value of $150,000 and adjusted basis of $20,000 to CCS. The land was encumbered by a $40,000 nonrecourse mortgage executed three years before. Recalling that CCS already had $60,000 in bank debt before Nicole's contribution, what tax bases do Nicole, Sarah, and Chanzz Inc. *initially* have in their CCS interests?

**Answer:** Their bases are $36,666, $146,666, and $146,666, respectively. Nicole, Sarah, and Chanzz Inc. would determine their initial tax bases as illustrated in the table below:

| Description | Nicole | Sarah and Chanzz Inc. | Explanation |
|---|---|---|---|
| (1) Basis in contributed land | $20,000 | | |
| (2) Cash contributed | $10,000 | $120,000 | Example 20-3. |
| (3) Members' share of $60,000 recourse bank loan | $20,000 | $ 20,000 | Example 20-3. |
| (4) Nonrecourse mortgage in excess of basis in contributed land | $20,000 | | Nonrecourse debt > basis is allocated only to Nicole. |
| (5) Remaining nonrecourse mortgage | $ 6,666 | $ 6,666 | 33.33% × [$40,000 − (4)]. |
| (6) Relief from mortgage debt | ($40,000) | | |
| Nicole's initial tax basis in CCS | $36,666 | $146,666 | Sum of (1) through (6). |

Although in many instances partners don't recognize gains on property contributions, there is an important exception to the general rule that may apply when property secured by debt is contributed to a partnership. In these situations, the contributing partner recognizes gain *only if* the cash deemed to have been received from

[16]§752(b).
[17]Reg. §1.752-3(a)(2).

a partnership distribution exceeds the contributing partner's tax basis in her partnership interest prior to the deemed distribution.[18] Any gain recognized is generally treated as capital gain.[19]

---

**Example 20-5**

**What if:** Assume Sarah and Chanzz Inc., but *not* Nicole, personally guarantee all $100,000 of CCS's debt ($60,000 bank loan + $40,000 mortgage on land). How much gain, if any, would Nicole recognize on her contribution to CCS and what would be the basis in her CCS interest?

**Answer:** Nicole would recognize $10,000 gain and have a $0 basis, computed as follows:

| Description | Amount | Explanation |
|---|---|---|
| (1) Basis in contributed land | $20,000 | Example 20-4. |
| (2) Cash contributed | $10,000 | Example 20-4. |
| (3) Nicole's share of debt | $ 0 | Sarah and Chanzz guaranteed all of CCS's debt. |
| (4) Debt relief | ($40,000) | Nicole was relieved of mortgage on land. |
| (5) Debt relief in excess of basis in contributed land and cash | ($10,000) | Sum of (1) through (4). |
| (6) Capital gain recognized | $10,000 | (5) with opposite sign. |
| Nicole's initial tax basis in CCS | $ 0 | (5) + (6). |

---

***Partner's holding period in partnership interest.*** Because a partnership interest is a capital asset, its holding period determines whether gains or losses from the disposition of the partnership interest are short-term or long-term capital gains or losses. The length of a partner's holding period for a partnership interest acquired by contributing property depends on the nature of the assets the partner contributed. When partners contribute capital assets or §1231 assets (assets used in a trade or business and held for more than one year), the holding period of the contributed property "tacks on" to the partnership interest.[20] Otherwise, it begins on the day the partnership interest is acquired.

---

**Example 20-6**

**What if:** Assume Nicole contributed land (no cash) that she had held for five years in exchange for her partnership interest. One month after contributing the property, she sold her partnership interest and recognized a capital gain. Is the gain long-term or short-term?

**Answer:** The gain is long-term because the five-year holding period of the land is tacked on to Nicole's holding period for her partnership interest. She is treated as though she held the partnership interest for five years and one month at the time she sold it.

---

***Partnership's tax basis and holding period in contributed property.*** Just as partners must determine their initial outside basis in their partnership interests after contributing property, partnerships must establish their inside basis in the contributed property.

---

[18]§731(a). However, §707(a)(2)(B) provides that deemed cash received from the relief of debt should be considered as sale proceeds rather than a distribution when circumstances indicate the relief of debt constitutes a disguised sale. Further discussion of disguised sale transactions is beyond the scope of this book.

[19]§731(a). This is equivalent to increasing what would have been a negative basis by the recognized gain to arrive at a zero basis. This mechanism ensures that partners will be left with an initial tax basis of zero anytime they recognize gain from a property contribution.

[20]Reg. §1.1223-1(a).

Measuring both the partner's outside basis and the partnership's inside basis is consistent with the entity theory of partnership taxation. To ensure built-in gains and losses on contributed property are ultimately recognized if partnerships sell contributed property, partnerships generally take a basis in the property equal to the contributing partner's basis in the property at the time of the contribution.[21] Like the adjusted basis of contributed property, the holding period of contributed assets also carries over to the partnership.[22] In fact, the only tax attribute of contributed property that *doesn't* carry over to the partnership is the character of contributed property. Whether gains or losses on dispositions of contributed property are capital or ordinary usually depends on the manner in which the partnership uses contributed property.[23]

## Example 20-7

**What if:** Assume CCS used the land Nicole contributed in its business for one month and then sold it for its fair market value of $150,000. What is the amount and character of the gain CCS would recognize on the sale (see Example 20-4)?

**Answer:** CCS recognizes $130,000 of §1231 gain and will allocate it to the member or members that will report it. Nicole's basis in the land prior to the formation of CCS was $20,000. Because CCS receives a carryover basis in the land of $20,000, it recognizes $130,000 of gain when the land is sold for $150,000 ($110,000 in cash and $40,000 of debt relief minus $20,000 basis in land). Also, because CCS used the land in its business and because Nicole's five-year holding period carries over to CCS, the land qualifies as a §1231 asset to CCS, and CCS recognizes §1231 gain when the land is sold. Note that $130,000 of gain is recognized regardless of whether Nicole sells the land and contributes cash to CCS, or CCS sells the land shortly after it is contributed.

In addition to tracking the inside basis of its assets for tax purposes, partnerships not required to produce GAAP financial statements may decide to use inside tax basis, as well as tax income and expense recognition rules, to maintain their books. Under this approach, a new partnership would prepare its initial balance sheet using the tax basis for its assets. In addition, it would create a **tax capital account** for each new partner, reflecting the tax basis of any property contributed (net of any debt securing the property) and cash contributions. Because each new partner's tax capital account measures that partner's equity in the partnership using tax accounting rules, it will later be adjusted to include the partner's share of earnings and losses, contributions, and distributions.

Besides satisfying bookkeeping requirements, a partnership's tax basis balance sheet can provide useful tax-related information. For example, we can calculate each partner's share of the inside basis of partnership assets by adding the partner's share of debt to her **capital account.** Also, partners who acquire their interests by contributing property (without having to recognize any gain) will have an *outside basis* equal to their share of the partnership's total inside basis. However, as we discuss more fully in the next chapter, partners' inside and outside bases will likely be different when they purchase existing partnership interests.

As another alternative to maintaining **GAAP capital accounts,** partnerships may also maintain their partner's capital accounts using accounting rules prescribed in the §704(b) tax regulations.[24] Partners set up **§704(b) capital accounts** in much the same

[21]§723.

[22]§1223(2).

[23]§702(b). However, §724 provides some important exceptions to this general rule for certain receivables, inventory, and capital loss property.

[24]Reg. §1.704-1(b)(2)(iv).

way as tax capital accounts, except that §704(b) capital accounts reflect the fair market value rather than the tax basis of contributed assets. Once a partnership begins operations, it can adjust §704(b) capital accounts so they continue to reflect the fair market value of partners' capital interests as accurately as possible. Partnerships may prefer this approach over simply maintaining tax capital accounts because §704(b) capital accounts are a better measure of the true value of partners' capital interests.

*continued from page 20-1 . . .*

Before forming CCS, its members agreed to keep its books using the tax basis of contributed assets and tax income and expense recognition rules. After receiving the cash and property contributions from its members and borrowing $60,000 from Nicole's bank, CCS prepared the tax basis balance sheet in Exhibit 20-2.

*to be continued . . .*

**EXHIBIT 20-2    Color Comfort Sheets, LLC**

| Balance Sheet March 31, 2009 | | |
| --- | --- | --- |
| | **Tax Basis** | **§704(b)/FMV*** |
| **Assets:** | | |
| Cash | $310,000 | $310,000 |
| Land | 20,000 | 150,000 |
| Totals | $330,000 | $460,000 |
| **Liabilities and Capital:** | | |
| Long-term debt | $100,000 | $100,000 |
| Capital-Nicole | (10,000) | 120,000 |
| Capital-Sarah | 120,000 | 120,000 |
| Capital-Chanzz Inc. | 120,000 | 120,000 |
| Totals | $330,000 | $460,000 |

*The §704(b)/FMV balance sheet is also provided to illustrate the difference in the two approaches to maintaining partners' capital accounts.

**Contribution of Services**    So far we've assumed partners receive their partnership interests in exchange for contributed property. They may also receive partnership interests in exchange for services they provide to the partnership. For example, an attorney or other service provider might accept a partnership interest in lieu of cash payment for services provided as part of a partnership formation. Similarly, ongoing partnerships may compensate their employees with partnership interests, to reduce compensation-related cash payments and to motivate employees to behave more like owners. Unlike property contributions, services contributed in exchange for partnership interests may create immediate tax consequences to both the contributing partner *and* the partnership, depending on the nature of the partnership interest received.[25]

---

[25]Rev. Proc. 93-27, 1993-2 CB 343 and Rev. Proc. 2001-43, 2001-2 CB 191. In 2005, the IRS issued Prop. Reg. §1.704-1, which will change certain elements of current tax law when it is adopted as a final regulation. The concepts and examples discussed here are consistent with both current law and the proposed regulation.

*continued from page 20-9...*

Once CCS was organized in March 2009, it built a small production facility on the commercial land Nicole had contributed, purchased and installed the equipment needed to produce sheets, and hired and trained workers—all before the actual production and marketing of the sheets. After production began on July 1, 2009, CCS started selling its sheets to local specialty bedding stores, but the local market was limited. To create additional demand for their product, the members of CCS decided to draw on Sarah's marketing expertise to develop an advertising campaign targeted at home and garden magazines. All members of CCS agreed Sarah would receive, on December 31, 2009, an additional *capital interest* in CCS with a liquidation value of $20,000 *and* an increase in her profit-and-loss-sharing ratio from 33.33 percent to 40 percent (leaving the other members each with a 30 percent share of profits and losses), to compensate her for the time she would spend on this additional project. At this point, CCS's debt remained at $100,000.

*to be continued...*

***Capital interests.*** Partners who receive unrestricted capital interests in exchange for services have the right to receive a share of the partnership's capital if it liquidates.[26] Because capital interests represent a current economic entitlement amenable to measurement, partners receiving capital interests for services must treat the amount they would receive if the partnership were to liquidate, or **liquidation value**[27] of the capital interest, as ordinary income.[28] In addition, the **service partner's** tax basis in the capital interest he receives will equal the amount of ordinary income he recognizes, and his holding period will begin on the date he receives the capital interest. The partnership either deducts or capitalizes the value of the capital interest, depending on the nature of the services the partner provides. For example, a real estate partnership would capitalize the value of a capital interest compensating a partner for architectural drawings used for a real estate development project.[29] Conversely, the same partnership would deduct the value of a capital interest compensating a partner for providing property management services. When the partnership deducts the value of capital interests used to compensate partners for services provided, it allocates the deduction only to the partners not providing services, or **nonservice partners,** because they have effectively transferred a portion of their partnership capital to the service partner.

| Example 20-8 | |
|---|---|

***What if:*** What are the tax consequences to Sarah and CCS if Sarah receives a capital interest (no profits interest) with a $20,000 liquidation value for her services?

**Answer:** As summarized below, Sarah has $20,000 of ordinary income, and CCS receives a $20,000 ordinary deduction. However, this deduction must be split equally between Nicole and Chanzz Inc. because, in effect, they transferred a portion of their capital to Sarah.

*(continued on page 20-11...)*

[26]Certain restrictions, such as vesting requirements, may be placed on partnership interests received for services. We limit our discussion here to unrestricted partnership interests.

[27]The proposed regulations in this area also allow the parties in this transaction to use the fair market value of partnership interests as a measure of value rather than liquidation value.

[28]The ordinary income recognized by the service partner is treated as a "guaranteed payment" by the service partner. Guaranteed payments are discussed more fully later in this chapter.

[29]§263(a).

| Description | Sarah | Nicole | Chanzz Inc. | Explanation |
|---|---|---|---|---|
| (1) Ordinary income | $20,000 | | | Liquidation value of capital interest. |
| Ordinary deduction | | ($10,000) | ($10,000) | Capital shift from nonservice partners. (1) × .5 |

**THE KEY FACTS**

**Other Acquisitions of Partnership Interests**

■ Contributing partner's tax basis and holding period in contributed property carries over to the partnership.

■ If service partners report ordinary income, the partnership either expenses or capitalizes the amount depending on the nature of the services provided.

■ The tax basis of a purchased partnership interest = purchase price + partnership debt allocated to partner, and the holding period begins on the purchase date.

***Profits interests.*** It's fairly common for partnerships to compensate service partners with profits rather than capital interests. Profits interests are fundamentally different from capital interests, because the only economic benefit they provide is the right to share in the future profits of the partnership. Unlike capital interests, they have no liquidation value at the time they are received. Nonservice partners generally prefer to compensate service partners with profits interests because they don't have to forgo their current share of capital in the partnership and may not ever have to give up anything if the partnership is ultimately unprofitable. Thus, a profits interest is more risky than a capital interest from the perspective of the service partner.

The tax rules applicable to profits interests differ from those pertaining to capital interests due to the fundamental economic differences between them. Because there is no immediate liquidation value associated with a profits interest, the service partner typically will not recognize income and the nonservice partners will not receive deductions.[30] However, future profits and losses attributable to the profits interest are allocated to the service partner (and away from the nonservice partners) as they are generated. In addition, the partnership must adjust debt allocations based on profit-and-loss-sharing ratios to reflect the service partner's new or increased share of profits and losses.

**Example 20-9**

***What if:*** Assuming Sarah received only a profits interest for her services instead of the capital interest she received in Example 20-8, what are the tax consequences to Sarah, Nicole, Chanzz Inc., and CCS?[31]

**Answer:** Sarah would not be required to recognize any income, and CCS would not deduct or capitalize any costs. As CCS generates future profits, Sarah will receive a greater share of the profits than she would have otherwise received, and the other two members will receive a correspondingly smaller share. In addition, with the increase in Sarah's profit-and-loss-sharing ratios from 33.33 percent to 40 percent, debt allocations among the partners will change to reflect Sarah's additional entitlement. Note that the debt allocations affect each partner's outside basis. The change in debt allocations is reflected in the table below:

| Description | Sarah | Nicole | Chanzz Inc. | Explanation |
|---|---|---|---|---|
| (1) Increase in debt allocation | $5,334 | | | Loss-sharing ratio increases from 33.33 percent to 40 percent or 6.67 percent [$60,000 recourse bank loan × 6.67% increase in loss-sharing ratio] + [$20,000 nonrecourse mortgage not allocated solely to Nicole × 6.67% increase in profit-sharing ratio]. |
| Decrease in debt allocation | | ($2,667) | ($2,667) | (1) × .5 |

[30]Rev. Proc. 93-27 indicates that income is recognized by the service partner "if the profits interest relates to a substantially certain and predictable stream of income," if the partner disposes if the profits interest within two years, or "the profits interest is a limited partnership interest in a publicly traded partnership."

[31]It is common for partnerships to grant a profits interests without an accompanying capital interest.

**Example 20-10**

What are the tax consequences to Sarah, Nicole, and Chanzz Inc. associated with the capital interest (liquidation value of $20,000) and profits interest Sarah receives for her services?

**Answer:** The tax consequences associated with giving Sarah *both* a capital and profits interest are summarized in the table below:

| Description | Sarah | Nicole | Chanzz Inc. | Explanation |
|---|---|---|---|---|
| (1) Ordinary income | $20,000 | | | Liquidation value of capital interest. |
| Ordinary deduction | | ($10,000) | ($10,000) | Capital shift from nonservice partners. (1) × .5 |
| (2) Increase in debt allocation | $ 5,334 | | | Loss-sharing ratio increases from 33.33 percent to 40 percent or 6.67 percent [$60,000 recourse bank loan × 6.67% increase in loss-sharing ratio] + [$20,000 nonrecourse mortgage not allocated solely to Nicole × 6.67% increase in profit-sharing ratio]. |
| Decrease in debt allocation | | ($2,667) | ($2,667) | (2) × .5 |

**Organization, Start-up, and Syndication Costs**  When partnerships are formed, they typically incur some costs that must be capitalized rather than expensed for tax purposes, because they will benefit the partnership over its entire lifespan. This category of expenses includes **organization costs** associated with legally forming a partnership (such as attorneys' and accountants' fees), **syndication costs** to promote and sell partnership interests, and **start-up costs** that would normally be deducted as operating expenses except that they are incurred before the start of active trade or business. However, with the exception of syndication costs,[32] which are never deductible, the partnership may elect to amortize these costs. Chapter 9 provides additional detail about immediately expensing or amortizing business organization and start-up costs.

## Acquisitions of Partnership Interests

After a partnership is formed and begins operating, new or existing partners can acquire partnership interests in exchange for contributing property and/or services, in which case the tax rules previously discussed in the context of forming a partnership still apply. Or new partners may purchase partnership interests from existing partners. Partners who purchase their partnership interests don't have to be concerned with recognizing taxable income when they receive their interests. However, in each of these scenarios they must still determine the initial tax basis and holding period in their partnership interests. Exhibit 20-3 summarizes the rules for determining the tax basis of partnership interests when they are received in exchange for contributed property or services, or when they are purchased.

---

[32]Syndication costs are typically incurred by partnerships whose interests are marketed to the public. Thus, syndication expenses are unusual in closely held partnerships.

**EXHIBIT 20-3**    Summary of Partner's Outside Basis and Holding Period By Acquisition Method

| Acquisition Method | Outside Basis | Holding Period |
|---|---|---|
| Contribute Property | Equals basis of contributed property − debt relief + debt allocation + gain recognized. | If property contributed is a capital or §1231 asset, holding period includes holding period of contributed property. Otherwise begins on date interest received. |
| Contribute Services | Equals liquidation value of capital interest + debt allocation. Equals debt allocation if only profits interest received. | Begins on date interest received. |
| Purchase | Equals cost basis[33] + debt allocation | Begins on date interest purchased. |

**Example 20-11**

CCS had overall operating losses from July 1, 2009 (when it began operating), through June 30, 2010. Because of the losses, Chanzz Inc. decided to sell its 30 percent interest in CCS (Chanzz Inc.'s original 33.33 percent interest in CCS was reduced to 30 percent at the end of 2009 when Sarah's interest was increased to compensate her for services provided) on July 1, 2010, to Greg Randall who, like Chanzz Inc., will be a nonmanaging member and guarantee a portion of CCS debt. Greg paid Chanzz Inc. $100,000 for its interest in CCS and was allocated a 30 percent share of CCS debt (CCS's debt remained at $100,000 on July 1, 2010). What is Greg's basis and holding period in CCS?

**Answer:** Greg's basis of $124,000 in CCS includes the $100,000 amount he paid to purchase the interest plus his $24,000 share of CCS's total $80,000 debt available to be allocated to all members ($60,000 recourse bank loan and $20,000 of nonrecourse mortgage remaining after allocating the first $20,000 to Nicole). Greg's holding period in his CCS interest begins on July 1, 2010.

# PARTNERSHIP ACCOUNTING PERIODS, METHODS, AND TAX ELECTIONS

**L03**

A newly formed partnership must adopt its required tax year-end and decide whether it intends to use either the cash or accrual method as its overall method of accounting. As you recall from Chapter 8, an entity's tax year-end determines the cutoff date for including income and deductions in a particular return, and its overall accounting method determines when income and deductions are recognized for tax purposes. Partnerships must frequently make other tax-related elections as well.

## Tax Elections

New partnerships determine their accounting periods and make tax elections including the election of overall accounting method, the election to expense a portion of organization and start-up costs, and the election to expense tangible personal property. Who formally makes all these elections? In theory, either the partnership or the partners themselves could do so. With just a few exceptions, the partnership tax rules rely on the entity theory of partnership taxation and make the partnership responsible for tax elections.[34] In many instances, the partnership does so in conjunction with filing its annual return. For example, it selects an accounting method

---

[33]§742.

[34]§703(b). Certain elections are made at the partner level.

and determines whether to elect to amortize start-up or organization costs by simply applying its elections in calculating ordinary business income on its first return. The partnership makes other tax elections by filing a separate document with the IRS, such as Form 3115 when it elects to change an accounting method.

---

**Example 20-12**

How will CCS elect its overall accounting method after it begins operations?

**Answer:** Nicole, Sarah, and Chanzz Inc. may jointly decide on an overall accounting method or, in their LLC operating agreement, they may appoint one of the members to be responsible for making this and other tax elections. Once they have made this decision, *CCS* makes the election by simply using the chosen accounting method when preparing its first information return.

---

### THE KEY FACTS

**Partnership Accounting Periods, Methods, and Tax Elections**

- Partnerships are responsible for making most tax elections.

- A partnership's taxable year is the majority interest taxable year, the common taxable year of the principal partners, or the taxable year providing the least aggregate deferral to the partners.

- Partnerships are generally eligible to use the cash method unless they have average gross receipts greater than $5 million and have corporate partners.

## Accounting Periods

**Required Year-Ends**    Because partners include their share of partnership income or loss in their taxable year ending with the partnership taxable year, or within which the partnership taxable year falls, any partnership tax year other than that of the partners will result in some degree of tax deferral for some or all of the partners.[35] Exhibit 20-4 reflects the tax deferral a partner with a calendar year-end would receive if the corresponding partnership had a January 31 year-end.

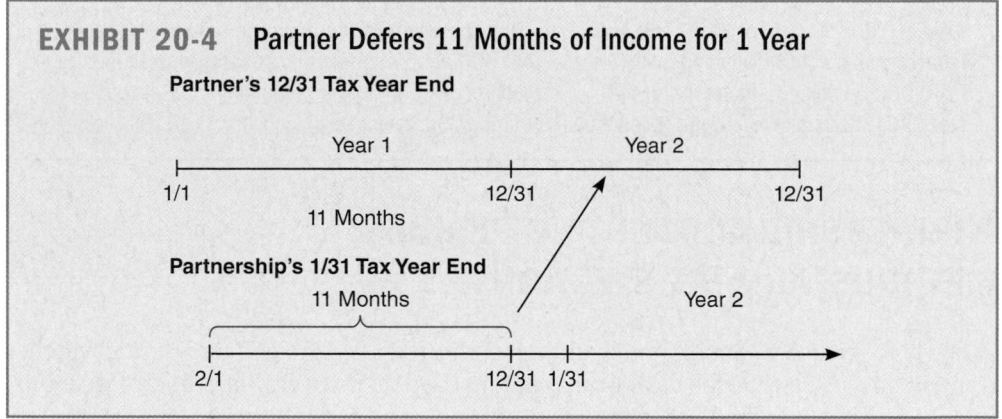

**EXHIBIT 20-4    Partner Defers 11 Months of Income for 1 Year**

Because the partner reports the partnership's year 1 income earned from February 1 until January 31 in the partner's second calendar year (the year within which the partnership's January 31 year-end falls), the partner defers reporting for one year the 11 months of income she was allocated from February 1 through December 31 of her first calendar year.

The government's desire to reduce the aggregate tax deferral of partners (the sum of the deferrals for each individual partner) provides the underlying rationale behind the rules requiring certain partnership taxable year-ends. Partnerships are generally required to use one of three possible tax year-ends.[36] As illustrated in Exhibit 20-5, they must follow a series of steps to determine the appropriate year-end.

The first potential required tax year is the **majority interest taxable year,** the taxable year of one or more partners who together own more than 50 percent of the capital and

---

[35]§706(a).

[36]Under certain circumstances, other alternative taxable years may be available to partnerships. See Rev. Proc. 2002-38, 2002-1 CB 1037 and §444 for additional information concerning these options.

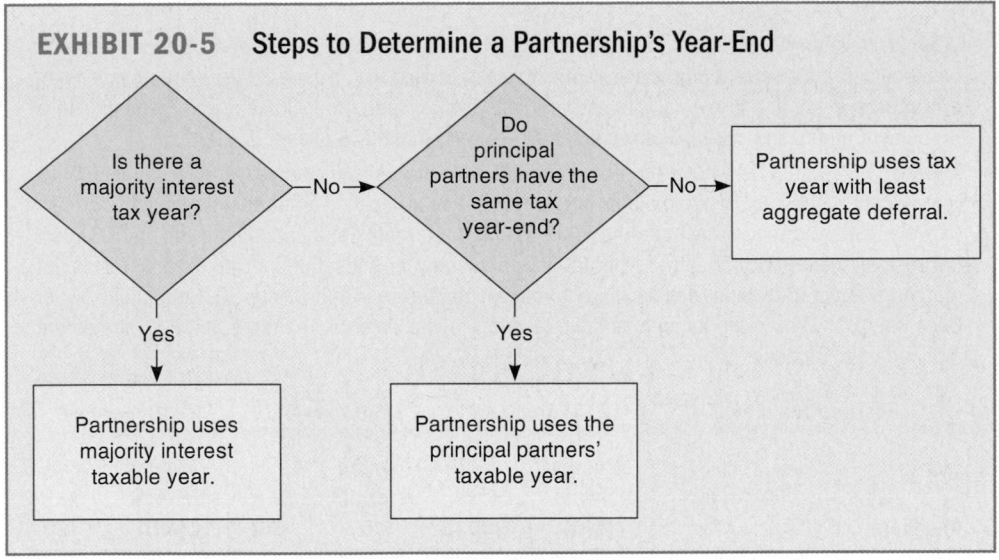

**EXHIBIT 20-5    Steps to Determine a Partnership's Year-End**

profits interests in the partnership.[37] However, there may not be a majority interest taxable year when several partners have different year-ends. For example, if a partnership has two partners with 50 percent capital and profits interests and each has a different tax year, there will be no majority interest taxable year. In that case, the partnership next applies the principal partners test to determine its year-end.

Under the **principal partners** test, the required tax year is the taxable year the principal partners *all* have in common. For this purpose, principal partners are those who have 5 percent or more interest in the partnership profits and capital.[38] Consider a partnership with two calendar-year partners, each with a 20 percent capital and profits interest, and thirty additional fiscal year-end partners, each with less than a 5 percent capital and profits interest. In this scenario, the required taxable year of the partnership is a calendar year corresponding with the taxable year of the partnership's only two principal partners. If, as in the earlier example, the partnership had two 50 percent capital and profits partners with different tax years, it would then use the tax year providing the "least aggregate deferral" to the partners, unless it is eligible to elect an alternative year-end.[39]

The tax year with the **least aggregate deferral** is the one among the tax years of the partners that provides the partner group as a whole with the smallest amount of aggregate tax deferral. Under this approach, we measure the total tax deferral achieved under each potential tax year mathematically by weighting each partner's months of deferral under the potential tax year by each partner's *profits* percentage and then summing the weighted months of deferral for all the partners.

| Example 20-13 |
| --- |

When CCS began operating in 2009, it had two calendar year-end members, Nicole and Sarah, and one member with a June 30 year-end, Chanzz Inc. What tax year-end must CCS use for 2009?

**Answer:** CCS was required to use the calendar year as its taxable year unless it was eligible for an alternative year-end. Although Chanzz Inc. had a June 30 taxable year, Nicole and Sarah both had calendar year-ends. Because Nicole and Sarah each initially own 33.33 percent of the capital and profits of CCS, and together they own greater than 50 percent of the profits and capital of CCS, the calendar year is the required taxable year for CCS because it is the majority interest taxable year.

(*continued on page 20-16...*)

---

[37] §706(b)(1)(B)(i).

[38] §706(b)(3).

[39] Reg. §1.706-1(b)(3).

**What if:** Assume CCS initially began operating with three members: Nicole, a calendar year-end member with a 20 percent profits and capital interest; Chanzz Inc., a June 30 year-end member with a 40 percent profits and capital interest; and Telle Inc., a September 30 year-end member with a 40 percent profits and capital interest. What tax year-end must CCS use for 2009?

**Answer:** CCS would be required to use a June 30 year-end unless it was eligible for an alternative year-end. CCS does not have a majority interest taxable year because no partner or group of partners with the same year-end owns more than 50 percent of the profits and capital interests in CCS. Also, because all three principal partners in CCS have different year-ends, the principal partner test is not met. As a result, CCS must decide which of three potential year-ends, June 30, September 30, or December 31, will provide its members the least aggregate deferral. The table below illustrates the required computations:

| Possible Year-Ends | | | 12/31 Year-End | | 6/30 Year-End | | 9/30 Year-End | |
|---|---|---|---|---|---|---|---|---|
| Members | % | Tax Year | Months Deferral* (MD) | % × MD | Months Deferral* (MD) | % × MD | Months Deferral* (MD) | % × MD |
| Nicole | 20% | 12/31 | 0 | 0 | 6 | 1.2 | 3 | .6 |
| Chanzz Inc. | 40% | 6/30 | 6 | 2.4 | 0 | 0 | 9 | 3.6 |
| Telle Inc. | 40% | 9/30 | 9 | 3.6 | 3 | 1.2 | 0 | 0 |
| Total aggregate deferral | | | | 6 | | 2.4 | | 4.2 |

*Months deferral equals number of months between the proposed year-end and partner's year-end.

June 30 is the required taxable year-end because it provides members with the least aggregate tax deferral (2.4 is less than 6 and 4.2).

## Accounting Methods

Although partnerships may use the accrual method freely, they may not use the cash method under certain conditions because it facilitates the deferral of income and acceleration of deductions. For example, partnerships with C corporation partners are generally not eligible to use the cash method.[40] However, if partnerships' average annual gross receipts for the three prior taxable years are less than $5 million, partnerships with C corporation partners may use the cash method if they otherwise qualify.[41] It should also be noted that entities generally eligible to use the overall cash method of accounting must nevertheless use the accrual method to account for the purchase and sale of inventory unless they meet certain exceptions provided by the IRS.[42]

**Example 20-14**

When CCS began operations, its members decided it should elect the cash method of accounting if eligible to do so. Would having a corporate member—Chanzz Inc.—prevent it from electing the cash method?

**Answer:** No. Although Chanzz Inc. was a founding member of CCS, its ownership share didn't affect the partnership's eligibility to use the cash method since CCS's average annual gross receipts were less than $5 million. If Chanzz Inc. had remained a member of CCS, the cash method might have been unavailable in future years if average annual gross receipts exceeded $5 million.

[40]§448(a)(2). In addition, §448(a)(3) prohibits partnerships classified as "tax shelters" from electing the cash method.

[41]§448(b)(3). If a partnership has not been in existence for at least three years, this test is applied based on the number of years it has been in existence.

[42]For example, Rev. Proc. 2001-10 2001-1 CB 272 exempts taxpayers with average annual gross receipts of $1 million or less from having to use the accrual method to account for the purchase and sale of inventory.

# REPORTING THE RESULTS OF PARTNERSHIP OPERATIONS  `LO4`

The first section in the Internal Revenue Code dealing with partnerships states emphatically that partnerships are flow-through entities: "A partnership as such shall not be subject to the income tax imposed by this chapter. Persons carrying on business as partners shall be liable for income tax only in their separate or individual capacities."[43] This feature of partnership taxation largely explains the popularity of partnerships over corporations, whose shareholders are subject to a double tax—once when the income is earned and again when it is distributed to shareholders as a dividend or when the shares are sold.

---

**Taxes in the Real World**

On March 22, 2007, Blackstone Group LP, one of the world's largest private equity firms, announced it would attempt to raise $4 billion through an initial public offering of limited partnership interests. This move was considered very unusual since Blackstone and other similar firms had historically been privately held.

Publicly traded firms are typically taxed as corporations even if they are legally structured as partnerships

or, in Blackstone's case, as limited partnerships. However, utilizing an arcane provision in the Tax Code, Blackstone was able to maintain its tax status as a partnership after its public offering.[44] Thus, investors purchasing Blackstone shares bought an investment subject to only one level of taxation but that, like shares in a corporation, could be readily traded in a public securities market.

---

## Ordinary Business Income (Loss) and Separately Stated Items

Although partnerships are not taxpaying entities, they are required to file information returns annually. They also distribute information to each partner detailing the amount *and* character of items of income and loss flowing through the partnership.[45] Partners must report these income and loss items on their tax returns even if they don't receive cash distributions from the partnership during the year.

When gathering this information for their partners, partnerships must determine each partner's share of **ordinary business income (loss)** and **separately stated items.** Partnership ordinary business income (loss) is all partnership income (loss) exclusive of any separately stated items of income (loss). Separately stated items share one common characteristic—they are treated differently from a partner's share of ordinary business income (loss) for tax purposes. To better understand why certain items must be separately disclosed to partners, consider how two particular separately stated items, dividend income and capital losses, might affect an individual partner's tax liability. Qualified dividend income allocated to individual partners is taxed at either a 0 percent or 15 percent rate, depending on individual partners' tax brackets.[46] In a similar vein, individual partners without capital gains during the year may deduct up to $3,000 in capital losses against their ordinary income, while other individual partners with capital gains may deduct more.[47] If a partnership's dividends and capital losses were simply buried in the computation of its overall income or loss for the year, the partner would be unable to apply these specific tax rules to her unique situation and determine her correct tax liability.

The Code specifically enumerates several common separately stated items, including short-term capital gains and losses, long-term capital gains and losses, §1231

**THE KEY FACTS**

**Reporting the Results of Partnership Operations**

- Partnerships file annual information returns reporting their ordinary business income (loss) and separately stated items.
- Ordinary business income (loss) = partnership overall income or loss exclusive of separately stated items.
- Separately stated items change partners' tax liabilities when they are separately stated.

---

[43]§701.
[44]§7704.
[45]Other items, such as tax credits, may also flow through the partnership to partners.
[46]§1(h).
[47]§1211.

gains and losses, charitable contributions, and dividends.[48] Many more items are considered under regulations issued by the IRS.[49] Exhibit 20-6 lists several other common separately stated items.

### EXHIBIT 20-6 Common Separately Stated Items

- Interest income
- Guaranteed payments
- Net earnings (loss) from self-employment
- Tax-exempt income
- Net rental real estate income
- Investment interest expense
- §179 deduction

---

**Example 20-15**

After constructing a building and purchasing equipment in its first year of operations ending on December 31, *2009,* CCS invested $15,000 of its remaining idle cash in stock and bonds. CCS's books reflected an overall loss for the year of $80,000. Included in the $80,000 loss were $2,100 of dividend income, $1,200 of short-term capital gains, and a $20,000 deduction for the capital interest given to Sarah at the end of 2009 (see Example 20-10). How much ordinary business loss and what separately stated items are allocated to the CCS members for the taxable year ended December 31, *2009?*

**Answer:** As reflected in the table below, CCS has $63,300 of ordinary business loss. In addition, it has $2,100 of dividend income, $1,200 in short-term capital gains, and $20,000 of ordinary deduction (related to the capital interest Sarah received) that are separately stated items. To Nicole, Sarah, and Chanzz Inc., CCS would report $21,100 of ordinary business loss, $700 of dividend income, and $400 of short-term capital gain. In addition, CCS would report $20,000 of ordinary income to Sarah for the capital interest she received, and a $10,000 deduction to Nicole and Chanzz Inc. reflecting the amount of partnership capital they relinquished.

| Description | CCS | Nicole $\left(\frac{1}{3}\right)$ | Sarah $\left(\frac{1}{3}\right)$ | Chanzz Inc. $\left(\frac{1}{3}\right)$ |
|---|---|---|---|---|
| 2009 overall net loss | ($80,000) | | | |
| Less: | | | | |
| Dividends | $2,100 | | | |
| Short-term capital gains | $1,200 | | | |
| Ordinary deduction for Sarah's capital interest | ($20,000) | | | |
| **Ordinary business loss** | **($63,300)** | **($21,100)** | **($21,100)** | **($21,100)** |
| **Separately stated Items** | | | | |
| Dividends | $2,100 | $700 | $700 | $700 |
| Short-term capital gains | $1,200 | $400 | $400 | $400 |
| Ordinary income for capital interest to Sarah | $20,000 | | $20,000 | |
| Ordinary deduction for capital interest to Sarah | ($20,000) | ($10,000) | | ($10,000) |

Nicole and Sarah will treat their shares of CCS's ordinary business loss as an *ordinary* loss and include it along with their shares of dividend income and short-term capital gain in their individual tax

(*continued on page 20-19...*)

---

[48]§702.
[49]Reg. §1.702-1(a).

returns for the year.[50] Chanzz Inc. will also include its share of these items in its annual tax return. But, because Chanzz is a corporation, different tax rules apply to its share of dividend income and short-term capital gains. For example, Chanzz will be entitled to the dividends received deduction, while Nicole and Sarah will pay tax on their share of dividend income at a 15 percent rate since their marginal rates on ordinary income are above 15 percent.

Notice that the character of separately stated items is determined at the partnership level rather than at the partner level.[51] This treatment reflects the entity theory.

**Example 20-16**

*What if:* Assume Chanzz Inc. is an investments dealer rather than a sports franchise operator. How would Chanzz Inc. classify its share of the $1,200 gain from the securities sold by CCS during 2009?

**Answer:** Chanzz Inc. would classify the $1,200 as short-term capital gains. Because the securities CCS sold were capital assets to it, the gain on the sale is a capital gain even though the securities are inventory (an ordinary asset) to Chanzz Inc. That is, we determine the character of the income at the partnership level, not the partner level.

**Guaranteed Payments**   In addition to dividends, capital gains, and other routine separately stated items, **guaranteed payments** are also very common items reported separately to the partners who receive them. As their name suggests, guaranteed payments are fixed amounts paid to partners regardless of whether the partnership shows a profit or loss for the year.[52] We can think of them—and some partnerships treat them—as economically equivalent to cash salary payments made to partners for services provided.[53] Specifically, they are typically deducted in computing a partnership's ordinary income or loss for the year. Though not eliminated from a partnership's ordinary business income (loss) computation, guaranteed payments must, nevertheless, be separately stated to the partners who receive them. This separate reporting serves the same purpose as providing W-2 forms to employees. Because guaranteed payments are similar to salary payments, partners treat them as ordinary income.

*continued from page 20-10. . .*

Because Sarah received an additional capital interest for marketing services she provided at the end of 2009, she held a 40 percent capital and profits interest and Nicole and Chanzz Inc. each held a 30 percent capital and profits interests at the beginning of 2010. After Sarah's initial work in formulating a marketing strategy in 2009, Nicole suggested they hire a permanent employee to oversee product marketing. However, because they were unable to find a suitable candidate, Sarah continued to shoulder the product marketing responsibilities in addition to her normal role as a managing member of CCS. To compensate Sarah for her additional workload, all members of CCS agreed to pay Sarah a $10,000 guaranteed payment for her marketing efforts in 2010. Exhibit 20-7 provides CCS's income statement for 2010. ■

---

[50]Nicole and Sarah would report their share of ordinary business loss on Schedule E, their share of dividend income on Schedule B, and their share of short-term capital gain on Schedule D of Form 1040.

[51]§702(b).

[52]§707(c).

[53]Fringe benefits that partners receive for services provided such as medical insurance and group-term life insurance are also treated as guaranteed payments. In addition to compensating partners for services provided, guaranteed payments are also made to partners for the use of capital.

**EXHIBIT 20-7** Color Comfort Sheets, LLC

| Income Statement December 31, 2010 | |
| --- | --- |
| Sales revenue | $40,000 |
| Cost of goods sold | (20,000) |
| Employee wages | (50,000) |
| Depreciation expense | (18,000) |
| Guaranteed payments | (10,000) |
| Miscellaneous expenses | (2,800) |
| Dividend income | 500 |
| Long-term capital gains | 300 |
| Overall net loss | ($60,000) |

**Example 20-17**

Given CCS's operating results for *2010* presented in Exhibit 20-7, how much ordinary business loss and what separately stated items will it report on its return for the year? How will it allocate these amounts to its members?

**Answer:** The table below displays CCS's ordinary business loss and separately stated items and the allocation of these amounts to CCS's members:

| Description | CCS | Nicole 30% | Sarah 40% | Chanzz Inc. 30% × 6/12* | Greg 30% × 6/12* |
| --- | --- | --- | --- | --- | --- |
| Sales revenue | $40,000 | | | | |
| Cost of goods sold | ($20,000) | | | | |
| Employee wages | ($50,000) | | | | |
| Depreciation expense | ($18,000) | | | | |
| Guaranteed payment to Sarah | ($10,000) | | | | |
| Miscellaneous expenses | ($2,800) | | | | |
| Ordinary business loss | ($60,800) | ($18,240) | ($24,320) | ($9,120) | ($9,120) |
| Separately stated to partners | | | | | |
| Dividends | $500 | $150 | $200 | $75 | $75 |
| Short-term capital gains | $300 | $90 | $120 | $45 | $45 |
| Guaranteed payment | | | $10,000 | | |

*As we noted in Example 20-11, Chanzz Inc. sold out to Greg Randall on July 1, 2010. Therefore, the items related to Chanzz Inc.'s original 30 percent interest must be allocated between Chanzz Inc. and Greg Randall.[54]

**Self-Employment Tax**  Individual partners, like sole proprietors, may be responsible for paying **self-employment taxes** in addition to income taxes on their share of earned income from partnerships.[55] The degree to which partners are responsible for self-employment taxes depends on their legal status as general partners, limited partners, or LLC members and their business activities. General partners report guaranteed payments for services they provide and their share of ordinary business income (loss)

[54]We assume here that the items are allocated based on the number of months the interest was held. See Chapter 21 for additional detail regarding methods to account for partners' varying interests in a partnership when a partnership interest is sold.

[55]Chapters 7 and 15 more fully discuss earned income and related self-employment taxes.

as self-employment income (loss) because they are actively involved in managing the partnership. Limited partners, on the other hand, are generally not allowed under state law to participate in the management of limited partnerships. Therefore, their share of ordinary business income (loss) is conceptually more like investment income than trade or business income. As a result, it is not subject to self-employment tax. However, if limited partners receive guaranteed payments for services provided to the partnership, they treat those payments as self-employment income.

Because LLC members may either be managing or nonmanaging members, the approach to taxing their share of ordinary business income (loss) for self-employment tax purposes ought to depend to some degree on their level of involvement in the LLC.[56] Tax rules in this area were developed before the popularity of LLCs, however, so no authoritative rules currently exist to help LLCs decide whether to characterize their members' shares of ordinary business income (loss) as self-employment income (loss). However, a proposed regulation issued by the IRS and later withdrawn can assist partnerships in drawing the line between aggressive and conservative positions in this area.[57] It provides that LLC members who have personal liability for the debts of the LLC by reason of being an LLC member, who have authority to contract on behalf of the LLC, *or* who participate more than 500 hours in the LLC's trade or business during the taxable year should be classified as general partners when applying the self-employment tax rules.

The lack of authoritative guidance in this area has resulted in a predictable diversity of practice. Some taxpayers and their advisors ignore the proposed regulations and claim that managing members of LLCs are similar to limited partners and shouldn't have to pay self-employment taxes at all. Others follow the spirit of the proposed regulation and take the approach that managing members are similar to general partners and should pay self-employment tax on part or all of their share of ordinary business income (loss), depending on their level of involvement in the LLC.[58]

---

**Example 20-18**

For *2010*, should CCS classify Sarah's $10,000 guaranteed payment as self-employment income?

**Answer:** Yes. The law is clear with respect to guaranteed payments to LLC members—they are always treated as self-employment income.

Using the proposed regulation, will CCS classify Sarah's $24,320 share of ordinary business loss for *2010* as a self-employment loss?

**Answer:** Yes. Under the proposed regulations, an LLC member who has personal liability for LLC debts or the ability to contract on behalf of the LLC, or who spends more than 500 hours participating in the business of the LLC, is classified as a general partner when applying the self-employment tax rules. Given Sarah's status as a managing member of CCS, at least one but probably all three criteria for classifying her share of CCS's ordinary business loss as self-employment loss will apply. Although these rules have not been finalized and are therefore not authoritative, the IRS would likely follow them because they represent its current thinking on the matter. Applying the law this way, CCS will report a $14,320 self-employment loss [($24,320) share of ordinary business loss + $10,000 guaranteed payment] as a separately stated item to Sarah so she can properly compute her self-employment tax liability on her individual return.

---

[56]Guaranteed payments to LLC members are clearly subject to self-employment tax because they are similar to salary payments.

[57]Proposed Reg. §1.1402(a)-2.

[58]Nonmanaging LLC members are so similar to limited partners that taxpayers and their advisors typically treat them as if they were limited partners for self-employment tax purposes.

**Example 20-19**

Using the proposed regulation, will CCS classify Nicole's $18,240 share of ordinary business loss for *2010* as self-employment loss?

**Answer:** Yes. Because Nicole, like Sarah, is involved in the day-to-day management of CCS, it will classify her entire share of ordinary business loss as self-employment loss, consistent with its classification of Sarah's share of ordinary business loss, and report the amount as a separately stated item to Nicole.

Under the proposed regulation, will CCS treat Greg's $9,120 share of ordinary business loss for 2010 as self-employment loss?

**Answer:** Yes. CCS will treat Greg's share of ordinary business loss as self-employment loss because he has guaranteed a portion of CCS's debt. CCS's total self-employment loss is $41,680 consisting of Sarah's $14,320 self-employment loss, Nicole's $18,240 self-employment loss, and Greg's $9,120 self-employment loss.

### Allocating Partners' Shares of Income and Loss

Partnership tax rules provide partners with tremendous flexibility in allocating overall profit and loss as well as specific items of profit and loss to partners, as long as partners agree to the allocations and they have "substantial economic effect." Partnership allocations designed to accomplish business objectives other than reducing taxes will generally have substantial economic effect.[59] If they are not defined in the partnership agreement or do not have substantial economic effect, allocations to partners must be made in accordance with the "partners' interests in the partnership."[60] Tax regulations presume the partners' interests in the partnership to be equal on a per capita basis but allow consideration for other factors reflecting the partners' economic arrangement, such as their capital contributions, distribution rights, and interests in economic profits and losses (if different from their interests in taxable income and loss). Partnership allocations inconsistent with partners' capital interests or overall profit-and-loss-sharing ratios are called **special allocations.**

Although special allocations are made largely at the discretion of partners, certain special allocations of gains and losses from the sale of partnership property are mandatory. Specifically, when property contributed to a partnership with built-in gains (fair market value greater than tax basis) or built-in losses (tax basis less than fair market value) is subsequently sold, the partnership must allocate, to the extent possible, the built-in gain or built-in loss (at the time of the contribution) solely to the contributing partner and then allocate any remaining gain or loss to all the partners in accordance with their profit-and-loss-sharing ratios.[61] This rule prevents contributing partners from shifting their built-in gains and built-in losses to other partners.

**Example 20-20**

*What if:* Assume that at the beginning of 2010, Nicole and Sarah decide to organize CCS's marketing efforts by region. Nicole will take responsibility for marketing in the western United States, and Sarah will take responsibility for marketing in the eastern United States. All members agree that CCS's provision for allocating profits and losses in the operating agreement should be amended to provide Nicole and Sarah with better incentives. Specifically, CCS would like to allocate the first 20 percent of profits or losses from each region to Nicole and Sarah. Then, it will allocate any remaining profits or losses

(*continued on page 20-23...*)

---

[59]Reg. §1.704-1 defines the requirements allocations must satisfy to have substantial economic effect.
[60]§704(b).

[61]§704(c). In addition to requiring built-in gains and losses to be specially allocated to contributing partners, §704(c) also requires depreciation to be specially allocated to noncontributing partners. Tax regulations permit partners to choose among several methods for making these required special allocations. Further discussion of these methods is beyond the scope of this book.

from each region among the members in proportion to their capital interests and profits interests at the end of 2010—40 percent to Sarah and 30 percent each to Nicole and Greg. Will CCS's proposed special allocation of profits and losses be accepted by the IRS?

**Answer:** Yes. Since CCS is a partnership for federal income tax purposes, it can make special allocations to members, and because they are designed to accomplish a business objective other than tax reduction, the IRS will accept them.[62]

*What if:* Assume the land Nicole contributed to CCS with a fair market value of $150,000 and tax basis of $20,000 was sold by CCS for $150,000 of consideration almost immediately after it was contributed. How would the resulting $130,000 gain be allocated among the members of CCS?

**Answer:** Nicole's built-in gain of $130,000 at the time of contribution must be allocated exclusively to her to prevent it from being shifted to other CCS members. Shifting the gain to other members could lower the overall tax liability of the CCS members if Sarah and Greg's marginal tax rates are lower than Nicole's marginal tax rate.

*What if:* Suppose CCS held the land Nicole contributed for one year and then sold it on March 31, 2010, for $180,000 instead of $150,000. How should the resulting $160,000 gain be allocated to Nicole, Sarah, and Chanzz Inc.?

**Answer:** The allocations are $139,000 to Nicole, $12,000 to Sarah, and $9,000 to Chanzz Inc., as reflected in the table below:

| Description | CCS | Nicole 30% | Sarah 40% | Chanzz Inc. 30% |
|---|---|---|---|---|
| Total gain from sale of land | $160,000 | | | |
| Less: Special allocation to Nicole of built-in gain | ($130,000) | $130,000 | | |
| Post-contribution appreciation in land | $ 30,000 | $ 9,000 | $12,000 | $9,000 |
| Total gain allocations | | $139,000 | $12,000 | $9,000 |

## Partnership Compliance Issues

Although partnerships don't pay taxes, they are required to file **Form 1065,** U.S. Return of Partnership Income, with the IRS by the 15th day of the 4th month after their year-end (April 15 for a calendar year-end partnership). Partnerships may receive an automatic five-month extension to file by filing **Form 7004** with the IRS before the original due date of the return.[63] Page 1 of Form 1065 details the calculation of the partnership's ordinary business income (loss) for the year, and page 3, **Schedule K,** lists the partnership's ordinary business income (loss) and separately stated items. In addition to preparing Form 1065, the partnership is also responsible for preparing a Schedule K-1 for each partner detailing her individual share of the partnership's ordinary business income (loss) and separately stated items for the year. Once prepared, Schedule K-1s are included with Form 1065 when it is filed, and Schedule K-1s are also separately provided to all partners (each partner receives a Schedule K-1 with her income and loss allocations). Exhibit 20-8, parts I through III, display CCS's information return, showing the operating results we summarized in Example 20-17 and Sarah's actual schedule K-1, reflecting the facts and conclusions in Examples 20-17 and 20-18.[64]

[62]Reg. §1.704-1(b)(5), Example 10, suggests that this type of special allocation would not violate the substantial economic effect rules.

[63]Under §6698, late filing penalties apply if the partnership fails to file by the normal or extended due date for the return.

[64]We use 2009 forms because 2010 forms were unavailable at the time the book was published.

**EXHIBIT 20-8 (PART I)**    Page 1 Form 1065
CCS's 2010 Ordinary Business Loss (on 2009 forms)

Form **1065**
Department of the Treasury
Internal Revenue Service

## U.S. Return of Partnership Income

For calendar year 2009, or tax year beginning _____, 2009, ending _____, 20 _____.
▶ See separate instructions.

OMB No. 1545-0099

**2009**

| | | |
|---|---|---|
| **A** Principal business activity | **Use the IRS label. Otherwise, print or type.** Name of partnership **Color Comfort Sheets** | **D** Employer identification number |
| **B** Principal product or service | Number, street, and room or suite no. If a P.O. box, see the instructions. **375 East 450 South** | **E** Date business started **April 1, 2009** |
| **C** Business code number | City or town, state, and ZIP code **Salt Lake City, UT 84608** | **F** Total assets (see the instructions) $ 370,000 |

**G** Check applicable boxes:  **(1)** ☑ Initial return  **(2)** ☐ Final return  **(3)** ☐ Name change  **(4)** ☐ Address change  **(5)** ☐ Amended return
**(6)** ☐ Technical termination - also check (1) or (2)

**H** Check accounting method:  **(1)** ☑ Cash  **(2)** ☐ Accrual  **(3)** ☐ Other (specify) ▶ _____

**I** Number of Schedules K-1. Attach one for each person who was a partner at any time during the tax year ▶    4

**J** Check if Schedules C and M-3 are attached . . . . . . . . . . . . . . . . . . . . . . . . ☐

**Caution.** Include **only** trade or business income and expenses on lines 1a through 22 below. See the instructions for more information.

### Income

| | | | | |
|---|---|---|---|---|
| **1a** | Gross receipts or sales . . . . . . . . . . . | **1a** 40,000 | | |
| **b** | Less returns and allowances . . . . . . . . . | **1b** | **1c** | 40,000 |
| **2** | Cost of goods sold (Schedule A, line 8) . . . . . . . . | | **2** | 20,000 |
| **3** | Gross profit. Subtract line 2 from line 1c . . . . . . . | | **3** | 20,000 |
| **4** | Ordinary income (loss) from other partnerships, estates, and trusts *(attach statement)* . . | | **4** | |
| **5** | Net farm profit (loss) *(attach Schedule F (Form 1040))* . . . . . | | **5** | |
| **6** | Net gain (loss) from Form 4797, Part II, line 17 *(attach Form 4797)* . . . . | | **6** | |
| **7** | Other income (loss) *(attach statement)* . . . . . . . . | | **7** | |
| **8** | **Total income (loss).** Combine lines 3 through 7 . . . . . . | | **8** | 20,000 |

### Deductions (see the instructions for limitations)

| | | | | |
|---|---|---|---|---|
| **9** | Salaries and wages (other than to partners) (less employment credits) . . . . . | | **9** | 50,000 |
| **10** | Guaranteed payments to partners . . . . . . . . . . | | **10** | 10,000 |
| **11** | Repairs and maintenance . . . . . . . . . . . . | | **11** | |
| **12** | Bad debts . . . . . . . . . . . . . . . . | | **12** | |
| **13** | Rent . . . . . . . . . . . . . . . . . . | | **13** | |
| **14** | Taxes and licenses . . . . . . . . . . . . . | | **14** | |
| **15** | Interest . . . . . . . . . . . . . . . . | | **15** | |
| **16a** | Depreciation *(if required, attach Form 4562)* . . . . . | **16a** | | |
| **b** | Less depreciation reported on Schedule A and elsewhere on return | **16b** | **16c** | 18,000 |
| **17** | Depletion **(Do not deduct oil and gas depletion.)** . . . . . | | **17** | |
| **18** | Retirement plans, etc. . . . . . . . . . . . . | | **18** | |
| **19** | Employee benefit programs . . . . . . . . . . . | | **19** | |
| **20** | Other deductions *(attach statement)* . . . . . . . . | | **20** | 2,800 |
| **21** | **Total deductions.** Add the amounts shown in the far right column for lines 9 through 20 . | | **21** | 80,800 |
| **22** | **Ordinary business income (loss).** Subtract line 21 from line 8 . . . . . . | | **22** | (60,800) |

**Sign Here**

Under penalties of perjury, I declare that I have examined this return, including accompanying schedules and statements, and to the best of my knowledge and belief, it is true, correct, and complete. Declaration of preparer (other than general partner or limited liability company member manager) is based on all information of which preparer has any knowledge.

May the IRS discuss this return with the preparer shown below (see instructions)? ☐ Yes ☐ No

▶ _____    ▶ _____
Signature of general partner or limited liability company member manager    Date

**Paid Preparer's Use Only**

| Preparer's signature | Date | Check if self-employed ▶ ☐ | Preparer's SSN or PTIN |
|---|---|---|---|
| Firm's name (or yours if self-employed), address, and ZIP code | | | EIN ▶ |
| | | | Phone no. |

**For Privacy Act and Paperwork Reduction Act Notice, see separate instructions.**    Cat. No. 11390Z    Form **1065** (2009)

**EXHIBIT 20-8 (PART II)**   Page 3 Form 1065
CCS's 2010 Schedule K (on 2009 forms)

Form 1065 (2009)                                                                                          Page **4**

| Schedule K | | Partners' Distributive Share Items | | Total amount |
|---|---|---|---|---|
| **Income (Loss)** | 1 | Ordinary business income (loss) (page 1, line 22) . . . . . . . . . . | 1 | (60,800) |
| | 2 | Net rental real estate income (loss) (*attach Form 8825*) . . . . . . . . . | 2 | |
| | 3a | Other gross rental income (loss) . . . . . . . . . . **3a** | | |
| | b | Expenses from other rental activities (*attach statement*) . **3b** | | |
| | c | Other net rental income (loss). Subtract line 3b from line 3a . . . . . . . | 3c | |
| | 4 | Guaranteed payments . . . . . . . . . . . . . . . . | 4 | 10,000 |
| | 5 | Interest income . . . . . . . . . . . . . . . . . . | 5 | |
| | 6 | Dividends:   a   Ordinary dividends . . . . . . . . . . . . | 6a | 500 |
| | | b   Qualified dividends . . . . . **6b**   500 | | |
| | 7 | Royalties . . . . . . . . . . . . . . . . . . . | 7 | |
| | 8 | Net short-term capital gain (loss) (*attach Schedule D (Form 1065)*) . . . | 8 | |
| | 9a | Net long-term capital gain (loss) (*attach Schedule D (Form 1065)*) . . . | 9a | 300 |
| | b | Collectibles (28%) gain (loss) . . . . . **9b** | | |
| | c | Unrecaptured section 1250 gain (*attach statement*) . . **9c** | | |
| | 10 | Net section 1231 gain (loss) (*attach Form 4797*) . . . . . . . . | 10 | |
| | 11 | Other income (loss) (*see instructions*)   Type ▶ _____ | 11 | |
| **Deductions** | 12 | Section 179 deduction (*attach Form 4562*) . . . . . . . . . | 12 | |
| | 13a | Contributions . . . . . . . . . . . . . . . . . . | 13a | |
| | b | Investment interest expense . . . . . . . . . . . . . | 13b | |
| | c | Section 59(e)(2) expenditures:   (1) Type ▶ _____   (2) Amount ▶ | 13c(2) | |
| | d | Other deductions (*see instructions*)   Type ▶ _____ | 13d | |
| **Self-Employ-ment** | 14a | Net earnings (loss) from self-employment . . . . . . . . . | 14a | (41,680) |
| | b | Gross farming or fishing income . . . . . . . . . . . | 14b | |
| | c | Gross nonfarm income . . . . . . . . . . . . . . . | 14c | |
| **Credits** | 15a | Low-income housing credit (section 42(j)(5)) . . . . . . . . | 15a | |
| | b | Low-income housing credit (other) . . . . . . . . . . . | 15b | |
| | c | Qualified rehabilitation expenditures (rental real estate) (*attach Form 3468*) . . | 15c | |
| | d | Other rental real estate credits (*see instructions*)   Type ▶ _____ | 15d | |
| | e | Other rental credits (*see instructions*)   Type ▶ _____ | 15e | |
| | f | Other credits (*see instructions*)   Type ▶ _____ | 15f | |
| **Foreign Transactions** | 16a | Name of country or U.S. possession ▶ _____ | | |
| | b | Gross income from all sources . . . . . . . . . . . | 16b | |
| | c | Gross income sourced at partner level . . . . . . . . . | 16c | |
| | | *Foreign gross income sourced at partnership level* | | |
| | d | Passive category ▶ _____   e General category ▶ _____   f Other ▶ | 16f | |
| | | *Deductions allocated and apportioned at partner level* | | |
| | g | Interest expense ▶ _____   h Other . . . . . . . ▶ | 16h | |
| | | *Deductions allocated and apportioned at partnership level to foreign source income* | | |
| | i | Passive category ▶ _____   j General category ▶ _____   k Other ▶ | 16k | |
| | l | Total foreign taxes (check one): ▶ Paid ☐   Accrued ☐ . . . . . | 16l | |
| | m | Reduction in taxes available for credit (*attach statement*) . . . . . | 16m | |
| | n | Other foreign tax information (*attach statement*) . . . . . . . | | |
| **Alternative Minimum Tax (AMT) Items** | 17a | Post-1986 depreciation adjustment . . . . . . . . . . | 17a | |
| | b | Adjusted gain or loss . . . . . . . . . . . . . . | 17b | |
| | c | Depletion (other than oil and gas) . . . . . . . . . . | 17c | |
| | d | Oil, gas, and geothermal properties—gross income . . . . . . | 17d | |
| | e | Oil, gas, and geothermal properties—deductions . . . . . . | 17e | |
| | f | Other AMT items (*attach statement*) . . . . . . . . . | 17f | |
| **Other Information** | 18a | Tax-exempt interest income . . . . . . . . . . . . | 18a | |
| | b | Other tax-exempt income . . . . . . . . . . . . . | 18b | |
| | c | Nondeductible expenses . . . . . . . . . . . . . | 18c | |
| | 19a | Distributions of cash and marketable securities . . . . . . | 19a | |
| | b | Distributions of other property . . . . . . . . . . . | 19b | |
| | 20a | Investment income . . . . . . . . . . . . . . . | 20a | |
| | b | Investment expenses . . . . . . . . . . . . . . | 20b | |
| | c | Other items and amounts (*attach statement*) . . . . . . . | | |

Form **1065** (2009)

**EXHIBIT 20-8 (PART III)** 2010 Schedule K-1 for Sarah Walker (on 2009 forms)
CCS Operates as an LLC

651109

| | | | |
|---|---|---|---|
| ☑ Final K-1 | ☐ Amended K-1 | | OMB No. 1545-0099 |

**Schedule K-1**
**(Form 1065)**

**20**09

Department of the Treasury
Internal Revenue Service

For calendar year 2009, or tax
year beginning _____, 2009
ending _____, 20 _____

**Partner's Share of Income, Deductions,**
**Credits, etc.** ▶ See back of form and separate instructions.

| **Part I** | **Information About the Partnership** |
|---|---|

**A** Partnership's employer identification number

**B** Partnership's name, address, city, state, and ZIP code

**Color Comfort Sheets**
**375 East 450 South**
**Salt Lake City, UT 84608**

**C** IRS Center where partnership filed return

**D** ☐ Check if this is a publicly traded partnership (PTP)

| **Part II** | **Information About the Partner** |
|---|---|

**E** Partner's identifying number

**F** Partner's name, address, city, state, and ZIP code

**Sarah Walker**
**549 Laurel Lane**
**Holiday, UT 84609**

**G** ☑ General partner or LLC member-manager     ☐ Limited partner or other LLC member

**H** ☐ Domestic partner     ☐ Foreign partner

**I** What type of entity is this partner? **Individual**

**J** Partner's share of profit, loss, and capital (see instructions):

| | Beginning | | Ending | |
|---|---|---|---|---|
| Profit | 40 | % | 40 | % |
| Loss | 40 | % | 40 | % |
| Capital | 40 | % | 40 | % |

**K** Partner's share of liabilities at year end:

| | | |
|---|---|---|
| Nonrecourse | $ | 12,000 |
| Qualified nonrecourse financing | $ | 8,000 |
| Recourse | $ | 24,000 |

| **Part III** | **Partner's Share of Current Year Income, Deductions, Credits, and Other Items** |
|---|---|

| No. | Item | Amount | No. | Item | Amount |
|---|---|---|---|---|---|
| 1 | Ordinary business income (loss) | (24,320) | 15 | Credits | |
| 2 | Net rental real estate income (loss) | | | | |
| 3 | Other net rental income (loss) | | 16 | Foreign transactions | |
| 4 | Guaranteed payments | 10,000 | | | |
| 5 | Interest income | | | | |
| 6a | Ordinary dividends | | | | |
| 6b | Qualified dividends | 200 | | | |
| 7 | Royalties | | | | |
| 8 | Net short-term capital gain (loss) | | | | |
| 9a | Net long-term capital gain (loss) | 120 | 17 | Alternative minimum tax (AMT) items | |
| 9b | Collectibles (28%) gain (loss) | | | | |
| 9c | Unrecaptured section 1250 gain | | | | |
| 10 | Net section 1231 gain (loss) | | 18 | Tax-exempt income and nondeductible expenses | |
| 11 | Other income (loss) | | | | |
| 12 | Section 179 deduction | | 19 | Distributions | |
| 13 | Other deductions | | | | |
| | | | 20 | Other information | |
| 14 | Self-employment earnings (loss) | (14,320) | | | |

**L05**

# PARTNER'S ADJUSTED TAX BASIS IN PARTNERSHIP INTEREST

Earlier in this chapter, we discussed how partners measure their initial tax basis in their partnership interests when they contribute property or services to partnerships in exchange for their partnership interests, or when they purchase partnership interests from an existing partner. Unlike the basis in a stock or other similar investment, which is usually fixed, the basis in a partnership is dynamic and must be *adjusted* as the partnership generates income and losses, changes its debt levels, and makes distributions to partners. These annual adjustments to a partner's tax basis are required to ensure partners don't double-count taxable income/gains and deductible

expenses/losses, either when they sell their partnership interests or when they receive partnership distributions. They also ensure tax-exempt income and nondeductible expenses are not ultimately taxed or deducted.

Partners make the following adjustments to the basis in their partnership interests, annually and in the order listed:[65]

- Increase for actual and deemed cash contributions to the partnership during the year.[66]
- Increase for partner's share of ordinary business income and separately stated income/gain items.
- Increase for partner's share of tax-exempt income.
- Decrease for actual and deemed[67] cash distributions[68] during the year.
- Decrease for partner's share of nondeductible expenses (fines, penalties, etc.).
- Decrease for partner's share of ordinary business loss and separately stated expense/loss items.

Basis adjustments that decrease basis may never reduce a partner's tax basis below zero.[69]

## Example 20-21

Given the events that affected CCS and its members during *2009*, what tax basis did Nicole, Sarah, and Chanzz Inc. have in their ownership interests at the end of 2009?

**Answer:** Their bases in CCS were $4,000, $152,000, and $114,000, respectively. Their individual tax basis calculations at the end of 2009 are illustrated in the table below:

| Description | Nicole | Sarah | Chanzz Inc. | Explanation |
|---|---|---|---|---|
| (1) Initial tax basis (including debt) | $36,666 | $146,666 | $146,666 | Example 20-4. |
| (2) Dividends | $ 700 | $ 700 | $ 700 | Example 20-15. |
| (3) Short-term capital gains | $ 400 | $ 400 | $ 400 | Example 20-15. |
| (4) Debt reallocation (deemed cash contribution/distribution) | ($2,666) | $ 5,334 | ($2,666) | Example 20-10. |
| (5) Sarah's capital interest | ($10,000) | $ 20,000 | ($10,000) | Examples 20-10, 20-15. |
| (6) CCS's ordinary business loss | ($21,100) | ($21,100) | ($21,100) | Example 20-15. |
| Tax basis on 12/31/09 | $ 4,000 | $152,000 | $114,000 | Sum of (1) through (6). |

(*continued on page 20-28...*)

### THE KEY FACTS

**Partner's Basis Adjustments**

▌A partner will increase the tax basis in her partnership interest for:
- Contributions.
- Share of ordinary business income.
- Separately stated income/gain items.
- Tax-exempt income.

▌A partner will decrease the tax basis in her partnership interest for:
- Cash distributions.
- Share of nondeductible expenses.
- Share of ordinary business loss.
- Separately stated expense/loss items.

▌A partner's tax basis may not be negative.

---

[65]Reg. §1.704-1(d)(2).

[66]Recall that partners are deemed to have made a cash contribution to the partnership when they are allocated an additional share of partnership debt.

[67]Recall that partners are deemed to have received a cash distribution from the partnership when they are relieved of partnership debt.

[68]Property distributions to partners are also treated as basis reductions. We discuss property distributions at length in Chapter 21.

[69]§705(a)(2).

**What if:** Suppose Sarah sold her LLC interest but forgot to include her share of short-term capital gains when computing her basis to determine her gain on the sale. What are the tax consequences of Sarah's mistake?

**Answer:** Sarah would be double-taxed on the amount of the short-term capital gain. She was initially taxed on her share of the short-term capital gain allocation, and she would be taxed a second time when she recognized $400 more gain on the sale than had she included her share of the gain in her basis.

**What if:** Assume Sarah was allocated $700 of tax-exempt municipal bond income instead of dividend income. What would happen if she neglected to increase her basis in CCS by the $700 tax-exempt income?

**Answer:** If Sarah were to sell her interest in CCS for a price reflecting the tax-exempt income received, she would, in effect, be converting tax-exempt income into taxable income.

---

## Example 20-22

In addition to the other events of *2010*, CCS increased its debt from $100,000 to $130,000 in the second half of the year. The $30,000 increase was attributable to accounts payable owed to suppliers. Unlike the case of the $60,000 bank loan, the members did not guarantee any of the accounts payable. Therefore, the accounts payable are considered nonrecourse debt because CCS is an LLC. Given this information, what are Nicole's, Sarah's, and Greg's tax bases in CCS at the end of *2010*?

**Answer:** Their bases are $0, $140,000, and $124,000, respectively. Nicole, Sarah, and Greg would determine their tax basis in CCS at the end of *2010* as illustrated in the table below:

| Description | Nicole 30% | Sarah[70] 40% | Greg 30% | Explanation |
|---|---|---|---|---|
| (1) Tax basis on 1/1/10 | $4,000 | $152,000 | | Example 20-21. |
| (1) Greg's purchase of Chanzz Inc.'s interest | | | $124,000 | Example 20-11. |
| (2) Dividends | $ 150 | $ 200 | $ 75 | Example 20-17. |
| (3) Long-term capital gains | $ 90 | $ 120 | $ 45 | Example 20-17. |
| (4) Increase in nonrecourse debt from accounts payable (deemed cash contribution) | $9,000 | $ 12,000 | $ 9,000 | $30,000 × member's profit-sharing ratio. |
| (5) CCS's ordinary business loss | ($18,240) | ($24,320) | ($9,120) | Example 20-17. |
| Preliminary tax basis | ($5,000) | $140,000 | $124,000 | Sum of (1) through (5). |
| Tax basis on 12/31/10 | $ 0* | $140,000 | $124,000 | *Nicole's basis can't go below zero. |

---

## Cash Distributions in Operating Partnerships

Even after a partnership has been formed, partners are likely to continue to receive actual and deemed cash distributions. For example, excess cash may be distributed to partners to provide them with cash flow to pay their taxes or simply for consumption, and deemed cash distributions occur as partnerships pay down their debts. The

---

[70]Recall that Sarah received a $10,000 cash guaranteed payment for services she performed in 2010. Cash guaranteed payments generally don't have a direct impact on the recipient partner's tax basis because they are similar to salary payments.

principles underlying the calculation of a partner's tax basis highlight the fact that partners are taxed on income as the partnership earns it instead of when it distributes it. If cash is distributed when partners have a positive tax basis in their partnership interests, the distribution effectively represents a distribution of profits that have been previously taxed, a return of capital previously contributed by the partner to the partnership, a distribution of cash the partnership has borrowed, or some combination of the three. Thus, as long as a cash distribution does not exceed a partner's tax basis before the distribution, it reduces the partner's tax basis but is not taxed. However, as we highlighted in our discussion of property contributions earlier in this chapter, cash distributions (deemed or actual) in excess of a partner's basis are taxable gains and are generally treated as capital gains.[71]

---

**Example 20-23**

**What if:** In Example 20-22, we determined that Sarah's basis in her partnership interest was $140,000. Assume that in addition to the facts provided in that example, Sarah received a $10,000 distribution in *2010*. What will her tax basis be at the end of the year?

**Answer:** Sarah's tax basis will be $130,000. After making only her positive adjustments for the year (positive adjustments come before negative adjustments such as distributions), she has a basis of $164,320, which is greater than the $10,000 distribution. Thus, the distribution would not have been taxable because it did not exceed her basis. Sarah would have also reduced her basis by the $10,000 distribution in addition to the $24,320 reduction for her share of the ordinary business loss, leaving her with an ending basis of $130,000 ($164,320 − $10,000 − $24,320).

What problem would be created if Sarah did not reduce her basis by the $10,000 distribution?

**Answer:** After she receives a $10,000 distribution, the value of Sarah's interest will decrease by $10,000. If she didn't reduce her tax basis by the distribution, selling her interest would produce a $10,000 artificial tax loss.

---

# LOSS LIMITATIONS

**LO6**

While partners generally prefer not to invest in partnerships with operating losses, these losses generate current tax benefits when partners can deduct them against other sources of taxable income. Unlike capital losses, which are of limited usefulness if taxpayers don't also have capital gains, ordinary losses from partnerships are deductible against any type of taxable income. However, they are deductible on the partner's tax return only when they clear three separate hurdles: (1) tax basis, (2) at-risk amount, and (3) passive activity loss hurdles. We discuss each hurdle below.

## Tax Basis Limitation

A partner's basis limits the amount of partnership losses the partner can use to offset other sources of income. In theory, a partner's basis represents the amount a partner has invested in a partnership (or may have to invest to satisfy her debt obligations). As a result, partners may not utilize partnership losses in excess of their investment or outside basis in their partnership interests. Any losses allocated in excess of their basis must be suspended and carried forward indefinitely until they have sufficient basis to utilize the losses.[72] Among other things, partners may create additional tax

[71]§731.
[72]§704(d).

basis in the future by making capital contributions, by guaranteeing more partnership debt, and by helping their partnership to become profitable.

**Example 20-24**

In Example 20-22 we discovered Nicole was allocated $5,000 of ordinary loss in excess of her tax basis for *2010*, leaving her with a basis of zero at the end of *2010*. What does Nicole do with this loss?

**Answer:** Nicole will carry forward all $5,000 of ordinary loss in excess of her tax basis indefinitely until her tax basis in CCS becomes positive. To the extent her tax basis increases in the future, the tax basis limitation will no longer apply to her ordinary loss. Even then, however, the at-risk and/or passive activity loss hurdles may ultimately apply to constrain her ability to deduct the loss on her future tax returns.

**What if:** Assuming Nicole is allocated $4,000 of income from CCS in 2011, how much of her $5,000 suspended loss will clear the tax basis hurdle in *2011*?

**Answer:** Nicole's basis will initially increase by $4,000. Then she can apply $4,000 of her suspended loss against this basis increase, leaving her tax basis at zero and holding a remaining suspended loss of $1,000. The $4,000 loss clearing the tax basis hurdle must still clear the at-risk and passive activity loss hurdles before Nicole can deduct it on her return.

## THE KEY FACTS

### Loss Limitations

■ Partnership losses in excess of a partner's tax basis are suspended and carried forward until additional basis is created.

■ Remaining partnership losses are further suspended by the at-risk rules to the extent a partner is allocated nonrecourse debt not secured by real property.

■ If a partner is not a material participant or the partnership is involved in rental activities, losses remaining after application of the tax basis and at-risk limitations may be used only against other passive income or when the partnership interest is sold.

## At-Risk Limitation

The at-risk hurdle or limitation is more restrictive than the tax basis limitation, because it excludes a type of debt normally included in a partner's tax basis. We have already highlighted the distinction between recourse and nonrecourse debt and noted that partners allocated recourse debt have economic risk of loss, while partners allocated nonrecourse debt have no risk of loss. Instead, the risk of loss on nonrecourse debt is borne by lenders. The **at-risk rules** in §465 were adopted to limit the ability of partners to use nonrecourse debt as a means of creating tax basis to use losses from tax shelter partnerships expressly designed to generate losses for the partners. The at-risk rules limit partners' losses to their amount "at risk" in the partnership—their **at-risk amount.** Generally, a partner's at-risk amount is the same as her tax basis except that, with one exception, the partner's share of certain nonrecourse debts is not included in the at-risk amount. Specifically, the only nonrecourse debts considered to be at risk are nonrecourse real estate mortgages from commercial lenders that are unrelated to borrowers. This type of debt is called **qualified nonrecourse financing.**[73] In addition to qualified nonrecourse financing, partners are considered to be at risk to the extent of cash and the tax basis of property contributed to the partnership. Further, partners are at risk for any partnership recourse debt allocated to them.

Partners apply the at-risk limitation after the tax basis limitation. Any partnership losses that would otherwise have been allowed under the tax basis limitation are further limited to the extent they exceed a partner's at-risk amount. Losses limited under the at-risk rules are carried forward indefinitely until the partner generates additional at-risk amounts to utilize the losses, or until they are applied to reduce any gain from selling the partnership interest.

**Example 20-25**

In Example 20-24 we discovered Nicole was allocated an ordinary business loss of $18,240. Of this loss, $13,240 cleared the tax basis hurdle and $5,000 did not. How much of the $13,240 ordinary business loss that clears the tax basis hurdle will clear the at-risk hurdle?

*(continued on page 20-31...)*

[73]§465(b)(6).

**Answer:** $4,240. The table below summarizes and compares Nicole's calculations to determine her tax basis and at-risk limitations for *2010*:

| Example | Description | Tax Basis | At-Risk Amount | Explanation |
|---------|-------------|-----------|----------------|-------------|
| 20-22 | (1) Nicole's tax basis on 1/1/10 | $ 4,000 | $4,000 | Nicole's tax basis and at-risk amount are the same because she was only allocated recourse debt and qualified nonrecourse financing. |
| 20-22 | (2) Dividends | $ 150 | $ 150 | |
| 20-22 | (3) Long-term capital gains | $ 90 | $ 90 | |
| 20-22 | (4) Nonrecourse accounts payable | $ 9,000 | $ 0 | |
| | (5) Tax basis and at-risk amount before ordinary business loss | $13,240 | $4,240 | Sum of (1) through (4). |
| 20-22 | (6) Ordinary business loss | ($18,240) | | |
| | (7) Loss clearing the tax basis hurdle | ($13,240) | | Loss limited to (5). |
| | Loss suspended by tax basis hurdle | ($5,000) | | (6) − (7). |
| | (8) Loss clearing tax basis hurdle | | ($13,240) | (7). |
| | **(9) Loss clearing at-risk hurdle** | | **($4,240)** | Loss limited to (5). |
| | Loss suspended by at-risk hurdle | | ($9,000) | (8) − (9). |

Although Nicole's $9,000 share of the nonrecourse accounts payable added in *2010* and her investment income of $990 allow her to create enough tax basis in *2010* to get $13,240 of her $18,240 ordinary business loss past the tax basis limitation, she is not at risk with respect to her $9,000 share of accounts payable because an LLC's accounts payable are general nonrecourse debt. Therefore, $9,000 of the $13,240 ordinary business loss clearing the tax basis hurdle is suspended under the at-risk limitation. As a result, Nicole has two separate losses to carry forward: a $5,000 ordinary loss limited by her tax basis and a $9,000 ordinary loss limited by the at-risk rules, leaving $4,240 of ordinary loss that overcomes both the tax basis and at-risk hurdles.

## Passive Activity Loss Limitation

Prior to 1986, partners with sufficient tax basis and at-risk amounts were able to utilize ordinary losses from their partnerships to offset portfolio income (that is, interest, dividends, and capital gains), salary income, and self-employment income from partnerships and other trades or businesses. During this time, a partnership tax shelter industry thrived by marketing to wealthy investors partnership interests designed primarily to generate ordinary losses they could use to shield other income from tax. To combat this practice, Congress introduced the **passive activity loss (PAL) rules.**[74] These rules were enacted as a backstop to the at-risk rules and are applied after the tax basis and at-risk limitations. Thus, depending on their situation, partners may

---

[74]§469. The passive activity loss rules apply primarily to individuals but also to estates, trusts, closely held C corporations, and personal service corporations.

have to overcome *three separate hurdles* before finally reporting partnership ordinary losses on their returns. In a nutshell, the passive activity loss rules limit the ability of partners in rental real estate partnerships and other partnerships they don't actively manage (passive activities) from using their ordinary losses from these activities (remaining after the application of the tax basis and at-risk limitations) to reduce other sources of taxable income.

**Passive Activity Defined** The passive activity rules define a passive activity as "any activity which involves the conduct of a trade or business,[75] and in which the taxpayer does not materially participate." According to the Code, participants in rental activities, including rental real estate[76] and limited partners are automatically deemed to be passive participants. In addition, participants in all other activities are passive unless their involvement in an activity is "regular, continuous, and substantial." Clearly, these terms are quite subjective and difficult to apply. Fortunately, regulations provide more certainty in this area by enumerating seven separate tests for material participation.[77] An individual other than a limited partner can be classified as a material participant in an activity by meeting any *one* of the seven tests in Exhibit 20-9.

**EXHIBIT 20-9** **Tests for Material Participation**

1. The individual participates in the activity more than 500 hours during the year.
2. The individual's activity constitutes substantially all the participation in such activity by individuals.
3. The individual participates more than 100 hours during the year and the individual's participation is not less than any other individual's participation in the activity.
4. The activity qualifies as a "significant participation activity" (individual participates for more than 100 hours during the year) and the aggregate of all other "significant participation activities" is greater than 500 hours for the year.
5. The individual materially participated in the activity for any 5 of the preceding 10 taxable years.
6. The activity involves personal services in health, law, accounting, architecture, and so on, and the individual materially participated for any three preceding years.
7. Taking into account all the facts and circumstances, the individual participates on a regular, continuous, and substantial basis during the year.

**Income and Loss Baskets** Under the passive activity loss rules, each item of a partner's income or loss from all sources for the year is placed in one of three categories or "baskets." Losses from *the passive basket* are not allowed to offset income from other baskets. The three baskets are (see Exhibit 20-10):

1. *Passive activity income or loss*—income or loss from an activity, including partnerships, in which the taxpayer is not a material participant.
2. *Portfolio income*— income from investments, including capital gains and losses, dividends, interest, annuities, and royalties.
3. *Active business income*—income from sources, including partnerships, in which the taxpayer is a material participant. For individuals, this includes salary and self-employment income.

[75]The term *trade or business* is also deemed to include property held for the production of income such as rental property.

[76]§469(b)(7) provides an important exception to the general rule that all real estate activities are passive. To overcome this presumption, taxpayers must spend more than half their time working in trades or businesses materially participating in real estate activities and more than 750 hours materially participating in real estate activities during the year. This exception benefits partners that spend a substantial amount of time in partnership activities like real estate development and construction. Moreover, §469(i) permits individual taxpayers to treat up to $25,000 of losses from rental real estate as active losses each year.

[77]Reg. §1.469-5T.

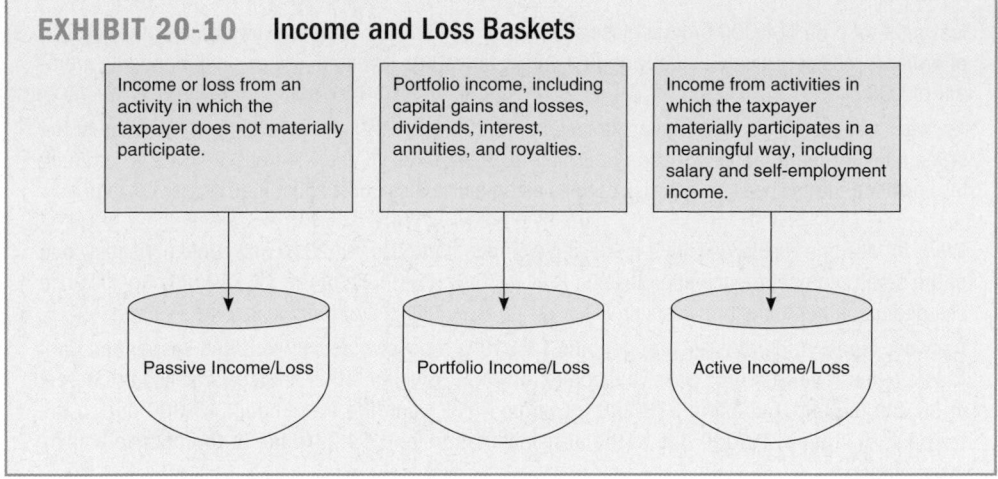

**EXHIBIT 20-10    Income and Loss Baskets**

| Income or loss from an activity in which the taxpayer does not materially participate. | Portfolio income, including capital gains and losses, dividends, interest, annuities, and royalties. | Income from activities in which the taxpayer materially participates in a meaningful way, including salary and self-employment income. |

Passive Income/Loss | Portfolio Income/Loss | Active Income/Loss

The impact of segregating a partner's income in these baskets is to limit her ability to apply passive activity losses against income in the other two baskets. In effect, passive activity losses are suspended and remain in the passive income or loss basket until the taxpayer generates current-year passive income, either from the passive activity producing the loss or from some other passive activity, or until the taxpayer sells the activity that generated the passive loss. On the sale, in addition to reporting gain or loss from the sale of the property, the taxpayer will be allowed to deduct suspended passive losses as ordinary losses.

**Example 20-26**

As indicated in Example 20-22, Greg was allocated a $9,120 ordinary loss for *2010* and had a $124,000 tax basis at year-end *after* adjusting his tax basis for the loss. Given that Greg was allocated $9,000 of nonrecourse debt from accounts payable during *2010,* what is Greg's at-risk amount at the end of the year?

**Answer:** $115,000. Greg's at-risk amount is calculated by subtracting his $9,000 share of nonrecourse debt from his $124,000 tax basis.

Given Greg's status as a silent or nonmanaging member of CCS, how much of his $9,120 ordinary loss can he deduct in *2010* if he has no other sources of passive income?

**Answer:** None. Because Greg's tax basis and at-risk amount are large relative to his $9,120 ordinary loss, the tax basis and at-risk hurdles don't limit his loss. However, Greg's $9,120 loss would be classified as a passive loss and suspended until Greg received passive income from another source—hopefully CCS—or until he disposes of his interest in CCS.

What could Greg do to deduct any losses from CCS in the future?

**Answer:** He could satisfy one of the seven tests in Exhibit 20-9 to be classified as a material participant in CCS, thereby converting his future CCS losses from passive to active losses. Or he could become a passive participant in some other activity producing trade or business income that could be offset by any future passive losses from CCS.

**Example 20-27**

From Example 20-25 we learned that Nicole would report $150 of dividend income and $90 of long-term capital gains from CCS on her *2010* tax return. Further, we learned that $4,240 of her $18,240 *2010* ordinary loss allocation from CCS cleared both the tax basis and at-risk hurdles,
*(continued on page 20-34...)*

leaving a total of $14,000 ordinary loss suspended and carried forward. How much of the $4,240 of ordinary loss can Nicole actually deduct on her tax return, given her status as a managing member of CCS?

**Answer:** Because Nicole is a managing member of CCS, it is likely she will satisfy at least one of the seven tests for material participation in Exhibit 20-9. As a result, she will treat the $4,240 ordinary loss clearing the tax basis and at-risk hurdles as an active loss and deduct it all on her tax return.

***What if:*** Assume Nicole was not a managing member of CCS during *2010* and could not satisfy one of the seven material participation tests in Exhibit 20-9. How much of the $4,240 ordinary loss can she deduct on her tax return, assuming she has no other sources of passive income?

**Answer:** None. Under this assumption, the $4,240 is a passive activity loss and suspended until Nicole either receives some passive income from CCS (or some other source) or sells her interest in CCS. In the end, her entire $18,240 loss from *2010* would be suspended: $5,000 due to the tax basis limitation, $9,000 due to the at-risk limitation, and $4,240 due to the passive activity loss limitation.

## CONCLUSION

This chapter explained the relevant tax rules pertaining to forming and operating partnerships. Specifically, we introduced important tax issues arising from partnership formations, including partner gain or loss recognition and calculating inside and outside basis. In addition, we explained accounting periods and methods, allocations of partners' ordinary income (loss) and separately stated items, basis adjustments, and loss limitation rules in the context of an operating partnership. Although it would seem that partnerships tax law should be relatively straightforward given that partnerships don't pay taxes, by now you may have come to realize quite the opposite is true. The next chapter continues our discussion of partnership tax law with a focus on dispositions of partnership interests and partnership distributions.

## SUMMARY

**LO1**   Determine whether a flow-through entity is taxed as a partnership or S corporation, and distinguish the entity approach from the aggregate approach for taxing partnerships.

- Unincorporated business entities with more than one owner are taxed as partnerships.
- Shareholders of certain corporations may elect to have them treated as flow-through entities by filing an S election with the IRS.
- Though partnerships and S corporations are both flow-through entities, the tax rules that apply to them differ.
- Partnership tax rules reflect both the aggregate and entity concepts.

**LO2**   Resolve tax issues applicable to partnership formations and other acquisitions of partnership interests, including gain recognition to partners and tax basis for partners and partnerships.

- As a general rule, partners don't recognize gain or loss when they contribute property to partnerships in exchange for a partnership interest.
- Partnership recourse debt is allocated to partners with ultimate responsibility for paying the debt, and nonrecourse debt is allocated to partners using profit-sharing ratios.
- Partners contributing property encumbered by debt may have to recognize gain, depending on the basis of the property and the amount of the debt.

- Partners contributing property to a partnership will have an initial tax basis in their partnership interest equal to the basis of contributed property less any debt relief plus their share of any partnership debt and any gain they recognize.

- Partners receiving partnership interests by contributing capital assets or §1231 assets have a holding period in their partnership interest that includes the holding period of the contributed property. If they contribute any other type of property instead, their holding period begins on the date the partnership interest is received.

- Partnerships with contributed property have a tax basis and holding period in the property equal to the contributing partner's tax basis and holding period.

- Partners who receive capital interests in exchange for services must report the liquidation value of the capital interest as ordinary income, and the partnership either deducts or capitalizes an equivalent amount depending on the nature of the services provided.

- Partners who receive profits interests in exchange for services don't report any income. However, they share in any subsequent partnership profits and losses.

- Partners who purchase partnership interests have a tax basis in their interests equal to the purchase price plus their shares of partnership debt, and their holding periods begin on the date of purchase.

Determine the appropriate accounting periods and methods for partnerships.　**LO3**

- Partnerships, rather than individual partners, are responsible for making most tax elections.

- The Code mandates that partners include their share of income (loss) or other partnership items for "any taxable year of the partnership ending within or with the taxable year of the partner."

- Partnerships must use a tax year-end consistent with the majority interest taxable year, the taxable year of the principal partners, or the year-end providing the least aggregate deferral for the partners.

- Partnerships with average annual gross receipts over $5 million that have corporate partners may not use the cash method of accounting. Otherwise, partnerships may use either the cash or accrual method of accounting.

Calculate and characterize a partnership's ordinary business income or loss and its separately stated items, and demonstrate how to report these items to partners.　**LO4**

- Partnerships must file Form 1065, U.S. Return of Partnership Income, with the IRS annually and must provide each partner with a Schedule K-1 detailing the partner's share of ordinary business income (loss) and separately stated items.

- Separately stated items include short-term and long-term capital gains and losses, dividends, §1231 gains and losses, and other partnership items that may be treated differently at the partner level.

- The character of separately stated items is determined at the partnership rather than at the partner level.

- Guaranteed payments are typically fixed payments made to partners for services provided to the partnership. They are treated as ordinary income by partners who receive them and are either deducted or capitalized by the partnership depending on the nature of services provided.

- Guaranteed payments to any type of partner (or LLC member) and general partners' shares of ordinary business income (loss) are treated as self-employment income (loss).

- Limited partners' shares of ordinary business income (loss) are not treated as self-employment income (loss).

- Though the tax law is uncertain in this area, all or a portion of LLC members' shares of ordinary business income (loss) should be classified as self-employment income (loss) if members are significantly involved in managing the LLC.

- Partnerships provide a great deal of flexibility because they may specially allocate their income, gains, expenses, losses, and other partnership items, as long as the allocations have "substantial economic effect" or are consistent with partners' interests in the partnership. Special allocations of built-in gain or loss on contributed property to contributing partners are mandatory.

**LO5** Explain the implications of a partner's tax basis and the adjustments that affect it.

- Partners must make specified annual adjustments to the tax basis in their partnership interests to ensure that partnership taxable income/gain or deductible expense/loss items are not double taxed or deducted twice, and that partnership tax-exempt income or nondeductible expense is not taxed or deducted.

- Partners increase the tax basis in their interests by their actual or deemed cash contributions, shares of ordinary business income, separately stated income/gain items, and shares of tax-exempt income.

- Partners decrease the tax basis in their interests by their actual or deemed cash distributions, shares of ordinary business loss, separately stated expense/loss items, and shares of nondeductible expenses.

- A partner's tax basis may never be reduced below zero.

- Cash distributions that are less than a partner's tax basis immediately before the distribution are not taxable. However, cash distributions in excess of a partner's tax basis immediately before the distribution are generally taxable as capital gain.

**LO6** Apply the basis, at-risk, and passive activity loss limits to losses from partnerships.

- In order for losses to provide tax benefits to partners, partnership losses must clear the tax basis, at-risk, and passive activity loss hurdles (in that order).

- Partnership losses in excess of a partner's tax basis are suspended and may be utilized only when additional tax basis is created.

- Losses clearing the tax basis hurdle may be utilized only to the extent of the partner's at-risk amount. A partner's at-risk amount generally equals her tax basis (before any reduction for current year losses) less her share of nonrecourse debt that is not secured by real estate.

- If a partner is not a material participant in the partnership or if the partnership is involved in rental activities, losses clearing the basis and at-risk hurdles may be reported on the partner's tax return only when she has passive income from the partnership (or other sources) or when she sells her partnership interest.

# KEY TERMS

§704(b) capital accounts (20-8)
aggregate approach (20-2)
at-risk amount (20-30)
at-risk rules (20-30)
built-in gain (20-3)
built-in loss (20-3)
capital account (20-8)
capital interest (20-3)
entity approach (20-2)
flow-through entities (20-2)
Form 1065 (20-23)
Form 7004 (20-23)
GAAP capital accounts (20-8)
general partnership (20-2)
guaranteed payments (20-19)
inside basis (20-4)
least aggregate deferral (20-15)

limited liability companies (20-2)
limited partnership (20-2)
liquidation value (20-10)
majority interest taxable year (20-14)
nonrecourse debt (20-4)
nonservice partner (20-10)
ordinary business income (loss) (20-17)
organization costs (20-12)
outside basis (20-4)
PAL (20-31)
partnership interest (20-3)
passive activity loss rules (20-31)
principal partner (20-15)
profits interest (20-3)
qualified nonrecourse financing (20-30)

recourse debt (20-4)
S corporations (20-2)
Schedule K (20-23)
self-employment taxes (20-20)
separately stated items (20-17)
service partner (20-10)
special allocations (20-22)
start-up costs (20-12)
Subchapter K (20-2)
Subchapter S (20-2)
syndication costs (20-12)
tax capital accounts (20-8)
taxable corporations (20-2)

# DISCUSSION QUESTIONS

1. **(LO1)** What is a *flow-through entity,* and what effect does this designation have on how business entities and their owners are taxed?
2. **(LO1)** What types of business entities are taxed as flow-through entities?
3. **(LO1)** Compare and contrast the aggregate and entity concepts for taxing partnerships and their partners.
4. **(LO2)** What is a partnership interest, and what specific economic rights or entitlements are included with it?
5. **(LO2)** What is the rationale for requiring partners to defer most gains and all losses when they contribute property to a partnership?
6. **(LO2)** Under what circumstances is it possible for partners to recognize gain when contributing property to partnerships?
7. **(LO2)** What is *inside basis* and *outside basis,* and why are they relevant for taxing partnerships and partners?
8. **(LO2)** What is recourse and nonrecourse debt, and how is each generally allocated to partners?
9. **(LO2)** How does the amount of debt allocated to a partner affect the amount of gain a partner recognizes when contributing property secured by debt?
10. **(LO2)** What is a tax basis capital account, and what type of tax-related information does it provide?
11. **(LO2)** Distinguish between a capital interest and a profits interest, and explain how partners and partnerships treat each when exchanging them for services provided.
12. **(LO2)** How do partners who purchase a partnership interest determine the tax basis and holding period of their partnership interests?
13. **(LO3)** Why do you think partnerships, rather than the individual partners, are responsible for making most of the tax elections related to the operation of the partnership?
14. **(LO3)** If a partner with a taxable year-end of December 31 is in a partnership with a March 31 taxable year-end, how many months of deferral will the partner receive? Why?
15. **(LO3)** In what situation will there be a common year-end for the principal partners when there is no majority interest taxable year?
16. **(LO3)** Explain the least aggregate deferral test for determining a partnership's year-end and discuss when it applies.
17. **(LO3)** When are partnerships eligible to use the cash method of accounting?
18. **(LO4)** What is a partnership's ordinary business income (loss) and how is it calculated?
19. **(LO4)** What are some common separately stated items, and why must they be separately stated to the partners?
20. **(LO4)** Is the character of partnership income/gains and expenses/losses determined at the partnership or partner level? Why?
21. **(LO4)** What are guaranteed payments and how do partnerships and partners treat them for income and self-employment tax purposes?
22. **(LO4)** How do general and limited partners treat their share of ordinary business income for self-employment tax purposes?
23. **(LO4)** What challenges do LLCs face when deciding whether to treat their members' shares of ordinary business income as self-employment income?
24. **(LO4)** How much flexibility do partnerships have in allocating partnership items to partners?

25. **(LO4)** What are the basic tax-filing requirements imposed on partnerships?
26. **(LO5)** In what situations do partners need to know the tax basis in their partnership interests?
27. **(LO5)** Why does a partner's tax basis in her partnership interest need to be adjusted annually?
28. **(LO5)** What items will increase a partner's basis in her partnership interest?
29. **(LO5)** What items will decrease a partner's basis in her partnership interest?
30. **(LO6)** What hurdles (or limitations) must partners overcome before they can ultimately deduct partnership losses on their tax returns?
31. **(LO6)** What happens to partnership losses allocated to partners in excess of the tax basis in their partnership interests?
32. **(LO6)** In what sense is the at-risk loss limitation rule more restrictive than the tax basis loss limitation rule?
33. **(LO6)** How do partners measure the amount they have at risk in the partnership?
34. **(LO6)** In what order are the loss limitation rules applied to limit partner's losses from partnerships?
35. **(LO6)** How do partners determine whether they are passive participants in partnerships when applying the passive activity loss limitation rules?
36. **(LO6)** Under what circumstances can partners with passive losses from partnerships deduct their passive losses?

## PROBLEMS

37. **(LO2)** Joseph contributed $22,000 in cash and equipment with a tax basis of $5,000 and a fair market value of $11,000 to Berry Hill Partnership in exchange for a partnership interest.

    a. What is Joseph's tax basis in his partnership interest?
    b. What is Berry Hill's basis in the equipment?

38. **(LO2)** Lance contributed investment property worth $500,000, purchased three years ago for $200,000 cash, to Cloud Peak LLC in exchange for an 85 percent profits and capital interest in the LLC. Cloud Peak owes $300,000 to its suppliers but has no other debts.

    a. What is Lance's tax basis in his LLC interest?
    b. What is Lance's holding period in his interest?
    c. What is Cloud Peak's basis in the contributed property?
    d. What is Cloud Peak's holding period in the contributed property?

39. **(LO2)** Laurel contributed equipment worth $200,000, purchased 10 months ago for $250,000 cash and used in her sole proprietorship, to Sand Creek LLC in exchange for a 15 percent profits and capital interest in the LLC. Laurel agreed to guarantee all $15,000 of Sand Creek's accounts payable, but she did not guarantee any portion of the $100,000 nonrecourse mortgage securing Sand Creek's office building. Other than the accounts payable and mortgage, Sand Creek does not owe any debts to other creditors.

    a. What is Laurel's initial tax basis in her LLC interest?
    b. What is Laurel's holding period in her interest?
    c. What is Sand Creek's initial basis in the contributed property?
    d. What is Sand Creek's holding period in the contributed property?

40. **(LO2)** Harry and Sally formed the Evergreen Partnership by contributing the
    following assets in exchange for a 50 percent capital and profits interest in
    the partnership:

■ **planning**

| | Basis | Fair Market Value |
|---|---|---|
| **Harry:** | | |
| Cash | $ 30,000 | $ 30,000 |
| Land | 100,000 | 120,000 |
| Totals | $130,000 | $150,000 |
| | | |
| **Sally:** | | |
| Equipment used in a business | 200,000 | 150,000 |
| Totals | $200,000 | $150,000 |

a. How much gain or loss will Harry recognize on the contribution?

b. How much gain or loss will Sally recognize on the contribution?

c. How could the transaction be structured a different way to get a better result
   for Sally?

d. What is Harry's tax basis in his partnership interest?

e. What is Sally's tax basis in her partnership interest?

f. What is Evergreen's tax basis in its assets?

g. Following the format in Exhibit 20-2, prepare a tax basis balance sheet for
   the Evergreen partnership showing the tax capital accounts for the partners.

41. **(LO2)** Cosmo contributed land with a fair market value of $400,000 and a tax
    basis of $90,000 to the Y Mountain Partnership in exchange for a 25 percent
    profits and capital interest in the partnership. The land is secured by $120,000
    of nonrecourse debt. Other than this nonrecourse debt, Y Mountain Partner-
    ship does not have any debt.

a. How much gain will Cosmo recognize from the contribution?

b. What is Cosmo's tax basis in his partnership interest?

42. **(LO2)** When High Horizon LLC was formed, Maude contributed the following
    assets in exchange for a 25 percent capital and profits interest in the LLC:

| | Basis | Fair Market Value |
|---|---|---|
| **Maude:** | | |
| Cash | $ 20,000 | $ 20,000 |
| Land* | 100,000 | 200,000 |
| Totals | $120,000 | $220,000 |

*Nonrecourse debt secured by the land equals $160,000

James, Harold, and Jenny each contributed $220,000 in cash for a 25 percent
profits and capital interest.

a. How much gain or loss will Maude and the other members recognize?

b. What is Maude's tax basis in her LLC interest?

c. What tax basis do James, Harold, and Jenny have in their LLC interests?

d. What is High Horizon's tax basis in its assets?

e. Following the format in Exhibit 20-2, prepare a tax basis balance sheet for
   the High Horizon LLC showing the tax capital accounts for the members.

43. **(LO2)** Kevan, Jerry, and Dave formed Albee LLC. Jerry and Dave each contributed $245,000 in cash. Kevan contributed the following assets:

| | Basis | Fair Market Value |
|---|---|---|
| **Kevan:** | | |
| Cash | $ 15,000 | $ 15,000 |
| Land* | 120,000 | 230,000 |
| Totals | $135,000 | $245,000 |

*Nonrecourse debt secured by the land equals $210,000

Each member received a one-third capital and profits interest in the LLC.

a. How much gain or loss will Jerry, Dave, and Kevan recognize on the contributions?
b. What is Kevan's tax basis in his LLC interest?
c. What tax basis do Jerry and Dave have in their LLC interests?
d. What is Albee LLC's tax basis in its assets?
e. Following the format in Exhibit 20-2, prepare a tax basis balance sheet for the Albee LLC showing the tax capital accounts for the members. What is Kevan's share of the LLC's inside basis?
f. If the lender holding the nonrecourse debt secured by Kevan's land required Kevan to guarantee 33.33 percent of the debt and Jerry to guarantee the remaining 66.67 percent of the debt when Albee LLC was formed, how much gain or loss will Kevan recognize?
g. If the lender holding the nonrecourse debt secured by Kevan's land required Kevan to guarantee 33.33 percent of the debt and Jerry to guarantee the remaining 66.67 percent of the debt when Albee LLC was formed, what are the members' tax bases in their LLC interests?

**research**

44. **(LO2)** Jim has decided to contribute some equipment he previously used in his sole proprietorship in exchange for a 10 percent profits and capital interest in Fast Choppers LLC. Jim originally paid $200,000 cash for the equipment. Since then, the tax basis in the equipment has been reduced to $100,000 because of tax depreciation, and the fair market value of the equipment is now $150,000.

a. Must Jim recognize any of the potential §1245 recapture when he contributes the machinery to Fast Choppers? {*Hint:* See §1245(b)(3).}
b. What cost recovery method will Fast Choppers use to depreciate the machinery? {*Hint:* See §168(i)(7).}
c. If Fast Choppers were to immediately sell the equipment Jim contributed for $150,000, how much gain would Jim recognize and what is its character? {*Hint:* See §1245 and 704(c).}

**research**

45. **(LO2)** Ansel purchased raw land three years ago for $200,000 to hold as an investment. After watching the value of the land drop to $150,000, he decided to contribute it to Mountainside Developers LLC in exchange for a 5 percent capital and profits interest. Mountainside plans to develop the property and will treat it as inventory, like all the other real estate it holds.

a. If Mountainside sells the property for $150,000 after holding it for one year, how much gain or loss does it recognize and what is the character of the gain or loss? {*Hint:* See §724.}
b. If Mountainside sells the property for $125,000 after holding it for two years, how much gain or loss does it recognize and what is the character of the gain or loss?
c. If Mountainside sells the property for $150,000 after holding it six years, how much gain or loss does it recognized and what is the character of the gain or loss?

46. **(LO2)** Claude purchased raw land three years ago for $1,500,000 to develop into lots and sell to individuals planning to build their dream homes. Claude intended to treat this property as inventory, like his other development properties. Before completing the development of the property, however, he decided to contribute it to South Peak Investors LLC when it was worth $2,500,000, in exchange for a 10 percent capital and profits interest. South Peak's strategy is to hold land for investment purposes only and then sell it later at a gain.

a. If South Peak sells the property for $3,000,000 four years after Claude's contribution, how much gain or loss is recognized and what is its character? {*Hint:* See §724.}

b. If South Peak sells the property for $3,000,000 five and one-half years after Claude's contribution, how much gain or loss is recognized and what is its character?

47. **(LO2)** Reggie contributed $10,000 in cash and a capital asset he had held for three years with a fair market value of $20,000 and tax basis of $10,000 for a 5 percent capital and profits interest in Green Valley LLC.

research

a. If Reggie sells his LLC interest thirteen months later for $30,000 when the tax basis in his partnership interest is still $20,000, how much gain does he report and what is its character?

b. If Reggie sells his LLC interest two months later for $30,000 when the tax basis in his partnership interest is still $20,000, how much gain does he report and what is its character? {*Hint:* See Reg. §1.1223-3.}

48. **(LO2)** Connie recently provided legal services to the Winterhaven LLC and received a 5 percent interest in the LLC as compensation. Winterhaven currently has $50,000 of accounts payable and no other debt. The current fair market value of Winterhaven's capital is $200,000.

a. If Connie receives a 5 percent capital interest only, how much income must she report and what is her tax basis in the LLC interest?

b. If Connie receives a 5 percent profits interest only, how much income must she report and what is her tax basis in the LLC interest?

c. If Connie receives a 5 percent capital and profits interest, how much income must she report and what is her tax basis in the LLC interest?

49. **(LO2)** Mary and Scott formed a partnership that maintains its records on a calendar-year basis. The balance sheet of the MS Partnership at year-end is as follows:

|  | Basis | Fair Market Value |
|---|---|---|
| Cash | $ 60 | $ 60 |
| Land | 60 | 180 |
| Inventory | 72 | 60 |
|  | $192 | $300 |
|  |  |  |
| Mary | $ 96 | $150 |
| Scott | 96 | 150 |
|  | $192 | $300 |

At the end of the current year, Kari will receive a one-third capital interest only in exchange for services rendered. Kari's interest will not be subject to a substantial risk of forfeiture and the costs for the type of services she provided are typically not capitalized by the partnership. For the current year, the income and expenses from operations are equal. Consequently, the only tax

consequences for the year are those relating to the admission of Kari to the partnership.

a. Compute and characterize any gain or loss Kari may have to recognize as a result of her admission to the partnership.

b. Compute Kari's basis in her partnership interest.

c. Prepare a balance sheet of the partnership immediately after Kari's admission showing the partners' tax capital accounts and capital accounts stated at fair market value.

d. Calculate how much gain or loss Kari would have to recognize if, instead of a capital interest, she received a profits interest.

50. **(LO2)** Dave LaCroix recently received a 10 percent capital and profits interest in Cirque Capital LLC in exchange for consulting services he provided. If Cirque Capital had paid an outsider to provide the advice, it would have deducted the payment as compensation expense. Cirque Capital's balance sheet on the day Dave received his capital interest appears below:

|  | Basis | Fair Market Value |
|---|---|---|
| **Assets:** | | |
| Cash | $150,000 | $ 150,000 |
| Investments | 200,000 | 700,000 |
| Land | 150,000 | 250,000 |
| Totals | $500,000 | $1,100,000 |
| | | |
| **Liabilities and capital:** | | |
| Nonrecourse debt | 100,000 | 100,000 |
| Lance* | 200,000 | 500,000 |
| Robert* | 200,000 | 500,000 |
| Totals | $500,000 | $1,100,000 |

*Assume that Lance's basis and Robert's basis in their LLC interests equal their tax basis capital accounts.

a. Compute and characterize any gain or loss Dave may have to recognize as a result of his admission to Cirque Capital.

b. Compute each member's tax basis in his LLC interest immediately after Dave's receipt of his interest.

c. Prepare a balance sheet for Cirque Capital immediately after Dave's admission showing the members' tax capital accounts and their capital accounts stated at fair market value.

d. Compute and characterize any gain or loss Dave may have to recognize as a result of his admission to Cirque Capital if he receives only a profits interest.

e. Compute each member's tax basis in his LLC interest immediately after Dave's receipt of his interest if Dave receives only a profits interest.

51. **(LO2)** Last December 31, Ramon sold the 10 percent interest in the Del Sol Partnership that he had held for two years to Garrett for $400,000. Prior to selling his interest, Ramon's basis in Del Sol was $200,000, which included a $100,000 share of nonrecourse debt allocated to him.

a. What is Garrett's tax basis in his partnership interest?

b. If Garrett sells his partnership interest three months after receiving it and recognizes a gain, what is the character of his gain?

52. **(LO3)** Broken Rock LLC was recently formed with the following members:

| Name | Tax Year-End | Capital/Profits % |
| --- | --- | --- |
| George Allen | December 31 | 33.33% |
| Elanax Corp. | June 30 | 33.33% |
| Ray Kirk | December 31 | 33.34% |

What is the required taxable year-end for Broken Rock LLC?

53. **(LO3)** Granite Slab LLC was recently formed with the following members:

| Name | Tax Year-End | Capital/Profits % |
| --- | --- | --- |
| Nelson Black | December 31 | 22.0% |
| Brittany Jones | December 31 | 24.0% |
| Lone Pine LLC | June 30 | 4.5% |
| Red Spot Inc. | October 31 | 4.5% |
| Pale Rock Inc. | September 30 | 4.5% |
| Thunder Ridge LLC | July 31 | 4.5% |
| Alpensee LLC | March 31 | 4.5% |
| Lakewood Inc. | June 30 | 4.5% |
| Streamside LLC | October 31 | 4.5% |
| Burnt Fork Inc. | October 31 | 4.5% |
| Snowy Ridge LP | June 30 | 4.5% |
| Whitewater LP | October 31 | 4.5% |
| Straw Hat LLC | January 31 | 4.5% |
| Wildfire Inc. | September 30 | 4.5% |

What is the required taxable year-end for Granite Slab LLC?

54. **(LO3)** Tall Tree LLC was recently formed with the following members:

| Name | Tax Year-End | Capital/Profits % |
| --- | --- | --- |
| Eddie Robinson | December 31 | 40% |
| Pitcher Lenders LLC | June 30 | 25% |
| Perry Homes Inc. | October 31 | 35% |

What is the required taxable year-end for Tall Tree LLC?

55. **(LO3)** Rock Creek LLC was recently formed with the following members:

| Name | Tax Year-End | Capital/Profits % |
| --- | --- | --- |
| Mark Banks | December 31 | 35% |
| Highball Properties LLC | March 31 | 25% |
| Chavez Builders Inc. | November 30 | 40% |

What is the required taxable year-end for Rock Creek LLC?

56. **(LO3)** Ryan, Dahir, and Bill have operated Broken Feather LLC for the last four years using a calendar year-end. Each has a one-third interest. Since they began operating, their busy season has run from June through August, with 35 percent of their gross receipts coming in July and August. The members would like to change their tax year-end and have asked you to address the following questions:

a. Can they change to an August 31 year-end and, if so, how do they make the change? {*Hint:* See Rev. Proc. 2002-38, 2002-1 CB 1037.}

b. Can they change to a September 30 year-end and, if so, how do they make the change? {*Hint:* See §444.}

**research**

57. **(LO3)** Ashlee, Hiroki, Kate, and Albee LLC each own a 25 percent interest in Tally Industries LLC, which generates annual gross receipts of over $10 million. Ashlee, Hiroki, and Kate manage the business, but Albee LLC is a nonmanaging member. Although Tally Industries has historically been profitable, for the last three years losses have been allocated to the members. Given these facts, the members want to know whether Tally Industries can use the cash method of accounting. Why or why not? {*Hint:* See §448(b)(3).}

58. **(LO4)** Turtle Creek Partnership had the following revenues, expenses, gains, losses, and distributions:

| | |
|---|---:|
| Sales revenue | $40,000 |
| Long-term capital gains | $ 2,000 |
| Cost of goods sold | ($13,000) |
| Depreciation—MACRS | ($3,000) |
| Amortization of organization costs | ($1,000) |
| Guaranteed payments to partners for general management | ($10,000) |
| Cash distributions to partners | ($2,000) |

Given these items, what is Turtle Creek's ordinary business income (loss) for the year?

59. **(LO4)** Georgio owns a 20 percent profits and capital interest in Rain Tree LLC. For the current year, Rain Tree had the following revenues, expenses, gains, and losses:

| | |
|---|---:|
| Sales revenue | $70,000 |
| Gain on sale of land (§1231) | $11,000 |
| Cost of goods sold | ($26,000) |
| Depreciation—MACRS | ($3,000) |
| §179 deduction* | ($10,000) |
| Employee wages | ($11,000) |
| Fines and penalties | ($3,000) |
| Municipal bond interest | $ 6,000 |
| Short-term capital gains | $ 4,000 |
| Guaranteed payment to Sandra | ($3,000) |

*Assume the §179 property placed in service limitation does not apply.

a. How much ordinary business income (loss) is allocated to Georgio for the year?
b. What are Georgio's separately stated items for the year?

60. **(LO4)** The partnership agreement of the G&P general partnership states that Gary will receive a guaranteed payment of $13,000, and that Gary and Prudence will share the remaining profits or losses in a 45/55 ratio. For year 1, the G&P partnership reports the following results:

| | |
|---|---:|
| Sales revenue | $70,000 |
| Gain on sale of land (§1231) | $ 8,000 |
| Cost of goods sold | ($38,000) |
| Depreciation—MACRS | ($9,000) |
| Employee wages | ($14,000) |
| Cash charitable contributions | ($3,000) |
| Municipal bond interest | $ 2,000 |
| Other expenses | ($2,000) |

a. Compute Gary's share of ordinary income (loss) and separately stated items to be reported on his year 1 Schedule K-1, including his self-employment income (loss).

b. Compute Gary's share of self-employment income (loss) to be reported on his year 1 Schedule K-1, assuming G&P is a limited partnership and Gary is a limited partner.

c. What do you believe Gary's share of self-employment income (loss) to be reported on his year 1 Schedule K-1 should be, assuming G&P is an LLC and Gary spends 2,000 hours per year working there full time?

61. **(LO4)** Hoki Poki, a cash-method general partnership, recorded the following items for its current tax year:

| | |
|---|---:|
| Rental real estate income | $ 2,000 |
| Sales revenue | $70,000 |
| §1245 recapture income | $ 8,000 |
| Interest income | $ 2,000 |
| Cost of goods sold | ($38,000) |
| Depreciation—MACRS | ($9,000) |
| Supplies expense | ($1,000) |
| Employee wages | ($14,000) |
| Investment interest expense | ($1,000) |
| Partner's medical insurance premiums paid by Hoki Poki | ($3,000) |

As part of preparing Hoki Poki's current year return, identify the items that should be included in computing its ordinary business income (loss) and those that should be separately stated. {*Hint:* See Schedule K-1 and related preparer's instructions at www.irs.gov.}

62. **(LO4)** On the last day of its current tax year, Buy Rite LLC received $300,000 when it sold a machine it had purchased for $200,000 three years ago to use in its business. At the time of the sale, the basis in the equipment had been reduced to $100,000 due to tax depreciation taken. How much did the members' self-employment earnings from Buy Rite increase when the equipment was sold? {*Hint:* See §1402(a)(3).}

63. **(LO4)** Jhumpa, Stewart, and Kelly are all one-third partners in the capital and profits of Firewalker general partnership. In addition to their normal share of the partnership's annual income, Jhumpa and Stewart receive an annual guaranteed payment of $10,000 to compensate them for additional services they provide. Firewalker's income statement for the current year reflects the following revenues and expenses:

| | |
|---|---:|
| Sales revenue | $340,000 |
| Interest income | 3,300 |
| Long-term capital gains | 1,200 |
| Cost of goods sold | (120,000) |
| Employee wages | (75,000) |
| Depreciation expense | (28,000) |
| Guaranteed payments | (20,000) |
| Miscellaneous expenses | (4,500) |
| Overall net income | $ 97,000 |

a. Given Firewalker's operating results, how much ordinary business income (loss) and what separately stated items [including the partners' self-employment earnings (loss)] will it report on its return for the year?

b. How will it allocate these amounts to its partners?

c. How much self-employment tax will each partner pay assuming none has any other source of income or loss?

64. **(LO4)** Lane and Cal each own 50 percent of the profits and capital of HighYield LLC. HighYield owns a portfolio of taxable bonds and municipal bonds, and each year the portfolio generates approximately $10,000 of taxable interest and $10,000 of tax-exempt interest. Lane's marginal tax rate is 35 percent while Cal's marginal tax rate is 15 percent. To take advantage of the difference in their marginal tax rates, Lane and Cal want to modify their operating agreement to specially allocate all of the taxable interest to Cal and all of the tax-exempt interest to Lane. Until now, Lane and Cal had been allocated 50 percent of each type of interest income.

a. Is HighYield's proposed special allocation acceptable under current tax rules? Why or why not? {*Hint:* See Reg. §1.704-1(b)(2)(iii)(b) and §1.704-1(b)(5) Example (5).}

b. If the IRS ultimately disagrees with HighYield's special allocation, how will it likely reallocate the taxable and tax-exempt interest among the members? {*Hint:* See Reg. §1.704-1(b)(5) Example (5)(ii).}

65. **(LO5)** Larry's tax basis in his partnership interest at the beginning of the year was $10,000. If his share of the partnership debt increased by $10,000 during the year and his share of partnership income for the year is $3,000, what is his tax basis in his partnership interest at the end of the year?

66. **(LO5)** Carmine was allocated the following items from the Piccolo LLC for last year:

> Ordinary business loss
> Nondeductible penalties
> Tax-exempt interest income
> Short-term capital gain
> Cash distributions

Rank these items in terms of the order they should be applied to adjust Carmine's tax basis in Piccolo for the year.

67. **(LO5)** Oscar, Felix, and Marv are all one-third partners in the capital and profits of Eastside General Partnership. In addition to their normal share of the partnership's annual income, Oscar and Felix receive annual guaranteed payments of $7,000 to compensate them for additional services they provide. Eastside's income statement for the current year reflects the following revenues and expenses:

| | |
|---|---:|
| Sales revenue | $420,000 |
| Dividend income | 5,700 |
| Short-term capital gains | 2,800 |
| Cost of goods sold | (210,000) |
| Employee wages | (115,000) |
| Depreciation expense | (28,000) |
| Guaranteed payments | (14,000) |
| Miscellaneous expenses | (9,500) |
| Overall net income | $ 52,000 |

In addition, Eastside owed creditors $120,000 at the beginning of the year but managed to pay down its debts to $90,000 by the end of the year. All partnership debt is allocated equally among the partners. Finally, Oscar, Felix and Marv had a tax basis of $80,000 in their interests at the beginning of the year.

a. What tax basis do the partners have in their partnership interests at the end of the year?

b. Assume the partners began the year with a tax basis of $10,000 and all the debt was paid off on the last day of the year. How much gain will the partners recognize when the debt is paid off? What tax basis do the partners have in their partnership interests at the end of the year?

68. **(LO5)** Pam, Sergei, and Mercedes are all one-third partners in the capital and profits of Oak Grove General Partnership. Partnership debt is allocated among the partners in accordance with their capital and profits interests. In addition to their normal share of the partnership's annual income, Pam and Sergei receive annual guaranteed payments of $20,000 to compensate them for additional services they provide. Oak Grove's income statement for the current year reflects the following revenues and expenses:

| | |
|---|---|
| Sales revenue | $476,700 |
| Dividend income | 6,600 |
| §1231 losses | (3,800) |
| Cost of goods sold | (245,000) |
| Employee wages | (92,000) |
| Depreciation expense | (31,000) |
| Guaranteed payments | (40,000) |
| Miscellaneous expenses | (11,500) |
| Overall net income | $ 60,000 |

In addition, Oak Grove owed creditors $90,000 at the beginning and $150,000 at the end of the year, and Pam, Sergei, and Mercedes had a tax basis of $50,000 in their interests at the beginning of the year. Also, Sergei and Mercedes agreed to increase Pam's capital and profits interest from 33.33 percent to 40 percent in exchange for additional services she provided to the partnership. The current liquidation value of the additional capital interest Pam received is $40,000.

a. What tax basis do the partners have in their partnership interests at the end of the year?

b. If, in addition to the expenses listed above, the partnership donated $12,000 to a political campaign, what tax basis do the partners have in their partnership interests at the end of the year assuming the liquidation value of the additional capital interest Pam received at the end of the year remains at $40,000?

69. **(LO6)** Alfonso began the year with a tax basis in his partnership interest of $30,000. His share of partnership debt at the beginning and end of the year consists of $5,000 of recourse debt and $5,000 of nonrecourse debt. During the year, he was allocated $40,000 of partnership ordinary business loss. Alfonso does not materially participate in this partnership and he has $1,000 of passive income from other sources.

a. How much of Alfonso's loss is limited by his tax basis?

b. How much of Alfonso's loss is limited by his at-risk amount?

c. How much of Alfonso's loss is limited by the passive activity loss rules?

70. **(LO5, LO6)** Juan Diego began the year with a tax basis in his partnership interest of $50,000. During the year, he was allocated $20,000 of partnership ordinary business income, $70,000 of §1231 losses, $30,000 of short-term capital losses, and received a cash distribution of $50,000.

a. What items related to these allocations does Juan Diego actually report on his tax return for the year? {*Hint:* See Reg. §1.704-1(d)(2) and Rev. Rul. 66-94.}

b. If any deductions or losses are limited, what are the carryover amounts and what is their character? {*Hint:* See Reg. §1.704-1(d).}

**■ research**
**■■**

71. **(LO6)** Farell is a member of Sierra Vista LLC. Although Sierra Vista is involved in a number of different business ventures, it is not currently involved in real estate either as an investor or as a developer. On January 1, year 1, Farell has a $100,000 tax basis in his LLC interest that includes his $90,000 share of Sierra Vista's general debt obligations. By the end of the year, Farell's share of Sierra Vista's general debt obligations has increased to $100,000. Because of the time he spends in other endeavors, Farell does not materially participate in Sierra Vista. His share of the Sierra Vista losses for year 1 is $120,000. As a partner in the Riverwoods Partnership, he also has year 1, Schedule K-1 passive income of $5,000.

    a. Determine how much of the Sierra Vista loss Farell will currently be able to deduct on his tax return for year 1, and list the losses suspended due to tax basis, at-risk, and passive activity loss limitations.

    b. Assuming Farell's Riverwoods K-1 indicates passive income of $30,000, determine how much of the Sierra Vista loss he will ultimately be able to deduct on his tax return for year 1, and list the losses suspended due to tax basis, at-risk, and passive activity loss limitations.

    c. Assuming Farell is deemed to be an active participant in Sierra Vista, determine how much of the Sierra Vista loss he will ultimately be able to deduct on his tax return for year 1, and list the losses suspended due to tax basis, at-risk, and passive activity loss limitations.

**research**

72. **(LO6)** Jenkins has a one-third capital and profits interest in the Maverick General Partnership. On January 1, year 1, Maverick has $120,000 of general debt obligations and Jenkins has a $50,000 tax basis (including his share of Maverick's debt) in his partnership interest. During the year, Maverick incurred a $30,000 nonrecourse debt that is not secured by real estate. Because Maverick is a rental real estate partnership, Jenkins is deemed to be a passive participant in Maverick. His share of the Maverick losses for year 1 is $75,000. Jenkins is not involved in any other passive activities, and this is the first year he has been allocated losses from Maverick.

    a. Determine how much of the Maverick loss Jenkins will currently be able to deduct on his tax return for year 1, and list the losses suspended due to tax basis, at-risk, and passive activity loss limitations.

    b. If Jenkins sells his interest on January 1, year 2, what happens to his suspended losses from year 1? {*Hint:* See §706(c)(2)(A), Reg. §1.704-1(d)(1), and *Sennett v. Commissioner* 80 TC 825 (1983).}

**planning**

73. **(LO6)** Suki and Steve own 50 percent capital and profits interests in Lorinda LLC. Lorinda operates the local minor league baseball team and owns the stadium where the team plays. Although the debt incurred to build the stadium was paid off several years ago, Lorinda owes its general creditors $300,000 (at the beginning of the year) that is not secured by firm property or guaranteed by any of the members. At the beginning of the current year, Suki and Steve had a tax basis of $170,000 in their LLC interests, including their share of debt owed to the general creditors. Shortly before the end of the year they each received a $10,000 cash distribution, even though Lorinda's ordinary business loss for the year was $400,000. Because of the time commitment to operate a baseball team, both Suki and Steve spent more than 1,500 hours during the year operating Lorinda.

    a. Determine how much of the Lorinda loss Suki and Steve will each be able to deduct on their current tax returns, and list their losses suspended by the tax basis, at-risk, and passive activity loss limitations.

    b. Assume that some time before receiving the $10,000 cash distribution, Steve is advised by his tax advisor that his marginal tax rate will be abnormally

high during the current year because of an unexpected windfall. To help Steve utilize more of the losses allocated from Lorinda in the current year, his advisor recommends refusing the cash distribution and personally guaranteeing $100,000 of Lorinda's debt, without the right to be reimbursed by Suki. If Steve follows his advisor's recommendations, how much additional Lorinda loss can he deduct on his current tax return? How does Steve's decision affect the amount of loss Suki can deduct on her current return and the amount and type of her suspended losses?

74. **(LO6)** Ray and Chuck own 50 percent capital and profits interests in Alpine Properties LLC. Alpine builds and manages rental real estate, and Ray and Chuck each work full time (over 1,000 hours per year) managing Alpine. Alpine's debt (both at the beginning and end of the year) consists of $1,500,000 in nonrecourse mortgages obtained from an unrelated bank and secured by various rental properties. At the beginning of the current year, Ray and Chuck each had a tax basis of $250,000 in his LLC interest, including his share of the nonrecourse mortgage debt. Alpine's ordinary business losses for the current year totaled $600,000, and neither member is involved in other activities that generate passive income.

■ **research**

a. How much of each member's loss is suspended because of the tax basis limitation?

b. How much of each member's loss is suspended because of the at-risk limitation?

c. How much of each member's loss is suspended because of the passive activity loss limitation? {*Hint:* See §469(b)(7).}

## COMPREHENSIVE PROBLEMS

75. Aaron, Deanne, and Keon formed the Blue Bell General Partnership at the beginning of the current year. Aaron and Deanne each contributed $110,000 and Keon transferred an acre of undeveloped land to the partnership. The land had a tax basis of $70,000 and was appraised at $180,000. The land was also encumbered with a $70,000 nonrecourse mortgage for which no one was personally liable. All three partners agreed to split profits and losses equally. At the end of the first year, Blue Bell made a $7,000 principal payment on the mortgage. For the first year of operations, the partnership records disclosed the following information:

| | |
|---|---|
| Sales revenue | $470,000 |
| Cost of goods sold | $410,000 |
| Operating expenses | $ 70,000 |
| Long-term capital gains | $  2,400 |
| §1231 gains | $    900 |
| Charitable contributions | $    300 |
| Municipal bond interest | $    300 |
| Salary paid as a guaranteed payment to Deanne (not included in expenses) | $  3,000 |

a. Compute the adjusted basis of each partner's interest in the partnership immediately after the formation of the partnership.

b. List the separate items of partnership income, gains, losses, and deductions that the partners must show on their individual income tax returns that include the results of the partnership's first year of operations.

c. (Optional) Using the information generated in answering parts a. and b., prepare Blue Bells' page 1 and Schedule K to be included with its Form 1065 for its first year of operations, along with Schedule K-1 for Deanne.

d. What are the partners' adjusted bases in their partnership interests at the end of the first year of operations?

76. The TimpRiders LP has operated a motorcycle dealership for a number of years. Lance is the limited partner, Francesca is the general partner, and they share capital and profits equally. Francesca works full-time managing the partnership. Both the partnership and the partners report on a calendar-year basis. At the start of the current year, Lance and Francesca had bases of $10,000 and $3,000, respectively, and the partnership did not carry any debt. During the current year, the partnership reported the following results from operations:

| | |
|---|---|
| Net sales | $650,000 |
| Cost of goods sold | $500,000 |
| Operating expenses | $160,000 |
| Short-term capital loss | $ 2,000 |
| Tax-exempt interest | $ 2,000 |
| §1231 gain | $ 6,000 |

On the last day of the year, the partnership distributed $3,000 each to Lance and Francesca.

a. What outside basis do Lance and Francesca have in their partnership interests at the end of the year?

b. To what extent does the tax basis limitation apply in restricting the partners' deductible losses for the year?

c. To what extent does the passive activity loss limitation apply in restricting their deductible losses for the year?

77. LeBron, Dennis, and Susan formed the Bar T LLC at the beginning of the current year. LeBron and Dennis each contributed $200,000 and Susan transferred several acres of agricultural land she had purchased two years earlier to the LLC. The land had a tax basis of $50,000 and was appraised at $300,000. The land was also encumbered with a $100,000 nonrecourse mortgage (i.e., qualified nonrecourse financing) for which no one was personally liable. The members plan to use the land and cash to begin a cattle-feeding operation. Susan will work full-time operating the business, but LeBron and Dennis will devote less than two days per year to the operation.

All three members agree to split profits and losses equally. At the end of the first year, Bar T had accumulated $40,000 of accounts payable jointly guaranteed by LeBron and Dennis and had made a $9,000 principal payment on the mortgage. None of the members have passive income from other sources.

For the first year of operations, the partnership records disclosed the following information:

| | |
|---|---|
| Sales revenue | $620,000 |
| Cost of goods sold | $380,000 |
| Operating expenses | $670,000 |
| Dividends | $ 1,200 |
| Municipal bond interest | $ 300 |
| Salary paid as a guaranteed payment to Susan (not included in expenses) | $ 10,000 |
| Cash distributions split equally among the members at year-end | $ 3,000 |

a. Compute the adjusted basis of each member's interest immediately after the formation of the LLC.

b. When does each member's holding period for his or her LLC interest begin?

c. What is Bar T's tax basis and holding period in its land?

d. What is Bar T's required tax year-end?

e. What overall methods of accounting are available to Bar T?

f. List the separate items of partnership income, gains, losses, deductions, and other items that will be included in each member's Schedule K-1 for the first year of operations. Use the proposed self-employment tax regulations to determine each member's self-employment income or loss.

g. What are the members' adjusted bases in their LLC interests at the end of the first year of operations?

h. What are the members' at-risk amounts in their LLC interests at the end of the first year of operations?

i. How much loss from Bar T, if any, will the members be able to deduct on their individual returns from the first year of operations?

# KAPLAN CPA SIMULATIONS

KAPLAN CPA REVIEW

**Please visit the Online Learning Center** (www.mhhe.com/spilker2011) to access the following Kaplan CPA Simulation:

The simulation for **Clark Co.** covers corporate tax and partnerships, including filing status; book-to-tax reconciliation; transactions with owners; and the tax impact of various partnership items.

chapter
21

# Dispositions of Partnership Interests and Partnership Distributions

## Learning Objectives

**Upon completing this chapter, you should be able to:**

**LO 1** Determine the tax consequences to the buyer and seller of the disposition of a partnership interest, including the amount and character of gain or loss recognized.

■

**LO 2** List the reasons for distributions, and compare operating and liquidating distributions.

■

**LO 3** Determine the tax consequences of proportionate operating distributions.

■

**LO 4** Determine the tax consequences of proportionate liquidating distributions.

■

**LO 5** Explain the significance of disproportionate distributions.

■

**LO 6** Explain the rationale for special basis adjustments, determine when they are necessary, and calculate the special basis adjustment for dispositions and distributions.

In January 2011*, Nicole and Sarah sit in the Color Comfort Sheets, LLC (CCS), office discussing the current state of business affairs over a cup of coffee. They both agree they are not doing as well as they had hoped after two years of running the business. Their main topic of discussion this morning is how to turn the business around. Both women know the viability of the business is at stake if they can't figure out how to make it profitable . . . and soon.

As Nicole and Sarah brainstorm various ideas, Nicole's administrative assistant interrupts to announce a phone call from Noprah Winsted, the media mogul. Nicole takes the call. On her top-rated television talk show Noprah occasionally promotes products to her viewers based on her successful experience with the product. Apparently, one of Noprah's viewers sent her a set of Color Comfort sheets. Noprah is so happy with the product that she wants to promote the sheets on her show in about two weeks. Nicole and Sarah are, of course, thrilled with this news. Products Noprah has endorsed in the past have become wildly successful. The focus of Nicole and Sarah's meeting changes dramatically. Now they have to figure out how they can gear up for an immediate increase in production. Nicole and Sarah's analysis of the accounting records reveals that CCS is in a precarious cash position—the business is down to its last $10,000.

| Storyline Summary | |
|---|---|
| *Taxpayer:* | Color Comfort Sheets, LLC |
| *Location:* | Salt Lake City, Utah |
| *Owners and interests:* | Nicole Johnson, managing member—30 percent interest Sarah Walker, managing member—40 percent interest Greg Randall, nonmanaging member—30 percent interest |

*To allow the storyline to continue from the previous example, this chapter begins in 2011. We assume the 2010 tax laws apply for 2011 and subsequent years.

Nicole and Sarah immediately call Greg to fill him in on the news. Greg is as thrilled as they are to hear that Noprah will promote their sheets and agrees to kick in an additional $30,000. Nicole says that she will contribute $30,000 and Sarah antes up another $40,000.

The following couple of weeks fly by in a whirlwind of work—phone calls, meetings with bankers, and production scheduling. After the show airs, Nicole and Sarah sit down to talk about the show and the CCS product promotion. Noprah's special guest for the show had been popular film star, Tom Hughes, promoting his soon-to-be-released movie *Global Warfare*. Tom had been good-natured and actually shown interest in the sheets. During the show, he announced he would order a set as soon as the broadcast was over. Nicole and Sarah anticipate orders will roll in. Sure enough, before Noprah had even said goodbye to her studio audience, CCS's Web site traffic picked up and the phone lines were hopping with new orders.

By the end of 2011, CCS's financial situation has completely turned around; business is booming, the accounting records show a healthy profit, and the partners feel comfortable the trend will continue. Greg decides it is time to talk to Nicole and Sarah about cashing out his investment.

*to be continued . . .*

This chapter explores the tax consequences associated with selling partnership interests and with distributing partnership assets to partners.

## L01    BASICS OF SALES OF PARTNERSHIP INTERESTS

As we've seen in previous chapters, owners of various business entities receive returns on their investments, either when the business makes distributions or upon the sale of their business interest. Corporate shareholders may sell their stock to other investors or back to the corporation. Likewise, partners may dispose of their interest in several ways: sell to a third party, sell to another partner, or transfer the interest back to the partnership. The payments in a disposition (sale) can come from either another owner of the partnership or a new investor; in either case, the sale proceeds come from outside the partnership.

Selling a **partnership interest** raises unique issues because of the flow-through nature of the entity. For example, is the interest a separate asset, or does the disposition represent the sale of the partner's share of each of the partnership's assets? (See Chapter 20 for a discussion of the entity and aggregate approaches to taxation of flow-through entities.) If the tax rules follow an entity approach, the interest is considered a separate asset and a sale of the partnership interest would be very similar to the sale of corporate stock. That is, the partner would simply recognize capital gain or loss on the sale, based on the difference between the sales price and the partner's tax basis in the partnership interest.

Alternatively, if the tax rules use the aggregate approach, the disposition represents a sale of the partner's share of each of the partnership's assets. This approach adds some complexity because of the differing character and holding periods of the partnership assets—ordinary, capital, and §1231. The selling partner also has the additional task of allocating the sales proceeds among the underlying assets in order to determine the gain or loss on each.

Rather than strictly following one approach, the tax rules end up being a mixture of the two approaches. When feasible, the entity approach controls; however, if the result distorts the amount or character of income, then the aggregate approach dominates. We discuss the tax consequences of sales of partnership interests by first taking the perspective of the seller (partner), then of the buyer (new investor).

### Seller Issues

The seller's primary tax concern in a partnership interest sale is calculating the amount and character of gain or loss on the sale. The selling partner determines the gain or loss as the difference between the amount realized and her **outside basis** in the partnership.[1] Because the selling partner is no longer responsible for her share of the partnership liabilities, any debt relief increases the amount the partner *realizes* from the sale under general tax principles.

---

| | **Example 21-1** |

Last year Chanzz Inc. sold its 30 percent interest in CCS on July 1 to Greg Randall, a wealthy local businessman, to limit its exposure to any further losses. Greg anticipated that CCS would become profitable in the near future and paid Chanzz Inc. $100,000 for its interest in CCS. Chanzz's share of CCS liabilities as of July 1 was $24,000. Chanzz Inc.'s basis in its CCS interest at the sale date was $105,000 (including its share of CCS's liabilities). What amount of gain did Chanzz recognize on the sale?

**Answer:** $19,000 gain, computed as follows:

| Description | Amount | Explanation |
|---|---|---|
| (1) Cash and fair market value of property received | $100,000 | |
| (2) Debt relief | 24,000 | |
| (3) Amount realized | $124,000 | (1) + (2). |
| (4) Basis in CCS interest | 105,000 | |
| Recognized gain | $ 19,000 | (3) − (4). |

---

> **THE KEY FACTS**
>
> Sale of Partnership Interest
>
> ■ Sellers' gain or loss calculation
>   Amount realized:
>     Cash and fair market value of property received plus
>     Debt relief
>   Less: Basis in partnership interest
>   Equals: Realized gain or loss
>
> ■ Buyer issues
>   · Outside basis—cost of the partnership interest plus share of partnership's liabilities.
>   · Inside basis—selling partner's inside basis at sale date.
>   · No changes to partnership asset bases (unless §754 election is in effect).
>   · Tax year closes with respect to selling partner.

The character of the gain or loss from a sale of a partnership interest is generally capital, because partnership interests are capital assets.[2] However, a portion of the gain or loss will be ordinary if a seller realizes any gain attributable to **unrealized receivables** or **inventory items**.[3] Practitioners often refer to these assets that give rise to ordinary gains and losses as **hot assets**.[4] Let's discuss that term further, because

---

[1]Partners determine their outside basis as discussed in the previous chapter. Importantly, the outside basis includes the selling partner's share of distributive income for the year to the date of the sale.

[2]§731 and §741.

[3]§751(a).

[4]There are actually two definitions of *inventory items* in §751. Section 751(a) inventory items are defined in §751(d) to include *all* inventory items. However under §751(b), the definition includes only *substantially appreciated* inventory. For purposes of determining the character of gain or loss from the sale of partnership interests, the term *inventory items* includes all inventory as in §751(a). However, these two definitions have created some confusion when using the term *hot assets*. In this chapter, we use the term *hot assets* to refer to unrealized receivables and all inventory items as in §751(a). The definition under §751(b) becomes more relevant when determining the tax treatment in a disproportionate distribution (discussed only briefly later in the chapter).

these assets are central to determining the tax treatment of many transactions in this chapter.

**Hot Assets**    As you might expect, unrealized receivables include the right to receive payment for (1) "goods delivered, or to be delivered"[5] or (2) "services rendered, or to be rendered."[6] For cash-method taxpayers, unrealized receivables include amounts earned but not yet received (accounts receivable). Accrual-method taxpayers, however, do not consider accounts receivable as unrealized receivables because they have already realized and recognized these items as ordinary income. Unrealized receivables also include items the partnership would treat as ordinary income if it sold the asset for its fair market value, such as depreciation recapture under §1245.[7]

Inventory items include classic inventory, defined as property held for sale to customers in the ordinary course of business, but also, more broadly, any assets that are *not* capital assets or §1231 assets, such as assets used in the business but not held for more than a year.[8] For example, all accounts receivable are considered inventory, even though only cash-method receivables are considered unrealized receivables. This broad definition means cash, capital assets, and §1231 assets are the only properties not considered inventory.[9]

---

### Example 21-2

CCS's balance sheet as of the date of Chanzz's sale of its CCS interest to Greg was the following:

**Color Comfort Sheets, LLC**
**July 1, 2010**

|  | Tax Basis | FMV |
|---|---|---|
| **Assets:** | | |
| Cash | $ 27,000 | $ 27,000 |
| Accounts receivable | 0 | 13,000 |
| Investments | 15,000 | 12,000 |
| Inventory | 1,000 | 1,000 |
| Equipment (cost = $100,000) | 80,000 | 86,000 |
| Building | 97,000 | 97,000 |
| Land | 20,000 | 150,000 |
| Totals | $240,000 | $386,000 |
| | | |
| **Liabilities and capital:** | | |
| Long term debt | $100,000* | |
| Capital—Nicole | (49,000) | |
| —Sarah | 108,000 | |
| —Chanzz | 81,000 | |
| Totals | $240,000 | |

*Of the $100,000 of long-term debt, $20,000 is allocated solely to Nicole. The remaining $80,000 is allocated to all three owners according to their profit-sharing ratios.

(continued on page 21-5...)

---

[5] §751(c)(1).
[6] §751(c)(2).
[7] §751(c).
[8] §751(d)(1).
[9] This broad definition of inventory includes all unrealized receivables except for recapture. Recapture items are excluded from the definition of inventory items simply because recapture is not technically an asset; rather, it is merely a portion of gain that results from the sale of property. Recapture is, however, considered an unrealized receivable (i.e., hot asset) under §751(a). This idea is important in determining whether inventory is substantially appreciated for purposes of determining the §751 assets for distributions as we discuss later in the chapter.

Which of CCS's assets are considered hot assets under §751(a)?

**Answer:** The hot assets are accounts receivables of $13,000 and $6,000 depreciation recapture (§1245) potential ($86,000 − $80,000) in the equipment. The accounts receivable is an unrealized receivable because CCS has not included it in income for tax purposes under CCS's cash accounting method. The depreciation recapture is also considered an unrealized receivable under §751(a). Inventory would be considered a hot asset; however, because the tax basis and fair market value are equal, it will not affect the character of any gain recognized on the sale.

---

**Example 21-3**

Review CCS's balance sheet as of the end of 2011.

**Color Comfort Sheets, LLC**
**December 31, 2011**

| | Tax Basis | FMV |
|---|---|---|
| **Assets:** | | |
| Cash | $390,000 | $ 390,000 |
| Accounts receivable | 0 | 40,000 |
| Inventory | 90,000 | 200,000 |
| Investments | 60,000 | 105,000 |
| Equipment (cost = $200,000) | 150,000 | 200,000 |
| Building (cost = $100,000) | 90,000 | 100,000 |
| Land—original | 20,000 | 160,000 |
| Land—investment | 140,000 | 270,000 |
| Totals | $940,000 | $1,465,000 |
| **Liabilities and capital:** | | |
| Accounts payable | $ 80,000 | |
| Long-term debt | | |
| Mortgage on original land | 40,000 | |
| Mortgage on investment land | 120,000 | |
| Capital—Nicole | 119,000 | |
| —Sarah | 332,000 | |
| —Greg | 249,000 | |
| Totals | $940,000 | |

What amount of CCS's assets are considered to be hot assets as of December 31, 2011?

**Answer:** The hot assets include inventory with a fair market value of $200,000, unrealized receivables of $50,000 of depreciation recapture potential on the equipment, and $40,000 of accounts receivable.

---

When a partner sells her interest in a partnership that holds hot assets, she modifies her calculation of the gain or loss to ensure the portion that relates to hot assets is properly characterized as ordinary income. The process for determining the gain or loss follows:

**Step 1:** Determine the total gain or loss by subtracting outside basis from the amount realized.

**Step 2:** Calculate the partner's share of gain or loss from hot assets as if the partnership sold these assets at their fair market value. This represents the ordinary portion of the gain or loss.

**Step 3:** Finally, subtract the ordinary portion of the gain or loss obtained in Step 2 from the total gain or loss from Step 1. This remaining amount is the capital gain or loss from the sale.[10]

---

[10]The partner must also determine if any portion of the capital gain or loss relates to collectibles (28 percent capital gain property) or to unrecaptured §1250 gains. This is typically referred to as the *look-through rule*.

## Example 21-4

In Example 21-1, Chanzz sold its interest in CCS to Greg Randall for $100,000 cash on July 1, 2010. As a result, Chanzz recognized a gain of $19,000 on the sale. What is the character of Chanzz's gain?

**Answer:** $5,700 of ordinary income and $13,300 of capital gain, determined as follows:

**Step 1:** Determine the total gain or loss: $19,000 from Example 21-1.

**Step 2:** Determine the ordinary gain or loss from hot assets:

| Asset | (1) Basis | (2) FMV | (3) Gain/Loss (2) − (1) | Chanzz's Share 30% × (3) |
|-------|-----------|---------|--------------------------|---------------------------|
| Accounts receivable | $    0 | $13,000 | $13,000 | $3,900 |
| Equipment | 80,000 | 86,000 | 6,000 | 1,800 |
| Total ordinary income | | | | $5,700 |

**Step 3:** Determine the capital gain or loss:

| Description | Amount | Explanation |
|-------------|--------|-------------|
| (1) Total gain | $19,000 | From Step 1. |
| (2) Ordinary income from §751(a) | 5,700 | From Step 2. |
| Capital gain | $13,300 | (1) − (2). |

## Example 21-5

**What if:** Assume the same facts as in Example 21-4, except Greg is willing to pay Chanzz only $82,800 cash for its interest in CCS. What is the amount and character of Chanzz's gain or loss?

**Answer:** $5,700 of ordinary income and capital loss of $3,900, determined as follows:

**Step 1:** Determine the total gain or loss:

| Description | Amount | Explanation |
|-------------|--------|-------------|
| (1) Cash and fair market value of property received | $  82,800 | |
| (2) Debt relief | 24,000 | Chanzz's share of CCS's allocable debt (30% × $80,000). |
| (3) Amount realized | $106,800 | (1) + (2). |
| (4) Basis in CCS interest | 105,000 | |
| Gain recognized | $    1,800 | (3) − (4). |

**Step 2:** Determine the ordinary gain or loss from hot assets:

| Asset | (1) Basis | (2) FMV | (3) Gain/Loss (2) − (1) | Chanzz's Share 30% × (3) |
|-------|-----------|---------|--------------------------|---------------------------|
| Accounts receivable | $    0 | $13,000 | $13,000 | $3,900 |
| Equipment | 80,000 | 86,000 | 6,000 | 1,800 |
| Total ordinary income | | | | $5,700 |

**Step 3:** Determine the capital gain or loss:

| Description | Amount | Explanation |
|---|---|---|
| (1) Total gain | $ 1,800 | From Step 1. |
| (2) Ordinary income from §751(a) | 5,700 | From Step 2. |
| Capital loss | $(3,900) | (1) − (2). |

## Buyer and Partnership Issues

A new investor in a partnership is of course concerned with determining how much to pay for the partnership interest. However, his primary tax concerns are about his inside and outside bases in the partnership. In general, for a sale transaction, the new investor's outside basis will be equal to his cost of the partnership interest.[11] To the extent that the new investor shares in the partnership liabilities, his share of partnership liabilities increases his outside basis.

### Example 21-6

When Greg Randall acquired Chanzz's 30 percent interest in CCS for $100,000 on July 1, 2010 (see Example 21-1), he guaranteed his share of CCS's debts just as Chanzz had done. As a result, Greg will be allocated his share of CCS's allocable debt in accordance with his 30 percent profit-sharing ratio. What is the outside basis of Greg's acquired interest?

**Answer:** $124,000, determined as follows:

| Description | Amount | Explanation |
|---|---|---|
| (1) Initial tax basis | $100,000 | Cash paid to Chanzz. |
| (2) Share of CCS's liabilities | 24,000 | 30% × CCS's allocable debt of $80,000. |
| Outside basis | $124,000 | (1) + (2). |

The partnership experiences very few tax consequences when a partner sells her interest.[12] The sale does not generally affect a partnership's **inside basis** in its assets.[13] The new investor typically "steps into the shoes" of the selling partner to determine his share of the partnership's inside basis of the partnership assets. Consequently, the new investor's share of inside basis is equal to the selling partner's share of inside basis at the sale date. Recall from the preceding chapter that each partner has a tax capital account that reflects the tax basis of property and cash contributed by the partner, the partner's share of earnings and losses, and distributions to the partner. In a sale of a partnership interest, the selling partner's tax capital account carries over to the new investor.[14]

---

[11]§1012. The outside basis will depend, in part, on how the new investor obtains the interest. For example, a gift generally results in a carryover basis whereas an inherited interest typically results in a basis equal to the fair market value as of the date of the decedent's death.

[12]Later in the chapter, we discuss situations in which the new investor's share of the partnership's asset bases are adjusted after a sale of a partnership interest under §754. Throughout this section, we assume that the partnership does not have a §754 election in effect.

[13]§743.

[14]An exception occurs when the selling partner contributed property with a built-in loss to the partnership. Only the contributing partner is entitled to that loss [see Chapter 20 and §704(c)(1)(C)]. Therefore, when a new investor buys a partnership interest from a partner that contributed built-in loss property, the new investor reduces his inside basis by the amount of the built-in loss at the contribution date.

### Example 21-7

Refer to Example 21-2 for CCS's balance sheet as of July 1, 2010. What is Greg's share of CCS's inside basis immediately after purchasing Chanzz's 30 percent interest in CCS?

**Answer:** Greg's share is $105,000: the sum of Chanzz' tax capital account of $81,000 and its share of CCS's liabilities of $24,000. Greg simply steps into Chanzz's place after the acquisition. In the preceding example, we determined Greg's outside basis to be $124,000. A sale of a partnership interest often results in a difference between the new investor's inside and outside bases because the outside basis is the price paid based on fair market value and the inside basis is the share of tax basis in the partnership assets.

**Varying Interest Rule**   If a partner's interest in a partnership increases or decreases during the partnership's tax year, the partnership income or loss allocated to the partner for the year must be adjusted to reflect her *varying interest* in the partnership.[15] Partners' interests increase when they contribute property or cash to a partnership[16] or purchase a partnership interest. Conversely, partners' interests decrease when they receive partnership distributions[17] or sell all or a portion of their partnership interests. Upon the sale of a partnership interest, the partnership tax year closes for the *selling* partner only. Regulations allow partners to choose between two possible methods for allocating income or loss to partners when their interests change during the year.[18] The first method allows the partnership to prorate income or loss to partners with varying interests, while the second method sanctions an interim closing of the partnership's books.[19]

### Example 21-8

CCS had a $60,000 overall operating loss for the 2010 calendar year. It closed its books as of July 1, 2010, for Chanzz *only* to determine its distributive share of income/loss as of the sale date. The issue of how to allocate the 2010 loss between Chanzz Inc. and Greg was easily resolved because CCS's operating agreement specifies the proration method to allocate income or loss when members' interests in CCS change during the year. How much of CCS's 2010 loss will Chanzz be allocated under the proration method?

**Answer:** Chanzz takes a loss of $9,000, which includes its share of CCS's loss but for only one-half the year ($60,000 × 30% share × 1/2 year) and will report it on its tax return. On the sale date, Chanzz decreases its basis in CCS by the $9,000 loss to determine its adjusted basis to use in calculating its gain or loss on the sale of its interest.

### Example 21-9

**What if:** If CCS's overall loss through June 30 was $20,000, how much of the $60,000 overall loss for 2010 will Chanzz and Greg Randall be allocated under an interim closing of the books?

**Answer:** CCS will allocate $6,000 of loss (30% × $20,000) to Chanzz and $12,000 of loss (30% × $40,000) to Greg.

---

[15]§706(d)(1).

[16]If all partners simultaneously contribute property or cash with a value proportionate to their interests, their relative interests will not change.

[17]If all partners receive distributions with a value proportionate to their interests, their relative interests will not change.

[18]Reg. §1.706-1(c).

[19]If within a 12-month period, there is a sale of 50 percent or more of the total capital and profits interest in the partnership, the partnership is terminated. When this occurs, the partnership tax year is closed for all partners, not just the selling partners. See §708(b).

---

**Taxes in the Real World**   *Changing the Way Companies Dispose*
*of a Business*

Corporate takeovers seemed to be the transaction du jour during the 1990s, but many practitioners are predicting joint ventures will be the defining deal for the current decade. We see regular articles in *The Wall Street Journal* describing how firms are starting up joint ventures or strategic alliances—or exiting them. For example, IBM recently announced plans to pull the plug on its enterprise printing systems. To do so, IBM formed a joint venture, named InfoPrint Solutions Company, with Ricoh Co., a Japanese printer and copier vendor. Ricoh paid IBM $725 million in cash for its initial 51 percent of the joint venture.

IBM retains the remaining 49 percent. Its ultimate goal is for Ricoh Co. to acquire its 49 percent of the joint venture over a period of three years.

The increase in the number of joint ventures and their possible dissolution or disposition brings an increasing need to understand the partnership tax rules and regulations. More than ever before, corporate tax executives find they must advise senior management on the opportunities and pitfalls of structuring joint ventures and investments as partnerships or LLCs under Subchapter K of the Internal Revenue Code.

---

# BASICS OF PARTNERSHIP DISTRIBUTIONS

**LO2**

Like shareholders receiving corporate dividend distributions, partners often receive distributions of the partnership profits, known as **operating distributions.** Recall that owners of flow-through entities are taxed currently on their business income regardless of whether the business distributes it. As a result, partners may require cash distributions in order to make quarterly estimated tax payments on their share of business income. Usually, the general partners (or managing members of LLCs) determine the amount and timing of distributions; however, the partnership (operating) agreement may stipulate some distributions.

Partners may also receive **liquidating distributions.** Because the market for partnership interests is much smaller than for publicly traded stock, partners may have a difficult time finding buyers for their interests. Partnership agreements also often limit purchasers of an interest to the current partner group, to avoid adding an unwanted partner. If the current partner group either cannot or does not want to purchase the interest, the partnership can instead distribute assets to terminate a partner's interest. These liquidating distributions are similar to corporate redemptions of a shareholder's stock. They can also terminate the partnership. We first explore the tax consequences of operating distributions, and then examine the tax treatment for liquidating distributions.

## Operating Distributions

**LO3**

A distribution from a partnership is an operating distribution when the partners continue their interests afterwards. Operating distributions are usually paid to distribute the business profits to the partners but can also reduce a partner's ownership. The partnership may distribute money or other assets. Let's look at the tax consequences of distributions of money, and then the tax consequences of property other than money.

**Operating Distributions of Money Only**   The general rule for operating distributions states that the partnership does not recognize gain or loss on the distribution of property or money.[20, 21] Nor do the general tax rules require a partner to recognize gain or

| THE KEY FACTS |
| --- |
| Operating Distributions |
| ■ **Gain or loss recognition:** Partners generally do not recognize gain or loss. One exception occurs when the partnership distributes money only and the amount is greater than the partner's outside basis. |
| (*continued*) |

---

[20]For distribution purposes, money includes cash, deemed cash from reductions in a partner's share of liabilities, and the fair market value of marketable securities.

[21]§731(b).

loss when she receives distributed property or money.[22] The partner simply reduces her (outside) basis in the partnership interest by the amount of the distribution. In doing so, she retains any gain or loss on her share of partnership assets represented by her outside basis.[23] In general, the partnership's basis in its remaining assets remains unchanged.[24]

---

### Example 21-10

(concluded)

■ **Basis of distributed assets:** Partners generally take a carryover basis in the distributed assets. If the partnership distribution includes other property and the combined inside bases is greater than the partner's outside basis, the bases of the other property distributed will be reduced.

■ **Remaining outside basis:** In general, partners reduce outside basis by money and other property distributed.

**What if:** Suppose CCS makes its first distribution to the owners on December 31, 2011: $250,000 each to Nicole and Greg and $333,333 to Sarah. After taking into account their distributive share of CCS's income for the year, the owners have the following predistribution bases in their CCS interests:

| Owner | Outside Basis |
|-------|---------------|
| Nicole | $205,000 |
| Sarah | $420,000 |
| Greg | $334,000 |

What are the tax consequences (gain or loss and basis in CCS interest) of the distribution to Sarah?

**Answer:** Sarah does not recognize any gain or loss on the distribution. She reduces her outside basis from $420,000 to $86,667 ($420,000 − $333,333) after the distribution.

---

The general rule of no gain is impractical when the partner receives a greater amount of money than her outside basis. She cannot defer gain to the extent of the excess amount because the outside basis is insufficient for a full reduction. Therefore, the partner reduces her outside basis to zero[25] and recognizes gain (generally capital) to the extent the amount of money distributed is greater than her outside basis.[26] A partner *never* recognizes a loss from an *operating* distribution.

---

### Example 21-11

**What if:** Suppose that in the December 31, 2011, distribution Nicole's distribution consists of $250,000 cash. Her outside basis is $205,000 before the distribution. What are Nicole's gain or loss and basis in her CCS interest after the distribution?

**Answer:** Nicole has $45,000 capital gain and $0 basis in CCS. Because she receives only money in the distribution, she decreases her outside basis to $0 and must recognize a $45,000 capital gain ($250,000 distribution less $205,000 basis). She recognizes gain because she receives a cash distribution in excess of her outside basis.

---

**Operating Distributions that Include Property Other Than Money**   If a partnership makes a distribution that includes property *other than money,* the partners face the problem of reallocating their outside basis between the distributed assets (including

---

[22]§731.

[23]The basis adjustment is a primary mechanism used to meet the overall tax objective of maintaining the partner's economic interest in the underlying partnership assets. We will see its use many times throughout this chapter.

[24]However, if the partnership has a §754 election in effect or if there is a substantial basis reduction, the partnership basis of its remaining assets must be adjusted following a distribution according to §734(a) and §755.

[25]§733.

[26]§731(a)(1).

money) and their continuing partnership interests.[27] Under the general rule, the partner takes a basis in the distributed property equal to the partnership basis in the property. This is called a **carryover basis**.[28] The tax rules define the order in which to allocate outside basis to the bases of distributed assets. First, the partner allocates the outside basis to any money received and then to other property as a carryover basis. The remainder is the partner's outside basis after the distribution.

---

**Example 21-12**

***What if:*** Suppose CCS's December 31, 2011, distribution to Sarah consists of $133,333 cash and investments (other than marketable securities), with a fair market value of $200,000 and an adjusted basis of $115,000. Sarah has a predistribution outside basis of $420,000. What are the tax consequences (Sarah's gain or loss, basis of distributed assets, and outside basis of CCS interest, and CCS's gain or loss) of the distribution?

**Answer:** Sarah recognizes no gain or loss on the distribution. To determine her bases in the distributed assets, she first allocates $133,333 to the cash and then takes a carryover basis in the investments so her basis in the investments is $115,000. Sarah reduces her outside basis by $248,333 ($133,333 cash + $115,000 basis of investments). Her outside basis after the distribution is $171,667 ($420,000 − $248,333). CCS does not recognize any gain or loss on the distribution.

---

When the partnership distributes property (other than money) with a basis that exceeds the remaining outside basis (after the allocation to any money distributed), the partner assigns the remaining outside basis to the distributed assets,[29] and the partner's outside basis is reduced to zero.[30] The first allocation of outside basis goes to money, then to hot assets, and finally to other property.[31] In this case, the partner's basis in the property received in the distribution will be less than the property's basis in the hands of the partnership.

---

**Example 21-13**

***What if:*** Suppose Nicole's December 31, 2011, distribution consists of $150,000 cash and investments (other than marketable securities) with a fair market value of $100,000 and an adjusted basis of $90,000. Her outside basis is $205,000 before the distribution. What are Nicole's tax consequences (gain or loss, basis of distributed assets, outside basis in CCS interest) of the distribution?

**Answer:** Nicole recognizes no gain or loss and takes a basis of $55,000 in the investments. Her outside basis in CCS is $0, computed as follows:

| Description | Amount | Explanation |
|---|---|---|
| (1) Nicole's outside basis | $205,000 | |
| (2) Cash distribution | 150,000 | |
| (3) Remaining basis | $ 55,000 | (1) − (2); remaining outside basis to be allocated to the distributed investments. |
| (4) Inside basis of investments | $ 90,000 | |
| (5) Basis in investments | $ 55,000 | Lesser of (3) or (4). |
| Nicole's outside basis in CCS | $     0 | (3) − (5). |

---

[27]In this context, money includes marketable securities [§731(c)(1)(A)]. The special rules in §731(c) for the treatment of distributed marketable securities are beyond the scope of this book.

[28]§732(a).

[29]§732(a)(2).

[30]§733.

[31]If multiple assets are distributed, then the outside basis will be allocated in accordance with §732(c). We discuss these rules later in conjunction with liquidating distributions.

Because a partner's outside basis includes her share of the partnership liabilities, the outside basis must reflect any changes in a partner's share of partnership debt resulting from a distribution. In essence, a partner treats a reduction of her share of debt as a distribution of money.[32] If the partner increases her share of debt, the increase is treated as a cash contribution to the partnership.

---

**Example 21-14**

**What if:** Suppose Greg receives land held for investment with a fair market value of $250,000 (adjusted basis is $140,000) as his distribution from CCS on December 31, 2011. He agrees to assume the $120,000 mortgage on the land after the distribution. His outside basis is $334,000 before considering the distribution. What are the tax consequences (gain or loss, basis of distributed assets, outside basis in her CCS interest) of the distribution to Greg?

**Answer:** Greg does not recognize any gain or loss on the distribution. His basis in the land is $140,000 and his outside basis in CCS is $278,000, determined as follows:

| Description | Amount | Explanation |
|---|---|---|
| (1) Greg's predistribution outside basis | $334,000 | |
| (2) Mortgage assumed by Greg | $120,000 | |
| (3) Greg's predistribution share of mortgage | $ 36,000 | (2) × 30% ownership. |
| (4) Deemed cash contribution from debt assumption | $ 84,000 | (2) − (3). |
| (5) Greg's outside basis after debt changes | $418,000 | (1) + (4). |
| (6) Greg's basis in distributed land | $140,000 | Carryover basis from CCS. |
| Greg's post-distribution outside basis | $278,000 | (5) − (6). |

Greg must first consider the effects of changes in debt before determining the effects of the distribution. The tax rules treat him as making a net contribution of $84,000 cash to the partnership, the difference between the full mortgage he assumes and his predistribution share of the debt. Greg then allocates $140,000 of his outside basis to the land and reduces his outside basis accordingly.

---

**L04**

## Liquidating Distributions

In contrast to operating distributions in which the partners retain a continuing interest in the partnership, liquidating distributions terminate a partner's interest in the partnership. If the current partners do not have sufficient cash or inclination to buy out the terminating partner, the partnership agreement usually allows the partnership to close out the partner's interest. At some point, all the partners may agree to terminate the partnership, either because they have lost interest in continuing it or it has not been profitable. In such cases, the partnership may distribute all its assets to the partners in complete partnership liquidation. This process is analogous to a complete corporate liquidation (discussed in Chapter 19).

The tax issues in liquidating distributions for partnerships are basically twofold: (1) to determine whether the terminating partner recognizes gain or loss and (2) to reallocate his or her entire outside basis to the distributed assets. The rationale behind the rules for liquidating distributions is simply to replace the partner's outside basis with the underlying partnership assets distributed to the terminating partner. Ideally, there would be no gain or loss on the distribution, and the asset bases would be the same in the partner's hands as they were inside the partnership. Of course, this case rarely occurs. The rules therefore are designed to determine when gain or loss must be recognized and to allocate the partner's outside basis to the distributed assets.

[32]§752(b).

**Gain or Loss Recognition in Liquidating Distributions**   In general, neither partnerships nor partners recognize gain or loss from liquidating distributions. However, there are exceptions. For example, when a terminating partner receives more money in the distribution than her outside basis, she will recognize gain.[33] See Example 21-11 for an illustration in the context of operating distributions.

In contrast to operating distributions, a partner may recognize a *loss* from a liquidating distribution, but only when two conditions are met. These conditions are (1) the distribution includes only cash, unrealized receivables, and/or inventory; *and* (2) the partner's outside basis is greater than the sum of the *inside bases* of the distributed assets.[34] The loss on the distribution is a capital loss to the partner.

Commonly, the terminating partner's share of partnership debt decreases after a liquidating distribution. Any reduction in the partner's share of liabilities is considered a distribution of money to the partner and reduces the outside basis available for allocation of basis to other assets, including inventory and unrealized receivables.

---

### Example 21-15

**What if:** Suppose on January 1, 2012, CCS liquidates Greg's interest in the LLC by distributing to him cash of $206,000 and inventory with a fair market value of $96,000 (adjusted basis is $43,000). Greg's share of CCS's liabilities as of the liquidation is $66,000. On January 1, 2012, Greg's outside basis in CCS is $334,000, including his share of CCS's liabilities. What is Greg's gain or loss on the liquidation of his CCS interest?

**Answer:** Greg recognizes a capital loss of $19,000 on the liquidation, computed as follows:

| Description | Amount | Explanation |
|---|---|---|
| (1) Outside basis before distribution | $334,000 | |
| (2) Debt relief | 66,000 | Deemed cash distribution. |
| (3) Outside basis after considering debt relief | $268,000 | (1) − (2). |
| (4) Basis of property distributed (cash + inventory) | 249,000 | |
| Gain (loss) on distribution | $(19,000) | (4) − (3). |

Greg recognizes a loss because he meets the two necessary conditions: (1) he receives only cash and inventory in the distribution *and* (2) the sum of the adjusted bases of the distributed assets is less than his basis in his CCS interest ($249,000 asset bases versus $268,000 CCS basis).

**THE KEY FACTS**

*Gain or Loss Recognition in Liquidating Distributions*

▌ **Generally:** Partners and partnerships do not recognize gain or loss.

▌ **Exceptions:**
· **Gain:** Partner recognizes gain when partnership distributes money and the amount exceeds the partner's outside basis in the partnership interest.
· **Loss:** Partner recognizes loss when two conditions are met: (1) Distribution consists of only cash and hot assets, and (2) the partner's outside basis exceeds the sum of the bases of the distributed assets.

---

**Basis in Distributed Property**   A key theme of the partnership tax rules is the idea that the partnership acts merely as a conduit for the partners' business activities. Thus, the rules attempt to keep the basis of the assets the same regardless of whether the partner or the partnership has possession of them. Moving assets in and out of the partnership should therefore have few tax consequences. The primary objective of the basis rules in liquidating distributions is to allocate the partner's entire outside basis in the partnership to the assets the partner receives in the liquidating distribution. The allocation essentially depends on two things: (1) the partnership's bases in distributed assets relative to the partner's outside basis and (2) the type of property distributed—whether it is money, hot assets, or other property. For purposes of distributions, hot assets include unrealized receivables and

---

[33]These rules are very similar to those for operating distributions. When a partner receives money only in complete termination of the partnership interest, any gain on distribution cannot be deferred through a basis adjustment. Therefore, the partner recognizes the gain.

[34]§731(a)(2).

inventory, as we've previously defined. We discuss each of the possible scenarios in Exhibit 21-1 in turn.

**EXHIBIT 21-1    Alternative Scenarios for Determining Basis in Distributed Property**

| Type of Property Distributed | Partner's outside basis is *greater* than inside bases of distributed assets | Partner's outside basis is *less* than inside bases of distributed assets |
|---|---|---|
| Money only | Scenario 1 | Scenario 3 |
| Money and hot assets | Scenario 1 | Scenario 4 |
| Other property included in distribution[35] | Scenario 2 | Scenario 5 |

### Partner's Outside Basis Is Greater Than Inside Basis of Distributed Assets

***Scenario 1: Distributions of money, inventory, and/or unrealized receivables.***    If the partnership distributes only money, inventory, and/or unrealized receivables (ordinary income property) and the partner's outside basis is greater than the sum of the inside bases of the distributed assets, the partner recognizes a capital loss.[36] The partner assigns a basis to the assets equal to the partnership basis in the assets and the remaining outside basis determines the recognized loss. To prevent a partner from converting a capital loss from her investment into an ordinary loss, the tax law prohibits increasing her basis in unrealized receivables and inventory and requires the partner to recognize a capital loss.[37]

---

**Example 21-16**

**What if:** Suppose Greg has an outside basis of $334,000, including his share of liabilities of $66,000. In a liquidating distribution, he receives $159,000 cash and inventory with a fair market value and basis of $49,000. Will Greg recognize a gain or loss? Why or why not?

**Answer:** Yes, Greg will recognize a capital loss of $60,000. In this case, Greg is unable to defer his loss without changing its character. Greg clearly cannot adjust the basis in the cash to defer the loss. *If* he increases his basis in the distributed inventory, he could defer the loss. However, this would produce an ordinary loss of $60,000 when Greg sells the inventory.[38] To prevent the conversion of a capital loss to an ordinary loss, Greg recognizes a $60,000 capital loss.

---

***Scenario 2: Other property included in distributions.***    Recall that in this scenario the liquidating partner must reallocate all her outside basis to the distributed assets. We determined in Scenario 1 that when the partnership distributes only money and/or hot assets and the distributed asset bases are less than the partner's outside basis, it

---

[35]This category includes distributions that include other property in addition to or instead of either money or unrealized receivables or inventory. For example, the distributions in this category can include any combination of money, unrealized receivables, and inventory as long as other property is also distributed.

[36]§731(a)(2).

[37]§732(c)(1) and §731(a)(2).

[38]If the inventory distributed to Greg is also considered inventory in his hands, the eventual sale of the inventory will generate ordinary income. If the inventory is a capital asset to Greg, a sale of the asset within five years of the distribution will generate ordinary income. After five years, the gain or loss would be capital.

was impossible to allocate the entire outside basis to the distributed assets without changing the character of a resulting loss. Thus, a partner never increases the bases of hot assets. However, when the partnership distributes other property, in addition to money and/or hot assets, the partner can adjust the basis of the *other* property without converting ordinary gains and losses to capital, and the liquidating partner will not recognize any gain or loss from the distribution.

**Example 21-17**

**What if:** Suppose CCS has no liabilities or hot assets and distributes $50,000 in cash and land with a fair market value of $160,000 and an adjusted basis of $20,000 to Greg in complete liquidation of his CCS interest. Greg has an outside basis of $268,000 prior to the distribution. What is Greg's recognized gain or loss on the distribution?

**Answer:** Greg does not recognize any gain or loss. He receives money and other property with a total basis of $70,000, which is less than his outside basis of $268,000. Greg first reduces his outside basis by the amount of money he receives, and he assigns his remaining outside basis to the land as follows:

| Description | Amount | Explanation |
|---|---|---|
| (1) Outside basis before distribution | $268,000 | |
| (2) Basis allocated to money distributed | 50,000 | |
| Remaining outside basis assigned to land | $218,000 | (1) − (2). |

Note that Greg increases the basis of the other property received in liquidation (land) from $20,000 to $218,000 in order to allocate his entire outside basis to the distributed assets. In some cases, "other" property might include personal assets for which the partner may never be able to recover the basis increase.

Example 21-17 illustrates the required basis increase in a very simple situation. In reality, liquidating distributions may include several types of assets. In these situations, to allocate the outside basis to the distributed assets, the partner completes the following, more detailed process:[39]

**Step 1:** The partner first assigns a basis to any money, inventory, and unrealized receivables equal to the partnership's basis in these assets. The partner also assigns a basis to the other distributed property in an amount equal to the partnership's basis in those assets.

**Step 2:** The partner then allocates the remaining outside basis (full outside basis less the amounts assigned in Step 1) to the other distributed property that has unrealized appreciation to the extent of that appreciation. Thus, if an asset has an adjusted basis to the partnership of $500 and a fair market value of $700, the partner will allocate the first $200 of remaining basis to that asset.[40]

**Step 3:** The partner allocates any remaining basis to all other property in proportion to the relative *fair market values* of the other property.

$$\text{Basis allocation} = \text{Remaining basis} \times \frac{\text{FMV}_{asset}}{\text{Sum of FMV}_{distributed\ other\ property}}$$

---

[39]§732(c)(2).

[40]If the remaining outside basis is insufficient to allocate the full amount of appreciation to the distributed assets in this step, then the partner will allocate the remaining basis in this step to the appreciated assets based on their relative appreciation.

## Example 21-18

**What if:** Suppose CCS makes the following distribution to Greg in liquidation of his CCS interest:

| Asset | CCS Tax Basis | Fair Market Value |
|---|---|---|
| Cash | $181,000 | $181,000 |
| Investment A | $  5,000 | $ 12,000 |
| Investment B | $ 10,000 | $ 13,000 |
| Inventory | $ 43,000 | $ 96,000 |

Greg's basis in his CCS interest as of the liquidation is $334,000, including his $66,000 share of CCS's liabilities. What is Greg's recognized gain or loss on the distribution? What is Greg's basis in the distributed assets following the liquidation?

**Answer:** Greg recognizes no gain or loss on the distribution. Greg's bases in the distributed assets are:

| | |
|---|---|
| Cash | $181,000 |
| Investment A | 21,120 |
| Investment B | 22,880 |
| Inventory | 43,000 |
| Total | $268,000 |

Because Greg receives other property in the distribution and the distributed asset bases are less than Greg's outside basis (Scenario 2), he will allocate his outside basis as follows:

First, Greg determines his allocable basis:

| Description | Amount | Explanation |
|---|---|---|
| (1) Basis in CCS before distribution | $334,000 | |
| (2) Debt relief | 66,000 | Greg's 30 percent share of CCS's debt. |
| Allocable basis | $268,000 | (1) − (2). |

Next, Greg allocates his remaining CCS basis of $268,000 to the distributed assets by following the three-step allocation process.

| Description | Amount | Explanation |
|---|---|---|
| **Step 1:** | | |
| (1) Allocable basis | $268,000 | See above. |
| (2) Basis assigned to cash | 181,000 | |
| (3) Basis assigned to inventory | 43,000 | |
| (4) Initial basis assigned to investment A | 5,000 | |
| (5) Initial basis assigned to investment B | 10,000 | |
| (6) Remaining allocable CCS basis | $ 29,000 | (1) − (2) − (3) − (4) − (5). |
| **Step 2:** | | |
| (7) Additional basis assigned to investment A | $  7,000 | Unrealized appreciation on investment A from example. FMV of $12,000 less basis of $5,000. |
| (8) Additional basis assigned to investment A | 3,000 | Unrealized appreciation on investment A from example. FMV of $13,000 less basis of $10,000. |
| (9) Remaining allocable CCS basis after Step 2 | $ 19,000 | (6) − (7) − (8). |

*Step 3:*

| | | |
|---|---|---|
| (10) Additional basis allocated to other property: investment A. | $ 9,120 | Basis allocation = $19,000 × ($12,000/$25,000) = $9,120. |
| (11) Additional basis allocated to other property: investment B. | $ 9,880 | Basis allocation = $19,000 × ($13,000/$25,000) = $9,880 |

In Step 3, Greg allocates the remaining basis to the distributed investments based on their relative fair market values using:

$$\text{Basis allocation} = \text{Remaining basis} \times \frac{\text{FMV}_{asset}}{\text{Sum of FMV}_{distributed\ other\ property}}$$

Thus, Greg's bases in the investments are:

| Description | Inv. A | Explanation | Inv. B | Explanation |
|---|---|---|---|---|
| (12) Initial basis assignment | $ 5,000 | From (4) above. | $10,000 | From (5) above. |
| (13) Basis assigned in Step 2 | 7,000 | From (7) above. | 3,000 | From (8) above. |
| (14) Basis assigned in Step 3 | 9,120 | From (10) above. | 9,880 | From (11) above. |
| Greg's bases in investments | $21,120 | (12) + (13) + (14). | $22,880 | (12) + (13) + (14). |

## Partner's Outside Basis Is Less Than Inside Basis of Distributed Assets

*Scenario 3: Distributions of money only.*   A partner recognizes a gain (generally capital) if the partnership distributes money (only) that exceeds the partner's outside basis. The gain equals the excess amount received over the outside basis. Example 21-11 illustrates the tax consequences for this scenario in the context of an operating distribution.

*Scenario 4: Distributions of money, inventory, and/or unrealized receivables.*   In liquidating distributions where the partner's outside basis is less than the inside basis of the distributed assets and the partnership distributes money and any property other than money, the partner reduces the basis in the distributed assets other than money but does not recognize gain or loss. Because the tax law does not restrict *reducing* bases of ordinary income assets, distributions of hot assets and other property will cause reductions in basis. However, the tax law does prescribe a particular sequence for the required reductions.

If the partnership distributes only money, inventory, and unrealized receivables, the partner reduces the basis of the hot assets distributed (assuming money doesn't exceed basis). The required decrease in the basis of the distributed assets is equal to the difference between the partner's outside basis and the partnership's inside basis in the distributed assets. The partner first assigns her outside basis to the assets received in an amount equal to the assets' inside bases (allocating to money first). Then the partner allocates the required *decrease* to the assets with unrealized depreciation, to eliminate any existing losses built into the distributed assets.[41] Finally, the partner allocates any remaining required decrease to the distributed assets in proportion to their *adjusted bases* (AB), after considering the previous steps using the following equation:

$$\text{Basis allocation} = \text{Required decrease} \times \frac{\text{AB}_{asset}}{\text{Sum of AB}_{distributed\ assets}}$$

---

[41]If the required decrease is insufficient to allocate the full amount of depreciation to the distributed assets in this step, then the partner will allocate the remaining required decrease in this step to the depreciated assets based on their relative unrealized depreciation.

## Example 21-19

*What if:* Suppose CCS makes the following distribution to Greg in liquidation of his CCS interest:

| Asset | CCS Tax Basis | Fair Market Value |
|---|---|---|
| Cash | $256,000 | $256,000 |
| Inventory A | 50,000 | $129,000 |
| Inventory B | 25,000 | $ 17,000 |
| Total | $331,000 | |

Greg's basis in his CCS interest as of the liquidation is $334,000, including his $66,000 share of CCS's liabilities. What is Greg's recognized gain or loss on the distribution? What is Greg's basis in the distributed assets following the liquidation?

**Answer:** Greg does not recognize any gain or loss. His basis in the cash is $256,000 and his basis in inventory A is $8,955 and in inventory B is $3,045, computed as follows:

First, Greg reduces his outside basis in CCS by his $66,000 debt relief, such that his outside basis allocable to distributed assets is $268,000 ($334,000 − $66,000). He must allocate this remaining basis to the distributed assets using the following steps:

| Description | Amount | Explanation |
|---|---|---|
| **Step 1:** | | |
| (1) Allocable basis | $268,000 | Basis in CCS of $334,000 − debt relief of $66,000. |
| (2) Basis assigned to cash | $256,000 | |
| (3) Initial basis assigned to inventory A | $ 50,000 | |
| (4) Initial basis assigned to inventory B | $ 25,000 | |
| (5) Required decrease | $ 63,000 | (2) + (3) + (4) − (1). Initial assignment of basis exceeds Greg's allocable CCS basis. |
| **Step 2:** | | |
| (6) Required decrease to inventory B | $ 8,000 | Unrealized depreciation on inventory B from example. FMV of $17,000 less basis of $25,000. |
| (7) Remaining required decrease | $ 55,000 | (5) − (6). |
| (8) Interim adjusted basis of inventory B | $ 17,000 | (4) − (6). |
| **Step 3:** | | |
| (9) Required decrease to inventory A | $ 41,045 | Basis reduction = $55,000 × ($50,000/$67,000). |
| (10) Required decrease to inventory B | $ 13,955 | Basis reduction = $55,000 × ($17,000/$67,000). |
| Final basis of inventory A | $ 8,955 | (3) − (9). |
| Final basis of inventory B | $ 3,045 | (8) − (10). |

In Step 3, Greg decreases the basis of the inventory in proportion to its relative adjusted bases determined in Step 2 using the following allocation:

$$\text{Basis allocation} = \text{Required decrease} \times \frac{AB_{asset}}{\text{Sum of } AB_{distributed\ assets}}$$

**Example 21-20**

**What if:** Suppose CCS makes the following distribution to Greg in liquidation of his CCS interest:

| Asset | CCS Tax Basis | Fair Market Value |
|-------|--------------|-------------------|
| Cash | $242,000 | $242,000 |
| Accounts receivable | 0 | $ 12,000 |
| Inventory | 74,000 | $120,000 |
| Total | $316,000 | |

Greg's basis in his CCS interest as of the liquidation is $334,000, including his share ($66,000) of CCS's liabilities. What is Greg's recognized gain or loss on the distribution? What is Greg's basis in the assets he receives in the liquidating distribution?

**Answer:** Greg does not recognize any gain or loss on the liquidation. His asset bases are:

| | |
|---|---|
| Cash | $242,000 |
| Accounts receivable | 0 |
| Inventory | 26,000 |
| Total | $268,000 |

Greg computes the basis as follows:

As a preliminary step to the allocation, he reduces his outside basis in CCS by his $66,000 debt relief, leaving an allocable outside basis of $268,000 ($334,000 − $66,000). He allocates this basis to the distributed assets using the following steps:

| Description | Amount | Explanation |
|-------------|--------|-------------|
| **Step 1:** | | |
| (1) Allocable basis | $268,000 | Basis in CCS of $334,000 − debt relief of $66,000. |
| (2) Basis assigned to cash | $242,000 | |
| (3) Initial basis assigned to accounts receivable | $ 0 | |
| (4) Initial basis assigned to inventory | $ 74,000 | |
| (5) Required decrease | $ 48,000 | (2) + (3) + (4) − (1). Initial assignment of basis exceeds Greg's allocable CCS basis. |
| **Step 2:** N/A because no assets have unrealized depreciation. | | |
| **Step 3:** | | |
| (6) Required decrease to accounts receivable | $ 0 | Basis reduction = $48,000 × ($-0-/$74,000). |
| (7) Required decrease to inventory | $ 48,000 | Basis reduction = $48,000 × ($74,000/$74,000). |
| Final basis of accounts receivable | $ 0 | (3) − (6). |
| Final basis of inventory | $ 26,000 | (4) − (7). |

In Step 3, Greg decreases the basis of the accounts receivable and inventory in proportion to their relative adjusted bases using the following allocation:

$$\text{Basis reduction} = \text{Required decrease} \times \frac{AB_{asset}}{\text{Sum of } AB_{distributed\ assets}}$$

Note that in this scenario, the tax rules re-characterize a portion ($48,000) of Greg's ultimate gain from capital gain to ordinary income. The sum of the bases of the distributed assets ($316,000) exceeds Greg's allocable outside basis ($268,000) by $48,000. Absent the allocation rules illustrated in Example 21-20, this would have been a capital gain to Greg. Instead, as we discuss below, the basis decrease to the hot assets will cause Greg to recognize any gain as ordinary upon sale of these assets.

***Scenario 5: Other property included in distributions.***   In our final scenario, the partnership distributes other property in addition to or instead of money and/or inventory and unrealized receivables, and the partner's outside basis is less than the combined inside bases of the distributed property. The terminating partner does not recognize gain or loss; rather, he decreases the basis in the other property distributed. The process for assigning basis to the distributed assets is similar to the method we described above, although the required basis decrease is focused on the other property rather than the hot assets.[42] The procedure is as follows:

**Step 1:** The partner first assigns a basis to any money, inventory, and unrealized receivables equal to the partnership's basis in these assets. The partner also assigns a basis to any other property equal to the partnership's basis in the other property distributed.

**Step 2:** The partner then allocates the required decrease (outside basis less partnership adjusted basis in distributed assets) to the other property that has unrealized depreciation to the extent of that depreciation to eliminate inherent losses. Thus, if an asset has an adjusted basis to the partnership of $700 and a fair market value of $600, the asset's basis is first reduced by $100 (unrealized depreciation).

**Step 3:** If any required decrease remains after accounting for the inherent losses in the distributed assets, the partner then allocates it to all other property in proportion to their *adjusted bases*. The adjusted bases used in this step are the bases from Step 2. We can determine the allocation as follows:

$$\text{Basis reduction} = \text{Required decrease} \times \frac{AB_{asset}}{\text{Sum of } AB_{\text{all distributed other property}}}$$

| Example 21-21 |
|---|

**What if:** Suppose CCS makes the following distribution to Greg in liquidation of his CCS interest:

| Asset | CCS Tax Basis | Fair Market Value |
|---|---|---|
| Cash | $187,000 | $187,000 |
| Investment A | 10,000 | $ 7,000 |
| Investment B | 10,000 | $ 18,000 |
| Inventory | 70,000 | $102,000 |
| Total | $277,000 | |

Greg's basis in his CCS interest as of the liquidation is $334,000, including his $66,000 share of CCS's liabilities of $66,000. What is Greg's recognized gain or loss on the distribution? What is Greg's basis in the distributed assets following the liquidation?

(*continued on page 21-21...*)

[42]§732(c)(3).

**Answer:** Greg does not recognize any gain or loss. His asset bases are as follows:

| | |
|---|---:|
| Cash | $187,000 |
| Investment A | 4,530 |
| Investment B | 6,470 |
| Inventory | 70,000 |
| Total | $268,000 |

Greg's basis in these assets is determined as follows:

Greg first determines his allocable basis of $268,000 by reducing his CCS basis ($334,000) for the deemed cash distribution relating to his $66,000 share of the reduction in CCS's debt.

| Description | Amount | Explanation |
|---|---:|---|
| **Step 1:** | | |
| (1) Allocable basis | $268,000 | Basis in CCS of $334,000 − debt relief of $66,000. |
| (2) Basis assigned to cash | $187,000 | |
| (3) Initial basis assigned to investment A | $ 10,000 | |
| (4) Initial basis assigned to investment B | $ 10,000 | |
| (5) Initial basis assigned to inventory | $ 70,000 | |
| (6) Required decrease | $ 9,000 | (2) + (3) + (4) + (5) − (1). Initial assignment of basis exceeds Greg's allocable CCS basis. |
| **Step 2:** | | |
| (7) Required decrease to investment A | $ 3,000 | Unrealized depreciation on investment A from example. FMV of $7,000 less basis of $10,000. |
| (8) Remaining required decrease | $ 6,000 | (6) − (7). |
| (9) Interim basis of investment A | $ 7,000 | (3) − (7). |
| **Step 3:** | | |
| (10) Required decrease to investment A | $ 2,470 | Basis reduction = $6,000 × ($7,000/$17,000). |
| (11) Required decrease to investment B | $ 3,530 | Basis reduction = $6,000 × ($10,000/$17,000). |
| Final basis of investment A | $ 4,530 | (9) − (10). |
| Final basis of investment B | $ 6,470 | (4) − (11). |

In Step 3, Greg decreases the basis of the other property (investments A and B) in proportion to their relative adjusted bases using the following allocation:

$$\text{Basis reduction} = \text{Required decrease} \times \frac{AB_{asset}}{\text{Sum of } AB_{\text{all distributed other property}}}$$

**Character and Holding Period of Distributed Assets**   For both operating and liquidating distributions, the character of the distributed assets usually stays the same for the partner as it was in the partnership, in order to prevent conversion of ordinary income to capital gain for both operating and liquidating distributions. The principal purpose of these rules is to prevent the partner from converting partnership ordinary income into capital gain simply by distributing assets. Thus, if a

partner sells certain assets with ordinary character after the distribution, the partner will recognize ordinary income from the sale.[43] These assets include inventory [§751(d)] and unrealized receivables [§751(c)]. For inventory items, the ordinary income "taint" will remain for five years after the distribution. For unrealized receivables, a subsequent sale at any time after the distribution will result in ordinary income. The reverse is not true, however. If a partnership distributes a capital asset that will be inventory to a terminating partner, the partner will have ordinary income from an eventual sale, not capital gain or loss. To ensure the character of any distributed long-term capital gain property retains its character to the partner, the partner's holding period generally includes the partnership's holding period.[44]

---

### Example 21-22

Greg has decided to cash out his investment in CCS in order to invest in another project in which he can more actively participate. After speaking to Nicole and Sarah about the options, the three owners decide Greg can cash out using one of two options.

*Option 1:* CCS will liquidate Greg's interest by distributing cash of $242,000; accounts receivable worth $12,000 (adjusted basis is $0); and inventory worth $120,000 (adjusted basis is $74,000).

*Option 2:* Nicole and Sarah will purchase Greg's interest in CCS. Nicole agrees to purchase two-thirds of Greg's interest for $249,333 cash and Sarah purchases the remaining one-third for $124,667 cash.

Greg's basis in his 30 percent CCS interest is $334,000, including his share of CCS's liabilities of $66,000. Either event would occur on January 1, 2012, when CCS's balance sheet is as follows:

**Color Comfort Sheets, LLC**
**January 1, 2012**

|  | Tax Basis | FMV |
|---|---|---|
| **Assets:** | | |
| Cash | $390,000 | $ 390,000 |
| Accounts receivable | 0 | 40,000 |
| Inventory | 90,000 | 200,000 |
| Investments | 60,000 | 105,000 |
| Equipment (cost = $200,000) | 150,000 | 200,000 |
| Building (cost = $100,000) | 90,000 | 100,000 |
| Land—original | 20,000 | 160,000 |
| Land—investment | 140,000 | 270,000 |
| Totals | $940,000 | $1,465,000 |
| | | |
| **Liabilities and capital:** | | |
| Accounts payable | $ 80,000 | |
| Long-term debt | 0 | |
| Mortgage on original land | 40,000 | |
| Mortgage on investment land | 120,000 | |
| Capital—Nicole | 119,000 | |
|     —Sarah | 332,000 | |
|     —Greg | 249,000 | |
| Totals | $940,000 | |

*(continued on page 21-23...)*

---

[43]§735(a).
[44]§735(b).

What are the tax consequences (amount and character of recognized gain or loss, basis in assets) for Greg under each option?

**Answer:** *Option 1:* Greg recognizes no gain or loss on the liquidation. His bases in the distributed assets are:

| | |
|---|---:|
| Cash | $242,000 |
| Accounts receivable | 0 |
| Inventory | 26,000 |
| Total | $268,000 |

*Option 2:* Greg recognizes ordinary income of $60,000 and a capital gain of $46,000.

We determine these tax consequences as follows:

*Option 1:* The distribution allows Greg to defer recognizing any gain or loss on the liquidation. Example 21-20 provides the details of the analysis. Greg has debt relief in an amount equal to his share of CCS's liabilities ($66,000). The debt relief is treated as a distribution of cash, so Greg reduces his outside basis by this amount from $334,000 to $268,000. The difference between the sum of the adjusted bases of the distributed property and his outside basis is $48,000 ($316,000 − $268,000) and represents a required *decrease* to the bases of assets distributed in liquidation. Greg follows the prescribed method illustrated in Example 21-20 to determine his asset bases.

The basis reduction for these assets allows Greg to defer recognizing a $48,000 gain on the liquidation. The cost to accomplish the deferral is that if Greg sells the inventory and the accounts receivable immediately after the distribution, he will recognize ordinary income of $106,000 as follows:

| | | |
|---|---:|---:|
| Amount realized: | | |
| Cash (equal to FMV of accounts receivable | $ 12,000 | |
| and inventory) | 120,000 | $132,000 |
| Less: Adjusted basis | | |
| Accounts receivable | 0 | |
| Inventory | 26,000 | 26,000 |
| Ordinary Income | | $106,000 |

The $106,000 ordinary income is $48,000 greater than the inherent gain on these assets of $58,000 ($132,000 − $74,000) had the partnership sold the assets. If Greg selects Option 1, he will not recognize income on the liquidation until he sells the inventory and collects (or sells) the accounts receivable, thereby leaving himself flexibility on the timing of gain recognition.

*Option 2:* In this option, Greg sells his CCS interest to Nicole and Sarah and receives cash of $374,000. Greg determines his total gain or loss as follows:

| | | |
|---|---:|---:|
| Amount realized: | | |
| Cash | $374,000 | |
| Debt relief | 66,000 | $440,000 |
| Less: Basis in CCS interest | | 334,000 |
| Realized and recognized gain | | $106,000 |

Next, Greg determines the character of the gain from the sale by first identifying the gain related to hot assets.

| Hot Asset — CCS | (1)<br>Basis | (2)<br>FMV | (3)<br>Gain/Loss<br>(2) − (1) | Greg's Share<br>30% × (3) |
|---|---:|---:|---:|---:|
| Accounts receivable | $ 0 | $ 40,000 | $ 40,000 | $12,000 |
| Inventory | 90,000 | 200,000 | 110,000 | 33,000 |
| Equipment | 150,000 | 200,000 | 50,000 | 15,000 |
| Total ordinary income | | | | $60,000 |

*(continued on page 21-24...)*

The final step for Greg is to determine the capital gain or loss by subtracting the ordinary portion from the total gain.

| | |
|---|---:|
| Total gain | $106,000 |
| Less: ordinary income from §751(a) | (60,000) |
| Capital gain | $ 46,000 |

If he chooses Option 2, Greg will recognize $60,000 of ordinary income and $46,000 of capital gain in 2012.

---

**Example 21-23**

Given the tax consequences to Greg in the previous example, should he have CCS liquidate his interest (Option 1) or sell his interest (Option 2)?

**Answer:** Under Option 1 (the liquidation), Greg is able to defer all recognition of gain until he later sells the distributed assets. This provides him flexibility in when he pays tax on the liquidation. However, when he recognizes any income upon subsequent sales, the character of the income will be ordinary and taxed at ordinary rates. Under Option 2, Greg must recognize income immediately upon the sale: $60,000 of ordinary income and $46,000 of capital gain. He has no future tax liability related to the transaction. The capital gain will be taxed at a maximum of 15 percent (the regular maximum tax rate for long-term capital gains). An additional consideration is that under Option 2 Greg receives cash, rather than a mixture of cash and other assets. If he wants to immediately invest the proceeds in another venture, he may prefer a pure cash payment.

---

*continued from page 21-2...*

Greg takes the liquidation option (Option 1) offered by CCS to avoid recognizing a gain currently. Although this option doesn't give him as much cash as a sale would have, Greg figures it is enough for another investment and he can avoid paying tax this year.

For the first time, CCS has only two owners—Nicole and Sarah. After liquidating Greg's interest, Nicole's interest has increased to 43 percent and Sarah's to 57 percent. Both women are happy with that outcome, though sorry to lose Greg's interest in the business. ∎

## L05    DISPROPORTIONATE DISTRIBUTIONS

Up to this point in the chapter, all our distribution examples have represented the partner's pro rata share of the partnership's ordinary assets and other property, as specified in the partnership agreement based on the partner's capital interests. In practice, distributions may not always reflect each partner's proportionate share.[45] Both operating and liquidating distributions can be **disproportionate distributions.** Without going into all the details of these complex rules, let's briefly discuss the implications of distributions in which partners receive either more or less of their share

---

[45]A thorough discussion of these issues is beyond the scope of this chapter. Therefore, we will abbreviate our discussion just to give a flavor for the issues and consequences of these disproportionate distributions.

of the so-called hot assets (assets defined in IRC §751(b) as **substantially appreciated inventory** and unrealized receivables).[46] Note that the definition of hot assets for purposes of disproportionate distributions includes only *substantially appreciated* inventory, not all inventory as is the case under §751(a), the definition we used to characterize the gain in dispositions of partnership interests. Inventory is considered substantially appreciated if its fair market value is more than 120 percent of its basis.

Suppose a partner receives less than her share of hot assets in a liquidating distribution. This may occur, for example, if a partner receives only cash in a liquidating distribution from a partnership with hot assets. Rather than applying the rules we discussed above, the disproportionate distribution rules require the partner to treat the distribution as a sale or exchange.[47] Basically, the rules treat the partner as having sold her share of hot assets to the partnership in exchange for "cold" [non-§751(b)] assets. This deemed sale generates an ordinary gain or loss to the partner on the deemed sale, essentially equal to her share of the appreciation or depreciation in the portion of hot assets not distributed to her. On the other hand, the partnership is deemed to have purchased the hot assets from the partner in exchange for cold assets. Therefore, the *partnership* recognizes a capital gain or loss equal to the remaining partners' inherent gain or loss in the distributed cold assets. The effects are reversed if a partner receives more than her share of the partnership's hot assets.[48] The rules guarantee that partners cannot convert ordinary income into capital gain through distributions. Thus, they require that partners will ultimately recognize their share of the partnership ordinary income regardless of the form of their distributions.

---

**THE KEY FACTS**

**Disproportionate Distributions**

■ **When?**
When distribution changes a partner's relative ownership of partnership hot assets.

■ **Why?**
To prevent partners from converting ordinary income into capital gains through distributions.

■ **How?**
Partner must treat distribution as a sale or exchange, which results in recognition of gain (or loss).

---

**Example 21-24**

*What if:* Suppose CCS distributes $374,000 in cash to Greg Randall on January 1, 2012, in complete liquidation of Greg's 30 percent interest in CCS. Greg's basis in his CCS interest before the distribution is $334,000. Assume CCS's balance sheet is as follows:

**Color Comfort Sheets, LLC**
**December 31, 2011**

|  | Tax Basis | FMV |
|---|---|---|
| **Assets:** | | |
| Cash | $700,000 | $ 700,000 |
| Inventory | 240,000 | 440,000 |
| Totals | $940,000 | $1,140,000 |
| | | |
| **Liabilities and capital:** | | |
| Liabilities | $240,000 | |
| Capital—Nicole | 119,000 | |
| —Sarah | 332,000 | |
| —Greg | 249,000 | |
| Totals | $940,000 | |

(continued on page 21-26...)

---

[46]Unrealized receivables includes the accounts receivable of a cash-method taxpayer, the excess of the fair market value over basis of accounts receivable for accrual-method taxpayers, and recapture of depreciation under §1245. The definition of substantially appreciated inventory is broader than simply goods primarily held for sale to customers. It also includes property that would not be classified as capital assets or §1231 assets if sold by the partnership. As a result, receivables are included as "inventory."

[47]§751(b).

[48]The partner would generally recognize capital gain on the deemed sale and the partnership would recognize ordinary income.

Is this distribution disproportionate? What are the implications of the distribution?

**Answer:** From CCS's balance sheet as of December 31, 2011, the fair market value of Greg's share of hot assets for purposes of disproportionate distributions [§751(b)] is $132,000 ($72,000 adjusted basis). This figure includes 30 percent of the fair market value of CCS's inventory of $440,000. Since Greg receives only cash in the distribution, he has not received a proportionate share of CCS's hot assets. Thus, the distribution will be a disproportionate one.

The tax law treats Greg as having sold his share of the hot assets for cold assets, and he will recognize ordinary income equal to his share of the appreciation on the hot assets not distributed, $60,000 ($132,000 − $72,000). CCS does not recognize any gain or loss because it has no appreciation in the assets (cash) used to "purchase" the hot assets.

**LO6**

## SPECIAL BASIS ADJUSTMENTS

Recall that when a partner sells her partnership interest, the partnership's inside basis is generally unaffected by the sale. This creates a discrepancy between the new investor's outside basis (cost) and her share of the partnership's inside basis, which artificially changes the potential income or loss at the partnership level. For example, earlier in the chapter Greg Randall purchased Chanzz's 30 percent interest in CCS for $82,800 (Example 21-5). Greg's outside basis after the acquisition is $106,800, reflecting the cash payment of $82,800 and his share of CCS's debt at the time of the acquisition, $24,000. However, Greg's share of CCS's inside basis in its assets is $105,000 (see Example 21-7). This is the outcome because the sale does not affect CCS's inside basis and Greg simply steps into Chanzz's shoes for determining his share of the inside basis. The discrepancy reflects Chanzz's unrecognized share of appreciation of CCS's assets (that Greg paid full value for) as of the sale date and causes Greg to be temporarily overtaxed when CCS sells these appreciated assets.

**Example 21-25**

**What if:** Suppose that immediately after Greg acquires his 30 percent interest in CCS for $82,800, CCS sells its accounts receivable for their fair market value of $13,000 (adjusted basis is $0). (See Example 21-2 for CCS's balance sheet as of July 1, 2010, the acquisition date.) What is the amount and character of gain Greg recognizes on the sale?

**Answer:** When CCS sells the accounts receivable, it recognizes $13,000 of ordinary income, of which $3,900 (30 percent) is allocated to Greg. However, when Chanzz sold its interest to Greg, Chanzz was already taxed on the $3,900 allocated portion of that ordinary income under §751(a), and Greg paid full value for his interest in the receivables when he acquired his 30 percent interest in CCS. This means Greg will be taxed on the $3,900 again in 2010, and his outside basis increases by $3,900. Because Greg paid fair market value for his share of the receivables, he should not have any income when they are sold at fair market value. Eventually, when Greg disposes of his CCS interest, his ultimate gain (or loss) on the disposition will be $3,900 less, because of the increase to his outside basis from this additional income; meanwhile, he is overtaxed on the receivables. Greg must report ordinary income today for an offsetting capital loss (or reduced capital gain) in the future when he disposes of his interest.

The tax rules allow the partnership to make an election for a **special basis adjustment** to eliminate discrepancies between the inside and outside bases and correct the artificial income or loss at the partnership level.[49] For the most part, basis discrepancies arise in two situations: following *sales* of partnership interests, and following *distributions* where a partner receives more (and in cases of a liquidating distribution, less) than her

---

[49]§754.

share of the inside basis in the partnership property and the partner recognizes a gain or loss on the distribution. Once a partnership makes a §754 election, the partnership is required to make the special basis adjustment for all subsequent sales of partnership interest and partnership distributions. The election can be revoked only with permission from the IRS.

Even without a §754 election in effect, the partnership must adjust its bases if the partnership has a **substantial built-in loss** at the time a partner sells her partnership interest. A substantial built-in loss exists if the partnership's aggregate adjusted basis in its property exceeds the property's fair market value by more than $250,000 when a transfer of an interest occurs.[50] An analogous event—a **substantial basis reduction**— may occur for distributions, which also triggers a mandatory basis adjustment.

Although the election is made under §754, the actual authorization of the special basis adjustment is governed by two separate code sections depending on which situation gives rise to the adjustment: (1) sale of partnership interest [§743(b)], or (2) distributions [§734(b)]. These two sections determine how much of an adjustment will be made, and §755 then stipulates how the adjustment is allocated among the partnership assets.

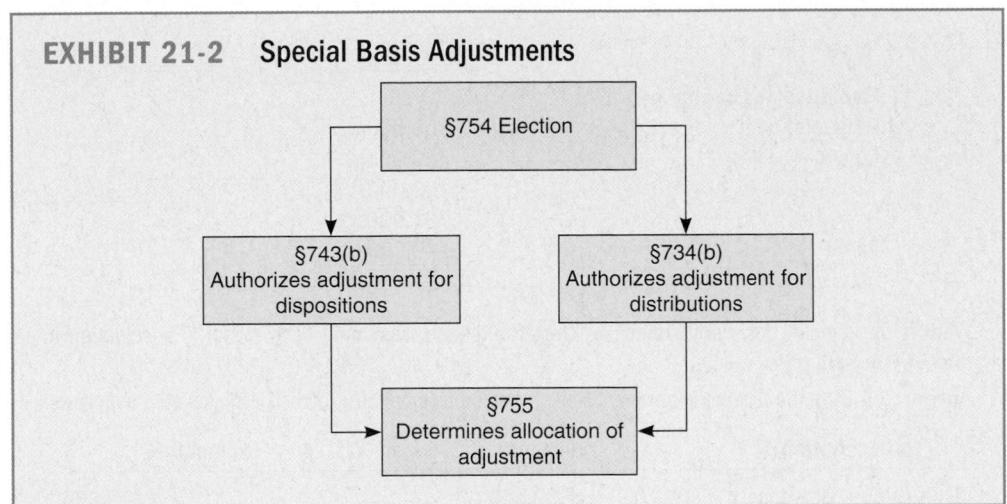

**EXHIBIT 21-2    Special Basis Adjustments**

## Special Basis Adjustments for Dispositions

The special basis adjustment the partnership makes when a partner sells her partnership interest is designed to give the new investor a share in the partnership assets equal to his outside basis. The basis adjustment in these cases applies *only* to the new investor. The inside bases of the continuing partners remain unchanged, so their income and losses will continue to be accurately allocated. The adjustment is equal to the difference between the new investor's outside basis and his share of inside basis.[51] The new investor's outside basis is generally equal to the cost of his partnership interest plus his share of partnership liabilities.[52] The special basis adjustment must

---

[50]§743(d)(1). In this context, a transfer generally refers to sales, exchanges, or transfers at death, not gift transfers.

[51]§743(b).

[52]A partner's share of inside basis is also labeled *previously taxed capital* [§1.743-1(d)]. The technical calculation is determined as follows (but generally equals the partner's tax capital account):

(1) the amount of cash the partner would receive on liquidation after an hypothetical sale of all the partnership assets for their fair market value after the sale of the partnership interest, plus

(2) the amount of taxable loss allocated to the partner from the hypothetical sale, less

(3) the amount of taxable gain allocated to the partner from the hypothetical sale.

then be allocated to the assets under allocation rules in §755, which are beyond the scope of this text.

**Example 21-26**

On July 1, 2010, Greg acquired Chanzz's 30 percent interest in CCS for $82,800. CCS's balance sheet as of the sale date is as follows:

**Color Comfort Sheets, LLC**
**July 1, 2010**

|  | Tax Basis | FMV |
|---|---|---|
| **Assets:** | | |
| Cash | $ 27,000 | $ 27,000 |
| Accounts receivable | 0 | 13,000 |
| Investments | 15,000 | 12,000 |
| Inventory | 1,000 | 1,000 |
| Equipment (cost = $100,000) | 80,000 | 86,000 |
| Building | 97,000 | 97,000 |
| Land | 20,000 | 150,000 |
| Totals | $240,000 | $386,000 |
| **Liabilities and capital:** | | |
| Long term debt | $100,000 | |
| Capital—Nicole | (49,000) | |
| —Sarah | 108,000 | |
| —Chanzz | 81,000 | |
| Totals | $240,000 | |

What is the special basis adjustment for Greg's purchase, assuming CCS had a §754 election in effect at the sale date?

**Answer:** $1,800, the difference between Greg's outside basis and inside basis, is calculated as follows:

| Description | Amount | Explanation |
|---|---|---|
| (1) Cash purchase price | $ 82,800 | |
| (2) Greg's share of CCS debt | 24,000 | $80,000 × 30%. |
| (3) Initial basis in CCS | $106,800 | (1) + (2). |
| (4) Greg's inside basis | 105,000 | Chanzz's tax capital ($81,000) plus share of CCS debt ($24,000) (See Example 21-7). |
| Special basis adjustment | $ 1,800 | (3) − (4). |

When a new investor's special basis adjustment is allocated to depreciable or amortizable assets, the new investor will benefit from additional depreciation or amortization. In some cases, the amounts can be quite substantial, and a new investor may be willing to pay more for a partnership interest when the partnership has a §754 election in place than for one without it.

## Special Basis Adjustments for Distributions

A similar potential problem exists when the partnership distributes assets to the partners that represent more (or in some cases, less) than their share of the inside basis in the partnership assets. This usually occurs when a partner recognizes a gain or loss on a distribution or when a partner's basis in the distributed property

is different from the partnership's basis in the property. In contrast to the special basis adjustment for sales of partnership interests, the special basis adjustment for distributions affects the common basis of *partnership* property and not merely one partner's basis.

The special basis adjustment can either increase or decrease the basis in the partnership assets. A **positive basis adjustment** will *increase* the basis in the partnership assets (1) when a partner receiving distributed property recognizes a gain on the distribution (for instance, in operating distributions where the partner receives money in excess of her outside basis), and (2) when a partner receiving distributed property takes a basis in the property less than the partnership's basis in the property. The positive adjustment will equal the sum of the gain recognized by the partners receiving distributed property and the amount of the basis reduction.

In Example 21-11, CCS distributed $250,000 cash to Nicole on December 31, 2011, as part of an operating distribution. Because Nicole's outside basis before the distribution was $205,000 and she received only money in the distribution, Nicole was required to recognize a $45,000 gain on the distribution. If CCS had a §754 election in effect, it would have a positive special basis adjustment from the distribution of $45,000.

A **negative basis adjustment** will *decrease* the basis in partnership assets (1) when a partner receiving distributed property in a liquidating distribution recognizes a loss on the distribution, and (2) when a partner receiving distributed property takes a basis in the property greater than the partnership's basis in the property.

The negative adjustment will equal the sum of the recognized loss and the amount of the basis increase made by the partners receiving the distribution. Recall from our previous discussion of distributions that negative adjustments can occur only in liquidating distributions. Only then does a partner recognize a loss or increase the distributed property basis from that of the partnership's basis.

In Example 21-15, CCS liquidated Greg's 30 percent interest by distributing cash of $206,000 and inventory with a fair market value of $96,000 (adjusted basis is $43,000). Because Greg's outside basis after considering his debt relief ($268,000) was greater than the sum of the bases of the property distributed ($249,000), Greg recognized a loss of $19,000 on the liquidation. If CCS had a §754 election in effect at the time of this liquidation, CCS would have a negative basis adjustment of $19,000.

As in the case of partnership dispositions, the allocation of the special basis adjustment among the partnership's assets for distributions is intended to offset any inequitable gain or loss the partners would have realized absent the adjustment. The process of allocating the adjustment for distributions is prescribed in §755, and these procedures are beyond the scope of this text.

## CONCLUSION

The tax rules for partnership dispositions and distributions are among the most complex in the Internal Revenue Code. This chapter provided an overview of these rules and in some cases plunged into the complexity. We discussed the calculation of gains and losses from the sale of a partnership interest, as well as the basis implications of the purchase to a new investor. In doing so, we discussed how *hot assets* might affect the gain or loss. The chapter also explained the basic rules for determining the tax treatment of partnership distributions.

We illustrated how partnership elections might affect the partnership's basis in assets following partnership interest dispositions or distributions. In general, the tax rules are designed to avoid having business owners make decisions based on tax rules rather than on business principles; however, making this goal a reality provides for some challenging applications.

## SUMMARY

**LO1**    Determine the tax consequences to the buyer and seller of the disposition of a partnership interest, including the amount and character of gain or loss recognized.

- Sellers are primarily concerned about their realized and recognized gain or loss on the sale of their partnership interest.
- Sellers' debt relief is included in the amount realized from the sale.
- Buyers' main tax concerns are determining their basis in the partnership interest they acquire and their inside bases of the partnership assets.
- A buyer's outside basis after an acquisition is generally his cost plus his share of partnership liabilities. A buyer's inside basis is generally the same as the seller's inside basis at the sale date.
- The sale of a partnership interest does not generally affect a partnership's inside basis.
- A partnership's tax year closes for the selling partner upon the sale of a partnership interest.
- Hot assets include unrealized receivables and inventory items.
- Unrealized receivables include the rights to receive payment for goods delivered or to be delivered, or services rendered or to be rendered, as well as items that would generate ordinary income if the partnership sold the asset for its fair market value, such as depreciation recapture.
- There are actually two definitions of inventory items. The first under §751(a) applies to sales of partnership interests and includes all classic inventory items and assets that are *not* capital or §1231 assets. The second definition of inventory [§751(b)] applies primarily to distributions and includes only substantially appreciated inventory.
- Sellers classify gains and losses from the sale of partnership interests as ordinary to the extent the gain relates to hot assets.
- Hot assets are also important to determine whether a distribution is proportionate or disproportionate.

**LO2**    List the reasons for distributions, and compare operating and liquidating distributions.

- Distributions from a flow-through entity are one mechanism to return business profits or capital to the owners of the entity.
- Distributions may also be used to liquidate an owner's interest in the business or to completely terminate the business.
- Operating distributions include distributions in which the owner retains an interest in the business.
- The purpose of liquidating distributions is to terminate an owner's interest in the business.

**LO3**    Determine the tax consequences of proportionate operating distributions.

- Partnerships do not generally recognize gain or loss on the distribution of property.
- Most operating distributions do not result in gain or loss to the partner receiving the distribution. Gains and losses are deferred through basis adjustments to the distributed assets and basis of the partnership interest.
- A partner recognizes a gain from an operating distribution if she receives a distribution of money that exceeds the basis in her partnership interest.
- Partners never recognize losses from operating distributions.

**LO4**    Determine the tax consequences of proportionate liquidating distributions.

- The tax issues in liquidating distributions are primarily twofold: (1) determining whether the liquidating partner recognizes a gain or loss, and (2) allocating the liquidating partner's basis in her partnership interest to the distributed assets.
- A partner recognizes a gain only when the partnership distributes more money than her basis in the partnership interest.
- A partner recognizes a loss only when the partnership distributes cash and hot assets and the partner's basis in the partnership interest is greater than the sum of the bases of the distributed assets.

- In all other cases, a partner does not recognize gains or losses from a liquidating distribution; rather, she will simply reallocate her basis in the partnership interest to the distributed assets.

- The key to the allocation process is to focus on two factors: (1) the type of property distributed, and (2) whether the total basis in distributed assets is larger or smaller than the partner's basis in the partnership interest.

- The character of the distributed assets usually stays the same to the partner as in the partnership.

Explain the significance of disproportionate distributions.

**L05**

- Disproportionate distributions occur when the assets distributed in either operating or liquidating distributions do not represent the partner's proportionate share of the partnership's hot and cold assets.

- A disproportionate distribution causes a shift in the proportion of ordinary income and capital gain income from the partnership. Therefore, the rules require the partner to treat a disproportionate distribution as a sale or exchange.

- If a partner receives more cold assets than her proportionate share in a distribution, she will generally recognize ordinary income in an amount equal to the appreciation of hot assets not distributed to her. If a partner receives more hot assets than her proportionate share, she will recognize capital gain equal to the appreciation of cold assets not distributed to her.

- The disproportionate distribution rules ensure that partners cannot convert ordinary income into capital gain through distributions.

Explain the rationale for special basis adjustments, determine when they are necessary, and calculate the special basis adjustment for dispositions and distributions.

**L06**

- Discrepancies between a partner's inside and outside basis may cause a partner to be overtaxed or undertaxed, at least temporarily. Special basis adjustment rules allow the partnership to eliminate discrepancies between inside and outside bases to correct the artificial income or loss at the partnership level.

- Basis discrepancies may occur following the acquisition of a partnership interest and following distributions where a partner receives more or less than her share of the inside basis in the partnership property.

- When a new investor purchases a partnership interest, she may make a special basis adjustment equal to the difference between her outside basis and her share of inside basis if the partnership has a §754 election in effect.

- A special basis adjustment is mandatory even without a §754 election in effect when a partner sells a partnership interest and the partnership has a substantial built-in loss at the time of the sale.

- When a partner recognizes a gain from a distribution or takes a basis in distributed property less than the partnership's basis in the property, the partnership will have a positive special basis adjustment to increase the partnership asset bases.

- When a partner recognizes a loss from a liquidating distribution or takes a basis in distributed property greater than the partnership's basis in the property, the partnership will have a negative special basis adjustment to decrease the partnership asset bases.

# KEY TERMS

carryover basis (21-11)

disproportionate distributions (21-24)

hot assets (21-3)

inside basis (21-7)

inventory items (21-3)

liquidating distributions (21-9)

negative basis adjustment (21-29)

operating distributions (21-9)

outside basis (21-3)

partnership interest (21-2)

positive basis adjustment (21-29)

special basis adjustment (21-26)

substantial basis reduction (21-27)

substantial built-in loss (21-27)

substantially appreciated inventory (21-25)

unrealized receivables (21-3)

## DISCUSSION QUESTIONS

1. **(LO1)** Joey is a 25 percent owner of Loopy LLC. He no longer wants to be involved in the business. What options does Joey have to exit the business?

2. **(LO1)** Compare and contrast the aggregate and entity approaches for a sale of a partnership interest.

3. **(LO1)** What restrictions might prevent a partner from selling his partnership interest to a third party?

4. **(LO1)** Explain how a partner's debt relief affects his amount realized in a sale of partnership interest.

5. **(LO1)** Under what circumstances will the gain or loss on the sale of a partnership interest be characterized as ordinary rather than capital?

6. **(LO1)** What are *hot assets* and why are they important in the sale of a partnership interest?

7. **(LO1)** For an accrual-method partnership, are accounts receivable considered unrealized receivables? Explain.

8. **(LO1)** Can a partnership have unrealized receivables if it has no accounts receivable?

9. **(LO1)** How do hot assets affect the character of gain or loss on the sale of a partnership interest?

10. **(LO1)** Under what circumstances can a partner recognize both gain and loss on the sale of a partnership interest?

11. **(LO1)** Absent any special elections, what effect does a sale of partnership interest have on the partnership?

research

12. **(LO1)** Generally, a selling partner's capital account carries over to the purchaser of the partnership interest. Under what circumstances will this not be the case?

13. **(LO2)** What distinguishes operating from liquidating distributions?

14. **(LO3)** Under what circumstances will a partner recognize a gain from an operating distribution?

15. **(LO3)** Under what circumstances will a partner recognize a loss from an operating distribution?

16. **(LO3)** In general, what effect does an operating distribution have on the partnership?

17. **(LO3)** If a partner's outside basis is less than the partnership's inside basis in distributed assets, how does the partner determine his basis of the distributed assets in an operating distribution?

18. **(LO4)** Under what conditions will a partner recognize gain in a liquidating distribution?

19. **(LO4)** Under what conditions will a partner recognize loss in a liquidating distribution?

20. **(LO4)** Describe how a partner determines his basis in distributed assets in cases in which a partnership distributes only money, inventory, and/or unrealized receivables in a liquidating distribution.

21. **(LO4)** How does a partner determine his basis in distributed assets when the partnership distributes other property in addition to money and hot assets?

planning

22. **(LO5)** SBT partnership distributes $5,000 cash and a parcel of land with a fair market value of $40,000 and a $25,000 basis to the partnership to Sam (30 percent partner). What factors must Sam and SBT consider in determining the tax treatment of this distribution?

23. **(LO5)** Discuss the underlying concern to tax policy makers in distributions in which a partner receives more or less than his share of the partnership hot assets.

24. **(LO5)** In general, how do the disproportionate distribution rules ensure that partners recognize their share of partnership ordinary income?

25. **(LO6)** Why would a new partner who pays more for a partnership interest than the selling partner's outside basis want the partnership to elect a special basis adjustment?

■ **planning**

26. **(LO6)** List two common situations that will cause a partner's inside and outside basis to differ.

27. **(LO6)** Explain why a partnership might not want to make a §754 election to allow special basis adjustments.

28. **(LO6)** When might a new partner have an upward basis adjustment following the acquisition of a partnership interest?

29. **(LO6)** Are special basis adjustments mandatory? If so, when?

## PROBLEMS

30. **(LO1)** Jerry is a 30 percent partner in the JJM Partnership when he sells his entire interest to Lucia for $56,000 cash. At the time of the sale, Jerry's basis in JJM is $32,000. JJM does not have any debt or hot assets. What is Jerry's gain or loss on the sale of his interest?

31. **(LO1)** Joy is a 30 percent partner in the JOM Partnership when she sells her entire interest to Hope for $72,000 cash. At the time of the sale, Joy's basis in JOM is $44,000 (which includes her $6,000 share of JOM liabilities). JOM does not have any hot assets. What is Joy's gain or loss on the sale of her interest?

32. **(LO1)** Allison, Keesha, and Steven each own equal interests in KAS Partnership, a calendar-year-end, cash-method entity. On January 1 of the current year, Steven's basis in his partnership interest is $27,000. During January and February, the partnership generates $30,000 of ordinary income and $4,500 of tax-exempt income. On March 1, Steven sells his partnership interest to Juan for a cash payment of $45,000. The partnership has the following assets and no liabilities at the sale date:

| | Basis | FMV |
|---|---|---|
| Cash | $30,000 | $30,000 |
| Land held for investment | 30,000 | 60,000 |
| Totals | $60,000 | $90,000 |

a. Assuming KAS's operating agreement provides for an interim closing of the books when partners' interests change during the year, what is Steven's basis in his partnership interest on March 1 just prior to the sale?

b. What is the amount and character of Steven's recognized gain or loss on the sale?

c. What is Juan's initial basis in the partnership interest?

d. What is the partnership's basis in the assets following the sale?

33. **(LO1)** Grace, James, Helen, and Charles each own equal interests in GJHC Partnership, a calendar-year-end, cash-method entity. On January 1 of the current year, James's basis in his partnership interest is $62,000. For the taxable year, the partnership generates $80,000 of ordinary income and $30,000 of dividend income. For the first five months of the year, GJHC generates $25,000 of

ordinary income. On June 1, James sells his partnership interest to Robert for a cash payment of $70,000. The partnership has the following assets and no liabilities at the sale date:

|                          | Basis     | FMV       |
|--------------------------|-----------|-----------|
| Cash                     | $ 27,000  | $ 27,000  |
| Land held for investment | 80,000    | 100,000   |
| Totals                   | $107,000  | $127,000  |

a. Assuming GJHC's operating agreement provides that the proration method will be used to allocate income or loss when partners' interests change during the year, what is James's basis in his partnership interest on March 1 just prior to the sale?

b. What is the amount and character of James's recognized gain or loss on the sale?

c. If GJHC uses an interim closing of the books, what is the amount and character of James's recognized gain or loss on the sale?

34. **(L01)** At the end of last year, Lisa, a 35 percent partner in the five-person LAMEC Partnership, has an outside basis of $60,000, including her $30,000 share of LAMEC debt. On January 1 of the current year, Lisa sells her partnership interest to MaryLynn for a cash payment of $45,000 and the assumption of her share of LAMEC's debt.

a. What is the amount and character of Lisa's recognized gain or loss on the sale?

b. If LAMEC has $100,000 of unrealized receivables as of the sale date, what is the amount and character of Lisa's recognized gain or loss?

c. What is MaryLynn's initial basis in the partnership interest?

35. **(L01)** Marco, Jaclyn, and Carrie formed Daxing Partnership (a calendar-year-end entity) by contributing cash 10 years ago. Each partner owns an equal interest in the partnership. Marco, Jaclyn, and Carrie each have an outside basis in his/her partnership interest of $104,000. On January 1 of the current year, Marco sells his partnership interest to Ryan for a cash payment of $137,000. The partnership has the following assets and no liabilities as of the sale date:

|                     | Basis     | FMV       |
|---------------------|-----------|-----------|
| Cash                | $ 18,000  | $ 18,000  |
| Accounts receivable | 0         | 12,000    |
| Inventory           | 69,000    | 81,000    |
| Equipment           | 180,000   | 225,000   |
| Stock investment    | 45,000    | 75,000    |
| Totals              | $312,000  | $411,000  |

The equipment was purchased for $240,000, and the partnership has taken $60,000 of depreciation. The stock was purchased seven years ago.

a. What are the *hot assets* [§751(a)] for this sale?

b. What is Marco's gain or loss on the sale of his partnership interest?

c. What is the character of Marco's gain or loss?

d. What are Ryan's inside and outside bases in the partnership on the date of the sale?

36. **(L01)** Franklin, Jefferson, and Washington formed the Independence Partnership (a calendar-year-end entity) by contributing cash 10 years ago. Each partner owns an equal interest in the partnership. Franklin, Jefferson, and

Washington each have an outside basis in his partnership interest of $104,000. On January 1 of the current year, Franklin sells his partnership interest to Adams for a cash payment of $122,000. The partnership has the following assets and no liabilities as of the sale date:

|  | Basis | FMV |
|---|---|---|
| Cash | $ 18,000 | $ 18,000 |
| Accounts receivable | 0 | 12,000 |
| Inventory | 69,000 | 81,000 |
| Equipment | 180,000 | 225,000 |
| Stock investment | 45,000 | 30,000 |
| Totals | $312,000 | $366,000 |

The equipment was purchased for $240,000, and the partnership has taken $60,000 of depreciation. The stock was purchased seven years ago.

a. What is Franklin's overall gain or loss on the sale of his partnership interest?

b. What is the character of Franklin's gain or loss?

37. **(LO1)** Travis and Alix Weber are equal partners in the Tralix Partnership, which does not have a §754 election in place. Alix sells one-half of her interest (25 percent) to Michael Tomei for $30,000 cash. Just before the sale, Alix's basis in her entire partnership interest is $75,000, including her $30,000 share of the partnership liabilities. Tralix's assets on the sale date are as follows:

|  | Basis | FMV |
|---|---|---|
| Cash | $ 40,000 | $ 40,000 |
| Inventory | 30,000 | 90,000 |
| Land held for investment | 80,000 | 50,000 |
| Totals | $150,000 | $180,000 |

a. What is the amount and character of Alix's recognized gain or loss on the sale?

b. What is Alix's basis in her remaining partnership interest?

c. What is Michael's basis in his partnership interest?

d. What is the effect of the sale on the partnership's basis in the assets?

38. **(LO1)** Newton is a one-third owner of ProRite Partnership. Newton has decided to sell his interest in the business to Betty for $50,000 cash plus the assumption of his share of ProRite's liabilities. Assume Newton's inside and outside basis in ProRite are equal. ProRite shows the following balance sheet as of the sale date:

|  | Basis | FMV |
|---|---|---|
| **Assets:** |  |  |
| Cash | $ 80,000 | $ 80,000 |
| Receivables | 25,000 | 25,000 |
| Inventory | 40,000 | 85,000 |
| Land | 30,000 | 20,000 |
| Totals | $175,000 | $210,000 |
| **Liabilities and capital:** |  |  |
| Liabilities | $ 60,000 |  |
| Capital—Newton | 38,333 |  |
| —Barbara | 38,334 |  |
| —Liz | 38,333 |  |
| Totals | $175,000 |  |

What is the amount and character of Newton's recognized gain or loss?

39. **(LO3)** Coy and Matt are equal partners in the Matcoy Partnership. Each partner has a basis in his partnership interest of $28,000 at the end of the current year, prior to any distribution. On December 31, they each receive an operating distribution. Coy receives $10,000 cash. Matt receives $3,000 cash and a parcel of land with a $7,000 fair market value and a $4,000 basis to the partnership. Matcoy has no debt or hot assets.

   a. What is Coy's recognized gain or loss? What is the character of any gain or loss?
   b. What is Coy's ending basis in his partnership interest?
   c. What is Matt's recognized gain or loss? What is the character of any gain or loss?
   d. What is Matt's basis in the distributed property?
   e. What is Matt's ending basis in his partnership interest?

40. **(LO3)** Justin and Lauren are equal partners in the PJenn Partnership. The partners formed the partnership seven years ago by contributing cash. Prior to any distributions, the partners have the following bases in their partnership interests:

| Partner | Outside Basis |
|---------|---------------|
| Justin | $22,000 |
| Lauren | $22,000 |

On December 31 of the current year, the partnership makes a pro rata operating distribution of:

| Partner | Distribution |
|---------|--------------|
| Justin | Cash $25,000 |
| Lauren | Cash $18,000 |
| | Stock $7,000 (FMV) |
| | ($2,000 basis to partnership) |

   a. What is the amount and character of Justin's recognized gain or loss?
   b. What is Justin's remaining basis in his partnership interest?
   c. What is the amount and character of Lauren's recognized gain or loss?
   d. What is Lauren's basis in the distributed assets?
   e. What is Lauren's remaining basis in her partnership interest?

41. **(LO3)** Adam and Alyssa are equal partners in the PartiPilo Partnership. The partners formed the partnership three years ago by contributing cash. Prior to any distributions, the partners have the following bases in their partnership interests:

| Partner | Outside Basis |
|---------|---------------|
| Adam | $12,000 |
| Alyssa | $12,000 |

On December 31 of the current year, the partnership makes a pro rata operating distribution of:

| Partner | Distribution |
|---------|--------------|
| Adam | Cash $16,000 |
| Alyssa | Cash $8,000 |
| | Stock $ 8,000 (FMV) |
| | ($6,000 basis to partnership) |

   a. What is the amount and character of Adam's recognized gain or loss?
   b. What is Adam's remaining basis in his partnership interest?

c. What is the amount and character of Alyssa's recognized gain or loss?

d. What is Alyssa's basis in the distributed assets?

e. What is Alyssa's remaining basis in her partnership interest?

42. **(LO3)** Karen has a $68,000 basis in her 50 percent partnership interest in the KD Partnership before receiving a current distribution of $6,000 cash and land with a fair market value of $35,000 and a basis to the partnership of $18,000.

a. What is the amount and character of Karen's recognized gain or loss?

b. What is Karen's basis in the land?

c. What is Karen's remaining basis in her partnership interest?

43. **(LO3)** Pam has a $27,000 basis in her 50 percent partnership interest in the Meddoc partnership before receiving any distributions. This year Meddoc makes a current distribution to Pam of a parcel of land with a $40,000 fair market value and a $32,000 basis to the partnership. The land is encumbered with a $15,000 mortgage (the partnership's only liability).

a. What is the amount and character of Pam's recognized gain or loss?

b. What is Pam's basis in the land?

c. What is Pam's remaining basis in her partnership interest?

44. **(LO3)** Two years ago, Kimberly became a 30 percent partner in the KST Partnership with a contribution of investment land with a $10,000 basis and a $16,000 fair market value. On January 2 of this year, Kimberly has a $15,000 basis in her partnership interest and none of her precontribution gain has been recognized. On January 2, Kimberly receives an operating distribution of a tract of land (not the contributed land) with a $12,000 basis and an $18,000 fair market value.

research

a. What is the amount and character of Kimberly's recognized gain or loss on the distribution?

b. What is Kimberly's remaining basis in KST after the distribution?

c. What is KST's basis in the land Kimberly contributed after Kimberly receives this distribution?

45. **(LO4)** Rufus is a one-quarter partner in the Adventure Partnership. On January 1 of the current year, Adventure distributes $13,000 cash to Rufus in complete liquidation of his interest. Adventure has only capital assets and no liabilities at the date of the distribution. Rufus's basis in his partnership interest is $18,500.

a. What is the amount and character of Rufus's recognized gain or loss?

b. What is the amount and character of Adventure's recognized gain or loss?

c. If Rufus's basis is $10,000 at the distribution date rather than $18,500, what is the amount and character of Rufus's recognized gain or loss?

46. **(LO4)** The Taurin Partnership (calendar-year-end) has the following assets as of December 31 of the current year:

|  | Basis | FMV |
| --- | --- | --- |
| Cash | $ 45,000 | $ 45,000 |
| Accounts receivable | 15,000 | 30,000 |
| Inventory | 81,000 | 120,000 |
| Totals | $141,000 | $195,000 |

On December 31, Taurin distributes $15,000 of cash, $10,000 (FMV) of accounts receivable, and $40,000 (FMV) of inventory to Emma (a one-third partner) in

termination of her partnership interest. Emma's basis in her partnership interest immediately prior to the distribution is $40,000.

   a. What is the amount and character of Emma's recognized gain or loss on the distribution?

   b. What is Emma's basis in the distributed assets?

   c. If Emma's basis before the distribution was $55,000 rather than $40,000, what is Emma's recognized gain or loss and what is her basis in the distributed assets?

47. **(LO4)** Melissa, Nicole, and Ben are equal partners in the Opto Partnership (calendar-year-end). Melissa decides she wants to exit the partnership and receives a proportionate distribution to liquidate her partnership interest on January 1. The partnership has no liabilities and holds the following assets as of January 1:

| | Basis | FMV |
|---|---|---|
| Cash | $18,000 | $18,000 |
| Accounts receivable | 0 | 24,000 |
| Stock investment | 7,500 | 12,000 |
| Land | 30,000 | 36,000 |
| Totals | $55,500 | $90,000 |

Melissa receives one-third of each of the partnership assets. She has a basis in her partnership interest of $25,000.

   a. What is the amount and character of any recognized gain or loss to Melissa?

   b. What is Melissa's basis in the distributed assets?

   c. What are the tax implications (amount and character of gain or loss and basis of assets) to Melissa if her outside basis is $11,000 rather than $25,000?

   d. What is the amount and character of any recognized gain or loss from the distribution to Opto?

48. **(LO4)** AJ is a 30 percent partner in the Trane Partnership, a calendar-year-end entity. On January 1, AJ has an outside basis in his interest in Trane of $73,000, which includes his share of the $50,000 of partnership liabilities. Trane generates $42,000 of income during the year and does not make any changes to its liabilities. On December 31, Trane makes a proportionate distribution of the following assets to AJ to terminate his partnership interest:

| | Basis | FMV |
|---|---|---|
| Inventory | $55,000 | $65,000 |
| Land | 30,000 | 25,000 |
| Totals | $85,000 | $90,000 |

   a. What are the tax consequences (gain or loss, basis adjustments) of the distribution to Trane?

   b. What is the amount and character of any recognized gain or loss to AJ?

   c. What is AJ's basis in the distributed assets?

   d. If AJ sells the inventory four years after the distribution for $70,000, what is the amount and character of his recognized gain or loss?

49. **(LO4)** David's basis in the Jimsoo Partnership is $53,000. In a proportionate liquidating distribution, David receives cash of $7,000 and two capital assets: land 1 with a fair market value of $20,000 and a basis to Jimsoo of $16,000; and land 2 with a fair market value of $10,000 and a basis to Jimsoo of $16,000. Jimsoo has no liabilities.

    a. How much gain or loss will David recognize on the distribution? What is the character of any recognized gain or loss?
    b. What is David's basis in the distributed assets?
    c. If the two parcels of land had been inventory to Jimsoo, what are the tax consequences to David (amount and character of gain or loss and basis in distributed assets)?

50. **(LO4)** Megan and Matthew are equal partners in the J & J Partnership (calendar-year-end entity). On January 1 of the current year, they decide to liquidate the partnership. Megan's basis in her partnership interest is $100,000 and Matthew's is $35,000. The two partners receive identical distributions, with each receiving the following assets:

| | Basis | FMV |
|---|---|---|
| Cash | $30,000 | $30,000 |
| Inventory | 5,000 | 6,000 |
| Land | 500 | 1,000 |
| Totals | $35,500 | $37,000 |

    a. What is the amount and character of Megan's recognized gain or loss?
    b. What is Megan's basis in the distributed assets?
    c. What is the amount and character of Matthew's recognized gain or loss?
    d. What is Matthew's basis in the distributed assets?

51. **(LO4)** Bryce's basis in the Markit Partnership is $58,000. In a proportionate liquidating distribution, Bryce receives the following assets:

| | Basis | FMV |
|---|---|---|
| Cash | $ 8,000 | $ 8,000 |
| Land A | $20,000 | $45,000 |
| Land B | $20,000 | $25,000 |

    a. How much gain or loss will Bryce recognize on the distribution? What is the character of any recognized gain or loss?
    b. What is Bryce's basis in the distributed assets?

52. **(LO1, LO5)** Bella Partnership is an equal partnership in which each of the partners has a basis in his partnership interest of $10,000. Bella reports the following balance sheet:

■ **planning**

| | Basis | FMV |
|---|---|---|
| **Assets:** | | |
| Inventory | $20,000 | $30,000 |
| Land | 10,000 | 15,000 |
| Totals | $30,000 | $45,000 |
| | | |
| **Liabilities and capital:** | | |
| Capital—Toby | $10,000 | |
|   —Kaelin | 10,000 | |
|   —Andrew | 10,000 | |
| Totals | $30,000 | |

a. Identify the *hot assets* if Toby decides to sell his partnership interest. Are these assets "hot" for purposes of distributions?

b. If Bella distributes the land to Toby in complete liquidation of his partnership interest, what tax issues should be considered?

53. **(LO1, LO6)** Michelle pays $120,000 cash for Brittany's one-third interest in the Westlake Partnership. Just prior to the sale, Brittany's interest in Westlake is $96,000. Westlake reports the following balance sheet:

| | Basis | FMV |
|---|---|---|
| **Assets:** | | |
| Cash | $ 96,000 | $ 96,000 |
| Land | 192,000 | 264,000 |
| Totals | $288,000 | $360,000 |
| | | |
| **Liabilities and capital:** | | |
| Capital–Amy | $ 96,000 | |
| –Brittany | 96,000 | |
| –Ben | 96,000 | |
| Totals | $288,000 | |

a. What is the amount and character of Brittany's recognized gain or loss on the sale?

b. What is Michelle's basis in her partnership interest? What is Michelle's inside basis?

c. If Westlake were to sell the land for $264,000 shortly after the sale of Brittany's partnership interest, how much gain or loss would the partnership recognize?

d. How much gain or loss would Michelle recognize?

e. Suppose Westlake has a §754 election in place. What is Michelle's special basis adjustment? How much gain or loss would Michelle recognize on a subsequent sale of the land in this situation?

54. **(LO4, LO6)** Cliff's basis in his Aero Partnership interest is $11,000. Cliff receives a distribution of $22,000 cash from Aero in complete liquidation of his interest. Aero is an equal partnership with the following balance sheet:

| | Basis | FMV |
|---|---|---|
| **Assets:** | | |
| Cash | $22,000 | $22,000 |
| Investment | 8,800 | 8,800 |
| Land | 2,200 | 35,200 |
| Totals | $33,000 | $66,000 |
| | | |
| **Liabilities and capital:** | | |
| Capital–Chris | $11,000 | |
| –Cliff | 11,000 | |
| –Cooper | 11,000 | |
| Totals | $33,000 | |

a. What is the amount and character of Cliff's recognized gain or loss? What is the effect on the partnership assets?

b. If Aero has a §754 election in place, what is the amount of the special basis adjustment?

55. **(LO4, LO6)** Erin's basis in her Kiybron Partnership interest is $3,300. Erin receives a distribution of $2,200 cash from Kiybron in complete liquidation

of her interest. Kiybron is an equal partnership with the following balance sheet:

|  | Basis | FMV |
|---|---|---|
| **Assets:** | | |
| Cash | $2,200 | $2,200 |
| Stock (investment) | 1,100 | 2,200 |
| Land | 6,600 | 2,200 |
| Totals | $9,900 | $6,600 |
| | | |
| **Liabilities and capital:** | | |
| Capital—Erin | $3,300 | |
| —Carl | 3,300 | |
| —Grace | 3,300 | |
| Totals | $9,900 | |

a. What is the amount and character of Erin's recognized gain or loss? What is the effect on the partnership assets?

b. If Kiybron has a §754 election in place, what is the amount of the special basis adjustment?

56. **(LO4, LO6)** Helen's basis in Haywood partnership is $270,000. Haywood distributes land to Helen in complete liquidation of her partnership interest. The partnership reports the following balance sheet just before the distribution:

|  | Basis | FMV |
|---|---|---|
| **Assets:** | | |
| Cash | $220,000 | $220,000 |
| Stock (investment) | 480,000 | 220,000 |
| Land | 110,000 | 220,000 |
| Totals | $810,000 | $660,000 |
| | | |
| **Liabilities and capital:** | | |
| Capital—Charles | $270,000 | |
| —Esther | 270,000 | |
| —Helen | 270,000 | |
| Totals | $810,000 | |

a. What is the amount and character of Helen's recognized gain or loss? What is the effect on the partnership assets?

b. If Haywood has a §754 election in place, what is the amount of the special basis adjustment?

## COMPREHENSIVE PROBLEMS

57. Simon is a 30 percent partner in the SBD Partnership, a calendar-year-end entity. As of the end of this year, Simon has an outside basis in his interest in SBD of $188,000, which includes his share of the $60,000 of partnership liabilities. On December 31, SBD makes a proportionate distribution of the following assets to Simon:

|  | Basis | FMV |
|---|---|---|
| Cash | $40,000 | $40,000 |
| Inventory | 55,000 | 65,000 |
| Land | 30,000 | 45,000 |
| Totals | $125,000 | $150,000 |

a. What are the tax consequences (amount and character of recognized gain or loss, basis in distributed assets) of the distribution to Simon if the distribution is an operating distribution?

b. What are the tax consequences (amount and character of recognized gain or loss, basis in distributed assets) of the distribution to Simon if the distribution is a liquidating distribution?

c. Compare and contrast the results from questions a and b.

■ **planning**

58. Paolo is a 50 percent partner in the Capri Partnership and has decided to terminate his partnership interest. Paolo is considering two options as potential exit strategies. The first is to sell his partnership interest to the two remaining 25 percent partners, Giuseppe and Isabella, for $105,000 cash and the assumption of Paolo's share of Capri's liabilities. Under this option, Giuseppe and Isabella would each pay $52,500 for half of Paolo's interest. The second option is to have Capri liquidate his partnership interest with a proportionate distribution of the partnership assets. Paolo's basis in his partnership interest is $110,000, including Paolo's share of Capri's liabilities. Capri reports the following balance sheet as of the termination date:

|  | Basis | FMV |
|---|---|---|
| **Assets:** | | |
| Cash | $80,000 | $80,000 |
| Receivables | 40,000 | 40,000 |
| Inventory | 50,000 | 80,000 |
| Land | 50,000 | 60,000 |
| Totals | $220,000 | $260,000 |
| | | |
| **Liabilities and capital:** | | |
| Liabilities | $50,000 | |
| Capital–Paolo | 85,000 | |
| –Giuseppe | 42,500 | |
| –Isabella | 42,500 | |
| Totals | $220,000 | |

a. If Paolo sells his partnership interest to Giuseppe and Isabella for $105,000, what is the amount and character of Paolo's recognized gain or loss?

b. Giuseppe and Isabella each have a basis in Capri of $55,000 before any purchase of Paolo's interest. What are Giuseppe's and Isabella's basis in their partnership interests following the purchase of Paolo's interest?

c. If Capri liquidates Paolo's partnership interest with a proportionate distribution of the partnership assets, what is the amount and character of Paolo's recognized gain or loss?

d. If Capri liquidates Paolo's interest, what is Paolo's basis in the distributed assets?

e. Compare and contrast Paolo's options for terminating his partnership interest.

59. Carrie D'Lake, Reed A. Green, and Doug A. Divot share a passion for golf and decide to go into the golf club manufacturing business together. On January 2, 2010, D'Lake, Green, and Divot form the Slicenhook Partnership, a general partnership. Slicenhook's main product will be a perimeter-weighted titanium driver with a patented graphite shaft. All three partners plan to

actively participate in the business. The partners contribute the following property to form Slicenhook:

| Partner | Contribution |
|---|---|
| Carrie D'Lake | Land, FMV $460,000 |
| | Basis $460,000, Mortgage $60,000 |
| Reed A. Green | $400,000 |
| Doug A. Divot | $400,000 |

Carrie had recently acquired the land with the idea that she would contribute it to the newly formed partnership. The partners agree to share in profits and losses equally. Slicenhook elects a calendar-year-end and the accrual method of accounting.

In addition, Slicenhook borrows $1,500,000 from BigBank at the time the contributions were made. Slicenhook uses the proceeds from the loan and the cash contributions to build a state-of-the-art manufacturing facility ($1,200,000), purchase equipment ($600,000), and produce inventory ($400,000). With the remaining cash, Slicenhook invests $45,000 in the stock of a privately owned graphite research company and retains $55,000 as working cash.

Slicenhook operates on a just-in-time inventory system so it sells all inventory and collects all sales immediately. That means that at the end of the year, Slicenhook does not carry any inventory or accounts receivable balances. During 2010, Slicenhook has the following operating results:

| | | |
|---|---|---|
| Sales | | $1,126,000 |
| Cost of goods sold | | 400,000 |
| Interest income from tax-exempt bonds | | 900 |
| Qualified dividend income from stock | | 1,500 |
| Operating expenses | | 126,000 |
| Depreciation (tax) | | |
| §179 on equipment | $39,000 | |
| Equipment | 81,000 | |
| Building | 24,000 | 144,000 |
| Interest expense on debt | | 120,000 |

The partnership is very successful in its first year. The success allows Slicenhook to use excess cash from operations to purchase $15,000 of tax-exempt bonds (you can see the interest income already reflected in the operating results). The partnership also makes a principal payment on its loan in the amount of $300,000 and a distribution of $100,000 to each of the partners on December 31, 2010.

The partnership continues its success in 2011 with the following operating results:

| | | |
|---|---|---|
| Sales | | $1,200,000 |
| Cost of goods sold | | 420,000 |
| Interest income from tax-exempt bonds | | 900 |
| Qualified dividend income from stock | | 1,500 |
| Operating expenses | | 132,000 |
| Depreciation (tax) | | |
| Equipment | 147,000 | |
| Building | 30,000 | 177,000 |
| Interest expense on debt | | 96,000 |

The operating expenses include a $1,800 trucking fine that one of its drivers incurred for reckless driving and speeding and meals and entertainment expense of $6,000.

By the end of 2011, Reed has had a falling out with Carrie and Doug and has decided to leave the partnership. He has located a potential buyer for his partnership interest, Indie Ruff. Indie has agreed to purchase Reed's interest in Slicenhook for $730,000 in cash and the assumption of Reed's share of Slicenhook's debt. Carrie and Doug, however, are not certain that admitting Indie to the partnership is such a good idea. They want at least to consider having Slicenhook liquidate Reed's interest on January 1, 2012. As of January 1, 2012, Slicenhook has the following assets:

|  | Tax Basis | FMV |
| --- | --- | --- |
| Cash | $ 876,800 | $ 876,800 |
| Investment–tax exempts | 15,000 | 18,000 |
| Investment stock | 45,000 | 45,000 |
| Equipment–net of dep. | 333,000 | 600,000 |
| Building–net of dep. | 1,146,000 | 1,440,000 |
| Land | 460,000 | 510,000 |
| Total | $2,875,800 | $3,489,800 |

Carrie and Doug propose that Slicenhook distribute the following to Reed in complete liquidation of his partnership interest:

|  | Tax Basis | FMV |
| --- | --- | --- |
| Cash | $485,000 | $485,000 |
| Investment stock | 45,000 | 45,000 |
| Equipment–net of dep. | 111,000 | 200,000 |
| Total | $641,000 | $730,000 |

Slicenhook has not purchased or sold any equipment since its original purchase just after formation.

a. Determine each partner's recognized gain or loss upon formation of Slicenhook.

b. What is each partner's initial tax basis in Slicenhook on January 2, 2010?

c. Prepare Slicenhook's opening tax basis balance sheet as of January 2, 2010.

d. Using the operating results, what are Slicenhook's ordinary income and separately stated items for 2010 and 2011? What amount of Slicenhook's income for each period would each of the partner's receive?

e. What are Carrie's, Reed's, and Doug's bases in their partnership interest at the end of 2010 and 2011?

f. If Reed sells his interest in Slicenhook to Indie Ruff, what is the amount and character of his recognized gain or loss? What is Indie's basis in the partnership interest?

g. What is Indie's inside basis in Slicenhook? What effect would a §754 election have on Indie's inside basis?

h. If Slicenhook distributes the assets proposed by Carrie and Doug in complete liquidation of Reed's partnership interest, what is the amount and character of Reed's recognized gain or loss? What is Reed's basis in the distributed assets?

i. Compare and contrast Reed's options for terminating his partnership interest.

# KAPLAN CPA SIMULATIONS

**KAPLAN** CPA REVIEW

**Please visit the Online Learning Center**    (www.mhhe.com/spilker2011) to access the following Kaplan CPA Simulation:

The simulation for **Clark Co.** covers corporate tax and partnerships, including filing status; book-to-tax reconciliation; transactions with owners; and the tax impact of various partnership items.

# chapter
# 22

# S Corporations

**Storyline Summary**

**Nicole Johnson, Sarah Walker, and Chance Armstrong**

*Location:*      Salt Lake City, Utah

*Status:*      Shareholders of newly formed Color Comfort Sheets, Inc. (CCS)

*Situation:*      Formed CCS as a corporation and have elected to have the entity taxed as an S corporation.

I n Chapter 15, we met Nicole Johnson, who turned her sheet-making hobby into a full-time business called Color Comfort Sheets (CCS). In this chapter, we assume Nicole formed CCS as a corporation, intending to elect S corporation tax status.

When starting the business, Nicole had cash to contribute to CCS but not enough to meet initial needs. She convinced her friend Sarah Walker to invest in CCS and, fortunately, after listening to Nicole and Sarah's proposal, local sports team owner Chance Armstrong also agreed to invest. Nicole and Sarah would take an active role in managing CCS; Chance would not. Nicole contributed a parcel of land and cash in exchange for one-third of CCS's stock. Sarah and Chance each contributed cash for one-third of the stock. With funding in place, CCS began operating on January 1, 2009. However, with the excitement (and turmoil) of starting the new business, it took Nicole, Sarah, and Chance a while to talk with their accountant about electing S corporation status. After several discussions, they filed their S election on May 1, 2009.

*to be continued . . .*

In this chapter, we discuss the tax and nontax characteristics of an **S corporation,** a hybrid entity that shares some characteristics with C corporations and some with partnerships.[1] S corporations are incorporated under state law and thus have the same legal protections as C corporations. They are governed by the same corporate tax rules that apply in the organization, liquidation, and reorganization of C corporations. However, unlike a C corporation, an S corporation is a flow-through entity and shares many tax similarities with partnerships. For example, basis calculations for S corporation shareholders and partners are similar, the income or loss of an S corporation flows through to its owners, and distributions are generally not taxed to the extent of the owner's basis.

Throughout this chapter, we highlight the tax similarities between S corporations and C corporations and between S corporations and partnerships, while focusing on the unique rules that apply to S corporations. These are more complex for S corporations that were once C corporations with **earnings and profits (E&P).**

## LO1

# S CORPORATION ELECTIONS

**THE KEY FACTS**

S Corporation
Qualification
Requirements

∎ Only U.S. citizens or
residents, certain trusts,
and certain tax-exempt
organizations may be
S corporation
shareholders.

∎ S corporations may
have no more than
100 shareholders.

∎ For purposes of the
100-shareholder limit,
family members and
their estates count as
only one shareholder.

## *Formations*

The same rules for forming and contributing property govern S and C corporations. As discussed in Chapter 19, §351 and related provisions apply when one or more persons transfer property to a corporation (C or S) in return for stock, and immediately after the transfer, these persons control the corporation. These rules allow shareholders meeting the requirements to defer gains they realize when they transfer appreciated property to the corporation in exchange for stock. Note that similar rules apply to formations and property contributions to partnerships under §721. One important difference, however, is that partnership tax rules do not impose a control requirement to defer gains (see Chapter 20 for partnership contributions).

## *S Corporation Qualification Requirements*

Unlike C corporations and partnerships, S corporations are limited as to type and number of owners (shareholders).[2] Only U.S. citizens or residents, certain trusts, and certain tax-exempt organizations may be shareholders, no corporations or partnerships.[3] S corporations may have no more than 100 shareholders; family members and their estates count as one. Family members include a common ancestor and her lineal descendants and their spouses (or former spouses). Thus, greatgrandparents, grandparents, parents, children, grandchildren, great-grandchildren, and the respective spouses are family members for this purpose. A practical implication of these limits is that large, publicly traded corporations cannot elect to be treated as S corporations.

---

[1]S corporations get their name from **Subchapter S** of the Internal Revenue Code, which includes code sections 1361–1379.

[2]§1361.

[3]Grantor trusts, qualified Subchapter S trusts, electing small business trusts, certain testamentary trusts, and voting trusts can own S corporation stock. A discussion of these trusts is beyond the scope of this chapter. Eligible tax-exempt shareholders include qualified retirement plan trusts or charitable, religious, educational, etc., organizations that are tax-exempt under §501.

**Example 22-1**

*What if:* Suppose CCS was formed with Nicole Johnson, Sarah Walker, and Chanzz Inc., a corporation owned by Chance Armstrong, as shareholders. Would CCS be eligible to elect S corporation status?

**Answer:** No. Because one of its shareholders is a corporation (Chanzz Inc.), CCS would not be eligible to elect S corporation status.

*What if:* Suppose Nicole, Sarah, and Chance recruited 97 U.S. residents to become shareholders of CCS. Meanwhile, Nicole gave several of her CCS shares to her grandfather and his bride as a wedding gift. After the transfer, CCS had 102 shareholders. Can CCS elect S corporation status?

**Answer:** Yes. Nicole (descendant of common ancestor), her grandfather (common ancestor), and her grandfather's wife (spouse of common ancestor) are treated as *one* shareholder for purposes of the 100-shareholder limit.

## S Corporation Election

An eligible corporation must make an affirmative election to be treated as an S corporation.[4] In addition to meeting the shareholder requirements above, it must:

- Be a domestic corporation (created or organized in the United States or under U.S. law or the law of any state in the United States).
- Not be a specifically identified ineligible corporation.[5]
- Have only one class of stock.

A corporation is considered to have only one class of stock if all of its outstanding shares provide identical distribution and liquidation rights. Differences in voting powers are permissible. In general, debt instruments do not violate the single class of stock requirement unless they are treated as equity elsewhere under the tax law.[6] In addition, §1361 provides safe-harbor rules to ensure that debt obligations are not re-characterized as a second class of stock.

> **THE KEY FACTS**
>
> **S Corporation Election**
>
> ■ An eligible corporation must make an affirmative election to be treated as an S corporation.
>
> ■ Eligible corporations meet the type and number of shareholder requirements, are domestic corporations, are not specifically identified as ineligible corporations, and have only one class of stock.
>
> ■ To elect S corporation status, the corporation makes a formal election using Form 2553.

**Example 22-2**

*What if:* Suppose Nicole was a resident of Toronto, Canada, and while she formed CCS in Canada under Canadian law, she still planned to do business in the United States. Is CCS eligible to elect S corporation status in the United States?

**Answer:** No. CCS would not be eligible for S corporation treatment because it was neither organized in the United States nor formed under U.S. laws.

*What if:* Suppose Nicole resided in Seattle and formed CCS under the state laws of Washington but planned to do a significant amount of business in Canada. Would CCS be eligible to elect S corporation status?

**Answer:** Yes, because CCS was formed under the laws of a U.S. state.

---

[4]§1362(a).

[5]Ineligible corporations include financial institutions using the reserve method of accounting under §585, insurance companies, corporations allowed a tax credit for income from Puerto Rico and from U.S. possessions under §936, corporations previously electing Domestic International Sales Corporation status, and corporations treated as a taxable mortgage pool.

[6]See §385 for factors considered in determining whether debt should be considered as equity for tax purposes.

To formally elect S corporation status effective as of the beginning of the current tax year, the corporation uses Form 2553, either in the prior tax year or within the first two and one-half months after the beginning of the current tax year.[7] Elections made after the first two and one-half months of a year are effective at the beginning of the following year. All shareholders on the date of the election must consent to the election.

### Example 22-3

**What if:** Suppose Nicole formed CCS as a C corporation in 2009 with a calendar tax year and finally got around to electing S corporation status on February 20, 2010. What is the earliest effective date of the S election?

**Answer:** January 1, 2010.

**What if:** Suppose Nicole formed CCS as a C corporation in 2009 with a calendar tax year and made the S election on March 20, 2010. When is the S election effective?

**Answer:** It is effective January 1, 2011, because Nicole made the election more than two and one-half months after the beginning of 2010.

Even when the corporation makes the election within the first two and one-half months after the beginning of its tax year, the election will not be effective until the subsequent year if (1) the corporation did not meet the S corporation requirements for each day of the current tax year before it made the S election, or (2) one or more shareholders who held the stock in the corporation during the current year and before the S corporation election was made did not consent to the election (for example, a shareholder disposes of his stock in the corporation in the election year before the election is made and fails to consent to the S election).[8]

### Example 22-4

**What if:** Suppose in 2009 Nicole formed CCS as a C corporation (calendar tax year) with Nicole, Sarah, and Chanzz Inc. (a corporation) as shareholders. On January 2, 2010, Chanzz Inc. sold all its shares to Chance Armstrong. On January 31, 2010, CCS filed an S corporation election, with Nicole, Sarah, and Chance all consenting to the election. What is the earliest effective date of the S election?

**Answer:** January 1, 2011. Because CCS had an ineligible shareholder (Chanzz Inc.) during 2010, the election is not effective until the beginning of 2011.

**What if:** Suppose in 2009 Nicole formed CCS as a C corporation (calendar tax year) with Nicole, Sarah, and Chance as shareholders. On January 30, 2010, Chance sold his shares to Nicole. On February 15, 2010, CCS filed an S election, with Nicole and Sarah consenting to the election. Chance, however, did not consent to the election. What is the earliest effective date of the S election?

**Answer:** January 1, 2011. Because Chance was a shareholder until January 30, 2010, and he did not consent to the S election in 2010, the S election is not effective until the beginning of 2011, the year after the election.

The timing of the election may be especially important for C corporations with net operating losses. The reason: Net operating losses attributable to C corporation years generally cannot be carried over to the S corporation. Thus, it may

---

[7]§1362(b). When the IRS determines that taxpayers have reasonable cause for making late elections, it has the authority to treat late elections as timely [§1362(b)(5)].

[8]§1362(b)(2).

be beneficial to delay the S election until the corporation has utilized its net operating losses.[9]

# S CORPORATION TERMINATIONS

Once the S election becomes effective, the corporation remains an S corporation until the election is terminated. The termination may be voluntary or involuntary.

## Voluntary Terminations

The corporation can make a *voluntary revocation* of the S election if shareholders holding more than 50 percent of the S corporation stock (including nonvoting shares) agree.[10] It files a statement with the IRS revoking the election made under §1362(a) and stating the effective date of the revocation and the number of shares issued and outstanding. In general, voluntary revocations made during the first two and one-half months of the year are effective as of the beginning of the year. A revocation after this period is effective the first day of the following tax year. Alternatively, a corporation may specify the termination date as long as the date specified is on or after the date the revocation is made.[11]

---

**Example 22-5**

**What if:** Suppose CCS was initially formed as an S corporation with a calendar year-end. After a couple of years, things were going so well that Nicole and Sarah (each one-third shareholders) wanted to terminate the S election and take CCS public. However, Chance (also a one-third shareholder) was opposed to the S election termination. Can Nicole and Sarah terminate the S election without Chance's consent?

**Answer:** Yes. To revoke the election, Nicole and Sarah need to own more than 50 percent of the shares, and together they own 66.7 percent.

**What if:** If Nicole and Sarah file the revocation on February 15, 2011, what is the effective date of the S corporation termination (assuming they do not specify one)?

**Answer:** January 1, 2011. If they file the S corporation revocation after March 15, 2011, it becomes effective January 1, 2012. CCS could have specified the effective date as long as it was on or after February 15, 2011 (the date it filed the revocation).

---

## Involuntary Terminations

Involuntary terminations can result from failure to meet requirements (by far the most common reason) or from an excess of passive investment income.

**Failure to Meet Requirements**    A corporation's S election is automatically terminated if the corporation fails to meet the requirements. The termination is effective on the date it fails the S corporation requirements. If the IRS deems the termination inadvertent, it may allow the corporation to continue to be treated as an S corporation if, within a reasonable period after the inadvertent termination, the corporation takes the necessary steps to meet the S corporation requirements.[12]

---

[9]Later in this chapter we discuss one exception to the rule that disallows net operating loss carryovers from C corporation to S corporation years. See the discussion of the S corporation built-in gains tax.

[10]§1362(d)(1)(B).

[11]§1362(d)(1)(D).

[12]§1362(f).

**Example 22-6**

> *What if:* Suppose CCS was formed as a calendar-year S corporation with Nicole Johnson, Sarah Walker, and Chance Armstrong as equal shareholders. On June 15, 2010, Chance sold his CCS shares to his solely owned C corporation, Chanzz Inc. Is CCS's S election still in effect at the beginning of 2011? If not, when was it terminated?
>
> **Answer:** No, the election was automatically terminated on June 15, 2010, when Chanzz Inc. became a shareholder because S corporations may not have corporate shareholders.

**Excess of Passive Investment Income**    If an S corporation has *earnings and profits* from a previous C corporation year (or through a reorganization with a corporation that has earnings and profits), its election is terminated if the S corporation has passive investment income in excess of 25 percent of gross receipts for three consecutive years. If the S corporation never operated as a C corporation or does not have C corporation earnings and profits (either by prior distribution of C corporate earnings and profits, or simply by not having earnings and profits at the effective date of the S election), this provision does not apply.

For purposes of the passive investment income test, **gross receipts** is the total amount of revenues received (including passive investment income and capital gains and losses) or accrued under the corporation's accounting method, *not* reduced by returns, allowances, cost of goods sold, or deductions. **Passive investment income (PII)** includes royalties, rents, dividends, interest, and annuities (not including capital gains or losses).[13] S corporation election terminations due to excess passive investment income are effective on the first day of the year following the third consecutive tax year with excess passive investment income.

**Example 22-7**

> *What if:* Suppose CCS was initially formed as an S corporation with a calendar year-end. During its first three years, it reported passive investment income in excess of 25 percent of its gross receipts. Is CCS's S election terminated under the excess passive investment income test? If so, what is the effective date of the termination?
>
> **Answer:** No, the excess passive investment income test does not apply to CCS in this situation because CCS has never operated as a C corporation; consequently, it does not have C corporation earnings and profits.
>
> *What if:* Suppose CCS was initially formed as a C corporation with a calendar year-end. After its first year of operations (very profitable), CCS elected S corporation status, effective January 1, 2010. During 2011, 2012, and 2013, it reported passive investment income in excess of 25 percent of its gross receipts. Is CCS's S election terminated under the excess passive investment income test? If so, what is the effective date of the termination?
>
> **Answer:** Yes, it is terminated. Because CCS has C corporation earnings and profits from 2009 and excess passive investment income for three consecutive years as an S corporation, its S election is terminated effective on January 1, 2014.

### Short Tax Years

S corporation election terminations frequently create an S corporation *short tax year* (a reporting year less than 12 months) and a C corporation short tax year. The corporation must then allocate its income for the full year between the S and the C corporation years, using the number of days in each short year (the daily method). Or it may use the

---

[13]PII excludes certain rents (e.g., rents derived from the active trade or business of renting property, produced film rents, income from leasing self-produced tangible property, temporary parking fees, etc.).

corporation's normal accounting rules to allocate income to the actual period in which it was earned (the specific identification method).[14] Both short tax year returns are due on the corporation's customary tax return due date (with normal extensions available).

---

### Example 22-8

**What if:** Suppose CCS was formed as a calendar-year S corporation with Nicole Johnson, Sarah Walker, and Chance Armstrong as equal shareholders. On June 15, 2010, Chance sold his CCS shares (one-third of all shares) to his solely owned C corporation, Chanzz Inc., terminating CCS's S election on June 15, 2010. Assume CCS reported business income for 2010 as follows:

| Period | Income |
|---|---|
| January 1 through June 14 (165 days) | $100,000 |
| June 15 through December 31 (200 days) | 265,000 |
| January 1 through December 31, 2010 (365 days) | $365,000 |

If CCS uses the daily method of allocating income between the S corporation short tax year (January 1–June 14) and the C corporation short tax year (June 15–December 31), how much income will it report on its S corporation short tax year return and its C corporation short tax year return for 2010?

**Answer:** S corporation short tax year = $165,000 ($365,000/365 days × 165 days); C corporation short tax year = $200,000 ($365,000/365 days × 200 days).

**What if:** If CCS uses the specific identification method to allocate income, how much will it allocate to the S corporation short year and C corporation short year?

**Answer:** S corporation short tax year, $100,000; C corporation short tax year, $265,000.

Note that if the entity wanted to minimize the income subject to taxation as a C corporation, it would use the daily method of allocating income.

---

## S Corporation Reelections

After terminating or voluntarily revoking S corporation status, the corporation may elect it again, but it generally must wait until the beginning of the fifth tax year *after* the tax year in which it terminated the election.[15] Thus, if the election was terminated effective the first day of the tax year, the corporation must wait five full years to again become an S corporation.

### THE KEY FACTS
**S Terminations and Reelections**

■ The S election may be revoked by shareholders holding more than 50 percent of the S corporation stock (including nonvoting shares).

■ A corporation's S election is automatically terminated if (1) the S corporation fails to meet the S corporation requirements, or (2) the S corporation has earnings and profits from a previous C corporation year and has passive investment income in excess of 25 percent of gross receipts for three consecutive years.

■ A corporation losing its S corporation status must wait until the beginning of the fifth year after the election was terminated to elect S corporation status again.

---

### Example 22-9

**What if:** Let's return to the facts of the previous example. CCS was formed as a calendar-year S corporation with Nicole Johnson, Sarah Walker, and Chance Armstrong as equal shareholders. On June 15, 2010, Chance sold his CCS shares (one-third of all shares) to his solely owned C corporation, Chanzz Inc., terminating CCS's S election on June 15, 2010. Absent permission from the IRS (see text below), what is the earliest date CCS may again elect to be taxed as an S corporation?

**Answer:** January 1, 2015. This is the fifth tax year after the year in which the termination became effective.

**What if:** Assume on February 1, 2010, CCS voluntarily elected to revoke its S corporation status effective January 1, 2011. Absent IRS permission, what is the earliest CCS may again elect to be taxed as an S corporation?

**Answer:** January 1, 2016. This is the fifth year after the year in which the termination became effective.

---

[14]If the S election termination is involuntary, the S corporation may not use the per day allocation method to allocate income between the short tax years if there is a sale or exchange of 50 percent or more of the corporation's stock during the year [§1362(e)(6)(D)].

[15]§1362(g).

The IRS may consent to an earlier election under a couple of conditions: (1) if the corporation is now owned more than 50 percent by shareholders who were not owners at the time of termination, or (2) if the termination was not reasonably within the control of the corporation or shareholders with a substantial interest in the corporation and was not part of a planned termination by the corporation or shareholders. Given the potential adverse consequences of an S election termination, the corporation should carefully monitor compliance with the S corporation requirements.

## L03

## OPERATING ISSUES

### Accounting Methods and Periods

Like partnerships, S corporations determine their accounting periods and make accounting method elections at the entity level. An S corporation makes most of its elections (like the §179 election) in conjunction with filing its annual tax return, and some by filing a separate request with the IRS. (For example, an application to change accounting methods is filed on Form 3115, separate from the S corporation's tax return.) For an S corporation previously operating as a C corporation, all prior accounting methods carry over to the S corporation.

Recall that both C corporations and partnerships face restrictions on using the cash method. S corporations do not. They may choose the cash, accrual, or hybrid method unless selling inventory is a material income-producing factor for them. In that case they must account for gross profit (sales minus cost of goods sold) using the accrual method, even if they are otherwise cash-method taxpayers. Hence, they would use the hybrid method.

Tax laws also specify permissible tax years for S corporations, but they are a little less cumbersome than for partnerships. S corporations must use a calendar year-end unless they can establish a business purpose for an alternative year-end or a natural business year-end. (For example, a business that receives 25 percent or more of gross receipts for the previous three years in the last two months of the year-end requested would qualify for a noncalendar year-end.)[16]

### Income and Loss Allocations

S corporations, like partnerships, are flow-through entities, and thus their profits and losses flow through to their shareholders annually for tax purposes. As we discussed in Chapter 20, partnerships have considerable flexibility in making special profit and loss allocations to their partners. In contrast, S corporations must allocate profits and losses pro rata, based on the number of outstanding shares each shareholder owns on each day of the tax year.[17]

An S corporation generally allocates income or loss items to shareholders on the last day of its tax year.[18] If a shareholder sells her shares during the year, she will report her share of S corporation income and loss allocated to the days she owned the stock using a pro rata allocation. If *all shareholders with changing ownership percentages* during the year agree, the S corporation can instead use its normal accounting rules to allocate income and loss (and other separately stated items, discussed below) to the specific periods in which it realized income and losses.

---

[16]§1378(b). In addition, S corporations, like partnerships, have the option of electing an alternative taxable year under §444.

[17]§1366(a), §1377(a).

[18]§1366(a).

**Example 22-10**

*What if:* Assume CCS was formed as a calendar-year S corporation with Nicole Johnson, Sarah Walker, and Chance Armstrong as equal (one-third) shareholders. On June 15, 2010, Chance sold his CCS shares to Nicole. CCS reported business income for 2010 as follows:

| Period | Income |
|---|---|
| January 1 through June 14 (165 days) | $100,000 |
| June 15 through December 31 (200 days) | 265,000 |
| January 1 through December 31, 2010 (365 days) | $365,000 |

How much 2010 income is allocated to each shareholder if CCS uses the daily method of allocating income?

**Answer:** Nicole's allocation is $188,333; Sarah's is $121,667; and Chance's is $55,000, calculated as follows.

| | **(1)**<br>**January 1–June 14** | **(2)**<br>**June 15–December 31** | **(1) + (2)**<br>**Total 2010**<br>**Allocation** |
|---|---|---|---|
| Nicole | $55,000<br>($365,000/365 × 165 × 1/3) | $133,333<br>($365,000/365 × 200 × 2/3) | **$188,333** |
| Sarah | $55,000<br>($365,000/365 × 165 × 1/3) | $66,667<br>($365,000/365 × 200 × 1/3) | **$121,667** |
| Chance | $55,000<br>($365,000/365 × 165 × 1/3) | $0 | **$ 55,000** |
| Totals | $165,000 | $200,000 | $365,000 |

How much 2010 income is allocated to each shareholder if CCS uses its normal accounting rules to allocate income to the specific periods in which it was actually earned?

**Answer:** Nicole's allocation is $210,000 ($100,000 × 1/3 + $265,000 × 2/3); Sarah's is $121,667 ($365,000 × 1/3); and Chance's is $33,333 ($100,000 × 1/3).

## Separately Stated Items

Like partnerships, S corporations are required to file tax returns (Form 1120S) annually. In addition, on Form 1120S, Schedule K-1, they supply information to each shareholder detailing the amount *and* character of items of income and loss flowing through the S corporation.[19] Shareholders must report these income and loss items on their tax returns even if they do not receive cash distributions during the year.

S corporations determine each shareholder's share of ordinary business income (loss) and separately stated items. Like partnerships, **ordinary business income (loss)** (also referred to as non-separately stated income or loss) is all income (loss) exclusive of any separately stated items of income (loss). **Separately stated items** are tax items that are treated differently from a shareholder's share of ordinary business income (loss) for tax purposes. The character of each separately stated item is determined at the S corporation level rather than at the shareholder level. The list of common separately stated items for S corporations is similar to that for partnerships, with a couple of exceptions. (For example, S corporations do not report self-employment income and do not have guaranteed payments.) Exhibit 22-1 lists several common separately stated items.

---

[19]Other items, such as tax credits and informational items such as AMT adjustments, may also flow through from the S corporation to its shareholders.

## EXHIBIT 22-1 Common Separately Stated Items

- Short-term capital gains and losses
- Long-term capital gains and losses
- Section 1231 gains and losses
- Dividends
- Interest income
- Charitable contributions
- Tax-exempt income
- Net rental real estate income
- Investment interest expense
- Section 179 deduction
- Foreign taxes

S corporations may hold stock in C corporations, and any dividends S corporations receive will flow through to their shareholders. However, S corporations are not entitled to claim the dividends received deduction (see Chapter 16 for a discussion of the dividends received deduction).

Assuming CCS operated as a C corporation in 2009 and an S corporation in 2010, Exhibit 22-2 presents the results of operations. CCS's S election was not effective until January 1, 2010, because the shareholders filed the S election after the required date for it to be effective in 2009.

## EXHIBIT 22-2

| Color Comfort Sheets Income Statement December 31, 2009 and 2010 | | |
| --- | --- | --- |
| | 2009, C Corporation | 2010, S Corporation |
| Sales revenue | $220,000 | $520,000 |
| Cost of goods sold | (50,000) | (115,000) |
| Salary to owners Nicole and Sarah | (70,000) | (90,000) |
| Employee wages | (45,000) | (50,000) |
| Depreciation expense | (15,000) | (20,000) |
| Miscellaneous expenses | (4,000) | (5,000) |
| Interest income | 3,000 | 6,000 |
| Dividend income | 1,000 | 3,000 |
| Overall net income | $ 40,000 | $249,000 |

### Example 22-11

Assume CCS was a C corporation for tax purposes in 2009 and an S corporation for 2010. Based on its operating results in Exhibit 22-2, how much ordinary business income and separately stated items are allocated to CCS's shareholders for 2009?

**Answer:** $0 ordinary business income and $0 separately stated items. Because CCS is a C corporation in 2009, its income does *not* flow through to its shareholders.

Based on the information in Exhibit 22-2, how much ordinary business income and separately stated items are allocated to CCS's shareholders for 2010?

**Answer:** See the following table for the allocations:

| Description | CCS | Allocations Nicole 1/3 | Sarah 1/3 | Chance 1/3 |
|---|---|---|---|---|
| 2010 overall net income | $249,000 | | | |
| Less: | | | | |
| Dividends | 3,000 | | | |
| Interest income | 6,000 | | | |
| Ordinary business income | $240,000 | $80,000 | $80,000 | $80,000 |
| Separately Stated Items: | | | | |
| Interest income | $  6,000 | $ 2,000 | $ 2,000 | $ 2,000 |
| Dividends | $  3,000 | $ 1,000 | $ 1,000 | $ 1,000 |

Nicole, Sarah, and Chance will treat their shares of CCS's ordinary business income as *ordinary* income and include it, along with their shares of interest and dividend income, in their individual tax returns for the year.[20]

## Shareholder's Basis

L04

Just as partners must determine their bases in their partnership interests, S corporation shareholders must determine their bases in the S corporation stock to determine the gain or loss they recognize when they sell the stock, the taxability of distributions, and the deductibility of losses.

**Initial Basis**    An S corporation shareholder calculates his *initial basis* upon formation of the corporation, like C corporation shareholders. (See Chapter 19 for a review.) Specifically, the shareholder's basis in stock received in the exchange equals the tax basis of the property transferred, less any liabilities assumed by the corporation on the property contributed (*substituted basis*). The shareholder's stock basis is increased by any gain recognized; it is reduced by the fair market value of any property received other than stock.[21] If, on the other hand, the shareholder purchased the S corporation stock from another shareholder, the new shareholder's basis is simply the purchase price of the stock.

**Example 22-12**

At the beginning of 2009, Nicole contributed $30,000 of cash and land with a fair market value of $130,000 and an adjusted basis of $125,000 to CCS. The land was encumbered by a $40,000 mortgage executed three years before. Sarah and Chance each contributed $120,000 of cash to CCS. What tax bases do Nicole, Sarah, and Chance have in their CCS stock at the beginning of 2009?

**Answer:** Nicole's basis is $115,000 ($30,000 cash + $125,000 adjusted basis of land − $40,000 mortgage assumed); Sarah's basis is $120,000; and Chance's is $120,000.

[20]Nicole, Sarah, and Chance would report their share of ordinary business income on Schedule E and their share of interest and dividend income on Schedule B of Form 1040.

[21]§358. This assumes the shareholder meets the §351 requirements. If the shareholder's exchange with the corporation does not meet these requirements, the shareholder's basis in the stock is its fair market value.

**Annual Basis Adjustments**    While C corporation rules govern the initial stock basis of an S corporation shareholder, subsequent calculations more closely resemble the partnership rules. Specifically, an S corporation shareholder's stock basis is dynamic and must be *adjusted* annually to ensure that: (1) taxable income/gains and deductible expenses/losses are *not* double-counted by shareholders either when they sell their shares or receive S corporation distributions (for example, because shareholders are taxed on the S corporation's income annually, they should not be taxed again when they receive distributions of the income), and (2) tax-exempt income and nondeductible expenses are not ultimately taxed or deducted.

S corporation shareholders make the following adjustments to their stock basis annually, in the order listed:

- Increase for any contributions to the S corporation during the year.
- Increase for shareholder's share of ordinary business income and separately stated income/gain items (including tax-exempt income).
- Decrease for distributions during the year.
- Decrease for shareholder's share of nondeductible expenses (fines, penalties).
- Decrease for shareholder's share of ordinary business loss and separately stated expense/loss items.

As with a partnership, adjustments that decrease basis may never reduce an S corporation shareholder's tax basis below zero.[22]

S corporation shareholders are not allowed to include any S corporation debt in their stock basis. Recall that partners *are* allowed to include their share of partnership debt in their basis. One implication of this difference is that, everything else equal, an S corporation shareholder's basis will be lower than a partner's basis, due to the exclusion of debt (however, see the discussion of *debt basis* for S corporation shareholders below).

---

### Example 22-13

Given the shareholders' 2009 bases in their CCS stock from the previous example (Nicole, $115,000; Sarah, $120,000; and Chance, $120,000), what basis does each have at the end of 2010, after taking into account the information in Exhibit 22-2 (but before taking into account any distributions, which are discussed below)?

**Answer:**  Nicole, $198,000; Sarah, $203,000; and Chance, $203,000, computed as follows:

| Description | Nicole | Sarah | Chance | Explanation |
|---|---|---|---|---|
| (1) Initial tax basis | $115,000 | $120,000 | $120,000 | Example 22-12. |
| (2) Ordinary business income | 80,000 | 80,000 | 80,000 | Exhibit 22-2. |
| (3) Interest income | 2,000 | 2,000 | 2,000 | Exhibit 22-2. |
| (4) Dividends | 1,000 | 1,000 | 1,000 | Exhibit 22-2. |
| Tax basis in stock at end of 2010 | $198,000 | $203,000 | $203,000 | (1) + (2) + (3) + (4). |

Note the shareholders do not include any portion of CCS's debt in their stock basis.

***What if:*** Suppose that, in addition to the amounts in Exhibit 22-2, CCS also recognized $1,200 of tax-exempt interest income in 2010. Nicole's share of this separately stated item is $400. Taking this allocation into account, what is Nicole's stock basis at the end of 2010?

**Answer:** It is $198,400 ($198,000 + $400). The tax-exempt income allocated to Nicole as a separately stated item increases her tax basis to ensure that she is never taxed on her share of the tax-exempt income.

---

[22]§1367(a)(2).

## Loss Limitations

S corporations have loss-limitation rules similar to those for partnerships. For an S corporation shareholder to deduct it, a loss must clear three separate hurdles: (1) tax basis, (2) at-risk amount, and (3) passive activity.[23]

**Tax Basis Limitation**   S corporation shareholders may not deduct losses in excess of their stock basis. Recall they are not allowed to include debt in their basis; partners are. This restriction makes it more likely that the tax basis limitation will apply to S corporation shareholders than to similarly situated partners. Losses not deductible due to the tax basis limitation are not necessarily lost. Rather, they are suspended until the shareholder generates additional basis. If the shareholder sells the stock before creating additional basis, the suspended loss disappears unused.

---

**Example 22-14**

*What if:* Suppose at the beginning of 2011, Nicole's basis in her CCS stock was $14,000. During 2011, CCS reported a $60,000 ordinary business loss and no separately stated items. How much of the ordinary loss is allocated to Nicole?

**Answer:** The loss allocation is $20,000 ($60,000 × 1/3).

How much of the $20,000 loss clears the tax basis hurdle for deductibility in 2011?

**Answer:** The amount of Nicole's basis in her CCS stock, or $14,000. The remaining $6,000 of loss does not clear the tax basis hurdle; it is suspended until Nicole generates additional basis.

---

Shareholders can mitigate the disadvantage of not including S corporation debt in their stock basis—by loaning money directly to their S corporations. These loans create **debt basis,** separate from the stock basis. Losses are limited first to the shareholders' tax bases in their shares *and then* to their bases in any direct loans made to their S corporations.[24] Specifically, if the total amount of items (besides distributions) that decrease the shareholder's basis for the year exceeds the shareholder's stock basis, the excess amount decreases the shareholder's debt basis. Like stock basis, debt basis cannot be decreased below zero. In subsequent years, any net increase in basis for the year *first restores the shareholder's debt basis* (up to the outstanding debt amount) and then the shareholder's stock basis. If the S corporation repays the debt owed to the shareholder before the shareholder's debt basis is restored, any loan repayment in excess of the shareholder's debt basis will trigger a taxable gain to the shareholder.

---

**Example 22-15**

*What if:* Suppose at the beginning of 2011, Nicole's basis in her CCS stock was $14,000. During 2011, Nicole loaned $8,000 to CCS and CCS reported a $60,000 ordinary business loss and no separately stated items. How much of the $20,000 ordinary loss allocated to Nicole clears the tax basis hurdle for deductibility in 2011?

**Answer:** All $20,000. The first $14,000 of the loss reduces her stock basis to $0, and the remaining $6,000 reduces her debt basis to $2,000 ($8,000 − $6,000).

*(continued on page 22-14...)*

---

[23]S corporations are also subject to the hobby loss rules in §183 that limit loss deductions for activities not engaged in for profit.

[24]§1366(d)(1)(B). These must be direct loans to the corporation. Thus, shareholders do not get debt basis when they guarantee a loan of the S corporation.

> **What if:** Suppose in 2012, CCS allocated $9,000 of ordinary business income to Nicole and no separately stated items. What are Nicole's CCS stock basis and debt basis at the end of 2012?
>
> **Answer:** Her stock basis is $3,000; her debt basis is $8,000. The income first restores debt basis to the outstanding debt amount and then increases her stock basis.

**At-Risk Limitation**    Like partners in partnerships, S corporation shareholders are subject to the *at-risk* rules. They may deduct S corporation losses only to the extent of their **at-risk amount** in the S corporation, as defined in §465. However, remember partners are at risk for recourse and certain nonrecourse debt of the partnership. In contrast, S corporation shareholders are deemed at risk only for direct loans they make to S corporations. With one notable exception, an S corporation shareholder's at-risk amount is the same as her stock basis.

The primary exception relates to nonrecourse loans: An S corporation share-holder taking out a nonrecourse loan to make a capital contribution to the S corpo-ration creates stock basis in the S corporation without increasing her amount at risk. If she takes out a nonrecourse loan to make a direct *loan* to the S corporation, the loan creates debt basis but does not increase her amount at risk. When the stock ba-sis plus debt basis is different from the at-risk amount, S corporation shareholders apply the tax basis loss limitation first, and then the at-risk limitation. Losses limited under the at-risk rules are carried forward indefinitely until the shareholder gener-ates additional at-risk amounts to utilize them or sells the S corporation stock.

**Post-Termination Transition Period Loss Limitation**    The voluntary or involuntary termination of a corporation's S election creates a problem for shareholders with suspended losses due to the basis and at-risk rules. The reason: These losses are gen-erally not deductible after the S termination date. Shareholders can obtain some re-lief provided by §1366(d)(3), which allows them to treat any suspended losses existing at the S termination date as occurring on the last day of the **post-termination transi-tion period (PTTP).** In general, the PTTP begins on the day after the last day of the corporation's last taxable year as an S corporation and ends on the later of (a) one year after the last S corporation day or (b) the due date for filing the return for the last year as an S corporation (including extensions).[25]

This rule allows the shareholder to create additional stock basis (by making ad-ditional capital contributions) during the PTTP and to utilize suspended losses based on her *stock* basis (not her debt basis) at the end of the period. Any suspended losses utilized at the end of the PTTP reduce the shareholder's basis in her stock. Any losses not utilized at the end of the period are lost forever.

**Example 22-16**

> **What if:** Suppose CCS terminated its S election on July 17, 2011. At the end of the S corporation's short tax year ending on July 17, Nicole's stock basis and at-risk amounts were both zero (she has never had debt basis), and she had a suspended loss of $15,000. In 2012, Nicole made additional capital contributions of $10,000 on February 20 and $7,000 on September 6. When does the PTTP end for CCS? How much loss may Nicole deduct, and what is her basis in the CCS stock at the end of the PTTP?
>
> *(continued on page 22-15...)*

---

[25]§1377(b)(1)(A). §1377(b) indicates that the PTTP also includes the 120-day period beginning on the date of a determination (not the date of the actual termination) that the corporation's S election had terminated for a previous taxable year.

**Answer:** For loss deduction purposes, CCS's PTTP ends on September 17, 2012. That date represents (b) in the "later of (a) or (b)" alternative—(a) one year after the last S corporation day, which would be July 17, 2012, or (b) the due date for filing the return for the last year as an S corporation, including extensions, which would be September 17, 2012 (September 15th falls on a Saturday), assuming CCS extends its tax return. (Note the short tax year S corporation return is due the same time as the short tax year C corporation return.) Nicole may deduct the entire $15,000 suspended loss because her basis at the end of the PTTP and before the loss deduction is $17,000. (That amount is calculated as a carryover basis of $0 on the last S corporation day plus $17,000 capital contributions during the PTTP.) Nicole's basis in CCS stock after the loss deduction is $2,000 ($17,000 basis at the end of the PTTP less the $15,000 loss deduction).

***What if:*** Suppose Nicole made her second capital contribution on October 22 instead of September 6. How much loss can Nicole deduct, and what is her basis in CCS stock at the end of the PTTP?

**Answer:** The loss deduction is $10,000: Nicole's stock basis at the end of the PTTP and before her loss deduction is only $10,000 because the $7,000 contribution occurred after the end of the PTTP. Nicole's basis in the CCS stock at the end of the PTTP and after the loss deduction is zero ($10,000 basis less $10,000 loss deduction). Her basis then increases to $7,000 on October 22, but the $5,000 suspended loss is lost forever.

**Passive Activity Loss Limitation**   S corporation shareholders, just like partners, are subject to the **passive activity loss rules.** There are no differences in the application of these rules for S corporations; the definition of a passive activity, the tests for material participation, the income and loss baskets, and the passive activity loss carryover rules described in Chapter 20 are exactly the same. Thus, as in partnerships, the passive activity loss rules limit the ability of S corporation shareholders to deduct losses unless they are involved in actively managing the business.[26]

**Example 22-17**

***What if:*** Suppose in 2012, CCS incurred an ordinary business loss and allocated the loss equally to its shareholders. Assuming Nicole, Sarah, and Chance all had adequate stock basis and at-risk amounts to absorb the losses, which of the three shareholders would be least likely to deduct the loss due to the passive activity limitation rules?

**Answer:** Chance. Because he is not actively involved in managing CCS's business activities, any loss allocated to him is a passive activity loss.

## Self-Employment Income

You might wonder whether an S corporation shareholder's allocable share of ordinary business income (loss) is classified as self-employment income for tax purposes. The answer is no, even when the shareholder actively works for the S corporation.[27]

In some cases, shareholders may work as employees of and receive a salary from the S corporation, which treats this salary payment like that made to any other employee: It withholds 7.65 percent of the shareholders' gross salary for Social Security taxes (subject to the wage limitation) and Medicare taxes, and it pays 7.65 percent of the shareholders' gross salary in payroll taxes—a combined tax rate of up to 15.3 percent on shareholders' salary payments.[28]

[26]§469.
[27]Rev. Rul. 59-221, 1955-1 CB 225.
[28]After the Social Security withholding limit has been reached, the S corporation would *withhold* 1.45 percent of the shareholder's gross salary for Medicare taxes, and the S corporation would also *pay* 1.45 percent of the shareholder's gross salary in Medicare taxes. In this situation, the combined payroll tax on the shareholder's salary is 2.9 percent.

Because of this stark contrast in the treatment of ordinary business income and shareholder salaries, S corporation shareholders may desire to avoid payroll taxes by limiting or even eliminating their salary payments. However, if they work as employees, they are required to pay themselves a reasonable salary for the services they perform. If they pay themselves an unreasonably low salary, the IRS may attempt to reclassify some or all the S corporation's ordinary business income as shareholder salary!

---

**Taxes in the Real World**    *Self-Employment Income*

Senator John Edwards, the Democratic Party's vice presidential candidate in 2004, was criticized by both *The Wall Street Journal* and *The New York Times* during the 2004 campaign for avoiding $591,112 in Medicare taxes, using what was arguably a legitimate tax planning strategy. Prior to becoming a senator, Edwards earned approximately $27 million as a personal injury attorney. During this time, his law practice converted from a general partnership to an S corporation, and Edwards began receiving a $360,000 annual salary from the S corporation. As a general partner, he would have seen his entire share of the *earnings* from his law partnership subject to Medicare taxes. However, by converting the law practice to an S corporation, he left only his $360,000 *salary* subject to Medicare taxes. Although the IRS might have argued that Edward's salary was unreasonably low, tax experts generally agreed it was reasonable under the circumstances.

*Source:* Kenneth A. Gary, "Edward's S Corporation Not an Abusive Tax Shelter," *Tax Notes,* July 26, 2004. Copyright © 2004 Tax Analysts. Reprinted with permission.

---

### Fringe Benefits

True to their hybrid status, S corporations are treated in part like C corporations and in part like partnerships with respect to tax deductions for qualifying employee fringe benefits.[29] For shareholder-employees who own 2 percent or less of the entity, the S corporation receives C corporation tax treatment. That is, it gets a tax deduction for qualifying fringe benefits, and the benefits are nontaxable to *all* employees. For shareholder-employees who own more than 2 percent of the S corporation, it receives partnership treatment.[30] That is, it gets a tax deduction, but the otherwise qualifying fringe benefits are taxable to the more than 2 percent shareholder-employees.[31]

Fringe benefits taxable to this group include employer-provided health insurance[32] (§106), group-term life insurance (§79), meals and lodging provided for the convenience of the employer (§119), and benefits provided under a cafeteria plan (§125). Examples of benefits that are nontaxable to more than 2 percent shareholder-employees (and partners in a partnership) include employee achievement awards (§74), qualified group legal services plans (§120), educational assistance programs (§127), dependent care assistance programs (§129), no-additional-cost services (§132), qualified employee discounts (§132), working condition fringe benefits (§132), *de minimis* fringe benefits (§132), on-premises athletic facilities (§132), and medical savings accounts (§220).

---

[29]Qualifying fringe benefits are nontaxable to the employee. Other fringe benefits (nonqualifying) are taxed as compensation to employees.

[30]§1372(a).

[31]The §318 attribution rules apply (see Chapter 18) for purposes of determining who is a more than 2 percent shareholder.

[32]Note, however, that more than 2 percent shareholder's are allowed to deduct their insurance costs as *for* AGI deductions [§162(l)].

# DISTRIBUTIONS

S corporations face special rules when accounting for distributions (operating distributions of cash or other property and liquidating distributions).[33]

## Operating Distributions

The rules for determining the shareholder-level tax consequences of operating distributions depend on the S corporation's history; specifically whether, at the time of the distribution, it has accumulated *earnings and profits* from a previous year as a C corporation. (See Chapter 18 for a discussion of C corporation earnings and profits.) We consider both situations—with and without accumulated earnings and profits.

### S Corporation with No C Corporation Accumulated Earnings and Profits
Two sets of historical circumstances could apply here: (1) An entity may have been an S corporation since inception, or (2) it may have been converted from a C corporation but does not have C corporation accumulated earnings and profits at the time of the distribution. In both cases, as long as there are no C corporation accumulated earnings and profits, the rules for accounting for the distribution are very similar to those applicable to distributions to partners. That is, shareholder distributions are tax-free to the extent of the shareholders' stock basis (determined after increasing the stock basis for income allocations for the year[34]). If a distribution exceeds the shareholder's stock basis, the shareholder has a capital gain equal to the excess distribution amount.

---

### Example 22-18

**What if:** Suppose CCS has been an S corporation since its inception. On June 1, 2012, CCS distributed $30,000 to Nicole. Her basis in her CCS stock on January 1, 2012, was $20,000. For 2012, Nicole was allocated $15,000 of ordinary income from CCS and no separately stated items. What is the amount and character of income Nicole recognizes on the distribution, and what is her basis in her CCS stock after the distribution?

**Answer:** Nicole has $0 income from the distribution and $5,000 basis in stock after the distribution ($35,000 − $30,000). Her stock basis for determining the taxability of the distribution was $35,000, or her beginning basis of $20,000 plus the $15,000 income allocation for the year (which is taxable to Nicole).

**What if:** Assume the same facts except that CCS distributed $40,000 to Nicole rather than $30,000. What is the amount and character of income Nicole recognizes on the distribution, and what is her basis in her CCS stock after the distribution?

**Answer:** Nicole has a $5,000 long-term capital gain (she has held her CCS stock more than one year) and $0 basis in her stock (the distribution reduced her stock basis to $0).

**What if:** Suppose CCS began in 2009 as a C corporation and elected to be taxed as an S corporation in its second year of operations. In 2009, it distributed all its earnings and profits as a dividend, so it did not have any earnings and profits at the end of 2009. In 2010, it distributed $30,000 to Nicole when her basis in her stock was $35,000. What is the amount and character of income she recognizes on the distribution, and what is her basis in her CCS stock after the distribution?

**Answer:** Nicole has $0 income on the distribution and $5,000 basis in stock after the distribution ($35,000 − $30,000). Because CCS did not have C corporation earnings and profits at the time of the distribution, her outcome is the same as if CCS had been taxed as an S corporation since inception.

#### THE KEY FACTS

**Cash Operating Distributions for S Corporations**

- For S corporations without E&P: Distributions are tax-free to the extent of the shareholder's stock basis. If a distribution exceeds the shareholder's stock basis, the shareholder has a capital gain equal to the excess distribution amount.

- For S corporations with E&P: Distributions are deemed to be paid from (1) the AAA account (tax-free to the extent of basis and taxed as capital gain thereafter), (2) existing accumulated E&P (taxable as dividends), and (3) the shareholder's remaining basis in the S corporation stock, if any (tax-free to the extent of basis and taxed as capital gain thereafter).

---

[33]The §302 stock redemption rules that determine whether a distribution in redemption of a shareholder's stock should be treated as a distribution or a sale or exchange apply to both C corporations and S corporations. See discussion on redemptions in Chapter 18.

[34]§1368(d).

**S Corporations with C Corporation Accumulated Earnings and Profits**    When there are accumulated earnings and profits (E&P) from C corporations at the time of the distribution, the distribution rules are a bit more complex. For S corporations in this situation, the tax laws require the corporation to maintain an **accumulated adjustments account (AAA)** to determine the taxability of S corporate distributions. The AAA represents the cumulative income or losses *for the period the corporation has been an S corporation.* It is calculated as:

> The beginning of year AAA balance
> + Separately stated income/gain items (excluding tax-exempt income)
> + Ordinary income
> − Separately stated losses and deductions
> − Ordinary losses
> − Nondeductible expenses that are not capital expenditures (except deductions related to generating tax-exempt income)
> − Distributions out of AAA[35]
> = End of year AAA balance

Unlike a shareholder's stock basis, the AAA may have a negative balance. However, the *reduction for distributions* may not cause the AAA to go negative or to become more negative. Also, unlike stock basis, the AAA is a corporate-level account rather than a shareholder-specific account.

---

**Example 22-19**

CCS was originally formed as a C corporation and reported 2009 taxable income (and earnings and profits) of $40,000 (see Exhibit 22-2). Effective the beginning of 2010, it elected to be taxed as an S corporation. In 2010, CCS reported $249,000 of overall income (including separately stated items—see Exhibit 22-2). What is the amount of CCS's AAA for 2010 before considering the effects of distributions?

**Answer:** $249,000, computed as follows:

| Description | Amount | Explanation |
|---|---|---|
| (1) Separately stated income | $ 9,000 | $6,000 interest income + $3,000 dividend (see Exhibit 22-2). |
| (2) Business income | 240,000 | Exhibit 22-2. |
| AAA before distributions | $249,000 | (1) + (2). |

**What if:** Assume that during 2010, CCS distributed $300,000 to its shareholders. What is CCS's AAA at the end of 2010?

**Answer:** AAA is $0, because the distribution cannot cause AAA to be negative.

**What if:** Instead of reporting $249,000 of income during 2010, assume that during 2010 CCS reported an ordinary business loss of $45,000, a separately stated charitable contribution of $5,000, and a $6,000 distribution to its shareholders. What is CCS's AAA at the end of 2010?

**Answer:** AAA is negative $50,000. CCS decreases its AAA by the $45,000 business loss and the $5,000 charitable contribution. AAA before distributions is negative $50,000. CCS does not decrease AAA by the $6,000 distribution because the distribution cannot cause AAA to be negative or make it more negative.

---

[35]If the current year income and loss items net to make a negative adjustment to the AAA, the net negative adjustments from these items is made to the AAA *after* any AAA reductions for distributions (that is, the reduction in AAA for distributions is made before the net negative adjustment for current year income and loss items). §1368(e)(1)(C).

S corporation distributions are deemed to be paid from the following sources in the order listed:[36]

1. The AAA account (to the extent it has a positive balance).[37]
2. Existing accumulated earnings and profits from years when the corporation operated as a C corporation.
3. The shareholder's stock basis.[38]

S corporation distributions from the AAA (the most common distributions) are treated the same as distributions when the S corporation does not have E&P. They are nontaxable to the extent of the shareholder's basis, and they create capital gains if they exceed the shareholder's stock basis. If an S corporation makes a distribution from accumulated E&P, the distribution is taxable to shareholders as a dividend. (See Chapter 18 for the calculation of corporate E&P.) Once an S corporation's accumulated E&P is fully distributed, the remaining distributions reduce the shareholder's remaining basis in the S corporation stock (if any) and are nontaxable. Any excess distributions are treated as capital gain.

## Example 22-20

**What if:** Assume at the end of 2010, before considering distributions, CCS's AAA was $24,000 and its accumulated E&P from 2009 was $40,000. Also assume Nicole's basis in her CCS stock is $80,000. If CCS distributes $60,000 on July 1 ($20,000 to each shareholder), what is the amount and character of income Nicole must recognize on her $20,000 distribution, and what is her stock basis in CCS after the distribution?

**Answer:** $12,000 dividend income and $72,000 stock basis after the distribution, computed as follows:

| Description | Amount | Explanation |
|---|---|---|
| (1) Total distribution | $ 60,000 | |
| (2) CCS's AAA beginning balance | $ 24,000 | |
| (3) Distribution from AAA | $ 24,000 | Lesser of (1) or (2). |
| (4) Distribution in excess of AAA | $ 36,000 | (1) − (3). |
| (5) Nicole's share of AAA distribution | $ 8,000 | (3) × 1/3 (nontaxable reduction of stock basis). |
| (6) Nicole's beginning stock basis | $ 80,000 | |
| **(7) Nicole's ending stock basis** | **$ 72,000** | (6) − (5). |
| (8) CCS's E&P balance | $ 40,000 | |
| (9) Dividend distribution (from E&P) | $ 36,000 | Lesser of (4) or (8). |
| **Nicole's share of dividend** | **$ 12,000** | (9) × 1/3. |

### THE KEY FACTS

**Property Distributions**

- S corporations recognize gains but not losses when they distribute property to their shareholders.

- For shareholders, the amount of the distribution is the fair market value of the property received (minus any liabilities the shareholder assumes on the distribution).

- The rules for determining the taxability of property distributions at the shareholder level are the same as those for cash distributions.

- Shareholders take a fair market value basis in the property received in the distribution.

---

[36]S corporations may elect to have distributions treated as being first paid out of existing accumulated earnings and profits from C corporation years to avoid the excess net passive income tax. We discuss the excess net passive income tax later in the chapter.

[37]Prior to 1983, S corporations' shareholders were taxed on undistributed taxable income as a deemed distribution. This undistributed income is referred to as *previously taxable income (PTI)*. For S corporations with PTI, distributions are considered to be paid out of PTI (if there is any remaining that has not been distributed) after any distributions out of their AAA. These distributions are also nontaxable to the extent of basis and reduce both the shareholder's basis and PTI.

[38]Technically, the distributions come from the Other Adjustments Account (OAA) and then any remaining shareholder equity accounts (e.g., common stock, paid-in capital). The OAA starts at zero at the S corporation's inception, is increased for tax-exempt income, and is decreased by expenses related to tax-exempt income, any federal taxes paid that are attributable to a C corporation tax year, and any S corporate distributions after the AAA and accumulated E&P have been reduced to zero. As with the AAA, the reduction for distributions may not cause the OAA to go negative or to increase a negative balance. Because from the shareholder's perspective distributions out of the OAA and equity accounts both reduce the shareholder's stock basis, we do not discuss the OAA or other equity accounts in detail.

**Property Distributions**    At times, S corporations distribute appreciated property to their shareholders. When they do so, S corporations recognize gain as though they had sold the appreciated property for its fair market value just prior to the distribution.[39] (This rule contrasts with the partnership provisions for property distributions but is consistent with the C corporation rules.) Shareholders who receive the distributed property recognize their distributive share of the deemed gain and increase their stock basis accordingly. On the other hand, S corporations do not recognize losses on distributions of property whose value has declined.

For the shareholder, the amount of a property distribution is the fair market value of the property received (minus any liabilities the shareholder assumes on the distribution). The rules we described above apply in determining the extent to which the amount of the distribution is a tax-free reduction of basis, a capital gain for a distribution in excess of basis, or a taxable dividend to the shareholder.[40] (See the rules for the taxability of distributions for S corporations with and without C corporation accumulated earnings and profits.) Shareholders take a fair market value basis in the property received in the distribution.

---

**Example 22-21**

*What if:* Assume that at the end of 2011, CCS distributes long-term capital gain property (fair market value of $24,000, basis of $15,000) to each shareholder (aggregate property distribution of $72,000 with an aggregate basis of $45,000). At the time of the distribution, CCS has no corporate E&P and Nicole has a basis of $10,000 in her CCS stock. How much gain, if any, does CCS recognize on the distribution? How much income does Nicole recognize as a result of the distribution?

**Answer:** CCS recognizes $27,000 of long-term capital gain and Nicole recognizes $14,000 of long-term capital gain, computed as follows:

| Description | Amount | Explanation |
|---|---|---|
| (1) FMV of distributed property | $ 72,000 | |
| (2) CCS's basis in distributed property | $ 45,000 | |
| **(3) CCS's LTCG gain on distribution** | **$ 27,000** | (1) − (2). |
| (4) Nicole's share of LTCG from CCS | $ 9,000 | (3) × 1/3. |
| (5) Nicole's stock basis after gain allocation | $ 19,000 | $10,000 beginning basis + (4). |
| (6) Distribution to Nicole | $ 24,000 | (1) × 1/3. |
| (7) Nicole's stock basis after distribution | $ 0 | (5) − (6) limited to $0. |
| (8) LTCG to Nicole on distribution in excess of stock basis | $ 5,000 | (6) in excess of (5). |
| **Nicole's total LTCG on distribution** | **$ 14,000** | (4) + (8). |

---

**Post-Termination Transition Period Distributions**    Recall the special tax rules relating to suspended losses at the S corporation termination date. Similarly, §1371(e) provides for special treatment of any S corporation distribution *in cash* after an S election termination and during the post-termination transition period (PTTP). Such

---

[39]§311(b). In addition, the S corporation may incur entity-level tax if the distributed property had built-in gains related to when the corporation converted to an S corporation. We discuss the built-in gains tax later in the chapter.

[40]Note that while S corporation shareholders reduce their stock basis by the fair market value of the property received, partners receiving property distributions from partnerships generally reduce the basis in their partnership interests by the adjusted basis of the distributed property.

cash distributions are tax-free to the extent they do not exceed the corporation's AAA balance and the individual shareholder's basis in the stock.

The PTTP for post-termination distributions is generally the same as the PTTP for deducting suspended losses, discussed above. For determining the taxability of distributions, the PTTP generally begins on the day after the last day of the corporation's last taxable year as an S corporation; it ends on the later of (a) one year after the last S corporation day or (b) the due date for filing the return for the last year as an S corporation (including extensions).[41]

### Liquidating Distributions

Liquidating distributions of a shareholder interest in an S corporation follow corporate tax rules rather than partnership rules. For a complete liquidation of the S corporation, the rules under §§331 and 336 (discussed in Chapter 19) govern the tax consequences. S corporations generally recognize gain *or* loss on each asset they distribute in liquidation (recall that S corporations recognize gain but not loss on operating distributions of noncash property). These gains and losses are allocated to the S corporation shareholders, increasing or decreasing their stock basis. In general, shareholders recognize gain on the distribution if the value of the property exceeds their stock basis; they recognize loss if their stock basis exceeds the value of the property.

## S CORPORATION TAXES, ACCOUNTING PERIODS AND METHODS, AND FILING REQUIREMENTS

**LO6**

Although S corporations are flow-through entities generally not subject to tax, three potential taxes apply to S corporations that previously operated as C corporations: the **built-in gains tax, excess net passive income tax,** and **LIFO recapture tax.** The built-in gains tax is the most common of the three and will be our starting point.

### Built-in Gains Tax

Congress enacted the built-in gains tax to prevent C corporations from avoiding corporate taxes on sales of appreciated property by electing S corporation status. The built-in gains tax applies only to an S corporation that has a *net unrealized built-in gain* at the time it converts from a C corporation. Further, for the built-in gains tax to apply, the S corporation must subsequently *recognize* net built-in gains during its first 10 years operating as an S corporation (first seven years for asset sales in 2009 and 2010), called the **built-in gains tax recognition period.**[42]

What exactly is a **net unrealized built-in gain?** Measured on the first day of the corporation's first year as an S corporation, it represents the net gain (if any) the corporation would recognize if it sold each asset at its fair market value. For this purpose, we net gains and losses to determine whether indeed there is a net unrealized gain at the conversion date. The corporation's accounts receivable and accounts payable are also part of the computation: Under the cash method, accounts receivable are gain items and accounts payable are loss items. If the S corporation has a net unrealized gain at conversion, it must compute its net recognized built-in gains for each tax year during its first 10 years as an S corporation (7 years for asset sales in 2009 and 2010) to determine whether it is liable for the built-in gains tax.

> **THE KEY FACTS**
>
> **Built-in Gains Tax**
>
> ■ The built-in gains tax applies only to S corporations that have a net unrealized built-in gain at the time they converted from C corporations and that recognize net built-in gains during their first 10 years operating as an S corporation (first 7 years for asset sales in 2009 and 2010).
>
> ■ The net unrealized built-in gain represents the net gain (if any) that the corporation would recognize if it sold each asset at its fair market value.
>
> *(continued)*

---

[41]§1377(b)(1)(A). For purposes of the taxability of distributions, the PTTP also includes: (1) the 120-day period that begins on the date of any determination (court decision, closing agreement, and so on) from an IRS audit that occurs after the S election has been terminated and adjusts the corporation's income, loss, or deduction during the S period; and (2) the 120-day period beginning on the date of a determination (not the date of the actual termination) that the corporation's S election had terminated for a previous taxable year [§1377(b)(1)(B) and (C)].

[42]§1374.

## Example 22-22

*(concluded)*

■ Recognized built-in gains (losses) include the gain (loss) for any asset sold during the year [limited to the unrealized gain (loss) for the specific asset at the S conversion date].

■ The net recognized built-in gain is limited to the lesser of (a) the net recognized built-in gain less any NOL and capital loss carryovers, (b) the net unrealized built-in gain not yet recognized, and (c) the corporation's taxable income for the year using the C corporation tax rules.

CCS uses the accrual method of accounting. At the beginning of 2010, it owned the following assets (but leased its manufacturing facility and its equipment):

| Asset | Fair Market Value (FMV) | Adjusted Basis (AB) | Built-in Gain (Loss) |
|---|---|---|---|
| Cash | $ 80,000 | $ 80,000 | $ 0 |
| Accounts receivable | 20,000 | 20,000 | 0 |
| Inventory (FIFO) | 130,000 | 110,000 | 20,000 |
| Land | 100,000 | 125,000 | (25,000) |
| Totals | $330,000 | $335,000 | $ (5,000) |

What is CCS's net unrealized built-in gain when it converts to an S corporation on January 1, 2010?

**Answer:** CCS has $0 net unrealized built-in gain. It has a net unrealized built-in loss, so it is not subject to the built-in gains tax.

**What if:** Suppose CCS's inventory is valued at $155,000 instead of $130,000. What is its net unrealized built-in gain?

**Answer:** It is $20,000. The $45,000 built-in gain on the inventory is netted against the $25,000 built-in loss on the land.

Recognized built-in gains for an S corporation year include (1) the gain for any asset sold during the year (limited to the unrealized gain for the specific asset at the S conversion date) and (2) any income received during the current year attributable to pre-S corporation years (such as collection on accounts receivable for cash-method S corporations). Likewise, recognized built-in losses for a year include (1) the loss for any asset sold during the year (limited to the unrealized loss for the specific asset at the S conversion date) and (2) any deduction during the current year attributable to pre-S corporation years (such as deductions for accounts payable for cash-method S corporations). The net recognized built-in gain for any year is limited to *the least of*:

1. The net of the recognized built-in gains and losses for the year.
2. The net unrealized built-in gains as of the S election date less the net recognized built-in gains in previous years. (This restriction ensures the net recognized built-in gains during the recognition period do not exceed the net unrealized gain at the S conversion date.)
3. The corporation's taxable income for the year, using the C corporation tax rules exclusive of the dividends received deduction and net operating loss deduction.

If taxable income limits the net recognized built-in gain for any year [item (3) above], we treat the excess gain as a recognized built-in gain in the next tax year. After the net recognized built-in gain to be taxed has been determined using the limitations above, it should be reduced by any net operating loss (NOL) or capital loss carryovers from prior C corporation years.[43] This base is then multiplied by the highest corporate tax rate (currently 35 percent) to determine the built-in gains tax. The built-in gains tax paid by the S corporation is allocated to the shareholders as a loss. We determine its character by allocating the loss proportionately among the recognized built-in gains giving rise to the tax.[44] For planning purposes, it is important to consider when to recognize built-in losses to reduce the S corporation's exposure to the built-in gains tax. That is, the S corporation could seek to recognize built-in losses in years with recognized built-in gains, in order to avoid the built-in gains tax.

---

[43]Capital loss carryovers only reduce built-in gains that are capital gains.
[44]§1366(f)(2).

**Example 22-23**

**What if:** Suppose CCS had a net unrealized built-in gain of $20,000. In addition to other transactions in 2010, CCS sold inventory it owned at the beginning of the year; that inventory had built-in gain at the beginning of the year of $40,000 (FMV $150,000; cost basis $110,000). If CCS had been a C corporation in 2010, its taxable income would have been $200,000. How much built-in gains tax must CCS pay in 2010?

**Answer:** It must pay $7,000 ($20,000 × 35%) in built-in gains tax. CCS must pay a 35 percent tax on the least of (a) $40,000 (recognized built-in gain on inventory), (b) $20,000 (initial net unrealized gain), and (c) $200,000 (taxable income computed as if CCS was a C corporation for 2010). It will reduce the amount of ordinary business income it would otherwise allocate to its shareholders by $7,000—the amount of the built-in gains tax—because the entire amount of the tax is due to inventory sales.

**What if:** Assume the same facts as above (an initial net unrealized gain of $20,000) except CCS sold two assets that had built-in gains at the time CCS became an S corporation. CCS sold a capital asset with a built-in gain of $10,000 and inventory with a built-in gain of $40,000. CCS would still pay a $7,000 built-in gains tax. This tax would be allocated as a loss to its shareholders. What is the character of the $7,000 loss?

**Answer:** It is a $1,400 capital loss [$7,000 × (10,000 capital gain/$50,000 total recognized built in gain)] and a $5,600 ordinary loss [$7,000 × ($40,000 ordinary income from inventory sale/$50,000 total recognized built-in gain)].

**What if:** Assume that in addition to the initial facts in the example, CCS also had a net operating loss from 2009 (the year it operated as a C corporation) of $15,000. How much built-in gains tax will CCS have to pay in 2010?

**Answer:** It will pay $1,750 ($5,000 × 35%). CCS is allowed to offset $15,000 of the $20,000 recognized portion of the initial net unrealized gain by its $15,000 net operating loss carryover from 2009.

**What if:** Suppose CCS had a net unrealized built-in gain of $20,000. In addition to other transactions in 2010, CCS sold inventory it owned at the beginning of the year; that inventory had built-in gain at the beginning of the year of $40,000 (FMV $150,000; AB $110,000). If CCS had been a C corporation in 2010, its taxable income would have been $4,000. How much built-in gains tax would CCS have to pay in 2010?

**Answer:** $1,400 ($4,000 × 35%). CCS must pay a 35 percent tax on the least of (a) $40,000 (recognized built-in gain on inventory), (b) $20,000 (initial net unrealized gain), and (c) $4,000 (taxable income computed as if CCS was a C corporation for 2010). Because the tax was limited due to the taxable income limitation, the excess gain of $16,000 ($20,000 recognized built-in gain minus $4,000 gain on which CCS paid tax) is treated as a recognized built-in gain in 2011.

## Excess Net Passive Income Tax

If an S corporation previously operated as a C corporation *and* has accumulated earnings and profits at the end of the year from a prior C corporation year, it may be subject to the *excess net passive income tax*.[45] Congress created this tax to encourage S corporations to distribute their accumulated earnings and profits from prior C corporation years. It does not apply to S corporations that never operated as a C corporation, or to S corporations without earnings and profits from prior C corporation years.

The tax is levied on the S corporation's **excess net passive income,** computed as follows:

$$\text{Excess net passive income} =$$
$$\frac{\text{Net passive}}{\text{investment income}} \times \frac{\text{Passive investment income} - (25\% \times \text{Gross receipts})}{\text{Passive investment income}}$$

[45]§1375.

**THE KEY FACTS**

**Excess Net Passive Income Tax**

- The excess net passive income tax applies only to S corporations that previously operated as C corporations *and* at the end of the year have accumulated earnings and profits from a prior C corporation year.

- This tax applies when passive investment income exceeds 25 percent of gross receipts.

- Passive investment income includes royalties, rents, dividends, interest (including tax-exempt interest), and annuities.

Note that an S corporation has excess net passive income only when (1) it has net passive investment income and (2) its passive investment income exceeds 25 percent of its gross receipts. For purposes of determining excess net passive income, *gross receipts* is the total amount of revenues (including passive investment income) received or accrued under the corporation's accounting method, and not reduced by returns, allowances, cost of goods sold, or deductions. Gross receipts also include capital gains and losses. As defined previously in the chapter, passive investment income includes royalties, rents, dividends, interest (including tax-exempt interest), and annuities (but not capital gains and losses). **Net passive investment income** is passive investment income decreased by any expenses connected with producing that income.

The excess net passive income tax is imposed on excess net passive income at the highest corporate tax rate (currently 35 percent). For purposes of computing the tax, excess net passive income is limited to taxable income computed as if the corporation were a C corporation (excluding net operating losses). The formula for determining the tax is:

$$\text{Excess net passive income tax} = 35\% \times \text{Excess net passive income}$$

Each item of passive investment income that flows through to shareholders is reduced by an allocable share of the excess net passive income tax. The portion of the tax allocated to each item of passive investment income is the amount of the item divided by the total amount of passive investment income.

The IRS may waive the excess net passive income tax in some circumstances, for example if the S corporation determined in good faith it did not have accumulated earnings and profits at the end of the tax year and within a reasonable period distributed earnings and profits it identified later.[46]

---

**Example 22-24**

During 2010 CCS reported the following income (see Exhibit 22-2):

|  | 2010 (S Corporation) |
|---|---|
| Sales revenue | $520,000 |
| Cost of goods sold | (115,000) |
| Salary to owners Nicole and Sarah | (90,000) |
| Employee wages | (50,000) |
| Depreciation expense | (20,000) |
| Miscellaneous expenses | (5,000) |
| Interest income | 6,000 |
| Dividend income | 3,000 |
| Overall net income | $249,000 |

What are CCS's passive investment income, net passive investment income, and gross receipts for 2010?

*(continued on page 22-25...)*

---

[46]§1375(d).

**Answer:** The amounts are $9,000 passive income ($6,000 interest income + $3,000 dividends); $9,000 net passive investment income (because CCS has $0 expenses in producing passive investment income); and $529,000 gross receipts ($520,000 sales revenue + $3,000 dividends + $6,000 interest income).

What is CCS's excess net passive income tax in 2010, if any?

**Answer:** Zero. CCS has accumulated earnings and profits from 2009 (See Exhibit 22-2), but it owes zero excess net passive income tax because its passive investment income is less than 25 percent of its gross receipts [$9,000 < $132,250 ($529,000 × 25%)].

*What if:* Suppose CCS has passive investment income of $180,000 ($120,000 interest + $60,000 dividends), expenses associated with the passive investment income of $20,000, and gross receipts of $700,000 ($520,000 + $180,000). Also, if CCS were a C corporation, its taxable income would have been $249,000; assume it had accumulated earnings and profits of $40,000. What is CCS's excess net passive income tax, if any? What effect, if any, would the excess net passive income tax have on interest and dividends allocated to the shareholders?

**Answer:** The base for the tax is limited to the lesser of (a) excess net passive income of $4,444 [($180,000 passive investment income minus $20,000 expenses associated with passive investment income) × ($180,000 − $700,000 × 25%)/$180,000] or $249,000 (CCS's taxable income if it had been a C corporation). Thus, the base for the tax is limited to $4,444, and the tax is $1,556 (35% × $4,444).

Interest and dividends allocated to the shareholders will be reduced by the excess net passive income tax. The interest income allocated to shareholders will be reduced by $1,037 [$1,556 tax × ($120,000 interest/$180,000 total passive investment income)], and dividend income will be reduced by $519 [$1,556 tax × ($60,000 dividend/$180,000)].

*What if:* Suppose CCS has passive investment income of $180,000, expenses associated with the passive investment income of $20,000, and gross receipts of $700,000 ($520,000 + $180,000). Also, if CCS were a C corporation, its taxable income would have been $2,000; assume it had accumulated earnings and profits of $40,000. What is CCS's excess net passive income tax, if any?

**Answer:** The base for the tax is limited to the lesser of (a) excess net passive investment income of $4,444 [$160,000 × ($180,000 − 25% × $700,000)/$180,000] or (b) $2,000 (taxable income if CCS had been a C corporation). So the tax is $700 (35% × $2,000).

Remember, if an S corporation pays the net excess passive income tax for three years in a row, its S election will be terminated by the excess passive income test.

## LIFO Recapture Tax

C corporations that elect S corporation status and use the LIFO inventory method are subject to the *LIFO recapture tax*. The purpose of this tax is to prevent former C corporations from avoiding built-in gains tax by using the LIFO method of accounting for their inventories.

Specifically, the C corporation must include the **LIFO recapture amount** in its gross income in the last year it operates as a C corporation.[47] That amount equals the excess of the inventory basis computed using the FIFO method over the inventory basis computed using the LIFO method at the end of the corporation's last tax year as a C corporation. In addition to being included in gross income (and taxed at

[47]§1363(d).

the C corporation's marginal tax rate), the LIFO recapture amount also increases the corporation's adjusted basis in its inventory at the time it converts to an S corporation. The basis increase reduces the amount of net unrealized gain subject to the built-in gains tax.

The corporation pays the LIFO recapture tax (technically a C corporation tax) in four annual installments. The first installment is due on or before the due date (not including extensions) of the corporation's last *C corporation* tax return. The final three annual installments are due each year on or before the due date (not including extensions) of the *S corporation*'s tax return.

The LIFO recapture tax does not preclude the S corporation from using the LIFO method, but it obviously does accelerate the gain attributable to differences between LIFO and FIFO for inventory existing at the time of the S corporation election.

---

### Example 22-25

**What if:** Suppose CCS uses the LIFO method of accounting for its inventory. Assume that at the end of 2009, the basis of the inventory under the LIFO method was $90,000. Under the FIFO method, the basis of the inventory would have been $100,000. Finally, regular taxable income in 2009 was $40,000. What amount of LIFO recapture tax must CCS pay?

**Answer:** CCS must pay $1,500 [($100,000 FIFO inventory basis − $90,000 LIFO inventory basis) × 15 percent]. The 15 percent tax rate is the marginal rate at which the additional $10,000 of income would have been taxed in 2009 under the corporate tax rate schedule. CCS would increase its basis in its inventory by $10,000 to $100,000 as of the end of 2009, its last year as a C corporation. This would reduce the unrealized net built-in gain on the inventory.

When is CCS required to pay the tax?

**Answer:** CCS must pay $375 by March 15, 2010; $375 by March 15, 2011; $375 by March 15, 2012; and $375 by March 15, 2013. March 15 is the annual tax return due date without extensions (see discussion below).

**What if:** Assume the same facts as above except CCS's regular taxable income from 2009 was $700,000. What amount of LIFO recapture tax is CCS required to pay?

**Answer:** CCS must pay $3,400 [($100,000 FIFO inventory basis − $90,000 LIFO inventory basis) × 34 percent]. The 34 percent tax rate is the marginal rate at which the additional $10,000 of income would have been taxed in 2009 under the corporate tax rate schedule. CCS must pay $850 by March 15 of 2010, 2011, 2012, and 2013.

---

### Estimated Taxes

The estimated tax rules for S corporations generally follow the rules for C corporations: S corporations with a federal income tax liability of $500 or more due to the built-in gains tax or excess net passive income tax must estimate their tax liability for the year and pay it in four quarterly estimated installments. However, an S corporation is not required to make estimated tax payments for the LIFO recapture tax.[48]

---

[48]Rev. Proc. 94-61, IRB 1994-38,56.

**EXHIBIT 22-3, PART I** CCS's Form 1120S, page 1

| Form **1120S** | | **U.S. Income Tax Return for an S Corporation** | | OMB No. 1545-0130 |
|---|---|---|---|---|

Department of the Treasury
Internal Revenue Service

► Do not file this form unless the corporation has filed or is attaching Form 2553 to elect to be an S corporation.
► See separate instructions.

**20 09**

For calendar year 2009 or tax year beginning , 2009, ending , 20

| **A** S election effective date **January 1, 2010** | Use IRS label. Other-wise, print or type. | Name **Color Comfort Sheets** | **D** Employer identification number **24-4681012** |
|---|---|---|---|
| **B** Business activity code number *(see instructions)* **314000** | | Number, street, and room or suite no. If a P.O. box, see instructions. **375 East 450 South** | **E** Date incorporated **January 1, 2009** |
| **C** Check if Sch. M-3 attached ☐ | | City or town, state, and ZIP code **Salt Lake City, UT 84103** | **F** Total assets *(see instructions)* $ **370,000** |

**G** Is the corporation electing to be an S corporation beginning with this tax year? ☑ Yes ☐ No   If "Yes," attach Form 2553 if not already filed

**H** Check if: **(1)** ☐ Final return  **(2)** ☐ Name change  **(3)** ☐ Address change
**(4)** ☐ Amended return  **(5)** ☐ S election termination or revocation

**I** Enter the number of shareholders who were shareholders during any part of the tax year . . . . . . . . . ►

**Caution.** *Include* **only** *trade or business income and expenses on lines 1a through 21. See the instructions for more information.*

| Income | | | | | | | |
|---|---|---|---|---|---|---|---|
| | **1a** | Gross receipts or sales | $520,000 | **b** Less returns and allowances | | **c** Bal ► **1c** | $520,000 |
| | **2** | Cost of goods sold (Schedule A, line 8) . . . . . . . . . . . | | | | **2** | 115,000 |
| | **3** | Gross profit. Subtract line 2 from line 1c . . . . . . . . . . | | | | **3** | 405,000 |
| | **4** | Net gain (loss) from Form 4797, Part II, line 17 *(attach Form 4797)* . . . . . | | | | **4** | |
| | **5** | Other income (loss) *(see instructions—attach statement)* . . . . . . . . | | | | **5** | |
| | **6** | **Total income (loss).** Add lines 3 through 5 . . . . . . . . . . ► | | | | **6** | $405,000 |

| Deductions (see instructions for limitations) | | | | |
|---|---|---|---|---|
| | **7** | Compensation of officers . . . . . . . . . . . . . . . . | **7** | $90,000 |
| | **8** | Salaries and wages (less employment credits) . . . . . . . . . | **8** | 50,000 |
| | **9** | Repairs and maintenance . . . . . . . . . . . . . . . | **9** | |
| | **10** | Bad debts . . . . . . . . . . . . . . . . . . . | **10** | |
| | **11** | Rents . . . . . . . . . . . . . . . . . . . . | **11** | |
| | **12** | Taxes and licenses . . . . . . . . . . . . . . . . | **12** | |
| | **13** | Interest . . . . . . . . . . . . . . . . . . . . | **13** | |
| | **14** | Depreciation not claimed on Schedule A or elsewhere on return *(attach Form 4562)* . . . . . | **14** | 20,000 |
| | **15** | Depletion **(Do not deduct oil and gas depletion.)** . . . . . . . . | **15** | |
| | **16** | Advertising . . . . . . . . . . . . . . . . . . . | **16** | |
| | **17** | Pension, profit-sharing, etc., plans . . . . . . . . . . . . | **17** | |
| | **18** | Employee benefit programs . . . . . . . . . . . . . . | **18** | |
| | **19** | Other deductions *(attach statement)* . . . . . . . . . . . | **19** | 5,000 |
| | **20** | **Total deductions.** Add lines 7 through 19 . . . . . . . . . ► | **20** | 165,000 |
| | **21** | **Ordinary business income (loss).** Subtract line 20 from line 6 . . . . . . . | **21** | $240,000 |

| Tax and Payments | | | | | |
|---|---|---|---|---|---|
| | **22a** | Excess net passive income or LIFO recapture tax *(see instructions)* . . | **22a** | | |
| | **b** | Tax from Schedule D (Form 1120S) . . . . . . . . . | **22b** | | |
| | **c** | Add lines 22a and 22b *(see instructions for additional taxes)* . . . | | | **22c** |
| | **23a** | 2009 estimated tax payments and 2008 overpayment credited to 2009 | **23a** | | |
| | **b** | Tax deposited with Form 7004 . . . . . . . . . . . | **23b** | | |
| | **c** | Credit for federal tax paid on fuels *(attach Form 4136)* . . . . | **23c** | | |
| | **d** | Add lines 23a through 23c . . . . . . . . . . . . . | | | **23d** |
| | **24** | Estimated tax penalty *(see instructions)*. Check if Form 2220 is attached . . . . . . . ► ☐ | | | **24** |
| | **25** | **Amount owed.** If line 23d is smaller than the total of lines 22c and 24, enter amount owed . . | | | **25** |
| | **26** | **Overpayment.** If line 23d is larger than the total of lines 22c and 24, enter amount overpaid . . | | | **26** |
| | **27** | Enter amount from line 26 **Credited to 2010 estimated tax** ► | Refunded ► | | **27** |

| **Sign Here** | Under penalties of perjury, I declare that I have examined this return, including accompanying schedules and statements, and to the best of my knowledge and belief, it is true, correct, and complete. Declaration of preparer (other than taxpayer) is based on all information of which preparer has any knowledge. | May the IRS discuss this return with the preparer shown below *(see instructions)?* ☐ Yes ☐ No |
|---|---|---|
| | ► Signature of officer        Date     ► Title | |

| **Paid Preparer's Use Only** | Preparer's signature ► | Date | Check if self-employed ☐ | Preparer's SSN or PTIN |
|---|---|---|---|---|
| | Firm's name (or yours if self-employed), address, and ZIP code ► | | EIN | |
| | | | Phone no. | |

**For Privacy Act and Paperwork Reduction Act Notice, see separate instructions.**   Cat. No. 11510H   Form **1120S** (2009)

**EXHIBIT 22-3, PART II**   CCS's 2010 partial Schedule K (2009 forms because 2010 forms were unavailable)

| Schedule K | Shareholders' Pro Rata Share Items | | | | Total amount |
|---|---|---|---|---|---|
| 1 | Ordinary business income (loss) (page 1, line 21) . . . . . . . . . . . . . | | | 1 | $240,000 |
| 2 | Net rental real estate income (loss) (*attach Form 8825*) . . . . . . . . . . | | | 2 | |
| 3a | Other gross rental income (loss) . . . . . . . . . | 3a | | | |
| b | Expenses from other rental activities (*attach statement*) . . . | 3b | | | |
| c | Other net rental income (loss). Subtract line 3b from line 3a . . . . . . . . . | | | 3c | |
| 4 | Interest income . . . . . . . . . . . . . . . . . . . | | | 4 | 6,000 |
| 5 | Dividends: **a** Ordinary dividends . . . . . . . . . . . . . . . . | | | 5a | 3,000 |
| | **b** Qualified dividends . . . . . . . . . | 5b | 3,000 | | |
| 6 | Royalties . . . . . . . . . . . . . . . . . . . . . | | | 6 | |
| 7 | Net short-term capital gain (loss) (*attach Schedule D (Form 1120S)*) . . . . . . . . | | | 7 | |
| 8a | Net long-term capital gain (loss) (*attach Schedule D (Form 1120S)*) . . . . . . . . | | | 8a | |
| b | Collectibles (28%) gain (loss) . . . . . . . . . | 8b | | | |
| c | Unrecaptured section 1250 gain (*attach statement*) . . . . | 8c | | | |
| 9 | Net section 1231 gain (loss) (*attach Form 4797*) . . . . . . . . . . . . . | | | 9 | |
| 10 | Other income (loss) (*see instructions*)   . .   Type ▶ | | | 10 | |

(left margin label: Income (Loss))

## Filing Requirements

S corporations are required to file **Form 1120S,** U.S. Income Tax Return for an S Corporation, with the IRS by the 15th day of the third month after the S corporation's year end (for example, March 15 for a calendar-year-end S corporation). S corporations may receive an automatic, six-month extension by filing **Form 7004** with the IRS prior to the original due date of the return.[49] Thus, the extended due date of an S corporation tax return is generally September 15.

Exhibit 22-3 presents page 1 of CCS's Form 1120S (for its 2010 activities), CCS's partial Schedule K, and Nicole's K-1 (we use 2009 forms because 2010 forms were unavailable at the time this book went to press). Note the K-1 from the 1120S is different from the K-1 of the 1065. In contrast to the 1065 Schedule K-1, the 1120S Schedule K-1 does not report self-employment income, does not allocate entity-level debt to shareholders, and does not allow for shareholders to have profit-and-loss-sharing ratios that are different from shareholders' percentage of stock ownership.

[49]Under §6698, late-filing penalties apply if the S corporation fails to file by the normal or extended due date for the return.

**EXHIBIT 22-3, PART III**    Nicole's 2010 Schedule K-1 (2009 forms because 2010 forms were unavailable)

671109

| | |
|---|---|
| ☐ Final K-1 | ☐ Amended K-1    OMB No. 1545-0130 |

**Schedule K-1**
**(Form 1120S)**
Department of the Treasury
Internal Revenue Service

**20**09

For calendar year 2009, or tax
year beginning _____ , 2009
ending _____ , 20 _____

**Shareholder's Share of Income, Deductions, Credits, etc.**    ▶ See back of form and separate instructions.

| **Part I** | **Information About the Corporation** |
|---|---|

**A**   Corporation's employer identification number
24-4681012

**B**   Corporation's name, address, city, state, and ZIP code
**Color Comfort Sheets**
**375 East 450 South**
**Salt Lake City, UT 84103**

**C**   IRS Center where corporation filed return
Ogden, UT

| **Part II** | **Information About the Shareholder** |
|---|---|

**D**   Shareholder's identifying number
123-45-9876

**E**   Shareholder's name, address, city, state, and ZIP code
**Nicole Johnson**
**811 East 8320 South**
**Sandy, UT 84094**

**F**   Shareholder's percentage of stock
ownership for tax year    _____ 33.33333 %

For IRS Use Only

| **Part III** | **Shareholder's Share of Current Year Income, Deductions, Credits, and Other Items** | | |
|---|---|---|---|
| **1** Ordinary business income (loss)    $80,000 | | **13** Credits | |
| **2** Net rental real estate income (loss) | | | |
| **3** Other net rental income (loss) | | | |
| **4** Interest income    $2,000 | | | |
| **5a** Ordinary dividends    $1,000 | | | |
| **5b** Qualified dividends    $1,000 | | **14** Foreign transactions | |
| **6** Royalties | | | |
| **7** Net short-term capital gain (loss) | | | |
| **8a** Net long-term capital gain (loss) | | | |
| **8b** Collectibles (28%) gain (loss) | | | |
| **8c** Unrecaptured section 1250 gain | | | |
| **9** Net section 1231 gain (loss) | | | |
| **10** Other income (loss) | | **15** Alternative minimum tax (AMT) items | |
| **11** Section 179 deduction | | **16** Items affecting shareholder basis | |
| **12** Other deductions | | | |
| | | **17** Other information | |
| * See attached statement for additional information. | | | |

For Paperwork Reduction Act Notice, see Instructions for Form 1120S.    Cat. No. 11520D    Schedule K-1 (Form 1120S) 2009

# COMPARING C AND S CORPORATIONS AND PARTNERSHIPS

Exhibit 22-4 compares tax consequences for C corporations, S corporations, and partnerships discussed in this chapter.

**EXHIBIT 22-4**   Comparison of Tax Consequences for C and S Corporations and Partnerships

| Tax Characteristic | C Corporation | S Corporation | Partnership |
|---|---|---|---|
| Forming or contributing property to an entity | No gain or loss on contribution of appreciated or depreciated property if transferors of property have control (as defined in §351) after transfer. | Same as C corporation. | Same as C and S corporations except no control requirement (§721 applies to partnerships). |
| Type of owner restrictions | No restrictions | Only individuals who are U.S. citizens or residents, certain trusts, and tax-exempt organizations. | No restrictions |
| Number of owner restrictions | No restrictions | Limited to 100 share-holders. (Family members and their estates count as one shareholder.) | Must have more than one owner. |
| Election | Default status if corporation under state law. | Must formally elect to have corporation taxed as S corporation. | Default status if unincorporated and have more than one owner. |
| Income and loss allocations | Not allocated to shareholders. | Income and loss flow through to owners based on ownership percentages. | Income and loss flow through to owners but may be allocated based on something other than ownership percentages (special allocations). |
| Entity debt included in stock (or partnership interest) basis | No | Generally no. However, loans made from shareholder to corporation create debt basis. Losses may be deducted to extent of stock basis and then debt basis. | Yes. All entity liabilities are allocated to basis of partners. |
| Loss limitations | Losses remain at corporate level. | Losses flow through but subject to basis limitation, at-risk limitation, and passive activity limitations. | Same as S corporations. |
| Self-employment income status of ordinary income allocations | Not applicable | Not self-employment income. | May be self-employment income depending on partner's status. |

*(continued)*

**EXHIBIT 22-4**    **Comparison of Tax Consequences for C and S Corporations and Partnerships (*concluded*)**

| Tax Characteristic | C Corporation | S Corporation | Partnership |
|---|---|---|---|
| Salary to owners permitted | Yes | Yes | Generally, no. Salary-type payments are guaranteed payments subject to self-employment tax. |
| Fringe benefits | Can pay nontaxable fringe benefits to owners. | Can pay nontaxable fringe benefits to owners who own two percent or less of stock. | May not pay nontaxable fringe benefits to owners. |
| Operating distributions: owner tax consequences | Taxable as dividends to extent of earnings and profits. | Generally not taxable to extent of owner's basis. | Same as S corporations. |
| Operating distributions: Entity tax consequences | Gain on distribution of appreciated property; no loss on distribution of depreciated property | Same as C corporations | Generally no gain or loss on distribution of property |
| Liquidating distributions | Corporation and shareholders generally recognize gain or loss on distributions. | Same as C corporations | Partnership and partners generally do not recognize gain or loss on liquidating distributions. |
| Entity-level taxes | Yes, based on corporate tax rate schedule. | Generally no, but may be required to pay built-in gains tax, excess passive investment income tax, or LIFO recapture tax if converting from C to S corporation. | No |
| Tax year | Last day of any month or 52-53 week year. | Generally calendar year. | Based on tax year of owners. |

# CONCLUSION

This chapter highlighted the rules specific to S corporations and compared S corporations to C corporations and partnerships. S corporations are a true hybrid entity: They share characteristics with C corporations (the legal protection of a corporation and the tax rules that apply in organizing and liquidating a corporation). They also share characteristics with partnerships (the flow through of the entity's income and loss to its owners, ability to make tax-free distributions to the extent of the owner's basis, and basis calculations for owners).

Although many S corporation attributes follow from the C corporation or partnership rules, several specific attributes unique to S corporations may be particularly important in choosing an entity form or operating an S corporation in a tax-efficient manner. These attributes include unique S corporation taxes, the rules for how debt enters into the basis calculations and loss limitation rules for S corporations, and the rules for how distributions are taxed for S corporations previously operating as C corporations.

# SUMMARY

**LO1**    Describe the requirements and process to elect S corporation status.

- Shareholders of S corporations are able to defer realized gains when they contribute property to the corporation if they have control of the corporation after the contribution.

- S corporations are limited in the type of owners they may have. Only individuals who are U.S. citizens or residents, certain trusts, and certain tax-exempt organizations may be shareholders of S corporations.

- S corporations may have no more than 100 shareholders. For this purpose, family members and their estates count as one shareholder. Family members include a common ancestor and her lineal descendants and their spouses (or former spouses).

- S corporations may have only one class of stock. The stock may have differences in voting rights between shares, but all stock must have identical rights with respect to corporate distribution and liquidation proceeds.

- The S corporation election is made on Form 2553. All shareholders on the date of the election must consent to the election.

- To be effective for the current year, the election must be filed in the prior tax year or within the first two and one-half months after the beginning of the year. Even then, the election may not be effective in certain circumstances.

**LO2**    Explain the events that terminate the S corporation election.

- The S corporation election may be voluntarily revoked by shareholders owning more than 50 percent of the S corporation stock. In general, revocations made within the first two and one-half months of the year are effective as of the beginning of the year and revocations after that date are effective on the first day of the next year. Alternatively, the shareholders may choose an alternate date that is not before the revocation election is filed.

- An S corporation's election is automatically terminated on the date it fails to meet the S corporation requirements.

- If an S corporation has earnings and profits from a previous C corporation year, its S election is terminated if it has passive investment income in excess of 25 percent of gross receipts for three consecutive years.

- When an S corporation election is terminated mid-year, the corporation files a short year tax return for the period it was an S corporation and a short year tax return for the portion of the year it was a C corporation. It can allocate the income on a per day basis or it may specifically identify the income to each period.

- When an S corporation's S election is terminated, it may not re-elect S status until the beginning of the fifth tax year after the tax year in which the election was terminated.

**LO3**    Describe operating issues relating to S corporation accounting periods and methods, and explain income and loss allocations and separately stated items.

- When C corporations elect to become S corporations, all prior accounting methods carry over to the S corporation.

- S corporations are generally required to use a calendar tax year.

- Income and losses are allocated to S corporation shareholders pro rata based on the number of outstanding shares each shareholder owns on each day of the tax year or, with shareholder consent, it may use its normal accounting rules to allocate income and loss to the shareholders.

- S corporations determine their ordinary business income and separately stated items for the year and allocate these to the shareholders during the year.

- Separately stated items are tax items treated differently at the shareholder level than a shareholder's share of ordinary business income.

Explain stock-basis calculations, loss limitations, determination of self-employment income, and fringe benefit rules that apply to S corporation shareholders.

**LO4**

- An S corporation's shareholder's initial basis in her stock is generally the basis of the property contributed to the corporation minus liabilities assumed by the corporation on the contribution.

- S corporation shareholders adjust their stock basis annually. They increase it for (in this order) contributions to the S corporation during the year and the shareholder's share of ordinary business income and separately stated income/gain items. They decrease it for distributions during the year, the shareholder's share of nondeductible expenses, and the shareholder's share of ordinary business loss and separately stated expense/loss items. The basis may not be reduced below zero.

- S corporation shareholders are not allowed to include the S corporation's debt in their stock basis. However, they are allowed to create *debt basis* for the amount of loans they make directly to the S corporation. Debt basis can absorb S corporation losses (see below).

- For an S corporation shareholder to deduct them, S corporation losses must clear three separate hurdles: (1) tax basis limitation in stock (and debt), (2) at-risk amount limitation, and (3) passive activity loss limitation.

- Losses suspended at a particular level remain suspended until the shareholder creates additional tax basis or at-risk amounts, clears the passive loss hurdle, or sells her stock in the S corporation.

- If a shareholder's stock and debt basis is reduced by loss allocations and then increased by subsequent income allocations, the income allocation first increases the debt basis to the debt's outstanding amount before increasing the stock basis.

- When an S corporation's S election is terminated, S shareholders can deduct their share of S corporation losses on the last day of the post-termination transition period as long as the losses are able to clear the three loss limitation hurdles.

- Allocation of ordinary business income is not self-employment income to S corporation shareholders.

- If S corporation shareholders are employees of the corporation, their wages are subject to employment taxes.

- Many fringe benefits that are nontaxable to other S corporation employees are taxable to employees who own more than 2 percent of the S corporation.

Apply the tax rules for S corporation operating distributions and liquidating distributions.

**LO5**

- Operating distributions from S corporations without accumulated earnings and profits from C corporation years are nontaxable to the extent of the shareholder's basis and then taxable as capital gain to the extent they exceed the shareholder's stock basis.

- Operating distributions from S corporations with accumulated earnings and profits from C corporation years are a nontaxable reduction in stock basis to the extent of the S corporation's accumulated adjustments account, a dividend to the extent of the corporation's earnings and profits, and then a nontaxable return of capital to the extent of the stock basis. Amounts in excess of the stock basis are capital gain.

- The accumulated adjustments account represents the cumulative income or losses for the period the corporation has been an S corporation.

- When S corporations distribute appreciated property to shareholders they must recognize gain on the distribution (the gain is allocated to the shareholders). When they distribute loss property, they are not allowed to deduct the losses. In either case, the fair market value of the property (reduced by liabilities) is the amount of the distribution to the shareholders.

- When an S election is terminated, cash distributions during the post-termination transition period are tax-free to the shareholder to the extent of the S corporation's accumulated adjustments account and the shareholder's stock basis.

- S corporations making liquidating distributions recognize gain or loss on the distributions. The gains or losses are allocated to the shareholders. The shareholders compare the amount received in the liquidating distribution to their stock basis to determine if they recognize gain or loss on the distributions.

**LO6** Describe the taxes that apply to S corporations, estimated tax requirements, and tax return filing requirements.

- S corporations that were formerly C corporations may be required to pay the built-in gains tax. The tax applies if the S corporation had a net unrealized built-in gain at the time it converted to an S corporation. It must pay the tax when it recognizes these net built-in gains during its first 10 years operating as an S corporation (first 7 years for asset sales in 2009 and 2010).
- The base for the tax is limited to the least of (1) the net of the recognized built-in gains and losses for the year, (2) the net unrealized built-in gains as of the date of the S election date less the net recognized built-in gains in previous years, and (3) the corporation's taxable income for the year using the C corporation tax rules (excluding the dividends received deduction and NOL deduction). The base is then reduced by any net operating loss (NOL) or capital loss carryovers from prior C corporation years.
- S corporations that were formerly C corporations and have C corporation earnings and profits must pay the excess net passive income tax when their passive investment income exceeds 25 percent of their gross receipts.
- The formula for the tax is 35 percent (the highest corporate tax rate) × (net passive investment income × [passive investment income − (25% × gross receipts)]/passive investment income).
- C corporations that elect to be taxed as S corporations and that use the LIFO method of accounting for inventories must pay the LIFO recapture tax. The tax is 35 percent times the excess of the inventory valued under the LIFO method over the inventory valued under the FIFO method at the time the S election became effective. The corporation pays one-quarter of the tax on its final C corporation tax return and the final three installments on its S corporation tax return for the first three years it is an S corporation.
- S corporations that must pay the built-in gains tax or the excess passive income tax generally must pay estimated taxes in four quarterly installments. They are not required to make estimated tax payments for the LIFO recapture tax.
- S corporations file Form 1120S by the 15th day of the third month after the tax year-end (generally March 15).
- S corporations may receive a six-month extension by filing Form 7004.
- On Form 1120S, S corporations report ordinary business income and separately stated items on Schedule K. Each shareholder's portion of items on the Schedule K is reported to the shareholder on her Schedule K-1.

## KEY TERMS

accumulated adjustments account (AAA) (22-18)

at-risk amount (22-14)

built-in gains tax (22-21)

built-in gains tax recognition period (22-21)

debt basis (22-13)

earnings and profits (E&P) (22-2)

excess net passive income (22-23)

excess net passive income tax (22-21)

Form 1120S (22-28)

Form 7004 (22-28)

gross receipts (22-6)

LIFO recapture amount (22-25)

LIFO recapture tax (22-21)

net passive investment income (22-24)

net unrealized built-in gain (22-21)

ordinary business income (loss) (22-9)

passive activity loss rules (22-15)

passive investment income (PII) (22-6)

post-termination transition period (PTTP) (22-14)

S corporation (22-2)

separately stated items (22-9)

Subchapter S (22-2)

## DISCUSSION QUESTIONS

1. **(LO1)** In general terms, how are C corporations different from and similar to S corporations?
2. **(LO1)** What are the limitations on the number and type of shareholders an S corporation may have? How are these limitations different from restrictions on the number and type of shareholders C corporations or partnerships may have?

3. **(LO1)**  Why can't large, publicly traded corporations be treated as S corporations?

4. **(LO1)**  How do the tax laws treat family members for purposes of limiting the number of owners an S corporation may have?

5. **(LO1)**  Super Corp. was organized under the laws of the state of Montana. It issued common voting stock and common nonvoting stock to its two shareholders. Is Super Corp. eligible to elect S corporation status? Why or why not?

6. **(LO1)**  Karen is the sole shareholder of a C corporation she formed last year. If she elects S corporation status this year on February 20, when will the election become effective and why? What if she had made the election on March 20?

7. **(LO1)**  JB Corporation is a C corporation owned 80 percent by Jacob and 20 percent by Bauer. Jacob would like JB to make an S election but Bauer is opposed to the idea. Can JB elect to be taxed as an S corporation without Bauer's consent? Explain.

8. **(LO1)**  In what circumstances could a calendar-year C corporation make an election on February 1, year 1, to be taxed as an S corporation in year 1 but not have the election effective until year 2?

9. **(LO2)**  Theodore, Alvin, and Simon are equal shareholders of Timeless Corp. (an S corporation). Simon wants to terminate the S election, but Theodore and Alvin disagree. Can Simon unilaterally elect to have the S election terminated? If not, what would Simon need to do to have the S election terminated?

10. **(LO2)**  Juanita is the sole shareholder of Belize Corporation (a calendar-year S corporation). She is considering revoking the S election. It is February 1, year 1. What options does Juanita have for timing the effective date of the S election revocation?

11. **(LO2)**  Describe the circumstances in which an S election may be involuntarily terminated.

12. **(LO2)**  Describe a situation in which a former C corporation that elected to be taxed as an S corporation may have its S election automatically terminated, but a similarly situated corporation that has always been taxed as an S corporation would not.

13. **(LO2)**  When a corporation's S election is terminated mid-year, what options does the corporation have for allocating the annual income between the S corporation short year and the C corporation short year?

14. **(LO2)**  On June 1, year 1, Jasper Corporation's S election was involuntarily terminated. What is the earliest Jasper may be taxed as an S corporation again? Are there any exceptions to the general rule? Explain.

15. **(LO3)**  Apple Union (AU), a C corporation with a March 31 year-end, uses the accrual method of accounting. If AU elects to be taxed as an S corporation, what will its year-end and method of accounting be (assuming no special elections)?

16. **(LO3)**  Compare and contrast the method of allocating income or loss to owners for partnerships and for S corporations.

17. **(LO3)**  Why must an S corporation report separately stated items to its shareholders? How is the character of a separately stated item determined? How does the S corporation report this information to each shareholder?

18. **(LO3)**  How do S corporations report dividends they receive? Are they entitled to a dividends received deduction? Why or why not?

19. **(LO4)**  Shawn receives stock in an S corporation when it is formed by contributing land with a tax basis of $50,000 and encumbered by a $20,000 mortgage. What is Shawn's initial basis in his S corporation stock?

20. **(LO4)**  Why is a shareholder's basis in an S corporate stock adjusted annually?

21. **(LO4)** What adjustments are made annually to a shareholder's basis in S corporation stock and in what order? What impact do these adjustments have on a subsequent sale of stock?

22. **(LO4)** Can a shareholder's basis in S corporation stock ever be adjusted to a negative number? Why or why not?

23. **(LO4)** Describe the three hurdles a taxpayer must pass if he wants to deduct a loss from his share in an S corporation.

24. **(LO4)** Is a shareholder allowed to increase her basis in her S corporation stock by her share of the corporation's liabilities, as partners are able to increase the basis of their ownership interest by their share of partnership liabilities? Explain.

25. **(LO4)** How does a shareholder create *debt basis* in an S corporation? How is debt basis similar and dissimilar to stock basis?

26. **(LO4)** When an S corporation shareholder has suspended losses due to the tax basis or at-risk limitation, is he allowed to deduct the losses if the S corporation status is terminated? Why or why not?

27. **(LO4)** When considering C corporations, the IRS checks to see whether salaries paid are too large. In S corporations, however, it usually must verify that salaries are large enough. Account for this difference.

28. **(LO4)** How does the tax treatment of employee fringe benefits reflect the hybrid nature of the S corporation?

29. **(LO4)** If a corporation has been an S corporation since inception, describe how its operating distributions to its shareholders are taxed to the shareholders.

30. **(LO4)** How are the tax consequences of a cash distribution different from those of a noncash property distribution to both the corporation and the shareholders?

31. **(LO5)** What role does debt basis play in determining the taxability of operating distributions to shareholders?

32. **(LO5)** What does the accumulated adjustments account represent? How is it adjusted year by year? Can it have a negative balance?

33. **(LO5)** If an S corporation with accumulated E&P makes a distribution, from what accounts (and in what order) is the distribution deemed to be paid from?

34. **(LO5)** Under what circumstances could a corporation with earnings and profits make a tax-free distribution to its shareholders after the S election termination?

35. **(LO5)** How do the tax consequences of S corporation liquidating distributions differ from the tax consequences of S corporation operating distributions at both the corporate and shareholder levels?

36. **(LO6)** When is an S corporation required to pay a built-in gains tax?

37. **(LO6)** When is an S corporation required to pay the excess net passive income tax?

38. **(LO6)** Is the LIFO recapture tax a C corporation tax or an S corporation tax? Explain.

39. **(LO6)** When must an S corporation make estimated tax payments?

40. **(LO6)** On what form does an S corporation report its income to the IRS? When is the tax return due? What information does the S corporation provide to shareholders to allow them to complete their tax returns?

41. **(LO6)** Compare and contrast S corporations, C corporations, and partnerships in terms of tax consequences at formation, shareholder restrictions, income allocation, basis calculations, compensation to owners, taxation of distributions, and accounting periods.

# PROBLEMS

42. **(LO1)** Julie wants to create an S corporation called J's Dance Shoes (JDS). Describe how the items below affect her eligibility for an S election.

   a. Because Julie wants all her shareholders to have an equal say in the future of JDS, she gives them equal voting rights and decides shareholders who take a more active role in the firm will have priority in terms of distribution and liquidation rights.

   b. Julie decides to incorporate under the state laws of Utah, since that is where she lives. Once she gets her business up and running, however, she plans on doing extensive business in Mexico.

43. **(LO1)** Lucy and Ricky Ricardo live in Los Angeles, California. After they were married, they started a business named ILL Corporation (a C corporation). For state law purposes, the shares of stock in ILL Corp. are listed under Ricky's name only. Ricky signed the Form 2553 electing to have ILL taxed as an S corporation for federal income tax purposes, but Lucy did not sign. Given that California is a community property state, is the S election for ILL Corp. valid?

   ■
   ■ **research**
   ■■

44. **(LO1)** Jane has been operating Mansfield Park as a C corporation and decides she would like to make an S election. What is the earliest the election will become effective under each of these alternative scenarios?

   a. Jane is on top of things and makes the election on January 1, 2010.

   b. Jane is mostly on top of things and makes the election on January 15, 2010.

   c. Jane makes the election on February 10, 2010. She needed a little time to convince a C corporation shareholder to sell its stock to a qualifying shareholder. That process took all of January, and she was glad to have it over with.

   d. Jane makes the election on March 14, 2010.

   e. Jane makes the election on February 5, 2010. One of the shareholders refused to consent to the S election. He has since sold his shares (on January 15, 2010) to another shareholder who approved the idea. But he never did consent to the election.

45. **(LO2)** Missy is one of 100 unrelated shareholders of Dalmatian, an S corporation. She is considering selling her shares. Under the following alternative scenarios, would the S election be terminated? Why or why not?

   a. Missy wants to sell half her shares to a friend, a U.S. citizen, so they can rename their corporation 101 Dalmatians.

   b. Missy's mother's family wants to be involved with the corporation. Missy splits half her shares evenly among her aunt, uncle, grandfather, and two cousins.

   c. Missy sells half her Dalmatian stock to her husband's corporation.

46. **(LO2)** Cathy, Heathcliff, and Isabelle are equal shareholders in Wuthering Heights (WH), an S corporation. Heathcliff has decided he would like to terminate the S election. In the following alternative scenarios, indicate whether the termination will occur and indicate the date if applicable (assume no alternative termination dates are selected).

   a. Cathy and Isabelle both decline to agree to the termination. Heathcliff files the termination election anyway on March 14, 2010.

   b. Isabelle agrees with the termination, but Cathy strongly disagrees. The termination is filed on February 16, 2010.

c. The termination seems to be the first thing all three could agree on. They file the election to terminate on March 28, 2010.

d. The termination seems to be the first thing all three could agree on. They file the election to terminate on February 28, 2010.

e. Knowing the other two disagree with the termination, on March 16, 2010, Heathcliff sells one of his 50 shares to his maid, who recently moved back to Bulgaria, her home country.

47. **(LO2)** Assume the following S corporations and gross receipts, passive investment income, and corporate E&P. Will any of these corporations have its S election terminated due to excessive passive income? If so, in what year? All became S corporations at the beginning of year 1.

a. Clarion Corp.

| Year | Gross Receipts | Passive Investment Income | Corporate Earnings and Profits |
|---|---|---|---|
| 1 | $1,353,458 | $250,000 | $321,300 |
| 2 | $1,230,389 | $100,000 | $321,300 |
| 3 | $1,139,394 | $300,000 | $230,000 |
| 4 | $1,347,039 | $350,000 | $100,000 |
| 5 | $1,500,340 | $400,000 | $ 0 |

b. Chanson Corp.

| Year | Gross Receipts | Passive Investment Income | Corporate Earnings and Profits |
|---|---|---|---|
| 1 | $1,430,000 | $247,000 | $138,039 |
| 2 | $ 700,380 | $200,000 | $100,000 |
| 3 | $ 849,000 | $190,000 | $100,000 |
| 4 | $ 830,000 | $210,000 | $ 80,000 |
| 5 | $1,000,385 | $257,390 | $ 80,000 |

c. Caillou Corp.

| Year | Gross Receipts | Passive Investment Income | Corporate Earnings and Profits |
|---|---|---|---|
| 1 | $1,000,458 | $250,000 | $0 |
| 2 | $ 703,000 | $300,480 | $0 |
| 3 | $ 800,375 | $400,370 | $0 |
| 4 | $ 900,370 | $350,470 | $0 |
| 5 | $ 670,000 | $290,377 | $0 |

d. Colline Corp.

| Year | Gross Receipts | Passive Investment Income | Corporate Earnings and Profits |
|---|---|---|---|
| 1 | $1,100,370 | $250,000 | $500 |
| 2 | $ 998,000 | $240,000 | $400 |
| 3 | $ 800,350 | $230,000 | $300 |
| 4 | $ 803,000 | $214,570 | $200 |
| 5 | $ 750,000 | $200,000 | $100 |

48. **(LO2)** Hughie, Dewey, and Louie are equal shareholders in HDL, an S corporation. HDL's S election terminates under each of the following alternative scenarios. When is the earliest it can again operate as an S corporation?

a. The S election terminates on August 1, year 2, because Louie sells half his shares to his uncle Walt, a citizen and resident of Scotland.

b.  The S election terminates effective January 1, year 3, because on August 1, year 2, Hughie and Dewey vote (2 to 1) to terminate the election.

49. **(LO3)** Winkin, Blinkin, and Nod are equal shareholders in SleepEZ, an S corporation. In the conditions listed below, how much income should each report from SleepEZ for 2010 under both the daily allocation and the specific identification allocation method? Refer to the following table for the timing of SleepEZ's income.

| Period | Income |
|---|---|
| January 1 through March 15 (74 days) | $125,000 |
| March 16 through December 31 (291 days) | 345,500 |
| January 1 through December 31, 2010 (365 days) | $470,500 |

a.  There are no sales of SleepEZ stock during the year.
b.  On March 15, 2010, Blinkin sells his shares to Nod.
c.  On March 15, 2010, Winkin and Nod each sell their shares to Blinkin.

**Use the following information to complete problems 50 and 51:**

| UpAHill Corporation (an S Corporation) Income Statement December 31, Year 1 and Year 2 | | |
|---|---|---|
| | **Year 1** | **Year 2** |
| Sales revenue | $175,000 | $310,000 |
| Cost of goods sold | (60,000) | (85,000) |
| Salary to owners Jack and Jill | (40,000) | (50,000) |
| Employee wages | (15,000) | (20,000) |
| Depreciation expense | (10,000) | (15,000) |
| Miscellaneous expenses | (7,500) | (9,000) |
| Interest income | 2,000 | 2,500 |
| Dividend income | 500 | 1,000 |
| Overall net income | $ 45,000 | $134,500 |

50. **(LO3)** Jack and Jill are owners of UpAHill, an S corporation. They own 25 and 75 percent, respectively.

a.  What amount of ordinary income and separately stated items are allocated to them for years 1 and 2 based on the information above?
b.  Complete UpAHill's Form 1120S, Schedule K, for year 1.
c.  Complete Jill's 1120S, Schedule K-1, for year 1.

51. **(LO3, LO4)** Assume Jack and Jill, 25 and 75 percent shareholders in UpAHill corporation, have tax bases in their shares at the beginning of year 1 of $24,000 and $56,000, respectively. Also assume no distributions were made. Given the income statement above, what are their tax bases in their shares at the end of year 1?

52. **(LO4)** Harry, Hermione, and Ron formed an S corporation called Bumblebore. Harry and Hermione both contributed cash of $25,000 to get things started. Ron was a bit short on cash but had a parcel of land valued at $60,000 (basis of $50,000) that he decided to contribute. The land was encumbered by a $35,000 mortgage. What tax bases will each of the three have in his or her stock of Bumblebore?

53. **(LO4)** Jessica is a one-third owner in Bikes-R-Us, an S corporation that experienced a $45,000 loss this year (year 1). If her stock basis is $10,000 at the beginning of the year, how much of this loss clears the hurdle for deductibility (assume at-risk limitation equals the tax basis limitation)? If she cannot deduct

the whole loss, what happens to the remainder? Is she able to deduct her entire loss if she sells her stock at year-end?

54. **(LO4)** Assume the same facts as in the previous problem, except that at the beginning of year 1 Jessica loaned Bikes-R-Us $3,000. In year 2, Bikes-R-Us reported ordinary income of $12,000. What amount is Jessica allowed to deduct in year 1? What are her stock and debt bases in the corporation at the end of year 1? What are her stock and debt bases in the corporation at the end of year 2?

55. **(LO4)** Birch Corp., a calendar-year corporation, was formed three years ago by its sole shareholder, James, who has operated it as an S corporation since its inception. Last year, James made a direct loan to Birch Corp. in the amount of $5,000. Birch Corp. has paid the interest on the loan but has not yet paid any principal. (Assume the loan qualifies as debt for tax purposes.) For the year, Birch experienced a $25,000 business loss. What amount of the loss clears the tax basis limitation, and what is James's basis in his Birch Corp. stock and Birch Corp. debt in each of the following alternative scenarios?

   a. At the beginning of the year, James's basis in his Birch Corp. stock was $45,000 and his basis in his Birch Corp. debt was $5,000.

   b. At the beginning of the year, James's basis in his Birch Corp. stock was $8,000 and his basis in his Birch Corp. debt was $5,000.

   c. At the beginning of the year, James's basis in his Birch Corp. stock was $0 and his basis in his Birch Corp. debt was $5,000.

**research**

56. **(LO4)** Timo is the sole owner of Jazz Inc., an S corporation. On October 31, 2010, Timo executed an unsecured demand promissory note of $15,000 and transferred the note to Jazz (Jazz could require Timo to pay it $15,000 on demand). When Timo transferred the note to Jazz, his tax basis in his Jazz stock was zero. On January 31, 2011, Timo paid the $15,000 to Jazz as required by the promissory note. For the taxable year ending December 31, 2010, Jazz incurred a business loss of $12,000. How much of the loss clears the stock and debt basis hurdles for deductibility?

57. **(LO4)** Chandra was the sole shareholder of Pet Emporium that was originally formed as an S corporation. When Pet Emporium terminated its S election on August 31, 2009, Chandra had a stock basis and an at-risk amount of zero. Chandra also had a suspended loss from Pet Emporium of $9,000. What amount of the suspended loss is Chandra allowed to deduct, and what is her basis in her Pet Emporium stock at the end of the post-termination transition period under the following alternative scenarios (assume Pet Emporium files for an extension to file its tax returns)?

   a. Chandra makes capital contributions of $7,000 on August 30, 2010, and $4,000 on September 14, 2010.

   b. Chandra makes capital contributions of $5,000 on September 1, 2010, and $5,000 on September 30, 2010.

   c. Chandra makes a capital contribution of $10,000 on August 31, 2010.

   d. Chandra makes a capital contribution of $10,000 on October 1, 2010.

**planning**

58. **(LO4)** Neil owns stock in two S corporations, Blue and Green. He actively participates in the management of Blue but maintains ownership in Green only as a passive investor. Neil has no other business investments. Both Blue and Green anticipate a loss this year, and Neil's basis in his stock of both corporations is zero. All else equal, if Neil plans on making a capital contribution to at least one of the corporations this year, to which firm should he contribute in order to increase his chances of deducting the loss allocated to him from the entity? Why?

59. **(LO4)** In the past several years, Shakira had loaned money to Shakira Inc. (an S corporation) to help the corporation keep afloat in a downturn. Her stock basis in the S corporation is now zero, and she had deducted $40,000 in losses that reduced her debt basis from $100,000 to $60,000. Things appear to be turning around this year, and Shakira Inc. repaid Shakira $20,000 of the $100,000 outstanding loan. What is Shakira's income, if any, on the partial loan repayment?

■ **research**
■■

60. **(LO4)** Adam Fleeman, a skilled carpenter, started a home improvement business with Tom Collins, a master plumber. Adam and Tom are concerned about the payroll taxes they will have to pay. Assume they form an S corporation and each earns a salary of $80,000 from the corporation; in addition, they expect their share of business profits to be $60,000 each. How much Social Security tax and Medicare tax (or self-employment tax) will Adam, Tom, and their corporation have to pay on their salary and profits?

61. **(LO4)** Using the facts in problem 60, could Adam and Tom lower their payroll tax exposure if they operated their business as a partnership? Why or why not?

■ **planning**

62. **(LO4)** Friends Jackie (0.5 percent owner), Jermaine (1 percent owner), Marlon (2 percent owner), Michael (86 percent owner), and Tito (10.5 percent owner) are shareholders in Jackson 5 Inc. (an S corporation). As employees of the company, they each receive health insurance ($10,000 per year benefit), dental insurance ($2,000 per year benefit), and free access to a workout facility located at company headquarters ($500 per year benefit). What are the tax consequences of these benefits for each shareholder and for Jackson 5 Inc.?

63. **(LO5)** Maple Corp., a calendar-year corporation, was formed three years ago by its sole shareholder, Brady, who immediately elected S corporation status. On December 31 of the current year, Maple distributed $30,000 cash to Brady. What is the amount and character of gain Brady must recognize on the distribution in each of the following alternative scenarios?

   a. At the time of the distribution, Brady's basis in his Maple Corp. stock was $35,000.

   b. At the time of the distribution, Brady's basis in his Maple Corp. stock was $8,000.

   c. At the time of the distribution, Brady's basis in his Maple Corp. stock was $0.

64. **(LO5)** Oak Corp., a calendar-year corporation, was formed three years ago by its sole shareholder, Glover, and has always operated as a C corporation. However, at the beginning of this year, Glover made a qualifying S election for Oak Corp., effective January 1. Oak Corp. did not have any C corporation earnings and profits on that date. On June 1, Oak Corp. distributed $15,000 to Glover. What is the amount and character of gain Glover must recognize on the distribution, and what is his basis in his Oak Corp. stock in each of the following alternative scenarios?

   a. At the time of the distribution, Glover's basis in his Oak Corp. stock was $35,000.

   b. At the time of the distribution, Glover's basis in his Oak Corp. stock was $8,000.

   c. At the time of the distribution, Glover's basis in his Oak Corp. stock was $0.

65. **(LO5)** Janna has a tax basis of $15,000 in her Mimikaki stock (Mimikaki has been an S corporation since inception). In 2010, Janna was allocated $20,000 of ordinary income from Mimikaki. What is the amount and

character of gain she recognizes from end of the year distributions in each of the following alternative scenarios, and what is her stock basis following each distribution?

a. Mimikaki distributes $10,000 to Janna.
b. Mimikaki distributes $20,000 to Janna.
c. Mimikaki distributes $30,000 to Janna.
d. Mimikaki distributes $40,000 to Janna.

66. **(LO5)** Assume the following year 2 income statement for Johnstone Corporation, which was a C corporation in year 1 and elected to be taxed as an S corporation beginning in year 2. Johnstone's earnings and profits at the end of year 1 were $10,000. Marcus is Johnstone's sole shareholder. What is Johnstone's accumulated adjustments account at the end of year 2, and what amount of dividend income does Marcus recognize on the year 2 distribution in each of the following alternative scenarios?

| Johnstone Corporation Income Statement December 31, Year 2 | |
|---|---|
| | Year 2 (S Corporation) |
| Sales revenue | $150,000 |
| Cost of goods sold | (35,000) |
| Salary to owners | (60,000) |
| Employee wages | (50,000) |
| Depreciation expense | (4,000) |
| Miscellaneous expenses | (4,000) |
| Interest income | 10,000 |
| Overall Net Income | $ 7,000 |

a. Johnstone distributed $6,000 to Marcus in year 2.
b. Johnstone distributed $10,000 to Marcus in year 2.
c. Johnstone distributed $16,000 to Marcus in year 2.
d. Johnstone distributed $26,000 to Marcus in year 2.

67. **(LO5)** At the end of the year, before distributions, Bombay (an S corporation) has an accumulated adjustments account balance of $15,000 and accumulated E&P of $20,000 from a previous year as a C corporation. During the year, Nicolette (a 40 percent shareholder) received a $20,000 distribution (the remaining shareholders received $30,000 in distributions). What is the amount and character of gain Nicolette must recognize from the distribution? What is her basis in her Bombay stock at the end of the year (assume her stock basis is $40,000 after considering her share of Bombay's income for the year but before considering the effects of the distribution)?

68. **(LO5)** Pine Corp., a calendar-year corporation, was formed three years ago by its sole shareholder, Connor, who has always operated it as a C corporation. However, at the beginning of this year, Connor made a qualifying S election for Pine Corp., effective January 1. Pine Corp. reported $70,000 of C corporation earnings and profits on the effective date of the S election. This year (its first S corporation year), Pine reported business income of $50,000. Connor's basis in his Pine Corp. stock at the beginning of the year was $15,000. What is the amount and character of gain Connor must recognize on the following

alternative distributions, and what is his basis in his Pine Corp. stock at the end of the year?

  a. Connor received a $40,000 distribution from Pine Corp. at the end of the year.

  b. Connor received a $60,000 distribution from Pine Corp. at the end of the year.

  c. Connor received a $130,000 distribution from Pine Corp. at the end of the year.

  d. Connor received a $150,000 distribution from Pine Corp. at the end of the year.

69. **(LO5)** Carolina Corporation, an S corporation, has no corporate E&P from its years as a C corporation. At the end of the year, it distributes a small parcel of land to its sole shareholder, Shadiya. The fair market value of the parcel is $70,000 and its tax basis is $40,000. Shadiya's basis in her stock is $14,000. Assume Carolina Corporation reported zero taxable income before considering the tax consequences of the distribution.

  a. What amount of gain or loss, if any, does Carolina Corporation recognize on the distribution?

  b. How much gain must Shadiya recognize (if any) as a result of the distribution, what is her basis in her Carolina Corporation stock after the distribution, and what is her basis in the land?

  c. What is your answer to (a) if the fair market value of the land is $25,000 rather than $70,000?

  d. What is your answer to (b) if the fair market value of the land is $25,000 rather than $70,000?

70. **(LO5)** Last year, Miley decided to terminate the S corporation election of her solely owned corporation on October 17, 2009 (effective immediately), in preparation for taking it public. At the time of the election, the corporation had an accumulated adjustments account balance of $150,000 and $450,000 of accumulated E&P from prior C corporation years, and Miley had a basis in her S corporation stock of $135,000. During 2010, Miley's corporation reported $0 taxable income or loss. Also, during 2010 the corporation made distributions to Miley of $80,000 and $60,000. How are these distributions taxed to Miley assuming the following?

  a. Both distributions are in cash, and the first was paid on June 15 and the second on November 15.

  b. Both distributions are in cash, and the first was paid on June 15 and the second on September 30.

  c. The same facts in (b) except the June 15 distribution was a property (non-cash) distribution (fair market value of distributed property equal to basis).

71. **(LO6)** Rivendell Corporation uses the accrual method of accounting and has the following assets as of the end of 2009. Rivendell converted to an S corporation on January 1, 2010.

| Asset | Adjusted Basis | FMV |
|---|---|---|
| Cash | $ 40,000 | $ 40,000 |
| Accounts receivable | 30,000 | 30,000 |
| Inventory | 130,000 | 60,000 |
| Land | 100,000 | 125,000 |
| Totals | $300,000 | $255,000 |

  a. What is Rivendell's net unrealized built-in gain at the time it converted to an S corporation?

b.  Assuming the land was valued at $200,000, what would be Rivendell's net unrealized gain at the time it converted to an S corporation?

c.  Assuming the original land value but that the inventory was valued at $85,000, what would be Rivendell's net unrealized gain at the time it converted to an S corporation?

72. **(LO6)** Virginia Corporation is a calendar-year corporation. At the beginning of 2010, its election to be taxed as an S corporation became effective. Virginia Corp.'s balance sheet at the end of 2009 reflected the following assets (it did not have any earnings and profits from its prior years as a C corporation).

| Asset | Adjusted Basis | FMV |
|---|---|---|
| Cash | $ 20,000 | $ 20,000 |
| Accounts receivable | 40,000 | 40,000 |
| Inventory | 90,000 | 200,000 |
| Land | 150,000 | 175,000 |
| Totals | $300,000 | $435,000 |

In 2010, Virginia reported business income of $50,000 (this would have been its taxable income if it were still a C corporation). What is Virginia's built-in gains tax in each of the following alternative scenarios?

a.  During 2010, Virginia sold inventory it owned at the beginning of the year for $100,000. The basis of the inventory sold was $55,000.

b.  Assume the same facts as (a), except Virginia had a net operating loss carryover of $24,000 from its time as a C corporation.

c.  Assume the same facts as (a), except that if Virginia were a C corporation, its taxable income would have been $1,500.

73. **(LO6)** Tempe Corporation is a calendar-year corporation. At the beginning of 2010, its election to be taxed as an S corporation became effective. Tempe Corp.'s balance sheet at the end of 2009 reflected the following assets (it did not have any earnings and profits from its prior years as a C corporation):

| Asset | Adjusted Basis | FMV |
|---|---|---|
| Cash | $ 20,000 | $ 20,000 |
| Accounts receivable | 40,000 | 40,000 |
| Inventory | 160,000 | 200,000 |
| Land | 150,000 | 120,000 |
| Totals | $370,000 | $380,000 |

Tempe's business income for the year was $40,000 (this would have been its taxable income if it were a C corporation).

a.  During 2010, Tempe sold all of the inventory it owned at the beginning of the year for $210,000. What is its built-in gains tax in 2010?

b.  Assume the same facts as in (a), except that if Tempe were a C corporation, its taxable income would have been $7,000. What is its built-in gains tax in 2010?

c.  Assume the original facts except the land was valued at $140,000 instead of $120,000. What is Tempe's built-in gains tax in 2010?

74. **(LO6)** Wood Corporation was a C corporation in 2009 but elected to be taxed as an S corporation in 2010. At the end of 2009, its earnings and profits were $15,500. The following table reports Wood's (taxable) income for 2010 (its first year as an S corporation).

**Wood Corporation**
**Income Statement**
**December 31, 2010**

| | |
|---|---:|
| Sales revenue | $150,000 |
| Cost of goods sold | (35,000) |
| Salary to owners | (60,000) |
| Employee wages | (50,000) |
| Depreciation expense | (4,000) |
| Miscellaneous expenses | (4,000) |
| Interest income | 8,000 |
| Dividend income | 2,000 |
| Overall net income | $   7,000 |

What is Wood Corporation's excess net passive income tax for 2010?

75. **(LO6)** Calculate Anaheim Corporation's excess net passive income tax in each of the following alternative scenarios:

a. Passive investment income, $100,000; expenses associated with passive investment income, $40,000; gross receipts, $120,000; taxable income if C corporation, $40,000; corporate E&P, $30,000.

b. Passive investment income, $100,000; expenses associated with passive investment income, $70,000; gross receipts, $120,000; taxable income if C corporation, $1,200; corporate E&P, $30,000.

c. Passive investment income, $100,000; expenses associated with passive investment income, $40,000; gross receipts, $120,000; taxable income if C corporation, $40,000; corporate E&P, $0.

76. **(LO5, LO6)** Mark is the sole shareholder of Tex Corporation. Mark first formed Tex as a C corporation. However, in an attempt to avoid having Tex's income double taxed, Mark elected S corporation status for Tex several years ago. On December 31, 2010, Tex reports $5,000 of earnings and profits from its years as a C corporation and $50,000 in its accumulated adjustments account from its activities as an S corporation (including its 2010 activities). Mark discovered that for the first time Tex was going to have to pay the excess net passive income tax. Mark wanted to avoid having to pay the tax but he determined the only way to avoid the tax was to eliminate Tex's E&P by the end of 2010. He determined that, because of the distribution ordering rules (AAA first), he would need to have Tex immediately (in 2010) distribute $55,000 to him. This would clear out Tex's accumulated adjustments account first and then eliminate Tex's C corporation earnings and profits in time to avoid the excess net passive income tax. Mark was not sure Tex could come up with $55,000 of cash or property in time to accomplish his objective. Does Mark have any other options to eliminate Tex's earnings and profits without first distributing the balance in Tex's accumulated adjustments account?

■ **planning**

■
■ **research**
■■

77. **(LO6)** Farve Inc. recently elected S corporation status. At the time of the election, the company had $10,000 of accumulated earnings and profits, and a net unrealized gain of $1,000,000 associated with land it had invested in (although some parcels had an unrealized loss). In the next couple of years, most of the income the company expects to generate will be in the form of interest and dividends (approximately $200,000 per year). However, in the future, the company will want to liquidate some of its current holdings in land and possibly reinvest in other parcels. What strategies can you recommend for Farve Inc. to help reduce its potential tax liability as an S corporation?

■ **planning**

78. **(LO6)** Until the end of year 0, Magic Carpets (MC) was a C corporation with a calendar year. At the beginning of year 1 it elected to be taxed as an S corporation. MC uses the LIFO method to value its inventory. At the end of year 0, under the LIFO method, its inventory of rugs was valued at $150,000. Under the FIFO method, the rugs would have been valued at $170,000. How much LIFO recapture tax must MC pay, and what is the due date of the first payment under the following alternative scenarios?

  a. Magic Carpets' regular taxable income in year 0 was $65,000.
  b. Magic Carpets' regular taxable income in year 0 was $200,000.

## COMPREHENSIVE PROBLEMS

■ planning

79. Knowshon, sole owner of Moreno Inc., is contemplating electing S status for the corporation. Provide recommendations related to Knowshon's election under the following alternative scenarios:

  a. At the end of the current year, Moreno Inc. has a net operating loss of $800,000 carryover. Beginning next year, the company expects to return to profitability. Knowshon projects that Moreno will report profits of $400,000, $500,000, and $600,000 over the next three years. What suggestions do you have regarding the timing of the S election? Explain.
  b. How would you answer (a) if Moreno Inc. had been operating profitably for several years and thus had no net operating loss?
  c. While several of Moreno Inc.'s assets have appreciated in value (to the tune of $2,000,000), the corporation has one property—some land in a newly identified flood zone—that has declined in value by $1,500,000. Knowshon plans on selling the loss property in the next year or two. Assume that Moreno does not have a net operating loss. What suggestions do you have for timing the sale of the flood zone property and why?

■ planning

80. Barry Potter and Winnie Weasley are considering making an S election on March 1, 2010, for their C corporation, Omniocular. However, first they want to consider the implications of the following information:

  • Winnie is a U.S. citizen and resident.
  • Barry is a citizen of the United Kingdom, but a resident of the United States.
  • Barry and Winnie each own 50 percent of the voting power in Omniocular. However, Barry's stock provides him with a claim on 60 percent of the Omniocular assets in liquidation.
  • Omniocular was formed under Arizona state law, but it plans on eventually conducting some business in Mexico.

  a. Is Omniocular eligible to elect S corporation status? If so, when is the election effective?

**For the remainder of the problem, assume Omniocular made a valid S election effective January 1, 2010. Barry and Winnie each own 50 percent of the voting power and have equal claim on Omniocular's assets in liquidation. In addition, consider the following information:**

  • Omniocular reports on a calendar tax year.
  • Omniocular's earnings and profits as of December 31, 2009, were $55,000.
  • Omniocular's 2009 taxable income was $15,000.

- Omniocular's assets at the end of 2009 are as follows:

| Omniocular Assets December 31, 2009 | | |
|---|---|---|
| Asset | Adjusted Basis | FMV |
| Cash | $ 50,000 | $ 50,000 |
| Accounts receivable | 20,000 | 20,000 |
| Investments in stocks and bonds | 700,000 | 700,000 |
| Investment in land | 90,000 | 100,000 |
| Inventory (LIFO) | 80,000* | 125,000 |
| Equipment | 40,000 | 35,000 |
| Totals | $980,000 | $1,030,000 |

*$110,000 under FIFO accounting.

- On March 31, 2010, Omniocular sold the land for $42,000.
- In 2010, Omniocular sold all the inventory it had on hand at the beginning of the year. This was the only inventory it sold during the year.

| Other Income/Expense Items for 2010 | |
|---|---|
| Sales revenue | $155,000 |
| Salary to owners | ($50,000) |
| Employee wages | ($10,000) |
| Depreciation expense | ($5,000) |
| Miscellaneous expenses | ($1,000) |
| Gain on sale of machinery | $12,000 |
| Interest income | $40,000 |
| Dividend income | $65,000 |

- Assume that if Omniocular were a C corporation for 2010, its taxable income would have been $88,500.

b. How much LIFO recapture tax is Omniocular required to pay and when is it due?

c. How much built-in gains tax, if any, is Omniocular required to pay?

d. How much excess net passive income tax, if any, is Omniocular required to pay?

e. Assume Barry's basis in his Omniocular stock was $40,000 on January 1, 2010. What is his stock basis on December 31, 2010?

**For the following questions, assume that after electing S corporation status Barry and Winnie had a change of heart and filed an election to terminate Omniocular's S election, effective August 1, 2011.**

- In 2011, Omniocular reported the following income/expense items:

| | January 1–July 31, 2011 (212 days) | August 1–December 31, 2011 (153 days) | January 1–December 31, 2011 |
|---|---|---|---|
| Sales revenue | $80,000 | $185,000 | $265,000 |
| Cost of goods sold | (40,000) | (20,000) | (60,000) |
| Salaries to Barry and Winnie | (60,000) | (40,000) | (100,000) |
| Depreciation expense | (7,000) | (2,000) | (9,000) |
| Miscellaneous expenses | (4,000) | (3,000) | (7,000) |
| Interest income | 6,000 | 5,250 | 11,250 |
| Overall net income (loss) | ($25,000) | $125,250 | $100,250 |

f.  For tax purposes, how would you recommend Barry and Winnie allocate income between the short S corporation year and the short C corporation year if they would like to minimize double taxation of Omnicular's income?

g.  Assume in part (f) that Omnicular allocates income between the short S and C corporation years in a way that minimizes the double taxation of its income. If Barry's stock basis in his Omnicular stock on January 1, 2011, is $50,000, what is his stock basis on December 31, 2011?

h.  When is the earliest tax year in which Omniocular can be taxed as an S corporation again?

81. Abigail, Bobby, and Claudia are equal owners in Lafter, an S corporation that was a C corporation several years ago. While Abigail and Bobby actively participate in running the company, Claudia has a separate day job and is a passive owner. Consider the following information for 2010:

- As of January 1, 2010, Abigail, Bobby, and Claudia each have a basis in Lafter stock of $15,000 and a debt basis of $0. On January 1, the stock basis is also the at-risk amount for each shareholder.
- Bobby and Claudia also are passive owners in Aggressive LLC, which allocated business income of $14,000 to each of them in 2010. Neither has any other source of passive income (besides Lafter, for Claudia).
- On March 31, 2010, Abigail lends $5,000 of her own money to Lafter.
- Anticipating the need for basis to deduct a loss, on April 4, 2010, Bobby takes out a loan using his car as collateral—he wants to limit his losses to the value of the automobile just in case he can't pay back the loan—to make a contribution of $10,000 to Lafter.
- Lafter has an accumulated adjustments account balance of $45,000 as of January 1, 2010.
- Lafter has C corporation earnings and profits of $15,000 as of January 1, 2010.
- During 2010, Lafter reports a business loss of $75,000, computed as follows:

| Sales revenue | $90,000 |
|---|---|
| Cost of goods sold | (85,000) |
| Salary to Abigail | (40,000) |
| Salary to Bobby | (40,000) |
| Business (loss) | ($75,000) |

- Lafter also reported $12,000 of tax-exempt interest income.

a.  What amount of Lafter's 2010 business loss of $75,000 tax loss are Abigail, Bobby, and Claudia allowed to deduct on their individual tax returns? What are each owner's stock basis and debt basis (if applicable) and each owner's at-risk amount with respect to the investment in Lafter at the end of 2010?

- During 2011, Lafter made several changes to its business approach and reported $18,000 of business income, computed as follows:

| Sales revenue | $208,000 |
|---|---|
| Cost of goods sold | (90,000) |
| Salary to Abigail | (45,000) |
| Salary to Bobby | (45,000) |
| Marketing expense | (10,000) |
| Business income | $ 18,000 |

- Lafter also reported a long-term capital gain of $24,000 in 2011.
- Lafter made a cash distribution on July 1, 2011, of $20,000 to each shareholder.

b.  What amount of gain/income does each shareholder recognize from the cash distribution on July 1, 2011?

82. While James Craig and his former classmate Paul Dolittle both studied accounting at school, they ended up pursuing careers in professional cake decorating. Their company, Good to Eat (GTE), specializes in custom-sculpted cakes for weddings, birthdays, and other celebrations. James and Paul formed the business at the beginning of 2009, and each contributed $50,000 in exchange for a 50 percent ownership interest. GTE also borrowed $200,000 from a local bank. Both James and Paul had to personally guarantee the loan. Both owners provide significant services for the business. The following information pertains to GTE's 2009 activities:

- GTE uses the cash method of accounting (for both book and tax purposes) and reports income on a calendar-year basis.
- GTE received $450,000 of sales revenue and reported $210,000 of cost of goods sold (it did not have any ending inventory).
- GTE paid $30,000 compensation to James, $30,000 compensation to Paul, and $40,000 of compensation to other employees (assume these amounts include applicable payroll taxes if any).
- GTE paid $15,000 of rent for a building and equipment, $20,000 for advertising, $14,000 in interest expense, $4,000 for utilities, and $2,000 for supplies.
- GTE contributed $5,000 to charity.
- GTE received a $1,000 qualifying dividend from a great stock investment (it owned 2 percent of the corporation distributing the dividend) and it recognized $1,500 in short-term capital gain when it sold some of the stock.
- On December 1, 2009, GTE distributed $30,000 to James and $30,000 to Paul.

**Required:**

a. Assume James and Paul formed GTE as an S corporation.

- Complete GTE's Form 1120S, page 1; Form 1120 S, Schedule K; and Paul's Form 1120S, Schedule K-1 (note that you should use 2009 tax forms).
- Compute the tax basis of Paul's stock in GTE at the end of 2009.
- What amount of Paul's income from GTE is subject to FICA or self-employment taxes?
- What amount of income, including its character, will Paul recognize on the $30,000 distribution he receives on December 1?
- What amount of tax does GTE pay on the $1,000 dividend it received?

b. Assume James and Paul formed GTE as an LLC.

- Complete GTE's Form 1065, page 1; Form 1065, Schedule K; and Paul's Form 1065, Schedule K-1 (note that you should use 2009 tax forms).
- Compute the tax basis of Paul's ownership interest in GTE at the end of 2009.
- What amount of Paul's income from GTE is subject to FICA or self-employment taxes?
- What amount of income, including its character, will Paul recognize on the $30,000 distribution he receives on December 1?
- What amount of tax does GTE pay on the $1,000 dividend it received?

c. Assume James and Paul formed GTE as a C corporation.

- Complete GTE's Form 1120, page 1 (note that you should use the 2009 tax form).
- Compute the tax basis of Paul's stock in GTE at the end of 2009.
- What amount of Paul's income from GTE is subject to FICA or self-employment taxes?
- What amount of income, including its character, will Paul recognize on the $30,000 distribution he receives on December 1?
- What amount of tax does GTE pay on the $1,000 dividend it received?

# chapter
# 23 State and Local Taxes

## Learning Objectives

**Upon completing this chapter, you should be able to:**

**LO 1** Describe the primary types of state and local taxes.

———————————————— ■ ————————————————

**LO 2** Determine whether a business has sales and use tax nexus and calculate its sales tax withholding responsibilities.

———————————————— ■ ————————————————

**LO 3** Identify whether a business has income tax nexus and determine its state income tax liabilities.

**Storyline Summary**

**Ken Brody**

*Location:*     Idaho

*Status:*     Sole owner of Wild West River Runners

*Situation:*     Ken owns retail stores in Idaho and Wyoming that sell merchandise locally; he must determine the company's state and local tax liabilities.

K en Brody owns Wild West River Runners, Incorporated (Wild West), an Idaho corporation. Wild West offers both guided white-water rafting adventures and retail sales of related equipment. It provides white-water rafting adventures in Idaho, Tennessee, Washington, and Wyoming; operates retail stores in Idaho and Wyoming; and runs an Internet-based retail store from Wyoming. Wild West's retail stores sell only locally (they never ship merchandise), but the salesclerks often refer customers to the Internet store (www.wildwestriverrunners.com). Most employees are teachers or college students during the school term; during the off-season, a few guides make sales visits with Ken and operate the retail stores. Ken attends the annual Raft and River show for 10 days each year in Phoenix, Arizona, and travels the country promoting Wild West's guided river adventures during the off-season.

Wild West's federal taxable income for the current year is $53,289, and it must determine its state and local tax liabilities. Because Wild West operates a multistate business, it must determine its sales and use tax withholding responsibilities and identify the states in which it must file returns. Once it makes these determinations, it must compute taxable income for each relevant state. ■

Like a lot of other businesses, Wild West is a multistate operation. From a business perspective, multistate businesses have access to a larger economic base than those operating in a single state. However, with this economic opportunity comes additional tax burdens.

## LO1  STATE AND LOCAL TAXES

The primary purpose of state and local taxes is to raise revenue to finance state governments. All 50 states and the District of Columbia have some combination of three primary revenue sources: sales and use tax, income or franchise tax, and property tax.[1]

This chapter focuses on sales and use taxes (excise taxes levied on the sale or use of tangible personal property within a state) and taxes based on *net* income (income taxes).[2]

Like federal tax law, state tax law includes legislative (state constitution and tax code), administrative (regulations and rulings), and judicial law (state and federal tax cases). While taxpayers deal with a single federal tax code, there are different tax codes for each state in which they are required to pay taxes. This makes state tax research particularly challenging. State tax agencies (such as the California Franchise Tax Board and New York Department of Finance and Taxation) administer the law and promulgate regulations for their particular states.[3] State and federal courts interpret the law when a state's tax authority and taxpayers cannot agree on its interpretation or constitutionality. Because of constitutionality questions, judicial law plays a significantly more important role in state tax law than in federal tax law.

It is impractical if not impossible to study each individual state statute in one text. Instead, this chapter addresses the most important state and local tax concepts.

The most important question Wild West, or any other taxpayer, must answer is whether it is subject to a state's taxing regime. The answer depends on the taxpayer's commercial domicile and whether the taxpayer has nexus in that state. **Commercial domicile** is the state where a business is headquartered and directs operations; this location may be different from the place of incorporation.[4] A business must always collect sales tax and pay income tax in the state where it is domiciled. **Nondomiciliary businesses** (businesses not domiciled in a state) are subject to tax only where they have nexus. **Nexus** is the sufficient (or minimum) connection between a business and a state that subjects the business to the state's tax system. The requirement for establishing nexus with a state depends on whether the tax is a sales and use tax, an income tax, or a nonincome-based tax. The nexus standard varies because the financial and administrative burdens vary across taxes. Sellers collect sales tax out of administrative convenience, but the sales tax burden belongs to the buyer in most states. In contrast, income tax is both owed and paid by the taxpayer earning the income.

Wild West's commercial domicile is Idaho because it is headquartered there, and it must collect and pay both Idaho sales tax and Idaho income tax. But as detailed in Exhibit 23-1, it has activities and sales in other states, so it must collect sales and use tax and pay income tax in the states in which it has nexus.

---

[1]State and local jurisdictions may also tax or levy the following: personal property, capital stock, business licensing, transfer taxes, incorporation, excise, severance, payroll, disability, unemployment, fuel, and telecommunication.

[2]This chapter discusses income and franchise taxes interchangeably. Franchise taxes are imposed for the right to conduct business within a state. Most franchise taxes (such as the California Franchise Tax) are net income based.

[3]A great resource for guidance and forms from specific states can be found on the Federation of Tax Administrator's Web site: www.taxadmin.org/fta/link/forms.html.

[4]Some companies (e.g., Hewlett-Packard) are incorporated in one state (e.g., Delaware) but domiciled or headquartered in another (e.g., California). These companies pay taxes in both (although sometimes just a capital stock tax applies in the state of incorporation if there are no activities other than incorporation within a state).

**EXHIBIT 23-1    Wild West's Activities and Sales by State**

| | | | Wild West In-State Activities | | |
|---|---|---|---|---|---|
| State | Sales | Employees | Property | Services | Commercial Domicile |
| Arizona | ✓ | | | | |
| California | ✓ | | | | |
| Colorado | ✓ | | | | |
| Idaho | ✓ | ✓ | ✓ | ✓ | ✓ |
| Tennessee | ✓ | ✓ | ✓ | ✓ | |
| Washington | ✓ | ✓ | ✓ | ✓ | |
| Wyoming | ✓ | ✓ | ✓ | ✓ | |

| | Wild West Sales | | |
|---|---|---|---|
| State | Goods | Services | Total |
| Arizona | $ 89,242 | $ 0 | $ 89,242 |
| California | 132,045 | 0 | 132,045 |
| Colorado | 75,002 | 0 | 75,002 |
| Idaho | 167,921 | 625,003 | 792,924 |
| Tennessee | 45,331 | 357,061 | 402,392 |
| Washington | 41,982 | 377,441 | 419,423 |
| Wyoming | 185,249 | 437,755 | 623,004 |
| Totals | $736,772 | $1,797,260 | $2,534,032 |

When a business sells tangible personal property in a state, it must collect and remit the **sales tax** on a periodic basis if it has nexus in that state.[5] Exhibit 23-2 provides an overview of who bears the burden (who must pay and who must collect and remit the tax) of sales and use taxes. Sales tax liability accrues on the sales of property within the state. For example, Wild West's Idaho retail store collects sales tax on

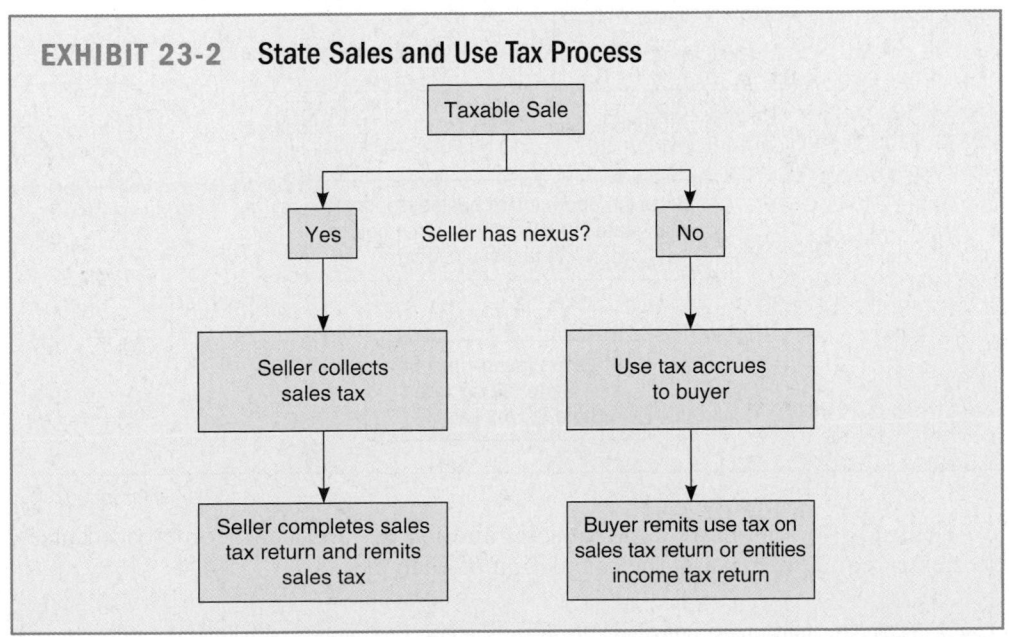

**EXHIBIT 23-2    State Sales and Use Tax Process**

[5]Businesses remit their sales and use tax liability on a monthly, quarterly, or annual basis depending on the size of the liability and the state law thresholds.

goods sold in Idaho stores and remits the tax to the Idaho state government. **Use tax** liability accrues in the state where purchased property will be used. The use tax only occurs when a seller in one state ships goods to a customer in a different state and the seller is not required to collect the sales tax (the seller does not have sales and use tax nexus in the state in which the goods are shipped to). For example, Colorado customers ordering through Wild West's Wyoming Internet store (which has no Colorado sales tax nexus) are required to accrue and pay the Colorado use tax (usually through their personal income tax returns).[6] Businesses with sales and use tax nexus in a state are responsible for paying the sales tax even if they fail to collect it.

Businesses engaged in **interstate commerce** also must deal with income-tax related issues. If a business meets certain requirements creating income tax nexus, it may be required to pay income tax to that state. The general process of determining a business's state income tax liability is highlighted in Exhibit 23-3. We compute the **state tax base** by making adjustments to federal taxable income. The adjustments are necessary to account for differences between federal income tax laws and state income tax laws. Then we divide the state tax base into **business income** and **nonbusiness income.** Business income (income from business activities) is subject to **apportionment** among states where nexus exists, based on the extent of the business's activities and property in various states. Nonbusiness income (all income but business income—generally investment income) is subject to **allocation** (assignment) directly to the business's state of commercial domicile. For states in which the business has nexus, state taxable income is the sum of the business income apportioned to that state plus the nonbusiness income allocated to that state. The business computes its state tax for that state liability by multiplying state taxable income by the state tax rate.

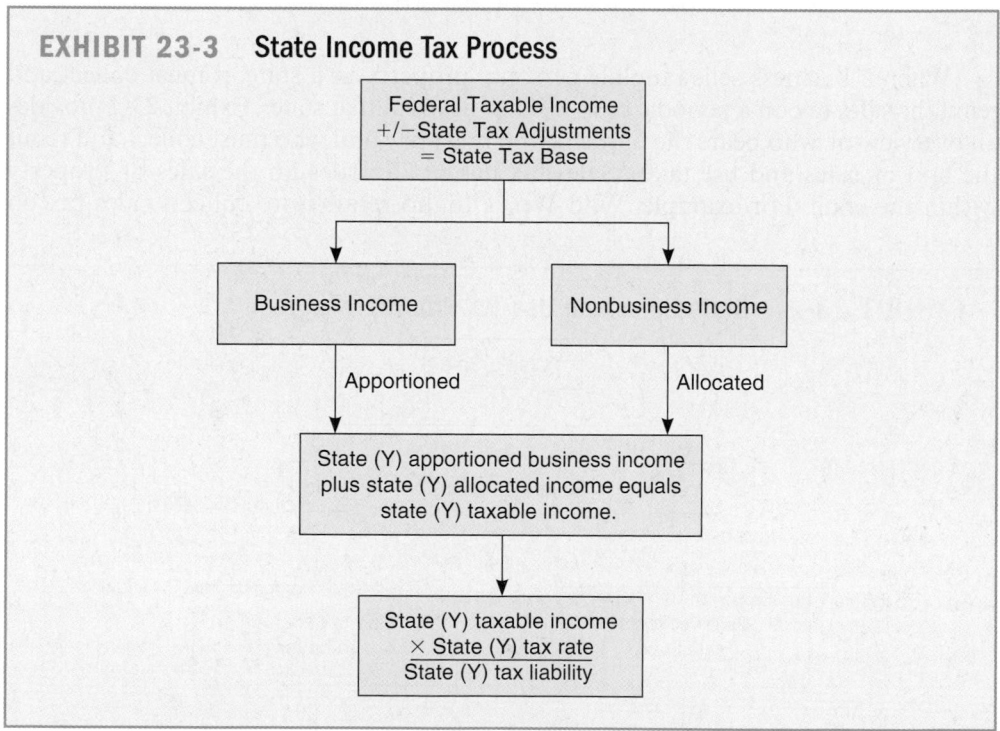

**EXHIBIT 23-3     State Income Tax Process**

Let's now look in more depth at sales and use tax and net income-based taxes, the nexus requirements, and the calculation of each tax.

---

[6]Use tax is paid by individuals completing the use tax liability line on their individual tax return. Alternatively, business entities collecting and remitting sales tax include the use tax on their sales tax return.

# SALES AND USE TAXES

Forty-five states and the District of Columbia impose sales and use taxes; Alaska, Delaware, Montana, New Hampshire, and Oregon do not. Generally, sales of tangible personal property are subject to the sales and use tax. Most states also tax restaurant meals, rental car use, and hotel room rentals (often at higher tax rates than general sales). Purchases of inventory for resale are exempt from the sales tax. For example, Wild West's rafting equipment purchases for resale are exempt from sales tax because inventory is taxed when sold, but its office furniture purchases for use in the business are taxable because they represent final sales. Taxable items vary from state to state. Many states exempt food (except prepared restaurant food) because taxing food is considered to be regressive; that is, it imposes a proportionally higher tax burden on lower-income taxpayers. Most states also exempt sales of real property, intangible property, and services. However, many states are expanding the types of services subject to sales tax.[7]

> **THE KEY FACTS**
>
> **Sales Tax Nexus**
>
> - Nexus is the sufficient connection between a business and a state that allows a state to levy a tax on the business.
>
> - Sales tax nexus is established through physical presence of salespeople or property in a state.

---

**Taxes in the Real World**    *Is It Candy or Is It Food?*

Items subject to the sales and use tax vary from state to state. Historically, New York taxed the sale of large marshmallows but exempted the sale of small marshmallows. Large and small marshmallows were treated differently because large marshmallows were considered to be candy, which was included in the sales tax base, while small marshmallows were considered to be a food ingredient and excluded from the sales tax base.

---

## Sales and Use Tax Nexus

Have you ever wondered why sometimes you pay tax on goods purchased over the Internet and sometimes you don't? The answer is nexus. A business is required to collect sales tax from customers in a state only if it has sales and use tax nexus with that state. For example, if you purchased this textbook from your local campus bookstore you paid tax (unless your state exempts educational materials), but if you purchased the book from Amazon.com you didn't pay sales tax unless you live in Washington state. Businesses without nexus or sales tax collection responsibility often use this as a comparative advantage, as indicated by the following excerpt from Amazon's 2008 annual report (see Exhibit 23-4).

Businesses that establish sales and use tax nexus with a state but fail to properly collect sales tax can create significant liabilities that may need to be disclosed for financial reporting purposes.[8] As a result, understanding when a business has nexus can be extremely important for profitability.

Businesses create sales tax nexus (the sufficient connection with a state that requires them to collect sales tax) when they have a *physical presence* in the state. Businesses have a physical presence in the state if (1) salespeople (or independent contractors representing a business) enter a state to obtain sales or if (2) tangible property (such as a company-owned truck making deliveries) is located within a state.[9]

The physical presence requirement is a judicial interpretation of the Commerce clause of the U.S. Constitution. Designed to encourage interstate commerce, this clause gives Congress power "To regulate Commerce with foreign Nations, and among the several States, and with the Indian Tribes." Because Congress has never

---

[7]For example, Connecticut taxes services such as tax preparation.

[8]Sales tax liabilities are ASC 450 contingencies.

[9]*Scripto, Inc. v. Carson, Sherriff,* et al, 362 U.S. 207. Scripto hired independent salesmen to represent the company in Florida. The Supreme Court held that these salesmen were agents of Scripto, who established the physical presence necessary to create nexus.

**EXHIBIT 23-4**   **Excerpt from Amazon's 2008 Annual Report**

*Taxation Risks Could Subject Us to Liability for Past Sales and Cause Our Future Sales to Decrease*

We do not collect sales or other taxes on shipments of most of our goods into most states in the U.S. Under some of our commercial agreements, the other company is the seller of record, and we are obligated to collect sales tax in accordance with that company's instructions. We may enter into additional agreements requiring similar tax collection obligations. Our fulfillment center and customer service center networks, and any future expansion of them, along with other aspects of our evolving business, may result in additional sales and other tax obligations. We collect consumption tax (including value added tax, goods and services tax, and provincial sales tax) as applicable on goods and services sold by us that are ordered on our international sites. One or more states or foreign countries may seek to impose sales or other tax collection obligations on out-of-jurisdiction e-commerce companies. A successful assertion by one or more states or foreign countries that we should collect sales or other taxes on the sale of merchandise or services could result in substantial tax liabilities for past sales, decrease our ability to compete with traditional retailers, and otherwise harm our business.

Currently, U.S. Supreme Court decisions restrict the imposition of obligations to collect state and local sales and use taxes with respect to sales made over the Internet. However, a number of states, as well as the U.S. Congress, have been considering initiatives that could limit or supersede the Supreme Court's position regarding sales and use taxes on Internet sales. If any of these initiatives were successful, we could be required to collect sales and use taxes in additional states. The imposition by state and local governments of various taxes upon Internet commerce could create administrative burdens for us, put us at a competitive disadvantage if they do not impose similar obligations on all of our online competitors and decrease our future sales.

---

exercised its right, the courts have determined the sales tax nexus threshold. In *National Bellas Hess,* the Supreme Court held that an out-of-state mail-order company did not have a sales tax collection responsibility because it lacked physical presence (even though it mailed catalogs and advertised in the state).[10] The mail order industry used this decision as a competitive advantage for several decades. In *Quill,* the Supreme Court reaffirmed that out-of-state (nondomiciliary) businesses must have a physical presence in the state before the state may require a business to collect sales tax from in-state customers.[11]

**Example 23-1**

Wild West sends promotional brochures from Idaho to its Colorado clients. Wild West generated sales of $75,002 to Colorado customers, but it has never collected Colorado sales and use tax or filed a Colorado sales and use tax return. Wild West has neither employees nor property in Colorado. Does it have sales and use tax nexus in Colorado?

**Answer:** No. Wild West lacks the physical presence required for Colorado nexus and therefore doesn't have Colorado sales and use tax collection responsibility.

**What if:** Assume that in addition to mailing promotional brochures, Ken visits Colorado on promotional trips. Does Wild West have sales and use tax nexus in Colorado under these circumstances?

**Answer:** Yes. The physical presence of Wild West's representatives, even for promotional trips, creates Colorado sales and use tax nexus.

**What if:** Assume Wild West's representatives (independent contractors) visit Colorado retail stores to solicit additional sales orders. Does Wild West have sales and use tax nexus in Colorado under these circumstances?

**Answer:** Yes. The physical presence of Wild West's representatives creates Colorado sales and use tax nexus.

---

[10]*National Bellas Hess, Inc. v. Department of Revenue of the State of Illinois,* 386 U.S. 753 (1967).
[11]*Quill Corporation, Petitioner v. North Dakota,* 504 U.S. 298 (1992).

Businesses selling products over the Internet have been able to avoid collecting sales and use tax because nexus is created through physical presence in the state of the buyer. In fact, Internet sales represent billions of dollars annually. As a result, the physical presence nexus standard has cost states substantial sales tax revenue. In 2008, New York implemented the so-called Amazon rule that requires Internet-based retailers to collect and remit New York sales tax; the rule is estimated to increase state revenues by $50 million per year. As you might expect, since this law is inconsistent with the Supreme Court's decision in *Quill,* Amazon has filed suit against the state of New York.[12]

### Sales and Use Tax Liability

Typically, sellers with nexus collect customers' sales tax liabilities. For example, Wild West collects sales tax on river-rafting equipment it sells from its retail store but not on river guiding *services* it provides. If the seller doesn't have nexus, then the customer is responsible for paying a use tax (at the same tax rate as sales tax) to the state in which the property is used.

---

**Example 23-2**

Wild West received $3,500 from a customer named Casey Jarvie residing in Sacramento, California. Of this amount, $500 was for personal rafting equipment shipped to Sacramento, where the sales tax rate is 7.75 percent. The remaining $3,000 was payment for a four-day river raft adventure on the Salmon River in Idaho. Wild West has neither salespeople nor property in California. Does Wild West have a responsibility to collect sales tax from Casey?

**Answer:** No. Wild West lacks physical presence and does not have sales and use tax nexus in California; therefore, it has no California sales tax collection requirement.

Because Wild West has no sales tax collection responsibility, does Casey have a use tax liability to the state of California? If so, in what amount?

**Answer:** Casey is responsible for remitting $38.75 of use tax ($500 × 7.75%) on his personal California state income tax return for the purchase and use of the rafting equipment in California. He is not required to pay California use tax on the river raft adventure purchase, because Wild West provided out-of-state services (no sales tax is due on the services in Idaho either).

***What if:*** If Casey had Wild West hold the goods until he arrived in Burley, Idaho, to pick them up (assume the sales tax rate in Burley, Idaho, is 6 percent), would Wild West have sales tax collection responsibility? If so, what is the sales tax amount?

**Answer:** Yes. Because Wild West has physical presence in Idaho, it is required to collect $30 ($500 × 6%) of sales tax and remit it to Idaho. Casey would also have an $8.75 use tax liability in California ($38.75 reduced by the $30.00 remitted to Idaho) in this scenario.

---

Large companies must often file sales and use tax returns in all 45 states that have sales and use taxes and the District of Columbia.[13] This administrative burden is further complicated by the fact that there are over 7,500 tax jurisdictions (including counties, cities, school districts, and other divisions) imposing sales and use taxes, and several hundred rates change annually at various times during the year.[14] The

---

[12]Amazon filed suit against New York in April 2008. Amazon lost the initial case and is currently awaiting a verdict at the appellate level.

[13]Some counties or political subdivisions of states without state sales taxes impose a local sales tax (such as Soldotna, Alaska).

[14]Software companies provide sales and use tax solutions that help companies with the administrative burden. However, they generally fail to indemnify businesses against errors in their software that result in uncollected sales taxes.

sales and use tax administrative burden can be large for small businesses as well. For example, a local pizzeria that delivers can sometimes be subject to a half-dozen sales tax rates if it crosses city, county, or school district boundaries.

---

**Example 23-3**

Recall from Exhibit 23-1 that Wild West has sales in Arizona, California, Colorado, Idaho, Tennessee, Washington, and Wyoming. Also, recall that it has property and employees in Idaho, Tennessee, Washington, and Wyoming. In which states does Wild West have sales and use tax nexus and, therefore, sales tax collection responsibility?

**Answer:** Wild West's physical presence of employees and property creates sales and use tax nexus in Idaho, Tennessee, Washington, and Wyoming.

How much sales and use tax must Wild West remit (assume the following sales tax rates: Idaho (6.00 percent); Tennessee (9.25 percent); Washington (7.70 percent); and Wyoming (6.00 percent)?

**Answer:** It must remit $28,616, computed as follows:

| State | (1)<br>Taxable Sales | (2)<br>Rate | (1) × (2)<br>Sales Tax Due |
|-------|-----------|------|---------------|
| Idaho | $167,921 | 6.00% | $10,075 |
| Tennessee | 45,331 | 9.25% | 4,193 |
| Washington | 41,982 | 7.70% | 3,233 |
| Wyoming | 185,249 | 6.00% | 11,115 |
| Totals | $440,483 | | $28,616 |

Remember, services are not generally subject to sales tax.

---

**Taxes in the Real World**   *The Streamlined Sales Tax Project*

Have you heard of the Streamlined Sales Tax Project? A lot of businesses have. The Streamlined Sales Tax Project is a multistate initiative to develop and implement a radically simplified sales and use tax system. The sole purpose is to lower the administrative burden of collecting sales tax enough so that sales and use tax can be imposed nationally on all businesses. While the project has helped create more uniformity in the items taxed from state to state, businesses are not required to comply with it.

The Streamlined Sales Tax Project sent letters to businesses (whether they had taxes or not) across the country implying that they must register and collect sales and use taxes for goods shipped to all member states. However, the *Quill* doctrine requires a business to have physical presence in a state before a state can require the collection of sales and use taxes for that state. Most professionals agree that businesses have no legal requirement to comply. However, Congress has considered several bills that would make the Streamlined Sales Tax system law.

You can find out more about the Streamlined Sales Tax Project at the following Web site: www.streamlinedsalestax.org.

---

**L03**

# INCOME TAXES

Forty-six states impose an income tax on corporations; Nevada, South Dakota, Washington, and Wyoming do not.[15] Forty-three states tax income from partnerships and S corporations; this chapter focuses on corporations, but the same

---

[15]Several states (such as California and New York) impose a franchise tax rather than an income tax. Since franchise taxes are generally based upon net income, they are essentially the same as income taxes.

principles apply to flow-through entities.[16] Businesses must pay income tax in their state of commercial domicile (where they are headquartered). For example, Wild West is both incorporated and domiciled in Idaho and is therefore subject to Idaho's income tax regime. Until a few decades ago, many businesses believed they were virtually exempt from state income taxes in states other than their state of commercial domicile. However, in *Complete Auto Transit,* the Supreme Court spelled out four criteria for determining whether states can tax nondomiciliary companies and to what extent.[17] First, a sufficient connection or nexus must exist between the state and the business. Second, a state may tax only a fair portion of a business's income. Businesses must be able to divide or apportion income among the states where nexus exists. Third, the tax cannot be constructed to discriminate against nonresident businesses. For example, states cannot impose a higher tax rate on nondomiciliary businesses than domiciliary businesses. Fourth, the taxes paid must be fairly related to the services the state provides.

To determine their state income tax liabilities, businesses must answer the following questions:

- In which states is the business required to file tax returns (in which states does it have nexus)?
- If the business is related to other entities, should it file separate state tax returns, or should it include the activities of the related entities on its state tax returns?
- What adjustments to federal taxable income must the business make to determine state taxable income for each state in which it is required to file?
- If income is taxable (nexus exists) in more than one state, how is it assigned among the various states in which the business is required to file tax returns?

### Income Tax Nexus

Businesses must file income tax returns in states where they have income tax nexus. However, the determination whether the business has established income tax nexus with a state depends on the nature of the business's activities in the state. Thus, the rules for determining income tax nexus are not necessarily the same as those for determining sales and use tax nexus. Physical presence creates income tax nexus for service providers, sellers of real property, and businesses licensing intangibles. However, physical presence does not create nexus for sellers of tangible personal property if their activities in the state are limited to "protected" activities as described by **Public Law 86-272.**

**Public Law 86-272**   In *Northwestern States Portland Cement,* the Supreme Court allowed Minnesota to tax an Iowa-based business.[18] By passing Public Law 86-272 in response, Congress acted to place limits on states' power to impose income taxes. Businesses are protected from income tax nexus in a particular state if (and only if) *all* the following apply:

- The tax is based on net income (not gross receipts or revenue).
- The taxpayer sells only tangible personal property in that state.
- The taxpayer's in-state activities are limited to **solicitation** of sales (see below for the definition of *solicitation*).

[16]Actually, these states tax individuals, and the income that flows through from partnerships and S corporations (although New Hampshire and Tennessee tax only dividends and interest); Alaska, Florida, Nevada, South Dakota, Texas, Washington, and Wyoming do not.
[17]*Complete Auto Transit, Inc. v. Brady,* 430 U.S. 274 (1977).
[18]*Northwestern Cement Co. v. Minnesota,* 358 U.S. 450 (1959). Widespread alarm from the business community following the case led to an intense lobbying effort, and seven months later Congress enacted Public Law 86-272.

- The taxpayer participates in interstate commerce.
- The taxpayer is nondomiciliary.
- The taxpayer approves orders outside the state.
- The taxpayer delivers goods from outside the state.

Businesses wishing to avoid nexus for taxes based on net income must sell only tangible personal property within the state.[19] Providing services along with property violates the criteria and creates nexus. For example, providing installation services with tangible personal property exceeds solicitation; in-state activities must be limited to solicitation of sales (discussed further in the next section). Only nondomiciliary companies engaging in interstate commerce are protected. Orders taken or received in-state must be sent out of state—say to regional sales offices or headquarters—for approval. The acceptance of orders in the state, or even the power to accept orders, exceeds the protection of Public Law 86-272. Accepted orders must be delivered by common carrier.[20] Delivery using the seller's truck violates the criteria and creates nexus, except as permitted by state law (New Jersey, Rhode Island, and South Carolina are among the states that list delivery by private vehicles as a protected activity).

| **Example 23-4** |
| --- |

**What if:** Assume that Wild West sends employees to Oregon to visit retail stores and solicit orders of rafting equipment only. Does the presence of Wild West's employees in Oregon create income tax nexus in Oregon?

**Answer:** No. Public Law 86-272 protects from nexus the physical presence of representatives soliciting sales of tangible personal property. Note, however, that this physical presence *would* create sales and use tax nexus for any sales generated by Wild West in Oregon.

**What if:** Assume that Ken or other Wild West sales representatives entered Oregon to solicit customers for both rafting equipment and white-water adventures. Does the presence of Wild West's employees create income tax nexus in Oregon?

**Answer:** Yes. Solicitation of *services* is not a protected activity under Public Law 86-272. Thus, soliciting services creates income tax nexus for Wild West in Oregon and creates an income tax filing requirement.

*Solicitation.*    Public Law 86-272 protects solicitation of tangible personal property but doesn't clearly define solicitation. In *Wisconsin v. Wrigley,* however, the Supreme Court addressed the definition.[21] Wrigley had salesmen and a regional manager in Wisconsin. Sales meetings were held both in the manager's basement and rented hotel space. The sales reps had company cars, a stock of gum, display racks, and promotional literature. The sales activities included handing out promotional materials, free samples, and free display racks; replacing stale gum; handling billing disputes; and occasionally filling orders from their stock of gum and issuing an agency stock check (a bill) to customers. All other orders were sent to Illinois for acceptance and were filled by common carrier from outside the state. The Supreme Court determined the following activities meet the definition of solicitation:

- Soliciting by any form of advertising.
- Carrying samples and promotional materials for display or distribution without charge.
- Passing inquiries or complaints to the home office.

---

[19]Taxes calculated based on gross receipts or other bases are not protected by Public Law 86-272.

[20]*Common carrier* is a general term referring to delivery businesses (such as FedEx, UPS, DHL, or USPS).

[21]*Wisconsin Department of Revenue v. William Wrigley, Jr. Co.,* 505 US 214 (1992).

- Checking customer's inventory for reorder.
- Maintaining a sample room for two weeks or less; this is known as the **trade show rule.**
- Recruiting, training, and evaluating salespeople using homes or hotels.
- Owning or furnishing personal property and autos used in sales activities.

The Supreme Court held the following activities do *not* meet the definition of solicitation and, therefore, create income tax nexus with the state in which they take place:

- Making repairs.
- Collecting delinquent accounts.
- Investigating creditworthiness.
- Installing or supervising the installation of property.
- Training for employees other than sales representatives.
- Approving or accepting orders.
- Repossessing property.
- Securing deposits.
- Maintaining an office other than in-home.

If sales reps know and understand these solicitation rules, they can help businesses avoid nexus in states where they want to avoid it.

---

**Example 23-5**

Assume that Wild West's Oregon salespeople give store employees free white-water gloves and pass on complaints to the home office. Do these activities create nexus for Wild West in Oregon?

**Answer:** No. Giving samples (without charge) and passing on complaints, suggestions, and customer inquiries are protected sales activities under Public Law 86-272. Therefore, Wild West is protected from Oregon income tax nexus.

*What if:* While in Oregon, several salespeople accepted checks for down payments on merchandise, repaired faulty merchandise, and performed credit checks. Do these activities create nexus in Oregon for Wild West?

**Answer:** Yes. Each of these activities is an unprotected sales activity, and any or all will create Oregon income tax nexus for Wild West.

---

Does a one-time sales activity violation create income tax nexus? Technically, yes. However, the *Wrigley* decision indicates that *de minimis* (immaterial) activities may be excluded. The determination of whether an activity is *de minimis* is a subjective one, based on relevant facts and circumstances.

---

**Example 23-6**

Assume that Wild West's salespeople occasionally investigate creditworthiness and occasionally repossess property in Oregon. Can Wild West avoid income tax nexus?

**Answer:** Possibly. Wild West must argue that these unprotected activities are *de minimis* because they were not material to its overall operations.

---

**Income Tax Nexus for Other Business Types or Nonincome-Based Taxes**    Public Law 86-272 does not protect service providers, sellers of real property, or businesses licensing intangibles. Further, it does not protect businesses from nonincome-based taxes. Establishing income tax nexus for nonprotected activities, and nexus for nonincome-based taxes, requires a physical presence just like establishing sales and use tax nexus.

## Example 23-7

*What if:* Assume that Ken and other Wild West employees visit Colorado retail stores and hold slideshows about summer rafting trips. After the slideshows, Ken and the other guides interact with and gather information from potential white-water rafting customers. Do these solicitation activities create income tax nexus?

**Answer:** Yes. Because white-water rafting trips are services rather than tangible personal property, the physical presence of Wild West employees creates income tax nexus in Colorado.

## Example 23-8

> **THE KEY FACTS**
>
> **Income Tax Nexus**
>
> ▪ Income tax nexus requirements vary depending on whether the business sells tangible personal property, services, or intangibles.
>
> ▪ Sellers of tangible personal property are protected from nexus under Public Law 86-272.
>  · Physical presence is protected as long as in-state activities are limited to solicitation.
>
> ▪ Sellers of intangibles, real property, and services establish nexus through physical presence of sales personnel or property.
>
> ▪ Several states are now asserting economic nexus.

*What if:* Assume that Wild West sends employees into Texas to visit retail stores and solicit orders of rafting equipment. Texas instituted a new tax, the Margin Tax, beginning in 2008. The tax is calculated on the lesser of gross margin or 70 percent of sales revenue. Would the presence of Wild West employees create nexus for the Texas Margin Tax?

**Answer:** Yes. Because the tax is not an income tax (it is not based on *net* income), Wild West is not protected by Public Law 86-272. Therefore, physical presence of salespeople soliciting sales of tangible personal property creates nexus (but it would *not* have created nexus if the tax were based on net income).

**Economic Income Tax Nexus** As we have discussed, businesses generally must have a physical presence in a state to establish income tax nexus with that state (P.L. 86-272 is the exception). However, many states are currently asserting a business without a physical presence in the state may establish income tax nexus if it has an economic presence in the state.[22] South Carolina was the first state to pursue economic nexus by disallowing the expenses of Toys R Us South Carolina to its subsidiary Geoffrey (a Delaware holding company). States asserting **economic nexus** claim they provide an infrastructure of phone and Internet connections to consumers (an economic base) that nonresident companies use to solicit business (this claim is analogous to providing roads for salespeople to visit the state's customers). For example, West Virginia asserted an income tax liability on a business (MBNA Bank) that merely solicited credit card customers through advertising and phone calls without having physical presence (employees or property) in the state. The West Virginia Supreme Court upheld the assertion, and the U.S. Supreme Court denied MBNA's *writ of certiorari*. However, most experts believe West Virginia's law to be unconstitutional, and the U.S. Supreme Court's refusal to hear the case was designed to urge Congress to resolve the uncertainty surrounding nexus issues.

## Example 23-9

*What if:* Assume that Wild West's Internet store receives and fills an order from a West Virginia customer. Wild West has no physical presence in West Virginia. Does Wild West have West Virginia income tax nexus?

**Answer:** Perhaps. West Virginia's assertion of economic nexus does not require physical presence. Therefore, Wild West could have economic income tax nexus, which would require it to file an income tax return in West Virginia.

---

[22]The Supreme Court's *Quill* decision created doubt on the standard for income tax nexus because in defining sales tax nexus it said that "nexus for other taxes may be different," which the states have interpreted as meaning that physical presence may not be required. Several recent cases have given de facto income tax nexus to businesses without the requisite physical presence [*Geoffrey, Inc. v. South Carolina Tax Commission,* S.C. Sup. Ct., 313 S.C. (1992); *Lanco, Inc. v. Director, Division of Taxation,* NJ Sup. Ct., Dkt. No.A-89-05 (2006); and *Tax Commissioner of West Virginia v. MBNA America Bank, N.A.,* 640 SE 2d 226 (WV 2006)].

Now that we've explored income tax nexus, let's determine Wild West's income tax nexus and filing requirements.

**Example 23-10**

Wild West is domiciled in Idaho and has physical presence through property and employees whose activities exceed protected solicitation in Idaho, Tennessee, Washington, and Wyoming. Recall from Example 23-4 that Wild West has sales in the following states: Arizona, California, Colorado, Idaho, Tennessee, Washington, and Wyoming. Where does Wild West have income tax nexus?

**Answer:** Wild West has income tax nexus in Idaho, Tennessee, Washington, and Wyoming. Nexus in Idaho because of commercial domicile, physical presence of retail stores (where orders are accepted), and provision of services. Nexus in Tennessee, Washington, and Wyoming because of physical presence of retail stores (where orders are accepted) and provision of services.

Where does Wild West have an income tax filing requirement?

**Answer:** Wild West will be required to file income tax returns in Idaho and Tennessee. Washington and Wyoming do not have a corporate income tax. Instead, Washington has a gross receipts tax (Business & Occupation tax). Wyoming does not tax corporations. As a result, Wild West will also file a Washington gross receipts return, as we discuss later.

---

**THE KEY FACTS**

**Entities Included on a Tax Return**

▪ Separate-return states require a separate return for each entity that has nexus in the state.

▪ Unitary states require members of a unitary group to file a single tax return reflecting the combined income of the unitary group.
· Any of three factors determine a unitary group: functional integration, centralization of management, and economies of scale.

---

## Entities Included on Income Tax Return

Some states require a **separate tax return** for each entity with income tax nexus in the state, and others require a **unitary tax return** (one return) for a group of related entities.[23]

**Separate Tax Returns** "Separate-return" states require only those businesses with nexus in a state to file an income tax return. This is generally true even when a group of companies file a federal consolidated tax return.[24] Most states east of the Mississippi River (except Illinois) are separate-return states.

**Example 23-11**

Wild West has nexus in Tennessee (a separate-return state) because its employees provide services within the state and it owns property there. Must Wild West file a separate Tennessee income tax return?

**Answer:** Yes. Wild West must file a separate Tennessee income tax return because it has nexus in Tennessee.

**What if:** Assume that Wild West splits into two separate corporations: one that runs retail stores (Wild West Retail) and one that provides the guided rafting services (Wild West Services). How would the split affect Wild West's Tennessee income tax filing requirements?

**Answer:** Wild West would file two separate income tax returns: one for Wild West Retail and one for Wild West Services. Both companies would have nexus in Tennessee because Wild West Retail's stores do more than solicit sales of tangible personal property and Wild West Service's activities are not protected activities under Public Law 86-272.

---

[23]The separate versus unitary discussion is a complex and controversial discussion even at the graduate tax level. However, a basic understanding of the terminology and concepts can be useful for all accounting professionals.

[24]Some states allow combined reporting, a setting where more than one corporation files together on the same income tax return. However, the tax is calculated as if each corporation filed a separate return and was taxed separately.

While separate tax returns are simple, the income reported on separate tax returns is potentially subject to manipulation through related-entity transactions (transfer pricing, for example). These "tax planning" opportunities are not available if the related entities are required to file a unitary tax return.

**Unitary Tax Returns** States west of the Mississippi River (and Illinois) are unitary return states. Whether a business must file one tax return with other businesses or entities depends on whether these businesses are considered to be a "unitary" group of entities.

In *Mobil,* the Supreme Court identified three factors that can be used to determine whether a group of businesses is unitary: functional integration (vertical or horizontal integration or knowledge transfer), centralization of management (interlocking directors, common officers, or rotation of management), and economies of scale (group discounts or other efficiencies due to size).[25] The unitary concept considers the integration and flow of value, rather than the business's legal form and ownership structure, in determining which companies file a tax return together. Taxpayers must consider each of the three factors to determine whether two (or more) businesses will be treated as one for state tax purposes.

The important concept here is that companies filing a federal consolidated tax return can be separated, and companies not filing a federal consolidated tax return can become a unitary group.[26] A unitary tax return group includes all members meeting the unitary criteria—whether they have nexus or not.[27] Unitary businesses usually have a flow of value between the various businesses. For example, raw materials or components can flow between businesses or one entity may borrow from another. The unitary concept pervades activities in the entire income tax system, including computing taxable income, computing apportionment percentages (discussed later in the chapter), and determining tax return filing requirements.

---

**Example 23-12**

**What if:** As in the previous example, assume that Wild West is divided into two separate corporations: Wild West Retail (WWR) and Wild West Services (WWS). Ken owns and manages both companies. The rafting services company purchases all its rafting equipment from the retail stores company. Guides for the rafting company stop at the retail store before trips so customers can purchase any necessary gear, and the store refers customers looking for guided rafting to the rafting company. Assume the two companies use the same marketing and accounting firms and receive discounts for having multiple bank accounts and insurance policies. Using the *Mobil* factors (functional integration, centralization of management, and economies of scale), are WWR and WWS part of a unitary group?

**Answer:** Yes. The retail store company and the rafting services company would likely be considered a unitary group and thus would combine income and file a single tax return. The two companies likely share some integration in that their customer bases have significant overlap, and the rafting services company purchases its equipment from the retail stores. They share centralization of management in that both are owned and operated by the same individual (Ken). The two companies have some economies of scale because they receive discounts for using the same accounting, banking, insurance, and marketing vendors. Businesses do not have to meet all three factors to be considered a unitary group, but WWR and WWS probably do. As a result, WWR and WWS would likely file a unitary (single) Idaho income tax return.

---

[25]In *Mobil Oil Corp. v. Vermont Tax Commissioner,* 445 U.S. 425 (1980), the U.S. Supreme Court held that the income of a multistate business can be apportioned if its intrastate and out-of-state activities form a part of a unitary business.

[26]In some cases, different divisions of a single corporation can be separated and in others a partnership and corporation can be joined.

[27]Entities without nexus usually have apportionment factors that are zero. While their incomes increase the unitary group's income, their zero apportionment factors decrease the apportionment factors to the state. Therefore, the inclusion of entities without nexus is nondiscriminatory.

## *State Taxable Income*

Companies doing business in multiple states must determine tax return due dates, procedures for filing tax return extensions, and other administrative requirements specific to each state. Businesses must also calculate state taxable income for each state in which they must file tax returns. Federal taxable income is generally the starting point for computing state taxable income. Just as corporations reconcile from book income to taxable income (see Chapter 16), businesses must reconcile from federal taxable income to state taxable income. This requires them to identify **federal/state adjustments** (differences) for *each specific state* before apportioning the income to a particular state where they have income tax nexus.

Rather than starting from scratch, many states conform to the federal tax law in some way. Most states "piggyback" their state tax laws on the federal tax laws (state tax codes generally follow the Internal Revenue Code).[28] Idaho generally conforms to the current Code. Consequently, Wild West will not report many federal/state adjustments. Other states adopt a specific version of the Code (the Code as of a specific date). California recently adopted the Code as of January 1, 2005 (previously it used the Code as of January 1, 2001), and Texas uses the Code as of January 1, 1996. This method causes more federal/state adjustments, because every subsequent change to the Internal Revenue Code results in less conformity between the state law and the federal tax law.

Because states do not tax federal interest income (interest from Treasury notes, for example), all states require a negative adjustment (reduction in federal income in adjusting to state income) for federal interest income. Most states require a positive adjustment for state income taxes, because they don't allow businesses to deduct state income taxes, and they require a positive adjustment for state and local bond interest income if the bond is from another state (they tax out-of-state bond interest income).[29]

States' tax instruction booklets generally describe common federal/state tax adjustments applicable for that state, but these descriptions are often incomplete, particularly problematic for states with low federal tax conformity. While it is impractical to identify all potential federal/state adjustments, Exhibit 23-5 provides a list of

**EXHIBIT 23-5   Common Federal/State Adjustments**

**Positive Adjustments (Increasing Taxable Income)**

State and local income taxes

State and local bond interest income from bonds in other states

Federal dividends received deduction

Federal income tax refunds (only in states where federal tax is allowed as a deduction)

Intercompany expenses associated with related parties (for separate-return states)*

MACRS depreciation over state depreciation

Federal bonus depreciation

Federal domestic production activities deduction

**Negative Adjustments (Decreasing Taxable Income)**

U.S. obligation interest income (T-bills, notes, and bonds)

State dividends received deduction

Foreign dividend gross up

Subpart F income

State income tax refunds included on federal return

State depreciation over federal depreciation

---

*Approximately 20 separate-return states require a positive adjustment of intercompany royalties, interest, and other expenses between related parties. The disallowance prevents companies from extracting profits from high-tax states and placing them in low- or no-tax states.

[28]Also, states may conform or not conform to administrative authority such as treasury regulations, revenue procedures, and revenue rulings.

[29]Thirty-three of the 46 states with an income tax require a positive adjustment for state and local expenses deducted on the federal return.

common federal/state adjustments and identifies each as positive adjustments (state income increasing) or negative adjustments (state income decreasing).

### Example 23-13

Wild West properly included, deducted, or excluded the following items on its federal tax return in the current year:

| Item | Amount | Federal Treatment |
|---|---|---|
| Idaho income tax | $27,744 | Deducted on federal return. |
| Tennessee income tax | $18,152 | Deducted on federal return. |
| Washington gross receipts tax | $ 6,201 | Deducted on federal return. |
| Idaho bond interest income | $ 5,000 | Excluded from federal return. |
| Federal T-note interest income | $ 1,500 | Included on federal return. |
| Domestic production activities deduction (DPAD) | $ 7,304 | Deducted on federal return. |

Given federal taxable income of $53,289, what is Wild West's state tax base for Idaho and for Tennessee?

**Answer:** The Idaho state tax base is $97,685; for Tennessee it is $109,989. Bases are calculated as follows:

| Federal Taxable Income | Idaho | Tennessee | Source |
|---|---|---|---|
| Wild West | $53,289 | $ 53,289 | Storyline |
| **Positive Adjustments** | | | |
| Idaho income tax | $27,744 | $ 27,744 | * |
| Tennessee income tax | 18,152 | 18,152 | * |
| State bond interest | 0 | 5,000 | States exempt their own interest only. |
| DPAD | 0 | 7,304 | Idaho conforms to federal law, Tennessee does not. |
| Total positive adjustments | $45,896 | $ 58,200 | |
| **Negative Adjustments** | | | |
| Federal interest | $ 1,500 | $ 1,500 | Federal interest is not taxable for state purposes. |
| Total negative adjustments | $ 1,500 | $ 1,500 | |
| State tax base | $97,685 | $109,989 | Federal + Positive − Negative. |

*Washington tax is deducted (it is not a positive adjustment) because it is not an income-based tax.

## Dividing State Tax Base among States

All state taxable income is taxed in the state of commercial domicile unless the business is taxable in more than one state. An interstate business must separate its business income (earned from business operations) from nonbusiness income (primarily from investments, including rents and royalties). The business must fairly *apportion* its business income among the states in which it conducts business, whereas it *allocates* or assigns nonbusiness income to a specific state (usually the state of commercial domicile).[30]

---

[30]The Multistate Tax Commission has provided guidance on the division of income between states in Article IV of its Compact. The Compact can be found at www.mtc.gov. Also, see the Uniform Division of Income Tax Purposes Act that many states have adopted.

**Business Income**   Business income includes all revenues earned in the ordinary course of business—sales less cost of goods sold and other expenses. Business income is fairly apportioned or divided across the states with nexus.[31] If a business has nexus with a state, it may apportion income to that state—even if the state does not actually impose a tax.[32]

---

**Example 23-14**

Recall from the preceding example that Idaho and Tennessee state tax bases were $97,685 and $109,989, respectively. Wild West's federal tax return shows the following investment income: dividends of $6,000, interest income of $14,505, and rental income of $18,000. What is Wild West's business income for Idaho and Tennessee?

**Answer:** Idaho and Tennessee business income amounts are $59,180 and $71,484, respectively, and calculated as follows:

|  | Idaho | Tennessee | Explanation |
|---|---|---|---|
| (1) State tax base | $97,685 | $109,989 | Example 23-13. |
| (2) Dividends | $ 6,000 | $ 6,000 | Federal tax return. |
| (3) Interest income | 14,505 | 14,505 | $11,005 (federal return) + $5,000 (state interest) − $1,500 (federal interest). |
| (4) Rental income | 18,000 | 18,000 | Federal tax return. |
| (5) Nonbusiness income | $38,505 | $ 38,505 | (2) + (3) + (4). |
| Business income | $59,180 | $ 71,484 | (1) − (5). |

---

*Apportionment formula.*   States determine the apportionment formula for income, and most rely on three factors: sales, payroll, and property. For each state in which it establishes income tax nexus, the business determines the factors as the ratio of (1) total sales, payroll, or property in a specific state to (2) total sales, payroll, or property everywhere. For example, the sales factor is:

$$\text{Sales factor in state } X = \frac{\text{Total sales in state } X}{\text{Total sales in all states}}$$

The sales factor includes all gross business receipts net of returns, allowances, and discounts.[33] The general rules for determining the amount of sales to include in the sales factor calculation are:

- Sales of tangible personal property are sourced (included) to the destination state (the location where the property is delivered to and used in).
- If the business does not have nexus in the destination state, sales are generally "thrown back" to the state from which the property is shipped; this is called the **throwback rule.**[34] For example, if a California business ships goods

---

[31]*Complete Auto Transit, Inc. v. Brady,* 430 U.S. 274 (1977).

[32]Creating nexus in states without an income tax creates "nowhere income"—income that is not taxed anywhere.

[33]There is some variation in the sales factor among states.

[34]Some states don't have a throwback rule and some states such as California have a double-throwback rule. This rule applies to drop shipments from a state without nexus. For example, if a California company ships goods from Arizona into Colorado and has nexus in neither Arizona nor Colorado, the sales are thrown back from Colorado into Arizona and then thrown back again from Arizona to California.

to Montana where it does not have nexus the sales are treated as if they are California sales.

- Dock sales (sales picked up by the customer) are generally sourced in the destination state rather than the state where they are picked up.
- Sales of services are sourced in the state where the services are performed (Illinois is an exception to this rule).
- Government sales are sourced in the state from which they were shipped.

## Example 23-15

Recall from Exhibit 23-1 that Wild West reported sales of $2,534,032. The sales are split between goods and services and sourced by state as follows:

| State | Wild West Sales | | |
|---|---|---|---|
| | Goods | Services | Total |
| AZ | $ 89,242 | $      0 | $    89,242 |
| CA | 132,045 | 0 | 132,045 |
| CO | 75,002 | 0 | 75,002 |
| ID | 167,921 | 625,003 | 792,924 |
| TN | 45,331 | 357,061 | 402,392 |
| WA | 41,982 | 377,441 | 419,423 |
| WY | 185,249 | 437,755 | 623,004 |
| Totals | $736,772 | $1,797,260 | $2,534,032 |

Recall from Example 23-10 that Wild West has nexus in Idaho, Tennessee, Washington, and Wyoming. Washington has a gross receipts tax and Wyoming does not tax corporations. What are the sales apportionment factors for Idaho and Tennessee?

**Answer:** The apportionment factors for Idaho and Tennessee are 31.29 percent and 15.88 percent, respectively, calculated from figures in the Total column in the sales table above:

$$\text{Idaho} \quad \frac{\$792,924}{\$2,534,032} = 31.29\%$$

$$\text{Tennessee} \quad \frac{\$402,392}{\$2,534,032} = 15.88\%$$

Payroll is generally defined as total compensation paid to employees.[35] The payroll factor is calculated as follows:

- Payroll includes salaries, commissions, bonuses, and other forms of compensation.
- Payroll does not include amounts paid to independent contractors.
- Payroll for each employee is apportioned to a single state (payroll for employees who work in more than one state is sourced to the state where they perform the majority of services).

---

[35]The payroll definition varies by state.

**Example 23-16**

Wild West's payments for wages are $737,021, sourced to the states as follows:

| Payroll State | Wild West Wages |
|---|---|
| Idaho | $201,032 |
| Tennessee | 148,202 |
| Washington | 115,021 |
| Wyoming | 272,766 |
| Total | $737,021 |

What are the payroll apportionment factors for Idaho and Tennessee?

**Answer:** The payroll apportionment factors for Idaho and Tennessee are 27.28 percent and 20.11 percent, respectively, calculated from the payroll table above:

$$\text{Idaho} \quad \frac{\$201,032}{\$737,021} = 27.28\%$$

$$\text{Tennessee} \quad \frac{\$148,202}{\$737,021} = 20.11\%$$

Property generally includes both real and tangible personal property, but not intangible property.[36] The general rules for determining the property factors are:

- Use the average property values for the year [(beginning + ending)/2].
- Value property at historical cost rather than adjusted basis (do not subtract accumulated depreciation in determining value).
- Include property in transit (such as inventory) in the state of destination.
- Include only business property (values of rented investment properties are excluded).
- Include rented or leased property by multiplying the annual rent by eight and adding this value to the average owned-property factor.

**Example 23-17**

The historical cost of Wild West's property (before subtracting accumulated depreciation) owned at the beginning and end of the year and rented during the year, by state, is as follows:

| State | Property Beginning | Ending | Rented |
|---|---|---|---|
| Idaho | $1,042,023 | $1,203,814 | $36,000 |
| Tennessee | 502,424 | 531,984 | 0 |
| Washington | 52,327 | 65,829 | 60,000 |
| Wyoming | 1,420,387 | 1,692,373 | 0 |
| Total | $3,017,161 | $3,494,000 | $96,000 |

(continued on page 23-20...)

[36]Property definitions may vary slightly by state.

What are the property apportionment factors for Idaho and Tennessee?

**Answer:** The property apportionment factors for Idaho and Tennessee are 35.07 percent and 12.85 percent, respectively, computed as follows:

$$\text{Idaho} \qquad \frac{\$1,410,919}{\$4,023,581} = 35.07\%$$

$$\text{Tennessee} \qquad \frac{\$517,204}{\$4,023,581} = 12.85\%$$

The average amount for each state from the subtotal property table is added to the inclusion amount from the subtotal rent table to reach the total property numerator for each state.

### Property and Rents Total

| State | Owned Property | | | Rented | |
| | Beginning | Ending | Average | Rents × 8 | Total |
|---|---|---|---|---|---|
| Idaho | $1,042,023 | $1,203,814 | $1,122,919 | $288,000 | $1,410,919 |
| Tennessee | 502,424 | 531,984 | 517,204 | | 517,204 |
| Washington | 52,327 | 65,829 | 59,078 | $480,000 | 539,078 |
| Wyoming | 1,420,387 | 1,692,373 | 1,556,380 | | 1,556,380 |
| Total | $3,017,161 | $3,494,000 | $3,255,581 | | $4,023,581 |

Historically, most states have used an equally weighted three-factor apportionment formula. This method adds together the sales, payroll, and property factors and divides the total by three to arrive at the apportionment factor (percentages) for each state. In recent years, many states have shifted to a double-weighted sales factor (doubling the sales factor, adding the payroll and property factors, and dividing the total by four). Both Idaho and Tennessee use the double-weighted sales factor for apportionment. Recently, some states have moved to a single-weighted sales factor that eliminates the payroll and property factors altogether. Oregon adopted a single-weighted sales factor beginning in 2008. All else equal, increasing the weight of the sales factor in the apportionment formula tends to decrease taxes on in-state businesses and increase taxes on out-of-state businesses. The reason is that in-state businesses tend to have high payroll and property factors relative to their sales factor in the state, and out-of-state businesses tend to have higher sales factors than payroll and property factors in that state.

### Example 23-18

Wild West must apportion its business income to Idaho and Tennessee. Its Idaho sales, payroll, and property factors are 31.29 percent, 27.28 percent, and 35.07 percent, respectively. Its Tennessee sales, payroll, and property factors are 15.88 percent, 20.11 percent, and 12.85 percent, respectively. These factors are aggregated from Examples 23-15 through 23-17. What are Wild West's apportionment factors in both states if they use a double-weighted sales factor?

**Answer:** The apportionment factors for Idaho and Tennessee are 31.23 percent and 16.18 percent, respectively.

| Factor | Idaho | Tennessee | Explanation |
|---|---|---|---|
| (1) Sales | 31.29% | 15.88% | |
| (2) Sales | 31.29% | 15.88% | |
| (3) Payroll | 27.28% | 20.11% | |
| (4) Property | 35.07% | 12.85% | |
| Apportionment factor | 31.23% | 16.18% | [(1) + (2) + (3) + (4)]/4 |

**What if:** Assume Tennessee uses an equally weighted three-factor apportionment formula. What are Wild West's apportionment factors?

**Answer:** The apportionment factors for Idaho and Tennessee are 29.06 percent and 16.28 percent, respectively. Idaho would be the same as above, and Tennessee's apportionment factor would now be calculated as follows:

| Factor | Tennessee | Explanation |
|---|---|---|
| (1) Sales | 15.88% | |
| (2) Payroll | 20.11% | |
| (3) Property | 12.85% | |
| Apportionment factor | 16.28% | [(1) + (2) + (3)]/3 |

**Nonbusiness Income**    We've said nonbusiness income is all income but business income. Here are common types of nonbusiness income, and the rules for allocating them to specific states:[37]

- Allocate interest and dividends to the state of commercial domicile (except interest on working capital, which is business income).
- Allocate rental income to the state where the property generating the rental income is located.
- Allocate royalties to the state where the property is used (if the business has nexus in that state; if not, allocate royalties to the state of commercial domicile).
- Allocate capital gains from investment property to the state of commercial domicile.
- Allocate capital gains from selling rental property to the state where the rental property was located.

**Example 23-19**

Wild West reports nonbusiness income as follows:

**Wild West**

| | | |
|---|---|---|
| Dividends | $ 6,000 | Federal tax return. |
| Interest | 14,505 | $11,005 (Federal return) + $5,000 (state and local interest) − $1,500 (Federal interest). |
| Rental income | 18,000 | Federal tax return. |
| Allocable total | $38,505 | |

Wild West's commercial domicile is in Idaho. Its rental income is for real property located in Wyoming. To which states should the firm allocate its nonbusiness income?

**Answer:** Wild West should allocate its nonbusiness income as follows:

**Wild West**

| | | |
|---|---|---|
| Idaho | $20,505 | $6,000 dividends + $14,505 interest income. |
| Nevada | 0 | |
| Tennessee | 0 | |
| Washington | 0 | |
| Wyoming | 18,000 | Rental income. |
| Total | $38,505 | |

[37]Multistate Tax Compact, Article IV, Division of Income, Paragraph 4.

### State Income Tax Liability

It is relatively easy to calculate a business's state taxable income and state tax after separating business and nonbusiness income, apportioning business income, and allocating nonbusiness income. Specifically, calculate state taxable income by multiplying business income by the apportionment factor and then adding any nonbusiness income allocated to the state.

---

**Example 23-20**

**What if:** Assume Idaho and Tennessee have a flat income tax rate of 7.6 percent and 6.5 percent, respectively. What is Wild West's income tax liability for Idaho and Tennessee?

**Answer:** Its liabilities are $2,963 and $752 in Idaho and Tennessee, respectively, computed as follows:

| Description | Idaho | Tennessee | Explanation |
|---|---|---|---|
| (1) State tax base | $97,685 | $109,989 | Example 23-14. |
| (2) Allocable income | ($38,505) | ($38,505) | Example 23-20. |
| (3) Business income | $59,180 | $ 71,484 | (1) − (2). |
| (4) Apportionment factor | 31.23% | 16.18% | Example 23-18. |
| (5) Apportioned income | $18,492 | $ 11,566 | (3) × (4). |
| (6) Allocable income | $20,505 | $ 0 | Example 23-19. |
| (7) State taxable income | $38,987 | $ 11,566 | (5) + (6). |
| (8) Tax rate | 7.6% | 6.5% | |
| Tax liability | $ 2,963 | $ 752 | (7) × (8). |

---

### Non (Net) Income-Based Taxes

Several states have nonincome-based taxes. Ohio has the Commercial Activity Tax, and Washington has the Business & Occupation Tax; these are both gross receipts taxes. Texas has the Margin Tax, the lesser of a gross margin tax or gross receipts tax. As we discussed earlier, Public Law 86-272 doesn't apply to nexus for nonincome-based taxes such as gross receipts taxes or property taxes; these are deductible for calculating taxable income for net income-based taxes.

---

**Example 23-21**

Wild West has nexus in Washington and is subject to that state's Business and Occupation (B&O) tax. The tax is .471 percent of gross receipts for retailers and 1.5 percent of gross receipts on services. Wild West's gross receipts from retail sales and services are $41,982 and $377,441, respectively (from Example 23-3). Calculate Wild West's B&O tax.

**Answer:** Wild West's B&O tax is $5,860, calculated as follows:

| Activity | (1) Receipts | (2) Rate | (1) × (2) Tax |
|---|---|---|---|
| Retailing | $ 41,982 | 0.471% | $ 198 |
| Services | $377,441 | 1.500% | 5,662 |
| B&O tax | | | $5,860 |

# CONCLUSION

In this chapter we discussed the fundamentals of state and local taxation with an emphasis on nexus, sales and use tax, and net income-based corporate taxes. State and local taxes currently make up a significant portion of many businesses' total tax burden and also consume a significant portion of the tax department's time.

Sales and use tax nexus is established through physical presence. Companies selling tangible personal property must collect sales tax from their customers (where nexus exists) and remit it to the various states. Income tax nexus requirements vary based on the type of goods or services provided by a business. Tangible personal property sales are protected from income tax nexus by Public Law 86-272 if certain criteria are met. For all other sales, nexus is created by physical presence, although some states are defining the concept of income tax nexus based on economic rather than physical presence.

Businesses subject to multijurisdictional taxation—taxation by more than one government—have many issues in common. A business located in San Diego, California, but also doing business in Tucson, Arizona, will be subject to California and Arizona tax. If it also does business in Rosarito, Mexico, it will be subject to both U.S. and Mexico taxes. State and local taxation and international taxation bring up many of the same issues. For both, businesses must determine which jurisdiction has the right to tax a transaction (nexus) and determine how to divide income among different jurisdictions. The next chapter examines multinational taxation.

## SUMMARY

Describe the primary types of state and local taxes.    **LO1**

- The primary purpose of state and local taxes is to raise revenue.
- Like federal tax law, state tax law is comprised of legislative, administrative, and judicial law.
- Judicial law plays a more important role in state tax law than federal tax law because constitutionality is a primary concern for state tax laws.
- The most important question any taxpayer must answer is whether it is subject to a state's taxing regime.
- Nexus is the connection between a business and a state sufficient to subject the business to the state's tax system.
- When a business sells tangible personal property, either sales or use tax is due. If the seller has nexus, the seller must collect and remit the tax to the state. Otherwise, the buyer is responsible for paying the use tax.
- Businesses engaged in interstate commerce that have nexus must pay income tax.

Determine whether a business has sales and use tax nexus and calculate its sales tax withholding responsibilities.    **LO2**

- Forty-five states and the District of Columbia impose sales and use taxes.
- The items subject to sales and use tax vary from state to state.
- Businesses are required to collect sales tax on sales only if they have sales and use tax nexus with that state.
- For nondomiciliary businesses, sales and use tax nexus is created through a physical presence (having salespeople or tangible property within the state, for example).

Identify whether a business has income tax nexus and determine its state income tax liabilities.    **LO3**

- Forty-six states impose an income tax on corporations, and 43 states tax the owners of partnerships and S corporations.
- Businesses must pay income tax in their state of commercial domicile, and nondomiciliary firms are subject to tax if they have nexus in the state.

- Businesses divide or apportion their income among the states where they have established nexus.
- Nexus requirements vary based on the nature of the business's activities: physical presence creates income tax nexus for service providers, sellers of real property, and businesses licensing intangibles; Public Law 86-272 protects solicitation of tangible personal property from nexus.
- Some states require a separate income tax return for each entity with nexus, and others require a unitary (one) tax return for a group of related entities as long as one of the entities has established nexus in the state.
- Businesses must calculate state taxable income for each state in which they must file a tax return—this requires businesses to identify federal/state adjustments.
- Firms adjust federal taxable income to arrive at their state taxable base.
- The state taxable base of an interstate business is separated into business and nonbusiness income: business income is apportioned across states using a general formula, and nonbusiness income is allocated to specific states using specific rules.
- Business income is apportioned using some variation of sales, payroll and property factors.

# KEY TERMS

allocation (23-4)

apportionment (23-4)

business income (23-4)

commercial domicile (23-2)

economic nexus (23-12)

federal/state adjustments (23-15)

interstate commerce (23-4)

nexus (23-2)

nonbusiness income (23-4)

nondomiciliary business (23-2)

Public Law 86-272 (23-9)

sales tax (23-3)

separate tax return (23-13)

solicitation (23-9)

state tax base (23-4)

throwback rule (23-17)

trade show rule (23-11)

unitary tax return (23-13)

use tax (23-4)

# DISCUSSION QUESTIONS

1. **(LO1)** Why do states and local jurisdictions assess taxes?
2. **(LO1)** Compare and contrast the relative importance of judicial law to state and local and federal tax law.
3. **(LO1)** Describe briefly the nexus concept and explain its importance to state and local taxation.
4. **(LO1)** What is the difference, if any, between the state of a business's commercial domicile and its state of incorporation?
5. **(LO1)** What types of property sales are subject to sales tax and why might a state choose to exclude the sales of certain types of property?
6. **(LO1)** In what circumstances would a business be subject to income taxes in more than one state?
7. **(LO1)** Describe how the failure to collect sales tax can result in a larger tax liability for a business than failing to pay income taxes.
8. **(LO2)** Discuss why restaurant meals, rental cars, and hotel receipts are often taxed at a higher-than-average sales tax rate.
9. **(LO2)** Compare and contrast general sales and use tax nexus and the new "Amazon" rule creating nexus in New York.
10. **(LO2)** What is the difference between a sales tax and a use tax?

11. **(LO2)** Renée operates Scandinavian Imports, a furniture shop in Olney, Maryland, that ships goods to customers in all 50 states. Scandinavian Imports also appraises antique furniture and has recently conducted in-home appraisals in the District of Columbia, Maryland, Pennsylvania, and Virginia. Online appraisals have been done for customers in California, Minnesota, New Mexico, and Texas. Determine where Scandinavian Imports has sales and use tax nexus.

12. **(LO2)** Web Music, located in Gardnerville, Nevada, is a new online music service that allows inexpensive legal music downloads. Web Music prides itself on having the fastest download times in the industry. It achieved this speed by leasing server space from 10 regional servers dispersed across the country. Discuss where Web Music has sales and use tax nexus.

13. **(LO2)** Discuss possible reasons why the Commerce clause was included in the U.S. Constitution.

14. **(LO2)** Describe the administrative burden businesses face in collecting sales taxes.

15. **(LO3)** Compare and contrast the rules determining where domiciliary and non-domiciliary businesses must file state income tax returns.

16. **(LO3)** Lars operates Keep Flying, Incorporated, a used airplane parts business, in Laramie, Wyoming. Lars employs sales agents that visit mechanics in all 50 states to solicit orders. All orders are sent to Wyoming for approval, and all parts are shipped via common carrier. The sales agents are always on the lookout for wrecked, abandoned, or salvage aircraft with rare parts because they receive substantial bonuses for purchasing and salvaging these parts and shipping them to Wyoming. Discuss the states where Keep Flying has income tax nexus.

17. **(LO3)** Explain changes in the U.S. economy that have made P.L. 86-272 partially obsolete. Provide an example of a company that P.L. 86-272 works well for and one that it does not work well for.

18. **(LO3)** Climb Higher is a distributor of high-end climbing gear located in Paradise, Washington. Its sales personnel regularly perform the following activities in an effort to maximize sales:

    • Carry swag (free samples) for distribution to climbing shop employees.
    • Perform credit checks of new customers to reduce delivery time of first order of merchandise.
    • Check customer inventory for proper display and proper quantities.
    • Accept returns of defective goods.

    Identify which of Climb Higher's sales activities are protected and unprotected from nexus under the *Wrigley* Supreme Court decision.

19. **(LO3)** Describe a situation in which it would be advantageous for a business to establish income tax nexus in a state.

20. **(LO3)** States are arguing for economic nexus; provide at least one reason for and one against the validity of economic nexus.

21. **(LO3)** Explain the difference between separate-return states and unitary-return states.

22. **(LO3)** Explain the rationale for the factors (functional integration, centralization of management, and economies of scale) that determine whether two or more businesses form a unitary group under the *Mobil* decision.

23. **(LO3)** Compare and contrast the reasons why book/tax and federal/state adjustments are necessary for interest income.

24. **(LO3)** Compare and contrast the ways a multistate business divides business and nonbusiness income among states.

25. **(LO3)** Contrast the treatment of government sales and dock sales for the sales apportionment factor.

26. **(LO3)** Most states have increased the weight of the sales factor for the apportionment of business income. What are some possible reasons?

27. **(LO3)** Compare and contrast federal/state tax differences and book/federal tax differences.

# PROBLEMS

28. **(LO2)** Crazy Eddie, Incorporated, manufactures baseball caps and distributes them across the northeastern United States. The firm is incorporated and headquartered in New York and sells to customers in Connecticut, Delaware, Massachusetts, New Jersey, New York, Ohio, and Pennsylvania. It has sales reps only where discussed in the scenarios below. Determine the states in which Crazy Eddie has sales and use tax nexus given the following:

   a. Crazy Eddie is incorporated and headquartered in New York. It also has property, employees, salespeople, and intangibles in New York.

   b. Crazy Eddie has a warehouse in Connecticut.

   c. Crazy Eddie has two customers in Delaware. Crazy Eddie receives orders over the phone and ships goods to its Delaware customers using FedEx.

   d. Crazy Eddie has independent sales representatives in Massachusetts who distribute baseball-related items for over a dozen companies.

   e. Crazy Eddie has salespeople who visit New Jersey. They follow procedures that comply with Public Law 86-272 by sending orders to New York for acceptance. The goods are shipped to New Jersey by FedEx.

   f. Crazy Eddie provides graphic design services to another manufacturer located in Ohio. While the services are performed in New York, Crazy Eddie's designers visit Ohio at least quarterly to deliver the new designs and receive feedback.

   g. Crazy Eddie receives online orders from its Pennsylvania client. Because the orders are so large, the goods are delivered weekly on Crazy Eddie's trucks.

29. **(LO2)** Brad Carlton operates Carlton Collectibles, a rare-coin shop in Washington, D.C., that ships coins to collectors in all 50 states. Carlton also provides appraisal service upon request. During the last several years the appraisal work has been done either in the D.C. shop or at the homes of private collectors in Maryland and Virginia. Determine the jurisdictions in which Carlton Collectibles has sales and use tax nexus.

30. **(LO2)** Melanie operates Mel's Bakery in Foxboro, Massachusetts, with retail stores in Connecticut, Maine, Massachusetts, New Hampshire, and Rhode Island. Mel's also ships specialty breads nationwide upon request. Determine Mel's sales tax collection responsibility and calculate the sales tax liability for Massachusetts, Connecticut, Maine, New Hampshire, Rhode Island, and Texas, using the following information.

   a. The Massachusetts stores earn $500,000 in sales. Massachusetts' sales tax rate is 6 percent; assume it exempts food items.

   b. The Connecticut retail stores have $400,000 in sales ($300,000 from in-store sales and $100,000 from catering) and $10,000 in delivery charges for catering activities. Connecticut sales tax is 6 percent and excludes food products but taxes prepared meals (catering). Connecticut also imposes sales tax on delivery charges on taxable sales.

   c. Mel's Maine retail store has $250,000 of sales ($200,000 for take-out and $50,000 of in-store sales). Maine has a 5 percent sales tax rate and a 7 percent sales tax rate on prepared food; it exempts other food purchases.

d. The New Hampshire retail stores have $250,000 in sales. New Hampshire is one of five states with no sales tax. However, it has a room and meals tax rate of 8 percent. New Hampshire considers any food or beverage served by a restaurant for consumption on or off the premises to be a meal.

e. Mel's Rhode Island stores earn $300,000 in sales. The Rhode Island sales tax rate is 7 percent and its restaurant surtax is 1 percent. Rhode Island considers Mel's a restaurant because its retail store has seating.

f. One of Mel's best customers relocated to Texas, which imposes an 8.25 percent state and local sales tax rate but exempts bakery products. This customer entertains regularly and ordered $5,000 of food items this year.

31. **(LO2)** Cuyahoga County, Ohio, has a sales tax rate of 7.75 percent. Determine the state, local, and transit (a local transportation district) portions of the rate. You can find resources on the State of Ohio Web site including the following link: www.tax.ohio.gov/divisions/tax_analysis/tax_data_series/sales_and_use/documents/salestaxmapcolor.pdf

■ **research**

32. **(LO2)** Kai operates the Surf Shop in Laie, Hawaii, which designs, manufacturers, and customizes surfboards. Hawaii has a 4 percent excise tax rate, technically paid by the seller. However, the state also allows "tax on tax" to be charged, which effectively means a customer is billed 4.166 percent of the sales price. Determine the sales and use tax the Surf Shop must collect and remit—or that the customer must pay—for each of the following orders:

a. Bronco, a Utah customer, places an Internet order for a $1,000 board that will be shipped to Provo, Utah, where the local sales tax rate is 6.25 percent.

b. Norma, a California resident, comes to the retail shop on vacation and has a $2,000 custom board made. Norma uses the board on vacation and then has the Surf Shop ship it to Los Angeles, California, where the sales tax rate is 8.5 percent.

c. Jim, an Ohio resident, places an order for a $2,000 custom board at the end of his vacation. Upon completion the board will be shipped to Columbus, Ohio, where the sales tax rate is 7 percent.

d. Bo, a Nebraska resident, sends his current surfboard to the Surf Shop for a custom paint job. The customization services come to $800. The board is shipped to Lincoln, Nebraska, where the sales tax rate is 7 percent.

33. **(LO2)** Last year, Pete, a Los Angeles, California, resident, began selling autographed footballs through Trojan Victory (TV), Incorporated, a California corporation. TV has never collected sales tax. Last year it had sales as follows: California ($100,000), Arizona ($10,000), Oregon ($15,000), New York ($50,000), and Wyoming ($1,000). Most sales are made over the Internet and shipped by common carrier. How much sales tax should TV have collected in each of the following situations:

■ **planning**

a. California treats the autographed football as tangible personal property subject to an 8.25 percent sales tax rate. Answer for California.

b. California treats the autographed football as part tangible personal property ($50,000) and part services ($50,000), and tangible personal property is subject to an 8.25 percent sales tax rate. Answer for California.

c. TV has no property or other physical presence in New York or Wyoming. Answer for New York and Wyoming.

d. TV has Pete deliver a few balls to fans in Arizona (5.6 percent sales tax rate) and Oregon (no sales tax) while attending football games there. Answer for Arizona and Oregon.

e. Related to part d, can you make any suggestions that would decrease TV's Arizona sales tax liability?

34. **(LO2)** Armstrong Incorporated, a Texas corporation, runs bicycle tours in several states. Armstrong also has a Texas retail store and an Internet store that ships to out-of-state customers. The bicycle tours operate in Colorado, North Carolina, and Texas, where Armstrong has employees and owns and uses tangible personal property. Armstrong has real property only in Texas and logs the following sales:

| Armstrong Sales | | | |
|---|---|---|---|
| State | Goods | Services | Total |
| Arizona | $ 34,194 | $ 0 | $ 34,194 |
| California | 110,612 | 0 | 110,612 |
| Colorado | 25,913 | 356,084 | 381,997 |
| North Carolina | 16,721 | 225,327 | 242,048 |
| Oregon | 15,431 | 0 | 15,431 |
| Texas | 241,982 | 877,441 | 1,119,423 |
| Totals | $444,853 | $1,458,852 | $1,903,705 |

Assume the following tax rates: Arizona (5.6 percent), California (7.75 percent), Colorado (8 percent), North Carolina (6.75 percent), Oregon (8 percent), and Texas (8.5 percent). How much sales and use tax must Armstrong collect and remit?

35. **(LO3)** Kashi Corporation is the U.S. distributor of fencing (sword fighting) equipment imported from Europe. It is incorporated in Virginia and headquartered in Arlington, Virginia; it ships goods to all 50 states. Kashi's employees attend regional and national fencing competitions where they maintain temporary booths to market their goods. Determine whether Kashi has income tax nexus in the following situations:

a. Kashi is incorporated and headquartered in Virginia. It also has property, employees, salespeople, and intangibles in Virginia. Determine whether Kashi has nexus in Virginia.

b. Kashi has employees who live in Washington, D.C., and Maryland but perform all their employment-related activities in Virginia. Does Kashi have nexus in Washington, D.C., and Maryland?

c. Kashi has two customers in North Dakota. It receives their orders over the phone and ships goods to them using FedEx. Determine whether Kashi has nexus in North Dakota.

d. Kashi has independent sales representatives in Illinois who distribute fencing and other sports-related items for many companies. Does Kashi have nexus in Illinois?

e. Kashi has salespeople who visit South Carolina for a regional fencing competition for a total of three days during the year. They send all orders to Virginia for credit approval and acceptance, and Kashi ships the goods into South Carolina by FedEx. Determine whether Kashi has nexus in South Carolina.

f. Kashi has sales reps who visit California for a national fencing competition and several regional competitions for a total of 17 days during the year. They send all orders to Virginia for credit approval and acceptance. The goods are shipped by FedEx into California. Does Kashi have nexus in California?

g. Kashi receives online orders from its Pennsylvania client. Because the orders are so large, the goods are delivered weekly on Kashi's trucks. Does Kashi have nexus in Pennsylvania?

h. In addition to shipping goods, Kashi provides fencing lessons in Virginia and Maryland locations. Determine whether Kashi has nexus in Virginia and Maryland.

i.  Given that Kashi ships to all 50 states, are there locations that would decrease Kashi's overall state income tax burden if nexus were created there?

■ planning

36. **(LO3)** Gary Holt LLP provides tax and legal services regarding the tax-exempt bond issues of state and local jurisdictions. Gary typically provides the services from his New York offices. However, for large issuances he and his staff occasionally travel to another state to complete the work. Determine whether the firm has income tax nexus in the following situations:

a.  Gary Holt LLP is a New York partnership and headquartered in New York. It also has property and employees in New York. Does it have income tax nexus in New York?

b.  Gary Holt LLP has employees who live in New Jersey and Connecticut and perform all their employment-related activities in New York. Does it have income tax nexus in New Jersey and/or Connecticut?

c.  Gary Holt LLP has two customers in California. Gary personally travels there to finalize the Alameda County bond issuance. Does it have income tax nexus in California?

37. **(LO3)** Root Beer Inc. (RBI) is incorporated and headquartered in Seattle, Washington. RBI runs an Internet business, makerootbeer.com, and sells bottling equipment and other supplies for making homemade root beer. It also has an Oregon warehouse from which it ships goods. Determine whether RBI has income tax nexus in the following situations:

a.  Root Beer is incorporated and headquartered in Washington and has property and employees in Oregon and Washington. Determine whether RBI has nexus in Oregon and Washington.

b.  Root Beer has hundreds of customers in California but no physical presence (no employees or property). Does it have nexus in California?

c.  Root Beer has 500 New York customers but no physical presence (no employees or property). Remember New York has the new Amazon rule. Determine whether RBI has nexus in New York.

38. **(LO3)** Rockville Enterprises manufactures woodworking equipment and is incorporated and based in Evansville, Indiana. Its real property is all in Indiana. Rockville employs a large sales force that travels throughout the United States. Determine whether each of the following is a protected activity in nondomiciliary states under Public Law 86-272:

a.  Rockville advertises using television, radio, and newspapers.

b.  Rockville's employees in Illinois check the credit of a potential customer.

c.  Rockville maintains a booth at an industry tradeshow in Arizona for 10 days.

d.  Sales representatives check the inventory of a customer to make sure it has enough in stock and that the stock is properly displayed.

e.  Rockville holds a management seminar for corporate executives over four days in Florida.

f.  Sales representatives supervise the repossession of inventory from a customer that is not making payments on time.

g.  Rockville provides automobiles to Idaho and Montana sales representatives.

h.  An Alabama sales representative accepts a customer deposit on a large order.

i.  Sales representatives carry display racks and promotional material that they place in customers' retail stores without charge.

39. **(LO3)** Software Incorporated is a sales and use tax software vendor that provides customers with a license to download and use its software on their machines. Software retains ownership of the software. It has customers in New Jersey and

■ research

West Virginia. Does Software have economic nexus in these states because of the following decisions: *Lanco, Inc. v. Director, Division of Taxation,* NJ Sup. Ct., Dkt. No.A-89-05; and *Tax Commissioner of West Virginia v. MBNA America Bank, N.A.,* 640 SE 2d 226 (WV 2006)?

40. **(LO3)** Peter, Inc., a Kentucky corporation, owns 100 percent of Suvi, Inc., a Mississippi corporation. Peter and Suvi file a consolidated federal tax return. Peter has income tax nexus in Kentucky and South Carolina; Suvi in Mississippi and South Carolina. Kentucky, Mississippi, and South Carolina are separate-return states. In which states must Pete and Suvi file tax returns? Can they file a consolidated return in any states? Explain. (*Hint:* Use South Carolina Form SC 1120 and the related instructions.)

41. **(LO3)** Use California Publication 1061 (2007) to identify the various tests California uses to determine whether two or more entities are part of a unitary group.

42. **(LO3)** Bulldog, Incorporated, is a Georgia corporation. It properly included, deducted, or excluded the following items on its federal tax return in the current year:

| Item | Amount | Federal Treatment |
|---|---|---|
| Georgia income taxes | $25,496 | Deducted on federal return. |
| Tennessee income taxes | $13,653 | Deducted on federal return. |
| Washington gross receipts tax | $ 3,105 | Deducted on federal return. |
| Georgia bond interest income | $10,000 | Excluded from federal return. |
| Federal T-note interest income | $ 4,500 | Included on federal return. |
| Domestic production activities deduction (DPAD) | $15,096 | Deducted on federal return. |

Use Georgia's Corporate Income Tax Form 600 and Instructions to determine what federal/state adjustments Bulldog needs to make for Georgia. Bulldog's federal taxable income was $194,302. Calculate its Georgia state tax base.

43. **(LO3)** Herger Corporation does business in California, Nevada, and Oregon, and has nexus in these states as well. Herger's California state tax base was $921,023 after making the required federal/state adjustments. Herger's state tax base contains the following items:

| Item | Amount |
|---|---|
| Federal T-note interest income | $ 5,000 |
| Nevada municipal bond interest income | $ 3,400 |
| California municipal bond interest income | $ 6,000 |
| Interest expense related to T-note interest income | $ 1,400 |
| Royalty income | $100,000 |
| Travel expenses | $ 9,025 |

Determine Herger's business income.

44. **(LO3)** Bad Brad sells used semitrucks and tractor trailers in the Texas panhandle. Bad Brad has sales as follows:

| Bad Brad | |
|---|---|
| State | Sales |
| Colorado | $ 234,992 |
| Oklahoma | 402,450 |
| New Mexico | 675,204 |
| Texas | 1,085,249 |
| Totals | $2,397,895 |

Bad Brad is a Texas corporation. Answer the questions in each of the following alternative scenarios.

a. Bad Brad has nexus in Colorado, Oklahoma, New Mexico, and Texas. What are the Colorado, Oklahoma, New Mexico, and Texas sales apportionment factors?

b. Bad Brad has nexus in Colorado and Texas. Oklahoma and New Mexico sales are shipped from Texas (a throwback state). What are the Colorado and Texas sales apportionment factors?

c. Bad Brad has nexus in Colorado and Texas. Oklahoma and New Mexico sales are shipped from Texas (a throwback state); $200,000 of Oklahoma sales were to the federal government. What are the Colorado and Texas sales apportionment factors?

d. Bad Brad has nexus in Colorado and Texas. Oklahoma and New Mexico sales are shipped from Texas (assume Texas is a nonthrowback state). What are the Colorado and Texas sales apportionment factors?

45. **(LO3)** Nicole's Salon, a Louisiana corporation, operates beauty salons in Arkansas, Louisiana, and Tennessee. These salon's sales by state are as follows:

| Nicole's Salon | |
|---|---|
| **State** | **Sales** |
| Arkansas | $ 130,239 |
| Louisiana | 309,192 |
| Tennessee | 723,010 |
| Total | $1,162,441 |

What are the payroll apportionment factors for Arkansas, Louisiana, and Tennessee in each of the following alternative scenarios?

a. Nicole's Salon has nexus in Arkansas, Louisiana, and Tennessee.

b. Nicole's Salon has nexus in Arkansas, Louisiana, and Tennessee, but $50,000 of the Arkansas amount is paid to independent contractors.

46. **(LO3)** Delicious Dave's Maple Syrup, a Vermont corporation, has property in the following states:

| | Property | |
|---|---|---|
| **State** | **Beginning** | **Ending** |
| Maine | $ 923,032 | $ 994,221 |
| Massachusetts | 103,311 | 203,109 |
| New Hampshire | 381,983 | 283,021 |
| Vermont | 873,132 | 891,976 |
| Total | $2,281,458 | $2,372,327 |

What are the property apportionment factors for Maine, Massachusetts, New Hampshire, and Vermont in each of the following alternative scenarios?

a. Delicious has nexus in each of the states.

b. Delicious has nexus in each of the states, but the Maine total includes $400,000 of investment property that Delicious rents out (unrelated to its business).

c. Delicious has nexus in each of the states, but also pays $50,000 to rent property in Massachusetts.

47. **(LO3)** Susie's Sweet Shop has the following sales, payroll and property factors:

| | Iowa | Missouri |
|---|---|---|
| Sales | 69.20% | 32.01% |
| Payroll | 88.00% | 3.50% |
| Property | 72.42% | 24.04% |

What are Susie's Sweet Shop's Iowa and Missouri apportionment factors under each of the following alternative scenarios?

a. Iowa and Missouri both use a three-factor apportionment formula.

b. Iowa and Missouri both use a four-factor apportionment formula that double-weights sales.

c. Iowa uses a three-factor formula and Missouri uses a single-factor apportionment formula (based solely on sales).

48. **(LO3)** Brady Corporation is a Nebraska corporation, but owns business and investment property in surrounding states as well. Determine the state where each item of income is allocated.

a. $15,000 of dividend income.

b. $10,000 of interest income.

c. $15,000 of rental income for South Dakota property.

d. $20,000 of royalty income for intangibles used in South Dakota (where nexus exists).

e. $24,000 of royalty income from Kansas (where nexus does not exist).

f. $15,000 of capital gain from securities held for investment.

g. $30,000 of capital gain on real property located in South Dakota.

49. **(LO3)** Ashton Corporation is headquartered in Pennsylvania and has a state income tax base there of $500,000. Of this amount, $50,000 was nonbusiness income. Ashton's Pennsylvania apportionment factor is 42.35 percent. The nonbusiness income allocated to Pennsylvania was $32,000. Assuming a Pennsylvania corporate tax rate of 8.25 percent, what is Ashton's Pennsylvania state tax liability?

# COMPREHENSIVE PROBLEMS

50. Sharon Inc. is headquartered in State X and owns 100 percent of Carol, Josey, and Janice Corps, which form a single unitary group. Assume sales operations are within the solicitation bounds of Public Law 86-272. Each of the corporations has operations in the following states:

| Domicile State | Sharon Inc.<br>State X<br>(throwback) | Carol Corp<br>State Y<br>(throwback) | Josey Corp<br>State Z<br>(nonthrowback) | Janice Corp<br>State Z<br>(nonthrowback) |
|---|---|---|---|---|
| Dividend income | $ 1,000 | $ 200 | $ 300 | $ 500 |
| Business income | $50,000 | $30,000 | $10,000 | $10,000 |
| Sales: State X | $70,000 | $10,000 | $10,000 | $10,000 |
| State Y | | $40,000 | $ 5,000 | |
| State Z | | $20,000 | $20,000 | $10,000 |
| State A | $20,000 | | | |
| State B | $10,000 | | | $10,000 |

(*continued*)

| Domicile State | Sharon Inc.<br>State X<br>(throwback) | Carol Corp<br>State Y<br>(throwback) | Josey Corp<br>State Z<br>(nonthrowback) | Janice Corp<br>State Z<br>(nonthrowback) |
|---|---|---|---|---|
| Property: State X | $50,000 | $20,000 | | $10,000 |
| State Y | | $80,000 | | |
| State Z | | | $25,000 | $20,000 |
| State A | $50,000 | | | |
| Payroll: State X | $10,000 | $10,000 | | |
| State Y | | $40,000 | | |
| State Z | | | $ 3,000 | $10,000 |
| State A | | | | $10,000 |

Compute the income reported, apportionment factors, and tax liability for State X assuming a tax rate of 15 percent.

51. Happy Hippos (HH) is a manufacturer and retailer of New England crafts headquartered in Camden, Maine. HH provides services and has sales, employees, property, and commercial domicile as follows:

| | | Happy Hippos In-State Activities | | | |
|---|---|---|---|---|---|
| State | Sales | Employees | Property | Services | Commercial Domicile |
| Connecticut | ✓ | ✓ | | ✓ | |
| Maine | ✓ | ✓ | ✓ | ✓ | ✓ |
| Massachusetts | ✓ | ✓ | | | |
| New Hampshire | ✓ | | | | |
| Rhode Island | ✓ | ✓ | | | |
| Vermont | ✓ | ✓ | ✓ | ✓ | |

Happy Hippos sales of goods and services by state are as follows:

| | Happy Hippos Sales | | |
|---|---|---|---|
| State | Goods | Services | Total |
| Connecticut | $ 78,231 | $ 52,321 | $130,552 |
| Maine | 292,813 | 81,313 | 374,126 |
| Massachusetts | 90,238 | | 90,238 |
| New Hampshire | 129,322 | | 129,322 |
| Rhode Island | 98,313 | | 98,313 |
| Vermont | 123,914 | 23,942 | 147,856 |
| Totals | $812,831 | $157,576 | $970,407 |

HH has federal taxable income of $282,487 for the current year. Included in federal taxable income are the following income and deductions: $12,000 of Vermont rental income; City of Orono, Maine, bond interest of $10,000; $10,000 of dividends; $2,498 of state tax refund included in income; $32,084 of state net income tax expense; and $59,234 of federal depreciation. Maine state depreciation for the year was $47,923, and Maine doesn't allow deductions for state net income taxes.

The employees present in Connecticut, Massachusetts, and Rhode Island are salespeople who perform only activities protected by Public Law 86-272.

Each of the states is a separate-return state.

HH's payroll is as follows:

| Payroll | |
| --- | --- |
| **State** | **Wages** |
| Connecticut | $ 94,231 |
| Maine | 392,195 |
| Massachusetts | 167,265 |
| Rhode Island | 92,391 |
| Vermont | 193,923 |
| Total | $940,005 |

HH's property is as follows:

| Property | | | |
| --- | --- | --- | --- |
| **State** | **Beginning** | **Ending** | **Rented** |
| Maine | $ 938,234 | $ 937,652 | |
| Vermont | 329,134 | 428,142 | $12,000 |
| Total | $1,267,368 | $1,365,794 | $12,000 |

a. Determine the states in which HH has sales and use tax nexus.
b. Calculate the sales tax HH must remit assuming the following sales tax rates: Connecticut (6 percent), Maine (8 percent), Massachusetts (7 percent), New Hampshire (8.5 percent), Rhode Island (5 percent), and Vermont (9 percent).
c. Determine the states in which HH has income tax nexus.
d. Determine HH's state tax base for Maine, assuming federal taxable income of $282,487.
e. Calculate business and nonbusiness income.
f. Determine HH's Maine apportionment factors using the three-factor method (assume that Maine is a throwback state).
g. Calculate HH's business income apportioned to Maine.
h. Determine HH's allocation of nonbusiness income to Maine.
i. Determine HH's Maine taxable income.
j. Calculate HH's Maine net income tax liability assuming a Maine income tax rate of 5 percent.

# The U.S. Taxation of Multinational Transactions

## Learning Objectives

**Upon completing this chapter, you should be able to:**

**LO 1** Understand the basic U.S. framework for taxing multinational transactions and the role of the foreign tax credit limitation.

■

**LO 2** Apply the U.S. source rules for common items of gross income and deductions.

■

**LO 3** Recall the role of income tax treaties in international tax planning.

■

**LO 4** Identify creditable foreign taxes and compute the foreign tax credit limitation.

■

**LO 5** Distinguish between the different forms of doing business outside the United States and list their advantages and disadvantages.

■

**LO 6** Comprehend the basic U.S. anti-deferral tax regime and identify common sources of subpart F income.

## Storyline Summary

**Detroit Doughnut Depot**

Privately held company located in Detroit, Michigan

Operated as a C corporation for U.S. tax purposes

Makes and sells fresh baked goods, homemade sandwiches, and premium coffee and tea drinks

**Lily Green**

Owner of Detroit Doughnut Depot (3D)

*Filing status:* Married filing jointly

*Dependents:* Two children

*Marginal tax rate:* 28 percent

L ily Green was excited about the growth of her coffee and baked goods business since she opened her store in downtown Detroit in 2005. From its humble beginnings, the Detroit Doughnut Depot (3D) had attracted a solid base of loyal customers who appreciated the freshness and organic ingredients that set the company's products apart from its competitors. Many of Lily's customers were commuters from nearby Windsor, Canada. They often asked Lily if she ever considered opening a store in Windsor, where they thought she would find a receptive customer base. Lily was intrigued by the idea of "going global" with her business, but she knew she needed to find someone to help her understand the U.S. and Canadian income tax implications of moving her business to Windsor. Her first questions dealt with how and when she would be subject to Canadian tax and whether her Canadian activities also would be subject to U.S. tax.

*to be continued . . .*

Lily Green is about to join a growing trend of expansion by U.S. businesses into international markets. In 1983, gross receipts of non-U.S. subsidiaries of U.S. multinational corporations totaled approximately $720 billion; by 2004, that number had risen to almost $3.5 trillion, a fivefold increase.[1] Before-tax profits increased from $57 billion in 1983 to more than $250 billion in 2004. Companies such as Google Inc. and McDonald's are reporting a significant amount of income from international operations. For example, Google Inc. reported pretax income from its international operations of $3.8 billion in 2008, approximately 55 percent of its total income before income taxes![2] McDonald's Corporation reported $23.5 billion of revenues in 2008, almost two-thirds of which came from outside the United States.

As dramatic as the outflow of investment from the United States has been, the inflow of investment by non-U.S. businesses and individuals into the United States has been just as impressive. According to the U.S. Bureau of Economic Analysis, the total amount of foreign-owned assets in the United States increased by more than 400 percent between 1980 and 2000.[3] U.S. subsidiaries of non-U.S. companies employed more than 5 million Americans in 2007.[4] Familiar non-U.S. companies with large U.S. operations include BP Global (United Kingdom), Toyota Motor Corporation (Japan), Honda Motor Corporation (Japan), Nissan Group (Japan), Nestle S.A. (Switzerland), Sony Corporation (Japan), GlaxoSmithKline PLC (United Kingdom), Volkswagen AG (Germany), Samsung Group (South Korea), BMW AG (Germany), Bridgestone Corporation (Japan), Bayer AG (Germany), and Philips Electronics N.V. (Netherlands).

This chapter provides a basic overview of the U.S. tax consequences related to transactions that span more than one national tax jurisdiction (in our storyline, the United States and Canada). We focus primarily on the U.S. tax rules that apply to **outbound transactions,** where a U.S. person engages in a transaction that occurs outside the United States or involves a non-U.S. person.[5] We also discuss briefly the U.S. tax rules that apply to **inbound transactions,** where a non-U.S. person engages in a transaction that occurs within the United States or involves a U.S. person. Most of the U.S. income tax rules that apply to multinational transactions are found in subchapter N of the Internal Revenue Code (§861–§999).

**L01**

# THE U.S. FRAMEWORK FOR TAXING MULTINATIONAL TRANSACTIONS

When a U.S. person engages in a transaction that involves a country outside the United States, there arises the issue as to which tax authority or authorities have jurisdiction (that is, the legal right) to tax that transaction. All governments (national, state, and local) must adopt a basis on which to claim the right to tax income. The criteria they choose to assert their right to tax a person or transaction is called **nexus.** At the national level, governments most often determine nexus by either the geographic source of the income **(source-based jurisdiction)** or the taxpayer's citizenship or residence **(residence-based jurisdiction).**

---

[1]Martin A. Sullivan, "A Challenge to Conventional International Wisdom," *Tax Notes* (December 11, 2006), pp. 951–961.

[2]As a reference point, Google Inc. reported a *loss* of $42.3 million in 2004 from international operations.

[3]Joint Committee on Taxation, *The Impact of International Tax Reform: Background and Selected Issues Relating to U.S. International Tax Rules and the Competitiveness of U.S. Businesses* (JCX-222-06), June 21, 2006.

[4]Mathew J. Slaughter, *Insourcing Mergers and Acquisitions* (Organization for International Investment, December 2007).

[5]As used in this chapter, a "person" includes an individual, corporation, partnership, trust, estate, or association. Section 7701(a)(1). The "United States," as used in this context, includes only the 50 states and the District of Columbia. §7701(a)(9).

Once nexus is established, a government must decide how a person's income and expenses are to be allocated and apportioned to its tax jurisdiction. Under a residence-based approach, a country taxes the worldwide income of the person earning the income. Under a source-based approach, a country taxes only the income earned within its boundaries. When applying a source-based approach, a government must develop source rules to allocate and apportion income and expenses to its jurisdiction. Within the United States, states use apportionment formulas that take into account sales, property, and payroll, or some combination of these factors, to apportion income and expenses to its tax jurisdiction.[6]

Income earned by a citizen or resident of one country that has its source in another country potentially can be taxed by both countries. The country where the taxpayer resides can assert residence-based jurisdiction, whereas the country where the income is earned can apply geographic source-based jurisdiction. To alleviate (mitigate) such double taxation and to promote international commerce, governments often allow their residents a tax credit for foreign income taxes paid on *foreign source* income. National governments also enter into bilateral income tax treaties with other national governments to mitigate the double taxation of income earned by residents of one country in the other country. Under a treaty, both countries may agree not to tax income earned within their boundaries by a resident of the other country.

The United States applies both residence-based jurisdiction and source-based jurisdiction in asserting its right to tax income. The U.S. government taxes *citizens* and *residents* on their worldwide income, regardless of source (residence-based jurisdiction).[7] In contrast, the U.S. government only taxes *nonresidents* on income that is "U.S. source" or is connected with the operation of a U.S. trade or business (source-based jurisdiction).

### U.S. Taxation of a Nonresident

U.S. source income earned by a nonresident is classified into two categories for U.S. tax purposes: (1) **effectively connected income** (ECI) and (2) **fixed and determinable, annual or periodic income** (FDAP). Income that is effectively connected with a U.S. trade or business is subject to *net taxation* (that is, gross income minus deductions) at the U.S. graduated tax rates. A nonresident reports such income and related deductions on a U.S. tax return, either a Form 1120F for a corporation or a Form 1040NR for an individual. FDAP income, which is generally passive income such as dividends, interest, rents, or royalties, is subject to a *withholding tax* regime applied to *gross income.* The payor of the FDAP income withholds the tax at the statutory rate (30 percent under U.S. tax law) or less under a treaty arrangement and remits it to the government. The recipient of the FDAP income usually does not have to file a tax return and does not reduce the FDAP income by any deductions. Most countries, including Canada, apply a similar tax regime to U.S. persons earning income within their jurisdiction.[8]

**Basic Framework for U.S. Taxation of Multinational Transactions**

- The United States taxes citizens and residents on their worldwide income and nonresidents on their U.S. source income.

- A noncitizen is treated as a U.S. resident for income tax purposes if the individual is a permanent resident (has a green card) or meets a substantial presence test.

- Nonresident income is characterized as either ECI or FDAP income.
  · ECI is taxed on a net basis using the U.S. graduated tax rates.
  · FDAP is taxed on a gross basis through a flat withholding tax.

- The U.S. allows citizens and residents a tax credit for foreign income taxes paid on foreign source income.

- The foreign tax credit is limited to the percentage of foreign source taxable income to taxable income times the precredit income tax on total taxable income.

**Example 24-1**

Lily decided to open a store in Windsor, Canada, from which she will sell baked goods and sandwiches made in her U.S. store and transported daily across the border. She elected to operate the store as a **branch** (an unincorporated division) of Detroit Doughnut Deport (3D) for Canadian tax purposes. Will 3D be subject to tax in Canada on any taxable income it earns through its Windsor store in 2010?

*(continued on page 24-4...)*

[6]See Chapter 23 for a more thorough discussion of how states apportion income.

[7]The United States is one of three countries (along with the Philippines and Bulgaria) that applies worldwide taxation based on citizenship as well as residency.

[8]Canada applies a 25 percent withholding tax rate on interest, dividends, and royalties unless reduced under a treaty.

**Answer:** Yes. 3D will have nexus in Canada because it operates a business there (residence-based jurisdiction). As a result, Canada and the Province of Ontario will tax the branch's Canadian-source taxable income.

How will Canada tax 3D's Canadian-source taxable income?

**Answer:** Canada will apply the appropriate corporate tax rate(s) to the branch's taxable income (gross income less deductions). For 2010, the general Canadian corporate tax rate is a flat 18 percent after abatements. The province of Ontario also will impose an income tax on the branch's taxable income.

*What if:* Assume 3D does not operate a business in Canada but owns stock in a Canadian company that pays the company a C$100 dividend each year.[9] How will Canada tax 3D on the dividend income it receives from its investment in the stock of a Canadian company?

**Answer:** Canada will apply a flat withholding tax on the gross amount of the dividend.[10]

## Definition of a Resident for U.S. Tax Purposes

An individual who is not a U.S. citizen is characterized for U.S. tax purposes as either a **resident alien** or a **nonresident alien.** An individual becomes a U.S. resident by satisfying one of two tests found in the IRC.[11] Under the first test, sometimes referred to as the *green card test,* an individual is treated as a resident if he or she possesses a permanent resident visa ("green card") at any time during the calendar year. Under the second test, sometimes referred to as the *substantial presence test,* an individual becomes a U.S. resident when he or she is *physically present* in the United States for 31 days or more during the current calendar year, *and* the number of days of physical presence during the current calendar year plus one-third times the number of days of physical presence during the first preceding year plus one-sixth times the number of days of physical presence during the second preceding year equals or exceeds 183 days.[12] As we will discuss later in the chapter, these rules are often modified by treaties between the United States and other countries to limit instances where an individual might be taxed as a resident by more than one country.

As always, there are a number of exceptions to the physical presence test. For example, international students and teachers generally are exempt from the physical presence test for five and two years, respectively. Individuals who are present in the United States during the current year for less than 183 days and who establish that they have a "closer connection" to another country can elect to be exempt from the physical presence test.[13] Other exemptions apply to unexpected medical conditions that arise while an individual is in the United States and to commuters from Canada and Mexico.

The residence of a corporation for U.S. tax purposes generally is determined by the entity's country of incorporation. For example, the parent company of Tyco International, Ltd., is now incorporated in Switzerland, although it is managed in the United States. For U.S. tax purposes, the parent company of Tyco is treated as a nonresident corporation, although its U.S. subsidiaries and U.S. branches are treated as U.S. residents. Some countries, such as the United Kingdom, determine a corporation's residence based on where central management of the company is located. U.K.

[9]The national currency of Canada is the Canadian dollar, abbreviated C$.

[10]Under the U.S.-Canada income tax treaty, the withholding tax on this dividend is 15 percent.

[11]§7701(b).

[12]For purposes of this test, a full day is considered any part of a day.

[13]An individual usually satisfies the closer connection test by demonstrating that he or she has a "tax home" in another country. A "tax home" is defined as the taxpayer's regular place of business or *regular place of abode.*

government would treat the parent company of Tyco as a U.S. resident because it is managed in the United States.

**Example 24-2**

*What if:* Assume for quality control purposes that Lily decided to do all of the baking for her Windsor store in Detroit. Every morning a Windsor employee drives a van to Detroit and picks up the baked goods for sale in Windsor. One of her employees, Stan Lee Cupp, made the 2-hour trip on 132 different days during 2010. He was not physically present in the United States prior to 2010. Will Stan be considered a U.S. resident in 2010 applying only the substantial presence test?

**Answer:** No. Although he is physically present in the United States for more than 30 days in 2010, he does not satisfy the 183-day test when applying the formula $[132 + (1/3 \times 0) + (1/6 \times 0) = 132]$.

*What if:* Assume Stan continues to be physically present in the United States for 132 days in 2011 and 2012. Will Stan be considered a U.S. resident in 2011 or 2012 applying only the substantial presence test?

**Answer:**

2011: No. He does not satisfy the 183-day test when applying the formula $[132 + (1/3 \times 132) + (1/6 \times 0) = 176]$.

2012: Yes. He now satisfies the 183-day test when applying the formula $[132 + (1/3 \times 132) + (1/6 \times 132) = 198]$.

Does Stan qualify for any exceptions that allow him to avoid being treated as a U.S. resident in 2012?

**Answer:** Yes. Stan can avoid being a U.S. resident under the closer connection test because he was physically present in the United States for less than 183 days in 2012 and his tax home is in Canada. If he is in the United States for 183 days or more, he will have to fall back on the U.S.-Canada income tax treaty to avoid being considered a U.S. resident for income tax purposes (to be discussed in more detail later in the chapter).

## Overview of the U.S. Foreign Tax Credit System

The United States mitigates the double taxation of foreign source income by allowing citizens and residents to claim a **foreign tax credit** (FTC) for foreign income taxes paid on their *foreign source* income. The goal of the FTC is to keep a U.S. taxpayer's worldwide *effective tax rate* (total income taxes paid/taxable income) from exceeding the U.S. statutory tax rate. The United States attempts to achieve this result through the **foreign tax credit limitation,** which is computed as follows:

$$\frac{\text{Foreign source taxable income}}{\text{Total taxable income}} \times \text{Precredit U.S. tax on total taxable income}$$

Currently, the foreign tax credit limitation is computed separately for two different categories of foreign source income—passive income and general income. We discuss the type of income put in each category in more detail later in this chapter. A taxpayer can carry any unused (excess) FTC for the current year to the previous tax year and then to the next 10 future tax years.

**Example 24-3**

Lily's store in Windsor was an immediate success and reported taxable income on its Canadian operations of C$25,000 for 2010. 3D paid a combined national and provincial income tax of C$8,000 on its taxable income (at a flat tax rate of 32 percent). Because 3D operates the Windsor store as a

*(continued on page 24-6...)*

branch, it also must report the income on its U.S. corporate income tax return along with taxable income from its Detroit operations. Assuming a translation rate of C$1:US$1, 3D reports the Canadian taxable income on its U.S. tax return as $25,000 and reports the Canadian income taxes as $8,000. 3D reported U.S. taxable income of $100,000. The company's U.S. income tax on $125,000 of taxable income is $32,000 before any credit for the income taxes paid to Canada (see the corporate tax rate schedule on the inside front cover).

Using the above facts, what is the foreign tax credit limitation that applies to 3D's Canadian income taxes for 2010?

**Answer:** $6,400, computed as $25,000/$125,000 × $32,000,

*where:*

$25,000  = Foreign source taxable income

$125,000 = Total taxable income

$32,000  = Precredit U.S. tax on total taxable income

What is 3D's net U.S. tax after subtracting the available foreign tax credit?

**Answer:** $25,600, computed as $32,000 − $6,400. 3D has an excess foreign tax credit of $1,600 ($8,000 − $6,400) that it can carry forward for 10 years.

What is 3D's effective tax rate on its total taxable income for 2010?

**Answer:** 26.9 percent, computed as ($8,000 + $25,600)/$125,000.

*What if:* Suppose the United States did not give 3D a foreign tax credit or a deduction for the Canadian taxes it paid on the Windsor operations. What would have been 3D's effective tax rate on its total taxable income for 2010?

**Answer:** 32 percent, computed as ($8,000 + $32,000)/$125,000.

*What if:* Assume 3D earned all of its $125,000 taxable income in the United States and paid no Canadian income taxes. What would have been the company's effective tax rate on its total taxable income for 2010?

**Answer:** 25.6 percent, computed as $32,000/$125,000.

*What if:* Assume 3D paid Canadian income taxes of C$5,000 for 2010 (a flat tax rate of 20 percent). What would have been its net U.S. tax after subtracting the available foreign tax credit?

**Answer:** $27,000, computed as $32,000 − $5,000.

What would have been 3D's effective tax rate on its total taxable income for 2010?

**Answer:** 25.6 percent, computed as ($5,000 + $27,000)/$125,000. In this example, 3D receives a full credit for the Canadian taxes in 2010 because the Canadian tax rate is less than the U.S. tax rate. The company's effective tax rate on its total taxable income is the same as if it had earned all of the income in the United States.

**L02**

# U.S. SOURCE RULES FOR GROSS INCOME AND DEDUCTIONS

Many of the U.S. tax rules that apply to multinational transactions require taxpayers to determine the jurisdictional (geographic) source (U.S. or foreign) of their gross income.[14] The source rules determine whether income and related deductions are

---

[14]The U.S. federal income tax source rules are found in §861–§865 and the accompanying regulations.

from sources within or without the United States. All developed countries have source-of-income rules, although most practitioners consider the U.S. rules to be the most complex in the world.

The U.S. source-of-income rules are important to *non-U.S. persons* because they limit the scope of U.S. taxation to only their U.S. source income. For *U.S. persons,* the primary purpose of the U.S. source-of-income rules is to calculate *foreign source taxable income* in the numerator of the foreign tax credit limitation. The United States imposes a tax on the worldwide income of U.S. persons, regardless of its source or the U.S. person's residence. The United States cedes *primary jurisdiction* to foreign governments to tax U.S. persons on income earned outside the United States while retaining the *residual* right to tax foreign source income to the extent it has not been "fully taxed" by the foreign government. The net result is that the United States taxes foreign source income earned by U.S. persons at a rate that theoretically reflects the difference between the U.S. tax rate and the foreign tax rate imposed on the income.

U.S. persons must understand the source-of-income rules in other situations. For example, U.S. citizens and residents employed outside the United States may be eligible to exclude a portion of their *foreign source earned income* from U.S. taxation under §911.[15] In addition, U.S. persons that pay U.S.-source FDAP income to foreign payees (for example, interest or dividends) usually are required to withhold U.S. taxes on such payments.[16]

The source-of-income rules are definitional in nature; they do not impose a tax liability, create income, or allow a deduction. Although their primary focus is on where the economic activity that generates income takes place, the U.S. government also uses the source rules to advance a variety of international tax policy objectives.

### Source of Income Rules

The Internal Revenue Code defines eight classes of gross income from sources within the United States[17] and eight classes of gross income from sources without the United States.[18] A summary of the general rules that apply to common sources of income follows. A detailed discussion of all of the exceptions to these rules is beyond the scope of this text.

**Interest**   As a general rule, the taxpayer looks to the *residence* of the party *paying* the interest (the borrower) to determine the geographic source of interest received. A borrower's residence is determined at the time the interest is paid. Factors that determine an individual's residence include the location of the individual's family; whether the person buys a home, pays foreign taxes, and becomes involved in social and community affairs; and the length of time spent in a country. Under these general rules, interest income is U.S. source if it is paid by the United States or the District of Columbia, a noncorporate U.S. resident, or a U.S. corporation. Although interest income paid by a U.S. bank to a nonresident (for example, an international student attending your university) is U.S.-source income, such interest is exempt from U.S. withholding or other income taxation.[19] This exception is designed to attract foreign capital to U.S. banks.

---

[15]If certain conditions are met, a U.S. individual can exclude up to $91,500 of earned income from U.S. taxation in 2010 plus additional earnings equal to excess "foreign housing expenses" under §911.

[16]§1441.

[17]§861(a).

[18]§862(a).

[19]§871(i)(2)(A) and §881(d).

**THE KEY FACTS**

**Source Rules**

■ The source rules determine if income or deductions are treated as U.S. source or foreign source.

■ For a U.S. taxpayer, the source rules primarily determine foreign taxable income in the calculation of the foreign tax credit limitation.

■ For a non-U.S. taxpayer, the source rules determine what income is subject to U.S. taxation.

**Example 24-4**

> 3D was dissatisfied with the 1 percent interest rate it received on its checking account at Bank of America in Detroit. Lily's investment adviser suggested the company invest $50,000 in 5-year bonds issued by the Canadian government with an interest rate of 3 percent. During 2010, 3D received C$1,500 in interest from the bonds. Per the U.S.-Canada treaty, the Canadian government did not withhold taxes on the payment. Assume the translation rate is C$1:US$1.
>
> What is the source, U.S. or foreign, of the interest Lily receives on the bonds?
>
> **Answer:** Foreign source. The source of interest income depends on the residence of the borrower at the time the interest is paid. The Canadian government is considered a resident of Canada for U.S. source rule purposes.

**Dividends** In general, the source of dividend income is determined by the *residence* of the corporation paying the dividend. Residence usually is determined by the corporation's country of incorporation or organization (in some countries, such as the United Kingdom, a corporation's residence is determined by where its central management is located).

**Example 24-5**

> As part of diversifying its investment portfolio, 3D purchased 200 shares of Scotiabank (Bank of Nova Scotia, Canada) for $50 per share in 2010. In 2010, Scotiabank paid 3D dividends of C$400. Scotiabank withheld C$60 in taxes (15 percent) on the payment. Assume the translation rate is C$1:US$1.
>
> What is the source, U.S. or foreign, of the dividend 3D receives on the stock?
>
> **Answer:** Foreign source. The source of dividend income depends on the residence of the payor of the dividend. Scotiabank is headquartered in Toronto, Canada, and is a resident of Canada for U.S. source rule purposes.

**Compensation for Services** The source of compensation received for "labor or personal services" is determined by the *location* where the service is performed. The IRS and the courts have held that the term includes activities of employees, independent contractors, artists, entertainers, athletes, and even corporations offering "personal services" (for example, accounting). The Code provides a limited **commercial traveler exception,** in which personal service compensation earned by nonresidents within the U.S. is *not* treated as U.S. source if the individual meets the following criteria:

- The individual was present in the United States for not more than 90 days during the current taxable year;[20]
- Compensation for the services does not exceed $3,000; and
- The services are performed for a nonresident alien, foreign corporation, or foreign partnership or for the foreign office of a domestic corporation.[21]

The United States frequently alters the limitations on length of stay and compensation through treaty agreements. In most cases, the 90-day limit is extended to 183 days, and no dollar limit is put on the amount of compensation received.

---

[20]For purposes of this test, a full day is considered to be any part of a day.
[21]§861(a)(3)(A)–(C).

Compensation for services performed within and outside the United States must be allocated between U.S. and foreign sources. An individual who receives compensation, other than compensation in the form of fringe benefits, as an employee for labor or personal services performed partly within and partly outside the United States is required to source such compensation on a *time basis*. An individual who receives compensation as an employee for labor or personal services performed partly within and partly outside the United States in the form of fringe benefits (for example, additional amounts paid for housing or education) is required to source such compensation on a *geographic basis* (that is, determined by the employee's principal place of work).

## Example 24-6

**What if:** Assume for quality control purposes that Lily decided to do all of the baking for her Windsor store in Detroit. Every morning a Windsor employee would drive a truck to Detroit and pick up the baked goods for sale in Windsor. One of her employees, Stan Lee Cupp, made the 2-hour trip on 120 different days during 2010 (240 hours spent in the U.S.). 3D paid Stan a salary of C$50,000 during 2010. He worked a total of 1,920 hours during 2010. Assume the translation rate is C$1:US$1. How much U.S. source compensation does Stan have in 2010? Base your computation on hours worked.

**Answer:** $6,250 (C$50,000 × 240/1,920 × $1). Stan sources his salary for U.S. tax purposes based on where he performed the services. Using hours worked, Stan spent 12.5 percent of his time performing services in the United States (240/1,920).

Using only the exception found in the IRC, will Stan be subject to U.S. tax on his U.S.-source wages in 2010?

**Answer:** Yes. Stan fails the commercial traveler exception. He is in the United States for more than 90 days during 2010.

**What if:** Assume Stan limits his trips to 90 days during 2010 (180 hours spent in the U.S.). Using only the IRC exception, will Stan be subject to U.S. tax on his U.S.-source salary in 2010?

**Answer:** Yes. Stan still fails the commercial traveler exception. Although he is in the United States for not more than 90 days, his U.S.-source salary is $4,688 (C$50,000 × 180/1,920 × $1), which exceeds $3,000.

As we discuss later in the chapter, the U.S.-Canada income tax treaty significantly liberalizes the commercial traveler exception to allow Stan to spend more time in the U.S. without being taxed.

---

**Taxes in the Real World**    *The Tax Court Strikes a Sour Note for a Noted Orchestra Conductor*

Noted French orchestra conductor Pierre Boulez, who was a resident of Germany at the time, argued that the $40,000 he received from CBS Records for conducting a recording session in the United States was really a "royalty" and not compensation for services. In this way, he hoped to take advantage of the U.S.-German income tax treaty that exempted royalty income from U.S. taxation. The IRS argued that the payment was compensation for services and was subject to U.S. tax because the services were performed in the United States. The Tax Court held for the IRS because Mr. Boulez had no ownership interest in the records he produced. *Boulez*, 83 T.C. 584 (1984).

**Rents and Royalties**    Rent has its source where the property generating the rent is located. Royalty income has its source where the intangible property or rights generating the royalty is used. Royalties include payments related to intangibles such as patents, copyrights, secret processes and formulas, goodwill, trademarks, trade brands, and franchises. An intangible is "used" in the country that protects the owner against its unauthorized use.

| **Example 24-7** | |
|---|---|

3D rented its Windsor store for C$2,500 per month, for a total of C$30,000 in 2010. Under the U.S.-Canada income tax treaty, 3D must withhold U.S. taxes at a 30 percent rate on rent payments that flow from the United States to Canada if the rent is U.S.-source income. Will 3D have to withhold taxes on the rent payments it makes in 2010?

**Answer:** No. The rent is considered foreign source income because the store that is rented is located in Canada.

**Gain or Loss from Sale of Real Property**   In general, gain or loss from the sale of realty has its source where the property sold is located.

**Gain or Loss from Sale of Purchased Personal Property**   Under the general rule, gain or loss from the sale of purchased personal (nonrealty) property[22] has its source based on the *seller's residence*. There are many exceptions to this general rule. In particular, gross income (sales minus cost of goods sold) from the sale of purchased *inventory* is sourced where *title passes*. Title is deemed to pass at the time when, and the place where, the seller's rights, title, and interest in the property are transferred to the buyer.

**Inventory Manufactured within the United States and Sold Outside the United States (§863 Sales)**   Taxable income derived from the manufacture of *inventory* within the United States and the sale of that inventory outside the United States has special apportionment rules found in regulations issued by the U.S. Treasury.[23] These regulations provide taxpayers with three elective methods for apportioning gross income (sales minus cost of goods sold) between U.S. and foreign sources, the one most frequently used being the *50/50 method*.

Under the 50/50 method, the taxpayer sources one-half of the gross income from sales based on where the inventory is manufactured and sources the other half based on where title passes to the inventory. Gross income from sales of inventory that is manufactured in the United States and sold outside the United States, with title passing outside the United States, is sourced 50 percent U.S. source and 50 percent foreign source.

The 50/50 method provides U.S. manufacturers with the opportunity to "create" foreign source income on export sales. This foreign source income generally is not taxed by the country in which the product is sold, unless the U.S. manufacturer has a physical presence in the foreign country. Adding zero-taxed foreign source income to the numerator of the FTC limitation ratio increases the foreign tax credit amount, which is especially helpful when the taxpayer is in an excess foreign tax credit position.

| **Example 24-8** | |
|---|---|

Return to the facts in Example 24-3. Lily's store in Windsor reported taxable income on its Canadian operations of C$25,000 for 2010. Detroit Doughnut Depot (3D) paid a combined national and provincial income tax of C$8,000 on its taxable income (at a flat tax rate of 32 percent). 3D reported the Canadian taxable income on its U.S. tax return as $25,000 and reported the Canadian income taxes

(*continued on page 24-11...*)

---

[22]Personal property under the source rules includes stock of a corporation. Sales of intangible property such as a patent, copyright, secret process, goodwill, trademark, trade brand, or franchise are subject to different source rules.

[23]The regulations are issued under §863(b), which is what gives these sales their name.

as $8,000. 3D's Detroit operations reported U.S. taxable income of $100,000. 3D's precredit U.S. tax liability was $32,000 on taxable income of $125,000. As computed in Example 24-2, 3D's FTC is limited to $6,400 ($25,000/$125,000 × $32,000), resulting in an excess FTC of $1,600 in 2010. 3D's tax adviser suggested that the company could eliminate ("absorb") some of the excess credit by selling additional baked goods it produced in Detroit to grocery stores in Windsor, with shipping terms as FOB: Destination (that is, title to the goods passes in Canada).

**What if:** Assume 3D is able to generate additional gross profit of C$25,000 by selling more baked goods to Windsor grocery stores in 2010, and the sales qualify as §863(b) sales. Canada does not impose any Canadian tax on the sales because they were not made out of the Windsor store. 3D's taxable income increases to $150,000, and its precredit U.S. tax increases to $41,750. What is 3D's FTC limitation for 2010 under this change in facts?

**Answer:** $10,438, computed as $37,500/$150,000 × $41,750,

*where:*

> $37,500   = Foreign source taxable income
>
> $150,000 = Total taxable income
>
> $41,750   = Precredit U.S. tax on total taxable income

3D increases the numerator in the FTC limitation ratio by $12,500 (50% × $25,000) because title passes in Canada. The denominator increases by $25,000, the additional taxable income generated by the §863(b) sales. 3D can now claim the entire FTC of $8,000 on its 2010 tax return.

## Source of Deduction Rules

After determining the source of gross income as being from U.S. or foreign sources, a taxpayer may be required to **allocate** and **apportion** allowable deductions to gross income from each geographical source to compute taxable income from U.S. and foreign sources. For a U.S. taxpayer, this allocation and apportionment process determines the foreign source deductions that are subtracted from foreign source gross income in computing foreign source taxable income in the numerator of the FTC limitation computation. A non-U.S. taxpayer with gross income that is effectively connected with a U.S. trade or business must determine the U.S. source deductions that are subtracted from U.S. gross income to compute U.S. taxable income.

U.S. and non-U.S. taxpayers can have different motivations in seeking to deduct (or not deduct) expenses from either foreign source or U.S. source gross income. A U.S. taxpayer seeking to maximize the foreign tax credit limitation will want to allocate as few deductions to foreign source gross income as possible, the goal being to make the ratio of foreign source taxable income to total taxable income as close to 100 percent as possible (or whatever ratio is needed to absorb any excess credits). Non-U.S. taxpayers operating in a low-tax-rate country (a tax rate less than the U.S. rate) have a tax incentive to allocate as many deductions to U.S. source income as possible to minimize their U.S. tax liability. Non-U.S. taxpayers operating in a high-tax-rate country (a tax rate greater than the U.S. rate) have a worldwide tax incentive to allocate as many deductions to foreign source income as possible to minimize their worldwide tax liability.

**General Principles of Allocation and Apportionment**    The IRC provides very broad language in describing how to allocate deductions to U.S. and foreign source gross income. The regulations attempt to match deductions with the gross income such deductions were incurred to produce.[24] Matching usually is done based on the "factual relationship" of the deduction to gross income. Deductions

---

[24]Reg. §1.861-8 provides the general rules for allocating and apportioning deductions to U.S. and foreign source gross income.

that can be directly associated with a particular item of income (for example, machine depreciation with manufacturing gross profit) are referred to as **definitely related deductions.** Deductions not directly associated with a particular item of gross income (for example, medical expenses, property taxes, standard deduction) are referred to as **not definitely related deductions** and are allocated to all gross income.

The regulations require the taxpayer to first allocate (associate) deductions to the class or classes of gross income such deductions were incurred to produce. The taxpayer then apportions the deduction between, in most cases, foreign source and U.S. source gross income. The regulations allow the taxpayer to apportion deductions using a method that reflects the factual relation between the deduction and the grouping of gross income. Examples include units sold, gross sales or receipts, and gross income.

| Example 24-9 | |
| --- | --- |

Return to the facts in Example 24-3. Lily's store in Windsor reported taxable income on its Canadian operations of C$25,000 for 2010. 3D paid a combined national and provincial income tax of C$8,000 on its taxable income (at a flat tax rate of 32 percent). The company reported the $25,000 taxable income on its U.S. corporate income tax return along with $100,000 of taxable income from its Detroit operations. 3D's U.S. income tax on $125,000 of taxable income is $32,000 before any credit for the income taxes paid to Canada. Included in the computation of taxable income was a deduction of $20,000 for advertising that 3D incurred to promote its stores in Detroit and Windsor. 3D elected to apportion the advertising deduction based on sales. For 2010, Detroit sales were $300,000 and Windsor sales were $100,000. How much of the $20,000 advertising deduction does 3D apportion to its foreign source taxable income for FTC purposes?

**Answer:** $5,000, computed as $100,000/$400,000 × $20,000,

*where:*

$100,000 = Canadian sales

$400,000 = Total sales

$20,000  = Advertising deduction

Using the above facts, what is the foreign tax credit limitation that applies to 3D's Canadian income taxes for 2010?

**Answer:** $5,120, computed as ($25,000 − $5,000)/$125,000 × $32,000,

*where:*

$25,000  = Foreign source gross income

$5,000   = Apportioned advertising deduction

$125,000 = Total taxable income

$32,000  = Precredit U.S. tax on total taxable income

Apportioning some of the advertising deduction to the numerator of 3D's FTC limitation ratio reduces the amount of foreign income taxes that are creditable in 2010.

**Special Apportionment Rules**  Special apportionment rules apply to nine categories of deductions, most notably interest, research and experimentation, state and local income taxes, losses on property disposition, and charitable contributions.[25] These special apportionment rules are very complicated, and the details are beyond the scope of this text. The basic rules for interest expense and research and experimentation are discussed below.

[25]The other deductions are stewardship expenses attributable to dividends received, supportive expenses, net operating losses, and legal and accounting fees.

Interest expense is allocated to all gross income using as a basis the assets that generated such income. Interest can be apportioned based on average tax book value or average fair market value for the year. Assets are attributed to income based on the source and type of income they generate, have generated, or may reasonably be expected to generate. Taxpayers may switch to the fair market value method at any time, but a switch back to the tax book value method requires permission from the commissioner. A taxpayer using the tax book value method can elect to use the alternative depreciation system on U.S. assets solely for purposes of apportioning interest expense.

<br>

**Example 24-10**

Expanding on the facts in Example 24-8, 3D borrowed $200,000 from Bank of America in Detroit and paid interest expense of $10,000 in 2010. 3D elected to apportion this interest expense between U.S. and foreign source income using average tax book value. 3D's U.S. assets had an average tax book value of $400,000 in 2010, and its foreign assets had an average tax book value of $100,000 in 2010. How much of the $10,000 interest deduction does 3D apportion to its foreign source taxable income for FTC purposes?

**Answer:** $2,000, computed as $100,000/$500,000 × $10,000,

*where:*

$100,000 = Average tax book value of Canadian assets

$500,000 = Total average tax book value of all of 3D's assets

$10,000  = Interest expense

<br>

Taking into account the apportioned advertising deduction and interest deduction, what is the foreign tax credit limitation that applies to 3D's Canadian income taxes for 2010?

**Answer:** $4,608, computed as ($25,000 − $5,000 − $2,000)/$125,000 × $32,000,

*where:*

$25,000  = Foreign source taxable income

$5,000   = Apportioned advertising expense

$2,000   = Apportioned interest expense

$125,000 = Total taxable income

$32,000  = Precredit U.S. tax on total taxable income

Allocation of a portion of the interest expense to the numerator of 3D's FTC limitation ratio further reduces the amount of foreign taxes that are creditable in 2010.

<br>

Research and experimental (R&E) expenditures must be apportioned between U.S. and foreign source income using either a sales method or a gross income method. Taxpayers can apportion a percentage of R&E based on where the research is conducted. The amount that can be sourced under this exclusive apportionment method is 50 percent if the sales method is elected and 25 percent if the gross income method is elected.

<br>

**Example 24-11**

Expanding on the facts in Example 24-9 and Example 24-10, 3D incurred $24,000 of research and experimentation (R&E) expenses in developing new flavors of doughnuts and coffee. 3D incurred these expenses in its Detroit bakery and deducted the amount in computing its taxable income. 3D elected to apportion this R&E expense between U.S. and foreign source income using the sales method. For 2010, Detroit sales were $300,000 and Windsor sales were $100,000. How much of
(*continued on page 24-14...*)

the $24,000 R&E expense does 3D apportion to its foreign source taxable income for FTC purposes?

**Answer:** $3,000, computed as $100,000/$400,000 × $12,000,

*where:*

> $100,000 = Canadian sales
>
> $400,000 = Total sales
>
> $12,000 = R&E expense not exclusively apportioned to U.S. sources

3D apportions 50 percent of the $24,000 to U.S. source taxable income under the exclusive apportionment method. The remaining $12,000 is apportioned between U.S. and foreign source income based on sales.

Taking into account the apportioned advertising deduction, interest expense, and R&E expense, what is the foreign tax credit limitation that applies to 3D's Canadian income taxes for 2010?

**Answer:** $3,840, computed as ($25,000 − $5,000 − $2,000 − $3,000)/$125,000 × $32,000,

*where:*

> $25,000 = Foreign source taxable income
>
> $5,000 = Apportioned advertising expense
>
> $2,000 = Apportioned interest expense
>
> $3,000 = Apportioned R&E expense
>
> $125,000 = Total taxable income
>
> $32,000 = Precredit U.S. tax on total taxable income

Allocation of a portion of the R&E expense to the numerator of 3D's FTC limitation ratio further reduces the amount of foreign taxes that are creditable in 2010.

*What if:* Assume 3D elected to use the gross income method to apportion R&E. For 2010, gross income from Detroit sales was $150,000 and gross income from Windsor sales was $37,500. How much of the $24,000 R&E expense does 3D apportion to its foreign source taxable income for FTC purposes?

**Answer:** $3,600, computed as $37,500/$187,500 × $18,000,

*where:*

> $37,500 = Canadian gross income
>
> $187,500 = Total gross income
>
> $18,000 = R&E expense not exclusively apportioned to U.S. sources

3D apportions 25 percent of the $24,000 to U.S. source taxable income under the exclusive apportionment method ($6,000). The remaining $18,000 is apportioned between U.S. and foreign source income based on gross income.

---

**THE KEY FACTS**

**Treaties**

■ Treaties are designed to encourage cross-border trade by reducing the double taxation of such income by the countries that are party to the treaty.

■ Treaties define when a resident of one country has nexus in the other country.

■ Treaties reduce or eliminate the withholding tax imposed on cross-border payments such as interest, dividends, and royalties.

The foreign tax credit limitation is computed on Form 1118 (corporations) or Form 1116 (individuals). Exhibit 24-1 presents a completed Form 1118 for the cumulative facts in Examples 24-9, 24-10, and 24-11.

**LO3**

## TREATIES

A tax treaty is a bilateral agreement between two contracting countries in which each agrees to modify its own tax laws to achieve reciprocal benefits. The general purpose of an income tax treaty is to eliminate or reduce the impact of double taxation so that residents paying taxes to one country will not have the full burden of taxes in the other country. The United States signed its first income tax treaty with France in 1939. The United States now has income tax treaties with 65 countries.

**EXHIBIT 24-1**    Form 1118: Foreign Tax Credit Corporations, Schedules A, B, F and H for 3D Corporation, cumulative facts from Examples 24-9, 24-10, and 24-11

Form **1118**
(Rev. June 2009)
Department of the Treasury
Internal Revenue Service

**Foreign Tax Credit—Corporations**
▶ Attach to the corporation's tax return.
▶ See separate instructions.

OMB No. 1545-0122

For calendar year 20____, or other tax year beginning ____, 20____, and ending ____, 20____

Name of corporation

**Detroit Doughnut Depot**

Employer identification number

Use a **separate** Form 1118 for each applicable category of income listed below. See **Categories of Income** on page 1 of instructions. Also, see **Specific Instructions** on page 5. Check only one box on each form.

☐ Passive Category Income
☑ General Category Income
☐ Section 901(j) Income: Name of Sanctioned Country ▶ _____
☐ Income Re-sourced by Treaty: Name of Country ▶ _____

**Schedule A    Income or (Loss) Before Adjustments** *(Report all amounts in U.S. dollars. See page 5 of instructions.)*

| 1. Foreign Country or U.S. Possession (Enter two-letter code from list beginning on page 11 of instructions. Use a separate line for each.) * | Gross Income or (Loss) From Sources Outside the United States (*INCLUDE* Foreign Branch Gross Income here *and* on Schedule F) | | | | | | | |
|---|---|---|---|---|---|---|---|---|
| | 2. Deemed Dividends (see instructions) | | 3. Other Dividends | | 4. Interest | 5. Gross Rents, Royalties, and License Fees | 6. Gross Income From Performance of Services | 7. Other (attach schedule) | 8. Total (add columns 2(a) through 7) |
| | (a) Exclude gross-up | (b) Gross-up (sec. 78) | (a) Exclude gross-up | (b) Gross-up (sec. 78) | | | | | |
| A | CN | | | | | | | | 25,000 | 25,000 |
| B | | | | | | | | | |
| C | | | | | | | | | |
| D | | | | | | | | | |
| E | | | | | | | | | |
| F | | | | | | | | | |
| **Totals** (add lines A through F) | | | | | | | | 25,000 | 25,000 |

\* For section 863(b) income, NOLs, income from RICs, and high-taxed income, use a single line (see **Schedule A** on page 5 of the instructions).

**Deductions (*INCLUDE* Foreign Branch Deductions here *and* on Schedule F)**

| | 9. Definitely Allocable Deductions | | | | 10. Apportioned Share of Deductions Not Definitely Allocable (enter amount from applicable line of Schedule H, Part II, column (d)) | 11. Net Operating Loss Deduction | 12. Total Deductions (add columns 9(e) through 11) | 13. Total Income or (Loss) Before Adjustments (subtract column 12 from column 8) |
|---|---|---|---|---|---|---|---|---|
| | Rental, Royalty, and Licensing Expenses | | (c) Expenses Related to Gross Income From Performance of Services | (d) Other Definitely Allocable Deductions | (e) Total Definitely Allocable Deductions (add columns 9(a) through 9(d)) | | | | |
| | (a) Depreciation, Depletion, and Amortization | (b) Other Expenses | | | | | | | |
| A | | | | 5,000 | 5,000 | 5,000 | | 10,000 | 15,000 |
| B | | | | | | | | | |
| C | | | | | | | | | |
| D | | | | | | | | | |
| E | | | | | | | | | |
| F | | | | | | | | | |
| **Totals** | | | | 5,000 | 5,000 | 5,000 | | 10,000 | 15,000 |

**For Paperwork Reduction Act Notice, see separate instructions.**    Cat. No. 10900F    Form **1118** (Rev. 06-2009)

---

Form 1118 (Rev. 06-2009)    Page **2**

**Schedule B    Foreign Tax Credit** *(Report all foreign tax amounts in U.S. dollars.)*

**Part I—Foreign Taxes Paid, Accrued, and Deemed Paid** *(see page 6 of instructions)*

| 1. Credit is Claimed for Taxes: | | 2. Foreign Taxes Paid or Accrued (attach schedule showing amounts in foreign currency and conversion rate(s) used) | | | | | | | | 3. Tax Deemed Paid (from Schedule C—Part I, column 10, Part II, column 8(b), and Part III, column 8) |
|---|---|---|---|---|---|---|---|---|---|---|
| ☐ Paid    ☐ Accrued | | Tax Withheld at Source on: | | | Other Foreign Taxes Paid or Accrued on: | | | | (h) Total Foreign Taxes Paid or Accrued (add columns 2(a) through 2(g)) | |
| Date Paid | Date Accrued | (a) Dividends | (b) Interest | (c) Rents, Royalties, and License Fees | (d) Section 863(b) Income | (e) Foreign Branch Income | (f) Services Income | (g) Other | | |
| A | | | | | | 8,000 | | | 8,000 | |
| B | | | | | | | | | | |
| C | | | | | | | | | | |
| D | | | | | | | | | | |
| E | | | | | | | | | | |
| F | | | | | | | | | | |
| **Totals** (add lines A through F) | | | | | | 8,000 | | | 8,000 | |

**Part II—Separate Foreign Tax Credit** *(Complete a **separate** Part II for **each** applicable category of income.)*

| | | |
|---|---|---|
| 1 | Total foreign taxes paid or accrued (total from Part I, column 2(h)) . . . . . . . . . . | 8,000 |
| 2 | Total taxes deemed paid (total from Part I, column 3) . . . . . . . . . . . . . . | |
| 3 | Reductions of taxes paid, accrued, or deemed paid (enter total from Schedule G) . . . . . . . ( _____ ) | |
| 4 | Taxes reclassified under high-tax kickout . . . . . . . . . . . . . . . . | |
| 5 | Total carryover of foreign taxes (attach schedule showing computation in detail—see page 6 of the instructions) . . | |
| 6 | Total foreign taxes (combine lines 1 through 5) . . . . . . . . . . . . . . . | 8,000 |
| 7 | Enter the amount from the applicable column of Schedule J, Part I, line 11 (see page 6 of instructions). If Schedule J is **not** required to be completed, enter the result from the "Totals" line of column 13 of the applicable Schedule A . . . . . . . | 15,000 |
| 8a | Total taxable income from all sources (enter taxable income from the corporation's tax return) . . . . . . | 125,000 |
| b | Adjustments to line 8a (see page 6 of instructions) . . . . . . . . . . . . . | |
| c | Subtract line 8b from line 8a . . . . . . . . . . . . . . . . . . | 125,000 |
| 9 | Divide line 7 by line 8c. Enter the resulting fraction as a decimal (see instructions). If line 7 is greater than line 8c, enter 1 . | .12 |
| 10 | Total U.S. income tax against which credit is allowed (regular tax liability (see section 26(b)) minus American Samoa economic development credit) . . | 32,000 |
| 11 | Credit limitation (multiply line 9 by line 10) (see page 6 of instructions) . . . . . . . . . | 3,840 |
| 12 | Separate foreign tax credit (enter the smaller of line 6 or line 11 here and on the appropriate line of Part III) . . . | 3,840 |

**Part III—Summary of Separate Credits** *(Enter amounts from Part II, line 12 for **each** applicable category of income. **Do not** include taxes paid to sanctioned countries.)*

| | | |
|---|---|---|
| 1 | Credit for taxes on passive category income . . . . . . . . . . . . . . . | |
| 2 | Credit for taxes on general category income . . . . . . . . . . . . . . . | 3,840 |
| 3 | Credit for taxes on income re-sourced by treaty (combine all such credits on this line) . . . . . . . | |
| 4 | Total (add lines 1 through 3) . . . . . . . . . . . . . . . . . . | 3,840 |
| 5 | Reduction in credit for international boycott operations (see page 6 of instructions) . . . . . . . | |
| 6 | **Total foreign tax credit** (subtract line 5 from line 4). Enter here and on the appropriate line of the corporation's tax return . . . . | 3,840 |

Form **1118** (Rev. 06-2009)

(continued)

**EXHIBIT 24-1    Form 1118: Foreign Tax Credit Corporations, Schedules A, B, F and H for 3D Corporation, cumulative facts from Examples 24-9, 24-10, and 24-11 (*concluded*)**

Form 1118 (Rev. 06-2009)

**Schedule F    Gross Income and Definitely Allocable Deductions for Foreign Branches**

| 1. Foreign Country or U.S. Possession (Enter two-letter code from Schedule A, column 1. Use a separate line for each.) | 2. Gross Income | 3. Definitely Allocable Deductions |
|---|---|---|
| A  CN | 25,000 | 10,000 |
| B | | |
| C | | |
| D | | |
| E | | |
| F | | |
| **Totals** (add lines A through F)* ▶ | 25,000 | 10,000 |

* **Note:** *The Schedule F totals are not carried over to any other Form 1118 Schedule. (These totals were already included in Schedule A.) However, the IRS requires the corporation to complete Schedule F under the authority of section 905(b).*

---

Form 1118 (Rev. 06-2009)                                                                                            Page **7**

**Schedule H    Apportionment of Deductions Not Definitely Allocable** (*complete only once*)

**Part I—Research and Development Deductions**

| | | (a) Sales Method | | | | (v) Total R&D Deductions Under Sales Method (add columns (ii) and (iv)) | (b) Gross Income Method—Check method used: ☐ Option 1 ☐ Option 2 (See page 9 of instructions.) | | (c) Total R&D Deductions Not Definitely Allocable (enter all amounts from column (a)(v) or all amounts from column (b)(vii)) |
|---|---|---|---|---|---|---|---|---|---|
| | | Product line #1 (SIC Code:          )* | | Product line #2 (SIC Code:          )* | | | (vi) Gross Income | (vii) Total R&D Deductions Under Gross Income Method | |
| | | (i) Gross Sales | (ii) R&D Deductions | (iii) Gross Sales | (iv) R&D Deductions | | | | |
| 1 | Totals (see page 9 of instructions) | 400,000 | 24,000 | | | | | | |
| 2 | Total to be apportioned | | 12,000 | | | 12,000 | | | |
| 3 | Apportionment among statutory groupings: | | | | | | | | |
| a | General category income | | 3,000 | | | | | | |
| b | Passive category income | | | | | | | | |
| c | Section 901(j) income* | | | | | | | | |
| d | Income re-sourced by treaty* | | | | | | | | |
| 4 | Total foreign (add lines 3a through 3d) | | 3,000 | | | | | | 3,000 |

* **Important:** See ***Computer-Generated Schedule H*** *in instructions.*                          Form **1118** (Rev. 06-2009)

---

Form 1118 (Rev. 06-2009)                                                                                            Page **8**

**Schedule H    Apportionment of Deductions Not Definitely Allocable** (*continued*)

**Part II—Interest Deductions, All Other Deductions, and Total Deductions**

| | | (a) Average Value of Assets—Check method used: ☐ Fair market value ☑ Tax book value ☐ Alternative tax book value | | (b) Interest Deductions | | (c) All Other Deductions Not Definitely Allocable | (d) Totals (add the corresponding amounts from column (c), Part I; columns (b)(iii) and (b)(iv), Part II; and column (c), Part II). Enter each amount from lines 3a through 3d below in column 10 of the corresponding Schedule A. |
|---|---|---|---|---|---|---|---|
| | | (i) Nonfinancial Corporations | (ii) Financial Corporations | (iii) Nonfinancial Corporations | (iv) Financial Corporations | | |
| 1a | Totals (see pages 9 and 10 of instructions) | 500,000 | | 10,000 | | | |
| b | Amounts specifically allocable under Temp. Regs. 1.861-10T(e) | | | | | | |
| c | Other specific allocations under Temp. Regs. 1.861-10T | | | | | | |
| d | Assets excluded from apportionment formula | | | | | | |
| 2 | Total to be apportioned (subtract the sum of lines 1b, 1c, and 1d from line 1a) | 500,000 | | 2,000 | | | |
| 3 | Apportionment among statutory groupings: | | | | | | |
| a | General category income | 100,000 | | 2,000 | | | |
| b | Passive category income | | | | | | |
| c | Section 901(j) income* | | | | | | |
| d | Income re-sourced by treaty* | | | | | | |
| 4 | Total foreign (add lines 3a through 3d) | 100,000 | | 2,000 | | | 5,000 |

* **Important:** See ***Computer-Generated Schedule H*** *in instructions.*                          Form **1118** (Rev. 06-2009)

Exhibit 24-2 provides a list of the countries with which the United States has income tax treaties. U.S. treaties generally do not affect the U.S. taxation of U.S. citizens, residents, and domestic corporations because such taxpayers are taxed on a worldwide basis.

**EXHIBIT 24-2    Countries with which the U.S. has Income Tax Treaties**

| | | |
|---|---|---|
| Australia | India | Philippines |
| Austria | Indonesia | Poland |
| Bangladesh | Ireland | Portugal |
| Barbados | Israel | Romania |
| Belgium | Italy | Russian Federation |
| Canada | Jamaica | Slovak Republic |
| China, Peoples Republic of | Japan | Slovenia |
| Commonwealth of Independent States | Kazakhstan | South Africa |
| Cyprus | Korea, Republic of | Spain |
| Czech Republic | Latvia | Sri Lanka |
| Denmark | Lithuania | Sweden |
| Egypt | Luxembourg | Switzerland |
| Estonia | Malta | Thailand |
| Finland | Mexico | Trinidad and Tobago |
| France | Morocco | Tunisia |
| Germany | Netherlands | Turkey |
| Greece | New Zealand | Ukraine |
| Hungary | Norway | United Kingdom |
| Iceland | Pakistan | Venezuela |

U.S. taxpayers can benefit from treaties that reduce the tax on designated items or classes of income. For example, most U.S. treaties provide a low withholding tax rate or an exemption from tax on various types of investment income (interest, dividends, gains from sale of stock, and royalties) that otherwise would be subject to a high withholding tax.[26] For individuals, U.S. treaties often provide exemption from taxation by the host country on wages or self-employment income earned in the treaty country, provided the individual does not spend more than 183 days in that other country. U.S. businesses generally are not taxed on business profits earned in the host treaty country unless they conduct that business through a **permanent establishment.** A permanent establishment generally is a fixed place of business such as an office or factory, although employees acting as agents can create a permanent establishment. Treaties also provide "tiebreaker" rules for determining the country in which an individual will be considered a resident for treaty purposes.

| Example 24-12 |
|---|

**What if:** Lily was trying to determine if 3D would be subject to Canadian taxation under two different scenarios: (1) open a store in Windsor and operate it as a branch of 3D or (2) make the baked goods in Detroit and ship them to Windsor-area grocery stores using the company's van. Article VII of the U.S.-Canada income tax treaty states that the business profits of a U.S. resident are taxed in Canada only if the business operates in Canada through a permanent establishment. Article V defines a permanent establishment as including a place of management, a branch, an office, a factory, and a

(continued on page 24-18...)

---

[26]Absent a treaty, the United States imposes a withholding tax rate of 30 percent on payments of FDAP income to nonresidents.

workshop. Under the U.S.-Canada treaty, will 3D be subject to Canadian tax on taxable income earned through its Windsor store?

**Answer:** Yes. A branch is defined as a permanent establishment. Canada can tax 3D's Canadian-source taxable income under Article VII of the U.S.-Canada treaty.

Under the U.S.-Canada treaty, will 3D be subject to Canadian tax on taxable income earned by selling goods to grocery stores in Windsor directly?

**Answer:** No. 3D does not have a permanent establishment in Canada on these sales. Canada will not tax income from these sales under Article VII of the U.S.-Canada treaty.

## Example 24-13

***What if:*** Assume for quality control purposes that Lily decided to do all of the baking for her Windsor store in Detroit. Every morning a Windsor employee drives a van to Detroit and picks up the baked goods for sale in Windsor. One of her employees, Stan Lee Cupp, made the 2-hour trip on 200 different days during 2010. Article IV of the U.S.-Canada income tax treaty states where an individual is considered a resident of both countries under their respective tax laws, the individual will be considered a resident of the country in which he or she has a permanent home. Stan has a home only in Canada, and Canada still considers him to be a Canadian resident. Will Stan be considered a U.S. resident in 2010 applying only the substantial presence test?

**Answer:** Yes. Stan is physically present in the United States for more than 30 days in 2010 and satisfies the 183-day test when applying the formula $[200 + (1/3 \times 0) + (1/6 \times 0) = 200]$.

Will Stan be considered a U.S. resident in 2010 applying the U.S.-Canada treaty?

**Answer:** No. Under the tiebreaker rules in the U.S.-Canada treaty, Stan is considered to be a resident of Canada only for income tax purposes because that is where he has his permanent home. The United States can tax Stan only on income that is considered to be from U.S. sources.

## Example 24-14

***What if:*** Assume that Stan made the 2-hour trip from Windsor to Detroit and back on 120 different days during 2010 (240 hours). 3D paid Stan a salary of C$50,000 during 2010. He worked a total of 240 days (1,920 hours) during 2010. Article XV of the U.S.-Canada income tax treaty states that a Canadian resident will be subject to U.S. tax on his U.S.-source compensation only if the compensation exceeds $10,000 or the individual is present in the United States for more than 183 days. Under the U.S.-Canada treaty, will Stan be subject to Canadian tax on his U.S.-source compensation in 2010?

**Answer:** No. Stan is exempt from U.S. tax on this compensation because under the apportionment rules for compensation discussed previously in Example 24-6, he has only $6,250 of U.S. compensation, computed as $(240/1,920) \times \$50,000$,

*where:*

$\qquad$ 240 = Number of hours worked in the United States

$\qquad$ 1,920 = Total number of hours worked

$\qquad$ $50,000 = Total compensation in U.S. dollars

***What if:*** Assume Stan received compensation of $86,000 in 2010. Under the U.S.-Canada treaty, will Stan be subject to Canadian tax on his U.S.-source compensation in 2010?

**Answer:** Yes. Although Stan was in the United States for less than 184 days, his U.S. compensation is $10,750, computed as $(240/1,920) \times \$86,000$.

# FOREIGN TAX CREDITS

The United States taxes the worldwide income of U.S. corporations, partnerships, trusts and estates, U.S. citizens, and resident aliens. As we have discussed, U.S. persons earning foreign source income may be subject to multiple taxation on such income by the United States and the country in which the individual resides or where the income is earned. For example, a U.S. citizen who is a resident of Great Britain and earns income in France may be subject to tax by all three governments. Without any relief from such multiple taxation, U.S. taxpayers would have little incentive to do business outside the United States.

## FTC Limitation Categories of Taxable Income

As we have previously discussed, the United States alleviates the multiple taxation of foreign source income earned by U.S. persons by allowing a tax credit for income taxes paid on such foreign source income. The foreign tax credit allowed in the current year is subject to a foreign tax credit limitation,[27] computed by multiplying the ratio of foreign source taxable income to total taxable income times precredit U.S. tax, as follows:

$$\frac{\text{Foreign source taxable income}}{\text{Total taxable income}} \times \text{Precredit U.S. tax}$$

The United States continuously struggles with whether, and to what extent, U.S. taxpayers should be required to segregate foreign source income subject to different tax rates and compute a separate FTC limitation for each category of income. Since 1976, the United States has required persons claiming the foreign tax credit to segregate foreign source income by category of income. Practitioners often refer to each income category as an **FTC basket.** Currently, there are two categories of FTC income, **passive category income** and **general category income.**[28] The "basket" approach limits blending opportunities (high-tax foreign source income and low-tax foreign source income) to income that is of the same character.

**Passive Category Income**    Passive category income generally is investment-type income that traditionally is subject to low foreign taxes (usually in the form of withholding taxes). Passive category income includes interest, certain dividends, rents, royalties, and annuities. Dividends received from 10–50 percent owned joint ventures and from more than 50 percent owned subsidiaries are subject to "look-through" rules. Under these rules, the dividend recipient characterizes the dividend for FTC basket purposes based on the source(s) of income from which the dividend is paid.

**General Category Income**    Income not treated as passive category income is defined as general category income. General category income includes gross income from an active trade or business, financial services income, and shipping income.

The application of the FTC limitation formula can result in an excess credit if the taxpayer's creditable foreign taxes exceed the FTC limitation amount. The United States allows taxpayers to carry back an excess FTC one year and carry forward an excess credit 10 years. Current year foreign tax credits are absorbed before any carryovers, which are absorbed on a first-in first-out basis.

## THE KEY FACTS

**Foreign Tax Credits**

- Only income taxes can be claimed as a credit on a U.S. tax return.
- A U.S. corporation owning 10 percent or more of a foreign corporation is eligible for an indirect FTC for taxes paid by the foreign corporation on dividends paid.
- The current year foreign tax credit cannot exceed the FTC limitation.
- The FTC limitation is applied to two separate categories (baskets) of foreign source income: passive and general.

---

[27]§904(d).
[28]§904(d).

**Example 24-15**

*What if:* Suppose 3D's branch operations in Windsor generated $25,000 of taxable income and paid Canadian tax of C$8,000. The branch income meets the definition of general category income for FTC purposes. In addition, 3D received a dividend of C$1,000 from its stock investment in Scotiabank. Under the U.S.-Canada treaty, Scotiabank withheld C$150 in taxes (15 percent) on the payment. The withholding tax is eligible for the foreign tax credit, and the dividend meets the definition of passive category income for FTC purposes. 3D has total taxable income of $200,000 in 2010 and has a precredit U.S. income tax of $61,250. In computing its FTC for 2010, can 3D combine the branch income with the dividend in calculating its FTC limitation?

*Answer:* No. The branch income and dividend cannot be "blended" because they are in different income categories for FTC limitation purposes.

How much of the C$8,000 in Canadian taxes can 3D claim as a FTC in 2010?

*Answer:* $7,806 ($7,656 + $150).

3D must compute separate FTC limitations for the branch income and dividend, as follows:

Branch income: $25,000/$200,000 × $61,250 = $7,656

Dividend income: $1,000/$200,000 × $61,250 = $306

3D can take a credit for the full amount of the withholding tax on the dividend ($150) but only a partial credit on the branch income. The separate basket approach prevents 3D from blending its high-tax income with its low-tax income.

What happens to the excess credit of $344 ($8,000 − $7,656) on the branch income?

*Answer:* 3D can carry back the excess FTC one year and then carry forward any remaining FTC for 10 years.

*What if:* Assume the branch income and dividend are both general category income. How much of the C$8,000 of Canadian taxes can 3D take as a credit in 2010?

*Answer:* $7,962 computed as $26,000/$200,000 × $61,250,

*where:*

$26,000 = Foreign source taxable income

$200,000 = Total taxable income

$61,250 = Precredit U.S. tax on total taxable income

The low tax dividend income absorbs an additional $156 of branch foreign taxes. The addition of the $1,000 dividend to the branch FTC limitation increases the FTC ratio from 12.5 percent to 13 percent. This 0.5 percent increase in the ratio increases the FTC limitation by $306 (0.5% × $61,250). The FTC on the dividend is $150, leaving an excess $156 to apply against the branch FTC.

### Creditable Foreign Taxes

The foreign tax credit is available only for foreign taxes the United States considers to be *income* taxes "in the U.S. sense." In general, a tax "resembles" the U.S. concept of an income tax when it is applied to net income.[29] Taxes that do not qualify as income taxes include property taxes, customs taxes, sales taxes, and value-added taxes. U.S. taxpayers can deduct noncreditable foreign taxes. On an annual basis, U.S. taxpayers also can elect to deduct foreign income taxes in lieu of claiming the credit. This election might make sense if the taxpayer does not expect to be able to use the credit during the 10-year carryforward period. Foreign taxes generally are translated into U.S. dollars using the average exchange rate for the year, regardless of when the

---

[29]There has been much litigation and many IRS rulings over whether a tax paid to another country qualifies as an income tax "in the U.S. sense."

tax is actually paid.[30] U.S. taxpayers can elect to translate withholding taxes using the exchange rate on the day the tax is withheld. This election makes translation of the withholding tax consistent with the translation of the payment (dividend, interest, royalty) into U.S. dollars, which is done using the exchange rate on the date of payment (referred to as the **spot rate**).

**Direct Taxes**   Direct foreign income taxes are income taxes paid directly by the U.S. taxpayer.[31] For example, income taxes paid by 3D to the Canadian government on its branch operations in Windsor would be direct foreign income taxes and eligible for a credit on the company's U.S. tax return.

**In Lieu of Taxes**   Taxes that do not qualify as income taxes can still be creditable if they are imposed "in lieu of" an income tax.[32] The most common example is a withholding tax imposed on gross income such as dividends, interest, and royalties. These taxes technically do not meet the definition of an income tax because they are imposed on gross, rather than net, income. However, most governments impose these taxes for administrative purposes in lieu of requiring the recipient of the income to file an income tax return.

**Indirect (Deemed Paid) Taxes**   Indirect taxes are foreign income taxes imposed on the income of a U.S.-owned **foreign subsidiary** or **foreign joint venture**.[33] These taxes are not considered direct taxes because they are not paid by the U.S. parent company or investor. Had the U.S. corporation conducted its foreign operations through a branch, the before-tax income of the branch would be reported on the corporation's U.S. tax return and a direct FTC would be claimed for any income taxes paid by the branch. The income of a foreign subsidiary is not reported on the U.S. tax return until it is distributed to the U.S. parent as a dividend or other payment. The dividend amount is net of the foreign income taxes imposed on that income.[34]

To put the U.S. tax consequences of a dividend distribution on equal footing with branch income, the United States allows certain U.S. corporations to "impute" a foreign tax credit for the income taxes paid by the foreign subsidiary on the dividend distributed. The U.S. corporation must "gross up" the dividend by the amount of the credit.[35] This gross up causes the U.S. corporation to report the pretax income of the subsidiary related to the dividend distributed, similar to what would have been reported had the subsidiary been operated as a branch.

---

**Example 24-16**

**What if:**  Let's say 3D operates its Windsor operations as a branch. The branch reported taxable income of C$25,000 for 2010 on which it paid a combined national and provincial income tax of C$8,000. Not including the branch income, 3D had taxable income of $125,000 from its U.S. operations in 2010. What amount of taxable income does 3D report on its U.S. tax return in 2010?

**Answer:**  $150,000. 3D includes the branch income with its U.S. taxable income.

(*continued on page 24-22...*)

---

[30]§986(a)(1)(A).

[31]Direct foreign income taxes are creditable under §901.

[32]In lieu of income taxes are creditable under §903.

[33]Indirect foreign income taxes are creditable under §902 or §960.

[34]As discussed in Chapter 18, dividends are payments out of earnings and profits, which is after-tax income of a corporation.

[35]§78.

What amount of foreign taxes are creditable for foreign tax credit purposes?

**Answer:** $8,000. The Canadian income taxes paid on the branch operations are considered a direct FTC because 3D pays the tax directly.

**What if:** Suppose 3D operates its Windsor operations as a subsidiary. The subsidiary reported taxable income of C$25,000 for 2010 on which it paid a combined national and provincial income tax of C$8,000. Assume for purposes of this example only that for U.S. tax purposes the subsidiary's earnings and profits is $17,000, computed as $25,000 − $8,000.[36] At the end of 2010, the subsidiary distributed all of its E&P to 3D as a dividend. Not including the dividend income, 3D had taxable income of $125,000 from its U.S. operations in 2010. Assume Canada did not impose a withholding tax on the dividend. What amount of foreign taxes are creditable for foreign tax credit purposes?

**Answer:** $8,000. 3D receives a deemed paid credit equal to the income taxes paid by the subsidiary on the dividend received.

What amount of taxable income does 3D report on its U.S. tax return as a result of the dividend in 2010?

**Answer:** $25,000. 3D grosses up the $17,000 dividend by the deemed paid credit of $8,000. The amount of taxable income reported from the dividend equals the taxable income reported from the branch operations.

Most subsidiaries and joint ventures do not pay out all of their current E&P as a dividend in the year earned. When a subsidiary distributes a portion of its total E&P as a dividend, the deemed paid credit is computed on a "blended" basis based on total income taxes paid on total E&P accumulated since 1987.[37] The amount of foreign income taxes deemed paid by the U.S. corporate shareholder on the receipt of a dividend is computed as follows:

$$\frac{\text{Dividends paid from post-1986 earnings and profits}}{\text{Total post-1986 earnings and profits}} \times \text{Post-1986 foreign taxes}$$

The post-1986 E&P is computed using the corporation's **functional currency** unless the corporation keeps its books in U.S. dollars.[38] The foreign corporation maintains its pool of post-1986 foreign income taxes in U.S. dollars.

**Example 24-17**

**What if:** Assume 3D organized its Windsor operations as a Canadian subsidiary of 3D, Canadian Doughnut Depot Company (CDD). CDD reported taxable income of C$25,000 for 2010, on which it paid a combined national and provincial income tax of C$8,000. Because CDD operates as a Canadian corporation, the Canadian taxable income is not reported on 3D's U.S. corporate income tax return (CDD is a nonresident with no U.S.-source income). Also assume for purposes of this example only, that CDD has post-1986 earnings and profits (E&P) of C$12,000, all of which is characterized as general category income. During 2010, CDD paid a dividend of C$6,000 to 3D. CDD withheld a Canadian withholding tax of C$300 (5 percent). Not including the dividend, 3D had taxable income of $140,000 in 2010. What is 3D's deemed paid credit on the dividend received from CDD in 2010?

*(continued on page 24-23...)*

---

[36]§964 requires a U.S. parent company to compute E&P for its foreign subsidiaries under U.S. tax rules. These rules are discussed in detail in Chapter 18.

[37]This computation was changed in the Tax Reform Act of 1986. Distributions received in taxable years prior to 1987 are treated as being paid out of the E&P for the year distributed assuming a LIFO assumption.

[38]§986(b). *Functional currency* is the currency in which the corporation conducts its transactions.

**Answer:** $4,000, computed as C$6,000/C$12,000 × $8,000,

*where:*

  C$6,000  = Dividend paid to 3D in CDD's functional currency

  C$12,000 = Post-1986 earnings and profits in CDD's functional currency

  $8,000   = Post-1986 foreign taxes in U.S. dollars

What amount of creditable foreign taxes does 3D have in 2010?

**Answer:** $4,300, computed as $4,000 + withholding taxes of $300.

What amount of gross income does 3D report as a result of the dividend from CDD?

**Answer:** $10,000, computed as $6,000 + $4,000. 3D must gross up the dividend ($6,000) by the deemed paid credit ($4,000) to compute the taxable income it reports from receiving the dividend. 3D's total taxable income for 2010 is $150,000 ($140,000 + $10,000), and its precredit U.S. tax is $41,750.

Assuming no deductions are subtracted from the foreign source gross income created by the dividend, what is 3D's FTC limitation for 2010?

**Answer:** $2,783, computed as $10,000/$150,000 × $41,750,

*where:*

  $10,000  = Foreign source taxable income from the dividend

  $150,000 = Total taxable income

  $41,750  = Precredit U.S. tax on total taxable income

3D has an excess FTC of $1,517 ($4,300 − $2,783).

---

A U.S. corporation must own directly 10 percent or more of the foreign corporation paying the dividend to be eligible for the deemed paid credit.[39]

### Example 24-18

**What if:** Assume 3D only owned 50 percent of CDD. CDD reported taxable income of C$25,000 for 2010 on which it paid a combined national and provincial income tax of C$8,000. For U.S. tax purposes, CDD has post-1986 earnings and profits (E&P) of C$12,000, all of which is characterized as general category income.[40] During 2010 CDD paid a dividend of C$3,000 to 3D. CDD withheld a Canadian withholding tax of C$150 (5 percent). Not including the dividend, 3D had taxable income of $140,000 in 2010. What is 3D's deemed paid credit on the dividend received from CDD in 2010?

**Answer:** $2,000, computed as C$3,000/C$12,000 × $8,000,

*where:*

  C$3,000  = Dividend paid to 3D in CDD's functional currency

  C$12,000 = Post-1986 earnings and profits in CDD's functional currency

  $8,000   = Post-1986 foreign taxes in U.S. dollars

What amount of creditable foreign taxes does 3D have in 2010?

**Answer:** $2,150, computed as $2,000 + withholding taxes of $150.

What amount of gross income does 3D report as a result of the dividend from CDD?

**Answer:** $5,000, computed as $3,000 + $2,000.

---

[39]Dividends paid to the foreign corporation from other foreign corporations can also be eligible for the deemed paid credit if certain direct and indirect ownership tests are met. This topic is beyond the scope of this text.

[40]§964 requires a U.S. parent company to compute E&P for its foreign subsidiaries under U.S. tax rules. These rules are discussed in detail in Chapter 18.

**L05**    # PLANNING FOR INTERNATIONAL OPERATIONS

*continued from page 24-1...*

After operating her Windsor store as a branch for the first year, Lily began to wonder if there were more tax-efficient ways to operate her Canadian operations. She was concerned that while the branch was easy to organize and operate, it might not provide the best tax advantages. Lily's tax adviser told her that Canada imposes a 10 percent "branch profits tax" on after-tax profits that exceed $500,000. Although the Windsor operations were a long way from reaching that level of profits, she hoped one day that she would reach that level of profitability. In addition, she wondered if it might be an advantage to have her Canadian operations identified as a Canadian company. Lily's tax adviser mentioned that operating as a Canadian corporation would provide deferral of her Canadian profits from U.S. taxation and would allow for some "transfer pricing" on the "sale" of her baked goods from the United States to Canada. ∎

The organizational form through which a U.S. person does business or invests outside the United States affects the timing and scope of U.S. taxation of foreign source income or loss reported by the business or investment. U.S. corporations conducting international operations directly (branch) or through a flow-through entity (partnership) are subject to U.S. tax or receive a U.S. tax benefit currently on income or loss from those operations. Foreign source income earned by a foreign corporation owned by U.S. persons (for example, a Canadian subsidiary of a U.S. corporation) generally is not subject to U.S. taxation until such income is repatriated to the U.S. shareholder as a dividend, interest, rent, royalty, or management fee (that is, U.S. taxation of such income is deferred to a future period).

The organizational form chosen can help a U.S. person reduce worldwide taxation through the following means:

- Defer U.S. taxation of foreign source income not repatriated to the United States.
- Maximize the foreign tax credit limitation on distributions.
- Reduce foreign taxes in high-tax jurisdictions through tax-deductible payments (for example, rent, interest, royalties, and management fees) to lower-tax jurisdictions.
- Take advantage of tax incentives provided by host jurisdictions (for example, a tax holiday on profits for a specified time period).
- Use transfer pricing to shift profits from a high-tax jurisdiction to a low-tax jurisdiction.
- Take advantage of tax treaties to reduce withholding taxes on cross-border payments

**Hybrid entities** such as limited liability companies can provide the U.S. investor with the legal advantages of corporate form (limited liability, continuity of life, transferability of interests) and the tax advantages of partnership or branch form (flow-through of losses and flow-through of foreign taxes to individual investors).

Each organizational form offers a U.S. person investing abroad with advantages and disadvantages. Most U.S. businesses operate abroad through either a subsidiary or hybrid entity. Corporation status provides the U.S. investor with protection against liabilities of the subsidiary, entitles the subsidiary to treaty benefits in its dealings outside the country of incorporation, and insulates its business income from

U.S. taxation until such income is repatriated back to the United States. Conversely, losses incurred in the subsidiary are not currently deductible on the investor's U.S. tax return.

### Check-the-Box Hybrid Entities

Through regulations, the U.S. Treasury allows U.S. taxpayers to elect the *U.S. tax status* of eligible entities by "checking the box" on Form 8832. Where the U.S. person owns 100 percent of the entity, the taxpayer can choose corporation status or branch status (the latter often is referred to as a **disregarded entity** because it is disregarded for U.S. tax purposes). Where more than one U.S. person owns the entity, the taxpayers can choose corporation status or partnership status. A multiple-person owned hybrid entity for which corporation status is elected is referred to as a **reverse hybrid entity.** Certain designated "per se" foreign entities are not eligible for this elective treatment. These ineligible entities tend to be entities that can be publicly traded in their host countries (for example, a German A.G., Dutch N.V., U.K. PLC, Spanish S.A., and a Canadian Corporation). The entire list is printed in the Instructions to Form 8832. In Canada, a U.S. corporation or individual must operate through an unlimited liability company (ULC) organized under the laws of Nova Scotia, Alberta, or British Columbia to achieve the benefits of operating through a hybrid entity.

Hybrid entities offer U.S. investors with much flexibility in avoiding the U.S. "anti-deferral" rules found in subpart F, which we discuss in the next section. However, there are drawbacks to operating through a hybrid entity. In particular, a hybrid entity organized outside the United States may not be eligible for treaty benefits because it is not recognized as a resident of the United States by the host country. For example, the U.S.-Canada treaty does not extend treaty benefits to distributions from a ULC to its U.S. investors. Distributions from a Nova Scotia ULC to its U.S. parent company in the form of dividends, interest, or royalties will be subject to a 25 percent withholding tax instead of a 5 percent, 0 percent, or 10 percent withholding tax, respectively, under the U.S.-Canada treaty. Exhibit 24-3 lists the advantages and disadvantages of operating outside the United States through different organizational forms.

> **THE KEY FACTS**
>
> Organizational Forms for Conducting International Operations
>
> ▌ A U.S. taxpayer doing business outside the United States can choose between a branch, partnership, corporation, or hybrid entity.
>
> ▌ A hybrid entity is an entity that is treated as a flow-through entity for U.S. tax purposes and a corporation for foreign tax purposes (or vice versa).
>
> ▌ A U.S. taxpayer elects the U.S. tax status of a hybrid entity by "checking the box" on Form 8832.
>
> ▌ Per se entities are not eligible for the check-the-box election.

---

## Example 24-19

Lily expects her Canadian operations to be profitable for the foreseeable future. She has plans to expand her operations throughout the province of Ontario and hopefully throughout all of Canada. Lily is trying to decide whether she should change the organizational form of her Canadian operations from a branch to a corporation or perhaps a hybrid entity. Can Lily organize her Canadian operations as a hybrid entity in Ontario for U.S. tax purposes?

**Answer:** No. Hybrid entities (unlimited liability companies) can only be organized in Canada in the provinces of Nova Scotia, Alberta, and British Columbia.

What are the primary income tax reasons for organizing the Canadian operations as a corporation for U.S. tax purposes?

**Answer:** There are several. Operating as a corporation allows for deferral from U.S. taxation on income earned by the Canadian operations until it is distributed to 3D as a dividend. In addition, 3D can loan money or lease its trademarks to the Canadian corporation and transfer income from Canada to the United States in the form of tax-deductible interest or royalties.

Are there any compelling nontax reasons for organizing the Canadian operations as a corporation for U.S. tax purposes?

**Answer:** Yes. Corporate form limits 3D's liability in Canada to its Canadian assets. In addition, operating as a corporation allows the company to hold itself out as a Canadian business to its customers and borrow money directly from Canadian banks.

**EXHIBIT 24-3** **Advantages and Disadvantages of Operating Outside the U.S. in Different Organizational Forms**

**Branch**

*Advantages*
- Foreign losses are currently deductible on the U.S. tax return.
- Foreign taxes imposed on income earned through the branch are eligible for the direct foreign tax credit.
- A branch qualifies as a permanent establishment and is eligible for treaty benefits.

*Disadvantages*
- Profits are subject to immediate U.S. taxation.
- The U.S. corporation must have 100 percent control over its international operations (joint ventures are not available).

**Subsidiary**

*Advantages*
- Separate entity status insulates the U.S. parent corporation against certain types of liabilities.
- Certain earnings are deferred from U.S. taxation until repatriation.
- Certain payments (management fees, royalties) made to the U.S. parent corporation may only be deductible in the host country if the payor is a corporation.

*Disadvantages*
- Losses are not deductible on the U.S. tax return for tax purposes.
- Certain foreign source income may be subject to the subpart F rules, which increases the administrative costs of operating as a subsidiary.

**Hybrid entity treated as a flow-through entity**

*Advantages*
- Foreign losses are currently deductible on the U.S. tax return.
- Foreign taxes imposed on income earned through the branch are eligible for the direct foreign tax credit.
- The U.S. corporation can operate as a joint venture.
- Certain payments (management fees, royalties, interest) made to the U.S. parent corporation are deductible in the foreign jurisdiction.

*Disadvantages*
- Profits are subject to immediate U.S. taxation.
- Dividend, interest, and royalty payments to the United States are not eligible for reduced treaty withholding taxes.

When drawing an organizational chart of a multinational company, the different organizational forms are often designated with different symbols. Exhibit 24-4 provides the symbols for each of the common organizational forms used by U.S. taxpayers to do business outside the United States and their tax status for U.S. tax purposes (we refer back to this exhibit in Exhibit 24-5).

## U.S. ANTI-DEFERRAL RULES

**LO6**

Deferral of U.S. taxation on all foreign source income earned through a foreign subsidiary would invite tax planning strategies that shift income to low-tax countries to minimize worldwide taxation. U.S. individuals and corporations could transfer investment assets to subsidiaries located in low- (no-) tax countries (**tax havens**) and earn low-tax or tax-exempt income until such time as it was repatriated to the United States.

The United States has debated whether to allow full deferral on all foreign earnings since 1937, when the U.S. government enacted its first "anti-deferral"

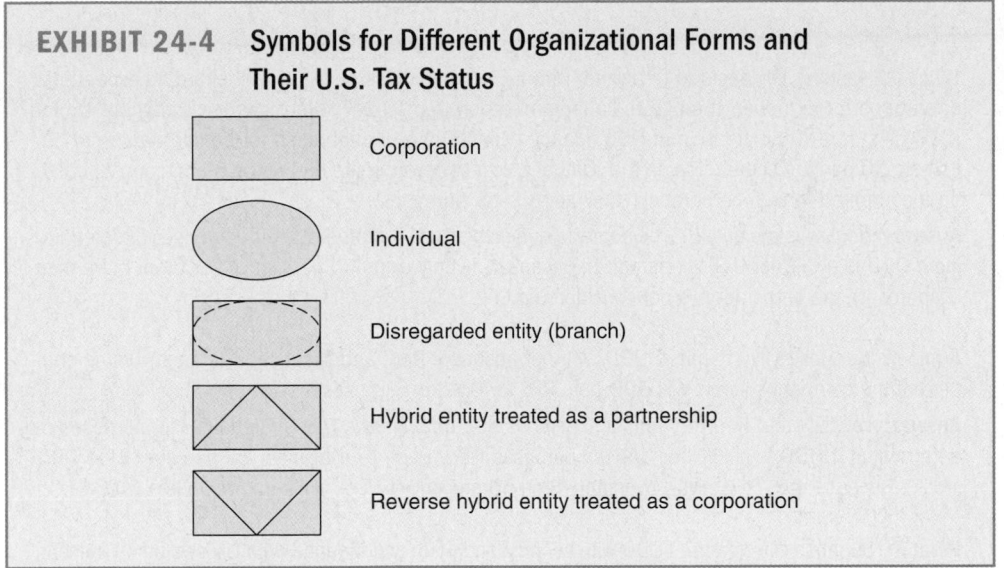

**EXHIBIT 24-4**    Symbols for Different Organizational Forms and Their U.S. Tax Status

Corporation

Individual

Disregarded entity (branch)

Hybrid entity treated as a partnership

Reverse hybrid entity treated as a corporation

rules applying to foreign personal holding companies. Congress, with urging from President Kennedy, enacted more expansive anti-deferral rules in subpart F of subchapter N of the Internal Revenue Code in 1962.[41]

In a nutshell, subpart F requires certain *U.S. shareholders* in a **controlled foreign corporation** (CFC) to include in their gross income currently their pro rata share of specified categories of "tainted" income earned by the CFC during the current year **(subpart F income)** regardless of whether such income is repatriated as a dividend (the income is treated as if it was paid out to the shareholders as a deemed dividend at the end of the CFC's taxable year). The deemed dividend is translated into U.S. dollars using the average exchange rate for the year. The technical rules that determine the amount of the deemed dividend to be included in income are among the most complex provisions in the Internal Revenue Code.

### Definition of a Controlled Foreign Corporation

A controlled foreign corporation is defined as any foreign corporation in which *U.S. shareholders* collectively own *more than* 50 percent of the total combined voting power of all classes of stock entitled to vote or the total value of the corporation's stock on *any day* during the CFC's tax year.[42] For purposes of subpart F, a *U.S. shareholder* is any *U.S. person* who owns or is deemed to own 10 percent or more of all classes of stock entitled to vote.[43] The term *United States person* means a citizen or resident of the United States, a domestic partnership, a domestic corporation, or any U.S. estate or trust, but it excludes certain residents of U.S. possessions.

Constructive ownership rules are used in the calculation of both the 50 percent test for determining CFC status and the 10 percent test for determining who is a U.S. shareholder.[44] These rules are similar to the constructive ownership rules found in subchapter C (Chapter 18) and include family attribution (spouse, children, grandchildren, and parents), entity-to-owner attribution, and owner-to-entity attribution. A detailed discussion of the other attribution rules is beyond the scope of this text.

[41]§§951–964.
[42]§957(a).
[43]§951(b).
[44]§958(b).

| | |
|---|---|
| **Example 24-20** | |

*What if:* Assume Lily decided to partner with a Canadian investor, Maurice Richard, to expand her operations into Quebec through a Canadian corporation to be called Quebec Doughnut Depot (QDD). As part of the creation of QDD, Maurice contributed enough cash to the corporation to become a 50 percent shareholder in the company, with Lily owning the remaining 50 percent. Will QDD be a controlled foreign corporation (CFC) for U.S. tax purposes?

**Answer:** No. Lily is the only U.S. person who qualifies as a U.S. shareholder for purposes of determining if QDD is a CFC for U.S. tax purposes. Because Lily only owns 50 percent of QDD (not *more* than 50 percent), the corporation is not considered a CFC.

*What if:* Suppose Lily organized QDD with her husband, Red, and Maurice, with each owning one-third of the company's stock. Will QDD be a CFC for U.S. tax purposes?

**Answer:** Yes. Lily and Red are both U.S. persons who qualify as a U.S. shareholder for purposes of determining if QDD is a CFC for U.S. tax purposes (they each own at least 10 percent of the QDD stock). Because they collectively own more than 50 percent of QDD, the corporation is a CFC.

*What if:* Suppose Lily organized QDD with her husband, Red, and Maurice, with Lily owning 49 percent, Red owning 2 percent, and Maurice owning 49 percent of the company's stock. Will QDD be a CFC for U.S. tax purposes?

**Answer:** Yes. Lily is deemed to own Red's 2 percent stock interest in QDD under the family attribution rules, making her a U.S. shareholder owning 51 percent of QDD's stock.

### Definition of Subpart F Income

Subpart F income generally can be characterized as low-taxed passive income or as "portable" income earned by a CFC. Passive income, otherwise referred to as **foreign personal holding company income,** includes interest, dividends, rents, royalties, annuities, gains from the sales of certain foreign property, foreign currency exchange rate gains, net income from certain commodities transactions, and income equivalent to interest. There are complex exceptions involving payments between CFCs in the same country, export financing interest, and rents and royalties derived in the active conduct of a trade or business. In addition, for tax years 2006–2009, subpart F income did not include dividends, interest, rents, and royalties received by one CFC from a related CFC to the extent the payment is attributable to non-subpart F income of the payor (the taxpayer "looks through" to payment to the income from which it was paid). Congress is considering extending this exception to 2010.

| | |
|---|---|
| **Example 24-21** | |

*What if:* Assume, as in Example 24-17, that 3D organized its Windsor operations as a wholly owned Canadian subsidiary, Canadian Doughnut Depot Company (CDD). CDD reported taxable income from its bakery operations of C$75,000 in 2010. CDD also purchased 1,000 shares of stock (less than 1 percent) in Cadbury PLC, a United Kingdom corporation. CDD purchased the stock because of its relations with Cadbury Beverages Canada, Inc., based in Mississauga, Ontario, which is Cadbury's Canadian subsidiary for beverage-related products. During 2010, CDD received dividends of £1,250, which translated into C$2,500.[45] Cadbury withheld £125 (C$250) of U.K. taxes on the payment

(continued on page 24-29...)

---

[45]The currency of the United Kingdom is the pound sterling, abbreviated £.

(a 10 percent withholding tax under the U.K.-Canada treaty). Does the dividend from Cadbury to CDD constitute subpart F income to 3D in 2010?

**Answer:** Yes. Dividends from investments in corporations that are not a CFC of 3D are considered foreign personal holding company income under subpart F.

Also included in subpart F income is foreign base company sales income, which is defined as income derived by a CFC from the sale or purchase of personal property (for example, inventory) to (or from) a related person, and the property is manufactured and sold outside the CFC's country of incorporation.[46] Similar rules apply to foreign base company services income.

This category of subpart F income was added because many countries offer incentives to multinational corporations to locate holding companies or sales companies within their borders by imposing no or a low tax on investment income or export sales. These companies are referred to as base companies because they operate primarily as profit centers and are located in a different country than where the economic activity (manufacture, sales, or service) takes place.

Without any anti-deferral rules, a U.S. multinational corporation could shift profits to a foreign base company by selling goods to the base company at an artificially low transfer price. The base company could then resell the goods at a higher price to the ultimate customer in a different country. The profit earned by the base company would be subject to the lower (or no) tax imposed by the tax haven country. The base company thus becomes a depository for the multinational company's excess funds, which can be invested in an active business or passive investment assets outside the United States.

**Example 24-22**

**What if:** Assume in 2011 that 3D set up a corporation in the Cayman Islands through which it intended to transfer its products from the United States to its operations in Canada. Under this plan, 3D would "sell" its products, made in the United States, to the subsidiary in the Cayman Islands at a low transfer price, after which the Cayman Islands subsidiary would resell the products to CDD at a high transfer price. The goal would be to locate as much profit as possible in a low-tax country (the Cayman Islands has no corporate income tax). Will profit from the sale of goods from the Cayman Islands subsidiary to CDD constitute subpart F income to 3D in 2011?

**Answer:** Yes. The Cayman Islands profit is considered foreign base company sales income under subpart F because the goods are manufactured outside the Cayman Islands by a related party (3D) and sold outside the Cayman Islands to a related party (CDD). 3D will be treated has having received a deemed dividend of the profit from the Cayman Islands subsidiary.

There are several exceptions that serve to exclude all or a portion of a CFC's subpart F income from current taxation to the U.S. shareholders. A *de minimis rule* excludes all gross income from being treated as foreign base company income if the sum of the CFC's gross foreign base company income is less than the lesser of 5 percent of gross income or $1 million. A *full inclusion rule* treats all of the CFC's gross income as foreign base company income if more than 70 percent of the CFC's gross income is foreign base company income. In addition, a taxpayer can *elect* to exclude "high-tax" subpart F income from the deemed dividend rules. High-tax subpart F income is taxed at an effective tax rate that is 90 percent or more of the highest U.S. statutory rate. For

[46]§954(d).

a U.S. corporation, the rate currently is 31.5 percent (90% × 35%). The calculation of the effective tax rate is complex and beyond the scope of this text.

---

**Example 24-23**

Return to the facts in Example 24-21, in which CDD reported taxable income from its bakery operations of C$75,000 in 2010 and received dividends of £1,250 from Cadbury PLC, which translated into C$2,500. Assume CDD has gross income of C$125,000 in 2011. In the previous example, we determined that the dividend constitutes subpart F income for U.S. tax purposes. Will 3D have a deemed dividend of this subpart F income in 2011?

**Answer:** No. The dividend is less than the lesser of 5 percent of CDD's gross income ($6,250) or $1 million and is not subject to the deemed dividend rules under the *de minimus* rule.

---

The subpart F rules apply only in years in which a corporation is a CFC for an uninterrupted period of 30 days or more during its taxable year. Only those U.S. shareholders who own stock in the CFC on the last day in the CFC's taxable year are treated as having received their pro rata share of any subpart F deemed dividend.

The computation of the deemed dividend under subpart F is exceptionally complicated and requires the CFC to allocate both deductions and taxes paid to subpart F gross income. The formula for this computation can be found in worksheets in the Instructions to Form 5471. In addition, the U.S. shareholder receives a deemed paid foreign tax credit similar to the indirect foreign tax credit available on actual dividend distributions.[47]

Earnings of the CFC treated as a deemed dividend under subpart F becomes *previously taxed income* and subsequently can be distributed to the shareholders without being included in the recipient's gross income a second time.

### Planning to Avoid Subpart F Income

U.S. multinational corporations expanding outside the United States often use hybrid entities as a tax-efficient means to avoid the subpart F rules. Tax aligning a U.S. corporation's international supply chain has become a frequent objective in international tax planning. Accomplishing this goal requires the formation of a foreign holding company (Foreign HoldCo) treated as a corporation for U.S. tax purposes (and thus eligible for deferral from U.S. taxation). The holding company owns the stock of hybrid entities set up to conduct each of the components of the company's foreign operations: financing (FinanceCo), manufacturing (OpCo), distribution (DistribCo), and intellectual property (IPCo). The holding company is strategically located in a country that lightly taxes dividend income paid by the hybrid entities. The hybrid entities also are strategically located in countries that tax the income from such operations (for example, interest or royalties paid by the operating company to the finance company or intellectual property company) at a low tax rate. For instance, Ireland taxes manufacturing and intellectual property income at 12.5 percent. By conducting these operations through hybrid entities, transactions between the entities (for example, a payment of interest, rents, or royalties from one entity to another), which otherwise would create subpart F income, are ignored for U.S. tax purposes but respected for foreign tax purposes because the hybrid entity is treated as a corporation in the country in which it is organized. This allows for the free flow of cash between foreign operations without the intrusion of the U.S. tax laws and the reduction of taxes in high-tax countries through cross-border payments that are deductible in the country in which the hybrid entity is located. Exhibit 24-5 provides a template for such an international operation.

---

[47]§960.

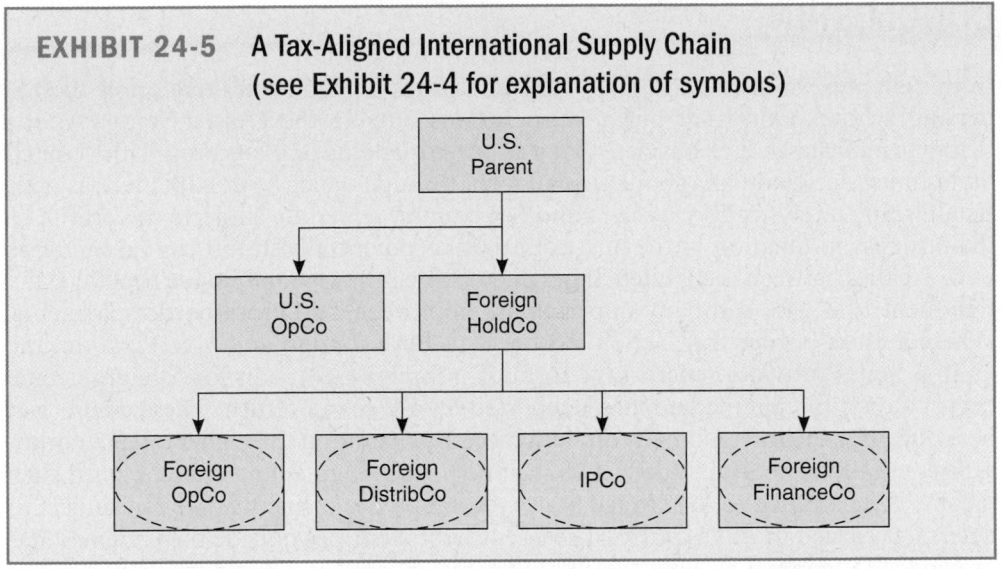

**EXHIBIT 24-5**   A Tax-Aligned International Supply Chain
(see Exhibit 24-4 for explanation of symbols)

---

**Taxes in the Real World**   *Lower Your Taxes: Move to Switzerland*

*Kerry Capell*
*September 10, 2009*

***BusinessWeek***
© 2009 McGraw-Hill, Inc.

As governments around the globe struggle to contain huge deficits, companies and executives are bracing for higher taxes. And increasingly they are turning to Switzerland for relief.

This isn't the Switzerland of shadowy private banking, the kind that got Zurich giant UBS (UBS) into trouble when it was forced to reveal details of American account holders suspected of tax evasion. Instead, Swiss cantons are openly and legally urging multinationals to relocate. This fall, U.S. fast-food giant McDonald's will move its European headquarters to Geneva from London,

joining Kraft Foods, Yahoo!, and Nissan. They've all relocated their main Europe offices to Switzerland in the last two years to take advantage of low corporate taxes.

A highly skilled workforce, leading universities, and strong intellectual-property laws also attract companies. Yet those low taxes are very much part of the lure. "There is a lot of interest from companies looking to shift their taxable profit to countries with lower rates," says Andreas Müller, an international corporate tax partner at KPMG in Zurich. Meanwhile, Britain and Ireland are increasing personal income tax rates for top earners. In the United States, tax hikes seem inevitable. Switzerland has no such plans, says Stéphane Garelli, professor of competitiveness at IMD Business School in Lausanne.

## PROPOSALS FOR CHANGE

In February 2010, President Obama proposed significant changes to the U.S. international tax laws that are intended to raise $122 billion in additional tax revenues over the period 2010 through 2019. Under one proposal, U.S. multinational corporations would be required to defer deducting interest expenses related to foreign source income until such income was recognized as income in the United States (for example, as a repatriated dividend). In addition, a U.S. company's direct and deemed-paid foreign tax credits would be computed based on the average rate of foreign tax paid on total foreign earnings. This would result in a blending of high- and low-tax foreign tax credit pools to compute an average global effective tax rate computation. A third proposal would be to treat "excessive returns" on income from intangibles shifted out of the United States as subpart F (non-deferred) income. President Obama dropped his previous proposal to repeal the check-the-box regime. These proposals are highly controversial and will be opposed by the majority of U.S. multinational companies.

## CONCLUSION

In this chapter we discussed some of the important U.S. tax rules that apply to U.S. persons who expand their business operations outside the United States. As the storyline indicates, a U.S. business that wants to expand its markets outside the United States must decide on an organizational form through which to conduct its business. Establishing a physical presence in another country generally subjects the profits of the business to taxation in the host country and potentially in the United States as well. Treaties between the United States and other countries can provide beneficial tax treatment to a U.S. company's operations, employees, and cross-border payments. Where a cross-border transaction is subject to both foreign and U.S. taxation, the United States provides relief in the form of a foreign tax credit for foreign income taxes paid on foreign income that is reported on a U.S. tax return. These credits can be reduced by the foreign tax credit limitation. By operating through a foreign corporation, a U.S. business can defer U.S. taxation on foreign source income until such income is repatriated to the United States. Certain types of income are not subject to deferral if earned through a CFC. The use of hybrid entities outside the United States provides U.S. companies with the ability to shift income and move cash across jurisdictions without being subject to deemed dividends under subpart F.

## SUMMARY

**L01**  Understand the basic U.S. framework for taxing multinational transactions and the role of the foreign tax credit limitation.

- Countries most often determine nexus by either the geographic source of the income (source-based jurisdiction) or the taxpayer's citizenship or residence (residence-based jurisdiction).
  - Under a residence-based approach, a country taxes the worldwide income of the person earning the income.
  - Under a source-based approach, a country taxes only the income earned within its boundaries.
- The U.S. government taxes citizens and residents on their worldwide income, regardless of source (residence-based jurisdiction).
  - An individual who is not a citizen will be treated as a U.S. resident for income tax purposes if he or she is considered a permanent resident (has a green card) or satisfies a substantial presence test.
- The U.S. government only taxes nonresidents on income that is "U.S. source" or is connected with the operation of a U.S. trade or business (source-based jurisdiction).
- To alleviate (mitigate) potential double taxation and to promote international commerce, governments often allow their residents a tax credit for foreign income taxes paid on foreign source income.

**L02**  Apply the U.S. source rules for common items of gross income and deductions.

- The U.S. source rules determine whether income and related deductions are from sources within or without the United States.
  - The U.S. source-of-income rules are important to non-U.S. persons because they limit the scope of U.S. taxation of their worldwide income.
  - For U.S. persons, the primary purpose of the U.S. source-of-income rules is to calculate foreign source taxable income in the numerator of the foreign tax credit limitation.
- The Internal Revenue Code defines eight classes of gross income from sources within the United States and eight classes of gross income from sources without the United States.
  - As a general rule, the taxpayer looks to the borrower's residence to determine the geographic source of interest received.

- In general, the source of dividend income is determined by the residence of the corporation paying the dividend.
  - The source of compensation received for labor or personal services is determined by the location where the service is performed.
  - Rent has its source where the property generating the rent is located.
  - Royalty income has its source where the intangible property or rights generating the royalty is used.
- After determining the source of gross income as being from U.S. or foreign sources, a taxpayer may be required to allocate and apportion allowable deductions to gross income from each geographical source to compute taxable income from U.S. and foreign sources.
  - The IRC provides very broad language in describing how to allocate deductions to U.S. and foreign source gross income.
  - The regulations attempt to match deductions with the gross income such deductions were incurred to produce, usually based on the "factual relationship" of the deduction to gross income.
  - Special apportionment rules apply to nine categories of deductions, most notably interest, research and experimentation, state and local income taxes, losses on property disposition, and charitable contributions.

Recall the role of income tax treaties in international tax planning.                        `LO3`

- A tax treaty is a bilateral agreement between two contracting countries in which each agrees to modify its own tax laws to achieve reciprocal benefits.
- The general purpose of an income tax treaty is to eliminate or reduce (mitigate) the impact of double taxation so that residents paying taxes to one country will not have the full burden of taxes in the other country.
- The United States currently has income tax treaties with 65 countries.
- Most U.S. treaties provide a low withholding tax rate or an exemption from tax on various types of investment income (interest, dividends, gains from sale of stock, and royalties) that would otherwise be subject to a high withholding tax.

Identify creditable foreign taxes and compute the foreign tax credit limitation.            `LO4`

- The foreign tax credit is available only for foreign taxes the United States considers to be income taxes.
- Creditable foreign income taxes can be direct, indirect, or "in lieu of" income taxes.
- Taxpayers must compute a separate FTC limitation for each category ("basket") of foreign source taxable income.
  - Passive category income generally is investment-type income that traditionally is subject to low foreign taxes (usually in the form of withholding taxes).
  - Income not treated as passive category income is defined to be general category income. General category income includes gross income from an active trade or business, financial services income, and shipping income.
  - A taxpayer computes the FTC limitation by multiplying the ratio of foreign source taxable income to total taxable income times precredit U.S. tax, as follows:

$$\frac{\text{Foreign source taxable income}}{\text{Total taxable income}} \times \text{Precredit U.S. tax}$$

Distinguish between the different forms of doing business outside the United States and list their advantages and disadvantages.                                                       `LO5`

- A U.S. person can do business outside the United States through a branch, partnership, corporation, or hybrid entity.
- A hybrid entity is an entity that is treated as a flow-through entity for U.S. tax purposes and a corporation for foreign tax purposes (or vice versa).
- A U.S. taxpayer elects the U.S. tax status of a hybrid entity by "checking the box" on Form 8832.
  - Certain designated per se foreign entities are not eligible for this elective treatment.

> **LO6**    Comprehend the basic U.S. anti-deferral tax regime and identify common sources of subpart F income.
>
> - Subpart F requires certain U.S. shareholders in a controlled foreign corporation (CFC) to include in their gross income currently their pro rata share of specified categories of "tainted" income earned by the CFC during the current year (*subpart F income*).
> - A controlled foreign corporation is defined as any foreign corporation in which U.S. shareholders collectively own more than 50 percent of the total combined voting power of all classes of stock entitled to vote or the total value of the corporation's stock on any day during the CFC's tax year.
>   - Constructive ownership rules are used in the calculation of both the 50 percent test for determining CFC status and the 10 percent test for determining who is a U.S. shareholder.
> - Subpart F income generally can be characterized as low-taxed passive income or "portable" income earned by a CFC.
>   - Foreign personal holding company income includes interest, dividends, rents, royalties, and gains from the sales of certain foreign property.
>   - Foreign base company sales income is income derived by a CFC from the sale or purchase of personal property to (or from) a related person and the property is manufactured and sold outside the CFC's country of incorporation.
> - There are several exceptions that serve to exclude all or a portion of a CFC's subpart F income from current taxation to the U.S. shareholders.
>   - A *de minimis rule* excludes all gross income from being treated as foreign base company income if the sum of the CFC's gross foreign base company income is less than the lesser of 5 percent of gross income or $1 million.
>   - A *full inclusion rule* treats all of the CFC's gross income as foreign base company income if more than 70 percent of the CFC's gross income is foreign base company income.

# KEY TERMS

allocate (24-11)

apportion (24-11)

branch (24-3)

commercial traveler exception (24-8)

controlled foreign corporation (24-27)

definitely related deductions (24-12)

disregarded entity (24-25)

effectively connected income (24-3)

fixed and determinable, annual or periodic income (24-3)

foreign joint venture (24-21)

foreign personal holding company income (24-28)

foreign subsidiary (24-21)

foreign tax credit (24-5)

foreign tax credit limitation (24-5)

FTC basket (24-19)

functional currency (24-22)

general category income (24-19)

hybrid entity (24-4)

inbound transaction (24-2)

nexus (24-2)

nonresident alien (24-4)

not definitely related deductions (24-12)

outbound transaction (24-2)

passive category income (24-19)

permanent establishment (24-17)

residence-based jurisdiction (24-2)

resident alien (24-4)

reverse hybrid entity (24-4)

source-based jurisdiction (24-2)

spot rate (24-21)

subpart F income (24-27)

tax haven (24-26)

# DISCUSSION QUESTIONS

1. **(LO1)** Distinguish between an outbound transaction and an inbound transaction from a U.S. tax perspective.
2. **(LO1)** What are the major U.S. tax issues that apply to an inbound transaction?
3. **(LO1)** What are the major U.S. tax issues that apply to an outbound transaction?

4. **(LO1)** How does a residence-based approach to taxing worldwide income differ from a source-based approach to taxing the same income.

5. **(LO1)** Henri is a resident of the United States for U.S. tax purposes and earns $10,000 from an investment in a French company. Will Henri be subject to U.S. tax under a residence-based approach to taxation? A source-based approach?

6. **(LO1)** What are the two categories of income that can be taxed by the United States when earned by a nonresident? How does the United States tax each category of income?

7. **(LO1)** Maria is not a citizen of the United States, but she spends 180 days per year in the United States on business-related activities. Under what conditions will Maria be considered a resident of the United States for U.S. tax purposes?

8. **(LO1)** Natasha is not a citizen of the United States, but she spends 200 days per year in the United States on business. She does not have a green card. True or False: Natasha will always be considered a resident of the United States for U.S. tax purposes because of her physical presence in the United States. Explain.

9. **(LO1)** Why does the United States allow U.S. taxpayers to claim a credit against their precredit U.S. tax for foreign income taxes paid?

10. **(LO1)** What role does the foreign tax credit limitation play in U.S. tax policy?

11. **(LO2)** Why are the income source rules important to a U.S. citizen or resident?

12. **(LO2)** Why are the income source rules important to a U.S. nonresident?

13. **(LO2)** Carol receives $500 of dividend income from Microsoft, Inc., a U.S. company. True or False: Absent any treaty provisions, Carol will be subject to U.S. tax on the dividend regardless of whether she is a resident or nonresident. Explain.

14. **(LO2)** Pavel, a citizen and resident of Russia, spent 100 days in the United States working for his employer, Yukos Oil, a Russian corporation. Under what conditions will Pavel be subject to U.S. tax on the portion of his compensation earned while working in the United States?

15. **(LO2)** What are the potential U.S. tax benefits from engaging in a §863 sale?

16. **(LO2)** True or False: A taxpayer will always prefer deducting an expense against U.S. source income and not foreign source income when filing a tax return in the United States. Explain.

17. **(LO2)** Distinguish between *allocation* and *apportionment* in sourcing deductions in computing the foreign tax credit limitation.

18. **(LO2)** Distinguish between a *definitely related deduction* and a *not definitely related deduction* in the allocation and apportionment of deductions to foreign source taxable income.

19. **(LO2)** Briefly describe the two different methods for apportioning interest expense to foreign source taxable income in the computation of the foreign tax credit limitation.

20. **(LO2)** Briefly describe the two different methods for apportioning R&E to foreign source taxable income in the computation of the foreign tax credit limitation.

21. **(LO2)** IBM incurs $250 million of R&E in the United States. How does the "exclusive apportionment" of this deduction differ depending on the R&E apportionment method chosen in the computation of the foreign tax credit limitation?

22. **(LO3)** What is the primary goal of the United States in negotiating income tax treaties with other countries?

23. **(LO3)** What is a *permanent establishment,* and why is it an important part of most income tax treaties?

24. **(LO3)** Why is a treaty important to a nonresident investor in U.S. stocks and bonds?

25. **(LO3)** Why is a treaty important to a nonresident worker in the United States?

26. **(LO4)** Why does the United States use a "basket" approach in the foreign tax credit limitation computation?

27. **(LO4)** True or False: All dividend income received by a U.S. taxpayer is classified as passive category income for foreign tax credit limitation purposes. Explain.

28. **(LO4)** True or False: All foreign taxes are creditable for U.S. tax purposes. Explain.

29. **(LO4)** What is an "indirect credit" for foreign tax credit purposes? What is the tax policy reason for allowing such a credit?

30. **(LO4)** What is a functional currency? What role does it play in the computation of an indirect credit for foreign tax credit purposes?

31. **(LO5)** What is a hybrid entity for U.S. tax purposes? Why is a hybrid entity a popular organizational form for a U.S. company expanding its international operations? What are the potential drawbacks to using a hybrid entity?

32. **(LO5)** What is a "per se" entity under the check-the-box rules?

33. **(LO6)** What are the requirements for a foreign corporation to be a *controlled foreign corporation* for U.S. tax purposes?

34. **(LO6)** Why does the United States not allow deferral on all foreign source income earned by a controlled foreign corporation?

35. **(LO6)** True or False: A foreign corporation owned equally by 11 U.S. individuals can never be a controlled foreign corporation? Explain.

36. **(LO6)** What is foreign base company sales income? Why does the United States include this income in its definition of subpart F income?

37. **(LO6)** True or False: Subpart F income is always treated as a deemed dividend to the U.S. shareholders of a controlled foreign corporation. Explain.

38. **(LO6)** True or False: Non-subpart F income always qualifies for tax deferral until it is repatriated back to the United States. Explain.

## PROBLEMS

39. **(LO1)** Camille, a citizen and resident of Country A, received a $1,000 dividend from a corporation organized in Country B. Which statement best describes the taxation of this income under the two different approaches to taxing foreign income?

    a. Country B will not tax this income under a residence-based jurisdiction approach but will tax this income under a source-based jurisdiction approach.

    b. Country B will tax this income under a residence-based jurisdiction approach but will not tax this income under a source-based jurisdiction approach.

    c. Country B will tax this income under both a residence-based jurisdiction approach and a source-based jurisdiction approach.

    d. Country B will not tax this income under either a residence-based jurisdiction approach or a source-based jurisdiction approach.

40. **(LO1)** Spartan Corporation, a U.S. corporation, reported $2 million of pretax income from its business operations in Spartania, which were conducted through a foreign branch. Spartania taxes branch income at 25 percent, and the United States taxes corporate income at 35 percent.

    a. If the United States provided no mechanism for mitigating double taxation, what would be the total tax (U.S. and foreign) on the $2 million of branch profits?

    b. Assume the United States allows U.S. corporations to exclude foreign source income from U.S. taxation. What would be the total tax on the $2 million of branch profits?

c. Assume the United States allows U.S. corporations to claim a deduction for foreign income taxes. What would be the total tax on the $2 million of branch profits?

d. Assume the United States allows U.S. corporations to claim a credit for foreign income taxes paid on foreign source income. What would be the total tax on the $2 million of branch profits? What would be your answer if Spartania taxed branch profits at 40 percent?

41. **(LO1)** Guido is a citizen and resident of Belgium. He has a full-time job in Belgium and has lived there with his family for the past 10 years. In 2008, Guido came to the United States for the first time. The sole purpose of his trip was business. He intended to stay in the United States for only 180 days, but he ended up staying for 210 days because of unforeseen problems with his business. Guido came to the United States again on business in 2009 and stayed for 180 days. In 2010 he came back to the United States on business and stayed for 70 days. Determine if Guido meets the U.S. statutory definition of a resident alien in 2008, 2009, and 2010 under the substantial presence test.

42. **(LO1)** Use the facts in problem 41. If Guido meets the statutory requirements to be considered a resident of both the United States and Belgium, what criteria does the U.S.-Belgium treaty use to "break the tie" and determine Guido's country of residence? Look at Article 4 of the 2006 U.S.-Belgium income tax treaty, which you can find on the IRS Web site, www.irs.gov.

■ **research**

43. **(LO1)** How does the U.S.-Belgium treaty define a *permanent establishment* for determining nexus? Look at Article 5 of the 2006 U.S.-Belgium income tax treaty, which you can find on the IRS Web site, www.irs.gov.

■ **research**

44. **(LO1)** Mackinac Corporation, a U.S. corporation, reported total taxable income of $5 million in 2010. Taxable income included $1.5 million of foreign source taxable income from the company's branch operations in Canada. All of the branch income is general category income. Mackinac paid Canadian income taxes of $600,000 on its branch income. Compute Mackinac's allowable foreign tax credit for 2010. Assume a U.S. corporate tax rate of 34 percent.

45. **(LO1)** Waco Leather Inc., a U.S. corporation, reported total taxable income of $5 million in 2010. Taxable income included $1.5 million of foreign source taxable income from the company's branch operations in Mexico. All of the branch income is general category income. Waco paid Mexican income taxes of $420,000 on its branch income. Compute Waco's allowable foreign tax credit for 2010. Assume a U.S. corporate tax rate of 34 percent.

46. **(LO2)** Petoskey Stone Inc., a U.S. corporation, received the following sources of income during 2010. Identify the source of each item as either U.S. or foreign.

a. Interest income from a loan to its German subsidiary.

b. Dividend income from Granite Corporation, a U.S. corporation.

c. Royalty income from its Irish subsidiary for use of a trademark.

d. Rent income from its Canadian subsidiary of a warehouse located in Wisconsin.

47. **(LO2)** Carmen SanDiego, a U.S. citizen, is employed by General Motors Corporation, a U.S. corporation. On April 1, 2010, GM relocated Carmen to its Brazilian operations for the remainder of 2010. Carmen was paid a salary of $120,000 and was employed on a 5-day week basis. As part of her compensation package for moving to Brazil, Carmen also received a housing allowance of $25,000. Carmen's salary was earned ratably over the 12-month period. During 2010 Carmen worked 260 days, 195 of which were in Brazil and 65 of which were in Michigan. How much of Carmen's total compensation is treated as foreign source income for 2010? Why might Carmen want to maximize her foreign source income in 2010?

48. **(LO2)** John Elton is a citizen and bona fide resident of Great Britain (United Kingdom). During 2010, John received the following income:

    - Compensation of $30 million from performing concerts in the United States.
    - Cash dividends of $10,000 from a French corporation stock.
    - Interest of $6,000 on a U.S. corporation bond.
    - Interest of $2,000 on a loan made to a U.S. citizen residing in Australia.
    - Gain of $80,000 on the sale of stock in a U.S. corporation.

    Determine the source (U.S. or foreign) of each item of income John received in 2010.

| Income | Source |
|---|---|
| Income from concerts | |
| Dividend from French corporation | |
| Interest on a U.S. corporation bond | |
| Interest of $2,000 on a loan made to a U.S. citizen residing in Australia | |
| Gain of $80,000 on the sale of stock in a U.S. corporation | |

49. **(LO2)** Spartan Corporation, a U.S. company, manufactures green eyeshades for sale in the United States and Europe. All manufacturing activities take place in Michigan. During the current year, Spartan sold 10,000 green eyeshades to European customers at a price of $10 each. Each eyeshade costs $4 to produce. All of Spartan's production assets are located in the United States. For each independent scenario, determine the source of the gross income from sale of the green eyeshades.

    a. Spartan ships its eyeshades F.O.B., place of destination.
    b. Spartan ships its eyeshades F.O.B., place of shipment.

■ planning

50. **(LO2)** Falmouth Kettle Company, a U.S. corporation, sells its products in the United States and Europe. During 2010, selling, general, and administrative (SG&A) expenses included:

| | |
|---|---:|
| Personnel department | $ 500 |
| Training department | 350 |
| President's salary | 400 |
| Sales manager's salary | 200 |
| Other general and administrative | 550 |
| Total SG&A expenses | $2,000 |

    Falmouth had $12,000 of gross sales to U.S. customers and $3,000 of gross sales to European customers. Gross income (sales minus cost of goods sold) from domestic sales was $3,000 and gross profit from foreign sales was $1,000. Apportion Falmouth's SG&A expenses to foreign source income using the following methods:

    a. Gross sales.
    b. Gross income.
    c. If Falmouth wants to maximize its foreign tax credit limitation, which method produces the better outcome?

■ planning

51. **(LO2)** Owl Vision Corporation (OVC) is a North Carolina corporation engaged in the manufacture and sale of contact lenses and other optical equipment. The company handles its export sales through sales branches in Belgium and Singapore. The average tax book value of OVC's assets for the year was $200 million, of which $160 million generated U.S. source income and $40 million generated foreign

source income. The average fair market value of OVC's assets was $240 million, of which $180 million generated U.S. source income and $60 million generated foreign source income. OVC's total interest expense was $20 million.

a. What amount of the interest expense will be apportioned to foreign source income under the tax book value method?

b. What amount of the interest expense will be apportioned to foreign source income under the fair market value method?

c. If OVC wants to maximize its foreign tax credit limitation, which method produces the better outcome?

52. **(LO2)** Freon Corporation, a U.S. corporation, manufactures air-conditioning and warm air heating equipment. Freon reported gross sales from this product group of $50,000,000, of which $10,000,000 was foreign source. The gross profit percentage for domestic sales was 15 percent, and the gross profit percentage from non-U.S. sales was 20 percent. Freon incurred R&E expenses of $6,000,000, all of which were conducted in the United States.

■ planning

a. What amount of the R&E expense will be apportioned to foreign source income under the sales method?

b. What amount of the R&E expense will be apportioned to foreign source income under the gross income method?

c. If Freon wants to maximize its foreign tax credit limitation, which method produces the better outcome?

53. **(LO3)** Colleen is a citizen and bona fide resident of Ireland. During 2010, she received the following income:

■ research

- Cash dividends of $2,000 from a U.S. corporation's stock.
- Interest of $1,000 on a U.S. corporation bond.
- Royalty of $100,000 from a U.S. corporation for use of a patent she developed.
- Rent of $3,000 from U.S. individuals renting her cottage in Maine.

Identify the U.S. withholding tax rate on the payment of each item of income under the U.S.-Ireland income tax treaty and cite the appropriate treaty article. You can access the 1997 U.S.-Ireland income tax treaty on the IRS Web site, www.irs.gov.

| Income | Withholding Tax Rate | Treaty Article |
|---|---|---|
| Cash dividends of $2,000 | | |
| Interest of $1,000 | | |
| Royalty of $100,000 | | |
| Rent of $3,000 | | |

54. **(LO4)** Gameco, a U.S. corporation, operates gambling machines in the United States and abroad. Gameco conducts its operations in Europe through a Dutch B.V., which is treated as a branch for U.S. tax purposes. Gameco also licenses game machines to an unrelated company in Japan. During the current year, Gameco paid the following foreign taxes, translated into U.S. dollars at the appropriate exchange rate:

| Foreign Taxes | Amount (in $) |
|---|---|
| National income taxes | 1,000,000 |
| City (Amsterdam) income taxes | 100,000 |
| Value-added tax | 150,000 |
| Payroll tax (employer's share of social insurance contributions) | 400,000 |
| Withholding tax on royalties received from Japan | 50,000 |

Identify Gameco's creditable foreign taxes.

■ **planning**

55. **(LO4)** Sombrero Corporation, a U.S. corporation, operates through a branch in Espania. Management projects that the company's pretax income in the next taxable year will be $100,000, $80,000 from U.S. operations and $20,000 from the branch. Espania taxes corporate income at a rate of 45 percent. The U.S. corporate tax rate is 35 percent.

    a. If management's projections are accurate, what will be Sombrero's excess foreign tax credit in the next taxable year? Assume all of the income is general category income.

    b. Management plans to establish a second branch in Italia. Italia taxes corporate income at a rate of 30 percent. What amount of income will the branch in Italia have to generate to eliminate the excess credit generated by the branch in Espania?

56. **(LO4)** Chapeau Company, a U.S. corporation, operates through a branch in Champagnia. The source rules used by Champagnia are identical to those used by the United States. For 2010, Chapeau has $2,000 of gross income, $1,200 from U.S. sources and $800 from sources within Champagnia. The $1,200 of U.S. source income and $700 of the foreign source income are attributable to manufacturing activities in Champagnia (general category income). The remaining $100 of foreign source income is passive category interest income. Chapeau had $500 of expenses other than taxes, all of which are allocated directly to manufacturing income ($200 of which is apportioned to foreign sources). Chapeau paid $150 of income taxes to Champagnia on its manufacturing income. The interest income was subject to a 10 percent withholding tax of $10. Assume the U.S. tax rate is 35 percent. Compute Chapeau's allowable foreign tax credit in 2010.

57. **(LO4)** Paton Corporation, a U.S. corporation, owns 100 percent of the stock of Tappan Ltd, a British corporation, and 100 percent of the stock of Monroe N.V., a Dutch corporation. Monroe has post-1986 undistributed earnings of €600 and post-1986 foreign income taxes of $400. Tappan has post-1986 undistributed earnings of £800 and post-1986 foreign income taxes of $200. During the current year, Tappan paid Paton a dividend of £100, and Monroe paid Paton a dividend of €100. The dividends were exempt from withholding tax under the U.S.-UK and U.S.-Netherlands income tax treaties. The exchange rates are as follows: €1:$1.50 and £1:$2.00.

    a. Compute Paton's deemed paid credit on the dividends it received from Tappan and Monroe.

    b. Assume this is Paton's only income and compute the company's net U.S. tax after allowance of any foreign tax credits.

■ **planning**

58. **(LO4)** Hannah Corporation, a U.S. corporation, owns 100 percent of the stock of its two foreign corporations, Red S.A. and Cedar A.G. Red and Cedar derive all of their income from active foreign business operations. Red operates in a low-tax jurisdiction (20 percent tax rate), and Cedar operates in a high-tax jurisdiction (50 percent tax rate). Red has post-1986 foreign income taxes of $200 and post-1986 undistributed earnings of 800u. Cedar has post-1986 foreign income taxes of $500 and post-1986 undistributed earnings of 500q. No withholding taxes are imposed on any dividends that Hannah receives from Red or Cedar. The exchange rate between all three currencies is 1:1. Assume a U.S. corporate tax rate of 35 percent. Under the look-through rules, all dividend income is treated as general category income.

    a. Compute the effect of an 80u dividend from Red on Hannah's net U.S. tax liability.

    b. Can you offer Hannah any suggestions regarding how it might eliminate the residual U.S. tax due on an 80u dividend from Red? Be specific in terms of the exact amounts involved in any planning opportunities you identify.

59. **(LO5)** Identify the "per se" companies for which a check-the-box election cannot be made for U.S. tax purposes in the countries listed below. Consult the Instructions to Form 8832, which can be found on the "Forms and Instructions" site on the IRS Web site, www.irs.gov.

   a. Japan
   b. Germany
   c. Netherlands
   d. United Kingdom
   e. People's Republic of China

60. **(LO5)** BP Inc., a U.S. corporation, intends to create a *limitada* in Brazil in 2010 to manufacture pitching machines. The company expects the operation to generate losses of US$2,500,000 during its first three years of operations. USCo would like the losses to flow through to its U.S. tax return and offset its U.S. profits.

   a. Can BP "check the box" and treat the *limitada* as a disregarded entity (branch) for U.S. tax purposes? Consult the Instructions to Form 8832, which can be found on the "Forms and Instructions" site on the IRS Web site, www.irs.gov.

   b. Assume management's projections were accurate and BP deducted $75,000 of branch losses on its U.S. tax return from 2010–2012. At 01/01/13, the fair market value of the *limitada's* net assets exceeded USCo's tax basis in the assets by US$5 million. What are the U.S. tax consequences of checking the box on Form 8832 and converting the *limitada* to a corporation for U.S. tax purposes?

61. **(LO6)** Identify whether the corporations described below are controlled foreign corporations.

   a. Shetland PLC, a UK corporation, has two classes of stock outstanding, 75 shares of class AA stock and 25 shares of class A stock. Each class of stock has equal voting power. Angus owns 35 shares of class AA stock and 20 shares of class A stock. Angus is a U.S. citizen who resides in England.

   b. Tony and Gina, both U.S. citizens, own 25 percent and 10 percent, respectively, of the voting stock of DaVinci S.A., an Italian corporation. Tony also owns 25 percent of the stock of Roma Corporation, an Italian corporation that owns 50 percent of the DaVinci stock.

   c. Pierre, a U.S. citizen, owns 45 of the 100 shares outstanding in Vino S.A., a French corporation. Pierre's father, Pepe, owns 8 shares in Vino. Pepe also is a U.S. citizen. The remaining 47 shares are owned by non-U.S. individuals.

62. **(LO6)** USCo owns 100 percent of the following corporations: Dutch N.V., Germany A.G., Australia PLC, Japan Corporation, and Brazil S.A. During the year, the following transactions took place:

   a. Germany A.G. owns an office building that it leases to unrelated persons. Germany A.G. engaged an independent managing agent to manage and maintain the office building and performs no activities with respect to the property.

   b. Dutch N.V. leased office machines to unrelated persons. Dutch N.V. performed only incidental activities and incurred nominal expenses in leasing and servicing the machines. Dutch N.V. is not engaged in the manufacture or production of the machines and does not add substantial value to the machines.

   c. Dutch N.V. purchased goods manufactured in France from an unrelated contract manufacturer and sold them to Germany A.G. for consumption in Germany.

   d. Australia PLC purchased goods manufactured in Australia from an unrelated person and sold them to Japan Corporation for use in Japan.

   Determine whether the above transactions result in subpart F income to USCo.

63. **(LO6)** USCo manufactures and markets electrical components. USCo operates outside the United States through a number of CFCs, each of which is organized in a different country. These CFCs derived the following income for the current year:

    a. F1 has gross income of $5 million, including $200,000 of foreign personal holding company interest and $4.8 million of gross income from the sale of inventory that F1 manufactured at a factory located within its home country.

    b. F2 has gross income of $5 million, including $4 million of foreign personal holding company interest and $1 million of gross income from the sale of inventory that F2 manufactured at a factory located within its home country.

    Determine the amount of income that USCo must report as a deemed dividend under subpart F in each scenario.

## COMPREHENSIVE PROBLEMS

64. Spartan Corporation manufactures quidgets at its plant in Sparta, Michigan. Spartan sells its quidgets to customers in the United States, Canada, England, and Australia.

    Spartan markets its products in Canada and England through branches in Toronto and London, respectively. Title transfers in the United States on all sales to U.S. customers and abroad (FOB: destination) on all sales to Canadian and English customers. Spartan reported total gross profit on U.S. sales of $15,000,000 and total gross profit on Canadian and U.K. sales of $5,000,000, split equally between the two countries. Spartan financed its Canadian operations through a $10 million capital contribution, which Spartan financed through a loan from Bank of America. During the current year, Spartan paid $600,000 in interest on the loan.

    Spartan sells its quidgets to Australian customers through its wholly owned Australian subsidiary. Title passes in the United States (FOB: shipping) on all sales to the subsidiary. Spartan reported gross profit of $3,000,000 on sales to its subsidiary during the year. The subsidiary paid Spartan a dividend of $670,000 on December 31 (the withholding tax is 0 percent under the U.S.-Australia treaty).

    a. Compute Spartan's foreign source gross income and foreign tax (direct and withholding) for the current year.

    b. Assume 20 percent of the interest paid to Bank of America is allocated to the numerator of Spartan's FTC limitation calculation. Compute Spartan Corporation's FTC limitation using your calculation from question a and any excess FTC or excess FTC limitation (all of the foreign source income is put in the general category FTC basket).

65. Windmill Corporation manufactures products in its plants in Iowa, Canada, Ireland, and Australia. Windmill conducts its operations in Canada through a 50 percent owned joint venture, CanCo. CanCo is treated as a corporation for U.S. and Canadian tax purposes. An unrelated Canadian investor owns the remaining 50 percent. Windmill conducts its operations in Ireland through a wholly owned subsidiary, IrishCo. IrishCo is a controlled foreign corporation for U.S. tax purposes. Windmill conducts its operations in Australia through a wholly owned hybrid entity (KiwiCo) treated as a branch for U.S. tax purposes and a corporation for Australian tax purposes. Windmill also owns a 5 percent interest in a Dutch corporation (TulipCo).

    During 2010, Windmill reported the following foreign source income from its international operations and investments.

|                   | CanCo    | IrishCo  | KiwiCo   | TulipCo  |
|-------------------|----------|----------|----------|----------|
| **Dividend income** |        |          |          |          |
| Amount            | $45,000  | $28,000  |          | $20,000  |
| Withholding tax   | 2,250    | 1,400    |          | 3,000    |
| **Interest income** |        |          |          |          |
| Amount            | $30,000  |          |          |          |
| Withholding tax   | 0        | 0        |          |          |
| **Branch income** |          |          |          |          |
| Taxable income    |          |          | $93,000  |          |
| AUS income taxes  |          |          | $31,000  |          |

Notes to the table:
1. CanCo and KiwiCo derive all of their earnings from active business operations.
2. The dividend from CanCo carries with it a deemed paid credit (§78 gross-up) of $30,000.
3. The dividend from IrishCo carries with it a deemed paid credit (§78 gross-up) of $4,000.

a. Classify the income received by Windmill and any associated §78 gross-up into the appropriate FTC baskets.

b. Windmill has $1,250,000 of U.S. source gross income. Windmill also incurred SG&A of $300,000 that is apportioned between U.S. and foreign source income based on the gross income in each basket. Assume KiwiCo's gross income is $93,000. Compute the FTC limitation for each basket of foreign source income. The corporate tax rate is 35 percent.

66. Euro Corporation, a U.S. corporation, operates through a branch in Germany. During 2010 the branch reported taxable income of $1,000,000 and paid German income taxes of $300,000. In addition, Euro received $50,000 of dividends from its 5 percent investment in the stock of Maple Leaf Company, a Canadian corporation. The dividend was subject to a withholding tax of $5,000. Euro reported U.S. taxable income from its manufacturing operations of $950,000. Total taxable income was $2,000,000. Precredit U.S. taxes on the taxable income were $680,000. Included in the computation of Euro's taxable income were "definitely allocable" expenses of $500,000, 50 percent of which were related to the German branch taxable income.

    Complete pages 1 and 2 of Form 1118 for just the general category income reported by Euro. You can use the fill-in form available on the IRS Web site, www.irs.gov.

67. USCo, a U.S. corporation, has decided to set up a headquarters subsidiary in Europe. Management has narrowed its location choice to either Spain, or Ireland, or Switzerland. The company has asked you to research some of the income tax implications of setting up a corporation in these three countries. In particular, management wants to know what tax rate will be imposed on corporate income earned in the country and the withholding rates applied to interest, dividends, and royalty payments from the subsidiary to the USCo.

    **research**

    To answer the tax rate question, consult KPMG's *Corporate and Indirect Tax Rate Survey 2009,* which you can access at http://www.kpmg.com/Global/en/IssuesAndInsights/ArticlesPublications/Documents/KPMG-Corporate-Indirect-Tax-Rate-Survey-2009.pdf. To answer the withholding tax questions, consult the treaties between the United States and Spain, Ireland, and Switzerland, which you can access at www.irs.gov (type in "treaties" as your search word).

# 25 Transfer Taxes and Wealth Planning

## Learning Objectives

**Upon completing this chapter, you should be able to:**

**LO 1** Outline the basic structure of federal transfer taxes.

—————■—————

**LO 2** Describe the federal estate tax and the valuation of transfers, and compute taxable transfers at death and the federal estate tax.

—————■—————

**LO 3** Summarize the operation of the federal gift tax and the calculation of the federal gift tax.

—————■—————

**LO 4** Apply fundamental principles of wealth planning and explain how income and transfer taxation interact to affect wealth planning.

| Storyline Summary | |
|---|---|
| *Taxpayers:* | Bob and Harry Smith, brothers, ages 69 and 63, respectively Frank's Frozen Pizza Inc. (FFP) is a family business. |
| *Description:* | Bob, recently deceased, was a widower and has a son, Nate (age 28). Harry is married to Wilma, age 38, and has a daughter, Dina (age 35), a son-in-law, Steve, and a grandson, George (age 6). |
| *Location:* | Ann Arbor, Michigan |
| *Employment status:* | Bob and Harry inherited shares in FFP in 1990. Bob and Harry have been employees of FFP. Bob retired from FFP and died earlier this year. Harry is planning to retire as CEO of FFP. |
| *Current situation:* | Nate is Bob's executor. |

**H**arry and Bob Smith were brothers and owners of a small privately held corporation, Frank's Frozen Pizzas Inc. (FFP). Their father, Frank, established the business 35 years ago, and Harry and Bob each inherited half of FFP's outstanding shares upon Frank's death. At the time of Frank's death in 1990, FFP shares were worth about $1 million, but the firm is now debt-free and has a value of $9 million. FFP's success didn't come easy. Over the years Harry and Bob were employed as executive officers and worked long, hard hours. After the death of his wife in 1995, Bob retired on his FFP pension. Over the years both Harry and Bob have transferred some of their FFP shares to other family members. Bob has given 20 percent of the shares in FFP to his son, Nate, and Harry has transferred a like amount to a trust established for Dina (his daughter) and George (his grandson).

Early this year Bob was injured in an auto accident. Unable to recover from his injuries, he died after two days in the hospital. Bob is survived by his son, Nate, executor of Bob's estate. Nate is now collecting his father's assets, and he would like help in preparing Bob's tax returns.

*to be continued . . .*

## L01  INTRODUCTION TO FEDERAL TRANSFER TAXES

This chapter discusses the basic elements of the federal transfer taxes. We begin by outlining transfer taxes and then proceed to a more detailed description of the federal estate tax. Finally, we survey the federal gift tax and conclude with an introduction to the principles of wealth planning.

### Beginnings

In 1916 Congress imposed an estate tax on transfers of property at death. Transfers at death are dictated by the **last will and testament** of the deceased and such transfers are called **testamentary transfers.** Shortly afterward, the transfer tax system was expanded to include a gift tax on lifetime transfers called **intervivos transfers** (from the Latin meaning "during the life of"). Eventually, a generation-skipping tax was also added.[1] Together, this trio of taxes represent one way of reducing the potential wealth society's richest families might accumulate over several generations. Remember, neither gifts nor inheritances are included in recipients' gross income.

Our discussion is limited to the current terrain of the transfer tax system. In 2001, Congress prospectively repealed the estate and generation-skipping taxes (but not the gift tax) effective *only* for the tax year 2010. Although both the generation-skipping and estate taxes are slated to be reinstated in 2011, At press time, Congress has yet to determine whether the current transfer tax system will be revised prior to 2011. In this chapter we assume that the estate and general-skipping taxes are not repealed, but that the provisions in effect for 2009 continue in effect for 2010. Stay tuned for the latest news.

### Common Features of Integrated Transfer Taxes

The two primary federal transfer taxes, the estate tax and the gift tax, were originally enacted separately and operated independently. In 1976 they were *unified* into a transfer tax scheme that applies a progressive tax rate schedule to cumulative transfers. In other words, the estate and gift taxes now are integrated into a common formula.

This integrated formula takes into account the cumulative effect of transfers in previous periods when calculating the tax on a transfer in a current period. Likewise, it takes lifetime transfers into account to determine the tax on assets transferred at death. As you'll see in the tax formulas, we add the taxable transfers in prior years to the current-year transfers and compute the tax on total (cumulative) transfers. Then, we subtract the tax on the earlier transfers from the total tax, to avoid taxing the earlier gifts twice. This calculation is designed to increase the likelihood that the most current transfers will be taxed at a higher marginal tax rate. However, the effect of this feature has been sharply reduced by recent reductions in the top tax rates. Exhibit 25-1 presents the unified transfer tax rate schedule for estate and gift taxes.

The first 11 tax brackets in Exhibit 25-1 are effectively offset by the second common feature of the integrated taxes, the **unified credit.** The unified credit was designed to prevent taxation of all but the largest cumulative transfers. The amount of cumulative taxable transfers a person can make without exceeding the unified credit is the **exemption equivalent.** As we'll discuss shortly, the unified credit currently eliminates tax on cumulative gifts up to $1 million and expands to eliminate tax on cumulative transfers up to $3.5 million at the time of death.[2]

A final important feature of the unified tax system is the application of two common deductions. Each transfer tax provides an unlimited charitable deduction

---

[1]As we'll explain shortly, an *estate* is a legal entity that comes into existence upon the death of an individual (the *decedent*) to transfer ownership of the property owned at death. Testamentary and intervivos transfers often involve *trusts,* another legal entity that we'll also discuss in this chapter.

[2]§2505 and §2010, respectively.

**EXHIBIT 25-1** Unified Transfer Tax Rates*

| Tax Base equal to or over | Not over | Tentative tax | plus | of amount over |
|---|---|---|---|---|
| 0 | $ 10,000 | 0 | 18% | 0 |
| $ 10,000 | $ 20,000 | $ 1,800 | 20% | $ 10,000 |
| $ 20,000 | $ 40,000 | $ 3,800 | 22% | $ 20,000 |
| $ 40,000 | $ 60,000 | $ 8,200 | 24% | $ 40,000 |
| $ 60,000 | $ 80,000 | $ 13,000 | 26% | $ 60,000 |
| $ 80,000 | $100,000 | $ 18,200 | 28% | $ 80,000 |
| $100,000 | $150,000 | $ 23,800 | 30% | $100,000 |
| $150,000 | $250,000 | $ 38,800 | 32% | $150,000 |
| $250,000 | $500,000 | $ 70,800 | 34% | $250,000 |
| $500,000 | $750,000 | $155,800 | 37% | $500,000 |
| $750,000 | $1 million | $248,300 | 39% | $750,000 |
| $1 million | $1.25 million | $345,800 | 41% | $1 million |
| $1.25 million | $1.5 million | $448,300 | 43% | $1.25 million |
| $1.5 million | | $555,800 | 45% | $1.5 million |

*Prior to 2007, the last bracket taxed transfers over $2 million at 46 percent. The estate tax is scheduled to be repealed for decedents dying in 2010, and for that year the top effective rate for the gift tax will be 35 percent for cumulative transfers over $1 million. The estate tax is scheduled to return in 2011 under a sunset provision.

**THE KEY FACTS**

**Common Features of the Unified Transfer Taxes**

- Property transfers, whether made by gift or at death, are subject to transfer tax using a progressive tax rate schedule.

- The unified credit exempts cumulative transfers by gift up to $1 million and cumulative transfers of $3.5 million at the time of death.

- Each transfer tax allows a deduction for transfers to charities and surviving spouses (the charitable and marital deductions, respectively).

for charitable contributions and a generous **marital deduction** for transfers to a spouse. The marital deduction allows almost unfettered transfers between spouses, treating a married couple as virtually a single taxpayer.

# THE FEDERAL ESTATE TAX

L02

The estate tax is designed to tax the value of property owned or controlled by an individual at death, the decedent. Because federal gift and estate taxes are integrated, taxable gifts affect the tax base for the estate tax. Exhibit 25-2 presents the estate tax formula.

**EXHIBIT 25-2** The Federal Estate Tax Formula

| | |
|---|---|
| | Gross Estate |
| *Minus:* | Expenses, Debts, and Losses |
| *Equals:* | Adjusted Gross Estate |
| *Minus:* | Marital and Charitable Deductions |
| *Equals:* | Taxable Estate |
| *Plus:* | Adjusted Taxable Gifts |
| *Equals:* | Estate Tax Base |
| *Times:* | Current Tax Rates |
| *Equals:* | Tentative Tax |
| *Minus:* | Gift Taxes Paid on Adjusted Taxable Gifts |
| *Minus:* | Unified Credit |
| *Equals:* | Estate Tax Payable |

## The Gross Estate

Property possessed by or owned (titled) by a decedent at the time of death is generally referred to as the **probate estate,** because the transfer of this property is carried out by a probate court. **Probate** is the process of gathering property possessed by or

titled in the name of a decedent at the time of death, paying the debts of the decedent, and transferring the ownership of any remaining property to the decedent's **heirs.** Property in the probate estate can include cash, stocks, jewelry, clothing, and realty owned by or titled in the name of the deceased at the time of death.

    The **gross estate** is broader than the probate estate. The gross estate consists of (1) the fair market value of property possessed or owned by a decedent at death *plus* (2) the value of certain automatic property transfers that take effect at death.[3] Property transfers that take effect only at death are not in the probate estate because the transfer takes place just as death occurs. Hence, the probate court does not need to affect a transfer. However, as discussed below, property subject to certain types of automatic transfers is specifically included in the gross estate because the transfer is a substitute for a testamentary transfer.

---

### Example 25-1

*What if:* Nate took an inventory of his father's property in preparation for distributing assets according to Bob's will. Nate must report this preliminary inventory of personal and investment property to the probate court; it includes the following:

|  | Fair Market Value |
|---|---|
| Auto | $ 33,000 |
| Clothes, furniture, and personal effects | 48,000 |
| Smith painting (original cost/initial estimated value) | 25,000 |
| Checking and savings accounts | 75,250 |
| FFP stock | 4,500,000 |
| Residence | 400,000 |
| Other investments | 8,200 |
| Total | $5,089,450 |

What amount of this property is included in Bob's gross estate?

**Answer:** Bob's gross estate includes the value of *all* the above property, or $5,089,450, because he owned these assets at his death.

*What if:* Suppose Bob was also entitled to a pension distribution of $15,000 but had not yet received the check at his time of death. Would this value also be included in Bob's probate estate and therefore gross estate?

**Answer:** Yes. Although Bob had not received the check, he was legally entitled to the property at the time of his death, and therefore it will be included in both his probate estate and gross estate.

---

**Specific Inclusions**    Besides property in the probate estate, the gross estate also includes property transferred automatically at the decedent's death. These testamentary transfers can occur without the help of a probate court because the ownership transfers by law at the time of death. A common example is property held in **joint tenancy with right of survivorship,** which legally transfers to the surviving tenant upon the joint tenant's death. Joint bank accounts are commonly owned in joint ownership with right of survivorship. In contrast, *tenants in common* hold divided rights to property and have the ability to transfer these rights during their life or upon death. Property held by tenants in common, such as real estate, does not automatically transfer at death and thus must be transferred via probate. Although the decedent's interest in jointly owned property (with the right of survivorship)

---

[3]§2033.

ceases at death, the value of the interest the decedent held in this property is still included in the gross estate.[4]

---

**Example 25-2**

Nate and his father jointly own two parcels of real estate not included in the inventory above. One parcel is a vacation home in Colorado. Nate owns this property jointly with Bob and the title is held in joint ownership with the right of survivorship. Will this property be included in Bob's probate estate and/or gross estate?

**Answer:** The property will *not* be included in Bob's *probate* estate, but it will be included in Bob's *gross* estate. When Bob died, Nate automatically became the sole owner of the property without going through probate. However, the property will be included in Bob's gross estate because it is an automatic transfer that is specifically included in the gross estate by law.

The second parcel is real estate in west Texas that Nate and Bob hold as equal tenants in common. Will it be necessary to probate this parcel of real estate to transfer ownership of Bob's share to the beneficiary named in Bob's will?

**Answer:** Yes. In addition, the value of Bob's one-half interest in the west Texas real estate is included in his gross estate.

---

Certain automatic property transfers are specifically included in the gross estate because, while the decedent didn't own the property at death, Congress deemed that the decedent controlled the ultimate disposition of the property. That is, the decedent effectively determined who would receive the property at the time of death. Another example of an automatic transfer is insurance on the life of the decedent. Proceeds of life insurance paid due to the death of the decedent are specifically included in the gross estate if either of two conditions is met. The proceeds are included in the gross estate if (1) the decedent owned the policy (or had "incidents" of ownership such as the right to designate the beneficiary) or (2) the decedent's estate or **executor** is the beneficiary of the insurance policy.

---

**Example 25-3**

Bob owned and paid annual premiums on an insurance policy that, on his death, was to pay the beneficiary of his choice $500,000. Bob named Nate the beneficiary, and the insurance company paid Nate $500,000 after receiving notification of Bob's death. Will Bob's gross estate include the value of the insurance proceeds paid to Nate?

**Answer:** Yes. The $500,000 of insurance proceeds is specifically included in Bob's estate despite the fact that it was paid directly to Nate and did not go through probate.

*What if:* Suppose Bob transferred ownership of the policy to Nate four years prior to his death. Nate had the power to designate the beneficiary of the policy, and he also paid the annual premiums. Will Bob's gross estate include the value of the insurance proceeds paid to Nate?

**Answer:** No. Bob had no incidents of ownership at his death (Nate controlled who is paid the proceeds upon Bob's death), and the proceeds were not paid to his estate.

---

*Jointly owned property.* The proportion of the value of jointly owned property included in the gross estate depends upon the type of ownership. When a decedent's interest is a **tenancy in common** (that is, there is no right of survivorship), a proportion of the value of the property is included in the gross estate that matches the decedent's

---

[4] §2040. There are a number of other transfers that are specifically included in the gross estate. For example, §2036 to §2039 and §2041 address transfers with retained life estates, transfers taking place at death, revocable transfers, annuities, and powers of appointment. A discussion of these provisions is beyond the scope of this text.

ownership interest. For example, consider a decedent who owned a one-third interest in property as a tenant in common. If the entire property is worth $120,000 at the decedent's death, then $40,000 is included in his gross estate.

The amount includible for property held as joint tenancy with the right of survivorship depends upon the marital status of the owners. When property is jointly owned by a husband and wife with the right of survivorship, *half the value* of the property is automatically included in the estate of the first spouse to die.[5] For *unmarried* co-owners, the value included in the decedent's gross estate is determined by the decedent's contribution to the total cost of the property. For example, consider a decedent who provided two-thirds of the total cost of property held as joint tenants with the right of survivorship. If the entire property is worth $240,000 at the decedent's death, then two-thirds ($160,000) is included in his gross estate.

---

**Example 25-4**

Bob and Nate originally purchased the Colorado vacation home seven years ago for $20,000 and held it as joint tenants with the right of survivorship. This property is not included in the list of property in Bob's probate estate because the title passes automatically to Nate upon Bob's death. Bob provided $15,000 of the purchase price, and Nate provided the remaining $5,000. The property was worth $400,000 at Bob's death. How much is included in his gross estate?

**Answer:** Bob's gross estate includes $300,000. For property held in joint tenancy with the right of survivorship, the amount included in the gross estate is equal to the proportion of the purchase price provided by the decedent. Bob provided 75 percent ($5,000 ÷ $20,000 = 75%). Hence, his gross estate will include $300,000 (75% × $400,000) of the value of the vacation home.

**What if:** Suppose Bob was married and owned the home with his wife as joint tenants with the right of survivorship. What amount would be included in Bob's gross estate?

**Answer:** The amount included in the estate is half the value of any property held with the surviving spouse as joint tenants with the right of survivorship, $200,000 in this case.

The west Texas land Bob and Nate owned is valued at $500,200. They owned it as tenants in common, with Bob holding a one-quarter interest and Nate holding the rest. What amount is included in Bob's gross estate?

**Answer:** The amount included in the estate is $125,050 ($500,200 × 25%), because Bob owned a one-quarter interest in the property.

---

Exhibit 25-3 summarizes the rules for determining the value of jointly owned property included in a decedent's gross estate.

**EXHIBIT 25-3** Amount of Jointly Owned Property Included in Gross Estate

| Ownership Form | Marital Status of Co-owners | Amount in Gross Estate |
| --- | --- | --- |
| Community property (discussed below) | Married | Half the fair market value |
| Joint tenancy with right of survivorship | Married | Half the fair market value |
| Joint tenancy with right of survivorship | Unmarried | Percentage of fair market value determined by decedent's contribution to total cost of the property |
| Tenancy in common | Married or unmarried | Percentage of fair market value determined by decedent's interest in the property |

---

[5]In some states joint tenancy with a right of survivorship between spouses is referred to as a **tenancy by the entirety.**

***Transfers within three years of death.***    Certain transfers, such as transfers of insurance policies, made within three years of the decedent's death are also included in the decedent's gross estate, valued as of the time of death. Without this provision, a simple but effective estate tax planning technique would be to transfer ownership in an insurance policy just prior to the decedent's death. This strategy, called *deathbed gifts,* would reduce the decedent's transfer taxes on the life insurance by the difference between its proceeds from the policy (the value at death) and its value on the date transferred.

Only certain transfers are specifically included under this provision, and they are often difficult to identify. Gift taxes paid on any taxable gifts during the three-year period preceding the donor's death are also included in the decedent's gross estate. This gross-up provision prevents donors from escaping estate tax on the amount of gift taxes paid within three years of death. In other words, the amount of gift taxes paid are included in the estate because these amounts would have been included in the estate had the decedent kept the property until death.

---

**Example 25-5**

**What if:** Suppose Bob owned a life insurance policy, and he transferred all incidents of ownership in the policy to his son one year before dying from a fatal disease. Would the life insurance proceeds be included in Bob's gross estate?

**Answer:** Yes. Bob's estate would include proceeds of the policy (grossed up for the gift taxes paid on the transfer), because Bob transferred the incidents of ownership within three years of his death.

---

**Valuation**    Property is included in the gross estate at the *fair market value* on the date of the decedent's death. While fair market value is simple in concept, it is very complicated to apply. Fair market value is defined by the **willing-buyer, willing-seller rule** as follows:

> The price at which such property would change hands between a willing buyer and a willing seller, neither being under any compulsion to buy or to sell, and both have reasonable knowledge of the relevant facts.[6]

We evaluate fair market value based on the facts and circumstances for each individual property. Determining value is relatively simple for properties that have an active market. For example, stocks and bonds traded on exchanges or over-the-counter are valued at the mean of the highest and lowest selling prices on the date of the decedent's death. Unfortunately, the valuation of many other properties, especially realty, is very difficult. The large number of court cases resolving contentious values testifies to the difficulties in applying the willing-buyer, willing-seller rule.

---

**Example 25-6**

At his death Bob owned an original landscape painting made in the late 1800s by one of his ancestors, Tully Smith. Bob purchased the Smith painting for $25,000 in 1980, and last year an expert estimated it was worth $210,000. Nate now has the painting appraised by another expert, who estimates its value at $250,000 based upon a painting by the same artist that sold at auction last month. What value should be placed on the painting for inclusion in the gross estate?

**Answer:** Nate should value the painting at $250,000 according to its specific characteristics and attributes (such as age, condition, history, authenticity, and so forth). Of course, the IRS might disagree with this value and seek to value the painting at a higher value.

---

[6]Reg. §25.2512-1.

The executor of an estate, however, can elect—irrevocably—to have all the property in the gross estate valued on an **alternative valuation date.** The alternative date for valuing the estate is six months after the date of death or on the date of sale or distribution of the property (if this occurs before the end of the six-month period). This election is available only if it reduces the value of the gross estate and the combined estate and generation-skipping taxes.[7]

---

**Example 25-7**

**What if:** Bob's shares of FPP are included in his estate at a value of $4.5 million. Suppose the value of the shares plummeted to $3 million several months after Bob's death. Could Nate as executor of Bob's estate opt to value these shares at the lower cost for estate tax purposes?

**Answer:** Nate could elect to value the shares on the alternate valuation date, six months after Bob's death. However, to qualify for this election, he must value *all* property in the estate on the alternate date, and the election must reduce the value of the entire gross estate as well as the combined estate and generation-skipping taxes.

---

*Valuation of remainders and other temporal interests.*    Assigning value to unique property is difficult enough, but sometimes we must also assign a value to a stream of payments over time or a payment to be made in the future. The right to currently enjoy property or receive income payments from property is a **present interest.** In contrast, the right to receive income or property in the future is a **future interest.** A present right to possess and/or collect income from property may not be permanent; if granted for a specific period of time or until the occurrence of a specific event, it is a **terminable interest.** For example, the right to receive income payments from property for 10 years is a terminable interest. A right to possess property and/or receive income for the duration of someone's life is called a **life estate.** The person whose life determines the duration of the life estate is called the **life tenant.**

At the end of a terminable interest, the property will pass to another owner, the person holding the future interest. In a **reversion,** it returns to the original owner. If it goes to a new owner, the right to the property is called a **remainder** and the owner is called a **remainderman.** For example, the right to own property after a 10-year income interest has ended is a future interest held by the remainderman. The right to property after the termination of a life estate is also called a remainder.

Future interests are common when property is placed in a trust. **Trusts** are legal entities established by a person called the **grantor.** Trusts are administered by a **trustee** and generally contain property called the trust **corpus.** The trustee has a **fiduciary duty** to manage the property in the trust for the benefit of a **beneficiary** or beneficiaries. This duty requires the trustee to administer the trust in an objective and impartial manner and not favor one beneficiary over another.

Since a future interest is essentially a promise of a future payment, we estimate the value of the remainder by discounting the future payment to a present value using a market rate of interest. For example, suppose property worth $100 is placed in a trust with the income to be paid to an income beneficiary each year for 10 years, after which time the property accumulated in the trust will be distributed. The remainder is a future interest with a value we estimate by calculating the present value of a payment of $100 in 10 years as follows:

$$\text{Value of remainder interest} = \frac{\text{Future payment}}{(1 + r)^n}$$

---

[7]§2032A. An executor can also elect to value certain realty used in farming or in connection with a closely held business at a special use valuation. Special use valuation allows realty to be valued at a current use that does not result in the best or highest fair market value. This election is available when the business is conducted by the decedent's family, constitutes a substantial portion of the gross estate, and the property passes to a qualifying heir of the decedent.

where $r$ is the market rate of interest, and $n$ is the number of years. The interest rate used for this calculation is published monthly by the Treasury as the **§7520 rate.**[8] If the §7520 rate is 6 percent, we calculate the value of a remainder of $100 placed in trust for 10 years as follows:

$$\text{Value of remainder interest} = \frac{\$100}{(1+.06)^{10}} = \frac{\$100}{(1.791)} = \$55.83$$

The value of property consists of the present interest (the right to income) and the future interest (the remainder). Hence, once we have estimated the value of the remainder, we compute the value of the income interest as the difference between the value of the remainder and the total value of the property.

$$\begin{aligned}\text{Value of income interest} &= \text{Total value} - \text{Value of remainder} \\ &= \$100 - \$55.83 \\ &= \$44.17\end{aligned}$$

If the terminable interest is a life estate, the valuation of the remainder is a bit more complicated, because payment of the remainder is delayed by the duration of the life estate. To estimate this delay, we base the calculation upon the number of years the life tenant is expected to live. To facilitate the calculation, the regulations provide a table that calculates the discount rate by including the life tenant's age. Exhibit 25-4 includes a portion of the table from the regulation with interest rates by column and the age of the life tenant by row.

> ### THE KEY FACTS
> **Valuation of Remainders and Income Interests**
> - Future interests are valued at present value, calculated by estimating the time until the present interest expires.
> - The present value calculation uses the §7520 interest rate published by the Treasury.
> - If the present interest is measured by a person's life (a life estate), then we estimate the delay by reference to the person's life expectancy as published in IRS tables.
> - We value a present interest such as an income interest or life estate by subtracting the value of the remainder interest from the total value of the property.

### EXHIBIT 25-4    Discount Factors for Estimating the Value of Remainders

| Regulation Section 20.2031-7(d)(7) Table S.—Based on Life Table 90CM Single Life Remainder Factors Applicable After April 30, 1999 [Interest rate] | | | | | | | | | |
| --- | --- | --- | --- | --- | --- | --- | --- | --- | --- |
| Age | 4.2% | 4.4% | 4.6% | 4.8% | 5.0% | 5.2% | 5.4% | 5.6% | 5.8% | 6.0% |
| 0 | .06752 | .06130 | .05586 | .05109 | .04691 | .04322 | .03998 | .03711 | .03458 | .03233 |
| 1 | .06137 | .05495 | .04932 | .04438 | .04003 | .03620 | .03283 | .02985 | .02721 | .02487 |
| 2 | .06325 | .05667 | .05088 | .04580 | .04132 | .03737 | .03388 | .03079 | .02806 | .02563 |
| 3 | .06545 | .05869 | .05275 | .04752 | .04291 | .03883 | .03523 | .03203 | .02920 | .02668 |
| 4 | .06784 | .06092 | .05482 | .04944 | .04469 | .04048 | .03676 | .03346 | .03052 | .02791 |
| 5 | .07040 | .06331 | .05705 | .05152 | .04662 | .04229 | .03845 | .03503 | .03199 | .02928 |
| 6 | .07310 | .06583 | .05941 | .05372 | .04869 | .04422 | .04025 | .03672 | .03357 | .03076 |
| 35 | .20592 | .19307 | .18121 | .17025 | .16011 | .15073 | .14204 | .13399 | .12652 | .11958 |
| 36 | .21312 | .20010 | .18805 | .17691 | .16658 | .15701 | .14814 | .13990 | .13225 | .12514 |
| 37 | .22057 | .20737 | .19514 | .18382 | .17331 | .16356 | .15450 | .14608 | .13825 | .13096 |
| 38 | .22827 | .21490 | .20251 | .19100 | .18031 | .17038 | .16113 | .15253 | .14452 | .13705 |
| 86 | .79805 | .79025 | .78258 | .77504 | .76764 | .76036 | .75320 | .74617 | .73925 | .73245 |
| 87 | .80904 | .80159 | .79427 | .78706 | .77998 | .77301 | .76615 | .75940 | .75277 | .74624 |
| 88 | .81962 | .81251 | .80552 | .79865 | .79188 | .78521 | .77865 | .77220 | .76584 | .75958 |
| 89 | .82978 | .82302 | .81636 | .80980 | .80335 | .79699 | .79072 | .78455 | .77847 | .77248 |

[8]The §7520 rate is 120 percent of the applicable federal midterm rate in effect during the month of the transaction.

**Example 25-8**

At the time of his death Bob owned a reversion in a trust he established for his niece, Dina. Under the terms of the trust, Dina is entitled to income for her life (a life estate), and Bob (or his **heir**) is entitled to the reversion. At the time of Bob's death, the trust assets were valued at $100,000, Dina was 35, and the §7520 interest rate was 6 percent. Should this reversion be included in Bob's gross estate and, if so, what value is placed on the future interest?

**Answer:** Bob's reversion interest is included in his estate because this is a property right he owned at his death. Under Table S in the regulations (Exhibit 25-4), based upon Dina's age and the current interest rate at the time of Bob's death, the percentage of the property that represents the value of Bob's reversion is 0.11958. Thus, his reversion is valued at $11,958 ($100,000 × 0.11958).

**What if:** Suppose the trust was established for George, age 6. Would this influence the value of Bob's reversion interest?

**Answer:** Yes. Under Table S in the regulations and based upon George's age and the current interest rate, the portion of the property that represents the value of Bob's reversion is 0.03076. Thus, Bob's reversion is valued at $3,076 ($100,000 × 0.03076).

The actuarial tables in the regulations are based upon common life expectancy tables from the latest U.S. Census data.[9] Generally, the value of a present interest, such as a life estate, does not depend on how the trustee invests the corpus (in growth stock or high-yield money market) because the fiduciary (the trustee or executor) has a duty to invest the property for the benefit of both the income beneficiary and the remainderman.

**Gross Estate Summary**  So far we've seen that the decedent's gross estate consists of the assets subject to probate as well as certain assets transferred outside probate. These latter assets include property owned by the decedent in joint tenancy with the right of survivorship as well as life insurance. The gross estate also includes certain property transferred by the decedent within three years of death and certain future interests owned by the decedent.

**Example 25-9**

Given previous examples, what is the value of Bob's gross estate?

**Answer:** It is $6,251,458, calculated as follows:

| Property | Value | Example |
|---|---|---|
| Auto | $    33,000 | 25-1 |
| Personal effects | 48,000 | 25-1 |
| Smith painting | 250,000 | 25-6 |
| Checking and savings accounts | 75,250 | 25-1 |
| FPP shares | 4,500,000 | 25-1 |
| Residence | 400,000 | 25-1 |
| Other investments | 8,200 | 25-1 |
| Life insurance proceeds | 500,000 | 25-3 |
| Colorado vacation home | 300,000 | 25-2 and 25-4 |
| West Texas land | 125,050 | 25-2 and 25-4 |
| Reversion interest in Dina Trust | 11,958 | 25-8 |
| Gross estate | $6,251,458 | |

[9]Reg. §20.2031-7(d)(6) presents the annuity tables for future interests vesting in a definite number of years, whereas Reg. §20.2031-7(d)(7) and IRS Publication 1457 present the annuity table for future interests vesting upon the death of one individual.

## The Taxable Estate

Referring to the estate tax formula in Exhibit 25-2, we calculate the taxable estate in two steps. The first consists of reducing the gross estate by deductions allowed for administrative expenses, debts of the decedent, and losses incurred during the administration of the estate. These deductions are allowed because Congress intends to tax the *net* amount transferred to beneficiaries. This step results in the **adjusted gross estate.** In the second step, we allow deductions for transfers to a decedent's spouse (the marital deduction) and to charities (the charitable deduction). These deductions result in the **taxable estate.** We discuss each type of deduction next.

**Administrative Expenses, Debts, Losses, and State Death Taxes** Debts of the estate, such as mortgages and accrued taxes, are deductible. Expenses incurred in administering the estate are also deductible, such as executor's fees, attorneys' fees, and the like. Funeral expenses are deductible, including any reasonable expenditure allowed under local law. Casualty and theft losses are deductible without any floor limitation. These losses must be incurred during the administration of the estate, otherwise the deduction belongs to the new owner of the property. Finally, death taxes imposed by the state are also deductible.[10]

---

**Example 25-10**

Nate paid $7,426 in funeral expenses for his father's services, and during the administration of his father's estate he paid executor's fees of $4,032 and attorney's fees of $9,500. In addition, Nate discovered Bob owed debts totaling $100,500. Since Michigan has no state death or inheritance taxes, no amounts were owed to the state. What is Bob's adjusted gross estate (gross estate minus expenses and debts)?

**Answer:** It is $6,130,000, calculated as follows:

| | | |
|---|---:|---:|
| Gross estate | | $6,251,458 |
| Funeral expenses | $ 7,426 | |
| Executor's fees and expenses | 4,032 | |
| Attorney's fees | 9,500 | |
| Debts of the decedent | 100,500 | |
| Total expenses and debts | | −121,458 |
| Adjusted gross estate | | $6,130,000 |

---

During the administration of the estate, the estate may collect income and will need to file an estate *income* tax return. The executor has the option of deducting administration expenses (but not funeral expenses) and casualty and theft losses on the estate tax return or on the estate's *income* tax return. While no double deduction is available, the choice is relatively simple. If the estate owes no estate taxes, then it should claim the deduction on the income tax return. If the estate owes estate taxes, the marginal estate tax rate is likely to be higher than the marginal income tax rate. Hence, it should probably claim the deduction on the estate tax return.

---

[10]§2053, §2054, and §2058 address expenses, losses, and state death taxes, respectively.

> **What if:** Suppose that during the administration of the estate a storm damaged the Colorado vacation home. Bob's share of the casualty loss to the home was $25,000. Would this be deductible in calculating Bob's taxable estate?
>
> **Answer:** Yes, although the executor can choose to deduct this loss on either the estate tax return or the estate's *income* tax return for the period that included the casualty. If the deduction is claimed on the estate tax return, the loss deduction is not subject to any floor limitations (such as the per casualty floor limitation ($500 in 2009 and $100 in 2010) and the 10 percent of AGI limits imposed on casualty losses claimed in individual income tax returns).

<table>
<tr><td>

**THE KEY FACTS**

**Estate Tax Deductions**

■ Estate tax deductions include the debts of the decedent, funeral expenses, and the costs of administering the estate, including casualty losses.

■ The value of property interests bequeathed to a surviving spouse is deductible if the interest is not terminable.

■ The value of property bequeathed to a qualified charity is deductible.

</td></tr>
</table>

**Marital and Charitable Deductions**   To avoid taxing a married couple's estate twice, Congress provides a deduction for bequests to a surviving spouse. To qualify for the marital deduction, the transferred property must be included in the estate of the deceased spouse, and the surviving spouse must receive the property from the decedent and control its ultimate disposition. For example, property that passes to the surviving spouse as a result of joint tenancy with the right of survivorship qualifies for the marital deduction, as would a direct bequest. However, property rights that are terminable do not generally qualify for the marital deduction. For example, suppose the decedent bequeaths the surviving spouse the right to occupy the decedent's residence until such time as the spouse remarries. The value of the right to possess the residence is a terminable interest and is not eligible for the marital deduction. In general, the estate tax marital deduction is unlimited in amount, so no tax is imposed even on a decedent who leaves her entire estate to a spouse.[11]

Charitable contributions of property are also deductible without any limitation. Charities are defined to include the usual public organizations (corporations organized exclusively for religious, charitable, scientific, literary, or educational purposes) but exclude certain nonprofit cemetery organizations. Interestingly, foreign charities qualify for the charitable deduction under the estate and gift tax but not under the income tax. No deduction is allowed unless the charitable bequest is specified under the last will and testament or is a transfer of property by the decedent before his death that is subsequently included in the decedent's estate. The amount of any bequest must be mandatory, although another person such as the executor can be given discretion to identify the charitable organization.

## Example 25-11

Not long after Bob's death, Nate gathered the Smith family for a reading of Bob's will. The will was relatively simple because Bob was unmarried at the time of his death. Bob had an adjusted gross estate of $6,130,000 and left all his property to Nate, with two exceptions. Bob bequeathed his remainder interest in the Dina Trust (value of $11,958) to Dina, and he bequeathed the Smith painting (value of $250,000) to the Midwest Museum in Ann Arbor (a qualified charity). Is either of these bequests deductible in calculating Bob's taxable estate? What is Bob's taxable estate?

*(continued on page 25-13...)*

---

[11]The terminable interest limitation is described in more detail for the marital deduction under the gift tax. *Qualified terminable interest properties* (*QTIPs* for short) are an exception to the nondeductibility of terminable interest property where the executor agrees to have qualifying terminable interests included in the estate of the surviving spouse. This exception is beyond the scope of this text.

**Answer:** The bequest to the museum qualifies for the charitable deduction because the museum is a qualified charity. Since Bob was unmarried at his death, none of the bequests qualify for the marital deduction. Bob's taxable estate is $5,880,000 calculated as follows:

| | |
|---|---|
| Adjusted gross estate | $6,130,000 |
| Charitable deduction | −250,000 |
| Taxable estate | $5,880,000 |

**What if:** Suppose Bob was married at the time of his death and left his FPP stock, valued at $4.5 million, to his surviving spouse. What amount of this transfer, if any, would qualify for the marital deduction?

**Answer:** Bob's estate would be entitled to a marital deduction of $4.5 million, the value of the entire spousal bequest. In the extreme, if Bob had left all his property to his spouse, then his taxable estate would be reduced to zero.

## Computation of the Estate Tax

Three additional steps are necessary to calculate the estate tax liability from the taxable estate. First, we increase the taxable estate by **adjusted taxable gifts** to determine the estate tax base. Next, we compute the tentative tax on the estate tax base, and finally, we reduce the tentative tax by credits. These credits are primarily composed of the tax on adjusted taxable gifts and the unified credit.

**Adjusted Taxable Gifts**    Adjusted taxable gifts are taxable gifts other than gifts already included in the gross estate. The objective of adding previously taxed transfers to the taxable estate is to allow the estate tax base to reflect all transfers, both intervivos and testamentary. Under a progressive tax rate schedule, this adjustment is designed to increase the marginal tax rate on the estate. Adjusted taxable gifts themselves, however, are not subject to tax in the estate formula. To prevent double taxation of prior taxable gifts, we reduce the tentative estate tax by a credit for the taxes that would have been payable on the adjusted taxable gifts under the current tax rate schedule. Thus, although prior gifts have a direct effect on the magnitude of cumulative taxable transfers, the estate tax is imposed only on cumulative transfers under the *current* rate schedule.

**Example 25-12**

After reviewing all Bob's records, Nate determined he had made only one taxable gift of FPP stock in 2002. This transfer resulted in a taxable gift of $1 million. Because the unified credit in 2002 offset cumulative gifts up to $1 million (the entire gift tax on this transfer), Bob did not pay any gift taxes at that time. Is this gift included in adjusted taxable gifts, and will it influence Bob's tentative estate tax calculated using the estate tax rate schedule in Exhibit 25-1? What is Bob's gross estate tax (tax prior to credits)?

**Answer:** Yes, the gift of stock in 2002 will be included in Bob's estate tax calculation as an adjusted taxable gift. Bob's gross estate tax is $2,976,800, calculated as follows:

| | | |
|---|---|---|
| Adjusted taxable gifts | $1,000,000 | prior gift |
| Taxable estate | 5,880,000 | taxable transfers in estate |
| Cumulative transfers | $6,880,000 | total taxable transfers |
| Tentative tax | $2,976,800 | tax on all transfers |
| Taxes payable on adjusted taxable gifts | −0 | tax paid due to 2002 gift |
| Gross estate tax | $2,976,800 | tax prior to credits |

*(continued on page 25-14...)*

**What if:** Suppose Bob had not made any taxable gifts prior to his death. Would this fact reduce his estate tax? What is his gross estate tax in this circumstance?

**Answer:** Without the gift of stock in 2002 Bob's estate tax would be significantly lower, because adding adjusted taxable gifts operates to increase the estate's marginal tax rate. Bob's gross estate tax would be $2,526,800, calculated as follows:

| | |
|---|---|
| Adjusted taxable gifts | $        0 |
| Taxable estate | 5,880,000 |
| Cumulative transfers | $5,880,000 |
| Tentative tax | $2,526,800 |
| Taxes payable on adjusted taxable gifts | −0 |
| Gross estate tax | $2,526,800 |

**What if:** Suppose Bob's 2002 gift of stock were valued at $1.25 million and the taxes on this gift (using the current tax rate schedule) were $102,500. What is Bob's gross estate tax?

**Answer:** $2,986,800, computed as follows:

| | |
|---|---|
| Adjusted taxable gifts | $1,250,000 |
| Taxable estate | 5,880,000 |
| Cumulative transfers | $7,130,000 |
| Tentative tax | $3,089,300 |
| Taxes payable on adjusted taxable gifts | −102,500 |
| Gross estate tax | $2,986,800 |

**Unified Credit**    Besides subtracting the credit for tax on adjusted taxable gifts, we reduce the gross estate tax by several other credits.[12] The most important is the unified credit, because it eliminates the estate tax on all but the largest estates. The unified credit was enacted in 1977 to apply to both gift and estate taxes. Its objective is to prevent the application of transfer tax to taxpayers who either would not accumulate a relatively large amount of property transfers during their lifetime and/or would not have a relatively large value of assets to pass to heirs upon their death. The amount of cumulative taxable transfers that can be made without exceeding the unified credit is called the exemption equivalent.

The amount of the unified credit and the exemption equivalent has changed over time, and Exhibit 25-5 presents the exemption equivalent amounts since 1986. The unified credit was the same amount for gift and estate tax purposes until 2004, at which time the unified credit for the gift tax was frozen at $345,800 ($1,000,000 exemption equivalent). The exemption equivalent for the estate tax was $3,500,000 in 2009, but it is scheduled to be temporarily repealed in 2010. After 2010, the unified credit is scheduled to return to an exemption equivalent of $1 million for both the estate and gift taxes.

Besides eliminating transfer taxes for relatively small cumulative transfers, the exemption equivalent also acts as the transfer requirement for filing an estate return. That is, an estate tax return (Form 706) must be filed if the gross estate plus adjusted taxable gifts equals or exceeds the exemption equivalent. Exhibit 25-6 presents the first page of Form 706 for Bob Smith. The deadline for the estate tax return is nine months after the decedent's death.[13]

[12]There are other credits that could also apply, but these are beyond the scope of this text. The credit for taxes on prior transfer is designed to adjust the tax for property that was subjected to estate tax within the last 10 years. There is also a credit for pre-1977 gift taxes paid on certain pre-1977 gifts that must be included in the gross estate. Both of these credits are equitable adjustments for potential multiple transfer taxes associated with sequential deaths and multiple inclusions, respectively. Prior to 2005, there was a credit for state death taxes.

[13]There is an automatic six-month extension to file the estate tax return, but an estimate of the tax due must be paid on the due date of the return.

**EXHIBIT 25-5    The Unified Credit and Exemption Equivalent**

| Year of Gift/Death | Unified Credit | Exemption Equivalent |
|---|---|---|
| 1986 | $ 155,800 | $ 500,000 |
| 1987–1997 | 192,800 | 600,000 |
| 1998 | 202,050 | 625,000 |
| 1999 | 211,300 | 650,000 |
| 2000–2001 | 220,550 | 675,000 |
| 2002–2003 | 345,800 | 1,000,000 |
| 2004–2005* | 555,800 | 1,500,000 |
| 2006–2008* | 780,800 | 2,000,000 |
| 2009* | 1,455,800 | 3,500,000 |
| 2010* | † | † |
| 2011 | 345,800 | 1,000,000 |

*The unified credit was the same amount for gift and estate tax purposes until 2004, at which time the unified credit for the gift tax was frozen at $345,800 ($1,000,000 exemption equivalent).
†The estate tax is scheduled to be temporarily eliminated in 2010.

**Example 25-13**

Bob died on February 7 of this year. What amount of estate tax must be paid on his estate, given his prior taxable gift of $1 million in 2002? What is the due date for Bob's estate tax return?

**Answer:** Estate tax of $1,521,000 is due after applying the unified credit, computed as follows:

| | |
|---|---|
| Tentative tax | $2,976,800 |
| Taxes payable on adjusted taxable gifts | −0 |
| Less: Unified credit | −1,455,800 |
| Estate tax due | $1,521,000 |

Bob's executor must file the estate tax return (Form 706 in Exhibit 25-6) or request an extension of time within nine months of Bob's death (by November 7 of this year).

**What if:** Suppose that Bob did not make any taxable gifts during his life. What amount of estate tax would be owed upon his death?

**Answer:** Bob's estate would only owe $1,071,000, computed as follows:

| | |
|---|---|
| Tentative tax | $2,526,800 |
| Taxes payable on adjusted taxable gifts | −0 |
| Less: Unified credit | −1,455,800 |
| Estate tax due | $1,071,000 |

**What if:** Suppose that during his life Bob made a $1.25 million taxable gift and paid gift taxes of $102,500 on this gift. What amount of estate tax would be owed upon his death?

**Answer:** Bob's estate would owe $1,531,000, computed as follows:

| | |
|---|---|
| Tentative tax | $3,089,300 |
| Taxes payable on adjusted taxable gifts | −102,500 |
| Less: Unified credit | −1,455,800 |
| Estate tax due | $1,531,000 |

**EXHIBIT 25-6    Page 1 of Form 706 Estate Tax Return for Bob Smith**

Form **706**
(Rev. September 2009)

Department of the Treasury
Internal Revenue Service

## United States Estate (and Generation-Skipping Transfer) Tax Return

OMB No. 1545-0015

**Estate of a citizen or resident of the United States (see separate instructions).**
**To be filed for decedents dying after December 31, 2008, and before January 1, 2010.**

### Part 1—Decedent and Executor

| | |
|---|---|
| **1a** Decedent's first name and middle initial (and maiden name, if any) <br> BOB | **1b** Decedent's last name <br> SMITH |

**2** Decedent's Social Security No. 000 ┊ 00 ┊ 0000

**3a** County, state, and ZIP code, or foreign country, of legal residence (domicile) at time of death
ANN ARBOR, WASHTENAW COUNTY MICHIGAN 48109

**3b** Year domicile established **1990**    **4** Date of birth **1940**    **5** Date of death **2010**

**6b** Executor's address (number and street including apartment or suite no.; city, town, or post office; state; and ZIP code) and phone no.
6305 TRAIL ROAD
ANN ARBOR, MICHIGAN 48109

**6a** Name of executor (see page 5 of the instructions)
NATE SMITH

**6c** Executor's social security number (see page 5 of the instructions)
000 ┊ 00 ┊ 0000

Phone no. ( 000 ) 000-0000

**7a** Name and location of court where will was probated or estate administered
WASHTENAW COUNTY PROBATE COURT

**7b** Case number
2010

**8** If decedent died testate, check here ▶ ☑ and attach a certified copy of the will.    **9** If you extended the time to file this Form 706, check here ▶ ☐

**10** If Schedule R-1 is attached, check here ▶ ☐

### Part 2—Tax Computation

| | | |
|---|---|---:|
| 1 | Total gross estate less exclusion (from Part 5—Recapitulation, page 3, item 12) | **1** 6,251,458 |
| 2 | Tentative total allowable deductions (from Part 5—Recapitulation, page 3, item 22) | **2** 371,458 |
| 3a | Tentative taxable estate (before state death tax deduction) (subtract line 2 from line 1) | **3a** 5,880,000 |
| b | State death tax deduction | **3b** 0 |
| c | Taxable estate (subtract line 3b from line 3a) | **3c** 5,880,000 |
| 4 | Adjusted taxable gifts (total taxable gifts (within the meaning of section 2503) made by the decedent after December 31, 1976, other than gifts that are includible in decedent's gross estate (section 2001(b))) | **4** 1,000,000 |
| 5 | Add lines 3c and 4 | **5** 6,880,000 |
| 6 | Tentative tax on the amount on line 5 from Table A on page 4 of the instructions | **6** 2,976,800 |
| 7 | Total gift tax paid or payable with respect to gifts made by the decedent after December 31, 1976. Include gift taxes by the decedent's spouse for such spouse's share of split gifts (section 2513) only if the decedent was the donor of these gifts and they are includible in the decedent's gross estate (see instructions) | **7** 0 |
| 8 | Gross estate tax (subtract line 7 from line 6) | **8** 2,976,800 |
| 9 | Maximum unified credit (applicable credit amount) against estate tax . **9** 1,455,800 | |
| 10 | Adjustment to unified credit (applicable credit amount). (This adjustment may not exceed $6,000. See page 6 of the instructions.) . . . . **10** | |
| 11 | Allowable unified credit (applicable credit amount) (subtract line 10 from line 9) | **11** 1,455,800 |
| 12 | Subtract line 11 from line 8 (but do not enter less than zero) | **12** 1,521,000 |
| 13 | Credit for foreign death taxes (from Schedule(s) P. (Attach Form(s) 706-CE.) . . . . **13** | |
| 14 | Credit for tax on prior transfers (from Schedule Q) **14** | |
| 15 | Total credits (add lines 13 and 14) | **15** |
| 16 | Net estate tax (subtract line 15 from line 12) | **16** 1,521,000 |
| 17 | Generation-skipping transfer (GST) taxes payable (from Schedule R, Part 2, line 10) | **17** |
| 18 | Total transfer taxes (add lines 16 and 17) | **18** 1,521,000 |
| 19 | Prior payments. Explain in an attached statement | **19** |
| 20 | Balance due (or overpayment) (subtract line 19 from line 18) | **20** 1,521,000 |

Under penalties of perjury, I declare that I have examined this return, including accompanying schedules and statements, and to the best of my knowledge and belief, it is true, correct, and complete. Declaration of preparer other than the executor is based on all information of which preparer has any knowledge.

**Sign Here**
▶ Signature of executor                    ▶ Date
▶ Signature of executor                    ▶ Date

**Paid Preparer's Use Only**
Preparer's signature ▶          Date          Check if self-employed ▶ ☐          Preparer's SSN or PTIN
Firm's name (or yours if self-employed), address, and ZIP code ▶          EIN ▶          Phone no. ( )

For Privacy Act and Paperwork Reduction Act Notice, see page 30 of the separate instructions for this form.    Cat. No. 20548R    Form **706** (Rev. 9-2009)

*continued from page 25-1 . . .*

Harry Smith and his new wife, Wilma, were vacationing in Europe when they were informed of Bob's accident, and they returned home in time to attend the funeral. His brother's death caused Harry to reconsider his priorities. This morning he announced to Wilma that he wants to retire and spend more time traveling and enjoying his family.

Harry wants FFP to continue under family ownership, but he was uncertain about who would manage the company. He previously transferred 20 percent of the FFP stock to a trust for Dina and her son, George. Harry now believes Nate would like to assume responsibilities as CEO, and Dina has agreed to support Nate's decisions. Harry plans to begin an orderly transfer of his FFP stock to Dina to provide a future source of support for her and George. Besides his FFP stock, Harry has accumulated considerable personal assets to help maintain his lifestyle during retirement. Although Wilma also has significant assets, Harry wants to provide for her support after his death. Finally, while Harry believes taxes and lawyers are necessary evils, he wants to avoid any unnecessary fees or taxes associated with the transfer of his assets. ∎

# THE FEDERAL GIFT TAX

**L03**

The gift tax is levied on individual taxpayers for all taxable gifts made during a calendar year. As we'll explain shortly, each *individual* (married couples cannot elect joint filing for gift tax returns) who makes a gift in excess of the annual exclusion amount must file a gift tax return (Form 709) by April 15 of the following year.[14] Exhibit 25-7 presents the complete formula for the federal gift tax in two parts. In the first part, we calculate taxable gifts for each donee, and in the second, we calculate the gift tax using the total taxable gifts for all donees. We begin by identifying transfers that constitute gifts.

**EXHIBIT 25-7    The Federal Gift Tax Formula**

| | |
|---|---|
| | *Part 1:* Calculate taxable gifts for each individual donee: |
| | Current Gifts |
| *Minus:* | ½ of split gifts (included in spouse's current gifts) |
| *Plus:* | ½ of split gifts by spouse |
| *Minus:* | Annual Exclusion ($13,000 per donee) |
| *Minus:* | Marital and Charitable Deductions |
| *Equals:* | Current Taxable Gifts |
| | |
| | *Part 2:* Sum taxable gifts for all donees and calculate tax: |
| | Total Current Taxable Gifts |
| *Plus:* | Prior Taxable Gifts |
| *Equals:* | Cumulative Taxable Gifts |
| *Times:* | Current Tax Rates |
| *Equals:* | Cumulative Tax |
| *Minus:* | Current Tax on Prior Taxable Gifts |
| *Minus:* | Remaining Unified Credit |
| *Equals:* | Gift Tax Payable |

[14]A gift tax return reporting taxable gifts must be filed by April 15th following year-end if a taxpayer has made *any* taxable gifts during the current calendar year *or wishes to elect gift-splitting*. When taxpayers request extensions for their individual income tax returns, they also receive a six-month extension for filing their gift tax returns.

## Transfers Subject to Gift Tax

The gift tax is imposed on intervivos **gifts,** lifetime transfers of property for less than adequate consideration. Typically, a gift is made in a personal context such as between family members. The satisfaction of an obligation is not considered a gift. For example, tuition payments for a child's education satisfy a support obligation and obligatory payments are not gifts. On the other hand, transfers motivated by affection or other personal motives, including transfers associated with marriage, are gratuitous and subject to the tax. The gift tax is imposed once a gift has been completed, and this occurs when the **donor** relinquishes control of the property and the **donee** accepts the gift.[15] For example, deposits made to a joint bank account are not completed gifts because the donor (depositor) can withdraw the deposit at any time. The gift will be complete at the time the *donee* withdraws cash from the account.

---

**Taxes in the Real World**    *Love and Taxes*

The small claims division of the Tax Court was asked to determine whether payments between former lovers constituted gifts or compensation. Jue-Ya Yang lived with her boyfriend, Howard Shih, who was an artist and calligrapher. While they were romantically involved, Mr. Shih made payments to Ms. Yang and later deducted these payments as wages.

Ms. Yang admitted doing housekeeping and cooking, but she argued that the payments were gifts.

Mr. Shih's testimony about the romantic relationship was evasive. He admitted on cross-examination that while their relationship was more than a professional one, Mr. Shih could not even recall taking Ms. Yang out on dates. The court concluded that Mr. Shih's testimony was untrue and held that the payments were gifts made with "detached and disinterested generosity."

Source: *Jue-Ya Yang*, TC Summary Opinion 2008-156 (12-15-08).

---

In some instances a donor may relinquish some control over transferred property but retain other powers that can influence the enjoyment or disposition of the property. If the retained powers are important, then the transfer will not be a complete gift.[16] For example, a transfer of property to a trust will not be a complete gift if the grantor retains the ability to revoke the transfer. If the grantor releases the powers, then the gift will generally be complete at that time, because the property is no longer subject to the donor's control. For example, a distribution of property from a revocable trust is a completed gift because the grantor no longer has the ability to revoke the distribution.

**Example 25-14**

On July 12th of this year Harry transferred $250,000 of FFP stock to the new Dina Trust. He gave the trustee directions to pay income to Dina for the next 20 years and then remit the remainder to her son George. Harry named a bank as trustee but retained the power to revoke the trust in case he should need additional assets after retirement. Is the transfer of the stock a completed gift?

**Answer:** No. Harry retains sufficient control that the transfer of the stock to the trust is an incomplete gift.

**What if:** Suppose that $15,000 of trust income were distributed to Dina at year-end. Is the transfer of the cash to Dina a completed gift?

**Answer:** Yes. With the payment Harry has relinquished control over the $15,000, and thus it is a completed gift.

**What if:** Suppose that Harry releases his power to revoke the trust at a time when the shares of FPP in the trust are valued at $225,000. Would this release cause the transfer of the stock to be a completed gift and, if so, what is the amount of the gift?

**Answer:** Yes. By releasing his powers Harry has relinquished control over the entire trust, and the value of the trust at that time ($225,000) would be a completed gift.

---

[15]If a donee refuses or disclaims a gift under §2518, the gift is not complete.

[16]§2514 addresses the treatment of general powers of appointment.

There are several important exceptions to the taxation of completed gifts. For example, political contributions are not gifts, and the payment of medical or educational expenses on behalf of another individual is not considered a gift if the payments are made directly to the health care provider or to the educational institution. To avoid confusing a division of property with a gift, we treat a transfer of property in conjunction with a divorce as nongratuitous (it is treated as a transfer for adequate consideration) if the property is transferred within three years of the divorce under a written property settlement.

In addition, special rules apply to transfers of certain types of property. To transfer life insurance policies, the donor must give the donee all the incidents of ownership, including the power to designate beneficiaries. An individual who creates a joint tenancy (either a tenancy in common or joint tenancy with right of survivorship) with someone who does not provide adequate consideration is deemed to make a gift at that time. The gift is the amount necessary to pay for the other party's interest in the property. For example, suppose the donor pays $80,000 toward the purchase of $100,000 in realty held as equal tenants in common with the donee (the donee provides only $20,000 of the purchase). The donor has made a gift of $30,000 to the donee, the difference between the value of the joint interest ($100,000 ÷ 2 = $50,000) and the consideration provided by the donee ($20,000).

---

**Example 25-15**

This year Harry helped purchase a residence for use by Dina and her husband Steve. The price of the residence was $250,000, and the title named Harry and Steve joint tenants with the right of survivorship. Harry provided $210,000 of the purchase price and Steve the remaining $40,000. Has Harry made a completed gift and, if so, in what amount?

**Answer:** Yes, Harry made a complete gift to Steve of $85,000, calculated by subtracting the amount paid by Steve from the price of his ownership interest ($125,000 minus $40,000).

*What if:* Suppose Steve didn't provide any part of the purchase price. What is the amount of the gift?

**Answer:** Harry made a complete gift to Steve of half the purchase price, $125,000.

---

**Valuation** Gifts are taxed at the fair market value of the donated property on the date the gift becomes complete. Remember, despite the valuation of a gift at fair market value, the donee generally takes a carryover basis for income tax purposes.[17] Virtually all the factors (and controversies) regarding valuation that we've already discussed with the estate tax apply to the valuation of gifts.

---

**Example 25-16**

Harry transferred $500,000 of FFP stock to the DG Trust, whose trustee is directed to pay income to Dina for her life and, upon Dina's death, pay the remainder to George (or his estate). At time of the gift, Dina was 35 years old and the §7520 interest rate was 5.8 percent. What are the values of the gift of the life estate and of the remainder interest?

**Answer:** Harry made a gift of the remainder to George and the life estate to Dina. Under Table S (see Exhibit 25-4), the percentage of the property that represents the value of George's remainder is 0.12652. Thus, George's remainder is valued at $63,260 ($500,000 × 0.12652). Dina's life estate is the remaining value of $436,740 ($500,000 − $63,260).

---

**The Annual Exclusion** One of the most important aspects of the gift tax is the **annual exclusion,** which operates to eliminate "small" gifts from the gift tax base. The

---

[17]The carryover basis may be increased for any gift tax paid (after 1976) on the appreciation of the property.

amount of the exclusion has been revised upwards periodically over the years and is now indexed for inflation.[18] In 2010 it is $13,000.

The annual exclusion is available to offset gifts made to *each* donee regardless of the number of donees in any particular year. For example, a donor could give $13,000 in cash to each of 10 donees every year without exceeding the annual exclusion. One important limitation to the annual exclusion is that it applies only to gifts of *present* interests; that is, a gift of a future interest is not eligible for an annual exclusion.

---

**Example 25-17**

When Harry transferred $500,000 of FFP stock to the DG Trust (Example 25-16), he simultaneously made two taxable gifts, a life estate to Dina and a remainder to George. What is the amount of the taxable gift of the life estate to Dina and the remainder interest to George, after taking the exclusion amount into account?

**Answer:** Dina's life estate is a present interest and would qualify for the annual exclusion. However, George's remainder is a future interest and will not qualify for the annual exclusion. Harry would file a Form 709 to report a taxable gift of $487,000 consisting of a $423,740 taxable gift to Dina ($423,740 less the annual exclusion of $13,000) and a taxable gift of $63,260 to George (no annual exclusion is available for a future interest).

| | Dina | George | Harry's Gift Tax Return |
|---|---|---|---|
| Current gifts | $436,740 | $63,260 | $500,000 |
| Annual exclusion | −13,000 | −0 | −13,000 |
| Taxable gifts | $423,740 | $63,260 | $487,000 |

---

Although most gifts will qualify for an annual exclusion only if the donee has a present interest (the ability to immediately use the property or the income from it), a special exception applies to future interests given to minors (under the age of 21). Gifts in trust for a minor are future interests if the minor does not have the ability to access the income or property until reaching the age of majority. These gifts will still qualify for the annual exclusion, however, as long as the property can be used to support the minor and any remaining property is distributed to the child once he or she reaches age 21.[19]

---

**Example 25-18**

Harry transferred $48,500 of cash to the George Trust. The trustee of the George Trust has the discretion to distribute income or corpus (principal) for George's benefit and is required to distribute all assets to George (or his estate) not later than George's 21st birthday. Is this gift eligible for the annual exclusion? If so, what is the amount of the taxable gift?

**Answer:** Yes, Harry will be entitled to an annual exclusion for the transfer despite the fact that George's interest is a future one, because the gift is in trust for the support of a minor and the property must distribute the assets to George once he reaches age 21. The amount of the gift is $48,500 reduced to a taxable gift of $35,500 after application of the $13,000 annual exclusion.

---

## Taxable Gifts

In part 1 of the formula in Exhibit 25-7, **current gifts** are accumulated for each donee, and this amount includes all gifts completed during the calendar year for each individual. Current gifts do not include transfers exempted from the tax, such as political

---

[18]The exclusion is indexed for inflation in such a way that the amount of the exclusion only increases in increments of $1,000.

[19]The courts have created another exception to the present interest rule called *Crummey power*. A discussion of this exception is beyond the scope of this text.

contributions. We make several adjustments to calculate current **taxable gifts** for each donee. As we've seen, each taxpayer is allowed an annual exclusion applied to the cumulative gifts of present interests made during the year to *each* donee. Next, if a married couple elects to split gifts (discussed below), half of each gift is included in current gifts of each spouse. The marital deduction for gifts to spouses and the charitable deduction for gifts to charity are the last adjustments to calculate taxable gifts for each donee. We discuss each in turn.

**Gift-Splitting Election**   Married couples have the option to *split gifts,* allowing them to treat *all* gifts made in a year as if each spouse had made one-half of each gift. In a **community property state,** both spouses automatically own equal shares in most property acquired during the marriage.[20] Hence, they make a gift of community property equally. In **common-law states,** one spouse can own a disproportionate amount of property because he or she earns most of the income. The **gift-splitting election** provides a mechanism for married couples in common-law states to achieve the same result as couples receive automatically in community property states.[21]

---

**Example 25-19**

Wilma and Harry live in Michigan, a common-law state. For the holidays Wilma gave cash gifts of $26,000 to Steve and $41,000 to Dina. Wilma and Harry did not elect to split gifts. What is the amount of Wilma's taxable gifts?

**Answer:** $41,000. After using her annual exclusion (both gifts are present interests), Wilma has made taxable gifts of $13,000 to Steve ($26,000 − $13,000) and $28,000 to Dina ($41,000 − $13,000).

*What if:* Suppose Wilma and Harry elect gift-splitting this year.

**Answer:** Both Wilma and Harry made taxable gifts of $7,500. Under gift-splitting, Wilma and Harry are each treated as making a gift of $13,000 to Steve and $20,500 to Dina. After the annual exclusion, neither Wilma nor Harry made a taxable gift to Steve [($26,000 ÷ 2) − $13,000 = $0]. However, both Wilma and Harry made a $7,500 taxable gift to Dina [($41,000 ÷ 2) − $13,000 = $7,500].

*What if:* Suppose Wilma and Harry lived in Texas (a community property state), and Wilma made the same gifts from community property.

**Answer:** Both Wilma and Harry made a taxable gift of $7,500. Under state law, each spouse is automatically treated as gifting half the value of any gifts made from community property. After the annual exclusion, neither Wilma nor Harry made a taxable gift to Steve [($26,000 ÷ 2) − $13,000] but each made a $7,500 taxable gift to Dina [($41,000 ÷ 2) − $13,000].

---

Besides increasing the application of the annual exclusion, a gift-splitting election also increases the likelihood that taxable gifts will be taxed at lower tax rates or offset by unified credits. To utilize gift-splitting, each spouse must be a citizen or resident of the United States, be married at the time of the gift, and not remarry during the remainder of the calendar year. Both spouses must consent to the election by filing a timely gift tax return. Taxpayers make this election annually and can apply it to all gifts completed by either spouse during the calendar year. As a result of the election, both spouses share a joint and several liability for any gift tax due.

---

[20]Depending upon state law, the ownership of property acquired by either spouse prior to a marriage is not automatically divided equally between the spouses. In other words, property owned prior to the marriage is not community property and continues to belong to the original owner.

[21]There are nine community property states: Arizona, California, Idaho, Louisiana, Nevada, New Mexico, Texas, Washington, and Wisconsin.

**Marital Deduction**  The marital deduction was originally enacted to equalize the treatment of spouses residing in common-law states. In community property states, the ownership of most property *acquired* during a marriage is automatically divided between the spouses. In common-law states, one spouse can own a disproportionate amount of property if he or she earns most of the income. Absent the marital deduction, in a common-law state, a transfer between the spouses to equalize the ownership of property would be treated as a taxable gift. However, because transfers to spouses are eligible for a marital deduction, no taxable gift results from such a transfer.

The marital deduction is subject to two limits. First, the amount is limited to the value of the gift after the annual exclusion. Second, transfers of **nondeductible terminable interests** do not qualify for a marital deduction. A nondeductible terminable interest is a property interest transferred to the spouse that terminates when some event occurs or after a specified amount of time, when the property is transferred to another.

## Example 25-20

After his decision to retire, Harry gave Wilma a piece of jewelry that is a family heirloom valued at $50,000. What is the amount of this taxable gift?

**Answer:** Zero. This gift will qualify for an annual exclusion, and the value after subtracting the annual exclusion qualifies for the marital deduction. The taxable gift is calculated below:

| | |
|---|---|
| Current gift | $50,000 |
| Less: Annual exclusion | −13,000 |
| Less: Marital deduction | −37,000 |
| Taxable gift | $      0 |

**What if:** Suppose Harry transferred $200,000 to a trust with directions to pay income to Wilma for her life (a life estate). After Wilma's death the corpus of the trust would then pass to Dina (the remainder). What is the amount of this taxable gift if Dina is age 38 at the time and the §7520 interest rate is 5 percent?

**Answer:** The total taxable gift is $187,000. This transfer is actually two gifts, a gift of a present interest to Wilma (a life estate) and a future interest to Dina (the remainder). The gift of the life estate is valued at $36,062 using the table in Exhibit 25-4 ($200,000 times .18031), and it qualifies for the annual exclusion. The gift of the remainder is a future interest valued at $163,938 ($200,000 minus $36,062) and does not qualify for an annual exclusion. The taxable gifts are calculated below:

| | Wilma | Dina |
|---|---|---|
| Current gifts | $36,062 | $163,938 |
| Less: Annual exclusion (life estate) | −13,000 | −0 |
| Less: Marital deduction | −0 | −0 |
| Taxable gift | $23,062 | $163,938 |

While the life estate is given to a spouse, it does not qualify for the marital deduction because it will terminate upon a future event (Wilma's death) and then pass to another person (Dina).

The limitation on the deductibility of terminable interests ensures that property owned by a married couple is subject to a transfer tax when the property is eventually transferred from the couple (as opposed to between the spouses). If a life estate were eligible for a marital deduction, it would not be taxed at the time of the gift nor would any value be taxed upon Wilma's death (the life estate disappears with her death). Hence, a marital deduction is available only for spousal transfers that will eventually be included in the recipient spouse's estate.[22]

---

[22]The limit is analogous to nondeductible terminable interests for the estate tax marital deduction.

**Charitable Deduction** The amount of the charitable deduction is also limited to the value of the gift after the annual exclusion. Requirements for an organization to qualify for the gift tax charitable deduction are quite similar to those for the income tax deduction (the entity must be organized for religious, charitable, scientific, educational, or other public purposes, including governmental entities). Unlike the income tax deduction, however, the charitable deduction has no percentage limitation. In addition, as long as the qualifying charity receives the donor's entire interest in the property, no gift tax return need be filed (assuming the donor has no other taxable gifts). Finally, a transfer to a charity also qualifies for an income tax deduction (subject to the AGI limits on the income tax charitable deduction).

**Example 25-21**

Harry donated $155,000 in cash to State University. What is the amount of the taxable gift?

**Answer:** Zero. The gift qualifies for the charitable gift tax deduction, as calculated below.

| | |
|---|---|
| Current gift | $155,000 |
| Less: Annual exclusion | −13,000 |
| Less: Charitable deduction | −142,000 |
| Taxable gift | $        0 |

Note that Harry can also claim an income tax deduction for the transfer.

## Computation of the Gift Tax

Part 2 of the formula in Exhibit 25-7 provides the method of calculating the gift tax. It begins by summing the taxable gifts made for all donees during a calendar year.

**Example 25-22**

Harry and Wilma did not make any gifts from community property and did not elect to gift-split this year (see Example 25-19). What is the amount of Harry's current taxable gifts this year?

**Answer:** Harry made $594,500 of taxable gifts, calculated using Part 1 of the formula in Exhibit 25-7 as follows:

| Gifted Property | Donee | Value | Example # |
|---|---|---|---|
| 1. Residence | Steve | $ 85,000 | 25-15 |
| Less: Annual exclusion | | −13,000 | |
| 2. DG Trust—life estate | Dina | 436,740 | 25-16 |
| Less: Annual exclusion | | −13,000 | |
| 3. DG Trust—remainder | George | 63,260 | 25-16 |
| 4. George Trust | George | 48,500 | 25-18 |
| Less: Annual exclusion | | −13,000 | |
| 5. Jewelry | Wilma | 50,000 | 25-20 |
| Less: Annual exclusion | | −13,000 | |
| Less: Marital deduction | Wilma | −37,000 | |
| 6. Donation | State University | 155,000 | 25-21 |
| Less: Annual exclusion | | −13,000 | |
| Less: Charitable deduction | State U | −142,000 | |
| Harry's current taxable gifts | | $594,500 | |

The amounts of the marital and charitable deductions are limited to the value of the property included in taxable gifts.

(continued on page 25-24...)

Will Wilma be required to file a gift tax return this year? If so, what is the amount of her taxable gifts?

**Answer:** Wilma must also file a gift tax return this year because her current gifts exceed the annual exclusion. Wilma's taxable gifts sum to $41,000, calculated as follows:

| Gifted Property | Donee | Value | Example # |
|---|---|---|---|
| Cash gift | Steve | $26,000 | 25-19 |
| Less: Annual exclusion | | −13,000 | |
| Holiday gift | Dina | 41,000 | 25-19 |
| Less: Annual exclusion | | −13,000 | |
| Wilma's Current Taxable Gifts | | $41,000 | |

*What if:* What is the amount of Harry and Wilma's taxable gifts if they elect to gift-split?

**Answer:** Harry and Wilma each made $285,250 of taxable gifts, calculated as follows:

| Gifted Property | Donee | Harry | Wilma |
|---|---|---|---|
| Harry's gift of a residence | Steve | $ 42,500 | $ 42,500 |
| Less: Annual exclusions | | −13,000 | −13,000 |
| Wilma's cash gift | Steve | 13,000 | 13,000 |
| Less: Annual exclusions | | −13,000 | −13,000 |
| Harry's transfer to DG Trust | Dina | 218,370 | 218,370 |
| Less: Annual exclusions | | −13,000 | −13,000 |
| Wilma's holiday gifts | Dina | 20,500 | 20,500 |
| Less: Annual exclusion | | −13,000 | −13,000 |
| DG Trust—remainder | George | 31,630 | 31,630 |
| George Trust | | 24,250 | 24,250 |
| Less: Annual exclusion | | −13,000 | −13,000 |
| Jewelry | Wilma | 50,000 | |
| Less: Annual exclusion | | −13,000 | |
| Less: Marital deduction | Wilma | −37,000 | |
| Donation | State U | 155,000 | |
| Less: Annual exclusion | | −13,000 | |
| Less: Charitable deduction | State U | −142,000 | 0 |
| Harry's current taxable gifts | | $285,250 | $285,250 |

Note that absent gift-splitting, Harry and Wilma made taxable gifts totaling $635,500 ($594,500 plus $41,000), but under gift-splitting that reduced to $570,500 ($285,250 plus $285,250) because Wilma was able to use two additional $13,000 annual exclusions from Harry for her portion of the gift to the George Trust and the DG Trust. Harry was able to use three additional annual exclusions from Wilma for her portion of the residence gift, the cash gift, and transfer to trust. However, if they elect to gift-split, Harry and Wilma will be jointly and severally liable for the gift taxes.

**Prior Taxable Gifts**    We compute the gift tax on cumulative taxable gifts by adding prior taxable gifts to current taxable gifts. The purpose of adding gifts from previous periods is to increase the tax base and thereby increase the marginal tax rate applying to current gifts. To prevent double taxation of prior taxable gifts, we subtract the gift tax on prior taxable gifts from the tax on total transfers. Note the tax on prior taxable gifts is the tax we computed on prior transfers under the *current* rate schedule after applying the unified credit used in prior periods.

**Unified Credit**    The last adjustment in the formula is the unused portion of the unified credit. We've seen that the unified credit eliminates the gift tax for individuals

who do not transfer a relatively large cumulative amount of property during their lifetime. The unified credit was originally the same for both the gift and estate taxes, but it has been adjusted many times and the exemption equivalent for the gift tax is now $1 million (see Exhibit 25-5). A gift tax return must be filed by each individual (no joint filing) who has made taxable gifts during the calendar year or who elects to split gifts, even if no tax is due because of the unified credit.

---

**Example 25-23**

Harry made a taxable gift of $1,000,000 in 1997, when he utilized a unified credit of $192,800. Otherwise, neither Wilma nor Harry has made previous taxable gifts. What is Harry's gift tax due this year?

**Answer:** Harry owes $99,525 of gift taxes, calculated using Part 2 of the formula in Exhibit 25-7, as follows:

| | | |
|---|---|---|
| Current taxable gifts | $ 594,500 | |
| Prior taxable gifts | 1,000,000 | |
| Cumulative taxable gifts | $1,594,500 | |
| Tax on cumulative gifts | | $598,325 |
| Less: Current tax on prior taxable gifts | | −345,800 |
| Tax on current taxable gifts | | $252,525 |
| Unified credit | $ 345,800 | |
| Less: Unified credit used previously | −192,800 | |
| Less: Unused unified credit | | −153,000 |
| Gift tax due | | $ 99,525 |

What is Wilma's gift tax due this year?

**Answer:** Zero. Wilma's gift tax is offset by her unified credit and is calculated as follows:

| | | |
|---|---|---|
| Wilma's current taxable gifts | | $41,000 |
| Less: Prior taxable gifts | | −0 |
| Cumulative gifts | | $41,000 |
| Tax on cumulative gifts | $4,020 | |
| Less: Current tax on prior taxable gifts | −0 | |
| Tax on current taxable gifts | | $ 4,020 |
| Less: Unused unified credit | | −345,800 |
| Gift tax due | | $ 0 |

Note Wilma's unused unified credit available for future gifts is $341,780 ($345,800 minus $4,020).

---

The gift tax formula requires donors to keep track of the portion of the unified credit they used to offset prior taxable gifts, in order to prevent multiple applications of the credit. We compute the gift tax on previous gifts using the current tax rate schedule and ignoring the use of the unified credit. This amount does *not* represent the amount of gift tax paid—just the gifts previously subject to tax. The unused portion of the unified credit then reduces the total gift tax to reach the gift tax due. We must track the amount of unified credit used to offset prior gifts from each period, because the gift tax on previous periods ignores the amount of gift tax actually paid. Exhibit 25-8 presents the first page of the completed gift tax return Form 709 for Harry Smith.

**EXHIBIT 25-8    Page 1 of Form 709 Gift Tax Return for Harry Smith**

Form **709**

Department of the Treasury
Internal Revenue Service

**United States Gift (and Generation-Skipping Transfer) Tax Return**

(For gifts made during calendar year 2009)

▶ **See separate instructions.**

OMB No. 1545-0020

**2009**

## Part 1—General Information

| 1 Donor's first name and middle initial | 2 Donor's last name | 3 Donor's social security number |
|---|---|---|
| HARRY | SMITH | 000-00-000 |

| 4 Address (number, street, and apartment number) | 5 Legal residence (domicile) |
|---|---|
| 2813 ELMWOOD | WASHTENAW, MICHIGAN |

| 6 City, state, and ZIP code | 7 Citizenship (see instructions) |
|---|---|
| ANN ARBOR, MICHIGAN 48109 | UNITED STATES |

| | | Yes | No |
|---|---|---|---|
| 8 | If the donor died during the year, check here ▶ ☐ and enter date of death _____ , _____ | | |
| 9 | If you extended the time to file this Form 709, check here ▶ ☐ | | |
| 10 | Enter the total number of donees listed on Schedule A. Count each person only once. ▶        6 | | |
| 11a | Have you (the donor) previously filed a Form 709 (or 709-A) for any other year? If "No," skip line 11b . . . . . . . | ✓ | |
| b | If the answer to line 11a is "Yes," has your address changed since you last filed Form 709 (or 709-A)? . . . . . . . | | ✓ |
| 12 | **Gifts by husband or wife to third parties.** Do you consent to have the gifts (including generation-skipping transfers) made by you and by your spouse to third parties during the calendar year considered as made one-half by each of you? (See instructions.) (If the answer is "Yes," the following information must be furnished and your spouse must sign the consent shown below. **If the answer is "No," skip lines 13–18 and go to Schedule A.**) . . . | | ✓ |
| 13 | Name of consenting spouse | 14 SSN | |
| 15 | Were you married to one another during the entire calendar year? (see instructions) . . . . . . . . . . . | | |
| 16 | If 15 is "No," check whether ☐ married ☐ divorced or ☐ widowed/deceased, and give date (see instructions) ▶ | | |
| 17 | Will a gift tax return for this year be filed by your spouse? (If "Yes," mail both returns in the same envelope.) . . . . | | |
| 18 | **Consent of Spouse.** I consent to have the gifts (and generation-skipping transfers) made by me and by my spouse to third parties during the calendar year considered as made one-half by each of us. We are both aware of the joint and several liability for tax created by the execution of this consent. | | |

Consenting spouse's signature ▶                                                    Date ▶

## Part 2—Tax Computation

| | | | |
|---|---|---|---|
| 1 | Enter the amount from Schedule A, Part 4, line 11 . . . . . . . . . | 1 | 594,500 |
| 2 | Enter the amount from Schedule B, line 3 . . . . . . . . . . . | 2 | 1,000,000 |
| 3 | Total taxable gifts. Add lines 1 and 2 . . . . . . . . . . . | 3 | 1,594,500 |
| 4 | Tax computed on amount on line 3 (see *Table for Computing Gift Tax* in separate instructions) . . | 4 | 598,325 |
| 5 | Tax computed on amount on line 2 (see *Table for Computing Gift Tax* in separate instructions) . . | 5 | 345,800 |
| 6 | Balance. Subtract line 5 from line 4 . . . . . . . . . . . | 6 | 252,525 |
| 7 | Maximum unified credit (nonresident aliens, see instructions) . . . . . . . . | 7 | 345,800 | 00 |
| 8 | Enter the unified credit against tax allowable for all prior periods (from Sch. B, line 1, col. C) . . | 8 | 192,800 |
| 9 | Balance. Subtract line 8 from line 7 . . . . . . . . . . . | 9 | 153,000 |
| 10 | Enter 20% (.20) of the amount allowed as a specific exemption for gifts made after September 8, 1976, and before January 1, 1977 (see instructions) . . . . . . . . | 10 | |
| 11 | Balance. Subtract line 10 from line 9 . . . . . . . . . . | 11 | 153,000 |
| 12 | Unified credit. Enter the smaller of line 6 or line 11 . . . . . . . . | 12 | 153,000 |
| 13 | Credit for foreign gift taxes (see instructions) . . . . . . . . | 13 | |
| 14 | Total credits. Add lines 12 and 13 . . . . . . . . . . | 14 | 153,000 |
| 15 | Balance. Subtract line 14 from line 6. Do not enter less than zero . . . . . . | 15 | 99,525 |
| 16 | Generation-skipping transfer taxes (from Schedule C, Part 3, col. H, Total) . . . . | 16 | |
| 17 | Total tax. Add lines 15 and 16 . . . . . . . . . . . | 17 | 99,525 |
| 18 | Gift and generation-skipping transfer taxes prepaid with extension of time to file . . . . | 18 | |
| 19 | If line 18 is less than line 17, enter **balance due** (see instructions) . . . . . . | 19 | 99,525 |
| 20 | If line 18 is greater than line 17, enter **amount to be refunded** . . . . . . . . . | 20 | |

**Sign Here**

Under penalties of perjury, I declare that I have examined this return, including any accompanying schedules and statements, and to the best of my knowledge and belief, it is true, correct, and complete. Declaration of preparer (other than donor) is based on all information of which preparer has any knowledge.

May the IRS discuss this return with the preparer shown below (see instructions)? ☐ Yes ☐ No

▶ _____
Signature of donor                    Date

**Paid Preparer's Use Only**

| Preparer's signature ▶ | Date | Check if self-employed ☐ | Preparer's SSN or PTIN |
|---|---|---|---|
| Firm's name (or yours if self-employed), address, and ZIP code ▶ | | | EIN |
| | | | Phone no. |

*Attach check or money order here.*

For Disclosure, Privacy Act, and Paperwork Reduction Act Notice, see page 12 of the separate instructions for this form.    Cat. No. 16783M    Form **709** (2009)

# WEALTH PLANNING CONCEPTS

**LO4**

Wealth planning coordinates both income and transfer tax strategies with nontax objectives. Before we explore transfer tax strategies, recall the third transfer tax, the generation-skipping tax, and the potential for income taxation of fiduciary entities such as estates and trusts. While these topics are certainly not unimportant, we note them only in passing because their complexity is beyond the scope of this text.

## The Generation-Skipping Tax

The **generation-skipping tax (GST)** is a supplemental tax designed to prevent the avoidance of transfer taxes (both estate and gift tax) through transfers that skip a generation of recipients. For example, a grandparent could give a life estate in property to a child, with the remainder to a grandchild. When the child dies and the grandchild inherits the property, no transfer tax is imposed because nothing remains in the child's estate (the life estate terminates at death). In this way, the grandparent pays one transfer tax (on the initial gift) to transfer the property down two generations.

The GST is triggered by the transfer of property to someone more than one generation younger than the donor or decedent—a grandchild rather than a child. A transfer to a grandchild is not subject to GST, however, if the grandchild's parents are dead. The GST is very complex and can be triggered directly by transfers or indirectly by a termination of an interest. Fortunately, the GST is not widely applicable because it does not apply to transfers that qualify for an annual gift tax exclusion and each donor/decedent is entitled to a relatively generous aggregate exemption ($3.5 million in 2010).

## Income Tax Considerations

A **fiduciary** entity is a legal entity that takes possession of property for the benefit of a person. An **estate** is a fiduciary that comes into existence upon a person's death to transfer the decedent's real and personal property. Likewise, a *trust* is also a fiduciary whose purpose is to hold and administer the corpus for other persons *(beneficiaries)*. While an estate exists only temporarily (until the assets of the decedent are distributed), a trust may have a prolonged or even indefinite existence. Because fiduciaries can exist for many years, special rules govern the taxation of income realized on property they hold. These rules are complex and relate to how fiduciaries account for income under state law. A detailed discussion is beyond the scope of this text, but we can give a useful general outline.

Trusts and estates may have discretion whether to accumulate income within the fiduciary (for future distribution) or distribute it currently. In general, income retained by the fiduciary is taxed as income to the fiduciary, and consequently it must file an income tax return. In contrast, income distributed currently by the fiduciary is taxed as income to the beneficiary. To accomplish this flow-through of income, fiduciaries are granted a deduction for current distributions of income that eliminates the potential for double taxation. Granting a fiduciary discretion over income distributions appears to provide an opportunity to split income (by creating yet another taxpayer). However, the fiduciary income tax rates are generally as high as or higher than the tax rates for individual beneficiaries. Hence, the potential income tax benefits from splitting income between fiduciaries and beneficiaries are typically negligible.

## Transfer Tax Planning Techniques

Transfer tax planning strategies are the same as those employed for income tax planning: timing, shifting, and conversion. Like income tax planning, wealth planning is

primarily concerned with accomplishing the client's goals in the most efficient and effective manner after considering *both* tax and nontax costs. For the most part, wealth planning is directed to maximizing after-tax wealth to be transferred from an older generation to a younger generation. A critical constraint in this process, however, is determining how tax strategies can achieve the client's ultimate (nontax) goals. Before attempting to integrate tax and nontax considerations, let's survey a few basic techniques for transfer tax planning.

**Serial Gifts**    A **serial gift** strategy converts a large taxable transfer into a tax-exempt transfer by dividing the transfer into multiple intervivos gifts. As long as the gifts qualify as present interests and do not exceed the annual exclusion, the transfers are exempt from all transfer taxes. Although serial gifts are an easy and low-cost planning strategy, this technique is limited in scope because only $13,000 ($26,000 if married) can be transferred each year tax-free to any specific donee. Hence, serial gifts can move significant amounts of wealth only if employed by multiple donors over multiple years and multiple donees.

---

**Example 25-24**

Suppose Harry and Wilma decide to begin transferring wealth to Dina and George. To what extent can serial gifts accomplish this goal without triggering gift taxes?

**Answer:** Harry and Wilma could make annual gifts of $13,000 each to Dina and George. These gifts would remove $52,000 per year from the Smiths' estate without triggering any transfer taxes (gift tax or generation-skipping tax). They could include any type of property as long as Dina and George can presently enjoy the property or income generated by it.

---

**Bypass Provisions**    In retirement, many individuals are concerned about keeping sufficient wealth to support a comfortable lifestyle for themselves and a surviving spouse. Indeed, it is common for a spouse to leave all of his or her property to the surviving spouse for this very reason. This type of plan will avoid all estate taxes on the estate of the first spouse to die (assuming the estate contains no terminable interests). However, it may not minimize total transfer taxes when we consider the estates of *both* spouses. The deceased spouse who leaves all property to the surviving spouse has no taxable estate (because of the marital deduction) and his or her unified credit goes unused. A **bypass provision** in the will of the deceased spouse will use the unified credit by transferring some property to beneficiaries other than the surviving spouse. As in the following example, this reduces total estate taxes because both spouses use their unified credits.

---

**Example 25-25**

*What if:* Suppose that Harry and Wilma have made no taxable gifts and Harry dies with a taxable estate of $10 million. Several years later, Wilma dies holding only the property she inherited from Harry. To isolate the estate tax savings, let's also assume that after Harry's death Wilma consumes any income from the property, and the value of the property remains constant. In addition, let's ignore the time value of money. What amount of transfer taxes will Harry and Wilma save if Harry uses a bypass provision to bequeath $3.5 million to Dina and the rest to Wilma?

**Answer:** They will save $1.575 million, per the following computation:

|  | Alternative 1<br>No Bypass | Alternative 2<br>Bypass |
|---|---|---|
| Harry's gross estate | $10,000,000 | $10,000,000 |
| Marital deduction | −10,000,000 | −6,500,000 |
| Taxable transfer | $          0 | $ 3,500,000 |
| Harry's estate tax (assumed) | 0 | $ 1,455,800 |
| Unified credit (assumed) | −0 | −1,455,800 |
| Estate tax on Harry | $          0 | $          0 |
| Wilma's taxable estate | $10,000,000 | $ 6,500,000 |
| Wilma's estate tax (assumed) | $ 4,380,800 | $ 2,805,800 |
| Unified credit (assumed) | −1,455,800 | −1,455,800 |
| Total estate tax (Wilma only) | $ 2,925,000 | $ 1,350,000 |
| Total estate tax savings | | $ 1,575,000 |

The total estate tax savings from a bypass provision can be significant. However, absent special provisions in the will, any property transferred to bypass the spouse will not be available to support the surviving spouse. Hence, taxpayers should consider a bypass provision only after estimating the amount of support required by the surviving spouse.

**The Step-Up in Tax Basis**   Timing is an important component in tax planning. Generally, a good tax strategy delays payment of tax, thereby reducing the present value of the tax paid. While deferral is important, transfer tax planning must also consider the potential appreciation of assets transferred, and the effect of the income tax that could apply if and when the appreciation is realized. Gifted property generally retains the donor's basis in the property (the donee takes a **carryover basis**), whereas inherited property takes a tax basis of fair market value.[23] The advantage of gifting property is that the donor eliminates the transfer tax on any additional future appreciation on the gifted property. The disadvantage is that the unrealized appreciation of the gifted property will eventually be taxed (although at the donee's income tax rate). Thus, gifting appreciating property reduces future transfer taxes but at the cost of additional future income taxes imposed on the donee. In contrast, for inherited property, past appreciation (up to the date of death) will never be subject to income tax but instead is subject to transfer tax at the time of the transfer.

**Example 25-26**

**What if:** Harry currently owns 30 percent of the outstanding shares of FFP. These shares have a basis of $300,000 but are worth in excess of $2.7 million. Suppose Harry intends to transfer his FPP shares to his daughter Dina who, in turn, intends to sell them after Harry's death. To what extent should income tax considerations influence whether Harry transfers these shares via intervivos gift or testamentary transfer? Estimate the total tax savings if Harry delays the transfer of the shares until

(continued on page 25-30...)

---

[23]An exception to the step-up for inherited property currently exists for certain property transferred by persons who die in 2010. For this year, the estate tax is scheduled to be repealed and the step-up in basis is supposed to be replaced by a carryover basis (except for the property of decedents with relatively small estates).

his death three years hence. Assume that the transfer (whether by gift or inheritance) will be taxed at the top transfer rate of 45 percent, while when Dina sells the shares in three years the gain will be taxed at a capital gains tax rate of 15 percent. Let's also assume that the FPP shares will not appreciate and the prevailing interest rate is 6 percent.

**Answer:** The total tax savings is $592,084 if Harry delays the transfer until his death rather than gifting the shares to Dina immediately. See the following discussion and computations:

|  | Gift | Inheritance | Explanation |
| --- | --- | --- | --- |
| Gift tax paid | $1,215,000 | | 45% times $2.7 million |
| Time value of gift tax | × 1.191 | | $(1.06)^3$ |
| Future value of gift tax | $1,447,084 | | value of gift tax paid |
| Estate tax paid | | $1,215,000 | 45% times $2.7 million |
| Dina's capital gain tax 15% | $ 360,000 | 0 | gain of $2.4 million on gift due to carryover basis |
| Total Taxes Paid | $1,807,084 | $1,215,000 | $592,084 of tax savings |

If a sale is planned, then the step-up in tax basis becomes critical to avoid being taxed on the accumulated appreciation. In this scenario, a testamentary transfer provides a step-up in tax basis and delays payment of the transfer tax for three years.

**What if:** Suppose Dina has no interest in selling the family business and intends to eventually transfer the shares to George. Moreover, suppose Harry believes the FFP shares will appreciate to $3.5 million within three years. To what extent should income tax considerations influence whether Harry transfers these shares immediately via intervivos gift or in three years via testamentary transfer? Estimate the total tax savings if Harry transfers the shares immediately rather than delaying the transfer until his death.

**Answer:** The tax savings is $127,916 if Harry transfers property immediately rather than delaying the transfer until his death. See the following discussion and computations:

|  | Gift | Inheritance | Explanation |
| --- | --- | --- | --- |
| Gift tax paid | $1,215,000 | | 45% times $2.7 million |
| Time value of gift tax | × 1.191 | | $(1.06)^3$ |
| Future value of gift tax | $1,447,084 | | value of gift tax paid |
| Estate tax paid | | $1,575,000 | 45% times $3.5 million |
| Total taxes paid | $1,447,084 | $1,575,000 | $127,916 of tax savings |

If Dina plans to hold the shares indefinitely and the property is rapidly appreciating, then an intervivos gift avoids having future appreciation taxed in Harry's estate. Although a gift of the shares would accelerate the imposition of transfer taxes, any unused unified credit could minimize the amount of taxes due on the transfer. In this scenario, an intervivos transfer reduces total transfer taxes even though the gift tax is paid three years before an estate tax would be due.

Timing becomes critical in determining how to trade off income tax savings (the step-up in tax basis) against transfer tax costs (paying gift tax now or paying estate taxes on additional appreciation later). Most tax advisors will suggest that elderly clients sell business assets or investments with unrealized losses, because upon death the basis of these assets will be adjusted downward to fair market value. In other words, the adjustment to basis can be a step-down as well as a step-up, and a sale prevents the elimination of the loss deduction.

## Integrated Wealth Plans

A client can have many nontax goals associated with the ultimate disposition of wealth, and some are very personal. It is often difficult to ascertain and prioritize them for planning purposes. However, an effective wealth plan must identify and integrate these personal objectives with tax costs. Often, the primary nontax objective of wealth planning is to preserve value during the transfer of control (management) of business assets. Thus, an essential nontax element of any effective wealth plan is to identify a safe mechanism to support the older generation in a specific lifestyle while transferring control to the younger generation.

Trusts are common vehicles for tax planning, in large part because these fiduciaries can be structured to achieve a great variety of tax and nontax objectives, including the support of specific beneficiaries.[24] The trustee is responsible for managing property in the trust, but the grantor also gives the trustee discretionary powers to provide flexibility. These powers can include the discretion to distribute income or corpus among beneficiaries. In addition grantors can retain powers, including the ability to revoke the trust, select the trustee (original or successor), terminate beneficial interests, and add to the corpus. The most important aspect of an irrevocable trust is that the provisions (including powers and guidelines for the exercise of discretionary powers) cannot be changed once the trust instrument has been executed.

Specific types of trusts are common to many wealth transfer plans. For example, a **bypass trust** is used in lieu of a bypass provision in the will to maximize the unified credit of the first spouse to die. This is accomplished by leaving the surviving spouse with a terminable interest (a life estate in investment property, for example) that won't qualify for the marital deduction in the amount of the exemption equivalent. A **life insurance trust** is funded with an irrevocable transfer of a life insurance policy, and the trustee is given the power to name beneficiaries and redesignate them in case of divorce or death. Upon the death of the grantor, the amount of the policy is paid into the trust but not included in the grantor's estate. Moreover, an immediate cash distribution from the trust is not taxable income to the beneficiaries.

---

**Example 25-27**

Harry is planning to purchase a $2 million life insurance policy. He wants to use the proceeds to support Wilma after his death and have any remaining funds paid to his surviving children. How would Harry structure a bypass trust to accomplish these goals?

**Answer:** Harry should transfer the policy to an irrevocable trust that directs the trustee to hold the policy and pay the premiums until Harry's death. At that time, the trustee should be directed to invest the $2 million proceeds and pay income to Wilma for the remainder of her life or until she remarries. At that time, the trust will terminate and pay the remainder to Harry's surviving children or their estates.

**What if:** Suppose Harry transfers the policy to an irrevocable trust and dies four years later. Will the use of this bypass trust trigger any estate taxes at that time?

**Answer:** Harry's transfer of the policy to the trust will be a taxable gift today to the extent of the value of the transfer. However, the $2 million proceeds from the policy will not be included in Harry's estate upon his death.

---

[24]Trusts are also popular because the trust property transfers outside probate, thereby avoiding both the costs and the publicity associated with probate.

Donors often use partnerships to transfer assets and for the control of a business in a systematic manner that also provides them with income and security. One specific form of partnership, the **family limited partnership,** divides a family business into various ownership interests, representing control of operations and future income and appreciation of the assets. These limited partnerships were sometimes used to transfer appreciation to members of a younger generation while allowing the older generation to effectively retain control of the business. Obviously, the intent of the estate and gift taxes is to recognize transfers of assets that also represent control of the assets. Hence, it was not surprising that Congress revised the law to restrict the ability of family limited partnerships to effectively transfer appreciation in business assets and operations to younger generations without also transferring control.

## CONCLUSION

In this chapter we learned to identify taxable transfers whether made at death (testamentary transfers) or during life (intervivos transfers). We also learned how to calculate estate and gift taxes, and we introduced some fundamental transfer tax planning techniques. The simplest and most effective wealth planning technique is serial giving. As long as the gifts are restricted to present interests under the annual exclusion, serial giving avoids all transfer taxes. Other methods, such as bypass trusts and family limited partnerships, can also be effective under the proper circumstances. In all cases, however, wealth planning should be carefully coordinated with other needs and objectives.

---

### SUMMARY

**L01**

Outline the basic structure of federal transfer taxes.

- Congress imposes a tax on transfers of property whether the transfer is a gift or occurs at death.
- The unified transfer tax scheme provides for a progressive tax rate schedule that applies to cumulative transfers. That is, transfers in all prior periods are taken into account when calculating the tax for a transfer in a current period.
- The unified credit offsets transfer tax on cumulative lifetime transfers (the exemption equivalent) of $1 million for gifts and $3.5 million for transfers at death.
- Each transfer tax shares two common deductions, an unlimited deduction for charitable contributions and a marital deduction that allows almost unfettered transfers between spouses.

**L02**

Describe the federal estate tax and the valuation of transfers, and compute taxable transfers at death and the federal estate tax.

- The gross estate includes property owned by the decedent at death (the probate estate) and certain property transfers taking effect at death.
- Property the decedent owned jointly is included in the gross estate. The value of the decedent's interest is included when property is held in joint tenancy, whereas half the value of the property in included when held with a spouse in joint tenancy with the right of survivorship.
- Property is included in the gross estate at fair market value (the value paid by a willing buyer to a willing seller), and value often depends upon the circumstances of the property.
- Temporal interests begin or end with the passage of time. The value of a future interest, such as a remainder, can be determined from IRS tables, and the value of a present interest, such as a life estate, is calculated at the difference between the value of the future interest and the current value of the property.

- The gross estate is reduced by administrative expenses, debts of the decedent, and losses incurred during the administration of the estate, resulting in the adjusted gross estate.

- The adjusted gross estate is reduced for certain transfers to a surviving spouse (the marital deduction) and for transfers to charities (the charitable deduction), resulting in the taxable estate.

- The taxable estate is increased by adjusted taxable gifts to determine cumulative transfers, and the tentative estate tax calculated using this tax base represents transfer tax on total transfers.

- Calculate the estate tax due by reducing the tentative tax by the estate tax calculated using adjusted taxable gifts and the unified credit.

Summarize the operation of the federal gift tax and the calculation of the federal gift tax. **LO3**

- Lifetime transfers of property for no (or inadequate) consideration are taxed as gifts if the transfer is complete and irrevocable.

- Contributions to political parties or candidates, and medical and educational expenses paid on behalf of an unrelated individual, are excluded from gift taxation.

- Gifts are taxed at the fair market value of the donated property on the date the gift becomes complete, and small gifts are reduced by the annual exclusion ($13,000) if they are present interests.

- With gift-splitting, married couples can elect to treat all gifts made in a year as if each spouse made one-half of each gift.

- Calculate taxable gifts by adjusting current gifts for exclusions and gift-splitting, and then deducting the marital deduction (for qualifying gifts to a spouse) and the charitable deduction.

- Transfers of terminable interests in property, such as a life estate, will not generally qualify for the marital deduction.

- Compute the gift tax on cumulative taxable gifts by adding prior taxable gifts to current taxable gifts.

- Reduce the gift tax on cumulative gifts by the gift tax on prior taxable gifts calculated, after applying the unified credit actually used in prior periods.

- Then reduce the gift tax by the *unused* portion of the unified credit.

- The generation-skipping tax is a supplemental tax designed to prevent the avoidance of transfer taxes (both estate and gift tax) through transfers that skip a generation of recipients.

Apply fundamental principles of wealth planning and explain how income and transfer taxation interact to affect wealth planning. **LO4**

- Trusts and estates are fiduciary taxpayers taxed on accumulated (undistributed) income via a fiduciary income tax return.

- Because fiduciary income tax rates are generally as high as or higher than the tax rates for individual beneficiaries, the income tax benefits from splitting income between fiduciaries and beneficiaries are typically negligible.

- A serial gift strategy saves gift taxes by converting a potentially large taxable transfer into a tax-exempt transfer of multiple smaller gifts that qualify for the annual exclusion of the donor.

- Bypass provisions in a will or bypass trusts reduce estate taxes by using the unified credit of the deceased spouse through a transfer of some property to beneficiaries other than the surviving spouse.

- Testamentary transfers allow a step-up in tax basis to fair market value, thereby eliminating the income tax on unrealized appreciation. In contrast, appreciation of property transferred via intervivos transfers may be eventually realized and taxed as income. However, a gift eliminates transfer taxes on expected future appreciation.

## KEY TERMS

adjusted gross estate (25-11)
adjusted taxable gifts (25-13)
alternative valuation date (25-8)
annual exclusion (25-19)
beneficiary (25-8)
bypass provision (25-28)
bypass trust (25-31)
carryover basis (25-29)
common-law states (25-21)
community property states (25-21)
corpus (25-8)
current gifts (25-20)
donee (25-18)
donor (25-18)
estate (25-27)
executor (25-5)
exemption equivalent (25-2)
family limited partnership (25-32)
fiduciary (25-27)

fiduciary duty (25-8)
future interest (25-8)
generation-skipping tax (GST) (25-27)
gift (25-18)
gift-splitting election (25-21)
grantor (25-8)
gross estate (25-4)
heirs (25-4)
intervivos transfers (25-2)
joint tenancy with the right of survivorship (25-4)
last will and testament (25-2)
life estate (25-8)
life insurance trust (25-31)
life tenant (25-8)
marital deduction (25-3)
nondeductible terminable interests (25-22)
present interest (25-8)

probate (25-3)
probate estate (25-3)
remainder (25-8)
remainderman (25-8)
reversion (25-8)
§7520 rate (25-9)
serial gift (25-28)
taxable estate (25-11)
taxable gifts (25-21)
tenancy by the entirety (25-6)
tenancy in common (25-5)
terminable interest (25-8)
testamentary transfers (25-2)
trust (25-8)
trustee (25-8)
unified credit (25-2)
willing-buyer, willing-seller rule (25-7)

## DISCUSSION QUESTIONS

1. **(LO1)** Identify the features common to the gift tax formula and the estate tax formula.

2. **(LO1)** Explain why Congress felt it necessary to enact a gift tax to complement the estate tax.

3. **(LO1)** Describe the unified credit and the purpose it serves in the gift and estate tax.

4. **(LO1)** Fred is retired and living on his pension. He has accumulated almost $1 million of property he would like to leave to his children. However, Fred is afraid much of his wealth will be eliminated by the federal estate tax. Explain whether this fear is well founded.

5. **(LO2)** Explain why the gross estate includes the value of certain property transferred by the decedent at death, such as property held in joint tenancy with the right of survivorship, even though this property is not subject to probate.

6. **(LO2)** Identify the factors that determine the proportion of the value of property held in joint tenancy with the right of survivorship that will be included in a decedent's gross estate.

7. **(LO2)** Define fair market value for transfer tax purposes.

8. **(LO2)** Harold owns a condo in Hawaii that he plans on using for the rest of his life. However, to ensure his sister Maude will own the property after his death, Harold deeded the remainder of the property to her. He signed the deed transferring the remainder in July 2009 when the condo was worth $250,000 and his life estate was worth $75,000. In January 2010 Harold died, at which time the condo was worth $300,000. What amount, if any, is included in Harold's gross estate? Explain.

9. **(LO2)** Paul is a widower with several grown children. He is considering transferring his residence into a trust for his children but retains a life estate in it.

Comment on whether this plan will prevent the value of the home from being included in Paul's gross estate when he dies.

10. **(LO2)** Explain how a remainder and an income interest are valued for transfer tax purposes.

11. **(LO2)** Explain why the fair market value of a life estate is more difficult to estimate than an income interest.

12. **(LO2)** Describe a reason why transfers of terminable interests should not qualify for the marital deduction.

13. **(LO2)** True or False: Including taxable gifts when calculating the estate tax subjects these transfers to double taxation. Explain.

14. **(LO2)** People sometimes confuse the unified credit with the exemption equivalent. Describe how these terms differ.

15. **(LO3)** Describe the requirements for a complete gift, and contrast a gift of a present interest with a gift of a future interest.

16. **(LO3)** Describe a property transfer or payment that is not, by definition, a transfer for inadequate consideration.

17. **(LO3)** Describe a situation in which a transfer of cash to a trust might be considered an incomplete gift.

18. **(LO3)** Identify two types of transfers for inadequate consideration that are specifically excluded from imposition of the gift tax.

19. **(LO3)** Under what circumstances will a deposit of cash to a bank account held in joint tenancy be considered a completed gift?

20. **(LO3)** Explain how a purchase of realty could result in a taxable gift.

21. **(LO3)** Describe the conditions for using the annual exclusion to offset an otherwise taxable transfer.

22. **(LO3)** List the conditions for making an election to split gifts.

23. **(LO3)** Describe the limitations on the deduction of transfers to charity.

24. **(LO3)** Explain the purpose of adding prior taxable gifts to current taxable gifts and show whether these prior gifts could be taxed multiple times over the years.

25. **(LO4)** Describe a reason why a generation-skipping tax was necessary to augment the estate and gift taxes?

26. **(LO4)** Explain why an effective wealth transfer plan necessitates cooperation between lawyers, accountants, and investment advisors.

27. **(LO4)** Describe how to initiate the construction of a comprehensive and effective wealth plan.

28. **(LO4)** List two questions you might pose to a client to find out whether a program of serial gifts would be an advantageous wealth transfer plan.

29. **(LO4)** A client in good health wants to support the college education of her teenage grandchildren. The client holds various properties but proposes to make a gift of cash in the amount of the annual exclusion. Explain to the client why a direct gift of cash may not be advisable and what property might serve as a reasonable substitute.

30. **(LO4)** An elderly client has a life insurance policy worth $40,000 that upon her death pays $250,000 to her sole grandchild (or his estate). The client still retains ownership of the policy. Outline for her the costs and benefits of transferring ownership of the policy to a life insurance trust.

31. **(LO4)** Describe the conditions in which a married couple would benefit from the use of a bypass provision or a bypass trust.

32. **(LO4)** Explain how a transfer of property as a gift may have income tax implications to the donee.

## PROBLEMS

33. **(LO2)** Hal and Wendy are married, and they own a parcel of realty, Blackacre, as joint tenants with the right of survivorship. Hal owns an additional parcel of realty, Redacre, in his name alone. If Hal should die when Blackacre is worth $800,000 and Redacre is worth $750,000, what value of realty would be included in his probate estate, and what value in his gross estate?

34. **(LO2)** Walter owns a whole-life insurance policy worth $52,000 that directs the insurance company to pay the beneficiary $250,000 on Walter's death. Walter pays the annual premiums and has the power to designate the beneficiary of the policy (it is currently his son, James). What value of the policy, if any, will be included in Walter's estate upon his death?

35. **(LO2)** Many years ago James and Sergio purchased property for $450,000. Although they are listed as equal co-owners, Sergio was able to provide only $200,000 of the purchase price. James treated the additional $25,000 of his contribution to the purchase price as a gift to Sergio. If the property is worth $900,000 at Sergio's death, what amount would be included in his estate if the title to the property was tenants in common? What if the title were joint tenancy with right of survivorship?

36. **(LO2)** Terry transferred $500,000 of real estate into an irrevocable trust for her son, Lee. The trustee was directed to retain income until Lee's 21st birthday and then pay him the corpus of the trust. Terry retained the power to require the trustee to pay income to Lee at any time, and the right to the assets if Lee predeceased her. What amount of the trust, if any, will be included in Terry's estate?

37. **(LO2)** Last year Robert transferred a life insurance policy worth $45,000 to an irrevocable trust with directions to distribute the corpus of the trust to his grandson, Danny, upon his graduation from college, or to Danny's estate upon his death. Robert paid $15,000 of gift tax on the transfer of the policy. Early this year, Robert died and the insurance company paid $400,000 to the trust. What amount, if any, is included in Robert's gross estate?

■research

38. **(LO2)** Willie purchased a whole-life insurance policy on his brother, Benny. Under the policy, the insurance company will pay the named beneficiary $100,000 upon the death of the insured, Benny. Willie names Tess the beneficiary, and upon Benny's death, Tess receives the proceeds of the policy, $100,000. Identify and discuss the transfer tax implications of this arrangement.

39. **(LO2)** Jimmy owns two parcels of real estate, Tara and Sundance. Tara is worth $240,000 and Sundance is worth $360,000. Jimmy plans to bequeath Tara directly to his wife Lois and leave her a life estate in Sundance. What amount of value will be included in Jimmy's gross estate and taxable estate should he die now?

40. **(LO2)** Roland had a taxable estate of $4.5 million when he died this year. Calculate the amount of estate tax due (if any) under the following alternatives.

    a. Roland's prior taxable gifts consist of a taxable gift of $1 million in 2005.

    b. Roland's prior taxable gifts consist of a taxable gift of $1.5 million in 2005.

    c. Roland's prior taxable gifts consist of a taxable gift of $2 million in 2007.

41. **(LO3)** Raquel transferred $100,000 of stock to a trust, with income to be paid to her nephew for 18 years and the remainder to her nephew's children (or their estates). Raquel named a bank as independent trustee but retained the power to determine how much income, if any, will be paid in any particular year. Is this transfer a complete gift? Explain.

42. **(LO3)** This year Gerry's friend, Dewey, was disabled. Gerry paid $15,000 to Dewey's doctor for medical expenses and paid $12,500 to State University for college tuition for Dewey's son. Has Gerry made taxable gifts and, if so, in what amounts?

43. **(LO3)** This year Dan and Mike purchased realty for $180,000 and took title as equal tenants in common. However, Mike was able to provide only $40,000 of the purchase price and Dan paid the remaining $140,000. Has Dan made a complete gift to Mike and, if so, in what amount?

44. **(LO3)** Last year Nate opened a savings account with a deposit of $15,000. The account was in the name of Nate and Derrick, joint tenancy with the right of survivorship. Derrick did not contribute to the account, but this year he withdrew $5,000. Has Nate made a complete gift and, if so, what is the amount of the taxable gift and when was the gift made?

45. **(LO3)** Barry transfers $1,000,000 to an irrevocable trust with income to Robin for her life and the remainder to Maurice (or his estate). Calculate the value of the life estate and remainder if Robin's age and the prevailing interest rate result in a Table S discount factor for the remainder of 0.27.

46. **(LO3)** This year Jim created an irrevocable trust to provide for Ted, his 32-year-old nephew, and Ted's family. Jim transferred $70,000 to the trust and named a bank as the trustee. The trust was directed to pay income to Ted until he reaches age 35, and at that time the trust is to be terminated and the corpus is to be distributed to Ted's two children (or their estates). Determine the amount, if any, of the current gift and the taxable gift. If necessary, you may assume the relevant interest rate is 6 percent and Jim is unmarried.

47. **(LO3)** This year Colleen transferred $100,000 to an irrevocable trust that pays equal shares of income annually to three cousins (or their estates) for the next eight years. At that time, the trust is terminated and the corpus of the trust reverts to Colleen. Determine the amount, if any, of the current gifts and the taxable gifts. If necessary, you may assume the relevant interest rate is 6 percent and Colleen is unmarried. What is your answer if Colleen is married and she elects to gift-split with her spouse?

48. **(LO3)** Sly wants to make annual gifts of cash to each of his four children and six grandchildren. How much can Sly transfer to his children if he makes the maximum gifts eligible for the annual exclusion, assuming he is single?

49. **(LO3)** Jack and Liz live in a community property state and their vacation home is community property. This year they transferred the vacation home to an irrevocable trust that provides their son Tom a life estate in the home and their daughter Laura the remainder. Under the terms of the trust, Tom has the right to use the vacation home for the duration of his life, and Laura will automatically own the property after Tom's death. At the time of the gift the home was valued at $500,000, Tom was 35 years old, and the §7520 rate was 5.4 percent. What is the amount, if any, of the taxable gifts? Would your answer be different if the home were not community property and Jack and Liz elected to gift-split?

50. **(LO3)** David placed $80,000 in trust with income to Steve for his life and the remainder to Lil (or her estate). At the time of the gift, given the prevailing interest rate, Steve's life estate was valued at $65,000 and the remainder at $15,000. What is the amount, if any, of David's taxable gifts?

51. **(LO3)** Stephen transferred $15,000 to an irrevocable trust for Graham. The trustee has the discretion to distribute income or corpus for Graham's benefit but is required to distribute all assets to Graham (or his estate) not later than Graham's 21st birthday. What is the amount, if any, of the taxable gift?

52. **(LO3)** For the holidays, Marty gave a watch worth $25,000 to Emily and jewelry worth $40,000 to Natalie. Has Marty made any taxable gifts and, if so, in what amounts? Does it matter if Marty is married to Wendy and they live in a community property state?

53. **(LO3)** This year Jeff earned $850,000 and used it to purchase land in joint tenancy with a right of survivorship with Mary. Has Jeff made a taxable gift to Mary and, if so, in what amount? What is your answer if Jeff and Mary are married?

54. **(LO3)** Laura transfers $500,000 into trust with the income to be paid annually to her spouse, William, for life (a life estate) and the remainder to Jenny. Calculate the amount of the taxable gifts from the transfers.

55. **(LO3)** Red transferred $5,000,000 of cash to State University for a new sports complex. Calculate the amount of the taxable gift.

56. **(LO3)** Casey gave $500,000 of stock to both Stephanie and Linda in 2005, 2006, and 2007. Calculate the amount of gift tax due and the marginal gift tax rate on the next $1 of taxable transfers under the following conditions:

    a. In 2005, the annual exclusion was $11,000. Casey was not married and has never made any other gifts.

    b. In 2006, the annual exclusion was $12,000. Casey was not married and the 2005 gift was the only other gift he has made.

    c. In 2007, the annual exclusion was $12,000. Casey was married prior to the date of the gift. He and his spouse, Helen, live in a common-law state and have elected to gift-split. Helen has never made a taxable gift, and Casey's only other taxable gifts were the gifts in 2005 and 2006.

**planning**

57. **(LO4)** Jones is seriously ill and has $2,000,000 of property that he wants to leave to his four children. He is considering making a current gift of the property (rather than leaving the property to pass through his will). Assuming any taxable transfer will be subject to the highest transfer tax rate, determine how much gift tax Jones will owe if he makes the transfers now. How much estate tax will Jones save if he dies after three years, during which time the property appreciates to $2,200,000?

58. **(LO4)** Angelina gave a parcel of realty to Julie valued at $210,000 (Angelina purchased the property five years ago for $88,000). Compute the amount of the taxable gift on the transfer, if any. Suppose several years later Julie sold the property for $215,000. What is the amount of her gain or loss, if any, on the sale?

**research**

59. **(LO4)** Several years ago Doug invested $21,000 in stock. This year he gave his daughter Tina the stock on a day it was valued at $20,000. She promptly sold it for $19,500. Determine the amount of the taxable gift, if any, and calculate the amount of taxable income or gain, if any, for Tina. Assume Doug is not married and does not support Tina, who is 28.

60. **(LO4)** Roberta is considering making annual gifts of $13,000 of stock to each of her four children. She expects to live another five years and to leave a taxable estate worth approximately $1,000,000. She requests that you justify the gifts by estimating her estate tax savings from making the gifts.

61. **(LO4)** Harold and Maude are married and live in a common-law state. Neither have made any taxable gifts and Maude owns (holds title) all their property. She dies with a taxable estate of $10 million and leaves it all to Harold. He dies several years later, leaving the entire $10 million to their three children. Calculate how much estate tax would have been saved if Maude had used a bypass provision in her will to direct $4 million to her children and the remaining $6 million to Harold. Ignore all credits in this problem except for the unified credit.

## COMPREHENSIVE PROBLEMS

**planning**

62. Suppose Vince dies this year with a gross estate of $15 million and no adjusted prior gifts. Calculate the amount of estate tax due (if any) under the following *alternative* conditions:

    a. Vince leaves his entire estate to his spouse, Millie.

    b. Vince leaves $10 million to Millie and the remainder to charity.

    c. Vince leaves $10 million to Millie and the remainder to his son, Paul.

    d. Vince leaves $10 million to Millie and the remainder to a trust whose trustee is required to pay income to Millie for her life and the remainder to Paul.

63. Hank possessed a life insurance policy worth $50,000 that will pay his two children a total of $400,000 upon his death. In 2006, Hank transferred the policy and all incidents of ownership to an irrevocable trust that pays income annually to his two children for 15 years and then distributes the corpus to the children in equal shares.

    a. Calculate the amount of gift tax due (if any) on the 2006 gift, given Hank has made only one prior taxable gift of $1.5 million in 2005.

    b. Estimate the amount of estate tax due if Hank were to die more than three years after transferring the insurance policy. At the time of his death, Hank estimates he will have a probate estate of $10 million to be divided in equal shares between his two children.

    c. Estimate the amount of estate tax due if Hank were to die within three years of transferring the insurance policy. At the time of his death, Hank estimates he will have a probate estate of $10 million to be divided in equal shares between his two children.

64. Jack made his first taxable gift of $1,000,000 in 1997, at which time the unified credit was $192,800. Jack made no further gifts until 2005, at which time he gave $250,000 each to his three children and an additional $100,000 to State University (a charity). The annual exclusion in 2005 was $11,000. Recently Jack has been in poor health and would like you to estimate his estate tax should he die this year. He estimates his taxable estate (after deductions) will be worth $5.4 million at his death. Assume Jack is single and has paid the proper amounts of tax in past years.

65. Montgomery has decided to engage in wealth planning and has listed the value of his assets below. The life insurance has a cash surrender value of $120,000, and the proceeds are payable to Montgomery's estate. The trust is an irrevocable trust created by Montgomery's brother 10 years ago and contains assets currently valued at $800,000. The income from the trust is payable to Montgomery's faithful butler, Walen, for his life, and the remainder is payable to Montgomery or his estate. Walen is currently 37 years old, and the §7520 interest rate is currently 5.4 percent. Montgomery is unmarried and plans to leave all his assets to his surviving relatives.

| Property | Value | Adjusted Basis |
|---|---|---|
| Auto | $ 20,000 | $ 55,000 |
| Personal effects | $ 75,000 | $ 110,000 |
| Checking and savings accounts | $ 250,000 | $ 250,000 |
| Investments | $2,500,000 | $ 770,000 |
| Residence | $1,400,000 | $ 980,000 |
| Life insurance proceeds | $1,000,000 | $ 50,000 |
| Real estate investments | $5,125,000 | $2,800,000 |
| Trust | $ 800,000 | $ 80,000 |

    a. Calculate the amount of the estate tax due (if any), assuming Montgomery dies this year and has never made any taxable gifts.

    b. Calculate the amount of the estate tax due (if any), assuming Montgomery dies this year and made one taxable gift in 2006. The taxable gift was $1 million, and Montgomery used his unified credit to avoid paying any gift tax.

    c. Calculate the amount of the estate tax due (if any), assuming Montgomery dies this year and made one taxable gift in 2006. The taxable gift was $1 million, and Montgomery used his unified credit to avoid paying any gift tax. Montgomery plans to bequeath his investments to charity and leave his remaining assets to his surviving relatives.

# Tax Forms

| | | |
|---|---|---|
| **Form 1040** | U.S. Individual Income Tax Return | A-2 |
| **Schedules A & B** | Itemized Deductions; Interest and Ordinary Dividends | A-4 |
| **Schedule C** | Profit or Loss from Business | A-6 |
| **Schedule D** | Capital Gains and Losses | A-8 |
| **Schedule E** | Supplemental Income and Loss | A-10 |
| **Schedule SE** | Self-Employment Tax | A-12 |
| **Form 1065** | Return of Partnership Income | A-14 |
| **Schedule K-1** | Partner Share of Income, Deductions, Credits, etc. | A-16 |
| **Form 1120** | Corporation Income Tax Return | A-17 |
| **Form 1120S** | Income Tax Return for an S Corporation | A-18 |
| **Schedule K-1** | Shareholder's Share of Income, Deductions, Credits, etc. | A-19 |
| **Schedule M-3** | Net Income (Loss) Reconciliation for Corporations | A-20 |
| **Form 706** | Estate (and Generation-Skipping Transfer) Tax Return | A-23 |
| **Form 709** | Gift (and Generation-Skipping Transfer) Tax Return | A-26 |

All tax forms can be obtained from the IRS Web site: www.irs.gov.

Form **1040**   Department of the Treasury—Internal Revenue Service
**U.S. Individual Income Tax Return**   20**09**   (99)   IRS Use Only—Do not write or staple in this space.

| | |
|---|---|
| For the year Jan. 1–Dec. 31, 2009, or other tax year beginning , 2009, ending , 20 | OMB No. 1545-0074 |

**Label**

(See instructions on page 14.)

**Use the IRS label.**

Otherwise, please print or type.

L A B E L   H E R E

Your first name and initial      Last name

If a joint return, spouse's first name and initial      Last name

Home address (number and street). If you have a P.O. box, see page 14.      Apt. no.

City, town or post office, state, and ZIP code. If you have a foreign address, see page 14.

Your social security number

Spouse's social security number

▲ You **must** enter your SSN(s) above. ▲

Checking a box below will not change your tax or refund.

**Presidential Election Campaign**   ► Check here if you, or your spouse if filing jointly, want $3 to go to this fund (see page 14) ►   ☐ You   ☐ Spouse

**Filing Status**

Check only one box.

1 ☐ Single
2 ☐ Married filing jointly (even if only one had income)
3 ☐ Married filing separately. Enter spouse's SSN above and full name here. ►
4 ☐ Head of household (with qualifying person). (See page 15.) If the qualifying person is a child but not your dependent, enter this child's name here. ►
5 ☐ Qualifying widow(er) with dependent child (see page 16)

**Exemptions**

6a ☐ **Yourself.** If someone can claim you as a dependent, **do not** check box 6a . . . . .
  b ☐ **Spouse** . . . . . . . . . . . . . . . .
  c Dependents:

| (1) First name   Last name | (2) Dependent's social security number | (3) Dependent's relationship to you | (4) ✓ if qualifying child for child tax credit (see page 17) |
|---|---|---|---|
| | | | ☐ |
| | | | ☐ |
| | | | ☐ |
| | | | ☐ |

If more than four dependents, see page 17 and check here ► ☐

  d Total number of exemptions claimed . . . . . . . . . . . .

Boxes checked on 6a and 6b

No. of children on 6c who:
• lived with you
• did not live with you due to divorce or separation (see page 18)

Dependents on 6c not entered above

Add numbers on lines above ►

**Income**

**Attach Form(s) W-2 here. Also attach Forms W-2G and 1099-R if tax was withheld.**

If you did not get a W-2, see page 22.

Enclose, but do not attach, any payment. Also, please use Form 1040-V.

| 7 | Wages, salaries, tips, etc. Attach Form(s) W-2 . . . . . . . | 7 | |
| 8a | **Taxable** interest. Attach Schedule B if required . . . . . . | 8a | |
| b | **Tax-exempt** interest. **Do not** include on line 8a . . . | 8b | | |
| 9a | Ordinary dividends. Attach Schedule B if required . . . . . | 9a | |
| b | Qualified dividends (see page 22) . . . . . . | 9b | | |
| 10 | Taxable refunds, credits, or offsets of state and local income taxes (see page 23) . . | 10 | |
| 11 | Alimony received . . . . . . . . . . . . | 11 | |
| 12 | Business income or (loss). Attach Schedule C or C-EZ . . . . | 12 | |
| 13 | Capital gain or (loss). Attach Schedule D if required. If not required, check here ► ☐ | 13 | |
| 14 | Other gains or (losses). Attach Form 4797 . . . . . . | 14 | |
| 15a | IRA distributions . | 15a | | b Taxable amount (see page 24) | 15b | |
| 16a | Pensions and annuities | 16a | | b Taxable amount (see page 25) | 16b | |
| 17 | Rental real estate, royalties, partnerships, S corporations, trusts, etc. Attach Schedule E | 17 | |
| 18 | Farm income or (loss). Attach Schedule F . . . . . . . | 18 | |
| 19 | Unemployment compensation in excess of $2,400 per recipient (see page 27) . . . | 19 | |
| 20a | Social security benefits | 20a | | b Taxable amount (see page 27) | 20b | |
| 21 | Other income. List type and amount (see page 29) _____ | 21 | |
| 22 | Add the amounts in the far right column for lines 7 through 21. This is your **total income** ► | 22 | |

**Adjusted Gross Income**

| 23 | Educator expenses (see page 29) . . . . . . | 23 | | |
| 24 | Certain business expenses of reservists, performing artists, and fee-basis government officials. Attach Form 2106 or 2106-EZ | 24 | | |
| 25 | Health savings account deduction. Attach Form 8889 . | 25 | | |
| 26 | Moving expenses. Attach Form 3903 . . . . . | 26 | | |
| 27 | One-half of self-employment tax. Attach Schedule SE . | 27 | | |
| 28 | Self-employed SEP, SIMPLE, and qualified plans . | 28 | | |
| 29 | Self-employed health insurance deduction (see page 30) | 29 | | |
| 30 | Penalty on early withdrawal of savings . . . . . | 30 | | |
| 31a | Alimony paid  b Recipient's SSN ► _____ | 31a | | |
| 32 | IRA deduction (see page 31) . . . . . . | 32 | | |
| 33 | Student loan interest deduction (see page 34) . . . | 33 | | |
| 34 | Tuition and fees deduction. Attach Form 8917 . . . | 34 | | |
| 35 | Domestic production activities deduction. Attach Form 8903 | 35 | | |
| 36 | Add lines 23 through 31a and 32 through 35 . . . . . . . . | 36 | |
| 37 | Subtract line 36 from line 22. This is your **adjusted gross income** . . . . . ► | 37 | |

**For Disclosure, Privacy Act, and Paperwork Reduction Act Notice, see page 97.**   Cat. No. 11320B   Form **1040** (2009)

| | | | | |
|---|---|---|---|---|
| **Tax and Credits** | 38 | Amount from line 37 (adjusted gross income) . . . . . . . . . . | 38 | |
| | 39a | Check if: ☐ **You** were born before January 2, 1945, ☐ Blind. ☐ **Spouse** was born before January 2, 1945, ☐ Blind. } Total boxes checked ▶ 39a | | |
| | **b** | If your spouse itemizes on a separate return or you were a dual-status alien, see page 35 and check here ▶ 39b ☐ | | |
| **Standard Deduction for—** | 40a | **Itemized deductions** (from Schedule A) **or** your **standard deduction** (see left margin) . . | 40a | |
| | **b** | If you are increasing your standard deduction by certain real estate taxes, new motor vehicle taxes, or a net disaster loss, attach Schedule L and check here (see page 35) . ▶ 40b ☐ | | |
| • People who check any box on line 39a, 39b, or 40b **or** who can be claimed as a dependent, see page 35. | 41 | Subtract line 40a from line 38 . . . . . . . . . . . . . | 41 | |
| | 42 | **Exemptions.** If line 38 is $125,100 or less and you did not provide housing to a Midwestern displaced individual, multiply $3,650 by the number on line 6d. Otherwise, see page 37 . . | 42 | |
| | 43 | **Taxable income.** Subtract line 42 from line 41. If line 42 is more than line 41, enter -0- . . | 43 | |
| • All others: | 44 | **Tax** (see page 37). Check if any tax is from: **a** ☐ Form(s) 8814 **b** ☐ Form 4972 . | 44 | |
| Single or Married filing separately, $5,700 | 45 | **Alternative minimum tax** (see page 40). Attach Form 6251 . . . . . . . | 45 | |
| | 46 | Add lines 44 and 45 . . . . . . . . . . . . . . . . ▶ | 46 | |
| | 47 | Foreign tax credit. Attach Form 1116 if required . . . . | 47 | | |
| Married filing jointly or Qualifying widow(er), $11,400 | 48 | Credit for child and dependent care expenses. Attach Form 2441 | 48 | | |
| | 49 | Education credits from Form 8863, line 29 . . . . | 49 | | |
| | 50 | Retirement savings contributions credit. Attach Form 8880 | 50 | | |
| Head of household, $8,350 | 51 | Child tax credit (see page 42) . . . . . . . | 51 | | |
| | 52 | Credits from Form: **a** ☐ 8396 **b** ☐ 8839 **c** ☐ 5695 | 52 | | |
| | 53 | Other credits from Form: **a** ☐ 3800 **b** ☐ 8801 **c** ☐ | 53 | | |
| | 54 | Add lines 47 through 53. These are your **total credits** . . . . . . . | 54 | |
| | 55 | Subtract line 54 from line 46. If line 54 is more than line 46, enter -0- . . . . ▶ | 55 | |
| **Other Taxes** | 56 | Self-employment tax. Attach Schedule SE . . . . . . . . . . | 56 | |
| | 57 | Unreported social security and Medicare tax from Form: **a** ☐ 4137 **b** ☐ 8919 | 57 | |
| | 58 | Additional tax on IRAs, other qualified retirement plans, etc. Attach Form 5329 if required . . | 58 | |
| | 59 | Additional taxes: **a** ☐ AEIC payments **b** ☐ Household employment taxes. Attach Schedule H | 59 | |
| | 60 | Add lines 55 through 59. This is your **total tax** . . . . . . . . ▶ | 60 | |
| **Payments** | 61 | Federal income tax withheld from Forms W-2 and 1099 . . | 61 | | |
| | 62 | 2009 estimated tax payments and amount applied from 2008 return | 62 | | |
| | 63 | Making work pay and government retiree credits. Attach Schedule M | 63 | | |
| If you have a qualifying child, attach Schedule EIC. | 64a | **Earned income credit (EIC)** . . . . . . | 64a | | |
| | **b** | Nontaxable combat pay election | 64b | | | |
| | 65 | Additional child tax credit. Attach Form 8812 . . . . | 65 | | |
| | 66 | Refundable education credit from Form 8863, line 16 . . . | 66 | | |
| | 67 | First-time homebuyer credit. Attach Form 5405 . . . . | 67 | | |
| | 68 | Amount paid with request for extension to file (see page 72) . | 68 | | |
| | 69 | Excess social security and tier 1 RRTA tax withheld (see page 72) | 69 | | |
| | 70 | Credits from Form: **a** ☐ 2439 **b** ☐ 4136 **c** ☐ 8801 **d** ☐ 8885 | 70 | | |
| | 71 | Add lines 61, 62, 63, 64a, and 65 through 70. These are your **total payments** . . . . ▶ | 71 | |
| **Refund** | 72 | If line 71 is more than line 60, subtract line 60 from line 71. This is the amount you **overpaid** | 72 | |
| Direct deposit? See page 73 and fill in 73b, 73c, and 73d, or Form 8888. | 73a | Amount of line 72 you want **refunded to you.** If Form 8888 is attached, check here ▶ ☐ | 73a | |
| | ▶ **b** | Routing number [          ] ▶ **c** Type: ☐ Checking ☐ Savings | | |
| | ▶ **d** | Account number [                    ] | | |
| | 74 | Amount of line 72 you want **applied to your 2010 estimated tax** ▶ | 74 | | |
| **Amount You Owe** | 75 | **Amount you owe.** Subtract line 71 from line 60. For details on how to pay, see page 74 . ▶ | 75 | |
| | 76 | Estimated tax penalty (see page 74) . . . . . . . | 76 | | |

| | |
|---|---|
| **Third Party Designee** | Do you want to allow another person to discuss this return with the IRS (see page 75)? ☐ **Yes.** Complete the following. ☐ **No** |
| | Designee's name ▶ — Phone no. ▶ — Personal identification number (PIN) [     ] |

**Sign Here**

Joint return? See page 15. Keep a copy for your records.

Under penalties of perjury, I declare that I have examined this return and accompanying schedules and statements, and to the best of my knowledge and belief, they are true, correct, and complete. Declaration of preparer (other than taxpayer) is based on all information of which preparer has any knowledge.

| | | | |
|---|---|---|---|
| Your signature | Date | Your occupation | Daytime phone number |
| Spouse's signature. If a joint return, **both** must sign. | Date | Spouse's occupation | |

**Paid Preparer's Use Only**

| | | | |
|---|---|---|---|
| Preparer's signature ▶ | | Date | Check if self-employed ☐ | Preparer's SSN or PTIN |
| Firm's name (or yours if self-employed), address, and ZIP code ▶ | | EIN | |
| | | Phone no. | |

**SCHEDULE A**
**(Form 1040)**

Department of the Treasury
Internal Revenue Service (99)

# Itemized Deductions

▶ **Attach to Form 1040.**          ▶ **See Instructions for Schedule A (Form 1040).**

OMB No. 1545-0074

20**09**

Attachment
Sequence No. **07**

Name(s) shown on Form 1040

Your social security number

---

**Medical and Dental Expenses**

**Caution.** Do not include expenses reimbursed or paid by others.

1  Medical and dental expenses (see page A-1) . . . . . .  | 1
2  Enter amount from Form 1040, line 38 | 2 |
3  Multiply line 2 by 7.5% (.075)  | 3
4  Subtract line 3 from line 1. If line 3 is more than line 1, enter -0- . . . . . . . . .  | **4**

**Taxes You Paid**

(See page A-2.)

5  State and local  **(check only one box):**
   a ☐ Income taxes, **or**  | 5
   b ☐ General sales taxes
6  Real estate taxes (see page A-5) . . . . . . . . .  | 6
7  New motor vehicle taxes from line 11 of the worksheet on back. Skip this line if you checked box 5b . . . . . .  | 7
8  Other taxes. List type and amount ▶ _____  | 8
9  Add lines 5 through 8 . . . . . . . . . . . . . .  | **9**

**Interest You Paid**

(See page A-6.)

**Note.**
Personal interest is not deductible.

10  Home mortgage interest and points reported to you on Form 1098  | 10
11  Home mortgage interest not reported to you on Form 1098. If paid to the person from whom you bought the home, see page A-7 and show that person's name, identifying no., and address ▶
_____
_____  | 11
12  Points not reported to you on Form 1098. See page A-7 for special rules . . . . . . . . . . . . .  | 12
13  Qualified mortgage insurance premiums (see page A-7) .  | 13
14  Investment interest. Attach Form 4952 if required. (See page A-8.)  | 14
15  Add lines 10 through 14 . . . . . . . . . . . .  | **15**

**Gifts to Charity**

If you made a gift and got a benefit for it, see page A-8.

16  Gifts by cash or check. If you made any gift of $250 or more, see page A-8 . . . . .  | 16
17  Other than by cash or check. If any gift of $250 or more, see page A-8. You **must** attach Form 8283 if over $500 . . .  | 17
18  Carryover from prior year  | 18
19  Add lines 16 through 18 . . . . . . . . . . . .  | **19**

**Casualty and Theft Losses**

20  Casualty or theft loss(es). Attach Form 4684. (See page A-10.) . . . . . . . . .  | **20**

**Job Expenses and Certain Miscellaneous Deductions**

(See page A-10.)

21  Unreimbursed employee expenses—job travel, union dues, job education, etc. Attach Form 2106 or 2106-EZ if required. (See page A-10.) ▶ _____  | 21
22  Tax preparation fees . . . . . . . . . . . .  | 22
23  Other expenses—investment, safe deposit box, etc. List type and amount ▶ _____
_____  | 23
24  Add lines 21 through 23 . . . .  | 24
25  Enter amount from Form 1040, line 38 | 25 |  | 25
26  Multiply line 25 by 2% (.02) . . . . . . . .  | 26
27  Subtract line 26 from line 24. If line 26 is more than line 24, enter -0- . . . . . .  | **27**

**Other Miscellaneous Deductions**

28  Other—from list on page A-11. List type and amount ▶ _____
_____  | **28**

**Total Itemized Deductions**

29  Is Form 1040, line 38, over $166,800 (over $83,400 if married filing separately)?
☐ **No.**   Your deduction is not limited. Add the amounts in the far right column for lines 4 through 28. Also, enter this amount on Form 1040, line 40a. | ▶ | **29**
☐ **Yes.**  Your deduction may be limited. See page A-11 for the amount to enter.
30  If you elect to itemize deductions even though they are less than your standard deduction, check here . . . . . . . . . . . . ▶ ☐

---

For Paperwork Reduction Act Notice, see Form 1040 instructions.          Cat. No. 17145C          Schedule A (Form 1040) 2009

**SCHEDULE B**
(Form 1040A or 1040)

Department of the Treasury
Internal Revenue Service (99)

# Interest and Ordinary Dividends

▶ **Attach to Form 1040A or 1040.**     ▶ **See instructions on back.**

OMB No. 1545-0074

2009

Attachment
Sequence No. **08**

Name(s) shown on return

Your social security number

---

## Part I
## Interest

(See instructions on back and the instructions for Form 1040A, or Form 1040, line 8a.)

**Note.** If you received a Form 1099-INT, Form 1099-OID, or substitute statement from a brokerage firm, list the firm's name as the payer and enter the total interest shown on that form.

| | | Amount |
|---|---|---|
| **1** | List name of payer. If any interest is from a seller-financed mortgage and the buyer used the property as a personal residence, see instructions on back and list this interest first. Also, show that buyer's social security number and address ▶ | **1** |
| **2** | Add the amounts on line 1 . . . . . . . . . . . . . | **2** |
| **3** | Excludable interest on series EE and I U.S. savings bonds issued after 1989. Attach Form 8815 . . . . . . . . . . . | **3** |
| **4** | Subtract line 3 from line 2. Enter the result here and on Form 1040A, or Form 1040, line 8a . . . . . . . . . . ▶ | **4** |

**Note.** If line 4 is over $1,500, you must complete Part III.

---

## Part II
## Ordinary Dividends

(See instructions on back and the instructions for Form 1040A, or Form 1040, line 9a.)

**Note.** If you received a Form 1099-DIV or substitute statement from a brokerage firm, list the firm's name as the payer and enter the ordinary dividends shown on that form.

| | | Amount |
|---|---|---|
| **5** | List name of payer ▶ | **5** |
| **6** | Add the amounts on line 5. Enter the total here and on Form 1040A, or Form 1040, line 9a . . . . . . . . . . . . ▶ | **6** |

**Note.** If line 6 is over $1,500, you must complete Part III.

---

## Part III
## Foreign Accounts and Trusts

(See instructions on back.)

You must complete this part if you **(a)** had over $1,500 of taxable interest or ordinary dividends; **(b)** had a foreign account; or **(c)** received a distribution from, or were a grantor of, or a transferor to, a foreign trust.

| | | Yes | No |
|---|---|---|---|
| **7a** | At any time during 2009, did you have an interest in or a signature or other authority over a financial account in a foreign country, such as a bank account, securities account, or other financial account? See instructions on back for exceptions and filing requirements for Form TD F 90-22.1 . . . . . . . . . . . . . . . . . . . . . . . . | | |
| **b** | If "Yes," enter the name of the foreign country ▶ | | |
| **8** | During 2009, did you receive a distribution from, or were you the grantor of, or transferor to, a foreign trust? If "Yes," you may have to file Form 3520. See instructions on back . . . . . . | | |

**For Paperwork Reduction Act Notice, see Form 1040A or 1040 instructions.**     Cat. No. 17146N     Schedule B (Form 1040A or 1040) 2009

**SCHEDULE C**
**(Form 1040)**

Department of the Treasury
Internal Revenue Service (99)

# Profit or Loss From Business

(Sole Proprietorship)

► **Partnerships, joint ventures, etc., generally must file Form 1065 or 1065-B.**
► **Attach to Form 1040, 1040NR, or 1041.**    ► **See Instructions for Schedule C (Form 1040).**

OMB No. 1545-0074

**2009**

Attachment
Sequence No. **09**

Name of proprietor

Social security number (SSN)

| A | Principal business or profession, including product or service (see page C-2 of the instructions) | **B** Enter code from pages C-9, 10, & 11 ► |
|---|---|---|
| C | Business name. If no separate business name, leave blank. | **D** Employer ID number (EIN), if any |

E    Business address (including suite or room no.) ►

City, town or post office, state, and ZIP code

F    Accounting method:    **(1)** ☐ Cash    **(2)** ☐ Accrual    **(3)** ☐ Other (specify) ►

G    Did you "materially participate" in the operation of this business during 2009? If "No," see page C-3 for limit on losses    ☐ Yes  ☐ No

H    If you started or acquired this business during 2009, check here    ►  ☐

## Part I    Income

| 1 | Gross receipts or sales. **Caution.** See page C-4 and check the box if: <br>• This income was reported to you on Form W-2 and the "Statutory employee" box on that form was checked, or <br>• You are a member of a qualified joint venture reporting only rental real estate income not subject to self-employment tax. Also see page C-3 for limit on losses. ►☐ | 1 | |
|---|---|---|---|
| 2 | Returns and allowances | 2 | |
| 3 | Subtract line 2 from line 1 | 3 | |
| 4 | Cost of goods sold (from line 42 on page 2) | 4 | |
| 5 | **Gross profit.** Subtract line 4 from line 3 | 5 | |
| 6 | Other income, including federal and state gasoline or fuel tax credit or refund (see page C-4) | 6 | |
| 7 | **Gross income.** Add lines 5 and 6 ► | 7 | |

## Part II    Expenses.    Enter expenses for business use of your home **only** on line 30.

| 8 | Advertising | 8 | | 18 | Office expense | 18 | |
|---|---|---|---|---|---|---|---|
| 9 | Car and truck expenses (see page C-4) | 9 | | 19 | Pension and profit-sharing plans | 19 | |
| 10 | Commissions and fees | 10 | | 20 | Rent or lease (see page C-6): | | |
| 11 | Contract labor (see page C-4) | 11 | | a | Vehicles, machinery, and equipment | 20a | |
| 12 | Depletion | 12 | | b | Other business property | 20b | |
| 13 | Depreciation and section 179 expense deduction (not included in Part III) (see page C-5) | 13 | | 21 | Repairs and maintenance | 21 | |
| | | | | 22 | Supplies (not included in Part III) | 22 | |
| | | | | 23 | Taxes and licenses | 23 | |
| | | | | 24 | Travel, meals, and entertainment: | | |
| | | | | a | Travel | 24a | |
| 14 | Employee benefit programs (other than on line 19) | 14 | | b | Deductible meals and entertainment (see page C-6) | 24b | |
| 15 | Insurance (other than health) | 15 | | 25 | Utilities | 25 | |
| 16 | Interest: | | | 26 | Wages (less employment credits) | 26 | |
| a | Mortgage (paid to banks, etc.) | 16a | | 27 | Other expenses (from line 48 on page 2) | 27 | |
| b | Other | 16b | | | | | |
| 17 | Legal and professional services | 17 | | | | | |

| 28 | **Total expenses** before expenses for business use of home. Add lines 8 through 27 ► | 28 | |
|---|---|---|---|
| 29 | Tentative profit or (loss). Subtract line 28 from line 7 | 29 | |
| 30 | Expenses for business use of your home. Attach **Form 8829** | 30 | |
| 31 | **Net profit or (loss).** Subtract line 30 from line 29. <br>• If a profit, enter on both **Form 1040, line 12,** and **Schedule SE, line 2,** or on **Form 1040NR, line 13** (if you checked the box on line 1, see page C-7). Estates and trusts, enter on **Form 1041, line 3.** <br>• If a loss, you **must** go to line 32. | 31 | |

32    If you have a loss, check the box that describes your investment in this activity (see page C-7).

• If you checked 32a, enter the loss on both **Form 1040, line 12,** and **Schedule SE, line 2,** or on **Form 1040NR, line 13** (if you checked the box on line 1, see the line 31 instructions on page C-7). Estates and trusts, enter on **Form 1041, line 3.**

• If you checked 32b, you **must** attach **Form 6198.** Your loss may be limited.

**32a** ☐ All investment is at risk.
**32b** ☐ Some investment is not at risk.

**For Paperwork Reduction Act Notice, see page C-9 of the instructions.**    Cat. No. 11334P    Schedule C (Form 1040) 2009

| Part III | Cost of Goods Sold (see page C-8) |

**33** Method(s) used to
value closing inventory:   **a** ☐ Cost    **b** ☐ Lower of cost or market    **c** ☐ Other (attach explanation)

**34** Was there any change in determining quantities, costs, or valuations between opening and closing inventory?
If "Yes," attach explanation . . . . . . . . . . . . . . . . . . . . . . . . ☐ Yes    ☐ No

| | | | |
|---|---|---|---|
| **35** | Inventory at beginning of year. If different from last year's closing inventory, attach explanation . . . | **35** | |
| **36** | Purchases less cost of items withdrawn for personal use . . . . . . . . . . . . . . | **36** | |
| **37** | Cost of labor. Do not include any amounts paid to yourself . . . . . . . . . . . . . | **37** | |
| **38** | Materials and supplies . . . . . . . . . . . . . . . . . . | **38** | |
| **39** | Other costs . . . . . . . . . . . . . . . . . . . | **39** | |
| **40** | Add lines 35 through 39 . . . . . . . . . . . . . . . . | **40** | |
| **41** | Inventory at end of year . . . . . . . . . . . . . . . . | **41** | |
| **42** | **Cost of goods sold.** Subtract line 41 from line 40. Enter the result here and on page 1, line 4 . . . | **42** | |

| Part IV | **Information on Your Vehicle.** Complete this part **only** if you are claiming car or truck expenses on line 9 and are not required to file Form 4562 for this business. See the instructions for line 13 on page C-5 to find out if you must file Form 4562. |

**43** When did you place your vehicle in service for business purposes? (month, day, year) ▶ ____ / ____ / ____

**44** Of the total number of miles you drove your vehicle during 2009, enter the number of miles you used your vehicle for:

**a** Business _____    **b** Commuting (see instructions) _____    **c** Other _____

**45** Was your vehicle available for personal use during off-duty hours? . . . . . . . . . . . . ☐ Yes    ☐ No

**46** Do you (or your spouse) have another vehicle available for personal use?. . . . . . . . . . ☐ Yes    ☐ No

**47a** Do you have evidence to support your deduction? . . . . . . . . . . . . . . . . ☐ Yes    ☐ No

**b** If "Yes," is the evidence written? . . . . . . . . . . . . . . . . . . . . . . ☐ Yes    ☐ No

| Part V | **Other Expenses.** List below business expenses not included on lines 8–26 or line 30. |

| | | |
|---|---|---|
| -------------------------------------- | | |
| -------------------------------------- | | |
| -------------------------------------- | | |
| -------------------------------------- | | |
| -------------------------------------- | | |
| -------------------------------------- | | |
| -------------------------------------- | | |
| -------------------------------------- | | |
| **48** Total other expenses. Enter here and on page 1, line 27 . . . . . . . . . . . . . | **48** | |

**SCHEDULE D**
**(Form 1040)**

Department of the Treasury
Internal Revenue Service (99)

# Capital Gains and Losses

► **Attach to Form 1040 or Form 1040NR.** ► **See Instructions for Schedule D (Form 1040).**
► **Use Schedule D-1 to list additional transactions for lines 1 and 8.**

OMB No. 1545-0074

**2009**

Attachment
Sequence No. **12**

Name(s) shown on return

Your social security number

---

**Part I    Short-Term Capital Gains and Losses—Assets Held One Year or Less**

| (a) Description of property (Example: 100 sh. XYZ Co.) | (b) Date acquired (Mo., day, yr.) | (c) Date sold (Mo., day, yr.) | (d) Sales price (see page D-7 of the instructions) | (e) Cost or other basis (see page D-7 of the instructions) | (f) Gain or (loss) Subtract (e) from (d) |
|---|---|---|---|---|---|
| **1** | | | | | |
| | | | | | |
| | | | | | |
| | | | | | |
| | | | | | |

**2** Enter your short-term totals, if any, from Schedule D-1, line 2 . . . . . . . . . . . . . . . . . . . . **2**

**3** **Total short-term sales price amounts.** Add lines 1 and 2 in column (d) . . . . . . . . . . . . . . . **3**

**4** Short-term gain from Form 6252 and short-term gain or (loss) from Forms 4684, 6781, and 8824 . . . **4**

**5** Net short-term gain or (loss) from partnerships, S corporations, estates, and trusts from Schedule(s) K-1 . . . . . . . . . . . . . . . . . . . . **5**

**6** Short-term capital loss carryover. Enter the amount, if any, from line 10 of your **Capital Loss Carryover Worksheet** on page D-7 of the instructions . . . . . . . . . . . . . . **6** ( )

**7** **Net short-term capital gain or (loss).** Combine lines 1 through 6 in column (f) . . . . . . **7**

---

**Part II    Long-Term Capital Gains and Losses—Assets Held More Than One Year**

| (a) Description of property (Example: 100 sh. XYZ Co.) | (b) Date acquired (Mo., day, yr.) | (c) Date sold (Mo., day, yr.) | (d) Sales price (see page D-7 of the instructions) | (e) Cost or other basis (see page D-7 of the instructions) | (f) Gain or (loss) Subtract (e) from (d) |
|---|---|---|---|---|---|
| **8** | | | | | |
| | | | | | |
| | | | | | |
| | | | | | |
| | | | | | |

**9** Enter your long-term totals, if any, from Schedule D-1, line 9 . . . . . . . . . . . . . . . . . . . . **9**

**10** **Total long-term sales price amounts.** Add lines 8 and 9 in column (d) . . . . . . . . . . . . . . . **10**

**11** Gain from Form 4797, Part I; long-term gain from Forms 2439 and 6252; and long-term gain or (loss) from Forms 4684, 6781, and 8824 . . . . . . . . . **11**

**12** Net long-term gain or (loss) from partnerships, S corporations, estates, and trusts from Schedule(s) K-1 . . . . . . . . . . . . . . . . . . . . **12**

**13** Capital gain distributions. See page D-2 of the instructions . . . . . . . . . . . . . **13**

**14** Long-term capital loss carryover. Enter the amount, if any, from line 15 of your **Capital Loss Carryover Worksheet** on page D-7 of the instructions . . . . . . . . . . . **14** ( )

**15** **Net long-term capital gain or (loss).** Combine lines 8 through 14 in column (f). Then go to Part III on the back . . . . . . . . . . . . . . . . . . . . **15**

---

For Paperwork Reduction Act Notice, see Form 1040 or Form 1040NR instructions.    Cat. No. 11338H    Schedule D (Form 1040) 2009

**Part III**    **Summary**

**16**  Combine lines 7 and 15 and enter the result . . . . . . . . . . . . . . . . . .    **16**

If line 16 is:
- A **gain**, enter the amount from line 16 on Form 1040, line 13, or Form 1040NR, line 14. Then go to line 17 below.
- A **loss**, skip lines 17 through 20 below. Then go to line 21. Also be sure to complete line 22.
- **Zero**, skip lines 17 through 21 below and enter -0- on Form 1040, line 13, or Form 1040NR, line 14. Then go to line 22.

**17**  Are lines 15 and 16 **both** gains?
☐ **Yes.** Go to line 18.
☐ **No.** Skip lines 18 through 21, and go to line 22.

**18**  Enter the amount, if any, from line 7 of the **28% Rate Gain Worksheet** on page D-8 of the instructions . . . . . . . . . . . . . . . . . . . . . . . . . ▶   **18**

**19**  Enter the amount, if any, from line 18 of the **Unrecaptured Section 1250 Gain Worksheet** on page D-9 of the instructions . . . . . . . . . . . . . . . . . . . . . ▶   **19**

**20**  Are lines 18 and 19 **both** zero or blank?
☐ **Yes.** Complete Form 1040 through line 43, or Form 1040NR through line 40. Then complete the **Qualified Dividends and Capital Gain Tax Worksheet** on page 39 of the Instructions for Form 1040 (or in the Instructions for Form 1040NR). **Do not** complete lines 21 and 22 below.

☐ **No.** Complete Form 1040 through line 43, or Form 1040NR through line 40. Then complete the **Schedule D Tax Worksheet** on page D-10 of the instructions. **Do not** complete lines 21 and 22 below.

**21**  If line 16 is a loss, enter here and on Form 1040, line 13, or Form 1040NR, line 14, the **smaller** of:

- The loss on line 16 or
- ($3,000), or if married filing separately, ($1,500)    } . . . . . . . . . . . . .    **21**  (                          )

**Note.** When figuring which amount is smaller, treat both amounts as positive numbers.

**22**  Do you have qualified dividends on Form 1040, line 9b, or Form 1040NR, line 10b?

☐ **Yes.** Complete Form 1040 through line 43, or Form 1040NR through line 40. Then complete the **Qualified Dividends and Capital Gain Tax Worksheet** on page 39 of the Instructions for Form 1040 (or in the Instructions for Form 1040NR).
☐ **No.** Complete the rest of Form 1040 or Form 1040NR.

**SCHEDULE E**
**(Form 1040)**

Department of the Treasury
Internal Revenue Service (99)

Name(s) shown on return

# Supplemental Income and Loss

(From rental real estate, royalties, partnerships,
S corporations, estates, trusts, REMICs, etc.)

▶ **Attach to Form 1040, 1040NR, or Form 1041.** ▶ See Instructions for Schedule E (Form 1040).

OMB No. 1545-0074

2009

Attachment
Sequence No. **13**

Your social security number

**Part I**    **Income or Loss From Rental Real Estate and Royalties**   **Note.** If you are in the business of renting personal property, use **Schedule C** or **C-EZ** (see page E-3). If you are an individual, report farm rental income or loss from **Form 4835** on page 2, line 40.

**1**   List the type and address of each **rental real estate property:**

A ----------------------------------------------------------

B ----------------------------------------------------------

C ----------------------------------------------------------

**2** For each rental real estate property listed on line 1, did you or your family use it during the tax year for personal purposes for more than the greater of:
- 14 days **or**
- 10% of the total days rented at fair rental value?
(See page E-3)

| | Yes | No |
|---|---|---|
| A | | |
| B | | |
| C | | |

**Income:**

| | | | Properties | | | Totals |
|---|---|---|---|---|---|---|
| | | | A | B | C | (Add columns A, B, and C.) |
| **3** | Rents received | 3 | | | | 3 |
| **4** | Royalties received | 4 | | | | 4 |

**Expenses:**

| | | | | | | |
|---|---|---|---|---|---|---|
| **5** | Advertising | 5 | | | | |
| **6** | Auto and travel (see page E-4) | 6 | | | | |
| **7** | Cleaning and maintenance | 7 | | | | |
| **8** | Commissions | 8 | | | | |
| **9** | Insurance | 9 | | | | |
| **10** | Legal and other professional fees | 10 | | | | |
| **11** | Management fees | 11 | | | | |
| **12** | Mortgage interest paid to banks, etc. (see page E-5) | 12 | | | | 12 |
| **13** | Other interest | 13 | | | | |
| **14** | Repairs | 14 | | | | |
| **15** | Supplies | 15 | | | | |
| **16** | Taxes | 16 | | | | |
| **17** | Utilities | 17 | | | | |
| **18** | Other (list) ▶ ----------- <br> ----------- <br> ----------- <br> ----------- | 18 | | | | |
| **19** | Add lines 5 through 18 | 19 | | | | 19 |
| **20** | Depreciation expense or depletion (see page E-5) | 20 | | | | 20 |
| **21** | Total expenses. Add lines 19 and 20 | 21 | | | | |
| **22** | Income or (loss) from rental real estate or royalty properties. Subtract line 21 from line 3 (rents) or line 4 (royalties). If the result is a (loss), see page E-5 to find out if you must file **Form 6198**. | 22 | | | | |
| **23** | Deductible rental real estate loss. **Caution.** Your rental real estate loss on line 22 may be limited. See page E-5 to find out if you must file **Form 8582.** Real estate professionals **must** complete line 43 on page 2 | 23 | ( ) | ( ) | ( ) | ( ) |
| **24** | **Income.** Add positive amounts shown on line 22. **Do not** include any losses | | | | 24 | |
| **25** | **Losses.** Add royalty losses from line 22 and rental real estate losses from line 23. Enter total losses here | | | | 25 | ( ) |
| **26** | **Total rental real estate and royalty income or (loss).** Combine lines 24 and 25. Enter the result here. If Parts II, III, IV, and line 40 on page 2 do not apply to you, also enter this amount on Form 1040, line 17, or Form 1040NR, line 18. Otherwise, include this amount in the total on line 41 on page 2 | | | | 26 | |

For Paperwork Reduction Act Notice, see page E-8 of the instructions.     Cat. No. 11344L     **Schedule E (Form 1040) 2009**

Schedule E (Form 1040) 2009 | Attachment Sequence No. **13** | Page **2**

Name(s) shown on return. Do not enter name and social security number if shown on other side. | **Your social security number**

**Caution.** The IRS compares amounts reported on your tax return with amounts shown on Schedule(s) K-1.

**Part II  Income or Loss From Partnerships and S Corporations**  **Note.** If you report a loss from an at-risk activity for which **any** amount is **not** at risk, you **must** check the box in column **(e)** on line 28 and attach **Form 6198.** See page E-1.

**27**  Are you reporting any loss not allowed in a prior year due to the at-risk or basis limitations, a prior year unallowed loss from a passive activity (if that loss was not reported on Form 8582), or unreimbursed partnership expenses? If you answered "Yes," see page E-7 before completing this section.  ☐ **Yes**  ☐ **No**

**28**

| (a) Name | (b) Enter P for partnership; S for S corporation | (c) Check if foreign partnership | (d) Employer identification number | (e) Check if any amount is not at risk |
|---|---|---|---|---|
| **A** | | ☐ | | ☐ |
| **B** | | ☐ | | ☐ |
| **C** | | ☐ | | ☐ |
| **D** | | ☐ | | ☐ |

| | Passive Income and Loss | | Nonpassive Income and Loss | | |
|---|---|---|---|---|---|
| | (f) Passive loss allowed (attach **Form 8582** if required) | (g) Passive income from **Schedule K–1** | (h) Nonpassive loss from **Schedule K–1** | (i) Section 179 expense deduction from **Form 4562** | (j) Nonpassive income from **Schedule K–1** |
| **A** | | | | | |
| **B** | | | | | |
| **C** | | | | | |
| **D** | | | | | |
| **29a** Totals | | | | | |
| **b** Totals | | | | | |

**30**  Add columns (g) and (j) of line 29a . . . . . . . . . . . . . . . . | **30** |

**31**  Add columns (f), (h), and (i) of line 29b . . . . . . . . . . . . | **31** ( | ) |

**32**  **Total partnership and S corporation income or (loss).** Combine lines 30 and 31. Enter the result here and include in the total on line 41 below . . . . . . . . . . . . . . | **32** |

**Part III  Income or Loss From Estates and Trusts**

**33**

| (a) Name | (b) Employer identification number |
|---|---|
| **A** | |
| **B** | |

| | Passive Income and Loss | | Nonpassive Income and Loss | |
|---|---|---|---|---|
| | (c) Passive deduction or loss allowed (attach **Form 8582** if required) | (d) Passive income from **Schedule K–1** | (e) Deduction or loss from **Schedule K–1** | (f) Other income from **Schedule K–1** |
| **A** | | | | |
| **B** | | | | |
| **34a** Totals | | | | |
| **b** Totals | | | | |

**35**  Add columns (d) and (f) of line 34a . . . . . . . . . . . . . . . | **35** |

**36**  Add columns (c) and (e) of line 34b . . . . . . . . . . . . . . | **36** ( | ) |

**37**  **Total estate and trust income or (loss).** Combine lines 35 and 36. Enter the result here and include in the total on line 41 below . . . . . . . . . . . . . . . . . . . | **37** |

**Part IV  Income or Loss From Real Estate Mortgage Investment Conduits (REMICs)—Residual Holder**

**38**

| (a) Name | (b) Employer identification number | (c) Excess inclusion from **Schedules Q,** line 2c (see page E-8) | (d) Taxable income (net loss) from **Schedules Q,** line 1b | (e) Income from **Schedules Q,** line 3b |
|---|---|---|---|---|
| | | | | |

**39**  Combine columns (d) and (e) only. Enter the result here and include in the total on line 41 below | **39** |

**Part V  Summary**

**40**  Net farm rental income or (loss) from **Form 4835.** Also, complete line 42 below . . . . . . | **40** |

**41**  Total income or (loss). Combine lines 26, 32, 37, 39, and 40. Enter the result here and on Form 1040, line 17, or Form 1040NR, line 18 ▶ | **41** |

**42**  **Reconciliation of farming and fishing income.** Enter your **gross** farming and fishing income reported on Form 4835, line 7; Schedule K-1 (Form 1065), box 14, code B; Schedule K-1 (Form 1120S), box 17, code U; and Schedule K-1 (Form 1041), line 14, code F (see page E-8) | **42** |

**43**  **Reconciliation for real estate professionals.** If you were a real estate professional (see page E-2), enter the net income or (loss) you reported anywhere on Form 1040 or Form 1040NR from all rental real estate activities in which you materially participated under the passive activity loss rules . . | **43** |

Schedule E (Form 1040) 2009

**SCHEDULE SE**
**(Form 1040)**

Department of the Treasury
Internal Revenue Service (99)

# Self-Employment Tax

► **Attach to Form 1040.**     ► **See Instructions for Schedule SE (Form 1040).**

OMB No. 1545-0074

**2009**

Attachment
Sequence No. **17**

Name of person with **self-employment** income (as shown on Form 1040)

Social security number of person
with **self-employment** income ►

## Who Must File Schedule SE

You must file Schedule SE if:

- You had net earnings from self-employment from **other than** church employee income (line 4 of Short Schedule SE or line 4c of Long Schedule SE) of $400 or more, **or**
- You had church employee income of $108.28 or more. Income from services you performed as a minister or a member of a religious order **is not** church employee income (see page SE-1).

**Note.** Even if you had a loss or a small amount of income from self-employment, it may be to your benefit to file Schedule SE and use either "optional method" in Part II of Long Schedule SE (see page SE-4).

**Exception.** If your only self-employment income was from earnings as a minister, member of a religious order, or Christian Science practitioner **and** you filed Form 4361 and received IRS approval not to be taxed on those earnings, **do not** file Schedule SE. Instead, write "Exempt—Form 4361" on Form 1040, line 56.

## May I Use Short Schedule SE or Must I Use Long Schedule SE?

**Note.** Use this flowchart **only if** you must file Schedule SE. If unsure, see *Who Must File Schedule SE,* above.

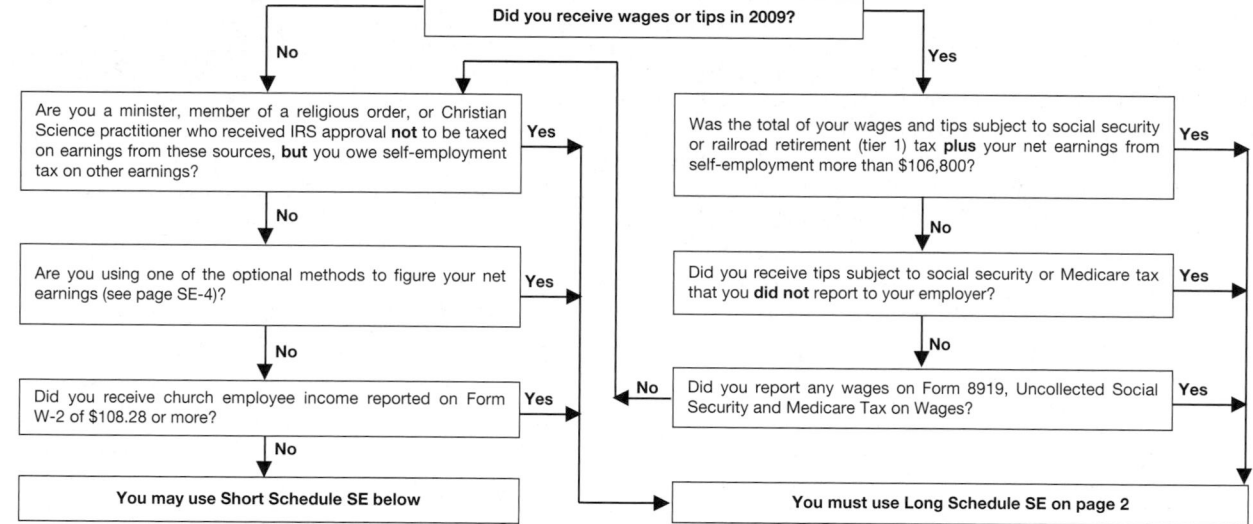

---

**Section A—Short Schedule SE. Caution.** Read above to see if you can use Short Schedule SE.

| | | |
|---|---|---|
| **1a** Net farm profit or (loss) from Schedule F, line 36, and farm partnerships, Schedule K-1 (Form 1065), box 14, code A . . . . . . . . . . . . . . . . . . | **1a** | |
| **b** If you received social security retirement or disability benefits, enter the amount of Conservation Reserve Program payments included on Schedule F, line 6b, or listed on Schedule K-1 (Form 1065), box 20, code Y | **1b** ( | ) |
| **2** Net profit or (loss) from Schedule C, line 31; Schedule C-EZ, line 3; Schedule K-1 (Form 1065), box 14, code A (other than farming); and Schedule K-1 (Form 1065-B), box 9, code J1. Ministers and members of religious orders, see page SE-1 for types of income to report on this line. See page SE-3 for other income to report . . . . . . . . . . | **2** | |
| **3** Combine lines 1a, 1b, and 2 . . . . . . . . . | **3** | |
| **4** **Net earnings from self-employment.** Multiply line 3 by 92.35% (.9235). If less than $400, **do not** file this schedule; you do not owe self-employment tax . . . . . . . . . . . ► | **4** | |
| **5** **Self-employment tax.** If the amount on line 4 is: <br> • $106,800 or less, multiply line 4 by 15.3% (.153). Enter the result here and on **Form 1040, line 56.** <br> • More than $106,800, multiply line 4 by 2.9% (.029). Then, add $13,243.20 to the result. <br> Enter the total here and on **Form 1040, line 56.** . . . . . . . . . . | **5** | |
| **6** **Deduction for one-half of self-employment tax.** Multiply line 5 by 50% (.50). Enter the result here and on **Form 1040, line 27** \| **6** \| | | |

For Paperwork Reduction Act Notice, see Form 1040 instructions.     Cat. No. 11358Z     Schedule SE (Form 1040) 2009

Attachment Sequence No. **17**    Page **2**

| Name of person with **self-employment** income (as shown on Form 1040) | Social security number of person with **self-employment** income ▶ |
|---|---|

## Section B—Long Schedule SE

### Part I    Self-Employment Tax

**Note.** If your only income subject to self-employment tax is **church employee income,** skip lines 1 through 4b. Enter -0- on line 4c and go to line 5a. Income from services you performed as a minister or a member of a religious order **is not** church employee income. See page SE-1.

**A**   If you are a minister, member of a religious order, or Christian Science practitioner **and** you filed Form 4361, but you had $400 or more of **other** net earnings from self-employment, check here and continue with Part I . . . . . . . ▶ ☐

| | | | | |
|---|---|---|---|---|
| **1a** | Net farm profit or (loss) from Schedule F, line 36, and farm partnerships, Schedule K-1 (Form 1065), box 14, code A. **Note.** Skip lines 1a and 1b if you use the farm optional method (see page SE-4) | **1a** | | |
| **b** | If you received social security retirement or disability benefits, enter the amount of Conservation Reserve Program payments included on Schedule F, line 6b, or listed on Schedule K-1 (Form 1065), box 20, code Y | **1b** | ( | ) |
| **2** | Net profit or (loss) from Schedule C, line 31; Schedule C-EZ, line 3; Schedule K-1 (Form 1065), box 14, code A (other than farming); and Schedule K-1 (Form 1065-B), box 9, code J1. Ministers and members of religious orders, see page SE-1 for types of income to report on this line. See page SE-3 for other income to report. **Note.** Skip this line if you use the nonfarm optional method (see page SE-4) . . . . . . . . . . . . . . | **2** | | |
| **3** | Combine lines 1a, 1b, and 2 . . . . . . . . . . . . . . | **3** | | |
| **4a** | If line 3 is more than zero, multiply line 3 by 92.35% (.9235). Otherwise, enter amount from line 3 | **4a** | | |
| **b** | If you elect one or both of the optional methods, enter the total of lines 15 and 17 here . . | **4b** | | |
| **c** | Combine lines 4a and 4b. If less than $400, **stop;** you do not owe self-employment tax. **Exception.** If less than $400 and you had **church employee income,** enter -0- and continue ▶ | **4c** | | |
| **5a** | Enter your **church employee income** from Form W-2. See page SE-1 for definition of church employee income. . . . . .   **5a** | | | |
| **b** | Multiply line 5a by 92.35% (.9235). If less than $100, enter -0- . . . . . . . . . | **5b** | | |
| **6** | **Net earnings from self-employment.** Add lines 4c and 5b . . . . . . . . . | **6** | | |
| **7** | Maximum amount of combined wages and self-employment earnings subject to social security tax or the 6.2% portion of the 7.65% railroad retirement (tier 1) tax for 2009 . . . . . . | **7** | 106,800 | 00 |
| **8a** | Total social security wages and tips (total of boxes 3 and 7 on Form(s) W-2) and railroad retirement (tier 1) compensation. If $106,800 or more, skip lines 8b through 10, and go to line 11   **8a** | | | |
| **b** | Unreported tips subject to social security tax (from Form 4137, line 10)   **8b** | | | |
| **c** | Wages subject to social security tax (from Form 8919, line 10)   **8c** | | | |
| **d** | Add lines 8a, 8b, and 8c . . . . . . . . . . . . . . . | **8d** | | |
| **9** | Subtract line 8d from line 7. If zero or less, enter -0- here and on line 10 and go to line 11   . ▶ | **9** | | |
| **10** | Multiply the **smaller** of line 6 or line 9 by 12.4% (.124) . . . . . . . . | **10** | | |
| **11** | Multiply line 6 by 2.9% (.029) . . . . . . . . . . . . . | **11** | | |
| **12** | **Self-employment tax.** Add lines 10 and 11. Enter here and on **Form 1040, line 56.** . . . | **12** | | |
| **13** | **Deduction for one-half of self-employment tax.** Multiply line 12 by 50% (.50). Enter the result here and on **Form 1040, line 27** .   **13** | | | |

### Part II    Optional Methods To Figure Net Earnings (see page SE-4)

**Farm Optional Method.** You may use this method **only** if **(a)** your gross farm income[1] was not more than $6,540, **or (b)** your net farm profits[2] were less than $4,721.

| | | | | |
|---|---|---|---|---|
| **14** | Maximum income for optional methods | **14** | 4,360 | 00 |
| **15** | Enter the **smaller** of: two-thirds ($^2/_3$) of gross farm income[1] (not less than zero) **or** $4,360. Also include this amount on line 4b above . . . . . . . . . . . . . . | **15** | | |

**Nonfarm Optional Method.** You may use this method **only** if **(a)** your net nonfarm profits[3] were less than $4,721 and also less than 72.189% of your gross nonfarm income,[4] **and (b)** you had net earnings from self-employment of at least $400 in 2 of the prior 3 years. **Caution.** You may use this method no more than five times.

| | | | | |
|---|---|---|---|---|
| **16** | Subtract line 15 from line 14 . . . . . . . . . . . . . | **16** | | |
| **17** | Enter the **smaller** of: two-thirds ($^2/_3$) of gross nonfarm income[4] (not less than zero) **or** the amount on line 16. Also include this amount on line 4b above . . . . . . . . . . | **17** | | |

[1] From Sch. F, line 11, and Sch. K-1 (Form 1065), box 14, code B.

[2] From Sch. F, line 36, and Sch. K-1 (Form 1065), box 14, code A— minus the amount you would have entered on line 1b had you not used the optional method.

[3] From Sch. C, line 31; Sch. C-EZ, line 3; Sch. K-1 (Form 1065), box 14, code A; and Sch. K-1 (Form 1065-B), box 9, code J1.

[4] From Sch. C, line 7; Sch. C-EZ, line 1; Sch. K-1 (Form 1065), box 14, code C; and Sch. K-1 (Form 1065-B), box 9, code J2.

# Form **1065**

Department of the Treasury
Internal Revenue Service

## U.S. Return of Partnership Income

For calendar year 2009, or tax year beginning _____ , 2009, ending _____ , 20 _____ .

▶ See separate instructions.

OMB No. 1545-0099

**2009**

| | | |
|---|---|---|
| **A** Principal business activity | **Use the IRS label. Other-wise, print or type.** | Name of partnership |
| **B** Principal product or service | | Number, street, and room or suite no. If a P.O. box, see the instructions. |
| **C** Business code number | | City or town, state, and ZIP code |

**D** Employer identification number

**E** Date business started

**F** Total assets (see the instructions)
$

**G** Check applicable boxes: **(1)** ☐ Initial return  **(2)** ☐ Final return  **(3)** ☐ Name change  **(4)** ☐ Address change  **(5)** ☐ Amended return
　**(6)** ☐ Technical termination - also check (1) or (2)

**H** Check accounting method: **(1)** ☐ Cash  **(2)** ☐ Accrual  **(3)** ☐ Other (specify) ▶ _____

**I** Number of Schedules K-1. Attach one for each person who was a partner at any time during the tax year ▶ _____

**J** Check if Schedules C and M-3 are attached . . . . . . . . . . . . . . . . . . . . . . . ☐

**Caution.** *Include **only** trade or business income and expenses on lines 1a through 22 below. See the instructions for more information.*

| | | |
|---|---|---|
| **Income** | **1a** Gross receipts or sales . . . . . . . . . . . | **1a** |
| | **b** Less returns and allowances . . . . . . . . . | **1b** ／ **1c** |
| | **2** Cost of goods sold (Schedule A, line 8) . . . . . . . . . . | **2** |
| | **3** Gross profit. Subtract line 2 from line 1c . . . . . . . . . . | **3** |
| | **4** Ordinary income (loss) from other partnerships, estates, and trusts *(attach statement)* . . | **4** |
| | **5** Net farm profit (loss) *(attach Schedule F (Form 1040))* . . . . . . | **5** |
| | **6** Net gain (loss) from Form 4797, Part II, line 17 *(attach Form 4797)* . . . . . | **6** |
| | **7** Other income (loss) *(attach statement)* . . . . . . . . . . | **7** |
| | **8** **Total income (loss).** Combine lines 3 through 7 . . . . . . . . | **8** |
| **Deductions** (see the instructions for limitations) | **9** Salaries and wages (other than to partners) (less employment credits) . . . . . . | **9** |
| | **10** Guaranteed payments to partners . . . . . . . . . . | **10** |
| | **11** Repairs and maintenance . . . . . . . . . . . | **11** |
| | **12** Bad debts . . . . . . . . . . . . . . | **12** |
| | **13** Rent . . . . . . . . . . . . . . . | **13** |
| | **14** Taxes and licenses . . . . . . . . . . . . | **14** |
| | **15** Interest . . . . . . . . . . . . . . | **15** |
| | **16a** Depreciation *(if required, attach Form 4562)* . . . . . . **16a** | |
| | **b** Less depreciation reported on Schedule A and elsewhere on return **16b** | **16c** |
| | **17** Depletion **(Do not deduct oil and gas depletion.)** . . . . . . | **17** |
| | **18** Retirement plans, etc. . . . . . . . . . . . | **18** |
| | **19** Employee benefit programs . . . . . . . . . . | **19** |
| | **20** Other deductions *(attach statement)* . . . . . . . . | **20** |
| | **21** **Total deductions.** Add the amounts shown in the far right column for lines 9 through 20 . | **21** |
| | **22** **Ordinary business income (loss).** Subtract line 21 from line 8 . . . . . . . . | **22** |

**Sign Here**

Under penalties of perjury, I declare that I have examined this return, including accompanying schedules and statements, and to the best of my knowledge and belief, it is true, correct, and complete. Declaration of preparer (other than general partner or limited liability company member manager) is based on all information of which preparer has any knowledge.

▶ _____
Signature of general partner or limited liability company member manager

▶ _____
Date

May the IRS discuss this return with the preparer shown below (see instructions)? ☐ Yes ☐ No

**Paid Preparer's Use Only**

| | | Date | | Preparer's SSN or PTIN |
|---|---|---|---|---|
| Preparer's signature | | | Check if self-employed ▶ ☐ | |
| Firm's name (or yours if self-employed), address, and ZIP code | ▶ | | EIN ▶ | |
| | | | Phone no. | |

**For Privacy Act and Paperwork Reduction Act Notice, see separate instructions.**

Cat. No. 11390Z

Form **1065** (2009)

Form 1065 (2009)                                                                          Page **2**

## Schedule A    Cost of Goods Sold (see the instructions)

| | | | |
|---|---|---|---|
| 1 | Inventory at beginning of year | 1 | |
| 2 | Purchases less cost of items withdrawn for personal use | 2 | |
| 3 | Cost of labor | 3 | |
| 4 | Additional section 263A costs (*attach statement*) | 4 | |
| 5 | Other costs (*attach statement*) | 5 | |
| 6 | **Total.** Add lines 1 through 5 | 6 | |
| 7 | Inventory at end of year | 7 | |
| 8 | **Cost of goods sold.** Subtract line 7 from line 6. Enter here and on page 1, line 2 | 8 | |

**9a** Check all methods used for valuing closing inventory:

    **(i)** ☐ Cost as described in Regulations section 1.471-3

    **(ii)** ☐ Lower of cost or market as described in Regulations section 1.471-4

    **(iii)** ☐ Other (specify method used and attach explanation) ▶ _____

  **b** Check this box if there was a writedown of "subnormal" goods as described in Regulations section 1.471-2(c)    ▶ ☐

  **c** Check this box if the LIFO inventory method was adopted this tax year for any goods (*if checked, attach Form 970*)   ▶ ☐

  **d** Do the rules of section 263A (for property produced or acquired for resale) apply to the partnership?      ☐ Yes   ☐ No

  **e** Was there any change in determining quantities, cost, or valuations between opening and closing inventory?    ☐ Yes   ☐ No
     If "Yes," attach explanation.

## Schedule B    Other Information

| | | Yes | No |
|---|---|---|---|
| **1** | What type of entity is filing this return? Check the applicable box: | | |

  **a** ☐ Domestic general partnership          **b** ☐ Domestic limited partnership

  **c** ☐ Domestic limited liability company     **d** ☐ Domestic limited liability partnership

  **e** ☐ Foreign partnership                 **f** ☐ Other ▶ _____

**2**   At any time during the tax year, was any partner in the partnership a disregarded entity, a partnership (including an entity treated as a partnership), a trust, an S corporation, an estate (other than an estate of a deceased partner), or a nominee or similar person?

**3**   At the end of the tax year:

  **a** Did any foreign or domestic corporation, partnership (including any entity treated as a partnership), trust, or tax-exempt organization own, directly or indirectly, an interest of 50% or more in the profit, loss, or capital of the partnership? For rules of constructive ownership, see instructions. If "Yes," attach Schedule B-1, Information on Partners Owning 50% or More of the Partnership

  **b** Did any individual or estate own, directly or indirectly, an interest of 50% or more in the profit, loss, or capital of the partnership? For rules of constructive ownership, see instructions. If "Yes," attach Schedule B-1, Information on Partners Owning 50% or More of the Partnership

**4**   At the end of the tax year, did the partnership:

  **a** Own directly 20% or more, or own, directly or indirectly, 50% or more of the total voting power of all classes of stock entitled to vote of any foreign or domestic corporation? For rules of constructive ownership, see instructions. If "Yes," complete (i) through (iv) below

| (i) Name of Corporation | (ii) Employer Identification Number (if any) | (iii) Country of Incorporation | (iv) Percentage Owned in Voting Stock |
|---|---|---|---|
| | | | |
| | | | |
| | | | |
| | | | |

  **b** Own directly an interest of 20% or more, or own, directly or indirectly, an interest of 50% or more in the profit, loss, or capital in any foreign or domestic partnership (including an entity treated as a partnership) or in the beneficial interest of a trust? For rules of constructive ownership, see instructions. If "Yes," complete (i) through (v) below

| (i) Name of Entity | (ii) Employer Identification Number (if any) | (iii) Type of Entity | (iv) Country of Organization | (v) Maximum Percentage Owned in Profit, Loss, or Capital |
|---|---|---|---|---|
| | | | | |
| | | | | |
| | | | | |
| | | | | |

Form **1065** (2009)

651109

☐ Final K-1          ☐ Amended K-1          OMB No. 1545-0099

**Schedule K-1**
**(Form 1065)**

20**09**

Department of the Treasury
Internal Revenue Service

For calendar year 2009, or tax

year beginning _____ , 2009

ending _____ , 20 _____

## Partner's Share of Income, Deductions,
## Credits, etc.          ► See back of form and separate instructions.

| **Part I** | **Information About the Partnership** |
|---|---|

**A**    Partnership's employer identification number

**B**    Partnership's name, address, city, state, and ZIP code

**C**    IRS Center where partnership filed return

**D**    ☐ Check if this is a publicly traded partnership (PTP)

| **Part II** | **Information About the Partner** |
|---|---|

**E**    Partner's identifying number

**F**    Partner's name, address, city, state, and ZIP code

**G**    ☐ General partner or LLC          ☐ Limited partner or other LLC
         member-manager                        member

**H**    ☐ Domestic partner               ☐ Foreign partner

**I**    What type of entity is this partner? _____

**J**    Partner's share of profit, loss, and capital (see instructions):

|  | **Beginning** | **Ending** |
|---|---|---|
| Profit | _____ % | _____ % |
| Loss | _____ % | _____ % |
| Capital | _____ % | _____ % |

**K**    Partner's share of liabilities at year end:

Nonrecourse . . . . . . . $ _____

Qualified nonrecourse financing . $ _____

Recourse . . . . . . . $ _____

**L**    Partner's capital account analysis:

Beginning capital account . . . $ _____

Capital contributed during the year $ _____

Current year increase (decrease) . $ _____

Withdrawals & distributions . . $ ( _____ )

Ending capital account . . . . $ _____

☐ Tax basis     ☐ GAAP     ☐ Section 704(b) book
☐ Other (explain)

**M**    Did the partner contribute property with a built-in gain or loss?
☐ Yes          ☐ No
If "Yes", attach statement (see instructions)

| **Part III** | **Partner's Share of Current Year Income, Deductions, Credits, and Other Items** |
|---|---|

| 1 | Ordinary business income (loss) | 15 | Credits |
|---|---|---|---|
| 2 | Net rental real estate income (loss) | | |
| 3 | Other net rental income (loss) | 16 | Foreign transactions |
| 4 | Guaranteed payments | | |
| 5 | Interest income | | |
| 6a | Ordinary dividends | | |
| 6b | Qualified dividends | | |
| 7 | Royalties | | |
| 8 | Net short-term capital gain (loss) | | |
| 9a | Net long-term capital gain (loss) | 17 | Alternative minimum tax (AMT) items |
| 9b | Collectibles (28%) gain (loss) | | |
| 9c | Unrecaptured section 1250 gain | | |
| 10 | Net section 1231 gain (loss) | 18 | Tax-exempt income and nondeductible expenses |
| 11 | Other income (loss) | | |
| | | 19 | Distributions |
| 12 | Section 179 deduction | | |
| 13 | Other deductions | 20 | Other information |
| 14 | Self-employment earnings (loss) | | |

*See attached statement for additional information.

For IRS Use Only

| Form **1120**<br>Department of the Treasury<br>Internal Revenue Service | **U.S. Corporation Income Tax Return**<br>For calendar year 2009 or tax year beginning _____ , 2009, ending _____ , 20 _____<br>▶ See separate instructions. | OMB No. 1545-0123<br>**2009** |
|---|---|---|

**A  Check if:**

1a Consolidated return (attach Form 851) . ☐
 b Life/nonlife consolidated return . . ☐
2 Personal holding co. (attach Sch. PH) . ☐
3 Personal service corp. (see instructions) . ☐
4 Schedule M-3 attached ☐

**Use IRS label. Otherwise, print or type.**

Name

Number, street, and room or suite no. If a P.O. box, see instructions.

City or town, state, and ZIP code

**B** Employer identification number

**C** Date incorporated

**D** Total assets (see instructions)
$

**E** Check if: **(1)** ☐ Initial return  **(2)** ☐ Final return  **(3)** ☐ Name change  **(4)** ☐ Address change

### Income

| | | |
|---|---|---|
| **1a** | Gross receipts or sales _____ **b** Less returns and allowances _____ c Bal ▶ | **1c** |
| **2** | Cost of goods sold (Schedule A, line 8) . . . . . . . . . . . . . . . | **2** |
| **3** | Gross profit. Subtract line 2 from line 1c . . . . . . . . . . . . . . | **3** |
| **4** | Dividends (Schedule C, line 19) . . . . . . . . . . . . . . . . | **4** |
| **5** | Interest . . . . . . . . . . . . . . . . . . . . . . . | **5** |
| **6** | Gross rents . . . . . . . . . . . . . . . . . . . . . | **6** |
| **7** | Gross royalties . . . . . . . . . . . . . . . . . . . . | **7** |
| **8** | Capital gain net income (attach Schedule D (Form 1120)) . . . . . . . . . | **8** |
| **9** | Net gain or (loss) from Form 4797, Part II, line 17 (attach Form 4797) . . . . . . | **9** |
| **10** | Other income (see instructions—attach schedule) . . . . . . . . . . . | **10** |
| **11** | **Total income.** Add lines 3 through 10 . . . . . . . . . . . . ▶ | **11** |

### Deductions (See instructions for limitations on deductions.)

| | | |
|---|---|---|
| **12** | Compensation of officers (Schedule E, line 4) . . . . . . . . . . ▶ | **12** |
| **13** | Salaries and wages (less employment credits) . . . . . . . . . . . . | **13** |
| **14** | Repairs and maintenance . . . . . . . . . . . . . . . . . | **14** |
| **15** | Bad debts . . . . . . . . . . . . . . . . . . . . . | **15** |
| **16** | Rents . . . . . . . . . . . . . . . . . . . . . . | **16** |
| **17** | Taxes and licenses . . . . . . . . . . . . . . . . . . | **17** |
| **18** | Interest . . . . . . . . . . . . . . . . . . . . . . | **18** |
| **19** | Charitable contributions . . . . . . . . . . . . . . . . . | **19** |
| **20** | Depreciation from Form 4562 not claimed on Schedule A or elsewhere on return (attach Form 4562) . . . | **20** |
| **21** | Depletion . . . . . . . . . . . . . . . . . . . . . | **21** |
| **22** | Advertising . . . . . . . . . . . . . . . . . . . . . | **22** |
| **23** | Pension, profit-sharing, etc., plans . . . . . . . . . . . . . . | **23** |
| **24** | Employee benefit programs . . . . . . . . . . . . . . . . | **24** |
| **25** | Domestic production activities deduction (attach Form 8903) . . . . . . . . | **25** |
| **26** | Other deductions (attach schedule) . . . . . . . . . . . . . . | **26** |
| **27** | **Total deductions.** Add lines 12 through 26 . . . . . . . . . . ▶ | **27** |
| **28** | Taxable income before net operating loss deduction and special deductions. Subtract line 27 from line 11 . . | **28** |
| **29** | **Less: a** Net operating loss deduction (see instructions) . . . . . . **29a** | |
| | **b** Special deductions (Schedule C, line 20) . . . . . . . . **29b** | **29c** |

### Tax, Refundable Credits, and Payments

| | | |
|---|---|---|
| **30** | **Taxable income.** Subtract line 29c from line 28 (see instructions) . . . . . . . . | **30** |
| **31** | **Total tax** (Schedule J, line 10) . . . . . . . . . . . . . . . | **31** |
| **32a** | 2008 overpayment credited to 2009 . . **32a** | |
| **b** | 2009 estimated tax payments . . . . **32b** | |
| **c** | 2009 refund applied for on Form 4466 . . **32c** ( _____ ) d Bal ▶ **32d** | |
| **e** | Tax deposited with Form 7004 . . . . . **32e** | |
| **f** | Credits: **(1)** Form 2439 _____ **(2)** Form 4136 _____ **32f** | |
| **g** | Refundable credits from Form 3800, line 19c, and Form 8827, line 8c . . . **32g** | **32h** |
| **33** | Estimated tax penalty (see instructions). Check if Form 2220 is attached . . . . . . . ▶ ☐ | **33** |
| **34** | **Amount owed.** If line 32h is smaller than the total of lines 31 and 33, enter amount owed . . . . | **34** |
| **35** | **Overpayment.** If line 32h is larger than the total of lines 31 and 33, enter amount overpaid . . . . . | **35** |
| **36** | Enter amount from line 35 you want: **Credited to 2010 estimated tax** ▶ _____ Refunded ▶ | **36** |

**Sign Here** ▶

Under penalties of perjury, I declare that I have examined this return, including accompanying schedules and statements, and to the best of my knowledge and belief, it is true, correct, and complete. Declaration of preparer (other than taxpayer) is based on all information of which preparer has any knowledge.

_____    _____    ▶ _____
Signature of officer              Date                Title

May the IRS discuss this return with the preparer shown below (see instructions)? ☐ **Yes** ☐ **No**

**Paid Preparer's Use Only**

| Preparer's signature ▶ | Date | Check if self-employed ☐ | Preparer's SSN or PTIN |
|---|---|---|---|
| Firm's name (or yours if self-employed), address, and ZIP code ▶ | | EIN | |
| | | Phone no. | |

**For Privacy Act and Paperwork Reduction Act Notice, see separate instructions.**    Cat. No. 11450Q    Form **1120** (2009)

Form **1120S**

Department of the Treasury
Internal Revenue Service

# U.S. Income Tax Return for an S Corporation

▶ Do not file this form unless the corporation has filed or is attaching Form 2553 to elect to be an S corporation.
▶ See separate instructions.

OMB No. 1545-0130

**2009**

For calendar year 2009 or tax year beginning _____ , 2009, ending _____ , 20 ___

| | |
|---|---|
| **A** S election effective date | **Use IRS label. Otherwise, print or type.** |
| **B** Business activity code number *(see instructions)* | |
| **C** Check if Sch. M-3 attached ☐ | |

Name

Number, street, and room or suite no. If a P.O. box, see instructions.

City or town, state, and ZIP code

**D** Employer identification number

**E** Date incorporated

**F** Total assets *(see instructions)*
$

**G** Is the corporation electing to be an S corporation beginning with this tax year? ☐ Yes ☐ No   If "Yes," attach Form 2553 if not already filed

**H** Check if: **(1)** ☐ Final return **(2)** ☐ Name change **(3)** ☐ Address change
**(4)** ☐ Amended return **(5)** ☐ S election termination or revocation

**I** Enter the number of shareholders who were shareholders during any part of the tax year . . . . . . . . . . ▶

**Caution.** *Include **only** trade or business income and expenses on lines 1a through 21. See the instructions for more information.*

## Income

| | | | |
|---|---|---|---|
| **1a** | Gross receipts or sales [_____] **b** Less returns and allowances [_____] **c** Bal ▶ | **1c** | |
| **2** | Cost of goods sold (Schedule A, line 8) . . . . . . . . . . . . | **2** | |
| **3** | Gross profit. Subtract line 2 from line 1c . . . . . . . . . . . | **3** | |
| **4** | Net gain (loss) from Form 4797, Part II, line 17 *(attach Form 4797)* . . . . | **4** | |
| **5** | Other income (loss) *(see instructions—attach statement)* . . . . . . . | **5** | |
| **6** | **Total income (loss).** Add lines 3 through 5 . . . . . . . . . . . ▶ | **6** | |

## Deductions (see instructions for limitations)

| | | | |
|---|---|---|---|
| **7** | Compensation of officers . . . . . . . . . . . . . . . | **7** | |
| **8** | Salaries and wages (less employment credits) . . . . . . . . . . | **8** | |
| **9** | Repairs and maintenance . . . . . . . . . . . . . . . | **9** | |
| **10** | Bad debts . . . . . . . . . . . . . . . . . . . | **10** | |
| **11** | Rents . . . . . . . . . . . . . . . . . . . . | **11** | |
| **12** | Taxes and licenses . . . . . . . . . . . . . . . . | **12** | |
| **13** | Interest . . . . . . . . . . . . . . . . . . . | **13** | |
| **14** | Depreciation not claimed on Schedule A or elsewhere on return *(attach Form 4562)* . . | **14** | |
| **15** | Depletion **(Do not deduct oil and gas depletion.)** . . . . . . . . | **15** | |
| **16** | Advertising . . . . . . . . . . . . . . . . . . | **16** | |
| **17** | Pension, profit-sharing, etc., plans . . . . . . . . . . . . | **17** | |
| **18** | Employee benefit programs . . . . . . . . . . . . . . | **18** | |
| **19** | Other deductions *(attach statement)* . . . . . . . . . . . | **19** | |
| **20** | **Total deductions.** Add lines 7 through 19 . . . . . . . . . ▶ | **20** | |
| **21** | **Ordinary business income (loss).** Subtract line 20 from line 6 . . . . . . | **21** | |

## Tax and Payments

| | | | | |
|---|---|---|---|---|
| **22a** | Excess net passive income or LIFO recapture tax *(see instructions)* . . | **22a** | | |
| **b** | Tax from Schedule D (Form 1120S) . . . . . . . . | **22b** | | |
| **c** | Add lines 22a and 22b *(see instructions for additional taxes)* . . . . | | **22c** | |
| **23a** | 2009 estimated tax payments and 2008 overpayment credited to 2009 | **23a** | | |
| **b** | Tax deposited with Form 7004 . . . . . . . . . | **23b** | | |
| **c** | Credit for federal tax paid on fuels *(attach Form 4136)* . . . . | **23c** | | |
| **d** | Add lines 23a through 23c . . . . . . . . . . . . . ▶ | | **23d** | |
| **24** | Estimated tax penalty *(see instructions)*. Check if Form 2220 is attached . . . . . . . ▶ ☐ | | **24** | |
| **25** | **Amount owed.** If line 23d is smaller than the total of lines 22c and 24, enter amount owed . . | | **25** | |
| **26** | **Overpayment.** If line 23d is larger than the total of lines 22c and 24, enter amount overpaid . . | | **26** | |
| **27** | Enter amount from line 26 **Credited to 2010 estimated tax** ▶ [_____] **Refunded** ▶ | | **27** | |

**Sign Here**

Under penalties of perjury, I declare that I have examined this return, including accompanying schedules and statements, and to the best of my knowledge and belief, it is true, correct, and complete. Declaration of preparer (other than taxpayer) is based on all information of which preparer has any knowledge.

▶ _____   _____   ▶ _____
Signature of officer                Date                Title

May the IRS discuss this return with the preparer shown below *(see instructions)*? ☐ Yes ☐ No

**Paid Preparer's Use Only**

| | | | |
|---|---|---|---|
| Preparer's signature ▶ | Date | Check if self-employed ☐ | Preparer's SSN or PTIN |
| Firm's name (or yours if self-employed), address, and ZIP code ▶ | | EIN | |
| | | Phone no. | |

**For Privacy Act and Paperwork Reduction Act Notice, see separate instructions.**   Cat. No. 11510H   Form **1120S** (2009)

671109

☐ Final K-1    ☐ Amended K-1    OMB No. 1545-0130

**Schedule K-1**
**(Form 1120S)**
Department of the Treasury
Internal Revenue Service

20**09**

For calendar year 2009, or tax
year beginning _____, 2009
ending _____, 20_____

**Shareholder's Share of Income, Deductions, Credits, etc.**    ▶ See back of form and separate instructions.

| Part I | Information About the Corporation |
| --- | --- |

**A**  Corporation's employer identification number

**B**  Corporation's name, address, city, state, and ZIP code

**C**  IRS Center where corporation filed return

| Part II | Information About the Shareholder |
| --- | --- |

**D**  Shareholder's identifying number

**E**  Shareholder's name, address, city, state, and ZIP code

**F**  Shareholder's percentage of stock
ownership for tax year _____ %

For IRS Use Only

| Part III | Shareholder's Share of Current Year Income, Deductions, Credits, and Other Items |
| --- | --- |

| | | | |
| --- | --- | --- | --- |
| 1 | Ordinary business income (loss) | 13 | Credits |
| 2 | Net rental real estate income (loss) | | |
| 3 | Other net rental income (loss) | | |
| 4 | Interest income | | |
| 5a | Ordinary dividends | | |
| 5b | Qualified dividends | 14 | Foreign transactions |
| 6 | Royalties | | |
| 7 | Net short-term capital gain (loss) | | |
| 8a | Net long-term capital gain (loss) | | |
| 8b | Collectibles (28%) gain (loss) | | |
| 8c | Unrecaptured section 1250 gain | | |
| 9 | Net section 1231 gain (loss) | | |
| 10 | Other income (loss) | 15 | Alternative minimum tax (AMT) items |
| 11 | Section 179 deduction | 16 | Items affecting shareholder basis |
| 12 | Other deductions | | |
| | | 17 | Other information |

\* See attached statement for additional information.

For Paperwork Reduction Act Notice, see Instructions for Form 1120S.    Cat. No. 11520D    Schedule K-1 (Form 1120S) 2009

| | | |
|---|---|---|
| **SCHEDULE M-3**<br>**(Form 1120)**<br><br>Department of the Treasury<br>Internal Revenue Service | **Net Income (Loss) Reconciliation for Corporations**<br>**With Total Assets of $10 Million or More**<br>► **Attach to Form 1120 or 1120-C.**<br>► **See separate instructions.** | OMB No. 1545-0123<br><br>20**09** |

| Name of corporation (common parent, if consolidated return) | Employer identification number |
|---|---|
| | |

Check applicable box(es):   (1) ☐ Non-consolidated return   (2) ☐ Consolidated return (Form 1120 only)

(3) ☐ Mixed 1120/L/PC group   (4) ☐ Dormant subsidiaries schedule attached

**Part I**   **Financial Information and Net Income (Loss) Reconciliation** (see instructions)

**1a** Did the corporation file SEC Form 10-K for its income statement period ending with or within this tax year?
   ☐ **Yes.**  Skip lines 1b and 1c and complete lines 2a through 11 with respect to that SEC Form 10-K.
   ☐ **No.**   Go to line 1b. See instructions if multiple non-tax-basis income statements are prepared.

  **b** Did the corporation prepare a certified audited non-tax-basis income statement for that period?
   ☐ **Yes.**  Skip line 1c and complete lines 2a through 11 with respect to that income statement.
   ☐ **No.**   Go to line 1c.

  **c** Did the corporation prepare a non-tax-basis income statement for that period?
   ☐ **Yes.**  Complete lines 2a through 11 with respect to that income statement.
   ☐ **No.**   Skip lines 2a through 3c and enter the corporation's net income (loss) per its books and records on line 4a.

**2a** Enter the income statement period: Beginning  MM/DD/YYYY   Ending  MM/DD/YYYY

  **b** Has the corporation's income statement been restated for the income statement period on line 2a?
   ☐ **Yes.**  (If "Yes," attach an explanation and the amount of each item restated.)
   ☐ **No.**

  **c** Has the corporation's income statement been restated for any of the five income statement periods preceding the period on line 2a?
   ☐ **Yes.**  (If "Yes," attach an explanation and the amount of each item restated.)
   ☐ **No.**

**3a** Is any of the corporation's voting common stock publicly traded?
   ☐ **Yes.**
   ☐ **No.**   If "No," go to line 4a.

  **b** Enter the symbol of the corporation's primary U.S. publicly traded voting common stock . . . . . . . . . . . . . . . . . . . . . . . . . . ☐☐☐☐☐

  **c** Enter the nine-digit CUSIP number of the corporation's primary publicly traded voting common stock . . . . . . . . . . . . . . . . . . . . . ☐☐☐☐☐☐☐☐☐

| | | | |
|---|---|---|---|
| **4a** | Worldwide consolidated net income (loss) from income statement source identified in Part I, line 1 . . | **4a** | |
| **b** | Indicate accounting standard used for line 4a (see instructions):<br>(1) ☐ GAAP   (2) ☐ IFRS   (3) ☐ Statutory   (4) ☐ Tax-basis   (5) ☐ Other (specify) _____ | | |
| **5a** | Net income from nonincludible foreign entities (attach schedule) . . . . . . . . . . . . | **5a** | (        ) |
| **b** | Net loss from nonincludible foreign entities (attach schedule and enter as a positive amount) . . . . | **5b** | |
| **6a** | Net income from nonincludible U.S. entities (attach schedule) . . . . . . . . . . . . | **6a** | (        ) |
| **b** | Net loss from nonincludible U.S. entities (attach schedule and enter as a positive amount) . . . . . | **6b** | |
| **7a** | Net income (loss) of other includible foreign disregarded entities (attach schedule) . . . . . . | **7a** | |
| **b** | Net income (loss) of other includible U.S. disregarded entities (attach schedule) . . . . . . | **7b** | |
| **c** | Net income (loss) of other includible entities (attach schedule) . . . . . . . . . . . . | **7c** | |
| **8** | Adjustment to eliminations of transactions between includible entities and nonincludible entities (attach schedule) . . . . . . . . . . . . . . . . . . . . . . . . . . . . . | **8** | |
| **9** | Adjustment to reconcile income statement period to tax year (attach schedule) . . . . . . . | **9** | |
| **10a** | Intercompany dividend adjustments to reconcile to line 11 (attach schedule) . . . . . . . | **10a** | |
| **b** | Other statutory accounting adjustments to reconcile to line 11 (attach schedule) . . . . . . . | **10b** | |
| **c** | Other adjustments to reconcile to amount on line 11 (attach schedule) . . . . . . . . . | **10c** | |
| **11** | **Net income (loss) per income statement of includible corporations.** Combine lines 4 through 10 . . . | **11** | |

**Note.** Part I, line 11, must equal the amount on Part II, line 30, column (a), and Schedule M-2, line 2.

**12** Enter the total amount (not just the corporation's share) of the assets and liabilities of all entities included or removed on the following lines.

| | Total Assets | Total Liabilities |
|---|---|---|
| **a** Included on Part I, line 4 . . . . . . . ► | | |
| **b** Removed on Part I, line 5 . . . . . . . ► | | |
| **c** Removed on Part I, line 6 . . . . . . . ► | | |
| **d** Included on Part I, line 7 . . . . . . . ► | | |

**For Paperwork Reduction Act Notice, see the Instructions for Form 1120.**   Cat. No. 37961C   **Schedule M-3 (Form 1120) 2009**

Schedule M-3 (Form 1120) 2009                                                                                          Page **2**

| Name of corporation (common parent, if consolidated return) | Employer identification number |
|---|---|

Check applicable box(es): **(1)** ☐ Consolidated group  **(2)** ☐ Parent corp  **(3)** ☐ Consolidated eliminations  **(4)** ☐ Subsidiary corp  **(5)** ☐ Mixed 1120/L/PC group

Check if a sub-consolidated: **(6)** ☐ 1120 group  **(7)** ☐ 1120 eliminations

| Name of subsidiary (if consolidated return) | Employer identification number |
|---|---|

### Part II  Reconciliation of Net Income (Loss) per Income Statement of Includible Corporations With Taxable Income per Return (see instructions)

| Income (Loss) Items (Attach schedules for lines 1 through 11) | (a) Income (Loss) per Income Statement | (b) Temporary Difference | (c) Permanent Difference | (d) Income (Loss) per Tax Return |
|---|---|---|---|---|
| 1 Income (loss) from equity method foreign corporations | | | | |
| 2 Gross foreign dividends not previously taxed . . | | | | |
| 3 Subpart F, QEF, and similar income inclusions . | | | | |
| 4 Section 78 gross-up . . . . . . . . . . | | | | |
| 5 Gross foreign distributions previously taxed . . | | | | |
| 6 Income (loss) from equity method U.S. corporations . | | | | |
| 7 U.S. dividends not eliminated in tax consolidation | | | | |
| 8 Minority interest for includible corporations . . | | | | |
| 9 Income (loss) from U.S. partnerships . . . . . | | | | |
| 10 Income (loss) from foreign partnerships . . . . | | | | |
| 11 Income (loss) from other pass-through entities . | | | | |
| 12 Items relating to reportable transactions (attach details) . . . . . . . . . . . . . . | | | | |
| 13 Interest income (attach Form 8916-A) . . . . | | | | |
| 14 Total accrual to cash adjustment . . . . . . | | | | |
| 15 Hedging transactions . . . . . . . . . | | | | |
| 16 Mark-to-market income (loss) . . . . . . . | | | | |
| 17 Cost of goods sold (attach Form 8916-A) . . . | ( ) | | | ( ) |
| 18 Sale versus lease (for sellers and/or lessors) . . | | | | |
| 19 Section 481(a) adjustments . . . . . . . | | | | |
| 20 Unearned/deferred revenue . . . . . . . | | | | |
| 21 Income recognition from long-term contracts . | | | | |
| 22 Original issue discount and other imputed interest | | | | |
| 23a Income statement gain/loss on sale, exchange, abandonment, worthlessness, or other disposition of assets other than inventory and pass-through entities | | | | |
| b Gross capital gains from Schedule D, excluding amounts from pass-through entities . . . . . | | | | |
| c Gross capital losses from Schedule D, excluding amounts from pass-through entities, abandonment losses, and worthless stock losses . . . . . | | | | |
| d Net gain/loss reported on Form 4797, line 17, excluding amounts from pass-through entities, abandonment losses, and worthless stock losses | | | | |
| e Abandonment losses . . . . . . . . . . | | | | |
| f Worthless stock losses (attach details) . . . . | | | | |
| g Other gain/loss on disposition of assets other than inventory | | | | |
| 24 Capital loss limitation and carryforward used . . | | | | |
| 25 Other income (loss) items with differences (attach schedule) | | | | |
| 26 **Total income (loss) items.** Combine lines 1 through 25 | | | | |
| 27 **Total expense/deduction items** (from Part III, line 36) | | | | |
| 28 Other items with no differences . . . . . . | | | | |
| 29a Mixed groups, see instructions. All others, combine lines 26 through 28 . . . . . . . . . . | | | | |
| b PC insurance subgroup reconciliation totals . . | | | | |
| c Life insurance subgroup reconciliation totals . . | | | | |
| 30 **Reconciliation totals.** Combine lines 29a through 29c | | | | |

**Note.** Line 30, column (a), must equal the amount on Part I, line 11, and column (d) must equal Form 1120, page 1, line 28.

Schedule M-3 (Form 1120) 2009

| Name of corporation (common parent, if consolidated return) | Employer identification number |
|---|---|
| | |

Check applicable box(es): **(1)** ☐ Consolidated group   **(2)** ☐ Parent corp   **(3)** ☐ Consolidated eliminations   **(4)** ☐ Subsidiary corp   **(5)** ☐ Mixed 1120/L/PC group

Check if a sub-consolidated: **(6)** ☐ 1120 group   **(7)** ☐ 1120 eliminations

| Name of subsidiary (if consolidated return) | Employer identification number |
|---|---|
| | |

**Part III** **Reconciliation of Net Income (Loss) per Income Statement of Includible Corporations With Taxable Income per Return—Expense/Deduction Items** (see instructions)

| Expense/Deduction Items | (a) Expense per Income Statement | (b) Temporary Difference | (c) Permanent Difference | (d) Deduction per Tax Return |
|---|---|---|---|---|
| **1** U.S. current income tax expense | | | | |
| **2** U.S. deferred income tax expense | | | | |
| **3** State and local current income tax expense | | | | |
| **4** State and local deferred income tax expense | | | | |
| **5** Foreign current income tax expense (other than foreign withholding taxes) | | | | |
| **6** Foreign deferred income tax expense | | | | |
| **7** Foreign withholding taxes | | | | |
| **8** Interest expense (attach Form 8916-A) | | | | |
| **9** Stock option expense | | | | |
| **10** Other equity-based compensation | | | | |
| **11** Meals and entertainment | | | | |
| **12** Fines and penalties | | | | |
| **13** Judgments, damages, awards, and similar costs | | | | |
| **14** Parachute payments | | | | |
| **15** Compensation with section 162(m) limitation | | | | |
| **16** Pension and profit-sharing | | | | |
| **17** Other post-retirement benefits | | | | |
| **18** Deferred compensation | | | | |
| **19** Charitable contribution of cash and tangible property | | | | |
| **20** Charitable contribution of intangible property | | | | |
| **21** Charitable contribution limitation/carryforward | | | | |
| **22** Domestic production activities deduction | | | | |
| **23** Current year acquisition or reorganization investment banking fees | | | | |
| **24** Current year acquisition or reorganization legal and accounting fees | | | | |
| **25** Current year acquisition/reorganization other costs | | | | |
| **26** Amortization/impairment of goodwill | | | | |
| **27** Amortization of acquisition, reorganization, and start-up costs | | | | |
| **28** Other amortization or impairment write-offs | | | | |
| **29** Section 198 environmental remediation costs | | | | |
| **30** Depletion | | | | |
| **31** Depreciation | | | | |
| **32** Bad debt expense | | | | |
| **33** Corporate owned life insurance premiums | | | | |
| **34** Purchase versus lease (for purchasers and/or lessees) | | | | |
| **35** Other expense/deduction items with differences (attach schedule) | | | | |
| **36** **Total expense/deduction items.** Combine lines 1 through 35. Enter here and on Part II, line 27, reporting positive amounts as negative and negative amounts as positive | | | | |

Form **706**
(Rev. September 2009)

Department of the Treasury
Internal Revenue Service

# United States Estate (and Generation-Skipping Transfer) Tax Return

OMB No. 1545-0015

Estate of a citizen or resident of the United States (see separate instructions).
To be filed for decedents dying after December 31, 2008, and before January 1, 2010.

## Part 1—Decedent and Executor

| **1a** Decedent's first name and middle initial (and maiden name, if any) | **1b** Decedent's last name | **2** Decedent's Social Security No. |
|---|---|---|

| **3a** County, state, and ZIP code, or foreign country, of legal residence (domicile) at time of death | **3b** Year domicile established | **4** Date of birth | **5** Date of death |
|---|---|---|---|

**6b** Executor's address (number and street including apartment or suite no.; city, town, or post office; state; and ZIP code) and phone no.

**6a** Name of executor (see page 5 of the instructions)

**6c** Executor's social security number (see page 5 of the instructions)

Phone no. (    )

**7a** Name and location of court where will was probated or estate administered

**7b** Case number

**8** If decedent died testate, check here ▶ ☐ and attach a certified copy of the will.  **9** If you extended the time to file this Form 706, check here ▶ ☐

**10** If Schedule R-1 is attached, check here ▶ ☐

## Part 2—Tax Computation

| | | |
|---|---|---|
| **1** | Total gross estate less exclusion (from Part 5—Recapitulation, page 3, item 12) . . . . . . . | **1** |
| **2** | Tentative total allowable deductions (from Part 5—Recapitulation, page 3, item 22) . . . . . | **2** |
| **3a** | Tentative taxable estate (before state death tax deduction) (subtract line 2 from line 1) . . . . | **3a** |
| **b** | State death tax deduction . . . . . . . . . . . . . . . . . . | **3b** |
| **c** | Taxable estate (subtract line 3b from line 3a) . . . . . . . . . . . . . | **3c** |
| **4** | Adjusted taxable gifts (total taxable gifts (within the meaning of section 2503) made by the decedent after December 31, 1976, other than gifts that are includible in decedent's gross estate (section 2001(b))) | **4** |
| **5** | Add lines 3c and 4 . . . . . . . . . . . . . . . . . . . | **5** |
| **6** | Tentative tax on the amount on line 5 from Table A on page 4 of the instructions . . . . . . | **6** |
| **7** | Total gift tax paid or payable with respect to gifts made by the decedent after December 31, 1976. Include gift taxes by the decedent's spouse for such spouse's share of split gifts (section 2513) only if the decedent was the donor of these gifts and they are includible in the decedent's gross estate (see instructions) . . . . . . . . . . . . . . . . . . . | **7** |
| **8** | Gross estate tax (subtract line 7 from line 6) . . . . . . . . . . . . . | **8** |
| **9** | Maximum unified credit (applicable credit amount) against estate tax . | **9** |
| **10** | Adjustment to unified credit (applicable credit amount). (This adjustment may not exceed $6,000. See page 6 of the instructions.) . . . . | **10** |
| **11** | Allowable unified credit (applicable credit amount) (subtract line 10 from line 9) . . . . . . | **11** |
| **12** | Subtract line 11 from line 8 (but do not enter less than zero) . . . . . . . . . . | **12** |
| **13** | Credit for foreign death taxes (from Schedule(s) P). (Attach Form(s) 706-CE.) . . . . . . . . . . . . . | **13** |
| **14** | Credit for tax on prior transfers (from Schedule Q) . . . . . . | **14** |
| **15** | Total credits (add lines 13 and 14) . . . . . . . . . . . . . . . | **15** |
| **16** | Net estate tax (subtract line 15 from line 12) . . . . . . . . . . . . . | **16** |
| **17** | Generation-skipping transfer (GST) taxes payable (from Schedule R, Part 2, line 10) . . . . . . | **17** |
| **18** | Total transfer taxes (add lines 16 and 17) . . . . . . . . . . . . . | **18** |
| **19** | Prior payments. Explain in an attached statement . . . . . . . . . . . . | **19** |
| **20** | Balance due (or overpayment) (subtract line 19 from line 18) . . . . . . . . . . | **20** |

Under penalties of perjury, I declare that I have examined this return, including accompanying schedules and statements, and to the best of my knowledge and belief, it is true, correct, and complete. Declaration of preparer other than the executor is based on all information of which preparer has any knowledge.

**Sign Here**

▶ Signature of executor                    ▶ Date

▶ Signature of executor                    ▶ Date

**Paid Preparer's Use Only**

| Preparer's signature ▶ | Date | Check if self-employed ▶ ☐ | Preparer's SSN or PTIN |
|---|---|---|---|
| Firm's name (or yours if self-employed), address, and ZIP code ▶ | | EIN ▶ | |
| | | Phone no. (    ) | |

**For Privacy Act and Paperwork Reduction Act Notice, see page 30 of the separate instructions for this form.**    Cat. No. 20548R    Form **706** (Rev. 9-2009)

Form 706 (Rev. 9-2009)

| Estate of: | Decedent's Social Security Number |
|---|---|

## Part 3—Elections by the Executor

*Please check the "Yes" or "No" box for each question (see instructions beginning on page 7).*

**Note.** Some of these elections may require the posting of bonds or liens.

|  |  | | Yes | No |
|---|---|---|---|---|
| **1** | Do you elect alternate valuation? . . . . . . . . . . . . . . . . . . . . . . . . | **1** | | |
| **2** | Do you elect special-use valuation? . . . . . . . . . . . . . . . . . . . . . . . . . .<br>If "Yes," you must complete and attach Schedule A-1. | **2** | | |
| **3** | Do you elect to pay the taxes in installments as described in section 6166? . . . . . . . . .<br>If "Yes," you must attach the additional information described on pages 10 through 12 of the instructions.<br>**Note. By electing section 6166, you may be required to provide security for estate tax deferred under section 6166 and interest in the form of a surety bond or a section 6324A lien.** | **3** | | |
| **4** | Do you elect to postpone the part of the taxes attributable to a reversionary or remainder interest as described in section 6163? . . . . . . . . . . . . . . . . . . . . . . | **4** | | |

## Part 4—General Information    (Note. Please attach the necessary supplemental documents. **You must attach the death certificate.**)

(see instructions on page 12)

Authorization to receive confidential tax information under Regs. sec. 601.504(b)(2)(i); to act as the estate's representative before the IRS; and to make written or oral presentations on behalf of the estate if return prepared by an attorney, accountant, or enrolled agent for the executor:

| Name of representative (print or type) | State | Address (number, street, and room or suite no., city, state, and ZIP code) |
|---|---|---|
| | | |

I declare that I am the ☐ attorney/ ☐ certified public accountant/ ☐ enrolled agent (you must check the applicable box) for the executor and prepared this return for the executor. I am not under suspension or disbarment from practice before the Internal Revenue Service and am qualified to practice in the state shown above.

| Signature | CAF number | Date | Telephone number |
|---|---|---|---|
| | | | |

**1** Death certificate number and issuing authority (attach a copy of the death certificate to this return).

**2** Decedent's business or occupation. If retired, check here ▶ ☐ and state decedent's former business or occupation.

**3** Marital status of the decedent at time of death:

☐ Married

☐ Widow or widower—Name, SSN, and date of death of deceased spouse ▶ - - - - - - - - - - - - - - - - - - - - - - - - - - - - - - - - - - - - - - - - - - - - - - - - - - - - - - - - - - - - - - - - - - - - - - - - -

☐ Single

☐ Legally separated

☐ Divorced—Date divorce decree became final ▶

| **4a** Surviving spouse's name | **4b** Social security number | **4c** Amount received (see page 12 of the instructions) |
|---|---|---|
| | | |

**5** Individuals (other than the surviving spouse), trusts, or other estates who receive benefits from the estate (do not include charitable beneficiaries shown in Schedule O) (see instructions).

| Name of individual, trust, or estate receiving $5,000 or more | Identifying number | Relationship to decedent | Amount (see instructions) |
|---|---|---|---|
| | | | |
| | | | |

| All unascertainable beneficiaries and those who receive less than $5,000 . . . . . . . . . . . . . . . ▶ | |
|---|---|

| **Total** . . . . . . . . . . . | |
|---|---|

*Please check the "Yes" or "No" box for each question.*

|  |  | Yes | No |
|---|---|---|---|
| **6** | Does the gross estate contain any section 2044 property (qualified terminable interest property (QTIP) from a prior gift or estate) (see page 12 of the instructions)? . . . . . . . . . . . . . . . . . . . . . . . . . . . . . | | |
| **7a** | Have federal gift tax returns ever been filed? . . . . . . . . . . . . . . . . . . . . . .<br>If "Yes," please attach copies of the returns, if available, and furnish the following information: | | |

| **7b** Period(s) covered | **7c** Internal Revenue office(s) where filed |
|---|---|
| | |

|  |  | Yes | No |
|---|---|---|---|
| **8a** | Was there any insurance on the decedent's life that is not included on the return as part of the gross estate? . . . . . . | | |
| **b** | Did the decedent own any insurance on the life of another that is not included in the gross estate? . . . . . . . . | | |

*(continued on next page)*

Form 706 (Rev. 9-2009)

## Part 4—General Information (continued)

| | If you answer "Yes" to any of questions 9–16, you must attach additional information as described in the instructions. | Yes | No |
|---|---|---|---|
| 9 | Did the decedent at the time of death own any property as a joint tenant with right of survivorship in which (a) one or more of the other joint tenants was someone other than the decedent's spouse, and (b) less than the full value of the property is included on the return as part of the gross estate? If "Yes," you must complete and attach Schedule E . . . . . . . . . . . | | |
| 10a | Did the decedent, at the time of death, own any interest in a partnership (for example, a family limited partnership), an unincorporated business, or a limited liability company; or own any stock in an inactive or closely held corporation? . . . . . . . . . | | |
| b | If "Yes," was the value of any interest owned (from above) discounted on this estate tax return? If "Yes," see the instructions for Schedule F on page 20 for reporting the total accumulated or effective discounts taken on Schedule F or G . . . . . . . . | | |
| 11 | Did the decedent make any transfer described in section 2035, 2036, 2037, or 2038 (see the instructions for Schedule G beginning on page 15 of the separate instructions)? If "Yes," you must complete and attach Schedule G . . . . . . . . . | | |
| 12a | Were there in existence at the time of the decedent's death any trusts created by the decedent during his or her lifetime? . . | | |
| b | Were there in existence at the time of the decedent's death any trusts not created by the decedent under which the decedent possessed any power, beneficial interest, or trusteeship? . . . . . . . . . . . . . . . . . . . . . . | | |
| c | Was the decedent receiving income from a trust created after October 22, 1986, by a parent or grandparent? . . . . . | | |
| | If "Yes," was there a GST taxable termination (under section 2612) upon the death of the decedent? . . . . . . . . | | |
| d | If there was a GST taxable termination (under section 2612), attach a statement to explain. Provide a copy of the trust or will creating the trust, and give the name, address, and phone number of the current trustee(s). | | |
| e | Did the decedent at any time during his or her lifetime transfer or sell an interest in a partnership, limited liability company, or closely held corporation to a trust described in question 12a or 12b? . . . . . . . . . . . . . . . . | | |
| | If "Yes," provide the EIN number to this transferred/sold item. ▶ | | |
| 13 | Did the decedent ever possess, exercise, or release any general power of appointment? If "Yes," you must complete and attach Schedule H | | |
| 14 | Did the decedent have an interest in or a signature or other authority over a financial account in a foreign country, such as a bank account, securities account, or other financial account? . . . . . . . . . . . . . . . . . . . | | |
| 15 | Was the decedent, immediately before death, receiving an annuity described in the "General" paragraph of the instructions for Schedule I or a private annuity? If "Yes," you must complete and attach Schedule I . . . . . . . . . . . | | |
| 16 | Was the decedent ever the beneficiary of a trust for which a deduction was claimed by the estate of a pre-deceased spouse under section 2056(b)(7) and which is not reported on this return? If "Yes," attach an explanation . . . . . . . . | | |

## Part 5—Recapitulation

| Item number | Gross estate | | Alternate value | Value at date of death |
|---|---|---|---|---|
| 1 | Schedule A—Real Estate . . . . . . . . . . . . . . . . . . . . | 1 | | |
| 2 | Schedule B—Stocks and Bonds . . . . . . . . . . . . . . . . . | 2 | | |
| 3 | Schedule C—Mortgages, Notes, and Cash . . . . . . . . . . . . . | 3 | | |
| 4 | Schedule D—Insurance on the Decedent's Life (attach Form(s) 712) . . . | 4 | | |
| 5 | Schedule E—Jointly Owned Property (attach Form(s) 712 for life insurance) . | 5 | | |
| 6 | Schedule F—Other Miscellaneous Property (attach Form(s) 712 for life insurance) . | 6 | | |
| 7 | Schedule G—Transfers During Decedent's Life (att. Form(s) 712 for life insurance) | 7 | | |
| 8 | Schedule H—Powers of Appointment . . . . . . . . . . . . . | 8 | | |
| 9 | Schedule I—Annuities . . . . . . . . . . . . . . . . . . . . | 9 | | |
| 10 | Total gross estate (add items 1 through 9) . . . . . . . . . . . . . | 10 | | |
| 11 | Schedule U—Qualified Conservation Easement Exclusion . . . . . . . | 11 | | |
| 12 | Total gross estate less exclusion (subtract item 11 from item 10). Enter here and on line 1 of Part 2—Tax Computation . . . . . . . . . . . . | 12 | | |

| Item number | Deductions | | Amount |
|---|---|---|---|
| 13 | Schedule J—Funeral Expenses and Expenses Incurred in Administering Property Subject to Claims . . . . | 13 | |
| 14 | Schedule K—Debts of the Decedent . . . . . . . . . . . . . . . . . . . . | 14 | |
| 15 | Schedule K—Mortgages and Liens . . . . . . . . . . . . . . . . . . . . | 15 | |
| 16 | Total of items 13 through 15 . . . . . . . . . . . . . . . . . . . . . . | 16 | |
| 17 | Allowable amount of deductions from item 16 (see the instructions for item 17 of the Recapitulation) | 17 | |
| 18 | Schedule L—Net Losses During Administration . . . . . . . . . . . . . . . . | 18 | |
| 19 | Schedule L—Expenses Incurred in Administering Property Not Subject to Claims . . . . . . . | 19 | |
| 20 | Schedule M—Bequests, etc., to Surviving Spouse . . . . . . . . . . . . . . . | 20 | |
| 21 | Schedule O—Charitable, Public, and Similar Gifts and Bequests . . . . . . . . . . | 21 | |
| 22 | Tentative total allowable deductions (add items 17 through 21). Enter here and on line 2 of the Tax Computation | 22 | |

# Form 709

Department of the Treasury
Internal Revenue Service

## United States Gift (and Generation-Skipping Transfer) Tax Return

(For gifts made during calendar year 2009)

► See separate instructions.

OMB No. 1545-0020

**2009**

## Part 1—General Information

| | |
|---|---|
| **1** Donor's first name and middle initial | **2** Donor's last name |
| **3** Donor's social security number | |

**4** Address (number, street, and apartment number)

**5** Legal residence (domicile)

**6** City, state, and ZIP code

**7** Citizenship (see instructions)

| | | Yes | No |
|---|---|---|---|
| **8** | If the donor died during the year, check here ► ☐ and enter date of death _____ , _____. | | |
| **9** | If you extended the time to file this Form 709, check here ► ☐ | | |
| **10** | Enter the total number of donees listed on Schedule A. Count each person only once. ► | | |
| **11a** | Have you (the donor) previously filed a Form 709 (or 709-A) for any other year? If "No," skip line 11b | | |
| **b** | If the answer to line 11a is "Yes," has your address changed since you last filed Form 709 (or 709-A)? | | |
| **12** | **Gifts by husband or wife to third parties.** Do you consent to have the gifts (including generation-skipping transfers) made by you and by your spouse to third parties during the calendar year considered as made one-half by each of you? (See instructions.) (If the answer is "Yes," the following information must be furnished and your spouse must sign the consent shown below. **If the answer is "No," skip lines 13–18 and go to Schedule A.**) | | |
| **13** | Name of consenting spouse     **14** SSN | | |
| **15** | Were you married to one another during the entire calendar year? (see instructions) | | |
| **16** | If 15 is "No," check whether ☐ married ☐ divorced or ☐ widowed/deceased, and give date (see instructions) ► | | |
| **17** | Will a gift tax return for this year be filed by your spouse? (If "Yes," mail both returns in the same envelope.) | | |

**18** **Consent of Spouse.** I consent to have the gifts (and generation-skipping transfers) made by me and by my spouse to third parties during the calendar year considered as made one-half by each of us. We are both aware of the joint and several liability for tax created by the execution of this consent.

Consenting spouse's signature ►                     Date ►

## Part 2—Tax Computation

| | | | |
|---|---|---|---|
| **1** | Enter the amount from Schedule A, Part 4, line 11 | **1** | |
| **2** | Enter the amount from Schedule B, line 3 | **2** | |
| **3** | Total taxable gifts. Add lines 1 and 2 | **3** | |
| **4** | Tax computed on amount on line 3 (see *Table for Computing Gift Tax* in separate instructions) | **4** | |
| **5** | Tax computed on amount on line 2 (see *Table for Computing Gift Tax* in separate instructions) | **5** | |
| **6** | Balance. Subtract line 5 from line 4 | **6** | |
| **7** | Maximum unified credit (nonresident aliens, see instructions) | **7** | 345,800 00 |
| **8** | Enter the unified credit against tax allowable for all prior periods (from Sch. B, line 1, col. C) | **8** | |
| **9** | Balance. Subtract line 8 from line 7 | **9** | |
| **10** | Enter 20% (.20) of the amount allowed as a specific exemption for gifts made after September 8, 1976, and before January 1, 1977 (see instructions) | **10** | |
| **11** | Balance. Subtract line 10 from line 9 | **11** | |
| **12** | Unified credit. Enter the smaller of line 6 or line 11 | **12** | |
| **13** | Credit for foreign gift taxes (see instructions) | **13** | |
| **14** | Total credits. Add lines 12 and 13 | **14** | |
| **15** | Balance. Subtract line 14 from line 6. Do not enter less than zero | **15** | |
| **16** | Generation-skipping transfer taxes (from Schedule C, Part 3, col. H, Total) | **16** | |
| **17** | Total tax. Add lines 15 and 16 | **17** | |
| **18** | Gift and generation-skipping transfer taxes prepaid with extension of time to file | **18** | |
| **19** | If line 18 is less than line 17, enter **balance due** (see instructions) | **19** | |
| **20** | If line 18 is greater than line 17, enter **amount to be refunded** | **20** | |

Attach check or money order here.

**Sign Here**

Under penalties of perjury, I declare that I have examined this return, including any accompanying schedules and statements, and to the best of my knowledge and belief, it is true, correct, and complete. Declaration of preparer (other than donor) is based on all information of which preparer has any knowledge.

May the IRS discuss this return with the preparer shown below (see instructions)? ☐ Yes ☐ No

► _____     _____
Signature of donor                          Date

**Paid Preparer's Use Only**

| Preparer's signature ► | Date | Check if self-employed ☐ | Preparer's SSN or PTIN |
|---|---|---|---|
| Firm's name (or yours if self-employed), address, and ZIP code ► | | EIN | |
| | | Phone no. | |

For Disclosure, Privacy Act, and Paperwork Reduction Act Notice, see page 12 of the separate instructions for this form.     Cat. No. 16783M     Form **709** (2009)

Form 709 (2009)                                                            Page **2**

## SCHEDULE A   Computation of Taxable Gifts (Including transfers in trust) (see instructions)

**A**  Does the value of any item listed on Schedule A reflect any valuation discount? If "Yes," attach explanation . . . . . . . Yes ☐  No ☐

**B**  ☐ ◀ Check here if you elect under section 529(c)(2)(B) to treat any transfers made this year to a qualified tuition program as made ratably over a 5-year period beginning this year. See instructions. Attach explanation.

**Part 1—Gifts Subject Only to Gift Tax.** Gifts less political organization, medical, and educational exclusions. (see instructions)

| A<br>Item<br>number | B<br>• Donee's name and address<br>• Relationship to donor (if any)<br>• Description of gift<br>• If the gift was of securities, give CUSIP no.<br>• If closely held entity, give EIN | C | D<br>Donor's adjusted<br>basis of gift | E<br>Date<br>of gift | F<br>Value at<br>date of gift | G<br>For split<br>gifts, enter<br>½ of<br>column F | H<br>Net transfer<br>(subtract<br>col. G from<br>col. F) |
|---|---|---|---|---|---|---|---|
| 1 | | | | | | | |
| *Gifts made by spouse —complete **only** if you are splitting gifts with your spouse and he/she also made gifts.* | | | | | | | |
| | | | | | | | |

**Total of Part 1.** Add amounts from Part 1, column H . . . . . . . . . . . . . . . . . . . . . . . . . . . ▶ |

**Part 2—Direct Skips.** Gifts that are direct skips and are subject to both gift tax and generation-skipping transfer tax. You must list the gifts in chronological order.

| A<br>Item<br>number | B<br>• Donee's name and address<br>• Relationship to donor (if any)<br>• Description of gift<br>• If the gift was of securities, give CUSIP no.<br>• If closely held entity, give EIN | C<br>2632(b)<br>election<br>out | D<br>Donor's adjusted<br>basis of gift | E<br>Date<br>of gift | F<br>Value at<br>date of gift | G<br>For split<br>gifts, enter<br>½ of<br>column F | H<br>Net transfer<br>(subtract<br>col. G from<br>col. F) |
|---|---|---|---|---|---|---|---|
| 1 | | | | | | | |
| *Gifts made by spouse —complete **only** if you are splitting gifts with your spouse and he/she also made gifts.* | | | | | | | |
| | | | | | | | |

**Total of Part 2.** Add amounts from Part 2, column H . . . . . . . . . . . . . . . . . . . . . . . . . . . ▶ |

**Part 3—Indirect Skips.** Gifts to trusts that are currently subject to gift tax and may later be subject to generation-skipping transfer tax. You must list these gifts in chronological order.

| A<br>Item<br>number | B<br>• Donee's name and address<br>• Relationship to donor (if any)<br>• Description of gift<br>• If the gift was of securities, give CUSIP no.<br>• If closely held entity, give EIN | C<br>2632(c)<br>election | D<br>Donor's adjusted<br>basis of gift | E<br>Date<br>of gift | F<br>Value at<br>date of gift | G<br>For split<br>gifts, enter<br>½ of<br>column F | H<br>Net transfer<br>(subtract<br>col. G from<br>col. F) |
|---|---|---|---|---|---|---|---|
| 1 | | | | | | | |
| *Gifts made by spouse —complete **only** if you are splitting gifts with your spouse and he/she also made gifts.* | | | | | | | |
| | | | | | | | |

**Total of Part 3.** Add amounts from Part 3, column H . . . . . . . . . . . . . . . . . . . . . . . . . . . ▶ |

*(If more space is needed, attach additional sheets of same size.)*                         Form **709** (2009)

**Part 4—Taxable Gift Reconciliation**

| | | | |
|---|---|---|---|
| 1 | Total value of gifts of donor. Add totals from column H of Parts 1, 2, and 3 . . . . . . . . . . | **1** | |
| 2 | Total annual exclusions for gifts listed on line 1 (see instructions) . . . . . . . . . . . . | **2** | |
| 3 | Total included amount of gifts. Subtract line 2 from line 1 . . . . . . . . . . . . . . . | **3** | |

**Deductions** (see instructions)

| | | | | |
|---|---|---|---|---|
| 4 | Gifts of interests to spouse for which a marital deduction will be claimed, based on item numbers _____ of Schedule A . . | **4** | | |
| 5 | Exclusions attributable to gifts on line 4 . . . . . . . . . . . | **5** | | |
| 6 | Marital deduction. Subtract line 5 from line 4 . . . . . . . . . . | **6** | | |
| 7 | Charitable deduction, based on item nos. _____ less exclusions . | **7** | | |

| | | | |
|---|---|---|---|
| 8 | Total deductions. Add lines 6 and 7 . . . . . . . . . . . . . . . . . . . . | **8** | |
| 9 | Subtract line 8 from line 3 . . . . . . . . . . . . . . . . . . . . . . . | **9** | |
| 10 | Generation-skipping transfer taxes payable with this Form 709 (from Schedule C, Part 3, col. H, Total) . . | **10** | |
| 11 | **Taxable gifts.** Add lines 9 and 10. Enter here and on page 1, Part 2—Tax Computation, line 1 . . . . | **11** | |

**Terminable Interest (QTIP) Marital Deduction.** (See instructions for Schedule A, Part 4, line 4.)

If a trust (or other property) meets the requirements of qualified terminable interest property under section 2523(f), and:

    **a.** The trust (or other property) is listed on Schedule A, and

    **b.** The value of the trust (or other property) is entered in whole or in part as a deduction on Schedule A, Part 4, line 4,
then the donor shall be deemed to have made an election to have such trust (or other property) treated as qualified terminable interest property under section 2523(f).

If less than the entire value of the trust (or other property) that the donor has included in Parts 1 and 3 of Schedule A is entered as a deduction on line 4, the donor shall be considered to have made an election only as to a fraction of the trust (or other property). The numerator of this fraction is equal to the amount of the trust (or other property) deducted on Schedule A, Part 4, line 6. The denominator is equal to the total value of the trust (or other property) listed in Parts 1 and 3 of Schedule A.

If you make the QTIP election, the terminable interest property involved will be included in your spouse's gross estate upon his or her death (section 2044). See instructions for line 4 of Schedule A. If your spouse disposes (by gift or otherwise) of all or part of the qualifying life income interest, he or she will be considered to have made a transfer of the entire property that is subject to the gift tax. See *Transfer of Certain Life Estates Received From Spouse* on page 4 of the instructions.

**12  Election Out of QTIP Treatment of Annuities**

    ☐ ◀Check here if you elect under section 2523(f)(6) **not** to treat as qualified terminable interest property any joint and survivor annuities that are reported on Schedule A and would otherwise be treated as qualified terminable interest property under section 2523(f). See instructions. Enter the item numbers from Schedule A for the annuities for which you are making this election ▶ _____

| SCHEDULE B | Gifts From Prior Periods |
|---|---|

If you answered "Yes" on line 11a of page 1, Part 1, see the instructions for completing Schedule B. If you answered "No," skip to the Tax Computation on page 1 (or Schedule C, if applicable).

| A<br>Calendar year or calendar quarter (see instructions) | B<br>Internal Revenue office where prior return was filed | C<br>Amount of unified credit against gift tax for periods after December 31, 1976 | D<br>Amount of specific exemption for prior periods ending before January 1, 1977 | E<br>Amount of taxable gifts |
|---|---|---|---|---|
| | | | | |
| | | | | |
| | | | | |
| | | | | |
| **1** Totals for prior periods . . . . . . . . . . . **1** | | | | |

| | | | |
|---|---|---|---|
| 2 | Amount, if any, by which total specific exemption, line 1, column D is more than $30,000 . . . . . . | **2** | |
| 3 | Total amount of taxable gifts for prior periods. Add amount on line 1, column E and amount, if any, on line 2. Enter here and on page 1, Part 2—Tax Computation, line 2 . . . . . . . . . . . . . . | **3** | |

*(If more space is needed, attach additional sheets of same size.)*                                                 Form **709** (2009)

## SCHEDULE C    Computation of Generation-Skipping Transfer Tax

**Note.** Inter vivos direct skips that are completely excluded by the GST exemption must still be fully reported (including value and exemptions claimed) on Schedule C.

### Part 1—Generation-Skipping Transfers

| A<br>Item No.<br>(from Schedule A,<br>Part 2, col. A) | B<br>Value (from Schedule A,<br>Part 2, col. H) | C<br>Nontaxable<br>portion of transfer | D<br>Net Transfer (subtract<br>col. C from col. B) |
|---|---|---|---|
| 1 | | | |
| | | | |
| | | | |
| | | | |
| | | | |
| | | | |

Gifts made by spouse (for gift splitting only)

| | | | |
|---|---|---|---|
| | | | |
| | | | |
| | | | |
| | | | |
| | | | |

### Part 2—GST Exemption Reconciliation (Section 2631) and Section 2652(a)(3) Election

Check here ▶ ☐   if you are making a section 2652(a)(3) (special QTIP) election (see instructions)

Enter the item numbers from Schedule A of the gifts for which you are making this election ▶ _____

| | | |
|---|---|---|
| **1** | Maximum allowable exemption (see instructions) . . . . . . . . . . . . . . | 1 |
| **2** | Total exemption used for periods before filing this return . . . . . . . . . | 2 |
| **3** | Exemption available for this return. Subtract line 2 from line 1 . . . . . . | 3 |
| **4** | Exemption claimed on this return from Part 3, column C total, below . . . . | 4 |
| **5** | Automatic allocation of exemption to transfers reported on Schedule A, Part 3 (see instructions) . . . . . | 5 |
| **6** | Exemption allocated to transfers not shown on line 4 or 5, above. **You must attach a "Notice of Allocation."** (see instructions) . . . . . . . . . . . . . . . . | 6 |
| **7** | Add lines 4, 5, and 6 . . . . . . . . . . . . . . . . . . . | 7 |
| **8** | Exemption available for future transfers. Subtract line 7 from line 3 . . . . . . . . . . . . | 8 |

### Part 3—Tax Computation

| A<br>Item No.<br>(from Schedule<br>C, Part 1) | B<br>Net transfer<br>(from Schedule C,<br>Part 1, col. D) | C<br>GST Exemption<br>Allocated | D<br>Divide col. C<br>by col. B | E<br>Inclusion Ratio<br>(subtract col. D<br>from 1.000) | F<br>Maximum Estate<br>Tax Rate | G<br>Applicable Rate<br>(multiply col. E<br>by col. F) | H<br>Generation-Skipping<br>Transfer Tax<br>(multiply col. B by col. G) |
|---|---|---|---|---|---|---|---|
| 1 | | | | | 45% (.45) | | |
| | | | | | 45% (.45) | | |
| | | | | | 45% (.45) | | |
| | | | | | 45% (.45) | | |
| | | | | | 45% (.45) | | |
| | | | | | 45% (.45) | | |

Gifts made by spouse (for gift splitting only)

| | | | | | | | |
|---|---|---|---|---|---|---|---|
| | | | | | 45% (.45) | | |
| | | | | | 45% (.45) | | |
| | | | | | 45% (.45) | | |
| | | | | | 45% (.45) | | |
| | | | | | 45% (.45) | | |
| | | | | | 45% (.45) | | |

| | | | |
|---|---|---|---|
| Total exemption claimed. Enter here and on Part 2, line 4, above. May not exceed Part 2, line 3, above . . . . . . . . | | **Total generation-skipping transfer tax.** Enter here; on page 3, Schedule A, Part 4, line 10; and on page 1, Part 2—Tax Computation, line 16 . . . . . . . . . . . . . | |

*(If more space is needed, attach additional sheets of same size.)*

# Tax Terms Glossary

**§83(b) election**   a special tax election that employees who receive restricted stock or other property with ownership restrictions can make to accelerate income recognition from the normal date when restrictions lapse to the date when the restricted stock or other property is granted. The election also accelerates the employer's compensation deduction related to the restricted stock or other property.

**§1231 assets**   depreciable or real property used in a taxpayer's trade or business owned for more than one year.

**§1231 gain**   this amount is 20 percent of the lesser of the gain realized or the accumulated depreciation on the asset.

**§1231 look-back rule**   a tax rule requiring taxpayers to treat current year net §1231 gains as ordinary income when the taxpayer has deducted a §1231 loss as an ordinary loss in the five years preceding the current tax year.

**§1245 property**   tangible personal property and intangible property subject to cost recovery deductions.

**§1250 property**   real property subject to cost recovery deductions.

**§162(m) limitation**   the $1 million deduction limit on nonperformance based salary paid to certain key executives.

**§179 election**   an incentive for small businesses that allows them to immediately expense a certain amount of tangible personal property placed in service during the year.

**§197 purchased intangibles**   intangible assets that are purchased that must be amortized over 180 months regardless of their actual useful lives.

**§263A Cost (or UNICAP)**   certain book expenses that must be capitalized into inventory for tax purposes.

**§291 depreciation recapture**   the portion of a corporate taxpayer's gain on real property that is converted from §1231 gain to ordinary income.

**§338 election**   an election by a corporate buyer of 80-percent-or-more of a corporation's stock to treat the acquisition as an asset acquisition and not a stock acquisition.

**§338(h)(10) election**   a joint election by the corporate buyer and corporate seller of the stock of a subsidiary of the seller to treat the acquisition as a sale of the subsidiary's assets by the seller to the buyer.

**§481 adjustment**   a change to taxable income associated with a change in accounting methods.

**§7520 rate**   interest rate set at 120 percent of the applicable Federal midterm rate (published monthly by the Treasury) and used to calculate the value of temporal interests.

**12-month rule**   regulation that allows prepaid business expenses to be currently deducted when the contract does not extend beyond 12 months and the contract period does not extend beyond the end of the tax year following the year of the payment.

**30-day letter**   the IRS letter received after an audit that instructs the taxpayer that he or she has 30 days to either (1) request a conference with an appeals officer or (2) agree to the proposed adjustment.

**90-day letter**   the IRS letter received after an audit and receipt of the 30-day letter that explains that the taxpayer has 90 days to either (1) pay the proposed deficiency or (2) file a petition in the U.S. Tax Court to hear the case. The 90-day letter is also known as the *statutory notice of deficiency.*

**704(b) capital accounts**   partners' capital accounts maintained using the accounting rules prescribed in the Section 704(b) regulations. Under these rules, capital accounts reflect the fair market value of property contributed to and distributed property from partnerships.

# A

**Abandoned spouse**   a married taxpayer whose spouse has left home for the last six months of the year. The taxpayer may qualify for head of household filing status if the taxpayer maintains a household for qualifying child.

**Accelerated Cost Recovery System (ACRS)**   the depreciation system enacted by Congress in 1981 that is based on the concept of set recovery periods and accelerated depreciation methods.

**Accountable plan**   an employer's reimbursement plan under which employees must submit documentation supporting expenses to receive reimbursement and reimbursements are limited to legitimate business expenses.

**Accounting method**   an approach for determining the taxable year in which a business recognizes a particular item of income or deduction thereby dictating the timing of when a taxpayer reports income and deductions.

**Accounting period**   a fixed period in which a business reports income and deductions, generally referred to as a tax year.

**Accrual method**   method of accounting that generally recognizes income in the period earned and recognizes deductions in the period that liabilities are incurred.

**Accrued market discount**   a ratable amount of the market discount at the time of purchase (based on the number of days the bond is held over the number of days until maturity when the bond is purchased) that is treated as interest income when a bond with market discount is sold before it matures.

**Accumulated adjustments account (AAA)**   an account that reflects the cumulative income or loss for the time the corporation has been an S corporation.

**Accumulated earnings and profits**   undistributed earnings and profits from years prior to the current year.

**Acquiescence**   issued after the IRS loses a trial-level or circuit court case when the IRS has decided to follow the court's adverse ruling in the future. It does not mean that the IRS agrees with the court's ruling. Instead, it simply means that the IRS will no longer litigate this issue.

**Acquisition indebtedness**   debt secured by a qualified residence that is incurred in acquiring, constructing, or substantially improving the residence.

**Acquisition subsidiary** a subsidiary used by the acquiring corporation in a triangular merger to acquire the target corporation.

**Action on decision** an IRS pronouncement that explains the background reasoning behind an IRS acquiescence or nonacquiescence.

**Active participant in a rental activity** an individual who owns at least 10% of a rental property and participates in the process of making management decisions, such as approving new tenants, deciding on rental terms, and approving repairs and capital expenditures.

**Ad valorem tax** a tax based on the value of property.

**Adjusted basis** the cost basis of an asset that has yet to be recovered by a business through cost recovery deductions. Adjusted basis can be computed by subtracting the accumulated depreciation, amortization, or depletion from the asset's initial cost basis.

**Adjusted current earnings (ACE)** a version of a corporation's current year earnings that more closely represents a corporation's economic income for the year than do regular taxable income or alternative minimum taxable income.

**Adjusted gross estate** gross estate reduced by administrative expenses, debts of the decedent, and losses, and state death taxes.

**Adjusted gross income (AGI)** gross income less deductions for AGI. AGI is an important reference point that is often used in other calculations.

**Adjusted tax basis** the taxpayer's acquisition basis (for example, cost) plus capital improvements less depreciation or amortization.

**Adjusted taxable gifts** cumulative taxable gifts from previous years other than gifts already included in the gross estate valued at date of gift values.

**After-tax rate of return** a taxpayer's before-tax rate of return on an investment minus the taxes paid on the income from the investment. The formula for an after-tax rate of return that is taxed annually is the before tax rate of return $\times$ (1 − marginal tax rate) [i.e., $r = R \times (1 - t)$]. A taxpayer's after-tax rate of return on an investment held for more than one tax period is $r = (FV/I)^{1/n} - 1$, where r is the after-tax rate of return, FV is the after-tax future value of the investment, I is the original investment amount, and n is the number of periods the investment is held.

**Aggregate approach** a theory of taxing partnerships that ignores partnerships as an entities and taxes partners as if they directly owned partnership net assets.

**Alimony** a support payment of cash made to a former spouse. The payment must be made under a written separation agreement or divorce decree that does not designate the payment as something other than alimony, and the payments must cease no later than when the recipient dies.

**All-inclusive income concept** definition of income that says that gross income means all income from whatever source derived.

**Allocate** as used in the sourcing rules, the process of associating a deduction with a specific item or items of gross income for purposes of computing foreign source taxable income.

**Allocation** the method of dividing or sourcing non-business income to specific states.

**Alternative minimum tax** a tax on a broader tax base than the base for the "regular" tax; the additional tax paid when the tentative minimum tax (based on the alternative minimum tax base) exceeds the regular tax (based on the regular tax base). The alternative minimum tax is designed to require taxpayers to pay some minimum level of tax even when they have low or no regular taxable income as a result of certain tax breaks in the tax code.

**Alternative minimum tax adjustments** adjustments (positive or negative) to regular taxable income to arrive at the alternative minimum tax base.

**Alternative minimum tax base (AMT base)** alternative minimum taxable income minus the alternative minimum tax exemption.

**Alternative minimum tax exemption** a deduction to determine the alternative minimum tax base that is phased out based on alternative minimum taxable income.

**Alternative minimum tax system** a secondary or parallel tax system calculated on an *alternative* tax base that more closely reflects economic income than the regular income tax base. The system was designed to ensure that taxpayers generating income pay some *minimum* amount of income tax each year.

**Alternative valuation date** date nine months after the decedent's date of death.

**Amortization** the method of recovering the cost of intangible assets over a specific time period.

**Amount realized** the value of everything received by the seller in a transaction (cash, FMV of other property, and relief of liabilities) less selling costs.

**Annotated tax service** a tax service arranged by code section. For each code section, an annotated service includes the code section; a listing of the code section history; copies of congressional committee reports that explain changes to the code section; a copy of all the regulations issued for the specific code section; the service's unofficial explanation of the code section; and brief summaries (called annotations) of relevant court cases, revenue rulings, revenue procedures, and letter rulings that address issues specific to the code section.

**Annual exclusion** amount of gifts allowed to be made each year per donee (regardless of the number of donees) to prevent the taxation of relatively small gifts ($13,000 per donee per year in 2009).

**Annualized income method** a method for determining a corporation's required estimated tax payments when the taxpayer earns more income later in the year than earlier in the year. Requires corporations to base their first and second required estimated tax installments on their income from the first three months of the year, their third installment based on the their taxable income from the first six months of the year, and the final installment based on their taxable income from the first nine months of the year.

**Annuity** a stream of equal payments over time.

**Applicable tax rate** the tax rate or rates used to measure a company's deferred tax asset or liability. In general, it is the enacted tax rate that is expected to apply to taxable income in the period in which the deferred tax asset or liability is expected to be recovered or settled. For U.S. tax purposes, the applicable tax rate is the regular tax rate.

**Apportion** as used in the sourcing rules, the process of calculating the amount of a deduction that is associated with a specific item or items of gross income for purposes of computing foreign source taxable income.

**Apportionment** the method of dividing business income of an interstate business among the states where nexus exists.

**Arm's-length transaction** transactions among unrelated taxpayers, where each transacting party negotiates for his or her own benefit.

**Articles of incorporation** a document, filed by a corporation's founders with the state describing the purpose, place of business, and other details of the corporation.

**Articles of organization** a document, filed by a limited liability company's founders with the state describing the purpose, place of business, and other details of the company.

**Asset and liability approach** the approach taken by ASC Topic 740 that focuses on computing a company's current taxes payable (refundable) and deferred tax assets and liabilities on the balance sheet. The income tax provision recorded on the income statement is

the amount needed to adjust the beginning of the year balance sheet amounts to the end of the year balance sheet amounts.

**Assignment of income doctrine**   the judicial doctrine holding that earned income is taxed to the taxpayer providing the service, and that income from property is taxed to the individual who owns the property when the income accrues.

**At-risk amount**   an investor's risk of loss in a worst case scenario. In a partnership, an amount generally equal to a partner's tax basis exclusive of the partner's share of nonrecourse debt.

**At-risk rules**   tax rules limiting losses flowing through to partners or S corporation shareholders to their at risk amount.

**Average tax rate**   a taxpayer's average level of taxation on each dollar of taxable income. Specifically,

$$\text{Average Tax Rate} = \frac{Total\ Tax}{Taxable\ Income}$$

# B

**Bargain element (of stock options)**   the difference between the fair market value of the employer's stock and the amount employees pay to acquire the employer's stock.

**Barter clubs**   organizations that facilitate the exchange of rights to goods and services between members.

**Basis**   a taxpayer's unrecovered investment in an asset that provides a reference point for measuring gain or loss when an asset is sold.

**Before-tax rate of return**   a taxpayer's rate of return on an investment before paying taxes on the income from the investment.

**Beneficiary**   person for whom trust property is held and administered.

**Bond**   a debt instrument issued for a period of more than one year with the purpose of raising capital by borrowing.

**Bond discount**   the result of issuing bonds for less than their maturity value.

**Bond premium**   the result of issuing bonds for more than their maturity value.

**Book equivalent of taxable income**   a company's pretax income from continuing operations adjusted for permanent differences.

**Book or financial reporting income**   the income or loss corporations report on their financial statements using applicable financial accounting standards.

**Book–tax difference**   a difference in the amount of an income item or deduction item taken into account for book purposes compared to the amount taken into account for the same item for tax purposes.

**Boot**   property given or received in an otherwise nontaxable transaction such as a like-kind exchange that may trigger gain to a party to the transaction.

**Bracket**   a subset (or portion) of the tax base subject to a specific tax rate. Brackets are common to graduated taxes.

**Branch**   an unincorporated division of a corporation.

**Bright line tests**   technical rules found in the tax law that provide the taxpayer with objective tests to determine the tax consequences of a transaction.

**Brother-sister controlled group**   a form of controlled group consisting of two or more corporations if five or fewer persons own more than 50 percent of the voting power or stock value of the corporation on the last day of the year.

**Built-in gain**   the difference between the fair market value and tax basis of property owned by an entity when the fair market value exceeds the tax basis.

**Built-in gains tax**   a tax levied on S corporations that were formerly C corporations. The tax applies to net unrealized built-in gains at the time it converted from a C corporation to the extent they are recognized during the first ten years (first seven years for asset sales in 2009 and 2010) it operates as an S corporation (the built-in gains tax recognition period). The applicable tax rate is 35 percent.

**Built-in gains tax recognition period**   the first ten years a corporation operates as an S corporation after converting from a C corporation (first seven years for asset sales in 2009 and 2010).

**Built-in loss**   the difference between the fair market value and tax basis of property owned by an entity when the tax basis exceeds the fair market value.

**Bunching itemized deductions**   a common planning strategy in which a taxpayer pays two year's worth of itemized expenses in one year to exceed the standard deduction in that year.

**Business activity**   a profit-motivated activity that requires a relatively high level of involvement or effort from the taxpayer to generate income.

**Business income**   income derived from business activities.

**Business purpose doctrine**   the judicial doctrine that allows the IRS to challenge and disallow business expenses for transactions with no underlying business motivation.

**Business tax credits**   nonrefundable credits designed to provide incentives for taxpayers to hire certain types of individuals or to participate in certain business activities.

**Bypass provision**   provision in the will of a deceased spouse that transfers property to nonspousal beneficiaries to maximize the value of the decedent's unified credit.

**Bypass trust**   trust used in lieu of a bypass provision to transfer property to nonspousal beneficiaries to maximize the value of the unified credit of the first spouse to die.

# C

**C corporation**   a corporate taxpaying entity with income subject to taxation. Such a corporation is termed a "C" corporation because it is subject to the provisions of subchapter C of the Internal Revenue Code.

**Cafeteria plan**   an employer plan that allows employees to choose benefits from a menu of nontaxable fringe benefits or receive cash compensation in lieu of the benefits.

**Capital account**   an account reflecting a partner's share of the equity in a partnership. Capital accounts are maintained using tax accounting methods or other methods of accounting, including GAAP, at the discretion of the partnership.

**Capital asset**   in general, an asset other than an asset used in a trade or business or an asset such as an account or note receivable acquired in a business from the sale of services or property.

**Capital gain property**   any asset that would have generated a long-term capital gain if the taxpayer had sold the property for its fair market value.

**Capital interest**   an economic right attached to a partnership interest giving a partner the right to receive cash or property in the event the partnership liquidates. A capital interest is synonymous with the liquidation value of a partnership interest.

**Capital loss carryback**   the amount of a corporation's net capital loss from one year that it uses to offset net capital gains in any of the three preceding tax years.

**Capital loss carryover**   the amount of a corporation's or an individual's net capital loss from one year that it may use offset net capital gains in future years.

**Capitalization**   recording an expenditure as an asset on the balance sheet rather than expensing it immediately.

**Carryover basis**   the basis of an asset the transferee takes in property received in a nontaxable exchange. The basis of the asset carries over from the transferor to the transferee.

**Cash method**   the method of accounting that recognizes income in the period in which cash, property, or services is received and recognizes deductions in the period paid.

**Cash surrender value**   the amount, if any, the owner of a life insurance policy receives when the policy is cashed in before the death of the insured individual.

**Cash tax rate**   the tax rate computed by dividing a company's taxes paid during the year by its pretax income from continuing operations.

**Casualty**   an unexpected, unforeseen event driven by forces outside the control of the taxpayer (such as "fire, storm, or shipwreck or other event or theft") that damages or destroys a taxpayer's property.

**Casualty loss**   a loss arising from a *sudden, unexpected,* or *unusual* event such as a "fire, storm, or shipwreck" or loss from theft.

**Ceiling**   limitations that are maximum amounts for adjustments to taxable income (or credits). The amounts in excess of the ceiling are either lost or carried to another tax year.

**Certainty**   one of the criteria used to evaluate tax systems. Certainty means taxpayers should be able to determine when, where, and how much tax to pay.

**Certificate of deposit**   an interest-bearing debt instrument offered by banks and savings and loans. Money removed from the CD before maturity is subject to a penalty.

**Certificate of limited partnership**   a document limited partnerships must file with the state to be formerly recognized by the state. The document is similar to articles of incorporation or articles or organization.

**Charitable contribution deduction modified taxable income** taxable income for purposes of determining the 10% of taxable income deduction limitation for corporate charitable contributions. Computed as taxable income before deducting (1) any charitable contributions, (2) the dividends received deduction, (3) net operating loss carrybacks, and (4) the domestic production activities deduction.

**Circular 230**   regulations issued by the IRS that govern tax practice and apply to all persons practicing before the IRS. There are three parts of Circular 230: Subpart A describes who may practice before the IRS (e.g., CPAs, attorneys, enrolled agents) and what practicing before the IRS means (tax return preparation, representing clients before the IRS, etc.). Subpart B describes the duties and restrictions that apply to individuals governed by Circular 230. Subpart C explains disciplinary proceedings for practitioners violating the Circular 230 provisions.

**Citator**   a research tool that allows one to check the status of several types of tax authorities. A citator can be used to review the history of the case to find out, for example, whether it was subsequently appealed and overturned, and to identify subsequent cases that cite the case. Citators can also be used to check the status of revenue rulings, revenue procedures, and other IRS pronouncements.

**Civil penalties**   monetary penalties imposed when tax practitioners or taxpayers violate tax statutes without reasonable cause—for example, as the result of negligence, intentional disregard of pertinent rules, willful disobedience, or outright fraud.

**Cliff vesting**   a qualified plan provision allowing for benefits to vest all at once after a period of time has passed.

**Collectibles**   a work of art, a rug or antique, a metal or gem, a stamp or coin, an alcoholic beverage, or other similar items held for investment for more than one year.

**Combined controlled group**   a form of a controlled group consisting of three or more corporations each of which is a member of either a parent-subsidiary or brother-sister controlled group and one of the corporations is the parent in the parent-subsidiary controlled group and also is in a brother-sister controlled group.

**Commercial domicile**   the state where a business is headquartered and directs operations; this location may be different from the place of incorporation.

**Commercial traveler exception**   a statutory exception that exempts nonresidents from U.S. taxation of compensation from services if the individual is in the United States 90 days or less and earns $3,000 or less.

**Common-law states**   the 41 states that have not adopted community property laws.

**Community-property states**   nine states (Arizona, California, Idaho, Louisiana, Nevada, New Mexico, Texas, Washington, and Wisconsin) that automatically equally divide the ownership of property acquired by either spouse during a marriage.

**Community property systems**   systems in which state laws dictate how the income and property is legally shared between a husband and a wife.

**Commuting**   traveling from a personal residence to the place of business.

**Conglomerate**   a group of corporations in different businesses under common ownership.

**Consolidation**   the combining of the assets and liabilities of two or more corporations into a new entity.

**Constructive dividend**   a payment made by a corporation to a shareholder that is recharacterized by the IRS or courts as a dividend even though it is not characterized as such by the corporation.

**Constructive ownership**   rules that cause stock not owned by a taxpayer to be treated as owned by the taxpayer for purposes of meeting certain stock ownership tests.

**Constructive receipt doctrine**   the judicial doctrine that provides that a taxpayer must recognize income when it is actually or constructively received. Constructive receipt is deemed to have occurred if the income has been credited to the taxpayer's account or if the income is unconditionally available to the taxpayer, the taxpayer is aware of the income's availability, and there are no restrictions on the taxpayer's control over the income.

**Continuity of business enterprise (COBE)**   a judicial (now regulatory) requirement that the acquiring corporation continue the target corporation's historic business or continue to use a "significant" portion of the target corporation's historic business assets to be tax-deferred.

**Continuity of interest (COI)**   a judicial (now regulatory) requirement that the transferors of stock in a reorganization collectively retain a continuing ownership (equity) interest in the target corporation's assets or historic business to be tax-deferred. The Regulations provide that COI is met when the shareholders of the target corporation, in the aggregate, receive equity equal to 40-percent-or-more of the value of the total consideration received.

**Contribution to capital**   a shareholder's or other person's contribution of cash or other property to a corporation without receipt of an additional equity interest in the corporation.

**Controlled foreign corporation**   a foreign corporation that is more than 50 percent owned by U.S. shareholders.

**Controlled group**   a group of corporations owned by the same individual shareholders; it can either be brother-sister corporations or parent-subsidiary corporations.

**Convenience**   one of the criteria used to evaluate tax systems. Convenience means a tax system should be designed to facilitate the collection of tax revenues without undue hardship on the taxpayer or the government.

**Corpus**   the principal or property transferred to fund a trust or accumulated in the trust.

**Correspondence examination**   an IRS audit conducted by mail and generally limited to one or two items on the taxpayer's return. Among the three types of audits, correspondence audits are generally the most common, the most narrow in scope, and least complex. The IRS typically requests supporting documentation for one or more items on the taxpayer's return (e.g., documentation of charitable contributions deducted).

**Cost depletion**   the method of recovering the cost of a natural resource that allows a taxpayer to estimate or determine the number of units that remain in the resource at the beginning of the year and allocate a pro rata share of the remaining basis to each unit of the resource that is extracted or sold during the year.

**Cost recovery**   the method by which a company expenses the cost of acquiring capital assets. Cost recovery can take the form of depreciation, amortization, or depletion.

**Coupon rate**   the interest rate expressed as a percentage of the face value of the bond.

**Covenant not to compete**   a contractual promise to refrain from conducting business or professional activities similar to those of another party.

**Criminal penalties**   penalties commonly charged in tax evasion cases (i.e., willful intent to defraud the government). They are imposed only after normal due process, including a trial. Compared to civil cases, the standard of conviction is higher in a criminal trial (beyond a reasonable doubt). However, the penalties are also much higher, such as fines up to $100,000 for individuals plus a prison sentence.

**Current earnings and profits**   an account maintained by a corporation to determine if a distribution is a dividend. Earnings and profits is computed for the current year by adjusting taxable income to make it more closely resemble economic income.

**Current gifts**   gifts completed during the calendar year that are not already exempted from the gift tax, such as political contributions.

**Current income tax expense or benefit**   the amount of taxes paid or payable (refundable) in the current year.

**Current tax liability or asset**   the amount of taxes payable or refundable in the current year.

**Cutback**   a phase-out limit that gradually reduces, but does not completely eliminate, deductions, credits, or other adjustments to taxable income.

# D

***De minimis* fringe benefit**   a nontaxable fringe benefit that allows employees to receive occasional or incidental benefits tax free.

**Debt basis**   the outstanding principal of direct loans from an S corporation shareholder to the S corporation. Once taxpayers deduct losses to the extent of their stock basis, they may deduct losses to the extent of their debt basis. When the debt basis has been reduced by losses, it is restored by income/gain allocations.

**Deductible temporary differences**   book-tax differences that will result in deductible amounts in future years when the related deferred tax asset is recovered.

**Deductions**   amounts that are subtracted from reduce gross income in calculating taxable income.

**Deductions above the line**   *for* AGI deductions or deductions subtracted from gross income to determine AGI.

**Deductions below the line**   *from* AGI deductions or deductions subtracted from AGI to calculate taxable income.

**Deductions *for* AGI**   deductions subtracted from gross income to determine AGI.

**Deductions *from* AGI**   deductions that do not affect AGI. *From* AGI deductions consist of itemized deductions, standard deductions, and exemptions.

**Deferral items, deferred income, or deferrals**   realized income that will be taxed as income in a subsequent year.

**Deferred like-kind exchange**   a like-kind exchange where the taxpayer transfers like-kind property before receiving the like-kind property in exchange. The property to be received must be identified within 45 days and received with 180 days of the transfer of the property given up.

**Deferred tax asset**   the expected future tax benefit attributable to deductible temporary differences and carryforwards.

**Deferred tax liability**   the expected future tax cost attributable to taxable temporary differences.

**Defined benefit plan**   employer-provided qualified plans that spell out the specific benefit employees will receive on retirement.

**Defined contribution plan**   employer-provided qualified plans that specify the maximum annual contributions employers and/or employees may contribute to the plan.

**Definitely related deductions**   deductions that are associated with the creation of a specific item or items of gross income.

**Dependency exemption**   a fixed deduction allowed for each individual who qualifies as a "dependent" of the taxpayer.

**Dependent**   a person for whom a taxpayer may claim a dependency exemption. To qualify as a dependent a person must be a qualifying child or qualifying relative of the taxpayer.

**Dependent care benefit**   a nontaxable fringe benefit that allows employees to receive up to $5,000 of care for children under age 13 or for a spouse or other dependent with physical needs.

**Depletion**   the cost recovery method to allocate the cost of natural resources as they are removed.

**Depreciation**   the cost recovery method to allocate the cost of tangible personal and real property over a specific time period.

**Depreciation recapture**   the conversion of §1231 gain into ordinary income on a sale (or exchange) based on the amount of accumulated depreciation on the property at the time of sale or exchange.

**Determination letters**   rulings requested by the taxpayer, issued by local IRS directors, and generally not controversial. An example of a determination letter is the request by an employer for the IRS to rule that the taxpayer's retirement plan is a "qualified plan."

**DIF (Discriminant Function) system**   the DIF system assigns a score to each tax return that represents the probability that the tax liability on the return has been underreported (a higher score = a higher likelihood of underreporting). The IRS derives the weights assigned to specific tax return attributes from historical IRS audit adjustment data from the National Research Program. The DIF system then uses these (undisclosed) weights to score each tax

return based on the tax return's characteristics. Returns with higher DIF scores are then reviewed to determine if an audit is the best course of action.

**Direct conversion**    when a taxpayer receives noncash property as a replacement for property damaged or destroyed in an involuntary conversion rather than a cash payment.

**Direct write-off method**    required method for deducting bad debts for tax purposes. Under this method, businesses deduct bad debt only when the debt becomes wholly or partially worthless.

**Disability insurance**    sometimes called sick pay or wage replacement insurance, pays the insured for wages lost due to injury or disability.

**Discharge of indebtedness**    debt forgiveness.

**Discount factor**    the factor based on the taxpayer's rate of return that is used to determine the present value of future cash inflows (e.g., tax savings) and outflows (taxes paid).

**Disproportionate distributions**    partnership distributions that change an owners' relative ownership of hot assets.

**Disqualifying disposition**    the sale of stock acquired using incentive stock options prior to satisfying certain holding period requirements. Failing to satisfy the holding period requirements converts the options into nonqualified stock options.

**Disregarded entities**    unincorporated entities with one owner that is an entity rather than an individual.

**Dividend**    a property distribution made by a corporation to a shareholder out of earnings and profits.

**Dividends received deduction**    a corporate deduction for part or all of a dividend received from other taxable, domestic corporations.

**Dividends**    distributions to shareholders of money or property from the corporation's earnings and profits.

**Document perfection program**    a program under which all tax returns are checked for mathematical and tax calculation errors.

**Domestic production activities deduction (DPAD)**    a deduction for businesses that manufacture goods in the United States.

**Donee**    person receiving a gift.

**Donor**    person making a gift.

**Double taxation**    the tax burden when an entity's income is subject to two levels of tax. Income of C corporations is subject to double taxation. The first level of tax is at the corporate level and the second level of tax on corporate income occurs at the shareholder level. Income of flow-through entities is generally not subject to double taxation.

**DRD modified taxable income**    taxable income for purposes of applying the taxable income limitation for the dividends received deduction. Computed as the dividend receiving corporation's taxable income before deducting the dividends received deduction, any net operating loss deduction, the domestic manufacturing deduction, and capital loss carrybacks.

**Dynamic forecasting**    the process of forecasting tax revenues that incorporates into the forecast how taxpayers may alter their activities in response to a tax law change.

# E

**Earmarked tax**    a tax assessed for a specific purpose (e.g., for education).

**Earned income**    compensation and other forms of income received for providing goods or services in the ordinary course of business.

**Earned income credit**    a refundable credit designed to help offset the effect of employment taxes on compensation paid to low

income taxpayers and to encourage lower income taxpayers to seek employment.

**Earnings and profits**    a measure of a corporation's earnings that is similar to its economic earnings. Corporate dividends are taxable to shareholders to the extent they come from earnings and profits.

**Economic nexus**    the concept that businesses without a physical presence in the state may establish income tax nexus in the state through an economic presence there.

**Economic performance test**    the third requirement that must be met for an accrual method taxpayer to deduct an expense currently. The specific event that satisfies the economic performance test varies based on the type of expense.

**Economy**    one of the criteria used to evaluate tax systems. Economy means a tax system should minimize its compliance and administration costs.

**Educational assistance benefit**    a nontaxable fringe benefit that allows an employer to provide a certain amount of education benefits on an annual basis.

**Effective tax rate**    the taxpayer's average rate of taxation on each dollar of total income (taxable and nontaxable income). Specifically,

$$\text{Effective Tax Rate} = \frac{Total\ Tax}{Taxable\ Income}$$

**Effectively connected income**    net income that results from the conduct of a U.S. trade or business by a nonresident.

**Employee**    a person who is hired to provide services to a company on a regular basis in exchange for compensation and who does not provide these services as part of an independent business.

**Employment taxes**    taxes consisting of the Old Age, Survivors, and Disability Insurance (OASDI) tax, commonly called the Social Security tax, and the Medical Health Insurance (MHI) tax known as the Medicare tax.

**Enacted tax rate**    the statutory tax rate that will apply in the current or a future period.

**Entity approach**    a theory of taxing partnerships that treats partnerships as entities separate from partners.

**Equity**    one of the criteria used to evaluate a tax system. A tax system is considered fair or equitable if the tax is based on the taxpayer's ability to pay; taxpayers with a greater ability to pay tax, pay more tax.

**Escrow account (mortgage-related)**    a holding account with a taxpayer's mortgage lender. The taxpayer makes mortgage payments to the lender that includes payment for the interest and principal and payments for property taxes. The lender maintains the payments for property taxes in the escrow account and uses the funds in the account to pay the property taxes when the taxes are due.

**Estate**    fiduciary legal entity that comes into existence upon a person's death and is empowered by the probate court to gather and transfer the decedent's real and personal property.

**Estate tax**    a tax based on the fair market values of wealth transfers upon death.

**Estimated tax payments**    quarterly tax payments that a taxpayer makes to the government if the tax withholding is insufficient to meet the taxpayer's tax liability.

**Excess net passive income**    net passive investment income × passive investment income in excess of 25% of the S corporation's gross receipts divided by its passive investment income.

**Excess net passive income tax**    a tax levied on S corporations that have accumulated earnings and profits from years in which it operated as a C corporation if the corporation reports excess net passive income.

**Exchanged basis**   the basis of an asset received in a nontaxable exchange. An exchanged basis is generally the basis of the asset given up in a nontaxable exchange.

**Excise taxes**   taxes levied on the retail sale of particular products. They differ from other taxes in that the tax base for an excise tax typically depends on the *quantity* purchased, rather than a monetary amount.

**Excluded income** or **exclusions**   realized income that is exempted from income taxation.

**Ex-dividend date**   the relevant date for determining who receives a dividend from a stock. Anyone purchasing stock before this date will receive current dividends. Otherwise, the purchaser must wait until subsequent dividends are declared before receiving them.

**Executor**   person who takes responsibility for collecting the assets of the decedent, paying the decedent's debts, and distributing the remaining assets to the rightful heirs.

**Exemption**   a fixed deduction that eliminates a certain amount of income from the income tax.

**Exemption equivalent**   amount of cumulative taxable transfers a taxpayer can make without exceeding the unified credit.

**Exercise date**   the date employees use their stock options to acquire employer stock at a discounted price.

**Exercise price**   the price at holders of stock options may purchase stock in the corporation issuing the option.

**Explicit tax**   a tax directly imposed by a government.

# F

**Face value**   a specified final amount paid to the owner of a coupon bond on the date of maturity. The face value is also known as the maturity value.

**Facts and circumstances test**   a test used to make subjective determination such as whether the amount of salary paid to an employee is reasonable. The test requires the taxpayer and the IRS to consider all the relevant facts and circumstances surrounding the situation in order to make a decision. The relevant facts and circumstance are situation specific.

**Family limited partnership**   partnership designed to save estate taxes by dividing a family business into various ownership interests representing control of operations and future income and appreciation of the assets.

**Favorable book-tax difference**   a book-tax difference that requires a subtraction from book income in determining taxable income.

**Federal/state adjustments**   amounts added to or subtracted from federal taxable income when firms compute taxable income for a particular state.

**Federal short-term interest rate**   the quarterly interest rate used to determine the interest charged for tax underpayments (federal short-term rate plus 3 percent).

**FICA taxes**   FICA (Federal Insurance Contribution Act) taxes are a term used to denote both the Social Security and Medicare taxes upon earned income. For self-employed taxpayers, the terms "FICA tax" and "self-employment tax" are synonymous.

**Fiduciary**   person or legal entity that takes possession of property for the benefit of beneficiaries.

**Fiduciary duty**   requirement that a fiduciary act in an objective and impartial manner and not favor one beneficiary over another.

**Field examination**   the least common audit. The IRS conducts these audits at the taxpayer's place of business or the location where the taxpayer's books, records, and source documents are maintained.

Field examinations are generally the broadest in scope and most complex of the three audit types. They can last many months to multiple years and generally are limited to business returns and the most complex individual returns.

**FIFO**   first-in, first-out method; an accounting method that values the cost of assets sold under the assumption that the assets are sold in the order purchased (i.e., first purchased, first sold).

**Filing status**   filing status places taxpayers into one of five categories (married filing jointly, married filing separately, qualifying widow or widower, head of household, and single) by marital status and family situation as of the end of the year. Filing status determines whether a taxpayer must file a tax return, appropriate tax rate schedules, standard deduction amounts, and several deduction and credit limitation thresholds.

**Final regulations**   regulations that have been issued in final form, and thus, until revoked, they represent the Treasury's interpretation of the Code.

**Financial reporting income**   see book income.

**Fiscal year**   a year that ends on a day other than December 31.

**Fixed and determinable, annual or periodic income**   U.S. source passive income earned by a nonresident.

**Flat tax**   a tax in which a single tax rate is applied throughout the tax base.

**Flexible spending account**   a plan that allows employees to contribute before-tax dollars that may be used for unreimbursed medical expenses or dependent care.

**Flipping**   a term used to describe the real estate investment practice of acquiring a home, repairing or remodeling the home, and then immediately, or soon thereafter, selling it (presumably at a profit).

**Floor limitation**   a minimum amount that an expenditure (or credit or other adjustment to taxable income) must meet before any amount is allowed.

**Flow-through entities**   legal entities like partnerships, limited liability companies, and S corporations that do not pay income tax. Income and losses from flow-through entities are allocated to their owners.

**For the convenience of the employer benefits**   nontaxable benefits employers provide to employees and employee spouses or dependents in the form of meals or lodging if provided on the employer's premises and are provided for a purpose that is helpful or convenient for the employer.

**Foreign joint venture**   a 50 percent or less owned foreign entity.

**Foreign personal holding company income**   a category of foreign source passive income that includes interest, dividends, rents, royalties, and gains from sale of assets.

**Foreign subsidiary**   a more than 50 percent owned foreign corporation.

**Foreign tax credit**   a credit for income taxes paid to a foreign jurisdiction.

**Foreign tax credit limitation**   the limit put on the use of creditable foreign taxes for the current year.

**Form 1065**   the form partnerships file annually with the IRS to report partnership ordinary income (loss) and separately stated items for the year.

**Form 1120S**   the form S corporations file annually with the IRS to report S corporation ordinary income (loss) and separately-stated items for the year.

**Form 7004**   the form C corporations, partnerships, and S corporations file to receive an automatic extension to file their annual tax return.

**Forward triangular merger**   an acquisition in which the acquired (target) corporation merges into an acquisition subsidiary of the acquiring corporation, after which the acquired corporation becomes part of the acquisition subsidiary of the acquiring corporation.

**Form W-2**   used to report wages paid to employees and the taxes withheld from them. The form is also used to report FICA taxes to the Social Security Administration.

**Form W-4**   a form used by a taxpayer to supply her employer with the information necessary to determine the amount of tax to withhold from each paycheck.

**Fringe benefits**   noncash benefit provided to an employee as a form of compensation. As a general rule, fringe benefits are taxable. However, certain fringe benefits are excluded from gross income.

**FTC basket**   a category of income that requires a separate FTC limitation computation.

**Full-inclusion method**   the method for accounting for advance payments for goods that requires that electing businesses immediately recognize advance payments as taxable income.

**Full-month convention**   convention that allows owners of intangibles to deduct an entire month's amortization in the month of purchase and month of disposition.

**Functional currency**   the currency of the primary economic environment in which an entity operates (that is the currency of the jurisdiction in which an entity primarily generates and expends cash).

**Future interest**   the right to receive property in the future.

# G

**GAAP capital accounts**   partners' capital accounts maintained using generally accepted accounting principals.

**General category income**   foreign source income that is not considered passive category income for foreign tax credit purposes (generally income from an active trade or business).

**General partnership**   a partnership with partners who all have unlimited liability with respect to the liabilities of the entity.

**Generation-skipping tax (GST)**   supplemental transfer tax designed to prevent the avoidance of estate and gift taxes through transfers that skip a generation of recipients.

**Gift**   a transfer of property where no consideration (or inadequate consideration) is paid for the property.

**Gift tax**   a tax based on the fair market values of wealth transfers by gift.

**Golsen rule**   the rule that states that the U.S. Tax Court will abide by the circuit court's rulings that has appellate jurisdiction for a case.

**Goodwill**   the value of a business in excess of the fair market value of identifiable assets.

**Graded vesting**   a qualified plan rule that requires an increasing percentage of plan benefits to vest with each additional year of employment.

**Graduated taxes**   taxes in which the tax base is divided into a series of monetary amounts, or brackets, where each successive bracket is taxed at a different (gradually higher or gradually lower) percentage rate.

**Grant date (stock options)**   the date on which employees receive stock options to acquire employer stock at a specified price.

**Grantor**   person creating a trust.

**Gross estate**   property owned by the decedent at death and certain property transfers taking effect at death.

**Gross income**   realized income reduced for any excluded or deferred income.

**Gross receipts (for purposes of net passive investment income tax calculation)**   the total amount of revenues (including passive investment income) received or accrued under the corporation's accounting method, not reduced by returns, allowances, cost of goods sold, or deductions. It also includes capital gains and losses.

**Group-term life insurance**   term life insurance provided by an employer to a group of employees.

**Guaranteed payments**   payments made to partners or LLC members that are guaranteed because they are not contingent on partnership profits or losses. They are economically similar to shareholder salary payments.

# H

**Haircut**   a phase-out limit that gradually reduces, but does not completely eliminate, deductions, credits, or other adjustments to taxable income.

**Half-year convention**   a depreciation convention that allows owners of tangible personal property to take one-half of a year's worth of depreciation in the year of purchase and in the year of disposition regardless of when the asset was actually placed in service or sold.

**Head of household**   one of five primary filing statuses. A taxpayer may file as head of household if s/he is unmarried as of the end of the year *and* pays more than half of the cost to maintain a household for a qualifying dependent who lives with the taxpayer for more than half of the year; or, s/he pays more than half the costs to maintain a household for a parent who qualifies as the taxpayer's dependent.

**Heirs**   persons who inherit property from the deceased.

**Hobby**   a revenue-generating activity that is motivated by personal motives rather than profit objectives.

**Home-equity indebtedness**   debt (except for acquisition indebtedness) secured by the taxpayer's qualified residence to the extent it does not exceed the fair market value of the residence over the acquisition indebtedness. Interest paid on up to $100,000 of home-equity indebtedness is allowed as an itemized deduction.

**Home office deduction**   deductions relating to the use of an office in the home. When the taxpayer qualifies, expenses are allocated between personal use and business use of the home.

**Horizontal equity**   one of the dimensions of equity. Horizontal equity is achieved if taxpayers in similar situations pay the same tax.

**Hot assets**   unrealized receivables or inventory items defined in §751(a) that give rise to ordinary gains and losses. The exact definition of hot assets depends on whether it is in reference to dispositions of a partnership interest or distributions.

**Hybrid entity**   an entity for which an election is available to choose the entity's tax status for U.S. tax purposes.

# I

**Impermissible accounting method**   an accounting method prohibited by tax laws.

**Implicit tax**   indirect taxes that result from a tax advantage the government grants to certain transactions to satisfy social, economic, or other objectives. They are defined as the reduced

before-tax return that a tax-favored asset produces because of its tax advantaged status.

**Imputed income** income from an economic benefit the taxpayer receives indirectly rather than directly. The amount of the income is based on comparable alternatives.

**Inbound transaction** a transaction conducted by a foreign person that is subject to U.S. taxation.

**Incentive stock option** a type of stock option that allows employees to defer the bargain element for regular tax purposes until the stock acquired from option exercises is sold. The bargain element is taxed at capital gains rates provided the stock is retained long enough to satisfy certain holding period requirements. Employers cannot deduct the bargain element as compensation expense.

**Income effect** one of the two basic responses that a taxpayer may have when taxes increase. The income effect predicts that when taxpayers are taxed more (e.g., tax rate increases from 25 to 28 percent), they will work harder to generate the same after-tax dollars.

**Income tax** a tax in which the tax base is income. Income taxes are imposed by the federal government and by most states.

**Independent contractor** a person who provides services to another entity, usually under terms specified in a contract. The independent contractor has more control over how and when to do the work than does an employee.

**Indirect conversion** the receipt of money or other property as a replacement for property that was destroyed or damaged in an involuntary conversion.

**Individual retirement account (IRA)** a tax-advantaged account in which individuals who have earned income can save for retirement.

**Information matching program** a program that compares the taxpayer's tax return to information submitted to the IRS from other taxpayers (e.g., banks, employers, mutual funds, brokerage companies, mortgage companies). Information matched includes items such as wages (e.g., Form W-2 submitted by employers), interest income (e.g., Form 1099-INT submitted by banks), dividend income (e.g., Form 1099-DIV submitted by brokerage companies), and so forth.

**Inheritance** a transfer of property when the owner is deceased (the transfer is made by the decedent's estate).

**Initial public offering** the first sale of stock by a company to the public.

**Inside basis** partnership or LLC's tax basis in its assets.

**Inside tax basis** the tax basis of an entity's assets and liabilities.

**Installment sale** a sale for which the taxpayer receives payment in more than one period.

**Institutional shareholder** an entity with large amounts to invest in corporate stock, such as investment companies, mutual funds, brokerages, insurance companies, pension funds, investment banks and endowment funds.

**Intangible assets** assets that do not have physical characteristics. Examples include goodwill, covenants not to compete, organizational expenditures, and research and experimentation expenses.

**Internal Revenue Code of 1986** the codified tax laws of the United States. Although the Code is frequently revised, there have only been three different codes since the Code was created in 1939 (i.e., the IRC of 1939, IRC of 1954, and IRC of 1986).

**Interpretative regulations** the most common regulation; they represent the Treasury's interpretation of the Code and are issued under the Treasury's general authority to interpret the Code.

**Interstate commerce** business conducted between parties in two or more states.

**Intervivos transfers** gifts made by a donor during his or her lifetime.

**Inventory items** (for sale of partnership interest purposes) classic inventory defined as property held for sale to customers in the ordinary course of business, but also assets that are not capital assets or § 1231 assets, which would produce ordinary income if sold by the entity. There are actually two definitions of inventory items in §751. §751(a) inventory items are defined in §751(d) to include all inventory items. The §751(b) definition includes only substantially appreciated inventory.

**Investment activities** a profit-seeking activity that is intermittent or occasional in frequency including the production or collection of income or the management, conservation, or maintenance of property held for the production of income.

**Investment expenses** expenses such as safe deposit rental fees, attorney and accounting fees that are necessary to produce portfolio income. Investment expenses are allowed for individuals as miscellaneous itemized deductions subject to the two percent of AGI floor limitation.

**Investment income** income received from portfolio type investments. Portfolio income includes capital gains and losses, interest, dividend, annuity, and royalty income not derived in the ordinary course of a trade or business. When computing the deductibility of investment interest expense, however, capital gains and dividends subject to the preferential tax rate are not treated as investment income unless the taxpayer elects to have this income taxed at ordinary tax rates.

**Investment interest expense** interest paid on borrowings or loans that are used to fund portfolio investments. Individuals are allowed an itemized deduction for qualified investment interest paid during the year.

**Involuntary conversion** a direct or indirect conversion of property through natural disaster, government condemnation, or accident that allows a taxpayer to defer realized gain if certain requirements are met.

**Itemized deductions** certain types of expenditures that Congress allows taxpayers to deduct as from AGI deductions.

# J

**Joint tenancy with the right of survivorship** title to property that provides the co-owners with equal rights to it and that automatically transfers to the survivor at the death of a co-owner.

# K

**Kiddie tax** a tax imposed at the parent's marginal rate on a child's unearned income.

# L

**Last will and testament** document that directs the transfer of ownership of the decedent's assets to the heirs.

**Late filing penalty** penalty assessed if a taxpayer does not file a tax return by the required date (the original due date plus extension).

**Least aggregate deferral** an approach to determine a partnership's required year-end if a majority of the partners don't have the same

year-end and if the principal partners don't have the same year-end. As the name implies, this approach minimizes the combined tax deferral of the partners.

**Legislative grace**   the concept that taxpayers receive certain tax benefits only because Congress writes laws that allow taxpayers to receive the tax benefits.

**Legislative regulations**   the rarest type of regulation, issued when Congress specifically directs the Treasury Department to create regulations to address an issue in an area of law. In these instances, the Treasury is actually writing the law instead of interpreting the Code. Because legislative regulations actually represent tax law instead of an interpretation of tax law, legislative regulations have more authoritative weight than interpretative and procedural regulations.

**Life estate**   right to possess property and/or collect income from property for the duration of someone's life.

**Life insurance trust**   trust funded with an irrevocable transfer of a life insurance policy and that gives the trustee the power to re-designate beneficiaries.

**LIFO**   last-in, first-out method; an accounting method that values the cost of assets sold under the assumption that assets are sold in the reverse order in which they are purchased (i.e., last purchased, first sold).

**LIFO recapture amount**   the excess of a C corporation's inventory basis under the FIFO method in excess of the inventory basis under the LIFO method in its final tax year as a C corporation before it becomes an S corporation.

**LIFO recapture tax**   a tax levied on C corporations that elects to be taxed as an S corporation when it is using the LIFO method for accounting for inventories.

**Like-kind exchange**   a nontaxable (or partially taxable) trade or exchange of assets that are similar or related in use.

**Limited liability company (LLC)**   a type of flow-through entity for federal income tax purposes. By state law, the owners of the LLC have limited liability with respect to the entity's debts or liabilities. Limited liability companies are taxed as partnerships for federal income tax purposes.

**Limited partnership**   a partnership with at least one general partner with unlimited liability for the entity's debts and at least one limited partner with liability limited to the limited partner's investment in the partnership.

**Liquidating distributions**   distribution that terminates an owner's interest in the entity.

**Liquidation value**   the amount a partner would receive if the part-nership were to sell all its assets, pay its debts, and distribute its remaining assets to the partners in exchange for their partnership interests.

**Listed property**   business assets that are often used for personal purposes. Depreciation on listed property is limited to the business use portion of the asset.

**Local tax**   taxes imposed by local governments (cities, counties, school districts, etc.).

**Long-term capital gain property**   property that would generate long-term capital gain if it were sold. This includes capital assets held for more than a year.

**Long-term capital gains or losses**   gains or losses from the sale of capital assets held for more than 12 months.

**Luxury automobile**   an automobile on which the amount of annual depreciation expense is limited because the cost of the automobile exceeds a certain threshold.

# M

**M adjustments**   see definition of Schedule M adjustments.

**Ms**   see definition of Schedule M adjustments.

**Majority interest taxable year**   the common tax year of a group of partners who jointly hold greater than 50% of the profits and capital interests in the partnership.

**Marginal tax rate**   the tax rate that applies to the *next additional increment* of a taxpayer's taxable income (or to deductions). Specifically,

$$\text{Marginal Tax Rate} = \frac{\Delta Tax}{\Delta Taxable\ Income}$$

$$= \frac{(New\ Total\ Tax - Old\ Total\ Tax)}{(New\ Taxable\ Income - Old\ Taxable\ Income)}$$

"old" refers to the current tax and "new" refers to the revised tax after incorporating the additional income (or deductions) in question.

**Marital deduction**   deduction for transfers of qualified property to a spouse.

**Market discount**   the difference between the amount paid for a bond in a market purchase rather than at original issuance when the amount paid is less than the maturity value of the bond.

**Market premium**   the difference between the amount paid for a bond in a market purchase rather than at original issuance when the amount paid is greater than the maturity value of the bond.

**Marriage benefit**   the tax savings married couples receive by filing a joint return relative to the tax they would have paid had they each filed as single taxpayers. This typically occurs when one spouse is either not working or earns significantly less than the other spouse.

**Marriage penalty**   the extra tax cost a married couple pays by fil-ing a joint return relative to what they would have paid had they each filed as single taxpayers. This typically occurs when both spouses earn approximately the same amount of income.

**Married filing jointly**   one of five primary filing statuses. A taxpayer may file jointly if s/he is legally married as of the end of the year (or one spouse died during the year and the surviving spouse did not remarry) and both spouses agree to jointly file. Married couples filing joint returns combine their income and deductions and share joint and several liability for the resulting tax.

**Married filing separately**   one of five primary filing statuses. When married couples file separately, each spouse reports the income he or she received during the year and the deductions he or she paid on a tax return separate from the other spouse.

**Maturity**   the amount of time to the expiration date, or maturity date, of a debt instrument. The maturity of a debt instrument is generally the life of the instrument at which a payment of the face value is due or the instrument terminates.

**Maturity value**   the amount paid to a bondholder when the bond matures and the bondholder redeems the bond for cash.

**Medicare tax**   the Medical Health Insurance (MHI) tax. This tax helps pay medical costs for qualifying individuals. Employees pay the Medicare tax at a rate of 1.45% on all wages. Self-employed tax-payers pay Medicare taxes at a rate of 2.9% of net-earnings from self employment. There is no limit of the amount of wages subject to the Medicare tax.

**Merger**   the acquisition by one corporation (acquiring) of the assets and liabilities of another (target) corporation. No new entity is created in the transaction.

**Mid-month convention** a convention that allows owners of real property to take one-half of a month's depreciation during the month when the property was placed in service and in the month it was disposed of.

**Mid-quarter convention** a depreciation convention for tangible personal property which allows for one-half of a quarter's worth of depreciation in the quarter of purchase and in the quarter of disposition. This convention must be used when more than 40% of tangible personal property is placed into service in the fourth quarter of the tax year.

**Minimum tax credit** credit available in certain situations for the alternative minimum tax paid. The credit can be used only when the regular tax exceeds the tentative minimum tax.

**Miscellaneous itemized deductions** deductions representing the sum of certain itemized deductions, such as unreimbursed employee business expenses, investment expenses, and tax preparation fees, that are subject to a special floor limitation.

**Mixed-motive expenditures** activities that involve a mixture of business and personal objectives.

**Modified Cost Recovery System (MACRS)** the current tax depreciation system for tangible personal and real property. Depreciation under MACRS is calculated by finding the depreciation method, the recovery period, and the applicable convention.

**Municipal bond** the common name for state and local government debt.

**Mutual fund** a diversified portfolio of securities owned and managed by a regulated investment company.

# N

**Negative basis adjustment** (for special basis adjustment purposes) the sum of the recognized loss and the amount of the basis increase made by an owner receiving the distribution.

**Net capital gain** the net gain resulting when taxpayers combine net long-term capital gains with net short-term capital losses.

**Net earnings from self-employment** the amount of earnings subject to self-employment income taxes. The amount is 92.35% of the net income from a taxpayer's Schedule C (for self-employed taxpayers).

**Net investment income** gross investment income reduced by deductible investment expenses.

**Net long-term capital gain** the net gain resulting when taxpayers combine long-term capital gains and losses for the year.

**Net long-term capital loss** the net loss resulting when taxpayers combine long-term capital gains and losses for the year.

**Net operating loss (NOL)** the excess of allowable deductions over gross income.

**Net operating loss carryback** the amount of a current year net operating loss that is carried back to offset income in a prior year.

**Net operating loss carryover** the amount of a current year net operating loss that is carried forward for up to 20 years to offset taxable income in those years.

**Net passive investment income** passive investment income less any expenses connected with producing it.

**Net short-term capital gain** the net gain resulting when taxpayers combine short-term capital gains and losses for the year.

**Net short-term capital loss** the net loss resulting when taxpayers combine short-term capital gains and losses for the year.

**Net unearned income** unearned income in excess of a specified threshold amount of a child under the age of 19 or under the age of 24 if a full-time student.

**Net unrealized built-in gain** the net gain (if any) an S corporation that was formerly a C corporation would recognize if it sold each asset at its fair market value. It is measured on the first day of the corporation's first year as an S corporation.

**Nexus** the connection between a business and a tax jurisdiction sufficient to subject the business to the tax jurisdiction's tax system. Also, the connection that required to exist between a jurisdiction and a potential taxpayer such that the jurisdiction asserts the right to impose a tax.

**No-additional-cost services** a nontaxable fringe benefit that provides employer services to employees with little cost to the employer (e.g., airline tickets or phone service).

**Nonacquiescence** issued after the IRS loses a trial-level or circuit court case when the IRS has decided to continue to litigate this issue.

**Nonbusiness income** all income except for business income—generally investment income and rental income.

**Nondeductible terminable interests** transfers of property interests to a spouse that do not qualify for a marital deduction, because the interest of the spouse terminates when some event occurs or after a specified amount of time and the property is then transferred to another person.

**Nondomiciliary business** a business operating in a state other than its commercial domicile.

**Non-performance based compensation** compensation paid to an employee that does not depend on the employee's performance or the corporation's performance or success. It usually is straight salary.

**Nonqualified deferred compensation** compensation provided for under a nonqualified plan allowing employees to defer compensation to a future period.

**Nonqualified stock option** a type of stock option requiring employees to treat the bargain element from options exercised as ordinary income in the tax year options are exercised. Correspondingly, employers may deduct the bargain element as compensation expense in the tax year options are exercised.

**Nonrecognition provisions** tax laws that allow taxpayers to permanently exclude income from taxation or to defer recognizing realized income until a subsequent period.

**Nonrecognition transaction** a transaction where at least a portion of the realized gain or loss is not currently recognized.

**Nonrecourse debt** debt for which no partner bears any economic risk of loss. Mortgages on real property are a common form of nonrecourse debt.

**Nonrefundable credits** tax credits that reduce a taxpayer's gross tax liability but are limited to the amount of gross tax liability. Any credit not used in the current year is lost.

**Nonresident alien** an individual that does not meet the criteria to be treated as a resident for U.S. tax purposes.

**Nonservice partner** a partner who receives a partnership interest in exchange for property rather than services.

**Nontaxable fringe benefit** an employer provided benefit that may be excluded from an employee's income.

**Not definitely related deductions** deductions that are not associated with a specific item or items of gross income.

# O

**Office examination** the second most common audit. As the name suggests, the IRS conducts these audits at the local IRS office. These audits are typically broader in scope and more complex than correspondence examinations. Small businesses, taxpayers operating sole proprietorships, and middle- to high-income individual taxpayers are more likely, if audited, to have office examinations.

**Operating distributions**   payments to the owners from an entity that represent a distribution of entity profits. Distributions generally fall into the category of operating distributions when the owners continue their interests in the entity after the distribution.

**Operating income**   the annual income from a trade or business or rental activity.

**Operating loss**   the annual loss from a trade or business or rental activity.

**Option exercise**   the use of a stock option to acquire employer stock at a specified price.

**Ordinary and necessary expense**   interpreted as an expense that is normal or appropriate and that is helpful or conducive to the business activity.

**Ordinary asset**   an asset created or used in a taxpayer's trade or business (e.g. accounts receivable or inventory) that generates ordinary income (or loss) on disposition.

**Ordinary business income (loss)**   a partnership's or S corporation's remaining income or loss after separately stated items are removed. It is also referred to as non-separately stated income (loss).

**Ordinary income property**   property that if sold would generate income taxed at ordinary rates.

**Organization costs**   costs associated with legally forming a partnership (such as attorneys' and accountants' fees)

**Organizational expenditures**   expenses that are (1) connected directly with the creation of a corporation or partnership, (2) chargeable to a capital account, and (3) generally amortized over 180 months (limited immediate expensing may be available).

**Original issue discount**   a type of bond issued for less than the maturity or face value of the bond.

**Outbound transaction**   a transaction conducted outside the United States by a U.S. person that is subject to U.S. taxation.

**Outside basis**   owner's tax basis of partnership (or LLC) interest. Outside basis includes an owner's share of the entity's debt.

**Outside tax basis**   an investor's tax basis in the stock of a corporation.

# P

**PAL**   an acronym for "passive activity loss." Losses allocated to partners who are not material participants in the partnership are passive activity losses.

**Parent-subsidiary controlled group**   a form of controlled group consisting of one corporation that owns at least 80% of the voting power or stock value of another corporation on the last day of the year.

**Partial liquidation**   a distribution made a corporation to shareholders that results from a contraction of the corporation's activities.

**Partnership agreement**   an agreement among the partners in a partnership stipulating the partners' rights and responsibilities in the partnership.

**Partnership interest**   an intangible asset reflecting the economic rights a partner has with respect to a partnership including the right to receive assets in liquidation of the partnership called a capital interest and the right to be allocated profits and losses called a profits interest.

**Passive activity**   an activity in which the taxpayer does not materially participate.

**Passive activity income or loss**   income or loss from an activity in which the taxpayer does not materially participate.

**Passive activity loss rules**   tax rules designed to limit taxpayers' ability to deduct losses from activities in which they don't materially participate against income from other sources.

**Passive category income**   foreign source personal holding company such as interest, dividends, rents, royalties, annuities, and gains from sale of certain assets that is combined in computing the FTC limitation.

**Passive investment income (PII)**   royalties, rents, dividends, interest (including tax exempt interest), and annuities. It does not include capital gains and losses.

**Passive investments**   direct or indirect investments (other than through a taxable corporation) in a trade or business or rental activity in which the taxpayer does not materially participate.

**Payment liability**   liabilities of accrual method businesses for which economic performance occurs when the business actually *pays* the liability for, among others: worker's compensation; tort; breach of contract or violation of law; rebates and refunds; awards, prizes and jackpots; insurance, warranties, and service contracts provided *to* the business; and taxes.

**Percentage depletion**   method of recovering cost of natural resource that allows a taxpayer to recover or expense an amount based on a statutorily determined percentage.

**Permanent book-tax differences**   items of income or deductions for either book purposes or for tax purposes during the year but not both. Permanent differences do not reverse over time so over the long run the total amount of income or deduction for the item is different for book and tax purposes.

**Permanent establishment**   generally, a fixed place of business through which an enterprise carries out its business. Examples include a place of management, a branch, an office, and a factory.

**Permissible accounting method**   accounting method allowed under the tax law. Permissible accounting methods are adopted the first time a taxpayer uses the method on a tax return.

**Person**   an individual, trust, estate, partnership, association, company, or corporation.

**Personal exemption**   a fixed deduction allowed for an individual taxpayer, and spouse if filing a joint tax return.

**Personal expenses**   expenses incurred for personal motives. Personal expenses are not deductible for tax purposes.

**Personal property tax**   a tax on the fair market value of all types of tangible and intangible property, except real property.

**Personal property**   all tangible property other than real property.

**Phase-outs**   limitations that gradually eliminate deductions, credits, or other adjustments to taxable income typically done ratably over a phase-out range (based on AGI or related income measure).

**Point**   one percent of the principal amount of a loan. A home buyer might pay points to compensate the lender for services or for a lower interest rate. Points paid to compensate the lender for services are not deductible. Points paid to the lender to reduce the rate of the loan are generally deductible (1) immediately if the loan is an original home loan or (2) over the life of the loan if the loan is a refinance.

**Portfolio investments**   investments producing dividends, interest, royalties, annuities, or capital gains.

**Positive basis adjustment**   (for special basis adjustment purposes) the sum of the gain recognized by the owners receiving distributed property and the amount of any required basis reduction.

**Post-termination transition period (PTTP)**   the period that begins on the day after the last day of a corporation's last taxable year as an S corporation and generally ends on the later of (a) one year after the

last S corporation day, or (b) the due date for filing the return for the last year as an S corporation (including extensions).

**Preferential tax rate**  tax rates lower than the tax rate applied to ordinary income.

**Preferentially taxed income**  income taxed at a preferential rate such as long-term capital gains and qualified dividends.

**Present interest**  right to presently enjoy property or receive income from the property.

**Present value**  the concept that $1 today is worth more than $1 in the future. For example, assuming an investor can earn a 5% after-tax return, $1 invested today should be worth $1.05 in one year. Hence, $1 today is equivalent to $1.05 in one year.

**Primary authority**  official sources of the tax law generated by the legislative branch (i.e., statutory authority issued by Congress), judicial branch (i.e., rulings by the U.S. District Court, U.S. Tax Court, U.S. Court of Federal Claims, U.S. Circuit Court of Appeals, or U.S. Supreme Court), or executive/administrative branch (i.e., Treasury or IRS pronouncements).

**Principal partner**  a partner having a 5% interest or more in partnership capital or profits.

**Principal residence**  the main place of residence for a taxpayer during the taxable year.

**Private activity bond**  bond issued by a municipality but proceeds of bond are used to fund privately owned activity.

**Private letter rulings**  IRS pronouncements issued in response to a taxpayer request for a ruling on specific issues for the taxpayer. They are common for proposed transactions with potentially large tax implications. For the requesting taxpayer, a private letter ruling has very high authority. For all other taxpayers, private letter rulings have little authoritative weight.

**Private nonoperating foundations**  privately sponsored foundations that disburse funds to other charities.

**Private operating foundations**  privately sponsored foundations that actually fund and conduct charitable activities.

**Probate**  process in the probate court of gathering property possessed by or titled in the name of a decedent at the time of death, paying the debts of the decedent and transferring the ownership of any remaining property to the decedent's heirs.

**Probate estate**  property possessed by or titled in the name of a decedent at the time of death.

**Procedural regulations**  regulations that explain Treasury Department procedures as they relate to administering the Code.

**Profits interest**  an interest in a partnership giving a partner the right to share in future profits but not the right to share in the current value of a partnership's assets. Profits interests are generally not taxable in the year they are received.

**Progressive tax rate structure**  a tax rate structure that imposes an increasing marginal tax rate as the tax base increases. As the tax base increases, both the marginal tax rate and the taxes paid increase.

**Prohibited interest**  an interest in the corporation maintained by a taxpayer after a complete redemption that does not allow the taxpayer to waive the family attribution rules.

**Proportional tax rate structure**  also known as a flat tax, this tax rate structure imposes a constant tax rate throughout the tax base. As the tax base increases, the taxes paid increase proportionally.

**Proposed regulations**  regulations issued in proposed form; they do not carry the same authoritative weight as temporary or final regulations. All regulations are issued in proposed form first to allow public comment on them.

**Public Law 86-272**  federal law passed by Congress that provides additional protection for sellers of tangible personal property against income tax nexus.

**Publicly traded corporations**  corporations whose stock is publicly traded on a stock exchange.

## Q

**Qualified debt**  (for mortgage interest expense deduction purposes) the amount of debt on which qualified residence interest is paid. This includes debt up to $1,000,000 of acquisition indebtedness and up to $100,000 of home-equity indebtedness.

**Qualified dividends**  paid by domestic or certain qualified foreign corporations that are eligible for lower capital gains rates.

**Qualified educational expenses**  consist of tuition and related costs for enrolling the taxpayer, spouse, or a dependent at a post-secondary institution of higher education.

**Qualified educational loans**  loans whose proceeds are used to pay qualified education expenses.

**Qualified employee discount**  a nontaxable fringe benefit that provides employer goods at a discount (but not below the employer's cost) and services to employees at up to a 20% discount.

**Qualified moving expense reimbursement**  a nontaxable fringe benefit that allows employers to pay moving related expenses on behalf of employees.

**Qualified nonrecourse financing**  nonrecourse debt secured by real property from a commercial lender unrelated to the borrower.

**Qualified production activities income (QPAI)**  the *net* income from selling or leasing property that was manufactured in the United States.

**Qualified replacement property**  property acquired to replace property damaged or destroyed in an involuntary conversion. It must be of a similar or related use to the original property even if the replacement property is real property (rental real estate for rental real estate).

**Qualified residence**  the taxpayer's principal residence and one other residence.

**Qualified residence interest**  interest paid on acquisition indebtedness and on home-equity indebtedness that is secured by a qualified residence.

**Qualified retirement accounts**  plans meeting certain requirements that allow compensation placed in the account to be tax deferred until the taxpayer withdraws money from the account.

**Qualified retirement plans**  employer-sponsored retirement plans that meet government imposed funding and anti-discrimination requirements.

**Qualified small business stock**  stock received at original issue from a corporation with a gross tax basis in its assets both before and after the issuance of no more than $50,000,000 and with 80% of the value of its assets used in the active conduct of certain qualified trades or businesses.

**Qualified transportation fringe benefit**  a nontaxable fringe benefit provided by employers in the form of mass transit passes, parking, or vanpool benefits.

**Qualified tuition plans (529 plans)**  a state-sponsored program designed to help parents finance education expenses by generating tax free income. 529 plans are administered by certain investment companies and are subject to contribution requirements and investment guidelines.

**Qualifying child**  an individual who qualifies as as dependent of a taxpayer by meeting a relationship, age, residence, and support test with respect to the taxpayer.

**Qualifying relative**   an individual who meets a relationship, support, and gross income test may qualify to be a dependent of another taxpayer.

**Qualifying widow or widower**   one of five primary filing statuses. Applies for up to two years after the year in which the taxpayer's spouse dies (the taxpayer files married filing jointly in the year of the spouse's death) as long as the taxpayer remans unmarried and maintains a household for a dependent child.

**Question of fact**   a research question that hinges upon the facts and circumstances of the taxpayer's transaction.

**Question of law**   a research question that hinges upon the interpretation of the law, such as interpreting a particular phrase in a code section.

# R

**Real property**   land and structures permanently attached to land.

**Real property tax**   a tax on the fair market value of land and structures permanently attached to land.

**Realization**   gain or loss that results from an exchange of property rights in a transaction.

**Realization principle**   the proposition that income only exists when there is a transaction with another party resulting in a measurable change in property rights.

**Realized gain or loss**   the difference between the amount realized and the adjusted basis of an asset sold or otherwise disposed of.

**Realized income**   income generated in a transaction with a second party in which there is a measurable change in property rights between parties.

**Recognition**   gain or loss included in the computation of taxable income.

**Recognized gain or loss**   the gain or loss included in gross income on a taxpayer's tax return. This is usually the realized gain or loss unless a nonrecognition provision applies.

**Recourse debt**   debt held by partnership for which at least one partner has economic risk of loss.

**Recovery period**   a length of time prescribed by statute in which tangible business property is depreciated.

**Refinance**   when a taxpayer pays off a current loan with the proceeds of a second loan.

**Refundable credits**   credits that are not limited to the amount of the gross tax liability. If the credit exceeds the gross tax liability, the taxpayer receives a refund for the excess credit.

**Regressive tax rate structure**   a tax rate structure that imposes a decreasing marginal tax rate as the tax base increases. As the tax base increases, the taxes paid increases, but the marginal tax rate decreases.

**Regulations**   the Treasury Department's official interpretation of the Internal Revenue Code. Regulations are the highest authority issued by the IRS.

**Related-party transaction**   financial activities among family members, among owners and their businesses, or among businesses owned by the same owners.

**Remainder**   right to ownership of a property that transfers to a new owner, the remainderman, following a temporary interest.

**Remainderman**   person entitled to a remainder interest.

**Reorganization**   a tax-deferred transaction (acquisition, disposition, recapitalization, or change of name or place of incorporation) that meets one of the seven statutory definitions found in §368(a)(1).

**Research and experimentation costs**   expenses for research including costs of research laboratories (salaries, materials, and other related expenses). Taxpayers can elect to amortize research and development costs over not less than 60 months from the time benefits are first derived from the research.

**Residence-based jurisdiction**   taxation of income based on the taxpayer's residence.

**Resident alien**   an individual who is not a U.S. citizen but is treated as a resident for U.S. tax purposes.

**Restricted stock**   stock employees receive as compensation that may only be sold after the passage of time or after certain performance targets are achieved. Because employees are not entitled to immediately sell the restricted stock they receive, the value of the stock is generally not taxable to employees or deductible by employers until the selling restrictions lapse.

**Return of capital**   the portion of proceeds from a sale (or distribution) representing a return of the original cost of the underlying property.

**Revenue procedures**   second in administrative authoritative weight after regulations. Revenue procedures are much more detailed than regulations and explain in greater detail IRS practice and procedures in administering the tax law. Revenue procedures have the same authoritative weight as revenue rulings.

**Revenue rulings**   second in administrative authoritative weight after regulations. Revenue rulings address the specific application of the Code and regulations to a specific factual situation. Revenue rulings have the same authoritative weight as revenue procedures.

**Reverse hybrid entity**   a "check-the-box" entity owned by multiple persons for which corporation status is elected.

**Reverse triangular merger**   an acquisition in which an acquisition subsidiary of the acquiring corporation merges into the acquired (target) corporation, after which the acquired corporation becomes a subsidiary of the acquiring corporation.

**Reversion**   terms by which ownership of property returns to the original owner following a temporary interest.

**Rollover**   a transfer of funds from a qualified retirement plan to another qualified retirement plan, from a qualified retirement plan to a Roth or traditional IRA, or from a traditional IRA to a Roth IRA.

**Roth 401(k)**   a type of defined contribution plan that allows employees to contribute on an after-tax basis and receive distributions tax free.

**Roth IRA**   an individually-managed retirement plan permitting individuals to contribute on an after-tax basis and receive distributions tax free.

**Roth qualified retirement plans**   retirement plans meeting the requirements for qualified plans but not allowing employees a current deduction for contributions. Distributions from Roth qualified retirement plans are tax free.

**Royalties**   payments taxpayers receive for allowing others to use their tangible or intangible property.

# S

**S corporation**   a corporation under state law that has elected to be taxed under the rules provided in subchapter S of the Internal Revenue Code. Under subchapter S, an S corporation is taxed as a flow-through entity.

**Safe-harbor provision**   provision of the tax law that reduces or eliminates a taxpayer's liability under the law if the taxpayer meets certain requirements.

**Sales tax**   a tax imposed on the retail sales of goods (plus certain services). Retailers are responsible for collecting and remitting the tax; typically sales tax is collected at the point of sale.

**Same-day sale**   phrase used to describe a situation where a taxpayer exercises stock options and then immediately sells the stock received through the option exercise.

**Schedule C**   a schedule on which a taxpayer reports the income and deductions for a sole-proprietorship.

**Schedule K**   a schedule filed with a partnership's annual tax return listing its ordinary income (loss) and its separately stated items.

**Schedule M adjustments**   book-tax differences that corporations report on the Schedule M-1 or M-3 of Form 1120 as adjustments to book income to reconcile to taxable income.

**Schedule M-1**   a schedule on Form 1120 that reconciles book income to taxable income before special deductions. Book-tax differences are reported in a general way.

**Schedule M-3**   a schedule on Form 1120 that reconciles book income to taxable income for corporations with total assets of $10 million or more. The schedule M-3 includes much more detail than the Schedule M-1 including identifying whether each book tax difference is a temporary difference or a permanent book-tax difference.

**Secondary authority**   unofficial tax authorities that interpret and explain the primary authorities, such as tax research services, tax articles, newsletters, and textbooks. Secondary authorities may be very helpful in understanding a tax issue, but they hold little weight in a tax dispute (hence, the term *unofficial* tax authorities).

**Secured loan**   a loan for which property is used as collateral for the loan. If the loan goes into default, the lender is only allowed to take possession of the property securing the loan.

**Security**   a financial instrument including an equity interest in business organizations and creditor interests such as savings accounts, notes, and bonds.

**Self-employment taxes**   Social Security and Medicare taxes paid by the self employed on a taxpayer's net earnings from self employment. For self-employed taxpayers, the terms "self-employment tax" and "FICA tax" are synonymous.

**SEP IRA**   a simplified employee pension that can be administered through an individual retirement account.

**Separate tax return**   a state tax return methodology requiring that each related entity with nexus files a separate tax return.

**Separately stated items**   income, expenses, gains, losses, credits and other items that are excluded from a partnership's or S corporation's operating income (loss) and disclosed to partners in a partnership or shareholders of an S corporation separately because their tax effects may be different for each partner or shareholder.

**Serial gift**   transfer tax strategy that uses the annual exclusion to convert a potentially large taxable transfer into a tax-exempt transfer by dividing it into multiple intervivos gifts spread over several periods or donees.

**Service partner**   partners who receive their partnership interest by contributing services rather than cash or property.

**Settlement statement**   a statement that details the monies paid out and received by the buyer and seller in a real estate transaction.

**Short-term capital gains or losses**   gains or losses from the sale of capital assets held for one year or less.

**Sin taxes**   taxes imposed on the purchase of goods (e.g., alcohol, tobacco products, etc.) that are considered socially less desirable.

**Single**   one of five primary statuses available. A taxpayer files as single if s/he is unmarried as of the end of the year and does not qualify for any of the other filing statuses. A taxpayer is considered single if s/he is unmarried or legally separated from his or her spouse under a divorce or separate maintenance decree.

**Single member LLC**   a limited liability company with only one member. Single member LLCs with individual owners are taxed as sole proprietorships and as disregarded entities otherwise.

**Social Security Tax**   the Old Age, Survivors, and Disability Insurance (OASDI) tax. The tax is intended to provide basic pension coverage for the retired and disabled. Employees pay Social Security tax at a rate of 6.2% on the wage base (employers also pay 6.2%). Self-employed taxpayers are subject to a Social Security tax at a rate of 12.4% on their net earnings from self employment. The base on which Social Security taxes are paid is limited to an annually determined amount of wages and/or net earnings from self employment.

**Sole proprietorship**   a business entity that is not legally separate from the individual owner of the business. The income of a sole proprietorship is taxed directly to the owner.

**Solicitation**   selling activities or activities ancillary to selling that are protected under Public Law 86-272.

**Source-based jurisdiction**   taxation of income based on where the income is earned.

**Special allocations**   allocations of income, gain, expense, or loss, etc. that are allocated to the owners of an entity in a manner out of proportion with the owners' interests in the entity. Special allocations can be made by entities treated as partnerships for federal income tax purposes.

**Special basis adjustment**   an optional (sometimes mandatory) election to adjust the entity asset bases as a result of an owner's disposition of entity interest or of distributions from the entity to its owners.

**Specific identification method**   an elective method for determining the cost of an asset sold. Under this method, the taxpayer specifically chooses the assets that are to be sold.

**Split-gift election**   election that allows spouses to treat all gifts made in a year as if each spouse made one-half of each gift.

**Spot rate**   the foreign currency exchange rate on a specific day.

**Standard deduction**   a fixed deduction offered in lieu of itemized deductions. The amount of the standard deduction depends on the taxpayer's filing status.

*Stare decisis*   a doctrine meaning that a court will rule consistently with (a) its previous rulings (i.e., unless, due to evolving interpretations of the tax law over time, they decide to overturn an earlier decision) and (b) the rulings of higher courts with appellate jurisdiction (i.e., the courts their cases are appealed to).

**Start-up costs**   expenses that would be classified as business expenses except that the expenses are incurred before the business begins. These costs are generally capitalized and amortized over 180 months but limited immediate expensing may be available.

**State tax**   a tax imposed by one of the fifty U.S. states.

**Statements on Standards for Tax Services (SSTS)**   standards of practice for tax professionals issued by the AICPA. Currently, there are seven SSTS that describe the tax professional standards when recommending a tax return position, answering questions on a tax return, preparing a tax return using data supplied by a client, using estimates on a tax return, taking a tax return position inconsistent with a previous year's tax return, discovering a tax return error, and giving tax advice to taxpayers.

**Static forecasting**   the process of forecasting tax revenues based on the existing state of transactions while ignoring how taxpayers may alter their activities in response to a tax law change.

**Statute of limitations**   defines the period in which the taxpayer can file an amended tax return or the IRS can assess a tax deficiency for

a specific tax year. For both amended tax returns filed by a taxpayer and proposed tax assessments by the IRS, the statute of limitations generally ends three years from the *later* of (1) the date the tax return was actually filed or (2) the tax return's original due date.

**Step-transaction doctrine**   judicial doctrine that allows the IRS to collapse a series of related transactions into one transaction to determine the tax consequences of the transaction.

**Stock dividend**   a dividend made by a corporation of its own stock.

**Stock-for-stock acquisition**   an exchange of solely voting stock by the acquiring corporation in exchange for stock of the target corporation, after which the acquiring corporation controls (owns 80-percent-or-more of) the target corporation. Often referred to as a "Type B reorganization."

**Stock redemption**   a property distribution made to shareholders in return for some or all of their stock in the distributing corporation that is not in partial or complete liquidation of the corporation.

**Stock split**   a stock redemption in which a corporation sends each shareholder 2 shares of stock for each share held by the shareholder.

**Strike price**   see exercise price.

**Structural tax rate**   the tax rate computed by dividing a company's income tax provision adjusted for nonrecurring permanent differences by its pretax income from continuing operations.

**Student loans**   loans where the proceeds are used for qualified educational expenses, but do not include home equity loans.

**Subchapter K**   the portion of the Internal Revenue Code dealing with partnerships tax law.

**Subchapter S**   the portion of the Internal Revenue Code containing tax rules for S corporations and their shareholders.

**Subpart F income**   income earned by a controlled foreign corporation that is not eligible for deferral from U.S. taxation.

**Substance-over-form doctrine**   judicial doctrine that allows the IRS to consider the transaction's substance regardless of its form and, where appropriate, reclassify the transaction according to its substance.

**Substantial authority**   the standard used to determine whether a tax practitioner may recommend and a taxpayer may take a tax return position without being subject to IRS penalty under IRC Sec. 6694 and IRC Sec. 6662, respectively. A good CPA evaluates whether supporting authority is substantial or not based upon the supporting and opposing authorities' weight and relevance. Substantial authority suggests that the probability that the taxpayer's position is sustained upon audit or litigation is in the 40 plus percent range or above.

**Substantial basis reduction**   negative basis adjustment of more than $250,000 resulting from a distribution from the entity to its owners.

**Substantial built-in loss**   exists when a partnership's adjusted basis in its property exceeds the property's fair market value by more than $250,000 when a transfer of an interest occurs.

**Substantially appreciated inventory**   (for partnership disproportionate distributions purposes) inventory whose fair market value exceeds its basis by more than 120%.

**Substituted basis**   the transfer of the tax basis of stock or other property given up in an exchange to stock or other property received in return.

**Substitution effect**   one of the two basic responses that a taxpayer may have when taxes increase. The substitution effect predicts that when taxpayers are taxed more, rather than work more, they will substitute nontaxable activities (e.g., leisure pursuits) for taxable ones because the marginal value of taxable activities has decreased.

**Sufficiency**   a standard for evaluating a good tax system. Sufficiency is defined as assessing the aggregate size of the tax revenues that must be generated and ensuring that the tax system provides these revenues.

**Syndication costs**   costs partnerships incur to promote the sale of partnership interests to the public. Syndication expenses must be capitalized and are not amortizable.

# T

**Tacks**   the adding on of the transferor's holding period of property to the transferee in a tax-deferred exchange.

**Tax**   a payment required by a government that is unrelated to any specific benefit or service received from the government.

**Tax accounting balance sheet**   a balance sheet that records a company's assets and liabilities at their tax bases instead of their financial accounting bases.

**Tax avoidance**   the legal act of arranging one's transactions or affairs to reduce taxes paid.

**Tax base**   the item that is being taxed (e.g., purchase price of a good, taxable income, etc.).

**Tax basis**   the amount of a taxpayer's unrecovered cost of or investment in an asset.

**Tax benefit rule**   holds that a refund of an amount deducted in a previous period is only included in income to the extent that the deduction reduced taxable income.

**Tax bracket**   a range of taxable income taxed at a specified rate.

**Tax capital accounts**   partners' capital accounts initially determined using the tax basis of contributed property and maintained using tax accounting income and expense recognition principles.

**Tax carryforwards**   tax deductions or credits that cannot be used on the current year tax return and that can be carried forward to reduce taxable income or taxes payable in a future year.

**Tax contingency reserve**   a company's reserve for taxes it has not paid, but it expects to pay, in the future for positions taken on the current and prior year income tax returns.

**Tax credits**   items that directly reduce a taxpayer's tax liability.

**Tax evasion**   the willful attempt to defraud the government (i.e., by not paying taxes legally owed). Tax evasion falls outside the confines of legal tax avoidance.

**Tax haven**   generally, a country offering very favorable tax laws for foreign businesses and individuals.

**Tax rate**   the level of taxes imposed on the tax base, usually expressed as a percentage.

**Tax rate schedule**   a schedule of progressive tax rates and the income ranges to which the rates apply that a taxpayer may use to compute her gross tax liability.

**Tax shelter**   an investment or other arrangement designed to produce tax benefits without any expectation of economic profits.

**Tax tables**   IRS provided tables that specify the federal income tax liability for individuals with taxable income within a specific range. The tables differ by filing status and reflect tax rates that increase with taxable income.

**Tax treaties**   agreements negotiated between countries that describe the tax treatment of entities subject to tax in both countries (e.g., U.S. citizens earning investment income in Spain). The U.S. president has the authority to enter into a tax treaty with another country after receiving the Senate's advice.

**Tax year**   a fixed period in which a business reports income and deductions, generally referred to as an accounting period.

**Taxable corporations**   corporations that file a tax return and pay corporate income taxes on their earnings. Taxable corporations are sometimes referred to as "C corporations."

**Taxable estate**   adjusted gross estate reduced by the marital deduction and the charitable deduction.

**Taxable fringe benefit**   a noncash fringe benefit provided by employers to an employee that is included in taxable income (e.g., auto allowance or group-term life over $50,000).

**Taxable gifts**   amount left after adjusting current gifts for gift splitting, annual exclusions, the marital deduction, and the charitable deduction.

**Taxable income**   the tax base for the individual income tax.

**Taxable temporary differences**   book-tax differences that will result in taxable amounts in future years when the related deferred tax liability is settled.

**Technical advice memorandum**   ruling issued by the IRS national office, requested by an IRS agent, and generally for a completed transaction.

**Temporary book-tax differences**   book-tax differences that reverse over time such that over the long-term, corporations recognize the same amount of income or deductions for the items on their financial statements as they recognize on their tax returns.

**Temporary regulations**   regulations issued with a limited life (three years for regulations issued after November 20, 1988). During their life, temporary regulations carry the same authoritative weight as final regulations.

**Tenancy by the entirety**   ownership by husband and wife similar to joint tenancy with right of survivorship.

**Tenancy in common**   ownership in which owners hold divided rights to property and have the ability to transfer these rights during their life or upon their death.

**Tentative minimum tax**   the tax on the AMT tax base under the alternative minimum tax system.

**Term insurance**   a form of life insurance without an investment or savings feature.

**Terminable interest**   right to property that terminates at a specified time or upon the occurrence of a specified event, such as a life estate.

**Testamentary transfers**   transfers that take place upon the death of the donor.

**Third-party intermediaries**   people or organizations that facilitate the transfer of property between taxpayers in a like-kind exchange. Typically, the intermediary receives the cash from selling the property received from the taxpayer and uses it to acquire like-kind property identified by the taxpayer.

**Throwback rule**   the rule that sales into a state without nexus are included with sales from the state the property was shipped from.

**Topical tax service**   a tax service arranged by subject (i.e., topic). For each topic, topical services identify tax issues that relate to each topic, and then explain and cite authorities relevant to the issue (code sections, regulations, court cases, revenue rulings, etc.).

**Trade or business**   a profit-motivated activity characterized by a sustained, continuous, high level of individual involvement or effort.

**Trade show rule**   a rule that permits businesses to have physical presence at conventions and trade shows for up to two weeks a year without creating nexus.

**Traditional 401(k)**   a popular type of defined contribution plan with before-tax employee and employer contributions and taxable distributions.

**Traditional IRA**   an individually managed retirement account with deductible contributions and taxable distributions.

**Transfer taxes**   taxes on the transfer of wealth from one taxpayer to another. The estate and gift taxes are two examples of transfer taxes.

**Travel expenses**   expenditures incurred while "away from home overnight," including the cost of transportation, meals, lodging, and incidental expenses.

**Treasury bond**   a debt instrument issued by the U.S. Treasury at face value, at a discount, or at a premium, with a set interest rate and maturity date that pays interest semiannually. Treasury bonds have terms of 30 years.

**Treasury note**   a debt instrument issued by the U.S. Treasury at face value, at a discount, or at a premium, with a set interest rate and maturity date that pays interest semiannually. Treasury notes have terms of 2, 5, or 10 years.

**Triple i agreement**   a 10-year agreement filed with the IRS in which the taxpayer agrees to notify the IRS that he or she has acquired a prohibited interest after waiving the family attribution rules in a complete redemption.

**Trust**   fiduciary entity created to hold and administer the property for other persons according to the terms of a trust instrument.

**Trustee**   person responsible for administering a trust.

# U

**U.S. Circuit Courts of Appeal**   the first level of appeals courts after the trial-level courts. There are 13 U.S. Circuit Courts of Appeal; one for the Federal Circuit and 12 assigned to hear cases that originated from a specific circuit (e.g., the 11th Circuit Court of Appeals only hears cases originating within the 11th Circuit).

**U.S. Constitution**   the founding law of the United States, ratified in 1789.

**U.S. Court of Federal Claims**   one of the three trial-level courts. It is a national court that only hears monetary claims against the federal government.

**U.S. District Court**   one of three trial-level courts. It is the only court that allows a jury trial. There is at least one district court in each state.

**U.S. savings bonds**   debt instruments issued by the U.S. Treasury at face value or at a discount, with a set maturity date. Interest earned from U.S. bonds is paid either at maturity or when the bonds are converted to cash before maturity.

**U.S. Supreme Court**   the highest court in the United States. The Supreme Court hears only a few tax cases a year with great significance to a broad cross-section of taxpayers or cases litigating issues in which there has been disagreement among the circuit courts. For most tax cases, the Supreme Court refuses to hear the case (i.e., the *writ of certiorari* is denied) and, thus, litigation ends with the circuit court decision.

**U.S. Tax Court**   a national court that only hears tax cases and where the judges are tax experts. The U.S. Tax Court is the only court that allows tax cases to be heard *before* the taxpayer pays the disputed liability and the only court with a small claims division (hearing claims involving disputed liabilities of $50,000 or less).

**Uncertain tax positions**   a company's reserve for taxes it has not paid, but expects to pay in the future for positions taken on the current and prior year income tax returns.

**Underpayment penalty**   the penalty that applies when taxpayers fail to adequately prepay their tax liability. The underpayment penalty is determined by multiplying the federal short-term interest rate plus three percentage points by the amount of tax underpayment per quarter.

**Unearned income**   income from property that accrues as time passes without effort on the part of the owner of the property.

**Unemployment tax**   the tax that pays for temporary unemployment benefits for individuals terminated from their jobs without cause.

**Unfavorable book-tax difference**   any book-tax difference that requires an add back to book income in computing taxable income. This type of adjustment is unfavorable because it increases taxable income relative to book income.

**Unified credit**   amount of credit designed to prevent transfer taxation of smaller cumulative transfers.

**Uniform cost capitalization rules (UNICAP rules)**   specify that inventories must be accounted for using full absorption rules to allocate the indirect costs of productive activities to inventory.

**Unitary tax return**   a state tax return methodology requiring the activities of a group of related entities to be reported on a single tax return. The criteria for determining whether a group of entities must file a unitary tax return are functional integration, centralization of management, and economies of scale.

**Unrealized receivables**   the rights to receive payment for (1) goods delivered, or to be delivered or (2) services rendered, or to be rendered. Unrealized receivables also include items the entity would treat as ordinary income if it sold the asset for its fair market value.

**Unrecaptured §1231 losses**   a net §1231 loss that is deducted as an ordinary loss in one year and has not caused subsequent §1231 gain to be taxed as ordinary income.

**Unrecaptured §1250 gain**   gain from the sale of real estate held by a noncorporate taxpayer for more than one year in a trade or business or as rental property attributable to tax depreciation deducted at ordinary tax rates. This gain is taxable at a maximum 25% capital gains rate.

**Use tax**   a tax imposed on the retail price of goods owned, possessed or consumed within a state that were *not* purchased within the state.

## V

**Valuation allowance**   the portion of a deferred tax asset for which it is more likely than not that a tax benefit will not be realized on a future tax return.

**Value-added tax**   a tax imposed on the producer of goods (and services) on the value of goods (services) added at each stage of production. Value-added taxes are common in Europe.

**Vertical equity**   one of the dimensions of equity. Vertical equity is achieved when taxpayers with greater ability to pay tax, pay more tax relative to taxpayers with a lesser ability to pay tax.

**Vest**   to become legally entitled to receive a particular benefit without risk of forfeiture; to gain ownership.

**Vesting period**   period of employment over which employees earn the right to own and exercise stock options.

## W

**Wash sale**   the sale of an investment if that same investment (or substantially identical investment) is purchased within 30 days before or after the sale date. Losses on wash sales are deffered.

**Wherewithal to pay**   the ability or resources to pay taxes due from a particular transaction.

**Whole life insurance**   a form of life insurance with an investment or savings component.

**Willing-buyer, willing-seller rule**   guideline for determining fair market value as "the price at which such property would change hands between a willing buyer and a willing seller, neither being under any compulsion to buy or to sell, and both have reasonable knowledge of the relevant facts."

**Withholdings**   taxes collected and remitted to the government by an employer from an employee's wages.

**Working condition fringe benefit**   a nontaxable fringe benefit provided by employers that would be deductible as an ordinary and necessary business expense if paid by an employee (e.g., reimbursement for professional dues).

*Writ of certiorari*   a document filed to request the U.S. Supreme Court to hear a case.

## Z

**Zero coupon bond**   a type of bond issued at a discount that pays interest only at maturity.

# Comprehensive Tax Return Problems

## INDIVIDUAL TAX RETURN PROBLEM 1

**Required:**

- Use the following information to complete Paul and Judy Vance's 2009 federal income tax return. If information is missing, use reasonable assumptions to fill in the gaps.
- You may need the following forms and schedules to complete the project: Form 1040, Schedule A, Schedule B, Schedule C, Schedule D, Schedule E, Schedule SE, Form 2106-EZ, Form 4562 (for the dental practice), Form 4562 (for the rental property), Form 4797, and Form 8863. The forms, schedules, and instructions can be found at IRS Web site (www.irs.gov). The instructions can be helpful in completing the forms.

**Facts:**

1. Paul J. and Judy L. Vance are married and file a joint return. Paul is self-employed as a dentist, and Judy is a college professor. Paul and Judy have three children. The oldest is Vince who lives at home. Vince is a law student at the University of Cincinnati and worked part-time during the year, earning $1,500, which he spent for his own support. Paul and Judy provided $6,000 toward Vince's support (including $4,000 for Vince's fall tuition). They also provided over half the support of their daughter, Joan, who is a full-time student at Edgecliff College in Cincinnati. Joan worked part-time as an independent contractor during the year, earning $3,200. Joan lived at home until she was married in December of 2009. She filed a joint return with her husband, Patrick, who earned $20,000 during the year. Jennifer is the youngest and lived in the Vance's home for the entire year. The Vances provide you with the following additional information:

   - Paul and Judy would like to take advantage on their return of any educational expenses paid for their children.
   - The Vances do not want to contribute to the presidential election campaign.
   - The Vances live at 621 Franklin Avenue, Cincinnati, OH 45211.
   - Paul's birthday is 3/5/1955 and his Social Security number is 333-45-6666.
   - Judy's birthday is 4/24/1958 and her Social Security number is 566-77-8888.
   - Vince's birthday is 11/6/1986 and his Social Security number is 576-18-7928.
   - Joan's birthday is 2/1/1990 and her Social Security number is 575-92-4321.
   - Jennifer's birthday is 12/12/1997 and her Social Security number is 613-97-8465.
   - The Vances do not have any foreign bank accounts or trusts.

2. Judy is a lecturer at Xavier University in Cincinnati, where she earned $30,000. The university withheld federal income tax of $3,375, state income tax of

$900, Cincinnati city income tax of $375, $1,860 of Social Security tax and $435 of Medicare tax. She also worked part of the year for Delta Airlines. Delta paid her $10,000 in salary; and withheld federal income tax of $1,125, state income tax of $300, Cincinnati city income tax of $125, $620 for Social Security tax, and $145 for Medicare tax.

3. The Vances received $800 of interest from State Savings Bank on a joint account. They received interest of $1,000 on City of Cincinnati bonds they bought in January with the proceeds of a loan from Third National Bank of Cincinnati. They paid interest of $1,100 on the loan. Paul received a dividend of $540 on General Bicycle Corporation stock he owns. Judy received a dividend of $390 on Acme Clothing Corporation stock she owns. Paul and Judy received a dividend of $865 on jointly owned stock in Maple Company. All of the dividends received in 2009 are qualified dividends.

4. Paul practices under the name "Paul J. Vance, DDS." His business is located at 645 West Avenue, Cincinnati, OH 45211, and his employer identification number is 01-2222222. Paul's gross receipts during the year were $111,000. Paul uses the cash method of accounting for his business. Paul's business expenses are as follows:

| | |
|---|---:|
| Advertising | $ 1,200 |
| Professional dues | 490 |
| Professional journals | 360 |
| Contributions to employee benefit plans | 2,000 |
| Malpractice insurance | 3,200 |
| Fine for overbilling State of Ohio for work performed on welfare patient | 5,000 |
| Insurance on office contents | 720 |
| Interest on money borrowed to refurbish office | 600 |
| Accounting services | 2,100 |
| Miscellaneous office expense | 388 |
| Office rent | 12,000 |
| Dental supplies | 7,672 |
| Utilities and telephone | 3,360 |
| Wages | 30,000 |
| Payroll taxes | 2,400 |

In June, Paul decided to refurbish his office. This project was completed and the assets placed in service on July 1. Paul's expenditures included $8,000 for new office furniture, $6,000 for new dental equipment (seven-year recovery period), and $2,000 for a new computer. Paul elected to compute his cost recovery allowance using MACRS. He did not elect to use Section 179 immediate expensing and he chose to not claim any bonus depreciation.

5. Judy's mother, Sarah, died on July 2, 2004, leaving Judy her entire estate. Included in the estate was Sarah's residence (325 Oak Street, Cincinnati, OH 45211). Sarah's basis in the residence was $30,000. The fair market value of the residence on July 2, 2004, was $155,000. The property was distributed to Judy on January 1, 2005. The Vances have held the property as rental property and have managed it themselves. From January 1, 2005, until June 30, 2009, they rented the house to the same tenant. The tenant was transferred to a branch office in California and moved out at the end of June. Since they did not want to bother finding a new tenant, Paul and Judy sold the house on June 30, 2009. They received $140,000 for the house and land ($15,000 for the land and $125,000 for the house), less a 6 percent commission charged by the broker. They had

depreciated the house using the MACRS rules and conventions applicable to residential real estate. To compute depreciation on the house, the Vances had allocated $15,000 of the property's basis to the land on which the house is located. The Vances collected rent of $1,000 a month during the six months the house was occupied during the year. They incurred the following related expenses during this period:

| | |
|---|---:|
| Property insurance | $500 |
| Property taxes | 800 |
| Maintenance | 465 |
| Depreciation (to be computed) | ? |

6. The Vances sold 200 shares of Capp Corporation stock on September 3, 2009, for $42 a share (minus a $50 commission). The Vances received the stock from Paul's father on June 25, 1979, as a wedding present. Paul's father originally purchased the stock for $10 per share in 1965. The stock was valued at $14.50 per share on the date of the gift. No gift tax was paid on the gift.

7. Judy is required by Xavier University to visit several high schools in the Cincinnati area to evaluate Xavier University students who are doing their practice teaching. However, she is not reimbursed for the expenses she incurs in doing this. During the spring semester (January through April, 2009), she drove her personal automobile 6,800 miles in fulfilling this obligation. Judy drove an additional 6,700 personal miles during 2009. She has been using the car since June 30, 2008. Judy uses the standard mileage method to calculate her car expenses.

8. Paul and Judy have given you a file containing the following receipts for expenditures during the year:

| | |
|---|---:|
| Prescription medicine and drugs (net of insurance reimbursement) | $ 376 |
| Doctor and hospital bills (net of insurance reimbursement) | 2,468 |
| Penalty for underpayment of last year's state income tax | 15 |
| Real estate taxes on personal residence | 4,762 |
| Interest on home mortgage (paid to Home State Savings & Loan) | 8,250 |
| Interest on credit cards (consumer purchases) | 595 |
| Cash contribution to St. Matthew's church | 3,080 |
| Payroll deductions for Judy's contributions to the United Way | 150 |
| Professional dues (Judy) | 325 |
| Professional subscriptions (Judy) | 245 |
| Fee for preparation of 2008 tax return paid April 14, 2009 | 500 |

9. The Vances filed their 2008 federal, state, and local returns on April 14, 2009. They paid the following additional 2008 taxes with their returns: federal income taxes of $630, state income taxes of $250, and city income taxes of $75.

10. The Vances made timely estimated federal income tax payments of $1,500 each quarter during 2009. They also made estimated state income tax payments of $300 each quarter and estimated city income tax payments of $160 each quarter. The Vances made all fourth quarter payments on December 31, 2009. They would like to receive a refund for any overpayments.

# INDIVIDUAL TAX RETURN PROBLEM 2

### Required:
- Use the following information to complete Paige Turner's 2009 federal income tax return. If information is missing, use reasonable assumptions to fill in the gaps.
- You may need the following forms and schedules to complete the project: Form 1040, Schedule A, Schedule B, Schedule C, Schedule D, Schedule E, Schedule SE, Form 2106, Form 4562, Form 4684, and Form 8283. The forms, schedules, and instructions can be found at IRS Web site (www.irs.gov). The instructions can be helpful in completing the forms.

### Facts:
1. Paige Turner is single and has two children from her previous marriage. Ali lives with Paige and Paige provides more than half of her support. Leif lives with his father, Will (Lief lived with Will for all of 2009). Will provides more than half of Leif's support. Paige pays "alimony" of $400 per month to Will. The payments are to continue until Leif reaches age 18, when they will be reduced to $150. Paige provides you with the following additional information:
   - She uses the cash method of accounting and a calendar year for reporting.
   - She wishes to contribute to the presidential election campaign.
   - Paige lives at 523 Essex Street, Bangor, Maine (04401).
   - Paige's birthday is May 31, 1971.
   - Ali's birthday is October 5, 2000.
   - Leif's birthday is December 1, 1998.
   - Paige's Social Security number is 007-16-4727.
   - Ali's Social Security number is 005-61-7232.
   - Leif's Social Security number is 004-23-3419.
   - Will's Social Security number is 006-45-6333.
   - She does not have any foreign bank accounts or trusts.
2. Paige is employed as a nuclear engineer with Atom Systems Consultants, Inc. (ASCI). Her annual salary is $70,000. ASCI has an extensive fringe benefits program for its employees. Paige's pay stubs indicate that she had $7,230 withheld in federal taxes, $4,987 in state taxes, $4,495 in Social Security taxes, and $1,051 in Medicare taxes. Her taxable compensation includes the following:

| | |
|---|---|
| Salary (before subtracting her 401k and flexible spending plan contributions) | $70,000 |
| – Personal contribution to 401k account | (7,000) |
| – Flexible spending plan contributions | (3,600) |
| + Group term life insurance | 97 |
| + Whole life insurance | 300 |
| + Payment of educational costs | See a below |
| + Free parking | See b below |
| + Health club dues | 900 |
| + Disability pay (see #7 below) | 1,200 |

Paige furnishes you with the following description of the fringe benefits she received from ASCI in 2009.

a. Taking advantage of ASCI's educational assistance program, during the fall Paige enrolled in two graduate engineering classes at a local college. ASCI paid her tuition, fees, and other course-related costs of $2,300.

b.  Paige also received free parking in the company's security garage that would normally cost $200 per month.

3. Paige manages the safety program for ASCI. In recognition of her superior handling of three potential crises during the year 2009, Paige was awarded the "Employee Safety Award" on December 15, 2009. The cash award was $500.

4. On January 15, 2009, Paige's father died. From her father's estate, she received stock valued at $30,000 (his basis was $12,000) and her father's house valued at $90,000 (his basis in the house was $55,000).

5. Paige owns several other investments and in February 2010 received a statement from her brokerage firm reporting the interest and dividends earned on the investments for 2009. (See Exhibit A.)

## EXHIBIT A    Forms 1099 and 1098

This is important tax information and is being furnished to the Internal Revenue Service.

| 1099-Div Dividends & Distributions | | |
|---|---|---|
| **Entity** | **Description** | **Amount** |
| General Dynamics | Gross qualified dividends | $300 |
| **1099-Int Interest** | | |
| **Entity** | **Description** | **Amount** |
| New Jersey Economic Development Bonds | Gross interest | $300 |
| IBM bonds | Gross interest | 700 |
| State of Nebraska Bonds | Gross interest | 200 |
| **1098-Mortgage Interest Statement** | | |
| **Entity** | **Description** | **Amount** |
| Sunbelt Credit Union | Mortgage interest | $7,100 |
| Northeast Bank | Home equity loan interest | 435 |

Grubstake Mining & Development: preliminary report (preliminary K-1) to Paige for the 2009 tax year

| | |
|---|---|
| Distribution to shareholder | $1,000 |
| Ordinary income (1% of $200,000) | $2,000 |

6. In addition to the investments discussed above, Paige owns 1,000 shares of Grubstake Mining & Development common stock. Grubstake is organized as an S corporation and has 100,000 shares outstanding (S corp. ID number 45-4567890). Grubstake reported taxable income of $200,000 and paid a distribution of $1.00 per share during the current year. Paige tells you that Grubstake typically does not send out its K-1 reports until late April. However, its preliminary report has been consistent with the K-1 for many years. (See Exhibit A.) Paige does not materially participate in Grubstake's activities.

7. Paige slipped on a wet spot in front of a computer store last July. She broke her ankle and was unable to work for two weeks. She incurred $1,300 in medical costs, all of which were paid by the owner of the store. The store also gave her $1,000 for pain and suffering resulting from the injury. ASCI continued to pay her salary during the two weeks she missed because of the accident. ASCI's plan also paid her $1,200 in disability pay for the time she was unable to work. Under this plan ASCI pays the premiums for the disability insurance.

8. Paige received a Form 1099-B from her broker for the sale of the following securities during 2009.

| Security | Sale Date | Purchase Date | Sales Price | Commission Paid on Sale | Her Basis |
|---|---|---|---|---|---|
| Nebraska Bonds | 03/14/09 | 10/22/09 | $2,300 | $160 | $1,890 |
| Cassill Corp (500 shares) | 10/20/09 | 02/19/09 | $8,500 | $425 | $9,760 |

9. In addition to the taxes withheld from her salary, she also made timely estimated federal tax payments of $175 per quarter and timely estimated state income tax payments of $150 for the first three quarters. The $150 fourth quarter state payment was made on December 28, 2009. Paige would like to receive a refund for any overpayment.

10. Because of her busy work schedule, Paige was unable to provide her accountant with the tax documents necessary for filing her 2008 state and federal income tax returns by the due date (April 15, 2009). In filing her extension on April 15, 2009, she made a federal tax payment of $750. Her return was eventually filed on June 25, 2009. In August 2009, she received a federal refund of $180 and a state tax refund of $60. Her itemized deductions for 2008 were $12,430.

11. Paige found a renter for her father's house on August 1. The monthly rent is $400, and the lease agreement is for one year. The lease requires the tenant to pay the first and last months' rent and a $400 security deposit. The security deposit is to be returned at the end of the lease if the property is in good condition. On August 1, Paige received $1,200 from the tenant per the terms of the lease agreement. In November, the plumbing froze and several pipes burst. The tenant had the repairs made and paid the $300 bill. In December, he reduced his rental payment to $100 to compensate for the plumbing repairs. Paige provides you with the following additional information for the rental in 2009.

| | |
|---|---|
| Property taxes | $770 |
| Other maintenance expenses | 285 |
| Insurance expense | 495 |
| Management fee | 350 |
| Depreciation (to be computed) | ? |

The rental property is located at 35 Harvest Street, Orono, Maine 04473. Local practice is to allocate 12 percent of the fair market value of the property to the land. (See #4.) Paige makes all decisions with respect to the property.

12. Paige paid $2,050 in real estate taxes on her principal residence. The real estate tax is used to pay for town schools and other municipal services.

13. Paige drives a 2009 Acura TL. Her car registration fee (based on the car year) is $50 and covers the period 1/1/09 through 12/31/09. In addition, she paid $280 in property tax to the town based on the book value of the car.

14. In addition to the medical costs presented in #7, Paige incurred the following unreimbursed medical costs:

| | |
|---|---|
| Dentist | $ 310 |
| Doctor | 390 |
| Prescription drugs | 215 |
| Over-the-counter drugs | 140 |
| Optometrist | 125 |
| Emergency room charges | 440 |
| LASIK eye surgery | 2,000 |
| Chiropractor | 265 |

15. On March 1, Paige took advantage of low interest rates and refinanced her $75,000 home mortgage with her original lender. The new home loan is for 15 years. She paid $215 in closing costs and $1,500 in discount points (prepaid interest) to obtain the loan. The house is worth $155,000 and Paige's basis in the house is $90,000. As part of the refinancing arrangement, she also obtained a $10,000 home equity loan. She used the proceeds from the home equity loan to reduce the balance due on her credit cards. Paige received several Form 1098 statements from her bank for interest paid by her in 2009. Details appear below. (See also Exhibit A on page C-4.)

| | |
|---|---|
| Primary home mortgage | $7,100 |
| Home equity loan | 435 |
| Credit cards | 498 |
| Car loan | 390 |

16. On May 14, 2009, Paige contributed clothing to the Salvation Army. The original cost of the clothing was $740. She has substantiation valuing the donation at $360. The Salvation Army is located at 350 Stone Ridge Road, Bangor, Maine 04401. In addition, she made the following cash contributions and received a statement from each of the following organizations acknowledging her contribution:

| | |
|---|---|
| Larkin College | $850 |
| United Way | 125 |
| First Methodist Church | 790 |
| Amos House (homeless shelter) | 200 |
| Local Chamber of Commerce | 100 |

17. On April 1, 2009, Paige's house was robbed. She apparently interrupted the burglar because all that's missing is an antique brooch she inherited from her grandmother (June 12, 2002) and $300 in cash. Unfortunately, she didn't have a separate rider on her insurance policy covering the jewelry. Therefore, the insurance company reimbursed her only $500 for the brooch. Her basis in the brooch was $6,000 and its fair market value was $7,500. Her insurance policy also limits to $100 the amount of cash that can be claimed in a theft.

18. Paige sells real estate in the evening and on weekends. She runs her business from a rental office she shares with several other realtors (692 River Road Bangor, Maine 04401). The name of her business is Turner Real Estate and the Federal identification number is 05-8799561. Her business code is 531210. Paige has been operating in a business-like way since 1999 and has always shown a profit. She had the following income and expenses from her business:

| | |
|---|---|
| Commissions earned | $21,250 |
| Expenses: | |
| Advertising | 2,200 |
| Telephone | 95 |
| Real estate license | 130 |
| Rent | 6,000 |
| Utilities | 600 |

She has used her Toyota Camry in her business since June 1, 2008. During 2009, she properly documented 6,000 business miles (500 miles each month). The total mileage on her car (i.e., business and personal-use miles) during the year was 15,000 miles (including 200 miles commuting to and from the real estate office). In 2009, Paige elects to use the standard mileage method to calculate her car expenses. She spent $45 on tolls and $135 on parking related to the real estate business.

19. Paige's company has an accountable expense reimbursement plan for employees from which Paige receives $12,000 for the following expenses:

| | |
|---|---|
| Airfare | $4,700 |
| Hotel | 3,400 |
| Meals | 2,000 |
| Car rentals | 600 |
| Entertainment | 900 |
| Incidentals | 400 |

20. During 2009, Paige also paid $295 for business publications other than those paid for by her employer and $325 for a local CPA to prepare her 2008 tax return.

# CORPORATE TAX RETURN PROBLEM 1

### Required:

- Complete Alvin's Music Inc.'s (AMI) 2009 Form 1120, Schedule D, and Schedule G (if applicable) using the information provided below.
- Neither Form 4562 for depreciation nor Form 4797 for the sale of the equipment is required. Include the amount of tax depreciation and the tax gain on the equipment sale given in the problem (or determined from information given in the problem) on the appropriate lines on the first page of the Form 1120.
- Assume that AMI does not owe any alternative minimum tax.
- If any information is missing, use reasonable assumptions to fill in the gaps.
- The forms, schedules, and instructions can be found at the IRS website (www.irs.gov). The instructions can be helpful in completing the forms.

### Facts:

Alvin's Music, Inc. (AMI) was formed in 2006 by Alvin Jones and Theona Smith. Alvin and Theona officially incorporated their store on June 12, 2006. AMI sells (retail) all kinds of music-related products including musical instruments, sheet music, CDs, and DVDs. Alvin owns 60 percent of the outstanding common stock of AMI and Theona owns the remaining 40 percent.

- AMI is located at 355 Music Way, East Palo Alto, CA 94303.
- AMI's Employer Identification Number is 29-5748859.
- AMI's business activity is retail sales of music-related products. Its business activity code is 451140.
- Officers of the corporation are as follows:
  - Alvin is the chief executive officer and president (Social Security number 123-45-6789).
  - Theona is the executive vice president (Social Security number 978-65-4321).
  - Gwen Givens is the vice president over operations (Social Security number 789-12-3456).
  - Carlson Bannister is the secretary (Social Security number 321-54-6789).
- All officers devote 100% of their time to the business and all officers are U.S. citizens.
- Neither Gwen nor Carlson owns any stock in AMI.
- AMI uses the accrual method of accounting and has a calendar year-end.
- AMI made four equal estimated tax payments of $70,000 each. Its tax liability last year was $175,000. If it has overpaid its federal tax liability, AMI would like to receive a refund.
- AMI paid a dividend of $80,000 to its shareholders on December 1. AMI had ample earnings and profits (E&P) to absorb the distribution.

The following is AMI's audited income statement for 2009:

| AMI Income Statement For year ending December 31, 2009 | |
|---|---:|
| Revenue from sales | $3,420,000 |
| Sales returns and allowances | (40,000) |
| Cost of goods sold | (834,000) |
| **Gross profit from operations** | $2,546,000 |
| **Other income:** | |
| Capital gains | 8,000 |
| Gain from disposition of fixed assets | 2,000 |
| Dividend income | 12,000 |
| Interest income | 15,000 |
| Gross Income | $2,583,000 |
| **Expenses:** | |
| Compensation | (1,300,000) |
| Depreciation | (20,000) |
| Bad debt expense | (15,000) |
| Meals and entertainment | (5,000) |
| Maintenance | (5,000) |
| Charitable donations | (27,000) |
| Property taxes | (45,000) |
| State income taxes | (60,000) |
| Other taxes | (56,000) |
| Interest | (62,000) |
| Advertising | (44,000) |
| Professional services | (32,000) |
| Pension expense | (40,000) |
| Supplies | (6,000) |
| Other expenses | (38,000) |
| Total expenses | (1,755,000) |
| Income before taxes | 828,000 |
| Federal income tax expense | (260,000) |
| Net Income after taxes | $ 568,000 |

**Notes:**

1. AMI has a capital loss carryover to this year from last year in the amount of ($5,000).

2. AMI's inventory-related purchases during the year were $1,134,000. It values its inventory based on cost using the FIFO inventory cost flow method. Assume the rules of §263A do not apply to AMI.

3. Of the $15,000 interest income, $2,500 was from a City of Fremont bond that was used to fund public activities (issued in 2007), $3,500 was from a Pleasanton City bond used to fund private activities (issued in 2006), $3,000 was from a U.S. Treasury bond, and the remaining $6,000 was from a money market account.

4. AMI sold equipment for $10,000. It originally purchased the equipment for $12,000 and, through the date of the sale, had recorded a cumulative total of $4,000 of book depreciation on the asset and a cumulative total of $6,000 of tax depreciation. For tax purposes, the entire gain was recaptured as ordinary income under §1245.

5. AMI's dividend income came from Simon's Sheet Music. AMI owned 15,000 shares of the stock in Simon's Sheet Music (SSM) at the beginning of the year. This represented 15% of the SSM outstanding stock.

6. On July 22, 2009, AMI sold 2,500 shares of its Simon's Sheet Music Stock for $33,000. It had originally purchased these shares on April 24, 2005, for $25,000. After the sale, AMI owned 12.5% of Simon's Sheet Music.

7. AMI's compensation is as follows:

   • Alvin $210,000
   • Theona $190,000
   • Gwen $110,000
   • Carlson $90,000
   • Other $700,000

8. AMI wrote off $10,000 in accounts receivable as uncollectible during the year.

9. Regular tax depreciation was $31,000. None of the depreciation should be claimed on Schedule A.

10. Of the $62,000 of interest expense, $56,000 was from the mortgage on AMI's building and the remaining $6,000 of interest is from business-related loans.

11. The pension expense is the same for both book and tax purposes.

12. Other expenses include $3,000 for premiums paid on term life insurance policies for which AMI is the beneficiary. The policies cover the lives of Alvin and Theona.

The following are AMI's audited balance sheets as of January 1, 2009 and December 31, 2009.

| | 2009 | |
| --- | --- | --- |
| | January 1 | December 31 |
| **Assets** | | |
| Cash | $ 240,000 | $ 171,000 |
| Accounts receivable | 600,000 | 700,000 |
| Allowance for doubtful accounts | (35,000) | (40,000) |
| Inventory | 1,400,000 | 1,700,000 |
| U.S. government bonds | 50,000 | 50,000 |
| State and local bonds | 140,000 | 140,000 |
| Investments in stock | 300,000 | 275,000 |
| Building and other depreciable assets | 1,500,000 | 1,600,000 |
| Accumulated depreciation | (200,000) | (216,000) |
| Land | 900,000 | 900,000 |
| Other assets | 250,000 | 270,000 |
| Total assets | $5,145,000 | $5,550,000 |
| **Liabilities and Shareholders' Equity** | | |
| Accounts payable | 250,000 | 220,000 |
| Other current liabilities | 125,000 | 120,000 |
| Mortgage | 800,000 | 790,000 |
| Other liabilities | 200,000 | 162,000 |
| Capital stock | 600,000 | 600,000 |
| Retained earnings | 3,170,000 | 3,658,000 |
| Total liabilities and shareholders' equity | $5,145,000 | $5,550,000 |

# CORPORATE TAX RETURN PROBLEM 2

**Required:**

- Complete Blue Catering Service Inc.'s (BCS) 2009 Form 1120, Schedule D and Schedule G (if applicable) using the information provided below.
- Form 4562 for depreciation is not required. Include the amount of tax depreciation given in the problem on the appropriate line on the first page of the Form 1120.
- Assume that BCS does not owe any alternative minimum tax.
- If any information is missing, use reasonable assumptions to fill in the gaps.
- The forms, schedules, and instructions can be found at the IRS website (www.irs.gov). The instructions can be helpful in completing the forms.

**Facts:**

Cara Siler, Janna Funk, and Valerie Cloward each own one-third of the common stock of Blue Catering Services Inc. (BCS). BCS was incorporated on February 4, 2007. It has only one class of stock outstanding and operates as a C corporation for tax purposes. BCS caters all types of social events throughout southern California.

- BCS is located at 540 Waverly Way, San Diego, CA 92101.
- BCS's Employer Identification Number is 38-4743474.
- BCS's business activity is catering food and services. Its business activity code is 722300.
- The shareholders also work as officers for the corporation as follows:
    - Cara is the chief executive officer and president (Social Security number 231-54-8976).
    - Janna is the executive vice president and chief operating officer (Social Security number 798-56-3241).
    - Valeri is the vice president of finance (Social Security number 879-21-4536).
- All officers devote 100% of their time to the business and all officers are U.S. citizens.
- BCS uses the accrual method of accounting and has a calendar year-end.
- BCS made four equal estimated tax payments of $20,000 each. Its tax liability last year was $70,000. If it has overpaid its federal tax liability, BCS would like to receive a refund.
- BCS paid a dividend of $30,000 to its shareholders on November 1. BCS had ample earnings and profits (E&P) to absorb the distribution.

The following is BCS's audited income statement for 2009:

| BCS Income Statement For year ending December 31, 2009 | |
| --- | --- |
| Revenue from sales | $1,800,000 |
| Sales returns and allowances | (5,000) |
| Cost of goods sold | (350,000) |
| **Gross profit from operations** | **$1,445,000** |
| **Other income:** | |
| Capital loss | (15,000) |
| Dividend income | 25,000 |
| Interest income | 10,000 |
| Gross income | $1,465,000 |

**BCS**
**Income Statement**
**For year ending December 31, 2009**

| Expenses: | |
| --- | ---: |
| Compensation | (950,000) |
| Depreciation | (10,000) |
| Bad debt expense | (15,000) |
| Meals and entertainment | (3,000) |
| Maintenance | (6,000) |
| Property taxes | (11,000) |
| State income taxes | (45,000) |
| Other taxes | (44,000) |
| Rent | (60,000) |
| Interest | (5,000) |
| Advertising | (52,000) |
| Professional services | (16,000) |
| Employee benefits | (32,000) |
| Supplies | (5,000) |
| Other expenses | (27,000) |
| Total expenses | (1,281,000) |
| Income before taxes | 184,000 |
| Federal income tax expense | (62,000) |
| Net income after taxes | $  122,000 |

**Notes:**

1. BCS's inventory-related purchases during 2009 were $360,000. It values its inventory based on cost using the FIFO inventory cost flow method. Assume the rules of §263A do not apply to BCS.

2. Of the $10,000 interest income, $1,250 was from a city of Irvine bond that was used to fund public activities (issued in 2005), $1,750 was from an Oceanside city bond used to fund private activities (issued in 2004), $1,000 was from a U.S. Treasury bond, and the remaining $6,000 was from a money market account.

3. BCS's dividend income came from Clever Cakes Inc. (CC). BCS owned 10,000 shares of the stock in Clever Cakes at the beginning of the year. This represented 10% of SSM outstanding stock.

4. On October 1, BCS sold 1,000 shares of its CC stock for $25,000. It had originally purchased these shares on April 18, 2007, for $40,000. After the sale, BCS owned 9% of CC.

5. BCS's compensation is as follows:

   • Cara $150,000
   • Janna $140,000
   • Valerie $130,000
   • Other $530,000

6. BCS wrote off $25,000 in accounts receivable as uncollectible during the year.

7. BCS's regular tax depreciation was $28,000. None of the depreciation should be claimed on Schedule A.

8. The $5,000 interest expense was from a business loan.

9. Other expenses include $6,000 for premiums paid on term life insurance policies for which BCS is the beneficiary. The policies cover the lives of Cara, Janna, and Valerie.

The following are BCS's audited balance sheets as of January 1, 2009, and December 31, 2009.

| | 2009 | |
| --- | --- | --- |
| | January 1 | December 31 |
| **Assets** | | |
| Cash | $ 180,000 | $ 205,000 |
| Accounts receivable | 560,000 | 580,000 |
| Allowance for doubtful accounts | (60,000) | (50,000) |
| Inventory | 140,000 | 150,000 |
| U.S. government bonds | 20,000 | 20,000 |
| State and local bonds | 120,000 | 120,000 |
| Investments in stock | 400,000 | 360,000 |
| Fixed assets | 140,000 | 160,000 |
| Accumulated depreciation | (50,000) | (60,000) |
| Other assets | 20,000 | 21,000 |
| Total assets | $1,470,000 | $1,506,000 |
| **Liabilities and Shareholders' Equity** | | |
| Accounts payable | 280,000 | 240,000 |
| Other current liabilities | 20,000 | 18,000 |
| Other liabilities | 40,000 | 26,000 |
| Capital stock | 400,000 | 400,000 |
| Retained earnings | 730,000 | 822,000 |
| Total liabilities and shareholders' equity | $1,470,000 | $1,506,000 |

# PARTNERSHIP TAX RETURN PROBLEM

**Required:**

- Using the information provided below, complete Arlington Building Supply's (ABS) 2009 Form 1065 and Schedule D. Also complete Jerry Johnson and Steve Stillwell's Schedule K-1.
- Form 4562 for depreciation is not required. Use the amount of tax depreciation and Section 179 expense provided in the income statement and the information in note 4 below to complete the appropriate lines on the first page and on Schedule K of the Form 1065.
- Form 4797 for the sale of trade or business property is not required. Use the amount of gain and loss from the sale of the truck and fork lifts in the income statement and the information provided in notes 4 and 5 below to complete the appropriate lines on the first page and on Schedule K of the Form 1065.
- If any information is missing, use reasonable assumptions to fill in the gaps.
- The forms, schedules, and instructions can be found at the IRS website (www.irs.gov). The instructions can be helpful in completing the forms.

**Facts:**

On January 1 of 1998, two enterprising men in the community, Jerry Johnson and Steve "Swiss" Stillwell, anticipated a boom in the local construction industry. They decided to sell their small businesses and pool their resources as general partners in establishing a retail outlet for lumber and other building materials, including a

complete line of specialty hardware for prefab tree-houses. Their general partnership was officially formed under the name of Arlington Building Supplies and soon became a thriving business.

- ABS is located at 2174 Progress Ave., Arlington, Illinois 64888.
- ABS's Employer Identification Number is 91-3697984.
- ABS's business activity is retail construction. Its business activity code is 444190.
- Both general partners are active in the management of ABS.
  - Jerry Johnson's Social Security number 500-23-4976. His address is 31 W. Oak Drive, Arlington, IL 64888.
  - Steve Stillwell's Social Security number 374-68-3842. His address is 947 E. Linder Street, Arlington, IL 64888.
- ABS uses the accrual method of accounting and has a calendar year end.

The following is ABS's 2009 income statement:

| ABI Income Statement For year ending December 31, 2009 | | |
|---|---:|---:|
| Sales (on account) | $410,000 | |
| Less: Sales returns | −20,000 | |
| | | $390,000 |
| Cost of goods sold | | −150,000 |
| Gross profit on sales | | $240,000 |
| Operating expenses | | |
| Salaries and wages (including partners guaranteed payments) | $79,000 | |
| Property taxes | 1,600 | |
| Payroll taxes | 2,450 | |
| Depreciation and 179 expense | 40,062 | |
| Advertising | 2,000 | |
| Bad debt expense | 3,850 | |
| Office expense | 1,800 | |
| Repairs | 2,150 | |
| Miscellaneous | 450 | |
| Fire insurance | 4,850 | 138,212 |
| Net operating income | | $101,788 |
| Other income | | |
| Gain on sale of securities | $ 1,350 | |
| Gain on sale of truck | 16,399 | |
| Dividend income | 695 | |
| Interest income | 4,260 | 22,704 |
| | | $124,492 |
| Other deductions | | |
| Interest on mortgage | $ 5,400 | |
| Interest on notes payable | 2,250 | |
| Charitable contributions | 5,000 | |
| Life insurance premiums | 3,000 | |
| Loss on sale of fork lifts | 466 | 16,116 |
| NET INCOME | | $108,376 |

**Notes:**

1. The partnership maintains its books according to the Section 704(b) regulations. Under this method of accounting, all book and tax numbers are equivalent except for life insurance premiums and tax exempt interest.

2. The partners' percentage ownership of original contributed capital is 30% for Johnson and 70% for Stillwell. They agree that profits and losses will be shared according to this same ratio. Any additional capital contributions must be made in these same ratios. The capital accounts may vary from these percentages from time to time as a result of withdrawals made by the partners, but in no event may the year-end capital account balances vary from the 30:70 ratio by more than 5 percent of total capital.

3. For their services to the company, the partners will receive the following annual guaranteed payments:

   | Johnson | $28,000 |
   |---------|---------|
   | Stillwell | $21,000 |

   Johnson is expected to devote all his time to the business, while Stillwell will devote approximately 75 percent of his.

4. Two forklifts were sold in September 2009. The old lifts were purchased new four years ago. Two new forklifts were purchased on September 1, 2009, for $32,000 and the partnership intends to immediately expense them under Section 179.

5. The truck sold this year was purchased several years ago. $16,099 of the total gain from the sale of the truck was recaptured as ordinary income under IRC Section 1245.

6. The partnership uses currently allowable tax depreciation methods for both regular tax and book purposes. Assume alternative minimum tax depreciation equals regular tax depreciation.

7. The partners decided to invest in a small tract of land with the intention of selling it about a year later at a substantial profit. On September 30, 2009, they executed a $50,000 note with the bank to obtain the $70,000 cash purchase price. Interest on the 18 percent note is payable quarterly, and the principal is due in one year. The first interest payment of $2,250 was made on December 30, 2009.

8. The note payable to the bank as well as the accounts payable are treated by the partnership as recourse debt. Assume the total recourse debt is allocated $28,776 to Jerry and $70,224 to Steve.

9. Some years after the partnership was formed, a mortgage of $112,500 was obtained on the land and warehouse from Commerce State Bank. Principal payments of $4,500 must be paid each December 31, along with eight percent interest on the outstanding balance. The holder of the note agreed therein to look only to the land and warehouse for his security in the event of default. Because this mortgage is nonrecourse debt, it should be allocated among the partners according to their profit sharing ratios.

10. The partnership values its inventory at lower of cost or market and uses the FIFO inventory method. Assume the rules of §263A do not apply to ABS.

11. During the year, the partnership bought three hundred shares of ABC, Ltd. for $6,100 on February 8, 2009. All the shares were sold for $6,650 on April 2, 2009.

12. Two hundred shares of XYZ Corporation were sold for $10,600 on September 13, 2009. The stock was purchased on December 1, 2003, and is not eligible for the 28% capital gains rate.

13. The following dividends were received:

| | |
|---|---|
| XYZ (qualified) | $400 |
| ABC, Ltd. (not qualified) | 295 |
| Total | $695 |

14. The partnership received interest income from the following sources:

| | |
|---|---|
| Interest on Illinois municipal bonds | $3,200 |
| Interest on savings | 560 |
| Interest on accounts receivable | 500 |
| Total | $4,260 |

15. The partnership donated $5,000 cash to the Red Cross.

16. Life insurance policies on the lives of Johnson and Stillwell were purchased in the prior year. The partnership will pay all the premiums and is the beneficiary of the policy. The premiums for the current year were $3,000, and no cash surrender value exists for the first or second year of the policy.

17. The partners withdrew the following cash amounts from the partnership during the year (in addition to their guaranteed payments):

| | |
|---|---|
| Johnson | $20,000 |
| Stillwell | $35,000 |

The following are ABS's book balance sheets as of January 1, 2009, and December 31, 2009.

| | | 12/31/09 | | 12/31/08 |
|---|---|---|---|---|
| **Assets** | | | | |
| Cash | | $ 70,467 | | $ 43,042 |
| Accounts receivable | | 76,000 | | 57,000 |
| Inventories | | 60,000 | | 50,000 |
| Investment in municipal bonds | | 50,000 | | 50,000 |
| Investment in XYZ common stock | | 40,200 | | 50,000 |
| Truck | | | $ 16,500 | |
| Less accumulated depreciation | | | 13,649 | |
| | | | | 2,851 |
| Machinery and equipment | $ 66,000 | | $ 50,000 | |
| Less accumulated depreciation | 58,697 | | 34,376 | |
| | | 7,303 | | 15,624 |
| Building | $120,000 | | $120,000 | |
| Less accumulated depreciation | 39,875 | | 36,798 | |
| | | 80,125 | | 83,202 |
| Land | | 90,000 | | 20,000 |
| TOTALS | | $474,095 | | $371,719 |
| **Liabilities and Capital** | | | | |
| Accounts payable | | $ 49,000 | | $ 45,500 |
| Notes payable | | 50,000 | | 0 |
| Mortgage payable | | 63,000 | | 67,500 |
| Capital: Jerry Johnson | | 94,553 | | 82,040 |
| Steve Stillwell | | 217,542 | | 176,679 |
| TOTALS | | $474,095 | | $371,719 |

# S CORPORATION TAX RETURN PROBLEM

**Required:**

- Using the information provided below, complete Salt Source Inc.'s (SSI) 2009 Form 1120S. Also complete Kim Bentley's Schedule K-1.
- Form 4562 for depreciation is not required. Include the amount of tax depreciation given in the problem on the appropriate line on the first page of the Form 1120S.
- If any information is missing, use reasonable assumptions to fill in the gaps.
- The forms, schedules, and instructions can be found at the IRS website (www.irs.gov). The instructions can be helpful in completing the forms.

**Facts:**

Salt Source Inc. (SSI) was formed as a corporation on January 5, 2006, by its two owners Kim Bentley and James Owens. SSI immediately elected to be taxed as an S corporation for federal income tax purposes. SSI sells salt to retailers throughout the rocky mountain region. Kim owns 70% of the SSI common stock (the only class of stock outstanding) and James owns 30%.

- SSI is located at 4200 West 400 North, Salt Lake City, Utah 84116.
- SSI's Employer Identification Numbers is 87-5467544.
- SSI's business activity is wholesale sales. Its business activity code is 424990.
- Both shareholders work as employees of the corporation
  - Kim is the president of SSI (Social Security number 312-89-4567). Kim's address is 1842 East 8400 South; Sandy, UT 84094.
  - James is the vice-president of SSI (Social Security number 321-98-7645). James's address is 2002 East 8145 South; Sandy, UT 84094.
- SSI uses the accrual method of accounting and has a calendar year end.

The following is SSI's 2009 income statement:

| SSI Income Statement For year ending December 31, 2009 | |
|---|---|
| Revenue from sales | $980,000 |
| Sales returns and allowances | (10,000) |
| Cost of goods sold | (110,000) |
| **Gross profit from operations** | $860,000 |
| **Other income:** | |
| Dividend income | 15,000 |
| Interest income | 5,000 |
| Gross income | $880,000 |
| **Expenses:** | |
| Compensation | (600,000) |
| Depreciation | (10,000) |
| Bad debt expense | (14,000) |
| Meals and entertainment | (2,000) |
| Maintenance | (8,000) |
| Business interest | (1,000) |

**SSI**
**Income Statement**
**For year ending December 31, 2009**

| | |
|---|---:|
| Property taxes | (7,000) |
| Charitable contributions | (10,000) |
| Other taxes | (30,000) |
| Rent | (28,000) |
| Advertising | (14,000) |
| Professional services | (11,000) |
| Employee benefits | (12,000) |
| Supplies | (3,000) |
| Other expenses | (21,000) |
| Total expenses | (771,000) |
| Net income | 109,000 |

**Notes:**

1. SSI's purchases during 2009 were $115,000. It values its inventory based on cost using the FIFO inventory cost flow method. Assume the rules of §263A do not apply to SSI.
2. Of the $5,000 interest income, $2,000 was from a West Jordan city bond used to fund public activities (issued in 2007) and $3,000 was from a money market account.
3. SSI's dividend income comes from publicly-traded stocks that SSI has owned for two years.
4. SSI's compensation is as follows:

   - Kim $120,000
   - James $80,000
   - Other $400,000.

5. SSI wrote off $6,000 in accounts receivable as uncollectible during the year.
6. SSI's regular tax depreciation was $17,000. AMT depreciation was $13,000,
7. SSI distributed $60,000 to its shareholders.
8. SSI is not required to compute the amount in its accumulated adjustments account.

The following are SSI's book balance sheets as of January 1, 2009, and December 31, 2009.

| | 2009 | |
|---|---|---|
| | January 1 | December 31 |
| **Assets** | | |
| Cash | $ 90,000 | $143,000 |
| Accounts receivable | 300,000 | 310,000 |
| Allowance for doubtful accounts | (60,000) | (68,000) |
| Inventory | 45,000 | 50,000 |
| State and local bonds | 38,000 | 38,000 |
| Investments in stock | 82,000 | 82,000 |
| Fixed assets | 100,000 | 100,000 |
| Accumulated depreciation | (20,000) | (30,000) |
| Other assets | 20,000 | 21,000 |
| Total assets | $595,000 | $646,000 |

| | 2009 | |
| --- | --- | --- |
| | January 1 | December 31 |
| **Liabilities and Shareholders' Equity** | | |
| Accounts payable | 60,000 | 55,000 |
| Other current liabilities | 5,000 | 8,000 |
| Other liabilities | 10,000 | 14,000 |
| Capital stock | 200,000 | 200,000 |
| Retained earnings | 320,000 | 369,000 |
| Total liabilities and shareholders' equity | $595,000 | $646,000 |

# GIFT TAX RETURN PROBLEM

Lamar Grabowski is a prosperous rancher who lives in Crawford, (Cherry County) Nebraska. Lamar is 60 years old and has been married to Elouisa (58 years old) for the past 37 years. Mildred and Charles are Lamar and Elouisa's adult children, ages 32 and 36, respectively. Over the years Lamar has considered making gifts to his children. Finally, in 2007 Lamar gave $250,000 each to Mildred and Charles. This year Lamar made the following gifts to Mildred and Charles:

| Property | Recipient | Market Value | Adjusted Basis |
| --- | --- | --- | --- |
| Cash from joint savings account | Mildred Jones | $1,380,000 | |
| 100 acres of ranch land near Crawford | Charles Grabowski | 1,640,000 | $125,000 |

In addition to these gifts, this year Lamar also made a gift of 20,000 shares of Acme Inc. stock to State University (a qualified educational institution). The stock is listed on a national exchange (CUSIP = 000123TP) and was valued at $800,000 on the date of the gift. Lamar purchased the Acme stock 34 years ago for $25,000, and he inherited the ranch land from his father in 1992 when it was valued at $600,000. Lamar's cash gifts are made from Lamar and Elouisa's joint savings account, and although Elouisa is a professional accountant, she has not contributed to the joint savings account.

Lamar filed a timely gift tax return for 2007 gifts offsetting a portion of each gift with his $12,000 annual exclusion and offsetting the remaining $147,640 of gift taxes with a portion of his unified credit. Lamar has engaged you to calculate the gift tax and prepare a draft of the gift tax return (pages 1–3).

# ESTATE TAX RETURN PROBLEM

Clark Griswold is wealthy engineer and inventor who retired to his residence in Fort Collins, (Larimer County) Colorado in 1994. Clark is married to Ellen Lamar and they have two adult children, Russell and Audrey. Clark passed away on March 22nd of this year at the age of 60, and his executor, Frank Shirley, has hired you to calculate the estate tax and prepare a draft of the estate tax return (pages 1 through 3). Clark's estate is being administered through the Larimer County Probate Court.

Frank has inventoried Clark's assets and has listed the value of his assets below. The auto, residence, and checking account were owned jointly (with the right of survivorship) with his wife, Ellen. Clark also owned a whole life insurance policy with a cash surrender value of $50,000. Ellen and Clark's estate were listed as beneficiaries on the insurance policy with Ellen receiving 1 million and the estate receiving the

remainder of the proceeds. The Ajax common stock, the real estate, and the patent were all owned by Clark rather than joint ownership. Frank also noted that the residence is subject to a $300,000 mortgage and the real estate is subject to a $500,000 mortgage. At his death Clark also owed $1,500 on his credit card.

| Property | Value | Adjusted Basis |
| --- | --- | --- |
| Auto | $ 20,000 | $ 55,000 |
| Personal effects | 75,000 | 110,000 |
| Checking account | 250,000 | 250,000 |
| 30,000 shares of Ajax common stock | 1,200,000 | 270,000 |
| Residence | 1,400,000 | 480,000 |
| Life insurance | 4,000,000 | 50,000 |
| Real estate | 1,000,000 | 2,100,000 |
| Patent | 1,225,000 | 100,000 |

Clark's will instructs Frank to distribute Clark's property as follows: Ellen inherits Clark's personal effects, Russell inherits the patent, and Audrey inherits 10,000 shares of the Ajax stock and the real estate. The will also instructs Frank to distribute 20,000 shares of the Ajax stock to State University (an educational institution), and after paying Clark's personal debts, the residual of the estate (if any) is divided equally between Russell and Audrey. The estate paid Clark's personal debts (credit card debt) and $4,300 of funeral expenses associated with Clark's burial. Finally, the estate paid Frank $27,000 in executor's fees associated with the administration of Clark's estate.

Clark's tax records indicate that in 2007 Clark gave $700,000 of Ajax stock to Russell and $500,000 of cash to Audrey. Clark filed a timely gift tax return (Form 709) and paid $82,000 in gift taxes.

# Code Index

Page numbers followed by n refer to footnotes.

**I.R.C. Sec.**
1(g), **7**-7n
1(g)(2)(A), **7**-7n
1(g)(4), **7**-7n
1(g)(5), **7**-7n
1(g)(7), **7**-7n
1(h), **4**-9n, **11**-14n, **11**-17n, **20**-17n
1(h)(7), **11**-12n
1(h)(11)(B), **7**-4n
1(h)(11)(B)(iii), **7**-4n
2(b), **4**-18n
21(e)(6), **7**-24n
24(a), **7**-22n
25A(b), **7**-25n
25A(d), **7**-27n
25A(f)(1), **7**-27n
25A(g)(3), **7**-25n
25A(i)(3), **7**-26n
25A(i)(4), **7**-26n
25A(i)(6), **7**-26n
25B(g), **13**-28n
26, **7**-31n
32, **7**-29n
32(i), **7**-29n
36, **14**-16n–17n
36A, **7**-28n
36(h), **14**-17n
38(c), **7**-31n
55(a), **16**-33n
55(d)(2), **16**-37n
55(e), **16**-33n
55(g)(1), **16**-36n
55(g)(2), **16**-36n
55(g)(4)(B)(iv), **16**-36n
56, **16**-34n
56(a)(C)(vi), **16**-34n
61(a), **4**-2n, **8**-2n
61(a)(12), **5**-19n
63(c)(1)(C), **6**-16n, **14**-15n
63(d), **6**-2n
66, **5**-9n
67(b)(10), **5**-12n
68, **6**-30n
68(f), **6**-36n
71(b), **5**-15n
71(c), **5**-15n
71(f), **5**-16n
72(a)(3), **5**-12n
72(d), **5**-11n
72(t), **13**-22n
72(t)(2)(F), **13**-23n

74(b), **5**-16n
74(c), **5**-17n
78, **24**-21n
79, **12**-23n, **12**-27n
83(a), **15**-14n
83(b), **19**-6n
85(a), **5**-10n
85(c), **5**-10n
86(b)(2)(A), **5**-18n
86(d), **5**-17n
101, **5**-21n, **5**-23n
104, **5**-25n
105(b), **12**-27n
106, **12**-27n
108(h), **14**-7n
111, **5**-5n
118, **19**-18n
119(a)(1), **12**-27n
119(a)(2), **12**-27n
121(a), **14**-3n
121(b)(4)(5), **14**-6n
125, **12**-31n
127(a)(2), **12**-28n
127(b)(2), **12**-28n
129, **12**-28n
132(a)(1), **12**-28n
132(a)(2), **12**-29n
132(a)(4), **12**-30n
132(a)(6), **12**-31n
132(c), **18**-17n
132(f)(1), **12**-30n
135(c)(4), **5**-23n
151(b), **4**-10
151(c), **4**-10
151(c)(2)(e), **4**-11n
151(c)(3)(B), **4**-11n
151(d)(3), **4**-14n
152, **4**-11n
152(c)(3)(A), **4**-11n
152(c)(4)(C), **4**-13n
152(e), **4**-13n
152(f), **4**-19n
152(f)(1), **4**-12n, **4**-14n
152(f)(2), **4**-11n, **13**-28n
152(f)(5), **4**-12n, **4**-14n
162, **6**-3n, **8**-2n
162(1), **6**-8n, **22**-16n
162(1)(2)(B), **6**-8n
162(a), **8**-3n
162(c), **8**-4n
162(e), **8**-5n

162(k), **18**-28n
163, **11**-30n
163(h), **14**-8n
163(h)(3)(E), **14**-12n
163(h)(4), **14**-8n
163(h)(4)(A)(iii), **14**-8n
164, **6**-16n
165, **6**-23n, **8**-14n
165(c)(3), **6**-23n
165(h)(5), **8**-14n
166(a), **8**-11n, **8**-28n
167(f), **9**-35–36n
168(d)(3)(B)(ii), **9**-18n
168(g)(2), **18**-6n
168(g)(3)(C), **9**-21n
168(i)(6), **9**-4n
168(i)(7)(B)(ii), **19**-17n
168(k)(1), **9**-19n
168(k)(2), **9**-20n
168(k)(2)(F)(i), **9**-23n
170, **16**-15n
170(a)(2), **16**-16n
170(c), **6**-18n
172(b)(1)(H), **16**-14n
174, **9**-35n
177(b)(2), **5**-22n
179(b)(6), **9**-25n
181, **11**-5n
183, **14**-24n, **22**-13n
195, **8**-5n, **9**-34n
197, **8**-5n, **9**-36n, **16**-8n, **19**-22n, **19**-24n
199, **8**-11n
199(d)(2), **8**-12n
212, **6**-3n, **8**-2n, **11**-29n
213(a), **6**-14n
213(d)(2), **6**-14n
213(d)(5), **6**-14n
213(d)(9)(A), **6**-14n
217, **6**-6
219(c), **13**-20n
221, **6**-9n
221(d)(2), **11**-25n
222, **6**-9n
222(c)(2)(A), **7**-27n
222(e), **6**-11n
243, **16**-18n
246(b)(1), **16**-19n
246(b)(2), **16**-20n
246(b)(3), **16**-19n
246(c), **16**-18n
248, **9**-32n

248(a)(1), **9**-32n
248(a)(2), **9**-33n
262(a), **8**-6n
263(a), **20**-10n
263A(a), **8**-21n
265, **11**-29n
267, **3**-12
267(a), **8**-28n, **10**-32n, **11**-19n
267(a)(2), **3**-11, **12**-6n
267(b), **8**-28n, **10**-14n, **11**-19n
267(c), **8**-28n, **10**-32n
274, **8**-7n, **8**-11n
274(c), **8**-9n
274(n), **12**-27n
275(a)(1), **16**-3n
280A, **14**-26n
280A(c)(5), **14**-20n, **14**-29n
280A(e), **14**-24n
280A(g), **14**-18n
280E, **8**-4n
280F(d)(5)(A), **9**-24n
301, **15**-19n
301(b), **18**-11n
301(c), **15**-20n, **18**-3n
301(d), **18**-11n
302, **18**-21n, **22**-17n
302(b)(1), **18**-22n, **18**-26–27n
302(b)(2), **18**-22n, **18**-27n
302(b)(3), **18**-22n, **18**-25n
302(b)(4), **18**-29n
302(c), **18**-26n
302(c)(2), **18**-26n
302(c)(2)(A)(iii), **18**-26n
302(e), **18**-30n
305(a), **18**-18n
305(b), **18**-19n
305, **11**-7n
307, **15**-19n, **18**-19n
311, **18**-12n
311(a), **18**-28n
311(b), **15**-20n, **18**-28n, **22**-20n
312, **18**-5n, **18**-12n
312(a), **18**-28n
312(n), **18**-6n, **18**-6n
312(n)(7), **18**-28n
317, **18**-3n
317(b), **18**-21n
318, **18**-24n, **22**-16n
331, **15**-23n, **19**-35n
332(a), **19**-36n
334(b)(1), **19**-36n
336, **15**-23n
336(a), **19**-36n
336(d)(1), **19**-36n
336(d)(2), **19**-38n
336(d)(3), **19**-39n
337(a), **19**-39n
351, **10**-31n, **19**-4n, **19**-7n, **22**-11n
351(a), **15**-13n
355, **19**-34n

357(a), **19**-12n
357(b), **19**-12n
357(c), **19**-13n
357(c)(3), **19**-13n
358, **19**-4n, **22**-11n
358(a), **19**-9n
358(a)(2), **19**-12n
362(a), **19**-14n
362(a)(2), **19**-18n
362(c)(1), **19**-18n
362(e)(2), **19**-16n, **19**-38n
368, **10**-32n
368(a)(1), **19**-26n
385, **22**-3n
402(g)(1), **13**-7n
402(g)(4), **13**-7n
404(a)(6), **13**-5n
404(h), **13**-26n
408(A)(c)(3), **13**-24n
408(A)(d)(2), **13**-23n
408(d)(3), **13**-23n
408(k), **13**-26n
408(m), **11**-11n
409A, **13**-18n
411(a), **13**-4n
411(c), **13**-8n
415(b)(1), **13**-3n
415(c)(1), **13**-7n
415(d)(1)(C), **13**-7n
422(a)(1), **12**-14n
441(e), **15**-15n
441(f), **15**-15n
443, **8**-15n
444, **22**-8n
446(a), **8**-17n
446(b), **8**-17n
448, **8**-29n, **16**-3n
448(a), **15**-15n
448(a)(2), **20**-16n
448(a)(3), **20**-16n
448(b)(3), **15**-15n, **20**-16n
453(A), **10**-29n
453(b)(1), **10**-29n
453(d), **10**-29n
453(i), **10**-31n
454(a), **5**-22n, **11**-5n
461, **8**-24n
461(c), **8**-26n
461(g)(2), **14**-12n
461(g), **8**-17n
461(h), **8**-24n
465(b)(6), **11**-34n, **20**-30n
465, **11**-34n, **11**-36n
469, **11**-35n, **20**-31n, **22**-15n
469(b)(7), **11**-38n, **20**-32n
469(g), **11**-37n
469(i), **14**-26n, **20**-32n
469(j), **14**-20n, **14**-26n
472(c), **8**-23n
501, **22**-2n

529(c)(3), **11**-25n
530(b), **11**-25n
531, **15**-13n, **18**-18n
541, **15**-13n
581, **15**-27n
585, **22**-3n
612, **9**-37n
613, **9**-38n
701, **20**-17n
702, **20**-18n
702(b), **20**-8n, **20**-19n
702(c), **20**-19n
703(b), **20**-13n
704(b), **15**-16n, **20**-22n
704(c), **20**-22n
704(c)(1)(C), **21**-7n
704(d), **20**-29n
705, **15**-19n
705(a)(2), **20**-27n
706, **8**-16n
706(a), **20**-14n
706(b)(1)(B), **15**-15n
706(b)(1)(B)(i), **20**-15n
706(b)(3), **20**-15n
706(d)(1), **21**-8n
707(a)(2)(B), **20**-7n
707(b)(2), **10**-13n
708(b), **21**-8n
709, **9**-32n
721, **10**-31n, **20**-3n
721(a), **15**-13n
722, **20**-4n
723, **20**-8n
724(b), **20**-8n
731, **15**-24n, **20**-29n, **21**-3n, **21**-10n
731(a), **15**-20n, **20**-7n
731(a)(1), **21**-10n
731(a)(2), **21**-13–14n
731(b), **15**-20n, **21**-9n
731(c), **21**-11n
731(c)(1)(A), **21**-11n
732(a), **21**-11n
732(a)(2), **21**-11n, **21**-14n
732(c), **21**-11n
732(c)(1), **21**-14n
732(c)(2), **21**-15n
732(c)(3), **21**-20n
733, **21**-10–11n
734(a), **21**-10n
735(a), **21**-22n
735(b), **21**-22n
741, **21**-3n
742, **20**-13n
743(b), **21**-27n
743(d)(1), **21**-27n
751, **15**-25n, **21**-3–4n
751(a), **15**-23n, **21**-3–4n
751(b), **21**-3n, **21**-25n
751(c), **21**-4n
751(c)(1), **21**-4n

751(c)(2), **21**-4n
751(d), **21**-3n
751(d)(1), **21**-4n
752(a), **20**-4n
752(b), **20**-6n, **21**-12n
753, **21**-7n
754, **21**-7n, **21**-10n, **21**-26n
755, **21**-10n
861, **24**-6n
861(a), **24**-7n
861(a)(3)(A), **24**-8n
862(a), **24**-7n
863(b), **24**-10n
865, **24**-6n
871(i)(2)(A), **24**-7n
881(d), **24**-7n
901, **24**-21n
902, **24**-21n
903, **24**-21n
904, **7**-31n
904(d), **24**-19n
911, **13**-28n, **24**-7n
911(b)(2), **5**-24
936, **22**-3n
951, **24**-27n
951(b), **24**-27n
954(d), **24**-29n
957, **24**-27n
958(b), **24**-27n
960, **24**-21n, **24**-30n
964, **24**-22–23n, **24**-27n
986(a)(1)(A), **24**-21n
986(b), **24**-22n
1001, **19**-3n
1001(a), **5**-5n, **10**-3n, **19**-3n
1001(b), **19**-3n
1001(c), **19**-4n
1011, **9**-3n
1012, **9**-3n, **15**-19n, **21**-7n
1014, **9**-5n
1015, **9**-4n
1015(d), **9**-4n
1031(a), **10**-24n
1031(a)(2), **10**-21n
1031(a)(3), **10**-23
1031(b), **10**-24n
1032, **19**-6n

1033, **10**-26n
1033(a)(2)(B), **10**-28n
1211, **10**-32n, **20**-17n
1211(a), **16**-11n
1211(b), **16**-11n
1212(a), **16**-11n
1212(a)(a)(A)(ii), **16**-12n
1221, **10**-5n, **11**-9n
1223(1), **19**-10n, **19**-15n
1223(2), **20**-8n
1223(4), **18**-19n
1231, **19**-11n
1239(a), **19**-11n
1244, **15**-23n
1245, **21**-25n
1250, **19**-11n
1272, **11**-4n
1276(a), **11**-5n
1278(b)(1), **11**-5n
1316, **22**-2n
1361, **15**-5n
1361(b), **15**-6n, **15**-13n, **15**-16n
1362(a), **15**-5n, **22**-3n
1362(b), **22**-4n
1362(b)(2), **22**-4n
1362(b)(5), **22**-4n
1362(d)(a)(B), **22**-5n
1362(d)(a)(D), **22**-5n
1362(e)(5)(D), **22**-7n
1362(f), **22**-5n
1362(g), **22**-7n
1363(d), **22**-25n
1366(a), **15**-16n, **22**-8n
1366(b)(2), **15**-19n
1366(d), **22**-13n
1366(f)(2), **22**-22n
1367, **15**-19n
1367(a)(2), **22**-12n
1368(b), **15**-20n
1368(d), **22**-17n
1368(e)(1)(C), **22**-18n
1372(a), **22**-16n
1374, **22**-21n
1375, **22**-23n
1375(d), **22**-24n
1377(a), **22**-8n
1377(b)(1)(A), **22**-14n, **22**-21n

1377(b)(1)(B), **22**-21n
1377(b)(1)(C), **22**-21n
1378, **8**-16n
1378(b), **15**-15n, **22**-8n
1402(a), **15**-17n
1441, **24**-7n
1502, **16**-28n
1504, **16**-19n
1504(a), **16**-28n
1561(a), **16**-25n
1563(a), **16**-24n
1563, **16**-24n
2010, **25**-2n
2032, **19**-14n
2032A, **25**-8n
2033, **25**-4n
2036, **25**-5n
2039, **25**-5n
2040, **25**-5n
2041, **25**-5n
2053, **25**-11n
2054, **25**-11n
2058, **25**-11n
2112, **6**-27n
2248, **8**-5n
2502, **25**-2n
2514, **25**-18n
2518, **25**-18n
6012, **2**-2, **7**-36n
6601, **7**-36n
6651, **7**-36n
6654, **7**-34n
6655, **16**-28n
6655(b)(2), **16**-32n
6655(c), **16**-28n
6655(d), **16**-29n, **16**-31n
6655(e), **16**-28–29n
6655(g)(2), **16**-31n
6694, **2**-26
6698, **20**-23n, **22**-28n
7520, **25**-9n
7701(a)(1), **19**-6n, **24**-2n
7701(a)(9), **24**-2n
7701(a)(43), **19**-14n
7701(a)(44), **19**-9n
7701(b), **24**-4n
7704, **15**-5n, **20**-17n

# PHOTO CREDITS

Chapter 1: Comstock Images/Jupiter Images
Chapter 2: ©James Hardy/Photo Alto
Chapter 3: Photodisc Collection/Getty Images
Chapter 4: Getty Images/Digital Vision
Chapter 5: Eric Audras/Photoalto/PictureQuest
Chapter 6: Eric Audras/Photoalto/PictureQuest
Chapter 7: Eric Audras/Photoalto/PictureQuest
Chapter 8: Creatas Images
Chapter 9: RF/Corbis
Chapter 10: ©Digital Vison/Punchstock
Chapter 11: PhotoDisc/Getty Images
Chapter 12: Banana Stock/Fotostock
Chapter 13: Banana Stock/Fotostock
Chapter 14: RF/Corbis
Chapter 15: ©PhotoAlto
Chapter 16: ©BananaStock
Chapter 17: ©BananaStock
Chapter 18: © RF/Corbis
Chapter 19: Jules Frazier/Getty Images
Chapter 20: ©PhotoAlto
Chapter 21: ©PhotoAlto
Chapter 22: ©PhotoAlto
Chapter 23: Brand X
Chapter 24: Ryan McVay/Getty Images
Chapter 25: BananaStock/Jupiterimages

# SUBJECT INDEX

Page numbers followed by n refer to footnotes.

## A

Abandoned spouses, 4-19
Academy Awards gift baskets, 2-5
Accelerated Cost Recovery System (ACRS), 9-5
Accelerated depreciation, 10-7n, 10-12
Accountable plan, 6-26
Accountants, unauthorized practice of law, 2-9
Accounting for income taxes
  complexity of, 17-3
  importance of, 17-3
  income tax provision process, 17-2–6
  objectives of, 17-2–6
Accounting method, 5-6–7, 8-16–33; see also Accrual method; Cash method
  adoption of, 8-30–31
  changing method of, 8-33
  choice of, 16-3
  corporations, 16-3
  entities overview, 15-15–16
  financial and tax accounting method, 8-17
  inventories, 8-21–23
  overall accounting method, 8-17
  partnership accounting, 20-14–16
  S corporations, 22-8
  stock option expense, GAAP vs. tax, 12-16
  tax consequences of method change, 8-33
Accounting periods, 8-15–16
Accounting Standards Codification (ASC) 718, stock compensation, 12-16n, 12-20n
Accrual income, 8-19
  advance payment for goods/services, 8-20
  all-events test for income, 8-19
  taxation of advance payments (prepaid income), 8-19–20
Accrual method, 3-5n, 3-11, 5-6–7, 8-11, 8-18–19, 16-3n
  accrual deductions, 8-24–28
  advance payment for goods/services, 8-20
  all-events test for deductions, 8-24
  bad debt expense, 8-27–28
  business expense deductions, 8-24

cash method vs., 8-29
  deductibility of salary payments, 12-6
  economic performance test, 8-24–27
  inventories, 8-21–23
  limitations on accruals to related parties, 8-28
  payment liabilities, 8-27
  prepaid income, 8-19–20
  revenue recognition, 8-19–20
Accrued market discount, 11-5
Accumulated adjustments account (AAA), 22-18
Accumulated earnings and profits, 18-4
Accumulated earnings tax, 15-13n
ACE (adjusted current earnings) adjustment, 16-35–36
Ackerman, Ruthie, 17-20
Acquiescence, 2-17
Acquisition indebtedness, 14-8–9
Acquisition subsidiary, 19-29
Acquisition tax model, 19-21–22
Actions on decisions, 2-17
Active business income, 20-32
Active participant, 14-26
Active participant in a rental activity, 11-39
Activities; see Business activities
Actuarial tables, 25-10
Ad valorem taxes, 1-14
Adjusted basis, 9-3, 10-2–3
Adjusted current earnings (ACE), 16-35–36
Adjusted gross estate, 25-11
Adjusted gross income (AGI), 4-2, 4-6, 7-5
  summary of deductions for, 6-12–13
Adjusted seasonal income method, 16-29n
Adjusted tax basis, 19-3
Adjusted taxable gifts, 25-13
Administrative expenses, taxable estate, 25-11
Administrative sources of the tax law, 2-9–10
  citations (examples), 2-10
  letter rulings, 2-16–17
  regulations, 2-15–16
  revenue rulings and revenue procedures, 2-15–16
  U.S. Treasury, 2-15–16

Adoption expense credit, 7-22, 7-32
Advance payment for goods/services, 8-20–21
Advance payment of income (prepaid income), 8-19–20
Affiliated group, 16-28
After-tax cost of contribution, defined contribution plans, 13-9
After-tax earnings distributed, 15-7–11
  individual shareholders, 15-7–9
After-tax earnings retained, 15-11
After-tax future value of an investment, 11-3
After-tax rate of return, 1-15, 3-3n, 3-17, 11-1–3, 11-21n
  defined contribution plans, 13-11–12
Age and/or blindness, 6-32
Age test, 4-11
  qualifying child, 4-11
Aggregate approach, 20-2
Alimony, 4-5–6, 5-14–16, 5-19
  front loading restrictions, 5-16
All-events test
  for deductions, 8-24
  for income, 8-19
All-inclusive definition of income, 4-2, 5-3, 5-14
Allocation, 23-4, 24-11
  general principles of, 24-11–12
Allowance method, 8-28
Alternative depreciation system (ADS), 9-5–6n, 9-21
Alternative minimum tax (AMT), 4-9, 7-8–14, 16-33, 16-35, 16-38–39; see also Corporate alternative minimum tax
  alternative minimum taxable income (AMTI), 7-9–12
  AMT computation, 7-12–13
  AMT exemption, 16-37–38
  AMT formula, 7-9
  AMT planning strategies, 7-14, 16-39
  common adjustments, 7-9–11
  depreciation for, 9-28
  exemptions and standard deduction, 7-10–12
  minimum tax credit, 16-39
  other considerations, 7-13–14
  tentative minimum tax (TMT), 7-12–13, 16-38

Alternative minimum tax (AMT) adjustments, **7**-9–11

Alternative minimum tax (AMT) base, **7**-9

Alternative minimum tax (AMT) exemption, **7**-11–12, **16**-37–38

Alternative minimum tax (AMT) formula, **7**-9

Alternative minimum taxable income (AMTI), **7**-9–11, **16**-36–37

Alternative recovery period, **9**-6n, **9**-21

Alternative tax systems; *see also* Tax system

evaluation of, **1**-16–21

Alternative valuation date, **25**-8

Amazon.com, **23**-7n

American Institute of CPAs (AICPA)

Code of Professional Conduct, **2**-23–24

Statements on Standards for Tax Services (SSTS), **2**-23–25

American Opportunity Credit (AOC), **7**-25–28, **7**-32, **12**-28

American Recovery and Reinvestment Act of 2009, **5**-10n, **6**-16

executive compensation, **12**-7n

Section 179 expensing, **9**-16–17

Amortization, **9**-2, **9**-30–37, **11**-4

corporate and Treasury bonds, **11**-4–5

organizational expenditures, **9**-32–34

patents and copyrights, **9**-35

research and experimentation expenditures, **9**-34–35

Section 197 intangibles, **9**-30–32

start-up costs, **9**-32–34

summary of amortizable assets, **9**-36

Amount realized, **19**-3

Amount realized (from dispositions), **10**-2

AMT adjustments, **7**-9–11

AMT base, **7**-9

AMT exemption, **7**-11–12, **16**-37–38

AMT formula, **7**-9

AMT preference item, **11**-12n

Anheuser-Busch Cos., **18**-29

Annotated tax services, **2**-18

Annual basis adjustments, **22**-12

Annual exclusion, gift tax, **25**-19–20

Annualized income method, **16**-29

Annuities, **5**-10–13

exclusion ratio, **5**-11

joint-life annuity, **5**-11

single-life annuity, **5**-11–12

unrecovered costs of, **5**-12n

Anti-stuffing provision, **19**-38

Apportion, **24**-11

Apportionment, **23**-4

general principles of, **24**-11–12

special apportionment rules, **24**-12–14

Appraisal, **9**-4

Appraisal value, **14**-15n

Arm's-length transactions, **3**-12, **8**-4

Articles of incorporation/organization, **15**-2

ASC 230, *Statement of Cash Flows,* **17**-2n

ASC 718 (formerly FAS 123R), **16**-10, **16**-10n, **16**-11–12

book/tax treatment of stock options, **16**-10, **16**-12

stock compensation, **12**-16n, **12**-20n

ASC 740 *Income Taxes,* **17**-1–2

accounting for uncertainty, **17**-23

application of, **17**-24–25

balance sheet classification, **17**-27–28

complexity of, **17**-3

computation/reconciliation of income tax provision, **17**-30–31

deductible temporary difference, **17**-9–10

deferred tax expense/liability, **17**-12

disclosure of uncertain tax positions, **17**-26–27

expected future taxable income, **17**-19

future reversals of temporary differences, **17**-18

income tax footnote disclosure, **17**-28–30

interest and penalties, **17**-26

international reporting standards convergence, **17**-32

measurement, **17**-24–25

objectives of, **17**-3–4

potential future taxable income, **17**-18

recognition and measurement, **17**-23–24

subsequent events, **17**-26

tax planning strategies, **17**-19

temporary differences, **17**-8–10

uncertain tax positions, **17**-24–27

valuation allowance for gross deferred tax assets, **17**-18–22

ASC 740-270, *Interim Reporting,* **17**-32

Assessments, **1**-4

Asset classes, **9**-6n

Asset depreciation range (ADR), **9**-6n

Asset dispositions, **4**-6, **5**-13, **9**-31n

Asset and liability approach, **17**-4

Asset values, **9**-4

Assets; *see also* Business assets

capital assets, **10**-5–6

cost recovery and, **9**-2–5

formula for calculating gain/loss, **5**-13

gain or loss on disposition, character of assets, **10**-4–7

listed property, **9**-20–22

losses on disposition of trade/business assets, **4**-6

ordinary assets, **10**-5

personal use assets, **6**-23

property dispositions, **5**-13

recovery period (depreciable "life"), **9**-5

Section 1231 assets, **10**-5–7

useful lives, **9**-5–6

Assignment of income doctrine, **3**-12, **5**-8, **7**-6

At-risk amount, **20**-30, **22**-14

At-risk limitation, **20**-30–31, **22**-14

At-risk rules, **20**-30

At risk/at-risk hurdle, **11**-33–36

Attribution from entities to owners or beneficiaries, **18**-25

Attribution from owners or beneficiaries to entities, **18**-25

Audits

audit selection, **2**-4–5

correspondence examinations, **2**-5

field examinations, **2**-6

hazards of litigation, **2**-6

office examinations, **2**-6

post-audit, **2**-6–9

statute of limitations and, **2**-4

types of, **2**-5–6

Automobiles depreciation limits, **9**-23–25

luxury automobiles, **9**-24

Average tax rate, **1**-6–7

Awards, **5**-16–17, **5**-19

**B**

Bad debt expense, **8**-11, **8**-27–28

Balance sheet, **17**-3

Balance sheet classification, ASC 740, **17**-27–28

Bargain element, **12**-11–12, **12**-13n, **16**-10

Bargain sales/leases of property, **18**-15

Barter clubs, **5**-4

Basis computation, entities overview, **15**-19

Basis (purchase price), **11**-5

Before-tax rate of return, **1**-15, **11**-1–2

Beneficiary, **25**-8, **25**-27

Berk, Christina Cheddar, **12**-25

Berkshire Hathaway Inc., **15**-12

Binomial pricing model, **12**-16n

Bittker, Boris I., **18**-27n

Black-Scholes option pricing model, **12**-16n

BNA Tax Management Portfolios, **2**-11, **2**-19

Bolton method, **14**-21n

*Bolton v. Commissioner,* **14**-21n

Bond, **11**-2

Bond discount/premium, **11**-4, **11**-5n

Bonus depreciation, **9**-19–20

Book equivalent of taxable income, **17**-8

temporary differences, **17**-8–9

Book or financial reporting income, **16**-3
Book-tax differences, **16**-4–9
  charitable contributions, **16**-15–17
  common permanent differences, **16**-4–5
  common temporary differences, **16**-6
  corporate-specific deductions, **16**-9–21
  dividends, **16**-7
  dividends received deduction, **16**-18–21
  federal income tax expense, **16**-5
  net capital losses, **16**-11–12
  net operating losses, **16**-13–15
  purchased goodwill, **16**-8
  stock options, **16**-9–11
Book treatment, **12**-16
Boot, **19**-6–7
  tax consequences of, **19**-10–12
Boot (not-like-kind property), **10**-24–26
Brackets, **1**-4
Branch, **24**-3
Breeding, training, or racing horses, **6**-28n
Bribes, **8**-4
Bright line test, **19**-27
  stock ownership tests, **18**-21, **18**-23
Brother-sister controlled group, **16**-24
Brown-Forman, **18**-30
Budget deficit, **1**-18
Buffett, Warren, **15**-12
Built-in gains/losses, **20**-3
Built-in gains tax, **22**-21–22
  recognition period, **22**-21
Bunching itemized deductions, **6**-2, **6**-33–34
Bush, George H. W., **1**-3
Business acquisitions, motivation for, **19**-21
Business activities, **6**-2–3
  deductions directly related to, **6**-3–6
  deductions indirectly related to, **6**-6–9
  deductions subsidizing specific activities, **6**-9–12
Business assets
  casualty losses, **8**-14–15
  listed property, **9**-20–22
  losses on disposition of, **4**-6, **6**-6, **8**-13–14
  for personal/business use, **8**-10
  recovery period for, **9**-7
Business casualty losses, **8**-14–15
Business deductions, **8**-2–4
  accrual method for, **8**-24
  bad debt expense, **8**-11
  capital expenditures, **8**-5
  casualty losses, **8**-14–15
  domestic manufacturing deduction, **8**-11–13

expenditures against public policy, **8**-4
expenses for production of tax-exempt income, **8**-5–6
limitations on, **8**-4–11
losses on disposition of business property, **8**-13–14
meals and entertainment, **8**-7
mixed-motive expenditures, **8**-7
as ordinary and necessary, **8**-3
personal expenditures, **8**-6
political contributions/lobbying costs, **8**-5
property use, **8**-10
as reasonable in amount, **8**-3–4
record keeping and other requirements, **8**-11
specific deductions, **8**-11–15
start-up costs and organizational expenditures, **8**-11–12
travel and transportation, **8**-8–10
Business entities; *see also* Entity tax characteristics
  accounting methods, **15**-15–16
  accounting periods, **15**-15
  basis computation, **15**-19
  contributions of property/services, **15**-13–14
  converting to other entity types, **15**-24–25
  deductibility of losses, **15**-21–22
  FICA and self-employment tax, **15**-16–18
  legal classification, **15**-2–3
  liquidating entities, **15**-23–24
  nontax characteristics, **15**-3–4
  number/type of owners, **15**-13
  responsibility for liabilities, **15**-3
  rights, responsibilities, legal arrangements, **15**-3–4
  selling ownership interests, **15**-22–23
  special allocations, **15**-16
  summary of, **15**-4, **15**-26
  tax classification, **15**-5–6
Business expenses, **3**-16, **4**-6, **8**-2–3
  associated with production of tax-exempt income, **8**-5–6
  employee vs. independent contractor, **7**-19–22
  as reasonable in amount, **8**-3–4
  typical ordinary and necessary expenses, **8**-3
  unreimbursed employee expenses, **6**-3
Business gross income, **8**-2
Business income, **4**-5, **5**-3, **23**-4
  income taxes, **23**-17–20
Business interest expense, **5**-19n
Business purpose doctrine, **3**-18
Business purpose test, **19**-27
Business tax credits, **7**-30–31
Business test, moving expenses, **6**-6–7

Business use of home, **8**-7, **14**-25–29
  direct vs. indirect expenses, **14**-27–28
  home office deductions, **14**-26–28
  limitations on deductibility of expenses, **14**-28–29
Buy-sell agreement, **18**-21
Bypass provisions, **25**-28–29
Bypass trust, **25**-31

**C**
C corporations, **8**-2, **8**-16, **8**-28–29, **15**-5, **16**-2, **18**-3n
  after-tax profits, **18**-2
  corporate tax formulas, **16**-2–3
  distributions from, **18**-2–3
  S corporations vs., **22**-30–31
Cafeteria plans, **12**-31
Calendar year, **8**-15
Callaway Golf 2009 Proxy Statement, **12**-8
Capell, Kerry, **24**-31
Capital accounts, **20**-8
Capital assets, **6**-19, **7**-4, **10**-5–6, **10**-5n, **11**-9
  tax advantages of, **11**-9
  tax planning strategies for, **11**-20–22
Capital expenditures, **8**-5
Capital gain property, **6**-19–20, **16**-15
Capital gains and losses, **6**-6, **10**-6, **11**-8–22
  classification by maximum applicable tax rates, **11**-12
  collectibles and Section 1202 gain, **11**-11–12
  limitations on capital losses, **11**-18–20
  netting process for, **11**-13–18
  personal-use assets, losses on, **11**-19
  portfolio income, **11**-8–10
  preferential tax rates for gains, **7**-4–6
  related parties sales, **11**-19
  reporting of capital gains, **11**-14
  review of, **10**-6
  summary for, **11**-20
  tax planning strategies, **11**-20–22
  types of, **11**-11
  unrecaptured Section 1250 gain, **11**-11
  wash sales, **11**-19
Capital gains tax rate, **3**-9, **7**-4–6
Capital-intensive industries, **9**-2
Capital interest, **20**-3, **20**-11
Capital loss carryback/carryover, **16**-11, **16**-16, **22**-22n
Capitalized tangible assets, **8**-5, **9**-2
Capitalizing the expenditure, **8**-5n
Carryback NOLs, **15**-21n
Carryover basis, **9**-4, **19**-14, **19**-17, **21**-11, **25**-19n, **25**-29
Cash contributions, **6**-18–19
Cash distributions, in operating partnerships, **20**-28–29

Cash guaranteed payments, **20**-28n
Cash inflows, **3**-4
Cash method, 3-5n, **3**-11, **5**-7, **8**-17–18, **16**-3n
  accrual method vs., **8**-29
  bad debt, **8**-29
  deductibility of salary payments, **12**-6
  deduction recognition, **8**-29
  expenditures for tangible/intangible assets, **8**-29
  income recognition, **8**-29
  inventories, **8**-21
  prepaid business expenses, **8**-29
  prepaid income for goods/services, **8**-20, **8**-29
  prepaid interest expense, **8**-29
  prepaid rental income, **8**-29
  12-month rule, **8**-17
Cash outflows, **3**-4
Cash surrender value, **11**-24
Cash tax rate, **17**-32
Casualties, **8**-14n
Casualty loss, **6**-23
  defined, **6**-23
Casualty and theft losses, **6**-23, **8**-14n
  business casualty losses, **8**-14–15
  comparison of, **8**-15
  deduction floor limitation, **6**-23–24
  as itemized deductions, **4**-7, **6**-23
Ceiling, **6**-21
Certainty in tax system, **1**-20–21
Certificate of limited partnership, **15**-2
Certificates of deposit (CDs), **6**-9, **11**-2
Certified public accountants (CPAs), **2**-23–26
Change-in-stock-ownership tests, **18**-22
Charitable contributions
  contributions of money, **6**-18–19
  corporations, **16**-15–17
  deduction limitations, **6**-21
  as itemized deductions, **4**-7, **6**-18–22
  limit modified taxable income, **16**-16
  summary of limitation rules, **6**-21
Charitable deductions, **24**-12, **25**-23
"Check the box" rules, **20**-2n
Child care credit, **4**-10
Child and dependent care credit, **7**-24–25
Child and dependent care expenses; *see also* Qualifying child; Qualifying relative
Child support payments, **5**-15, **5**-15n
Child tax credit, **7**-22–23, **7**-32
  phase-out threshold, **7**-22–23
Circular 230, **2**-23, **2**-25–26
Citator, **2**-20
Civil penalties, **2**-26–27
Class of stock, **19**-4n
Client letter
  analysis, **2**-22
  basic components of, **2**-22

closing, **2**-22
  facts, **2**-22
  research question and limitations, **2**-22
  sample client letter, **2**-23
Cliff vesting, **13**-4
Clinton, Bill, **1**-3
Closed facts, **2**-17
Closely held corporations/business, **18**-2
  dividend policies in, **18**-18
  stock redemption, **18**-21–22
Cloyd, C. B., **16**-3n
Collectibles, Section 1202 gain and, **11**-11–12
Combined controlled group, **16**-24
Commerce Clearing House (CCH)
  *Master Tax Guide,* **2**-10
  *Standard Federal Tax Reporter,* **2**-11, **2**-18
  *Tax Research Consultant,* **2**-11, **2**-19
Commercial domicile, **23**-2
Commercial traveler exception, **24**-8
*Commissioner v. Indianapolis Power & Light Co.,* **8**-20n
*Commissioner v. Lincoln Electric Co.,* **8**-3n
*Commissioner v. Newman,* **3**-18
*Commissioner v. Sullivan,* **8**-4n
Committee reports, **2**-10
Common carrier, **23**-10n
Common-law states, **25**-21
Community property states/systems, **4**-17n, **5**-8–9, **25**-21, **25**-21n
Commuting, **6**-25
Compensation, **3**-2, **3**-17, **4**-5, **5**-3, **12**-2
  to employee-owners, **3**-13–14
  equity-based compensation, **12**-10–22
  excess ("unreasonable") compensation, **18**-15
  fringe benefits, **12**-22–35
  multinational transactions, **24**-8–9
  salary and wages, **12**-2–9
  unreasonable compensation, **3**-15n, **12**-7n
Compensatory stock options, **12**-16n
*Complete Auto Transit, Inc. v. Brady,* **23**-9n, **23**-17n
Complete liquidation, **19**-34–39
  liquidating corporation, **19**-36–39
  tax consequences of, **19**-35–36
Compliance, **16**-25–32
  consolidated tax returns, **16**-7n, **16**-28
  corporate estimated taxes, **16**-28–32
  corporate tax return due dates, **16**-28–32
Consolidated tax return, **16**-7n, **16**-28
Consolidations, **19**-27
Constructive dividends, **18**-3, **18**-14–18
  examples of, **18**-15
Constructive ownership, **8**-28n, **10**-14n, **18**-24

Constructive receipt doctrine, **3**-10–11, **5**-7
Continuity of business enterprise (COBE), **19**-27
Continuity of interests (COI), **19**-26–27
Contra accounts, **17**-18
Contributed property/services, **15**-13–14, **21**-7n
Contribution limits, defined contribution plans, **13**-7–8
Contributions to capital, **19**-18–19
Control, **19**-5
  of the corporation, **19**-5
  Section 351 tax deferral, **19**-7–9
Controlled-foreign corporation (CFC), **24**-27
Controlled groups, **16**-24–25
  definitions for, **16**-24
Convenience in tax system, **1**-20–21
Conversion strategies, **3**-16–18
  limitations of, **3**-17–18
Cooper Industries, **3**-16
Copyrights, **9**-30, **9**-35–36
*Corliss v. Bowers,* **5**-7
Corporate acquisitions
  acquisition tax model, **19**-21–22
  computing tax consequences to parties, **19**-23–34
  motivations for, **19**-21
  tax model for, **19**-21–22
  taxable acquisitions, **19**-23–25
  taxable and tax-deferred, **19**-20–22
Corporate alternative minimum tax, **16**-33–39
  ACE adjustment, **16**-35–36
  adjustments, **16**-34–39
  alternative minimum taxable income (AMTI), **16**-36–37
  AMT exemption, **16**-37–38
  corporate AMT formula, **16**-34
  depreciation adjustment, **16**-34–35
  disposition of depreciable assets, gains/loss on, **16**-35
  preference items, **16**-33–34
  tax planning, **16**-39
  tentative minimum tax (TMT), **16**-38
Corporate AMT formula, **16**-34
Corporate bonds, **11**-2, **11**-4–5
Corporate dividends, shareholder taxation of, **18**-3
Corporate formations
  contributions to capital, **19**-18–19
  depreciable assets, **19**-17–18
  liabilities in excess of basis, **19**-13–14
  other issues related to, **19**-17–18
  requirements for tax deferral, **19**-5–7
  Section 351 tax deferral, **19**-6
  Section 1244 stock, **19**-19–19
  shareholder liabilities, assumption of, **19**-12

Corporate formations—*Cont.*
  tax-avoidance transactions, **19**-12–13
  tax-deferred transfers of property,
    **19**-4–19
Corporate inversions, **3**-16
Corporate liquidation, **19**-34–39
Corporate marginal tax rate, **15**-9
Corporate regular taxable income
  accounting periods and methods, **16**-3
  book-tax differences, **16**-4–9
  computation of, **16**-3–25
  controlled groups, **16**-24–25
  corporate-specific deductions, **16**-9–21
  regular tax liability, **16**-22–24
  taxable income summary, **16**-22–23
Corporate shareholders, **15**-4, **15**-7,
  **15**-9–10, **19**-36
  reducing corporate-level tax, **15**-11
Corporate tax return
  due dates, **16**-28–32
  estimated taxes, **16**-28–32
Corporate taxable income formula,
  **16**-2–3
Corporations, **15**-3; *see also*
  C corporations; S corporations
Corpus, **25**-8
Correspondence examinations, **2**-5
Cost basis, **9**-3, **10**-3
Cost depletion, **9**-37
Cost recovery, **9**-2–5; *see also*
  Amortization; Depletion;
  Depreciation
  assets and, **9**-2
  basis for, **9**-3–5
Cost segregation, **9**-26
"Coupon" rate, **11**-4
Covenants not to compete, **9**-30, **9**-36
Coverdell Education Savings Account
  (CESA), **5**-22, **6**-10n, **11**-26
Credits; *see also* Tax credits
  for elderly and disabled, **7**-32
  for increasing research activities, **7**-32
Criminal penalties, **2**-26
Cross-purchase agreement, **18**-21
*Crummey power,* **25**-20n
Cumulative difference, **8**-33
Current earnings and profits (E&P),
  **18**-4–5; *see also* Earnings and profits
  template for computing, **18**-8
Current gifts, **25**-20
Current income tax expense or
  benefit, **17**-11
Current tax liability or assets, **17**-3
Cutback, **6**-36

**D**
*Daily Tax Report,* **2**-11
Daimler-Chrysler merger, **3**-7–8
Date of the distribution, **18**-9
Date of grant, **12**-20

*De minimis* fringe benefits, **5**-21, **12**-26,
  **12**-30, **22**-16
*De minimis* rule, **19**-8
"Death tax," **1**-12
Debt basis, **22**-13
Debt instruments, **1**-18
Debts, taxable estate, **25**-11
Decedent, **25**-2n
Deductible temporary differences,
  **17**-9–10
Deductions, **4**-6–8, **5**-5, **6**-2; *see also*
  Business deductions; *For*
  AGI deductions; Itemized
  deductions
  above the line (*for* AGI), **4**-6–7, **5**-15,
    **6**-2–13
  below the line (*from* AGI), **4**-6–8,
    **6**-2, **6**-13–31
  for personal and dependency
    exemptions, **6**-34–35
  subsidizing specific activities, **6**-9–12
Deductions *for* AGI; *see For* AGI
  deductions
Deductions *from* AGI, **4**-6–8, **6**-2,
  **6**-13–31
Deemed asset purchase, **19**-25
"Defense of Marriage Act," **4**-17
Deferral items, **4**-5
Deferral method, **8**-20
Deferral period, **3**-8n
Deferral provisions, **5**-26
Deferral strategy, **3**-10
Deferred compensation; *see also*
  Nonqualified deferred
  compensation; Stock options
  individual retirement accounts
    (IRAs), **13**-18–24
  qualified retirement plans, **2**-16,
    **13**-2–3
  restricted stock, **12**-17–21
  self-employed retirement accounts,
    **13**-24–28
Deferred income, **4**-5, **5**-2
Deferred income tax expense or benefit,
  calculation of, **17**-22
Deferred like-kind exchange (Starker
  exchange), **10**-23
Deferred tax asset, **17**-2, **17**-18,
  **17**-27–28
Deferred tax liability, **17**-2, **17**-27–28
Defined benefit plans, **13**-3–5
  defined contribution plans vs., **13**-12
  distributions, **13**-5
  funding, accounting, and plan
    maintenance, **13**-5
  vesting, **13**-4
Defined contribution plans, **13**-3,
  **13**-5–15
  after-tax cost of contributions, **13**-9
  after-tax rate of return, **13**-11–12

  contribution limits, **13**-7–8
  defined benefit plan vs., **13**-12
  distributions, **13**-9–11
  employer matching, **13**-6–77
  nonqualified plans vs., **13**-15–16
  Roth 401(k) plans, **13**-13–15
  vesting, **13**-8–9
Definitely related deductions, **24**-12
Dependency exemptions, **4**-7–8,
  **4**-10–16, **6**-34
  deductions for, **6**-34–35
  dependency requirements, **4**-11, **4**-16
  maximum phase-out range, **6**-35
  qualifying child, **4**-11–13
  qualifying relative, **4**-13–16
Dependent, **4**-11
Dependent care benefits, **12**-31
Dependent care credit, **4**-10, **7**-24–25,
  **7**-32
Dependent child, unearned income of,
  **4**-9
Depletion, **9**-2, **9**-37–39
  percentage depletion, **9**-38
Depreciable asset, **10**-24n
Depreciable assets
  gains/loss on disposition of, **16**-35
  transferred to a corporation,
    **19**-17–18
Depreciation, **3**-6, **8**-5, **9**-2, **9**-5–29
  alternative minimum tax
    (AMT), **9**-28
  bonus depreciation, **9**-19–20
  conventions for, **9**-5, **9**-8–10
  corporate AMT adjustment, **16**-34–35
  half-year convention, **9**-8, **9**-11–13
  immediate expensing, **9**-15–20
  luxury automobiles, **9**-23–25
  methods of, **9**-5–6
  mid-quarter convention, **9**-8–10,
    **9**-13–15
  personal property depreciation,
    **9**-5, **9**-10
  real property, **9**-25–27
  recovery period, **9**-6–8
  summary (example), **9**-28–29
Depreciation conventions, **9**-5, **9**-8–10
Depreciation recapture, **3**-18, **6**-20n,
  **10**-7–12
  Section 1245 property, **10**-8–11,
    **10**-30–31
  Section 1250 for real property,
    **10**-11–12
Depreciation recovery period, **9**-6–8
Depreciation tables, **9**-5, **9**-26–27
Determination letters, **2**-16
DIF (Discriminant Function)
  system, **2**-4
Diller, Barry, **12**-16n
Direct conversions, **10**-27
Direct foreign income taxes, **24**-21n

Direct write-off method (business only), **8**-28
Disability insurance, **5**-25
Disabled individual, **4**-11, **7**-32
Discharge of indebtedness, **5**-19–20
Disclosures
 income tax footnote disclosure, **17**-28–30
 uncertain tax positions, **17**-26–27
Discount, **11**-4–5
Discount factor, **3**-3
 estimating value of remainders, **25**-9
Discount points, **14**-13
Dispositions, special basis adjustments for, **21**-27–28
Dispositions of business property, **8**-13–14; *see also* Property dispositions
Disproportionate distributions, **21**-24–26
Disqualified property, **19**-36–37
Disqualifying disposition, **12**-15
Disregarded entities, **15**-5, **24**-25
Distance test, **6**-6–7
Distributed assets, character and holding period of, **21**-21–24
Distributions, **13**-9–11, **13**-22–23, **15**-7n, **22**-17–21
 defined benefit plans, **13**-5
 defined contribution plans, **13**-9–11
 entities overview, **15**-20–21
 liquidating distributions, **22**-21
 noncash property to shareholders, **18**-11–14
 operating distributions, **22**-17–19
 post-termination transition period distributions, **22**-20–21
 property distributions, **22**-20
 Roth IRAs, **13**-22–23
 S corporations, **22**-17–21
 special basis adjustments for, **21**-28–29
 traditional IRAs, **13**-22
Dividend puzzle, **18**-17
Dividends, **3**-13, **3**-15, **4**-5, **5**-3, **5**-10, **11**-2–8, **18**-2
 book-tax differences, **16**-7
 constructive dividends, **18**-14–18
 corporate dividends, **18**-3
 from qualified foreign corporations, **7**-4n
 motivation to pay, **18**-17–18
 multinational transactions, **24**-8
 preferential tax rates for, **7**-4–6
 qualifying dividends, **4**-9, **7**-4
 stock dividends, **18**-18–20
 tax consequences to corporation for noncash property as, **18**-12
 tax consequences to shareholders, **18**-18–19
 tax law definition of, **18**-4

Dividends received deduction (DRD), **15**-10, **16**-16, **16**-18–21
 deduction limitation, **16**-19
 modified taxable income, **16**-19
Document perfection program, **2**-4–5
Domestic International Sales Corporation, **22**-3n
Domestic manufacturing deduction (DMD), **8**-11–13
Domestic production activities deduction (DPAD), **16**-16
Donee/donor, **25**-18
Double family attribution, **18**-24
Double taxation, **3**-13, **3**-14n, **15**-7, **15**-12, **18**-3
 exclusions to mitigate, **5**-23–24
 foreign-earned income, **5**-24
 gifts and inheritances, **5**-23
 life insurance proceeds, **5**-23
 mitigation of, **15**-11–13
 reducing corporate-level tax, **15**-11
 reducing shareholder-level tax, **15**-12–13
DRD (dividends received deduction) modified taxable income, **16**-19
Drucker, Jesse, **17**-27n
Dynamic forecasting, **1**-16–17

**E**
Earmarked tax, **1**-3
Earned income, **5**-9–10, **5**-14
Earned income credit, **4**-10, **7**-29, **7**-32
Earnings per share, **12**-11n
Earnings and profits (E&P), **22**-2
 adjustments to, **18**-5
 C corporation, **15**-20
 computation of, **18**-4–5
 deduction of certain expenses, **18**-6
 deferral/acceleration of income, **18**-6
 disallowance of certain expenses, **18**-5
 income excluded from taxable income, **18**-5
 negative current/accumulated E&P, **18**-10
 negative current/positive accumulated E&P, **18**-9
 noncash property distributions, **18**-3–14
 ordering of distributions, **18**-7
 positive current/accumulated E&P, **18**-7–8
 positive current/negative accumulated E&P, **18**-9
 template for computing, **18**-8, **18**-13
Economic benefit, **5**-3
Economic earnings, **18**-4
Economic nexus, **23**-12–13
Economic performance test, **8**-24–27
 goods/services from another party, **8**-24–25, **8**-27

payment liabilities, **8**-26–27
 providing goods/services to another party, **8**-26–27
 recurring items exception, **8**-27
 renting/leasing property from another party, **8**-25, **8**-27
Economy, **1**-21
Education credits, **6**-9, **7**-25–28
Education-related exclusions, **5**-22
 other subsidies, **5**-22–23
 scholarships, **5**-22
Educational assistance benefits, **12**-28
Educational expenses, **6**-9, **6**-11–12
Educational loans, interest on, **6**-9–11
Educational savings plans, **11**-25–26
Educational subsidies, **5**-22–23
Effective tax rate, **17**-7, **17**-31–32, **24**-5
 importance of, **17**-31–32
 interim period effective tax rate, **17**-32
 permanent differences, **17**-7
Effective tax rates, **1**-7–8, **1**-10
Effectively connected income (ECI), **24**-3
Elderly tax credit, **7**-32
Emergency Economic Stabilization Act of 2008, **12**-7n
Emerging Issues Task Force (EITF), **17**-2, **17**-2n
Employee, **7**-19, **12**-22
 nonqualified deferred compensation plans, **13**-16–18
 nontaxable fringe benefits, **12**-31–32
 restricted stock, considerations for, **12**-18–20
 self-employed (independent contractor) vs., **7**-19–22
 stock options, considerations for, **12**-13–15
 taxable fringe benefits, **12**-22–26
 unreimbursed employee expenses, **6**-3
Employee business expenses, **6**-4, **6**-25–26
 reimbursements, **6**-26
 travel and transportation, **6**-25–26
Employee educational assistance, **12**-28
Employee expense reimbursements, **6**-26
Employee FICA taxes payable, **7**-14–16
Employee-purchased disability policy, **5**-26
Employer
 deductibility of salary payments, **12**-6–9
 defined contribution matching, **13**-6–7
 meals and lodging for convenience of, **12**-26–28
 nonqualified deferred compensation plans, **13**-18–19
 nontaxable fringe benefits, **12**-31–32
 restricted stock, considerations for, **12**-20
 stock options, considerations for, **12**-15–17

Employer—*Cont.*
taxable fringe benefits, **12**-25
wages and salary considerations, **12**-6–9
Employer educational assistance benefits, **12**-28
Employer matching, **13**-6–77
Employer-provided child care credit, **7**-32
Employer-provided qualified plans, **13**-3
Employment-related forms, **12**-3
Employment taxes, **1**-11–12, **7**-14–22
employee FICA taxes payable, **7**-14–16
FICA (payroll) taxes, **7**-14–16, **12**-5–6, **12**-25
withholding taxes, **12**-2–4
Enacted tax rate, **17**-12, **17**-15
Energy credit, **7**-32
Enrolled agent, **2**-25
Entertainment deductions, **8**-7–8
Entity approach, **20**-2
Entity tax characteristics, **15**-6–25
accounting methods, **15**-15–16
accounting periods, **15**-15
after-tax earnings distributed, **15**-7–11
after-tax earnings retained, **15**-11
basis computation, **15**-19
contributions of property/services, **15**-13–14
converting to other entity types, **15**-24–25
deductibility of losses, **15**-21–22
distributions, **15**-20–21
double taxation and mitigation of, **15**-7, **15**-11–13
FICA and self-employment tax, **15**-16–18
liquidating entities, **15**-23–24
number/type of owners, **15**-13
selling ownership interests, **15**-22–23
special allocations, **15**-16
summary of, **15**-26
Entity tax classification, **15**-5–6
Equity-based compensation, **12**-10–22
restricted stock, **12**-17–21
stock options, **12**-10–12
summary of, **12**-21–22
Equity in tax system, **1**-19–20
horizontal vs. vertical equity, **1**-19–20
Escrow (holding) account, **14**-15
Estate, **2**-2, **25**-2n, **25**-27
Estate and gift taxes, **1**-11–12
adjusted taxable gifts, **25**-13
computation of, **25**-13–15
unified credit, **25**-14
Estimated taxes, **4**-10, **7**-20, **7**-33
annualized income method, **16**-29–30
corporations, **16**-28–32
payment penalty, **3**-7n
S corporations, **22**-26

Eustice, James E., **18**-26n
Everson, Mark, **2**-5
Excess net passive income, **22**-21, **22**-23–25
Excess ("unreasonable") compensation, **18**-15
Exchange traded funds (ETFs), **11**-21–22
Exchanged basis, **10**-24
Exchanged basis property, **19**-9n
Excise taxes, **1**-12–14
Exclusions, **4**-5, **5**-2, **5**-20–26; *see also* Income exclusion provisions
common exclusions, **5**-20–22
Ex-dividend date, **11**-7
Executor, **25**-5
Exemption equivalent, **25**-2, **25**-14
Exemptions, **4**-7, **6**-34
alternative minimum tax (AMT), **7**-11–12
standard deduction and, **6**-32–36
Exercise date, **12**-11, **12**-13
Exercise price, **12**-11, **16**-9
Expenditures against public policy, **8**-4
Expense deductions, **3**-16, **8**-2–3
Expenses
deducted from taxable income, **18**-5
excluded from taxable income, **18**-6
Explicit taxes, **1**-14, **11**-23
Extensions, **2**-2–3, **7**-36

**F**

Face value, **11**-3
Facts and circumstances test, **12**-7
Fair market value, **6**-19, **9**-5n, **25**-7
Fairness in tax system, **1**-19
Family attribution, **18**-24
Family limited partnership, **25**-32
FAS 5, *Accounting for Contingencies,* **17**-23, **23**-5n
FAS 109, *Accounting for Income Taxes,* **17**-2, **17**-4n, **17**-18n
uncertainty in income tax positions, **17**-18n, **17**-23
FAS 123(R), **17**-9
FAS 142 tests for annual impairment, **9**-36
FASB Accounting Standards Codification Topic 740, *Income Taxes; see* ASC 740 *Income Taxes*
FASB Concepts Statement No. 6, *Elements of Financial Statements,* **17**-4
FASB Interpretation (FIN) No. 48, *Accounting for Uncertainty in Income Taxes—An Interpretation of FASB Statement No. 109,* **17**-23, **17**-27, **23**-5n
Favorable book-tax differences, **16**-4, **17**-8n

Federal estate tax, **25**-3–17
adjusted taxable gifts, **25**-13–14
administrative expenses, debts, losses, **25**-11–12
estate tax computation, **25**-13–17
gross estate, **25**-3–4, **25**-10
jointly owned property, **25**-5–6
marital and charitable deductions, **25**-12–13
specific inclusions, **25**-4–7
state death taxes, **25**-11–12
taxable estate, **25**-11–12
transfers within 3 years of death, **25**-7
unified credit, **25**-14–15
valuation, **25**-7–10
Federal estate tax formula, **25**-3
Federal gift tax, **25**-17–26
annual exclusion, **25**-19–20
charitable deduction, **25**-23
computation of, **25**-23–24
gift-splitting election, **25**-21
marital deduction, **25**-22
nondeductible terminal interests, **25**-22
prior taxable gifts, **25**-24
taxable gifts, **25**-20–21
transfers subject to gift tax, **25**-18–19
unified credit, **25**-24–25
valuation, **25**-19
Federal gift tax formula, **25**-17
Federal income tax, **1**-4, **1**-11
Federal income tax computation, **7**-2–8
exceptions to basic computation, **7**-4–8
kiddie tax, **7**-6–8
marriage penalty or benefit, **7**-3–4
preferential rate for capital gains/dividends, **7**-4–6
tax rate schedules, **7**-2–3
Federal income tax expense, corporations, **16**-5
Federal Insurance Contributions Act (FICA), **7**-14–16, **12**-5–6, **12**-25
employee vs. independent contractor, **7**-19–22
entities overview, **15**-16–18
Federal short-term interest rate, **2**-3, **7**-35
*Federal Tax Weekly Alert,* **2**-11
Federal taxes, **1**-10–12
employment, **1**-11–12
estate and gift taxes, **1**-11–12
excise taxes, **1**-11–12
income taxes, **1**-4, **1**-11
transfer taxes, **1**-12
unemployment taxes, **1**-11–12
U.S. tax revenues, **1**-11
Federal transfer taxes
common features of, **25**-2–3
integrated transfer taxes, **25**-2–3
introduction to, **25**-2–3
origins of, **25**-2

Federal Unemployment Tax rate, **1**-12
Federal/state adjustments, **23**-15
Federation of Tax Administrator's Web site, **23**-2n
FedEx, **7**-20
Fiduciary/fiduciary duty, **25**-8, **25**-27
Field examinations, **2**-6
FIFO (first-in, first-out), **3**-6, **8**-22–23, **11**-10
50/50 method, **24**-10
52/53 week year, **8**-15
Filing requirements, **2**-2–4, **7**-36–37; *see also* Taxpayer filing requirements
  late filing penalty, **7**-36
  late payment penalty, **7**-36–37
  S corporations, **22**-28
Filing status, **2**-2, **4**-16–20, **7**-2
  gross income thresholds (2010), **2**-2
  head of household, **4**-18–20
  importance of, **4**-16
  married filing jointly, **4**-16–17
  married filing separately, **4**-16–17
  qualifying widow/widower, **4**-17–18
  single, **4**-20
  standard deduction amounts, **4**-7
  unmarried taxpayers, **4**-17
FIN 48; *see* FASB Interpretation (FIN) No. 48
Final regulations, **2**-10, **2**-16
Financial Accounting Standards Board (FASB), **17**-2–3
Financial statement disclosure
  balance sheet classification, **17**-27–28
  computation/reconciliation of income tax provision with hypothetical tax provision, **17**-30–31
  defined benefit plans, **13**-5
Financial and tax accounting methods, **8**-17
Fines, **1**-3, **8**-4
First-in, first-out (FIFO), **3**-6, **8**-22–23, **11**-10
First-time home buyer tax credit (FTHTC), **7**-32, **14**-16–17
Fiscal year, **8**-15
529 plans, **5**-22, **11**-25–26
Fixed and determinable, annual or periodic income (FDAP), **24**-3
Flat tax, **1**-4, **1**-8–9, **1**-20
Flexible spending accounts (FSAs), **6**-13, **6**-13n, **12**-31
Flipping, **14**-3
Floor limitation, **6**-15
Flow-through entities, **5**-14, **6**-6, **8**-2n, **8**-16, **11**-32, **15**-6–7, **20**-2
  aggregate and entity concepts, **20**-2
  losses from, **4**-6
  overview of, **20**-2

Flow-through losses, **15**-22, **15**-22n
*For* AGI deductions, **4**-6–7, **6**-2–13, **22**-16n
  alimony paid, **4**-6, **5**-15
  business expenses/activities, **4**-6, **6**-2–4, **6**-6–7
  common deductions, **4**-6
  flow-through entities, **6**-6
  flow-through entity losses, **4**-6
  health-insurance for self-employed, **4**-6, **6**-8
  investment asset losses, **4**-6
  losses on dispositions of business assets, **4**-6, **6**-6
  moving expenses, **4**-6, **6**-6–8
  penalty for early withdrawal of savings, **6**-9
  qualified education expenses, **6**-11–12
  qualified education loans, interest on, **6**-10
  qualified retirement account contributions, **4**-6
  rental and royalty expenses, **4**-6, **6**-5–6
  self-employment tax deduction, **4**-6, **6**-8–9, **7**-17–19
  subsidizing specific activities, **6**-9–12
  summary of, **6**-12–13
  trade or business expense, **6**-4
For the convenience of the employer benefits, **12**-27
Foreclosure of home mortgage, exclusion of gain from debt forgiveness, **14**-7
Foreign-earned income, **5**-24
Foreign housing expenses, **24**-7n
Foreign income taxes, **6**-16
Foreign joint venture, **24**-21
Foreign personal holding company income, **24**-28
Foreign shareholders, **15**-10–11
Foreign source income, **24**-3, **24**-5, **24**-7
Foreign subsidiary, **24**-21
Foreign tax credits (FTC), **7**-22, **7**-31–32, **24**-5, **24**-19–23
  creditable foreign taxes, **24**-20–23
  direct taxes, **24**-21
  FTC basket, **24**-19
  FTC limitation categories of taxable income, **24**-5, **24**-19
  general category income, **24**-19
  indirect (deemed paid) taxes, **24**-21–23
  in lieu of taxes, **24**-21
  overview of system, **24**-5–6
  passive category income, **24**-19
Foreign transportation expenses, **8**-9n
Form of receipt, **5**-4
Form of a transaction, **18**-15
Forward triangular merger, **19**-26, **19**-29–30, **19**-33

401(k) plan
  individual 401(k)s, **13**-26–28
  Roth 401(k) plans vs., **13**-15, **13**-24–25
Franchise taxes, **23**-2n, **23**-8n
Frieswick, Kris, **17**-1n
Fringe benefits, **5**-21, **12**-22–35, **15**-11n, **20**-19n; *see also* Nontaxable fringe benefits
  *de minimis* fringe benefits, **12**-30
  Disney example, **12**-34
  employee considerations for, **12**-22–24
  employer considerations for, **12**-25
  excluded from gross income, **5**-21
  group-term life insurance, **12**-23
  nontaxable fringe benefits, **12**-26–30
  qualified fringe benefit, **6**-8
  S corporations, **22**-16
  summary of, **12**-33–35
  tax planning with, **12**-32–33
  taxable fringe benefits, **12**-22
*From* AGI deductions; *see also* Itemized deductions
Front loading restrictions, **5**-16
"Fruit and tree" analogy, **3**-12, **5**-8n
"Full" depreciation recapture, **10**-8n
Full-inclusion method/rule, **8**-20, **24**-29
Full-month convention, **9**-30
Full-time students, **13**-28n
Functional currency, **24**-22, **24**-22n
Funding, accounting, and plan maintenance, defined benefit plans, **13**-5
Future interest, **25**-8
Future value of money, **3**-3

**G**
Gain or loss on disposition
  capital assets, **10**-5–6
  character of assets, **10**-4–7
  ordinary assets, **10**-5
  property use and holding period, **10**-5
  Section 1231 assets, **10**-6–7
Gambling winnings/losses, **4**-7, **5**-16–17, **6**-29
General category income, **24**-19
General Depreciation System (GDS), **9**-5n
General Dynamics Corporation, **18**-30
General Electric, **12**-29
General Motors, **17**-20
General partnership (GP), **15**-2, **20**-2
Generally accepted accounting principles (GAAP), **8**-17, **17**-2, **17**-12
  capital accounts, **20**-8
Generation-skipping tax (GST), **25**-2, **25**-27
*Geoffrey, Inc. v. South Carolina Tax Commission,* **23**-12n

Gift-splitting election, **25**-17n, **25**-21
Gift tax, **1**-12, **9**-4n
    transfers subject to, **25**-18–19
Gifts and inheritances, **4**-5, **5**-23, **25**-18
    adjusted taxable gifts, **25**-13
Golsen rule, **2**-15
Goodwill, **8**-5, **9**-31n, **9**-36
    acquired in asset acquisition, **16**-8
Government bonds, **11**-2
Graded vesting, **13**-4
Graduated taxes, **1**-4–5
Grant date, **12**-11, **12**-13
Grantor, **25**-8
Grantor trusts, **22**-2n
Gray, Steven, **13**-6
Green card test, **24**-4
*Gregory v. Helvering,* **19**-27n
Gross estate, **25**-3–10
    summary of, **25**-10
Gross income, **2**-2, **2**-13, **4**-5, **5**-2, **6**-2,
    **8**-2, **12**-22; *see also* Business
        gross income
    alimony, **5**-14–16
    defined, **5**-3
    discharge of indebtedness, **5**-19–20
    economic benefit, **5**-3
    flow-through entities, **5**-14
    form of receipt, **5**-4
    imputed income, **5**-18–19
    other sources of, **5**-14–20
    prizes, awards, and gambling
        winnings, **5**-16–17
    realization principle, **5**-3–4
    recognition, **5**-3–4
    recovery of amounts previously
        deducted, **5**-5
    return of capital principle, **5**-4–5
    Social Security benefits, **5**-17–18
    summary (example), **5**-26–27
    tax benefit rule, **5**-5
    U.S. source rules for, **24**-6–14
Gross income test, **4**-13, **6**-14n
    qualifying relative, **4**-14–16
Gross income thresholds (2010) by
    filing status, **2**-2
Gross profit percentage, **10**-30
Gross receipts, **22**-6, **22**-24
Gross-up, **12**-24
Gross Vehicle Weight Rating (GVWR),
    **9**-25n
Group-term life insurance, **12**-23, **12**-26
Guaranteed payments, **15**-17, **20**-10n,
    **20**-19–20, **20**-19n, **20**-21n

**H**
Haircut, **6**-36
Half-year convention, **9**-1–13
    MACRS tables, **9**-39
    for year of disposition, **9**-12
Hand, Learned, **3**-19

Hatch, Richard, **2**-5
Hazards of litigation, **2**-6
Head of household, **4**-7, **4**-18–20
    standard deduction, **6**-32
Health and accident insurance/benefits,
    **12**-26
Health care reimbursement, **5**-25
Health insurance coverage, **5**-21
Health insurance deduction for
    self-employed, **4**-6, **6**-8
Health insurance premiums, **6**-8n
Heirs, **25**-4
*Helvering v. Horst,* **5**-8n
Hobby, **6**-27, **8**-2
Hobby loss, **6**-27–28, **14**-24n, **22**-13n
Hobby loss limitation, **6**-27
Holding period, **7**-4n, **20**-13
Holmes, Oliver Wendell, **5**-7n
Home-equity indebtedness, **14**-8–9
    limitation on amount of, **14**-10
Home equity loans, **6**-10n, **11**-30n
Home office deductions, **14**-26–28; *see
    also* Business use of home
Home ownership; *see also* Personal
        residence; Rental use of home
    business use of home, **14**-25–29
    first time home buyer tax credit,
        **14**-16–17
    home sale exclusion in hardship
        circumstances, **14**-5–6
    interest expense on home-related
        debt, **14**-7–12
    mortgage insurance, **14**-12
    personal use of home, **14**-2
    points, **14**-12–14
    qualified residence interest, **14**-8
    real property taxes, **14**-15
    tax and nontax consequences of, **14**-2
Home-related debt, **14**-7–12
    acquisition indebtedness, **14**-9
    home-equity indebtedness, **14**-10
    interest deduction, **14**-9
    limitations on, **14**-9–12
    qualifying debt, **14**-10–15
HOPE scholarship credits, **4**-10, **6**-10n,
    **7**-22; *see* American opportunity
    credit (AOC)
Horizontal equity, **1**-19–20
Hospitals and long-term care
    facilities, **6**-15
Hot assets, **21**-3–6, **21**-3n
    determining gain/loss on, **21**-5–6
House of Representatives, Ways and
    Means Committee Report,
    **2**-10–13
Hybrid entities, **24**-24
"Hybrid" method of accounting, **3**-11n,
    **5**-7n
Hypothetical income tax expense,
    **17**-30n

**I**
Illegal kickbacks, **8**-4
Immediate expensing election, **9**-15–18
    choice of assets for, **9**-18–19
    limits on, **9**-16–17
Impermissible accounting method, **8**-30
Implicit taxes, **1**-14–16, **3**-16–17, **11**-23
Imputed income, **5**-18–19
Inbound transactions, **24**-2
Incentive stock, **12**-10–11
Incentive stock options (ISOs), **12**-13,
    **12**-15, **16**-9–10
Incidence of taxation, **1**-10
Income; *see also* Gross income; Income
        exclusion provisions
    alimony, **4**-5–6, **5**-14–16
    all-events test for, **8**-19
    all-inclusive income concept, **4**-2,
        **5**-3, **5**-14
    annuities, **5**-11–13
    assignment of income doctrine, **5**-8
    business income, **4**-5, **5**-3
    common income items, **4**-5
    compensation and fringe benefits,
        **4**-5, **5**-3
    deferred income, **4**-5
    discharge of indebtedness, **4**-5, **5**-19–20
    excluded income/exclusion
        provisions, **4**-5, **5**-20–26
    flow-through entities, **5**-14
    gains from property sales, **4**-5
    imputed income, **5**-18–19
    interest and dividends, **4**-5, **5**-3
    other sources of gross income,
        **5**-14–20
    prizes, awards, and gambling
        winnings, **5**-16–17
    property, **5**-10–11
    property dispositions, **5**-13
    realization and recognition of, **5**-2–9
    realized income, **4**-2
    rents and royalties, **4**-5, **5**-3
    retirement income, **4**-5
    services (earned income), **5**-9–10
    social security benefits, **5**-17–18
    substitution effects vs., **1**-17–19
    taxpayers recognition of, **5**-6–7
    types of, **5**-9–20
Income deferral, **5**-26
    timing strategies, **3**-6–8
Income effect, **1**-17
Income exclusion provisions, **5**-20–26
    common exclusions, **5**-20–26
    deferral provisions, **5**-26
    disability insurance, **5**-25
    education-related exclusions, **5**-22–23
    educational subsidies, **5**-22–23
    foreign-earned income, **5**-24
    fringe benefits, **5**-21
    gifts and inheritances, **5**-23

health care reimbursement, **5**-25
life insurance proceeds, **5**-23
municipal interest, **5**-21
personal injury payments, **5**-25
scholarships, **5**-22
sickness and injury-related
  exclusions, **5**-24–26
workers' compensation, **5**-24–25
Income and loss allocations, **20**-32–33
  S corporation, **22**-8–9
Income recognition, **3**-6–8, **5**-6–7, **8**-20
Income-shifting strategies, **3**-11–16
  corporate inversions, **3**-16
  family members, related-party
    transactions, **3**-12–13
  jurisdictions and limitations, **3**-15–16
  owners-business transactions, **3**-13–15
Income statement, **17**-3
Income tax accounting, asset and
  liability approach, **17**-3–4
Income tax footnote disclosure, **17**-28–30
Income tax planning, wealth planning
  and, **25**-27
Income tax positions, accounting for
  uncertainty in, **17**-23–25
Income tax provision process,
  **17**-2, **17**-6
  compute current income tax expense/
    benefit, **17**-11
  current and deferred income tax
    expenses/benefit, **17**-6–17
  ending balances in balance sheet
    deferred tax asset/liability
    accounts, **17**-12–17
  permanent differences adjustments,
    **17**-6–8
  steps in, **17**-6–22
  temporary differences/tax
    carryforward amounts, **17**-8–10
  valuation allowance, determining if
    needed, **17**-18–21
Income tax return, **23**-13
Income taxes, **1**-11, **1**-13, **23**-8–22;
  *see also* Corporate alternative
  minimum tax; Individual income
  tax computation
  accounting for, **17**-2–6
  business income, **23**-17–20
  calculation of, **4**-8–9
  as complex, **1**-20
  defined, **17**-3
  dividing state tax base among states,
    **23**-16–21
  economic nexus, **23**-12–14
  entities included, **23**-13–14
  nexus, **23**-9
  nonbusiness income, **23**-21
  non(net) income-based taxes, **23**-22–23
  Public Law 86-272, **23**-9–11
  separate tax returns, **23**-13–14

state income tax liability, **23**-22
state taxable income, **23**-15–16
unitary tax returns, **23**-14
Incorporating a business, **3**-13n
Independent contractor, **7**-19
Indirect conversions, **10**-28
Indirect foreign income taxes, **24**-21n
Individual 401(k)s, **13**-26–28
  nontax considerations, **13**-28
Individual income tax computation,
  **7**-2–8; *see also* Alternative
  minimum tax
  exceptions to, **7**-4–8
  kiddie tax, **7**-6–8
  marriage penalty or benefit, **7**-3–4
  preferential rates for capital gains/
    dividends, **7**-4–6
  tax rate schedules, **7**-2–3
Individual income tax formula, **4**-2–10,
  **16**-2
  common exclusions and deferrals, **4**-5
  deductions, **4**-6
  deductions *for* AGI, **4**-6–7
  deductions *from* AGI, **4**-7–8
  filing status, **4**-16–20
  income tax calculation, **4**-8–9, **7**-2–8
  other taxes, **4**-9
  personal and dependency
    exemptions, **4**-10–16
  realized income, exclusions, deferrals,
    and gross income, **4**-2–5
  summary of, **4**-20
  tax credits, **4**-9–10
  tax prepayments, **4**-10
Individual marginal tax rates, **15**-9
Individual retirement accounts (IRAs),
  **13**-19–24
  distributions, **13**-22
  rollover to Roth, **13**-23–24
  Roth IRAs, **13**-22–24
  saver's credit, **13**-28–29
  traditional IRAs, **13**-19–22, **13**-24–25
Individual tax formula, **4**-2
Individually managed qualified
  retirement plans, **13**-19–24
*Indopco v. Commissioner,* **8**-5n
Information matching program, **2**-4–5
Inheritance, **5**-23
Initial basis, S corporation, **22**-11
Initial public offering (IPO), **15**-3, **15**-4n
Inside basis, **20**-4, **21**-7
Installment sales, **4**-5, **5**-26, **10**-17,
  **10**-29–31
  gains ineligible for reporting, **10**-30–31
  gross profit percentage, **10**-30
Institutional shareholders, **15**-7, **15**-10
Intangible assets, **8**-5, **9**-2; *see also*
  Amortization
  amortizable intangible asset
    summary, **9**-36

Intangible property, **24**-10n
Integrated wealth plans, **25**-31–32
Interest, **4**-5, **5**-3, **5**-10, **11**-3–7
  dividends vs., **11**-3
  timing of payments and taxes, **11**-7
Interest expense
  home-related debt, **14**-7–9
  as itemized deduction, **4**-7, **6**-17–18
  multinational transactions, **24**-7, **24**-13
Interest and penalties, ASC 740, **17**-26
Interim period effective tax rates, **17**-32
Internal Revenue Code (IRC), **2**-10–11,
  **2**-13, **12**-7
  basic organization of, **2**-13
  example of code organization, **2**-14
  judicial doctrines, **3**-18
  Section 1(h), **15**-7n
  Section 162(b)(2), **2**-13
  subchapter C, **18**-3
  subchapter N, **24**-2
Internal Revenue Code of 1939, **2**-11
Internal Revenue Code of 1954, **2**-11
Internal Revenue Code of 1986, **2**-11,
  **2**-13, **16**-15n
Internal Revenue Code Section, **2**-18
Internal Revenue Service (IRS), **17**-3
  appeals/litigation process, **2**-7
  audit process, **2**-5–6
  audit selection, **2**-4–9
  Circular 230, **2**-23, **2**-25
  post-audit, **2**-6–9
  Web site of, **2**-18, **5**-14n
*IRS Form 10-K,* **17**-1n, **17**-3, **17**-32
*IRS Form 10-Q,* **17**-1n, **17**-32
*IRS Form 706:* United States Estate
  (and Generation-Skipping
  Transfer Tax Return), **25**-14, **25**-16
*IRS Form 709:* United States Gift (and
  Generation-Skipping Transfer)
  Tax Return, **25**-17, **25**-25–26
*IRS Form 870,* **2**-6
*IRS Form 966,* **19**-34
*IRS Form 1040,* **4**-2–4, **4**-21–22, **6**-2n,
  **6**-4, **6**-38n, **7**-38, **20**-19n
  Schedule A Itemized Deductions,
    **6**-13, **6**-31, **6**-38n, **14**-7
  Schedule B, **11**-3n, **11**-7n
  Schedule C Profit or Loss from
    Business, **6**-4, **6**-29, **7**-16, **13**-26n
  Schedule D, **10**-20, **11**-14–15
  Schedule E Rental or Royalty
    Income, **6**-5–5, **7**-16n, **14**-22–23
*IRS Form 1040NR,* **24**-3
*IRS Form 1065:* U.S. Return of
  Partnership Income, **5**-14n, **8**-2,
  **15**-5, **20**-23–25
*IRS Form 1099,* **7**-20n
*IRS Form 1099-DIV,* **2**-5, **11**-7
*IRS Form 1099-INT,* **2**-5
*IRS Form 1099-OID,* **11**-4

*IRS Form 1099R,* **13**-5n
*IRS Form 1116,* **24**-14
*IRS Form 1118:* Foreign Tax Credit
   Corporations, **24**-14–16
*IRS Form 1120,* **8**-2, **15**-5, **16**-25–26,
   **16**-27n, **17**-3, **17**-11, **17**-12n
*IRS Form 1120A,* **16**-25n
*IRS Form 1120F,* **24**-3
*IRS Form 1120S:* U.S. Income Tax
   Return for an S Corporation,
   **5**-14n, **8**-2, **15**-5, **22**-9, **22**-27–28
*IRS Form 1120X,* **17**-11n
*IRS Form 1139,* **17**-11n
*IRS Form 2210:* Underpayment of
   Estimated Tax by Individuals,
   Estates, and Trusts, **7**-35, **12**-4n
*IRS Form 2220,* **16**-32
*IRS Form 3115,* **8**-33, **9**-27n, **20**-14, **22**-8
*IRS Form 3903,* **6**-6n
*IRS AMT 4562,* **9**-29
*IRS Form 4626:* Alternative Minimum
   Tax—Corporations, **16**-33n,
   **16**-39–40
*IRS Form 4797:* Sales of Business
   Property, **10**-18–19
*IRS Form 4952,* **11**-30n
*IRS Form 5701,* **17**-11n
*IRS Form 6251,* **7**-9
*IRS Form 7004,* **17**-3n, **20**-23, **22**-28
*IRS Form 8814,* **7**-7
*IRS Form 8824,* **10**-27
*IRS Form 8829:* Expenses for Business
   Use of Your Home, **14**-29
*IRS Form 8832,* **24**-24–25
*IRS Form 8903,* **8**-12n
*IRS Form W-2,* **2**-5, **7**-20n, **7**-33,
   **12**-2–4, **12**-13n
*IRS Form W-4,* **7**-19n, **12**-2–4
*IRS Publication 15-B:* Employer's Tax
   Guide to Fringe Benefits, **12**-32
*IRS Publication 17:* Your Federal
   Income Tax, **4**-11n, **7**-36n
*IRS Publication 78:* Cumulative List of
   Organizations Described in Section
   170(c) of the Internal Revenue
   Code of 1986, **6**-18n, **16**-15n
*IRS Publication,* **2**-11
*IRS Publication 505:* Tax Withholding
   and Estimated Tax, **12**-3n
*IRS Publication 514:* Foreign Tax
   Credit for Individuals, **7**-31n
*IRS Publication 519,* **15**-13n
*IRS Publication 523:* Selling Your
   Home, **14**-3n
*IRS Publication 526,* **6**-18n
*IRS Publication 537:* Residential Rental
   Property (Including Rental of
   Vacation Homes), **14**-20n
*IRS Publication 542:* Corporations,
   **16**-33n

*IRS Publication 547:* Casualties,
   Disasters, and Thefts, **6**-23n
*IRS Publication 600,* **6**-16n
*IRS Publication 915,* **5**-29
*IRS Publication 936:* Home Mortgage
   Interest Deduction, **14**-8n
*IRS Publication 946,* **9**-5n
*IRS Publication 970:* Tax Benefits for
   Education, **5**-22n, **12**-28
*IRS Publication 972,* **7**-23
*IRS Publication 1457,* **25**-10n
*IRS Publication 1779:* Independent
   Contractor or Employee, **7**-19n
IRS Uniform Lifetime Table, **13**-10
International Accounting Standards
   Board (IASB), **17**-32
   IAS 12, *Accounting for Income Taxes,*
      **17**-32
International Financial Reporting
   Standards (IFRS), **16**-3n, **17**-32
International operations
   advantages/disadvantages of, **24**-26
   check-the-box hybrid entities, **24**-25–6
   planning for, **24**-24–26
International tax laws, proposals for
   change, **24**-31
Internet sales, **23**-6–7
   sales tax, **1**-14
Interpretative regulations, **2**-16
Interstate commerce, **23**-4
Intervivos transfers, **25**-2
Inventories, **8**-21–23, **15**-15n, **21**-3, **21**-3n
   inventory cost-flow methods, **8**-22–23
   manufactured within U.S. and sold
      abroad, **24**-10
   uniform capitalization (UNICAP
      rules), **8**-21–22
Inventory cost-flow methods, **8**-22–23
   FIFO, **8**-22
   LIFO, **8**-22
   specific identification, **8**-22
Inventory valuation allowances, **8**-21n
Investment activities, **6**-3–4
Investment advisory fees, **6**-27
Investment assets, losses on disposition
   of, **4**-6
Investment decisions, taxes and, **1**-15
Investment expenses, **3**-16, **6**-4, **6**-27,
   **8**-2n, **11**-28–32
   investment interest expense, **11**-30–32
   summary of, **11**-28
Investment income, **11**-2, **11**-31
Investment interest expense, **11**-28,
   **11**-30–31
Investment planning, **3**-10n, **3**-16
   income deferral, **3**-6–8
Investments; *see also* Capital gains
      and losses
   after-tax rate of return, **11**-1–3
   before-tax rate of return, **11**-1–2

corporate and Treasury bonds,
   **11**-4–5
dividends, **11**-7–8
educational savings plans, **11**-25–26
interest, **11**-3–4
investment expenses, **11**-28–29
life insurance, **11**-23–25
municipal bonds, **11**-22–23
overview of, **11**-2
portfolio income, **11**-2–8, **11**-26–27
savings bonds, **11**-5–7
tax-exempt income, **11**-22–26
Involuntary conversions, **5**-26, **10**-17,
   **10**-26–29
Involuntary termination
   failure to meet requirements, **22**-5
   S corporations, **22**-5–6
Itemized deductions, **4**-7; *see also*
      Business deductions
   alternative minimum tax (AMT) and,
      **7**-10–11
   bunching itemized deductions, **6**-2,
      **6**-33–34
   calculation of phase-out, **6**-36–37
   casualty and theft losses, **4**-7, **6**-23–24
   charitable contributions, **4**-7, **6**-18–22
   employee business expenses, **6**-25–26
   hobby losses, **6**-27–28
   interest expense, **4**-7, **6**-17–18
   investment expenses, **6**-27
   job expenses, **4**-7
   limitation on (2 percent of AGI
      floor), **6**-29
   medical and dental expenses, **4**-7,
      **6**-13–15
   miscellaneous deductions, **4**-7,
      **6**-25–31
   phase-out of, **6**-30
   primary categories of, **4**-7
   sales tax on purchase of qualified
      motor vehicles, **6**-16
   summary of, **6**-30
   tax preparation fees, **6**-27
   taxes, **4**-7, **6**-16–17

## J

Jackson Hewitt, **2**-27
JetBlue Airways, **12**-28
Job expenses, as itemized deductions,
   **4**-7
*John P. White,* **6**-24
Joint Committee on taxation, **24**-2n
Joint Conference Committee, **2**-12–13
Joint-life annuity, **5**-11
Joint tenancy with right of
   survivorship, **25**-4
Jointly owned property, **25**-5–6
*Journal of Accountancy,* **2**-11
*Journal of Taxation,* **2**-11
*J.R. Huntsman v. Comm.,* **2**-28, **14**-13n

Judicial sources of the tax law, **2**-9–10
  citations (examples), **2**-10
  courts, **2**-14–15
Jurisdictions, **3**-11

**K**

*Kearns v. Comm.,* **18**-15n
*Keenan v. Bowers* case, **6**-24
Keogh plans, **13**-25n
Kiddie tax, **3**-12n, **5**-8n, **7**-6–8

**L**

*Lanco, Inc. v. Director, Division of Taxation,* **23**-12n
Land, **9**-25
Last-in, first-out (LIFO), **3**-6, **8**-22–23
Last will and testament, **25**-2
Late filing penalty, **7**-36
Late payment penalty, **7**-36–37
Law reviews, **2**-11
Least aggregate deferral, **20**-15
Legal classification of business entity, **15**-2–3
Legislative grace, **4**-6
Legislative regulations, **2**-16
Legislative/statutory sources of the tax law, **2**-9, **2**-13
  Congress, **2**-11–13
  Internal Revenue Code, **2**-11, **2**-13
  tax laws legislation process, **2**-11–13
  tax treaties, **2**-13–14
  U.S. Constitution, **2**-11, **2**-13
Letter rulings, **2**-16–17
Liabilities, business entities, **15**-3
Life estate, **25**-8
Life insurance, **11**-23–25, **25**-5, **25**-19
Life insurance coverage, **5**-21
Life insurance premiums, **8**-6
Life insurance proceeds, **4**-5, **5**-23
Life insurance trust, **25**-31
Life tenant, **25**-8
Lifetime learning credits, **4**-10, **6**-10n, **7**-22, **7**-26n, **7**-27–28, **7**-32, **12**-28
LIFO (last-in, first-out), **3**-6, **8**-22–23
  recapture amount, **22**-25
  recapture tax, **22**-21, **22**-25–26
Like-kind exchanges, **3**-10n, **4**-5, **5**-26, **9**-4, **10**-17, **18**-6
  deferred like-kind exchange, **10**-23
  exchanged basis, **10**-26
  non-like-kind property (boot), **10**-24–26
  property use, **10**-22
  reporting of, **10**-26
  tax consequences of, **10**-24
  timing requirements for, **10**-22–23
Like-kind property
  defined, **10**-21
  personal property, **10**-21

property ineligible for treatment, **10**-21
  real property, **10**-21
Limited liability company (LLC), **15**-2–3, **15**-17, **20**-2
Limited liability corporations (LLCs), **20**-5n
Limited liability partnerships (LLPs), **15**-3n
Limited partners, **11**-34n, **15**-17, **20**-21n
Limited partnership (LP), **15**-2, **20**-2
Liquidating corporation, **19**-36–39
Liquidating distributions, **21**-9, **21**-11n, **21**-12–24, **22**-21
  basis in distributed property, **21**-13–14
  character/holding period of assets, **21**-21–24
  gain/loss recognition in, **21**-13
  outside basis greater than inside basis, **21**-14–17
  outside basis less than inside basis, **21**-17–21
Liquidating entities, **15**-23–24
Liquidation, **19**-34–39
Liquidation value, **20**-10
Listed property, **8**-10n, **9**-20–22
  business-use percentage, **9**-20–21
Loan origination fees, **14**-13
Loan secured by residence, **14**-8
Lobbying costs, **8**-5
Local taxes; *see* State and local taxes
Long-term capital gain property, **16**-15
Long-term capital gains or losses, **3**-16, **4**-9, **6**-19, **11**-11
  election to investment income, **11**-31–32
Look-through rule, **21**-5n
Loss harvesting, **11**-22
Loss limitations, **20**-29–34, **22**-13–15
  at-risk limitation, **20**-30
  income and loss baskets, **20**-32–34
  passive activity loss limitation, **20**-31–32
  tax basis limitation, **20**-29–30
Losses, **6**-6, **11**-33
  on dispositions of business property, **8**-13–14
  on rental property, **14**-24–26
  taxable estate, **25**-11
Lower of cost or market, **8**-21n
*Lucas v. Earl,* **3**-12, **5**-8n
Lump-sum distributions, **13**-20n
Luxury automobiles, **9**-24
  depreciation limits, **9**-24n
  depreciation rules, **3**-18, **9**-23–25

**M**

M adjustments, **16**-25
MACRS; *see* Modified accelerated cost recovery system (MACRS)
Majority interest taxable year, **20**-14

Making Work Pay Credit (MWPC), **7**-28–29, **7**-32
Marginal tax rate, **1**-4–6, **3**-8, **7**-4
Marital deductions, **25**-3, **25**-22
Market discount/premium, **11**-5
Marketable securities, **21**-11n
Marquardt, Katy, **11**-22
Marriage benefit/penalty, **7**-3–4
Married filing jointly, **4**-7, **4**-10, **4**-16–17
  standard deduction, **6**-32
Married filing separately, **4**-7, **4**-16–17
  standard deduction, **6**-32
Material participation, **11**-36
  tests for, **20**-32
Maturity, **11**-5
Maturity value, **11**-3
McDonald's, **18**-17–18
McGinn, D., **14**-19n
Meals and entertainment, **8**-7–8
Meals and lodging, **6**-25n
  for convenience of employer, **12**-26–28
Measurement, **17**-24
Medical and dental expenses, **4**-7, **6**-13–15
  deduction limitation, **6**-15
  health insurance coverage, **5**-21
  hospitals and long-term care facilities, **6**-15
  transportation and travel, **6**-14–15
Medical Health Insurance (MHI) tax, **1**-11
Medicare tax, **1**-10–12, **7**-14–17, **12**-5
Memorandum decision, **2**-10, **2**-15
Mergers, **19**-27
Microsoft, **12**-21n, **18**-21
Mid-month convention, **9**-25–26
Mid-point class life, **18**-6
Mid-quarter convention, **9**-8–10
  application of, **9**-13–14
  MACRS tables, **9**-39–40
  for year of disposition, **9**-15, **9**-27
Mileage test, **6**-6–7
Minimum distributions, **13**-6, **13**-10n
Minimum tax credit, **7**-13, **16**-39
Miscellaneous itemized deductions, **4**-7, **6**-25–31, **11**-29n–30n
  employee business expense, **6**-25–26
  gambling losses, **5**-17
  hobby losses, **6**-27–28
  investment expenses, **6**-27
  limitation on (2 percent of AGI floor), **6**-29
  not subject to AGI floor, **6**-30
  subject to AGI floor, **6**-25–28, **8**-3
  tax preparation fees, **6**-27
Mixed-motive expenditures, **8**-7, **8**-11
*Mobil Oil Corp. v. Vermont Tax Commissioner,* **23**-14n

Modified Accelerated Cost Recovery System (MACRS), **9**-1, **9**-5, **9**-14, **9**-28, **9**-39–42
 MACRS half-year convention, **9**-39
 MACRS tables, **9**-11n, **9**-39–42
 MACRS mid-quarter convention, **9**-39–40
 nonresidential real property mid-month convention, **9**-42
 residential rental property mid-month convention, **9**-41
Modified AGI, **5**-17–18, **6**-10, **8**-12n
"More likely than not" standard, **2**-24
Mortgage insurance, **14**-12
Moving expenses, **4**-6, **6**-6–8, **14**-6n
 business test, **6**-6–7
 distance test, **6**-6–7
 qualified reimbursements, **12**-30–31
"Ms," **16**-25
Multinational transactions
 nonresident taxation, **24**-3
 resident for tax purposes, **24**-4–5
 U.S. source rules for gross income and deductions, **24**-6–14
 U.S. taxing framework for, **24**-2–6
Multiple support agreement, **4**-14
Multistage Tax Commission, **23**-16n
*Multistage Tax Compact, Article IV, Division of Income,* **23**-21n
Municipal bonds, **1**-16, **3**-16, **3**-18, **4**-5, **5**-21, **11**-22–23
Municipal interest, **5**-20–21
Mutual funds, **11**-2, **11**-9n

**N**

*National Bellas Hess, Inc. v. Department of Revenue of the State of Illinois,* **23**-6n
National Research Program (NRP), **2**-4
Natural resources, **9**-2, **9**-37
Necessary expense, **8**-3
Negative basis adjustment, **21**-29
Negative income tax, **7**-29
Negative/positive evidence, **17**-19
Nelson, Daniel, **12**-7n
Net capital gain, **11**-13
Net capital losses, corporations, **16**-11–12
Net earnings from self-employment, **7**-16, **13**-25
Net investment income, **11**-30
Net long-term capital gain/loss, **11**-13
Net operating loss (NOL), **15**-21, **16**-13–15
 NOL carryback/carryover, **16**-13, **16**-16
Net passive investment income, **22**-24
Net short-term capital gain/loss, **11**-13
Net taxation, **24**-3
Net unearned income, **7**-7

Net unrealized built-in gain, **22**-21
Newsletters, **2**-11
Nexus, **23**-2, **23**-5–7, **23**-9, **24**-2
 economic nexus, **23**-12–13
 multinational transactions, **24**-2–3
Nicolaisen, Donald, **17**-3
90-day letter (statutory notice of deficiency), **2**-6–7
No-additional-cost services, **12**-28
"No business purpose" motive, **19**-13
Non-like-kind property (boot), **10**-24–26
Nonacquiescence, **2**-17
Nonbusiness bad debt, **11**-11n
Nonbusiness income, **23**-4, **23**-21
Noncash payments, **8**-17
Noncash property distributions, **18**-11–14
 as dividend, **18**-12
 effect on E&P, **18**-13–14
 fair market value of, **18**-12–14
 liabilities, **18**-12
Noncorporate shareholders, **19**-35
Nondeductible personal expense, **14**-27n
Nondeductible terminal interests, **25**-22
Nondomiciliary businesses, **23**-2
Nonliquidating distributions, **18**-2
Nonmanaging LLC members, **20**-21n
Non(net) income-based taxes, **23**-22–23
Nonqualified deferred compensation, **13**-2, **13**-15–19
 employee considerations, **13**-16–18
 employer considerations, **13**-18–19
 qualified defined contributions plans vs., **13**-15–16
Nonqualified preferred stock, **19**-7n
Nonqualified stock, **12**-10
Nonqualified stock options (NQOs), **12**-13–16, **16**-9, **17**-7n
Nonqualifying dividends, **15**-7n
Nonrecognition provisions, **5**-20
 reasons for, **5**-20
Nonrecognition transactions, **10**-17; *see also* Like-kind exchanges
 installment sales, **10**-29–31
 involuntary conversions, **10**-26–29
 other nonrecognition provisions, **10**-31–32
 related-party loss disallowance rules, **10**-32–33
Nonrecourse debt, **20**-4–5, **20**-5n
Nonrefundable personal tax credits, **7**-22–28, **7**-31n
Nonresidential property, **9**-25, **9**-42
Nonresidents, **24**-3
 nonresident aliens, **15**-13n, **24**-4
 U.S. taxation of, **24**-3–4
Nonservice partners, **20**-10
Nontax characteristics of business entities, **15**-3–4

Nontaxable compensation benefits, **3**-13, **3**-16
Nontaxable exchange, **9**-4
Nontaxable fringe benefits, **3**-2, **5**-21n, **7**-20, **12**-26–30
 cafeteria plans and flexible spending accounts (FSAs), **12**-31
 common forms of, **12**-26
 *de minimis* fringe benefits, **12**-30
 dependent care benefits, **12**-28, **12**-31
 educational assistance benefits, **12**-28
 employee educational assistance, **12**-28
 employee/employer considerations for, **12**-31–32
 group-term life insurance, **12**-23, **12**-26
 health and accident insurance/benefits, **12**-26
 meals/lodging for convenience of employer, **12**-26–28
 no-additional-cost services, **12**-28
 qualified employee discounts, **12**-29
 qualified moving expense reimbursements, **12**-30–31
 qualified transportation fringe, **12**-20
 working condition fringe benefits, **12**-29–30
Nontaxable gifts, **2**-5
Nontaxable liquidating distributions, **19**-39
Nontaxable stock dividends, **18**-18–19
Nontaxable transaction, special basis rules, **9**-3n, **9**-4
*Northwestern Cement Co. v. Minnesota,* **23**-9n
Not definitely related deductions, **24**-12
Novack, Janet, **8**-13

**O**

Obama, Barack, **24**-31
Office examinations, **2**-6
Old Age, Survivors, and Disability Insurance (OASDI) tax, **1**-11
150 percent declining balance, **9**-5
Open facts, **2**-17
Operating distributions, **21**-9–12
 of money only, **21**-9–10
 property other than money, **21**-10–12
Operating income/losses, **11**-2
Operating partnerships, cash distributions in, **20**-28–29
Option attribution, **18**-25
Option exercise, **12**-11
Ordinary asset, **10**-5
Ordinary business income/loss, **20**-17–19, **22**-9
 partnership operations, **20**-17–19
Ordinary and capital gains tax rates, **3**-9
Ordinary expense, **8**-3
Ordinary income, **3**-16
Ordinary income (loss), **20**-17

Ordinary income property, **6**-19–20, **10**-6n, **16**-15
Ordinary and necessary, **6**-4, **8**-3
Organization costs, **20**-12
Organizational expenditures, **8**-5, **8**-11–12, **9**-32–35
Organizational form of a business, **19**-2
Original cost of asset, **9**-5
Original issue discount (OID), **11**-4, **11**-5n
Other Adjustments Account (OAA), **22**-19n
Other fringe benefits, **22**-16n
Other temporal interests, **25**-8–10
Outbound transactions, **24**-2
Outside basis, **20**-4, **20**-13, **21**-3, **21**-7n
Ownership interests, **15**-22–23
Ownership test, **14**-3

**P**
PAL; *see* Passive activity loss
Parent-subsidiary controlled group, **16**-24
Partial depreciation recapture, **10**-12n
Partial liquidation, **18**-2, **18**-29–30
Parties to the reorganization, **19**-26
Partnership, **5**-14n, **8**-2, **8**-16, **15**-5–6
Partnership accounting, **20**-13–16
    accounting methods/periods, **20**-14–16
    allocating partners' shares of income/loss, **20**-22–23
    guaranteed payments, **20**-19–20
    ordinary business income/loss, **20**-17–19
    reporting results of, **20**-17–23
    required year-ends, **20**-14–16
    self-employment tax, **20**-20–21
    separately stated items, **20**-17–18
    tax elections, **20**-13–14
Partnership agreement, **15**-2
Partnership books, **20**-3n
Partnership compliance issues, **20**-23
Partnership distributions
    basics of, **21**-9–24
    liquidating distributions, **21**-12–24
    operating distributions, **21**-9–12
Partnership formations, **20**-3–13
    acquiring partnership interests, **20**-3–13
    contributions of property, **20**-3–9
    contributions of services, **20**-9–12
    holding period in partnership interest, **20**-7
    initial tax basis, **20**-4
    organization, start-up, and syndication costs, **20**-12
    rules for allocating partnership debt, **20**-5
    summary of outside basis/holding period, **20**-13

Partnership interest, **20**-3, **21**-2
    acquisitions of, **20**-12–13
    allocating partners' shares of income/loss, **20**-22–23
    basic of sales of, **21**-2–8
    buyer and partnership issues, **21**-7–8
    cash distributions in operating partnerships, **20**-28–29
    holding period in, **20**-7
    partner's adjusted tax basis in, **20**-26–29
    seller issues, **21**-3–4
Partnership returns, **2**-3
Passenger automobiles, **9**-23
Passive activity, defined, **11**-36, **20**-32
Passive activity income or loss, **11**-32–39, **14**-20n, **14**-24–26, **20**-32
    income and loss categories, **11**-36–38
    rental real estate exception, **11**-38–39, **14**-24–26
Passive activity loss (PAL) limitation, **20**-31–32, **22**-15
Passive activity loss (PAL) rules, **20**-31, **22**-15
Passive category income, **24**-19
Passive investment income (PII), **22**-6
    excess of, **22**-6
Passive investments, **11**-2
Patents, **8**-5, **9**-30, **9**-35–36
Pay-as-you-go basis, **7**-33
Payment liability, **8**-24, **8**-26
Payroll, **23**-18
Payroll taxes (FICA), **12**-5, **15**-3n
Penalties, **1**-3, **2**-26–27, **8**-4
    early withdrawal of savings, **6**-9
Pension Benefits Guaranty Corporation, **13**-6
Per diem rate, **8**-7n
Percentage depletion, **9**-38
Permanent book-tax differences, **16**-4–5
Permanent differences, **17**-6–8, **17**-22
    common permanent differences, **17**-7
Permanent establishment, **24**-17
Permissible accounting method, **8**-30
Person, **24**-2n
Personal exemptions, **4**-8, **4**-10, **6**-34
    maximum phase-out range, **6**-35
    phase-out computation, **6**-37–38
Personal expenses, **8**-6
Personal holding company tax, **15**-13n
Personal injury payments, **5**-25
Personal interest expense, **5**-19n
Personal property, **1**-14, **9**-5, **24**-10n
    calculating depreciation for, **9**-10
    depreciation conventions, **9**-8–10
    depreciation method, **9**-5–6
    like-kind exchanges, **10**-21
    mid-quarter depreciation table for, **9**-13
Personal property taxes, **1**-4, **1**-14, **4**-7, **6**-16

Personal residence; *see also* Business use of home
    business use of home, **14**-26–29
    debt forgiveness on foreclosure, exclusion of gain, **14**-7
    exclusion of gain on sale, **14**-2–7
    first-time home buyer tax credit, **14**-16–17
    home sale exclusion in hardship circumstances, **14**-5–6
    interest expense on home-related debt, **14**-7–9
    limitations on exclusion, **14**-5–7
    ownership test, **14**-3–4
    personal use and deemed personal use, **14**-18
    sale, exclusion of gain, **4**-5, **5**-20n
    use test, **14**-3–4
Personal-use assets, **9**-5
    casualty and theft losses, **6**-23–24
    losses on sale of, **11**-9n, **11**-19
Persons, **19**-5
Phase-outs of itemized deductions, **6**-30
Physical presence, **23**-5
Plan maintenance, defined benefit plans, **13**-5
Points, **14**-12–14
Political contributions, **8**-5, **25**-19
*Pollock v. Farmers' Loan and Trust Company,* **1**-11
Portfolio income, **20**-32
    capital gains and losses, **11**-8–22
    corporate and Treasury bonds, **11**-4–5
    dividends, **11**-7–8
    educational savings plans, **11**-25–26
    interest, **11**-2–7
    life insurance, **11**-23–25
    municipal bonds, **11**-22–23
    summary of, **11**-26–27
    tax exempt income, **11**-22–26
    U.S. savings bonds, **11**-5–7
Portfolio investment expenses, **11**-28–32
    investment expenses, **11**-28–29
    investment interest expense, **11**-30–32
Portfolio investments; *see* Investments
Positive basis adjustment, **21**-29
Post-termination transition period (PTTP), **22**-14
Post-termination transition period distributions, **22**-20–21
Post-termination transition period loss limitation, **22**-14
*Practical Tax Strategies,* **2**-11
Pratt, J., **16**-3n
Preference items, **7**-9
    corporate alternative minimum tax, **16**-34
Preferential tax rate, **7**-4, **7**-8
    for capital gains and dividends, **7**-4–6

Preferentially taxed income, 7-5
Premium, **11**-4–5
Prepaid expenses, 3-6, **8**-17–18
Prepaid income, **8**-19–20
Prepaid interest income, **8**-20
Prepaid rental income, **8**-20
Prepayments, 7-33–36
Present interest, **25**-8
Present value of money, 3-3–4
Previously taxable income (PTI), **22**-19n
Previously taxed capital, **21**-27n
Primary tax authorities, 2-9
   citations to, 2-10
   Congress, 2-9
   Courts, 2-9
   US. Treasury/IRS, 2-9
Principal partners, **20**-15
Principal residence, **14**-3
Private activity bonds, **11**-22n, **16**-34
Private letter rulings, 2-10, 2-16, 3-7
Private nonoperating foundations, **6**-21
Private operating foundations, **6**-21
Prizes, **5**-16–17
Probate/probate estate, **25**-3
Procedural regulations, 2-16
Production of income, **10**-5
Professional corporations (PCs), **15**-2n
Professional journals (examples), **2**-11
Professional limited liability companies (PLLCs), **15**-2n
Profit-motivated activities, **6**-3
Profits interest, **15**-14, **20**-3, **20**-3n, **20**-11
Progressive tax rate structure, 1-4, 1-8–10, 1-20
Prohibited interests, **18**-26
Property, **23**-19; *see also* Personal property; Real property
   capital gain property, **6**-19–20
   as charitable contribution, **6**-19
   gains from sale of, 4-5
   income from, **5**-10–11
   ordinary income property, **6**-19–20
   partnership formations, **20**-3–9
Property dispositions, **5**-13, **10**-2–4; *see also* Nonrecognition transactions
   adjusted basis, **10**-2–3
   amount realized, **10**-2
   realized gain or loss, **10**-3–4
   recognized gain or loss, **10**-4
   summary of formulas for gains/losses, **10**-4
Property distributions, **22**-20
   basic tax law framework, **18**-3
   corporate dividends, **18**-3
Property payments, **5**-16
Property taxes, **1**-13–14, **1**-20
Property transactions
   computing adjusted tax basis, **19**-3
   computing amount realized, **19**-3
   computing gain/loss realized, **19**-3

general tax rules for, **19**-3–4
tax-deferred transfers to corporation, **19**-4–19
Property use, **8**-10
Proportional tax rate structure, 1-4, 1-8, 1-10
Proposed regulations, 2-10, 2-16
Public Law 86-272, **23**-9–11
Publicly traded corporations, trends in stock redemption, **18**-28–29
Publicly traded partnerships, **20**-2, **20**-2n
Punitive damage, **5**-25
Purchase method, **19**-21n
Purchased goodwill, **16**-8
Purchased personal property, gain or loss from sale of, **24**-10

**Q**

Qualified debt, **14**-11
Qualified dividends, **11**-7
   election to investment income, **11**-31
Qualified educational expenses, **6**-9, **6**-12
   deductions for, **6**-11–12
   summary of limitations of, **6**-11
Qualified educational loans, **6**-9–11
   deduction for interest on, **6**-10
   summary of limitations on, **6**-10
Qualified employee discounts, **12**-29
Qualified exchange intermediary, **10**-23n
Qualified foreign corporations, **11**-7n
Qualified fringe benefit, **6**-8
Qualified moving expense reimbursements, **12**-30–31
Qualified nonrecourse financing, **11**-34, **20**-30
Qualified production activities income (QPAI), **8**-12
Qualified replacement property, **10**-28
Qualified residence, **14**-8
Qualified residence interest, **14**-13
Qualified retirement accounts, **5**-26
   contributions to, 4-6
Qualified retirement plans, 2-16, **13**-2–3
Qualified small business stock, **11**-11
Qualified terminable interest properties (QTIPs), **25**-12n
Qualified transportation fringe benefits, **12**-30
Qualified tuition plans (529 plan), **11**-25–26
Qualifying child, **4**-11–13
   age test, **4**-11
   children of divorced/separated parents, **4**-13
   dependency requirements summary, **4**-16
   relationship test, **4**-11
   residence test, **4**-11
   support test, **4**-12
   tiebreaking rules, **4**-12–13

Qualifying dividends, 4-9, 7-4
Qualifying fringe benefits, **22**-16n
Qualifying person, head of household filing status and, **4**-18
Qualifying relative, **4**-11, **4**-13–16
   dependency requirements summary, **4**-16
   gross income test, **4**-14–16
   relationship test, **4**-13
   support test, **4**-13–14
Qualifying widow or widower, 4-7, **4**-17–18
Question of fact, 2-19
Question of law, 2-19
Quick reference sources (examples), **2**-11
*Quill Corporation, Petitioner v. North Dakota,* **23**-6n, **23**-12n

**R**

Railroad retirement benefits, **5**-17n
Real estate taxes, 1-4, **6**-16
   as itemized deduction, 4-7, **6**-16
Real property, **1**-14, 9-5
   applicable convention/method, **9**-26
   cost segregation, **9**-26
   depreciation, **9**-25–27
   depreciation tables, **9**-26–27
   gain or loss from sale of, **24**-10
   like-kind exchanges, **10**-21
   mid-month convention for year of disposition, **9**-27
   recovery period for, **9**-25
Real property taxes, **1**-14, **14**-15
Realization principle, **5**-3–4, **19**-3
Realized gain or loss (on disposition), **10**-3–4
Realized income, **4**-2–5
Reasonable in amount, **8**-3
Reasonable basis, **2**-24
Recapture, **10**-9, **21**-4n
Recognition, 5-4, **17**-23–24, **19**-4
   FIN 48, **17**-23
   gain or loss on disposition, **10**-4
Record keeping, **8**-11
Recourse debt, **20**-4, **20**-5n
Recovery of amounts previously deducted, **5**-5
Recovery periods (depreciable life), **9**-5–8
   common business assets, **9**-7
Redemption agreement, **18**-21
Refinances/refinancing, **14**-9, **14**-13
Refundable credit, **7**-28
Refundable personal credits, **7**-28–30
   earned income credit, **7**-29–30
   making work pay credit (MWPC), **7**-28–29
   other refundable personal credits, **7**-30

Regressive tax rate structure, 1-4, 1-9–10
Regular decision, 2-10, 2-15
Regular federal income tax computation; see Federal income tax computation
Regular tax rates, 7-8
Regulations, 2-15
Rehabilitation credit, 7-32
Related-parties, 10-14, 10-14n, 11-19n, 18-22n, 19-36
  capital losses on sales to, 11-19
  gains on sale of depreciable property, 10-13–14
  limitations on accruals to related parties, 8-28
  loss disallowance rules, 10-32–33
Related-party transactions, 3-12, 3-14, 3-16, 12-6n
Related person, 19-36
Relationship test, 4-11, 4-13, 4-16
  qualifying child, 4-11
  qualifying relative, 4-13
Relevant authorities, 2-18
Remainder/remainderman, 25-8–10
Rental expenses, 11-29n
  by tier and deduction sequence, 14-20
  Tax Court vs. IRS method of allocating expenses, 14-21
Rental real estate
  losses on, 14-24–26
  nonresidence, 14-24
  passive activity loss exception, 11-38–39
  rental prior to sale, 14-4
Rental and royalties, 4-5–6, 5-3, 5-10, 6-3–6
  multinational transactions, 24-9
Rental use of home, 14-18–26
  expenses by tier and deduction sequence, 14-20
  flowchart of tax rules, 14-32–33
  losses on rental property, 14-24–26
  minimal rental use, 14-18–19
  minimal/no personal use, 14-18–19
  summary of tax rules, 14-25
  tax court vs. IRS method of allocating expenses, 14-20–21
  vacation home, 14-19–23
Reorganization, 19-26
  business purpose test, 19-27
  continuity of business enterprise (COBE), 19-27
  continuity of interests (COI), 19-26–27
  judicial principles of, 19-26 27
  summary of, 19-33
Research and experimental (R&E) expenditures, 9-30, 9-34–36
  multinational transactions, 24-13

Research Institute of America (RIA) United States Tax Reporter, 2-18
Research memo, 2-18, 2-20
  analysis, 2-22
  authority list, 2-22
  basic parts of, 2-20
  conclusion, 2-22
  facts, 2-20
  issues, 2-20–22
  sample memo, 2-21
Residence-based jurisdiction, 24-2
Residence test, 4-11, 4-16
  qualifying child, 4-11
Residency (primary residence), 11-22n
Resident, defined, for U.S. tax purposes, 24-4–5
Resident alien, 24-4
Residential energy efficient property credit, 7-32
Residential rental property, 9-25, 9-41
Restricted stock, 12-17–21
  Apple example, 12-20
  employee considerations for, 12-18–20
  employer considerations for, 12-20–21
  GAAP vs. tax expense, 12-21
  other nontax issues, 12-21
  sample timeline for, 12-17
  with/without Section 83(b) election, 12-18–20
Retirement income, 4-5
Retirement planning, 3-7, 3-10n
Retirement plans; see also Nonqualified deferred compensation
  after-tax rates of return, 13-11–12
  defined benefit plans, 13-3–6
  defined contribution plans, 13-5–15
  employer-provided qualified plans, 13-3
  individual retirement accounts, 13-19–22
  qualified plans vs. nonqualified plans, 13-19
  Roth 401(k) plans, 13-13–15
  saver's credit, 13-28–29
  self-employed retirement accounts, 13-24–28
Return of capital, 5-4–5, 5-11, 5-14, 10-4n
Revenue Act of 1913, 1-11
Revenue Act of 1921, 19-5
Revenue procedures, 2-10, 2-15–16, 9-17n
Revenue recognition, accrual method, 8-20
Revenue rulings, 2-10, 2-15–16
Reverse hybrid entity, 24-25
Reverse triangular merger, 19-26, 19-30–31, 19-33
Reversion, 25-8
*RIA Federal Tax Coordinator,* 2-11, 2-19

*RIA Federal Tax Handbook,* 2-10
*RIA United States Tax Reporter,* 2-11
Rollover, 13-20n, 13-23–24
Roth 401(k) plans, 13-13–15, 13-17n, 13-22n
  qualified distributions from, 13-14
  traditional 401(k) plan vs., 13-15
Roth IRAs, 5-20n, 13-19, 13-20, 13-20n, 13-22–24, 13-22n, 13-24n
  distributions, 13-22–23
  rollover from traditional IRA, 13-23–24
  traditional IRAs vs., 13-24–25
Routine maintenance, 9-3
Rowland, Robin, 8-5
Royalties, 5-10, 6-6n

**S**

S corporations, 5-14n, 8-2, 8-16, 8-28, 15-5–6, 15-19n, 15-27, 20-2, 22-2, 22-7n, 22-13n
  accounting methods and periods, 22-8
  built-in gains tax, 22-21–2
  C corporations vs., 22-18–19, 22-30–31
  corporation reelections, 22-7–8
  distributions, 22-17–21
  election/reelection of, 22-3–4, 22-7–8
  estimated taxes, 22-26
  excess net passive income tax, 22-23–25
  excess of passive investment income, 22-6
  filing requirements, 22-28
  formations, 22-2
  fringe benefits, 22-16
  income and loss allocations, 22-8
  involuntary termination, 22-5–6
  LIFO recapture tax, 22-25–26
  liquidating distributions, 22-21
  loss limitations, 22-13–15
  no C corporation accumulated earnings and profits, 22-17
  operating issues, 22-8–16
  property distributions, 22-20
  qualification requirements, 22-2
  self-employment income, 22-15–16
  separately stated items, 22-9–10
  shareholder's basis, 22-11–12
  short tax years, 22-6–7
  termination of, 22-5–8
  voluntary termination, 22-5
Safe-deposit box fees, 6-27
Safe-harbor provisions, 7-34
Safe-harbor rules, 22-3
Salary and wages, 12-2–9
  deductibility of salary payments, 12-6–9
  employee considerations for, 12-2
  employer considerations for, 12-6–9

Salary and wages—*Cont.*
  FICA (payroll taxes), **12**-5
  limits on salary deductibility, **12**-7–9,
    **13**-18
  withholding taxes, **12**-2–4
Sales tax, **1**-4, **1**-10, **1**-13–14, **1**-20
Sales and use taxes, **23**-3, **23**-5–8
  nexus, **23**-5–7
  tax liability, **23**-3n, **23**-5n, **23**-7–8
Salvage values, **9**-5
Same-day sale, **12**-14
Sarbanes-Oxley Act, **17**-1
Saver's credit, **7**-31n, **7**-32, **13**-28–29
Savings accounts, **11**-3
Savings Incentive Match Plans for
    Employees (SIMPLE) Ira, **13**-25n
*S. C. Chapin,* **10**-2n
Schedule A: Itemized Deductions, **6**-13,
    **6**-31, **6**-38n, **14**-7
Schedule B, **11**-3n, **11**-7n, **20**-19n,
    **22**-11n
Schedule C: Profit or Loss from Business,
    **6**-4, **7**-16, **8**-32, **13**-25n, **14**-27n
Schedule D, **10**-20, **11**-14–15, **20**-19n
Schedule E: Rental or Royalty Income,
    **6**-5–6, **7**-16n, **14**-22–23, **20**-19n,
    **22**-11n
Schedule K, **20**-23, **22**-28
Schedule K-1, **5**-14n, **20**-23, **20**-26,
    **22**-9, **22**-28–29
Schedule L, **17**-12n
Schedule M, **16**-25, **16**-27
Schedule M-1, **16**-25–28
Schedule M-3, **16**-25, **16**-28
Scholarships, **5**-22
*Scripto, Inc. v. Carson, Sherriff, et al.,*
    **23**-5n
Secondary tax authorities, **2**-10–11
  common secondary authorities, **2**-11
Section 83(b) election, **12**-18–20
Section 162(m) limitation, **13**-18
Section 179 expense, **9**-9n, **9**-15–18,
    **9**-30n–31n
  choice of assets for, **9**-18–19
  limits on, **9**-16–18
  luxury automobiles, **9**-25
Section 197 purchased intangibles,
    **9**-30–32, **9**-36
Section 291 depreciation recapture,
    **10**-12
Section 338 election, **19**-25
Section 351 tax deferral
  boot, tax consequences of, **19**-10–12
  computing tax basis of stock
    received, **19**-9
  control test of property, **19**-7–9
  qualifying stock, **19**-6–7
  requirements of, **19**-6–9
  shareholders, tax consequences to,
    **19**-9–10

tax basis of property received, **19**-15
  transfer of property to the
    corporation, **19**-6
  transferee corporation, **19**-14–17
Section 481 adjustment, **8**-33
Section 1031 exchange, **10**-17–19
Section 1202 gain, collectibles and,
    **11**-11–12
Section 1231 assets, **10**-6–7,
    **20**-7, **21**-25n
Section 1231 gains or losses, **10**-5,
    **10**-8n, **10**-9, **10**-13n, **10**-14–16,
    **11**-11n
  look-back rule, **10**-15–16
  netting process, **10**-14–16
Section 1231(b) assets, **6**-19n
Section 1239 recapture provision,
    **10**-13–14
Section 1244 stock, **15**-23n, **19**-19
Section 1245 property, **10**-8–11,
    **10**-30–31
Section 1250 property, **10**-11–12,
    **10**-15n
  unrecaptured gains for individuals,
    **10**-12–13, **11**-11, **14**-4n, **14**-29
Section 7520 rate, **25**-9, **25**-9n
Secured loan, **14**-8
Securities and Exchange Commission
    (SEC), **8**-17, **17**-1n, **17**-2
  Regulation S-X, **17**-29n
Self-created goodwill, **16**-8n
Self-created patents, **9**-35–36
Self-employed business expense, **6**-4
Self-employed individuals, **6**-3
  employee vs., **7**-19–22
  health insurance deduction, **4**-6, **6**-8
Self-employed retirement accounts,
    **13**-24–28
  individual 401(k)s, **13**-26–28
  simplified employee pension (SEP)
    IRA, **13**-26
Self-employment compensation, **12**-2n
Self-employment income, **13**-24n
  S corporation, **22**-15–16
Self-employment taxes, **1**-11, **4**-6,
    **4**-9, **6**-8–9, **7**-16–19, **15**-17n,
    **20**-20–21, **20**-21n
  computation of, **7**-17
  entities overview, **15**-16–18
  partnerships, **20**-20–21
Senate Finance Committee Report,
    **2**-10–13
SEP (simplified employee pension)
    IRA, **13**-26
Separate-return states, **23**-13–14
Separate tax return, **23**-13–14
Separate taxpaying entity, **15**-6
Separately stated items, **20**-17–18,
    **22**-9–10
  S corporations, **22**-9–10

Serial gifts, **25**-28
Series EE bonds, **5**-22–23, **11**-5,
    **11**-9n, **11**-25n
Series I bonds, **11**-5, **11**-25n
Service partner, **20**-10
Services
  income from, **5**-9–10
  partnership formations, **20**-3–9
Settlement statement, **14**-13, **14**-15,
    **14**-30–31
704(b) capital accounts, **20**-8–9
Shareholder liabilities, **19**-12
  liabilities in excess of basis, **19**-13–14
Shareholder tax, **15**-12n
Shareholders, **15**-3–4
  complete liquidation, **19**-35–36
  noncash property distributions,
    **18**-11–14
  reducing shareholder-level tax,
    **15**-12–13
  tax consequences in Section 351
    transaction, **19**-9–10
  tax consequences of stock dividend,
    **18**-18–19
Shareholder's basis
  annual basis adjustments, **22**-12
  S corporation, **22**-11–12
Sherin, Keith S., **12**-24
Short tax years, **22**-6–7
Short-term capital gains or losses,
    **11**-11
Sickness and injury-related exclusions,
    **5**-24–26
Sideways attribution, **18**-25
Signaling, **18**-20
Simple plans, **13**-25n
Simplified employee pension (SEP)
    IRA, **13**-26
  nontax considerations, **13**-26
Sin tax, **1**-3
Single filing status, **4**-7, **4**-20
  standard deduction, **6**-32
Single-life annuity, **5**-11–12
Single-member LLCs, **15**-5
Sixteenth Amendment, **1**-11, **2**-11, **2**-13
Slaughter, Mathew J., **24**-2n
Small business corporation, **19**-19
"Smell test," **3**-18
Smith, Adam, **1**-16n
Social Security benefits, **5**-17–19, **13**-2
Social Security tax, **1**-9–12, **6**-8–9,
    **7**-14–17, **12**-5
Social Security Trust Fund, **13**-2n
Social Security withholding, **22**-15n
Sole proprietorships, **3**-13, **8**-2,
    **8**-16, **9**-32n, **13**-24n, **15**-2–3,
    **15**-5–6, **20**-2n
Solicitation, **23**-9–11
Source-based jurisdiction, **24**-2
Source of deduction rules, **24**-11

Source of income rules, **24**-7–11
  compensation for services, **24**-8–9
  dividends, **24**-8
  for gross income and deductions, **24**-6–14
  interest, **24**-7
  inventory manufactured within and sold outside U.S., **24**-10
  non-U.S. persons, **24**-7
  rents and royalties, **24**-9
  sale of purchased personal property, **24**-10
  sale of real property, **24**-10
Special allocations, **15**-16, **20**-22
Special apportionment rules, **24**-12–14
Special basis adjustments, **21**-26–29
  for dispositions, **21**-27–28
  for distributions, **21**-28–29
Specific identification method, **8**-22, **11**-10
Split gifts, **25**-21
Spot rate, **24**-21
Standard deductions, **4**-7, **6**-32–36
  age and/or blindness, **6**-32
  Alternative Minimum Tax (AMT) and, **7**-10
  amounts (summary), **6**-32
  by filing status, **4**-7
  exemptions and, **6**-32–36
Standard mileage rate, **6**-26, **8**-8
Stanley Works, **3**-16
"Starbucks footnote," **8**-13
*Stare decisis* doctrine, **2**-15
Starker exchange (deferred like-kind exchange), **10**-23
Start-up costs, **8**-5, **8**-11–12, **9**-34–35, **20**-12
State death taxes, taxable estate, **25**-11–12
State income tax, **1**-4
State income tax liability, **23**-22
State income tax process, **23**-4
State and local taxes, **1**-13–14, **23**-2–4
  average revenues, **1**-13
  excise taxes, **1**-14
  income taxes, **1**-13
  as itemized deduction, **4**-7, **6**-16
  property taxes, **1**-14
  sales and use taxes, **1**-13–14
State sales and use tax process, **23**-3
State Street Bank 2009 Proxy Statement, **12**-8
State tax base, **23**-4
State taxable income, **23**-15–16
Statements on Standards for Tax Services (SSTS), **2**-23–25
Static vs. dynamic forecasting, **1**-17
Static forecasting, **1**-16–17
Statute of limitations, **2**-3–4
Statutory notice of deficiency, **2**-6

Statutory sources of the tax law, **2**-9–14
  citations (examples), **2**-10
  Congress, **2**-11–13
  Internal Revenue Code (IRC), **2**-11, **2**-13
  tax laws legislative process, **2**-11–13
  tax treaties, **2**-13–14
  U.S. Constitution, **2**-11, **2**-13
Step-transaction doctrine, **3**-18
Step-up in tax basis, **25**-29–30
Stock, T., **16**-3n
Stock, tax basis in Section 351 transaction, **19**-9–10
Stock dividends, **11**-7n, **18**-3, **18**-18–19
  nontaxable, **18**-18–19
  taxable stock dividends, **18**-19–20
Stock-for-stock acquisitions/reorganization, **19**-31–32
Stock-for-stock tax-free exchange, **3**-7
Stock options, **12**-10–12, **12**-16n
  Adobe's 2009 proxy statement, **12**-10
  ASC 718 (formerly FAS 123R), **16**-10, **16**-12
  book-tax differences, **16**-9–12
  employee considerations for, **12**-13–15
  employer considerations for, **12**-15–17
  expense treatment, GAAP vs. tax, **12**-16
  incentive stock options (ISOs), **12**-13, **12**-15, **16**-9–10
  non qualified options, **12**-15–16
  nonqualified stock options (NQOs), **12**-13–16, **16**-9, **17**-7n
  sample timeline for incentive/nonqualified options, **12**-12
  terminology of, **12**-10–11
Stock redemptions, **18**-2, **18**-20–29
  complete redemption, **18**-25–26
  contraction of ownership interest, **18**-22–27
  form of, **18**-21–22
  not essentially equivalent to a dividend, **18**-26–27
  substantially disproportionate to shareholder, **18**-22–25
  tax consequences to distributing corporation, **18**-28
  trends by publicly traded corporations, **18**-28–29
Stock split, **18**-18
Stone, L. M., **14**-5n
Straight-line method, **9**-5, **9**-21, **9**-30
Straight type A merger, **19**-26–27
Streamlined Sales Tax Project, **23**-8
Strike price, **12**-11
Structural tax rate, **17**-31
Subchapter C experts, **19**-6n
Subchapter K, **20**-2
Subchapter S, **20**-2, **22**-2n

Subpart F income, **24**-27–30
  planning to avoid, **24**-30–31
Subscriptions, **6**-27
Subsequent events, ASC 740, **17**-26
Substance-over-form doctrine, **3**-18
Substance of a transaction, **18**-15
Substantial authority standard, **2**-24, **2**-26
Substantial basis reduction, **21**-27
Substantial built-in loss, **21**-27
Substantial presence test, **24**-4
Substantially appreciated inventory, **21**-25
Substantially disproportionate with respect to the shareholder, **18**-22–25
Substituted basis, **19**-9, **22**-11
Substitution effect, **1**-17
Sufficiency of tax system, **1**-16–17
Sullivan, Martin A., **24**-2n
Support test, **4**-12–14, **4**-16
  qualifying child, **4**-12
  qualifying relative, **4**-13–14
Syndication costs, **20**-12, **20**-12n

**T**

Tangible assets, **8**-5, **9**-2
Tangible personal property, **6**-20, **9**-9
  immediate expensing, **9**-5–18
Tax and taxes
  calculation of, **1**-4
  defined, **1**-3
  earmarked tax, **1**-3
  employment/unemployment taxes, **1**-11–12
  excise taxes, **1**-12, **1**-14
  Federal taxes, **1**-10–12
  fundamental business decisions and, **1**-2
  general purpose of, **1**-3
  implicit taxes, **1**-14–16
  income taxes, **1**-11, **1**-13
  investment decisions and, **1**-15
  as itemized deductions, **4**-7, **6**-16
  personal financial decisions and, **1**-2
  pervasive role of, **1**-2
  political process and, **1**-2
  property taxes, **1**-14
  sales and use taxes, **1**-13–14
  sin taxes, **1**-3
  state and local taxes, **1**-13–14
  tax planning and, **3**-2
  three criteria necessary for, **1**-3
  transfer taxes, **1**-12
  types of, **1**-10–16
  understanding of, **1**-2–3
Tax accounting balance sheet, **17**-12, **19**-23
*Tax Adviser*, **2**-11
Tax avoidance vs. tax evasion, **3**-18–19
Tax-avoidance transactions, **19**-12–13

Tax base, **1**-4
Tax basis, **5**-4–5, **5**-13, **9**-3, **11**-9, **11**-35, **19**-4, **19**-15
  step-up in, **25**-29–30
Tax basis hurdle, **11**-34
Tax basis limitation, **20**-29–30, **22**-13–14
Tax benefit rule, **5**-5
Tax bracket, **7**-2
Tax capital accounts, **20**-8
Tax carryforwards, **17**-4, **17**-8–10
Tax code; *see* Internal Revenue Code
*Tax Commissioner of West Virginia v. MBNA America Bank, N. A.,* **23**-12n
Tax Court method, **14**-20–21, **14**-21n
Tax credits, **4**-9–10, **7**-22–33, **20**-17n, **22**-9n
  business tax credits, **7**-30
  child tax credit, **7**-22–23
  credit application sequence, **7**-31–33
  dependent care credit, **7**-24–25
  earned income credit, **7**-29–30
  education credits, **7**-25–28
  first-time home buyer credit, **14**-16–17
  foreign tax credit, **7**-31
  making work pay credit (MWPC), **7**-28–28
  nonrefundable personal credits, **7**-22–28
  refundable personal credits, **7**-28–30
  summary of, **7**-31–32
Tax deductions
  accelerating deductions, **3**-4–6
  timing strategies for, **3**-4–8, **3**-10
Tax deferral; *see also* Section 351 tax deferral
  in corporate formation, **19**-5–8
  Section 351 requirements, **19**-6–9
Tax-deferred acquisition, **19**-26
  forward triangular type A merger, **19**-26
  reverse triangular type A merger, **19**-26
  straight type A merger, **19**-26
Tax-deferred stock acquisition, **19**-31
Tax depreciation; *see* Depreciation
Tax elections, partnership accounting, **20**-13–14
Tax evasion, **2**-5, **3**-18–19
Tax-exempt investment income
  educational savings plans, **11**-25–26
  expenses associated with production of, **8**-5–6
  life insurance, **11**-23–25
  municipal bonds, **11**-22–23
Tax-exempt shareholders, **15**-10–11
Tax-favored asset, **1**-14–16
Tax haven, **3**-16, **24**-26
Tax home, **24**-4n

Tax law; *see also* Internal Revenue Code
  administrative sources, **2**-15–17
  judicial sources, **2**-14–15
  legislative process for, **2**-11–13, **3**-8
  letter rulings, **2**-16–17
  sources of, **2**-9–17
  tax treaties, **2**-13–14
*Tax Law Review* (New York University School of Law), **2**-11
Tax law sources, **2**-9–17
  Internal Revenue Code (IRC), **2**-11
  legislative process, **2**-11–13
  primary authorities, **2**-9–10
  secondary authorities, **2**-10
Tax legislative process, **3**-8
Tax loss, from casualties, **6**-23
*Tax Notes,* **2**-11
Tax penalty, **2**-3
Tax planning; *see also* Timing strategies
  ASC 740, **17**-19
  capital assets and, **11**-20–22
  conversion strategies, **3**-2, **3**-16–18
  fringe benefits and, **12**-32–33
  general AMT planning strategies, **7**-14
  income shifting, **3**-2
  income-shifting strategies, **3**-11–16
  judicial doctrines, **3**-18
  maximizing after-tax wealth, **3**-2
  overview of, **3**-2
  tax avoidance vs. tax evasion, **3**-18–19
  timing strategies, **3**-2–11
Tax practitioner, **2**-24
  penalties for tax violations, **2**-26–27
Tax preference items, **1**-19, **7**-9
Tax preparation fees, **6**-27
Tax prepayments, **4**-10
Tax professionals
  AICPA Code of Professional Conduct, **2**-23
  responsibilities of, **2**-23–26
Tax rate schedule, **1**-5, **4**-8, **7**-2
Tax rate structures, **1**-8–10
  key facts of, **1**-10
  progressive tax, **1**-8–10
  proportional tax, **1**-8–10
  regressive tax, **1**-9–10
Tax rates, **1**-4
  average tax rate, **1**-6–7
  effective tax rate, **1**-7–8
  kiddie tax, **7**-8
  marginal tax rates, **1**-4–6
  preferential tax rates, **7**-8
  regular tax rates, **7**-8
  ways to measure, **1**-4–8
Tax Reform Act of 1986, **16**-33, **24**-22n
Tax refund, **4**-10
Tax research, **2**-17–23
  analyzing tax authorities, **2**-19–20
  communicating the results, **2**-20–22
  identifying the issues, **2**-17–18

keyword searching, **2**-19
  locating relevant authorities, **2**-18–19
  steps in, **2**-17–23
  understanding the facts, **2**-17
Tax research services, **2**-10–11
Tax return due date, **2**-2–3
Tax shelters, **11**-35, **20**-16n
Tax summary, **7**-37
Tax system
  certainty in, **1**-20–21
  convenience of, **1**-20–21
  economy and, **1**-21
  equity of, **1**-19
  horizontal vs. vertical equity, **1**-19–20
  income vs. substitution effects, **1**-17–19
  static vs. dynamic forecasting, **1**-17
  sufficiency of, **1**-16–17
  trade-offs in, **1**-21
Tax tables, **4**-8, **4**-23, **7**-3, **7**-39
Tax treaties, **2**-11, **2**-13–14
Tax violations
  civil penalties for, **2**-26–27
  criminal penalties for, **2**-26
Tax year, **8**-15
Taxable corporations, **11**-32, **15**-5–6, **20**-2; *see also* C corporations; S Corporations
Taxable estate, **25**-11–12
Taxable fringe benefits, **12**-22
  employee considerations for, **12**-22–24
  employer considerations for, **12**-25
Taxable gifts, **25**-20–21
Taxable income, **4**-2
  expected future income exclusive of reversals/carryforwards, **17**-19
  income excluded from, **18**-5
  in prior carryback year(s), **17**-19
  summary, **6**-35–36
  tax planning strategies, **17**-19
  timing strategies for, **3**-4–8, **3**-10
Taxable stock dividends, **18**-18–19
Taxable and tax-deferred corporate acquisitions, **19**-20–22
Taxable temporary difference, **17**-9
Taxpayer Compliance Measurement Program, **2**-4
Taxpayer filing requirements, **2**-2–4, **7**-37
  extensions, **2**-2–3
  late filing penalty, **7**-36
  late payment penalty, **7**-36–37
  statute of limitations, **2**-3–4
  tax return due date, **2**-2–3
Taxpayer penalties, **2**-26–27
  late filing penalty, **7**-36
  late payment penalty, **7**-36–37
  underpayment penalties, **7**-34–36
Taxpayer prepayments, **7**-33–36
  underpayment penalties, **7**-34–36

Taxpayers, when to recognize income, **5**-6–7

Technical advice memorandum, **2**-10, **2**-16

Temporary book-tax differences, **16**-4, **16**-6–7
  dividends, **16**-76
  goodwill acquired in asset acquisition, **16**-8
  unfavorable/favorable charitable contributions, **16**-17

Temporary differences, **17**-8–10
  common temporary differences, **17**-9
  deductible temporary differences, **17**-9–10
  defined (ASC 740), **17**-8
  expense/losses that are deductible, **17**-8–9
  future reversals of, **17**-18
  identification of, **17**-9–10
  revenue/gains that are taxable, **17**-8–9
  taxable temporary differences, **17**-9

Temporary regulations, **2**-10, **2**-15

10-year look-forward rule, **18**-26

Tenancy by the entirety, **25**-6n

Tenancy in common, **25**-4–5

Tentative minimum tax (TMT), **7**-9, **16**-38
  AMT computation and, **7**-12–13

Term insurance, **11**-24

Terminable interest, **25**-8, **25**-12n

Testamentary transfers, **25**-2

Theft losses, **4**-7, **8**-14–15

Third-party intermediaries, **10**-22, **10**-23n

30-day letter, **2**-6–7

*Thomas A. Curtis, M.D., Inc.,* **18**-15n

Throwback rule, **23**-17

Time value of money; *see* Present value of money

Timing requirements, like-kind exchange, **10**-22–23

Timing strategies, **3**-1–11
  changing tax rates and, **3**-8–10
  constant tax rates, **3**-5–8
  decreasing tax rates, **3**-10
  income deferral, **3**-6–8
  increasing tax rates, **3**-10
  interest payments and taxes, **11**-7
  limitation to, **3**-10–11
  present value of money, **3**-3–4
  tax deductions, **3**-4–6
  taxable income, **3**-4–6

*T.J. Starker, Appellant v. United States of America,* **10**-23n

Topical tax services, **2**-18–19

Trade or business, **6**-3, **20**-32n

Trade show rule, **23**-11

Trademarks, **9**-36

Traditional 401(k) plans, **13**-13
  Roth 401(k) plan vs., **13**-15

Traditional IRAs, **13**-19–22
  distributions, **13**-22
  rollover to Roth IRA, **13**-23–24
  Roth IRA vs., **13**-24–25

Transactions subject to tax deferral, **19**-5–8

Transfer pricing, **3**-15–16

Transfer of property to the corporation, **19**-6

Transfer tax planning techniques, **25**-27–28

Transfer taxes, **1**-12

Transferor, **5**-23

Transferred basis property, **19**-14n

Transfers within three years of death, **25**-7

Travel and transportation expenses, **8**-8–10
  employee business expenses, **6**-25–26
  for medical purposes, **6**-14–15

Treasury bonds, **11**-4–5

Treasury notes, **11**-4

Treaties, **24**-14–18

Trigger event, **18**-21

"Trilogy of the rings," **6**-24

Triple i agreements, **18**-26, **18**-28n

Troubled Asset Relief Program (TARP), **12**-7n

Trustee, **25**-8

Trusts, **25**-2n, **25**-8, **25**-27, **25**-31n

Tschetschot, George E., **6**-29n

12-month rule, **8**-17–18

200 percent (double) declining balance, **9**-5

Type A asset acquisitions, **19**-26–28, **19**-33

Type B stock-for-stock reorganizations, **19**-31–32

Type C reorganization, **19**-33

Type D reorganization, **19**-33

Type E reorganization, **19**-33

Type F reorganization, **19**-33

Type G reorganization, **19**-33

**U**

Uncertain tax positions, **17**-11, **17**-23
  ASC 740 application of, **17**-24–27
  ASC 740 disclosure requirements, **17**-26–27

Underpayment penalty, **7**-34–36

Unearned income, **5**-10

Unemployment compensation, **5**-10n, **5**-25

Unemployment taxes, **1**-11–12

Unfavorable book-tax difference, **16**-4, **17**-9n

Unified credit, **25**-2, **25**-14–15
  federal gift tax, **25**-24–25

Unified transfer tax rates, **25**-3

Uniform capitalization, **8**-21–22

Uniform cost capitalization rules (UNICAP rules), **8**-21–22

Uniform Division of Income Tax Purposes Act, **23**-16n

Uniforms or special clothing, **8**-6

Unincorporated entities, **20**-2n

Unitary tax returns, **23**-13–14

U.S. anti-deferral rules, **24**-26–31

U.S. Circuit Courts of Appeals, **2**-7–10, **2**-14–15
  citations (examples), **2**-10
  geographic boundaries for, **2**-8

U.S. Constitution, **2**-11, **2**-13
  Article 1, Section 7, **2**-11

U.S. Court of Federal Claims, **2**-6–10, **2**-15
  citations (examples), **2**-10

U.S. Department of the Treasury, history of taxation, **1**-2

U.S. District Courts, **2**-6–8, **2**-15
  citations (examples), **2**-10

U.S. President, **2**-12–13

U.S. savings bonds, **11**-5–7, **11**-25n
  Series EE bonds, **5**-22–23

U.S. Supreme Court, **2**-8–10, **2**-14
  citations (examples), **2**-10
  income tax, **1**-11

U.S. Tax Court, **2**-6–8, **2**-15
  memorandum decision, **2**-10, **2**-15
  regular decision, **2**-10, **2**-15

U.S. Treasury, **2**-15–16
  regulations, revenue rulings/procedures, **2**-15–16

U.S. Treasury bonds, **11**-4–5

*United States v. Davis,* **18**-27n

Unrealized receivables, **21**-3–4, **21**-25n

Unreasonable compensation, **3**-15n

Unrecaptured Section 1231 losses, **10**-15

Unrecaptured Section 1250 gains, **10**-12–13, **11**-11, **11**-11n, **14**-29, **21**-5n

Unrecovered costs of an annuity, **5**-12n

Unreimbursed employee business expenses, **6**-3

Use tax, **1**-13–14, **23**-4, **23**-4n

Use test, **14**-3

Useful life, **9**-5–6

**V**

Vacation homes, **14**-19–23

Valuation
  gross estate, **25**-7–10
  remainders and other temporal interests, **25**-8–10

Valuation allowance, **17**-18
  determining the need for, **17**-18–21
  expected future taxable income, **17**-19

Valuation allowance—*Cont.*
 future reversals of temporary
  differences, **17**-18
 negative/positive evidence allowance
  is needed, **17**-19
 tax planning strategies, **17**-19
 taxable income in prior carryback
  year(s), **17**-19
Value-added tax, **1**-10
Value of income interest, **25**-9
Value of remainder interest, **25**-8–9
 discount factors for, **25**-9
Varying interest rule, **21**-8
Vertical equity, **1**-19–20
Vest, **12**-11, **16**-9
Vesting, **13**-4
 defined benefit plans, **13**-4
 defined contribution plans, **13**-8–9
Vesting date, **12**-11
Vesting period, **16**-10
Vesting requirements, **20**-10n
*Virginia Tax Review* (University of
  Virginia School of Law), **2**-11

Voluntary revocation, **22**-5
Voluntary terminations, S corporation,
  **22**-5
Voting power, **19**-7, **19**-30
Voting stock, **19**-30

**W**

Wages; *see* Salary and wages
Wash sales, **11**-19
*Wealth of Nations, The* (Smith), **1**-16n
Wealth planning concepts, **25**-27–32
 bypass provisions, **25**-28–29
 generation-skipping tax, **25**-27
 income tax consideration, **25**-27
 integrated wealth plans, **25**-31–32
 serial gifts, **25**-28
 step-up in tax basis, **25**-29–30
 transfer tax planning techniques,
  **25**-27–28
*Welch v. Helvering,* **8**-3n
Welfare to work credit, **7**-32
Wherewithal to pay, **5**-4

Whole life insurance, **11**-23
*William H. Carpenter,* **6**-24
Willing-buyer, willing-seller rule, **25**-7
Wilson, Frank J., **8**-5
*Wisconsin Department of Revenue v.
  William Wrigley, Jr. Co.,* **23**-10n
Withholding, **4**-10, **7**-33
Withholding allowances, **12**-2
Withholding tables, **12**-3
Withholding taxes, **12**-2–4
Work opportunity credit, **7**-32
Worker, Homeownership, and Business
  Assistance Act of 2009, **16**-14n
Worker, Retiree, and Employer
  Recovery Act of 2008, **13**-6n
Workers' compensation, **5**-24–25
Working conditions fringe benefits,
  **12**-29–30
*Writ of certiorari,* **2**-8, **23**-12

**Z**

Zero-coupon bonds, **11**-4